JOY OF COOKING

by Irma S. Rombauer,
Marion Rombauer Becker,
and Ethan Becker

Illustrated by Laura Hartman Maestro

SCRIBNER

Joy's soul lies in the doing.

—WILLIAM SHAKESPEARE

SCRIBNER
1230 Avenue of the Americas
New York, NY 10020

Designed by Margery Cantor
Set in Minion
Manufactured in the United States of America

1 3 5 7 9 10 8 6 4 2

Library of Congress Cataloging-in-Publication Data is available.

ISBN 0-684-81870-1

To Granny Rom, Mom, and Pop—all of
whom gave life and soul to *Joy;*
and to the millions of friends who
have given *Joy* their love.

Contents

Foreword

My Granny Rom (known to the rest of the world as Irma Rombauer) wrote *Joy* in 1931 with her characteristic verve and zest for life. She wrote it for the times . . . when domestic help was fast becoming a thing of the past and women all over the country were once again heading to the kitchen. This book made cooking socially acceptable, fun and easy, and helped change the perception of cooking from a chore to a joy. Over the next twenty-two years, Irma revised the book, always keeping current with the times, even writing for the days of war rationing.

My mother, Marion, worked with Granny Rom from the first edition, and the transition of her stewardship was complete with the 1953 edition of *Joy*. When Granny Rom died in 1964, Mom carried on the tradition of *Joy*'s constant renewal and betterment using her keen intellect, scientific approach, and organizational bent. She oversaw several editions of the book, and her 1975 revision of the *Joy of Cooking* was the best-selling edition ever.

When Mom passed away in 1976, I was entrusted to oversee the tradition and future of *Joy*. I thought I would do just as she had done and her mother before her—sit down and write the next revision of the book. But as it turned out, my first task was to establish a relationship with publishing partners who had the resources and vision to help me produce the best possible book for the times.

And what times these are! Who would have thought twenty-five years ago that cooking would be a noble career choice and one of America's favorite pastimes? Since *Joy*'s last version, the food community has grown to thousands of experts, cooking magazines abound, and literally tens of thousands of cookbooks have been published.

Three years ago, Simon & Schuster and Scribner became my new partners in this new revised edition of the *Joy of Cooking*. They have vastly expanded the possibilities for this book's future and put the country's food experts within reach. Together, we have held fast to *Joy*'s revision focuses: provision of new recipes and the latest food and nutrition knowledge; collaboration with the best cooks; and, ultimately, a cookbook that is useful to the novice and experienced cook alike.

Using these guiding factors has resulted in the New, Improved, All-Purpose 1997 edition of the *Joy of Cooking*. We hope you find this to be the most comprehensive, best organized, and easiest-to-use *Joy* ever. The recipes include old favorites, recipes from Cockaigne (our family home), recipes for those fast and furious days, and recipes that reflect America's melting pot of culture and cuisine.

Overseeing the *Joy* has been both challenging and rewarding, and through it all, I have had the help of many people: my eternal friend, Joan Becker; my son, John, whose life has given mine so much meaning; and my brother Mark, his wife Jennifer, and their son Joe, who are all an important part of the family and the *Joy* tradition. My gratitude to the Koerner Rombauer family, *Joy*'s ambassadors in the Napa Valley. Thanks to Bob Epsteen, who stood by me many times when I was too tired to stand; to Fred Greenman, a trusted friend and adviser; to Anne Mendelson, who wrote the history of *Joy* in her thoughtful book, *Stand Facing the Stove*. Thanks to and God bless the late Sasha Vereschagin, a loyal friend and a man who lived life with a joyous heart. I want to express appreciation to my dear friends Matt and Alice MacLeid for their support, encouragement, and contributions; and thank-yous go to my old crew, Judy Bosio, Patty Eiser, Debbie Gibson, the late Dana Leonard, Betsy Glosik, and Nina Gannon.

Acknowledgment is due Jack Romanos and the people at Scribner and Simon & Schuster, who recognized the value of the *Joy of Cooking* and gave their all in the production of this new edition. I am especially appreciative of Carolyn Reidy and Susan Moldow, the visionary publishers I always dreamed of having.

It's difficult to express my feelings of gratitude to

Maria Guarnaschelli, who labored on this revision with the same passion and devotion as if she were a member of the family. Since the first day we began planning this edition, she has given me incredible support and encouragement. Working with her has truly been a privilege and a joy.

Many thanks to Kate Niedzwiecki for her efficient and professional assistance in New York; to Marah Stets, a lady whose contributions and work behind the scenes have been invaluable to *Joy;* and to Suzen O'Rourke, who really "cooks by the book." A special thanks to Gene Winick and Sam Pinkus, who are not only my agents, but my friends. My eternal appreciation goes to the many food experts and writers whose contributions and collaborations are at the heart of this *Joy.* Thanks are also due to Beth Wareham, who is working hard to spread *Joy* to the world.

Every day I am thankful to my assistant Mary Gilbert, ever-smiling and positive, whose work on the Menus chapter was first-rate.

And finally, my love and appreciation to Susan Cope Becker—my wife, my friend, and my happiness.

Ethan Becker
August 1997
Cockaigne
Cincinnati, Ohio

Introduction

I came to Scribner to build a library of enduring cookbooks, as I had done for nearly twenty years at another publishing house. I relished the challenge, especially when I learned that the centerpiece of the newly created cookbook list was to be a thoroughly revised edition of *Joy of Cooking.*

That was early in 1994, more than twenty years since a new edition of *Joy of Cooking* had been published. Ethan Becker, whose parents and grandmother created *Joy of Cooking,* guarded his birthright with rare courage and patience. He did not undertake a revision until he found an editor and publisher whose vision of *Joy* matched his own. When I learned that the monumental undertaking had fallen to me, I was so daunted that while going from the city to the country, hoping to sort out my thoughts, I drove my car straight into a trailer truck.

Then I got down to work. I knew that the book must show America's fascination with food and its embrace of cuisines from many cultures. Both of these come, I think, from our growing realization that what we eat can make us feel better and live longer. This means using the best and freshest ingredients. It also meant bringing *Joy*'s recipes from other countries—which had been in the book from the start—closer to their ethnic roots and not more "American." The 1964 edition of *Joy,* for instance, always ahead of its time, had a recipe for risotto; it called for chicken livers and beef stock, but made no mention of any special kind of rice. Today's edition includes notes on why medium-grain rice produces such a creamy risotto and has definitions of different rices. It gives instructions on how Italians prepare their favorite risotto Milanese; and a risotto with vegetable stock, fresh corn, and lime juice, which stunned me when I tasted it at a San Francisco restaurant while celebrating my thirtieth wedding anniversary. The new edition gives, in other words, basic information that helps a cook understand the essence of a dish, how to make its most classic version, and a recipe using the bright, sharp, fresh flavors that characterize our own way of cooking.

Every single recipe and every chapter has been reconceived, revamped, and retested. Yet this new edition will be both reassuringly familiar to longtime *Joy* lovers and more useful and accessible for today's cooks. We have kept Irma Rombauer's original, readable recipe style, indicating each ingredient at the point it is needed in the recipe. But we have been more specific about ingredients: eggs are large, and butter is unsalted and olive oil is extra-virgin where taste is paramount. Each chapter is now a world unto itself, providing explanations, illustrations, and recipes. Information about a recipe appears right in or right next to it, and recipes are free of symbols and cross-references wherever possible. We have kept the line-drawing style of illustration, which shows just what you need to know far more clearly than a photograph can. Every illustration is new, with special emphasis on basic techniques and the tools needed for almost every cooking process.

This *Joy* features a new system of organization within each chapter, beginning with easy recipes and proceeding gradually to more elaborate ones. The chapter on cakes, for instance, starts with one-bowl cakes and moves on to cakes of many parts. Individual techniques are explained where you need them, and explanatory material, formerly spread throughout the book, now appears where it most closely applies. Instructions on how to beat egg whites and sift flour are in the cake chapter; definitions of grains and beans, once in the chapter called Know Your Ingredients, now precede the recipes for grain and bean dishes. You need not read the introductory material to start in cooking.

New chapters reflect the new ways we eat. Today sandwiches, burritos, and pizzas can be the basis of a meal, and so they have their own chapter. So do Little Dishes, those piquant and often grain- or vegetable-based recipes, many of them from other countries like Mexico, China, and Thailand, which used to be thought of as side dishes. Separate chapters are now devoted to Beans and Tofu, Pasta and Noodles, and Grains, which all take a central role in our thinking of what makes a meal. Most of the recipes in the Soups and Salads chapters can be meals in themselves. All these chapters offer the option of using meat as a condiment rather than a main ingredient, in line with today's understanding of healthful eating. (I should also mention that we're particularly proud of the completely new and encyclopedic chapter on meats.)

Concerns about health are reflected everywhere in the book—but not in individual calorie counts or nutritional breakdowns in each recipe. The new chapter on nutrition gives sound and practical advice on healthful diets, and within chapters many reduced-fat alternatives are given. But the overriding concern is how each recipe tastes. People will only come back to food that tastes good: flavorful, wholesome, delicious food is what we have worked to deliver.

There was no way to do all that we have done and fully explore the subjects included in this book without eliminating a few topics found in previous editions. For that reason, we did not include chapters on long keeping, such as canning, preserving, and drying, in order to give everything that *is* included in this one volume all the space it deserves.

With Ethan Becker's enthusiastic support, I turned to scores of top cookbook writers and cooking teachers for help in preparing this edition. For three years we worked intensively with them. Every single writer, researcher, and recipe tester was excited and proud to have a part in a new *Joy of Cooking*—a book that helped reveal to them a world so rich and rewarding that they made it their lives. We can say with pride and awe that we believe the reading of this new edition will be guided by the century's greatest minds in food.

I hope this new edition will excite and inspire a whole new generation of cooks.

Maria Guarnaschelli
Vice President and Senior Editor

I would like to thank a few invaluable people for their tireless support. First I would like to thank Carolyn Reidy, who believed in my ability to do it, supported a revision that took much longer than she thought it would, and who was a vital source of encouragement—a brilliant publisher. I thank Susan Moldow for her caring presence every day; she truly understood the nuances of what it took to get this done and supported my very unconventional way of working. I thank Marah Stets, who has the ability to read my mind; she is objective, ferociously intelligent, fair minded, ever aware of the team, and deeply knowledgeable about food for someone so young. Thanks also to Kate Niedzwiecki, who possesses the true spirit of a team player and is compassionate and meticulous. Theresa Horner has the rare talent of identifying and understanding people's gifts, and brings them out with grace. Kimberly Werner is committed, scrupulous, and perfectionistic; she helped us achieve a vision we could not have without her. I thank M. C. Hald and Olga Leonardo for their dedicated and ever-ready help all along the way. My heartfelt gratitude goes to Beth Wareham, in whose capable, energetic, and dynamic hands *Joy* will soar. I thank Margery Cantor for her graceful and understated design which preserves the spirit of *Joy*. And thanks to Erich Hobbing who sensitively interpreted that design on this coast. Thanks to Paula Scher for modernizing the jacket design while carefully guarding the tradition of *Joy*. My gratitude to Laura Hartman Maestro, whose art is as important to this revision as the text it illustrates. Thanks also to Jacqueline Chwast and David Lance Goines.

I'd also like to thank a few friends and advisers. First thanks to Stephen Schmidt, an author and dear friend on whom I made huge demands—because of his endless generosity he was always there. It is he who kept me in touch with people outside of New York and with the history of American cookbooks and recipes. Molly Stevens is the hardest worker I've ever known. She went out of her way to give every inch of herself to this book, including a trip to Texas for an intensive course on meat. Thanks to Deirdre Davis, who was a vital part of the recipe development process; Didi was there whenever we needed her to test and retest recipes, right until the very end. Sylvia Thompson was our connection to the earth and former *Joys*. I offer my heartfelt thanks to Corby Kummer—devoted friend, trusted critic, and peerless editor. I thank Lynne Rosetto Kasper for her supporting, advising, and mentoring. And thanks to Pat Wells—adviser, trusted friend, and gifted teacher and cook. Special thanks to Nach Waxman for his resourceful help all along the way. I am grateful to Anne Mendelson, Susan Westmoreland, Pam Anderson, and Betty Fussell, who were there to help in the early days of planning the book. I thank Gene Winick and Sam Pinkus and their families for their vital love and support. And I offer my heartfelt thanks to Ethan Becker, whose friendship and insight have meant so much to me these past three years. Finally, my deep thanks go to my mother for teaching me to love food, and to my father for his appreciation of fine food.

There is no way we could ever have conquered a job of this magnitude without the help of many professionals. We owe our heartfelt thanks to a number of people who have given us invaluable help along the way in the form of research and information, recipe development and testing, consultation and editing, copyediting and designing.

Diet, Lifestyle & Health
Marion Nestle

Entertaining
Karen MacNeil

Menus
Mary Gilbert

Coffee, Tea & Hot Chocolate
Helen Gustafson, Corby Kummer

Stocks & Sauces
John Ash

Condiments, Marinades & Dry Rubs
Molly Stevens, Sylvia Thompson

Soups
Amy Cotler

Eggs
Elaine Corn, Margaret Fox

Hors d'Oeuvre
Amy Cotler

Little Dishes
Jody Adams, Samia Ahad, Elizabeth Andoh, Rick and Deann Bayless, Darra Goldstein, Stephen Johnson, Diane M. Kochilas, Stephanie Lyness, Nicole Routhier, Chris Schlesinger, Nina Simonds, Susan Stuck, Patricia Wells, Caroline Wheaton, John Willoughby

Sandwiches, Burritos & Pizzas
Chris Schlesinger, John Willoughby

Salads and Salad Dressings
Chris Schlesinger, John Willoughby

Grains
Nao Hauser, Marie Simmons

Beans & Tofu
Nao Hauser, Dana Jacobi, Marie Simmons

Pasta, Dumplings & Noodles
Bruce Cost, Erica De Mane, Lynne Rossetto Kasper, Nina Simonds

Vegetables
Betty Fussell, Nao Hauser, Deborah Madison

Fruits
Sylvia Thompson

Stuffing
Bruce Aidells, Pam Anderson, Denis Kelley

Shellfish
Arthur Boehm, Ed Brown, Shirley King, Susan Hermann Loomis

Fish
Arthur Boehm, Ed Brown, Shirley King, Susan Hermann Loomis

Poultry
Bruce Aidells, Denis Kelley, Stephen Schmidt, Pam Anderson

Game
John Ash, Janie Hibler

Meat
Bruce Aidells, Denis Kelley, Chris Schlesinger, Molly Stevens, Stephen Schmidt

Yeast Breads
Peter Reinhart, Madge Rosenberg, Nancy Ross Ryan

Quick Breads
Alice Medrich

Pancakes, Waffles, French Toast & Doughnuts
Dorie Greenspan

Cookies
Nancy Baggett

Candy
Lee E. Benning, Carole Bloom, Elaine Gonzalez

Pies & Tarts
Emily Luchetti, Alice Medrich, Stephen Schmidt

American Fruit Desserts
Jim Dodge

Puff Pastry, Strudel & Danish Pastries
Deirdre Davis, Emily Luchetti, Alice Medrich

Cakes, Tortes & Cupcakes and Frostings, Fillings & Glazes
Alice Medrich

Custards, Puddings, Mousses & Dessert Soufflés
Stephen Schmidt

Dessert Sauces
Stephen Schmidt

Cooking Methods
Rick and Deann Bayless, Chris Schlesinger, John Willoughby

Know Your Ingredients
Alice Arndt, Valerie Cipollone, Bruce Cost, Lee Hofstetter, Jennifer Humphries, Marion Nestle, Toby Oksman, Adam Rapoport, Peter Reinhart, Sylvia Thompson, Jonathan White, Marilyn Wilkenson, Virginia Willis

CONSULTANTS/RESEARCHERS
Rick and Deann Bayless, Jack Bishop, Polly Clingerman, Jane Spencer Davis, Betty Fussell, Jessica Harris, Nao Hauser, Mike Hughes, Lynne Rosetto Kasper, Phyllis Kohn, Loni Kuhn, Lori Longbotham, Linda Marino, Anne Mendelson, Russ Parson, Mardee Haidin Regan, Sarah Anne Reynolds, Jon Rowley, Stephen Schmidt, Cort E. Sinnes, Sue Spitler, Molly Stevens, Sylvia Thompson, Patricia Wells

EDITORS
Katherine Alford, Valerie Cipollone, Brian Crawley, Gail Damerow, Deirdre Davis, Susan Derecsky, Jennifer Humphries, Cindy Mushet, Virginia Willis

RECIPE CONTRIBUTORS
Selma Abrams, Rick Bayless, Abigail Johnson Dodge, Eva Forson, Gordon Hamersley, Hallie Harron, Larry Hayden, Joanne Killeen and George Germon, Mildred Kroll, Lori Longbotham, Maricel Presilla, Sue Spitler, Patricia Wells, Jasper White, Lisa Yockelson

TESTERS
Deirdre Allen, Phillip Andres, Brigit Legere Binns, Jean-Marie Brownson, Larry Catanzaro, Val Cipollone, Linda Dann, Deirdre Davis, Jane Davis, Abigail Johnson Dodge, Aurora Esther, Michele Fagerroos, Pat Haley, Melissa Hamilton, William Hay, Kate Hays, Tim Healea, Paula Hogan, Rosemary Howe, Jennifer Humphries, Fran Kennedy, Maya Klein, Virginia Lawrence, Jill Leigh, Karen Levin, Linda Marino, Kathleen McAndrews, Lisa Montenegro, Cindy Mushet, Joyce O'Neill, Suzen O'Rourke, Holly Pearson, Mary Placek, Marion K. Pruitt, Lisa Schumacher, Christopher Stoye, Jill Van Cleave, Laurie Wenk, Carla Williams, Deborah Winson

EDITORIAL ASSISTANTS
Diane Bridgford, Harriot Manley, Hanna McAndrews, Sukey Pett

COPYEDITORS
Annette Corkey, Virginia Croft, Catherine DeLury, Laurel Gillespie, Amy Handy, Mary Hogan Hearle, Jerilee Hundt, Jane Mollman, Jacinta Monniere, Katherine Ness, Barbara Ottenhoff, Susan Stuck, Judith Craig Sutton, Anne Treadwell, Kimberly Werner, Alicia Williams, Cynthia Wortmann

We would also like to thank Adobe Type Corporation for donating the fonts Minion and Penumbra for use in this book, Russell Crowell at NK Graphics, and Mary Kay Dunning at Bernardaud.

JOY
OF
COOKING

DIET, LIFESTYLE & HEALTH

Today, Americans enjoy a greater abundance and variety of food than ever before—more than most other people on earth. Nevertheless, many of our health and nutritional problems arise from unbalanced diets and overeating. We ingest too many calories and too much fat, cholesterol, sugar, and salt and not nearly enough fiber and other protective nutrients. At the same time, our lives have become increasingly sedentary; we drive rather than walk, watch television instead of playing tennis or gardening, park ourselves in front of the computer for hours at a time. This pattern predisposes us to heart disease, cancer, stroke, and diabetes—conditions that together account for nearly half the deaths in this country each year. Scientists may disagree on some of the particulars, but nearly everyone agrees that we could prevent or delay many of these illnesses if we ate more wisely and led more physically active lives.

But what, exactly, does eating wisely entail? As our markets are deluged with thousands of new products every year, we are equally deluged with claims of the miraculous health benefits these products are said to offer. At the same time, we hear conflicting, often sensationalized reports about the supposed dangers of one familiar food after another. How we long for some unimpeachable (but, we would hope, not unduly strict) authority to tell us once and for all what we should and should not eat, and in what quantity and combination!

To begin with, we should remember that the basis of wise eating is not nutrients but *foods,* eaten in a healthful pattern. The diet of much of the world's population is severely limited by poverty and the unavailability of ingredients; many must struggle simply to stay alive. In the United States, our principal concern should be to construct diets that avoid nutritional excesses and restore balance to our nutritional lives. To live in good health, we need proteins, fats, and carbohydrates, as well as more than forty vitamins, minerals, amino acids, and fatty acids. But ingesting too many vitamins and minerals can cause ill effects as surely as does consuming excessive quantities of fat, cholesterol, salt, and sugar.

The secret of a long and healthy life, an aged (and healthy) friend used to assure us, is to choose one's parents well. Good health depends, to a great extent, on genetic endowment—and plain good fortune. But if fortune, as Louis Pasteur reminded us, favors only the prepared mind, it seems likely that it may favor the well-kept body too. We are stuck with our genes, for better or for worse, but we can demonstrably and sometimes dramatically affect our health and well-being by our personal choices about exercise and diet.

The United States government issues official dietary guidelines (occasionally revised as new research becomes available) based on nutritional research. These describe an overall pattern of balanced diet and activity for good health. We are urged to eat a variety of foods; to balance the food we eat with physical activity in order to maintain or improve our weight; to choose a diet with plenty of grain products, vegetables, and fruits; to limit consumption of fats, sugars, and salts; and to drink alcoholic beverages in moderation, if at all. These dietary guidelines can be put into practice by following a Food Guide Pyramid (see below) that illustrates the relative importance of various food groups to the overall diet. The United States Department of Agriculture (USDA) has established five food groups as good sources of important nutrients and has calculated the number and size of servings from each group that its advisers believe must be eaten daily to meet general guidelines for good health, as well as Recommended Dietary Allowances (RDAs) established for specific nutrients. Food plants clearly constitute the foundation of healthful diets, so many servings of grains, vegetables, and fruits should be chosen daily. The dairy and meat groups are also important, but a relatively smaller number of servings is needed every day. At the pyramid's tip are fats and sweets, to be eaten less frequently.

FOOD GUIDE PYRAMID

GUIDE TO DAILY FOOD CHOICES

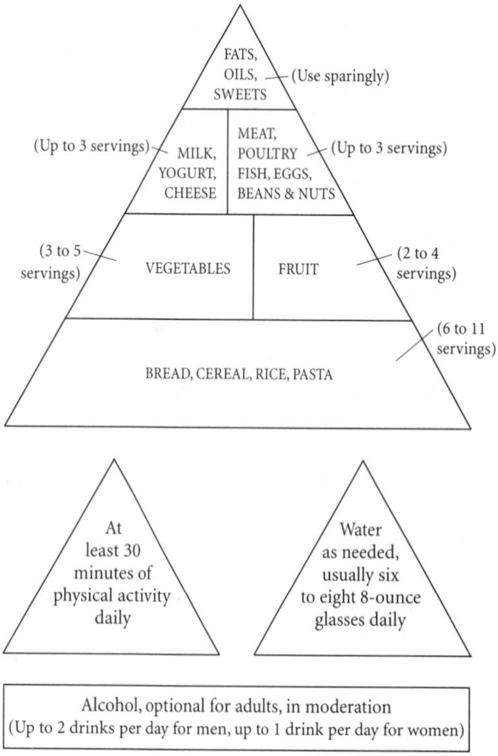

Depending on specific caloric needs, the pyramid recommends a certain number of servings daily of grains, vegetables, fruits, and meat and dairy products. If these recommendations seem unreasonable—who eats 6 to 11 servings of grain a day?—it's only because the USDA doesn't use the term *serving* the way most of us do. According to the agency, a serving of meat or fish weighs 2 to 3 ounces (which could mean one-quarter of a filleted trout or half a fast-food burger); a 1-inch cube of cheese counts as a serving of dairy; a single serving of cold breakfast cereal (a grain) measures 1 ounce. A 6-ounce muffin from the corner deli counts as 6 grain servings, enough for one day—and a 21-ounce restaurant dinner steak adds up to as much meat as most people should probably eat in a week.

It should be noted, however, that not all nutritionists accept the Food Guide Pyramid as gospel. Some critics of the USDA maintain that the recommended servings of meat and dairy products are too high, perhaps because of intense lobbying by the concerned industries. Proponents of the "Mediterranean diet"—based originally on traditional consumption patterns in Greece and southern Italy (where heart disease and related ailments are comparatively rare)—argue for a greater amount of fat, in the form of olive oil, cheese, and yogurt, than the USDA would like and a smaller intake of red meat. To show other healthful ways of eating, Oldways Preservation & Exchange Trust, a nonprofit educational organization based in Cambridge, Massachusetts, has developed alternative pyramids, including Asian, Latin American, and vegetarian.

But most of us don't eat according to charts and pyramids and government regulations. We don't want to take all the fun out of eating, and indeed we shouldn't. What's important is to develop sensible eating habits overall, skewing our diets in the right direction but not panicking over an occasional digression. If a bacon cheeseburger or a wedge of devil's food cake brings us pleasure, we should by all means enjoy it—once in a while. But we should also remember, whether we're eating burgers or barley, that bigger is not necessarily better when it comes to food—that we can usually satisfy cravings with smaller portions than we might be used to, thereby economizing on both cost and calories. If we eat foods that are chosen according to sensible guidelines, handled and cooked properly, and consumed in sensible amounts, all of our nutritional requirements will be met. Most of the portions given in this book are sensible—large enough, but not excessive.

WHAT COUNTS AS A SERVING?*

Grain Products Group (bread, cereal, rice, and pasta)
- 1 slice bread
- 1 ounce ready-to-eat cereal
- ½ cup cooked cereal, rice, or pasta

Vegetable Group
- 1 cup raw leafy vegetables
- ½ cup other vegetables—cooked or raw
- ¾ cup vegetable juice

Fruit Group
- 1 medium apple, banana, or orange
- ½ cup chopped, cooked, or canned fruit
- ¾ cup fruit juice

Milk group (milk, yogurt, and cheese)
- 1 cup milk or yogurt
- 1½ ounces natural cheese
- 2 ounces processed cheese

Meat and Beans Group (meat, poultry, fish, dried beans, eggs, and nuts)
- 2 to 3 ounces cooked lean meat, poultry, or fish
- ½ cup cooked dried beans or 1 egg counts as 1 ounce lean meat; 2 tablespoons peanut butter or ⅓ cup nuts counts as 1 ounce meat

Alcohol
- 12 ounces regular beer
- 5 ounces wine
- 1.5 ounces 80-proof distilled spirits

* Some foods fit into more than one group. Dried beans, peas, and lentils can be counted as servings in either the meat and beans group or the vegetable group. These "crossover" foods can be counted as servings from either one or the other group, but not both. Serving sizes indicated here are those used in the Food Guide Pyramid and are based on both suggested and usually consumed portions necessary to achieve adequate nutrient intake. They differ from serving sizes on the Nutrition Facts label, which reflect portions usually consumed.

(From *The 1995 Dietary Guidelines for Americans,* 4th edition. USDA, USDHHS. HG 232)

On the other hand, nutritious food does not depend on quantifiable factors alone. What some scientists are only just now beginning to acknowledge is that it's not only what we eat that affects our health, but also how we eat—the mood or spirit, the beauty of the table, however simple, and the company with whom we enjoy the food. When the very long-lived, those who reach 90 or 100 in sprightly good health, are interviewed about the "secrets" of their longevity, they often cite (as one recent study put it) "a sense of humor and an active life." To quote our good friend and food writer Patricia Wells, "Several times every day, food offers each of us the promise of short-term happiness. As a source of satisfaction, joy, discovery, and renewal, few daily rituals have such extraordinary potential as the act of preparing and sharing a good meal." This is not to say that we should disregard the counsel of nutritionists and doctors—just that good eating depends as much on factors that cannot be measured in a laboratory.

VEGETARIAN DIETS

Many of the world's populations follow vegetarian diets, usually for religious reasons, or near-vegetarian ones, mandated by the scarcity of meat and other animal products in certain areas. In the United States, people may choose vegetarian diets of varying rigor (some American "vegetarians" happily consume fish and poultry, drawing the line only at the dreaded "red meat") for reasons of religion, philosophy, or health. Some follow a vegan diet, which rules out all animal products, including such vegetarian staples as eggs and cheese. Most vegetarian diets follow healthful dietary patterns and, as long as calories are adequate and food sources vary, are very nutritious. A well-balanced vegetarian diet provides all essential nutrients and is ample in protein. Vegans, however, must find a supplemental source of vitamin B_{12} (fermented soybeans, for example). Vegetarian diets are also appropriate for children as long as they contain enough fats and calories and a sufficient variety of foods to support growth.

FOOD LABELS

Fresh natural foods are nearly always more flavorful than packaged foods, with greater nutritional value. Some packaged products, however, have uses and values of their own (canned tuna is essential, for instance, for salade Niçoise), and almost everybody keeps at least some packaged goods on hand for the sake of convenience. Before buying processed or other packaged foods, read the government-mandated Nutrition Facts information on the label. This lists the percentage and weight of calories, fat, fatty acids, cholesterol, sodium, carbohydrates, fiber, sugar, protein, and some vitamins and minerals, compared with the Daily Values (DV) established by the Food and Drug Administration. A low DV percentage is better for fat, saturated fat, cholesterol, sugar, and sodium, but higher DVs are preferable for fiber, vitamins, and minerals. Bear in mind that the Nutrition Facts are based on diets containing 2,000 or 2,500 calories a day, and the serving sizes reflect those that are reported by national surveys as *usually* consumed. These may be smaller, sometimes much smaller, than what you are served outside the home or are used to eating.

FOOD ADDITIVES

If you read food labels, you'll notice that many processed foods contain various additives. Some, like vitamin C or calcium, make nutritional sense; others, like artificial colors, flavor enhancers, and emulsifiers or other texturizers, are used to mask "cosmetic" deficiencies. Most additives pose no health risks in the small amounts commonly used. As a general rule, the more additives a product contains, the lower its nutritional value. Sugar substitutes such as sorbitol, saccharin, and aspartame, though they may be useful for people who must restrict sugar intake and will do no harm to others in small quantities, provide no nutritional benefit. Keep in mind, too, that products containing artificial sweeteners may still be high in calories from other components.

FOOD ALLERGIES

Many everyday foods—among them milk, wheat, nuts, soy and other beans, fish and shellfish, chicken, corn, citrus fruits, and yeasts—contain proteins that may prove allergenic to a small segment of the population. The only way to avoid allergic reactions in most cases is to define the offending ingredient and then avoid it. Sometimes allergy tests can help with identification, but not always. Compare records of food intake with symptoms. Many allergists recommend an elimination diet that removes suspicious foods one at a time, several days apart, or an addition diet that starts with white rice and adds food one at a time. Once you identify the allergenic food, simply seek out recipes that do not call for it.

FOOD SAFETY

Microbes can be friendly creatures, helping us to make bread, cheese, and alcohol; they can also be very unfriendly, particularly when they release toxins into our meat, poultry, dairy products, even fruit juices, causing uncomfortable reactions, illness, and sometimes death. For the most part, the effects of unfriendly microbes are caused by the improper handling of foods and thus are usually preventable. Microbes are ubiquitous in raw foods, but most are harmless, and nearly all are destroyed by cooking. Remember, though, that microbes proliferate rapidly at room temperature; problems often occur as a result of poor temperature control during production, storage, or preparation. As a basic safety rule, separate raw from cooked foods; keep hot foods hot and cold foods cold; wash your hands, utensils, and cutting boards frequently and thoroughly; and refrigerate leftovers soon after cooking. Please read carefully the specific sections in this book for recommendations on optimum handling and storage conditions for eggs, poultry, and other foods that require special considerations in this regard.

PESTICIDES

Pesticides, insecticides, herbicides, and fungicides are widely used in U.S. agriculture to protect food crops from worms, insects, weeds, or fungi that may affect their quality and their profitability. Most of the produce we buy in the supermarket—virtually everything that isn't labeled "organic"—has been grown with one or more of these agents.

Careful buying and cleaning of produce is clearly important. Whenever practical, buy organic produce—which by definition has been grown without pesticides and their relatives. It is not always cosmetically perfect, but it is free of potentially harmful substances and may even be more flavorful than mass-produced fruit and vegetables.

ABOUT CALORIES

The metabolism of food protein, fat, and carbohydrate produces energy that is measured in kilocalories (kcal), more commonly known as calories. One kcal is the amount of heat needed to raise the temperature of 1 liter (a bit more than a quart) of water 1 degree centigrade. Translated into food values, each gram of protein in food is worth 4 calories; each gram of carbohydrate, 4 calories; and each gram of fat about 9 calories. Alcohol also contributes calories—7 per gram of beer, wine, or spirits. The calories in alcohol, as well as those in pure sugar, are called "empty," however, because these foods have no other nutritional value. Nutrient composition tables give the caloric content of standard portions of food and ingredients (see page 1081). Healthful, balanced diets typically provide 15 to 20 percent of calories from protein, 20 to 30 percent from fat, and 50 to 65 percent from carbohydrates. Most adults require about 2,000 to 3,000 calories each day, depending on weight, musculature, and activity level. Muscle tissue uses more calories than fat tissue, so a heavy, muscular, active man requires more calories than a small, inactive woman. Pregnancy and lactation do not require "eating for two," because they increase caloric requirements by only a small amount.

To maintain ideal body weight, calories consumed must be offset by calories expended. A pound of fat in food, or in our bodies, is worth about 3,500 calories. To lose one pound each week requires a daily deficit of 500 calories, from eating less, being more active, or both. Because fat is highly caloric, eating less of it makes sense. Although this is not a diet book, the fat content of many of our recipes is consistent with health and weight concerns. Be careful, though. A reduced-fat diet will not lead to reduced weight if other foods compensate; many foods advertised as low in fat may be high in calories from carbohydrates. Beware, too, of diet plans that promise quick results from eating unusual combinations of foods or nutrients. No matter what their source, calories are calories, and the only way to lose weight is to eat fewer calories in proportion to your level of activity. Focus instead on the activity side of the weight equation to expend energy, increase the proportion of body muscle to fat, and raise the metabolic rate—all of which ultimately reward those of us who love food by permitting us to eat more without gaining weight. Personal trainers and punishing exertions are not required; walking, cycling, yoga, and dancing, among other pleasurable activities, all count.

ABOUT NUTRIENTS

Very little of what we eat is wasted. Our bodies efficiently use the proteins, fats, and carbohydrates from almost everything we ingest. Digestive enzymes take apart these structures piece by piece, splitting proteins into amino acids, carbohydrates into sugars, fats into fatty acids. We absorb these smaller pieces and reassemble them into our own structures or metabolize them to produce energy. Vitamins and minerals take part in these metabolic processes.

Eating too little or too much of almost any nutrient can be harmful, however. To discover the optimal range for nutrient consumption, look to the government's Recommended Dietary Allowances (RDAs). RDAs refer to nutrients, not food, and are established at deliberately high levels; people with average nutrient requirements can eat much less than the RDAs and still be healthy. The RDAs vary by age, body size, and sex; those for infants and children are lower, and those for adolescents and pregnant and lactating women are higher, than the usual adult standards.

PROTEIN

Protein is essential for its nitrogen and amino acids, which are the building blocks for muscles, skin, connective tissues, and almost every other body part. The chief components of protein are twenty amino acids that are needed to build tissue properly. Of these twenty, eleven are "nonessential," as the body is able to synthesize them on its own; the remaining nine cannot be synthesized and must be ingested regularly. These nine are known as essential amino acids. As important as protein is, however, Americans may consume too much of it. The adult RDA for protein ranges from 50 to 60 grams per day, but many of us consume almost twice that—all too often combined with excessive fat. Even in the leanest cuts of meats, which can offer 50 percent of their calories from protein, the rest of the calories come from fat. Proteins from vegetable sources such as whole grains, nuts, seeds, and legumes can satisfy all of our protein needs without meat consumption at all. International cuisines always contain vegetable protein sources, such as beans, tortillas, rice, tofu, chickpeas, and couscous (to name a few).

FAT

When health authorities encouraged us to reduce our fat intake to an achievable 30 percent of calories or less, they could hardly have imagined that so many Americans would interpret this sensible advice as a call to avoid fat entirely. While Americans consume entirely too much fat, avoiding it altogether is neither beneficial nor desirable. We *must* eat fats (or lipids) to provide our bodies with energy, supply the fatty acids necessary for many of the body's chemical activities, and carry the four fat-soluble vitamins, A, D, E, and K. Finally, fat makes eating more pleasurable—because it usually tastes very good indeed, and because it acts as a hospitable medium for other pleasant flavors.

All food fats are mixtures of saturated, monounsaturated, and polyunsaturated fatty acids, but in different proportions. The fats from meats and dairy foods are highly saturated and are solid at room temperature. The fats from olive oil are largely monounsaturated and are liquid at room temperature but solidify somewhat when refrigerated. The fats from seed oils are largely polyunsaturated and remain liquid even when refrigerated. These distinctions have important implications for health. Diets high in foods containing saturated fats raise levels of cholesterol in the blood and increase the risk for heart disease; they may also increase the risk of certain cancers. In contrast, diets that substitute monounsaturated and polyunsaturated fats for saturated fats reduce blood cholesterol levels. For example, populations that consume olive oil as the principal fat display very low rates of heart disease and cancer. Regardless of type, all food fats are highly caloric and contribute about 120 calories per tablespoon. (Butter actually contains somewhat fewer calories than other fats because of its water content.) Meat, dairy foods, vegetable oils, and table fats are the chief fat sources in American diets. To avoid excess fat, be aware of hidden fat sources and eat fats in small amounts, taking smaller portions of meat and high-fat dairy foods, using table and cooking fats judiciously, and eating more fruits, vegetables, and grains.

CHOLESTEROL

Cholesterol is not, in itself, a bad thing. We need it to form vitamin D, cell membranes, and sex hormones. Our bodies produce it, usually in sufficient quantities for our needs. But we also take in additional cholesterol when we eat animal products—meat and dairy, including eggs. (Cholesterol is produced only by animals, in fact. Those bottles of olive oil and packages of other vegetable products whose labels boast "No Cholesterol!" are a bit of a cheat; to borrow a popular soft drink slogan, "Never had it, never will.") Excess blood cholesterol gets deposited in arteries and can eventually cause blockages. A good way to lower the risk of heart disease is to eat smaller portions of food high in saturated fat, including meat, high-fat dairy products, and processed foods made with animal fats. For reasons we can't fathom, eating saturated fat raises blood cholesterol levels even more than eating cholesterol.

CARBOHYDRATES

At first glance, carbohydrates seem to be found in a bewildering array of foods, from those we tend to consider healthful—fruits, whole grains, pasta, and bread—to those with a less salubrious reputation, like candy or potato chips. Plant-based diets high in complex carbohydrates are linked to low rates of chronic disease. Simple carbohydrates are monosaccharides, occurring in fruits and honey, and disaccharides, such as common table sugar. Complex carbohydrates, or polysaccharides, are starch (present in rice, grains, and beans) and fiber, which is not digested. All digestible carbohydrates perform the important function of providing energy to the brain, muscles, and nervous system in the form of glucose, or blood sugar. If we do not eat enough carbohydrates, muscles and fat break down to form products that we can use to make glucose. Too much carbohydrate is also undesirable; it has fewer calories than fat, but the calories still count. Sugars and corn sweetener provide only empty calories and should be limited in our diets. Our taste preference for sweetness is innate, however, and an occasional dessert or sweet drink in moderation is a fine indulgence.

FIBER

Only food plants provide fiber—the carbohydrate components of leaves, roots, and seeds that cannot be digested by salivary or intestinal enzymes. Fiber adds bulk, absorbs water, and aids elimination from the intestine. Food fiber is classified as soluble or insoluble. Soluble fiber includes pectins and other indigestible starches from fruits, oats, and beans; it helps reduce levels of blood cholesterol and control fluctuations in blood glucose levels. Insoluble fiber comes from the outside layers of wheat and other grains and promotes the health of the digestive tract. Eating more fiber simply means eating more fruits, vegetables, and whole grains.

VITAMINS AND MINERALS

Our bodies require at least thirteen vitamins and sixteen minerals from food for efficient daily operation. Vitamins are classed as fat-soluble (A, D, E, and K) or water-soluble (the various B vitamins and C). Fat-soluble vitamins must be eaten along with fat in order to be absorbed. They can be stored by the body and, if overconsumed, can build up to harmful levels. Water-soluble vitamins dissolve readily in water and so are easily excreted; they must be supplied frequently to the diet, and excessive intake rarely causes problems. Diets that contain a sufficient quantity and variety of foods easily meet our daily requirements for most of the essential minerals. Sodium is a notable exception, in that we often consume much *more* than the small quantity we need, in the form of salt, much of it added to processed foods. Many studies link high blood pressure at least in part to excessive use of salt and recommend moderating its use.

WATER

Water makes up one-half to three-fourths of the body's weight and is indispensable for virtually every body function—digestion, absorption, transportation of nutrients, building tissue, and maintaining temperature. The average adult consumes about 2 to 3 quarts of water a day, in the form of drinking water and other fluids as well as the considerable moisture contained in foods. Under normal circumstances, the amount of water we lose each day through perspiration, expiration of water vapor from the lungs, and elimination of water in urine is easily compensated for by the water we ingest. The best indication (though not an infallible one) of the body's need for water is thirst.

NUTRITIONAL SUPPLEMENTS

All of the nutrients we need are readily available from food. If dietary guidelines are followed properly and foods are eaten in the proper proportions, nutritional supplements should be unnecessary. The one exception concerns vegans, who may need to take a vitamin B_{12} supplement. However, supplements never contain the valuable components of whole foods in their entirety, and an overabundance of any one vitamin, mineral, or other nutrient might do more harm than good.

ABOUT ALCOHOL

Though wine and beer contain trace elements of some nutrients, alcohol's calories are mostly empty. And since alcohol's caloric value is comparatively high—150 calories for a standard 12-ounce beer, 100 calories for a 5-ounce glass of wine or a 1.5-ounce shot of spirits—it's obvious that excessive consumption, whatever else it might do to the body, is a pretty inefficient way of nourishing yourself. Nonetheless, alcohol, like fat and salt and sugar, brings pleasure to the palate, and those who have no compelling medical or behavioral reason to avoid it may enjoy it, in moderation, without guilt. Many studies have pointed out the salutary effects of wine in particular; among other things, it aids digestion and acts as a mild natural sedative. Research also shows that people who drink moderately—on the order of up to one standard drink per day for women and two for men—have a lower risk of heart disease than teetotalers (and those who drink to excess). This benefit does not necessarily outweigh the possible increase in the risk of breast cancer in women who drink even modest amounts of alcohol, however, or the damage to health and society caused by alcohol abuse. If you drink alcohol, do so responsibly. If you don't now drink alcoholic beverages, there is no reason to begin, as the risk of heart disease can be reduced by other healthful habits, such as frequent exercise.

THE FUTURE OF FOOD

The global food environment is changing constantly, affected by factors as diverse as the growing world population, developments in genetic engineering (which may turn out to be boon or bane), the widespread increase in meat consumption (which means, among other things, more precious cropland devoted to the comparatively inefficient raising of animal fodder), the continuing use of drugs on animals to prevent the diseases rampant in feedlots and batteries, and the popularity of seed hybridization, which reduces biological diversity. Agriculture is concentrated more and more in the hands of large corporations, and governments support this trend through water and land subsidies and tax abatements. As a result, we are now able to buy almost any kind of "seasonal" food all year round, and often at very low prices. But there are hidden costs: the impact of the overuse of fertilizers and pesticides on the quality of our land, water, and air; the despoiling of tropical forests and jungles to produce our meat and winter vegetables; and the damage done to the birds, frogs, and pollinating insects with whom we share our ecosystem. New methods of using and conserving land and water are badly needed.

We can look with some relief to the slow but steady increase in interest in organic farming methods; to the proliferation of Integrated Pest Management; to the increasing availability of organically grown produce, meat, and milk; to the growing number of urban farmers' markets; and to the success of cooks, bakers, and food purveyors who use locally and organically produced ingredients skillfully, thus winning over more and more of the general population. Some guarded optimism might be appropriate. But to ensure that these trends continue, as Marion Nestle, professor and chair of Nutrition and Food Studies at New York University, reminds us, every one of us ought to take an active interest in the way our food is produced and processed. Pay attention to proposed legislative changes affecting food labeling, food safety, agricultural production, and the quality of our land, air, and water, and let your legislators know how you feel about them. The political arena is full of lobbyists representing enterprises that would like to weaken regulation or shift the burden of compliance from industry to understaffed agencies. If we are what we eat, we need to do everything we can to protect our precious food resources.

ENTERTAINING

Since the first caveman invited a neighbor to share a haunch of roasted mastodon, there have been hosts and guests. The relationship is a natural and mutually satisfactory one, and over the centuries, human society has made an art out of "having people over"—whether that means offering a hungry traveler a bowl of soup or staging a wedding banquet for a thousand of one's daughter's closest friends. Entertaining guests is an act of friendship and an expression of generosity. It is perhaps our oldest social ritual, and our most universal—but, like everything else, it has changed with the times.

The elaborate entertaining of the past—developed when even middle-class families had servants and heirloom troves of silverware and good china—no longer seems to have much of a place in daily life. As the twenty-first century unfolds, in fact, we're convinced that the two most important elements of successful entertaining are simplicity and creativity. In short, to entertain well, be yourself. Offer your guests the things you both like and can manage well. Do this with a little imagination and a sense of style, remember a few basic rules and you'll be an excellent host.

Above all, don't overdo it. Nothing is more disconcerting to a guest than the impression that his or her presence is causing a household commotion. Confine all noticeable efforts for your guests' comfort and refreshment to the period preceding their arrival. Be prepared but be flexible. Satisfy yourself that you have anticipated every possible emergency—the howling child, your mate's exuberance, your helper's ineptness, your own last-minute qualms—and then relax and enjoy your guests. If, at the last minute, something does happen to upset your well-laid plans, rise to the occasion. A minor catastrophe could be the making of your party. Remember that the poet Horace, back in Roman times, once observed that "a host is like a general; it takes a mishap to reveal his genius."

ABOUT OUTDOOR ENTERTAINING

The backyard barbecue—shades of roasted mastodon!—is perhaps the easiest and most comfortable way we have of entertaining and for that reason might well serve as a model for entertaining of all types. "Come on over for burgers!" we say casually, remembering (at least for the moment) that the elementary urge to welcome guests and feed them well is at the heart of entertaining. As with any entertaining, however, the host should consider the guests' comfort at an outdoor party and anticipate potential problems. What's the weather likely to be? If rain is possible, is there an indoor alternative? If it could be very hot, is there plenty of shade and plenty of drinking water? If swimming is available, does everybody know so that they can come equipped? What protection can you offer against insects if they're likely to be a problem (screened porches, citronella candles, electric "zappers," etc.)? If the affair will go on after dark, are there floodlights, hurricane candles, or some other adequate light sources available? It is expected, of course, that the menu at a barbecue will be simple, but will there be something for the kids to eat (if kids there are) and something for those who might not favor meat? Plastic glasses and utensils and paper plates and napkins are perfectly acceptable, and even preferable if there are small children about (or if the party is poolside, where broken glass or china can mean disaster), but if you'll be serving grown-ups on a terrace or in a screened porch, real glasses, silver, china, and cloth napkins add undeniable flair to the proceedings—even if the food is corn on the cob, hot dogs, and spareribs.

Picnics don't usually count as "entertaining." They're one-on-one affairs (the original picnic, after all, was a jug of wine, a loaf of bread, and thou) or informal family gatherings. But for small groups of people, an excursion to the park or the beach or a handy meadow with baskets of food and drink in hand (or, alternately, a stand-and-nibble "tailgate party" at a sporting event or county fair) can be a delightful affair. Ask yourself the same questions about weather, insects, and so on that you would for a backyard barbecue and leave highly perishable foods at home or carry them in well-chilled coolers (deviled eggs and other dishes with mayonnaise—potato salad included—need to be kept cool). Again, if appropriate, real wine glasses and silverware and such can add elegance to this informal means of entertaining. Because you're not at home (as you would be with a backyard party), it's a good idea to bring along a strictly practical "picnic kit" containing a corkscrew, a small sharp knife, a serving spoon, a can opener, matches, a small salt-and-pepper set, a package of small napkins, tablecloth clips, an oven mitt, a screwdriver, plastic bandages, sunblock, and safety pins.

ABOUT BUFFETS

Buffets are a good choice for large, casual get-togethers when dining-table space is limited. Choose a colorful, varied array of foods and display them on a handsomely appointed table. Make sure you have ample backup portions of everything served, so you can replenish dishes as needed. Cater generously, for guests are apt to take larger portions at buffets. Label any food that isn't easily identifiable with a small tent card placed beside the dish. If you're having more than a dozen guests, set up two identical buffet lines so that guests can serve themselves quickly and still have the chance to sample everything—and make sure that there are cutlery and plates for both lines. If you are low on casseroles or hot plates, restrict the number of hot foods to those you can serve quickly straight from the pot or a hot serving dish or obtain more serving vessels from a party rental company. Everything offered on a buffet should be easily eatable with a fork or with fingers—no knife-cutting required.

ABOUT COCKTAIL PARTIES

The cocktail party is an estimable but endangered social institution. Its demise may be blamed on factors as various as the waning popularity of hard liquor, the regrettable decline of the sibling arts of conversation and flirtation, and the growing acceptance in this country of the European idea that dinner by itself is sufficient diversion for an evening. (The cocktail party, remember, is an American invention.) We steadfastly defend the cocktail party, however, both as an abstract notion and as an uncomplicated and extremely pleasant means of entertaining. And we can't help pointing out that it is also a relatively painless means of entertaining business contacts and of discharging social obligations to those with whom you may not care to share an entire meal.

A good cocktail party begins with good liquors (and wines and beers if you like); "house" brands reflect on the quality of the house. Unless you plan to hire a professional bartender or the number of guests is so small that you or a volunteer guest can handle mixology duties without missing the fun, it's best to serve just one type of cocktail, made up in batches—pitchers of martinis or margaritas, for example. Or simply display exemplars of the four "basic" liquors (Scotch, bourbon, gin, and vodka) with an assortment of appropriate mixes, a bucket of ice, glasses in several sizes, and a long-handled bar spoon, and let guests serve themselves highballs and "rocks" drinks. Mixes aside, there should always be something nonalcoholic available; sparkling mineral water is practically de rigueur these days, and freshly squeezed orange juice is never out of place.

There must always be food at a cocktail party, of course, or the cocktails will quickly overwhelm the party. The food offered need not be complicated, nor even homemade. Pâtés and terrines purchased from a specialty food shop or an assortment of well-chosen cheeses, in either case served with crackers or sliced breads of good quality, are sufficient for an informal gathering. More sophisticated cocktail parties call for elegant hors d'oeuvre or, perhaps, an attractive service of smoked salmon or even caviar. In general, cocktail parties shouldn't last more than two hours, and those two hours should be found somewhere between 5 and 8 P.M.—never later, unless enough food is being served to constitute a light dinner. A shorter cocktail period is appropriate if it is a prelude to another event—a dinner out with the same guests, for instance, or an expedition to the theater. In this case, keep both drinks and food as simple as possible: Champagne and smoked salmon would be perfect.

A variation on the cocktail party, usually specific to the year-end holidays, is the open house. The same basic rules apply, but such an event may run for three to four hours or even more, with the expectation that guests will drop by at their convenience during that period of time but rarely stay more than an hour or so. This means of entertaining is particularly appropriate for busy holiday weekends, for which guests may be expected to have several invitations; it also permits the host to invite a larger number of people than might fit comfortably in the available quarters at one time. Because of the inevitable ebb and flow of guests, passed finger foods are inappropriate to an open house of any size and duration, and food tends to be rather more substantial than at a simple cocktail party. A modified buffet table is more appropriate, probably involving nothing that needs to be kept warm; baked ham, turkey, and a whole poached salmon make attractive and satisfying centerpieces for the array.

ABOUT BRUNCH

The meal we call "brunch" is an easy meal to prepare. Bakery scones, muffins, bagels, and fancy breads are perfectly acceptable—and a good way for beginners to practice their entertaining skills. Brunches may be served buffet style or may more closely resemble a light lunch. Choose your menu carefully, keeping things simple and avoiding complicated egg dishes that might be difficult to prepare for a crowd—individual omelets or eggs Benedict, for example. The popularity at brunchtime of quiche lorraine and such other make-ahead egg-based specialties as frittatas and tortilla Español is understandable. It is customary to serve something alcoholic with brunch, but keep this simple, too; white wine, Champagne (or the combination of Champagne and orange juice known as the Mimosa), or a pitcher of Bloody Marys or Screwdrivers will usually be sufficient.

ABOUT LUNCH

Lunch is another endangered institution in the United States. Businessmen and businesswomen boast about "brown bagging" as an indication of their professional dedication; stay-at-home moms and dads are too busy with children, volunteer work, and exercise programs—and are probably on diets anyway. Students and young professionals, alas, seem to prefer fast food to real food. This is a pity, because the sit-down lunch, even when it's light and simple, is an immensely civilized respite from the rigors of the day. The basic rules governing table settings, seating, and serving for a sit-down dinner party, 11, apply, but a modern lunch should rarely have more than three courses (a modest appetizer, a straightforward main course, and perhaps a light dessert), and two will frequently suffice. Multi-ingredient salads, medium-bodied soups (hot or cold), and unelaborate fish or fowl dishes are suitable luncheon dishes, and elegant sandwiches are not to be eschewed. Alcoholic beverages are usually less appropriate at lunch than at dinner for a variety of reasons, but a token quantity of white or light red wine, depending on the food served, should be offered in most cases. On occasion, particularly over holiday periods when no one has work to do in the afternoon, a full-scale "serious" lunch might be enjoyed. This is basically a sit-down dinner held during daylight hours, and sit-down dinner rules apply, for the menu as for all else. If eating and drinking seriously at lunchtime seems decadent, incidentally, take solace in the fact that doctors and nutritionists agree that it's much healthier to dine well during the day than shortly before retiring for the night.

ABOUT AFTERNOON TEA

Like the sit-down luncheon, the tea party might seem to some to be unsuited to the modern world—too time-consuming, with too much of an air of the raised pinkie about it. The truth is, though, that offering guests a well-brewed pot of tea is almost as easy as pouring them mugs of coffee. And tea complements a wide range of accompanying snacks—the traditional scones, to be sure, but also any kind of quick bread, muffins, or cookies (especially rolled and icebox cookies) or buttered, simply filled sandwiches on crustless, thin-sliced bread. A proper afternoon tea is served between 4 and 6 P.M. Set a tea table as you would a buffet table, putting out cups on their saucers and teaspoons to one side, along with small cloth napkins. No other silverware should be necessary, unless you are serving jam, butter, or clotted cream to accompany scones or other baked goods. This may be the time to present butter molded into attractive designs. If you are offering a wide variety of foods, also set butter plates. It is more elegant to arrange tea cakes and sandwiches on small plates than on large serving platters. At an informal tea party, the host pours the tea, adjusting its strength to each guest's taste with hot water from a second pot. At a more formal tea, the guest of honor "does the honors."

ABOUT DINNER PARTIES

The most traditional form of entertaining, and to our mind the most satisfying, is the sit-down dinner party. At good dinner parties, conversation flourishes, friendships are forged or reinforced, and good food and drink can be appreciated and discussed. In no other form of entertaining does the host so unequivocally display respect for the guests and convivial concern for their welfare. It has been said that the ideal number at the dinner table is somewhere between the Three Graces and the Eight Muses; we find that the most easily managed and successful number of guests is between six and eight—enough to encourage social intercourse in numerous configurations but not so many that conversation turns to din. Select friends you think will genuinely enjoy each other, whether or not they've ever met. Written invitations are always preferable, as they make guests feel honored even in advance—but the telephone is far more common today and is perfectly acceptable. Invitations to a dinner party should go out two to three weeks in advance; for a party on or near a major holiday (the Fourth of July or Christmas, for instance), send invitations at least a month ahead of time.

ABOUT THE MENU

If you are cooking the meal yourself, remember these two important rules: Choose food that can be prepared ahead of time, so that you can spend more time at the table than over the stove, and never, ever, make a dish for company that you haven't made before and mastered. Beyond that, let common sense prevail: Plan enough courses to show that you've gone to some trouble, but not so many that guests will feel overwhelmed. Offer a varied but coherent and well-balanced progression of dishes, considering the colors, textures, and flavors of each one and how they will fit together. Let the menu reflect the climate, serving lighter dishes in hot weather and heartier ones when it's cold. Follow the seasons, buying what's best and freshest in the markets. Unless you know your guests' food preferences well, avoid daunting animal parts or overly spicy foods; inquire discreetly about food allergies or vegetarian tendencies if you think it's appropriate. Don't be afraid to serve guests what you like to eat yourself. Serving something you enjoy, and are confident making, is part of sharing yourself—even if that something is only meat loaf or spaghetti and meatballs. It is also perfectly acceptable to serve at least some prepared food bought from an outside source. The French think nothing of stopping at a *traiteur* for a pâté or some lobster in aspic as a first course or at a *pâtisserie* for a strawberry tart or a gâteau Saint-Honoré for dessert—and there's no reason why we shouldn't import a big platter of appetizers from a good gourmet store or a spectacular chocolate cake from a favorite bakery. And no guest has ever been known to object to a serving of top-quality store-bought ice cream and cookies. One of the best hosts we know has a ready answer if a guest asks, "Did you make this?" She replies, "I made it possible."

ABOUT TABLE SETTINGS

An inviting table is as important to a successful dinner as inviting food. Table decorations can be as natural or whimsical as you like, but make sure they don't interfere with the passing of serving dishes or block guests' views of one another—and remember that they should be suited in color and scale to the foods served. Don't make the effects so stagey that your guests' reaction is "You went to a lot of trouble." Make them say, rather, "You had a lot of fun doing it!"

Flowers should have no detectable scent, and neither should you; heavy perfumes of any kind fight with the flavors of the food. Arrange flowers in small bouquets or consider floating rosebuds or other flowers in shallow bowls or custard cups. (It's a good idea to have an empty vase or two on hand in case guests bring flowers with them, as guests are wont to do. Such flowers needn't go on the dinner table but can be placed on the sideboard or in the living room.) Nothing helps establish a romantic or elegant mood at the dinner table more than candlelight. Buy dripless, unscented candles (beeswax produces particularly lovely light) and make sure that the height of the candle flame is either below or substantially above the eye level of seated guests.

An attractive tablecloth adds graciousness to any dinner party, although for casual dinners, cloth or rush placemats look good on a wood table (preferably newly polished with odorless wax). Cotton or linen napkins are essential for a formal dinner party; polyester and other artificial fabrics are less absorbent and unpleasant to the touch. Fanciful napkin folding is best left to restaurants. Even at the most formal dinners, napkins should be simply folded into quarters and then in half into rectangles. The exposed corners face the bottom left, making it easy for the seated diner to pick up the napkin by one corner, let it drop and unfold completely, and place it on his or her lap. A napkin folded into quarters and then in half to form a triangle is also simple and elegant; the corners should be placed facing the guest on top of the plate, unless a plated first course is waiting at each plate. Napkin rings are fine for everyday use but are out of place at a formal dinner party. Small, elegant salt and pepper shakers should be placed on the table—one set for every four to six guests. Saltcellars are often considered even more elegant; these are tiny, shallow, open bowls filled with salt to be pinched up with the fingers or transported from bowl to food with miniature spoons.

At formal dinners, there is always a plate in front of every guest. When diners are seated, each place should be set with a service plate—a decorative plate larger than the dinner plates. (In order to ensure that each guest has sufficient elbowroom, there should be at least thirty inches from the center of one service plate to the center of the next.) The service plate usually remains on the table for the first course or two; the appetizer plate and soup bowl are set on top of it. The service plate is always removed before the main course, which should be served on hot plates (unless, of course, it's a cold summertime entrée such as poached salmon or cold roast beef). The dinner plates from your "good" china can be used as service plates, and those from your everyday china, which might better withstand heating, used for dinner. To heat dinner plates, place them on the rack in a 175°F oven for about 15 minutes, then remove them with a potholder. The drying cycle of a dishwasher will also heat plates, or you can simply run them under hot tap water and dry them just before serving. Traditionally the plates for any one course match each other, no matter how many patterns and kinds of plates appear throughout the meal—but confident hosts freely mix patterns even at the same course.

Most soups should be served in wide, shallow bowls with broad rims. Consommés and cream soups, however, are classically presented in small, deep bowls, like two-handled teacups; the soup may be sipped directly from the bowl. Salad plates and cups and saucers are never set in advance; they are brought to the table as needed. Some Europeans maintain that butter plates have no place at formal dinners and that bread—usually in the form of hard-crusted rolls to be eaten unbuttered—should be placed directly on the tablecloth to the left of the plate. If you wish to serve butter, as many hosts do, then set butter plates at the upper left of each place setting. Finger bowls may seem like an archaic affectation today, but they will be much appreciated if you're serving foods meant to be eaten with the fingers. These are shallow, rimless glass or silver bowls filled with tepid water in which floats a lemon slice (traditional if seafood is being served), a scented geranium leaf or rose petal, or a sprig of fragrant herb. Guests dip only their fingertips into the water, then dab them dry with their napkins. Finger bowls are often brought to the table on top of the dessert plates, with the dessert fork and spoon resting on the plate on either side of the bowl; the guest places the fork and spoon to either side of the plate and puts the finger bowl opposite the water glass, to the upper left. Or finger bowls may be set, on a saucer or not, to the left of each diner's plate after the appropriate course has been cleared.

As is usual in the much maligned art of etiquette, practicality guides both host and guest in both the setting and the use of silverware. The simple rule is to work from the outside in. As each course is finished, the accompanying silverware is removed, and the guest may be confident in using the implement(s) now found on the outside. The table setting for a simple meal of knife-and-fork appetizer and main course is shown below. (Europeans often set forks with the tines facing down; if your silver is handsomer face down than up, feel free to expose that side. The French also sometimes add to each setting a *porte-couteau* or knife rest—a small bar, usually of glass or silver, on which the blade of a sauce-streaked knife may be propped; these can be handsome but are archaic and unneces-

Table setting for a simple meal of knife-and-fork appetizer and main course

Table setting for a meal that includes soup and dessert

sary if cutlery is to be changed with each course.) Add soup and dessert to the menu, and you'll need a soup-spoon and a fork or spoon or both, depending on the dessert, arranged as shown above. (If you're using both, the fork points right, the spoon left.)

Seafood forks are placed on the right, outside the knife.

Other than dessert utensils positioned above the plate, forks are placed to the left of the plate and knives (with the knife blade facing inward) and spoons to the right—with these exceptions: seafood forks (for clams, oysters, etc., not fish forks) are placed on the right, outside the knife, shown above. When no knife is set, the fork goes on the right by itself (for instance, in

When no knife is set, as for pie and coffee, the fork goes on the right inside the spoon.

Beverage spoons are placed to the right of all other implements. Small coffee spoons, however, should rest on the demitasse saucer.

the setting for a chopped luncheon salad) or on the right inside the spoon (as for a piece of pie with a cup of coffee, shown below, left). Beverage spoons, like those for iced tea, are placed to the right of all other implements, shown above. Coffee spoons belong on the far right, too, except the small ones served with demitasse or espresso cups and saucers, which should rest on the saucer itself, shown above. If you're setting a butter plate, and have butter knives, these should be placed on each butter plate in a position mimicking that of the main-course knife, shown below. (If you don't set butter knives, it is perfectly acceptable for guests to use their main-course knives for butter.) Steak knives may be set with steaks, chops, racks of meat, and certain game birds whose flesh might be difficult to cut, but these should be in addition to the regular setting, not a replacement for the main-course knife. The classic rule is to set no more silverware beside each plate than is required for three courses (plus dessert silverware above the plate, if appropriate). If four or more savory courses are to be served, the host should set new silverware after the first three.

Butter knives should be placed on each butter plate in a position mimicking that of the main-course knife.

If you have fish forks and knives—the former squat, thick tined, and tridentlike, the latter assuming a sort of elegant, elongated trowel shape—by all means set them for any fish course. The configuration of the knife blade makes the implement suitable for filleting small fish at the table, if they're served on the bone. In the absence of these items, however, salad forks and luncheon knives are more than adequate substitutes. Elegant French restaurants often set sauce spoons, which look rather like soup spoons with their bowls nearly flattened out, to enable diners to genteelly scoop up sauce from the plate (instead of mopping it up ungenteelly, for instance, with bread); these are rarely used at home, but again, if you have them (and are serving a sauced dish), set them. The ultimate rule for cutlery, however, is to use what you have. A guest, we presume, would rather be invited to share dinner with you now than wait until you fill out your set of silver.

If you are serving Asian-style rice or noodle dishes, you may wish to set chopsticks—the tools with which several billion of the world's citizens eat their daily fare. Unless you are serving a group of known specialists, these should be set in addition to, not instead of, other tableware; although eating with chopsticks is not difficult, below, it does take a bit of practice, and some guests may wish to stick with more familiar means of transporting food from plate to mouth. If chopsticks are set, they should be placed to the right of the outermost spoon in the table setting. Do not set cheap paper-wrapped wooden chopsticks at a sit-down dinner, though these would be acceptable for a casual lunch. Unwrapped chopsticks are placed side by side, usually with their tips slightly elevated on a small rest (similar to a *porte-couteau*). Although the two are identical in shape and size, each of the chopsticks has its own function: the lower one remains stationary, while the upper one is pressed against the lower, moving up and down to complete a tonglike action to grasp the food. To eat with chopsticks, hold them by the upper portion (often squared off but always thicker than the tip), placing the lower stick in the crease of the thumb,

Place the lower chopstick in the crease of the thumb and brace it firmly against the ring finger.

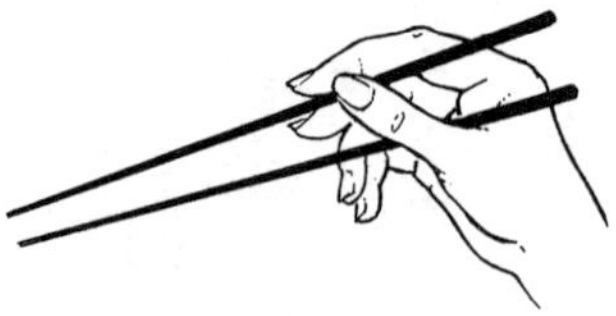

Position the upper stick as you would hold a pencil.

shown below left, with the lower end of the chopstick braced firmly against the soft inner surface of the last joint of the ring finger as shown. Then position the upper stick much as you would hold a pencil, with the point of the stick approximately even with the lower stick when pressed together at the point, shown above. For westerners, these tools automatically bring at first a leisured pace of consumption, and it is a comfort to know that in eating rice and noodles, it is not bad form to bring the bowl up just under the chin—a maneuver that facilitates matters greatly for the uninitiated.

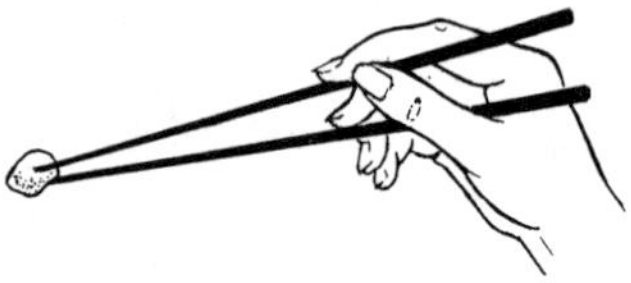

When pressed together the points of the two chopsticks should be approximately even.

This is perhaps the place to mention that some foods may be eaten—*demand* to be eaten—with nothing more than the utensils we were born with: our fingers. It is perfectly acceptable, even in the most formal circumstances, for instance, to pick up chicken legs and pieces of small birds such as squab or quail. Corn on the cob, spareribs, clams and oysters on the half shell, and crab and lobster still in their shells are also appropriate finger fare. If asparagus is served without sauce, it may be picked up; with sauce, a fork and knife is neater. Eat fruit with your hands unless a fork and fruit knife are set.

Separate glasses for white and red wine dress up a table setting but are hardly essential. A good-sized wine glass with a rounded or slightly elongated bowl is fine for both. Clear, long-stemmed glasses, uncut or etched, are best. Water glasses should hold more than wine glasses and are usually of a different shape. Both wine and water glasses are set before the meal; no more than three wine glasses should be positioned at the same time, no matter how many wines are being served. The wine glass to be used during the main course should be

Wine and water glasses are placed on a northwestern to southeastern diagonal, with the main-course wine glass about a half inch above the point of the main-course knife.

The water goblet is placed above all the wine glasses, closest to the inside of the table.

placed about a half inch above the point of the main-course knife. All other wine glasses are then placed on a northwestern to southeastern diagonal from this point, according to when they will be used, shown above. (Wine is poured from the right, directly into the glass.) Wine baskets can be handsome objects but serve no practical purpose; wine coasters, on the other hand, help keep dribbles of red wine from embellishing the tablecloth. The water goblet is placed above all the wine glasses, closest to the inside of the table, shown above right. If you are setting a tall tumbler for iced tea, lemonade, or another beverage in place of wine, place it where the main-course wine glass would have gone.

ABOUT SEATING AND SERVING

Experienced hosts swear that the key to a successful dinner party is the seating. Think which friends might share similar hobbies or professions (but let them discover these, rather than using that surefire conversation-stopper, "I know you'll have lots to talk about"). Spouses should be seated apart, unless it's a family occasion. Although "boy-girl-boy-girl" is one of the first seating rules everybody learns, strict alternation of men and women is often impossible—and may be impractical if you want to match guests with similar interests. Tradition holds that the guest of honor, if female, sits to the right of the host, or, if male, sits to the left of the hostess. Further, it is said, at a formal dinner party hosted by a woman with a woman guest of honor, the two women sit at opposite ends of the table; the same rule applies to two men. These directions may be taken with the proverbial grain of salt. When an English writer friend of ours was invited to Sandringham Castle for dinner with the Prince of Wales not long ago, he was startled (and ultimately charmed) to find that the prince himself assumed a seat in the very middle of one side of the long table, making himself available for conversation with as many guests as possible. Place cards are helpful at a dinner of more than eight or ten. They go directly atop the napkin if it is centered on the plate or just above the plate and in the center of the place setting if it is not. The hosts do not have place cards. If the party is small, simply indicate where each guest will sit. Clear place cards with the first course so guests aren't left wondering what to do with them, unless you're hosting a large party with guests unknown to one another—in which case they may be left on the table to ease mutual identification.

Styles of serving food have evolved over the centuries, but in the dining rooms of the Western world today, these fall into two main categories. Historically, so-called French service was a version of what we might consider family style: many dishes of food were put in the middle of the table, and it was up to the person nearest each serving dish to see that the guests around him got a bit of whatever they wanted. (No one tasted everything; there were too many dishes.) In the middle of the nineteenth century, a new style of service came into fashion in Paris. Introduced to Parisians at the Russian embassy, it came to be called Russian service: food was arranged on individual plates in the kitchen, and everyone was offered the same amount of the same food.

For most modern dinner parties, a combination of several types of service might be appropriate. Intricate appetizers might be plated in the kitchen, for instance, and platters of roasted meat passed around the table either by servers or by the guests themselves. In addition, certain courses might be arranged on a sideboard for buffet service. This is particularly appropriate for mixed appetizer courses or for assorted desserts. If you are an accomplished carver, consider practicing your art at the table, impressing your guests with your deftness and offering each one the cut he or she prefers. On the other hand, if you don't want your guests to see you wrestle with a turkey or a leg of lamb, carve safely out of sight and quickly bring the platter to the table. Unless the food was first plated, seconds are always offered, with each dish served the same way it was the first time. With any method of service, guests ask for the salt, pepper, or any sauce or condiment they require, all of which are left on the table; the person closest to the desired object passes it, choosing a route by which it will pass through the fewest hands possible.

When dinner is done, clear no more than two plates at a time, scraping and stacking out of view of guests. Resist the urge to do any extensive cleaning up while your guests are still present; your job (and your pleasure) as host is to spend as much time as possible with your friends. Resist, as well, the kind of good-intentioned rush to help that often turns a dinner's aftermath into a volunteer free-for-all. On the other hand, cohosts may share preliminary clean-up duties, and there's nothing wrong with accepting an unobtrusive dependable assist from one good friend who knows his or her way around the house and is cooperatively disposed. In general, though, the more people who remain at the table at meal's end the better—and that includes you.

Before dessert is served, clear all plates, serving dishes, and condiments, including salt and pepper, from the table, and brush off crumbs with a tightly folded clean napkin. Set dessert plates if you are using them. It is the American custom to take coffee or tea with dessert, though the European practice is to offer them afterward, accompanied perhaps by chocolate truffles or amaretti. Coffee and tea, like all drinks, are poured from the right, and cream and sugar are offered from the left; if the creamer and sugar bowl have been placed on the table, they are passed counterclockwise. Invite guests to have after-dinner beverages in the living room, if you wish. Often, though, the conversation is at its best and most expansive during and after dessert, and guests would rather stay at the table. The Spanish even have an admiring term for this portion of the dinner party—the *sobremesa* or "over the table"; it is widely reckoned on the Iberian peninsula to be the best part of the meal. At this point in the evening, in whatever room the party has settled, hostly duties now taper off, limited to refilling guests' cups or liqueur glasses. For the host, these are the best moments of the evening.

A FINAL NOTE

We've been to small dinner parties at which at least half a dozen of the rules and recommendations offered above were blithely disregarded—and everybody had a wonderful time. We can offer reasoned counsels and repeat the lessons of experience and tradition, but the truth is that if the table is attractive and clean, the food and drink honest and good, the company amiable and interesting, and the host generous and calm, an affair can be a resounding success no matter where the glasses go or who is sitting where. And that is our last word on entertaining.

MENUS

Combining dishes in a single meal is planning a menu—and in doing so we like to recall the aphorism of the great French gastronome Brillat-Savarin: *Menu malfait, diner perdu*—"A badly made menu means a lost dinner." The best meals, whether simple or elaborate, are built on principles of harmony, flow, and balance. In planning a meal, first consider the season, the climate, the time of day, and, of course, the likely likes and dislikes of those at table. When entertaining people whose tastes one does not know, it is not a bad idea to consider familiar foods that almost everyone loves.

THE CHEESE COURSE

Cheese has been eaten as a snack or as part of a light meal all over Europe since the days of the ancient Greeks—but the presentation of a formal cheese course at the end of a meal, before or instead of dessert, is a French notion of relatively recent vintage, adopted widely by other Europeans, but never as popular in America as perhaps it should be. Cheese, being salty to a greater or lesser degree but also usually possessing a certain milky sweetness, makes an ideal bridge between savory and sweet courses. It is also richly satisfying enough to stand on its own as the coda to a good dinner. The French believe, with scientific evidence to back them up, that cheese contains beneficial enzymes and bacteria that aid in digestion—and even that much of its fat content remains unabsorbed by the body, so that it is not as nutritionally daunting as it might look. The best reason to eat cheese, of course, after dinner or any other time, is simply that it is one of our most delicious foods. To do it justice at the table, follow these simple guidelines.

Selection: The cheese tray at a good French restaurant is a thing of wonder, commonly displaying twenty to thirty perfectly ripened specimens, from tiny cork-shaped fresh goat cheeses to runny wedges of Brie to huge slabs of Cantal or Beaufort the color of old ivory. Even if you could reproduce such an array at home, you wouldn't want to, any more than you'd put a dozen different wines on the table and expect your guests to choose between them. An ideal home "cheese tray" should include no more than three or four cheeses. Generally, these should be of different types: for instance, one fresh goat cheese; one soft fermented cheese (Brie, Camembert, Pont-l'Évêque, etc.—the rind, incidentally, is edible); one blue-veined cheese (the classics are Roquefort from France, Gorgonzola from Italy, and Stilton from England, but there are many others, including a splendid American example called Maytag Blue); and one firm cheese (farmhouse Cheddar, caerphilly, good-quality provolone, Gruyère, Gouda, Manchego, etc.). If your guests are cheese connoisseurs, you might want to try a comparative tasting—three goat cheeses, or three blues, or perhaps a selection of cheddars from England, Vermont, Wisconsin, and California. Alternately, a single perfect cheese may be served: irregular chunks of crumbly Parmigiano-Reggiano, for example, or a ripe whole Brie, or a cylinder of Stilton soft enough to be scooped out with a spoon.

Accompaniment: The one essential accompaniment to cheese at the end of a meal is an offering of bread or crackers, served on a separate tray. This can be simply good French bread or a country-style loaf; thick slices of toasted whole grain bread or pumpernickel; slices of walnut or homemade raisin bread (as is served in many good French restaurants); an array of good-quality commercially made crackers (the bland English round ones called water biscuits are good with blues and other strong cheeses); or that great British favorite, the thin, crisp oat-based crackers called oatcakes. Softened butter should always be served with a cheese course, though true cheese connoisseurs rarely use it. Fruit marries well with cheese, and a bowl of assorted apples, pears, and grapes would be appropriate with the cheese after a casual meal—though a few small wedges of apple on each plate might be more appropriate for a more formal dinner. Dried fruits, especially figs, go nicely with cheese, too. Walnuts and even roasted chestnuts are other possible accompaniments, and the English sometimes serve pale inner stalks of celery with Stilton or Cheddar.

Utensils: Although Parmigiano-Reggiano may be picked up in the fingers and nibbled after informal Italian meals, a small knife is proper for almost every other kind of cheese. Butter knives are inappropriate unless you're serving nothing but fresh and/or very ripe soft cheeses; if you don't have smaller versions of your dinner knives, use the dinner knives themselves. Cheese is nearly always spread or placed on bread or crackers, but you may want to offer diners small forks so that they have the option of eating bits of cheese by themselves.

Wines: The art of matching wine and cheese is an arcane one, and some connoisseurs go to great pains (or, perhaps one should say, pleasures) sampling various combinations in search of perfect mates. Suffice it to say that, though red wine is the traditional accompaniment to cheese (the cheese course may have been invented in the first place to use up red wine left over from the main course), white wine goes very well with certain kinds—fresh goat cheese, for instance—and sweet wines often complement blue cheeses and other strong cheeses. The French sometimes drink Sauternes with Roquefort, for example, and the British favor port with Stilton.

Ripeness and Serving Temperature: An Englishman of our acquaintance used to maintain that there were three stages of maturity for brie: firm, soft, and "Quick, Mabel, it's heading out the door!" In fact, there is a perfect point of ripeness (or rather there are several perfect points, depending on individual taste) for every cheese, and the watchful storage of cheese until it reaches its optimum condition—which the French call *affinage,* or refining—is a complicated art. Unless you train yourself to become a specialist, we recommend finding and cultivating a good cheese merchant, and, for company at least, buying cheeses that are ready to eat. Unless you're going to serve it the day you buy it, cheese should be stored, loosely wrapped, in the refrigerator. But cheese should always be removed from cold storage at least 3 hours before being served; cold cheese is wasted cheese, deprived of much of its flavor and aroma.

HOLIDAY

Thanksgiving

Stuffed Celery, 151
Crudités, 161
Oyster Stew, 112, **or**
Butternut Squash Soup, 94, **or**
Mushroom Soup, 96
Roasted Turkey, 614, with Miles Standish Stuffing, 484, and Giblet Gravy, 614, **or**
Roasted Stuffed Chicken or Capon, 581, **or**
Steamed Lobster, 512
Pan-Fried Golden Potatoes with Rosemary and Lemon, 409
Mashed Sweet Potatoes, 427
Maple Glazed Parsnips, 394
Green Beans with Sautéed Mushrooms, 345
Creamed Onions, 391
Chestnut Puree, 366
Whole Cranberry Relish, 64
Golden Glow Gelatin Salad, 233
Tart Green Salad, 207
Parker House Rolls, 750
Chocolate Pecan Pie, 889
Mince Pie, 877
Fresh Ginger Cake, 935
Indian Pudding, 1024
Pumpkin Cheesecake, 983
Pears in Red Wine, 475

Christmas

Gravlax, 563, **or**
Oysters on the half shell with Mignonette Sauce, 506
Make-Ahead Goat Cheese and Walnut Soufflés, 139
Slow-Roasted Beef Rib Roast, 649, with Yorkshire Pudding, 787, **or**
Baked Ham, 706, with Orange Molasses Glaze, 90, **or**
Roasted Stuffed Goose with Giblet Gravy, 622, and Mashed Potato Stuffing, 485, **or**
Roasted Whole Salmon, 552
Grated Butternut Squash Gratin, 425, **or**
Celery Root and Potato Gratin, 363
Roasted Radicchio, 375
Brussels Sprouts Cockaigne, 353
Barley and Mushroom "Risotto," 246
Mixed Greens with Cheese Crisp, 208
Vienna Rolls, 752
Ginger Crème Brûlée, 1018
Plum Pudding, 1026
Trifle, 966
Cranberry Crunch, 901
Kourambiedes, 832
Mexican Wedding Cakes, 832
Mother Kroll's Lebkuchen, 820
Bourbon Balls, 841

Kwanzaa

Georgia Peanut Soup, 103
Doro Wat, 601, with Basic Cooked White Rice, 255, **or**
Caribbean Callaloo, 114, **or**
Grill-Smoked Jamaican Jerk Chicken, 610
Sautéed Okra with Roasted Red Peppers, 388
Kale with Bacon, 379
Portobello Pizzas, 385
Basic Rolled Biscuits, 789
Sweet Potato Pudding, 888
Benne Seed Wafers, 831
Rich Rolled Sugar Cookies, 827
Gingerbread People, 828

New Year's Eve

Caviar, 174, **or**
Salmon Pâté, 161
Fettuccine Alfredo, 310
Pan-Seared Duck Breasts with Fig and Red Wine Sauce, 621
Roasted Jerusalem Artichokes, 378
Spinach with Currants and Pine Nuts, 416
Creamy Leeks, 382
Broiled Mushroom Caps, 385
Endive and Walnut Salad, 211
Baked Alaska, 965
Individual Molten Chocolate Cakes, 960
Grand Marnier Soufflé, 1034
Basic Angel Cake, 952

Easter

Deviled Eggs, 126
Creamy Cucumber Gelatin Salad, 233
Cream of Asparagus Soup, 96, **or**
Tuscan-Style Stuffed Artichokes, 341
Roasted Loin of Lamb, 714, **or**
Baked Ham, 706, **or**
Spicy Maple Roasted Quail, 628, **or**
Roasted Whole Blackfish, Grouper, or Other Fish with Mediterranean Flavors, 552
Sautéed Tiny New Potatoes, 412
Braised Peas, 396
Pea, Pea-Pod, and Pea Shoot Salad, 219
Joined Finger Rolls, 750
Banana Brown Betty, 902
Chocolate Marble Cake, 942
Coeurs à la Crème, 454
Almond Torte Cockaigne, 959

Passover

Matzo Ball Soup, 107, **or**
Gefilte Fish, 564
Sweet & Sour Brisket, 675, with Tzimmis with Potato Knaidle, 676, **or**
Roasted Chicken with Herbs and Garlic, 580
Cold Asparagus Salad wtih Sesame Seeds, 219, **or**
Sicilian Salad, 220
Passover Nut Sponge Cake, 947
Strawberries Romanoff, 454

SPECIAL MENUS

Wedding Buffet

Smoked Trout Canapés with Horseradish Cream, 148
Pesto Cheesecake, 149
Baked Honey Shrimp, 154
Anchovy Toasts, 162
Stuffed Dates, 463
Vichyssoise, 103
Stuffed Butterflied Filet or Tenderloin of Beef, 653
Roasted Monkfish with Garlic and Herbs, 552
Spicy Peanut Sesame Noodles, 326
Couscous Salad with Pine Nuts and Raisins, 227
Roasted Asparagus, 343

Sautéed Cherry Tomatoes, 432
Green Beans with Slivered Almonds, 345
Gratin Dauphinois, 412
Cheese Course, 17, with Grapes and Pears
Three-Tier White Wedding Cake, 975
Chocolate-Covered Strawberries, 455
Lemon Curd Bars Cockaigne, 819
Candied Citrus Peel, 461
White Jordan Almonds

Barbecue

Pulled Pork Sandwiches, 693
Barbecued Spareribs, 701
Country-Style Ribs Baked in Barbecue Sauce, 701
Cole Slaw, 222
American Potato Salad, 220
Black Bean, Corn, and Tomato Salad, 224
Hushpuppies, 780
Tart Corn Relish, 65, **or**
Chow-Chow, 63
Southern Corn Bread, 777
Buttermilk Biscuits, 790
Chess Pie, 889
Peach Pie, 875
Chocolate Sheet Cake, 932

Picnic

Hard-Boiled Eggs, 125
Fried Chicken, 601
Tabbouleh, 227
Penne Salad with Feta and Olives, 226
Three-Bean Salad, 224
Fresh Fruit Cup or Fruit Salad, 443
Brownies Cockaigne, 816
Oatmeal Chocolate Chip Cookies, 821

VEGETARIAN SIDE- AND MAIN-COURSE IDEAS

Fresh Corn Chowder, 110
Cold Avocado Soup, 95
Tuscan Bread and Tomato Soup, 98
Roasted Red Pepper Soup, 98

Brown Rice and Tofu Salad with Orange Sesame Dressing, 290
Spinach Salad with Grapefruit, Orange, and Avocado, 213
Pita Salad, 217
Carrot and Raisin Salad, 218
Romaine and Red Onion Salad with Corn Bread Croutons, 211
Greek Spinach and Cheese Pie (Spanakopita), 417
Baked Chiles Rellenos with Cheese, 405
Individual Baked Shells with Red Pepper Puree, 317
Cauliflower, Potato, and Spinach Curry, 361
Vegetable Pot Pie with a Cheddar Biscuit Crust, 426
Red Peppers Stuffed with Saffron Rice and Pine Nuts, 404
Wild Caribbean Black Bean Chili, 276
Vegetarian Chili, 282
Sweet Potato and Peanut Stew, 428
Mushroom Ragout, 386, over Oven-Baked Polenta, 249
Roasted Red Pepper and Herb Goat Cheese Lasagne, 315
Baked Zucchini Stuffed with Couscous, 267
Red Beans and Lima Succotash, 282
Lentils with Spinach and Soy Sauce, 280
Quinoa-Stuffed Acorn Squash, 254
Kidney Bean Casserole, 283
Curried Chickpeas with Vegetables, 277
Eggplant Parmigiana, 373

ETHNIC DINNERS

Mexican

Roasted Cactus Salad, 357
Turkey in Simple Red Mole, 617
Stuffed Jalapeños, 405
Jicama Salad, 220
Trembleque (Coconut Milk Pudding), 1019

New Orleans

Louisiana Court-Bouillon, 113
Red Beans and Rice, 282
Blackened Fish Steaks or Fillets, 561
Louisiana-Style Chayote, 365
New Orleans Bread Pudding, 1023, **or**
Pineapple with Hot Buttered Rum Sauce, 474

Indian

Tandoori Chicken, 611, **or**
Saag Paneer, 417
Dal, 284
Basic Cooked White Rice, 255
Raita I or II, 82
Fresh Mint-Cilantro Chutney, 66
Naan, 753
Sliced Mango

Italian

Penne with Vodka, 309
Florentine Boneless Roast Pork, 689

Peas with Prosciutto and Onions, 396
Classic Tuscan Saltless Loaf, 759
Sicilian Salad, 220
Panna Cotta, 1039
Tiramisù, 966
Classic Biscotti, 834

Asian

Hot and Sour Soup, 102
Chinese Roasted Duck, 621, **or**
Teriyaki Grilled Salmon, Tuna, or Swordfish, 545
Stir-Fried Bok Choy with Mushrooms, 1349
Shanghai Noodles with Eggplant and Fresh Seasonal Vegetables, 329
Basic Cooked White Rice, 255
Litchis, Mangoes, and Loquats

Mediterranean

Fennel à la Grecque, 376, on toast
Broiled or Grilled Shrimp or Scallops, Basque Style, 507
Ratatouille, 374
Baklava, 918, **or**
Fruit Crostata, 882, **or**
Baked Figs with Ricotta, 464

Latin America

Latin Roasted Pork Shoulder, 693
Black Beans and Rice, 276
Golden Sautéed Plantain Slices, 406
Trembleque (Coconut Milk Pudding), 1019
Latin Sponge Cake with "Three Milks," 967

French

Warm Leeks Vinaigrette, 382
Cassoulet, 286, **or**
Salmi of Squab, 630
Field Salad with Fresh Herbs, 207
Baguette, 740
Tarte Tatin, 880, with Crème Fraîche, 1071
Chocolate Pots de Crème, 1015

German

Prune Compote, 464
Braised Pork with Sauerkraut, 701
Spätzle, 322, **or**
Mashed Potatoes, 408
Basic Rye Bread, 745
Schaumtorte, 957

East European

Cherry Soup, 109
Hungarian Goulash, 670, **or**
Chicken Paprikash, 598
Poppy-Seed Noodles, 319
Roasted Cauliflower with Paprika, 361
Palatschinken, 807

BRUNCH IDEAS

Watermelon Fruit Basket, 469
Roasted Nectarines with Raspberry Vinegar Glaze, 469
Buttered Apple Slices, 448
Melon and Prosciutto, 469
Fruit Soup, 109

Spaghetti alla Carbonara, 311
Kedgeree, 565
Crabcakes, 1520
Steak or Chicken Fajitas, 194
Grilled Vegetable Burritos, 195
Liver and Onions, 728
Artichoke Fritatta for a Crowd, 135
Tomato and Goat Cheese Quiche, 141
Fried Eggs, 128, with Baked Cheese Grits, 250
Huevos Rancheros, 128
Western or Denver Omelet, 134
Eggs Benedict, 130, or Eggs Beatrice, 129
Gratinéed Eggs Florentine, 130
Scrambled Eggs, 130, with Summer Squash Sautéed with Parsley and Garlic, 419
Bagels and Lox, 188
Basic Breakfast Strata, 142
Matzo Brei, 131
Chicken and Apple Sausage, 727
Broiled or Grilled Ham Steak, 707
Hash Brown Potatoes, 410

Sweet Cheese Blintzes, 806
Belgian Waffles, 802
Lemon Poppy Seed Pancakes, 799
Four-Grain Flapjacks, 796
Filled French Toast, 808
Eggless Maple French Toast, 809
Crêpe Cake, 806
Deluxe Sunday Morning Coffeecake, 781
Fresh Fruit Kuchen, 902
Cinnamon Cream Cheese Strata, 142
Orange Loaf with Dried Cranberries or Apricots and Pecans, 774
Apple Walnut Muffins, 784

Chocolate Chip Orange Scones, 792
Sticky Buns, 769

LUNCH MENUS

Chicken Consommé, 107
Sautéed Sweetbreads with Bacon and Curly Endive, 732
Raspberry Gratin, 453

Thai Fish Cakes, 562
Asian Cole Slaw, 223
Melon with Prickly Pear Sauce, 476, or Mango Fool, 467

Anchovy Toasts, 162
Grilled Scallop & Fennel Salad, 215
Apple Galette, 883

Spinach Fettuccine with Smoked Salmon and Asparagus, 311
Field Salad with Fresh Herbs, 207
Fresh sliced melon and strawberries

French Onion Soup, 95
Tart Green Salad, 207
Apple Crisp, 900, or Tarte Tatin, 880

Roasted Red Pepper Soup, 98
Chard Tart, 364
Orange Rum Cake, 933

Grilled Vegetable Roll-Ups, 191
Black Bean, Corn, and Tomato Salad, 224
Chocolate Chip Cookies Cockaigne, 830

Slow-Baked Salmon Fillets with Herbed Olive Oil, 550
Roasted Asparagus, 343
Fresh Corn Risotto with Basil, Tomato, and Lime, 261
Peach Pie, 875

Greek Salad, 210
Stuffed Grape Leaves, 163
Mediterranean Olive Bread, 776
Baklava, 918

Bruschetta with Mozzarella and Fresh Oregano, 168
Minestrone, 100
Zabaglione, 1036, with Tuiles, 822

Cold Avocado Soup, 95
Escabèche of Fish, 563
Latin American Flan with Condensed Milk, 1016

Grilled or Broiled Swordfish and Nectarine Skewers, 547
Quick Couscous, 267
Bittersweet Chocolate Tart, 892, or Chocolate-Glazed Caramel Tart, 892

Grilled Open-Faced Steak Sandwich with Quick Pickled Onions, 659
No-Fail French Fries, 411
Strawberry Rhubarb Cobbler, 896

Spinach with Seared Shrimp, Bacon and Roasted Bell Peppers, 213
Focaccia, 753
Lemon Tart, 891

Mediterranean White Bean Soup, 104
Spice-Dusted Shrimp or Other Shellfish on Greens, 518
Tiramisù, 966

Baked Chiles Rellenos with Cheese, 405
Spanish Rice, 258
Latin Sponge Cake with "Three Milks," 967

Baked Chicken with Onions, Garlic & Rosemary, 585
Couscous Salad with Pine Nuts and Raisins, 227
Blueberry Pie, 874

DINNER MENUS

Mixed Greens with Cheese Crisp, 208
Porcini and Red Wine Sauce, 308, over Fettuccine
Fresh Ginger Cake, 935

Melon Soup, 109
Hoisin-Glazed Skirt Steak wtih Scallion Ginger Slaw, 663
Thai Coconut Rice, 259
Stir-Fried Asparagus, 343
Ginger Crème Brûlée, 1018

Beef Stew, 669
Roasted Whole Garlic Heads, 378, with Baguette, 740
Apple Spice Cake, 933

Tart Greens with Apples, Pecans, and Buttermilk Honey Dressing, 211

Veal Rib Roast with Garlic Crumbs and Mustard Cream, 681
Anna's Lima Beans, 281
Pan-Fried Golden Potatoes with Rosemary and Lemon, 409
Bananas Foster, 450

Potato Patties, 165
Almond-Crusted Roasted Boneless Pork Loin, 690
Flageolets and Tomatoes with Buttered Crumbs, 285
Wild Rice and Barley, 269
Sweet-and-Sour Glazed Small Onions, 392
Apple Crisp, 900

Creamed Mushrooms with Dried Porcini, 387, over Toast
Sautéed Pork Tenderloin Medallions, 696
Roasted Potatoes, Beets, and Onions Vinaigrette, 348
Field Salad with Fresh Herbs, 207
Linzertorte, 881

Zucchini Pancakes with Mint and Feta Cheese, 420
Lamb Chops with Roasted Garlic and Cognac, 715
Pommes Anna, 412
Turnip Puree, 435
Pears in Cream and Kirsch, 473

Grilled Ratatouille Salad, 374
Mixed Shellfish in Tomato Sauce, 516, over pasta
Classic Tuscan Saltless Loaf, 759
Melon with Port, 468

Warm Leeks Vinaigrette, 382
Cabbage Rolls Stuffed with Salmon and Wild Rice, 356
Quick Beer Bread, 775
Yogurt Cake, 941

Greek Lemon Soup, 105
Broiled Salmon with Tomatoes, Basil, and Mint, 546
Simplest Risotto, 260
Key Lime Pie, 891

Bruschetta with Tomatoes and Basil, 168
Roasted Monkfish with Garlic and Herbs, 552
Broiled Tomatoes, 431
Basic Cooked Lentils, 279
Blueberry Pandowdy, 895

Pan-Grilled Fish Fillets or Steaks with Sorrel Sauce, 557
Oven-Baked Polenta, 249
Sautéed Cherry Tomatoes, 432
German Chocolate Cake, 944

Sunday Supper Fish Cakes with Horseradish Cream, 565
Peas and Carrots, 396, with Crispy Shallots, 415
Oven-Baked White Rice, 256
Sour Cream Chocolate Chip Cake, 931

Lobster Bisque, 112
Roasted Pheasant, 628
Two-Grain Date Pilaf, 258
Brussels Sprouts with Brown Butter and Toasted Nuts, 353
Velvet Spice Cake, 942

Braised Marinated Rabbit with Prunes, 632
Basic Cooked Wild Rice, 268
Gooseberry Fool, 452

Gorgonzola-Stuffed Chicken Breasts, 590
Roasted Carrots, 359
Barley with Toasted Buttered Pecans, 246
Individual Baked Rice Puddings, 1021

Potato and Chicken Bake, 413
Sautéed Broccoli with Garlic and Red Pepper Flakes, 351
Baked Apples, 447

COFFEE, TEA & HOT CHOCOLATE

ABOUT COFFEE

Coffee has always thrived on adversity. In the Arab world, where the coffee plant was first cultivated commercially in the fifteenth century, coffee was widely consumed by the populace but condemned by Islamic leaders for its supposed intoxicating effects. Coffee was banned repeatedly as it traveled from Constantinople to Venice and then to Vienna and other European capitals. The beans were initially sold by pharmacists and then in cafés—which became notorious hotbeds of revolution and enlightened thinking. These days, the coffee controversy continues, as new studies seem to be published weekly, alternately decrying coffee as a health hazard or informing us that, no, it's all right to drink after all.

Coffee beans are the seed of a fruit, picked green, and do not acquire their familiar brown color and intoxicating aroma until they are roasted, as Corby Kummer has written in his authoritative book, *The Joy of Coffee.* All commercial coffee beans belong to one of two main species, Arabica and robusta. Arabica beans, named for the Arabs (who first grew them), are the better of the two, producing the finest flavors when grown at high altitudes in semitropical climates, near but not at the equator. Robusta beans, which require less care and thrive in low altitudes and equatorial climates, have about twice the caffeine of Arabicas but less flavor. Most of what goes into supermarket coffee blends is robusta, often with a small percentage of Arabica beans added for flavor. Almost all beans sold in coffee specialty shops, on the other hand, are Arabica. Words such as *excelso* and *supremo,* sometimes found on coffee packages, sound impressive but are essentially meaningless grading terms.

Coffee grows mostly in three regions of the world: Africa, Indonesia, and Central and South America. There is also a tiny quantity grown in the Hawaiian Islands—the only coffee grown on American soil—and some in Yemen on the Red Sea. Africa, the birthplace of coffee, still grows beans with wild flavors that coffee lovers prize. The best of these are the true Mochas, named for the Yemeni port from which coffees were once shipped to the rest of the world. (The word *mocha* has come to mean a flavor combination of coffee and chocolate, of course, but this has nothing to do with Mocha beans.) True Mochas are rare and expensive, although the name still appears as half of the most famous coffee blend, Mocha-Java—which, incidentally, rarely contains either a bean of real Mocha or coffee from the Indonesian island of Java. Some Ethiopian beans have the same fruity, winy flavors as Mochas; they are often called Harrar and Djimmah, for the regions where they grow. The other star of African coffees is from Kenya, a country that produces many superlative beans. Indonesian coffees are famous for their body—a rich, mouth-coating sensation—and for their musky, earthy (not "dirty") flavors. Among the most common is Sumatra. The island of Sulawesi (the former Celebes, a name coffee merchants still use) also produces prized beans, and those of Java, while less sought after than they once were, are still of high quality. Many good coffees also come from the island of Papua New Guinea, whose coffee industry is young and progressive. Central and South America and the Caribbean produce many noteworthy coffees. Of chief interest to connoisseurs are those of Central America, particularly Guatemala and Costa Rica. Many of the beans from these regions offer the balance and smoothness that made Jamaica's Blue Mountain coffee legendary. Genuine Blue Mountain is almost impossible to find in the United States today, since the Japanese buy nearly all the tiny annual production, and it is impossibly expensive when it does appear. Brazil grows fully one-third of the coffee drunk in the world, but almost none of it is of interest to connoisseurs. Colombia, like Kenya, has put money and research into its coffee industry and so produces reliable coffees; unlike those of Kenya, however, its beans are seldom exceptional.

Flavored coffees have recently become extremely popular. Enjoy them if you like, but remember that such coffees are usually based on bland, mediocre beans that are stirred with chemical flavoring essences after roasting. And be aware that grinding these beans and brewing them at home will impart their flavors, possibly forever, to your grinder and brewing apparatus. (You can sometimes clean a propeller-blade grinder successfully by whirring 2 to 3 tablespoons sugar in it for 30 seconds, then wiping out the chamber and washing the lid.) Even storing flavored beans close to unflavored ones can be dangerous, because the aromas of the flavored beans can easily penetrate anything near them. A better bet for flavored coffee is to brew good coffee from good, unflavored beans and then dose it modestly with one or more of the flavoring essences available at many gourmet shops. These are very potent; stir them into pots or cups of coffee by the ¼ teaspoon.

ABOUT STORING COFFEE

To ensure the best coffee at home, buy whole beans roasted within the past week and grind them just before you brew. It is always best to buy a small amount of coffee at a time. Odd as it may sound, the surest way to obtain recently roasted coffee is to order it by mail, since companies usually ship a day or two after roasting. Air and moisture are the enemies of coffee beans. Virtually all canned coffee is preground, meaning that by the time the buyer opens the can, the coffee is probably on the road to staleness. Even "vacuum-packed" cans almost always retain a small amount of oxygen—enough to start turning the coffee stale. A better solution is the valve-lock bag, which has a one-way valve to allow carbon dioxide to escape without letting in oxygen. These give coffee a shelf life of 3 months at the most, but that's only if the bag remains unopened.

The best way to store coffee beans, ground or whole, is in an opaque, airtight canister just big enough to hold them, with as little air at the top as possible. Keep the coffee at room temperature and use it within 10 days if possible. Many people store coffee in the refrigerator or freezer. The problem is that the beans—and, even more so, ground coffee—can absorb food odors in the refrigerator. (Bags of ground coffee are so absorbent, in fact, that they were once recommended as refrigerator refresheners—the precursor to baking soda.) The freezer is a better option, though ground coffee can absorb odors even there—and the oils in beans congeal when frozen, possibly affecting the body of the brewed coffee.

ABOUT GRINDING COFFEE BEANS

It is essential to use the right grind of coffee for your brewing method. As a rule of thumb, the shorter the brewing time, the finer the grind must be. Espresso, which brews in 30 seconds or less, requires a very fine grind. Plunger-pot coffee, in which coffee grounds steep in water, like tea leaves, for a full 6 minutes, requires a very coarse grind. Propeller-blade grinders, shown 26 (bottom left), the kind most people have, are not ideal, for they produce an uneven grind and if whirred too long heat the beans, releasing aromatic substances that should go into your cup and not into the air. Cool, precise tearing apart of the beans is called for, and it's best done in a "burr mill," which has two notched blades whose position can be set for the desired fineness of grinds, shown 26 (bottom right). Home burr mills are noisy and slow, but you can grind as much or as little as you like and get a reliably consistent result. Follow the manufacturer's instructions for grinding times. Instructions are also provided for cleaning the machine, but this can be complicated. It's usually much easier to have the grinder cleaned professionally at an appliance repair shop. The hand-cranked grinders of yore—often seen converted to

RATIO OF GROUND COFFEE TO WATER

GROUND COFFEE	WATER	BREWED COFFEE
¼ cup (2 scoops)	1 cup (8 ounces)	¾ cup (6 ounces)
6 tablespoons (3 scoops)	2 cups (16 ounces)	1½ cups (12 ounces)
½ cup (4 scoops)	3 cups (24 ounces)	2¼ cups (18 ounces)
½ cup plus 2 tablespoons (5 scoops)	3½ cups (28 ounces)	2¾ cups (22 ounces)
¾ cup (6 scoops)	4 cups (32 ounces)	3 cups (24 ounces)
¾ cup plus 2 tablespoons (7 scoops)	4½ cups (36 ounces)	3½ cups (28 ounces)
1 cup (8 scoops)	5½ cups (44 ounces)	4½ cups (36 ounces)
1 cup plus 2 tablespoons (9 scoops)	6¼ cups (50 ounces)	4¾ cups (38 ounces)

lamps—are also burr mills. (If these are clean and in good condition, they work fine for grinding coffee beans even today.) If you don't own a burr mill, you can use one of the professional ones commonly found at supermarkets and even convenience stores. These suffer from heavy and often careless use, however. Always assume that the grind will be one or two settings coarser than is promised by the little pictures on the dial and always run a few fresh beans through before you begin, to get rid of stale flavors.

If you must use a propeller-blade grinder, grind the beans slightly coarser than you think you'll need, grind in 10-second bursts, and never whir the beans for more than 30 seconds, which will overheat them badly. Try not to grind more than 4 scoops at a time, because the chamber is rarely big enough to do a decent job on more than that. Lift the machine off the counter and shake it while it grinds. Always unplug the grinder after each use, wipe out the grinding chamber with a damp paper towel or sponge, and wash the plastic top in hot water. Here are approximate grinding times for propeller-blade grinders: 10 seconds for the plunger pot, 13 seconds for flat-bottomed paper filters (which generally fit into American electric drip brewers) or wedge-shaped gold filters, and 16 seconds for wedge-shaped paper filters. The grounds should resemble coarse-ground cornmeal for a plunger pot and granulated sugar for a drip brewer.

ABOUT BREWING COFFEE

The ratio of ground coffee to water is vital: The general rule is to use 1 standard coffee scoop, which holds 2 tablespoons ground coffee, for every 6 ounces water. The problem is that coffee scoops tend to vary greatly in capacity. Measure the capacity of your scoop and adjust your subsequent coffee measurements accordingly. If you prefer weaker coffee than the two-to-six rule provides, make it at full strength and then dilute it to taste with hot water or milk. The chart above shows the ratios of ground coffee to water that we find make the best brewed coffee for any filtering method.

There are a number of good ways to brew coffee, but the percolator is not one of them. Percolators violate two of the cardinal rules of good coffee brewing: they boil the coffee, extracting bitter and sour substances that should play no part in coffee, and they pour water that is too hot over the grounds repeatedly, instead of just-right water only once. Here are the recommended methods of coffee brewing:

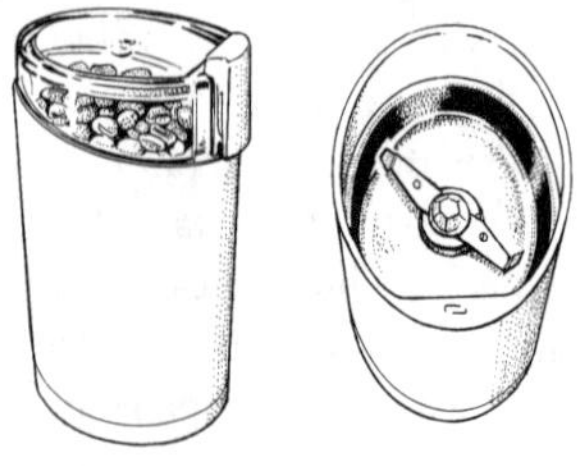

Propeller-blade grinders are common, but not ideal.

Burr mills have two notched blades whose position can be set for the desired fineness of grinds.

Filter cone and glass pot

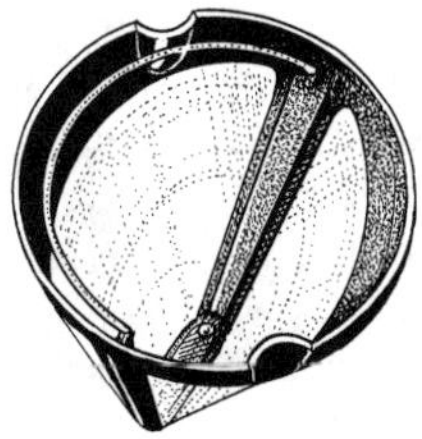

Gold-washed metal filter

Electric drip machine with flat-bottomed filter

Filter Cones: This method—which involves pouring hot water through ground coffee measured into a filter set inside a cone, shown above left, to drip into a glass or vacuum pot—has become increasingly popular in recent years. Paper filters are convenient to use, but connoisseurs believe they rob coffee of some of its desirable texture. Gold-washed metal filters are preferred, shown above center, and these are available for most filter brewers, manual and electric. They can go into the dishwasher and will withstand several years of constant use—after which their gold plating will have worn away and they will need to be replaced. If you do use paper filters, don't store them near strong spices, as the paper absorbs odors easily. To make drip coffee manually, bring water to a rolling boil and remove it immediately from the heat. Wait about 15 seconds, then slowly drip just enough water over the ground coffee to moisten it thoroughly; this ensures that the rest of the water will pass evenly through the coffee, not encountering dry spots that will rob the finished brew of flavor. Wait another 30 seconds or so, then pour in the correct amount of water all at once (or in stages if necessary). It is best to drip coffee directly into a thermal carafe that has been preheated with hot tap water. (Never repour brewed coffee through spent grounds to get stronger coffee; what you will get instead is everything you wanted to leave behind in the grounds.)

Electric Drip Machines: These operate on the same principle as manual filter cones, but they pour water over the coffee electrically from a premeasured reservoir. In buying an electric drip machine, shown above right, look for power as expressed in wattage; the higher it is, the stronger the heater and, thus, the better the coffee. The flat-bottomed cupcake-shaped filter is generally preferred to the cone shape, as it is thought to allow the water to saturate the ground coffee more evenly. If you will not be serving the whole pot you brew within 10 or 15 minutes, transfer the coffee to a warmed thermal carafe—do not leave it cooking on the warmer. Electric coffee machines should be cleaned every few months; this is done by running a solution of cleaning powder, available in coffee emporiums, through the machine. (A mixture of one part white vinegar to four parts water will also work.) Always run three or four batches of plain water through the machine after cleaning.

Metal Drip Pots: The commonest version of these is the old-fashioned stovetop pot divided, top to bottom, into chambers for hot water, ground coffee, and brewed coffee, shown (bottom right). Theoretically this is an

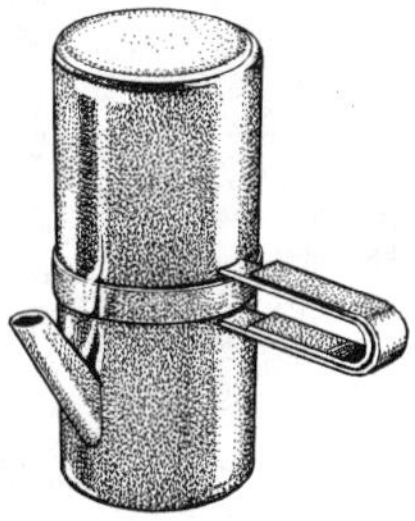

Flip-drip, or Neopolitan pot

Metal drip pot with chambers for hot water, ground coffee, and brewed coffee

excellent brewing method, producing coffee full in body and flavor, but beware of aluminum pots, which interact with the acids in coffee and with time can impart off flavors. The Italian version of this pot, called a flip-drip or Neapolitan pot, shown 27 (bottom left), eliminates the need to add hot water separately. The water boils in the bottom compartment, the pot is turned upside down, and the water drips through the coffee grounds into what was the top compartment. Both kinds of metal pot offer the convenience of a premeasured capacity of ground coffee and water, but the ratio of coffee to water is more generous in the Italian version, so the results are more flavorful. As with machine-brewed coffee, always transfer the brewed coffee to a prewarmed thermal carafe if you're not going to drink it immediately.

Plunger Pots: Also called French press pots, these, shown below left, operate in a unique manner: ground coffee (relatively coarse) goes into the pot (usually glass), hot water is added to the grounds, which are allowed to steep, and then a metal screen attached to a plunger is pushed down slowly, forcing the coffee grounds to the bottom of the pot. The resulting coffee has a thick texture that is preferred by many and is particularly appropriate to the flavors of dark-roasted coffees. Use the same proportions of ground coffee to water recommended for filter drip coffee. Because the coffee cools quickly with this method, rinse the pot before use with hot water, wrap it in a terrycloth towel as the coffee steeps, and transfer the coffee to a prewarmed thermal carafe when done.

Middle Eastern Coffee Makers: Probably every nation of the eastern Mediterranean brews coffee with a very simple method thought to have originated in the coffeehouses of Cairo in the fifteenth century: Very finely ground, presweetened coffee is lightly boiled several times in a medieval-looking long-handled brass or copper vessel called a *cezve* in Turkish and *ibrik* or *briki* in Greek. The coffee is not filtered, but the grounds stay in the bottom of the pot; some sediment always finds its way into each cup, where it sinks to the bottom and remains. This is often dumped onto the saucer with one smart rap after the coffee is consumed and is then used to tell fortunes. To brew Middle Eastern coffee, start with specially ground coffee and a special pot from a Greek or Middle Eastern market. Rinse demitasse cups in hot water to preheat them. Measure 2 teaspoons coffee into the pot for each ½ cup water. Stir in sugar to taste (in the Middle East, the ratio is often equal parts sugar and coffee) and a pinch of ground cardamom if you like. Bring the coffee to a frothing simmer over medium heat. Just as it puffs and is about to boil over, remove the pot from the stove and pour a bit of foam into each of the waiting cups. Return the pot to the heat for two or three brief boilings, removing it quickly each time as it is about to boil over. Divide the rest of the brewed coffee among the cups, distributing the remaining foam equally.

Espresso Makers: The term *espresso* correctly refers to the brewing method, not a coffee bean or degree of roast, and it's the brewing method that gives the fullest-bodied coffee by far. Espresso machines force hot but not boiling water through finely ground coffee at high pressure. The pressure produces a syrupy body impossible to achieve by any other means and a pleasantly bittersweet flavor that lingers on the palate. The tradeoff for the matchless concentration of flavor that espresso provides is that you get only a very small amount at a time. A properly brewed cup of espresso measures just 1½ to 2 ounces, as compared with the 6 ounces in a standard cup of coffee as calculated by the coffee industry.

Plunger pot

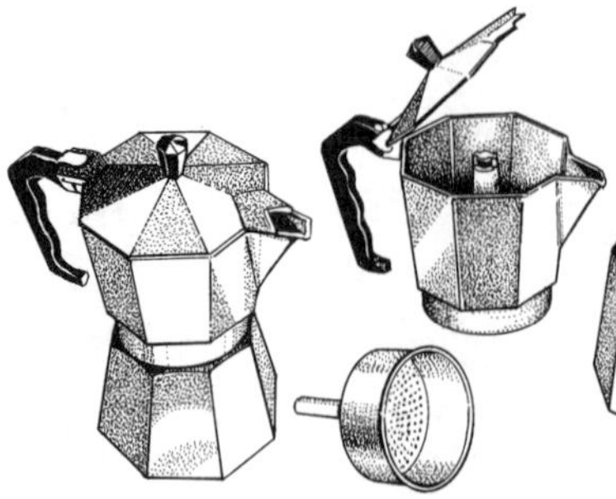
Moka pot

Pump espresso maker

There are two ways to make espresso at home. Italians use a stovetop apparatus called the moka pot, shown 28 (bottom center), which yields coffee that is roughly halfway between drip coffee and true espresso in body and flavor. In the moka pot, water boils in a tightly sealed bottom chamber, steam pressure forces hot water up through a central filter basket containing ground coffee, and the brewed coffee drips out of a central tube into the upper chamber, from which it is poured. The pots are inexpensive and easy to maintain, requiring only the periodic replacement of a rubber gasket. To make coffee in a moka pot, fill the bottom with cold water to the level of the safety valve. Set the metal filter in it and fill it with dark-roasted coffee ground medium-fine. Screw on the upper chamber and set the moka over medium-low heat. After about 3 minutes, coffee will begin to hiss and dribble out two holes at the sides of the tube in the upper compartment. As soon as a small dark pool collects in the bottom of the chamber, turn off the heat. This will safeguard against burning the bottom of the pot.

Devoted espresso enthusiasts often prefer pump espresso makers, shown 28 (bottom right), to mere moka pots. Although not quite on a par with professional machines, they do force hot water through ground coffee at a high enough pressure to achieve the syrupy body of true espresso. Unfortunately, they are expensive, require frequent cleaning, and brew no more than two small cups of espresso at a time. Follow the manufacturer's instructions for each machine, but in general it's always a good idea to preheat the metal filter and its holder by running hot water through them and into the espresso cup (this also primes the pump). Also be sure to use a sufficiently fine grind of coffee—in this case buying preground coffee unless you have invested in a high-quality burr grinder. If the machine is functioning properly, the flow of espresso begins in a gently curving steady black drip, like honey from a spoon. After 5 to 10 seconds, the drip should become a pour and the color will lighten. Finally, if all goes well, a pure golden "crema" comes out—a thin layer of foam with very fine bubbles and a warm straw color that is the essential sign of well-made espresso.

ABOUT CAPPUCCINO AND CAFFÈ LATTE

Cappuccino—named for the brown robes of Capuchin monks, whose color it is thought to resemble—is the glory of the Italian coffee bar. Don't expect powdered cinnamon or cocoa, though, for true cappuccino is just espresso and steamed milk crowned by a head of satiny foam—with coffee, milk, and foam in approximately equal proportions. (Steamed milk is simply milk that has been heated with an injection of steam, usually through a tube connected to the boiler of an espresso machine.) To make cappuccino, first steam the milk (follow the manufacturer's instructions on your espresso machine or simply scald the milk in a saucepan, making certain that it does not come to a boil), aiming for a warm, liquidy combination of milk and foam that is a bit under twice the volume of the milk you started with. Then brew espresso into a larger cup than usual, making sure the cup is hot. Using a large spoon to block the foam so that hot milk comes out of the pitcher first, pour no more than ½ cup milk over the waiting espresso—¼ cup steamed milk and ¼ cup foam is ideal. Spread the foam gently over the top of the espresso with the back of the spoon so that it holds its shape just enough to leave visible a brown rim around the edge.

Caffè latte is basically an oversized cappuccino in the United States, but in Italy it is one part espresso diluted with four parts scalded or steamed milk, with no foam on top. Caffè macchiato is espresso "marked" with just a tablespoon or two of foam. In Italy, coffee with milk is considered a breakfast beverage; after lunch or dinner, Italians drink espresso.

COFFEE DRINKS

Coffee by itself or with nothing more than sugar and cream is probably the closest thing we have to a national beverage. But coffee also blends well with alcohol and other flavorings to produce a variety of deliciously assertive and warming drinks.

CAFÉ DIABLO

8 servings

This festive coffee bowl requires a darkened room for full effect. For individual servings, and an easier version of this recipe, put a small sugar cube in a coffee spoon, saturate it with brandy, and ignite. When the sugar is melted, lower the spoon into a partially filled demitasse of hot coffee. Add a lemon twist and 1 or 2 cloves, then stir the mixture with a cinnamon stick. Also, you can simply stir a teaspoon of warmed light rum or whiskey into a small cup of hot coffee, adding a twist of lemon peel and sweetening to taste.

Rinse and dry:

1 small orange

Stud it with:

20 whole cloves

Combine in a deep silver bowl:

Peel of 1 orange, thinly sliced

Peel of 1 lemon, thinly sliced
Two 3-inch cinnamon sticks
10 small sugar cubes

Heat (but do not boil) and pour into the bowl:

6 ounces brandy

Place the bowl on a tray and bring the bowl, the orange, and a flameproof ladle to the table. Carefully ignite the brandy and ladle the liquid repeatedly over the spices until the sugar is melted. Pour into the bowl:

4 cups hot strong coffee

Now fill the ladle with:

2 ounces Cointreau

Set the studded orange in the Cointreau, ignite the liqueur, and lower the flaming ladle into the bowl, allowing the orange to float. Ladle the coffee into demitasse cups.

CREMAT (FLAMING COFFEE) *4 to 6 servings*

This showpiece party drink is served outdoors on summer evenings on Spain's Costa Brava, often to the tune of the soft Cuban-inspired songs called *habaneras.* Combine in a flameproof 4- to 6-quart bowl:

8 ounces Spanish brandy, warmed
12 ounces dark rum, warmed
3 tablespoons sugar
Peel of 1 lemon, thinly sliced
Three 5-inch cinnamon sticks

Stir, then carefully ignite the mixture, holding a long wooden match near the surface (do not immerse the match). Stir with a long spoon while slowly adding:

4 cups hot strong coffee

When all the coffee has been added and the flame is extinguished, ladle into cups.

IRISH COFFEE *1 serving*

This internationally popular coffee drink was invented not in Ireland but at San Francisco's Buena Vista Café. In a warmed Irish coffee glass or other heatproof glass mug, stir together:

1½ ounces Irish whiskey
6 ounces hot strong coffee
1 teaspoon sugar

Top with:

1 tablespoon sweetened whipped cream

If desired, pour over the top of the cream:

Dash of green crème de menthe (optional)

JAMAICAN COFFEE *1 serving*

In a warmed glass mug, stir together:

1 ounce Jamaican dark rum
1 ounce Tía Maria
6 ounces hot strong coffee

Top with:

1 tablespoon sweetened whipped cream

KIOKI COFFEE *1 serving*

In a warmed glass mug, stir together:

1 ounce Kahlúa (coffee liqueur)
½ ounce brandy
6 ounces hot strong coffee

ABOUT TEA

Tea—the leaves of *Camellia sinensis,* an evergreen shrub related to the familiar domestic camellia—was first cultivated in China well over two thousand years ago. At first it was used as medicine and in Buddhist rituals, but in the fifth or sixth century A.D., it began to be drunk for pleasure. Today China remains a major producer of tea, but tea is also grown in appreciable quantities in Japan, India, Sri Lanka, and several parts of Africa. (There is also a tiny production in South Carolina, a tentative revival of a thriving colonial-era industry.) There are countless varieties of tea, and—as with coffee or wine—soil, climate, and the altitude at which the leaves are grown yield differences in flavor and aroma. But how tea leaves are processed accounts for enormous differences as well.

There are three principal methods of processing tea leaves, the results of which are known as green tea, black tea, and oolong tea. All start in more or less the same way: Tea leaves are brittle when fresh and must be "withered," either in sunlight or in warm air, to be made supple enough to handle. They are then rolled, twisted, and lightly broken, usually by machine. The essential oils that give tea its flavor come to the surface at this point. If the process is now stopped by "firing," or heating, the leaves, the tea is called green, even though its color may range from olive green to warm cream. All Japanese tea and most Chinese tea is green. Until the 1830s Americans drank only green tea, but consumption declined steadily after that to the point that it virtually ceased here. Today green tea is coming into fashion again, not only for its delicacy and flavor but also for its apparent health benefits. It is high in vitamins (especially C) and in antioxidants that some researchers believe might help prevent cancer and heart disease.

Tea leaves turn black if their flavor-giving oils are exposed for longer periods to air—usually very humid air—and allowed to oxidize. Oxidation not only darkens the color of the leaves but also allows them to develop new flavor compounds—among them the astringent ones technically called polyphenols but commonly known as tannins. Black tea is what most Westerners drink most of the time. (The Chinese call it red tea after the color of the brewed liquid.) When the British planted tea in India in the early 1800s, and in Ceylon slightly later, almost all of what was harvested was processed as black tea. Americans eventually inherited the British taste for tea processed this way.

The third main way to process tea is to allow it to oxidize only partially, so that some of the fresh flavors of green tea and some of the deeper flavors of black tea are combined. This kind of tea, called oolong, is produced in China and Taiwan; Taiwan's former name, Formosa, is still used for the oolong produced there, which some connoisseurs consider to be the best.

Almost all tea sold commercially is blended, and there are often as many as twenty or more varieties in a blend—most of them black. The names of these blends can be confusing. "Pekoe" and "orange pekoe," for example, were originally grading terms but today are used by individual tea packers to describe house blends. English breakfast tea, supposedly blended for consumption by that nationality at that meal, traditionally contains a measure of richly aromatic Keemun, the best known of the many black teas produced in northern China. Keemun is sometimes packaged under its own name, as is Yunnan, the best-known black tea from southern China. Yunnan's deep, full flavor, sometimes said to suggest mocha coffee, has made it a favorite black tea all over the world. The black tea of Assam, in northeastern India, usually forms the basis of Irish breakfast tea, which is known for its hearty character. (The Irish, who drink more tea per capita than any other nation, like their tea dark and full-bodied, and they are famously expert tea blenders.) Darjeeling is India's most highly prized tea, but the term is sometimes used to describe a blend of less expensive black teas in the Darjeeling style.

ABOUT FLAVORED TEAS

The most famous flavored tea is Earl Grey, a blend of black teas—from whatever country the packer chooses—flavored with oil of bergamot, a variety of citrus fruit whose oils are commonly used in perfumes. Jasmine tea is the world's most widely consumed flavored tea. Technically it is a scented tea, classically made by rubbing jasmine petals into the steamed leaves of green or semifermented tea as many as seven times; today the flowers are usually tumbled with the tea in containers under controlled conditions of temperature and humidity. Lapsang Souchong is smoked tea, cured in rooms where pine logs burn slowly, and has been compared to Scotch whisky, which also gets its flavor from charred wood. Chai, a generic name for any spiced Indian tea drink containing milk and sugar, is becoming popular in the United States. It almost always includes cinnamon, cardamom, cloves, and white or black peppercorns, sometimes with fresh ginger added. Mint tea, as it is drunk throughout the day in northern Africa, especially Morocco, and in Turkey (typically heavily sugared), is green or black tea mixed with mint leaves, dried or fresh.

ABOUT HERBAL TEAS

These are not really teas but rather infusions (the French call them tisanes) made not with tea leaves but with herbs. Both soothing and refreshing, herbal teas traditionally have been used medicinally. Among the most popular herbal teas are chamomile (a reputed stomach settler), peppermint, rose hips, *tilleul* (the French word for leaves of the European linden, or lime, tree), and lemon verbena (*verveine*). These are brewed alone or in blends. Feel free to create your own blends, including whatever spices you like or bits of fresh lemon grass and ginger.

ABOUT TEA BAGS

Tea bags are said to be an American invention, developed out of the little silk bags a New York City importer named Thomas Sullivan used for sending tea samples in the early years of this century. It is possible to make excellent tea with a tea bag, but not easy. Most tea bags are filled with "fannings" or "dust"—two sorting grades describing size and not quality. Although most packers use lesser-quality teas for bags than for loose tea, sometimes the fannings or dust can be quite good. The problem is that tea bags are rarely packed in airtight containers, and because the leaves are so finely chopped or pulverized, they grow stale more quickly than loose tea does. Also the paper used for most bags can impart a flavor of its own to the tea. If you buy tea bags, store them in an opaque, tightly sealed container, away from heat such as stoves and radiators. And do not keep any tea, in bags or loose, for more than 6 months.

HOW TO BREW TEA

All you need to brew tea well is the best tea you can find and hot water—and the water is almost as important as the tea. If the water that goes into your tea does not taste good, neither will the finished product. Do not use distilled water, for the minerals, essential for flavor, have been removed. Filtered water, on the other hand, is ideal. Filter pitchers are now widely available and inexpensive.

Your teapot should have a wide mouth, for getting tea in and out of the pot, and a handle that stays cool, shown below right. Asians tend to prefer clay or iron pots; "brown betty" pots of English clay work well, too. Avoid aluminum or any uncoated metal, which will interact with the tea and produce off flavors. Tea should never steep in hot water for longer than 5 minutes or it will be bitter.

The traditional measure for tea is 1 teaspoon tea per cup and one for the pot, but in fact, the amount of tea should vary according to your own taste and the kind of tea you are using. The less the tea has been processed, the more of it you will need. As a starting point, use the above measure for black tea, half again as much for oolong tea, and twice as much for green tea. Length of brewing time should also vary according to tea type—as well as whether the tea is loose or in bags. (Tea bags steep the fastest.) *Tea is not ready when its color changes.* This is one of the commonest mistakes people make in brewing tea. Tea bags should steep for at least 3 minutes and no more than 5; oolongs, Darjeelings, and delicate black teas usually require 3 to 4 minutes; other black teas need 4 to 5 minutes; green teas should steep for only 1 to 2 minutes.

It is simple to remove tea bags, of course. One possibility for decanting tea is to brew it in a separate pot or even a clean saucepan set over very low heat and then to pour it through a clean strainer into the serving pot. The easier way to remove spent tea leaves is to first place the tea in a ball or wire-mesh basket. Tea balls are usually made of inexpensive, uncoated metal and are awkward to open and close; worse, they are rarely big enough to allow the leaves to more than double in volume, as they must do during brewing. The only kind of efficient tea ball is a globe of wire mesh, shown below left, which usually shuts with a hinge; the problem is finding a pot that has an opening large enough to accommodate the globe.

Our favorite pot contains a wide and deep inset basket, which gives plenty of room for the leaves to expand and can be lifted out as soon as the tea is ready. Individual metal tea filters are also available and useful. Look for the ones with cylinders that extend to the bottom of the cup and offer the most water-tea contact.

Always preheat the teapot, with either boiling water or very hot tap water. Water for brewing most teas must be boiling hot; the exception is green tea, for which the water should be hot but not boiling (170° to 190°F). Always bring the teapot to the kettle, not vice versa, so the water will not have time to cool. To keep tea warm both during and after brewing, you can wrap the teapot in a tea cozy or thick towel. Once you've removed the leaves, the tea can be transferred to a thermal carafe—less elegant than a teapot but a more practical way to serve it fresh and hot. (Do not use a carafe you've put coffee in, however, or your tea will take on a coffee flavor.) To serve tea to a crowd, brew in advance a pot using twice as much tea as usual, then fill each cup or pot with half of this tea essence and half hot water.

WHAT TO PUT IN TEA

"Milk or lemon?" "Neither, thank you," purists will reply. But milk goes well with black tea, for its sweetness counteracts the astringency of the tannins. The old-fashioned English dictate "milk in first," or "MIF"—supposedly a sign of good breeding—was simply a way to prevent thin porcelain in typically cold English houses from cracking at the touch of hot tea. Sugar also makes black tea palatable. The tradition in Russia, when drinking tea from a samovar, is to sip it from a glass with a sugar cube held between the teeth or to add a generous teaspoon of raspberry or other preserves directly to the liquid. Honey is also a fine way to sweeten tea and give it flavor. Neither milk nor sweetener, however, is traditionally added to smoky Lapsang Souchong or to delicate green tea. Although lemon will overpower a fine Darjeeling, it is not only traditional but also wonderfully refreshing in most iced black tea.

ABOUT SERVING TEA

Many centuries ago, Japanese Zen Buddhists evolved a tea ceremony, full of intricate steps and requirements,

Wire mesh globe

Teapot with inset basket

that is still practiced to this day; as they wait for the tea to be brewed and served, a ritual that can last for several hours, both the server and the served try to achieve a state of fruitful contemplation. In England, on the other hand, afternoon tea became popular as a way to stave off hunger between lunch and dinner. And since it was simple enough to be served to friends by the mistress of the house, without help from her servants, it provided an opportunity for gossip safe from overhearing. This is not to be confused with high tea, named for the later hour at which it was served (usually at six or seven o'clock); also called meat tea, high tea was supper for workers who took their main meal at lunch. High tea as an institution is dying out, but afternoon tea remains a pleasant way to entertain and offers the opportunity of serving light savory foods rather than the sweet ones traditionally associated with coffee.

SPICED TEA *8 servings*

Combine in a saucepan and bring to a boil:

½ cup sugar
¾ cup water

Remove from the heat and add:

4 strips orange zest
6 whole cloves
4 cardamom seeds, crushed
One 3-inch cinnamon stick

Meanwhile, prepare the tea (see How to Brew Tea, 31), using:

3 tablespoons plus 1 teaspoon loose black tea
5 cups water

Pour the hot infusion into a heavy crystal bowl. Strain the steeped tea over the mixture and serve at once in punch cups or teacups.

LEMON VERBENA (VERVEINE) *3 to 5 servings*

This infusion method can be used for all herb teas.
Bring to a boil:

3 cups water

Remove from the heat and immediately pour over:

½ cup dried lemon verbena (*verveine*) leaves

set in a strainer insert (see How to Brew Tea, 31) or in a teapot. Let steep for 10 to 20 minutes. Remove the insert or strain out the leaves and serve at once in teacups.

ICED TEA *8 servings*

Rombauer family legend has it that this beverage originated in our native city of St. Louis—even though the inventor was actually an Englishman who hit upon the idea out of desperation. The year was 1904; the place, the St. Louis World's Fair; the circumstance, the indifference of the general public in the sweltering midwestern heat to Richard Blechynden's hot tea concession.

Prepare the tea (see How to Brew Tea, 31), using twice the quantity of leaves suggested. Stir, strain, and let cool to room temperature. Pour over ice cubes in tall glasses.

Serve with your choice of:

Lemon slices
Mint sprigs or bruised mint leaves
Sugar or honey
1 teaspoon rum per serving

COCOA AND HOT CHOCOLATE

The cacao tree, which produces the beans that eventually become cocoa, is native to the area around the Amazon River. The Aztecs learned how to roast and crush the beans to make a beverage they called *xocolatl*. The beans were considered so valuable that they were used as money, and the drink was reserved for royalty. The Spanish conquerors who pillaged the Aztec empire in the early 1500s brought the cocoa bean back to Spain; it was almost certainly the Spanish who first blended it with sugar, creating drinkable chocolate as we know it.

Cocoa powder, from which most hot chocolate (more correctly, hot cocoa) is made, is often sold premixed with powdered milk and sugar. And because cocoa powder does not dissolve instantly in liquid but tends to form lumps that must be smoothed by vigorous stirring, commercial mixes are treated to increase solubility. You will have much better hot chocolate if you start with unsweetened cocoa powder, sweeten it to taste, and mix it with fresh milk. Some cocoa powder has been "Dutched" by the addition of an alkaline agent. Dutch-processing darkens the natural whitish brown hue of cocoa powder to a lustrous mahogany color and helps make the powder more soluble, but it does not necessarily improve the flavor. In Mexico, a special wooden stirrer called a *molinillo* is used to fluff chocolate drinks just before serving. This also inhibits the formation of the cream "skin" that often appears on top. If you want this aerated effect, try a wire whisk or rotary beater. Serve the hot beverage in a deep, narrow chocolate cup to retain the heat, and spoon whipped cream on top if desired. You can also add marshmallows; use miniature ones or snip the larger kind into bits using scissors dipped in cold water.

AMERICAN HOT COCOA

1 cup

In the United States, we like the soothing character of milk and are accustomed to a relatively thin cocoa about the consistency of milk—especially if we are drinking it before bedtime. The proportions suggested here will produce a cocoa richer in flavor but far less sweet than you will get from most commercial mixes. Skim or low-fat milk can be substituted for whole milk, and so can half-and-half.

Stir together in a small, heavy saucepan:

1 tablespoon unsweetened cocoa
1 teaspoon sugar

Vigorously stir in, first by tablespoons and then in a slow, steady stream:

¾ cup milk

Heat, stirring constantly and scraping the bottom of the pan, over medium heat just until bubbles appear at the sides. Remove from the heat and stir in:

⅛ teaspoon vanilla, or ½ teaspoon Kahlúa or Grand Marnier (optional)

Top with:

Ground nutmeg or cinnamon
Whipped cream or marshmallows

ITALIAN HOT COCOA

2½ cups

Italians like a very dense cocoa and thicken it with cornstarch so that it attains an almost puddinglike or chocolate sauce consistency. For a thinner version, add more milk, water, or half-and-half or mix in some strong brewed coffee or espresso.

Stir together in a medium, heavy saucepan:

½ cup unsweetened cocoa
⅓ cup sugar
1 teaspoon cornstarch or arrowroot

Stir in thoroughly and set over low heat:

½ cup water

Stir in:

½ cup water
1 cup milk

Cook, stirring, over medium-low heat until the mixture is thickened and coats a spoon, about 10 minutes. Stir in:

⅛ teaspoon vanilla, or ½ teaspoon Kahlúa or Grand Marnier (optional)

Top each serving with:

Ground nutmeg or cinnamon
Whipped cream or marshmallows

ITALIAN MOCHA

Prepare Italian Hot Cocoa, above, substituting 1 cup strong brewed coffee, or ½ cup water and ½ cup espresso, for the water.

FRENCH HOT CHOCOLATE

6 cups

This is a much richer, sweeter beverage than cocoa—in truth, an opulent liquefied confection. Whipped cream, in this case, is superfluous.

In a medium, heavy saucepan, bring to a rolling boil:

1 cup light or heavy cream

Immediately remove from the heat and whisk in:

8 ounces bittersweet or semisweet chocolate, cut into ¼-inch pieces

Strain the mixture through a fine-mesh sieve or tea strainer, pushing it through with a rubber spatula or wooden spoon. Refrigerate the chocolate concentrate in a covered jar for up to 10 days.

For each cup of hot chocolate, stir together:

¼ cup chocolate concentrate
¼ cup milk, water, or coffee

Heat over low heat, or in a microwave on high for 45 to 60 seconds, until warm but not boiling. Stir in:

⅛ teaspoon vanilla, or ½ teaspoon Kahlúa or Grand Marnier (optional)

Top each serving with:

Ground nutmeg or cinnamon
Whipped cream or marshmallows

STOCKS & SAUCES

ABOUT STOCKS

Stocks are a vital ingredient in many sauces, soups, and other foods, and no store-bought variety can compare with a well-tended homemade version. Stock making is different from other kinds of cooking. Instead of calling for tender, young ingredients, stocks are best made with meat from older animals and mature vegetables, cooked slowly for a long time to extract every vestige of flavor. Purists may insist on using only fish stock in a fish soup or beef stock in a beef stew, but today's household rarely has the luxury of such precision. Since chicken and vegetable stocks are the mildest in flavor and the easiest to prepare, they have become our most popular—and can be used for, among other things, both fish soup and beef stew if necessary. Certainly, full-flavored beef stock or savory white veal stock is still worth making if you have the time.

The characteristics of any good stock are flavor, body, and clarity. Of the three, flavor is paramount, and the way to get it is by using a high proportion of ingredients to water. The most flavorful stocks are made with only enough water to cover the bones, shells, or vegetables. Additional water is needed only when it evaporates below the level of the ingredients before the stock is fully cooked. Follow the recipes for ideal ratios of liquid to solids, but the principle is simple: keep the solids covered while cooking. Cooking times for stocks depend on how long it takes to extract all the flavor from the ingredients. While it takes at least 8 hours for raw beef bones to give up all their richness and flavor, chicken bones only need to be boiled for half that time. Vegetable and fish stocks rarely require more than an hour to cook. In fact, their delicate flavors deteriorate if overcooked. When preparing ingredients for stock making, it is important to chop vegetables and bones to size according to their cooking times—large for long cooking and small for quick cooking—to allow their flavors to be fully extracted.

Simmering the stock past the recommended cooking time can produce an unpleasant bitter taste. A stock should be strained when all the flavors and goodness have been fully extracted from the meat, bones, and vegetables. If in doubt, retrieve a meaty bone from the simmering stock. If the meat still has some flavor, allow the stock to simmer for longer. If the meat is entirely tasteless and the bone joints are falling apart, it is time to strain the stock.

If a stock tastes weak after straining, remove and discard the fat, then simmer the stock briskly to reduce the water content and concentrate the flavor. This technique, known as reduction and used extensively in sauce making (see page 38), does produce a more deeply flavored stock, but in the process much of the

Stockpot

aromatic, fresh taste of the vegetables is lost. For this reason, we do not recommend reducing vegetable stock. In addition, not all dishes require a deep, concentrated flavor. A light stock is sometimes more appropriate for its subtlety. In instances when you want a hearty stock, first roast the bones and vegetables in a hot oven. Then transfer the bones and vegetables to the stockpot, pour off any excess grease, and add water or wine to the hot roasting pan to release the intensely flavored caramelized cooking juices—a step known as deglazing. Add the liquid to the stockpot. The resulting brown stock is darker and richer than a stock made by straight simmering, which is referred to as a white stock. This technique can be used for meat, poultry, fish, or vegetable stocks.

When choosing meat or bones for the stockpot, understand that meat adds flavor, while bones contribute body. Bones, especially those from the joints (knuckles and shoulders) of young animals, contain gelatin, which gives a stock body and a rich, smooth texture. Always use a combination of bones and meat, or look for particularly meaty bones. By definition, a stock is made with more bones than meat, while a broth is made from meat. For economy's sake, meat or poultry used for stock making can be removed from the pot before the stock is ready (while the meat still has flavor) and reserved for another meal; see Express Chicken Broth, 42. The resulting light stock can be used as is, or the bones can be returned to the pot and the stock cooked further. Raw ingredients produce the best stock, but in a pinch, leftover meat or vegetables will do. Leftover carcasses, such as turkey, broken up and pushed under the water, make a fine stock, 39.

The clarity of a stock is more than an aesthetic concern. A clear stock tastes clean and fresh, while a cloudy one will often seem greasy and muddled. The secret to a clear stock is to start with cold water, allow it to come slowly to a boil, then immediately lower the temperature to the slightest simmer while you carefully skim any impurities, froth, or fat that rises to the surface. This technique not only brings the most flavor out of the ingredients but also draws out impurities in the meat and bones that would otherwise cloud your stock. If a stock is permitted to boil, these impurities, in the form of the scum that forms on the surface of the stock, will be incorporated into the liquid instead. If you do not have enough time to simmer a stock gently, consider preparing one of the express broth recipes in this chapter.

TOOLS FOR MAKING STOCK

The most important tool is the most obvious—a stockpot, shown above. The best type is narrow, tall, and heavy-bottomed, to allow the stock to simmer gently without too much evaporation and to facilitate skimming. An 8- to 10-quart stockpot is ideal for making 2- to 4-quart batches of stock, but a smaller pot can be called into service for lesser quantities. Just be sure the pot is large enough to accommodate all of the solids (bones, shells, or vegetables) with room to cover them with 2 inches of water. Dutch ovens or wide soup pots also work, as long as you monitor the simmering stock and add more water whenever the level drops below the solids. Avoid aluminum pots, which may react with the ingredients and affect the flavor. A second large pot is handy for cooling strained stock; plastic containers work, but they insulate, and so the stock will not cool as quickly.

For making brown stocks, it is also essential to have a large roasting pan, preferably with handles. Sieves are another must—ideally two of them, one coarse and one fine. The long-handled conical kind, called a chinois or China cap, is ideal, but you can improvise a fine-mesh sieve by lining a colander with a double layer of cheesecloth, a dampened layer of paper towels, or a coffee filter. Gravy separators, also called fat separators, are a convenient way to remove excess fat from stock when there is no time to chill the stock and let the fat solidify.

SEASONING STOCK

Stocks are usually meant to be comparatively unassertive in flavor, so that they can be used for a number of purposes. Onions, carrots, and celery, the traditional mixture of aromatic vegetables for stock, known as a *mirepoix* in French, should be added sparingly about 30 minutes after the stock has begun to simmer and the impurities have been removed. Different styles of cooking alter this classic mixture; in Louisiana, for instance, the standard vegetable mixture

RULES FOR STOCK MAKING

The higher the ratio of solids to water, the more flavorful the stock. The water should just barely cover the ingredients. Too much water will make a watery stock. Add water during cooking if necessary.

Cut the ingredients into small pieces for quick-cooking stocks and larger pieces for long-cooking stocks. Express stocks use the smallest-cut ingredients, followed by fish stock, then vegetable stock, then poultry, and lastly meat.

Start with cold water and bring it slowly to a simmer. Never rush a stock. Simmer gently so bubbles just barely break on the surface. Never allow a stock to boil.

Skim the impurities that rise to the surface as the stock simmers—often during the first 30 minutes, and then once an hour or so. Have two bowls nearby, one filled with water to set the skimmer in so that it does not get covered with congealed fat and impurities, and a second bowl to collect what you skim off.

Stop cooking the stock when there is no flavor left in the ingredients.

Adjust the flavor. If the stock tastes too thin, simmer it until it is flavorful. As the water evaporates, the stock reduces in volume and its flavor is concentrated. Vegetable stock becomes bitter when overreduced.

A well-made stock contains very little fat. Begin by trimming all meat and bones of visible fat, and finish by either skimming the stock carefully while still warm or chilling the stock so the fat forms a solid layer and is easily removed. Alternatively, and easiest yet, use an inexpensive gravy separator.

Many variables affect the yield of a stock recipe, such as the size of the pot and the kind of meat or bones used. Ultimately, a good flavor is more important than achieving the exact yield.

includes onions, green peppers, and celery. Mushrooms and leeks are also common. The discreet use of either fresh or dried seasonings, including parsley, thyme, bay leaves, and peppercorns, in the form of a bouquet garni, below, is equally important. Salt is almost never added to stock. The reduction process, during both the original simmering and any subsequent cooking, would concentrate the salt and ruin the results. Vegetable stocks are an exception to the rule. Because they are generally lighter in flavor and are rarely reduced, some cooks prefer to add a small amount of salt during cooking to bring out the flavors. For express broth or quick-cooking stocks, there is no need to tie the seasonings in a bundle—they may simply be tossed in with the vegetables.

BOUQUET GARNI

Since herbs tend to float and get in the way as you skim the surface of a stock, we recommend tying them together in a little packet, known as a bouquet garni. Vary the contents to suit your dish, with additions such as whole cloves, dill, lemon zest, or garlic. For express broth or quick-cooking stocks, there is no need to tie the seasonings in a bundle—they may simply be tossed in with the vegetables.

Wrap in a 4 x 4-inch piece of cheesecloth:

Small bunch of parsley or parsley stems
8 sprigs fresh thyme, or 1 teaspoon dried
1 bay leaf
2 or 3 celery leaves (optional)

Tie the cheesecloth securely with a piece of cotton twine or omit the cheesecloth and simply tie the herbs together at their stems.

Refrigerate in a tightly covered container until ready to use.

STRAINING AND STORING STOCK

When the stock has finished cooking, strain it through a fine-mesh sieve (or a colander lined with a double layer of cheesecloth or a coffee filter) into another pot or a large heatproof container and discard the solids. Pressing heavily on the solids while straining may cloud the stock. We have recommended it for the vegetable stock recipes, where the extra flavor from the cooked vegetables is needed. Do not let the stock sit out at room temperature for long as it is a good breeding ground for bacteria. Speed up the cooling process by placing the hot pot, uncovered, in a sink of ice water and stirring it a few times. Once the stock cools enough so that it will not raise the temperature of your refrigerator, cover it tightly and chill it. When the stock is chilled, any fat will rise in a solid mass that must be removed before reheating. While cold, this fat layer actually protects the stock. Stock will keep for 3 to 5 days in the refrigerator. If refrigerated for longer, after 3 days skim the solidified fat from the surface and boil the stock for 10 minutes, then refrigerate it for another 3 to 5 days. For prolonged storage, transfer stock to pint or quart plastic containers or plastic freezer bags and freeze it. Small amounts of stock can also be frozen in ice cube trays. See also Reducing Stock to a Glaze, below, for other storage possibilities.

REDUCING STOCK TO A GLAZE

Meat, poultry, and fish (but not vegetable) stocks can be cooked down, or reduced, until they become a thick, syrupy glaze that is both potent and delectable. Although the lengthy reduction takes patience and care, the end product becomes a wonderfully convenient "secret ingredient" for seasoning and finishing; see About Gravy and Pan Sauces, 51. When it is fully reduced, a glaze is just 10 to 15 percent of the volume of original stock and it will last for months tightly covered in the refrigerator. Reduced stock can also be a practical solution to a shortage of refrigerator or freezer space, as it takes up less room. Reduced fish stock tends to be too strong for most tastes.

Prepare:

4 cups Brown Beef Stock, 40, Brown Veal Stock, 41, or Brown Chicken Stock, 39

Degrease the stock well and place it in a large pot over medium-high heat. Allow the stock to simmer vigorously. Skim any foam that rises to the surface and transfer the stock to gradually smaller pots as it reduces in volume. Lower the heat when the stock begins to get noticeably thicker and more concentrated to avoid burning. The glaze is ready when it coats the back of a spoon and only about 1 cup remains, anywhere from 2 to 4 hours depending on the shape of the pan. Remove from the heat and let cool. The glaze will solidify and feel rubbery to the touch. Cover and refrigerate, or cut into small squares equivalent to 1 tablespoon or more and freeze for use in preparing sauces, soups, or stews.

VEGETABLE STOCK

About 4 cups

Vegetable stock can be used in place of chicken or fish stock. Beyond the standard recipe, below, vegetable stocks allow for much improvisation. Good additions include onions, carrots, potatoes, corncobs, fennel, fresh herbs, ginger, garlic, washed organic vegetable skins, and even a few tablespoons of lentils. A small amount of soy sauce, a pinch of ground black pepper or red pepper flakes, and/or some salt can also be added. Vegetables to avoid include those in the cabbage family (except when used deliberately and with discretion), eggplant, and most strong greens (with the exception of kale); too many carrots or parsnips will turn the stock overly sweet (we like to include a small turnip to add complexity to the stock and to offset the sweetness of the carrot). When possible, tailor the ingredients to suit the recipe the stock will be used in. For example, a stock accented with ginger and garlic would be good in many Asian recipes. In general, 5 cups vegetables to 6 cups water makes about 3 to 4 cups stock.

Combine in a stockpot:

1 medium onion, sliced
1 leek, white part only, cleaned thoroughly and sliced
1 carrot, peeled and sliced
1 small turnip, peeled and sliced
6 cloves garlic, peeled and smashed
6 cups cold water
1 bouquet garni, 37

Simmer gently, partially covered, until the vegetables are completely softened, 45 to 60 minutes. Strain into a clean pot or heatproof plastic container, pressing down on the vegetables to extract the juices. Season with:

Salt and ground black pepper to taste (optional)

Let cool, uncovered, then refrigerate until ready to use.

VEGETABLE BROTH

Use this method to extract the most flavor from the vegetables. Prepare Vegetable Stock, above, first cooking the vegetables over medium heat in 2 tablespoons unsalted butter or oil, stirring occasionally, until they are wilted, about 15 minutes. Add the water and seasonings and continue as directed.

ROASTED VEGETABLE STOCK

About 4 cups

This is a more robust vegetable stock.

Preheat the oven to 400°F. Lightly grease a roasting pan.

Toss together in the prepared pan and roast until well browned, about 1 hour:

8 ounces mushrooms or mushroom stems, wiped clean
1 onion, quartered
2 carrots, peeled and cut into 2-inch pieces
8 cloves garlic, peeled and smashed
1 small turnip, peeled and cut into 2-inch pieces

Remove the vegetables to a stockpot, then deglaze the hot roasting pan by adding:

1 cup cold water

Scrape up any browned bits, then add to the pot along with:

6 cups cold water

1 bouquet garni, 37, including a pinch of red pepper flakes

Simmer gently, uncovered, until the vegetables are completely softened, 45 to 60 minutes. Strain into a clean pot or heatproof plastic container, pressing down on the vegetables to extract the juices. Season with:

Salt to taste

Let cool, uncovered, then refrigerate until ready to use.

COURT BOUILLON *4 cups*

Court bouillon is a seasoned liquid cooked for only a short time (*court* is French for *short*) and is especially useful when you haven't the time to make an actual stock or when your recipe requires only a lightly flavored broth. The composition can vary, but most contain some type of acid (lemon juice or wine vinegar), to help keep delicate fish firm during poaching, and an assortment of aromatic vegetables and herbs. Sometimes the bouillons are used only as a blanching and cooking medium and then discarded. Other times they become a sauce base after being used to poach fish or shellfish. Court Bouillon and Vegetable Stock, 38, are generally interchangeable, but vegetable stock has no lemon juice or vinegar.

Combine in a stockpot over medium heat:

6 cups cold water

½ cup chopped onions

½ cup chopped celery

¼ cup chopped leeks, tender white part only, washed thoroughly

¼ cup chopped carrots

1 bouquet garni, 37

Bring to a boil, reduce the heat, and let simmer gently, uncovered, until the vegetables are tender, about 20 minutes. Add:

3 tablespoons lemon juice or white wine vinegar

Simmer for another 10 minutes. Strain into a clean pot or heatproof plastic container. If desired, season with:

Salt and ground black pepper to taste

Use immediately to poach fish or vegetables or let cool, uncovered, then refrigerate until ready to use.

CHICKEN STOCK *About 8 cups*

Using the lesser amount of chicken suggested below will result in a lighter stock, which will reinforce the flavor in many dishes without adding a pronounced chicken taste; the greater amount will yield a richer one, to give backbone to soups and sauces.

Combine in a stockpot over medium heat:

4 to 5½ pounds chicken parts (backs, necks, wings, legs, or thighs), or 1 whole 4- to 5½-pound roasting chicken, well rinsed

16 cups cold water (or just enough to cover)

Bring to a boil, reduce the heat, and simmer gently. Skim often until impurities no longer appear, about 30 minutes. Add:

1 onion, coarsely chopped

1 carrot, peeled and coarsely chopped

1 celery stalk, coarsely chopped

1 bouquet garni, 37

Simmer, uncovered, for 3 hours, adding water as needed to cover. Strain into a clean pot or heatproof plastic container. Let cool, uncovered, then refrigerate. Remove the fat when ready to use.

BROWN (OR ROASTED) CHICKEN STOCK

This chicken stock variation has a richer flavor than "white" chicken stock.

Preheat the oven to 425°F. Prepare Chicken Stock, above, first combining the chicken parts and vegetables, without the bouquet garni, in a heavy roasting pan and roasting, stirring occasionally, until well browned, about 1 hour. Remove the chicken and vegetables to a stockpot and deglaze the hot roasting pan by adding 1 cup water and scraping up any browned bits. Add the liquid to the pot along with water to cover, about 16 cups, and the bouquet garni. Continue as directed.

TURKEY STOCK *12 to 20 cups*

This stock is the perfect use for a leftover Thanksgiving turkey carcass and the accompanying bits of meat. If the carcass is very large, break it into pieces before adding it to the pot. Turkey stock can be substituted in any dish calling for chicken stock.

Barely cover with cold water in a large stockpot over medium heat:

1 meaty turkey carcass, from a 12- to 25-pound turkey, broken up

Bring to a boil, reduce the heat, and simmer gently. Skim often until impurities no longer appear, about 30 minutes. Add:

1 onion, quartered

1 carrot, peeled and cut into 1-inch pieces

1 celery stalk, cut into 1-inch pieces

1 bouquet garni, 37

Simmer, uncovered, for 3 hours. Skim any impurities that rise and add water as needed to cover. Strain into a clean pot or heatproof plastic container. Let cool, uncovered, then refrigerate. Remove the fat when ready to use.

GAME STOCK *About 8 cups*

This stock can be made with rabbit or with duck, guinea hen, or other small game birds.

Combine in a stockpot over medium heat:

One 3-pound rabbit or fowl, or 3 pounds meaty game bones, rinsed and drained
16 cups cold water

Bring to a boil, reduce the heat, and simmer gently. Skim often until impurities no longer appear, about 30 minutes. Add:

1 medium onion, coarsely chopped
1 carrot, peeled and cut into 1-inch pieces
1 celery stalk, cut into 1-inch pieces
1 bouquet garni, 37

Simmer, uncovered, for 2½ hours, adding water as needed to cover. Strain into a clean pot or heatproof plastic container. Let cool, uncovered, then refrigerate. Remove the fat when ready to use.

BROWN BEEF STOCK *About 10 cups*

The combination of beef shanks and chicken bones produces a hearty stock in half the time it takes to make Classic Beef Stock, below.

Preheat the oven to 425°F. Lightly oil a roasting pan. Place in the prepared pan and roast for 15 minutes:

3 pounds meaty beef shanks, cut into 2-inch pieces, or oxtails, split into chunks, or a combination

Add:

1 pound chicken parts (backs, necks, wings, legs, or thighs), well rinsed
2 medium onions, quartered
2 carrots, peeled and thickly sliced
2 celery stalks, cut into 2-inch pieces

Roast, stirring occasionally to prevent the vegetables from burning, until the bones are well browned, about 40 minutes. Transfer the meat and vegetables to a stockpot, carefully pour off any excess grease without discarding the caramelized cooking juices, and add to the hot roasting pan:

2 cups cold water

Scrape up any browned bits, then add the liquid to the pot along with:

14 cups cold water (or just enough to cover)

Bring to a boil over medium heat, skim off the impurities, reduce the heat, and simmer gently. Skim often until impurities no longer appear, about 30 minutes. Add:

1 leek, split lengthwise, cleaned thoroughly, and cut into 2-inch pieces
1 bouquet garni, 37, including 1 whole clove

Simmer, uncovered, for 4 hours, skimming as necessary and adding water as needed to cover. Strain into a clean pot or heatproof plastic container. Let cool, uncovered, then refrigerate. Remove the fat when ready to use.

CLASSIC BEEF STOCK

Prepare Brown Beef Stock, above, substituting 5 pounds beef bones, preferably knucklebones, for the beef shanks and chicken. Cut the vegetables into larger pieces and simmer the stock for 8 hours.

LAMB STOCK *About 7 cups*

Good for boosting the flavor in lamb soups, stews, and sauces. Do not use in recipes calling for fowl or other kinds of meat, as the distinctive lamb character will overpower other flavors.

Prepare Brown Beef Stock, above, substituting 2 pounds lamb shoulder chops, well trimmed, for the beef and chicken and decreasing the onions, carrots, celery, and water by one-half. Omit the leek. Simmer for 3 hours.

WHITE VEAL STOCK *About 8 cups*

The comparatively mild flavor of this stock makes it highly versatile. Blanching the veal breast and bones by briefly boiling them and discarding the water helps create a clear stock. Ask your butcher to split the veal bones.

Cover with cold water in a stockpot over high heat:

1½ pounds veal breast
1½ pounds veal knucklebones, split

Bring to a boil. Immediately drain and rinse the veal, the bones, and the pot. Return the veal breast and bones to the pot along with:

12 ounces chicken parts (backs, necks, wings, legs, or thighs), well rinsed
12 cups cold water (or just enough to cover)

Bring to a boil, skim off the impurities, and reduce the heat. Simmer gently for about 20 minutes. Add:

2 large onions, coarsely chopped
2 medium leeks, white and tender green parts, cleaned thoroughly and chopped
2 carrots, peeled and coarsely chopped
1 celery stalk, coarsely chopped
1 bouquet garni, 37

Simmer, uncovered, for 3 to 4 hours, adding water as needed to cover. Strain into a clean pot or heatproof plastic container. Let cool, uncovered, then refrigerate. Remove the fat when ready to use.

BROWN VEAL STOCK

Preheat the oven to 425°F. Lightly grease a roasting pan. Proceed as for White Veal Stock, above, but first roast the veal in the prepared pan for 15 minutes; add the chicken and vegetables, without the bouquet garni, and roast until well browned, about 1 hour. Remove the meat and vegetables to a stockpot, carefully pour off any excess grease without discarding the caramelized cooking juices, and add 1 cup cold water or wine (red or white) to the hot roasting pan. Scrape up any browned bits, then add the liquid to the pot along with cold water to cover. Bring to a boil, reduce the heat, and simmer gently, skimming often for the first 30 minutes. Add the bouquet garni and continue as directed.

FISH STOCK

About 6 cups

Fish heads and bones are available from your fishmonger. Be sure they smell fresh, and take the time to remove all traces of blood and viscera before making stock. If bones are unavailable, use inexpensive whole fish, like porgies or small bass. For a mild-tasting, all-purpose fish stock, avoid oily fish such as salmon or herring.

Combine in a stockpot over medium heat:

2 pounds fish heads and bones, or whole fish, scaled, gutted, gills and viscera removed, rinsed well and drained
1 small onion, sliced
1 large leek, white and tender green parts, cleaned thoroughly and sliced
½ bulb fennel, sliced (optional)
1 to 2 cloves garlic (optional)
1 cup dry white wine (optional)
6 cups cold water (or just enough to cover)
1 bouquet garni, **37**

Bring to a boil, reduce the heat, and simmer gently. Cook, uncovered, skimming often, for 30 to 40 minutes. Strain into a clean pot or heatproof plastic container. Let cool, uncovered, then refrigerate until ready to use.

FISH FUMET

This is a richer-tasting fish stock.

Prepare Fish Stock, above, first cooking the vegetables over medium-low heat in 2 tablespoons butter until they begin to soften, about 5 minutes. Add the fish heads and bones and cook, stirring once or twice, until they begin to turn opaque, 5 minutes more. Be sure not to let the vegetables or fish brown. Add the wine, cold water, and bouquet garni and continue as directed.

SHRIMP STOCK

About 3 cups

Shrimp shells can be accumulated in the freezer until you have enough to make this stock. The heads have the most flavor, so include them if possible. Leftover lobster heads and shells also make great additions. For a clear stock, omit the tomato paste.

Heat in a stockpot over medium-high heat:

2 tablespoons vegetable oil

Add and cook, stirring occasionally, until the shells are bright pink and aromatic, about 15 minutes:

3 cups uncooked shrimp shells, well rinsed and drained (from about 2 pounds shrimp)
2 small onions, diced
2 small carrots, peeled and diced
2 celery stalks, diced

Stir in:

2 tablespoons tomato paste (optional)

Add:

6 cups cold water
1 bay leaf
½ tablespoon lightly crushed black peppercorns
Splash of Pernod or ¼ teaspoon fennel seeds (optional)

Bring almost to a boil, reduce the heat, and simmer gently, partially covered, for 20 minutes. Strain into a clean pot or heatproof plastic container, pressing down on the shells to extract all the liquid. Let cool, uncovered, then refrigerate until ready to use.

DASHI

About 4 cups

One of the bases of traditional Japanese cuisine, this stock is made quickly, from just two ingredients—*kombu,* or kelp, and *katsuobushi,* or dried bonito flakes, also referred to as smoky fish flakes—both of which can be found in Asian markets or health food stores. Dashi should be used within 4 to 5 days of preparation. It should not be boiled or cooked for too long, and it does not freeze well. When reheating, do not boil.

Combine in a stockpot over high heat:

One 5 x 4-inch piece *kombu* (kelp)
4½ cups cold water

Bring almost to a boil. Immediately remove from the heat and stir in:

⅓ cup loosely packed *katsuobushi* (dried bonito flakes)

Let stand until the flakes begin to sink, 2 to 3 minutes. Remove the *kombu* with tongs. Strain the stock at once into a clean pot or heatproof plastic container. Let cool, uncovered, then refrigerate until ready to use.

CHICKEN-ENRICHED DASHI (TORI-GARA DASHI)

About 4 cups

Cover with cold water in a stockpot over high heat:

1 pound chicken parts (backs, necks, wings, legs, or thighs), well rinsed

Bring to a boil. Immediately drain and rinse the chicken parts and the pot. Return the chicken to the pot along with:

One 5 x 4-inch piece *kombu* (kelp)

6 cups cold water

Bring to a boil, reduce the heat, and simmer gently. Cook, uncovered, skimming often, for 20 to 25 minutes. Season with:

1 tablespoon soy sauce

Remove from the heat and stir in:

⅓ cup loosely packed *katsuobushi* (dried bonito flakes)

Let stand until the flakes begin to sink, 2 to 3 minutes. Remove the *kombu* with tongs. Strain the stock into a clean pot or heatproof plastic container. Let cool, uncovered, then refrigerate until ready to use.

ABOUT BROTHS

Unlike stocks, which are made primarily from bones, broths are made from meat (except for vegetable broth), and they cook for shorter periods of time. The resulting liquid has a fresher, more definable flavor but less body than a stock. For this reason, broths are ideal for soups. Most of the canned stocks sold today are closer to broths and are best used in soups, not sauces, since they are often seasoned with salt and other seasonings, which makes it inadvisable to boil them down.

CHICKEN BROTH

About 12 cups

Once this fine-tasting broth is made, the chicken can be removed from the pot and used in soup or any other dish calling for cooked chicken.

Combine in a stockpot over medium heat:

One whole 3½- to 4-pound chicken, well rinsed

12 cups cold water

Bring almost to a boil, reduce the heat, and simmer gently, skimming often until impurities no longer appear. Meanwhile, pulse in a food processor until finely chopped:

1 medium onion, cut into eighths

1 carrot, peeled and cut into 2-inch pieces

1 celery stalk, cut into 2-inch pieces

Add the chopped vegetables to the pot. Simmer, uncovered, until the chicken is cooked, about 40 minutes. Remove the chicken and reserve. Strain the broth into a clean pot or heatproof plastic container. Let cool, uncovered, then refrigerate. Remove the fat when ready to use.

EXPRESS CHICKEN BROTH

About 4 cups

This broth can also be made with canned beef broth or consommé; just omit the giblets.

Combine in a heavy saucepan:

Three 14½-ounce cans ready-to-serve reduced-sodium chicken broth

Any chicken giblets, trimmings, or bones on hand (optional)

Contents of 1 bouquet garni, 37 (no need to wrap)

Cut into 1-inch pieces and pulse in a food processor until finely chopped:

1 small onion

1 small carrot

1 small celery stalk, with leaves

1 leek, white part only, cleaned thoroughly, or 3 whole scallions

1 small garlic clove (optional)

Bring almost to a boil over medium-high heat, reduce the heat, and simmer gently for about 30 minutes. Strain into a clean pot or heatproof plastic container. Let cool, uncovered, then refrigerate. Remove the fat when ready to use.

EXPRESS BEEF BROTH

About 4 cups

This is not clear, like a long-simmered stock, but it has a good, beefy flavor.

Combine in a stockpot over medium heat:

1½ pounds boneless beef chuck, cut into 1-inch cubes and pulsed in a food processor until coarsely chopped

5 cups cold water

Bring almost to a boil, reduce the heat, and simmer gently, skimming often until impurities no longer appear. Add:

1 onion, cut into 1-inch pieces

1 large leek, white and tender green parts, cleaned thoroughly and chopped

1 carrot, peeled and sliced

1 tablespoon tomato paste

5 parsley stems

½ teaspoon dried thyme

3 black peppercorns, lightly crushed

1 whole clove

Simmer, uncovered, for 1 hour. Strain into a clean pot or heatproof plastic container. Let cool, uncovered, then refrigerate. Remove the fat when ready to use. The stock will separate, so whisk before using.

EXPRESS FISH BROTH *About 4 cups*

When you have neither the time nor the inclination to procure fish bones for fish stock, the combination of bottled clam juice and canned chicken broth or stock provides a decent-tasting substitute. If you have any fish trimmings on hand, throw them in as well.

Heat in a medium, heavy skillet:

½ tablespoon olive oil

Add:

1 carrot, peeled and finely chopped
1 small onion or large leek, finely chopped
1 clove garlic, finely chopped

Cook, stirring, over medium-high heat until soft. Add:

½ cup dry vermouth

Stir for about 1 minute, then blend in:

Four 8-ounce bottles clam juice
1½ cups mild chicken broth
Any fish trimmings on hand (optional)
¼ small lemon (optional)

Simmer for 20 minutes, skimming and stirring occasionally. Strain into a clean pot or heatproof plastic container. Let cool, uncovered, then refrigerate until ready to use.

EXPRESS SHELLFISH CHIPOTLE BROTH *About 2½ cups*

This light but highly flavorful broth is good enough to be used as a sauce. Ladle an ounce or two over vegetables, legumes, or seafood immediately before serving.

Combine in a large saucepan over medium heat:

1½ cups uncooked shrimp shells, well rinsed and drained (from about 1 pound shrimp)
2 teaspoons tomato paste
½ teaspoon chopped chipotle peppers in adobo sauce, or to taste
Large pinch of saffron
½ cup dry white wine

Bring almost to a boil, reduce the heat, and simmer gently, partially covered, for 5 to 10 minutes. Add:

2½ cups Chicken Stock, 39

Simmer for 10 minutes more. Strain through a fine-mesh sieve and let the stock rest for a few minutes to allow any solids to settle. Carefully transfer to a clean saucepan or heatproof plastic container, leaving the solids behind. Use immediately or let cool, uncovered, then refrigerate until ready to use.

ABOUT SAUCES

The French chefs, who codified sauces, defined a sauce as any liquid or semiliquid embellishment that enhances, gives moisture to, and/or adds richness to the food it accompanies. The classic French sauces—based on an intricate but logical system of stocks and other *fonds de cuisine,* or kitchen basics—are not the end of the story. Every cuisine has sauces of its own, sometimes quite different from anything the French would recognize, and Americans have adopted and adapted many of these, adding our own ideas where appropriate. We also use sauces differently from the French, at least some of the time, and in so doing have redefined what a sauce can be. A sauce no longer needs to be perfectly smooth or so mild that it can be eaten by itself almost like a soup (once an ideal for sauce).

ABOUT FLAVOR BASES

Many sauce recipes begin by sautéing a mix of aromatic vegetables, spices, herbs, or other savory ingredients to develop a *flavor base.* Cooking these first in a bit of butter, olive oil, or other fat releases their flavors so that as you add other ingredients—stock, wine, tomatoes, for example—the entire sauce becomes infused with the character of the flavor base.

This universal cooking technique forms the foundation for dishes all across the globe. The first step in a Chinese stir-fry is to cook a smashed wedge of ginger and some crushed or chopped garlic in hot oil in a wok. In southern parts of Africa, chopped onions and garlic are sautéed in peanut oil with cayenne or chili peppers. The French have *mirepoix*—onions, carrots, and celery cooked gently in butter to bring out their inherent sweetness (a *white mirepoix* for light-colored dishes substitutes the white part of leeks for the carrots); a *matignon* adds mushrooms and chopped ham to the standard *mirepoix* to create a more assertive base. The Italian version, *soffritto,* usually consists of onions, carrots, and celery sautéed in olive oil in place of butter; a *soffritto* can also include fennel, leeks, garlic, or chopped herbs such as parsley.

TOOLS FOR SAUCE MAKING

For sauce making, the most important utensil is a good, heavy-bottomed, 1½- to 3-quart saucepan. Saucepans with sloping slides, sometimes called Windsor pans, are excellent for reducing or cooking down sauces to concentrate flavor: they allow sauces to boil down quickly, and the slanted sides facilitate whisking and stirring. As with stockpots, avoid aluminum, which may react with some ingredients. Other useful tools include a skimmer, or wide, saucer-shaped flat ladle (a large flat spoon is a good substitute); an assortment of ladles in various sizes; a whisk (vital for emulsified sauces such as hollandaise and mayonnaise)—preferably the elongated pear-shaped kind or a flat whisk, which easily gets into corners and smoothes out roux-based sauces; an assortment of wooden spoons; and both flat wooden spatulas (called "chef's spatulas") and rubber ones for scraping sauces from bowls or saucepans. A double boiler can be used to make some sauces and their variations, but a stainless-steel bowl placed over a saucepan works just as well. A blender or food processor can be used for making emulsified sauces and many condiments. A good-quality fine-mesh sieve is a must for straining. A food mill is very useful for making vegetable and bean purees.

ABOUT THICKENERS FOR SAUCE

Not all sauces need to be thick enough to coat food, but those that do are usually thickened with an added agent of some kind. The following are the most common thickeners:

Roux: A roux is a mixture of fat and flour, cooked together, usually in equal amounts. Although exact amounts of fat and flour are called for in recipes, it is solely the amount of flour that determines the thickness of the sauce. Fat lubricates and smooths the flour so it does not form lumps when combined with stock or other liquid. The preferred fat is butter, but it could also be chicken or other poultry fat, rendered meat drippings, oil, or margarine. A roux is started by melting butter or other fat, adding flour, and cooking the two together over low heat, whisking or stirring constantly to prevent scorching. During this process, which takes only a few minutes, the starch in the flour expands as it blends with the fat; if a roux cooks too quickly, the resulting mixture will be grainy. (If the fat floats to the top, the roux has separated; this happens rarely, but if it does, there is nothing to do but to throw out the roux and start over.) There are three types of roux—white, blond, and brown, each with a different cooking time. White roux, used to make traditional white sauce, should be cooked just until the butter and flour are evenly incorporated and smooth and should be removed from the heat before the roux begins to darken at all, 3 to 5 minutes. Blond roux, used in velouté-based sauces and cream soups, cooks for a little longer, until it begins to give off a faint nutty aroma and turns an ivory color, 6 to 7 minutes. Brown roux, basic to Cajun and Creole cooking, cooks the longest—8 to 15 minutes and sometimes longer—until it is a dark brown and has a strong nutty fragrance. (The longer you cook a roux, the less it will thicken. The heat eventually breaks down the starch in the flour.) Whether making white, blond, or brown roux, let it cool slightly before slowly whisking in the stock or other liquid. If you have made the roux in advance, it is important to first warm either it or the liquid to be added to it. Despite the legendary rule to add hot liquid to cold roux and cold liquid to hot roux, almost any combination will work. Simply avoid trying to combine cold roux and cold liquid, which would become lumpy, or hot roux and hot liquid, which would spatter and cause burns. Once the roux and liquid are combined, stir constantly until the sauce is thickened and comes to a simmer. Once it has thickened, stir and skim often during the slow, gentle cooking needed to reduce the sauce to the desired consistency. Any trace of a floury taste will disappear after 10 minutes of slow simmering. If lumps do appear, strain the sauce through a fine-mesh sieve before proceeding with the recipe.

Kneaded Butter (Beurre Manié): This is a convenient last-minute thickener, added to a cooked liquid just before serving, such as a sauce or a stew that has not become as thick as desired. Kneaded butter is simply softened butter mixed with an equal proportion of flour and kneaded by hand or with a fork. It is shaped into balls the size of a pea that can be whisked into a simmering liquid. Once you have added the butter, bring the sauce back to a simmer and remove the pan from the heat; extended cooking or boiling may cause the sauce to separate. Since the flour is not cooked, it can leave a raw flour taste, so kneaded butter should be used sparingly.

Flour Paste: Sometimes called whitewash, flour paste is made from one part flour and two parts cold water or stock whisked together and then added as needed to the simmering stock or pan drippings. Let the sauce heat until it is thickened and simmer for about 3 minutes, stirring, to eliminate the raw taste of the flour.

Cornstarch: Food critics sometimes express their disapproval of certain dishes by noting that they seem to have been thickened with cornstarch. Why this is considered undesirable is beyond us; cornstarch is an excellent and relatively unobtrusive thickening agent. A pure starch with almost twice the thickening power of flour, cornstarch thickens sauces and soups while giving them a glossy and somewhat translucent appearance familiar from many sweet desserts and Chinese sauces. Unlike flour, cornstarch adds no floury taste. It is dissolved in a small amount of cold liquid before being whisked into the simmering sauce at the last minute. Cornstarch thickens immediately, allowing you to easily judge the amount needed. One tablespoon cornstarch will thicken about 1½ to 2 cups liquid. Overheating will thin a cornstarch-thickened sauce.

Arrowroot: Arrowroot, a pure starch derived from a tropical American plant by the same name, performs much like cornstarch when dissolved in cold liquid and whisked in at the last moment to thicken a sauce, making it shiny and glossy. Arrowroot has a bit more thickening power than cornstarch, and it is less likely to thin out if overheated. Buy only small amounts; it begins to lose its effectiveness when stored for more than 1 or 2 months.

Potato Starch: Preferred by some cooks as a starch thickener but somewhat difficult to find, potato starch is the pure starch derived from potatoes. Like cornstarch and arrowroot, potato starch, when dissolved in cold liquid and added to a simmering stock, thickens immediately and gives the sauce some translucency. Overheating the sauce, however, will thin it out. One tablespoon of potato starch will moderately thicken 1 cup of liquid.

Tapioca Flour: Tapioca is derived from the South American cassava root. Its flour is sometimes used for thickening sauces, clear fruit glazes, and fruit fillings, especially those intended to be served cold or frozen as it does not break down when frozen, the way flour-thickened sauces do. Beware of overcooking liquids thickened with tapioca flour. Never let them boil as the tapioca will become stringy. Once the liquid begins to simmer, remove it from the heat and let it sit for 15 minutes, stirring only once or twice during the first 5 minutes, and the sauce will set. Use 1 tablespoon tapioca flour per cup of liquid.

Breadcrumbs and Ground Nuts: Finely ground breadcrumbs and pulverized nuts, especially almonds, have been used since the Middle Ages to add texture and thickness to sauces. Today we commonly thicken a pesto with ground pine nuts, and breadcrumbs add body to the spicy Mediterranean mayonnaise known as rouille, 75.

Filé Powder: Filé powder, the classic thickener of Creole gumbos, is derived from the bark of the sassafras tree. *Filé* translates to the word *string*, an apt description of its thickening ability. Filé powder is added at the last minute to a pot of simmering gumbo. Besides adding texture, it lends a distinct, earthy, somewhat musty flavor, making it unsuitable as a universal thickening agent. It is rarely found in anything besides filé gumbo.

Egg Yolks: Egg yolks do not thicken a sauce as dramatically as the starch-based thickeners, but they add body and richness and give the sauce a smooth, satiny quality. They are never added directly to hot liquid but are stirred into a bit of milk, cream, or stock, to which some of the sauce itself is then added; the sauce is then removed from the heat and this mixture is stirred in. Finally, the sauce is returned to low heat and stirred constantly until it has thickened slightly. (The sauce should never boil.) This technique, known as tempering the yolks, prevents them from curdling. Two yolks with ¼ to ⅓ cup cream will enrich and thicken about 1½ cups of sauce.

Cream and Crème Fraîche: Cream functions as a thickener when it is first simmered to reduce its volume. This can be done directly in the sauce, as in a gravy or pan sauce, or separately and then added to the sauce. In either case, use a large heavy-bottomed pan so that the cream will not boil over, and let the cream simmer until it is reduced by about half its original volume. Reduced cream can be used in large amounts for white sauces or in small doses to add a satiny finish to almost any other sauce. Crème fraîche can be spooned directly into a simmering sauce to add body, richness, and a subtle tangy flavor. While it is as thick as sour cream or clotted cream to begin with, crème fraîche will not separate if the sauce is boiled down.

Butter: Using butter is one of the most common and easiest ways to give a beautiful, silky finish to a sauce, while slightly thickening it and improving its flavor. To finish a sauce with butter, remove the pan from the heat, then add softened—not melted—butter bit by bit, moving the pan in a circular motion so that the butter swirls around in the sauce (or whisk it in gradually). Once the butter is added, the sauce cannot be reheated or held for very long. About 1 tablespoon butter is used to finish 1 cup of sauce. Flavored butters, 76 to 78, can also be used when their flavors are appropriate.

Purees: Purees of cooked vegetables and fruits are an excellent way to add body and flavor to a sauce. The puree can be very smooth or slightly chunky. Starchy vegetables, such as potatoes or white beans, will make a sauce quite thick, while other vegetables and fruits, such as roasted red peppers, stewed onions, or pureed apples, will thicken it only slightly. (Purees, of course, are much lower in fat and calories than most other thickeners.)

Reduction: Reducing a sauce means simply concentrating what is already there. When a meat or poultry stock is simmered until it is thick and syrupy, the gelatin from the bones and meat in the stock will thicken any sauce. Remember not to add salt and pepper until after a sauce is fully reduced or you may find it overseasoned.

ABOUT MOTHER SAUCES

The great French sauces, each with infinite possibilities for variation, are based on just a few basic formulas. To understand this orderly system of classic French sauces, it is necessary to come to know the leading sauces, also called Mother Sauces, from which all other sauces are born. These leading sauces include Sauce Béchamel; Velouté Sauce; Brown Sauce, or Espagnole; and Hollandaise. Once you master these, it is a simple matter of adding flavor accents and ingredients to turn out an exciting array of delectable sauces.

SAUCE BÉCHAMEL (WHITE SAUCE)

About 1 cup

Named for Louis de Béchamel, a seventeenth-century French financier and courtier, this French sauce is prized for its unassertive character and smooth texture, which make it the ideal agent to thicken and bind a wide range of dishes and to coat many kinds of foods. Make your béchamel a little thicker than you think it should be, because it is easier to thin it out than to thicken it. When combining béchamel sauce with other ingredients, use 1 cup sauce for every 2 cups solids, and use a light hand with the seasoning until you taste the mixture. The sauce can be refrigerated or kept warm in the top of a double boiler. Place a piece of wax paper directly on the surface of the sauce to prevent a skin from forming.

Combine in a small saucepan over very low heat:

1¼ cups milk
¼ onion with 1 bay leaf stuck to it using 2 whole cloves
Pinch of freshly grated nutmeg (optional)

Simmer gently for 15 minutes, uncovered, to infuse flavor into the milk. Discard the onion, bay leaf, and cloves. Meanwhile, melt in a medium, heavy saucepan over low heat:

2 tablespoons unsalted butter

Stir in:

2 tablespoons all-purpose flour

Cook, uncovered, stirring occasionally with a wooden spoon or spatula, over medium-low heat until the roux is just fragrant but not darkened, 2 to 3 minutes. Remove from the heat and let cool slightly. Slowly whisk in the warm milk and return the saucepan to the heat. Bring the sauce slowly to a simmer, whisking to prevent lumps, and cook, stirring often and skimming any skin that forms on the surface, over low heat, without boiling, until it reaches the consistency of thick cream soup, 8 to 10 minutes. Strain through a fine-mesh sieve, if desired. Season with:

Salt and ground white pepper to taste

Use as an ingredient in another recipe or proceed with one of the sauce variations described below or with one of your own inspiration.

THIN BÉCHAMEL SAUCE

Use as a quick base for cream soups by adding pureed vegetables.

Prepare Sauce Béchamel, above, decreasing the butter to 1 tablespoon and the flour to 1 tablespoon. The finished sauce should be thick enough to coat the back of a spoon.

THICK BÉCHAMEL SAUCE

Use as a soufflé base or to bind a runny casserole.

Prepare Sauce Béchamel, above, increasing the butter to 3 tablespoons and the flour to 3 tablespoons.

SAUCE AURORE (BÉCHAMEL WITH TOMATO FLAVORING)

A lovely rosy sauce with a hint of acidity.

Prepare Sauce Béchamel, above, stirring in a tablespoon or two of concentrated tomato paste or sun-dried tomato paste before straining. Just before serving, whisk in 2 tablespoons softened unsalted butter.

SAUCE MORNAY (CHEESE SAUCE)

For poached or baked eggs; steamed vegetables; poached poultry, fish, or seafood; filled crêpes; and an elegant macaroni and cheese. The sauce can also be smoothed over these foods and browned in the oven or under a broiler.

Prepare Sauce Béchamel, above, adding ¼ cup firmly packed finely grated cheese—2 tablespoons Gruyère and 2 tablespoons Parmesan is traditional, but any aged cheese is very good, alone or in combination. Try Swiss, Cheddar, or blue cheeses such as Gorgonzola,

Roquefort, and Stilton. Cook, stirring, just until the cheese is melted—the cheese can turn stringy. Season with salt, and, in place of pepper, a pinch of ground red pepper and a few grains of mace or nutmeg. Should the sauce become stringy, bring it just to a simmer and whisk in a few drops of dry white wine or lemon juice, then remove from the heat.

MUSTARD SAUCE

For broiled fish or ham.

Prepare Sauce Béchamel, above, adding 2 to 4 tablespoons Dijon, grainy French, or brown English mustard to taste.

SAUCE SOUBISE (ONION SAUCE)

For fish, veal, sweetbreads, lamb, or main-dish vegetables.

Prepare Sauce Béchamel, above, and set aside. Combine 1 chopped large onion and 2 tablespoons stock in a heavy 1-quart saucepan. Cover and cook over low heat, shaking occasionally, until the onions are tender but not browned, about 12 minutes. Stir in the Sauce Béchamel, cover, and cook over low heat for 15 minutes, stirring frequently. Press through a fine sieve (reserve the onions for a soup). The sauce will be thick. Return to low heat and slowly whisk in 2 to 4 tablespoons cream or milk to the desired consistency. Add salt and ground white pepper to taste.

SAUCE HONGROISE (ONION AND PAPRIKA SAUCE)

For chicken, game birds, veal, beef, fish, noodles, and hearty vegetables.

Prepare Sauce Béchamel, above, and set aside. In a heavy 1-quart saucepan, melt 1 tablespoon butter over low heat. Stir in ½ cup minced onions, cover, and cook, stirring often, over low heat until the onions are thoroughly tender but not browned, about 20 minutes. Add ½ tablespoon sweet or hot paprika and stir, uncovered, for about 30 seconds to cook the spice. Stir in the Sauce Béchamel and simmer gently, stirring often, for 10 minutes. Strain through a fine-mesh sieve, then whisk in 2 to 4 tablespoons sour cream, light or heavy cream, milk, or stock to the desired consistency. If you wish, whisk in 2 tablespoons softened butter just before serving.

CURRY SAUCE

An American invention, especially good for leftovers.

Prepare Sauce Béchamel, above, and set aside. In a small skillet, heat 2 tablespoons butter. Add 1 finely chopped large onion and 1½ to 2½ teaspoons curry powder to taste. Cook over low heat until the onions are tender, about 2 minutes, stirring often. Blend into the Sauce Béchamel. Add salt and ground white pepper to taste.

À LA KING SAUCE

For a quick use of leftovers, stir this sauce into 3 cups diced chicken or turkey and serve it hot over toast or in a puff pastry shell. Prepare Sauce Béchamel, above, and set aside. In a heavy 1-quart saucepan, heat 1 tablespoon butter. Add 1 minced green bell pepper and cook, stirring, over low heat until tender, about 5 minutes. Stir in 1 pimiento or red bell pepper, cut into matchsticks, and sprinkle with 4 teaspoons dry sherry. Stir in the Sauce Béchamel. Add salt and ground white pepper to taste.

YOGURT AND OLIVE OIL BÉCHAMEL

About 3 cups

This is a contemporary version of classic béchamel from gifted Greek cook Aglaia Kremezi.

Whisk together in a saucepan over medium heat:

4 tablespoons olive oil
4 tablespoons all-purpose flour

Cook, whisking, for about 1 minute until the mixture starts to froth. Remove from the heat, whisk for a couple of minutes, then pour in, whisking constantly:

2 cups cold whole milk

Whisk in:

1 cup whole-milk yogurt

Set over the heat and, whisking, bring to a boil to thicken. The mixture may look curdled, but it will smooth out once it has boiled and thickened. Stir in:

⅔ cup grated Gruyère cheese
Sea salt to taste
Pinch of ground black or white pepper

FLOURLESS WHITE SAUCE

1 cup

For years, chefs and home cooks have looked for ways to avoid the starchy flour-thickened sauces they associate with heavy French cooking. This luxurious sauce, popularized by James Peterson in his authoritative book *Sauces,* depends on boiling down stock and heavy cream to give it body.

The result is not as thick as the traditional white sauce, but it is intensely rich and creamy. Use a saucepan large enough to allow the cream to foam up, and whisk the sauce from time to time to keep it from becoming grainy. Do not attempt to boil the cream more than recommended, or it will lose its delicacy and curdle. Use this in place of Sauce Béchamel for any of the variations, except when the recipe relies on the binding or browning ability of the sauce, as in soufflés, casseroles, and croquettes. Do not use for a gratin either; if exposed to the high heat of a broiler, the sauce will separate and break.

Boil in a small, heavy saucepan over high heat until cooked down to ½ cup:

2 cups Chicken Stock, 39

Set aside. Meanwhile, boil in a small, heavy saucepan over medium-high heat, whisking to prevent it from boiling over, until reduced by half:

1 cup heavy cream

Whisk the cream into the stock and add:

Salt and ground white pepper to taste

TOMATO CREAM SAUCE

Serve this sauce on meats, poultry, or fish.

Prepare Flourless White Sauce, above, and stir in 4 tablespoons of your favorite tomato sauce, such as Italian Tomato Sauce, 304, Sun-Dried Tomato Sauce, 305, Red Pesto Sauce, 308, or 1½ tablespoons tomato paste. Simmer for 2 minutes and serve warm.

CHILI CREAM SAUCE

Serve this with beef, lamb, pork, or poultry.

Remove the stems and seeds from 1 or 2 large dried chili peppers, such as pasillas or anchos, cover the chilies with hot water and let soak until softened, about 20 minutes. Drain. Either chop the chili peppers by hand or puree in a food processor. Prepare Flourless White Sauce, above, and add the chilies to the sauce. Simmer gently over low heat for 3 minutes. Season with salt and ground red pepper to taste.

NO-CREAM WHITE SAUCE

About 2½ cups

A puree of starchy rice replaces the look and feel of heavy cream in this deceptively smooth and rich-tasting reduced-fat sauce base. Add seasonings and herbs to make it a sauce on its own, or use as an ingredient in casseroles and soups.

Heat in a saucepan over medium heat:

2 tablespoons olive oil

Add and cook, stirring, until softened:

½ cup chopped onions

Add and cook, stirring constantly, for 2 minutes more:

⅓ cup rice (preferably medium- or short-grain)

Add:

⅔ cup Chicken Stock, 39, or Vegetable Stock, 38

1 cup dry white wine

Cover and simmer until the liquid is almost absorbed and the rice is very soft, about 25 minutes. Let cool slightly, then transfer to a blender or food processor and puree until smooth. With the machine running, add until you reach the desired consistency:

Up to 1½ cups more stock

Season with:

Salt and ground black pepper to taste

VELOUTÉ SAUCE

About 2 cups

The difference between Sauce Béchamel and Velouté Sauce is only one of ingredients—the techniques are identical. Instead of milk, a velouté, named for its velvety texture, is made exclusively with any "white" or light-colored stock—chicken, veal, fish, even vegetable. The resulting velouté sauce is more ivory-colored than béchamel and is slightly translucent. Traditionally, a velouté is served with the same kind of food that was used in the stock—for example, chicken with chicken, fish with fish. But this need not be the case. Any stock you find compatible with the dish you are preparing is fine, and vegetable-based veloutés are versatile indeed. Allowing the sauce to simmer gently for an extra 15 minutes will remove any trace of a floury taste. The sauce can be refrigerated or kept warm in the top of a double boiler. Stir occasionally to prevent a skin from forming.

Heat, stirring occasionally, in a small saucepan over medium heat until hot:

2½ cups White Veal Stock, 40, Chicken Stock, 39, Fish Stock, 41, or Vegetable Stock, 38

Meanwhile, melt in a medium, heavy saucepan over low heat:

3 tablespoons butter, preferably unsalted

Stir in:

3 tablespoons all-purpose flour

Cook over low heat, stirring constantly with a wooden spoon or spatula, until the roux is fragrant and ivory colored or just lightly darkened, about 6 minutes. Remove from the heat and let cool for 1 minute. Gradually whisk in the stock along with:

¼ cup minced mushrooms (optional)

Return the saucepan to the heat and bring the sauce slowly to a simmer, whisking to prevent lumps. Cook the sauce, stirring often and skimming any skin that forms on the surface, over medium-low heat, without boiling, until it is thick enough to coat the back of a spoon, about 20 minutes. Strain through a fine-mesh sieve, if desired. Season with:

Salt and ground white pepper to taste

Just before serving, whisk in:

1 to 2 tablespoons unsalted butter, softened

Or proceed with one of the sauce variations described below or with one of your own inspiration.

FLAVORED BUTTER VELOUTÉ

A quick way to dress up any velouté.

Prepare Velouté Sauce, above. Just before serving, whisk in 2 tablespoons of any slightly softened flavored butter, 76 to 78.

SAUCE SUPRÊME (CREAM SAUCE)

Best with chicken or vegetables.

Prepare Velouté Sauce, above, adding ¾ cup heavy cream to the saucepan along with the stock. Just before serving, whisk in 2 tablespoons more heavy cream and, if desired, 2 tablespoons softened unsalted butter.

SAUCE BERCY (SHALLOT AND WINE SAUCE)

Named for the old wine-merchants' section of Paris, this sauce is often made with fish stock velouté as an accompaniment to fish, but it can also be prepared with chicken stock and served with chicken.

Prepare Velouté Sauce, above. Melt 1 tablespoon unsalted butter in a heavy saucepan over medium heat. Stir in 2 tablespoons minced shallots and cook until softened but not browned. Add 1 cup dry white wine and cook until the liquid is reduced by half. Stir in 1 tablespoon chopped fresh parsley and stir the mixture into the velouté.

SAUCE SMITANE

Serve this sauce with roasted poultry or game birds.

Prepare Velouté Sauce, above. Melt 1 tablespoon butter, preferably unsalted, in a heavy saucepan over medium heat. Stir in ¼ cup finely chopped onions and cook until softened but not browned. Add 1 cup dry white wine and cook until the liquid is reduced by half. Then stir in 1 cup of the velouté and simmer for 5 minutes. Remove from the heat and stir in 1 cup sour cream. Season to taste with salt, ground black pepper, and fresh lemon juice if desired.

ABOUT BROWN SAUCES

In the world of grand French sauces, the stock-based brown sauces are usually held in the highest regard. With either Sauce Espagnole, below, or Sauce Demi-Glace, 50, as a starting point, these sauces are more time-consuming than other sauces, but their flavor and texture are incomparable. For the most complex and compelling sauces, different liquids (wine, stock, juice, for example) and savory ingredients (onions, chopped ham, herbs, to name a few) are added at intervals and allowed to cook down and concentrate before the next is added. Although it is often necessary to save time by adding the liquids and ingredients all at once, the resulting sauce will not offer as many luscious layers of flavor.

The best sauces begin with good stock, but if you find the flavor of either your stock or your sauce a bit pale, try adding a spoonful or two of meat glaze, 000, to the sauce as it simmers. The wines used in these sauces should be of good quality, especially any that are added close to the end of cooking. Do not attempt to produce brown sauces that are as thick as béchamels, 46, or veloutés, 48; they will only become sticky and unappealing. Instead, stop cooking when the sauce has reached the consistency of heavy cream. Stir with a spoon rather than a whisk—whisking lightens the color by incorporating air. A swirl of softened butter at the end adds a sheen to these sauces while enriching their flavor. Brown sauces can be refrigerated for 4 to 5 days or frozen for 3 months and are best stored topped with a thin film of sherry.

SAUCE ESPAGNOLE (BASIC BROWN SAUCE)

About 6 cups

In classic French cuisine, this most fundamental of brown sauces, from which legions of other sauces were made, required pounds and pounds of beef and bones and would occupy a kitchen burner for days. This method takes much less time but produces a very flavorful sauce if you start with good stock. Four slices of bacon can be chopped, cooked to render their fat, and then this fat can be substituted for the butter. Finish according to one of the recipes that follow or according to your own taste, and serve with meats or poultry.

Melt in a large, heavy saucepan or Dutch oven over medium-high heat:

8 tablespoons (1 stick) unsalted butter or ½ cup beef or veal drippings

Add and cook, stirring, until the vegetables are caramelized and browned:

½ cup finely chopped onions
¼ cup finely chopped carrots
¼ cup finely chopped celery

Reduce the heat to medium and add, stirring:

½ cup all-purpose flour

Cook, stirring constantly, to make a brown roux, 44, about 10 minutes. Gradually stir in:

8 cups cold Brown Beef Stock, 40

2 cups drained canned peeled tomatoes

½ cup coarsely chopped fresh parsley, including stems

1 bouquet garni, 37

Bring just to a simmer. Immediately reduce the heat to low and cook, uncovered, at a bare simmer, stirring occasionally and skimming the fat and any skin that forms on the surface, until the sauce is reduced by half, 2 to 2½ hours. It should be the consistency of heavy cream, no thicker. Strain through a fine-mesh sieve. Stir the sauce occasionally as it cools to prevent a skin from forming. Refrigerate, make into one of the brown sauce variations that follow, or season to taste.

QUICK BROWN SAUCE

About 4 cups

Prepared in about 30 minutes, this sauce makes the wonders of brown sauce much more accessible to many of our kitchens. For a vegetarian version, it can be made with vegetable stock. This recipe is easily halved.

Heat in a large, heavy skillet, preferably nonstick, over high heat:

2½ tablespoons butter, preferably unsalted

1 tablespoon vegetable oil

Add and cook, stirring, until well browned, about 3 minutes:

2 large red onions, minced

Sprinkle with:

2 tablespoons sugar

Cook, stirring, until the sugar is deeply browned and smells as if it is beginning to burn. Remove from the heat and whisk in:

½ cup dry red wine

Bring to a boil and boil for 2 to 3 minutes. Whisk in:

6½ cups Brown Beef Stock, 40, Chicken Stock, 39, or Vegetable Stock, 38, or a combination

¼ cup mushroom powder or ½ ounce dried mushrooms ground in a blender

½ teaspoon dried thyme

Bring to a rolling boil over high heat and boil for 4 minutes. Strain through a fine-mesh sieve into a heatproof bowl and set aside. Heat in the same skillet over medium heat:

3 tablespoons butter, preferably unsalted

Make a roux by whisking in:

¼ cup all-purpose flour

Cook, stirring, until the mixture is walnut brown, 5 to 8 minutes. Whisk in the strained stock along with:

2 tablespoons port

¼ teaspoon ground black pepper

Bring to a boil, whisking, and boil until it is the consistency of heavy cream, 8 to 10 minutes. Strain again, if desired, and blend in:

1 tablespoon butter, preferably unsalted, softened (optional)

Salt to taste

SAUCE DEMI-GLACE

About 4 cups

Described by the French master chef George-Auguste Escoffier as "Sauce Espagnole taken to the extreme limit of perfection," this sauce takes time and is worth making only if the basic stock is of the highest quality.

Combine in a large, heavy saucepan or Dutch oven over medium heat:

4 cups Sauce Espagnole, 49, or Quick Brown Sauce, above

4 cups Brown Beef Stock, 40, or Brown Chicken Stock, 39

½ cup chopped mushrooms

Simmer gently, uncovered, stirring occasionally, until cooked down by half, 2 to 2½ hours. Strain through a fine-mesh sieve and return to a clean saucepan. Stir in over very low heat:

½ cup port, Madeira, or dry sherry

Salt and ground black pepper to taste

Just before serving, whisk in:

2 to 4 tablespoons butter, preferably unsalted, softened (optional)

SAUCE MADÈRE (MADEIRA SAUCE)

About 1 cup

Dry sherry or port can be substituted for the Madeira. Serve with poultry, game, beef, veal, or ham.

Combine in a medium, heavy saucepan over medium-high heat and simmer, uncovered, until cooked down to 1 cup:

1 cup Sauce Espagnole, 49, Quick Brown Sauce, above, or Sauce Demi-Glace, above

¼ cup Madeira

1 teaspoon meat glaze, 38 (optional)

Strain through a fine-mesh sieve and stir in:

⅓ cup Madeira, dry sherry, or port

Salt and ground black pepper to taste

Just before serving, whisk in:

1 tablespoon butter, preferably unsalted, softened (optional)

SAUCE CHASSEUR (HUNTER'S SAUCE)

About 2 cups

Traditionally served with game, this sauce is also delectable with roasted meats, poultry, steaks, or chops.

Melt in a medium, heavy saucepan over medium heat:

2 tablespoons butter, preferably unsalted

Add and cook, stirring, until softened:

2 tablespoons minced shallots or onions

Add and cook, stirring, until lightly browned, about 5 minutes:

1 cup sliced mushrooms

Add and simmer, uncovered, until cooked down by half:

¼ cup dry white wine

2 tablespoons brandy

Add and cook, stirring occasionally, for 5 minutes:

1 cup Sauce Espagnole, 49, Quick Brown Sauce, 50, or Demi-Glace, 50

½ cup tomato puree

Salt and ground black pepper to taste

Just before serving, stir in:

1 tablespoon minced fresh parsley

1 tablespoon minced fresh chervil or tarragon (optional)

1 to 2 tablespoons butter, preferably unsalted, softened (optional)

SAUCE BORDELAISE (RED WINE AND MARROW SAUCE)

About 1½ cups

Though it takes its name from the Bordeaux wine traditionally used to make it, any robust dry red wine can be used. Serve it with broiled or roasted meats or poultry, sweetbreads, chops, or game. This sauce is also delicious, though a little less rich, without the poached marrow.

Combine in a small, heavy saucepan over medium-high heat and simmer, uncovered, until cooked down by three-quarters:

¼ cup sherry vinegar or red wine vinegar

1 shallot, minced

1 sprig fresh thyme

1 sprig fresh parsley

½ bay leaf

4 black peppercorns

Add:

½ cup dry red wine

Cook down again until reduced by three-quarters. Strain through a fine-mesh sieve into a medium saucepan and discard the solids. Place over medium heat and stir in:

1 cup Sauce Espagnole, 49, Quick Brown Sauce, 50, or Demi-Glace, 50

Simmer, uncovered, for 15 minutes. Just before serving, stir in:

¼ cup diced beef marrow, poached for a few minutes and drained (optional)

2 teaspoons minced fresh parsley

Salt and ground black pepper to taste

SAUCE MARCHAND DE VIN (MUSHROOM WINE SAUCE)

About 2 cups

Serve this "wine merchant's" sauce with broiled steak.

Melt in a medium, heavy saucepan over medium heat:

2 tablespoons butter, preferably unsalted

Add and cook, stirring, until softened and the liquid is evaporated:

1 cup thinly sliced mushrooms

Stir in and simmer for 10 minutes:

½ cup Brown Beef Stock, 40, Brown Chicken Stock, 39, or Brown Veal Stock, 41

½ cup dry red wine

Stir in and simmer for 20 minutes:

1 cup Sauce Espagnole, 49, Quick Brown Sauce, 50, or Sauce Demi-Glace, 50

Just before serving, season with:

Fresh lemon juice to taste (optional)

Salt and ground black pepper to taste

SAUCE PIQUANT (BROWN SAUCE WITH PICKLES AND CAPERS)

About 1¼ cups

Serve this with grilled meats, pork, liver, tongue, or tripe and with leftover meats.

Melt in a medium, heavy saucepan over medium heat:

1 tablespoon butter, preferably unsalted

Add and cook, stirring, until lightly browned:

2 tablespoons minced shallots

Stir in and cook over medium-high heat until the liquid is almost evaporated:

2 tablespoons dry white wine

2 tablespoons white wine vinegar

Stir in and simmer, uncovered, for 10 minutes:

1 cup Sauce Espagnole, 49, Quick Brown Sauce, 50, or Sauce Demi-Glace, 50

Just before serving, stir in:

1 tablespoon chopped fresh parsley or a mixture of fresh parsley, tarragon, and chervil

1 tablespoon minced cornichons or sour gherkins

1 tablespoon chopped drained capers (optional)

Salt and ground black pepper to taste

ABOUT GRAVY AND PAN SAUCES

Gravy and pan sauces are made from the pan drippings of meat or poultry after it has been roasted or sautéed. They are the quick and lively descendants of the ancestral brown sauces. While a traditional gravy is thickened with flour, a pan sauce is not.

Both gravy and pan sauce begin with the deglazing of a hot pan to capture all the caramelized cooking juices and bits of flavor that have been released during cooking and are sticking to the bottom of the pan. (There are fewer delicious bits in a nonstick pan, of course.) Some cooks prefer to deglaze the roasting pan and then pour all the liquid into a saucepan to finish the sauce. It is important to always begin by pouring off all but the smallest amount of grease or fat from the pan before deglazing or your sauce will be greasy. Depending on the quantity of fat or cooking juices, use a spoon, a skimmer, a ladle, or a gravy separator, or simply pour off the fat. Pan drippings from quickly sautéed foods will not have the same intensity as those from long-roasted meats and poultry. To compensate for this lack of flavor, we recommend adding flavorings such as shallots, onions, ginger, and/or garlic to the hot pan before deglazing and giving them a chance to brown first.

To deglaze properly, make sure the pan is hot, then add ¼ cup or more liquid. While water is certainly appropriate, flavor will be increased by the use of wine juice, stock, cream, cider, beer, spirits, or almost any other appropriate liquid or combination of liquids. Gravies and pan sauces can be thickened with cream, roux, or cornstarch. See page 44 for a description of possible thickeners. If you decide to use a roux, pour off the cooking juices, make the roux directly in the pan, and then whisk the juices back in.

PAN GRAVY FOR MEAT *About 1 cup*

This is based on a roux made right in the pan. To be sure there is enough gravy to go around for a big occasion, have warm stock and melted butter, or bacon fat, on hand and multiply the recipe accordingly.

After roasting the meat, remove it to a platter and keep warm. Pour off the fat from the roasting pan and reserve 2 tablespoons. Also, pour off the degreased pan juices and reserve separately. Place the roasting pan on a burner over medium heat and pour in:

2 tablespoons reserved fat from roasting pan or rendered bacon fat

Stir in:

1 to 2 tablespoons all-purpose flour

Cook, whisking or stirring constantly and scraping up the browned bits from the bottom and sides of the pan, for several minutes to remove the raw taste of the flour and smooth the mixture. Add:

Reserved pan juices and enough wine, juice, stock, water, cream, cider, beer, spirits, or a combination to make 1 cup
Fresh or dried minced herbs of your choice
Finely grated lemon zest (optional)
Salt and ground black pepper to taste

Cook, whisking or stirring, until the gravy is thickened to the desired consistency. Strain through a fine-mesh sieve, if desired, and serve hot.

PAN GRAVY FOR POULTRY *About 2 cups*

Another roux-thickened sauce. This recipe may be doubled.

After roasting the poultry, remove it to a platter and keep warm. Pour off the fat from the roasting pan and reserve ¼ cup. Also, pour off the degreased pan juices and reserve separately. Place the roasting pan on a burner over medium heat and pour in:

2 to 4 tablespoons reserved fat from roasting pan, melted butter, or rendered bacon fat

Stir in:

2 to 4 tablespoons all-purpose flour

Cook, whisking or stirring constantly and scraping up the browned bits from the bottom and sides of the pan, for several minutes to remove the raw taste of the flour and smooth the mixture. Add:

Reserved pan juices and enough Chicken Stock, 39, or other liquid to make 2 cups
Chopped cooked giblets (optional)
¼ cup or more light or heavy cream (optional)
Salt and ground black pepper to taste

Cook, whisking or stirring, until the gravy is thickened to the desired consistency. Strain through a fine-mesh sieve, if desired, and serve hot.

BASIC HERB PAN SAUCE *½ cup*

A bright and lively sauce for lamb, pork, or chicken. The mustard will make the sauce thinner, so leave it out if you prefer a thicker sauce. This sauce can also be made without pan drippings.

After cooking lamb chops, pork chops, or chicken breasts, remove them to a platter and keep warm. Pour off the fat and heat the skillet over medium-high heat. Add:

⅓ cup Chicken Stock, 39, Express Chicken Broth, 42, apple cider, wine, or other liquid

Stir with a wooden spoon to loosen and dissolve any browned bits, bring to a boil, and add:

¼ cup minced shallots
1 bay leaf

2 teaspoons Dijon mustard (optional)
1½ teaspoons fresh lemon juice, white wine vinegar, or Cognac, or to taste
Salt and ground black pepper to taste

Cook, stirring occasionally, over medium-high heat until slightly thickened, 1 to 2 minutes. Add and cook until reduced by about half, 3 to 5 minutes:

¼ cup heavy cream (optional)

Remove the pan from the heat. Strain the sauce through a fine-mesh sieve, if desired, and stir in:

1 tablespoon minced fresh herbs (parsley, thyme, and/or rosemary)

Swirl in:

1 tablespoon butter, preferably unsalted, softened (optional)

Arrange the meat on plates, spoon the sauce over, and just before serving, garnish with:

Fresh herb sprigs (optional)

PAN SAUCE WITH LEEKS, ORANGE, AND ROSEMARY

½ cup

The combination of citrus and rosemary adds a welcome dimension to almost any sautéed meat or poultry.

After cooking steak, lamb chops, pork chops, or chicken breasts, remove them to a platter and keep warm. Pour off all but about 1 teaspoon fat and heat the skillet over medium heat. Add:

1 small leek (white part only), cleaned thoroughly and thinly sliced

Cook, stirring, until just starting to soften and brown and add:

⅓ cup fresh orange juice

Boil, stirring with a wooden spoon to loosen and dissolve any browned bits, and cook for 2 to 3 minutes. Add:

⅓ cup Chicken Stock, 39, or Express Chicken Broth, 42
Two 2-inch strips orange zest
1 sprig fresh rosemary

Cook, stirring often, until reduced by about half and thickened, 4 to 5 minutes. Discard the zest and rosemary. Season with:

Salt and ground black pepper to taste

Swirl in:

1 tablespoon butter, preferably unsalted, softened (optional)

Arrange the meat on plates, spoon the sauce over, and sprinkle with:

2 teaspoons minced fresh parsley

RED WINE AND SOUR CHERRY PAN SAUCE

⅓ cup

Sun-dried cherries mirror the flavors of many red wines. This sauce makes a fine accompaniment to pork, beef, or chicken.

After cooking steak, pork chops, or chicken breasts, remove them to a platter and keep warm. Pour off all but 1 teaspoon fat and heat the skillet over medium-high heat. Add:

⅓ cup finely diced red onions

Cook, stirring, until just starting to soften and brown. Add:

¼ cup dry red wine

Bring to a boil, stirring with a wooden spoon to loosen and dissolve any browned bits, and cook for 2 to 3 minutes. Add:

¼ cup Chicken Stock, 39, Express Chicken Broth, 42, or water
⅓ cup dried sour cherries
One 2-inch strip lemon zest
1 teaspoon packed light brown sugar
½ teaspoon balsamic vinegar
½ teaspoon fresh thyme leaves

Cook, stirring often, over high heat until reduced by half and thickened, about 3 minutes. Discard the zest. Season with:

Salt and ground black pepper to taste

Swirl in:

1 tablespoon butter, preferably unsalted, softened (optional)

Arrange the meat or poultry on plates and spoon the sauce over the chops.

ABOUT PAN SAUCES MADE WITHOUT PAN DRIPPINGS

Many modern pan sauces are made without pan drippings. Instead, the base begins with a few shallots or other onion relative sautéed in fat, and then the recipe proceeds as for standard pan sauces. Layers of flavor can come from successive additions of aromatic ingredients and liquids, such as wine, stock, or juice. These simple and pure sauces are almost always left unthickened and can be quite low in fat. The key to success is to simmer a good-quality, fresh-tasting meat or poultry stock until it begins to take on a saucelike character. Do not overcook, but feel free to add seasonings—and if fat is not a concern, a swirl of butter at the last minute will add richness and give a beautiful sheen. Any of the preceding pan sauces can be made according to this technique: begin by heating 1 tablespoon butter, olive oil, or other fat in a small skillet and cooking 2 to 4 tablespoons minced shallots, garlic, or onions until softened and lightly browned, and then proceed with the recipe.

Another alternative is to gently warm a vinaigrette dressing, either in the skillet after cooking meat, poultry, or fish or in a separate saucepan. Whether rich and creamy or citrusy and bright, vinaigrettes are a quick and flavorful way to sauce anything from roasted meats to grilled vegetables.

MUSHROOM WINE SAUCE *¾ cup*

Using meat glaze will give this sauce more depth of flavor and body; without it, the woodsy mushroom flavor dominates.

Heat in a skillet over high heat:

2 tablespoons olive oil

Add and cook until soft, about 10 minutes:

8 ounces mushrooms, wiped clean and thickly sliced
1 shallot, minced

Add, bring to a boil, and cook until reduced by half, about 10 minutes:

1½ cups dry red wine, such as Merlot or Zinfandel
1 tablespoon meat glaze, 38 (optional)

Remove from the heat, skim the surface, and swirl in:

4 tablespoons (½ stick) butter, preferably unsalted, softened

Season with:

Salt and ground black pepper to taste

Serve warm.

OLIVE AND SUN-DRIED TOMATO PAN SAUCE *½ cup*

Serve this boldly flavored sauce with beef, lamb, or chicken. You can also make this sauce directly in the skillet after sautéing the main course—it will have a richer flavor.

Heat in a small saucepan over medium-high heat:

1 cup Chicken Stock, 39, or Express Chicken Broth, 42
¼ cup chopped pitted black oil-cured olives
¼ cup chopped drained sun-dried tomatoes in oil

Boil until slightly syrupy, 5 to 10 minutes, stirring in any accumulated juices from the resting meat if desired. Stir in:

1 tablespoon minced fresh parsley
1 teaspoon balsamic vinegar, or to taste
Salt and ground black pepper to taste

Serve warm.

CITRUS SAUCE *½ cup*

A perfect sauce for grilled foods, especially fish.

With a sharp knife, remove the peel and all the white pith from:

2 navel oranges
1 small lemon

Holding the fruit over a bowl to catch the juices, use a knife to free the orange and lemon sections with as little membrane as possible; let the sections fall into the bowl. Squeeze out the remaining juice after removing all the sections. Stir in:

¼ cup extra-virgin olive oil
Salt and ground white pepper to taste

Serve at room temperature, or cover and refrigerate for up to 1 day.

BLACKBERRY SAGE SAUCE *1½ cups*

Serve with beef, venison, or other game.

Heat in a saucepan over medium heat:

1 tablespoon olive oil

Add and cook, stirring, until very lightly browned:

¼ cup chopped shallots

Add, increase the heat to high, and boil until reduced by half:

2 cups hearty red wine

Add and continue to boil until the sauce reaches a light saucelike consistency:

3 cups Brown Chicken Stock, 39, Brown Veal Stock, 41, or Game Stock, 40
1¾ cups fresh or frozen blackberries
¼ cup chopped fresh sage, or 1½ tablespoons dried

Add:

1 tablespoon honey, or to taste
Salt and ground black pepper to taste

Strain through a fine-mesh sieve, pressing the solids to extract all the liquid. Serve warm.

ORANGE AND GINGER SAUCE *1½ cups*

The addition of cream gives this sauce a very smooth texture. This sauce can be made without stock, but it will be lighter in flavor and body. Use this technique as a model for a world of sauces, substituting different seasonings and wines. Try this version with poultry or wildfowl.

Melt in a saucepan over medium heat:

1 tablespoon butter, preferably unsalted

Add and cook, stirring, until very lightly browned:

¼ cup chopped shallots or scallions
¾ cup chopped mushrooms

Add, increase the heat to high, and boil until reduced by half:

1 cup dry white wine
2 tablespoons chopped peeled fresh ginger

Add and continue to boil until reduced by half:

3 cups Chicken Stock, 39, or Express Chicken Broth, 42 (optional)
¾ cup fresh orange juice

Add and cook until the sauce reaches a light saucelike consistency:

¾ cup heavy cream

Strain through a fine-mesh sieve. Stir in:

1 tablespoon grated orange zest
Fresh lemon juice to taste
Salt and ground black pepper to taste

Serve warm.

ABOUT HOLLANDAISE SAUCE AND BÉARNAISE SAUCE

These famous French sauces (the first named for Holland and the second for the southwestern French region of Béarn, home of the beloved monarch Henri IV) transform the plainest cooked vegetables or broiled, grilled, or roasted meats into something special. As emulsified sauces, both are close cousins of mayonnaise, though both are prepared and served hot. Professional chefs often make these sauces over a low direct heat. We strongly recommend using a double boiler or—better yet—a stainless-steel bowl set over a saucepan holding about 1½ inches of water. The advantage of the bowl is that its shape gives you plenty of room to whisk air into the sauce, making a lighter, more voluminous sauce. Whichever method you choose, the water in the bottom of the double boiler should simmer, not boil, and it should never touch the bottom of the bowl or pan. Remove the bowl or top of the double boiler from the heat if you feel that the sauce is getting too hot; whisk until the sauce cools slightly, then put it back over the heat to continue.

The most critical stage in the making of hollandaise or béarnaise is the initial whipping and cooking of the egg yolks. Begin by whisking the yolks and liquid (lemon juice or water) off the heat until light and frothy. Then, over the barely simmering water, continue to whisk vigorously to gently warm the yolks. They will become pale yellow and expand to three or four times their original volume.

Next, remove the yolks from the heat and begin to dribble in the warm—not hot—clarified butter. As the sauce begins to thicken, add the butter in a steady trickle. Do not let the sauce or butter cool too much as you whisk as the butter will begin to harden and thicken. Add a few drops of warm water if this happens. If at any point the sauce looks as if it is about to separate, immediately whisk in a couple of tablespoons of cold heavy cream or water. If it does separate, all is not lost: simply whisk 1 new yolk in a clean bowl, then slowly whisk this yolk into the broken sauce to re-form the emulsion. Hollandaise and béarnaise sauces must be served promptly, for they will curdle if reheated.

HOLLANDAISE SAUCE

About 1 cup

Place in the top of a double boiler or in a large stainless-steel bowl set up as a double boiler:

3 large egg yolks
1½ tablespoons cold water

Off the heat, whisk the egg mixture until it becomes light and frothy. Place the top of the double boiler or the bowl over—not in—barely simmering water and continue to whisk until the eggs are thickened, 2 to 4 minutes, being careful not to let the eggs get too hot. Remove the pan or bowl from over the water and whisk to slightly cool the mixture. Whisking constantly, very slowly add:

½ cup warm (not hot) clarified butter, 1069

Whisk in:

1 to 3 teaspoons fresh lemon juice
Dash of hot red pepper sauce (optional)
Salt and ground white pepper to taste

If the sauce is too thick, whisk in a few drops of warm water. Serve immediately or keep the sauce warm for up to 30 minutes by placing the bowl in warm (not hot) water.

BLENDER HOLLANDAISE SAUCE

About 1 cup

Less fluffy but a great time-saver. The clarified butter should be very warm, since the sauce is not reheated.

Place in a blender or food processor:

3 large egg yolks
2 teaspoons fresh lemon juice, or to taste
Ground white pepper or hot red pepper sauce to taste
Salt to taste

Process on high speed for 1 minute. With the machine running, add in a slow, steady stream:

½ cup very warm to hot clarified butter, 1069

By the time all the butter is poured in—about 1 minute—the sauce should be thickened. If not, process on high speed for about 20 seconds more. Taste and adjust the seasonings. Serve immediately or keep warm by submerging the blender container in warm (not hot) water. Serve warm.

SAUCE MOUSSELINE

A lighter version of hollandaise that is good with poached fish or vegetables.

Prepare Hollandaise Sauce, above, or Blender Hollandaise Sauce, above. Just before serving, gently fold in ½ cup whipped cream.

SAUCE MALTAISE

Make this sauce with blood oranges, if possible, and serve it on lightly steamed asparagus.

Prepare Hollandaise Sauce, above, or Blender Hollandaise Sauce, above, preferably without the lemon juice. In a small saucepan over low heat, cook ¼ cup fresh orange juice, 2 large strips orange zest, and, if desired, ½ teaspoon sugar, stirring until thickened, about 4 minutes. Let the orange mixture cool, then strain and fold into the hollandaise.

THREE-CITRUS HOLLANDAISE

Prepare Sauce Maltaise, above, substituting a combination of fresh orange, lemon, and lime juices and zests for the orange juice and zest.

ANCHO CHILE HOLLANDAISE

Prepare Hollandaise Sauce, above, or Blender Hollandaise Sauce, above. Stir together 1 to 2 teaspoons ground ancho chili pepper, ¼ teaspoon ground cumin, and about 1 tablespoon water. Stir this mixture into the hollandaise and add fresh lime or lemon juice to taste.

BÉARNAISE SAUCE

About 1 cup

A cousin of hollandaise, béarnaise gets its special flavor from a reduction of white wine, vinegar, and tarragon. Served mostly with grilled meat and fish, béarnaise is good with its traditional companion, filet mignon.

Combine in a small saucepan over medium heat and simmer, uncovered, until cooked down by two-thirds:

3 tablespoons dry white wine
3 tablespoons tarragon vinegar or white wine vinegar
1 shallot, minced
6 sprigs fresh tarragon, leaves removed and reserved
8 black peppercorns, lightly crushed

Remove the tarragon sprigs from the reduction and reserve the liquid. Place in the top of a double boiler or in a large stainless-steel bowl set up as a double boiler:

3 large egg yolks
1½ teaspoons cold water

Off the heat, whisk the egg mixture until it becomes light and frothy. Place the top of the double boiler or the bowl over—not in—barely simmering water and whisk until the eggs are thickened, 2 to 4 minutes, being careful not to let the eggs get too hot. Remove the pan or bowl from over the water and whisk to slightly cool the mixture. Whisking constantly, very slowly add:

½ cup warm (not hot) clarified butter, 1069

Stir in the reserved tarragon leaves, chopped, and the reduced liquid, to taste, along with:

Salt and ground white pepper to taste

If the sauce is too thick, thin it slowly with a few drops of the reserved vinegar-wine reduction or warm water. Serve immediately or keep the sauce covered until serving to prevent a skin from forming. Serve warm.

BLENDER BÉARNAISE SAUCE

About ¾ cup

For a true béarnaise flavor, make the hollandaise base using water and no lemon juice.

Combine in a small saucepan over low heat, and simmer until reduced to about 1 tablespoon:

2 tablespoons dry white wine
2 tablespoons tarragon vinegar
1 tablespoon minced shallots
½ teaspoon chopped fresh tarragon
4 black peppercorns, lightly crushed

Strain through a fine-mesh sieve and let the liquid cool. Stir the liquid to taste into:

Blender Hollandaise Sauce, 55, made with water in place of the lemon juice

Stir in:

½ teaspoon minced fresh tarragon, or more to taste

Taste and adjust the seasonings. Serve immediately.

SAUCE FOYOT OR VALOIS

Serve with grilled or sautéed meats.

Prepare Béarnaise Sauce, above, or Blender Béarnaise Sauce, above. Stir in about 1 tablespoon slightly warm meat glaze, 38.

SAUCE PALOISE

Prepare Béarnaise Sauce, above, or Blender Béarnaise Sauce, above, substituting fresh mint for the tarragon.

SAUCE CHORON

Prepare Béarnaise Sauce, above, or Blender Béarnaise Sauce, above. Just before serving, stir in 1 tablespoon tomato paste.

FRESH HERB BÉARNAISE SAUCE

Prepare Béarnaise Sauce, above, or Blender Béarnaise Sauce, above, substituting fresh cilantro, parsley, basil, thyme, chives, or sage for the tarragon.

ABOUT BUTTER SAUCES

A few well-loved sauces depend on butter almost entirely. For these, nothing less than the freshest butter will do—unsalted is best, because it will not interfere with any other seasonings. The simplest of these, Brown Butter, below, and Beurre Meunière, below, are nothing more than seasoned butter cooked until it begins to brown and takes on marvelous nutty and toasty flavors. The slightly more complicated Beurre Blanc, below, derives its velvety smoothness from whisking in the butter so that it blends into and thickens the sauce without melting outright.

BEURRE NOISETTE (BROWN BUTTER)

About 5 tablespoons

Make this quickly in the same skillet you have cooked fish in and serve it over the fish—or make it separately to use as a sauce for green vegetables.
Melt in a small skillet over medium-low heat:

4 to 5 tablespoons butter, preferably unsalted

Cook slowly, shaking or stirring so that it cooks evenly. Watch as the butter begins to foam; it can burn easily. Remove the butter from the heat when it becomes light brown and smells nutty. Stir in:

1 teaspoon white wine vinegar or fresh lemon juice
Salt and ground black pepper to taste

Serve immediately.

BEURRE MEUNIÈRE (LEMON BUTTER)

Prepare Beurre Noisette, above, using lemon juice and 1 tablespoon finely chopped fresh parsley.

BEURRE NOIR (BLACK BUTTER)

In old-fashioned French slang, *un oeil au beurre noir*—"an eye with black butter"—is a black eye. Delicious against the light flavor of sautéed fish such as sole, cod, or skate.
Prepare Beurre Noisette, above, allowing the butter to cook until it is dark brown.

SAUCE POLONAISE (BROWN BUTTER CRUMB SAUCE)

5 tablespoons

A traditional topping for vegetables, especially cauliflower.
Heat in a small skillet over medium heat:

Beurre Meunière, above

Add and cook, stirring, until softened:

1 tablespoon minced shallots

Add and cook, stirring, until evenly golden brown:

¼ cup fine dry unseasoned breadcrumbs

Taste and adjust the seasonings. Garnish the vegetable you are serving with:

Finely chopped hard-boiled eggs

Pour the sauce over the vegetable and serve immediately.

BEURRE BLANC (WHITE BUTTER SAUCE)

⅓ cup

Said to have been invented either in the Anjou region of France or in the vicinity of Nantes, and popularized in Paris by a restaurateur named Mère Michel, beurre blanc is among the most refined of French sauces. The only real trick to making a perfect sauce is to whisk in the butter without letting it melt completely. Cutting the butter into small cubes helps, as does removing the simmering liquid from the heat and whisking it constantly. The addition of a bit of heavy cream is added insurance that the sauce will hold together. Beurre blanc can be flavored by substituting various stocks for all or part of the wine, by adding herbs or citrus zest, or by replacing all or part of the butter with a flavored butter, 76 to 78. Beurre blanc is traditional with fish, especially shad, but it is also served on chicken breasts, squab, asparagus, artichokes, and leeks, among other foods. Some chefs strain the beurre blanc before serving, but it is not essential.
Combine in a small skillet over medium heat and simmer, uncovered, until cooked down by three-quarters:

6 tablespoons dry white wine
2 tablespoons white wine vinegar
3 tablespoons minced shallots
Salt and ground white pepper to taste

Stir in:

1 tablespoon heavy cream

Remove from the heat and add, whisking constantly, 1 piece at a time until the sauce is creamy and whitened:

8 tablespoons (1 stick) cold butter, preferably unsalted, cut into at least 8 pieces

If you need a bit more heat to soften the butter, hold the pan briefly over very low heat. Never let the butter melt completely, or the sauce will separate. Strain through a fine-mesh sieve, if desired, season to taste, and serve immediately.

BEURRE ROUGE (RED BUTTER SAUCE)

Prepare Beurre Blanc, above, substituting dry red wine and red wine vinegar for the dry white wine and white wine vinegar.

LEMON BEURRE BLANC

Prepare Beurre Blanc, above, stirring the grated zest of 1 small lemon into the wine mixture before reducing it.

MUSTARD BEURRE BLANC

Prepare Beurre Blanc, above. Just before serving, whisk in ½ teaspoon Dijon mustard, ½ teaspoon French whole-grain mustard, and fresh lemon juice to taste.

ABOUT TOMATO SAUCES

If there were ever to be an American mother sauce from which endless progeny spring forth, it would be tomato sauce. While the tomato itself is indigenous to the Americas, we borrow from the cultures of the world in how we use it. From the Italians we get our rich family of pasta sauces and pizza toppings; from England and Asia we have adopted our most famous condiment, ketchup; and from Mexico come our bright and fresh salsas. Tomatoes can be used raw or cooked, pureed or coarsely chopped, as a backdrop for other ingredients or on their own, to produce a range of vibrant sauces. Their sharp flavor and juicy texture make them ideal for creating sauces without the broth or stock that so many other sauces depend on. In fact, many tomato sauces are made without any meat at all. Tomato sauces need not be restricted to pasta and pizza; use them on meats, poultry, fish, and vegetables. Top baked chicken breasts with Simplest Italian Tomato Sauce Marinara, 305, or Tomato Concassé, 433, or pair the Puttanesca Sauce, 305, with sautéed pork medallions. In Pasta, Dumplings, & Noodles, 295, you will find more sauce ideas and also non-tomato-based sauces that should not be limited to pasta: Porcini and Red Wine Sauce, 308, can easily be served with a beef roast, or Pesto Sauce, 307, with grilled fish.

ABOUT VEGETABLE, LEGUME, AND FRUIT PUREES

Creating flavorful sauces from purees is a simple matter of controlling texture and taste. Choose either foods that have been softened by cooking or naturally tender foods like fruit and use a blender, food processor, or food mill to transform them into smooth pastes. Add stock, water, juice, cooking liquid, or other appropriate liquid to turn the puree into a sauce as thick or thin as desired. Whether you start with the savory vegetables from the bottom of a roasting pan or a pot of white beans cooked until tender, pureed sauces have enormous flavor potential.

ROASTED RED PEPPER SAUCE

1 cup

Serve this deeply flavored, almost sweet sauce with roasted or grilled meats, chicken, or fish.

Heat in a medium, heavy pan over medium heat:

2 tablespoons olive oil

Add:

1½ cups chopped onions

Cook, stirring often, until lightly browned, 5 to 10 minutes. Stir in:

3 large or 4 medium red bell peppers, roasted, 402, peeled, and coarsely chopped
2 tablespoons minced garlic
1 tablespoon sweet paprika
¼ teaspoon ground cinnamon
⅛ to ¼ teaspoon ground red pepper, to taste

Cook for 1 minute more. Add:

1½ cups beef stock and 1 cup water, or 2 cups water

Bring to a boil. Reduce the heat, partially cover, and very slowly simmer the sauce for about 1½ hours. Puree the mixture in a blender or food processor. Season with:

Salt and ground black pepper

Serve warm.

ROASTED TOMATILLO SPINACH SAUCE

1½ cups

Use this technique with almost any vegetable to create a range of vibrant sauces. Simply roast the vegetables until they are soft and beginning to caramelize and then puree the hot vegetables in a blender or food processor along with all their cooking juices, a bit of stock, and seasonings to match.

Preheat the oven to 400°F. Oil a baking pan.

Place in a single layer in the prepared pan and roast until soft and golden brown, 15 to 20 minutes:

2 pounds tomatillos, husked and rinsed
2 medium poblano or Anaheim peppers, seeded
1 large onion, quartered
12 cloves garlic

Place the vegetables, including the juices, in a blender or food processor along with:

1¼ cups coarsely chopped fresh spinach, washed and dried (optional)
⅓ cup chopped fresh cilantro
¾ cup Chicken Stock, 39, Vegetable Stock, 38, or more as needed
Salt and ground black pepper to taste

Pulse until smooth, adding more stock if necessary to make a medium-bodied sauce. Reheat gently in a small saucepan and serve immediately or store, covered, in the refrigerator for up to 2 days.

SIMPLE RED LENTIL SAUCE
6 servings

This is an almost nonfat sauce that uses pureed lentils to give it richness and body. Substitute other types of lentils and experiment with seasonings such as chili powder, toasted curry powder, and chopped herbs.

Heat in a large saucepan over medium heat:

1 tablespoon olive or vegetable oil

Add and cook, stirring, until softened, 5 to 7 minutes:

½ cup minced onions

Add and cook, stirring, for 1 minute:

2 teaspoons minced garlic

Add and bring to a boil:

4½ cups Chicken Stock, 39, Vegetable Stock, 38, or water

¾ cup red lentils, rinsed and sorted

Reduce the heat, cover, and simmer gently until the lentils are very tender, 20 to 25 minutes. Puree in a blender or food processor along with:

Stock or water to yield a saucelike consistency

Salt and ground black pepper to taste

Serve immediately or store, covered, in the refrigerator for up to 2 days.

MANGO MUSTARD SEED SAUCE
1½ cups

A delicious fresh sauce for grilled chicken and fish.

Place in a small dry skillet over medium heat and toast until they just begin to pop:

1½ tablespoons yellow or black mustard seeds

Remove from the heat and combine in a blender or food processor along with:

2 ripe mangos, peeled and cut into small cubes

1 medium, ripe banana, chopped

2 tablespoons finely minced peeled fresh ginger

1 teaspoon finely minced garlic

½ teaspoon curry powder

½ cup grapefruit juice

2 teaspoons sherry vinegar

1½ teaspoons hot chili oil

1 teaspoon honey, or to taste

Salt and ground black pepper to taste

Process briefly to produce a smooth sauce. Serve immediately or store, covered, in the refrigerator, for up to 3 days.

ABOUT VEGETABLE JUICE SAUCES

Juice-based sauces are fast and delicious. An electric juicer is essential to extract the juice and remove the pulp from the fresh vegetables. Consider appearance as well as taste, and imagine the possibilities from carrots and beets to red and yellow bell peppers. To add body to the finished sauce, simmer the juice to reduce it a bit or whisk in a few tablespoons of extra-virgin olive oil.

FRESH BEET SAUCE
¾ cup

This simple method can be used for any number of fresh vegetable sauces—spinach, carrot, bell pepper, and so on.

Pour into a saucepan and bring to a boil:

1¾ cups fresh beet juice (from about 2 pounds peeled beets)

Cook over high heat until reduced to about ¾ cup. Remove from the heat and add in a slow, steady stream, whisking constantly to slightly thicken the sauce:

2 to 4 tablespoons olive oil

Whisk in:

1 teaspoon white wine vinegar

Salt and ground black pepper to taste

Serve immediately or store, covered, in the refrigerator for up to 2 days.

CARROT GINGER SAUCE
¾ cup

Juice in an electric juicer:

1½ pounds carrots, peeled

¼ cup chopped shallots

2 tablespoons chopped peeled fresh ginger

Transfer to a saucepan and stir in:

1 tablespoon curry powder

Pinch of red pepper flakes (optional)

Bring to a boil and cook over high heat until reduced to about ¾ cup. Add in a slow, steady stream, whisking constantly to slightly thicken the sauce:

2 to 4 tablespoons olive oil

Season with:

Several drops of lemon juice

Serve immediately or store, covered, in the refrigerator for up to 2 days.

CONDIMENTS, MARINADES & DRY RUBS

Salsas, chutneys, dipping sauces, relishes, quick pickles, sambals, flavored butters and mayonnaises, even barbecue sauces, spice rubs, and glazes, all come under the heading of condiments. Whereas they differ widely in what they contain and how they are used, each occupies the same location in the culinary firmament, somewhere between a single spice and a side dish to be eaten on its own.

The characteristics of condiments tend to shift over time, but they do share a few attributes. All are used to provide flavor for food; all contain more than a single ingredient; all can be made in advance and most can be stored for at least a day or two, often much longer; and all stand alone, created independently and therefore able to add their distinctive flavors to a range of different dishes. (This last characteristic distinguishes them from pan sauces, which draw much of their flavor from the browned bits left in the pan after cooking poultry or meat.)

Condiments possess qualities that make them particularly useful for today's cooks. Most of them are quick and easy to prepare, and their intense flavors can make even a plain broiled chicken breast an interesting meal. Also, since the recipes for condiments are flexible, a cook can adjust the flavor by adding more or less garlic, chili pepper, vinegar, spices, lime juice, and so on, depending on personal preference and on what the condiment will accompany.

Serve these condiments as a garnish for soups or stews, on steamed vegetables, with grains and beans, with pasta, grilled dishes, tortilla chips, breads, or crackers—or, perhaps best of all, put them out on the table so your guests can help themselves.

ABOUT CANNING CONDIMENTS

The following condiments may be safely put up in a boiling water canner. We make these large old-fashioned recipes for gifts. Halving the amounts is not recommended, as simmering in smaller batches detrimentally affects flavor, texture, and the critical acid content. Here are the recommended headspaces and processing times:

Tomato Ketchup and Blender Tomato Ketchup: 1/8 inch, 15 minutes

Chili Sauce, Chow Chow, Piccalilli, Green Tomato Relish, and Tart Corn Relish: 1/2 inch, 15 minutes

Green Mango Chutney, Apple Chutney, Pear Chutney, and Tomato Chutney: 1/4 inch, 10 minutes

For the canner, any large pot will do, as long as it is at least 2 1/2 inches taller than the jars being processed and has a lid. Place a rack or folded towel on the bottom (to let water circulate and keep the glass from cracking against the bottom). Set the pot over just one burner, fill half full with hot water, and bring to a simmer (180°F). Use only Mason-type jars manufactured in this country specifically for home canning, free of defects. Also use only the two-piece vacuum caps that come with the jars. The lids must be brand-new, but the rings can be reused until they rust or warp. Condiments are best packed in pint or half-pint jars (timing is the same for both). Heat the jars by filling them with very hot water; pour simmering water over the lids in a bowl. Fill and cap one jar at a time. Pack lightly with hot food, leaving the required headspace (the pocket of air measured on the inside of the jar from the rim down to the food). Force out any air bubbles by sliding a clean narrow nonmetallic spatula between the food and the sides of the jar. Wipe the rim and threads of the jar with a clean damp cloth. Set on the lid and screw the ring on firmly—stop turning when you feel resistance. Immediately lower the jar into the kettle with a jar lifter or tongs. Jars should not touch.

Process the jars at once. If necessary, add or remove boiling water so the level remains 1 inch above the jar tops. Cover the kettle and bring to a rolling boil over highest heat. When the water boils, set the timer. Times given are for 0 to 1,000 feet elevation. For 1,001–3,000 feet, add 5 minutes; 3,001–6,000 feet, add 10 minutes; 6,001–8,000 feet, add 15 minutes; 8,001–10,000 feet, add 20 minutes. Adjust the heat to maintain a gentle boil, and maintain the water level. When the jars have boiled for the recommended time, turn off the heat and lift the jars onto a towel in a draft-free place, placing them at least 1 inch apart. Do not tighten the rings. Let the jars cool for at least 8 hours, then check the seal: every lid should curve down slightly in the center and should stay depressed when pressed with a finger. If this is not the case, refrigerate the jar at once and serve the contents within a few days. Label the sealed jars and store in a cool, dark, dry place.

ABOUT TABLE SAUCES

Every cuisine has its own special sauce that at mealtime is pulled from a cool place or prepared fresh and brought to the table (in some cultures, even at breakfast). Some of these sauces, such as salsa and ketchup, go over food. Some, such as wasabi and Thai peanut sauce—and, in most cases, mustard and mayonnaise—are for dipping. Chefs have given us many wonderful innovations for these sauces, but most of the recipes remain simple.

ABOUT SALSAS

Salsa translates as "sauce" from both Italian and Spanish, and in these countries, "salsa" can apply to everything from creamy white sauce to brown gravy. Still, when we hear the word *salsa,* it is the Latino tomato-and-chili-pepper-based mixes that spring to mind. Like ketchups, salsas can go over just about everything on the plate. Although some ingredients can be cooked, the sauce itself should be raw, cool, and garden fresh.

In many instances, the raw onions in these recipes are finely chopped, then rinsed under cold water and sometimes sprinkled with citrus juice before combining with the other ingredients. Hand chopping gives superior texture, and rinsing mellows the onion wonderfully, avoiding any biting aftertaste that may overpower the other flavors of the sauce.

Tomatoes can be seeded, 430, but this is not the traditional way to prepare these fresh, unfussy salsas. When removing the blender's lid after grinding condiments containing chili peppers, avert your face—chili fumes are powerful.

For extra dimension in a salsa, mix in a splash of light tequila or dark rum. Salsas are best served at room temperature soon after they are made. For most recipes, allow 2 to 4 tablespoons per serving.

SALSA FRESCA

About 2 cups

This recipe for Mexican salsa is easily doubled or tripled, but try to make only as much as you will use immediately, as it loses its texture on standing and the chili peppers increase in heat. Regional variations include using scallions or white or red onions, water instead of lime juice, and in Yucatán, sour-orange juice instead of lime juice. Any sort of fresh chili pepper can be used—each contributes its distinctive character. Rinsing the chopped onions eliminates the biting aftertaste that could otherwise overwhelm the other ingredients. As you can see, precise amounts are less important than the happy marriage of flavors, so taste as you go. Salsa Fresca complements everything from tacos to hot grills to cool vegetables. In American-style Mexican food, this type of salsa is sometimes called *pico de gallo.*

Combine in a medium bowl:

½ small white or red onion or 8 slender scallions, finely chopped, rinsed, and drained
2 tablespoons fresh lime juice or cold water

Prepare the following ingredients, setting them aside, then add all together to the onion mixture:

2 large ripe tomatoes, or 3 to 5 ripe plum tomatoes, seeded, if desired, and finely diced
¼ to ½ cup chopped fresh cilantro (leaves and tender stems)
3 to 5 serrano or fresh jalapeño peppers, or ¼ to 1 habanero pepper, or to taste, seeded and minced
6 radishes, finely diced (optional)
1 medium clove garlic, minced (optional)

Stir together well. Season with:

¼ teaspoon salt, or to taste

Serve immediately.

SALSA VERDE CRUDA *About 2 cups*

Intensely fresh, pungent, and herbal, this tomatillo salsa is the easiest salsa of all. It is especially good with fish, chicken, steamed or roasted vegetables, and eggs. However, since the onion is not rinsed and everything is whirled to a puree, it must be served within an hour of preparing for optimum quality. If left to sit, the raw onion will overpower the sauce.

Combine in a food processor or blender and coarsely puree, leaving the mixture a little chunky:

8 ounces tomatillos, husked, rinsed, and coarsely chopped
1 small white or red onion, coarsely chopped
3 to 5 fresh green chili peppers (such as serrano or jalapeño), seeded and coarsely chopped
1 clove garlic, peeled (optional)
3 to 4 tablespoons fresh cilantro sprigs

Remove to a medium bowl and stir in enough cold water to loosen the mixture to a saucelike consistency. Stir in:

1 teaspoon salt, or to taste
¾ teaspoon sugar (optional)

Serve immediately.

CORN, CHERRY TOMATO, AND AVOCADO SALSA *About 2 cups*

Boil in salted water to cover for 1 minute, drain, and remove the kernels from:

2 ears sweet corn, husked and silk removed

Place the corn kernels in a medium bowl along with:

8 small cherry tomatoes, seeded, if desired, and halved
1 small ripe avocado, peeled and coarsely chopped
¼ cup coarsely chopped fresh basil
½ small red onion, finely diced, rinsed, and drained
2 tablespoons vegetable oil
2 tablespoons fresh lime juice, or to taste
1 clove garlic, finely chopped
1 to 3 fresh jalapeño peppers, seeded and finely chopped
Salt and ground black pepper to taste

Stir together well and serve immediately. This salsa will keep, covered and refrigerated, for 1 day.

ROASTED TOMATO-CHIPOTLE SALSA *About 2 cups*

Tomatoes—and the salsa they create—take on a deeper flavor when roasted. This salsa is particularly good with grilled chicken and lamb.

Build a medium-low fire in your grill or preheat the broiler.

Place on the grill or on a broiler pan:

6 medium, ripe tomatoes, seeded, if desired, and halved

Grill or broil (broil as close to the heat as possible), turning as needed, until the skins are blackened in spots and slightly softened, about 5 minutes each side on the grill and slightly less time in the broiler. When cool enough to handle, remove the skins and coarsely chop the tomatoes, put them in a medium bowl, and stir in:

1 small onion, finely chopped, rinsed, and drained
¼ cup coarsely chopped fresh cilantro
3 tablespoons fresh lime juice, or to taste
2 tablespoons olive oil
2 cloves garlic, finely chopped
1½ teaspoons finely chopped canned chipotle pepper, or to taste
1 teaspoon ground cumin
Salt to taste

Serve immediately.

ROASTED TOMATILLO SALSA *About 2 cups*

Roasting the tomatillos first gives this salsa an irresistible depth of flavor and smooth texture.

Preheat the broiler. Line a baking sheet with aluminum foil. Place in a single layer on the baking sheet:

1 pound tomatillos, husked and rinsed

Broil until darkened and softened on one side, about 4 minutes; turn the tomatillos over and broil on the other side, 5 to 6 minutes more. Let cool completely. Place the roasted tomatillos (and any juice that has accumulated around them) in a blender or food processor along with:

3 fresh hot green chili peppers (such as serrano or jalapeño), seeded and chopped
1 small clove garlic, minced (optional)

Coarsely puree, leaving the mixture a little chunky. Remove to a medium bowl, and stir in:

¼ cup water
1 small white onion, finely chopped, rinsed, and drained
3 to 4 tablespoons chopped fresh cilantro
1 teaspoon salt
¾ teaspoon sugar

To thin the salsa to a medium consistency, add:

Up to ¼ cup water

Let the salsa stand for a few minutes before serving to allow the flavors to develop.

ROASTED TOMATO-JALAPEÑO SALSA

About 2 cups

Heat the broiler. Arrange on a rimmed baking sheet:

1 pound red, ripe tomatoes

Broil 4 inches from the heat until they blister, darken, and soften on one side, about 4 minutes; turn them over and broil the other side until blistered and darkened, 5 to 6 minutes. Meanwhile, heat a dry cast-iron griddle or skillet over high heat, and add:

2 large fresh jalapeño peppers
3 cloves garlic, unpeeled

Shake them in the pan until their skins are soft and charred here and there, 5 to 10 minutes for the jalapeños, about 15 minutes for the garlic. Let cool, then peel the tomatoes, reserving the juices, pull the stems off the jalapeños, and peel the garlic. Place the jalapeños and garlic in a food processor or blender with:

¼ teaspoon salt

Process to a coarse paste. Add the tomatoes and process a few times until you have a coarse-textured puree. Stir in:

½ small white onion, finely chopped, rinsed, and drained
Generous ⅓ cup loosely packed chopped fresh cilantro
About 1½ teaspoons cider vinegar (optional)

Add 2 to 4 tablespoons water, if necessary, to give the salsa a fairly thick but easily spoonable consistency. Taste and season with:

Salt

Serve immediately.

MANGO SALSA

About 3 cups

Use this as a master recipe for fruit salsas—wonderful with just about any food but particularly with grilled or sautéed fish. Papaya, pineapple, peaches, or apricots can be substituted for the mango; basil or parsley can stand in for the cilantro; and pineapple or guava juice is a good alternative to the orange juice.

Combine in a large bowl:

1 small red onion, chopped, rinsed, and drained
¼ cup fresh lime juice

Prepare the following ingredients, setting them aside, then add all together to the onion mixture:

1 large ripe mango, peeled, pitted, and coarsely chopped
1 small red bell pepper, cut into thin strips
¼ cup coarsely chopped fresh cilantro
1 clove garlic, minced
¼ cup fresh orange juice
1 fresh jalapeño or other small chili pepper, finely chopped

Stir together well. Season with:

Salt and cracked black peppercorns to taste

Serve immediately. This salsa will keep, covered and refrigerated, for 1 day.

FRUIT SALSA WITH BLACK BEANS

Dots of purply-black catch the eye, and their sweetness is pleasant with every fruit.

Prepare Mango Salsa, above, adding ¼ to ⅓ cup rinsed and drained canned small black beans.

ABOUT RELISHES AND CHUTNEYS

Nearly every cuisine has created small dishes to be served on the side, designed to enhance the main dishes. Whether called relishes, sambals, chutneys, or garnishes, most are in the realm of condiments, being savory, piquant, spicy, or salty. When selecting a relish to serve, look for contrast—colors, textures, shapes, and flavors different from the main dish. Temperature can contrast, but it need not. Most relishes are best cold or at room temperature, but fruit relishes can be flavorful when warm.

Fresh Indian chutneys are the traditional Indian chutney—long-cooked chutneys are a British invention. Fresh chutneys are quickly made, brilliantly seasoned, and enormously refreshing. A cross between a relish and a table sauce, they can be spooned over everything from simply cooked vegetables to elaborate composed dishes.

CHOW-CHOW

9 to 10 pint jars

In nineteenth-century India and China, *chow-chow* was slang for a mix. This marvelous relish was the first recipe in the pickle section in the first edition of this book. The vegetables are in a thick mustard sauce, so chow-

chow can be served as a creamy relish or a crunchy cool sauce. Please see About Canning Condiments, 60.
Remove a thin slice from each end, and then slice crosswise 1/4 inch thick:

2 pounds unpeeled tender small cucumbers

Stir together in a large bowl until the salt is dissolved:

5 cups cold water
1/2 cup salt

Add the cucumbers, stir well, cover, and let stand in a cool place for 12 hours. Keep covered until ready to use. For the sauce, combine in a 6-quart nonreactive saucepan and stir until the sugar is dissolved:

2 1/2 quarts cider vinegar
2 1/2 cups sugar

Stir together in a medium bowl until smooth:

1 1/2 cups all-purpose flour
6 tablespoons dry mustard
1 1/2 tablespoons ground turmeric
3 tablespoons celery seeds

Slowly whisk about 2 cups of the vinegar mixture into the flour mixture, then whisk until smooth. Bring the remaining vinegar mixture to a simmer over low heat. Slowly whisk in the flour mixture. Cook, whisking constantly, until smooth and simmering. Remove from the heat, cover, and reserve. Cut into 1/2-inch pieces or dice, to make 3 quarts:

1 1/2 pounds firm green tomatoes, cored
1 1/2 pounds green bell peppers
1 pound tender young snap peas, trimmed

Combine them in a large saucepan with:

1 1/2 pounds tender cauliflower, cut into bite-sized florets
1/2 pound bite-sized boiling onions, blanched for 1 minute and peeled

Pour boiling salted water (1 teaspoon salt to 4 cups water) over the vegetables to cover. Return to a boil, then drain thoroughly. Also drain thoroughly the reserved cucumbers. Add them to the vegetables and stir together well. Heat the mustard sauce to boiling and stir into the hot vegetables. Season with:

Salt to taste

Can while hot; or let cool, then cover and refrigerate for up to 1 month.

PICCALILLI *About 10 cups*

Once, the vegetables for this classic Southern relish were cut into slices. If they are chopped, the relish is more useful because it can easily be spread. Please see About Canning Condiments, 60.
Remove a thin slice from each end, then chop:

5 pounds tender small cucumbers

Combine them in a large bowl with:

1 1/3 pounds green bell peppers, chopped
1 1/3 pounds onions, chopped

Stir together in another bowl until the salt is dissolved:

2 1/2 quarts cool water
1 cup salt

Add the brine to the vegetables, stir well, cover, and let stand for 12 hours in a cool place. Drain well. Combine in a 6-quart nonreactive saucepan and bring just to the boiling point, stirring until the sugar is dissolved:

1 quart cider vinegar
4 cups sugar

Tie in a moist square of cloth and add:

3 tablespoons whole mixed spices, such as pickling spices
1 1/2 teaspoons celery seeds
1 1/2 teaspoons mustard seeds

Add the drained vegetables. Return to the boiling point. Stir in, if desired:

1 tablespoon plus 2 teaspoons red pepper flakes

Can while hot; or let cool, remove the spices, then cover and refrigerate for up to 1 month.

WHOLE CRANBERRY RELISH *About 3 cups*

The Thanksgiving classic.
Combine in a large skillet:

1 pound cranberries, picked over
2 cups sugar
1/2 cup water
1/2 cup orange juice
2 teaspoons grated orange zest

Cook, uncovered, over medium heat until most of the cranberries pop open and the mixture is somewhat thickened, 7 to 10 minutes. If desired, add:

1/2 cup blanched almonds, slivered

Let cool and serve or refrigerate for up to 1 day.

UNCOOKED CRANBERRY-ORANGE RELISH *About 2 1/2 cups*

This tart and refreshing relish is an excellent companion not only to the Thanksgiving turkey, but to any meat or fowl. Since you use the whole orange, including the rind, it is important to allow the relish to mellow for at least 2 days before serving.
Pick over:

One 12-ounce package cranberries

Cut into eighths and remove the seeds from:

1 orange, unpeeled

Place half of the cranberries and half of the orange in a food processor fitted with the steel blade and pulse until the mixture is evenly chopped but not pureed.

Transfer to a medium bowl. Repeat with the remaining cranberries and orange. Stir in:

1 cup sugar

Cover and refrigerate for at least 2 days or up to 2 weeks. Serve chilled or at room temperature.

GREEN TOMATO RELISH
About 6 pint jars

Delicious, and invaluable for salvaging unripened tomatoes before frost. Please see About Canning Condiments, 60.

Combine in a large bowl:

8 pounds green tomatoes, thinly sliced
2¾ pounds onions, thinly sliced

Sprinkle with:

½ cup salt

Stir together well, cover, and refrigerate for 12 hours. Rinse in cold water and drain. Combine in a 4-quart nonreactive saucepan and bring to a boil, stirring until the sugar is dissolved:

1½ quarts cider vinegar
2 pounds brown sugar

Stir in:

2 pounds green bell peppers, sliced
1 pound red bell peppers, diced
6 cloves garlic, minced
1 tablespoon dry mustard
1½ teaspoons salt

Add the tomatoes and onions and stir together well. Tie in a moist square of cloth and add:

1 tablespoon whole cloves
1 tablespoon ground ginger
1½ teaspoons celery seeds
One 3-inch cinnamon stick, broken

Simmer, stirring often, until the tomatoes are translucent, about 1 hour. Can while hot; or let cool, remove the spice bag, then cover and refrigerate for up to 1 month.

CORN AND TOMATO RELISH
About 3½ cups

This relish, based on the piccalillis or pickle relishes of the American South, goes particularly well with pork. If you wish, you can use thawed frozen corn, but use only good-quality ripe tomatoes.

Boil in salted water to cover for 1 minute, drain, and remove the kernels from:

3 ears sweet corn, husked and silk removed

Place the corn kernels in a small bowl along with:

2 ripe tomatoes, finely diced
1 small red onion, finely diced
¼ cup diced sweet pickles
½ cup cider vinegar
1 tablespoon sugar
1 tablespoon celery seeds
Salt and cracked black peppercorns to taste

Mix together well, cover, and refrigerate until ready to serve. This relish will keep, covered and refrigerated, for 4 to 5 days.

TART CORN RELISH
About 10 pints

Crunchy corn and bright colors and flavors make this relish especially prized in winter. (Do not make it in winter with frozen corn—it will be disappointing. Wait until summer.) Please read About Canning Condiments, 60.

Blanch for 5 minutes in boiling salted water (1 teaspoon salt to every 1 quart water):

18 medium ears yellow or bicolor corn, husked and silk removed

Dip in cold water, then pat dry. Cut the kernels from the cobs, without scraping, into a very large container. Add:

1 pound red bell peppers, chopped
8 ounces green bell peppers, chopped
4 ounces mild green chili peppers, seeded and chopped
1½ pounds red onions, chopped
12 ounces green or red cabbage, chopped
5 cups cider vinegar
1 cup sugar
1 cup water
½ cup fresh lemon juice
3 tablespoons chopped fresh dill, or 1½ teaspoons dried dill weed
2 tablespoons salt
2 teaspoons yellow mustard seeds
2 teaspoons ground turmeric
1 teaspoon celery seeds

Mix until well blended. Whisk until smooth in a small bowl:

1 cup water
½ cup all-purpose flour

Cook the vegetables in 2 batches in a nonreactive saucepan. Bring half of the vegetables to a boil over high heat, then reduce the heat and simmer, stirring often, for 10 minutes. Stir in half the reserved flour mixture, and cook, stirring occasionally until the mixture thickens, then more often, for 10 minutes more. Repeat with the remaining vegetables and flour mixture. Can while hot; or let cool, then cover and refrigerate for up to 1 month.

QUICK RED ONION PICKLE
About 2 cups

A perfect accompaniment to grilled chicken or steak.

Combine in a medium bowl:

⅓ cup red wine vinegar
2 tablespoons sugar
1 tablespoon grenadine (optional)
1 tablespoon cracked black peppercorns

Add and let marinate for 2 hours:

2 red onions, cut into ¼-inch-thick slices and separated into rings

Serve immediately. This pickle will keep, covered and refrigerated, for up to 2 days.

RED ONION MARMALADE

About 2 cups

Onion marmalade—sometimes called confit—is wonderful with roasted meats.

Combine in a medium nonreactive saucepan over low heat:

3½ large red onions, cut into ¼-inch-thick slices, slices halved crosswise
⅓ cup dry red wine
⅓ cup red wine vinegar
¼ cup packed light brown sugar
¼ cup mild honey

Cook, stirring, until the sugar is dissolved; then simmer, stirring often, until the consistency of marmalade, about 30 minutes. Stir in:

1 tablespoon orange juice
1 tablespoon lemon juice

Continue to cook, stirring, until the juices are absorbed. Let cool, then cover and refrigerate for up to 3 weeks. Serve at room temperature.

FRESH MINT CHUTNEY

About ⅔ cup

Delicious with fish, green and root vegetables, and poultry and veal. In India, mint chutney is prized for its digestive properties, and accompanies fried and highly spiced dishes. Peppermint leaves are best, but another mint can be used; if it is not strongly flavored, add more leaves. Seeded fresh chili peppers can be added, if desired, but then add a bit more water to make a thin puree.

Combine in a food processor or blender and process to a coarse puree, stopping to scrape down the sides as needed:

1 cup fresh peppermint or other mint leaves
¼ large onion, cut into 1-inch pieces
5 tablespoons cold water
2 tablespoons fresh lime or lemon juice
2 teaspoons sugar
¼ teaspoon coarse salt
⅛ teaspoon ground red pepper, or to taste

Cover and refrigerate, but do not keep for more than 1 day. Serve in a small bowl.

FRESH MINT-CILANTRO CHUTNEY

About 1 cup

This is prepared fresh daily by an Indian grocer in Los Angeles for her clients to eat with her potato samosas, 165. It is hot, complex, and marvelous.

Combine in a food processor or blender and puree, stopping to scrape down the sides as needed:

1 cup lightly packed fresh mint leaves
½ cup lightly packed fresh cilantro leaves
½ cup coarsely chopped onions
3 small scallions, cut into small pieces
3 fresh jalapeño peppers, seeded and cut into small pieces
3 tablespoons water
1½ tablespoons fresh lemon juice
¼ teaspoon salt

Cover and refrigerate for up to 1 day.

FRESH PINEAPPLE CHUTNEY

About 2½ cups

This is lovely, and although Indonesian, could be paired with food from Mexico to Morocco.

Prepare, 474, and quarter lengthwise:

1 ripe sweet pineapple (about 2½ pounds)

Core each quarter and discard, cut into bite-sized chunks, then cut each chunk in half, cutting with the grain. Combine in a medium nonreactive saucepan with:

2 fresh red or green serrano peppers, seeded and minced
2 tablespoons sugar
¼ teaspoon ground cinnamon
¼ teaspoon salt
Pinch of ground cloves

Bring to a simmer, stirring often, over medium heat. Continue to cook, stirring often, until the pineapple is just tender, 15 to 20 minutes. Serve hot or at room temperature. This chutney will keep, covered and refrigerated, for up to 12 hours.

FRESH TAMARIND CHUTNEY

About 1½ cups

This Indian sweet-sour-spicy chutney has the consistency of a thin dipping sauce and is traditionally served with kebabs and fried foods. Find tamarind in Asian or Hispanic markets or specialty food stores.

Combine in a small saucepan and let stand for 30 minutes:

4 ounces tamarind pulp
1 tablespoon finely chopped peeled fresh ginger
2½ cups hot water

While the tamarind is soaking, spread in a small dry skillet over medium-high heat and toast, shaking the pan often to prevent burning, until very aromatic, about 2 minutes:

1 tablespoon cumin seeds

Remove the cumin to a small bowl and let cool completely. Grind to a fine powder in a spice grinder, coffee grinder, or blender, or with a mortar and pestle. Remove the tamarind from the water and place it in a strainer over a saucepan. Mash it thoroughly with a fork to separate the seeds and fibers from the peel. Strain the pulp, pressing down on it to squeeze out all the juice. Add the soaking liquid and stir in:

6 tablespoons packed light brown sugar
1 to 2 fresh jalapeño or other chili peppers, seeded and finely chopped

Bring the mixture to a boil, reduce the heat, and cook, stirring, at a bare simmer for 15 minutes. Remove to a food processor or blender and puree until smooth, adding just a bit of water if necessary to create a thin-sauce consistency. Return the tamarind mixture to the saucepan and stir in the ground cumin along with:

1 teaspoon curry powder
Salt and ground red pepper to taste (optional)

Cook, stirring, over the lowest possible heat for 5 minutes. Strain the mixture through a coarse-mesh sieve, pressing hard on the solids with a rubber spatula. Thin the sauce to the desired consistency with:

Up to ½ cup water

Cover and refrigerate for up to 3 weeks.

ABOUT LONG-SIMMERED CHUTNEYS

In the beginning, cooked chutney was prepared in India exclusively for the English, and almost exclusively of green mangoes. Then creative cooks made chutneys out of everything from plums to rhubarb. Chutneys are an exception to the rule that sweet preserves are best cooked in small batches. You can make an enormous quantity, as long as you have a large, heavy-bottomed saucepan and a strong stirring arm. (As with all long-simmering mixtures, the wider the base of the saucepan, the more evenly the chutney will cook.) With its wealth of vinegar, sugar, and spices, a tightly closed jar of chutney can hold its quality—even improve—in the refrigerator for several months. The chutneys that follow have quite different characteristics. As delectable as they are with curries, their deep, complex flavors are superb with grills and roasts.

GREEN MANGO CHUTNEY

About 6½ pint jars

This is the exotic fruit that is most associated with the word *chutney*. Good with chicken, veal, pork, and fish. A flame tamer mutes the heat of the stove burner and disperses it evenly over the bottom of the pot—perfect for slow simmering over a long period of time. Please see About Canning Condiments, 60.

Cut into ½-inch-thick slices, separating the flesh from the seeds:

6½ pounds green mangoes, peeled

Cut the slices in half crosswise, and combine in a 4-quart nonreactive saucepan with:

4 cups cider vinegar

Simmer, covered, until the mangoes are barely tender, about 20 minutes. Remove from the heat and stir in:

4 cups packed light brown sugar
8 ounces dried currants

Grind to a coarse powder in a spice grinder, coffee grinder, or blender, or with a mortar and pestle:

2½ tablespoons toasted yellow mustard seeds

Transfer to a blender or food processor. Cut into small pieces and add:

2 ounces fresh jalapeño or serrano chili peppers, cored and seeded
2 ounces garlic cloves, peeled
2 ounces fresh ginger, peeled

Pulse until finely chopped. Stir in, then pulse to a coarse paste:

3 tablespoons ground turmeric
2 tablespoons ground ginger
1½ tablespoons ground nutmeg
1 tablespoon ground allspice
2 teaspoons ground mace
2 teaspoons ground red pepper
2 teaspoons salt

Thoroughly stir this mixture into the mangoes. Bring to a simmer, stirring often, over low heat. Reduce the heat to the lowest setting and set the saucepan on a flame tamer. Cook, partially covered, until the mixture is the color of dark brown sugar and as thick as jam, about 3 hours. Stir every 10 minutes—more often toward the end—to prevent scorching. Can while hot; or let cool, cover, and refrigerate for up to 1 month.

APPLE CHUTNEY

About 6 pint jars

This can also be made with green tomatoes. Wonderfully tangy. Please see About Canning Condiments, 60.

Stir together well in a 4-quart nonreactive saucepan:

10 medium-large juicy green apples, peeled, cored, and chopped
4 red bell peppers, chopped
3 cups seeded Muscat or large dark seedless raisins
2 thin-skinned lemons, seeded and finely chopped
½ cup chopped peeled fresh ginger
2 cloves garlic, minced

4½ cups packed light brown sugar
4 cups cider vinegar
2 teaspoons salt, or to taste
½ teaspoon ground red pepper

Bring to a simmer, stirring often, over low heat; then simmer, partially covered, until thick, about 2 hours. Stir often—especially toward the end—to prevent scorching. Can while hot; or let cool, then cover and refrigerate for up to 1 month.

PEAR CHUTNEY

About 5 pint jars

Ideal with pork, turkey, and game birds. This recipe is from Sylvia Thompson, a great friend of *Joy*. Please read About Canning Condiments, 60.

Remove the zest with a zester or finely shred the zest, then juice:

6 large oranges

Combine the zest and juice in a 4-quart nonreactive saucepan with:

2½ cups cider vinegar
2 pounds dark brown sugar
2 tablespoons ground coriander
2 tablespoons yellow mustard seeds
Four 3-inch cinnamon sticks, broken into 1-inch pieces
One 3- inch dried red chili pepper, crumbled
½ teaspoon ground cloves
½ teaspoon salt

Add:

4 pounds underripe flavorful pears, peeled, cored, and cut into ½-inch-thick slices

Stir the slices to coat them with the syrup. Add:

1 pound ripe tomatoes, peeled, seeded, and chopped, or drained canned plum tomatoes, chopped
12 ounces dark raisins
12 ounces golden raisins
1 large onion, minced
2 ounces fresh ginger, peeled and finely chopped
4 large cloves garlic, minced

Stir together well. Bring to a simmer, stirring often, over low heat; then simmer, partially covered, stirring often, pushing the pears beneath the syrup. After about 1½ hours, stir in:

1 cup frozen concentrated unsweetened apple juice, thawed
1 cup water

Simmer, uncovered, stirring often, until the mixture is thick, dark, and syrupy and the pears are translucent, 1½ hours more. If desired, stir in:

1 tablespoon ground coriander (optional)

Can while hot; or let cool, then cover and refrigerate for up to 1 month.

TOMATO CHUTNEY

About 18 pint jars

A California heirloom given to us by good friend Lida Schneider, this has uncommon depth. It is our favorite chutney, superb with any meat, poultry, fish, or winter squash, sweet potatoes, and potatoes. Please read About Canning Condiments, 60.

Combine in a 20-quart nonreactive saucepan:

8 quarts chopped peeled ripe tomatoes
1 quart chopped onions
1 quart chopped peeled tart, juicy green apples
1 pound seeded Muscat raisins or large dark seedless raisins
1 pound golden raisins
1½ pounds dark brown sugar
1½ pounds light brown sugar
1½ quarts cider vinegar
¼ cup yellow mustard seeds
2 tablespoons ground cloves
1 tablespoon ground allspice
1½ teaspoons ground red pepper
3 tablespoons salt, or to taste

Stir together well. Bring to a simmer, stirring often, over low heat; then simmer, partially covered, until very thick and dark, 3 to 5 hours. Stir often—espeically toward the end—to prevent scorching. Can while hot; or let cool, then cover and refrigerate for up to 1 month.

SPICY CUCUMBER SAMBAL

About 4 cups

In Malaysia, sambals may be pastelike relishes similar to those in Indonesia, but they are also sometimes mixtures of grated raw fruits or vegetables seasoned with vinegar and chili peppers—like this one—and served with fish and shellfish.

Stir together well in a small bowl:

3 small or 2 medium cucumbers, peeled, halved, seeded, and finely diced
1 small red onion, finely diced
3 tablespoons to ⅓ cup minced fresh chili peppers of your choice
2 tablespoons minced garlic
2 tablespoons minced peeled fresh ginger
2 tablespoons ground white pepper (you can substitute black)
2 tablespoons sugar
½ cup coarsely chopped fresh cilantro

¼ cup fresh lime juice
¼ cup fish sauce (optional)
Salt to taste

Cover and refrigerate until ready to serve. This sambal will keep, covered and refrigerated, for up to 1 week.

INDONESIAN GINGER SAMBAL (SAMBAL CUKA)

About ½ cup

Indonesian sambals are a kind of relish, very concentrated in flavor and usually quite fiery. They are typically served in very small amounts to accompany meat, poultry, or fish.

Process in a food processor until finely chopped:

One ½-inch piece fresh ginger, peeled
3 cloves garlic

With the machine still running, add and process to a fine paste:

6 to 8 fresh or dried hot chili peppers, seeded, if desired, and coarsely chopped

Stop the machine, add, and process until smooth:

3 tablespoons white vinegar
2 teaspoons packed light brown sugar
Salt to taste

Cover and refrigerate until ready to serve. This sambal will keep, covered and refrigerated, for up to 3 weeks.

ABOUT KETCHUPS

We got our ketchup from the British in the nineteenth century, and they got theirs from the Far East long before. The word is derived from the Malay word *kechap,* a fish sauce. No other food so familiar to Americans seems to have so many spellings. In England, it is both pronounced and written "ketchup," while both "catsup" and "ketchup" are used in the United States. In the beginning, ketchups resembled today's unsweetened Asian seasoning sauces—thin, sharp, and dark. Some were concocted from tomato juice, but many were based on mushrooms, walnuts, anchovies, or oysters. The Mushroom Ketchup in this section, 70, an English sauce, gives a sense of the early ketchups. Sugar was not added until the end of the last century. Today's ketchups are a wonderful balance of tangy and sweet.

TOMATO KETCHUP

About 10 pint jars

In commercial ketchups, sweetening is the second ingredient—after tomato concentrate and before the garlic and onion powders. One taste of a true tomato ketchup simmered from fresh ingredients will make you understand why people savor homemade ketchup not just with hamburgers and French fries but with steaks as well.

Combine in a large nonreactive pot over medium heat and simmer, stirring occasionally, until very soft:

14 pounds ripe tomatoes, peeled and chopped
8 medium onions, sliced
2 red bell peppers, diced

Puree through the medium blade of a food mill or push through a coarse-mesh sieve, then return to the pot. Stir in:

¾ cup packed light brown sugar
½ teaspoon dry mustard

Tie in a moist square of cloth and add to the tomato mixture:

One 3-inch cinnamon stick
1 tablespoon whole allspice
1 tablespoon whole cloves
1 tablespoon ground mace
1 tablespoon celery seeds
1 tablespoon black peppercorns
2 bay leaves
1 clove garlic, peeled

Bring the mixture to a rolling boil, then reduce to a simmer. Continue to cook, stirring often and carefully so it does not scorch, until the sauce is reduced by half. Remove and discard the spice bag. Stir in:

2 cups cider vinegar
Canning or pickling salt to taste
Ground red pepper to taste (optional)

Reduce the heat and simmer, stirring almost constantly, for 10 minutes. Can while hot; or let cool, then cover and refrigerate for up to 1 month.

BLENDER TOMATO KETCHUP

About 9 pint jars

The flavoring and cooking make this an old-fashioned ketchup without the old-fashioned work of putting it through a food mill or sieve.

In manageable batches, process in a blender until pureed, about 5 seconds each batch:

24 pounds ripe tomatoes, peeled and quartered
2 pounds onions, quartered
1 pound red bell peppers, cut into strips
1 pound green bell peppers, cut into strips

Remove to a large nonreactive saucepan. Stir together well and bring to a boil, stirring often, over medium heat. Boil gently, stirring often and thoroughly, for 1 hour. Stir in:

9 cups cider vinegar
9 cups sugar
¼ cup canning or pickling salt

Tie in a moist square of cloth and add to the tomato mixture:

- 3 tablespoons dry mustard
- 1½ tablespoons sweet or hot paprika
- 1½ tablespoons whole allspice
- 1½ tablespoons whole cloves
- Two 3-inch cinnamon sticks

Continue boiling gently and stirring until the mixture is reduced by half and mounds up on a spoon with no separation of liquid and solids. Remove and discard the spice bag. Can while hot; or let cool, then cover and refrigerate for up to 1 month.

RED ONION-GARLIC KETCHUP *About 3 cups*

The rich, deep, robust flavors of this ketchup are perfect with steak or roast beef.

Heat in a large nonreactive skillet over medium heat:

- ⅓ cup olive oil

Add and cook, stirring often, until well browned, about 10 to 20 minutes:

- 5 large red onions, thinly sliced

Stir in and cook until the garlic and ginger are softened, about 3 minutes:

- ¼ cup minced garlic
- 1 tablespoon minced peeled fresh ginger
- 1 medium, ripe tomato, finely diced

Add:

- 1 teaspoon hot red pepper sauce, or to taste
- 5 tablespoons Worcestershire sauce
- ½ cup light or dark molasses
- ¾ cup cider vinegar
- 1 teaspoon ground allspice

Reduce the heat to low and cook, stirring occasionally, until slightly thickened, about 15 minutes. Remove from the heat and season with:

- Salt and ground black pepper to taste

Let cool to room temperature. Once the mixture has cooled, place it in a blender or food processor and puree. Serve warm or cold. This will keep, covered and refrigerated, for up to 1 month.

MUSHROOM KETCHUP *About 3½ cups*

Mushrooms bring the woodsy fragrances of the forest to the table. Unlike our thick, sweet, tomato-based ketchups, this English condiment for robust meats and game is a thin, pungent, deeply flavored sauce.

Wipe clean and chop coarsely on a large baking sheet (with rim) lined with several layers of wax paper:

- 4 pounds mushrooms, preferably cremini

Spread out and sprinkle with:

- 7 tablespoons coarse salt

Cover and refrigerate, stirring and squeezing with your hands occasionally, for 2 to 3 days. Drain the mushrooms and rinse well, discarding the liquid. Combine in a large nonreactive saucepan with:

- 1 cup red wine vinegar
- ⅔ cup cider vinegar
- 1 medium red onion, finely chopped
- 1 clove garlic, finely chopped
- ½ teaspoon ground black pepper
- ¼ teaspoon ground ginger
- ¼ teaspoon ground allspice
- ¼ teaspoon ground mace or nutmeg

Bring to a boil, reduce the heat, and simmer, uncovered, stirring often, until very fragrant and flavorful, about 30 minutes. Strain into a clean saucepan, pressing out all the liquid. Bring to a simmer, then strain through a dampened cloth. Can while hot, or let cool, then cover and refrigerate for up to 1 month.

CHILI SAUCE *About 8 pint jars*

The difference between Tomato Ketchup and Chili Sauce is that the first is smooth and mild, the second textured and zesty. This recipe can be halved.

Grind together in batches through the medium blade of a food mill or chop medium-fine in a food processor:

- 6 red bell peppers, coarsely chopped
- 6 large onions, coarsely chopped

Remove to a 6-quart nonreactive saucepan and stir in:

- 14 pounds ripe tomatoes, peeled, seeded, and chopped
- 3 cups cider vinegar
- 2 cups packed light brown sugar
- 2 tablespoons salt
- 2 tablespoons dry mustard (optional)
- 1 tablespoon ground black pepper
- 1 tablespoon ground allspice
- 1 teaspoon ground cloves
- 1 teaspoon ground ginger
- 1 teaspoon ground cinnamon
- 1 teaspoon ground nutmeg
- 1 teaspoon celery seeds

Stir to blend thoroughly, then bring to a boil over medium heat. Simmer, stirring often to prevent scorching, until as thick as desired, about 3 hours. Taste and adjust the seasonings, especially the salt. Can while hot; or let cool, then cover and refrigerate for up to 1 month.

COCKTAIL SAUCE *About 1 cup*

This wonderful old recipe makes a lively dunking sauce for seafood. For a contemporary sauce, add finely chopped cilantro, red onions, green chili peppers, and/or lime juice.

Stir together well in a small bowl:

½ cup ketchup
½ cup chili sauce
¼ cup finely grated horseradish

Stir in:

Hot red pepper sauce to taste
Fresh lemon juice to taste

Serve at room temperature. This will keep, covered and refrigerated, for up to 1 week.

ABOUT HOMEMADE MUSTARDS

Preparing your own mustard from seeds is a cooking adventure—and a source of gifts from your kitchen. Somehow, homemade mustard is even more impressive to most people than homemade preserves, although it is far easier to prepare—it is simply stirred, not cooked. Mustards have good keeping power in the refrigerator, and mellow with time.

GRAINY OR SMOOTH FRENCH-STYLE MUSTARD

About 2 cups

Use this mustard paste as is, or add one of the various recommended flavorings. It is very sharp when new, but mellows over time; we suggest leaving it in the refrigerator, covered, for several days before serving it. This is wonderful spread in cold meat sandwiches, particularly roast beef, corned beef, or cold pork. If you want a smooth mustard, leave out the mustard seeds and triple the amount of dry mustard.

Grind in a spice grinder, coffee grinder, or blender, or with a mortar and pestle, until about the texture of coarse cornmeal:

1 cup yellow mustard seeds

Remove to a medium bowl. Add and stir well to combine:

3 tablespoons dry mustard
1 cup water
½ cup cider vinegar
½ cup dry white wine

Let stand for 2 hours, then stir well again.

Season with:

Salt and ground black pepper to taste

Cover and refrigerate until ready to use. This mustard will keep, covered and refrigerated, for up to 2 to 3 weeks.

IDEAS FOR FLAVORING MUSTARD

Prepare Grainy or Smooth French-Style Mustard, above, and stir in one of the following to blend:

½ cup dried fruit (such as nectarines, apricots, or plums), plumped, 463, and finely diced, plus 2 tablespoons honey, or to taste
½ cup minced or finely snipped fresh herbs (such as tarragon, rosemary, thyme, or chives) plus 1 tablespoon packed brown sugar
Juice of 1 lemon plus 1 tablespoon ground coriander
1 teaspoon each ground cloves, ground nutmeg, and ground cinnamon
1 tablespoon drained horseradish plus 1 teaspoon dill seeds
Finely minced garlic to taste

UNCOOKED HOT CHINESE MUSTARD

Catch-in-the-throat Chinese and German mustards seem mysterious, but they are no more complicated than mustard seeds ground to a powder—dry mustard—and blended to a paste with a cold liquid such as water, flat beer, or vinegar. The liquid gives these mustards character.

Experiment and find the blend that suits your palate by adding 2 to 3 tablespoons cold liquid to about ¼ cup dry mustard. If this is too hot, smooth it out with a little olive or peanut oil and a few grains of sugar. Keep at room temperature, not in the refrigerator, for up to 2 weeks.

COOKED HOT MUSTARD

Place in a heatproof glass bowl about 2 ounces dry mustard. Bring some water to a rolling boil and pour over the mustard to cover it. Set over, not in, rapidly boiling water. Before covering, see that the mustard has been stirred into a paste but is still covered with the hot liquid, and drain off any excess water. Cover and cook for 15 minutes. You can add 1 teaspoon sugar and ¼ to ½ teaspoon salt. For a brightly colored mustard, add ¼ teaspoon ground turmeric. Place in a jar and let cool, uncovered, for 1 to 2 hours. Cap tightly. Keep this mustard at room temperature, not refrigerated, for up to 2 weeks.

ABOUT HOMEMADE MAYONNAISE

If you are accustomed to store-bought mayonnaise, your first taste of homemade will be a surprise. Homemade mayonnaise is an elegant French sauce, not a sandwich spread (although you can make it thick enough to spread). The flavor is bright with lemon juice or vinegar and nutty with good oil. Homemade mayonnaise is elegant, and can be made quickly.

Mayonnaise, like hollandaise and béarnaise, is an emulsion—a stable liquid mixture in which one liquid is suspended in tiny globules throughout another, as with egg yolks in oil (mayonnaise) or in butter (hollandaise). The oil you choose will be the predominant flavor in your mayonnaise. Made entirely with a robust olive or walnut oil, the sauce will suit equally full-flavored foods—rich meats and aromatic vegetables, for example. For delicate foods such as poached fish, a milder oil is recommended. When mayonnaise is to be the base for other flavors, make it with mild-tasting peanut, safflower, grape-seed, or corn oil. For general use, a balance of fruity and mild oils is most satisfying. Usually three parts mild to one part fruity oils is about right, although sometimes it can be half and half. The oil must be very fresh. One tinge of rancidity (common in oil that has been on the shelf), and the sauce is all but inedible, so taste the oil before you start. The eggs must also be very fresh; as eggs age, they lose their ability to stabilize an emulsion.

Making the sauce in a food processor or blender or with an electric mixer is practically foolproof, and the sauce has greater volume and a fluffier texture than when made by hand. For the finest and silkiest texture of all, make the sauce by hand.

Ingredients at room temperature emulsify more readily than cold ones, so start by covering the eggs in their shells with hot water to warm them briefly. If the oil was refrigerated, warm to room temperature. To be certain of success when improvising your own formula, bear in mind that 1 egg yolk can emulsify up to about ¾ cup oil, no more. One-half cup is even safer.

Problems with mayonnaise are simple to fix. If the mayonnaise starts to separate, place a fresh egg yolk in a small clean bowl. Slowly add the separated mayonnaise, drizzling it and whisking it in as you first did with the oil. You may need to add more oil to compensate for the extra yolk. If the mayonnaise is too thick for your taste, thin it with a little water or cream.

Mayonnaise can be flavored in many ways. Add herbs, dried spices, flavored vinegars, and dry mustard to the yolks at the start. Though lemon juice and wine vinegar are classic, other citrus juices and most other vinegars can also be used. If you know you will be adding liquid flavorings, use extra oil to make an extra-thick sauce.

Homemade mayonnaise can be kept, tightly covered in the refrigerator, for a day or two, but it will lose some of its sheen after a few hours. Mayonnaise does not freeze well. When serving homemade mayonnaise and all foods containing it, keep track of the time it spends outside the refrigerator. Because raw egg contains microorganisms that start multiplying above 40°F, the maximum time mayonnaise should be out of the refrigerator is 2 hours—and when the air temperature is 85°F or above, it is 1 hour. When salmonella from raw eggs is a concern, make the Sabayon-Style Mayonnaise, 74.

To perk up store-bought mayonnaise for a sauce in a pinch, fold in an equal amount of sour cream or beat an equal amount of chilled heavy cream and fold it in.

TRADITIONAL MAYONNAISE *About 1 cup*

This is our basic mayonnaise, from which all of our variations can be prepared. It will stand up best as Mayonnaise Collée, 76. It can be whisked to a lighter consistency by gradually adding an appropriately flavored stock, vegetable juice, or even spirits. Use a ceramic, glass, or stainless-steel bowl—aluminum or copper will react with the acid and affect the color and even the flavor of the sauce.

Whisk together in a medium bowl until smooth and light:

2 large egg yolks
1 to 2 tablespoons fresh lemon juice or white wine vinegar
¼ teaspoon salt
Pinch of ground white pepper

Whisk in by drops until the mixture starts to thicken and stiffen:

1 cup vegetable oil, at room temperature

As the sauce begins to thicken—when about one-third has been added—whisk in the oil more steadily, making sure each addition is thoroughly blended before adding the next. Should the oil stop being absorbed, whisk vigorously before adding more. Stir in:

Up to 1½ teaspoons Dijon mustard (optional)
Salt and ground black pepper to taste

Serve immediately or refrigerate in a covered jar for 1 to 2 days.

BLENDER MAYONNAISE *About 1 cup*

If using a food processor, use the plastic blade if you have one, as it seems to make a slightly lighter sauce. Egg white is needed in machine-made mayonnaise. Beat 1 egg well with a fork to blend the yolk and white, let it settle a few seconds, then measure. This recipe can be doubled, in which case, just use 1 large egg.

Combine in a blender or food processor:

2 tablespoons well-beaten egg
1 large egg yolk
¼ teaspoon dry or Dijon mustard

Process on high speed until well blended, about 5 seconds in a blender, 15 seconds in a food processor fitted with the plastic blade, 30 seconds in a food processor fitted with the steel blade. Scrape down the sides, then sprinkle the mixture with:

1 teaspoon fresh lemon juice and/or white wine vinegar or rice vinegar

¼ teaspoon salt

Process for about 2 minutes in a blender, 15 seconds in a food processor fitted with the plastic blade, 7 to 8 seconds in a food processor fitted with the steel blade. Have ready in a small spouted measuring pitcher:

¾ cup oil, at room temperature

With the machine running, add the oil in the thinnest possible stream. After about one-third of the oil has been added—the mixture will have swollen and stiffened—add the oil in a slightly thicker stream. Stop the machine when all has been added and scrape down the sides and around the blade, mixing in any unabsorbed oil. If you want a thicker sauce, add as before:

Up to ¼ cup oil, at room temperature

Should the sauce be too thick, add as needed:

Light or heavy cream, milk, or water, at room temperature

Taste the mayonnaise and stir in:

1½ to 3 teaspoons fresh lemon juice or white wine vinegar

½ to 1 teaspoon dry or Dijon mustard

Salt and ground white pepper to taste

Serve immediately, or refrigerate in a covered jar for 1 to 2 days.

YOGURT MAYONNAISE

A marvelously tangy light sauce to use in all the ways you would use mayonnaise.

Prepare Traditional Mayonnaise, above, or Blender Mayonnaise, above, and combine with ½ to 1 cup yogurt (nonfat is fine). Season to taste with salt and ground white pepper.

CURRY MAYONNAISE

Superb with cold vegetables, eggs, fish, poultry, and meats (everything!).

Prepare Traditional Mayonnaise, above, Blender Mayonnaise, above, or Yogurt Mayonnaise, above, and set aside. In a small skillet, stir 2 tablespoons best-quality curry powder in 2 tablespoons mild-tasting oil over low heat for 30 to 60 seconds—until you start to smell it. Let cool and whisk into the mayonnaise—Yogurt Mayonnaise, is especially good. Season to taste with salt and ground black pepper.

MUSTARD MAYONNAISE

For cold poultry, meats, fish, and strong-flavored vegetables; traditional with cracked crab.

Prepare Traditional Mayonnaise, above, or Blender Mayonnaise, above, and stir in 1 tablespoon mustard—yellow is lightest and best for fish and seafood; stronger Dijon suits poultry and meats. Season to taste with salt and ground black pepper.

MAYONNAISE WITH GREEN HERBS

Beautiful with cold shellfish, fish, vegetables, and cold poached meats.

Prepare Traditional Mayonnaise, above, or Blender Mayonnaise, above, and stir in 2 to 3 tablespoons minced fresh herbs, such as tarragon, basil, chervil, chives, parsley, and oregano. Season to taste with salt and ground black pepper.

TARTAR SAUCE

Prepare Traditional Mayonnaise, above, or Blender Mayonnaise, above, and stir in 1 tablespoon minced scallions (or onions or shallots), 1½ teaspoons minced sour gherkins or dill pickles, 1½ teaspoons drained capers, and 1½ teaspoons drained sweet pickle relish or minced sweet pickles, if desired. Heighten the flavors with a dash or two of fresh lemon juice or hot red pepper sauce. Serve sprinkled with 1 tablespoon minced fresh parsley and 1 tablespoon finely snipped fresh chives.

SAUCE RÉMOULADE

This French classic is marvelous with salads, vegetables, cold meats, poultry, and shellfish.

Prepare Traditional Mayonnaise, above, or Blender Mayonnaise, above, and stir in 1 hard-boiled egg, finely chopped; 1 tablespoon minced cornichons or sour gherkins; 1 tablespoon drained capers; 1 tablespoon chopped fresh parsley; 1½ teaspoons chopped fresh tarragon; 1 small clove garlic, minced; and ½ teaspoon Dijon mustard. Season to taste with salt and ground black pepper.

RUSSIAN HORSERADISH CREAM

Piquant and suave, this is superb with cold beef, tongue, ham, game, and root vegetables.

Prepare Traditional Mayonnaise, above, or Blender Mayonnaise, above, and stir in ½ cup sour cream and 3 to 4 tablespoons finely grated fresh horseradish or drained prepared horseradish. Blend thoroughly, then taste as you stir in 1 to 2 teaspoons cider vinegar, salt, and, if desired, a sprinkling of sugar.

SAUCE ANDALOUSE (TOMATO AND PIMIENTO OR ROASTED RED PEPPER)

For vegetables, beef, fish, and eggs.

Prepare Traditional Mayonnaise, above, or Blender Mayonnaise, above, and stir in 1 small plum tomato, peeled, seeded, and finely diced, and 1 roasted red pepper, finely diced, or 1 bottled pimiento, drained and finely diced. Season to taste with salt and ground white pepper.

CHIPOTLE PEPPER MAYONNAISE

A zesty sauce for meat and poultry.

Prepare Traditional Mayonnaise, above, or Blender Mayonnaise, above, and stir in 1 tablespoon minced canned chipotle peppers, 1 teaspoon minced garlic, 1 tablespoon tomato puree, 2 tablespoons chopped fresh cilantro, and 2 tablespoons fresh lime juice. Season to taste with salt and ground black pepper.

SABAYON-STYLE MAYONNAISE *About 1 cup*

Using the technique for preparing soft custard Sabayon, 1044, yolks are sufficiently cooked in this mayonnaise so there is no concern about salmonella. This mayonnaise is wonderfully light, and all the usual mayonnaise flavorings can be added. Once you have practiced cooking the yolks a couple of times, the sauce will go quickly. In this formula, less oil than usual is added, and it is added rapidly, since too much beating will deflate the sauce. However, like sabayon, its beauty is fleeting. Use the least amount of water or stock for small yolks, and proportionately more liquid for larger yolks.

Combine in a medium stainless-steel bowl or a medium saucepan with sloping sides (so you can whisk efficiently):

3 egg yolks
3 to 4½ tablespoons cold water or stock

Whisk together vigorously until frothy, 30 to 60 seconds. Hold the bowl with a pot holder and set it over medium heat. Immediately start whisking, and whisk nonstop until the mixture is frothy and beginning to stiffen and you can glimpse the bottom of the bowl as you whisk. Immediately remove from the heat and whisk for another 20 seconds to cool the yolks. Immediately add in a thick stream:

½ cup oil, at room temperature

Whisk just until all the oil is incorporated—do not overbeat. Remove to a clean bowl and let cool, uncovered. Stir in:

1½ to 3 teaspoons fresh lemon juice and/or white wine vinegar
½ to 1 teaspoon dry or Dijon mustard, or to taste
Salt and ground white pepper to taste

Cover, refrigerate, and serve within 2 to 3 hours.

CREAM CHEESE MAYONNAISE (SAUCE PARISIENNE) *About 1 cup*

A traditional French sauce for cold asparagus that contains no eggs and relatively little oil. When prepared with reduced-fat cream cheese, it contains about one-fourth the calories and cholesterol and about one-half the fat of standard mayonnaise but has none of the disappointments of many substitutes. However, it does have a tendency to separate. To prevent this, serve well chilled, and, if necessary, whirl for a minute or two in the food processor, then serve at once.

Process in a food processor until smooth and creamy:

5 ounces Neufchâtel or low-fat or regular cream cheese
¼ teaspoon sweet or hot paprika (optional)

With the machine running, pour through the feed tube in a slow, steady stream:

5 tablespoons mild-tasting oil, at room temperature

Add in a slow, steady stream:

1½ tablespoons fresh orange juice
1½ tablespoons fresh lemon juice
½ teaspoon salt
½ teaspoon ground white pepper

Stop the machine and scrape the sauce together. Taste and adjust the seasonings. Transfer to a bowl, cover, and chill. This mayonnaise will keep, covered and refrigerated, for 1 week. For a true *Sauce Parisienne,* stir in before serving:

2 tablespoons chopped fresh chervil

GARLIC MAYONNAISE (AÏOLI) *About 1 cup*

Sometimes called beurre de Provence—the butter of Provence—aïoli is traditionally served slightly chilled as a sauce for cold poached fish, vegetables, meat, or eggs. It also makes a luxurious garnish for hot and cold soups. Aïoli is a contraction of the Provençal words for garlic and oil.

Whisk together in a medium bowl until smooth and light:

2 large egg yolks
4 to 6 cloves garlic, finely minced
Salt and ground white pepper to taste

Whisk in by drops until the mixture starts to thicken and stiffen:

1 cup olive oil, or part olive and part safflower or peanut oil, at room temperature

As the sauce begins to thicken, whisk in the oil more steadily, making sure each addition is thoroughly blended before adding the next. Gradually whisk in:

1 teaspoon fresh lemon juice, or to taste

½ teaspoon cold water

Taste and adjust the seasonings. Serve immediately or refrigerate in a jar for 1 to 2 days.

POTATO GARLIC MAYONNAISE (SKORDALIA)

Both Provençals and Greeks use the trick of cutting the richness of mayonnaise by replacing some of it with a smooth cooked potato puree.

Prepare Aïoli (above) and whisk in ½ cup lukewarm pureed cooked potatoes—blend well, but not more than necessary. If the sauce is too thick, whisk in a compatible stock. This variation is good with all the same things as aïoli. The puree can also be blended into a plain mayonnaise or one with another flavor.

SAFFRON GARLIC MAYONNAISE (ROUILLE)

About 1 cup

This thick, garlicky, bright-gold sauce is the essential finish for Bouillabaisse, 115, and other Provençal fish soups and stews. It is also wonderful with fish, seafood, meats, poultry, and vegetables from the oven or grill. All rouilles are brilliant in color. Some cooks use pureed roasted red peppers, but we vote for saffron.

Stir together in a small bowl, cover, and let stand for 10 minutes:

¾ teaspoon saffron threads, or ⅛ teaspoon powdered saffron

2 tablespoons hot stock from the soup to be garnished, or water

Process in a food processor to fine crumbs:

1 fresh French roll (not sourdough), crust trimmed

Add ¾ cup of the breadcrumbs to the saffron infusion. Mash with a fork to a loose paste, stirring in, if necessary:

Up to 1 tablespoon hot stock or water

Place in a mortar or small bowl:

1 large dried red chili pepper, seeded

Vigorously pound to a powder with a pestle or sturdy wooden spoon. Add and pound until the garlic is pureed:

3 small cloves garlic, peeled

⅛ teaspoon coarse salt

Stir in:

1 large egg yolk

Stir in the bread paste bit by bit, then work vigorously until blended and smooth. Following the method for adding oil to mayonnaise, 72, add:

About ¾ cup olive oil, or part olive and part safflower oil, at room temperature

Let the oil fall to one side of the mortar, very slowly at first, while you stir it in without stopping. (If the sauce should start to curdle, simply stir in a little hot stock or water.) When the mixture has absorbed all the oil it can, season with:

Salt to taste

Cover and refrigerate. Use the same day.

ABOUT DECORATING COLD FOOD

The time may come when you wish to present guests with a magnificent chilled poached chicken, whole fish, veal rolls, or arrangement of vegetables. This is the time to add gelatin to mayonnaise and light stock and use the mixtures for decoration. Mayonnaise collée is mayonnaise containing enough gelatin so that it sets with a shiny surface. It is generally used to form an opaque coating over cold food. The instant it is ready—it tends to set even at room temperature—spread it as you would frosting, with broad firm strokes of a spatula, working quickly. Chill the dish uncovered (and, to make sure the refrigerator has no odors that will be absorbed by the mayonnaise, place a saucer heaped with baking soda on each shelf).

Once the mayonnaise has set, you can gently press over the surface of the food thin stalks of herb leaves; edible flowers and buds; cutouts (using cookie or canapé cutters or a small sharp knife) from leek leaves, scallion rings, pimientos, carrots, radishes, turnips, zucchini and yellow summer squash, cucumbers, asparagus, snap beans, all sorts of peppers, tomatoes, edible pea pods, celery sprigs and leaves, hard-boiled egg whites, citrus zest, black olives, eggplant skins, lotus root; or slices of kiwi fruit, citrus, or strawberries—anything decorative and compatible with the food beneath.

If you plan to glaze the surface with a jelled stock (aspic glaze), cut the pieces thin and flat. If the pieces do not lie flat, boil them in water to cover just enough to relax them, then pat dry and set on the mayonnaise again. Thickish or heavy pieces are best dipped in liquid aspic glaze—that way, they will stay in place. Long, thin-tipped tweezers are very helpful if the decoration is elaborate. If you make a dent in the set mayonnaise, smooth it out with a table knife dipped in hot water—or patch by smoothing over a little soft mayonnaise collée. Chill again when the decorating is finished—the surface must be cold when applying the glaze.

Pour liquid glaze from the tip of a spoon, holding the spoon close to the surface so the aspic won't splatter but will stay more or less where it lands—it will start to set almost instantly. If you must smooth it, dip a table knife in very hot water and shake off excess drops. Apply the aspic in thin, even coats—two thin coats work better than one thick coat. Chill the food after the first coat, then, if necessary, apply a second coat and chill again. After the glaze has set, you can pipe thick mayonnaise decoratively on the food or along the point where the food meets the platter, making a finished border. At serving time, adding a border of chopped clear aspic, below, seems to make the whole platter shimmer.

One thing to bear in mind is that mayonnaise collée is so fresh and light that on hot days, or when the food must wait under hot lights, the mayonnaise does not hold up. At such times, try a less delicate form of decoration.

JELLED MAYONNAISE (MAYONNAISE COLLÉE)

Version I of this mayonnaise yields about 1¼ cups; Version II yields about 3 cups.

I. Use the smaller amounts of gelatin and stock to use the mayonnaise for masking food, the larger amount for piping the mayonnaise through a pastry tube.

Stir together in a small saucepan or microwave-safe bowl and let stand for 5 minutes:

1½ to 2 teaspoons unflavored gelatin
1½ to 2 tablespoons Vegetable Stock, 38, Chicken Stock, 39, or water

Cook, stirring, over low heat or briefly microwave until the gelatin is dissolved and the mixture is a clear syrup. When lukewarm, whisk into:

1 cup Traditional Mayonnaise, 72, or any style mayonnaise, 72 to 75, made with 2 to 4 tablespoons extra oil, to be thick

The gelatin must be thoroughly distributed through the mayonnaise. To color the sauce pink, stir in:

Up to 1 tablespoon tomato puree

To color it green, stir in:

Up to 1 tablespoon cooked thick spinach puree

Use immediately, as directed above.

II. Prepare:

Aspic Glaze, below

While still lukewarm and liquid, beat ¼ cup of the glaze into:

1 cup Traditional Mayonnaise, 72, or any style mayonnaise, 72 to 75, made with 2 to 4 tablespoons extra oil, to be thick

Use immediately, as directed above.

ASPIC GLAZE

About 2 cups

You can use this glaze to mask food directly, and omit the mayonnaise collée completely.

Stir together in a small saucepan or microwave-safe bowl and let stand for 5 minutes:

1 tablespoon unflavored gelatin
½ cup White Veal Stock, 40, Chicken Stock, 39, or Vegetable Stock, 38

Cook, stirring, over low heat or briefly microwave until the gelatin is dissolved and the mixture is a clear syrup. Stir in:

1½ cups stock
Salt and ground white pepper to taste

Chill and use when the liquid thickens to the consistency of egg white.

ABOUT FLAVORED BUTTERS (BEURRES COMPOSÉS)

Made by blending herbs or other flavorings into plain butter, these are versatile, quick to make, and easy to store. Flavored butters are served either cold or at room temperature, as decorative garnishes or as instant sauces. They can also be used in place of plain butter for bread or rolls and as an ingredient in complex sauce recipes. There are two basic types of flavored butters, cooked and uncooked. Cooked ones are browned to various degrees, mixed with other ingredients, and usually served warm as simple sauces for sautéed, grilled, broiled, or steamed foods. Uncooked flavored butters are simply softened butter mixed with spices, herbs, or other pureed or chopped ingredients. The butter can be used immediately while still soft, or rolled into cylinders in pieces of wax or parchment paper, plastic wrap, or aluminum foil, then refrigerated for 1½ to 2 hours, or frozen, and sliced into thin rounds to garnish dishes just before serving. Allow about 1 tablespoon per serving. (Flavored butters can be frozen for several weeks, but they should not be refrigerated for more than 24 hours.) For both kinds of flavored butters, start with fresh butter of the highest quality, preferably unsalted.

For guests, we smooth the butter into a small bowl in which it just fits and run a fork over the top in a decorative swirl or crosshatch. The butter is served at room temperature with a butter knife.

BASIC FLAVORED BUTTER

About ¼ cup

In a small bowl, cream with a fork or wooden spoon:

4 tablespoons (½ stick) butter (preferably unsalted), softened

Gradually stir in flavorings as desired along with:

Salt and ground white pepper to taste

Roll the mixture into a cylinder in a piece of wax or parchment paper, plastic wrap, or aluminum foil (or shape as desired, above), and refrigerate or freeze until firm enough to slice. Or refrigerate in a small bowl or ramekin and spoon on just before serving.

MAÎTRE D'HÔTEL BUTTER (LEMON AND PARSLEY)

Traditionally served over broiled steak.

Prepare Basic Flavored Butter, above, and add 1 tablespoon finely chopped parsley and ¾ to 1½ tablespoons fresh lemon juice.

GARLIC BUTTER

For vegetables, steaks, chops, chicken, fish, shellfish, snails, and bread. Blanched garlic has a sweeter, milder flavor than raw garlic.

Prepare Basic Flavored Butter, above, and add 1 to 3 cloves garlic, boiled, if desired, in water to cover for 5 to 6 minutes, or left raw, mashed to a paste (with salt if using raw). If desired, add 1 teaspoon minced fresh herbs, such as oregano, marjoram, basil, chervil, or parsley—or a combination.

SNAIL BUTTER (SHALLOTS OR SCALLIONS)

A milder, more interesting form of garlic butter but with the same uses—traditionally for snails.

Prepare Basic Flavored Butter, above, and add 2 tablespoons minced shallots or scallions (white part only); 1 to 2 cloves garlic, mashed to a paste with ½ teaspoon salt; 1 tablespoon minced fresh parsley; ground black pepper to taste; and, if desired, 1 tablespoon fresh lemon juice and 1 tablespoon minced celery.

ANCHOVY BUTTER

For broiled fish, steak, and lamb chops and as a canapé spread.

Prepare Basic Flavored Butter, above, and add 1 teaspoon anchovy paste, ¼ teaspoon fresh lemon juice, or to taste, and salt and ground red pepper to taste.

CRESS OR ARUGULA BUTTER

Wonderfully zippy with root vegetables and other strong flavors.

Prepare Basic Flavored Butter, above, and add 1½ teaspoons finely chopped watercress or arugula and a dash of fresh lemon juice.

ORANGE BUTTER

For fish and vegetables.

Prepare Basic Flavored Butter, above, and add the finely grated zest of 1 orange, 1 tablespoon strained fresh orange juice, or to taste, a pinch of ground red pepper, and salt to taste.

NUT BUTTER

Often used to finish cream sauces, and delicious on sautéed chicken and delicate fish.

Prepare Basic Flavored Butter, above. Pulse in a food processor or pound with a mortar and pestle ¼ cup toasted whole blanched almonds, hazelnuts, pistachios, walnuts, or pecans until very fine but not a paste. Add 1 teaspoon water if the nuts seem too dry or in danger of turning into nut butter. Stir into the butter.

SOY SAUCE BUTTER

For grilled fish, chicken, and beef, especially in an Asian-style menu.

Prepare Basic Flavored Butter, above, and whisk in 2 to 3 teaspoons soy sauce.

RED CAVIAR BUTTER

Prepare Basic Flavored Butter, above, and blend in one 2-ounce jar red lumpfish caviar, 1 heaping teaspoon minced scallions, and ½ teaspoon fresh lemon juice.

MUSTARD BUTTER

About ⅔ cup

While a simple mustard butter is nothing more than a few spoons of mustard mashed into softened butter, this combination of roasted garlic and herbs is irresistible. We find it excellent as a rub for small game birds or served on meats and roasted poultry.

Combine in a small bowl:

8 tablespoons (1 stick) unsalted butter, slightly melted
¼ cup Dijon mustard
2 teaspoons honey
1 tablespoon mashed roasted garlic, 378
1 teaspoon minced fresh savory or oregano
2 teaspoons fresh lemon juice
Salt and ground black pepper to taste

Use immediately to baste poultry, or refrigerate in a small bowl or ramekin and spoon on just before serving.

CHILI BUTTER

About ⅓ cup

Rub this butter under the skin of poultry or wildfowl before roasting to keep it moist and flavorful.

Heat in a small skillet over medium heat:

2 tablespoons olive oil

Add and cook, stirring, until softened:

½ cup minced shallots or scallions
4 cloves garlic, finely chopped

Remove to a small bowl and let cool. Stir in:

4 tablespoons (½ stick) unsalted butter, softened
½ teaspoon ground cinnamon
½ teaspoon ground cumin
1½ tablespoons chili powder
2 tablespoons minced fresh cilantro and/or parsley
1 tablespoon fresh lemon juice
Salt and ground black pepper to taste

Use immediately, or refrigerate in a small bowl or ramekin and spoon on just before serving.

SHRIMP OR LOBSTER BUTTER

About ½ cup

For added flair, put in a dash of Pernod and some crushed fennel seeds. Use as a sauce for shellfish, as a spread for canapés, or for finishing béchamel or velouté sauces served with fish.

Dry in a 250°F oven for 10 to 20 minutes:

Uncooked or cooked shells from 1 pound shrimp or crayfish or from one 1½- to 2-pound lobster, well rinsed and drained

Break up the shells as finely as possible with a wooden mallet or rolling pin. Melt in the top of a double boiler over simmering water:

8 tablespoons (1 stick) unsalted butter

Add the shells and simmer gently for 10 minutes; *do not let the butter boil.* Set aside for 20 minutes to allow the flavors to infuse. Strain through a fine-mesh sieve lined with several layers of cheesecloth into a bowl. Place the bowl in a larger bowl of ice water to cool quickly. Refrigerate and skim off the butter when the mixture is solidified. Discard the liquid.

ABOUT FLAVORED OILS

Light oils infused with the flavors of herbs, spices, and fruits are a refreshing and more healthful alternative to butter and other fats. Flavored oils are simple to make and add depth of flavor as well as moisture and a sensual touch to finished dishes. They are not for cooking but for seasoning, just as you would drizzle olive oil over vegetables, noodles, or pastas. The purest and easiest technique is a cold infusion—such as Portuguese Chili Oil, below. Allow ½ to 3 tablespoons per serving. Flavored oils must be refrigerated, and most will hold their quality for at least 1 month. Prepare only as much as you will use in that time. For optimum flavor, bring the amount of oil you will be serving to room temperature. Leftover warmed oil that has been prepared with fresh (that is, not dried) ingredients must be discarded.

PORTUGUESE CHILI OIL

About ¾ cup

Piri-Piri is a staple of Portuguese cooking, and demonstrates the easy cold-infused method.

Fill a dry, scrupulously clean 8- to 10-ounce bottle or jar with:

¼ to ⅓ cup small dried red chili peppers, slightly crumbled

Fill to the top with:

Extra-virgin olive oil or a less fruity blend of oils

Cap tightly and store in the refrigerator to steep for 1 month before using. If desired, strain and discard the chili peppers. This keeps in the refrigerator for up to 1 month.

ORANGE OIL

About 1 cup

Drizzle over poached shellfish or grilled fish, chicken, or vegetables just before serving. You may substitute lemon, lime, grapefruit, or a combination of zests for the orange zest. Use these proportions to make an infused oil with any fresh ingredients, unless they are unusually bland or strong. You may have to experiment with amounts—or infuse for a shorter time; do not leave fresh ingredients in oil for more than 4 days.

Combine in a dry, scrupulously clean 8- or 10-ounce jar:

Grated zest of 3 oranges, about ¼ cup
1 cup mild olive, walnut, peanut, or other mild oil

Cover and shake the jar gently, then steep in the refrigerator for up to 4 days. Strain through a dampened paper coffee filter (paper towels can taste of chemicals). Keep this oil covered and refrigerated for up to 2 weeks, then discard.

CHILI OIL

About ¾ cup

Exceedingly hot—use sparingly. A few drops are superb in dipping sauces for dumplings, or in dressings for Asian vegetable dishes.

Coarsely chop in a blender or spice grinder:

1 cup dried chili peppers, preferably Thai

Transfer to a stainless-steel saucepan and add:

¾ cup peanut oil

Cook over medium heat until the peppers begin to foam. Remove from the heat when some of the smallest flecks on the side of the pan blacken. Cover, and let sit for 4 to 6 hours. Strain through a dampened paper coffee filter into a scrupulously clean jar or bottle. This keeps, covered and refrigerated, for up to 1 month.

SPICE OIL

Grinding your own spices ensures the most intense flavors.

Prepare Chili Oil, above, substituting ground caraway, cardamom, cumin, cinnamon, fennel, or saffron for the chili peppers.

AN INTERNATIONAL SAMPLER OF COLD SAUCES

AMERICAN HORSERADISH CREAM

About 1¼ cups

An unexpected combination, a particular delight with hot roast beef, but also good with cold meats.

Beat until stiff:

½ cup chilled heavy cream

Gradually add, beating constantly:

3 tablespoons fresh lemon juice or cider vinegar
2 tablespoons grated horseradish or drained prepared white horseradish
¼ teaspoon salt
Pinch of ground red pepper

Chill for 30 to 60 minutes, then serve.

BAVARIAN APPLE AND HORSERADISH SAUCE

About 1 cup

Delightfully simple, and a marvelous accompaniment for hot sausages or cold boiled beef. Make this fresh each time.

Stir together well in a medium bowl:

⅓ cup grated fresh horseradish or drained prepared horseradish
⅓ cup peeled and finely grated sour green apples
2½ tablespoons fresh lemon juice
½ teaspoon sugar
¼ teaspoon salt

Cover and let stand for 15 to 30 minutes to allow the flavors to develop. Stir in:

¼ cup sour cream

Sprinkle with:

1 teaspoon minced fresh parsley

Serve immediately.

HONEY-MUSTARD DIPPING SAUCE

About ¾ cup

This simple sauce is especially good with fried chicken or fish.

Stir together well in a small bowl:

6 tablespoons honey
¼ cup Dijon mustard
Ground red pepper to taste

Serve at room temperature. This sauce will keep, covered and refrigerated, for up to 1 month.

MOJO

About 1 cup

The national table sauce of Cuba, mojo is a colorful version of the familiar vinaigrette. Traditionally made with the fresh juice of the sour orange, it can also be made with fresh lime juice, and for variation, grapefruit or pineapple juice. Unlike most vinaigrettes, mojo is briefly cooked to bring out the full flavor of the garlic. Use caution when adding the juice to the hot oil, as it may splatter. A deep saucepan is a wise precaution. Mojo can be stored for a few days, but it is best when served fresh.

Heat in a saucepan over medium heat:

½ cup olive oil

Add and cook until fragrant but not browned, 20 to 30 seconds:

8 cloves garlic, minced

Remove from the heat and let cool 5 minutes. Carefully stir in and bring to a boil:

¾ cup fresh lime, grapefruit, or pineapple juice
¾ teaspoon ground cumin
Salt and ground black pepper to taste

Let cool and serve at room temperature. This sauce will keep, covered and refrigerated, for up to 3 days.

SCANDINAVIAN MUSTARD-DILL SAUCE

About 1 cup

Especially good with Gravlax, 563, this sauce can also be served with other smoked, grilled, sautéed, or poached fish.

Whisk together in a medium bowl until smooth:

3 tablespoons Swedish or Dijon mustard
2 tablespoons snipped fresh dill
1 to 2 tablespoons sugar
2 tablespoons fresh lemon juice or red wine vinegar, or to taste
Salt and ground black pepper to taste
Pinch of ground cardamom

Gradually add, whisking constantly, until blended and smooth:

½ cup vegetable oil

Cover and let stand for 2 to 3 hours before serving to allow the flavors to develop. Serve at room temperature or chilled. This sauce will keep, covered and refrigerated, for up to 2 days.

CHIMICHURRI

About 1¼ cups

The Argentineans are enthusiastic meat eaters, and often serve grilled or roasted meat with this slightly spicy sauce on the side.

Whisk together thoroughly in a small bowl:

½ cup olive oil
¼ cup red wine vinegar

Stir in:

1 small onion, finely chopped
⅓ cup finely chopped fresh parsley or cilantro
4 cloves garlic, finely chopped
1 tablespoon finely chopped fresh oregano (optional)
Salt to taste
¼ teaspoon ground red pepper, or to taste
¼ teaspoon ground black pepper, or to taste

Cover and let stand for 2 to 3 hours before serving to allow the flavors to develop. This sauce will keep, covered and refrigerated, for up to 2 days.

ENGLISH FRESH MINT SAUCE *About ½ cup*

In England, roasted lamb with mint sauce is as much a tradition as mint jelly is here. The sauce is thin and sprightly—a refreshing change from sweet jelly. The original recipe calls for dark vinegar, but we find a lighter vinegar—white wine vinegar or rice vinegar—more appealing.

Stir together in a small bowl until the sugar is dissolved:

1 tablespoon turbinado sugar (packed light brown can be substituted)
2 tablespoons boiling water

Stir in:

2 tablespoons minced fresh young mint leaves
8 to 10 tablespoons white wine vinegar or rice vinegar

Cover and let stand for 2 to 3 hours before serving to allow the flavors to develop. This sauce will keep, covered and refrigerated, for up to 2 days.

ENGLISH CUMBERLAND SAUCE *About ¾ cup*

Many feel this is the best of all sauces for cold meat and poultry, and hot ham and tongue. It is quick and easy, but you may have trouble finding the red currant jelly. If so, substitute plum or cherry jelly (not jam).

Drop into a small saucepan of boiling water:

Zest of 1 large orange, removed in large strips
Zest of 1 large lemon, removed in large strips

Boil until the pieces are soft, 5 to 10 minutes. Drain, discarding the water, and cut into thin strips and return to the saucepan. Add:

½ cup red currant or plum jelly
Juice of 1 lemon
1 tablespoon port
1 tablespoon powdered sugar (optional)
1 to 2 teaspoons Dijon mustard
Pinch of ground ginger
Ground white pepper to taste

Cook, stirring, over lowest heat until the jelly is melted—be careful not to scorch the sauce. Remove from the heat and whisk until smooth. The sauce will thicken as it cools; for a slightly thinner sauce, whisk in additional:

Port

Cover and refrigerate until cold. Serve cold, whisking to blend. This sauce will keep, covered and refrigerated, for up to 1 week.

PISTOU *About 1 cup*

The Provençal version of Italy's pesto, made without nuts, makes a great addition to soups and stews.

Vigorously pound to a paste with a mortar and pestle, or process in a food processor or blender until the garlic is minced:

4 to 6 large cloves garlic, peeled
Pinch of coarse salt

Gradually add and pound, or process, to a dark green paste:

2 cups packed fresh basil leaves

Add in 4 batches and pound, or pulse, to the consistency of soft butter:

½ cup grated Parmesan or Gruyère cheese

Gradually add and pound, or with the machine running, pour through the feed tube in a slow, steady stream, until the sauce has the consistency of coarse mayonnaise:

⅓ cup olive oil, preferably extra virgin

Season with:

Salt and ground black pepper to taste

Serve at room temperature or store, covered and refrigerated, for up to 2 days.

PICADA *About ½ cup*

This is one of the "secret ingredients" of the cooking of the Catalonia region of Spain—not really a sauce, and never served by itself, but a condiment to be stirred directly into stews, soups, and sauces a few minutes before they are finished cooking. Picadas destined to be used with meat, poultry, or game dishes often include a bit of chocolate; those to be used with fish sometimes have fish roe or livers added.

Heat in a small skillet over medium heat:

1 tablespoon extra-virgin olive oil

Add and brown:

One ½-inch-thick slice French or Italian bread

Crumble and place in a mortar or small food processor or blender. Pound with a pestle or process along with:

½ cup whole blanched almonds, skinned hazelnuts, and pine nuts, or all almonds, coarsely chopped and toasted
2 cloves garlic, halved
8 black peppercorns (optional)
Salt to taste
Pinch of toasted saffron threads (optional)

Remove the mixture to a bowl and thoroughly work in with a fork:

3 tablespoons extra-virgin olive oil, or as needed
1 teaspoon finely chopped fresh parsley

Let stand until the picada holds together in a thick paste, about 30 minutes. The picada will keep, covered and refrigerated, for up to 2 days.

SALSA VERDE

About 1 cup

This classic Italian tart green sauce is traditionally served with braised meats, fried calamari, and grilled fish dishes.

Place in a food processor:

⅔ cup parsley leaves
2½ tablespoons drained capers
6 anchovy fillets (optional)
½ teaspoon finely chopped garlic
½ teaspoon strong mustard
½ teaspoon red wine vinegar or 1 tablespoon freshly squeezed lemon juice
½ cup extra-virgin olive oil
Salt to taste

Blend to a uniform consistency, but do not overprocess. Adjust the seasonings. Serve at room temperature or store, covered and refrigerated, for up to 1 week.

TUNA SAUCE

About 2 cups

One of Italy's most delectable summer inventions is *Vitello Tonnato,* Cold Poached Veal with Tuna Sauce. Cold poached chicken is equally sublime, and a lot easier. Hot, room temperature, or cold grilled or roasted vegetables with tuna sauce make a superb light luncheon. This recipe is simpler and less rich than most. Use part lime juice for a wonderful tang.

Combine in a food processor or blender and process until smooth, 30 seconds to 1 minute, stopping to scrape down the sides as needed:

One 6-ounce-can Italian tuna packed in oil, drained
1 cup mayonnaise
5 anchovy fillets, finely chopped, or 2 teaspoons anchovy paste, or to taste
3 tablespoons drained capers
3 tablespoons fresh lemon juice
Freshly ground black pepper

Remove to a medium bowl, cover, and refrigerate until needed. To serve, thinly slice the cold meat or chicken and arrange, overlapping, on a platter. Pour the sauce over and sprinkle the arrangement with:

Chopped parsley

This sauce will keep, covered and refrigerated, for up to 2 days.

AVGOLEMONO

About 1¼ cups

This favorite Greek sauce is good with lamb or green vegetables, or can be added to soups, stews, and casseroles—anything, say the Greeks, that is not made with garlic or tomatoes.

Stir together in a small bowl:

1 tablespoon cold water
1 teaspoon cornstarch

Whisk together in a small, heavy stainless-steel saucepan over low heat just until warm:

3 large egg yolks
3 to 4 tablespoons fresh lemon juice

Pour the cornstarch mixture into the egg mixture. Gradually add, stirring or whisking constantly:

1 cup Vegetable Stock, 38, or Express Chicken Broth, 42

Cook, stirring constantly, over medium-low heat until thick and creamy and the sauce coats the back of a spoon; do not let the sauce get too hot, or the eggs will curdle. Remove the sauce from the heat and stir in:

Salt and ground black pepper to taste

Serve immediately.

LEMON EGG SAUCE

About 1 cup

This version of Greek Avgolemono, above, is trickier to make because there is no cornstarch to thicken it, but the lighter flavor and silkier texture are well worth the effort.

Combine in a small, heavy stainless-steel saucepan over high heat and boil until reduced by half:

1½ cups Chicken Stock, 38, or Express Chicken Broth, 42
⅓ cup dry white wine

Whisk together in a medium bowl:

2 large egg yolks
3 tablespoons fresh lemon juice

Slowly whisk the reduced stock into the egg mixture, being very careful not to curdle the eggs. Return the mixture to the saucepan and cook, stirring constantly, over medium-low heat until the sauce is slightly thickened. Immediately strain through a fine-mesh sieve. Season with:

Salt and ground black pepper to taste

1 tablespoon finely snipped fresh chives

Serve immediately, or keep warm for up to 1 hour before serving.

GEORGIAN GARLIC AND WALNUT SAUCE

About 1¾ cups

Georgia, in the former Soviet Union, is a mountainous country that grows citrus fruits and tea. It is also rich in walnut groves. Serve this sauce with grilled chicken or anything else from the grill. It is also delicious with cucumbers, tomatoes, red beans, asparagus, spinach, and beets. You can increase the amount of spices, if desired.

Combine in a food processor and process until finely ground:

1 cup whole walnuts, toasted

3 small cloves garlic, coarsely chopped

Remove to a stainless-steel, ceramic, or glass bowl. Add and stir well to combine:

3 tablespoons minced fresh cilantro

2 teaspoons fresh lemon juice or red wine vinegar

¼ teaspoon ground coriander

¼ teaspoon ground red pepper, or to taste

¼ teaspoon ground turmeric

¼ teaspoon ground fenugreek (optional)

Thin the sauce to the consistency of light cream with:

About ¾ cup Chicken Stock, 39, or Vegetable Stock, 38

Cover and refrigerate for several hours or up to 2 days before serving. Serve at room temperature.

TURKISH GARLIC AND HAZELNUT SAUCE

Great with cold shellfish.

Prepare Georgian Garlic and Walnut Sauce, above, substituting hazelnuts for the walnuts.

HARISSA

About ⅓ cup

In North Africa, this fiery pepper paste is stirred into black olives, seafood stews, soups, herb salads, and vegetable dishes, or used as an ingredient in sauces for brochettes, *tagines,* and couscous.

Combine in a small dry skillet over medium heat and toast, shaking the pan often to prevent burning, until very aromatic, 2 to 3 minutes:

1 teaspoon caraway seeds

1 teaspoon coriander seeds

½ teaspoon cumin seeds

Remove from the heat, let cool to room temperature, and grind to a fine powder in a spice grinder, coffee grinder, or blender, or with a mortar and pestle. Add and grind again until smooth:

2 cloves garlic, quartered

Salt to taste

Add and grind until all the ingredients are well combined:

3 tablespoons sweet paprika

1 tablespoon red pepper flakes

1 tablespoon olive oil

The harissa will be very thick and dry. Transfer the paste to a small jar and cover with:

Olive oil

Store, covered, in the refrigerator; it will keep for 6 months.

RAITA I (INDIAN YOGURT SALAD)

About 1½ cups

Serve this condiment alongside spicy meats, fish, poultry, or vegetarian entrees. It helps cool down the mouth, and is the main source of protein in an Indian vegetarian meal. Raita is best made and served fresh, but it can be prepared ahead and refrigerated, covered, for up to 2 hours.

Stir together well in a small bowl:

1 cucumber, halved, seeded, and finely chopped

1 cup yogurt, or ½ cup yogurt and ½ cup sour cream

1 tablespoon finely chopped fresh mint

¼ teaspoon ground cumin

1 small jalapeño pepper, seeded and diced (optional)

RAITA II

Stir together well in a small bowl:

1 ripe banana, peach, or nectarine, finely chopped, or ½ cup fresh pineapple chunks

1 cup yogurt, or ½ cup yogurt and ½ cup sour cream

1 tablespoon golden raisins (optional)

2 tablespoons chopped blanched almonds or macadamia nuts

Up to 4 tablespoons sugar or honey, depending on the tartness of the fruit

Pinch of ground nutmeg or ground cardamom

NAM PRIK (THAI HOT SAUCE)

About ⅔ cup

Nam Prik, which translates as "pepper water," is the traditional table sauce of Thailand, where there are any number of variations on the recipe. It is served with vegetables in every form, stirred into soups, and used as a sauce for rice or noodles. The sauce is best a day or two after making, and keeps well for several weeks in the refrigerator. If dried shrimp and fish sauce are not available, add more fresh or dried chili peppers and lime juice.

Pound to a paste with a mortar and pestle or process in a small food processor or blender:

18 tiny dried shrimp, chopped
4 small dried red chili peppers, seeded, if desired, and crumbled
4 cloves garlic, chopped
2 tablespoons fresh lime juice
1 tablespoon fish sauce

Stir in:

3 small red or green serrano peppers, seeded, if desired, and finely chopped
Chopped fresh cilantro to taste
A little brown sugar (optional)

Cover and refrigerate for at least 1 day before serving.

THAI CHILE-LIME DIPPING SAUCE

About ¾ cup

Pass this fiery sauce, best made only 15 minutes or so before serving, as a dip for grilled meats or fish.

Coarsely chop together:

6 fresh jalapeño peppers, seeded
6 cloves garlic, peeled

Place in a small bowl and stir in:

6 to 8 tablespoons fresh lime juice
Salt to taste

Let stand at room temperature until ready to serve.

SOUTHEAST ASIAN PEANUT DIPPING SAUCE

About 1⅔ cups

Some version of this simple, spicy sauce is served all over southeast Asia, with the small skewers of meat and chicken known as *satays*. It is also delicious as a dipping sauce for many other dishes, from spring rolls to grilled meats.

Heat in a small saucepan over medium heat:

2 teaspoons vegetable oil

Add and cook, stirring, for 5 seconds:

4 cloves garlic, finely chopped
1 small fresh chili pepper, seeded and minced

Add and cook, stirring, until thickened, about 4 minutes:

1 cup water
¼ cup soy sauce
⅓ cup chunky peanut butter, preferably unsweetened
1 teaspoon packed light brown sugar, or to taste
3 tablespoons chopped unsalted roasted peanuts (optional)

Remove from the heat and stir in, if desired:

1 tablespoon finely chopped fresh mint leaves

Serve warm or at room temperature. This sauce will keep, covered and refrigerated, for up to 1 week.

NUOC CHAM

About 1 cup

This all-purpose sauce is nearly always on the table in Vietnam, both at home and in restaurants. It might be called the Vietnamese ketchup.

Combine in a small bowl and let stand for 5 minutes:

1 fresh hot Asian chili or jalapeño pepper (preferably red), seeded and finely chopped
6 tablespoons fresh lime juice, or 2 tablespoons fresh lime juice and ¼ cup rice vinegar

Stir in:

¼ cup fish sauce
3 tablespoons sugar, or to taste
2 tablespoons coarsely shredded carrot
1 tablespoon coarsely shredded daikon radish (optional)
3 to 5 cloves garlic, finely chopped

Serve at room temperature. This sauce will keep, covered and refrigerated, for up to 6 days.

ASIAN BLACK BEAN SAUCE

About ½ cup

This sauce can be rubbed on fish or shellfish before steaming, or served as a condiment with the finished dish.

Mash to a paste with a fork in a small bowl:

3 tablespoons preserved black beans

Add:

2 scallions, finely chopped

Stir in:

2 tablespoons soy sauce
2 tablespoons dry sherry
4 cloves garlic, finely chopped
2 teaspoons peanut or other vegetable oil
2 teaspoons toasted sesame oil
2 teaspoons finely chopped peeled fresh ginger
Salt and cracked black peppercorns to taste

Serve at room temperature. This sauce will keep, covered and refrigerated, for up to 6 days.

JAPANESE WASABI SOY SAUCE

About ½ cup

Wasabi, the pale green paste traditional with sushi and sashimi, is the ground root of a plant in the mustard family. Its flavor resembles that of horseradish, but it is more aromatic. Wasabi paste, small portions pinched into mounds for individual servings, is always accompanied on the table by a small beaker of soy sauce. Often the two are combined into a pungent dipping sauce for strong-tasting fish and beef. Wasabi soy sauce is best eaten right away, for it loses its pungency as it sits.

The powders and pastes at Asian groceries labeled "wasabi" are not the true root and are sharper in taste. If you can buy the fresh root, peel it, remove the knots, and grate in a circular motion on the finest blade of a grater.

Finely grate peeled fresh wasabi root to make:

1 tablespoon grated wasabi root

Or mix together with a fork to make a smooth paste:

1 tablespoon wasabi powder
2 to 3 drops of lukewarm water

Cover and let stand for 10 minutes to allow the flavors to develop. Stir in:

½ cup dark soy sauce, preferably low-sodium

Serve individually in small, shallow bowls.

GINGER SOY SAUCE

Prepare Japanese Wasabi Soy Sauce, above, substituting 1 tablespoon grated peeled fresh ginger for the wasabi. Use immediately for fish, chicken, or meat.

ABOUT MARINADES, DRY RUBS, AND PASTES

An easy way to enhance the flavor of meat, poultry, fish, and vegetables is to season them with a savory mixture in the form of a dry rub, paste, or marinade before cooking. The food absorbs the essential oils from the herbs and spices, and when citrus juice, wine, or vinegar is used, the flesh of meat, poultry, fish, or vegetables becomes tenderer. Fruity oils, sweetening sugar, and aromatic vegetables also contribute to a more vibrant, more intense taste.

ABOUT MARINADES

A marinade is a seasoned liquid used to flavor meat, poultry, fish, or vegetables before cooking. While marinades may be cooked or uncooked, almost all contain some type of acidic ingredient, such as wine, vinegar, citrus juice, or other fruit juice, that acts to tenderize the surface of meats, fish, and poultry and to encourage the transfer of flavors. Many marinades, especially those used on vegetables, lean fish, and poultry, often include some olive oil, melted butter, or other fat in order to baste the food as it cooks. Some cooks find that strong-flavored spirits such as brandy and rum overpower a food's natural flavor, but juniper-enhanced gin and corn-sweet bourbon can make barbecue marinades come alive.

Marinate only in glass, stainless steel, or food-grade plastic, so the container will not react with the acid. (The glaze on a ceramic container may contain lead—you have no way of telling if it does—and acid will draw the toxic lead from the glaze into the food.) To avoid making more marinade than you actually need, use a container just large enough to hold the food.

Tender foods can be marinated with delicious results, but avoid marinating them too long, or they will turn stringy, even mushy. Refrigerate food while it marinates. Cubed meats marinate for just 2 to 3 hours; a whole 5- to 10-pound piece, for 12 to 24 hours. Some traditional stews marinate for as long as 2 to 3 days. Use a stainless-steel or wooden spoon to turn the food and to stir the marinade from time to time. Sizes, shapes, and textures of meats are variable, but a general rule is to allow 6 to 8 tablespoons of marinade for every 1 pound of food. Sometimes marinades are cooked first. Chill these before adding to the meat, so they will not raise the temperature of the meat. Some marinades are also suitable as a finishing sauce. *Never use the marinade in which raw meat, poultry, or fish has steeped for basting cooked food or as a sauce without first bringing it to a boil to kill any harmful bacteria from the raw food.* Marinades are usually best when prepared fresh. Vinaigrettes, 236 to 239, also make flavorful marinades.

Finally, sprinkling salt over the food before placing it in the marinade ensures that the food is seasoned evenly. Food to be browned needs to be drained and patted dry after marinating; wet food will not brown properly. To intensify the full flavors of the marinade in the finished dish, use it as a braising liquid or to baste the food as it cooks. Just be sure to cook it thoroughly by boiling first.

CITRUS HERB MARINADE

About ½ cup

This is among the simplest and most satisfying ways to give fish, poultry, meat, and large vegetables lively flavor before applying heat. Suit the herbs to the food.

Combine in a dish and blend with a fork:

¼ cup mild-tasting olive or nut oil
2½ tablespoons fresh lemon juice
1½ tablespoons fresh orange juice or dry red wine
⅓ cup chopped fresh parsley, preferably flat-leaf
1½ teaspoons dried thyme leaves or other appropriate herb
½ bay leaf, very finely crumbled
1 clove garlic, minced (optional)
1 teaspoon salt
¼ teaspoon ground black or white pepper, or to taste

Use immediately, or cover and refrigerate for up to 1 week.

QUICK CITRUS MARINADE

Prepare Citrus Herb Marinade, above, omitting the herbs and optional garlic, blending the oil, lemon juice, and orange juice or wine, then seasoning with salt and ground black or white pepper to taste. Use immediately. Marinate for 2 to 3 hours, turning the pieces often.

WHITE WINE MARINADE *About ¾ cup*

Especially good with grilled or broiled fish, poultry, or meat.

Whisk together thoroughly:

- ¼ cup white wine (it can be dry or fruity)
- ¼ cup vegetable oil
- ¼ cup minced shallots or onions
- ¾ teaspoon minced fresh tarragon, chervil, or thyme, or ¼ teaspoon dried
- ½ teaspoon ground white pepper
- ¼ teaspoon salt, or to taste

Let stand at room temperature for 1 hour to allow the flavor to develop. Whisk to blend and use immediately, or cover and refrigerate for up to 1 week.

TANDOORI MARINADE *About 1⅓ cups*

In Indian cooking, chicken and meats are always marinated in an aromatic mixture of yogurt and spices before they are cooked in a tandoor, a fiercely hot, charcoal-fire vertical oven. The acidity in the yogurt tenderizes the exterior of the meat and can actually overtenderize if left for more than 4 hours. This marinade is traditionally tinted with a natural dye, which imparts to tandoori chicken its characteristic orange-yellow color.

Whisk together thoroughly:

- 1 cup yogurt
- 2 to 3 tablespoons vegetable oil
- 2 teaspoons finely minced garlic
- 2 teaspoons finely minced peeled fresh ginger
- 1 teaspoon ground coriander
- 1 teaspoon ground cumin
- 1 teaspoon ground red pepper
- 1 teaspoon Garam Masala, 1061, or ¼ teaspoon ground cinnamon
- ½ teaspoon ground turmeric
- ½ teaspoon salt
- 1 tablespoon yellow food coloring (optional)
- 1½ teaspoons red food coloring (optional)

Use immediately.

SOY AND SHERRY MARINADE *About 1¼ cups*

The combination of soy sauce and dry sherry produces an aromatic and delicious flavor in broiled or grilled chicken and game hens when marinated for only 2 to 3 hours.

Whisk together thoroughly:

- ½ cup soy sauce
- ½ cup dry sherry
- 2 tablespoons Dijon mustard
- 1 tablespoon hot red pepper sauce
- ¼ cup vegetable oil

Use immediately, or cover and refrigerate for up to 1 month.

BEER MARINADE *About 2 cups*

A pungent mixture for broiling, grilling, and roasting.

Whisk together thoroughly:

- 1½ cups beer
- ¼ cup any citrus or ginger marmalade
- 1 tablespoon dry mustard
- 1 tablespoon minced peeled fresh ginger, or 1 teaspoon ground
- 2 cloves garlic, minced
- ¼ teaspoon salt
- 1 teaspoon sugar or honey

Use immediately, or cover and refrigerate for up to 1 week.

RED WINE MARINADE *About 2¼ cups*

A cooked marinade, excellent for red meats.

Combine in a medium saucepan over low heat and simmer for 2 minutes:

- 2 cups dry red wine
- 1 small onion (preferably red), thinly sliced
- 2 cloves garlic, finely minced
- 3 sprigs fresh parsley
- 2 sprigs fresh thyme
- 6 black peppercorns, cracked
- 1 small bay leaf
- 2 whole cloves

Remove from the heat and season with:

- Salt to taste

Chill to use as a marinade. This marinade will keep, covered and refrigerated, for up to 1 week.

VINEGAR MARINADE FOR GAME AND GAME BIRDS

Prepare Red Wine Marinade, above, substituting water for the wine and omitting the garlic and cloves. Add ¼ cup red wine vinegar or cider vinegar, 6 whole allspice or juniper berries, and increase the bay leaves to 2½.

TERIYAKI MARINADE AND SAUCE

About 1 cup

In Japanese, *teri* means "gloss" and *yaki* are broiled foods. In Japan, *teriyaki* refers to a lustrous sweet glaze that is brushed over fish, poultry, beef, and pork at the end of broiling, grilling, or pan frying. In this country, we use the mixture the same way but often steep the food in the marinade for a few hours first. The recipe can be multiplied, as it keeps indefinitely in the refrigerator. Sake and mirin are available at Asian markets, and more and more where other wines are sold.

Combine in a small saucepan over medium heat and cook, stirring, until the sugar is dissolved:

⅓ cup sake
⅓ cup mirin
⅓ cup soy sauce, preferably low-sodium
2¼ teaspoons sugar

You can use the hot mixture immediately as a sauce, or chill it for a marinade. The teriyaki will keep, covered and refrigerated, for up to 1 month.

ABOUT DRY RUBS AND PASTES

A dry rub is a compatible blend of dried herbs and spices that is rubbed on food before cooking. When a dry rub is moistened with oil or ground fresh ginger or garlic, it becomes a paste, which is even easier to use, because it clings nicely to the food. Ingredients for rubs are ideally ground by hand with a mortar and pestle—there is less risk of overprocessing, and the herbs and spices seem to be most completely expressed. You can use a sturdy bowl and a wooden spoon if it suits you. The next most efficient tools are a spice grinder or coffee grinder or a blender. Their bowls are better shaped for small batches than those of a food processor; however, a good mini food processor can work. Pastes are best ground in a blender or food processor.

To use a dry rub or paste, simply rub the mixture over the entire surface of the food, using enough pressure to make sure that an even layer adheres. Naturally, a mild mixture can be applied more thickly than one that is spicy or hot. (Wash your hands well after rubbing, as some spices can irritate the skin.) Although a rub or paste smeared on just before cooking still adds flavor, apply it to the food up to 24 hours before cooking, so the flavor will be more than skin deep. Turn the food several times as it rests, and leave the seasoning in place for cooking. (Some seasonings produce a handsome dark-colored finish and some create a tasty crunchy crust, especially in grilling or sautéing.) Keep any unused rubs and pastes refrigerated for up to a week in tightly covered small jars. *Discard any that have come into contact with raw poultry, fish, or meat.*

PEPPERY DRY RUB

About 3½ cups

Fantastic on steaks and other red meats.

Stir together well in a small bowl:

2 cups coarsely cracked black peppercorns
¼ cup coarsely cracked white peppercorns
2 tablespoons ground coriander
2 to 4 tablespoons red pepper flakes
¼ cup packed light or dark brown sugar
½ cup salt

This rub will stay potent, covered and kept in a cool, dark, dry place, for up to 6 weeks.

CAJUN DRY RUB

About ¼ cup

This spice mix, best known as "blackening spice," can be rubbed generously on chicken, fatty fish, steaks, or vegetables before pan broiling, grilling, or sautéing. It will transform into a tangy, deeply caramelized crust as the food cooks. Expect the spices to smoke some during cooking.

Stir together well in a small bowl:

1 tablespoon cracked black peppercorns
1 tablespoon salt
2 teaspoons crushed fennel seeds
1 teaspoon dried thyme
1 teaspoon sweet or hot paprika
1 teaspoon dry mustard
1 teaspoon garlic powder
½ teaspoon ground red pepper
1 teaspoon ground sage

This rub will stay potent, covered and kept in a cool, dark, dry place, for up to 6 weeks.

SOUTHERN DRY RUB FOR BARBECUE

About 2 cups

Southern barbecue chefs rub spice mixtures like this one into pork or beef before it starts the long, slow cooking that will transform it into barbecue.

Spread in a small dry skillet over medium heat and toast, shaking the pan often to prevent burning, until fragrant, 2 to 3 minutes:

¼ cup cumin seeds

Remove from the heat, let cool to room temperature, and grind to a fine powder in a spice grinder, coffee grinder, or blender, or with a mortar and pestle. Transfer to a small bowl and add:

¼ cup packed light or dark brown sugar
½ cup sweet or hot paprika
¼ cup chili powder
2 tablespoons ground red pepper
1 teaspoon ground mace
¼ cup salt
¼ cup cracked black peppercorns

Stir together well. This rub will stay potent, covered and kept in a cool, dark, dry place, for up to 6 weeks.

TOASTED WHOLE SPICE DRY RUB *About 2 cups*

This rub is delicious with duck, game hen, and pork.

Combine in a large dry skillet over medium heat and toast, shaking the pan often to prevent burning, until fragrant, 2 to 3 minutes:

Two 3-inch cinnamon sticks
8 cardamom pods
¼ cup white peppercorns
½ cup coriander seeds
¼ cup cumin seeds
1 tablespoon whole cloves
1 tablespoon whole allspice
2 small dried red chili peppers of your choice
4 whole star anise

Remove from the heat, let cool to room temperature, and grind to a fine powder in a spice grinder, coffee grinder, or blender, or with a mortar and pestle. This rub will stay potent, covered and kept in a cool, dark, dry place, for up to 6 weeks.

WEST INDIES DRY RUB *About 1¾ cups*

This rub goes well on poultry, pork, lamb, or beef.

Combine in a small dry skillet over medium heat and toast, shaking the pan often to prevent burning, until fragrant, 2 to 3 minutes:

¼ cup cumin seeds
¼ cup coriander seeds

Remove from the heat. Let cool to room temperature, and grind to a fine powder in a spice grinder, coffee grinder, or a blender or with a mortar and pestle. Transfer to a small bowl and add:

¼ cup curry powder
¼ cup ground white pepper
¼ cup ground ginger
¼ cup salt
2 tablespoons ground allspice
2 tablespoons ground red pepper

Stir together well. This rub will stay potent, covered and kept in a cool, dark, dry place, for up to 6 weeks.

JAMAICAN JERK PASTE *About 1¼ cups*

The cornerstone of all jerk dishes is this vinegary, intensely hot paste of dried herbs and habanero or Scotch bonnet peppers, which are some five times hotter than jalapeños. If you cannot find these peppers, a habanero-based hot sauce makes a good substitute. This is traditional with pork or chicken.

Puree in a food processor or blender:

⅓ cup fresh lime juice
10 fresh habanero or Scotch bonnet peppers, or ¼ cup habanero-based hot sauce
2 tablespoons white vinegar
2 tablespoons fresh orange juice (optional)
3 scallions, coarsely chopped
2 tablespoons dried basil
2 tablespoons dried thyme
2 tablespoons yellow mustard seeds, or 1 tablespoon dry mustard
2 teaspoons ground allspice
1 teaspoon ground cloves
1 teaspoon salt
1 teaspoon ground black pepper

The mixture should have the consistency of thick tomato sauce. If needed, thin with additional:

Lime juice, vinegar, or orange juice

MEDITERRANEAN GARLIC HERB PASTE *About 1½ cups*

This paste is wonderful on grilled and roasted vegetables, fish, lamb, and beef.

Combine in a blender or food processor and coarsely puree, leaving the mixture a little chunky:

2 cups mixed fresh herbs (parsley, sage, rosemary, thyme, basil, and/or oregano)
10 cloves garlic
1 tablespoon red pepper flakes
½ cup olive oil
2 tablespoons salt
¼ cup cracked black peppercorns

Cover and refrigerate until ready to use. This paste will keep, covered and refrigerated, for up to 1 week.

MUSTARD PASTE FOR ROASTED MEATS *About ⅔ cup*

This is equally delicious on lamb, beef, rabbit, and chicken, and gives a gilded finish.

Stir together well in a small bowl:

½ cup Dijon or brown mustard, whole-grain or smooth
2 tablespoons dry white wine

1 clove garlic, minced (optional)
1 tablespoon minced fresh herbs, or 1 teaspoon dried (use rosemary for lamb; thyme for beef; or tarragon for chicken or rabbit)
1 teaspoon minced peeled fresh ginger, or ¼ teaspoon ground

Use immediately.

CHILI-GARLIC SPICE PASTE *About 2 cups*

This paste is good with poultry, firm-textured fish, shrimp, and vegetables.

Combine in a blender or food processor until smooth:

¾ cup minced fresh jalapeño peppers
½ cup cloves garlic, peeled
½ cup olive oil
2 tablespoons grated lemon or lime zest
2 tablespoons cracked black peppercorns
1 tablespoon salt
2 teaspoons chili powder

Use immediately, or cover and refrigerate for up to 1 week.

ASIAN GINGER SPICE PASTE *About 2⅓ cups*

This fragrant herb paste suits poultry, game birds, full-flavored fish, pork, beef, and roasted vegetables.

Combine in a blender or food processor and coarsely puree, leaving the mixture a little chunky:

½ cup minced peeled fresh ginger
⅓ cup sesame oil
1 tablespoon red pepper flakes
¼ cup chopped fresh cilantro
¼ cup chopped fresh mint
¼ cup chopped fresh basil
2 tablespoons salt
2 tablespoons cracked white peppercorns

Cover and refrigerate until ready to use. This paste will keep, covered and refrigerated, for up to 1 week.

THAI GREEN CURRY PASTE *About 1 cup*

This fragrant and spicy paste is excellent on meats and seafood, or stirred into soups, rice, pasta, and other grain dishes.

Combine in a small dry skillet over medium heat and toast, shaking the pan often to prevent burning, 2 to 3 minutes:

2 teaspoons coriander seeds
1 teaspoon cumin seeds
1 teaspoon fennel seeds
1 teaspoon black peppercorns

Remove from the heat, let cool to room temperature, and grind to a fine powder in a spice grinder, coffee grinder, or blender or with a mortar and pestle. Transfer to a small bowl.

Combine in a blender or food processor and process until finely chopped, about 4 minutes:

⅓ cup tightly packed fresh cilantro leaves
Two ¼-inch slices galangal or fresh ginger, peeled
1 stalk lemon grass, bottom third only, chopped
12 serrano peppers or 6 fresh jalapeño peppers, seeded and chopped
2 large shallots, chopped
4 cloves garlic, chopped
Grated zest of 1 lime
1 teaspoon shrimp paste (optional)
1½ teaspoons salt
1 teaspoon freshly grated or ground nutmeg

Add the spices and, with the machine running, slowly pour in:

¼ cup peanut oil

Cover and refrigerate until ready to use. This paste will keep, covered and refrigerated, for up to 1 week.

RED CURRY PASTE

Prepare Thai Green Curry Paste, above, substituting fresh or reconstituted dried red chili peppers for the fresh green ones.

MOROCCAN HERB PASTE (CHARMOULA) *About 1½ cups*

Charmoula is used to flavor fish before or after grilling, roasting, or baking. Its consistency is between a paste and a marinade.

Stir together well in a small bowl:

⅓ cup finely chopped fresh parsley
⅓ cup finely chopped fresh cilantro
2 tablespoons olive oil
2 tablespoons fresh lemon juice
2 cloves garlic, finely chopped

Grind to a fine powder in a spice grinder, coffee grinder, or blender or with a mortar and pestle:

1 teaspoon coriander seeds
1 teaspoon cumin seeds
12 black peppercorns
1 teaspoon red pepper flakes
Generous pinch of saffron threads, toasted and crumbled (optional)

Add to the herb mixture along with:

1 medium onion, finely chopped
1 teaspoon hot or sweet paprika
Salt and ground red pepper to taste

Stir together well, then drizzle over the top:

Olive oil

Cover and refrigerate until ready to use. This paste will keep, covered and refrigerated, for up to 1 week.

ABOUT BASTES, GLAZES, AND BARBECUE SAUCES

A baste is a liquid that is brushed onto foods during cooking. It is especially useful when foods are exposed to high temperatures, as in roasting, grilling, and broiling. The simplest bastes to brush on are pan drippings, but anything that moistens can be used. Bastes should contain a good proportion of fat. Oil, butter, and drippings keep surfaces from drying out while contributing to a handsome, browned finish. Seasonings add interest to a baste but are not necessary if surfaces have been seasoned before cooking. Avoid adding sweet ingredients (honey, sugar, fruit juice), since sugars scorch easily and may burn before the food is cooked.

Sweet ingredients do, however, belong in a glaze. A glaze is a liquid that adds luster and gloss to foods while cooking. The sheen comes from some form of melted sugar. Depending on the heat of the oven, the sweetness of the sauce, and the size of the piece of meat, apply a glaze during the last 15 to 45 minutes of cooking. A big ham, for instance, should be glazed during the last 45 minutes of baking. Glazes should be thick enough to paint on a surface without dripping. A quick final coating of glaze is often brushed on just before the food is served, and glazes can be passed as dipping sauces at the table. In addition to being sweet, glazes are typically fruity and/or spicy.

Barbecue sauces can be tomato-based or made with a variety of other ingredients. Although purists maintain that the only true barbecue is made with a dry spice rub, many prefer to add deep spicy flavor with a sauce. A form of glaze, barbecue sauce should be applied when you would a glaze—judging by the oven temperature, the sweetness of the sauce, and the size of the food. A nonsweet sauce can be brushed on from start to finish. Be sure to serve extra barbecue sauce at the table.

ORANGE-PINEAPPLE-CHIPOTLE BASTE

About 3 cups

This lively baste also makes a tasty marinade or dipping sauce for grilled meats and all poultry.

Combine in a medium saucepan over medium-high heat:

4 cups pineapple juice
2 cups orange juice
2 cups white vinegar
3 tablespoons pureed canned chipotle peppers, or to taste
2 tablespoons ground cumin

Bring to a boil, reduce the heat to medium, and simmer, uncovered, until reduced by about two-thirds, 45 to 60 minutes. Remove from the heat and stir in:

¼ cup fresh lime juice
½ cup chopped fresh cilantro
Salt and cracked black peppercorns to taste

Use hot or at room temperature. This baste will keep, covered and refrigerated, for about 1 month.

VERMOUTH BASTE

About 1 cup

Dry vermouth makes a delicious baste, especially for lamb. It can also be used as a marinade.

Whisk together thoroughly:

½ cup dry vermouth
½ cup olive oil, or use part walnut or good peanut oil
1 tablespoon fresh lemon juice

Use immediately, or cover and refrigerate for up to 1 month.

SOUTHWESTERN APRICOT GLAZE

About 1 cup

This sweet and spicy mixture works well on a wide variety of foods, but is particularly good brushed on chicken.

Combine in a small saucepan over medium heat:

1 cup apricot preserves
½ cup red wine vinegar
One 2-inch cinnamon stick, broken, or ¼ teaspoon ground cinnamon
2 tablespoons minced fresh chili peppers of your choice

Bring to a boil and cook until the mixture is slightly thickened, 5 to 7 minutes. Use hot or at room temperature. This glaze will keep, covered and refrigerated, for about 1 month.

ORANGE MOLASSES GLAZE

About 2½ cups

Paint this dark, rich glaze on large cuts of beef or game several hours before roasting and then baste the meat generously with it as it cooks.

Heat in a medium saucepan over medium heat:

1 tablespoon olive oil

Add and cook, stirring, until just beginning to color:

1¼ cups finely minced onions
3 tablespoons finely minced garlic

Stir in and bring to a boil:

1 tablespoon cracked black peppercorns
½ cup balsamic vinegar
2 cups fresh orange juice
1 tablespoon grated orange zest
½ cup light or dark molasses
1 tablespoon coriander seeds, crushed (toasted, if desired)
¼ cup yellow mustard seeds
1 teaspoon salt

Reduce the heat and simmer, uncovered, until the glaze is slightly thickened, 10 to 15 minutes. Let cool to room temperature. This glaze will keep, covered and refrigerated, for 3 to 4 days.

GLAZES FOR BAKED HAM AND ROASTED POULTRY

Remove a ham from the oven about 45 minutes before it is to be served. Score the fat on top in any pattern, stud with whole cloves, and brush with the glaze. Return to the oven to finish baking. Depending on size, wait until 15 to 30 minutes before the end of cooking to glaze poultry—the smaller the size, the shorter the time. These glazes can be used to cook turkey parts as well.

Brown Sugar: Use your fingers to mix ¾ cup packed light brown sugar (work out the lumps) and 2 teaspoons dry mustard. Slowly stir in fresh orange juice until a spreading consistency.

Cranberry: Stir until blended and of a spreading consistency ¾ cup jellied cranberry sauce, ⅓ cup packed light brown sugar (work out the lumps), and 1½ tablespoons fresh lemon juice, or to taste.

Marmalade: If necessary, briefly heat ¾ cup orange, lemon, ginger, pineapple, or any desired marmalade to make it spreading consistency.

Mustard: Stir together ½ cup packed light brown sugar (work out the lumps), ¼ cup yellow mustard, and 2 tablespoons honey or light molasses.

Pineapple: Stir together ½ cup finely chopped fresh or drained canned crushed pineapple, ¾ cup packed light brown sugar, and ½ teaspoon ground ginger.

BARBECUE SAUCE *About 2 cups*

When cooking at high temperatures, either under the broiler or on the grill, apply this sauce during the last 15 minutes of cooking.

Combine in a medium saucepan over medium heat and cook, stirring often, until the sauce comes to a simmer:

1½ cups ketchup, preferably Tomato Ketchup, 69
1 cup cider vinegar or red wine vinegar
¼ cup Worcestershire sauce
¼ cup soy sauce
1 cup packed light or dark brown sugar
2 tablespoons dry mustard
4 tablespoons chili powder, or to taste
1 tablespoon grated, peeled fresh ginger, or 1 teaspoon ground
2 cloves garlic, minced
2 tablespoons vegetable oil
3 slices lemon

Simmer, stirring often, for 5 minutes.

Remove the lemon slices if desired. This sauce will keep, covered and refrigerated, for up to 2 weeks.

CHIPOTLE PEPPER GLAZE/ KETCHUP/BARBECUE SAUCE *About 2 cups*

This is a basic "all-purpose" sauce/condiment. We also use this as a basis for vinaigrettes, and to flavor mayonnaise.

Heat in a large saucepan over medium-high heat:

1 tablespoon olive oil

Add and cook, stirring, until lightly colored:

1 cup chopped onion
2 teaspoons minced garlic

Stir in, cover, and simmer until the chili peppers are very soft, about 30 minutes:

½ cup dried apricots
¾ cup dry white wine
¾ cup Vegetable Stock, 38, or Chicken Stock, 39
½ cup fresh orange juice
2 large dried California or New Mexico (red Anaheim) peppers, seeded and torn into small pieces
1 or 2 dried or canned chipotle peppers, coarsely chopped

Let cool slightly and puree in a blender along with:

¼ cup pure maple syrup
2 tablespoons Dijon mustard

Strain through a fine-mesh sieve and season with:

Salt to taste

Depending on its use, if desired, thin with additional:

Stock or orange juice

Let cool to room temperature. This sauce will keep, covered and refrigerated, for up to 2 weeks.

SOUPS

If any food seems inherently calming, and even consoling, it is soup. Soup feels good when the weather gets cold. It restores our spirit and our vigor. (The first "restaurants" were eighteenth-century Parisian establishments that served rich soups to restore, or *restaurer,* the hungry citizenry.) In the old days, when a "soup bunch" of vegetables and herbs cost a nickel and bones were free from the butcher, American home cooks routinely made soups from scratch. Today, the smell of soup simmering still symbolizes home cooking.

ABOUT EQUIPMENT

A wooden spoon and a ladle are the only implements that are really essential for making soup—and, of course, a pot. An 8- to 10-quart pot is required for making stock (see About Stocks, 35) or large batches of soup. A 4-quart pot is about right for everyday use.

Some soups in this chapter are pureed to make them smooth; others are partially pureed to give them a "creamier" texture. Here are the pros and cons to using commonly available kitchen equipment to adjust the texture of a soup.

Food Processor: This tool is especially good for thick soups. Beware of overloading, as liquids can leak out the bottom or overflow. Depending on the size of your food processor, it may be best to puree soups in two batches. Or you can puree the solid ingredients with just enough liquid to keep the blade from clogging; return the puree to the pot, and stir or whisk to blend.

Blender: A blender works well for pureeing thinner soups. When blending hot soup, do not fill the blender more than one-third full. Wrap a dish towel around the lid and start on a low speed, then gradually increase the speed.

Hand-Held Immersion Blender: This tool is exceptionally convenient, because it is portable and easy to clean. It is simple to control: just immerse the blade end in the soup and turn it on, moving it around the soup until you achieve the desired texture. The solid

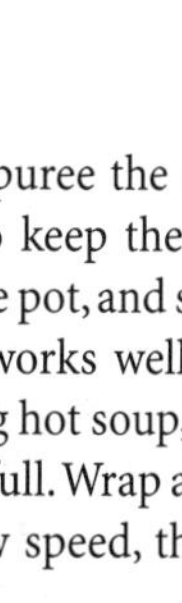

Immersion blender

ingredients must be very soft for the blender to work, and it can never create a completely silken texture. But it is still an excellent tool for soups that are only partially pureed, such as some bean soups.

Food Mill: Once a soup is cooked until the ingredients are quite soft, the food mill purees and strains simultaneously. Interchangeable disks help the cook control the final texture of the soup. A food mill also strains out tomato seeds.

Food mill

SERVING SOUP

Of course, you can serve soup in anything that will hold it. But over the centuries certain bowls have become traditional for certain soups, and for practical reasons. First-course soups are usually presented in smaller bowls than hearty main-course versions. Cream soups and consommés, which cool quickly, are traditionally served in comparatively deep bowls, looking literally like two-handled teacups with matching saucers; occasionally an elegant broth is served in actual demitasse cups and sipped like espresso.

The bowls of cream-soup spoons are deep and nearly rounded so that they can hold a reasonable quantity of liquid, shown below. Chowders, fish soups, and other soups with numerous ingredients, which are slower to cool, are usually served in shallow, broad-rimmed dishes or in underplates; the appropriate spoons for these are long-handled with shallow oval-shaped bowls that can hold plenty of chunks, shown below. If you can, serve Asian soups in Chinese or Japanese lacquer or ceramic bowls with those distinctive open-handled ceramic Asian soup spoons, and use ovenproof bowls or crocks for a soup such as French onion, which requires time in the oven. Any tablespoon will do, but soup is best eaten with a large spoon with an elongated bowl.

As for serving size, consider 1 cup of soup an appetizer, and 1½ to 2 cups a main course.

IS STOCK NECESSARY?

It depends on the soup.

Some soups need stock for taste and body. French Onion Soup, 95, derives its rich color and deep flavor from beef stock, and Hot and Sour Soup, 102, would be nothing other than hot and sour were it not made with a rich chicken stock. Similarly, most single-vegetable soups need the depth of flavor that a savory liquid brings. In some cases, stock is the very soul of the soup: Matzo Ball Soup, 107, is really chicken stock with matzo balls in it.

But when the main ingredients of a soup are full of character, you may not want to mask their flavors by adding stock. The beets in New York Deli Borscht, 96, the vegetables in Provençal Vegetable Soup, 100, the meat in Oxtail Soup, 118, need nothing more than water to carry their powerful flavors. Likewise, most soups based on beans and legumes, 103 to 105, do not require stock, their main ingredients being rich and earthy. A few soups can be prepared either with stock or without. Minestrone, 100, with its garden abundance, may have a warmer flavor with chicken stock, but it is also fine with water. Smooth Potato Leek Soup, 102, is delicious with stock or without.

A classic stock—composed of many ingredients, simmered for hours, strained, and reduced—is essential only for soups where the broth is the main component, as in Chicken Noodle Soup, 106. For most other

A deep cream-soup bowl and deep rounded spoon are perfect for a soup that cools quickly.

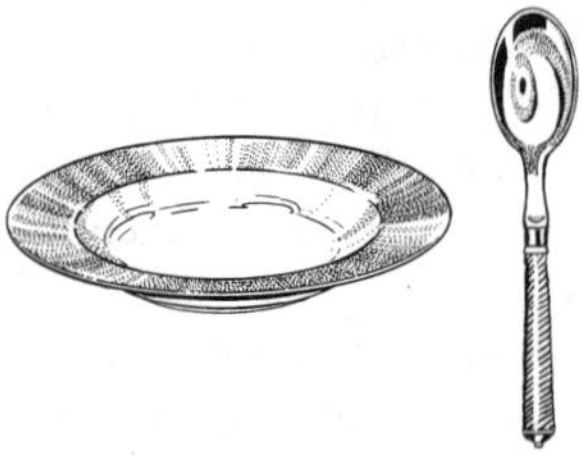

A shallow soup dish and long-handled, shallow spoon are ideal for a soup with numerous ingredients.

soups, an express broth, 42 to 43, will work perfectly well. So will a canned stock. Low-sodium canned stocks are always preferable, because the lack of salt leaves the cook freer to adjust the seasonings and to use more stock without worrying about the saltiness.

If you prefer a lighter soup or a vegetarian soup, any of the all-vegetable stocks, 38 to 39, or Vegetable Broth, 38, can replace a meat, poultry, fish, or seafood stock in soup. When you need a substitute for beef stock, it is worth your time to prepare Roasted Vegetable Stock, 38, which has a similar depth of flavor.

Finally, remember that no matter what the soup, a small quantity of salt pork, a ham hock, or a few slices of bacon will add meaty flavor and depth to soups in a short time.

ABOUT SUBSTITUTIONS

Soups that begin by sautéing vegetables in oil or butter can be adapted by cutting the fat in half and adding ¼ cup water or stock, which sweats the vegetables rather than sautés them. The same vegetables can also be cooked directly in the soup liquid with no previous sautéing at all. Even if you are not concerned about fat, stock should always be degreased before use (see About Stocks, 35) for purely aesthetic reasons. If meat is cooked in a soup, trim it thoroughly; after it has cooked, carefully ladle the fat from the surface—or, better yet, refrigerate the soup overnight so that the fat rises to the top and solidifies, then carefully remove it from the soup's surface. (Many soups taste better the second day anyway.)

Most recipes calling for cream can be made with less cream than the recipe specifies or with none at all, but before you decide against a recipe calling for cream, divide the total amount of cream into the number of servings. Most of the time, a cup of the soup will contain only a few tablespoons of cream. If the soup is not boiled, you can often substitute low-fat milk, yogurt, or a touch of sour cream (which has half the fat of regular cream).

Japanese clear-soup bowl with cover

STORING SOUP

Soup keeps beautifully, tightly covered in the refrigerator, improving in flavor. The exception is soup made with fish and seafood. The delicate flavors of the fish have finest quality as soon as they are cooked. Fruit soups and soups made with meat, poultry, milk, cream, or eggs keep for up to 3 days. Soups made purely of vegetables and legumes keep for up to 4 days.

Refrigerate soup when it has completely cooled and cover tightly. Always store soup in a container that it completely fills—air is the enemy. For the same reason, leave any fat on top of the soup until serving time, as the layer seals the soup beneath.

All soups can be frozen. Those that contain chunks of vegetables that do not freeze well—root vegetables, for example—can be pureed after thawing, then heated with enough stock or milk to loosen. Pureed soups hold their quality for up to 3 months. Other soups are best served within 1 month of freezing. In busy households, it may be useful to freeze main-dish soups in individual portions.

VEGETABLE SOUPS

If you live near a farmers' market and have the time, shop there. As a general seasonal guide, prepare soups using root vegetables and hearty vegetables, such as winter squash, during the cold months; soups using more perishable produce, such as tomatoes and corn, are best cooked during the warm months. Pureed green-vegetable soups should not cook long, or they will turn gray.

Chinese soup bowl with flat-bottomed spoon

An ovenproof bowl is used for a soup such as French onion.

Cut vegetables are often an integral part of a mixed-vegetable soup. Cut them uniformly, to help ensure even cooking. When improvising a soup using cut vegetables, bear in mind that some vegetables take longer than others to cook. Long-cooking vegetables, such as potatoes, should be added first, followed by vegetables such as carrots and green beans, leaving quick-cooking greens, such as spinach and chard, for last (see Chicken Soup with Variations, 106).

OLD-FASHIONED VEGETABLE SOUP

About 4 cups

Vary the vegetables in this soup. For the 3 cups of stock in the recipe, use 2 cups diced vegetables.

Bring to a boil over high heat, in a soup pot:

3 cups Classic Beef Stock, 40, Brown Beef Stock, 40, Chicken Stock, 39, or Vegetable Stock, 38
¼ cup diced onions
¼ cup diced carrots
¼ cup sliced celery
¼ cup diced potatoes
¼ cup 1-inch pieces green beans
¼ cup corn kernels
¼ cup baby peas
¼ cup baby lima beans
¼ cup chopped green cabbage (optional)
1 clove garlic, minced
1½ teaspoons tomato paste or ½ cup chopped drained canned or stewed tomatoes

Reduce the heat to low and simmer for 10 minutes. Stir in:

2 tablespoons chopped fresh parsley
Salt and ground black pepper to taste

Ladle into warmed bowls and serve.

CABBAGE SOUP

About 8 cups

We sampled this soup in a Paris bistro, where we discovered that a garnish of Roquefort adds just the right finish.

Heat in a soup pot over medium-low heat:

2 tablespoons olive or other vegetable oil

Add and cook, stirring, until tender but not browned, 5 to 10 minutes:

2 small leeks (white part only), cleaned thoroughly and chopped
2 medium onions, diced
2 tablespoons chopped garlic

Stir in:

4 cups Chicken Stock, 39
2 cups water
2 large carrots, sliced
¾ teaspoon caraway seeds, or 1 teaspoon if garnishing with Roquefort cheese

Bring to a boil and stir in:

2 small potatoes, peeled and diced

Reduce the heat and simmer until the potatoes are cooked, about 15 minutes. Stir in:

4 cups shredded green cabbage

Continue to simmer until the cabbage is wilted, about 15 minutes, adding a little water to cover, if necessary. Stir in:

1 teaspoon salt
¼ teaspoon ground black pepper, or to taste
¼ cup chopped fresh parsley

Ladle into warmed bowls. Sprinkle each serving with:

1 tablespoon crumbled Roquefort or other blue cheese (optional)

BUTTERNUT SQUASH SOUP

About 9 cups

Although this soup calls for butternut squash, almost any winter squash—including delicata, hubbard, and acorn squash, and pie pumpkins—can be substituted. For an unusual garnish, rinse and dry the squash seeds, toss them in 1½ teaspoons oil to lightly coat, and bake them along with the squash until browned, then sprinkle them on the soup just before serving.

Preheat the oven to 400°F.

Place cut side down on an oiled baking sheet:

1 medium to large butternut squash (about 3½ pounds), halved and seeded

Bake until the squash can easily be pierced with a fork, about 1 hour. Let cool, then scoop the pulp from the squash skin and discard the skin. Melt or heat in a soup pot, over medium-low heat:

3 tablespoons unsalted butter or vegetable oil

Add and cook, stirring, until tender but not browned, 5 to 10 minutes:

2 large leeks (white part only), cleaned thoroughly and chopped
4 teaspoons minced peeled fresh ginger

Stir in the squash along with:

4 cups Chicken Stock, 39, or any vegetable stock, 38 to 39

Bring to a simmer and cook, stirring and breaking up the squash with a spoon, for 20 minutes. Puree until smooth. Return to the pot and stir in:

2 cups chicken or vegetable stock
1½ teaspoons salt

Heat through. Ladle into warmed bowls. Garnish with:

Chopped fresh parsley or cilantro
Croutons
Toasted squash seeds (optional)

FRENCH ONION SOUP

About 8 cups

The secret to this beloved classic is long, slow cooking of the onions to allow their natural sugars to caramelize; this gives the soup its characteristic depth of flavor and rich mahogany color.

Heat in a soup pot over medium-low heat until the butter is melted:

2 tablespoons unsalted butter
2 tablespoons olive oil

Add and stir to coat:

5 medium onions, thinly sliced
Pinch of dried thyme

Cook, stirring occasionally, and keeping a vigilant eye on the onions so they do not scorch, over medium heat. As soon as they start to brown, after about 15 minutes, reduce the heat to medium-low and continue to cook, covered, stirring more often, until the onions are a rich brown color, about 40 minutes. Stir in:

2 tablespoons dry sherry or cognac

Increase the heat to high and cook, stirring constantly, until all the sherry has cooked off. Stir in:

3½ cups Brown Beef Stock, 40, Roasted Vegetable Stock, 38, or Brown Chicken Stock, 39

Bring to a boil, reduce the heat, and simmer, partially covered, for 20 minutes. Season with:

1 to 1½ teaspoons salt
¼ to ½ teaspoon ground black pepper

Place 8 ovenproof soup bowls or crocks on a baking sheet. Ladle the hot soup into the bowls and top each serving with:

1 to 3 slices French bread, toasted if fresh

Sprinkle each bowl with:

3 tablespoons grated Gruyère cheese

Broil or bake in a 450°F oven until the cheese is melted and starting to brown. Serve immediately.

COLD AVOCADO SOUP

About 4 cups

Flavorful ripe Hass avocados, the kind with the bumpy skins, are best for this colorful summer soup, which is made in minutes.

Puree in a food processor until smooth:

2 ripe Hass avocados (about 1 pound), peeled and pitted
1 small clove garlic, chopped

Stir in:

2 cups buttermilk
4 teaspoons fresh lime juice
¼ teaspoon salt
Pinch of ground red pepper

Remove to a bowl and refrigerate until cold. Thin, if necessary, with:

¼ to ½ cup buttermilk or water

Taste and adjust the seasonings. Ladle the soup into chilled bowls and garnish with:

1½ cups Salsa Fresca, 61
2 tablespoons sour cream or yogurt (optional)
½ pound fresh lump crabmeat, picked over, or cooked shrimp (optional)

CREAM OF CAULIFLOWER SOUP

About 6 cups

This recipe is a blueprint for a multitude of vegetable soups, all delicious even without the cream or milk. To retain the color in green vegetables, such as broccoli, do not cover or overcook the soup.

Heat in a soup pot over medium-low heat until the butter is melted:

¼ cup water or stock
1 tablespoon unsalted butter (optional)

Add and cook, covered, stirring occasionally, until tender but not browned, 5 to 10 minutes:

1 medium onion, coarsely chopped
2 cloves garlic, sliced
⅛ teaspoon ground nutmeg (optional)

Stir in:

4½ cups Chicken Stock, 39, or any vegetable stock, 38 to 39
1½ cups white wine (optional)
1½ pounds trimmed cauliflower, coarsely chopped

Bring to a boil, reduce the heat, and simmer until the cauliflower is tender, 15 to 20 minutes. Puree until smooth. Return to the pot and stir in:

¼ to ½ cup heavy cream, half-and-half, or milk
½ to 1 teaspoon salt
⅛ teaspoon ground white or black pepper

Simmer briefly and ladle into warmed bowls. Garnish with:

Chopped fresh parsley or snipped fresh dill or chives

Serve with:

Croutons or crackers

CREAM OF CARROT SOUP

Follow the recipe for Cream of Caulifower Soup, above, substituting carrots for the cauliflower, 1 tablespoon minced peeled fresh ginger for the garlic, and ½ teaspoon curry powder for the nutmeg; using 4 cups stock and 1 cup fresh orange juice; and omitting the wine. Simmer for 15 minutes. Puree the soup, adding ¼ to ½ cup heavy cream or half-and-half, salt to taste, and ⅛ teaspoon ground black pepper. Simmer briefly. Ladle into warmed bowls and serve.

CREAM OF ASPARAGUS SOUP

Follow the recipe for Cream of Caulifower Soup, above, omitting the nutmeg and using 4 cups chicken stock and ½ cup dry vermouth or white wine (optional). Trim 1½ pounds asparagus, discarding the tough ends and reserving the tips. Chop the stalks and add to the stock. Simmer for 5 minutes. Puree the soup, adding ¼ to ½ cup heavy cream or half-and-half, salt to taste, ⅛ teaspoon ground black pepper, and the reserved asparagus tips. Simmer for 3 to 5 minutes. Ladle into warmed bowls and serve.

CREAM OF BROCCOLI SOUP

Follow the recipe for Cream of Caulifower Soup, above, substituting broccoli for the cauliflower. Simmer the broccoli until tender but still brightly colored, 5 to 8 minutes. Proceed with the basic recipe, using ground black, not white, pepper.

NEW YORK DELI BORSCHT

About 5 cups

About the only thing deli borscht has in common with traditional Russian borscht, 116, is the presence of beets. This quick version is light and contains no fat. It is usually served cold but is also satisfying hot. To make a more substantial dish, add warm and quartered new potatoes to either the hot or cold version. If you find unwilted greens attached to your beets, wash and dry them, then chop and stir them in at the last minute for an untraditional touch. This borscht can be pureed if a smooth soup is desired. A dollop of sour cream on each portion is deli tradition.

Combine in a soup pot:

- **3 cups water**
- **1 pound beets, peeled and cut into thin strips**
- **1 large carrot, peeled and cut into thin strips (optional)**
- **1 clove garlic, minced**

Bring to a boil, reduce the heat, and simmer until the beets are tender, 5 to 10 minutes. Stir in:

- **2 tablespoons fresh lemon juice**
- **1½ teaspoons salt**
- **⅛ teaspoon ground black pepper**

Serve hot or cold, garnished with:

- **Sour cream**
- **Snipped fresh dill**

MUSHROOM SOUP

About 6 cups

Slice rather than chop the mushrooms for a meaty texture and a handsome look.

Heat in a soup pot, over high heat, until the butter is melted:

- **3½ tablespoons extra-virgin olive oil**
- **1 tablespoon unsalted butter or additional olive oil**

Add:

- **1½ pounds mushrooms (preferably at least 12 ounces wild), wiped clean and tough stems removed, sliced**
- **½ cup chopped shallots**

Cook, stirring often, until the mushrooms are wilted, about 5 minutes. Add:

- **3 tablespoons dry sherry or Madeira**
- **5 tablespoons all-purpose flour**
- **1 teaspoon dried thyme, or 1 tablespoon chopped fresh thyme**

Reduce the heat to low and cook, stirring constantly and scraping the bottom of the pan, for 5 minutes. Stir in:

- **4½ cups Brown Chicken Stock, 39, or any vegetable stock, 38 to 39**
- **½ to 1 teaspoon salt**
- **¾ teaspoon ground black pepper**

Bring to a boil, reduce the heat to medium, and simmer until slightly thickened, about 20 minutes. Ladle into warmed bowls. Garnish with:

- **Chopped fresh parsley or fresh thyme leaves**

CREAM OF MUSHROOM SOUP

Prepare Mushroom Soup, above. Stir in ½ cup heavy cream and ½ teaspoon salt. Simmer briefly, taste and adjust the seasonings, and serve.

MUSHROOM BARLEY SOUP

About 4 cups

Combine and let stand until the mushrooms are softened, about 20 minutes:

- **¼ ounce dried mushrooms, such as porcini or shiitake (about 3)**
- **1 cup hot water**

Remove the mushrooms and squeeze dry with paper towels. Reserve the soaking liquid. Dice the mushrooms finely and reserve. Heat in a soup pot over medium-low heat until the butter is melted:

- **1 tablespoon unsalted butter**
- **1 tablespoon vegetable oil**

Add and cook, stirring, until tender but not browned, 5 to 10 minutes:

- **5 ounces mushrooms, wiped clean and tough stems removed, coarsely chopped**
- **1 small leek (white part only), cleaned thoroughly and diced**
- **1 small onion, diced**
- **1 medium celery stalk, diced**
- **1 small carrot, diced**
- **2 cloves garlic, minced**

Increase the heat slightly and add:

⅓ cup pearl barley

Cook, stirring, until lightly toasted, about 5 minutes. Stir in the reserved diced mushrooms. Strain the soaking liquid through a fine-mesh sieve lined with a dampened paper towel and stir it into the vegetable mixture along with:

4 cups Brown Beef Stock, 40, or Roasted Vegetable Stock, 38

Bring to a boil, reduce the heat, and simmer, partially covered, until the barley is tender, about 40 minutes. Season with:

1 tablespoon snipped fresh dill
½ teaspoon salt
½ teaspoon ground black pepper

Ladle into warmed bowls and serve immediately.

FRESH TOMATO SOUP

About 4 cups

A simple, clean-tasting soup.

Heat in a soup pot, over medium-low heat:

2 tablespoons olive oil, preferably extra virgin

Add and cook, stirring, until tender but not browned, 5 to 10 minutes:

1 medium onion, coarsely chopped

Stir in:

3 pounds ripe tomatoes, peeled, seeded, and chopped, with juices

Simmer until the tomatoes are covered in their own liquid, about 25 minutes. Puree until smooth. Return to the pot and stir in:

¾ teaspoon salt
¼ teaspoon ground black pepper

Serve hot or cold.

CREAM OF FRESH TOMATO SOUP

Prepare Fresh Tomato Soup, above. Stir in ¼ cup heavy cream and, if you like, 1 tablespoon Pesto Sauce, 307. Gently heat through. Serve immediately.

GRILLED TOMATO SOUP

About 4 cups

A rustic-style, intensely flavored soup that is delicious either hot or cold. The grilling brings out the sweetness of the tomato as well as adding a light smoky flavor. If you cannot grill the tomatoes, broil them as close as you can to the heating element. The soup may thicken more when it is cold than when it is hot. If thinning is desired, add a little more stock or a bit of water.

Preheat the grill or broiler.

Halve through the circumference and seed:

3 pounds ripe tomatoes

Brush both sides with:

Olive oil, preferably extra virgin

If grilling, simply place on the grill. If broiling, arrange skin side up in a roasting pan. Grill or broil the tomatoes on both sides until golden and slightly charred. Remove to a platter or leave in the roasting pan. Heat in a soup pot, over medium-low heat:

2 tablespoons olive oil, preferably extra virgin

Add and cook, stirring often, until tender but not brown, 5 to 10 minutes.:

1 medium onion, coarsely chopped

Add the tomatoes and stir, breaking up the tomatoes with the spoon. Stir in:

1 cup Chicken Stock, 39
1 tablespoon dry white wine
1 clove garlic, minced

Simmer until the tomatoes are softened and have released their juices, 25 to 30 minutes. Puree until smooth. Strain, if you wish, to remove the skin. Stir in:

¾ teaspoon salt
¼ teaspoon ground black pepper

Let cool to room temperature and refrigerate until cold. Just before serving, stir in:

2 tablespoons fresh lemon juice
1 teaspoon balsamic vinegar
2 tablespoons chopped fresh basil

Adjust the seasonings, ladle into bowls, and garnish with:

1 sprig fresh basil
1 thin slice lemon, seeded (optional)

TOMATO JALAPEÑO CHILAQUILES

About 4 cups

This soup is Mexican soul food at its simplest—a hearty pot of slightly chewy tortillas simmered with a highly flavored tomato-jalapeño stock. Somewhat like a rustic pasta dish, *chilaquiles* are served most often at *almuerzo* (late morning breakfast or brunch). Sliced chard or coarsely shredded cooked chicken can be added for a more substantial version. This recipe was given to us by Rick Bayless, the talented authority on Mexican cooking, who serves it at his Chicago restaurant, the Frontera Grill.

Heat a medium, heavy skillet or griddle (preferably cast iron) over medium heat until hot. Place in the skillet:

1 to 2 fresh jalapeño peppers
2 large cloves garlic, unpeeled

Roast, turning occasionally, until the chili peppers are blistered and blackened on all sides and the garlic is soft to the touch, 10 to 15 minutes. When cool enough to handle, peel the garlic. Place in a food processor or blender with the chili peppers. Coarsely chop using on-off pulses. Add:

One 28-ounce can whole tomatoes, drained

Process until the mixture is coarsely pureed. Heat in a soup pot over medium heat:

1½ teaspoons vegetable oil

Add and cook until nicely browned, about 8 to 10 minutes:

½ small onion, thinly sliced

Increase the heat to medium-high and add the tomato mixture. Cook, stirring, until the mixture is darkened and slightly thickened, about 5 minutes. Reduce the heat to medium-low and stir in:

3 cups Chicken Stock, 39, Chicken Broth, 42, Vegetable Stock, 38, or Vegetable Broth, 38

Simmer, stirring occasionally, for 15 minutes. Season with:

½ to 1 teaspoon salt (depending on the saltiness of the broth)

Just before serving, bring the mixture to a boil and add:

8 ounces thick homemade-style tortilla chips

Stir to coat the chips well, then increase the heat to medium-high and boil rapidly, stirring gently and often, until the chips are softened (but are still a little chewy) and the sauce is reduced to a medium-thick consistency, 2 to 3 minutes for thinner chips, 4 to 5 minutes for thicker chips. Immediately spoon the *chilaquiles* onto a warm deep platter. Serve garnished with:

¼ cup finely crumbled queso fresco or grated Monterey Jack cheese
2 tablespoons chopped fresh cilantro (optional)
2 tablespoons sour cream thinned with a little milk (optional)

TUSCAN BREAD AND TOMATO SOUP (PAPPA AL POMODORO)

About 4 cups

From the days when bread was the heart and soul of the kitchen—and not a scrap was wasted—comes this favorite of Tuscany's country soups. Make it with fresh tomatoes in high summer and eat it at room temperature, or prepare it with canned tomatoes in winter and serve hot. To stay true to the goodness of the soup, use a bread made without sugar.

Preheat the oven to 200°F.

Dry in the oven for 15 to 20 minutes:

2 or 3 thick slices country bread

Alternatively, use stale bread. Heat in a soup pot, over medium heat:

3 tablespoons extra-virgin olive oil

Add and cook, stirring, until beginning to color, about 10 minutes:

1 medium red onion, coarsely chopped
Salt and ground black pepper to taste

Meanwhile, rub the bread on both sides with:

1 clove garlic, halved

Coarsely chop together:

4 large cloves garlic, peeled
⅓ cup tightly packed fresh basil leaves

Reduce the heat to medium-low, stir in the garlic mixture, and cook until the garlic barely colors, 2 to 3 minutes. Add:

1½ pounds ripe tomatoes, peeled, seeded, and coarsely chopped, or one 28-ounce can whole tomatoes, drained and chopped
Pinch of red pepper flakes

Cook, stirring, over medium-high heat until thick and fragrant, about 5 minutes. Stir in:

2 cups Chicken Stock, 39, or Vegetable Stock, 38

Boil for 2 minutes. Taste and adjust the seasonings. Break up the bread in the bottom of soup bowls. Ladle in the hot soup and top each serving with:

4 fresh basil leaves, torn
Drizzle of extra-virgin olive oil
Parmesan cheese shavings

Serve hot or at room temperature.

ROASTED RED PEPPER SOUP

About 8 cups

This is a rustic-style soup that is full of texture and sweet red pepper flavor. If fresh fennel is not available, use an equal amount of chopped celery and increase the fennel seeds to 1¼ teaspoons. Serve either hot or cold with grilled garlic toasts.

Preheat the broiler.

Arrange skin side up in a roasting pan:

6 large red bell peppers, quartered and seeded

Trim if necessary so the peppers lay flat and brush them lightly with:

Olive oil

Place under the broiler and cook until the skins are thoroughly blistered and blackened. Remove the pan to a rack. When cool enough to handle, peel the peppers, discarding the skins, and cut into long strips. Heat in a soup pot over medium-low heat:

3 tablespoons olive oil

Add and cook, stirring, until tender but not browned, 10 to 15 minutes:

2 cups chopped onion
1 cup diced carrots
1 cup chopped fennel bulb

Stir in:

5 cups Chicken Stock, 39, or Vegetable Stock, 38
1 cup dry white wine
3 tablespoons medium-grain rice, preferably Arborio
2 tablespoons chopped fresh basil, or 2 teaspoons dried
1 tablespoon chopped fresh rosemary, or 1 teaspoon dried
1 teaspoon fennel seeds
1/8 teaspoon red pepper flakes

Bring to a boil, reduce the heat, and simmer partially covered, until the peppers and rice are very tender, about 30 minutes. Meanwhile, make the garlic toasts. Preheat the grill or broiler.

Arrange on a baking sheet:

8 slices Italian bread or 16 slices French bread

Lightly brush the slices on both sides with:

Olive oil, preferably extra virgin

Rub on both sides with:

1 to 2 cloves garlic, halved

Grill or broil the bread on both sides until golden. When the soup is done, puree until smooth. Return the soup to the pot and season with:

Salt and ground black pepper to taste
2 to 3 drops balsamic vinegar

Ladle into bowls or let cool to room temperature and refrigerate. Serve with the garlic toasts. If serving chilled, taste cold and adjust the seasonings.

CHEDDAR CHEESE SOUP

About 6 cups

Serve this soup as a main course.

Melt in a soup pot, over medium heat:

6 tablespoons (3/4 stick) unsalted butter

Add and cook until tender, but not browned, 5 to 10 minutes:

1 cup diced onions
1 cup diced celery
3/4 cup diced carrots

Sprinkle with:

1/4 cup all-purpose flour

Cook, stirring, for 3 to 4 minutes more. Slowly whisk in:

4 cups Chicken Stock, 39

Bring the soup to a boil, whisking constantly. Reduce the heat to a simmer and cook until thickened, about 45 minutes. Puree until smooth. Return to the pot, bring to a simmer, and stir in:

1 cup heavy cream or half-and-half
8 ounces Cheddar cheese, grated
1 teaspoon dry mustard

Reduce the heat to low and stir until the cheese is melted. (Do not let the soup boil: if the soup is too hot, the cheese will break down.) Season with:

Hot red pepper sauce to taste (optional)
Worcestershire sauce to taste (optional)
Salt and ground black pepper to taste

If you prefer a thinner soup, thin with additional:

Stock or cream

Garnish with:

Croutons
Finely chopped smoked ham
Chopped cooked broccoli

GAZPACHO

About 6 cups

There are numerous varieties of gazpacho in Spain—a white one from Málaga, made with garlic, bread, and almonds and garnished with green grapes; a cumin-scented one from Granada; even a stewlike game-filled version (called *gaspatxos*) from Alicante. The most familiar version is this one—an Andalusian "pureed salad" of summery vegetables. Classic gazpachos are thickened with bread, although many contemporary recipes, like this one, omit it. On the other hand, we have added a nontraditional jalapeño pepper for more bite. Gazpacho is better served the day it is made, but if preparing it for the following day, use half the jalapeño, as the heat increases with time.

Finely chop, but do not puree, in a food processor or blender:

1 medium cucumber, peeled, seeded, and coarsely chopped
1 medium green bell pepper, coarsely chopped

Remove to a large bowl. Finely chop in the processor:

1 small onion, coarsely chopped
1/3 cup packed fresh parsley leaves

Remove to the bowl. Add to the processor and finely chop:

2 1/2 pounds ripe tomatoes, peeled, seeded, and coarsely chopped

Remove to the bowl. Add:

1 cup tomato juice
1/4 cup red wine vinegar
3 tablespoons extra-virgin olive oil
2 cloves garlic, minced
1 fresh jalapeño pepper, seeded and minced, or a dash of hot pepper sauce (optional)
2 teaspoons salt

Stir well. Refrigerate for at least 2 hours. Serve in chilled bowls.

MINESTRONE *About 10 cups*

Minestrone embraces a legion of hearty vegetable and bean soups from Italy. This one is a melding of styles and is equally good served hot or warm.

Heat over medium heat in a large soup pot, until the pancetta or bacon has released its fat, 2 to 3 minutes:

2 tablespoons extra-virgin olive oil
1 ounce pancetta or 2 slices bacon, chopped (optional)

Add and cook, stirring, until the greens are beginning to wilt, 5 to 10 minutes:

1 medium onion, chopped
1 large carrot, peeled and chopped
2 medium celery stalks with leaves, minced
One 4-inch sprig fresh rosemary, or 1 teaspoon dried
¼ cup tightly packed fresh basil leaves, chopped
¼ cup tightly packed fresh parsley leaves, chopped
2 cloves garlic, minced
½ small head green cabbage, chopped
3 Swiss chard leaves washed, dried, and chopped

Cover, and cook until the vegetables are tender, about 10 minutes. Stir in:

One 14-ounce can whole tomatoes, drained and broken into pieces

Cook, stirring, over medium-high heat for 3 to 5 minutes. Stir in:

One 16-ounce can *borlotti* or pinto beans, rinsed and drained, half of them mashed
10 cups Chicken Stock, 39, or water

Bring to a boil, reduce the heat, and simmer, partially covered, for 30 minutes. Remove the rosemary sprig, if used. Stir in:

4 ounces orzo

Continue to simmer for 15 minutes. Ladle into warmed bowls and drizzle over each serving:

Extra-virgin olive oil

Sprinkle with:

Ground black pepper to taste

PROVENÇAL VEGETABLE SOUP (SOUPE AU PISTOU) *About 10 cups*

This signature dish of the south of France is a light and flavorful vegetable soup.

Heat in a large soup pot, over medium-low heat:

2 tablespoons olive oil, preferably extra virgin

Add and cook, stirring, until tender but not browned, 5 to 10 minutes:

1 medium onion, chopped
1 small leek (white and tender green parts), cleaned thoroughly and chopped
1 medium carrot, peeled and chopped
1 large celery stalk, chopped

Stir in:

2 medium, ripe tomatoes, peeled, seeded, and chopped
1 small potato, peeled and chopped
8 cups water
2 teaspoons salt
Pinch of saffron threads (optional)

Bring to a boil, reduce the heat, and simmer until the potatoes are tender, about 30 minutes. Stir in:

One 15½- or 19-ounce can cannellini, great Northern, or other white beans, rinsed and drained, or 1 to 2 cups cooked (⅓ to ⅔ cup dried), 271
Small handful of thin spaghetti, broken up, or short macaroni
1 small zucchini, quartered lengthwise and sliced
4 ounces green beans, cut into 1-inch pieces

Simmer just until the pasta is tender. Meanwhile, make the pistou: Puree in a blender, until smooth:

2 cups fresh basil leaves
2 cloves garlic, chopped
¼ cup extra-virgin olive oil

Remove the soup from the heat. Immediately stir in the pistou along with:

⅔ cup coarsely grated Parmesan cheese
1 teaspoon ground black pepper

Ladle into warmed bowls to serve hot, or serve at room temperature or cold.

MULLIGATAWNY SOUP *About 5 cups*

The predecessors of this version of Mulligatawny were created by local cooks in southern India. The countless variations of this soup are all curried and then smoothed with coconut milk or cream.

Skin, bone, and cut into bite-sized pieces:

2 pounds chicken thighs

Heat over medium-high heat in a soup pot:

3 tablespoons vegetable oil

Add and cook, stirring, until golden brown, 7 to 8 minutes:

1 medium onion, thinly sliced

Add and cook, stirring, for 30 seconds:

2 cloves garlic, finely minced
One 1-inch piece fresh ginger, peeled and finely minced
1 tablespoon curry powder

Add the chicken along with:

2 tablespoons water

Cook, stirring, until the chicken loses its raw color and the oil sizzles and pools around the meat, 3 to 4 minutes.

Stir in:

4 cups Chicken Stock, 39
½ teaspoon salt

Bring to a boil, reduce the heat to medium, and simmer until the chicken is cooked through, 20 to 30 minutes. Stir in:

1 cup unsweetened coconut milk (optional)

Simmer for 5 minutes more. Divide among 4 bowls:

½ cup hot cooked rice

Ladle the soup on top and garnish with:

Fresh coriander leaves
Lemon wedges
Chopped apples

BARLEY SOUP WITH SAUSAGES (MINESTRA D'ORZO)

About 16 cups (4 quarts)

This soup is inspired by the foods of Italy's mountainous Tyrol at Austria's border. On its native turf, it would be flavored with "speck," meaty chunks of pork deeply smoked and cured with salt, juniper, garlic, and spices. Smoked kielbasa or bratwurst can be substituted. Serve with thick slices of country bread.

Cook in a medium skillet, or on a medium-hot outdoor or stovetop grill, until browned on all sides and heated through:

6 ounces deeply smoked sausages

Slice the sausages thinly and place in a large soup pot along with:

16 cups (4 quarts) Vegetable Stock, 38, or Chicken Stock, 39
1¼ cups pearl barley
2 large bay leaves, crumbled

Bring to a boil, reduce the heat, and simmer, partially covered, for 30 minutes. Meanwhile, heat in a large skillet over medium heat:

2 tablespoons extra-virgin olive oil

Add:

½ large head green cabbage, chopped

Cook, stirring, until the cabbage begins to color, 5 to 10 minutes. Add:

2 medium onions, finely chopped
1 large carrot, peeled and finely chopped
1 large celery stalk with leaves, finely chopped
3 tablespoons tightly packed fresh parsley leaves, minced
Two 3-inch sprigs fresh rosemary, or 2 teaspoons dried

Cook, stirring often, until the onions are browned, 10 to 15 minutes. Stir in:

3 tablespoons tightly packed fresh marjoram leaves, minced, or 1 tablespoon dried
1 large clove garlic, minced

Add 1 cup liquid from the soup pot and scrape the bottom of the skillet to loosen any browned bits. Stir the contents of the skillet into the soup pot along with:

2 red or white new potatoes, peeled and diced

Cover and simmer gently until the barley is tender but not mushy and the potatoes are cooked but firm, about 30 minutes more. If the soup is too thick, thin with water as needed. Season with:

2½ teaspoons salt
1 teaspoon ground black pepper

Ladle into warmed bowls. Sprinkle each serving with:

1 to 2 tablespoons shredded aged Montasio or imported provolone cheese

PORTUGUESE GREENS SOUP (CALDO VERDE)

About 10 cups

This hearty soup is from the province of Minho, Portugal, which is famous for its cooking. *Caldo verde* was brought to us by the Portuguese communities in Cape Cod, Rhode Island, and other parts of the eastern seaboard.

Heat in a large soup pot, over medium-low heat:

1½ tablespoons olive or other vegetable oil

Add and cook, stirring, until tender but not browned, 5 to 10 minutes:

1 medium onion, chopped
2 cloves garlic, minced

Stir in:

8 cups water, or 6 cups water and 2 cups Chicken Stock, 39
4 medium potatoes, peeled and thinly sliced
1½ teaspoons salt
½ teaspoon ground black pepper

Bring to a boil, reduce the heat, and simmer until the potatoes are soft, about 20 minutes. Remove the pot from the heat. Using a potato masher, lightly mash the potatoes right in the pot. (This will give the soup a chunky texture.) Heat in a medium skillet, over medium-high heat:

½ teaspoon vegetable oil (optional)

Add and cook, stirring, until browned:

6 ounces Portuguese linguiça or chorizo sausage, thinly sliced

Add to the soup pot. Pour 1 cup of the soup into the skillet. Scrape up the browned bits and return the liquid and browned bits to the soup. Simmer for 5 minutes. Stir in:

4 cups shredded kale, Swiss chard, or collard leaves (from a 6- to 8-ounce bunch), washed and dried

Simmer for 5 minutes. Stir in:

2 tablespoons fresh lemon juice

Ladle into warmed bowls.

HOT AND SOUR SOUP

About 5 cups

A bowl of this bracing soup—which originated in northern China and now seems to be eaten almost everywhere in the United States—works wonders for the spirit. Freezing the pork chop for 15 minutes will make it easier to slice into thin strips. Wood or cloud ear mushrooms and tiger lily buds are available in Asian markets.

Combine in a medium bowl and let stand until the mushrooms are softened, about 20 minutes:

10 dried wood or cloud ear mushrooms (optional)
4 dried shiitake mushrooms (8 if not using wood ears)
10 tiger lily buds (optional)
1½ cups hot water

Meanwhile, combine in a small bowl:

5 tablespoons rice vinegar
3 tablespoons soy sauce
1 tablespoon cornstarch
4 ounces center-cut pork chop, cut into ¼-inch strips

Remove the mushrooms and lily buds. Reserve the soaking liquid. Remove any tough pieces of the mushrooms and slice into strips. Discard the tough ends of the lily buds and cut in half. Combine. Cut into strips about the same size as the pork:

4 ounces firm tofu, well drained

To prepare the soup, strain the reserved mushroom soaking liquid through a fine-mesh sieve lined with a dampened paper towel. Bring to a boil in a soup pot along with:

4 cups Chicken Stock, 39, Brown Chicken Stock, 39, or any vegetable stock, 38 to 39

Add the mushroom mixture, reduce the heat, and simmer for 3 minutes. Stir together in a small bowl:

3 tablespoons cornstarch
3 tablespoons water

Add to the soup and simmer, whisking constantly, until slightly thickened. Add the meat and tofu along with:

¾ to 1 teaspoon ground black pepper

Bring back to a simmer, then stir into the soup in a wide circle:

1 large egg, well beaten

Remove from the heat and add:

1 tablespoon toasted sesame oil

Ladle into warmed bowls. Garnish with:

Sliced scallion greens

Pass at the table for those who like their soup very hot and sour:

Rice vinegar
Chili oil

SCALLION AND MUSHROOM SOUP

About 7 cups

This soup uses the whole scallion with stunning results. The inspiration for this recipe comes from Crème Olga. Beat with a wooden spoon until light and fluffy:

4 tablespoons (½ stick) unsalted butter, softened

Add and stir together well:

5 bunches scallions, very finely chopped

Remove to a soup pot and season with:

1 teaspoon salt
½ teaspoon ground white pepper

Cook, covered, over low heat for about 10 minutes. Do not brown the scallions. Remove the pot from the heat. Stir in:

2 tablespoons all-purpose flour

Cook for 1 minute. Whisk in:

4 cups Chicken Stock, 39

Bring to a boil, whisking, over medium heat. Reduce the heat and simmer for 10 minutes. Meanwhile, wipe clean, remove the tough ends of the stems only, and very thinly slice:

12 ounces mushrooms with stems

Remove the soup from the heat and stir in two-thirds of the mushrooms. Immediately push through a sieve or food mill. Stir in:

¼ to ½ cup half-and-half

Gently heat the soup until hot, then stir in the remaining mushrooms. Ladle into warmed bowls. Top each serving with:

Sprinkle of ground red pepper
Dollop of sour cream

POTATO LEEK SOUPS

Potatoes and leeks make magic together. This divine synergy is reflected in these two soups, one a simple stock- or water-based soup, the other a smooth, cream-enriched version.

SMOOTH POTATO LEEK SOUP (POTAGE PARMENTIER)

About 8 cups

Thin this soup, if necessary, with a bit more water or stock. For extra smoothness, push through a sieve after it has been pureed in a food processor.

Melt in a soup pot, over low heat:

3 tablespoons unsalted butter, or 1 tablespoon butter and ¼ cup water

Add and cook, stirring, until tender but not browned, about 20 minutes:

8 large leeks (white part only), cleaned thoroughly and chopped

Stir in:

3 medium or 2 large baking potatoes, peeled and thinly sliced

5 cups Chicken Stock, 39, Vegetable Stock, 38, or water

Bring to a boil, reduce the heat, and simmer until the potatoes are soft, about 30 minutes. Puree until smooth. Season with:

Salt to taste

¼ teaspoon ground white or black pepper

Thin, if necessary, with additional:

Stock or water

Reheat gently, then ladle into warmed bowls.

VICHYSSOISE

The "classic French" soup was actually invented by French chef Louis Diat around 1910, when he worked at New York's Ritz-Carlton Hotel. During the Second World War, when the French spa town of Vichy became the capital of the collaborationist government, this soup was served in the United States under a variety of different names.

Prepare Smooth Potato Leek Soup, above, adding ½ to 1 cup heavy cream, or a combination of milk and cream. Season with salt and ground black pepper to taste and thin if necessary. Garnish with snipped fresh chives, if desired. Serve hot or cold.

ABOUT LEGUME SOUPS

For the contemporary cook, legume soups have many advantages, besides their great nutrition: they are easy to prepare in large batches, they freeze well, the raw materials are easily kept on hand, and they require little attention while cooking. For additional information, see Beans & Tofu, 270.

Pureed bean soups can be passed through a sieve or food mill to eliminate the skins. If a legume soup becomes too thick during long simmering, simply thin it with a bit of water or stock. Do not puree for a chunkier soup.

CUBAN BLACK BEAN SOUP (SOPA DE FRIJOL NEGRO)

About 8 cups

When accompanied with the traditional condiments of rice, egg, lemon, and onion, this soup makes a colorful and complete dinner. A food mill will leave a coarse texture and eliminate the skins. For a chunky texture, puree just 2 cups of the finished soup.

Pick over, rinse, and soak, 270:

1 pound dried black beans (about 2½ cups)

Heat in a large soup pot over medium-low heat:

2 tablespoons vegetable oil

Add and cook, stirring, until tender but not browned, 5 to 10 minutes:

2 medium onions, chopped

3 medium celery stalks, diced

4 cloves garlic, minced

½ Scotch bonnet pepper or 2 to 3 fresh jalapeño peppers, seeded and diced

Drain and add the black beans along with:

11 cups water

1 large ham hock (optional)

Bring to a boil, reduce the heat, and simmer until the beans are tender, about 2 hours. Remove the ham hock if using. Discard the bone, skin, and fat; dice the meat. Puree the beans in a food processor or by passing them through a food mill. Return to the pot. Stir in the meat along with:

¼ to ½ cup dry sherry or rum

2 teaspoons salt (less if using the ham hock)

Simmer for several minutes to heat through. Thin with additional water if necessary. Stir in:

2 tablespoons fresh lemon juice (optional)

Garnish at the table with any or all of the following:

Lemon wedges

Chopped onions

Steamed white rice

Chopped hard-boiled eggs

Chopped scallions

GEORGIA PEANUT SOUP

About 4 cups

Peanuts, or groundnuts, are among the many culinary treasures brought to the United States by slaves from Africa. If you are preparing this dish a day or so ahead, use less ground red pepper and hot red pepper sauce, as the heat intensifies over time.

Heat in a soup pot, over medium-low heat until the butter is melted:

2 tablespoons unsalted butter

1 tablespoon vegetable oil

Add and cook, stirring, until tender but not browned, about 5 to 10 minutes:

1 small onion, chopped

2 medium celery stalks, chopped

Stir in:

2 tablespoons all-purpose flour

Reduce the heat to low and cook, stirring, for 5 minutes. Stir in:

4 cups Chicken Stock, 39, or Brown Chicken Stock, 39

Simmer, stirring often, until the soup begins to thicken, about 5 minutes. Stir in:

1 cup unsalted smooth peanut butter
¼ cup heavy cream or half-and-half
1½ teaspoons salt
1 teaspoon ground red pepper
1 teaspoon hot red pepper sauce

Heat through but do not boil. Stir in:

2 teaspoons fresh lemon juice

Ladle into warmed bowls. Garnish with:

3 tablespoons chopped dry-roasted peanuts
¼ cup chopped scallion greens

LENTIL SOUP

About 10 cups

Heat in a large soup pot, over medium-low heat:

3 tablespoons olive oil

Add and cook, stirring, until tender but not browned, 5 to 10 minutes:

3 medium carrots, peeled and diced
3 medium celery stalks, diced
1 large onion, diced
3 cloves garlic, minced
2 ounces prosciutto or pancetta, or 4 slices bacon, diced (optional)

Stir in:

8 cups water
2 cups lentils, picked over and rinsed
One 14½-ounce can diced tomatoes, drained
1 teaspoon dried thyme

Bring to a boil, reduce the heat, and simmer until the lentils are tender, 30 to 45 minutes. Stir in:

1½ teaspoons balsamic vinegar
2 teaspoons salt (1 teaspoon if using the meat)
1 teaspoon ground black pepper

Ladle into warmed bowls.

LENTIL SOUP WITH SAUSAGE AND POTATO

Any type of sausage can be added to this soup, including chorizo, kielbasa, and frankfurters.

Prepare Lentil Soup, above, adding after the lentils have been cooking for 30 minutes 1 large potato, peeled and diced. Cook for 10 minutes, then add 6 ounces sausage, sliced, and ½ cup water. Simmer until the potatoes are tender and the sausages are just heated through, about 5 minutes.

LENTIL SOUP WITH GREENS

Prepare Lentil Soup, above. Trim (remove the center rib if tough), wash and dry 1 bunch greens (about 10 ounces), such as kale or spinach, then cut the leaves into strips. Add to the finished soup and cook until tender but still bright green.

MEDITERRANEAN WHITE BEAN SOUP

About 6 cups

Simple and aromatic, this is what used to be called a "pantry soup," because it uses household staples. Feel free to add a touch of extra chopped fresh herbs with the parsley, such as thyme, fennel leaves, or sage.

Pick over, rinse, and soak, 270:

1 cup large dried white beans, such as great Northern or cannellini

Drain and place in a soup pot along with:

7 cups water
¾ teaspoon dried rosemary
8 cloves garlic, chopped or sliced

Bring to a boil, reduce the heat, and simmer until the beans are tender, 1 to 1½ hours. Stir in:

½ cup chopped ripe tomatoes
¼ cup chopped fresh parsley
¼ cup extra-virgin olive oil
4 teaspoons red wine vinegar
2 teaspoons salt
½ teaspoon ground black pepper

Ladle into warmed bowls.

U.S. SENATE BEAN SOUP

About 6 cups

This soup has been on the U.S. Senate restaurant menu since 1901.

Pick over, rinse, and soak, 270:

1¼ cups small dried white beans, such as pea or navy

Drain and place in a soup pot along with:

7 cups cold water
1 small ham hock

Bring to a boil, reduce the heat, and simmer until the beans are tender, about 1¼ hours. Remove the ham hock. Discard the bone, skin, and fat; dice the meat. Return it to the pot along with:

1 large onion, diced
3 medium celery stalks with leaves, chopped
1 large potato, peeled and finely diced
2 cloves garlic, minced
1½ teaspoons salt
½ teaspoon ground black pepper

Simmer until the potatoes are quite soft, 20 to 30 minutes. Remove from the heat and mash with a potato masher until the soup is a bit creamy. Stir in:

2 tablespoons chopped fresh parsley

Ladle into warmed bowls.

SPLIT PEA SOUP *About 6 cups*

Try this on a cold winter day, seasoned with plenty of freshly ground black pepper.

Combine in a soup pot:

8 cups cold water
1 small ham hock
1 pound split green peas (about 2 cups)

Bring to a boil, reduce the heat, and simmer for 1 hour. Stir in:

1 large carrot, peeled and diced
1 large celery stalk, diced
1 medium onion, diced
2 cloves garlic, minced
1 bouquet garni, 37

Simmer until the ham hock and peas are tender, about 1 hour more. Season with:

Salt and lots of ground black pepper to taste

Remove the ham hock. Discard the bone, skin, and fat; dice the meat. Return it to the soup. For a thicker soup, simmer to the desired consistency. Stir to blend before serving. Ladle into warmed bowls. Garnish with:

Croutons

ABOUT CLEAR STOCKS WITH ADDITIONS

This is one category of soups for which a tasty, full-bodied homemade stock is strongly recommended. You can intensify the flavor of a light stock by simmering it to evaporate some of the water. Or simmer it with chopped vegetables—finely diced carrots, celery, and onions—and perhaps fresh herbs, then strain out the vegetables. The ultimate broth is consommé, 107, enriched with both meat and vegetables and clarified with egg whites.

Many of the recipes in this section call for chicken stock, because it is easy to prepare and seems to have the most universal appeal; feel free to substitute any of the stocks provided in the Stocks and Sauces chapter.

CHINESE EGG DROP SOUP *About 4 cups*

A simple, delicate soup.

Combine in a large saucepan and simmer, partially covered, for 15 minutes:

4 cups Chicken Stock, 39
2 large slices fresh ginger
2 large cloves garlic, smashed and peeled

Discard the ginger and garlic. Stir together in a small bowl:

1 tablespoon cornstarch
3 tablespoons water

Bring the soup to a low simmer and add the cornstarch mixture. Stir until the soup is slightly thickened. Stir in:

1 teaspoon salt
1/8 teaspoon ground black pepper

Whisk together thoroughly in a small bowl:

1 large egg
1 teaspoon vegetable oil

Bring the soup to a very low simmer and pour the egg mixture in a large circle on the surface of the soup. Once the egg sets, stir gently. Stir in:

2 scallions, diagonally sliced
2 tablespoons chopped fresh cilantro

Ladle into warmed bowls.

ITALIAN PARMESAN AND EGG SOUP (STRACCIATELLA) *About 3 cups*

A Roman specialty, *stracciatella* derives its name from the word *straccetti,* little rags—describing the strands of cooked egg that float in the broth.

Bring to a simmer in a medium saucepan:

3 cups Chicken Stock, 39

Meanwhile, whisk together until blended:

1 large egg
1½ tablespoons grated Parmesan cheese
1 tablespoon dry unseasoned breadcrumbs
2 tablespoons chopped fresh parsley
1 small clove garlic, finely minced

Stir this mixture rapidly into the simmering stock and stir until the egg is set, 30 to 60 seconds. Garnish with:

Freshly grated or ground nutmeg or grated lemon zest

Ladle into warmed bowls.

GREEK LEMON SOUP *About 4 cups*

Unlike *stracciatella,* where the eggs are supposed to separate, here the eggs are blended to create a smooth, creamy texture. This is done by adding a little of the hot stock to the eggs before they are added to the soup to prevent them from curdling.

Bring to a rolling boil in a medium saucepan,:

3 cups Chicken Stock, 39
½ cup long-grain rice

Reduce the heat, cover, and simmer until the rice is tender, about 20 minutes. In a medium bowl, whisk just enough to combine and be uniform in color:

2 large eggs
¼ cup fresh lemon juice

Stir 2 tablespoons of the hot stock into the egg mixture. To prevent curdling, gradually pour the egg mixture into the hot, not boiling, soup while stirring constantly. Season with:

1 to 2 tablespoons fresh lemon juice (optional)
Salt and ground black pepper to taste

Ladle into warmed bowls. Garnish with:

Chopped fresh parsley or snipped fresh dill

SPANISH GARLIC SOUP WITH EGGS (SOPA DE AJO)

About 4 cups

This soup is traditionally made with water, but chicken stock imparts a richer flavor. If available, use a robust, fruity olive oil.

Heat in a soup pot, over low heat:

3 tablespoons extra-virgin olive oil

Add and cook, stirring, just until beginning to color, 5 to 10 minutes:

1 head garlic, separated into cloves and peeled (about 16 cloves)

Remove with a slotted spoon to a small bowl. Cook, stirring, in the oil on both sides over medium-high heat until golden, 1 to 2 minutes each side:

4 slices French or country bread

Rub both sides with:

1 clove garlic, halved

Stir into the pot:

1 tablespoon sweet or hot paprika
¼ teaspoon cumin seeds

Stir in the cooked garlic along with:

4 cups Chicken Stock, 39
½ teaspoon salt
¼ teaspoon ground black pepper

Bring to a boil, reduce the heat, and simmer until the garlic is tender, about 20 minutes.

Preheat the oven to 400°F.

Remove the garlic with a slotted spoon and mash with a fork. Return it to the pot, then bring the soup to a low simmer. Set 4 ovenproof bowls or crocks on a baking sheet and ladle the soup into the bowls. One at a time, break into a small bowl, then slide each into a bowl of soup:

4 large eggs

Carefully slide the baking sheet into the oven. Cook just until the egg whites are set (the yolks should still be runny), about 3 minutes. Top each serving with a garlic crouton, allowing the bread to soak into the soup.

CHICKEN NOODLE SOUP

About 4 cups

Using homemade stock in this recipe makes all the difference, transforming a dependable standard into a great soup. If you do make your own stock, remove some of the chicken meat from the bones when the stock is done and return it to the soup. For variety, try stirring in a peeled, seeded, and diced tomato and a teaspoon of chopped fresh herb, such as tarragon, parsley, dill, or basil, just before serving the soup.

Bring to a boil in a medium saucepan,:

4 cups Chicken Stock, 39, or Brown Chicken Stock, 39

Stir in:

1 cup fine egg noodles or 2 ounces thin fresh or dried pasta

Cook until the pasta is tender but firm, 4 to 5 minutes. Season with:

2 tablespoons chopped fresh parsley
Salt to taste
Pinch of ground black pepper

Ladle into warmed bowls.

CHICKEN SOUP WITH VARIATIONS

With simple additions, flavorful homemade chicken stock can be transformed into a multitude of other simple soups. Here are some examples. (Vegetarians can substitute Vegetable Stock, 38.) If you are adding both grains and vegetables, add the vegetables when the grains are almost cooked.

CHICKEN RICE OR BARLEY SOUP

About 4 cups

Bring to a simmer in a medium saucepan:

4 cups Chicken Stock, 39, or Brown Chicken Stock, 39
½ teaspoon salt

Stir in:

3 tablespoons long-grain rice or 2 tablespoons pearl barley

Simmer until tender, about 15 minutes for rice, 30 to 45 minutes for barley.

CHICKEN SOUP WITH RAVIOLI OR TORTELLINI

Prepare Chicken Rice or Barley Soup, above, substituting ravioli or tortellini (quantity to taste) for the rice or barley. Simmer until tender but firm, 5 to 10 minutes.

Any of the following can be added to or substituted for the additions above:

- Stir in 5 minutes before the soup is fully cooked:
  1½ cups sliced mixed vegetables, such as carrots, celery, tomatoes, and/or onions
- Stir in 1 to 2 minutes before the soup is fully cooked:
  1 cup thinly sliced greens (such as escarole, kale, or spinach), trimmed, washed, and dried
- Stir in any of the following just before serving:
  1 tablespoon dry sherry or white wine
  Chopped fresh tarragon, basil, or parsley, or snipped fresh dill
  Pinch of ground black pepper

MATZO BALL SOUP *About 6 cups; 12 to 14 large balls*

This simple classic is wonderful with or without the optional additions.

Beat on medium speed for 1 minute:

4 large eggs
1 teaspoon salt

If desired, stir in:

½ cup finely diced fennel; 2 tablespoons snipped fresh dill and 4 teaspoons snipped fresh or dried chives; or 2 tablespoons chopped fresh parsley and 2 tablespoons snipped fresh dill (optional)

Stir in:

⅓ cup plus 1 tablespoon soda water

Fold in until well blended:

1 cup matzo meal
¼ teaspoon ground black pepper
1 teaspoon curry powder (optional)
1 to 2 teaspoons finely chopped peeled fresh ginger, or 1 teaspoon ground (optional)

Cover and refrigerate for 1 to 4 hours.

With wet hands, form the matzo balls. Drop the balls into a large pot of boiling salted water, cover, reduce the heat, and simmer for 20 minutes. When the matzo balls are almost finished, heat in a soup pot:

6 cups Chicken Stock, 39

Season with:

1¼ teaspoons salt
¼ teaspoon ground black pepper (optional)

When the matzo balls are finished, add them to the stock. Ladle the stock into warmed bowls and add 2 matzo balls to each serving.

CHICKEN OR BEEF CONSOMMÉ *About 6½ cups*

Clear, intensely flavorful consommé, one of the glories of classical French cooking, makes an elegant start to a formal dinner party. For a clear consommé, the stock must be completely free of grease. For particularly strong consommé, simmer 16 cups (4 quarts) of degreased stock until reduced by half before clarifying it.

Combine in a food processor:

1 small onion, quartered
1 small carrot, peeled and cut into 2-inch pieces
1 small celery stalk, cut into 2-inch pieces
2 tablespoons packed fresh parsley leaves
½ teaspoon fresh thyme leaves

Pulse until coarsely chopped. Add:

1 pound boneless, skinless chicken breasts, fat trimmed, cut into 2-inch pieces, or 1½ pounds beef round or rump steak, fat trimmed, cut into 1-inch pieces

Pulse until chopped but not pureed. Remove to a medium bowl. Add:

3 large egg whites

Stir together well. Warm in a soup pot, over low heat:

8 cups Chicken Stock, 39, or Classic Beef Stock, 40, or Brown Beef Stock, 40, thoroughly degreased

Whisk in the vegetable mixture. Very slowly bring to a simmer without boiling, occasionally stirring and scraping the bottom of the pot to prevent burning until the egg foam rises to the surface, about 30 minutes. (Be careful not to stir after the broth reaches a simmer.) When the egg foam starts to solidify, make a small hole in the center with the end of a wooden spoon. Continue to simmer very gently until the egg foam mixture is solid, about 30 minutes more. Remove the pot from the heat. Line a sieve with a slightly dampened cheesecloth or dish towel. Gently move the foam to the side of the pot and ladle out the consommé. Strain the consommé through the sieve into a large saucepan. Season with:

1 teaspoon salt, or to taste

Heat through, then ladle into warmed bowls.

CONSOMMÉ BRUNOISE

In classical French cooking, a brunoise is a mixture of finely diced vegetables. In this case, three of the vegetables most basic to the French kitchen are added directly to the finished consommé, making a very attractive presentation.

Prepare Chicken or Beef Consommé, above, adding with the salt: 2 tablespoons very finely diced leeks (white part only), 2 tablespoons very finely diced carrots, and 2 tablespoons very finely diced celery. Simmer gently until the vegetables are tender, about 5 minutes. Ladle into warmed bowls.

MISO SOUPS

Miso soups—miso is fermented bean curd—are an essential part of the traditional Japanese breakfast, though soups thickened with miso also appear at lunch and dinner. In Japan, there are many varieties of miso. Here are two basic miso soups, one based on the light-colored, mellow miso that is popular in Kyoto and Osaka, and the other a dark-colored, pungent red miso that is favored in the region of Tokyo.

LIGHT-COLORED MISO SOUP WITH SIMMERED VEGETABLES *About 4½ cups*

Bring to a simmer in a medium saucepan:

4 cups Dashi, 41

Season with:

1 teaspoon soy sauce
Splash of sake (optional)

Stir in and simmer until barely tender, 2 to 3 minutes:

1 small carrot, peeled, halved lengthwise, and thinly sliced
One 2-inch piece daikon radish, peeled, halved lengthwise, and thinly sliced

Place in a small bowl:

3 tablespoons light-colored miso, such as shiro mugi miso (barley-enriched miso)

Add about ¼ cup of the warm dashi and whisk to dissolve the miso; then whisk this mixture back into the soup. Divide among 4 bowls:

1 small scallion, chopped
2 ounces firm tofu, cut into small cubes

Ladle the hot miso-thickened broth and vegetables into the bowls. Serve immediately.

DARK-COLORED MISO SOUP WITH SAUTÉED VEGETABLES *About 4½ cups*

Soak in cold water for 10 minutes:

1½ teaspoons dried *wakame* bits (optional)

Drain, squeeze out the excess liquid, and divide the *wakame* among 4 soup bowls. Heat in a medium saucepan over high heat:

1 teaspoon vegetable oil

Add and cook, stirring, until slightly browned, about 1 minute:

2 to 3 fresh shiitake mushroom caps, thinly sliced
1 small leek (white part only), cleaned thoroughly and thinly sliced on a diagonal

Add:

Pinch of salt
½ teaspoon sake (optional)

Cook, stirring, until the leeks are wilted, about another minute. Stir in:

4 cups Dashi, 41
1 teaspoon soy sauce

Cook over medium-low heat until warm. Place in a small bowl:

3 to 3½ tablespoons red miso

Add about ¼ cup of the warm dashi and whisk to dissolve the miso; then whisk this mixture back into the soup. Ladle the hot miso-thickened broth and vegetables over the *wakame*. Serve immediately.

MONGOLIAN HOT POT *About 8 cups; 6 to 8 servings*

A hot pot is a round basin with a sort of chimney in the middle containing smoldering coals to heat stock, shown below. This device can be found in Asian shops or specialty cookware stores, but a fondue pot or electric skillet, while not as dramatic, can easily be substituted. In China, diners cook their own meat and vegetables in the sizzlingly hot stock, then dip them into a sauce they assemble from a selection of seasonings set out on the table. When all the meat and vegetables have been eaten, the guests sip the remaining soup. This is a wonderful party dish. The meat is easier to slice thinly if frozen for 20 minutes first.

For the dipping sauce, puree in a blender:

½ cup rice vinegar
⅓ cup sugar or ¼ cup honey
½ cup soy sauce
⅓ cup red miso or rinsed fermented black beans
¼ cup toasted sesame oil
1 tablespoon minced peeled fresh ginger
2 teaspoons chili oil, or more to taste
3 cloves garlic, chopped

Pour the sauce into individual serving bowls and garnish with:

Chopped scallions (about 3 scallions)
Chopped fresh cilantro
Snipped fresh chives

Arrange decoratively on a platter:

2 pounds beef sirloin steak or lamb loin, fat trimmed, thinly sliced
3 cups sliced Napa cabbage
8 ounces firm tofu, cut into 16 pieces
8 ounces spinach, trimmed, washed, and dried

To serve, bring the sauce and platter to the table. Bring to a boil:

Mongolian hot pot

8 to 10 cups Brown Beef Stock, 40

Pour the hot stock into a hot pot, fondue pot, or electric skillet at the table and keep at a simmer. With chopsticks or forks, diners hold the meat or vegetables in the simmering stock until done, then dip it into the sauce and eat. When the ingredients on the platter are finished, combine and let stand for 10 minutes:

4 ounces rice sticks, broken into small pieces
6 cups hot water

Drain and add the noodles to the stock. Ladle the stock and noodles into each bowl over the remaining sauce.

FRUIT SOUPS

We include recipes for fruit soups that are traditionally served as first courses. Feel free to present them as desserts, however. Whichever place they occupy on your menu, they are easy to make, and they cleanse the palate.

FRUIT SOUP

About 6 cups

In many Scandinavian homes in the Midwest, this soup is served before the main course, or set out on the buffet table. It can be made the day before and refrigerated. It is good hot or cold.

Combine in a large saucepan and let stand for 45 minutes:

¾ cup dried apricots or peaches, quartered
¾ cup dried prunes, pitted and quartered
3 tablespoons raisins
2 tablespoons dried currants
Two 3-inch cinnamon sticks
Grated zest of 1 orange
3 tablespoons quick-cooking tapioca
4 cups apple juice, cranberry juice, or water

Stir in:

Up to ¼ cup of sugar

Bring to a boil, reduce the heat to low, and simmer, stirring occasionally, until the fruit is softened and the soup is thickened, about 30 minutes. Stir in:

2 red apples, peeled, cored, and cut into 1-inch pieces

Cook until the apple is tender, about 8 minutes. Let cool and remove the cinnamon sticks. Serve warm or cold, garnished with:

Crème fraîche, sour cream, or heavy cream

CHERRY SOUP

About 6 cups

Here is a sweet-tasting fruit soup eaten as a first course in eastern Europe. We make this in the summer with fresh cherries and serve it cold before the main course. In the winter, we use canned or bottled cherries and serve it heated.

Have ready:

2 pounds cherries, stemmed and pitted, or 4 cups stemmed and pitted canned cherries, drained

Place half of the cherries in a soup pot, along with:

2 cups water
2 cups Gewürztraminer or medium-dry white wine

Bring to a boil, reduce the heat, and simmer until the cherries are soft, about 15 minutes. Puree until smooth. Stir together in a small bowl:

¼ cup sugar
4 teaspoons cornstarch

Add 3 tablespoons of the cherry mixture to the cornstarch and sugar and stir well. Return the cherry puree and the cherry paste to the pot and cook over high heat, whisking until thickened, about 5 minutes. Reduce the heat and stir in the reserved cherries along with:

1 tablespoon fresh orange juice
1 tablespoon fresh lemon juice
1 teaspoon grated orange zest

Simmer until warmed through. Taste for sweetness; if not sweet enough, add additional:

Sugar

If too sweet, add additional:

Lemon juice

Serve warm or cold, garnished with:

Dollop of sour cream or yogurt
Fresh mint sprigs

MELON SOUP

About 8 cups

Ripe cantaloupe and freshly squeezed juices are essential to this no-cook summer soup.

Puree in a food processor until smooth:

2 medium very ripe and sweet cantaloupes or other orange-fleshed melons, peeled, seeded, and cut into chunks

Pour into a large bowl and stir in:

1 cup fresh orange juice
¼ cup fresh lime juice
2 tablespoons fresh lemon juice

Refrigerate until cold, about 2 hours. When ready to serve, prepare:

¼ cup freshly grated peeled ginger

Using a cheesecloth or your hands, squeeze out the ginger juice into a small bowl. Stir 4 teaspoons of the juice into the soup. Serve in chilled bowls, garnished with:

Thinly sliced kiwi fruit or strawberries
Fresh mint sprigs

CHOWDER

The word *chowder* usually conjures up images of a steaming bowl of New England clam chowder. In nineteenth-century New England, "chowder masters," famous for their skill, as well as home cooks, prepared versions of the soup for gatherings on the beach or at home.

The word derives from the French *chaudière,* a type of cauldron, but regional chowders have become an American culinary tradition. Early settlers made chowder from household staples: rendered salt pork was simmered in water with local fish or seafood, then thickened with sea biscuits or bread. In the nineteenth century, potatoes replaced the crackers, and milk and cream came to be added to chowder. Other milk chowders then evolved, including corn chowder.

FRESH CORN CHOWDER

About 6 cups

Place in a soup pot and cook, stirring, over medium-low heat until it releases all of its fat and is beginning to crisp, 10 to 15 minutes:

4 slices bacon, chopped

Leaving the bacon in the pan, spoon off all but 2 tablespoons of fat. Add and cook, stirring, until tender and slightly browned, 10 to 15 minutes:

1 small onion, chopped
2 medium celery stalks, diced

Remove the kernels from:

6 small ears of corn

Reserve the kernels and add the cobs to the soup pot along with:

4½ cups milk
2 medium potatoes, peeled and diced

Push the corn cobs into the milk to fully submerge them. Bring the milk to a boil. Reduce the heat and simmer, covered, until the potatoes are tender, 10 to 15 minutes. Remove the cobs. Stir in the reserved corn kernels along with:

1½ teaspoons salt
½ teaspoon ground white or black pepper

Simmer gently until the corn is tender, about 5 minutes. With a slotted spoon, remove 1½ cups solids from the soup and puree until smooth. Return to the soup and add:

1 tablespoon unsalted butter

Let stand until the butter is melted, then stir. Ladle into warmed bowls.

CORN CHOWDER WITH CHILI PEPPERS

About 5 cups

A spicy, meatless corn chowder.

Heat in a soup pot, over medium-low heat until the butter is melted:

1 tablespoon unsalted butter
1 tablespoon vegetable oil

Add and cook, stirring, until tender but not browned, 5 to 10 minutes:

1 medium onion, diced
1 medium poblano pepper, seeded and diced
2 cloves garlic, minced
½ fresh jalapeño pepper, seeded and diced

Stir in:

3 cups milk
2 cups fresh corn kernels (from 2 to 3 ears)
1 teaspoon salt

Bring to a boil, reduce the heat, and simmer gently until the corn is tender, about 3 minutes. Stir in:

1 large ripe tomato, peeled, seeded, and coarsely chopped

Simmer gently for about 2 minutes to marry the flavors. With a slotted spoon, remove 1½ cups solids from the soup and puree until smooth. Return to the soup. Heat gently just to warm through. Stir in:

1 tablespoon chopped fresh cilantro

Ladle into warmed bowls. If you like, pass at the table:

Lime wedges

NEW ENGLAND CLAM CHOWDER

About 4 cups

This recipe from Boston chef Jasper White gets its creamy thickness from heavy cream and the starch in the potatoes.

Scrub individually with a vegetable brush:

5 pounds quahogs or other hard-shell clams

Place in a sink or large soup pot, cover with cold water, and stir in:

¼ cup salt

Let stand for 30 minutes to rid the clams of sand. Rinse and drain in a colander. Place the clams in a large soup pot and add:

1 cup water
Any scraps of onion, celery, thyme, or bay leaf (optional)

Cover and steam over high heat until the clams are completely open, 10 to 15 minutes. Discard any that do not open. Pour the cooking liquid through a fine-mesh sieve and set aside. When the clams are cool enough to handle, remove from their shells and coarsely chop into ⅜-inch pieces.

Place in a soup pot and cook, stirring, over medium heat until slightly crisp:

2 slices bacon or 2 ounces salt pork, diced

Stir in:

1 medium onion, cut into ½-inch dice
1 bay leaf
½ tablespoon chopped fresh thyme
1 tablespoon unsalted butter

When the onions are translucent, add the reserved cooking liquid along with:

3 red or white new potatoes, cut into ½-inch dice

Bring to a boil, reduce the heat, and simmer until the potatoes are tender, about 12 minutes. Stir in the chopped clams along with:

1 cup heavy cream

Simmer for 5 minutes. Season with:

Ground black pepper to taste
1 tablespoon chopped fresh parsley

Ladle into soup dishes or cups. Serve with:

Cream Biscuits, 790, or common crackers

MANHATTAN CLAM CHOWDER *About 10 cups*

Salt pork, onions, seafood, potatoes, and, most of the time, milk make a traditional chowder. Manhattan clam chowder substitutes tomatoes for the milk. Some consider this blasphemy, others say it simply is not chowder, others want nothing else.

Scrub individually with a vegetable brush:

10 to 12 pounds quahogs or other hard-shell clams, preferably 2 to 3 inches across

Place in a sink or large soup pot, cover with cold water, and stir in:

¼ cup salt

Let stand for 30 minutes to rid the clams of sand. Rinse and drain in a colander. Place the clams in a large soup pot and add:

2 cups water

Cover and steam over high heat until the clams are completely open, 10 to 15 minutes. Discard any that do not open. Pour the cooking liquid through a fine-mesh sieve and set aside. When the clams are cool enough to handle, remove from the shell and chop finely. Heat in a large skillet, over medium heat:

1 tablespoon vegetable oil

Add and cook, stirring occasionally, until browned:

3 slices bacon, finely chopped

Add and cook, stirring, until tender but not browned, 5 to 10 minutes:

2 medium onions, chopped
½ green bell pepper, diced
1 large celery stalk, diced

Stir in the reserved cooking liquid along with:

One 28-ounce can whole plum tomatoes, with juice, chopped
3 cups Fish Fumet, 41, or Express Fish Broth, 43

Bring to a boil. Stir in:

1 pound potatoes, peeled and cut into 1-inch dice

Reduce the heat to medium-low and simmer until the potatoes are tender, about 20 minutes. Stir in the chopped clams and season with:

½ teaspoon ground black pepper
2 tablespoons chopped fresh parsley

Simmer briefly, then ladle into warmed bowls.

RHODE ISLAND (PORTUGUESE-STYLE) CLAM CHOWDER

As unconventional as Manhattan clam chowder, but very tasty.

Prepare Manhattan Clam Chowder, above, substituting 2 tablespoons olive oil for the bacon and adding along with the clams 6 ounces thinly sliced Portuguese linguiça or chorizo and ¼ to ½ teaspoon red pepper flakes. Simmer over low heat for 10 minutes. Ladle into warmed bowls.

PACIFIC NORTHWEST SALMON CHOWDER *About 5 cups*

This chowder is enriched with a cream reduction.

In a small saucepan, simmer, whisking occasionally, until reduced to ⅔ cup:

1 cup heavy cream

Meanwhile, melt in a soup pot over medium heat:

1 tablespoon unsalted butter

Add and cook, stirring, until the leeks are tender but not browned, 5 to 10 minutes:

2 medium leeks (white part only), cleaned thoroughly and chopped
¼ cup dry vermouth
1 clove garlic, minced

Stir in:

3 cups Fish Stock, 41, Fish Fumet, 41, or Express Fish Broth, 43
2 red or white new potatoes, diced
½ teaspoon salt

Bring to a boil, reduce the heat, and simmer until the potatoes are cooked, 10 to 15 minutes. Reduce the heat to low. Add the reduced cream along with:

1 salmon fillet (about 12 ounces)
¼ teaspoon ground black or white pepper

Simmer just until the salmon is cooked, 8 to 10 minutes, depending on the thickness of the fish. Gently break apart the fillet with a wooden spoon. Serve immediately, garnished with:

Small dill sprigs

LANDLUBBER'S FISH CHOWDER

12 to 14 cups; 8 to 10 servings

Use salmon, monkfish, tautog, cod, or wolffish here. Flaky fish, such as flounder, mackerel, or sea bass, tend to fall apart too easily. Serve as a main course for lunch or dinner. For a reduced-fat fish chowder, omit the cream.

Remove any excess skin and, using tweezers, pick out any bones from:

3½ pounds boneless, skinless fish fillets

If you have to use a knife to cut out the bones, be sure to leave the fillets in pieces as large as possible. Place in a large soup pot and cook, stirring, over low heat until it is beginning to crisp, 10 to 15 minutes:

4 ounces meaty salt pork or 4 slices bacon, cut into ¼- to ½-inch dice

Add and cook, stirring, until the onions are tender but not browned, 10 to 15 minutes:

4 tablespoons (½ stick) unsalted butter
2 large onions, cut into 1-inch dice
3 bay leaves
1 tablespoon chopped fresh thyme

Stir in:

3 large Maine or other boiling potatoes, peeled, halved lengthwise, and cut into ¼-inch-thick slices
3 cups Fish Stock, 41, Fish Fumet, 41, or Express Fish Broth, 43

Bring to a boil, reduce the heat, and simmer until the potatoes are tender, about 20 minutes. Remove the bay leaves and stir in the fish fillets along with:

2 cups heavy cream

Simmer until the fish is cooked through and beginning to flake, 8 to 10 minutes. Season with:

Salt and ground black pepper to taste
2 tablespoons chopped fresh parsley and/or chervil

Remove from the heat. Ladle into soup dishes. Top each serving with:

Dollop of butter

Serve with:

Cream Biscuits, 790, or common crackers

FISH AND SEAFOOD SOUPS

Fish and seafood lend themselves to soups and stews, because they stay moist and tender when cooked at a low temperature and closely watched. But they are easy to overcook, so serve or remove from the heat as soon as the fish is cooked. A light chicken stock is often a better substitute for fish fumet than many commercial fish or clam broths, which may add a fishy taste to the soup. With the exception of most chowders, which tend to sit well overnight, generally fish soups are best eaten as soon as they are cooked.

OYSTER STEW

About 4 cups

A double boiler prevents overcooking of the oysters. In many New England homes, this is often served before the turkey at Thanksgiving.

Combine in the top of a double boiler set directly over medium-low heat:

2 to 4 tablespoons unsalted butter
1 tablespoon or more grated onions or leeks, a sliver of garlic, or ½ cup minced celery

Cook, stirring, until the butter is melted and the onion is tender but not browned, about 5 minutes. Stir in:

1 to 1½ pints shucked oysters, with their liquor
1½ cups milk
½ cup light cream
½ teaspoon salt
⅛ teaspoon ground white pepper or sweet or hot paprika

Place the top of the double boiler over, not in, boiling water. When the milk is hot and the oysters are floating, stir in:

2 tablespoons chopped fresh parsley

Ladle into warmed bowls.

OYSTER BISQUE

Prepare Oyster Stew, above, but before adding the parsley, remove the stew from the heat and pour a small quantity over 2 beaten egg yolks. After mixing, add them slowly to the hot stew. Heat over low heat for 1 minute, but do not allow to boil. Serve immediately.

LOBSTER BISQUE

About 8 cups

A classic lobster bisque derives its deep flavor and dusky-pink color from beef stock and its distinctive, velvety body from rice. The soup should be thick but not too thick, so thin it as necessary before serving.

Combine in a wide, deep pot or Dutch oven and bring to a boil over high heat:

5 cups water
2 cups dry white wine
2 cups Fish Stock, 41, or Fish Fumet, 41
1 cup Classic Beef Stock, 40, or Brown Beef Stock, 40

Place in the pot back side down:

2 live lobsters (1¼ to 1½ pounds each)

Cover the pot tightly, return the liquid to a boil, and cook for 6 minutes. Turn the lobsters with tongs, cover the pot, and cook for 6 minutes more. Remove from the heat. Remove the lobsters from the broth. When cool enough to handle, remove the meat from the shells and discard the coral and green matter (tomalley). Cover and refrigerate the meat. Chop the shells and bodies, return to the broth, and simmer, uncovered, for 45 minutes. Strain through a fine-mesh sieve and discard the solids. You need 6 cups of broth. If you have more, boil it over high heat until reduced to 6 cups. If you have less, add water to make 6 cups. Melt in a large saucepan over medium heat:

3 to 4 tablespoons unsalted butter

Add and cook, stirring, until tender but not browned, 5 to 10 minutes:

1 cup finely chopped onions
⅓ cup finely chopped carrots
⅓ cup finely chopped celery

Stir in the 6 cups of broth along with:

1½ cups chopped, seeded, peeled tomatoes, fresh or canned
⅓ cup long-grain rice
1 bay leaf
1½ teaspoons minced fresh tarragon, or ½ teaspoon dried
1 teaspoon sweet or hot paprika
½ teaspoon minced garlic
½ teaspoon salt
¼ teaspoon dried thyme
⅛ teaspoon ground red pepper

Bring to a boil, reduce the heat, and simmer, partially covered, for 40 minutes. Meanwhile, cut the lobster meat into ¼-inch dice. Melt in a medium skillet over medium heat:

2 to 4 tablespoons unsalted butter

Add the lobster meat and cook, stirring, until heated through. Stir in:

¼ cup Cognac or brandy
¼ teaspoon salt
¼ teaspoon ground white pepper, preferably freshly ground

Cook, stirring, until nearly all of the liquid is evaporated. Set aside ⅓ cup of the meat for garnish. Add the rest of the meat and any juices to the soup mixture. Remove the bay leaf. In a food processor or, preferably, a blender, puree the soup in small batches until smooth. Return the soup to the saucepan and stir in the reserved lobster meat along with:

½ to 1 cup heavy cream

Heat the bisque through over low heat. Thin, if necessary, with:

Clam broth or milk

Remove from the heat and season with:

Drops of fresh lemon juice to taste
Salt and ground white pepper to taste
Ground red pepper to taste

If you wish, garnish each serving with:

2 tablespoons minced fresh tarragon or parsley

SHRIMP BISQUE

Prepare Lobster Bisque, above, substituting 1 pound shell-on shrimp for the lobsters. Steam the shrimp until the shells turn pink and curl, about 2 minutes, and simmer the shells for only 30 minutes.

LOUISIANA COURT-BOUILLON *About 7 cups*

A court-bouillon is a light-flavored broth used for cooking food, primarily fish, but also vegetables and meat. This is not a classic court-bouillon but a spicy Cajun fish and tomato stew that is sometimes served as a soup. Redfish or snapper is often used in this dish, but you can use any white flaky fish. For variety, we have added shrimp, but feel free to omit or to add your favorite shellfish.

Heat in a large skillet over medium heat:

3 tablespoons vegetable oil

Add and cook, stirring, until lightly browned, about 5 minutes:

3 tablespoons all-purpose flour

Add and cook, stirring, just until softened, about 3 minutes:

½ cup diced green bell peppers
½ cup diced celery
½ cup diced onions
2 cloves garlic, minced
½ teaspoon dried thyme

Stir in:

One 28-ounce can whole plum tomatoes, drained and coarsely chopped
2 cups Fish Stock, 41, Fish Fumet, 41, or Express Fish Broth, 43

Bring to a boil, reduce the heat to medium-low, and simmer for 10 minutes. Stir in:

1 pound flaky white fish fillets (such as haddock or snapper), cut into 2-inch pieces
12 small shrimp (about ¼ pound), peeled and deveined

Cover and cook until the fish is opaque in the center, about 3 minutes. Season with:

2 teaspoons Worcestershire sauce
1 teaspoon salt
¾ to 1¼ teaspoons hot red pepper sauce

Stir in:

½ to ¾ cup cooked long-grain rice

Taste and adjust the seasonings, adding more Worcestershire and hot red pepper sauce as desired. Ladle into warmed bowls.

CHARLESTON CRAB SOUP
About 4 cups

From South Carolina's low country, this quick and easy soup makes an elegant first course or light main course. It is called she-crab soup when made with female crabs and their flavorful, colorful roe.

Melt in a large saucepan, over low heat:

3 tablespoons unsalted butter

Whisk in:

3 tablespoons all-purpose flour

Cook, whisking, until the flour smells toasted but is not browned, about 3 minutes. Gradually whisk in:

3 cups milk
1 teaspoon Worcestershire sauce
¾ teaspoon hot red pepper sauce

Bring to a boil, whisking, reduce the heat, and simmer for about 5 minutes. Reduce the heat to low and stir in:

1 pound lump crabmeat, picked over for shells and cartilage, with roe if available
1 to 2 tablespoons dry sherry
¾ teaspoon salt

Taste and adjust the seasonings, adding more hot red pepper sauce if desired. Heat gently just until the crab is warmed through. Ladle into warmed bowls. Garnish with:

Thinly sliced scallion greens

CREAM OF MUSSEL SOUP (BILLI BI)
About 4 cups

This is a French mussel soup made with cream and white wine. The secret to this soup is to strain the mussel cooking liquid through several layers of cheesecloth to make sure you trap every possible grain of sand. You will find the optional curry powder at the end to be a perfect accent against the creamy broth.

Scrub individually with a vegetable brush:

3 pounds small mussels

Remove the beards. Discard any damaged mussels or those that do not close with a sharp tap on the counter. Place the mussels in a large soup pot along with:

1½ cups dry white wine
⅓ cup chopped shallots
5 sprigs fresh parsley
3 sprigs fresh thyme

Cover and steam over medium heat until the mussels are completely open. Discard any that do not open. Pour the cooking liquid through a sieve lined with several layers of dampened cheesecloth or paper towels into a medium saucepan. Bring to a low simmer. When the mussels are cool enough to handle, remove from their shells. Whisk together in a small bowl:

1 cup heavy cream or half-and-half
1 large egg yolk

Gradually whisk about 1 cup of the cooking liquid into the egg mixture, then whisk back into the saucepan. Heat gently, but do not boil. Season with:

Salt to taste
Pinch of ground red or white pepper
½ teaspoon curry powder (optional)

Ladle into warmed bowls. Garnish with the reserved mussels and sprinkle with:

Snipped fresh chives

CARIBBEAN CALLALOO
About 12 cups

Callaloo is the name given to a family of plants favored in the Caribbean for their tart green leaves. Callaloo leaves are occasionally found canned in Caribbean markets, but fresh spinach and Swiss chard are good substitutes. This soup can also be served over rice as a main course.

Place in a soup pot and cook, stirring, over medium heat until almost crisp:

3 slices bacon, thinly sliced crosswise

Leaving the bacon in the pot, pour off all but 1 teaspoon of the fat and add:

8 ounces ham, cubed
1 medium onion, chopped
1 clove garlic, minced
3 scallions, thinly sliced

Cook, stirring, until the onions are tender but not browned, 5 to 10 minutes.

Stir in:

1 pound callaloo, spinach, or Swiss chard, trimmed, washed, dried, and coarsely chopped
5 cups Chicken Stock, 39
¼ teaspoon dried thyme

Cover, bring to a boil, and simmer for 5 minutes. Reduce the heat, remove the cover, and add:

8 ounces lump crabmeat, picked over for shells and cartilage, or sliced raw shrimp
8 ounces white fish fillets (such as tilefish, cod, grouper, or sea bass), cooked or raw

½ teaspoon salt
8 ounces fresh okra, sliced, or frozen sliced okra
1 cup unsweetened coconut milk
Ground black pepper to taste

Simmer until the okra and fish are cooked, about 10 minutes. The fillets will break up as they cook. Serve immediately.

SARDINIAN SEAFOOD STEW (CASSOLA)

About 8 cups; 4 to 6 servings

This differs from other seafood stews in that its base integrates the flavor of squid, which needs to braise a bit. But you can prepare the dish up to 1 day in advance up to that point. If making ahead, keep refrigerated.

Soak in a small amount of hot water to cover for 30 minutes:

5 sun-dried tomato halves, preferably packed in oil

Drain and reserve the soaking liquid. Chop the tomatoes and reserve.

Scrub individually with a vegetable brush:

1 pound small mussels

Remove the beards. Discard any damaged mussels or those that do not close with a sharp tap on the counter. Place the mussels in a large soup pot, along with:

1 cup dry white wine

Lift the mussels from the pot and remove most of them from their shells, but reserve a few in the shells for garnish. Continue to cook the cooking liquid until reduced to about 1 cup. Pour through a sieve lined with several layers of dampened cheesecloth or paper towels, and set aside. Place in a large saucepan along with the drained sun-dried tomatoes:

1 tablespoon olive oil
1 medium onion, chopped
½ cup chopped fresh basil

Cook, stirring, over medium heat until the onions are golden, 10 to 15 minutes. Add:

½ pound squid, cleaned, 503, and cut into bite-sized pieces

Increase the heat to high and cook, stirring almost constantly, until the squid begins to brown, 3 to 4 minutes. Add the reserved tomato soaking liquid along with:

1 teaspoon minced garlic
1 dried red chili pepper

Cook, stirring, until the liquid is evaporated, about 2 minutes. Stir in the reserved mussel cooking liquid along with:

3 cups chopped, seeded, peeled tomatoes, fresh or canned
2 cups Fish Stock, 41, Fish Fumet, 41, Express Fish Broth, 43, or water

Bring to a boil, reduce the heat to medium-low, and simmer, stirring occasionally, until the squid is tender, about 1 hour. Remove the chili pepper and stir in:

2 tablespoons red wine vinegar

Add:

1 pound shrimp, peeled, deveined, if desired
1 pound firm white-fleshed fish fillets or steaks, such as snapper, halibut, grouper, or monkfish

Cover and cook until the fish is tender, 5 to 10 minutes. The fish fillets will break up as they cook. Add the shelled mussels to the pot and cook just until heated through. Season with:

Salt and ground black pepper to taste

Garnish with the reserved mussels in their shells and sprinkle with:

Minced fresh parsley

Serve with:

Crusty French bread

BOUILLABAISSE

About 8 cups; 4 to 6 servings

In this classic Provençal fisherman's stew, the only rule is that it should be a mix of different kinds of fish and shellfish paired with a combination of garlic, tomato, saffron, and fennel. The seafood suggestions in this recipe are only a guide. Feel free to substitute whatever you can find very fresh at the market. Well-scrubbed clams, mussels, shrimp, all in the shell, can be added, as can a number of fish types: snapper, halibut, and perch, to name a few. Remember that bouillabaisse should capture the flavor of the freshest catch of the day, and need not adhere to strict rules.

Heat in a large saucepan, over medium heat until the butter is melted:

1 tablespoon olive oil
1 tablespoon unsalted butter

Add and cook, stirring occasionally, until the vegetables are tender but not browned, 5 to 10 minutes:

1 medium leek (white and green parts), cleaned thoroughly, halved lengthwise, and cut into ½-inch pieces
1 small fennel bulb, quartered, cored, and thinly sliced
1 medium celery stalk, cut into thin diagonal slices
1 bay leaf
1 star anise, or ¼ teaspoon anise seeds or fennel seeds (optional)
¼ teaspoon saffron threads
½ teaspoon salt

Add:

3 cloves garlic, minced

Cook, stirring, for 2 minutes more. Reduce the heat if the bottom begins to scorch. Add:

1 tablespoon tomato paste

Cook, stirring, for 1 minute. Stir in:

½ cup dry white wine

Bring to a gentle boil and cook for 3 minutes. Stir in:

1½ cups canned whole tomatoes, with juice, broken into pieces

2 cups Fish Stock, 41, Fish Fumet, 41, or Express Fish Broth, 43

½ teaspoon ground red pepper

¾ teaspoon salt

Bring to a boil, reduce the heat, cover, and simmer for 20 minutes. The bouillabaisse broth can be made a day in advance.

Bring to the smoking point in a large soup pot over high heat:

2 tablespoons olive oil

Add:

12 littleneck clams, well scrubbed

Cook, stirring, for 2 to 3 minutes. Keep the oil from smoking. Remove the star anise if using, and add the reserved broth. Bring to a boil, reduce the heat, and simmer for 3 minutes. Stir in:

¾ pound monkfish, sea bass, red snapper, or halibut fillets, or a combination, cut into 1½-inch pieces

Continue to cook, covered, for 1 minute. Stir in:

12 sea scallops (about ½ pound)

Cook just until the seafood is done, 2 to 3 minutes more. Discard any clams that are not open. Stir in:

2 tablespoons Pernod or anisette (optional)

Serve with:

Croutons

Rouille, 75

BOURRIDE OF MONKFISH AND CLAMS

About 8 cups

This is a modern take on the classic fish soup from Provence. In honoring the dish's origins, we have stirred the local mayonnaise (aïoli) right into the fish broth. This is an easy dish to prepare and a great dish for company. Shell the clams for a more elegant presentation or arrange them in their shells over the top of the bourride.

Heat in a large nonreactive skillet over medium-high heat:

¼ cup olive oil

Have ready:

2 pounds monkfish fillets, cut into 2 x 1-inch pieces

Sprinkle with:

Ground black pepper to taste

Place the fish in the skillet in an even layer and cook until browned on one side, 5 to 7 minutes. Turn the monkfish over and stir in:

24 small littleneck clams, well scrubbed

3 medium leeks (white and tender green parts), cleaned thoroughly and cut crosswise into ¼-inch-thick slices

1 teaspoon chopped fresh thyme

¼ teaspoon saffron threads

Pinch of red pepper flakes

1½ cups dry white wine

Cover the skillet, reduce the heat to medium, and cook until the clams are completely open, 8 to 15 minutes. Discard any that do not open. Remove from the heat and remove the clams from the skillet. Shell the clams and return them to the skillet. If leaving clams in the shell, add them. Add:

1 cup Aïoli, 74, using the larger amount of garlic

Gently shake the skillet and stir the sauce with a wooden spoon until it is thickened and coats the fish and clams. Stir in:

1 teaspoon fresh lemon juice

Season with:

Ground black pepper to taste

Ladle into warmed shallow bowls and sprinkle with:

1 tablespoon chopped fresh parsley

Pass separately to float atop the soup:

Garlic croutons

ABOUT MEAT SOUPS AND POULTRY SOUPS

Many of these robust soups can be served as a full meal. All the meat soups here require long simmering. This allows economical cuts of meat to become tender and impart their full flavor to the soup.

Tough but flavorful stewing hens are difficult to find, so the poultry soups in this section are made with chicken. Because chicken cooks fast, it is easy to prepare substantial soup quickly. All chicken, especially white meat, becomes dry and stringy with overcooking. So reheat the soup gently, just until hot. Improvise your own versions with seasonal ingredients on hand.

BORSCHT

About 8 cups

This is the original Russian borscht, meaty and brimming with tomatoes and cabbage. The beets in this version are roasted instead of boiled, for added flavor. For a complete meal, serve with black bread and butter.

Preheat the oven to 400°F.

Scrub:

12 ounces beets

Wrap the beets together in aluminum foil and roast on a baking sheet until they can easily be pierced with a fork, about 1 hour. Let cool, peel, then slice and cut into thin strips.

While the beets are roasting, prepare:

1 pound boneless beef chuck, cubed, or 1½ pounds pork spareribs, cut into single ribs

Lightly dredge with:

All-purpose flour

Heat in a soup pot, over medium-high heat:

2 tablespoons vegetable oil

Add the meat and brown on all sides. Stir in:

4½ cups Brown Beef Stock, 40, or water
One 28-ounce can whole plum tomatoes, drained and chopped

Bring to a boil, reduce the heat, and simmer, partially covered, until the meat is almost tender, about 30 minutes. Stir in:

2 cups shredded green or red cabbage
1 medium onion, chopped
2 medium carrots, peeled and sliced
2 medium celery stalks, sliced
1½ teaspoons tomato paste

Simmer, partially covered, until the vegetables and meat are tender, about 30 minutes. Stir in the beets along with:

2 tablespoons red wine vinegar
2 teaspoons fresh lemon juice
2 cloves garlic, minced
½ teaspoon salt, or to taste
¾ teaspoon ground black pepper
1½ teaspoons sugar (optional)

Simmer, partially covered, for 15 minutes. Thin the soup with water if necessary. Ladle into warmed bowls. Garnish with:

Sour cream
Snipped fresh dill

FRENCH SIMMERED BEEF AND VEGETABLES (POT-AU-FEU)

About 10 cups broth; 4 to 6 servings

This hearty French boiled dinner features a variety of meats, mostly beef, and vegetables. The cooking broth is strained, seasoned, and served first in warmed bowls, then the meat and marrow bones are presented on a platter, accompanied by mustard and cornichons (French pickles), and toast on which to spread the succulent marrow.

Combine in a large soup pot, and cover with cold water:

4 beef short ribs (about 2½ pounds)
4 beef marrowbones, wrapped in cheesecloth
2 pounds beef shank, cut into 2-inch-thick slices

Bring to a boil, reduce the heat to low, and simmer, partially covered, for 2 hours. Stir in:

4 chicken thighs, skin removed
12 ounces whole sausage
4 medium carrots, cut into 1-inch pieces
4 medium leeks (white and tender green parts), cleaned thoroughly, halved lengthwise, and cut into 1-inch pieces
2 medium turnips, peeled and cut into 1-inch pieces
3 medium celery stalks, cut into 1-inch pieces

Simmer, partially covered, until the chicken is cooked, 30 to 40 minutes. Remove and reserve the meat and vegetables. Strain the broth and return it to the pot. Reduce to 10 cups over high heat. Slice the beef shank and sausage, then arrange the meat, vegetables, and marrowbones on a platter. Cover with aluminum foil and keep warm in a 200°F oven. Skim the fat off the surface of the broth with a ladle. Season with:

1½ teaspoons salt
Ground black pepper to taste

Heat the broth and ladle into warmed bowls. Serve the meat platter accompanied with:

Dijon or whole-grain mustard
Coarse salt
Cornichons
Toasted sliced French bread

VIETNAMESE BEEF NOODLE SOUP (PHO BO)

About 12 cups; 4 to 6 servings

In North Vietnam, this light, flavorful, visually exciting soup is a favorite for breakfast, lunch, and dinner. It has given rise to numerous *pho* restaurants all over the United States. The broth can be made in advance and easily refrigerated or frozen. But, when served, be sure the meat is thinly sliced and the broth boiling hot.

BEFORE COOKING

Have ready:

¼ cup thinly sliced peeled fresh ginger
1 medium onion, sliced
3½ pounds oxtail, cut into 2-inch pieces (have your butcher do this)
One 3-inch cinnamon stick
6 star anise
1 tablespoon salt
1 teaspoon soy sauce
One 1-inch piece Chinese yellow rock sugar (optional)

Place on a plate:

12 ounces round steak, sliced as thinly as possible (more easily done if partially frozen)

Place on a second plate:

2 serrano peppers, thinly sliced
24 fresh basil leaves, halved
¼ cup 2-inch pieces scallion, halved lengthwise

Place on a third plate:

2 cups bean sprouts
3 tablespoons coarsely chopped fresh basil
Lime wedges
3 fresh chili peppers, coarsely chopped

TO COOK:

Heat a large soup pot over medium-high heat. When fairly hot, turn in the ginger and onion slices. Cook, stirring, until fragrant.

Add the oxtail and cook, stirring, briefly. Stir in:

3½ quarts cold water

Bring to a boil. Skim off the impurities that rise to the surface.

Stir in the cinnamon, star anise, salt, soy sauce, and rock sugar if using.

Reduce the heat and simmer the soup for 2½ to 3 hours, skimming as needed. Strain and reserve.

About 30 minutes before the broth is done, soak in cold water to cover:

12 ounces dried flat rice stick noodles (*banh pho*)

Bring to a boil in a large pot:

4 quarts water

Add the rice stick noodles. Cook for about 1 minute. Drain.

TO SERVE:

Divide the noodles among individual soup bowls.

Add the slices of raw beef to each bowl, arranging them attractively.

Divide the serrano peppers, basil leaves, and scallions among the bowls.

While arranging the individual soup bowls, bring the beef broth to a boil over high heat. Immediately fill each bowl with the boiling broth and serve. If the broth is added at the table, diners have the pleasure of watching it cook the beef and noodles.

Place the plate of bean sprouts, basil, lime, and chili peppers on the table, allowing diners to help themselves.

OXTAIL SOUP

About 5 cups

One story claims this rich meaty soup was born of necessity during the French Reign of Terror in 1793. During that period of privation, hides were delivered to the tanneries complete with tails. These were commonly thrown away, until one day a hungry nobleman pleaded for a tail and made it into soup.

Heat in a soup pot over medium-high heat:

1½ tablespoons extra-virgin olive oil

Add and brown on all sides:

2 pounds oxtail (about 1 disjointed oxtail)

Stir in:

6 cups water
1 large carrot, peeled and diced
1 large celery stalk, diced
1 large onion, diced
2 cloves garlic, peeled
4 black peppercorns

Bring to a boil, reduce the heat, and simmer, partially covered, until the meat comes effortlessly from the bone, 3 to 4 hours. As the water evaporates during cooking, add only enough water to keep the meat submerged. Remove the oxtail from the soup. Discard the fat and bones and reserve the meat. Refrigerate the soup until cold, then remove the fat.

When ready to serve, return the meat to the soup. Heat and season with:

¼ teaspoon salt

Ladle into warmed bowls. Garnish with:

Chopped fresh parsley

Pass at the table:

Ground black pepper

OXTAIL SOUP WITH VEGETABLES

Prepare Oxtail Soup, above, adding with the salt: 1 medium leek (white part only), cleaned thoroughly and cut into thin strips; 1 small carrot, cut into thin strips; 1 small celery stalk, cut into thin strips; ¼ teaspoon additional salt. Simmer until the vegetables are tender, about 15 minutes. Add the meat and complete as directed.

SCOTCH BROTH

About 6 cups

This Scottish classic is hundreds of years old in origin.

Bring to a boil in a soup pot:

6 cups water
1½ pounds lamb shoulder, trimmed of fat and cut into ½-inch pieces

Reduce the heat, and simmer for 10 minutes. Skim the impurities from the surface. Stir in:

½ cup pearl barley
3 medium leeks (white part only), cleaned thoroughly and chopped

1 large carrot, peeled and diced
1 large celery stalk, diced
½ teaspoon salt

Bring to a boil, reduce the heat, and simmer, partially covered, until the meat is tender, about 1½ hours. Replenish the water as needed. Spoon off the fat from the surface and season with:

Salt and ground black pepper to taste
2 tablespoons chopped fresh parsley

CHICKEN SOUP COCKAIGNE

About 10 cups

This classic chicken soup has a few surprises in it. The sweet taste of parsnips adds a wonderful note, as does the hint of ground mace. Vary the vegetables using your favorites and substitute ¼ cup rice or 2 ounces egg noodles for the potatoes, if desired.

Bring to a boil in a soup pot:

8 cups Chicken Stock, 39
1 whole chicken (about 3 pounds), cut into serving pieces, or 3 pounds chicken parts
3 large carrots, diced
3 parsnips or 2 small purple-top turnips, peeled and diced (optional)
3 large celery stalks, diced
3 medium onions, coarsely chopped
2 medium leeks (white part only), cleaned thoroughly and sliced
2 large garlic cloves, minced
1 bouquet garni, 37
¼ teaspoon ground black pepper
¼ teaspoon ground mace (optional)

Reduce the heat and simmer until the chicken is well cooked, about 1 hour. Remove the chicken to a plate and let cool. Meanwhile, add to the soup pot:

2 medium Maine or new potatoes, diced

Simmer until tender, 15 to 20 minutes. Discard the bouquet garni and turn off the heat. When the chicken is cool enough to handle, remove and discard the skin and bones. Shred the meat and add to the soup. Reheat over medium heat and season with:

¼ cup chopped fresh parsley
Salt and ground black pepper to taste

Ladle into warmed bowls.

CHICKEN GUMBO

About 10 cups

Quingombo, an African Congo word for okra, became "gumbo" in Louisiana and came to be known as a thick soup/stew thickened either with okra or with filé powder (ground sassafras root). This version gets its distinctive taste from a dark roux of oil and flour and a mix of dried spices. Make it a day or two ahead if you can, for it only improves with time.

Combine in a small bowl and reserve:

½ cup chopped celery
½ cup chopped onions
½ cup chopped green bell peppers

Combine in a plastic or paper bag:

2 teaspoons ground red pepper
1½ teaspoons salt
1 teaspoon ground black pepper
1 teaspoon garlic powder

Add and shake until completely covered:

1 whole chicken (about 3 pounds), cut into serving pieces

Add and shake again:

½ cup all-purpose flour

Heat in a large cast-iron or other skillet over medium heat:

2 to 4 tablespoons vegetable oil

Add and brown the chicken pieces on all sides, 5 to 10 minutes. Remove and set aside. Add to the skillet, scraping up the browned bits:

½ cup vegetable oil

Whisk in:

½ cup all-purpose flour

Cook, stirring often, over medium-low heat until the roux turns reddish brown, 5 to 6 minutes. Gently stir with a long-handled wooden spoon, using caution, because the roux is extremely hot and sticks to the skin. (If black specks appear, the roux is burned—so begin again in a clean pot.) Remove from the heat, add the reserved vegetables, and stir until the roux stops bubbling, 1 to 2 minutes. Carefully add the roux and vegetable mixture to a soup pot. Whisk in:

8 cups Chicken Stock, 39, or Brown Chicken Stock, 39

Bring to a boil, whisking. Reduce the heat and add the chicken. Simmer until the chicken is cooked through, about 30 to 45 minutes. Remove the chicken from the pot and discard the skin and bones, shred the meat, and reserve. Stir into the soup pot:

12 ounces andouille or chorizo sausage, cut into thin slices or small cubes
1 tablespoon chopped garlic

Simmer until the sausage is cooked through, about 10 minutes. Stir in the reserved chicken meat along with:

½ cup chopped scallions
Salt to taste
Hot red pepper sauce to taste

Ladle into warmed bowls. Garnish with:

Sliced scallion greens

PENNSYLVANIA DUTCH CHICKEN CORN SOUP

About 6 cups

Use any type of wide egg noodle in this soup, or make your own, 318. Some recipes call for a garnish of popcorn to reinforce the corn flavor and to add some crunch to the soup.

Bring to a boil in a soup pot:

6 cups water, or 3 cups water and 3 cups Chicken Stock, 39
1½ to 2 pounds chicken parts, or ½ whole chicken, cut into serving pieces
1 teaspoon salt (½ teaspoon if using chicken stock)
⅛ teaspoon ground black pepper

Skim the impurities from the surface. Reduce the heat and simmer, covered, until the chicken is well cooked, about 1 hour. Remove the chicken, discard the skin and bones, shred the meat, and set aside. (At this point you can remove the surface fat with a small ladle.) Bring the stock to a boil. Stir in:

1¾ cups short, wide egg noodles
1 cup fresh or frozen corn kernels

Cook, stirring occasionally, until the noodles are tender but firm. Stir in the shredded chicken along with:

1 hard-boiled egg, chopped
1½ tablespoons chopped fresh parsley

Ladle into warmed bowls.

PUERTO RICAN CHICKEN RICE SOUP (ASOPAO DE POLLO)

About 9 cups

This dish is traditionally made with annatto seeds, which give the soup its characteristically yellow color; this recipe uses ground annatto, but it can be omitted. Serve this soup/stew as soon as it cooks, before the rice absorbs the broth.

For the adobo seasonings, combine:

1½ teaspoons garlic powder
1½ teaspoons onion powder
1½ teaspoons dried oregano
¾ teaspoon salt
¾ teaspoon ground black pepper

Rub the spices into the skin of:

1 whole chicken (about 3 pounds), cut into serving pieces

Heat in a soup pot, over medium-low heat:

3 tablespoons vegetable oil

Add and cook, stirring, until tender but not browned, 5 to 10 minutes:

1 medium onion, diced
1 medium green bell pepper, diced
½ cup diced ham
1 Scotch bonnet pepper or 2 fresh jalapeño peppers, seeded and diced
2 cloves garlic, minced

Stir in the chicken along with:

6 cups water
One 14½-ounce can diced tomatoes, drained
2 teaspoons ground annatto seeds (optional)

Bring to a boil, reduce the heat, and simmer, partially covered, for 25 minutes. Stir in:

½ cup long-grain rice

Continue to simmer until the chicken and rice are cooked, about 20 minutes. Remove the chicken, discard the skin and bones, and shred the meat. Return it to the soup and stir in:

1 cup fresh or frozen peas
½ cup chopped fresh cilantro
½ cup pimiento strips or sliced green olives stuffed with pimientos
Salt to taste

Simmer gently until the peas are just cooked through, 2 to 3 minutes. Ladle into warmed bowls.

THAI CHICKEN AND COCONUT SOUP

About 6 cups

If they are available, simmer kaffir lime leaves or lemongrass in the coconut milk first for a delicate citrus flavor.

Bring to a boil in a soup pot:

3 cups Chicken Stock, 39
2⅔ cups unsweetened coconut milk

Reduce the heat and stir in:

2 small Thai peppers or 3 fresh jalapeño peppers, seeded and sliced
3 tablespoons Thai fish sauce (*nam pla*) or soy sauce
1 teaspoon minced peeled fresh ginger
⅛ teaspoon salt

Simmer for 10 minutes, then stir in:

1 pound boneless, skinless chicken breasts, thinly sliced
2 tablespoons fresh lime juice

Simmer, stirring occasionally, until the chicken is no longer pink, about 5 minutes. Ladle into warmed bowls. Garnish with:

Chopped fresh cilantro

EGGS

The egg is nature's perfect shape. It is not surprising that so elegant a container should turn out to hold a small treasure of balanced nutrients—protein, fats, vitamins, and minerals. The egg's unique properties give it a unique versatility. Eggs bind ground meats, pureed vegetables, and doughs; they lighten cakes and breads; they thicken custards, tenderize timbales, and provide richness to mousses and puddings. Eggs emulsify mayonnaise, thicken sauces, and clarify or enrich soups. They are used to glaze breads and rolls, insulate pie doughs against sogginess, and create ethereal meringues.

It is essential to understand exactly how eggs behave under certain conditions precisely because they are so diverse. The important point is that eggs are extremely sensitive. Unlike some culinary mishaps, mistakes with eggs are most often irreversible and it is usually necessary to start over with fresh eggs.

COMPOSITION AND NUTRITION

The egg's shell is made of hard but slightly porous calcium carbonate and lined on the inside and outside with protective membranes. Most eggs are washed before coming to market, which removes the outside membrane or cuticle; a light coating of mineral oil is often applied to replace it. The color of the shell is an indication of the breed of the hen and has no connection with the quality of the egg or of its flavor. Brown shells are preferred by some cooks, particularly in the Northeast—and certain species of chickens lay yellow or even light pink, green, or blue eggs.

A single egg white from a large egg weighs about 1 ounce, provides about 17 calories, is almost 90 percent water, and is otherwise made up mostly of protein, with only trace amounts of vitamins and minerals. The yolk of the same egg, although smaller in size (weighing about ½ ounce), is far denser and is richer in calories (about 60), nutrients, and flavor. Besides providing fat, cholesterol, vitamins, and minerals, the yolk offers a bit of protein and a measure of lecithin—the compound with the ability to make sauces, like mayonnaise, thick and smooth. A whole egg contains all of the essential amino acids, an essential fatty acid called linoleic acid, 6 grams of protein, 4.5 grams of fat (1.5 grams of which are saturated), 213 milligrams of cholesterol, 1 gram of carbohydrate, 60 milligrams of potassium, and 65 milligrams of sodium, as well as 13 vitamins—almost all except C and niacin.

Besides shell, yolk, and white, an egg has several other parts: the chalazae, or chalazae cords, the twisted, slightly elastic strands of egg white that anchor the yolk to the ends of the shell so that it stays neatly in the middle (most prominent in very fresh eggs, these do not interfere with the taste or cooking of eggs but are strained out of custards before baking so they do not form tiny lumps; the germ cell, or germinal spot—the tiny, pinhead-sized white spot that sits on top of a fresh egg yolk and carries the chicken's genetic information—which has no effect on the quality of an egg; and the air cell, or slight space between the egg membrane and the eggshell at the wide end of every egg (the larger the air pocket, the older the egg; a very old egg will actually shrivel up inside its shell). The dark spots you sometimes see in egg yolks are nothing more than blood from capillaries that burst when the egg was formed. These spots are harmless and can easily be removed with the tip of a knife.

EGGS AND CHOLESTEROL

Americans have been eating far fewer eggs in the last twenty years, in large part because of concern over cholesterol, which is found in ample supply in egg yolks. (Egg whites contain no cholesterol.) Recent studies, however, suggest that eating eggs in moderation has little effect on the level of blood cholesterol, and most nutritionists agree that eggs have a place in a well-rounded, well-balanced diet. If cholesterol is a concern, see About Egg Substitutes, 123.

ABOUT EGG QUALITY, HANDLING, AND SAFETY

The quality of an egg is largely a matter of how old it is; the best eggs are the freshest. Age is not the only determining factor, however. The shell naturally protects an egg, and if it is cracked or damaged, the contents will deteriorate rapidly; eggs with cracked, damaged, or dirty shells should not be used. Also important are the variables of temperature (eggs should be stored at less than 40°F), humidity (the ideal range is 70 to 80 percent), and handling (which means prompt and frequent gathering, along with washing and oiling of the shell by the producer). A week-old egg, properly stored, can be fresher than an egg left at room temperature for just one day. Look for the date or freshness code required on the carton of any USDA-inspected eggs. Always buy eggs from a refrigerated case rather than a room-temperature display.

A fresh egg has a round, shapely, high-standing yolk surrounded by a thick, translucent white. The chalazae cords that anchor the yolk in place should be clearly evident. As an egg ages, the yolk flattens out. The white, cloudy when extremely fresh, becomes clear, thin, and runny. If you are unsure of the age of your eggs, just before using them, place them in a bowl of cold water. Those that float—a sign that the egg inside has shrunk through extended moisture loss—are not usable. You can also break an egg into a clean bowl and smell it. An old or stale egg will smell like damp grass or straw and will taint any delicate or pure egg dishes.

Caution: The bacteria *Salmonella enteritidis,* which can cause illness and even death, is occasionally found in raw eggs, even uncracked eggs. While the risk remains extremely low (it is estimated that 1 in 10,000 eggs is infected, and even infected eggs may not cause problems if properly stored and cooked), we recommend handling eggs carefully, particularly when cooking for young children, the elderly, pregnant women, or anyone with a compromised immune system. Buy refrigerated eggs and get them to your own refrigerator as quickly as possible. Never use a doubtful egg. When cracking or separating eggs, make sure that the fresh egg never touches the exterior of the shell, which is more apt to carry contamination. Before and after handling eggs, wash your hands and any utensils or equipment that may come into contact with either the shell or the contents.

When eggs are cooked, either alone or combined with other ingredients, to a temperature of 140°F, all harmful bacteria will be killed. An instant-read thermometer with a thin probe is the easiest way to check the temperature of many dishes. For preparations of eggs on their own, fried or poached eggs for example, you can use your eyes. Egg whites firm and set at 160°F, and yolks begin to thicken and set at 145°F. Eggs have reached the safe zone when the white is set and the yolk is just starting to firm but may remain runny in the center. For whole-egg dishes such as scrambled eggs or omelets, the mixed egg will set at around 165°F—well above the safety margin. The addition of other ingredients, especially fat, will raise the temperature at which eggs set, meaning scrambled eggs made with additional cream and/or butter will stay soft and moist at higher temperatures, making them both safe and succulent. For dishes like casseroles and quiche, the eggs are sufficiently cooked when a knife inserted in the center comes out clean.

Of greater concern to some are a number of classic recipes that depend on raw or only lightly cooked eggs—among them mayonnaise, dessert mousse, eggnog, and Caesar salad. Some cooks now substitute pasteurized liquid eggs (available both whole and separated into yolks and whites) or dried egg whites. The liquid eggs most closely resemble fresh eggs and are only slightly less efficient than fresh eggs for emulsifying or whipping purposes. Dried whites are best for lightly cooked meringues. Some cooks refuse to compromise and continue using fresh eggs, raw or lightly cooked, without incident. If you are of this school, minimize risk by using the freshest eggs possible and storing them at temperatures below 40°F. It is essential to serve egg dishes immediately or to chill them quickly and then refrigerate. Never hold any dish containing raw eggs for more than a few hours in the refrigerator.

STORING EGGS

Fresh eggs, if refrigerated without interruption, should retain their quality for at least 1 month, although the whites will become noticeably thinner. Because they are repeatedly exposed to warm air, eggs stored in those handy slots in the refrigerator door will deteriorate more quickly than those kept in their carton, set on an inside shelf. Keep raw cut garlic and onions, pungent cheeses, and highly spiced foods tightly wrapped and away from fresh eggs. While eggs in the shell last longer than most fresh foods, once out of their shells they deteriorate quickly and require special handling. If storing eggs out of the shell, it's best to separate the whites from the yolks. Egg whites will keep in the refrigerator, tightly covered, for up to a week with little change in character or quality. Yolks, however, are much more susceptible to spoilage and tend to dry out or turn gelatinous when stored. In a tightly covered container, unbroken egg yolks will keep in the refrigerator for up to 2 days.

EGG GRADES AND SIZE

Most eggs sold in the supermarkets are labeled either grade AA or grade A. These are the top two classifications of the USDA's voluntary system for indicating an egg's quality before it is shipped to the marketplace. These grades have no bearing on size or freshness. Rather, both AA and A indicate eggs that had high, round yolks and firm, thick whites when they were first laid. While eggs graded AA are a bit more shapely, the difference between the two grades is slight, and in time, no matter what its grade, any egg yolk will flatten out and the white will turn watery.

The most common egg size sold today is large, and our recipes, unless they state otherwise, use large eggs. Eggs of any size may be used for preparations such as fried, boiled, or poached—when the size of the egg has no effect on the overall recipe. The typical serving size is 1 to 2 eggs per person. For recipes such as soufflés, custards, and cakes that depend on an exact number of large eggs, use the Egg Sizes and Weights chart that follows to substitute smaller or larger eggs.

Sometimes it is convenient or necessary to weigh or measure eggs out of the shell. Any time you need only part of an egg, beat the egg slightly to make it easier to measure. Use the following conversions:

1 large egg white = 1 ounce = 2 tablespoons
1 large egg yolk = ½ ounce = 1 tablespoon

ABOUT EGG SUBSTITUTES

Most egg-replacement products are 98 to 99 percent egg whites and thus lack the yolk-rich taste of whole eggs. Egg whites are also apt to dry out when cooked, becoming tough and rubbery—so cook egg substitutes gently, adding seasonings (hot sauce or chopped fresh herbs are good) if appropriate to add flavor. You can make your own egg substitute by gently mixing together 12 egg whites, 1 tablespoon vegetable oil, and ¼ teaspoon salt. For a more egglike color, add 6 drops of yellow food coloring. About ⅓ cup of this mixture is the equivalent volume of a whole egg. Another way to reduce the fat and cholesterol and still retain some of the taste of a whole egg is to substitute egg whites for up to half of the whole eggs in a recipe. Figure 1½ egg whites (or a scant 3 tablespoons) for every whole egg you omit.

ABOUT COOKING EGGS

When heated, an egg's remarkable transformation from a thin, runny liquid into a firm, opaque food is the result of a simple process. When eggs are heated, their proteins begin to unravel and bond with one another. At relatively low temperatures, the proteins remain loose and supple, allowing the egg to set while remaining moist and tender. Excessive heating, however, causes the proteins to fuse into a hard, tough mass. In the case of plain egg dishes, such as fried, poached, or hard-boiled eggs, the result is a rubbery white and a dry, crumbly yolk. In the case of custards, quiches, and egg-thickened sauces and soups, the result is a grainy, watery consistency—a state described as curdled. (See About Baked Custards, 1013.) The key to cooking eggs successfully is to avoid overcooking. Cream, butter, and cheese are especially welcome in egg dishes, not only because they add their own creamy richness but also because fat counteracts the tendency toward curdling.

Since eggs cook so quickly and, once cooked, can never return to their liquid state, you need to be very careful when you combine them with a hot mixture. Condition the eggs first by whisking a small quantity of the hot mixture into the beaten eggs, then add the eggs to the rest of the hot mixture. This technique,

EGG SIZES AND WEIGHTS

Use this chart to replace the large eggs called for in recipes with eggs of another size. The amounts in parentheses are the weights of an egg in the shell.

LARGE (2 OUNCES)	JUMBO (2½ OUNCES)	X-LARGE (2¼ OUNCES)	MEDIUM (1¾ OUNCES)	SMALL (1½ OUNCES)
1	1	1	1	1
2	2	2	2	3
3	2	3	3	4
4	3	4	5	5
5	4	4	6	7
6	5	5	7	8

referred to as tempering, is used in many sauces, soups, soufflés, and custards.

SEPARATING EGGS

Separating eggs can be done with an egg separator, shown below, or by hand. To use an egg separator, place the device on the rim of a cup or small bowl. Crack the egg carefully into the center. The white will run through the horizontal slits around the sides into the container below, while the yolk will sit in the depression of the separator. To separate by hand, have three bowls ready. Holding an egg in one hand, tap the egg lightly but sharply on the edge of one of the bowls to make an even, crosswise break. Holding the egg in both hands over a bowl, pull the edges apart until the eggshell is broken into halves. Some of the egg white will immediately flow into the bowl underneath. Pour the remaining egg back and forth from one half-shell to the other, letting more of the white flow into the bowl each time until only the yolk remains in the shell. During this shifting process, you will be able to tell quickly if there is any discoloration or off odor, in which case you should discard the entire egg immediately. Should the yolk break during this process, you can try to remove any yolk particles from the white with the corner of a paper towel moistened with cold water. If this fails, the white may still be used for anything other than beaten egg whites; even the smallest speck of yolk can prevent egg whites from frothing. If the white is fresh and speckless, transfer it to the second bowl, the yolk to the third, and continue. See How to Beat Egg Whites, 928, and How to Fold Egg Whites, 929.

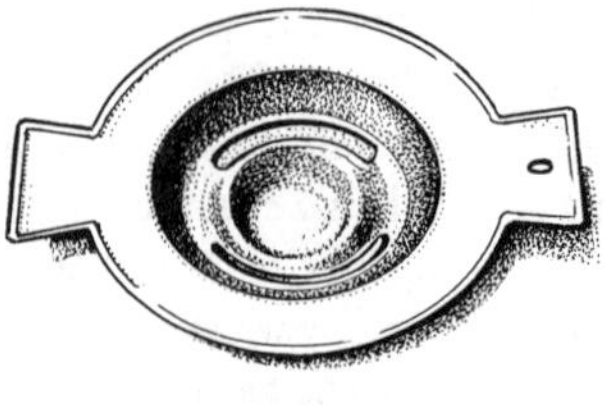

Egg separator

ABOUT SOFT- AND HARD-BOILED EGGS

The most basic way of cooking eggs is directly in their shells. As simple as this method is, it requires a certain amount of precision and technique to achieve perfection. To begin with, "boiled eggs" is a misleading term. Eggs should *never* be boiled—they should be cooked gently at no more than a bare simmer. Higher heat overcooks the proteins, leaving the egg white tough and rubbery. In addition, the vigorous action of boiling water bashes the eggs around, often cracking the shells and causing them to leak. We recommend cooking eggs by lowering them into already simmering water—enough to cover them by at least an inch. It is important to have a saucepan large enough to accommodate all the eggs in a single layer and enough water so that the temperature is not dramatically lowered when the eggs are added. A colander or fry basket makes easy work of lowering the eggs in all at once and then pulling them out quickly when the egg timer rings. Some cooks prick a small hole in the ends of the eggshells with a pin or special gadget known as an egg pricker. This helps prevent the eggshell from cracking, but it is not essential.

The difference between soft-boiled and hard-boiled eggs is merely one of timing. After the eggs have been added to the pot, start the timer once the water returns to a simmer. A soft-boiled egg takes 3 to 5 minutes, depending on size, and has a fully set white and a warm, slightly runny yolk. Hard-boiled eggs take 12 to 15 minutes to become firm throughout, with a yolk that remains bright yellow and moist. An overcooked hard-boiled egg will have a rubbery white and a pale, dry, chalky yolk. Overcooking may also cause a greenish black rim to form between the yolk and the white. Quickly cool hard-boiled eggs by plunging them into cold water to arrest the cooking and help prevent this discoloration.

The simplest way to serve a soft-boiled egg is in an eggcup, wide end down. Use a table knife or teaspoon to crack off the top third of the eggshell, then season with salt and ground black pepper. Another presentation is to spoon them out of the shell, using a folded towel to protect your hand from the heat, and serve them in a small bowl with buttered toast. If you are nimble, you can peel soft-boiled eggs entirely and serve them much as you would poached eggs, on toast or English muffins with any number of garnishes.

Much discussion swirls around the best way to peel a hard-boiled egg. Very fresh eggs (less than 3 days old) are the most difficult to peel. The older the egg, the larger the air cell, and the neater it peels. Thoroughly chilling hard-boiled eggs before peeling helps by firming the white. Holding an egg under a stream of cool water as you peel removes any bits of broken shell. Some cooks advocate a two-step method that involves plunging the cooked egg into ice water for 2 minutes, then reboiling it for exactly 30 seconds and peeling it immediately.

Hard-boiled eggs can be served in any number of ways—among them chopped, seasoned, and mixed with mayonnaise for Egg Salad, 230, halved and stuffed as in Deviled Eggs, 126, or sliced and served warm on toast with a creamy sauce.

Hard-boiled eggs are best stored in their shells in the refrigerator, where they will keep for 2 to 3 weeks. A hard-boiled egg out of its shell should be stored, tightly sealed, in the refrigerator for no more than 1 week. If you lose track and are not sure whether an egg in your refrigerator is hard-boiled or raw, set it on a countertop and give it a spin. A hard-boiled egg will spin evenly like a top, while a raw egg will wobble and topple as the yolk sloshes around inside.

SOFT-BOILED EGGS (BASIC RECIPE)

When boiling many eggs at one time, be sure the pan is large enough to hold them in a single layer. Please read About Soft- and Hard-Boiled Eggs, 124.

Bring to a boil in a saucepan over high heat:

2 to 4 quarts water, enough to cover a single layer of eggs by 1 inch

Gently lower into the water with a slotted spoon or in a colander or fry basket:

Unshelled eggs

Return the water to a boil and immediately reduce the heat to a simmer. Start timing, allowing 4 minutes for large eggs, 3½ minutes for small and medium eggs, and 4½ minutes for extra-large and jumbo eggs. Serve immediately.

HARD-BOILED EGGS (BASIC RECIPE)

Prepare as for Soft-Boiled Eggs, above, allowing 14 minutes for large eggs, 12 minutes for small and medium eggs, and 15 minutes for extra-large and jumbo eggs. Plunge hard-boiled eggs into cold water to prevent further cooking.

CODDLED EGG

1 serving

An egg is said to be coddled when it is gently cooked, either in or out of the shell, so that it remains soft and tender. You can coddle eggs in the shell for use as an ingredient in another recipe, such as Caesar Salad, 209, by gently boiling them for 2 minutes. To enjoy coddled eggs on their own, you can cook them in egg coddlers, specially designed cups of porcelain, heatproof glass, or pottery with a screw-on top. For best results, place the cups on a rack or a folded dish towel to keep them off the bottom of the pan. (The towel will not burn in simmering water.) Make sure the level of the water covers the porcelain part of the coddler.

Have ready a saucepan that will accommodate an egg coddler and a rack or folded dish towel. Fill a saucepan with enough water to reach the rim of the egg coddler and bring to a boil over high heat. Butter the insides of the egg coddler and break in:

1 egg

Top with:

½ teaspoon butter (optional)
2 teaspoons light or heavy cream (optional)
Pinch of salt
Pinch of ground black pepper

Screw the top on tightly. Set the filled coddler on the rack or the towel in the boiling water, cover, and immediately reduce the heat to a simmer. Simmer for 6 to 8 minutes for a medium-set egg. Lift the cup from the water by the ring, but unscrew the top by grasping the entire lid with a pot holder. Do not unscrew from the ring or it may break. If you want the egg cooked further, replace the lid, return it to the simmering water, and cook for 1 to 2 minutes more. Serve the egg directly from the cup with buttered toast.

CODDLED EGG WITH HAM, CHEESE, OR HERBS

Prepare Coddled Egg, above, adding 1 to 3 teaspoons chopped ham, crumbled cooked bacon, grated cheese, diced pâté, chopped anchovies, or minced fresh herbs to the coddler before adding the egg. Cook for 1 to 2 minutes longer.

QUICK HARD-BOILED EGG WITH WHITE SAUCE

1 serving

A snap to make for lunch or supper.

Prepare:

⅓ cup Sauce Béchamel, 46, or Sauce Mornay, 46, warmed
1 hard-boiled egg, 125, sliced
1 slice bread, toasted and lightly buttered

Arrange the sliced egg on the toast and top with the sauce. Serve as is or sprinkle with:

Grated Swiss or Parmesan cheese (optional)

and place under the broiler until the cheese is melted.

CREAMED EGGS AU GRATIN

2 to 3 servings

Serve with warm crusty bread and a green salad for a quick, easy, satisfying meal.

Preheat the oven to 350°F.

In a small sauté pan, heat together over low heat:

1 tablespoon butter
1 tablespoon olive oil

Add and sauté until softened but not browned, about 5 minutes:

½ cup minced shallots or onions

Set aside to cool. Combine in a bowl:

4 hard-boiled eggs, 125, chopped or sliced
1 cup Sauce Béchamel, 46
2 tablespoons chopped fresh herbs, such as parsley, tarragon, chervil, and chives
¾ teaspoon Dijon mustard
½ teaspoon minced garlic
¼ teaspoon salt
⅛ teaspoon ground black pepper
Pinch of freshly grated or ground nutmeg

Add the reserved shallots. Stir to blend. Transfer the mixture to 1 medium-sized or 2 or 3 smaller baking dishes. Sprinkle with:

¾ cup fresh breadcrumbs
1 tablespoon butter, cut into small pieces

Bake until heated through, 10 to 20 minutes. Place briefly under the broiler to brown and crisp the crumbs.

CURRIED EGGS

Prepare Creamed Eggs au Gratin, above, adding 1 teaspoon curry powder to the sautéing shallots or onions.

CREAMED EGGS WITH ASPARAGUS TIPS

Prepare Creamed Eggs au Gratin, above, adding ¾ cup asparagus tips, cooked and drained, to the sauce.

STUFFED EGGS

4 servings

Almost any cooked meat, fish, or vegetable can be cut into small cubes, stirred into the mashed yolks, and seasoned to make a tasty filling. Just be sure to use enough mayonnaise or other creamy medium to keep the mixture moist and light.

Slice lengthwise in half:

4 hard-boiled eggs, 125, cooled and shelled

Carefully remove the yolks, leaving the whites intact. Place the yolks in a bowl, mash, and add:

2 tablespoons mayonnaise or sour cream
2 teaspoons minced fresh herbs, such as chives, tarragon, chervil, parsley, and basil
1 to 2 teaspoons Dijon mustard, to taste
1 teaspoon vinegar (any type)
1 teaspoon minced shallots
¼ teaspoon salt
⅛ teaspoon Worcestershire sauce
⅛ teaspoon ground black pepper
Pinch of curry powder

Spoon the filling into the whites, mounding it slightly to resemble a whole egg, or pipe the filling into the whites using a pastry tube with a star tip for a more elegant effect. Keep the eggs refrigerated until serving time; remove them from the refrigerator about 15 minutes before serving.

DEVILED EGGS

Prepare Stuffed Eggs, above, adding 3 drops hot red pepper sauce, or more to taste, to the yolks. Garnish with paprika.

BAKED STUFFED EGGS

4 servings

A lunch or supper dish.

Preheat the oven to 425°F. Grease a shallow 8- to 9-inch baking dish.

Arrange in the baking dish:

4 Stuffed Eggs, 126 (8 halves total), made with 2 tablespoons Sauce Béchamel, 46, or heavy cream in place of the mayonnaise

Pour over them:

1 cup Sauce Béchamel, 46, or Simplest Italian Tomato Sauce Marinara, 305

Top with:

Fresh breadcrumbs or grated cheese

Bake until golden brown and warmed through, 10 to 15 minutes.

SCOTCH EGGS

6 servings

This dish is traditionally deep-fried, but here it is updated by baking in the oven. Try substituting basil or marjoram for any of the herbs specified in the recipe.

Position a rack in the lower third of the oven and preheat the oven to 400°F. Lightly grease a 13 x 9-inch baking dish.

Combine thoroughly in a bowl:

12 ounces ground pork
1 large egg
1 tablespoon chopped fresh parsley
1 teaspoon grated lemon zest (optional)
1 teaspoon salt
¾ teaspoon chopped fresh savory, or ¼ teaspoon dried
¾ teaspoon chopped fresh sage, or ¼ teaspoon dried
¾ teaspoon chopped fresh thyme, or ¼ teaspoon dried
¼ teaspoon ground black pepper
¼ teaspoon ground coriander
¼ teaspoon freshly grated or ground nutmeg

Place on a plate:

2 tablespoons all-purpose flour

Place in a bowl and beat:

1 large egg

Place on another plate:

1 cup fresh breadcrumbs

Divide the pork mixture into 6 equal portions and form into patties. With your hands, mold each patty around one of:

6 hard-boiled eggs, 125, shelled, rinsed, and patted dry

Rub your hands lightly with cold water before shaping each egg; this helps prevent the meat from sticking to you. Roll each egg in the flour to coat and shake off the excess. Dip in the egg, then roll in the breadcrumbs to cover completely. Place in the prepared baking dish. Bake for 30 minutes, turning the eggs over halfway through the cooking time. Let rest for 5 to 10 minutes and eat hot, or let cool to room temperature. You may also enjoy these chilled.

DYED EASTER EGGS

Think of these eggs as art, not food, since they often sit at room temperature for long periods and their interiors will not be edible. The acidity of the vinegar sets the colors. Make separate small batches for each color. Rubbing the colored eggs with vegetable oil after they have dried gives them a pretty luster.

Prepare and place in a bowl:

Hard-boiled white eggs, 125, cooled, washed, and dried

Bring to just under a boil over high heat:

Enough water to cover the eggs

Add:

1 tablespoon white vinegar for each cup of water
Several drops of food coloring, depending on the intensity of color you wish to obtain

Pour the colored water over the eggs. Let the eggs sit until the water cools. The longer they sit, the richer the color. Remove the eggs from the dye and let them air-dry. Once dry, rub the exterior of the shells, if desired, with:

Vegetable oil

DYED HOLLOW EASTER EGGS

For an egg that will last for years and pose no danger of spoiling, begin by emptying the shell of its contents. Use a large trussing needle or ice pick to punch a hole through each end of a raw egg. It is easier if the egg is more than a week old. Stick the needle into the center of the egg to break the yolk membrane. Blow hard into one hole to push the egg out the other end. Once the shell is empty, wash and gently dry, then proceed as directed in Dyed Easter Eggs, above, draining the shells, if necessary, after dyeing, and omitting the vegetable oil.

ABOUT FRIED EGGS

Fried eggs are actually sautéed eggs—cooked in a small amount of fat, usually butter, but sometimes bacon fat or olive or other vegetable oil. Fried eggs, like eggs cooked other ways, will quickly turn tough and rubbery if the heat is too high. Some cooks like the brown, crispy edges of a fast-cooked fried egg, but a lower temperature yields a tender, more delicate egg. Truly fresh grade AA eggs make the best-looking fried eggs, with their neat, compact shape and high, well-centered yolk.

FRIED EGGS SUNNY-SIDE-UP

2 to 4 servings

Use enough butter or other fat to generously coat the bottom of the pan—though a nonstick skillet makes it easier to slide the cooked eggs onto a plate. Covering the eggs while they cook ensures a fully cooked egg without sacrificing the pleasure of a tender white and runny yolk.

Melt in a large skillet over medium-low heat:

1 to 2 tablespoons butter, bacon fat, or olive oil

When hot, break into the skillet:

4 eggs

Season with:

Scant 1/8 teaspoon salt

Pinch of ground black pepper, or to taste

Cover and cook until the whites are completely set and the yolks are just barely beginning to thicken around the edges, 4 to 6 minutes. Serve immediately on warmed plates with buttered toast or English muffins.

BASTED EGGS

For sunny-side-up eggs that are more cooked on top, cook the eggs in 2 to 3 tablespoons butter or other fat. As the eggs cook, use a spoon to collect the hot fat from the edges of the pan and dribble it over the tops of the eggs. Baste the eggs in this manner 2 or 3 times. Cover the pan with a lid between bastings.

FRIED EGGS OVER EASY

Follow the procedure for Fried Eggs Sunny-Side-Up, above, but do not cover. Instead, when the whites are completely set and the yolks are nearly set, flip each egg carefully by sliding a slotted spatula under the egg, supporting the yolk, and cautiously turning it over in the skillet. Cook just long enough to set a film over the yolk without browning, no more than 30 seconds more.

FRIED EGGS OVER HARD

For those who like a yolk nearly set. Follow the procedure for Fried Eggs Over Easy, above, allowing the egg to cook for about 1 minute after flipping.

FRIED EGG SANDWICH

1 serving

Preheat the broiler.

Prepare:

1 or 2 over-easy or over-hard fried eggs, above

Season with:

Salt and ground black pepper to taste

Red pepper flakes to taste (optional)

Place on:

1 slice bread or ½ English muffin, toasted

Cover with:

1 to 2 tablespoons grated cheese, such as Cheddar or Swiss

Place under the broiler to melt the cheese for a few seconds. Garnish, if desired, with:

Ketchup

Lettuce

Bacon

Thinly sliced ham

Cover with:

1 slice bread or ½ English muffin, toasted

EGG IN A HOLE

1 or 2 servings

Young eaters get a big kick out of this dish.

Using a 2½-inch biscuit cutter or small glass, cut a round hole out of the center of:

2 slices sandwich bread

Melt in a large skillet over medium heat:

2 tablespoons butter

Add the bread slices and cook for about 30 seconds. Crack into the holes:

2 eggs

Do not worry if some of the white remains on top of the bread. Add more butter if needed. When the egg begins to set, 2 to 3 minutes, flip the bread and egg using a spatula. Fry the other side until the eggs are done to your liking. Serve on a warmed plate. Fry the leftover rounds of bread and serve them as well.

HUEVOS RANCHEROS

4 servings

In this classic Mexican dish, fried eggs are placed on a tortilla, then smothered with a spicy, rustic tomato chili pepper sauce. Typically, these eggs are accompanied with refried beans.

Prepare and keep warm:

2 cups Roasted Tomato–Jalapeño Salsa, 63, or Roasted Tomato–Chipotle Salsa, 62

In a large, nonstick skillet, heat over medium-high heat:

1 to 2 tablespoons vegetable oil

When hot, add 1 at a time and quick-fry for 2 to 3 seconds each side:

4 corn tortillas

Remove to paper towels to drain, then wrap in foil and keep warm in a 200°F oven. Set the skillet over medium-low heat (or use two skillets if the eggs will not all fit at once) and add a bit more oil if needed. Break into the skillet:

4 to 8 eggs

Let cook until set, sunny-side-up. Cover the pan for a minute or so for the most even cooking. Season with:

Salt and ground black pepper to taste

Set a tortilla on each of 4 warmed plates and top with 2 eggs. Spoon a generous ½ cup of the warm tomato-jalapeño sauce around each serving. Serve immediately sprinkled with:

Finely crumbled Mexican queso fresco, farmer's cheese, or feta cheese

Chopped fresh cilantro

EGGS BEATRICE *4 servings*

Serve these eggs with sautéed vegetables on the side as an interesting and lighthearted alternative to eggs Benedict.

Heat in a large skillet over medium heat:

2 tablespoons butter

Add and cook until heated through:

4 large tomato slices, ¼ to ½ inch thick

Remove from the skillet and place 1 slice on each of:

4 English muffins halves, toasted, or 4 potato pancakes, 410, each about 3 inches in diameter

Quickly wipe out the pan with a paper towel. Add:

1 tablespoon butter

When the butter is foaming, break into the skillet:

4 eggs

Season with:

Scant ⅛ teaspoon salt

Pinch of ground black pepper

Cover and cook until the whites are completely set and the yolks are just barely beginning to thicken around the edges, 4 to 6 minutes. Place the eggs on top of the tomatoes. Increase the heat to high and add to the skillet:

2 tablespoons butter

1 tablespoon minced shallots or scallions

3 tablespoons red wine vinegar

Boil the mixture until slightly reduced. Stir in:

2 tablespoons chopped mixed fresh herbs, such as parsley, tarragon, and chives

Taste and adjust the seasonings. Pour the sauce over the eggs and serve immediately on warmed plates.

ABOUT POACHED EGGS

Poached eggs should be *poached,* not simmered or boiled. Start with fresh grade AA eggs cracked just moments before cooking; these have the most compact shape. Eggs more than a week old are likely to have sprawling whites and uncentered yolks. Choose a large pan so that the eggs will not be crowded. For a more elegant presentation, some cooks drain the cooked eggs against a clean dish towel and use scissors or a small knife to trim away any straggly white bits. While water is certainly the most common medium for poaching eggs, other liquids, including stock, wine, cream, milk, sauce, or soup, can be used. In some recipes these more flavorful poaching liquids are then thickened and used as a sauce for the eggs. Eggs are also sometimes poached and served directly in a soup. If you are serving a crowd, poached eggs can be transferred as they finish cooking to a wide, shallow bowl of water warmed to 150°F and held for up to 30 minutes. They can also be poached ahead of time and refrigerated for up to 24 hours; transfer to a bowl of ice water the moment they are done, then, when ready to serve, carefully transfer to a large bowl full of 150°F water, cover, and let stand for 15 minutes. Alternatively, place the chilled eggs on a bed of thick sauce or creamed or pureed vegetables in a baking dish, top with Sauce Béchamel, 46, or one of its derivatives, and bake at 350°F until heated through, 10 to 20 minutes.

Molded eggs—made by cracking fresh eggs into individual buttered molds that are then set above gently simmering water until the white is set and the yolk is just beginning to firm up—are often used in place of poached eggs, since their perfectly round shape makes an attractive presentation.

POACHED EGGS (BASIC RECIPE) *4 servings*

In this updated method, poached eggs are held at 150°F for 15 minutes to ensure a perfectly safe egg with a soft yolk and tender white.

Heat 2 to 3 inches of water in a large saucepan over medium heat until almost boiling. Add:

1 tablespoon vinegar (any type)

Crack into 4 small cups and slide one by one from the cup into the simmering water:

4 eggs

If an egg sinks to the bottom, wait until it is nearly set before attempting to dislodge it with a slotted spoon so the yolk does not break. Maintain the water just below a simmer, reducing the heat to low if necessary. Cook until the whites are set and the centers are still soft. Remove with a large slotted spoon and set in a second pot of water warmed to 150°F. Cover and let stand for 15 minutes; reheat if the temperature falls below 145°F. Drain each egg with a slotted spoon and hold it against a clean, dry dish towel to absorb as much water as possible. If desired, use scissors to trim away any ragged edges. Serve the poached eggs on warmed plates with buttered toast or English muffins, or use in any recipe calling for poached eggs.

EGGS BENEDICT *2 to 4 servings*

This enduring brunch specialty was apparently invented at the famed Delmonico's restaurant in New York City in the 1920s. The original base may have been toast rather than English muffins. Then, as now, Hollandaise Sauce, 55, was considered essential; a fancy interpretation added a slice of black truffle on top of each sauced egg. The basic construction lends itself to improvisation. In place of ham or Canadian bacon, the eggs can be placed on top of creamed spinach, fried tomatoes, or artichoke bottoms, and set upon a base of thick-cut toast, cornbread, or potato pancakes. The sauce might be Maltaise, 56, Béarnaise, 56, or Mornay, 46—and the eggs can even be fried or medium-boiled and carefully peeled instead of poached. Here is the standard recipe.

Place on warmed plates or a warmed serving platter:

2 English muffins, split, toasted, and buttered

Arrange on the muffins:

4 thick slices ham or Canadian bacon, warmed

Set on each slice of ham one of:

4 poached eggs, 129, well drained

Divide among the 4 eggs to coat:

½ cup Hollandaise Sauce, 55

Serve immediately, passing extra sauce on the side if desired.

EGGS WITH SMOKED SALMON

Arrange very thin slices of smoked salmon on 4 buttered toasted slices of light rye or pumpernickel bread. Top each with 1 poached egg and cover with Hollandaise Sauce, 55, or Scandinavian Mustard-Dill Sauce, 79, if desired. Sprinkle with snipped fresh dill.

POACHED EGGS BLACKSTONE

Fry 4 slices of bacon until crisp, then crumble and set aside. Fry four ½-inch-thick slices tomato, coated with seasoned flour, in the bacon fat until lightly browned. Arrange 1 poached egg on each tomato slice. Top with crumbled bacon and Hollandaise sauce, 55, or Béarnaise Sauce, 56.

GRATINÉED EGGS FLORENTINE

Cover the bottom of a buttered shallow baking dish with 1 cup Creamed Spinach, 416. Arrange 4 poached eggs on top, cover with ½ cup Sauce Mornay, 46, and sprinkle with ¼ cup grated Swiss or Parmesan cheese. Brown quickly under a hot broiler.

ABOUT SCRAMBLED EGGS

It takes both patience and a bit of technique to make great looking and tasting scrambled eggs. The first step is to beat the eggs until the whites and yolks are completely blended. The addition of cream, butter, milk, or even water will keep the eggs more tender when cooked to medium doneness. But the liquid can also separate out and turn the eggs watery, especially if they are cooked too quickly—gentle heat is essential for producing soft, delectable eggs. The lower the heat, the longer it takes the eggs to cook, and the creamier the result. The French technique, explained below, takes this principle to an extreme by cooking scrambled eggs in a double boiler. Also important to the texture of the finished eggs is how often they are stirred. Infrequent stirring will produce large, uneven curds; more constant, careful stirring and scraping of the bottom of the pan will keep the heat evenly distributed and result in more delicate, billowy curds and creamier eggs. Vigorous stirring will produce small curds. Finally, scrambled eggs must be served immediately. We recommend transferring them to warmed plates while they are still slightly underdone. They will continue to cook and firm up to perfection on their way to the table.

SCRAMBLED EGGS (BASIC RECIPE) *2 servings*

You can use a nonstick pan and cut back on the butter if you prefer.

Beat together until the whites and yolks are completely combined:

3 to 4 eggs
Scant ¼ teaspoon salt
⅛ teaspoon ground black pepper or paprika, or a few drops of hot red pepper sauce

Melt in a skillet over low heat:

1 to 2 tablespoons butter

When the butter begins to foam, pour in the egg mixture. With a wooden spoon or a heatproof rubber or metal spatula, push the eggs gently as they set, folding and stirring them into soft curds. Stir more quickly as the eggs thicken. Continue to cook until the eggs are just set, creamy, and still moist, 2 to 5 minutes. They will continue to cook and firm up for several seconds off the heat. Transfer the eggs to warmed plates and serve immediately.

FRENCH SCRAMBLED EGGS (BASIC RECIPE) *2 servings*

These eggs are velvety smooth, with creamy, soft curds. For an elegant appetizer, top them with caviar or cubes of foie gras.

Melt in the top of a double boiler over—not in—boiling water:

1 tablespoon butter

Beat together until the whites and yolks are completely combined:

3 to 4 eggs
2 tablespoons butter, cut into small pieces
¼ teaspoon salt
⅛ teaspoon ground black pepper

Pour the eggs into the double boiler and stir with a wooden spoon as the butter melts. Continue stirring, scraping the bottom and sides of the pan, until the eggs have thickened into soft, creamy curds, 10 to 15 minutes. If desired, place the eggs in individual prebaked tartlet shells, 866, or bouchées, 911. Serve immediately on warmed plates.

IDEAS FOR SCRAMBLED EGGS

Scrambled eggs are the perfect medium for the improvisational cook. Additions should be at room temperature, and vegetables that contain a lot of moisture—tomatoes, zucchini, and mushrooms for example—must be cooked first so the eggs do not become watery. Stir the following into the eggs after the curds have begun to form, figuring 1 teaspoon to 1 tablespoon of added ingredients per egg:

- Grated or crumbled cheese
- Cottage cheese
- Crème fraîche or sour cream
- Roasted bell peppers
- Sautéed red, green, or yellow bell peppers
- Finely chopped scallions
- Small pieces of broiled or sautéed sausage or ham
- Strips of smoked salmon and sautéed onions
- Chopped fresh herbs, especially fines herbes (tarragon, chives, parsley, and chervil)
- Cubed herbed cream cheese
- Cooked asparagus tips
- Sautéed mushrooms
- Black or white truffles (let beaten eggs and truffle slices sit together in a bowl in the refrigerator for 1 hour)

MATZO BREI (BASIC RECIPE)

For centuries when Passover came, Jewish cooks around the world invented different ways to prepare matzo, unleavened bread. Below is a recipe for matzo and eggs that can compete with any brunch pancakes or waffles.

For each person use:

2 unsalted matzos

1 large egg, well beaten

Hold the matzos under hot running water to quickly wet both sides without making them soggy. Place in a colander to drain. Tear the matzos into 2½- to 3-inch pieces and set in a bowl. Add the egg(s) and gently stir to coat the matzo pieces. Season to taste with:

Salt

Heat in a large skillet:

⅛ inch vegetable oil or chicken fat

Spread the matzo mixture in the skillet in a very thin layer, spreading it with a large spoon or spatula. Cook, turning the pieces as they brown, until medium-brown and crispy. If making a large quantity for a crowd, use 2 pans and keep the cooked matzo brei warm in a 200°F oven. Serve warm, passing the salt shaker or a combination of sugar and cinnamon.

ABOUT BAKED EGGS (EGGS EN COCOTTE)

There are several advantages to baking eggs. First, the heat of the oven cooks eggs slowly and evenly, eliminating many of the challenges of stovetop cooking. Next, it is both convenient and attractive to serve eggs in the little ramekins, gratin dishes, or casseroles in which they were baked (the French call this presentation *en cocotte*). Finally, and perhaps most important, this method is wonderfully flexible. Classically speaking, baked, or shirred, eggs are cooked in buttered molds with nothing more than salt and pepper and a little butter or cream, but consider this only a starting point. Sautéed vegetables, cooked breakfast meats, or smoked fish can be added to the molds to create main courses, or the eggs can be topped with sauces of various kinds or cheese. (If you wish to cut back on fat, eliminate the butter or cream and simply cover each dish to trap the steam and prevent the surface from drying out.)

For tender, evenly cooked eggs, we recommend placing them in a water bath. Four-ounce ramekins, which hold one egg, are commonly used, but you can use something larger—6-ounce custard cups, ovenproof coffee cups, dessert bowls, or large muffin tins, for instance. For a water bath, choose a roasting pan large enough to accommodate the molds without them touching one another or the sides of the pan. Either set a cake rack in the pan or cover the bottom of the pan with a dish towel or several layers of paper towels so that the molds do not sit directly on the hot pan bottom. Slide the ramekin-filled pan into the hot oven, and immediately pour in enough hot water to come one-half to two-thirds up the sides of the ramekins—enough to reach the level of the eggs. Baked eggs should be cooked until the whites are set and the yolks just beginning to set. Care should be taken not to overcook the eggs: the ramekins will retain heat and continue to cook the eggs after they are removed from the oven.

The French prepare *oeufs sur le plat*—literally "eggs on the plate"—in small gratin dishes and bake them directly on the oven rack, not in a water bath. *Oeufs sur le plat* cook a bit more quickly than baked eggs and have a texture not unlike that of sunny-side-up fried eggs.

BAKED EGGS (BASIC RECIPE) *1 serving*

To bake 2 eggs, use a 6-ounce ramekin, double all other ingredients, and bake for about 18 minutes.

Preheat the oven to 350°F. Lightly butter a 4-ounce ramekin and sprinkle it with:

Pinch of salt

Pinch of ground black pepper

Crack into it:

1 egg

Drizzle over the top:

1 teaspoon to 1 tablespoon heavy cream

½ teaspoon melted butter (optional)

If you do not use cream or butter, loosely cover the top of the ramekin with foil. Bake in a water bath until the white is firm and the yolk is thickened, about 15 minutes. Serve directly from the ramekin with buttered toast.

BAKED EGGS IN BACON RINGS

Prepare Baked Eggs, above, lining the buttered dish with 1 slice lightly cooked bacon before adding the egg. Drizzle 1 teaspoon melted butter over the top and sprinkle with salt and paprika. After baking, unmold the egg onto a round of toast and garnish with parsley if desired.

BAKED EGGS WITH RATATOUILLE

Prepare Baked Eggs, above, placing 1 tablespoon Ratatouille, 374, in the bottom of the dish before adding the egg. Drizzle ½ teaspoon olive oil over the top before baking. Serve topped with another tablespoon of warmed ratatouille.

ABOUT OMELETS

There are three basic types of omelets: rolled, flat, and souffléed. All are made from beaten eggs cooked so that the exterior is firm and smooth while the inside remains somewhere between runny and barely moist. Unlike most egg dishes, omelets are cooked over high heat. The classic omelet, known as a French omelet, is rolled or folded, typically around some type of savory filling. The flat omelet is made much like a large pancake. Souffléed omelets are made puffy and light by separating the eggs and beating the egg whites until airy and light.

ABOUT OMELET PANS

In making omelets, the right pan makes an enormous difference. Purists insist on a special heavy-gauge omelet pan, shown below, used solely for omelet making and never washed—it is simply rubbed with soft toweling and a handful of salt. While these pans do produce superior omelets, not many of us have the luxury of a kitchen stocked with single-purpose equipment. In truth, any slope-sided, heavy-based pan with a smooth surface will do. Nonstick pans are excellent for cooking all types of eggs, omelets included, and allow you to reduce the amount of cooking fat.

An omelet is easiest to manage and looks best when prepared in the proper size pan. For a 2-egg omelet, a pan with a 6- to 8-inch diameter is best. A 3- to 5-egg omelet needs an 8- to 9-inch pan, and if you insist on showing off with a 6- to 8-egg omelet, wield a 10- to 12-inch pan. Small is beautiful for French omelets: cutting a large rolled omelet into many servings inevitably results in a sloppy mess. If you do want to attempt a large omelet, try a flat omelet or frittata, 134 to 135.

ABOUT COOKING OMELETS

The success of any omelet demands that the fat in the pan be hot enough to gently set the exterior of the omelet at once, but not so hot as to toughen it before the rest of the egg cooks. With the pan at the proper heat, a 2-egg omelet takes less than 1½ minutes to cook from the time the beaten egg hits the hot pan until the finished omelet is rolled out onto a warmed plate. For this reason, you will want to have all your ingredients—and diners—ready when you start cooking. When making more than one omelet, beat the total number of eggs you will need, and use a ladle or measuring cup to pour 3½ ounces, or a scant ¼ cup, for each 2-egg omelet. Keep melted butter and filling ingredients by the stove and move quickly, making the omelets one by one. Serve them as they are ready, or keep them warm in a 200°F oven and serve when all are finished. If you have more than four to make, use another pan or two. Attention to more than one pan at a time is a skill that needs to be developed, so practice before your debut. Stagger the different pans' "schedules" so that the omelets are not all at the same stage at once.

Omelet pan

ABOUT FRENCH OR ROLLED OMELETS

A perfectly executed French omelet requires a certain practiced rhythm. The eggs should be beaten only enough to thoroughly blend the whites and yolks, not enough to incorporate air or make them frothy. Add the eggs to the hot pan the moment the butter's bubbling begins to subside but before it starts to brown. Grasp the handle of the pan and shake the eggs back and forth while stirring the eggs with your other hand, shown below. The best tool for stirring is a table fork, held flat so it does not touch the pan bottom. In as little as 20 to 30 seconds, the eggs will begin to form curds and set firmly along the bottom, while the surface will remain moist and custardy. This is your cue to stop stirring and, with the back of the fork, shape the omelet into a neat circle by gently spreading the eggs evenly around the pan. With the surface still moist, quickly add any filling you might want (see below).

Roll the omelet with what can be described as a soft fold. Tilt the pan away from you at about a 45-degree angle and use the fork to coax the top third of the omelet away from the handle and down over onto itself (and the filling if there is one). If you prefer an omelet with a lightly browned surface, let it sit for a few seconds, once folded, on the burner. With a warm plate waiting, slant the pan to 90 degrees or more. Make a second fold by sliding the omelet out of the pan until it lies seam side down on the plate. Straighten the edges of the omelet to form a neat oval and serve immediately.

An omelet's filling should complement the delicate flavor of the eggs, not overwhelm it. The classic French omelet is sometimes made with only eggs and salt and pepper; or ingredients such as chopped herbs and finely diced meats may be added directly to the beaten eggs, while more substantial fillings may be placed in the middle of the omelet just before it is rolled up. To fill a 2-egg omelet, have ready ⅓ to ½ cup of cooked or prepared filling. Place 2 tablespoons in the omelet while it is still in the pan and before you have rolled it, aiming for a line along the middle third. Reserve the remainder for a final garnish on top. Or fold the omelet without a filling and then, after it is on the plate, cut an incision along the top and fill it with the warm garnish. Garnishes should be fully cooked (if cooking is necessary at all) and neither too cold nor too hot when added to an omelet. Here are some suggested fillings for French omelets:

Red or black caviar and sour cream
Duxelles, 387
Caramelized Onions, 391

FRENCH OMELET

1 serving

Please read About Omelets, 132, and About French or Rolled Omelets, above.

Combine and beat with a fork until the whites and yolks are blended:

2 large eggs
Scant ⅛ teaspoon salt
Pinch of ground black pepper

Melt in a 6- to 8-inch skillet over medium-high heat:

1 tablespoon butter

Tilt the skillet to coat the sides and bottom thoroughly. When the butter is hot and the foam has subsided, pour in the eggs. Shake the pan back and forth while stirring the eggs with your other hand, using a fork held flat, just above the pan bottom. If adding a filling, do so once the bottom has set, placing it in a line in the center of the omelet. Use the fork to begin to roll the edge of the omelet toward the center, all the while tilt-

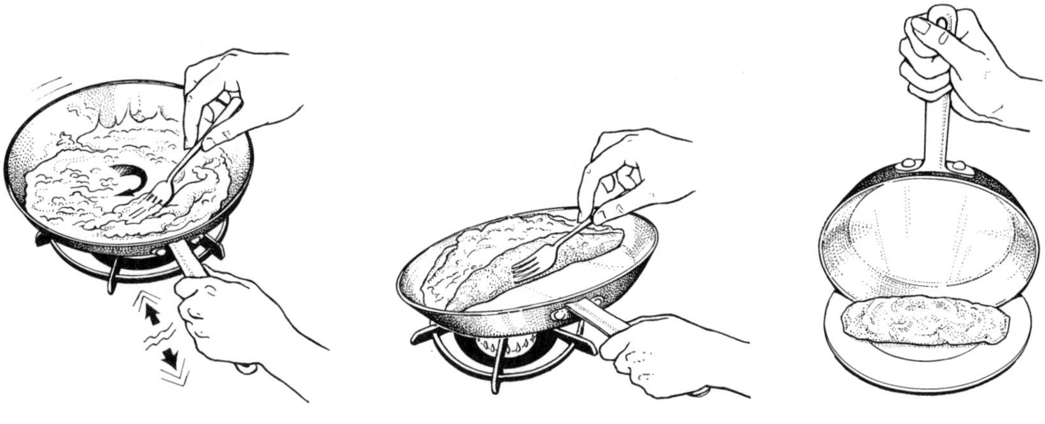

Rolled omelet

ing the pan to fold the omelet against the pan wall. Check to see if the underside of the omelet is as browned as you wish. If not, leave on the heat for a few seconds more before serving. With a warmed plate at the ready, tilt the pan up until the omelet makes a second fold and slips seam side down onto the plate. Serve immediately or keep warm in a 200°F oven.

FOLDED OMELET

For a beginner, the firmer texture of this omelet is a bit more manageable. It is neatly folded in half and does not require the tricky shaking and stirring action of the French omelet.

Prepare French Omelet, above, using 2 eggs and adding 2 tablespoons milk, cream, or stock to the beaten eggs. As the omelet cooks, instead of stirring and shaking the pan, lift the edges of the omelet with a pancake turner and tilt the skillet to allow the uncooked egg mixture to run to the bottom. When all is an even consistency, place any filling on the bottom half and fold the omelet in half, forming a half-moon shape. Serve immediately on a warmed plate.

EGG-WHITE OMELET

For anyone on a low-cholesterol, reduced-fat diet, it is possible to modify egg recipes to eliminate the yolks. Since the yolks carry the richness and flavor of the egg, we recommend compensating by adding more in the way of seasonings and fillings.

Prepare Folded Omelet, above, substituting 3 egg whites for the 2 whole eggs, eliminating the milk, cream, or stock, and using vegetable oil in place of butter. Add chopped herbs and plenty of seasonings to the whites before adding them to the pan. Choose a moist, zesty filling.

ABOUT FLAT OMELETS

In flat omelets, eggs assume a supporting role, binding the savory ingredients and adding richness while the emphasis is on the filling. A flat omelet can be thick or thin, but it is always too hearty and awkward to roll or fold; instead, it is served in wedges, much like an open-faced pizza. Flat omelets can be made ahead and served at room temperature.

The most direct method for making a flat omelet is to sauté the filling ingredients, often vegetables, in a skillet over high heat, and then to pour the beaten eggs directly onto the vegetables. The only trick to this method is to be sure that none of the vegetables stick to the pan—or the eggs will stick too. Guard against this by using a generous amount of fat or a nonstick pan. The second method is to combine the lightly beaten eggs and prepared ingredients and then to pour them directly into a hot buttered pan. When the eggs first hit the pan, let them sit, undisturbed, for about 5 seconds to allow the bottom to begin to set. Then use a wooden spatula to gently push the eggs toward the center, tilting the pan to allow uncooked egg to run to the bottom of the pan.

Whichever method you use, once the eggs form a cohesive, semifirm omelet, stop moving them, reduce the heat slightly if the bottom is browning, and decide how you prefer to cook the still-runny top side. There are three choices: first, flip the omelet with a bold toss-and-catch motion that requires some practice; second, cover the skillet with a lightly buttered heatproof plate, invert it to release the omelet, and slide the "flipped" omelet back into the skillet; or third, place the skillet under a hot broiler for a few seconds until the top is firm.

WESTERN OR DENVER OMELET *2 servings*

This flat omelet is often served in sandwich form on buttered white toast or a toasted bun.

Melt in a medium skillet, preferably nonstick, over medium heat:

1 tablespoon butter

Add and cook until soft, about 10 minutes:

⅓ cup minced onions
⅓ cup minced green bell peppers

Add and cook for another 5 minutes:

⅓ cup finely diced ham

Meanwhile, mix together:

4 eggs
1 tablespoon milk
⅛ teaspoon ground black pepper
Scant ⅛ teaspoon salt

Pour the eggs into the hot pan over the cooked vegetables and ham. Let cook, undisturbed, for about 5 seconds, then use a wooden spatula to slowly move the eggs toward the center, tilting the pan to allow uncooked egg to run to the bottom of the pan. Stop moving the eggs as they set. Flip the omelet and cook the other side for a few seconds, or refer to About Flat Omelets, 134, for alternative ways to cook the top side. When served, the omelet should still be a bit soft in the center. Divide the omelet in half. Serve on warmed plates.

HANGTOWN FRY *4 servings*

According to legend, a miner who struck it rich back in 1849 rushed into the best restaurant in Hangtown, California, and demanded a dish made with the two most expensive ingredients he could imagine: oysters and

eggs. The cook suggested adding bacon for good measure—and Hangtown Fry was born. (Hangtown now bears the considerably less colorful name of Placerville.)
Mix together:

¾ cup all-purpose flour
½ teaspoon salt
¼ teaspoon ground black pepper

Dredge with the seasoned flour:

1 dozen oysters, shucked, 500

Dip them in:

1 egg, lightly beaten

and then roll them in:

¾ to 1 cup fresh or dry breadcrumbs

Heat in a medium skillet over high heat:

2 tablespoons butter

Add the breaded oysters and fry them until golden and crisp. Add to the skillet:

8 eggs, lightly beaten
¼ teaspoon salt
⅛ teaspoon ground black pepper

Reduce the heat to medium and let cook, undisturbed, for about 5 seconds, then use a wooden spatula to slowly move the eggs toward the center, tilting the pan to allow uncooked egg to run to the bottom of the pan. Stop moving the eggs as they set. Flip the omelet and cook the other side for a few seconds, or refer to About Flat Omelets, 134, for alternative ways to cook the top side. When served, the omelet should still be a bit soft in the center. Divide the omelet into quarters. Serve on warmed plates with:

Crisp bacon (optional)

ZUCCHINI FRITTATA *4 servings*

A frittata is the Italian version of an omelet. It is more robust than the classic French omelet and a bit easier to handle. Frittatas are cooked in a heavy skillet over low heat until they are firm—not runny like a French omelet—and they are left open-faced, not folded. Instead of trying to flip the frittata, we recommend popping it into the oven or under the broiler to cook the top side. Served in wedges, frittatas are delicious hot, warm, or at room temperature.
Heat in a large skillet over medium heat:

2 tablespoons olive oil

Add and cook, stirring, until golden brown:

1 cup thinly sliced onions

Add and cook until lightly browned, about 10 minutes:

3 medium zucchini, thinly sliced

Season with:

¼ teaspoon salt
⅛ teaspoon ground black pepper

Transfer the vegetables to a strainer to drain off the excess oil. Let cool completely.
Preheat the broiler.
Meanwhile, beat together until smooth:

5 eggs
½ teaspoon salt
Pinch of ground black pepper

Add the cooled zucchini and onion mixture along with:

½ cup grated Parmesan cheese (optional)
1 tablespoon finely shredded fresh basil
1 tablespoon minced fresh parsley

Heat in a large, ovenproof skillet over medium heat:

2 tablespoons olive oil or butter

When hot, pour in the egg mixture. Reduce the heat and cook until the bottom is set, then place under the broiler for 30 to 60 seconds to finish cooking or refer to About Flat Omelets, 134, for alternative ways to cook the top side. A traditional frittata is not browned. Loosen the frittata with a spatula and slide it onto a plate.

ASPARAGUS FRITTATA

Prepare Zucchini Frittata, above, substituting ¾ to 1 cup lightly steamed asparagus tips and pieces for the sautéed zucchini and onions. Omit the basil.

ARTICHOKE FRITTATA FOR A CROWD *8 servings*

Serve as an appetizer—it keeps a small crowd happy while dinner is cooking. If the crowd is larger than 8, make 2 frittatas and keep one warm. A well-seasoned skillet is essential for removing the slices easily. If you don't have one, try a large nonstick pan with a heatproof handle.
Cut off the stem and top two-thirds of:

6 medium artichokes

Place the artichokes bottom side up on the work surface and cut away the dark green outer leaves with quick, short strokes, beginning at the stem and working out. Once the white flesh is exposed, trim off all the remaining leaves. Scoop out the center choke area with a grapefruit spoon or teaspoon and cut the artichoke bottom into 8 pieces.
Melt in large, well-seasoned cast-iron skillet over medium heat:

3 tablespoons unsalted butter

Add and cook, stiring, until softened but not browned, about 5 minutes:

2 medium leeks, cleaned thoroughly and chopped
1 large clove garlic, chopped

Add the artichoke pieces along with:

¾ cup water

1 tablespoon fresh lemon juice

Cover and simmer over medium-low heat until the artichoke hearts are just tender, 12 to 15 minutes. Add more water if needed. Meanwhile roast, 402, peel, seed, and thinly slice:

1 red bell pepper

Whisk together:

12 large eggs

1¼ cups half-and-half

1 cup grated Parmesan cheese

½ cup chopped fresh basil

1 teaspoon salt

Ground black pepper to taste

Preheat the broiler.

When the artichokes are just tender, remove the lid and cook until the liquid is evaporated. Add:

2 tablespoons butter

Swirl to melt and coat the pan. Give the egg mixture a quick whisking and add to the pan. Stir in the roasted peppers. Cook the frittata over medium-low heat until the center is almost set, about 18 minutes. Cook the frittata under the broiler until browned, about 2 minutes. Cool to warm and serve from the skillet in thin slices.

ABOUT SOUFFLÉED OMELETS

These impressive creations are made by separating eggs and beating the whites until stiff, as you would for a soufflé. The omelet is then cooked in an omelet pan until puffy and light and can be either left flat or folded over to envelop a filling. We especially like sweet fillings, such as fruit or preserves, with these omelets, but savory cheese or herb fillings can also be delicious. Whatever your choice, do not overdo it. Use no more than ⅓ cup prepared fruit or a few tablespoons of jam thinned with a teaspoon of liquor for 4 eggs. A properly executed souffléed omelet has a lovely brown, firm, dry exterior enveloping a soft, creamy, airy center. With the added volume of the beaten whites, you get more servings from fewer eggs and 1 egg per person satisfies most appetites. For a 4-egg omelet, you will need a 10- to 12-inch pan for a full rise.

The first step in making a souffléed omelet is to separate the eggs and beat the whites until stiff, 928. The beaten yolks are then quickly but gently folded into the whites, and the mixture is immediately poured into a moderately hot ovenproof omelet pan. The pan should be hot enough to set the underside of the omelet, but not so hot that it browns right away. Souffléed omelets are not shaken or stirred; simply spread the egg mixture evenly and smooth the surface with a spatula. Covering the pan with a lid whose underside has been buttered to prevent sticking helps trap the heat and cook the top side. After about 5 minutes, remove the cover and slide the half-cooked omelet into a hot oven until the top sets to your liking. Then, either place a filling on one side of the cooked omelet and gently fold it into a half-moon shape, or slide the omelet directly onto a warm plate and garnish with a sauce or filling.

SOUFFLÉED OMELET (BASIC RECIPE)

4 servings

Please read About Souffléd Omelets, above.

Preheat the oven to 375°F.

Combine and whisk until thick and light:

4 large egg yolks

3 tablespoons sugar

In a separate bowl, beat until stiff but not dry, 928:

4 large egg whites

Pinch of salt

Fold the yolk mixture gently into the whites. Melt in a 10-inch ovenproof skillet over medium heat:

1 to 2 tablespoons butter

When the foam has subsided, pour the batter into the pan, spread evenly, and smooth the top. Shake the pan after a few seconds to discourage sticking and then cover the pan with a lid whose underside has been buttered to prevent sticking. Reduce the heat and cook for about 5 minutes. Remove the cover and place the skillet in the oven until the top is set, 3 to 5 minutes. Either fold the omelet in half or slide it out onto a warmed plate and sprinkle with:

Powdered sugar

Serve immediately.

JAM-FILLED SOUFFLÉED OMELET

Prepare Souffléed Omelet, above, but before folding the omelet, fill with 2 tablespoons warm apricot jam mixed with 1 teaspoon rum or brandy, or 2 tablespoons raspberry jam mixed with 1 teaspoon lemon juice.

ABOUT SOUFFLÉS

A well-made soufflé is the triumph of egg cooking. A soufflé has two components—stiffly beaten egg whites and a thick, well-seasoned or flavored base. In a traditional savory soufflé recipe, the base is a thick Sauce Béchamel, 46, to which flavorings such as chopped vegetables, cheese, or cooked meats or fish are added along with egg yolks for richness and flavor. Whatever the ingredients, they should be finely chopped or grated and well seasoned—the base needs to have enough flavor to compensate for the blandness of the egg whites. In place of the traditional béchamel sauce, other thick sauces and purees can be used, as long as they are not so dense as to weigh down the soufflé or so thin as to be runny. Whatever the base, it can be made up to 2 days in advance and held in the refrigerator until it is time to make the soufflé. About 45 minutes before you plan to serve the soufflé, warm the base to lukewarm, beat the egg whites, and proceed with the rest of the recipe. In addition to the flavorings in the sauce, some ingredients, such as grated cheese, can be sprinkled over the whites as they are folded into the base.

The air trapped inside the fluffy, cloudlike foam of well-beaten egg whites is responsible for the lightness of any soufflé. It expands in the hot oven and forces the featherlight mixture to rise. For this reason, many cooks add 1 or 2 additional egg whites for every 4 whole eggs to ensure an impressive rise. In any case, proper beating of the whites is crucial to the success of any soufflé. Please read How to Beat Egg Whites, 928. Once the whites have reached stiff peaks, immediately fold them into the waiting sauce or flavored base by first stirring in a quarter of the whites to lighten the base and then carefully folding in the rest so as not to deflate the mixture.

Small 8-ounce ramekins are ideal for individual soufflés to be served as a first course or the main course for a luncheon, brunch, or light supper. To make one large soufflé that you can proudly carry to the table, use a 6-cup soufflé mold for 4 to 5 egg whites, enough for 4 servings, or an 8-cup mold for 6 to 7 egg whites, enough for 6 servings. While specially designed soufflé molds are ideal, any straight-sided baking dish will do as long as it is not too shallow. Some cooks deliberately use a soufflé mold that is too small for the volume of eggs and then extend it with a 4-inch "collar" of buttered foil, parchment paper, or brown or wax paper, tied around the outside of the baking dish with string, shown 1028. This allows the production of very tall, narrow soufflés.

The final height of the soufflé depends greatly on how well you prepare the mold. It should be generously buttered with soft, not melted, butter, then liberally sprinkled with dry breadcrumbs, finely grated dry cheese, or cornmeal. Tilt the mold in all directions until the bottom and sides are well coated, then invert the mold and tap out any excess. The crumbs, cheese, or cornmeal will help the soufflé rise up straight and tall and, as an added benefit, will produce a deliciously crunchy golden crust. The mold can be prepared in advance, but be careful not to smudge the coatings. Whether you are making small or large soufflés, fill to just below the rim. If it is any fuller, you will need to make a collar to support the extra height as it rises.

The soufflé is most fragile as it first rises, so keep the oven door closed for at least the first half of the baking time. As the soufflé bakes, it gets firmer and a bit more resilient, allowing you to open the door to check on it without ill effect. A savory soufflé should be tested for doneness when it has risen a good 3 to 4 inches above the rim and the crust is golden. First, touch the top of the soufflé lightly with your hand. If it feels firm, with a slight wobble in the middle, it is done. Ideally, a soufflé should remain somewhat moist and creamy inside while dry and firm on the outside. If you prefer a drier soufflé, leave it in the oven for a bit longer, but bear in mind that an overcooked soufflé will begin to deflate. Soufflés can also be baked in a water bath. They will not rise as high, and their texture will be more dense and custardlike, but they will hold their loft longer after baking, giving the cook a little extra breathing space. Prepare any soufflé recipe, 137 to 139, baking in a water bath until risen and brown. This will take 5 to 10 minutes longer than if baked directly in the oven. Please read About Baked Custards, 1013.

Once baked, a soufflé waits for no one and should immediately be whisked to the table. It will begin its inevitable descent within a minute or two of leaving the oven. Soufflés are sometimes accompanied with a sauce, which can be passed separately or spooned directly into a hole created in the center of the soufflé.

CHEESE SOUFFLÉ

6 servings

Please read About Soufflés, above.

Preheat the oven to 375°F. Generously butter an 8-cup soufflé dish or six 8-ounce ramekins and dust the insides with:

¼ to ½ cup dry breadcrumbs or grated Parmesan cheese

Shake out the excess. Heat in a small skillet over medium heat:

1 tablespoon butter

Add and cook until softened, then set aside:

2 tablespoons minced shallots

Prepare:

1½ cups Thick Béchamel Sauce, 46, at room temperature or slightly warmed

Remove from the heat and add the sautéed shallots, along with:

1¼ cups lightly packed grated Swiss, Cheddar, or a combination of Swiss and Parmesan cheese

⅛ teaspoon ground black pepper

RULES FOR SOUFFLÉS

1. Soufflés are best baked in straight-sided molds—so they can rise up tall and erect—that are generously buttered with soft, not melted, butter and dusted with grated cheese or dry breadcrumbs.

2. The well-seasoned savory soufflé base of Thick Béchamel Sauce can be made up to 2 days in advance and stored in the refrigerator. Simply warm it to lukewarm about 1 hour before you plan to serve the soufflés (45 minutes is adequate when making individual soufflés).

3. Adding 1 or 2 additional egg whites for every 4 whole eggs used will produce a soufflé with more height and a lighter texture.

4. The egg whites must be folded into the base as soon as they are whipped to stiff, but not dry, peaks.

5. Soufflé molds should be filled to within 1 to ½ inch of the rim—if higher, the soufflé may spill over the sides during baking.

6. Before baking, run your thumb around the inside rim of the mold, making a 1-inch groove (make a ½-inch groove for individual molds), or moat, in the soufflé mixture. This will promote an even rise and give the cooked soufflé a top-hat appearance.

7. Bake the soufflés on a baking sheet for ease moving them in and out of the oven, and set the sheet on the bottom rack of the oven to make room for the soufflés' anticipated rise.

8. For the fluffiest soufflés, bake them as soon as they are assembled, but they can sit at room temperature, covered with an inverted bowl, for up to 30 minutes before baking if necessary.

½ teaspoon salt
Pinch of ground red pepper
Pinch of freshly grated or gound nutmeg
6 large egg yolks, added one by one

Beat vigorously to blend and set aside. Beat until stiff but not dry, 928:

6 large egg whites
Pinch of salt

Stir one-quarter of the whites into the soufflé base to lighten it, then fold in the rest. Pour into the prepared soufflé dish or ramekins. Bake until the soufflé is risen and golden brown on top, 40 to 45 minutes (20 to 25 minutes for individual soufflés). Remove from the oven and serve immediately.

HAM AND CHEESE SOUFFLÉ

Prepare Cheese Soufflé, 137, reducing the cheese to 1 cup. Add ¾ cup finely chopped smoked ham and 1 tablespoon grated onions to the finished soufflé base before folding in the egg whites.

BLUE CHEESE AND PARMESAN SOUFFLÉ

Prepare Cheese Soufflé, 137, using ½ cup crumbled blue cheese and ½ cup grated Parmesan cheese for the cheese.

SPINACH SOUFFLÉ

6 servings

Please read About Soufflés, 137.

Preheat the oven to 375°F. Generously butter an 8-cup soufflé dish or six 8-ounce ramekins and dust the insides with:

¼ to ½ cup dry breadcrumbs or grated Parmesan cheese

Shake out the excess. Combine in a bowl or large saucepan:

1½ cups Thick Béchamel Sauce, 46, at room temperature or slightly warmed
¾ teaspoon salt
⅛ teaspoon ground nutmeg or red pepper
Pinch of ground white pepper

Beat ½ cup of the mixture into:

6 large egg yolks
¾ cup grated Parmesan or Swiss cheese, or a combination

Combine with the rest of the sauce, beating vigorously to blend. Add:

1½ cups cooked spinach, squeezed dry and finely chopped

Beat until stiff but not dry, 928:

6 large egg whites
Pinch of salt

Stir one-quarter of the whites into the soufflé base to lighten it, then fold in the rest. Pour into the prepared soufflé dish or ramekins. Bake until the soufflé is risen and golden brown on top, 40 to 45 minutes (20 to 25 minutes for individual soufflés). Remove from the oven and serve immediately.

MUSHROOM SOUFFLÉ

Prepare Spinach Soufflé, above, substituting sautéed finely chopped mushrooms (preferably cremini) for the spinach. If desired, ½ to 1 cup grated Gruyère cheese can be substituted for the Parmesan. For additional herbs, try 1½ teaspoons chopped fresh marjoram or rosemary.

MAKE-AHEAD GOAT CHEESE AND WALNUT SOUFFLÉS

8 servings

These are more substantial than traditional soufflés, but they are wonderful in their own right. Serve them on a lightly dressed bed of field greens. Please read About Soufflés, 137.

Preheat the oven to 350°F.

Combine:

¾ cup walnuts, toasted and finely chopped
¼ cup cornmeal

Generously butter eight 6-ounce ramekins or custard cups and sprinkle the insides with the cornmeal mixture, tilting in all directions until completely coated. Scatter any nuts that do not adhere over the bottoms of the dishes.

Melt in a saucepan over medium heat:

3 tablespoons unsalted butter

Stir in until smooth:

¼ cup all-purpose flour

Cook, stirring, for 1 minute. Remove from the heat and stir in:

⅔ cup milk

Return to the heat and, stirring very briskly, bring to a boil. (The mixture will be very thick.) Scrape into a bowl. Add and mash until the cheese is melted:

10 ounces fresh unripened goat cheese

Beat in:

4 large egg yolks
2 cloves garlic, very finely minced
¼ teaspoon dried thyme
¼ teaspoon salt
¼ teaspoon ground white pepper

Beat until stiff but not dry, 928:

5 large egg whites
¼ teaspoon cream of tartar

Stir one-quarter of the whites into the soufflé base to lighten it, then fold in the rest. Pour into the prepared ramekins and smooth the tops. Place the ramekins in a water bath. Bake until a skewer inserted in the center comes out almost clean, about 30 minutes. Let stand for 15 minutes in the water bath, then invert onto a greased baking sheet. The soufflés can be served immediately or cooled, covered tightly with plastic wrap, and refrigerated for up to 3 days.

When ready to serve, heat the soufflés in a 425°F oven until warmed through, 5 to 7 minutes.

ABOUT TIMBALES, QUICHES, AND OTHER SAVORY CUSTARDS

Savory custards rely on the gradual cooking of the egg proteins to form silky-smooth, tender-set dishes. The final texture of a custard depends largely on the proportion of eggs to liquid. More whole eggs or egg whites produce a firm, well-set custard, while extra liquid or additional yolks give a softer, creamier custard.

Timbale is the French word for kettle drum and is commonly used to refer to any savory custard baked in a small, high-sided, tapered drum-shaped mold. In its modern usage, a timbale is any savory custard, or bound mixture of grains, meat, or seafood, that is cooked in an individual mold and then inverted and unmolded before serving.

The most famous of savory custards is quiche, a custard containing small bits of vegetables, fish, meats, and/or cheese baked in a tart or pie crust. The basic proportions are 3 to 4 whole eggs for every 2 cups of milk. Using cream in place of milk or replacing one whole egg with 2 yolks gives you a richer, more custardy quiche. Quiche is traditionally prepared in a prebaked tart shell brushed with egg yolk to help prevent it from becoming soggy. For a more elegant presentation, it can also be baked in individual tart shells. We have also had great success with crustless quiche baked in well-buttered molds. The advantages of these are twofold: you do not need to make a crust, and a crustless quiche can be baked in a water bath, giving it a softer, denser texture, much like that of a timbale.

VEGETABLE TIMBALE

4 servings

Position a rack in the lower third of the oven. Preheat the oven to 325°F. Lightly grease four 6-ounce ramekins or custard cups.

Steam or blanch until crisp-tender:

2 cups coarsely chopped cauliflower florets, broccoli florets, or zucchini or 2 cups corn kernels

Drain thoroughly and either finely chop or pulse in a food processor. Transfer to a bowl. Melt in a small skillet over medium heat:

1 tablespoon unsalted butter

Add and cook, stirring, until softened, 2 to 3 minutes:

¼ cup minced shallots (about 2)

Add to the vegetables and season with:

2 tablespoons Madeira (optional)
½ teaspoon salt
⅛ teaspoon freshly grated or ground nutmeg
Ground black pepper to taste

Heat almost to a boil:

1 cup light or heavy cream

Whisk into the vegetables:

3 large eggs

Slowly whisk in the hot cream and ladle the custard into the prepared dishes. Sprinkle the tops with:

¼ cup grated Parmesan cheese (optional)

Place the custard in a water bath (see About Baked Custards, 1013). Cover the pan with aluminum foil and bake until the custard is set two-thirds of the way to the center of the dishes, 25 to 30 minutes. Remove from the oven, loosen the cover but leave it on, and return to the oven to cook for another 10 minutes. Let cool for 10 minutes, then run a knife around the inside edge of the ramekins. Invert the timbales onto serving plates. Serve sprinkled with:

Chopped fresh parsley or snipped chives (optional)

VEGETABLE TIMBALES II *4 servings*

Including a fair amount of breadcrumbs will give you a less custardlike timbale that is especially tolerant of improvisation. The breadcrumbs temper the egg's sensitivity to excess moisture and offer an elegant means to use up leftover pureed vegetables or small amounts of soups.

Preheat the oven to 325°F. Lightly butter four 4-ounce ramekins and line the bottoms with wax or parchment paper.

Stir together in a large bowl until well combined:

1½ cups cooked, seasoned, and chopped vegetables (such as spinach, broccoli, asparagus, mushrooms, tomatoes); or cooked, pureed, and seasoned carrots or winter squash
2 large eggs
⅓ cup lightly packed fresh breadcrumbs
¼ cup grated Swiss, Cheddar, or Parmesan cheese
3½ tablespoons heavy cream
1 tablespoon grated onions
1 tablespoon chopped fresh parsley
½ teaspoon salt
⅛ teaspoon ground black pepper
Dash of hot red pepper sauce (optional)

Fill the ramekins up to three-quarters full and place them in a water bath (see About Baked Custards, 1013). Bake until set, golden brown, and a knife inserted in the center comes out clean, 35 to 40 minutes. Let cool for 10 minutes, then run a knife around the inside edge of the ramekins. Invert the timbales onto serving plates. If desired, serve with:

Simplest Italian Tomato Sauce Marinara, 305, or Sauce Mornay, 46

QUICHE LORRAINE *One 9-inch quiche; 4 to 6 servings*

This brunch and lunch classic is a specialty of the Lorraine region of northeastern France, where it was first made as early as the sixteenth century. Traditional quiche Lorraine contains no cheese.

Preheat the oven to 375°F.

Prepare and bake in a 9½- or 10-inch two-piece tart pan and glaze with egg yolk:

Flaky Pastry Dough, 862

Cook in a heavy skillet over medium heat, stirring constantly, until the fat is almost rendered but the bacon is not yet crisp:

4 ounces sliced bacon, cut into 1-inch pieces

Drain on paper towels. Beat together:

3 large eggs, lightly beaten
1½ cups crème fraîche, heavy cream, or half cream and half milk
½ teaspoon salt
¼ teaspoon ground black pepper
Pinch of freshly grated or ground nutmeg

Arrange the bacon on the bottom of the shell and pour the custard into it. Bake until the filling is browned and set, 25 to 35 minutes.

HAM AND CHEESE QUICHE

Prepare Quiche Lorraine, above, substituting 1 cup chopped ham for the cooked bacon and spreading 1 cup grated Gruyère or other cheese on the bottom of the pie shell before adding the custard.

BROCCOLI QUICHE

Sauté ½ red onion, chopped, and 1 clove garlic, minced, in olive oil until soft. Blanch and drain ⅔ cup broccoli florets. Prepare Quiche Lorraine, above, omitting the bacon. Spread the onions, broccoli, and ¾ cup grated Gruyère or other cheese on the bottom of the pie shell before adding the custard.

CRUSTLESS QUICHE *One 10-inch quiche; 6 servings*

Any quiche can be made crustless with the following recipe. If you use cheese, toss it with a tablespoon of all-purpose flour first to coat.

Position a rack in the center or upper third of the oven. Preheat the oven to 400°F. Butter a 10-inch glass pie pan or ceramic quiche pan.

Prepare the fillings for Quiche Lorraine, Ham and Cheese Quiche, or Broccoli Quiche, all above, and set aside. In a bowl beat together until well combined:

4 large eggs
1½ cups light cream

1 tablespoon chopped fresh herbs, or 1 teaspoon dried (optional)
½ teaspoon salt
¼ teaspoon freshly grated or ground nutmeg
Ground black pepper to taste

Add the reserved filling and stir well to distribute evenly in the custard. Pour the mixture into the prepared dish and bake until set, golden, and a knife inserted in the center comes out clean, about 30 minutes. Let rest for 10 minutes to settle, then cut into wedges and serve.

REDUCED-FAT QUICHE

Please read The Role of Fat in Custards, 1014.

Prepare Crustless Quiche, above, substituting 3 egg whites for 2 of the whole eggs and 1¼ cups milk plus ¼ cup light cream for the cream. Bake the quiche at 325°F in a water bath (see About Baked Custards, 1013) until set in the center and a knife inserted in the center comes out clean, 40 to 55 minutes. If desired, place the quiche briefly under the broiler to brown the top before serving.

TOMATO AND GOAT CHEESE QUICHE

One 9-inch quiche; 6 servings

Prepare:

½ recipe Flaky Pastry Dough, 859, or Deluxe Butter Flaky Pastry Dough, 862

Roll out the dough ⅛ inch thick and fit into a buttered 9-inch quiche, tart, or pie pan. Refrigerate while you prepare the filling.

Set a rack in the lowest position in the oven. Preheat the oven to 400°F.

Prepare and set aside:

1 pound plum tomatoes (about 6), cored, quartered lengthwise, and seeded

Crumble into a bowl:

4 ounces fresh goat cheese

Slowly mash in with the back of a wooden spoon until smooth:

¾ cup half-and-half or heavy cream
½ cup milk

Add and whisk until smooth:

3 large eggs
1 tablespoon chopped fresh parsley
1½ teaspoons chopped fresh thyme or savory or 3 tablespoons chopped fresh basil
¼ teaspoon salt
Plenty of ground black pepper

Remove the pastry shell from the refrigerator and arrange the tomato quarters in the shell like the spokes of a wheel, with the pointed end (blossom end) toward the center of the quiche. Fill in the center with more quarters. Pour the cheese mixture over the tomatoes and bake until the pastry and top are golden brown, 40 to 45 minutes. Let the quiche rest for 10 minutes to settle, then cut into wedges and serve.

LEEK TART (FLAMICHE AUX POIREAUX)

One 9-inch tart; 6 servings

This is a rich leek and cream pie from northern France.

Prepare:

½ recipe Flaky Pastry Dough, 859, or Deluxe Butter Flaky Pastry Dough, 862

Roll out the dough ⅛ inch thick and fit into a buttered 9-inch quiche, tart, or pie pan. Refrigerate while you prepare the filling.

Melt in a medium skillet over medium heat:

2 tablespoons unsalted butter

Add:

2 pounds leeks (white and tender green parts only), split lengthwise, cleaned thoroughly, and cut into ¼-inch-thick slices
½ teaspoon salt
Ground black pepper to taste

Cover and cook until the leeks are very soft, with little color, reducing the heat as they cook, about 30 minutes.

After about 15 minutes of cooking time, set a rack in the lowest position in the oven. Preheat the oven to 400°F.

In a bowl, beat together until well combined:

2 large eggs
½ cup heavy cream, half-and-half, or light cream
¼ teaspoon freshly grated or ground nutmeg
Salt and ground black pepper to taste

Remove the pastry shell from the refrigerator. When the leeks are done, add to the custard and transfer to the prepared pastry shell. Bake until golden and the custard is set, 20 to 30 minutes. Let rest for 10 minutes to settle, then cut into wedges and serve.

BASIC BREAKFAST STRATA

6 to 8 servings

This one-dish egg casserole is somewhere between a baked custard and French toast. Layers of day-old buttered bread form the base, and the addition of sausage, cheese, vegetables, or whatever strikes your fancy gives it character and flavor. An egg custard is then slowly poured over the top, and the whole thing is left in the refrigerator overnight to meld. The next morning, simply bake it while the coffee brews.

Butter a 2½-quart soufflé dish or casserole. Heat a large, heavy skillet over medium-high heat and add:

1½ pounds bulk Country or Breakfast Sausage, 727, or store-bought sausage

Brown the sausage for 5 minutes, breaking it up with a fork as it cooks. Add:

2 cups sliced mushrooms
½ cup finely chopped onions

Cook for 5 minutes, stirring frequently. Set aside. In a large bowl, combine:

4 large eggs, lightly beaten
2 cups milk

Place in the bottom of the prepared baking dish a layer of:

1 large loaf day-old Italian bread, cut into 18 to 20 slices, crusts removed, buttered if desired

Top with half of the sausage mixture and sprinkle with one-third of:

1½ cups grated Swiss or Cheddar cheese

Repeat with another layer of bread, the other half of the sausage, and another ½ cup cheese. Cover with a third layer of bread. Slowly pour the milk and egg mixture over the top and sprinkle with the last ½ cup grated cheese. Let the strata stand for at least 1 hour or cover and refrigerate for up to 24 hours.

Preheat the oven to 350°F.

Set a baking sheet on the lowest rack of the oven to catch any drips and bake the strata until the top is nicely browned and bubbly, about 1 hour.

CINNAMON CREAM CHEESE STRATA

Prepare Basic Breakfast Strata, above, omitting the sausage, onions, and mushrooms and substituting cinnamon-raisin bread for the Italian bread. Use 5 ounces cream cheese, cut into small cubes, in place of the cheese, and add 2 teaspoons ground cinnamon and ¼ cup pure maple syrup to the egg mixture.

EGGNOGS

UNCOOKED EGGNOG

About 40 servings

A rich and extravagant version.

In a large bowl, beat until light in color:

12 large egg yolks

Gradually beat in:

1 box (1 pound) powdered sugar

Add very slowly, beating constantly:

2 cups dark rum, brandy, bourbon, or rye, or a combination

Let stand, covered, for 1 hour to dispel the eggy taste. Add, beating constantly:

2 to 4 cups chosen liquor(s)
8 cups heavy cream

Refrigerate, covered, for 3 hours. In another large bowl, beat until the peaks are stiff but not dry:

8 to 12 large egg whites

Fold the egg whites gently into the other ingredients. Serve the eggnog sprinkled with:

Freshly grated or ground nutmeg

COOKED EGGNOG

About 18 servings

Lightly cooking this eggnog kills any possibly dangerous bacteria in the eggs. Two tablespoons of vanilla can replace the spirits. Do not double this recipe.

Combine and set aside:

1 cup milk
1 cup heavy cream

Whisk just until blended:

12 large egg yolks
1⅓ cups sugar
1 teaspoon freshly grated or ground nutmeg

Whisk in:

2 cups milk
2 cups heavy cream

Transfer the mixture to a large, heavy saucepan and place over low heat, stirring constantly, until the mixture becomes a little thicker than heavy cream (about 175°F). Do not overheat, or mixture will curdle. Remove from the heat and immediately stir in the reserved milk and cream. Pour through a strainer into a storage container. Chill thoroughly, uncovered, then stir in:

1½ cups brandy, Cognac, dark rum, or bourbon

Cover and refrigerate for at least 3 hours or up to 3 days. Serve sprinkled with:

Freshly grated or ground nutmeg

HORS D'OEUVRE

Hors d'oeuvre, or as we usually spell and say it, "hors d'oeuvres," are small portions of food served before a meal to accompany drinks, alcoholic or otherwise. In the United States, we tend to use the term *hors d'oeuvre* interchangeably with *appetizer.* Hors d'oeuvre, literally translated, means "outside the work" of the main meal, and it is important to remember that the hors d'oeuvre course should not forecast any of the joys that are to follow. If you serve pickled beets or anchovy eggs on tomatoes with the preliminary drinks, forget the very existence of beet and tomato when planning the dinner. This is a central concept in good menu planning.

Hors d'oeuvre can be dips, spreads, pastries, olives, or nuts; they can be based on eggs, fruits, cheeses, meats, vegetables, seafood, breads. Almost anything served in portions that can be eaten with the fingers will qualify. Canapés are a specific type of hors d'oeuvre consisting of a thin bread, cracker, or pastry base, a spread, one or more toppings, and a garnish—in effect, tiny open-faced sandwiches. Hors d'oeuvre may be served hot, at room temperature, or cold. The selection is important, so plan the hors d'oeuvre menu with the whole dinner menu in mind, striking a balance between tastes and textures and degrees of richness. If the meal that follows is to be rich, serve an array of simple, light hors d'oeuvre. If your menu is plainer, try more complex items with stronger flavors. Before a dinner party, two or three kinds of hors d'oeuvre of the lighter variety are usually sufficient; you want to stimulate guests' appetites, not sate them. For a cocktail party without dinner to follow, prepare five or six different hors d'oeuvre, including some more substantial foods. For a reception or party that will take the place of dinner, serve six to eight hors d'oeuvre with lots of variety and with heartier kinds added. As a general rule, figure two pieces per person of each hors d'oeuvre at any type of party. (These loose guidelines do not include dips, which may always be included.) Whether setting out a buffet table laden with hors d'oeuvre or passing trays of bite-sized foods, vary the shapes, sizes, colors, and textures to make the selections visually enticing.

Hors d'oeuvre can often be prepared ahead of time and refrigerated, or in a few cases even frozen, for future use. Hors d'oeuvre made with pastry, 151–153, are especially convenient.

It is usually best to choose hors d'oeuvre that don't require last-minute cooking, so that you can spend some time with your guests before you need to finish the main meal. If you are serving hot hors d'oeuvre, pass them after all of your guests have arrived so that everyone has the opportunity to taste them. A microwave can speed preparation time; use it to reheat precooked hors d'oeuvre or heat dips and sauces. Hors d'oeuvre based on bread, however, do not reheat successfully in a microwave.

CHIPS

Crunchy and delicious, these may well be America's favorite food. The most common chips are made from potatoes, but delicious recipes for fried root chips and tortilla chips can also be found below.

POTATO OR SARATOGA CHIPS *4 servings*

Properly fried chips are light, without any greasy feel. It helps to use a deep-fat fryer with a basket, and it's important not to let the chips brown too quickly, or they'll be limp once removed from the fat. It should take them about 3 minutes to turn from white to gold. Since many conditions affect how rapidly anything cooks and browns, from altitude to the exact condition of the potato, adjust the temperature to get the timing right on the first few, then continue with the rest. For waffled potato chips, use the waffle-cut attachment on a mandoline, 411—a mandoline also produces thin, even slices for regular chips.

Soak in cold water for 2 hours, changing the water twice:

1 pound baking potatoes, peeled and sliced as thinly as possible

Drain and dry very well between clean dish towels.

Heat in a deep fryer or deep, heavy pot to 380°F:

3 inches vegetable or olive oil

Slowly drop a handful of potatoes into the oil. Poke them several times with a spoon so they don't stick to one another. Cook until golden, 2 to 3 minutes. Remove to paper towels to drain. Sprinkle, if desired, with:

Salt to taste

ROOT CHIPS *6 servings*

Though the potato crisps most successfully, other root vegetables can also be turned into chips, providing varied flavors and colors.

With a sharp knife, vegetable peeler, or food processor, peel, then slice as thinly as possible, at most 1/8 inch thick, any combination of the following, about 1 1/2 pounds total:

Baking potatoes
Celery root
Carrots
Parsnips
Rutabagas
Sweet potatoes
Red or golden beets

Place the potatoes, celery root, parsnips, and rutabagas in cold water after slicing to prevent discoloring. Heat in a deep fryer or deep, heavy pot to 370° to 380°F:

2 inches vegetable oil

Drain the vegetables and pat them dry. Fry each type of vegetable separately, adding just a few at a time so as not to overcrowd. Poke the slices with a chopstick to prevent them from sticking. Cook until golden brown. The time will vary slightly for each individual vegetable. Remove to paper towels to drain. Season with:

Salt to taste

Serve hot.

CRISPY POTATO SKINS *16 skins; 4 servings*

For a spicy variation, sprinkle these browned potato wedges with grated Monterey Jack and/or Cheddar cheese, broil, and serve with one of the salsas for dipping, 61 to 63.

Scoop out the flesh (reserving it for another use) from:

4 baking potatoes, baked and quartered lengthwise

Preheat the oven to 500°F.

Melt in a large skillet over medium-high heat:

2 tablespoons butter

Add half the potato wedges and cook, stirring, until golden brown. Remove to paper towels to drain. Spread the insides with:

Garlic Butter, 77, Chili Butter, 77, Sesame Ginger Butter, or other flavored butter, 76 to 78

Place on a baking sheet and crisp in the oven for about 5 minutes. Serve hot. Repeat with the remaining potato wedges.

TORTILLA CHIPS *48 chips*

Homemade tortilla chips based on top-quality store-bought or homemade corn tortillas are a real treat.

Quarter:

12 Corn Tortillas, 754

Heat in a medium skillet to 375°F:

2 cups vegetable oil

Add as many tortilla quarters as will fit in a single layer and fry, turning once, until browned and crisp. Remove to paper towels to drain. Repeat with the remaining tortillas. Sprinkle immediately with:

Salt

NACHOS *10 to 12 servings*

Nachos were apparently invented by, and named for, Ignacio "Nacho" Anaya at a restaurant called the Victory Club in the Mexican border town of Piedras Negras (just across the Rio Grande from Eagle Pass, Texas) in 1946 or 1947. The original "Nacho's Special" was nothing more than fried tortilla chips topped with cheese

and sliced jalapeños. These nachos are slightly more complicated than Nacho's original, but they're addictively good. There are many types of canned chili peppers available, from mild to fiery, so choose carefully.
Preheat the broiler. On an 11- or 12-inch round heatproof platter, spread:

4 ounces tortilla chips (about 4 cups)

(They can be slightly overlapping.) Sprinkle with:

1½ cups grated sharp Cheddar cheese
1½ cups grated Monterey Jack cheese
One 4-ounce can chopped mild green chili peppers, drained

Broil 5 to 6 inches from the heat until the cheese is melted, 2 to 3 minutes. Top with your choice of:

Sour cream
Sliced pitted black olives
Chopped scallions
Chopped jalapeño pepper rings
Chopped fresh cilantro

Serve immediately.

DIPS

Dips have become a staple American hors d'oeuvre. Quick and easy to prepare, they offer the opportunity for endless flavor combinations and can be built on a number of bases, including sour cream, crème fraîche, yogurt, soft cheeses, mayonnaise, and cream cheese. To lower the fat in the recipes, use reduced-fat versions of these products or try vegetable- or bean-based recipes instead, such as Black-Bean Salsa Dip, below, or any of the salsas in Condiments, Marinades & Dry Rubs, 60. Flavored mayonnaises also make great dips, 73 to 75. Prepare cold dips at least 1 hour ahead of time or even a day in advance to allow the flavors to blend. Hot dips can be assembled ahead, covered, and kept refrigerated until ready to cook. Serve cold dips in small bowls, hollowed-out large round loaves of bread, or vegetable "containers," such as cabbage leaves or bell peppers. In warmer weather, place the dip container in crushed ice when serving. Accompany dips with an assortment of cut-up raw vegetables, crackers, assorted breads (toasted or otherwise), chips, seafood, or cubes of cheese or meat. Plan on about 1 cup dip to serve 4 people.

RED ONION DIP

About 2 cups

A great improvement on the standard onion dip.
Stir together in a large nonstick skillet over medium-high heat:

3 small red onions, finely chopped (about 2 cups)
2 cups beef stock
1½ tablespoons minced peeled fresh ginger
3 cloves garlic, minced
1 teaspoon fresh thyme leaves or minced fresh parsley, or scant ½ teaspoon dried
Salt and ground black pepper to taste

Bring to a boil, stirring, until almost all of the stock has been absorbed by the onion, about 15 minutes; watch it carefully at the end so that it doesn't burn. Remove to a bowl and stir in:

1 teaspoon balsamic vinegar

Let cool completely, then stir in:

1 cup sour cream

Serve slightly chilled.

SPINACH YOGURT DIP

2 cups

For a creamier consistency, drain the yogurt by placing it in a sieve lined with a clean dish towel or coffee filter for about 30 minutes.
Thaw, squeezing as dry as possible:

One 10-ounce package frozen chopped spinach

Mince in a food processor:

3 scallions, chopped
1 to 2 cloves garlic, chopped

Add the spinach along with:

2 cups low-fat yogurt, or 1 cup full-fat or low-fat yogurt and 1 cup nonfat cottage cheese
2 tablespoons grated Parmesan cheese
2 tablespoons sour cream (optional)
⅛ teaspoon freshly grated or ground nutmeg
Salt to taste

Pulse until smooth. Refrigerate for at least 1 hour or up to 24 hours. Serve in a bowl with:

Cut-up raw vegetables
Sliced bread

SPINACH YOGURT DIP IN A BREAD BOWL

Prepare Spinach Yogurt Dip, above. To make the bread bowl, cut the top inch off a crusty round loaf of bread (about 1 pound). Pull the bread out of the center to hollow it. Spoon the dip in and serve the removed bread chunks for dipping.

BLACK-BEAN SALSA DIP

About 1¼ cups

This no-fat dip can be served with tortilla chips or spooned into Masa Boats, 171, and garnished with any or all of the suggestions below.
Puree in a food processor until smooth:

One 15½-ounce can black beans, rinsed and drained
6 tablespoons medium-hot or hot salsa
1½ tablespoons fresh lime juice
1 small clove garlic, minced

Garnish with:

Diced tomatoes, chopped fresh cilantro, and/or diced red bell peppers

Serve with:

Tortilla chips

BAKED ARTICHOKE DIP

About 2½ cups

Preheat the oven to 400°F.

Stir together in a medium bowl:

1 cup mayonnaise
1 cup grated Parmesan cheese
½ cup finely chopped onions

Pulse in a food processor until finely chopped:

One 13¾-ounce can artichoke hearts, well drained

Stir into the cheese mixture along with:

1 tablespoon fresh lemon juice or dry white wine
¼ to ½ teaspoon ground black pepper

Scrape into a small baking dish or ovenproof crock. Combine and sprinkle over the dip:

3 tablespoons dry unseasoned breadcrumbs
1 teaspoon olive oil

Bake until the top is browned, about 20 minutes. Serve with:

Crackers or toast

HOT CRAB DIP

2 cups

Preheat the oven to 325°F. Butter a 2-cup ovenproof bowl.

Puree in a food processor until smooth:

8 ounces cream cheese, softened
¾ cup mayonnaise
2 tablespoons minced onions
1 teaspoon drained horseradish
1 teaspoon Worcestershire sauce
¼ teaspoon salt

Scrape into the bowl. Fold in:

One 6-ounce can crabmeat, drained

If desired, sprinkle with:

Slivered almonds

Bake until heated through, about 25 minutes. Serve with:

Crackers

SEVEN-LAYER DIP

20 servings

This substantial appetizer is best warm but can be served at room temperature. Assemble and serve it in a glass dish to display the layers.

Preheat the broiler.

In a 13 x 9-inch glass baking dish, evenly spread:

One 16-ounce can refried beans

Mash together and spread over the beans:

3 large ripe Hass avocados, peeled and pitted
3 tablespoons fresh lime juice

Mix together and spread over the avocado layer:

2 cups sour cream
1 envelope (1 ounce) taco seasoning

In the order listed, sprinkle with:

3 tablespoons drained chopped canned mild green chili peppers
One or two 5¾-ounce cans pitted black olives, drained and sliced
8 ripe plum tomatoes, chopped (about 4 cups)
2 cups grated sharp Cheddar cheese

Broil about 4 inches from the heat just until the cheese is melted, 1 to 2 minutes. If desired, sprinkle the top with:

Chopped fresh cilantro or scallions

Serve with:

Sturdy tortilla chips or toasted wedges of pita bread

SPREADS

Spreads are a bit thicker than dips and are sometimes served already atop crackers, toast, or sliced vegetables. Most spreads can be turned into dips by thinning slightly with cream, lemon juice, vinegar, or mayonnaise. Because spreads keep well, they can be made a day ahead and refrigerated until just before serving. If you do not plan to serve spreads on crackers or toast, offer them in small bowls or ramekins with the crackers alongside. Figure 1 to 2 tablespoons of spread per person.

LIPTAUER CHEESE

1 cup

This is Hungary's famous spiced cheese spread.

Stir together until thoroughly blended:

8 ounces cream cheese, softened
2 teaspoons sweet Hungarian paprika

Stir in:

2 tablespoons finely minced onions
2 teaspoons drained capers, chopped
¾ teaspoon caraway seeds

Scrape into a small bowl and serve with:

Thinly sliced black or rye bread
Radishes (optional)

BLUE CHEESE SPREAD WITH WALNUTS

1¼ cups

If serving with fruit slices, soak the fruit in a bowl of water mixed with a squeeze of lemon juice to prevent browning.

Puree in a food processor until smooth:

8 ounces cream cheese, softened

2 ounces blue cheese
2 tablespoons port (optional)

Scrape into a small bowl. Sprinkle with:

1 tablespoon chopped walnuts, toasted

Serve with:

Sliced French bread
Sliced apples and/or pears
Quartered fresh figs

CREAM-CHEESE CHUTNEY SPREAD *1½ cups*

This old-fashioned spread is especially good with whole-wheat crackers.

Pulse in a food processor until combined:

8 ounces cream cheese, softened
6 tablespoons mango chutney

Scrape into a small bowl. Sprinkle with:

1 tablespoon chopped walnuts, toasted

Serve with:

Crackers

SALMON MOUSSE *3 cups*

This easy mousse can also be piped through a pastry bag with a large fluted tip onto or into sliced bread, Cucumber Cups, 232, or cucumber slices.

Stir together in a saucepan or microwave-safe cup:

¼ cup fresh lemon juice
2¼ teaspoons (1 envelope) unflavored gelatin

Let stand for 5 minutes to soften. Heat for 1 to 2 minutes over medium heat or in a microwave, covered, on high until dissolved, about 40 seconds. Let cool for a few minutes, then stir in:

¼ cup mayonnaise
¼ cup sour cream

Combine in a food processor:

One 15-ounce can red salmon, drained, skin and bones removed
¼ cup chopped fresh dill
1 shallot, minced
1 tablespoon drained capers, chopped cornichons, or pickle relish
1 teaspoon sweet paprika
Ground red or white pepper to taste

Pulse briefly just until combined. Do not overprocess. Add the gelatin mixture and pulse once just to combine. Beat until stiff peaks form:

¾ cup heavy cream

Gently fold the salmon mixture into the cream. Oil a decorative fish mold or a stainless-steel bowl. Transfer the salmon mixture to the oiled container, smooth the top, cover, and refrigerate until firm, 2 to 3 hours. To unmold, submerge two-thirds of the mold in very hot water for 20 to 30 seconds and immediately invert the mousse onto a serving platter. Garnish with:

Watercress sprigs, thinly sliced cucumber, or lemon wedges

CRACKERS, BISCUITS, AND OPEN-FACED SANDWICHES

Crackers, biscuits, and breads are easy to dress up into hors d'oeuvre. Try these contemporary classics or make up your own. See also Ideas for Tea Sandwiches, 184.

LEMON CRACKERS *About 44 crackers*

These can be frozen, thawed, and then sliced and baked when company arrives.

Whisk together in a bowl:

1½ cups finely grated Parmesan cheese
¾ cup all-purpose flour
1 teaspoon finely grated lemon zest
¾ teaspoon coarsely ground black pepper

Add and cut in with 2 knives or a pastry blender until the mixture resembles coarse crumbs:

4 tablespoons (½ stick) cold butter, cut into small pieces

Make a well in the center and add:

1½ tablespoons water
1 teaspoon fresh lemon juice

Stir with a fork just until the mixture forms a dough. Briefly knead the dough just until combined. Transfer to a sheet of wax paper and, using the wax paper as an aid, shape it into a squared-off log, about 11 inches long. Wrap in the wax paper and refrigerate until firm enough to slice, about 1 hour. (The dough can be prepared up to this point 2 days in advance.)

Preheat the oven to 375°F.

Cut the dough into ¼-inch-thick slices and arrange 1 inch apart on baking sheets. Bake one sheet at a time until the crackers are golden around the edges, about 10 minutes. Transfer carefully with a spatula to a rack and let cool completely. Sprinkle with:

Coarsely ground black pepper

HAM BISCUITS *24 biscuits; 8 servings*

This popular southern treat can be served already assembled, or you can let guests put together their own.

Preheat the oven to 425°F.

Prepare the dough for:

Basic Rolled Biscuits, 789, or Beaten Biscuits, 791

adding:

¼ cup snipped fresh chives (optional)

Roll out the dough into a circle or rectangle about ¾

inch thick. Cut into 2-inch rounds, hearts, or diamonds with a biscuit or cookie cutter. Place 1 inch apart on ungreased baking sheets and brush the tops with:

Melted butter

Bake until golden on top, about 15 minutes. Meanwhile, for honey mustard, whisk together in a small bowl:

½ cup whole-grain mustard
2 tablespoons honey, or to taste
1 tablespoon Dijon mustard

Or have ready for spreading:

4 tablespoons (½ stick) butter

When the biscuits are cool enough to handle, split them, spread with the honey mustard or butter, and make sandwiches with:

12 ounces thinly sliced smoked or baked ham or prosciutto

Serve warm or at room temperature.

TURKEY BISCUITS WITH CHUTNEY BUTTER

24 biscuits; 8 servings

Cress or Argula Butter, 77, Nut Butter, 77, or any other flavored butter can be substituted for the chutney butter in these biscuits.

Prepare the biscuits for Ham Biscuits, above. While the biscuits are baking, stir together:

8 tablespoons (1 stick) butter, softened
3 tablespoons mango chutney
Pinch of curry powder
Pinch of salt

When the biscuits are cool enough to handle, split them, spread with the chutney butter, and make sandwiches with:

12 ounces sliced turkey breast

Serve warm or at room temperature, or to serve the assembled biscuits hot, heat on a baking sheet in a 350°F oven until warmed through, about 10 minutes.

FILET MIGNON CANAPÉS

About 90 small canapés

Served on thin slices of baguette, a little filet goes a long way. A wide variety of flavored spreads can be applied; some of them are suggested below.

Prepare:

Roasted Filet or Tenderloin of Beef (High-Temperature Method), 625, or Beef on a String, 655, using 2½ pounds beef

Meanwhile, thinly slice:

3 thin baguettes

(Wider baguettes will yield fewer canapés.) Spread the baguette slices evenly with:

1¼ to 1½ cups Snail Butter, 77, Maître d'Hôtel Butter, 77, flavored butter, 76 to 78, honey mustard, whole-grain mustard, or a flavored mayonnaise, 73 to 75

Cut the filet lengthwise into quarters and thinly slice each quarter. Top each bread slice with a slice of filet. If desired, top each one with:

1 small sprig fresh parsley, dill, or watercress
Capers
Sliced or diced raw or roasted yellow or red bell peppers
Diced onions
Dab of Caramelized Onions, 391

SMOKED TROUT CANAPÉS WITH HORSERADISH CREAM

75 small canapés

Using a vegetable peeler, cut lengthwise stripes into:

2 English cucumbers

Cut the cucumbers into seventy-five ¼-inch-thick slices and lay these out on baking sheets. Stir together:

½ cup sour cream
4 teaspoons drained horseradish, or more to taste

Using a measuring spoon, dollop about ¼ teaspoon of the horseradish cream on the center of each cucumber slice. Divide among the cucumber slices:

8 ounces boneless smoked trout, skinned and broken into small pieces about the size of almonds

These can be stored for up to 3 hours in the refrigerator, lightly covered with dampened paper towels. Before serving, garnish each canapé with:

1 tiny sprig fresh dill

Serve on a tray, garnished with:

Lemon wedges

CHEESE AS HORS D'OEUVRE

In addition to these simple cheese-based delights, consider serving a cheese platter as an hors d'oeuvre. Choose at least two varieties and no more than eight or ten, depending on the size of your guest list. Arrange the cheeses on a large board or tray with or without fruit. Select complementary cheeses, and present them whole to be sliced (or scooped up) as desired by the guests. Make sure you have the proper serving utensils (cheese knives, etc.), and enough of them. Offer a variety of mustards, breads, biscuits, and/or crackers on the side. See The Cheese Course, 17.

MARINATED GOAT CHEESE WITH FRESH THYME

8 to 10 servings

Goat cheese marinated in olive oil with herbs is a staple of the Mediterranean larder.

Place in a shallow bowl:

One 7-ounce log goat cheese
2 tablespoons extra-virgin olive oil
1½ teaspoons fresh thyme leaves

Turn the cheese to coat. Marinate in the refrigerator, turning once or twice, for at least 1 hour or up to 5 days. Let warm to room temperature before serving, about 30 minutes. Serve with:

Sliced French bread, toasted

GOAT CHEESE WITH CRACKED PEPPER

8 to 10 servings

Crack with the bottom of a heavy pot:

½ teaspoon whole black peppercorns

Roll in the peppercorns:

One 7-ounce log goat cheese

Set the cheese on a plate and drizzle over the top:

2 tablespoons extra-virgin olive oil

If desired, sprinkle with:

6 sun-dried tomato halves in oil, drained and chopped

Serve at room temperature with:

Sliced French bread, toasted

PESTO CHEESECAKE

20 servings

This "cheesecake," a kind of vegetarian pâté, was the centerpiece at Ethan and Susan Becker's wedding reception.

Prepare:

Pesto Sauce, 307

Preheat the oven to 375°F. Lightly butter an 8-inch springform pan. Dust the bottom and sides of the pan with:

Seasoned dry breadcrumbs

Mix together in a large bowl ½ cup of the pesto along with:

1 pound ricotta cheese
½ cup sour cream
4 large eggs
1 teaspoon salt
½ teaspoon grated lemon zest
½ teaspoon freshly grated or ground nutmeg
½ teaspoon ground black pepper

Pour into the prepared pan. Bake in a water bath, 1013, until set, 30 to 35 minutes. Remove from the water bath and transfer the pan to a rack to cool completely. Cover and refrigerate until cold, 6 to 12 hours. Slide a thin-bladed knife around the outside of the cake and remove the outer ring. Spread the remaining pesto around the sides of the cheesecake. Spread the top with an even layer of:

½ cup sour cream

If desired, arrange on the top:

12 sun-dried tomato halves in oil, drained and chopped

Serve cold or at room temperature with:

Sliced French bread, toasted

CHEESE BALL

One 7-inch ball

In a large bowl, blend with a mixer:

Two 8-ounce packages cream cheese, softened
⅓ cup grated Parmesan cheese
¼ cup mayonnaise
2 tablespoons finely chopped onions
2 tablespoons finely chopped carrots
2 tablespoons finely chopped celery
1 teaspoon drained horseradish
½ teaspoon salt

Place the mixture on a large piece of plastic wrap. Bring up the edges of the wrap and form the mixture into a ball. Place in a small, deep bowl to help it hold its shape and refrigerate for at least 1 hour. If desired, when firm, roll the cheese ball in:

1¼ cups chopped walnuts

Press the nuts to make them adhere. Serve with:

Crackers

The cheese ball can be stored in the refrigerator for up to 3 days.

BRIE BAKED IN PASTRY

28 servings

Let warm to room temperature, 30 minutes to 1 hour:

One 17½-ounce package frozen puff pastry sheets

Unfold the two 9-inch squares and, on a lightly floured surface, gently roll out each into a 12-inch square. Center 1 sheet in a 9-inch pie pan. Top with:

One 1-kilogram Brie wheel (2.2 pounds, 8 inches in diameter)

If desired, spread the top of the cheese with:

3 to 4 tablespoons sweet chutney, finely chopped, or sweet preserves

Fold the pastry up and over the Brie, pleating the excess and trimming it to 1 inch over the top rim of the cheese. Cut the second pastry sheet into a circle the diameter of the Brie, using the top of the cheese box as a template. Lay the pastry circle on top of the Brie, gently roll the top and bottom edges together, and crimp to seal. Refrigerate for at least 30 minutes or up 24 hours.

Preheat the oven to 400°F.

Stir together in a small bowl:

1 large egg yolk
1 tablespoon milk

Using a pastry brush, gently brush the egg wash over the pastry. Bake for 10 minutes. Reduce the oven temperature to 350°F and bake until golden and puffy, 30 to 40 minutes. Let stand for 1 hour before serving. Serve in the pie pan or gently remove to a plate. Cut a small wedge and partially remove. Set out the Brie with a knife, surrounded by:

Sliced fresh or dried fruit
Sliced French bread

FRUIT AS HORS D'OEUVRE

Fruit offers a light, refreshing counterpoint to savory hors d'oeuvre. During the summer months, when a greater variety of fruit is available all over the country, the colorful bounty of a large fruit platter can be truly magnificent. Keep the pieces large and arrange them according to size, color, and shape rather than tossing them together like a salad. Mix styles on the same platter by combining cut melons, pineapple, or other fruit with some whole fruit with stems, like berries, small clusters of seedless grapes, or cherries on the stem. Use fruit leaves for garnish if available. For a spicy arrangement, make a platter of sliced peeled honeydew melon, watermelon, cantaloupe, mango, green apple, and jícama (though a vegetable, it is a lovely addition to a fruit platter) and just before serving, sprinkle the platter with lime juice or a mixture of salt and chili powder. Also consider skewered fruits served with a sweetened dip—for instance, a mixture of vanilla yogurt, honey, mint, and lemon zest. Grilled fruits such as pineapple, plums, peaches, and bananas, served on or with skewers or toothpicks, are another possibility. Single fruit trays are also dramatic. Try serving a large basket of strawberries with a bowl of sour cream and another of brown sugar, or melon balls or strawberries wrapped in prosciutto. In the winter months, try a platter of red-skinned pear wedges served with a soft blue cheese for spreading.

VEGETABLES AS HORS D'OEUVRE

Cooked or raw vegetables make some of the most colorful and appreciated hors d'oeuvre. In addition to the recipes that follow, remember that a large basket of assorted raw vegetables, often called crudités, makes a pretty centerpiece. Please see page 161 for ideas and consider any of the dips in this chapter in addition to the dipping suggestions there.

NEW POTATOES STUFFED WITH BACON AND CHEESE

24 little potato skins

Look for small new potatoes or cut larger ones crosswise into thirds; use the two ends for potato skins and save the middle slices in water to cover for another use.

Preheat the oven to 425°F.

Whisk together in a medium bowl:

2 tablespoons butter, melted (optional)
1 teaspoon Dijon mustard

Halve:

Twelve 1½- to 2-inch new potatoes

With the large end of a melon baller, hollow out each half, leaving ¼-inch shells. Immediately toss the halves in the mustard mixture. Roast, cut side down, on a lightly oiled baking sheet until nicely browned, 20 to 30 minutes. Sprinkle with:

Coarse salt

Turn the potatoes upright and distribute equally among the skins:

¾ cup grated pepper Jack cheese

Sprinkle equally with:

8 slices bacon, cooked until crisp and crumbled

At this point, the potatoes can be held at room temperature for up to 2 hours before serving. Return the potatoes to the oven and bake until hot, about 5 minutes. If desired, garnish with:

Sour cream
Sliced scallion greens

NEW POTATOES STUFFED WITH SOUR CREAM AND CAVIAR

24 little potatoes

Prepare the potatoes as directed for New Potatoes Stuffed with Bacon and Cheese, above, omitting the mustard or, if desired, omitting both the butter and the mustard and roasting them cut side up. If you would rather not scoop the potatoes out, slice them instead and top with the sour cream and caviar. Let the potatoes cool for 5 minutes, then sprinkle with:

Coarse salt

Spoon or pipe into each potato skin:

1 teaspoon sour cream or crème fraîche

Top each potato with:

⅛ to ½ teaspoon caviar or other roe

Sprinkle generously with:

Snipped fresh chives

MUSHROOMS STUFFED WITH BREADCRUMBS AND HERBS

24 mushrooms

These may be frozen unbaked for up to 2 weeks, but for best results, cook them fresh. If frozen, thaw for 1 hour, then bake as directed.

Preheat the oven to 375°F.

Remove and reserve the stems from:

20 ounces mushrooms, wiped clean

Count out 24 same-sized mushroom caps and toss with:

1 to 2 tablespoons butter, melted, or olive oil

Slice the remaining caps. Rinse and chop the stems. Heat in a medium skillet:

2 tablespoons butter or olive oil

Add the sliced and chopped mushrooms along with:

1 large shallot, minced

½ teaspoon dried thyme

Cook, stirring occasionally, over medium heat for 5 minutes. Stir in:

¾ cup dry or fresh unseasoned breadcrumbs

3 tablespoons snipped fresh chives or chopped fresh basil or tarragon

2 tablespoons dry vermouth or sherry

Transfer to a food processor and coarsely chop. Season with:

Salt and ground black pepper to taste

Fill each mushroom cap with 1 heaping teaspoon of the filling. Place on a baking sheet. Sprinkle with:

2 to 3 tablespoons grated Parmesan cheese

Bake until the top is bubbling, about 15 minutes. Serve warm.

MUSHROOMS STUFFED WITH SAUSAGE

24 mushrooms

Heat a medium skillet over medium heat. Add:

12 ounces sweet or hot sausage links, casings removed, or bulk sausage

2 teaspoons minced garlic

Cook for 5 minutes, stirring to break up the meat. Stir in:

½ cup dry or fresh unseasoned breadcrumbs

¼ cup chopped roasted red peppers or pimientos

3 tablespoons minced fresh parsley

Prepare Mushrooms Stuffed with Breadcrumbs and Herbs, above, discarding the mushroom stems and substituting the sausage mixture for the mushroom filling. Sprinkle with cheese and bake as directed.

STUFFED CELERY

24 pieces

Depending on the filling, use a spoon, pastry bag, or plastic bag with a cut corner to stuff the celery.

Fill the hollows of:

Twenty-four 3-inch-long pieces celery, leaves intact where possible

with 1¼ to 1½ cups of any of the following:

Cream cheese, softened

Salmon Mousse, 147

Blue Cheese Spread with Walnuts, 146

Garnish with:

Chopped walnuts or fresh parsley

PASTRY HORS D'OEUVRE

Phyllo (also called filo) pastry dough leaves, basic to a number of cuisines all over the Middle East, eastern Europe, and Greece, can be found in the frozen food section of your supermarket. Thin and fragile, the pastry can be quite intimidating to the uninitiated, but it is easy to use if you follow these rules: Thaw the pastry in the refrigerator or at room temperature, remove it from the box, open the sheets out flat (they will be rolled in the package), and immediately cover the stack with a damp clean dish towel. Use one sheet at a time, keeping the rest covered. Brush each layer and the tops of the formed pastry with melted butter to keep it from drying and flaking. Don't worry about small tears.

Because it keeps so well in the freezer, pastry is a perfect choice for elegant hors d'oeuvre that can be at least partially prepared in advance. Pastry dough, for instance, can be rolled, cut, shaped, and frozen, then removed from the freezer at the proper time, filled, and baked. Phyllo pastries, such as those below and on pages 917 to 919, can be completely assembled and then frozen later to be baked straight from the freezer. Choux paste (pâte à choux), 919, can be frozen in its uncooked state and removed the day before the party to thaw overnight in the refrigerator. The morning of the party, pipe the dough into shapes and bake the puffs. For specific details on handling choux paste and puff pastry, please see the Pies and Pastry chapter.

MUSHROOM TRIANGLES

36 triangles

You may end up with about 30 triangles.

Combine in a small bowl:

½ ounce dried porcini or other dried mushrooms, such as shiitake

1 cup hot water or white wine

Let stand for 30 minutes. Strain the liquid through a fine-mesh sieve lined with a dampened paper towel, reserving the liquid, and finely chop the mushrooms. Melt in a medium skillet over medium heat:

2 tablespoons butter

Add and cook, stirring constantly, for 1 minute:

2 tablespoons minced shallots

1 teaspoon minced garlic

Add the chopped dried mushrooms along with:

6 ounces cremini, shiitake, or button mushrooms, wiped clean, stems trimmed, coarsely chopped

Cook, stirring occasionally, until the mushrooms begin to wilt, about 3 minutes. Add:

3 tablespoons reserved mushroom soaking liquid

2 tablespoons minced fresh parsley

½ teaspoon salt
¼ teaspoon ground black pepper, or to taste

Cook, stirring occasionally, until the mixture is almost dry, about 5 minutes. Transfer to a bowl and let cool completely. If desired, stir in:

2 ounces goat cheese

Preheat the oven to 375°F.

Melt in a small saucepan:

4 tablespoons (½ stick) butter

Cover with a damp towel on a work surface:

8 sheets frozen phyllo dough, thawed

Remove 1 sheet and brush it with melted butter. Lay another sheet over the first and cut lengthwise into 9 strips. Working with 1 strip at a time, spoon 1 teaspoon of the filling at the bottom left corner of the strip. Fold the bottom end over the filling to meet the right-hand edge, making a triangle; continue to fold, as if folding a flag, all the way to the top. Place on a baking sheet. Repeat with the remaining strips. Brush the tops with melted butter. Repeat with the remaining phyllo and filling. Bake until golden brown, about 15 minutes. Serve hot.

SPINACH AND FETA TRIANGLES
36 triangles

This is a classic Greek combination.

Melt in a small skillet over medium heat:

2 tablespoons butter

Add and cook, stirring, for about 5 minutes:

¼ cup minced onions

Add:

One 10-ounce package frozen chopped spinach or mustard greens, thawed and well drained (about 1 cup)

Cook over medium heat until the juices are evaporated, about 5 minutes. Remove to a medium bowl and let cool. Stir in:

4 ounces feta cheese, crumbled
1 teaspoon fresh lemon juice
½ teaspoon ground black pepper

Proceed as for Mushroom Triangles, 151, substituting the spinach mixture for the mushroom filling.

PARMESAN STRAWS
32 straws

Cheese straws are a perfect way to use puff pastry scraps.

Roll out into a 17 x 9-inch rectangle:

1 pound Food Processor Puff Pastry, 908

Transfer the pastry to an ungreased baking sheet. Cover and refrigerate the dough for at least 30 minutes or wrap airtight and freeze until ready to use.

If the dough is frozen, let it thaw for a few minutes before cutting. Quickly transfer the pastry to a cutting board, trim ½ inch from all the sides to make a 16 x 8-inch rectangle, and cut into two 8-inch squares. Lightly brush the squares with:

1 egg, lightly beaten

Sprinkle over 1 square:

½ cup grated dry cheese, such as Parmesan, pecorino, aged Asiago, or a combination
Salt and ground black pepper to taste

Roll lightly with the rolling pin to embed the cheese. Brush any cheese that clings to the rolling pin back onto the pastry. Place the second square, egg side down, on top of the cheese. Roll the cheese-filled dough into a 17 x 9-inch rectangle. Return to the baking sheet and refrigerate for 30 minutes.

Transfer the dough to a cutting board. Butter the baking sheet generously. Trim the pastry ½ inch all around, then cut the dough crosswise into 8 x ½-inch strips. Twist each strip by holding one end on the work surface and twisting the other end about 3 revolutions. Place the twisted strips at least 1 inch apart on the baking sheet, pressing the ends down firmly so that they don't untwist. Refrigerate or freeze until firm while the oven preheats.

Position a rack in the lower third of the oven. Preheat the oven to 425°F.

Bake the cheese straws until they are light brown, 12 to 15 minutes. Remove the sheet to a rack and let cool completely before serving.

PEPPER CHEESE STRAWS

Prepare Parmesan Straws, above, combining the cheese with 2 to 3 tablespoons cracked black peppercorns and salt to taste.

FOOD PROCESSOR CHEESE STRAWS

Preheat the oven to 350°F.

Place in the bowl of a food processor:

8 tablespoons (1 stick) unsalted butter, softened
8 ounces sharp cheese, such as sharp Cheddar or blue cheese, cut into chunks

Add:

1½ cups all-purpose flour
¼ teaspoon salt
¼ to ½ teaspoon ground red pepper
1 teaspoon Worcestershire sauce

Process until the mixture comes together; then press the dough together, wrap it in plastic, and chill for 30 minutes. Divide the dough into 4 equal pieces and roll each piece out between 2 sheets of wax paper to ⅛ inch thick. Cut into 6 x ½-inch strips. Twist, if desired, or form into other shapes. Arrange the pieces on 1 or 2 ungreased cookie sheets. Or, if desired, use a cookie press outfitted with a houndstooth or star dispenser. Push the dough out onto an ungreased cookie sheet to make individual "straws." Bake until crisp and lightly browned, about 15 minutes. For a darker color, cook a bit longer. Remove the sheet to a rack and let cool completely before serving.

CHOUX PUFFS WITH LOBSTER SALAD

24 small puffs

Baked choux puffs can also be filled with other salads such as Egg Salad, 230, Shrimp Salad, 231, Chicken or Turkey Salad, 229, with a chutney. Creamy fillings like Chicken Liver Pâté, 725, and Salmon Mousse, 147, can be piped into the bottom of unsplit puffs using a pastry bag fitted with a wide plain tip.

Prepare:

½ recipe Choux Paste, 919

Form into twenty-four 1-inch puffs on a baking sheet. Bake as directed and cool. Split and fill with:

1 to 1½ cups Lobster Salad, 231

Serve immediately.

SEAFOOD AS HORS D'OEUVRE

Fish and shellfish are always appreciated as hors d'oeuvre and are easy to prepare, since most of the work can be done ahead of time. No-Fail Boiled Shrimp, 514, can be cooked a day ahead and stored in the refrigerator until ready for presentation with cocktail sauce—making shrimp cocktail. Take care to arrange the shrimp in the same direction to create a more impressive look. Serve Coconut Shrimp, 154, on a tray sprinkled with coconut flecks. Dips and sauces should be made a day ahead to let the flavors blend. Use bowls, hollowed-out lemon halves, cleaned oyster shells, or whole crab shells to hold dips. You can turn broiled or grilled shrimp or scallops, 507, or any of its variations into a dramatic hors d'oeuvre by threading the seafood on skewers before grilling. Oysters and clams should be opened as close to serving time as possible.

ANGELS ON HORSEBACK

24 pieces

This dish is a classic British savory.

Preheat the oven to 400°F.

Butter and lightly toast:

Twenty-four 2-inch bread rounds (cut from 8 pieces firm bread)

Shuck:

24 medium oysters

Cut crosswise in half:

12 slices bacon

If desired, spread one side of the bacon lightly with:

Anchovy paste

Wrap a half slice of bacon, anchovy side in, around each oyster and secure with toothpicks. Place on a baking sheet. Bake until the bacon is crisp, about 10 minutes. Drain on paper towels. Place the oysters on the toasts and sprinkle with:

3 tablespoons minced fresh parsley

Serve immediately.

OYSTERS ROCKEFELLER

24 oysters

Preheat the oven to 450°F.

Shuck, 502, and place on the half shell:

24 medium oysters

Combine in a food processor just until minced, about 30 seconds:

1½ cups well-drained cooked spinach
⅓ cup fresh breadcrumbs
¼ cup chopped scallions
2 tablespoons crumbled cooked bacon
2 teaspoons chopped fresh parsley
½ teaspoon salt
4 drops hot red pepper sauce

Add:

3 tablespoons olive oil or butter, softened
1 teaspoon anisette liqueur

Process for 10 seconds more. Spoon 1 heaping teaspoon of the spinach mixture over each oyster. Sprinkle a baking sheet liberally with:

Coarse salt

Nestle the oysters into the salt to steady them. Bake until plumped, about 10 minutes, then broil until the tops are browned, about 2 minutes. Serve hot.

CLAMS CASINO

24 clams

Preheat the broiler.

Combine in a food processor or blender until smooth, about 1 minute:

4 tablespoons (½ stick) butter, softened
1 scallion, chopped
1½ tablespoons minced fresh parsley
1 tablespoon fresh lemon juice
¼ teaspoon salt

Shuck, 497, and place on the half shell:

24 cherrystone clams

Spoon about 1 teaspoon of the butter mixture on top of each clam. Top with:

6 slices bacon, cooked until crisp and crumbled

Broil until the butter is bubbling, about 3 minutes.

BAKED HONEY SHRIMP *6 first-course servings; 12 to 15 hors d'oeuvre servings*

Mix together in a small bowl:

1 tablespoon chopped fresh parsley
1 teaspoon grated lemon zest

Cover and refrigerate until ready to use. Whisk together in a medium bowl:

Juice of 2 lemons
½ cup olive oil
2 tablespoons soy sauce
2 tablespoons honey
2 tablespoons Cajun seasoning
1 tablespoon chopped fresh parsley
¼ teaspoon ground red pepper

Add to the bowl:

2 pounds large shrimp, shelled and deveined, if desired, 490

Toss well in the dressing, cover, and let marinate in the refrigerator for 1 hour, stirring occasionally.

Position a rack in the center of the oven. Preheat the oven to 450°F.

Transfer the shrimp to a baking pan or sheet large enough to hold them in 1 layer. Bake the shrimp until they are firm, 8 to 10 minutes. Sprinkle the shrimp with the reserved lemon zest and parsley mixture, and serve with:

Sliced French bread

FRIED SHRIMP

Frying is a perfect way to cook shrimp because the succulent juices remain sealed inside the crisp crust. A simple squeeze of lemon juice adds the perfect acid balance to any fried seafood, but richer sauces can be used as well, such as Rémoulade, 73, or Tartar Sauce, 73.

CAJUN POPCORN *12 to 15 servings*

This recipe can be made with clams, oysters, baby shrimp, or, as it is traditionally done in Louisiana, with crayfish. In Louisiana the shells are sometimes left on, adding more crunch. These baby shrimp can be scooped up and eaten as easily as a handful of popcorn, so make sure you have plenty.

Stir together in a medium bowl:

1 cup all-purpose flour
1 teaspoon sugar
1 teaspoon salt
½ teaspoon onion powder
½ teaspoon garlic powder
½ teaspoon ground white pepper
½ teaspoon ground black pepper
½ teaspoon ground red pepper
½ teaspoon dried thyme

Make a well in the center. Gradually pour into the well, whisking constantly:

1½ cups milk
2 large eggs, lightly beaten

Let stand for 30 minutes. Meanwhile, heat to 365°F in a deep fryer or deep, heavy pot:

2 cups vegetable oil

Stir into the batter:

2 pounds baby Gulf shrimp, shelled

Remove with a slotted spoon and lightly toss with:

2 cups dry unseasoned breadcrumbs or fine cornmeal

Immediately add to the hot oil in batches and fry until crisp and lightly browned, 2 to 3 minutes. Remove with a slotted spoon to paper towels. Serve immediately with:

Garlic Mayonnaise, 74

BEER-BATTER SHRIMP *6 first-course servings; 12 to 15 hors d'oeuvre servings*

Shell, leaving the tails:

2 pounds medium shrimp

With a paring knife, open each shrimp along the back and remove the intestinal vein. Open the shrimp down the back without cutting all the way through to butterfly it, then press flat. Stir together in a large bowl:

1 cup all-purpose flour
2 teaspoons salt
1 teaspoon baking powder
½ teaspoon ground red pepper

Whisk in:

¾ cup beer
½ cup milk
2 large eggs

Add the shrimp and let stand for 30 minutes. Heat in a deep fryer or deep, heavy pot to 365°F:

3 cups vegetable oil

Remove the shrimp 1 at a time from the batter and fry in small batches, turning twice to ensure they are golden brown and crispy, about 4 minutes total. Using tongs, remove the shrimp to paper towels to drain. Serve as is or with:

Sauce Rémoulade, 73

COCONUT SHRIMP

Prepare Beer-Batter Shrimp, above, substituting ½ cup orange juice for the beer. After the shrimp are dipped in the batter, press them into a mixture of 3 cups shredded unsweetened dried coconut and 1 cup dry unseasoned breadcrumbs. Fry as directed. Serve as is or with Mango Salsa, 63.

CHICKEN AS HORS D'OEUVRE

Chicken hors d'oeuvre can be passed on trays with small dipping bowls if there is a sauce (don't forget to follow with a small basket to collect bones, napkins, and skewers) or served in paper-lined baskets on the table. Serve with more than one dip or sauce for variety. For chicken wings, some cooks prefer to substitute the lower-fat chicken "tenders" (breast pieces), though these are less flavorful. If you skewer them after cooking, they make an elegant presentation.

BUFFALO CHICKEN WINGS *24 pieces*

These were invented at the Anchor Bar in Buffalo, New York, in 1967.

Preheat the oven to 350°F.

Remove and discard the wing tips from:

1½ pounds chicken wings

Separate each wing into 2 pieces at the joint; trim excess fat and skin. Stir together on a plate:

⅓ cup all-purpose flour

1 teaspoon salt

½ teaspoon ground black pepper

Coat the wings with the flour mixture and shake off the excess. Heat in a deep fryer or deep, heavy pot to 375°F:

3 cups vegetable oil

Heat over medium heat until a corner of a wing held in the oil makes a lively sizzle. Add as many wings as will fit in a single layer without crowding; fry, turning once, until golden brown and cooked through, about 10 minutes. Drain on paper towels and keep warm on a baking sheet in the oven. Repeat with the remaining wings. Heat in a small saucepan over low heat until foaming:

3 tablespoons butter

Remove from the heat and stir in:

2 tablespoons red wine vinegar

2 tablespoons hot red pepper sauce, or to taste

Transfer the wings to a large mixing bowl, pour the sauce over the wings, and toss until evenly coated. Taste and adjust the seasonings. Serve hot with:

Celery sticks

Creamy Blue-Cheese Dressing, 240

DEVILED CHICKEN WINGS *24 pieces*

Preheat the oven to 400°F. Grease a large baking sheet with:

2 tablespoons vegetable oil

Remove and discard the wing tips from:

1½ pounds chicken wings

Separate each wing into 2 pieces at the joint; trim excess fat and skin. Stir together in a large bowl:

½ cup honey

3 tablespoons whole-grain mustard

2 tablespoons Dijon mustard

1 tablespoon cider vinegar

Combine on a plate:

⅔ cup dry unseasoned breadcrumbs

1 teaspoon dried thyme

½ teaspoon ground red pepper, or more to taste

Toss the wings in the honey mixture. Add 1 at a time to the crumb mixture and turn to coat completely, shaking off the excess.

Spread the wings on the prepared baking sheet. Bake, shaking the pan twice during the cooking or turning the wings with tongs, until the wings are well browned and crispy, 20 to 30 minutes. Serve hot or at room temperature.

LEMON ROSEMARY CHICKEN ON SKEWERS *16 pieces*

Cubed chicken breast is marinated, skewered, then broiled or grilled. When grilling, make sure to cover the exposed skewers with foil, or they will burn. Alternatively, cook the chicken unskewered, and skewer it afterward to serve it. If you prefer more of a glaze, you can sauté the marinated chicken in a pan with a little oil, then skewer the pieces afterward. Grilled or sautéed pieces of fruit or vegetables can be added to the skewers for color and flavor contrast. For another skewered chicken dish, prepare Beef Satay, 179, using chicken.

Stir together in a medium bowl:

3 tablespoons olive oil

2 tablespoons fresh lemon juice

2 teaspoons grated lemon zest

1 teaspoon chopped fresh rosemary

1 teaspoon minced garlic

½ teaspoon salt

¼ teaspoon ground black pepper

Cut into 16 pieces by cutting each half into 8 pieces:

1 boneless, skinless chicken breast

Add the chicken to the marinade and stir to coat. Cover and refrigerate for 1 to 2 hours.

When you are ready to cook, prepare a medium-hot charcoal grill or preheat the broiler.

Thread the chicken pieces onto 16 skewers, covering the exposed wood with aluminum foil. Grill or broil just until cooked through, about 2 minutes on each side. Serve hot or at room temperature.

CHICKEN FINGERS

6 to 8 servings

Whisk together in a large bowl:

½ cup milk
1 large egg
1 tablespoon vegetable oil
1 tablespoon water

Stir together on a plate:

½ cup dry seasoned breadcrumbs
½ cup cornmeal
½ cup all-purpose flour
1 teaspoon salt
½ to 1 teaspoon ground red or black pepper

Coat in the milk mixture:

1 pound chicken tenders (breast fillets)

Roll the tenders 1 at a time in the crumb mixture. Place in a single layer on a baking sheet. (At this point, the chicken can be refrigerated for several hours before frying.) Heat in a deep fryer or large deep, heavy pot to 375°F:

2 inches vegetable oil

Place a few tenders in the oil so the pan is not crowded and cook until golden brown, 2 to 3 minutes on each side. Drain on paper towels. Fry the remaining tenders and drain. Serve warm or at room temperature with any of the following sauces and dips:

Southeast Asian Peanut Dipping Sauce, 83
Creamy Blue-Cheese Dressing, 240
Italian Tomato Sauce, 304
Pesto Sauce, 307
Ranch Dressing, 241
Reduced-Fat Yogurt Dill Dressing (Reduced Fat), 242
Honey-Mustard Dipping Sauce, 79

MEATS AS HORS D'OEUVRE

Filled and rolled sliced meats have become a popular hors d'oeuvre because they can be prepared quickly and hold well. Make and arrange these small hors d'oeuvre on trays lined with greens or fresh herbs and garnished with fresh fruit. Cover the trays well and refrigerate until just before serving. Make hors d'oeuvre-sized Swedish Meatballs, 723, ahead and reheat in the microwave, on top of the stove, or in the oven. Marinate and skewer Rumaki, 157, well ahead of the party, cover and refrigerate, and slide under the broiler when you're ready to serve.

HAM ROLLS WITH ASPARAGUS AND HONEY MUSTARD

20 to 25 pieces

Lay out on a work surface:

5 medium-thin slices smoked ham or prosciutto (about 8 ounces)

Carefully spread the slices with a thin layer of:

Honey mustard (about 2 teaspoons total)

Along one edge of each slice, lay:

1 cooked asparagus stalk

Roll the ham around the asparagus to form a long cylinder. Cover with plastic wrap and refrigerate until firm, 1 to 3 hours. When ready to serve, slice each roll crosswise into 4 or 5 pieces, about 1 inch long. Stand the slices, cut side up, on a platter, alone or with other rolled meats. Garnish with:

Orange slices
Watercress sprigs

SMOKED TURKEY AND ARUGULA ROLLS

32 pieces

Peppery arugula stands up nicely to smoked turkey. If your supermarket doesn't carry arugula, substitute watercress.

Stir together:

½ cup mayonnaise
1 tablespoon Pesto Sauce, 307

Lay out on a work surface:

8 medium-thin slices smoked turkey (about 8 ounces)

Carefully spread a thin layer of the pesto mayonnaise over the slices. Cut each slice crosswise in half, then in half the opposite way to form four triangles. Top each with:

1 arugula or watercress leaf, trimmed

Roll up each triangle to form a cone with a little green peeking out. Stand the pieces up on a platter, alone or with other rolled meats.

PIGS IN A BLANKET

16 pieces

Kids love these and enjoy helping to roll them as well. Packaged dough allows variations on the classic—just make sure to gently push the perforations together to seal.

Preheat the oven to 375°F.

Carefully unroll:

One 8-ounce can refrigerated crescent roll dough

Separate into 4 equal rectangles, ignoring the corner-to-corner perforations. Cut each rectangle into four 3-inch-long strips. Brush each strip lightly with:

Dijon mustard

Top each strip with:

1 cocktail frank (16 franks total)

Roll the dough around each frank, pushing together at the ends to seal. Place seam side down on an ungreased baking sheet, about 2 inches apart. Whisk together, then brush on the dough:

1 large egg

1 tablespoon milk

Bake until the dough is puffy and golden brown, about 15 minutes. Serve with a dipping bowl of:

Honey-Mustard Dipping Sauce, 79, or mustard

KIELBASA IN QUILTS

32 pieces

Prepare Pigs in a Blanket, 156, substituting 1 pound kielbasa for the cocktail franks. Divide the dough into 4 rectangles (do not cut into strips) and cut the kielbasa into 4 pieces. Brush the dough with the mustard, and roll each rectangle around a kielbasa section, pinching the seam together to seal. Refrigerate for 15 minutes to make slicing easier. Place on a work surface, seam side down, and slice each roll crosswise into 8 rounds. Place the rounds, meat side up, on an ungreased baking sheet, brush with the egg wash, and bake as directed.

RUMAKI

18 pieces

These can be assembled ahead of time and broiled just before serving.

Trim well and cut in half:

8 ounces chicken livers, rinsed

Whisk together in a mixing bowl:

2 tablespoons soy sauce

2 tablespoons sake or dry sherry

1 tablespoon grated peeled fresh ginger

2 teaspoons light brown sugar

Add the livers and toss until coated. Cover and marinate in the refrigerator for 1 to 2 hours.

Preheat the broiler.

Lay out on a work surface:

6 thick slices bacon (about 8 ounces), cut crosswise into thirds

Lay 1 piece of chicken liver on each piece of bacon and roll up. Secure with a toothpick speared through the overlapping ends of the bacon and out the other side. Place on a broiler rack set on a drip pan. Broil 4 inches from the heat, turning once, until the bacon is crisp and the livers are cooked but still slightly pink inside, 5 to 6 minutes. Drain briefly on paper towels, transfer to a platter, and serve hot.

WATER CHESTNUT RUMAKI

36 pieces

These are a little less awkward to roll and still have a wonderful taste.

Mix together and marinate for 20 minutes:

One 8-ounce can whole water chestnuts, rinsed and drained

2 tablespoons teriyaki sauce

Preheat the broiler.

Lay out on a work surface:

12 thick slices bacon (about 1 pound), cut crosswise into thirds

Lay 1 water chestnut on each piece of bacon and roll up. Secure with a toothpick speared through the overlapping ends of the bacon and out the other side. Place on a broiler rack set on a drip pan. Broil 4 to 6 inches from the heat, turning once, until the bacon is cooked but not crisp, about 3 minutes. Drain briefly on paper towels. Serve hot on a bed of:

Kale

LITTLE DISHES

In the United States and many European countries, the tradition has developed of structuring meals in a regular pattern: small appetizer, larger main course with accompaniments, small dessert. Sometimes one end or the other is lopped off, and sometimes more courses are added, but the form remains more or less the same. It scarcely need be said that not all the world eats this way. Most cuisines provide some sort of mealtime structure, of course, but the size of courses does not necessarily vary in accordance with their place in the meal, and in those regions where a variety of foodstuffs is available, many "little dishes" are often preferred to one or more bigger ones. These may even redefine the very nature of mealtime. In Spain, for example, *tapas* provide the underpinning for an informal but intensely sociable lifestyle; Cantonese *dim sum* fuel regular business or family gatherings; in Greece, Turkey, and the Middle East the array of small dishes known as *mezethes* or *meze* embodies a centuries-old heritage of hospitality, as does the *zakuska* table of Russian tradition. Everywhere they are found, small dishes are the foods of good fellowship and ease, almost invariably linked with drinking (wine, spirits, or tea) and the international embodiment of what we now call "comfort foods."

This style of eating became something of a fad in the United States in the 1980s under the name "grazing." Instead of always following our old-fashioned mealtime traditions, we might well find it very pleasant indeed to "graze" on a bite of this or two bites of that—or to combine several "little dishes" into a full meal.

CHINA

The little dishes favored by the Cantonese are known collectively as *dim sum,* which literally means "dot the heart," a phrase we have always thought implied small, pointed pleasures. Dim sum are associated with *yam cha,* or tea taking—the long, leisurely morning ritual of sitting and talking, sipping and nibbling. Originally the participants were men doing their business—real or imagined—but today the whole family enjoys the process. Dim sum restaurants tend to be cavernous; servers circulate with carts containing a wide assortment of dumplings, prepared meats and vegetables, and other items, both sweet and savory, arrayed on little plates. Summoned by a beckon or nod, servers deposit the plates on the table, then move on to the next; one's bill is calculated by the number of empty plates accumulated. The essential beverage with dim sum is tea. Even in areas of China where the dim sum tradition as such does not exist, street vendors offer snacks such as sweetened nuts, and eggs cooked in a flavorful tea mixture and little dishes such as scallion pancakes and pickled vegetables are widely popular.

BABY RIBLETS *32 riblets*

Whisk together in a bowl:

½ cup soy sauce
1 tablespoon minced peeled fresh ginger
1 tablespoon minced fresh cilantro or 1 teaspoon ground coriander
2 teaspoons minced garlic
½ teaspoon ground black pepper
¼ teaspoon coarse salt

Whisk in:

2 tablespoons peanut oil
1 tablespoon toasted sesame oil

Pour the marinade into a wide, shallow pan. Add and turn to coat evenly:

2 racks pork baby back ribs, halved

Marinate for at least 45 minutes at room temperature.

Meanwhile, preheat the oven to 400°F.

Lay the ribs out on baking sheets. Bake until still slightly pink, about 30 minutes.

Prepare a medium-hot charcoal fire or preheat the broiler.

Grill or broil the ribs until they are deep brown and glazed, about 3 minutes each side. Baste with the marinade, cut into individual riblets, and serve hot.

CHINESE DUMPLINGS *About 20 dumplings*

Dumpling skins are available in all Chinese markets and, these days, in many supermarkets. If you live near a Chinese market, it is probably the best place to buy your dumpling skins, since the skins sold there will tend to be thinner and therefore slightly less doughy. Alternatively, you can use 6½-inch square egg roll wrappers, and trim the corners to make 4½-inch circles.

You can substitute ground turkey for the pork in these dumplings if you wish or, for a vegetarian version, leave out the meat and add about a cup of mung bean sprouts.

Combine in a large bowl:

2½ cups finely chopped Chinese (Napa) cabbage
1 teaspoon salt

Let stand for 30 minutes to draw out the water, then squeeze as much water as possible from the cabbage.

Combine with:

8 ounces lean ground pork
1½ cups minced leeks
4 teaspoons minced garlic
1 tablespoon soy sauce
2½ teaspoons toasted sesame oil
2 teaspoons cornstarch
1½ teaspoons sake
⅛ teaspoon ground black pepper

Stir vigorously with a fork to break up the meat. If the mixture seems loose, mix in:

½ teaspoon cornstarch

Place 2 packed tablespoons of the filling in the center of each of:

20 round dumpling skins

Brush the edge with water and fold in half to make a half-moon shape, pressing out the air and sealing the edges together. If desired, form small peaks along the rounded edge using the thumb and index finger of one hand. (The straight edge of the dumpling will bend in a semicircle to conform to the shape of the pleated edge.) Place the sealed dumplings on a baking sheet lightly dusted with:

Cornstarch

Bring to a boil in a large pot over high heat:

12 cups water

Add half the dumplings, stir once or twice to prevent them from sticking, return to a boil, and boil for 7 minutes. Remove with a strainer, drain, and repeat with the remaining dumplings.

Combine:

½ cup soy sauce
1 tablespoon minced garlic

and serve alongside the hot dumplings.

SCALLION PANCAKES *4 pancakes*

These pancakes, another Chinese specialty, can be served whole as an appetizer or side dish, or cut into wedges and served as a snack. You can make them up to 8 hours ahead of time, then reheat for 5 minutes in a 350°F oven just before serving.

Mix well in a medium bowl:

1½ cups cake flour
½ cup all-purpose flour
1½ teaspoons salt

Add:

1½ tablespoons corn oil
1 cup boiling water

Stir to form a rough dough. If the dough is too soft, knead in up to:

¼ cup flour

Turn the dough onto a lightly floured surface and knead until smooth, about 5 minutes, adding more flour as needed. Cover with a cloth or wrap in plastic and let stand for 20 minutes. Turn out the dough onto a floured work surface and divide it into 4 equal portions. Roll out 1 portion into a 6 x 8-inch rectangle. Brush with:

1 teaspoon toasted sesame oil

Sprinkle with:

1 tablespoon chopped scallion greens

From the long side, roll the dough into a cylinder and pinch the ends to seal. Flatten the roll slightly with a rolling pin and coil into a snail shape, with the seam on the inside. Pinch the end to secure and set aside while rolling and shaping the remaining portions. Let the pancakes stand for 30 minutes. Flour the work surface and roll out the coiled pancakes into 8-inch rounds.

Heat in a medium, heavy skillet over medium heat:

3 tablespoons safflower or corn oil

Add 1 pancake and fry, turning once, until golden brown and crisp on both sides, 2 to 3 minutes per side. Remove to paper towels to drain. Transfer to a baking sheet and keep warm in a 200°F oven while frying the remaining pancakes, using more oil as needed.

Mix together:

½ cup soy sauce
1 tablespoon minced peeled fresh ginger
1 tablespoon chopped scallion greens
1 teaspoon toasted sesame oil (optional)

Serve the pancakes immediately with this dipping sauce.

TEA EGGS

20 eggs

Wedges of these beautiful, flavorful eggs make a great cocktail snack.

Place in a large pan with cold water to cover:

20 large eggs

Bring to a boil over high heat, reduce the heat to low, and simmer, uncovered, for 10 minutes. Drain, let cool in cold water, and drain again. Lightly tap the shells on a hard surface to crack them but do not remove the shells. Place in a large, heavy pan:

10 cups water
½ cup loose black tea leaves
¼ cup sake
3 tablespoons soy sauce
6 quarter-sized slices fresh ginger, peeled and smashed with the flat side of a cleaver
Peel of 2 oranges
Two 3-inch cinnamon sticks or 1 teaspoon ground cinnamon
3 star anise
1½ tablespoons salt

Bring to a boil over high heat, reduce the heat to low, and simmer, uncovered, for 20 minutes. Add the cooked eggs and continue to simmer for 45 minutes. Remove from the heat and let the eggs cool completely in the tea mixture. Remove the eggs from the liquid and their shells. Serve warm or chilled, cut into wedges.

CANTONESE-STYLE PICKLED VEGETABLES

6 appetizer servings

Halve lengthwise and seed:

6 small pickling cucumbers or 2 English cucumbers

Cut each cucumber half lengthwise into thirds, then roll-cut, 334, into 1-inch pieces. Place in a large bowl along with:

1½ pounds peeled baby carrots, trimmed
1 tablespoon salt

Toss lightly and let stand for 2 hours. Drain off any water that has collected, then pat the vegetables dry.

Whisk together until the sugar is dissolved:

½ cup sugar
½ cup rice vinegar

Add the vinegar mixture to the vegetables along with:

12 quarter-sized slices fresh ginger, peeled and smashed with the flat side of a cleaver

Toss lightly to coat, cover, and refrigerate for at least 3 hours or up to 24 hours before serving.

CRISP PECANS

6 appetizer servings

Walnut halves can be substituted in this recipe.

Bring to a boil in a large, heavy saucepan over high heat:

½ cup sugar
1 teaspoon salt
4 cups water

Add:

1 pound pecan halves

Return to a boil, reduce the heat to medium, and simmer, uncovered, for 15 minutes. Drain the pecans well, then spread in a single layer on a baking sheet and let dry for about 1 hour, tossing occasionally.

Preheat the oven to 300°F. Lightly grease a baking sheet with:

Corn or safflower oil

Spread the nuts in a single layer on the baking sheet and roast, stirring occasionally, until crisp and golden brown, about 45 minutes. Let cool completely, then transfer to a serving bowl. The pecans will keep, stored in a tightly covered container, for up to 1 week.

FRANCE

Although French food has the reputation of being formal and the concept of snacking is foreign in traditional French culinary life, there is a rich repertoire of light, simple dishes in France, served either as appetizers (or, in some restaurants, as the "pre-appetizers" called *amuse-bouches,* mouth-amusers) or as constituents of a casual lunch or supper. These are not "little dishes" in the cultural sense perhaps, but they can be happily adapted to the purpose. Many of these *petits plats* come from the region of Provence—among them the caper-olive paste known as tapenade and little toasts topped with anchovy spread (both of which, not coincidentally, are pungent enough to stand up to the customary aperitif of the region, the anise-flavored liquor known as pastis)—but every part of France makes its contribution.

CRUDITÉS *6 to 8 appetizer servings*

Crudités literally means "rawnesses" and refers to an assortment of raw vegetables. In France, this usually means a kind of untossed salad, with portions of, for instance, quartered tomatoes and shredded carrots, both moistened with vinaigrette, celery root dressed with sauce rémoulade, and some neatly trimmed long radishes, all sharing a small plate. In the United States, the term has come to mean an assortment of raw vegetables, often cut into chunks or strips, with a dip on the side. The best vegetables for any selection of crudités are those that are freshest in the market (or your garden) on the day you are making it. For maximum visual effect, arrange the vegetables in a large basket or on a platter, interspersing those with brighter colors (radishes, bell peppers, carrots) among those of a more subdued hue (scallions, celery, cauliflower, mushrooms). For a casual affair, a single dip or salad dressing for drizzling over the vegetables is sufficient. If the crudités are the centerpiece of a buffet of little dishes, you might want to offer several dipping options.

Decoratively arrange in a large basket or on a platter:

About 6 cups assorted vegetables, rinsed, seeded, and trimmed as needed (any combination of cauliflower florets, radishes, carrot sticks, celery sticks, cucumber spears, zucchini strips, mushrooms, snow peas, bell peppers cut into eighths, fennel strips, blanched green beans, romaine lettuce hearts, scallions, cherry tomatoes, strips of cooked beets, and so on)

Garnish as desired with:

Green and/or black olives
Large fresh parsley and/or rosemary sprigs

Set out one or more of the following for dipping and drizzling over the top:

Any salad dressing, 234 to 242
Any dipping sauce, 145 to 147
Any flavored mayonnaise, 73 to 74, or Garlic Mayonnaise, 74
Tapenade, below

SALMON PÂTÉ *4 to 6 appetizer servings*

Combine in a small saucepan:

4 ounces skinless salmon fillets, cut into bite-sized pieces
½ cup dry white wine

Bring to a boil over medium heat. Remove from the heat and drain, discarding the wine. In a small saucepan, heat over medium heat:

1 tablespoon olive oil

Add the salmon and cook until opaque, about 5 minutes; do not let it brown. Add:

2 tablespoons brandy or Cognac
Salt and ground black pepper to taste

Remove from the heat and set aside. In a small saucepan, melt over medium heat:

3 tablespoons unsalted butter

Add and cook, stirring, until opaque, 3 to 5 minutes:

4 ounces smoked salmon

Let cool, then puree the smoked salmon in a food processor along with:

3 tablespoons unsalted butter

Using a fork, combine the fresh salmon and the smoked salmon mixtures until well blended. Taste and adjust the seasonings. Cover and refrigerate for at least 12 hours before serving. Remove from the refrigerator about 30 minutes before serving. Serve on:

Thin slices of warm toast

TAPENADE (CAPER OLIVE PASTE)

About 2¾ cups

Based on its name, the one essential ingredient in this popular spread is the caper—*tapeno* in Provençal. Tapenade made without capers or with only a hint of them is sometimes called *olivade.*

Combine in a food processor:

2 cups black olives, preferably oil cured, pitted
3 anchovies, rinsed and patted dry (optional)
3 tablespoons drained capers
3 tablespoons extra-virgin olive oil
2 tablespoons brandy or fresh lemon juice
2 cloves garlic, coarsely chopped
2 teaspoons fresh thyme leaves, or 1 teaspoon dried
Salt and ground black pepper to taste

Pulse until the mixture is still coarse but of a uniform consistency. Serve with:

Crusty French bread or Crudités, above

TUNA TAPENADE *1 cup*

With a fork, flake and transfer to a food processor:

One 6-ounce can tuna packed in olive oil, drained (if tuna packed in olive oil is not available, use white tuna packed in water, drained)

Add:

4 tablespoons (½ stick) unsalted butter, softened
1 cup best-quality green olives (such as Picholine), pitted
¼ cup minced fresh basil
Grated zest of 1 lemon
2 tablespoons fresh lemon juice

Process just until blended; the mixture should remain slightly coarse. If desired, season with:

Ground black pepper to taste

Transfer to a medium bowl and serve at room temperature. The tapenade can be stored, covered and refrigerated, for up to 3 days.

ANCHOVY TOASTS *4 appetizer servings*

Soak for 10 minutes in cold water to cover:

4 ounces anchovies, drained

Drain, pat dry, and mince. Combine well with:

3 tablespoons extra-virgin olive oil
1 tablespoon red wine vinegar
3 tablespoons chopped fresh parsley
2 cloves garlic, minced
Ground black pepper to taste

Preheat the broiler.

Place on a baking sheet:

16 slices French bread, cut on a diagonal from a baguette or other narrow loaf

Broil until golden, about 3 minutes each side. Spread the toasts with the anchovy mixture and broil just until warm, about 1 minute. Serve immediately.

GOUGÈRES (CHEESE PUFFS) *About 48 puffs*

These Burgundian cheese puffs, as light as air when made properly, are an elegantly simple hors d'oeuvre. Pass them on a pretty tray and serve with Champagne.

Stir:

1 cup grated Gruyère cheese

into:

1 recipe Choux Paste, 920

Pipe as directed for profiteroles, 921. Sprinkle with:

About ½ cup grated Gruyère cheese

Bake as directed for profiteroles, 921. Do not poke the bottoms. Serve warm.

CHEESE CHIPS *25 to 30 chips*

Preheat the broiler.

Grate into a small bowl:

4 ounces imported French sheep's milk cheese, Dutch Gouda, or Monterey Jack cheese, rind removed

Sprinkle 1 tablespoon of the grated cheese into a 2-inch round metal cookie cutter placed on a nonstick baking sheet. Take care to spread the cheese as thinly as possible so that it will cook evenly. Continue, leaving enough space between rounds to allow the cheese to spread as it cooks. Place the baking sheet under the broiler about 3 inches from the heat. Keeping the oven door slightly ajar, watch the cheese very carefully as it bubbles, turns lacy, and browns slightly, 1 to 2 minutes. When the bubbling subsides, the baking sheet can be removed from the oven. If some of the chips are not fully cooked on the edges, rotate the pan and keep them under the heat until they are done. (If making the chips in batches, take care that the baking sheet is cooled before the next batch.) Remove the baking sheet from the oven and allow the chips to cool and firm up, 1 to 2 minutes. Using a spatula, carefully transfer the chips to a rack. The chips can be stored in an airtight container for up to 1 week.

GREECE AND THE MIDDLE EAST

In Greece, when friends gather in *tavernas* or *ouzerís* to socialize over glasses of potent anise-flavored ouzo or resinated wine, the table is always cluttered with plates full of little snacks called *mezethes.* These might include a creamy feta cheese dip, a puree of roasted eggplant, or the pureed fish roe known as taramasalata—all to be eaten on triangles of pita bread—or such items as stuffed grape leaves or assorted phyllo pastries stuffed with olives, greens, or cheese. Likewise, in Turkey and the Middle East, similar preparations appear in arrays of *meze,* served less as cocktail-hour snacks (since the predominantly Muslim population in these regions does not consume alcohol) than as appetizers before a meal—or even, in sufficient quantity and variety, as a substitute for more formal main dishes.

WHIPPED FETA WITH ROASTED PEPPERS

About 2 cups

This dip is a specialty of Macedonia.

Combine in a food processor:

1 pound Greek feta cheese, crumbled
2 tablespoons extra-virgin olive oil

Pulse until the feta is creamy. Add:

1 red bell pepper, roasted, 403, peeled, seeded, and coarsely chopped
2 or 3 fresh jalapeño peppers, seeded and minced
2 pickled pepperoncini, rinsed, seeded, and minced
Several grindings of black pepper

Pulse until the mixture is well combined while gradually adding:

3 tablespoons extra-virgin olive oil
2 tablespoons fresh lemon juice

The feta should be creamy and spreadable. Taste and add more olive oil and/or lemon juice if desired. Serve with:

Crackers or pita bread

SMALL OLIVE PASTRIES *About 36 pastries*

Heat in a large, heavy skillet over medium heat:

3 tablespoons extra-virgin olive oil

Add and cook, stirring often, until wilted, 5 to 7 minutes:

1 small fennel bulb, trimmed and coarsely chopped (about ⅔ cup)
1 cup coarsely chopped red onions

Remove to a medium bowl and add:

2 cups pitted Kalamata olives, rinsed and coarsely chopped
2 teaspoons chopped fresh oregano
½ teaspoon ground fennel seeds or 2 tablespoons ouzo

Toss well to combine and let stand at room temperature for 20 minutes.

Meanwhile, preheat the oven to 375°F. Lightly oil 2 baking sheets.

Unroll onto a dry work surface:

1 pound phyllo dough, thawed if frozen

Cover with a dry cloth and cover the dry cloth with a damp cloth. Removing 1 sheet of phyllo at a time, place the phyllo in front of you, cut it lengthwise in half, and brush each half lightly with:

Extra-virgin olive oil

Fold each strip lengthwise in half, so each is about 3 inches wide and brush again lightly with oil. Place 1 scant tablespoon filling on the bottom of each strip. Fold the bottom corner to the other side to make a triangle and continue folding to the end of the strip, as if folding a flag. Place seam side down on a baking sheet. Repeat with the remaining phyllo and filling. Bake until the phyllo is golden brown, about 15 minutes. Serve warm or at room temperature.

TARAMASALATA (PUREED FISH ROE)

About ½ cup

This rich, creamy mixture is usually served as a spread with bread or crackers. True *taram,* the salted and dried roe of gray mullet, is difficult to find. Smoked cod or carp roe is a good substitute; rinse under cold running water to remove excess salt.

Combine in a food processor or blender:

4 ounces smoked cod or carp roe or dried gray mullet roe
Juice of 1 large lemon

Add:

2 slices firm white bread, trimmed, soaked briefly in water, and squeezed dry

With the machine running, gradually pour in:

½ to ⅔ cup olive oil

Taste and add more lemon juice if desired. Transfer to a small bowl and stir in:

½ small onion, grated and squeezed dry with a paper towel

Refrigerate and serve chilled.

STUFFED GRAPE LEAVES *About 40 pieces*

For a vegetarian version of this classic dish, omit the lamb, double the amount of rice, and add ½ cup dried currants and 2 tablespoons pine nuts to the filling mixture, then pour an additional 1 cup of liquid into the pan before cooking.

Drain:

Two 8-ounce jars grape leaves in brine

Separate the leaves in a large bowl and cover with boiling water. Let soak for 1 hour, changing the water (use cold water) twice to remove excess salt. Drain them and gently pat dry. Mix together until well combined:

1½ pounds lean ground lamb
1 medium onion, grated or finely chopped
½ cup finely chopped mixed fresh herbs (any combination of parsley, dill, and mint)
⅓ cup white rice
1 tablespoon salt
1 teaspoon dried thyme
Ground black pepper to taste

Line a Dutch oven or other large saucepan with several grape leaves, using the small or torn ones. To stuff the remaining leaves, place each one vein side up on a plate. Put a heaping tablespoon stuffing on the leaf near the stem end. Fold this end over the stuffing, then fold in the 2 sides and roll up the leaf like a small cigar, tucking in the edges to make a neat package. Squeeze gently and place seam side down in the prepared pan. Continue stuffing the leaves in the same manner, packing them in tightly together in a single layer. Repeat with a second layer. (Leave a few leaves unstuffed.) Drizzle over the top:

3 tablespoons olive oil

Pour in:

2 cups chicken or beef stock or water

Cover the top with more grape leaves and weight with a small plate. Cover the pan and simmer over low heat until the lamb is cooked and the packages are hot, about 30 minutes. Serve hot or cold, accompanied, if desired, with:

Plain yogurt

HERBED LABAN (YOGURT CHEESE)

About 20 balls

These tangy rounds are often served for breakfast in the Middle East, but they make an excellent appetizer when served on a platter with ripe tomatoes, marinated olives, and cucumber spears and accompanied with wedges of pita bread.

Mix well:

2 cups low-fat yogurt
2 teaspoons salt

Scrape into a colander lined with a triple layer of cheesecloth and let drain at room temperature for 24 hours. Turn out onto several layers of paper towels on a plate and refrigerate until almost dry to the touch, 6 to 10 hours. Mix together:

2 tablespoons minced fresh mint, or 1 tablespoon dried crumbled
1 tablespoon sweet paprika

Form the yogurt cheese into balls slightly larger than golf balls. Roll the balls in the mint mixture. Serve at once, or place in a jar and cover with:

Olive oil

Refrigerate until ready to use.

HUMMUS (MIDDLE EASTERN CHICKPEA AND SESAME DIP)

About 2 cups

If using canned chickpeas, rinse 2 cups (one 16-ounce can) and puree as directed, using water to thin the puree. In Egypt, hummus is flavored with cumin; use ½ teaspoon ground cumin for this quantity.

Pick over, rinse, and soak, 270:

¾ cup dried chickpeas

Drain and place in a pan with water to cover by 2 inches. Bring to a boil, reduce the heat, and simmer until very tender, about 1½ hours. Drain, reserving the cooking liquid. Remove the chickpeas to a food processor or blender and add:

⅓ cup fresh lemon juice
3 tablespoons tahini
2 cloves garlic, finely minced
Salt to taste

Puree until smooth, adding 2 to 3 tablespoons of the cooking liquid as needed to obtain a soft, creamy consistency. Remove to a shallow serving bowl and garnish with:

1 tablespoon olive oil
Sprinkling of hot or sweet paprika
1 tablespoon finely chopped fresh parsley

Serve with:

Warm pita bread

BABA GHANOUSH (ROASTED EGGPLANT DIP)

About 2 cups

You can stir ½ cup yogurt into the eggplant puree just before serving, then garnish.

Preheat the oven to 400°F.

Pierce in several places:

3 medium eggplants (about 4 pounds)

Roast on a baking sheet until the skins are dark mahogany in color and the flesh feels soft, 45 to 60 minutes. Let stand until cool enough to handle. Split the eggplants and scoop the flesh into a colander. Press lightly to extract the excess liquid. Remove to a food processor and add:

1½ tablespoons tahini
2 cloves garlic, chopped
Juice of 1 large lemon
½ teaspoon salt

Pulse until smooth. Taste and adjust the seasonings. Remove to a shallow serving bowl and garnish with:

1 tablespoon olive oil
1 tablespoon finely chopped fresh parsley
Several pitted black olives (optional)

Serve with:

Warm pita bread

INDIA

In a traditional meal in India, all the dishes are served at one time, and there is little appetizer/main-dish hierarchy. The small dishes of Indian cooking, then, are just parts of the whole. Perhaps the most popular small dishes of India are the little savory pastries called *samosas,* which can be filled with potatoes and other vegetables or with a meat mixture. Another well-liked dish is the spicy fruit or potato salad called *chat,* traditionally served not as part of a meal but as a snack, often from little shops specializing in it. Barbecued meat skewers and spicy chicken bites are other popular snacks among more well-to-do Indians, while the bedrock staple lentil dishes called dal, 284, can be eaten at any time.

SAMOSAS WITH POTATOES AND PEAS

About 60 samosas

These little pastries freeze very well when wrapped in plastic and can be baked frozen—simply add 5 minutes to the baking time.

Preheat the oven to 375°F. Butter 2 baking sheets. Unroll on a dry work surface:

1 pound phyllo dough, thawed if frozen

Cover with a dry towel and cover the dry towel with a damp towel. Prepare the mixture for:

Potato Patties, 165

Fold into the potato mixture:

1 cup frozen peas, thawed

Melt:

8 tablespoons (1 stick) butter

Remove 1 sheet of the phyllo and lay it on the work surface, with a long side facing you. Brush lightly with melted butter, lay a second sheet on top, and brush it with melted butter. Cut the sheets vertically into 2½-inch-wide strips (the last strip will be only 2 inches). Cover the strips with a sheet of wax paper or plastic wrap and cover that with a damp towel. Working with 1 strip at a time, scoop up a rounded teaspoon of the potato mixture and pat it over the bottom right-hand corner of the strip, so that it fills the entire corner, not just the center. Fold the corner to the other side to make a triangle and continue folding to the end of the strip, as if folding a flag. Place on a baking sheet and brush the top with melted butter. Repeat with the remaining phyllo and filling. Bake until lightly browned, about 15 minutes. Serve immediately.

CHAT (POTATO AND CHICKPEA SALAD WITH TAMARIND)

4 appetizer servings

Tamarind provides a unique tangy flavor to this dish, but it might be hard to find. You can substitute equal parts molasses, lime juice, and Worcestershire sauce for the tamarind water.

Combine in a 1-cup measure:

½ cup warm water

1 golf-ball-sized lump tamarind pulp

Drop into boiling water to cover:

2 medium boiling potatoes

Cover and cook until tender, 25 to 30 minutes. Meanwhile, prepare the *chat masala*. Toast in a heated skillet over medium heat until a shade darker and fragrant, 1 to 2 minutes:

1 tablespoon cumin seeds

2 teaspoons coriander seeds

Finely grind in a spice mill or coffee grinder along with:

1 teaspoon black peppercorns

Combine with:

2 teaspoons kosher salt

Drain the potatoes and let cool to room temperature. Remove the skins and cut the potatoes into ½-inch cubes. Combine with:

1 cup canned chickpeas, rinsed and drained

1 plum tomato, chopped

1 small onion, chopped (about ½ cup)

1 serrano pepper, seeded and minced

2 tablespoons chopped fresh cilantro

Mash the softened tamarind pulp with a fork or use your fingers. The water should become dark brown and thick with tamarind pulp. Strain, discarding the pulp. Measure 3 tablespoons tamarind water and add to the salad along with the *chat masala*. Toss gently with a fork and serve.

POTATO PATTIES

About twenty-four 1½-inch patties

If shaped into slightly larger patties (3 to 4 inches in diameter), these can also be served as a side dish with grilled meat.

Drop into boiling water to cover:

1½ pounds boiling potatoes (6 to 8 potatoes)

Cover and cook until tender, 25 to 30 minutes. Drain, remove the skins, and mash. Heat in a medium skillet over high heat:

1 tablespoon canola or other vegetable oil

Add and stir-fry until they pop:

1 teaspoon black or yellow mustard seeds

Add and stir-fry for 20 seconds more:

3 cloves garlic, thinly sliced

Stir the garlic mixture into the mashed potatoes along with:

1 small onion, chopped (about ½ cup)

¼ cup chopped fresh cilantro

1 serrano or jalapeño pepper, if desired, seeded and minced

2 tablespoons fresh lemon juice

1¼ teaspoons salt

Shape the mixture into 1½-inch patties and cook in batches, without crowding, in a lightly oiled skillet until lightly browned on both sides, 1 to 2 minutes each side. Serve at once, accompanied with:

Fresh Mint-Cilantro Chutney, 66

BARBECUED KEBABS *9 skewers*

Prepare a medium-hot charcoal fire or preheat the broiler.

Combine:

1½ pounds lean ground beef or lamb
1 large onion, very finely minced (about 1 cup)
½ cup chopped fresh cilantro
One 2½-inch piece fresh ginger, peeled and minced (about ¼ cup)
1 large clove garlic, minced
2 tablespoons chopped fresh mint
2 serrano or jalapeño peppers, seeded and minced
1 tablespoon ground coriander
1 teaspoon ground red pepper
1 teaspoon salt

Shape the mixture with lightly oiled hands into 9 flattened sausages, about 4 inches long, 1½ inches wide, and 1 inch thick. Carefully thread a skewer through each sausage. Grill until browned and just cooked through, about 2 minutes each side, or broil on a slotted broiling tray for 3 to 5 minutes each side. Serve with:

Pita bread or Naan, 753
Raita I, 82, or Raita II, 82

ITALY

Although Italy is known for the *abbondanza* (abundance) of its table and for its respect for mealtime as a definitive social and family occasion, the measured pace of life in that country also lends itself to small dishes eaten casually. In fact, so habitual is the practice of enjoying informal repasts midmorning and midafternoon that they have specific names—*spuntini* for the morning snack, *merende* for the afternoon. But Italian small dishes are perhaps most familiar to us in the form of the antipasto—which does not mean "before the pasta" but simply "before the meal." This is not necessarily the platter of assorted vegetables and cold cuts that often goes by the name in the United States. Antipasto can be a simple appetizer—melon or figs with prosciutto, prosciutto or air-dried beef alone, fresh mozzarella with tomatoes, anchovies with roasted peppers, and the like. Or it can be a buffet assortment of cold delights from which the diner may freely choose. The selection might include any of the above, as well as squid salad, all manner of pickled or grilled vegetables, marinated olives, various salads, wedges of the room-temperature flat omelets called *frittate,* zucchini or onions stuffed with meat or with breadcrumbs and herbs, and so on. The best arrays of antipasto offer a variety of flavors, textures, and colors but add up to something light enough to serve as a prelude to the feast to come. Nobody says, of course, that you cannot enjoy antipasto by itself and forget the feast.

AFFETTATO (ITALIAN CURED MEATS)

A traditional *affettato* includes five or six kinds of assorted cured meats, or *salumi,* Italian for what the French call *charcuterie.* This includes *salame* (known as salami to Americans) itself, which is simply firm, dry-aged sausage, usually made of pork and pork fat, though sometimes of beef or a mixture of beef and pork. (In Italy, there are also versions made from the meat of wild boar, horse, or even donkey!) The texture of the ground meat may vary from very fine to coarse; flavorings always include salt and black pepper and usually garlic, while some versions also have cloves, nutmeg, cinnamon, or other spices or herbs. So-called Genoa salami, common in American delicatessens, is medium-fine in texture. Another type of *salame* is sopressata, which is dry-aged sausage made of meat and fat from pigs' heads, compressed and tied into square lengths. Pepperoni, a small, firm, spicy salami well known to American pizza lovers, is unknown in Italy (where *pepperoni* are sweet bell peppers), but it may be added to *affettato* if desired. No Italian-made sausages can be imported into the United States at this time, but there are good versions of these meats made in this country and Canada—as well as some Hungarian salami, which can be more than acceptable. Mortadella, which is cooked (rather than dry-aged) sausage, is a puree of pork stuffed into a natural casing. In Bologna, where it is made, it is studded with cracked peppercorns and cubes of creamy fat. Soft in texture and subtle in flavor, some domestic varieties are very good and feature pistachios.

Salumi also include the superb prosciutto di Parma, one of the rare meat products that can be imported from Italy and an essential element in any top-notch *affettato.* Good-quality cooked ham, coppa (a fat-marbled, compressed round of pork neck meat), speck (slow-smoked, spice-cured boneless hog's leg), and bresaola (boneless air-dried beef) are also found on an *affettato* platter.

To serve an *affettato,* arrange the thinly sliced meats attractively on a large platter, rolling some, folding some into loose triangles, and leaving others flat. (In general, salamis are cut on the diagonal, and those that are narrow in diameter should be sliced slightly thicker than those that are wide.) Figure about 4 ounces of meat per person for a generous serving. Accompany the platter with slices of good Italian-style bread and little curls of butter.

TUSCAN DIPPING SAUCE FOR RAW VEGETABLES

Pinzimonio, the Italian name of this sauce, is longer than the recipe. Pure and rustic, *pinzimonio* traditionally accompanies a platter of mixed vegetables at the start of a meal. Offer the freshest, finest seasonable vegetables, for example, quartered baby artichokes or leafy celery hearts, eighths of fennel bulbs or colorful bell peppers, slender young asparagus spears or carrots, tender snap beans, shelled fava beans, and small radishes with leaves. Prepare and chill them for no more than an hour or two in advance.

Set at each place a small dish containing:

Extra-virgin olive oil

After passing the vegetable platter, pass for sprinkling into the oil:

Ground white pepper
Coarse salt

MELON AND FIGS WRAPPED IN PROSCIUTTO

6 appetizer servings

Seed, thinly slice, and remove the rind from:

1 small honeydew melon or large cantaloupe

Halve through the stem end:

6 fresh figs

Wrap each melon slice and fig half separately in:

1 paper-thin slice prosciutto (about 8 ounces total)

Serve at room temperature.

FENNEL WRAPPED IN PROSCIUTTO

12 appetizer servings

Trim the top and ¼ inch from the bottom of:

1 fennel bulb (about 1 pound)

Cut in half vertically, then cut crosswise into about thirty-six ¼-inch slices. Wrap each fennel piece in:

1 paper-thin slice prosciutto (about 4 ounces total)

Arrange on a serving platter and sprinkle with:

2 ounces Parmesan cheese, thinly shaved

Sprinkle over the top:

1 tablespoon extra-virgin olive oil
Ground black pepper to taste

Serve at room temperature.

BOCCONCINI (MARINATED MOZZARELLA)

6 to 8 appetizer servings

Warm in a medium skillet over medium heat:

1 cup olive oil

Add:

2 cloves garlic, thinly sliced
12 black peppercorns
3 large sprigs fresh rosemary
¼ teaspoon salt
Pinch of red pepper flakes

Remove from the heat and let cool to room temperature. Remove the rosemary sprigs. Pour the oil over:

12 ounces fresh mozzarella, cut into 1-inch cubes

Let stand at room temperature for several hours or cover and refrigerate for up to 4 days. If refrigerated, bring to room temperature before serving.

WHITE BEAN AND ROASTED GARLIC PUREE

4 servings

Pick over, rinse, and soak, 270:

1 cup dried cannellini, white kidney, great Northern, baby lima, or other white beans

Drain. Place in a large saucepan with enough water to cover by 2 inches and add:

1 bay leaf
1 sprig fresh thyme
1 thick onion wedge

Bring to a boil. Reduce the heat to low and cook, covered, until the beans are tender, about 1 hour. Drain, reserving ½ cup of the cooking liquid. Discard the bay leaf and thyme.

Meanwhile, preheat the oven to 325°F.

Combine in an 8-ounce custard cup or small baking dish:

6 large cloves garlic, crushed
2 tablespoons olive oil, preferably extra virgin

Cover with aluminum foil and bake until golden but not browned, about 35 minutes. Let cool slightly. In a food processor, puree the reserved cooking liquid with:

1 cup ½-inch cubes peeled baking potatoes
½ cup packed fresh basil leaves
1 teaspoon salt

Add the cooked beans and roasted garlic with oil. Process until smooth. Stir in:

⅛ teaspoon ground black pepper

Serve hot with roasted meats or chicken.

BRUSCHETTA WITH TOMATOES AND BASIL

8 slices

From the Italian word meaning "roasted over coals," bruschetta is the original garlic bread. In its simplest form, it is nothing more than grilled country bread rubbed with garlic cloves and brushed with olive oil.

(The Tuscans call it *fett'unta,* meaning "under oil.") Bruschetta can also serve as the foundation for a wide variety of toppings, however. A single bruschetta makes a good appetizer, while two or three will make a nice lunch when accompanied with a simple salad. If you follow the same process with smaller pieces of bread, you will be making *crostini,* or little toasts, which are traditionally served as appetizers.

Prepare a medium-hot charcoal fire or preheat the broiler.

Place on the grill or under the broiler:

8 thick slices crusty firm Italian bread or other country-style bread

Grill or broil, turning once, until golden brown, about 3 minutes each side. Remove from the heat and rub the surface with:

2 large cloves garlic, halved

Brush with:

3 to 4 tablespoons extra-virgin olive oil

Combine well:

4 medium, ripe tomatoes, cored and diced

½ cup slivered fresh basil leaves

Salt and ground black pepper to taste

Divide the tomato mixture among the bruschetta and serve immediately.

BRUSCHETTA WITH MOZZARELLA AND FRESH OREGANO

Grill or broil the bread, rub with garlic, and brush with oil as directed for Bruschetta with Tomatoes and Basil, 167. Top each slice with shredded mozzarella cheese (about 8 ounces total). Broil just until the cheese is bubbling. Top with diced fresh tomatoes (about 1 large tomato total) and chopped fresh oregano (about 2 tablespoons total).

JAPAN

The cuisine of Japan is renowned for its spare, elegant presentation; for its reliance on, and glorification of, seafood (and lesser but still important appreciation of seaweed); and for its full appreciation of each individual ingredient in a dish. The small dishes of this cuisine, which may be accompanied with sake, beer, or tea, reflect all three of these important qualities—particularly in such carefully arranged dishes as Shrimp and Scallop Dumplings. The simplicity of ingredients and precise construction of Beef and Scallion Rolls and the delicacy of flavor found in Chicken Dumplings are further evidence of the care that goes into the "little dishes" of Japanese cooking.

CHICKEN DUMPLINGS

About 60 dumplings

The dumplings can be made in advance and frozen in the soy mixture. Thaw, reheat, and thicken the sauce with cornstarch as directed.

Warm in a small skillet over medium heat:

1½ teaspoons vegetable oil

Add and cook until softened but not browned:

1 small clove garlic, minced

Let cool, then remove to a food processor. Add:

10 ounces boneless, skinless chicken breasts

10 ounces boneless, skinless chicken legs or thighs

Process just enough to chop the meats. Add:

2 tablespoons shiro miso (light fermented bean paste)

1 large egg yolk

Process just until smooth. Sprinkle in:

2 tablespoons all-purpose flour

Process to blend well. To make the poaching liquid, bring to a boil in a wide saucepan:

8 cups water

1 tablespoon sake

In a second wide saucepan, combine and gently simmer:

2 cups water

¾ cup soy sauce

⅓ cup sugar

¼ cup sake

2 tablespoons mirin

Moisten your hands with cold water and form the chicken mixture into ¾-inch balls. Drop a half or a third of the dumplings into the poaching liquid. Simmer until they rise to the surface, about 1½ minutes. Remove with slotted spoon to the simmering soy mixture and simmer for 5 minutes. Remove to a plate or bowl and repeat with the remaining dumplings. Just before serving, thicken the soy mixture with a paste made from:

3 tablespoons cornstarch

⅓ cup cold water

Serve the dumplings hot or at room temperature with the sauce.

BEEF AND SCALLION ROLLS (NEGI MAKI)

About 30 rolls

Freeze for 20 minutes to make slicing easier:

1¼ pounds boneless beef sirloin steak, trimmed of fat

Meanwhile, trim and cut into 2-inch lengths, then divide into 15 bundles of 3 to 5 pieces each:

7 to 8 scallions

Cut the beef into 15 very thin slices. Place each slice between 2 sheets of plastic wrap and pound lightly with the bottom of a small skillet to an even thinness. (If the beef should tear, patch it with another piece on top.) Roll a piece of beef snugly around each scallion bundle, wrapping it 2 to 3 times. Secure the roll by threading a wooden toothpick lengthwise through the meat. Heat in a large skillet over high heat:

1½ tablespoons vegetable oil

Add the rolls seam side down and sear. Once the seams have sealed, turn and brown the rolls on all sides. After about 1 minute, when the beef has changed color, add:

2 tablespoons sake
2 tablespoons soy sauce
1 tablespoon sugar

Reduce the heat slightly and cook for 1 minute, shaking the pan to keep the rolls from sticking. Remove the skillet from the heat and let the rolls cool slightly. To remove the toothpicks, twist in place, then pull out gently. If there is a lot of sauce left in the skillet, reduce over high heat to 2 tablespoons. Just before serving, return the rolls to the skillet over high heat and shake to glaze them with the sauce. Slice each roll crosswise in half and serve warm.

SHRIMP AND SCALLOP DUMPLINGS

About 25 dumplings

Process in a food processor until finely chopped:

5 ounces fresh bay or sea scallops, rinsed and patted dry
3 ounces fresh shrimp, shelled and deveined

Add and pulse until smooth:

1 tablespoon sake
Pinch of salt

Sprinkle with:

2 teaspoons cornstarch

Process to a smooth paste. Lightly oil a heatproof plate that will fit in your steamer. Moisten your hands with cold water and divide the seafood mixture into 25 equal portions. Roll each portion into a ball, flatten between the heels of your hands to a 1½-inch disk, and set it down on the oiled plate. (Do this in batches if necessary.) In the center of each dumpling, place a few bits of:

Beni shoga (red pickled ginger), finely minced

With a toothpick, press it lightly into the seafood mixture. Bring the water in the bottom of the steamer to a boil, then adjust the heat so the water simmers steadily. Set the plate in the steamer and steam the dumplings for 1 to 2 minutes. They will puff up as they steam but deflate to their original shape when removed. With a spatula, transfer the dumplings to a plate and garnish with:

Chopped parsley

Serve warm or at room temperature, accompanied with a dipping sauce made from:

2 to 3 tablespoons soy sauce
1 to 2 tablespoons fresh lime or ginger juice (extracted by pressing grated fresh ginger)

MEXICO AND LATIN AMERICA

The cuisines of the American nations south of the United States are rich and varied, and small dishes play an important part in them. In Mexico, many of the dishes we sometimes take, quite wrongly, to make up Mexican cuisine—tacos, quesadillas, empanadas, and the like—in fact belong to a class of dishes known collectively as *antojitos,* or "little whims" (or "cravings"). Into this category, too, might be placed fried tortilla chips eaten with the now-familiar avocado mixture called guacamole (from the Nahuatl words meaning "avocado" and "sauce").

TACOS FILLED WITH GROUND BEEF, TURKEY, OR CHICKEN

4 appetizer servings

Tacos are simply food wrapped in tortillas. Until recently, the tacos we saw in the United States were thin, crackly, machine-made tortilla folders filled with ground beef, grated cheese, lettuce, and perhaps some salsa. In fact, though, the tortillas for tacos can be folded or rolled around the filling, and they can be served soft or fried either before or after they have been filled. The range of possible fillings is as wide as the range of American sandwich fixings. Here are a few suggestions.

Have ready:

12 fresh Corn Tortillas, 754, or store-bought corn tortillas

If using fresh tortillas, warm them 1 at a time in a skillet over medium heat, flipping them once or twice, for about 15 seconds; wrap in a dish towel and keep warm in a 250°F oven. If using store-bought tortillas, wrap them in a dish towel, place in a steamer over simmering water, cover, and steam for 1 minute. Turn off the heat and let stand in the covered steamer for 20 minutes. Meanwhile, heat in a medium skillet over medium heat until hot but not smoking:

2 tablespoons vegetable oil

Add:

½ medium red onion, minced

Cook, stirring often, until softened, 4 to 5 minutes. Increase the heat to medium-high and add:

1 pound ground beef, turkey, or chicken

Cook, breaking up the meat with a wooden spoon, until no longer pink, about 3 minutes. Stir in:

1 to 3 cloves garlic, minced
1 tablespoon chili powder
2 teaspoons ground cumin
2 teaspoons ground coriander
Pinch of anise seeds, lightly crushed (optional)
Salt to taste

Cook, stirring, for 30 seconds. Add:

1 cup tomato sauce
Minced fresh jalapeño or other chili peppers or hot red pepper sauce to taste

Cook, stirring occasionally, over low heat for 10 minutes. Meanwhile, place on the serving table in separate bowls or on a large platter.

2 cups shredded romaine lettuce, washed and dried
4 ounces queso fresco or Monterey Jack cheese, shredded
Salsa Fresca, 61
Corn, Cherry Tomato, and Avocado Salsa, 62

If necessary, reheat the meat mixture and transfer to a serving bowl. Place the warmed tortillas in a basket and serve immediately, allowing each guest to layer ingredients into his or her own taco as desired. Or layer each tortilla with the ground meat mixture, lettuce, cheese, and a generous dollop of one of the salsas, fold over, and serve 3 to each guest.

GRILLED FISH TACOS

4 servings

Place in a shallow baking dish just large enough to hold them in a single layer:

2 pounds swordfish, halibut, monkfish, or other firm fish, cut into 1-inch cubes (22 to 26 pieces)

Mix well:

1/3 cup fresh sour orange, ooo, or lime juice
3 tablespoons coarsely chopped fresh cilantro or oregano
1 to 2 tablespoons minced jalapeños or other fresh chili peppers
1 teaspoon salt
1 teaspoon ground black pepper

Pour the marinade over the fish, cover, and refrigerate for at least 1 hour or up to 3 hours.

Prepare a medium-hot charcoal fire.

Have ready:

12 fresh Corn Tortillas, 754, or store-bought corn tortillas

If using fresh tortillas, warm them 1 at a time in a skillet over medium heat, flipping them once or twice, for about 15 seconds; wrap in a dish towel and keep warm in a 250°F oven. If using store-bought tortillas, wrap them in a dish towel, place in a steamer over simmering water, cover, and steam for 1 minute. Turn off the heat and let stand in the covered steamer for 20 minutes.

Meanwhile, remove the fish from the marinade and thread it onto skewers. Grill over the hot fire, turning it once, until the fish is opaque in the center, 4 to 5 minutes each side. Remove from the heat and slide the fish off the skewers onto a platter. Place on the table along with:

2 cups shredded romaine lettuce, washed and dried
1 cup thinly sliced radishes
Corn, Cherry Tomato, and Avocado Salsa, 62

Place the warmed tortillas in a basket and serve immediately, allowing each guest to layer ingredients into his or her own taco as desired. Or layer each tortilla with the fish, lettuce, radishes, and a generous dollop of the salsa, fold up, and serve 3 to each guest.

GRILLED SHRIMP TACOS

Prepare Grilled Fish Tacos, above, substituting 1½ pounds medium shrimp, shelled and deveined, for the fish. Grill the shrimp until opaque in the center, 3 to 4 minutes each side. Serve with the corn tortillas, 2 cups shredded cabbage, and Roasted Tomato-Chipotle Salsa, 62.

CRISP SHREDDED CHICKEN TACOS OR FLAUTAS

4 appetizer servings

To make these crispy deep-fried tacos into *flautas*, or "flutes," spread the filling down the center of the tortillas, then roll them up in a tubular fashion.

Preheat the oven to 350°F.

Remove the skin from:

1½ pounds chicken legs and thighs

Prepare and rub the meat generously with:

Chili-Garlic Spice Paste, 88

Place in a roasting pan and roast until the meat pulls away from the bone easily, about 40 minutes. Let stand until cool enough to handle. Pull the meat off the bones and chop or shred it into bite-sized pieces. In a medium bowl, mix the chicken with enough of the remaining garlic chili paste just to moisten it. Heat in a large, heavy skillet over medium-high heat until hot but not smoking:

½ inch vegetable oil

Add 1 at a time and fry for 3 to 4 seconds to soften:

12 fresh Corn Tortillas, 754, or store-bought corn tortillas

Drain on several layers of paper towels. Place about 2½ tablespoons of the chicken mixture in the center of each tortilla and roll up firmly. Reheat the oil in the skillet over medium-high heat. Place 3 or 4 of the tacos in the hot oil and fry until the bottom is crispy, about 2 minutes. Turn and crisp the second side, 1 to 2 minutes. Remove from the oil, drain on paper towels, and repeat with the remaining tacos. Place on individual plates or a serving platter. Top each taco with a dollop of:

Salsa Fresca, 61

CRISP SHREDDED PORK TACOS OR FLAUTAS

Prepare Crisp Shredded Chicken Tacos or Flautas, above, substituting shredded barbecued pork prepared as directed for North Carolina Pulled Pork Sandwich, 694, for the chicken.

CRISP BLACK BEAN TACOS OR FLAUTAS

Prepare Crisp Shredded Chicken Tacos or Flautas, above, substituting Refried Beans, 276, for the chicken. Sprinkle the filling in each taco with about 2 teaspoons grated Monterey Jack cheese before rolling it up.

SHRIMP AND AVOCADO TOSTADAS

4 tostadas

Another of the delicious Mexican snacks based on the tortilla, tostadas are crisp-fried tortillas laid out flat and covered with a filling. Seafood is a popular topping for tostadas on the coasts of Mexico.

Heat in a medium skillet over medium-high heat until hot but not smoking:

¾ inch vegetable oil

Add 1 at a time and fry, turning once, until crisp, about 30 seconds each side:

4 fresh Corn Tortillas, 754, or store-bought corn tortillas

Shake off the excess oil and drain on paper towels. Whisk together in a large bowl:

¼ cup vegetable oil
2 tablespoons fresh lime juice
2 tablespoons minced fresh cilantro
1 teaspoon ground cumin
1 teaspoon ground coriander
Salt to taste
Hot red pepper sauce to taste

Add:

1 pound medium shrimp, cooked, 490, shelled, and deveined
1 cup fresh or thawed frozen corn kernels
4 ounces queso fresco or Monterey Jack cheese, grated
1 ripe avocado, peeled and coarsely chopped
2 plum tomatoes, chopped
½ medium red onion, minced
Salt to taste
Hot red pepper sauce to taste

Refrigerate until ready to serve. When ready to serve, top the tortillas with:

½ small head romaine or iceberg lettuce, washed, dried, and finely shredded

Divide the shrimp mixture over the lettuce and garnish with:

Fresh cilantro sprigs

CHICKEN OR TURKEY TOSTADAS

4 tostadas

Heat in a medium skillet over medium-high heat until hot but not smoking:

¾ inch vegetable oil

Add 1 at a time and fry, turning once, until crisp, about 30 seconds each side:

4 fresh Corn Tortillas, 754, or store-bought corn tortillas

Shake off the excess oil and drain on paper towels. Combine in a bowl:

3 cups shredded romaine lettuce, washed and dried
1½ cups diced cooked chicken or turkey
1 cup grated queso fresco or Monterey Jack cheese
1 cup cooked black beans (about ⅓ cup dried), 271, rinsed if canned, drained
1 small red or yellow bell pepper, cut into bite-sized pieces

Add and toss to coat:

About ½ cup Lime Vinaigrette, 237, or ¾ cup Guacamole Dressing, 242

Place the tortillas on plates and top with the turkey mixture. Serve immediately with:

Sour cream
Salsa Fresca, 61, or other salsa of your choice

MASA BOATS WITH ASSORTED TOPPINGS

12 appetizer servings; 24 pieces

Snack food takes on a new meaning when you taste these Mexican classics with all their flavor and pleasingly crunchy textures. Those *sopes* can be filled with just about anything, from simple cheese, to scrambled eggs, to shredded meats, fish, and poultry. The shells are made from masa harina (the dried, powdered fresh corn masa used to make tortillas), found in many Mexican markets and large supermarkets; they can be made a day or two in advance and kept tightly covered before their final frying and filling. Queso añejo is a hard, pungent, and salty aged goat cheese. Pecorino Romano and Parmesan make good substitutes.

Thoroughly combine in a large bowl:

2¼ cups masa harina
1½ cups hot water

Cover and let stand for 20 minutes. Mix in (knead with your hands if desired) until thoroughly combined:

⅓ cup plus 1 tablespoon all-purpose flour
2 tablespoons solid vegetable shortening or lard
1 teaspoon baking powder
¾ teaspoon salt

Divide the dough into 12 pieces and roll each into a ball. Place on a plate and cover with plastic wrap. Heat a griddle or large skillet over medium heat until hot. Press 1 ball at a time between sheets of plastic wrap into a disk about ⅜ inch thick. Place the disks in a single layer on the hot griddle and bake until lightly browned but still soft in the middle, about 2 minutes each side. Remove the browned disks to a cutting board and slice crosswise in half (as you would an English muffin). With the cooked side down, pinch a ¼-inch-high edge all around each disk, molding the pliable masa from the center. Cover tightly with plastic wrap. Have ready:

1 cup cooked or canned black beans, coarsely mashed and warmed
½ cup finely crumbled cooked sausage, preferably Mexican chorizo, warmed
About 1 cup Salsa Fresca, 61
½ cup grated Mexican queso añejo or Parmesan cheese

Heat to 360°F in a large saucepan or deep skillet over medium heat:

¾ inch vegetable oil

Add 2 or 3 shells at a time to the hot oil. Fry until lightly browned but not hard, about 45 seconds. Drain on paper towels and keep warm in a 200°F oven while you fry the rest. To serve, fill each hot shell with 2 teaspoons beans, 1 heaping teaspoon sausage, a spoonful of salsa, and a generous sprinkling of cheese. Serve immediately, garnished with:

Fresh cilantro leaves

GRIDDLE-BAKED QUESADILLAS

6 appetizer servings

These delicious tortilla snacks can be stuffed with all kinds of Mexican flavors, from melting cheese and the traditional herb epazote to slivers of cooked meat, fish, or poultry. Here, a simple combination of cheese with roasted peppers and fried onions is baked in your choice of flour or corn tortillas.

Heat in a medium skillet over medium heat until hot:

1½ teaspoons vegetable oil

Add and cook until nicely browned, about 8 minutes:

1 small white onion, halved and thinly sliced

Stir in:

1½ cups roasted pepper strips, such as fresh poblano or Anaheim peppers, canned green chili peppers, or bottled roasted peppers
¼ teaspoon salt, or to taste

Heat through, then remove from the heat. Have ready:

2 cups grated Mexican Chihuahua, Monterey Jack, or brick cheese
6 Flour Tortillas, 754, or very fresh Corn Tortillas, 754

Lightly oil a griddle and heat over medium heat. Place as many tortillas as will fit in a single layer on the hot griddle. Top each with ⅓ cup of the cheese and about 2 tablespoons of the roasted pepper mixture. Bake on the griddle until the cheese begins to melt, about 1 minute, then fold the tortillas in half. Continue griddle-baking until crispy on both sides, another minute or two. Serve immediately, accompanied with:

Salsa Fresca, 61, or Guacamole, 173

EMPANADAS

10 to 12 large empanadas

These flaky meat pies are a much-loved snack all through Latin America. Although they can be filled with anything from fish to fruit, a meat filling is most common. Lard makes the most flavorful, flaky crust.

For the dough, place in a large bowl or food processor:

3 cups all-purpose flour
1½ teaspoons baking powder
1 teaspoon salt

Mix with a fork or pulse until combined. Add:

10 tablespoons (1¼ sticks) cold unsalted butter, cut into small pieces
½ cup lard or solid vegetable shortening, cut into small pieces

Cut the butter and lard into the flour mixture using a pastry blender or pulse in the food processor until the mixture resembles coarse crumbs. If using the food processor, transfer the mixture to a large bowl. Drizzle over the top:

11 to 13 tablespoons ice water

Mix gently with a fork until the flour mixture is dampened enough to gather into a ball. Shape into a flat disk, wrap tightly in plastic, and refrigerate for at least 1 hour. For the filling, heat in a large nonstick skillet over medium heat:

1 tablespoon vegetable oil

Add:

1 medium onion, diced
2 cloves garlic, minced

Cook, stirring, until the onion is translucent, about 5 minutes. Stir in:

1 pound lean ground beef

Cook until the beef is lightly browned, about 8 minutes. Stir in:

1 cup diced peeled potatoes
1 large tomato, cored and chopped
¼ cup raisins (optional)
¼ cup coarsely chopped pitted green olives (optional)
1 teaspoon dried oregano
½ teaspoon salt
½ teaspoon ground black pepper
¼ teaspoon dried thyme

Cook, covered, over medium heat until the potatoes are tender, about 10 minutes. Uncover the pan, increase the heat to medium-high, and cook briefly to evaporate any pan juices. Remove from the heat and let cool completely.

Preheat the oven to 400°F.

To shape the empanadas, roll out the dough ⅛ inch thick on a lightly floured surface. Cut 6-inch rounds from the dough. (You will have to reroll the scraps to get 10 to 12 rounds.) Spoon about ¼ cup of the filling onto one side of each round. Moisten the edges of the rounds with water, fold each one in half, and press the edges together to completely enclose the filling. Use the tines of a fork to decoratively seal the edges. Place 2 inches apart on a baking sheet. Mix together and brush over the tops of the empanadas:

1 large egg, lightly beaten
1 tablespoon milk
Pinch of salt

Bake until nicely browned, about 15 minutes. Let cool slightly on a rack and serve warm.

GUACAMOLE
About 2 cups

Use a large fork or a potato masher to gently crush ripe avocados into this classic Mexican avocado relish. Serve guacamole as an accompaniment to tacos, tortilla chips, cut-up raw vegetables (such as jícama, cucumber, and radish slices), and grilled fish or poultry.

Using the coarsest side of a four-sided grater, grate into a medium bowl:

½ small white onion
1 or 2 fresh jalapeño peppers, or to taste
1 medium, firm, ripe tomato

Using a large knife, halve:

2 large or 3 medium, ripe avocados, preferably Hass

Remove the avocado pits, then use a large spoon to scoop the flesh into the bowl with the onion mixture. Use a large fork or potato masher to coarsely mash the avocados together with the onion mixture. Stir in:

2 tablespoons chopped fresh cilantro
1 tablespoon fresh lime juice
½ teaspoon salt, or to taste

Cover with plastic wrap placed directly on the surface of the mixture and let stand for a few minutes. Serve garnished with:

Fresh cilantro sprigs

NORTH AFRICA

In Tunisia, Algeria, and Morocco—the countries that together make up what is called the Maghreb (literally, "the West")—food is both sustenance and ritual. Spices are used imaginatively, and mindful attention is paid to the careful juxtaposition of not only flavors but also aromas. Typical "little dishes" include the brochettes of lamb that are sold everywhere in the *souks,* or markets, and the wealth of fruit and vegetable salads that begin meals in private homes. Richly exotic but accessible, the little dishes of North Africa provide an easy introduction to a set of interconnected but distinct cuisines that are among the world's best.

LAMB BROCHETTES WITH NORTH AFRICAN SPICES
4 appetizer servings

Prepare a medium-hot charcoal fire.

Mix well:

2 tablespoons caraway seeds
1 tablespoon ground cumin
1½ teaspoons ground coriander
1½ teaspoons ground black pepper
1 teaspoon red pepper flakes, or to taste
1 teaspoon salt

Thoroughly rub the spice mixture over:

8 ounces boneless leg of lamb, cut into ½-inch chunks (about 16 cubes)

Thread the lamb onto 4 skewers and grill until the lamb is done to your liking, 5 to 7 minutes each side for medium-well done. Serve warm or at room temperature, accompanied, if desired, with:

Grilled pita wedges
Harissa, 82

TUNISIAN-STYLE CARROT SALAD

4 appetizer servings

To add extra bite to this salad, stir in 2 diced radishes just before serving.

Peel and coarsely grate into a large bowl:

4 medium carrots

Add:

2 red bell peppers, cut into thin matchsticks

12 Kalamata or other olives, pitted and quartered

Mix well:

½ cup orange juice

2 tablespoons olive oil

1 tablespoon fresh lemon juice

1 teaspoon ground coriander

1 teaspoon ground cumin

¼ teaspoon ground cinnamon

¼ teaspoon red pepper flakes, or to taste

Salt and ground black pepper to taste

Add to the carrot mixture, toss well, and serve, accompanied, if desired, with:

Grilled pita wedges

LEMON-FLECKED OLIVES

1 cup

Mince and place in small bowl:

3 slices North African Preserved Lemons plus 1 tablespoon liquid from the jar, 458

Add:

1 cup best-quality anchovy-stuffed green olives, drained, or Picholine olives, pitted

Toss to coat the olives. Store, covered tightly and refrigerated, for up to 1 month.

HARISSA-SEASONED BLACK OLIVES

2 cups

In a bowl, combine and toss to blend:

2 cups best-quality unpitted black olives (such as Nyons), drained

2 tablespoons Harissa, 82, or to taste

Spoon the olives into a jar and shake to blend again. Store, covered and refrigerated, for at least 1 day before sampling and up to 1 month. To serve, bring to room temperature.

RUSSIA AND GEORGIA

In Russia, little dishes take the form of *zakuski* (from the word *kus*, meaning "morsel"), a flavorful array of hot and cold appetizers eaten with icy vodka as a snack or to precede the main meal. The tradition developed in response to Russia's harsh climate and bad roads, as a way of offering guests ready-made appetizers to take the edge off their hunger after a long and arduous journey. At the great estates, *zakuski* could include up to two dozen different dishes, while simple family suppers would make do with only one or two offerings, most likely some smoked fish and a vegetable salad. A larger *zakuski* selection should balance hot and cold dishes and a few salty and pickled foods, and there should always be plenty of black bread (and chilled vodka) on hand. Ready-made *zakuski* include caviar, smoked salmon or sturgeon, marinated herring, cured ham, pickled hot peppers, half-sour dill pickles, and hard cheese. The following *zakuski* are excellent prepared at home.

CAVIAR

All fish produce roe, or eggs, and fish roe is greatly appreciated in many cuisines—from the *taramasalata* (pureed and seasoned gray mullet or cod roe) of Greece and the *bottarga* (dried and salted tuna or gray mullet roe) of Italy to the *tobiko* (flying fish roe) favored in sushi bars or the salmon roe found in hors d'oeuvre assortments from San Francisco to St. Petersburg. It is only the luxurious roe of the sturgeon, however, that can be labeled "caviar" in this country—and no other roe comes close in flavor and delicate consistency. The sturgeon is an ancient fish, dating back to prehistoric times, and its eggs have been processed and eaten at least since the time of the Egyptians. Although sturgeon is or was found in rivers and lakes all over America, Europe, and Asia, it is that of the Caspian Sea, bordered by Russia and Iran, that has traditionally produced the world's best caviar. Caviar comes principally from three species of sturgeon and is sold under their names: beluga is considered the finest; the eggs are comparatively large and gray, with a mild but pronounced flavor; osetra (or oscietre) caviar is more strongly flavored, with large golden brown, black, gray, dark green, or blue-white grains; sevruga is small grained and black or dark gray in color and forthright but still delicate on the palate. The legendary "golden caviar," supposedly once reserved for tsars and shahs, is apparently not a separate variety but the eggs of either a particularly old or an albino fish; it indeed has a golden cast to it and is very mild—some say too mild—in flavor. (Malossol is not a sturgeon type but the Russian term for "lightly salted"; in general, only the finest grades of caviar, usually beluga, bear this name.)

Both Russia and Iran export Caspian caviar; Iran's is slightly less salty and sometimes very slightly less oily. Buy caviar only from a reputable source and read labels well. If at all possible, taste before buying. Avoid crunchy whitefish and lumpfish roes colored to resemble sturgeon caviar. No caviar should taste excessively salty or truly fishy. Unopened jars of caviar can be stored in the refrigerator at 35°F to 36°F for at least 2 months. Once opened, caviar should be kept in the refrigerator and eaten within a day or two. Do not freeze caviar.

Caviar is classically served either in small crystal bowls or directly from its tin, on ice, with an ivory or mother-of-pearl spoon. (Any small nonreactive implement will work.) Traditional accompaniments include separately chopped hard-boiled egg whites and yolks; chopped flat-leaf parsley; crème fraîche; and brioche toast points (toasted thinly sliced white bread is fine too, but crackers are too brittle). Some connoisseurs eschew all but the toast, and most avoid chopped onions, capers, and lemon juice, which interfere with caviar's delicate flavor. Champagne is often linked with caviar in the public imagination, perhaps because both are such emblematic luxury products, but we prefer ice-cold vodka (unflavored) or aquavit, which nicely offsets the richness of the sturgeon eggs.

PIROZHKI *About 48 dumplings*

The name for these little dumplings comes from the word *pir,* meaning "feast." They are found everywhere in Russia—they are sold from street carts, offered with hearty soups in cafés, and form an integral part of the *zakuski* table in private homes.

In a large bowl, combine and let stand until the yeast is dissolved:

1 envelope (2¼ teaspoons) active dry yeast
¼ cup lukewarm water

Add:

1 cup milk, at room temperature
6 tablespoons (¾ stick) butter, softened
2 large eggs, at room temperature
1 tablespoon sugar
1 teaspoon salt

Mix well, then make a soft dough by adding:

4 to 5 cups all-purpose flour

Turn out the dough onto a floured surface and knead until smooth and elastic. Place in a greased bowl, cover, and let rise in a warm, draft-free place until doubled in volume, about 1½ hours. While the dough is rising, prepare the filling. Heat in a large skillet over medium heat:

2 tablespoons vegetable oil

Add and cook, stirring, until golden, about 7 minutes:

2 large onions, finely chopped

Add and cook, stirring occasionally, until browned, about 5 minutes:

1 pound lean ground beef

Remove from the heat and stir in:

2 hard-boiled eggs, finely chopped
2 tablespoons sour cream
2 tablespoons beef stock
2 tablespoons minced fresh dill
1 tablespoon minced fresh parsley
2 teaspoons salt
Ground black pepper to taste

Lightly oil 2 baking sheets. Punch down the dough and divide into 48 balls. Roll each ball out on a floured surface to a 3½-inch round. Place a heaping tablespoon of the filling in the center of each circle. Moisten one side of the round, fold it in half, and pinch together. Gently shape each pie into an oval. Place the pies on the baking sheets, cover, and let rise until puffy, 30 to 40 minutes.

Meanwhile, preheat the oven to 350°F.

Lightly beat:

1 large egg

Brush the tops of the dumplings with the egg wash. Bake until golden, about 20 minutes. Serve warm or at room temperature.

EGGPLANT CAVIAR *8 to 10 appetizer servings*

This dish from the Caucasus was originally created as a tasty substitute for those who could not afford the luxury of real caviar.

Preheat the oven to 375°F.

Pierce in several places and roast on a baking sheet until soft, 45 to 60 minutes:

2 pounds eggplant (about 2 large)

Let stand until cool enough to handle. Peel the eggplants and finely chop. Heat in a large skillet over medium heat:

6 tablespoons olive oil

Add and cook, stirring occasionally, until soft, about 7 minutes:

2 medium onions, finely chopped
1 green bell pepper, finely chopped
2 tablespoons minced garlic

Add the eggplant along with:

One 28-ounce can plum tomatoes, drained and finely chopped
2 teaspoons salt
Ground black pepper to taste

Bring the mixture to a boil, reduce the heat to low, and simmer, covered, for 1 hour. Remove the cover and continue to simmer, stirring frequently, until the excess liquid is evaporated; the mixture should be thick but not dry. Stir in:

2 tablespoons fresh lemon juice

Taste and adjust the seasonings. Let cool, then cover and refrigerate for several hours before serving on:

Black or rye bread

GEORGIAN KIDNEY BEAN SALAD

6 to 8 appetizer servings

The cooking of Georgia is the spiciest—and many say the best—in all of the former Soviet Union. It is said that Georgians measure a stranger by the gusto (and capacity) with which he or she eats. You can replace the cooked beans with one 19-ounce can kidney beans, rinsed and drained.

Pick over, rinse, and soak, 270:

8 ounces dried red kidney beans

Drain and place the beans in a saucepan. Add water to cover by 2 inches along with:

1 small onion, peeled and halved
1 clove garlic, peeled
1 bay leaf

Bring to a boil over high heat, reduce the heat to low, and simmer, covered, until the beans are tender but not mushy, about 1 hour. Drain and discard the onion, garlic, and bay leaf. Remove the beans to a medium bowl. Stir in:

1/3 cup plum jam
2 tablespoons red wine vinegar
1 to 2 tablespoons minced fresh cilantro
1 tablespoon fresh lemon juice
1/2 small fresh jalapeño or other small chili pepper, seeded and minced
1 clove garlic, minced
1/2 teaspoon salt
1/4 teaspoon ground coriander
Ground black pepper to taste

Taste and adjust the seasonings and serve at room temperature.

SALTED MUSHROOMS

6 to 8 servings

For a more distinct flavor, try using your favorite wild mushrooms in this recipe.

Wipe clean and trim:

1 pound mushrooms

Trim, rinse, and divide in half:

1 bunch fresh dill

Have ready a clean 2-quart crock or glass jar. Coarsely chop half the dill with:

3 cloves garlic

Sprinkle a portion of the remaining dill in the bottom of the crock or jar. Top with a layer of mushrooms, stems up. Combine:

2 to 3 bay leaves, broken into small pieces
2 teaspoons juniper berries
1/2 teaspoon black peppercorns
1/2 teaspoon whole cloves

Sprinkle a portion of the spice mixture, a portion of the dill and garlic mixture, and a portion of the remaining fresh dill over the mushrooms. Continue layering in this fashion until all the mushrooms have been used. Stir together to dissolve the salt:

1 to 2 cups water
2 tablespoons pickling salt

Pour the salted water over the mushrooms, cover with a small plate, and weight the plate with a heavy can to make sure the mushrooms are not exposed to air. Let stand at cool room temperature for 48 hours, then transfer to the refrigerator. The mushrooms will be ready to eat in 2 to 3 days and can be kept, covered and refrigerated, for up to 1 month.

GARLIC CHEESE

About 2 cups

This spread is delicious on black bread. Try adding a slice of ham or a few sprigs of watercress.

Shred into a medium bowl:

8 ounces Havarti or domestic Muenster cheese

Add:

2 large cloves garlic, finely minced
3 to 4 tablespoons mayonnaise
1 tablespoon snipped fresh chives
Pinch of salt (optional)

Mix well to combine, then taste and adjust the seasonings. Cover and refrigerate for at least 4 hours. Before serving, return to room temperature. Serve on squares of:

Black bread

SCANDINAVIA

The great Scandinavian contribution to the category of little dishes is the smorgasbord, or bread and butter table. A typical smorgasbord includes a great deal more than sandwiches, though. It is a veritable groaning board (or bord) of a variety of salads, sliced meats, pickled or marinated fish (herring in more than one form is essential), cooked and raw vegetables, hot dishes, and desserts. It is a whole meal of little dishes, accompanied with aquavit and beer.

POTATO AND HERRING SALAD

6 appetizer servings

Place in a medium pot with enough cold salted water to cover:

12 ounces red or other boiling potatoes

Bring to a boil, reduce the heat, and simmer until the potatoes are tender when pierced with a fork, 20 to 25 minutes. Drain, peel, and cut into bite-sized pieces. Toss gently with:

1¼ cups diced marinated or pickled herring fillets
¾ cup chopped celery with leaves
6 tablespoons sour cream
1½ tablespoons fresh lemon juice
1 tablespoon minced fresh parsley
1 tablespoon snipped fresh chives
1 teaspoon sweet paprika

Refrigerate the salad until chilled and serve in:

Lettuce cups

SMOKED SALMON AND EGG SANDWICHES

4 large or 8 small sandwiches

Lay on a work surface:

4 thin slices dark rye bread

Spread generously with:

Unsalted butter, softened

Divide among the bread slices:

4 large slices smoked salmon (about 4 ounces total)

Lay diagonally in a strip across each piece of bread:

About ¼ cup firm scrambled eggs, at room temperature

Sprinkle with:

Snipped fresh dill

Cut in half, if desired, and serve.

DANISH SHRIMP SANDWICH

4 large or 8 small sandwiches

Lay on a work surface:

4 thick slices light rye or white bread

Spread generously with:

Unsalted butter, softened

Cover each bread slice with:

About 25 tiny bay shrimp, well drained

Sprinkle generously with:

Ground black pepper

Cut in half, if desired, and serve with:

Lemon wedges for squeezing

SPAIN

Spain's famed *tapas* developed in the nineteenth century (some scholars think even earlier) in Andalusia in southern Spain. Andalusia is sherry country, and the story is that drinkers in local taverns took to placing slices of bread atop their glasses between sips to keep the flies out (*tapas* derives from the verb *tapar*, "to cover"). Some enterprising bartender then put a slice of ham or sausage on the bread. Soon tiny plates were being used as covers and a variety of foods were spooned onto them—and the habit spread throughout Spain. Today some tapas bars specialize in one or two items, such as ham, salt cod, or fried fish, while others offer stunning displays of dishes both complex and simple. In fact, virtually anything can be a *tapa*, from marinated olives or bread rubbed with tomato pulp to a small serving of stewed tripe or paella. *Tapas* are bar food par excellence, and to nibble them without a glass of sherry, wine, or beer at hand would be unthinkable to the Spanish. Nearly as unthinkable would be nibbling *tapas* on the run; the *tapeo*, or tapas ritual, demands many hours of relaxed conversation punctuated by food and drink, usually consumed in a succession of places. Eating *tapas* is not "grazing"—it is enjoying life.

BREAD STICKS WITH SERRANO HAM

6 appetizer servings

Wrap:

12 long, thin bread sticks, 741

with:

12 very thin slices serrano ham

Secure with toothpicks and serve at room temperature, accompanied, if you wish, with:

Extra-virgin olive oil for dipping
Roasted almonds

SAUSAGES WITH FRESH FIGS

6 appetizer servings

Prepare a medium-hot charcoal fire or preheat the broiler.

Simmer in salted water to cover until medium-rare in the center, about 6 minutes:

3 pounds fresh pork sausages with garlic

Drain well and brush lightly with:

Olive oil

Grill or broil, turning every 2 minutes or so, until lightly browned, 8 to 10 minutes total. Meanwhile, lightly brush:

15 ripe green figs, halved

with:

Olive oil

Grill or broil just until they begin to soften, about 3 minutes. Be careful not to overcook the figs. Place the figs and sausages on a platter and sprinkle with:

Extra-virgin olive oil
1 teaspoon aged sherry vinegar

Serve warm or at room temperature.

TORTILLA ESPAÑOLA (POTATO OMELET)

6 servings

In the United States, when we make a Spanish omelet, it is a rolled one filled with peppers and tomatoes—but this authentic Spanish version is flat (but usually thick) and filled with potatoes and onions. *Tortilla* means "little cake" and in this case has nothing to do with the "little cakes" of corn or wheat flour called tortillas in Mexico and Central America.

Heat in a large skillet over medium heat:

2 tablespoons olive oil

Add:

1 large onion (about 8 ounces), cut into 1/8-inch-thick slices
Salt and ground black pepper to taste

Cook until the onions are soft and golden, reducing the heat as they cook, about 20 minutes. Remove to a large bowl. Heat in the same skillet over high heat:

1/4 cup olive oil

Add:

1 pound red-skinned potatoes, peeled and cut into 1/8-inch-thick slices

Cook until golden brown, 10 to 12 minutes. Reduce the heat to medium-high if the oil gets too hot and smoky. Toss the potatoes often with a metal spatula, separating the slices that stick together. Some will stick together no matter what you do, and that is fine. Remove the potatoes with a slotted spoon to paper towels to drain. Set aside the pan with the oil in it. Add to the onions and mix together:

6 large eggs
1/2 teaspoon salt
Ground black pepper to taste

Sprinkle the potatoes with:

Salt and ground black pepper to taste

Add the potatoes to the egg mixture and toss to coat the slices well with the egg. Return the skillet to high heat to heat the remaining oil in the pan. When hot, add the egg mixture and immediately reduce the heat to low. Let the omelet cook for 3 to 4 minutes, undisturbed, until the bottom is golden and the egg is two-thirds to three-quarters set. Shake the pan from time to time to make sure the omelet does not stick. If it does, slide a metal spatula under the egg to free it from the pan and continue cooking. Place a lightly oiled large heatproof plate upside down over the omelet and flip the skillet to turn the omelet over, or refer to About Flat Omelets, 134, for alternative ways to cook the top side. Slide the omelet back into the pan to cook the second side. Cook until golden and set, 2 to 3 minutes more. Shake the omelet loose from the pan and slide onto a clean plate. Cut into 6 wedges and serve hot or at room temperature.

MIXED MARINATED OLIVES, SPANISH STYLE

4 cups

Combine in a small saucepan:

1 cup Spanish olive oil
2 sprigs fresh rosemary
3 cloves garlic, very finely minced
2 bay leaves
1/2 teaspoon coarsely ground black pepper
Pinch of red pepper flakes

Bring to a bare simmer over medium heat. Immediately remove from the heat, stir once or twice, and let cool to room temperature. Meanwhile, rinse with warm water, drain, and dry well with paper towels:

2 cups brine-cured green olives
1 cup oil-cured black olives
1 cup small brine-cured black olives

Place the olives in a glass or earthenware container and pour the oil over them. Let cool completely, then cover and keep in a cool place for up to 1 week. Bring to room temperature before serving.

SOUTHEAST ASIA

In Singapore, Thailand, Vietnam, and elsewhere in Southeast Asia, street food—grilled marinated meats, fried dumplings, attractively dressed fruit—is raised to an art. The many small dishes of the cuisines of the region are characteristically flavored with chili peppers, garlic, coconut, fish sauce, and the herb trio of fresh mint, cilantro, and basil. Cooking time is minimal in these dishes, but the complex mix of flavors is captivating.

VIETNAMESE SUMMER ROLLS

4 to 6 appetizer servings

If the rice paper you are using is especially fragile and is tearing, use 2 sheets for each summer roll. Immerse them as directed, then overlap 2 sheets in the middle by 4 inches.

Bring to a rapid boil in a medium saucepan:

4 cups water
1 bundle Japanese somen noodles (about 2 1/2 ounces), broken in half

Boil until the noodles are just firm to the bite, about 2 minutes. Use tongs or a slotted spoon to remove the noodles to a colander; rinse with cold water. Add to the still-boiling water:

16 medium shrimp, in their shells

Boil until they turn pink and float to the surface, about 2 minutes. Drain in a colander, refresh with cold water, then shell and cut lengthwise in half. Rinse with cold water to remove the veins and drain on paper towels. Place the noodles and shrimp on a small baking sheet along with:

4 large leaves red-leaf or Boston lettuce, torn lengthwise in half and central ribs removed
1 large carrot, shredded
1 cup bean sprouts
½ cup fresh mint leaves
½ cup fresh cilantro leaves
16 chives

Lay out and cover with a damp cloth:

Eight 12-inch round sheets rice paper

Lay a damp kitchen towel in front of you and have a large bowl of hot water (115° to 120°F) at hand. Dip 1 sheet of rice paper into the hot water, being sure to immerse it completely. It will immediately become pliable. Quickly remove it and place on the towel. Place a piece of lettuce along the bottom edge of the rice sheet about 2 inches from the edge. Top the lettuce with one-eighth of the cooked noodles, carrots, sprouts, mint, cilantro, and chives, then with 4 shrimp halves. Fold the sides of the rice paper over the filling, then roll up tightly into a neat cylinder. Set seam side down on a large platter and cover with a damp towel to keep moist. Repeat with the remaining rice paper and filling ingredients. To serve, cut each roll crosswise into 4 even pieces. Serve immediately or the rice paper will toughen up. Pass for dipping:

Southeast Asian Peanut Dipping Sauce, 83

GRILLED FIVE-SPICE RIBS

6 to 8 appetizer servings

Peel and discard the rough outside husks, then thinly slice the tender core of:

2 stalks fresh lemon grass

Place in a blender or food processor along with:

3 tablespoons sugar
2 tablespoons chopped shallots
2 tablespoons minced garlic
2 tablespoons fish sauce
2 tablespoons soy sauce
2 tablespoons toasted sesame oil
2 tablespoons peanut oil
2 tablespoons five-spice powder
1 teaspoon chili bean paste

Process until finely pureed, then remove to a large bowl. Add:

3 pounds spareribs or baby back ribs, separated into individual ribs, rinsed, and patted dry

Toss to coat each rib thoroughly. Cover and let stand at room temperature for 1 hour or refrigerate for up to 24 hours.

Prepare a medium-hot charcoal fire or preheat the broiler.

Grill or broil the ribs, turning frequently, about 6 inches from the heat until the ribs are nicely browned and cooked through, 15 to 20 minutes. Serve immediately, sprinkled, if desired, with:

2 tablespoons sesame seeds, toasted

BEEF SATAY WITH PEANUT SAUCE

6 to 8 appetizer servings

You can substitute strips of boneless chicken breast for the beef in this recipe. Grill the chicken longer than the beef, about 3 minutes each side. Before removing the satay from the grill, cut into one of the pieces of chicken to be sure it is cooked all the way through.

Process in a blender or food processor until smooth:

½ cup canned unsweetened condensed milk
⅓ cup minced shallots
2 tablespoons brown sugar
2 tablespoons soy sauce
1 tablespoon minced garlic
1 teaspoon ground cumin
1 teaspoon ground coriander

Place in a shallow dish:

1 pound boneless beef sirloin, cut across the grain into strips about 3 x 1½ inches

Add the marinade, toss to coat the beef strips thoroughly, cover, and let stand for 1 hour at room temperature or refrigerate for up to 24 hours.

Prepare a medium-hot charcoal fire or preheat the broiler.

Combine in a medium saucepan:

1 cup canned unsweetened coconut milk
½ cup creamy peanut butter
4 teaspoons firmly packed light brown sugar
1 tablespoon fish sauce
1 tablespoon soy sauce
1 tablespoon canned Thai Massaman curry paste
½ teaspoon curry powder

Whisk in thoroughly:

½ cup hot water

Simmer, stirring occasionally, over low heat until the flavors are well blended, 15 to 20 minutes. Stir in:

2 teaspoons fresh lime juice

Keep warm while you grill the meat. Thread a 6-inch-long bamboo skewer through each strip of meat. Lightly brush the skewered meat on both sides with:

Vegetable oil

Grill or broil, turning once, until golden brown, 2 to 3 minutes. Serve immediately, passing the warm peanut sauce on the side for dipping.

SWITZERLAND

CHEESE FONDUE *2 to 3 cups; 4 to 6 servings*

Legend has it that fondue was invented during a sixteenth-century siege of Zurich, when inhabitants had to feed themselves on a small stock of available ingredients—which fortunately included bread, cheese, and wine. The dish later became a tradition throughout German-speaking Switzerland and in the mountainous French region of Savoie. It was popular party fare in the United States in the 1950s and 1960s, and after a period in culinary disrepute is now enjoying a revival here.

Tear into bite-sized pieces:

1 loaf white country bread

Rub the interior of a medium stainless-steel pot with:

1 clove garlic, peeled and halved

Discard the garlic and add to the pot:

1¼ cups Swiss fendant or other dry white wine

Bring to a simmer over medium heat. Add:

1 pound Gruyère cheese, chopped

Pinch of freshly grated or ground nutmeg

Cook, stirring with a wooden spoon, until the cheese is melted (the cheese and wine will not yet be blended). Mix together thoroughly in a small bowl:

1 tablespoon cornstarch

2 tablespoons kirsch

Stir into the cheese mixture. Continue to stir and simmer until the cheese mixture is smooth, about 5 minutes. Season with:

Salt and ground black pepper

If the fondue is too thick, add up to:

¼ cup Swiss fendant or other dry white wine

To serve, transfer to a fondue pot or chafing dish set over a flame. To eat, spear bread pieces with fondue forks and dip in the cheese, continuing to stir the mixture with the forks as you dip.

SANDWICHES, BURRITOS & PIZZAS

John Montague, an eighteenth-century English diplomat and the fourth Earl of Sandwich, was an inveterate card player who disliked being taken away from his game for anything so mundane as lunch. When hunger panged, he would ask his servants for a piece of meat on top of (and perhaps also beneath) a slice of bread so he could eat without laying down his hand. Thus the sandwich got its name, and unlike so many other tales of culinary origins, this one is apparently quite true.

Even though Montague may have been responsible for naming the sandwich, he certainly did not invent it. Almost every culture has its "sandwich," whether the burritos of Mexico, the filled pita pockets of the Middle East, or the calzones (and, by extension, pizzas—open-faced sandwiches) of Italy. Pizzas, in fact, have become America's great one-dish meal, and with our typical ingenuity, we have found a way to improve on something great, by putting pizza on the grill, 196.

Nothing will ever be simpler, though, or more appropriate at any hour, than the kind of sandwich that kept Montague at the gaming table. Because sandwiches are so simple and straightforward, the fresher and better the ingredients, the better the end result. Do not be afraid to experiment with breads and fillings, but do consider the flavor and texture of both the filling and the bread. A moist, chunky filling will burst out of soft bread; a dryish one will get lost inside a crusty roll.

If you are making a lot of sandwiches for company, you might want to save time by arranging the ingredients so that you can prepare the sandwiches on an assembly line. Line up the bread in rows, pairing slices so they will match. Make sure the dressing (especially if it is butter) is soft enough to spread and extend it all the way to the edges of the bread. If the filling is spreadable, gently extend it to the edges of the bread too. Then put the slices together and press gently. Sturdy sandwiches like heros and subs can be made ahead of time, then wrapped in plastic storage bags, plastic wrap, or aluminum foil and stored in the refrigerator for up to 4 hours. This is not advisable for delicate sandwiches or those with particularly moist fillings. When cutting sandwiches, use a very sharp knife to avoid squashing and ragged edges.

IDEAS FOR SIMPLE SANDWICHES AND THEIR RELATIVES

FILLINGS/DRESSING/BREAD

Roast Beef

Basic sandwich: Iceberg or romaine lettuce and sliced tomatoes / Mustard or mayonnaise / Kaiser roll or rye, white, or whole-wheat bread

Watercress and sliced red onions / Bavarian Apple and Horseradish Sauce, 79 / Sourdough bread

Swiss cheese / Green Goddess Dressing, 240 / Whole-wheat bread

Quick Red Onion Pickle, 65 / Thousand Island Dressing, 240 / Kaiser roll

Sun-dried tomatoes / Roasted Red Pepper Dressing, 238 / Olive bread, see page 744

Frisée (curly endive) and sliced cucumbers / Tzatziki, 219 / Italian bread

Sliced radishes and Bibb lettuce / Rosemary mustard, see page 71 / Baguette

Roasted red peppers / Red-Onion–Garlic Ketchup, 70 / Focaccia, 753, or ciabatta

Blue cheese / Chimichurri, 80 / Rye or pumpernickel bread

Romaine lettuce and fontina cheese / Green Peppercorn Vinaigrette, 237 / Onion rolls

Roast Lamb

Basic sandwich: Sliced onions and romaine lettuce / Red Onion Marmalade, 66, or mayonnaise / Kaiser roll or toasted white or whole-wheat bread

Sliced red onions and roasted red peppers / Fresh Herb Vinaigrette, 237 / Focaccia, 753, or ciabatta

Goat cheese / Apricot Dressing, 239 / White or whole-wheat pita bread

Watercress / Roasted Red Pepper Dressing, 238 / Sourdough bread

Feta cheese and romaine lettuce / Garlic Mayonnaise, 74 / Potato or hearth bread

Monterey Jack cheese / Roasted Tomato–Chipotle Salsa, 62 / Tortillas or pita bread

Baby mustard greens or watercress / Fruit Salsa with Black Beans, 63 / Tortillas or pita bread

Roasted garlic / Mayonnaise with Green Herbs, 73 / Sesame roll

Sliced tomatoes / Tapenade, 161 / Baguette

Mesclun / Harissa, 82 / Italian or pita bread

Roast Pork

Basic sandwich: Romaine or iceberg lettuce and gherkins / Mustard / Whole-wheat or rye bread

Cole Slaw, 222 / Barbecue Sauce, 90 / White bread

Arugula, roasted garlic, and chives / Mustard / Italian bread

Thinly sliced apples / English Cumberland Sauce, 80 / Rye bread

Romaine lettuce / Mango Salsa, 63 / Tortillas or pita bread

Thinly sliced red onions / Pear Chutney, 68 / Potato bread or chapatis

Watercress / Corn and Tomato Relish, 65 / White bread

Ham or Tongue

Basic sandwich: Iceberg lettuce, sliced tomatoes, and Swiss cheese / Yellow mustard / Rye, white, or whole-wheat bread

Cheddar cheese and bread-and-butter pickles / Dijon mustard / Kaiser roll

Swiss cheese / Chow-Chow, 63 / Onion roll

Cranberry sauce / Apricot mustard, see page 71 / Rye or pumpernickel bread

Havarti cheese / Fresh Pineapple Chutney, 66 / Rye bread

Gruyère cheese / Garlic Butter, 77 / Olive bread

Half-sour pickles and Boston lettuce / Tzatziki, 219 / Potato bread

Crabmeat / Russian Horseradish Cream, 73 / Pumpernickel bread

Fontina cheese and alfalfa sprouts / Anchovy Butter, 77 / Kaiser roll

Brie / Mustard / Pumpernickel bread

Sliced Chicken or Turkey

Basic sandwich: Romaine or iceberg lettuce and sliced tomatoes / Mayonnaise / White, whole-wheat, or rye bread

Stuffing / Whole Cranberry Relish, 64 / Thick-sliced white bread

Bacon and Cheddar cheese / Thousand Island Dressing, 240 / Potato bread

Romaine lettuce / Tuna Sauce, 81 / Kaiser roll

Sliced red onions and spinach / Sauce Rémoulade, 73 / White bread

Walnuts / Hummus, 164 / Pita or *lavash*

Prosciutto and radicchio / Garlic Mayonnaise, 74 / Focaccia, 753

Thinly sliced cucumbers / Tabbouleh, 227 / Pita bread

Sliced tomatoes / Georgian Garlic and Walnut Sauce, 82 / Pumpernickel bread

Sliced avocados and sprouts / Honey Mustard Vinaigrette, 237 / Wheat or multigrain bread

Grilled onions / Barbecue Sauce, 90 / Kaiser roll

Sun-dried tomatoes and sliced black olives / Pesto Sauce, 307 / Focaccia, 753

Chicken or Turkey Salad

Basic sandwich: Iceberg or romaine lettuce and sliced tomatoes / White, whole-wheat, or rye bread

Thinly sliced radishes and scallions / Garlic Mayonnaise, 74 / White or light rye bread

Sliced celery and pine nuts / Mayonnaise with Green Herbs, 73 / Pita or potato bread

Romaine lettuce and minced fresh oregano / Guacamole Dressing, 242 / Tortillas or pita bread

Sliced avocados and Bibb lettuce / Sour cream / Bagels

Sliced scallions, cashews, and currants / Mayonnaise mixed with mango chutney / Toasted sourdough bread

Sliced green grapes / Orange Butter, 77 / Walnut bread

Orange segments / Butter / Limpa or pumpernickel bread

Egg Salad

Basic sandwich: Romaine or iceberg lettuce and sliced tomatoes / Whole-wheat, rye, or white bread

Sun-dried tomatoes / Tapenade, 161 / Italian bread

Thinly sliced green and black olives / Basic Herb Vinaigrette, 236 / Kaiser roll

Roasted red peppers / Lemon Caper Vinaigrette, 237 / Toasted white bread

Sardines / Anchovy Butter, 77 / Rye bread or toasted English muffin

Bacon and sliced tomatoes / Cress or Arugula Butter, 77 / Toasted brioche or challah

Thinly sliced avocados and tomatoes / Mayonnaise / Whole-wheat bread

Thinly sliced red onions and watercress / Sour cream and Quick Red Onion Pickle, 65 / Black bread

Steamed asparagus / Mayonnaise with Green Herbs, 73 / Whole-wheat bread

Seafood Salads (Tuna, Salmon, Shrimp, Crab, or Lobster)

Basic sandwich: Romaine lettuce / Hot dog, hamburger, or Kaiser roll; pita bread; or white, whole-wheat, or rye bread

Bibb lettuce / Classic Russian Dressing, 240 / Whole-wheat bread

Sliced tomatoes / Cress or Arugula Butter, 77 / Brioche

Sliced avocados / Garlic Mayonnaise, 74 / Pumpernickel bread

Sliced scallions and cucumbers / Guacamole, 173 / Tortillas

Thinly sliced shallots / Mustard Mayonnaise, 73 / White bread

Thinly sliced fennel / Tzatziki, 219 / Pita or white bread

Cilantro or basil leaves / Apple Chutney, 67 / Sourdough bread

Bacon or Canadian bacon / Butter / Toasted brioche or challah

Peanut Butter (or Other Nut Butter)

Basic sandwich: Marshmallow Fluff / White bread

Jelly / White or whole-wheat bread or toasted English muffin

Bacon / None or hot pepper jelly / Whole-wheat bread

Sliced bananas / White or raisin bread

Thinly sliced celery / Rye crackers

Walnut halves or whole peanuts / Cream cheese / Rye bread or raisin bagel

Honey / Bagel

Thinly sliced apples / Apple butter / Cracked-wheat bread

Granola / Butter / Sourdough bread

Grilled or Braised Vegetables

Basic sandwich: Mozzarella cheese / Fresh Herb Vinaigrette, 237 / Focaccia, 753, or French or Italian bread

Prosciutto / Garlic Mayonnaise, 74 / Focaccia, 753

Sprouts of your choice / Hoisin sauce / Pita bread or rice paper

Sliced mangoes / Fresh Tamarind Chutney, 66 / Pita bread

Grated lemon zest / Cream cheese / Thick-sliced white bread

Watercress or arugula / Sauce Andalouse, 74 / Sourdough bread

Monterey Jack cheese / Salsa Verde Cruda, 62 / Tortillas or Italian bread

Romaine lettuce / Red Onion Marmalade, 66 / Focaccia, 753, or French bread

Grilled Fish

Basic sandwich: Romaine lettuce and sliced tomatoes and onions / Garlic Mayonnaise, 74 / French bread

Frisée (curly endive) or arugula / Tapenade, 161 / Potato bread or Focaccia, 753
Sliced radishes and shredded lettuce / Salsa Verde Cruda, 62 / Flour Tortillas, 754
Watercress / Corn and Tomato Relish, 65 / Kaiser roll
Thinly sliced fennel / Sauce Andalouse, 74 / White or French bread
Grilled scallions or onions / Mustard Mayonnaise, 73 / Kaiser roll
Bibb lettuce and sliced cucumbers / Red Caviar Butter, 77 / Italian bread

Cheeses

Basic sandwich: Sliced avocados, tomatoes, and lettuce / Mayonnaise / White bread or bagel
Thinly sliced plums / Honey Mustard Vinaigrette, 237 / Walnut bread
Romaine lettuce / Quick Red Onion Pickle, 65 / Onion roll
Watercress / Sauce Rémoulade, 73 / Kaiser roll
Arugula / Basil Chive Vinaigrette, 237 / Olive bread, see page 744, or herb bread
Alfalfa sprouts / Hummus, 164 / Pita or sourdough bread
Sopressata or other hard salami / Roasted Red Pepper Dressing, 238 / Italian bread
Frisée (curly endive) / Piccalilli, 64 / Whole-wheat bread
Country ham / Mustard flavored with horseradish / Rye or whole-wheat bread
Roasted red peppers / Mayonnaise / White bread

Sandwiches Made from Leftover Main Courses

Basic sandwich: Classic Italian American Tomato Sauce I or II, 306 / Halved loaf of Italian bread or hero roll
Meat loaf, 722, or Ham Loaf, 722 / Barbecue Sauce, 90, or ketchup / Halved loaf of Italian bread or hero roll
Chicken Parmigiana, 589, or Veal Parmigiana, 683 / Italian Tomato Sauce, 304 / Halved loaf of Italian bread or hero roll
Eggplant Parmigiana, 373 / Italian Tomato Sauce, 304 / Halved loaf of Italian bread or hero roll
Beef Pot Roast, 667 / Ketchup or mustard / Kaiser roll

IDEAS FOR TEA SANDWICHES

The bread used for these sandwiches is always sliced very thinly and usually has the crusts trimmed off. Once the sandwiches are assembled, cut them into quarters for serving.

FILLINGS / SEASONING / DRESSING / BREAD

Cream cheese / Date Nut Bread, 775
Thinly sliced cucumbers / Butter / White bread
Thinly sliced red onions and finely snipped chives / Pinch of ground cloves / Butter / Brioche
Very thinly sliced Cheddar cheese / Chopped fresh cilantro / Green Mango Chutney, 67 / Whole-wheat bread
Watercress / Nasturtium or chive flowers / Butter or flavored butter, 76 to 78 / Milk Bread, 746, or white bread
Thinly sliced tomatoes and chopped fresh basil / Pinch of ground cumin / Mayonnaise or Garlic Mayonnaise, 74 / Whole-wheat or potato bread
Thinly sliced radishes and mint leaves / Grated lemon zest / Mayonnaise with Green Herbs, 73 / Brioche
Brie and thinly sliced almonds / Pinch of ground allspice / Butter / Pumpernickel bread
Smoked salmon / Minced fresh dill / Horseradish / Black bread
Smoked ham / Pinch of ground cloves / Orange marmalade / Whole-wheat bread
Thinly sliced poached shrimp / Celery seeds / Sour cream / White bread
Thinly sliced strawberries / Dash of balsamic vinegar / Crème fraîche / Brioche
Thinly sliced hard-boiled eggs / Capers / Dijon mustard / Rye bread
Chicken and thinly sliced Granny Smith apples / Minced scallions / Curry Mayonnaise, 73 / White bread
Crabmeat and thinly sliced avocados / Pinch of sweet paprika / Mayonnaise / Black bread
Blue cheese and thinly sliced pears / Pinch of ground nutmeg / Butter / Baguette rounds
Caviar / Minced onions / Russian dressing / Pumpernickel bread
Thinly sliced peeled lemons / Ground black pepper / Red Caviar Butter, 77 / White bread
Thinly sliced fontina cheese / Fresh thyme leaves / Anchovy Butter, 77 / Potato bread
Belgian endive and escarole / Minced fresh tarragon / Creamy Chili Dressing, 241 / White bread
Thinly sliced pimiento-stuffed green olives / Snipped fresh chives / Cream cheese / White bread

CLASSIC CLUB SANDWICH *4 sandwiches*

This all-American sandwich, invented in the late nineteenth century—quite possibly at the Saratoga Club in Saratoga Springs, New York—is now found everywhere, from diners to room-service menus to fancy restaurants. The bread is best toasted and allowed to dry slightly after toasting; it is also a good idea to cut the top slice into halves or quarters before adding it, to avoid mashing everything together as you bear down with the knife. This is the original, classic club, but many variations are possible: Try grilled fish, chicken salad, tuna salad, egg salad, sliced hard-boiled eggs, rare roast beef, or crab or lobster salad in place of the sliced chicken. Watercress, basil, arugula, or spinach may be substituted for the lettuce, and roasted red peppers, grilled vegetables, or tender young asparagus spears are tasty additions. A flavored mayonnaise can be used for dressing.

Lay out on a work surface:

12 slices firm white bread, toasted until crisp, crusts removed if desired

Spread the bread lightly on 1 side with:

Mayonnaise (about 1/4 cup total)

Divide among 4 slices, spread side up:

4 Bibb, Boston, or iceberg lettuce leaves
8 ounces thinly sliced cooked white chicken or turkey

Top with another 4 slices toast, spread side up. Divide among the 4 sandwiches:

4 Bibb, Boston, or iceberg lettuce leaves
1 medium tomato, very thinly sliced
16 slices bacon, cooked until crisp
1/2 cucumber, peeled, seeded, and very thinly sliced (optional)

Top with another 4 slices toast, spread side down. Press the sandwiches gently together and cut each one into 4 triangles. Pierce each triangle with a toothpick or skewer to hold it together.

HOT BROWN *4 servings*

Developed at the Brown Hotel in Louisville, Kentucky, in 1920, this delight remains on the menu to this day.

Preheat the broiler.

In each of 4 small gratin dishes, place:

1 slice white toast, cut in half diagonally (4 slices total)

Top each with:

2 tomato slices (8 slices total)
2 slices bacon, cooked until crisp (8 slices total)
2 ounces thinly sliced turkey (8 ounces total)

Pour over each:

1/4 to 1/3 cup Sauce Mornay, 46

Broil until bubbling and serve immediately.

THE HERO *4 sandwiches*

The hero—also known as the bomber, the grinder, the wedge, the zep, the hoagie, and the submarine (some say for its shape; others, because a deli near the U.S. submarine base in Groton, Connecticut, made a particularly famous version), among other things—is essentially a long, wide roll filled with Italian-style deli meats and cheese. We've heard rumors that some hero makers used to wrap the sandwiches in cloth towels and invite children to sit on them in the car on the way to a picnic, so that the sandwiches would compress, blending their flavors. A less colorful but more genteel method of achieving the same effect is to weight the sandwiches under cast-iron skillets filled with cans. They can also be eaten without flattening, of course.

Split in half lengthwise:

1 loaf Italian or French bread

Moisten generously with:

Fresh Herb Vinaigrette, 237, Lemon Caper Vinaigrette, 237, or other vinaigrette of your choice

Arrange in layers on the bread:

About 1 pound Italian deli meats (a combination of 3 or more of Genoa salami, prosciutto, mortadella, capocollo, pepperoni, or sopressata)
4 to 8 ounces sliced provolone cheese
8 to 12 pickled hot peppers
2 to 3 bell peppers, roasted, 402, and sliced
1/2 cup fresh basil leaves and/or finely shredded lettuce

Cover with the top of the bread and serve immediately, or wrap tightly in aluminum foil and let stand for 30 minutes, under weights if desired, before serving to meld the flavors. Cut into 4 pieces for serving.

SAUSAGE AND PEPPER SUB *4 sandwiches*

This is another approach to the submarine sandwich.

Brown in a large nonstick skillet over medium heat, shaking the pan to turn:

12 ounces sweet Italian sausage links, turkey sausage links, or other sausage links of your choice

Add and cook, covered, for 10 minutes:

1/3 cup chicken stock

Remove the sausage to a plate. Pour off all but 1 to 2 tablespoons of the liquid in the pan. Add:

2 tablespoons olive oil
1 large onion, thinly sliced
3 cloves garlic, minced

Cook, stirring, until softened, 6 to 7 minutes. Add:

1 large red bell pepper, thinly sliced
1 large green bell pepper, thinly sliced
1½ teaspoons minced fresh oregano (optional)
Salt and ground black pepper to taste

Cook until the peppers are softened, about 5 minutes. Return the sausages to the pan and cook for 3 minutes. Stir in:

1 tablespoon balsamic vinegar (optional)

Adjust the seasonings and spoon the mixture into:

4 hero rolls, split lengthwise and warmed

Gently press the sandwiches together and serve warm.

THE HOT DOG

4 hot dogs

An American beach and backyard grill classic, hot dogs can be dressed up with a variety of add-ons or eaten with your favorite condiments. Since they are precooked, all you need to do is heat them up. For a reduced-fat hot dog, use chicken or turkey frankfurters and do not butter the buns.

Spread each of:

4 hot dog buns, toasted if desired

with:

2 teaspoons butter (8 teaspoons total)

Place in a saucepan and simmer in water to cover for 5 minutes; or grill or broil until well seared, about 3 minutes each side; or slice lengthwise almost all the way through, open up to flatten, and cook in a teaspoon or two of butter until browned, about 4 minutes each side:

4 frankfurters

Place on the prepared buns. Add your choice of:

Ketchup
Mustard
Green Tomato Relish, 65
Piccalilli, 64
Chopped red or white onions
Tart Corn Relish, 65

Serve at once.

IDEAS FOR HOT DOGS

German Dog: Top each hot dog with about 3 tablespoons prepared sauerkraut.

Cheese Dog: Top each hot dog with 1 or 2 slices of American cheese or 2 tablespoons of cheese spread.

Mexican Dog: Top each hot dog with 2 tablespoons Salsa Fresca, 61, ½ jalapeño pepper, coarsely chopped, and 1 tablespoon grated Monterey Jack cheese.

Yuppie Dog: Top each hot dog with about 3 tablespoons Caramelized Onions, 391, and 1 tablespoon Dijon mustard.

Chili Dog: Top each hot dog with about ¼ cup chili.

Cincinnati Five-Way Chili Dog: Top each hot dog with about ¼ cup chili, 2 tablespoons cooked kidney beans, 2 tablespoons chopped onions, 2 tablespoons shredded American cheese, and a pinch of ground red pepper.

THE HAMBURGER

4 burgers

The hamburger gets its name from the German city of Hamburg, where the idea of eating raw shredded beef (steak tartare) is said to have been introduced by sailors returning from Russia. Some enterprising Hamburger apparently got the idea of cooking the delicacy—and the next thing anyone knew, there were McDonald's in Moscow and Beijing. (The first American appearance of the burger is, not surprisingly, a matter of some debate, but many historians trace it to St. Louis, Missouri, which has a large German-derived population, in 1904.) It is a mistake to make burgers with lean beef, for they need some fat for flavor and moistness. The ideal burger meat is 100 percent ground chuck, with about 20 percent fat—enough to produce a juicy burger but not so much that you will have a lot of fat left in the pan. If you are a real burger fanatic, you might consider grinding your own meat just before making the patties: cut a chuck roast into 2-inch pieces, then grind in a food processor using the metal blade.

Mix together in a large bowl with your hands or a wooden spoon:

1¼ pounds ground chuck
Salt and ground black pepper to taste

Divide the meat into 4 equal portions and form each into a burger about 1 inch thick. Cook, flipping once, by grilling over a hot fire, broiling under a preheated broiler, or cooking in a preheated skillet over medium-high heat. For all three methods, it will take about 3 minutes each side for rare, 4 minutes each side for medium, and 5 minutes each side for well-done. Place the burgers between:

4 hamburger rolls or other rolls, halved, or 8 slices bread of your choice

Add your choice of:

Tomato ketchup or other ketchup of your choice, 69 to 70
Mustard
Green Tomato Relish, 65
Piccalilli, 64
Chow-Chow, 63

Serve at once.

CHEESEBURGER

Prepare The Hamburger, above, topping each burger, after flipping it, with 1 or 2 thin slices of American cheese, aged Cheddar, or other cheese of your choice. For a Bacon Cheeseburger, top each cooked cheeseburger with 2 or 3 crisp cooked slices bacon.

DOUBLE-CHEESE TOMATO BURGER

Prepare The Hamburger, above, topping the burgers, after flipping them, with 1½ cups grated Gruyère cheese, 2 sliced ripe plum tomatoes, and 2 tablespoons grated Parmesan cheese. When cooked, sprinkle each burger with 1 tablespoon minced fresh parsley.

BLUE CHEESE AND BACON BURGER

Prepare The Hamburger, above, topping the burgers, after flipping them, with four 1-ounce slices Saga or other blue cheese and 4 crisp cooked slices bacon, cut crosswise in half.

CALIFORNIA BURGER

Prepare The Hamburger, above. On each bun, place 1 thin slice of red onion. Top with the cooked burger, then with a thick slice of ripe tomato and a leaf or two of Boston lettuce or other mild lettuce of your choice.

TEX-MEX BURGER

Prepare The Hamburger, above, adding several dashes of hot red pepper sauce to the meat before shaping the burgers. Serve the cooked burgers topped with Guacamole, 173, and Salsa Fresca, 61.

CHILI BURGER

Prepare The Hamburger, above, topping each cooked burger with several tablespoons of the chili of your choice and about 2 teaspoons minced onions.

BARBECUE BURGERS

Prepare The Hamburger, above, topping each cooked burger with 1 to 2 tablespoons of barbecue sauce of your choice.

MUSHROOM BURGER

4 burgers

Heat in a large skillet over medium heat:

2 tablespoon butter

Add:

2 small onions, sliced

Cook, stirring, for 5 minutes. Add:

8 ounces mushrooms, wiped clean and sliced
1 yellow or red bell pepper, diced (optional)
1 teaspoon fresh thyme leaves
Salt and ground black pepper to taste

Cook, stirring, for 10 minutes. Keep warm while you prepare:

The Hamburger, 186

Top the cooked burgers with the mushroom mixture.

BECKER BURGERS

4 burgers

The traditional way of serving these in the Becker home is as open-faced sandwiches on whole-wheat toast with the pan juices poured over the burgers.

Divide into 4 equal portions and form each into a burger about ¾ inch thick:

1½ pounds lean ground beef

Heat in a heavy skillet over medium-high heat:

2 tablespoons olive oil

Add the burgers and cook for 2 minutes. Turn and cook on the other side for 4 minutes for medium-rare. Sprinkle the burgers generously with:

Ground black pepper
2 tablespoons soy sauce
2 tablespoons port
Several drops hot pepper sauce

Remove the skillet from the heat, cover, and let stand for 5 minutes. Serve at once.

CHUTNEY TURKEY BURGER

4 burgers

For the simplest turkey burgers, simply shape a pound of ground turkey into 4 patties, season to taste with salt and pepper, then grill, broil, or pan-fry and serve on a bun with thick slices of red onion. For added moisture and flavor, we suggest combining the meat with other ingredients.

Stir together in a small bowl:

½ cup Tomato Chutney, 68, or Green Mango Chutney, 71, large pieces chopped
1 tablespoon Dijon mustard
2 teaspoons fresh lemon juice, or to taste

Combine in another bowl:

1 pound ground turkey
3 tablespoons Green Mango Chutney, 67, large pieces chopped
2 scallions, minced
1 teaspoon ground cumin
1 teaspoon ground coriander
Salt and ground black pepper to taste

Shape into 4 patties and grill, broil, or pan-fry, turning once, just until cooked through, 4 to 5 minutes each side. Meanwhile, spread the chutney mixture over:

8 thick (½-inch) slices sourdough bread, toasted

Top 4 slices of the bread with:

Arugula leaves
4 very thin slices red onions

Place the burgers on top, top with the remaining bread, and serve hot.

SLOPPY JOE *6 sandwiches*

The Sloppy Joe—known as "loosemeat" in certain parts of the country—dates from the 1950s. Why "Joe," it is not possible to say with surety, but "sloppy" is obvious enough.

Heat in a large skillet, preferably nonstick, over medium heat:

1 tablespoon vegetable oil

Add:

1 small onion, finely diced
1 small red or yellow bell pepper, finely diced
4 cloves garlic, minced
1 large celery stalk, finely diced
1 teaspoon fresh thyme leaves (optional)
Salt and ground black pepper to taste

Cook, stirring frequently, until the onion is softened but not browned, about 10 minutes. Transfer the onion mixture to a plate. Add to the skillet and increase the heat slightly:

1¼ pounds ground beef chuck or sirloin

Cook, breaking up any lumps with a wooden spoon, just until browned, 3 to 4 minutes. Add the onion mixture along with:

½ cup Chili Sauce, 70
½ cup beer or water
3 tablespoons Worcestershire sauce
Hot red pepper sauce to taste

Partially cover and simmer, stirring occasionally, until the flavors are blended and the sauce is slightly thickened, about 15 minutes. Toast, cut side up, under a broiler:

6 large seeded rolls or six 6-inch lengths French bread, halved

Sprinkle the Sloppy Joe mixture with:

3 tablespoons minced scallion greens

Spoon onto the bottom halves of the rolls and cover with the tops. Serve hot.

OPEN-FACED HOT ROAST BEEF SANDWICH *4 sandwiches*

Served with a big helping of mashed potatoes, gravy, and some steamed green beans, this is one of the great American diner traditions. Do not try to dress up the sandwich with good European-style bread; this is one case where spongy American white bread is right at home.

Very thinly slice:

About 1 pound cold roast beef

Prepare and keep very hot:

1 cup Basic Brown Sauce, 49

Beat together until blended:

2 tablespoons butter, softened
¼ teaspoon yellow mustard or 1 teaspoon drained horseradish

Spread this mixture over:

4 thick (½-inch) slices white or other soft bread of your choice

Layer the roast beef on top of the bread, douse generously with the hot brown sauce, and serve immediately.

OPEN-FACED HOT TURKEY SANDWICH

Prepare Open-Faced Hot Roast Beef Sandwich, above, substituting thinly sliced cooked turkey for the roast beef and Basic Bread Stuffing, 482, for the beaten butter mixture.

OPEN-FACED HOT CHICKEN SANDWICH

Prepare Open-Faced Hot Roast Beef Sandwich, above, substituting thinly sliced cooked chicken breast for the roast beef. Omit the butter mixture and substitute 1 cup White Sauce, 46, flavored, if desired, with 1 tablespoon fresh thyme leaves, for the Basic Brown Sauce.

GRILLED CHEESE SANDWICH *4 sandwiches*

The grilled cheese sandwich is probably the most popular hot American sandwich after the hamburger. Sliced tomatoes and crisp bacon or ham are traditionally added. But it can also be dressed up with an interesting topping like mango chutney, Salsa Verde, 81, Tapenade, 161, or apricot mustard, see page 71.

Lay out on a work surface:

8 slices white sandwich bread or other bread of your choice, crusts removed if desired

Top 4 slices of bread with:

1 pound thinly sliced or grated Cheddar, American, or fontina cheese

Top with the remaining bread and press together gently. Heat in a large skillet over medium heat until the foam subsides:

3 tablespoons butter
1 tablespoon vegetable oil

Add the sandwiches, in batches if necessary, and cook, turning once, until the outside is golden brown and the cheese is just melted and has started to ooze slightly, 7 to 8 minutes. Cut the sandwiches in half and serve hot.

BAGELS AND LOX

4 open-faced sandwiches; 2 closed sandwiches

The combination of bagels, cream cheese, and smoked salmon (either lox or Nova Scotia) is a Jewish delicatessen classic. Smoked sable, whitefish, or sturgeon is also traditional in place of the salmon.

Cut in half horizontally and toast if desired:

2 bagels

Spread 1 half of each bagel with:

About 2 tablespoons cream cheese

Top each with:

1 thin slice Bermuda or red onion
1 thin slice ripe tomato
2 paper-thin slices (about 1 ounce) lox or Nova Scotia smoked salmon
Scandinavian Mustard-Dill Sauce, 79 (optional)

Serve either open-faced or form into 2 closed sandwiches.

DELI-STYLE CORNED BEEF AND TONGUE TRIPLE-DECKER SANDWICH

4 triple-decker sandwiches

This recipe is adapted from New York City's Carnegie Deli, where show biz is the daily bread. On the menu, this sandwich is called "Tongue's for the Memory."

Lay out on a work surface:

12 slices rye bread

Generously spread 8 of the slices on one side with:

Classic Russian Dressing, 240

Divide on top of the dressing on 4 slices of the bread:

About 4 ounces sliced beef tongue
About 3/4 cup Cole Slaw, 222

Top with the 4 remaining dressing-spread slices, dressing side up. Divide on top:

About 8 ounces sliced corned beef
About 4 ounces sliced imported Swiss cheese

Slice the remaining 4 slices bread in half and place on top of the sandwiches. Slice the sandwiches in half to match the top slices and serve.

DELI-STYLE PASTRAMI AND CORNED BEEF TRIPLE-DECKER SANDWICH

Prepare Deli-Style Corned Beef and Tongue Triple-Decker Sandwich, above, substituting thinly sliced pastrami for the tongue and drained sauerkraut for the cole slaw.

DELI-STYLE ROAST BEEF AND LIVER TRIPLE-DECKER SANDWICH

Prepare Deli-Style Corned Beef and Tongue Triple-Decker Sandwich, above, substituting Sautéed Calf's Liver, 728, for the corned beef and roast beef for the tongue. Layer dill pickles on top of the cheese.

DELI-STYLE BRAUNSCHWEIGER SANDWICH

4 sandwiches

Braunschweiger is the most popular of the liverwursts, a family of soft, precooked sausages that all contain at least 30 percent pork liver. Named after a German town, Braunschweiger is smoked for added flavor. Any other type of liverwurst can be substituted.

Lay out on a work surface:

8 slices pumpernickel or rye bread

Generously spread 4 slices on one side with:

Drained horseradish

Spread the other 4 slices with:

Spicy mustard

Layer on top of the horseradish-spread slices:

About 8 ounces Braunschweiger or other liverwurst, thinly sliced
1/2 red onion, thinly sliced
1/2 cucumber, peeled, seeded, and thinly sliced
8 slices bacon, cooked until crisp, or 8 anchovy fillets

Cover with the remaining bread, mustard side down. Press the sandwiches gently together and serve.

WESTERN SANDWICH

1 sandwich

This diner staple brings breakfast to the dinner table.

For each sandwich, mix together the following:

1 large egg, lightly beaten
2 tablespoons milk
2 tablespoons chopped cooked ham or bacon
1 tablespoon minced onions
1 tablespoon finely chopped green or red bell peppers
Salt and ground black pepper to taste

Melt in a medium skillet over medium heat:

1 teaspoon butter

Pour the egg mixture into the hot pan and cook until almost set; flip it over and cook for 1 minute more. Serve on:

1 large Kaiser or hard roll, split and warmed

WELSH RAREBIT

6 to 8 servings

Welsh rarebit—a British dish served on toast or crackers as lunch or supper—should really be Welsh rabbit. The idea is that melted cheese on toast is what the Welsh rabbit hunter has to eat when he comes home empty-handed. This is a traditional recipe, made with beer; some experts insist on stale ale.

Grate:

3 cups aged Cheshire, Cheddar, or Colby cheese (about 1 pound)

Melt in the top of a double boiler set over boiling water:

1 tablespoon butter

Stir in and heat until warm:

1 cup beer

Add the cheese and cook, stirring constantly with a fork, until the cheese is melted. Stir in:

1 large egg, lightly beaten
1 teaspoon Worcestershire sauce
1 teaspoon salt
½ teaspoon sweet paprika
¼ teaspoon dry mustard
¼ teaspoon curry powder (optional)
Several grains of ground red pepper

Cook for 1 minute, stirring, until slightly thickened. Serve at once on top of:

6 to 8 slices beer, cheese, rye, or other bread of your choice, toasted, or sesame flatbread or crackers

THE MACKIE

Prepare Welsh Rarebit, above, topping toasted slices of white bread with sliced tomatoes and crisp bacon before covering with the cheese mixture.

BLUSHING BUNNY

Prepare Welsh Rarebit, above, substituting tomato juice or canned tomato soup for the beer.

BLT

4 sandwiches

This all-time favorite demonstrates the American genius for combining flavors. To dress it up, add slices of avocado and some bean sprouts, substitute brioche for the white bread, or slip in some thinly sliced cooked shrimp or lobster.

Lay out on a work surface:

8 slices crisp dry white toast

Spread the bread lightly on one side with:

Mayonnaise (about 3 tablespoons total)

Divide among 4 slices, spread side up:

2 beefsteak or other meaty tomatoes, sliced about ¼ inch thick
8 Bibb, Boston, or red-leaf lettuce leaves
12 slices bacon, cooked until crisp
Salt and ground black pepper to taste

Top with the remaining 4 slices toast, press together gently, and serve.

CHIPPED BEEF AND CHEESE SANDWICH

6 sandwiches

Chipped beef—very thin slices of salted, smoked, dried beef packed in jars—has long been an essential part of the American pantry.

Stir together well:

¼ cup grated sharp Cheddar cheese
2 tablespoons mayonnaise

Finely shred and stir in:

4 ounces chipped beef

Add and mix well:

¼ cup finely chopped sweet-and-sour pickles
2 tablespoons minced fresh parsley or celery leaves
1 tablespoon minced onions
1 to 3 teaspoons yellow, hot, or whole-grain mustard or Worcestershire sauce
Salt and ground black pepper to taste

Spread over:

6 slices potato bread or other bread of your choice

Add, if desired:

Lettuce leaves
Tomato slices

Top with:

6 slices bread

Serve at once.

TUNA MELT

4 open-faced sandwiches

You can substitute Cheddar, fontina, or any other melting cheese for the Monterey Jack.

Preheat the broiler.

Prepare Tuna Salad, 230. Divide the salad among:

4 slices rye or other bread of your choice, toasted

Top with:

4 ounces Monterey Jack cheese, grated

Broil the open-faced sandwiches in a shallow baking pan about 4 inches from the heat until the cheese is melted and golden, 1 to 2 minutes. Serve hot.

SHRIMP OR LOBSTER MELT

4 open-faced sandwiches

Preheat the broiler.

Prepare:

Shrimp Salad, 231, or Lobster Salad, 231

Divide the salad among:

4 slices brioche or challah, lightly toasted

Top with:

4 ounces Parmesan cheese, grated

Broil the sandwiches in a shallow baking pan about 4 inches from the heat until the cheese is melted and golden, 1 to 2 minutes. Serve hot.

REUBEN SANDWICH *6 open-faced sandwiches*

One theory holds that this quintessential deli sandwich was created by New York delicatessen proprietor Arthur Reuben in 1941 to honor an actress named Annette Seelos (why it is not the Annette Sandwich, we cannot guess). Another theory gives credit to a grocer from Omaha, Nebraska, who supposedly invented it during a card game in 1955. Our vote goes to New York. If you wish, rather than broiling the open-faced sandwich, you can top it with another slice of rye and grill it the way you would a grilled cheese sandwich, 188.

Preheat the oven to 400°F.

Toast:

6 slices rye bread

Spread thinly with:

Butter, softened

Classic Russian Dressing, 240

Divide among the slices:

About 1¼ pounds thinly sliced lean corned beef

About 12 ounces well-drained sauerkraut or Cole Slaw, 222

6 slices Swiss cheese

Arrange on a baking sheet and bake until the cheese begins to melt, 5 to 7 minutes. Heat the broiler and broil the sandwiches until the cheese is lightly browned, about 1 minute. Serve immediately, accompanied with:

Dill or half-sour pickles (optional)

RACHEL SANDWICH

Prepare Reuben Sandwich, above, substituting thinly sliced turkey for the corned beef.

CROQUE MONSIEUR *6 sandwiches*

This French grilled ham-and-cheese sandwich is standard Parisian café fare.

Preheat the broiler.

Lay out on a work surface:

12 slices home-style white bread or *pain de mie*, 759

Spread 1 side of 6 of the slices with:

Unsalted butter, softened (3 tablespoons total)

Grainy or Smooth French-Style Mustard, 71 (optional)

Place on the buttered sides:

6 thin slices good-quality ham (about 12 ounces)

Cover with the remaining slices of bread. Place the sandwiches under the broiler and grill until golden. Remove the sandwiches, turn, and cover each with:

4½ ounces Gruyère cheese, grated

Return to the broiler and grill until the cheese is bubbling and golden. Cut into halves or quarters and serve warm.

CROQUE MADAME

Prepare Croque Monsieur, above. When the sandwich is almost golden, remove from the broiler and cut a small round out of the top piece of the cheese-covered bread, exposing the ham. Reserve the round. Break a small egg into the hole and place under the broiler until the egg is set, 2 to 3 minutes. To serve, top the egg with the cheese-covered round.

MONTE CRISTO

Prepare Croque Monsieur, above, substituting very thinly sliced chicken for the ham and Swiss cheese for the Gruyère.

CUBAN SANDWICH *4 sandwiches*

The classic Cubano is pressed with a sandwich iron, but you can achieve the same effect with a heavy cast-iron skillet.

Preheat the oven to 400°F.

Split in half lengthwise:

One 24-inch-long loaf Cuban bread or French baguette

Spread 1 side lightly with:

Butter, softened

Spread the other side generously with:

Whole-grain mustard

Layer on the bottom half:

8 ounces thinly sliced ham

8 ounces thinly sliced Swiss or Muenster cheese

8 ounces roasted pork, thinly sliced

Sliced sour pickles

Cover with the top half of the bread and slice crosswise into 4 sandwiches. Wrap each sandwich tightly in a sheet of aluminum foil. Place the sandwiches in a large cast-iron skillet and place another heavy ovenproof skillet on top to press them down. Bake the sandwiches until very hot and the cheese is melted, 20 to 25 minutes. Unwrap carefully and serve hot.

TURKEY AND AVOCADO ROLL-UPS *4 sandwiches*

Inspired by rolled snacks from around the world, Americans have recently created the "roll-up"—almost any combination of ingredients rolled up in a piece of flatbread of one kind or another and eaten out of hand. It is the sandwich redesigned.

Lay out on a work surface:

4 flatbreads, such as pita bread, *lavash,* or Flour Tortillas, 754

Divide among the flatbreads, leaving a 1-inch border:

12 ounces sliced turkey breast
2 avocados, thinly sliced
2 carrots, peeled and grated
1 medium tomato, chopped
2 scallions, finely chopped
1 cup sprouts of your choice (optional)
Salt and ground black pepper to taste

Drizzle over the filling:

Tahini Dressing, 241, Reduced-Fat Blue-Cheese Dressing, 240, or Tangerine Shallot Dressing, 239

On 2 opposite sides of the flatbread, fold over ½ inch, then roll up tightly, starting at 1 of the unfolded sides and serve.

GRILLED VEGETABLE ROLL-UPS *4 sandwiches*

Grill:

2 red bell peppers, halved
2 green bell peppers, halved
1 small eggplant, cut lengthwise into ½-inch-thick slices
2 medium red onions, cut into thick slices
1 zucchini or summer squash, cut lengthwise into ½-inch-thick slices
8 mushrooms, wiped clean

Let stand until cool enough to handle. Chop all the grilled vegetables into ¼-inch pieces and combine in a bowl with:

2 tablespoons coarsely chopped fresh basil, parsley, or cilantro
Salt and ground black pepper to taste
About ¼ cup Mojo, 79, Sauce Andalouse, 74, or a vinaigrette of your choice

Divide among:

4 flatbreads, such as pita bread, *lavash,* or Flour Tortillas, 754

Roll up as directed for Turkey and Avocado Roll-Ups, 191.

OYSTER PO' BOY *4 sandwiches*

Even a poor boy feels like a king when eating one of these sandwiches, say our New Orleans friends. Bacon makes a nice addition to this version, or you can substitute fried catfish, Louisiana andouille sausages, fried eggs, chicken salad, or even pot-roasted beef and gravy for the oysters.

Pour into a deep fryer or deep, heavy pot and heat to 375°F:

1½ inches vegetable oil

Meanwhile, combine:

½ cup yellow cornmeal
1 teaspoon salt
1 teaspoon ground black pepper

Dredge in this mixture:

24 oysters, shucked

Shake gently to remove the excess cornmeal, then deep-fry in batches of 6, turning occasionally, until golden brown and just cooked through, 1 to 2 minutes. Remove with a slotted spoon to paper towels to drain.

Halve crosswise, then lengthwise:

Two 15-inch loaves soft-crusted French bread

Spread the cut sides of each piece of bread generously with:

Tartar Sauce, 73, or Cocktail Sauce, 70

Divide among the bottom halves of the bread:

1 large tomato, sliced ¼ inch thick
About 1 cup shredded iceberg lettuce

Top with the oysters, cover with the top halves of the bread, and press together gently. Serve warm.

PHILADELPHIA CHEESE STEAK *4 sandwiches*

Philadelphia fast food, circa 1930. Purists insist on using pasteurized cheese spread instead of real grated cheese.

Wrap in aluminum foil and warm in a 350°F oven:

4 French rolls, split lengthwise

Slice ⅛ to ¼ inch thick, then into ¼-inch-wide strips:

1 pound beef sirloin, tip steak, or top round steak

Heat in a large nonstick skillet over medium heat until hot but not smoking:

3 tablespoons vegetable oil

Add:

2 medium onions, thinly sliced
1 small red bell pepper, cut into thin strips
1 small green bell pepper, cut into thin strips

Cook, stirring, until the onions are softened, 4 to 5 minutes. Add the beef and cook, stirring, to the desired doneness, about 2 minutes for medium-rare. Season with:

Salt to taste
Hot red pepper sauce to taste

Divide the beef mixture among the bottom halves of the rolls and top with:

½ cup shredded provolone or mozzarella cheese

Return to the oven to melt the cheese. Cover with the top halves of the rolls, press together gently, and serve hot.

LOBSTER ROLL *4 sandwiches*

A, perhaps *the,* basic New England summer sandwich. The beach shack version is served on commercial hot dog buns, but there is no reason not to use brioche sandwich rolls or other rolls.

Combine:

1 pound boiled or steamed lobster meat, coarsely chopped
¼ cup mayonnaise
¼ cup minced celery
Salt and ground black pepper to taste

Divide the lobster mixture among the bottom halves of:

4 brioche sandwich rolls or hot dog buns, split lengthwise and lightly toasted

Divide on top of the lobster mixture:

12 ripe tomato slices (optional)
12 fresh basil leaves (optional)

Cover with the top halves of the rolls, or press the buns together gently, and serve immediately.

FRIED CLAM ROLL *4 to 6 servings*

You can also make this sandwich with fried mussels or oysters.

Preheat the oven to 425°F.

Pour into a deep fryer or deep, heavy pot and heat to 375°F:

1½ to 2 inches vegetable oil

Meanwhile, split in half lengthwise:

One 12-inch loaf French or Italian bread

Remove some of the center of the bread to make room for the filling. Brush the inside of the loaf with:

Melted butter

Toast in the oven until golden brown, 5 to 6 minutes. Slather with:

Tartar Sauce, 73, or Sauce Rémoulade Sauce, 73

Arrange on the bottom half of the bread:

Shredded lettuce
Sliced ripe tomatoes

Top with:

Fried Clams, 521 to 522

Cover with the top of the loaf, press together gently, and serve warm.

MUFFULETTA *6 sandwiches*

This sandwich's name comes from an Italian dialect word for a certain kind of bread, but it is strictly a New Orleans specialty. Ingredients may vary, like those for a hero, but chopped green and black olive salad is essential.

Combine well in a small bowl:

1 cup finely chopped pitted brine-cured green olives, such as Picholine
1 cup finely chopped pitted brine-cured black olives, such as Kalamata
½ cup extra-virgin olive oil
⅓ cup finely chopped fresh parsley
2 teaspoons minced fresh oregano, or scant ¾ teaspoon dried
1 clove garlic, minced
1 red bell pepper, roasted, 402, peeled, seeded, and finely chopped
Juice of ½ lemon, or to taste

Cover and refrigerate for at least 8 hours. Split horizontally in half:

1 large round loaf (8 to 9 inches) Italian or French bread

Remove most of the soft inner bread, creating a cavity inside each half. Drain the olive mixture, reserving the marinade. Brush the insides of both halves of the loaf generously with the marinade, then spread half of the olive mixture in the bottom half. Add in layers:

About 2 cups shredded lettuce, arugula, or other salad greens
About 4 ounces thinly sliced mortadella or other soft salami
About 4 ounces thinly sliced sopressata or other hard salami
About 4 ounces thinly sliced provolone, fontina, or fresh mozzarella cheese
1 cup coarsely chopped fresh tomatoes, or ½ cup chopped drained sun-dried tomatoes in oil

Top with the remaining olive salad, cover with the top half of the loaf, and wrap tightly in plastic. Place on a large plate, cover with another plate, and weight with several pounds of canned goods. Refrigerate for at least 30 minutes or up to 6 hours. To serve, unwrap the loaf and cut into wedges.

PASTIES *6 pasties*

When the copper boom was at its peak in Michigan's Upper Peninsula in the nineteenth century, immigrants from Finland and from Cornwall in southern England flooded the area to work in the mines. One or the other of these groups (or perhaps both) brought with them the pastry-enclosed meat pies that are now known as pasties. Basically beef stew in a closed pastry shell, these could be baked fresh in the morning and carried down into the mines for lunch. The Michigan copper boom is long over, but pasties are still popular in the state's upper reaches.

Combine well:

1¼ pounds beef round steak, cut into ½-inch cubes, or ground chuck
2½ cups ½-inch cubes peeled rutabagas or turnips
2½ cups ½-inch cubes peeled potatoes
1 cup ½-inch cubes peeled carrots
2 medium onions, coarsely chopped
Salt and ground black pepper to taste

Cover and set aside. Mix together in a large bowl:

4 cups all-purpose flour
1 tablespoon sugar
½ teaspoon salt

Cut in with a pastry blender or 2 knives until the mixture resembles coarse crumbs:

1¾ cups solid vegetable shortening

Mix together:

½ cup water
1 large egg
1 tablespoon white vinegar

Add the liquid ingredients to the dry ingredients and mix just until combined. Turn out onto a floured work surface. Divide into 6 portions and roll each out to form an 8-inch round.

Preheat the oven to 400°F.

Divide the filling among the 6 rounds, spooning the filling onto half of each dough round. Fold the dough over the filling and tuck it under the filling. Moisten the exposed edge and bring it up to meet the tucked edge, pinching the dough together to seal it. (Each pasty should resemble a small football, flattened on the bottom side.) Cut a slit in the top of each pasty and place on an ungreased baking sheet. Bake until the crust is golden, 50 to 60 minutes. Serve warm or at room temperature.

GRILLED EGGPLANT AND ROASTED RED PEPPER PANINI

4 sandwiches

Panini literally means "little breads," but it is a common Italian word for sandwiches.

Prepare a medium-hot charcoal fire or preheat the broiler.

Combine well:

6 fresh basil leaves, chopped
2 tablespoons balsamic vinegar
1 to 3 cloves garlic, minced
2 red bell peppers, roasted, 402, peeled, seeded, and cut into strips about ¼ inch thick

Cut crosswise into ½-inch-thick slices:

1 medium eggplant

Brush the eggplant slices on both sides with:

2 tablespoons olive oil

Grill the eggplant over the hot coals or broil 4 inches from the heat just until tender, about 4 minutes each side. Remove from the heat. Split in half horizontally:

Four 4-inch squares Focaccia, 753

Spread the bottom halves generously with:

Tapenade, 161

Arrange on top:

4 ounces sliced fresh mozzarella or crumbled feta or goat cheese
1 large ripe tomato, sliced

Divide the eggplant and the pepper mixture on top and cover with the top halves of the focaccia. Press together gently and serve.

PROSCIUTTO, MOZZARELLA, AND BASIL PANINI

4 sandwiches

Try making this with focaccia or any other flatbread instead of ciabatta.

Split in half horizontally and toast lightly:

4 pieces ciabatta, each about 5 x 4 inches

Drizzle the bottom halves lightly with:

Extra-virgin olive oil
Balsamic vinegar

Layer each bottom half with:

4 very thin slices prosciutto (about 8 ounces total)
About 2 ounces mozzarella cheese, thinly sliced (about 8 ounces total)
6 fresh basil leaves
Salt and ground black pepper to taste

Cover with the top halves, press together gently, and serve.

STEAK FAJITAS

4 servings

Little known outside their native Texas until not very long ago.

Arrange in a single layer in a roasting pan just large enough to hold it:

1 pound skirt steak, cut into 3-inch strips

Whisk together:

Juice of 3 limes
2 scallions, minced
3 cloves garlic, minced
3 tablespoons minced fresh cilantro
2 teaspoons vegetable oil
½ to 1 teaspoon red pepper flakes
¼ teaspoon ground coriander
¼ teaspoon ground anise seeds

Pour the marinade over the steak, cover, and refrigerate for 12 to 24 hours, tossing several times.

Prepare a medium-hot charcoal fire or preheat the broiler.

Remove the steak from the marinade, discarding the marinade, and grill or broil until it is cooked to your liking, 2 to 3 minutes each side for medium-rare. Meanwhile, wrap in aluminum foil:

Four 7-inch flour tortillas

Place under the broiler or off on one side of the grill until heated through, about 4 minutes. Unwrap the tortillas and top each one with the steak, along with a spoonful or two of:

Salsa Fresca, 61

Roll up the tortillas and serve hot.

CHICKEN FAJITAS

Prepare Steak Fajitas, above, substituting 2 whole chicken breasts, skinned, boned, split, and cut diagonally into 1-inch-thick strips, for the skirt steak. Marinate for only 1 to 3 hours. Broil the chicken about 6 inches from the heat until firm to the touch and cooked through, about 5 minutes. Substitute Roasted Tomato–Chipotle Salsa, 62, for the Salsa Fresca.

CLASSIC BEAN BURRITOS

4 servings

These Mexican-American "roll-ups" differ from tacos primarily because flour rather than corn tortillas are used.

Preheat the oven to 350°F.

Divide into 2 batches and wrap in aluminum foil:

8 flour tortillas

Warm in the oven for 15 to 20 minutes. Remove from the oven and lay the tortillas flat on a work surface. Spoon down the middle of each, dividing evenly and leaving a margin of about 1½ inches at the bottom edge:

4 cups Refried Beans, 276

Sprinkle with:

2 cups grated Monterey Jack cheese
½ cup grated Cheddar cheese
½ cup minced onions
Minced jalapeño or other fresh chili peppers to taste

Fold the bottom of the tortilla up, then roll it from one side into a cylinder. Place the burritos on a baking sheet and bake until the cheese is melted, about 5 minutes. Serve at once. If desired, garnish with:

Sour cream
Minced scallions or snipped fresh chives

SHREDDED PORK BURRITOS

Prepare Classic Bean Burritos, above, substituting 1 cup shredded barbecued pork, prepared as directed for North Carolina Pulled Pork Sandwich, 694, for 1 cup of the refried beans.

GRILLED VEGETABLE BURRITOS

Prepare Classic Bean Burritos, above, reducing the refried beans to 1 cup and omitting the cheeses, onions, and peppers. Top the beans on each tortilla with about ½ cup coarsely chopped mixed grilled red bell peppers, zucchini, and scallions, 337. There is no need to heat this one—just top with 1 to 2 tablespoons Salsa Verde, 81, roll up, and serve.

PIZZAS AND CALZONE

We remember when "pizza pie" was still a novelty in the United States, little seen outside southern Italian neighborhoods. Today pizza is an American commonplace—often in forms that would amaze its Italian progenitors.

PIZZA WITH TOMATO SAUCE, MOZZARELLA, AND ASSORTED TOPPINGS

Two 12-inch pizzas

This is the type of pizza that most of us first encountered, a relatively thick crust topped with tomato, cheese, and assorted other ingredients. We advise not overloading your pizza with toppings; two or three, besides the basic tomato and cheese, are usually sufficient.

Prepare as directed:

Basic Pizza Dough, 752, or Bread Machine Pizza Dough, 760

Spread in an even layer on each pizza, leaving a ½-inch border:

½ cup Italian Tomato Sauce, 304

Sprinkle each with:

6 ounces mozzarella cheese, shredded
Other toppings as desired (suggestions follow)

If using a baking stone, slide the pizza off the baker's peel onto the baking stone in the preheated oven. If making the pizza on a baking sheet, place the pan and pizza in the oven on the bottom rack. Bake until the crust is browned and the cheese is golden, about 12 minutes. Remove from the oven, slice, and serve at once.

TOPPING IDEAS FOR PIZZA WITH TOMATO SAUCE

There are no rules for pizza toppings except to combine ingredients that you like together. Here are some classic combinations and some new suggestions.

Pizza Margherita: Layer the pizza with 1¾ cups diced plum tomatoes, ½ cup coarsely chopped fresh basil, 2 to 3 tablespoons grated Parmesan cheese, and 2 tablespoons extra-virgin olive oil. Season to taste with salt and ground black pepper and bake as directed.

Pizza Romano: Layer the pizza with 1¼ cups thinly sliced mushrooms; 2 green bell peppers, thinly sliced; and 1 onion, thinly sliced. Season to taste with salt and ground black pepper and bake as directed.

Seattle Pizza: Layer the pizza with about 12 very thin slices prosciutto or 8 thin rounds Canadian bacon, halved, and about 25 canned pineapple chunks, well drained. Season to taste with salt and ground black pepper and bake as directed.

Italian Sausage and Onions: Top the pizza with 12 ounces hot or mild Italian sausages, casings removed, browned in a skillet over medium heat for about 5 minutes. Very thinly slice 1 onion and scatter the slices over the sausage. Season to taste with salt and ground black pepper and bake as directed.

Mushroom, Sausage, and Pepperoni: Layer the pizza with 8 ounces Italian sausages with fennel, casings removed, browned in a skillet over medium heat for about 5 minutes; 1¼ cups thinly sliced mushrooms; and about 40 pepperoni slices. Season to taste with salt and ground black pepper and bake as directed.

Prosciutto, Artichoke Hearts, and Black Olives: Layer the pizza with about 12 very thin slices prosciutto; 10 drained marinated artichoke hearts, quartered; and about 20 Kalamata or other brine-cured black olives, pitted and sliced. Season to taste with salt and ground black pepper and bake as directed.

Fennel, Onion, and Asiago Cheese: Sauté 1 medium onion, sliced; 1 fennel bulb, trimmed and sliced; and 2 cloves garlic, minced, in 2 tablespoons olive oil along with ½ teaspoon dried marjoram and ¼ teaspoon red pepper flakes until the onions are translucent, 5 to 7 minutes. Spread evenly over the pizza. Season to taste with salt and ground black pepper and bake as directed. Five minutes before the pizza is done, sprinkle ½ cup grated Asiago cheese over the top.

Grilled Eggplant, Mushrooms, and Sun-Dried Tomatoes: Layer the pizza with 1 small eggplant, grilled, 194, and thinly sliced; ¾ cup thinly sliced mushrooms of your choice; 1 red onion, very thinly sliced; and 8 oil-packed sun-dried tomatoes, drained and thinly sliced. Season to taste with salt and ground black pepper and bake as directed.

WHITE PIZZA

Two 12-inch pizzas

According to American labeling laws, if it does not have tomato sauce, you cannot call it pizza. This would astonish Italians, who frequently eat pizza with just a touch of tomato or even none at all.

Prepare as directed:

Basic Pizza Dough, 752, or Bread Machine Pizza Dough, 760

Brush each generously with:

Extra-virgin olive oil

Top each with:

Toppings as desired (suggestions follow)

If using a baking stone, slide the pizza off the baker's peel onto the baking stone in the preheated oven. If making the pizza on a baking sheet, place the pan and pizza in the oven on the bottom rack. Bake until the crust is golden brown, about 12 minutes. Remove from the oven, slice, and serve at once.

TOPPING IDEAS FOR WHITE PIZZA

Any of the topping combinations suggested for Pizza with Tomato Sauce can also be used for white pizzas. Other ideas include:

Fresh Tomatoes, Basil, and Feta Cheese: Top the pizza with 2 vine-ripened tomatoes, very thinly sliced. Sprinkle with 3 tablespoons coarsely chopped fresh basil, then crumble 3 ounces feta cheese over the top. Season to taste with salt and ground black pepper and bake as directed.

Caramelized Onions, Black Olives, and Rosemary: Spread 1½ cups Caramelized Onions, 391, evenly over the pizza. Scatter about 20 sliced pitted Kalamata or other brine-cured black olives over the onions and sprinkle with 2 teaspoons dried or 4 teaspoons finely chopped fresh rosemary. Season to taste with salt and ground black pepper and bake as directed.

Fresh Clams and Garlic: Sprinkle the pizza with 2 dozen shucked fresh littleneck clams, 3 cloves garlic, minced, and about 2 teaspoons coarse salt. Bake as directed. When the pizza comes out of the oven, sprinkle it with about 2 tablespoons chopped fresh parsley.

Spicy Shrimp and Roasted Red Peppers: Sauté 12 medium shrimp, shelled, in 2 tablespoons olive oil over medium-high heat until cooked through, 3 to 4 minutes each side. Coarsely chop the shrimp and scatter evenly over the top of the pizza. Cut 2 roasted bell peppers, 402, into thin strips and arrange over the top. Sprinkle with ½ teaspoon red pepper flakes and ½ teaspoon dried thyme. Season to taste with salt and ground black pepper and bake as directed.

Portobello Mushrooms and Goat Cheese: Thinly slice 2 large portobello mushrooms or 8 to 10 button mushrooms. Sauté with 1 red onion, thinly sliced, and 3 cloves garlic, minced, in 1 tablespoon olive oil until the mushrooms are tender, about 5 minutes. Spread evenly over the pizza. Sprinkle ½ teaspoon dried thyme over the mushrooms, then crumble 4 ounces goat cheese over the top. Season to taste with salt and ground black pepper and bake as directed.

Chicken and Broccoli: Top the pizza with 2 grilled or sautéed boneless chicken breasts, cut into small bite-sized pieces; arrange between the pieces of chicken 2 cups drained blanched broccoli florets, each about 1 inch across; scatter over the top 1 onion, very thinly sliced, and 1 cup shredded mozzarella cheese. Season to taste with salt and ground black pepper and bake as directed.

Potatoes and Sage: Boil or oven-roast 8 ounces potatoes and very thinly slice them while still warm. Scatter the potatoes over the pizza and sprinkle with 2 teaspoons dried or 2 tablespoons coarsely chopped fresh sage and 2 tablespoons extra-virgin olive oil. Season to taste with salt and ground black pepper and bake as directed.

GRILLED PIZZA

Many culinary discoveries happen by accident. Grilled pizza is one of them. While trying to reproduce the taste and texture of the thin-crusted pizzas they had enjoyed in Italy, Johanne Killeen and George Germon, chef/owners of Al Forno Restaurant in Providence, Rhode Island, realized that the characteristics they loved so much came from the high heat and smoke of the live fire in wood-burning brick ovens. Having only a wood-fired grill in his own kitchen, George decided to try his luck grilling pizza. Much to his surprise, the dough did not fall through the grate but instead stiffened and cooked almost immediately. With a little experimentation, George developed a technique for a pizza he thought surpassed the benchmark in Italy. On the grill, the pizza comes into direct contact with fire. The smoke curls around the dough, leaving its delicate perfume on its surface.

GRILLING TIPS

To grill pizza successfully, you will need patience and some extra dough to master the technique.

You can use your favorite pizza dough or try ours. We recommend using an all-purpose unbleached flour. It has the right amount of gluten to produce a dough that stretches easily with just a little resistance.

Grilling pizza requires a hot fire started with kindling and fueled with hardwood charcoal. Build your fire on one side of the grill. For cooking, you will want a cool area on the grill in order to add the toppings without burning the bottom of the crust. If you have a hibachi, build the fire on one side. For kettle-type grills, create a center line with two or three bricks laid end to end and bank the charcoal on one side. A large grill is more convenient than a small one, but if your grill cannot accommodate a 12-inch round of dough, simply divide the dough and make 2 or 3 small pizzas.

Set up your work area as close to the grill as possible. The dough, olive oil, and a variety of topping ingredients should be close at hand and ready before you begin. The crispy, chewy texture of the grilled pizza comes from the irregularity of the dough stretched by hand rather than with a rolling pin. When you transfer the dough from the work surface to the grill, it has a tendency to stretch and sag a bit, so it is a good idea to work very close to the grill. Stretch and grill the pizzas one at a time.

When choosing toppings for the pizza, keep in mind that less is more. If the ingredients on top are too thick, the dough will burn before the top has a chance to cook. The pizza should cook in 5 to 8 minutes. If after 8 minutes the cheese is not melted and the toppings are not bubbling, either your fire is not hot enough or you have placed an excess of ingredients on top. More time on the grill will only dry out and toughen the pizza.

GRILLED PIZZA WITH TOMATO AND THREE CHEESES

One 10- to 12-inch pizza

The following recipe will serve four as an appetizer or one as a main course. The dough can easily be doubled or tripled.

Combine in a mixing bowl or in the bowl of a heavy-duty mixer:

1 teaspoon active dry yeast
2 tablespoons warm (105° to 115°F) water

Let stand until the yeast is dissolved and the water is foamy on the surface, about 5 minutes. Add:

⅔ cup cool water
2 cups unbleached all-purpose flour
1½ teaspoons coarse salt

Mix until the dough comes together. Knead by hand or with the dough hook on medium speed until the dough is smooth and elastic, about 10 minutes. Brush a large bowl with:

Olive oil

Add the dough and brush the surface with:

Olive oil

Cover the bowl with plastic wrap and let rise in a warm place away from drafts until doubled in volume, about

2 hours. Punch the dough down. Cover with plastic wrap and let rise for at least 45 minutes at room temperature or overnight in the refrigerator.
While the dough is rising, prepare a hot charcoal fire, setting the grill rack 3 to 4 inches above the coals.
Prepare the topping ingredients. Brush the back side of a large baking sheet with:

1 tablespoon olive oil

Place 1 ball of dough on the pan and turn it over to coat with oil. With your hands, spread and flatten the pizza dough into a 10- to 12-inch freeform circle, ¼ inch thick. You may end up with a rectangle rather than a circle; the shape is unimportant. If the dough shrinks back into itself, let it stand for a few minutes, then continue to spread and flatten the dough. Do not make a lip. Take care not to stretch the dough so thin that it tears. If this happens, all is not lost; rather than try to repair the holes, simply avoid them when adding the toppings.
When the fire is hot (you will be able to hold your hand 5 inches above the fire for only 3 to 4 seconds), use your fingertips to lift the dough gently by the 2 corners closest to you and drape it onto the coolest part of the grill rack. Catch the loose edge on the grill first and guide the remaining dough into place over the fire. Cover, and within 2 to 3 minutes, the dough will puff slightly, the underside will stiffen, and grill marks will appear. Using spring-loaded tongs and a spatula, immediately flip the crust over onto the coolest part of the grill. Quickly brush the grilled surface with:

2 teaspoons olive oil

Spread over the entire surface of the pizza:

¼ cup grated Parmesan cheese
⅓ cup grated fontina cheese
2 tablespoons grated pecorino cheese

Spoon in dollops on top:

6 tablespoons chopped canned tomatoes in heavy puree

Top with:

1 tablespoon chopped fresh parsley
1 teaspoon ground black pepper

Sprinkle on top:

1 to 2 tablespoons olive oil

After the toppings have been added, slide the pizza back toward the hot coals so that about half of the pizza is directly over the heat. Rotate the pizza frequently so that different sections receive high heat and check the underside by lifting the edge with tongs to be sure it is not burning. The pizza is done when the top is bubbling and the cheese is melted. Garnish with:

5 fresh basil leaves, torn by hand

Serve immediately.
Continue stretching the dough balls and grilling pizzas using the above topping ingredients or the following suggestions.

ADDITIONAL TOPPING IDEAS FOR GRILLED PIZZA

Anchovy and Mozzarella: Rinse 3 anchovy fillets in warm water, pat dry with paper towels, and coarsely chop. Combine the anchovies with 3 tablespoons olive oil. Brush a liberal amount of the anchovy oil on the grilled side of the pizza. Top with a 3-inch ball of fresh mozzarella, thinly sliced and patted dry on paper towels; 1 tablespoon chopped fresh mint; and 1 tablespoon chopped fresh parsley. Sprinkle with the remaining anchovy oil. Finish grilling as directed. Anchovy lovers might want to add more anchovy fillets.

Grilled Pizza Bolognese: Liberally brush the grilled side of the pizza with olive oil, top with ¼ cup grated Parmesan cheese and ⅓ cup grated fontina cheese. Spread with ⅓ to ½ cup of Bolognese Sauce, 307, or other leftover meat sauce from pasta, drizzle 2 tablespoons olive oil over the top, and finish grilling as directed.

Mixed Herbs and Cheese: Liberally brush the grilled side of the pizza with olive oil. Top with ½ cup grated fontina cheese, 2 tablespoons grated pecorino cheese, ½ teaspoon minced fresh garlic, ¼ cup chopped mixed fresh herbs (oregano, thyme, basil, rosemary), and ¼ cup chopped fresh parsley. Drizzle 2 to 3 tablespoons olive oil over the top. Finish grilling as directed. This pizza can be eaten as is or it can become a meal when topped with a tossed salad of arugula and summer tomatoes.

OTHER POSSIBILITIES

Tuna and capers
Sausage, radicchio, and ricotta salata
Spicy peppers, tomato, and goat cheese
Garlic and herbs
Tapenade, 161, and crème fraîche
Sicilian-style: Piquant Tomato Sauce, 305, garlic, cumin-scented ricotta, raisins, and imported black or green olives
Broccoli rabe, sausage, and cheese, such as fontina
Julienned asparagus with Parmesan cheese and chopped hard-boiled eggs

CALZONE WITH ASSORTED FILLINGS

2 calzones; 4 servings

Calzone, literally "pant leg," is a pizza folded onto itself—a closed envelope of dough with the toppings on the inside. As with sandwiches, the possibilities for calzone fillings are endless. Be careful not to make the fillings too moist, however, since these will steam and render the calzone dough mushy. Also, it makes sense to cut the ingredients for the fillings into relatively small pieces, since this makes the calzone easier to eat. Prepare through the first rise:

Basic Pizza Dough, 752, or Bread Machine Pizza Dough, 760

Preheat the oven to 450°F. Lightly grease a baking sheet.

Divide the dough in half and form each half into a ball. Place on a lightly floured work surface, sprinkle with flour, and cover with a dish towel or plastic wrap. Let stand for 20 minutes. Meanwhile, prepare:

Fillings as desired (suggestions follow)

Shape each ball of dough into a thick disk and let stand for about 5 minutes. Roll each one into a 10-inch round. Divide the filling among the rounds. Fold the dough over, making a half circle, and tightly seal the edges with your fingertips. Reduce the oven temperature to 400°F. Place the calzones on the baking sheet and bake until nicely browned, 30 to 35 minutes. Serve hot or at room temperature.

FILLING IDEAS FOR CALZONE

Any of the topping combinations suggested for Pizza with Tomato Sauce, Mozzarella, and Assorted Toppings, 195, can be used to fill the calzones. To do so, simply chop the ingredients coarsely and combine with 6 ounces shredded mozzarella cheese. Other good calzone fillings include the following:

Prosciutto and Three Cheeses: Combine well 1 cup finely chopped prosciutto, ¾ cup grated Parmesan cheese, ¾ cup ricotta cheese, ¾ cup diced mozzarella cheese, ¼ cup finely chopped fresh parsley, and salt and ground black pepper to taste.

Pepperoni, Onion, and Peppers: Thinly slice 1 red bell pepper, 1 green bell pepper, and 1 onion; sauté in 2 teaspoons olive oil until softened, about 5 minutes. Coarsely chop and combine with 8 ounces thinly sliced pepperoni and salt and ground black pepper to taste.

Sausage and Caramelized Onions: Combine well 8 ounces sweet Italian sausages, casings removed, cooked over medium heat until browned, 5 to 8 minutes; 2 onions, thinly sliced and caramelized, 391; ½ cup ricotta cheese; ½ cup diced mozzarella cheese; and salt and ground black pepper to taste.

Chicken, Black Olives, and Sun-Dried Tomatoes: Combine well 2 grilled, roasted, or sautéed chicken breasts, cut into small bite-sized pieces; 20 Kalamata or other brine-cured black olives, pitted and thinly sliced; 8 oil-packed sun-dried tomatoes, drained and thinly sliced; ¼ cup thinly sliced fresh basil; and salt and ground black pepper to taste.

SALADS

Although the term *salad* once meant nothing more than lettuce tossed with oil and vinegar, today's salads are made from almost every sort of vegetable, meat, poultry, fish, pasta, grain, or legume, raw or cooked, cold or warm, tied together by a flavorful dressing. Every step in creating a salad, from selecting ingredients to serving it, allows for the cook's imagination.

A simple green salad is an excellent way to refresh the palate after the main course of a large dinner and a perfect preparation for the dessert to come. A plate of marinated vegetables will spark the appetite before the main course. Salads can also replace vegetable side dishes. Tangy cole slaw and creamy potato salad make perfect partners to barbecued foods. And finally, there are more and more instances where salad becomes the entire meal. Innovative combinations of salad greens paired with grilled or roasted meat or fish are gaining ground as full-fledged entrées in our quest for healthful ways of eating.

All this freedom can be seen as a tribute to American independence and creativity as well as to the variety of foods available to us. However, it is at its best practiced with some restraint. Care should be taken not to pack too many diverse ingredients into one salad. Each element should be chosen for its unique contribution of flavor, texture, and appearance. Too many tastes combined without thought results in a clamor of flavors and textures that no one will enjoy.

ABOUT TOSSED SALADS

The relatively simple effort required to produce an outstanding salad is nowhere more evident than in the mother of all salads—the tossed salad. Tossed salads are often referred to as green salads, garden salads, or mixed salads, and while there may be other additions—croutons, herbs, cheese—the greens are paramount. All too often we are served limp greens topped with a dollop or two of bottled dressing, a few croutons, and a wedge of tomato, all crowded onto an undersized plate. Anyone who has ever enjoyed a garden-fresh mix of cool, crisp greens dressed with a light coat of a well-balanced vinaigrette understands the distinction. A well-made tossed salad is never an afterthought but rather a carefully orchestrated part of the meal.

In its simplest form, a green salad is composed of one kind of fresh lettuce dressed with the best-quality oil and vinegar you can manage. In a more complex presentation, it is a mix of carefully selected greens garnished with seasonings, vegetables, meat, or fish and tossed with a specially tailored dressing. Whatever the case, keep in mind that the type of tossed salad you prepare should depend on where it falls in your menu.

For a picnic or a camping trip, wash and dry the

PREPARING GREENS FOR A SALAD

To begin with, buy the freshest greens with crisp leaves, free of brown spots on leaves or stems. When available, greens still attached to their roots are usually more intense in flavor than those severed at the stem. Use greens as soon as possible after buying them. If you have to store them, remove any leaves that are wilted or show signs of decay and take off any rubber or metal bands holding greens together. Unwashed greens will keep for 3 to 4 days at most. (If the greens wilt slightly, they can often be revived by soaking them in ice-cold water for 3 to 5 minutes, drying them well, then placing them in the refrigerator for 30 minutes or so.) Store greens in the vegetable bin of your refrigerator in a plastic bag with holes poked in it. Properly washing, drying, and chilling salad greens is the indispensable first step in any salad. No marvel of ingredients or perfection of dressing can mask or make up for sand or dirt on salad greens. Likewise, inadequately dried greens, left full of water, will render the entire salad soggy and flavorless, since dressing can cling only to dry leaves. Unchilled greens rapidly become limp and lose their flavor.

Always handle greens carefully, so as not to bruise them. The easiest way to wash them is to separate the leaves and place them in a large bowl or sink full of cold water, swish them around for 30 seconds or so, then lift them from the water gently so that the dirt and grit remain in the water. Repeat the process until the water is clear; one dunking may do for relatively clean greens such as red-leaf lettuce, while spinach, which is notoriously sandy, may take three or four. If you are in doubt, the surest way to remove sand and grit is to expose the entire surface of each leaf to cold running water for a brief time. This takes a bit longer but yields the reward of an entirely sand-free salad from even the grittiest greens.

For drying, salad spinners are a wonderful convenience. Overcrowding a salad spinner, however, will both bruise the greens and hinder the device's ability to dry them adequately. A spinner about one-half to two-thirds full will work perfectly every time. Alternatively, dry greens by tossing lightly in a colander, tapping your fingers against the underside of the colander to make sure all the water runs out. In either case, it will probably be necessary to wrap them in absorbent paper towels for the final drying. Whatever the method, once dried, the greens should be well chilled to render them crisp.

Once they are washed and dried, store greens in whole form, tearing or cutting them only when you are about to make the salad. They should be placed in the coolest part of the refrigerator, which is usually one of the vegetable storage bins, where they will keep well for 2 but not more than 3 days. If you are serving the salad the same day, the ideal container for washed and dried greens is your salad bowl. Line it with paper towels, add the greens, cover with two layers of moistened paper towels, and seal the bowl tightly with plastic wrap or aluminum foil. Otherwise, put them into a plastic bag with holes poked in it.

To assemble the salad, sort through the greens, discarding any tough stems or wilted spots, and gently tear them by hand into uniform pieces. The pieces should be small enough to be speared with a fork and folded politely into the mouth, about 1½ to 2 inches across. Small leaves can be left whole. Iceberg lettuce, cabbages, and other especially crisp greens can be sliced or shredded with a knife.

greens (iceberg lettuce will stay crispest the longest), then chill them in a large plastic bag. Take the dressing along in a separate container.

Specialty dressings are included with some of the salad recipes in this chapter, but see Salad Dressings, 234, for others. As a general rule, thick, creamy dressings work better with sturdy greens, and simple dressings often match up best with complex salads with many ingredients. Allow 1½ to 2 cups loosely packed washed and dried greens and 2 to 3 tablespoons dress-

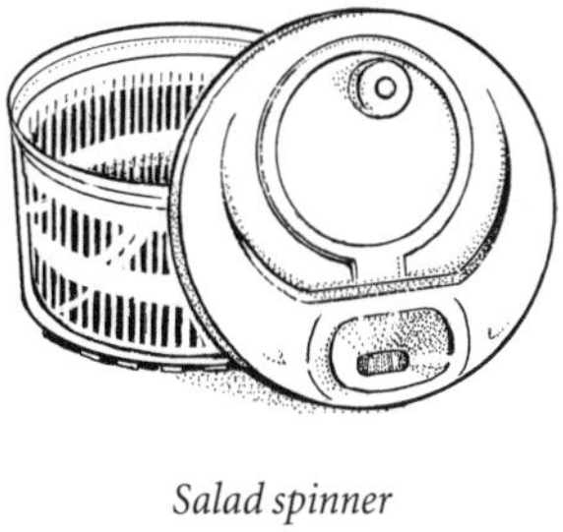

Salad spinner

ABOUT DRESSING SALADS

The time to dress green salads is always at the very last minute. Once dressed, greens lose their charm by becoming limp if they sit too long.

To dress a salad, place the greens in a bowl large enough to hold them spaciously. Whether combined beforehand or actually mixed in the bowl, pour the dressing or its ingredients down the side of the bowl so that it forms a puddle at the bottom. The tossing can now be done with clean hands, a pair of tongs, a couple of ordinary wooden kitchen spoons, or the oversized fork and spoon known as a salad set. Whatever implements you choose, the tossing action is always the same. In all cases, reach into the bottom of the bowl and gently lift the greens upward so that the topmost greens fall to the bottom. Gently repeat this action until all the leaves have had their turn moving across the bottom of the bowl and all the dressing is distributed. If salt, pepper, or any other dry condiments are to be added, sprinkle them lightly over the greens as you toss. Each leaf should glisten with just enough dressing to enhance its flavor. Too much dressing will overcome the greens and destroy the bright freshness that is a hallmark of a good salad. It is always best to start with too little dressing and add more if necessary.

ing per person (less for vinaigrettes and more for creamy dressings). Since we often prepare salads for more than one, figure ½ cup vinaigrette (or ¾ cup creamy style) for 4 servings.

ABOUT SALAD BOWLS

Well-seasoned wooden salad bowls are sometimes ascribed a sacred inviolability by salad fanciers. Soap and a sponge supposedly must never touch them. We think this idea is mistaken. The residue left after wiping the bowl with only a damp cloth tends to become rancid and can mar the flavor of subsequent salads. We recommend a bowl made of glass or of pottery with a glazed surface. A wooden bowl that is sealed with a food-grade varnish will also work well. All should be scrupulously cleaned after each use.

ABOUT SERVING TOSSED SALADS

Simple salads belong after the main course or as a side dish, while more complex salads come first as an appetizer or stand on their own as a main course. Some type of bread, breadstick, or cracker complements most salads. In all except the most informal settings, serve separate salad plates or bowls to keep the dressing from running into other flavors in the meal and vice versa. Chilling the plates or bowls helps maintain the desired crisp, cool character of the greens. Generally, serve all salads in large plates or bowls so that one's salad does not tumble onto the table or one's lap.

GREENS

Arugula: Also called Italian cress and found across the United States, arugula is a member of the mustard family. (The Italians call it rucola, the French roquette, and the English rocket.) It has a tender leaf, a pungent peppery bite, and the scent of pine. Some varieties have smooth-edged leaves and others have serrated leaves. The spiciness of arugula intensifies as it ages and also varies considerably from bunch to bunch. Dark green in color, arugula is delicious alone or as an

Arugula

Amaranth

Beet greens

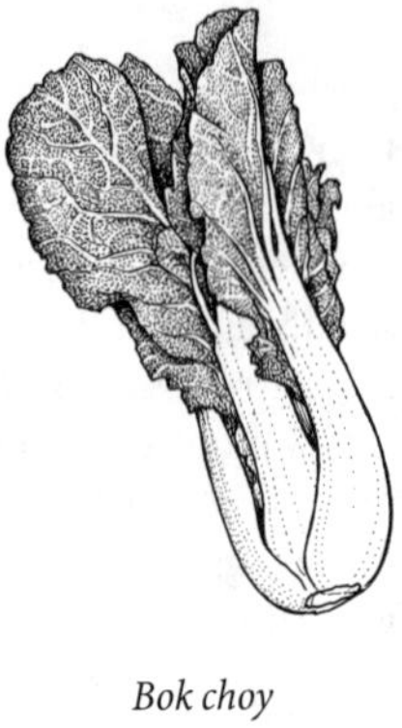

Bok choy

accent in mixed green salads. It also combines well with legumes, especially white beans, and other vegetables. Tiny arugula blossoms are gorgeous, white or yellow with brown markings, and are not to be missed. They make a handsome, pungent addition to salads.

Baby Greens: Many leafy green vegetables are served in cooked form when they attain maturity. They are also sold in their infant stage, when they are delicate in texture and flavor. They can then be eaten raw in salads. Try some of the following. **Amaranth:** Young green-leaf amaranth is tender, with an intense spinachy taste (another name for it is Chinese spinach). The red varieties have the same flavor and brighten a salad nicely. **Beet Greens:** Only the tiniest of these can be eaten raw, for they soon become too tough to be palatable. If you have a garden, trim them when you thin the beets and add them to salads. They provide a fresh taste and a faint echo of the flavor of beets. **Bok Choy:** Also called pak choi, this is a member of the mustard cabbage family; it comes in loose heads of fleshy stalks and broad leaves, with stalks that are white or green, thin or broad. Leaves may be light to dark green, thick or thin, cupped or flat. Baby bok choy is a miniature, delicately flavored bunch of leaves with small stalks, about 4 inches long. The yellow-flowering shoots are delicious too. **Collards:** These flat, blue-green, cabbage-flavored leaves are sweetest when grown in cold climates and picked after a frost. **Kale:** Most culinary kales have ragged or frilled blue, magenta, or grayish leaves. Kales have a delicate cabbage taste and, like collards, are sweetest after a frost. Kale makes a beautiful garnish when mature and can be used as a green when very young. **Komatsuna:** Also known as mustard spinach, this Japanese green has thick dark green leaves. Its flavor combines the blandness of cabbage and the bite of mustard. The young stalks are also delicious. **Mustard Greens:** This term is a catchall for any leafy green in the mustard family not otherwise identified by name. They may be broad and smooth or fringed and curled, dark green or light green or purple, hot and pungent or mild and sweet. Tightly curled, rather stiff green mustard varieties and flat-leaf purple varieties are among the most popular. Mustards can be eaten raw only when very small. They add a strong peppery flavor to a salad. Mustard-green flowers add a colorful accent to salads. **Swiss Chard:** This green has long, flat, celerylike stalks with large, coarse leaves at the top. Red Swiss chard, also known as rhubarb chard, has ruby-colored stalks. The stems have a delicate, celery-like taste, and the leaves have a hearty, spinachlike flavor. Chard has an affinity with citrus, so use a lemon dressing or add segments of orange or grapefruit to the salad. **Turnip Greens and Broccoli Rabe (Rapini, Broccoli Rape, Broccoli Raab, Broccoli di Rape):** These are forms of turnip leaves (*rapa* means turnip in Italian) and, when young, can be used like arugula. They have a mustardy bite, sometimes with a touch of sweetness.

Belgian Endive: This is actually the blanched head of a variety of chicory known as *witloof* (Dutch for "white leaf"), which is grown in darkness to preserve its very light color and mild flavor. The heads resemble young unshucked corncobs, creamy white with pale yellow tips. The leaves are both tender and crisp and have a distinctly clean, mildly bitter flavor. Belgian endive blends well with tart greens like radicchio and arugula and contrasts equally well with soft, delicate lettuces like Boston or Bibb. The outer leaves can serve as receptacles for crabmeat salad and can be eaten as an hors d'oeuvre.

Cabbage: Because green cabbages tend to be bitter in spring and summer, care should be exercised in mixing them with other tart greens. Winter cabbages, especially Savoy cabbage, are sweeter. Finely shredded red cabbage is a salad basic, used for color and texture for years before radicchio and other exotic greens

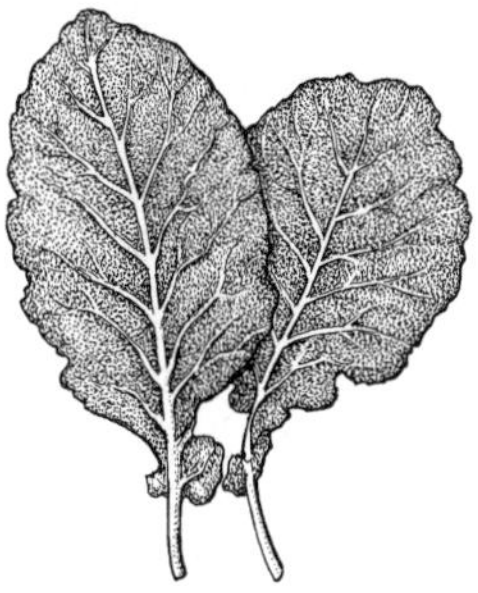

Collards

Kale

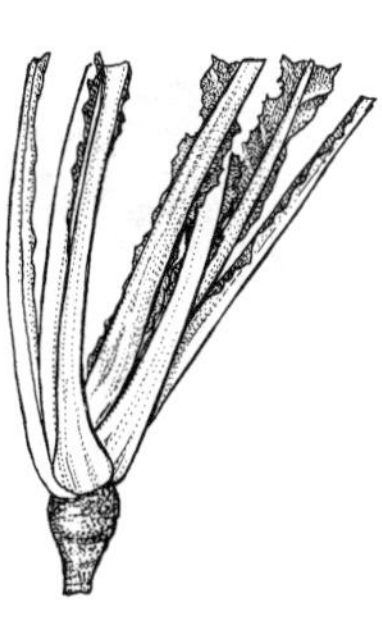

Komatsuna stalks

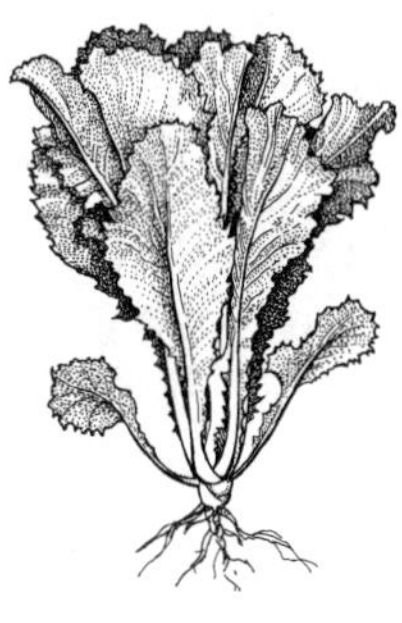

Mustard greens

appeared in our markets. Among the varieties of Chinese cabbage that are suitable for salads are michihili, whose crisp, mild, dark green leaves grow in a cylinder like a tall, slender head of romaine lettuce, and Napa or Nappa, whose pale ruffled leaves and crunchy ribs have a mild, slightly nutty flavor.

Celery Leaves: Chopped celery stalks appear in many kinds of salads, but the leaves are also good-tasting and leave a hint of pepper. The pale whitish green ones at the heart of the celery are best.

Celtuce: Also known as stem or asparagus lettuce, this is an Asian lettuce grown for its thick, succulent stalk. It tastes a bit like water chestnuts. Very young leaves can be used like lettuce in salads.

Chicory: The term applies to a group of bitter greens in the Sunflower family. The roasted and ground roots of one variety are turned into the bitterish extender or substitute for coffee still favored in New Orleans. See Belgian Endive, Curly Endive, Escarole, and Radicchio.

Cresses: Common cresses, which belong to the Mustard family, have leaves ranging from faintly peppery to searing hot in character. Watercress, the mildest and most familiar form, has crisp stems and glossy, dime-sized, dark green leaves. The stems as well as the leaves are edible, but use only tender ones. Garden cress is softer in texture but similar to watercress in taste. Curly cress leaves are lacy, like those of flat-leaf parsley, but extremely pungent. Upland cress is similar to watercress, but if grown in hot weather, it becomes so strong as to be nearly inedible.

Curly Endive: A variety of chicory, this has coarse, prickly, dark green leaves with a pleasant tang. The terms *curly endive* and *frisée* are used interchangeably, though most often what is labeled "frisée" has small, tender, lacy, pale green leaves with white centers and has a mild tartness and a more delicate taste than other chicories.

Dandelion Greens: A very tart green with jagged-edged leaves that look like arrows. Young, tender leaves less than 6 inches long are the least tart and are ideal in salads. Both raw and cooked, dandelion greens have a rich, bracing flavor and are worth buying when they appear in the market.

Escarole: Eaten both raw and cooked, this member of the chicory family has broad, irregularly shaped flat leaves with slightly curled edges, like the leaves of butterhead lettuce. The leaves are dark green at the top and grow paler as they approach the stem. The sturdy leaves have a pronounced tartness and a firm, chewy texture.

Good King Henry: Also called allgood or wild spinach, these spade-shaped leaves, often the first greens of spring, have a faint spinachlike flavor but are not related to spinach. The flowering tips are also edible. Good King Henry mixes nicely with tender red-leaf lettuces.

Herbs and Flowers: Add leaves or blossoms whole, tear them into bite-sized pieces, or cut them into ribbons. To add in quantity as a salad green: angelica, any basil, chervil, cilantro, dill, Florence fennel leaves, lemon balm, lovage, marjoram, any mint, any parsley, any sage, salad burnet, sweet cicely, tarragon. To use sparingly as an accent: ambrosia, anise, anise hyssop, caraway, epazote, garlic, garlic chives, Greek oregano, hyssop, Mexican oregano, mitsuba, perilla or shiso, rosemary, any savory, any thyme, Vietnamese coriander. In addition to the flowers of the herbs above, these flowers add flavor: clove pinks, elderberry, lavender (sparingly), lemon, mustard, nasturtium, rose, rosemary, scented geranium, society garlic, sweet woodruff, violets. If you like, use herbs with flowers to add an instant garnish—the flowers of basil and chives are especially beautiful.

Swiss chard

Turnip greens

Broccoli rabe

Belgian endive

Lettuces: There are hundreds of individual varieties of lettuce. Many come in both red and green, and avid gardeners will have dozens of favorites among looseleaf varieties, such as Black-Seeded Simpson, Deer Tongue, Lollo Rossa, and Salad Bowl. But no matter what the variety, they are all from one of four general categories, classified by the shape and growth habit of the lettuce. **Butterhead:** These tender lettuces are delicately flavored, with soft ruffled leaves gathered together into small, round, rather loose heads. Familiar varieties include Bibb, Boston, butter, limestone, and red tip. Bibb is more delicate-tasting than the larger Boston. The subtly sweet, buttery flavor of these lettuces combines well with stronger-flavored greens and is also lovely on its own. **Iceberg:** Also known as crisphead, iceberg lettuce was developed in the United States in this century. It has a compact, smooth round head that varies from pale green in the center to medium green on the outside and is dependably crisp, crunchy, very heavy in the hand, tightly packed, and compact. This lettuce has a distinct and attractive flavor, ships well, and can be torn, shredded, or sliced like cabbage. It is also available year-round. **Looseleaf:** Tender, mild, mellow, and soft, these lettuces are also known as "bunching" or "cutting" lettuces. They have sprawling, crisp yet tender leaves with sweet and refined flavors and are at their best in the spring. The leaves grow loosely bunched and may have ruffled edges and/or red tips. The many varieties of looseleaf lettuces include green leaf, red leaf, and oakleaf, a loose lettuce with divided leaves that look similar to real oak leaves. These lettuces are wonderful to eat on their own and also blend well with stronger-tasting greens. **Romaine or Cos:** This is a cylindrical, upright lettuce with stiff, elongated leaves, crisp center ribs, a rather juicy but relatively coarse texture, and a pleasantly assertive taste. The outer leaves are usually darker in color than the inner leaves and have a stronger flavor. It is also available in red.

Mâche: A member of the chicory family, this exceptional green is also called rapunzel, feldsalat, lamb's lettuce, and corn salad because it often grows in cornfields. Very delicate, sweet, and nutty, it is also very expensive because it is highly perishable. The clusters are small, made up of smooth, velvety, tongue-shaped green leaves. It is marvelous served alone or in combination with other delicate greens and herbs. It can be cooked like spinach and makes a BLT fit for a king.

Mesclun: This is not a type of green, but the name given to a mixture of salad greens that has recently become very popular. The term comes from the Provençal word for "mixture," and the idea comes from the practice common throughout Europe of gathering a variety of young field greens and mixing them in a salad. In the United States, mesclun has become a catchall term, meaning almost any assortment of edible greens, along with the occasional edible flowers or whole herb leaves, that are delicate and mild enough to be eaten raw. The idea is to create a balance between strong-flavored greens, such as arugula or mizuna, and more subtle greens, such as baby lettuces.

Miner's Lettuce: Also called claytonia, these are small, slightly cupped, triangular-shaped leaves with tiny flowers in their centers. Their flavor is fresh, rather like mild spinach.

Mizuna: Of Asian origin, and one of the most delicately flavored of the mustards, mizuna has dark green, feathery leaves that are delightful tossed with flowers and a light dressing flavored with sesame oil. Related is mibuna, which is similar in flavor but slightly stronger and quite distinctive in appearance, with a clump of long, narrow, densely packed stems that explode into a spray of leaves. Baby mizuna is an essential ingredient in mesclun.

Orach: These arrow-shaped leaves, sometimes called mountain spinach, have a mild spinach flavor.

Pea Shoots: The first 3 to 5 inches of a snow pea vine, including the vine itself, tendrils, leaves, pods, and

Green cabbage

Red cabbage

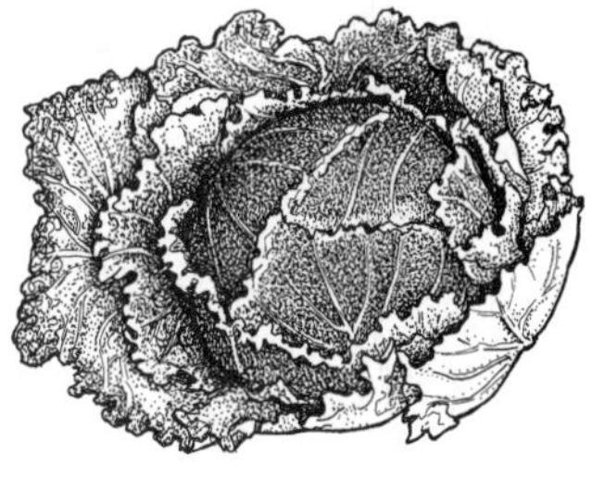

Savoy cabbage

sometimes flowers, are considered the pea shoot. They are popular in the cooking of Shanghai and Vietnam and now appear in our markets. Freshly picked, these are crisp, with a light pea flavor. They are exquisite in salads and, though delicate, hold their own with stronger flavors.

Purslane: Although considered a weed in most of the United States, this green has been eaten for centuries throughout India, Turkey, and parts of the Middle East. It resembles a small creeping jade plant. Leaves of the Goldgelber variety are large and golden. Purslane has juicy stalks and small oval leaves with a tart lemony flavor. Snap stems into sprigs and add to salads.

Radicchio: There are two varieties of this Italian chicory, one with a round head that resembles a small tender cabbage, the other with elongated leaves. Both are a beautiful magenta-mauve color with ivory streaks, and both have a pleasantly bitter, slightly peppery flavor. Radicchio combines well with both mild and assertive greens and adds stunning color to any salad.

Shungiku, or Chrysanthemum Leaves: Also known as garland chrysanthemum, these are the uniquely tasty, almost perfumed leaves of a type of chrysanthemum.

Sorrel: Garden sorrel comes up early in spring and lasts until snow crushes its stalks; where winters are mild, sorrel is green all year long. The leaves and stalks look like bright green spinach, but its flavor is its own—intensely lemony. It is wonderful in salads, but use it discreetly, both because its flavor can overwhelm and because its concentration of oxalic acid can be mildly toxic in large doses.

Spinach: With its clean, astringent freshness, the flavor of spinach is the reference point for many green leaves. Whether crinkled or flat (the latter are more delicate in flavor), spinach leaves are a versatile, valuable salad green. Include the stems, chopping them neatly, and if the pink roots are still attached, drop them in too for their crunch.

Sprouts: The long translucent wisps emerging from alfalfa, radish, mung bean, and other sprouted seeds are embryonic roots and stalks. The smallest sprouts are preferable for salads (they will quickly grow to the stir-fry stage). To sprout your own, see page 273.

Tatsoi: A ground-hugging member of the mustard family, this is also known as rosette bok choy because its leaves grow like rose petals. The rounded leaves are thick and very dark green and have a richly assertive mustard flavor particularly esteemed by the Chinese.

BASIC MIXED GREEN SALAD

The ultimate after-dinner salad. Many markets sell premixed greens, but for a more personalized salad, select an assortment of the freshest salad greens available. Combine greens with contrasting pungencies, textures, and appearances for the most interest. Use the stronger-tasting tart greens as an accent; otherwise, they may dominate the entire salad.

Follow the advice in About Tossed Salads, 200, allowing about 2 cups assorted greens per person. Toss the salad with just enough Basic Vinaigrette, 236, or one of the variations to coat the leaves lightly but thoroughly (1/4 to 1/3 cup for 2 servings). Serve immediately on chilled plates.

GREEN SALAD

4 to 6 servings

Combine in a salad bowl:

2 large heads Boston or Bibb lettuce, washed, dried, and torn into bite-sized pieces
1 tablespoon chopped fresh parsley (optional)
1 tablespoon snipped fresh chives (optional)

Toss well to coat with:

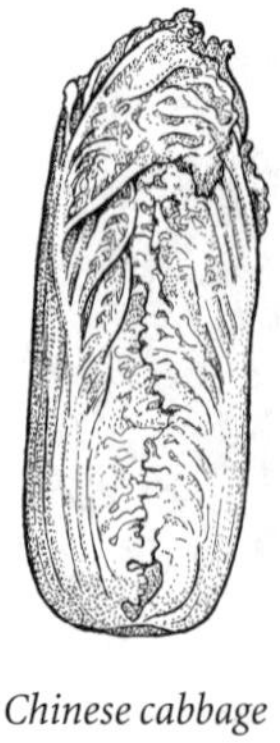

Chinese cabbage

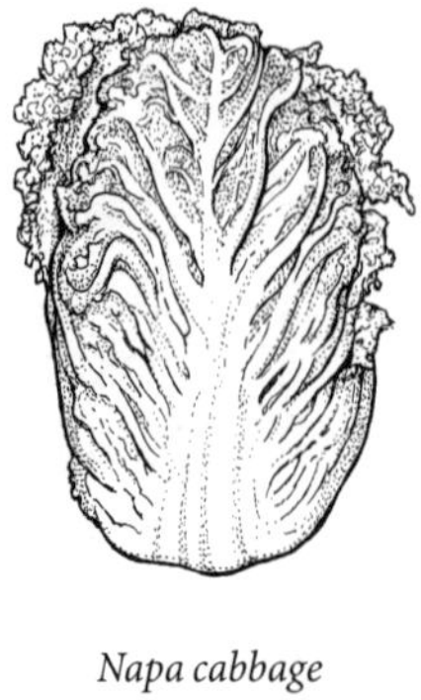

Napa cabbage

Celery with leaves

Celtuce

GREENS SUBSTITUTION CHART

If you cannot locate a particular green called for in the salad recipes, you can almost always find a substitute.

MILD GREENS

Butterhead Lettuces
Crisphead Lettuces
Looseleaf Lettuces
Romaine Lettuces
Celery Leaves
Celtuce
Mâche, or Corn Salad

SLIGHTLY TART GREENS

Arugula
Belgian Endive
Collards
Curly Endive
Dandelion Greens
Escarole
Kale
Mizuna
Watercress
Young Romaine Lettuce Hearts

TART GREENS

Arugula
Broccoli Rabe
Curly Cress
Curly Endive
Escarole
Mustard Greens
Radicchio
Radish Leaves
Turnip Greens
Upland Cress

MILD CABBAGES

Bok Choy
Collards
Kale
Komatsuna

SPINACH

Amaranth
Beet Greens
Chard
Good King Henry
Komatsuna
Miner's Lettuce

CRISP GREENS

Cabbages
Iceberg Lettuce
Pea Shoots
Purslane

½ to ¾ cup Basic Vinaigrette, 236, or one of the variations

Serve immediately.

TART GREEN SALAD

4 to 6 servings

Combine in a salad bowl:

2 bunches arugula, tough stems trimmed, washed, dried, and torn into bite-sized pieces
3 Belgian endives, washed, dried, cores removed, and cut crosswise into 1½-inch-thick slices
1 small head radicchio, washed, dried, and torn into bite-sized pieces

Toss well to coat with:

½ to ¾ cup Fresh Herb Vinaigrette, 236

Serve immediately.

FIELD SALAD WITH FRESH HERBS

4 to 6 servings

The idea of using whole herbs as salad greens seems rather novel to us today, but it has a long and noble history.

Combine in a salad bowl:

1 cup fresh herb leaves (any combination of chervil, sage, tarragon, dill, basil, marjoram, flat-leaf parsley, and mint)

Watercress

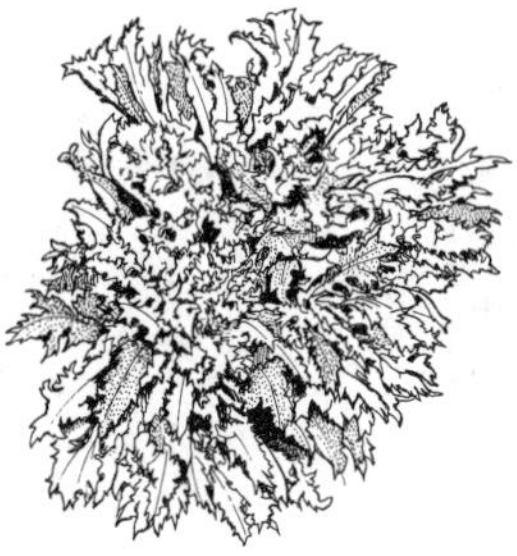

Curly endive

Dandelion greens

4 cups bite-sized pieces salad greens (any combination of curly endive, radicchio, watercress, mâche, dandelion greens, and arugula), washed and dried

Toss well to coat with:

⅓ to ½ cup Basic Vinaigrette, 236

Serve immediately.

MIXED GREENS WITH CHEESE CRISP

4 servings

Toss together in a small bowl:

½ cup grated Gruyère cheese

1 tablespoon grated Parmesan cheese

Sprinkle in an even layer in a large nonstick skillet to form an 8-inch disk. Cook over medium heat, spooning off the fat, until lightly browned, about 4 minutes. Using a spatula, carefully lift the pancake onto a paper-towel-lined baking sheet and blot dry.

Place in a salad bowl:

6 cups bite-sized pieces salad greens (any combination of romaine lettuce, Boston lettuce, and escarole), washed and dried

Toss well to coat with:

⅓ to ½ cup Basic Vinaigrette, 236

Divide among 4 salad plates and crumble the cheese crisp on top.

ABOUT GARNISHED GREEN SALADS

A green salad is easily transformed into an enticing appetizer or even a main course with the addition of a few ingredients chosen for texture, taste, and visual appeal. The greens remain dominant in these salads, so avoid the temptation to overwhelm them with too many bits of this and that. Think in terms of balance and harmony. Too many assertive garnishes, such as olives, garlic, and crumbled bacon, will cancel each other out. On the other hand, too many sweet flavors—fruit, soft cheese, carrots, and tomatoes—may become cloying. Begin by tasting the greens. If they are strong and pungent, they can support more flavor; mild and tender greens tolerate less.

IDEAS FOR GARNISHING GREEN SALADS

The simplest way to enhance a green salad is to add condiments or seasonings to the salad while or after you toss it with the dressing. Be sure to give the greens a few extra tosses to integrate the additions well. With a light coat of dressing on the greens, small accents such as croutons, nuts, cheese, and olives will cling to the salad and are less apt to fall to the bottom of the bowl. For more substantial additions like grilled chicken, sliced beef, or the multiple ingredients of a Greek salad, everything gets tossed together at once. Following are some additions:

Tomatoes: There are those who say that it is unwise to add cut-up tomatoes to a tossed salad, as their juices will thin the dressing. If this possibility concerns you, prepare them separately and use them to garnish the salad bowl or cut the tomatoes into vertical slices instead of horizontal rounds, since they bleed less this way. Cherry tomatoes can be left whole. Even cut in half (vertically from the stem), they release little juice. Many cooks believe that a bit of tomato skin is as much out of place at the dinner table as a bowie knife, while others prefer their fresh vegetables as unadulterated as possible. See Tomatoes, 429.

Croutons: Croutons are valued as much for their crunchy texture as for their flavor. Add these at the very last minute to prevent them from becoming soggy and leave them out if the salad is served alongside a starchy meal, such as pasta, potatoes, or rice.

Nuts and Seeds: Nuts and seeds add crunch and can complement the greens and the dressing. Simply place them in a dry skillet over medium heat and cook, stirring or shaking the pan often to prevent burning,

Escarole

Good King Henry

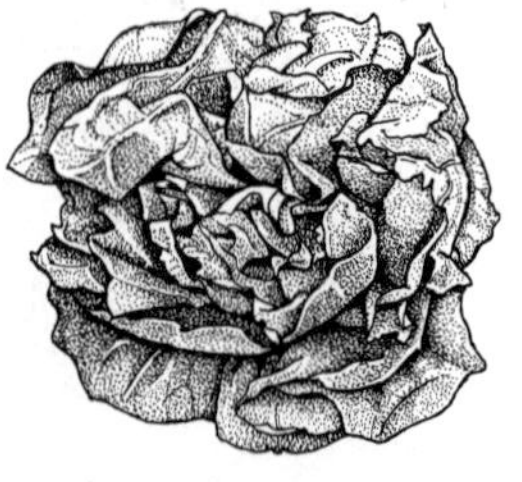

Butterhead lettuce

Iceberg lettuce

until they just begin to release their fragrance, about 4 minutes.

Vegetables: Thinly slice, shred, grate, or julienne raw vegetables such as carrots, cabbage, celery, cucumbers, bell peppers, fennel, and mushrooms so that they mix with the greens and do not fall like dead weight to the bottom of the bowl.

Garlic: Garlic is perhaps the most influential seasoning. There are two ways of giving to a salad a delicate touch of this pungent flavor. Halve a clove of garlic, rub the inside of a salad bowl with the cut sides, then discard the clove. Or rub a rather dry crust of bread on all sides with a halved clove of garlic (this is called a *chapon*) and place it in the salad bowl under the greens. Add the dressing and toss the salad lightly to distribute the flavor; remove the *chapon* and serve the salad at once. The *chapon* itself can be served to a garlic enthusiast. If you wish to have a slightly stronger flavor, mash a clove of garlic at the bottom of the salad bowl with the other seasonings and add the dressing to the bowl before the greens.

Ideas for Salad Garnishes:

Avocados, sliced
Bacon, crumbled
Cheese, sliced or crumbled
Chickpeas, kidney beans, or other cooked legumes
Fresh herbs
Hard-boiled eggs, chopped
Ham or other cured meats, thinly sliced
Smoked or cured fish (salmon, trout, mackerel), flaked
Marinated artichoke hearts, whole or sliced
Olives, pitted
Orange or grapefruit slices, peel and pith removed
Dried fruit (raisins, currants, cranberries, cherries)
Apples, sliced
Mangoes, sliced
Pears, sliced

CAESAR SALAD

6 servings

The Caesar is said to have been invented in 1924 by Caesar Cardini at his restaurant in Tijuana, Mexico, where it was made with whole leaves of romaine lettuce and eaten with the fingers. Long a staple ceremoniously tossed at tableside in Continental restaurants, the Caesar is now a salad of choice in restaurants of every type. Whether or not to include anchovies in the salad once was the main point of discussion. Today the question is whether to top the Caesar with chicken breast, shrimp, or sliced beef. Any of these make a fine addition, turning a first course into an entrée, but we retain an affection for the pure and genuine article. First coddling, or gently boiling, the egg helps to thicken the dressing.

Preheat the oven to 350°F.

Heat in a small saucepan over medium heat until the butter is melted:

2 tablespoons butter
2 tablespoons extra-virgin olive oil
2 cloves garlic, halved lengthwise
Salt and ground black pepper to taste

Remove from the heat and let stand for 10 minutes. Discard the garlic. Toss with the butter mixture:

3 cups ½-inch cubes French or Italian bread

Spread on a baking sheet and bake, shaking the pan once or twice, until golden brown, 12 to 15 minutes.

Mash together in a small bowl until a paste is formed:

4 cloves garlic, peeled
½ teaspoon salt

Whisk in:

2 teaspoons fresh lemon juice
1 teaspoon Worcestershire sauce
Salt and ground black pepper to taste

Red-leaf lettuce

Oakleaf lettuce

Green-leaf lettuce

2 to 4 anchovy fillets, rinsed, patted dry, and mashed to a paste (optional)

Add in a slow, steady stream, whisking constantly:

½ cup extra-virgin olive oil

In a salad bowl, toss the croutons and dressing with:

2 small heads romaine lettuce (preferably young or inner pale green leaves), washed, dried, and torn into bite-sized pieces

2 large eggs, boiled gently for 2 minutes, or added raw (see About Egg Quality, Handling, and Safety, 122)

Sprinkle with:

½ cup Parmesan cheese shavings

Serve immediately.

REDUCED-FAT CAESAR SALAD

6 servings

This is a reasonable stand-in for the classic Caesar for those who are concerned about fat intake.

Preheat the oven to 350°F.

Toss to combine well:

3 cups ½-inch cubes sourdough bread
5 spritzes olive oil spray
2 cloves garlic, finely minced
Salt and ground black pepper to taste

Spread on a baking sheet and bake, shaking the pan once or twice, until golden brown, about 10 minutes. Let cool.

Mash together in a small bowl until a paste is formed:

1 clove garlic, peeled
Pinch of salt

Whisk in:

2 tablespoons chicken stock
1 tablespoon grated Parmesan cheese
1 tablespoon minced fresh parsley
2 teaspoons sherry vinegar
1 teaspoon Dijon mustard
1 teaspoon fresh thyme leaves
2 anchovy fillets, rinsed, patted dry, and mashed to a paste (optional)

Add in a slow, steady stream, whisking constantly:

2 tablespoons extra-virgin olive oil

In a salad bowl, toss the croutons and dressing with:

2 small heads romaine lettuce (preferably young or inner pale green leaves), washed, dried, and torn into bite-sized pieces
3 tablespoons grated Parmesan cheese
Salt and ground black pepper to taste

Sprinkle with:

1 tablespoon freshly grated Parmesan cheese

Serve immediately.

GREEK SALAD

4 to 6 servings

Combine in a salad bowl:

2 large or 3 small heads Boston, romaine, or iceberg lettuce, washed, dried, and torn into bite-sized pieces
8 cherry tomatoes or tomato wedges
½ cup coarsely crumbled feta cheese
6 thin slices red onion
½ cucumber, peeled and sliced
8 Kalamata olives, pitted
¾ cup diagonally sliced celery hearts
4 scallions, cut into 1-inch pieces
8 firm radishes, sliced
One 2-ounce can anchovy fillets, rinsed, patted dry, and halved lengthwise

Whisk together:

6 to 7 tablespoons olive oil
2 tablespoons fresh lemon juice or red wine vinegar
1 teaspoon finely minced garlic
1 teaspoon dried oregano
Salt and ground black pepper to taste

Pour the dressing over the salad and toss well. Serve immediately.

Romaine lettuce

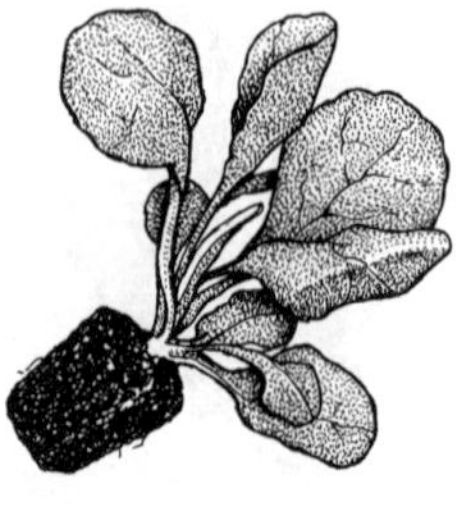

Mâche

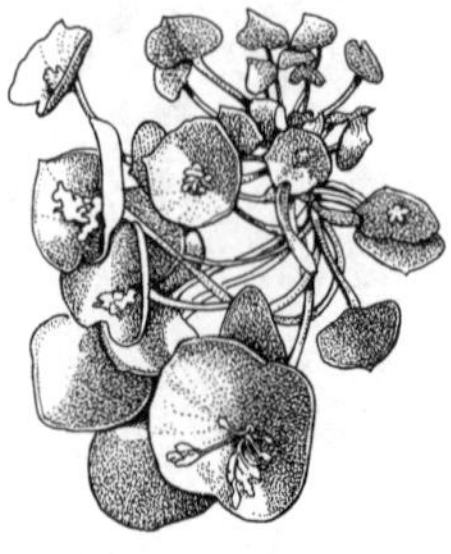

Miner's lettuce

ROMAINE AND RED ONION SALAD WITH CORN BREAD CROUTONS

4 servings

Croutons made from good rye or whole-wheat herb bread can be substituted for ones made with corn bread.

Preheat the oven to 350°F.

Toss together on a baking sheet:

- **2 cups ½-inch cubes corn bread (about 2 large pieces)**
- **2 tablespoons extra-virgin olive oil**

Bake, shaking the pan once or twice, until golden, about 10 minutes. Transfer to a salad bowl and let cool.

Whisk together in a small bowl:

- **2 cloves garlic, minced**
- **2 tablespoons grated Parmesan cheese**
- **2 tablespoons balsamic vinegar**
- **2 tablespoons chicken stock**
- **1 teaspoon chopped fresh basil or parsley, or to taste**
- **Salt and ground black pepper to taste**

Add in a slow, steady stream, whisking constantly:

- **¼ cup olive oil**

In a salad bowl, toss the croutons and dressing with:

- **2 small heads romaine lettuce, washed, dried, and torn into bite-sized pieces**
- **1 small red onion, thinly sliced**

Sprinkle with:

- **Parmesan cheese shavings**

Serve immediately.

TART GREENS WITH APPLES, PECANS, AND BUTTERMILK HONEY DRESSING

4 to 6 servings

Whisk together in a small bowl:

- **¼ cup cider vinegar**
- **¼ cup sour cream**
- **¼ cup buttermilk**
- **3 tablespoons honey**
- **1 teaspoon minced garlic**
- **1 scallion, minced**
- **Pinch of ground red pepper**
- **Salt and ground black pepper to taste**

Add in a slow, steady stream, whisking constantly:

- **½ cup olive oil**

Combine in a salad bowl:

- **4 cups bite-sized pieces arugula, washed and dried**
- **1 small head radicchio, washed, dried, and torn into bite-sized pieces**
- **2 Belgian endives, washed, dried, and sliced lengthwise into long strips**

Stir the dressing well, add just enough to moisten the greens, and toss to coat. Divide the greens among salad plates and top with:

- **2 Granny Smith or other tart apples, cored and very thinly sliced**
- **½ cup pecan halves, toasted**

Serve immediately.

ENDIVE AND WALNUT SALAD

4 servings

Whisk together in a salad bowl:

- **1 tablespoon red wine vinegar**
- **1 tablespoon minced shallots**
- **½ teaspoon Dijon mustard**
- **Salt and ground black pepper to taste**

Add in a slow, steady stream, whisking constantly:

- **2 tablespoons walnut oil**
- **2 tablespoons vegetable oil**

Add:

- **8 Belgian endives, washed, dried, cores removed, cut crosswise into ½-inch-thick slices**
- **½ cup walnut halves, toasted**
- **¼ cup crumbled Gorgonzola or other blue cheese (optional)**

Toss well to coat. Serve immediately.

ARUGULA WITH SUMMER VEGETABLES

4 to 6 servings

Use this recipe as a rough guideline, substituting whatever summer vegetables are most plentiful in the mar-

Mizuna

Orache

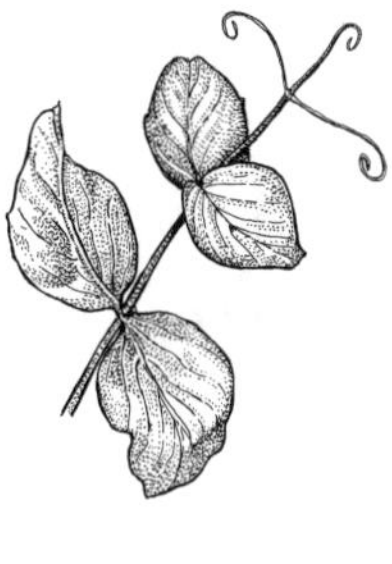

Pea shoots

ket. Baby turnip or beet greens or Swiss chard leaves can be substituted for the mâche and/or arugula.
Prepare:

Basic Vinaigrette, 236, or one of the variations

Cook in a large pot of boiling water for about 1 minute:

1 small summer squash, cut into ½-inch cubes

Remove with a large slotted spoon, refresh in ice water, and drain well. Add to the boiling water:

8 ounces thin green beans, trimmed

Cook just until crisp-tender, about 1 minute. Remove with a large slotted spoon, refresh in ice water, and drain well. Combine the summer squash and green beans in a salad bowl along with:

2 cups cherry tomatoes, halved
1 small red onion, halved and very thinly sliced
⅓ cup minced fresh basil

Toss well with enough of the vinaigrette to coat. Taste and adjust the seasonings. Divide among salad plates:

4 cups bite-sized pieces arugula and romaine lettuce, washed and dried

Spoon the vegetables on top. Drizzle more dressing over the salads and garnish with:

Fresh basil leaves (optional)

Serve immediately.

SALAD OF GRILLED CHICKEN AND TART GREENS

4 to 6 servings

This is a good way to use up leftover chicken.
Prepare:

Apricot Dressing, 239, or other fruit-based dressing

Combine in a salad bowl:

10 to 12 cups bite-sized pieces bitter greens (any combination of arugula, escarole, young dandelion greens, curly endive, mizuna, watercress, and radicchio), washed and dried

Toss well with just enough dressing to lightly coat the greens. Slice diagonally 1 inch thick:

2 whole boneless, skinless chicken breasts (about 1¼ pounds), grilled, 608, or broiled, 583

Divide the greens among salad plates and arrange the chicken on top. If desired, drizzle more dressing over the salads and serve immediately.

THAI BEEF SALAD

6 servings

Refreshing, aromatic salads are typical of Thai cooking.
Bring to a boil in a large pot:

12 cups water

Add:

1½ pounds beef tenderloin, trimmed of fat and tied

Cover and cook at a steady simmer for 15 to 18 minutes for medium-rare. Remove the beef, cover with a damp dish towel, and let cool to room temperature. Meanwhile, combine in a salad bowl:

3 bunches watercress, tough stems trimmed, washed and dried
1¼ cups fresh mint leaves
1¼ cups fresh cilantro leaves
2 bunches radishes, thinly sliced
1 medium red onion, thinly sliced
2 tablespoons thin strips lemon zest

Cover and refrigerate until ready to serve. Whisk together in a small bowl:

½ cup vegetable oil
½ cup fresh lime juice
3 tablespoons fish sauce (optional)
1 tablespoon soy sauce
1½ teaspoons sugar
Red pepper flakes to taste
Salt and ground black pepper to taste

Slice the beef crosswise ½ inch thick, then cut into ½-inch-thick strips. Add the beef and dressing to the watercress mixture, toss to coat and combine, and serve immediately.

Purslane

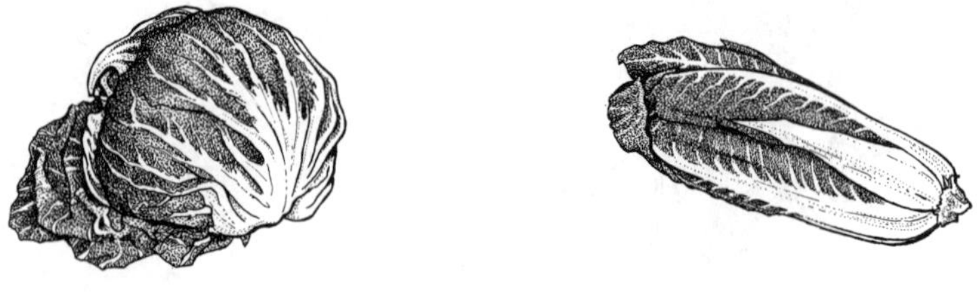

Round and oblong radicchio

SPINACH SALAD *4 servings*

Tender young spinach leaves are ideal for this classic salad. Young mustard greens or young dandelion leaves make delicious substitutes.

Cook in a skillet over medium-high heat until crisp:

4 slices bacon

Drain on paper towels and crumble. Combine well:

¼ cup cider vinegar or vinegar of your choice
2 tablespoons olive or vegetable oil
2 teaspoons yellow mustard seeds (optional)
2 teaspoons minced fresh parsley, or a combination of other fresh herbs
1 teaspoon grated onion
1 teaspoon sugar

Place in a salad bowl:

1 large bunch young spinach, trimmed, washed, and dried

Pour the dressing over the spinach and toss well. Sprinkle with the crumbled bacon and garnish with:

2 or 3 hard-boiled eggs, sliced into rounds

Serve immediately.

WARM SPINACH SALAD

Prepare Spinach Salad, above, substituting 2 tablespoons of the bacon drippings for the oil if desired. Heat the dressing until just before it begins to boil and pour over the spinach greens. Garnish with the hard-boiled eggs and crumbled bacon and serve immediately.

SPINACH WITH SEARED SHRIMP, BACON, AND ROASTED BELL PEPPERS *4 servings*

This is an elegant elaboration on the classic spinach salad. Use baby spinach leaves if you can find them. Bell peppers are easily roasted in the kitchen, but you can use canned as long as you rinse them well.

Roast, 402:

2 bell peppers, preferably 1 each red and yellow

Peel, seed, and cut into thin strips. Heat in a medium skillet over medium heat until hot but not smoking:

2 tablespoons olive oil

Add:

1 pound medium shrimp, shelled and deveined, with tails left on
Salt and ground black pepper to taste

Cook, stirring, until the shrimp have a little color on the outside and are opaque throughout, 3 to 4 minutes each side. Remove from the pan, let cool, and chill. Meanwhile, return the skillet to the heat and cook until crisp, 6 to 8 minutes:

8 slices bacon

Drain on paper towels and coarsely crumble. Whisk together in a small bowl:

¼ cup sherry vinegar
1 tablespoon Dijon mustard
1 tablespoon chopped shallots
1 teaspoon chopped fresh thyme
½ to 1 teaspoon red pepper flakes

Add in a slow, steady stream, whisking constantly:

¾ cup olive oil

Combine the peppers, shrimp, and bacon in a salad bowl with:

4 cups bite-sized pieces spinach (preferably baby leaves), washed and dried

Stir the dressing well, add just enough to moisten the ingredients, and toss to coat and combine. Taste and adjust the seasonings. Serve immediately.

SPINACH SALAD WITH GRAPEFRUIT, ORANGE, AND AVOCADO *2 to 4 servings*

Toast briefly in a small skillet over medium heat:

3 tablespoons sesame seeds

Toss together in a salad bowl:

Shungiku (or chrysanthemum leaves)

Sorrel

Curly-leaf spinach

3 generous handfuls (about 6 cups) baby spinach leaves, washed and dried
2 to 3 pinches of salt
3 to 4 tablespoons Tangerine Shallot Dressing, 239

Divide the spinach among salad plates and arrange on top:

1 grapefruit, peeled and sectioned, 457
1 navel orange, peeled and sectioned, 457
1 ripe avocado, peeled and sliced

Sprinkle with the sesame seeds and season with:

Ground black pepper to taste

Serve immediately.

LOBSTER SALAD VINAIGRETTE *4 to 6 servings*

This salad can also be made with cooked crabmeat or shrimp. It makes an opulent appetizer or light main course.

Preheat the oven to 425°F.

Toss together on a baking sheet:

6 thick slices French bread, cut into 1-inch cubes
3 tablespoons extra-virgin olive oil

Bake, shaking the pan once or twice, until golden brown, about 10 minutes. Prepare:

Basil Chive Vinaigrette, 237

Combine in a salad bowl:

2 cups watercress, with tender stems, washed and dried
2 cups mesclun or baby romaine leaves, washed and dried
1½ cups thinly sliced Belgian endive, washed and dried

Toss well with just enough vinaigrette to coat the greens. Divide the greens among salad plates.

Toss together, adding just enough vinaigrette to coat:

10 to 12 ounces cooked lobster meat, cut into ½-inch chunks

Flat-leaf spinach

1 ripe avocado, peeled and diced
½ red bell pepper, diced
½ yellow bell pepper, diced

Spoon the lobster mixture over the greens and garnish with the croutons along with:

2 ripe plum tomatoes, peeled, seeded, and diced

Drizzle more vinaigrette over the salads if desired.

ABOUT WARM OR WILTED SALADS

Despite our earlier insistence on the crispness of the leaf in green salads, there is virtue in the wilted or warm salad. In the classic Warm Spinach Salad, 213, a hot dressing partially cooks the greens, rendering them succulent and tender. In others, a warm garnish, such as baked goat cheese or fresh tuna hot off the grill, is placed on a bed of cool, crisp greens, producing a dramatic contrast of temperature and texture. These salads make an impressive first course or a memorable entrée. Whatever your choice, serve warm salads immediately, because they lose their appeal as the greens become soggy.

BISTRO SALAD *6 servings*

This classic, known in France as *frisée aux lardons,* can be served without the eggs. Thick-cut bacon, which will not need blanching, can be substituted for the salt pork.

Preheat the oven to 350°F.

Have ready:

10 slices French bread

Sprinkle both sides with:

2 to 3 tablespoons olive oil
Salt and ground black pepper to taste

Cut the bread into ½-inch cubes. Spread on a baking sheet and bake, shaking the pan once or twice, until golden brown, about 10 minutes.

Boil in water to cover for 2 minutes:

8 ounces salt pork, diced

Drain, rinse with cold water, and pat dry. Heat in a skillet over medium heat until hot but not smoking:

1 tablespoon vegetable oil

Add the salt pork and cook, stirring, until browned, 6 to 8 minutes. Remove with a slotted spoon and drain on paper towels. Pour ½ cup of the fat in the skillet into a small bowl and whisk in:

2 shallots, thinly sliced crosswise
3 tablespoons red wine vinegar
1 tablespoon minced fresh parsley
2 cloves garlic, minced
1 teaspoon fresh thyme leaves
Salt and ground black pepper to taste

In a salad bowl, toss the salt pork and croutons with:

2 large heads frisée (curly endive), washed, dried, and torn into bite-sized pieces

Toss well with just enough dressing to coat. Divide among 6 salad plates and top with:

6 large eggs, poached, 129, and trimmed

Minced fresh parsley (optional)

Serve immediately.

BAKED GOAT CHEESE AND BABY GREENS

4 servings

In Provence, France, where this salad is popular, mesclun includes many different salad greens and herbs, each varying in flavor, texture, and color. A mix might contain red- and green-tipped oakleaf lettuce, arugula, romaine lettuce, chervil, colorful red radicchio, curly white as well as green endive, escarole, and bitter dandelion greens. Add fresh herbs to this mixture (sage, dill, and tarragon are our favorites), top with baked goat cheese, and you have a delicious lunch or supper dish.

Preheat the oven to 400°F. Grease a small baking dish. Refrigerate in a salad bowl:

6 cups mixed baby greens or mesclun, washed and dried

Stir together in a shallow bowl:

1 cup fine dry unseasoned breadcrumbs

1 teaspoon dried thyme

Pour into another shallow bowl:

¼ cup extra-virgin olive oil

Coat first with the olive oil and then with the breadcrumbs:

4 rounds fresh goat cheese, each about 2½ inches in diameter and ½ inch thick

Place the cheese on the baking dish and bake until golden brown and lightly bubbling, about 6 minutes. Meanwhile, prepare:

Basic Vinaigrette, 236

Toss the greens with just enough vinaigrette to coat and divide among 4 salad plates. Place a round of baked cheese in the center of each salad and serve at once.

MIXED GREENS WITH GRILLED TUNA, LEEKS, AND TOMATOES

4 servings

This salad makes an elegant main course. Grilling the tuna, leeks, and tomatoes creates a rich smoky flavor that offsets the slightly bitter tang of the greens. If you cannot locate mesclun, substitute romaine lettuce.

Prepare a medium-hot charcoal fire.

Boil in water to cover just until tender, about 3 minutes:

4 leeks, root ends carefully trimmed (to keep leeks whole), tough greens trimmed, cleaned thoroughly

Drain, refresh in ice water, and drain again. Meanwhile, have ready along with the leeks:

Four 1½-inch-thick tuna steaks (about 4 ounces each)

2 large ripe tomatoes, cored and cut into 1-inch-thick slices

Lightly brush the leeks, tuna, and tomatoes with:

Olive oil

Sprinkle with:

Salt and ground black pepper to taste

Grill the tuna for 4 to 5 minutes each side for medium-rare. Grill the leeks cut side down for 4 minutes and the tomatoes for 2 minutes each side, just until lightly browned. Divide among 4 serving plates:

2 cups bite-sized pieces salad greens (any combination of mizuna, frisée, escarole, or arugula), washed and dried

1 bunch watercress, tough stems trimmed, washed and dried

Arrange the grilled tuna, leeks, and tomatoes on top of the lettuce. Drizzle over the salads:

⅓ to ½ cup Creamy Caraway Dressing, 241

Sprinkle with:

Snipped fresh chives

Serve immediately.

GRILLED SCALLOP AND FENNEL SALAD

4 servings

Like greens, foods cooked over a live fire have a kind of immediacy, a direct connection to the outdoors, that is particularly welcome during summer months. Here we combine creamy grilled scallops with smoky fennel and slightly bitter arugula, then add an herb vinaigrette to bind it all together.

Prepare a medium-hot charcoal fire.

Wash and pat dry:

1 pound sea scallops

Remove the fronds, trim the base, and cut lengthwise into ½-inch-thick slices:

2 fennel bulbs

Sprinkle lightly with:

Olive oil

Salt and ground black pepper to taste

Grill the scallops on one side until the outside is crispy, 2 to 3 minutes. Turn and grill until the other side is crispy and the center is opaque, 2 to 3 minutes more.

Grill the fennel just until tender, about 3 minutes each side. Whisk together in a small bowl:

¼ cup fresh lemon juice
1 tablespoon Dijon mustard
1 tablespoon minced shallots
1 tablespoon minced fresh tarragon
1 tablespoon chopped fresh parsley
1 teaspoon chopped fresh thyme
Salt and ground black pepper to taste

Add in a slow, steady stream, whisking constantly:

½ cup olive oil

Combine the scallops and fennel in a salad bowl along with:

4 cups bite-sized pieces arugula or romaine lettuce, washed and dried
1 small red onion, thinly sliced
2 ripe tomatoes, cored and cut into wedges

Stir the dressing well, add just enough to moisten the ingredients, toss to coat, and serve.

GRILLED SWORDFISH, TANGERINE, AND JÍCAMA SALAD

4 servings

Tangerines, particularly seedless ones, are excellent in salads. Here their slightly tart sweetness adds just the right counterpoint to the meaty swordfish. This salad is just as good with grilled tuna or grilled boneless chicken thighs.

Prepare a medium-hot charcoal fire.

Whisk together in a small bowl:

½ cup olive oil
2 tablespoons fresh lime juice
2 tablespoons red wine vinegar
2 tablespoons coarsely chopped fresh parsley
1 tablespoon Dijon mustard
1½ teaspoons honey
2 teaspoons ground cumin
Salt and cracked black peppercorns to taste

Have ready:

Four 1- to 1½-inch-thick swordfish steaks (8 to 10 ounces each)

Brush with:

4 teaspoons vegetable oil

Sprinkle with:

Salt and ground black pepper to taste

Grill just until opaque in the center, about 5 minutes each side. Combine in a salad bowl:

1 head Boston lettuce, tough outer leaves removed, inner leaves trimmed, washed, dried, and torn into bite-sized pieces
2 tangerines, seeded and separated into sections (sections peeled if desired, 457)
1 medium jícama or celery root, peeled and cut into thin strips
1 red bell pepper, thinly sliced
Salt and ground black pepper to taste

Stir the dressing well, add just enough to moisten the ingredients, and toss to coat. Place the swordfish on top, drizzle any remaining dressing over the salad, and serve.

ABOUT VEGETABLE SALADS AND SAVORY FRUIT SALADS

Nowadays vegetable salads and savory fruit salads attractively arranged and dressed are a much appreciated alternative to green salads. The variety of textures and tastes in vegetables and fruits gives these salads a greater range of possibilities than their leafy cousins. Whatever the recipe, select produce at the peak of freshness, for there is no hiding inferior ingredients in these pure and simple creations. Vegetable salads are made from raw or cooked vegetables, solo or combined with others. And do not limit yourself to just the recipes on these pages, delicious though they may be. Almost any vegetable makes an interesting and often elegant salad when steamed or blanched and paired with a dressing. Try combining green beans, snap peas, artichokes, asparagus, or leeks with Spicy Walnut Vinaigrette, 238, or Tangerine Shallot Dressing, 239, or any of the vinaigrettes on pages 236 to 238. Fruits are left uncooked and sometimes mixed with other fruits and vegetables. Serve these salads to spark the appetite before a meal or as a refreshing side dish or include several on a buffet table.

TOMATO SALAD

6 to 8 servings

It is hard to beat a salad of freshly harvested, juicy, ripe summer tomatoes dressed with a bit of good olive oil and vinegar and some parsley—nothing more. Choose the best tomatoes you can find—fully ripe but not too soft. Combine red and yellow tomatoes for a colorful effect.

Arrange so that they overlap around or across a chilled platter:

6 large ripe tomatoes (preferably vine ripened), cut into ½-inch-thick slices or wedges

Drizzle over the tomatoes:

½ cup extra-virgin olive oil, or more to taste
Splash of balsamic vinegar

Sprinkle with:

¼ cup minced fresh parsley
Salt and ground black pepper to taste

Do not refrigerate. Serve immediately.

TOMATO AND BASIL SALAD

Prepare Tomato Salad, above, substituting ¼ cup fresh basil leaves, chopped or left whole, for the parsley.

TOMATO AND ONION SALAD

Prepare Tomato Salad, above, alternating thin slices of red onion with the tomato slices.

TOMATO SALAD VINAIGRETTE

Prepare Tomato Salad, above, substituting Basic Vinaigrette, 236, or any of the variations for the oil, vinegar, parsley, and seasonings.

TOMATO AND MOZZARELLA SALAD (INSALATA CAPRESE)

4 to 6 servings

Named for the island of Capri, where it was perhaps first made, this gloriously simple salad is popular all over Italy and is increasingly so in the United States.

Arrange, alternating slices, on a platter:

4 large ripe tomatoes, cut into ½-inch-thick slices
12 ounces mozzarella cheese, cut into ¼-inch-thick slices

Sprinkle with:

1½ cups fresh basil leaves

Drizzle over the salad:

½ cup olive oil, preferably extra virgin
Salt to taste

Serve at once or let stand at room temperature for up to 1 hour before serving. In either case, do not refrigerate the salad.

BREAD AND TOMATO SALAD (PANZANELLA)

8 to 10 servings

Traditionally, stale bread in Italy (and in many homes throughout the world) was never thrown away. It was grated into breadcrumbs and added to savory fillings or used as the basis for salads like this one. Here country-style Italian or French bread is lightly toasted to make it dry enough to soak up the dressing.

Preheat the oven to 350°F.

Spread on a baking sheet:

5 cups 1-inch bread cubes

Bake, shaking the pan once or twice, until browned, 10 to 15 minutes. Whisk together in a small bowl:

½ cup extra-virgin olive oil
½ cup red wine vinegar
¼ cup fresh lemon juice
¼ cup minced fresh parsley
1 teaspoon minced garlic
Salt and cracked black peppercorns to taste

In a salad bowl, toss the croutons and dressing with:

3 cucumbers, peeled, seeded, and cut into ½-inch cubes
3 large ripe tomatoes, cut into ½-inch cubes
1 large red onion, cut into ½-inch cubes
½ cup pitted Kalamata or other brine-cured black olives
½ cup fresh basil leaves

Add the dressing, toss well, and remove to a large platter. Sprinkle with:

½ cup Parmesan cheese shavings

Serve at once.

PITA SALAD (FATTOUSH)

4 servings

This is a refreshing Syrian salad. If you are in a hurry, replace the cucumber with pieces of washed and dried romaine or cos lettuce.

Toss together in a colander:

1 small cucumber, peeled, seeded, and cut into ½-inch cubes
1 teaspoon salt

Let stand to drain for 30 minutes.

Preheat the oven to 350°F.

Open on a baking sheet and bake until crisp and lightly browned, about 10 minutes:

Two 7-inch pita breads

Break into bite-sized pieces. Press the excess water out of the cucumbers, rinse quickly, and blot dry. Combine the cucumbers in a medium bowl with:

3 medium ripe tomatoes, chopped
1 small green bell pepper, diced (optional)
6 scallions, white and tender green parts, finely chopped
⅓ cup chopped fresh parsley
2 tablespoons chopped fresh cilantro
1 tablespoon finely chopped fresh mint

Whisk together in a small bowl:

⅓ cup olive oil, preferably extra virgin
Juice of 1 large lemon (about ¼ cup)
1 clove garlic, crushed
¼ teaspoon salt

Pour the dressing over the vegetables and toss well. Add the pita toasts, toss again, and serve immediately.

AVOCADO SLICES

4 to 6 servings

The soft, buttery texture and taste of avocados combine beautifully with the sharp, tangy flavors of citrus and vinaigrettes. Serve lightly dressed avocado slices as a garnish for grilled meats and fish or arrange them on a bed of crisp lettuce as a sprightly first course. Select only ripe fruit.

Cut crosswise on a slight angle into ¼-inch-thick slices:

2 ripe avocados, chilled and peeled

Marinate for 5 minutes in:

½ to ¾ cup Basic Vinaigrette, 236, or one of the variations

Arrange the slices in an overlapping fan shape on a bed of lettuce. Sprinkle with:

Chopped fresh parsley, chives, or mint

Serve immediately.

AVOCADO AND CITRUS SALAD

Prepare Avocado Slices, above, alternating the avocados with sections of grapefruit and orange.

AVOCADO AND MANGO SALAD

4 servings

This salad is luscious with either mango or papaya—choose whichever you can find the ripest. The mango and the avocado are the centerpieces here, not the greens.

Halve:

1 lemon

Halve, peel, and thinly slice lengthwise:

2 ripe Hass avocados

Gently rub the slices with the lemon halves. Slice vertically into segments:

1 ripe mango or papaya, peeled

Combine in a small bowl:

1 large red onion, thinly sliced
½ cup fresh lemon juice
Pinch of salt

Whisk together in a small bowl:

½ cup olive oil
2 tablespoons fresh lemon juice
Salt and ground black pepper to taste

Toss with half of the dressing:

2 cups arugula leaves, washed and dried

Divide among chilled salad plates. Around the arugula, alternate slices of avocado and mango. Spoon the remaining dressing over the slices. Arrange the onion over the arugula. Serve immediately.

CARROT AND RAISIN SALAD

4 servings

If you have the time, crisp the peeled carrots on ice for an hour before grating.

Combine in a medium bowl:

4 large carrots, peeled and coarsely grated
½ cup raisins
½ cup coarsely chopped pecans or unsalted roasted peanuts
1 tablespoon fresh lemon juice
2 teaspoons grated lemon zest
¾ teaspoon salt
Ground black pepper to taste

Pour over:

1 cup sour cream, or ½ cup sour cream and ½ cup mayonnaise

Toss well and serve.

WALDORF SALAD

4 to 6 servings

Created by Chef Oscar Tschirky of the Waldorf-Astoria Hotel in New York in the late 1890s, this salad was considered the height of sophistication in the early years of this century. Originally it contained nothing more than apples, celery, and mayonnaise. Chopped walnuts and seeded grape halves came later. A version popular with children includes miniature marshmallows.

Combine in a medium bowl:

1 cup diced celery
1 cup diced firm apples
½ cup coarsely chopped walnuts (optional)
½ cup seedless red grapes, halved (optional)

Stir in:

½ to ¾ cup mayonnaise

Serve at room temperature or cold.

ABOUT CUCUMBERS

Be sure to select firm, hard cucumbers. Unless you are dealing with the roundish "apple" cucumber, yellowness is an undesirable trait, as is flabbiness. Both signify age, a pithy interior, and a tough skin. Otherwise, the skin is edible, sometimes even by allergic people who cannot tolerate the pulp alone. The skin should have a slight sheen; if highly polished, however, the cucumber has probably been waxed and should then be peeled. If you wish to make the cucumbers more decorative, leave them unpeeled and score them with a fork, shown below, before slicing.

CUCUMBER SALAD

4 servings

Combine in a small bowl:

¼ cup rice vinegar
4 teaspoons sesame seeds, toasted
2 teaspoons superfine sugar

For a decorative effect, score the cucumber skin with a fork.

Add and toss to coat:

1 large cucumber, scrubbed or peeled if waxed, halved crosswise, and cut into thin strips or thinly sliced crosswise

Cover and refrigerate until the salad is cold, about 1 hour. Serve.

CUCUMBER AND YOGURT SALAD (TZATZIKI)

4 to 6 servings

Set a very fine mesh sieve or a colander lined with a coffee filter or several layers of cheesecloth over a bowl. Add and let drain at room temperature for at least 2 hours or, covered, in the refrigerator for up to 24 hours:

2 cups yogurt

Toss together in a colander:

1 large cucumber, peeled, seeded, and diced
1 teaspoon salt

Let stand to drain for 30 minutes. Press the excess water out of the cucumbers, rinse quickly, and blot dry. Mash together until a paste is formed:

2 cloves garlic, peeled
2 to 3 pinches of salt

Combine the yogurt, cucumbers, and garlic in a medium bowl along with:

2 to 3 teaspoons white wine vinegar
2 teaspoons chopped fresh mint
2 teaspoons snipped fresh dill
Salt and ground white pepper to taste

Drizzle over the salad:

1 tablespoon olive oil, preferably extra virgin

COLD ASPARAGUS SALAD WITH SESAME SEEDS

4 to 6 servings

Whisk together in a small bowl:

3 tablespoons toasted sesame oil
4 teaspoons white wine vinegar
4 teaspoons soy sauce
2½ tablespoons sugar

Toast in a small skillet until golden brown:

4 teaspoons sesame seeds

Immediately stir into the dressing. Place in a large pot of boiling water:

1½ pounds asparagus, peeled and cut diagonally into 2-inch pieces

Cook for no more than 1½ minutes for thin asparagus or 2½ minutes for thicker. Immediately drain and refill the pot with cold running water until all the heat has left the asparagus. Drain again and dry thoroughly. Cover and refrigerate until the salad is cold, about 1 hour. Toss with the dressing. Serve.

PEA, PEA-POD, AND PEA SHOOT SALAD

Prepare the dressing for Cold Asparagus Salad with Sesame Seeds, above. Cook 1 cup sugar snap peas in a large saucepan of boiling salted water for 2 minutes. Add ½ cup snow peas and ½ cup fresh or thawed frozen tiny green peas and cook for 1 minute. Drain, rinse, and drain again as for the asparagus. Pat dry. Toss the peas and dressing together in a bowl along with 6 cups pea shoots, washed and dried. Serve immediately.

CREAMY BEET SALAD

4 to 6 servings

Toss the salad while the beets are still warm so that they thoroughly absorb the dressing. The recipe can be prepared 3 to 4 hours in advance:

Cut into ¾-inch cubes and place in a medium bowl:

3 to 4 medium beets, cooked and peeled

Whisk together in a small bowl:

2 teaspoons red wine vinegar
Salt to taste

Gradually whisk in until well blended:

2 tablespoons olive oil
1 tablespoon vegetable oil

Stir in:

2 tablespoons heavy cream
1 tablespoon drained horseradish
Ground white pepper to taste

Pour the dressing over the beets and toss to coat evenly. Garnish with:

Snipped fresh dill (optional)

FENNEL AND MUSHROOM SALAD

6 to 8 servings

If you have a mandoline, 411, with which to slice the mushrooms and fennel, this salad comes together quickly.

Whisk together in a small bowl:

3 tablespoons extra-virgin olive oil
1 clove garlic, finely minced
½ to 1 tablespoon chopped fresh tarragon (optional)
Salt and ground black pepper to taste

Stir together in a medium bowl until the salt is dissolved:

¼ cup fresh lemon juice
Salt to taste

Add and toss to combine:

8 ounces mushrooms, wiped clean and thinly sliced
1 fennel bulb, thinly sliced

Pour the dressing over the vegetables and toss to coat evenly. Sprinkle with:

½ cup Parmesan cheese shavings

CELERY ROOT RÉMOULADE

4 to 6 servings

This also makes an interesting hors d'oeuvre.
Wash well, peel, and cut into ¼-inch-thick rounds:

2 medium celery roots

Boil in salted water to cover for 3 to 4 minutes. Drain and let cool. Cut into very thin strips. Cover with:

Sauce Rémoulade, 73

allowing about ½ cup of sauce for every 2 cups celery root. Chill well and serve on a bed of:

Watercress, tough stems trimmed, washed and dried

JÍCAMA SALAD

8 servings

The lime and ground chili peppers in this recipe are the perfect complements to jícama's slightly sweet flavor. Its juicy, porous texture is reminiscent of an apple, though it is never mealy. Peel and halve lengthwise:

1 medium jícama (about 1 pound)

Lay each half on its cut side, slice ¼ inch thick, and cut the slices diagonally in half. Cut diagonally into ¼-inch-thick slices:

2 small cucumbers, halved lengthwise and seeded

Cut a slice off the stem and blossom ends of:

3 medium navel oranges

Stand the oranges on a cutting board and cut away the peel and all the white pith. Halve lengthwise, then cut crosswise into ¼-inch-thick slices. In a large bowl, toss the jícama, cucumbers, and oranges along with:

6 radishes, thinly sliced
1 small red onion, thinly sliced
Juice of 2 limes (about ⅓ cup)

Let stand for 20 minutes, then season with:

Salt to taste

To serve, spoon the salad onto a platter and drizzle the accumulated juices on top. Sprinkle with:

About 2 teaspoons ground chili pepper, preferably ancho or guajillo
About ⅓ cup coarsely chopped fresh cilantro

SICILIAN SALAD

4 to 6 servings

This is an easy salad to make and is just as good when made without the fennel or olives.
Cut a slice off the stem and blossom ends of:

4 medium navel oranges

Stand the oranges on a cutting board and cut away the peel and all the white pith. On a plate cut crosswise into ¼-inch-thick slices. Arrange the slices on a platter and pour the juice over them. Arrange with the orange slices:

1 small red onion, thinly sliced
3 small fennel bulbs, thinly sliced (optional)
½ cup pitted black Gaeta olives (optional)

Sprinkle with:

6 fresh mint leaves, finely chopped
Ground black pepper to taste

Drizzle over the salad:

2 tablespoons olive oil, or more to taste

Let stand for about 2 hours at room temperature before serving.

ABOUT POTATO SALAD

The best potatoes for any salad are waxy, or low-starch, potatoes, as opposed to the starchy tubers known as russet, or baking, potatoes. Waxy potatoes hold their shape once cooked and will not crumble when sliced or diced. Red Bliss and Yellow Finn are popular varieties for salads. New potatoes are also favored because their thin skins do not need peeling. See Potatoes, 406.

Potato salad is best prepared from scrubbed potatoes cooked in their jackets just until soft enough to be easily pierced with a fork. Overcooking destroys the potato's texture, while undercooking dampens the potato's flavor. The skins are easily removed after cooking if desired. Cut potatoes for salad into either large dice or thick slices as soon as they are cool enough to handle. Potatoes absorb the maximum flavor from a dressing when still warm; so with the exception of mayonnaise- or cream-based dressings, which can separate or spoil, toss just-cooked potatoes with the dressing and serve the salad either warm or after it has cooled to room temperature. For mayonnaise- and cream-based salads, allow the potatoes to cool slightly but *do not refrigerate them before you put the dressing on,* as they will lose much of their down-to-earth savor. In either case, toss potatoes gently to keep them intact.

AMERICAN POTATO SALAD

6 to 8 servings

Many cooks customize their potato salad with such additions as hard-boiled eggs, sweet pickle relish, black olives, crumbled crisp cooked bacon, mint, pimientos, whole-grain mustard, or halved cherry tomatoes—not all of these at once, of course.
Bring to a boil in a large pot with enough salted cold water to cover:

2 pounds red or other waxy potatoes

Reduce the heat and simmer, uncovered, until the potatoes are tender when pierced with a fork, 20 to 25 minutes. Drain, peel if desired, and cut into bite-sized pieces. In a medium bowl, toss the still-warm potatoes with:

1 medium celery stalk, diced

2 tablespoons finely snipped fresh chives, or 2 scallions, minced, or 2 tablespoons minced red onion

¼ cup minced fresh parsley

Stir together:

¾ to 1 cup mayonnaise

2 tablespoons milk or red wine vinegar

Add the mayonnaise mixture to the warm potato mixture and toss gently to coat. Season with:

Salt and ground black pepper to taste

Serve at room temperature or chilled.

FRENCH POTATO SALAD

6 to 8 servings

The French like to bathe their potatoes in a simple vinaigrette. This needs to be done while the potatoes are still warm so they can absorb all the flavors in the dressing.

Place in a medium bowl while still warm:

2 pounds red or other waxy potatoes, prepared as directed for American Potato Salad, above

Whisk together in a small bowl:

6 tablespoons red or white wine vinegar, or ¼ cup white wine vinegar and 2 tablespoons dry white wine

1 shallot, minced, or ½ red onion, minced, or 3 tablespoons finely snipped fresh chives

2 tablespoons minced fresh parsley

2 tablespoons drained capers (optional)

1 tablespoon whole-grain mustard

1 tablespoon minced fresh tarragon, mint, dill, or thyme (optional)

Salt and ground black pepper to taste

Add in a slow, steady stream, whisking constantly:

6 tablespoons olive oil

Pour the dressing over the potatoes, toss gently to combine, and serve warm, at room temperature, or chilled.

GERMAN POTATO SALAD

6 servings

German potato salad is traditionally served warm or even hot, but leftovers are good cold as well.

Place in a medium bowl while still warm:

2 pounds red or other waxy potatoes, prepared as directed for American Potato Salad, above

Cook in a skillet over medium heat until crisp, 6 to 8 minutes:

4 slices bacon

Drain the bacon on paper towels, crumble it, and add it to the potatoes. Pour all but 2 tablespoons of the bacon fat out of the pan. Cook in the remaining fat over medium heat until golden, about 4 minutes:

1 small onion, diced

1 cup chopped celery with leaves (optional)

Add:

1 dill pickle, chopped (optional)

Add and bring just to a boil:

½ cup chicken stock, beef stock, or water

¼ cup white wine vinegar or cider vinegar

1 teaspoon sugar

1 teaspoon sweet paprika

1 teaspoon dry mustard (optional)

Salt and ground black pepper to taste

Pour the dressing over the potatoes, toss gently to coat, and garnish with:

Chopped fresh parsley and/or snipped fresh chives

Serve immediately.

TZATZIKI POTATO SALAD

6 servings

Tzatziki, a Greek yogurt sauce, makes a superb and unexpected dressing, low in fat but high in flavor.

Set a very fine mesh sieve or a colander lined with a coffee filter or several layers of cheesecloth over a bowl. Add and let drain at room temperature for at least 2 hours or, covered, in the refrigerator for up to 24 hours:

2 cups low-fat yogurt

Meanwhile, toss together in a colander set over a bowl and let drain at room temperature for at least 1 hour or, covered, in the refrigerator for up to 24 hours:

1 cucumber, scrubbed or peeled if waxed, seeded, and finely diced

1 teaspoon salt

Squeeze the cucumber in a dish towel to remove as much liquid as possible, then dry completely on paper towels. Combine the yogurt and cucumber in a large bowl along with:

2 tablespoons extra-virgin olive oil

1 tablespoon finely snipped fresh dill

1 tablespoon minced fresh mint

1 tablespoon red wine vinegar, or more to taste

Ground black pepper to taste

Mash together until a paste is formed:

2 cloves garlic, peeled

½ teaspoon salt

Stir into the yogurt mixture. Let stand for 1 hour or refrigerate, covered, for up to 24 hours. Meanwhile, place in a medium bowl while still warm and let cool to room temperature:

2 pounds red or other waxy potatoes, prepared as directed for American Potato Salad, above

Salt and ground black pepper to taste

Add the tzatziki and toss gently to coat evenly. Cover

and refrigerate. Serve chilled or at cool room temperature, garnished with:

Thin cucumber slices
Fresh dill sprigs
Fresh mint sprigs

PERUVIAN POTATO SALAD

4 servings; about 1⅓ cups sauce

Peruvian potato salad is most flavorful when the potatoes are warm, but it is equally enjoyable when chilled. Use Peruvian blue potatoes if available, but any all-purpose or boiling potato will work.

Heat in a small skillet over medium heat:

1 tablespoon peanut oil

Add:

½ medium onion, chopped
1 clove garlic, chopped

Cook until soft and lightly browned, 5 to 7 minutes. Transfer to a blender and add:

½ cup roasted unsalted Spanish peanuts, skins removed
½ cup milk
⅓ cup crumbled ricotta salata or farmer's cheese
1½ tablespoons peanut oil
1 fresh jalapeño or other chili pepper, quartered and seeded
½ teaspoon salt
¼ teaspoon ground turmeric

Blend the sauce until smooth and set aside. Cover with cold water and bring to a boil:

4 to 6 Peruvian blue, Yellow Finn, or boiling potatoes (about 1½ pounds)

Cook until tender when pierced with the tip of a sharp knife, about 25 minutes. Drain and, when cool enough to handle, peel and slice into rounds. Arrange on 4 salad plates:

Lettuce leaves

Top the lettuce with the potato slices and, if desired, season with:

Salt and ground black pepper

Spoon the reserved sauce over the potatoes. Garnish each plate with:

Hard-boiled eggs
Pickled onions
Black olives
Cooked corn on the cob, sliced into 2-inch-thick rounds

ABOUT COLE SLAW

There are probably as many versions of cole slaw as there are people who make it. The one constant is raw cabbage (the name itself comes from the Dutch *koolsla,* meaning "cabbage salad"). After that, all bets are off. The cabbage may be red, white, or green; the dressing may be vinaigrette or have a base of mayonnaise or sour cream; and the salad may contain a vast array of other ingredients, among them bacon, carrots, bell peppers, pineapple, pickles, onions, and herbs. Soaking the shredded cabbage in ice-cold water for an hour before draining and dressing renders it refreshingly crisp.

COLE SLAW

6 servings

A basic recipe for an American favorite; improvisations on the theme are encouraged.

Stir together until well blended:

¾ cup Traditional Mayonnaise, 72, or Blender Mayonnaise, 72
¼ cup white vinegar
1 tablespoon sugar

Alternatively, prepare:

½ to 1 cup Basic Vinaigrette, 236, other vinaigrette of your choice, 237 to 238, or Sour Cream Dressing, 242

Finely shred or chop:

1 small head chilled green or red cabbage, cored and outer leaves removed

Stir in just enough dressing to moisten the cabbage. Season with:

Salt and ground black pepper to taste

If desired, add any of the following:

Dill, caraway, or celery seeds, or a combination
Chopped fresh parsley, chives, or other herb
Crumbled crisp bacon
Pineapple chunks
Grated peeled carrots
Coarsely chopped onions, bell peppers, or pickles

Stir again and serve immediately.

TANGY REDUCED-FAT COLE SLAW

4 servings

This cole slaw has less than 75 calories per serving and excellent flavor. Drained yogurt can be substituted for sour cream in almost any recipe.

Set a very fine mesh sieve or a colander lined with a coffee filter or several layers of cheesecloth over a bowl. Add and let drain at room temperature for at least 2 hours or, covered, in the refrigerator for up to 24 hours:

½ cup nonfat yogurt

Transfer the yogurt to a bowl. Add and whisk together until smooth:

1½ tablespoons cider vinegar
1 tablespoon sugar

1 tablespoon snipped fresh dill
1 teaspoon drained horseradish
½ teaspoon dry mustard
Salt and ground black pepper to taste

Combine in a large bowl:

4 cups finely shredded green or red cabbage
1 cup grated peeled carrots

Add the dressing to the cabbage mixture and toss to coat evenly. Refrigerate, covered, for at least 1 hour. Serve chilled.

ASIAN COLE SLAW

4 to 6 servings

This is a cross between cole slaw and the Korean pickled, fermented cabbage staple called *kimchee*. Letting the cabbage stand with salt draws out some of its moisture so that the salad remains crunchy.

Toss together in a colander:

½ head green or red cabbage, cored and outer leaves removed, finely shredded
1 tablespoon salt

Place a plate on top of the cabbage and weight it with heavy cans or a bag of sugar or flour. Let drain at room temperature for 3 hours. Whisk together in a large bowl until the sugar is dissolved:

1 cup rice vinegar
1 cup sugar
2 tablespoons minced peeled fresh ginger
1 teaspoon red pepper flakes, or to taste

Rinse and drain the cabbage and dry it well. Add it to the vinegar mixture along with:

1 cup finely shredded peeled carrots

Toss well. Cover and refrigerate for at least 8 hours or up to 24 hours. Serve cold, garnished with:

Fresh cilantro leaves

HOT APPLE SLAW

4 to 6 servings

This is a fine autumn salad. Granny Smith and other similarly tart apples work especially well here, though any cooking apple will do.

Cook in a large skillet over low heat until crisp:

6 slices thick-cut bacon

Drain the bacon on paper towels and crumble. Add to the fat in the skillet:

3 tablespoons cider vinegar
2 tablespoons water
1 tablespoon light or dark brown sugar
1 teaspoon caraway seeds, lightly crushed
Salt to taste

Bring to a boil, reduce the heat to a simmer, and stir in:

3 cups finely shredded red or green cabbage
1 large cooking apple, peeled, cored, and grated

Simmer for 2 minutes. Serve hot, garnished with the bacon.

ABOUT BEAN, RICE, PASTA, AND GRAIN SALADS

The mild flavors and chewy textures of beans, rice, pasta, and other grains are a perfect backdrop for a variety of salads. Fresh vegetables, seasonings, meat, and poultry are added for contrast and flavor, making these versatile side dishes or healthy meals unto themselves. These salads take a bit of advance preparation, since the beans, rice, pasta, and grains must first be cooked, but once made, they hold up well. If the salad has been refrigerated, let it stand at room temperature for a bit before serving, taste and adjust the seasonings (starches tend to absorb seasonings over time), and serve at room temperature.

The salads that follow are best made from beans, rice, pasta, and grains that are cooked to firm-tender. Boost the flavor of rice, grains, and beans by cooking in stock or broth with a few aromatic vegetables. Pastas should be cooked until tender but firm. Canned beans can easily be substituted for dried. Whatever the base, be sure everything is well drained, lest it dilute the dressing, and, as with potatoes, toss these salads while still warm to absorb the most flavor from the dressing. Some pastas are rinsed in cool water to rid them of excess starch.

CHICKPEA SALAD

4 servings

Chickpeas are rich in vitamins A and C, high in fiber, and a good source of calcium and iron.

Combine in a medium bowl:

2 cups canned chickpeas, rinsed and drained
½ small red onion, minced
3 tablespoons minced fresh parsley
2½ tablespoons fresh lemon juice
2 tablespoons extra-virgin olive oil
1 teaspoon Dijon mustard
1 to 2 cloves garlic, minced
Salt and ground black pepper to taste

On a platter, make a bed of:

4 cups shredded chicory, escarole, or romaine lettuce, washed and dried

Spoon the chickpea salad on top and serve at room temperature.

CHICKPEA AND ROASTED RED PEPPER SALAD

Prepare Chickpea Salad, above, adding 2 red bell peppers, roasted, 402, peeled, and diced, or one 7-ounce jar roasted red peppers, drained and diced, along with the onion.

WHITE BEAN SALAD WITH GREEN OLIVES

4 to 6 servings

Add a can of tuna to this salad and you can set the table for lunch or supper.

Combine in a medium bowl:

3 cups cooked white kidney beans (about 1 cup dried), 275, or other white beans, rinsed and drained if canned
2 small celery stalks, thinly sliced
15 Spanish olives, pitted and sliced
2 tablespoons chopped fresh tarragon or parsley

Whisk together:

1 tablespoon red wine vinegar
1 clove garlic, minced
½ teaspoon sweet paprika
¼ teaspoon salt

Whisk in:

3 to 4 tablespoons olive oil, preferably extra virgin

Pour the dressing over the bean mixture and toss gently to coat. Season with:

Ground black pepper to taste

Serve at room temperature.

THREE-BEAN SALAD

4 to 6 servings

This American salad-bar classic actually tastes better the next day.

Boil in salted water to cover until tender but still slightly crunchy, about 2 minutes:

1 cup ½-inch pieces green beans
1 cup ½-inch pieces yellow wax beans

Drain and place in a large bowl. Add and stir to combine:

One 16-ounce can kidney beans, rinsed and drained
½ cup chopped green bell pepper
½ cup chopped onion

Whisk together in a small bowl or shake in a small covered jar:

½ cup vegetable oil
½ cup tarragon vinegar or red wine vinegar
¾ cup sugar
1 teaspoon minced fresh tarragon, or ½ teaspoon dried
1 teaspoon salt
½ teaspoon ground black pepper

Pour the dressing over the bean mixture and toss well to coat. Cover and refrigerate for at least 6 hours or overnight. Serve cold. If desired, serve in:

Lettuce cups, 232

BLACK BEAN, CORN, AND TOMATO SALAD

6 servings

Boil in water to cover for 1 minute:

1½ cups corn kernels (cut from 3 ears corn)

Drain and rinse under cold water. Whisk together in a small bowl:

2 tablespoons red wine vinegar
1 clove garlic, minced
⅛ teaspoon salt
Ground black pepper to taste

Gradually whisk in:

5 tablespoons olive oil, or to taste
¼ cup snipped or sliced fresh basil

Toss with most of the dressing in a serving bowl:

3 cups cooked black beans (about 1 cup dried), 273, rinsed and drained if canned

With the remaining dressing, toss the corn along with:

8 ounces cherry tomatoes, halved
1 cup chopped red onions

Stir gently into the beans. Serve garnished with:

Fresh basil leaves

LENTIL AND RED POTATO SALAD WITH WARM SHERRY VINAIGRETTE

4 servings

Make this close to serving time so that it can be consumed while still warm. It goes well with grilled or broiled sausages and braised escarole or other greens.

Cook in boiling water until tender, about 15 minutes:

12 ounces small red potatoes, halved if larger than 1 inch in diameter

Drain and cut into small cubes when cool enough to handle. Combine in a large bowl:

½ cup thinly sliced scallions
½ cup chopped fresh parsley

Add the potato cubes along with:

4½ cups warm cooked green or brown lentils (about 1½ cups dried), 274

Whisk together in a small saucepan:

¼ cup extra-virgin olive oil
3 tablespoons sherry vinegar
1 clove garlic, very finely minced
½ teaspoon salt
⅛ teaspoon ground black pepper

Heat, stirring, until warm. Pour over the lentil mixture and serve.

RICE SALAD WITH CHICKEN AND BLACK OLIVES

4 servings

This recipe can be used as a blueprint for many kinds of rice salads. Simmer the rice in chicken stock for more flavor. As a general rule, use 3 cups cooked rice for roughly an equal amount of other ingredients (vegetables, fruit, chicken, seafood, etc.), cooked, if necessary, and chopped into bite-sized pieces. Toss with about ½ cup dressing of your choice.

Stir together in a medium bowl:

1½ cups diced cooked chicken
½ cup diced peaches (about 1 medium)
½ cup coarsely chopped pitted oil-cured black olives
½ cup diced red or yellow bell peppers

Add while still warm:

3 cups cooked long-grain white rice (about 1½ cups uncooked)
½ cup Fresh Herb Vinaigrette, 237

Toss well to combine. Serve warm, at room temperature, or chilled.

RICE SALAD WITH CHICKEN AND PISTACHIOS

Prepare the rice for Rice Salad with Chicken and Black Olives, above. Toss with 3 cups diced cooked chicken; ¾ cup shelled unsalted pistachios; 1 medium red onion, finely diced; ½ cup chopped flat-leaf parsley; 6 fresh basil leaves, chopped; ¼ cup drained capers; ⅓ cup olive oil; the grated zest and juice of 1 lemon; and salt and ground black pepper to taste. Serve at room temperature.

RICE SALAD WITH SUN-DRIED TOMATOES

Prepare the rice for Rice Salad with Chicken and Black Olives, above. Whisk together 6 oil-packed sun-dried tomato halves, minced; 6 tablespoons olive oil; 3 tablespoons balsamic vinegar; 1 clove garlic, minced; 1 teaspoon chili powder; ¼ teaspoon ground cumin; and ¼ teaspoon ground coriander. Stir into the warm rice along with 4 more sun-dried tomato halves, diced; ¼ cup pine nuts, toasted; 4 scallions, minced; and salt and ground black pepper to taste. Serve warm or at room temperature.

WILD RICE SALAD WITH SAUSAGE

4 to 6 servings

The nutty taste of wild rice balances the sweet grapes and savory sausage. Serve this salad on a bed of lightly dressed Boston lettuce or curly-leaf lettuce as a lunch or supper entrée.

Whisk together in a small bowl:

2 tablespoons Champagne vinegar or white wine vinegar
1 tablespoon Dijon mustard

Whisk in:

⅓ cup olive oil
Salt and ground black pepper to taste

Cook, stirring, in a medium skillet over medium heat until cooked through, breaking up with the side of a spoon:

1 pound sweet Italian sausage, casings removed

Drain on paper towels, pat dry, let cool, and remove to a large bowl. Combine with:

2¼ cups cooked wild rice (about ¾ cup uncooked), rinsed and drained
2¼ cups cooked long-grain white rice (about ¾ cup uncooked), rinsed and drained
3 inner celery stalks with leaves, thinly sliced
12 ounces seedless green or red grapes, halved (optional)

Add the dressing and toss well to coat. Taste and adjust the seasonings. Serve at room temperature.

BROWN RICE SALAD WITH DATES AND ORANGES

4 servings

This salad takes its flavor inspiration from North Africa.

Stir together in a large bowl:

3 cups cooked brown rice (about 1 cup uncooked)
16 dates, pitted and diced
2 large navel oranges, peeled, divided into segments, each segment cut into thirds
2 scallions, minced
¼ cup dark or golden raisins
¼ cup minced fresh parsley
¼ cup extra-virgin olive oil
2 tablespoons fresh lemon juice
¼ teaspoon ground cinnamon
¼ teaspoon ground cumin
Pinch of red pepper flakes
Salt to taste

Serve at room temperature.

PASTA SALAD (BASIC RECIPE)

4 to 6 servings

Try substituting fresh or reconstituted dried chili peppers for the red pepper flakes, using different fresh herbs, or adding diced cheese, such as fontina, or diced cooked meat, such as ham, chicken, or lamb, to the mix. If you prefer a creamy pasta salad, substitute ½ cup mayonnaise for the vinaigrette.

Combine in a large bowl while the pasta is still warm:

8 ounces elbow macaroni, penne, wagon wheel, or other pasta, cooked until tender but firm, rinsed with cool water, and drained
3 tablespoons extra-virgin olive oil
3 tablespoons white wine vinegar

2 tablespoons chicken stock
Salt and ground black pepper to taste

Let cool to room temperature. Stir in:

12 cherry tomatoes, halved
12 yellow plum tomatoes, quartered
½ cup finely diced red onion
12 oil-cured black olives, pitted and coarsely chopped
¼ cup minced fresh basil
¼ cup minced fresh parsley
2 tablespoons minced fresh mint
1 teaspoon finely grated lemon zest

Taste and adjust the seasonings. Serve at room temperature.

CREAMY MACARONI SALAD (REDUCED FAT)

4 servings

This salad has less than 140 calories per serving.

Set a very fine mesh sieve or a colander lined with a coffee filter or several layers of cheesecloth over a bowl. Add and let drain at room temperature for at least 2 hours or covered in the refrigerator for up to 24 hours:

½ cup plus 2 tablespoons nonfat yogurt

Transfer the yogurt to a bowl. Add and whisk together:

1 clove garlic, minced
1½ teaspoons red wine vinegar
1 teaspoon sugar
Salt and ground black pepper to taste

Add and toss to coat:

4 ounces elbow macaroni, cooked until tender but firm, rinsed with cool water, and drained

Stir in:

½ cup finely chopped red, yellow, or orange bell peppers, or a combination
½ cup very thinly sliced fennel
3 tablespoons minced red onions
2 tablespoons minced fresh basil

Taste and adjust the seasonings. Serve at room temperature or slightly chilled.

PENNE SALAD WITH FETA AND OLIVES

4 to 6 servings

Since both feta and capers are salty, taste this salad before adding any salt.

Mince together:

½ cup fresh parsley leaves
2 tablespoons drained capers (optional)
1 tablespoon fresh oregano leaves
1 small fresh jalapeño or other chili pepper, seeded if less heat is desired
2 cloves garlic

Place in a serving bowl along with:

⅓ cup extra-virgin olive oil

Stir in:

5 to 6 ounces feta cheese, coarsely crumbled
About 12 Kalamata olives, pitted and finely chopped
Salt if needed and ground black pepper to taste

Cook in a large pot of boiling salted water until tender but firm:

1 pound penne

Place in a colander:

½ small red onion, cut into rings

Drain the pasta onto the onion in the colander and immediately add both to the feta mixture. Toss gently to coat and combine. Serve at room temperature.

PASTA SALAD WITH GRILLED CHICKEN AND AVOCADO

4 to 6 servings

A thoroughly American treatment for pasta using favorite foods—grilled chicken and avocado. The dish can also be made with leftover baked or broiled chicken.

Combine well in a large serving bowl:

3 boneless, skinless chicken breast halves (about 1 pound), grilled, and cut into thin strips
1 pound fusilli, cooked until tender but firm, rinsed with cool water, and drained
1 large ripe Hass avocado, peeled and finely diced
3 medium ripe tomatoes, seeded and chopped
4 scallions, thinly sliced
2 cloves garlic, finely minced
¼ cup drained capers
¼ cup chopped fresh basil, cilantro, or parsley
¼ cup olive oil, or more to taste
Juice of 1 lemon
Salt and ground black pepper to taste

Serve at room temperature. It is best to serve this salad soon after it is made because the avocado tends to darken. If you need to make it ahead, dice and add the avocado just before serving.

PASTA SALAD WITH SHRIMP, ROASTED RED PEPPERS, AND BLACK OLIVES

4 to 6 servings

Shrimp is so good cold, it is a natural for a light pasta salad. For more flavor in the salad, boil the shrimp in the shell first and then use the same water to cook the pasta. This salad refrigerates well, but bring it closer to room temperature before serving.

Roast, 402:

4 red bell peppers

Peel, seed, and cut into thin strips. Toss together in a large bowl:

1 pound penne, fusilli, or other pasta, cooked until tender but firm, rinsed with cool water, and drained
1/3 cup olive oil
1 clove garlic, minced

Add the roasted peppers along with:

1 pound medium shrimp, boiled, 514, shelled, and deveined
1/2 cup pitted oil-cured black olives
1/2 cup chopped fresh flat-leaf parsley
1/4 cup pine nuts, toasted
Pinch of ground red pepper
Salt and ground black pepper to taste

Toss well to coat and combine. Serve at room temperature.

TORTELLINI (OR RAVIOLI) SALAD

4 to 6 servings

Toss together gently in a large bowl:

1 pound tortellini or small cheese ravioli, cooked until tender but firm, rinsed with cool water, and drained
2 pounds ripe tomatoes, peeled, seeded, and very coarsely chopped
One 16-ounce jar marinated artichoke hearts, drained and quartered
1/2 cup Niçoise or other oil-cured black olives, pitted and coarsely chopped
3 tablespoons drained capers (optional)
About 40 small fresh basil leaves, torn into pieces

Season with:

2 to 3 drops red wine vinegar
Salt and ground black pepper to taste

Let cool for several minutes, then add:

4 ounces mozzarella cheese (preferably fresh), cut into 1/2-inch cubes

Toss again. Serve warm or at room temperature.

COUSCOUS SALAD WITH PINE NUTS AND RAISINS

4 servings

Fine bulgur, like couscous, can also be steamed, 266, and used in this recipe. You can also mix couscous and bulgur together for an interesting variation.

Toss together:

3 cups cooked couscous (about 1 1/3 cups uncooked)
1/4 cup Lime Vinaigrette, 237, prepared with cumin seeds

Add and toss to combine:

1/4 cup pine nuts, toasted
1 yellow bell pepper, very finely diced
6 dried apricots, finely chopped
3 tablespoons golden raisins
2 tablespoons dried currants
2 tablespoons chopped fresh cilantro or snipped fresh chives

Season with:

Salt to taste

Add more dressing if desired.

QUINOA SALAD

Prepare Couscous Salad with Pine Nuts and Raisins, above, substituting 3 cups cooked quinoa (about 1 cup uncooked) for the couscous.

TABBOULEH

4 to 6 servings

Tabbouleh is a popular Middle Eastern salad and makes a particularly refreshing summer dish. The following recipe is fairly standard, but there are many variations using chopped cucumber, red onion, dill, and basil, even crumbled feta cheese. Traditionally tabbouleh is scooped up and eaten with leaves of romaine lettuce.

Combine in a large bowl:

1 cup medium bulgur
2 cups boiling water

Cover with an inverted plate and let stand for 30 minutes. Drain in a sieve, pressing with the back of a large spoon to remove the excess moisture, and return to the bowl. Add:

4 large ripe tomatoes, finely chopped
2 cups fresh parsley sprigs, finely chopped
1 cup packed fresh mint sprigs, finely chopped
1 cup packed purslane, washed, dried, and finely chopped (optional)
1 bunch scallions, finely chopped
1 medium onion, finely chopped

Stir in:

1/2 teaspoon ground allspice (optional)
1/2 teaspoon salt
1/4 teaspoon ground black pepper

Whisk together:

1/3 cup fresh lemon juice
1/3 cup olive oil

Add to the bulgur and toss to coat. Spoon the salad onto a platter and surround with:

1 head romaine lettuce, separated into leaves, washed, and dried

Serve at room temperature.

ABOUT COMBINATION SALADS

Combination salads, also called composed salads, are the culmination of all salad making. These savory marvels can contain almost any food—vegetables, fruits, leafy greens, starches, cheeses, meats, poultry, and seafood—bound together by one or more dressings, and are often decoratively, if not formally, arranged. There are no fixed rules for combination salads; some of the best creations are inspired by a trip to the farmers' market or an excess of leftovers. When improvising, begin by settling on a dominant ingredient or flavor and then add foods that will enhance by way of complement or contrast in flavor, texture, and appearance. Select only fresh and appealing foods. Leftover chicken or red meat can make an ideal base for these salads, but avoid refrigerated cooked vegetables that have lost all their crunch and flavor.

Many elements of a combination salad can be prepared in advance, but it is best to assemble the salad just before serving in order to distribute the dressing and adjust the seasonings. When lettuce is a part of a combination salad, as either a bed, border, or constituent, it should always be added at the last possible moment so it remains cool and crisp.

CHEF'S SALAD

4 to 6 servings

Place on a large platter:

About 10 cups bite-sized pieces salad greens of your choice, washed and dried

Prepare one of the following and add just enough (about ¾ cup) to lightly coat the greens:

Basic Vinaigrette, 236, Creamy Blue-Cheese Dressing, 240, or Thousand Island Dressing, 240

Arrange on top, preferably in triangular sections like slices of pizza:

1 cup long, thin strips cooked chicken or turkey breast meat

About 4 ounces smoked or baked ham, cut into long, thin strips, or prosciutto, very thinly sliced and rolled into cigar shapes

About 5 ounces Swiss, Cheddar, Gruyère, or other firm cheese, cut into long, thin strips

Also add:

2 ripe tomatoes, cut into wedges

2 or 3 hard-boiled eggs, quartered lengthwise

12 brine-cured black olives, pitted

Sprinkle with:

½ cup minced fresh parsley

Salt and ground black pepper to taste

Serve immediately.

REDUCED-FAT CHEF'S SALAD

6 servings

Stir together in a small serving bowl:

½ cup low-fat mayonnaise

1 large shallot, minced

3 tablespoons chili sauce

3 tablespoons pickle relish

1 tablespoon minced fresh parsley

Salt and ground black pepper to taste

Chop together until of uniform consistency:

1 hard-boiled egg white, chopped

1 tablespoon minced fresh parsley leaves

Place in a large shallow bowl:

About 10 cups bite-sized pieces salad greens of your choice, washed and dried

Arrange on top of the greens:

6 ounces reduced-fat Swiss cheese, cut into thin strips

6 ounces smoked turkey breast, cut into thin strips

6 ounces ham, cut into thin strips

Also add:

10 cherry tomatoes, halved

1 small English cucumber, cut into thin strips

Sprinkle with the egg white mixture and serve, passing the dressing separately.

COBB SALAD

4 to 6 servings

This close cousin to Chef's Salad, above, was created in the mid-1920s by restaurateur Bob Cobb at his Brown Derby Restaurant in Los Angeles.

Mash together in a small bowl until a paste is formed:

1 clove garlic, peeled

¼ teaspoon salt

Whisk in:

⅓ cup red wine vinegar

1 tablespoon fresh lemon juice

¼ cup Roquefort or other blue cheese, crumbled

Salt and ground black pepper to taste

Add in a slow, steady stream, whisking constantly:

⅔ cup olive oil

Line a platter with:

1 head Bibb lettuce, separated into leaves, washed, and dried

Arrange on top of the lettuce leaves:

1 large bunch watercress, tough stems trimmed, washed, dried, and coarsely chopped

1 ripe avocado, peeled and diced

4 to 6 cups diced cooked chicken or turkey breast

6 to 8 slices bacon, cooked until crisp and crumbled

3 hard-boiled eggs, diced

3 medium tomatoes, coarsely chopped

¼ cup finely snipped fresh chives

¼ cup crumbled Roquefort or other blue cheese

Lightly drizzle the vinaigrette over the salad and serve, passing the remaining vinaigrette separately.

REDUCED-FAT COBB SALAD
6 servings

Whisk together until smooth:

½ cup low-fat mayonnaise
½ cup buttermilk
2 shallots, minced
2 tablespoons minced fresh parsley
1 teaspoon minced fresh tarragon
Salt and ground black pepper to taste

Toss with half of the dressing:

1 small head Bibb lettuce, washed, dried, and shredded
1 cup fresh parsley leaves
1 small bunch watercress, tough stems trimmed, washed, dried, and coarsely chopped

Place the greens on a platter and arrange in rows on top:

1 whole chicken breast, poached, 604, skinned, boned, and shredded
4 plum tomatoes, peeled, seeded, and diced
½ ripe avocado, peeled and diced
¼ cup finely snipped fresh chives

Drizzle the remaining dressing over the salad and sprinkle with:

4 slices turkey bacon, cooked until crisp and crumbled
2 tablespoons finely crumbled Roquefort or other blue cheese

Serve immediately.

SALADE NIÇOISE
4 to 6 servings

You can depart from tradition and substitute grilled fresh tuna, salmon, or swordfish for the canned tuna.

Cook in a large pot of boiling salted water until tender, about 20 minutes:

6 small red new potatoes

Remove with a slotted spoon, let cool, cut into ½-inch-thick slices, and place in a medium bowl. Meanwhile, add to the pot and boil until bright green but still crisp, 2 to 3 minutes:

1 pound green beans, trimmed

Drain, refresh under cold running water, drain again, and add to the potatoes. Whisk together in a small bowl:

3 tablespoons red wine vinegar
2 teaspoons Dijon mustard
Salt and ground black pepper to taste

Add in a slow, steady stream, whisking constantly:

6 tablespoons olive oil, preferably extra virgin

Drizzle about one-quarter of the dressing over the potatoes and beans and gently toss to coat, being careful not to break the potato slices. Arrange on a large platter:

1 head Boston lettuce, separated into leaves, washed, and dried

Arrange on top of the lettuce:

2 large ripe tomatoes, cut into 8 wedges each

Drizzle another quarter of the dressing on top. Arrange the green beans and potatoes on the platter along with:

5 hard-boiled eggs, halved lengthwise

Place in the center of the salad:

One 6-ounce can tuna, preferably oil packed, drained and flaked

Drizzle the remaining dressing over all. Scatter over the top:

½ cup Niçoise olives
¼ cup minced fresh parsley
2 tablespoons drained capers
2 to 4 anchovy fillets, rinsed and patted dry (optional)
Salt and ground black pepper to taste

Serve immediately.

CHICKEN OR TURKEY SALAD
4 to 6 servings

For the ultimate chicken or turkey salad, roast the poultry on the bone, let it cool enough to handle, and shred or chop the meat into bite-sized pieces or large chunks. Be sure to include plently of both dark and light meat for best flavor.

Combine in a medium bowl:

2 cups diced cooked chicken or turkey
1 cup diced celery

Combine with:

½ to 1 cup mayonnaise
Salt and ground black pepper to taste

Serve on a bed of:

Lettuce leaves

If desired, garnish with:

1 tablespoon chopped fresh parsley or tarragon (optional)

CURRIED CHICKEN OR TURKEY SALAD

Prepare Chicken or Turkey Salad, above, replacing the celery with ¼ cup each raisins and chopped toasted walnuts or almonds and 2 chopped scallions. Use Curry Mayonnaise, 73.

SOUTHWESTERN CHICKEN SALAD
4 servings

To turn this salad into a snack, omit the bed of cabbage and serve it with tortilla chips.

Toss to combine in a large bowl:

2 whole chicken breasts, poached (see Creamed Chicken or Turkey, 604) or baked, 585, skinned, boned, and shredded or diced
1 small red onion, minced
2 plum tomatoes, seeded and diced

1 ripe avocado, peeled and diced
½ cup minced fresh cilantro
¼ cup olive oil
¼ cup fresh lime juice
½ teaspoon grated lime zest
1 teaspoon ground cumin
½ teaspoon chili powder, or to taste
Salt and ground black pepper to taste

Cover and refrigerate for at least 1 hour to allow the flavors to blend. Combine and divide among 4 salad plates:

2 cups finely shredded red cabbage
2 cups finely shredded green cabbage

Top with the chicken salad and sprinkle with:

½ cup coarsely chopped roasted peanuts

Serve immediately.

CHINESE CHICKEN SALAD

4 servings

Be sure to reserve some of the juice from the mandarin oranges, as it adds a delicious sweet tang to the dressing. Combine in a large bowl:

4 cups thin strips cooked chicken (about 1 pound cooked)
1 cup canned mandarin oranges, drained, juice reserved
⅔ cup sliced scallions
½ cup chopped roasted unsalted peanuts

Whisk together in a small bowl until well blended:

⅔ cup reserved mandarin orange juice
½ cup peanut oil
2 tablespoons fresh lemon juice
1½ teaspoons chili oil (optional)
1 teaspoon minced peeled fresh ginger
½ teaspoon salt, or to taste
¼ teaspoon ground Szechuan peppercorns

Pour ½ cup dressing over the chicken mixture and toss to combine. Taste and adjust the seasonings. Serve the salad over:

4 cups shredded Chinese (Napa) cabbage

Top with:

½ cup chopped roasted unsalted peanuts
1 cup chow mein noodles

Drizzle the remaining dressing over the salad and serve.

TURKEY SALAD WITH CHUTNEY AND CASHEWS

4 servings

This salad is delicious anytime, but it is a particularly good way to use leftover Thanksgiving turkey. You can use your favorite prepared mango chutney or make your own, 68.

Whisk together in a large bowl:

½ cup mayonnaise
½ cup sour cream
3 tablespoons mango chutney, coarsely chopped
2 teaspoons curry powder
Salt and ground black pepper to taste

Add and toss to coat:

3 cups thin strips cooked turkey meat
3 scallions, minced
2 celery stalks, thinly sliced
½ cup coarsely chopped roasted cashews
⅓ cup dried currants

Cover and refrigerate until cold. If desired, serve on a bed of:

Salad greens, washed and dried

EGG SALAD

4 servings

Combine in a medium bowl:

6 hard-boiled eggs, finely chopped
¼ to ⅓ cup mayonnaise
2 tablespoons minced onions (optional)
2 tablespoons minced celery (optional)
Salt and ground black pepper to taste
Pinch of curry powder (optional)

Refrigerate until cold.

TUNA SALAD

4 servings

Among the extra ingredients that can be added to this recipe are coarsely chopped toasted cashews, pecans, or walnuts; cubes of Cheddar or Monterey Jack cheese; diced green and/or red bell peppers; minced red onions or finely snipped chives; roasted red peppers and pitted black or green olives; or bean sprouts and diced water chestnuts.

Flake with a fork into a medium bowl:

One 6-ounce can water-packed tuna, drained, or 1 cup leftover grilled, poached, or sautéed tuna

Add and stir together well:

½ cup diced celery or diced seeded, peeled cucumber
¼ cup mayonnaise, or to taste
1 tablespoon drained capers (optional)
1 tablespoon minced fresh parsley (optional)
1 teaspoon fresh lemon juice
Salt and ground black pepper to taste

Refrigerate until cold and serve on a bed of:

Lettuce leaves, washed and dried

LOBSTER SALAD

2 servings

This elegant and subtle salad makes a splendid lunch for two.

Combine in a medium bowl:

2 cups chopped or shredded cooked lobster meat
½ cup sour cream, mayonnaise, or yogurt

⅔ cup thinly sliced seeded, peeled cucumber (optional)
1 hard-boiled egg, chopped (optional)

Stir in:

3 tablespoons slivered blanched snow peas
1 tablespoon finely snipped fresh chives
1 tablespoon minced fresh parsley
1 teaspoon minced fresh tarragon
1 teaspoon fresh lemon juice
¼ teaspoon grated lemon zest

Serve immediately on chilled plates lined with:

Boston lettuce leaves or mixed greens, washed and dried

Garnish with:

Snipped fresh chives
Lemon wedges

SHRIMP SALAD

Prepare Lobster Salad, above, substituting cooked medium shrimp, cut lengthwise in half, for the lobster.

SEAFOOD SALAD

6 to 8 servings

Be sure that all the seafood you use for this Italian salad is very fresh.

Stir together well in a large bowl:

½ cup olive oil
¼ cup fresh lemon juice
1½ tablespoons Dijon mustard
1 tablespoon minced garlic
1 tablespoon drained capers
1 red bell pepper, cut into thin strips
6 green olives, pitted and quartered
6 oil-cured black olives, pitted and quartered
¼ cup coarsely chopped fresh parsley

Add and toss well:

1 pound squid, cooked, bodies cut into ¼-inch-thick rings, and tentacles separated
12 ounces medium shrimp, cooked, shelled, deveined, and halved crosswise
4 ounces sea scallops, cooked, and halved
12 cherrystone clams, cooked, and removed from the shells
12 mussels, cooked, and removed from the shells

Season with:

Salt and cracked black peppercorns to taste

Let stand at room temperature for at least 30 minutes or up to 1 hour, toss again, and serve.

CRAB LOUIS

4 servings

This salad was created by the chef at the Olympic Club in Seattle in the late nineteenth century.

Arrange on a platter or in a salad bowl:

Boston or Bibb lettuce leaves, washed and dried

Place on top:

About 1 cup thin strips Boston, Bibb, or red-leaf lettuce, washed and dried

Heap on top of these:

2 cups cooked lump crabmeat, preferably fresh

Pour over the crab:

1 cup Sauce Louis, 241

Garnish with:

2 hard-boiled eggs, sliced (optional)
Snipped fresh chives

Serve at once.

ABOUT VEGETABLE AND FRUIT SALAD CUPS

The bright, fresh, colorful nature of salads makes them feasts for the eyes as well as the palate. One of our favorite ways to present vegetable, grain, rice, bean, meat, poultry, and seafood salads is in hollowed-out cases made from vegetables and fruits.

AVOCADO SALAD CUPS

Avocados have an unexpected affinity with shrimp, crab, and lobster, making them the perfect vehicle for serving these salads, above.

To prepare avocado cups, chill the avocados, then cut lengthwise in half. Place the avocado between the palms of your hands and gently twist the halves apart. Tap the large pit with the edge of a knife and give it a twist to free it, then lift it out. To prevent the fruit from darkening after cutting, sprinkle it with lemon juice. Mound the salad of your choice in the hollows left by the pits and garnish with parsley sprigs. Serve at room temperature, allowing 1 filled avocado half per person.

COLD STUFFED TOMATOES

Tomatoes can be cut and stuffed in a variety of ways to add a splash of color to any salad buffet. Almost any vegetable, grain, or combination salad goes well in tomatoes, but the best begin with ripe, good-tasting tomatoes. Whether or not to peel the tomatoes before stuffing is a personal choice. Keep in mind, however, that peeled tomatoes (particularly vine-ripened beauties) are especially delicate and best used to hold loosely packed vegetable salads such as Cucumber Salad, 218, and cold Asparagus Salad with Sesame Seeds, 219. Other good choices for filling tomatoes are a rice salad, 225, Couscous Salad with Pine Nuts and Raisins, 227, a cole slaw, 222, Tabbouleh, 227, Seafood Salad, above, Lobster Salad, above, Egg Salad,

230, Chicken Salad, 229, Tuna Salad, 230, and cottage cheese flavored with fresh herbs.

To prepare tomato cases, first peel the tomatoes, 430, if you wish. Slice off the round top of the tomato and, using a small serrated knife, cut around the inside to remove the core, pulp, and seeds, being careful to leave a thick-enough wall to support the case. The chopped tomato pulp can be mixed right into many salad recipes. You can also cut the tomatoes crosswise in half in a zigzag fashion and fill them, or fill hollowed-out halves separately. Before filling, salt the hollows lightly, invert the tomatoes, and let drain for 20 minutes. Chill and fill, allowing 1 stuffed tomato per person.

CUCUMBER CUPS

Cucumbers are refreshing on a luncheon plate or as an hors d'oeuvre, and their smaller size makes them more appropriate as a garnish than as a main course. Suitable fillings include Chicken Salad, 230, any seafood salad, 231, and any rice salad, 225, or other salad of small grains.

To prepare cucumber cups, first refrigerate small, shapely cucumbers until cold. Either peel the cucumbers or, for a more decorative effect, score the peel with a fork, shown 218. Waxed cucumbers should be peeled. Cut the cucumbers lengthwise in half, scoop out the seeds, and fill the halves. Alternatively, slice the whole cucumbers crosswise into 2- to 3-inch pieces and hollow the pieces from one end, leaving enough on the bottom to prevent the filling from falling out.

LETTUCE AND CABBAGE CUPS

A bit more formal than serving a combination salad on a bed of greens, lettuce cups make a neat display. The small, round, rather loosely bunched butterhead lettuces are ideal for salad cups. We also like the deep color of radicchio and red cabbage. Separate the leaves from the head carefully without tearing; wash and dry the leaves, sorting through to find enough evenly shaped ones for stuffing. Any imperfect leaves can go into the salad bowl. Just before serving, fill the leaves with any suitable salad you can think of, such as Chicken Salad, 229, Lobster Salad, 231, or any of the grain or bean salads, 223 to 225.

MELON CUPS

Ideal for a light luncheon, stuffed melon offers the cool refreshment of fruit combined with the savory substance of a meat or poultry salad.

To prepare melon cups, cut a cantaloupe or other melon in half. Remove the seeds and scallop the edges, if desired, for a more decorative effect. Refrigerate until cold. Just before serving, fill the melon with Chicken Salad, 229, Turkey Salad with Chutney and Cashews, 230, or a fruit salad.

BASIC SAVORY ASPIC

4 to 6 servings

Although clarifying the stock with egg whites and/or eggshells and then straining the mixture results in an aspic that is slightly clearer, we have omitted that step here, opting for ease of cooking rather than an absolutely clear aspic. (If you want to take the time to do this, please read about clarifying consommé, 107.) In addition to meat, poultry, or seafood, ingredients such as chopped raw celery, pitted olives, or toasted nuts make nice additions to this aspic.

Let stand in a medium bowl for 5 minutes to soften:

1 tablespoon unflavored gelatin
¼ cup cold water

Add and stir until the gelatin is dissolved:

¼ cup boiling seafood, chicken, or meat stock

Stir in:

1½ cups cold seafood, chicken, or meat stock
2 tablespoons white wine vinegar, or 1½ tablespoons fresh lemon juice, or to taste
Salt to taste

Cover and refrigerate until partially set (about as thick as raw egg whites). Stir in:

1½ to 2 cups diced savory ingredients of your choice (cooked shrimp, lobster, or other seafood if using seafood stock; cooked chicken or turkey if using chicken stock; cooked beef or lamb if using meat stock)

Rinse a 4-cup mold or bowl, then shake out the excess water. Pour in the aspic, cover, and refrigerate until set, about 3 hours. Unmold, 1037, onto a platter and surround with:

Lettuce leaves, washed and dried

Serve cold.

TOMATO ASPIC

6 servings

Combine in a medium saucepan and simmer for 30 minutes:

4 cups tomato juice
½ cup tomato puree
½ cup chopped onions
2 celery stalks, chopped
2 tablespoons fresh lemon juice
1 tablespoon balsamic vinegar (optional)
2 teaspoons sugar
2 teaspoons dried basil or tarragon, or 2 tablespoons minced fresh

1 teaspoon salt
1 teaspoon black peppercorns
1 whole clove
1 bay leaf

Let stand in a large bowl for 5 minutes to soften:

4½ teaspoons (2 envelopes) unflavored gelatin
½ cup cold water

Strain the hot tomato juice mixture into the gelatin. Measure the volume and stir in enough water to make a total volume of 4 cups liquid. Chill the aspic. When it is the consistency of raw egg whites, add 1 to 2 cups of any combination of the following:

1 Hass avocado, peeled and cut into ½-inch pieces
1 cup diced yellow bell peppers
1 fresh jalapeño pepper, seeded and minced (optional)
1 cup lump crabmeat, flaked
1 tablespoon chopped fresh cilantro or basil

Rinse a 6- to 8-cup mold or bowl, then shake out the excess water. Pour in the aspic, cover, and refrigerate until set, about 3 hours. Unmold, 1037, garnish with:

Sliced vegetables

and serve.

CREAMY CUCUMBER GELATIN SALAD

6 to 8 servings

This is one of the most sophisticated gelatin molds we have come across.

Combine in a medium bowl and let stand for 10 minutes:

1 medium cucumber, peeled, seeded, and diced
4 cups water
2 teaspoons salt

Drain the cucumbers, then toss with:

1 tablespoon lemon juice

Let stand in a small bowl for 5 minutes to soften:

2¼ teaspoons (1 envelope) unflavored gelatin
2 tablespoons cold water

Add and stir until the gelatin is dissolved:

¼ cup scalded milk

Add the gelatin mixture to the cucumbers along with:

1 teaspoon white wine tarragon vinegar
½ teaspoon salt

Whip until stiff peaks form and fold into the cucumbers in 2 additions:

1 cup heavy cream

Rinse a 4-cup ring mold or bowl, then shake out the excess water. Spoon in the cucumber mixture and smooth the top. Refrigerate for 12 hours.

Combine in a medium bowl 1 hour before serving:

1 pound medium cooked shrimp, shelled and deveined
3 tablespoons minced fresh parsley
½ cup Basic Vinaigrette, 236

Unmold, 1037, top with the cooked shrimp, and serve.

GOLDEN GLOW GELATIN SALAD

8 servings

Drain, reserving the juice:

One 20-ounce can crushed pineapple

Add enough water to the reserved juice to make 2 cups total and bring to a boil in a small saucepan. Place in a medium bowl:

One 3-ounce package orange-flavored gelatin
One 3-ounce package pineapple-flavored gelatin

Add the hot liquid and stir until the gelatin is dissolved. Stir in:

2 cups cold water

Refrigerate until the gelatin is as thick as raw egg whites, 1 to 1½ hours. Fold in the reserved pineapple along with:

4 cups grated carrots

Rinse an 8-cup mold or bowl, then shake out the excess water. Pour in the gelatin mixture, cover, and refrigerate until set, about 3 hours. Unmold, 1037, or serve from the bowl.

SALAD DRESSINGS

A salad dressing is best described as an uncooked sauce and, like all sauces, its role is to enhance the flavor of the food. The dressing can be plain or fancy—as simple as a squeeze of citrus juice or dash of vinegar and a splash of oil, or as complex as an emulsion of oil and acid flavored with herbs, spices, chives or shallots, eggs, stock or vegetable juice, even such weighty substances as relish, salsa, chutney, tapenade, or pesto. Whatever its style, however, a well-made salad dressing is a balancing act. It should possess a distinct character but never steal the show. A dressing should be well seasoned (typically with a tang of acidity to deliver zest to the food) but not so assertive that it overwhelms the taste of the more delicate salad. And, finally, a salad dressing should have enough body to lightly coat the salad but never be so heavy that the greens collapse under its weight. Before using any dressing, taste it on a lettuce leaf or other element of the salad itself and adjust the seasonings and consistency as necessary.

Salad dressings, like their close cousins mayonnaise and hollandaise sauce, are prepared independently and then matched with a certain food, almost as a sort of condiment. This independence means that dressings are not tied to any particular food or presentation and are thus ripe for improvisation and interpretation. Many dressings can be converted into sauces, marinades, or glazes for grilled or roasted meat, fish, or poultry; into dips for crudités or chips; or into sandwich spreads—or they can be used to make an impromptu meal out of leftover cold meats, poultry, or fish. See Stocks & Sauces, 35, for more on using vinaigrettes as savory sauces.

ABOUT DRESSINGS

The easiest way to dress a salad is to simply add oil and vinegar or citrus juice directly in with the greens and season with salt and freshly ground black pepper. While this does season the greens, it requires a well-trained sense of proportion. Most cooks prefer to make up a dressing beforehand so that its flavors are more thoroughly blended and so that the oil-acid balance can be more easily adjusted if necessary. The most basic concoction of this kind is the classic French dressing called vinaigrette, which is nothing but a combination of three to four parts oil (usually olive) and one part acid (usually wine vinegar), seasoned with salt and pepper and often spiced with mustard and/or garlic.

While the ingredients in a vinaigrette are few and quite simple, the technique for combining them requires a bit of understanding. Left alone, the elements in a simple vinaigrette do not mix—they separate—making it difficult to dress a salad evenly. The oil rises to the top and the vinegar, which behaves like water, sinks to the bottom. To create a dressing with an even distribution of oil and vinegar, the two elements must be combined in some sort of an emulsion, meaning that the two repellent ingredients become mixed. This is achieved by adding the oil to the vinegar and vigorously shaking or whisking until they temporarily blend together. In its most basic form, an oil and vinegar emulsion will hold together long enough to pour over the salad. Many cooks, however, prefer a thicker, more stable emulsion that doesn't separate as quickly when left to stand, allowing time to attend to other parts of the meal. Adding other ingredients to the vinegar—such as mustard, garlic, onions, pureed vegetables, olive paste, or cream, to name a few—helps to thicken a salad dressing and make the emulsion more stable. These additional ingredients also allow more room to stray away from the classic three-to-one or four-to-one oil-to-vinegar ratio. Apart from vinaigrette-based dressings, creamy-style dressings typically get their thick, smooth consistency not from an oil and vinegar emulsion but from some element that easily produces a smooth, thick consistency—for instance, mayonnaise, yogurt, buttermilk, sour cream, crème fraîche, heavy cream, or tahini.

ABOUT MAKING A VINAIGRETTE

The most surefire way to make a thick, well-emulsified vinaigrette is to first whisk together the vinegar or lemon juice and the seasonings (salt, minced shallots or other members of the onion tribe, and mustard) in a small bowl. Then slowly add the oil, drop by drop, whisking as you go, until the dressing begins to thicken. Add the oil in more of a steady stream as the dressing becomes noticeably thicker. An alternative, and perhaps more convenient, technique is to place the vinegar or lemon juice and seasonings in a small jar with a tight-fitting lid and shake to blend. Then add the oil in three or four additions, shaking vigorously between additions. A third and equally popular method is to mix the vinegar and seasonings in a blender and then add the oil in a slow, steady stream with the machine running.

Vinaigrette can be stored, tightly covered, in the refrigerator for up to 2 weeks. Always whisk dressings briskly just before adding them to salads so that the ingredients are well mixed and in balance, and don't add more vinaigrette than is necessary to lightly coat the salad.

ABOUT OIL AND ACID

Although the ingredients in a vinaigrette are ordinary—oil and acid—the flavor possibilities are extraordinary, thanks to the abundant variety of oils and vinegars available to us. The salad oil par excellence is extra-virgin olive oil, but this varies greatly in both quality and character, depending on the place of origin and the producer. We recommend you sample as many oils as possible (specialty food shops sometimes offer tastings) to find one you like. Many olive oil connoisseurs argue that the best olive oils should merely be drizzled over foods and not mixed into dressings. They claim that whisking or vigorous blending destroys the fruity, delicate character of extra-virgin olive oil. We find that the benefits of a good olive oil in a dressing outweigh this claim. Oil labeled simply "virgin" (without the "extra") is rarely seen in the United States but is usually fine for salad dressing. Pure olive oil, less delicate in flavor and higher in acidity, is generally preferred for cooking rather than dressing—though there are those who feel that it is adequate for complexly flavored dressings.

Flavored olive oils are also widely available, especially those infused with lemon, garlic, or various herbs. These additions sometimes mask inferior oil, but certain of these products (usually the more expensive ones) are quite good for specialized uses. In multi-ingredient dressings, you may wish to avoid olive oil altogether and use a less expensive and more neutral-tasting oil, such as canola, corn, peanut, sunflower, or safflower. On the other hand, for certain salads, such strongly flavored oils as walnut, almond, hazelnut, and toasted sesame oil are appropriate. Since nut oils tend to be very assertive, temper them by adding only a few tablespoons to a dressing and filling out the remainder with a more neutral oil. For more information, see About Oils, 1067.

Vinegars vary greatly in acidity and in flavor and different types will have different effects on your dressing. Again, let your nose and palate be your guide to find what you like. Wine vinegar, the most readily available kind, is most popular for salad dressings. The most complex and flavorful wine vinegar is that made in Spain from sherry; it has high acidity and a very strong, robust flavor—richer, nuttier, and more complex than that of other wine vinegars—and has long been a favorite vinegar of good cooks.

As for the popular balsamic vinegar, if you find one you like, by all means blend a bit of it into salad dressings as a seasoning. If you are lucky enough to come into possession of some true *aceto balsamico tradizionale*—it is packaged in tiny bottles and can cost a hundred dollars or more for a few ounces—please don't use it in salad dressing! Drizzle a few drops over cooked asparagus or thinly sliced raw mushrooms, over a simply grilled piece of fish or meat, on shards of Parmigiano-Reggiano, or on fresh strawberries. See About Vinegar, 1066, for more information.

Citrus juice makes a good alternative to vinegar in salad dressings. Lemon juice is the most versatile, but for certain dressings, lime, orange, or even grapefruit juice might be appropriate. Bear in mind that citrus juice is less acidic than most vinegar, which means that you can make dressing with a ratio closer to two parts oil to one part acid. Some cooks like to combine a bit of lemon juice and a bit of vinegar. With its lower acidity, a salad dressed with citrus juice is more "wine friendly" than one dressed with vinegar. No true connoisseur would dream of serving wine with a vinegar-anointed course. As a French friend of ours once put it, "Wine and vinegar should never be on the same table together, if only because it is very bad manners to remind the wine that a member of its family has gone astray."

OTHER INGREDIENTS

Beyond the use of different oils and vinegars, there are countless ways to create distinctive and delicious salad dressings. As more flavorings and ingredients take center stage, the dressing loses the strict character of an oil-and-vinegar-based vinaigrette. These dressings, featuring anything from pureed vegetables to shredded cheese to chopped nuts, add textural interest as well as flavor to a salad. Bear in mind that more is not always better, and sometimes the best creations are sublimely simple. It is best to begin with a flavor principle, or theme, and stick with it. Also, be sure to coordinate the consistency of the dressing with the style of the salad. Sturdy vegetables, meat, and poultry can stand up to a thicker dressing, while delicate tender greens require something lighter. As a general rule, seasonings and finely chopped or pureed ingredients are added to the acid at the start, and then the oil is mixed in. Liquid additions, including stock, juice, cream, and buttermilk, are generally added after the oil and often result in a slightly thinner dressing. Here is a list of some of our favorite additions:

Freshly Ground Black Pepper: For many, a tossed salad is not complete without a few turns of a pepper grinder.

Herbs: Finely chopped or pureed. Dressings made with hearty herbs, such as rosemary, oregano, and thyme, should be allowed to sit for several hours for the flavors to infuse.

Assertive Ingredients: Chopped olives, pickles, anchovies, capers, mustard, tapenade, pesto, relish, Worcestershire sauce, and garlic. Use these with care in dressings made with flavorful oils, such as extra-virgin olive oil or nut oils, because their flavors may clash. Too many assertive flavors in one dressing will cancel each other out. Bear in mind that you may want to cut back on salt and vinegar when you add salty, briny ingredients.

Savory Flavors: Some of the most delectable salad dressings are made with the savory pan drippings from a roast, a dash of soy sauce, a bit of reduced meat or poultry glaze, or even a few tablespoons of fresh, flavorful stock. Since a well-made stock contains no fat, substituting stock for three-quarters of the oil is a delicious way to make a reduced-fat dressing. See Reduced-Fat Vinaigrette, 237.

Wine and Spirits: A splash of good-quality red or white wine or spirits, such as port, whiskey, or brandy, adds an exciting dimension to a basic vinaigrette.

Fruit or Vegetable Purees and Juices: Purees add flavor, body, and visual appeal to dressings. Be sure to squeeze any excess water from the puree before adding it to the vinegar. Vegetable and fruit juices are also used but, like stock, may result in a thinner dressing.

Cheese: Soft and crumbly cheeses can be blended into the vinegar. Hard cheese should be grated first.

Sweeteners: Honey, pure maple syrup, pomegranate juice, molasses. A touch of sweet can nicely balance some salads, but don't overdo it. The days of candy-sweet salads are, we hope, gone forever.

BASIC VINAIGRETTE OR FRENCH DRESSING

About 1½ cups

Vinaigrette is the preferred dressing in France for green salads, avocados, artichokes, and many kinds of sliced, shredded, or chopped vegetables. It is also the starting point for a host of more complicated dressings and accepts a variety of accents with additional ingredients. The optional ingredients in this recipe not only add flavor but also help maintain the emulsion of oil and vinegar that is essential to a good vinaigrette.

If garlic flavor is desired, mash together until a paste is formed:

1 small clove garlic, peeled
2 to 3 pinches of salt

Remove to a small bowl or a jar with a tight-fitting lid. Add and whisk or shake until well blended:

⅓ to ½ cup red wine vinegar or fresh lemon juice
1 shallot, minced
1 teaspoon Dijon mustard (optional)
Salt and ground black pepper to taste

Add in a slow, steady stream, whisking constantly, or add to the jar and shake until smooth:

1 cup extra-virgin olive oil

Taste and adjust the seasonings. Use at once or cover and refrigerate.

REDUCED-FAT VINAIGRETTE *About 1½ cups*

This recipe uses chicken stock to replace much of the oil. While this dressing will never be as emulsified as a standard vinaigrette, it is much lower in calories. Use only fresh, flavorful stock.

Whisk together in a small bowl or shake in a jar with a tight-fitting lid:

3 tablespoons red wine vinegar or fresh lemon juice
1 tablespoon Dijon mustard
1 clove garlic, minced
Salt and ground black pepper to taste

Add in a slow, steady stream, whisking constantly, or add to the jar and shake until smooth:

¾ cup Chicken Stock, 39
3 tablespoons extra-virgin olive oil

Taste and adjust the seasonings. Use at once or cover and refrigerate.

FRESH HERB VINAIGRETTE

Prepare Basic Vinaigrette, 236, or Reduced-Fat Vinaigrette, above, adding ⅓ cup minced or finely snipped fresh herbs (basil, dill, parsley, chives, and/or thyme).

BASIL CHIVE VINAIGRETTE

Prepare Basic Vinaigrette, 236, or Reduced-Fat Vinaigrette, above, adding ⅓ cup minced fresh basil, ⅓ cup finely snipped fresh chives, and, if desired, 1 tablespoon walnut oil.

GREEN PEPPERCORN VINAIGRETTE

Prepare Basic Vinaigrette, 236, or Reduced-Fat Vinaigrette, above, adding 2 tablespoons minced drained green peppercorns or 1 tablespoon cracked dried green peppercorns.

LIME VINAIGRETTE

Prepare Basic Vinaigrette, 236, or Reduced-Fat Vinaigrette, above, substituting ¼ cup fresh lime juice for the vinegar or lemon juice and, if desired, adding a large pinch of toasted cumin seeds.

HORSERADISH VINAIGRETTE

Prepare Basic Vinaigrette, 236, or Reduced-Fat Vinaigrette, above, substituting cider vinegar for the red wine vinegar or lemon juice and adding 1 tablespoon drained horseradish.

LEMON CAPER VINAIGRETTE

Prepare Basic Vinaigrette, 236, or Reduced-Fat Vinaigrette, above, with fresh lemon juice and add 1 tablespoon minced drained capers, 1 tablespoon minced fresh parsley, and ½ teaspoon finely grated lemon zest.

BLACK PEPPER VINAIGRETTE

Prepare Basic Vinaigrette, 236, or Reduced-Fat Vinaigrette, above, adding 1 teaspoon finely grated lemon zest and 2 teaspoons cracked black peppercorns, or to taste.

HONEY MUSTARD VINAIGRETTE *About ¾ cup*

Whisk together in a small bowl or shake in a jar with a tight-fitting lid:

2 tablespoons fresh lemon juice
1 tablespoon white wine vinegar
1 teaspoon honey, or to taste
1 teaspoon whole-grain mustard, or to taste
Salt and ground black pepper to taste

Add in a slow, steady stream, whisking constantly, or add to the jar and shake until smooth:

6 tablespoons extra-virgin olive oil

Taste and adjust the seasonings. Use immediately or cover and refrigerate.

TOMATO MINT VINAIGRETTE *About 2 cups*

Puree in a food processor until smooth, about 1 minute:

1 ripe tomato, peeled and seeded

Add and process for 15 seconds:

½ cup chopped fresh mint
1 shallot, chopped
2 tablespoons red wine vinegar
2 tablespoons fresh lime juice
1 teaspoon Dijon mustard
1 clove garlic, minced
Salt and ground black pepper to taste

With the machine running, slowly pour through the feed tube and process until smooth:

½ cup olive oil

Taste and adjust the seasonings. Use immediately or cover and refrigerate.

SPICY WALNUT VINAIGRETTE

About 1¼ cups

Whisk together in a small bowl or shake in a jar with a tight-fitting lid:

1 shallot, minced
3 tablespoons balsamic vinegar, or to taste
2 tablespoons minced walnuts
2 teaspoons Dijon mustard
Salt to taste
Hot red pepper sauce to taste

Add in a slow, steady stream, whisking constantly, or add to the jar and shake until smooth:

⅓ cup extra-virgin olive oil
⅓ cup walnut oil

Taste and adjust the seasonings. Use immediately or cover and refrigerate.

CHUNKY BLUE-CHEESE VINAIGRETTE

About 1⅔ cups

If you like a smoother consistency, crumble the cheese more finely.

Whisk together in a small bowl:

¼ cup cider vinegar
¼ cup coarsely chopped fresh parsley
6 dashes of Worcestershire sauce
Salt and ground black pepper to taste

Add in a slow, steady stream, whisking constantly, until smooth:

¾ cup olive oil

Whisk in:

⅓ cup coarsely crumbled blue cheese

Taste and adjust the seasonings. Use immediately or cover and refrigerate.

FENNEL PARMESAN VINAIGRETTE

About 1½ cups

Whisk together in a small bowl or shake in a jar with a tight-fitting lid:

⅓ cup balsamic vinegar
3 tablespoons grated Parmesan cheese
1 teaspoon fennel seeds, lightly crushed
1 shallot, minced
1 clove garlic, minced
Salt and ground black pepper to taste

Add in a slow, steady stream, whisking constantly, or add to the jar and shake until smooth:

1 cup olive oil

Taste and adjust the seasonings. Use immediately or cover and refrigerate.

GINGER SOY VINAIGRETTE

About 1 cup

This Asian-inspired, slightly spicy dressing is particularly nice with watercress salads.

Mash together until a paste is formed:

1 clove garlic, peeled
2 to 3 pinches of salt

Remove to a small food processor or a blender. Add and puree:

¼ cup rice vinegar
¼ cup minced shallots
2 tablespoons minced peeled fresh ginger
1 tablespoon soy sauce
½ teaspoon toasted sesame oil
Salt to taste
Hot red pepper sauce to taste

With the machine running, slowly pour through the feed tube and process until smooth:

½ cup peanut or vegetable oil

Taste and adjust the seasonings. Use immediately or cover and refrigerate.

THAI VINAIGRETTE

About ⅔ cup

This vinaigrette, in which the high acidity is balanced by a touch of sweetness, also makes a particularly good marinade for fish or chicken.

Whisk together in a small bowl or shake in a jar with a tight-fitting lid:

¼ cup fresh lime juice
2 tablespoons fish sauce
1 teaspoon sugar
Salt to taste
Ground red pepper to taste

Add in a slow, steady stream, whisking constantly, or add to the jar and shake until smooth:

6 tablespoons vegetable oil

Taste and adjust the seasonings. Use immediately or cover and refrigerate.

ROASTED RED PEPPER DRESSING

About 1¾ cups

Roast, 402:

2 red bell peppers

Peel, seed, and coarsely chop. Puree in a food processor or blender. Add and pulse to blend:

¼ cup balsamic vinegar
¼ cup finely chopped fresh basil, thyme, or oregano, or a combination
2 teaspoons minced garlic
Salt and ground black pepper to taste

With the machine running, slowly pour through the feed tube and process until smooth:

¾ cup olive oil

Taste and adjust the seasonings. Use immediately or cover and refrigerate.

TANGERINE SHALLOT DRESSING

About 1½ cups

This dressing is especially good on any salad with chicken or even just drizzled over grilled chicken.

Mash together until a paste is formed:

- 1 clove garlic, peeled
- 2 to 3 pinches of salt

Remove to a small bowl or a jar with a tight-fitting lid. Add and whisk or shake until well blended:

- ¼ cup fresh tangerine or clementine juice
- 2 tablespoons fresh lemon juice
- 2 small shallots, minced

Add in a slow, steady stream, whisking constantly, or add to the jar and shake until smooth:

- ⅔ cup vegetable oil

Taste and adjust the seasonings. Use immediately or cover and refrigerate.

APRICOT DRESSING

About 1½ cups

Especially good on salads of Asian greens or any salad that has pork or lamb in it.

Whisk together in a medium bowl or shake in a jar with a tight-fitting lid until smooth:

- ¼ cup apricot nectar
- 3 tablespoons balsamic vinegar
- 3 tablespoons minced dried apricots
- 3 tablespoons coarsely chopped fresh parsley
- 2 teaspoons minced garlic
- 2 teaspoons whole-grain mustard
- 1 teaspoon sugar
- Salt and cracked black peppercorns to taste

Add in a slow, steady stream, whisking constantly, or add to the jar and shake until smooth:

- ¼ cup olive oil

Taste and adjust the seasonings. Use immediately or cover and refrigerate.

ROASTED GARLIC DRESSING

About 1 cup

Preheat the oven to 400°F.

Place on a piece of heavy-duty aluminum foil:

- 1 head garlic, top third cut off and loose papery peel removed
- 2 shallots, loose papery peel removed

Sprinkle with:

- 2 tablespoons olive oil

Wrap and seal tightly. Roast for 1 hour. Remove the package from the oven, open carefully, and let the contents cool. When cool enough to handle, squeeze the garlic and the shallots from their peels into a small food processor or a blender. Add and puree:

- 2 tablespoons extra-virgin olive oil
- 1 tablespoon fresh lemon juice
- 1 tablespoon white wine vinegar
- 1 teaspoon Dijon mustard
- 1 teaspoon fresh thyme leaves
- 1 teaspoon minced fresh rosemary
- Salt and ground black pepper to taste

With the machine running, slowly pour through the feed tube and process until smooth:

- 6 tablespoons olive oil

Taste and adjust the seasonings. Use immediately or cover and refrigerate.

SUN-DRIED TOMATO DRESSING

About ¾ cup

This simple dressing, which works well on salads that include arugula, also makes an excellent simple pasta sauce.

With the food processor running, drop through the feed tube and process until finely chopped:

- 2 small shallots, quartered
- 1 or 2 cloves garlic, halved

Stop the machine, add, and process until finely minced:

- 6 sun-dried tomato halves in oil, drained and coarsely chopped
- 6 brine-cured black olives, pitted
- 2 tablespoons balsamic vinegar
- 1 tablespoon fresh thyme leaves or chopped fresh basil
- Salt and ground black pepper to taste

With the machine running, slowly pour through the feed tube and process until smooth:

- ½ cup olive oil

Taste and adjust the seasonings. Use immediately or cover and refrigerate.

POPPY SEED HONEY DRESSING

About ⅔ cup

This dressing is an old favorite for salads that combine greens and fruit.

Whisk together in a small bowl or shake in a jar with a tight-fitting lid until smooth:

- ¼ cup honey
- 3 tablespoons cider vinegar or other fruit vinegar
- 2 tablespoons olive oil
- 1 small shallot, minced
- 2 teaspoons Dijon mustard
- 1 teaspoon poppy seeds
- Salt and ground black pepper to taste

Taste and adjust the seasonings. Use immediately or cover and refrigerate.

FETA DRESSING (REDUCED FAT) *About ½ cup*

Feta is lower in fat than many other cheeses but still has plenty of flavor.

Process in a blender or food processor until smooth:

- 2 ounces feta cheese, crumbled
- ¼ cup red wine vinegar
- 1 teaspoon minced fresh oregano
- Salt and ground black pepper to taste

With the machine running, slowly pour through the feed tube and process until smooth:

- 2 tablespoons extra-virgin olive oil

Taste and adjust the seasonings. Use immediately or cover and refrigerate.

CLASSIC RUSSIAN DRESSING *About 1¾ cups*

An American invention despite its name, this dressing goes well with composed salads, eggs, shellfish, and chicken salad and provides a wonderful spread for deli sandwiches.

Stir together in a small bowl until well blended:

- 1 cup Traditional Mayonnaise, 72, or Blender Mayonnaise, 72
- ¼ cup Chili Sauce, 70, or Tomato Ketchup, 69
- 1 tablespoon freshly grated horseradish
- 1 teaspoon Worcestershire sauce
- 1 tablespoon minced fresh parsley (optional)
- 1 teaspoon grated onions
- Salt and ground black pepper to taste

Taste and adjust the seasonings. Use immediately or cover and refrigerate.

THOUSAND ISLAND DRESSING *About 1½ cups*

An obvious relative of Russian dressing, Thousand Island is great on a wedge of iceberg lettuce and makes a good sandwich spread.

Stir together in a small bowl until well blended:

- 1 cup Traditional Mayonnaise, 72, or Blender Mayonnaise, 72
- ¼ cup Chili Sauce, 70, or Tomato Ketchup, 69
- 1 hard-boiled egg, chopped
- 2 tablespoons minced gherkins or pickle relish
- 1 tablespoon minced fresh onions
- 1 tablespoon finely snipped fresh chives
- 1 tablespoon minced fresh parsley
- Salt and ground black pepper to taste

Taste and adjust the seasonings. Use immediately or cover and refrigerate.

GREEN GODDESS DRESSING *About 2 cups*

This creamy, herby dressing was invented at the historic Palace Hotel in San Francisco in the 1920s in honor of William Archer's hit play *The Green Goddess.* It enjoyed great success, especially in California, for decades and, in our opinion, is worth a revival.

Stir together in a small bowl until well blended:

- 1 cup Traditional Mayonnaise, 72, or Blender Mayonnaise, 72
- ½ cup sour cream
- ¼ cup snipped fresh chives or minced scallions
- ¼ cup minced fresh parsley
- 1 tablespoon fresh lemon juice
- 1 tablespoon white wine vinegar
- 3 anchovy fillets, rinsed, patted dry, and minced
- Salt and ground black pepper to taste

Taste and adjust the seasonings. Use immediately or cover and refrigerate.

CREAMY BLUE-CHEESE DRESSING *About 2 cups*

Good-quality blue cheese, such as Roquefort, turns this into a truly distinctive dressing.

Puree in a food processor or blender until smooth:

- 1 cup Traditional Mayonnaise, 72, or Blender Mayonnaise, 72
- ½ cup sour cream
- ¼ cup finely chopped fresh parsley
- 1 to 2 tablespoons fresh lemon juice or red wine vinegar
- 1 teaspoon minced garlic
- 6 dashes of Worcestershire sauce
- Salt and ground black pepper to taste
- Pinch of ground red pepper, or to taste

Add and process to the desired consistency:

- 4 ounces blue cheese

Taste and adjust the seasonings. Use immediately or cover and refrigerate.

REDUCED-FAT BLUE-CHEESE DRESSING *About 1½ cups*

Puree in a small food processor or blender:

- ¾ cup buttermilk
- ¼ cup fat-free mayonnaise
- ¼ cup crumbled blue cheese
- 1 clove garlic, minced (optional)
- Ground red pepper to taste

Transfer to a bowl and stir in:

- 1 tablespoon snipped fresh chives

Thin, if necessary, with additional:

- Buttermilk or water

Taste and adjust the seasonings. Use immediately or cover and refrigerate.

SAUCE LOUIS *About 2 cups*

Originally created for Crab Louis, 231, this dressing is also especially relished with salads that include artichokes, shrimp, or lobster.

Stir together in a small bowl until well blended:

- **1 cup Traditional Mayonnaise, 72, or Blender Mayonnaise, 72**
- **¼ cup heavy cream or Crème Fraîche, 1071 (optional)**
- **¼ cup Chili Sauce, 70**
- **¼ cup finely chopped red or yellow bell peppers**
- **¼ cup finely chopped scallions**
- **2 tablespoons fresh lemon juice**
- **1 teaspoon Worcestershire sauce**
- **Salt and ground black pepper to taste**

Taste and adjust the seasonings. Use immediately or cover and refrigerate.

CREAMY CARAWAY DRESSING *About 1⅓ cups*

Although it won't have quite the same rich flavor, you can make this dressing with equal parts yogurt and sour cream instead of crème fraîche.

Whisk together in a small bowl:

- **½ cup fresh lemon juice**
- **½ cup Crème Fraîche, 1071**
- **2 tablespoons caraway seeds, lightly toasted**
- **1 tablespoon whole-grain mustard**
- **1 tablespoon chopped shallots**
- **1 teaspoon chopped fresh thyme**

Add in a slow, steady stream, whisking constantly until smooth:

- **2 tablespoons extra-virgin olive oil**

Season with:

- **Salt and ground black pepper to taste**

Taste and adjust the seasonings. Use immediately or cover and refrigerate.

CREAMY CHILI DRESSING *About 1½ cups*

Whisk together in a small bowl or combine in a blender:

- **½ cup olive oil**
- **¼ cup sour cream**

Add and whisk together or blend to combine:

- **¼ cup fresh lime juice**
- **¼ cup coarsely chopped fresh cilantro**
- **2 tablespoons chili powder**
- **2 teaspoons ground cumin**
- **Salt and cracked black peppercorns to taste**

Taste and adjust the seasonings. Use immediately or cover and refrigerate.

MIDWESTERN CREAM DRESSING *About ¾ cup*

This is a classic—a legacy from early farming days, when oil was too rare to be used on salads. It is particularly good on soft leaf lettuces and on potato salads and slaws.

Whisk together in a small bowl:

- **¼ cup cider vinegar or white wine vinegar**
- **¼ cup sugar**
- **2 tablespoons light cream**
- **2 teaspoons celery seeds or poppy seeds**
- **Salt and cracked black peppercorns to taste**

Taste and adjust the seasonings. Use immediately or cover and refrigerate.

TAHINI DRESSING *About 2¼ cups*

Tahini, the sesame-seed paste that is a staple of Middle Eastern cooking, is available in specialty food stores. This dressing goes especially well with salads that include chickpeas and makes a great dip for crudités.

Whisk together in a small bowl:

- **1 cup tahini**
- **½ cup water**
- **Juice of 2 lemons, or to taste**
- **3 cloves garlic, minced**
- **1 tablespoon minced fresh cilantro, or to taste**
- **1 teaspoon ground coriander**
- **½ teaspoon ground cumin**
- **Salt to taste**
- **Ground red pepper to taste**

Thin with water as necessary, especially when using as a dressing. Taste and adjust the seasonings. Use immediately or cover and refrigerate.

RANCH DRESSING *About 1 cup*

The original version of this now-ubiquitous condiment was created at the Hidden Valley Guest Ranch in Santa Barbara in the 1950s. The formula was subsequently purchased by the Clorox company, which uses the Hidden Valley name to this day, but "ranch" has become a generic name not just for a dressing but for a buttermilky flavor (as in ranch-flavored corn chips). Here's a fresh homemade version. If you prefer a less runny dressing, stir in ⅓ to ½ cup of mayonnaise or sour cream.

Mash together until a paste is formed:

- **1 clove garlic, peeled**
- **2 to 3 pinches of salt**

Remove to a small bowl or a jar with a tight-fitting lid. Add and whisk or shake until well blended:

- **¾ cup buttermilk**
- **2 to 3 tablespoons fresh lime juice**

1 tablespoon minced fresh cilantro or parsley
1 tablespoon snipped fresh chives
Salt and ground black pepper to taste

Taste and adjust the seasonings. Use immediately or cover and refrigerate.

GOAT CHEESE DRESSING (REDUCED FAT)

About 1 cup

Whisk together in a small bowl:

4 ounces soft fresh goat cheese, at room temperature
¼ cup buttermilk
2 teaspoons white wine vinegar
1 teaspoon Dijon mustard
1 teaspoon minced fresh thyme
1 teaspoon minced fresh parsley
Pinch of grated lemon zest
Salt and ground black pepper to taste

Thin, if necessary, with additional:

Buttermilk or water

Taste and adjust the seasonings. Use immediately or cover and refrigerate.

YOGURT DILL DRESSING (REDUCED FAT)

About ¾ cup

Vary this all-purpose creamy, reduced-fat dressing by using other fresh herbs, such as thyme, oregano, or mint, in place of the dill; substituting chives for the shallots; or adding a generous pinch of curry powder, ground cumin, or ground red pepper.

Whisk together in a small bowl:

½ cup nonfat yogurt
2 shallots, minced
2 tablespoons finely snipped fresh dill
2 teaspoons Dijon mustard
Salt and ground black pepper to taste

Taste and adjust the seasonings. Use immediately or cover and refrigerate.

SOUR CREAM DRESSING FOR VEGETABLE SALADS

About 1¼ cups

Use as a dressing or a dip. For a reduced-fat version, substitute low-fat yogurt for the sour cream.

Whisk in a small bowl until smooth:

1 cup sour cream

Stir in:

2 tablespoons minced red bell peppers
1 teaspoon grated onions
1 teaspoon celery seeds or dill seeds
Salt and ground black pepper to taste

Taste and adjust the seasonings. Use immediately or cover and refrigerate.

GUACAMOLE DRESSING

About 2 cups

This dressing goes well with any salad that includes seafood, particularly grilled salmon. You can also use it as a dip for tortilla chips, just like guacamole itself.

Whisk together in a medium bowl:

¼ cup fresh lime juice
¼ cup finely chopped fresh cilantro or parsley
2 teaspoons ground cumin
1 teaspoon minced garlic
1 teaspoon minced fresh chili peppers

Add in a slow, steady stream, whisking constantly, until smooth:

½ cup olive oil

Stir in:

2 avocados, peeled and finely diced
1 medium, ripe tomato, finely diced
Salt and cracked black peppercorns to taste

Taste and adjust the seasonings. Use immediately or cover and refrigerate.

GRAINS

They say love comes when you least expect it, and that's what's been happening with grains. People pampered their whole lives with thick steaks, flashy salads, and rich desserts are suddenly finding that what they really crave are homely little wheat berries, bowls of cornmeal mush, even tiny amaranth.

GRAINS AND NUTRITION

The quest for low-fat, high-fiber fare led to a much closer look at grains, which provide complex carbohydrates, protein, a very small amount of fat, many of the B-complex vitamins, and an essential array of minerals. By eating the six to eleven daily servings of grains recommended in federal dietary guidelines, you can consume the recommended amount of protein found in one to three small portions of meat, without the saturated fat and with much more fiber. The nutrition is more reliable if the grains are whole, varied, and supplemented by beans and some dairy products, meat, or fish; grains are somewhat low in one or another essential amino acid and lack vitamin B_{12}, which is found only in foods derived from animals.

But nobody ever fell in love because it was good for them. In the case of grains, no small amount of glamour was bestowed by foreign cuisines, sampled in travels abroad or in ethnic American restaurants. Rice seduced as sushi and risotto, corn as polenta and tamales, wheat as tabbouleh and couscous.

All true grains are fruits of grasses, and thus whole kernels are sometimes called berries. They are composed of three basic parts, shown below: the nutrient-dense germ, or seed, which contains protein and some oil; the endosperm, comprising carbohydrates and protein; and the bran, or high-fiber outer layer. Rice, barley, and oats also have an inedible outer husk; wheat, rye, and corn do not. If you eat all parts of the grain, other than the husk, you get all the vitamins, minerals, and other nutrients it contains—all the nourishment the seed needs to become a plant. It is common practice, however, to remove the bran and the

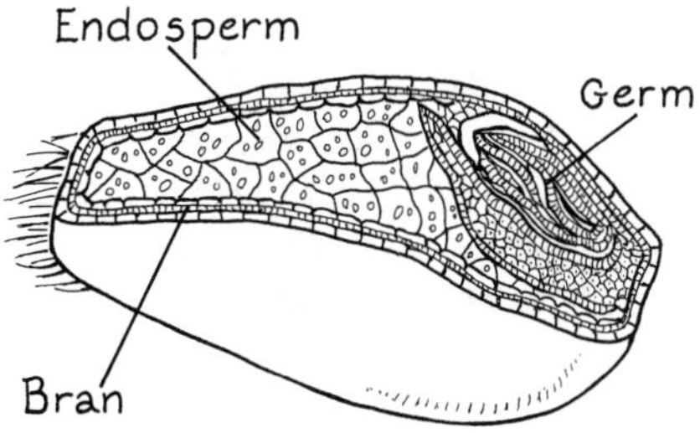

The three basic parts of whole grain kernels

germ and consume only the endosperm. White rice, for example, is endosperm only. So is the part of the wheat that is ground into white flour. Both these products are enriched with B vitamins and iron to replace, and even increase, the amounts lost when the bran and germ are discarded, but some things, including the vitamin E and fiber of the original, are left out.

Grains are much more alike than unalike, both in the cooking and the nutrition. Good health food stores and some supermarkets will stock more than a dozen distinct grains, including buckwheat and quinoa, which are not true grains, botanically speaking, but are similar enough to be treated as such. You'll find separate discussions of each grain and its forms, with cooking information, in this chapter.

BUYING AND STORING GRAINS

An important general consideration is freshness. Any whole grain, for example, whether brown rice or millet, is much more perishable than a refined product such as white rice or pearl barley. So it is wise to buy these in a store that does a heavy volume of business in whole grains and perhaps even keeps them in a specially cooled section. Products high in oil content, especially quinoa and wheat germ, turn rancid fast and should be refrigerated once you get them home or break the vacuum seal of the jar. Buy other whole grains in amounts you can use within 1 month and store them in tightly covered jars in the pantry or refrigerate or freeze them in freezer bags or sealed containers for up to 2 months. Signs of rancidity are an off odor before cooking and a bitter taste when cooked. Grains purchased loose usually need to be rinsed and picked over for bits of chaff or debris. Place the grain in a large fine-mesh sieve set in a pot large enough to hold it; rinse under cold water, raking the grain with your fingers. Let debris rise to the surface and remove it. Drain well. Grains sold in boxes are generally clean and ready for the pot.

COOKING GRAINS

Cooked grains can be refrigerated for at least 3 days—and a few days longer if cooked with water and not stock or other perishable ingredients. They reheat beautifully in the microwave. Spread portions on individual plates, cover with plastic wrap, and microwave on high for 1 to 2 minutes per serving. To reheat a bowlful, sprinkle the surface lightly with water, cover with plastic wrap or a lid, and microwave on high for about 1½ minutes per cup; stir before serving. To reheat on the stovetop, put a thin layer of water in a saucepan, add the grain, and simmer, covered, over medium heat until hot.

Toasting a grain before you simmer it in liquid brings out the fragrance. You can spread it in a heavy saucepan or skillet and heat over medium heat, stirring often, until the grain smells rich and toasted, usually just a few minutes; be careful not to scorch the smallest grains, such as amaranth and millet. Heating or melting some oil or butter in the pan before you stir in and toast the grain will add flavor and help keep the kernels separate, for fluffier texture, when they cook; this preparation is called a pilaf and often includes vegetables lightly browned with the grain. To toast a cup of grain in the microwave, spread it in a wide flat-bottomed casserole or pie plate and microwave, uncovered, on high for 3 to 6 minutes, depending on the size of the kernel, stirring every 2 minutes. To toast grains in the oven, spread them on a baking sheet and bake in a preheated 350°F oven for about 10 minutes, stirring once only.

Another way to enhance flavor is to cook the grain with a well-seasoned liquid instead of plain water. Stocks made from chicken, meat, dried mushrooms, and vegetables can be substituted. So can canned tomatoes with enough of their juice to equal the amount of water required. The possibilities extend to apple juice and milk, substituted for part or all of the water, with breakfast cereals. With grains that need to simmer a while, including brown rice and barley, you can add chopped onions, mushrooms, carrots, and/or celery to the water with the grain; the vegetables will cook long enough to season the liquid. With faster-cooking grains such as white rice, simmer chopped onions or carrots in the water for 10 to 15 minutes before adding the grain. A grain cooked in plain water will be too bland for most tastes unless you add about ⅛ teaspoon salt per serving to the pot; taste while the grain is still hot, when it will more readily absorb a little more salt than if allowed to cool. Some grains, such as cornmeal and buckwheat, tend to need as much as ¼ teaspoon per serving.

Combining two or three grains in one dish yields a sum greater than its parts in mingled fragrances and textures. This is easiest to do with grains that cook in roughly the same amount of time and with similar amounts of liquid. Some examples: brown rice and pearl barley; basmati or other long-grain white rice and bulgur; bulgur and buckwheat; cornmeal and amaranth; hulled barley and wheat berries. Grains that require different amounts of cooking can be added to the pot sequentially; they will need a little less water together than they do separately because there is less evaporation. Be sure to use a pot big enough for both grains and add water if needed, ¼ cup at a time, toward the end.

Grains can be simmered on the stovetop, in the oven, or in the microwave, which won't save time but will yield predictably good texture, with no pot to wash. The pressure cooker can be a big time-saver with long-cooking wheat berries and hulled barley, but it is important to consult your owner's manual for instructions; some recommend against cooking any grains, and others require that the grain be cooked in an aluminum-foil-covered bowl to prevent the possibility that loose bits of hull or starch will clog the steam vent.

Wheat berries and other large whole grains are commonly presoaked for 8 hours or overnight to hasten their cooking time. A soaking shortcut is to heat the grain and liquid to a full boil on top of the stove and simmer for 2 minutes; remove from the heat and let stand, covered, for 1 hour, until some kernels begin to split. Or microwave the grain and liquid in a covered casserole on high for 10 minutes and then on medium for 5 minutes; let stand, covered, for 1 hour. Either way, cooking the grain in the soaking water retains nutrients. Note that presoaking is not always called for when the grain is to be used in a salad, because a firmer texture is desired.

Be generous with the size and the width of the pot when cooking grains, as they will cook fluffier if not clumped together. With more than 1 cup grain, you will get fluffier results if you use a wide saucepan, a Dutch oven, or even a deep skillet with a tight lid. Fine-textured and small grains, such as cornmeal and amaranth, tend to stick to the pot and scorch if not stirred often, especially if cooked without fat. Using a double boiler or the microwave reduces the risk, as well as the need to stir as much, by removing the grain from direct heat. Oven baking yields consistently dry, fluffy results with rice and barley if the casserole is wide and heavy enough, because the heat comes from all sides and not just the bottom of the pot.

Any grain makes a nutritious hot breakfast cereal, but most people prefer the soft consistency of a ground or rolled grain cooked with plenty of liquid. See recipes under Oats, Corn, and Wheat for specific preparations; also consider fine-grain buckwheat groats, amaranth, millet, teff, and spelt or whole-wheat couscous, all of which can be cooked as directed in the basic methods detailed in this chapter, with additional water if porridge consistency is desired, and served with warmed milk or some butter and honey or brown sugar. Conversely, any grain with even a little chewiness can be turned into a wonderful salad. See recipes under Barley, Rice, Rye, Triticale, and Wheat for specific preparations. Feel free to substitute another grain of similar size in a salad. Toss the grain with the dressing while it is still warm or at room temperature for best absorption and least stickiness.

AMARANTH

The Aztecs revered amaranth as a giver of strength. The grain has once again gained recognition as a giver of strength, because its protein, iron, magnesium, and phosphorus are somewhat higher than those of other grains and its amino acid balance is somewhat better, supplying the lysine that is deficient in other grains, especially corn. Amaranth kernels are very flavorful, somewhat like sesame seeds but also a little bit peppery; when cooked, they turn shiny and resemble a small-grain brown caviar.

Because of their very small size, they clump together like a porridge and also tend to stick to the pot. So use a nonstick saucepan, a double boiler, or the microwave to cook amaranth. Or mix with other grains: ⅓ cup amaranth with ⅔ cup toasted quinoa simmered in 2 cups water for 15 to 20 minutes yields a tempting blend. Also substitute amaranth for part of the cornmeal in polenta recipes to boost flavor and nutrients.

For 4 servings (3 to 4 cups), cook 1 cup amaranth with 2 cups water for firm, chewy kernels or 3 cups water for porridge consistency; only a little salt is needed, about ¼ teaspoon, especially if you use only 2 cups water. On the stovetop, bring the amaranth, water, and salt to a boil in a nonstick saucepan, reduce the heat to low, and simmer, covered, for 20 to 25 minutes, depending on the amount of water used.

Microwave 1 cup amaranth, 2 or 3 cups water (as directed above), and ¼ teaspoon salt in a covered casserole on high for 5 minutes, then on medium-low for 15 to 20 minutes. Let stand, covered, for 5 minutes.

BARLEY

Funny how barley, a crop traced back to 7000 B.C., continues to surprise and delight, as if every dish it appears in reinvents its roasted-nut taste. Lately it has ventured beyond its supporting role in mushroom barley soup and Scotch broth to a starring role in dishes such as risotto and in salads. The off-white oval kernels most commonly sold as pearl barley have had the tough husk, bran, and germ ground away, yielding the endosperm, a kernel that cooks much faster than hulled, or whole, barley. Pearl barley will keep for at least 6 months in an airtight container in a cool pantry. Scotch, or pot, barley has more of the bran left on, and therefore more fiber, phosphorus, and potassium are retained. Barley is processed into several quick-cooking forms, including steamed and rolled into flakes or cut into grits for breakfast cereal.

The amount of liquid used to cook pearl barley varies according to the desired texture. Cook 1 cup pearl barley with 3 cups water for a firm, chewy texture, or use 4 cups water for a softer texture, adding ½ to ¾ teaspoon salt to the water. Pearl barley can be substituted for brown rice in Oven-Baked Brown Rice with Mushrooms, 256 (increase the stock to 3 cups) and for white rice in Risotto Milanese, 260 (increase the stock to 6 cups, or as needed). Both hulled and Scotch barley should be soaked for 8 hours or overnight, then simmered until tender, 1 to 1½ hours, in a ratio of 1 cup barley to 4 to 5 cups liquid.

Microwave 1 cup pearl barley with 2¾ cups water and ½ teaspoon salt in a covered casserole on high for 5 minutes, then on medium-low for 42 to 45 minutes. Let stand, covered, for 5 minutes. Microwave the same way ½ cup pearl barley and ½ cup long-grain brown rice.

BASIC COOKED PEARL BARLEY

Scant 2 cups; 2 to4 servings

This recipe can be doubled; use the lesser amount of water for a firmer grain.

Bring to a boil in a large saucepan:

2 to 2½ cups water
½ cup pearl barley
½ teaspoon salt

Reduce the heat to low and cook, covered, until the barley is tender and the water is absorbed, about 45 minutes. Drain off any excess water.

BARLEY WITH TOASTED BUTTERED PECANS

3 to 4 servings

Toasted nuts, especially pecans, transform this unassuming grain into a special dish.

Prepare:

Basic Cooked Pearl Barley, above

Melt in a small skillet over medium heat:

2 tablespoons butter

Add:

¼ cup broken pecan pieces

Cook, stirring, until toasted, about 3 minutes. Stir into the cooked barley and serve warm.

BARLEY AND MUSHROOM "RISOTTO"

8 servings

This is not a real risotto because it does not contain rice, but it is made in the same way. To serve this dish as a main course for 4 people, omit the salt and stir in ½ to 1 cup grated Parmesan cheese just before serving.

Heat in a large, deep skillet over medium heat until the foam subsides:

4 to 6 tablespoons (½ to ¾ stick) butter

Add and cook, stirring, until tender but not brown, about 7 minutes:

1⅓ cups finely chopped onions

Stir in and cook until softened:

8 ounces shiitake mushrooms, stems removed and caps diced

Reduce the heat to medium-low. Add and stir until glazed with butter:

1 cup pearl barley

Add and cook, stirring, until the liquid is absorbed:

⅔ cup dry white wine
1 tablespoon mashed or finely minced garlic
½ teaspoon salt
½ teaspoon ground black pepper

Warm, but do not allow to simmer, in a saucepan set over very low heat:

6 cups chicken stock

Keep the stock warm. Stir 2 cups of the chicken stock into the barley. Simmer slowly, stirring occasionally, until the stock is almost absorbed. Add the remaining stock ½ cup at a time, allowing each addition to be absorbed before adding the next and stirring often. The barley needs 45 to 60 minutes' cooking to become tender. If you run low on stock while the barley is still very underdone, reduce the heat. If you do run out of stock, finish cooking with hot water. This risotto can be made 4 days ahead. Let cool completely, then cover and refrigerate. Reheat in a skillet over low heat, adding a little water and stirring frequently.

BARLEY, MUSHROOM, AND ASPARAGUS SALAD

4 to 6 servings

Cook in a large pot of boiling salted water until tender, about 40 minutes:

1 cup pearl barley

While the barley is cooking, heat in a small skillet over medium heat:

3 tablespoons olive oil

Add:

2 shallots, minced

Cook, stirring, until softened, about 2 minutes. Add:

1 cup sliced fresh morel or other wild and/or cultivated mushrooms

Cook, stirring, until the mushrooms have released their liquid and are softened and the liquid is evaporated, about 3 minutes. Stir in:

1 tablespoon fresh lemon juice
1 tablespoon minced fresh parsley
½ teaspoon finely grated lemon zest
Salt and ground black pepper to taste

Remove from the heat. When the barley is tender, add to the pot and cook until bright green and crisp-tender, about 4 minutes:

6 ounces pencil-thin asparagus, cut diagonally into 1-inch pieces

Drain the barley and asparagus thoroughly in a colander. Combine the mushroom and barley mixtures; taste and adjust the seasonings. Serve warm.

BUCKWHEAT

Buckwheat gets right to the heart of whole-grain flavor. The complexity of the flour distinguishes Brittany's crêpes and Japan's soba noodles, and the nuttiness of the kernels makes Russia's roasted groats, or kasha, irresistible. Botanically, buckwheat is not a grain at all but the seed of a plant related to rhubarb. Buy kasha, commonly sold in supermarkets, for deepest flavor, or choose unroasted groats, found in health food stores, for blander delicacy. Since the taste difference is quite pronounced, be certain of the one you want. Both are available as whole groats or cracked to various degrees of fineness. Whole groats cook to chewy, separate kernels; the finest milling yields a porridge. Whole kasha groats can be combined and steamed with white rice; the amounts of liquid and cooking time for the two are roughly the same. Kasha is commonly mixed with an egg and/or toasted in a saucepan with butter or oil before steaming to keep the grains firm and separate. You can skip this step if microwaving. Cooking in stock instead of water will boost the flavor without adding fat.

Microwave 2 cups chicken or beef stock and ¼ to ½ teaspoon salt, depending on the saltiness of the stock, in a 2-quart covered casserole on high for 5 minutes; stir in 1 cup whole or coarse-grind kasha and microwave, covered, on medium until the liquid is absorbed, about 10 minutes. Let stand, covered, for 5 minutes, fluff with a fork, and let stand for 5 minutes more. If desired, first microwave 1 tablespoon butter in the casserole on high for 1 minute; stir in 1 small onion, finely chopped; and microwave, uncovered, on high for 4 minutes, stirring after 2 minutes. Add the stock and proceed as directed.

BASIC COOKED KASHA

About 4 cups; 4 servings

Rinse and drain:

1 cup kasha (whole roasted buckwheat groats)

Combine with:

1 large egg or egg white, well beaten

Stir until blended. Let stand for 5 minutes. Heat a large skillet over medium heat until hot enough to evaporate a drop of water. Add the kasha and cook, stirring, until the grains are separate and toasted, about 3 minutes. Or, instead, heat in the skillet:

1 tablespoon vegetable oil

Add the kasha and cook, stirring, until the grains are toasted, about 3 minutes. Stir in:

2 cups water or any stock
½ teaspoon salt, or to taste

Bring to a boil, reduce the heat to low, and simmer, covered, until the kasha is fluffy, about 15 minutes. Remove from the heat and let stand, covered, for 10 minutes.

BOWTIES WITH KASHA (KASHA VARNISHKES)

4 to 8 servings

Kasha Varnishkes is a traditional eastern European dish that is low in calories and delicious. The trick to making tender but firm, not mushy, kasha is to coat it with egg and stir it over high heat until toasted and the grains are separate. The nutty flavor of the kasha is a wonderful foil for the creamy taste of pasta. In the summer, we turn this dish into a pasta salad using whatever fresh vegetables can be found and toss with a vinaigrette dressing. Rigatoni or small shells work well here too.

Brown in a medium nonstick skillet over medium-high heat:

2 to 3 tablespoons chicken fat or vegetable oil
2 large onions, cut into ½-inch pieces
2 cups sliced mushrooms (button, shiitake, or portobello, or a combination), optional
1 clove garlic, minced
Salt and ground black pepper to taste

Remove to a large bowl. Cook in a large pot of boiling salted water until tender but firm:

6 ounces bowtie pasta

Drain the noodles and toss with the onion mixture. Beat in a small bowl:

1 large egg

Add:

1 cup whole kasha (whole roasted buckwheat groats)

Stir until the grains are well coated. Wipe out the skillet and heat it over high heat. Transfer the kasha mixture to the skillet and cook, stirring, until the grains are toasted and separate, 2 to 3 minutes. Reduce the heat to low and add:

2 cups hot chicken stock

Stir, cover, and simmer until the stock is absorbed and the kasha is tender but not mushy, 7 to 8 minutes. Stir in the noodle mixture. Taste and adjust the seasonings. Garnish with:

2 tablespoons chopped fresh parsley

Serve immediately. The dish can be made 1 to 2 days in advance and reheated, uncovered, in a 350°F oven. If the mixture is dry, add ¼ cup more chicken stock.

CORNMEAL, GRITS, AND HOMINY

Corn on the cob, the only grain eaten fresh from the field, previews the subtle sweetness of dried corn in all its forms. The very sweetest dried corn comes from the same ears sold as fresh, but we have not seen it sold outside Pennsylvania Dutch farm areas, where the kernels are rehydrated as stewed or creamed corn. The corn raised for drying and milling and sold as cornmeal, hominy, and grits is starchier and much less sugary; yet its flavor recalls the opulence of a cornfield ripe for harvest. It is unmistakable also in popcorn, which is a type of corn with a hard hull but enough moisture inside to burst from its own steam pressure when heated; this favorite snack is a good source of fiber.

Dried corn is processed for hot breakfast cereal and side dishes in two basic ways. If it is simply ground, the product is cornmeal, and coarse, medium, or fine grind can be used in any recipe unless otherwise specified. If you buy stone-ground cornmeal, you are getting the oily germ with the starchy endosperm; the product has a much higher fiber and mineral content, and it must be refrigerated. The more commonly available enriched degerminated cornmeal has lost its germ and thus has a more stable shelf life.

Dried corn that has been treated with an alkali to remove its hulls is called hominy or slaked corn. The process makes the niacin in corn available as a nutrient and thus prevents pellagra. The Native Americans who first made hominy used wood ash or lime; today slaked lime or lye is most common. Cracked into a coarse meal, hominy becomes hominy grits; ground into flour, it is masa harina, used to make tortillas. Whole dried hominy made from white corn is also known as posole; cooked, it is available canned and, in some places, frozen. Hominy is sometimes available as golden (made from yellow corn) and white. Use a combination if available. To make hominy, see page 250.

Microwave 1 cup grits (not quick-cooking or instant), 3 cups water, and 1 teaspoon salt in a covered casserole on high until the water is absorbed, about 11 minutes, stirring after 7 minutes. Let stand, covered, for 5 minutes.

For polenta, microwave 3½ cups water or a combination of water and chicken stock in a 2-quart bowl on high until boiling, about 9 minutes. Gradually whisk in 1 cup yellow cornmeal and 1 teaspoon salt (or less, to taste, if using salted stock). Microwave, uncovered, on medium until thickened, about 4 minutes, whisking after 2 minutes. Whisk in butter and pepper to taste; let stand for 2 minutes. To make Polenta Toast, 249, spread the hot polenta on a baking sheet, refrigerate, and proceed as directed.

CORNMEAL MUSH

About 4 cups; 4 servings

Made with either white or yellow cornmeal, this is polenta's cousin from the southern United States and is a favorite breakfast food served with butter, molasses, sorghum, maple syrup, or honey.

Stir together in the top of a double boiler:

1 cup white or yellow cornmeal
½ cup cold water
1 teaspoon salt, or to taste

Gradually stir in:

4 cups boiling water, or 2 cups boiling water and 2 cups boiling milk

Stir until smooth. Place directly over the heat and cook, stirring, until the mixture boils, about 2 minutes. Place the top of the double boiler over boiling water. Cover and cook, stirring often, for 25 to 30 minutes. Spoon into bowls and drizzle over the top:

Melted butter
Molasses, pure maple syrup, sorghum, or honey

TAMALE PIE

8 to 10 servings

Unlike many tamale pies, which have a top crust only, this one is completely enclosed in a cornmeal crust. This dish can be baked up to 3 days ahead, kept covered in the refrigerator, and reheated in a 300°F oven for 20 minutes.

Crumble into a large skillet and cook over medium-high heat until the meat is no longer pink, thoroughly breaking up the meat with the back of a spoon:

1½ pounds lean ground beef or ground turkey

If necessary, tilt the skillet and spoon out any fat. Stir in:

3 cups tomato salsa
½ cup chopped pimiento-stuffed green olives
1 tablespoon chili powder
1 tablespoon ground cumin
½ teaspoon ground cinnamon

Bring the mixture to a simmer. Reduce the heat to low and simmer gently, stirring occasionally, for 10 minutes. Remove from the heat. Bring just to a boil in a small saucepan:

1⅓ cups water
1 cup vegetable or chicken stock

Cover and remove from the heat. Whisk together in a large bowl:

2 teaspoons baking powder
1½ teaspoons salt

Whisk in:

⅓ cup vegetable oil

Then stir in, mixing until all the cornmeal is coated with the oil:

3 cups yellow cornmeal

Add the reserved stock mixture and stir well. Let the batter stand for 5 minutes. Mix in:

2 large eggs

Position a rack in the center of the oven. Preheat the oven to 400°F. Generously grease a 13 x 9-inch baking dish, preferably glass.

Remove 1½ cups of the cornmeal batter and reserve. Using a rubber spatula, spread the remaining batter evenly over the bottom and all the way up the sides of the pan. Gently spoon the beef filling over the crust, then cover evenly with:

12 ounces grated sharp Cheddar cheese (about 3 packed cups)

Stir into the reserved batter:

¼ cup hot water

Then spread it in a thin, even layer over the top of the pie. The batter will blend lightly with the cheese. Bake the pie until nicely browned, about 40 minutes. Let stand for 15 minutes. Cut the pie lengthwise in half, then cut each half crosswise into 4 or 5 equal pieces.

POLENTA

The traditional Italian technique for making polenta is to add the dry cornmeal in a thin, steady stream to a pot of boiling salted water or stock, stirring constantly to prevent lumps. Another way to prevent lumps is to mix the cornmeal with cold liquid before adding it, gradually, to boiling liquid.

SOFT POLENTA WITH BUTTER AND CHEESE

About 4 cups; 4 servings

This is the basic formula for stirred soft polenta. For more flavor, replace up to half of the water with chicken stock.

Melt in a large saucepan over medium heat:

3 tablespoons butter

Add and cook, stirring, until translucent, about 5 minutes:

½ cup finely chopped onions

Stir in and bring to a boil:

3 cups water

Stir together:

1 cup water
1 cup yellow cornmeal

Gradually stir into the boiling water, reduce the heat to low, and cook, stirring constantly with a wooden spoon, until the cornmeal is very thick and leaves the side of the pan as it is stirred, about 25 minutes. Sprinkle with:

2 tablespoons to ½ cup grated Parmesan cheese
1 teaspoon salt, or to taste

OVEN-BAKED POLENTA

6 servings

In this version of polenta, the preliminary cooking can be cut in half because the polenta finishes cooking as it bakes in the oven. This recipe can be made ahead and reheated the next day. Serve with Italian sausage or as a vegetarian main dish with steamed greens.

Melt or heat in a large saucepan over medium heat:

2 tablespoons butter or olive oil

Add and cook, stirring, until translucent, about 5 minutes:

½ cup finely chopped onions

Stir in and bring to a boil:

3 cups water, or 1½ cups chicken stock and 1½ cups water

Stir together:

2 cups water, or 1 cup chicken stock and 1 cup water
1½ cups yellow cornmeal

Gradually stir into the boiling water; cook, stirring constantly, over low heat until the cornmeal is thickened, about 15 minutes.

Preheat the oven to 350°F. Lightly butter a shallow 2-quart baking dish.

Pour half of the polenta into the baking dish. Smooth with a spatula. Have ready:

4 ounces Gruyère cheese, thinly slivered
4 ounces mozzarella cheese, thinly slivered
½ cup grated Parmesan cheese

Top the layer of polenta with half of the cheese. Spread the remaining polenta on top and sprinkle with the remaining cheese. Pour over:

½ cup heavy cream, half-and-half, or milk

Bake until the top is browned and bubbly, 35 to 45 minutes. Let stand for 10 minutes before serving.

POLENTA TOAST

4 servings

Thin layers of cold polenta can be cut into squares or triangles and browned in melted butter on top of the stove or in the oven. They can be served as an appetizer with roasted peppers or mushrooms, as an accompaniment to stews, in soups, or under grilled meats. Make the polenta ahead, cover, and store in the refrigerator up to 1 day before cutting, browning, and serving.

Prepare:

Soft Polenta with Butter and Cheese, 249, decreasing the butter to 2 tablespoons and using 2 tablespoons of cheese

Lightly oil a 13 x 9-inch baking pan. Spread the polenta in an even layer in the pan and let cool slightly. Cover and refrigerate for at least 3 hours or up to 24 hours, until cold and set.

About 45 minutes before serving, preheat the oven to 425°F. Lightly brush a nonstick baking sheet with olive oil.

Cut the polenta into 3-inch squares, then diagonally into triangles. Carefully transfer the pieces to the baking sheet. Bake until the bottoms are browned, about 15 minutes. Remove the baking sheet from the oven and carefully turn the toasts over. Bake until the second side is browned, about 10 minutes. Alternatively, cook the polenta toasts in olive oil or butter on a griddle or in a large, heavy skillet until browned on both sides.

BAKED CHEESE GRITS

4 servings

Grits are a favorite dish throughout the American South, where they were eaten by Native Americans long before the colonists arrived. They can be cooked plain and served by the spoonful straight from the pot, eaten with any number of toppings (like pasta), or enriched with butter, onions, garlic, and cheese and baked in a casserole, as they are here.

Bring to a boil in a large saucepan:

5 cups water

Meanwhile, melt in a small skillet over medium heat:

4 tablespoons (½ stick) butter

Add and cook, stirring, until translucent, about 5 minutes:

½ cup chopped onions

Stir in and cook for 1 minute more:

1 clove garlic, finely minced

Remove from the heat. Stir into the boiling water:

1 cup grits

1 teaspoon salt

Cover and cook, stirring occasionally, over low heat until thickened, about 20 minutes.

Preheat the oven to 350°F. Butter a 2-quart casserole or soufflé dish.

Add the onion mixture to the grits along with:

2 cups grated Cheddar cheese

Whisk together until blended:

½ cup milk

2 large eggs

¼ teaspoon ground red pepper

Gradually stir into the grits. Transfer to the casserole. Bake until a toothpick inserted in the center comes out clean, 50 to 60 minutes.

SOUFFLÉD CHEESE GRITS

Prepare Baked Cheese Grits, above, substituting 2 large egg whites for the eggs. Beat the egg whites until soft peaks form, then fold into the grits just before spooning into the casserole. Bake as directed.

HOMINY

8 cups

By far the most common and easiest form of hominy to prepare is canned and needs only to be rinsed. The next most common is dried whole hominy. To cook purchased dried hominy, soak 1 cup whole dried hominy for at least 8 hours or overnight in water to cover. Drain, add fresh water to cover by 2 inches, and bring to a boil. Reduce the heat to low, cover, and simmer until tender, 1½ to 2 hours. Drain. This will yield 3 cups cooked hominy.

Here is how to make hominy from dried whole-kernel corn. This method takes the most time and trouble, but some cooks swear that the flavor merits the work.

Combine in a large saucepan and let stand for 12 hours:

4 cups dried whole-kernel corn

8 cups water

2 tablespoons baking soda

Bring to a boil, reduce the heat to low, and cook, covered, for 3 hours, replenishing the water as needed. Drain and plunge the corn into a large bowl of cold water. Rub the corn to remove the hulls, drain, and rinse. Return the corn to the saucepan and cover with:

8 cups water

Bring to a boil and drain. Rinse with cold water and rub to remove any hulls. Drain again. Return to the saucepan and add:

8 cups water

1 tablespoon salt

Bring to a boil, drain, and toss with:

Melted butter to taste

BAKED HOMINY

4 to 6 servings

Bake this with chopped baked ham or substitute chopped apples for the ham, which adds a nice sweetness to the casserole.

Preheat the oven to 375°F. Heat in a medium skillet over medium heat:

1 tablespoon vegetable oil

Add and cook, stirring, until the onions are softened:

1 cup chopped onions

½ cup chopped baked ham or peeled apples

Stir in:

2½ cups hominy, above, drained canned hominy, or thawed frozen hominy

One 14½-ounce can diced tomatoes, with juice

½ teaspoon salt

⅛ teaspoon ground black pepper

Combine:

1 cup fine fresh breadcrumbs

1 cup grated Cheddar cheese

Spoon half of the hominy into a 2-quart casserole. Sprinkle with half of the breadcrumb mixture. Spoon the remaining hominy mixture on top and sprinkle with the remaining breadcrumb mixture. Dot the top with:

1 tablespoon butter, cut into small pieces

Bake until the top is browned, about 15 minutes.

POSOLE

4 servings

Posole is a hearty Latin American stew served on feast days and other special occasions. This is one of many variations on a piquant Southwest classic. The day before cooking the posole, start the chili paste. Place in a bowl and cover with boiling water by 1 inch.

6 to 8 dried New Mexico (red Anaheim) peppers, seeded

6 to 8 dried chili negro (also called chilaca) peppers, seeded

Soak for at least 8 hours or overnight. Drain and finely chop in a food processor, then press through a food mill or sieve. Refrigerate until ready to use.

For the posole, heat in a large saucepan over medium heat:

1 tablespoon olive oil

Add and cook, stirring, until translucent, about 5 minutes:

1 cup chopped onions

Add and cook, stirring, until the bell peppers are softened, about 3 minutes:

½ cup chopped red bell peppers

1 tablespoon chopped garlic

½ teaspoon dried oregano

Stir in:

2 cups hominy, above, drained canned hominy, or thawed frozen hominy

2 cups chicken or vegetable stock

Bring to a boil. Stir in ¼ to ⅓ cup (to taste) of the chili paste along with:

¼ cup chopped seeded fresh Anaheim peppers or canned green chilies

1 tablespoon chopped seeded fresh jalapeño peppers

Simmer, partially covered, over low heat for 30 minutes. Just before serving, stir in:

⅓ cup fresh orange juice

2 tablespoons fresh lemon juice

1 teaspoon salt, or to taste

Serve over rice.

CHICKEN AND CHEESE TAMALES

8 tamales; 4 servings

A tamale is a Mexican dish of cornmeal wrapped in cornhusks or banana leaves and baked or steamed. Tamales may be filled with chicken, meat, beans, or cheese, or they may be sweet. If you cannot find fresh corn in husks, you can use dried cornhusks, available in Mexican food stores; they must be soaked an extra 2 hours. If neither fresh nor dried cornhusks are available, rectangular pieces (about 9 x 7 inches) of aluminum foil or parchment paper can be used instead. Just make sure to wrap loosely so that the cornmeal has space to expand as it cooks. When using cornhusks, tie with long, narrow strips of the husks or kitchen string to keep the tamales intact while steaming. If using foil, crimp the edges; if using parchment, fold under the ends and secure with string.

Cut 1 inch from the stem ends of:

4 medium ears fresh unhusked corn

Husk the corn, discarding the silks. Cover the husks with boiling water and soak for 30 minutes. Cut the kernels from the corn and measure 1½ cups for the filling. Puree 1 cup of the corn in a food processor. Combine on a plate:

½ teaspoon ground cumin

½ teaspoon chili powder

½ teaspoon salt

¼ teaspoon ground red pepper

Coat with the seasoning:

1 boneless, skinless whole chicken breast (about 8 ounces)

Melt in a large skillet over low heat:

1 tablespoon butter

Add and cook, stirring, over low heat until tender but not browned:

½ cup slivered onions

Add the chicken and brown lightly on both sides. Cover and cook over low heat until cooked through, about 5 minutes. Let cool. Cut into thin shreds; there should be about 1½ cups. Stir together in a large bowl until blended:

⅔ cup instant grits
⅔ cup yellow cornmeal
1 tablespoon sugar
1½ teaspoons baking powder
½ teaspoon salt

Stir in until smooth:

1¼ cups boiling water

Beat in until incorporated:

6 tablespoons (¾ stick) butter or lard, softened

Whisk in the pureed corn and stir in the ½ cup whole kernels along with:

2 tablespoons minced seeded fresh jalapeño peppers

Drain the cornhusks and pat dry. Tear 16 thin strips from 2 or 3 pieces of husk to tie the tamales. Arrange 2 husks, slightly overlapping, side by side, and alternating the tips and stem ends to form a rectangle about 9 x 7 inches. Repeat until 8 rectangles are arranged. Top each with about ⅓ cup of the corn mixture. Dividing evenly, top each with the shredded chicken along with a total of:

½ cup grated Monterey Jack cheese

Fold the long edges of the cornhusks over the filling, slightly overlapping the edges. Twist the ends and tie each end tightly with a strip of cornhusk to form a packet. Place a steaming rack large enough to hold the tamales in a single layer over 1 inch boiling water; use 2 racks and pans if necessary. Cover and steam, adding more boiling water as needed, until the corn filling is puffed up inside the cornhusks, about 35 minutes. Let cool slightly and serve warm.

MILLET

Millet has been a staple in Africa and Asia at least since biblical times. Unlike the millet sold as birdseed, the grain marketed for people has its humanly indigestible hull removed and cooks fairly quickly, yielding a fluffy side dish that looks like couscous but has its own delicate taste. The flavor of millet becomes full and rich when well toasted, with or without butter or oil; it takes well to garlic, chili peppers, Parmesan cheese, and other counterpoints to its mildness. It also benefits from mixing with other grains, especially rice. Millet is known for its storage durability, but you should refrigerate it to be sure of preventing rancidity.

Microwave 1 tablespoon butter or oil in a flat-bottomed 2-quart casserole on high for 1 minute. Stir in 1 cup millet; microwave, uncovered, on high until golden, 3½ to 4 minutes, stirring after 2 minutes. Stir in 2½ cups water and ½ teaspoon salt. Microwave, covered, on high for 5 minutes, then on medium until the liquid is absorbed, about 15 minutes. Let stand, covered, for 5 minutes. Microwave the same way ½ cup millet and ½ cup quinoa or white rice, decreasing the liquid to 2¼ cups.

BASIC COOKED MILLET

4 to 4½ cups; 4 to 6 servings

I. Bring to a boil in a medium saucepan:

2½ cups water

Stir in:

½ teaspoon salt
1 cup millet

Cover and cook over low heat until the water is absorbed, 25 to 30 minutes. Let stand, covered, for 5 minutes before serving.

II. Melt or heat in a large saucepan over medium-low heat:

2 tablespoons butter or olive oil

Add and cook, stirring, until toasted and golden, about 3 minutes:

1 cup millet

Stir in:

2½ cups boiling water or stock
½ teaspoon salt

Cover and cook over low heat until the water is absorbed, 25 to 30 minutes. Let stand, covered, for 5 minutes before serving.

OATS

Oats deserve attention for their nutritional value, especially for their fiber, half of which is the insoluble type that aids digestion and the other half the soluble type that lowers cholesterol.

All oats are milled to remove an inedible hull but, after that, may be processed either as groats, usually cut, or steamed and rolled to hasten cooking and prolong their shelf life. Oat groats, which we know more commonly as steel-cut or Scotch oats or Irish oatmeal, contain enough fat to warrant refrigeration; because they are less processed, they yield a chewier cereal that is less likely to turn to mush. The more oats are steamed, rolled, and cut, the faster they cook and the softer they turn. The flavor benefits of mixing oats with other grains are evident in multigrain breads and several of the cereals and granolas that follow, for the oats bring a sweetness to the mix.

To microwave 1 serving of old-fashioned oatmeal, combine in a large cereal bowl ¾ cup water, ⅓ cup old-fashioned rolled oats, a pinch of salt, and 1 teaspoon sugar or honey if desired. Microwave, uncovered, on medium for 5 minutes, stirring halfway through. Cover with a plate and let stand for 1 minute.

To microwave 1 serving of steel-cut oats (not quick cooking), use a large casserole and some butter to prevent the cereal from boiling over. Mix in a 2-quart casserole 1 cup water, ¼ cup Scotch oats or Irish oatmeal, 1 teaspoon butter, and a pinch of salt. Microwave, covered, on high until the liquid is absorbed, about 12 minutes, stirring every 3 minutes. Let stand, covered, for 3 minutes. This recipe can be doubled in a 3-quart casserole; microwave and stir as directed for 6 to 9 minutes more.

OLD-FASHIONED ROLLED OATS WITH RAISINS AND SPICES

2½ cups

Oatmeal, the all-time favorite cooked cereal, is available as old-fashioned rolled, quick cooking, steel cut, and, of course, instant. This recipe and the two following cooked cereals are made with the old-fashioned flavors of brown sugar or maple syrup and spices.

Bring to a boil in a medium saucepan:

2 cups water

Stir in until blended:

1½ cups old-fashioned rolled oats
⅓ cup raisins
Pinch of salt

Reduce the heat and simmer, uncovered, for 10 minutes. Stir in:

1 teaspoon vanilla
½ teaspoon ground cinnamon
¼ teaspoon freshly grated or ground nutmeg

Top each serving with:

1 to 2 tablespoons light or dark brown sugar or pure maple syrup

QUICK-COOKING OATS WITH RAISINS AND SPICES

Prepare Old-Fashioned Rolled Oats with Raisins and Spices, above, substituting quick-cooking oats for the rolled oats and simmering for 3 minutes instead of 10 minutes.

STEEL-CUT OATS WITH RAISINS AND SPICES

3½ cups

Bring to a boil in a medium saucepan:

4 cups water

Stir in until blended:

1 cup steel-cut or Scotch oats or Irish oatmeal

Cook, stirring, until the mixture is thickened, about 3 minutes. Reduce the heat and simmer, uncovered, for 20 minutes, stirring the bottom of the pan often to discourage sticking. Stir in:

⅓ cup raisins
Pinch of salt
1 teaspoon vanilla
½ teaspoon ground cinnamon
¼ teaspoon freshly grated or ground nutmeg

Continue to simmer for 10 minutes. Top each serving with:

1 to 2 tablespoons light or dark brown sugar or pure maple syrup

MUESLI

3 cups

Muesli, also called Swiss oatmeal, was developed in the late nineteenth century by a Swiss physician for his patients. Treat it like a dry cereal and eat it warmed or at room temperature.

Stir together in a large bowl:

1 cup old-fashioned rolled oats
1 cup boiling water

Let stand, covered, overnight. The next morning, stir in:

½ cup raisins
⅓ cup chopped walnuts or unblanched almonds
¼ cup flaked unsweetened dried coconut
¼ cup chopped dried apricots
1 teaspoon light brown sugar

Spoon into bowls. (If desired, the cereal can be warmed in a small saucepan before serving.) Pour over each serving:

Warmed milk or cream to taste

UNSWEETENED DRIED FRUIT AND NUT GRANOLA

6 cups

No sugar or sweetener is added to this otherwise classic recipe for granola with dried fruits and nuts. Serve it spooned over plain yogurt along with fresh fruit or eat it as a cold cereal topped with milk or cream.

Preheat the oven to 300°F.

Pour into a 13 x 9-inch baking pan:

½ cup vegetable oil

Heat in the oven for about 10 minutes. Stir in:

2 cups old-fashioned rolled oats
1 cup wheat flakes
1 cup rolled rye

Bake, stirring often, until toasted, about 15 minutes. Stir in:

1 cup chopped walnuts, unblanched almonds, or hazelnuts
½ cup unsalted hulled sunflower seeds
½ cup raw wheat germ
2 tablespoons sesame seeds

Bake, stirring once or twice, until toasted, about 10 minutes. Stir in:

1 cup raisins

½ cup chopped dried apricots or other dried fruit

Let cool. Store in a tightly sealed container. Granola will keep for up to 5 days at room temperature or for up to 1 month in the refrigerator.

QUINOA

Quinoa's taste and texture tease with lightness and a very faint herbal quality. Its name, pronounced "keen-wa," puzzles at first, and its botanical origins are not truly those of a grain but of a weed related to lamb's quarters. Yet quinoa, cultivated in the Andes by Inca farmers hundreds of years ago, is an eminently practical grain for everyday eating, for it cooks fast and is high in protein and minerals. It becomes rancid quickly, so refrigerate it. Toast quinoa, with or without butter or oil, for best flavor. Quinoa can be substituted for bulgur or white rice in pilafs and salads and is especially good with toasted pecans or other nuts.

To microwave, spread 1 cup quinoa in a flat-bottomed 2-quart casserole. Microwave, uncovered, on high for 5 minutes, stirring halfway through. Stir in 2 cups water and ½ teaspoon salt, and ⅛ teaspoon chili powder if desired. Microwave, covered, on high for 5 minutes, then on medium-low for 15 minutes. Let stand for 5 minutes, then fluff with a fork. Microwave the same way ⅔ cup quinoa and ⅓ cup amaranth.

BASIC COOKED QUINOA *About 3 cups; 4 servings*

As a variation, substitute ⅓ cup chopped onions for the garlic and use chicken stock in place of the water. If you are cutting fat, omit the olive oil and garlic and toast the quinoa in a dry skillet over medium-low heat.

Rinse in a fine-mesh sieve and drain:

1 cup quinoa

Heat in a large, deep skillet over medium heat:

1 tablespoon olive oil

Add and cook, stirring constantly to avoid burning the garlic:

1 clove garlic, finely minced

Add the quinoa and cook, stirring constantly, until the grains are separate and golden. Stir in:

2 cups water

½ teaspoon salt

Bring to a boil, reduce the heat, and simmer until the liquid is absorbed, 12 to 15 minutes. Fluff with a fork.

QUINOA-STUFFED ACORN SQUASH *4 servings*

Halves of golden acorn squash stuffed with quinoa, Parmesan cheese, and toasted hazelnuts is an inspired combination. Excellent when made ahead and reheated. Serve as a vegetarian main dish or as a side dish with roasted meats or poultry.

Preheat the oven to 350°F.

Arrange cut side down in a baking pan:

3 acorn squash, halved and seeded

Add ½ inch water to the pan and cover with aluminum foil. Bake until the squashes are tender, 45 to 55 minutes. Leave the oven on. Let the squash cool. Heat in a large skillet over medium heat:

1 tablespoon butter

Add and cook, stirring, until golden, about 8 minutes:

½ cup chopped onions

Stir in:

½ cup quinoa, rinsed and drained

Heat, stirring, until toasted, about 3 minutes. Stir in:

1 cup chicken or vegetable stock

Bring to a boil, reduce the heat, and simmer, covered, for 15 minutes. Uncover and let cool slightly. Scoop out and dice the pulp of 2 squash halves. Turn the other 4 halves cut side up and season with:

½ teaspoon salt

⅛ teaspoon ground black pepper

Combine the quinoa and squash. Stir in:

¼ cup chopped hazelnuts or whole unblanched almonds, toasted

2 tablespoons chopped fresh parsley

2 tablespoons grated Parmesan cheese

Spoon into the squash cavities, distributing evenly. Sprinkle the tops with:

2 tablespoons grated Parmesan cheese

Bake until heated through, about 20 minutes.

RICE

A cook needs to know two things about rice. The first is whether or not the bran and germ are still attached. If so, it is brown rice (although in some instances, such as Thai black rice, the rice is another color.) The advantages of brown rice are its much higher fiber content and the presence of vitamins and minerals that are lost in white rice. The disadvantage is its longer cooking time and its perishability: brown rice must be refrigerated and used within a month. White rice offers two advantages: year-long shelf life and relatively quick cooking.

If rice is parboiled before the bran is removed, it retains more B vitamins. The resulting white rice is known as "converted" and takes a little more liquid and a little longer to cook than other white rice but shares the same shelf life. If rice is cooked and dried again before packaging, it becomes "instant," a less flavorful product with softer kernels but a convenience nevertheless, especially with brown rice.

The second thing is the length of the grain. A kernel of long-grain rice, brown or white, is three to five times longer than it is wide; the cooked kernels are fluffy and separate easily. Medium- and short-grain rice kernels are closer to oval in shape, less than twice as long as they are wide, and contain more amylopectin, a waxy starch molecule that makes the cooked rice denser and the kernels more apt to cohere. Short-grain rice is often called glutinous (although it has no gluten) or sticky rice in the Asian cuisines that favor it in dishes ranging from sushi to desserts. Medium- and short-grain rice, if steamed or simmered the same way as long-grain rice, need about ¼ to ½ cup less water per cup of rice and thus a few minutes less cooking time. Cooks around the world have devised myriad ways to highlight the starchy plumpness of medium and short kernels.

Numerous varieties of rice are called aromatic because they have a pronounced nutty fragrance due to a higher concentration of a natural compound found in all rice. The most famous of these is basmati, a long-grain rice, white or brown, grown in India, Pakistan, and now also the United States; it gives Indian pilafs their distinctive, and irresistible, fluffy texture and aroma. Jasmine is a long-grain white aromatic rice originally from Thailand and now grown in the United States as well; it cooks moist and tender but not fluffy, like a medium-grain rice, and has a lovely subtle perfume. Other popular American-grown aromatic rices are Texmati, white and brown, a type of basmati from Texas; Wehani, a long-grain brown variety from California; and Louisiana pecan, a white rice named for its aroma.

The best-known rices of Spain and Italy are medium-grain and much valued for their soft cooked texture. These are used for paella and risotto. The classic Spanish rice for paella comes from the province of Valencia. The Italian rices, grown in the Piedmont and Lombardy regions, include Arborio, Vialone Nano, and Carnaroli. American medium-grain rice can be substituted for these and can also be used to prepare Japanese-style rice.

Red and black rice have joined the basic white and brown on store shelves. These come in various grain sizes and may be aromatic or not. What the color does indicate, usually, is that the bran has been left on and therefore the rice will need longer cooking. Thai black rice turns purplish and sticky when cooked; it is deeply flavorful and often is cooked with coconut milk to make a pudding.

Electric rice cookers are ingenious devices that make preparing white or brown rice a snap. Most rice cookers have a large cooking chamber (often lined with a nonstick coating) that rests above an electric heating element. Most also come with a perforated insert that fits near the bottom of the cooking pot, transforming the rice cooker into a steamer for vegetables, fish, and other foods. Follow the manufacturer's instructions, but keep in mind that some rice cookers imported from Asia come with directions that assume the rice has been rinsed or soaked. When cooking dry—not rinsed or soaked—rice in a rice cooker, use ¼ to ½ cup less water per cup than you would in stovetop cooking.

Microwave 1 cup long-grain white rice with 1¾ to 2 cups water (1½ to 1¾ cups for American medium-grain) and ¼ to ½ teaspoon salt in a covered casserole on high for 5 minutes, then on medium for 15 minutes. Let stand, covered, for 5 minutes.

Microwave 1 cup long-grain brown rice with 2½ cups water (2 cups for short-grain) and ¼ to ½ teaspoon salt in a covered casserole on high for 5 minutes, then on medium-low for 40 to 45 minutes, with the shorter time for short-grain. Let stand, covered, for 5 minutes.

BASIC COOKED WHITE RICE *3 cups; 4 servings*

Use 2 cups water for soft, tender rice or 1¾ to 1⅞ cups for firmer grains. Use ¼ cup less, either way, when cooking medium-grain white rice. Do not stir except as directed, or the rice will turn gummy.

I. Bring to a boil in a medium saucepan:

1¾ to 2 cups water
1 tablespoon butter or vegetable oil (optional)
¼ to ½ teaspoon salt

Add and stir once:

1 cup long-grain white rice

Cover and cook over very low heat until all the water is absorbed, 15 to 18 minutes. Do not lift the cover before the end of cooking. Let stand, covered, for 5 to 10 minutes before serving.

II. This method is popular in the American South, Latin America, and parts of Europe.

Spread in a large, broad, shallow, heavy saucepan to a depth of only 2 or 3 grains:

1 cup long-grain or medium-grain white rice

Add just enough liquid to cover the rice by ½ inch or the thickness of your hand. Bring to a gentle boil and stir once. Cook, uncovered, over low heat until the liquid is almost absorbed, about 5 minutes. Cover the saucepan and continue to cook for 15 to 18 minutes. Do not lift the cover before the end of cooking. Let stand, covered, for 5 to 10 minutes before serving.

BASIC COOKED CONVERTED RICE

Prepare Basic Cooked White Rice, Method I, above, using converted long-grain white rice and increasing the water to 2¼ cups. Simmer for 25 minutes.

BASIC COOKED BROWN RICE *3½ cups; 4 servings*

Use 2¼ to 2½ cups water for long-grain brown rice or 2 to 2¼ cups water for short-grain brown rice; the larger amount yields softer, slightly stickier rice. Short-grain brown rice cooks a little faster than long-grain. Do not stir except as directed.

Bring to a boil in a medium saucepan:

2 to 2½ cups water
1 tablespoon butter (optional)
¼ to ½ teaspoon salt

Add and stir once:

1 cup brown rice

Cover and cook over very low heat until all the water is absorbed, 35 to 45 minutes. Do not lift the cover before the end of cooking. Let stand, covered, for 5 to 10 minutes before serving.

OVEN-BAKED WHITE RICE *4 servings*

Perfect rice every time, because the temptation to stir is not easily satisfied. (Stirring makes rice sticky.) This foolproof rice goes well with roasted chicken or broiled or baked fish.

Preheat the oven to 350°F.

Melt or heat in a 2-quart stovetop-to-oven casserole over medium heat:

1 tablespoon butter or olive oil

Add and cook, stirring, until softened, 3 to 5 minutes:

½ cup chopped onions

Add and stir until well coated:

1 cup long-grain white rice

Add:

2 cups chicken stock
¼ teaspoon salt

Bring to a boil. Cover and bake until the rice is tender and the stock is absorbed, 20 to 25 minutes. Let stand, covered, for 5 minutes before serving.

OVEN-BAKED BROWN RICE WITH MUSHROOMS *4 to 6 servings*

Brown rice and mushrooms share the same deep, earthy flavor. Serve this simple preparation topped with broccoli or a mixture of cooked vegetables as part of a vegetarian meal. Or serve as a side dish with meat or chicken.

Preheat the oven to 350°F.

Melt or heat in a 2-quart stovetop-to-oven casserole over medium-high heat:

3 tablespoons butter or olive oil

Add and cook, stirring, until the mushrooms are lightly browned, about 8 minutes:

1½ cups coarsely chopped mushrooms
½ cup chopped onions
1 clove garlic, finely chopped

Add and stir until coated:

1 cup long-grain brown rice
⅛ teaspoon ground black pepper

Add:

2¼ cups chicken or vegetable stock
¼ teaspoon salt

Bring to a boil. Cover and bake until the rice is tender and the stock is absorbed, about 45 minutes. Let stand, covered, for 10 minutes before serving.

FRIED RICE *4 servings*

Fried rice is considered snack food by the Chinese and is never served as the main course at a Chinese meal. Americans like to eat fried rice as a main dish. It is popular as much for its taste as for its rapid preparation and versatility. Remember to always begin with cold cooked rice (a mixture of part white and part brown is excellent).

The variations are endless. Add small amounts (about ½ cup) of cooked cut-up broccoli, carrots, green beans, squash, or sweet potatoes; thawed frozen green peas; diced or slivered cooked chicken or pork; or chopped uncooked or leftover cooked shrimp or flaked fish to the finished dish. For additional flavor, sprinkle with toasted sesame seeds or chopped peanuts. Drizzle with a little toasted sesame oil or soy sauce at the table.

Whisk together:

4 eggs
½ teaspoon salt

Heat a large nonstick skillet or wok over medium heat until hot enough to evaporate a drop of water on contact. Pour in and tilt the skillet to coat:

1 tablespoon vegetable oil

Heat until very hot. Add the eggs all at once and as they bubble up around the edges, push them to the center, tilting the skillet to cook the eggs evenly. Break the cooked eggs into clumps. When the eggs are set, remove to a bowl. Pour into the hot skillet and heat until hot:

2 tablespoons vegetable oil

Add and cook, stirring to coat the grains with oil, for 3 minutes:

3 to 4 cups cold cooked rice (1 to 1⅓ cups uncooked)
1 teaspoon minced peeled fresh ginger

Stir in the cooked eggs along with:

½ cup thin diagonal scallion slices

Serve immediately.

RED RICE
4 servings

At the height of tomato season, make this dish with fresh tomatoes that have been peeled and pressed through a food mill. Other times of the year, use good-quality canned tomatoes, also pressed through a food mill.

Heat in a large saucepan or deep skillet over medium heat:

2 tablespoons vegetable oil or bacon fat

Add and cook, stirring, until softened, about 5 minutes:

½ cup chopped onions

Stir in:

One 28-ounce can whole tomatoes, drained, or 2 cups chopped peeled fresh ripe tomatoes, pressed through a food mill
½ cup chicken stock

Bring to a boil. Add:

4 cups cooked long-grain rice (1⅓ cups uncooked)
½ teaspoon salt, or to taste

Stir until blended. Cook, covered, over medium-low heat until the rice has absorbed all the tomato, about 12 minutes. Uncover and cook off any excess moisture over medium-high heat, about 2 minutes. Season with:

Salt and ground black pepper to taste

HOPPIN' JOHN (CAROLINA RICE AND BEAN PILAU)
8 to 10 servings

Pilau, that is, a rice dish made with meat or vegetables, was probably brought to the Carolinas in the early seventeenth century by the Huguenots, French Protestants who came to America in order to escape persecution in their homeland. Pilau is Middle Eastern, not French, but it had come to be made in Provence during the late Middle Ages, when Muslims settled widely throughout Mediterranean Europe. When French-style Middle Eastern pilau came to America, it blended with rice dishes made by African Americans, who were experts at cooking rice. What resulted were various American pilaus—or pilafs, purlows, perlews, and so on—of which Hoppin' John is today the best known. Southerners traditionally serve Hoppin' John at New Year's, but it is delicious at any time.

Pick over and rinse:

8 ounces dried black-eyed peas (about 1¼ cups)

Turn the peas into a large ovenproof pot and add enough cold water to cover by 1 inch. Boil rapidly for 1 minute, then remove from the heat, cover, and let stand for 1½ hours. Drain the peas and rinse thoroughly. Return the peas to the pot and add:

3 cups water
1½ cups chopped onions
1 tablespoon minced garlic (optional)
4 ounces smoked ham, diced
½ teaspoon dried thyme
½ teaspoon red pepper flakes
2 large bay leaves

Simmer gently, uncovered, just until tender, 20 to 30 minutes. Drain, reserving the cooking liquid. Discard the bay leaves. Season the peas and ham with:

Salt and ground black pepper to taste

Cover and set aside. Let the pea cooking liquid settle for 5 minutes, then pour it into a 4-cup measure, discarding the residue at the bottom of the pot. Add to make 2¾ cups:

½ to 1¼ cups chicken stock

Position a rack in the center of the oven. Preheat the oven to 325°F.

Set the same pot you used to cook the peas over medium heat and add:

2 tablespoons butter
2 to 4 slices bacon, diced

Cook, stirring, until the bacon has released most of its fat and has begun to crisp. Stir in:

1½ cups long-grain rice
1 teaspoon salt

Cook, stirring to coat the grains with fat, for 1 minute. Add the pea cooking liquid and bring to a simmer. Stir once with a fork, then cover and bake until the rice has absorbed all the liquid, 20 to 25 minutes. Scatter the peas and ham over the top, cover, and return to the oven for 3 minutes. Sprinkle with:

¼ cup minced fresh parsley

Toss lightly with a fork until the rice is fluffed and all the ingredients are mixed. Cover and let stand for 10 to 30 minutes before serving. Hoppin' John can be made 1 day ahead, covered, and refrigerated. Bring to room temperature, then bake, covered and without stirring, in a 275°F oven just until warmed through.

BASIC PILAF
4 servings

Rice stirred in hot butter or oil before simmering is very flavorful and fluffy, especially if you use basmati rice. The preparation is known as a pilaf, and it traditionally calls for seasonings to be sautéed in the pot with the rice. The name can be traced to the Persian *pilau.* All kinds of variations are found in the Middle East, the Caucasus, and India.

Melt in a large saucepan or deep skillet over low heat:

2 tablespoons butter

Add and cook, stirring, until golden, about 8 minutes:

½ cup chopped onions

Add and cook, stirring, until coated, about 3 minutes:

1 cup white basmati rice

Stir in:

2 cups water or chicken stock

½ teaspoon salt (if using water)

Bring to a boil. Stir once, cover, and cook over low heat until the liquid is absorbed and the rice is tender, about 15 minutes. Do not stir. Let stand, covered, for 5 minutes before serving. Sprinkle with:

2 tablespoons chopped walnuts, toasted, or 2 tablespoons chopped fresh parsley

SPICED BROWN RICE PILAF *4 servings*

Basmati, which in Sanskrit means "Queen of Fragrance," has an alluring nutlike aroma and flavor. Between the flavor of basmati and the perfume of the cinnamon, this dish is simply irresistible.

Melt in a large saucepan or deep skillet over medium-low heat:

2 tablespoons butter

Add and cook, stirring, until golden, about 8 minutes:

½ cup chopped onions

Add and cook, stirring, for 1 minute:

1 clove garlic, finely chopped

Add:

1 cup brown basmati rice

2 tablespoons raisins or dried currants

One 2-inch cinnamon stick

Stir to combine. Add:

3 cups chicken stock

Bring to a boil. Stir once, cover, and cook over medium-low heat until the stock is absorbed and the rice is tender, about 50 minutes. Uncover and let stand for 5 minutes before serving.

TWO-GRAIN DATE PILAF *4 to 6 servings*

Rice and bulgur spiced with a cinnamon stick and topped with a few chopped dates make this recipe an especially exotic pilaf.

Melt in a large saucepan or deep skillet over medium heat:

2 tablespoons butter

Add and cook, stirring, until golden, about 8 minutes:

½ cup chopped onions

Add:

1 cup white basmati rice

1 cup bulgur or cracked wheat

One 1-inch cinnamon stick

Stir to coat with the butter. Add:

4 cups water or chicken stock

1 teaspoon salt (if using water)

Bring to a boil. Stir once, cover, and cook over medium-low heat until the liquid is absorbed and the rice is tender, about 20 minutes. Uncover and let stand for 5 minutes. Meanwhile, melt in a small skillet over medium heat:

1 tablespoon butter

Add and cook, stirring, until heated through, about 1 minute:

¼ cup diced dates

Spoon the pilaf into a serving dish and top with the dates. Serve immediately.

LENTIL AND RICE PILAF WITH TOASTED CUMIN SEEDS *4 to 6 servings*

Lentils are the fastest-cooking dried legume and, for that reason, can be cooked with white rice into an interesting pilaf. Whole cumin seeds lend a wonderful aroma to the dish. Serve as a side dish or as a main course topped with cooked vegetables.

Stir into a medium saucepan of boiling water:

½ cup lentils, picked over and rinsed

Boil, uncovered, for 10 minutes; drain. Heat in a large saucepan or deep skillet over low heat:

2 tablespoons vegetable oil

Add and cook just until sizzling, about 1 minute:

1 clove garlic, finely chopped

½ teaspoon cumin seeds

Add the lentils along with:

1 cup white basmati rice

Stir to combine. Add:

2 cups chicken stock

¼ to ½ teaspoon salt

Bring to a boil. Stir once, cover, and cook over medium-low heat until the stock is absorbed and the rice and lentils are tender, about 15 minutes. Uncover and let stand for 5 minutes. Meanwhile, toast in a small skillet over medium heat:

¼ cup chopped walnuts

Sprinkle over the pilaf and serve.

SPANISH RICE *4 to 6 servings*

This rice is delicious served with chicken or pork and, because it is oven baked, is a foolproof rice dish for any occasion.

Preheat the oven to 350°F.

Combine in an ovenproof skillet or casserole:

2 slices bacon, minced
½ cup chopped onions
½ cup chopped green bell peppers
1 clove garlic, minced

Cook, stirring, over medium heat until the onions are golden, about 5 minutes. Add:

1 cup long-grain white rice

Stir until well coated. Add:

1¾ cups chicken stock
1 cup chopped drained canned tomatoes
½ teaspoon sweet or hot paprika
¼ teaspoon ground black pepper

Bring to a boil. Stir once, cover, and bake until the stock is absorbed and the rice is tender, about 25 minutes. Uncover and let stand for 5 minutes before serving.

PERSIAN RICE

4 to 6 servings

Persian rice dishes are cooked so that there is a delicious crust on the bottom of the pot (called *tah dig*) that is lifted out and served either on top of the soft cooked rice or as a side dish. Persian rice can be prepared in a nonstick skillet so that the rice can be inverted as a large pancake with the crisp rice on top and the soft cooked rice, perfumed with spices, snuggled underneath. Persian cooks rinse the rice in several changes of water, and often soak it as well, before cooking. The secret to success here is the butter. In Persian cooking, ghee, or clarified butter, is used.

Preheat the oven to 350°F.

Bring to a boil in a large pot:

16 cups (4 quarts) water
1 tablespoon salt

Stir in:

2 cups white basmati rice
One 1-inch cinnamon stick
3 whole cloves
3 black peppercorns
¼ teaspoon cardamom seeds

Cook, uncovered, stirring occasionally, until the rice is almost tender, about 10 minutes. Drain and let stand in a sieve until ready to use. (Leave the spices in the rice.)

Melt in a large ovenproof nonstick skillet over medium heat:

8 tablespoons (1 stick) butter

Spoon off 3 tablespoons and reserve. Add to the remaining butter in the skillet:

1 cup thinly sliced onions
¼ teaspoon saffron threads

Cook, stirring, over medium heat until the onions are golden, about 8 minutes. Spread the onions in an even layer in the skillet. Stir into the cooked rice:

2 tablespoons diced dried apricots
2 tablespoons dried sweet or sour cherries or golden raisins

Spoon the rice over the onions; smooth the top of the rice with the back of a large spoon and press down very firmly to pack it. Drizzle the reserved butter evenly over the top. Cover with a double layer of aluminum foil, crimping the edges and pressing down on the top. Bake for 1 hour. Let stand, covered, for 10 minutes. Uncover and invert a large round platter over the skillet. Protecting your hands with a dish towel, turn the skillet and platter over, allowing the rice to drop onto the platter. Sprinkle with:

¼ cup chopped shelled pistachios

THAI COCONUT RICE

4 to 6 servings

Thai, or jasmine, rice is a long-grain rice with a soft, slightly sticky consistency. Often sold as street food throughout Asia, the rice is cooked in spiced coconut milk and wrapped in a banana leaf, making it a handy package—very much the Far Eastern version of fast food. Make your own coconut milk by grinding small pieces of fresh peeled coconut in a food processor with boiling water and then squeezing the liquid through a cheesecloth. Canned unsweetened coconut milk is available in many supermarkets or wherever Asian groceries are sold and is much more convenient. If using the canned coconut milk (make sure it is unsweetened), dilute it by half with water. If using domestically grown jasmine rice, there is no need to rinse it. Imported jasmine rice should probably be rinsed.

Bring to a boil in a large saucepan:

2 cups coconut milk, or 1 cup canned unsweetened coconut milk and 1 cup water
1 cup jasmine rice
1 thin slice peeled fresh ginger
¾ teaspoon salt

Stir once, cover, and cook over very low heat until the liquid is absorbed and the rice is tender, about 20 minutes. Meanwhile lightly toast, stirring, in a small skillet over medium-low heat:

⅓ cup flaked or shredded unsweetened dried coconut

Sprinkle over the cooked rice along with:

Fresh cilantro leaves (optional)

CONGEE WITH CHICKEN AND SCALLIONS

4 servings

Cook this plain, as in the first step, and you have Chinese-style breakfast porridge. Add the chicken and scallions, and you have a thick, whole-meal soup.

Bring to a boil in a large saucepan:

6 cups water
1 cup medium-grain rice
1 thin slice peeled fresh ginger
1 scallion (white part only)
1 teaspoon salt

Reduce the heat to low and cook, uncovered, stirring occasionally, until the rice is very soft and the soup is thick, 20 to 25 minutes. Stir in:

8 ounces boneless, skinless chicken breasts, thinly sliced crosswise

Cook, covered, until the chicken is no longer pink in the center, about 5 minutes. Meanwhile, lightly toast, stirring, in a small skillet over medium-low heat:

1 tablespoon sesame seeds

Discard the ginger and scallion from the soup. To serve, ladle the soup into warmed bowls and sprinkle with the sesame seeds along with:

1 tablespoon thinly sliced scallion greens

ABOUT RISOTTO

Risotto is Italy's contribution to the art of rice cooking. A technique as well as a dish, risotto exists in no other culture. Creamy yet resilient to the bite and with big round flavors, a risotto is not merely cooked, it is built. The process is simple and the guidelines few. Follow them, using the best stock, rice, and cheese possible, and prepare yourself for a treat.

SIMPLEST RISOTTO (RISOTTO IN BIANCO)

6 to 8 first-course servings; 4 to 6 main-course servings; halve recipe to serve 2

This is the easiest of all risottos to make. Even with canned stock it shines as an enticing opening to a special dinner or as a memorable one-dish meal needing only a good salad and a light dessert. Risotto takes about 20 minutes to cook once the first liquid is added.

Melt in a large, heavy saucepan over medium heat:

2 tablespoons butter or extra-virgin olive oil

Add and cook, stirring, over low heat until soft and translucent but not browned:

1 medium onion, minced

Meanwhile, simmer over medium heat:

8 cups chicken stock

Increase the heat under the onions to medium and stir in:

2 cups Italian rice or American medium-grain rice

Using broad strokes, stir the rice until it looks chalky and you can see a white dot in the center of each grain, about 3 minutes. Stir in:

½ cup dry white wine

Stir to prevent sticking as the wine is absorbed by the rice. Then start stirring in the stock, 1 cup at a time. Each cup must be absorbed before the next is added. Stir the risotto continuously to keep it from sticking. When 6 cups stock have been absorbed, add the stock ½ cup at a time and start tasting the rice. It should be tender but still a little firm to the bite, never mushy. Take the risotto off the heat when the rice still has a little more resistance than you would like. Fold in:

1 tablespoon butter

Gently fold in:

⅔ to 1 cup grated Parmesan cheese

Season with:

Salt and ground black pepper to taste

Let the risotto stand for a moment or two. Spoon the risotto into warmed soup dishes and serve immediately.

RISOTTO MILANESE

8 first-course servings; 6 main-course servings

The most famous of the numerous Italian risottos, this dish is always flavored with saffron. Use this basic technique to create a variety of risottos using leftover meats or seafood, small quantities of sauces, sausage, vegetables, or even fruits.

Combine and let stand for 10 minutes:

3 generous pinches of saffron threads
1 cup hot chicken stock

Melt in a large, heavy saucepan over medium heat:

3 tablespoons butter

Stir in:

1 medium onion, minced

Cook over low heat until soft and clear. Meanwhile, simmer over medium heat:

9 cups chicken stock

Increase the heat under the onions to medium and stir in:

1 pound Italian rice or American medium-grain rice

Cook, stirring often, until the rice is chalky in appearance, about 5 minutes. Add:

½ cup dry white wine

Stir until absorbed. Add the saffron mixture and simmer, uncovered, stirring often, until absorbed. Add the chicken stock, 1 cup at a time, and simmer and stir continuously until absorbed. (If desired, when half of the stock has been used and the rice is still quite firm, the

RULES FOR RISOTTO

Use a large, heavy saucepan and never cover the cooking risotto. Anticipate about 20 minutes' cooking time.

Use a medium-grain rice, never long-grain. First choices are Italian imports, always "superfino" grade—Arborio, Carnaroli, Vialone Nano, Roma, or Balso. Second choice is American medium-grain rice.

Add small quantities of simmering stock to the risotto and stir almost constantly.

At the end of cooking, the rice should be creamy in consistency and tender to the taste but still have a little "bite." Let the risotto stand off the heat for a few minutes before serving.

risotto can be removed from the heat and refrigerate, covered, for up to 2 days. To finish the risotto, reheat and continue.)

Add the remaining stock, 1 cup at a time, until the rice is tender but still has some "bite." It should be creamy and not stiff. Fold in:

1 to 1½ cups grated Parmesan cheese

Season with:

Salt and ground black pepper to taste

Let rest for a few minutes, then serve in warmed soup dishes. If desired, serve with:

Grated Parmesan cheese

SPRING OR SUMMER RISOTTO WITH VEGETABLES (PRIMAVERA OR D'ESTATE)

Prepare Risotto Milanese, above, adding sautéed pieces of artichoke, asparagus, peas, zucchini, onion, eggplant, broccoli, cauliflower, or green beans after folding in the Parmesan cheese. For added dimension, sauté half of the vegetables with the onion, adding the other half midway through cooking.

CLASSIC VENETIAN RICE AND PEAS (RISI E BISI)

Prepare Risotto Milanese, above, adding 2 ounces minced pancetta with the onion. Omit the saffron, but use the stock. When the rice is half cooked, add 1½ pounds chopped sugar snap peas in their pods, ½ cup coarsely chopped fresh flat-leaf parsley, and 2 tablespoons chopped fennel greens or 1 teaspoon ground fennel seeds. Finish with the cheese, 2 tablespoons butter, and a generous amount of pepper. Although usually served as a first course, this makes a fine one-dish supper.

RISOTTO WITH SEAFOOD

Prepare Risotto Milanese, above, adding chunks of fish or shellfish for the last 5 to 10 minutes of cooking. The saffron is optional. Tomato is a good addition along with parsley and other fresh herbs. Traditionally cheese is not used with fish. Fish or vegetable stock can be substituted for the chicken stock.

Another approach is to sauté chunks of seafood with flavorings (garlic, shallot, herbs, wine, etc.) until almost completely cooked, then stir this in at the end of the cooking time.

FRESH CORN RISOTTO WITH BASIL, TOMATO, AND LIME

4 to 6 servings

Make this delicate fresh corn, tomato, and basil risotto at the height of the corn season. The lime juice adds a distinctive flavor when combined with the natural acidity of the tomato and the sweet, starchy taste of the corn and the rice.

Combine:

1 cup diced seeded peeled ripe tomatoes
2 tablespoons chopped fresh basil
1 tablespoon fresh lime juice
¼ teaspoon salt, or to taste

Bring to a simmer:

5 cups chicken stock

Cut:

2 cups corn kernels from 4 or 5 large ears

Puree 1 cup of the corn kernels in a food processor. Heat in a large saucepan or deep skillet over medium heat until the foam subsides:

2 tablespoons butter, preferably unsalted

Add and cook, stirring, until translucent, about 5 minutes:

½ cup finely chopped scallions (white part only)

Add:

1½ cups Italian rice or American medium-grain rice

Stir to coat with the butter. Add:

½ cup dry white wine

Cook, stirring, until absorbed. Add 1 cup of the simmering stock and cook, stirring, over medium-low heat until the stock is absorbed. Add the remaining stock, ½ cup at a time, cooking and stirring until the liquid is almost completely absorbed before adding more. Continue adding the remaining stock, in ½-cup additions, stirring and cooking over medium-low heat, until the rice is almost tender, about 15 minutes. Stir in the reserved pureed corn and another ½ cup stock; continue to cook, stirring and adding stock as needed, until the rice is tender but with a slight firmness to the center of the grain, 5 to 10 minutes more, or longer, depending on the rice. Stir in the corn kernels and the fresh tomato mixture. Season with:

Salt and ground black pepper to taste

Spoon into warmed soup bowls and sprinkle each serving with:

Grated Parmesan cheese

LEFTOVER RISOTTO PANCAKE (RISOTTO AL SALTO)

4 servings

This large pancake of leftover risotto is prepared with Risotto Milanese, above, but this is such a great use for leftover risotto that there is really no reason not to use any risotto, providing any added chunks are not too large, causing the pancake to break when turned. It is best to use a well-seasoned or nonstick skillet, a thin spatula for turning, and plenty of butter. *Risotto al salto* is traditionally made into one large, thin pancake, which takes some skill to turn; it is easier to make more than one in smaller sizes, from silver dollars to 4- or 5-inch rounds.

Place in a large bowl:

1 to 2 cups cold leftover risotto, 260 to 261

Stir in, 1 tablespoon at a time:

1 large egg, lightly beaten

If the risotto is very soft, do not add all of the egg. Heat in a large nonstick skillet over medium-low heat until foamy:

2 tablespoons butter

Add the risotto mixture by tablespoonfuls for small pancakes or by ½- to 1-cup measures for larger pancakes. Cook, undisturbed, until the bottoms are browned and crisp, about 5 minutes. Carefully turn and brown the second side, about 5 minutes. If making small pancakes, several can be fried at once, but fry larger pancakes 1 at a time. Before serving, sprinkle the pancakes with:

Grated Parmesan cheese

PAELLA VALENCIANA

4 to 6 servings

Paella gets its name from the broad, shallow pan (paella or paellera) traditionally used to cook this classic dish, born in the Valencia region of Spain. It was originally a dish not of the seaside but of the *huertas,* or market gardens, of the interior, and it was always cooked outdoors. True paella Valenciana is made not with seafood at all, but with chicken, rabbit, several kinds of beans, and sometimes snails. More elaborate versions of the dish, including fish, shellfish, other vegetables, and sometimes pork or sausage, have become popular all over Spain and the Hispanic Caribbean—all over the world, for that matter.

Paella is made with rice similar to that used for risotto, and, in fact, risotto rices can be substituted for the authentic Valencia variety used in Spain. The method of cooking is very different from that for risotto, however: while risotto must be stirred constantly, paella should never be stirred once its ingredients have been mixed together. The best way to cook paella is outside, on a round grill. Cooking time will vary according to the intensity of heat, distance between pan and fire, and so on. Here is a genuine Valencian paella with directions for stovetop cooking.

Heat in a large paella pan or large, shallow skillet over medium heat:

¼ cup olive oil

Add and brown in batches:

1½ pounds chicken parts, cut into small serving pieces

8 ounces rabbit, cut into small serving pieces (or substitute 8 ounces chicken)

As the chicken and rabbit pieces are done, remove them to several layers of paper towels to drain. Pour off all but a tablespoon of fat from the pan, then in the remaining fat, cook, stirring often, over very low heat for about 30 minutes:

1 medium onion, chopped

3 ripe tomatoes, peeled, seeded, and chopped

Return the chicken and rabbit to the pan and stir well to coat. Pour in:

4½ cups hot chicken stock

Simmer for 10 minutes. Add:

1 cup cooked white kidney beans (about ⅓ cup dried), 275, rinsed and drained if canned

1 cup cooked butter beans

1 cup cooked green beans, preferably Italian-style flat beans

1 teaspoon fresh rosemary leaves

Salt to taste

Stir well, then stir in:

1 pound Valencia rice, Italian rice, or American medium-grain rice

Make sure the ingredients are well distributed and gently pat down the top. Cook, uncovered and without stirring, over medium-high heat until the rice is done and the liquid is evaporated, 20 to 25 minutes. If the liquid evaporates too quickly, add more hot stock as needed. Do not allow the rice to burn; however, a dark brown crust on the bottom of the pan is considered desirable. When the paella is done, let stand for 10 to 15 minutes before serving.

SHELLFISH PAELLA

Prepare Paella Valenciana, above, omitting the rabbit and rosemary and decreasing the amount of chicken to about 1 pound. With the beans, add 12 scrubbed mussels, 1 pound deveined peeled raw shrimp (preferably with tails on), 8 ounces Spanish (not Mexican) chorizo, diced (optional), 1 tablespoon sweet paprika, and 6 to 8 saffron threads, crumbled. Proceed as directed. When the paella is done, use tongs to retrieve the mussels and shrimp and arrange them on top of rice.

CHICKEN JAMBALAYA

4 servings

Jambalaya is a popular dish throughout the American South but is most often associated with the cooking of New Orleans. It is made with rice and pork, ham, chicken, shrimp, and any variety of other additions and seasonings. Jambalaya has some remarkable similarities to pilaf, and there is much discussion as to the origin of the word *jambalaya.* Some say the name derives from *jambon,* the French word for ham. There are many different styles of jambalaya and probably as many recipes as there are cooks in New Orleans.

Melt or heat in a large skillet over medium heat:

2 tablespoons butter or vegetable oil

Add and cook, turning often, until browned on all sides, about 10 minutes:

1 broiler-fryer chicken (about 2½ pounds), cut into serving pieces

Remove to a plate and season with:

Salt and ground black pepper to taste

Add to the drippings in the skillet:

1 medium green bell pepper, diced
½ cup diced celery
1 cup long-grain white rice
⅛ teaspoon ground red pepper

Stir to coat with the drippings. Stir in:

3 cups boiling water
¼ cup chopped fresh parsley
¾ teaspoon salt
¼ teaspoon dried thyme
⅛ teaspoon ground black pepper
1 bay leaf

Return the chicken to the skillet. Top with:

1 cup slivered cooked ham (about 1 ounce) or 2 ounces chorizo sausage, thinly sliced

Cook, covered, over medium-low heat until the water is absorbed and the chicken is cooked through, about 20 minutes. Cook, uncovered, until any excess moisture is evaporated, about 3 minutes.

PLAIN COOKED JAPANESE RICE (GOHAN)

6½ cups

Here is the basic recipe for cooking rice for sushi. It becomes the backdrop for most Japanese meals and is the basis for all sushi (vinegared rice) dishes. To achieve superior taste and texture, use Japanese-style short- or medium-grain rice grown in California for the Japanese market and sold in large bags in Asian markets or wherever Asian groceries are sold. The Japanese prefer their rice rinsed well, until the water runs clear. Adding *kombu* (kelp) to the cooking pot will enhance the natural flavor of the rice, which is particularly important for making sushi. If using an electric rice cooker, follow the manufacturer's instructions.

Place in a bowl with cold water to cover:

3 cups Japanese-style short- or medium-grain rice

Stir vigorously to remove the excess starch. Drain the rice and rinse again in fresh cold water until the water runs clear. This usually takes several rinsings. Drain the rice well after the final rinsing. Place the drained rice in a large pot along with:

3 cups plus 2 tablespoons cold water
One 1-inch-square piece *kombu* (kelp), optional

Let the rice stand in the water for 10 minutes. Cover the pot with a tight-fitting lid and bring to a boil over high heat. It is best not to remove the lid to check on the progress; instead, rely on other clues: you can hear the bubbling noises and see the lid begin to dance. This should take about 5 minutes. Reduce the heat to medium and continue to cook until the water is absorbed, about 5 minutes. Increase the heat to high again for 30 seconds to dry off the rice. Remove the pot from the heat and let stand, still tightly covered, for at least 10 minutes or up to 30 minutes. This final step makes more tender grains of rice.

To make less rice, use the following amounts:

1 cup rice and 1 cup plus 1½ tablespoons water yields a generous 2 cups
2 cups rice and 2 cups plus 2 tablespoons water yields a generous 4 cups
2½ cups rice and 2½ cups plus scant 2½ tablespoons water yields 5¼ cups

RYE

The stuff of robust breads and whiskey, rye has a surprisingly mild identity as a whole grain, labeled rye berries or simply rye grain. The long gray-brown kernels take time to simmer to chewy softness, but not as much time as wheat or triticale berries. They usually are not soaked before being cooked, although they can be to hasten the process. Rye is a good source of thiamine, iron, phosphorus, and potassium and has been considered a weight-loss aid because it retains water, swells more than other grains in the stomach, and digests more slowly, prolonging the feeling of fullness. Mix cooked rye berries into white rice for complementary flavor and chewy contrast. Stir some into rye bread dough or rye bread stuffings for a more substantial texture. Substitute rye berries in any wheat berry salad or in Garlic-Sesame Triticale Salad, below, and serve warm as a bed for roasted poultry.

For 4 servings (3 cups), bring 1 cup rye berries, 3 cups water, and ½ teaspoon salt to a boil. Reduce the heat to low and simmer, covered, until some berries have burst and all are tender, 45 to 60 minutes. Drain.

Microwave 1 cup rye berries, 2¾ cups water, and ½ teaspoon salt in a covered casserole on high for 10 minutes, then on medium-low for 45 to 60 minutes.

RYE BERRY SALAD WITH ROASTED PEPPER DRESSING

4 to 6 servings

Cook until tender, above:

½ cup rye berries

Meanwhile, mash together to form a paste:

1 clove garlic, peeled
¼ teaspoon salt

Remove to a blender or food processor and add:

One 7½-ounce jar roasted red peppers, drained
6 tablespoons olive oil
2 tablespoons fresh lemon juice, or to taste
2 tablespoons white wine vinegar
1 shallot, chopped
1 tablespoon ground cumin
Salt and ground black pepper to taste
Pinch of ground red pepper

Puree until smooth. Drain the rye berries in a colander, transfer to a large bowl, and add just enough dressing to moisten. Stir to coat. Stir in:

1 large carrot, peeled and diced
2 small celery stalks with leaves, diced
6 to 8 radishes, diced
1 medium zucchini, diced
½ fennel bulb, diced
1 small yellow bell pepper, diced
½ small red onion, finely diced
2 tablespoons minced fresh cilantro
Salt and ground black pepper to taste

Add enough additional dressing to coat. Taste and adjust the seasonings. Serve at room temperature.

TEFF

The world's tiniest grain, teff has one of the biggest flavors. It smells like molasses while cooking, and if mixed with butter, it tastes like cake. Only the size of celery seeds, the iron-rich kernels have a high surface-to-center ratio, which makes them high in fiber. Teff is best known as the staple grain of Ethiopia, where it is turned into a spongy flat bread called *injera.* In the United States it is sold as a flour, in a pasta, and as a whole grain. The tiny kernels naturally clump together, making the cooked grain dense. Serve it as a breakfast porridge, topped with warmed milk, or use it as a "seasoning" grain—cooking it and then stirring it into cooked brown rice, millet, or barley for rich taste. Food writer Nao Hauser suggests that teff, cooked like porridge, with three parts water to one part grain, can be spread while warm in a baking pan, refrigerated, cut into squares or triangles, and baked or fried like Polenta Toast, 249.

For 4 servings (3½ to 4 cups), toast 1 cup teff in 2 tablespoons butter or vegetable oil in a large saucepan over medium heat, stirring often. Gradually stir in 2½ to 3 cups boiling water and add 1 teaspoon of salt. Reduce the heat to low and simmer, covered, until tender, about 15 minutes. Use the smaller amount of liquid for firmer grains and the larger amount for a porridge texture.

To microwave, heat 1 tablespoon butter or vegetable oil in a flat-bottomed 3-quart casserole on high for 1 minute. Stir in 1 cup teff; microwave, uncovered, on high for 3 minutes, stirring after 2 minutes. Stir in 2⅓ to 2¾ cups water and 1 teaspoon salt. Microwave, covered, on high for 5 minutes, then on medium for 15 minutes. Let stand for 5 minutes. Stir well with a fork to fluff, and let stand, uncovered, for 5 minutes more.

TRITICALE

A hybrid of wheat (*triticum* in Latin) and rye (*secale* in Latin), triticale was invented in Scotland over a century ago. Triticale flour has more gluten than rye but not nearly as much as wheat, and so it is best mixed with wheat flour in bread recipes. Triticale berries are a little larger than wheat berries and lighter in taste but can be cooked the same way, 266, and substituted in wheat berry recipes. Toast them first in a skillet or in the oven, to bring out more of their subtle flavor.

GARLIC-SESAME TRITICALE SALAD *4 servings*

Rye, wheat, or spelt berries can be substituted here.

Cook in a large pot of boiling salted water until tender, about 1 hour:

1 cup triticale berries

Drain and remove to a large bowl. Heat in a small skillet over medium heat until hot but not smoking:

3 tablespoons vegetable oil

Add and cook, stirring, until very fragrant, 2 to 3 minutes:

2 scallions, minced
1 tablespoon minced peeled fresh ginger
1 or 2 cloves garlic, minced

Stir in:

½ teaspoon toasted sesame oil
Salt to taste
Red pepper flakes to taste

Stir into the triticale berries. Taste and adjust the seasonings. Serve warm or at room temperature, garnished with:

½ cup coarsely chopped dry-roasted cashews or peanuts

WHEAT

Wheat, the grain of ancient Mediterranean civilizations, came to dominate the world's crops with the farming of North America's Great Plains and is essential, because of its uniquely stretchable protein, to risen breads, our "staff of life."

Whole kernels, with bran and germ intact, are called wheat berries. They hold all the nutrients wheat has to offer. Wheat is classified as winter or spring wheat, depending on when it is sown, and soft, hard, or durum, depending on its protein content. These factors affect the flour much more than the berries, but most wheat berries sold are hard red winter wheat. Two exceptions are spelt and kamut, both examples of the thousands of types of wheat that have been neglected over the millennia in favor of others better suited to bread making. Spelt has a magnificent wheaty flavor; a similar Italian grain, called *farro* (actually yet another old wheat whose English name is emmek), is softer and therefore faster cooking and stickier than American-grown spelt. Kamut cooks up to yellow-beige kernels—much larger than those of other wheats—for a very attractive and delicious contrast with other wheat berries or grains in pilafs and salads. All wheat berries can be used interchangeably. Adjust the cooking time for the desired finished texture.

For very firm berries for salads, cook, without presoaking, in boiling water for about 1 hour. For softer, chewier berries for salads or pilafs, either double the cooking time or presoak overnight. Discard the soaking water only if the grain is dirty; otherwise, use it as part of the cooking liquid. You can mix cooked wheat berries with other raw grains and cook them longer or bake them in stuffings, and they will remain chewy. The sturdy texture of the berries makes them a welcome addition to salads and cereals made with softer grains, as well as to salads made with beans.

Milled wheat berries are called cracked wheat. If the milling is coarse, the wheat can be cooked like white rice and used in salads and pilafs; if finely ground, the wheat can be added for texture to bread doughs and batters. Either way, cracked wheat tastes better toasted.

When wheat berries are triple-processed—steamed, dried, and then milled—the result is bulgur, which retains much of the nutrition of whole wheat. Bulgur cooks up flavorful and fluffy as a pilaf but does not need to be cooked at all, just softened in boiling water.

Traditional couscous is coarsely ground semolina—a hard-wheat flour used for pasta—that is mixed with water and salt into a dough and then rolled into tiny balls that steam to fluffiness. This form of pasta is a mainstay of several North African cuisines and is also found in Sicily and other Mediterranean areas. The couscous sold in the United States has usually been presteamed and dried before packaging; quick-cooking couscous can be either reconstituted in boiling water for the sake of speed or steamed the traditional way for a fluffier texture. Although it is technically a pasta, couscous is interchangeable with bulgur and other tiny grains in many soups and salads, and so we include it here.

Wheat germ contains almost as much fiber as wheat bran and more vitamins and minerals. Consider adding a teaspoon or two per serving of toasted wheat germ to any breakfast cereal and to doughs and batters, as it tastes mildly sweet and is high in the antioxidant vitamin E. Because there is oil in the germ, it must be refrigerated after opening. To toast wheat bran, stir constantly in a heavy skillet over medium heat until it is slightly darkened and smells nutty.

Microwave 1 cup wheat berries of any kind with 3¾ cups water in a 3-quart covered casserole on high for 10 minutes, then on medium for 5 minutes. Let stand, covered, for 1 hour. Stir in ½ teaspoon salt. Microwave, covered, on high for 10 minutes, then on medium-low for 45 to 55 minutes.

For wheat berries with brown rice, microwave ½ cup wheat berries (kamut and spelt are especially good) with 1¾ cups water; microwave and let stand for 1 hour as directed above. Stir in ¾ teaspoon salt, 1 cup long-grain brown rice, and 2 cups water; microwave, covered, on high for 5 minutes, then on medium-low for 45 minutes.

Microwave 1 cup bulgur, 2 cups water, and ½ teaspoon salt in a covered casserole on high for 5 minutes, then on medium for 15 minutes. Let stand, covered, for 5 minutes and fluff with a fork. Microwave the same way ½ cup bulgur and ½ cup long-grain or basmati white rice, stirring in ¼ cup dried currants if desired.

To microwave whole-wheat or spelt couscous (quick-cooking couscous doesn't need any cooking—it should only be reconstituted, see above), heat 1½ cups salted water in a covered casserole to a rolling boil, about 5 minutes on high. Stir in 1 cup whole-wheat or spelt couscous and microwave, covered, on medium-low for 4 minutes. Let stand, covered, for 10 minutes and fluff with a fork. If desired, boil ¼ cup dried currants with the salted water.

BASIC COOKED WHEAT, KAMUT, OR SPELT BERRIES

1½ cups

Whole-grain berries swell into tender but slightly chewy morsels when they are cooked. Cover the berries with plenty of water and simmer gently for 1½ to 2 hours. Berries that have been soaked for at least 8 hours cook in half the time.

Soak in water to cover by 2 inches:

½ cup wheat, kamut, or spelt berries

Let stand overnight. Drain if needed and add to:

4 cups boiling salted water

Gently simmer, uncovered, until tender but still chewy, 45 to 60 minutes. Drain. Use in salads, soups, cereals, stuffings, or pilaf, alone or mixed with other grains.

WHOLE-GRAIN BERRIES WITH SAUTÉED ONIONS AND DRIED FRUITS

4 servings

Fully cooked wheat, kamut, and spelt berries make an excellent side dish or stuffing for poultry when tossed with golden sautéed onions and plumped diced dried fruits. Add a cinnamon stick to the mixture for the final heating, and the warm, sweet, spicy aroma will permeate the grains. Use any mixture of grains; even wild rice, brown rice, Wehani, or other blends will work well as part of the mixture. This is particularly good with roasted pork.

Melt or heat in a large skillet over medium heat:

2 tablespoons butter or olive oil

Add and cook, stirring, until golden, 8 to 10 minutes:

1 cup chopped onions

Add:

1 cup diced mixed dried fruits, such as dried apricots, pitted prunes, golden or dark raisins, dried currants, dried cherries, and/or dried cranberries

Stir to blend. Stir in:

3 cups cooked wheat, spelt, or kamut berries, above, or a combination of cooked berries, cooked millet, 252, and cooked brown and/or wild rice

One 2-inch cinnamon stick

½ cup chicken stock or water

Cover and cook, stirring once or twice, over low heat until the flavors are blended, about 10 minutes. Season with:

¼ teaspoon salt

⅛ teaspoon ground black pepper

If desired, sprinkle with:

¼ cup chopped blanched almonds, walnuts, or pecans, toasted

BASIC COOKED BULGUR

Because bulgur is steamed before it is dried and cracked, it can be softened and made ready to eat by soaking in boiling water without cooking. This method is often used for salads. Bulgur is available in fine, medium, and coarse grinds. Here are three methods for preparing basic bulgur:

I. Place 1 cup bulgur in a bowl. Stir in 2½ cups boiling water and ½ teaspoon salt. Cover with an inverted plate and let stand until the liquid is absorbed, about 30 minutes. Drain; press out the excess moisture or squeeze dry in a dish towel. The bulgur will be slightly chewy and good in salads. Yield: 3 cups.

II. Bring 2 cups water or stock to a boil in a small saucepan. Stir in 1 cup bulgur and ½ teaspoon salt. Cook, covered, over low heat for 15 minutes. Drain if needed. The bulgur will be soft and fluffy. Yield: 3 cups.

III. Melt 1 tablespoon butter in a small saucepan over medium heat. Add 1 cup bulgur and cook, stirring, until lightly toasted and coated with butter, about 1 minute. Add 2 cups water or stock, and ½ teaspoon salt if needed. Bring to a boil. Cover and cook over low heat until the liquid is absorbed and the bulgur is tender, about 20 minutes. The bulgur will be soft and slightly sticky. Yield: 3 cups.

TRADITIONAL STEAMED COUSCOUS

About 3 cups; 4 servings

Steaming is the traditional North African way to cook couscous, with the couscous removed from the steamer and fluffed several times. This recipe calls for fluffing with the fingertips only once but still yields feather-light couscous. Line the steamer with dampened cheesecloth if the perforations are too large. Any kind of couscous can be used in this recipe.

Rinse in a sieve with tap water:

1 cup couscous

Let stand for 10 minutes. Rub the damp couscous between your fingertips to break up any clumps. To cook the couscous, use a *couscoussière* or two-tiered vegetable steamer. Half fill the compartment (bottom) with water; do not let it touch the perforated steamer above. Lightly brush the inside of the steamer (or the cheesecloth liner) with vegetable oil. Bring the water to a boil. Place the moistened couscous in the steamer. After 20 minutes of cooking, remove the couscous to a platter and spread it out with a fork. Let cool slightly. Sprinkle with:

¼ cup cold water

½ teaspoon salt

Lightly oil your fingertips and use them to gently fluff the couscous, loosening any clumps and separating the grains. Return the couscous to the steamer. Cover and cook for 20 minutes more. Remove to a platter, cover with aluminum foil, and let stand for 10 minutes before serving.

QUICK COUSCOUS

About 3 cups; 4 servings

Not as light and fluffy as steamed couscous but very quick and convenient. Quick-cooking whole-wheat and spelt couscous should be stirred into the boiling liquid in the pan, covered, cooked over low heat for 5 minutes, and then allowed to stand for 10 minutes.

Place in a medium bowl:

1¼ cups quick-cooking couscous

Pour in:

1½ cups boiling water or stock

Cover with an inverted plate and let stand for 10 minutes. Uncover and fluff with a chopstick or fork.

WINTER VEGETABLE COUSCOUS

10 to 12 servings

This dish is delicious served with harissa, the Moroccan chili-pepper condiment. Ras El Hanout is added both to the vegetables and to the couscous.

Heat in medium skillet until moderately hot but not smoking:

¼ cup olive oil

Add and cook, stirring, until softened and just beginning to brown:

3 portobello mushrooms, wiped clean, gills removed, and thickly sliced

Remove from the heat and set aside. Heat in a large, heavy pan until moderately hot but not smoking:

¼ cup olive oil

Add:

1 red onion, quartered

1 celery root, cut into large chunks

2 white turnips, peeled and quartered

1 rutabaga, peeled and cut into 2-inch pieces

2 leeks (white and green parts), cleaned thoroughly and cut into ¼-inch-thick slices

1 medium head cauliflower, separated into florets

½ teaspoon dried thyme

½ teaspoon dried marjoram

Stir in:

1 tablespoon Ras El Hanout, 1062

Cook, covered, over medium heat until partially cooked, about 10 minutes. Stir in:

3 cups vegetable stock

Continue cooking until the vegetables are tender but not overdone, 20 to 30 minutes. At the end of the cooking, the flavors of the vegetables should have blended together well, but each one should hold together and be distinct. During the last 10 minutes of cooking, stir in the reserved portobello mushrooms along with:

2 cups cooked chickpeas (about ⅔ cups dried), 273, rinsed and drained if canned

Season with:

Salt and ground black pepper to taste

Rinse in a sieve with tap water:

5 cups couscous

Stir in:

2 tablespoons Ras El Hanout, 1062

Salt to taste

Let stand for 20 minutes, then rub the couscous through your hands to separate the grains. Ten minutes before serving, stir in:

2 cups vegetable stock

Cook, covered, over medium heat to steam and heat through. To serve, mound the couscous in the center of a large platter and surround it with the vegetables. Garnish with:

10 fresh mint leaves

BAKED ZUCCHINI STUFFED WITH COUSCOUS

4 servings

Vegetables stuffed with grains (couscous, bulgur, rice, or any of the many grains available) are very popular throughout the Mediterranean region. The flavors (cinnamon, dried fruit, garlic, olive oil, and pine nuts) in this stuffed zucchini dish suggest the cuisines of Morocco, Tunisia, Greece, Sicily, and Turkey.

Preheat the oven to 400°F. Lightly oil a baking dish.

Trim the stems and halve lengthwise:

2 medium zucchini

Sprinkle with:

Salt and ground black pepper to taste

Place the zucchini cut side down in the baking dish. Bake until the cut side is lightly browned, 10 to 12 minutes. Reduce the oven temperature to 350°F. Let the zucchini cool slightly. Using a teaspoon, scoop out the centers of the zucchini, leaving four ¼-inch-thick shells. Finely chop the pulp. Heat in a large skillet over medium heat:

1 tablespoon extra-virgin olive oil

Add and cook, stirring, until golden, about 5 minutes:

¼ cup chopped onions

Add the chopped zucchini along with:

⅓ cup quick-cooking, whole-wheat, or spelt couscous
1 clove garlic, finely minced

Cook, stirring, until coated with the oil. Stir in:

¾ cup chicken stock
1 tablespoon dried currants
½ teaspoon ground cinnamon

Bring to a boil. Cover and cook over low heat for 5 minutes. Uncover and let cool to room temperature. Stir in:

1 tablespoon pine nuts, toasted

Spoon the couscous mixture into the zucchini boats, dividing it evenly. Arrange in the baking pan and cover with aluminum foil. Bake until heated through, about 20 minutes. Serve hot.

COUSCOUS WITH ZUCCHINI AND CHERRY TOMATOES

6 servings

Heat in a large saucepan over medium-low heat:

2 tablespoons olive oil

Add and cook, stirring, until golden, about 5 minutes:

1 medium onion, chopped

Add and cook, stirring, for 1 minute:

2 cloves garlic, minced

Stir in:

2½ cups chicken or vegetable stock
1½ pounds medium zucchini, trimmed and cut into ½-inch-thick slices

Bring to boil. Cook until the zucchini is tender but not soft, 3 to 5 minutes. Stir in:

2 tablespoons chopped fresh thyme, or 2 teaspoons dried

Stir in:

1½ cups quick-cooking couscous
1 tablespoon butter or olive oil

Remove from the heat. Cover and let stand until the stock is absorbed, about 10 minutes. Fluff the couscous with a fork. Stir in:

24 cherry tomatoes

Serve.

COUSCOUS SALAD

4 to 6 servings

Combine in a large bowl:

1 box (about 1¾ cups) quick-cooking couscous
2¼ cups boiling water

Cover and let stand until the water is absorbed and the couscous has expanded, about 15 minutes. Fluff with a fork. As soon as the couscous is cool enough to handle, rub your hands with olive oil and gently rub the couscous between your fingertips to make sure all the lumps are out. Stir in:

½ cup diced peeled carrots
½ cup diced celery
1 tablespoon grated lemon or lime zest
2 tablespoons chopped fresh mint
2 tablespoons chopped fresh parsley
2 teaspoons ground cumin
Salt and ground black pepper to taste

Whisk together until smooth:

¼ cup olive oil
3 tablespoons lemon juice
1 teaspoon ground turmeric

Add to the salad, stir well to moisten, and serve warm or chilled.

WILD RICE

Only very distantly related to regular rice, wild rice is native to the Great Lakes region and holds a rather regal place among other New World foods. Because it is unique in its complex taste of nuts and wine, cooks put up with its forbidding price and unpredictable cooking time. No longer wild, but cultivated, wild rice may be hand- or machine-harvested and is priced higher or lower accordingly. The price also rises with the length of the kernels; the longest are the most prized. The kernels are heated and partially hulled after harvest; the amount of this processing, as well as the length of the kernel, affects how much water and time will be needed for cooking. The strong flavor and chewiness of wild rice make it, like wheat berries, a good match with any kind of rice or barley.

BASIC COOKED WILD RICE

3½ cups; 4 to 6 servings

It is a good idea to rinse wild rice before cooking to remove any bits of hull that sometimes cling to the grain after processing. Cooking time will vary depending on the rice. Wild rice is done when most of the kernels are cracked, revealing the fluffy white interior. If the water evaporates before the rice is done, simply add more water, about ¼ cup at a time.

Combine in a large saucepan:

3 cups water
1 cup wild rice, rinsed and drained
1 teaspoon salt (optional)

Bring to a boil. Stir once, cover, and simmer over low heat until the water is absorbed and the rice is fluffy and tender, 35 to 55 minutes. Let stand, covered, for 10 minutes before serving.

WILD RICE WITH SAUTÉED MUSHROOMS

4 to 6 servings

Use any combination of exotic and/or cultivated mushrooms in this simple side dish. Try shiitake, cremini, oyster, hen-of-the-woods, porcini, or any combination of mushrooms available, or simply use button mushrooms.

Prepare:

Basic Cooked Wild Rice, above

About 10 minutes before the rice is done, heat in a large saucepan or deep skillet over medium-high heat:

¼ cup olive oil

Add and cook, stirring, until lightly browned, 5 to 8 minutes:

2 cups sliced button or cremini mushrooms
1 cup sliced shiitake or porcini mushroom caps
1 cup chopped onions

Add and cook, stirring, until combined, about 2 minutes:

¼ cup finely chopped fresh parsley
2 cloves garlic, finely chopped
1 teaspoon fresh thyme leaves, or ¼ teaspoon dried

Stir in the cooked wild rice along with:

Salt and ground black pepper to taste

Cover and cook over medium heat until heated through, about 5 minutes. If desired, sprinkle with:

¼ cup sliced unblanched almonds, toasted

WILD RICE AND BARLEY

4 to 6 servings

Barley and wild rice or other grains that take about an hour to cook can be used interchangeably in this simple dish.

Heat in a large saucepan or deep skillet over medium heat:

2 tablespoons extra-virgin olive oil

Add and cook, stirring, until lightly browned, about 5 minutes:

10 ounces mushrooms, wiped clean and chopped
1 cup chopped onions

Add and cook, stirring, for 1 minute:

½ cup wild rice
½ cup pearl barley
1 clove garlic, finely chopped (optional)
1 teaspoon fresh thyme leaves, or ½ teaspoon dried

Stir in:

4 cups chicken or beef stock
¼ to ½ teaspoon salt

Bring to a boil. Cover and cook, without stirring, until the stock is absorbed, 50 to 60 minutes. Let stand, covered, for 5 minutes.

BEANS & TOFU

Jazz great Louis Armstrong sometimes closed his letters with "Red beans and ricely yours"—an image as big and warm as his smile.

Ham-simmered red beans spooned over rice is a signature dish of New Orleans, where Armstrong grew up. If he had come from Boston, he might have signed off with baked beans and brown bread; from Mexico, with black beans and tortillas; from India, with dal and basmati; from Italy, with pasta e fagioli.

An excellent source of protein, vitamins, minerals, and fiber, beans are what nutritionists like to call a "powerhouse"—a food that is unusually rich in nutrients but relatively low in calories. Because they are digested slowly, and thus raise blood sugar very gently, they are sometimes recommended for diabetics. Their high fiber content, both water soluble and nonsoluble, has been linked to lower blood cholesterol. And it is suspected that beans contain some compounds that protect against cancers.

"Heirloom" beans, old types that were previously spurned by commercial growers, are now being revived. As dramatic as some of these look, however, with their bright colors and vivid patterns, they are all related to the kidney beans, black beans, great Northern beans, and others that have long dominated American bean fields. Most are variations of the common bean, or *Phaseolus vulgaris*—descendants of the beans that can be traced back eight thousand years to Central American origins. Sharing the same genus, but a different species, are lima beans, a historical contemporary of the common bean first grown in the Andes. Another branch of the *Phaseolus* genus yields scarlet runner beans and their kin, which bear flashy red flowers. All these Western Hemisphere natives were unknown to the rest of the world before Columbus.

Six types of legumes—a category that includes peas and lentils as well as beans—were cultivated for thousands of years on other continents. Those native to the Near East are lentils, peas, chickpeas, and fava beans, which are also known as broad beans. Those that have long been grown in China are mung beans (actually native to India), which are ancestors of black-eyed peas and soybeans. Now an enormous American commercial crop, soybeans are processed mostly into other products and rarely eaten straight from the pot. See Soybeans, 287, for a separate discussion.

ABOUT SOAKING BEANS

Whether or not to soak beans before cooking is a hot topic today. Many noted food professionals, whose opinions we hold in high regard, argue that fresh dried beans do not benefit from presoaking before cooking. Heating the legumes to boiling and then simmering them until they swell with water and soften can be done in one continuous process. After years of investigative research, Russ Parson, noted food authority and writer, believes that unsoaked legumes produce a richer, thicker broth and a meatier cooked bean with incomparable flavor. As for the digestive issues of nonsoaked beans, his research proves that soaking beans removes only 5 to 10 percent of the gas-producing sugars that can cause digestive problems for some people. He believes that if Americans ate beans on a more regular basis, they wouldn't be adversely affected by those sugars at all. In order to ensure success with this method, the beans must be of high quality and fresh. Given the limited availability of high-quality fresh beans, presoaking the beans first is kinder, both to the bean and to the cook. Not only does it save anywhere from 30 minutes to over an hour on the stove, but it also treats the seed coat more gently than steady simmering, so that the shape of the bean holds without breaking. At high elevations, where simmering times will be extended by the lower temperature of the boiling water, soaking for up to 24 hours is good time-saving insurance.

Before you prepare any legumes, spread them in a pan or large colander and remove any tiny stones that may have accompanied them out of the field. Then rinse the beans very well under cold water, raking them with your fingers to get rid of any clumps of dirt.

Our preferred soaking method is to heat the soaking water, which hastens the swelling of the beans. For a gentle quick-soak, pour boiling water over the beans to cover by 2 inches, cover, let stand until the beans have swelled to at least twice their size and have absorbed most of the water, and then drain, discarding the soaking liquid. This will take at least an hour and possibly longer, but the beans will remain firm and keep their shape when cooked.

Another way to soak beans is to place them in a large bowl or pot and add water to cover by at least 2 inches. Cover and let stand for up to 24 hours; refrigerate to prevent fermentation if the kitchen is very warm. The beans will swell to triple their dried size. Drain well and discard the soaking liquid.

A third method, which risks breaking some bean skins, is to place the beans in a saucepan, add water to cover by 2 inches, and heat to boiling; then reduce the heat and simmer for 2 minutes. Let stand, covered, for 1 hour. Or microwave 1 pound beans and 4 cups water in a covered 3- to 4-quart casserole on high to boiling, 12 to 17 minutes, and then on medium for 2 minutes. Stir and let stand, covered, for 1 hour. Either way, rinse and drain the beans before the final cooking.

ABOUT COOKING BEANS

To cook beans, place them in a large pot and add cold water to cover by 2 inches. Bring to a boil over high heat; skim off the foam that rises to the surface. Reduce the heat to low and cover; simmer, stirring and skimming occasionally, until the beans are tender. Do not boil rapidly or the abrasion will loosen the bean skins. If the pot threatens to boil over, partially remove the cover. Cook beans uncovered if you have seasoned the liquid and want some of it to evaporate to concentrate the flavor or to thicken the dish. Baking is an alternative to boiling, especially with black, red, and white beans (see the recipes); the benefits are better shape and creamier texture.

Beans readily absorb seasonings from water. A classic way to add flavor is to bury one or two smoked ham hocks or a ham bone in the beans; smoked turkey can be substituted. Add a couple of bay leaves and an onion studded with a half- dozen cloves to the ham or turkey, and the beans will taste smoky and slightly spicy. Simmer beans with chopped onions and carrots to sweeten them; use at least a cup of each with a pound of beans, because the water will dilute their impact. Whole allspice and a piece of cinnamon stick are especially good with black or red beans; wrap spices in cheesecloth or place in a tea ball for easy removal. Whole bay leaves and dried thyme or rosemary bring nice herbal notes to white and lima beans. The possibilities are infinite and come with only a few caveats. First, expect that any salty ingredients, such as smoked meats, will slow the cooking a little; do not add plain salt until near the end, when the beans have already softened. Do not add tomatoes, citrus, vinegar, molasses, or any other acidic ingredients until near the end, after the beans are tender; acid, like salt, prevents the beans from softening. This principle is conveniently applied in reverse when you make Boston baked beans: the precooked beans do not turn mushy when baked for hours in the oven because the added molasses and tomatoes keep the skins firm.

If you want relatively firm beans, for a salad or side dish or to use in recipes that call for further cooking without acidic ingredients, remove a few beans and pinch them for tenderness at the low end of the cooking time range suggested in About Bean Varieties, 273. If you want very soft beans for a soup, you may decide to cook them longer than suggested. If so, be sure there is enough water in the pot to keep the beans from drying out. Add more as needed, for the beans will not continue to soften without more water to absorb.

ABOUT PRESSURE-COOKING BEANS

The pressure cooker performs brilliantly when extracting all the flavor from a smoked ham hock or smoked turkey part cooked with beans. It will also cook beans much faster than is otherwise possible. Put the two together, with enough water to cover, and you can have saucy, seasoned beans in as little as 10 to 15 minutes of cooking at 15 pounds pressure. Pressure-cooker manufacturers commonly recommend two precautions for beans: do not fill the cooker more than half full, and add 1 tablespoon vegetable oil per cup of beans to prevent frothing. To these we add another warning: be skeptical of the cooking times suggested in your owner's manual, as they can be much too long. For firm texture, cook presoaked beans at 15 pounds pressure for one-fifth to one-quarter of the minimum cooking time listed in About Bean Varieties, 273; you can always simmer the beans longer without pressure if needed. Some cooks do not bother presoaking beans that will go into the pressure cooker and just add 5 minutes (or 10 minutes for chickpeas and other long-cooking types) to compensate; if you choose to follow suit, remember to use at least 4 cups water and 1 tablespoon oil per cup of beans. But we do not recommend this practice, as it is likely to split the bean skins, diminishing the texture of the beans and increasing the risk of clogging the steam vent.

ABOUT MICROWAVING BEANS

Microwave cooking also saves time. Microwave to boiling and then soak 1 pound beans, or soak them for up to 24 hours, as directed in About Soaking Beans, 270. Then place the rinsed and drained beans in a large microwave-safe bowl or 3- to 4-quart casserole with 3 cups water (3½ cups for chickpeas, which may need to cook a little longer) and any desired herbs and spices; add ½ cup chopped onions and/or carrots if desired. Be aware that beans are apt to boil over; to help prevent this, add 2 teaspoons vegetable oil and cover the bowl tightly with 2 layers plastic wrap. Microwave the beans on high to boiling, 12 to 17 minutes, then on medium for 30 to 45 minutes, stirring twice. Begin checking for doneness at 20 minutes if the beans are the fast-cooking type and you want them firm for salad. If cooking black-eyed peas or black beans without presoaking, microwave only 1 cup at a time; proceed as for other beans, using 3 cups water. Microwave 1 cup presoaked beans the same way but reduce the water to 2½ cups and reduce the cooking times on both high and medium by about one-third.

The microwave method is slightly different for lentils and split peas. Because there is no presoaking, these legumes need to cook with almost twice as much water per cup as presoaked beans. So it is more convenient to cook only about 1 cup at a time, to allow enough room in the bowl for the water to boil; the same holds true for unsoaked black-eyed peas and black beans. Combine 1 cup brown or green lentils or green or yellow split peas and 2½ to 3 cups water or chicken stock (using the smaller amount of water for firm texture) in a large bowl or 3- to 4-quart casserole. Tightly cover with plastic wrap and microwave on high for 10 minutes, then on medium for about 20 minutes for firm texture or 30 minutes for very soft texture. Let stand for 10 minutes. With faster-cooking red or yellow lentils, microwave the same way, but reduce the time on medium to 3 minutes; let stand, covered, for a full 20 minutes for further absorption of water. Because lentils and split peas have thin skins or no skins at all, you can salt the water; other seasonings that work well are a piece of cinnamon stick, bay leaves, chili powder, and chopped onions.

One pound of dried beans equals 2 to 2½ cups. Each 1 cup of dried beans cooks to 3 cups, or 4 servings. Cooked beans can be refrigerated for up to 2 days, or a day longer if the refrigerator is kept very cold. Store with some of the cooking liquid for reheating on the stovetop. If reheating in the microwave, cover only loosely to prevent the skins from splitting. Cooked beans freeze well for up to 6 months.

ABOUT SUBSTITUTING CANNED BEANS

Canned beans can be substituted cup for cup in recipes that call for cooked beans, but they are almost always softer and less flavorful. Since brands vary in quality, it is worth trying different ones. Rinsing canned beans improves the taste a little and removes excess salt. To rinse well, put the beans in a large sieve set in a pot or bowl and let cold water run over the beans until the pot is filled, raking the beans with your fingers, and drain, repeat, and then drain well. For a full 2 cups cooked beans, you will need to start with a large can, 19 or 20 ounces. The smaller 15- or 16-ounce can holds only 1½ to 1¾ cups.

ABOUT SPROUTING BEANS

The most fundamental bean transformation is sprouting, or turning the bean and its embryo into the beginnings of a plant. Almost all organically grown beans, if not too old, can be sprouted, but do not sprout fava beans, for there may be some risk in eating these raw. Lentils and adzuki and mung beans are good choices, because small beans tend to sprout more readily than large ones. Small amounts of sprouts can be eaten raw—in a sandwich or sprinkled over a salad, for example—but if you are using more than a large handful, heat them briefly to improve digestibility. You can add them toward the end of cooking to other vegetables, grains, and stir-fries.

To make 1½ cups sprouts, start with 3 tablespoons dried beans. Seeds, such as alfalfa, wheat, and radish (but never tomato or potato), can be sprouted the same way, following these steps:

1. Pick over and rinse the beans. Place the beans in a large bowl and cover with about 2 inches warm (not hot) water. Let stand for up to 24 hours; then drain and rinse.
2. Place the beans in a sterile 1-quart glass jar. Cover the jar with a double layer of cheesecloth (or a finer-weave cloth if you are sprouting very small seeds, such as mustard) and secure with a rubber band.
3. Rinse the beans twice a day by filling the jar with cool water and draining it off through the cheesecloth. Be sure to drain well, as water left standing in the jar can cause mold.
4. Pale shoots should appear within 5 days (or a few days longer with some vegetable seeds). They are ready to harvest when about an inch long. Before harvesting, place the jar in the sun for a few hours to encourage the shoots to produce chlorophyll. Not all beans will sprout; discard those that do not. See Bean Sprouts, 346, for storage and nutrition information.

ABOUT BEAN VARIETIES

Look for shiny beans of uniform size and color when buying dried beans. Faded color indicates age, lack of uniformity means they will cook unevenly, and tiny pinholes are evidence of insect damage. Be aware that the colors and markings on some beans will likely fade as the bean simmers and swells with water. Dried beans can be stored in airtight packaging or covered jars in a cool, dry place away from light for up to 6 months—or a year if conditions are perfect.

Adzuki Beans: Also called aduki or azuki beans, these small, claret red, mild-tasting beans are used to make the red bean paste used in Chinese buns and other sweets. They add color contrast to grain salads, and can be substituted for small red beans, although they are more fragile in texture and much lighter in taste. Their flavor is faintly reminiscent of black-eyed peas. Both adzukis and black-eyed peas are in the Mung Bean family. Simmer, covered, for 30 to 40 minutes.

Anasazi Beans: These kidney bean relatives were cultivated by the Anasazi natives of the American Southwest a thousand years ago. Their medium to small oval shape is colored deep burgundy and spotted with white. They turn dark pink when cooked and can be used in any red bean recipe. Simmer, covered, for 30 to 40 minutes.

Appaloosa Beans: Another red kidney bean relative, these have black and brown spots on a light background, like Appaloosa ponies. The color darkens and markings fade with cooking. Use in red bean recipes. Simmer, covered, for 1 to 1½ hours.

Black Beans: See the black bean recipes. Simmer soaked or unsoaked beans, covered, for 30 to 60 minutes.

Black-eyed Peas: See the black-eyed pea recipes; also see Vegetables, 344, for fresh. Simmer soaked or unsoaked beans, covered, for 30 to 60 minutes.

Calypso Beans: A black bean hybrid, the calypso is a medium-sized white bean with a large black splotch that fades slightly with cooking. Substitute for white beans or in black bean salads. Simmer, covered, for 30 to 40 minutes.

Cannellini Beans: See the white bean recipes. Simmer, covered, until tender with a little bite, about 30 minutes.

Chickpeas: See the chickpea recipes. Simmer, covered, for 1½ to 2 hours.

Christmas Limas: See the lima bean recipes. Simmer, covered, for 1 to 1½ hours.

Cranberry Beans: Putty colored with burgundy markings, these very flavorful kidney bean kin turn pinkish brown when cooked. They are variously known as October beans, shelly or shellout beans, Roman beans, and, in Italy, *borlotti.* Use in red bean or white bean recipes; see Vegetables, 344, for fresh. Simmer, covered, for 45 to 90 minutes.

European Soldier Beans: These oval ivory-colored beans are distinguished by a reddish dappling along one side that is said to resemble a toy soldier. The markings remain after cooking. Use in white bean and kidney bean recipes. Because the skins tend to split, simmer gently, covered, for about 45 minutes.

Fava Beans: See the fava bean recipes; also see Vegetables, 344, for fresh. There are two ways to prepare fava beans for cooking: either boil gently in water to cover for 15 minutes, or cover with plenty of cold water and let stand for up to 24 hours. Drain, then lift off the skins with your fingertips or a small paring knife. Simmer the skinned beans, covered, until tender (some beans will become mushy), 25 to 60 minutes.

Flageolets: Dried immature kidney beans favored in France, flageolets are medium, slender ovals ranging in color from white to light mint green. They retain their shape and color after cooking. Use in white bean recipes. Simmer, covered, until tender with a little bite, 25 to 30 minutes.

French Navy Beans: A type of navy bean with a rounded egg shape and a light green ridge along one side, these are interchangeable with the larger marrow bean. Use in white bean recipes. Simmer, covered, for about 40 minutes.

Great Northern Beans: See the white bean recipes. Simmer, covered, for 1 to 1½ hours.

Jackson Wonder Beans: Medium, flat ovals, these start out coral brown with reddish whorls and turn reddish brown when cooked. They are a type of kidney bean developed in Atlanta in the 1880s by Thomas Jackson. Use in red bean recipes. Simmer, covered, for about 45 minutes.

Lentils: See the lentil recipes. No soaking needed. Simmer green or brown lentils for 20 to 30 minutes. Simmer Beluga lentils for 10 to 20 minutes. Simmer red or yellow lentils for 5 to 8 minutes; they do not hold their shape and are best spooned over rice or used in soup.

Lima Beans: See the lima bean recipes; also see Vegetables, 344, for fresh. Simmer, covered, for 50 to 90 minutes.

Marrow Beans: A classic baking bean, the marrow is medium sized, oval, and ivory; it remains firm yet creamy after cooking. Use in white bean recipes. Simmer, covered, for 35 to 45 minutes.

Mung Beans: Small, round mung beans are most often encountered as bean sprouts, but Indian cooks use mung beans, whole or split, with skins or without, in soups and sauces. Skinless, split mung beans, called *moong dal,* can be found in Indian groceries and cooked as dal, 284. Mung bean flour is used to make cellophane noodles. The whole bean is commonly green with a yellow interior but can also be yellow, brown, or black. No soaking needed. Simmer whole beans for about 1 hour.

Navy Beans: See the white bean recipes. Simmer, covered, for 1½ to 2 hours.

Peas, Whole and Split: See the split pea recipes. Soak whole peas but not split peas. Simmer, covered, for 35 to 60 minutes.

Pigeon Peas: A staple of many Caribbean cuisines, these are related to black-eyed peas, which are cousins of mung beans, but have their own earthy flavor. Pigeon peas, also called *gandules* or *gungo* beans, are used fresh and dried in soups and stews, and are often mixed into well-seasoned rice. They are small and light gray to yellow in color, with tough skins. Simmer, covered, for 50 to 90 minutes.

Pink Beans: See the red bean recipes. Simmer, covered, for 1 hour.

Pinto Beans: See the red bean recipes. Simmer, covered, for 50 to 60 minutes.

Rattlesnake Beans: A kidney bean hybrid named for the snakelike way its pod coils around the vine, the rattlesnake bean is medium to small, with brown markings that pale but remain visible after cooking. Use in red bean recipes, especially chili. Simmer, covered, for 40 to 45 minutes.

Red Kidney Beans: See the red bean recipes. Simmer, covered, for 1 to 1½ hours.

Rice Beans: These are related to kidney beans but look like fat grains of rice. They are mild but very slightly bitter, like pine nuts, and fit well in casseroles, salads, or soups, especially those with delicate, creamy flavors. Simmer, covered, for 30 to 50 minutes.

Scarlet Runner Beans: Large mauve beans with purple-black markings, scarlet runners are named for their showy red flowers. Their color deepens when they're cooked, but the markings remain. Popular in Europe, scarlet runners are wonderful tossed with fruity olive oil, fresh herbs, scallions, and a touch of vinegar. Use them instead of cranberry or pinto beans; also see the red bean recipes. White emergo beans, also called sweet white runners, and black runner beans are cousins and can be used interchangeably. Simmer, covered, for about 1 hour.

Small Red Beans: See the red bean recipes. Simmer, covered, for 1 to 1½ hours.

Steuben Yellow-eye Beans: These medium, cream-colored beans hold their shape and retain their distinctive caramel splotch after cooking. Like navy beans, their kin, they are excellent baked. Use in white bean recipes. Simmer, covered, for 40 to 60 minutes.

Swedish Brown Beans: Relatives of the kidney bean, these medium, caramel-colored beans became popular in Sweden as good bakers that retain their character when combined with assertive flavors and hold their color when cooked. Use instead of great Northern, navy, or pinto beans. Simmer, covered, for 30 to 45 minutes.

Tepary Beans: Cultivated since ancient times in central Mexico, tepary beans are small but full of flavor. They are usually tan or white but can be gold, black, or speckled and retain their color during cooking. Substitute in recipes that call for navy, pinto, or black beans, according to the color of the bean; tepary beans are especially appropriate in recipes with Mexican or Southwest seasonings. Simmer, covered, for 40 to 60 minutes.

Tongues-of-Fire Beans: Related to cranberry beans, tongues-of-fire are medium, plump, oval beige beans with maroon markings that turn dusky during cooking. Called *borlotti lingua di fuoco* in Italian, they are often found in highly seasoned Italian and Portuguese dishes and are good for baking. Substitute for cranberry or pinto beans. Simmer, covered, for 40 to 50 minutes.

Trout Beans: Also known as Jacob's Cattle beans and, in Germany, as *forellen,* the word for trout, these reveal their kidney bean kinship in their shape but are white to pale purple in color and mottled with darker purple markings that fade somewhat with cooking. Use instead of pinto or pink beans. Simmer gently, covered, as the skins are thin, for 45 to 60 minutes.

White Kidney Beans: See the white bean recipes. Simmer, covered, for 1 to 1½ hours.

BLACK BEANS

From Mexico to Cuba to Brazil, black beans, also called turtle beans, signify the rich flavors of Latin American cooking. So identified are they with Hispanic cuisines that they are often called *frijoles negros,* "black beans" in Spanish. They have a wonderful earthiness that stands up to lots of onions and garlic, chili peppers and spices, and smoked meats. Medium sized, with a white dot along one edge, they hold their black color in cooking and color the liquid too. Because they are thin skinned, they soften to thick-soup consistency if cooked long enough. For the same reason, they cook quickly and should be watched carefully if you want firm beans for a salad. They can be mixed with chopped mangoes or papayas, white onions, and chili peppers to make a salsa or can be substituted in chili recipes. They cook more evenly and break up less if not soaked.

CLASSIC BLACK BEANS (FRIJOLES NEGROS)

6 servings

These are delicious served with nothing more than a spoonful of sour cream or yogurt and some diced avocados, but they are also very good served in warm tortillas, as a topping for nachos, over warm rice, or thinned with stock and served as a soup garnished with cilantro leaves. Pinto, pink, kidney, and navy beans can be substituted for the black beans.

Pick over and rinse:

1 pound dried black beans (about 2½ cups)

Drain. Heat in a large saucepan over medium heat:

3 tablespoons vegetable oil or bacon drippings

Add:

1 medium onion, diced

Cook, stirring often, until deep golden brown, about 10 minutes. Stir in the beans along with:

8 cups water
1 large sprig fresh epazote (optional)
1 fresh jalapeño pepper or dried chipotle pepper, halved and seeded (optional)

Remove any beans that float. Bring to a boil. Reduce the heat to medium-low and simmer, partially covered, until the beans are thoroughly tender, about 1 hour. Stir the beans regularly and add water as needed to keep the liquid a generous ½ inch above the level of the beans. Season with:

Salt and ground black pepper to taste

Simmer for another 10 to 15 minutes for the beans to absorb the seasoning, then remove from the heat. Serve hot.

BRAZILIAN BLACK BEANS

6 servings

The texture of this spicy Brazilian dish falls in between a soup and a stew. Cook it down if you prefer it thicker.

Pick over and rinse:

2 cups black beans

Drain the beans and transfer to a soup pot. Add:

4 cups water

Bring to a boil, reduce the heat, and simmer, partially covered, stirring occasionally, for 1½ hours. Meanwhile, bring a medium saucepan of water to a boil. Pierce in several places with a fork:

8 ounces hot Italian sausage (optional)

Add to the pot and boil until an instant-read thermometer inserted in the center of a sausage registers 160°F, about 45 minutes. Drain, rinse with cold water, and slice into ¼-inch-thick rounds. Set aside. Heat in a medium skillet over medium-low heat:

¼ cup olive oil

Add:

1 onion, chopped
1 green bell pepper, chopped
4 cloves garlic, minced

Cook until the vegetables are tender but not brown, 7 to 10 minutes. Add:

1 teaspoon ground cumin
¾ teaspoon red pepper flakes
¾ teaspoon ground cardamom

Stir and cook for 1 minute, remove from the heat, and add to the beans after they have cooked for 1½ hours. Cook until the beans are very tender, about 30 minutes more. Add:

¾ cup orange juice
¼ cup dry sherry
1 to 2 teaspoons salt, or to taste
Ground black pepper to taste

Cook for 15 minutes more, or longer if desired. Garnish with:

Sour cream

BLACK BEANS AND RICE *4 servings*

In the Spanish-speaking Caribbean, this classic is known as *Moros y Cristianos,* or Moors and Christians; the black beans supposedly represent the dark-skinned Moors, who ruled much of Spain for centuries. Leftover cooked black beans can be used to make this dish.

Heat in a large saucepan over medium heat:

2 tablespoons olive oil

Add:

1 cup chopped onions
2 cloves garlic, finely chopped
1 habanero or other fresh chili pepper, seeded and chopped, or ¼ teaspoon red pepper flakes, or more to taste

Cook, stirring, until tender, 5 to 8 minutes. Stir in:

1 cup diced tomatoes (optional)
2½ cups cold water
1 cup long-grain rice
1 teaspoon salt

Bring to a boil. Stir in:

2 cups cooked black beans (about ⅔ cup dried), 273, rinsed and drained if canned, or leftover Classic Black Beans, 275

Cover and cook over medium-low heat until the water is absorbed and the rice is tender, about 20 minutes. Remove from the heat and let stand, covered, for 10 minutes before serving.

REFRIED BEANS *6 servings*

A classic Mexican side dish. The beans are easier to mash if they are warm.

Heat in a large skillet over medium-high heat:

2 tablespoons vegetable oil or bacon drippings

Add:

1 medium white onion, chopped

Cook, stirring often, until deep golden brown, about 10 minutes. Add:

4 cloves garlic, minced

Cook, stirring, for 1 minute. Add with a slotted spoon 1 cup at a time:

4 cups undrained Classic Black Beans, 275, or cooked black beans (about 1⅓ cups dried), 273, undrained if canned

Mash each addition of beans to a coarse puree with a potato masher or the back of a large spoon before adding the next cupful. Stir in:

1 cup cooking liquid or water

Cook, stirring often, over medium to low heat until the beans are a little soupier than you would like to serve them—they will thicken as they sit. The whole mashing and cooking process will take 10 to 15 minutes. Season with:

Salt to taste

Serve warm with:

Crumbled queso fresco, feta, or grated Parmesan cheese
Tortilla chips

WILD CARIBBEAN BLACK BEAN CHILI *8 to 10 servings*

To the traditional chili seasonings of cumin and chili powder, this Caribbean-inspired black bean version adds the tang of citrus and the blistering floral heat of the habanero pepper.

Pick over and rinse:

4 cups dried black beans

Drain. Combine the beans in a large pot with water to cover by 2 inches. Bring to a boil. Reduce the heat to low and simmer, partially covered, until almost tender, about 1 hour. Drain. Heat in the same large pot over medium heat until hot but not smoking:

¼ cup vegetable oil

Add:

4 medium onions, finely diced

Cook, stirring occasionally, until just starting to brown, 8 to 10 minutes. Add:

¼ cup minced garlic
1 to 2 tablespoons minced habanero peppers or 6 to 8 tablespoons minced fresh jalapeño peppers

Cook, stirring, for 1 minute. Add, stir together well, and bring to a simmer:

¼ cup chili powder
¼ cup ground cumin
2 tablespoons sugar
2 teaspoons salt
2 teaspoons ground black pepper
1½ cups fresh orange juice
¾ cup fresh lime juice
3 teaspoons grated orange zest
2 teaspoons grated lime zest
One 28-ounce can crushed tomatoes
6 cups water

Stir in the reserved black beans. Return to a simmer, cover, and reduce the heat to low. Cook, partially covered, checking occasionally and adding more water as needed, until the beans are just soft to the bite, 1½ to 2 hours. Adjust the seasonings and serve, garnished, if desired, with:

Sour cream
Chopped fresh cilantro
Minced scallions
Lime wedges for squeezing

BLACK-EYED PEAS

Black-eyed peas, or their cousins cowpeas, are members of the mung bean family. They have a fuller vegetable flavor than most beans. A small black dot, which remains visible after cooking, names the cream-colored beans, which are also known as black-eye Susans and are very closely related to yellow-eye and crowder peas. Soaking is not necessary, because black-eyed peas have thin skins. If you wish to substitute fresh or frozen black-eyed peas for dried, use triple the cup amount called for and cook just until the beans are tender, 15 to 30 minutes, depending on the maturity and whether they are frozen.

WARM BLACK-EYED PEAS AND GREENS

4 servings

Beans and greens are combined in cuisines all over the world. This particular dish is inspired by two Southern specialties—collards cooked with salt pork and black-eyed peas cooked with a ham hock.

Combine in a large pot:

1½ cups dried black-eyed peas, drained and rinsed
1 smoked meaty ham hock (about 12 ounces)
1 small whole onion
1 small carrot, peeled
1 leafy celery top
1 bay leaf
1 clove garlic, peeled
6 cups water

Bring to a boil. Reduce the heat and simmer, covered, until the peas are tender, about 45 minutes. Drain, reserving about 1 cup of the cooking liquid. Discard the bay leaf, onion, garlic, and celery. Return the peas to the pot along with the reserved cooking liquid. Shred the meat from the ham hock and add the meat to the peas. Cut the carrot into ½-inch chunks and add to the peas. Stir in:

1 head escarole, curly endive, collard greens, or Swiss chard, washed, dried, and coarsely chopped

Bring to a boil. Reduce the heat to medium and simmer, covered, until the greens are tender, 10 to 15 minutes. Stir in:

1 tablespoon red wine vinegar
½ teaspoon salt, or to taste
¼ teaspoon ground black pepper

Serve warm or at room temperature.

CHICKPEAS

Chickpeas seem indestructible. They come out of a can firmer than other beans, hold up well in stews and salads, and can withstand grinding to make Falafel, 278, or baking for a pop-in-your-mouth snack. They are also known as garbanzos and ceci beans; a smaller variety is sold skinless and split as *chana dal* in Indian groceries and can be used instead of split peas to make dal, 284. Chickpeas are a constant in Mediterranean cuisines, from Middle Eastern hummus to Moroccan couscous, imparting a mild nutty flavor to all.

CURRIED CHICKPEAS WITH VEGETABLES

4 servings

This simple skillet dish makes a perfect meatless entrée.

Heat in a large skillet over medium heat until sizzling:

¼ cup vegetable oil
2 teaspoons cumin seeds

Add:

1 tablespoon minced peeled fresh ginger
1 tablespoon minced garlic

Cook, stirring, over low heat for 1 minute; do not brown. Stir in:

2 teaspoons curry powder

Cook for 1 minute. Stir in:

1¾ cups cooked chickpeas (about ⅔ cup dried), 273, rinsed and drained if canned
2 cups ½-inch cubes peeled sweet potatoes
2 cups cauliflower florets
1 cup 1-inch pieces green beans
1 cup chicken stock
½ to 1 teaspoon salt
Ground black pepper to taste

Cover and cook over medium heat until the vegetables are tender, about 10 minutes. Stir together:

1 cup yogurt
2 tablespoons all-purpose flour

Add to the vegetables along with:

1 tablespoon finely chopped fresh jalapeño peppers

Cook, stirring, over low heat until heated through; do not boil. Toast in another skillet over medium-low heat:

2 tablespoons shredded dried coconut, preferably unsweetened

Sprinkle over the vegetables. Top with:

¼ cup chopped roasted unsalted cashews or peanuts

COUSCOUS WITH CHICKPEAS *4 servings*

Heat in a large skillet over medium heat:

3 tablespoons olive oil

Add:

1 cup sliced blanched almonds

Cook, stirring, just until lightly golden, 2 to 3 minutes. Add:

3 cloves garlic, finely chopped

Cook, stirring, for about 1 minute. Stir in:

1 teaspoon sweet or hot paprika
1 teaspoon ground cumin
1 teaspoon ground coriander
½ to 1 teaspoon hot red pepper sauce

Cook until heated through, about 1 minute more. Stir in:

2½ cups chicken or vegetable stock or water
2 cups cooked chickpeas (about ⅔ cup dried), 273, rinsed and drained if canned
1 cup chopped raisins or whole dried currants

Bring to a boil and stir in:

1¼ cups quick-cooking couscous

Cover, remove from the heat, and let stand for 5 minutes. Fluff the couscous with a fork. Season with:

Salt and ground black pepper to taste

Garnish with:

¼ cup chopped fresh parsley or cilantro

FALAFEL *4 servings*

Falafel—the original "veggie burger"—is popular street food in the Middle East and New York City. The beans are soaked, ground, and fried rather than boiled.

Pick over, rinse, and soak, 270:

1¼ cups dried chickpeas

Drain thoroughly. Place in a food processor and finely chop. Add:

½ cup chopped onions
¼ cup packed fresh parsley leaves
2 cloves garlic, chopped
2 teaspoons ground cumin
1½ teaspoons salt
½ teaspoon coriander seeds, crushed, or ½ teaspoon ground coriander
½ teaspoon baking soda
¼ teaspoon ground red pepper

Process until the mixture is coarsely pureed. Remove to a bowl and stir in:

2 tablespoons all-purpose flour

With wet hands, form the chickpea mixture into 4 patties, each about 3 inches in diameter. Let stand for 15 minutes.

Meanwhile, preheat the oven to 350°F.

Pour into a deep skillet:

½ inch vegetable oil

Fry the chickpea patties until golden on both sides, about 4 minutes each side. Drain on paper towels. Stir together:

¼ cup tahini
¼ cup cold water
1 tablespoon fresh lemon juice
Pinch of salt

Wrap in aluminum foil:

4 pita breads

Heat in the oven until warmed, about 10 minutes. Open one edge of each pita bread and distribute among the pockets:

2 cups thinly sliced crisp lettuce (such as romaine or iceberg), washed and dried
4 thin tomato slices

Add a falafel to each pita and drizzle the tahini sauce over the falafel. Add:

Hot red pepper sauce to taste

OVEN-ROASTED CHICKPEAS *4 servings*

Coated with olive oil and garlic and oven-roasted until golden brown, these chickpeas are great as a snack, tossed in a salad, or sprinkled over rice pilaf.

Preheat the oven to 350°F.

Toss to coat and combine:

2 cups cooked chickpeas (about ⅔ cup dried), 273, rinsed and drained if canned
¼ cup olive oil, preferably extra virgin
2 cloves garlic, finely minced

Spread in a 13 × 9-inch baking pan. Bake, stirring often, until the chickpeas are golden, 30 to 40 minutes. Sprinkle with:

½ teaspoon salt

Serve warm or at room temperature.

FAVA BEANS

Dried fava beans present many obstacles. Their tough skins, if not removed, keep the beans from softening unless boiled for several hours; they have a hint of bitterness, unlike the sweet mildness of common beans; and they are indigestible to some people, particularly those of Mediterranean background, who carry a genetic sensitivity to the toxicity of the undercooked bean and the plant's pollen. Yet dried fava beans, also called broad or horse beans, are beloved for their bitter-edged, winy taste—somewhat reminiscent of olives—and dense texture. The dried bean is large, flat, and reddish brown; a smaller variety, called *ful,* is used in the famous Egyptian dish of garlic- and lemon-seasoned beans called *ful medames.* After peeling and cooking, dried favas do not hold their shape and so are commonly served as a spread or puree. Do not substitute cooked dried for fresh fava beans, which are much milder and firmer.

FAVA BEAN PUREE *4 servings*

Spread this bean puree on coarse or toasted bread, use as a dip for pita toasts or raw vegetables, or spoon onto crisp greens as a salad. The celery, parsley, lemon, olive oil, and garlic marry well with the distinctively earthy taste of the fava beans. Lima or white beans can be substituted, but they will need to be cooked a bit longer.

Pick over, rinse, and soak, 270:

1¼ cups dried fava, lima, or white kidney beans

If using fava beans, use your fingertips or a small paring knife to lift off the tough outer skins. Combine the beans in a large saucepan with water to cover by 2 inches. Stir in:

1 clove garlic, halved
1 bay leaf
½ teaspoon fresh oregano leaves, or ¼ teaspoon dried
½ teaspoon fresh thyme leaves, or ¼ teaspoon dried
¼ teaspoon red pepper flakes

Bring to a boil. Reduce the heat to low and cook, partially covered, until the beans are very tender, 30 to 45 minutes (up to 1½ hours if using lima beans). Drain and let cool slightly. Discard the bay leaf. Combine the beans with:

1 cup diagonally sliced celery
¼ cup coarsely chopped fresh parsley
3 tablespoons extra-virgin olive oil
1 tablespoon fresh lemon juice
1 clove garlic, finely minced
½ teaspoon salt
⅛ teaspoon ground black pepper

Stir with a fork until blended and the beans are coarsely mashed.

LENTILS

Whole lentils are thin skinned, require no soaking, and cook relatively quickly. The olive-drab lentils sold everywhere are sometimes called green, other times brown, and are actually shades of both; they cook to a soft texture and taste. French green lentils (Le Puy are the finest example) are about half the size of the more common lentils, are much darker green, and have a deeper flavor. They are cooked the same way as common lentils but remain firmer, making them a good choice for salads. Beluga lentils are tiny and black like caviar and deeply flavored; they cook in about half the time of other lentils, hold their shape, and offer a novel appearance on the plate. More colorful and very quick cooking are red (which turn golden when cooked) and yellow lentils; both of these are skinless and, whether whole or split, dissolve into a puree as they cook.

BASIC COOKED LENTILS *6 to 8 servings*

Vary seasonings by adding a pinch of dried thyme and/or oregano, a chopped carrot, a leafy green celery top, or even a slice of fresh ginger. Plainly cooked lentils make a perfect side dish, or you can use them in salads and side dishes, combined with cooked vegetables and/or rice if desired. The yield from 1 pound (2½ cups) dried lentils is about 7½ cups cooked. The recipe can be halved.

Combine in a large saucepan:

1 pound brown or green lentils (about 2½ cups), picked over and rinsed
8 cups water
½ small onion
1 clove garlic, peeled
1 bay leaf

Bring to a boil. Reduce the heat and simmer, uncovered, until the lentils are tender, 20 to 30 minutes. Drain and let cool. Remove the onion, garlic, and bay leaf. Season with:

Salt and ground black pepper to taste

Serve or reserve for another recipe.

SESAME STIR-FRIED LENTILS AND VEGETABLES *4 to 6 servings*

Lentils are used in this recipe much as plain cooked rice would be used in fried rice or in a skillet dish of rice heated with vegetables. Serve over rice for a meatless dinner.

Toast in a small skillet over medium heat for about 1 minute:

1 tablespoon sesame seeds

Place in a vegetable steaming basket over boiling water:

1 cup diagonally sliced peeled carrots
2 cups broccoli florets
1 cup ½-inch cubes yellow squash
1 cup trimmed snow peas

Cover and steam until crisp-tender, about 5 minutes. Rinse with cool water to stop the cooking. Heat in a large skillet over medium-high heat:

2 tablespoons vegetable oil

Add:

½ cup ½-inch pieces red bell peppers

Cook, stirring, for about 2 minutes. Add:

1 tablespoon finely chopped garlic
1 tablespoon finely chopped peeled fresh ginger
¼ teaspoon red pepper flakes (optional)

Cook, stirring, until sizzling, about 30 seconds. Add the steamed vegetables along with:

3 cups cooked brown or green lentils (about 1 cup dried), 274
½ cup thinly sliced scallions
3 tablespoons soy sauce
2 teaspoons toasted sesame oil

Cook, stirring, just until heated through, about 3 minutes. Sprinkle with the toasted sesame seeds. Serve hot.

LENTILS WITH SPINACH AND SOY SAUCE

4 to 6 servings

For the best flavor, cook 1 cup lentils as directed for Basic Cooked Lentils, 279, using the same seasonings and 4 cups water.

Heat in a large saucepan or deep skillet over medium-low heat:

2 tablespoons olive oil

Add:

1 cup diced peeled carrots

Cook, stirring, until tender, about 10 minutes. Add:

1 clove garlic, finely minced

Stir to blend. Add:

3 cups cooked brown or green lentils (about 1 cup dried), 274
One 12-ounce bunch or one 10-ounce bag spinach, trimmed, washed, and dried
1 tablespoon soy sauce

Stir well, cover, and cook over low heat until the spinach is wilted, 3 to 5 minutes. Serve with:

Hot cooked rice

LENTILS WITH TURKEY AND GREEN OLIVES

4 to 6 servings

This recipe was given to us by Gordon Hamersley, one of Boston's outstanding chefs. It is a dish that is great for stretching just a little meat a long way and is also delicious with duck legs in place of the turkey.

Preheat the oven to 350°F.

Have ready:

3 turkey drumsticks (about 2 pounds)

Sprinkle with:

Salt and ground black pepper to taste

Heat in a large, nonreactive, ovenproof skillet over medium-high heat:

2 tablespoons vegetable oil

Add the drumsticks to the skillet and cook until browned on one side, about 10 minutes. Turn and brown the other side, about 5 minutes more. Remove to a platter and pour off all but 2 tablespoons of the fat. Add:

1 medium onion, chopped

Cook, stirring, just until softened, about 3 minutes. Return the turkey to the skillet and add:

2 cups dry white wine

Sprinkle with:

½ cup water
1 tablespoon chopped fresh thyme

Cover and bring to a boil. Bake in the oven until the turkey is tender, about 1½ hours. Meanwhile, melt in a large saucepan over medium heat:

1 tablespoon butter

Add:

2 medium carrots, peeled and diced
1 medium celery stalk, diced
1 medium leek (white and tender green parts), cleaned thoroughly and diced

Cook, stirring occasionally, just until softened, about 5 minutes. Stir in:

3 cups brown or green lentils, picked over and rinsed
10 cups water

Bring to a boil. Reduce the heat and simmer, partially covered, until the lentils are tender, about 30 minutes. Drain. Remove the drumsticks to a plate, cover with aluminum foil, and keep warm. Add to the skillet:

3 cups coarsely chopped spinach, trimmed, washed, and dried
1 cup pitted brine-cured green olives, chopped
1½ tablespoons fresh lemon juice

Cook over medium heat until the spinach is wilted, about 6 minutes. Stir in the lentils. Season with:

Salt and ground black pepper to taste

Spoon the lentil mixture into a large, shallow bowl, arrange the turkey on top, and serve.

COTECHINO WITH BRAISED LENTILS

6 servings

This is a New Year's celebration dish from northern Italy, made with juicy cotechino (an Italian fresh pork sausage) and lentils that can be braised ahead.

Bring to a gentle simmer in a pot large enough to hold the sausage:

12 cups water

Pierce in several places with a fork:

One 1½- to 2-pound cotechino sausage

Add to the pot and adjust the heat so the water stays just below a simmer. Cook, covered, until an instant-read thermometer inserted in the center of the sausage registers 160°F, about 45 minutes. Turn off the heat and keep warm. Meanwhile, bring to a boil in a large saucepan:

10 cups water

Add:

1 pound brown or green lentils (about 2½ cups), picked over and rinsed

Reduce the heat and simmer, partially covered, until barely tender, about 20 minutes. While the lentils cook, heat in a large skillet over medium heat:

3 tablespoons extra-virgin olive oil

Add:

1 medium red onion, minced
1 medium carrot, peeled and minced
1 small celery stalk with leaves, minced
1 large bay leaf

Cook, stirring, until golden brown, about 10 minutes. Stir in:

1 large clove garlic, minced
2 teaspoons fresh marjoram leaves

Cook for 30 seconds. Stir in:

One 14- to 16-ounce can whole tomatoes, drained and crushed
1 cup chicken stock

Cook over medium-high heat until very thick, 10 to 15 minutes. Drain the lentils, stir into the tomato mixture, and cook until tender, about 10 minutes. Season with:

Salt and ground black pepper to taste

Spread the hot lentils in a shallow mound on a serving platter. Cut the hot sausage into ¼-inch-thick slices and arrange the slices over the lentils. Serve very hot.

LENTILS AND TOMATO SAUCE WITH ELBOW MACARONI AND FRIED ONIONS

6 to 8 servings

This recipe is adapted from a popular Syrian and Egyptian dish often called *rishta*. The name refers to thin homemade noodles, but this version calls for dried macaroni.

Heat in a large skillet over medium-high heat:

3 tablespoons olive oil

Add:

3 cups diced onions

Cook, stirring, until the onions are dark golden brown, about 20 minutes. Remove half of the onions and reserve. Stir into the remaining onions:

2 cloves garlic, minced

Cook for 1 minute. Stir in:

1½ cups brown or green lentils, picked over and rinsed
3 cups water

Cover and bring to a boil. Reduce the heat to medium-low and cook until the lentils are tender, about 25 minutes. Stir in:

One 28-ounce can whole tomatoes, with juice
1 teaspoon ground cumin
½ teaspoon ground coriander
¼ teaspoon ground allspice

Cover and cook for 10 minutes. Uncover and simmer, stirring to break up the tomatoes, until the mixture is thickened, about 10 minutes. Season with:

1 teaspoon salt
¼ teaspoon ground black pepper

Meanwhile, cook in plenty of boiling salted water until tender but firm, about 10 minutes:

2 cups elbow macaroni or ditalini

Drain. Quickly dry the pasta cooking pot and add the reserved onions along with:

½ teaspoon cumin seeds

Cook, stirring, over medium-high heat until the onions are sizzling. Add the drained macaroni and stir to combine. Taste and adjust the seasonings. To serve, spoon the macaroni into individual bowls and top with a ladleful of the spiced lentils. Sprinkle with:

Red pepper flakes to taste

LIMA BEANS

Dried limas display a softer and milder side of the firm, pale green, frozen limas we tend to eat more often. Small lima beans, also called baby limas or sieva beans, are actually a different species from the large ones, which are also known as butter beans or Fordhook limas. The large limas can be used in any white bean recipe, and the size makes them good in stews and in mixtures of beans for soups and chilies. For a change of pace from the whiteness of dried limas, find Christmas limas, a large bean with brownish red mottling that remains visible after cooking. Do not substitute cooked dried limas for fresh or frozen ones, because the taste and texture are considerably different.

ANNA'S LIMA BEANS *8 servings*

This dish is the creation of Anna Amendolara Nurse, a New York cooking teacher.

Pick over, rinse, and soak, 270:

1 pound large dried lima beans

Drain. Combine in a large saucepan with water to cover by 2 inches. Bring to a boil. Reduce the heat and simmer, covered, until the beans are almost tender, 30 to 50 minutes. Drain, reserving 2 cups of the cooking liquid (add water if necessary to make 2 cups).

Preheat the oven to 300°F.

Combine the beans and cooking liquid in a 3- to 4-quart casserole along with:

6 cups water
1 large onion, chopped
8 ounces thick-cut bacon, diced
½ cup chili sauce
⅓ cup dark molasses
1 tablespoon cider vinegar
2 teaspoons salt
½ teaspoon dry mustard

Cover and bake until tender, about 30 minutes.

RED BEANS

When we think of beans that fill us up, with both flavor and meaty texture, it is red beans that first come to mind—in chili recipes, in a thick blanket of ham-suffused red beans on rice, and even in three-bean salad. All the common red beans—kidney, pinto, pink, small red, and cranberry—are related, but each has a distinct personality. Kidney beans, deep reddish brown or sometimes light red, have a fill-your-mouth quality due in part to their large size. They keep their shape when cooked, which makes them well suited to chunky chili. Pinto beans, beige and dappled with brown, are meaty as well but thinner skinned than kidney beans and thus well suited to refried beans and soupier chilies. Pink beans start out looking like pale, half-sized kidney beans; however, with cooking their color deepens, and their texture is firmer and denser than kidney beans. Small red beans are also known as chili beans and Mexican red beans, denoting their favored use and origins. Their robust taste, similar to that of kidney beans, makes them good in any long-simmered, well-seasoned bean dish.

RED BEAN AND LIMA SUCCOTASH *4 servings*

Succotash takes its name from the Narragansett word *msickquatash,* meaning "boiled kernels of corn." The most popular form of succotash today combines corn with lima beans—but red kidney or cranberry beans work superbly too.

Pick over, rinse, and soak, 274:

½ cup dried red kidney or cranberry beans

Drain. Combine in a medium saucepan with water to cover by 2 inches. Bring to a boil. Reduce the heat and simmer, covered, until the beans are very tender, about 1½ hours. Add water as needed to keep the beans moist. Drain. Bring to a boil in a large saucepan:

1 cup heavy cream

Boil over medium heat until reduced to about ½ cup, being careful not to let it overflow. Add the cooked beans along with:

1½ cups fresh, canned, or frozen corn kernels
1 cup cooked fresh or frozen baby lima beans

Cover and cook over low heat for 10 minutes. Stir in:

1 tablespoon butter
1 teaspoon fresh thyme leaves (optional)
½ teaspoon salt
⅛ teaspoon ground black pepper

Taste and adjust the seasonings. Serve hot.

RED BEANS AND RICE *6 to 8 servings*

A southern staple with many variations.

Pick over, rinse, and soak, 274:

1 pound dried red kidney, pinto, or small red beans (about 2 cups)

Combine in a large pot:

8 cups water
2 ham hocks (2 to 3 pounds)
1 cup finely chopped celery
1 cup finely chopped onions
1 cup finely chopped green bell peppers
2 teaspoons chopped garlic
2 bay leaves
1 teaspoon dried thyme
1 teaspoon dried oregano
1 teaspoon ground white pepper
½ teaspoon ground red pepper

Bring to a boil. Reduce the heat and simmer, covered, stirring occasionally, until the ham hocks are tender, about 1 hour. Remove the ham hocks and let cool. Drain the beans, add them to the pot, and return to a boil. Reduce the heat and simmer, covered, until the beans are tender, about 30 minutes. Add water as needed to keep the beans covered. Remove the meat from the ham hocks and add it to the pot along with:

1 pound smoked andouille or smoked kielbasa sausage, cut diagonally into ½-inch-thick slices

Warm through. Serve over:

4 cups hot cooked rice

VEGETARIAN CHILI

8 servings

Heat in a large saucepan over medium heat:

2 tablespoons olive oil

Add:

1 cup chopped peeled carrots
1 cup chopped red bell peppers
1 cup chopped green bell peppers
1 cup chopped onions
2 cloves garlic, minced

Cook, stirring, until the onions are golden, 12 to 15 minutes. Add:

1 to 2 fresh green chili peppers, seeded and finely chopped, or 1 chipotle pepper in adobo sauce, minced
1 tablespoon ground ancho chili pepper
1 tablespoon ground cumin

Cook, stirring, for 2 minutes. Stir in:

One 28-ounce can plum tomatoes, with juice, coarsely chopped
One 16-ounce can red kidney beans, rinsed and drained, or 1½ cups cooked (about ½ cup dried), 274
One 16-ounce can cannellini beans, rinsed and drained, or 1½ cups cooked (about ½ cup dried), 273
One 16-ounce can black beans, rinsed and drained, or 1½ cups cooked (about ½ cup dried), 273
1 cup tomato juice
Salt to taste

Bring to a boil. Reduce the heat to medium-low and simmer, uncovered, stirring occasionally, until the flavors are blended, adding more tomato juice or water as needed, about 45 minutes. Taste and adjust the seasonings. Ladle into bowls and serve with:

Sour cream
Salsa Fresca, 6
Chopped fresh cilantro

CARIBBEAN RED BEAN STEW WITH PORK

4 to 6 servings

This is one of the best possible ways to stretch a small amount of meat.

Pick over, rinse, and soak, 270:

1½ cups dried red kidney, pinto, or small red beans

Drain. Combine the beans in a large saucepan with:

8 cups water
1 small onion
1 leafy celery top
1 bay leaf
1 clove garlic, peeled
One 3-inch cinnamon stick

Bring to a boil. Reduce the heat and simmer, covered, until the beans are tender, about 1 hour. Drain, reserving 4 cups of the cooking liquid. Discard the vegetables and seasonings. Heat in a large saucepan over medium heat:

1 tablespoon olive oil

Add and brown on all sides:

1 pound trimmed boneless pork cut into 1-inch cubes

Add:

1 large onion, cut into ½-inch cubes
1 green bell pepper, cut into 1-inch pieces
2 cups 1-inch cubes peeled sweet potato
1 tablespoon coarsely chopped garlic
1 teaspoon salt

Cook, stirring, until the onions are golden, 12 to 15 minutes. Add:

2 teaspoons hot paprika

Stir to blend. Add the cooked beans and the reserved cooking liquid. Bring to a boil. Reduce the heat and simmer, uncovered, until the pork is tender and the stew is thick, about 1 hour. Serve hot.

KIDNEY BEAN CASSEROLE

4 to 6 servings

This is an old-fashioned bean casserole. You can add bacon if you wish, finely chopping a slice or two and cooking it along with the onions; decrease the vegetable oil by half.

Preheat the oven to 350°F. Oil a 2-quart casserole or soufflé dish.

Have ready:

4 ounces sharp Cheddar cheese, grated

Heat in a large skillet over medium heat:

2 tablespoons vegetable oil

Add:

1 cup chopped onions
2 cloves garlic, finely chopped

Cook, stirring, until the onions are golden, 12 to 15 minutes. Stir in:

2 teaspoons chili powder

Cook for 1 minute. Stir in:

4 cups cooked red kidney beans or other beans of your choice (about 1⅓ cups dried), 274, rinsed and drained if canned
One 28-ounce can whole tomatoes, drained and coarsely chopped
½ teaspoon salt
¼ teaspoon ground black pepper

Spread half of the bean mixture in the casserole and sprinkle with half of the cheese. Add the remaining bean mixture and then the remaining cheese. Bake, uncovered, until the top is browned, about 25 minutes. Serve hot.

SPLIT PEAS

Green split peas remind us how good peas taste, with a flavor more intense than that of young green peas and a much denser texture. Yellow split peas are similar but blander, providing a more neutral backdrop for all kinds of seasonings. Both cook to a thick, creamy texture that is perfect for soups and sauces. The technique of steaming dried peas to loosen their skins, then peeling and splitting them to hasten cooking, has been practiced in India for thousands of years. The resulting products, shiny green and yellow split peas, are so convenient to use that they have largely displaced dried whole peas, with their gray-green skins, on supermarket shelves. Whole dried peas need soaking; split peas do not. Because they have no skins, split peas lose their shape in the pot; for the same reason, they can be cooked with salt, for there are no skins to toughen.

INDIAN LENTIL PUREE (DAL) *4 to 6 servings*

Dal is the Hindi word for both an array of legumes used in Indian cooking and a preparation of legumes that is a staple of Indian cuisine. In Indian households where meat is either too expensive or prohibited by religion, dal is likely to be on the table at every meal as the protein. If the dal is pureed, it is soupy or "wet" and eaten with rice; if not pureed, the dal is "dry" and eaten with bread. A pureed dal may be thick or thin, as the cook chooses.

Pick over, rinse, and place in a large saucepan:

1 cup yellow split peas or red lentils

Add:

2 cups water
1 small onion, sliced
¾ teaspoon minced garlic
¾ teaspoon minced peeled fresh ginger
½ teaspoon ground turmeric

Simmer, covered, until the split peas are tender, 20 to 25 minutes. Puree through a food mill and return to the saucepan. Stir in:

1 cup water
¾ teaspoon salt

Simmer, partially covered, until the dal is thickened to the consistency of split pea soup, about 20 minutes. Stir in:

2 fresh serrano or jalapeño peppers, seeded and cut into thirds
1 plum tomato, diced
2 tablespoons chopped fresh cilantro

Serve with:

Hot cooked rice

WHITE BEANS

These are the beans glazed with molasses in traditional baked beans, simmered with a ham bone for U.S. Senate Bean Soup, 106, and braised with meats in a French cassoulet. Great Northern beans are about twice the size of navy (or pea) beans; these two are the most commonly available white beans and are excellent baked or in soups. Cannellini are often called white kidney beans, but the two are different though related; white kidney beans are like red kidney beans in size and texture, while cannellini are slimmer and creamier when cooked. All of these white beans, part of the kidney bean clan, can be used interchangeably, with consideration given to the size of the bean if relevant to the recipe. Flageolets are white to pale green immature kidney beans. Both their color and delicate flavor place them firmly in the White Bean family, but they taste slightly more like fresh beans and hold their shape very well when cooked. Use them like other white beans but favor them especially for their firmness in salads. Perhaps because they are so mild to begin with, white beans seem to stand up less well to canning than other beans.

CLASSIC TUSCAN BEANS *6 to 8 servings*

Tuscans love beans so much that the rest of Italy calls them *mangia fagioli*, "the bean eaters." Tradition and goodness come together in this simplest of cooking methods—simmering dried beans seasoned with fresh sage, garlic, and olive oil. Dried cannellini beans are a first choice for their sweet, creamy character. More readily available pinto or cranberry beans come close. Serve hot or at room temperature, drizzling a thread of olive oil over the beans at the table.

Pick over, rinse, and soak, 270:

1 pound dried cannellini, pinto, or cranberry beans (about 2 cups)

Drain. Combine in a large pot with:

12 fresh sage leaves or whole dried sage leaves
3 cloves garlic, halved
1 tablespoon extra-virgin olive oil

Add water to cover by 3 inches. Bring to a simmer, partially cover, and simmer gently until tender, about 1 hour. Drain. Season to taste with:

Salt and ground black pepper

Serve hot, warm, or at room temperature, seasoning each portion with about:

1 teaspoon extra-virgin olive oil, preferably Tuscan

BOSTON BAKED BEANS

10 to 12 servings

A not-too-sweet version of the classic New England dish that lets the flavor of the bean shine through. The beans become darker in color and richer in flavor if the dish is made a day ahead. The recipe can be halved; cooking times remain the same. For a meaty, smoky flavor, you can substitute 12 ounces of diced thick-cut bacon for the salt pork.

Pick over and rinse:

2 pounds small dried white beans or navy beans (about 4½ cups)

Combine in a large ovenproof pot or Dutch oven with:

16 cups water

Bring to a boil over high heat and boil for 2 minutes. Turn off the heat, cover tightly, and let stand for 1 hour. Uncover, return the beans to a boil, and boil for 2 minutes. Remove from the heat, cover tightly, and let stand for 1 hour. Uncover, return the beans to a boil over high heat, then reduce the heat so the water no longer bubbles. Cook, uncovered, until the beans are soft and creamy in the center but still completely intact, without frayed skins, 45 to 60 minutes. Carefully turn the beans into a colander. Tilt but do not shake the colander to drain off as much liquid as possible.

Position a rack in the center of the oven. Preheat the oven to 250°F.

Bring to a boil in the same pot:

3 cups water

Stir in to blend thoroughly:

1 cup light or dark molasses

1 tablespoon salt

2 teaspoons ground black pepper, or to taste

½ teaspoon ground cloves

Gently stir in the beans along with:

8 ounces salt pork (including the rind), cut into ½-inch cubes

2 cups chopped onions

Either leave the mixture in the pot or transfer it to a 6- to 8-quart bean pot. If necessary, stir in enough hot water to come just to the top of the beans. Cover the pot and bake until the bean liquid is thickened, 4 to 5 hours. Serve hot with:

Brown Bread, 773

The beans can be refrigerated for up to 1 week or frozen for up to 6 months.

HONEY-GLAZED BAKED BEANS

8 servings

This is a wonderful basic formula for baked beans.

Pick over, rinse, and soak, 270:

1 pound dried pinto beans (about 2 cups)

Drain. Combine in a large saucepan with:

10 cups water

Bring to a boil. Reduce the heat and simmer, covered, until the beans are almost tender, about 45 minutes.

Preheat the oven to 300°F.

Drain the beans, reserving the cooking liquid. Combine the beans in a 5- to 6-quart casserole with:

2 medium onions, diced

8 ounces bacon, diced, or 1 ham hock

2 cloves garlic, minced

Stir into the cooking liquid:

1 cup honey or pure maple syrup

2 tablespoons ground ginger

1 teaspoon dry mustard

1 teaspoon salt

½ teaspoon ground black pepper

Pour the liquid over the beans. Cover and bake until the beans are tender, about 2½ hours. If you used a ham hock, shred the meat and stir into the baked beans.

CAMPFIRE BEANS

6 servings

We have always found a way to go on camping trips where these were served.

Have ready at least 2 to 3 quarts hot coals. Dig a hole deep enough and wide enough to hold a covered cast-iron kettle, allowing about 4 extra inches to the depth of the hole. Prepare Honey-Glazed Baked Beans, above, in the kettle. Put half the coals in the bottom of the hole. Sink the covered kettle. Cover the lid with a large piece of aluminum foil to keep out the dirt. Cover with the rest of the coals. Now fill in the hole with the dirt, making sure there is at least 3 inches dirt on the top of the kettle. Do not dig in to peek for at least 4 hours.

FLAGEOLETS AND TOMATO WITH BUTTERED CRUMBS

6 servings

This is a faster, almost meatless version of cassoulet, the baked bean and duck confit dish of southwestern France, the recipe for which follows on page 286.

Pick over, rinse, and soak, 270:

1¼ cups dried flageolet or other small white beans

Drain the beans. Combine in a large saucepan with:

6 cups water

1 sprig fresh oregano, or ½ teaspoon dried

1 sprig fresh thyme, or ¼ teaspoon dried

½ small onion

1 clove garlic, peeled

Bring to a boil. Reduce the heat and simmer, uncovered, until the beans are tender, 35 to 45 minutes. Drain.

Discard the herb stems if using. Meanwhile, combine in a large skillet:

2 tablespoons diced salt pork or thick-sliced bacon

½ cup chopped onions

Cook, stirring, over low heat until the bacon is crisp and the onions are tender, about 10 minutes. Stir in:

1 clove garlic, finely minced

Cook for 1 minute. Add:

One 28-ounce can whole tomatoes, with juice

Cook, breaking up the tomatoes with the side of a spoon, over medium-low heat until thickened, about 20 minutes. Stir in the beans along with:

1½ teaspoons salt

⅛ teaspoon ground black pepper

Taste and adjust the seasonings.

Preheat the oven to 350°F.

Transfer the bean mixture to a shallow 1¾-quart baking dish. Stir together:

1 cup coarse fresh breadcrumbs (from firm sliced bread)

2 tablespoons butter, melted

Spread evenly over the beans. Bake until the crumbs are golden and the beans are heated through, about 25 minutes.

BEANS AND CABBAGE WITH SHRIMP

4 to 6 servings

This may not sound like much, but we have heard this dish called "phenomenal."

Heat in a large saucepan over medium heat:

2 tablespoons olive oil

Add:

1 cup minced onions

2 cloves garlic, minced

Cook, stirring, until the onions are soft and translucent, 5 to 8 minutes. Stir in:

2 cups chicken or fish stock

1 bay leaf

Cook, uncovered, over medium to low heat until partially reduced, about 8 minutes. Stir in:

4 cups thinly sliced Savoy cabbage

2 cups cooked navy beans, 274, or cooked cannellini beans, 273 , rinsed and drained if canned

1 cup thinly sliced peeled carrots

2 teaspoons chopped fresh thyme, or ½ teaspoon dried

Cover and cook until the vegetables are wilted and tender, about 8 minutes. Remove the bay leaf. Stir in:

1 pound medium to large shrimp, shelled and deveined

Cook until pink, 3 to 4 minutes. Sprinkle with:

¼ cup chopped fresh parsley

Salt and ground black pepper to taste

Serve warm.

CASSOULET

8 servings

Cassoulet is a dish of slow-baked beans and various meats, usually including confit (duck or goose cooked in fat). Classic cassoulet requires several days' preparation. Our shortcut version from southwestern France can be made and served the same day if you have homemade, 624, or store-bought confit on hand or if you omit the confit. Serve this cold-weather party dish with red wine, crusty bread, and a green salad. This recipe is from Boston chef Gordon Hamersley.

Pick over, rinse, and soak, 270:

4 cups dried great Northern or flageolet beans

Have ready:

16 cups (4 quarts) chicken stock

2 medium onions, cut into ½-inch cubes

4 duck or 2 goose confit legs, 624

Heat in a large pot over medium heat until hot but not smoking:

1 tablespoon olive or other vegetable oil

Add:

8 ounces thick-cut smoked bacon, cut into 2-inch pieces

Cook, stirring, for 2 minutes. Add 1 cup of the onions and cook, stirring, for 2 minutes. Stir in 8 cups of the stock. Drain and add the beans, cover, and simmer until the beans are almost tender, about 1 hour. Drain and reserve the beans and cooking liquid separately.

Preheat the oven to 350°F.

Melt in a large ovenproof pot over medium heat:

1 tablespoon fat from the confit

Add:

1 pound butt pork, trimmed of fat, cut into 2-inch cubes

Sear until brown, about 3 minutes. Discard the fat left in the pot. Stir in the remaining onions along with:

10 cloves garlic, peeled

4 teaspoons chopped fresh thyme

3 tablespoons tomato paste

Season with:

Salt and ground black pepper to taste

Stir in 4 cups of the stock along with:

One-half 750-ml bottle dry white wine

Cover and bring to a boil. Transfer to the oven and bake for 1 hour. Stir in the beans and duck legs along with:

8 ounces mild Italian sausage

Bake the cassoulet for 30 minutes more. Check the cassoulet occasionally and add as much of the remaining stock as needed. Sprinkle with:

1 cup dry unseasoned breadcrumbs

Continue to bake, uncovered, until the breadcrumbs form a golden brown crust, about 20 minutes. To serve, bring the cassoulet to the table and spoon some of the beans and meat onto each plate.

SOYBEANS

It is easy to consume soybeans every day and never see a single bean. Because soybeans are higher in fat than other legumes (with the exception of peanuts) and supply almost twice as much protein as other beans, the huge American crop is valued mostly for its oil and its use as animal feed. The cooked beans are very bland; they do not tempt with the earthiness of common beans or the nuttiness of lentils and chickpeas.

But there are reasons to pay attention to soybeans. They contain substances thought to help prevent breast and other cancers, as well as Omega-3 fatty acids, which reduce the risks of heart disease. These assets are preserved when soybeans are turned into soy milk, tofu, and tempeh.

Cook soybeans and mix them with other cooked beans in recipes such as baked beans and soups to reap the benefits of their nutrients and counter their blandness. Black soybeans are lighter and more nuanced in taste than yellow ones; both need presoaking to reduce lengthy cooking times. Place either one in a large bowl and pour boiling water over to cover by 2 inches; let stand for 12 hours. Drain and rinse well. Place in a pot with water to cover by 2 inches and bring to a boil, skimming foam from the surface. Reduce the heat, cover, and simmer for 1¾ to 3 hours.

Soybeans can also be roasted for a mild-tasting, crunchy snack. Soak yellow soybeans as for cooking, above, and drain well. Spread the beans in shallow pans, allowing plenty of room, and roast at 250°F, stirring occasionally, until browned and beginning to crisp, about 1 hour 10 minutes. Sprinkle with salt, if desired, while still warm.

Most soy-based foods are created by manipulating the bean in one of two ways, either by grinding and cooking the beans and then filtering out the liquid to make soy milk (the bean fiber remaining, called okara, is sometimes used as a vegetable protein substitute for meat) and tofu; or by fermenting the beans to produce tempeh or one of many seasonings. The foremost fermented seasoning is soy sauce, which is best if made from whole soybeans—not soy meal or soy proteins—with the addition of only water, wheat, and salt; this is often called tamari. Fermented black beans, a favorite sauce ingredient in southern China, are made by cooking and fermenting small black soybeans with salt and spices; refrigerate these indefinitely in a covered jar and chop or crush lightly when adding to recipes to release their tangy aroma.

In Japan, fermented soybeans are omnipresent in the form of miso, a paste used to season and thicken sauces, marinades, and, most commonly, miso soup, 110. Miso varies in strength but is always salty; use about 1 tablespoon miso to season 4 cups liquid or food and always blend the paste with a few tablespoons of the liquid before stirring it into the rest of the dish. Intense heat destroys the healthful enzymes in miso, so when appropriate add it at the end of cooking and avoid boiling. Many varieties of miso are commonly characterized as white, sweet, and mild (*shiro* in Japanese); medium golden or tan in color *(chu);* or pungent, dark red or brown *(aka),* which is good for marinades and should not be cooked a long time. Refrigerate miso in a covered container for up to a few months but use it within a few weeks for best flavor.

Soy milk and other soy dairy imitations are a boon for lactose-intolerant people and those who do not eat animal products, as the fermenting bacteria are a source of vitamin B_{12}. Be aware of two things: soy milk, though rich in protein, lacks the calcium and vitamin D of cow's milk; and soy milk may be fattened with oil and sweeteners. While soy milk can be used instead of cow's milk in recipes (it darkens slightly with cooking), other soy dairy substitutes do not necessarily behave like their dairy counterparts when heated. Soy cream cheese works in baking, but soy sour cream does not. Soy cheese will not melt like cheese unless it contains casein, a cow's-milk derivative. Refrigerate soy dairy substitutes like those made with cow's milk, for they are just as perishable.

SOY MILK

6 cups

This soy milk is naturally sweet and rich. To flavor it, add a vanilla bean while the milk is simmering and discard it after the milk has cooled. The chilled milk can also be flavored with honey. Use a blender with a metal, glass, or heatproof plastic container and lid; if the container is glass, warm it with hot water before using to prevent cracking.

Pick over, rinse, and soak, 270:

1 cup dried soybeans

in:

5 cups cold water

Drain and divide the soybeans into 3 equal portions. Process 1 portion of the soybeans at high speed in a blender with:

¾ cup boiling water

With the blender running, remove the center cap and slowly pour through the lid:

1⅓ cups boiling water

Continue processing until the mixture is very smooth. Remove to a sieve lined with a dish towel or several layers of fine cheesecloth and set over an 8-cup glass measure or large bowl. Repeat the procedure 2 times with the remaining soybeans. Mash the soybean mixture against the side of the sieve with a wooden spoon to extract as much liquid as possible. Gather the towel or cheesecloth around the mixture and squeeze to extract the remaining liquid. Remove the soy milk to a large saucepan. Cook over medium-high heat, stirring constantly to prevent scorching, until the mixture foams up. Remove from the heat and let stand for 1 minute. Return the saucepan to the burner and reduce the heat to medium or medium-low. Simmer gently for 10 minutes, stirring often. Remove from the heat and let cool, stirring occasionally to prevent a film from forming on the top. Measure the soy milk and add water, if necessary, to make 6 cups. Refrigerate the soy milk for up to 5 days, or chill and freeze for up to 1 month. (Thawed soy milk may need to be whipped in a blender or food processor to restore its smoothness.)

ABOUT TOFU

Tofu is the humble soybean's leap toward culinary art, especially in the cuisines of China, where it was invented more than a thousand years ago, and Japan. Tofu (also called bean curd and dofu) is made like cheese, by coagulating soy milk until it forms curds, which are broken up and then pressed. But tofu is unlike cheese in that it rarely stands on its own. Instead, it bathes in the flavors of soups, sauces, marinades, and dressings. Its smoothness can range from as soft as custard to as chewy as a bread dumpling. A 4-ounce serving provides up to one-quarter of a day's protein requirement (softer tofu contains more water and thus fewer nutrients per ounce), about 10 grams of fat, and no cholesterol. Since most tofu is coagulated with a calcium compound, it also provides a goodly amount of that mineral.

Tofu is as perishable as dairy foods and highly susceptible to bacterial contamination, so wash your hands and work surfaces and keep the tofu refrigerated as you would chicken. When buying refrigerated tofu, check the expiration date. You can leave it in its tub or pouch, but it is better to open the package, discard the liquid, and pour in fresh water; change the water daily. It will keep this way for up to a week, depending on its freshness when purchased. Because of the risk of contamination, it is best to avoid tofu sold from open tubs, even if it is refrigerated.

The tofu called "silken," often sold in aseptic boxes, is labeled soft or firm, but either one is much more fragile than regular tofu. Made more like yogurt than like cheese, silken tofu is coagulated from thick soy milk and not pressed. The delicacy of silken tofu makes cubes of it, cut with great care, a welcome garnish for light clear soups, but the big advantage of silken tofu is that it purees beautifully in a food processor or blender. Pureed soft silken tofu has the consistency of yogurt and can be used in dressings, sauces, dips, cream soups, and puddings. Refrigerate pureed tofu and stir well before using. Be aware that it will darken slightly to a beige or grayish color as it stands, so use it with ingredients that will mask the color. For a dessert topping, use brown sugar or maple syrup instead of white sugar. Be sure to add 1 to 2 teaspoons fresh lemon or lime juice to any pureed tofu dish to perk up the taste.

The tofu used for cooking, sometimes called "cotton" tofu, is labeled soft, firm, or extra firm, depending on how much liquid was drained off during processing. Firm and extra firm hold together better in the pot. Cooks commonly firm up tofu by pressing it under a weight for 30 to 60 minutes, depending on how much water the tofu starts out with and the desired firmness. The curd becomes denser and chewier, holds together better when sliced or cubed, and releases less flavor-diluting water when simmered in a sauce or soup. If you press soft (but not silken) tofu, you can substitute it for firm.

To press a 1-pound block of tofu, cut it horizontally in half to make two slabs, each about 1 inch thick. Place a sheet of aluminum foil over a cutting board large enough to hold both slabs side by side. To allow the water to drain off, place one end of the board over the edge of the sink or on a baking sheet and prop up the other end with a ¼-cup measure or an inch-thick box. Place the tofu on the board and cover with another sheet of foil. Place a second cutting board or similarly shaped weight over the tofu and let stand for 10 minutes to compact somewhat. The sides of the tofu should bulge very slightly, but be careful not to overweight soft tofu before it has compacted, or it may split. After 10 minutes, add more weight, evenly distributed; a cast-iron skillet or Dutch oven with two or three large cans in it, several nested heavy skillets, or several large books will do the job. Check the weighted tofu for firmness after 30 minutes; if desired, turn the slabs over, replace the weight, and press for an additional 15 to 30 minutes. Refrigerate pressed tofu in a bowl of water; it will not reabsorb water and can be kept for 2 to 3 days if you change the water daily. While some of the recipes that follow call for pressed tofu, this extra step is not essential, just a textural refinement.

Freezing pressed tofu removes even more moisture. The thawed tofu can be cut into cubes and used like other tofu, but the dryness makes it chewier and better able to absorb marinades and sauces. It can be crumbled over salads or soups, and the crumbles can mimic the texture of hard-boiled egg whites in a mock egg salad. Pressed firm or extra-firm tofu works best, but soft tofu can also be frozen.

Pressed or not, tofu can be cut into cubes or slices and sautéed in oil to brown and crisp it before adding to stir-fries or stews. Tofu can also be red-cooked in the Chinese style (see Red-Cooked Pork Shoulder, 702), in other words very slowly braised in dark soy sauce, with star anise if desired, to color, season, and firm it; use red-cooked tofu in stir-fries. But the flexibility of tofu—its ability to take on so many textures and flavors—should not detract from the ease of cooking it simply. It is excellent cubed and tossed into stir-fried asparagus, for example, or with cellophane noodles and mixed vegetables. Tofu is, after all, a convenience food—one that provides all the nutrients of soybeans with very little preparation.

Smoked tofu is exceptionally convenient, because it tastes good straight from the package, like a semifirm smoked cheese. Slice it for a sandwich or mix cubes of it into a chopped vegetable salad.

Please note that tofu package sizes vary widely. In the following recipes, you can use any size package that approximates the weight indicated.

SZECHUAN SPICED TOFU

4 servings

Vary the hotness of this dish by adjusting the amount of chili paste. As with all stir-fries, have all the ingredients measured, chopped, and ready before beginning to cook.

Heat in a wok or large skillet over medium-high heat:

1 tablespoon peanut or vegetable oil

Add:

2 teaspoons minced peeled fresh ginger
1 teaspoon minced garlic

Stir-fry for 1 minute. Add:

One 8-ounce can flower-cut baby corn, drained
4 cups ½-inch-thick slices bok choy
½ small onion, sliced

Stir-fry until the bok choy is slightly wilted, 3 to 4 minutes. Combine and stir in:

½ cup chicken or vegetable stock
2 tablespoons soy sauce
1 tablespoon black bean sauce or black bean paste
1 tablespoon dry sherry
2 teaspoons chili paste
1 tablespoon cornstarch
½ teaspoon sugar
¼ teaspoon Szechuan peppercorns, lightly cracked if desired

Boil, stirring, until thickened, about 1 minute. Stir in:

One 10½-ounce package extra-firm tofu, pressed if desired, 288, and cubed

Heat through for 2 to 3 minutes. Arrange on a serving platter:

One 12-ounce package Chinese-style egg noodles, cooked

Spoon the tofu mixture over the noodles and garnish with:

¼ cup shredded peeled carrots
2 tablespoons sliced scallions

SOUTHEAST ASIAN CURRIED VEGETABLE STEW

6 servings

Curry seasonings and coconut milk are combined in this fragrant vegetable stew. Shredded cooked chicken can be added if desired.

Heat in a wok or large saucepan over medium heat:

1 tablespoon vegetable oil

Add:

1½ teaspoons cumin seeds

Cook, stirring, for 1 to 2 minutes. Process in a food processor to a smooth paste:

½ medium onion, coarsely chopped
One 1-inch piece fresh ginger, peeled and quartered
4 cloves garlic, peeled
1 to 2 medium fresh jalapeño peppers, seeded
1 teaspoon ground turmeric
2 tablespoons water

Add the paste to the cumin seeds and cook, stirring often, over medium-low heat for 3 to 5 minutes. Stir in:

One 14-ounce can unsweetened coconut milk
½ cup chicken or vegetable stock
1 pound sweet potatoes, peeled and cut into ¾-inch cubes

Bring to a boil. Reduce the heat and simmer, covered, for 8 minutes. Stir in:

3 cups broccoli florets and cut stems

One 10½-ounce package firm tofu, or 8 ounces tempeh, cut into ¾-inch cubes

Simmer, covered, until the broccoli is tender, about 10 minutes. Add and bring to a boil:

1 large tomato, coarsely chopped

Combine and stir in:

3 tablespoons fresh lime juice

2 tablespoons water

2 tablespoons all-purpose flour

Boil, stirring, until thickened, about 1 minute. Stir in:

½ to 1 teaspoon chili paste

Salt and ground black pepper to taste

Arrange on a serving platter:

6 cups hot cooked brown or white rice

Spoon the vegetable curry over the rice and sprinkle generously with:

Finely chopped fresh cilantro

Chopped cashews (optional)

SMOKED TOFU BURGERS

6 servings

This flavorful patty mixture can also be baked as a loaf in a small loaf pan at 350°F for 40 to 45 minutes.

Soak in warm water to cover until softened, about 20 minutes:

½ ounce dried shiitake mushrooms

Drain, discarding the liquid, and squeeze out the excess water from the mushrooms. Chop the mushrooms, discarding the tough centers and stems. Heat in a large skillet over medium heat:

2 to 3 teaspoons chili sesame oil

Add the shiitakes along with:

1 cup finely chopped broccoli florets and stems

⅓ cup finely chopped red bell peppers

¼ cup sliced scallions

2 teaspoons finely chopped peeled fresh ginger

1½ teaspoons minced garlic

Cook, stirring, until tender, 4 to 5 minutes. Combine with:

One 6-ounce package smoked tofu, finely chopped

1 cup cooked brown rice

⅔ cup dry unseasoned breadcrumbs

2 large eggs, lightly beaten

1 tablespoon soy sauce

Remove to a food processor and pulse several times, until a spoonful of the mixture can be pressed into a ball. Shape the mixture into 6 patties (or burgers), using about ½ cup for each. Cook in a lightly greased skillet over medium heat until browned, 3 to 5 minutes each side. Serve hot on rolls.

BROWN RICE AND TOFU SALAD WITH ORANGE SESAME DRESSING

6 servings

Smoked tofu is also an excellent choice for this salad. Black beans or any other preferred beans can be substituted for the adzukis.

Shake together in a tightly covered jar:

½ cup canola oil

4 teaspoons toasted sesame oil

⅓ cup orange juice

⅓ cup seasoned rice vinegar

1 small fresh jalapeño pepper, seeded and minced

1 teaspoon minced peeled fresh ginger

1 teaspoon minced garlic

Chill. Combine in a large bowl:

4 cups warm cooked brown basmati rice

One 10½-ounce package extra-firm tofu, pressed if desired, 288, and cut into ¾-inch cubes

1½ cups cooked adzuki beans (about 3 cups dried), 273, rinsed and drained if canned

½ cup chopped red onions

1 cup chopped bell peppers, preferably half red and half green

¼ cup finely chopped fresh cilantro

Shake the dressing well, pour over the rice mixture, and toss well to coat. Season with:

Salt and ground black pepper to taste

Line a serving platter with:

Lettuce leaves

Spoon the salad on the leaves and sprinkle with:

1 tablespoon sesame seeds, toasted

ABOUT TEMPEH

Because of its firm, chewy texture and mushroomlike flavor, tempeh is very easy to cook with. It substitutes for meat when marinated or sauced and briefly sautéed, stir-fried, or steamed. Originating in Indonesia and a staple there, tempeh is made by inoculating cooked skinless split soybeans with *Rhizopus oligosporus* bacteria, shaping the beans into cakes, and allowing them to ferment for about 24 hours. The resulting supple slabs are sealed and refrigerated, ready for sale. Often a grain such as rye or millet is mixed with the soybeans to make a milder tempeh, without the slightly bitter edge of the straight soybean product; sesame seeds, seaweed, or dried vegetables can be added for seasoning.

Tempeh is as perishable as tofu, so check the freshness date. The product should look firm and delicately veined with white mold. Patches of black mold are fine—they indicate the bacteria are still active—and can be trimmed away before cooking. Signs of spoilage in tempeh are red, yellow, or green mold, sliminess, and the smell of ammonia. Cut tempeh into strips, cubes, or cutlets as desired. Steaming softens tempeh's texture; sautéing browns and crisps it.

MOO SHU TEMPEH

12 pancakes; 6 servings

Mandarin pancakes are delicate and delicious. The pancakes can be cooled, stacked with plastic wrap, and refrigerated for up to 24 hours or frozen for up to 2 months. If cooking time does not allow this preparation, warm flour tortillas will substitute nicely.

Stir together until crumbly:

⅓ cup boiling water

1 cup all-purpose flour

Shape into a ball and knead on a lightly floured surface until the dough is very smooth, about 10 minutes. Let stand, covered, for 30 minutes. Divide the dough into 12 equal pieces. Roll each piece into a ball, then into a 3-inch disk. Brush the top of 1 disk lightly with:

Sesame or vegetable oil

Top with a second disk. Roll out both disks together into a 6-inch pancake, being careful not to wrinkle the dough when rolling. Cook the pancakes in a lightly greased small skillet over medium to medium-high heat until the surface blisters and turns the color of parchment; turn often with chopsticks or tongs. Remove from the skillet and immediately separate the pancakes, using a sharp knife. Repeat with the remaining disks. Keep the pancakes warm, loosely covered, in a 200°F oven. At this point, the pancakes can be wrapped well and stored in the refrigerator or freezer. To reheat, arrange the pancakes slightly overlapping on a baking sheet and bake, covered, at 300°F until warm, 10 to 15 minutes.

Combine and let stand until the mushrooms are softened, 15 to 20 minutes:

1½ cups hot water

1 ounce dried shiitake mushrooms

¼ ounce dried wood or cloud ear mushrooms

Drain, reserving the liquid, and squeeze out the excess water from the mushrooms. Slice the mushrooms, discarding the tough centers and stems. Combine:

One 8-ounce package tempeh, cut into thin strips

1 tablespoon soy sauce

Heat in a wok or large skillet over medium heat:

1 teaspoon toasted sesame oil

Add:

3 large eggs, lightly beaten

Cook, without stirring, until set but still moist. Remove the egg pancake and cut into small pieces. Heat in the wok:

1 tablespoon toasted sesame oil

Add the tempeh mixture and stir-fry until lightly browned. Add the mushrooms along with:

One 8-ounce can bamboo shoots, drained and sliced

¼ cup sliced scallions

2 teaspoons minced peeled fresh ginger

Stir-fry for 2 to 3 minutes. Strain the mushroom soaking liquid through a fine-mesh sieve lined with dampened paper towels, measure it, and add water as needed to make ¾ cup. Combine with:

3 tablespoons soy sauce

3 tablespoons dry sherry

1 tablespoon cornstarch

1 teaspoon sugar

Pour into the wok and boil, stirring, until thickened, about 1 minute. Gently stir in the egg pieces. Spread each pancake with:

2 to 3 teaspoons plum sauce

Top each with about ⅓ cup of the tempeh mixture and then with:

1 scallion

Roll up, folding in the bottom end for eating.

SZECHUAN-STYLE "HACKED" TEMPEH

4 servings

Tempeh replaces the chicken in this traditional dish. Served chilled, the ingredients are tossed with a peanut sauce.

Combine and let stand for 15 to 30 minutes:

One 8-ounce package tempeh, cut into ½-inch cubes

2 tablespoons soy sauce

2 to 3 teaspoons minced peeled fresh ginger

1 teaspoon minced garlic

½ teaspoon Szechuan peppercorns, cracked

Heat in a wok or medium skillet over medium heat:

1 tablespoon vegetable oil

Add the tempeh mixture and cook, stirring, until browned. Let cool, then refrigerate until chilled.

Combine and arrange on a serving platter:

2 cups sliced seeded peeled cucumbers

½ cup chopped red bell peppers

¼ cup sliced scallions

Spoon the tempeh mixture over the vegetables. Stir together until smooth and drizzle over the tempeh mixture:

- ¼ cup smooth peanut butter
- 2 tablespoons soy sauce
- 2 tablespoons rice vinegar
- 1 tablespoon dry sherry
- 3 to 4 teaspoons toasted sesame oil
- 1 teaspoon chili paste

Garnish with:

- ½ cup chopped red bell peppers
- ¼ cup sliced scallions
- ¼ cup chopped salted peanuts

Toss just before serving. If desired, serve with:

- Chilled cooked rice noodles

ABOUT SOY PROTEIN

The high-protein content of soybeans has inspired American manufacturers to make it available in rather anonymous forms, without the distinct character of tofu or tempeh, for use as a meat substitute or diet supplement. Textured vegetable protein, or TVP, is the most widely used as a meat substitute. Made from compressed defatted soy flour, the tan granules swell in tomato juice, stock, or water to twice their volume; with cooking, the texture approaches that of ground meat. Soak 1 cup textured vegetable protein to equal the volume of 1 pound ground meat; use it to replace part or all of the meat in loaves, spaghetti sauce, chili, or other highly seasoned ground meat preparations. A meat loaf made with textured vegetable protein will come out of the oven softer than one made with meat but will firm up to meat texture if refrigerated overnight. Such loaves, like meat loaf itself, freeze well.

Textured soy concentrate, or TSP, is defatted soy flour concentrate processed to remove the natural bean sugars that can cause gas. The product is extruded into chunks and dried; rehydrate the chunks in hot stock or water and then add to stews, curries, or other saucy dishes as they simmer to absorb the seasonings. Soy isolate is soy protein in the form of a white powder. It is most often used industrially to add texture and protein to products ranging from imitation meat to bodybuilding drinks, but it is also sold retail as a food supplement. Stir 2 tablespoons soy isolate into orange juice, milk, or yogurt to add 20 grams soy protein, about the same amount as is in 4 ounces tempeh or tofu or ¾ cup cooked soybeans.

DINNER LOAF, TEX-MEX STYLE *8 to 10 servings*

The flavor of this loaf is even better the next day. Leftovers make terrific sandwiches too.

Combine and let stand until softened, 15 to 20 minutes:

- ½ cup boiling water
- 1 dried ancho chili pepper

Preheat the oven to 350°F. Grease a 9 × 5-inch (8-cup) loaf pan.

Drain, discarding the liquid, and squeeze out the excess water from the chili pepper. Chop the chili pepper, discarding the seeds and membranes. Combine with:

- 1 cup textured vegetable protein
- One 15-ounce can Mexican-style tomato sauce
- One 15-ounce can black beans, rinsed and drained
- ¾ cup water
- 1 large egg, lightly beaten
- ¼ cup raisins
- 1 small onion, chopped
- 1 small fresh jalapeño pepper, seeded and minced, or 2 mild or hot canned chili peppers, drained and chopped
- ¾ cup corn bread stuffing crumbs
- ⅓ cup all-purpose flour
- ¼ cup finely chopped fresh cilantro
- 2 teaspoons salt
- 1 teaspoon ground cumin

Pack the loaf mixture into the pan. Loosely cover with aluminum foil and bake for 45 minutes. Uncover and bake until set, 15 to 30 minutes. Let stand in the pan on a rack for 5 minutes, then invert onto a serving platter.

LION'S HEAD *4 servings*

Traditionally, the loaf mixture is made with pork, but this version is made with textured vegetable protein and served with a stir-fry of Asian vegetables. It is also delicious cold.

Soak in warm water to cover until softened:

- ⅓ ounce dried wood or cloud ear mushrooms

Preheat the oven to 350°F.

Drain, discarding the liquid, and squeeze out the excess water from the mushrooms. Chop the mushrooms. Combine:

- ¾ cup textured vegetable protein
- ¾ cup water
- 3 tablespoons soy sauce
- 2 tablespoons dry sherry
- 2 teaspoons minced peeled fresh ginger
- 1½ teaspoons minced garlic
- 1 teaspoon chili sesame oil
- ½ teaspoon chili paste

Let stand for 5 minutes, then add the mushrooms along with:

1/3 cup chopped bamboo shoots
1/3 cup chopped water chestnuts
1/3 cup cooked brown rice
1/3 cup dry unseasoned breadcrumbs
1/3 cup all-purpose flour
1/4 cup sliced scallions
1 large egg, lightly beaten

Stir until well blended and shape on a baking pan into a round loaf about 8 inches in diameter. Bake until set, about 45 minutes.

Heat in a wok or large skillet over medium heat:

1 tablespoon peanut or vegetable oil

Add:

1/3 cup chopped red bell peppers
1/4 cup sliced scallions
2 teaspoons minced garlic
2 teaspoons minced peeled fresh ginger

Cook, stirring, for 1 to 2 minutes. Add:

6 cups 1/4-inch-thick slices Napa cabbage

Cook, stirring, until crisp-tender, 3 to 4 minutes. Stir together and pour into the wok:

3/4 cup chicken or vegetable stock
1 tablespoon soy sauce
1 tablespoon dry sherry
1 tablespoon cornstarch

Boil, stirring, until thickened, about 1 minute. Place the cooked loaf in the center of a serving platter and spoon the stir-fried vegetables around it. Cut the loaf into wedges to serve.

SEITAN

Also called wheat gluten or wheat meat, seitan is another protein-rich Asian meat substitute, but one that uses wheat instead of soy. It was invented by Buddhist monks centuries ago to bring the texture and protein of meat to their vegetarian diet. It is made by kneading and washing a dough of very-high-protein flour to develop the wheat's gluten and remove its starch and bran. Shaped into chunks, balls, cutlets, or a large sausage, the grayish gluten is then simmered gently in stock for several hours. It swells, absorbs flavor, and becomes firm with cooking. You can shortcut the iffy process of making seitan at home by starting with a packaged mix or buying ready-to-use seitan in jars or refrigerated tubs or packages. Check the expiration date on refrigerated seitan; refrigerate for no longer than a week after opening or freeze it for 3 to 4 weeks. Ready-made seitan is commonly sold in the stock it was cooked in, which may be flavored with soy sauce and ginger or with Mexican, Italian, Thai, or other seasonings.

Seitan can be prepared in any way that will disguise its grayness but should not be cooked much longer than necessary to heat and sauce it thoroughly, as lengthy cooking brings out a bitter taste. Small chunks or cutlets can be pan-fried or lightly battered and deep-fried for appealing crispness. Thin slices can be simmered in a sauce and do indeed have the texture of braised meat. Chop seitan in a food processor or grind through a meat grinder and use it like ground beef in spaghetti sauce and sloppy joes.

Seitan provides 16 grams protein per 4-ounce serving, has no fat, and is rich in iron. It should be avoided by anyone sensitive to gluten, especially those with celiac disease.

ROOT VEGETABLE AND SEITAN STEW

8 servings

Vary the vegetables for the stew depending upon availability and preference. Turnips, rutabagas, sweet potatoes, kohlrabi, and fennel are other delicious choices.

Heat in a large Dutch oven or heavy pot over low heat:

2 tablespoons vegetable oil

Add:

1 cup sliced onions
1 cup sliced leeks (white part only)
1 cup sliced peeled carrots
5 cloves garlic, minced

Cook, covered, stirring occasionally, until very soft, about 20 minutes. Stir in:

1 tablespoon sugar

Cook, uncovered, stirring occasionally, over medium to medium-low heat until the onions are caramelized, 10 to 15 minutes. Stir in:

4 cups chopped mixed mushrooms, such as portobello, shiitake, and/or oyster mushrooms

Cook for 3 to 4 minutes, then stir in:

3 tablespoons all-purpose flour

Cook for 1 minute. Cut into 3/4- to 1-inch cubes and add:

1 medium baking potato
1 medium parsnip, peeled
1 small butternut squash, peeled and seeded

Stir in:

2 1/2 cups vegetable stock
1/2 cup dry white wine or vegetable stock
1/2 teaspoon dried rosemary
1/2 teaspoon dried thyme
2 or 3 pinches of freshly grated or ground nutmeg

Bring to a boil. Reduce the heat and simmer, covered, for 20 minutes. Stir in:

1 1/2 cups halved small Brussels sprouts
1 1/2 cups chopped plum tomatoes

1½ cups chopped unpeeled Jerusalem artichokes
1 pound seitan, cut into 1-inch cubes

Simmer, covered, for 20 minutes more. Season with:

Salt and ground black pepper to taste

If desired, serve over:

Hot cooked bulgur or brown rice

SEITAN KIBBE
4 servings

Serve these delicious Middle Eastern–style "meatballs" with Cucumber and Yogurt Salad, 219, and warm pitas.

Combine in a large bowl and let stand for 10 to 15 minutes:

1 cup fine bulgur
1⅓ cups cold water

Preheat the oven to 350°F. Generously oil a baking pan. Drain off the excess water from the bulgur and stir in:

4 cups ground seitan
1⅓ cups finely chopped fresh parsley
⅔ cup finely chopped onions
4 large cloves garlic, minced
2 large eggs, lightly beaten
1 cup all-purpose flour
1½ teaspoons dried mint
½ teaspoon salt
½ teaspoon ground black pepper

Divide the mixture into 16 equal parts, about ¼ cup each. Cut into sixteen ½-inch cubes:

2 ounces feta cheese

Heat in a small skillet over medium heat:

1 teaspoon vegetable oil

Add and toast until lightly browned:

½ cup pine nuts

Place 1 cube cheese and 4 or 5 pine nuts in the center of each seitan portion and shape the mixture around the filling, forming "meatballs." Place about 1 inch apart in the prepared pan and bake until browned and hot in the center, about 20 minutes. Serve hot.

PASTA, DUMPLINGS & NOODLES

Nowhere is our tendency to mix and match world flavors more evident than in our passion for pasta and noodles. From lo mein to linguine, from spätzle to soba, pasta and noodles make up one of the largest and richest chapters in American cooking.

Certainly Italy has made the greatest contribution. Italy's influence on our love affair with noodles is so great that the Italian word *pasta* has become a part of our everyday language. In this chapter, we use *pasta* to refer to noodles of Italian origin and *noodles* when referring to eastern European and Asian dishes.

PASTA AND NUTRITION

Pasta is made from wheat. From a nutritional standpoint, it joins other grain foods as the foundation of healthful diets and is the basis of many traditional cuisines. Many people believe that pasta is fattening and try to avoid eating it. This is a misunderstanding, as pasta is composed mainly of starch and protein, both relatively low in calories compared to fat. Most pasta dishes contain sauce, cheese, meat, or vegetables that balance the starch and prevent unusual fluctuation in blood sugar levels. People who are concerned about calories should keep the portion sizes within reasonable limits, use tomato rather than cream sauces, and add just small amounts of meat or cheese.

ABOUT DRIED AND FRESH PASTA

Dried pasta and fresh pasta are not better or worse, only different. That venerable favorite, spaghetti, is always a dried pasta made of the strongest durum wheat and water, never egg. On the other hand, fettuccine are flour and egg noodles that are best when fresh. However, in every case, a box of good-quality dried pasta is far better than any mediocre fresh pasta. Although some high-quality fresh pastas are available, most cannot compare with what you can produce in your own kitchen. Making your own pasta provides the pleasure and satisfaction of working with your hands to master a craft, and the results make for memorable eating.

ABOUT COOKING PASTA

Fresh or dried, pasta should always be cooked in a large quantity of fiercely boiling salted water. Use about 1 tablespoon salt per 3 quarts water. Estimate 6 quarts water per 1 pound pasta, except for delicate filled pastas and very large noodles such as lasagne, which will need 9 to 12 quarts water. In either case, cooking more than 2 pounds of pasta at once invites problems of uneven cooking and draining. Adequate water and frequent stirring are the two keys to eliminating the problem of pasta sticking together. Adding oil to the water has little effect except to keep the pot

RULES FOR COOKING PASTA

Pasta should be cooked and eaten; never prepare it ahead. Cook and immediately toss with sauce.

Count on 6 quarts boiling water seasoned with about 1 tablespoon salt per pound of pasta. Eliminate salt only if absolutely necessary. Delicate filled pastas or large pieces need 9 to 12 quarts water. Do not use oil—it achieves nothing.

Unless outrageously long, do not break pasta before cooking.

Cook pasta at a fierce boil, stirring often. Fresh pasta cooks in several seconds to several minutes, while dried pasta takes longer. Taste for doneness. There should be no raw flour taste and some firmness to the bite (Italians call this al dente*). Soft, mushy pasta is thrown out, never eaten.*

Immediately drain cooked pasta into a large colander and toss to rid it of all water. Then quickly combine with sauce.

Never rinse pasta unless it will be baked or served cool in a salad. Starches clinging to the surface of the noodles help them meld with the sauces.

Pasta is best hot, so warm up its serving bowl and dishes if at all possible.

Pasta salads are best cool or at room temperature, not cold.

from boiling over. Unless the strands are outrageously long and cannot fit into the pot without cracking, do not break pasta before cooking.

Since pasta cooks quickly and is at its best as soon as it is cooked, have everything ready before you start—the sauce prepared, a large colander set in the sink for draining, and a serving bowl and dishes warming in the oven. Once the salted water is rapidly boiling, add the pasta all at once. As soon as the pasta softens slightly, give it a stir, partially cover the pot, and let it continue to boil vigorously, stirring often to keep it from sticking together.

Different pastas have different cooking times, and the only test for doneness is to lift a piece from the pot and taste it. Italians consider the ideal state *al dente* (to the tooth), which means tender but firm—no raw flour taste and enough firmness to give a pleasing resistance to the bite. Start testing fresh pasta and very thin shapes after about 30 seconds, spaghetti and linguine after 4 minutes, and thick macaroni after 8 minutes. Once the pasta tastes done, do not waste a moment—empty the pot immediately into the colander and quickly toss the colander to rid the pasta of as much water as possible. In a few recipes, some of the pasta water is ladled from the pot just before draining and blended into the sauce. Usually these are sauces based on sautés of seasonings, such as garlic and olive oil, or sautés of vegetables. The starch, salt, and liquid extend the sauce and bring seasoning and body to it. Adding more oil would make the sauce too unctuous and heavy. The small amount of starch in the pasta water also encourages these light sauces to cling to the pasta.

Combine the drained pasta with its sauce over heat if possible for maximum flavor, or simply toss the hot pasta and sauce in a warmed serving bowl. Either way, pasta is best eaten hot without delay. Rinse pasta only if it is destined to be baked (for example, in lasagne or stuffed shells) or to be eaten cool in a salad. The starch that clings to unrinsed pasta helps the hot pasta meld with the sauce.

ABOUT SAUCES FOR ITALIAN PASTA

The simplest pasta sauce consists of little more than olive oil with the addition of garlic. *Aglio e olio* (simply garlic and oil) is a southern Italian classic. The simple vegetable sauces of southern Italy are made by adding zucchini, cauliflower, broccoli rabe, bell peppers, beans, and other local vegetables to the olive oil base; other typical additions include anchovies, red chili peppers, and fresh herbs. Pesto, the classic sauce of Genoa, is made by mixing fresh basil, cheese, and pine nuts with that region's fragrant olive oil and garlic.

Marinara sauce consists simply of oil and garlic with chopped tomatoes added; its many variations include puttanesca (with olives and capers) and red clam sauce.

Because most Americans are familiar with southern Italian cooking, we think of Italy as a land of tomato sauce. In parts of northern Italy where butter prevails, you will likely come across egg pasta tossed with nothing more than the local butter and maybe a little cream

RULES FOR EATING PASTA

Italians eat pasta without accompaniment either as a first course or a main course. They claim that it is so complex in the mouth that it would be compromised if served as a side dish or with an accompaniment.

Figure on 2 ounces dried pasta for a first-course serving (3 ounces fresh) and at least 4 ounces dried pasta for a main-course serving (5 ounces fresh). One pound dried pasta equals about 1¼ pounds fresh and serves 6 to 8 as a first course or 4 or 5 as a main course.

Keep pasta hot by serving it in bowls rather than on flat plates. Warm the bowls beforehand in a 200°F oven.

Most Italians favor eating pasta with a fork, not a fork and spoon. Eat long pastas gracefully by taking up only a few strands with your fork; brace the fork on the inside rim of your pasta bowl, and twirl until all the strands are wrapped around it.

Knives and pasta do not go together. Long pastas are twirled onto the fork; baked or filled pastas are cut with the side of a dinner fork.

Holding a napkin over your chest to shield your shirt from pasta sauce gone astray is in perfectly good form. Tucking the napkin into a collar is more of a family style of eating.

Italians rarely use cheese with seafood pasta, adamantly claiming that cheese overwhelms the delicate flavors of many fish and other seafoods.

Leftover pasta can be very good when reheated with a little olive oil or butter in a skillet over medium heat. Some cooks add a bit of water to guard against scorching or sticking. This is family snacking and never the way pasta is first served.

and grated Parmesan, the local cheese. The sauce in Fettuccine Alfredo, the classic restaurant dish from Rome, is made with just these three ingredients alone. Many of the country's meat-based sauces contain very little tomato, even in the south. A ragù from Bologna will typically include veal, beef, butter, and a little milk or cream. In Tuscany, beef sauces are flavored with olive oil and sometimes red wine. Rome is famous for its lamb ragù. The classic Neapolitan meat sauce is based on pork and usually contains just a hint of tomato. All these long-cooked sauces develop complex flavors from a reduction of wine and meat stocks.

CHEESE FOR PASTA

Seek out good Italian cheeses in your area, and always taste before buying. (The cheese may be Italian, but if it is of poor quality or does not taste good, do not buy it.) When good-quality imported Italian cheeses are not available, domestic substitutions are possible, but the most obvious choices are not always the best. The trick is to keep the taste and sense of the food as close to the original as possible. Here are some guidelines.

Parmigiano-Reggiano: This mouth-filling cow's milk cheese with a complex and pleasing aftertaste is made in a small, legally designated area of Emilia-Romagna in northern Italy. It is the only true Parmesan. All the others are imitations. Older is *not* better. Today's Parmigiano-Reggiano usually reaches its peak at about two years. Before World War II, when different cows gave Parmigiano-Reggiano milk, the cheese successfully aged longer. Surprisingly, a Vella dry Jack and a Wisconsin Asiago are closer in flavor than American and Argentinian Parmesans.

Mozzarella: Premium mozzarella, a cow's milk cheese, is always fresh and kept in a liquid bath, has a creamy center, and tastes of fresh milk with a little tang. Buffalo milk mozzarella, made from the milk of water buffalos, is a highly prized specialty of the area around Naples. If fresh mozzarella is impossible to find, use the low-moisture mozzarella found in most supermarkets. For more flavor, try scamorza cheese instead.

Romano, Pecorino, Pecorino Romano: *Pecorino* means sheep's milk cheese; it is made in almost every area of Italy. The cheeses range from hard, salty, sharp, and mainly used for grating (Pecorino Romano, sheep cheese from Rome, is the best known); to nutty and round in flavor and ideal for eating or grating; to fresh and creamy with an earthy undertaste. Locatelli Romano is a brand of Pecorino Romano and not a different cheese. Romano and Parmigiano-Reggiano are not interchangeable even if recipes sometimes claim they are: one is sharp, the other bold and round in flavor.

If Pecorino Romano is not available, try an aged domestic sheep's milk cheese or a *sharp* domestic provolone. For a nutty medium-aged sheep's milk cheese with some tang, use domestic fontinella or kasseri. For a fresh, creamy, and tangy pecorino, try very mild domestic goat's milk cheese or Italian ricotta salata.

Ricotta: Most supermarket ricotta lacks the creamy, sweet, and silken quality of fine ricotta. Seek out the freshest possible in specialty stores, or blend ¼ cup heavy cream into each pound of supermarket ricotta. Sheep's milk ricotta is highly prized, especially in southern Italian sweets and pasta fillings, but difficult to find.

Ricotta Salata: Imported from central and southern Italy, this salted fresh sheep's milk ricotta is pressed into cylinders about 7 × 4 inches. It tastes clean, sweet-salty, and fresh. Use wherever a lively, refreshing quality is needed. Shave or crumble it over pastas and salads, substitute it for feta cheese in recipes, or serve it as an antipasto with roasted peppers, olives, and rustic bread. You can find ricotta salata in some supermarkets and specialty stores.

Mascarpone: This intensely rich fresh cow's milk cheese from northern Italy, resembling very thick whipped cream, is found in many stores these days, probably due to the popularity of the Italian dessert tiramisù, 966. It can be imitated by stirring together until smooth 8 ounces cream cheese, softened, ½ cup sour cream, and ¼ cup heavy cream.

ABOUT MATCHING PASTA SHAPES AND SAUCES

Italy claims at least three hundred different pasta shapes (some authorities assert as many as a thousand). With all these possibilities, it helps to remember a basic rule for pairing pasta and sauce—the chunkier and more robust the sauce, the bolder the pasta shape. Hollow maccheroni, wide, thick lasagnette, and broad ribbons of pappardelle take to sauces with big flavors and bite-sized chunks of vegetables or meats. Ethereal angel hair is best in soups or light sauces. Remember that pasta needs to be moistened with sauce, not drowned in it: you want to taste the pasta as well as the sauce.

The same pasta may go by different names in different parts of Italy. A corkscrew shape may be called fusilli or rotelle; filled square or rectangular pastas are tortelli in some areas, agnolotti in others, and ravioli elsewhere.

ABOUT PASTA IN SOUP

Italy's pasta soups fall into two major categories: filled or other pastas cooked in stock and garnished only with grated cheese (usually Parmigiano-Reggiano) and brothy home-style soups with tiny or broken pasta and vegetables or other ingredients.

Italian home cooks use whatever is at hand, boiling up broth and dropping into it whatever pasta is handy; by the time the pasta is tender, the vegetables are just right. For more substance, they beat together an egg or two with grated cheese and stir it into the soup about a minute before taking it off the stove.

Tiny pastas are used in several styles of soups: cook them in the stock and finish the soup with minced fresh herbs and/or grated cheese and/or beaten egg stirred in at the last moment. Add pasta with vegetables or other ingredients for brothy soups.

- Small shapes: Meloni, orzo, pastine, tubetti, ditalini, anellini (little rings), stelline, avene (oats), tempestine (little tempests), and quadrettini.
- Break these long strands into clear soups to whatever size you need: pappardelle, lasagnette, maltagliati, lasagne, bucatini, capellini, vermicelli, spaghetti, and linguine.

ABOUT FREEZING FRESH PASTA

Fresh Pasta: Unfilled fresh pasta is best not frozen but allowed to dry at room temperature. Until it is dried, make sure the pieces do not touch. Hang it from a rack or spread it on shallow baskets, or when it is partially dry, sprinkle it with semolina flour and roll into loose coils. The dried pasta will keep for several days; it may crack if held longer, but the flavor will not be changed.

Filled Pasta: Pastas with moist fillings or stuffed with fresh or creamy cheese do not freeze well. Pastas stuffed with firm meat fillings or others that are essentially dry will freeze well.

To freeze pasta, line a large baking sheet with aluminum foil. Spread out the filled pasta so that the pieces do not touch. Freeze overnight. Gently drop the pieces into heavy freezer bags and seal, leaving some air in the bag to protect the pasta from being crushed. Freeze for up to 3 months.

GUIDE TO ITALIAN PASTA SHAPES AND USES

SHAPE & NAME	COOKING TIME	SUBSTITUTIONS	GOES WITH
Bigoli 	8 to 15 minutes	Bucatini, Perciatelli	Chunky meat, seafood, or vegetable sauces: Chicken Ragù, 307
Bucatini/Perciatelli *Little Mouths* 	10 to 18 minutes	Bigoli, Sedani, Long Fusilli	Chunky and/or robust sauces: Piquant Tomato Sauce, 305 Fresh Tomato Sauce with Mozzarella, 305
Capelli d'Angelo/ Capellini *Angel Hair* 	2 to 4 minutes	Vermicelli, Spaghettini	Delicate, light sauces: Garlic and Oil, 308 Butter and Cheese, 309 Fresh Herbs, 309
Cavatelli 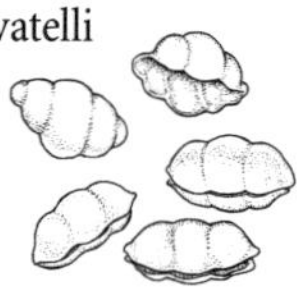	9 to 13 minutes	Small Gnocchi, Malloreddus, Sedanini	Sauces with full flavors but not large pieces: Bolognese Sauce, 307 Fresh Tomato Sauce, 305 Shrimp and Fresh Chili Peppers, 311
Maccheroni alla Chitarra *Guitar Pasta* 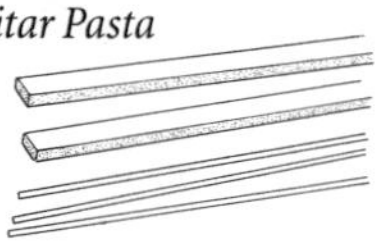	6 to 8 minutes	Spaghetti, Bigoli	Medium- to full-bodied sauces: Tomato Sauces, 304 to 307 Canned Tuna Sauce, 308
Conchiglie *Shells* 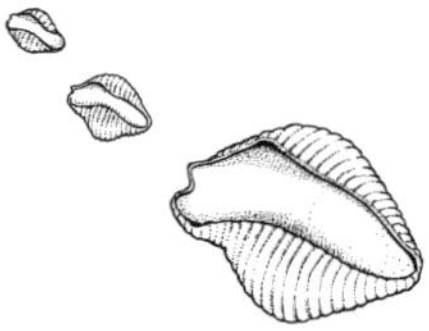	8 to 20 minutes	Ziti, Penne, Fusilli, Orecchiette	Mini shells in soups: Minestrone, 100 Small shells with sauces: Sun-Dried Tomato Sauce, 305 Chicken Ragù, 307 Tomato Sauces, 304 to 307 Large stuffed shells: All fillings, 313 to 314 All: Tuna Noodle Casserole, 321
Farfalle *Butterflies* or *Bow Ties* 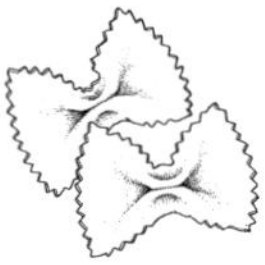	9 to 12 minutes	Shells, Short Fusilli, Sedani, Penne	Chunky sauces with bold flavors: Spicy Chicken Bits and Broccoli, 312 Chicken Ragù, 307
Fettuccine *Ribbons* 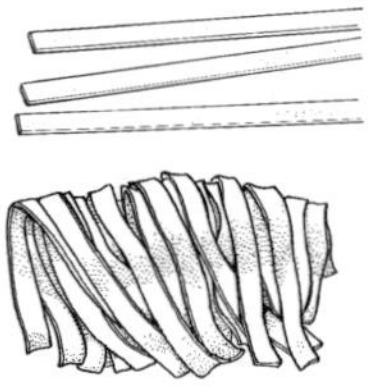	7 to 9 minutes	Tagliatelle	Creamy sauces and chunky medium- to full-bodied sauces: Fettuccine Alfredo, 310 Fresh Herbs, 309 Tomato Sauces, 304 to 307 Bolognese Sauce, 307 Chicken Ragù, 307

SHAPE & NAME	COOKING TIME	SUBSTITUTIONS	GOES WITH
Fusilli *Corkscrews* 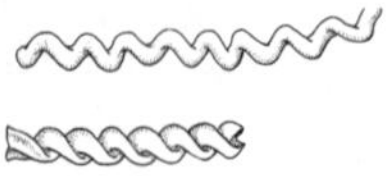 *Long and short*	Long: 8 to 12 minutes Short: 10 to 15 minutes	Penne, Bigoli, Bucatini, Sedani, Medium Shells, Farfalle, Rotelle	Chunky sauces with bold flavors: Long: Porcini and Red Wine Sauce, 308 Pesto Sauce, 307 Shrimp and Fresh Chili Peppers, 311 Short: Baked Macaroni and Cheese, 320 Tuna Noodle Casserole, 321
Gnocchi *Dumplings*  *Potato* *Semolina*	Potato: 6 minutes Semolina: Baked 25 minutes	Potato: Hollow and Shaped Maccheroni Semolina: No substitutions	Light to bold sauces: Bolognese Sauce, 307 Chicken Ragù, 307 Tomato Sauces, 304 to 307 Butter and Cheese, 309 Porcini and Red Wine Sauce, 308
Lasagne 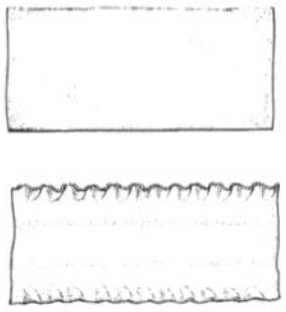	8 to 14 minutes	Maltagliati, Pappardelle	Lasagne, 314 to 317
Lasagnette *Little Lasagne* 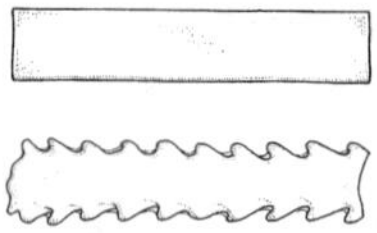	9 to 15 minutes	Pappardelle, Maltagliati, Broken Lasagne	Big, bold-flavored sauces: Bolognese Sauce, 307 Chicken Ragù, 307
Linguine *Little Tongues* 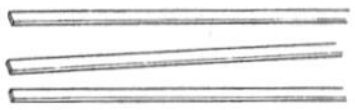	5 to 8 minutes	Spaghetti, Trenette, Maccheroni alla Chitarra	Smooth to chunky sauces, light to medium bodied: Pesto Sauce, 307 Red Pesto Sauce, 308 Fresh Tomato Sauce, 305
Maltagliati *Bad Cuts* 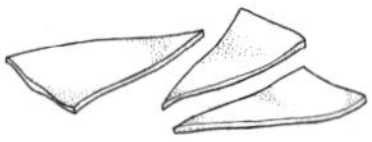	2 to 5 minutes	Broken Pappardelle For chunky sauces: Broken Lasagne, Farfalle, Penne	Light to bold sauces: Tomato Sauces, 304 to 307 Bolognese Sauce, 307 Chicken Ragù, 307
Melloni *Melon Seeds* 	5 to 8 minutes	Orzo, Broken Spaghetti, Linguine, Vermicelli	Soups: Minestrone, 100, and other bean or vegetable soups, 93 to 104 Clear Soups, 105 to 107
Orecchiette *Little Ears* 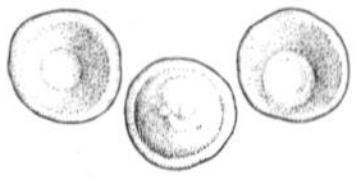	10 to 15 minutes	Shells, Farfalle	Bold, chunky sauces: Sausage and Broccoli Rabe, 312 Bolognese Sauce, 307 Chicken Ragù, 307 Piquant Tomato Sauce, 305

SHAPE & NAME	COOKING TIME	SUBSTITUTIONS	GOES WITH
Orzo *Barley Kernels* 	10 to 13 minutes	Melloni	Soups, 94 to 120 Fresh Herbs, 309
Pappardelle 	9 to 13 minutes	Lasagnette, Maltagliati, Broken Lasagne, Tagliatelle, Fettuccine	Robust sauces: Bolognese Sauce, 307 Puttanesca Sauce, 305
Penne *Quills or Pens* 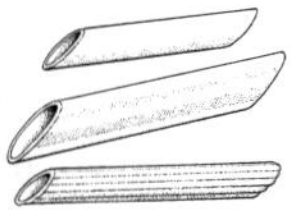	10 to 15 minutes	Sedani, Shells, Short Fusilli	Chunky sauces, casseroles, tomato and vegetable sauces: Porcini and Red Wine Sauce, 308 Bolognese Sauce, 307
Pizzoccheri *Buckwheat Ribbons* 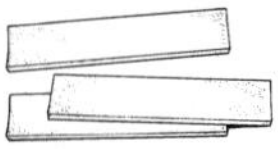	10 to 14 minutes	Whole-Wheat Pasta, Fettuccine, Tagliatelle, Pappardelle, Fusilli	Deep-flavored, robust sauces: Sausage and Broccoli Rabe, 312
Rigatoni *Big Ribs* 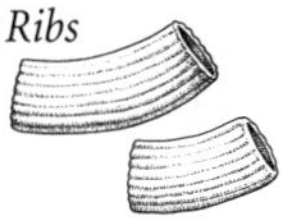	10 to 16 minutes	Ziti, Short Fusilli, Penne, Sedani, Strozzapreti	Sturdy sauces with big flavors: Puttanesca Sauce, 305 Shrimp and Fresh Chili Peppers, 311
Sedani, Sedanini *Celery, Little Celery* 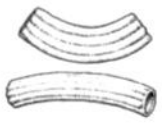	8 to 14 minutes	Penne, Short Fusilli, Shells	Robust sauces and vegetable sauces: Canned Tuna Sauce, 308 Red Pesto Sauce, 308 Fresh Tomato Sauce with Black Olives, 305 Puttanesca Sauce, 305
Spaghetti *Little Strings* 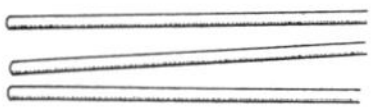	7 to 8 minutes	Linguine, Maccheroni alla Chitarra, Trenette	Medium-bodied sauces: Tomato Sauces, 304 to 307 Puttanesca Sauce, 305 Classic Italian American Tomato Sauce II, 306
Tagliatelle *Little Cuts* 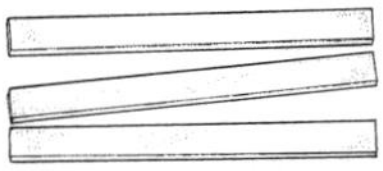	7 to 10 minutes	Fettuccine	Substantial sauces with chunky vegetables: Bolognese Sauce, 307 Primavera, 309 Italian Tomato Sauce, 304
Trenette 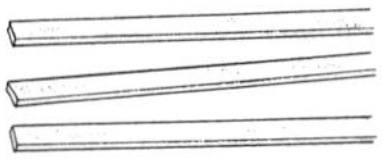	7 to 10 minutes	Tagliatelle, Linguine	As for Tagliatelle

SHAPE & NAME	COOKING TIME	SUBSTITUTIONS	GOES WITH
Vermicelli *Little Worms* 	4 to 6 minutes	Capellini	Light sauces: Butter and Cheese, 309 Garlic and Oil, 308 Fresh Herbs, 309
Ziti *Bridegrooms* 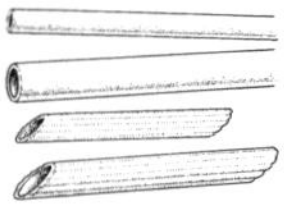	12 to 18 minutes	Rigatoni, Broken Lasagne, Penne	Big sauces with deep flavors: Puttanesca Sauce, 305 Bolognese Sauce, 307 Shrimp and Fresh Chili Peppers, 311

FRESH EGG PASTA (BASIC RECIPE)

About 1¾ pounds

Fresh pasta is generally made with unbleached all-purpose flour rather than the durum semolina flour used for dried pasta. Whole eggs, egg whites, and water and/or wine are used to moisten the flour, and sometimes seasonings, salt, and olive oil are also added. Fresh pasta should rest for at least an hour after cutting and before cooking. For leftovers, see About Freezing Fresh Pasta, 298.

Pour onto a clean counter, shape into a mound, and make a well in the center of:

3½ cups unbleached all-purpose flour, preferably stone-ground organic

Add to the well in the flour:

5 large eggs or 7 large egg whites
1 teaspoon salt (optional)
1 teaspoon extra-virgin olive oil (optional)

Beat the eggs lightly with a fork, drawing in some flour as you go, until the eggs are mixed and slightly thickened. Using the fingertips of one hand, gradually incorporate the flour into the eggs and blend everything into a smooth, not too stiff dough. If the dough feels too dry and crumbly, add water as needed.

Alternatively, process the ingredients in a food processor just until blended, 15 to 20 seconds, being careful not to overheat the dough.

Knead the dough until satiny and very elastic, about 10 minutes. Divide the dough into 4 pieces and wrap the pieces loosely in plastic or cover with an inverted bowl. If you have time, let the dough rest for 30 minutes before rolling it out.

SPINACH PASTA

Cook 10 ounces fresh spinach, trimmed, washed, and dried, or thaw 6 ounces frozen spinach. Squeeze the spinach dry and mince it very fine. Prepare Fresh Egg Pasta, above, decreasing the eggs to 2. Add the spinach to the flour with the eggs.

HERB PASTA

Prepare Fresh Egg Pasta, above, adding ½ cup minced strong fresh herbs (sage, rosemary, thyme, oregano, or marjoram) or 1½ cups minced mild fresh herbs (basil, chives, parsley, or scallions) to the flour with the eggs.

ESPECIALLY STRONG PASTA

Use this recipe for moist fillings and light-bodied ribbon noodles.

Prepare Fresh Egg Pasta, above, substituting ½ cup cool water or white wine for 3 of the eggs.

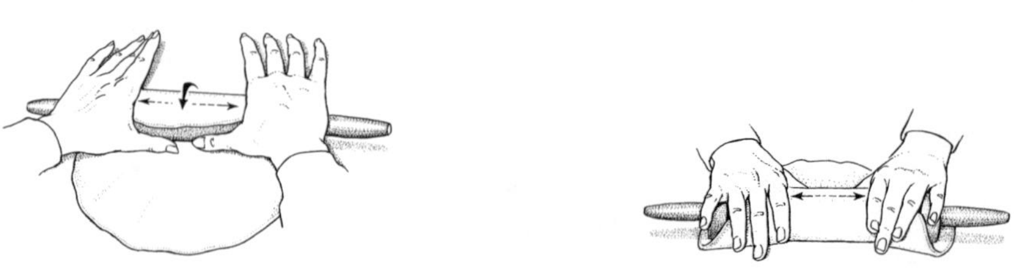

Stretch the dough sideways: wind it around the pin a quarter of the way toward yourself and run your palms over it from the pin's center outward.

WHOLE-WHEAT PASTA

Prepare Fresh Egg Pasta, above, substituting 1 to 1½ cups whole-wheat flour for the same amount of all-purpose flour. This dough may need a little more liquid.

ABOUT ROLLING OUT FRESH PASTA

The key to light, resilient pasta is gently stretching and pulling the sheet of dough as you roll it thinner and thinner. Whether working with a rolling pin or a hand-cranked pasta machine, work with only a quarter of the pasta at a time, leaving the rest loosely covered. Avoid automatic pasta machines that mix and then extrude finished pasta—the results are inferior to pasta rolled by hand or through a hand-cranked pasta machine.

Working by Hand: Lightly flour a large surface and use a rolling pin to roll out 1 piece of the dough, repeatedly turning it a quarter turn as the circle grows. When the pasta is about ⅛ inch thick, pick it up and wind it around the rolling pin a quarter of the way toward yourself. At the same time, stretch the dough gently sideways by running your palms over it from the pin's center outward. Unroll the dough, turn the round a quarter of a turn, and repeat this winding and sideways stretching three more times. Then stretch the dough from the center by winding a third of it back onto the pin and gently pushing the pin away from yourself; keep the rest of the dough in place with the palm of your other hand. Turn the dough a quarter turn and repeat until the entire circle of dough is stretched and the dough reaches the desired thickness. For ribbon pastas, such as fettuccine, tagliatelle, maltagliati, and others, the dough should be about 1/32 inch thick, thin enough to detect the outline of your hand through it. For filled pasta, the sheets should be thinner still—sheer enough to clearly see your hand through it.

Working with a Pasta Machine: Set the machine's rollers at the widest setting. Lightly flour 1 of the 4 pieces of dough. Pass the dough through the rollers three times, folding it over onto itself each time. Sprinkle flour on the dough any time it threatens to stick. Guide the dough as it comes out of the rollers with the palm of your hand, held flat to protect the dough from being punctured by your fingers. Set the rollers one notch closer together and repeat the process another two or three times. Stop flouring the dough when it is no longer sticky. The dough should go from lumpy and even holey to a satiny sheet. As this happens, begin to stretch the dough gently as it emerges from the rollers. Continue to notch the rollers closer together and roll the pasta through them until you reach the desired thickness, 1/32 inch for ribbon pastas, such as fettuccine, tagliatelle, maltagliati, and others; the dough must be paper thin for filled shapes.

Making Shapes: Ribbons and unfilled shapes are cut pasta sheets that have partially dried. Before cutting, let the pasta sheet dry on a clean counter until it feels leathery but not at all stiff, about 20 minutes. Use a sharp knife or pizza cutter to cut it into ribbons, strips, or squares. Dry the cut pasta further in an airy area—on large flat baskets covered with dish towels, or separate the strands and drape them over dowels or broom handles—until it is no longer moist and sticky. Semidry ribbon pastas can be dusted with semolina flour to prevent sticking, wrapped in coils, and set on racks or in baskets for drying. If not using the pasta immediately, dry it thoroughly and store in sealed containers. Do not freeze. Although it is best cooked the same day, dried homemade pasta is very good indeed several days later.

Farfalle: Cut pasta into rectangles about 1½ x 1 inch and pinch each one together at the center.

Fettuccine: Cut long strands a little wider than ⅛ inch.

Lasagne: Cut into rectangles about 8 x 4 inches.

Lasagnette: Cut into 1-inch-wide strips.

Pappardelle: Cut ribbons ¾ inch wide.

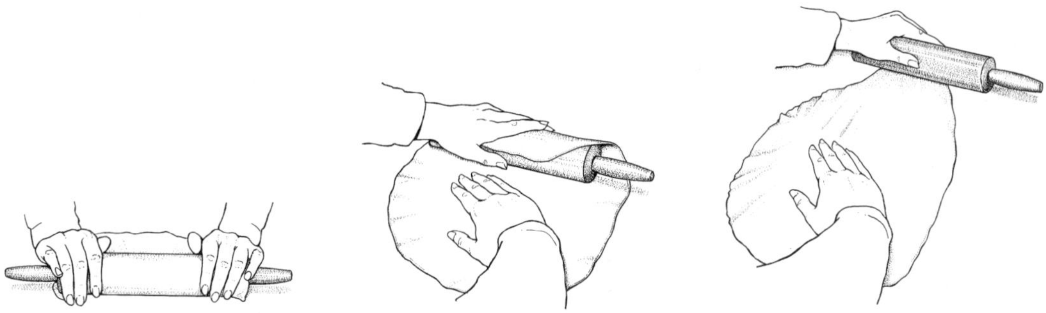

Stretch the dough from the center: wind a third of it back onto the pin and gently push the pin away from yourself.

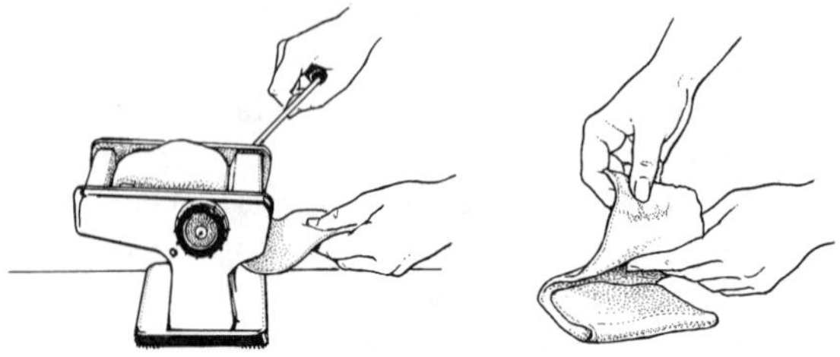

Pass the dough through the rollers three times, folding it over on itself each time.

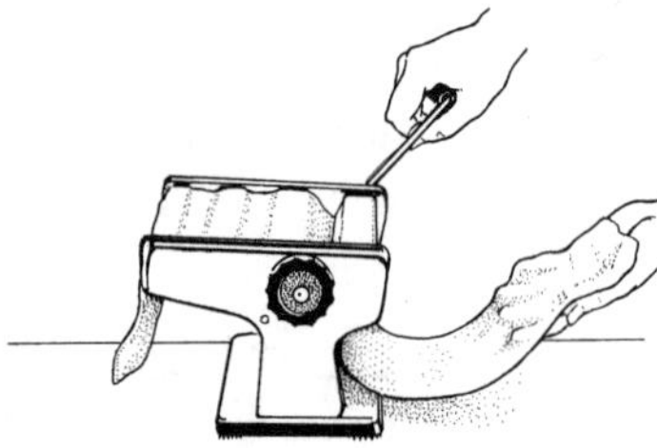

Guide the dough as it comes out of the rollers with the palm of your hand.

Tagliatelle: Cut ribbons just under ⅜ inch wide.
Trenette: Roll out the dough a little thicker than usual and cut strands ¼ inch wide.

ABOUT TOMATO SAUCE

Most tomato sauce recipes invite improvisation, but no matter what other ingredients eventually find their way into the sauce, the best begin with good tomatoes—superbly ripe with deep flavor and a nice balance of sweet and acid. When fresh tomatoes are available, trust your own palate and taste them before buying if you can. Vine ripening does not guarantee good flavor. For both globe and plum types, peeling fresh tomatoes for briefly cooked sauces is a matter of preference and tradition. Many cooks like the texture and taste of a good tomato's peel.

When flavorful fresh tomatoes are unavailable, choose good-quality canned whole tomatoes for best flavor. Cans of crushed and pureed tomatoes often contain generous amounts of inferior tomato paste, which can impart a heavy, metallic taste. Do not assume imported canned tomatoes are best; several of our brands of domestic tomatoes are as good as and sometimes better than imported varieties.

The faster a tomato sauce is cooked, the fresher and brighter its flavor; hence, we prefer wide skillets that let liquids evaporate quickly rather than saucepans that slow down the process. When generous amounts of aromatic vegetables and other seasonings enter a recipe, a longer simmer (20 to 30 minutes) in a saucepan encourages flavors to unfold and meld. Likewise, meat-based tomato sauces often cook longer still.

Tomato paste and sugar are optional ingredients. The first, used in small quantities, boosts tomato flavor, while a little of the second smooths out excess acidity. When shopping for prepared sauces, look for those with the fewest preservatives—they will have the freshest flavor—and rely on your own taste until you find one or two you like. Simple tricks to boost the flavor of a store-bought sauce are

A drizzle of good olive oil and a sprinkling of ground black pepper
A handful of fresh mushrooms, sliced and sautéed
A few good-quality pitted olives and drained capers
A can of tuna fish, drained
A mixture of fresh herbs, minced

ITALIAN TOMATO SAUCE (BASIC RECIPE)

Enough for 1 pound pasta

This classic tomato sauce and any of its variations can be kept in the refrigerator for up to 4 days or frozen for up to 3 months.

Heat in a large skillet over medium heat:

2 to 3 tablespoons extra-virgin olive oil

Add:

⅓ cup finely chopped fresh parsley
1 medium onion, finely chopped
1 small carrot, peeled and finely chopped
1 celery stalk with leaves, finely chopped

Cook, stirring, until the onions are golden brown, about 5 minutes. Add:

2 cloves garlic, minced
½ cup packed fresh basil leaves, chopped, or 1 sprig each fresh rosemary, sage, and thyme

Cook, stirring, for about 30 seconds. Stir in:

2½ pounds ripe tomatoes, peeled, if desired, seeded, and coarsely chopped, or one 28-ounce can and one 14-ounce can whole tomatoes, with juice, crushed between your fingers as you add them to the pan
1 tablespoon tomato paste (optional)
Salt and ground black pepper to taste

Simmer, uncovered, until the sauce is thickened, about 10 minutes. Remove the herb sprigs.

PIQUANT TOMATO SAUCE

Prepare Italian Tomato Sauce, above, substituting 1 whole dried red chili pepper for the carrots and celery and decreasing the basil to just a few leaves. Remove the chili pepper before serving.

SUN-DRIED TOMATO SAUCE

Put ½ cup sun-dried tomatoes (not in oil) in a small bowl, add boiling water to cover, and let soak until softened, about 20 minutes. Drain well and finely chop. Prepare Italian Tomato Sauce, above, decreasing the fresh tomatoes to 2 pounds or the canned tomatoes to 34 ounces, and adding the sun-dried tomatoes along with the garlic.

SIMPLEST ITALIAN TOMATO SAUCE MARINARA

Enough for 1 pound pasta

Bring to a simmer in a large saucepan over medium-low heat:

2 pounds ripe tomatoes, peeled, if desired, seeded, and coarsely chopped, or one 28-ounce can whole tomatoes, with juice, crushed between your fingers as you add them to the pan
⅓ cup extra-virgin olive oil
3 cloves garlic, halved
6 sprigs fresh basil
6 sprigs fresh parsley

Simmer, uncovered, until the sauce is thickened, about 10 minutes. Pass through a food mill and season with:

Salt and ground black pepper to taste

MARIA'S TWENTY-MINUTE TOMATO SAUCE

Enough for 1 pound pasta

Heat in a medium saucepan over medium heat:

2 tablespoons extra-virgin olive oil

Add:

1 medium onion, minced
2 medium carrots, peeled and minced
2 cloves garlic, minced

Cook, stirring, until softened, about 5 minutes. Stir in:

One 28-ounce can whole tomatoes, with juice, broken into pieces
1 tablespoon dried basil
1 to 2 teaspoons dried oregano

Simmer, uncovered, until the sauce is thickened, about 10 minutes. Remove to a food processor and pulse until smooth. Return to the saucepan and stir in:

1 to 2 teaspoons sugar
½ to 1 teaspoon red pepper flakes
Salt and ground black pepper to taste

Heat through, about 5 minutes.

FRESH TOMATO SAUCE

Enough for 1 pound pasta

Summer's best. Make this easy sauce when you can get juicy, ripe tomatoes.

Drain in a colander for 20 minutes:

5 large ripe tomatoes, seeded and finely diced

Remove to a large bowl and stir in:

½ cup fresh basil leaves, finely chopped
3 tablespoons extra-virgin olive oil
2 cloves garlic, finely minced
Salt and ground black pepper to taste

Let stand for at least 30 minutes. Serve the sauce at room temperature. If serving over hot pasta, sprinkle each portion with:

1 to 2 teaspoons balsamic vinegar

FRESH TOMATO SAUCE WITH MOZZARELLA

Prepare Fresh Tomato Sauce, above. Add 8 ounces fresh mozzarella cheese, cut into small cubes, to the hot pasta and toss before adding the tomato sauce.

FRESH TOMATO SAUCE WITH BLACK OLIVES

Prepare Fresh Tomato Sauce, above. Stir in ½ cup pitted Ligurian black or Kalamata olives to the sauce.

FRESH TOMATO SAUCE WITH FRESH OREGANO OR PARSLEY

Prepare Fresh Tomato Sauce, above, substituting fresh oregano or parsley for the basil.

FRESH TOMATO SAUCE WITH HOT CHILI PEPPER

Prepare Fresh Tomato Sauce, above. Stir in 1 small fresh chili pepper, seeded and finely minced.

PUTTANESCA SAUCE

Enough for 1 pound pasta

Spicy, savory, and exciting, Puttanesca, or Streetwalker's, Sauce is ready to toss with pasta in minutes.

Heat in a large skillet over medium heat:

¼ cup extra-virgin olive oil

Add:

2 large cloves garlic, minced
1 dried red chili pepper

Cook, stirring and crushing the pepper with the back of a spoon, just until the garlic is pale blond, about 30 seconds. Stir in:

1 cup oil-cured black olives, such as Gaeta, pitted and coarsely chopped
6 anchovy fillets, soaked in water to cover for 5 minutes and drained
½ teaspoon dried oregano

Cook for about 30 seconds, then stir in:

1½ pounds ripe tomatoes, peeled, if desired, seeded, and chopped, or one 28-ounce can whole tomatoes, with juice, crushed between your fingers as you add them to the pan

Simmer, uncovered, until the sauce is thickened, about 5 minutes. Stir in:

3 tablespoons packed minced fresh parsley
2 tablespoons drained capers

Season with:

Salt and ground black pepper to taste

CLASSIC ITALIAN AMERICAN TOMATO SAUCE I (NEAPOLITAN RAGÙ)

Enough for 1 pound pasta

This is the sauce Italian grandmothers had simmering on the stove for half a day.

Heat in a large Dutch oven over medium-high heat:

2 tablespoons olive oil, preferably extra virgin

Add:

1½ pounds boneless pork loin or beef bottom round, in 1 piece

Brown on all sides. Add:

2 cups diced onions
4 ounces prosciutto or pancetta, chopped
2 cloves garlic, minced

Reduce the heat to medium and cook, stirring the vegetables and prosciutto around the piece of meat, until the onions are softened, about 10 minutes. Stir in:

1 cup water

Cook until the water is almost evaporated and has made a little bit of sauce around the onions, 20 to 25 minutes. Stir in:

3½ pounds ripe tomatoes, peeled, if desired, seeded, and chopped, or two 28-ounce cans whole tomatoes, with juice, crushed between your fingers as you add them to the pan
1 cup red wine
¼ cup tomato paste
1 sprig fresh basil or oregano, or 1 teaspoon dried

Bring to a boil, reduce the heat, and simmer, uncovered, stirring often, turning the meat halfway through the cooking time, until the meat offers no resistance when pierced with the tip of a sharp knife and is fall-apart tender, 3 to 4 hours. Remove the meat and set aside to cool. Cook down the sauce if it is not thick, and season with:

Salt and ground black pepper to taste

Place in a medium skillet over medium heat:

1 pound sweet Italian sausage

As soon as the sausage has released some of its fat, increase the heat to medium-high to help with the browning. Cut the sausage into ¼-inch-thick slices and stir into the sauce. Finely chop the reserved piece of meat or process in a food processor until finely chopped but not a paste. If chopping by hand, remove to a bowl. Add to either the bowl or processor:

2 large eggs
¾ cup fresh breadcrumbs
½ cup chopped fresh parsley
½ cup grated Parmesan cheese
½ teaspoon salt
Ground black pepper to taste

Stir together well or process just to mix, then shape into 1-inch meatballs. Heat in a large skillet over medium-high heat:

2 tablespoons olive oil

Brown the meatballs in batches, about 1 minute each side, adding more oil as needed. Stir into the sauce.

CLASSIC ITALIAN AMERICAN TOMATO SAUCE II

Enough for 1 pound pasta

Unsurpassed in its ability to please family and friends. The meatballs and sauce also make a fine dish on their own or tucked into crusty rolls.

With the machine running, drop through the feed tube of a food processor:

1 clove garlic, peeled
½ cup packed fresh parsley leaves
4 ounces Parmesan or Asiago cheese, cut into coarse chunks

Process until the cheese is finely grated. Add:

1 medium onion, halved

Process until finely grated. Remove to a large bowl. Add and blend well:

1 pound lean ground beef, or 8 ounces lean ground beef and 8 ounces ground turkey
½ cup fresh breadcrumbs
1 large egg, lightly beaten
3 tablespoons dry red wine
2 tablespoons tomato paste
½ teaspoon salt
⅛ teapoon ground black pepper

Shape into about fourteen 2- to 3-inch meatballs. Dredge lightly with:

All-purpose flour

Heat in a large skillet over medium-high heat:

2 to 3 tablespoons extra-virgin olive oil

Add the meatballs and brown on the bottom. Turn and sprinkle with:

1 medium onion, finely chopped

Brown the meatballs on all sides. Pour off the fat in the skillet and add:

- **1 clove garlic, minced**
- **¼ teaspoon dried oregano**

Stir in:

- **One 28-ounce can whole tomatoes, with juice, crushed between your fingers as you add them to the pan**

Bring to a simmer and cover the pan. Reduce the heat and simmer gently until the meatballs are cooked and the sauce is thickened, about 30 minutes.

ITALIAN-STYLE MEATBALLS

Prepare the meat mixture for Classic Italian American Tomato Sauce II, above. Shape into meatballs ½ to ¾ inch in diameter. Brown in olive oil, then simmer in a little white wine and chicken stock for about 20 minutes. Serve hot as an antipasto or a main course without the tomato sauce.

BOLOGNESE SAUCE (RAGÙ BOLOGNESE)

Enough for 1 pound pasta

With beef as the main ingredient and surprisingly little tomato, the many subtle tastes in this famous sauce come together beautifully.

Heat in a large saucepan over medium-low heat:

- **3 tablespoons extra-virgin olive oil**
- **1 ounce pancetta, finely chopped (optional)**

Cook, stirring, until the pancetta releases its fat but is not browned, about 8 minutes. Increase the heat to medium and add:

- **1 large carrot, peeled and minced**
- **2 small celery stalks, minced**
- **½ medium onion, minced**

Cook, stirring, until the onions are translucent, about 5 minutes. Add and brown:

- **1¼ pounds coarsely ground beef skirt steak or very lean ground chuck**

Stir in:

- **¾ cup chicken or beef stock**
- **⅔ cup dry white wine**
- **2 tablespoons tomato paste**

Reduce the heat to low and simmer gently, partially covered and skimming occasionally, until the sauce is the consistency of a thick soup, about 2 hours. From time to time as the sauce simmers, add, 2 tablespoons at a time:

- **1½ cups whole milk**

Let cool, cover, and refrigerate for up to 24 hours. Skim the fat off the top before reheating.

CHICKEN RAGÙ

Enough for 1 pound pasta

Pappardelle is traditionally served with a sauce made from game, but chicken makes a delicious substitute in this richly flavored sauce. To freeze the sauce, prepare up to sautéing the mushrooms. Cook and blend in the mushrooms shortly before serving.

Heat in a large Dutch oven over low heat:

- **3 tablespoons extra-virgin olive oil**

Add:

- **2 ounces salt pork, diced**
- **1 medium onion, finely chopped**
- **1 carrot, peeled and finely chopped**
- **1 celery stalk, finely chopped**

Cook, stirring occasionally, until the vegetables are softened and beginning to brown, about 8 minutes. Add to the Dutch oven:

- **1 pound boneless chicken thighs, diced**

Season with:

- **Salt and ground black pepper to taste**

Increase the heat to medium and brown on all sides, about 5 minutes. Stir in and cook until almost evaporated:

- **½ cup dry white wine**

Stir in:

- **1 cup chicken stock**
- **One 28-ounce can whole plum tomatoes, drained and chopped**

Reduce the heat to low and simmer, partially covered, until the chicken is tender, about 1½ hours. Sprinkle with:

- **6 fresh sage leaves, chopped**
- **Salt and ground black pepper to taste**

Melt in a medium skillet over medium heat:

- **3 tablespoons butter**

Add and cook, stirring, until browned:

- **8 ounces mushrooms, wiped clean and halved**
- **Salt and ground black pepper to taste**

Add the mushrooms to the sauce.

PESTO SAUCE

Enough for 1 pound pasta

This classic sauce from Genoa needs to be made with fresh basil. Pesto is traditionally tossed with trenette, a flat ribbon pasta similar to linguine but fresh. Sometimes green beans and sliced potatoes are cooked along with the pasta in the same water, making the dish more robust. If freezing, add the nuts and cheese after thawing.

Process to a rough paste in a food processor:

- **2 cups loosely packed fresh basil leaves**
- **⅓ cup pine nuts**
- **2 medium cloves garlic, peeled**
- **½ cup grated Parmesan cheese**

With the machine running, slowly pour through the feed tube:

½ cup extra-virgin olive oil

If the sauce seems dry (it should be a thick paste), add a little more olive oil. Season with:

Salt and ground black pepper to taste

Use immediately or store in a covered glass jar in the refrigerator for up to 1 week.

RED PESTO SAUCE

Enough for 1 pound pasta

Sun-dried tomatoes may have originated in Italy, but American cooks have invented uses barely conceived of across the Atlantic. Even yellow sun-dried tomatoes are good here. Toss this pesto with pasta, spread it on bruschetta, 167, or pizza, 195, or serve it with grilled poultry or seafood. If serving with pasta, reserve ½ cup of the pasta cooking water to stir into the pesto. Otherwise, just add hot water to thin it to the desired consistency.

Combine in a small saucepan with enough water to cover:

⅓ cup chopped drained water-packed sun-dried tomatoes
1 clove garlic, peeled
6 fresh basil leaves

Bring to a boil, remove from the heat, and let stand for 20 minutes. With the machine running, drop through the feed tube of a food processor:

1 large clove garlic, peeled
1 cup packed fresh basil leaves
¼ cup extra-virgin olive oil
⅓ cup grated Parmesan cheese

Drain the tomato mixture, add to the processor, and finely chop. Season with:

Salt and ground black pepper to taste

Stir in:

½ cup pasta cooking water or hot water

PORCINI AND RED WINE SAUCE

Enough for 1 pound pasta

A robust and meaty-tasting sauce with little or no meat and the haunting woodsy taste of porcini mushrooms.

Soak in hot water to cover until softened, for about 20 minutes:

1½ ounces dried porcini mushrooms, thoroughly rinsed

Remove the mushrooms with a slotted spoon and chop. Strain the soaking liquid through a sieve lined with a paper towel. Heat in a large skillet over medium-high heat:

2 tablespoons extra-virgin olive oil
2 ounces pancetta, finely chopped (optional)

Add:

½ medium onion, minced
Zest of ½ lemon, cut into very thin strips
4 fresh or dried sage leaves

Cook, stirring, until the onions are softened. Add the porcini along with:

8 ounces button mushrooms, wiped clean and thinly sliced

Increase the heat to high and cook, stirring, until the mushrooms are golden brown. Stir in:

1 clove garlic, minced

Stir in the porcini soaking liquid. Simmer briskly until the liquid is reduced to a glaze. Stir in and reduce again to a glaze:

1 cup dry red wine

Stir in:

1 cup chicken stock

Season with:

Salt and ground black pepper to taste

CANNED TUNA SAUCE

Enough for 1 pound pasta

Slow-cooked garlic gives this sauce its deep flavors. If you can, use tuna packed in olive oil. If serving with pasta, reserve ½ cup of the pasta cooking water to stir into the sauce.

Heat in a large skillet over medium-low heat:

¼ cup extra-virgin olive oil

Add:

2 tablespoons chopped fresh parsley
8 large cloves garlic, halved

Cook, stirring, until the garlic is softened, about 20 minutes. Do not let the garlic darken further than blond, or it will be bitter. Stir in:

3 anchovy fillets, rinsed, patted dry, and chopped
1 cup oil-cured black olives, pitted and coarsely chopped
½ cup pasta cooking water or hot water
½ teaspoon fennel seeds, crushed (optional)
Generous pinch of red pepper flakes

Cook for 1 minute, remove from the heat, and stir in:

One 6-ounce can tuna, drained and flaked
1 tablespoon drained capers (optional)
1 tablespoon chopped fresh parsley
Salt and ground black pepper to taste

SPAGHETTI WITH GARLIC AND OIL (AGLIO E OLIO)

8 first-course servings; 4 main-course servings

A simple sauce of olive oil and garlic is one of the purest ways of enjoying good-quality spaghetti or other skinny ribbon-shaped pasta. A little bit of the pasta cooking water helps the sautéed garlic cling to the pasta.

Bring to a rolling boil in a large pot:

6 quarts water

2 tablespoons salt

Add and cook until tender but firm:

1 pound spaghetti

Meanwhile, heat in a large skillet over medium heat:

3 tablespoons extra-virgin olive oil

Add:

3 large cloves garlic, thinly sliced

1 dried red chili pepper (optional)

Cook, stirring, until the garlic is pale blond, about 2 minutes. Remove the chili pepper. Drain the spaghetti, reserving ½ cup of the cooking water. Add the cooking water and hot pasta to the garlic mixture and toss to combine. Season with:

Salt and ground black pepper to taste

Serve hot. No cheese should be served with this dish.

FETTUCCINE WITH BUTTER AND CHEESE

8 first-course servings; 4 main-course servings

Use freshly grated Parmigiano-Reggiano for the best flavor.

Bring to a rolling boil in a large pot:

6 quarts water

2 tablespoons salt

Add and cook until tender but firm:

1¼ pounds fresh fettuccine or tagliatelle, or 1 pound dried

Drain and toss the hot pasta with:

8 tablespoons (1 stick) unsalted butter, softened, or ⅓ cup extra-virgin olive oil

1½ cups grated Parmesan cheese

Season with:

Salt and ground black pepper to taste

Serve immediately.

LESS BUTTERY BUTTER AND CHEESE SAUCE

Boil 1½ cups chicken stock until reduced by half. Stir in 3 tablespoons unsalted butter. Meanwhile, prepare Fettuccine with Butter and Cheese, above. Toss the stock mixture with the hot pasta and Parmesan cheese. Season with salt and ground black pepper to taste.

PENNE WITH VODKA

8 first-course servings; 4 main-course servings

Here is a modern Italian pasta dish that is elegant enough to begin a formal dinner.

Melt or heat in a large skillet over medium heat:

3 tablespoons butter or olive oil

Add:

1 onion, finely chopped

Cook, stirring, until softened, about 5 minutes. Add:

2 large cloves garlic, finely minced

Cook, stirring, until just starting to color, about 1 minute. Stir in:

One 28-ounce can whole plum tomatoes, lightly drained and chopped by hand or in a food processor

¼ cup vodka

¼ teaspoon red pepper flakes

Simmer briskly for 10 minutes. Stir in:

½ cup heavy cream

Heat through. Stir in:

12 fresh basil leaves, chopped (optional)

Salt and ground black pepper to taste

Meanwhile, bring to a rolling boil in a large pot:

6 quarts water

2 tablespoons salt

Add and cook until tender but firm:

1 pound penne

Drain and remove to a large serving bowl. Toss with the sauce and serve very hot. Grated cheese is not usually served with this sauce.

FETTUCCINE WITH FRESH HERBS

8 first-course servings; 4 main-course servings

Bring to a rolling boil in a large pot:

6 quarts water

2 tablespoons salt

Add and cook until tender but firm:

1¼ pounds fresh fettuccine, or 1 pound dried

Meanwhile, rub a warmed serving bowl with:

1 clove garlic, halved

Combine in the bowl:

3 to 4 tablespoons extra-virgin olive oil

1 cup loosely packed fresh basil leaves, finely chopped

1 cup finely snipped fresh chives or chopped scallion tops

¼ cup fresh oregano or marjoram leaves, finely chopped

1 cup grated Parmesan cheese, or 1½ cups ricotta or ricotta salata, crumbled

Salt and ground black pepper to taste

Drain the pasta and toss it with the herb mixture. Serve hot.

FETTUCCINE PRIMAVERA

8 first-course servings; 4 main-course servings

Any seasonal vegetable can be added or substituted in this easy but elegant sauce; just make sure they are all cut about the same size so the sauce has a uniform look. You might try sugar snap peas, artichokes, green beans, spring scallions, or zucchini.

Bring to a rolling boil in a large pot:

6 quarts water

2 tablespoons salt

Add and cook for 1 minute:

6 asparagus, tough ends trimmed, finely diced, tips left whole

1 small bunch broccoli, stemmed and cut into very small florets

Remove the vegetables with a sieve and rinse under cold water to stop the cooking. Reserve the vegetable cooking water. Heat in a large skillet over medium heat:

2 tablespoons olive oil

3 tablespoons butter

Add:

1 large onion, finely diced

2 medium carrots, peeled and finely diced

Cook, stirring, until softened, about 5 minutes. Add the blanched asparagus and broccoli along with:

¾ cup fresh or thawed frozen peas

Salt and ground black pepper to taste

Cook, stirring, until all the vegetables are tender. Return the vegetable cooking water to a boil. Add and cook until tender but firm:

1 pound fresh fettuccine, or 12 ounces dried

Stir into the vegetables:

1 cup heavy cream

Simmer over medium heat while the pasta is cooking. Drain the pasta and add it to the sauce along with:

12 fresh basil leaves, chopped

½ cup grated Parmesan cheese

Toss to coat over low heat. Serve very hot.

PASTA AND BEANS (PASTA E FAGIOLI)

8 first-course servings; 4 main-course servings

More a soup than a stew, *pasta e fagioli* is a beloved dish in Italy, the ultimate in nutritious peasant food. Every household in every region has a version.

Heat in a large saucepan over medium heat:

2 tablespoons extra-virgin olive oil

Add:

1 medium onion, finely chopped

1 small carrot, peeled and finely chopped

1 medium celery stalk with leaves, finely chopped

2 tablespoons packed finely chopped fresh parsley

Cook, stirring, until the onions are golden brown, about 10 minutes. Stir in:

2 large cloves garlic, minced

Cook for 1 minute. Add:

One 14-ounce can whole tomatoes, with juice, crushed between your fingers as you add them to the pan

Boil, stirring, until thickened, about 3 minutes. Stir in:

One 15- to 19-ounce can cannellini, great Northern, or pinto beans, rinsed and drained

2 cups chicken stock

1 cup 1-inch pieces green beans

1 cup frozen small lima beans

Return to a boil. Stir in:

2 cups packed 1-inch piece escarole, curly endive, or Swiss chard, washed and dried

Partially cover and simmer for 5 minutes. Stir in:

1 cup elbow macaroni

Salt to taste

Cook until the macaroni is tender but firm, about 15 minutes. Thin, if needed, with additional:

Stock

Season with:

Ground black pepper to taste

Just before serving, stir in:

¼ cup grated pecorino cheese

Ladle into bowls and serve immediately, passing:

Additional grated pecorino cheese on the side

FETTUCCINE ALFREDO

8 first-course servings; 4 main-course servings

This simple, classic dish is extraordinary when made with fresh egg fettuccine, heavy cream, and authentic Parmigiano-Reggiano cheese.

Bring to a rolling boil in a large pot:

6 quarts water

2 tablespoons salt

Add and cook until tender but firm:

1¼ pounds fresh fettuccine, or 1 pound dried

Melt in a large skillet over medium heat:

8 tablespoons (1 stick) unsalted butter

Drain the pasta and add it to the skillet along with:

1 cup heavy cream

1 cup freshly grated Parmesan cheese

Salt and ground black pepper to taste

Toss over low heat until the pasta is well coated. Serve immediately.

LINGUINE WITH WHITE CLAM SAUCE

8 first-course servings; 4 main-course servings

Made for years up and down Italy's coast. In some areas a little tomato is added, in others chili pepper or herbs and white wine, but the constant is the freshest of clams.

Boil in a large skillet for 5 minutes:

2 cups water
¼ cup dry white wine
½ teaspoon dried oregano
5 parsley stems
1 bay leaf
Pinch of red pepper flakes (optional)

Add:

4 pounds small clams (such as littlenecks), scrubbed

Simmer, covered, until the shells open. Remove the clams from the broth, discarding any unopened ones, and shuck them, reserving any juice. Strain the broth and reserve. Wipe out the skillet. Cook, stirring, for a few minutes:

2 tablespoons olive oil
1 large clove garlic, minced
2 tablespoons packed finely chopped fresh parsley

Meanwhile, bring to a rolling boil in a large pot:

6 quarts water
2 tablespoons salt

Add and cook until tender but firm:

1 pound linguine

Drain. Add the pasta, reserved clams with juice, and broth to the skillet. Toss with:

2 tablespoons chopped fresh parsley

Serve immediately.

LINGUINE WITH RED CLAM SAUCE

Prepare Linguine with White Clam Sauce, above, adding 1 cup thoroughly drained canned whole tomatoes, crushing them between your fingers, when the garlic is barely colored. Simmer, stirring, for 3 minutes. Proceed as directed.

PENNE WITH SHRIMP AND FRESH CHILI PEPPERS

8 first-course servings; 4 main-course servings

Ready in the time it takes to boil the pasta. The orange zest adds a pleasant zing to this spicy dish.

Bring to a rolling boil in a large pot:

6 quarts water
2 tablespoons salt

Add and cook until tender but firm:

1 pound penne

Meanwhile, heat in a large skillet over medium heat:

¼ cup olive oil

Add and cook until the garlic turns blond:

8 cloves garlic, chopped
Zest of 1 orange, minced
1 to 2 mild to hot fresh chili peppers, seeded and diced

Add:

1 pound shrimp, peeled, deveined, and diced

Cook, stirring, until the shrimp are barely firm, about 3 minutes. Remove ½ cup of the pasta cooking water and stir it into the shrimp. Drain the pasta and toss it with the sauce. Season with:

Salt and ground black pepper to taste

Serve hot.

SPINACH FETTUCCINE WITH SMOKED SALMON AND ASPARAGUS

8 first-course servings; 4 main-course servings

Smoked salmon, although not an Italian ingredient, is now often found in pasta sauces in both Italy and the United States. A little goes a long way. Any thicker, uneven end cuts are perfect for this sauce.

Bring to a rolling boil in a large pot:

6 quarts water
2 tablespoons salt

Add and cook until tender but firm, 1 to 4 minutes depending on their thickness:

1 pound fresh asparagus, tough ends trimmed, cut into 1-inch pieces

Scoop out the asparagus with a sieve and rinse under cold water to stop the cooking and preserve the bright green color. Return the cooking liquid to a rolling boil. Add and cook until tender but firm:

1¼ pounds fresh spinach fettuccine, or 1 pound dried

Meanwhile, melt in a large skillet over medium heat:

3 tablespoons unsalted butter

Add the asparagus and cook, stirring, just to coat with butter, about 1 minute. Stir in and heat through:

1 cup heavy cream
Grated zest of 1 lemon

Drain the pasta and add it to the skillet along with:

4 ounces smoked salmon, cut into thin strips, or cooked fresh salmon, cut into small pieces
¼ cup snipped fresh chives
¼ cup chopped fresh parsley
Salt and ground black pepper to taste

Toss to combine and serve immediately.

SPAGHETTI ALLA CARBONARA

8 first-course servings; 4 main-course servings

Italian bacon (pancetta) and cheese-flavored eggs tossed with spaghetti, this is another Roman tradition made in no time and an old favorite with Americans as Sunday brunch fare.

Heat in a large skillet over medium-high heat:

1 tablespoon extra-virgin olive oil

Add and cook, stirring, until crisp:

6 ounces pancetta or bacon, finely diced

Pour off all but 3 tablespoons fat from the pan. Meanwhile, bring to a rolling boil in a large pot:

6 quarts water

2 tablespoons salt

Add and cook until tender but firm:

1 pound spaghetti

Reserve ⅓ cup of the pasta cooking water and combine it with:

4 large eggs, lightly beaten

⅓ cup grated pecorino cheese

Drain the pasta and add it while very hot to the skillet. Add the egg mixture and toss over medium heat until the eggs are firm. Season with:

Ground black pepper to taste

Serve hot, passing separately:

1 to 2 cups grated pecorino cheese

ORECCHIETTE WITH SAUSAGE AND BROCCOLI RABE

8 first-course servings; 4 main-course servings

Broccoli rabe, or rapini, is a pleasantly bitter vegetable similar to one used often in southern Italy, especially in Puglia. It is available in many stores, but broccoli can be substituted. For the most authentic sauce, find good-quality mild Italian pork sausages.

Heat in a large skillet over medium heat:

¼ cup olive oil, preferably extra virgin

Add:

4 sweet Italian sausages (about 1 pound), casings removed

Cook, breaking the meat up with a spoon, until nicely browned, about 5 minutes. Stir in:

3 large cloves garlic, finely minced

¼ teaspoon red pepper flakes

Cook for 1 minute more. Stir in:

1 large bunch broccoli rabe, washed, dried, and coarsely chopped, or 1 to 1½ pounds broccoli, stems peeled, coarsely chopped

Cover and cook just until tender, about 5 minutes. Meanwhile, bring to a rolling boil in a large pot:

6 quarts water

2 tablespoons salt

Add and cook until tender but firm:

1 pound orecchiette or other short dried pasta

Drain the pasta, leaving some water clinging to the noodles, and add it to the skillet over low heat. Toss to coat and combine, then remove to a large serving bowl. Season with:

Salt and ground black pepper to taste

Sprinkle with:

¼ cup grated pecorino or domestic kasseri cheese

Serve immediately, passing additional:

Grated cheese

BOW TIES WITH SPICY CHICKEN BITS AND BROCCOLI

8 first-course servings; 4 main-course servings

A quick and zesty supper or first course.

Bring to a rolling boil in a large pot:

6 quarts water

2 tablespoons salt

Add and cook until tender but firm:

1¼ pounds fresh farfalle, or 1 pound dried

Meanwhile, combine in a large bowl:

4 boneless, skinless chicken breast halves, cut into bite-sized pieces

2 cups broccoli pieces (florets and peeled stems)

2 teaspoons grated lemon zest

¼ teaspoon ground red pepper

¼ teaspoon ground black pepper

Pinch of salt

Heat in a large skillet over high heat:

3 tablespoons olive oil, preferably extra virgin

Add the chicken mixture and cook, stirring, until browned, about 5 minutes. Stir in:

½ cup dry white wine

½ cup tomato puree

1 cup pitted oil-cured black olives, preferably Italian

2 tablespoons drained capers

Simmer, uncovered, for 5 minutes. Drain the pasta and toss it with the sauce. Serve immediately with:

Grated pecorino cheese

POTATO GNOCCHI

About 80 pieces; 4 to 6 servings

Gnocchi are a pasta for potato lovers and well worth the effort. Make them ahead for a special occasion and bring them out of the freezer just before the guests arrive. For Italians, they are a pasta, cooked and sauced in the same way and eaten as a first course or one-dish meal.

Preheat the oven to 400°F.

Scrub well:

2 pounds baking potatoes

Prick each potato in a dozen places with a fork. Bake directly on an oven rack until easily pierced with a fork, about 1 hour. While the potatoes are still hot, split them lengthwise and scoop out the pulp. Push it through a potato ricer or force through a sieve with the back of a spoon. There should be about 2⅔ packed cups. Combine the potatoes in a bowl with:

1⅓ cups all-purpose flour

1 teaspoon salt

¼ teaspoon freshly grated or ground nutmeg

Stir vigorously, then turn out onto a work surface and knead until smooth and blended. Bring 3 to 4 inches of well-salted water to a simmer in a large pot. Have ready:

3 tablespoons butter, melted, or olive oil

Roll about 2 tablespoons of the dough into a cylinder ¾ inch wide. Cut it into pieces ¾ inch long. Roll each piece against the tines of a fork while pressing a small dent on the opposite side with your finger. Drop the gnocchi into the simmering water and cook until they float, about 2 minutes. They should hold a firm shape and be chewy to the bite. If they turn out slimy and soft, knead into the dough:

3 tablespoons all-purpose flour

Then test again. When the dough is right, roll it into 3 or 4 ropes ¾ inch wide, cut the ropes into ¾-inch pieces, and form the pieces as gnocchi. Drop one-third to one-half of the gnocchi into the pot and simmer, uncovered, until they float, then remove with a slotted spoon or skimmer to a wide bowl. Drizzle some of the melted butter over the gnocchi. Toss to coat. Repeat until all the gnocchi are done. Serve at once with:

Additional melted butter and grated Parmesan cheese, a tomato sauce or ragù, or Pesto Sauce, 307

To make gnocchi ahead, spread the uncooked gnocchi on a lightly floured baking sheet and refrigerate, covered with plastic wrap, for up to 12 hours. To keep them longer, freeze the gnocchi on the baking sheet until hard, then remove to a freezer bag or container. Gnocchi will keep frozen for up to 1 month. Cook directly from the freezer, adding about 1 minute to the cooking time.

FILLED AND BAKED PASTAS

It is best to have the filling prepared before making the pasta, since you need to fill and shape the pasta while it is still moist. When working with ravioli, tortelli, tortelloni, agnolotti, and mostaccioli, let your imagination play a bit.

Making Filled Pasta by Hand: For the pasta, make Fresh Egg Pasta, 302, or Especially Strong Pasta, 302, if the filling is moist. The fresh pasta sheets must be filled and shaped immediately after they are rolled out, while they are still moist. Roll the pasta thin enough to see your hand through it and keep the sheets moist by covering them with plastic wrap as you work. Please read About Freezing Fresh Pasta, 298.

Ravioli: Cover half a sheet of freshly rolled pasta with mounds of ½ teaspoon each of the chosen filling spaced 1 inch apart. Dip your finger in water and run it around the filling. Fold over the unfilled half of the pasta sheet, taking care to cover each mound so that no air is trapped. With the side of your hand, press firmly to seal. Use a zigzag cutter to cut the sheet into squares or rectangles, checking that each piece is well sealed.

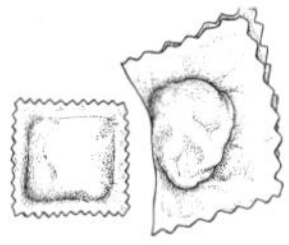

Ravioli

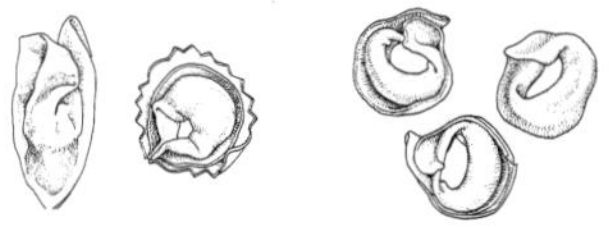

Cappelletti *Tortellini*

Tortellini, Cappelletti: To create these little doughnuts of filled pasta, cut freshly rolled sheets of pasta into 1¾-inch rounds. Place ¼ teaspoon filling in the center of each round, fold each round in half, and seal the edges. Bring the tails of the half circle together, overlapping them, and twist one over the other. Tortellini are traditionally filled with meat, while cappelletti are filled with cheeses or other fillings, depending on the region.

Cooking Filled Pastas: For each pound of pasta, bring 8 quarts salted water to a rolling boil. Add the pasta, reduce the heat, and simmer, uncovered, so as not to break apart the delicate shapes. Most filled pastas will float to the surface when they are done. Be careful not to overcrowd the pot; if you must, cook the pasta in batches. To cook frozen pasta, simply slip the still-frozen pieces into the boiling water and cook for an extra minute or two.

Some pasta shapes, such as lasagne, manicotti, and cannelloni, are cooked before they are filled and baked in a casserole. These pastas can be found in the section on baked pasta, 314 to 318, but many of the fillings can be used for the filled pastas here.

SIMPLE CHEESE FILLING

Enough to fill 100 to 150 pieces

Use this filling in a variety of filled and stuffed pastas. It is also wonderful as a stuffing for vegetables, such as mushrooms, peppers, zucchini, and tomatoes.

Stir together in a large bowl:

1½ cups good-quality ricotta cheese
1¼ cups grated Parmesan, Asiago, kasseri, or fontinella cheese
1 generous cup shredded fresh mozzarella cheese
¼ medium onion, finely chopped
6 scallions, finely chopped
¼ cup tightly packed fresh oregano leaves, finely chopped
¼ cup tightly packed fresh basil leaves, finely chopped (optional)
1 clove garlic, minced
Salt and ground black pepper to taste

Taste and adjust the seasonings, then add:

1 large egg, lightly beaten

Store, covered, in the refrigerator for up to 24 hours.

VEGETABLE CHEESE FILLING

Enough for 1 pound large pasta

Perfect for manicotti, this savory cheese filling works beautifully for large shells, ravioli, lasagne, or ziti.

Soak in warm water to cover for 20 minutes:

1 tablespoon dried currants (optional)

Drain and set aside. Meanwhile, bring to a rolling boil in a large pot:

1 cup water

Add and simmer, uncovered, until softened:

8 ounces fresh spinach or 12 ounces Swiss chard, trimmed, or 6 ounces curly endive, escarole, or radicchio, washed and dried

Drain, squeeze dry, and finely chop. Heat in a medium skillet over medium-high heat:

1 tablespoon extra-virgin olive oil

Add and cook until browned:

¼ cup minced onions
1 ounce pancetta or prosciutto, minced (optional)

Stir in:

1 small clove garlic, minced

Cook for 30 seconds (be careful not to burn the garlic). Stir in the greens and cook for 2 minutes. Let cool, then blend with the drained currants and:

1 cup ricotta cheese
¾ cup grated Parmesan cheese
1½ tablespoons pine nuts, toasted
Freshly grated or ground nutmeg to taste
Salt and ground black pepper to taste

Taste and adjust the seasonings, then stir in:

1 large egg, lightly beaten

This filling will keep, covered and refrigerated, for up to 24 hours.

MEAT FILLING

Enough to fill 100 to 150 pieces

Use this blend of sautéed meats, cheese, and prosciutto to fill ravioli, tortellini, or cappelletti, or spread it over lasagne. You can omit the pork if you wish, and add instead 6 more ounces of poultry.

Have ready:

1½ cups grated Parmesan cheese

Melt or heat in a medium skillet over medium-high heat:

1 to 2 tablespoons butter or extra-virgin olive oil

Add:

4 to 5 ounces boneless, skinless turkey, chicken, or capon breast, thinly sliced
One 1-inch-thick pork loin chop (8 to 9 ounces), boned, trimmed, and thinly sliced
2 tablespoons finely chopped onions
Salt and ground black pepper to taste

Cook, stirring often, until browned and cooked through, 4 to 5 minutes. Stir in:

¼ cup dry white wine

Bring to a boil, scraping up the browned bits on the bottom of the pan. Remove from the heat, let cool, and remove to a food processor. Add 1 cup of the cheese along with:

4 ounces mortadella
3 ounces prosciutto
Pinch of ground nutmeg
Salt and ground black pepper to taste

Process until finely chopped and well blended. (The meats can also be chopped by hand.) Taste and adjust the seasonings. There should be just a hint of nutmeg. Stir in the remaining cheese. At this point, the filling can be covered and refrigerated for up to 2 days.

ABOUT BAKED PASTA

Baked pasta dishes, sometimes casually referred to as casseroles, range from traditional Italian lasagne with sheets of homemade pasta to macaroni and cheese. They have long been popular as company dishes. For all these dishes, both the sauce and the filling can be made a day ahead. Since the pasta is cooked twice in these recipes, boil it only long enough to be pliable and barely tender.

CLASSIC ITALIAN AMERICAN LASAGNE

8 to 10 servings

This was the festive holiday lasagne that leaped from Italian American tables all over the United States. Do not mix the cooked sliced sausage directly into the sauce—it is layered with the meatballs in this lasagne.

Have ready:

Classic Italian American Tomato Sauce I or II, 306

1 pound ricotta cheese

1 pound mozzarella cheese (preferably fresh), thinly sliced or shredded

Preheat the oven to 375°F. Lightly oil a 13 x 9 x 3-inch baking or lasagne pan. Bring to a rolling boil in a large pot:

8 quarts water

2 tablespoons salt

Add and cook until barely tender:

1 pound fresh lasagne, or 1 pound dried

Drain and separate the noodles. Arrange a layer of noodles over the bottom of the pan. Spread with one-third of the ricotta. Scatter one-quarter of the mozzarella over the ricotta and season with:

Salt and ground black pepper to taste

Arrange one-third of the meatballs in the pan, either whole or cut in half, and scatter one-third of the sausage slices over the meatballs. Save 2 cups of the sauce for the top of the lasagne, then spoon about 1 cup of sauce over the meat in the pan. Add another layer of noodles and continue layering the lasagne until all the ingredients are used. You will have 4 layers of pasta with 3 layers of filling. Spread the reserved 2 cups of sauce over the top layer of noodles. Sprinkle the final one--quarter of the mozzarella over the sauce along with:

¼ cup grated Parmesan cheese

Bake until well browned and bubbly, about 45 minutes. Let stand for 15 minutes before serving.

LASAGNE BOLOGNESE

8 to 10 servings

This classic meat lasagne is utterly lush. Manage your time by making the béchamel and meat sauces a day or so ahead.

Have ready:

Bolognese Sauce, 307

1 cup grated Parmesan cheese

Melt in a large pot over medium heat:

2 tablespoons butter

Add:

2 tablespoons all-purpose flour

Cook, stirring with a wooden spoon, until well blended. Gradually whisk in:

3½ cups milk

Stir in:

1 small onion, halved

½ carrot, peeled and coarsely chopped

4 celery leaves

2 whole cloves

Simmer gently, stirring often, until reduced by one-third, about 15 minutes. Season with:

Freshly grated or ground nutmeg to taste

Salt and ground black pepper to taste

Strain the béchamel sauce into a bowl, pressing against the vegetables with a wooden spoon. Discard the vegetables. Cover the surface of the sauce with plastic wrap. The béchamel can be made ahead and refrigerated for up to 3 days; bring to room temperature before proceeding.

Bring to a rolling boil in a large pot:

8 quarts water

2 tablespoons salt

Add and cook until barely tender:

1¼ pounds fresh spinach lasagne, or 1 pound dried

Drain and separate the noodles. Keep in a bowl of ice water. Meanwhile, warm the meat sauce.

Preheat the oven to 350°F. Lightly oil a 13 x 9 x 3-inch baking or lasagne pan.

Spread a thin layer of meat sauce over the bottom of the dish. Cover with a layer of pasta, overlapping the noodles by ½ inch. Spread a thin layer of béchamel over the noodles and top with a thin layer of meat sauce. Sprinkle with about 1½ tablespoons grated cheese and top with another layer of pasta. Repeat the layers, reserving ⅓ cup béchamel and ¼ cup cheese to cover the final layer of pasta. Loosely cover with aluminum foil and bake for 40 to 50 minutes. Let stand for 10 minutes before serving.

ROASTED RED PEPPER AND HERB GOAT CHEESE LASAGNE

8 to 10 servings

The goat cheeses available in stores vary so much, from dry and crumbly to smooth and creamy, that you may need as little as ¼ cup or as much as 1 cup heavy cream to make the filling in this recipe spreadable. This meatless lasagne is easily assembled ahead of time and is ideal for buffets.

Have ready:

1½ recipes Simplest Italian Tomato Sauce Marinara, 305

6 large red bell peppers, roasted, 402, peeled, seeded, and coarsely chopped

½ cup grated Parmesan cheese

Combine in a food processor:

1 clove garlic, chopped

3 scallions, or ½ small onion, chopped

¼ cup packed mixed fresh herbs, such as basil and parsley, or 1 tablespoon mixed dried oregano and parsley

Two 10- to 11-ounce logs fresh mild goat cheese
Up to ¼ cup heavy cream
Salt and ground black pepper to taste

Process until creamy and smooth. The filling should be easy to spread. If it is too stiff, add:

Up to ¾ cup heavy cream

Bring to a rolling boil in a large pot:

8 quarts water
2 tablespoons salt

Add and cook until barely tender:

1 pound fresh lasagne, or 1 pound dried

Preheat the oven to 375°F. Lightly oil a 13 x 9 x 3-inch baking or lasagne pan.

Spread a thin layer of the tomato sauce over the bottom of the dish. Cover the sauce with a layer of pasta, overlapping the noodles by ½ inch. Spread with one-quarter of the cheese filling and top with one-quarter of the red peppers. Ladle enough tomato sauce to just barely cover the layer and sprinkle with one-quarter of the Parmesan cheese. Repeat the layers 3 more times until all the ingredients are used, finishing with tomato sauce and Parmesan cheese (4 layers total). Cover the dish with aluminum foil and bake until bubbly on top, 20 to 30 minutes for fresh pasta, 45 to 50 minutes for dried pasta. Remove the foil for the last 10 to 15 minutes of baking. Remove from the oven and let stand for 10 minutes before serving.

ROASTED VEGETABLE LASAGNE *8 to 10 servings*

The vegetables in this meatless lasagne are first roasted, giving them extra flavor and character. They can be prepared a day ahead and stored in the refrigerator, making assembly of the lasagne simple. This version is made without the traditional tomato sauce, incorporating fresh tomatoes into the layers instead. The zucchini and eggplant are roasted together, divided between two pans, while the tomatoes are roasted in their own pan because they release a lot of juice, which would inhibit browning of the zucchini and eggplant. If your oven will hold two pans side by side, then you will be able to roast everything at the same time on two racks. If not, roast the tomatoes as a separate batch. The lasagne is covered during a portion of the baking time because there is no tomato sauce; use a layer of breadcrumbs if desired.

Position a rack in the lower third of the oven and another in the upper third. Preheat the oven to 450°F. Lightly oil a 13 x 9 x 3-inch baking or lasagne pan.

Place in a large bowl:

2 medium-large eggplants (about 3 pounds), quartered and cut into ½-inch-thick slices
6 medium zucchini (about 3 pounds), cut into ½-inch-thick slices

Pour over the vegetables:

½ cup olive oil, preferably extra virgin
1 teaspoon salt
½ teaspoon ground black pepper

Toss well to coat all the vegetable pieces with oil and remove to 2 roasting pans. Position the pans side by side in the oven or place 1 on each rack if they do not fit side by side. Roast for 20 minutes. Toss the vegetables with a metal spatula, scraping up the browned bits. Continue to roast until well browned and soft, about 20 minutes more. Remove to a large bowl. Place in a roasting pan:

3 pounds ripe tomatoes, halved crosswise

Drizzle over the tomatoes:

2 tablespoons olive oil, preferably extra virgin
Generous amount of salt
Ground black pepper to taste

Roast the tomatoes until soft and slightly golden, about 45 minutes. Remove the tomatoes with their juice and all the oil to the bowl with the vegetables and stir together well.

Reduce the oven temperature to 375°F.

Bring to a rolling boil in a large pot:

8 quarts water
2 tablespoons salt

Meanwhile, stir together well in a medium bowl:

1 pound ricotta cheese
2 large eggs
½ cup grated Parmesan cheese
½ teaspoon salt, or to taste
Ground black pepper to taste
Ground nutmeg to taste (optional)

Have ready:

1 pound mozzarella cheese (preferably fresh), shredded

When the water boils, add and cook until barely tender:

1 pound fresh, or 1 pound dried lasagne

Drain and separate the noodles. Keep in a bowl of ice water. To assemble the lasagne, arrange a layer of noodles over the bottom of the pan. Spread with one-third of the ricotta mixture. Sprinkle one-quarter of the mozzarella over the ricotta mixture along with:

2 tablespoons Parmesan cheese
Ground black pepper to taste

Spoon one-third of the roasted vegetables on top. Add another layer of noodles and continue layering the lasagne until all the ingredients are used. You will have 4 layers of pasta and 3 layers of filling. Sprinkle the final one-quarter of the mozzarella over the top along with:

2 tablespoons Parmesan cheese
1 cup fresh breadcrumbs (optional)

Cover the pan with aluminum foil and bake for 30 minutes. Uncover and continue to bake until golden and bubbly, about 15 minutes more. Let stand for 15 minutes before serving.

PESTO VEGETABLE LASAGNE *8 to 10 servings*

If you like pesto, you will love this country-style lasagne, an American improvisation on some of our favorite flavors.

Soak in warm water to cover for 20 minutes:

1 tablespoon dried currants (optional)

Drain and set aside. Have ready:

1½ recipes Pesto Sauce, 307

In a large pot with only the water that clings to the leaves, cook over medium heat until wilted:

1¼ pounds spinach or 1½ pounds Swiss chard, trimmed, washed, and dried

Drain and let cool in a colander, squeeze dry, and finely chop. Heat in a medium skillet over medium-high heat:

2 tablespoons olive oil

Stir in and cook until browned:

½ cup minced onions
Two ⅛-inch-thick pancetta or Genoa salami slices, minced (optional)
3 tablespoons pine nuts

Add the currants and greens along with:

1 small clove garlic, minced

Cook, stirring, for about 2 minutes. Let cool, then blend with:

1 pound whole-milk or skim-milk ricotta cheese
1½ cups grated Parmesan cheese
1 large egg
Freshly grated or ground nutmeg to taste
Salt and ground black pepper to taste

Taste and adjust the seasonings. Bring to a rolling boil in a large pot:

8 quarts water
2 tablespoons salt

Add and cook until barely tender:

1 pound fresh lasagne, or 12 ounces dried

Drain and separate the noodles. Keep in a bowl of ice water.

Preheat the oven to 350°F. Lightly oil a 2½-quart shallow baking dish or a 13 x 9 x 3-inch baking or lasagne pan.

Line the bottom of the dish with a single layer of the lasagne. Spread with one-quarter of the cheese mixture. Spread with one-quarter of the pesto. Repeat the layers 3 more times, until all the ingredient are used. Cover with aluminum foil. Bake for 35 minutes. Uncover and bake until the pasta is heated through, about 15 minutes more. Let stand for 5 minutes before serving.

INDIVIDUAL BAKED SHELLS WITH RED PEPPER PUREE *6 to 8 appetizer servings*

This recipe is from Johanne Killeen and George Germon of Al Forno restaurant in Providence, RI.

Preheat the oven to 500°F.

Bring a medium pot of water to a boil. Add and cook for 8 minutes:

2 hot or sweet Italian sausages

Remove and discard the casings and coarsely chop the sausages. Meanwhile, puree in a blender:

4 medium red bell peppers, roasted, 402, peeled, and seeded

You should have about 1 cup puree. In a large bowl, combine the sausage and the red pepper puree along with:

½ cup chopped canned tomatoes in heavy puree
2 cups heavy cream
½ cup grated pecorino cheese
½ cup coarsely shredded fontina cheese
2 tablespoons ricotta cheese
½ teaspoon salt

Bring to a rolling boil in a large pot:

5 quarts water
2 tablespoons salt

Add and cook for 4 minutes:

1 pound pasta shells

Drain the pasta, add to the ingredients in the bowl, and toss to combine. Divide the pasta mixture among 6 to 8 individual gratin dishes (1½- to 2-cup capacity). Dot with:

4 tablespoons (½ stick) unsalted butter, cut into small pieces

Bake until bubbly and browned on top, 7 to 10 minutes.

BAKED MANICOTTI *6 to 8 servings*

Have ready:

Italian Tomato Sauce, 304

Bring to a rolling boil in a large pot:

8 quarts water
2 tablespoons salt

Add and cook until barely tender

1 pound manicotti

Preheat the oven to 350°F. Lightly oil a 3-quart shallow baking dish.

Using a small spoon, fill the pasta tubes with:

Simple Cheese Filling, 313, or Vegetable Cheese Filling, 314

Arrange the rolls side by side in the baking dish. At this point, the dish can be covered and refrigerated for up to 24 hours. Just before baking, spoon the tomato sauce over the manicotti and sprinkle with:

½ cup shredded fresh mozzarella cheese

3 tablespoons grated Parmesan or Asiago cheese

Cover with aluminum foil and bake until heated through, about 40 minutes. Let stand for 10 minutes in the turned-off oven with the door open. Serve hot.

CRESPELLE

6 servings

Have ready:

Eight 7-inch Savory Crêpes, 805, or Buckwheat Crêpes, 805

Simple Cheese Filling, 313, Meat Filling, 314, or Vegetable Cheese Filling, 314

Italian Tomato Sauce, 304

Preheat the oven to 350°F. Grease a 2½-quart shallow baking dish.

Spread the filling over the crêpes. Roll up and arrange side by side in the dish. Cover with aluminum foil and bake for 15 minutes. Pour the tomato sauce over the crêpes and bake, uncovered, until the sauce is bubbling and the crêpes are heated though, about 10 minutes more. Serve hot.

ABOUT AMERICAN NOODLE DISHES

Some of our first noodle dishes came to the United States with the Dutch and German settlers. Later we adopted a broad array of other noodle favorites from Russia, Hungary, and Ukraine. While we may not necessarily remember their origins, these dishes, with their quirky names, variable shapes, and soft to chewy textures, offer a great deal of pleasure and nourishment.

EGG NOODLES

1 pound

These are rich and savory egg noodles.

By Hand:

In a large bowl, cut together with a pastry blender or your fingers to form fine crumbs:

1½ cups all-purpose flour

1 tablespoon plus 1 teaspoon cold unsalted butter

⅛ teaspoon salt

Make a well in the center. Lightly beat together and add to the well:

2 large egg yolks

2 large eggs

Using a fork, gradually mix the flour mixture into the eggs, and continue to mix until the dough comes together. Divide the dough into quarters. Start rolling out 1 piece of the dough with a rolling pin, stretching it a little more with each roll. Between each rolling and stretching, continue to sprinkle it with flour if needed to keep it from sticking. Repeat this procedure until the dough is paper thin and translucent. Repeat with the remaining dough. Let it dry on a pasta rack or makeshift dowel for about 20 minutes. Avoid drying the noodles too much. Roll the noodle sheets up and cut to the desired thickness. The noodle dough can also be rolled and cut with a hand-cranked pasta machine; follow the manufacturer's instructions.

In a Food Processor: Cut the butter into very small pieces and place in the bowl with the flour and salt. Pulse 2 or 3 times to mix. Add the eggs and pulse again to mix the dough. The dough should form a ball around the blade. Do not overmix. Roll out as directed above.

BUTTERED EGG NOODLES

6 to 8 servings

This very quick and easy noodle recipe will keep the kids at the supper table.

Bring to a rolling boil in a large saucepan:

12 cups water

1 tablespoon salt

Add cook until tender but firm:

1 pound Egg Noodles, above, or 1 pound dried egg noodles

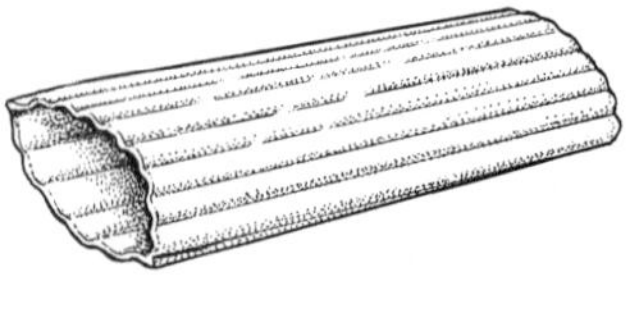

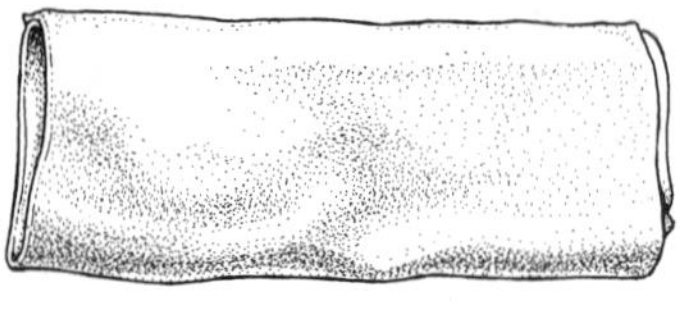

Manicotti

Fresh noodles will take as long as 5 minutes, depending upon how thick they are. If using dried noodles, follow the package directions. Drain the noodles and return to the pot. Add:

8 tablespoons (1 stick) unsalted butter, melted
Salt and ground black pepper to taste

Toss to coat and serve in warmed bowls or as a side dish.

EGG NOODLES WITH GARLIC AND BREADCRUMBS
6 to 8 servings

Melt in a medium skillet until the foam subsides:

4 to 8 tablespoons (½ to 1 stick) unsalted butter

Add:

1 cup dry unseasoned breadcrumbs
1 to 2 cloves garlic, minced

Cook, stirring, until the breadcrumbs begin to brown. Stir in:

1 tablespoon chopped fresh parsley

Toss with:

1 pound Egg Noodles, 318, or 1 pound dried egg noodles, cooked until tender but firm

Serve immediately.

POPPY-SEED NOODLES
6 to 8 servings

Toss together:

1 pound Egg Noodles, 318, or 1 pound dried egg noodles, cooked until tender but firm
½ cup unsalted butter, melted
2 tablespoons poppy seeds, or to taste
1 teaspoon sugar (optional)

Serve immediately.

EGG NOODLES WITH POT CHEESE
6 to 8 servings

Toss together in the noodle cooking pot:

1 pound Egg Noodles, 318, or 1 pound dried egg noodles, cooked until tender but firm
8 tablespoons (1 stick) unsalted butter, melted
1 pound pot or cottage cheese
Salt and ground black pepper to taste

Heat through over low heat. Serve garnished with:

Crumbled bacon (optional)
Chopped fresh parsley or snipped fresh dill

EGG NOODLES WITH SOUR CREAM AND CHIVES
6 to 8 servings

Combine in a medium saucepan:

8 tablespoons (1 stick) unsalted butter, melted
8 ounces sour cream or yogurt
¼ cup minced onions
2 tablespoons finely snipped fresh chives
2 tablespoons chopped fresh parsley
1 clove garlic, minced

Cook gently for about 5 minutes. Toss with:

1 pound Egg Noodles, 318, or 1 pound dried egg noodles, cooked until tender but firm

Serve immediately.

MUSHROOM WALNUT NOODLE PUDDING (KUGEL)
10 to 12 servings

A wonderful addition to any cook's repertoire, this kugel can be served as a side dish with meat or poultry or as a main dish for brunch or lunch. It is also a great addition to a buffet table.

Preheat the oven to 350°F. Grease a 13 x 9-inch baking pan with vegetable shortening.

Bring to a rolling boil in a large pot:

Two 14½-ounce cans chicken broth
4 cups water

Add and cook just until tender, 6 to 7 minutes:

12 ounces fresh or dried egg noodles

Drain. Meanwhile, heat in a large skillet over medium-high heat:

½ cup vegetable oil

Add:

2 medium onions, thinly sliced

Cook, stirring, until golden brown, about 10 minutes. Remove with a slotted spoon. Mix 2 tablespoons of the onion cooking oil with the drained noodles to keep them from sticking. Heat the baking pan in the oven for 15 minutes. To the remaining oil in the skillet, add:

1 large portobello mushroom cap, wiped clean, sliced, and cut into 1-inch pieces
8 ounces button mushrooms, wiped clean and sliced
Salt and ground black pepper to taste

Cook, stirring, over medium-high heat until browned, about 10 minutes. Beat well but not until frothy:

5 large eggs, at room temperature

Add the eggs to the noodles and stir together well. Stir in the onions, mushrooms, and oil from the skillet along with:

¾ cup coarsely chopped walnuts

Pour the noodle mixture into the hot baking pan. Bake until the noodles are lightly browned, about 45 minutes. Serve hot or warm.

SWEET NOODLE PUDDING (LUKSHENKUGEL)
12 to 14 servings

Some variety of noodle pudding is served at most traditional Jewish holiday meals, and there are countless recipes for them. The custom was to serve a sweet pudding as a second main course on the Sabbath to symbolize prosperity and abundance. Fat-free dairy products can be substituted. *Lukshenkugel* is wonderful hot, warm, or cold.

Preheat the oven to 325°F. Butter a 13 x 9-inch baking pan.

Bring to a rolling boil in a large pot:

6 quarts water

2 tablespoons salt

Add and cook until tender but firm:

1 pound Egg Noodles, 318, or 1 pound dried egg noodles

Drain. Stir together in a large bowl:

2 cups sour cream

1 pound cottage cheese

1 pound cream cheese

3 large eggs

½ cup sugar

2 teaspoons vanilla

1 teaspoon ground cinnamon

½ teaspoon salt

Add the noodles and stir together well. Pour into the baking pan. Bake for 1½ hours. Meanwhile, stir together in a small bowl with a fork or your fingers:

½ cup packed dark brown sugar

½ cup chopped walnuts

2 tablespoons all-purpose flour

2 teaspoons ground cinnamon

2 tablespoons butter, softened

Sprinkle over the top of the casserole and bake for 30 minutes more.

BAKED MACARONI AND CHEESE

4 to 6 main-course servings; 8 to 10 side-dish servings

An especially good rendition of a timeless classic. The sauce can be made ahead and blended with just-cooked noodles before baking, or the entire casserole can be assembled a day in advance.

Preheat the oven to 350°F. Grease a 1½-quart deep baking dish.

Bring to a rolling boil in a medium saucepan:

6 cups water

1½ teaspoons salt

Add and cook just until tender:

2 cups elbow macaroni (8 ounces)

Drain and remove to a large bowl. Have ready:

2¼ cups grated sharp Cheddar or Colby cheese

Melt in a large saucepan over medium-low heat:

2 tablespoons butter

Whisk in and cook, whisking, for 3 minutes:

2 tablespoons all-purpose flour

Gradually whisk in:

2 cups whole or skim milk

Stir in:

½ medium onion, minced

1 bay leaf

¼ teaspoon sweet paprika

Simmer gently, stirring often, for 15 minutes. Remove from the heat and stir in two-thirds of the cheese. Season with:

Salt and ground black pepper to taste

Stir in the macaroni. Pour half of the mixture into the baking dish and sprinkle with half of the remaining cheese. Top with the remaining macaroni and then the remaining cheese. Melt in a small skillet over medium heat:

1 tablespoon butter

Add and toss to coat:

½ cup fresh breadcrumbs

Sprinkle over the top of the macaroni. Bake until the breadcrumbs are lightly browned, about 30 minutes. Let stand for 5 minutes before serving.

BAKED MACARONI AND CHEESE (REDUCED FAT)

Prepare Baked Macaroni and Cheese, above, using skim milk and substituting one 8-ounce package Neufchâtel cheese for the Cheddar cheese. Cut the Neufchâtel into 1-inch cubes and add it to the sauce all at once before seasoning with salt and ground black pepper to taste.

STOVETOP MACARONI AND CHEESE

4 to 6 main-course servings; 8 to 10 side-dish servings

Very creamy and very cheesy. The size of the pot is essential in this recipe—it must be big for the sauce to thicken correctly. If you do not have a 7-quart pot, you can cook the elbow macaroni in any pot, then prepare the cheese sauce and finish the dish in a 12-inch skillet.

Bring to a rolling boil in a large pot:

12 cups water

1 tablespoon salt

Add and cook just until tender:

2 cups elbow macaroni (8 ounces)

Drain and return to the pot. Add:

4 tablespoons (½ stick) unsalted butter, cut into small pieces

Stir until well blended. Add and stir together until smooth:

One 12-ounce can evaporated milk

12 ounces extra-sharp Cheddar cheese, grated

2 large eggs, lightly beaten

1 teaspoon dry mustard dissolved in 1 teaspoon water
¾ teaspoon salt
½ teaspoon ground red pepper, or to taste

Set the pot over very low heat and, stirring constantly, bring the mixture to the first bubble of a simmer, 5 to 10 minutes. It should thicken noticeably. This may take several minutes. Increase the heat slightly if the sauce is still soupy after 5 minutes, but watch it very carefully. Do not overheat (above 170°F), or the sauce will curdle. Serve immediately. If you are not ready to serve, remove the pot from the heat, cover the surface with plastic wrap, cover the pot, and let stand at room temperature.

TUNA NOODLE CASSEROLE *4 to 6 servings*

This tuna noodle casserole is made with a cheese sauce studded with vegetables. It takes only a few more minutes to make than the condensed-soup kind.

Position a rack in the center of the oven. Preheat the oven to 375°F. Butter a 1½- to 2-quart shallow baking dish.

Melt in a medium saucepan over medium heat until fragrant and bubbly:

4 tablespoons (½ stick) unsalted butter

Add:

¾ cup thinly sliced mushrooms
¼ cup finely diced red or green bell peppers
¼ cup finely chopped onions

Cook, stirring occasionally, until the vegetables are just tender, about 5 minutes. Stir in:

¼ cup all-purpose flour

Cook for 1 minute. Remove from the heat and whisk in:

2½ cups milk

Return the saucepan to the heat and cook, whisking, until the sauce comes to a boil and is thickened, about 10 minutes. Remove from the heat, add, and whisk until melted:

¾ to 1 cup grated Cheddar cheese

Drain thoroughly:

Two 6-ounce cans water- or oil-packed white tuna

Turn the tuna into a large bowl and break into flakes with a fork. Do not mince. Stir in the hot cheese sauce, then add:

2 cups cooked egg noodles
¼ cup minced fresh parsley
Salt and ground black pepper to taste

Stir together well. Pour the mixture into the baking dish. Mix together and sprinkle over the top:

½ cup dry unseasoned breadcrumbs, fine cracker crumbs, or crushed corn flakes
2 tablespoons unsalted butter, melted

Bake until bubbly and browned on top, 25 to 35 minutes.

ABOUT DUMPLINGS

Simple, satisfying, and a particular treat in cold-weather months, dumplings take many forms. The English word *dumpling* originally meant something that was hollow. This idea of the dumpling still survives today in desserts such as Apple Dumplings, 899, which consist of pastry or biscuit crusts wrapped around whole apples. Modern savory dumplings, however, are solid, made with a base of flour or cooked potatoes. There are two principal types. European dumplings such as Potato Gnocchi, 312, Spätzle, 322, and Nockerln, 322, are similar to fresh pasta in taste and texture. Although these dumplings are sometimes cooked in a soup or stew, they are more commonly simmered in water and then added to a dish or combined with butter or a sauce after they have been fully cooked. Most American dumplings, by contrast, are light, fluffy, and dry, akin to biscuits or cake. They are cooked on top of a stew, potpie, or casserole and served directly out of the dish.

When cooking dumplings of either type, start with plenty of liquid, as dumplings absorb a lot. The liquid should be simmering—but not boiling—when the dumplings are dropped in, and kept at a simmer throughout cooking. Otherwise, the dumplings may become soggy or even disintegrate. You can usually cook European-style dumplings in advance and then add them to a hot soup or stew just before serving. To prevent the dumplings from turning soft and sticky, drain them well, lightly coat them with oil or melted butter, and store them in a single layer, covered, in the refrigerator for up to 2 days. American-style dumplings must be served as soon as they are done, or they will become heavy.

DUMPLINGS *6 to 8 servings*

These easy-to-make dumplings are the richest and fluffiest we know.

Mix together:

2 cups all-purpose flour
1 tablespoon baking powder
¾ teaspoon salt

Bring just to a simmer in a small saucepan:

3 tablespoons butter
1 cup milk

Add to the dry ingredients. Stir with a fork or knead by hand 2 to 3 times until the mixture just comes together. Divide the dough into about 18 puffy dumplings. Roll each piece of dough into a rough ball. Gently lay the formed dumplings on the surface of your stew, cover, and simmer for 10 minutes. Serve immediately.

POTATO DUMPLINGS (KARTOFFELKLÖSE)

6 to 8 servings

These are light and tender, especially good with a roast and gravy. They are traditional with Sauerbraten, 668.

Cook in a large pot of boiling water until tender:

6 medium baking potatoes, unpeeled

When cool enough to handle, peel and rice the potatoes. Combine with:

2 large eggs
½ cup all-purpose flour
1½ teaspoons salt

Beat the batter with a fork until fluffy. Lightly shape into 1-inch balls. Bring to a gentle boil in a large pot:

6 quarts water
2 tablespoons salt

Drop the balls into the water and cook for 10 minutes. Drain. Stir together:

8 tablespoons (1 stick) butter, melted, or bacon drippings
¼ cup dry unseasoned breadcrumbs

Sprinkle the crumbs over the dumplings and serve.

CORNMEAL DUMPLINGS

4 to 6 servings

Bring to a simmer:

5 to 6 cups beef or chicken stock

Meanwhile, sift together:

¾ cup all-purpose flour
½ cup cornmeal
2 teaspoons baking powder
½ teaspoon salt

Cut in with a fork or pastry blender:

1 tablespoon cold butter

Whisk together:

1 large egg
⅓ cup milk

Stir into the dry ingredients just until blended. Gently drop teaspoonfuls of the batter into the simmering stock. Tightly cover the pan. Simmer the dumplings for 20 minutes. Serve them hot with the stock.

SPÄTZLE

4 or 5 servings

Spätzle, *spätzen,* or, more plainly, German egg dumplings are often served alongside a goulash or stew and are particularly welcome next to roasted veal. Substituting milk for the water produces a richer, if slightly denser, dumpling. Spätzle are also delicious when pan-seared in a buttered skillet until the edges are crisp.

Combine:

1½ cups all-purpose flour
½ teaspoon baking powder
¾ teaspoon salt
Pinch of freshly grated or ground nutmeg

Beat together:

2 large eggs
½ cup milk or water

Add to the flour mixture. Beat well with a wooden spoon to create a fairly elastic batter. Bring to a simmer in a large saucepan:

6 cups salted water or chicken stock

Drop small bits of the batter from a spoon into the bubbling liquid, or force the batter through a spätzle machine or colander to produce strands of dough that will puff into irregular shapes. Spätzle are done when they float to the surface. They should be delicate and light, although slightly chewy. If the first few taste heavy and dense, add more drops of milk or water to the batter before continuing. Lift the cooked spätzle from the saucepan with a strainer or slotted spoon. Serve spätzle as a side dish, drizzled with:

Melted butter

Or melt in a small skillet over medium heat:

1 tablespoon butter

Add and cook, stirring, until toasted, 3 to 5 minutes:

⅓ cup fresh breadcrumbs

Sprinkle over the hot spätzle.

CHEESE SPÄTZLE

Prepare Spätzle, above, drain, and remove to a shallow baking dish. Top with ¼ cup grated mild cheese. Broil until the cheese is melted, about 1 minute.

NOCKERLN

About 1 cup

An Austrian dumpling, a bit lighter than spätzle.

Beat until creamy:

4 tablespoons (½ stick) unsalted butter, softened
1 large egg

Stir in:

1 cup all-purpose flour
⅛ teaspoon salt

Gradually stir in until a firm batter is formed:

About 6 tablespoons milk

Shape teaspoonfuls of the batter into small balls. Drop them into boiling water or directly into the clear soup in which they will be served. Reduce the heat and simmer, covered, for 10 minutes. For a stew, cook the nockerln in water, drain, and drop them into the meat mixture just before serving.

ABOUT ASIAN NOODLES

In over two thousand years of noodle making, cooks in China, Japan, Thailand, Vietnam, and other Asian countries have come up with a wondrous variety of recipes. Today, many of these—pan-fried noodles, ramen noodle soup, pad thai, and lo mein—are becoming favorites in our busy lives.

Asian noodles are best understood by the type of flour or starch with which they are made. When looking for substitutes, choose noodles in the same starch family. Today, the most common Asian noodles are made with wheat or rice; some are also made from mung bean starch and buckwheat. In general, ignore the recipe directions on the package and follow the advice given here, along with your own good sense. Asians prefer noodles long and uncut, because they symbolize longevity, especially when served at birthday celebrations. Eating noodles in Asia can be a noisy affair: it is not impolite to slurp them up.

ASIAN NOODLES

Chinese Wheat-Flour Noodles: Fresh wheat noodles come in a variety of shapes and thicknesses, including a spaghetti shape and a thick oval-shaped strand, known as Shanghai style, similar to the Japanese udon. More unusual, but equally delicious, is the flat, wide wheat *chow fun.* Dried Chinese wheat noodles are packaged in straight 12-inch lengths or, in the case of thinner noodles, in nests. Generally, Chinese wheat-flour noodles are used in soups and sometimes in stir-fried dishes. Cook by dropping the noodles into a large pot of boiling water (without salt or oil) until softened, about 4 minutes (longer for dried). The Chinese like to cook their noodles until they are very tender. Before stir-frying, pan-frying, or adding to soup, rinse the cooked noodles under cold water and toss with a little oil to prevent them from clumping.

Chinese Egg Noodles: Fresh and dried egg noodles are made with wheat flour and eggs. The best are pale yellow in color (an unnaturally bright yellow indicates color additives) and have a dry, fresh look. Chinese egg noodles are popularly sold as *mein.* Regular *mein,* about ⅛ inch thick, resembles spaghetti and is used for stir-frying (as in lo mein), for pan-frying, or in cold noodle dishes. Egg noodles are also available thin or extra thin for soups. A flat, fettuccine-like noodle is best stir-fried or cooked and topped with a sauce. Similar egg noodles are called *ramen* in Japan and *ba mee* in Thailand. Cook egg noodles according to the directions for Chinese Wheat-Flour Noodles, above.

Dried Rice-Flour Noodles: Noodles made with rice flour and water are among the most popular of all Asian noodles. They are sold in 1-pound packages in Chinese, Thai, and Vietnamese markets in two basic styles—rice sticks and rice vermicelli.

Rice Stick Noodles: These thin, flat, translucent noodles should be soaked for 30 minutes in cold water, then boiled for 4 to 7 minutes before being added to any dish. They are most commonly used in pad thai and other stir-fried dishes and soups. Rice sticks are known as *banh pho* in Vietnam and *jantabon* in Thailand.

Rice Vermicelli: These delicate, extra-thin noodles are used in soups, salads, and stir-fried dishes. Soak them in cold water for 30 minutes, rinse, and then boil for 2 minutes before using. Rice vermicelli can also be deep-fried to make a light, crisp nest on which to serve other foods. If they are to be deep-fried, do not soak or rinse; simply drop the dry noodles into very hot oil, where they will puff and crisp up nicely. Rice vermicelli are *bun* in Vietnam and *san mee* in Thailand.

Fresh Rice Noodles: Most often sold in 1-pound sheets, called *sha he fen* by the Chinese, these can be cut to any width and used in any dish calling for rice noodles. These will keep refrigerated for up to 2 weeks. After rinsing briefly in warm water, the fresh rice noodles can be stir-fried or added directly to soups.

Mung Bean Noodles: Called cellophane noodles or bean threads, these translucent dried noodles are made from the starch of the mung bean (the same bean sold as bean sprouts) and sold in small bundles. Popular in soups and occasionally stir-fried, these threadlike noodles have a more slippery texture than either rice or wheat noodles. Cellophane noodles also puff up into a crisp nest when deep-fried. These should be soaked in hot water to soften for 15 to 30 minutes before using (unless headed to the deep fryer) and then can be added directly to a soup or stir-fry.

Soba, or Japanese Buckwheat Noodles: Enjoyed in northern Japan, these thin brownish noodles are made from wheat flour and buckwheat, a hardy plant that grows well in harsh climates. The dried noodles are expensive, but there is no real substitute for their slightly nutty, appealing taste (in some recipes udon or Chinese wheat-flour noodles can be used). Often a course unto itself, soba is traditionally served cold in a square wooden box with a dipping sauce made of dashi (Japanese sea stock) seasoned with soy sauce and mirin, a sweet, syrupy rice wine. Cook soba noodles according to the directions for Japanese noodles, below.

Japanese Udon: Thick, plump, white noodles made of wheat flour, salt, and water, udon come both flat and round, dried and fresh, and are first cousins to the Shanghai-style wheat-flour noodle. Typically served in broth and sprinkled with chopped scallions and a fiery spice mixture called *shichimi,* these hearty noodles also work well in gutsy stews and casseroles. Cook udon according to the directions for Japanese noodles, below.
Japanese Somen: These delicate white noodles, made from hard wheat flour and a touch of sesame oil, are sold dried in neat 8-ounce bundles elegantly tied with ribbon. They are typically served cold with a dipping sauce. Somen and soba are sometimes found in a shade of pale green, the result of powdered green tea mixed into the flour. Cook somen noodles according to the directions for Japanese noodles, below.
Japanese Ramen: Japan's most popular noodle, ramen is simply another name for the spaghetti-like Chinese egg noodle called *mein.*
To Cook Japanese Noodles (Soba, Udon, Somen): Bring a large quantity of water (at least 12 cups per pound) to a rolling boil in a large pot. Add the noodles gradually, so the water does not stop boiling. Stir slowly to keep the noodles from sticking to the bottom of the pot. When the water returns to a rolling boil, add 1 cup cold water. Cook until just past the al dente stage (check by tasting). Drain the noodles and rinse briefly under cold water.

CHICKEN LO MEIN

4 servings

Lo mein simply means sautéed noodles. Fresh Chinese egg noodles are traditional, but any spaghetti-shaped noodle works well. Almost any combination of meat and vegetables can be added.

BEFORE COOKING:

Stir together in a medium bowl:

1 teaspoon cornstarch
½ teaspoon salt
1 teaspoon toasted sesame oil

Cut across the grain to make very thin slices (more easily done if the chicken is partially frozen):

1 boneless, skinless chicken breast (about 6 ounces)

Toss in the cornstarch mixture and let marinate for 10 to 20 minutes. Place on a plate:

4 ounces bok choy, cut crosswise into 3-inch pieces
¼ cup bamboo shoots, sliced
3 scallions, cut into 2-inch pieces
¼ cup sliced mushrooms
1 teaspoon finely minced garlic

Stir together in a small bowl:

¼ cup chicken stock
2 tablespoons oyster sauce
1 tablespoon soy sauce
1½ teaspoons sugar

Have ready:

¼ cup bean sprouts

TO COOK:

Bring to a rolling boil in a large pot:

16 cups (4 quarts) water

Add and cook until softened:

6 ounces fresh Chinese egg noodles or dried spaghetti

Drain and rinse under cold water until cool. Drain again and toss thoroughly with:

1 teaspoon toasted sesame oil

Heat a wok or large skillet over high heat. When hot, pour in:

⅓ cup peanut oil

Swirl around the wok until very hot but not smoking. Add the chicken, quickly stirring and flipping in the oil to separate the slices, and cook lightly. Drain in a sieve or colander.

Reheat the wok over high heat. When hot, pour in:

3 tablespoons peanut oil

Swirl until very hot but not smoking. Add all the ingredients on the plate with the bok choy. Stir and toss vigorously until the vegetables are well coated with oil, about 45 seconds.

Pour the chicken stock mixture down the side of the wok. Stir and cover, allowing the vegetables to steam in the sauce, for 1 minute.

Uncover and add the noodles and the chicken. Stir and toss for about 30 seconds.

Add the bean sprouts and stir for about 30 seconds. Pour into a serving dish. Sprinkle with:

½ teaspoon cracked black peppercorns

Serve immediately.

BEEF CHOW FUN

4 servings

Chow fun usually implies pan-fried broad rice noodles. This dish is typical Chinese noodle-house fare.

BEFORE COOKING:

Soak in hot water to cover until softened, about 20 minutes:

8 ounces ½-inch-wide dried rice noodles

Stir together well in a medium bowl:

2 teaspoons soy sauce
1 teaspoon cornstarch

Stir in:

1 teaspoon toasted sesame oil

Cut across the grain to make very thin 2 x 1-inch slices (more easily done if the meat is partially frozen):

8 ounces flank steak

Toss in the soy mixture and let marinate for 20 to 30 minutes.

Place on a saucer or small plate:

2 teaspoons Chinese salted black beans, lightly mashed

2 teaspoons finely minced garlic

4 teaspoons finely minced peeled fresh ginger

Place on a separate plate:

8 ounces green beans, trimmed and cut into 2-inch pieces

Place on another plate:

3 fresh red chili peppers, or ½ red bell pepper for less heat, cut into thin strips

½ cup 2-inch pieces scallion

Stir together in a small bowl:

½ cup chicken stock

¼ cup oyster sauce

2 tablespoons Chinese cooking wine or dry white wine

2 tablespoons soy sauce

2 teaspoons sugar

Stir together well in a cup, leaving the stirring spoon in for later:

2 teaspoons cornstarch

2 tablespoons cool water

Have ready:

1 teaspoon toasted sesame oil

TO COOK:

Heat a wok or large skillet over high heat. When hot, pour in:

½ cup peanut oil

Swirl around the wok until very hot but not smoking. Add the beef, quickly stirring and flipping in the oil to separate the slices, and cook lightly. Drain in a sieve or colander.

Drain the noodles well. Reheat the wok or skillet over high heat. When hot, pour in:

¼ cup peanut oil

Swirl until hot. Add the noodles. From time to time, stir and toss until some surfaces brown slightly. Remove to a plate. Discard the oil.

Reheat the wok over high heat. When hot, pour in:

¼ cup peanut oil

Swirl until very hot but not smoking. Scrape in the black beans, garlic, and ginger. Stir briefly until the garlic browns very slightly.

Add the green beans and toss for 1 minute. Add the chili peppers and scallions and stir well for 1 minute more.

Stir the chicken stock mixture and add. Stir and toss until completely hot.

Return the beef and noodles to the wok. Stir and toss quickly to mix completely.

Stir the cornstarch mixture. Pour it slowly into the sauce while stirring. Stir until the mixture is thickened and the noodles are glazed and shiny. Add the sesame oil and give a final stir.

Pour into a serving dish. Top with:

Fresh cilantro leaves

Serve immediately.

SINGAPORE NOODLES *4 servings*

This popular Chinese version of a Malaysian dish uses curry powder and thin rice noodles. Traditionally it is made with Chinese barbecued pork, *cha siu;* here we use pork loin.

BEFORE COOKING:

Soak in hot water to cover until softened, about 10 minutes:

8 ounces thin rice vermicelli

Drain. Cut into thin slices and then into thin strips (more easily done if the meat is partially frozen):

4 ounces pork loin

Combine in a small bowl with:

2 teaspoons soy sauce

Toss and let stand.

Place on one side of a plate:

¼ cup thinly sliced onions

1 teaspoon thin strips fresh red chili pepper

Warm in a small skillet over low heat:

2 tablespoons curry powder

Stir in:

¼ cup unsweetened coconut milk

1 teaspoon salt

½ teaspoon sugar

Cook, stirring, for 30 to 45 seconds. Scrape the mixture into a second small bowl.

Stir together in a third small bowl:

¼ cup chicken stock

1 tablespoon oyster sauce

1 teaspoon salt

Place on the other side of the plate:

¼ cup roasted peanuts, chopped

1 teaspoon red pepper flakes

2 tablespoons dried shrimp, very finely chopped (optional)

Stir together well in a fourth small bowl:

1 cup bean sprouts
2 tablespoons chopped fresh basil
Juice of ½ lemon

TO COOK:

Heat a wok or large skillet over high heat. When hot, pour in:

¼ cup peanut oil

Swirl around the wok until very hot but not smoking. Add the pork, quickly stirring and flipping to separate the strips. Cook until they are no longer pink but not browned. Remove with a slotted spoon. To the wok add:

1 tablespoon peanut oil

Swirl until very hot. Add the onions and chili peppers. Cook and stir until the onions are softened, about 5 minutes. Remove with a slotted spoon, leaving as much oil as possible in the wok. Set aside atop the pork strips. Add the curry mixture to the wok. Stir and cook very briefly. Quickly add the chicken stock mixture and heat through, stirring constantly.

Add the noodles, seared pork strips, and onion mixture to the wok, stirring constantly until heated through. Add the peanuts, pepper flakes, and dried shrimp if using, and stir thoroughly.

Add the bean sprout mixture and stir for about 30 seconds, until all the ingredients are thoroughly mixed. Pour into a serving dish. Serve immediately.

SPICY PEANUT SESAME NOODLES

4 to 6 servings

This traditional Chinese dish is served at room temperature as an appetizer, a lunch, or a light supper. It is a delight of taste and texture, with soft noodles, creamy sauce, spicy chili peppers, and the crunch of raw cucumbers.

BEFORE COOKING:

Thoroughly blend in a food processor:

2 cups natural unsalted smooth peanut butter
½ cup rice or white vinegar
¼ cup light soy sauce
2 teaspoons dark soy sauce
2 tablespoons small pieces garlic
2 to 6 serrano or other fresh chili peppers, cut into pieces
3 tablespoons sugar
2 teaspoons salt

Remove the peanut butter mixture to a medium bowl. Stir in:

½ cup toasted sesame oil
2 tablespoons chili oil

Gradually stir in until smooth:

1 cup freshly brewed black tea

The sauce can be covered and refrigerated for 1 to 2 days. Allow to return to room temperature before using.

TO COOK:

Bring to a rolling boil in a large pot,

4 to 4½ quarts water

Add:

1 pound fresh Chinese egg noodles or dried spaghetti

Cook until softened. Drain and rinse under cold water until cool. Drain and toss thoroughly with:

2 teaspoons toasted sesame oil

TO SERVE:

Place the noodles in a serving dish, top with all the sauce, and stir together slightly. Or serve on individual dinner plates and top with 3 to 4 generous tablespoons sauce per serving. Garnish with:

Peeled, seeded cucumber, cut into thin strips
Fresh cilantro leaves

SPICY PEANUT SESAME NOODLES WITH CHICKEN

Prepare Spicy Peanut Sesame Noodles, above. Poach 2 boneless skinless chicken breast halves in boiling water for 5 to 7 minutes. Let cool, shred, and stir into the final stage of the sauce.

SHRIMP PAD THAI

4 servings

Rapidly becoming very popular in the United States, there are many versions of this Thai specialty. This is a good one.

BEFORE COOKING:

Soak in hot water to cover until softened, 20 to 30 minutes:

6 ounces dried rice stick noodles

Drain and cover. Stir together well in a medium bowl:

1 teaspoon cornstarch
1 teaspoon toasted sesame oil

Peel, devein, and halve lengthwise:

8 ounces large shrimp

Toss in the cornstarch mixture and let marinate for 15 to 20 minutes.

Place in a small bowl:

3 large eggs, well beaten

Place on a saucer or small plate:

½ cup 1½-inch pieces scallion (white part only)
2 to 3 fresh red chili peppers, chopped
2 tablespoons finely minced garlic

Place on another saucer or small plate:

4 ounces firm tofu, cut into ½-inch cubes (optional)

Stir together in another small bowl:

¼ cup Thai fish sauce (*nam pla*)
¼ cup fresh lemon juice
3 tablespoons sugar

On a plate, place clockwise from the "top" in the following order:

½ cup bean sprouts
⅓ cup roasted peanuts, coarsely chopped
¼ cup fresh basil leaves, cut into thin strips
¼ cup fresh cilantro leaves
2 teaspoons dried shrimp, finely ground (optional)
½ teaspoon red pepper flakes
½ teaspoon ground black pepper

TO COOK:

Heat a wok or skillet over high heat. When hot, pour in:

⅓ cup peanut oil

Swirl around the wok until very hot but not smoking. Add the shrimp and cook, stirring vigorously, until translucent, 30 to 45 seconds. Drain in a sieve or colander.

Reheat the wok over high heat. Pour in:

2 tablespoons peanut oil

Swirl briefly. Stir the beaten eggs. Slowly pour the eggs into the wok and cook, stirring vigorously, until the eggs have set. Remove to a plate.

Reheat the wok over high heat. When hot, pour in:

3 tablespoons peanut oil

Swirl until very hot but not smoking. Add the scallion mixture and stir briefly until the garlic browns very slightly.

Add the tofu if using. Stir gently for 1 to 2 minutes.

Add the noodles. Stir until well coated.

Add the fish sauce mixture. Stir well.

Add the shrimp. Add the eggs. Stir well.

Add the ingredients on the plate in clockwise order, stirring as you go. Pour into a serving dish. Serve immediately.

BEIJING NOODLES WITH MEAT SAUCE

4 servings

Some claim this simple, ancient noodle dish was the original spaghetti with meat sauce. In fact, it is delicious made with spaghetti.

BEFORE COOKING:

Stir together well in a small bowl:

½ cup Chinese black bean sauce
2 tablespoons sugar

Place on a saucer or small plate:

½ cup 2-inch pieces scallion

Have ready:

1 tablespoon toasted sesame oil

TO COOK:

Heat a wok or large skillet over high heat. When hot, pour in:

3 tablespoons peanut oil

Swirl around the wok until very hot but not smoking. Add:

1 pound ground pork

Break up, stir well, and cook until the pork is well separated and no longer pink but not browned.

Add the bean sauce mixture. Stir well.

Add the scallions and sesame oil. Stir well.

Remove the wok from the heat.

While cooking the pork, bring to a rolling boil in a large pot:

4 to 4½ quarts water

Add:

1 pound fresh Chinese egg noodles or dried spaghetti

Cook until softened. Drain and pour into a large bowl. If necessary, briefly reheat the meat sauce. Pour over the noodles and stir together well. Serve immediately.

TO SERVE:

Stir together in each of 4 small bowls:

¼ cup red wine vinegar
1 teaspoon chili oil

Place on the table to be sprinkled onto individual portions to taste.

SPICY SZECHUAN NOODLES

4 servings

A pork and noodle dish in the Szechuan style, with plenty of fresh ginger, garlic, and chili peppers.

BEFORE COOKING:

Place on a saucer or small plate:

2 tablespoons finely minced peeled fresh ginger
1 tablespoon finely minced garlic
1 to 2 tablespoons coarsely chopped fresh chili peppers
¼ cup coarsely chopped bamboo shoots

Stir together well in a small bowl:

¼ cup chicken stock
1 tablespoon soy sauce
2 tablespoons Chinese black bean sauce
2 teaspoons sugar

Place on another saucer or small plate:

½ cup 2-inch pieces scallion

TO COOK:

Heat a wok or large skillet over high heat. When hot, pour in:

⅓ cup peanut oil

Swirl around the wok until very hot but not smoking. Add all the ingredients on the saucer with the ginger. Stir briefly until the garlic browns very slightly.

Add:

1 pound ground pork

Break up, stir well, and cook until the pork is well separated and no longer pink but not browned.

Add the chicken stock mixture. Stir well and cook for 1 to 2 minutes.

Add the scallions and stir briefly.

Remove the wok from the heat.

While cooking the pork, bring to a rolling boil in a large pot:

4 to 4½ quarts water

Add:

1 pound fresh Chinese egg noodles, or 1 pound dried spaghetti

Cook until softened. Drain and pour into a large bowl. If necessary, briefly reheat the meat sauce. Pour over the noodles. Season with:

½ teaspoon toasted sesame oil

Stir together well. Serve immediately.

PAN-BROWNED NOODLE CAKE WITH SHRIMP AND BEEF

4 servings

A home-style dish with a noodle "cake" that is golden and crisp on the outside and soft on the inside. It is best made with fresh Chinese egg noodles.

BEFORE COOKING:

In a large pot, bring to a rolling boil:

4 to 4½ quarts water

Add:

1 pound fresh Chinese egg noodles

Cook until softened. Drain. Stir together well in a medium bowl:

1 teaspoon soy sauce
1 teaspoon cornstarch

Stir in:

1 teaspoon toasted sesame oil

Cut across the grain to make very thin 2 x 1-inch slices (more easily done if the meet is partially frozen):

8 ounces flank steak

Toss in the soy mixture and let marinate for 20 to 30 minutes. Stir together well in another medium bowl:

1 teaspoon cornstarch
1 teaspoon toasted sesame oil

Peel, devein, 490, and halve lengthwise:

8 ounces large shrimp

Toss in the cornstarch mixture and let marinate for 15 to 20 minutes.

Place on a large plate:

¼ cup sliced mushrooms
1 cup small bok choy leaves
¼ cup sliced bamboo shoots

Stir together well in a small bowl:

1 cup chicken stock
2 teaspoons soy sauce
1 teaspoon salt
1 teaspoon sugar

Stir together well in a cup, leaving the mixing spoon in for later:

2 teaspoons cornstarch
2 tablespoons cool water

Have ready:

½ teaspoon toasted sesame oil

TO COOK:

Heat a wok or a round-bottomed pan over high heat. When hot, pour in:

½ cup peanut oil

Swirl around the wok until hot. Add the noodles, heaping them together loosely in a flat mound in the round bottom of the wok. Cook without disturbing until the bottom turns golden brown and the "cake" has become firm. With a slotted spoon or spatula, gently lift the noodle cake out. Invert it onto a serving platter. Keep warm in a 175°F oven.

Heat a clean wok or large skillet over high heat. When hot, pour in:

3 tablespoons peanut oil

Swirl around the wok until very hot but not smoking. Add the beef, quickly stirring and flipping in the oil to separate the slices, and cook lightly. Drain in a sieve or colander.

Reheat the wok over high heat. When hot, pour in:

3 tablespoons peanut oil

Swirl until very hot but not smoking. Add the shrimp and cook, stirring vigorously, until translucent, 30 to 45 seconds. Drain in a sieve or colander.

Reheat the wok over high heat. When hot, pour in:

¼ cup peanut oil

Swirl until very hot but not smoking. Add the mushrooms, bok choy, and bamboo shoots. Stir and toss vigorously until the vegetables are well coated with oil, about 45 seconds.

Add the chicken stock mixture. Stir occasionally until the mixture boils gently.

Add the beef and shrimp. Stir well.

Stir the cornstarch mixture. Pour slowly into the sauce while stirring. Stir until the mixture is thickened and the contents are glazed and shiny.

Stir in the sesame oil. Pour on top of the noodle "cake."

Sprinkle with:

½ teaspoon cracked black peppercorns

Serve immediately.

SHANGHAI NOODLES WITH EGGPLANT AND FRESH SEASONAL VEGETABLES

4 servings

Traditionally this dish calls for thick hand-cut oval noodles called Shanghai style. They are available fresh in Chinese markets, but good-quality fettuccine or spaghetti are fine substitutes.

BEFORE COOKING:

Combine in a small bowl:

4 dried mushrooms, preferably Chinese black
2 cups warm water

Let stand until the mushrooms are softened, 30 to 45 minutes. Drain and squeeze the mushrooms dry with paper towels. Snip off and discard the woody stems. Slice into thin strips. Peel and cut into 3-inch-long "French-fry" sticks, about ⅓ inch thick:

1 small eggplant

Heat a wok or large skillet over high heat. When hot, pour in:

1 cup peanut oil

Swirl around the wok until very hot but not smoking. Add the eggplant sticks, moving them gently in the oil to separate. When golden brown, drain in a sieve or colander and immediately set on paper towels.

Place on a large plate:

4 ounces bok choy, washed, dried, and halved lengthwise if necessary
12 fresh snow peas
¼ cup sliced bamboo shoots
3 scallions, cut into 2-inch pieces

Stir together well in a small bowl:

¼ cup chicken stock
2 tablespoons oyster sauce
1 tablespoon soy sauce
1½ teaspoons sugar
½ teaspoon salt

Have ready:

½ cup bean sprouts

TO COOK:

Bring to a rolling boil in a large pot:

16 cups (4 quarts) water

Add:

7 ounces Shanghai-style noodles

Cook just until tender. Drain and rinse under cold water until cool. Drain and toss thoroughly with:

2 teaspoons toasted sesame oil

Heat a wok or large skillet over high heat. When hot, pour in:

3 tablespoons peanut oil

Swirl around the wok until very hot but not smoking. Add the mushroom strips and stir briefly. Add all the ingredients on the plate with the bok choy. Stir and toss vigorously until the vegetables are well coated with oil, about 45 seconds.

Pour the chicken stock mixture down the side of the wok. Stir and cover, allowing the vegetables to steam in the sauce until slightly wilted.

Uncover and add the noodles. Stir and toss for about 30 seconds.

Add the bean sprouts. Stir for about 30 seconds.

Pour into a serving dish. Distribute the eggplant sticks over the top. Sprinkle with:

¼ teaspoon cracked black peppercorns

Serve immediately.

JAPANESE NOODLES IN BROTH

4 to 6 servings

Simplicity itself—freshly cooked noodles in a flavorful broth garnished with scallions and spice. Cooking the noodles first and then reheating them in boiling water guarantees that they will not get soft and mushy sitting in the broth.

BEFORE COOKING:

Have ready:

2 cups 2-inch pieces scallions
Japanese seven-spice mix (*shichimi*), available in small shakers in Japanese markets, or Chinese five-spice mix (optional)

TO COOK:

Bring to a rolling boil in a large pot:

3½ to 4 quarts water

Add and cook until softened:

1 pound dried udon noodles

Drain and rinse under cold water until cool.

Bring to a boil in a large pot over high heat:

8 cups chicken stock
¼ cup Japanese soy sauce
2 tablespoons sugar
1 tablespoon salt

The broth can be prepared in advance and refrigerated but must be served boiling hot.

TO SERVE:

Bring a generous amount of water to a boil in a large pot. Place the noodles in a sieve and dip them into the boiling water to reheat. Divide the noodles among individual soup bowls. Sprinkle with the scallions. Ladle 1½ to 2 cups seasoned broth into each bowl. Sprinkle on the spice mix, if using, to taste.

JAPANESE NOODLES IN DASHI

Prepare Japanese Noodles in Broth, above, substituting Dashi, 41, for the chicken stock, seasoned with 5 tablespoons soy sauce, 2 tablespoons sugar, and 2 tablespoons mirin.

MOON-VIEWING NOODLES

Traditionally eaten with the first full moon in September.

Prepare Japanese Noodles in Broth, above

Top each bowl with a carefully poached egg.

COLD SOBA NOODLES IN A BASKET

4 servings

This is the classic way the Japanese eat their buckwheat noodles—chilled and with spicy condiments, including wasabi, the green horseradish paste familiar to sushi eaters. The noodles are usually served in a small, flat noodle basket or slotted box, but an attractive salad plate works just as well.

BEFORE COOKING:

Combine in a medium saucepan over medium heat:

2½ cups Dashi, 41
½ cup plus 2 tablespoons Japanese soy sauce
¼ cup mirin
1 teaspoon sugar

Bring to a gentle boil. Stir in:

3 cups dried bonito flakes (available in Japanese markets)

Remove from the heat. After the flakes are wet, about 15 seconds, strain the liquid and let cool to room temperature. This will keep, covered and refrigerated, for up to 24 hours.

Using scissors, cut into fine shreds and place on a saucer or small plate:

1 sheet nori (a dark, thin sheet of seaweed, available in Japanese markets)

Arrange on a plate:

2 tablespoons wasabi paste (available in Japanese markets; follow instructions for reconstituting with water)
½ cup 2-inch pieces scallion
⅓ cup grated radishes, preferably daikon

TO COOK:

Bring to a rolling boil in a large pot:

8 to 12 cups water

Add and cook until nearly tender:

8 ounces dried soba noodles

Drain and rinse under cold water until cool, swishing the noodles with your hand to rinse well.

TO SERVE:

Divide the noodles among 4 baskets, bowls, or salad plates. Sprinkle each serving with the nori shreds. Divide the dipping sauce among 4 small bowls and place beside each serving. Place the plate with the wasabi on it within easy reach.

SPICY PEPPER PESTO SOBA

4 to 6 servings

Soba is a captivating noodle. Once it is cooked, you can toss the noodles with all different types of fresh herb pastes or dressings.

BEFORE COOKING:

Bring to a boil in a medium pot:

8 cups water

Add:

2 boneless, skinless chicken breast halves

Poach for 5 to 7 minutes. Drain. Let cool, shred, and reserve on a saucer or small plate.

Bring to a boil in a medium saucepan:

8 cups water

Add and quickly remove 10 to 15 seconds after:

6 ounces snow peas, ends trimmed

Rinse immediately under cold water until cool. Place on a plate. Place on the same plate:

1 red bell pepper, cut into 2-inch-long thin strips
1 yellow bell pepper, cut into 2-inch-long thin strips

Stir together well in a large bowl:

½ cup Japanese soy sauce

- 3½ tablespoons mirin or sake
- 3 tablespoons Chinese black vinegar or Worcestershire sauce
- 2½ tablespoons sugar
- 1 tablespoon safflower or corn oil

Add the chicken, snow peas, and red and yellow pepper strips. Toss to coat thoroughly.

Mince in a food processor or blender:

- 6 cloves garlic, peeled
- 2 fresh jalapeño peppers, seeded
- 1 cup fresh cilantro leaves
- ½ cup fresh parsley leaves
- 1 tablespoon toasted sesame oil

TO COOK:

Bring to a rolling boil in a large pot:

- 4 to 4½ quarts water

Add and cook until nearly tender, 3 to 4 minutes:

- 12 ounces dried soba noodles

Drain and rinse under cold water until cool. Drain. Pour into a large bowl.

Add the garlic mixture to the noodles and toss to coat thoroughly. Stir the chicken and vegetable mixture and arrange attractively atop the noodles. Serve immediately.

VEGETABLES

It is a glorious time for vegetable lovers. Farmers at their markets, exporters, and seedsmen are showering us with tastes, textures, and aromas we had never even heard of a few years ago. Science keeps confirming the age-old maternal admonition to eat your vegetables. The specific diseases you can avoid and the miracle micronutrient of the moment might change with each new study, but the general advice stays the same: vegetables are good for you. Every vegetable contains every nutrient—every vitamin (with the exception of vitamin B_{12}, which vegetarians can obtain easily from dairy products), every mineral, every kind of dietary fiber. It is less important to worry about which vegetable has the higher amount of one vitamin or antioxidant than to eat as many vegetables as you can, the fresher the better.

ABOUT BUYING AND KEEPING FRESH VEGETABLES

Avoid vegetables that look dry or wrinkled, bruised or badly blemished, lackluster. If two vegetables are of equal size and one is heavier, the heavier vegetable, which retains more moisture, will be more succulent. A good rule to follow is to select vegetables as close to the same size as possible—this ensures even cooking, even when pieces are cut up.

Because vegetables are generally less fragile than fruits, they are permitted to ripen before harvest. Fresh vegetables are still very much alive when you bring them into the kitchen. A cold, moist environment helps keep their tissues vibrant. For most vegetables, the shelter of a sealed perforated plastic bag (sold as "vegetable" bags) in a closed refrigerator crisper is ideal. However, if there is too much moisture, tissues start to deteriorate. For this reason, wait until just before cooking them to wash vegetables.

A few fine points for storing fresh vegetables. *Buds and stems:* Plunge the stalks of artichokes, asparagus, broccoli, and cauliflower and any long-stemmed greens in a pitcher of water, then refrigerate. *Greens without stems:* Whether for salad or cooking, wrap in barely moist paper towels, then place in a perforated vegetable bag. *Roots:* Cut off any greens on top, leaving 2 to 3 inches of stems. Wrap the greens separately. Leaves draw moisture from their roots—an advantage for the leaves, but not the roots. *Mushrooms:* Wrap these in a loose paper bag.

If the vegetable comes wrapped in cellophane, remove the wrapper and place the vegetable in a perforated plastic bag. The following vegetables are best stored in a cool, dry place—ideally somewhere between 45° and 50°F, but a warmer temperature is better than a colder one: boniatos, eggplants, garlic, onions,

RULES FOR VEGETABLES

1. When possible, buy vegetables that have been organically raised. Give preference to domestically raised vegetables in their seasons. Even better, try to buy vegetables from your part of the country—they will not have been stressed by shipping a long distance, and their nutrients will be intact.

2. Inspect vegetables piece by piece to make sure all you take home are of prime quality. Choose vegetables with a radiant appearance—and without blemishes.

3. Get a book from the library and learn the names of heritage varieties of vegetables you like. Then you will know that the funny-looking ruffled tomatoes at the farmers' market are Costoluto Genovese and superior in flavor, not some poorly raised contemporary stock.

4. Look for the sign that should be displayed stating which vegetables have been waxed or sprayed. If there is no sign, ask that it be put up, then urge the produce manager to provide unwaxed, unsprayed fruits.

5. Do not wash vegetables until you are ready to cook them. Those that you suspect have been waxed or sprayed, wash with a mild detergent, rinse thoroughly, then peel. When the edible skins of vegetables have not been treated, do not remove them—they are a source of flavor, nutrients, texture, and fiber.

6. Wherever you store vegetables, give them a quick check daily. When a piece shows any sign of spoilage—sliminess, softness, mold, or oozing—remove it. Spoilage is infectious and will quickly ruin surrounding pieces.

7. As a general rule, store whole onions, garlic, shallots, chayotes, plantains, winter squashes, tomatoes, and thick-skinned tubers and roots in a cool cupboard—once cut, they must be refrigerated. When there are leaves on root vegetables, cut them off and store separately. Plunge vegetables with stalks into a container of cold water and refrigerate. Most other vegetables are best stored in a perforated plastic bag in the refrigerator crisper.

8. When cooking vegetables, retain maximum nutrition by cooking quickly and using as little liquid as possible. Save cooking liquids and use them in soups or to cook another vegetable.

9. Because most vegetables contain acid to some degree, all tools and pans should be made of nonreactive materials—stainless steel, enameled cast iron, or nonstick coated.

plantains, potatoes, winter squashes, sweet potatoes, taro roots, tomatoes, yams, and yuca roots.

ABOUT PREPARING VEGETABLES

Prepare vegetables as close to cooking time as possible. All vegetables grown commercially and most you grow yourself—even organically raised vegetables—should be washed before preparing. Only the insides of layered vegetables (lettuces, cabbages, onions) can be presumed to be free of dust and the errant insect. Wash vegetables no more than is needed to remove dust and dirt. Root vegetables whose peel you will retain should be scrubbed with a fairly stiff brush—you can see the soil melt away. Do not use a woven plastic or metal pad to scrub vegetables, as brittle bits of the pad can break off and get buried, unseen, in the food. In bunches of greens where soil gathers at the base, cut off the base, separate the leaves, and drop them into a sinkful of tepid, not cold, water. Tepid water relaxes the leaves just enough for them to let down hidden grains of sand. Swish gently with your hands. Individual leaves such as those of mustard greens can be rinsed individually. Lift the greens into a colander; empty the water and check for sand at the bottom of the sink; rinse the sink and repeat until the bottom is clean. With some greens, it will be necessary to repeat several times. If you suspect the vegetable has been treated with wax and/or pesticide, the best approach is to wash it, peel it, and wash it again. Pesticide residue cannot be washed off most vegetables.

The skin is a vegetable's seal, keeping nutrients in and microorganisms out. Break that seal—do whatever cutting and slicing is needed—as close to cooking as possible. If necessary, vegetables can be cut up and refrigerated in an airtight container several hours in advance, as in the morning for an evening meal. Packaged precut vegetables such as carrot sticks at the market usually have been treated with an antispoilage solution, and sensitive palates can taste it. Leave the skin on a vegetable whenever possible, unless you suspect it has been sprayed or waxed. The most efficient tool for peeling thin skin is a carbon-steel swivel-bladed peeler, which keeps its sharp edge over time; supermarket swivel-bladed peelers are fine but should be replaced every few months. Pare as thinly as possible. A paring knife invariably takes more flesh of the vegetable along with it than is necessary. If the vegetable is cooked whole and then peeled and sliced, maximum nutrients and flavor are retained, and the skin is easier to remove. A few vegetables, notably potatoes, artichokes, salsify, celery root, Jerusalem artichokes, and some tropical roots, darken when their flesh is exposed to air. With these vegetables, use only a stainless-steel blade—carbon steel will react with the flesh and darken it instantly. Darkened flesh is harmless, but to prevent susceptible flesh from discoloring, drop the pared vegetable into cold water mixed with lemon or lime juice or vinegar (1 tablespoon juice or vinegar to 4 cups water). It is best not to keep vegetables in water for more than 20 minutes, lest nutrients and flavor start leaching out.

Cut surfaces release flavorful juices, as when you are chopping tomatoes for a sauce or onions for a soup. The smaller the pieces are, the more quickly the juices will be released. For soups and sauces, pieces need not be uniform, so you can use a food processor—just be sure to scrape all the liquid from the workbowl into the pan. For uniform pieces that will finish cooking at the same time, cut by hand, with the slicing disk on a food processor, or with a mandoline, shown 441. When a vegetable has two parts with distinctly different shapes and textures, as broccoli does, you must cut the denser, slower-cooking part into smaller pieces than the more tender part if both are to cook in the same amount of time. The same is true when cooking two or more vegetables together, as when steaming rutabagas and potatoes before mashing them. Chop them into pieces—the rutabagas slightly smaller, as they take a little longer to cook than potatoes—and arrange them in the steamer. Another reason for cutting vegetables is to expose just the right amount of surface to the seasoning you have in mind. If you want to serve the vegetable with a light sauce, you might decide to cut it into small pieces or thin slices so that the butter you are using can coat as much surface as possible. But if the sauce will be thick and rich, such as a hollandaise, you may want to cut it in larger pieces so that the vegetable will not be overwhelmed.

All hand cutting begins with slicing. Many chopping and slicing devices are available, but nothing can replace a skilled, relaxed wrist and a sharp, heavy knife. Practice with a mushroom, which is yielding and not slippery when placed cap down, and work up to an onion, which can be both resistant and evasive.

The point of the knife is never lifted from the cutting board; instead it forms a pivot. The handle end of the knife is raised high enough to be eased gently up and down, its wide blade guided by the perpendicular forefinger and midfinger of the free hand, which holds and guides the vegetable being cut. As the slicing progresses, inch a slow retreat with the free hand, which should keep a firm grasp on the object. When roll-cutting, make a diagonal cut straight down, roll the carrot (or turnip or potato) a quarter turn, and slice again. Repeat until all of the carrot is cut.

It is easier to slice a round vegetable, like a potato, if you first cut a thin slice off the bottom to create a flat surface to rest on the cutting board (the resulting slices will not be completely round, however). For attractive diagonal slices of a thin vegetable, such as green beans or asparagus, hold the knife at an angle to either the vegetable or the cutting board. For most everyday cooking, vegetables are simply sliced crosswise; they can first be cut lengthwise into halves or quarters if they are very thick. But if you want to turn slices into more elegant strips or cubes, cut long vegetables, like zucchini, into 2-inch chunks and then slice the pieces lengthwise (for the tidiest appearance, first cut a straight edge on all sides of chunks and discard the scraps—or save them for the stockpot). Round vegetables, like turnips, can be sliced crosswise or lengthwise, depending on which will yield the longer slice. To

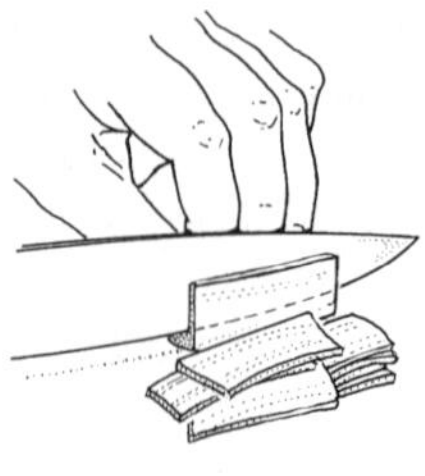

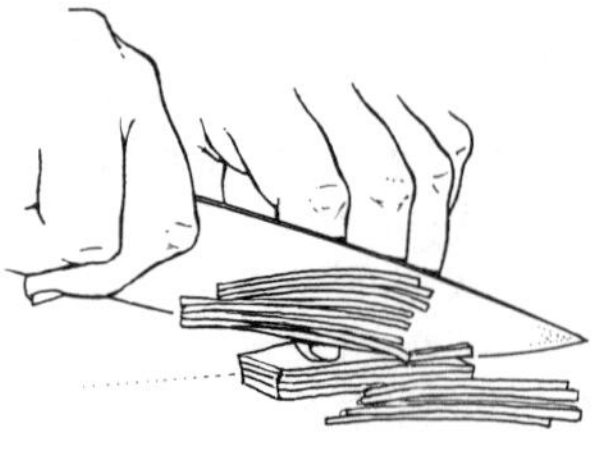

Cutting into julienne

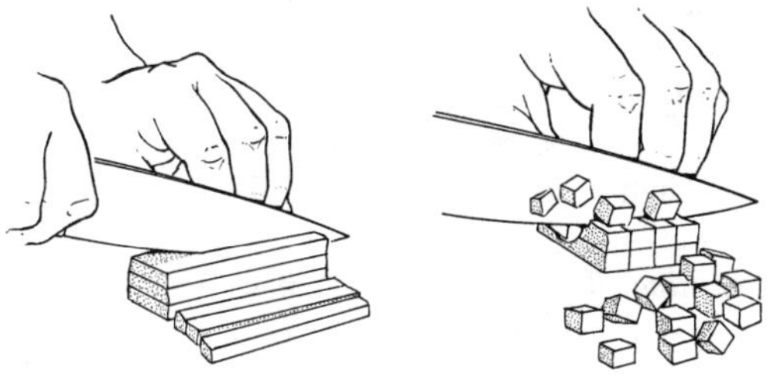

Dicing a vegetable

cut slices into smaller pieces, stack them, a few at a time, then cut them into very thin strips (less than ⅛ inch thick) to make a julienne, shown 334, slightly wider strips (about ⅛ inch thick) to make matchsticks, or much wider strips (about ¼ inch thick) to make batons. To dice the vegetable, shown above, cut first into ½-inch-wide strips, then hold them together and cut across them to make ½-inch cubes. If you cut tiny ⅛-inch cubes, they are called a brunoise and traditionally added to consommé.

Cutting an onion chef's style keeps pieces from scattering all over the board and gives you control of the size of the pieces, shown below. Halve the peeled onion lengthwise. Lay the halves cut side down on the board. Steady the piece lightly with the tips of the fingers of your assisting hand (the rest of your hand safely turned under, so just the first joints of the hand are exposed to the knife). Slice the onion lengthwise in parallel cuts up to, but not through, the root. (For slices, now cut off the root.) Next, make several horizontal cuts of the desired thickness parallel to the board up to, but not through, the root. (For matchsticks, now cut off the root.) For diced or chopped pieces, cut through the onion at right angles to the last cuts at the desired thickness, then cut through the root. For round onion slices, slice crosswise.

Many large leaves—such as those of chard and some of the Chinese cabbages—have fleshy ribs in the center. The leafy parts will cook faster than the ribs and should be separated, although they can be combined again for serving. Fold the leaves lengthwise in half, and either use the tip of a small, sharp knife to slice the green leaves away from the center stalk, or hold the top of the stalk and rip the two leafy parts off the stalk from top to bottom. Often the stalks can be cut up as another vegetable—the ribs of chard can be chopped and cooked like celery.

ABOUT COOKING VEGETABLES

There is more than one cooking method for every vegetable, and no one method is superior. Some vegetable enthusiasts go so far as to suggest that vegetables are best if not cooked at all. To preserve nutrients, flavors, and textures, cook vegetables as quickly as possible in a covered pot. To preserve color, cook in an uncovered pot—acids, which all vegetables contain, collect on the underside of the lid and then drop back into the pot, darkening colors. Color should never be maintained by the addition of baking soda, for this alkali not only destroys nutrients but makes vegetables mushy. Colors also may be lost through cooking in hard water. Salting early in cooking helps retain bright colors.

The degree of doneness is a matter of personal taste. Some enjoy vegetables like green beans slightly undercooked—the crisp-tender stage. However, cabbage, onions, and rutabaga grow sweeter when cooked until soft. Fibrous greens become easier to digest as their fibers soften. And sometimes a little extra cooking will release enough natural juices to allow the cook to reduce the amount of butter, salt, or other seasoning needed. As with cooking so many other foods, when you start *smelling* the vegetables, they are at the point of being fully cooked. Most vegetables should be lightly salted before they are cooked; seasoning to taste

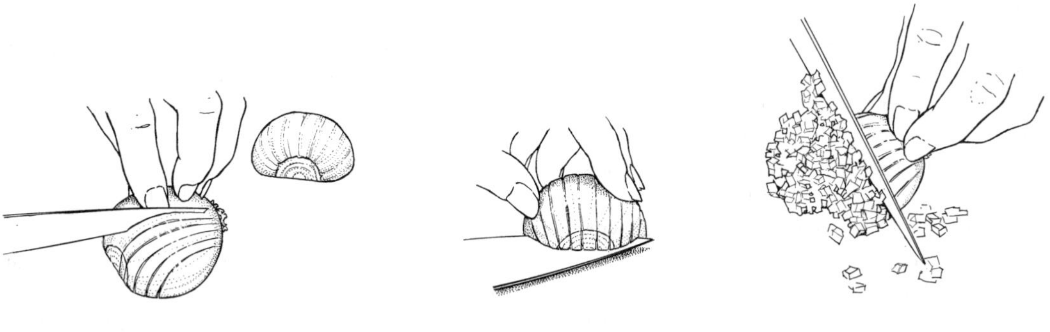

Chopping an onion

requires considerably less salt if it is done during cooking and not afterward, and the flavor seems deeper somehow. Allow about ½ tablespoon salt per 4 cups cooking water, or ⅛ to ¼ teaspoon salt per serving of vegetables not cooked in water.

Here are all sorts of ways to cook, heat, and serve vegetables.

Boiling: When green vegetables are dropped into a big uncovered pot of boiling salted water that is rapidly brought back to a boil, their color is instantly set. Given ample space in the water, each piece cooks quickly. For retaining flavor and texture, this method is superb. Boiling time in a recipe is counted from the time the water returns to a boil after the vegetables have been added. This sort of boiling is also useful for tough vegetables, like fibrous green beans or large leaves.

Fill a stockpot with 16 cups (4 quarts) water, unless otherwise noted. Add 1½ tablespoons salt. Cover and bring to a boil over high heat. Drop the vegetables into furiously boiling water and start counting for specified cooking times from the time the water returns to the boil. Do not leave the pot for long, as most vegetables cook quickly. Soon after the water returns to a boil, pull out a sample vegetable with tongs or a long-handled strainer and taste. Do this frequently until the vegetable is a shade less than the desired degree of doneness, then drain. Since the temperature at which water boils decreases at high altitudes, vegetables will take longer to boil to doneness, and water may need to be added during prolonged cooking.

Quickly plunging vegetables into boiling water is the method of choice for setting color and partially cooking vegetables that will be finished another way or frozen or canned. In this partial boiling—called blanching or parboiling—the vegetables are cooled quickly unless the finishing cooking follows immediately. For more information on blanching and parboiling, see page 1052.

Braising and Stewing: Slow cooking in a flavorful liquid is ideal for vegetables like potatoes, carrots, turnips, rutabagas, cabbages, and Brussels sprouts, which can all absorb stock or another seasoning liquid. They can be tossed first over medium-high heat in hot butter or another fat and then simmered, partially submerged in the cooking liquid, until the vegetables are soft and the liquid is reduced to a saucelike consistency. Since the "sauce," or pot liquor, is eaten with the vegetables, the vitamins and minerals that dissolve in it are not lost. Braising can be done on top of the stove or in the oven; either way requires a heavy pot and will caramelize some of the juices of a sweet vegetable, like carrots, to yield deep and delicious flavor.

Broiling: One advantage to broiling over grilling is that for vegetables like mushroom caps, butter or oil can be placed in the hollow to moisten the flesh without running out.

Creaming, Buttering, and Saucing: Practically any vegetable can be served in or with a sauce. However the vegetable is cooked, drain it thoroughly before combining with a sauce or butter. The amount to use depends on the richness of both the vegetable and the sauce—as little as 1 teaspoon butter to ¼ cup cream sauce per cup of cooked vegetables. Consider the amount, too, if the vegetables are to be presented in individual bowls or spooned from a serving bowl onto a plate. If you are moistening vegetables in a casserole—perhaps in layers—spoon over just enough sauce to cover them. Such casseroles are often finished off with a layer of buttered breadcrumbs, sometimes mixed with cheese and browned.

Deep-Frying: Because success depends so largely on the quality of the fat and avoiding its excess absorption, please read Deep-Frying, 1050. Check to see that the vegetables are dry before applying a coating. It is also best to let the coating dry for about 10 minutes before immersing the food in fat, which should be heated to between 350° and 375°F. Cook until the vegetables are golden. Vegetables suitable for coating or battering and deep-frying are long green beans; ⅓-inch-thick eggplant slices barely nicked with a thin knife at ½-inch intervals all around the bands of skin; mushrooms and tiny bell peppers, whole or halved; cucumber, squash, zucchini, or sweet potato rounds; sliced lotus roots or bamboo shoots; small bundles of julienned onions or thin scallions; asparagus tips; cauliflower or broccoli florets; artichoke hearts or stems.

Glazing: Root vegetables cooked by this method are suitable for garnishing and require no further saucing. Choose:

2 cups young vegetables (onions, carrots, turnips, or potatoes), halved or quartered to uniform size

Combine in a very shallow, heavy pan with:

1 cup chicken or mild vegetable stock
2 tablespoons butter
2 teaspoons sugar
½ teaspoon salt

Simmer, covered, until the vegetables are nearly done and the liquid has been almost absorbed. Uncover and cook, shaking the pan constantly over high heat, until coated with a golden glaze. Serve at once.

Grilling: Vegetables are usually halved or sliced for grilling to speed up cooking, and the cut surfaces need to be coated with oil or a vinaigrette, which will protect against drying and also promote browning. The popular practice of cooking foil-wrapped packets of cut-up vegetables on the grill is actually a form of steaming and works with any vegetable that steams well, although carrots and other hard vegetables can take twice as long as they would being steamed on the stove. For campfires and barbecues, here are two simple potless ways to cook vegetables. For the first, use frozen or sliced and washed vegetables. Place them on heavy-weight aluminum foil and seal them. Cook the foil-wrapped vegetables on a grill or under or on hot coals for 10 to 15 minutes. For the second method, place thick slices of tomato, mushroom, pepper, or parboiled onion directly on a greased grill rack above the coals. Cover with an inverted colander and cook until tender.

High-Altitude Vegetable Cooking: In baking vegetables at high elevations, use approximately the same temperatures and timing given for sea-level cooking. In cooking vegetables at high altitude by any process involving moisture, both more liquid and a longer cooking time are needed, as the vegetables boil at lower temperatures. If the vegetables are more thinly sliced or cut into smaller pieces, they will cook in less time. Make these adjustments as an approximate time guide: For each 1000 feet of elevation, add to the recipe's cooking time about 10 percent for carrots and onions and about 7 percent for green beans, squash, green cabbage, turnips, and parsnips. In cooking frozen vegetables at high altitudes, whole carrots and beans may require as much as 5 to 12 minutes of additional cooking, while other frozen vegetables may need only 1 to 2 more minutes. Do not be surprised if whole potatoes, beets, and yams need considerably more time than at sea level.

Microwave Cooking: For speed of cooking and maximum preservation of nutrients, the microwave is matchless. Colors and flavors are vibrant and, with careful attention, textures can be too. Timing in these recipes is for food on a turntable in a 750- to 1050-watt oven. In the range of time given, the shorter cooking time is for the higher wattage. A turntable is essential for even cooking. If your oven has no built-in turntable, buy a wind-up turntable in the housewares section of a department store. Generally, a 2-quart baking dish is called for. An 8 x 8 x 2-inch glass dish is ideal, with a lid or microwave plastic wrap sealed all around the dish except at one corner, where it is folded back to make a vent. For liquid, use vegetable, chicken, or beef stock, or lightly salted water. No matter what the recipe timing says, as soon as you can smell the vegetables, stop the oven and taste a sample piece, because they are close to ready. The importance of standing time to finish the cooking cannot be overemphasized. Microwaving works best for vegetables with quantities of about 1 pound; otherwise the cooking can be uneven. Nevertheless, it is often faster to microwave two successive batches and mix them together than it is to cook a vegetable by a slower method. Do use the microwave to melt butter or make a simple sauce right in the serving dish, no matter which way you have cooked the vegetable.

Pressure-Cooking: The pressure cooker offers another fast way of steaming vegetables. It is a boon for dense vegetables like roots and winter squashes, but green vegetables are almost invariably overcooked. We do not recommend pressure-cooking any vegetable that requires less than 5 minutes' conventional cooking. The quantity of food in the pan does not affect timing, so the pressure cooker offers an advantage when there is a quantity of potatoes, for example, to cook. Always use the trivet that comes with the pan (or, if necessary, a round cake rack). Follow the pan manufacturer's booklet regarding timing. Also note within this chapter which vegetables *cannot* be pressure-cooked. After cooking fresh vegetables, cool the cooker at once by placing it under cold running water.

Pureeing: A potato masher or food mill will yield a coarse puree; a hand-held mixer or potato ricer will produce a smooth puree. More nutrients are retained if the vegetables are cooked before blending. You can heat the puree briefly in butter or cream before serving.

Refreshing: To instantly stop hot food from further cooking—as when vegetables are pulled from a pot of boiling water—it is plunged into ice water or placed under cold running water.

Roasting or Baking: In the dry heat of the oven with no added liquid, nutrients are preserved and flavors are concentrated. Oven cooking takes time but is convenient, especially with vegetables that have a thick exterior, such as potatoes and winter squashes. Watery vegetables like eggplant cook so soft that they can easily be scooped from the shell. Remember to pierce the skin of any whole roasting vegetable with a knife tip in several places, or the vegetable may explode from built-up steam. Vegetables that do not have a protective skin must be sheltered from drying on the outside, either by coating the flesh with oil or by roasting at a temperature low enough to cook the inside before the outside dries out (see instructions for individual vegetables). An easy way to roast vegetables is to cook them with roasting poultry or meat. Set whole small potatoes, or larger ones halved or quartered—or vegetables of similar size—in the pan and turn occasionally to keep moistened with drippings. They may overcook a little, but they will be delectable.

Sautéing: Like stir-frying, this involves stirring vegetables in hot fat over fairly high heat. In sautéing, however, the heat can be a little lower and vegetables need not be cut up. The aim is to season the vegetable with butter or oil as it cooks and, in many cases, to brown it. Please read more about sautéing on page 1051.

Simmering and Poaching: Cooking vegetables at a temperature below that of boiling water is sometimes useful. Use stock for added flavor and follow the method on page 1052.

Steaming: Steaming is fast and convenient (you can easily check the progress), and it protects water-soluble nutrients, which do not dissolve in the steam. An electric steamer is faster than steaming on top of the stove. A collapsible steamer basket placed in a large pot with a tight-fitting lid or in an electric skillet or a metal insert made to fit a specific pan or pot, or a metal or bamboo Chinese steamer also works well with most vegetables. Make sure the water level does not rise above the level of the basket; heat the water to boiling, add the vegetables, cover tightly, and cook to desired doneness. Vegetables that do not fit easily into steamers, such as asparagus spears, can be placed directly in a pan filled with about ⅜ inch boiling water or stock; cover tightly and at least once during steaming reposition the spears or other pieces to lift the parts that are submerged. Another method of steaming greens, which results in darker colors but maximum nutrients, is to cook them, covered, in ¼ to ½ inch boiling stock or salted water until tender, stirring occasionally.

Stir-Frying: Vegetables cut in small, even pieces and stirred over intensely high heat with a modicum of fat and liquid cook through in the fastest possible time. Stir-frying is most efficient when the pieces of food have plenty of room to move in the pan, allowing surfaces constant exposure to heat. Work in several batches, if necessary, to prevent vegetables from being crowded and steaming in their own moisture, which prevents browning and dilutes flavor. Many vegetables are best stir-fried until golden or brown and then finished with steam by adding liquid and covering the pan. This method reduces the amount of fat needed to finish cooking dense vegetables and yields excellent taste.

For best results, the vegetables should be sliced to uniform thickness. Cut those that tend to stringiness on a diagonal. Stem ends and midribs should be removed from coarse-leaf vegetables, then sliced and cooked separately. Use 1 to 2 tablespoons cooking oil—peanut oil is a great favorite—per pound of vegetables. Heat the wok or large, heavy skillet until almost smoking hot. Add the oil and heat to the point of fragrance. You can add a slice or two of garlic or fresh ginger briefly, then discard it before the vegetables are put in the pan. If meat and vegetables are to be cooked together, the meat is cooked first. Remove it from the pan and add it again when the vegetables are nearly finished. Stir the vegetables rapidly with a large, flat spatula, coating them with oil, until they show signs of wilting slightly. Some cooks like to season at this point with a dash of soy sauce and stock. When the vegetables are just tender, stir in additional stock if needed. Succulent vegetables such as cucumbers, tomatoes, summer squash, spinach, Chinese cabbage, and leafy greens release so much liquid themselves that they usually do not need additional stock. Cover the pan briefly until the sauce comes to a boil, stir vigorously, then serve at once.

Stuffing Vegetables: Naturally large and hollow vegetables are easy to shape into delicious and decorative cases for stuffing; these include tomatoes, peppers, squashes, cucumbers, onions, and mushrooms. It is

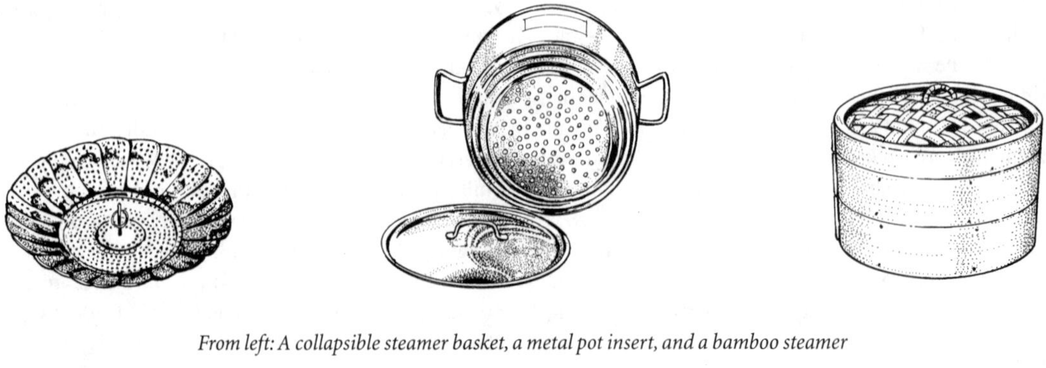

From left: A collapsible steamer basket, a metal pot insert, and a bamboo steamer

best to parboil the cases until nearly tender before stuffing, as stuffing mixtures generally cook faster than the vegetable. Experiment with using parboiled vegetable cases in place of individual baking dishes, filling the vegetable with pasta mixtures, soufflé batters, other vegetable combinations—anything that contrasts in color, flavor, and texture with the case. The classic stuffing for bell peppers, 404, can be used to stuff other vegetables. Raw foods that need long cooking should not be ingredients in vegetable stuffings.

After parboiling and draining the cases, fill the vegetables and place them on a rack in a pan containing about ¼ inch water. Bake the stuffed vegetables in a 400°F oven until thoroughly hot, unless otherwise indicated.

Sweating: To release delicious flavor from finely chopped aromatic vegetables (onions, garlic, shallots, carrots, and celery, for example) before they are simmered in a sauce, stew, or braise, "sweat" them in a small amount of butter or oil in a covered pan over medium to low heat. After a few minutes—when the vegetables are tender but not browned and their juices are released—they are ready. For a lower-fat technique, butter and oil can be replaced with stock.

ABOUT VEGETABLES IN THE MENU

The government's nutrition guidelines, which recommend three to five servings of vegetables daily, regard one serving as ½ cup of a cooked vegetable. Put this amount on a dinner plate, and you will see how small it is. A more common portion is closer to 1 cup; the recommended daily intake is actually quite simple to achieve. Although yield varies, the rule of thumb is that 1 pound of vegetables yields three or four servings. With spinach and other leaves, the yield is closer to two servings per pound.

Like many other nonvegetarians, we long ago discovered the pleasure of lightening the week's menus with one or two vegetarian dinners. And instead of hot cereal on a chilly morning, sometimes we heat stuffed baked potatoes, 411 to 412, or a slice of Chard Tart, 364, or boniatos mashed with apples for breakfast. Fresh creamed corn for breakfast on a summer's morning is fast and heavenly. Vegetables also make excellent seasonings, providing a nutritional two-fer. Stir browned onions or mushrooms into rice; sauce green beans with braised tomatoes; use diced peppers or ribbons of arugula or grated carrots as a garnish. Between meals, grab a stalk of raw broccoli or a handful of radishes or roasted pumpkin seeds instead of sugary sweets.

Try serving leftover vegetables in a salad—cold food is as nutritious as hot.

ARTICHOKES

Artichokes, one of springtime's earliest vegetables, are the immature flower buds of a thistle plant. Whether an artichoke is round and green or tulip-shaped and purple, its edible parts are at the base of the leaf and just above the stem, in the saucer-shaped piece called the heart. Artichoke flesh has a firm but velvety texture. Its flavor is a unique blend of earthy root and sweet green shoot—something between celery root and asparagus. You may occasionally find them referred to as *globe* artichokes to distinguish them from Jerusalem artichokes, to which they are not related.

Select tightly closed buds that feel heavy for their size. If they are part of the smaller autumn crop, they may be streaked with brown—this is the result of frost and not harmful. (In fact, some frost sweetens the buds.) If the stems are long enough, plunge them into a bowl of water and refrigerate. Otherwise, store the artichokes in a perforated plastic vegetable bag in the refrigerator crisper. When harvested plum sized, all but the outer leaves are edible. To eat these baby artichokes, hold the artichoke by the stem, place the top in your mouth, bite down, and the luscious center will pop out. Look for these artichokes in markets with specialty produce.

To Prepare: If you are in a hurry, you can cook larger artichokes as is. However, a little trimming makes a big difference in appearance and ease of eating. Have on hand a lemon half or two; its juice rubbed over cut surfaces will keep the flesh from discoloring. After rinsing, use scissors to trim off the tough, thorny tops of the outside layers of leaves. You can either bend each leaf back and snap off the top, European style (a hand-finished look) or snip it off with scissors in the American style—the only method that works with tough end-of-the-season artichokes. Rub cut surfaces frequently with lemon. When you reach the thin inner leaves that are green at the top but celery yellow at the base, lay the artichokes on their sides on a cutting board, 000. With a sharp, heavy, stainless-steel knife or a serrated knife (artichoke darkens carbon steel), trim off the top inch or so of the inner leaves, 340. Pull out the immature prickly, pinkish leaves in the center, shown 340, and use the tip of a spoon or a grapefruit knife to scrape up the thicket of fuzz beneath, called the choke—it is a thistle, remember. It will lift up in small pieces. Be careful not to cut into the heart, the buried treasure beneath. The stems are as delicious as the hearts. Italians leave as much as 3 inches of stems attached and serve artichokes stalk up. But American growers trim stems much closer to the bud, and our way of serving is to snap or slice off the stems close to the base so the artichoke will sit squarely on the plate. To prepare baby artichokes, please see the recipe on page 341.

For cooked whole artichoke hearts, prepare the artichokes as above, cook as desired, then simply remove the stems and leaves, retrieving the heart. Trim away any rough places with a paring knife.

Artichokes retain the most nutrients when they are microwaved or steamed, but they are equally tasty boiled, braised, and fried. For braising and frying, see the recipes on page 341.

To Boil: Artichokes should be boiled in a large pot so that they have plenty of room. Whether cooking several baby or 1 large artichoke, place in a stockpot 16 cups (4 quarts) water, ¼ cup cider vinegar or lemon juice, and 1½ tablespoons salt. Bring to a boil over high heat and drop in the prepared artichokes right side up; you can also add 1½ tablespoons olive oil and ½ crushed garlic clove for each serving if desired. Rapidly return the water to a rolling boil and cook, uncovered, until the artichokes test tender when pierced with a thin skewer and a leaf comes away easily from the base of the largest artichoke. Once the water returns to a boil, allow 12 to 15 minutes for baby artichokes, 20 to 25 minutes for medium artichokes, 25 to 35 minutes for large globes. Drain upside down in a colander.

To Steam: Place the artichokes bottom side up in a steaming basket over 1 to 2 inches boiling water. Cook, covered, until all test tender when pierced with a thin skewer. Allow 15 to 20 minutes for baby artichokes, 25 to 35 minutes for medium, and up to 45 minutes for large globe artichokes. Cooking times vary considerably according to the age of the artichokes.

To Microwave: Place 2 medium artichokes in a 2-quart baking dish. Add 2 tablespoons stock or lightly salted water, cover, and cook on high until tender enough to pierce all the way through with a thin skewer, 5 to 8 minutes. Let stand, covered, for 5 minutes.

To Pressure-Cook: Large artichokes can be pressure-cooked with 1 cup liquid at 15 pounds pressure for 10 minutes. Cool the cooker at once.

Simply cooked artichokes are most flavorful at room temperature or a little warmer. To serve, offer a small dish of melted butter, hollandaise sauce, or vinaigrette. Be sure there is room on the plate for the spent leaves, or set an empty plate or bowl. Starting at the bottom, pluck one leaf at a time from the bud, dip into the sauce, then draw its meaty end through your teeth to extract the flesh. When the leaves are finished, cut the heart into bite-sized pieces and dip.

To prepare cooked artichoke cups for filling hot with cooked vegetables, or cold with seafood or a salad, prepare as directed above but slice off the top third of the buds instead of the top 1 inch. To prepare artichokes for frying or to include them in a stew or casserole, prepare as for filling, then cut into quarters or thinner pieces, as desired.

Artichokes have a curious property. They contain an acid, called cynarin, that for some people distorts the flavors of accompanying food and drink. When serving a special wine, it is best to keep artichokes off the menu. Artichokes go well with sharp flavors such as lemon, orange, wine and fruit vinegars, dark olives, and capers, and they are also delicious with ham and garden peas. Garlic, shallots, bay, cilantro, parsley, sage, tarragon, fennel, basil, oregano, and coriander seeds are especially good with artichokes. Allow 1 medium to large or 6 to 9 baby artichokes per person.

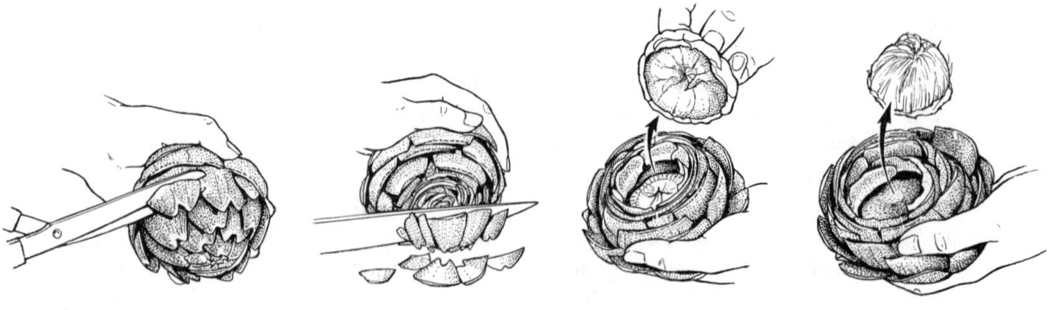

Trimming an uncooked artichoke and removing the choke

ROASTED ARTICHOKE STEMS AND HEARTS

4 servings

Preheat the oven to 400°F.

Trim, leaving most of the stem on, quarter, and remove the chokes from:

5 medium artichokes

As you work, rub the cut surfaces with:

1 lemon, halved

Bring to a boil in a stockpot:

12 cups water
1½ tablespoons fresh lemon juice
2 teaspoons salt

Add the artichokes and boil, uncovered, until tender but firm, about 5 minutes. Drain, pat dry, then slice the quarters into halves or thirds. Toss them in a 13 x 9-inch baking dish with:

2½ tablespoons extra-virgin olive oil
1 large clove garlic, slivered
½ teaspoon salt
¼ teaspoon ground black pepper

Cook, stirring twice, until the artichokes have begun to color and crisp in places, about 30 minutes. Remove and serve just as they are, or sprinkle with a mixture of:

¼ cup chopped fresh parsley, chervil, or tarragon
1 teaspoon finely grated lemon zest (optional)
1 small clove garlic, minced (optional)

Or serve at room temperature, accompanied by individual dipping bowls of:

Tuna Sauce, 81, Southeast Asian Peanut Dipping Sauce, 83, or Mustard Mayonnaise, 73

FRIED ARTICHOKES

4 servings

Fried artichokes are a specialty of Roman Jewish cooking, in which they are fried whole and weighted, upside down, so that they resemble a flower; they are popular throughout the Middle East.

Trim down to the pale green leaves, leaving most of the stem on, quarter, and remove the chokes from:

4 medium artichokes

As you work, drop them into a bowl of water with lemon juice added. Heat in a large skillet over medium-high heat until hot:

1 cup extra-virgin olive oil

Meanwhile, drain the artichokes and pat them dry. Mix in a shallow bowl:

½ cup all-purpose flour
Salt and ground black pepper to taste

Lightly beat together in a second shallow bowl:

2 large eggs

Toss the artichokes in the seasoned flour to coat them, then dip them into the eggs. When the oil is hot, fry several at a time, turning often, until they are golden and tender, 5 to 6 minutes. Drain briefly on paper towels, then pile them on a platter and season with:

Sea salt

Serve with:

Lemon wedges

TUSCAN-STYLE STUFFED ARTICHOKES

6 appetizer servings

Preheat the oven to 375°F.

Trim by snapping off the outer leaves until you reach the leaves that are green only at the tip (you will be removing 5 or 6 layers of leaves):

6 medium artichokes

Slice the tops off, pull out the sharp inner leaves, and scrape out the fuzzy choke. Trim the dark green outer skin from the base and stem. To prevent discoloration, rub all the cut surfaces with:

½ lemon

Combine well:

6 tablespoons extra-virgin olive oil
6 tablespoons fresh breadcrumbs, toasted
¼ cup minced fresh parsley
3 cloves garlic, minced
3 tablespoons grated Parmesan cheese
Salt and ground black pepper to taste

Using a teaspoon, fill the cavities of the artichokes with this mixture. Place the stuffed artichokes in a baking dish in which they fit snugly. Pour ½ inch of water into the bottom of the dish and add to it:

Juice of ½ lemon
1 tablespoon extra-virgin olive oil

Cover the dish with aluminum foil and bake until the artichokes are tender, about 45 minutes. Serve warm or at room temperature.

BRAISED BABY ARTICHOKES AND PEAS

4 to 6 servings

From Brittany to Sicily, spring's chokeless artichokes and young peas are combined to make an incomparable dish. This makes a fine first course. For a vegetarian main dish, serve generously topped with grated mild cheese. To eat baby artichokes, hold each by the stem and bite down at your fingertips.

Have ready a bowl of cool water with a splash of lemon juice. Rinse and thoroughly dry:

24 walnut-sized artichokes, stems trimmed but not removed

Pull off all tough outer leaves and trim the stems flush with the bottoms, dropping the artichokes into the water to keep them from darkening. In a medium, deep skillet, heat:

2 tablespoons olive oil

Add:

1 small onion, chopped

Stir over medium heat until the onion browns. Add the artichokes and sauté over moderately high heat, shaking the pan, until they are browned all over, about 10 minutes. Stir in:

2 large cloves garlic, minced
2 cups shelled young peas (about 2 pounds unshelled)
2 tablespoons butter
2 tablespoons stock or water
Salt and ground black pepper to taste

Bring to a simmer, cover, and cook over low heat until the artichokes and peas are tender, 10 to 15 minutes. Occasionally shake the skillet, holding the lid. Check to see if more stock is needed toward the end. Taste for salt and pepper, then stir in:

2 teaspoons fresh lemon juice
2 tablespoons shredded fresh basil

Serve immediately.

JUNE VEGETABLE RAGOUT

4 servings

You can substitute four 9-ounce packages of frozen artichoke hearts, thawed and quartered, for the fresh artichokes in this recipe.

Trim:

8 large artichoke hearts, quartered, or 16 baby artichokes, trimmed and quartered

As you work, drop them into a bowl of water with lemon juice added. Cut lengthwise in half and peel:

2 medium onions

Place each half, cut side down, on a cutting board and cut crosswise into very thin slices. In an unheated large skillet, combine the onions with:

6 tablespoons extra-virgin olive oil
1 plump head garlic, separated into cloves and peeled, cloves halved lengthwise
1 small bunch summer savory or stems and sprigs of thyme and parsley, tied with kitchen string
Salt to taste

Toss to coat the ingredients with the oil. Cover and sweat over low heat until the onions are softened, about 10 minutes. Drain and add the artichokes and:

2 pounds fava beans blanched, refreshed, and shelled
3 tomatoes, peeled, seeded, and coarsely chopped
1½ cups dry white wine

Simmer, uncovered, for 10 minutes to evaporate the alcohol. Add:

2 pounds fresh peas in their pods, shelled, blanched, and refreshed, 1052 (about 2 cups)
20 asparagus tips, blanched and refreshed, 1052

Cook until the green vegetables are heated through, about 2 minutes more. Remove the pan from the heat and immediately stir in until creamy:

2 tablespoons cold unsalted butter, cut into small pieces

Remove and discard the bundle of savory. Taste for seasoning. Serve immediately with crusty bread.

ASPARAGUS

Asparagus spears poke through the earth in spring. If not picked, these young shoots grow into tall ferny branches with bright red berries. The thinner the shoot, the younger and, usually, the tenderer. The shoots can be green, purple, or green and purple; cream-colored shoots, should you find them, have been raised deprived of sunlight. Select crisp, tightly closed stalks whose cut ends are not dry. Asparagus is perishable, so plan to serve it the day of harvesting or purchase. In the meantime, submerge the ends of the spears in a pitcher of water and refrigerate.

To Prepare: After rinsing, hold each spear with one hand at the base of the stalk and the other hand an inch or two farther toward the tip. Bend the spear. It will break at the point where the tender stalk starts to toughen. If it does not snap, move your hand a little farther up the stalk and bend again until the stalk breaks. Tough ends can be chopped and simmered in water to cover to make a broth for soup. Stalks thinner than your little finger will probably not need paring; if the bottom end is at all tough and fibrous, use a vegetable peeler to remove the skin up to and stopping at the tip.

Thin asparagus is best steamed, boiled, sautéed, stir-fried, or microwaved (white asparagus generally takes a few minutes longer than green). The fleshy spears of thicker asparagus are suited to roasting and grilling. Cook asparagus quickly. It is done when it turns bright green and is tender, with a trace of crispness. Even 1 minute of overcooking will start turning it dull. Whatever the cooking method, remove the pieces as they are ready.

To Boil: Use a medium, deep skillet wide enough so the spears can be laid flat. For every 12 thick or 18 pencil-slim spears (about 10 ounces, prepared weight), bring 5 cups water and ½ tablespoon salt to a boil. Gently lay in the asparagus, rapidly return to a boil, and boil until the spears are tender with a hint of crispness, 4 to 5 minutes for thin spears, 6 to 7 minutes for medium spears, and 8 to 10 minutes for thick spears. Stir thick spears after 4 minutes. Immediately lift out with tongs, place on a plate, and pour off any water on the plate.

To Steam: Stand whole spears upright without crowding in a tall steamer, or lay flat in a steamer basket or in a wide bamboo steamer. Place over 1 to 2 inches boiling water and cover. Steaming asparagus tips takes 3 to 4 minutes; pencil-slim asparagus takes 4 to 5 minutes, medium asparagus 6 to 7 minutes, and thick asparagus 7 to 10 minutes. Spears can be cut into pieces and steamed; start checking for doneness at 5 minutes. Pieces are done when they are tender with a hint of crispness.

To Microwave: Place 1 pound thin to medium trimmed spears in a 2-quart baking dish. Add 2 tablespoons stock or lightly salted water. Cover and cook on high until crisp-tender, 4 to 9 minutes, rearranging every 3 minutes. Let stand, covered, for 2 minutes.

To Grill: Rinse, drain, pat dry, and brush thick spears generously with olive or nut oil. Place the spears over a slow wood or charcoal fire. Never taking your eyes off them, turn them frequently until you can smell the asparagus and one tastes cooked through.

Serve cooked asparagus hot or at room temperature. Drizzle hot asparagus with melted butter, seasoned olive oil, Hollandaise Sauce, 55, or Basic Vinaigrette, 236, and sprinkle chopped hard-boiled egg on top. Asparagus has affinities with the same flavors as artichokes, 340, and also with most fish, eggs, and sharp cheeses such as Parmesan and pecorino. Allow about 5 ounces per serving.

ROASTED ASPARAGUS

4 servings

It is surprising how delicious these delicate spears can be when roasted in a very hot oven. A fine first course.

Preheat the oven to 500°F.

Snap off the bottoms and peel the lower halves of:

1 pound asparagus

Arrange the spears in a single layer in a shallow baking dish and drizzle over them very lightly:

Extra-virgin olive oil

Toss the spears to coat lightly. Roast until tender but still slightly firm, 8 to 10 minutes. Sprinkle with:

Salt and ground black pepper to taste
Extra-virgin olive oil
2 tablespoons minced fresh parsley, tarragon, and/or chives

Serve as a first course at room temperature, garnished with:

Lemon wedges

STIR-FRIED ASPARAGUS

4 to 6 servings

Stir-frying seems to bring out flavors in asparagus that are not released by boiling or steaming.

Snap off the bottoms and cut into 2-inch pieces:

2 pounds asparagus

Warm a wok over high heat, then add:

2 tablespoons peanut or vegetable oil

Swirl the oil around the sides of the wok, then add the asparagus along with:

1 tablespoon slivered peeled fresh ginger

Stir-fry for 2 to 3 minutes, then add:

2 cloves garlic, slivered
⅛ teaspoon salt

Stir-fry for 1 minute, then add:

¼ cup chicken stock

Cover the wok, reduce the heat, and cook gently until the asparagus is tender, about 5 minutes. Serve sprinkled with:

1½ tablespoons white or black sesame seeds, toasted
¼ teaspoon toasted sesame oil

ASPARAGUS WITH ORANGE AND HAZELNUTS

4 servings

Roast, steam, or boil:

1 pound asparagus, bottoms snapped off

Place a large skillet over medium heat and add:

2 tablespoons butter
1½ tablespoons grated orange zest
¼ cup chopped hazelnuts, toasted
Juice of ½ orange

Cook until the butter is slightly browned, then add the cooked asparagus. Toss several times to heat through, then add:

Salt and ground black pepper to taste

Serve warm as a side dish or salad.

ASPARAGUS WITH MUSTARD MISO

4 to 6 servings

Miso, or fermented bean curd, is available in many varieties. The mustard-miso dressing here is made with light-colored (white) miso, a milder style. If you prefer a more pungent dressing, use the stronger dark-colored (red) miso.

Bring to a boil in a stockpot:

12 cups water

1½ tablespoons salt

Add and cook for 1½ to 5 minutes, depending on size:

2 pounds asparagus, bottoms snapped off, cut diagonally into 2-inch pieces

When the asparagus is tender with a slight crunch remaining, drain and rinse under cold water to stop the cooking. Drain well, dry, transfer to a bowl, and set aside. Mix in a small bowl:

1 teaspoon dry mustard

1 teaspoon cold water

Let sit for 10 minutes to develop the flavor of the mustard. Add:

1 tablespoon light-colored (white) miso

Vigorously whisk together to break up the miso until it is smooth. Add:

2 tablespoons minced scallions

1 tablespoon fresh lemon juice

1 tablespoon rice vinegar

2 teaspoons soy sauce or tamari

Pour the dressing over the reserved asparagus and toss well together. Serve chilled or at room temperature.

BAMBOO SHOOTS

Rinse canned bamboo shoots well before using; if you cannot use the whole can, transfer the remaining shoots to a covered container of fresh water and try to change the water daily. Fresh bamboo shoots, the new growth of bamboo stalks, are a marvelous addition to stir-fries. These are usually available only in winter and are hard to find even then. Unpeeled fresh shoots will keep for a week in the refrigerator. To use, peel away the outer leaves, cut off and discard the base, and cook the edible inner core, whole or sliced, in boiling water for at least 5 minutes to remove a toxin, hydrocyanic acid. If the shoot still tastes bitter, boil it again. Drain, rinse, and refrigerate in water as for canned.

Bamboo shoots are so bland that their value is texture rather than flavor. They blend especially well with other Asian vegetables, ancient companions. In a mix, allow about 2 ounces per serving.

GREEN BEANS AND FRESH SHELL BEANS

In terms of eating, there are three stages in a bean's life. The first stage comes in early summer and lasts through the fall, when the bean pod, from a day to a week old, is tender enough to snap when folded in half. Pods can be rounded and skinny, like French filet beans or haricots verts; broad, flat, and thick, like Italian Romanos; or round, slender, and long as your arm, like Asian yard-long beans. The pod of every sort of bean can be picked and cooked at this young stage, and some, like America's great Blue Lakes and Kentucky Wonders, have been developed for eating as pods. Edible-pod beans come in green, purple, yellow, and assorted colors in between (the purple turn green in cooking). Store them in a perforated plastic vegetable bag in the refrigerator crisper. Green beans can be superb after freezing but must be prepared with attention to detail and eaten sooner rather than later.

Nobody notices the beans in edible pods because the beans are mere nubbins. When they have grown large enough to be distinctly visible through the skin, their time has come. At this second stage, the pods are too leathery to eat but the beans are plump and tender and rich with flavor. They are called fresh shell beans, or shellies. Lima beans, butter beans, French flageolets, and horticultural beans are best as shell beans; black-eyed peas, fava beans, cannellini beans, and cranberry beans are superb at this stage. Refrigerate shell beans in their pods as for green beans, for no more than a few days, and shell them just before cooking. If you buy them already shelled, cook them within a day. We like to braise shell beans with butter, broth, or chopped tomatoes and herbs. Both cooked pods and shell beans are also delectable tossed with vinaigrette, served hot or at room temperature. You can steam or parboil shell beans and use them in any recipe that calls for cooked dried beans. Thawed frozen shell beans are as delicious as when freshly cooked.

A bean's third stage is when it has matured and nearly all its moisture has evaporated. The once-soft pod is so brittle and dry that eventually it snaps open, flinging its mature seeds onto the earth. These beans—dried beans—are delicious after being slowly cooked. Please see Beans & Tofu, 270.

To Prepare Green Beans: All fresh green (or yellow or purple) beans except yard-long beans are good raw. When serving them cooked, it is easiest to do nothing to the pods but rinse and cook them. Some people do not enjoy green beans unless the tops and tails have been removed; to trim the rinsed beans, gather them into a bunch, level one end of the bunch on the counter, and use a strong, sharp knife to cut off one end; repeat on the other end. Some heritage varieties of beans must have their strings removed. Top and tail the bean, pulling the string attached to the end along the side.

Green beans are best boiled, steamed, stir-fried, and microwaved. Fleshy pods such as Romanos can also be braised and stewed. Allow 4 to 6 ounces per serving.

To Boil Green Beans: This method gives bright color, plump texture, and full flavor. For every 1 pound prepared beans, bring to a boil 12 cups water and 1½ tablespoons salt in a stockpot. Drop in the beans, rapidly return the water to a boil, and give the pot a good stir. Beans are done when they are tender but still crisp. Skinny filet beans will be done in 2 to 4 minutes; rounded or fleshy flat pods will take 4 to 8 minutes. Immediately drain in a colander. To cook in advance for reheating at serving time, plunge the beans into a bowl of ice water until they are cold, 3 to 4 minutes. Drain and wrap in a towel, then refrigerate for up to 8 hours.

To Steam Green Beans: Place prepared beans in a steaming basket (preferably in a single layer) over 1 to 2 inches boiling water. Cover and cook until tender but still crisp. Steaming time for a single layer of skinny filet beans is 5 to 7 minutes; for rounded or fleshy pods, 8 to 12 minutes. When beans are more than a single layer deep, allow 3 to 5 minutes more, and stir halfway through the steaming time—those on top steam fastest.

To Microwave Green Beans: Cut 1 pound tender bean pods into 1½-inch pieces. Place in a 2-quart baking dish. Add ¼ cup stock or lightly salted water. Cover and cook on high until tender but still crisp, 9 to 13 minutes, stirring twice. Let stand, covered, for 2 minutes.

Green beans can also be cut into ½-inch pieces and stir-fried.

Edible-pod beans have a great affinity with butter in every form—cool and flavored, 76 to 78, or hot and flavored, 57 to 58. Chopped toasted nuts are marvelous too, especially almonds and hazelnuts. Special green bean herbs are dill, mint, chervil, parsley, and lovage.

To Prepare Shell Beans: Look for shell beans in late summer. To shell most pods, squeeze them open and split them along the seam with your thumbnail or a knife tip. Fresh green soybeans differ from other shell beans in that they should be cooked and served in the pod, to be popped out by each diner. Allow 8 ounces unshelled or 4 to 5 ounces shelled beans per serving.

Small fresh fava beans, available in early spring, should be used the same way as fresh peas; their interior skin can be bitter and should be removed. Plunge shelled fava beans into boiling water for 30 to 60 seconds, lift out, drop into cold water to cool, then drain. To peel fava beans, run a thumbnail along a bean, cutting the skin, then pinch it to pop the bean out of its skin.

To Boil Shell Beans: For every 1 pound fresh shelled beans (around 2½ cups), bring 8 cups and ½ tablespoon salt to a boil in a large saucepan. Add the beans, stir, and rapidly return the water to a boil. Boil, uncovered, until tender. Fresh green soybeans in their pods will take 10 to 15 minutes. Small limas, butter beans, crowder peas, and fava beans will take 20 to 30 minutes; black-eyed peas can take up to 40 minutes. Stir occasionally. Drain.

To Steam Shell Beans: This is a good way to cook fresh shelled beans, as they will not burst, as sometimes happens in boiling. Place in a steaming basket over 1 to 3 inches boiling water, cover, and steam until thoroughly tender, about 15 minutes for small tender beans, 20 to 35 minutes for larger or older beans. Stir once or twice.

To Microwave: Place 1½ cups shell beans in a 1-quart baking dish. Add 1 tablespoon stock or lightly salted water. Cover and cook on high until tender, 6 to 9 minutes, stirring once. Let stand, still covered, for 2 minutes.

Shell beans always taste richer when seasoned with something from the onion family, and some of their many affinities are with tomatoes, carrots, peppers, ham, sausages, mild cheeses, chili peppers, garlic, summer savory, marjoram, sage, parsley, celery, thyme, and bay.

GREEN BEANS WITH SAUTÉED MUSHROOMS

3 or 4 servings

Steam until tender, 10 to 15 minutes:

1 pound green beans, trimmed, halved if desired

Meanwhile, heat in a large nonstick skillet:

1 tablespoon extra-virgin olive oil

Add:

8 ounces mushrooms, wiped clean and sliced
1 tablespoon minced shallots or onions

Cook over medium heat until the mushrooms are tender, 3 to 5 minutes. Add the steamed beans to the skillet along with:

Salt and ground black pepper to taste

Toss the mixture well to heat the beans through, then serve.

GREEN BEANS WITH SLIVERED ALMONDS

Prepare Green Beans with Sautéed Mushrooms, above, substituting ¼ cup slivered almonds for the mushrooms and shallots. Cook the almonds in the oil over medium heat until lightly browned, 2 to 3 minutes, before adding the steamed beans and, if desired, 1 tablespoon fresh lemon juice. Alternatively, toast the almonds before adding them directly to the steamed beans with 1 tablespoon melted butter and 2 teaspoons fresh lemon juice.

GREEN BEANS WITH ONIONS, TOMATOES, AND DILL *4 servings*

This dish, especially well suited to the substantial Blue Lake or Romano beans, calls for long, slow cooking and yields a richly flavored, tender stew.

Warm in a large skillet or Dutch oven:

2 tablespoons olive oil

Add:

1 white onion or 10 scallions, finely diced
1 large clove garlic, thinly sliced
¼ teaspoon dill seeds

Cook gently over medium heat until the onions have softened, about 4 minutes. Add:

1 pound slender green beans, trimmed
2 large tomatoes, peeled and finely chopped
¼ cup water, vegetable stock, or tomato juice
1 tablespoon chopped fresh dill
1 tablespoon chopped fresh parsley

Simmer, covered, until the beans are tender, about 20 minutes. Season with:

¼ teaspoon salt, or to taste

Serve warm.

STIR-FRIED YARD-LONG BEANS WITH GINGER AND GARLIC *4 servings*

Yard-long beans, available in Asian markets, keep their firm-crunchy texture when stir-fried. They are related to black-eyed peas and share their pungent flavor. Select thin, dark green beans—as opposed to the lighter-colored beans—for best flavor. Heat a wok over high heat for 30 seconds. Add:

2 tablespoons peanut oil

Swirl the wok to coat it with the oil and heat until the oil is hot. Add:

1 pound yard-long beans or green beans, trimmed and cut to the desired length
1 tablespoon minced peeled fresh ginger
2 teaspoons minced fresh garlic
¼ teaspoon salt, or to taste

Stir-fry until the beans are bright green, 5 to 6 minutes. Do not allow the garlic to burn. Add:

3 to 4 tablespoons rich stock or water

Cover and simmer gently until the beans are tender, 8 to 10 minutes.

PUREED LIMA BEANS WITH FRESH THYME *3 or 4 servings*

Combine in a medium saucepan:

2 cups shelled fresh lima beans, or one 10-ounce package frozen
1 cup vegetable or chicken stock or water

Bring to a boil. Reduce the heat, cover, and simmer until the beans are very tender, about 15 minutes. Transfer the beans and liquid to a blender or food processor and add:

3 tablespoons heavy cream, half-and-half, or milk
1 tablespoon butter
1 teaspoon minced fresh thyme
¼ teaspoon salt
⅛ teaspoon ground black pepper

Puree until smooth. Taste and adjust the seasonings. Serve hot.

FAVA BEANS ROMAN STYLE *4 to 6 servings*

Many Roman vegetable dishes are made with olive oil, garlic, and a zippy accent of red pepper flakes. Fava beans, however, are more likely to be stewed with onions and herbs, a softer style of cooking. Peas are also very good cooked this way.

Remove from their pods, then blanch and peel unless very small:

3 pounds fava beans

Warm in a large skillet or Dutch oven:

¼ cup extra-virgin olive oil

Add:

½ cup finely diced white onions or scallions
1 tablespoon chopped fresh parsley

Cook gently over medium-low heat until the onions have softened, about 4 minutes. Stir in:

2 slices bacon, diced and blanched (optional)

Cook 4 to 5 minutes more, then add the beans along with:

¾ cup water or light chicken stock
½ teaspoon salt
Ground black pepper to taste

Bring to a boil, then simmer for 10 to 20 minutes. The beans should be done by the time the liquid is reduced, leaving just a little sauce to coat them. Taste for salt and pepper before serving.

BEAN SPROUTS

The threadlike mung bean sprouts common in Chinese cooking add delicate crunchiness to stir-fried dishes. Asian markets often also carry soybean sprouts, which are thicker and longer and have yellow heads. Unlike mung bean sprouts, which can be enjoyed raw, soybean sprouts should be cooked briefly—either stir-fried, steamed, or parboiled for 1 minute—to rid them of enzymes that inhibit digestibility. They remain crunchy despite the cooking, with a slightly nutty taste. Be sure sprouts are perky fresh when you buy them, without wilting or browning. Refrigerate in a perforated plastic vegetable bag in the refrigerator crisper and use them within a few days, rinsing and spinning them dry in a salad spinner.

The vivid variety of sprouted legumes also available—more bean than sprout in most cases—make good snacks and salad ingredients. They also contribute texture and color to rice; add them, without stirring, for the last few minutes of cooking. For more about sprouts, please read About Sprouting Beans, 272. Allow 4 to 6 ounces per serving.

STIR-FRIED BEAN SPROUTS *4 servings*

A lightning-fast dish.

Rinse and freshen in cold water, snapping off any dark ends:

1 pound fresh bean sprouts

Have ready:

3 scallions, cut into 1-inch pieces
1¼ teaspoons salt
1 teaspoon soy sauce
2 teaspoons white vinegar

Heat a wok or medium skillet over high heat. When hot, add and swirl until very hot but not smoking:

¼ cup peanut oil

Add the bean sprouts, stir, and flip very quickly for 30 seconds. Add the scallions and continue to stir for another 30 seconds. Add the salt and soy sauce and stir for 30 seconds more. Add the vinegar while continuing to stir vigorously for a final 60 seconds. Pour into a serving bowl and serve immediately.

BEETS AND BEET GREENS

A source of sugar, beets are an intensely sweet vegetable, but a trace of sharpness keeps their flavor from being cloying. Once there was just the crimson beet, but now beets are also gold, orange, white, and candy striped; they can be perfectly round or long and slender, no bigger than the tip of your thumb or as big as your fist. Beets are available most of the year but are best from summer through early winter. When selecting a bunch of beets, if all the roots are equally fine, choose the bunch with the smallest leaves that are in the best condition (not yellowing or tattered). The greens are an indication of freshness for the roots; if they look moist and fresh, the roots will be too. If you are buying beets without leaves, avoid any that look dry, cracked, or shriveled.

Beets go especially well with lemon and orange, vinegar, any form of cream, onions, walnuts, parsley, caraway seeds, dill, tarragon, and mustard. Allow about 5 ounces per serving.

To Prepare: Cut off the leaves, leaving 1 to 2 inches stem on the beets, and keep the rootlets, or tails, in place. Pack the beets and leaves separately in perforated plastic vegetable bags and store in the refrigerator crisper (see page 201 for wrapping greens). Scrub beets well just before cooking but do not remove the skin.

In cooking, both roots and leaves bleed their colors into any dish they are in—except for golden beets, which hold their color. When handling cooked red beets, you may want to wear rubber gloves, as red beet juice can stain the hands for hours. Cooked beets are wonderful hot or cold. Serve small beets whole; slice larger ones into sections or rounds. Young, tender beets are delightful grated raw into a salad. Beets of any size are delicious steamed, baked, and microwaved.

To Boil: For every 1 pound prepared beets, bring 12 cups water and 1½ tablespoons salt to a boil in a stockpot. Add the beets, rapidly return the water to a boil, then cook, covered, until tender when pierced through with a thin skewer or knife tip. Allow about 20 minutes for small and baby beets, 30 to 35 minutes for medium, and 45 to 60 minutes for large beets. Drain, then plunge into cold water to cool. When cool enough to handle, slice off the stems and rootlets and slip off the skins.

To Steam: Arrange the prepared beets in a single layer in a steaming basket over 1 to 2 inches boiling water. Cover and steam until tender when pierced through with a thin skewer or knife tip, 25 to 30 minutes for small and baby beets, 35 to 40 minutes for medium, and up to 60 minutes for large beets. Add boiling water to the steamer as needed.

To Microwave: Place 5 medium unpeeled beets in a 2-quart baking dish. Add ¼ cup stock or lightly salted water. Cover and cook on high until tender when pierced with a thin skewer, 12 to 18 minutes, stirring every 5 minutes. Let stand, still covered, for 3 minutes.

To Pressure-Cook: Whole unpeeled 2½-inch beets can be pressure-cooked with 1½ cups liquid at 15 pounds pressure for 15 minutes. Cool the cooker at once.

To Cook Beet Greens: Beets are a close relative to chard, and the leaves share chard's bite. You can cook beet greens, covered, in ¼ to ½ inch boiling stock or salted water until tender but still crisp, 8 to 15 minutes, stirring occasionally. Otherwise, prepare, cook, and serve as you would chard, 363 to 365.

BAKED OR ROASTED BEETS *4 servings*

Convenient when the stovetop is crowded. Serve hot or at room temperature.

Preheat the oven to 350°F.

Leaving the rootlets, trim all but 1 inch of the stems, then wash:

1 pound beets

Place them in an 8 x 8-inch baking pan and add ½ cup water. Seal the pan tightly with foil and bake until the beets are easily pierced with a thin skewer or knife tip, about 45 minutes for small beets, 1 hour for medium, and 1¼ hours for large beets. Slip off the skins when ready to serve. Leave the beets whole or slice into rounds or wedges. Season with:

Salt and ground black pepper or paprika to taste

Toss with:

2 tablespoons butter or olive or walnut oil
1 tablespoon chopped fresh parsley or snipped fresh chives or dill
Fresh lemon or lime juice to taste

ROASTED POTATOES, BEETS, AND ONIONS VINAIGRETTE

6 servings

This is more an approach than a hard-and-fast recipe. We love the color, flavor, and texture mix of potatoes, beets, and onions, but eggplant, asparagus, or carrots could be added or substituted. If you do not have access to baby vegetables, quarter and roast large ones, adjusting the cooking time accordingly.

Preheat the oven to 375°F.

Toss together and arrange in a single layer in a baking pan:

12 fingerling or creamer potatoes, halved or quartered lengthwise
12 cloves garlic, unpeeled
2 tablespoons olive oil
Fresh rosemary or thyme sprigs
Salt and ground black pepper to taste

Toss together and arrange in another baking pan:

8 ounces cipolline or pearl onions, peeled
1 tablespoon olive oil
Salt and ground black pepper to taste

Toss together and arrange in a third baking pan:

12 ounces baby red, chiogga, or golden beets, trimmed and scrubbed
1 tablespoon olive oil
Salt and ground black pepper to taste

Tightly cover each pan with foil and roast the vegetables until tender, 35 to 40 minutes; uncover the potatoes and garlic after 20 minutes to allow them to brown and crisp slightly. Reserve any juices from the beets and onions and stir into:

Basic Vinaigrette, 236

While the beets are still warm, gently rub their skins off, using paper towels. Arrange the roasted vegetables around a mound of:

1 cup loosely packed mixed fresh herbs

Drizzle the vinaigrette over the vegetables. Serve at room temperature.

SWEET-AND-SOUR BEETS WITH APPLES

4 servings

Preheat the oven to 350°F. Lightly butter a 13 x 9-inch baking pan.

Combine in the pan:

2 cups ½-inch cubes cooked beets (about 5 medium)
2 cups diced unpeeled Granny Smith apples
½ cup thinly sliced onions
2 tablespoons fresh lemon juice
1 teaspoon salt
Generous grating of nutmeg

If the apples are exceedingly tart, sprinkle them with:

1 tablespoon light brown sugar

Dot with:

2 tablespoons unsalted butter

Cover and bake for 30 minutes; stir well and bake until very tender, about 15 minutes more. Serve warm.

SAUTÉED BEET GREENS

4 servings

Remove the stems and wash:

1½ pounds beet greens

Leave whole if the leaves are small, or cut them into wide ribbons. Shake off as much water as possible. Heat in a large skillet:

2 tablespoons butter or extra-virgin olive oil

Add and cook over medium heat until softened:

1 large shallot, finely diced, or 2 tablespoons diced onions

Add the beet greens and sprinkle with:

Salt to taste

Cook, tossing the greens in the pan, until wilted and tender, 3 to 4 minutes. Serve with:

Balsamic vinegar or lemon wedges

BOK CHOY, OR PAK CHOI

It is confusing and frustrating when bok choy is called pak choi—and the reverse. They are the same vegetable. Bok choy is a Cantonese term for one of the Chinese cabbages; pak chois/bok choys are mild-flavored Asian cabbages. Select medium-sized bunches with the brightest colors and firmest stalks. Very small bunches will be labeled baby bok choy. In spring and summer, you may find flowering bok choy, bunches with small broccoli-like florets. Store in perforated plastic vegetable bags in the refrigerator crisper.

Affinities are the same as for other Asian mustard cabbages. Allow 8 ounces per serving.
To Prepare: Separate the stems and rinse well. Tear or cut the leafy greens from the ribs, 335, and cook the leaves and stems separately.
To Boil: Cook as for chard, 364, boiling large leaves for 2 to 4 minutes, ½-inch pieces of stems and stalks for 4 to 6 minutes, baby bok choy leaves for 6 to 8 minutes, thinly sliced baby bok choy heads for 3 to 5 minutes.
To Steam: Cook leaves and stems as for chard, 364.
To Braise: Cook as for chard, 364. Large leaves will cook in the same amount of time as chard.

STIR-FRIED BOK CHOY WITH MUSHROOMS

4 to 6 servings

Place in a small bowl:

6 dried black or shiitake mushrooms

Pour over the mushrooms:

½ cup boiling water

Let soak for 20 minutes, stirring the mushrooms occasionally. While the mushrooms soak, prepare, keeping the stems separate from the leafy parts:

1½ to 2 pounds bok choy, bottoms trimmed, stalks washed, and cut into 2-inch pieces

In a small saucepan, warm over medium-low heat:

1 cup chicken stock
½ teaspoon salt
½ teaspoon sugar

Remove the mushrooms from their soaking liquid and reserve the liquid. Cut the mushrooms into ¼-inch-thick slices and set aside. In a small bowl, mix:

2 tablespoons reserved mushroom soaking liquid, strained
1 tablespoon Scotch whiskey or Shaoxing wine
2 teaspoons cornstarch
¾ teaspoon ground white white pepper

Heat in a wok or a large skillet over high heat:

3 tablespoons peanut oil

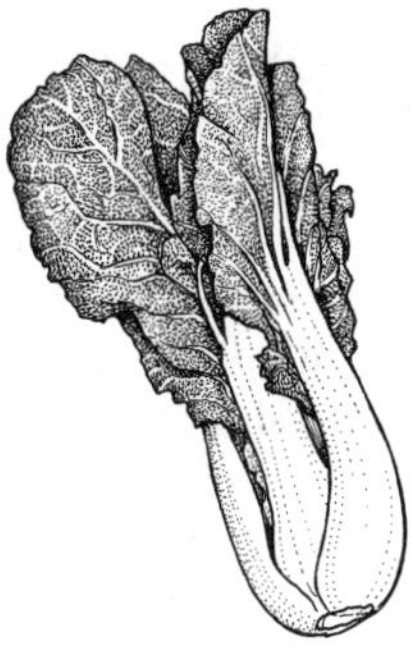

Bok choy

Add the reserved mushrooms and bok choy stems and cook, stirring often, for 3 to 5 minutes to soften. Add the reserved bok choy leaves and warmed chicken stock, cover, and steam until the leaves wilt, 1 to 2 minutes. Uncover and transfer the vegetables with a slotted spoon to a serving dish. Stir the reserved cornstarch mixture and whisk into the chicken stock. Bring to a boil, whisking, and add:

2 teaspoons toasted sesame oil

Stir well, pour the sauce over the vegetables, and serve.

BABY BOK CHOI WITH SOY GINGER SAUCE

2 to 4 servings

These tender little heads cook in minutes. Allow 1 or 2 per person.
Rinse, then cut lengthwise in half:

4 baby bok choi

Steam cut side down over boiling water for 4 to 5 minutes. Remove with a pair of tongs to a platter. Mix thoroughly in a small bowl:

¼ cup soy sauce
¼ cup balsamic vinegar
2 tablespoons water
1 tablespoon slivered peeled fresh ginger

Spoon the sauce over the bok choi.

BONIATO

Boniato, also called *batata,* looks like the potato that it is. It is harvested year-round in Florida and other tropical areas. The blotchy skin may be purplish or reddish, and the inside is white or creamy and slightly mealy in consistency when cooked. The taste, less sweet than that of orange sweet potatoes, suggests roasted chestnuts. Boniato bruises and rots very easily, so choose carefully, avoiding any with soft spots, and store in a cool, dark place for no more than a day or two. When exposed to air, the flesh of boniato discolors quickly, so drop peeled pieces into cold water and cook them in boiling water to cover to prevent contact with air—or bake them whole in their skins. Boniato goes well with apples, butter, and cream.

SWEET OR SAVORY BAKED BONIATO

4 servings

Serve as you would a baked potato.
Preheat the oven to 400°F.
Bake until tender when pierced with the tip of a knife, 45 to 55 minutes:

4 boniatos, scrubbed

Slit open the tops and fluff the pulp with a fork. Mix together and season each boniato with:

1 tablespoon unsalted butter
1 tablespoon sour cream
½ teaspoon sugar
¼ teaspoon ground cinnamon

Or with:

1 tablespoon snipped fresh chives
Salt and ground black pepper to taste

If desired, top with one of the following:

Maître d'Hôtel Butter, 77, Cajun Dry Rub, 86, Red Onion Marmalade, 66, or Salsa Fresca, 61

BREADFRUIT

The exterior of these melon-sized round fruits is covered with hundreds of scaly bumps. Unripe, they are green and their flesh resembles a potato—hard, white, and starchy. Like plantains, breadfruit is used in savory and sweet dishes according to its ripeness. For savory purposes, choose one that is evenly green. At this stage, it can be cooked like a potato or sweet potato—steamed, boiled, baked, fried, or roasted—but it must be served hot, or it will be unappetizingly waxy. When slightly ripe, the outside is partly green. Baked at this stage, its flesh is slightly sticky, somewhat fruity, but spongy like bread, making it good for sopping up a spicy sauce. When ripe, the exterior is tender and brownish, and the flesh is creamy and sticky but still starchy and rather bland in flavor. It can be used in place of sweet potatoes in Candied Sweet Potatoes, 428. The fruits are available year-round in markets with a Caribbean and West Indian clientele. The 2- to 5-pound globes are sold from water-filled drums or in tightly closed plastic bags. Choose fruits that are heavy for their size. White speckled patches are normal, but avoid those with soft and dark spots or any hard knotty places. Breadfruit is extremely perishable. Cook it at once if you buy it green and want to eat it that way, or let it ripen, uncovered, at room temperature to the degree you wish. Once it is ripe, refrigerate it for no more than a day before cooking. Pare and remove the stem and seedy core before or after cooking, depending on how you cook it. Breadfruit has affinities with piquant and spicy seasonings, as well as cream and coconut.

ROASTED BREADFRUIT *6 servings*

You may wish to serve the breadfruit mashed or pureed. The flesh absorbs butter and liquid to an astonishing degree.

Preheat the oven to 375°F.

Place in an 8 x 8-inch baking pan:

1 unpeeled green breadfruit

Add 1½ cups water to the pan to prevent the breadfruit from burning—add more if necessary during cooking. Bake until tender, about 1 hour. Pull out the stem and core (they should come out easily) and discard them. Cut the breadfruit in half and season with:

Salt and ground black pepper to taste, or sugar and butter

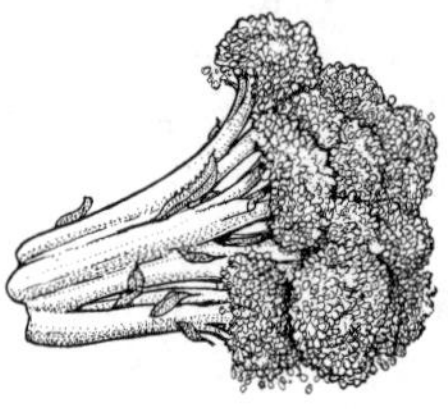

Broccoli

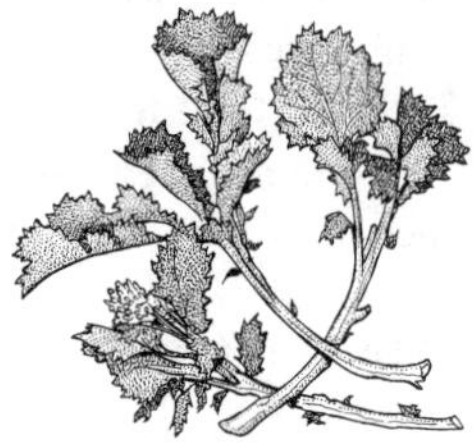

Rapini

BROCCOLI, CHINESE BROCCOLI, RAPINI, AND BROCCOLI RABE

A head of broccoli is an intricate bouquet of tiny flower buds. Each small green stalk is called a floret and contains hundreds of buds. Cooked correctly, broccoli tastes slightly mustardy and is crunchy, a delectable vegetable for sauces—and indeed, it is a member of the valuable mustard family. Although it is available year-round, broccoli's natural season is from late fall through early spring. When choosing broccoli, run an eye over the selection and pick the head with the tiniest buds. Their color will be dark green with a purple or blue haze. Any yellowish heads are on their way to blooming and should be avoided. Given two heads of equal fineness, choose the one with the most leaves, as the leaves are highly nutritious. Cook and serve them as you would chard leaves, 364 to 365. If the stalks are long enough, plunge them in a container of water and refrigerate; otherwise, store in perforated plastic vegetable bags in the refrigerator crisper.

The vegetable sold as either purple broccoli or purple cauliflower or broccoflower closely resembles broccoli in shape and flavor. Romanesco is a form of broccoli with a conical head formed of small peaks of buds in a beautiful chartreuse. Prepare these as you would broccoli—they will turn deep green when cooked.

Chinese broccoli is also known as Chinese kale. It is closely related to both broccoli and our common kale, and its season is from early summer to early winter. Like all mustards, it sprouts flower buds, and they look like broccoli's—but their flavor is like kale, mild and cabbagey. Rapini, a springtime green, is another mostly leafy plant and is often confused with broccoli rabe. Rapini leaves and buds have a mustardy bite, much like turnip greens, which they resemble. Broccoli rabe's leaves and buds are mustardy but sweet; it is an autumn green. Store, prepare, cook, and serve all these buds as you would broccoli, and the leaves as you would kale, 379, turnip greens, 436, or chard, 364 to 365.

To Prepare: For optimum eating quality, cut the thick stalk and the florets to approximately the same size. Cut off the stalk at the base. Cut off the florets at the base of their small stalks. If some florets are much larger than others, cut them to match the rest. Use a paring knife to cut off the tough, fibrous skin of the stalk down to the moist, tender flesh, then cut the stalk into matchsticks about the same size as the stalks of the florets.

To Boil: Boiling broccoli uncovered in a large amount of salted water results in the mildest possible flavor and brightest color. For each 1 pound prepared broccoli, bring 16 cups (4 quarts) water and 1½ tablespoons salt to a rolling boil in a stockpot. Drop in the pieces and rapidly return to a boil. Boil, uncovered, until tender but still crisp, 2 to 4 minutes for florets, 6 to 8 minutes for a whole head. Drain.

To Steam: Place florets and tender stalk pieces in a steaming basket over 1 to 2 inches boiling water, cover, and steam until the pieces are tender but still crisp, 3 to 5 minutes for florets and stalk pieces, up to 10 minutes for whole bouquets. Another way is to stand the bottoms of whole bouquets of uniform size, stalks peeled, in a small, deep saucepan. Add 1½ cups cold water. Bring to a boil, cover the pot, and cook until the bouquets are crisp-tender, 10 to 15 minutes. This way, the thickest parts of the base will boil while the florets steam. Drain.

To Microwave: Arrange broccoli spears in a spoke pattern so that the stems are all pointing toward the center of the dish and the heads are along the outside edge. Salt lightly, cover, and microwave on high until tender, 6 to 8 minutes, but let stand, uncovered, for 3 minutes before serving. To microwave florets and matchsticks of stalks, place 1 pound in a baking dish. Salt lightly. Cover and cook on high until tender but still bright, about 5 minutes, rearranging the pieces after 3 minutes. Let stand, uncovered, for 2 minutes before serving.

Cooked broccoli is delicious hot or at room temperature. When carefully prepared and frozen, broccoli and broccoflower may be slightly soft but have good flavor. These closely related vegetables all have affinities with lemon, orange, butter in any form, olive oil, nut oils, breadcrumbs crisped in butter, vinaigrette dressings, Hollandaise Sauce, 55, Sauce Maltaise, 56, Basic Vinaigrette, 236, and Yogurt Mayonnaise, 73, as well as garlic, capers, olives, sweet peppers, mild cheeses, crumbled hard-boiled egg, dill, and marjoram. Allow 5 to 8 ounces per serving.

SAUTÉED BROCCOLI WITH GARLIC AND RED PEPPER FLAKES

4 servings

A southern Italian way of fixing all kinds of vegetables—especially good with members of the cabbage family. You can toss the cooked broccoli with pasta, pitted black olives, and grated Parmesan or pecorino cheese to make a main course.

Remove the florets, then peel and dice the stems of:

2 pounds broccoli

Steam or boil until barely tender, then drain. If not finishing the dish until later, cool the broccoli under cold running water. Heat in a large skillet:

3 tablespoons extra-virgin olive oil

Add and cook, stirring over medium heat until their aromas are released:

2 cloves garlic, thinly sliced or chopped

2 good pinches of red pepper flakes or 1 small dried red chili pepper, crumbled

Add the broccoli and cook until heated through and tender, 3 to 4 minutes longer. Season with:

Salt and ground black pepper to taste

GINGER WINE BROCCOLI STIR-FRY

4 servings

Bring to a rolling boil in a stockpot:

16 cups (4 quarts) water

1 tablespoon salt

Remove the florets from:

1 large head broccoli

Save the stalks for another use. Boil the florets until crisp-tender, about 2 minutes. Drain and set aside. Stir together in a small bowl until smooth:

2 teaspoons cornstarch

2 tablespoons water

Place a wok or large skillet over high heat. When hot, add and swirl until very hot but not smoking:

3 tablespoons peanut oil

Add:

4 slices peeled fresh ginger

4 large cloves garlic, crushed

Stir and press until the garlic is lightly golden, then remove the ginger and garlic and discard. Add the broccoli florets and stir until all the pieces are lightly coated with the oil. Combine in a small bowl and add by pouring down the side of the wok or skillet:

⅓ cup Shaoxing wine or pale dry sherry
3 tablespoons soy sauce
2 tablespoons light brown sugar
1 teaspoon toasted sesame oil

Toss to blend well. Reduce the heat to medium, cover, and cook for 30 seconds. Stir the cornstarch mixture, add it to the wok, and combine thoroughly. Cook, uncovered, until the sauce thickens, 1 to 2 minutes. Pour into a serving dish and serve immediately.

GRATIN OF BROCCOLI WITH CHEDDAR CHEESE

4 to 6 servings

Position a rack in the upper third of the oven. Preheat the oven to 425°F. Butter a 2-quart gratin dish.
Sprinkle the dish with:

2 tablespoons fresh breadcrumbs, toasted

Boil, 000:

2 pounds broccoli, florets and stalks cut into pieces

Drain and return to the cooking pot. Gently fold in:

Sauce Mornay, 46, made with Cheddar cheese

Spread evenly in the baking dish and cover the top with:

2 tablespoons butter, softened, cut into small pieces
¼ cup fresh breadcrumbs

Bake until bubbly and lightly browned on top, about 20 minutes.

STIR-FRIED CHINESE BROCCOLI WITH OYSTER SAUCE

2 to 4 servings

If you wish to substitute regular broccoli, use the larger amount of stock and cook longer, as indicated. Vegetarians can replace the oyster sauce with hoisin sauce.
Trim off the ends and any yellow leaves, cut stalks into 1½-inch pieces, and thoroughly rinse:

1 large bunch Chinese broccoli (about 1 pound) or 1 pound regular broccoli

Heat a wok or large skillet over high heat, then add:

1 tablespoon peanut or vegetable oil
3 cloves garlic, minced
1 tablespoon minced peeled fresh ginger
¼ teaspoon red pepper flakes or ½ teaspoon chili paste with garlic

Stir-fry for a few seconds, but do not allow the garlic to brown. Add the broccoli with the water that still clings to its leaves. Stir-fry for 2 minutes more, then add:

¼ cup chicken stock, or ⅓ cup for regular broccoli

Cover the wok tightly and cook for 4 minutes. Uncover and add:

¼ cup oyster sauce

Stir-fry over medium-high heat until the broccoli is crisp-tender, about 3 minutes (8 minutes for regular broccoli). Sprinkle with:

3 or 4 drops toasted sesame oil

Serve immediately.

GARLIC-BRAISED BROCCOLI RABE OR RAPINI

4 servings

Bring to a rolling boil in a stockpot:

16 cups water
1½ tablespoons salt

Thinly slice the greens, peel the stems, and cut into 1-inch pieces:

1 bunch broccoli rabe or rapini (about 1 pound)

Boil for 2 minutes, then drain and squeeze the moisture out of the leaves. Heat in a large skillet over medium heat:

2 tablespoons extra-virgin olive oil

Add:

1 clove garlic, thinly sliced
1 small dried red chili pepper (optional)

Add the broccoli rabe and cook over medium heat until tender, about 4 minutes. Remove the chili pepper and season with:

Salt and ground black pepper to taste

Serve hot.

BRUSSELS SPROUTS

Brussels sprouts are bite-sized green cabbages, juicy with a nutty-sweet cabbage flavor. Like larger cabbages, most are green, but there are purply red Brussels sprouts too. They are in season from late fall through winter. If you are lucky enough to find Brussels sprouts still attached to their stalks, choose the smallest stalk—it will be younger and its sprouts sweetest. When sprouts are sold loose, select those that are heavy for their size and tightly closed, without any touch of yellow or blemish. (If the sprouts come packaged in a basket, have no qualms about opening the basket to inspect its contents.) Store Brussels sprouts in a perforated plastic vegetable bag in the refrigerator crisper.

To Prepare: If you have found a stalk, pluck the sprouts free. Pull off loose leaves from around the stem of each sprout and trim the stems. Rinse and drain. To cook sprouts fastest and most evenly, slice them in half from top to bottom. To eat the leaves separately—they seem most delicious this way—trim out the core with a small sharp knife and gently pull the leaves apart. The tightly connected center leaves should be thinly sliced.

To Boil: As with broccoli, boiling Brussels sprouts in a large quantity of water results in the mildest flavor and most vivid color. With the tip of a paring knife, cut an X in the bottom of each sprout to help them cook quickly and evenly. For each 1 pound prepared sprouts, bring 16 cups (4 quarts) water and 1½ tablespoons salt to a rolling boil in a stockpot. Drop in the sprouts and rapidly return to a boil. Boil, uncovered, until a thin skewer or sharp knife pierces a sprout all the way through, 6 to 12 minutes for whole sprouts, 4 to 7 minutes for halves, depending on size. Drain. If desired, return the sprouts to the pot and shake over high heat until they are dry, 30 to 60 seconds.

To Steam: With the tip of a paring knife, cut an X in the bottom of each sprout to help them cook quickly and evenly. Arrange sprouts of uniform size in a steamer basket. Place over 1 to 2 inches boiling water and cover. Steam until tender when pierced with a thin skewer or the tip of a knife, 8 to 15 minutes for whole sprouts, 4 to 8 minutes for halves, depending on size.

To Roast: Preheat the oven to 375°F. Boil halved Brussels sprouts as directed above just until tender. Drain and toss with 2 tablespoons olive oil, ¼ teaspoon salt, and ground black pepper to taste. Lightly brush a baking sheet with olive oil and arrange the sprouts on it cut side down. Roast until the sprouts are lightly browned on their cut sides, about 20 minutes.

To Microwave: Place 4 cups whole sprouts in a 2-quart baking dish. Add ¼ cup stock or lightly salted water. Cover and cook on high until tender when pierced with a thin skewer, 6 to 8 minutes, stirring after 2 minutes. Let stand, covered, for 3 minutes.

To Sauté Leaves: Separate leaves are best quickly sautéed in butter or a nut oil until tender, about 4 minutes.

Brussels sprouts have affinities with all the same flavors that cabbage does, 354, but they are as delicious with the buttery-lemony sauces that are good with broccoli, 351. Allow 4 to 5 ounces per serving.

BRUSSELS SPROUTS WITH BROWN BUTTER AND TOASTED NUTS

4 to 6 servings

Place in a large skillet:

3 tablespoons butter
¼ cup chopped hazelnuts, almonds, or pecans, toasted

Heat over low heat until the butter begins to brown and take on a nutty smell. Steam in another pan until tender, 15 to 20 minutes:

1 pound Brussels sprouts, trimmed

Add them to the pan with the brown butter and toss over low heat with:

Salt and ground black pepper to taste

BRUSSELS SPROUTS WITH CHESTNUTS

6 servings

If possible, use fresh chestnuts in this recipe; canned ones are so soft that they add little to the finished dish.

Place in a large skillet:

2 tablespoons melted butter or bacon drippings
4 plump shallots, halved, or 12 boiling onions
1 pound fresh chestnuts, peeled, 366

Roll the chestnuts around the pan, then cook over medium heat, gently shaking the pan occasionally, until both the shallots and the chestnuts are lightly browned, about 10 minutes. Add and bring to a boil:

1 cup chicken or vegetable stock or water
1 bay leaf
1 sprig fresh thyme
Several sprigs fresh parsley
3 tablespoons port or dry sherry (optional)
¼ teaspoon salt
⅛ teaspoon ground black pepper
1 pound Brussels sprouts, halved

Reduce the heat to medium, cover, and simmer until the Brussels sprouts are tender, about 15 minutes. Remove the bay leaf, thyme sprigs, and parsley sprigs before serving.

BRAISED BRUSSELS SPROUTS AND SHALLOTS

About 4 servings

Prepare Brussels Sprouts with Chestnuts, above, omitting the chestnuts, using 1 pound shallots in all, and using stock. Serve sprinkled with minced fresh parsley or chervil.

BRUSSELS SPROUTS COCKAIGNE

2 to 4 servings

Ethan Becker was always disappointed by Brussels sprouts—until he tried these.

Rinse, pat dry, and slice in half lengthwise:

12 Brussels sprouts

Warm in a medium skillet over medium-low heat:

3 tablespoons butter, or 1½ tablespoons butter and 1½ tablespoons olive oil

Add and cook, stirring, until beginning to brown:

1 to 2 cloves garlic, crushed

Remove the garlic from the skillet with a slotted spoon and discard. Place the sprouts cut side down in the garlic butter. Cover and cook over low heat until tender, 15 to 20 minutes. Arrange on a warm platter and drizzle with any remaining butter. Serve with:

Freshly grated Parmesan cheese (optional)

BURDOCK

Burdock is a root that grows more than 3 feet deep but is rarely more than ½ inch wide. Like carrots, it is a member of the parsley family, and the white flesh is mildly sweet. Young shoots and large soft leaves are slightly bitter and nice in salads. The Japanese are fond of burdock, and it is always part of a mixed vegetable tempura when it is in season, which is most of the year. Look for the roots in Asian groceries. They will probably be dirty on the outside, but that is just good earth. Select firm, crisp roots with no soft spots. Wrap, unwashed, in moist paper towels, then place in a perforated plastic vegetable bag and keep in the refrigerator crisper. It will keep for a week or two.

When ready to cook, rinse off the soil. The skin has the most flavor, so scrub it gently but thoroughly with a stiff brush. Snip off any hairy rootlets. Burdock can be cooked any way carrots can, so slice or cut accordingly. Because the flesh quickly discolors when cut, immediately drop the pieces into cold water containing a splash of cider vinegar or lemon. (Sometimes burdock that has been out of the ground for a while turns bitter—soaking in the acidulated water for an hour or so should eliminate this.) With its neutral flavor, burdock is a useful addition to stews. Depending on the dish, allow 2 to 4 ounces per serving.

CABBAGE

Although they are in the market year-round, if you watch closely you will see that cabbages change with the seasons. Early or summer cabbages, harvested June through October, are cone shaped; they weigh 2 to 2½ pounds and have tender, juicy, mild leaves. Cabbages that mature from mid-October through March have flat or round heads and weigh 3 to 15 pounds; their flavor is well developed. Those picked after a hard autumn frost are sweetest. Fineness of flavor in cabbages is indicated by thickness of leaves—the thinner, the better. Savoy cabbages—those with ruffled crinkly leaves—have the thinnest leaves and incomparable flavor. As pretty as they are, red cabbages have thicker leaves than green cabbages, and their flavor is less interesting. Select cabbages that are heavy for their size and have bright, crisp leaves with no signs of yellowing, cuts, or bruises. Store cabbage in perforated plastic vegetable bags in the refrigerator crisper.

To Prepare: Remove any wilted leaves, then rinse. To cut, use a large, heavy knife to halve or quarter the cabbage through the stem. Cut around the core and remove it. Cut the head into wedges or slice it into thin shreds or ribbons. Red cabbage requires longer cooking, but can be prepared in the same way as green cabbage. Cabbage is most flavorful steamed, braised, or stir-fried.

To Boil: For the mildest flavor, boil cabbages in quarters or large wedges. For each 1 pound prepared cabbage, bring 16 cups (4 quarts) water and 1½ tablespoons salt to a rolling boil in a stockpot. Drop in the wedges, rapidly return to a boil, and cook, uncovered, until the pieces can be pierced with a thin skewer, 12 to 15 minutes for red cabbage, 9 to 11 minutes for green cabbage, and 4 to 6 minutes for Napa cabbage. Shreds of cabbage should be boiled until tender but still crisp, 3 to 5 minutes. Whole leaves can be boiled for stuffing—allow 8 to 10 minutes for red cabbage leaves, 3 to 4 minutes for green, and 2 to 3 minutes for Napa cabbage leaves. Drain.

To Steam: Steam cabbage in shreds, wedges, or whole leaves. Allow 15 to 17 minutes for red cabbage wedges, 12 to 15 minutes for green, and 6 to 8 minutes for Napa cabbage. Heap cabbage shreds in the steamer basket over 1 to 2 inches boiling water, cover, and steam until they are tender but still crisp, 8 to 10 minutes for red cabbage, 12 to 14 for green, and 6 to 8 minutes for Napa cabbage shreds. Whole leaves will steam to pliability in approximately 15 minutes for red cabbage, 5 to 7 minutes for green, and 3 to 5 minutes for Napa cabbage.

To Microwave: Spread 1 pound shredded cabbage in a 2-quart baking dish. Add 2 tablespoons stock or lightly salted water. Cover and cook on high until tender but still crisp, 8 to 12 minutes, stirring after 4 minutes. Let stand, covered, for 2 minutes. One pound cabbage wedges can be cooked the same way; rearrange the pieces after 5 minutes and cook until tender, 12 to 14 minutes. Let stand, covered, for 3 minutes.

Do not freeze cooked cabbage; most thawed cabbage is watery and of poor quality.

Cabbage is especially good accompanying rich meats, salted and smoked meats, game, and all root vegetables. It goes well with red wine, sage, thyme, caraway, dill, fennel, horseradish, apples, onions, chestnuts, juniper berries, and sour cream. Allow 4 to 5 ounces per serving.

CREAMED CABBAGE

4 servings

The cream mingles with water from the cabbage, resulting in a thin but very flavorful sauce.

Bring to a rolling boil in a stockpot:

16 cups (4 quarts) water
1½ tablespoons salt

Remove the outer leaves from:

1 pound green cabbage, preferably Savoy

Cut into quarters, remove the core, and cut crosswise into thin slices. Cook, uncovered, for 3 minutes, then drain and press out the excess water. Melt in a large skillet:

2 tablespoons butter

Add the cabbage along with:

½ cup crème fraîche or heavy cream
1 tablespoon snipped fresh dill, 1 teaspoon caraway seeds, or 10 juniper berries
1 teaspoon salt
Ground black pepper to taste

Toss well, then simmer until the cabbage is tender but not mushy, about 15 minutes. Season to taste with:

Several drops dry sherry or red wine vinegar
Salt to taste

BRAISED CABBAGE WITH DILL

4 servings

If you wish to omit the cream, simmer the carrots for an extra 5 minutes to maximize their sweetness.

Bring to a boil in a covered skillet:

8 ounces carrots, peeled and thinly sliced
1 cup chicken stock or water
1 tablespoon butter

Reduce the heat and simmer until the carrots are crisp-tender, about 7 to 9 minutes. Add:

1 pound shredded cabbage
2 tablespoons heavy cream (optional)
1 tablespoon snipped fresh dill, 1 teaspoon dried dill, or 1 teaspoon dill seeds

Cook, covered, over low heat until the cabbage wilts, about 10 minutes. Uncover, stir well, and cook until the cabbage is tender and the pan juices are reduced to a syrupy consistency, about 10 minutes more. Stir in:

¼ cup minced fresh parsley
Salt and ground black pepper to taste

CABBAGE GRATIN

4 to 6 servings

A delicate and subtle dish.

Preheat the oven to 375°F. Butter a 2-quart gratin dish. Dust the dish with:

½ cup grated Parmesan cheese or toasted fresh breadcrumbs

Bring to a rolling boil in a stockpot:

16 cups (4 quarts) water
1½ tablespoons salt

Add and cook for 5 minutes:

6 cups shredded cabbage (about 1 pound)

Drain and press out as much water as possible. Whisk together in a large bowl:

2 large eggs
1 cup milk or light cream
½ cup grated Emmentaler or Gruyère cheese
¼ cup all-purpose flour
1 teaspoon salt
½ teaspoon caraway seeds, toasted
⅛ teaspoon ground cardamom

Add the drained cabbage, pour into the gratin dish, and cover the top with:

¼ cup grated Parmesan or Gruyère cheese

Bake until golden on top, 40 to 50 minutes.

CABBAGE AND POTATOES WITH SMOKED HAM

4 to 6 servings

This is reminiscent of a New England boiled dinner. Crinkled Savoy cabbage adds visual plushness and delicate flavor.

Bring to a boil in a large saucepan:

8 cups water
4 boiling or Yellow Finn potatoes (about 1 pound), peeled and quartered
2 teaspoons salt

When the water is boiling, add:

1 small green cabbage (about 1 pound), cut into sixths and cored

Simmer, uncovered, until the potatoes are tender, 12 to 15 minutes. Drain and toss immediately with:

6 ounces smoked ham, coarsely chopped
3 tablespoons chopped fresh parsley
Ground black pepper to taste

Arrange on a platter and serve with:

Lemon wedges or a cruet of vinegar
Horseradish and/or mustard, or Pear Chutney, 68

STUFFED CABBAGE ROLLS

6 to 8 servings

Traditionally, stuffed cabbage rolls, also called *parkkas* or *holishkes,* were favorites in eastern and central European countries at harvest time. At the Jewish holiday of Succoth, they were among many stuffed vegetables served to symbolize the wish for a plentiful harvest. These days in this country, stuffed cabbage makes a satisfying cold-weather party dish—wonderful with potato pancakes or mashed potatoes. The rolls are even better when prepared 2 to 3 days in advance. They can be frozen for up to 1 month. Sour salt is citric acid, the same as used in pickling and canning. It can be found in drugstores or in supermarkets that have a section of kosher foods.

Combine in a large bowl:

1 pound ground beef, chicken, or turkey
1 large egg
½ cup seasoned dry breadcrumbs
½ cup white rice

½ cup water
1 large carrot, peeled and grated
1 onion, finely chopped
1 clove garlic, minced
Salt and ground black pepper to taste

Bring to a rolling boil in a stockpot:

16 cups (4 quarts) water
1½ tablespoons salt

Cut out the core with a small, sharp knife, then drop stem side down into the water:

1 Savoy or other green cabbage (about 2 pounds)

Boil for 5 to 10 minutes and remove the softened outer leaves. Return the cabbage to the simmering water to continue to soften as you begin to fill the leaves. (Alternatively, freeze the whole cabbage for 24 hours, then remove and separate the leaves.) Trim off the back spine of each leaf so it will be supple. With the core end of a leaf near you, hollow side up, place an inch-thick roll of stuffing at the bottom of the leaf, leaving a 1½-inch margin at either side. Fold the right margin over and roll up the leaf loosely—the rice will expand. Tuck the left end into itself, closing the opening. Repeat with the other leaves until all the filling is used. Chop enough of the remaining cabbage leaves to make 1 cup. Heat in an 8- to 10-quart, heavy pot:

3 tablespoons vegetable oil

Add the chopped cabbage along with:

1 medium onion, chopped

Cook, stirring, over medium-high heat until golden brown. Add:

½ cup dry white wine

Simmer over low heat for 5 minutes. Add:

One 28-ounce can plum tomatoes in puree, broken or cut up
1 cup water
½ cup raisins (optional)
¼ to ½ cup packed brown sugar
8 gingersnaps (2 inches across)
Juice of 1 large lemon
2 chunks sour salt, or ½ teaspoon powdered

Bring to a boil. Place the cabbage rolls seam side down in the sauce; if the sauce does not cover the rolls, add a little water. Reduce the heat, cover, and simmer for 1½ hours, shaking the pan every 30 minutes to prevent sticking. Serve hot with:

Sour cream or crème fraîche

CABBAGE ROLLS STUFFED WITH SALMON AND WILD RICE

6 servings (12 cabbage rolls)

A special version of stuffed cabbage. You can use canned salmon (one 6-ounce can); simply cook the vegetables in the oil and add the canned salmon, drained, along with the cooked wild and white rice. Prepare and have ready for stuffing, above:

12 large cabbage leaves, preferably Savoy

Cook in separate pots until done and set aside:

⅓ cup long-grain white rice
⅓ cup wild rice

Heat in a small skillet over high heat:

2 tablespoons olive oil or unsalted butter

Add:

6 ounces salmon, skinned and cut into 1-inch chunks

Sear the salmon, turning frequently, for about 2 minutes. Stir in:

¼ cup chopped leeks or sliced scallions (white part only)
8 medium shiitake mushrooms, thinly sliced
2 teaspoons chopped fresh tarragon, or 1 teaspoon dried

Lower the heat to medium-high and cook the mixture for 4 to 5 minutes, stirring frequently. Transfer the mixture to a bowl and add the reserved cooked white and wild rice (and canned salmon, if using). Season with:

1½ teaspoons grated lemon zest
Salt and ground black pepper to taste

Preheat the oven to 350°F. Lay the reserved cabbage leaves out on a work surface and place about ¼ cup of rice stuffing on each leaf. Fold in the sides of the leaves over the stuffing, then roll the leaves to make a package enclosing the stuffing. Place the rolls seam side down in a baking dish that will hold them in 1 layer. Bring a tea kettle of water to a boil and pour around the leaves to a depth of ¼ inch. Cover the baking dish and cook the stuffed cabbage until heated through, 25 to 30 minutes. Serve with:

Avgolemono, 81

BRAISED RED CABBAGE WITH APPLES

4 servings

Immerse briefly in a bowl of cold water:

1 small head red cabbage (about 2 pounds), quartered, cored, and thinly sliced crosswise

In a large nonreactive skillet or Dutch oven, cook over low heat until the fat is rendered:

2 slices bacon, diced, or use 2 tablespoons butter or vegetable oil

Add and cook over medium-low heat until golden:

3 tablespoons finely chopped onions

Lift the cabbage out of the water and add it to the pan along with:

1 large green apple, peeled, cored, and cut into matchsticks
3 tablespoons red wine vinegar
2 tablespoons honey
¼ teaspoon salt if bacon is used, or 1 teaspoon if butter or oil is used
⅛ teaspoon caraway seeds

Cover the pan and cook over medium-low heat until the cabbage is very soft, 1 to 1½ hours, adding boiling water if needed during cooking.

ALSATIAN SAUERKRAUT *6 servings*

Traditional with frankfurters, other sausages, roast pork, and spareribs, sauerkraut should be served raw or barely heated through to retain its full flavor. But for milder flavor, cook for a longer time, as directed in this recipe. For a vegetarian main dish, serve this with roasted root vegetables and applesauce.

Heat in a large ovenproof skillet:
2 tablespoons butter, bacon drippings, or vegetable oil

Add and cook, stirring frequently, over medium heat until translucent:
½ cup sliced onions or shallots

Add and cook for about 5 minutes:
4 cups homemade or deli-case sauerkraut, drained (2 pounds)

Stir in:
1 medium, tart apple, peeled and grated
1 to 2 teaspoons caraway seeds

Cover the sauerkraut with:
Boiling beef or vegetable stock or water
¼ cup dry white wine

Cook, uncovered, for 30 minutes.
Preheat the oven to 325°F.
Cover the skillet and bake for about 30 minutes. If desired, season with:
1 to 2 tablespoons brown sugar

CACTUS PADDLE

In the Southwest and Mexico, the large, flat, fleshy, oval green pads of the nopal cactus are prepared as a vegetable. When cooked, pieces have the color and translucence of cooked bell pepper, but they are also viscid, like okra. The flavor is something between bell pepper and artichoke or asparagus or okra—unique and delectable. They are available all year in Hispanic markets. Select paddles that are about 4 inches wide and under ¼ inch thick. They will probably have had their prickers removed or be a so-called spineless variety. Choose paddles that are bright colored and somewhat stiff—never limp. Pack in perforated plastic vegetable bags in the refrigerator crisper.

To Prepare: Use a vegetable peeler to trim the outside edges and any eyes where prickers were—examine closely because there may be some in spineless paddles. If the prickers have not been removed, wear a glove on your working hand. Hold the pad firmly with tongs and use a small sharp knife to shave off the little bumps containing the thorns. Leave on as much skin as you can, since it is tasty. (If you should catch a thorn in your hand, press sticky tape over the spot and pull up.) Rinse the paddles well. If the thick base is still attached, cut it off and discard. Cactus pads can be oiled and slowly grilled whole (flavorful but a little chewy). Usually they are cut into ¼- to ½-inch squares and boiled until tender, then added to salads, beans, and other vegetables.

To Boil: Bring a saucepan of cold salted water to a boil and drop in the pieces, adding a handful of coarsely chopped scallion greens if desired (the greens reduce the mucilaginous quality). Boil, uncovered, until tender but not soft, 10 to 15 minutes, depending on the thickness. Drain and rinse several times in cold water until the stickiness is gone.

Perhaps in the market you will find a package of paddles that have already been diced. They are fine if they are fresh and not discolored. Cactus paddles have affinities with Tex-Mex and Mexican flavors. Allow about 4 ounces per serving.

ROASTED CACTUS SALAD *4 cups; 8 servings*

Preheat the oven to 375°F.
Have ready:
7 fresh medium cactus paddles

Holding a cactus paddle gingerly between the nodes of the prickly spines, trim off the edge that outlines the paddle, including the blunt end where the paddle was severed from the plant. Slice or scrape off the spiny nodes from both sides. Cut into ¾-inch squares; there will be about 3 cups. Remove the cactus to a baking sheet and toss with:
1 tablespoon olive oil

Sprinkle with:
Salt to taste

Roast, stirring occasionally, until tender and all exuded liquid has evaporated, about 20 minutes. (After 5 minutes in the oven, the cactus will begin to leak its sticky liquid, but as it continues to roast, the liquid will evaporate.) Let cool.

Combine the cooled cactus with:
1½ cups Salsa Fresca, 61
1 tablespoon olive oil

Season with:

½ teaspoon salt, or to taste

Line a serving bowl with:

Several romaine lettuce leaves

Add the salad mixture. Before serving, sprinkle with:

2 tablespoons crumbled Mexican queso añejo, dry feta, or grated Parmesan cheese

CARDOONS

Cardoons are the thick, fleshy stalks of a plant in the Thistle family, very similar to artichokes. The stalks look like very large, coarse, matte-gray celery. The dull color is the result of "blanching"—the growing stalks are wrapped and deprived of sunlight for many weeks. Depending on the climate and the care in blanching, a cardoon's flavor can be mild or bittersweet and a little or a lot like artichoke. Depending on the area, cardoons may be available from late spring to late summer, or late winter through early spring. They are grown in California or imported from Italy; look for them in Italian markets. Select crisp, unbruised stalks—the smaller, the better. Wrap the base of the stalks in a moist paper towel and store in a perforated plastic vegetable bag in the refrigerator crisper for up to a week.

To Prepare: First discard any tough stalks, trim off any leaves, and scrape off any strings with a vegetable peeler. Cut stalks into 2- to 3-inch pieces, stopping where the stalk resists the knife. Immediately soak the pieces in water mixed with lemon or lime juice (1 tablespoon juice for every 4 cups) for about 30 minutes. If the pieces are tender, you can serve them raw for dipping, as for *pinzimonio,* 167, or with another sauce for raw vegetables. Because cardoon tends to darken, boiling in water with lemon juice is the preferred basic cooking method; steaming is not recommended.

To Boil: For every 1 pound prepared cardoons, bring to a boil in a large saucepan 8 cups water with the juice of ½ lemon and 2½ teaspoons salt. Drop in the pieces and boil, uncovered, until the thickest can be pierced with a thin skewer. For tender but still crisp cardoons, boil gently for 15 to 30 minutes; for thoroughly tender pieces, boil for up to 1 hour. Drain well.

The pieces can be covered and refrigerated for a few hours. They are delicious sautéed in butter or oil until hot and sprinkled with a grated robust cheese. and they make delectable fritters. Cardoons have all the affinities artichokes do, 340. Allow about 5 stalks for 2 servings.

CARROTS

At the supermarket, buy carrots with their tops on, selecting only those with crisp, bright leaves. The sealed plastic bags in which most carrots are sold may help retain their moisture, but the bag makes selection frustrating. A cross-hatching of orange lines printed on the bag gives the illusion that the carrots are more orange than they are, and bands printed across the top and bottom of the bag cover up the stem ends—first to show signs of spoilage. Unless they have just been set out, loose carrots in an unrefrigerated bin are of the poorest quality of all. Among vegetables, carrots are second only to beets in sugar content. Depending on the variety, large carrots are often sweeter than skinny ones. Avoid carrots tinged with green (green is bitter), those that are cracked (hiding places for microorganisms), those with softness or mold at the stem end, and those that are rubbery or shriveled. Most carrots are treated with pesticide as they grow, so buy organically raised carrots when you can. Store carrots, their green tops twisted off, in perforated plastic vegetable bags in the refrigerator crisper. Carrots are related to parsley, and their green tops, though apt to be chewy, can be

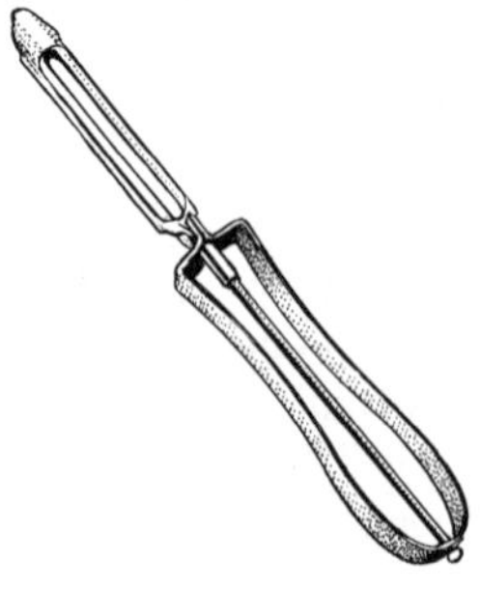

Vegetable peeler

Vegetable brush

chopped and added to vegetable soup. The greens are perhaps most valuable as an indication of the freshness of the carrots. Store them in their own vegetable bag in the crisper.

Cook carrots until tender but still crisp or until fully tender, according to taste. Carrots become sweeter as they cook, which makes them valuable in soups or stews.

Carrots go well with peas, potatoes, beef, brown sugar, raisins and currants, lemon and orange, thyme, dill, mint, parsley, chervil, ginger, and nutmeg. Allow about 4 ounces per serving.

To Prepare: Having been covered with soil, carrots need a thorough scrubbing with a vegetable brush or a light paring with a vegetable peeler before cooking. Carrots will cook fastest when cut lengthwise in half or in rounds or diagonal slices about ¼ inch thick.

To Boil: For each 1 pound prepared carrots, bring to a boil 16 cups (4 quarts) water with 1½ tablespoons salt in a stockpot. Add the carrots and rapidly return to a boil. Boil, uncovered, until tender but still crisp, 4 to 6 minutes for matchsticks, dice, or slices; 7 to 10 minutes for halved carrots; or 12 to 15 minutes for whole carrots. Allow a few minutes longer to cook until tender if they are to be mashed.

To Steam: Arrange carrots in a steamer basket. Cover and steam over 1 to 2 inches boiling water. Depending on the number of layers, allow 7 to 10 minutes for matchsticks, dice, and slices; 16 to 20 minutes for halved or whole carrots.

To Microwave: Spread 2 cups sliced carrots in a 1-quart baking dish. Add 2 tablespoons stock or lightly salted water. Cover and cook on high until tender but still crisp, or completely tender, 5 to 8 minutes, stirring after 3 minutes. Let stand, covered, for 3 minutes.

To Pressure-Cook: Whole large (1¼-inch diameter) carrots can be pressure-cooked with 1 cup liquid at 15 pounds pressure for 4 to 8 minutes. Cool the cooker at once.

ROASTED CARROTS
4 servings

Preheat the oven to 400°F.
Toss together:

1½ pounds medium or large carrots, whole or cut into large chunks of equal size
Enough olive or vegetable oil to lightly coat
⅛ teaspoon dried thyme, or several sprigs fresh
Salt and ground black pepper to taste

Spread the carrots in a single layer in a baking dish and bake until golden and tender, about 1 hour.

PARSLIED CARROTS
4 to 6 servings

A family favorite.
Steam or boil in salted water until tender, 000:

6 large carrots (about 1½ pounds), peeled and thinly sliced into rounds

Drain and rinse to stop the cooking. Cook in a large skillet over medium heat until softened:

2 tablespoons finely diced shallots or onions
2 tablespoons butter

Add the cooked carrots along with:

½ teaspoon fresh lemon juice
Salt to taste
Paprika or ground black pepper to taste

When the carrots are warmed through, toss them with:

2 tablespoons chopped fresh parsley

BRAISED CARROTS
4 servings

Place in a sauté pan that has a lid and is wide enough to hold the carrots in a single layer:

1 pound carrots, peeled, quartered lengthwise, and cut into even sticks
½ cup water or chicken or beef stock
1½ tablespoons butter
1 teaspoon sugar or brown sugar
½ teaspoon salt

Simmer, covered, over medium heat until the carrots are tender and most of the liquid has been absorbed, 15 to 20 minutes. When the pan is almost dry, continue to cook the carrots for a few minutes more, then season with:

1 tablespoon chopped fresh parsley, chervil, tarragon, or thyme
Ground black pepper to taste

Or top with:

Grated Gruyère or Parmesan cheese or Cress Butter, 77

GLAZED CARROTS

Serve as a side dish or to garnish a roast.
Prepare Braised Carrots, above, omitting the salt and increasing the sugar to 1½ tablespoons and the butter to 2 to 3 tablespoons—1 tablespoon brandy may also be added. Cook until a syrupy glaze forms on the bottom of the pan. Roll the carrots around in the pan until they are well coated, then turn them into a dish and garnish with chopped fresh mint or parsley.

CREAMED CARROTS

Prepare Braised Carrots, above, adding ½ cup light cream when the carrots are tender. Simmer just until the cream lightly cloaks the carrots, then season with ground black pepper to taste and a pinch of grated nutmeg or chopped fresh parsley, chervil, tarragon, or snipped chives.

OVEN-BRAISED CARROTS AND PARSNIPS

4 servings

Preheat the oven to 375°F.
Place in a shallow baking dish:

1 pound medium carrots, peeled, quartered lengthwise, and cut into 1½-inch pieces
8 ounces medium parsnips, peeled, quartered, and cut into 1½-inch pieces
¾ cup chicken stock or water
2 tablespoons butter, cut into small pieces
½ teaspoon salt

Cover tightly with aluminum foil and bake until tender, about 45 minutes. Shake the pan once or twice during baking. Uncover and bake until the vegetables begin to brown, 10 to 15 minutes more. Season with:

Chopped fresh parsley or tarragon
Ground black pepper to taste

ROOT VEGETABLE PUREE

4 to 6 servings

The potatoes lend this puree a light texture and delicate flavor.
Place in a large saucepan:

8 ounces all-purpose or baking potatoes, peeled and thinly sliced

Add water to cover generously, bring to a boil, and cook for 5 minutes. Add:

1 pound carrots, peeled, halved, and cut into thick slices

Continue cooking until both vegetables are completely tender, about 25 minutes. Drain and return the vegetables to the pan. Working over low heat, mash the vegetables with a potato masher or beat with a hand-held mixer until very smooth. Mix in:

½ cup milk or light or heavy cream
1½ tablespoons butter, softened
½ teaspoon salt
¼ teaspoon ground white pepper

Taste and adjust the seasonings and cook just until heated through. Serve piping hot. If desired, top with:

Cress Butter, 77, or Beurre Noisette, 57

CELERY ROOT PUREE

Prepare Root Vegetable Puree, above, substituting 2 medium celery roots (about 1½ pounds total), peeled, quartered, and thinly sliced, for the carrots. Flavor with a little Dijon mustard and minced fresh thyme or snipped fresh chives.

PARSNIP PUREE

Prepare Root Vegetable Puree, above, substituting 1 pound parsnips for the carrots. If desired, add a small piece of peeled fresh ginger with the parsnips; remove the ginger before mashing the vegetables. If desired, top with Nut Butter, 77, made with cashews.

RUTABAGA PUREE

Prepare Root Vegetable Puree, above, substituting 1 medium rutabaga, peeled and cut into 1-inch cubes, for the carrots. Season generously with ground black pepper. If desired, top with Orange Butter, 77.

CAULIFLOWER

Cauliflower's flavor has a lovely nutlike quality beneath a sweet cabbage taste. Like broccoli, it is a cold-weather member of the Mustard family. At the farmers' market, you may find cauliflower in its natural cloak of leaves. These shelter the hundreds of tiny flowers from the sun, keeping them snowy white. (If you ever see a patch of gray on a head of cauliflower, it is a spot the sun reached—just trim it off.) Select heads that feel firm, whose florets are tightly packed and without a trace of black—the beginning of spoilage. Loose florets are also a sign of aging. Store in perforated plastic vegetable bags in the refrigerator crisper.

Milder in flavor than broccoli, cauliflower still has similar affinities, 351. It is especially good with cheese sauce, sautéed almonds, ham, celery, curry, nutmeg, and mace. Allow about 4 ounces per serving.

To Prepare: To cut into florets, cut the head in half or quarters, remove the core from each piece, and then cut or break the florets into pieces of the desired size.

To Boil: Cauliflower's flavor is mildest when boiled in a large quantity of water. Bring 16 cups (4 quarts) water, 1½ tablespoons salt, and the juice of 1 lemon to a rolling boil in a stockpot. Add the cauliflower, either whole or separated into florets. If boiling the cauliflower whole, place it in the pot stem side up. Boil, uncovered, until a thin skewer easily pierces the stalk of a whole head, 10 to 15 minutes, or the largest floret is tender but still crisp, 3 to 5 minutes. Drain.

To Steam: Place the cauliflower in a single layer in a steaming basket over 1 to 2 inches boiling water. Cover and cook until tender but still crisp, 6 to 9 minutes for florets, up to 20 minutes for a whole head.

To Microwave: Spread 2 cups florets in a 1-quart baking dish. Add 1 tablespoon stock or lightly salted water. Cover and cook on high until crisp-tender or completely tender, 3 to 5 minutes, stirring after 2 minutes. Let stand, covered, for 2 minutes. Or remove the core and place a whole head in a 2-quart casserole with 2 tablespoons water; cover and cook the same way.

STEAMED CAULIFLOWER WITH PARSLEY AND GARLIC
4 servings

Steam, 360, until nearly tender, 6 to 10 minutes:

1 medium head cauliflower (1½ pounds), cut into small florets

Meanwhile, melt in a small skillet over medium heat:

2 to 4 tablespoons butter

Add:

2 small cloves garlic, minced

Cook, stirring, until the garlic is tender and the butter is just slightly browned, 2 to 4 minutes. Place the hot cauliflower in a serving bowl and toss with the butter mixture along with:

2 to 4 tablespoons minced fresh parsley
Salt and ground black pepper to taste

SAUTÉED CAULIFLOWER
4 servings

Steam, 360, for 5 minutes:

1 small head cauliflower (1¼ pounds), cut into florets

Heat in a large skillet over medium heat until the garlic just begins to color:

3 tablespoons olive oil
2 cloves garlic, slivered

Add the cauliflower along with:

¼ teaspoon red pepper flakes

Increase the heat to high and sauté until the cauliflower begins to brown in places, about 6 minutes. Toss with:

2 tablespoons chopped fresh parsley
¼ teaspoon salt
Grated Parmesan cheese to taste

Serve with:

Lemon wedges

Or omit the salt and cheese and garnish with:

Anchovy Butter, 77

ROASTED CAULIFLOWER WITH PAPRIKA
4 servings

Not the usual treatment for this vegetable, but one that deepens its flavor effectively.

Preheat the oven to 400°F.

Toss together:

1 large head cauliflower (about 2 pounds), cut into large florets
Enough vegetable oil to lightly coat
Salt and ground black pepper to taste

Spread in a single layer in a baking dish. Add:

2 tablespoons water

Bake until the stems are tender when pierced with a knife and beginning to brown, about 25 minutes. Remove and toss with:

Butter or olive oil to taste
Salt to taste
2 teaspoons sweet paprika
1 tablespoon chopped fresh parsley or tarragon

Or in place of the paprika and herb, serve with one of the following:

Fruit Salsa with Black Beans, 63, Sauce Aurore, 46, or Sauce Bercy, 49

SCALLOPED CAULIFLOWER
4 servings

A delectable dish when you use a fine-quality cheese, such as Gruyère, aged Cheddar, or Italian Parmesan.

Preheat the oven to 350°F. Butter a 2-quart gratin dish. Boil, 360:

2 pounds cauliflower, cut into small florets

Drain well and spread in the gratin dish. Sprinkle with half of:

⅔ cup grated cheese

Spoon over:

1½ cups Sauce Béchamel, 46, mixed with ½ teaspoon grated or ground nutmeg or 1 tablespoon Dijon mustard

Sprinkle over the top the remaining cheese along with:

½ cup plain or buttered fresh breadcrumbs

Bake until bubbly and browned on the top, about 25 minutes. Serve sprinkled with:

Paprika, ground red pepper, or red pepper flakes

CAULIFLOWER, POTATO, AND SPINACH CURRY
4 servings

The word *curry* has two meanings: it refers either to the aromatic leaves of the south Indian kari plant (curry leaves) or to a stew flavored with a blend of fragrant spices, often a premixed curry powder. Most American cooks are surprised to learn that a curry does not exist in traditional Indian cooking. The word is a British corruption of one or another Indian dish; perhaps of *kahri,* a Tamil word meaning sauce, or of *karhi,* a soupy north Indian dish of yogurt thickened with chickpea flour, or of *kari,* a south Indian technique of stir-frying vegetables. Eventually a very simple gravied dish called a *salan* was renamed *kari,* or curry, and the term was thus integrated into Indian cooking and culture.

This is a very popular vegetable curry combination. You can substitute peas for the spinach if desired. Cooking the curry powder and flour eliminates any starchy taste in the spice mixture, adds color to the dish, and intensifies the flavor of the spices.

Boil, 360, for 5 minutes:

½ head cauliflower, cored and cut into florets

Remove from the water with a slotted spoon and transfer to a bowl of cold water. Add to the boiling water and cook for 5 minutes:

2 medium potatoes, cut into ½-inch cubes

Drain, rinse in cold water, drain well again, and transfer to a bowl. Drain the cauliflower and add to the potatoes. Set them aside. Place in a food processor:

1 large tart apple, peeled, cored, and sliced
3 large cloves garlic, sliced
One 2-inch piece fresh ginger, peeled and sliced
2 hot fresh chili peppers, such as jalapeño or serrano, seeded and sliced (optional)

Process together until minced but not pureed and set aside. Coarsely chop:

2 medium onions

Heat in a large, heavy pot or Dutch oven over medium heat:

¼ cup vegetable oil or clarified butter

Add the onions and reserved apple mixture and cook until the vegetables are softened and starting to color, 5 to 7 minutes. Add:

2 tablespoons curry powder
1 tablespoon all-purpose flour

Cook for 3 to 5 minutes to lightly brown the curry powder and flour. Add:

One 14-ounce can unsweetened coconut milk
½ cup water or vegetable or chicken stock
1 teaspoon salt

Bring to a boil over high heat, stirring, then add, along with the reserved cauliflower and potatoes:

One 16-ounce can chickpeas, drained

Lower the heat to medium, cover, and cook for 15 minutes. Stir in, cover, and cook until wilted, about 3 minutes:

12 ounces fresh spinach, stemmed, washed, and torn into pieces, or one 10-ounce package frozen peas

Season to taste with more salt if needed and:

Ground black pepper to taste

Serve the curry over:

Hot cooked rice

CELERY

When choosing bunches of celery, the lightest color with the shiniest surface will have the finest flavor. Darker green stalks may be stringy. You might find Chinese celery, which has thinner stalks than regular celery and a remarkably intense flavor. Select a well-shaped bunch of any celery that is heavy for its size, with moist, bright-colored leaves. Stalks should have no cracks, cuts, bruises, or trimmed patches. Store the whole bunch in a perforated plastic vegetable bag in the refrigerator crisper.

To Prepare: Separate the stalks and rinse them well, giving a light scrub to the bases where sand has gathered. Trim off the remnants of the root at the base. Sometimes there will be a soft white heart at the bottom—the cook's treat. Pare off any strings from the surface of outer stalks with a vegetable peeler. The leafy tips starting at the point where each main stalk bursts into multiple stalks may be tougher, but they should not be discarded. Chop the tips up and then toss them into salads and soups and use to flavor stocks. Should stalks be limp after storage—or should you want them to be super-crisp, for serving raw—soak them in ice water until they firm up. Unless the bunch is very young and tender, the outer stalks are best used in cooking. The paler center ones, also called the heart, are best served raw.

Celery is a flavorful addition to stir-fries. Or simmer thin slices in a tightly covered heavy skillet in ½ inch milk and a little butter until tender but still crisp. For a refreshing first course called Celery Victor, trim tender, tightly packed hearts to 6 inches in length and then halve lengthwise; steam until crisp-tender, place in a dish, and toss with vinaigrette while still hot. Refrigerate and serve at room temperature.

After thawing, frozen celery loses its crispness but can still be useful as a seasoning in cooking. Celery goes well with every sort of cheese, cream, lemon, dill, chives, parsley—and who can resist a stalk filled with peanut butter? Allow 4 to 5 ounces per serving.

To Microwave: Cut 1 pound celery stalks into 2- to 3-inch pieces. Place in a 2-quart baking dish. Add 2 tablespoons stock or lightly salted water. Cover and cook on high until tender but still crisp, 8 to 12 minutes, stirring after 4 minutes. Let stand, covered, for 2 minutes.

BRAISED CELERY HEARTS

4 servings

A luscious accompaniment to roasted meats.

Arrange in a large skillet or Dutch oven:

1½ pounds celery hearts, washed, trimmed, and cut into 3- to 4-inch lengths

Top with:

½ cup chicken or veal stock
3 tablespoons fresh lemon juice
2 tablespoons butter, cut into small pieces
1 tablespoon sugar
½ teaspoon salt

Bring the liquid to a boil, then cover closely with parchment paper or aluminum foil and then the lid. Simmer until tender, about 25 minutes. Transfer the celery to a platter and keep warm. Boil the remaining liquid over medium-high heat until reduced to about ½ cup. Add and cook for 1 minute:

1 tablespoon butter or Kneaded Butter, 44

Pour this glaze over the celery and serve.

CELERY ROOT

More or less round and orange in size, celery root has a daunting appearance—knobby, grimy, and perhaps tangled at the roots. Ah, but beneath the skin is tender, cream-colored flesh with an exquisite nutty taste. An autumn and winter vegetable, celery root is also called celeriac and turnip-rooted celery. Select small to medium knobs, the heaviest for their size. They should have no cuts, bruises, or soft spots. If there are stalks on top, they should be crisp and fresh. You can use the stalks for seasoning—they have the concentrated flavor of Chinese celery. Leave on any stalks and store in perforated plastic vegetable bags in the refrigerator crisper.

To Prepare: Scrub well all over with a stiff brush under cold running water. Cut off bits of roots. When peeling, have ready a bowl of acidulated water (1 tablespoon vinegar or lemon juice to 4 cups cold water) to drop the pieces in, because the flesh discolors when exposed to the air. Using a large stainless-steel knife, cut off the top and the bottom. Use a sharp stainless-steel paring knife to cut off the thick skin. Cut out any pits and pockets; you can cut the root any way you would a potato.

To Boil: Boiling the whole root in its jacket keeps the creamy color and delicate flavor intact. However, this method is best for small to medium roots—the outside would overcook on a large root. For every 1 pound scrubbed whole unpeeled celery root, bring 12 cups cold water with 1½ tablespoons salt to a boil in a stockpot. Drop in the roots, return to a boil, and cook until easily pierced with a thin skewer, 35 to 45 minutes. Drain. The root can be peeled and prepared for serving at once or wrapped and refrigerated for up to 8 hours. To boil cut-up pieces, cut each peeled root into 8 wedges and cook for 8 to 10 minutes. Serve at once.

To Steam: Place 1-inch cubes of peeled celery root that have been kept in acidulated water into a steaming basket in a single layer over 1 to 2 inches boiling water. Steam until easily pierced with a thin skewer, 8 to 10 minutes. If there are several layers, stir once or twice and allow an extra 5 to 10 minutes of cooking time. Serve at once.

Celery root makes marvelous salad dressed with mayonnaise or vinaigrette; use it raw in place of or with cooked potato in salad. For a delicious accompaniment to roasted meats, combine two parts cooked celery root and one part cooked potato and mash with butter, salt, and pepper. Celery root's affinities are the same as those of celery, 362, with the additions of mustard, celery seeds, and apples. Allow 4 to 5 ounces per serving.

ROASTED CELERY ROOT

4 servings

Usually the skin is too tough to eat, but wait and see—it can be tender. The roots are served like baked potatoes.

Preheat the oven to 350°F.

Scrub:

2 medium unpeeled celery roots (about 1¼ pounds)

Trim off any rootlets and fibers. Pat the roots dry. Brush the roots with:

2 tablespoons olive oil

Place in an 8 x 8-inch baking pan and roast, uncovered, in the middle of the oven until tender all through when pierced with a thin skewer, about 1 hour. Turn the roots over with tongs after 30 minutes. Immediately slice the roots in half through the middle, then trim the tops and bottoms as needed so that each half will sit squarely on a plate. Mash the center just enough to absorb the sauce, and drizzle with:

Mustard Beurre Blanc, 58, or Beurre Noisette, 57

Sprinkle with:

Minced fresh parsley

CELERY ROOT AND POTATO GRATIN

6 to 8 servings

Prepare Gratin Dauphinois, 412, substituting 1 medium celery root (1 pound), peeled, quartered, and thinly sliced, for 1 pound of the potatoes.

CHARD

When you see the large, ruffled, rich green leaves of Swiss chard at the market, you might imagine they have a flamboyant flavor to match. In fact, chard has a more delicate taste than spinach, and very young chard leaves are as mild as lettuce. The *Swiss* is a puzzlement; there is nothing Swiss about this close relative of beets. But there is more to this vegetable than leaves. The fleshy ribs can be prepared separately; they taste like earthy celery. Chard leaves may be green with white ribs or burgundy with crimson ribs. Select the bunch with the smallest, crispest, brightest leaves and no yellowing, tears, or holes. Store in perforated plastic vegetable bags in the refrigerator crisper.

Chard is best steamed, wilted, sautéed, microwaved, or braised. Dress cooked greens with oil and vinegar or butter and lemon juice. Very young chard can be added to salads, but usually this green is cooked. Cooked stems are excellent with any cream sauce. They also make a delightful gratin.

All leafy greens seem to have affinities for butter, lemon, sweet basil, nutmeg, parsley, garlic, pine nuts, and mushrooms. Allow about 8 ounces per serving.

Spinach beets or Perpetual beets have leaves similar to chard. Prepare, cook, and serve them as you would spinach, 415 to 418.

To Prepare: Separate the stems from the leaves and rinse in warm water. The leaves can be left whole, torn into pieces, or cut into strips by stacking the leaves, rolling them up, and slicing into ¼- to ½-inch ribbons. Cut chard stems crosswise into ¼- to ½-inch slices.

To Boil: To retain their bright color, chard greens can be blanched if needed for another use (such as a pasta filling, 313 to 314). Cook only 1 pound prepared leaves and stem pieces at a time. Bring 16 cups (4 quarts) water to a rolling boil with 1½ tablespoons salt in a stockpot. Drop in the leaves, rapidly return the water to a boil, then boil, uncovered. For blanching, cook until the leaves are wilted, about 2 minutes; for boiling, cook 3 to 4 minutes for leaves, 5 to 7 minutes for ½-inch pieces of stems. Scoop the chard out with a strainer. Drain and squeeze out as much moisture as possible.

To Wilt: To retain the most nutrients and flavor (although the color will darken), place leaves with the water that clings to them from rinsing in a medium skillet. Sprinkle with ⅛ teaspoon salt for each pound. Cook, turning the leaves with tongs every few seconds, for 3 to 4 minutes, then cover the pan and continue to cook for 3 to 4 minutes more.

To Steam: Whole leaves can be steamed, covered, in steamer basket over 1 to 2 inches boiling water until tender but still crisp, about 8 minutes. Stem pieces take 8 to 10 minutes to steam until tender but still crisp.

To Braise: Bring to a boil 4 cups of water or stock and 1 teaspoon salt in a medium skillet. Add 1 pound prepared chard leaves and cook, covered, until tender but still crisp, 3 to 6 minutes. Dress with oil and vinegar or with butter.

To Microwave: Coarsely chop 1 pound leafy greens and spread in a 3-quart baking dish. Cover and cook on high until tender but still crisp, 5 to 7 minutes, stirring after 3 minutes. Let stand, still covered, for 2 minutes. If not tender enough for your taste, finish cooking in a skillet in a little olive oil. Serve sprinkled with fresh lemon juice.

CHARD SAUTÉED WITH GARLIC

4 to 6 servings

Remove the stems from:

2 medium bunches red or green chard (about 1½ pounds)

Cut the stems into ½-inch pieces. Coarsely chop the leaves; rinse well, but do not dry. Heat in a large skillet over medium-low heat until the oil smells good and the garlic is just beginning to color:

2 tablespoons extra-virgin olive oil
2 cloves garlic, thinly sliced
1 small dried red chili pepper, crumbled, or ¼ to ½ teaspoon red pepper flakes (optional)

Add the chard stems and season with:

Salt to taste

Cook, stirring occasionally, until the stems are nearly tender, about 2 minutes. Add the chard leaves and cook, partially covered, until both the leaves and the stems are tender, 3 to 5 minutes more. Season with:

Juice of ½ lemon or 1½ tablespoons red wine vinegar

Taste again for salt. Serve in a bowl, surrounded with:

Lemon wedges

Or instead of salt and lemon, dot with:

Soy Sauce Butter, 77

CHARD TART

One 11-inch tart

A springtime tradition in many parts of Italy and France. Escarole leaves, spinach, or other spring vegetables can be mixed in or substituted for the chard.

To prepare the pastry, combine in a medium bowl:

2 cups all-purpose flour
½ teaspoon salt

Stir in until thoroughly blended:

½ cup water
½ cup extra-virgin olive oil

Knead the mixture briefly. The dough will be very moist and difficult to roll, so press it into an 11-inch tart pan with a removable rim. Refrigerate for at least 1 hour or until needed.

Cook in a large skillet over medium-low heat until well softened, about 15 minutes:

2 tablespoons olive oil
1 red onion, finely diced

Add and cook until tender, 8 to 10 minutes:

1 pound chard leaves or other greens, stems removed, leaves well washed and chopped

Season with:

2 tablespoons chopped fresh basil, or 1½ teaspoons dried, finely crumbled
¼ teaspoon salt
⅛ teaspoon ground black pepper

Position a rack in the lower third of the oven. Preheat the oven to 375°F.

Combine in a bowl:

3 large eggs
⅓ cup heavy cream or half-and-half
1 cup grated Parmesan cheese

Add the chard mixture, then scrape the mixture into the prepared tart shell. Bake until the crust is golden and the filling is firm, 40 to 45 minutes. Let cool to room temperature before serving.

CHAYOTE

Pear shaped and pale or apple green, chayote is a tropical form of summer squash. Also called mirliton and christophene, the squash has deep lengthwise ridges and a large center seed, like an avocado. The harder the squash and the darker the green, the better the flavor will be. Chayote keeps for up to 1 month unwrapped in a cool, dark, dry place. It also can be stored in perforated plastic vegetable bags in the refrigerator crisper, but for only 1 week.

Chayote has good quality when frozen. It has the same affinities as other summer squashes, 419, but it is especially good with cheese. Allow ½ squash per serving.

To Prepare: If the chayote is small, its skin will not be tough and will not require peeling. If the skin is thick, pare the chayote with a vegetable peeler, working under running water to prevent being irritated by the sticky substance just under the skin, which disappears in cooking. Use a sharp paring knife to cut out the skin in the ridges. Cut off the stem and halve the squash lengthwise to remove the seed.

To Boil: For every 1 pound prepared chayotes, bring 5 cups cold water with a generous 1¾ teaspoons salt to a rolling boil in a saucepan. Add the chayotes and boil gently, uncovered, until tender but still firm, about 45 minutes for halves, 30 minutes for lengthwise quarters, 20 minutes for ¾-inch-thick slices.

To Steam: Place chayotes in a steamer basket over 1 to 2 inches boiling water and cover. Steam until tender when pierced with a thin skewer, 10 to 15 minutes for halves, or 4 to 6 minutes for ¼-inch-thick slices.

To Microwave: Place peeled ¼-inch-thick slices of 1 chayote in a 2-quart baking dish. Add 3 tablespoons stock or lightly salted water. Cover and cook on high until tender or crisp-tender, 5 to 6 minutes, stirring after 2 minutes. Let stand, covered, for 2 minutes.

LOUISIANA-STYLE CHAYOTE *6 servings*

Boil in salted water to cover until tender but firm, about 6 to 10 minutes:

3 chayotes, halved and seeds removed

Remove, set upside down to cool, then scoop out the insides, leaving a shell ⅓ inch thick. Pat dry and place the shells in a 13 x 9-inch baking dish. Chop the pulp.

Preheat the oven to 375°F.

Sauté in a large nonstick skillet over high heat until the shrimp are bright pink:

1 tablespoon olive or safflower oil
6 large shrimp (about 3 ounces), peeled and deveined

Remove the shrimp with a slotted spoon, let cool, and finely chop. Add the squash pulp to the same pan along with:

1 large scallion, chopped (about ¼ cup)
1 clove garlic, minced
⅓ cup finely diced red bell pepper
⅓ cup chopped fresh flat-leaf parsley
¼ cup finely diced ham
1 teaspoon chopped fresh thyme
Salt and ground black pepper to taste
Pinch of ground red pepper, or to taste

Cook over medium-high heat until no liquid remains and everything is dry, about 4 minutes. Stir in the shrimp. Divide the filling among the 6 squash shells and sprinkle each one with:

1 tablespoon plain dry or toasted fresh breadcrumbs

Bake until heated through and browned on top, about 35 minutes.

CHESTNUTS

With their smooth, creamy texture and rich, earthy taste, chestnuts traditionally have been served as a vegetable. The flattish, plum-sized nuts with glossy brown shells are harvested in fall. Soon their starch turns to sugar, which gives them their characteristic sweetness. Refrigerate in perforated plastic bags. Chestnuts are always cooked before serving, having been peeled first.

A handful of cooked whole chestnuts is delightful added to braised cabbage dishes, and they are a classic ingredient for stuffing, 483. One pound chestnuts yields a little more than 8 ounces peeled, or 2 cups.

To Prepare: Use the tip of a sharp paring knife to cut an X on the flat side of each nut. Drop into a pot of boiling water, let the water return to a boil, and boil for 5 minutes. Turn off the heat. Remove a few nuts at a time and peel off the outer shell and inner papery layers. If some resist peeling, return them to the pot to soak longer. Reboil if necessary. Now the chestnuts are ready to be cooked.

To Boil: Place peeled whole chestnuts in a large, heavy skillet or saucepan. For every 1 pound, add 5 cups boiling water and 1¾ teaspoons salt. Return to a boil, and boil, uncovered, until easily pierced with a thin skewer, 30 to 40 minutes. Milk (and no salt) can be used if the chestnuts will be sweetened, or stock can be used if the chestnuts will be in a savory dish. Place chestnuts in a buttered baking dish, cover with stock, cover the dish, and bake at 325°F until tender, about 1 hour.

CHESTNUT PUREE *6 to 8 servings*

Small portions of this rich puree, which can be extended with ½ cup or more mashed potatoes, are ample It is a standard accompaniment to game, especially venison.

Remove the shells and skins, above, from:

1½ pounds chestnuts

Place in a pot along with:

Enough water or stock to cover

Simmer, uncovered, until softened, 30 to 40 minutes. Drain, reserving the liquid. Mash the chestnuts with a fork until smooth, or pass through a food mill. Stir in:

2 tablespoons butter
Pinch of freshly grated or ground nutmeg
Salt and ground black pepper to taste
Light or heavy cream to taste (optional)

Keep warm in the top of a double boiler until ready to serve. Stir in the reserved cooking liquid or cream if necessary to thin the puree.

CHINESE CABBAGES

The so-called Chinese cabbages compare to our common cabbage as romaine lettuce compares to iceberg. Like icebergs, common cabbages have round heads with thick, crunchy, mild-tasting leaves. Like romaines, Chinese cabbages have oblong heads with thin, juicy, full-flavored leaves. The Chinese cabbage we see more and more in the supermarket is pale green Napa cabbage. These are referred to as "hearted" or "barrel shaped" to distinguish them from the long "cylindrical" shape of Michihili cabbages. You will find both Napa and Michihili at Asian markets, and their flavors and uses in cooking are much the same. Select, store, prepare, and cook as for common cabbage, 354, but do not overcook, or their lovely flavor and texture will be destroyed. When the midrib is well developed on a leaf, separate it and cook as for chard ribs, 364. Affinities are for other Asian vegetables and flavors. Allow 8 ounces per serving.

STIR-FRY OF NAPA CABBAGE AND CARROTS *4 servings*

Heat a wok or large skillet over high heat. Add and stir-fry for a few seconds, but do not allow the garlic to brown:

1 tablespoon peanut or vegetable oil
2 cloves garlic, minced
1 tablespoon minced peeled fresh ginger

Add and stir-fry for 3 minutes:

8 ounces carrots, shredded

Then add and stir-fry until the cabbage is tender, about 3 more minutes:

1 medium-large head Napa cabbage (about 2 pounds), rinsed and thinly sliced

Add and stir well to mix:

2 tablespoons soy sauce
1 teaspoon toasted sesame oil
½ teaspoon chili paste with garlic or ¼ teaspoon red pepper flakes (optional)

Serve immediately, sprinkled with:

Minced fresh cilantro or parsley

COLLARD GREENS

Collards' large, smooth, dark green leaves have a flavor somewhere between cabbage or kale and turnip greens, fellow members of the Mustard family. De-

Chinese cabbage

Napa cabbage

pending on their size and age, they can be mild and sweet or mustardy. Collards do not form a head but grow on stalks that are too tough to eat. The leaves cook fairly quickly. Choose crisp bunches with no yellow or torn leaves. Store in perforated plastic vegetable bags in the refrigerator crisper.

Collards are superb seasoned just with vinegar and hot pepper sauce, but they also have affinities with garlic, onions, chili peppers, lemon, and other piquant flavors. Allow about 8 ounces per serving.

To Prepare: After rinsing in lukewarm water, strip the leaves from the inedible stalks. Stack the leaves, roll them up, and slice into very thin strips for fastest cooking or cut into wider ribbons and then chop.

To Boil: Follow the method for mustard greens, 388, and cook the prepared leaves until tender but not mushy, 10 to 15 minutes, depending on the age and thickness of the leaves. Baby greens will cook very quickly. Drain.

To Braise: Follow the method for mustard greens, 388, and cook the prepared leaves until tender but not mushy, 12 to 15 minutes, though baby greens will cook very quickly. Drain. Collards can also be braised with bacon, like kale, 379.

To Microwave: In a 3-quart baking dish, place 1¼ pounds whole leaves with the water that clings to them from rinsing. Cover and cook on high until tender, 7 to 10 minutes, stirring after 3 minutes. Let stand, covered, for 2 minutes.

SOUTHERN COLLARD GREENS *6 servings*

All greens on the tough side, such as turnip greens, mustards, and dandelions, can be cooked by this method.

Boil gently, uncovered, in a large pot until the broth is flavorful, 30 to 40 minutes:

10 cups water

5 ounces salt pork or smoked pork neck bones

Tear into small pieces:

3 pounds collard greens, well washed

Add to the pot along with:

1 small dried red chili pepper, seeds removed (optional)

Simmer, uncovered, just until tender, 15 to 30 minutes, stirring occasionally. Drain and remove the salt pork or neck bones. Serve with:

Red wine Vinegar or Southeast Asian Peanut Dipping Sauce, 83

COLLARDS WITH RICE *4 servings*

Medium-grain rice yields a denser texture than long-grain, but any uncooked white rice can be used.

Heat in a medium saucepan:

2 tablespoons olive oil

Add and cook until tender, about 5 minutes:

1 large sweet onion, chopped, or 1 bunch scallions, coarsely chopped

Add:

1 bunch collard greens (about 12 ounces), well washed, patted dry, stemmed, leaves coarsely chopped

Cover and cook gently for 10 minutes. Then stir in:

1 cup medium-grain rice

Cook, stirring, until the rice is well coated with oil and starting to look opaque, 3 to 5 minutes. Stir in:

1¾ cups very hot chicken stock or water

2 tablespoons minced fresh dill, or 2 teaspoons dried

½ teaspoon salt

¼ teaspoon ground black pepper

Bring to a boil. Reduce the heat to low and simmer, tightly covered, for 15 minutes. Check a grain of rice, and if it seems nearly done, remove the pot from the heat. Let stand, covered, for 5 to 10 minutes. (If it is far from done, cook for 3 to 5 minutes more, then let it stand.) Serve with:

Hot red pepper sauce

CORN

The variety of corn we call sweet corn, which nowadays is the only type we eat fresh, has undergone radical change, becoming sweeter every year. Corn geneticists have engineered a bundle of sugar-enhanced and supersweet hybrids that are designed to remain sweet and nonstarchy while shipped and stored for supermarket sales. That is why we now get fresh supermarket corn, grown commercially in Florida, all winter long. Compared to most summer corn, winter corn lacks moisture, creaminess, tenderness, and all signs of just-picked freshness. Even these qualities, it must be added, vary widely in fresh summer corn, according to the variety. Use fresh winter corn, then, as an alternative to frozen or canned corn rather than as a substitute for fresh summer corn, which is in a category of its own.

We recommend that you give fresh ears of corn no more than a quick dip in a large quantity of boiling water, just long enough to heat them but short enough to keep them sweet, crisp, and tender. Remember that the kernels of these sweet corns taste delicious raw—in salads, salsas, garnishes, purees. They do not need to be cooked for flavor or digestibility, although cooking them slightly will intensify flavor.

Corn goes well with butter, cheese, peas, shell beans, bacon, chili peppers and chili powder, paprika, and oregano.

The soft black fungus rarely discovered on an ear of market corn is anathema to growers, but its sweet earthy flavor and creamy texture make it a great culinary treat. Americans call it corn smut and most farmers destroy it, but in Mexico, ears containing *huitlacoche* are sold in markets. Store the ears as usual and consult a Mexican cookbook for cooking details.

To Prepare: First remove the husks and silks. To remove kernels from the cob, hold the ear firmly with the bottom end placed on a counter or in a shallow soup bowl to keep the kernels from splattering. If you want to retain the shape and texture of the whole kernel, cut straight down the cob with a sharp knife, cutting two or three rows at a time. If you are after the inner creaminess of the kernel, cut off just the tops of the kernels. Then, with the back of your knife, scrape down the cob to press out the base of the kernels and the corn "milk," which gives body and moisture to corn purees and creamy corn dishes.

It is impossible to estimate precisely the cup volume of kernels per ear of corn because corn varies so widely. To err on the side of caution, in our recipes we have adopted the formula of one ear corn to equal ½ cup kernels.

To Microwave: Place 1 to 4 unhusked ears parallel on the turntable, alternating tips and ends. Cook on high until you can smell the corn, 6 to 9 minutes for 2 ears, 12 to 14 for 3 or 4 ears. For 3 or 4 ears, rotate the ear(s) in the center with those on the outside halfway through cooking. After cooking, cover with a folded dish towel and let stand for 5 minutes. Use a fresh towel to protect your hands from the steamy husks when shucking the corn.

Popcorn is a different subspecies from sweet corn. It dries in a way that encloses a dot of moisture in the kernel's center. When the kernel gets hot enough, the moisture dries suddenly, causing the kernel to explode.

To Pop Corn: Heat 1 tablespoon vegetable oil in a large, heavy skillet over high heat. Add 1 corn kernel. When it pops, add ¼ cup popcorn, cover, and reduce the heat to medium. Shake the pan nonstop until the corn stops popping. At once turn it into a bowl and sprinkle with ¼ to ½ teaspoon salt and about 2 tablespoons melted butter; stir quickly to mix well. Yield is about 7 cups popped corn. The secret of fully popped corn is moisture in the kernels. If ¼ cup kernels yields 5 cups or less, add 1 tablespoon water to a 1-pound jar of the same kernels, shake well, and store in a cool, dry place for a few days before popping again.

CORN ON THE COB

Allow 1 to 3 ears per person, depending on appetites. Today's corn needs only to be warmed through. If you immerse but 2 or 3 ears at a time in a large amount of boiling water, so that the water stays at a boil, a dip of only 30 to 60 seconds is enough to heat the ears. Sweet corn should be firm but tender to the bite. If you want it slightly softer and more cooked, leave the ears in the water for 2 to 3 minutes—but no more.

Husk the corn and remove the silks if you like, but we prefer to boil corn in the husks. Remove only the thickest outside husks to leave a tight covering inside, which steams the ear within and intensifies the corn flavor. You do not need to remove the silks first—once heated, they will come off with the remaining husks.

Remove only the coarsest outside husks from:

Fresh ears of sweet corn

Drop them 1 at a time into a large pot of boiling water. Cook for at least 30 seconds or up to 3 minutes. Remove from the water with tongs, then strip back the husks, if you have left them on, leaving them attached to the ends of the cobs.

Pile the ears on a platter and serve with:

Salt and ground black pepper

Butter, herbed butter or oil, or chili butter

Lime juice, herbed mayonnaise, barbecue sauce, or coconut milk spiced with ground red pepper

GRILLED CORN IN THE HUSKS

Soak ears of corn in their husks in cold water for 2 to 3 hours before putting them on the grill. For a stronger grilled or roasted taste, do not soak the ears. Do not worry about removing the silks, for they will come off later with the husks. Lay the ears directly on a hot grill rack, on ash-covered coals, or on a rack in a 450°F oven. Grill, turning the ears with a pair of tongs so that they roast evenly on all sides, for 8 to 15 minutes, depending on the heat. Serve with any of the flavorings suggested for Corn on the Cob, above.

ROASTED CORN WITHOUT HUSKS

To intensify the taste of grilled corn and to caramelize the sugar in sweet corn, remove the husks and silks and lay the ears directly on a grill over very hot coals. Grill, turning the ears to brown them evenly, for 5 to 7 minutes. Season with lime juice and ground red pepper, butter or olive oil, and/or chopped fresh herbs.

ROASTED CORN IN FOIL

This method steams the ears inside a foil wrapper.
Remove the husks and silks from 1 to 2 ears sweet corn per person. Rub lightly with an herb paste or other savory flavored butter or oil or sauce. Wrap each ear in a piece of aluminum foil. Bake in a 450°F oven, on a grill, or directly on the coals, turning a few times, for 8 to 10 minutes.

SAUTÉED CORN

4 servings

Cut and scrape the kernels from:

6 ears sweet corn (about 3 cups)

Melt in a medium nonstick skillet until bubbly:

2 tablespoons olive oil

Add the corn and cook, stirring often to keep it from sticking, over medium heat until heated through, 3 to 4 minutes. Season with:

Salt and ground black pepper to taste

Stir in any of the following:

Minced fresh parsley
1 tomato, seeded and chopped
Chopped fresh tarragon, basil, cilantro, thyme, or marjoram
Pinch of chili powder
Diced fresh jalapeño or serrano peppers, chopped roasted poblano peppers, or chopped Anaheim peppers
1 or 2 slices cooked bacon, crumbled

SAUTÉED CORN WITH OTHER VEGETABLES

Prepare Sautéed Corn, above, sautéing any of the following in the butter until softened, about 4 minutes, before adding the corn:

¾ cup finely diced red or green bell pepper
¾ cup diced zucchini
¾ cup diced onion

CREAMED CORN

4 servings

Cut and scrape the kernels from:

5 ears sweet corn (about 2½ cups)

Melt in a medium nonstick skillet:

1 tablespoon butter

Add and cook over low heat until softened, 3 to 4 minutes:

¼ cup thinly sliced scallions or diced shallots

Add the corn along with:

½ cup half-and-half, heavy cream, or crème fraîche

Cook over low heat, stirring as little as possible, until thickened, about 2 minutes. Season with:

Salt and ground black pepper to taste
1 tablespoon chopped fresh tarragon, basil, or parsley (optional)

CORN FRITTERS

4 servings

Cut and scrape the kernels from:

5 ears sweet corn (about 2½ cups)

Place the corn and pulp in a large bowl and stir in:

2 large egg yolks, lightly beaten
2 tablespoons all-purpose flour
1 tablespoon sugar
¼ teaspoon salt
⅛ teaspoon ground black pepper

Beat until the peaks are stiff but not dry:

2 large egg whites

Fold the egg whites into the corn mixture. Heat in a large nonstick skillet over high heat until hot:

2 tablespoons butter or vegetable oil

Drop in the batter, a heaping tablespoon at a time. Reduce the heat to medium and cook until browned on the bottom, 2 to 3 minutes. Turn once (do not pat the fritters down) and cook the second side until browned. Take care not to overcook them. Serve immediately.

CORN PUDDING COCKAIGNE

4 servings

For variation, add a little chopped fresh tarragon, thyme, basil, or mint.
Preheat the oven to 325°F. Butter an 8 x 8-inch baking dish.
Cut and scrape the kernels from:

4 ears sweet corn (about 2 cups)

Combine with:

½ to ¾ cup heavy cream
1 teaspoon sugar (optional)
Salt and ground white pepper to taste

Spread the corn mixture in the baking dish. Dot the top with:

1 tablespoon butter, cut into small pieces

Bake until the pudding is set, 30 to 40 minutes.

CORN PUDDING WITH ROASTED POBLANO PEPPERS

6 servings

This side dish is rich enough to serve in larger portions as a main dish.
Position a rack in the center of the oven. Butter a 1½-quart gratin or soufflé dish.
Roast, 402:

3 poblano or New Mexico green chili peppers

Peel, remove the seeds and veins, then chop.
Cut and scrape the kernels from:

4 ears sweet corn (about 2 cups)

Heat in a large skillet over medium heat:

2 tablespoons butter or corn oil

Add and cook for 5 minutes:

1 onion, diced
2 teaspoons minced garlic
½ teaspoon dried oregano

Stir in the corn kernels and roasted peppers. Cook for 3 minutes, then let cool. Combine in another bowl:

4 large eggs, lightly beaten
¾ cup grated Monterey Jack or Muenster cheese
½ cup grated sharp Cheddar cheese
Salt and ground black pepper to taste

Add the cooled corn mixture and scrape into the prepared dish. Bake until puffed and golden, about 30 minutes.

CHEESE, CHILI, CORN SQUARES

About 7 dozen small squares

Quick and easy.
Preheat the oven to 350°F. Generously butter a 9 x 9-inch baking pan.
Cut and scrape the kernels from:

3 ears sweet corn (about 1½ cups)

Combine with:

1 pound Monterey Jack cheese, grated
6 large eggs, lightly beaten
3 fresh jalapeño peppers, seeded and finely chopped
2 tablespoons ground dried medium-hot chili peppers
Salt and ground black pepper to taste

Scrape the mixture into the prepared pan. Bake until the top is nicely browned, about 30 minutes. Let cool until it hardens sufficiently to be cut, then cut into 1-inch squares.

BAKED FRESH CORN TAMALE TERRINE

12 to 16 servings

In Mexico, *tamales d'elotes* made from fresh young corn ears are especially prized.
Cut and scrape the kernels from:

6 ears sweet corn (about 3 cups)

Reserve the green husks. Puree half the kernels (1½ cups) in a food processor and reserve the rest. Dry-roast in their skins in a heavy skillet over low heat until golden brown but not charred, about 10 minutes:

3 cloves garlic

Let cool, then remove the skins and add the garlic to the processor. Heat in the same skillet:

1 tablespoon vegetable oil

Add and cook until the onion is softened:

1 white onion, finely chopped
2 tablespoons ground dried medium-hot chili peppers
1 teaspoon salt

Add the mixture to the processor and puree. Stir in the reserved corn kernels and set aside.
Preheat the oven to 350°F. Line two 9 x 5-inch loaf pans with some of the corn husks.
Mix together to make a smooth dough:

1½ cups masa harina
1 cup hot water

Let cool. Beat with an electric mixer until fluffy:

8 tablespoons (1 stick) butter, softened
2 tablespoons lard or solid vegetable shortening

Beat in alternately the tamale dough and the corn puree, and continue to beat until light and spongy. Add:

1 teaspoon baking powder

Beat until well mixed. Spread half the dough over the husks in the pan. Sprinkle over the dough, dividing evenly:

1 cup grated Muenster or Monterey Jack cheese

Lay over the cheese:

1½ cups diced roasted, 402, poblano peppers
3 tablespoons chopped fresh cilantro

Cover the peppers with the remaining dough, then cover the dough with a layer of corn husks. Cover and seal the top of each pan tightly with aluminum foil. Bake for 1½ hours. Remove the foil and the top layer of husks and let the loaves cool for 30 minutes to firm up. Unmold each loaf carefully onto a serving platter. Remove the remaining husks and cut the loaves into thick slices.

DEE'S CORN AND TOMATO SALAD

4 servings

We were first served this wonderful expression of summer's tastes by our friend Dee Schmid.
Cut the kernels from:

6 ears sweet white corn, briefly blanched and cooled

Combine in a bowl with:

1 large tomato, diced
½ red onion, diced
1 to 2 tablespoons chopped fresh basil

Barely wet with:

Basic Vinaigrette, 236

Serve chilled or at room temperature within 2 to 3 hours, garnished with:

Fresh basil leaves

CUCUMBERS

These quenching vegetables—about 96 percent water—are cucurbitas, part of a huge family that includes squashes. They may be field or hothouse grown, long and slender or stubby or round, and nearly seedless or filled with seeds. We eat them when they are green and immature. The round lemon cucumber, however, we eat when mature and pale yellow. Pickling cucumbers, by contrast, have thick skins and have been bred to keep their crispness and to absorb liquid especially well. Small gherkins and cornichons are just pickling cucumbers bred to taste good when picked at the baby stage. West Indian gherkins, however, are a different subspecies; sometimes called prickly fruited gherkins, they are olive shaped and covered with soft spines, and they make excellent pickles. Cucumbers' season is summer and early autumn, although they are nearly always in the market. Because slicing cucumbers are very often waxed, you may have to peel the skin. Select only cucumbers that are a rich green and completely sound and firm—no soft spots, bruises, cuts, or withered places. Lemon cucumbers should be about 2 inches in diameter with yellow-green skin. Usually the smallest cucumbers will be the least mature and therefore will have the smallest seeds. Store in perforated plastic vegetable bags in the refrigerator crisper.

To Prepare: If you leave the skin on, an attractive finish for slicing is to run a salad fork down the length of the cucumber all around. Although the seeds are tender and a source of fiber, you may wish to remove them. Halve the cucumber lengthwise and scrape them out with the tip of a spoon. If a sample of the cucumber tastes bitter, cut off the ends and peel it. Sprinkle cider vinegar all over it, then add a pinch of salt and a pinch of sugar. Let stand for up to 30 minutes, then rinse well. Europeans enjoy cooked cucumbers much more often than we do. The texture and flavor of a cooked cucumber is tender and mild. Cook cucumbers as you would zucchini, remembering that the flesh is considerably more watery.

Cucumbers go well with sour cream, yogurt, raw onions, and fresh tomatoes, and they are particularly delicious flavored with lemon, vinegar, soy sauce, dill, chervil, cumin, basil, parsley, tarragon, oregano, mint, lemon grass, garlic, and toasted sesame seeds. Allow ½ medium cucumber per serving.

SAUTÉED CUCUMBERS WITH FRESH HERBS

4 servings

Both the expensive shrink-wrapped "gourmet" cucumbers and ordinary garden varieties work well here if you first salt them to disgorge their considerable liquid. Tender-skinned garden cucumbers need not be peeled. Scoop out the seeds, then cut crosswise into slices about ⅜ inch thick:

3 large cucumbers or 2 English cucumbers, peeled and halved lengthwise

Sprinkle with:

Salt

Let drain in a colander for at least 15 minutes. Rinse briefly with water, then press out the excess liquid. Melt in a large skillet:

1½ tablespoons butter

Add and cook over medium heat until softened, about 3 minutes:

1 shallot, finely diced (optional)

Add the cucumbers and cook until warm, about 1 minute. Add:

2 to 3 tablespoons water or chicken stock

Reduce the heat and cook until tender but firm, about 4 minutes more. Toss with:

2 teaspoons snipped fresh dill, chives, or chopped parsley

Salt and ground white pepper to taste

CREAMED CUCUMBERS WITH FRESH HERBS

Prepare Sautéed Cucumbers with Fresh Herbs, above, omitting the herb and substituting ½ cup heavy cream or crème fraîche for the water or stock. Cook until heated through and the cucumbers are tender but firm, about 5 minutes. Garnish with snipped fresh chives or chopped fresh lemon thyme, dill, chervil, lovage, or tarragon.

EGGPLANT

Eggplants are native to Africa and Asia, and in many parts of those continents, they have come to be regarded as a satisfying substitute for meat. The soft, sweet flesh holds its shape when carefully cooked and is compatible with all sorts of sauces and seasonings. In this country, eggplant once meant the beautiful inky-purple teardrop- and globe-shaped fruits so beloved in the south of France and Italy. Influenced by these cuisines, we acquired the habit of sprinkling the slices with salt before cooking, to draw out excess moisture and bitter juices from the flesh. Traditionally eggplant was fried to brown it—browning enhances its color and deepens its flavor. A great deal of oil is needed in frying, because the flesh soaks up oil at an astonishing rate. Nowadays, many cooks brown eggplant in a veil of oil, and only older eggplants are bitter; avoid these by not buying any whose flesh does not bounce back when lightly pressed. If young eggplants are not available, do salt sliced eggplant, below. Otherwise, today salting is rarely necessary. Asian eggplants, which are easily identifiable by their large, plump zucchini shape, and standard eggplants come in beautiful shades of purple, green, and white. Breeders are giving us smaller and smaller sizes of both types. As a group, Asian eggplants have thinner skin, creamier flesh, and fewer and smaller seeds, and they are more perishable than the standard sort. A third group of eggplants is available in markets with a Thai and Vietnamese clientele. These eggplants may resemble a bunch of green grapes, red fluted tomatoes, cream-colored eggs, or bright green-and-white-striped plums. Small ones can be very seedy and therefore crunchy. Red ones can be exceedingly bitter. Egg shapes may have the tender skin and flesh of Asian eggplants, or be relatively tough and bitter.

Eggplants may be available year-round, but their peak season is midsummer to midautumn. Select eggplants of whatever sort that are heavy for their size, with taut skin, a fresh, green cap and stem, and not a single soft spot, cut, or bruise. In standard and Asian types, the skin should be glossy (Thai eggplants have a matte finish). As a rule, small to medium eggplants are the choicest, being the youngest. Store unwrapped in a cool place or in a perforated plastic bag in the refrigerator crisper. Be careful not to bruise eggplant, for its skin can be fragile. Standard and Asian eggplants can be used interchangeably in recipes. All eggplants are tastiest baked, grilled, sautéed, and braised, and large standard eggplants make good shells for stuffing and baking.

Eggplant goes well with lamb, tomatoes, mushrooms, onions, peppers, cheese, cream sauces, oregano, marjoram, soy sauce, and garlic. Allow about 5 ounces per serving.

To Prepare: Trim stems. Leave the skin on, unless it is thick or unless the flesh will be mashed or pureed. If the skin is tough, peel with a thin, sharp knife. Cut into slices, cubes, or halves. Eggplant discolors when cut with a carbon-steel knife, so use a stainless-steel one and cook in a nonreactive pan.

To Salt: If the eggplant seems old and the flesh is dark, it may need salting to draw out bitterness. Generously sprinkle pieces (cut as called for in the recipe) with coarse salt. Place them in a nonreactive colander and let drain for 30 to 60 minutes. Turn onto a thick towel and gently press out excess moisture. Lightly rub the pieces in the towel to rub off the salt and dry them.

To Brown Eggplant: Brush a cast-iron skillet with a film of oil, and heat until hot but not smoking over medium-high heat. Add cubes and smallish slices of eggplant and toss and turn with a pancake turner until nicely browned. Or brush cut pieces with oil, arrange on an oiled baking sheet, and brown in a 400°F oven until they are the color you wish. Set the sheet on a preheated baking stone if you have one, and stir or turn the pieces once or twice.

To Microwave: For puree, cut several deep slits in the skin of a whole 1-pound eggplant with a knife tip. Place in a baking dish. Cover and cook on high until tender, 6 to 8 minutes, turning it over after 3 minutes. Let stand, covered, for 2 minutes. To microwave ½-inch-thick slices for use in casseroles and other dishes, arrange in a single layer on a paper-towel–lined plate and season as desired. Microwave, uncovered, on high to desired tenderness, about 6 minutes per 8 ounces. Let stand for 2 minutes.

ROASTED WHOLE EGGPLANT

Roasting eggplant produces a puree-tender pulp that can be used for all kinds of dips. You also can grill whole eggplants, allowing them to char for a distinctive smoky flavor. A 1-pound eggplant will yield about 1½ cups pureed pulp.

Preheat the oven to 400°F.

Make several slits with a knife tip in:

1 eggplant

Fill the cuts with:

Garlic slivers

Set in an 8 x 8-inch baking dish. Bake until the eggplant has collapsed, 30 minutes to 1 hour, depending on size. Remove to a colander so that any juices can drain off, then cut in half and scoop out the pulp. Leave it coarse or mash it to a puree. Use this for eggplant dips, such as Baba Ghanoush, 164, or season to taste with:

Extra-virgin olive oil, melted butter, or toasted sesame oil
Chopped fresh herbs such as marjoram or basil
Fresh lemon juice or a vinaigrette
Yogurt
Salt and ground black pepper

BAKED EGGPLANT

4 servings

The small, oblong Italian and Asian varieties of eggplant are a perfect size and shape for this dish, and they do not require prior salting.

Preheat the oven to 375°F.

Halve lengthwise:

4 oblong eggplants (about 6 ounces each)

Score the cut surfaces with a knife without cutting through the skin. Heat in a large skillet until hot:

¼ cup light olive or vegetable oil

Add the eggplants cut side down. Reduce the heat to medium and cook until golden, about 5 minutes. Turn and cook on the second side for several minutes. Remove and arrange cut side up and top to tail in a shallow baking dish. Sprinkle with:

Ground black pepper to taste
3 ounces feta cheese, crumbled

Wipe out the skillet and heat in it:

2 teaspoons light olive or vegetable oil

Add:

4 plum tomatoes, peeled, seeded, and chopped

Cook, stirring, until broken down into a rough sauce, 5 to 10 minutes. Season with:

Salt and ground black pepper to taste

Spoon the tomatoes over the eggplants. Cover and bake until the eggplants are tender, about 35 minutes. Uncover and sprinkle the tops with:

½ teaspoon dried oregano

Bake for 5 minutes more.

ROLLED STUFFED EGGPLANTS

4 servings

A great summer side dish, appetizer, or vegetarian entrée. The rolls can be formed well in advance and refrigerated before baking.

Preheat the oven to 400°F. Lightly oil a 13 x 9-inch baking dish.

Combine in a bowl:

¾ cup shredded provolone or mozzarella cheese
¾ cup ricotta cheese
2 tablespoons grated Parmesan cheese
2 tablespoons chopped fresh marjoram or basil
1 small clove garlic, minced

Cut lengthwise into ¼-inch-thick slices:

1 large eggplant (about 1¼ pounds)

Brush both sides of the slices with:

Olive oil

Cook the eggplant in batches in a skillet until golden, about 5 minutes each side, then remove to a platter. Spread a mound of the cheese mixture at the base of each eggplant slice, then roll it up. Arrange the rolls seam side down in the baking dish. Cover the dish and bake until heated through and the cheese is melted, about 20 minutes. Remove the rolls to warmed plates. Serve surrounded with:

Fresh Tomato Sauce, 305
Fresh basil leaves

EGGPLANT PARMIGIANA

3 to 4 main-dish servings; 6 side-dish servings

Prepare:

1 recipe Fresh Tomato Sauce, 305

Peel and cut into ½-inch-thick rounds:

2 medium eggplants (about 1 pound each)

Salt, 372.

Dredge in:

⅓ cup all-purpose flour

Shake off the excess. Whisk together, then dredge the eggplant in:

2 large eggs
1 tablespoon olive oil

Then dredge in:

1¼ cup fresh breadcrumbs

Arrange the eggplant slices on a rack and let dry for 10 to 30 minutes. Pour into a large skillet and heat until it shimmers:

¼ cup olive oil, or more if needed

Add the eggplant and cook, in batches if necessary, over medium-high heat for 4 to 5 minutes on each side, turning with a spatula. Keep warm in a 200°F oven while you finish cooking the rest. You may have to add more oil to the skillet if you fry the eggplant in 2 batches. Season with:

Salt and ground black pepper to taste

Meanwhile, position a rack in the upper third of the oven. Preheat the oven to 425°F.

Coat a 17 x 11-inch rimmed baking sheet with half of the tomato sauce.

Arrange the fried eggplant slices in a single layer or slightly overlapping, if necessary, on the baking sheet and top with the remaining tomato sauce and:

2 teaspoons dried oregano
¼ teaspoon ground black pepper

Combine and sprinkle over the eggplant:

1½ cups shredded whole-milk mozzarella cheese
⅔ cup grated Parmesan cheese

Sprinkle over the top:

2 teaspoons chopped fresh parsley

Bake until the cheese is melted and bubbly, about 10 minutes. Serve at once.

CAPONATA (EGGPLANT RELISH)

About 4 cups

A Sicilian condiment, good on its own or served as a side dish.

Peel and cut into ½-inch cubes:

1 medium eggplant

Salt, 372.

Heat in a large, heavy skillet over medium heat until hot but not smoking:

2 tablespoons olive oil

Add:

1 cup finely chopped celery

Cook, stirring often, until softened, about 4 minutes. Add:

1 medium onion, finely chopped
1 clove garlic, minced

Cook, stirring often, until the onion is soft and lightly colored, about 5 minutes. Remove with a slotted spoon to a bowl. Add to the skillet:

2 tablespoons olive oil

Add the eggplant cubes and cook, stirring constantly, until lightly browned, 5 to 7 minutes. Add the celery mixture along with:

1½ cups canned plum tomatoes, drained and coarsely chopped
12 green olives, pitted and coarsely chopped
1½ tablespoons drained capers
2 tablespoons red wine vinegar
1 tablespoon tomato paste
2 teaspoons sugar
1 teaspoon minced fresh oregano
1 teaspoon salt
Ground black pepper to taste

Bring to a boil, reduce the heat to low, and simmer, uncovered, until thickened, about 15 minutes. Taste and adjust the seasonings with additional salt, pepper, and vinegar if needed. Remove to a serving bowl and garnish with:

2 tablespoons minced fresh parsley

Serve at room temperature with:

Toasted sliced crusty bread

RATATOUILLE

4 to 6 servings

This Provençal vegetable mélange can be served chilled with a splash of lemon or herb vinegar. Or serve it warm as an accompaniment to lamb or chicken or as a vegetarian entrée with saffron rice. It tastes even better the second day.

Sauté in a large skillet or Dutch oven over high heat until the vegetables are golden and just tender, 10 to 12 minutes:

¼ cup olive oil
1 medium eggplant (about 1 pound), peeled and cut into 1-inch cubes
1 pound zucchini, cut into 1-inch cubes

Remove the vegetables and reduce the heat to medium-high. In the same pan, cook until the onions are slightly softened:

2 tablespoons olive oil
1½ cups sliced onions

Add and cook, stirring occasionally, until the vegetables are just tender but not browned, 8 to 12 minutes:

2 large red bell peppers, cut into 1-inch squares
3 cloves garlic, chopped

Season with:

Salt and ground black pepper to taste

Add:

1½ cups chopped seeded peeled fresh tomatoes
2 to 3 sprigs fresh thyme
1 bay leaf

Reduce the heat to low, cover, and cook for 5 minutes. Add the eggplant and zucchini and cook until everything is tender, about 20 minutes more. Taste and adjust the seasonings. Stir in:

¼ cup chopped fresh basil

GRILLED RATATOUILLE SALAD

6 servings

Prepare a medium-hot charcoal fire.
Combine in a bowl:

2 to 4 tablespoons olive oil
2 to 3 tablespoons red wine vinegar, to taste

When the coals are covered with gray ash, coat with the oil mixture:

Twelve ½-inch-thick eggplant slices
2 fennel bulbs, quartered lengthwise
2 medium zucchini, cut lengthwise into thick slices
4 plum tomatoes
3 slender leeks (white part only), split up to the root ends and washed thoroughly
3 red, orange, or yellow bell peppers, or a combination
½ head garlic, unpeeled

Grill the vegetables, turning as needed, until the tomatoes and peppers are charred on the outside and the other vegetables are tender, about 5 minutes for the zucchini, up to 20 minutes for the garlic. Remove from the grill and let cool slightly. Peel, seed, and dice the tomatoes and bell peppers. Dice the fennel and zucchini into ½-inch pieces. Trim the root ends from the leeks and slice. Squeeze the garlic cloves from their skins and mash. Combine the vegetables, except the eggplant slices, in a bowl. Just before serving, stir in:

3 tablespoons minced fresh basil
1 tablespoon extra-virgin olive oil
Pinch of grated orange zest
Salt and ground black pepper to taste

Arrange the eggplant slices on a platter, top with the ratatouille, and serve at room temperature.

ENDIVE, ESCAROLE, AND RADICCHIO

These are all chicories and have in common firm leaves and a refreshing touch of bitterness. See also Greens, 202, for they are usually eaten raw. Cooking tames the bitterness slightly and softens the leaves, yielding a perfect counterpoint to the richness of meats. All can be torn into pieces or sliced into ribbons and sautéed like chard, 364. Because Belgian endive and radicchio have compact heads, they also can be baked, roasted, or quickly grilled. Radicchio brings gorgeous red color to the plate. Store in perforated plastic vegetable bags in the refrigerator crisper. Good flavor combinations for these bitter greens are with spicy cheeses, salty meats like ham and bacon, piquant flavors like capers and olives, and hard-boiled eggs. Allow about 8 ounces per serving.

BELGIAN ENDIVE AU GRATIN *4 servings*

Many people are surprised that Belgian endive can be cooked as a vegetable—and how good it tastes. It is an excellent accompaniment to grilled fish or meats.

Position a rack in the center of the oven and preheat the oven to 325°F. Lightly butter an 8 x 8-inch baking dish. Place half of each in a layer in the baking dish:

8 medium Belgian endives, rinsed, trimmed of any bruised outer leaves, and halved lengthwise
3 tablespoons unsalted butter, cut into pieces
2 tablespoons fresh lemon juice

Repeat to make a second layer. Pour over the top:

¼ cup boiling chicken stock or water

Cover and bake for 45 minutes. Uncover and sprinkle over the top:

½ cup fresh breadcrumbs
2 tablespoons grated Parmesan cheese

Increase the oven temperature to 375°F and bake until the endives are browned, about 20 minutes more.

BRAISED RADICCHIO *4 to 6 servings*

Braised radicchio can be finely chopped and tossed with fresh pasta.

Cook in a large skillet over medium heat for 3 minutes:

1 tablespoon extra-virgin olive oil
2 ounces lean pancetta, chopped

Increase the heat to high and add:

1 pound radicchio, any wilted leaves trimmed, cut into wedges (about 6 per head)
1 medium onion, finely chopped
½ small carrot, finely chopped

Cook, turning often, until the radicchio is wilted and nicely browned on all sides. Add:

½ cup dry white wine

Simmer over medium heat until evaporated, turning the radicchio once or twice. Pour in:

½ to ⅔ cup chicken stock
2 tablespoons heavy cream

Simmer for about 3 minutes, scraping up any browned bits in the pan. Season with:

Salt and ground black pepper to taste

ROASTED RADICCHIO *4 servings*

Preheat the oven to 425°F. Lightly brush a 13 x 9-inch baking dish with olive oil.

Cut into wedges 2 to 3 inches wide at the center:

2 medium heads radicchio

Brush the wedges generously with:

Olive oil

Season with:

Salt and ground black pepper to taste

Place the wedges in a single layer in the baking dish and bake for 10 minutes. Using tongs, turn them and bake until tender, 10 to 15 minutes more. Check for doneness by piercing them with a paring knife—it should just go through without too much resistance.

Serve with:

Balsamic vinegar, fresh lemon juice, or Aïoli, 74

Fennel bulb

FENNEL

A bulb of fennel looks like a bunch of celery with a wide, round base. The individual stalks, which are beautifully plaited, are broad and thin, while the tops are round and fleshy. Fennel leaves are ferny, and the flavor of the whole plant is like licorice. (Some markets label it anise, which it is not.) Fennel is a rare cool-weather vegetable—it is harvested from midautumn through midspring. Select sparkling white bulbs with crisp, bright greens—no cuts, dark patches, or bruises. The rounder bulbs seem to be more tender than those that are really flat. Store in a perforated plastic vegetable bag in the refrigerator crisper.

To Prepare: To separate the stalks, cut off the base

where they are connected, then pull the stalks apart gently. To cut the bulb into wedges, trim the base no more than necessary, then carefully quarter the bulb lengthwise. If left exposed to the air for very long, the flesh can discolor. Either rub cut parts with a lemon half or place for no longer than 30 minutes in cold water mixed with a splash of vinegar.

Fennel's feathery leaves make a nice garnish or can be chopped and used as an herb. The top round stalks can be added to a stock for seasoning—they are usually too tough to eat. Fennel is delightful raw, dipped in light sauces, and it is a lovely addition to all sorts of salads. It is best roasted, braised, grilled, and sautéed. Or it can be lightly simmered in a seasoned stock.

Fennel is lovely with fish, and it is wonderful with tomatoes, oranges, apples, walnuts, cheeses, lemon, and dill. Allow about ½ bulb per serving.

Note that if you wish to grow fennel, select Florence fennel for the edible bulb; common fennel will give you tasty leaves and, ultimately, fennel seeds, but the stalks are liable to be very tough and stringy.

To Boil: Bring to a boil 16 cups (4 quarts) stock or water and 1½ tablespoons salt in a stockpot. Add 2 to 3 bulbs of prepared fennel and cook until tender when tested with a thin skewer or knife tip; it should still have a hint of crispness. This will take about 4 to 6 minutes for ¼-inch-thick slices, 6 to 8 minutes for ½-inch-thick slices, 10 to 15 minutes for quarters, and 15 to 20 minutes for large whole bulbs.

To Blanch: Use this method when the bulb needs to be softened but will require further cooking, as in Roasted Fennel, below. Follow the boiling method, using whole bulbs only, and cook for 9 to 10 minutes. Drain.

ROASTED FENNEL

4 to 6 servings

Remember to add fennel to the dish when you roast chicken. It adds immeasurably to the flavor of the pan juices, and the juices, in turn, add depth to the fennel.

Preheat the oven to 375°F.

Trim, blanch, above, and drain:

2 medium fennel bulbs

Cut lengthwise into ¼-inch-thick slices. Brush a baking pan with:

1 tablespoon olive oil

Arrange the fennel slices in a single layer in the pan. Brush the tops with:

2 tablespoon olive oil

Roast for about 15 minutes, then turn and roast on the other side until the slices can easily be pierced with a thin skewer or knife tip and are lightly browned, 15 to 20 minutes more. Season with:

Salt and ground white pepper to taste

Serve hot or at room temperature, sprinkled with:

Lemon juice or finely shredded Parmesan cheese

FENNEL À LA GRECQUE

4 to 6 servings or more

Serve cold as part of an antipasto plate or hot with fish or poultry.

Combine in a large nonreactive pan, bring to a boil, cover, and simmer for 10 minutes:

1½ cups water
½ cup dry white wine or vermouth
1 small onion, minced
3 cloves garlic, minced
3 tablespoons extra-virgin olive oil
Juice of 1 lemon (about 3 tablespoons)
1 teaspoon white wine vinegar
1 teaspoon salt
1 teaspoon coriander seeds
½ teaspoon fennel seeds, lightly crushed
½ teaspoon peppercorns
1 sprig fresh thyme
1 bay leaf

Add:

3 small fennel bulbs, trimmed and quartered but still attached at the base

If there is not enough liquid, add water to cover. Simmer, uncovered, until the fennel is tender when pierced with a knife, 15 to 20 minutes. Let cool in the liquid. To serve, remove the fennel with a slotted spoon to a serving dish and sprinkle with:

Chopped fennel greens
1 teaspoon minced fresh cilantro (optional)

Serve the quarters whole or thinly slice them.

GRILLED FENNEL AND TOMATOES WITH BLACK OLIVES AND BASIL

4 servings

Prepare a medium-hot charcoal fire.

Rub:

2 fennel bulbs, trimmed and cut lengthwise into ½-inch-thick wedges
4 plum tomatoes, halved

with:

¼ cup olive oil
Salt and ground black pepper to taste

Place on the grill and cook until the fennel is slightly soft and the tomatoes are nicely browned, 3 to 4 minutes each side. Remove from the grill and place in a large bowl along with:

½ cup coarsely chopped pitted imported black olives
⅓ cup coarsely chopped fresh basil
¼ cup extra-virgin olive oil

Juice of 1 lemon

Salt and ground black pepper to taste

Toss lightly and serve at once.

GRATIN OF FENNEL AND ZUCCHINI

4 to 6 servings

Combine in a large skillet:

1 tablespoon olive oil

3 to 4 medium fennel bulbs (about 2 pounds), trimmed and finely chopped

1 large onion, finely chopped

Season with:

Salt and ground black pepper to taste

Cook, uncovered, over very low heat for 1 hour, stirring often.

In another large skillet, heat over high heat:

1 tablespoon olive oil

Add:

2 medium zucchini (about 1 pound), thinly sliced

Sauté just until cooked through, 3 to 4 minutes. Remove the zucchini and drain. In the skillet in which you cooked the zucchini, heat:

1 tablespoon olive oil

Add:

2 pounds fresh tomatoes, peeled, seeded, and finely chopped

Cook, stirring often, over medium-high heat until the pieces cook down and the sauce is quite thick, about 15 minutes. Season with:

Salt and ground black pepper to taste

Preheat the broiler.

Spoon the fennel mixture into a 12-inch oval gratin dish and decoratively arrange the zucchini on top of the fennel. Season lightly with:

Salt and ground black pepper to taste

Broil for 2 to 3 minutes. Remove from oven and mound the tomato sauce in the center of the gratin.

FIDDLEHEAD FERNS

The new shoots of the ostrich fern, fiddleheads have a flavor reminiscent of asparagus and artichoke—some say with a touch of green beans. If you are lucky enough to live in a part of the country where these come to market in spring, choose those that are bright green and tightly coiled, and use them the same day.

To Prepare: Trim the "tail" to the same thickness as the coil. Immerse the ferns in cold water and swirl gently to clear and rub away any fuzzy brown covering, then rinse well.

To Boil and Steam: Cook as for asparagus, 342, just until tender when pierced with a thin skewer, 10 to 15 minutes. Serve (on toast, if desired) with melted butter and lemon juice. Caution: Some people are allergic to ferns. And do not pick fiddleheads in the wild, since only the ostrich fern is considered completely safe for eating.

GARLIC AND ELEPHANT GARLIC

Fresh crops of garlic come to market from California in summer and from Mexico in spring, but this member of the Onion (and thus of the Lily) family is available all year. Choose plump, firm heads of cloves with tight, papery skins that may be white, purplish, or tinged with red. Store away from light at room temperature. Avoid using cloves with brown spots or green sprouts—they are past their prime. The bunches of green garlic you may find at the farmers' market are garlic at the immature stage—just as scallions are the immature stage of cooking onions. The flavor of the immature bulbs and tender green leaves is exquisite. Prepare and store it as you would scallions, but use as you would garlic.

Elephant garlic is not true garlic but a form of leek. Its white- or purple-skinned cloves are the size of brazil nuts, and their flavor is mild enough not to require cooking. Peel the cloves as you would an onion and use as you would garlic.

To Peel: To loosen the skin from a true garlic clove, lay the clove on a board and press down gently but firmly with the side of a large, heavy knife. The skin will burst and is easily pulled off. Or use a tubular garlic peeler, available in kitchen supply stores; simply put a clove or two in the tube and roll on a hard surface. The skin comes right off and often stays behind in the peeler.

To Mince: Slice a peeled clove lengthwise, cut through once or twice horizontally, then chop crosswise into very fine pieces.

To Mash to a Paste: Hold the blade almost flat against the minced pieces and crush them while pulling the knife back and forth through the pulp until it becomes as smooth as you can make it. Although a garlic press is wasteful—some of the clove remains in it—it must be used when raw garlic is part of a very smooth mixture and even mincing and mashing is not fine enough.

To Press: Crush the garlic clove through a garlic press.

To Cook: Garlic becomes milder when cooked. Blanch unpeeled cloves in a small pot of boiling water until tender; peel and continue with the recipe. When sautéing, beware of burning garlic, which will make it strong and acrid. Whole heads of garlic, roasted with all but their outermost papery skin intact, turn soft and sweet enough to be spread on bread. You also can squeeze the roasted garlic cloves from their skins and spread over grilled or roasted meats for delicious seasoning, or use them in salad dressings and pasta sauces.

We often take a tip from Chinese and Indian cuisines by heating oil or butter with whole or peeled cloves of garlic, then scooping them out the minute they start to change color; this delicately flavors the oil and butter. The French and Italians often just rub the salad bowl with garlic, then remove it before adding the greens.

Garlic has great freshness when frozen as a paste, and cloves dry very well. When used with a light hand, garlic can enhance nearly every savory food.

ROASTED WHOLE GARLIC HEADS

4 to 6 servings

To eat this as a first course, squeeze the pulp from each clove and spread on slices of buttered, toasted French bread. Serve with assorted olives and fresh goat cheese, if desired.

Preheat the oven to 325°F.

To expose the cloves, cut the top third from:

4 large heads garlic

Place in an 8 x 8-inch baking dish and add:

Enough chicken stock or water to come one-third up the sides of the heads

Drizzle over the heads:

2 tablespoons olive oil or chicken stock

Place on top of each head:

1 sprig fresh thyme (optional)

Cover with aluminum foil and bake until the garlic is soft and tender, about 1 hour. Serve hot or at room temperature.

JERUSALEM ARTICHOKES, OR SUNCHOKES

These knobby little tubers taste something like artichoke hearts, although they are not artichokes at all; when raw, they are as crisp as jícama and water chestnuts. Their season is late fall through midspring. Select the smoothest tubers (some varieties are scarcely knobby at all), with tight-fitting skins of uniform color, firm and free of discoloration or mold. Store in perforated plastic vegetable bags in the refrigerator crisper. Jerusalem artichokes are delicious raw in salads or on a raw vegetable tray. They are also good steamed, stir-fried, sautéed, braised, and roasted. Be vigilant when cooking them, because they can turn to mush in an instant.

To Prepare: Whenever possible, leave the skin on, since most of the nutrients lie just beneath it. The flesh of Jerusalem artichokes discolors quickly. Use a stainless-steel knife and toss pieces with an acidic dressing immediately if you plan to serve them in salad, or keep in acidulated water (1 tablespoon vinegar mixed with 4 cups cold water) for up to 30 minutes before cooking.

To Cook: Do not cook the tubers in aluminum or iron, as these metals also discolor their flesh.

With their neutral flavor, Jerusalem artichokes are compatible with most flavors, in the manner of potatoes. They are especially good with lemon and tarragon but can also be glazed like carrots, 359. Allow about 4 ounces per serving.

GOLDEN PAN-FRIED JERUSALEM ARTICHOKES

4 servings

Heat in a medium skillet until hot:

1/8 to 1/4 inch sunflower or olive oil

Add:

1 pound Jerusalem artichokes, scrubbed and cut into 1/4-inch-thick rounds

Cook, shaking the pan occasionally, over medium heat until golden, 8 to 10 minutes. Drain on paper towels, then transfer to a serving dish and toss with:

Salt and ground black pepper to taste

Minced fresh parsley, dill, or tarragon

Serve with:

Lemon wedges

ROASTED JERUSALEM ARTICHOKES

4 servings

Preheat the oven to 425°F.

Place in a 13 x 9-inch baking dish large enough to hold them in a single layer:

1 pound Jerusalem artichokes, scrubbed, peeled if desired, and cut into 1 1/2-inch cubes

Toss with:

2 tablespoons olive or vegetable oil

1/4 teaspoon salt

1/8 teaspoon ground black pepper, or to taste

Add:

A few sprigs fresh thyme or rosemary

2 bay leaves

Bake, stirring occasionally, until tender when pierced with a knife and quite brown, about 40 minutes.

JÍCAMA

The uninspiring appearance of a jícama—like a rough, brown-skinned turnip—belies its sweet, water-crisp, white flesh. Because its flesh holds its color and texture, jícama is a favorite for the raw vegetable tray and salad bowl. It is best quickly cooked—coin-shaped pieces of jícama make a fine substitute for water chestnuts in stir-fries. Jícamas are shipped from Mexico or warm parts of this country all year. Select small to medium tubers that are uniformly hard, heavy for their size, with no sign of shriveling or drying. Store unpeeled and unwrapped in the refrigerator crisper.

To Prepare: Before serving, scrub well, then use a sharp stainless-steel paring knife to peel—the thin skin pulls right off. Next, remove the thin, fibrous layer beneath. Cut into slices, wedges, cubes, or matchsticks.

Jícama's mild sweetness needs the contrast of lime, lemon, or orange juice. It also has an affinity with ground red pepper or hot pepper sauce. Allow about 4 ounces per serving.

KALE

Kale deserves to be appreciated as much as spinach. Its crisp, curled, crinkly, or deeply cut leaves (in dark green, blue-green, or purple-red) have a rich but delicate cabbage taste and hold their texture in cooking. Select crisp, moist bunches with no torn or yellowing leaves. Store in perforated plastic vegetable bags in the refrigerator crisper.

Kale has the same affinities as cabbage, 354. Allow about 8 ounces per serving.

To Prepare: Rinse in lukewarm water, then strip the greens from the stems and discard the stems. Stack the greens, roll up, and slice into ribbons. Thin, tender ribbons can go in salads.

To Boil: Follow the method for mustard greens, 388, and cook prepared leaves until tender but not mushy, 6 to 8 minutes for thin leaves, 18 to 25 minutes for densely curled leaves. Baby leaves will cook very quickly. Begin testing for doneness early—do not overcook. Drain.

To Braise: Follow the method for mustard greens, 388, and cook prepared leaves until tender but not mushy. The timing will depend upon the thickness of the leaves, from 7 to 8 minutes for thin leaves to 20 to 25 minutes for densely curled leaves. Baby greens will cook very quickly. Drain.

To Microwave: Microwave kale leaves like cabbage, 354.

KALE WITH BACON

2 to 4 servings

If desired, omit the bacon and use 2 tablespoons olive oil.

Strip the leaves from the stems, discard the stems, wash well, and coarsely chop:

1 large bunch kale (about 1 pound)

Cook in a large skillet until crisp, then remove to paper towels to drain:

1 or 2 slices bacon, diced

Pour off all but 1 tablespoon of the drippings, then add to the skillet:

1 tablespoon olive oil
1 small onion, finely chopped
1 clove garlic, chopped

Cook over medium heat until the onions are golden brown, then add as much kale as will fit in the skillet and sprinkle with:

Salt

When the kale cooks down, add the rest. Cover and cook over medium heat until the kale is tender, 15 to 20 minutes. Season with:

Salt and ground black pepper to taste

Toss with the reserved bacon along with:

1 tablespoon red wine vinegar

KALE AND POTATO GRATIN

6 servings

Preheat the oven to 350°F. Butter a 2-quart gratin dish. Have ready:

4 medium Yukon gold or all-purpose potatoes (about 1¼ pounds), peeled and cut into ⅛-inch-thick rounds
2 small onions, cut into ⅛-inch-thick slices

Steam until almost tender, 8 to 10 minutes:

1 large bunch (about 1 pound) kale, stemmed and washed

Drain and let stand until cool enough to handle. Press out the excess water and coarsely chop. In the gratin dish, build up alternating layers of potatoes, onions, and kale, beginning and ending with the potatoes. Dot each onion layer with:

1 tablespoon butter, cut into pieces
½ teaspoon minced fresh tarragon
¼ teaspoon salt
⅛ teaspoon ground black pepper

Pour over the layers:

1½ cups milk or half-and-half

Cover and bake until the potatoes are tender and almost all the liquid is absorbed, 30 to 45 minutes. Broil, if desired, to brown the top. Serve.

KOHLRABI

Kohlrabis look like vegetables at an early stage of evolution—hard green or magenta turnips, with cabbagey leaves on long stems sprouting out all over them. The word *kohlrabi* means "cabbage turnip" in German, and kohlrabis are related to cabbage. However, kohlrabi is neither a root nor a leafy vegetable but a swollen stem. They grow perched on top of the ground, and their flavor is not earthy but that of a delicate, sweet, nut-flavored cabbage. And kohlrabi is wonderfully crisp.

Young leaves are also sweet but have a slightly stronger taste of cabbage. Kohlrabi's season is summer through autumn. Select them plum sized or smaller, with leaves attached if possible, and firm, unblemished, with glowing colors. Snip off the stalks and store with the bulbs in perforated plastic vegetable bags in the refrigerator crisper.

The quality of frozen kohlrabi is acceptable. Kohlrabi has special affinities for tomatoes, cream, cheese, chives, parsley, chervil, and dill. Allow ½ small kohlrabi bulb per serving.

To Prepare: Tender bulbs do not need peeling. Shreds are wonderful in salad, as are kohlrabi sticks (cut like carrot sticks) on the raw vegetable tray. Just scrub and trim the bulb evenly. The stalks are nippy, like radishes, and also can be chopped for salads.

To Boil: For 1 pound prepared kohlrabi, bring 8 cups water and 2 teaspoons salt to a rolling boil in a large saucepan. Add the kohlrabi, return to a boil, and cook until tender but still crisp, 7 to 9 minutes for matchsticks, 9 to 10 minutes for ¼-inch-thick slices.

To Steam: Place the prepared kohlrabi in a steamer basket over 1 to 2 inches boiling water. Cover and cook until tender but still crisp, 9 to 11 minutes for matchsticks, 12 to 14 minutes for ¼-inch-thick slices. If more than 1 layer, stir occasionally and allow a few extra minutes.

To Cook Leaves: If you are lucky enough to find kohlrabi with the leaves still attached, they can be cooked like mustard greens, 388. Cut the leaves into ribbons and cook until tender, 10 to 20 minutes, depending on age and thickness. Drain.

To Microwave: Spread 1 pound kohlrabi slices in a 2-quart baking dish. Add ¼ cup stock or lightly salted water. Cover and cook on high until tender but still crisp or completely tender, 6 to 8 minutes, stirring after 3 minutes. Let stand, covered, for 2 minutes.

KOHLRABI WITH PARMESAN CHEESE

4 servings

A delicate vegetable deliciously finished.

Peel and cut into matchsticks:

2 small kohlrabi bulbs

Cook in boiling water, above, or in the microwave oven, above, until tender. Drain, then toss with:

1 to 2 tablespoons butter

Immediately sprinkle with:

4 ounces Parmesan cheese, grated

Ground black pepper to taste

Serve at once.

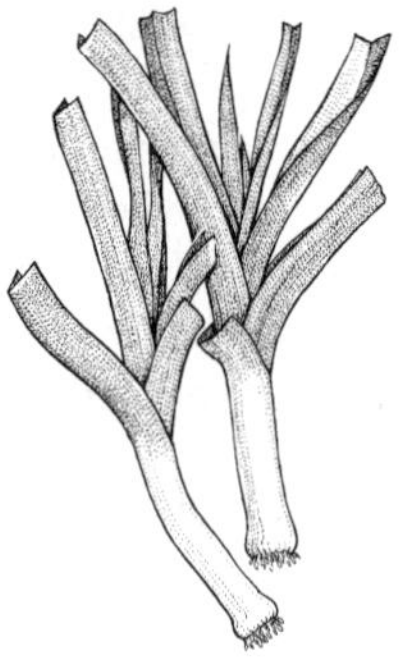

Leeks

LEEKS

Looking like enormous scallions with flat rather than hollow leaves, leeks are an ancient member of the Onion family, milder and sweeter than any others in the clan. Leeks are in season from fall to spring, but they are in the market most of the year. When leeks start to send up flowers in spring, their centers become solid and inedible, but the outside leaves are still useful. When buying a bunch, try to choose leeks all the same size, preferably small. Be sure the leaves are bright, crisp, and not torn and the white parts are not discolored. Store in perforated plastic vegetable bags in the refrigerator crisper.

Wild leeks, also called ramps, are harvested in spring. They can be cooked like cultivated leeks but smell much stronger until the heat mellows them. Store wild leeks tightly wrapped in plastic to contain their aroma.

Leeks are compatible with many foods, but they taste especially good with lemon, butter, cheese, cream, fennel, potatoes, garlic, chicken, ham, dill, nutmeg, parsley, and chives. Allow 10 to 12 ounces untrimmed leeks per serving.

To Julienne or Slice: Trim off the root and the dark green leaves; if the pale green part is tender, leave about 1 inch attached to the white part. For julienne, cut the leek lengthwise in half, then cut the halves into 2-inch lengths and slice lengthwise for julienne. For slices, cut the halves crosswise into half slices.

To Wash: The layers of a leek can contain dirt, since the white stalks are "blanched," buried in earth to keep them pale. Swish julienned or sliced leeks in a large bowl of cool water. Let them stand a few minutes while the dirt falls to the bottom, then lift them out with a strainer. Repeat if there is a lot of dirt left in the bowl. If you are using leeks that are simply halved lengthwise, soak them in water for 15 minutes to loosen the dirt, gently swish them around, and rinse under cool water, fanning the leaves open as you rinse if they are especially dirty.

Slender leeks are especially nice sliced into salads, grilled and served hot, or steamed and served at room temperature. Thicker leeks are wonderful braised or in soups and stews. Be careful not to overcook leeks, as the layers are very thin.

To Steam: Leeks of any thickness can be steamed whole, trimmed to the white bulb, or halved, sliced, or julienned. Arrange prepared pieces in a steamer basket in a single layer over 1 to 2 inches boiling water. Steam, covered, until a thin skewer easily pierces the thickest part. Depending on thickness and age, steaming times will be 10 to 25 minutes for whole leeks, 6 to 8 minutes for halves, and 3 to 5 minutes for slices or whole baby leeks. Begin testing for doneness early, as they overcook quickly.

To Microwave: Place 1 pound halved leeks in a single layer in a 2-quart baking dish with the water that clings to them from rinsing. Cover and cook on high until softened, 3 to 4 minutes, turning the leeks over after about 1½ minutes. Let stand, covered, for 2 minutes.

BRAISED LEEKS
4 servings

Once cooked, these leeks can be served with simple finishing touches of olive oil or butter and chopped herbs, turned into a succulent gratin, grilled, or served cold with a mustard or shallot vinaigrette. Vegetarians can simmer the leeks in water enhanced with a bouquet garni and vegetables. Whether you use water or stock, the liquid that remains is excellent to use in risottos and soups.

Bring to a simmer in a medium skillet:

3 cups chicken stock, or 3 cups water with 2 bay leaves, 2 sprigs fresh thyme, 1 celery stalk, thinly sliced, 1 carrot, thinly sliced, and 1 teaspoon salt

Trim the ends and dark green leaves, halve lengthwise, and wash:

4 medium to large leeks

Cut the leeks to fit the pan. Add the leeks to the simmering stock, cover, and simmer until tender when the cut sides are pierced with a knife, about 15 minutes. Press the leeks down into the liquid several times as they cook so that they do not dry out. When done, carefully remove each leek, draining off the excess stock. Place them cut side up on a platter. Drizzle or sprinkle over the top:

Basic Vinaigrette, 236, butter, extra-virgin olive oil, or herb-flavored olive oil

Chopped fresh chervil, chives, tarragon, and/or parsley

Salt and ground black pepper to taste

SLOW-ROASTED LEEKS
4 to 6 servings

Here are leeks gently—sweetly—roasted.

Preheat the oven to 300°F.

Trim the dark green leaves from:

12 slender leeks (about 1 inch thick)

Halve lengthwise, trimming off the rootlets but leaving the base intact so most of the layers will hold together; wash thoroughly. Bring to a boil in a large skillet:

1½ cups meat, chicken, or vegetable stock

Add the leeks and return to a boil. Cover and cook for 2 minutes, occasionally shaking the skillet. Drain (save the stock for soup). Brush a 13 x 9-inch baking dish with:

1 tablespoon butter, melted

Lay in the leeks, cut sides up. Brush the tops with:

5 tablespoons butter, melted

Sprinkle with:

Salt and ground white pepper to taste

Roast, uncovered, until the leeks are easily pierced with a thin skewer, 40 to 60 minutes, brushing occasionally with the buttery juices. Serve hot as a first course or side dish, sprinkled with the pan juices blended with:

Lemon juice to taste

Garnish with:

Minced fresh parsley, chervil, or tarragon

GRILLED LEEKS
4 servings

If you have very thin leeks, leave them whole but split them lengthwise two-thirds of the way down to wash them.

Prepare a medium-hot charcoal fire or preheat the broiler.

Trim the dark green leaves, halve lengthwise, thoroughly wash, and pat dry:

4 medium leeks (white part only)

Place cut sides up on a platter and brush with:

Olive oil

Make sure the oil gets into the insides of the leaves. Season with:

Salt and ground black pepper to taste

Grill the leeks, cut side facing the heat, until lightly browned, about 7 minutes. Turn them over once and grill for a few minutes more. The exact time will depend on the heat of the fire—just take care not to burn them. When done, remove to a platter and season with any one of the following:

Extra-virgin olive oil and finely minced fresh parsley or tarragon

Mustard Butter, 77

Basic Vinaigrette or French Dressing, 236

Green Goddess Dressing, 240

CREAMY LEEKS

4 servings

Melt in a large skillet over medium-low heat:

2½ tablespoons butter

Add and cook for 2 to 3 minutes without letting them brown:

4 cups julienned leeks (about 12 ounces or 3 large leeks), 380

Add:

1 cup chicken stock, or 1 cup water and ½ teaspoon salt

1 sprig fresh thyme

Cover and simmer until the leeks are tender, about 5 minutes. Uncover, increase the heat to medium-high, and add:

¼ cup dry white wine

Boil until the liquid is reduced by half, 10 to 15 minutes. Stir in:

2 tablespoons heavy cream

½ teaspoon curry powder or 1 pinch of freshly grated or ground nutmeg (optional)

Cook until the cream is absorbed. Season with:

Salt and ground black pepper to taste

If you use curry, serve the leeks garnished with:

Finely snipped fresh chives

If you use nutmeg, serve with:

Chopped fresh parsley or chervil

WARM LEEKS VINAIGRETTE

4 servings

Use thin leeks in this classic French first course. The cooking liquid is turned into a mustard vinaigrette.

Heat in a large skillet over medium-high heat until hot but not smoking:

¼ cup olive oil

Add:

16 slender leeks (about 1 inch thick), trimmed and cleaned thoroughly

Cook, turning, until golden brown, about 10 minutes. Stir in:

1 cup chicken stock

¼ cup dry red wine

Cook, covered, turning occasionally, until the leeks are tender when pierced, about 10 minutes. Transfer to a serving platter. Add to the skillet:

¼ cup chicken stock

2 teaspoons red wine vinegar, or to taste

Cook, stirring, until slightly thickened. Remove the skillet from the heat and stir in:

2 teaspoons minced fresh parsley

1 teaspoon Dijon mustard

Salt and ground black pepper to taste

Pour the vinaigrette over the leeks and let cool. Serve at room temperature, garnished with:

Snipped fresh chives

LETTUCE

Salads are the best showcase for lettuces of all kinds. See Salads, 200, for selection and storage information. If you have an abundance of butterhead lettuce, stir it into a creamed soup or use it in Braised Lettuce, below. Slice romaine lettuce into ribbons to mix and cook with sturdier greens such as dandelions, 204. Cook any kind of lettuce leaves as for Stuffed Cabbage Rolls, 355, and use to wrap whole fish or fillets for steaming. To keep a whole chicken or fish moist during roasting, place a bed of shredded lettuce and a little chicken stock in the bottom of the pan.

BRAISED LETTUCE

6 servings

A highly flavored and unexpected vegetable to serve with roasted meats.

Cook, uncovered, in a large skillet with a lid over low heat for 10 minutes:

1 thick slice bacon (about 2 ounces), finely diced, or 2 tablespoons olive oil

¾ cup diced onions

¾ cup diced carrots

Meanwhile, drop into a large pot of boiling water and cook for 2 minutes:

3 large heads butter lettuce, washed and outer leaves removed

Drain, then cut lengthwise in half. Set the lettuces cut side down over the vegetables and add enough water to come slightly less than halfway up the sides. Season with:

Salt and ground black pepper to taste

Bring to a boil. Reduce the heat, cover, and simmer for 15 minutes. Remove the lettuce with a slotted spoon to a warmed platter. Keep warm. Remove the lid and reduce the liquid over high heat to a syrupy sauce. Pour over the lettuce. Serve immediately.

LOTUS ROOT

The lotus plant is a tropical water lily that grows throughout Asia. Its sensuous, peony-like pink or white flowers, buds, large waxy leaves, and brown seeds can all be eaten. But it is the crisp, fine-grained rhizome (commonly called root) that is cooked in many ways in China and Japan. A plump oblong (5 to 8 inches long and about 2½ inches wide), the rhizome is perforated with air holes—a crosswise slice looks like an ivory carving. Lotus rhizomes are in Asian markets year-round. Select firm, buff-colored pieces without soft spots, blemishes, or bruises. Size has no effect on texture or flavor. Store the roots in a cool, dark place as you would potatoes; they will not keep as long.

To Prepare: The flesh darkens rapidly when exposed to the air, so have a bowl of acidulated water ready (4 cups water mixed with 1 tablespoon vinegar). Pare off the skin, then slice and drop into the water. Cook quickly. For example, stir-fry thin slices until they begin to soften. Sprinkle with sake, soy sauce, and sugar, and stir over medium heat until tender. Season with red pepper flakes and serve with rice. Consult Chinese and Japanese cookbooks for detailed recipes for steaming and braising lotus root and preparing it for salads, soups, and desserts.

MUSHROOMS

Mushrooms lend both elegance and earthiness to a dish. While we are grateful for the abundance of cultivated small button mushrooms, wild mushrooms have considerably more character, and an assortment of them is available in specialty groceries and supermarkets. Choose mushrooms that are heavy for their size, with dry, firm caps and stems—nothing damp or shriveled, no dark or soft spots, and all close to the same size. If the gills are open, the mushrooms are more mature and their flavor will be stronger, and with a wild mushroom, this may be a plus. Open-gilled mushrooms should be used as soon as possible. A trick: When a costly mushroom is needed to flavor a dish, buy one or two, depending on the intensity of its flavor, then fill in with neutral-tasting button mushrooms.

White button or commercial mushrooms are rounded, plump, creamy, and mild. Select only those with closed caps. If they are very small, use them whole.

Porcini, also called cèpes or boletes, look like very large button mushrooms with thick stalks and reddish caps. They are among the tastiest of wild mushrooms, something to enjoy simply in a risotto or sauté of mixed mushrooms. Brush large ones with olive oil and lemon juice and broil or grill as you would meat. Look for fresh porcini in late spring and fall.

Chanterelles, or girolles, resemble a curving trumpet. Their golden or orange-brown caps and slender stems can hint of apricots or be delicately earthy. They have an affinity with cream, whether over toast, pasta, chicken, or polenta. The similarly shaped black mushrooms variously called black trumpets, horns of plenty, or trumpets of death are closely related and similar in taste but have thinner flesh. Both are gathered from summer into winter.

Creminis, or Italian browns, are the same as button mushrooms, only grown outdoors and bigger. They have light brown caps and a naturally more developed flavor.

Enoki are as slender as bean sprouts and, with their tiny dots of caps, look like an ivory sea creature. They are a pretty salad ingredient, adding a faintly sweet taste. They are also lovely barely heated and served in broth. To use, trim off the spongy base and separate the strands.

Morels are small, with dark brown, conical, sponge-like caps. The honeycombed surface that allows them to soak up sauces can also harbor sand. Swish morels around in a bowl of water, being sure to pat them dry thoroughly before using. Morels have a special affinity with tender young vegetables.

Oyster mushrooms can be cultivated or wild. They grow in clusters of small fan-shaped caps with short stems, cream colored to grayish brown. Their texture is smooth, and their flavor can have a touch of the sea.

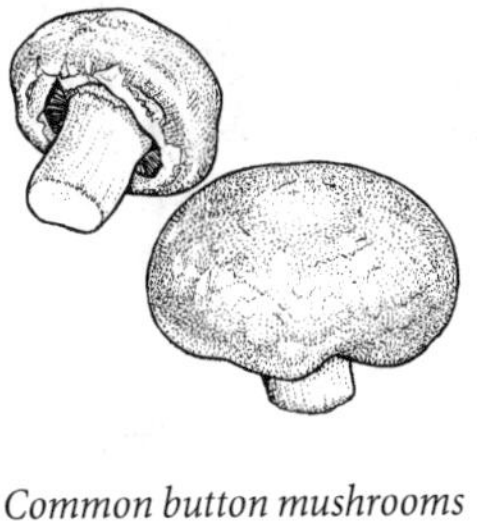

Common button mushrooms

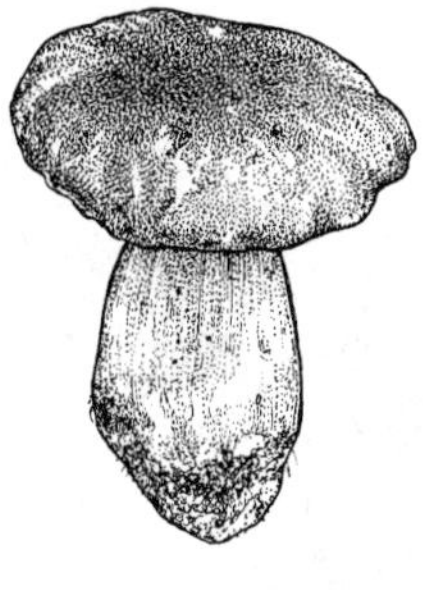

Porcino, also called cèpe or bolete

Chanterelles, also called girolles

Portobellos are cultivated mushrooms, full-blown creminis (above). They are generous in size (up to 6 inches wide), meaty, and robustly flavored (although they have no wild taste). Their open gills and large, flat caps make them naturals for grilling and broiling. They are also useful in sautés.

Shiitakes are umbrella shaped, brown or brown-black. They are cultivated on logs and have a distinctive earthy taste. Save the tough stems to simmer in stock.

Wood or cloud ear mushrooms are the dark, very thin, almost crunchy mushrooms that give so many Chinese dishes a subtly woodsy taste. Unlike other fresh mushrooms, these should look damp. They are available in Asian markets.

Mushrooms go well with cream, lemon, garlic, shallots, onions, cheese, fennel, fish, chicken, veal, peas, dill, chervil, parsley, tarragon, basil, oregano, and capers. Allow 4 to 5 ounces per serving.

Caution! A number of poisonous forms of wild mushrooms, during various stages of their development, resemble edible forms. Take the time to become familiar with the mushrooms you wish to pick—accompany someone you are absolutely sure is an experienced forager until you know your mushrooms as well as he or she does.

To Store: Wrap unwashed mushrooms in a loosely closed paper bag or wrap loosely in damp paper towels. Leave packaged mushrooms in their unopened package. Store on a refrigerator shelf, not in the crisper (too much moisture hastens spoilage).

To Prepare: Clean mushrooms with a soft brush or wipe with a damp cloth. Or if the mushrooms are truly grimy, rinse them quickly under cold running water and pat dry. Never soak mushrooms—their delicate tissues will absorb water. If desired, slice ⅛ inch off the bottom of the stems to refresh them but do not discard the flavorful stems. If only caps are called for in a recipe, cut the stem flush with the cap. Either chop the stems fairly fine, toss them until lightly browned in a little butter, and add them to the dish or use within a day to flavor something else. As a general rule, use intense heat when cooking mushrooms, and cook just enough to lightly brown them and heat them through. The best methods are sautéing, stir-frying (for 3 to 4 minutes), grilling, and broiling.

To Brown: When mushrooms are to be added to a soup or stew, never add them raw. Mushrooms simmered from the raw state always seem to have a raw flavor. Bring out their flavor by browning them first in a little butter or oil, tossing them in a skillet over high heat just until you can smell them. To brown without fat, heat a cast-iron skillet very hot. Add whole small mushrooms, quarters, or large slices and stir over high heat without stopping until the pieces have lightly browned. Remove at once. Be sure to scrape all pan juices into the dish.

To Use Dried Mushrooms: Dried mushrooms provide intensified mushroom flavor in a sauce, soup, or stew. Soak dried mushrooms in lukewarm water to cover until softened, at least 15 minutes, then rinse well and remove the hard stems. To make a stock base for a sauce or stew, simmer dried mushrooms for an hour in stock or water to cover by several inches with a pinch each of salt and sugar. Strain the soaking liquid through a damp coffee filter, paper towel, or cheesecloth to remove sand.

ROASTED PORTOBELLO MUSHROOMS, FINES HERBES

About 4 servings

Brief high-heat roasting draws out just enough moisture to intensify the good flavor of these fine mushrooms. Any large, thick, fleshy caps roast successfully—thin mushrooms can turn leathery. Choose clean caps—water can be absorbed by the tissues, diluting the flavor.

Black trumpets, also called horns of plenty or trumpets of death

Cremini

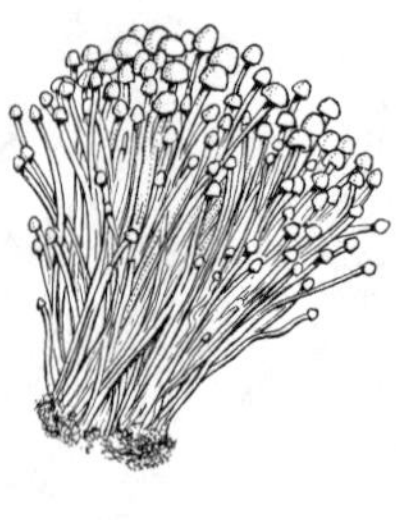

Enoki

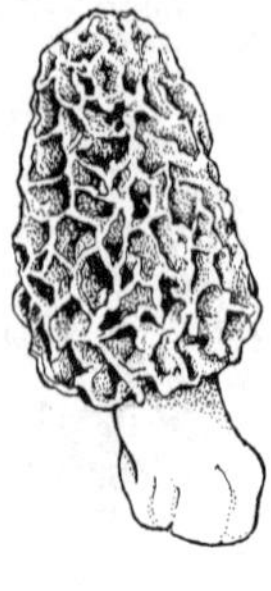

Morel

Position a rack in the center of the oven. Preheat the oven to 500°F.

Gently wipe the tops of:

Four 4-ounce portobello or 1 pound cremini mushrooms

Trim off the stems at the caps (save for another use). Brush the bottom of a rimmed baking sheet and the tops of the caps with:

About 4 tablespoons (½ stick) unsalted butter, melted, or olive oil

Arrange the caps rounded side up in the pan and roast for 6 minutes. Remove from the oven, closing the oven door, and quickly turn the caps over with tongs, rearranging cremini mushrooms in the pan. Sprinkle with:

2 tablespoons melted lard, melted unsalted butter, or olive oil

Salt and ground black pepper to taste

Return to the oven and roast until the caps look evenly roasted, 5 to 6 minutes more. Serve as a first course on small hot plates, rounded side up, drizzled with pan juices (if any) and sprinkled with a portion of the following mixture:

1 tablespoon chopped fresh chives
1 tablespoon chopped fresh chervil
1 tablespoon chopped fresh parsley
1 tablespoon chopped scallions
1 tablespoon chopped fresh tarragon

SAUTÉED MUSHROOMS

2 or 3 servings

Use a large skillet and give the mushrooms plenty of room so that they will brown instead of steam in their own juices. These are great over steak or grilled fish, stirred into 2 cups cooked pasta or rice, or as an omelet filling.

Heat in a very large skillet over high heat:

2½ to 3 tablespoons butter or olive or vegetable oil, or a combination

Add:

1 pound any variety or combination of mushrooms, wiped clean and sliced

Cook, tossing constantly, until the mushrooms begin to color, 5 to 7 minutes. Add:

¼ to ⅓ cup chopped fresh parsley
2 to 3 cloves garlic, chopped

Cook for 1 minute more. Season with:

Salt and ground black pepper to taste

Serve immediately.

BROILED MUSHROOM CAPS

4 small servings

Preheat the broiler.

Carefully remove the stems from:

12 medium mushrooms, wiped clean

Brush with:

Melted butter or olive oil

Season with:

Salt to taste

Broil stem side down for 2½ minutes, then remove and turn them over. Fill each mushroom cap with any one of the following:

Boursin, cream cheese, or fresh goat cheese mixed with chopped garlic and herbs
Snail Butter, 77
Maître d'Hôtel Butter, 77
Shrimp or Lobster Butter, 78
Creamed Spinach, 416

Broil until the filling is hot and bubbling, another 2 minutes. Serve plain or on:

Thinly sliced toast

PORTOBELLO PIZZAS

If the caps you have are small, these are wonderful appetizers—if large, a main course!

Preheat the oven to 350°F. Lightly oil a baking sheet.

Remove the stems from:

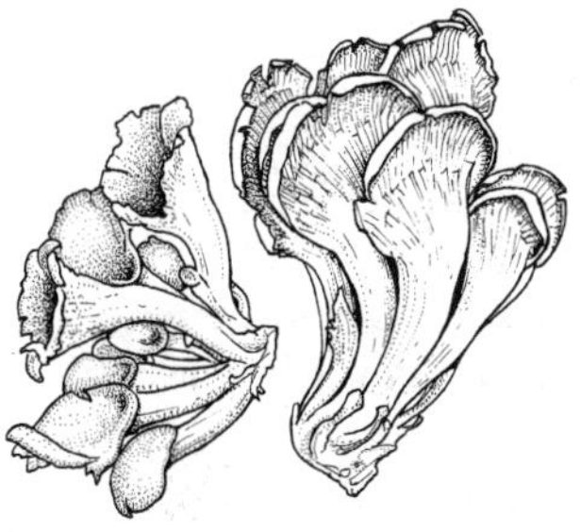

Oyster mushrooms, also called pleurottes or shimeji

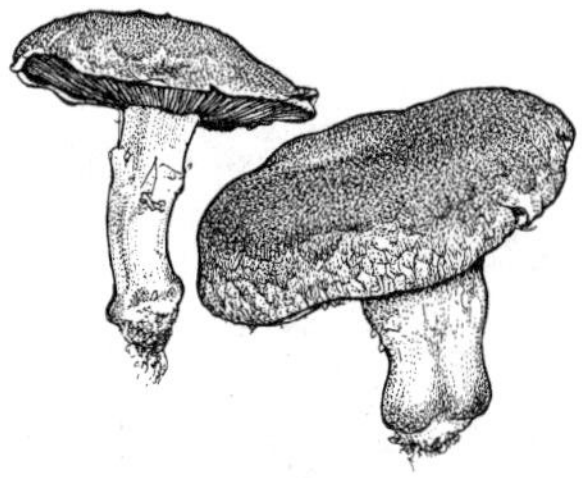

Portobello mushrooms

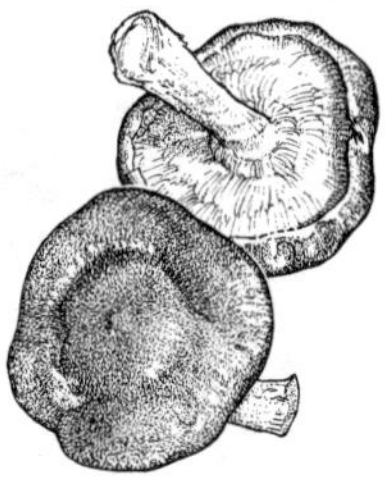

Shiitake mushrooms

Portobello mushrooms

Arrange the mushrooms stem side up on the sheet. Layer the caps with:

Finely chopped garlic
Thinly sliced plum tomatoes
Diced smoked ham or hard salami

Top with:

Grated Parmesan, Romano, or provolone cheese
Freshly ground black pepper
A sprinkling of thyme, oregano, or basil, fresh if possible

Bake for 5 minutes. Then place under the broiler until the cheese is the consistency you like.

BROILED MUSHROOMS, ITALIAN STYLE

4 to 6 servings

Toss together:

1 pound large portobello, cremini, button, or other mushrooms, wiped clean and thickly sliced
2 to 3 tablespoons extra-virgin olive oil
1 large clove garlic, minced
1 tablespoon minced fresh rosemary or 3 tablespoons minced fresh flat-leaf parsley
Ground black pepper to taste

Let stand for 15 to 20 minutes.
Place the broiler rack as close to the heat source as possible and preheat the broiler for 10 minutes.
Spread the mushrooms in a single layer on a broiler pan. Broil until crisp on one side, about 90 seconds; turn and crisp the other side. Serve hot, seasoned with:

Salt to taste

GRILLED MUSHROOMS

6 first-course servings

The best mushrooms for grilling are portobello, shiitake, and oyster mushrooms.
Prepare a medium-hot charcoal fire.
Remove the stems from:

6 large portobello or 12 large shiitake mushrooms, wiped clean

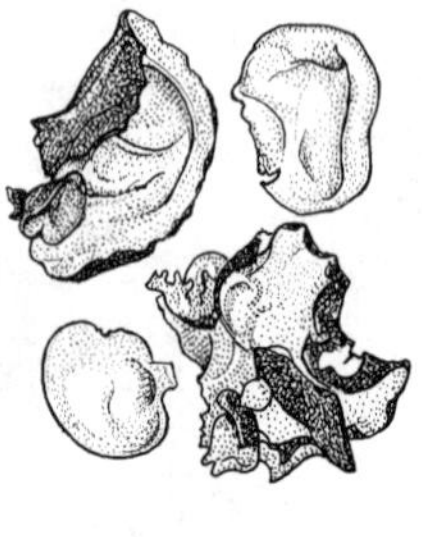

Wood ears, also called cloud ears

Brush both sides with:

Olive oil

Season with:

Salt and ground black pepper to taste

Place the mushrooms stem side up on the grill rack and grill, turning once, until seared and tender, 5 to 8 minutes each side. Place on a large platter and garnish with:

6 sprigs flat-leaf parsley, chopped

Grill to toast:

6 or 12 thick slices Italian bread

Rub with:

2 cloves garlic, halved

Brush lightly with:

Olive oil

Place the toast around the mushroom platter to soak up the mushroom juices, or place 1 large mushroom on each slice of toast.

GRILLED MUSHROOMS WITH GARLIC OR NUT BUTTER

Prepare Grilled Mushrooms, above, omitting the toast and substituting Garlic Butter, 77, or Nut Butter, 77, for the olive oil. Slice and serve as a side dish.

MUSHROOM RAGOUT

4 servings

Serve over soft polenta, rice, garlic-rubbed croutons or popovers. For more intense flavor, soak ½ ounce dried mushrooms, chop, and add with the fresh mushrooms; use the soaking water for part of the liquid.
Heat over medium-high heat in a large saucepan:

1 tablespoon olive oil

Add and cook until golden, about 10 minutes:

1 onion, diced

Remove and set aside. Heat in the same pan over medium heat:

1 tablespoon olive oil

Add and cook until they begin to release their liquid:

1 pound assorted fresh mushrooms, wiped clean and thickly sliced

Add the onions along with:

2 cloves garlic, finely chopped
1 teaspoon chopped fresh rosemary, or scant ½ teaspoon dried
Salt and cracked black peppercorns to taste

Cook until the mushrooms begin to brown, another 3 to 4 minutes. Stir in:

1 tablespoon tomato paste

Increase the heat to high and cook, stirring, for 1 to 2 minutes more. Add:

1½ cups vegetable stock, chicken stock, or water

Reduce the heat and simmer for 10 minutes. Stir in to form a sauce:

2 tablespoons cold butter, cut into pieces
1½ teaspoons balsamic vinegar

Garnish with:

Grated Parmesan cheese (optional)
Chopped fresh parsley

CREAMED MUSHROOMS WITH DRIED PORCINI

4 servings

A very rich side dish or sauce, or an opulent first course when spooned over toast.

Soak in warm water just to cover until softened, about 15 minutes:

1 ounce dried porcini mushrooms

Drain, reserving ¼ cup liquid. Finely chop the mushrooms. Heat in a large skillet:

2 tablespoons butter
2 tablespoons olive oil

Add and cook over medium heat until translucent, about 5 minutes:

½ cup finely diced onions

Add the chopped porcini along with:

1 pound assorted fresh mushrooms, wiped clean and thinly sliced

Increase the heat to medium-high and cook, stirring often, until the mushrooms release and then reabsorb their juices, about 5 minutes. Add the reserved mushroom liquid along with:

½ cup heavy cream or crème fraîche
2 cloves garlic, minced
1½ teaspoons fresh thyme leaves
Salt and ground black pepper to taste

Reduce the heat to medium and simmer until the sauce is slightly thickened. Taste and adjust the seasonings, then add:

2 tablespoons chopped fresh parsley

DUXELLES

About ½ cup

This mushroom flavoring is delicious on toast, in scrambled eggs or omelets, stuffed under the skin of chicken, or folded into mashed potatoes. It is important to squeeze all the moisture out of the chopped mushrooms or they will not brown properly.

Chop very fine or pulse in a food processor until they resemble coarse sand:

8 ounces mushrooms, wiped clean

Squeeze about ¼ cup of the mushrooms at a time in dampened cheesecloth or a thin cotton towel and wring them very hard to extract their bitter juices. The mushrooms will be in a solid lump if you have squeezed hard enough. Heat in a medium skillet until the foam subsides:

1½ tablespoons butter
1 teaspoon vegetable oil

Add and cook briefly over medium heat:

2 tablespoons very finely minced shallots or scallions (white part only)

Add the mushrooms and cook, stirring often, over medium-high heat until they have begun to brown and there is very little liquid, 5 to 6 minutes. Stir in:

1 tablespoon dry sherry or Madeira

Cook until completely evaporated. Add:

¼ cup heavy cream (optional)
Salt and ground black pepper to taste
Pinch of dried thyme or grated or ground nutmeg

Let cool, then refrigerate in a covered container for up to 10 days or freeze for up to 3 months.

BECKER DUXELLES

About 1 cup

An especially luxurious variation, created by Ethan Becker on his return from the Cordon Bleu cooking school in Paris.

Prepare Duxelles, above, using 2 tablespoons butter and 3 tablespoons olive oil. Substitute ½ cup very finely chopped onions for the shallots and cook until translucent. Add 2 minced cloves garlic with the mushrooms. Omit the dry sherry and add instead 2 tablespoons port or dry red wine, ½ teaspoon ground black pepper, and ¼ teaspoon grated lemon zest (optional). Season to taste with salt.

MUSTARD GREENS

This term technically applies to all leafy greens in the Mustard family, but usually it refers to whatever mustard greens happen to have been grown and offered for sale. Their season is January through April, although many may be available other times of the year. Mustards with broad, smooth leaves loosely formed in heads are called broadleaf mustards; they are pungent, whether mustardy or sweet. Coarse, large leaves with pinked edges are common, or leaf, mustards; their flavor is the mildest of the greens. Fringed and curled leaves are called curled mustards, and their flavor is spicy hot. You can add tender leaves to salads or cook them like chard, 364, but it is best to mix them with milder greens for balance. Select them as you do other greens; look for crisp, bright leaves with no yellowing or tears. Store in perforated plastic vegetable bags in the refrigerator crisper.

Mustard greens have the same affinities as collards, 367. Allow about 8 ounces per serving.

To Prepare and Cook: Preparation and cooking methods are the same as for others in the family—collards, 367, kale, 379, and turnip greens, 436. Timing varies, because some leaves are tender and some are tough. See each recipe for specific cooking times.

To Boil: Bring 16 cups (4 quarts) water and 1½ tablespoons salt to a rolling boil in a stockpot. Add 1 to 1½ pounds prepared mustard greens and quickly bring the water back to a boil. Cook, uncovered, until tender but not mushy, 5 to 10 minutes, depending on the age and thickness of the leaves. Baby greens will cook very quickly. Drain.

To Braise: Bring 4 cups water or stock and 1 teaspoon salt to a boil in a medium skillet with lid. Add 1 pound mustard leaves and turn them with a pair of tongs until they wilt down and fit easily in the pan. Cover and cook, stirring occasionally, until the greens are tender but not mushy, 9 to 11 minutes, depending on age and thickness. Baby greens will cook very quickly. Drain.

BRAISED MUSTARD GREENS WITH BACON

4 servings

Wash thoroughly and chop into 1-inch pieces:

2½ pounds mustard greens

In a large pot suitable for cooking the greens, cook until crisp:

6 slices bacon, cut into 1-inch pieces

Add the greens along with:

⅔ cup chopped onions (optional)

Cook, stirring with a wooden spoon, until the greens are coated with fat. Cover the greens with water and season with:

Salt to taste

Bring to a boil. Cover the pot, reduce the heat, and simmer gently until the greens are tender, 1 hour or longer. Stir occasionally and add water if they threaten to scorch. When the greens are done, increase the heat to medium-high and, stirring often, boil off nearly all the cooking liquid. Add:

1 or 2 dashes of cider vinegar or red wine vinegar

Season with:

Salt and ground black pepper to taste
Sugar to taste

Serve very hot.

MUSTARD GREENS WITH CHICKPEAS AND CURRY

4 servings

Serve over rice to turn this side dish into a main course for two.

Heat in a large skillet:

2 tablespoons melted butter, ghee, ooo, or vegetable oil

Add:

2 medium onions, chopped
4 cloves garlic, minced
½ teaspoon ground cumin

Cook, stirring, over medium heat until the onions are softened, about 5 minutes. Stir in:

1 large bunch mustard greens (about 12 ounces), washed, trimmed, and chopped

Cook until wilted, about 5 minutes. Stir in:

1 tablespoon mild curry powder
½ teaspoon ground ginger
½ teaspoon ground coriander
¼ teaspoon ground red pepper
¼ cup vegetable or chicken stock or water

Bring to a boil. Reduce the heat to a simmer and add:

One 15-ounce can chickpeas, drained and rinsed
One 14-ounce can diced tomatoes, with juice
½ teaspoon salt

Cook, stirring often, until the greens are tender, about 10 minutes.

OKRA

The okra pods beloved in the South are the young seedpods of a beautiful plant related to hollyhocks and hibiscus (okra blossoms are edible). Southerners know that okra can be cooked in two ways with distinctly different results. Whole pods, untouched by a knife, are steamed or sautéed for just 3 to 5 minutes. The pods emerge tender but still crisp and full of rich flavor. The pods are not gummy—repeat, are not sticky, slimy, or gummy. For a soup or stew, the pods are cut into thick slices so they can release their sweet mucilaginous ingredient for a natural thickening. The secret to superb eating is to choose pods no longer than your little finger. Pods should be heavy for their size, moist and plump, blemish free, with stems intact. Do not cook okra pods in an aluminum, iron, or unlined copper pot. Small pods and sliced large pods can be deep-fried.

Okra goes well with tomatoes, peppers, onions, garlic, seafood, ham, chicken, rice, hot sauce, curry powder, and a tangy touch of lemon, lime, or vinegar. Allow 4 to 5 ounces per serving.

SAUTÉED OKRA WITH ROASTED RED PEPPERS

4 servings

Trim the ends from and cut into ½-inch-thick slices:

1 pound small fresh okra, or two 10-ounce packages frozen whole okra

Heat a large, heavy skillet (preferably seasoned cast iron) over medium heat until hot. Add:

1½ tablespoons olive oil

Heat until hot. Add:

1 small red onion, halved and thinly sliced

Cook, stirring, until tender but still crisp and translucent, about 4 minutes. Add the okra in a single layer and cook until the slices are bright green and crisp-tender, 3 to 5 minutes. Stir in:

2 cloves garlic, minced

2 red bell peppers, roasted, 402, peeled, seeded, and cut into ¼-inch-wide strips

¼ teaspoon salt

Cook, stirring, until the okra is tender, about 2 minutes more. Serve immediately, sprinkled with:

1 tablespoon minced fresh cilantro or parsley

OKRA STEW

4 to 6 servings

Soaking the okra in the vinegar helps reduce its sticky juices.

Combine in a bowl and marinate for 30 minutes:

1 pound fresh or thawed frozen whole okra, stems trimmed

½ cup red wine vinegar

2 tablespoons salt

Drain and rinse under cold running water. Heat in a large skillet over medium heat:

3 tablespoons olive or vegetable oil

Add:

2 onions, chopped

2 cloves garlic, minced

Cook until lightly colored around the edges, 4 to 5 minutes. Add:

1 pound fresh or canned tomatoes, peeled, seeded, and diced

1 teaspoon sugar

Cook over medium-low heat until thick, about 30 minutes. Add the okra and season with:

Salt and ground black pepper to taste

Cook until the okra is tender, about 10 minutes more. Serve in bowls or over:

Grits, 250, or Polenta, 249

ONIONS

As they are one of the most versatile seasonings in a cook's repertory, it pays to know your onions.

Fresh Onions

The most common fresh onions are scallions, called green onions in some parts of the country. They are essentially seedling onions, long, slender, and supple. Their white parts may be sweet or hot, but their hollow bright green leaves are generally sweet—a fine substitute for chives. There are white, yellow, and red scallions, but the flesh of most is white, no matter what the skin color. Scallions are available year-round. (Tip: When a recipe calls for shallots and you are fresh out, combine the white parts of scallions with an equal amount of garlic.) *Bunching onions* are a different type of green onion. They may look like scallions at first glance, but scallions have slightly rounded bulbs at the roots, while bunching onions are straight as an arrow. There are Japanese and Welsh bunching onions. Both produce meaty stalks that are superb in cooking, especially grilled or broiled. The Japanese use only bunching onions in cooking. Their flavor is slightly more bitter than common scallions. For any scallions or bunching onions, select those with the crispest leaves with no yellowing or tears, and with shiny, bright, clean stalks. Store in perforated plastic vegetable bags in the refrigerator crisper. *Sweet onions* are mostly grown during the winter in warm climates. They are full-size but do not keep well. Sweet onions also tend to be juicy, and their moisture content adds to their perishability. Here are the Vidalias, Granos, Granexes, and Mauis you can eat raw with pleasure in spring. (So-called

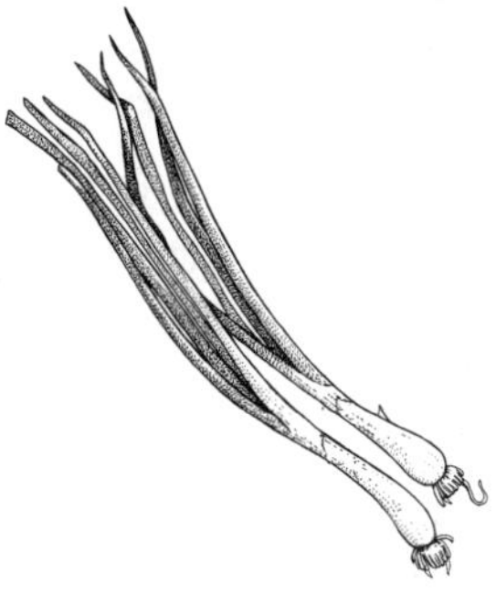

Scallions

Vidalia onion

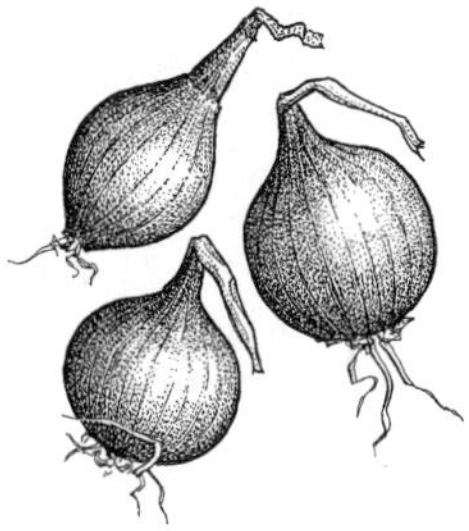

Pearl onions

Spanish onion

Bermuda onions are in this group too.) Washington State's Walla Wallas are in season in July and August. Use crisp sweet onions in salads and sandwiches and as a garnish. Sometimes they are referred to as slicing onions, in contrast to cooking onions, which follow. Due to their sugar content, sweet onions caramelize beautifully when simmered, but be careful that they do not scorch. However you use them, do so within a few days of purchase. Select only firm, crisp, unblemished onions and store in perforated plastic vegetable bags in the refrigerator crisper.

Dried or Storage Onions

The yellow, red, and white onions at the supermarket—from pearl to baseball in size—have been cured, that is, dried. After reaching maturity, they are harvested and spread out in the air. As their skins dry to translucence, the hollow centers at their necks close tight, sealing them against spoilage. Although an onion just pulled from the earth is juicier, a dried onion's flavor is more concentrated. These onions are also sharper tasting. Dried onions are ready in autumn, but they will keep for months. *Pearl* and *boiling onions* are common large onions harvested when tiny or small—the perfect size for martinis and creamed or glazed onions. They may be white, red, or yellow. To peel, pour boiling water over them and let cool. Use a knife to cut off the roots, pull off the skin, then cut a shallow X in the root end. This will hold the outer layers together in cooking. Snip off any leaves on top. You can soak the onions in ice water to cover for 30 minutes at this point if you want to crisp them. Small onions were made to be swathed in white sauces. *Cooking onions* are the common medium to large yellow, red, and white onions that never fail us at the market and, when cooking, send up one of the kitchen's most seductive aromas. Skin color has less to do with the flavor of a cooking onion than its variety and where it was grown. Very generally speaking, yellow onions are richly flavored but on the sharp side when raw. Most sweeten beautifully when carefully cooked. White onions are often pungent when raw—sometimes breathtakingly so—but there are mild varieties like White Sweet Spanish. In some parts of the country, Spanish is understood to mean a very large, mild, yellow onion. Actually, breeders can attach the word *Spanish* to mild onions of every size and color. Red onions are usually on the sweet side and can be cooked the same way as most yellow and white onions. As a class, they do not store as well. Some red onions are red only down through the first layer; when you find a market that stocks onions that are red through and through, stick with them. Cooking onions of all kinds should be tightly closed and very firm, without soft spots or black, powdery patches of mold. To store dried onions, spread them out—do not heap—in a cool, dry place. Keep them away from potatoes, which give off moisture that hastens spoilage. Wrap cut onions tightly in plastic wrap and refrigerate in the vegetable crisper.

Onions have special affinities with sugar, cream, mushrooms, potatoes, beef, liver, peas, cheese, all greens, tomatoes, oranges, beets, beans (all stages), cucumbers, walnuts, dill, caraway, thyme, sage, mint, parsley, and chervil. Allow 4 to 5 ounces per serving if served on their own.

To Prepare: Tears can be reduced by chilling onions before peeling or by peeling them under running water and chopping them in the food processor. Hand chopping, however, keeps pieces drier and more uniform in size. To peel, use the tip of a sharp paring knife to pull the skin off the onion, then pull off any membrane beneath. To cut whole slices or to chop in a food processor or by hand, trim off the root end, which is tough. The only time to leave the root end is when slicing or dicing chef's style, described on page 334. After working with onions, scrub the cutting board well or rub it with lemon; otherwise, the next food chopped may pick up the aroma.

To Cook: Onions are best cooked quickly with as little liquid as possible. That means baking, grilling, broiling, stir-frying, and microwaving. When you cook onions with little liquid, be careful to stir often so that the edges do not burn. (Burned onions taste acrid.)

Boiling onion

Red onion

To Parboil Onions: Bring 16 cups (4 quarts) water and 1½ tablespoons salt to a rolling boil in a stockpot. Add 1 to 2 pounds peeled onions and cook, uncovered, just until tender when pierced with a thin skewer or knife tip. Allow 5 to 10 minutes for pearl or boiling onions, 30 minutes for medium whole onions, and up to 1 hour for large whole onions. Onions sliced ¼ inch thick will cook in about 5 minutes.

ROASTED WHOLE ONIONS

4 servings

Nothing could be easier than this dish of onions. They can be eaten hot, like a baked potato, with butter, salt, and pepper, or cold with a vinaigrette. Whole onions also can be wrapped in aluminum foil and roasted on the grill for the same amount of time.

Preheat the oven to 375°F.

Leaving their skins on, nestle into a baking dish:

4 medium onions (any type)

Bake, uncovered, until tender when pierced with a knife, 1 to 1½ hours. Remove, halve lengthwise, and arrange the onion halves on a platter. Place in their centers:

Butter or extra-virgin olive oil

Salt and ground black pepper to taste

Pinch of finely chopped fresh parsley, thyme, or sage

Balsamic or sherry vinegar (optional)

SAUTÉED ONIONS

2 to 4 servings

Cooked quickly over high heat, onions emerge lightly browned and crisp on the outside and moist on the inside—perfect for topping a mashed potato, burger, or steak.

Heat in a large skillet:

2 tablespoons olive oil, butter, or a combination

Add:

4 medium onions, halved and thinly sliced or cut into ½-inch or larger squares

Sauté over high heat until lightly browned around the edges. Season well with:

Salt and ground black pepper to taste

Dash of dry red wine or balsamic vinegar (optional)

CARAMELIZED ONIONS

About 4 cups

If you cook onions over low heat so that they wilt without browning, they are said to be sweated. At this stage, their taste is gentle but not sweet. If you continue cooking, the onions will caramelize, or turn brown and quite sweet. The onions cook down to about half their volume and can be refrigerated for a few days or frozen. Caramelized onions are used as the basis for stews and sauces in many cuisines, from Spanish to Burmese.

Heat in a very large skillet until the butter is melted:

2 tablespoons butter

2 tablespoons olive oil

Add:

3 pounds onions, thinly sliced

Sprinkle with:

1 teaspoon salt

Cook over the lowest possible heat for 1 hour, turning the onions several times. Do not be tempted to increase the heat—the onions need to be thoroughly soft before they begin to brown. Once they are soft, increase the heat to medium and cook, stirring constantly, until well browned, or caramelized, about 25 minutes more. If the residue from the juices has built up in the pan, add:

½ cup dry white wine or water

Scrape the pan to dissolve the browned bits. They will immediately mix into the onions, darkening them further. Remove from the heat and season well with:

Salt and plenty of ground black pepper to taste

If serving as a side dish, you might want to add:

Grated Parmesan cheese

CREAMED ONIONS

4 servings

Considered essential on many Thanksgiving tables.

Preheat the oven to 350°F.

Drop into a large saucepan half filled with cold water:

1 pound pearl onions

Bring to a boil and boil for 1 minute. Using a slotted spoon, remove the onions, peel, and return them to the boiling water. Simmer until tender, about 10 minutes. Drain, reserving ⅓ cup of the cooking liquid. Remove the onions to a shallow 2-quart baking dish. Melt in a small saucepan over medium heat:

1½ tablespoons butter

Stir in:

1½ tablespoons all-purpose flour

Cook, stirring occasionally, over low heat until fragrant but not darkened, about 3 minutes. Add the reserved cooking liquid along with:

½ cup milk

½ cup half-and-half or evaporated skim milk

½ teaspoon salt

¼ teaspoon ground black pepper

Cook, whisking constantly, until thickened, about 3 minutes. Pour the mixture over the onions and sprinkle with:

1 cup grated Swiss cheese (optional)

Bake until bubbly, about 15 minutes.

SWEET-AND-SOUR GLAZED SMALL ONIONS

4 to 6 servings

Good with roast turkey or pork.
Peel:

1 pound boiling onions or pearl onions

Heat in a large, heavy skillet:

1 tablespoon butter or olive oil

Add the onions and cook, shaking the pan every few minutes, over medium heat until lightly browned, about 5 minutes. Stir in:

1 cup water
2 tablespoons dark or golden raisins, or a combination
1 tablespoon dark or light brown sugar
1 small sprig fresh rosemary
1 ripe plum tomato, diced

Simmer, covered, until the onions are tender when pierced with a knife, about 20 minutes. Add:

2 tablespoons red wine vinegar or sherry vinegar

Increase the heat and cook until the liquid has evaporated to a thick glaze, 7 to 9 minutes. Season with:

Salt and ground black pepper to taste

BAKED STUFFED ONIONS WITH SAUSAGE

4 servings

Position a rack in the center of the oven. Preheat the oven to 375°F. Butter a baking dish just large enough to hold the onions.
Slit from top to bottom with the point of a sharp paring knife and peel:

4 large yellow globe onions (about 2½ pounds)

Do not cut off either the stem or the root ends. Place the onions in an 8-quart pot and cover with 16 cups (4 quarts) water and 1½ tablespoons salt. Bring to a moderate simmer and cook, partially covered, until the onions are tender enough to be pierced by a skewer but still feel crunchy and slightly resistant, 15 to 20 minutes. Remove the onions from the saucepan with a slotted spoon and set root end down on a flat baking dish. Let stand until cool enough to handle.
To hollow the onions, slice off the top fourth of each onion at the stem end, reserving the tops. Using a small pointed knife, make several cuts into the center of the onion, going about two-thirds of the way down to the bottom and cutting to within 3 or 4 of the outermost layers. When the center of the onion has been well scored and the interior layers feel loose, hollow out the center with a teaspoon or small fork, leaving a wall 3 layers (about ¼ inch) thick. Coarsely chop the centers along with reserved onion tops. If there is a hole in the wall of an onion, simply cover it with a piece scraped from the middle.
Crumble into a medium skillet and brown well over medium heat:

½ cup (about 4 ounces) well-seasoned fresh sausage

Without draining off the fat, add the chopped onion tops and centers and cook, stirring, until the onions are golden and very soft, about 10 minutes. Squeeze dry, finely chop, and add to the sausage mixture:

One 10-ounce package frozen spinach, thawed, or 8 ounces fresh spinach leaves, steamed

Cook slowly for 5 minutes. Pour in:

⅔ cup heavy cream

Cook for 1 minute more; the mixture should be quite thick. Remove from the heat and stir in:

3 to 4 tablespoons fresh breadcrumbs, or enough to make the stuffing hold its shape on a spoon

Stir in:

⅛ teaspoon freshly grated or ground nutmeg
⅛ teaspoon ground sage (optional)

Season with:

Salt and ground black pepper to taste

Arrange the scooped-out onions in the baking dish. Pile in the sausage stuffing, mounding it over the centers. Sprinkle with:

2 tablespoons fresh breadcrumbs
1 tablespoon butter, cut into small pieces

Bake until lightly browned on top, 20 to 25 minutes. Let stand for a few minutes before serving.

GRILLED SWEET ONIONS

4 servings

Large red onions can be used when sweet onions are unavailable. These are great with hamburgers.
Prepare a medium-hot charcoal fire.
Prepare:

3 large Vidalia or other sweet onions, peeled and sliced into 1-inch-thick rounds

Secure each slice with a skewer so they do not fall apart. Rub with:

¼ cup olive oil
Salt and ground black pepper to taste

Place the onion slices on the grill rack and grill until nicely browned, about 6 minutes each side. Remove from the grill and remove the skewers. Serve plain or with:

Fresh Herb Vinaigrette, 237, Aïoli, 74, or Chili Butter, 77

FRIED ONION RINGS

4 to 6 servings

Use traditional fritter batter if you like onions thickly coated, or try a mixture of club soda and flour for a light, crisp coating, or use the seasoned club soda batter from Fried Zucchini in Herb Batter, 420. Try dusting the hot onions with ground red pepper as well as salt.

Combine in a bowl:

4 large white onions (about 3 pounds), sliced ¼ inch thick and separated into rings
1½ cups milk
1½ cups water

Let soak for 1 hour, turning frequently. Remove the onion rings and drain on paper towels. Meanwhile, prepare:

Fritter Batter for Vegetables, Meat, and Fish, 1051

Pour into a deep fryer or deep, heavy pot and heat to 365°F:

3 inches peanut oil

Pick up several rings at once on a fork, dredge in the batter, and let the excess batter drip off. Drop them into the oil and fry until light brown. Drain on paper towels, then sprinkle with:

Salt to taste
Ground red pepper or chili powder to taste (optional)

GRILLED SESAME SCALLIONS *4 servings*

The scallions can also be broiled in a baking pan until browned on both sides.

Prepare a medium-hot charcoal fire.

Trim the root ends and leave 5 inches of green on:

16 scallions

Rub with:

2 tablespoons toasted sesame oil
Salt and ground black pepper to taste

Place the scallions on the grill rack and grill, turning several times, until golden brown, 3 to 5 minutes.

PALM HEARTS

Today groves of palms are raised commercially in Florida and other tropical climates specifically for hearts, which are taken while the palms are tiny. A trimmed palm heart resembles a large carrot formed of layers of rings, like an onion. It has the whiteness of salsify and a flavor resembling a canned artichoke heart. Until now hearts of palm were only available canned, but since they are now a commercial crop, fresh hearts will be increasingly available, theoretically year-round. Most are sent to market trimmed of their fibrous exterior layer. Select fresh hearts that show moistness at both ends and no signs of cracking, dehydration, or separation of layers. They are very perishable, so store in perforated plastic vegetable bags in the refrigerator crisper and use as soon as possible.

Whether cool or hot, these delicate pieces are best served simply—any way you would serve asparagus or artichoke hearts. They make a superlative pureed soup. However, a squeeze of lemon, a drizzle of olive oil, and a little chopped garlic are flavoring enough. Allow 3 to 4 ounces per serving.

To Prepare: Hearts of palm can be served raw or cooked. Rinse and, if necessary, pare away any fibrous material to reach the tender white heart.

To Prepare Raw for Salads: Slice crosswise into rounds about ½ to ¼ inch thick and soak in ice water for an hour. Drain well and pat dry. The pieces will be crunchy and can be dressed with vinaigrette and served on a bed of greens (ideally, some of them bitter for contrast) or added to a mixed salad. (For more salad ideas, please see the salads chapter.)

To Steam: Steaming the heart whole retains the best color and flavor. Place in a steaming basket over 1 to 2 inches boiling water and cover tightly. Steam the hearts until tender when pierced with a thin skewer, about 7 minutes for small hearts or 9 minutes for larger hearts. Immediately lift out with tongs and drop into a big bowl of ice water to stop the cooking. When cool, slice and finish as desired.

PARSNIPS

These roots look like large cream-colored carrots and are as sweet as carrots, but they have a delightful spicy nip beneath the sweetness. Their cooked texture is like potatoes—they make a velvety puree. A winter vegetable, parsnips add pizzazz to carrot and potato dishes. Select small to medium roots (large parsnips can have woody cores), crisp, plump, and unblemished. Store in perforated plastic vegetable bags in the refrigerator crisper.

Parsnips have great affinities with cream, butter, and nutmeg. Allow 4 to 5 ounces per serving.

To Prepare: Peel before using. The dense core will soften when cooked unless it is very tough, in which case the thickest part of the core should be cut out and discarded. Cut into cubes, slices, or matchsticks.

To Boil and to Steam: Cut 1 pound prepared roots into ½-inch cubes or ¼-inch-thick slices and boil or steam as for turnips, 434. For boiling, allow 4 to 5 minutes to cook until tender. Steamed cubes and slices will cook in 5 to 6 minutes.

To Roast: Preheat the oven to 375°F. Cut 1 pound peeled roots into ½-inch cubes. Toss with 2 tablespoons olive oil, ¼ teaspoon salt, and ground black pepper. Place in

a 13 x 9-inch baking pan and roast for 30 to 40 minutes, until lightly browned and tender when pierced with a thin skewer or knife tip.
To Microwave: Follow the microwave instructions for carrots, 359.
To Pressure-Cook: Whole large (2-inch diameter) parsnips can be pressure-cooked with 1 cup liquid at 15 pounds pressure for 10 minutes. Cool the cooker at once.

GLAZED PARSNIPS
4 to 6 servings

With a vegetable peeler, strip the skins from:

1½ pounds parsnips

Trim the root and stem ends. Cut the parsnips crosswise in half and cut the large halves lengthwise down the middle. If the core in the large pieces is wider than ½ inch or woody looking and very dark yellow, pry it out with the tip of a knife; this will not be necessary unless the parsnips are large and overmature. If not cooking them immediately, cover the parsnips with ice water to prevent discoloration; do not let stand for more than 1 hour.
In a large skillet, combine the parsnips with:

2 cups water
3 tablespoons butter
2 teaspoons sugar
1 teaspoon salt
¼ teaspoon ground white pepper

Bring to a slow boil. Cover and cook over medium heat until tender, 10 to 12 minutes. They should suggest a thoroughly cooked sweet potato in texture. Uncover the skillet, increase the heat to high, and boil the cooking liquid down to a syrupy glaze that coats the parsnips, stirring often. Be careful not to scorch.

MAPLE GLAZED PARSNIPS

Prepare Glazed Parsnips, above, adding 3 tablespoons maple syrup at the end. Cook for about 1 minute more, stirring gently to coat the parsnips with the syrup. Add a pinch of freshly grated or ground nutmeg.

PARSNIP PUREE WITH SHERRY OR MADEIRA

Prepare Glazed Parsnips, above, and puree in a food processor or blender; if using a blender, you will have to perform this step in several batches. Turn the puree into a heavy saucepan, place over low heat, and gradually beat in 4 tablespoons (½ stick) softened butter. Remove from the heat. Add 2 to 3 tablespoons medium-dry sherry or Madeira and beat in 2 to 6 tablespoons hot milk or cream, just enough to give the puree the consistency of mashed potatoes. Season to taste with salt, pepper, and just a few drops of fresh lemon juice.

CURRIED PARSNIPS
4 to 6 servings

Serve these parsnips as an accompaniment to ham or pork chops or as a vegetarian entrée over rice or lentils. Peel, core, and cut into large matchsticks (batons):

1½ pounds parsnips

Drop into a pot of boiling salted water and boil for 2 minutes; drain. Cook in a large skillet over medium heat until softened, about 5 minutes:

3 tablespoons butter or vegetable oil
½ onion, finely diced

Add and cook, stirring constantly, for 1 minute:

1 tablespoon curry powder

Stir in:

½ cup chicken or vegetable stock or whole milk

Add the parsnips and simmer, covered, over low heat until tender, about 10 minutes. Stir in but do not boil:

½ cup yogurt

Season with:

Salt and ground black pepper to taste

Garnish with:

4 slender scallions (including 2 inches of green), thinly sliced
Fresh cilantro sprigs (optional)

OVEN-BRAISED PARSNIPS
4 servings

Parsnips, which are drier than most root vegetables, turn chewy and tough when dry-roasted but stay moist when braised. Allow them to color a little at the end, once they are cooked.
Preheat the oven to 375°F.
Peel, quarter lengthwise, and remove the cores from:

1½ pounds parsnips

Combine them in a shallow baking dish with:

¾ cup water or stock
2 tablespoons butter, cut into small pieces
½ teaspoon salt

Cover and bake until tender, 35 to 45 minutes. Give the pan a shake once or twice during baking. Remove the cover and bake until the parsnips begin to color a little, 10 to 15 minutes more. Serve, seasoned with:

Ground black pepper to taste
Chopped fresh parsley or tarragon

PEAS

Fresh Peas

Fresh peas are plush, meaty, and rich. Next time you see peas in the pod at the market—from spring through early summer—treat yourself to a feast. Select medium-sized pods that are bright green, moist, firm, and filled end to end with fat peas. Avoid those that are blemished and puffy. Petits pois are baby peas in which the bumps under the pod are developed but tiny. Store peas in their pods in perforated plastic vegetable bags in the refrigerator crisper.

Allow ¾ to 1 pound pods per serving (to yield ¾ to 1 cup peas).

To Prepare: At cooking time, rinse the pods, then shell the peas into a bowl. Snap off the stem and pull it down the side—a string will come with it, unlocking the seal. Press the pod at the seam, pulling it open on either side, and the peas will pop out. No need to rinse them. (Reserve some pods for sweetening soup stock.)

To Sweat: For every 1 cup peas, place the peas in a heavy skillet with 2 or 3 empty pods. Add 3 tablespoons stock or water, 1½ tablespoons butter, 1 tablespoon minced scallions or onions, ½ tablespoon minced fresh parsley or mint, ½ teaspoon sugar, ¼ teaspoon salt (if using unsalted stock or water), and a pinch of ground white pepper. Stir, bring to a simmer, then arrange a handful of finely shredded lettuce on top (1 handful is enough, regardless of the volume of peas). Cover and simmer, shaking the pan frequently, until tender, 5 to 10 minutes. Add a little more liquid if needed during cooking.

To Boil: Bring 8 cups water and 2 teaspoons salt to a rolling boil in a large saucepan. Add shelled garden peas, return to a boil, and cook, uncovered, just until tender, 4 to 10 minutes, depending on size and age. Older, starchier garden peas will cook in 7 to 10 minutes.

To Steam: Place the peas in a steamer basket over 1 to 2 inches of boiling water and cook, covered, until tender, 5 to 10 minutes. If there is more than 1 layer, stir once or twice during cooking.

To Microwave: Place 2 cups fresh peas in a 1-quart baking dish. Add ¼ cup stock or lightly salted water. Cover and cook on high until tender, 4 to 6 minutes, stirring after 3 minutes. Let stand, covered, for 3 minutes.

Edible Pod Peas

Fresh peas are like shell beans, halfway in development between immature pods and brittle pods full of dried peas. Like green beans, edible-pod peas have only suggestions of seeds inside. All pods are edible at this stage, but not all are tender. The strain we call snow peas (and also sugar peas, Mennonite peas, or Chinese pea pods) are most delicate. We call them Chinese because the pods are a staple of stir-fries, and stir-frying is probably the tastiest and most nutritious way to cook them.

Snow peas are available in Asian markets most of the year; buy snow peas only where the turnaround is brisk, for they can be rubbery if old. In the 1970s, sugar snap peas were developed from snow peas. These pods are as plump as those of shelling peas because they contain peas of a good size, but they are as sweet and tender as snow peas. A remarkable vegetable. Select and store them the same way as above. Sugar snaps are usually available early spring to early summer.

In spring at Asian markets, look for a bin containing small dark green leaves on slender stalks, some with fine tendrils and white pea blossoms. These are pea shoots, leaves at the tips of stalks on snow pea plants (probably a variety of snow pea bred for its leaves). Leaves at the market are larger and tougher than those you would harvest were you raising them; still they are special. Choose the smallest and brightest with the thinnest stems. The whole branch has a sweet pea flavor. Remove the leaves, tendrils, and flowers from the stalk (unless the stalk is very tender, discard it). Pea shoots make a beautiful salad but can be briefly cooked as for any delicate green. They are extremely perishable and must be used the day you bring them into the kitchen. To store, plunge the ends into a jar of water and refrigerate.

To Prepare: Unless they are stringless varieties, sugar snap peas and snow peas must have their strings removed. Snow peas may need just the string removed from the thicker seam, but sugar snaps will probably need strings from both seams removed. Some cooks have found that edible pods strung after cooking (when they will be served cool) are all the sweeter.

To Boil: Bring 8 cups water and 2 teaspoons salt to a boil in a large saucepan. Add 2 cups pea pods, return to a boil, and cook, uncovered, until crisp-tender. Start testing at 30 seconds, though they may take as long as 1 to 2 minutes.

To Steam: Place the prepared edible-pod peas in a steamer basket over 1 to 2 inches boiling water and cook, covered, until tender but still crisp, 2 to 5 minutes. If there is more than 1 layer, stir once or twice during cooking.

To Microwave: Cook as for fresh peas.

Peas in all forms go well with cream, mint, parsley, chervil, sage, thyme, lovage, carrots, onions, mushrooms, potatoes, turnips, celery, rice, lamb, ham, chicken, and fish.

YOUNG PEAS (PETITS POIS) *4 servings*

This method works well with peas that need little cooking.

Place in a saucepan or skillet:

2 cups small shelled fresh or frozen peas

Add enough water to barely cover. Cook over medium-high heat until heated through, about 3 minutes; do not let the pan dry completely. Stir in:

2 tablespoons butter, heavy cream, or crème fraîche

Cook, shaking the pan, until the butter is melted or the cream is bubbling; you do not want the peas to fry in the butter or the cream to dry out, so add an extra teaspoon or so of water if needed. When done, turn off the heat and season with:

Salt and ground black pepper to taste

Serve as is or stir in:

1 teaspoon finely chopped fresh mint or chervil or torn fresh basil; snipped fresh chives and chive blossoms; chopped fresh parsley; or several drops fresh lemon juice

BRAISED PEAS

4 to 6 servings

This method of cooking is especially suited to mature peas.

Bring to a boil in a medium saucepan:

2 cups large shelled fresh peas (about 2 pounds unshelled)
⅔ cup chicken stock
¼ cup finely chopped scallions
1 tablespoon butter
¼ teaspoon sugar (optional)
Pinch of salt

Reduce the heat and cover the pan. Simmer, stirring occasionally, until the peas are tender, 15 to 25 minutes, depending on their size and maturity. Season with:

Salt and ground black pepper to taste
Finely minced fresh parsley

STIR-FRIED SNOW PEAS

4 to 6 servings

This dish also can be made with sugar snaps or a combination.

Remove the stems and strings from:

1 pound snow peas or sugar snap peas or a combination

Heat a wok over high heat, then add:

1 tablespoon peanut oil

Heat until almost smoking and add:

1 tablespoon minced peeled fresh ginger

Stir-fry for 30 seconds, then add the peas and stir-fry vigorously until all are shiny and coated with the oil. Sprinkle with:

1 tablespoon chopped fresh basil or lemon basil
½ teaspoon salt

Cook until the peas are hot, another minute or two. Serve immediately.

FRESH PEAS AND ONIONS

4 servings

With the popularity of farmers' markets, there is now a chance of using newly pulled onions and fresh peas. If the only fresh peas available are chalky and dry, you are better off using frozen ones.

Melt in a large skillet over medium heat:

2 tablespoons butter

Add and cook until limp:

1 large sweet onion, quartered and thinly sliced
2 tablespoons water

Add:

2 cups large shelled fresh peas (about 2 pounds unshelled)
4 fresh basil leaves, thinly sliced
⅓ cup water or chicken stock
Pinch of salt

Cook until the peas are tender, about 3 minutes. Season with:

Salt and ground black pepper to taste

PEAS AND CARROTS

A classic.

Combine in any proportion:

Hot cooked carrots
Hot cooked green peas

Drain the vegetables well. Pour over them:

Melted butter
Chopped fresh parsley

Season with:

Salt and ground black pepper to taste

Serve at once.

PEAS WITH PROSCIUTTO AND ONIONS

4 to 6 servings

Heat in a large skillet over medium heat:

3 tablespoons olive oil

Add and brown lightly:

24 pearl onions, peeled

Add:

3 tablespoons water

Cover and cook over low heat until tender, about 5 minutes. Stir in:

2 cups shelled fresh peas (about 2 pounds unshelled) or one 10-ounce package frozen baby peas, thawed
4 ounces prosciutto or ham, finely diced
1 to 2 teaspoons water if using fresh peas
Salt and ground black pepper to taste

Cover and cook until the peas are tender, 5 to 8 minutes. If you are using frozen peas, cook for only 3 to 5 minutes. Taste and adjust the seasonings and serve immediately.

PEPPERS

Popular Fresh Peppers:

(The words *pepper* and *chili* are used interchangeably.)

Anaheim: These long green chilies grow abundantly in the American Southwest and are likely the ones you will find in a can labeled "green chilies." They also grow in northern Mexico. When fresh, they are light lime green to red. The flavor is reminiscent of bell peppers and green apples. They have a tough skin and a heat level that varies from mild to hot, depending on the cultivar. Delicious when roasted and peeled and used in stews and sauces, they can also be stuffed or eaten raw in salads. Most measure 6 to 7 inches in length and 1½ inches wide at the stem end, tapering slightly before coming to a rather pointy tip. Other names: California long green, Hatch, verde.

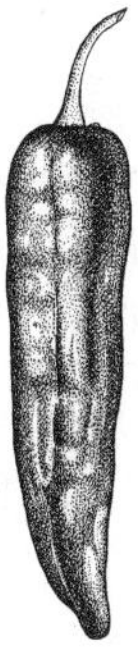

Anaheim pepper

Banana: These pale yellow to orange-red crisp peppers range from sweet to very piquant and are easy to grow. Their flesh makes them hard to roast and peel. Use them raw or roasted and peeled in salads and stews, or pickle them. They measure 5 to 6 inches in length, 1½ inches wide at the stem end, and taper to a point. Other names: güero, sweet banana, Hungarian wax.

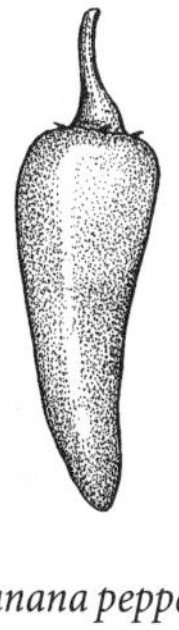

Banana pepper

Bell: From dark green to red, bright orange, bright yellow, pale yellow, and dark purple, bell peppers are the best known and most common sweet pepper used in this country. Although there are many cultivars available, the four-lobed bell-shaped fruits without any piquancy are the most popular. These thick-fleshed peppers are used in soups, stews, salads, relishes, sauces, and casseroles and often are stuffed as well. Roasting these peppers changes their flavor and softens the crisp, juicy flesh. Popular with some home gardeners is a slightly spicy cultivar known as Mexi-Bell. Bell peppers measure 4 to 6 inches in length and 3 to 4 inches wide at the stem end.

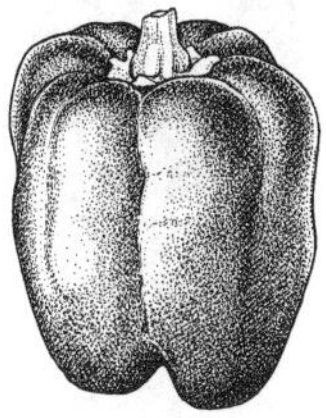

Bell pepper

Cayenne: These long, curved, slightly wrinkled, very spicy fruits have become the most common type of capsicum grown in the world. They are used throughout Asia in meat and vegetable dishes and in great quantities in Cajun specialties in this country. Dried, they are kept whole or are ground into powder for cooking and spice blends; they also are used as a table condiment in the form of bottled hot sauces. The slender, green to red pods are elongated, measuring about

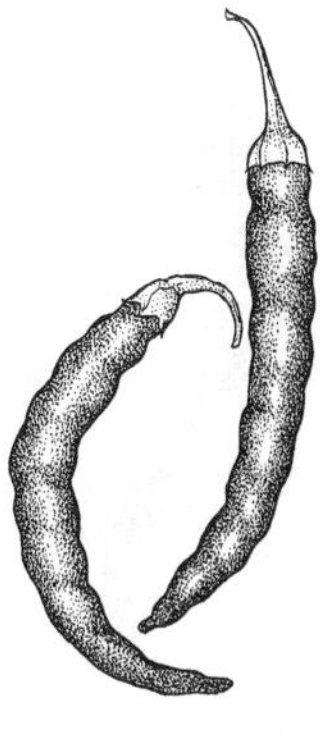

Cayenne pepper

½ inch wide and 5 to 10 inches in length. Other names (or similar peppers): finger, long hot.

Cherry: Named for their large, cherry-shaped pods, these peppers range from mild to hot and are commonly pickled whole in their green and red stages. These fleshy peppers have many seeds, a slightly sweet taste, and tough skin. They measure about 1 inch in length and 1 to 1½ inches wide at the stem end. Do not confuse them with the spicy cascabel chili—a similarly shaped pepper used dried in Mexico. Other names: hot cherry, sweet cherry, Hungarian cherry.

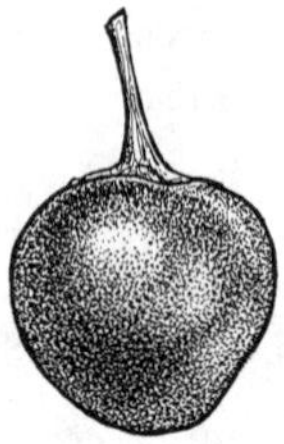

Cherry pepper

Chilaca: These delicious, smoky-tasting, somewhat twisted black-green chilies are not very well known in the United States but are common in western Mexico. They have a thick, slightly wrinkled, tough skin with medium-thin flesh that ranges from mild to medium hot. They are excellent sliced and fried, as well as roasted (although peeling them can be tedious), and are used in soups, salads, sauces, and vegetable dishes and anywhere else the more common poblano pepper appears. They measure about 8 inches in length and 1 inch wide all the way from the stem end to the blunt tip.

Cubanelle: Glossy peppers ranging in color from yellow-green to orange and red, sweet-tasting cubanelles

Chilaca pepper

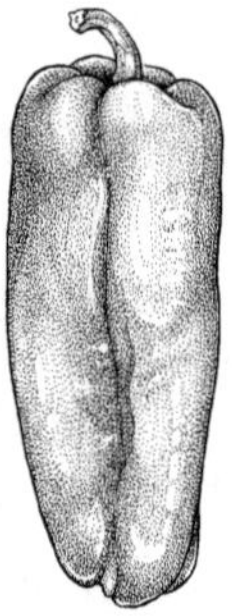

Cubanelle pepper

are popular as a condiment in Italian dishes, in which they are sautéed with olive oil and garlic. They can be used wherever a bell pepper is called for—in salads, as a vegetable, or stuffed. They measure about 6 inches in length by 2 inches wide at the stem end, tapering slightly to a rather blunt tip. Other name: Italian.

Fresno: Similar to Santa Fe Grande and Floral Gem, these yellowish green to fire-engine-red peppers resemble jalapeños and are sometimes mistaken for them. Slightly hotter than jalapeños, they are deliciously floral and can be substituted for jalapeños in salsas and cooked dishes. They measure about 3 inches long by 1½ inches wide at the stem end, tapering sharply to a point.

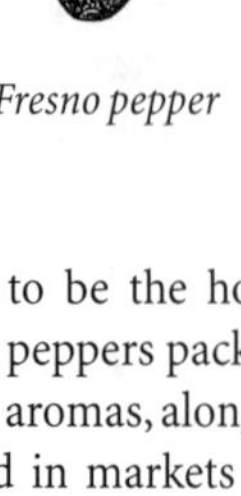

Fresno pepper

Habanero: Reputed to be the hottest of all chilies, these lantern-shaped peppers pack tremendous fruity and floral flavors and aromas, along with an incredible punch. Usually found in markets colored green, yellow-orange, or bright orange, habaneros are sometimes mislabeled as the equally hot but less floral Scotch bonnet. Used extensively in the Yucatán, they have become increasingly popular in this country in salsas, sauces, and condiments. They measure about 1½ inches long and 1½ inches wide at the stem end.

Habanero peppers

Jalapeño: These stubby green to red chilies are widely available and can vary considerably in their heat from totally mild (a new heatless jalapeño is now being grown for use in commercial American salsa) to quite hot varieties found in farmers' markets and their homeland of Veracruz, Mexico. This pepper's bright green, juicy, grassy taste works well in many dishes, from raw salsas to soups and stews, and even stuffed and fried. When mature jalapeños are smoked and dried, they are known as chipotles. Fresh jalapeños measure about 2½ inches in length and ¾ inch wide at the stem end and taper a little before coming to a rather blunt tip.

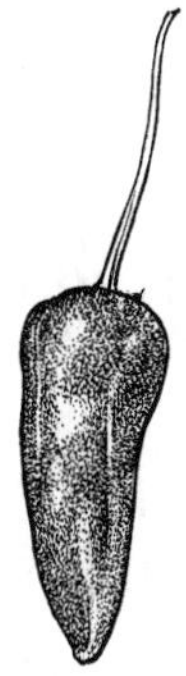

Jalapeño pepper

Manzano: These highly aromatic, plump, lantern-shaped, juicy chilies have a lush tropical flavor and aroma. The exterior is usually yellow to deep orange or red, and the interior seeds are jet black. Use manzanos

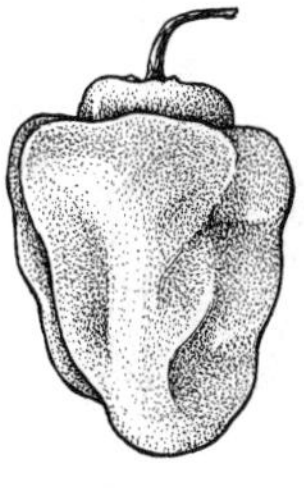

Manzano pepper

in salsas and cooked dishes in place of jalapeños, poblanos, or habaneros, but know that they are quite intensely piquant. They measure 2 inches long and 1½ inches wide at the stem end and look rather boxy, though most will have a little point or nipple at the tip. Other names: apple, peron (pear).

Peperoncini: These sweet to mildly piquant pale green to red peppers are best known as a pickled pepper used in Italian dishes. They rarely are found fresh in markets but are popular with many home gardeners. They measure about 3 inches in length and ¾ inch wide at the stem end, sloping gently to a point.

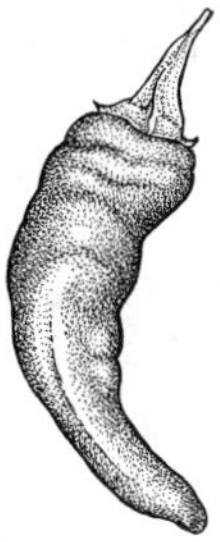

Peperoncini

Pimiento: These fleshy peppers, which range from sweet to hot, are used mostly in the red-ripe stage for commercial canning. Pimientos can range up to 5 inches in length and 3 inches wide at the stem end, and they have a rather boxy appearance that culminates in a small point. Other name: pimento.

Pimiento pepper

Poblano: Dark green, rich-tasting poblanos are used extensively throughout Mexico and are gaining in popularity in this country. The pepper's flesh has a compact texture with a good (but varying) amount of heat. Use them roasted and peeled in soups, sauces, and stews or whole as an edible vessel for a pork or cheese filling, as in chiles rellenos. When dried, they usually

Poblano pepper

are known as ancho chilies. Poblanos measure 4 to 5 inches long and about 2½ inches wide at the stem end, tapering to a sharp point. Other name: pasilla.

Scotch bonnet: These bright yellow, orange, green, or red peppers can be distinguished from habanero (with which they are often confused) by their squashed lantern shape and slightly smaller size. Extremely hot, these intensely aromatic, flavorful chilies are used extensively in the Caribbean in hot sauces and condiments. They measure 1 to 2 inches long by 1 to 1½ inches wide at the stem end. Other name: Scot's bonnet.

Scotch bonnet pepper

Serrano: These tapering, bullet-shaped chilies are prized among cooks for their consistent heat level and pure, fresh chili taste. Serranos are such a staple in Mexican cooking that they are often called simply *chiles verdes,* or green chilies. Use them fresh, pickled, or roasted anywhere their spicy, green, hot pepper qualities are wanted. Serranos are mostly sold green, but greenish yellow to red ones can occasionally be found. They measure 1½ to 2 inches long and ½ inch wide at the stem end. Other name: verde.

Serrano peppers

Tabasco: This pale green to yellow-orange to red hot pepper was developed by the McIlhenny family of Avery Island, Louisiana, for use in Tabasco, their popular fermented hot sauce. Home gardeners prize these for their intense heat.

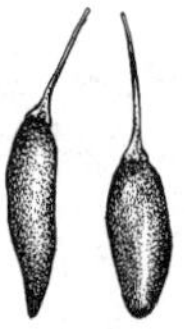

Tabasco peppers

Thai: Although there are many different peppers in Asian markets labeled "Thai peppers," perhaps the most common in this country are the small, elongated, pointy green to red peppers sold with their stems attached. These intensely hot peppers measure about 1½ inches long and only ¼ inch wide. Other names: bird, bird's-eye.

Thai peppers

Popular Dried Peppers:
(The words *pepper* and *chili* are used interchangeably.)

Ancho: These very dark peppers (dried poblanos) have a rich, earthy flavor with lots of sweet, fruity overtones and medium piquancy. They are used through-

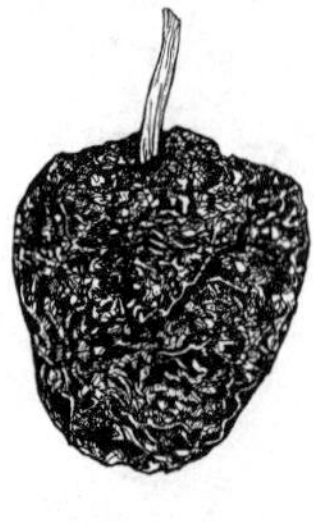

Dried ancho pepper

out Mexico in sauces, moles, and soups and are available in Mexican markets and specialty groceries in this country. They are wrinkled looking, roughly heart shaped, and measure about 4 inches long and 2 to 3 inches wide at the stem end. Other name: pasilla.

Arbol: Fiery hot, these pointy, bright red chilies have a shiny skin, and usually their stems are attached. They are used in hot sauces or ground into powder. Fresh arbol peppers occasionally show up frozen in Latin markets. They measure about 3 inches in length and ¾ inch wide.

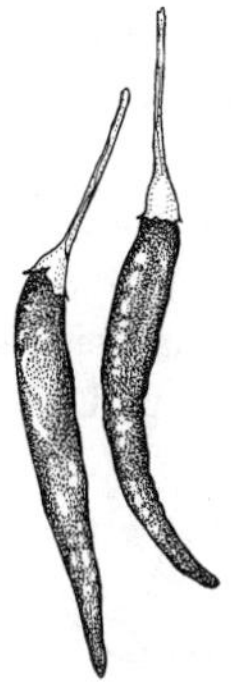

Dried arbol peppers

Cascabel: These round, dull cranberry-red peppers have seeds that rattle when the pepper is shaken (hence the name *cascabel,* or jingle bell) and are rich, spicy, and aromatic. Use them in salsas, sauces, soups, and stews. They measure about 1 inch in diameter. Other name: bolita.

Dried cascabel peppers

Cayenne: See description under fresh peppers.

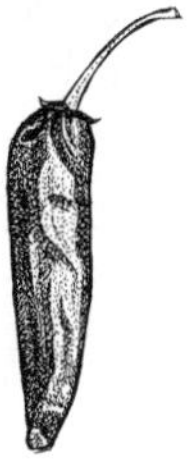

Dried cayenne pepper

Chipotle: Chipotle peppers (dried, smoked jalapeños) have made great gains in popularity in this country for their intense rich, smoky flavor. These days they show up everywhere, from canned tomato sauce (adobo) to salsas, sauces, pickles, stews, soups, and more. There are two types of chipotles, both made from different cultivars of the jalapeño. The first is the black-red chili chipotle (also know as the chipotle colorado, mora, or morita); this small chipotle (1 to 1½ inches long and ½ inch wide) is prized for its sweet, smoked flavor and its dark, rosewood red color. The second type, usually called chipotle meco, is larger (3 to 4 inches long by 1 inch wide) and pale brown in color, with a more tobacco-like taste and usually less heat.

Dried chipotle pepper

Guajillo: Smooth skinned, dark, translucent, Bing cherry red, with bright flavor, lots of tang, and a medium to hot piquancy, guajillos are the workhorse peppers of the Mexican kitchen. The thin-fleshed peppers are used commonly in sauces, soups, stews, and moles. They measure about 5 inches in length and 1 to 1½ inches wide at the stem end, tapering gently to a

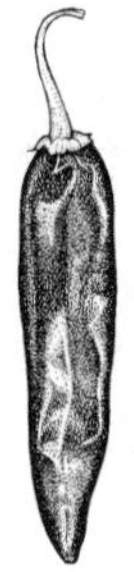

Dried guajillo pepper

point. They are often confused with the less flavorful New Mexico, or California, chilies.

Mulato: These very dark, black-red chilies often are mistaken for anchos. Once you taste them you will notice a deeper, dark flavor—almost chocolatey—but with less sweetness. They are used in sauces, moles, and stews.

Dried mulato pepper

New Mexico: Similar to the popular guajillo chili in appearance, the New Mexico chili is the one often strung in ristras (swags) or clustered into decorative wreaths. But these translucent red, mild to medium-hot chilies (known as long green, New Mexico, or red Anaheim chilies when fresh) are not just for decoration. They are delicious in soups, stews, and sauces and make a tasty ground chile powder. They measure about 5 inches in length and 1½ inches wide at the stem end. Other names: colorado, ristra, California.

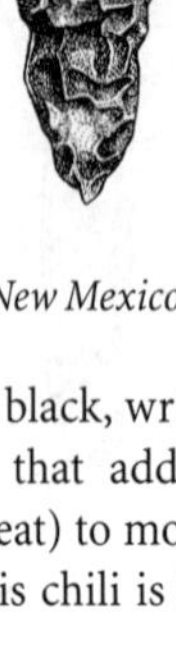

Dried New Mexico pepper

Pasilla: These nearly black, wrinkled peppers have a dark, woodsy flavor that adds a uniqueness (and medium amount of heat) to moles, sauces, soups, and stews. When fresh, this chili is known as the chilaca.

Dired pasilla pepper

Pasillas measure 8 to 10 inches long and about 1 inch wide. Other names: negro, pasilla mexicana.

Pequin: These little red ovals, about ½ inch long, have a relentless heat with a rich, complex, tangy flavor. They are used in salsas and sauces and fried whole as a condiment. Other name: piquín.

Pequin peppers

ROASTING PEPPERS

Roasting provides the best way to remove the skin of peppers. In addition, it softens their flesh, tempers the raw taste, and adds a delicious smokiness. Thick-walled peppers can be taken a step further and charred. Thinner-walled peppers—this includes most chilies—are better if blistered but not completely charred, or they will lose flesh when you peel them. Red peppers tend to char faster than green ones, having more sugars in their flesh. Once they are blistered, lay peppers in a bowl and cover with a towel or plate. Leave for a few minutes. Their heat will create steam, which will loosen the skins. Try not to rinse peppers after roasting, for much of the smoky flavor is on the surface. Scrape off the skins with a knife. If the peppers were whole, make a slit down one side, then run the tip of a small serrated knife around the stem underneath its base. Remove the top and the core and seeds that come with it, then scrape away remaining seeds and cut away the membranes. Add any juices in the bottom of the bowl to the dish you are making, or blend them into a vinaigrette dressing. Roasting and peeling can be done a day or two in advance; wrap the peppers airtight and refrigerate.

Stove-Roasting Fresh Peppers: This is the simplest method. Place whole peppers directly in the flames of your gas burner on its highest setting. (If you do not have a gas burner, set the peppers on a grill called an asador, one that rests above the burner, or use the broiler method.) Keep an eye on the peppers and turn them frequently with tongs, letting the peppers blister or char (do not pierce with a cooking fork, as juices will be lost). Continue until the entire surface is blistered.

Many cooks quickly toast, or stove-roast, dried chili peppers before rehydrating them. As in toasting bread, a flash of intense heat deepens and rounds out flavors.

Broiler-Roasting Fresh Peppers: Line a broiler pan with aluminum foil. Place whole peppers on the foil and brush with olive oil. Broil, turning as needed, until blackened on all sides. You can also flatten the peppers, see below. To Cut Peppers into Pieces: Brush the skin with oil. Place the pepper skin side up on a broiling pan and set the pan 5 to 6 inches under the broiler. Broil until the skin starts to blister and brown in places, watching it at every moment. Let the pieces char if you wish the flesh to be well cooked.

Grill-Roasting Fresh Peppers: This is the most flavorful method. Set whole peppers on a rack over ash-covered coals, a hot but dying fire. Let them sit in one place until they are blistered or charred, then turn them and repeat until the whole pepper is done.

Griddle- or Skillet-Roasting Fresh Peppers: This is for small fresh chilies such as serranos and jalapeños. Heat a dry cast-iron griddle or skillet over high heat, add the whole peppers, and shake them around the skillet until their skins are soft and charred here and there. These chilies are customarily not peeled after roasting, but they may be.

Griddle- or Skillet-Roasting Dried Peppers: This method gives the greatest control; overtoasted dried peppers turn acrid. For small chilies, heat a dry cast-iron griddle or skillet over medium heat until medium-hot. Add the chilies and press with a pancake turner, then turn and press until you can smell them—this will take just a few seconds. When the pods are lightly browned at the points where they touched the heat, remove them from the griddle. When cool, break off the stem, shake out the seeds, and discard them. For large chilies, remove the stems, slit the pod down one side, open up the pod, shake out the seeds, and break into pieces that will lie flat. If the pod is brittle and breaks, just shake out the seeds and break it into large pieces. Heat the dry griddle as above and press the pieces with the pancake turner, again until you can smell them—this, too, will take only seconds. Turn and repeat on the other side, then remove the pieces to a dish.

Rehydrating Dried Chilies: After roasting, rehydrate dried chilies by covering them with hot (not boiling) water, submerging the pieces in the bowl with a saucer, and letting them soak until pliant, 15 to 20 minutes. Longer soaking can leach out flavor. You can use the soaking liquid, but taste it to be sure it is not bitter.

PREPARING PEPPERS

To Cut Peppers into Pieces: For every shape but rings, use a small, sharp knife to cut around the stem at its base on top. Lift out the top and the core and seeds. Slice off a bit of the bottom, then make a lengthwise cut down one side. Open up the pepper into one flat piece. The skin is usually tough and glassy, making it easy for a knife to slip off—the inside is easier to work on. Set the pepper skin side down on your board, then scrape away the seeds and cut away the membranes. Now you can slice the pepper into whatever pieces the recipe calls for. For rings, cut out the stem, then cut crosswise into slices as thick as desired. Use a small, sharp knife to cut away the membranes and seeds from each slice.

To Prepare a Whole Pepper for Stuffing from the Top: Slice the top ½ inch from the pepper, then scrape out the seeds and membranes with a spoon. If the pepper does not stand straight, trim the bottom to level it (but do not make a hole, or the juices from the stuffing will run out). Chop the flesh from the top slice and add it to the stuffing if appropriate (or use it in salad). Huge peppers should be halved lengthwise through the stem. Leave the stem intact (it is needed to hold in the stuffing), but scrape out the seeds and membranes.

Bell peppers are delicious additions to salads. Rings of bell peppers in any color make a gay garnish. To cook bell peppers, sauté, grill, stir-fry, stew, or stuff and bake them. Roasted peppers can be frozen for up to 1 month. Leave their skins on, then peel when thawed. The peppers will lose texture but are good in sauces.

Bell peppers have special affinities with rice, lamb, onions, tomatoes, cheese (especially creamy sorts), oregano, chili powder, and celery seeds. Chili peppers seem to have an affinity with nearly every savory food. Allow 1 small to medium sweet pepper per serving, but figure chili peppers according to taste.

SAUTÉED PEPPERS

4 to 6 servings

Use primarily red, yellow, orange, and other sweet, fleshy bell peppers for this simple sauté. Include a green bell or green chili pepper for piquancy if desired. This dish is also delicious when made with green bell peppers alone. Serve warm or at room temperature.

Heat in a large skillet over high heat until nearly smoking:

2 to 3 tablespoons extra-virgin olive oil

Add:

4 bell peppers (about 2 pounds), preferably 2 red, 1 orange, and 1 yellow, cut into ¼-inch-wide strips, leaving the seeds in if desired

1 Anaheim or 2 serrano peppers, seeded and diced (optional)

Sauté until they begin to color in places. Reduce the heat to medium and season with:

Salt to taste

Cover the pan and cook until the peppers are softened, about 10 minutes. Increase the heat and add:

2 tablespoons aged red wine vinegar

Cook, tossing, until it evaporates. Remove from the heat and immediately stir in:

2 tablespoons chopped fresh marjoram, basil, or mint

1 tablespoon chopped fresh parsley

1 or 2 cloves garlic, finely chopped

If serving at room temperature, garnish the peppers with:

Niçoise, Gaeta, or Kalamata olives; strips of anchovies and quartered hard-boiled eggs; or drained capers (optional)

GRILLED RED BELL PEPPERS AND RED ONIONS

4 servings

Prepare a medium-hot charcoal fire.

Prepare:

2 red bell peppers, halved lengthwise and seeded

2 small red onions, trimmed and halved crosswise

Brush with:

¼ cup olive oil

Sprinkle with:

Salt and ground black pepper to taste

Place on the grill rack and cook until well browned, about 5 minutes each side. Remove and let stand until cool enough to handle. Cut the peppers into ½-inch-thick slices and separate the onion rings. Toss in a large bowl along with:

¼ cup extra-virgin olive oil

¼ cup balsamic vinegar

¼ cup coarsely chopped fresh parsley

1 teaspoon minced garlic

Salt and ground black pepper to taste

Serve immediately.

MEAT-STUFFED BELL PEPPERS

4 servings

An update of an American classic, based on ground beef and rice. A vegetarian version can be made by sautéing 1 pound firm tofu, drained and crumbled.

Preheat the oven to 375°F. Oil a baking dish in which the peppers will fit snugly.

Prepare for stuffing, 403:

4 bell peppers (any color)

Steam over boiling water for 10 minutes. Heat in a large skillet:

2 tablespoons olive or vegetable oil

Add and sauté over medium heat until the beef is lightly colored, about 10 minutes:

8 ounces ground beef

½ onion, finely chopped

½ teaspoon dried thyme

Add:

1 cup hot cooked rice

1 ripe tomato, peeled, seeded, and finely chopped

2 large eggs, lightly beaten

1 clove garlic, minced

1 teaspoon dried basil or marjoram, crumbled

Worcestershire sauce or red pepper flakes to taste

Salt and ground black pepper to taste

Fill the peppers with the meat mixture and set them in the baking dish. Combine and sprinkle over the tops:

½ cup fresh breadcrumbs

1 tablespoon olive oil or melted butter

Bake until the peppers are tender and the filling hot, about 25 minutes. If necessary, brown the tops under the broiler.

RED PEPPERS STUFFED WITH SAFFRON RICE AND PINE NUTS

4 to 6 servings

Halve lengthwise, keeping the stems intact, and seed:

2 large or 3 medium red bell peppers

Steam over boiling water until slightly softened, 8 to 10 minutes. Heat in a wide saucepan:

2 tablespoons olive oil

Add and cook over medium heat until softened:

6 scallions (white part and 1 inch of green), chopped

3 cloves garlic, minced

⅛ teaspoon crushed saffron threads

Add and stir briefly to coat with oil:

1½ cups long-grain white rice

Add and bring to a boil:

1¾ cups water or chicken stock

Stir, reduce the heat to low, and cover. Cook for 10 minutes, then let stand, covered, for 10 minutes more.

Preheat the oven to 350°F.

Fluff the rice, turn it into a large bowl to cool, then add:

2 cups shredded provolone cheese

⅓ cup pine nuts, toasted

¼ cup chopped fresh parsley

2 tablespoons chopped fresh marjoram or basil

Mix well and season with:

Salt and ground black pepper to taste

Place the peppers in a baking dish in which they fit snugly. Spoon the filling into each pepper half, mounding the top. Add to the bottom of the dish:

½ cup chicken stock or water

Cover lightly with aluminum foil and bake until heated through, about 35 minutes. Serve sprinkled with:

Chopped fresh parsley

BAKED CHILES RELLENOS WITH CHEESE

6 servings

In San Antonio, they wrap a chile relleno in a large warm flour tortilla for a Tex-Mex sandwich.

Grill or broil, turning occasionally, over a burner or 4 inches below a preheated broiler until blistered and blackened on all sides and slightly softened, 5 to 10 minutes:

6 medium poblano peppers

Peel the charred skin from the peppers and rinse them briefly. Make a long slit in the side of each pepper and carefully remove the seeds and veins. Pat dry and place on a baking sheet.

Preheat the oven to 350°F.

Mix together:

8 ounces Mexican Chihuahua, Monterey Jack, brick, or mild Cheddar cheese, coarsely shredded

2 large scallions, minced

Form into 6 ovals, then stuff the ovals into the center of the peppers and gently reshape them. Bake for 15 minutes to thoroughly heat through. Serve hot with:

Warmed chunky salsa

Chopped fresh cilantro

STUFFED JALAPEÑOS

8 or 9 appetizer servings

Chiles rellenos are usually made with poblano chiles, but we like the extra spiciness and bite-sized allure that jalapeños provide.

Prepare:

1 cup plus 2 tablespoons Picadillo, 720 (about ½ recipe)

Make a T-shaped slit in the sides of:

18 large fresh jalapeño peppers, stems intact

The top of the T should be just below and parallel with the top of the pepper (and no wider than ½ inch); the long part of the T should extend from the stem to the point. Fill a large saucepan with about 3 inches water and add:

¼ cup dark brown sugar

½ teaspoon salt

Bring to a boil, stir until the sugar is dissolved, and add the jalapeños. Simmer very gently over medium-low heat, stirring occasionally, until the peppers are almost tender, 5 to 6 minutes. With a slotted spoon, remove the peppers from the liquid. Drain cut side down for a minute or two, then carefully scrape the seeds out with a small spoon. Stuff each jalapeño with about 1 tablespoon of the picadillo, pressing it and molding it roughly into its original shape. At this point, it is highly recommended that the jalapeños be put in the freezer for at least 30 minutes, but no longer than 60 minutes, to firm them up.

Heat in a medium, heavy, deep skillet until very hot (about 375°F on a deep-fry thermometer):

¾ inch vegetable oil

While the oil is heating, spread on a shallow plate:

¼ cup all-purpose flour

Separate, letting the whites fall into the bowl of an electric mixer and collecting the yolks in a small dish:

3 large eggs, preferably at room temperature

Add to the egg whites:

¼ teaspoon salt

Beat at medium speed until they hold stiff peaks. With the mixer running, add:

1 tablespoon all-purpose flour

Then add the yolks 1 at a time, letting each be fully incorporated before adding the next. Working quickly (so the batter will not deflate) and in groups of 3 or 4 (so the pan will not get crowded), dredge a jalapeño in the plate of flour, then dip it into the egg batter to coat evenly and lay it in the hot oil. After about 2 minutes, use a spoon to very gently bathe the tops of the jalapeños with the hot oil. When they are golden underneath, use the same spoon to turn them over. Fry on the other side (no need to baste this time), then use a slotted spoon to remove them to a baking sheet lined with several layers of paper towels. Keep the fried peppers warm in a 200°F oven until all are done. Spoon onto individual serving plates:

2 cups salsa

Set the warm chilies on top and decorate with:

Chopped fresh cilantro (optional)

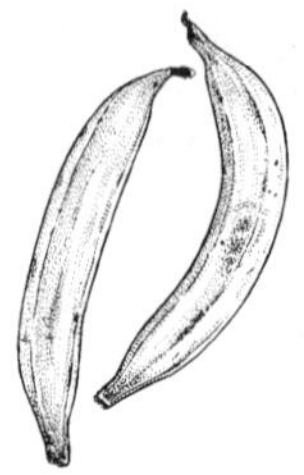

Plantains

PLANTAINS

Plantains are a close relation of bananas, but they are starchier and therefore always cooked. The form and degree of cooking depends on a plantain's stage of ripeness. When green, it is very hard, not sweet, and barely banana flavored. Green plantains are cooked like potatoes, in their skins, and the timing is similar. When the skin is yellow, the plantains are half-ripe. Cook them with the skin on as for potatoes; the flesh will be creamy and have a delicate banana taste. When the skin is brown to black, cook plantains as you would a banana—the flesh will be soft but firmer than a banana's. In Mexico, plantain is preferred at this stage, and it is often fried in thick rounds in oil and served with rice.

Plantains are available year-round in Hispanic groceries. Green and half-ripe plantains can be ripened like bananas at room temperature; this will take several days. Once ripe, plantains will keep for a few days at room temperature or in the refrigerator.

Plantains have affinities with butter, lime juice, rice, and other tropical fruits. Allow ½ plantain per serving.

To Bake: The easiest way to eat the fruit is to bake it in its skin. Perforate the peel in a few places with a fork, then bake in a 400°F oven until the flesh is fork-tender, about 40 minutes. Serve in its skin with butter as you would a baked potato, also sprinkling with lime juice and hot sauce if desired.

To Peel: To remove the stiff, thick peel of green and yellow plantains, cut the fruit crosswise into 2 to 4 pieces, slit the skin along each of its ridges, then pull off the peel from a corner of each section. To peel ripe plantain, cut off the ends, cut a slit the length of the skin, and remove it.

GOLDEN SAUTÉED PLANTAIN SLICES

4 servings

Serve these hot. They can be reheated, if needed, in a skillet or the oven. Especially good with fried chicken or baked ham.

Cut the ends off:

4 small brown to black, ripe plantains

Make a shallow slit down the length of each plantain just deep enough to cut through the skin. Peel off the skin and cut the plantains into ¼-inch-thick slices. Heat in a large nonstick skillet until hot:

2 tablespoons butter
1 tablespoon vegetable oil

Add half the plantain slices in a single layer. Cook, turning once, over medium-low heat until nicely golden on both sides, 6 to 8 minutes. Remove to a plate and keep warm while frying the remaining slices. Sprinkle with:

Coarse salt and ground black pepper to taste
Chopped fresh cilantro

TOSTONES

6 servings

An innovative California chef of our acquaintance uses these as "toast" to serve with caviar—an unorthodox but surprisingly good combination.

Cut the ends off:

4 small brown to black, ripe plantains

Make a shallow slit down the length of each plantain just deep enough to cut through the skin. Peel off the skin and cut the plantains into ¼-inch-thick slices. Heat in a deep fryer or deep, heavy pot to 325°F:

2 inches vegetable oil

Deep-fry the plantain slices, a few at a time, until golden. Drain well on paper towels. Place the fried slices in a single layer on a baking sheet and flatten each slice with a meat mallet to an even ⅛-inch thickness. Reheat the oil to 350°F and refry the plantain slices a few at a time until golden and crisp, 2 to 3 minutes. Drain well on paper towels and serve immediately, sprinkled with:

Coarse salt

POTATOES

Potatoes fall into three types. Potatoes containing relatively high moisture and low starch are described as waxy and are called *boilers.* These are the potatoes that hold their shape as cubes and slices in potato salads, gratins, and stews. At the market, they are the smooth round reds, round whites, and oblong White Roses. Potatoes low in moisture and high in starch are described as mealy and are called *bakers.* When cooked, their flesh is dry and fluffy, exactly right for baking, frying, and mashing (even though they are boiled). These are the knobby, tuber-shaped russets, or Idahos, at the market. While a baking potato will crumble in a potato salad, boiling potatoes are superb baked. They will not be fluffy, but their skins will be crisp and their flesh will absorb pan juices or butter beautifully. A baking potato is the one to use in soup to give it body—it will fall apart gracefully, as in Vichyssoise, 103. Russets are also the recommended type for frying. They have the ability to release their starch, given ample soaking and rinsing. Starch absorbs fat and, if not flushed out of the potato, results in heaviness. Russets can make crisp-on-the-outside and fluffy-on-the-inside fries. Russet potatoes that are either baked or boiled for mashing should be eaten or mashed right away, because they will lose their fluffy texture if left to stand. Keep potatoes out of aluminum and iron pots, where they will turn gray. The flesh of some potatoes is between waxy and mealy, having moderate moisture and starch. Called *all-purpose,* a few of these potatoes match the quality of the best boilers and bakers.

Potatoes are next classed according to age—whether they are *new* or *storage.* New potatoes are babies, harvested before they develop the potential their variety prescribes. No matter what the variety, new potatoes are boiler types, because they have not had enough time to develop much starch. (The opposite is not the case, however. Some of the potatoes that take longest to mature, called late-season, are also low in starch. The variety is the determining factor.) New potatoes are best steamed or roasted, always in their skins, and served with melted butter and chopped herbs or swathed in cream sauce. Purple-skinned, white-fleshed Caribes make especially delicious new potatoes. Somewhere in this vast country, potatoes are freshly dug and sent to market every month. That means when the sign at the market in January says, "New Potatoes," you should be able to rub the skin off with your fingers. If you cannot, it is a storage potato, no matter how small its size. Storage potatoes have been cured in the sun, their skins toughened, and held in cold storage for weeks, sometimes months.

Like heritage apples, old-fashioned American and favorite continental varieties of potatoes are being grown again. White Rose is a pleasant potato, but there are many that are far more flavorful. Thus far, the most flavorful potatoes we have tasted are Yellow Finn and Bintje; the best boilers, Butterfinger and Russian Banana; the best bakers, Russet Burbank and Lemhi Russet; the best all-purpose, Red Gold. The most beautiful has to be All Blue, with its sparkling lilac-blue flesh.

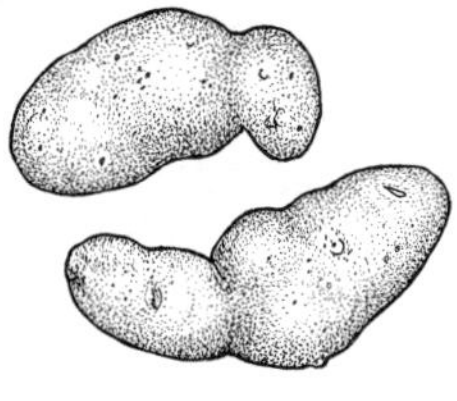

Fingerling potatoes

Look for the following colors at farmers' markets, and ask your supermarket produce manager to find some.

Blue potatoes through and through are All Blue (round all-purpose). Purple through and through is Purple Peruvian (fingerling baker). Yellow through and through are Yellow Finn (flat, round, or pear-shaped all-purpose), German Butterball (round to oblong all-purpose), and Yukon gold (standard all-purpose). Red through and through is All Red (round boiler). Red and yellow—red skin, yellow flesh—are Rose Finn Apple and Ruby Crescent (both fingerling boilers), Desiree (round to oblong all-purpose) and Red Gold (standard all-purpose). White flesh with buff skin is Anoka (standard boiler).

Select potatoes that are firm and heavy for their size, with taut skin and no cuts, dark spots, cracks, mold, or other sign of spoilage. If there is a greenish cast to the potato or a green patch on it, avoid it—the green part was exposed to the sun and will be bitter (even mildly toxic). Avoid those that have sprouted; they will be soft and even bitter. Store potatoes, unwashed and unwrapped, in a cool, dark, dry, well-ventilated place. After storing, should you find your potatoes have turned green or begun to sprout, cut off the green or sprout with 1/4 inch of the flesh beneath it (or discard them).

Potatoes have great affinities with butter, cream in any form, cheese, chives, dill, onions, garlic, parsley, chervil, rosemary, sage, oregano, bacon, mushrooms. Allow about 6 ounces per serving.

To Prepare: Leave skins on whenever possible—the skin is valuable nutritionally and packs a great amount of a potato's earthy flavor. If it is essential to peel, use a swivel peeler. Flesh exposed to air will darken if not cooked soon, so work quickly or drop pieces in a bowl of cold water mixed with a few drops of lemon juice or vinegar. Also use a stainless-steel knife, for carbon steel will discolor the flesh. When baking whole potatoes, be sure to prick the skin in several places to avoid steam buildup, which can cause a potato to explode in the oven.

To Boil: Place 1 or 2 pounds potatoes in a large pot and add enough cold water to cover by 1 inch. Add 1 teaspoon salt for each quart of water. Bring to a boil and cook until tender when pierced with a thin skewer or knife tip. Allow 10 to 15 minutes for whole small or baby potatoes, 20 to 25 minutes for medium, and 35 to 45 minutes for whole large potatoes. Slices ¼ inch thick will cook in 5 to 7 minutes.

To Steam: Place whole potatoes or slices in a steaming basket over 1 to 2 inches boiling water and cook, covered, until tender all the way through when pierced with a thin skewer or knife tip. For whole potatoes, allow 15 to 20 minutes for small or baby potatoes, 30 to 35 minutes for medium, and 35 to 45 minutes for large potatoes. Slices ¼ inch thick will cook in 10 to 15 minutes, a few minutes longer if there are layers.

To Bake: Set whole potatoes on an oven rack or a baking sheet. A baking nail or thick skewer through the center will carry heat evenly through the flesh, but it is not necessary. Do pierce the potato in several places to make sure that it does not explode in baking. Halved and quartered potatoes bake faster and have wonderfully crisp surfaces. Bake at 400°F until tender when tested with a thin skewer, 45 to 60 minutes for whole potatoes.

To Microwave: Microwaved potatoes are, to our taste, a last resort. Peel and quarter 4 medium baking potatoes and arrange in a 2-quart baking dish. Cover and cook on high until tender, 9 to 12 minutes, stirring after 5 minutes. Let stand, covered, for 3 minutes. Immediately mash a microwaved potato if your goal is a fluffy texture.

To Pressure-Cook: Whole large (2½-inch-diameter) potatoes can be pressure-cooked with 1½ cups liquid at 15 pounds pressure for 15 minutes; 1½-inch-diameter potatoes need just 1 cup liquid and 10 minutes' cooking; ¾-inch-thick slices need 1 cup liquid and 5 minutes' cooking. Cool the cooker at once.

MASHED POTATOES

6 servings

A food mill or ricer ensures a smooth puree. An electric mixer, a potato masher, or a fork takes more elbow grease but can do the job. The food processor is too hard on potatoes, leaving them with an unappetizing gluey texture. Baking potatoes make the best mashed potatoes. Mashed potatoes are best when served at once, for they lose their fluffiness when held or reheated. In a pinch, they can be kept hot for up to 30 minutes by covering the serving bowl with aluminum foil and placing it in a larger pan of hot water over a low burner. Or smooth the potatoes in a buttered baking dish, run a film of hot cream over the top, cover loosely with aluminum foil, and keep in a 300°F oven; the cream may brown.

Steam, boil, or microwave, above, until tender:

2 pounds potatoes (about 6 medium), peeled and cut into large chunks

If desired, you can include in the pan or microwave dish:

2 cloves garlic, thinly sliced
1 onion slice or 2 chopped scallions (white part only)
1 small celery stalk, with leaves
1 small bay leaf or 1 sprig fresh thyme or parsley

Drain thoroughly (save the liquid for soup). Remove any large pieces of vegetables or herbs. Place the potatoes in a large, heavy skillet or return to the pan and shake over medium heat until the pieces are mealy and dry. Cover to keep hot while you heat in a small pan over low heat:

6 tablespoons cream, half-and-half, milk, or buttermilk
3 tablespoons butter, preferably unsalted

Cover the pan loosely and be careful not to let the mixture boil. Meanwhile, quickly puree or mash the hot po-

POTATO RICER

A potato ricer is the best tool for preparing light, even-textured mashed potatoes. Look for a sturdy metal ricer with at least a 2-cup perforated bowl for holding the boiled potatoes and two long handles that, when squeezed together, force the potatoes through holes in the bottom of the cup. A good ricer should come with two disks of different sized perforations that can be inserted into the cup. One has smaller holes for finely riced potatoes. The other disk has larger holes that can be used to press out spätzle or to remove excess moisture from cooked greens or other vegetables.

Potato ricer

tatoes, working out every lump. Whip with a fork while pouring in the hot milk and butter, then take about 30 seconds to whip the mixture until fluffy. Stir in:

Salt and ground white pepper to taste

Serve at once, topped with:

1 to 2 tablespoons butter, softened

Some Savory Additions to Mashed Potatoes

1 head roasted garlic, 378
2 pinches saffron threads diluted in 2 tablespoons warm water or light cream
½ cup Duxelles, 387
⅓ cup chopped fresh basil or other fresh herb
½ cup grated Gruyère, Swiss, or Cheddar cheese, or soft goat cheese

BUTTERMILK MASHED POTATOES *4 servings*

These potatoes are a wonderful reduced-fat version of an all-American favorite. The buttermilk adds a pleasant lemony-tart flavor. The potatoes can be baked or boiled. If baking, use russet (Idaho) potatoes; if boiling, use red, new, or all-purpose potatoes. Russet potatoes are starchier, so they will need more buttermilk; use the larger amount called for in this recipe. Add ingredients to the potatoes gently; whipping or beating hard results in gummy potatoes.

For baking, preheat the oven to 400°F.

Place directly on the oven rack:

1 pound russet (Idaho) potatoes, about the same size, scrubbed and pricked with a fork

Bake until tender when pierced with the tip of a sharp knife, about 1 hour. Let cool slightly, then peel them. Place the potatoes in a pan and mash with a potato masher or fork. If you like lump-free potatoes, press the potatoes through a ricer.

For boiling, place in a medium saucepan:

1 pound red-skinned new or all-purpose potatoes, peeled and cut into 1-inch pieces

Cover the potatoes with cold water and bring to a boil. Boil, uncovered, until tender, 15 to 20 minutes. Drain and return to the pan. Mash as described in Mashed Potatoes, above.

Add to the mashed potatoes:

½ to ⅔ cup buttermilk
1 tablespoon olive oil (optional)
½ teaspoon salt, or to taste
Ground black pepper to taste
Freshly grated or ground nutmeg to taste (optional)

Gently mix the potatoes with a spoon, taking care not to whip or beat hard or they will become gummy. Reheat if necessary and serve.

MASHED POTATOES WITH CABBAGE AND SCALLIONS (COLCANNON) *6 to 8 servings*

This is an Irish favorite.

Place in a large saucepan or Dutch oven:

2 pounds Yellow Finn, Yukon gold, or all-purpose potatoes, peeled and cut into 1½-inch chunks

Add cold water just to cover. Pile on top of the potatoes:

2 bunches scallions (white part only), sliced
1 small head green cabbage (about 1 pound), cored and chopped into 1-inch pieces

Bring to a boil, then reduce the heat to maintain a gentle boil. Cook, covered, until the potatoes are fork-tender, about 20 minutes. Drain and return the potatoes, cabbage, and scallions to the pot. Mash the mixture over low heat while adding:

½ cup milk or half-and-half, warmed
4 to 8 tablespoons (½ to 1 stick) butter, softened
1 scant teaspoon salt
¼ teaspoon ground black pepper

When the mixture is coarsely mashed, taste and adjust the seasonings and serve.

SMASHED POTATOES WITH BASIL PESTO *4 to 6 servings*

Smashing or crushing potatoes instead of mashing them has become popular in contemporary American restaurants. Try leaving the peels on some of the potatoes for added texture.

Boil, 407, in salted water to cover until very tender:

3 pounds red-skinned or Yellow Finn potatoes

Drain well and return to the pan. Place back on the burner and shake to dry the potatoes. Peel all or half the potatoes, then smash with a large spoon or fork, blending in:

½ cup milk
1 tablespoon butter

Add:

½ cup Pesto Sauce, 307
Salt and ground black pepper to taste

Serve hot. The potatoes can be placed in an oiled baking dish and reheated in a 375°F oven just before serving.

PAN-FRIED GOLDEN POTATOES WITH ROSEMARY AND LEMON *4 to 6 servings*

Heat in a large nonstick or cast-iron skillet:

2 tablespoons olive oil

Add:

1½ pounds Yellow Finn or all-purpose potatoes, peeled and sliced into ¼-inch-thick rounds

Cook over medium-high heat until golden and crisp on the bottom. Using a thin flat spatula so as not to break them, turn and cook until the second side is golden and crisp. Toss with:

2 teaspoons finely minced fresh rosemary
Finely grated zest of 1 lemon
Salt and ground black pepper to taste

HASH BROWN POTATOES
4 servings

There are two kinds of hash browns: those made with raw potatoes and those made with boiled ones. The kind with boiled potatoes stick together better and cook more quickly, but some prefer the texture of those that begin raw. If you use raw potatoes, cover the pan while they are cooking on the first side to hasten the cooking.

Toss together:

1½ pounds boiled or raw all-purpose potatoes, peeled and finely diced (about 4 cups)
2 tablespoons finely chopped onions (optional)
½ teaspoon salt
Ground black pepper to taste

Heat in a large, heavy skillet over medium-high heat:

3 tablespoons vegetable oil

Add the potatoes, toss them a few times, then spread them evenly in the pan and press down with a spatula. Reduce the heat to medium and cook slowly, pressing down several more times, until browned on the bottom, about 15 minutes. As the potatoes cook, give the pan a gentle shake a few times to make sure they are not sticking. Cut the cake down the middle, then, using 2 spatulas, turn each side over. Do not worry if they do not turn evenly—this is a "hash"! If the pan seems too dry, add a little more oil before you return the potatoes. Cook the second side until golden brown. Serve piping hot.

POTATO PANCAKES
About twelve 3-inch cakes

Use baking or all-purpose potatoes for their starch content, which helps hold the potato shreds together. You can substitute a second root vegetable, such as parsnip, carrot, or celery root, for one-quarter of the potatoes.

Wrap in a clean dish towel and wring to squeeze out as much moisture as possible:

2 cups coarsely grated peeled potatoes

Combine in a bowl with:

3 large eggs, lightly beaten
1½ tablespoons all-purpose flour
1 tablespoon grated onions
1¼ teaspoons salt

Heat in a large, heavy skillet over medium-high heat until hot:

¼ cup vegetable oil or butter

Drop spoonfuls of the potato mixture in the skillet, then spread into 3-inch cakes about ¼ inch thick. Fry until browned on the bottom, reducing the heat to medium, if needed, to prevent scorching. Turn and cook the second side until crisp, 3 to 5 minutes each side. Drain briefly on paper towels. Serve with:

Sour cream or Yogurt Cheese, 1071
Snipped fresh chives or applesauce

GOLDEN POTATO PANCAKES (RÖSTI)
2 or 3 servings

Rösti is the classic Swiss potato pancake. Like hash browns, it can be made with either raw or boiled potatoes (the latter being somewhat easier).

Toss together:

1 pound all-purpose potatoes, baked, cooked, peeled, and coarsely grated, or 1 pound raw all-purpose potatoes, peeled, cut into thin strips, rinsed, and dried
½ teaspoon salt

Melt in a medium, heavy skillet over medium heat:

2 tablespoons butter

Add the potatoes and cook for 4 to 5 minutes, turning frequently so that the shreds are all lightly coated with butter. Press together to form a cake, reduce the heat to low, and cook until golden on the bottom, about 20 minutes. Turn the cake out onto a plate, then slide it back into the pan and cook the second side. If desired, sprinkle the top with:

1½ tablespoons grated Gruyère cheese

When the second side is golden, slide the potato cake onto a serving plate. Cut into 2 or 3 pieces and serve plain or garnished with:

Snipped fresh chives

POTATO GALETTE
4 to 6 servings

Use a well-seasoned cast-iron skillet or a heavy nonstick pan, and be careful when turning this golden potato cake.

In a well-seasoned large, heavy skillet, melt over low heat:

3 tablespoons butter

Pour out and reserve all but 1 tablespoon of the butter. Arrange in concentric circles in the skillet:

1½ pounds baking potatoes, peeled and thinly sliced

As you build layers, sprinkle them with the reserved melted butter and season with:

Salt and ground black pepper to taste

Cover tightly and cook until the potatoes are golden on the bottom, 20 to 25 minutes. Turn the cake out onto a plate, then slide it back into the pan to brown the second side, about 15 minutes. Pierce with a knife to make sure the slices are tender all the way through. If not, continue to cook over low heat for 5 minutes more.

NO-FAIL FRENCH FRIES

4 to 6 servings

For crisp, golden fries, use starchy baking potatoes and fry in two stages. The first frying can be done in advance, but the second frying should be done just before serving. Please read Deep-Frying, 1050.

Place in a bowl and soak in cold water to cover for 30 minutes:

4 large baking potatoes, peeled and sliced into 2¼ x ⅜-inch strips

Drain and dry very well, because excess water will spatter in the fat.

Pour into a deep fryer or deep, heavy pot and heat to 330°F:

3 inches peanut or other vegetable oil

Drop in the potatoes about 1 cup at a time and fry until the spattering ceases, about 2 minutes. Skim out the potatoes with a slotted spoon and drain on paper towels. They will be rather pale and limp and easy to crush with your fingertips. Let cool for at least 5 minutes before starting the second frying.

For the second frying, heat the oil to 365°F. Fry the potatoes in small batches in a frying basket, if you have one, to ensure quick and easy removal. Fry until the potatoes are golden brown, 2 to 3 minutes, then remove the basket, shake off the excess oil, and turn the fries onto paper towels. Serve them at once, piled on a plate or in a basket lined with a napkin. Do not cover them or they will turn limp.

SHOESTRING POTATOES

4 to 6 servings

A mandoline, shown below, makes perfect shoestrings, but you can also use a knife or a food processor to cut the potatoes. They should brown in 2 to 3 minutes during the second frying; do not let them brown faster or they will end up limp.

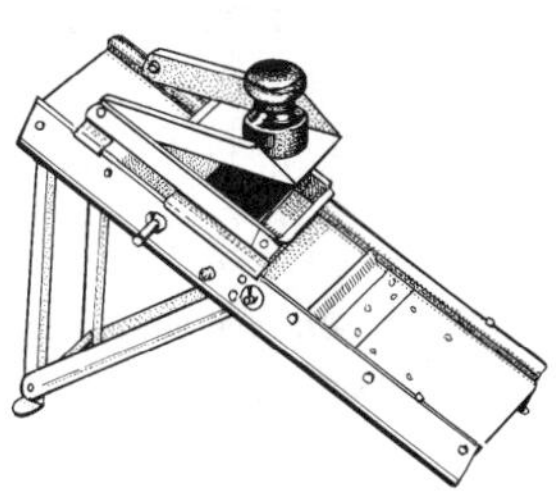

Mandoline

With a knife, mandoline, or food processor, cut into julienne strips no more than 3/16 inch thick:

4 large baking or Yukon gold potatoes, peeled

Let soak in a bowl of ice water for 30 minutes. Drain, shake off the excess water, and dry well. Double-fry them in peanut or light olive oil, as for No-Fail French Fries, above. When done, pile onto a plate and sprinkle lightly with:

Salt to taste

Ground red pepper (optional)

FRANCONIA, OR BROWNED POTATOES

4 servings

We love browned potatoes but have an aversion to the hard-crusted, grease-soaked variety so often served. Boil these first to ensure a tender crust.

Boil in salted water to cover until they are not quite done, so there is resistance to the testing fork:

6 all-purpose potatoes, about 2 inches in diameter, scrubbed

Preheat the oven to 350°F.

Heat in a small, heavy, ovenproof skillet until hot but not quite to the point of fragrance:

3 tablespoons butter

3 tablespoons vegetable oil

Add the potatoes, cover, and bake for about 20 minutes, turning occasionally for even browning. Sprinkle with:

2 tablespoons finely chopped fresh parsley

Bake, uncovered, about 10 minutes more.

BAKED POTATOES WITH CHEESE AND BACON

2 servings

These are also known as twice-baked potatoes. Omit the bacon if you wish.

Preheat the oven to 400°F.

Wash, dry, and pierce in several places:

2 large baking potatoes

Rub the potatoes generously with:

Olive or vegetable oil

Bake on an oven rack until softened, 45 to 55 minutes.

Meanwhile, in a small bowl, mix together:

½ cup finely grated Monterey Jack or brick cheese

¼ cup sour cream

2 slices cooked bacon, crumbled, or 2 ounces cooked ham, chopped

1 to 2 scallions, minced

1 teaspoon Dijon mustard

¼ to ½ teaspoon hot red pepper sauce

When the potatoes are cooked, cut a long slit in the top of each. Squeeze the potato open and scoop out the pulp, leaving a ½-inch-thick shell. Mix the cooked potato with the cheese mixture. Place the shells in an 8 x 8-inch baking dish and mound the cheese mixture in them. Bake until the cheese is nicely melted, about 15 minutes. Serve sprinkled generously with:

Minced fresh parsley

TEX-MEX POTATOES

Prepare Baked Potatoes with Cheese and Bacon, above, substituting pepper Jack cheese for the Monterey Jack, ½ teaspoon ground cumin for the mustard, and cilantro for the parsley.

BLUE CHEESE AND BACON POTATOES

Prepare Baked Potatoes with Cheese and Bacon, above, substituting ¼ cup finely crumbled blue cheese for the Monterey Jack.

OVEN-ROASTED "FRENCH FRIES" *4 servings*

Rutabagas and turnips also can be cooked this way.

Preheat the oven to 450°F.

Peel and cut lengthwise into ⅜-inch-wide strips:

4 medium baking potatoes (about 1 pound)

Let soak in cold water for 10 minutes, then drain and dry well. Toss the potatoes with:

2 tablespoons vegetable or olive oil

Spread on a baking sheet and bake, turning several times, until golden, 30 to 40 minutes. Turn the potatoes onto paper towels to drain briefly, then sprinkle with:

½ teaspoon salt
Paprika or ground black pepper to taste (optional)

POMMES ANNA *6 to 8 servings*

There is a tinned baking pan designed just for this glorious, rich cake of potatoes, but a cast-iron skillet works perfectly well. A mandoline, shown 411, or an inexpensive plastic version, often called a V-slicer, makes preparation of this dish a breeze.

Position a rack in the center of the oven. Preheat the oven to 425°F.

Have ready:

12 tablespoons (1½ sticks) butter, clarified, 1069

Pour the butter into an 8-inch cast-iron skillet to a depth of ¼ inch. Set over low heat and layer in:

2½ to 3 pounds potatoes, preferably Yukon gold, peeled and sliced ⅛ inch thick

Build the bottom layer especially carefully with overlapping, nicely shaped slices. As you assemble the cake, sprinkle each layer with:

Salt and ground black pepper to taste
Melted butter (optional)

When all the potatoes are in the pan, lightly butter or oil a pot lid slightly smaller than the pan, and press it firmly on top of the potatoes to compress them. Cover the pan and put in the oven over a baking sheet to catch any drips. Bake for 20 minutes, remove the cover, and press down firmly on the potatoes. Bake, uncovered, until the sides are visibly browned and crisp, 20 to 25 minutes more. Holding the lid firmly against the potatoes, tilt the pan and pour off any melted butter that has not been absorbed. To serve, invert the potatoes onto a plate and cut into wedges.

GRATIN DAUPHINOIS *6 to 8 servings*

Use whatever proportion of milk and half-and-half suits you, depending on the richness you desire in the final product. We suggest starting with 2 cups half-and-half to 1 cup milk.

Preheat the oven to 350°F. Rub a 12-inch gratin dish or a shallow 3-quart baking dish with:

1 clove garlic, halved

Let dry, then coat with:

1 tablespoon butter, softened

Combine in a large saucepan or Dutch oven:

2½ pounds baking potatoes, peeled and very thinly sliced
3 cups milk or half-and-half or a combination
1 teaspoon salt
¼ teaspoon ground black pepper
Pinch of freshly grated or ground nutmeg

Bring the mixture to a gentle boil over medium heat, then cook and stir until the liquid thickens slightly, about 5 minutes. Pour the mixture into the prepared dish. Press down on the top layer to submerge the potatoes. Sprinkle with:

1 cup grated Gruyère or Fontinella cheese

Bake until the top is golden and the potatoes are tender, 45 minutes to 1 hour.

SAUTÉED TINY NEW POTATOES *4 servings*

Watch your farmers' market for the first little new potatoes arriving around July. They make this simple dish superlative.

Scrub well and pat dry:

24 very small new potatoes, about the same size

Heat in a large, heavy skillet:

2 tablespoons olive oil or clarified butter, 1069

Roll the potatoes around the pan to coat them, then cover and cook over low heat until tender, about 25 minutes. Every so often give the pan a gentle shake so that they brown evenly. Sprinkle with:

Salt and ground black pepper to taste
Snipped fresh chives, chopped fresh parsley, or other fresh herb (optional)

POTATO AND CHICKEN BAKE *4 servings*

In France, many people used to bring one-pot dinners like this to the village to cook in the baker's oven while they attended church on Sunday. Typically, a leg of lamb or a whole chicken was placed over a bed of potatoes. Here the dish is made with very large chicken breasts; smaller breasts will overcook and dry out before the potatoes are done. For a change, try this dish with a whole chicken, split in half; adjust the cooking time accordingly.

Position a rack in the lower third of the oven. Preheat the oven to 375°F. Lightly grease a shallow 2-quart baking dish with:

Olive oil

Whisk together in a small bowl:

3 tablespoons balsamic vinegar
3 tablespoons olive oil
2 large cloves garlic, minced
1 tablespoon chopped fresh parsley
1 tablespoon chopped fresh basil, chervil, or tarragon, or 1½ teaspoons dried
1 tablespoon chopped fresh savory or thyme, or 1½ teaspoons dried
¼ teaspoon salt
Ground black pepper to taste

Prepare:

1 pound russet or Yukon gold potatoes, peeled and very thinly sliced
1 large sweet onion (about 8 ounces), thinly sliced

Arrange half of the potatoes in the baking dish. Season well with:

Salt and ground black pepper to taste

Spoon one-quarter of the vinaigrette over the potato slices and spread the herbs with a fork. Arrange the onion slices over the potatoes and top with the remaining potato slices. Season and spoon another one-quarter of the vinaigrette over them, spreading the herbs evenly. Top the potatoes with:

4 large chicken breast halves (about 4 pounds), boned but not skinned

Spoon the remaining vinaigrette over the chicken breasts. Bake, uncovered, until the potatoes are tender and the chicken juices run clear when pierced in the thickest part with the tip of a sharp knife, 50 to 60 minutes. Spoon the potatoes, onions, and chicken onto plates and drizzle the pan juices over the chicken.

RADISHES (INCLUDING DAIKON)

Spring and summer radishes—with names like Cherry Belle, Sparkler, and Easter Eggs—are the familiar round radishes, mostly red accents for salads and garnishes. As summer grows hot, so does the flesh of our radishes. The elongated forms, icicles or French Breakfast types, tolerate heat better than the round shapes, which is why they turn up through summer. White icicle radishes are carrot shaped, with milder flesh than red radishes. The name French Breakfast refers to the French custom of swiping a radish through a pot of sweet butter before taking a bite, a refreshing idea at any meal. Spring and summer radishes are best served well rinsed, well chilled, with their leaves on and the rootlet nipped off. A dish of coarse salt is all that is needed for seasoning. If radishes are not thoroughly crisp, they can be revived by soaking in ice water.

By autumn, the large radishes, mostly Asian varieties, are ready. Chinese radishes are round or oval and green and can weigh a pound. Their flesh may be white, green, rose, or all three colors. They are served raw, often carved into delicate roses and other flowers. Autumn also brings enormous (foot-long) pure white, carrot-shaped, juicy radishes called daikon in Japan and mooli in India. Unlike our spring and summer radishes, daikon/mooli radishes are mild in flavor and a valued part of the daily diet—often pickled, added to soup, or grated and cooked with other vegetables and spices. In winter come the turnip-shaped black radishes, black on the outside and snow white on the inside. Their flesh is pungent and relatively dry. Black radishes are a favorite in Russia for slicing or cutting into matchsticks and adding to mixed vegetable salad dressed with sour cream. All these radishes are available in Asian markets.

Raw radishes are excellent with unsalted butter, coarse salt, and cold beer. Allow 3 to 4 small radishes per serving; for large roots in cooking, allow 3 to 4 ounces.

To Prepare: Choose firm, flawless roots and bright, crisp greens. Trim the leaves from the roots and store separately in perforated plastic vegetable bags in the refrigerator crisper. Radish leaves have a shorter keeping life than the roots. The leaves are as tasty and nutritious as turnip greens. Cook them the same way or add them to a tossed salad. Tender, juicy radishes can be prepared in the same ways as turnips. In fact, some varieties of turnips, as babies, are indistinguishable from round white radishes.

To Boil and to Steam: Cook as for turnips, 434.

RED RADISHES WITH SCALLIONS *4 servings*

Trim the leaves and any excessively long roots from:

2 bunches red radishes, well scrubbed

Cut any especially large ones in half or quarters. Melt in a large skillet:

1 tablespoon butter

Cook gently over medium heat until softened, 2 or 3 minutes:

2 bunches scallions (white part and 1 inch of green), cut into ½-inch pieces

Add the radishes along with:

½ cup chicken stock

Cover the pan and simmer until the radishes are tender, 3 to 4 minutes. Uncover, increase the heat to medium-high, and boil rapidly to reduce the pan juices while shaking the pan back and forth a few times. Season with:

Salt to taste

SALSIFY AND SCORZONERA

These are two roots resembling big carrots and parsnips. Botanically, they are unrelated to each other—salsify has beige skin, and scorzonera's skin is nearly black. In terms of texture and flavor, however, they are almost identical, with white to cream-colored flesh hinting of the sea (another name for salsify is oyster plant). Their season is late autumn through winter. If they are homegrown, add their tender leaves to salads. Use only firm, unblemished roots and store in perforated plastic vegetable bags in the refrigerator. The roots sweeten during cold storage.

To Prepare: Because the flesh darkens when exposed to air, and because much of scorzonera's flavor is in its skin, the roots are best cooked unpeeled and whole.

To Steam: Place in a steaming basket over 1 to 2 inches of boiling water. Cover and steam until they can be easily pierced with a thin skewer, about 10 minutes. Be careful not to overcook, or the flesh will be mushy.

To savor their unique delicate flavor, mash cooked salsify or scorzonera with a fork and add butter, salt, pepper, and a pinch of mace or nutmeg. They also can be prepared any way parsnips are and simple ways potatoes are. Allow about 5 ounces per serving.

SALSIFY WITH HERBS *4 servings*

Combine in a bowl:

Juice of 2 lemons

2 cups water, or as needed to cover

Peel, cut into 3-inch lengths, and immediately put into the water:

2 pounds salsify

Bring to a boil in a medium saucepan:

8 cups water

1 tablespoon all-purpose flour

2 tablespoons fresh lemon juice

1 teaspoon salt

Drain the salsify and add to the pan. Boil, uncovered, until tender when pierced with a knife, 10 to 20 minutes. Drain, then toss with:

2 tablespoons butter or olive oil

1½ tablespoons chopped fresh parsley

1½ tablespoons chopped fresh tarragon

2 teaspoons snipped fresh chives

Lemon juice or white wine vinegar to taste

SALSIFY WITH BROWNED BUTTER

Prepare Salsify with Herbs, above, substituting 3 tablespoons Beurre Noisette, 57, for the butter, and 2 tablespoons chopped fresh parsley and 1 clove garlic, chopped, or ¼ cup toasted chopped hazelnuts or almonds for the herbs.

Shallot bulb

SHALLOTS

These are members of the Onion family, usually the size of small boiling onions, with copper, gold, or gray-brown skin. Their flesh can be white, yellow, or pink. Sometimes what appears to be one round shallot will be two half rounds; merely pull them apart. The flavor of a shallot is milder than that of any other onion, but warm and intense. The French use shallots for seasoning far more than onions. In this country, that would be prohibitive. Shallots are expensive because their growing habit makes using machinery impossible—people must care for shallots in the field. Shallots are available year-round because they store well, but they are best when freshly harvested—from mid- to late summer. Select firm bulbs that fill their skins and have no sprouts on top (unless you wish to grow greens).

To Prepare: Trim off the top and base with a small, sharp knife. If you will be chopping or slicing the bulb, cut it lengthwise in half and carefully pull off the skin. If it will be cooked whole, peel, using the tip of the knife. The flesh of shallots can react badly to rough handling. When crushed, it exudes liquid, which may result in the flavor of the shallot going bitter. So chop with care.

Season with shallots in cooking as you would onions but do not brown them—their flavor can be bitter. Best to first soften them in butter, wine, or vinegar. Whole shallots can be cooked like small boiling onions. Shallots go well with butter, white and red wine, vinegar, mushrooms, fish, chicken, and beef.

ROASTED SHALLOTS

About 4 servings

A delectable garnish for simply cooked fish, poultry, meat, and main-dish vegetables.

Preheat the oven to 450°F.

Peel and trim:

1 pound sweet-flavored shallots, about the same size

Using an 8 x 8-inch baking dish or a pan in which the shallots just fit in a single layer, brush the bottom of the dish and the shallots all over with:

3 to 4 teaspoons melted lard, olive oil, or walnut oil

Arrange the shallots in the dish rounded side down. Roast in the middle of the oven for 15 minutes, shaking the dish once or twice to move the bulbs around. Use tongs to turn the shallots over, return to the oven, and roast until 1 or 2 can easily be pierced with a thin skewer, 4 to 5 minutes more. Sprinkle with:

Salt and ground white pepper to taste

Serve at once.

CRISPY SHALLOTS

About ½ cup

Use these crisp, sweet shallots to garnish Asian noodles, stir-fries, rice, and sautéed greens. They will keep for a month in a covered container.

Heat in a small, heavy pan until hot but not smoking:

½ cup peanut oil

⅛ teaspoon ground turmeric

Drop in:

4 large shallots, sliced in thin rounds

Simmer in the oil until they turn light gold, then stir in:

½ teaspoon sugar

Cook until the onions just begin to brown, another 3 to 4 minutes. Remove with a slotted spoon and drain on paper towels. When dry, store in a covered container.

SORREL

Sorrel's leaves look like bright green spinach, but that is where the resemblance ends. Spinach has an earthy green flavor; sorrel is piercingly sour. When spinach cooks, the leaves crumple into a dark green heap that can be chopped or creamed. Cooked sorrel leaves dissolve and turn khaki green. However, used as a seasoning rather than a vegetable, sorrel is exhilarating on the tongue and complementary to everything from potatoes to fish. Sorrel is in season spring, summer, and fall, but its leaves are most tender in spring. Pick the smallest and crispest leaves, with no wilting, soft spots, or tears. Store in perforated plastic vegetable bags in the refrigerator crisper as for greens, 332.

Sorrel ribbons are delightful in salads. Like spinach, the leaves contain a considerable amount of oxalic acid, so do not make a steady diet of raw leaves. Sorrel is delicious with cream in any form, butter, fish, potatoes, chervil, and chicken. Allow 2 to 4 ounces per serving.

To Prepare: Rinse and nip off the stems at the base of the leaves (the stems can contain annoying fibers). Either strip the leafy greens from the ribs and cut them crosswise into thin ribbons or keep tender leaves whole. Sorrel needs very little cooking (be sure to use a pan that is not aluminum, or the pan will discolor). For soup, add ribbons of greens to the pot during the last 3 to 4 minutes of cooking. For a sauce, cook ribbons in a little butter, stock, or water in an uncovered skillet, stirring, until the leaves have completely wilted and changed color. Whole leaves may need to be pureed through a food mill.

SPINACH

Spinach is available all year at the market, but its peak season is the cool of spring and fall. As with all greens, choose only those that are crisp, bright, and unblemished—no soft spots, wet places, wilting, yellowing, or tears. Store unwashed in perforated plastic vegetable bags in the refrigerator crisper.

Spinach has great affinities not just with butter, cream, and cheese but also with lemon, vinegar, eggs, garlic, dill, parsley, basil, nutmeg, onion, mushrooms, bacon, anchovies, and fish. Allow 5 to 8 ounces per serving.

To Prepare: Wash thoroughly just before serving. Twist off the pink root ends (called crowns), and rinse and save them for tossing in salad. Nip off stems at the base of the leaves and chop the tender stems for soup. Either use leaves whole, or stack and cut crosswise into thin ribbons, or tear into small pieces.
To Boil: Cook as for chard, 364, until just wilted, 1 to 2 minutes.
To Steam: Cook as for chard, 364, until just wilted, 3 to 4 minutes, turning the leaves every minute so they cook evenly.
To Wilt: Cook as for chard, 364, just until tender, about 2 minutes.
To Microwave: Place 1 pound rinsed leaves in a 3-quart baking dish. Cover and cook on high until tender, 5 to 7 minutes, stirring after 3 minutes. Let stand, covered, for 5 minutes.

WILTED SPINACH OR CHARD *2 or 3 servings*

Combined with ricotta cheese, this makes an excellent filling for ravioli.
Wash thoroughly but do not dry:

12 well-packed cups spinach or chard leaves or a combination

Coarsely chop, then place in a large skillet. Season with:

Salt to taste

Cook, stirring frequently, over medium heat until completely wilted but still bright green, about 5 minutes. Remove to a serving dish and toss with:

Extra-virgin olive oil
Dash of white wine vinegar, red wine vinegar, or lemon juice
Ground black pepper to taste

Or serve plain with:

Georgian Garlic and Walnut Sauce, 82

Serve immediately.

CREAMED SPINACH *4 to 6 servings*

Small portions are filling. Creamed spinach also serves as a filling for mushrooms and zucchini, cannelloni, ravioli, and pancakes or crêpes.
Wash thoroughly but do not dry:

1½ to 2 pounds spinach, stemmed

Place in a large saucepan over medium heat and cook, covered, in the water clinging to the leaves until wilted, 4 to 5 minutes. Remove to a colander, rinse quickly, and press out as much water as possible. Finely chop. Bring to a boil in a large skillet:

½ cup heavy cream

Add the cooked spinach and season with:

½ teaspoon salt
Freshly grated or ground nutmeg to taste
Ground black pepper to taste

Cook over medium heat until the cream has reduced, about 3 minutes. If the cream reduces more than you want, making the spinach a little dry, moisten it again by adding:

2 to 3 tablespoons milk, light cream, or water

Serve hot, garnished with one of the following:

Hard-boiled eggs, sliced, chopped, or pressed through a sieve
Crumbled cooked bacon
Buttered small croutons
White sauce or Sauce Mornay, 46
Hollandaise Sauce, 55
Beurre Blanc, 57

PUREED SPINACH

Prepare Creamed Spinach, above, then remove the mixture to a food processor and process until smooth, leaving a little texture or not, as you wish.

GARLICKY SPINACH *2 or 3 servings*

Heat in a large, heavy skillet:

1½ tablespoons olive oil

Add:

2 or 3 cloves garlic, minced
2 anchovies, rinsed, patted dry, and finely chopped (optional)

Cook over medium-low heat until the garlic is just beginning to color, 30 to 60 seconds. Add:

1 pound fresh spinach, stemmed, washed well, and shaken dry, or two 10-ounce packages frozen

Cover the pan and cook over high heat until steam appears. Reduce the heat and simmer, covered, until tender, 2 to 3 minutes. Season with:

Salt and ground black pepper to taste

Or pass a bowl of:

Nam Prik (Thai Hot Sauce), 82, or Ginger Soy Sauce, 84

SPINACH WITH CURRANTS AND PINE NUTS *4 to 6 servings*

This unusual combination is much appreciated in portions of the Mediterranean, from Catalonia to Sicily to Greece.
Wash thoroughly but do not dry:

2 pounds spinach, stemmed

Coarsely chop and place the wet spinach in a large saucepan. Season with:

Salt to taste

Cover and cook over medium heat until the spinach is just wilted, about 5 minutes. Drain well. Heat in a large skillet over medium heat:

¼ cup olive oil

Add:

¼ cup pine nuts

Cook just until they begin to color, about 2 minutes. Add:

2 cloves garlic, finely minced

Cook another minute. Add the spinach along with:

¼ cup dried currants

Salt and ground black pepper to taste

Cook, stirring frequently, about 5 minutes more. Serve hot.

SAAG PANEER

4 servings

Saag Paneer, which literally translates as "spinach cheese," is a typical Indian vegetarian combination of vegetables and protein, in this case a fresh cheese. Our recipe is a variation on the traditional recipe—the spinach is stir-fried quickly rather than cooked to a puree. Be sure to use a nonstick pan to fry the cheese so it does not stick.

In a medium, heavy saucepan, bring to a boil:

4 cups whole milk

Remove the pan from the heat and add:

3 tablespoons fresh lemon juice

Stir until the milk curdles and separates into bits of solid curd floating in the liquid whey. Let stand for 5 minutes, then pour through a fine-mesh sieve lined with a double layer of cheesecloth. Let stand until cool enough to handle, then pull the corners of the cloth together over the curd and squeeze out as much liquid as possible. Flatten the curd, still in the cheesecloth, to a thickness of ½ to 1 inch. Set it on a plate and top with another plate. Weight with a can and let stand for 20 minutes, then cut the cheese into ½-inch cubes.

Coarsely chop:

Two 10-ounce bunches spinach, stemmed and washed well

Heat in a large nonstick skillet over medium-high heat:

¼ cup canola oil

Add and cook until lightly browned, about 15 seconds:

1 teaspoon cumin seeds

Add the cheese cubes and sauté, shaking the pan every now and then to turn the cubes, until golden brown, 3 to 4 minutes. Remove the cheese and set aside. Add to the oil in the pan:

1 medium onion, thinly sliced

Cook until softened and translucent, 3 to 4 minutes. Add and sauté for 1 minute:

4 cloves garlic, thinly sliced

2 small dried red chili peppers

Add as much chopped spinach as will comfortably fit into the pan, cover, and cook until wilted enough to add more spinach. Add a few more handfuls of spinach, cover, and continue until all the spinach is wilted. Sprinkle with:

½ teaspoon salt

Cook, uncovered, until all the water is evaporated. Fold in the fried cheese, remove the red peppers, and serve hot.

GREEK SPINACH AND CHEESE PIE (SPANAKOPITA)

About thirty 2-inch squares or diamonds

Stem, wash well, and coarsely chop:

2 pounds (or three 10-ounce bags) spinach

Heat in a large skillet over medium heat:

2 tablespoons olive oil

Add and cook until softened, 5 to 7 minutes:

1 large onion, finely chopped

4 scallions, finely chopped

Add the chopped spinach a handful at a time. Cook until the spinach is wilted and the liquid is released, 5 minutes. Increase the heat to high and cook, stirring often, until the liquid has evaporated and the spinach is dry, 7 to 10 minutes. Stir in:

¼ cup snipped fresh dill or chopped fresh parsley

Let stand until cool enough to handle, then squeeze to remove the excess liquid. In a medium bowl, lightly beat:

4 large eggs

Add the cooked spinach mixture along with:

8 ounces feta cheese, crumbled

2 tablespoons grated kefalotiri (Greek grating cheese) or Parmesan cheese

½ teaspoon salt

Several grinds of black pepper

Pinch of freshly grated or ground nutmeg

Lightly oil a 13 x 9-inch baking pan. Melt:

8 tablespoons (1 stick) butter

Unroll on a dry work surface:

1 pound phyllo dough, thawed if frozen

Trim 1 inch from the edges of the phyllo dough. Cover with a dry towel and cover the dry towel with a damp towel. Lay 1 sheet of phyllo in and up the sides of the prepared pan and brush lightly with melted butter. Top with 7 more phyllo sheets, brushing each one lightly with butter. Spread the spinach mixture over the layered phyllo. Top with 8 more sheets, brushing each one with butter, including the top sheet. Roll the overhanging phyllo from the sides to form a border all the way around. With a thin, sharp knife, cut the pie into squares or diamonds, but do not cut through the bottom or the filling will leak onto the pan. Refrigerate for 30 minutes.

Preheat the oven to 375°F.

Bake the spinach pie until crisp and golden, about 45 minutes. Remove from the oven and let stand for a few minutes. Cut the squares or diamonds right through to the bottom and serve.

SPINACH AND CHEESE TIROPITES

About 45 triangles

Prepare the spinach filling for Greek Spinach and Cheese Pie, above. Brush 1 sheet of phyllo with melted butter. Place another sheet on top of the first and brush with butter. Cut lengthwise into 3-inch-wide strips. Put a heaping tablespoon of filling at one end about 1 inch from the edge and fold the corner over it to make a triangle. Continue to fold, as you would a flag, until the whole strip is folded into a triangular packet. Brush with melted butter. Repeat with the remaining filling and phyllo. Bake the tiropites on a baking sheet until golden brown, 15 to 20 minutes. Tiropites can be assembled in advance, frozen, and baked just before serving.

SUMMER SQUASH AND SQUASH BLOSSOMS

Summer squash is another vegetable picked at an immature stage, as green beans and sweet corn are. Let a zucchini grow until its shell is hard, and you can treat it like a winter squash. Over the years, farmers, gardeners, and cooks have harvested in summer those winter squash that taste best when their skin is still thin. In fact, as long as we are eating squash young, we should pick them very young. Most French and Italian cooks feel a summer squash is over the hill if it has no blossom attached. Squash cross-pollinate very easily, and breeders are also constantly working on new forms. In addition, a gene called *precocious yellow* has been threaded into the genes of traditional shapes, giving us bright yellow pattypans and zucchini with deep, sweet, buttery flavor.

Look for the following squash at farmers' markets (better still, grow them yourself). All but tromboncino belong to the group that gives us acorn winter squash and most pumpkins; tromboncino comes from the group that gives us butternut winter squash. Cocozelle is a heritage Italian-style zucchini, pale green with light ridges; fine-grained, nutty, superbly flavored flesh; 4 to 6 inches long and slender. Cousa is a heritage Middle Eastern–style zucchini, very light green, 3 to 4 inches long and blocky, with mild, lightly sweet flesh. Marrow is an English-style zucchini, pure white, fine textured, and tapered 6 to 8 inches long. Pattypan or scallop squash are flattened rounds with scalloped edges, picked 3 inches wide or less. Their flavor is lighter and nuttier than zucchini. Heritage pattypans are pale green. Hybrids are more rounded and can be gold (Sunburst, with the precocious yellow gene) or dark green. Tromboncino is an intriguing pale green heirloom—long, thin, trombone shaped, picked at 8 to 12 inches, with sweet, fine-grained flesh. Yellow crookneck are heritage American squash with bright yellow, bumpy skin on bulbous-shaped squash with slender curved necks 4 to 5 inches long, and incomparable sweet flavor. Pattypan and yellow crookneck squash, because of their sweeter flavor, are good mashed. Straightneck squash have the same flavor but look like yellow zucchini. Zucchini nowadays are thin, dark green, and 6 to 8 inches long; similarly long and thin

Crookneck squash

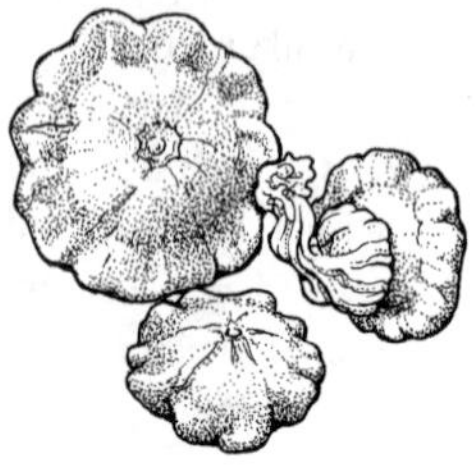

Pattypan squash

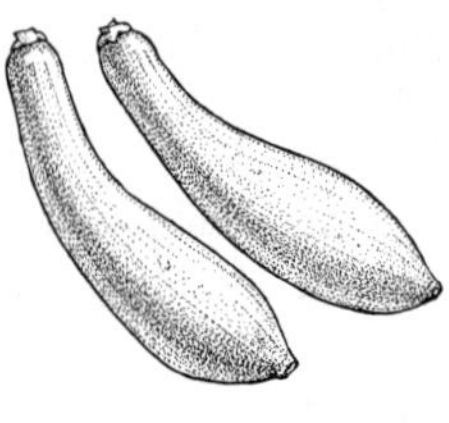

Yellow squash

Zucchini with blossom

but bright gold (Gold Rush); and nutty 1- to 4-inch rounds.

Select the smallest, firmest, glossiest squash, heaviest for their size, without soft spots or other blemishes. Store in perforated plastic vegetable bags in the refrigerator crisper.

With their mild, sweet flesh, summer squash are excellent with most of summer's flavors, especially tomatoes, onions, peppers (both sweet and chili), garlic, oregano, marjoram, basil, parsley, dill, rosemary, sage, and tarragon, as well as lemon, cheese, butter, olive oil, and capers. Allow about 5 ounces per serving.

To Prepare: Simply rinse. The stalks are edible if tender enough; otherwise, trim them off. Never peel summer squash. Small cubes or matchsticks are delicious in salads and on the raw vegetable tray—in fact, young squash can often be prepared the same way as cucumbers. The best way to preserve the flavor and texture of these delicate vegetables is to cook them as quickly as possible in as little liquid as possible.

To Boil: Bring 16 cups (4 quarts) water and 1½ tablespoons salt to a rolling boil in a stockpot. Add the prepared squash and cook just until tender but still crisp. Whole baby squash, ½-inch cubes, ¼-inch slices, and matchsticks will cook in 2 to 4 minutes; squash quarters or halves in 6 to 8 minutes, depending on thickness. Drain.

To Steam: Place prepared squash in a steamer basket over 1 to 2 inches boiling water. Cook, covered, just until tender but still crisp. Whole baby squash, ½-inch cubes, ¼-inch slices, and matchsticks will cook in 4 to 6 minutes; squash quarters or halves in 7 to 10 minutes, depending on thickness. If cooking more than 1 layer, stir gently about halfway through.

To Microwave: Place 2 cups slices in a 1-quart baking dish. Cover and cook on high just until tender, 2 to 4 minutes, stirring after 2 minutes. Let stand, covered, for 1 minute.

Squash blossoms (taken from both summer and winter squash) are sometimes available at the market. Rush them home and prepare them as soon as possible, for they wilt quickly. To pick your own, choose excess male blossoms (with no rounding at the base) just before using. Flowers will last in perforated plastic vegetable bags in the refrigerator crisper for a few hours if necessary. Do not wash unless the blossoms are dusty. Remove the stem and calyx if they seem tough. Inspect for insects. Squash blossoms are delightful stuffed and baked, and they make lovely sweet or savory fritters. Allow three per person.

SAUTÉED SUMMER SQUASH WITH PARSLEY AND GARLIC

4 servings

Give squash plenty of space in a hot skillet so it can sear and brown before giving up its juices. If you find ½-inch-thick baby squashes, just leave them whole.

Dice or slice into ½-inch-thick pieces:

1½ pounds summer squash

Heat in a large skillet over high heat:

3 tablespoons olive oil

Drop in the squash a handful at a time, and let each gain a little color before adding the next handful. Sauté until all the squash is golden and tender, about 7 minutes. Remove to a serving dish and toss with:

3 tablespoons chopped fresh parsley
2 large cloves garlic, finely chopped
1 teaspoon grated lemon zest (optional)
Salt and ground black pepper to taste

SUMMER SQUASH AND PASTA

4 to 6 servings

Steam until tender:

1 pound summer squash, cut into ½-inch-thick batons or dice

Toss in a bowl with:

1 pound mostaccioli, penne, or macaroni, cooked and drained
½ to ¾ cup Pesto Sauce, 307

BRAISED CROOKNECK SQUASH WITH ONIONS AND HERBS

4 servings

The squash should be of similar size so that they cook in the same amount of time; cut larger squash into pieces if necessary.

Cook in a large skillet over medium heat until the onion is wilted, about 4 minutes:

2 to 3 tablespoons butter or olive oil, or a combination
1 small onion, finely diced

Add:

1½ pounds small crookneck squash or mixed summer squash, rinsed and halved lengthwise

Increase the heat to high and sauté until heated through. Reduce the heat to medium and add:

¾ cup water or chicken stock

Cover and cook until the squash is tender, about 10 minutes, depending on size. Season with:

1 tablespoon chopped fresh tarragon, dill, or opal basil, or 2 teaspoons chopped fresh marjoram
Salt and ground black pepper to taste

ZUCCHINI WITH CORN AND CHILI PEPPERS

8 servings

Known in the Southwest and Mexico as *calabacitas*, this side dish also can be served as a vegetarian entrée, accompanied by beans and tortillas.

Heat in a large skillet over medium heat:

3 tablespoons corn oil or butter

Cook, stirring, until softened, about 8 minutes:

1 white onion, finely chopped

2 pounds summer squash, zucchini, or a combination, diced

Add:

2 cups corn kernels, preferably fresh (from 4 large ears)

3 New Mexico (red Anaheim) or poblano peppers, roasted, 402, and chopped

½ cup water, milk, or light cream

½ teaspoon salt

1 to 2 serrano peppers (optional), roasted, 402, and chopped

Cover and simmer for 8 minutes. Season with:

Salt and ground black pepper to taste

Garnish with:

4 scallions, thinly sliced

2 tablespoons chopped fresh cilantro or parsley

ZUCCHINI PANCAKES WITH MINT AND FETA CHEESE

About 19 pancakes; 6 to 8 servings

Shred on the large holes of a grater or in a food processor:

2½ pounds green or golden zucchini

Sprinkle lightly with:

Salt

Mix together in a bowl:

2 large eggs

½ cup crumbled feta cheese

½ cup dry unseasoned breadcrumbs

¼ cup all-purpose flour

1 bunch scallions (white part and 2 inches of green), slivered

2 cloves garlic, minced

½ cup chopped fresh parsley

3 tablespoons chopped fresh mint or 1½ tablespoons chopped fresh marjoram

Salt and ground black pepper to taste

Quickly rinse the squash, then, using your hands or a towel, squeeze out the excess liquid. Add the squash to the batter.

Preheat the oven to 200°F.

Heat in a large skillet:

2 tablespoons olive oil

Drop in the batter, using ¼ cup for a 4-inch cake. Fry over medium heat until golden brown on the bottom, about 4 minutes. Turn and brown the second side. Keep the fried pancakes warm in the oven while you fry the remaining batter, adding more oil if needed.

FRIED ZUCCHINI IN HERB BATTER

4 servings

Mushrooms, bell pepper strips, and thin sweet potato slices also are good fried in this batter.

Slice into ¼-inch-thick rounds:

4 medium zucchini (6 to 7 inches each)

Mix together in a bowl:

1 cup all-purpose flour

¾ cup club soda

3 tablespoons chopped fresh flat-leaf parsley

2 tablespoons minced fresh thyme, chives, marjoram, and/or sage

½ teaspoon salt

If the batter is too thick, stir in:

Up to ¼ cup club soda

Add the zucchini slices and coat them in the batter. Pour into a deep fryer or deep, heavy pot and heat to 350°F.

2 inches vegetable or peanut oil

Add the zucchini, a few slices at a time, to the hot oil. Deep-fry, stirring the slices, until golden, 2 to 3 minutes. Remove with a slotted spoon and drain on paper towels. Serve immediately, sprinkled with:

Sea salt to taste (optional)

Fresh lemon juice or cider vinegar

If desired, accompany with:

Tart Corn Relish, 65

ZUCCHINI CASSEROLE

4 main-course servings

This casserole is best if allowed to cool for 20 to 30 minutes before serving. It is also very good at room temperature or even cold.

Preheat the oven to 350°F. Butter a 10 x 8-inch baking dish.

Coarsely grate:

1½ pounds zucchini

Remove to a colander and stir in:

2 teaspoons coarse salt

Weight the zucchini and let drain for 30 minutes. Squeeze the zucchini between your hands to remove as much liquid as possible. Meanwhile, thinly slice:

2 medium onions

2 ounces (about 6 medium) shiitake mushrooms, wiped clean, stems removed

Heat in a medium skillet over medium heat:

2 tablespoons olive oil

Add the onions and mushrooms and sprinkle with:

½ teaspoon coarse salt

Cook, stirring occasionally, until the onions are softened but not browned, about 20 minutes. Meanwhile, peel and grate:

12 ounces baking or Yukon gold potatoes

Put the potatoes into a bowl and immediately stir in:

3 large eggs, well beaten
⅛ teaspoon ground black pepper
Pinch of ground red pepper

Stir in the drained zucchini, the onion mixture, and half of:

½ cup grated Gruyère cheese
¼ cup grated Parmesan cheese

Scrape the mixture into the baking dish and smooth the top. Sprinkle with the remaining cheeses and drizzle over the top:

1 tablespoon olive oil

Cover with aluminum foil and bake until set, about 1 hour. Remove the foil and broil to brown the top. Let stand for at least 20 minutes before serving.

SQUASH BLOSSOMS STUFFED WITH CHEESE AND HERBS

4 servings

The blossoms of zucchini and other squash are much appreciated around the Mediterranean and in Latin America. Use the stems as handles and eat these by hand, or serve them with a light tomato sauce.

Remove the pistils, leaving the stems on:

12 large squash blossoms

Mince together:

1 clove garlic, peeled
¼ teaspoon salt

Transfer to a bowl and mix with:

¾ cup fresh goat cheese, ricotta, or shredded mozzarella or Monterey Jack cheese (about 3 ounces)
½ cup grated Parmesan cheese
1 tablespoon chopped fresh parsley
1 tablespoon chopped fresh basil or 2 teaspoons chopped fresh thyme
Ground black pepper to taste

Carefully open the petals of each blossom and stuff about 1 tablespoon of the mixture into the base. Twist the tops of the petals together. Dip the blossoms 1 at a time into:

1 large egg, lightly beaten

Then coat with:

All-purpose flour

Shake off any excess. Heat in a medium skillet:

½ inch light olive oil

Fry the blossoms 3 or 4 at a time, turning occasionally, over medium heat until golden, 2 to 4 minutes. Drain briefly on paper towels. Serve right away.

BAKED STUFFED ZUCCHINI

2 to 4 servings

A side dish for four, a vegetarian main dish for two. These can be made hours ahead of time.

Preheat the oven to 400°F.

Halve lengthwise:

2 medium zucchini (6 to 7 inches each)

With a small spoon, carefully scrape out the pulp, leaving a ⅜-inch-thick shell. Steam, 338, the shells cut side down for 5 minutes. Coarsely chop the pulp. Heat in a small skillet until softened, about 3 minutes:

2 teaspoons olive oil or butter
3 tablespoons finely chopped onions or scallions

Meanwhile, squeeze the moisture out of the chopped zucchini, then add it to the pan along with:

1 clove garlic, minced

Cook for 2 minutes more. Turn into a bowl and combine with:

1 large egg, lightly beaten
½ cup grated Parmesan or aged Monterey Jack cheese
⅓ cup dry unseasoned bread crumbs
2 tablespoons chopped fresh parsley
2 teaspoons chopped fresh marjoram, tarragon, basil, or thyme
½ teaspoon grated lemon zest
Salt and ground black pepper to taste

Spoon the filling into the zucchini shells and set them in a baking dish. Drizzle the tops with:

Olive oil

Add water to come ⅛ inch up the sides of the shells. Bake until the zucchini is tender and the top is browned, about 30 minutes. Let cool for a few minutes before serving.

BAKED SQUASH WITH PARMESAN AND HERBS

4 to 6 servings

Baking squash, once it is steamed, gives the top layer texture and color and concentrates the vegetable's flavor.

Preheat the oven to 375°F. Lightly butter or oil a large gratin dish.

Steam over boiling water for 4 minutes:

1¼ pounds squash, thinly sliced

Make a layer of the steamed squash in the dish. Season with:

Salt and ground black pepper to taste

Sprinkle with half of:

2 tablespoons grated Parmesan cheese

1 tablespoon chopped fresh marjoram, 1 tablespoon Pesto Sauce, 307, or 1 teaspoon dried herbes de Provence

Repeat with a second layer of squash, seasonings, and the remaining Parmesan and herbs. Sprinkle the top with:

2 tablespoons olive oil or butter or Anchovy Butter, 77, cut into small pieces

Bake until heated through, about 25 minutes. Serve with:

Lemon wedges

SUMMER SQUASH GRATIN *6 servings*

This crumbly, golden gratin is irresistible. Try it with straightneck or pattypan squash or whatever summer squash is available.

Preheat the oven to 350°F. Lightly butter a 10-inch gratin dish.

Steam until tender, about 10 minutes:

1¼ pounds yellow squash, cut into ½-inch cubes

Remove to a medium bowl. Cook in a small skillet until softened:

1 tablespoon butter or olive oil

½ small onion, finely diced

Add to the squash along with:

⅔ cup diced Monterey Jack, raclette, Swiss, or Teleme cheese

⅓ cup crème fraîche

2 tablespoons grated Parmesan cheese

1 tablespoon white vermouth or dry white wine

1 teaspoon ground coriander

Salt and ground white pepper to taste

Pour into the prepared dish. Combine and sprinkle over the top:

½ cup fresh breadcrumbs

1 tablespoon melted butter

Bake until bubbling and golden, about 35 minutes.

SUMMER SQUASH, SWEET PEPPER, AND POLENTA CASSEROLE *4 servings*

This firm-textured casserole, full of garden-fresh vegetables, can be sliced like a pie and served at room temperature.

Position a rack in the center of the oven. Preheat the oven to 350°F. Generously butter a 9-inch round baking dish.

Heat in a large, heavy skillet over medium-high heat:

½ tablespoon unsalted butter

½ tablespoon olive oil

Add and cook, stirring, for 3 minutes:

1 small onion, coarsely chopped

1 red bell pepper, cut into ½-inch pieces

2 small red-skinned new potatoes, peeled and cut into ½-inch cubes

Stir in and cook until the vegetables are partially softened but not browned, about 2 minutes:

2 large cloves garlic, minced

Add and cook, stirring, until almost tender, 4 to 5 minutes:

1 medium yellow squash, cut into ¾-inch cubes

1 medium zucchini, cut into ¾-inch cubes

In a large bowl, toss together:

½ cup cornmeal

¼ cup all-purpose flour

¼ cup grated Parmesan cheese

1 tablespoon fresh thyme leaves

1 teaspoon salt

1 teaspoon ground black pepper

In a separate bowl, whisk together:

1 cup milk

2 large eggs

Whisk the egg mixture into the cornmeal mixture until combined. Stir the vegetables into the loose batter and spread it in the prepared baking dish. Bake until firm, 25 to 30 minutes. Sprinkle with:

6 tablespoons grated Gruyère cheese (about 2 ounces)

Bake until golden around the edges, about 7 minutes more. Serve hot or at room temperature.

WINTER SQUASH (INCLUDING PUMPKIN)

Native to this hemisphere, many of our noble squash are of ancient heritage. Many are brilliantly colored, beautifully shaped, and of a generous size. The texture of cooked winter squash is thick and velvety. It can taste intensely sweet and rich or bland. If you are planning to bake pies and/or cakes with winter squash and have a choice, choose a squash with dry flesh. For the table, moist-fleshed squash are preferred. A selection of the following squash should be available in winter and spring.

Acorn squash are a deeply ridged acorn shape, in black, dark green, or orange. They weigh 1 to 3 pounds, convenient for 1 to 2 servings. Their flesh is yellow to orange, moderately sweet, but relatively bland. Orange acorns often are sweetest and have the best flavor. Ambercup is a 3-pound hybrid with a red-orange color and shape and extra-sweet, dry flesh. Banana is a huge (10 to 75 pounds) cylinder with ivory to pink rind and dense orange flesh that is moderately sweet and tasty. Buttercup and Kabocha, or green hokkaido, are more or less drum shaped, 3 to 5 pounds, with rinds that can be dark green to black. Their flesh is deep orange, immensely rich and sweet, and on the dry side, even flaky. Kabocha/green hokkaido was developed in Japan from buttercup. Butternut is tan and long necked with a bulb at one end; inside, the orange flesh is rich, sweet, dry, and superb. These 4- to 6-pound squash have the least waste of any winter squash, since the neck is solid and just the bulb contains seeds. Cushaw is pear shaped, and different varieties come in sizes from 12 to 40 pounds. Usually the shell is a shade of green and the flesh is yellow, thick, fine grained, and sweet. It is excellent for pies. Delicata and Sweet Dumpling are two different forms of the same squash. Delicata is cylindrical and Sweet Dumpling is round. Both are deeply ridged and ivory to yellow with green stripes. They weigh about 8 ounces and are charming baked for a single serving. Their moist orange flesh is reminiscent of sweet potatoes—in fact, they are sometimes called Sweet Potato Squash. Hokkaido, or orange hokkaido, is red-orange, with a globe or teardrop shape, weighing 4 to 7 pounds. It was developed in Japan from Hubbard squash, which its flesh resembles. Hubbard is another richly flavored squash. Shaped like an old-fashioned top, the shell can be green, blue-gray, or gold and is often warted. Traditional Hubbards weight 8 to 20 pounds, but now there are 2½- to 4-pound sizes. The flesh is deep orange, fine grained, sweet, and dry. Pumpkin is the name we have given orange winter squash with rounded shapes, usually ridged, containing orange flesh. No pumpkin is a specific type, the way the rest of these squash are, but no matter. The finest all-purpose pumpkin—good for mashing, pies, and jack-o'lanterns—is Connecticut Field. It reaches 15 to 25 pounds. Small Sugar is considered the finest pie pumpkin, around 7 pounds. (Connecticut Field has been a favorite since before 1700, and Small Sugar was introduced before the Civil War.) New pumpkins include many that are palm sized, but these are strictly for decoration. Vegetable Spaghetti, usually called spaghetti squash, is yellow and cylindrical, with pale yellow, translucent fibers that behave like spaghetti on the plate—and has pasta's bland taste. It is fun to eat, a favorite with children.

To select winter squash, even if a cut piece, choose one that is heavy for its size, with a thick, hard shell showing no soft spots, mold, cuts, or bruises. Store whole squash unwrapped in a cool, dark, dry place with good ventilation. Store cut pieces in plastic wrap and refrigerate.

Winter squash are delicious not only baked and mashed but also added to soups, stews, gratins, and savory tarts and combined with other vegetables in purees. They have good quality when frozen mashed. Squash are tasty with butter, cream, garlic, spicy cheeses, thyme, sage, mushrooms, pork, and toasted nuts. On average, 1 pound untrimmed squash yields a generous 13 ounces edible flesh or 1¾ cups cooked puree. Allow 8 to 12 ounces untrimmed squash per serving.

To Prepare: Scrub the squash before cooking. If baking whole, leave as is. If baking in pieces, leave the peel on. For all other cooking techniques, peel the squash by cutting in half or in pieces if large. Cutting into the thick, hard shell of a long-stored winter squash can be difficult, if not dangerous. Use a strong, sharp, heavy knife, preferably serrated. It is best if someone can steady the squash for you. If not, set the squash on a

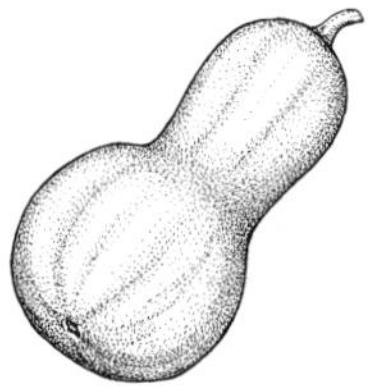

Butternut squash

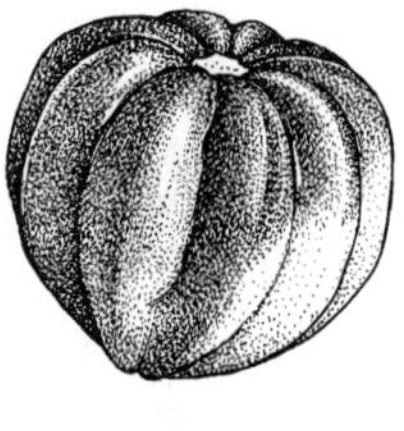

Acorn squash

Pumpkin

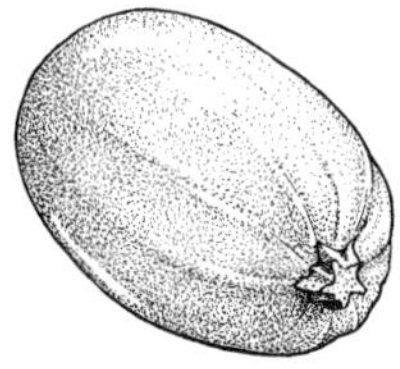

Spaghetti squash

thick towel. Cut slowly and deliberately, plunging in the tip of the knife first, then pulling down on the rest of the blade—you may have to hammer it with a mallet. Rather than try to saw your way through, lift the knife out and start again. Remove the seeds and strings, and peel with a vegetable peeler or a paring knife. Cut the squash into chunks, cubes, or slices.

To Steam: Place prepared squash cut side down in a steaming basket over 1 to 2 inches boiling water. Cook, covered, until easily pierced with a thin skewer or knife tip, 12 to 15 minutes for 1-inch cubes, 15 to 20 minutes for small squash halves like Delicata or Sweet Dumpling, 25 to 30 minutes for large pieces of squash.

To Roast or Bake Whole: Scrub the squash before cutting. Squash that will comfortably fit into your oven can be baked whole quite successfully. This saves the most nutrients and is an easier way to deal with a hard shell than trying to cut it. Deeply pierce the squash in 4 to 5 places around the top with a knife—air vents to keep the squash from exploding. Set the squash in a baking dish or on a rimmed baking sheet (it may ooze sugary juices) and bake in the middle of a 375°F oven until the flesh tests tender when pierced with a thin skewer or knife. A small squash may take 45 minutes; a whole butternut, 1½ hours. Cut in half through the stem, scoop out seeds and strings, and serve as desired.

To Roast or Bake Pieces: Large squash must be cut into pieces for cooking. Bake halves, quarters, or slabs of winter squash cut side down on a rimmed baking sheet. Remove the seeds and strings before baking. Add ¼ inch water to the pan and cover the pan with aluminum foil. Bake in a 400°F oven until tender when pierced with a thin skewer. Halfway through the baking, pieces can be turned over with tongs, brushed with butter or mild oil, and sprinkled with brown sugar and nutmeg or other spice. Allow 30 to 45 minutes for small pieces. Serve in the shell.

To Microwave: A whole acorn squash can be microwaved. Pierce the squash in 4 or 5 places with a sharp knife. Place on a paper towel. Cook on high until tender, 7 to 10 minutes, turning the squash over after 4 minutes. Cover with a cloth and let stand for 5 minutes. For squash cut into 1-inch cubes, place in a 2-quart baking dish. Cover and cook on high until tender, 6 minutes, stirring after 3 minutes. Let stand, covered, for 2 minutes. For slices, cover and cook on high heat until tender, 7 minutes, stirring after 3 minutes. Let stand, covered, for 2 minutes.

To Pressure-Cook: Winter squash can be pressure-cooked if cut into 1-inch-thick cubes or slices. Cook with 1½ cups liquid at 15 pounds pressure for 12 minutes. Cool the cooker at once.

To Bake Seeds: Winter squash seeds are a tasty bonus. To roast them, separate them from the strings but do not wash. Toss the seeds with 1 tablespoon vegetable oil per 1 cup seeds and a little salt, if desired. Spread the seeds on a baking sheet and bake at 250°F until dry, about 1½ hours. The seeds then may be seasoned and toasted in a 350°F oven.

SWEET OR SAVORY WINTER SQUASH PUREE

All winter squashes are good for pureeing.

Bake until softened, above:

Whole small winter squash or pieces of large ones

Remove the seeds and fibers, then measure the pulp and scrape it into a bowl. For a sweet puree, add for every 1 cup pulp:

1 tablespoon butter
1 teaspoon brown sugar or maple syrup
¼ teaspoon ground ginger, or to taste
Salt and ground black pepper to taste

For a savory puree, add for every 1 cup pulp:

1 tablespoon butter or olive oil
1 small clove garlic, minced (optional)
1 tablespoon chopped fresh parsley or sage
Salt and ground black pepper to taste

Beat in with a spoon, adding enough to make a smooth, soft puree:

Warm heavy cream or orange juice

Serve plain or top with:

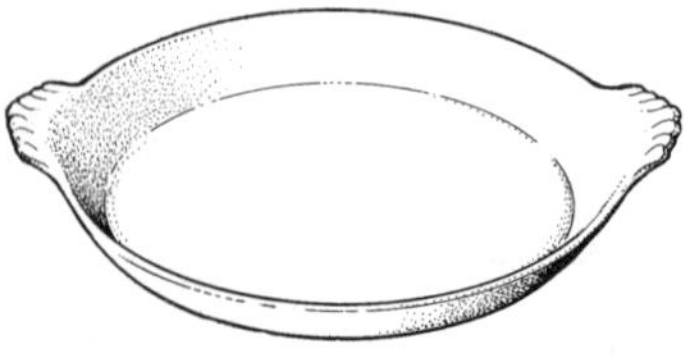

Gratin dish

Casserole

Sautéed Onions, 391, fine shreds of lemon zest, mascarpone or sour cream, or grated Parmesan or Gruyère cheese

SPAGHETTI SQUASH "SPAGHETTI"

4 to 6 servings

This odd squash really does produce long, spaghetti-like strands that can be tossed with butter or tomato sauce, like pasta.
Pierce generously with a knife tip to keep it from exploding:

1 medium spaghetti squash (about 2 pounds)

Place it on the turntable of a microwave and cook on high until tender when pressed with your fingers or pierced with a thin skewer, about 15 minutes. If you do not have a turntable, rotate the squash every 5 minutes during the cooking time. Let cool for 10 minutes before cutting the squash. Halve the squash and remove the seeds, then scrape the strands into a bowl and separate them with a fork to make "spaghetti." Toss with:

Butter or olive oil
Grated Parmesan cheese
Salt and ground black pepper to taste
Red pepper flakes (optional)

GRATED BUTTERNUT SQUASH GRATIN

4 servings

While many vegetable gratins make excellent vegetarian main-course dishes, because of its fine, rather uniform texture, this gratin is better served as a side dish. The straight, long neck of the butternut squash is easiest to peel and grate.
Preheat the oven to 375°F. Rub a 10-inch gratin dish with:

1 clove garlic, crushed

Butter the dish. Chop what is left of the garlic and combine it in a saucepan with:

1½ cups milk or half-and-half, scalded

Let stand. Slice the neck from:

1 large butternut squash

You should have about 12 ounces. Peel it, then grate on the large holes of a four-sided grater or in a food processor. Toss the shreds with:

2 tablespoons all-purpose flour
1 teaspoon salt
Ground black pepper to taste
½ cup shredded fontina or Gruyère cheese (optional)

Spread the squash in the gratin dish and pour the hot milk over it. Cover and bake for 40 minutes. Remove the cover and continue baking until all the liquid is absorbed and the top has begun to brown, about 20 minutes more. Garnish with:

Chopped fresh parsley or chervil

BAKED ACORN SQUASH WITH PEAR AND APPLE

4 servings

Preheat the oven to 325°F. Butter a baking pan.
Place cut side down in the baking pan:

2 medium acorn squash, halved and seeded

Add ¼ inch hot water to the pan. Bake for 45 minutes. Meanwhile, mix in a medium bowl:

2 large apples, peeled, cored, and diced
1 ripe pear, peeled, cored, and diced
¼ cup dried currants or raisins
2 tablespoons packed dark brown sugar
Grated zest of 1 small orange
¼ teaspoon ground cinnamon
⅛ teaspoon freshly grated or ground nutmeg

Heat in a large skillet over medium heat until melted:

2 tablespoons butter

Add the apple mixture and cook until the fruit is golden brown, about 5 minutes. Stir in:

¼ cup apple cider or orange juice
1 tablespoon bourbon or dark rum (optional)

Simmer, stirring often, until the fruit is tender, about 8 minutes. Remove the squash from the oven; pour off the water from the pan and turn the squash cut side up. Fill the squash with the apple mixture. Bake until the squash is tender, about 15 minutes more.

BAKED BUTTERNUT SQUASH STUFFED WITH SAUSAGE AND APPLES

4 servings

Position a rack in the center of the oven. Preheat the oven to 375°F. Lightly oil a baking dish large enough to hold the squash.
Halve lengthwise and remove the seeds and strings from:

2 butternut squash (about 1 pound each)

Arrange the squash cut side up in the baking dish and brush lightly with:

1 tablespoon vegetable oil

Cover with a lid or aluminum foil and bake until almost tender, 30 to 40 minutes. Keep the oven on.
Meanwhile, crumble into a skillet and cook over medium heat until no longer pink:

1 cup well-seasoned fresh bulk sausage (about 8 ounces)

Without draining off the fat, add:

1 large tart green apple, peeled, cored, and cut into ¼-inch cubes

Cook, stirring, for several minutes, just until crisp-tender. Remove from the heat. When the squash is cooked, let it cool slightly, then scoop out most of the flesh, leaving ⅜-inch-thick shells. Lightly mix the squash pulp into the sausage mixture, breaking up the squash as little as possible. Mix in:

2 tablespoons butter, softened
1 tablespoon packed dark brown sugar
¼ teaspoon ground sage
Salt and ground black pepper to taste

Pile the stuffing into the squash halves. Dot with:

1 tablespoon butter, cut into small pieces
1 tablespoon packed dark brown sugar

Bake, uncovered, until piping hot and brown and crusty on top, 20 to 25 minutes. Let cool for several minutes before serving.

VEGETABLE POTPIE WITH CHEDDAR BISCUIT CRUST

8 to 12 servings

This dish makes wonderful party food because it serves a crowd and the vegetables can be prepared up to 1 day ahead: Cut up, brown, and place the vegetables in the baking dish. The crust can be made up to 2 hours ahead and kept covered at room temperature. Keep the vegetables in large chunks so that they remain intact and do not cook down to a puree.

Prepare and keep each vegetable in separate bowls:

2 medium red onions (about 1 pound), cut into thick slices
3 medium carrots, peeled and cut into 1-inch pieces
3 parsnips, peeled and cut into 1-inch pieces
1 celery root, peeled and cut into 1-inch pieces
1 butternut squash (about 2½ pounds), peeled and cut into 1-inch pieces
1 acorn squash (about 1½ pounds), peeled and cut into 1-inch pieces
8 ounces portobello mushrooms, cut into thick slices and slices halved crosswise

Have ready:

3 or 4 tablespoons olive oil
3 or 4 tablespoons unsalted butter

Heat ½ tablespoon oil and ½ tablespoon butter in a large skillet over medium-high heat. Add the onion slices and cook until browned, about 3 minutes on each side. Transfer to a large bowl and season with:

Salt and ground black pepper to taste

Add a bit more oil and butter to the pan, then add the carrots and parsnips. Brown, stirring frequently, for 5 to 7 minutes, transfer to the bowl, and season with salt and pepper. Repeat, adding oil and butter as needed, with the celery root and squashes, browning them all separately and seasoning with salt and pepper as you place them in the bowl. Finally, add the mushrooms to the pan with more oil and butter if needed, turn the heat to high, and brown them well, tossing frequently, about 5 to 7 minutes. Add to the bowl and season with salt and pepper.

Preheat the oven to 400°F.

Add to the vegetables:

2 tablespoon chopped fresh marjoram, or 1 tablespoon dried

Gently mix the herb and vegetables together, transfer to a 13 x 9-inch baking dish, and spread evenly in 1 layer. Pour over the vegetables:

4 cups vegetable or chicken stock

Cover the dish and bake until the vegetables are just tender when pierced with the tip of a sharp knife, 30 to 45 minutes. While the vegetables bake, prepare:

1 recipe Basic Rolled Biscuits, 789

using heavy cream in place of the milk and adding with the cream:

¾ cup grated Cheddar cheese
2 teaspoons minced garlic (optional)
¼ teaspoon cracked black pepper

Set aside. After the vegetables have cooked for 30 to 45 minutes, uncover the dish and spoon dollops of biscuit dough over the vegetables. Continue baking until the biscuits are browned, 20 to 25 minutes more. Remove from the oven, let stand for 10 minutes, and serve.

SWEET POTATOES, YAMS, AND TRUE YAMS

When we say "sweet potatoes," we mean the ones with yellow-gray to brown skin and yellowish to white, dry, mealy flesh. When we say "yams," we mean the ones with copper to purple skins and very sweet, moist, orange flesh. The simple difference between sweets and yams is variety. True yams, however, are not related to any of these sweet potatoes. They are tropical tubers with crisp, bland, white to yellow flesh. Available in Hispanic groceries, the tuber can be boiled, baked, fried, or prepared in any potato way except pureed, which emphasizes its mucilaginous qualities.

Shape is not an indication of quality. All can be round or torpedo shaped, knobby or sleek. When choosing potatoes, select firm tubers with uniformly bright skin, heavy for their size, free of soft spots, dark spots, and mold. Although available year-round, the potatoes are harvested fresh fall through winter. Store the potatoes unwrapped in a cool, well-ventilated, dark, dry place. Cooked yams should be refrigerated; they reheat better than white potatoes.

Some particularly good pairings are with orange, pineapple, apples, pecans, sweet spices, butter, cream, brown sugar, maple sugar and syrup, and rich meats such as pork, duck, and game birds. Hispanic cooks contrast the sweetness of these potatoes with chili peppers, bell peppers, cilantro, scallions, tomatoes, garlic, lemon, and lime.

To Prepare: Scrub well. If peeling is necessary, it is easiest to do so after cooking. Yams and sweets are best baked, steamed, grilled, or microwaved.

To Boil: Boil whole sweet potatoes in their jackets for flavor and color. Place scrubbed whole potatoes of uniform size in a broad pot. Measuring the water, add cold water to cover by 1 inch. Add ½ tablespoon salt for every quart of water, bring to a boil, then cover and boil until a thin skewer can easily pierce to the center—tender but not soft. Depending on size, allow 15 to 35 minutes. Drain.

To Steam: Steam whole, unpeeled sweet potatoes, covered, in a steaming basket over 1 to 2 inches boiling water until tender, 30 to 45 minutes. Steam halves until tender, 15 to 20 minutes; 13 to 18 minutes for 1- to 2-inch cubes.

To Bake: Pierce the skin in several places. For soft skin, rub the potato with butter or oil; for crisp skin, just pat the potato dry. Place the potatoes in a single layer on a rimmed baking sheet (the potatoes may ooze syrup) and bake, uncovered, at 400°F until softened, 45 to 60 minutes, depending on size. Yellow sweet potatoes are also good grilled.

To Microwave: Pierce as many as 4 whole medium potatoes in several places. Place on a paper towel in a spoke pattern. Cook on high until tender, 5 to 9 minutes for 2 potatoes, 10 to 13 minutes for 4 potatoes, turning them over and rearranging after 5 minutes. Cover with a towel and let stand for 5 minutes.

To Pressure-Cook: Whole large sweet potatoes can be pressure-cooked with 1 cup liquid at 15 pounds pressure for 10 minutes. Cool the cooker at once.

To Make Sweet Potato Chips: See Root Chips, 144.

MASHED SWEET POTATOES

4 to 6 servings

Boil, above, until thoroughly tender:

2 pounds sweet potatoes or yams, scrubbed

Drain and let stand until cool enough to handle. Remove the skins, then mash, rice, or put the sweet potatoes through a food mill. Add:

4 tablespoons (½ stick) butter, softened, or to taste
Salt to taste

Thin with:

Warm heavy cream or fresh orange, tangerine, or lemon juice

If desired, season additionally with any of the following:

½ cup chopped pineapple, or to taste
½ cup pecans or ¼ cup black walnuts, toasted
3 tablespoons diced crystallized ginger, or ½ teaspoon ground
2 tablespoons light or dark brown sugar
1 tablespoon bourbon or dry sherry
1 teaspoon grated orange or lemon zest
Pinch of ground cloves or ½ teaspoon ground cinnamon

Beat the potatoes with a fork or whisk until very light. Serve immediately or reheat at 375°F in a buttered baking dish. Garnish with:

Fine shreds of orange zest

STUFFED SWEET POTATOES

4 servings

Bake, above:

2 large sweet potatoes or yams, scrubbed

Halve lengthwise, then, grasping them with a towel, scoop out the pulp, leaving a ¼-inch shell. Mash or puree the flesh, then season and beat until light, as for Mashed Sweet Potatoes, above. Fill the shells, swirling the top. Serve immediately, or dot with butter and broil until a light crust is formed, about 5 minutes.

DEEP-FRIED SWEET POTATOES

Please read Deep-Frying, 1050.

Boil in water to cover for 10 minutes:

4 large sweet potatoes or yams, scrubbed

Peel, then cut them into strips about ⅜ inch thick. Pour into a deep fryer or deep, heavy pot and heat slowly to 365°F:

3 inches vegetable oil

Deep-fry the strips about 1 cup at a time until golden brown. Drain on paper towels. Sprinkle to taste with:

Brown sugar (optional)
Salt
Freshly grated or ground nutmeg

Offer a dipping sauce, if desired:

Southeast Asian Peanut Dipping Sauce, 83, or Nam Prik (Thai Hot Sauce), 82 (optional)

SWEET POTATOES WITH APPLES AND BROWN SUGAR

6 servings

Heat in a large skillet:

2 tablespoons butter
1 tablespoon vegetable oil

Add and toss together:

1½ pounds sweet potatoes or yams, peeled and cut into ¼-inch-thick rounds
3 red apples, cored and cut into rounds
⅓ cup packed light or dark brown sugar
½ teaspoon salt

Add:

¼ cup apple juice or water

Cover and cook over low heat until the sweet potatoes are tender, about 30 minutes. Uncover, increase the heat to medium, and cook about 5 minutes more, turning the potatoes and apples every so often so that they are well caramelized but not burned. The juices should boil away. When done, season with:

Ground black pepper to taste

CANDIED SWEET POTATOES *6 to 8 servings*

Thanksgiving would not seem complete without these.
Boil, 427, until nearly tender when pierced with a knife, 20 to 25 minutes:

3 pounds sweet potatoes, scrubbed

Drain the potatoes and let stand until cool enough to handle.

Preheat the oven to 350°F. Butter a 13 x 9-inch baking dish.

Peel, then cut the potatoes lengthwise into quarters. Layer in the baking dish, seasoning each layer with:

Salt and ground black pepper or paprika to taste
1 teaspoon butter, cut into small pieces
2 to 3 tablespoons packed light or dark brown sugar or pure maple syrup

Dot the top layer with:

2 tablespoons butter

Pour over the dish:

⅓ cup apple cider or water

Cover and bake until well glazed and very soft, about 45 minutes.

GRILLED SWEET POTATOES WITH SWEET CHILI GLAZE *4 to 8 servings*

Omit the chili pepper if you want the sweetness without the heat.

Prepare a medium-hot charcoal fire.

Cook in a large pot of boiling salted water until easily pierced with a fork but still firm, 5 to 8 minutes:

4 medium sweet potatoes, peeled and cut lengthwise into 1-inch-thick slices

Remove, drain, and let cool to room temperature.
Meanwhile, mash together until well combined:

6 tablespoons light or dark molasses
2 tablespoons light or dark rum
1 tablespoon butter
1 teaspoon minced fresh jalapeño or other chili pepper (optional)
Pinch of ground mace
Salt and ground black pepper to taste

Place the sweet potatoes on the grill rack and grill until browned, 4 to 5 minutes each side. Brush with the molasses mixture, cook for about 30 seconds more each side, remove, and serve.

SWEET POTATO AND PEANUT STEW *6 servings*

Omit the ground beef or turkey for a vegetarian version.
Heat in a large, heavy saucepan over medium-low heat:

¼ cup peanut oil

Add:

1 onion, chopped
1 red or green bell pepper, chopped
1 fresh jalapeño or serrano pepper, seeded and minced

Cook until the vegetables are tender but not brown, 7 to 10 minutes. Add:

4 cloves garlic, minced
1 packed tablespoon minced peeled fresh ginger

Cook for another 2 to 3 minutes and stir in:

1 tablespoon chili powder
1 teaspoon ground cumin
½ teaspoon red pepper flakes

Cook for 1 minute and add:

2 sweet potatoes, peeled and cut into 1½-inch pieces
⅓ cup tomato paste
Salt and ground black pepper to taste

Add enough water to barely cover the vegetables and mix well. Bring to a boil, lower the heat, cover, and simmer for 45 minutes, stirring occasionally. While the stew cooks, heat in a medium skillet over high heat:

1 teaspoon peanut oil

Add:

12 ounces ground beef or turkey

Sauté, turning often, until browned. Transfer to a plate with a slotted spoon and set aside until the stew has cooked for 45 minutes. When ready, add the meat to the stew along with:

2 small zucchini (1 inch in diameter), trimmed and sliced

Cook for another 15 minutes. Place in a small bowl:

½ cup peanut butter (chunky or smooth), preferably unsalted

Stir in 1 cup of the stewing liquid until smooth and add

the peanut butter mixture to the pot. Mix well and cook another 15 minutes. Season with:

Salt and ground black pepper to taste

Serve plain or with:

Hot cooked rice or couscous

SPICY BAKED TRUE YAMS

4 servings

Try these instead of potatoes.

Preheat the oven to 375°F.

Rinse and pat dry:

2 pounds true yams, peeled and cut into 1-inch pieces

Put the pieces in a large roasting pan along with:

2 tablespoons light olive or vegetable oil
½ teaspoon salt
¼ teaspoon ground black pepper
¼ teaspoon chili powder

Turn the pieces to coat well. Bake, turning often, until browned on all sides, 40 to 45 minutes. Add ½ inch water to the pan and bake until softened, about 15 minutes more.

Serve with:

Orange Butter, 77, Nut Butter, 77, or Beurre Noisette, 57

TARO OR DASHEEN

Taro is the umbrella name for a number of starchy tropical roots that are staples in parts of Asia, Africa, the Caribbean, and South America. You may find one or another in groceries with customers from these areas. A common taro has brown skin and white or lavender flesh that tastes like potato. Select firm roots, heavy for their size, with no soft spots or blemishes. Peel before or after cooking.

To Boil or Steam: Cook as for potatoes, 407.

To Bake: Remove loose fibers and boil the unpared root in water to cover for 15 minutes. Then bake as for potatoes, but be sure the oven temperature is not higher than 375°F.

Serve taro hot, because the flesh turns sticky when cool. Allow about 5 ounces per serving.

TOMATILLOS

Tomatillos look like small shiny green, yellow-green, or lavender tomatoes encased in parchment-paper husks. Tomatillos are picked underripe. They are related to tomatoes, but tomatillos have a lemony tang rather than the sharpness of green tomatoes. This tang lends sprightliness to sauces in Mexican cooking. Tomatillos may be sporadically available at the supermarket, but they are always for sale at Hispanic groceries. Select fruits that are firm and fill their husks, and avoid any that have come out of them. Store them, unwashed and unhusked, loose in the refrigerator crisper—they will keep for weeks.

Tomatillos go well with tomatoes, avocados, chili peppers, cilantro, lime, fish, seafood, and almost all Hispanic flavors. Allow about 4 ounces per person.

To Prepare: Peel off and discard the husks, rinse off the sticky covering, then trim out the stems. Do not peel. Tomatillos can be quartered and added raw to salads, but even when a Mexican sauce is called *cruda,* or raw, tomatillos are cooked because cooking intensifies their flavor.

To Boil: Bring 8 cups water and 2 teaspoons salt to a rolling boil in a large saucepan. Add 1 pound husked tomatillos and cook just until softened, 3 to 5 minutes, depending on size.

To Steam: Place husked tomatillos in a steaming basket over 1 to 2 inches boiling water. Cook, covered, just until softened, 5 to 10 minutes, depending on size.

To Roast: Flavor is greatly enhanced by a touch of roasting. They can be roasted on a hot dry griddle in the manner of chili peppers, 402, cooking until the skin is slightly charred and the fruits have softened. This can be tricky because the skin has a tendency to burn before the flesh softens.

To Broil: Broil tomatillos on a rimmed baking sheet 4 inches under a very hot broiler until they blister, darken, and soften on one side, about 4 minutes; turn them over and broil the other side for 5 to 6 minutes.

TOMATOES

Tomatoes come in two shapes, round and plum, and in many sizes. Cherry tomatoes are usually the first round tomatoes in season. Their skins are relatively tough, but their flesh is sweet and juicy. Cherry tomatoes may be red, gold, orange, or yellow-green. They are heavenly tossed in a little oil or butter until heated through, then served on everything from English muf-

Tomatillo

fins to pasta to pizza. Currant tomatoes, the shape and size of currants, are the closest thing to wild tomatoes that most of us will ever taste. They have not been fiddled with by breeders but come straight from South America. Their flavor is ultrasweet, especially the yellow ones. Most standard round tomatoes are as juicy as cherry tomatoes and as easily used raw. At the market, round tomatoes are round tomatoes. But gardeners can choose to grow salad tomatoes, which are small to medium in size and only moderately juicy—ideal for salads. And they can grow slicing tomatoes, large to beefsteak tomatoes, which are wonderfully rich and juicy. Look for them at the farmers' market. Also look for heritage tomatoes that may be ruffled or in a rainbow of colors.

The other basic shape tomatoes take is called plum or pear. Oval or teardrop in shape, these tomatoes are small to medium, about the same size as salad tomatoes. Their value lies in cooking because their flesh is thick, meaty, almost dry. Sometimes they are called paste or Roma tomatoes because they are the ones to use in classic tomato paste, and Roma is the best-known variety of plum tomatoes. Without juices that must be evaporated in long simmering, the fresh, tangy-sweet flavor of a plum tomato immediately goes into a soup, sauce, gratin, stew, or any cooked tomato dish. You also can use plum tomatoes raw in salads and uncooked sauces, as well as whenever juiced tomatoes are called for—just skip the juicing step.

Botanically fruits and impossible to ship when fully ripe, most tomatoes are picked at the hard, green, relatively indestructible stage, then ripened with gas (no sun in sight). Green tomatoes, like green bell peppers, are unripe and come in every size and shape. They may be puckery tart, with crisp flesh not unlike that of a tart green apple.

Years ago, commercially raised tomatoes were red, period. Now red, yellow, gold, and orange tomatoes come to market. Flavor, for the most part, is determined by the variety, but on the whole we find gold and orange tomatoes much sweeter than red tomatoes. Some can be positively fruity, as though a strain of apricots had been mixed in.

Tomatoes are in the market all year, but in most parts of the country, tomato season is midsummer till frost. Out of season, most market tomatoes have been grown in a greenhouse or hydroponically—in water rather than soil. They look like tomatoes, they slice like tomatoes, but they have no tomato taste. However, when you see plum tomatoes out of season, look around for the box they came in. If they came from Mexico, they will probably be tasty, but they should be peeled because they will probably have been sprayed.

Tomatoes continue to develop their mature color off the vine, but since sugars do not materially increase, flavor does not improve. The finest commercial tomatoes are called "vine ripened." They are not mature when picked, but they have begun to show their finished color. Select firm, bright tomatoes that are heavy for their size. Scarring around the stem end is harmless. When there are leaves attached, they must be moist and fresh looking. If the tomato smells like a tomato, grab it. Homegrown tomatoes should be picked when they are fragrant and then eaten on the spot—or at least the same day. Store underripe to firm ripe tomatoes at room temperature, unwrapped. Store ripe tomatoes—those that yield to the touch—in the refrigerator, unwrapped, on a shelf, not in the moist crisper.

Tomatoes have great affinities with butter, olive and nut oils, cream and cheese in any form, onions, garlic, any basil, oregano, sage, thyme, dill, parsley, chervil, tarragon, rosemary, cilantro, cumin, rice, seafood, avocados, cucumbers, peppers, eggplant, okra, beans, summer squash, eggs, bread, potatoes, walnuts, olives, and capers. Allow 4 to 8 ounces per serving.

To Peel: Cut a small X in the bottom of the tomatoes—do not cut the flesh. Ease the tomatoes one by one into a pot of boiling water. Leave ripe tomatoes in for about 15 seconds, barely ripe tomatoes in for twice as long. Lift them out with a sieve and drop into a bowl of ice water to stop the cooking. Pull off the skin with the tip of the knife. If the skin sticks, return the tomato to the boiling water for another 10 seconds and repeat. If the dish can use a touch of smoky flavor and if you have a gas burner, an easier way to peel tomatoes is to hold the tomato on a long-handled fork over the burner, turning it until the skin splits. Do not plunge in water, but after cooling, peel as above.

To Seed and Juice: To seed and juice a tomato, cut it crosswise in half (between the top and bottom). Squeeze each half gently, cut side down, over a strainer set in a bowl to catch the juice, which you can add to soup. Now run the tip of a finger into each of the cavities and flick out the mass of seeds.

Tomatoes are marvelous baked or roasted, stewed, sautéed, broiled, and grilled.

To Roast: Roast tomatoes under the broiler as you would tomatillos, 429. They are done when the skin is charred but the flesh beneath is still soft. Peel with a sharp paring knife (but not meticulously—a bit of char is delicious). Roasted tomatoes are especially suited to soups, sauces, and stews.

To Sweat: Quarter them and place in a saucepan with a small lump of butter and a pinch each of sugar and salt for each tomato. Bring to a simmer, stirring, then cover the pan, adjust the heat so the tomatoes continue to simmer, and cook until tender, 5 to 15 minutes. Minced onion and sweet basil also can be added. An old country trick was to add big cubes of thick pieces of toast when the tomatoes were juicy. Serve hot.

To Microwave: Place tomato halves in a round dish. Cover and cook on high, 2 to 4 minutes for 2 medium tomatoes, 10 to 13 minutes for 4 medium tomatoes, rearranging once halfway through. Let stand, still covered, for 2 minutes.

BROILED TOMATOES *4 servings*

Serve as a side dish or place on thin slices of toast rubbed with a halved clove of garlic for a warm open-faced sandwich.

Preheat the broiler. Lightly oil a rimmed baking sheet.

Slice horizontally into slices ½ to 1 inch thick:

4 large tomatoes, ripe but not too soft

Season with:

1 teaspoon salt

¼ teaspoon ground black pepper

Place on the baking sheet and sprinkle with:

½ cup grated Parmesan cheese (optional)

2 tablespoons olive oil

Broil about 5 inches from the heat until golden on top and heated through, about 5 minutes. If the cheese has been omitted, serve with:

Sauce Rémoulade, 73, or Spicy Cucumber Sambal, 68

TOMATOES BROILED WITH BLUE CHEESE *4 servings*

Preheat the broiler. Lightly oil a gratin dish or glass pie pan.

Halve crosswise (through the equator):

4 medium, ripe tomatoes

Arrange the tomato halves cut side up in the dish. Sprinkle with:

About 4 ounces blue cheese, Gorgonzola, or other veined cheese, crumbled

2 teaspoons chopped fresh marjoram or oregano, or scant 1 teaspoon dried oregano

Ground black pepper to taste

Drizzle over the tops:

Extra-virgin olive oil

Broil about 6 inches from the heat until the cheese has begun to brown, about 7 minutes. Serve hot or let cool slightly.

GRILLED TOMATOES *6 servings*

Grilled ripe tomatoes are fragile. They are easiest grilled whole, then pureed. Their smoky undertaste adds an incomparable dimension to sauces and soups. Set whole firm ripe tomatoes over a low fire and turn with tongs as the skin chars. When charred all over, cool, then puree with the skin. Green tomatoes grill beautifully.

Prepare a medium-hot charcoal fire.

Cut into ½-inch-thick slices:

6 large green tomatoes

Brush all over with:

Olive or other vegetable oil

Coat with:

Cornmeal mixture for Fried Green Tomatoes, 433

omitting the thyme and paprika and adding, if desired:

⅛ teaspoon ground red pepper

Grease the grill rack and add the tomatoes. Grill, turning once with tongs, just until they begin to soften, 4 to 6 minutes. Serve hot, plain or with:

Mayonnaise with Green Herbs, 73

SLOW-ROASTED TOMATOES *2 to 4 servings*

Baking tomatoes for a long time at low heat gradually concentrates their flavor to a rich tomato sauce. Heavenly tossed with pasta.

Preheat the oven to 250°F. Spread out on a rimmed baking sheet lined with parchment paper:

4 to 5 large ripe tomatoes, cut into ¾-inch-thick slices

Combine:

1 teaspoon powdered sugar

1 teaspoon salt

1 teaspoon ground black pepper

Sprinkle over the tomatoes. Drizzle over:

Olive oil

Sprinkle with:

Chopped fresh basil, thyme, or other herb of your choice

Bake for 2 hours, then let cool to room temperature.

TOMATOES PROVENÇAL *4 servings*

If necessary, cut a thin slice from the bottom of each tomato so that it stands upright.

Preheat the oven to 350°F. Lightly oil a 13 x 9-inch baking dish.

Combine in a small bowl:

½ cup fresh breadcrumbs
2 tablespoons grated Parmesan cheese
2 tablespoons chopped fresh flat-leaf parsley
2 tablespoons chopped fresh basil
2 cloves garlic, finely chopped
2 teaspoons extra-virgin olive oil

Halve crosswise, then gently squeeze the seeds from:

4 medium, firm ripe tomatoes

Arrange cut side up in the baking dish and season with:

Salt and ground black pepper to taste

Spoon the breadcrumb mixture over the tomatoes, gently patting it into a dome. Drizzle over the tops:

Olive oil

Bake until the breadcrumbs are golden and the tomatoes are softened, about 50 minutes.

STEWED TOMATOES *4 servings*

Stewed tomatoes are a favorite accompaniment to macaroni and cheese and are also good with fish, chicken, and lamb. Since they are juicy, serve stewed tomatoes in separate dishes or small bowls rather than on dinner plates with other foods.

Peel, 430:

8 medium-large very ripe tomatoes (about 3½ pounds)

Cut the tomatoes crosswise in half. Gently squeeze out the seeds and cut out the cores, leaving the tomato halves as intact as possible. Place in a large, heavy saucepan:

3 to 4 tablespoons unsalted butter or flavorful olive oil or a blend of both

Heat over medium heat until the butter melts or the oil becomes fragrant. Add the tomatoes, stir gently to coat with the fat, and cover. Cook, stirring gently from time to time, until the tomatoes become soft but still retain their shape, 6 to 8 minutes. Season with:

Salt and ground black pepper to taste
2 tablespoons minced fresh parsley or finely shredded fresh basil (optional)

If you like, pass the tomatoes with:

Grated Swiss, Cheddar, or Parmesan cheese

Stewed tomatoes are best when served at once but can be refrigerated in a covered container for up to 3 days. Rewarm over gentle heat.

SCALLOPED TOMATOES *8 to 10 servings*

An old-fashioned, thoroughly delicious way to make use of the summer's bounty of fresh tomatoes. For a more substantial dish, mix 1 cup finely diced ham or cooked chicken with the tomatoes.

Position a rack in the center of the oven. Preheat the oven to 350°F. Lightly butter a shallow 10-inch round baking dish, quiche pan, or pie pan.

Peel and seed, 430, then cut into ¼-inch dice:

3 pounds tomatoes (about 4 cups)

Melt in a large skillet over medium heat:

2 tablespoons unsalted butter

Stir in:

1½ cups fine dry breadcrumbs

Cook, stirring constantly, until fragrant and nicely toasted, 3 to 6 minutes. Scrape the crumbs into a mixing bowl and set aside. Return the skillet to medium heat and add:

3 tablespoons unsalted butter

Heat until the foam begins to subside, then add:

1 cup finely chopped onions
1 large red or green bell pepper, finely chopped

Cook, stirring occasionally, until the vegetables are tender and just beginning to color, about 10 minutes. Add the vegetables to the crumbs along with:

1 tablespoon sugar
¾ teaspoon salt
½ teaspoon ground black pepper

Mix well. Distribute half of the crumb mixture over the bottom of the baking dish. Cover evenly with the tomatoes and sprinkle lightly with:

Salt and ground black pepper to taste

Sprinkle the remaining crumb mixture evenly over the top. Bake until the tomatoes are bubbly in the center and the top is richly browned, about 40 minutes. Sprinkle with:

Chopped fresh parsley

SAUTÉED CHERRY TOMATOES *4 servings*

Use a colorful mixture if you wish, leaving the tiniest, currant-sized ones whole.

Heat in a large skillet:

1½ tablespoons extra-virgin olive oil

Add:

2 shallots, finely diced, or 4 scallions (white part only), sliced

Cook, stirring, until softened, just a few minutes. Increase the heat to high and add:

4 cups red or yellow cherry tomatoes or a combination, halved or quartered

Sauté just until they are warmed through, no longer, about 2 minutes. Remove from the heat and season with:

1 tablespoon chopped fresh flat-leaf parsley
1 tablespoon chopped fresh tarragon, marjoram, basil, lemon basil, thyme, or lovage

Salt and ground black pepper to taste
Or omit the herbs and accompany with:
Fresh Mint Chutney, 66

TOMATO CONCASSÉ
1 cup

This is a wonderful condiment for grilled chicken or fish. Prepare only as much as you need of this basic preparation, as it does not keep well.
Peel, seed, and juice, 430:
2 large ripe tomatoes
Dice the pulp very finely.

FRIED GREEN TOMATOES
6 servings

This is the traditional solution to the problem of tomatoes that do not have time to ripen before the first frost. They are a traditional southern side dish but make a great sandwich too.
Remove the stem ends, then cut crosswise into ½-inch-thick slices:
6 large green tomatoes
Combine in a shallow bowl:
2 cups fine cornmeal
½ cup all-purpose flour
1 tablespoon chopped fresh parsley
1 tablespoon chopped fresh thyme
1 teaspoon paprika
Salt and ground black pepper to taste
Dip the tomato slices 1 at a time into:
1 cup milk
Then coat with the cornmeal mixture. Shake off the excess and set on a plate. Heat in a large skillet until hot enough to sizzle a drop of water:
1 cup vegetable oil
Add as many tomatoes as will fit in a single layer and fry until golden and crisp, turning once. Repeat with the remaining tomatoes, adding oil as needed. Serve immediately, plain or with:
Harissa, 82, or Garlic Mayonnaise, 74

TRUFFLES

The great French writer Alexandre Dumas once proposed that if the truffle could speak, it would declare, "Eat me and adore God." A truffle is simply the underground flowering of a fungus typically found around oak or hazelnut trees, with whose roots it has a symbiotic relationship. There are said to be at least 70 species of truffles in all, but in the culinary canon the only two that matter are the black truffle (*Tuber melanosporum*), harvested primarily in France and a bit in Italy and Spain, and the white truffle (*Tuber magnatum*), found mostly in the Piedmont region of Italy. The two are vastly different in character: Black truffles (which are sometimes more brown than black) have a nutty character and a faint but distinct aroma; they are usually cooked or at least marinated or macerated (typically in Cognac) before use. Black truffles are essential to the classic French Périgourdine sauce, are often added to pâtés and terrines (especially of foie gras), and are frequently combined with eggs and potatoes. White truffles are positively pungent, with a racy, almost primal perfume so strong that, in Italy, it is against the law to carry them on public transportation. White truffles are almost never cooked but are instead shaved raw over pasta, risotto, fonduta (the Piedmontese version of fondue), egg dishes, and salads. They are often stored (briefly) nestled in closed containers of risotto rice, to which they lend a vivid truffle flavor; the truffle can be used elsewhere, as it does not give all its flavor to the rice.

Entrepreneurs have long tried to raise truffles by inoculating forest soil with fungus spores, and some claim limited success—but in general truffles must be hunted in the wild. This work is traditionally done by dogs in Italy and pigs in France, though dogs are also making inroads in France because they do not eat the truffles when they dig them up, whereas pigs do.

Less expensive than classic black and white truffles are the so-called summer truffle (*Tuber aestivum*), a pleasant but mild-flavored black variety, and a pungent but not particularly interesting white variety (*Tuber gibbosum*) found in northern California and southern Oregon. Truffles sold in jars or cans vary widely in quality but can be quite good.

If you are so fortunate as to be able to buy (and afford) a fresh truffle, choose one that is firm to the touch, with a pronounced aroma. Spongy, bland-smelling truffles are too old. To clean fresh truffles, brush them lightly with a soft kitchen brush or wipe them gently with a soft cloth. Do not wash them unless they are coated with dirt—which those imported from France and Italy will not be.

TURNIPS AND RUTABAGAS

The moment you taste glazed young turnips or buttery potatoes mashed with golden rutabagas, you will understand their appeal. Closely related roots in the Mustard family, both turnips and rutabagas have the shape of a top. Turnips are generally smaller and more slender and have white skin with purple tops and white flesh. Rutabagas have creamy gold skin with purple tops and yellow flesh and are firmer than turnips. Both are crisp and peppery sweet when raw but meltingly soft and wonderfully sweetened when cooked. Rutabagas are harvested in autumn, but they are customarily dipped in wax and then stored in a cool, dark, dry place for use over winter (keep an eye out for mold on the wax). Turnips are best when freshly harvested, spring and fall. Select firm, unblemished roots, heavy for their size—the smaller, the sweeter. Store roots from the market in perforated plastic vegetable bags in the refrigerator crisper.

Cooked turnips and rutabagas can be mashed and served any way potatoes are. They are especially satisfying when blended in equal parts with potatoes or sweet potatoes. Turnips and rutabagas go well with cream, butter, lemon, nutmeg, garlic, spicy cheeses, crisp bacon, thyme, parsley, and chervil. Allow 8 ounces per serving.

To Prepare: No need to peel small, thin-skinned young turnips, but older turnips should be thinly pared. Scrub the rutabaga, then peel with a sharp paring knife to remove the thick skin and any wax. Cut into slices, wedges, cubes, or matchsticks. Young turnips are delicious raw. The earthy taste of cooked rutabagas and older turnips makes it possible to use them interchangeably in recipes.

To Boil: Bring 8 cups water and 2 teaspoons salt to a rolling boil in a large saucepan. Add 1 pound turnips or rutabagas, peeled and cut into ½-inch cubes, and cook until tender when pierced with a thin skewer or knife tip. Allow 6 to 8 minutes for turnips, 12 to 14 minutes for rutabagas. Drain.

To Steam: Place prepared roots in a single layer in a steamer basket over 1 to 2 inches boiling water. Cook, covered, until tender when pierced with a thin skewer or knife tip. After 2 minutes, lift the lid briefly to allow sulfurous compounds to escape. For turnips, allow 7 to 9 minutes for matchsticks; for rutabaga matchsticks, 10 to 12 minutes; for ½-inch turnip cubes, 10 to 13 minutes; for rutabaga cubes, 18 to 20 minutes; for medium turnip quarters, 17 to 20 minutes; for rutabaga quarters 35 to 45 minutes; and for whole medium turnips, 35 to 40 minutes.

To Roast: Preheat the oven to 375°F. Peel and cut medium turnips into 6 wedges, rutabagas into ½-inch cubes. For each 1 pound prepared roots, toss with 2 tablespoons olive oil, ¼ teaspoon salt, and ground black pepper to taste. Place in a single layer in a roasting pan and cook until tender when pierced with a thin skewer or knife tip, 35 to 45 minutes for turnips, 55 to 65 minutes for rutabagas.

To Microwave: Place 1 pound ½-inch peeled cubes in a 2-quart baking dish. Add 3 tablespoons stock or lightly salted water. Cover and cook on high until tender, 7 to 9 minutes, stirring after 3 minutes. Let stand, covered, for 3 minutes.

BRAISED TURNIPS *4 servings*

Boil, above, uncovered, over high heat for about 6 minutes:

1½ pounds white turnips, peeled, left whole if small, quartered if large

Drain. Pour into a large, heavy skillet and bring to a boil over high heat:

1 cup chicken stock

Add:

3 tablespoons butter
½ teaspoon salt, or more to taste
Ground black pepper to taste

Stir until the butter is melted. Add the blanched turnips. The stock should come about ¾ inch up the side of the turnips; add more stock or water if needed. Reduce the heat, cover the skillet, and simmer until the turnips are tender but still slightly resistant to the tip of a sharp knife, 10 to 20 minutes. Remove the turnips to a serving dish. Boil the cooking liquid over high heat until reduced to a thin, syrupy glaze. Pour it over the turnips and serve immediately.

Turnip

Rutabaga

BRAISED TURNIPS WITH PANCETTA AND LEEKS *4 servings*

Melt in a medium skillet over medium-low heat:

1 tablespoon butter

Add:

3 large leeks (white part plus 1 inch of green), cleaned thoroughly and chopped

Cook for 1 minute, then add:

2 cloves garlic, minced

⅓ cup chopped pancetta

Cook gently for 10 minutes. Stir in:

1 pound turnips, peeled and cut into ¼-inch matchsticks

½ cup chicken stock or water

Cover and simmer over low heat until tender, 15 to 20 minutes. Stir in:

2 teaspoons red wine vinegar

1 teaspoon chopped fresh thyme or 2 teaspoons chopped fresh parsley

½ teaspoon salt

Ground black pepper to taste

Serve hot.

TURNIP PUREE *4 to 6 servings*

Mashed potatoes soften the aggressive edge that winter turnips can have and make a much better puree. You can simply boil the turnips and mash them, but they taste better if braised first. Keep the puree hot and work quickly, as reheating deflates the light texture.

Prepare:

Braised Turnips, 434

adding, if desired:

1 leek (white part only), cleaned thoroughly and chopped

Puree until smooth. Beat the puree into:

1 to 2 cups Mashed Potatoes, 408

Add:

Butter to taste, softened, or ¼ cup heavy cream

1 tablespoon chopped fresh parsley

1 teaspoon minced fresh thyme

Salt and ground black pepper to taste

Whip with a fork until fluffy, about 30 seconds. Pile into a warmed serving bowl and top with:

1 to 2 tablespoons butter, softened

SCANDINAVIAN RUTABAGA PUREE

Prepare Turnip Puree, above, substituting rutabaga for the turnip and omitting the leek and potatoes. After pureeing, beat in the cream instead of butter and replace the herbs with 2 tablespoons packed brown sugar and 1 teaspoon ground ginger.

WINTER ROOT VEGETABLE BRAISE *4 main-dish servings*

Serve this winter vegetable stew in soup plates with pieces of garlic-rubbed toast and a shower of parsley to lift its subtle colors, or surround it with mashed potatoes. In addition to the vegetables listed, you could also include fennel, salsify, parsley root, artichokes, and Jerusalem artichokes.

Heat in a large skillet or Dutch oven over medium heat:

1½ tablespoons olive oil

1 tablespoon butter

1 bay leaf

1 large sprig fresh thyme

Add:

2 onions, diced

Cook, stirring occasionally, until the onions begin to brown and have left a sugary residue on the bottom of the pan, about 12 minutes. Add and cook for 3 minutes more:

4 large mushrooms, wiped clean and thickly sliced

2 cloves garlic, minced

Pour in:

½ cup dry white wine

Increase the heat and boil, scraping the bottom of the pan, until the liquid is reduced to a syrup, about 5 minutes. Add:

8 ounces turnips, peeled and quartered

8 ounces small rutabagas, peeled and cut into 1-inch cubes

1 pound celery root, peeled and cut into 1-inch cubes

1 tablespoon all-purpose flour

½ teaspoon salt

Stir the vegetables together, then pour in:

2½ cups chicken stock

Bring to a boil. Reduce the heat and simmer, covered, until the vegetables are tender, 20 to 25 minutes. Mix together:

3 tablespoons heavy cream

1 tablespoon Dijon mustard

Pour this into the stew and stir well. Season with:

Ground black pepper to taste

Fresh thyme leaves or chopped fresh parsley

OVEN-ROASTED TURNIPS WITH SQUASH AND SHALLOTS *6 to 8 servings*

Perfect for a holiday dinner to accompany roast turkey, chicken, pork, or beef.

Preheat the oven to 375°F.
Place in a 13 x 9-inch baking pan and toss together:

- **2 pounds turnips or rutabagas, peeled and cut into ¾-inch chunks**
- **1 small butternut squash (1½ pounds), peeled, seeded, and cut into ¾-inch chunks**
- **12 to 18 small shallots or pearl onions, peeled**
- **3 tablespoons rendered fat from roasted turkey, chicken, pork, or beef, or olive or vegetable oil**
- **1 tablespoon melted butter**
- **1 tablespoon minced fresh rosemary**
- **¼ teaspoon salt**
- **Ground black pepper to taste**

Roast, stirring occasionally, until the vegetables are fork-tender, about 1½ hours. Season with:

- **Salt and ground black pepper to taste**
- **Chopped fresh parsley or snipped fresh chives**

TURNIP GREENS

Cut the stalks off turnips a few inches above the roots and store the greens in perforated plastic vegetable bags in the refrigerator crisper.

Turnip greens are especially good cooked with other greens, like collards, in water flavored with salt pork or a ham bone. They are traditionally seasoned with sprinklings of oil, vinegar, hot sauce or ground red pepper, and sugar. They have the same affinities as collards, 367. Allow 6 to 8 ounces per serving.

To Prepare: After rinsing, pull tender leaves off ribs and tear large pieces into bite-sized ones. Discard stalks.

To Boil: Follow the method for mustard greens, 388, and cook prepared leaves until tender but not mushy, 8 to 13 minutes, depending on the age and thickness of the leaves. Baby leaves will cook very quickly. Drain.

To Braise: Follow the method for mustard greens, 388, and cook prepared leaves until tender but not mushy, 11 to 13 minutes. After cooking for 2 minutes, lift the lid to release sulfurous compounds, then cover again and finish cooking. Drain.

To Microwave: As for cabbage, 354.

TURNIP GREENS WITH SALT PORK

4 to 6 servings

To Northerners, it seems as though Southerners cook greens like these forever—but the result of long cooking is a very rich flavor. Two or three types of greens can be cooked together if desired. Traditionally, greens are served with the cooking liquid, or pot liquor, to be soaked up with Southern Corn Bread, 777.

Coarsely chop together:

- **4 ounces salt pork**
- **4 slices bacon**

Bring to a boil in a pot large enough to hold the greens:

- **6 cups water**

Add the pork and bacon and simmer, covered, for 30 minutes. Meanwhile, remove the thick stems and discolored leaves from:

- **3 pounds turnip greens**
- **1 pound mustard greens**

Wash the leaves very well, then add to the simmering pork. Simmer, covered, for 1 hour. Season with:

- **1 teaspoon salt**
- **¼ teaspoon ground black pepper**
- **4 to 5 dashes of hot red pepper sauce**

Serve hot in bowls with plenty of the cooking liquid.

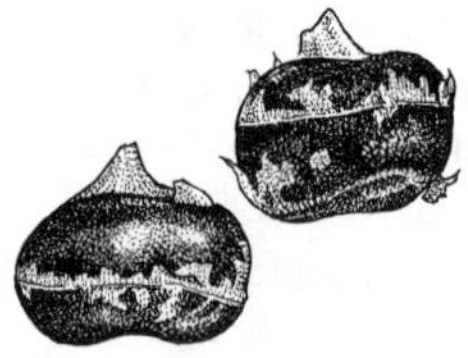

Water chestnuts

WATER CHESTNUTS

The fresh water chestnuts sold in Chinese markets have a seductive delicacy not found in the straightforward crunch of the canned. They are not chestnuts at all but resemble them in size and in the brown color of their papery skin. Choose firm ones without soft spots or signs of yellowing; refrigerate them in a paper bag for up to 2 weeks. Store opened canned water chestnuts like canned bamboo shoots, 344; to reduce their tinny taste, boil for 1 minute and drain well before using. Water chestnuts grow in muddy water; fresh ones must be washed before you peel them. Their crisp, white flesh will discolor, so drop the peeled pieces into a bowl of water if not cooking at once. Water chestnuts can be eaten raw but become more flavorful with cooking, without losing their crispness. Slice and add to stir-fries or chop and mix into ground meat or grains prior to cooking. For use in salads, boil them for 5 minutes, drain, and chill. Allow 3 ounces of water chestnuts per serving.

STIR-FRIED WATER CHESTNUTS

4 servings

Stir-fry shrimp or diced chicken breasts with the red peppers to turn this colorful dish into a main course.

Drop into a pot of boiling water and cook for 5 minutes (1 minute for canned):

8 ounces fresh water chestnuts, peeled and sliced, or two 8-ounce cans sliced water chestnuts, drained

Combine in a small bowl:

3 tablespoons soy sauce
2 teaspoons minced or crushed garlic
2 teaspoons minced peeled fresh ginger
2 teaspoons toasted sesame oil
1 teaspoon sugar
1 teaspoon chili paste with garlic or ¼ teaspoon red pepper flakes

Heat a wok or large skillet, then add:

1 tablespoon vegetable oil

Heat until hot. Add:

2 large red bell peppers, cut into thin matchsticks

Stir-fry over medium-high heat for 2 minutes. Stir in:

1 pound fresh snow peas, strings removed

Stir-fry until tender but still crisp, about 2 minutes. Add the water chestnuts and stir-fry until all the vegetables are tender, another 1 to 3 minutes. Stir in the soy sauce mixture over high heat. Cook, stirring to coat thoroughly, until the sauce is slightly reduced, about 2 minutes more.

Stir in:

1 cup bean sprouts (optional)

Serve hot, sprinkled with:

2 tablespoons minced fresh cilantro
1 scallion, minced

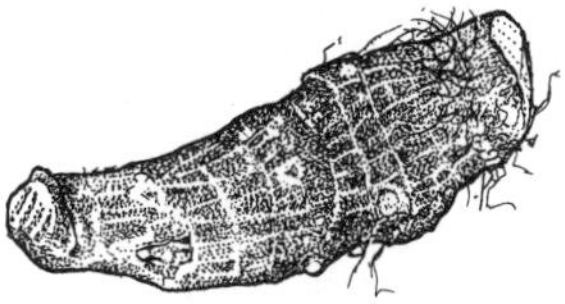

Yautia

YAUTIA

Yautia, also known as malanga, stands out among tropical tubers for its strong, earthy taste. Simmer it as you would taro or yuca roots or yams. Look carefully for relatively thin, chestnut-colored skin with no softness or withering when you select yautia, as the root does not keep well; store at room temperature for no longer than a couple of days. Peel with a paring knife; the flesh will be slippery and may be white, creamy yellow, or streaked with pink. Rinse well and drop into cold water until ready to cook. Leave pared yautia whole or cut into 3- to 4-inch pieces; simmer until tender when pierced, about 25 minutes. Watch the pot for the last few minutes, as the root begins to disintegrate quickly once cooked through. Like other tropical roots, yautia also can be cooked as chips or fritters. Allow about 5 ounces per serving.

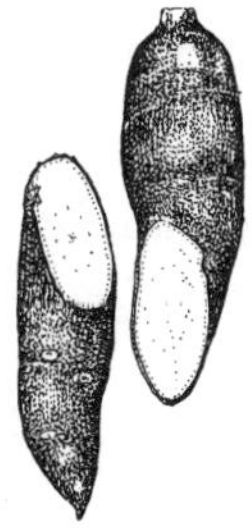

Yuca

YUCA ROOT

Also called cassava, manioc, or tapioca, the root known as yuca in Spanish has a rich, buttery taste. The texture of its fresh is that of a rather flaky boiled potato, and it is good in stews, anointed with garlicky olive oil, or dabbed with fresh salsa. Its shiny, barklike brown skin conceals hard, pure white flesh that turns yellowish and almost translucent when cooked. Yuca root does not store well, so make sure it smells fresh and has no mold or cracks when you buy it. Keep it at a cool room temperature and cook it as soon as possible, or freeze peeled raw chunks tightly wrapped in plastic for up to 1 month.

Yuca is higher in calories than potatoes and quite filling in small portions; it provides much potassium and some iron. Allow 6 to 8 ounces per serving.

To Prepare: Cut the tapered root into chunks, slit the skin with a paring knife, then use the blade to peel away the skin and its underlayer in one piece. Halve chunks lengthwise and pull out the thin, fibrous core that runs down the center of the root. Rinse well and hold in cold water.

To Cook: Simmer yuca root in salted water to cover until tender, about 20 minutes for 2-inch pieces.

CUBAN-STYLE YUCA ROOT WITH CITRUS AND GARLIC

6 servings

Use a paring knife to remove the outer peel and fibrous underlayer from:

3 pounds yuca roots, scrubbed and cut into 3-inch sections

Rinse well and place in a pot of cold water to cover. Bring to a boil and add:

½ teaspoon salt

Reduce the heat and simmer, covered, until the root is easily pierced with a fork, about 30 minutes.

Meanwhile, heat in a large skillet:

2 tablespoons vegetable oil

Add and cook until translucent, about 4 minutes:

1 small onion, minced

Stir in:

6 cloves garlic, minced
⅓ cup fresh grapefruit or lemon juice
⅓ cup fresh orange juice
¼ teaspoon salt

Cook gently until the garlic is tender, 10 to 15 minutes. Stir in:

2 tablespoons chopped fresh parsley or cilantro
1 teaspoon crumbled dried oregano

Drain the yuca. Combine with the sauce and serve immediately.

FRUITS

Fruits are pure pleasure—when they are ripe. Vitamins, minerals, and fibers have no more persuasive salesman than a juicy, honey-sweet peach. Eating fruit is good for everyone, of course: every fruit, like every vegetable, contains all vitamins (except B_{12}, which is found in any dairy product), minerals, and phytochemicals—those nutrients whose health-promoting properties are forever being newly discovered. As always, the best advice is to eat the most fresh fruit you can, and preferably to eat fruit that is local, in season, and perfectly ripe.

SHOPPING FOR FRESH FRUITS

Most of the fruits in these pages can be found at a market in some part of the country—if not the supermarket, then a farmers' market, fancy grocery, or ethnic market. As much as possible, buy fruits in their domestic season, and buy fruits for canning, freezing, and preserving at the peak of the season. Produce is most reasonable in price when plentiful, nutrition is greatest when fruits have not traveled for long, and flavor is richest when fruits reach the peak of their reproductive cycle. In the summer and early fall, farmers' markets and roadside stands offer the greatest variety and generally the most flavorful selection. When, in cold weather, it is back to the supermarket, make friends with the produce manager so that when you want to sample a fruit before buying it, he or she will readily give you a taste.

The way to shop for fruits is not to make a list at home but to wait until you get to the market and see and smell what is best. This is especially true when composing a fruit mixture. Here is the usual choice in a well-stocked market:

Dependably Available All Year: apples, avocados, bananas, coconuts, dates, dried fruits, grapefruit, grapes, kiwis, lemons, limes, oranges, pears, pineapple.

Usually Dependably Available (the season will be longer some places, and more fruits will be available both regionally and from imported sources):

January: mandarins

February and March:—

April: rhubarb, strawberries

May: apricots, papayas, rhubarb, strawberries

June: apricots, blackberries, blueberries, cherries, figs, mangoes, papayas, raspberries, strawberries

July: apricots, blackberries, blueberries, cherries, mangoes, nectarines, peaches, plums, raspberries

August: blackberries, blueberries, figs, melons, nectarines, peaches, plums, watermelons

September: melons, watermelons

October: cranberries, persimmons, pomegranates, quinces

RULES FOR FRUIT

1. When possible, buy fruit grown organically. Select domestically raised fruit in its season. Fruit raised in your region is even better because nutrition is greatest when fruits have not traveled for long.

2. Choose healthy-looking fruit—bright, plump, and sound. Become familiar with which fruits have been waxed or sprayed and urge the produce manager to provide unwaxed, unsprayed fruits.

3. Do not wash fruit until serving time, then wash especially well any commercially raised fruits or fruits you suspect have been sprayed.

4. To Ripen Fruit: Underripe fruits can be ripened most efficiently in a brown paper bag. Do not crowd the fruits in the bag. Place the bag at room temperature out of the sun. Turn the bag over every day so fruits can ripen evenly. Adding an apple or banana will speed the process because these fruits emit a harmless gas that enhances ripening.

5. After ripening, most fruits keep best when stored in a perforated plastic bag in the refrigerator crisper drawer. The exceptions—avocados, bananas, citrus fruits, pineapples, and melons—can be refrigerated, but their quality is best preserved in a dark, cool (50° to 65°F) place.

6. Wherever you keep them, give fruits a quick check daily. When a piece shows any sign of spoilage—mold or softness or oozing—remove it. Spoilage is infectious and will quickly ruin surrounding fruits.

7. Peeling Fruit: In general, do not peel fruit if you can avoid it. More often than not, the peel is a rich source of flavor, interesting texture, and valuable nutrients. However, in certain recipes or preparations, peeling is desirable. To peel fruits with loosely attached skin, dip them in boiling water for 20 to 60 seconds, transfer to a bowl of cold water to cool, then slip off the skin.

8. To Keep Fruits from Darkening: When preparing fruits whose flesh turns brown upon exposure to air, rub surfaces with the cut edge of a citrus fruit—lemon, orange, mandarin, grapefruit, or lime. A quantity of fruit can be kept in a bowl of acidulated water—mix ½ to 1 tablespoon lemon juice or white vinegar into 1 quart water. Do not keep fruit in this bath for more than 20 minutes.

9. When cooking fruit, retain nutrients by cooking quickly and using as little liquid as possible. Save cooking liquids and turn them into a syrup or blend some into your breakfast fruit juice.

10. Because fruits are acidic, all tools and pans should be made of nonreactive materials—stainless steel, enameled cast iron, or nonstick coated.

11. Dried fruits such as raisins, currants, and dried cherries benefit by being plumped before being added to a recipe. Plump them by soaking in warmed or boiling spirits, fruit juice, or any liquid in the recipe they are to be used in for 10 to 15 minutes before use.

November: cranberries, mandarins, persimmons, quinces
December: cranberries, mandarins

IDEAS FOR FRUIT SUBSTITUTIONS

When a fruit called for in a recipe is unavailable, by all means substitute. If the fruits will be cooked, you will have best results using something of the same type, since it will have similar physical characteristics. The following are botanical types within which fruits are virtually interchangeable in a recipe:

Pome Fruits (contain a central core with small seeds): apples, pears, quinces. Quinces must be cooked and take the longest time of the three fruits. Pears cook the fastest.

Stone Fruits (contain a single pit): apricots, cherries, nectarines, peaches, plums.

Berries (contain small seeds with juicy flesh): The brambles—all forms of blackberries and raspberries—are easily interchangeable. Remember that raspberries are hollow and cook faster than solid-centered blackberries. Blueberries, huckleberries, and cranberries make up another group; currants and gooseberries, another. Cape gooseberries, elderberries, and grapes are related to no other berry in this group but can be substituted for others.

Citrus (segments of juicy pulp with tough seeds beneath aromatic, leathery skin): oranges, mandarins, grapefruit, pomelos, lemons, limes, and all their crosses.

Melons (round to oblong fruits with hard rinds and seeds): Dessert melons include cantaloupe, casaba, Crenshaw, honeydew, Persian, and the tropical melons; kiwano is a close relative. Watermelons are another melon group. All melons are interchangeable; watermelons contain 5 percent more water than dessert melons and are coarser in texture.

CHARACTERISTICS OF FRUITS

How to tell when a fruit is ripe? First, use your nose. Most fruits let us know they are ready to eat by emitting a tantalizing fragrance. A pear is not ripe until it smells like a pear. Still, a few mature fruits keep their scent to themselves—not until you slice one open will you smell it. With them, use your touch. Hold the fruit between your palms and gently apply pressure. Even if the whole fruit is not supposed to be soft, somewhere there will be a soft spot that indicates ripeness—the tip of a peach, the dent in a cantaloupe where the stem was. Occasionally your ear will guide you. Shake a coconut—the more its milk sloshes inside, the better.

Every type of fruit has seeds inside, which is what distinguishes fruits from vegetables. Yes, that means peas, corn, cucumbers, peppers, and tomatoes are fruits. Over time, culinary custom has overridden botany, and a food is regarded as fruit if it seems more sweet than savory.

Sweetness is a fruit's great attraction. Fruits are rich in fructose, sucrose, and glucose and relatively low in calories because they contain so much water. Most fruits are at least 80 percent water; bananas are 74 percent, avocados 66 percent. The water makes fruit juicy and refreshing.

And, of course, fruits are enormously nutritious. They are a major source of vitamins, fiber, minerals, and antioxidant nutrients that protect against disease. Citrus peel and the white membrane beneath it contain more vitamin C than the flesh, as well as valuable pectin. Many fruits are excellent sources of dietary fiber.

The Food Guide Pyramid recommends two to four servings of fruit daily. Thoughtful nutritionists urge a minimum of three to five.

PREPARING FRUITS

For their nutrients and fiber, leave peels on the fruit when you can. However, if the fruit was not organically grown, there is a chance the skin or rind contains pesticide residue. Apples may have been sprayed up to a dozen times before reaching the supermarket—and then given a coat of wax in storage. Pears, peaches, and citrus fruits may also have been waxed. Apart from their cosmetic glow, edible waxes seal in moisture, which retards spoilage and helps protect fruit in shipping and handling. Waxes also seal in any fungicide or pesticide residue present. Federal law requires markets to post notice of waxed produce, but posting is on the honor system, since there are no funds to enforce the law. Washing with soap or detergent does not remove the wax. If a child is going to eat the fruit or if your diet is rich in fiber, peel waxed fruit, then wash it in clear water. Peeling removes all the fungicide or pesticide residue from apricots, bananas, and pears. Washing in water containing a mild dishwashing detergent can eliminate at least 30 percent of residue. When a child will be eating nonorganically grown berries and fruits that cannot be peeled, wash the fruit in a pint of water containing a few drops of pure soap, then rinse thoroughly.

Wait to rinse fruits until just before serving. The moist tissues of fruit are susceptible to molds, so during storage they must be kept as dry as possible. Virtually all fresh fruits lose their flavor rapidly when soaked in water, so always rinse them quickly and gently and dry at once.

To peel by blanching: Apricots, peaches, nectarines, plums, and other fruits with loosely attached skins can be peeled by blanching the way you peel tomatoes. Dip the fruit in boiling water for 20 to 60 seconds, depending on the size and density of the fruit, lift out and drop in cold water to cool, then slip off the skin. The skin of underripe fruit may not come off so easily—either return it to the boiling water for another minute or remove the skin with a vegetable peeler. To avoid discoloration, use sharp serrated stainless-steel knives when working with fruit.

When exposed to air, the flesh of apples, apricots, avocados, bananas, peaches, nectarines, pears, some yellow plums, and quinces turns brown. The fruit may not darken immediately, and if you work quickly, often no treatment is needed. If you are interrupted after treating the fruit, wrap it airtight in plastic wrap and refrigerate. Here are two solutions to help prevent fruit from browning: Sprinkle lemon, orange, lime, grapefruit, or pineapple juice over the fruit and gently toss to coat all surfaces; or mix in a bowl ½ to 1 tablespoon lemon juice or white vinegar for every quart of water—amounts are not crucial—and add the fruit directly to the water as you peel and cut it. Rinse the pieces in cold water within 20 minutes and shake or pat dry.

COOKING FRUITS

For maximum nutritional value, eat fruit raw. To retain nutrients, minimize the loss of heat-sensitive vitamins, such as vitamin C, by cooking quickly by steaming, stir-frying, or simmering in as little liquid as possible—microwaving is also excellent.

Because of their acidity, fruits discolor when cooked

in aluminum and iron pots and pans. Keep to stainless-steel, enameled cast-iron, and nonstick vessels.

Baking: The all-embracing heat of the oven is an incomparable way of cooking soft-firm and firm fruits like apricots, peaches, nectarines, plums, figs, pineapple, apples, pears, and quinces. Bake unpeeled halves or quarters of soft-firm fruits at 325°F until hot and tender, basting frequently. For every 1½ to 2 pounds prepared fruit, use a mixture of 2 tablespoons each melted butter, honey, and fresh lemon or lime juice.

Broiling: Allow 3 to 6 inches between the fruit and the source of heat, depending on the thickness of the fruit being cooked and its sugar content. A concentration of sugar will cause the fruit to blacken before it is warmed through. It is best to broil thin pieces so that you do not have to turn them. Never take your eyes off broiling fruit.

Cooking Purees: Purees are most delicate if cooked covered over gentle heat in a broad pan so that all the fruit cooks evenly, or in a double boiler, which ensures no scorching. Stir often.

Flamed or Flambéed: For best results, use at least 2 ounces alcoholic spirits and remember that unless the temperature of the fruit is at least 75°F, you may not get any effect at all. Heat the fruit over mild heat or in a covered chafing dish or electric skillet on low. Warm the spirits too, but do not let them simmer. Sprinkle the fruit lightly with sugar and, after pouring the warmed spirits over the warmed fruit, cover the pan again for a moment before lighting.

Gratinéeing: The appeal of a gratin is its contrast of temperatures and textures: cool fruit beneath warm, creamy topping, with a caramelized top.

Grilling: The grill gives a luscious outdoor flavor to fruits, and it is easy to fit pieces on the grill around whatever meat, poultry, or fish is also cooking. Small pieces should be threaded on skewers so they do not fall through the slats. When skewering, cut the pieces so that all will finish at the same time—soft fruits in larger chunks, firm fruits in smaller ones.

Microwaving: The microwave poaches prunes, pineapple, apricots, and plums quickly and beautifully. Rules are the same as for cooking vegetables, except you will cook fruits until thoroughly tender, not crisp-tender. Use less sugar than you expect to need, since sugar molecules attract the waves, and they need to reach the fruit too.

Poaching: Boiling does not suit fruit; it is too violent a method. But cooking in liquid just below or at a gentle simmer preserves the delicate texture of fruits and is suited to nearly all fruits that can be cooked. For soft-textured fruits, such as berries and peaches, the fruit should not actually be cooked, just heated through. So that the heat will reach all pieces quickly and evenly, soft fruit should be poached in a single layer. Use a skillet rather than a saucepan, and poach in batches if necessary. Prepare Light Syrup for Poaching Fruit, below. Bring the syrup to a simmer and gently place the fruit in the syrup using a spoon. Reduce the heat at once and cook with the liquid barely bubbling until the fruit is hot or barely tender. Immediately remove the pan from the heat and lift out the pieces with a slotted spoon so they will not continue to cook. Another method is to cook the fruit until not quite heated through or tender, then remove the pan from the heat and let the fruit finish cooking in the cooling syrup.

Poached fruit can be kept in its syrup in the refrigerator for a day or two before serving. You can use the syrup again for a compatible fruit—it will keep refrigerated for up to 1 week. If you prefer, you can remove the fruit from the syrup and boil the syrup over high heat until reduced to a thicker consistency. Cool and return the fruit to the syrup.

LIGHT SYRUP FOR POACHING FRUIT *1 quart*

Fruit poaches successfully in every liquid, from dense syrup to plain water. A lightly sweetened syrup is traditionally used for poaching because it helps preserve texture and shape in cooking without overwhelming flavor. These are the proportions of the 30 percent syrup so useful in canning.

In a quart measuring pitcher, combine:

1¼ cups sugar
Water, wine, or a combination to make 1 quart

Stir until the sugar is dissolved. If necessary, cook uncovered in the microwave, stirring every 2 minutes, until clear. Depending on the fruit you are poaching, you may wish to add one of the following:

½ vanilla bean, halved lengthwise
Zest of 1 lemon or small orange, in a long curl or finely shredded
Thin slices of ½ lemon or orange, unpeeled
1 to 2 tablespoons grated fresh ginger
1 cinnamon stick
Fresh or dried herbs or spices, whole or finely chopped
1 to 2 tablespoons balsamic or fruit vinegar (if wine has not been used in the syrup)

Pressure-cooking: Because you have no quick way to stop the cooking and because most fruits have delicate flesh, we do not recommend pressure-cooking any fresh fruits. In addition, apples, rhubarb, and cranberries especially tend to sputter and clog the vent. They can be explosive if every vestige of steam is not expelled before removal of the cover.

Sautéing: This gives a buttery finish and slight glaze to pieces and is delicious for firm-fleshed fruits. Allow about 2 tablespoons melted butter for every cup of sliced fruit, turning very gently two or three times with a spatula, until the pieces are hot but still holds its shape, 2 to 5 minutes. Sprinkle with 2 to 3 teaspoons fresh lemon or lime juice and the same amount or more of sugar, usually light brown, and serve at once. Apples are never more delicious than when slowly cooked in butter with a little sugar until tender and caramelized.

Steaming: This method preserves nutritional content and gives the fruit a silken finish. Place thin (up to ½ inch) pieces of fruit on a rimmed plate so that no juices will be lost. Use tongs to turn the pieces once. Depending on the fruit, the plate, and the source of steam, steaming may be quicker or take a bit longer than simmering. Dried fruits are a natural for cooking in the steamer.

Stewing: This is cooking fruit in a covered pan in just enough liquid to keep it moist, an excellent method for all sorts of fruits.

FLAVORING FRUIT

When you have had your fill of fruit on its own, enjoy it with powdered sugar and cream. Or add a spirit that intensifies the flavor. The spirit can be added in a syrup or directly.

Classic spirits for fruit are wines—dry, sweet, and fortified (like port and Marsala), plain brandy (distilled from grape wine), fruit brandy (distilled from other fermented fruits), and liqueurs (brandy infused with fruit or herbs, then sweetened). A splash of good-quality plain brandy adds elegance to every fruit. But if there were to be one bottle in the cupboard for fruit, our choice would be maraschino, a smooth liqueur distilled from sweet black cherries. Kirsch, an alternative, is cherry brandy, considerably drier (it is often labeled kirschwasser). Since orange lifts almost every fruit flavor, a second choice would be Triple Sec (most affordable), Cointreau, Grand Marnier, or Dutch curaçao, liqueurs flavored with the peel of bitter orange, a separate variety.

Vinegar can also lift the flavors of fruit, particularly fresh fruit and particularly fruit vinegars like raspberry and strawberry. A good-quality balsamic vinegar is startlingly good with strawberries and cherries.

FRESH FRUIT CUP OR FRUIT SALAD

10 to 12 servings

You can be sure a mix of fresh fruits will be pleasing when you base it on year-round favorites, then add bright colors and flavors from fruits of the season (good proportions are about 2 pounds foundation fruits and 1½ to 2 pounds seasonal fruits). To keep the mixture from looking like a hash, cut pieces in a variety of shapes, none smaller than bite-sized. Although it should be served to guests within a few hours, you can enjoy the fruits for a day or two—citrus juices and honey keep them from darkening.

Add the following fruits and ingredients in the order given to a large mixing bowl, stirring gently every once in a while:

2 sweet oranges, peeled, seeded, and cut into bite-sized chunks
Juice of 1 large lemon
⅓ cup mild honey, preferably orange blossom, or sugar
2 green eating apples, cored and cut into medium dice
1 large ripe pear, cored and cut into bite-sized chunks
1 large banana, thinly sliced

Add 3 or 4 seasonal fruits, about 8 ounces each. Choose from:

Kiwis, peeled, cut lengthwise in half, and sliced
Strawberries, hulled and quartered lengthwise
Whole raspberries, blueberries, or blackberries
Pitted sweet cherries
Melon or watermelon balls
Peaches, nectarines, apricots, or plums, pitted and sliced
Seedless red grapes, stemmed

MACÉDOINE OF FRESH FRUITS

A macédoine is a fresh fruit cup flavored with spirits. Clear cherry-flavored maraschino liqueur is incomparable with mixed fruit.

Prepare Fresh Fruit Cup or Fruit Salad, above, adding ½ cup maraschino liqueur or ⅓ cup orange liqueur with the honey or sugar. Cover, and refrigerate for about 4 hours before serving for the flavors to blend and mellow.

HEAVY SYRUP FOR CHILLING FRUIT *2 cups*

As the syrup surrounds pieces of fruit, it efficiently transmits the cold. Do not serve fruit so cold, however, that its flavor is obscured.

Combine:

1⅔ cups sugar
1 cup water

Stir until the sugar is dissolved. If necessary, heat, uncovered, in the microwave, stirring every 2 minutes, until clear.

FRUIT FONDUE

8 to 10 servings

Fresh, sweet fruit served with warm melted chocolate sauce for dipping is one combination that never disappoints. Wash, dry well, and hull:

2 pints ripe strawberries

Peel and cut into 2-inch lengths:

6 ripe bananas

Trim, peel, and cut crosswise into 1-inch-thick slices:

1 large ripe pineapple

Using an apple corer, small cookie cutter, or a sharp knife, cut out the core in each ring, then cut the ring into 4 pieces. Arrange the fruit on a platter with:

American Sponge Cake, 946, or Hot-Milk Sponge Cake, 947, cut into cubes (optional)

Prepare:

4 cups Chocolate Sauce, 1045, or Chocolate Custard Sauce, 1041

Serve the sauce warm in a bowl or fondue pot with the fruit and cake.

APPLES

When buying apples, look for fruit with flesh that feels firm and tight beneath the skin. There should be no soft spots, dark bruises, or holes. Do not be deceived by size. Larger apples tend to mature faster and thus can be mealier than small ones. For fast ripening, keep apples at room temperature. For longest keeping, refrigerate sound apples in perforated plastic bags or keep in a dry, cold place—32°F to 40°F.

To peel an apple, use a swivel-bladed vegetable peeler—a knife takes too much flesh. To core, cut in quarters lengthwise and then cut out the core from each piece with a down-and-up motion. To core a whole apple, push an apple corer through the center from the top, aimed at the blossom end below.

Superbly flavored apples should be served cool. Apples that are light on flavor, like Red Delicious, are best cold—twice as crisp as at room temperature.

Mellow the flavor of cooking apples by leaving them at room temperature for a day or two before using. An apple of poor flavor can be improved with the addition of lemon juice and a pinch of cinnamon in cooking, but remember that nothing can really compensate for natural flavor. To make applesauce without having to peel or add sugar, use naturally sweet Braeburns and Golden Delicious. In cooking, unless you are working with one of the great eating apples, a blend of sweet and tart, spicy and mild, will give dimension to flavor and often texture. And when you have time, buy two or three types of each of the eating apples available and have a taste test, making different combinations until you find something terrific. Consider that there are hundreds of flavor and aroma molecules in every bite. Apples can be baked, broiled, frittered, grilled, poached, sautéed, steamed, and stir-fried. Apples have a special affinity for vanilla and almond, apricots and quinces, cinnamon, cloves, nutmeg, cardamom, coriander, rosemary, sage, and lemon.

Apples are classed according to how they are used. *Eating* (dessert) apples are, as a rule, crisp or crunchy, juicy, sweet or sweet-tart, with an intriguing aroma and complex flavor. *Cooking* (or culinary) apples are usually firmer and on the tart side, although they may be juicy and touched with sweetness. Most apples contain between 10 and 14 percent sugar. Tart apples just contain more malic acid, which blunts their sweetness. The texture of an apple's cooked flesh can be fluffy, as in a baked Rome Beauty; tender but intact, as in a Jonagold; or thick, as in Newton Pippin applesauce. A few splendid varieties like Golden Delicious and Gravenstein are suited to both eating and cooking. True cider apples—like Kingston Black and Fox Whelp—are high in acid and tannin and thus not fit for eating fresh but give cider sparkling flavor and depth. There are also a few apples good for both cider and cooking, like McIntosh, Northern Spy, and Cortland. Crab apples are a

Golden Delicious apple

Rome Beauty apple

McIntosh apple

different species altogether. They are tiny—an inch or so wide—and very tart; they are excellent for pickling and jellying because they contain so much pectin.

Knowing the characteristics of the apples at the market saves time and energy and spares frustration over collapsed baked apples, mushy slices in pie, and bland applesauce. Here are some favorite apples grown domestically—uses are in order of what the apple does best.

Akane: juicy, crisp, tart, white flesh. Eating, sauce (cook with the skin on, then strain), drying; use within 4 weeks.

Arkansas Black: crisp, firm, juicy, fragrant, golden flesh. Eating, sauce, cider; keeps 6 months or more, gaining in flavor.

Baldwin: crisp, coarse, juicy, spicy, yellow flesh. Cider, pie, sauce, eating; keeps up to 6 months.

Black Gilliflower or Sheepnose: rich and sweet. Excellent for drying, can be baked; use within 2 months.

Braeburn: crisp, firm, rich, sweet-tart, yellow flesh. Eating, sauce, pie; keeps 6 months or more.

Bramley or Bramley's Seedling: England's favorite cooking apple—firm, coarse, juicy, tangy-sweet flesh high in vitamin C; baking, sauce, cider; keeps 6 months or more.

Calville Blanc d'Hiver: sixteenth-century apple, a French favorite—tender, lightly tart, spicy, yellowish white flesh, higher in vitamin C than oranges. Eating, tarts, sauce, cider; keeps at least 3 months, its flavor mellowing.

Cortland: crisp, very juicy, fragrant, tangy, white flesh. Eating, salad (the flesh stays white), pie, sauce, cider, drying; keeps at least 2 months.

Cox's Orange Pippin: firm, juicy, richly flavored. Eating, pie, sauce, cider; keeps about 3 months.

Empire: crisp, juicy, sweet-tart, creamy white flesh. Eating, cider; keeps 4 to 6 weeks.

Esopus Spitzenberg: Thomas Jefferson's favorite apple—crisp, fine-grained, juicy, fragrant, spicy, yellow flesh. Connoisseur's eating apple, also for baking; keeps 6 months or more.

Fuji: crisp, fine-grained, juicy, sweet, white flesh. Eating; keeps 6 months or more.

Gala: crisp, firm, fragant, sweet and mildly tart. Eating, cooking in butter, drying; keeps 3 months or more.

Golden Delicious: juicy, fragrant, and honey sweet. Eating, salad, sauce, tarts, cooking in butter, cider; keeps at least 2 months.

Granny Smith: crisp, juicy, from mildly tart to tart, white flesh. Pie, sauce, juice, baking; keeps up to 6 months.

Gravenstein: crisp, fine-grained, juicy, slightly tart. Unexcelled for pie, sauce, baking, cider, and fine for eating; keeps 4 to 6 weeks.

Grimes Golden: fine-grained, juicy, fragrant, spicy, yellow flesh. Eating, sauce, pie, cider, drying, freezing; keeps about 3 months.

Idared: tender, juicy, fragrant, and lightly tart. Pie, sauce, baking, cooking, canning; keeps 6 months or more.

Jonagold: crisp, juicy, sweet-tart, yellow flesh. Eating, juice, pie, baking; keeps about 3 months.

Jonathan: crisp, fine-grained, juicy, slightly tart. Eating, sauce, pie, cider; use within 4 to 6 weeks.

Lady or Christmas Apple: very small, crisp, juicy, intensely sweet, white flesh. Eating, baking, cider (and centerpieces and wreaths); keeps 4 months or more.

Lodi or Improved Yellow Transparent: crisp, juicy, sweet-tart, white flesh. Sauce, pie; use within 2 weeks.

Macoun: firm, fragrant, juicy, white flesh, surpasses parent McIntosh's flavor. Eating, pie, sauce; keeps about 3 months.

McIntosh: tender, juicy, fragrant, spicy, tart. Eating, cider, sauce; keeps at least 2 months.

Melrose: rather coarse, juicy, sweet, white flesh. Pie, wait until after Christmas for eating; keeps up to 6 months.

Mutsu or Crispin: crisp, juicy, spicy, lightly tart, white flesh. Eating, sauce, cider; keeps 6 months or more.

Red Delicious apple

Whitney crab apple

Newton Pippin or Pippin: moderately fine-grained, aromatic, and tart. Eating, pie, sauce, cider; keeps 5 months.
Northern Spy: very juicy, sprightly and sweet, high in vitamin C. Eating, baking, pie, sauce, cider, drying; keeps up to 5 months.
Red Delicious: crisp, juicy, mildly tart. Eating, cider; keeps 6 months or more.
Rhode Island Greening or Greening: an early American apple—crisp, juicy, rich, tart, greenish white flesh. Pie, sauce, drying, eating, cider; keeps 6 months or more.
Rome Beauty: crisp, firm, juicy, mildly tart. Baking, drying, cider; keeps at least 2 months.
Roxbury Russet: seventeenth-century American apple—crisp, coarse-textured, tart-sweet, yellow-green flesh. Eating, pie, sauce, cider; keeps up to 6 months.
Spartan: crisp, firm, sweet-tart, white flesh. Superb eating; keeps up to 3 months, improving in flavor.
Stayman Winesap: firm, juicy, fragrant, winy, greenish yellow flesh. Baking, sauce, cider; keeps at least 2 months.
Summer Rambo: sixteenth-century French apple—crisp, very juicy, winy. Eating, sauce, drying, pie; use within 4 weeks.
Wealthy: very juicy, fragrant, winy, sweet. Eating, pie, sauce, cider, baking, preserves, freezing. Keeps up to 3 months.
Winesap: crisp, firm, very juicy, winy, yellow flesh. Eating, cider, sauce, pie; keeps 6 months or more.
Wolf River: soft, slightly tart, creamy white flesh. Excellent for drying; use within 4 weeks.
York or York Imperial: crisp, coarse-grained, fragrant, mildly tart. Pie, sauce, baking, cider; keeps 2 months.

APPLESAUCE

4 to 6 servings

This can be chunky or smooth. A blend of 2 or 3 apples makes the best-tasting sauce. Begin with a tart-sweet apple like Gravenstein or Newton Pippin, then mix in spicy McIntosh with Gravensteins or winy Staymans with Pippins. Golden Delicious adds sunny sweetness to any blend. This recipe doubles easily.

Place in a large, heavy skillet or saucepan:

3 pounds cooking apples, peeled if desired, cut into ½-inch-thick slices

Apple corer

½ to ¾ cup apple cider or apple juice, depending on juiciness of apples
1 to 1½ tablespoons fresh lemon juice, depending on tartness of apples
1 large cinnamon stick

Cover and simmer, stirring often, over low heat until tender but not mushy, about 20 minutes. Stir in:

Scant ½ cup white or turbinado sugar or 6 tablespoons mild honey
1 teaspoon ground ginger (optional)
½ teaspoon ground mace (optional)
½ teaspoon ground nutmeg

Cook, stirring, until the sweetener is dissolved and blended, about 1 minute. Remove from the heat. Discard the cinnamon stick. For chunky applesauce, break up the apples with a wooden spoon. For medium texture, crush with a potato masher. For smooth sauce, pass it through a food mill or coarse sieve. Serve warm or chilled. If desired, accompany with:

Heavy cream or yogurt

For a new flavor, sprinkle each serving with:

Anise or fennel seeds, toasted and crushed

BERRY APPLESAUCE

Prepare Applesauce, above, substituting 3 cups cranberries,* picked over, for 1 pound of the apples and increasing the apple cider or apple juice to ¾ to 1 cup. Taste and add more sugar if needed. Pass the sauce through a food mill or coarse sieve to remove the seeds.

Another way with berries is to prepare Applesauce, above, reducing all amounts by one-third. When the sauce is finished, stir in 1 pound fresh strawberries, raspberries, or loganberries. Taste and add more sugar if needed. Pass through a food mill or coarse sieve to remove the seeds. Top with whole fresh berries just before serving.

FRENCH APPLESAUCE

Prepare Applesauce, above, substituting 2 tablespoons unsalted butter for 2 tablespoons of the cider. Omit the nutmeg and blend ¾ to 1 teaspoon vanilla into the finished sauce. Serve with Custard Sauce, 1041, or Fresh Strawberry or Raspberry Sauce, 1048.

INSTANT APPLESAUCE

4 to 6 servings

As the apples are uncooked, the texture of this applesauce is crispy-crunchy and the flavor wonderfully fresh. Kids love this.

Scrub well:

2 pounds firm, sweet, or tart-sweet apples with tender skins, such as Golden Delicious, Fuji, Gala, or Lodi

Quarter, core, and cut the apples into eighths. Puree in batches in a food processor or blender along with:

3 tablespoons fresh lemon juice

Stop to push down the pieces as needed. Remove to a bowl and stir in:

¼ cup white or packed brown sugar or maple sugar, or 3 tablespoons honey or maple syrup, or ¼ cup finely chopped pitted dates or soft raisins, or to taste

¾ to 1 teaspoon ground cinnamon (optional)

Serve at once or refrigerate until chilled.

BAKED APPLES

4 to 6 servings

Seemingly simple, baked apples can become an elegant dessert or brunch dish. Seasonings can vary widely: any nut or fruit, ginger in any of its forms, white sugar, maple syrup, honey, or preserves for sweetening. The most important thing is to choose a variety of apple that is firm, tart, and full of character.

Preheat the oven to 350°F.

Core through the top, stopping ½ inch from the bottom:

4 large or 6 small, firm, tart apples, such as Rome Beauty, McIntosh, Jonagold, or Granny Smith

Set the apples in a shallow 1- to 1½-quart baking dish, just large enough to hold them without touching. Combine:

⅓ cup packed brown sugar
¼ cup chopped walnuts, lightly toasted
¼ cup raisins (optional)
Grated zest of ½ lemon
½ teaspoon ground nutmeg
¼ teaspoon ground cinnamon

Spoon the mixture into the apples and scatter any that is left into the pan. Dot on top of the apples:

1½ tablespoons unsalted butter, cut into small pieces

Pour into the pan:

⅔ cup water or fresh sweet cider if available

Cover tightly with a lid or aluminum foil. Bake the apples for about 30 minutes. Uncover, baste with the syrup in the bottom of the pan, and bake until they are tender but not mushy, about 10 minutes more, depending on the variety. Place the apples on serving plates and spoon the syrup over the apples. Serve warm or at room temperature. If desired, accompany with:

Heavy or light cream or vanilla ice cream

BAKED APPLES WITH ORANGE SAUCE

8 servings

Make these with fat, juicy, sweet-tart apples like Rome Beauty, McIntosh, Jonagold, or Granny Smith.

Preheat the oven to 375°F.

Beat together:

10 tablespoons unsalted butter, softened
⅔ cup packed light brown sugar

Cut out the cores, stopping ½ inch from the bottom and being careful not to pierce the base with a knife, from:

8 medium baking apples (about 2¾ pounds)

Use a vegetable peeler to peel the skin from the top one-quarter of each apple. Push the butter mixture into the centers, then spread the remainder over the exposed flesh. Set the apples in a shallow 2-quart baking dish. Slice a little off the bottom as needed if an apple is lopsided. Pour into the dish:

1 cup apple juice

Bake, uncovered, in the center of the oven for 20 minutes, then use a bulb baster to baste the apples with the juices. Bake for 10 minutes more, then baste again. Bake until the apples are just tender when tested with a thin skewer, 10 to 15 minutes more.

Meanwhile, make a glaze by blending together in the order listed:

½ cup packed light brown sugar
1½ tablespoons all-purpose flour
2 tablespoons thawed frozen orange juice concentrate
¾ teaspoon ground nutmeg
¼ teaspoon ground cinnamon

Remove the dish from the oven. Smooth the glaze over the exposed flesh of the apples and bake 10 more minutes. Cool for at least 15 minutes before serving warm with the sauce in the dish.

BUTTERED-RUM BAKED APPLES

Prepare Baked Apples with Orange Sauce, above, substituting ¼ cup dark rum for the apple juice and adding ⅔ cup water to the dish. When making the glaze, substitute 1½ tablespoons water for the orange juice concentrate.

CANDIED APPLES

5 servings

These are best within 24 hours of preparing.

Line a baking sheet with parchment or wax paper. Flatten 5 paper cupcake liners on the baking sheet. Remove the stems and insert a wooden skewer into the stem end of each of:

5 medium red apples

Combine in the top of a double boiler or a saucepan that will fit over another pan:

2 cups sugar
1 cup water
⅔ cup light corn syrup
One 2-inch cinnamon stick

Stir until the sugar is dissolved. Bring to a boil; boil without stirring for about 3 minutes, brushing down any crystals on the sides of the pan with a pastry brush dipped in hot water. Boil until the syrup reaches 290°F on a candy thermometer, the soft-crack stage (see The Stages of Cooked Syrup, 846). Remove the cinnamon stick. Add:

3 or 4 drops red food coloring (optional)

Set the pan over—not in—boiling water. Working quickly, dip in the apples, one at a time, and coat evenly with the glaze. Twirl the apple at the end so the extra drips off. Set each apple on a cupcake liner.

CARAMEL APPLES
5 servings

Line a baking sheet with parchment or wax paper. Flatten 5 paper cupcake liners on the baking sheet. Remove the stems and insert a wooden skewer into the stem end of each of:

5 medium red apples

Combine in the top of a double boiler or a heatproof bowl set over—not in—boiling water:

1 pound store-bought caramels
2 tablespoons water

Heat, stirring until the caramels are melted and smooth. Working quickly, dip in the apples, one at a time, scraping the excess off on the side of the pan. If desired, dip the bottom in:

½ cup chopped unsalted peanuts

Set each apple on a cupcake liner. If refrigerated, the caramel will set in a few minutes.

BUTTERED APPLE SLICES
4 breakfast servings or 8 garnish servings

Perfect alongside roast pork or fresh ham.

Melt in a large skillet over medium-low heat until foamy:

2 tablespoons butter

Add in a single layer:

2 firm, tart apples, cored and cut into ⅜-inch slices

Cook until the bottoms are golden. Turn and cook the second side until golden, a few minutes longer, depending on the firmness of the apples. Do not let them turn soft.

To glaze, especially if they are very tart, sprinkle over the surface:

2 tablespoons sugar

Let stand until the sugar melts. Serve warm.

APPLE FRITTERS
6 servings

Mix together in a medium bowl:

1 cup all-purpose flour
2 tablespoons sugar
1½ teaspoons baking powder
¼ teaspoon salt

Whisk together in another bowl:

⅔ cup milk
1 egg yolk
1 tablespoon butter, melted

Gradually stir into the dry ingredients until smooth.

Pour into a shallow baking dish:

Juice of 1 lemon

Add and turn to coat:

4 large firm apples, peeled, cored, and cut into ¼-inch slices

Pour into a deep fryer or deep, heavy pot and heat to 375°F:

3 inches vegetable oil

Beat in a medium bowl until the peaks are stiff but not dry:

2 large egg whites, at room temperature

Fold the egg whites into the batter. Working with a few apples at a time, shake off the lemon juice and dip them into the batter, letting the excess drip off. Immediately drop the slices into the hot oil and deep-fry, turning once, until golden brown and puffed. Drain the fritters on paper towels and keep warm in a 250°F oven until all are finished. Serve the apple fritters sprinkled with:

Powdered sugar or pure maple syrup

SPICED CRAB APPLES
About 4 cups

Combine in a large saucepan:

2 cups sugar
1½ cups white vinegar or red or white wine vinegar

Cover and boil until the sugar is dissolved, about 5 minutes. Add:

1 pound unblemished whole crab apples (preferably red), with stems

Simmer over low heat, uncovered, just until tender, 3 to 5 minutes, depending on their size and firmness. Do not let them get mushy. Remove the apples from the syrup to a 1-quart jar. Add to the syrup:

One 1-inch piece cinnamon stick
6 allspice berries
4 whole cloves

Boil over high heat until the syrup is thickened and

seasoned to your taste. Let cool, then strain and pour over the apples. Cover and keep refrigerated for up to 1 month.

APRICOTS

If you live where winters are cold, summers are hot and dry, and there are few late frosts, you know about luscious tree-ripened apricots. Should you come across ripe apricots of one of the great varieties—Royal or Blenheim—enjoy them out of hand or cut into a fruit cup, for these soft fruits are costly to pack and ship. If you live elsewhere, the best-tasting fruit will be the barely ripe ones you cook.

In selecting fruit, size is less important than variety and ripeness. If apricots are soft, juicy, and fragrant, eat them the same or next day. They will ripen after picking, but fruit that is greenish yellow or does not have an apricot aroma will not have enough time to develop good flavor before it spoils. Ripen fruits by the paper bag method, 440. They will keep in the refrigerator for up to 1 week.

Cooked apricots are delicious, since heat intensifies their flavor. For cooking, use just-ripe fruit. Cook apricots only long enough to soften them, for they are mushy if overcooked. Apricots can be baked or grilled, but poaching preserves their delicacy. Most recipes for peaches, nectarines, and plums apply to apricots. As with other stone fruits, a little orange juice or zest emphasizes the apricot flavor. Apricots have a special affinity for apples and almonds, close relatives in the rose family.

APRICOT COMPOTE

4 servings

When fruit is steeped in sugar, the sugar draws out its juice, forming a syrup. Here apricots are poached in their own syrup, brightened with orange. This results in a particularly rich apricot flavor. The skins toughen slightly in cooking.

If desired, peel by blanching, 440:

10 sweet firm ripe apricots (1¼ pounds)

Cut each apricot in half along the seam line and remove the pit. Arrange cut sides up in a large shallow bowl. Spoon a little of the following into each cavity, in the order given:

¼ cup fresh orange juice

¼ cup sugar

Cover and let stand in a cool place until the sugar is dissolved, about 2 hours. Turn the fruit cut sides down with their syrup into a heavy nonstick skillet. Bring to a simmer over medium heat. Reduce the heat to low, cover, and cook until the apricots are tender when tested with a thin skewer, 7 to 8 minutes. They will continue cooking out of the pan, so do not overcook. Turn into a serving bowl cut sides up and pour the syrup over them. Cover and refrigerate for 1 hour, if desired. Serve warm or cool, sprinkled with:

Chopped pistachios or slivered almonds, toasted

Serve with:

Crème Anglaise, 1041

AVOCADOS

Grown in southern California and Florida, avocados are available year-round. California specializes in the Hass, a purplish black, pebbly skinned avocado of the Guatemalan type. Hass avocados weigh about 8 ounces and have superior flavor. Their flesh is so rich and buttery because it contains twice as much fat as the smaller, smooth-skinned, green Mexican type of avocados that are grown in Florida. (California's other avocado, smooth green Fuerte, is probably a Guatemalan-Mexican hybrid.) Although fat means calories, most fat in avocados is monounsaturated, the friendly sort found in olives. From southern Florida and Hawaii also comes the yellow-skinned West Indian avocado. Should you find 1- to 2-ounce cocktail avocados (they are Fuertes or Mexican fruits with no seed, remnants of dropped pollinated flowers), prepare as usual.

Choose an unblemished fruit that is heavy for its size, ideally one that is tender when gently pressed between your hands. Ripe avocados are rare at the market, so plan to buy them about 3 days before you will need them. Until it is cut, a stone-hard avocado will ripen by the paper bag method, 440, in about that much time. Slightly overripe fruit can be used for mashing but not slicing. Refrigerate ripe fruits for up to 2 days.

Avocado flesh quickly darkens when exposed to air. This does not affect quality or flavor but mars the beauty of the fruit. To prevent darkening, immediately rub cut surfaces with a slice of citrus or blend citrus juice into mashed avocado—the more, the better. When preparing mashed avocado in advance, press heavy-duty plastic wrap on top and smooth out any air bubbles. Leaving the pit in an avocado half works because air cannot reach where the seed is, but placing a pit in a bowl of guacamole has no effect.

Avocados turn bitter when cooked, so enjoy them raw. When adding avocado to cooked dishes, do it at the last minute, off the heat.

BANANAS

The banana is close to being the perfect fruit. It satisfies hunger pangs from the time its tips are green and its flesh is firm and faintly tart until its golden skin is speckled with brown and the fruit is creamy sweet. Most bananas at the market are from Central America and are abundant year-round. They are picked when fully developed but green. This is done even when fruits will be eaten locally, because the fruit ripens most satisfactorily off the tree. Two principal varieties come to us. The Gros Michel is big and long with a tapered tip and thick yellow skin. Connoisseurs describe its flavor as "adequate." The Cavendish is shorter, squatter, and curved, with thinner yellow skin. Its flavor is preferred. However, there are over a hundred varieties of cultivated bananas across the world, and more and more are available here. Handsome red-skinned bananas have sweet, faintly pink flesh. Sabas and Brazilians are very straight and ripen to tartness. Finger-sized Manzano (or apple or finger) bananas have a sweet-sharp taste.

Whatever the color, select plump bananas with vibrant-looking skin. If the skin looks dull, the fruit may have been damaged by cold and will not ripen. Bananas are susceptible to bruising, but superficial brown lines on the skin indicating nicks and scratches probably have not harmed the fruit inside. When a whole area on the skin is dark, it indicates the bruise is more than skin deep. Be sure the skin is intact—an opening in the envelope invites spoilage. Ripen bananas out of the sun at room temperature, turning them daily. For faster ripening, use the paper bag method, 440. Ripe bananas can be refrigerated, although their skins will blacken. To prepare a banana, just peel it and remove the fibrous strings. When cutting up a banana, coat the pieces with citrus juice to keep them from darkening. Bananas are even sweeter after cooking. Green-tipped fruits hold their shape best—try them baked, grilled, broiled, and sautéed. Use fully ripe fruits for mashing and stirring into batters. Bananas can be frozen and also dried. See also Plantains, 406.

BANANAS FOSTER

4 servings

This classic recipe is from Brennan's restaurant in New Orleans. If you enjoy chafing-dish cooking, prepare this at the table before your guests.

Peel and cut in half lengthwise:

4 firm ripe bananas

Cut each length into 4 pieces. In a large, heavy skillet, melt:

2 tablespoons butter

Place the bananas in the skillet cut sides down. Cook over low heat for 5 minutes, then turn with a spatula and cook for another 5 minutes, just until fork-tender—do not overcook. Sprinkle with:

3 tablespoons light brown sugar
¼ teaspoon ground cinnamon
⅛ teaspoon ground nutmeg

Transfer the bananas to a heatproof serving dish and arrange in a single layer. Add to the skillet:

½ cup dark rum
1 tablespoon brandy (optional)

Over medium heat, use a spatula to loosen caramelized bits while the spirits heat. When the tip of a finger tells you they are hot, ignite with a long wooden match, then pour over the bananas. Spoon over:

Vanilla ice cream

GRILLED BANANAS

4 servings

Fun for the end of a barbecue.

Prepare a medium-hot charcoal fire.

Peel and cut lengthwise in half:

4 ripe bananas

Cut each half on a diagonal into 3 pieces. Heat in a microwave oven or small saucepan until very fluid:

¼ cup honey

Toss the bananas with the honey in a shallow bowl until all are coated. This can be done 1 to 2 hours in advance.

Arrange the banana pieces crosswise on the grill over hot coals. Grill until marked on the bottom. Turn and grill just until the second side is marked. Arrange on a platter and dust lightly with:

Ground cinnamon
Ground ginger (optional)

Serve immediately.

These also can be pan-grilled in a ridged cast-iron skillet. Heat the skillet over high heat until very hot but not smoking. Quickly arrange about half the banana pieces crosswise on the ridges. Turn the pieces when they are marked on the bottom and remove them when marked on the second side, about 30 seconds to 1 minute each side. Repeat with the remaining bananas.

BERRIES

Select berries that are glossy, plump, the deepest color of their variety, and with no sign of mushiness or mold. When berries are sold by the box, turn it upside down to make sure there is no stain or moisture on the bottom, indicating an overripe berry or two has dissolved. Inspect for mold—one small spot can make every berry in the box taste moldy. When you get home, immediately spread the berries on a towel and remove any that are not perfect. Eat any crushed berries soon. Refrigerate the rest, *unwashed,* layered between paper towels. Just before serving, place the berries in a colander, dip into a quantity of cool water, and gently swish; then lift out, shake off the water, and gently pat dry on a cloth.

Blackberries: Picked firm, the many offspring of the wild Pacific blackberry are tart—good for canning and pies. Picked fully ripe, they are soft, fragrant, sweet, and best eaten raw. One form of blackberry or another is in season from June through mid-September. Select all forms as for red raspberries. They do not last for more than a day.

Boysenberries are long, maroon, and almost seedless. Their flavor is sweet-tart, rather like raspberries, with a distinctive fragrance. They are of excellent quality and good for all forms of cooking and preserving. Loganberries may be a cross of red raspberry and blackberry. Most people who have tasted them think these large, juicy, slightly tart, burgundy-red berries are the finest flavored of all berries and the best for cooking. Marion and olallie berries are medium to large, shiny black, and sweet, with the hint of a wild blackberry flavor. Marion is the most popular blackberry, especially fine in desserts. Sylvan berries are a cross between boysenberry and marion berry. They are large, shiny black, mild, and very sweet. Tayberries are another raspberry and blackberry cross. Very large, purple-red, and cone shaped with solid centers, tayberries must be enjoyed where they grow, as they are too soft to ship. Youngberries are purple-black, similar to boysenberries but sweeter. They make a refreshing juice.

Blueberries: Blueberries are sweet with enough tang to make them interesting—close your eyes and you taste plum. Blue on the outside and light green on the inside, cultivated berries are much larger than their wild forebears. Maine's wild low-bush blueberries are small but intensely flavored. Choose plump, sound berries nicely covered with bloom, a whitish coating that preserves the moisture in blueberries and helps them keep longer than most other berries. As delicious as blueberries are raw, they are the perfect baker's berry—from pies to pancakes to muffins to cheesecake topping. Blueberries both freeze and dry superbly and are good canned as well. They have little pectin but make luscious preserves and jams.

Brambles (More): These are close relatives of blackberries and raspberries. American dewberries are round to oblong, bluish black, glossy, and sweet but milder than blackberries. Japanese wineberries are small, orange-red, shaped like raspberries, and have a tart flavor that makes good wine. Thimbleberries are bright reddish orange, thimble shaped, small, and seedy but also rich, tangy, and tasty.

Cranberries: Cultivated cranberries come in shades of red from light to dark to nearly black—the assorted reds do not represent degrees of ripeness but varieties. Fresh cranberries appear sometime in October and stay through December. Cranberries are rich in pectin—one reason why the relish they make is so popular, for it unmolds flawlessly. The berries are remarkable keepers, both in the refrigerator and freezer. Preparation is simply a matter of rinsing and checking for bits of leaves and twigs. Try cranberries in any recipes calling for red currants.

CRANBERRY CONSERVE

About six ½-pint jars

This is a luxurious form of cranberry sauce, with uncommon beauty, texture, and flavor.

Chill, then slice very thinly on a plate, removing any seeds:

12 ounces unpeeled oranges

Cut the slices in half. Place with their juice in a small skillet with:

½ cup apple cider or juice

Cover and simmer until the orange peel is soft, 15 to 20 minutes. Peel, core, and cut into ½-inch chunks to make 1½ cups:

1 pound fresh pineapple

Pick over:

1 pound cranberries

Combine all the fruits in a large saucepan along with:

4 cups sugar
½ cup lemon juice
Scant 1 teaspoon ground cinnamon
¾ teaspoon whole cloves

Bring to a boil, reduce the heat, and simmer, stirring often, until thick, about 35 minutes. Pour into a shallow dish, cover loosely with wax paper, and let stand in a cool place overnight. The following day, bring the conserve to a boil, whisk well to combine, and ladle into clean jars. The conserve will keep, tightly covered, in the refrigerator for up to 3 weeks.

Currants: In northern Europe, tangy red currants are turned into colorful preserves and elegant sauces for meat. Black currants are cultivated for rich dark jams, syrups, and liqueurs like crème de cassis. Currants look like small, shiny, round buttons. They are scarce in this country, but from mid-June through August, pester the supermarket produce manager and growers at the farmers' market to find some for you.

Red and black currants are different species. The red are juicy, with a brilliant fruity sharpness. Black currants are larger than red—over ½ inch in diameter. They are not quite as juicy and their flavor is muted. Yellow currants might be a variety of black or a native berry. Pink currants are a variant of red. There are opalescent white currants, which may have come from either the red or the black species. Light-colored fruits are less acidic and are translucent when cooked. Currants are very high in pectin, a soluble fiber.

The berries grow in clusters, and if yours are still on the stem, gently tease them off with a fork. The flavor is so tart that currants, like cranberries, are almost always cooked. They have small hard seeds that are marginally edible. It is best, but a labor of love, to seed them raw. Poke a thin skewer through the stem end and push the seeds out the other side, holding back the pulp with your other hand. Or cook the berries until softened, then pass through a food mill or sieve.

Elderberries: Tiny, purple-black elderberries are not often eaten on their own but are instead used in cooking to flavor other fruits. No other fruit will give an apple pie more verve. The berries grow in broad loose clusters following June's creamy white elderflowers. The round berries have a tart, spicy, winy taste. In August, elderberries might be found at a farmers' market but are more likely to be found growing in a tall shrub by a country road. Select sprays with the darkest berries. Once home, freeze the sprays on baking sheets, then shake them into a deep bowl—the berries will fall off (this will also dispatch any small insects clinging to the sprays). Either pack in a freezer bag and return to the freezer or rinse the berries and cook them as you would blueberries. Elderberries have long been prized for making wine, jam, and jelly. To add to a 9-inch apple pie, mix a heaping 3 cups berries into the prepared apples, then blend in the sugar and spices. Elderberries must always be cooked, since the small amount of a poisonous alkaloid they may contain is destroyed in cooking. The cooked berries can also be frozen.

Gooseberries: Gooseberries are usually the size of large blueberries but rounder, although some are ovals, some are teardrops, and some are as big as quail eggs. The berries are the same translucent color all through, whether white, gold, purple-red, burgundy, rose, or the standard lime green. When underripe, gooseberries have a clean sharp taste like sour grapes. As they ripen, a touch of muscat creeps in, softening the sharpness. Gooseberries are in season from May through August but are most widely available in June. Choose the firmest and shiniest berries at the market. When picking, remember that the ripe berries are those that fall from the bush when touched. Gooseberries are good keepers when refrigerated.

The ripest, sweetest berries are wonderful raw, but most gooseberries are cooked with sugar. The English cook elderflowers with gooseberries to bring out the muscat in the berries; a splash of muscat wine has the same effect. Gooseberries can be cooked well in advance; because they are so acid, they never discolor. To prepare for cooking, "top and tail" the berries—use a thumbnail to nip off the remnants of stem at the top end and blossom at the tail end. For a cooked puree, this step can be omitted because the ends will be caught in the sieve. Like lemon, the acidity of gooseberries in a sauce makes an excellent foil for fatty fish and meat. Gooseberries make heavenly puddings, tarts, and pies. The berries freeze and can well and make superlative preserves.

GOOSEBERRY FOOL

4 to 5 servings

In seventeenth-century England, fruit fools were custard blended with stewed fruit. Now, in this country, they are equal parts pureed fruit and whipped cream mixed together. Gooseberries make a classic fool, their lively sourness playing against sweet cream. We leave the seeds in for texture, but you may prefer to strain them out.

If you do not plan to strain the berries, top and tail:

Generous 3 cups gooseberries (1 pound)

Cook in a medium, heavy pan over low heat, crushing the berries with a potato masher when they soften, until thoroughly soft, 10 to 15 minutes. Puree in a blender or food processor. Strain if you wish, then blend in:

¼ cup wine, such as muscatel (optional)

2 tablespoons sugar, or more to taste (keep it tangy)

Cover and refrigerate for up to 3 days.

Up to 3 hours before serving, whip until soft peaks form:

1¼ cups cold heavy cream

Whitesmith and Achilles gooseberries

Cover and refrigerate until just before serving. Gently fold the gooseberry puree into the cream. If you have not used wine, add:

½ teaspoon vanilla

Taste for sweetness and vanilla. Mound in stemmed glasses and serve immediately.

Huckleberries: Huckleberries resemble blueberries in appearance and flavor but are much seedier and therefore not grown commercially. Several fruits are called huckleberries. One of the most commonly gathered is the Black huckleberry, an eastern native. It is glossy black and has ten seedlike nuts. It is not a berry but a drupe, a fruit with a pit, like a peach. Another is the Evergreen huckleberry, which grows along the Pacific Coast. It is a true berry, black and tart. Huckleberries ripen in late summer. Pick the darkest, ripest, soundest berries and refrigerate them until using. Keep for up to 2 days in the refrigerator. Substitute huckleberries for blueberries in recipes in which the seeds are strained out—syrups, dessert sauces, and jams. The berries may be frozen and canned.

Mulberries: Like coconuts, mulberries fall ripe off the tree. They are purple, very soft, and very juicy. They also stain everything they touch, including fingers. Mulberries look like a type of blackberry and are sweet-tart. Because they have been on the ground, they must be carefully rinsed. To preserve their shape, place them in a colander and dip them in and out of cool water. The berries are best with cream but can be used in any way that blackberries or black currants are. In England, mulberries are pureed and served as a sauce for roast lamb. They make beautiful ice cream. Mulberries may be frozen and canned.

Raspberries: In Roman times, red raspberries were available only gathered from the wild. When perfectly ripe, a raspberry's flavor is ambrosial—sweet but tangy. Taste large raspberries before you buy them; they may be bland. The berry becomes hollow after picking, as its stem and core remain on the stalk. Most raspberries are red, but yellow (or amber) raspberries are mutations from the red. Some yellow raspberries are delicious, but others are flavorless; most are unusually soft. In preserves, yellow raspberries may not cook to an appealing color—experiment with a small amount before committing to a batch and, if necessary, mix in red raspberries to lift the color. Black or Blackcap raspberries are glossy purple black and almost round, very much like red raspberries but with a more pronounced flavor—and more seeds. They are excellent for all uses. Purple raspberries are a cross between black and red raspberries. Their color is dull dark red when raw, but they cook to a rich red. They usually taste like tangy red raspberries. Their tartness makes them especially good in preserves. The berries are larger than red raspberries and tend to be soft.

Raspberries have two seasons. Depending on the area of the country, locally grown early raspberries appear in late spring through midsummer, and late berries in midsummer through autumn. To eat them fresh, sprinkle with sugar if they are tart and serve with softened vanilla ice cream or heavy cream. Raspberries are so soft that they easily dissolve into a fragrant scarlet sauce when heated. Cooked raspberries have a special affinity with red currants. Raspberries freeze but do not can well.

RASPBERRY GRATIN

8 servings

This simple, beautiful dessert shows off raspberries at their best. If you like, add other fruits, such as more berries or sliced peaches. Sour cream or crème fraîche can be used in place of sabayon.

Divide between 8 individual gratin dishes or ramekins:

2 cups fresh raspberries

Spread over the top, allowing some of the fruit to show through:

Sabayon with White Wine Sauce, 1044

Sprinkle over the sabayon:

4 to 6 tablespoons dark brown sugar, lumps broken up

Preheat the broiler.

Just before serving, broil the gratins 3 inches from the heat for about 3 minutes to melt the sugar. Watch closely to see that it does not burn. Serve immediately.

Strawberries: Two hundred years ago or so, the modern strawberry began its evolution from small wild strawberries, called wood strawberries. Today the tiny wood strawberry—*fraise des bois*—is still unsurpassed for fragrance and flavor. The slightly larger Alpine strawberry was derived from wood strawberries. However, breeders are delivering more and more luscious varieties, even some very large strawberries that are superb. Modern strawberries can be heart shaped, conical, rounded, squarish, or teardrops.

Local berries are most plentiful between midspring and midsummer; wood and Alpine berries come in midsummer. Rinse the berries before serving only if they were commercially raised or if, in your garden, they got muddy or have been exposed to sprays. Do not rinse tiny berries at all if you can help it. A gentle shake in a towel removes dust while saving the fragile flesh from losing flavor to the rinse water. Keep caps on berries until serving time, as the gash left after removing them exposes the berry to spoilage. To hull the berries, we are of the thumbnail school—a quick nip and the cap comes off. Even the tip of a small spoon catches some of the berry with it. But if you are hulling hundreds of berries for preserves or freezing, the tip of a spoon or a strawberry huller, shown 455, is most practical. In fruit cups and salads, leave berries whole only if they are bite-sized: it is awkward to pop an enormous berry in the mouth and frustrating to try to steady a berry in order to cut it with a fork or spoon. If strawberries must wait more than an hour or two before serving, sprinkle them with sugar, cover tightly, and refrigerate. Strawberries' greatest affinity is for cream in any form. Other good pairings are red wine and orange.

An idiosyncrasy of most strawberries is that they tolerate no middle ground in terms of cooking. Their bright flavor and color pale and their texture droops in the baked crisps and slumps in which blueberries and blackberries excel. Only in sweet preserves, when strawberries are boiled at full tilt and every element is intensified, are they a match for eating fresh. Strawberries freeze well—best as a puree. They are not good canned but may be dried. Strawberry juice is tasty when freshly made.

STRAWBERRIES ROMANOFF
6 servings

There are many versions of this French recipe, named after the Russian royal family. This one is luscious.

Wash if necessary, dry thoroughly, hull, and slice lengthwise into a shallow bowl:

1½ pounds ripe strawberries

Sprinkle over them:

1 cup fresh orange juice
2 tablespoons sugar

Stir gently to mix. Cover and refrigerate for 2 to 3 hours. Whip until soft peaks form:

½ cup cold heavy cream

Cover and refrigerate for up to 2 hours.

Before serving, let stand at room temperature for 10 minutes:

1 pint vanilla ice cream

Mash the ice cream in a bowl and let stand until soft and fluffy but not soupy. Meanwhile, drain the strawberries and remove to a glass serving bowl (save the juice for breakfast). Add and toss until blended:

5 to 6 tablespoons orange liqueur
¼ cup powdered sugar

Fold the ice cream and whipped cream together until blended. Pile in the center of the strawberries and serve at once.

COEURS À LA CRÈME
6 servings

Coeurs à la crème, literally "hearts of cream," are the perfect Valentine's Day dessert. The consistency of cheese custard, the desserts are allowed to set in heart-shaped baskets or in molds with perforated bottoms (to allow moisture to drain). Coeur à la crème molds are available in specialty food stores. The dessert can also be molded in custard cups or ramekins after letting it drain in a cheesecloth-lined sieve. Although French coeur à la crème contains no sugar, many people find it more tempting with a little powdered sugar stirred in.

Traditional recipes call for *fromage blanc* or *fromage frais*—fresh cheeses that have a consistency similar to yogurt but none of the tang. Our substitute works well, but if you have a source for the fresh cheese, buy 1 pound and mix it with the ½ cup heavy cream. Above all, do not try to use reduced-fat ingredients in this recipe—the mixture may not set if you do.

Puree in a food processor for 30 seconds:

1 cup creamy small-curd cottage cheese
½ cup sour cream
2 tablespoons plain yogurt

Scrape into a bowl and fold in:

½ cup heavy cream, whipped

Fraise de bois

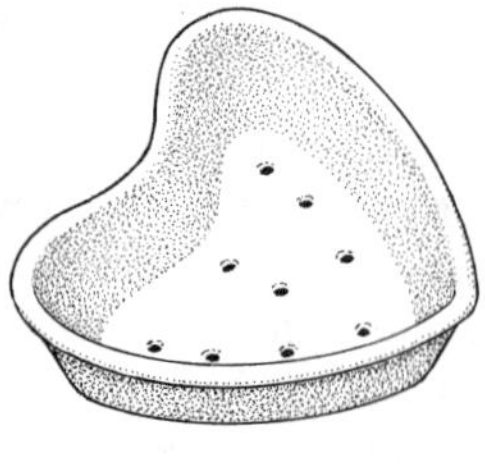

Coeur à la crème mold

Cut a sheet of cheesecloth into six 7-inch squares, dampen with cold water, and line coeur-à-la-crème molds with the cheesecloth. Pack the cheese mixture into the molds, fold the excess cheesecloth over the tops, and place the molds on a plate. If you are not using molds, place the cheese mixture in a sieve lined with a triple thickness of damp cheesecloth. Let drain in the refrigerator for 24 hours. If not using molds, pack the mixture into cheesecloth-lined custard cups or ramekins. To serve, unmold onto plates and peel off the cheesecloth. Serve with:

Sliced fresh strawberries

Fresh Strawberry Sauce, 1048 (optional)

STRAWBERRY CHEESECAKE SURPRISES

2 pints

Wash if necessary, dry thoroughly, and hull, so that the entire stem and center are removed:

2 pints ripe strawberries

Cut a thin sliver from the bottom of the berries so they stand upright. Mix together until smooth:

8 ounces cream cheese or Neufchâtel cheese

2 tablespoons sour cream or heavy cream

3 tablespoons powdered sugar

1 teaspoon vanilla

Pipe the cream cheese mixture into the center of the strawberries. Cover and refrigerate for at least 30 minutes before serving.

CHOCOLATE-COVERED STRAWBERRIES

About 32 strawberries

Surprisingly easy to prepare, especially with our quick chocolate tempering method, these are always a delight. Because you need to temper a little extra chocolate to dip the strawberries, you will have some chocolate left over. It will have berry juices in it and will not be good for retempering and dipping other fruits or candies in, so make bark or nut clusters: Simply add nuts or other crunchy treats, mix, and spread, or drop by the teaspoonful on a wax paper-lined baking sheet. Refrigerate 10 minutes and break into pieces.

Wash and dry thoroughly:

2 pints strawberries

Temper, 849:

1 pound bittersweet or semisweet chocolate

Holding the strawberries by their stems, dip them into the chocolate one by one. Place on a baking sheet lined with wax paper. Refrigerate until set, about 20 minutes. Serve immediately.

CHERRIES

A big bowl of unstemmed sweet cherries, perhaps sparkling with crushed ice, is one of the joys of early summer. Bings are the favorite of commercial growers because they grow easily, taste good, and travel well. Fresh light-skinned Royal Anns and Rainiers are more fragile than Bings and are seen outside of cherry country only for short periods. Pitted raw sweet cherries are incomparable in salads, cold soups, fruit cups, quick breads, cakes, and sauces. But for a hot dessert or for filling a tart, briefly poach the fruits until their flesh is slightly softened. Sweet cherries are available late May through July; August fruits are from cold storage or of inferior quality.

Pie, tart, or sour cherries, another variety, are tastier after cooking, since they are very acid and heat helps them absorb sweetening. Although most commercial sour cherries are canned, you may find fresh morellos, delightful with their red juice, or amarelles, with their clear juice, close to where they are grown. Sour cherries ripen a couple of weeks after sweet cherries. Montmorency, a morello, is the principal sour cherry in this country. It is predominantly grown in New England, around the Great Lakes, and on the Great Plains. Heart-shaped Duke cherries are a sweet-and-sour cross. Their sprightly yellow flesh is good for cooking and for preserves.

All cherries are sent to market ripe. Choose them individually (never prepackaged) after tasting one for flavor. Select the largest, glossiest, plumpest, and firmest with the greenest stems. For sweet cherries, choose the darkest; for sour cherries, the brightest. Avoid stemless cherries—the wound is an invitation to bacteria, as evidenced when there is brown around the stem scar. If there are soft or spoiling cherries in a bin,

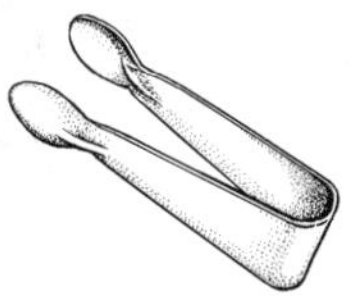

Strawberry huller

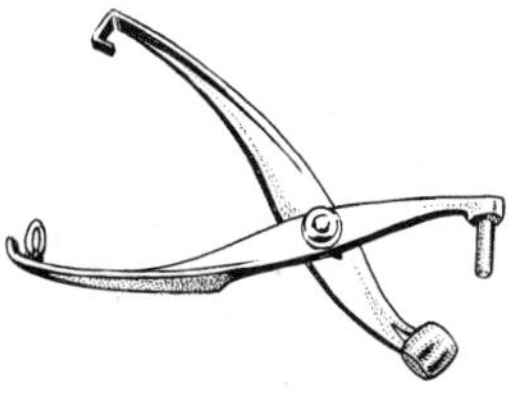

Cherry pitter

do not buy any. The taste of mold can permeate surrounding fruit. To keep cherries, arrange them, without rinsing, in a single layer between paper towels and wrap in plastic. To prepare, rinse, stem, and pit with a cherry pitter (an inexpensive tool found in cookware stores, shown 455 (bottom right)). Push the plunger through the stem scar, pitting one by one into a small empty bowl. All fresh cherries may be canned, frozen, or dried, and all go well with poultry and pork.

Candied and maraschino cherries are pitted sweet cherries that have been bleached until colorless and then dyed red or green.

CHERRIES WITH CREAM AND CHOCOLATE

6 servings

Cherries and chocolate are one of the great flavor combinations in fruit. These cherries are also delicious warm under ribbons of Warm White Chocolate Sauce, 1046.

Remove the stems from:

2 pounds fat, ripe, sweet cherries

Arrange the cherries in a single layer in a large nonstick skillet. Sprinkle evenly with:

¼ cup sugar

Over high heat, shake the skillet and turn the cherries until the sugar melts and the cherries are heated through, about 5 minutes. Remove from the heat and sprinkle over:

1 tablespoon crème de cacao, maraschino liqueur, or kirsch

Shake the pan over high heat for a few seconds until you can smell the spirits. Remove the cherries and juices to a serving bowl. Let cool, then remove the pits from the cherries with your fingers, cover, and refrigerate for 1 to 2 hours.

Meanwhile, prepare Sour Cream Whipped Topping, 1040, or Whipped Cream, 995.

Cover and refrigerate. To serve, divide the cherries and their liquid among 6 shallow dessert bowls. Put a dollop of whipped cream on top of each bowl. Dividing evenly, sprinkle with:

1½ ounces bittersweet chocolate, finely grated

CITRUS FRUITS

The first time you see an ugli fruit or pomelo or kaffir lime, you may not know what is inside, but you know it is citrus because of its skin. The genus of subtropical fruit called citrus is botanically described as aromatic, leathery-skinned berries with eight to fifteen internal segments containing juicy pulp.

Unless organically grown, citrus fruits usually are thinly coated with wax. If you want to use the zest, we urge you to use organically grown fruits. Fruits are supposed to be picked fully ripe, which is usually the case, because the ripeness of oranges, for example, is regulated by law in citrus-producing states. Choose citrus that is heavy for its size—it will be the juiciest. Ignore the color of the rind, since it may have no bearing on the interior quality. (Some mature but green oranges may have been dipped in orange vegetable dye. This must be stamped on the box.) Tasting a fruit is the only sure test of quality. As with all fruit, superficial marks are of no importance, but avoid pieces with deep bruises, soft spots, or mold and any that feel spongy or shriveled. All ripe citrus except limes and grapefruits can be stored at room temperature for about 2 weeks. Room-temperature fruits yield the most juice and the most perfume. For longer keeping, wrap in perforated plastic bags and store in the refrigerator crisper.

Most preparation of citrus fruits is simple. To extract the juice, pierce the fruit with a knife and microwave for 30 seconds or place the fruit in hot water for a few minutes. Then roll each piece under your palm on a hard surface until the inside feels soft. Both heat and pressure release juice from the cells. To quickly juice a small fruit or two, hold the cut side of the half against the palm of your hand and squeeze firmly. Seeds will be trapped inside. To juice several fruits, you can choose between a citrus press, shown below, which often has a built-in strainer, or a wooden reamer, shown 457 (bottom left) which is handy but necessitates straining the seeds from the juice. Store citrus juices in a dark glass jar with a screw lid for maximum preservation and keep it cold. Stored this way, freshly squeezed juice retains nearly all its vitamin C for about 24 hours, although its flavor will deteriorate.

In grating or peeling citrus zest, remove just the top colored layer, as the white pith beneath is bitter. However, this white membrane—the albedo—is very rich in pectin (soluble fiber). When peeling citrus, include as much of the white membrane as you can bear to eat;

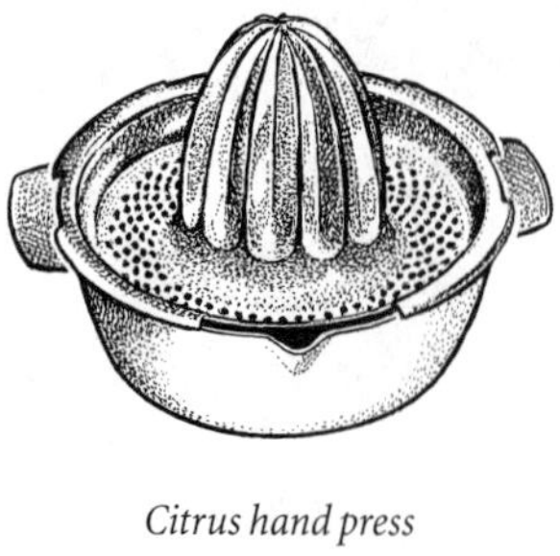

Citrus hand press

its flavor is not so bitter as to ruin the flavor of the fruit. When juicing citrus to drink, stir the pulp back in if your press has strained it out.

The only fussy preparation of citrus is segmenting the fruit for a salad or dessert. This takes not skill but time—and it is worth it. Without its tough bitter casing, the delicate citrus pulp sparkles—chefs call these sections *supremes.* Slice off the top and bottom of the round fruit, down to the flesh. Stand the fruit on a grooved cutting board (to catch juices) and use a serrated knife to cut off the rind in even slices, shown 458 (bottom left). Trim away any remaining white membrane. Free each segment by cutting down against the membrane on either side. Lift out the segment and remove any seeds. Squeeze all the juice from the membranes into a bowl. The best way to slice citrus very thin is to have the fruit chilled and use a thin, sharp serrated knife.

Citrus both cans and freezes well, and the peel dries beautifully.

Grapefruit and Pomelos: There are two types of grapefruit, white fleshed (pink) and pigmented (red). Fresh grapefruit of both types can be found in the market year-round because the fruits ripen at different times in Texas, Florida, California, and Arizona. Select heavy, firm, round, or slightly flattened fruits with smooth skins. Russeted fruits—those with a brownish texture on the rind—often have the best flavor. Avoid fruits with rough, puffy rinds. Marsh is the most popular white-fleshed grapefruit. It has fine flavor and few or no seeds. Star Ruby, Rio Red, and Flame are pigmented fruits of excellent quality with few to no seeds.

Grapefruit whets the appetite, and makes an ideal first course. Segments are delicious in fruit salads, as garnish for poultry, in ices, and as decorations for desserts. Grapefruit is marvelous in a tossed green salad. It is especially flavorful sweetened with honey. The tangy fruit goes especially well with avocado, shellfish, and other citrus, and grapefruit makes canned tuna and salmon seem fresher. Grapefruit cans and freezes well.

Pomelo, ancestor of today's grapefruit, is the largest citrus fruit—grapefruit sized and bigger. It can be round or pear shaped, with firm white or pink flesh. Pomelo is a favorite fruit in Asia and is seen more and more in this country. The flesh is not as juicy as that of grapefruit, but Chandler, the most common pomelo, has delicious sweet pink flesh, usually with few seeds. (Seediness in many citrus varieties depends on whether there is a similar tree—a pollinator—close by. No pollinator, few or no seeds.) Pomelos are traditionally served in skinless segments. To prepare, slice off each end of the fruit, down to the flesh. Score the rind in four or five places without cutting into the flesh. Pull off the rind, then cut away as much white membrane as desired. Pull the fruit apart in halves, then slice each half in half. Stand a quarter upright and slice off the thin edge of the wedge, the fibrous white membrane. Use the technique shown on page 458 (bottom right) to free each segment, then serve any way you would serve grapefruit segments. Shaddock is another name for this fruit.

Pomelo-grapefruit crosses offer us Oroblanco and Melogold, supersweet fruits with no bitterness and no seeds. Look for these cantaloupe-sized fruits winter through spring.

Kumquats: These birds'-egg-sized fruits are unique among citrus and are actually in a different genus from the rest. Kumquats' size also makes them unique—each makes a bite. The kumquat for eating fresh, rind and all, is Meiwa. It is round with sweet, spicy flesh and rind. Nagami, the other kumquat that comes to market, is oblong. Nagami's rind is sweet, but its flesh is sour, which is a pleasing combination for preserves and marmalades. Both types vary in color from gold to orange. Kumquats are available in early winter, and the freshest supply will be at an Asian market. Select fruits that are thoroughly plump, not shriveled at an end. For eating, just rinse well. Eating the small seeds should not be a problem. To eat Nagamis out of hand, pinch the fruit, rolling it slightly between your fingers, to release some of the rind's sweetness into the tart flesh. Add whole kumquats to simmering stews just long enough to soften the rind. In fruit cups and compotes, if the fruits are small enough, leave them whole; other-

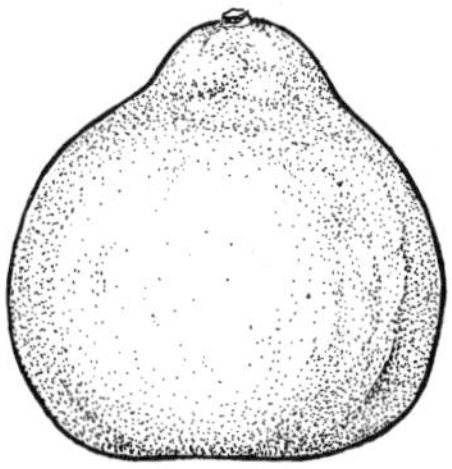

The Reinking pomelo has a slightly lemony flavor.

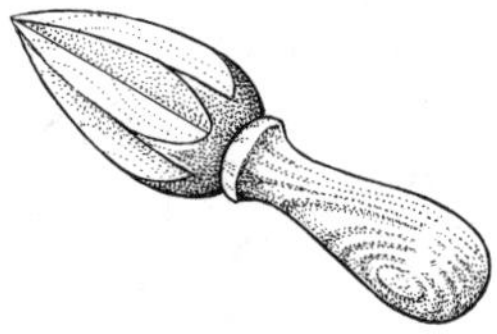

Citrus reamer

wise, slice lengthwise in half. Whole bright kumquats also make a charming garnish.

Lemons and Citrons: Fresh lemons are in the market all year. Supermarket lemons are either bright yellow Eurekas or Lisbons. Meyer lemons are a cross between lemon and mandarin. Their rind is bright yellow and very thin. Their juicy flesh is warm gold with a tangy sweet flavor hinting of citrus blossoms. It can be mimicked with half lemon and half orange juice, although the flowery element will be missing. Meyer lemons ripen all year, but your best chance of finding them is in specialty markets winter through spring. Use them as lemons, but also look for ways to use them as a fruit to eat. Chilled halves of Meyer lemons can be sliced paper thin and added to fruit cups, compotes, and salads. Bite-sized chunks of the lemon add a delicious dimension to long-cooking meat stews, particularly rich ones. The enormous Ponderosa lemon is a hybrid between lemon and citron. It is difficult to peel, but its juice is highly acidic and can be used as standard lemon juice. The best of all these lemons will have smooth, thin rind and be heavy for their size. Avoid lemons brushed with green, for they will be tarter but less flavorful.

Fresh citrons will not be found at the supermarket, but in citrus-growing parts of the country, they may turn up at a farmers' market. Citrons are in season through the year but predominantly in autumn. The Etrog citron looks like an elongated lemon; Buddha's Hand has long thick fingers, a curiosity. Citron is a venerable fruit, the hadar or goodly fruit of the Bible. Just one fruit with its intense, long-lasting fragrance can perfume room after room. The peel is so thick it takes up half the fruit. In fact, the peel is what is used: candied citron peel is a mainstay of holiday baking.

NORTH AFRICAN SALT-PRESERVED LEMONS

One 1-quart jar

Prepare these remarkable pickles for a Moroccan tagine or to flavor a seafood soup, a vegetable salad, a poached chicken, or a stuffing. Preserved lemons will keep for 1 year as long as they are completely covered with salted juice and not contaminated by bacteria. For this reason, remove the lemons not with your fingers but with clean, dry tongs.

Measure:

⅓ cup salt, preferably coarse salt

Spoon 2 tablespoons of the salt into a sterilized wide-mouthed quart jar. Wash, dry, remove any stem bits, and set in a warm oven for 5 minutes to finish drying (moisture in the peel can cause spoilage):

2 pounds ripe, juicy lemons

Roll the lemons on the counter to release their juice. Quarter a lemon lengthwise, stopping ½ inch from the bottom so the quarters fan out but remain attached at one end. Gently open the lemon and sprinkle the 8 surfaces with ½ teaspoon of the salt. Carefuly squeeze the lemon's juice into a bowl—a wooden reamer is the ideal tool, or squeeze with your hands. Close the lemon, pack into the jar, and add its juice. Continue with the remaining lemons, sprinkling each layer with 1½ teaspoons salt. If the juice does not cover the lemons when all are in the jar, it is imperative to add:

Lemon juice to cover

Leave a ½-inch space at the top of the jar. Force out the air bubbles by sliding a narrow spatula between the lemons and the side of the jar. Slowly turn the jar while moving the spatula up and down, forcing up any bubbles of air. Be sure the lemons are still covered with liquid and there is only a ½-inch head space. If necessary, add more liquid and force out the bubbles again. Wipe the rim of the jar. Fold a square of plastic wrap to make 4 layers and place over the top, then tightly cap the jar. Place on a saucer in a warm place—it can be in the sun—and cure for 1 month. Each day, turn the jar upside down to redistribute the salted juice. After the curing period, refrigerate, or keep in a cool, dry place. To serve a lemon, rinse under cold running water. When the lemons are all gone, add the juice to salad dressing.

Limes: There are two if not three types of true limes. One group, called the Bartender's lime, is made up of

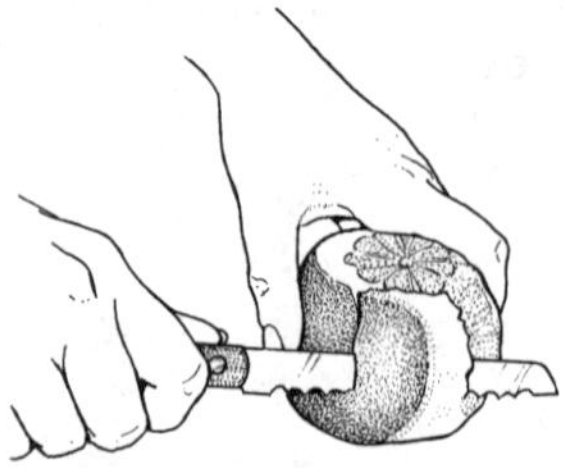

Cut off citrus rind with a serrated knife.

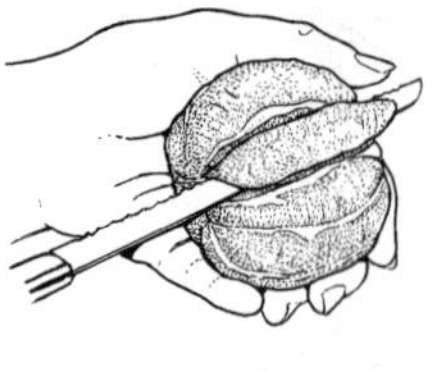

To free each segment, cut down toward the center against the membrane.

Mexican limes, Key limes, and West Indian limes. They are small and oval. Commercially, they are picked green when they are at their most sour. When they turn yellow-orange, they are mature. Their pulp is pale with a splendidly tart, aromatic flavor. Seedless Bearss limes are larger, the size of a small lemon. For the most flavor select Bearss when green—ripe, they are greenish yellow inside and out. Their flavor is bright but less intense than that of the Mexican lime group. Some feel Bearss is a separate type, and some regard it as a variety of Persian or Tahitian lime because it is almost identical. Some form of true lime is available year-round. Select firm, glossy, heavy fruits—the heavier, the juicier. Refrigerate immediately in perforated plastic bags in the crisper.

Preparation is the same as for lemons. In summer, when limes are less expensive than lemons—a bargain, in fact—we find new ways to use them in place of lemons in recipes. True limes have a light, clean freshness in their tang. Their juice can often rescue a dull dish better than lemon or orange juice because their flavor is more distinctive. By the same token, lime juice does not blend with other flavors as well, so it must be used with restraint. Lime peel can be tough, so taste a piece or two before using it. A brief blanching may be needed to tenderize it.

Rangpur limes are probably very sour mandarins, and they look it. They are round, loose skinned, and deep orange with orange pulp. They are available in November and December. The Otaheite orange, a florists' potted tree with miniature oranges with undistinguished sweet juice, is a dwarf form. Use as limes or lemons. Indonesian limes (sometimes referred to as kaffir limes) are shaped like some mandarins—round with a topknot. Their green skin is wrinkled in ridges and valleys. The fruit smells delicious, but the scant juice is acrid. The leaves are used to flavor Southeast Asian soups and curries.

Mandarins (Tangerines): Loose skinned and easily peeled, mandarins look like small oranges, but their flesh is tarter and usually seedier. They are fun to eat out of hand because the segments come apart effortlessly. Select fruits heavy for their size, free of bruises and soft spots. Color is not always to be trusted, and russeted skins can cover especially good fruit. Satsumas, among the choicest of mandarins, sometimes can be eaten when the rind is green. When ripe, their rind is bright orange. Satsumas are sweet with tangy overtones and seedless. They are first to come to the market in November and are available through January. Owaris are the most widely available satsumas. Common mandarins include clementines, a group of very small to medium fruits, very juicy, sweet, and aromatic, variously seedy and seedless. Clementines are called Algerian mandarins in California and are in season the earliest, from late November into December through April, if you include those from North Africa and Spain. Fairchild is a juicy mandarin-tangelo cross with superb flavor, ripening in November and December. Mandarins are often called tangerines, but the term has no botanical significance.

To peel mandarins, just push a thumb into the center on the top and pull back the rind. If you wish to peel their segments, separate them, then pull off the membrane individually. Use a knife tip to flick out seeds. Mandarin segments add a brilliant touch to fruit cups, salads of all sorts, and fruit desserts. Touches of orange in a rich meat or vegetable stew are a delicious surprise—stir in segments at the last moment, just enough to heat them through. Use mandarins as you would orange segments or slices. This is a versatile fruit that wants exploring.

Oranges: Because the thickness of the orange rind depends on both the variety and the climate in which it was grown, thin skin, while desirable, may not be an option. Between a large, light fruit and a small, heavy one, choose the small one. As for color, oranges grown in Florida are not as brightly colored as those from California, but quality is equal. Florida oranges may also be russeted—have brownish patches all over. As with apples, this can be a sign of especially juicy, tasty fruit.

Fresh sweet oranges are available year-round at the market, but varieties come and go. Each variety has its unique characteristics. Valencias, the monarch of juice oranges, begin in early February and last into October. They are sweet with few or no seeds and are equally marvelous eaten out of hand—over the sink. When Valencias are finished, navel oranges come in. They are the favorite eating orange because they are richly flavored, easy to peel, and seedless. Look for Cara Cara Pink navels, with stunning reddish pink flesh, as well as the trusty standard Washington navel. They begin in November and last into May. Sweet Jaffas, similar to Valencias, may appear from Israel in winter, and seedy but aromatic Pineapple oranges may appear in January and February. Blood oranges have raspberry-colored flesh and juice. Indeed, they taste as if the fruit were steeped in berry juice. Whether Moro, Sanguinelli, or Tarocco, blood oranges are available toward the end of the navel season, March through May.

Sour oranges are not grown on a wide scale commercially, but in late winter and early spring they can be found in Hispanic markets and farmers' markets in citrus-growing country. These are marmalade oranges, Seville, Bouquet de Fleurs, and Chinotto. Often the fruits are called bitter oranges, and this is more to the point. While acidic, they have a bitter aftertaste that is the hallmark of orange marmalade. Their juice is delightful when used for lemon juice in recipes, being sour and bitter and orange all at once.

A straightforward way to eat an orange is to slice it in half, then in half the other way, then cut each quarter in half. This makes nice chunks that you can sink your teeth into, pulling out every speck of sweetness and juice. When peeling a whole orange to eat out of hand, if there is a knife around, score the fruit lengthwise in quarters, then pull off the rind. Otherwise, just pull off the rind in pieces. For a company dish, use a small serrated knife and remove the peel in a spiral, being careful not to cut into the flesh more than necessary. Orange slices make a fast alternative to peeled segments. After removing the peel, simply slice the orange crosswise. For a garnish, leave the slices whole. For adding to a mixture, cut the slices in half; check for seeds. Oranges are at their best raw. They hold their own with robust flavors like spinach, chicories, onions, garlic, tomatoes, and beef. In Provence, orange is one of the best-loved flavorings for savory foods. Use orange juice in place of lemon juice occasionally to discover new nuances of flavor in a composition. Orange juice is almost as marvelous a flavor enhancer as lemon, and a little should always be added to red and yellow fruits.

Tangelos: These are mandarin-grapefruit crosses. Minneola is the most popular tangelo, available December through April. Its rind is deep orange-red, and the fruit has a prominent neck, which makes it easy to recognize. Select it as for a mandarin. It is easy to peel, the flesh is wonderfully juicy and rich but tart, and there are few to many seeds. Whereas Minneola looks like a mandarin, ugli resembles the grapefruit side of the family. It has a thick, bumpy, orange-green rind but sweet, juicy flesh with few seeds. The segments separate easily and can be used all the ways grapefruit segments are. Ugli fruit are available in spring.

Tangors: Tangors are orange and mandarin crosses. They resemble mandarins and are selected and used the same way. Available January to March, Temple is regarded as a tangor, but it may be a cross between orange and pomelo. The rind is deep orange-red, and the flesh is spicy and juicy. Temples are also seedy and comparatively hard to peel. Murcott, in season from January to March, has unknown parentage. It is referred to as a mandarin, but some specialists think it is a mandarin-orange cross. Murcotts have bright orange rind and rich flavor. They are easy to peel and have many seeds.

WINTER FRUIT SALAD

3 to 4 servings

Peel and section, 456, into a bowl, adding all the juices:

1 grapefruit
1 orange

Refrigerate until cold. Not long before serving, add:

1 apple, quartered, cored, and thinly sliced
1 banana, sliced

Stir to coat the flesh with citrus juice to prevent discoloration. Stir in:

1 small bunch seedless red grapes, stemmed and halved

Spoon the fruit salad into serving bowls.

CITRUS SALAD

6 servings

Grate 3 tablespoons zest from:

4 navel oranges
2 tangelos or 3 mandarins
2 grapefruit

Peel and section the fruit, 456, and combine with the zest and all the citrus juices. Add:

Sugar to taste (optional)
2 tablespoons orange liqueur (optional)

Cover and refrigerate until ready to serve.

AMBROSIA

6 servings

Peel and section, 456, into a bowl, adding all the juices:

6 navel oranges

Add and gently combine:

3 bananas, sliced
½ pineapple, cut into ½-inch cubes
½ cup miniature marshmallows (optional)
½ cup shredded sweetened dried coconut
3 tablespoons orange liqueur (optional)

Cover and refrigerate until ready to serve.

BROILED GRAPEFRUIT

4 servings

This delicious old-fashioned way with grapefruit can be served as a first course or for dessert. Pink grapefruit is preferred for its appealing color. These can be

Grapefruit knife

prepared many hours in advance, then sugared and broiled just before serving.

Adjust the broiler rack so the grapefruit will be about 4 inches below a gas flame or 3 inches below an electric element. Preheat the broiler.

Cut horizontally in half:

2 grapefruit, preferably pink

Remove any large seeds. If desired, snip out the tough centers. Loosen each section by cutting along the membranes and skin with a small serrated knife or grapefruit knife. Place the halves on a small rimmed baking sheet. Sprinkle with:

1 tablespoon sugar

¼ teaspoon ground star anise or ground ginger (optional)

Leaving the broiler door slightly ajar, broil the grapefruit until the tops begin to brown, about 5 minutes. Remove. For garnish, quickly place in the center of each half:

1 small berry

Serve at once.

CANDIED CITRUS PEEL

About 2 cups

Candied citrus peel can be nibbled on its own or dipped into chocolate, and it makes a bright, flavorful addition to other desserts; for instance, it can be finely chopped and folded into cheesecake, gingerbread batter, even ice cream. This recipe is easily doubled.

Place in a saucepan:

Peel of 3 oranges, 2 grapefruits, or 6 lemons, removed in large strips

Add water to cover and simmer for 30 minutes. Drain, cover with fresh cold water, and simmer until tender. Drain, refresh under cold water, and remove any remaining pulp or pith by scraping it away with a spoon. Cut the peel into 2 x ¼-inch strips. Combine in a large, heavy saucepan:

1 cup sugar

3 tablespoons light corn syrup

¾ cup water

Stir over low heat until the sugar is dissolved. Brush down the sides of the pan with a pastry brush dipped in warm water. Add the fruit peel and cook very gently over low heat until most of the syrup is absorbed. Cover and let stand overnight. Bring to a simmer again, then let cool slightly and drain. Spread several layers of paper towels on a counter and spread on them:

1 cup sugar

Roll the citrus peel in the sugar until well coated. Transfer the peel to a sheet of wax or parchment paper and let it dry for at least 1 hour. Store between layers of wax or parchment paper in an airtight container in the refrigerator for up to 4 months.

CHOCOLATE-DIPPED CANDIED CITRUS PEEL

Prepare Candied Citrus Peel, above. Temper, 849, 1 pound bittersweet or semisweet chocolate. Holding each strip of peel at one end, dip the citrus strips into the chocolate. Let dry on wax or parchment paper until the chocolate is set, about 1 hour. Store as directed.

COCONUTS

If you live in coconut country, you know the delight of using the flower sap as well as the green and the mature fruit of this graceful palm. The kernel of the fruit—the part we enjoy—is encased in a smooth tan husk. It is usually removed before the coconut is sent to market, and what we buy is a round, hard, fibrous brown shell. Under the shell lies a thin skin. The white creamy meat beneath surrounds a pool of milky, faintly sweet liquid, refreshing to drink. (Many call this liquid coconut milk. Do not confuse it with the coconut milk called for in recipes, which is an infusion, 462.) As the fruit matures, the liquid diminishes. When they are ripe, coconuts fall from the tree. Fresh ripe coconuts are available year-round, with their peak season October through December.

When you want to make coconut layer cake, you will not regret the extra time and trouble given to dealing with a coconut. You will find the freshest coconuts in Asian and Hispanic groceries. Select the coconut heaviest for its size and the one whose liquid makes the loudest sound when you shake it—for its meat will be moistest. Whole coconuts can be stored at cool room temperature, but once one is opened, the meat and liquid must be refrigerated.

To open a coconut, if it has a husk, drop it onto a hard surface. If it does not crack open enough so that the husk pulls away, repeat until it does or use a hand ax or hatchet. If the shell inside is green, the top can be lopped off with a large, heavy knife. The liquid within will be clear, and the greenish jellylike pulp makes ideal food for small children and invalids. To open the hard brown shell of a mature nut, pierce the two or three "eyes" at one end with a clean screwdriver, hammering it into them. Drain and refrigerate the liquid, being certain to use or freeze it within 24 hours. The liquid can be drunk as is over ice or used in piña coladas and similar drinks. (It is unlikely but possible that the liquid will taste sour instead of sweet—this indicates a spoiled coconut; discard it.)

Now tap the shell briskly all over with a hammer. The shell usually splits lengthwise, and the halves can be used as containers for serving food. If this does not work, the shell can be opened with heat (but this will fracture the shell). Bake the drained coconut at 375°F until it starts to crack, 20 to 25 minutes. When cool enough to handle, tap it all over with the hammer to release the meat, then set crack side up, cover with a towel, and hit the coconut hard on the crack. It will break open, and the meat will separate from the shell. Use the screwdriver to free any meat stuck to the shell. Remove the skin with a vegetable peeler, then hand-grate. Or cut into 1-inch pieces and pulse in a blender or food processor. To measure, pack coconut shreds lightly in the cup.

You may wish to make fresh coconut milk, the ingredient that makes so many Asian soups, sauces, curries, drinks, desserts, and candies incomparably suave. The milk is the infusion of grated mature coconut and boiling water or milk. The milk is similar to cow's milk to the extent that its fat rises to the top, the fat is saturated (most often true of animal fats), and it must be refrigerated—it has the same storage life as cow's milk. Pour 1 cup boiling water or milk (whole, low fat, or skim) over 1 packed cup fresh coconut shreds. Stir well, cover, and let steep for 30 minutes. To coax every sweet drop from the coconut, process the mixture (no more than 3 cups at a time) in a blender or food processor for 1 minute. Pour all the shreds and milk into a damp clean cloth and press the liquid into a bowl, squeezing until the shreds are dry. This first pressing is referred to as thick coconut milk, and the yield is about 1 cup. A second, even a third and fourth, infusion can be made from the same shreds, but the results will be increasingly thin. For economy's sake, milk from several batches can be combined, but for quality's sake, stop at three infusions. Cover, refrigerate, and use within 3 days.

Coconut cream is what rises to the top when coconut milk has been refrigerated and left to set. It can be skimmed off and refrigerated. Coconut butter is made from coconut cream by beating with a rotary beater or in a blender. When the solid mass rises, force any excess water out of it with the back of a spoon. Wrap and refrigerate. Coconut milk, cream, and butter are very sensitive to high heat. Add them to hot foods at the last minute or cook in a double boiler over hot water. You can substitute these products for their dairy equivalents, but be aware that coconut is much lower in protein and much higher in fat than cow's milk.

To use the spent shreds, mix 2 tablespoons sugar into every 1 cup coconut and stir in a heavy pan over low heat until they turn golden. Store in a tightly covered jar and sprinkle over cereals, fruits, and desserts.

Freshly grated and canned or packaged dried shredded or flaked coconut are interchangeable in recipes if you substitute 1 cup freshly grated for 1⅓ cups dried canned or vice versa. If your grated fresh coconut seems dry, soak it in milk to cover for several hours in the refrigerator, then drain and pat dry before using. To remove the sugar from commercially sweetened coconut or to plump packaged (not canned) dried coconut, soak it in a combination of half milk and half water to cover for an hour or two in the refrigerator, then drain and pat dry. To toast grated, flaked, or shredded coconut, thinly spread it on a baking sheet and bake for about 10 minutes in a 325°F oven, stirring often. Coconut meat freezes well.

DATES

Perhaps because of their brown color and wrinkled skins, dates are typically regarded as dried fruit. However, many that are packaged are fresh; it is the nature of some varieties to ripen with little moisture in their flesh, which is why dates are classed as soft, semisoft, and dry. Dates are harvested in late fall and early winter. You will have the best selection during winter and can be surest the dates are fresh. But with their remarkable keeping qualities, the fruits are available and delicious year-round. Nearly three-quarters of their weight may be in fruit sugar, which explains why the fruits are relatively high in calories.

Deglet Noor is far and away the most plentiful date available. Khadrawy is a richly flavored date that ripens early. Barhi is the softest date, hinting of caramel. Plush Medjool can be enormous, a meal in two or three dates. Thoory, the driest date, is terrific for camping and trekking.

It is difficult to know whether the dates in the package you buy are fresh or dried. It does not matter, really, unless you get very old dates. Supermarket dates are most likely dried. If you can, buy in bulk where the stock has a brisk turnover. A market with a Middle Eastern clientele is a good bet. When you are selecting dates, even though the skin may be wrinkled, the fruit should be plump and have a sheen. Avoid dates that are hard or broken or that have a fermented odor. Although surface sugar crystals are harmless, avoid dates with those too. Pass up dates in prechopped or any "quick and easy" form. In our experience, unpitted dates are unrivaled in quality, both for eating and for cooking. They have not been handled by a machine and are as sound as the day they were picked. Dates will keep at cool room temperature in a tightly closed container for at least a month. They keep best in the refrigerator, but wrap them well because they absorb the odors of other foods.

To pit dates, make a slit in the top, open the sides, lift out the seed, then press the date closed again—if looks matter. For small pieces, chop or slice with a heavy knife, frequently rinsing the blade with water and wiping it dry. If you need to prepare a lot of dates, pit them, then freeze them on a baking sheet for an hour; they will be firmer and easier to slice. If you should have dates that are dry and hard, steam them briefly until softened. Finely chopped dates are delicious in place of sugar or honey to sweeten cereals, in peanut butter and cream cheese sandwiches, fruit dishes, pies, and similar desserts. Add them sparingly, tasting as you go. Sprinkle sliced dates in savory meat and vegetable stews for a sweet depth of flavor. Dates freeze beautifully.

STUFFED DATES

30 stuffed dates

Combine in the top of a double boiler:

30 pitted dates
¼ cup brandy
2 tablespoons fresh orange juice

Cover and cook over simmering water, turning once, until the dates are plump and softened and their skins are curling off, 15 to 20 minutes. Let the dates cool somewhat and peel off the skins while they are still warm. Stuff the dates with:

30 blanched whole almonds

Mix together in a small bowl:

¼ cup sugar
1 teaspoon ground cinnamon
Grated zest of 1 orange

Roll the stuffed dates in the spiced sugar and let them dry on a plate for a few hours. Pack them layered between sheets of wax paper or aluminum foil in an airtight tin. Let them dry for several days before eating. Stored in an airtight tin, these dates will keep for up to 3 months.

DRIED FRUITS

The high caloric and nutritive values of dried fruits can be readily grasped if you realize that it takes 5½ pounds fresh apricots to yield 1 pound dried. The fruits are suddenly not so expensive when you realize there is no waste except the pits in dried prunes and that you are getting concentrated food value.

When selecting dried fruits, look for the biggest and brightest, the plumpest, and those with uniform color. Avoid fruits with blemishes and packages containing bits and pieces of stalks or damaged fruits. Check for unnecessary additives. When a new box or package is opened, do not store the fruits in the opened container. Dried fruits should be stored in tightly covered glass containers in a cool (45° to 50°F), dark, dry place or the refrigerator. Glass is good because you can see if any moisture is collecting inside—moisture will cause dry foods to spoil. All varieties must be watched for insects. Store dried fruits far from pungent foods like onions and garlic, because the fruits readily absorb other odors. Should sugaring develop—crystals of sugar forming on the surface of the skin—you can dip the fruit in boiling water, drain thoroughly, and dry at once. This is not a concern, but a nuisance. A cool, dry atmosphere will keep it from happening.

Raisins, which, of course, are simply dried grapes, divide into seedless, which grow without seeds, and seeded, which have had the seeds removed. Dark seedless raisins are sun-dried principally from green Thompson Seedless grapes, the same ones we buy at the market. Monukka raisins are made from large green grapes with a richer flavor than Thompson. Golden seedless raisins are also Thompsons but have been oven dried and treated with sulfur dioxide to keep them from darkening. Their flavor is finer and warmer than the dark raisins. Sultanas are also golden, sweet, and seedless but are dried from a yellow-green Turkish grape. They are the standard pale raisin abroad and sometimes can be found in fancy groceries. Seeded muscat raisins are large and intensely fruity sweet. Their flavor comes from greenish gold muscat grapes, which must be seeded. The grapes are dried in the sun, the way dark seedless raisins are, and their color is often deep reddish brown. The finished raisins are treated with vegetable oil to keep them soft. Muscats are the finest cooking raisin available, but the few that are produced are shipped only around the holidays. We buy several boxes and freeze them for the rest of the year. Currants are made not from fresh currants but from the tiny grapes we call Champagne grapes and Europeans call Corinth, hence the name. As their flavors are quite different, when nuance of flavor is important, use the type of raisin called for in a recipe. In something like cookies or a family salad, it is fun to try different sizes and flavors of fruit.

Plumping dried fruits: Unless they are very fresh, raisins and currants profit by being plumped before using. This can be done by soaking them in the liquid in which they are to be cooked—such as the liquid called for in a cake—for 10 to 15 minutes before use.

Raisins and currants can also be plumped by rinsing briefly, draining, spreading on a flat pan, and then heating, tightly covered, in a 350°F oven until they puff up and are no longer wrinkled. In cooking other dried fruits, do not soak them first unless the processor so directs on the package. The less water used, the more natural sugars will be retained within the fruit.

To reconstitute dried fruits: A rule of thumb is that the longer it took the fruit to dry, the longer it will take to rehydrate it. Add water or apple juice at room temperature. For each cup of dried apples, use 1½ cups water; for pears, use 1¾ cups; for peaches, 2 cups water. Soak apples for up to 30 minutes, pears and peaches for up to 1¼ hours. Soaking too long can result in loss of flavor and texture. If you must soak the fruit longer, refrigerate it.

To cook, cover and simmer the soaked fruit in the same liquid. Because sugar has the effect of slowing down the absorption of water, wait to sweeten the simmering fruit until after it is tender. A little fresh citrus juice blended into the syrup before serving freshens the fruit. A few grains of salt, too, can bring out flavor. Strain any leftover cooking liquid through a damp cloth and refrigerate it for the next batch of dried fruits.

To use dried fruits—apples, for instance—in a recipe calling for fresh ones, reconstitute 1 pound dried for every 3½ to 4 pounds fresh.

Small dried fruits are often messy to cut or chop. If they are sticky, flour them, using for this purpose, when baking, a portion of the flour called for in the recipe. They also may be more easily cut if the scissors or the knife blade is heated. If you are chopping a large quantity, you may want to use a meat grinder instead. Heat the grinder very thoroughly in boiling water before feeding in the fruit.

Candied and preserved fruits are sometimes substituted for dried fruits. If large amounts of candied fruits are used, allow for their extra sugar content. With preserved fruits, compensate for both sugar and liquid. Should any of the fruits have dried out, steam them lightly—sprinkled with wine, juice, or water—in the top of a double boiler over, not in, boiling water; or prepare them for stuffing by steaming for 10 to 15 minutes in a colander over boiling water until tender enough to pit.

PRUNE COMPOTE

6 servings

These are stewed prunes to the nth degree. To stew plain prunes, omit the tea and orange juice. Cooked prunes will keep for at least 2 weeks in the refrigerator, improving in flavor.

Combine with just enough water to cover in a medium, heavy saucepan:

1 pound pitted prunes

Bring to a simmer. Reduce the heat to low, cover, and cook for 20 minutes. Gently stir in:

½ cup sugar

½ cup fresh orange juice

Add:

2 bags Earl Grey tea

Cover and cook until all the prunes are tender, about 10 minutes more. Remove from the heat and refresh the flavor by blending in another:

½ cup fresh orange juice

Discard the tea bags and remove the fruit and syrup to a container. Cover tightly and refrigerate for at least 3 hours before serving—the compote will be best the next day. Accompany with:

Cream, crème fraîche, sour cream, or yogurt

FIGS

A ripe fresh fig is so intensely sweet and rich it should either be eaten out of hand or sliced in half and accompanied with no more than a small scoop of ice cream, a paper-thin wrapping of prosciutto, or a twist of the peppermill. Figs from the June through July crop are generally the largest and most flavorful. The second crop in late summer is the most plentiful, but the quality is best for preserving and drying. Select tree-ripened figs if you can, but usually this delicate fruit is shipped unripe. Ripen uncovered at room temperature. Once ripe—soft to the touch with just a bit of resistance—figs rapidly lose quality, although they can be held in the refrigerator for a bit, layered between paper towels. There is nothing to trim on a fig but the stem. Grilled or roasted until barely heated through, whole figs make a superb garnish.

BAKED FIGS WITH RICOTTA

4 servings

Preheat the oven to 350°F.

Combine in a small saucepan:

6 tablespoons sugar

½ cup water

Bring to a boil, cover, and boil until the sugar is dissolved and the syrup is reduced to ¼ cup, about 5 minutes. Stir in:

½ cup sweet or dry Marsala

Snip the stems from:

8 fresh figs

Quarter the figs from the top down almost to, but not through, the bottoms. Press up from the bottom to spread the figs open and place in a shallow baking dish. Spoon the Marsala syrup over the figs. Bake until the figs are tender, about 20 minutes.

Meanwhile, mash together:

6 tablespoons ricotta or mascarpone cheese (2 ounces)
6 tablespoons heavy cream or milk
1 teaspoon sugar

When the figs are done, place them in serving dishes, dab some of the cheese mixture into the center of each fig flower, and spoon the syrup around. Serve warm or at room temperature. Garnish, if desired, with:

Shaved bittersweet chocolate

GRAPES

The grapes we enjoy come from three species. The most common are European or wine grapes; these are the thin-skinned grapes that grace our tables in fresh bunches, as raisins and dried currants, and in wine. The term table grape has come to be synonymous with the European species. Characteristically, the skin of European grapes clings to its pulp. Of the dozens of varieties grown for the table, a few seedless red and green varieties are the most popular, even though many varieties with seeds have more exciting flavors. Varieties of grapes used for wine have complex nuances of taste and are excellent for cooking, but, unfortunately, they are rarely sent fresh to market.

Grapes native to this country have comparatively thicker skin that slips easily from the pulp—they are often called slipskins. Fox grapes, native from New England to Georgia to Indiana, are the principal American species. Foxes may be sweet but are usually astringent, with a spicy musky aroma and a flavor that has come to be described as "foxy." Concords—the grapes of commercial jelly and purple juice—are a superlative example of fox grapes. The second American species is the muscadines, native from Delaware to Florida to Kansas. Most are sweet, and some are even muskier and more richly aromatic than foxes. Scuppernongs are perhaps the best-known muscadine; they are so sweet their jelly can taste like honey. American grapes ripen in September and October; they are usually too fragile to ship. Most are sent to factories to be turned into juice, sweet preserves, or wine.

Most European varieties are grown in California and are shipped all over the country. They mature at different times and some keep for months. Fresh domestic table grapes begin arriving in the market in late May and can last until March, although most have finished by January. The gap in late winter is filled with imported grapes.

Grapes are supposed to be picked ripe, but occasionally they are not quite so, and being a berry, they will not ripen off the vine. All the grapes on a bunch should be plump, sound, and the same size. A dusting of bloom—the powdery finish—is a sure sign of freshness. Color also tells. Look for green grapes with a gold cast. Darker grapes should have a uniformly deep tone. Stems must be green and moist (except for one or two varieties, like Emperor, which will have woody stems). It is easier to inspect free whole bunches, but wrapped bunches are better protected from bruising. At home, remove any grapes that are imperfect, and refrigerate the bunch in a perforated plastic bag for up to 3 days.

For the finest bouquet in table grapes, remove them from the refrigerator about an hour before serving. Rinse in a refreshing bath of cool water into which you have stirred a splash of lemon juice or wine vinegar. To serve as dessert, unless there are grape shears on the table, snip into portion-size clusters. Grapes plucked one by one soon make a noble bunch threadbare.

Frozen grapes make a delicious snack, and, of course, grapes are superb pressed into juice and dried into raisins and currants.

GUAVAS

There are a number of guavas in the world, but the common guava—the one most available here—resembles a pale smooth-skinned lemon. Its juicy flesh is a luscious shade of pink and has an intensely sweet flowery-fruity flavor. If you live in Florida or southern California, you may also find strawberry and lemon guavas at a farmers' market. They are smaller than the common variety but have the same rich flavor. If the guavas you find are still firm, they will continue to ripen at home. Choose blemish-free fruits, as yellow and soft as you can find, and ripen them at room temperature, out of the sun, or in a closed paper bag, 440. Ripening time is unpredictable, so check daily and turn the fruits often. When they are ripe, refrigerate in a perforated plastic bag.

Guavas are simple to serve. Just trim off the blossom end, slice in half either way, and eat with a spoon—the seeds of most guavas are edible. For fruit cups and salads, peel with a vegetable peeler and cut in slices. The four chambers filled with seeds and pulp make a lovely pattern in the slices. If you prefer, remove the seeds and pulp before slicing or cutting the flesh into chunks. Slightly underripe guavas are very good lightly cooked. Poach peeled cubes and add to a compote or puree them and use as a sauce for cold meats or other fruits.

JUJUBES OR CHINESE DATES

The size of dates and round to teardrop shaped, ripe jujubes have sweet, meaty brown flesh, reminiscent of dates. Like dates, jujubes contain a single pit. The fruits ripen in clusters on the tree in autumn. Some jujube varieties can be eaten green—they are as crisp as apples. For those that are best when brown, select them at the orange-red stage, when the first brown spot appears. Ripen uncovered at room temperature, turning occasionally. Refrigerate them in a perforated plastic bag when ripe.

The whole poached fruits add richness to a compote. Before poaching, puncture each jujube in several places with a skewer so the flesh can absorb the syrup through the tough skin. In China, the fruits are one of the elements in the classic festival dessert Eight-Treasure Rice Pudding. Jujubes make delicious candy, jelly, and fruit cheese. Dried jujubes are served like dates. The fruits also freeze well.

KIWI FRUIT

This is a dream fruit—with green flesh that is velvety, pineapple sweet, and elegantly beautiful. Kiwis are available year-round because they keep well in cold storage. Select unbruised firm fruits without shriveling or soft spots. A ripe kiwi is as soft as a ripe peach, but usually the fuzzy brown ovals at the market need ripening. Use the paper bag method, 440. Set wrapped ripe kiwis in the refrigerator away from other fruits, whose ethylene gas can overripen the kiwis. Kiwis can be peeled and sliced hours in advance; they never darken. Use a vegetable peeler, then slice crosswise, revealing a sunburst of tiny seeds between a pale center and halo of lime green. Do not cook kiwis, for they turn a woeful shade of green. Instead, imagine fresh kiwis are melons and use slices all the same ways. Hardy kiwis are ovals with smooth, opaque green skins (although there is a red variety), the size of large grapes. They taste like sweet kiwis and ripen in autumn. They are best for eating out of hand.

LITCHIS

A little like jellied incense, these fruits are protected by a fragile, round, brown shell. Out of their shells, the fruits are white and grapelike, but there is a large, smooth seed inside. Fresh litchis are found in Asian markets in summer. Select fruits with their stems attached in uncracked shells—the redder the shell and the heavier the fruit, the fresher. The unpeeled fruit keeps for up to 1 week in the refrigerator. To serve, peel the fruit and serve whole with a wedge of lemon or lime, perhaps three to five a person. Or use litchis in a tropical fruit cup. When dried, the fruit shrinks, turns dark brown, and has something of a raisin taste. Dried litchis, available in Asian markets, make a delicious after-dinner sweet. Canned, the fruit has dull flavor by comparison.

MANGOES

Mangoes come in ovals, kidney shapes, and rounds, usually the size of a large avocado. Their flavor is peach touched with lime or perhaps pineapple; their texture is much like that of a peach but sometimes fibrous. Mangoes may be available in January but are sweeter later in the season—June is the peak—and they may continue through August. Select plump fruits without blemishes, soft spots, or shriveled skin. Skin color differs according to variety; the Keitt mango can be solid green when ripe. However, avoid any green fruit with a grayish tinge, for it may not ripen properly. Mangoes are usually shipped underripe, as they ripen well after picking. Ripen them uncovered at cool room temperature out of the sun, turning occasionally; at warmer temperatures, they may ripen too quickly and the flavor may be altered. You also can ripen mangoes in a paper bag, 440. Mangoes are ripe when they are richly fragrant and yield when you gently press them between your hands. Black speckles on the skin are to be expected. Refrigerate ripe mangoes in a perforated plastic bag in the crisper for up to 2 days.

To cut up mangoes: you first must cut the flesh from the long, broad, thin-edged pit. Score the skin lengthwise in quarters and pull off the peel. For an oval mango, hold it on one thin edge on a grooved cutting board (to catch the juice). With a sharp serrated knife, slice down either side of the pit, which is about ½ inch

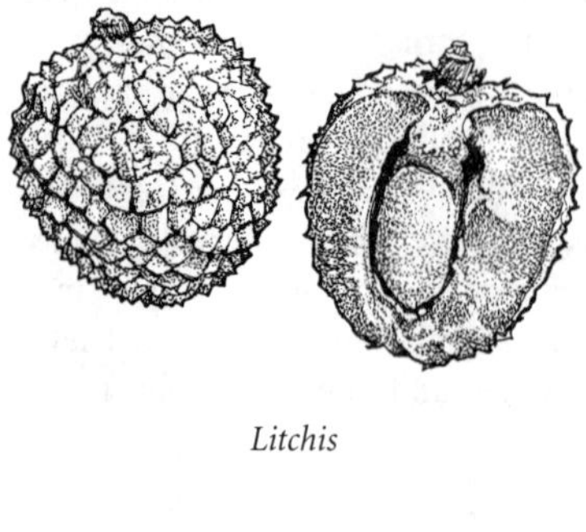

Litchis

thick, removing two thick pieces. Cut the remaining flesh from the pit. Cut the flesh as desired. For a round mango, peel the same way. Then, working on one side at a time, cut the fruit down to the pit in slices or cubes, slide the knife down underneath and cut the pieces free of the pit. Repeat on the other side.

Serve raw mangoes slightly chilled all the ways you would peaches and papayas. They are delicious cooked in chutney, sautéed with chicken and fish, or garnishing grilled meat and poultry. A touch of orange with mango—as with peaches—is lovely. Mangoes are very good canned and frozen.

MANGO FOOL

4 to 5 servings

The tropical-peach taste of mangoes makes an exquisite fool. In a pinch, simply puree the mango and fold into 1 pint of softened vanilla ice cream or frozen yogurt.

Quarter lengthwise and peel:

3 ripe mangoes (about 12 ounces each)

Cut the flesh off the pits into a bowl. Puree in a blender or food processor. Blend in:

⅔ to ¾ cup powdered sugar, depending on sweetness of the fruit

2 tablespoons lime juice

1 tablespoon orange juice

Cover and chill for up to 1 day. To serve, whip until soft peaks form (the cream may be whipped up to 3 hours in advance):

1¼ cups cold heavy cream

Fold the puree and cream together—you can blend them thoroughly or leave streaks of gold through the cream. Pile into stemmed glasses and top with:

Fresh mint sprigs

Serve at once.

MELONS

There are four types of dessert melons—the melons that are not watermelons. Unless otherwise noted, summer is their peak season. If a melon has no fruity perfume at the smooth (the blossom) end, do not buy it (unless it is a casaba, discussed below). There also should be a slight softness at the blossom end. Choose melons that are heaviest for their size, with no soft spots, mold, or cracks and no strong aroma indicating overripeness. If, when you gently shake a melon, seeds rattle, chances are the melon is too ripe. To know whether a melon will continue to ripen and what it ought to taste like, become familiar with the melon types, since characteristics differ.

The only melons that ripen slightly after picking are the smooth, or winter, group. "Smooth" describes the rind relative to other melons. Honeydew and Santa Claus or Christmas melons have genuinely smooth rinds, but Canary and Crenshaw melons are slightly wrinkled, and casabas have distinct wrinkles. "Winter" indicates the melons take longer to ripen than others. They are ready in the fall. The flavor of these melons is mild and their flesh pale—light orange in Crenshaw and green to white in the rest, although salmon pink honeydews have been bred. Smooth melons are fragrant when ripe, except for casaba. Casabas are ripe when golden yellow except at the stem end, which may be slightly greenish.

America's cantaloupe, muskmelon, nutmeg, and Persian melons are in the *netted* group. Choose those in which the netting is pronounced and the fragrance is as sweet as you expect the flavor to be. The melon's flesh should be musky and orange. In Europe, and botanically speaking, *true cantaloupes* have another shape. They have a smooth, hard rind and may be lightly fluted. Their orange, green, or pink flesh is intensely sweet and perfumed. The great French Charentais melon is the most prominent in this group. A small crack close to the stem indicates full ripeness.

Stunning fruits blended from all of the above are termed *tropical melons.* Here are Galia, Ha-Ogen, Passport, French Breakfast, as well as other exotically flavored fruits available mostly from the home garden.

To round out the ripening of smooth or winter melons, place them uncut in a paper bag, 440. Cut melons will not ripen. Ripe melons of other types will soften

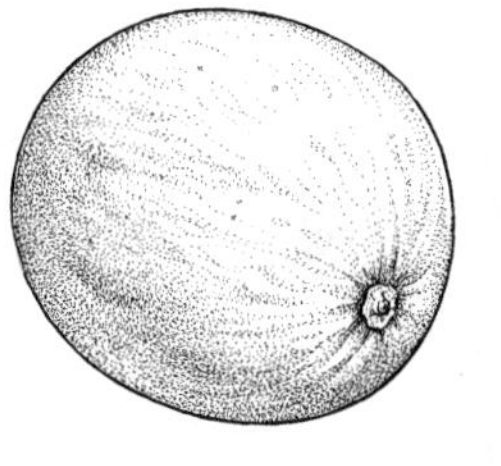

Honeydew melon

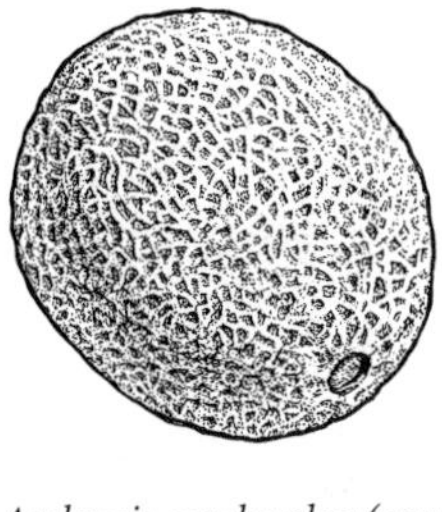

Ambrosia muskmelon (can-

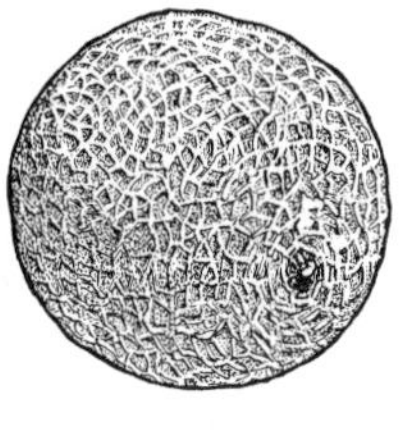

Galia melon

and may be a bit juicier if left at room temperature for a day or two. Refrigerate ripe or cut melons in tightly closed plastic bags—their aroma will affect everything around them in the refrigerator—and serve within 2 days.

Melons are usually eaten raw. To prepare, slice the melon in half through the stem end and scoop out the seeds and loose pulp or strings. At this point, half a small melon makes a first course or dessert decorated with a sprig of mint. For the main course, fill it with cottage cheese, berries, a fruit cup, or a salad of fruits, vegetables, or poultry. Or serve it for dessert with a scoop of ice cream. Or use a melon baller, shown 469, to scoop out balls, then add the remnants to a smoothie. To cut the melon into pieces, slice the half into 2-inch-thick wedges and cut off the rind at the point where it changes to the color of the flesh. When served peeled, no melon is wasted, although you can certainly serve unpeeled wedges to be eaten with a spoon. If desired, continue slicing peeled pieces into thin crescents or bite-sized chunks. Melon rings are appealing: Cut off the rind of a whole melon, then cut the melon crosswise into ½-inch-thick slices. Scrape out the seeds. A chilled melon is indeed refreshing, but perfume is lost to the cold. A ripe dessert melon needs no seasoning, but a shake of ginger or white pepper or a spritz of lemon or orange juice may add a pleasing note. Dessert melons freeze well.

Happily, there is just one type of watermelon, and it is glorious. These days there is no superior size, shape, or color of watermelon, and many have that old-fashioned honey-sweet taste. The flesh may be red, pink, orange, or gold; it may have seeds or be seedless; it may be the size of a small cantaloupe or a large ham.

For luscious eating, you are surest buying a cut melon. There should be a sweet watermelon fragrance emanating through the plastic wrap, the flesh should appear dense and firm, seeds should be dark (although a seedless variety may have small white seeds), and there should be no thin white streaks. If you need a whole melon, select one that is symmetrical with a waxy bloom on the rind, and check underneath to make sure it is yellowish—a sign it has ripened on the ground. Refrigerate the melon at once but take it out an hour before serving. To prepare watermelon, cut it lengthwise in half, then cut it crosswise in slices and remove the rind. You can also cut it with a melon baller if you wish. Watermelon slices sprinkled with mild rice vinegar make a delightful salad. Watermelons freeze well.

SUMMER FRUIT CUP

2 servings

Halve and seed:

1 perfectly ripe small cantaloupe

Using the small end of a melon baller, make round balls of the cantaloupe by pressing the baller deep into the flesh until juice comes out of the hole in the bottom of the baller, twisting to cut a whole ball, and removing. Combine the melon balls with:

½ cup fresh sweet cherries, pitted
1 tablespoon orange juice
1 tablespoon crème de cassis or orange liqueur

Scoop out the remaining craters of flesh from the cantaloupe halves to make a smooth container (save the flesh for another use). Just before serving, gently toss the melon mixture with:

½ cup fresh raspberries, blackberries, or blueberries

Divide the fruit between the melon shells. Garnish with:

Fresh mint sprigs

MELON WITH PORT

4 servings

Cut a thin slice from both stem and blossom end of:

2 perfectly ripe small cantaloupes or other dessert melons

Cut the melons horizontally in half, scoop out the seeds, place on individual serving plates, and pour into each half:

Charentais melon

Ha-Ogen melon

Up to ¼ cup ruby port

Cover loosely with plastic wrap and let stand at room temperature for 30 minutes before serving.

MELON AND PROSCIUTTO *4 to 6 servings*

The inspiration for combining wedges of melon and paper-thin slices of prosciutto just may have come from proximity. Some of Italy's finest cantaloupes are grown not far from where some of its finest Parma hams are cured. This is one of summer's most refreshing first courses.

Cut in half and scoop out the seeds from:

1 ripe cantaloupe or Crenshaw melon (about 3 pounds), cool but not chilled

Slice each half into 6 wedges and remove the rind. Place 2 or 3 wedges on each plate. Cut into wide strips:

8 ounces thinly sliced prosciutto or Serrano ham

Drape the ham over the slices—or wrap each piece of fruit in ham. Serve at once and pass the peppermill.

WATERMELON FRUIT BASKET *About 14 servings*

No matter how many times you may make this, it is always a thrill to serve. Everything can be prepared 3 to 4 hours in advance for combining at serving time. An icebox watermelon can be prepared the same way, using a proportionately smaller amount of fruit.

Rinse and wipe dry:

1 ripe 12- to 14-pound watermelon

With a long, sharp serrated knife, cut a thin, flat slice off one long side of the melon to keep it from wobbling. Slice the melon lengthwise in two, cutting about 1 inch above the center. Lift off the top. Remove the flesh in the heart of the melon with a melon baller, shown below or use a teaspoon to scoop out egg shapes. Cover and refrigerate 4 cups watermelon balls. Scoop out the rest of the flesh (save it for another purpose), leaving about ½ inch of red flesh lining the shell. Stand the shell upside down in a cool place to drain. Pour into a large mixing bowl:

2 cups fresh orange juice

You will need about 10 cups fruit in addition to the watermelon to fill the basket. For the most refreshing mix, use unpeeled summer fruits and berries, cut up no smaller than bite-sized. With the watermelon balls, we like richly colored, firm ripe fruits such as:

Whole small strawberries, hulled
Blackberries
Blueberries
Cantaloupe or honeydew melon balls
Sliced nectarines
Sliced plums of any color
Sliced kiwis or seedless green grapes

Cut up the fruits and toss with the orange juice to keep them from darkening. Cover and refrigerate. Sugar should not be necessary. Just before serving, add the watermelon to the other fruit along with:

3 tablespoons chopped fresh mint

Toss gently together with your hands and fill the melon shell (save the juices in the bowl to drink). If desired, top with:

14 scoops (about 3 pints) best-quality sorbet or sherbet

Serve at once, ladling into dessert bowls.

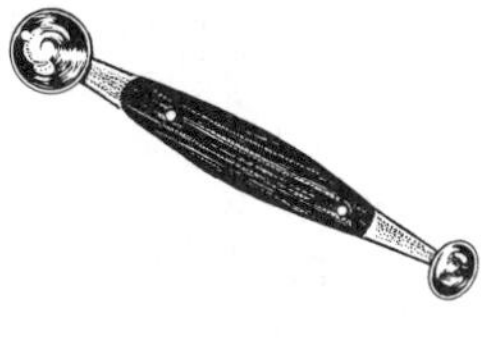

Melon baller

NECTARINES

Nectarines are peaches in plum clothing. They do not have legendary varieties, and, even at their best, they are not as juicy as peaches, but their flavors can be sublime. If you substitute nectarines in a recipe for peaches, add a small amount of orange or pineapple juice to fill in for the missing juice.

ROASTED NECTARINES WITH RASPBERRY VINEGAR GLAZE *4 servings*

Nectarines are delicious, but they are impossible to halve and pit neatly. It is the better part of valor to prepare them whole. When baked at high heat, their skins turn russet, and they make a handsome accompaniment for rich poultry, pork, venison, or other game.

Preheat the oven to 425°F.

With the tip of a knife, slash on 4 sides to prevent the skin from bursting:

4 firm ripe nectarines

Place in a 9-inch pie pan and set the pan on a baking sheet. Combine in a saucepan:

1 cup raspberry vinegar
1 cup packed light brown sugar
2 tablespoons butter

Heat, stirring, over low heat until the sugar is dissolved and the butter melted. Pour over the nectarines. Bake for 10 minutes and baste using a bulb baster. Bake for another 10 minutes, then turn the nectarines over with tongs. Bake until they test tender when pierced with a thin skewer, about 5 minutes more. Do not overcook. Carefully pour the glaze into a wide, heavy saucepan and boil it down until thickened, about 10 minutes. Loosely cover the nectarines with aluminum foil to keep warm. Stir into the glaze:

¼ teaspoon ground black pepper, or to taste

Pour over the nectarines in a serving dish and serve.

PAPAWS OR PAWPAWS

These fruits, native to the eastern United States, are sometimes called Michigan or Nebraska bananas. They look like stubby bananas, and their soft, pale flesh is creamy and sweet. Papaws ripen after the first heavy frost, turning from green gold to almost black. The ripe fruit is soft and does not keep, but papaws may be picked when underripe and refrigerated for longer keeping. Their flavor is like banana custard or vanilla custard with a touch of pear, mango, or pineapple. The ripe fruit smells uncommonly sweet and can be cloying; perhaps it is not wise to ripen the fruit indoors. Related to cherimoyas and sweetsops, papaws are best eaten raw with a spoon, discarding the large black seeds. Heat alters the delicate flavor, although they can be baked like bananas in cakes and puddings. Papaws dry well.

PAPAYAS

For drama at the table, slice a whole yellow-green papaya in half to reveal apricot-colored flesh and jet black seeds. Scoop all but a few of the seeds into a bowl and set a lime half in their place—a ripe papaya is delicately sweet and needs tang for balance. Most of the 1-pound fruits, shaped like short-necked pears, come from Hawaii. Those with salmon pink flesh are the Solo Sunrise variety—less juicy than golden Solo Waimanalo. If you see orange-fleshed papaya sold by the piece, it is from Mexico. This variety can weigh up to 10 pounds and is less sweet. In some parts of the country, papayas are available year-round, but in most parts they are generally available only in early summer.

Fully ripe Solo papayas are almost completely yellow and soft as a ripe peach. Select them when they are at least half yellow and yield slightly when pressed between your hands. Uncut papayas have no aroma, but the skin should be smooth. Ignore superficial blemishes. Mexican papayas should have a lightly sweet scent. Ripen a half-yellow papaya by the paper bag method, 440. Refrigerate for up to 1 day when ripe.

Peel ripe Solo papayas, cut lengthwise in half, and remove and rinse the seeds. They are spicy and can be used as you would capers, or you can dry them and coarsely grind them like peppercorns. Prepare papaya and serve as melon, with one exception. As with raw pineapple, the enzymes in papaya prevent gelatin from jelling. Papayas are most refreshing raw, but slightly underripe fruit—Mexican papayas especially—are good glazed and baked like winter squash, sautéed in inch-thick slices, grilled in quarters or cubes, or cooked in curries and soups. Papayas can and freeze well.

PEACHES

America's legendary peaches have sugary flesh that melts in the mouth, much of it creamy white and clingstone. (*Freestone, semi-freestone,* and *clingstone* are terms used to describe how easily the pit is removed. There is no correlation between qualities of the peach and how the flesh comes off the pit.) If you live in the Southwest, the small, red-fleshed clingstone peaches grown in arid lands are perhaps the sweetest peaches of all.

Peaches are in season at different times across the country but everywhere in July and August. When shopping for peaches, bring no preconceptions. Of course, avoid those with spots, bruises, and shriveled skins, but huge fruits that ought to be woody can have silky flesh. And unless it is green, the skin's color reflects variety, not ripeness. There is one cardinal rule in selecting peaches: "tree-ripened" is a necessity. Although underripe fruits soften and grow juicier at room temperature, they do not increase in sugar. A fully ripe peach is sweetly perfumed and gives slightly when gently pressed between your palms. If you must ripen peaches, use the paper bag method, 440. Refrigerate ripe fruits.

If you wish to leave the skin on a peach but rid it of its fuzz, rub off the fuzz under cold running water. To peel a peach, use the blanching method, 440. Because peach flesh darkens when exposed to air, peel a peach at the last minute or treat it with an antibrowning solution, 440. To remove the pit, cut around the peach on the seamline, twist the halves in opposite directions, and gently pull them apart. If the pit does not come out easily with the tip of a knife, slice or quarter the peach down to the stone, then lift or slice the pieces away.

Fresh peaches are good, but a little cooking deepens their flavor and is the only way to serve less-than-ripe fruit. Experiment with poaching, baking, sautéing, and grilling peaches. When there is an overflow, they do very well frozen, canned, dried, and pureed into nectar.

PEACHES IN PORT *4 servings*

Halve and remove the pits from:

2 ripe peaches

Cut each peach half into 4 slices. Place 4 slices in each of 4 stemmed glasses. Cover with:

Ruby port

Garnish with:

Fresh mint leaves

PEACH MELBA *4 servings*

The great French chef Escoffier created this beautiful dessert to honor the Australian soprano Nellie Melba at the Hotel Savoy in London in 1892.

Prepare:

Lemon-flavored Light Syrup for Poaching Fruit, 442

Add:

1 teaspoon vanilla

2 ripe perfect peaches

Poach over low heat until tender, about 5 minutes, depending on their ripeness. Let the peaches cool in the syrup, then cover and refrigerate until cold. (This can be done a day or two ahead.)

To serve, remove the peaches from the syrup, slip off the skins, cut the peaches in half along the seamline, and remove the pits. Put in each of 4 pretty goblets or dishes:

1 scoop vanilla ice cream

Top each with a peach half, pitted side down, and spoon on top:

Fresh Raspberry Sauce, 1048

PEARS

European pears—fragile when ripe but sturdy while green—are the ideal growers' fruit, since the pears must ripen off the tree. On the tree, the fruit turns mealy. Pears are available year-round, but their natural peak season is August through October. Sometimes you will find ripe pears at the market. A pear is ripe when it smells like a pear and gives to gentle pressure applied at the stem end. Because some pears will rot before they ripen, it is wise to select the ripest pears available. Examine pears carefully for bruises. Superficial scrapes and blemishes are not important, but avoid pears with dark or soft spots or any shriveling. For the most part (Anjou is an exception), yellow pears deepen from green to yellow as they ripen, but red pears are red before they are ripe. Bartlett, Comice, Concorde, and Seckel will ripen to melting softness, but serve Anjou, Bosc, and Red Clapp's Favorite, and cook Winter Nellis, while slightly crisp.

You can ripen pears at room temperature, then refrigerate them for a day or two before serving. Or you can refrigerate the fruits until a week before you want to serve them, then ripen at room temperature in a paper bag, 440. When refrigerating pears, perforated plastic bags are crucial, because when sealed airtight, the fruit darkens at the center. Turn and check the pears frequently wherever they are to watch for deterioration.

There are many fewer varieties of pears available than apples, but the pears we have differ in character, which keeps pear season interesting.

Anjou: Oval with melting white flesh, Anjou is blander than most. It is the most abundant winter pear, good for eating and cooking and keeps for up to 7 months.

Bartlett: The sweet, juicy flesh of this golden bell-shaped pear is equally delicious eaten out of hand, cooked, canned, and dried; it keeps for up to 8 weeks. (Bartlett is the old English pear, Williams' Bon Chretien, source of the elegant eau de vie Poire William.)

Bosc: Tapered, russeted Bosc has all the pear virtues—tender, aromatic, juicy, and rich—is lovely for eating, cooking, and drying, and keeps for up to 7 months.

Comice: Rounded in shape, sweet, rich Comice is the queen of dessert pears and keeps for up to 7 months.

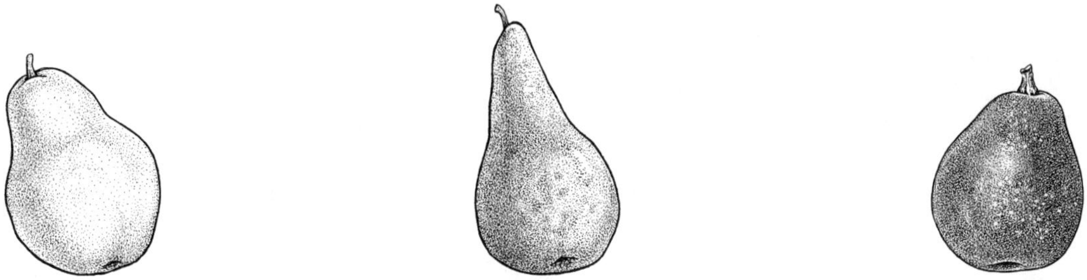

From left: Bartlett, Bosc, and Seckel pears

Concorde: This yellow-skinned, Bosc-shaped, European winter eating pear has Comice parentage; it keeps for up to 4 months.
Packham's Triumph: Said to be Australia's favorite eating pear, it is a Bartlett type and keeps for 3 to 4 months.
Red Clapp's Favorite: Large and elongated, this is a crimson dessert pear with sweet full flavor, but it only keeps for up to 2 weeks.
Seckel: Russeted, round Seckel is just 2 inches long but is juicy, spicy, tender, and aromatic—excellent for eating and incomparable for pickling and canning—but it only keeps for up to 8 weeks.
Winter Nellis: Affectionately called Nellies, this pear is fat and russeted, not gorgeous, but perhaps the best pear for cooking, although some enjoy it on its own. It keeps up for to 4 months.
Duchess, Forelle, Kieffer, and Moonglow are also excellent pears for canning.

To serve pears raw, leave the skins on. Eat out of hand or core as for apples, 444. After cutting the pear in half, you can scoop out the core with a teaspoon and serve the halves if you treat the cut sides for browning, 440. Raw pears and raw apples are virtually interchangeable in recipes, the main difference being the obvious one of texture—pears are soft, and apples are crisp. Pears have a particular affinity for cheese, nuts, and chocolate. Pears are delicious poached, sautéed, grilled, and baked. Slightly underripe pears are best for cooking, since they will hold their shape. When baking or poaching them whole, choose pears of uniform size with stems attached, then shave a thin slice from the bottom so they all stand upright. Warm pears bring out the zing in sweet spices like ginger, cinnamon, cardamom, nutmeg, mace, and cloves. Whether raw or cooked, pears have the best flavor when cool—neither hot nor cold. European pears are superb for canning and drying, but they do not freeze well.

Asian pears appear to be a cross between apple and European pear, but as round, juicy, and crisp as they are, they are still true pears. They are in season July through October, peaking in September. Only one or two varieties are usually seen, but Asian markets offer a more interesting selection. These pears are generally shipped ripe. There are essentially two colors. Most of the greenish type ripen to yellow green; russet pears deepen to rich golden brown. The fruits are good keepers. The Asian pear is milder in flavor than either an apple or a pear. They are best eaten raw and unpeeled. They are especially handsome served in whole crosswise slices—the seeds form a star. Dip in acidulated water, 440. These neither can nor freeze well.

POACHED PEARS

6 servings

Firm-fleshed cooking pears become meltingly soft when briefly poached in sugar syrup, and their flavor becomes rounder and sweeter. The handsomest way to present poached pears is whole and upright, with their stems on. However, the pears can also be cooked in halves or quarters. Work quickly, and you will not need to use antibrowning solution. The pears will whiten in the syrup.

Prepare in a large, heavy saucepan:

6 cups (1½ recipes) Light Syrup for Poaching Fruit, 442

Peel:

6 medium, firm ripe, sweet pears, stems attached (about 2 pounds)

Carefully cut out the core from the bottom, using a small, thin, sharp knife, or slice the pears in halves or quarters lengthwise, then cut out the cores. Bring the syrup to a boil and add the fruit. Simmer, uncovered, over low heat, turning frequently with a wooden spoon, until the flesh is tender when tested with a thin skewer. Start checking a fully ripe pear after 8 minutes, but it may take as long as 20 minutes. Lift out whole pears with a slotted spoon and set on a platter; cover loosely with plastic wrap and refrigerate. Turn pear pieces into a bowl, cover with syrup, wrap, and refrigerate. To serve whole pears, make a hole next to the stem and set in each:

1 sprig fresh mint

Serve halves and quarters in fruit salads, mixed compotes, or dusted with:

Pinch of ground mace

PEARS IN RED WINE

4 servings

Port or dry white wine would also be delicious here.

Combine in a saucepan large enough to hold 4 pears:

1½ cups dry red wine
1 cup sugar, or to taste
One 2-inch strip lemon zest
2 tablespoons fresh lemon juice
4 whole cloves, or 4 cardamom pods (preferably green), split open and tied in a muslin bag, or one 2-inch cinnamon stick

Bring to a boil. Reduce the heat to low and simmer, covered, until the sugar is dissolved, about 5 minutes. Meanwhile, core and peel, leaving the pears whole and the stems on and taking off as little flesh as possible:

4 firm ripe pears

Trim the bottoms to make a stable base. Place the pears in the syrup and poach over low heat, turning them occasionally, just until tender, about 10 minutes. Let cool in the syrup, still covered. Remove the spice. If you wish, refrigerate the pears, turning them occasionally so they color evenly. They will keep in the refrigerator for up to several days.

To serve, put each pear in a glass serving bowl. Strain the syrup through a fine sieve and pour several spoonfuls over each pear. You can boil the syrup down to concentrate it if you like, but this is not necessary.

POIRES HÉLÈNE

Marvelous together— pears, vanilla, and chocolate.

Prepare Poached Pears, above. Set a scoop of vanilla ice cream on a dessert plate and smooth it into a flat, round pedestal broader than the base of a whole pear. (The ice cream base may be frozen in advance.) To serve, set a cold whole poached pear on the ice cream. Pour a coating of warm Chocolate Sauce, 1045, over the top, garnish, if desired, with a mint sprig, and serve at once.

PEARS IN CREAM AND KIRSCH *6 servings*

Save this for those who appreciate understated elegance.

Position a rack in the center of the oven. Preheat the oven to 425°F.

Peel, quarter lengthwise, and core:

6 medium, firm ripe, sweet pears (about 2½ pounds)

Work quickly, and you will not need to worry that the flesh will darken—the pears will whiten in the kirsch. Melt over medium heat in your largest skillet, one in which the pears will just fit in a single layer:

2 tablespoons butter, preferably unsalted

Add the pears and sprinkle over:

3 tablespoons sugar

¼ cup kirsch

Cook over medium-low heat, turning the pears frequently with a wooden spoon, until they are tender when tested with a thin skewer, 5 to 20 minutes, depending on the ripeness of the pears. Arrange the pears, cut sides down, in a 9 x 9-inch baking dish. Add to the skillet:

¼ cup heavy cream

Boil this sauce over high heat until slightly thickened, 30 seconds to 2 minutes, then pour over the pears. Bake just until the cream on top sets into a skin, about 10 minutes. Serve at once. The dish will look plain but needs no garnish.

PERSIMMONS

Brilliant-orange persimmons herald autumn and see us through the winter holidays. A favorite fruit in Japan (called *kaki,* also their name in much of Europe), persimmons ought to be appreciated in this country at least for their jelly smoothness and apricot-rich taste. Hachiya persimmons are large and acorn shaped. Until they mature to silky soft ripeness, they are as astringent as a harsh tannic wine. By contrast, Fuyu persimmons, resembling orange tomatoes, are not at all astringent, even while firm and crisp. Fuyus are tannin free. If you can remember that acorns are bitter or tomatoes are sweet, you will never bite into the wrong persimmon. Any other variety of persimmon you see will have the shape of Hachiya or Fuyu, so proceed accordingly. Small reddish American persimmons are gathered in the wild and from a few varieties grown by passionate fans. But the fruit is inconsistent as to whether it ripens fully enough not to be unnervingly astringent. When the fruits are fully ripe, they can be honeylike and delicious.

Persimmons turn orange before they ripen, but richness of color is an indication of quality. Select the deepest-colored persimmons, heavy for their weight, with no cracks, and with all four sepals (heart-shaped leaves) green and attached. Ripen persimmons uncovered at room temperature or in a paper bag with an apple, 440, turning frequently. This can take weeks. To preserve ripe fruits that you cannot get to, freeze them whole.

All persimmons need for serving is rinsing, cutting out the sepals and cap, then slicing in half from top to bottom. Taste a bit of the peel: If it is bitter, scoop the pulp out of it with a spoon; otherwise, leave it. Serve Hachiyas in halves with a spoon. Fuyus can be sliced for adding to salad or fruit cups. We do not recommend cooking persimmons to be served on their own, for heat seems to turn their flesh bitter. However, ripe persimmons are wonderful in a batter for bread, pudding, or cake. Include the very finely chopped skin.

Pureed ripe persimmon makes a splendid sauce for cold poultry or nonrich desserts. It may need nothing more than a little lemon juice. Push halves or quarters of the fruit through a nylon sieve. Or puree cut-up persimmons in a food processor, but first check for seeds. When finely processed, the skin makes tiny darker flecks in the sauce, adding texture; strain them out if you wish. Persimmons freeze and dry well.

PINEAPPLES

These exotic American natives are available year-round, which seems miraculous in the chill of winter. Prices tend to be lowest in the spring through June—ideal timing for wedding breakfasts and graduation feasts. They also contain bromelain, an enzyme that breaks down protein, which means that fresh pineapple, like papaya, tenderizes meats. Make it the principal ingredient in a marinade. This brings up cautions: Add fresh pineapple to meat or poultry as a garnish or mix it into a meat or poultry salad not more than 10 minutes before serving, or the enzyme will make their flesh mushy. Since bromelain "digests" the protein in milk, fresh pineapple should not be added to cottage cheese or yogurt until just before serving. The protein in gelatin is also vulnerable. However, by bringing the fruit to a boil, you can deactivate the enzyme.

It is essential to bring home a pineapple that is perfectly ripe, since the fruit will soften but not grow sweeter after picking. Unfortunately, none of the traditional tests is trustworthy, except one. If the pineapple smells pineapple sweet, it is ripe. If the fruit is cold, though, the fragrance will be muted. The next best indication of ripeness and quality is a sticker that says the fruit was flown in from Hawaii. Fruits harvested elsewhere may have been picked underripe, and fruits brought in by boat may be too ripe and have the vinegary odor of fermenting pineapple. Choose plump fruit with rind that is neither shriveled dry nor soft, especially at the base. Leaves should be crisp and uniformly green. The larger the pineapple, the more edible flesh there will be in proportion to waste. If there are two or more large fragrant fruits, choose the one heaviest for its size. Store an underripe pineapple whole, at room temperature, away from sunlight, for up to 2 days. Keep a ripe whole fruit in the refrigerator in a perforated plastic bag. Store trimmed fruit in an airtight container.

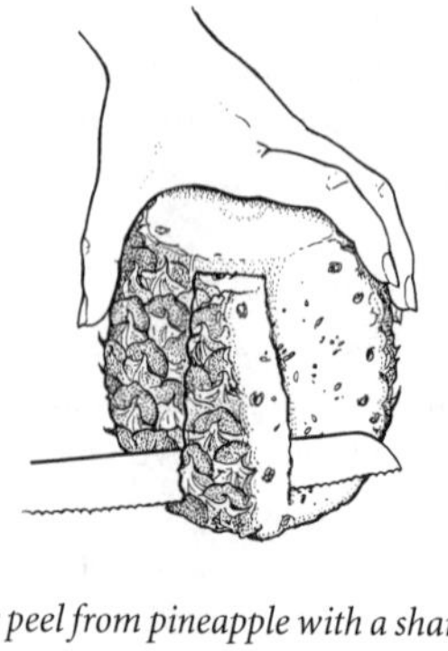

Slice the peel from pineapple with a sharp knife.

To prepare pineapple, cut off the leaves at their base, removing all traces of green. Using a large knife, slice off the bottom rind. Stand the pineapple on its base and cut off the rind from the sides, using wide downward strokes and catching as little flesh as possible while being sure to remove as much of the eyes as possible. The fruit can be sliced crosswise and the core of each slice cut out with a small knife. Or use a heavy knife to cut the pineapple lengthwise into quarters. Cut away the core, then slice the quarter in wedges or chunks. Do not throw away the core pieces without nibbling off all the good flesh around the edges. To shred the flesh, pull it apart with two forks. Pineapple is delicious baked, grilled, sautéed, and stir-fried. Pineapple is also good canned, frozen, dried, and candied.

GLAZED PINEAPPLE RINGS

8 to 10 rings

For garnishing ham. To decorate pork chops, chicken breasts, or other smaller cuts, cut the rings in half after broiling.

Preheat the broiler. Butter a broiling pan.

Trim, peel, and cut crosswise into ½-inch-thick slices, above:

1 large ripe pineapple

Using an apple corer, small cookie cutter, or a sharp knife, cut out the core in each ring. Arrange the rings on the buttered pan and drizzle with:

4 to 5 tablespoons melted butter

Sprinkle the rings with:

About ½ cup sugar

Broil, without turning, until hot and golden, 5 to 8 minutes. Serve hot.

PINEAPPLE IN HOT BUTTERED RUM SAUCE

4 servings

Combine in a wide, nonreactive skillet:

4 tablespoons (½ stick) unsalted butter
¼ cup packed dark brown sugar
¼ cup dark rum
½ teaspoon ground allspice

Heat, stirring, over low heat until the sugar is dissolved and the syrup is thick and bubbly. Add:

1 large ripe pineapple, peeled, cored, and cut into bite-sized chunks, above with juices

Heat, basting the pineapple with the syrup, until it is heated through. Divide the pineapple among 4 serving bowls, spoon the sauce over, and sprinkle with:

Crushed macaroon crumbs or unsweetened shredded coconut, lightly toasted

Serve immediately.

PLUMS

While there are only two or three species of peaches or apricots, we can choose from sixteen or more species of plums. Many are wild purple, red, or yellow American plums, ½ to 1 inch across, and named variously Beach, Sand, Wild Goose, and Sierra plums. They make superbly tart sauces, jams, and jellies. American plums are yours for the picking. European plums are a little larger, 1½ to 3 inches long, and usually oval, although some are round. Sugar-filled blue or purple common plums are usually dried for prunes, but they are also excellent stewed or baked in compotes and for canning. Recommended varieties are French Prune, Imperial, Italian Prune, Stanley, and Sugar. European plums include also golden dessert-quality Greengages, astringent blue Damsons, and small yellow Mirabelles, incomparable for preserves. Pits are usually freestone in European plums but clingstone in the Japanese type. Japanese plums are most of what we buy for eating out of hand and cooking. They are larger and juicier, with a richer tart-sweet flavor that is often spicy. Red-fleshed Santa Rosa and Elephant Heart are excellent dessert plums. Elephant Heart is also good for cooking, as are dark purple Friar, purplish red Wickson, and green Kelsey. There are fresh plums from mid-May to mid-October. Japanese plums come first, peaking in August, then the European sorts arrive for autumn.

Tree- or shrub-ripened plums are what you hope for, but the fruits are often picked underripe. They will soften at room temperature, although sugars will not increase, nor will flavors develop. The problem is that it is difficult to tell a fully ripe plum from one that has softened while waiting at the market, since both will give slightly when gently pressed between your hands. Here is another instance in which you must taste a sample before buying. Avoid fruit with cracks or moist soft spots near the stem area. If the plums need ripening, leave uncovered at room temperature or place in a paper bag out of the sun, turning daily.

Refrigerate ripe fruit in a perforated plastic bag for up to 3 days. Japanese plums are finest eaten out of hand, since they are so juicy. European plums are best for cooking, since they are drier and their pit comes away cleanly. To prepare European plums for cooking, rinse and slice in half around the seam, twist to open, and remove the pit. Use in halves or cut into quarters or slices. Leave the peel on for maximum flavor and nutrients, although it will add tang. If it must be removed, use the blanching technique, 440. Remember to add slices of firm plums to all sorts of salads. Small chunks of plums give a pleasing dimension to stews and braises; mix them in at the end and cook just enough to soften. Plums are marvelous poached or baked whole in a little sugar syrup, 442, with shreds of orange and a dash of cinnamon. Serve them cold. Plum cobblers, pies, and tarts are among the most delicious of desserts. Plums are excellent for canning, freezing, and—of course—drying.

POMEGRANATES

Pomegranates, with their tart-sweet ruby seeds, are in season autumn through December. Pomegranates are picked ripe. The fruits should be heavy for their size and burstingly plump. The crown should be slightly soft when gently pressed, and the leathery rind should be lustrous rather than dull and dry. When using the fruits in a centerpiece, leave them at room temperature as briefly as possible, for they dry out in warmth. However, refrigerated in a perforated plastic bag, the fruits keep for up to 2 weeks.

Most children are fascinated by pomegranates and love to pick out the jewellike morsels one by one (resulting, of course, in clothes stained scarlet). Use a serrated knife to slice off the blossom end of the fruit, including some of the white pith but none of the seeds. Score the rind lengthwise in 4 or 5 places. Place the fruit in a large container and cover with cool water. Let it soak for about 5 minutes. Keeping the pomegranate under water, gently break the fruit apart along the scoring lines. Pull back the rind and separate seeds from membranes. In the water, the light rind and pith will float and the heavy seeds sink. Use a sieve to skim off the debris, then pour the seeds and water into a colander. Pat the drained seeds dry and store, tightly covered, in the refrigerator until needed; they will stay fresh for at least a day or two.

Wonderful pomegranate

There are two ways to juice a pomegranate. (Although the stains usually come out, wear a big apron when doing this.) For jelly, you can cut the fruit in half and ream it on a juicer. The sugar and the method of cooking seem to keep the jelly from tasting bitter.

To prepare juice for drinks or syrups: crushing the membranes releases their tannin into the juice, resulting in juice that is woefully bitter. Rinse the fruits and firmly roll them around on something hard until they have softened somewhat; this helps release the juice inside. Slice the fruit in quarters over a bowl, remove and discard the rind, then pull out the seeds, placing them in the bowl and discarding the rest of the fruit. Wrap the seeds a handful at a time in a damp cloth and squeeze hard into a bowl. Squeeze out every drop. For crystal clarity (although you will lose volume), cover and refrigerate the juice for a day or two—up to a week—to let the surprising amount of sediment settle to the bottom. Pour off the clear juice carefully.

There are few foods in this world that a sprinkling of pomegranate seeds will not enhance—in fact, we have yet to find one. Pomegranates freeze well.

POMEGRANATE MOLASSES

About 1 pint

This dark tangy syrup is in the cupboards of fine cooks from the Mediterranean to the Caucasus. Simmered down to an essence, the fruit's sugars hint of molasses. The syrup has all molasses's uses except in baking, with an infinitely more appealing flavor. Use pomegranate molasses as the base for a cooling spritzer. Brush it over light meats and poultry before grilling or after sautéing. Stir a little into salad dressing. Use it for sweetening tropical fruits. Spoon it over cakes and desserts. Extracting the juice is a nuisance, but it is the only way to get juice that is not bitter. This syrup is a labor of love; the reward is its wonderfully rich flavor and that it keeps for several months.

Roll on the counter, pressing firmly, to free up the juices:

10 pounds juicy ripe pomegranates

1 pound juicy ripe lemons

Cut the pomegranates in half, peel off the rind, and pull the fruit apart into manageable chunks. Wrap a chunk in a square of damp towel or cheesecloth and press and squeeze out every drop of juice into a bowl. You should finish with about 8 cups. Pour into a clear container and set in a cool place for a few hours. About 2 cups sediment will sink to the bottom. Meanwhile, juice the lemons. Strain the lemon juice through damp cloth into a deep, heavy saucepan. Ladle the clear pomegranate juice into the pan and add:

1 cup sugar

Heat, stirring, over low heat until the sugar dissolves. Simmer the mixture, uncovered, until it is reduced to 2 cups; start measuring after 1½ hours. Pour into a sterilized bottle. Let cool, then cover and refrigerate. For a perfectionist's molasses, let it settle for a month or two, then pour off the clear syrup, leaving the sediment behind. The yield will be less.

PRICKLY PEARS

In this country, these juicy berries the size and shape of an egg are most often purplish red or deep yellow. In others parts of the world, they may be cream colored, chartreuse, pink, or even purple verging on black. They have many names: cactus or Indian or Barbary pear or Indian fig, tuna (Spanish), or sabra (Hebrew). The fruits are prickly outside but watermelon sweet inside. Prickly pears are filled with small seeds, and in some varieties, the seeds are edible. Most fruits are harvested in the West in August through December. The fruits grow with small rosettes of spines scattered over their peel. Select ripe fruits, but to test them, pick each one up with a folded paper bag, since there may be bits of needles still in their flesh. The spines are supposed to be removed before the fruit is shipped, but there is no guarantee. Those prickly pears that yield when gently pressed between your hands are ready. Store at cool room temperature out of the sun. When they are ripe, refrigerate in a perforated plastic bag for up to 2 days.

To prepare for eating—which is invariably raw—wear thick rubber gloves. Rinse, then cut off the ends and score with the tip of a knife lengthwise in quarters. Peel off the skin, then slice or cut into quarters, or scoop out the flesh and puree it, then strain out seeds. Serve prickly pear as a bright mild accompaniment with a wedge of lime or lemon, since the flesh lacks acid. The flesh freezes well as a puree, and scarlet prickly pear jelly is brilliant colored.

MELON WITH PRICKLY PEAR SAUCE

6 servings

The sauce is a ravishing scarlet, and its sweet-tart flavor combines deliciously with the honeyed taste of cantaloupe or Crenshaw melon. The sauce can be made and the melons prepared several hours in advance.

Remove the seeds and rind from:

3 pounds ripe sweet orange-fleshed melon or richly flavored honeydew

Slice into 6 wedges, wrap in plastic wrap, and refrigerate. Wearing rubber gloves, peel with a vegetable peeler:

3 ripe prickly pears (about 1 pound)

Cut into 1-inch chunks and puree in a food processor until smooth. Combine in a bowl with:

3 tablespoons strained fresh orange juice
2 tablespoons strained fresh lemon juice
2 tablespoons sugar

Cover and chill for at least 1 hour. To serve, set a melon wedge on each plate, then spoon a ribbon of the sauce across it through the center, then down onto the plate on either side. Garnish each with:

1 sprig fresh mint

QUINCES

To fill a room with sweet, rich fragrance, place a ripe gold quince in the middle of it. A member of the rose family, a quince looks like a pear that grew fat and lumpy with a stubby neck. Probably because they are too astringent to eat raw, quinces have fallen out of favor in this country. But when slices are poached until translucent and a deep shade of red, their flavor is reminiscent of rose and apple, with a touch of pineapple in the variety called Pineapple quince. Not every variety of quince reddens when cooked; some turn gold.

Quinces are available in October and November. Buy lots when you find them, as they keep for up to 2 weeks in a perforated plastic bag in the refrigerator. Select fruits with some fragrance, although they will ripen nicely at room temperature. Avoid those with spots, bruises, and tiny holes that could indicate worms. Handle gently, for, surprisingly, these fruits bruise easily.

The core of a quince is flint-hard. *To prepare:* Rub off any fuzz, peel with a vegetable peeler, and use a cleaver or heavy chef's knife to cut the fruit in half and then in quarters. With a paring knife, trim out the core, dipping down to remove all the white grains. Quinces cook just like apples except they can take up to twice the cooking time. For superb flavor, replace one-quarter to one-third of the apples in a recipe with quinces. In the Middle East, quinces are commonly baked and stewed with meat. Rich in pectin, the fruits make glorious sweet preserves and candy.

BAKED QUINCES

4 servings

Serve these sweet-scented fruits for breakfast or dessert. Quinces can be difficult to core, but the results are worth it. The flesh may darken while you are preparing them, but the orange and apple juices will refresh their color. These will keep in the refrigerator for several days.

Preheat the oven to 300°F.

Thinly slice crosswise, then cut the slices in half:

1 large orange

Scrub off any fuzz and peel:

4 medium ripe, fragrant quinces (about 1½ pounds)

Halve and then quarter, using a large, heavy knife and slowly pushing the blade down through the fruit. Cut out the cores with a small serrated knife, catching all the gritty parts (save the trimmings for jelly). Arrange a layer of quinces cut sides up in a deep 2-quart baking dish. Sprinkle with:

1 tablespoon sugar

Add a layer of orange slices. Continue layering to the top, finishing with orange slices. Add:

1 cup apple juice

Cover and bake until the quinces test tender when pierced with a thin skewer, 1½ to 3 hours. Remove from the oven and baste the top pieces with the juices. If the quinces are dry, cover them with more:

Apple juice (about 1 cup)

Serve warm or chilled with the juices in the dish. Accompany with:

Ice cream mixed with whipped cream (see Strawberries Romanoff, 454) **or heavy cream**

RHUBARB

Botanically a vegetable, rhubarb has stalks that look like cherry-red celery but are less watery. Their flavor is tartness itself with a fruity aftertaste. Field-grown rhubarb is available principally in April and May; hothouse rhubarb is available in some parts of the country year-round. Usually hothouse stalks are pink or pale red. They have a less tart flavor and are less stringy than field-grown stalks, which are a richer red with a richer flavor to match. When choosing rhubarb, pick crisp, firm stalks, ideally no more than an inch wide, and the deepest reds in the bin. If leaves are attached, they should be crisp. Slice the leaves off when you get home and discard them, since they are mildly toxic. Rhubarb does not ripen once harvested. Store whole stalks in perforated plastic bags in the crisper for up to 3 days.

Rhubarb is too tart to eat raw, but a little sugar or honey helps set its color in cooking and smoothes out the tang. To prepare, rinse and then trim the tops and bottoms of the stalks. If the stalks are stringy, peel them back with a small knife as for celery and remove the coarsest strings before cooking. If the stalks are over 1½ inches wide, slice them lengthwise in half. Cut crosswise into 1- to 2-inch pieces. If sugar is a concern, you can stew rhubarb without sugar, since it will be sweeter after cooking. Sprinkle the pieces with water in a heavy skillet and cook until tender, then stir in sugar to taste. Continue cooking until the desired texture is reached, remembering that rhubarb will continue to soften and cook as it cools. We find rhubarb most delicious when poached in Light Syrup for Poaching Fruit, 442, and simmered until the pieces are tender but still intact. Rhubarb is particularly delicious with oranges and strawberries, so we usually add one or the other to the cooking fruit. It also makes an excellent compote to serve with poultry and white meats. Rhubarb cans and freezes well and makes heavenly pies, preserves, and jelly.

RHUBARB COMPOTE

3 servings

Combine in a medium, heavy saucepan:

4 cups ½-inch pieces rhubarb
¼ to ½ cup sugar

Let stand at room temperature until the rhubarb exudes some juice, at least 15 minutes. Bring the mixture to a boil over medium-high heat, stirring constantly. Reduce the heat to low, cover, and simmer, stirring occasionally, until the rhubarb is tender and the liquid thickened, 10 to 12 minutes. Remove from the heat and let cool without stirring. Refrigerate for at least 2 hours or for up to 2 days. The compote will thicken when chilled.

TROPICAL EXOTICS

Look for these fruits as they become more and more available, especially in Asian and Hispanic markets.

Acerolas: Often called Barbados cherries, these are bright red and cherrylike, with three small pits. Their flesh is sweet to acid and tastes like tart apple when cooked.

Cape Gooseberries (Poha Berries, Golden Berries): Related to Chinese lanterns and tomatillos, these berries are sweet without being cloying and make delicious preserves. These gooseberry-sized berries grow individually in papery husks. When ripe, their skin glows like yellow tomatoes. They are sometimes available in spring from New Zealand, then again in the early fall from local plants. Select golden fruits, preferably still in their parchment-colored husks. Leave the berries in the husks, as the wrapping protects them from spoiling. Refrigerate—they are very long-keeping. To serve, pull the berry from the husk and discard the husk. Rinse lightly, for they are sticky. The berries are good raw but most delicious poached in Light Syrup for Poaching Fruit, 442, flavored with lemon. They will be tender in 3 minutes. They freeze and dry well. Some ground cherries resemble cape gooseberries enough to be twins.

Carambolas or Star Fruits: This tropical fruit with waxy yellow skin is an oval the size of a small cantaloupe. But rather than solid, it is airy, made of fleshy wings down its length. Thin crosswise slices of carambola reveal graceful pointed stars. The fruits are commercially grown in Florida and should be available autumn through winter. Carambolas are juicy, with the crisp succulence of an underripe plum. Depending on ripeness and the type (two are being grown), their flavor can be tart, sweet-tart, or watery. Some carambolas have reminded us of feijoas. Look for carambolas at Asian markets and fancy groceries. Ripe fruits are lightly brown along the tips of the ridge. Smell them: When only slightly overripe, a fruit can seem to be fermenting. If the fruit is deep yellow with no brown at the tips, it will ripen at room temperature. Avoid greenish fruits. Refrigerate ripe carambolas in a perforated plastic bag in the crisper. To serve, there is no need to peel or even to remove the thin seeds at the centers (although you may flick them out if you wish). Rinse, pat dry, and slice crosswise about ¼ inch thick. Carambolas do not freeze, but they can well.

Cerimans: This fruit of the split-leaf philodendron is also called a monstera. With rows of small hexagonal scales, the fruit looks like a long, thin, green pine cone. Wrap it in plastic wrap and ripen at room temperature until the entire rind is loose, 5 to 6 days. Remove it, then pull off the creamy pineapple-banana–flavored pulp with a fork and refrigerate. Serve alone or with ice cream.

Cherimoya

Cherimoyas or Custard Apples: From a distance, the green cherimoya looks like an upside-down artichoke with rounded leaves. Up close, you find that the "leaves" are imprints in the leathery skin. The white flesh is the texture of firm custard and tastes something like banana and pineapple. The season is from November through April, peaking in February and March. They are grown in California and may be found in Asian markets or fancy groceries. Select fruit heavy for its size with no bruises or discolorations. The fruits will probably require further ripening. Let stand at room temperature out of the sun, turning frequently. It may take a week until the cherimoya is as soft as a ripe peach. Refrigerate and serve cold and raw in unpeeled wedges, accompanied with a slice of your favorite citrus. If not serving at once, brush the flesh with citrus juice to keep it from browning. Eat with a spoon, discarding the seeds and sprinkling with tart juice to balance the sweet flesh. Cherimoya can also be cut into cubes and added to a fruit cup. This is not a cooking fruit, nor does it can or freeze well.

Durian

Durians: Durians are round, melon sized, and covered with sharp thorns and are ripe from April to July. As they approach maturity, their aroma becomes as repellent as rotting onions (in Indonesia, we are told, one cannot bring a durian onto a public bus). When ripe, the shell is split open and the buttery flesh scooped out. The flesh bears little echo of the odor of the fruit; some find almonds and vanilla in the taste. The large seeds can be roasted and eaten as a snack. Asian markets sell the flesh frozen, often under the name of jack fruit.

Feijoas: Pineapple guava is another name for this fruit, and it aptly reflects feijoa's delicious and complex flavor. Commercially grown feijoas are an egg's size and shape and have a waxy dark green peel with a light bloom. The soft-firm flesh is slightly gritty, like a pear's. It is greenish yellow with a jellylike center containing tiny edible seeds. Feijoas are in season from fall through early winter. Look for them in Hispanic groceries; select unblemished fruits—they will be underripe. Ripen at room temperature, uncovered, turning frequently. When they are as soft as a ripe pear and wonderfully fragrant, either eat them at once or refrigerate between paper towels. While you are at the market, buy some fresh cream cheese. Cut the ripe fruit in half, heap soft cheese in the center, and eat with a spoon out of the shell, taking a dab of cheese with each bite. If there will be any waiting, the cut flesh should be brushed with citrus juice to keep it from darkening. The skin is bitter, so peel it with a vegetable peeler. Cut the fruit into cubes or quarters and treat with an antibrowning solution, 440. Feijoas are often confused with common guavas, which tells you that you can use one fruit for the other in a recipe—but use only common or strawberry guavas when making guava jelly. Feijoas can be cooked, but they are best fresh in delicate dishes. They may be canned but do not freeze well.

Genips or Mamoncillos: These fruits are the size of grapes but are lime green on the outside and orange-pink on the inside, with a round pit (or two seeds fitted together). The gummy pulp is sweet and refreshing, reminiscent of grapes. Eat out of hand.

Kiwanos or African Horned Cucumbers or Melons: Like a small, spiky orange fruit from the sea, these relatives of melons and cucumbers have orange-green cucumberlike flesh with a mild cucumber flavor—disappointing for such a dramatic appearance. Kiwanos are in season in late summer. Cut off the rind and slice the flesh into chunks for salads.

Loquats: A loquat looks like a pear-shaped apricot with smooth skin. Inside, nearly half the fruit is given to large brown seeds. The flesh of a loquat is light to medium orange, moist, and tender yet firm. Depending on the variety, the flavor may be reminiscent of cherries, apricots, plums, grapes, or litchis, but it is always a blend of sweet and sharp. In Florida, they come in season in March and last through May; in California, they are available through June. However, sad to say, the fruits bruise so easily that they are rarely available far from where they grow. If you come across these special fruits, choose as many without stems as possible and pick the largest, heaviest, most fragrant fruits. Keep loquats at room temperature until they start to deteriorate, then refrigerate briefly in a perforated plastic bag. To serve, if there is a stem attached, snap or slice it off. To savor their complex flavor, enjoy loquats out of hand, dropping the seeds and perhaps the blossom end onto a small plate. Most loquats do not need peeling, but when they do, the skin pulls off easily. To add to fruit cups and salads, slice the fruits in half lengthwise, remove the seeds, and nip out blossom ends. If the pieces are large, cut them in half again. Loquats have a lovely flavor when poached in Light

Syrup for Poaching Fruit, 442, but be careful not to overcook. The fruits also make marvelous jam and jelly, and they freeze well in syrup.

Passion Fruits or Purple Granadillas: A ripe passion fruit looks like a small, crumpled, purply brown ball. Slice into the thin brittle rind and you will find a mass of small dark seeds, each enclosed in translucent yellowish pulp. The interior of the shell is white, veined and rimmed pomegranate red. The fruit is the seeds, in the same way that pomegranate fruit is seeds (*granadilla,* its Spanish name, means "little pomegranate"). The edible seeds are crunchy, and there are dark pink pulpy connectors beneath the seeds. Scraped together with a spoon, they have a citrus consistency. A passion fruit's flavor is tart, honeyed, and complex—often a mingling of strawberry, pineapple, and lemon. Grown in Hawaii, Florida, California, and New Zealand, the fruit is theoretically available all year. Choose the largest, heaviest fruits. If the shell is smooth, ripen the fruit at room temperature until the rind is deeply wrinkled but firm. Refrigerate in a perforated plastic bag or freeze whole. Without altering flavor, freezing softens the pulp and makes it easier to puree.

Open the fruit by slicing off the top. If it is your first passion fruit, enjoy the fruit on its own—spooned out of the shell, perhaps with drops of honey or an orange liqueur. To make a puree that will be passion fruit essence, scoop the pulp into a bowl, then press through a nylon sieve. For juice, turn the seeds into a damp cloth and squeeze the juice into a container. Each fruit probably will give less than 1 tablespoon juice, but it will be thick and strong and can be carefully diluted. Use it to flavor other drinks, fruit soups, fruit desserts, creams, or custards. The spent seeds are so well flavored, you can stir them into fruit juice to give it a passion fruit flavor. A spoonful of the puree in a fruit ice or creamy frozen dessert makes it otherworldly.

It is worth noting that this fruit is not named for its wildly sensual flavor. Instead the name comes from the passion flower that created it, which South American Jesuits found to be emblematic of the Passion of Christ.

Maypops are fruits of hardy passion flower vines and are mostly found in the wild. They are sometimes called apricot vines, as the 2-inch oval fruits are yellowish and the ripe yellowish pulp—seedy, similar to passion fruits—has a sweet-tart apricot taste.

PINEAPPLE WITH PASSION FRUIT

4 to 5 servings

Passion fruit's magenta, gold, and soft green are intriguing speckled through the cubes of yellow pineapple. Their flavors together are wonderfully exotic, and the passion fruit's seeds add a pleasant crunch. No added sugar is needed.

Slice off the leaves and rind of:

One 2½-pound ripe sweet pineapple

Cut lengthwise into quarters, slice off the hard core, then cut each quarter into bite-sized cubes. Slice in half over a bowl to catch the juice:

2½ to 3 ounces wrinkled passion fruits (about 2)

Scoop their pulp into a small bowl. Use your fingers or 2 forks to break up the pulp into small pieces. Combine them in a bowl with the pineapple and blend thoroughly. Cover and chill for 1 to 2 hours and serve garnished with:

Fresh mint sprigs

Tamarind

Tamarinds: The dark brown pulp scraped from inside tamarind seed pods is deliciously rich and acid—something like tangy pureed prunes. The pulp can be turned into fresh relishes and long-keeping chutneys and cooling drinks. In season from November to May, fresh tamarind pods are sporadically available in Hispanic and Asian markets. Almost always for sale are 8-ounce packets of pulp. Choose the softest one you can find and soak it in boiling water for 10 to 15 minutes. (As a general rule, measure ⅓ cup boiling water for a tablespoon of pulp.) Mash it thoroughly with a fork to separate the seeds and fibers from the pulp. Strain the pulp, pressing down on it to squeeze out as much juice as possible. Seal leftover pulp airtight and store in the refrigerator for up to 3 months or in the freezer for up to 1 year.

STUFFING

Most traditional stuffings begin with sautéed vegetables—always onions, usually celery, frequently bell peppers, and maybe a little garlic. Beyond that, regional and personal preferences produce countless variations. An occasional rice- or couscous-based version aside, stuffing is based on bread. Some cooks crumble corn bread, a few cut up French or Italian loaves, and many swear by plain old fluffy white bread or packaged bread cubes. Whatever the bread, stale or toasted breadcrumbs produce a drier stuffing that will soak up the savory juices of the roasting bird without becoming soggy and give added texture to the cooked stuffing. Soft, fresh, untoasted breadcrumbs yield a spongy, dense stuffing with a texture like mashed potatoes. Flavoring combinations might include oysters and pecans, dried cherries and walnuts, apricots and almonds, sausage and fennel, and chorizo and spicy peppers—among many others.

Plain, unflavored packaged breadcrumbs or bread cubes can be used in any recipe, though they often taste stale. If you use them, you may need to increase the stock called for in the recipe. If making a recipe that calls for fresh, soft breadcrumbs, a 1-pound loaf yields about 10 cups.

Some people like their bread stuffing dry, some moist, some fluffy. Melted fat is the best way to add moisture—so try melted butter, bacon, or other drippings. Fat does not dry out in heat and it does not make breads and grains gummy the way liquids may. The next best moisture to add is beaten whole eggs. They bake to a fluffy consistency. For a wetter texture, use stocks, broths, and juices, but with a light hand. Bread stuffing confined in a cavity or wrapped tightly in foil does not get drier as it bakes, so the mixture should be just moist enough so crumbs or cubes stick together when pinched.

Stuffing baked in a bird will absorb the bird's juices. Stuffing baked in an uncovered baking dish outside the bird, however, needs to be well moistened with stock or it will end up dry. Eggs are also sometimes added, giving both moisture and firmness. Moisten bread mixtures to be stuffed into a bird's cavity just enough so they stick together when pinched. When spooning the stuffing into the bird, do not overpack, as it may prevent the stuffing from cooking to a safe temperature. *Caution: The stuffing in a bird should register 160°F when a meat thermometer is inserted in the center of the cavity; otherwise it may not be safe to eat.* If the bird is roasted to perfection but your stuffing is not done, remove the bird from the oven, scoop the stuffing into a buttered casserole, and continue to bake it in the hot oven while the bird rests before carving.

STUFFING BAKED IN A DISH

Any remaining stuffing that does not fit into the cavity of the bird can be baked separately, or you may even prefer to bake all of the stuffing outside the bird. Stuffing baked outside the bird should first be moistened with ½ to 1 cup of stock, milk, or wine to make up for the missing juices that it would absorb when cooked inside a roasting bird. Spread the stuffing in a shallow layer in a large, shallow buttered casserole or gratin dish. Ladle over enough stock, milk, or wine to moisten the stuffing, cover with aluminum foil if you wish, and bake in a preheated 350°F oven for 30 to 45 minutes. If you have covered the stuffing with aluminum foil but would like a crispy brown crust, dot the top with butter and bake uncovered for the last 20 minutes. If you are roasting a bird at the same time, baste the stuffing with pan drippings a few times during baking. If you plan to serve stuffing as the starchy side dish, allow about ¾ cup per person.

MAKING STUFFING AHEAD

All stuffings can be made ahead and refrigerated for up to 2 days. Stuffing intended to be baked inside a bird should be reheated before you stuff the bird with it. If making stuffing ahead, do not add any egg to the mixture until you have reheated it and are ready to stuff. The simplest method for reheating a stuffing is on top of the stove, stirring gently so as not to turn the whole mixture to mush. Stuffings to be baked in a dish can go directly from the refrigerator to the oven.

ABOUT FORCEMEAT

Besides the popular bread and grain stuffings, there is a category of stuffings based on uncooked ground meat, poultry, fish, or shellfish known as forcemeat (a variant of the French word for stuffing, *farce*). Most recognizable to us today cooked on its own as meat loaf and pâté, forcemeat was once the standard mixture used to stuff poultry and other foods. The character of forcemeat depends largely on how the meat or fish has been ground. Some are finely textured and smooth, as in an elegant, truffled pâté; others are more rustic, as in Sausage and Fennel Stuffing, 487. As with all stuffings, there is a great deal of variance in how forcemeat stuffings are prepared, but all must be thoroughly cooked before serving.

DRESSING VS. STUFFING

The terms *stuffing* and *dressing* are used interchangeably despite the occasional argument that anything cooked in the bird is stuffing and anything baked separately must be called dressing. Stuffing is actually the original name, and the term *dressing* came from Victorian England when *stuffing* was thought to be a bit unseemly.

BASIC BREAD STUFFING

8 to 10 cups

This and the bread stuffing recipes that follow yield enough to stuff a 14- to 17-pound turkey. Many of the variations yield enough for an additional small casserole of stuffing. To stuff an oven roaster or 6 to 8 rock Cornish hens, halve the recipes. For a larger turkey, increase all the ingredients by half. The optional egg makes the stuffing firm. If you prefer the bread to be moist, skip the toasting step.

Position a rack in the center of the oven. Preheat the oven to 400°F.

Toast until golden brown:

1 pound sliced firm white sandwich, French, or Italian bread, including crusts, cut into ½-inch cubes, or 10 cups lightly packed bread cubes

Turn into a large bowl. Heat in a large skillet over medium-high heat until the foam subsides:

4 to 8 tablespoons (½ to 1 stick) unsalted butter

Add and cook, stirring, until tender, about 5 minutes:

2 cups chopped onions
1 cup finely chopped celery

Remove from the heat and stir in:

¼ to ½ cup minced fresh parsley
1 teaspoon dried sage, or 1 tablespoon minced fresh
1 teaspoon dried thyme, or 1 tablespoon minced fresh
¾ teaspoon salt
½ teaspoon ground black pepper
¼ teaspoon freshly grated or ground nutmeg
⅛ teaspoon ground cloves

Stir into the bread cubes and toss until well combined. Depending on how much butter you started with and how firm you want the stuffing, stir in, a little at a time, until the stuffing is lightly moist but not packed together:

⅓ to 1 cup chicken stock
1 to 2 large eggs, well beaten (optional)

Adjust the seasonings. To use as a stuffing, reheat just before spooning it into the bird(s). Or moisten with additional:

Stock and/or egg

and turn into a large, shallow buttered baking dish. Bake in a 350°F oven until the top has formed a crust and the stuffing is heated through, 25 to 40 minutes.

BREAD STUFFING WITH TOASTED NUTS OR CHESTNUTS AND DRIED FRUIT *About 12 cups*

Use shelled and roasted fresh chestnuts, or canned or frozen if desired; do not use chestnuts packed in syrup, which are too sweet for this dish.

Prepare Basic Bread Stuffing, above, adding ½ to 1 cup walnuts, pecans, or Brazil nuts, toasted and coarsely chopped, or 1½ cups chestnuts, boiled or toasted and coarsely chopped, and ½ cup dried fruit, such as raisins, cranberries, cherries, or diced prunes, when tossing the bread with the seasonings.

BREAD STUFFING WITH OYSTERS *About 12 cups*

Freshly shucked raw oysters are sweeter and milder than raw oysters already shucked and sold by the pint. Ask your fishmonger to shuck the oysters for you or shuck them yourself, saving the juices (known as the liquor) to moisten the stuffing.

Prepare Basic Bread Stuffing, above, adding 2 dozen shucked (or 1 pint raw) oysters, drained, when tossing the bread with the seasonings. Use the drained oyster liquor in place of, or in addition to, the chicken stock.

BREAD STUFFING WITH SAUSAGE AND APPLES *14 to 16 cups*

Twelve ounces of brown-and-serve sausages, thawed and cut into small pieces, can be substituted for the bulk sausage. Sauté the pieces with the apples, using butter in place of the sausage drippings.

Cook in a large skillet over medium-high heat, breaking up the meat with a slotted spoon as it cooks, until no longer pink, 8 to 10 minutes:

1 pound bulk pork sausage

Remove the sausage to a paper-towel-lined plate to drain. Pour off all but 2 tablespoons of the fat and return the skillet to the stove. Add and cook, stirring, until tender:

4 cups diced peeled green apples, such as Granny Smith

Prepare:

Basic Bread Stuffing, above

adding the sausage and apples when tossing the bread with the seasonings.

BREAD AND MUSHROOM STUFFING *10 to 12 cups*

Heat in a medium skillet over medium-high heat until the foam subsides:

2 tablespoons unsalted butter

Add and cook, stirring, until tender and the liquid is evaporated:

1 pound button or wild mushrooms, wiped clean and sliced

Prepare:

Basic Bread Stuffing, above

adding the mushrooms when tossing the bread with the seasonings.

PARSLEY AND BREADCRUMB STUFFING FOR FISH *About 2 cups*

This delicate, buttery stuffing can be used to stuff a range of seafood, from sole fillets to whole baked trout. Because fish cooks much more quickly than stuffed poultry, the bread for fish stuffings should be finely crumbed and the vegetables finely chopped. This recipe yields enough to stuff 4 servings of fish fillets, steaks, or whole dressed fish, or 2 pounds of fillets or steaks and 3 to 4 pounds of whole dressed fish.

Melt in a medium skillet over low heat:

6 tablespoons (¾ stick) butter

Add and cook, stirring, until tender but not brown, about 5 minutes:

½ cup finely chopped onions

½ cup finely chopped celery

Remove from the heat and stir in:

1½ cups fresh breadcrumbs

3 tablespoons finely chopped fresh parsley

Season with:

½ teaspoon lemon juice

¼ teaspoon salt

¼ teaspoon ground black pepper

Use as a stuffing.

BACON STUFFING FOR FISH

A savory stuffing for richer tasting fish such as trout, salmon, bluefish, and mackerel.

Prepare Parsley and Breadcrumb Stuffing for Fish, above, omitting the butter and instead first frying 12 slices bacon until crisp, removing the bacon, and cooking the vegetables in the rendered bacon fat. Finish the stuffing by adding the crumbled bacon. If desired, stir 3 tablespoons chopped pecans into the stuffing.

CRABMEAT STUFFING

A rich and spirited stuffing well suited for fish fillets such as cod, sole, or salmon.

Prepare Parsley and Breadcrumb Stuffing for Fish, above, adding ¼ cup finely chopped green bell peppers to the vegetables, decreasing the breadcrumbs to 1 cup, adding ½ cup chopped freshly cooked or well-drained canned crabmeat or lobster, increasing the lemon juice to 1 teaspoon, and adding ¼ teaspoon dry mustard.

BASIC CORN BREAD STUFFING *About 8 cups*

Any corn bread will work in this recipe. However, if you are making corn bread from scratch, choose Southern Corn Bread, 777, which is unsweetened. If you like the corn bread moist, skip the toasting step.

Position a rack in the center of the oven. Preheat the oven to 400°F.

Toast until golden brown:

8 cups cubed corn bread or 1 recipe Southern Corn Bread, 777

Turn into a large bowl. If you like a crumbly texture, break up the cubes with your fingers.

Heat in a large skillet over medium-high heat until the foam subsides:

4 to 8 tablespoons (½ to 1 stick) unsalted butter

Add and cook, stirring, until tender, about 5 minutes:

2 cups chopped onions
1 cup finely chopped celery
1 green bell pepper, cut into small dice (optional)
1 red bell pepper, cut into small dice (optional)
2 cloves garlic, minced (optional)

Remove from the heat and stir in:

¼ to ½ cup minced fresh parsley
1 teaspoon dried sage, or 1 tablespoon minced fresh
1 teaspoon dried thyme, or 1 tablespoon minced fresh
¾ teaspoon salt
½ teaspoon ground black pepper

Stir into the bread cubes and toss until well combined. Depending on how much butter you started with and how firm you want the stuffing, stir in, a little at a time, until the stuffing is lightly moist but not packed together:

⅓ to 1 cup chicken stock
1 to 2 large eggs, well beaten (optional)

Adjust the seasonings. To use as a stuffing, reheat just before spooning it into the bird(s). Or moisten with additional:

Stock and/or egg

and turn into a large, shallow buttered baking dish. Bake uncovered in a 350°F oven until the top has formed a crust and the stuffing is heated through, 25 to 40 minutes.

CORN BREAD STUFFING WITH SAUSAGE AND BELL PEPPERS *12 to 14 Cups*

Prepare Basic Corn Bread Stuffing, above, with the optional green and red bell peppers, adding 1 pound cooked hot or mild bulk sausage and, if desired, ¼ teaspoon ground red pepper when tossing the bread with the seasonings.

CORN BREAD STUFFING WITH OYSTERS AND TOASTED PECANS *10 to 12 cups*

Prepare Basic Corn Bread Stuffing, above, omitting the garlic and adding 2 dozen shucked (or 1 pint raw) oysters, drained, and/or 1 to 2 cups pecans, toasted and coarsely chopped, when tossing the bread with the seasonings. Use the drained oyster liquor in place of, or in addition to, the chicken stock.

CORN BREAD STUFFING WITH CUMIN AND HOT CHILI PEPPERS *10 to 12 cups*

Two 4-ounce cans of diced mild green chili peppers can be substituted for the poblano or Anaheim peppers.

Roast, 402, peel, seed, and chop:

4 poblano peppers or 8 Anaheim peppers
3 fresh jalapeño peppers

Prepare, using the optional bell peppers and garlic:

Basic Corn Bread Stuffing, above

Add the roasted peppers along with:

1 teaspoon ground cumin
1 teaspoon dried oregano
1 cup frozen, canned, or cooked fresh corn kernels

when tossing the bread with the seasonings.

MILES STANDISH STUFFING *20 to 22 cups*

Our editor's husband, who is obviously of Italian descent, claims this stuffing has its name because it was served aboard the *Mayflower* as it sailed west. He maintains it contains the Puritans' two favorite staples: pepperoni and mozzarella. Whatever its origins, this stuffing is a real victory for an American holiday.

This recipe yields enough to stuff a 25-pound turkey with a little left over for baking.

Toast until golden brown:

1 pound sliced fluffy white sandwich bread

Spread 1 side of each toasted slice with:

Butter

Cut into ½-inch cubes and turn into a large bowl. Toss with:

Generous sprinkling of salt and ground black pepper
2 tablespoons dried thyme
1 tablespoon dried sage
2 teaspoons dried rosemary

Heat in a large skillet over medium-high heat until the foam subsides:

8 tablespoons (1 stick) unsalted butter

Add and cook, stirring, until tender, about 7 minutes:

2 cups sliced onions

2 cups thinly sliced celery

Stir into the bread cubes and toss until well combined. Return the skillet to the stove and heat over medium-high heat until the foam subsides:

2 tablespoons unsalted butter

Add and cook, stirring, until browned, about 5 minutes:

1 turkey heart, cut into ½-inch cubes

1 turkey gizzard, cut into ½-inch cubes

Salt and ground black pepper to taste

Add the bread cubes along with:

1 pound bulk breakfast sausage, cooked and crumbled

12 ounces skim-milk mozzarella cheese, cut into ½-inch cubes

6 to 10 ounces spicy pepperoni, cut into ¼-inch cubes

Toss to combine. Generously moisten with:

⅔ to 1 cup chicken stock

Use as a stuffing or turn into a large, shallow buttered baking dish and bake in a 350°F oven until golden brown, 30 to 45 minutes.

MASHED POTATO STUFFING

5 to 6 cups

This surprisingly light stuffing, ideally made from left-over mashed potatoes, is excellent baked in a buttered casserole and served with roasted chicken, roast beef, or baked ham—but it also makes a very good stuffing for turkey, goose, pork, or capon.

Melt or heat in a large skillet over medium heat:

4 tablespoons (½ stick) unsalted butter or olive oil

Add and cook, stirring occasionally, until tender and beginning to caramelize, 10 to 15 minutes:

3 cups thinly sliced onions

Turn into a large bowl and toss with:

4 cups mashed potatoes

½ to 1 cup dry unseasoned breadcrumbs

½ cup minced fresh parsley

2 teaspoons dried sage, or 2 tablespoons minced fresh

½ teaspoon dried thyme, or 1½ teaspoons minced fresh

Salt and ground black pepper to taste

1 large egg, lightly beaten

½ to 1 cup milk or chicken stock, or a combination

Dot with:

2 tablespoons unsalted butter, cut into small pieces

Sprinkle with:

Grated Parmesan cheese

Use as a stuffing or turn into a large, shallow buttered baking dish and bake in a 350°F oven until browned and bubbly, 30 to 40 minutes.

SWEET POTATO AND APPLE STUFFING

About 8 cups

Serve this stuffing with Pork Crown Roast, 692, roasted turkey, or baked ham.

Bring to a boil in water to cover and simmer, covered, until tender:

2 pounds whole sweet potatoes or yams, unpeeled

Drain. When cool enough to handle, remove the skins and mash the potatoes in a large bowl. Heat in a large skillet over medium-high heat until the foam subsides:

2 tablespoons unsalted butter

Add and cook, stirring, until the vegetables are tender, about 5 minutes:

1½ cups chopped onions

½ cup chopped celery

½ teaspoon salt

¼ teaspoon ground black pepper

Add and cook, stirring, until the apples are tender but still firm, 3 to 4 minutes:

2 cups diced peeled green apples, such as Granny Smith or Golden Delicious

½ cup apple cider

¼ teaspoon ground cinnamon

¼ teaspoon ground nutmeg

¼ teaspoon ground cloves

Stir into the sweet potatoes along with:

2 cups dry unseasoned breadcrumbs, preferably homemade

Adjust the seasonings and moisten, if needed, with:

¼ cup chicken or vegetable stock

Dot with:

4 tablespoons (½ stick) unsalted butter, cut into small pieces

Use as a stuffing or turn into a large, shallow buttered baking dish and bake in a 350°F oven until browned and bubbly, 30 to 45 minutes.

RICE STUFFING WITH ALMONDS, RAISINS, AND MIDDLE EASTERN SPICES

About 4 cups

This intensely flavored stuffing goes well with rock Cornish hens, partridge, or quail. Baked in a casserole, it also makes a good side dish with grilled chicken or fish.

Heat in a large skillet over medium heat:

2 tablespoons olive oil

Add and cook, stirring, until tender, about 5 minutes:

1 cup chopped onions

Add and stir until well coated:

1 tablespoon minced garlic

½ teaspoon ground cumin

½ teaspoon ground coriander

½ teaspoon ground turmeric
½ teaspoon sweet paprika
½ teaspoon ground ginger
½ teaspoon ground black pepper
¼ teaspoon salt
1 cup medium-grain rice

Stir in and bring to a simmer:

1½ cups chicken stock

Reduce the heat to low, cover, and simmer until the rice is cooked, about 20 minutes. Turn the mixture into a large bowl, let cool slightly, and stir in:

¼ cup golden raisins
¼ cup diced pitted prunes
¼ cup slivered blanched almonds, toasted
1 teaspoon grated lemon zest
2 tablespoons fresh lemon juice
1 large egg, lightly beaten

Adjust the seasonings. Use as a stuffing or turn into a large, shallow buttered baking dish, cover, and bake in a 350°F oven until the flavors are blended and the stuffing is hot, 20 to 30 minutes.

COUSCOUS STUFFING WITH DRIED APRICOTS AND PISTACHIOS

About 4 cups

Best as stuffing for small, mild-flavored birds such as rock Cornish hens, poussins, or squab—or as a side dish for roasted or grilled lamb. For a sweeter stuffing, replace some of the apricots with finely diced dates.

Melt in a large saucepan over medium heat:

2 tablespoons unsalted butter

Add and cook, stirring, until tender, about 5 minutes:

½ cup finely chopped onions
½ cup finely diced carrots

Stir in and bring to a boil:

1½ cups chicken stock
½ cup finely chopped dried apricots
1 tablespoon chopped preserved lemons, 458 (optional)
¼ teaspoon salt
¼ teaspoon ground black pepper
Pinch of ground cinnamon
Pinch of ground ginger

Stir in:

1 cup quick-cooking couscous

Remove from the heat, cover, and let stand for 5 minutes. Fluff with a fork and stir in:

½ cup chopped pistachios, whole pine nuts, or slivered blanched almonds, toasted
¼ cup minced fresh parsley

Use as a stuffing or serve immediately.

WILD RICE AND PORCINI STUFFING

About 3 cups

This is the perfect accompaniment to wild game birds, venison, or braised beef. Use the strained mushroom soaking liquid as part of the liquid to cook the rice. A wild rice blend can be substituted for the wild rice.

Combine in a small bowl and let soak for 20 minutes:

1 ounce dried porcini mushrooms
1 cup hot water

Remove the mushrooms from the soaking liquid, coarsely chop, and place in a large bowl. Meanwhile, heat in a medium skillet over medium-high heat until the foam subsides:

2 tablespoons unsalted butter

Add and cook, stirring, until softened, about 5 minutes:

½ cup finely chopped onions
¼ cup finely chopped celery
¼ cup minced shallots
1 tablespoon minced garlic

Stir into the mushrooms along with:

2 cups cooked wild rice
¼ cup chopped fresh or frozen cranberries (optional)
¼ cup minced fresh parsley
½ teaspoon dried thyme, or 1½ teaspoons minced fresh
½ teaspoon dried sage

Sprinkle with:

Salt and ground black pepper to taste

Use as a stuffing or turn into a large, shallow buttered baking dish, cover, and bake in a 350°F oven until the flavors are blended and the stuffing is hot, about 20 minutes.

RICE STUFFING WITH CHORIZO AND HOT CHILI PEPPERS

About 6 cups

This is wonderful stuffed in chicken. One 4-ounce can of diced mild green chili peppers can be substituted for the poblano or Anaheim peppers.

Roast, 402, peel, seed, chop, and place in a medium bowl:

2 poblano peppers or 4 Anaheim peppers

Heat in a large skillet over medium-high heat:

2 tablespoons olive oil

Add and cook, stirring, until tender, about 5 minutes:

1 cup finely diced onions
1 tablespoon minced garlic

Add and cook, stirring, until no longer pink, about 10 minutes:

1¼ pounds chorizo, casings removed

Stir into the roasted peppers along with:

2 cups cooked white rice
1 large egg, lightly beaten (optional)
1 cup chopped scallions
¼ cup minced fresh cilantro
¼ teaspoon salt, or to taste
¼ teaspoon ground black pepper, or to taste

Use as a stuffing or turn into a large, shallow buttered baking dish, cover, and bake in a 350°F oven until the flavors are blended and the stuffing is hot, 20 to 30 minutes.

SPINACH-RICOTTA STUFFING *About 2 cups*

Stuff this well-seasoned mixture under the skins of chicken pieces or under the skin of a whole, butterflied, flattened bird, 569. If substituting frozen spinach for fresh, skip the cooking step; simply thaw a 10-ounce box of frozen spinach, squeeze it to remove excess liquid, chop it coarsely, then toss it with the breadcrumbs and ricotta cheese.

Heat in a large skillet or Dutch oven over medium-high heat until wilted:

One 12-ounce bunch or 10-ounce bag spinach, trimmed, washed, and coarsely chopped

Remove from the heat. When the spinach is cool enough to handle, squeeze out the excess liquid. Return the pan to medium heat and heat:

2 teaspoons olive oil

Add and cook, stirring, until tender, 3 to 4 minutes:

½ cup finely chopped onions
1 teaspoon minced garlic

Combine the spinach and sautéed vegetables in a large bowl and toss with:

1 cup ricotta cheese
½ cup soft breadcrumbs from day-old bread
2 tablespoons grated Parmesan cheese
2 teaspoons olive oil
½ teaspoon salt
¼ teaspoon ground black pepper
Pinch of freshly grated or ground nutmeg

Use as a stuffing.

SPINACH, MUSHROOM, AND GROUND MEAT STUFFING *About 8 cups*

Vary the meat in this stuffing, depending on what it is going into. Stuff veal breast, Crown Roast of Pork, 692, or lamb with ground trimmings from the same meat. For small birds, try bulk Italian or breakfast sausage.

Heat in a very large skillet over medium-high heat until the foam subsides:

6 tablespoons (¾ stick) unsalted butter

Add and cook, stirring occasionally, until tender but not brown, about 7 minutes:

3 cups finely chopped onions

Add and cook, stirring, until wilted:

1 pound mushrooms, wiped clean and finely chopped

Squeeze until almost dry:

Two 12-ounce bunches spinach, trimmed, washed, and coarsely chopped, or two 10-ounce packages frozen chopped spinach, thawed

Stir into the vegetable mixture and cook until all the liquid is evaporated and the pan looks dry. Turn the mixture into a large bowl and stir in:

1½ pounds ground veal or pork, or a combination
2 cups fine fresh breadcrumbs
1 cup finely chopped fresh parsley
1½ teaspoons dried thyme
1 teaspoon salt
1 teaspoon ground black pepper
½ teaspoon freshly grated or ground nutmeg
2 large eggs, lightly beaten

Use as a stuffing.

SAUSAGE AND FENNEL STUFFING *3 cups*

Use this tasty, meat-loaf-like mixture to stuff a 6- to 7-pound chicken or capon.

Melt in a small skillet over low heat:

1½ tablespoons butter

Add and cook, stirring, over medium heat until tender and lightly browned, 15 to 20 minutes:

1 chicken heart, cut into small dice
1 chicken gizzard, peeled and cut into small dice

Add and cook, stirring, for 2 to 3 minutes more:

1 chicken liver, cut into small dice (optional)
2 teaspoons fennel seeds
1 teaspoon dried rosemary, or 1 tablespoon minced fresh
¾ teaspoon salt
¼ teaspoon ground black pepper

Turn into a large bowl and stir in:

1 pound bulk sausage
1½ cups dry breadcrumbs
2 large eggs, lightly beaten

Use as a stuffing.

SHELLFISH

Shellfish are our most popular creatures of the sea. They are distinctive in both flavor and form. Although one often can be substituted for another in some recipes—shrimp for scallops, for example, and vice versa—one would never be mistaken for the other. Almost every shellfish has its own rules for buying, cleaning, and, sometimes, even eating.

WHERE DO SHELLFISH COME FROM?

Like finfish, shellfish come from saltwater and freshwater and are both wild and farmed. Nearly 50 percent of all shrimp we eat are farmed, as are increasing numbers of scallops. Most oysters and many clams and mussels are also cultivated—not farmed, strictly speaking, but "planted" and encouraged to grow in certain beds where they are easily harvested. And although shellfish take well to farming, it is important that they be handled correctly. Because fish farming is intensive—that is, there are more fish in a given area than there would naturally be—huge amounts of nutrients must be added to the water, usually in the form of pellets not unlike dry cat food in appearance and content. If this and other aspects of the process are done properly, the results are excellent; whereas farmed salmon is distinctively different from wild salmon, few could tell the difference between high-quality farmed and wild shrimp. The texture and taste are almost identical.

Some shellfish, especially shrimp, comes to us from all over the world. Some, such as most lobster and crab, is fairly local. But even the fact that many shellfish must be sold alive (unless they are cooked) no longer limits their distribution: Live Maine lobster is sold on the West Coast, just as dozens of varieties of West Coast oysters are sold in the East. Properly handled, many live shellfish can live for weeks out of the water and, although they are never as flavorful as they are when first harvested, their quality can remain fairly high.

Because shellfish are so different from one another, it is easier to give general buying and storing information for smaller groups of them, and even for individual species. But first a word about nomenclature: When we say "shellfish," we usually are talking about the members of three major groups:

- Mollusks, which include scallops, clams, mussels, oysters, and related species
- Crustaceans, which include crabs, lobsters, and shrimp
- Cephalopods, which include octopus, squid, and cuttlefish.

Individual species within each of these groups have their similarities and differences (as do individual species across groups; when it comes to cooking, scallops have more in common with shrimp than they do with oysters). In the information that follows, we have handled the individual species one at a time, grouping them roughly according to larger categories.

A NOTE ABOUT SHELLFISH SAFETY

Cooked shellfish are among the best animals you can eat. Much of what was written about finfish in the Fish chapter is true for shellfish as well. They are lean, they contain beneficial nutrients—protein without lots of fat; beneficial Omega-3 fatty acids, and micronutrients such as zinc—and they almost never contain additives such as antibiotics or growth hormones.

But the ever-popular mollusks feed by filtering the water in which they live through their bodies. If there are unsafe bacteria or toxic algae in that water, those pathogens end up in the mollusks. Even thorough cooking does not always destroy all of these. Eating mollusks raw, especially, presents a certain amount of risk. Generally, the risk is of nasty but not life-threatening gastrointestinal illness. Nevertheless, any illness can be life-threatening to children, the elderly, and people with immune deficiency diseases, and gastrointestinal distress is unpleasant at best.

Should you choose to eat raw clams or oysters (or mussels or scallops), there are some precautions worth taking. All legal mollusks are grown in licensed, regularly inspected areas; harvesters must tag their clams and oysters with their names and the areas from which the shellfish were gathered. You can ask to see these tags when buying fish in markets or restaurants.

Generally, neither supermarkets nor well-established restaurants can afford to buy clams or oysters taken illegally. It is more of a risk for the home cook to buy fish from parked trucks, temporary roadside stands, or other itinerant "shops." It is also risky to gather shellfish yourself, unless you consult the Coast Guard first. As long as the water is regularly tested and contains no more than the legal limit of harmful bacteria, your risks are minimal.

SHRIMP

Shrimp is the favorite seafood of most Americans (we eat more of it than any other except canned tuna). And why not? With lobsterlike flavor and texture at half the price, shrimp is easier to cook than steak and is among the most versatile forms of animal protein.

There are two important things to understand about shrimp: One, all shrimp is not the same. And two, because it has become an international commodity, bought and sold in huge quantities, because of its popularity, and because it freezes so well, almost all shrimp is frozen before sale. First, the differences among shrimp: About three-quarters of the shrimp we eat is imported from all over the world—Ecuador is a big supplier, as are Sri Lanka, Thailand, and China. Much of that imported shrimp is farm-raised, and under a variety of conditions. Some farm-raised shrimp eat only whatever the tides bring in, resulting in a fairly watery, insipid product, while others have their diet supplemented by feed, making them meatier.

An increasing amount of the domestic supply is also farm-raised, although it does not yet make up the majority. We still catch plenty of wild shrimp in the Gulf of Mexico, off the coast of California, and elsewhere. Shrimp is also caught in some other areas—off the coast of Maine, for example, and the Carolinas—but the catch remains small by national standards and, for the most part, is consumed locally. There are literally hundreds of species of shrimp (also called prawns) harvested and grown worldwide, but only a few are likely to appear in our fish stores and supermarkets. Here is how to tell which you are buying:

Gulf White: Usually wild, sometimes farm-raised. Almost always excellent. Can be very large. Pale shells.

Mexican (or Ecuadorian) White: Also very good, more frequently farm-raised. Similar in appearance to Gulf White.

Gulf Pink or Brown: Most often wild. Usually not as large as whites, with pinkish or brownish shells. Brown shrimp often taste of iodine, a taste that is enjoyed in various parts of the country.

Black Tiger: The most common shrimp in supermarkets these days. Almost always farm-raised, almost always from Asia. Reasonably high quality, although not as flavorful as any of the above species. Distinctive gray shells with black, red, or yellow feelers.

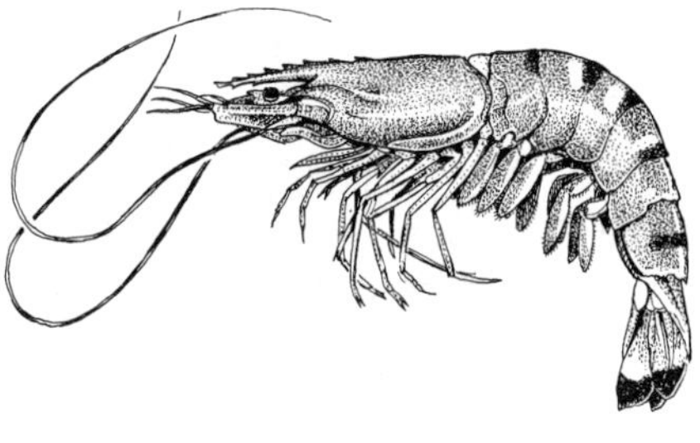

Black tiger shrimp

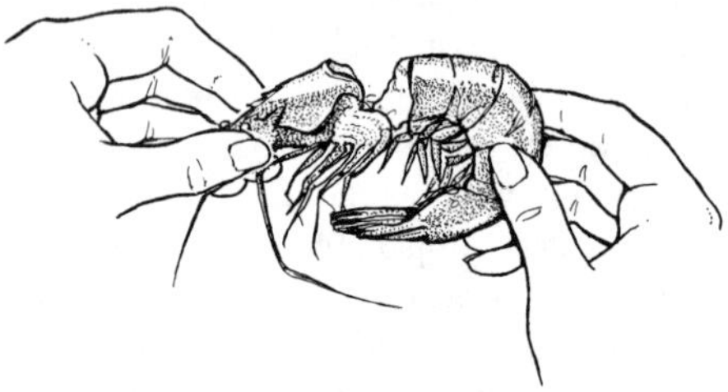

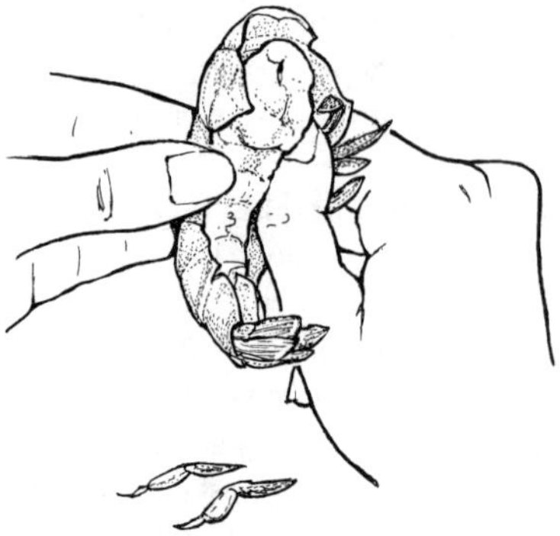

Peeling a shrimp

When a fishmonger or supermarket clerk tells you that his or her shrimp are "fresh," it probably means that they have been thawed only recently. Not that freezing shrimp is a problem; they keep brilliantly when frozen.

If you want to determine the species, ask to see the box; almost all shrimp are packed in 2-kilogram or 5-pound boxes. In addition to species, there are several other factors to consider in preparing shrimp:

Judging Quality: Except for black tiger shrimp, do not buy any with black spots on their shells, a sign of spoilage, or with yellow or gritty shells, which may have been bleached to remove black spots. Do not buy any shrimp with dry spots, which indicate freezer burn.

Size: Shrimp are measured by the number it takes to make a pound. U-8 (under 8 per pound) are huge; U-60 (under 60 per pound) are quite small. Given that it is best to peel shrimp yourself (the peels make excellent stock, 41), it makes sense to buy larger shrimp to make this somewhat tedious chore a bit less so. But that does not mean you need to buy the prohibitively expensive U-8 shrimp; stay with those in the 20- to 30-per-pound range for a good combination of economy, size, and relative ease of peeling.

Peeling: Do it yourself, shown above, for two reasons. Prepeeled shrimp have lost some of their flavor, and the shells make great stock, 41 (freeze them if you like, then make a big batch of stock when you have the shells from several pounds of shrimp). If you are grilling, broiling, or boiling shrimp, consider cooking them in their shells, for it protects the meat from drying out and helps them retain maximum flavor.

Deveining: The "vein" of a shrimp is actually its intestinal tract and can impart a bitter taste. To remove the vein, make a shallow cut along the back of a peeled shrimp and pull out the vein with the tip of the knife, shown below, center.

Butterflying: Lay an unpeeled shrimp on its side on a work surface. Starting about 1/4 inch away from the tail, make a horizontal cut along the inside curl of the shrimp (through the legs), shown below right, without cutting the shrimp or shell in half. With your fingers, open the shrimp and flatten it with the palm of your hand so it lies almost flat.

Cooking: Smaller shrimp are done as soon as they turn pink, usually in 3 to 5 minutes. Larger shrimp need an extra couple of minutes to cook all the way through. You can just press on the side of one and tell by its texture when it is done; it will be firm and not at all mushy. But it is just as easy to cut one open and check; shrimp are opaque when fully cooked.

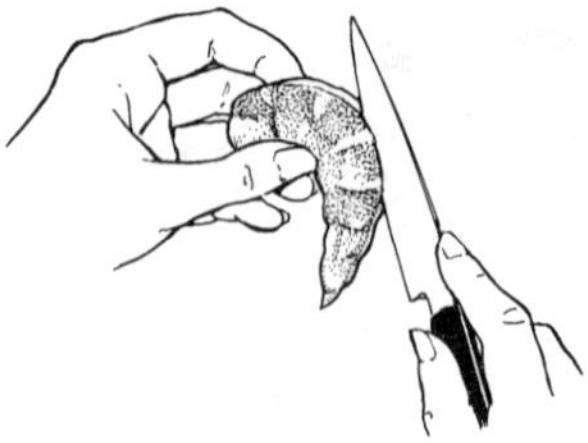

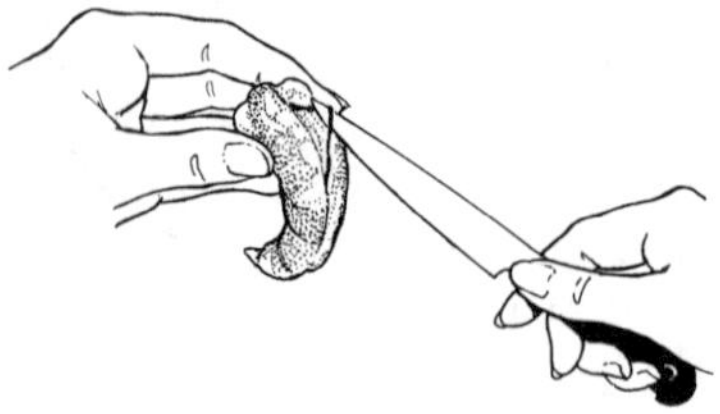

Deveining a shrimp

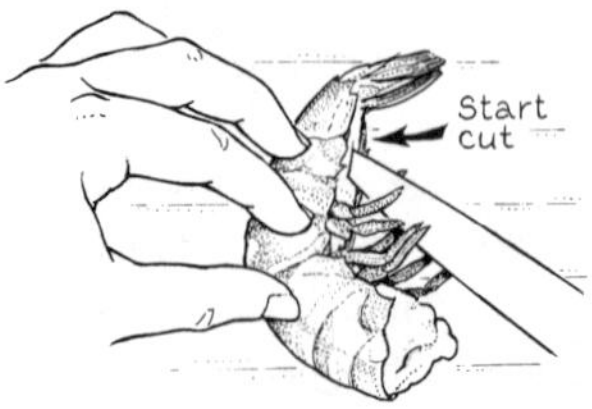

Butterflying a shrimp

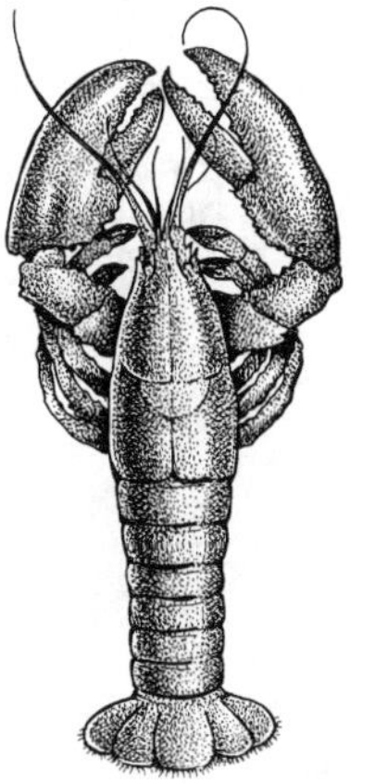

Northern lobster or homard

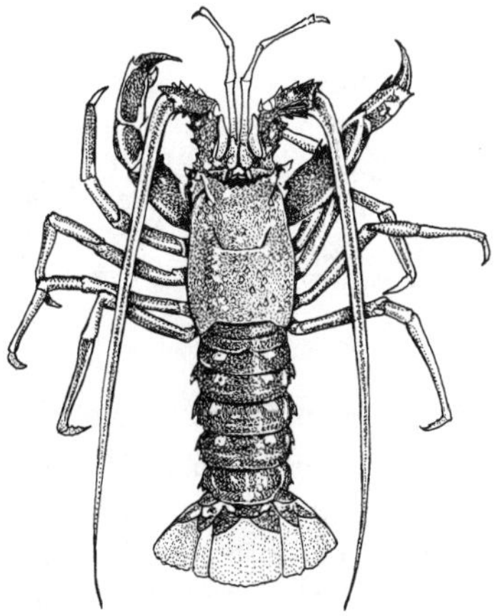

Rock or spiny lobster

Where found: Worldwide, and sold everywhere.
To store: Do not thaw frozen shrimp until the day before you are ready to cook them. Thaw by placing them in the refrigerator or in a bowl of running water. If fresh or thawed, store on or in a bed of ice, with drainage for melting ice. Keep iced until ready to cook.
To clean: Shrimp heads come off with a simple tug. Hold the shrimp in one hand, then separate the shell on the underside, using the legs or feelers to give you a grip. Usually, the shell can be removed in one piece. To devein, make a shallow cut with a sharp, thin knife along the outside curl and pick out the vein with your fingers or the tip of the knife.
Best cooking techniques: All methods.
Similar shellfish: Crayfish (very similar), scallops.

LOBSTERS

Northern (Maine) Lobster, European Lobster, Spiny Lobster

Although there are literally dozens of types of lobsters in the world, they fall neatly into two groups: those with edible claws and those without. Those with claws—on this continent commonly called Maine lobster even when taken from Canada or elsewhere on the North Atlantic coast—are generally agreed to be superior and are, in fact, true lobsters. Those without, which have excellent tail meat, most often are seen locally (in Florida, the Gulf States, and southern California) or in the form of frozen lobster tails. European lobsters, which are very similar to our Northern lobster, never make it to this side of the Atlantic. There are also European spiny lobsters; these, too, are eaten locally. All lobsters can be used interchangeably in recipes, although those without claws obviously have less meat.

Technically, all lobster sold is "wild," although many are held in pens for months at a time, which arguably is a form of domestication.

All lobsters should be bought alive (and absolutely kicking) or cooked. Steaming—the easiest cooking method—kills lobsters without much effort (and it is unlikely, say most experts, that lobsters feel pain). But if you want to kill a lobster without cooking it, pierce it behind the head with a sharp, heavy knife. Find the cross-hatch right behind the lobster's head. Plunge the point of a sturdy chef's knife straight down, shown below. To avoid muscular contractions, you can put the lobster in the freezer for a few minutes until it is still. If you wish to halve the lobster, place the cutting board on a baking sheet to collect the juices. Cut forward through the head and back through the body and tail, shown 492 (top).

If you are planning to use the lobster meat in a sautéed or stir-fried dish, parboil the lobster: Bring a full pot of water (3 quarts water per 1½- to 2-pound lobster) to a boil and add one or more lobsters—as many as will fit without crowding. Cover the pot and

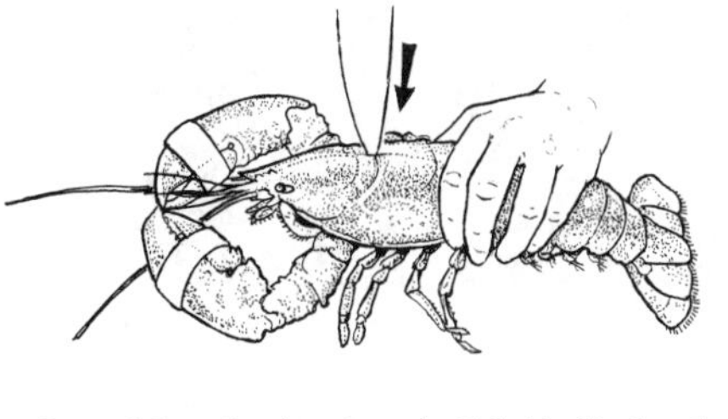

Killing a lobster by plunging a knife behind its head

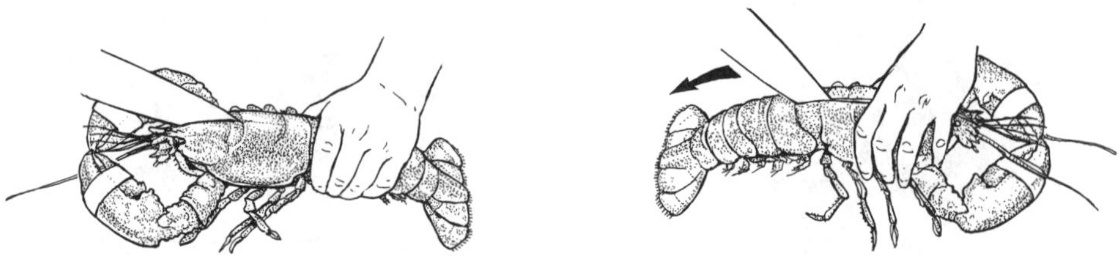

Halving a lobster

boil for about 3 minutes per pound (do not try this with lobsters that weigh more than 2 pounds, for they will boil unevenly); the lobster will have stopped moving and begun to turn red. Remove it from the water, let it cool for a few minutes, then cut it up (and remove the meat if you like). You then can refrigerate the lobster, well covered, for up to a day before cooking.

Live lobsters should squirm vigorously when removed from the tank, flipping their tails and moving their claws. A limp lobster (called a "sleeper" in the trade), with hanging claws, may die by the time you get to cook it. Lobster is expensive, so do not settle for half-alive specimens; the meat will be mushy and may even taste bad. You can also have lobsters shipped by air from Maine lobster farms—at a price. But for many landlocked cooks, this is probably the best option for buying a healthy lobster.

Lobsters, like crabs, shed their shells and grow new ones. The new shells are quite soft at first and, when a lobster is caught at this stage (in the summer), it is called a soft-shell (or sometimes a new-shell). Soft-shells are fun: You can break them easily with your hands and gobble them up as fast as shrimp. (Do not try eating the shells, though, as you would with a soft-shell crab—they are not that soft.) But soft-shells do not contain as much meat as do hard-shells, and they also contain a great deal of water. Generally speaking, the harder the shell, the more meat it contains. All

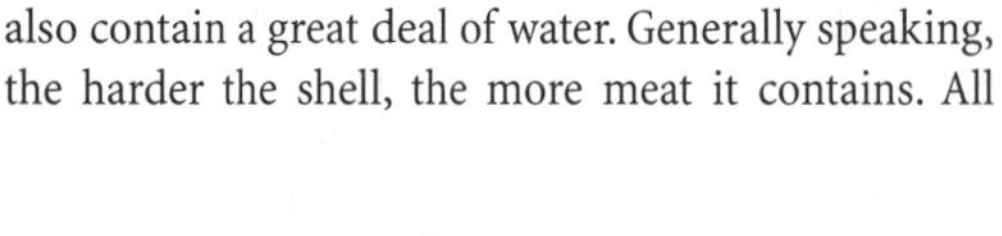

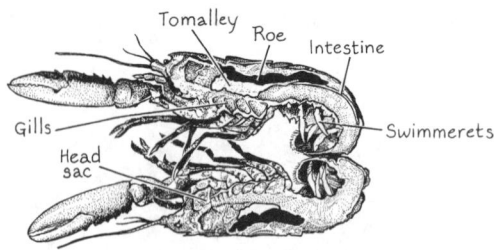

A halved lobster

parts of the lobster, with the exception of the head sac and the gills, are edible. The milky white substance is congealed blood, the creamy green is tomalley (or liver, which is wonderful spread on toasts and served with the lobster), and the fairly solid red (if you have bought a female) is roe or coral.

Size is another issue. Some people say that larger lobsters are tough, but that is not the case. In fact, there is a good argument to be made that a 3-pound lobster contains more edible meat than two 1½-pound lobsters. The larger a lobster gets, the more meat it contains in those difficult-to-reach parts of the claw and the body that make lobster eating so much fun. Yes, some lobster meat is occasionally tough and stringy, but this is usually the result of overcooking; size has nothing to do with it.

Lobsters can be too small, however; a lobster weighing less than 1¼ pounds will not contain enough meat for an average eater. Most people have little trouble consuming lobsters weighing 1½ pounds.

Finally, there is sex. Female lobsters are said to have more meat and more tender meat, but if they do, it is barely discernible. (It is true that most female lobsters are a bit broader through the top of the tail—the "hips"—than most males, which may make them weigh more. What females do have, sometimes at least, is coral or roe, the lovely red (reddish black when raw) egg sac that makes for delicious eating. Since female lobsters carry their eggs for as long as two years, the chance of one containing coral is good. With a practiced eye, you easily can learn to distinguish a male from a female lobster: the "swimmerets," the five pairs of small fins on the abdomen, are pointy and hard on male lobsters; on females, they are leathery and soft.

Where found: True lobsters: Along the northern Atlantic Coast, but shipped everywhere. Spiny lobsters: In warmer waters, usually eaten locally.

To buy: Alive and kicking. When lobsters are removed from the tank, they should flip their tails and wiggle their claws. Or buy them already cooked.

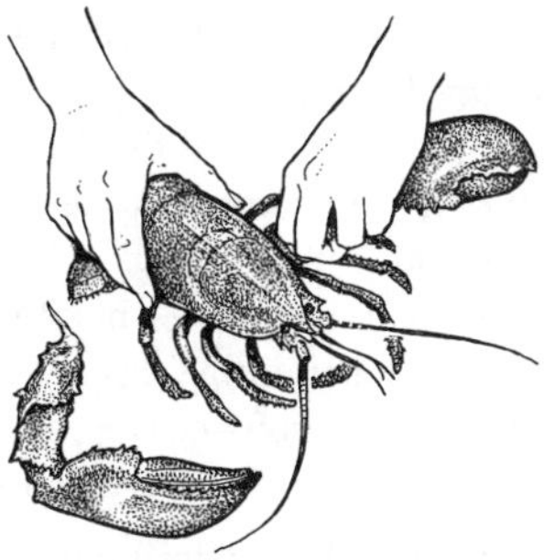

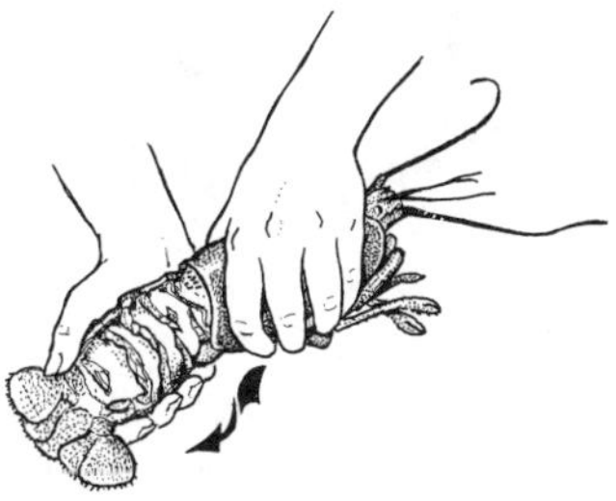

Snapping off the claws and tail of the lobster

To store: NOT in water; they will die. Best stored in the refrigerator, preferably on a bed of moist seaweed or newspaper.
To clean: When cooked whole, no cleaning is necessary. If lobsters are halved, pull the head sac out of both halves and remove the intestine (it will probably only be in one half) with your fingers or tweezers. To remove the meat from a parboiled or fully cooked lobster, start by twisting the knuckles and claws off the body. Next twist the tail off the carcass, shown below left. Roll the tail on a hard surface while pressing down with your hand to crack the shell, allowing you to peel it almost like a shrimp, shown below left. The tail contains the largest piece of meat in the lobster, and the tail fins contain small bits of tasty meat which can be squeezed out. Crack open the claws with a nutcracker or a swift blow with a heavy knife, shown below right. Remove the meat in the knuckles by cracking open the shells or cutting them with kitchen shears. Snap off the 8 legs; on larger lobsters, there is good meat in these. Snap each in half and use a skewer to push the meat out. There are also small bits of meat in the carcass. Lift the protective shell, or carapace, from where it met the tail—it should come right off. Crack open the carcass lengthwise and pick out the meat between the gills and the legs. The tomalley and roe, shown 492 (bottom), can also be removed.
Best cooking techniques: Steaming or boiling, grilling, stir-frying.
Substitute: Shrimp.
When is it done? Lobster doneness is judged most easily by time, about 10 minutes per pound.

CRAB

Blue Crab, King Crab, Snow Crab, Dungeness Crab, Stone Crab

As you can see already, there are many species of edible crab. The list above comprises only those crabs that are commonly sold in the United States. But there are literally thousands of others, many of them equally delicious. The above, plus a few other species that are seen only locally, seem to be enough to keep most Americans happy. We will discuss them one at a time, but first a mention of what they have in common: They all have white, delicious meat that is just as good cold as hot, and they all must be sold live or cooked.

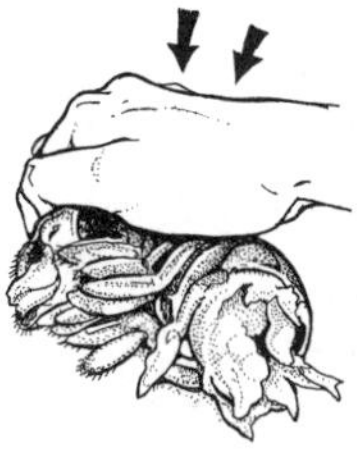

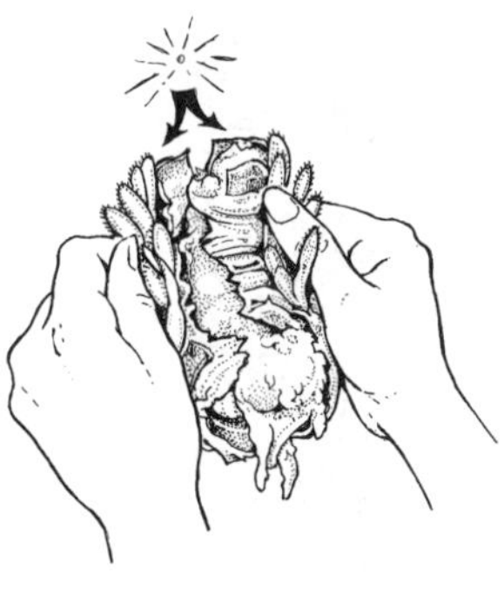

Cracking the lobster tail so that you can peel off the shell

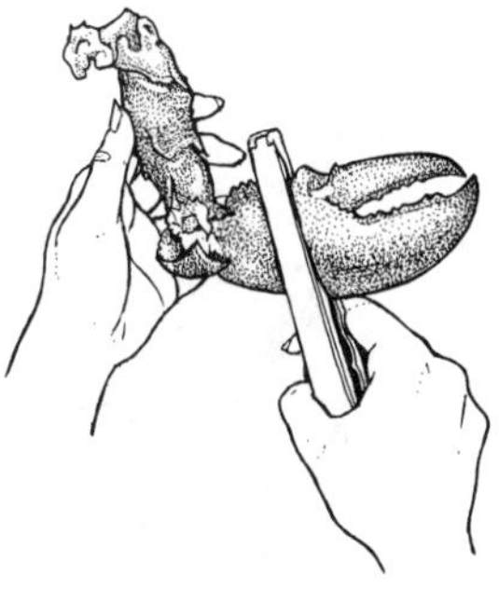

Cracking the lobster claws

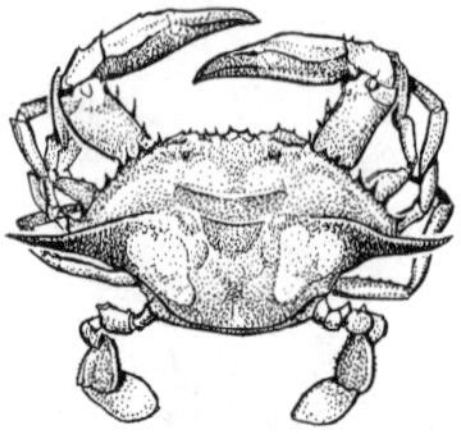

Blue crab

Blue Crab: The ubiquitous crab of the Atlantic and Gulf Coasts, these appear essentially in three forms: whole, most frequently sold live; soft-shell, sold live or very fresh; and as picked crabmeat. The last is probably the most familiar form for most shoppers. It is always worth it to buy the best meat, usually called lump crabmeat, which is made up of the relatively large chunks of meat found in the crab's body. Other grades—claw or flake—do not give as much satisfaction. If possible (and it is possible, especially in the big cities and seafood ports of the East Coast), buy fresh-picked rather than pasteurized crabmeat, for the flavor is noticeably better.

Whole blue crabs are sold in markets. They are a nuisance to clean and pick yourself; the yield is somewhere between 10 and 15 percent (you would have to pick 7 to 10 crabs to obtain 1 pound meat) and, unless you are highly skilled, each crab will take you about 10 minutes to clean. So if you want meat for recipes, buy prepicked lump crabmeat.

There are, however, two very good reasons to buy live blue crabs. One is that they make great additions to soups and sauces. Simply clean them and add them to any simmering soup, tomato sauce, or other sauce. When the dish is done, discard the crab; its meat will have added tremendous flavor. The other is to prepare traditional steamed crabs, 513.

Soft-shell crabs are blue crabs that have shed their old shells—they do so in order to grow—and whose new shells have not yet hardened. This window of opportunity lasts only a few hours, but if you remove the crabs from the water during that time, the shells remain soft. At that point, soft-shells are either shipped live or cleaned and frozen. Although you sometimes can get the fishmonger to do it for you, cleaning a live soft-shell is not difficult.

Where found: On the Atlantic and Gulf Coasts, but often shipped everywhere.

To buy: Whole blue crabs must be alive and kicking, or cooked. Soft-shells must be alive (packed in straw, paper, or seaweed, they will not be very active, but will smell wonderful), cooked, or frozen. Crabmeat is packed in containers, fresh (which is best), frozen, or pasteurized.

To store: Live crabs or soft-shells: In the refrigerator, on ice; use as quickly as possible. Picked crabmeat: In the refrigerator or frozen.

To clean: Soft-shells: Shown below. First, snip off the eyes and mouth with a pair of scissors. Pull back each side of the top shell and pull out and discard the inedible gills. Then turn the crab over and pull off the little flap called the "apron." Live blue crabs: Shown 495. Plunge into boiling water for 30 seconds or until dead. Twist off the apron. Pull off the top shell, then clean out the stringy gills, also called "dead man's fingers" found under both sides of the shell. Lift out the crabmeat, discarding any bits of shell or cartilage. Crack the claws with a mallet or rolling pin and pull out the meat. To eat cooked blue crabs, remove and crack open the two large front

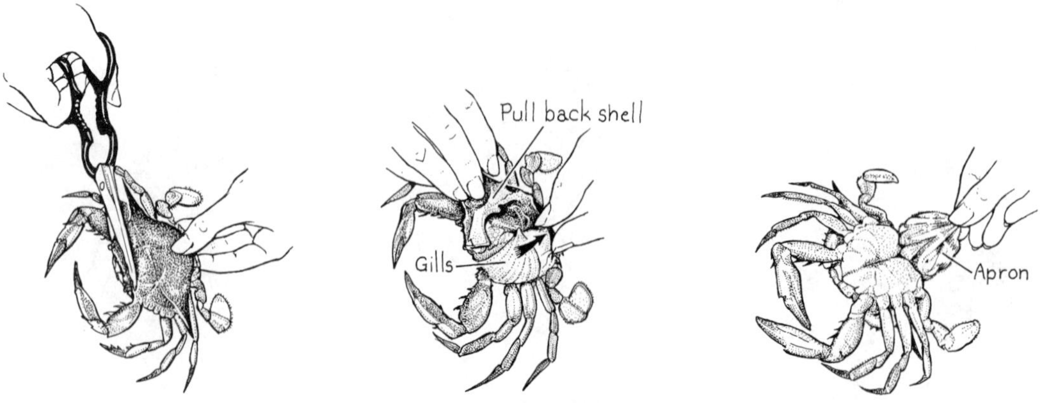

Cleaning a soft-shell crab

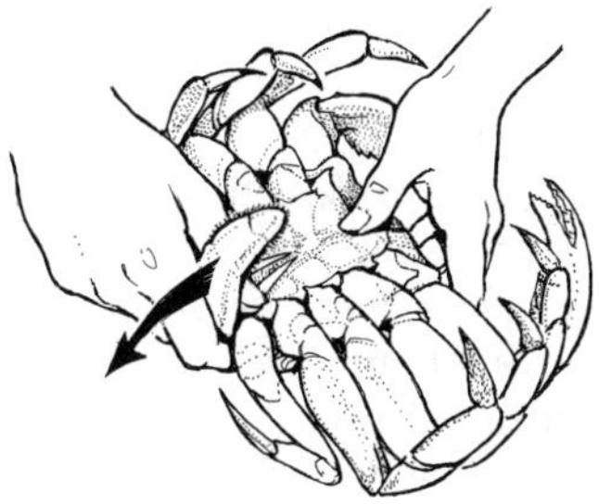

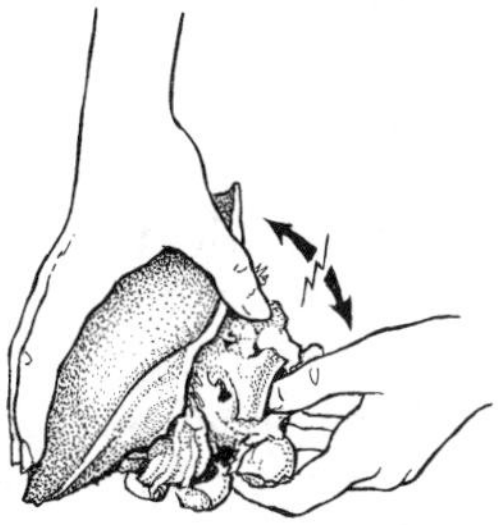

Cleaning a hard-shell crab

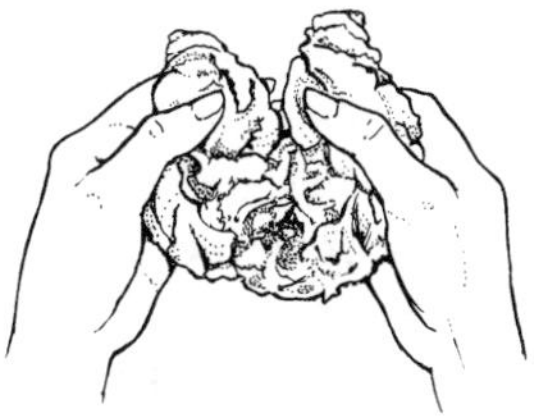

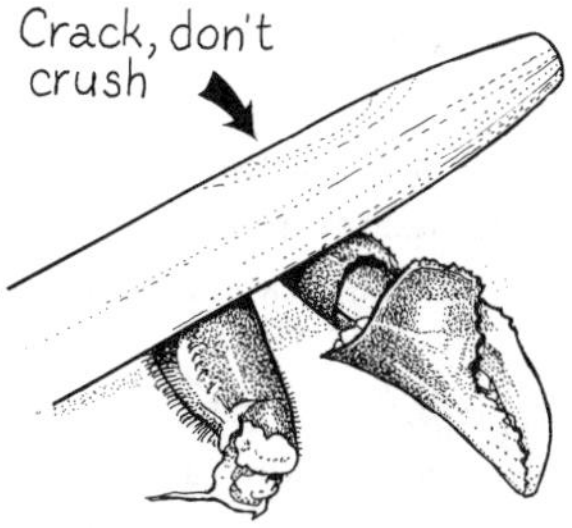

claws, then pull off the top shell and remove the two nuggets of meat toward the head. Pick out the meat between the gills and the legs and remove the tomalley and roe from the carcass.

Best cooking techniques: Soft-shells: Deep-frying, sautéing, or grilling. Live blue crabs: Boiling, steaming, or in sauces or soups. Crabmeat: In crab cakes, salads, or stir-fries.

Similar shellfish: Other crabs.

When is it done? Soft-shells: As soon as each side is crisp or red. Blue crabs: When the shell is bright pink. If boiled, about 5 minutes after the water returns to a boil.

King Crab: The huge crab of Alaska, its body contains little meat, and it is too big (up to 20 pounds) to ship live. Usually the legs and claws are cooked separately, then split, frozen, and shipped. This makes them perfect for a very quick meal; the legs can be thawed and heated up, or eaten cold, or even steamed for a few minutes without thawing. Buy legs, not claws—that is where the meat is.

Snow Crab: Smaller than king crab, snow crab is often sold the same way: cooked and frozen. Snow crab has a lower meat-to-shell ratio than king crab but is usually much less expensive.

Where found: Fished in Alaska, frozen or canned and shipped everywhere.

To buy: Look for split, frozen legs, without freezer burn.

To store: Store frozen, well wrapped, until ready to use. Thaw in the refrigerator or cook without thawing.

To clean: No cleaning is necessary.

Best cooking techniques: Steaming, grilling, roasting. Do not overcook or it will dry out.

Similar shellfish: Other crabs, lobster.

When is it done? As soon as it is hot; most king crab legs and snow crabs are sold precooked.

Dungeness Crab: The beautiful, sweet-tasting mid-sized crab of the West Coast, its meat is similar to that of lobster. Because keeping them alive is more difficult and costly than it is with lobster, these crabs—like king and snow crabs—are precooked and frozen. They often are thawed and simply served cold but, of course, can be steamed like lobster or other crabs.

Where found: Fished up and down the West Coast; cooked and frozen and shipped everywhere,

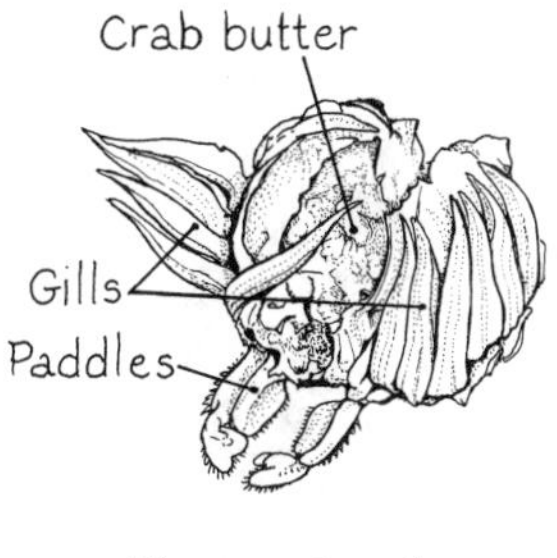

The parts of a crab

although far more common in the West than in the East.

To buy: Buy whole, well-wrapped crabs, without freezer burn.

To store: Store frozen, well wrapped, until ready to use. Thaw in the refrigerator or cook without defrosting.

To clean: No cleaning is necessary. To eat, twist off the apron, the folded part of the bottom shell. Pull off the top shell; remove and discard the gills, the stringy material near the tops of the legs. Break or cut into halves or quarters and pick out the meat; crack the claws with a nutcracker or rolling pin and pull out the meat. Snip off the shell on the legs and lift out the meat with a skewer.

Best cooking techniques: Precooked and often served cold. Can be steamed, broiled, roasted, or grilled.

Similar shellfish: Other crabs, lobster.

When is it done? As soon as it is thawed or hot; almost all Dungeness crabs are sold precooked.

Stone Crab: This is the "recyclable" crab of Florida. When the crab is caught, one claw is snapped off and the crab is returned to the water (it is illegal to take whole stone crabs), where it will grow another claw. As with West Coast crabs, the claw is almost always cooked immediately. You eat the claws by smacking the (very hard) shell with a hammer or similar implement and picking out the meat. They are good with Mustard Mayonnaise, 73, or any vinaigrette, 236 to 238.

Where found: Florida and the Gulf Coast; shipped elsewhere.

To buy: Cold, cooked, and sweet smelling.

To store: In the refrigerator; use as quickly as possible.

To clean: No cleaning is needed.

Best cooking techniques: They are already cooked. Eat cold, by smacking the shell with a hammer and picking out the meat.

Similar shellfish: Other crabs.

Crayfish

When is it done? Almost always precooked.

A Note about Surimi: Surimi, often sold as "crab food" or "seafood" or "sea legs," is not crab. Rather, it is a highly processed form of white fillets (usually, but not always, Pacific pollock) designed to look like crabmeat, which it does—right down to the pinkish red edges, which are dyed on. There is nothing wrong with surimi, as long as you know what it is: an inexpensive processed form of seafood. It is not a substitute for crab in any real sense, although, combined with mayonnaise, it makes a good salad or sandwich.

CRAYFISH

Crayfish, called crawfish in the South, are essentially freshwater shrimp, found and enjoyed all over the world; they look like miniature lobsters, right down to their little claws (which can pinch—beware). And, like lobster, crayfish is best bought live, stored live (for just a day or so), cooked live, and eaten simply. The only meat in a crayfish (other than that you might find with a microscope) is in its tail, so eating them is a simple affair: Twist the tail off the body and split it. The juices in the head are good too, and the creamy fat, usually orange or white, found between the body and the tail is delicious.

Where found: Worldwide; fished and farmed commercially on West and Gulf Coasts. Shipped live and frozen nationwide.

To buy: If alive, pick through to sort out dead ones. If frozen, the crayfish should be whole and individual.

To store: If alive, in the refrigerator, covered with a damp cloth or paper towel, for no more than a day or two.

To clean: Simply pick through and, again, discard any that are dead.

Best cooking techniques: Boiling.

Similar shellfish: Shrimp, lobster.

When is it done? Usually about 5 minutes after the water returns to a boil, or when red.

CLAMS

Soft-shell clams: Steamer, gaper, mud clam, geoduck (pronounced gooey-duck), razor clam, jackknife clam, etc.

Hard-shell clams: Quahogs (pronounced ko-hogs), littleneck, top neck, count neck, cherrystone, Manila clam, mahogany clam, chowder clam, sea clam, hard clam, cockle, surf clam, butter clam, etc.

There are dozens of types of clams, some usually eaten raw (see A Note about Shellfish Safety, 489),

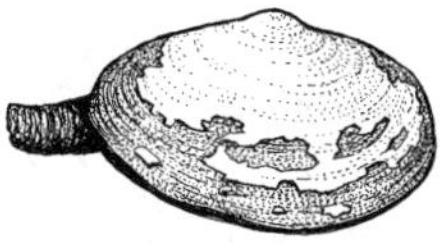

Soft-shell clam

Hard-shell clam

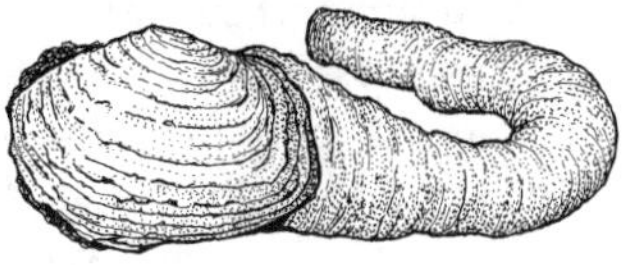

Geoduck

some always cooked. They fall, roughly, into two types: hard-shells and soft-shells. The differences are so great that they are worth treating separately.

Soft-shell clams: Soft-shell clams, shown above left, include the common steamers and the less frequently seen geoducks, razor clams, and several others with brittle, easily broken shells. Because they live with their shells partially open (a descriptive common name is "gapers"), and because they cannot close their shells once they are taken from the water (their "neck" or "foot" protrudes), they are usually so sandy that the meat itself must be purged of sand before eating. This can be accomplished by soaking in salted water (or seawater) for 2 hours or more, by repeated rinsing in fresh water, or—as is commonly done with steamers—by dunking the meat itself in clam broth (essentially the cooking water) after cooking.

Although they are easy to shuck, soft-shell clams are never eaten raw; the small varieties are usually steamed or deep-fried. Larger species, such as the enormous geoduck, are cut up and added to chowders and soups.

Where found: Worldwide.

To buy: Soft-shell clams must be alive (or cooked, canned, or frozen) when you buy them. The smell should be appealing, the shell should resist further opening, and the "neck" should move a bit when you touch it. Also, the less sand you feel, the easier they will be to clean.

To store: Not in a sealed plastic bag, where they will suffocate. Preferably in a bowl or mesh bag, in the refrigerator, covered lightly with a damp towel. Ice is not necessary; mollusks stay alive for days, at 40°F.

To clean: The best way, if you have the time, is to soak them in heavily salted water (about one part salt to ten parts water), refrigerated, for several hours or overnight. If you are in a rush or the clams are not too sandy (steam one and try it), just rinse them in several changes of fresh water until no sand falls to the bottom of the bowl. (This method is just fine for steamed clams, which you will rinse in clam broth before eating.)

To shuck: Cut open the shell with a knife as with oysters, 502, and cut the clam from the shell. Slit the skin of the "neck," or siphon, and pull off the tough neck skin.

Best cooking techniques: Steaming, deep-frying, in soups and chowders, cut up if large.

Substitute: Mussels.

When is it done? If steamed, when the shell pops open, usually 3 to 5 minutes after the steaming liquid boils. If fried, as soon as the crust is browned. In soups and chowders: whole, 3 to 5 minutes; cut up, almost instantly.

Hard-shell clams: Hard-shell clams, shown above center, vary more in size and color than in shape or form. But vary they do, from the tiny cockle (not, strictly speaking, a true clam but close enough for culinary purposes), less than an inch across, to the giant sea clam, which may weigh hundreds of pounds, and from the bleached white littlenecks and cherrystones of the Atlantic coast to the aptly named mahogany clam, harvested in deeper waters. All have firm, sometimes tough, meat with excellent, briny flavor. And all have the distinct advantage of being essentially free of grit internally.

There is some confusion about nomenclature of hard-shell clams, but the common names relate primarily to size:

Littlenecks: The smallest hard-shell, under 2 inches across (preferably considerably under). Good eaten raw or cooked. Manila clams are about the same size and are also good raw.

Cherrystones: In some areas, 2 to 3 inches across, in others, up to 4 inches. Can still be eaten raw, flavor is good, but may be tough. Excellent for cooking. Mahogany clams are the same size. There are also some excellent varieties that are steely gray, just about blue, in color.

Quahogs or chowder clams: In some areas, quahog is a generic name for hard-shells, but in others, it refers to those clams over 3 to 4 inches across. They are too tough for raw eating and too big for eating whole. Cut up and use in soups, stews, chowders.

Other hard-shell varieties are rarely sold in their shells but are cooked and cut up as clam meat for chowder or sauce.

Where found: There are more hard-shells found on the East Coast than the West, but all species ship well and are available throughout the country.

To buy: Hard-shell clams must be alive (or cooked, canned, or frozen) when you buy them. The smell should be appealing, and the shell should be intact and virtually impossible to pry open. Some hard-shell clams are farm-raised, but it is unlikely you will notice any difference.

To store: Not in a sealed plastic bag, where they will suffocate. Preferably in a bowl or mesh bag, in the refrigerator, covered lightly with a damp towel. Ice is not necessary; mollusks stay alive for days, at 40°F.

To clean: Rinse a few times. If the shell is very gritty, scrub with a vegetable brush.

To shuck: For use in recipes, shuck by steaming or microwaving, just until the shells pop open. To shuck raw, use a sturdy paring knife (or a clam knife) to pry open the clam opposite its hinge. Once the knife is in, take care to move it along the top shell so you do not cut the meat itself in half. Scrape the meat off the bottom shell, preserving as much of the juice as you can, shown below. If you are a novice, be aware that shucking raw hard-shells is an acquired skill, and requires patience.

Best cooking techniques: The smaller clams, which have the best flavor, are versatile: they can be enjoyed raw, lightly sautéed or grilled in their shells, or steamed. The larger ones are shucked by steaming and used—cut up if necessary—in soups, stews, and chowders.

Substitute: Oysters.

When is it done? Smaller clams: As soon as the shell pops open, usually about 5 minutes (if you prefer a firmer, less raw texture, steam, microwave, sauté, or grill for an extra minute or two). Larger cherrystones: Whole, a few minutes longer. In soups and chowders: Smaller clams, whole, 2 to 3 minutes; cut-up clams, almost instantly.

MUSSELS

Blue mussels, shown 499, are the most common variety. New Zealand green-lipped mussels, are also good and can be used interchangeably.

The quality of mussels is difficult to judge in the store, and their meat, is firm, plump, large, sweet, and clean at its best. You can be certain you are buying live mussels, but you cannot be certain you are buying delicious ones. A wise policy is to identify the source the next time you have good mussels and try to stay with it. Many retailers buy their mussels from the same source over and over, and they can be consistently fine. Some mussels are farm-raised (they are grown on ropes), and their advocates claim that these are more consistent than wild mussels.

You can gather your own mussels—they grow in temperate shallow water all over the world, and there are even freshwater varieties—but water quality is all-important. See A Note about Shellfish Safety, 489, and check with local health or game authorities before gathering mussels (or any other mollusk).

Where found: Worldwide in temperate waters.

To buy: Some mussel shells are beautifully clean and shiny; others are encrusted with barnacles and other evidence of life at sea. Neither is an indication of quality. Like clams and oysters, mussels must be alive (or cooked) at the time of purchase. The smell should be appealing and the shell intact. Reject any with broken shells or those that seem unusually light or heavy (they may be empty or filled with mud). Gaping is okay, but live mussels will close—slowly but surely—when you squeeze or tap the shell.

To store: Not in a sealed plastic bag, where they will suffocate. Preferably in a bowl or mesh bag, in the refrigerator, covered lightly with a damp towel. Ice is not necessary; mollusks stay alive for days at 40°F.

To clean: Remove the "beard," the hairy vegetative growth attached to the shell, shown 499 (top right). You can usually just tug it off or cut it with a knife.

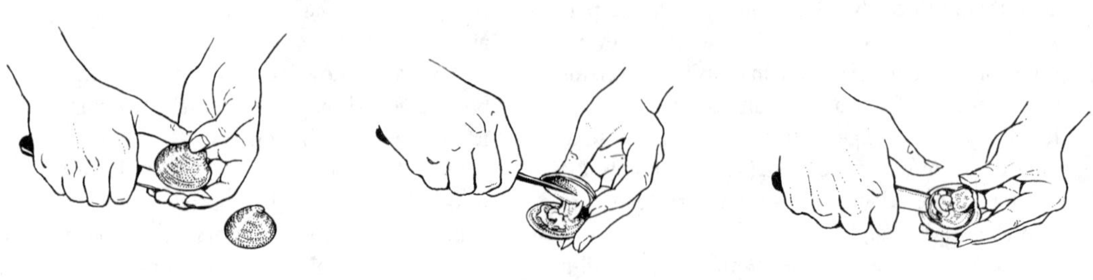

Shucking a clam

Black mussel

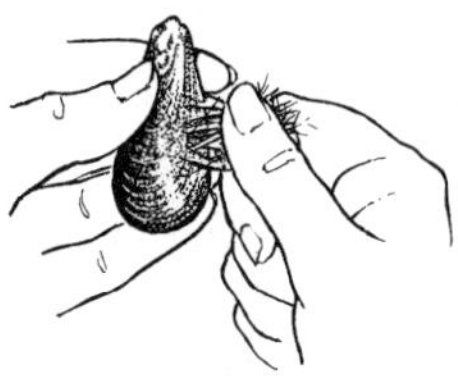

Removing the beard from a mussel

Wash the mussels in several changes of cold water (if time allows, place them in a pot and run a slow stream of cold water over them for an hour or so, no longer). Keep washing until the water runs clear. Sort through the mussels and discard any with damaged shells.

To shuck: Almost always done by steaming. You can cut raw mussels (see A Note about Shellfish Safety, 489) from the shell with a knife, too, but a light presteaming does no harm unless you are planning to eat them raw.

Best cooking techniques: Mussels are best steamed. They can also be grilled, roasted, or broiled.

Substitute: Soft-shell clams.

When is it done? As soon as the shells pop open and the meat firms up, less than 10 minutes after the steaming water returns to a boil. Discard any that refuse to open.

SCALLOPS

Calico Scallops, Sea Scallops, Bay Scallops, Pink Scallops

When you buy shucked scallops, you are buying the relatively huge abductor muscle that the scallop uses to open and shut its shell. The fact that scallops are shucked and cleaned almost immediately after capture is, in one way, a shame, for the red roe and ivory milt of scallops—loosely attached to the muscle and supremely creamy in texture when cooked—are exceptionally delicious. But it gives the muscle a longer shelf life, because it is not in contact with the more fragile innards. Scallops are the one mollusk most often sold shucked but not cooked. If you have a chance to buy live scallops still in their shell, do so; shucking is easy, and the meat will be wonderful, even raw (see A Note about Shellfish Safety, 489). Save the shells—they can be used and reused for serving scallops (you can also buy shells in many gourmet stores).

Scallop

Calico: These are the tiny scallops—smaller than the last joint on your pinkie—usually sold in supermarkets, frequently at very appealing prices. They can be good, but extreme care must be taken not to overcook them, for two reasons. One, their size makes shucking them by hand unprofitable, so they are steamed open, which means they are partly cooked when you buy them. And two, they are so small that they need only 2 to 3 minutes' cooking by most methods. Keep them tender and they are worth eating; overcook them and they turn to rubber.

Sea: These can be quite large (some shells are the size of salad plates) but remain tender no matter what the size. Those that are shucked at sea may be soaked in a bath of water and tripolyphosphate; this process both extends their shelf life and artificially increases the weight of the meat. You want to make every effort to buy unsoaked ("dry") scallops. They taste better, and they brown better (because they contain less water). Be suspicious of any sea scallops that are pure white, a good indication that they have been soaked; the natural color of sea scallops ranges from white to off-white to pale shades of orange, pink, and tan.

Individually quick frozen (IQF) sea scallops can be a good buy and usually retain most of their flavor—sometimes more than older "fresh" scallops.

Bay: Most people agree that these cork-shaped, off-white specimens are the most flavorful scallops. Their wild range is very, very small, concentrated in an area between Long Island and Cape Cod. This, combined with their short season—November through February—makes them scarce. But they are extraordinary and the best scallops for eating raw. Take care not to pay for bay scallops when you are buying calico scallops; the former are usually off-white, the latter flat white and much smaller.

About ten years ago, a group of Chinese entrepreneurs brought a bucket of bay scallops home from Nantucket and began to cultivate them. Now, these farm-raised bay scallops are sold everywhere and, although their flavor is not as superb as that of the wild variety, they are much less expensive and quite good. Just make sure you are buying true bays and not the much smaller, whiter calicos labeled as such.

Pink: From the Puget Sound, these are sold live, in the shell, and steamed open, like mussels. They are rarely seen outside of the Northwest.

Where found: Calicos and sea scallops are sold everywhere; wild bay scallops rarely make it out of the Northeast, but the farmed varieties are becoming quite common; pink scallops almost never leave the Northwest.

To buy: Select sweet-smelling scallops with no traces of dryness or browned edges.

To store: In the refrigerator, on ice if possible. Cook immediately. If you have live scallops, cook them or store whole in the refrigerator.

To clean: Shucked scallops have a small hinge on one side that is tough and chewy; if you like, peel it right off, shown below left (this is not necessary with small calicos). Rinse the meat very lightly to remove any sand.

To shuck: Since scallops gape naturally, they are easy to shuck. Open the shell with any knife, then scoop out the muscle (and red or white roe, if any). Discard the dark innards and remove the stark-white "hinge" attached to the side of the muscle.

Best cooking techniques: Truly fresh scallops are wonderful raw. Calicos are best very lightly sautéed. Sea and bay scallops can be cooked any way you like. Pink scallops are usually steamed.

Substitute: Shrimp.

When is it done? In the opinion of many, the interior of scallops should remain cool, creamy, and almost raw. Others prefer them cooked through, although not to the point of rubberiness. All scallops cook quickly; check calicos and pinks (by eating one) after 2 minutes. Check larger bays and seas after 3 to 4 minutes. No scallop will take longer than 6 to 8 minutes to cook.

OYSTERS

Eastern, Pacific or Japanese, European Flat, Olympia, Kumamoto

There are five species of oysters grown commercially in North America. Two are indigenous: The Eastern *Crassostrea virginica,* which is found from Nova Scotia to Texas, and the tiny Olympia *Ostrea lurida,* once plentiful from San Francisco to Washington State and now grown only in a few small bays in southern Puget Sound.

The European Flat *Ostrea edulis* is now raised by half-shell growers on both coasts. The Pacific oyster *Crassostrea gigas* was brought from Japan to Washington State in the 1920s to replace the Olympia oyster, which was near extinction at the time. The Pacific oyster is now the predominant oyster on the West Coast (and in Europe, since the 1970s).

The small, deep-cupped Kumamoto *Crassostrea sikamea* was brought to Washington State experimentally in 1947 as a replacement for the cherished but declining Olympia oyster. The Kumamoto is now thought to be extinct in the Kumamoto prefecture in southern Japan where it originated but is now grown by several West Coast half-shell growers and has become the sweetheart of the half-shell trade.

But—most people say, amazed—if there are only five kinds of oysters, what about Malpeque (P.E.I.),

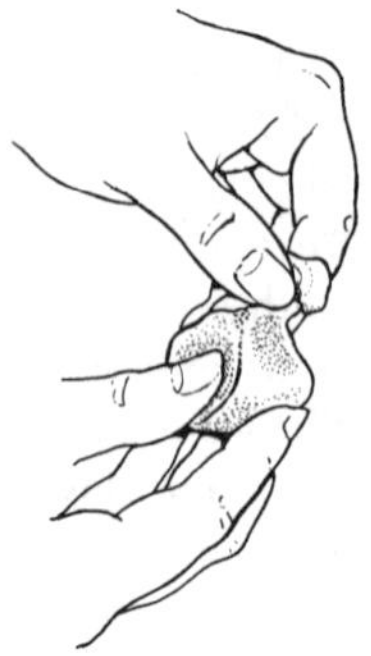

Peeling the hinge off the shucked scallop

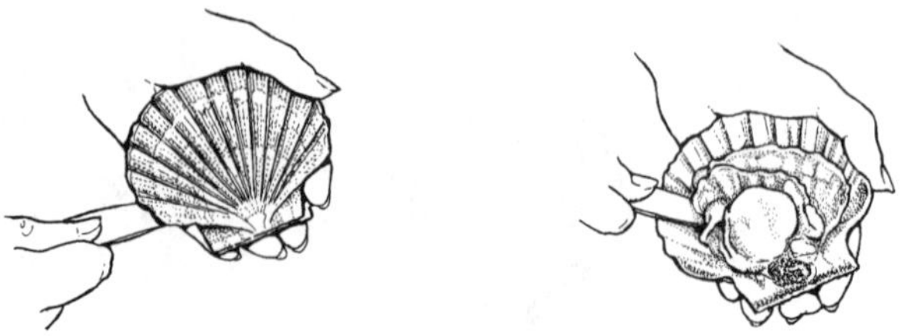

Shucking a scallop

Pine Island (NY), Apalachicola (FL), Steamboat Island (WA), Fisher's Island (NY), Cotuit (MA), Westcott Flat (WA), Pemaquid (ME), Snow Creek (WA), Hog Island (CA), Quilcene (WA), Holmes Harbor Flat (WA), Kegotauk Salts (VA), and the dozens of others heard of and seen?

According to two thousand years of history and tradition, oysters are named not by their species, but by the bay, town, or region in which they are grown. It is pretty simple, really, once you get the hang of it, and it helps you to pick favorites because—believe it or not—the flavor of oysters is so dependent on the water they filter through their bodies that Martha's Vineyard oysters usually taste quite different from Nantucket oysters.

These days oysters are shipped overnight from one coast to the other, making it possible to sometimes find all five species on a restaurant menu or in a fish store. To help clear up any confusion this may cause, many are using Latin names as well as the market names to distinguish one species from another. As for the "R" months rule—that is, only eat oysters in months which have an "r" in them, September through April—it remains a good guideline for oyster consumption. Oysters certainly can be eaten in the summer, but the risks from bacteria, which love the warmer water of summer, are greater. In addition, oysters in most areas are spawning, a process called "gameto genesis" when the stored glycogen, which gives the oyster its sweet taste and firm texture, is given over to gamete production. The texture changes from firm to milky, the taste from sweet to bitter. In the post-spawning recovery period, oysters are thin without sweetness or complexity and taste mostly of brine. The one notable exception to the "R" month rule is the Kumamoto, which is actually best in summer. They spawn in September or October.

As for the differences among the species:

Eastern: Grown all along the East and Gulf Coasts, this oyster, shown below, has an oval shell that is sometimes uneven in shape and form. At its best, the Eastern oyster is crisp and briny; it has little complexity but gives a delightful hit of strong, delicious, mineral-laden salt. Usually but not always, it is best from northern waters. Southern oysters tend to be larger, softer, and less flavorful; as a result, it is best to use them for cooking. Some typical names: Wellfleet, Apalachicola, or any other town, island, or body of water with clean growing waters along the East or Gulf Coasts.

Pacific or Japanese: Known for its fluted shell and unusual flavors, this is the oyster, shown below, that is most commonly grown on the West Coast and in Western Europe. Once you see it and the Eastern together, you will forever know the difference. The Pacific oyster's taste varies widely but is always distinctive, ranging from cucumber to watermelon but almost always with

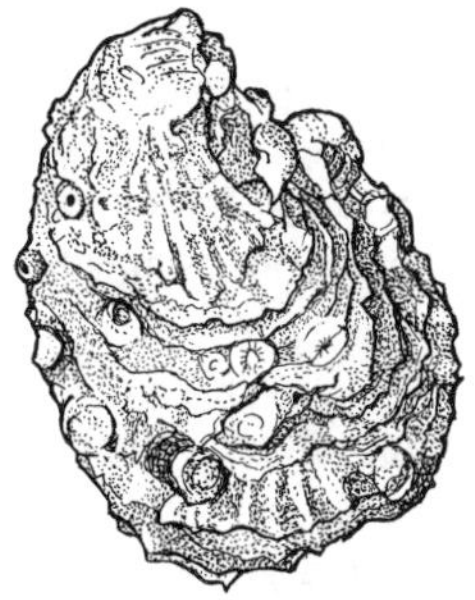

Eastern oyster

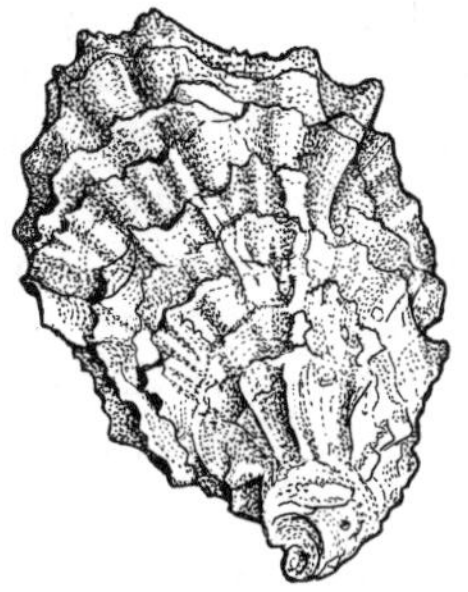

Pacific or Japanese oyster

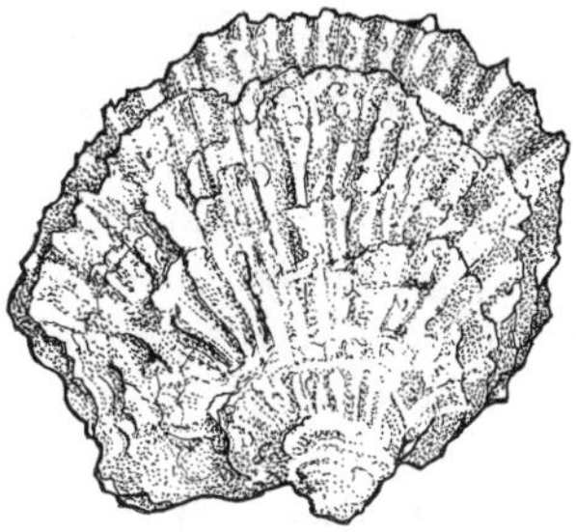

European flat oyster

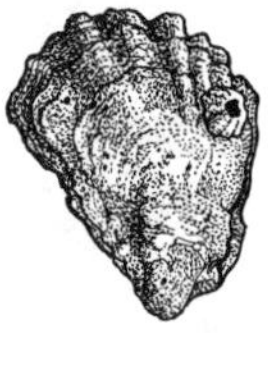

Olympia oyster

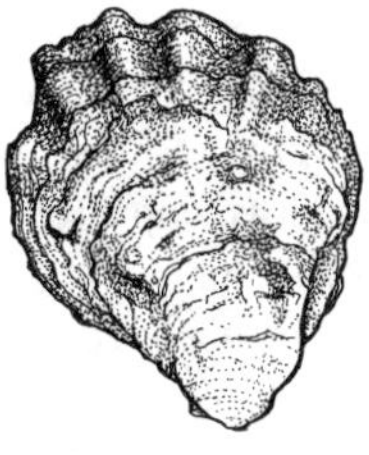

Kumamoto oyster

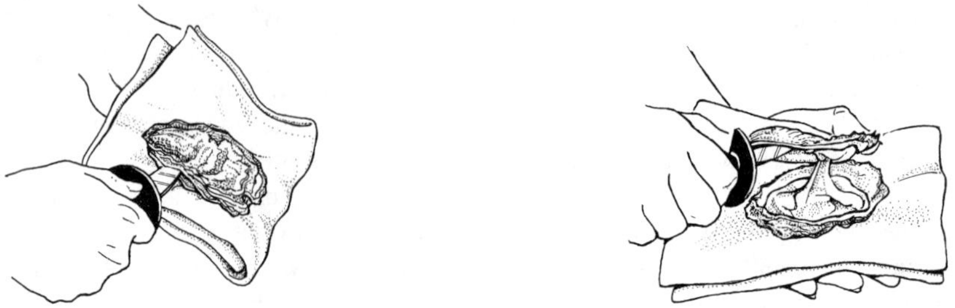

Shucking an oyster

a fruitiness that is not present in other oysters. Some typical names: Quilcene, Hama-Hama, or any other town, island, or body of water in the Pacific Northwest.
European Flat: The original and, some maintain, "true" oyster, shown 501, grown in Europe, the Northwest, and a few spots in Maine and elsewhere. It has a distinctively round, flat shell (it is most commonly called the flat or, in French, *plat*). The flavor is decidedly metallic—you either love it or hate it, but it is certainly worth trying. These are best enjoyed raw. Some typical names: Snow Creek Flats, Holmes Harbor Flats.
Olympia: The half-dollar-sized oyster, shown 501, is indigenous to the Northwest and grown only there. Not unlike the flat in flavor. So tiny that eating them is almost a game. Rarely seen outside of the Northwest except in restaurants.

Unquestionably, the best way to eat the finest oysters is raw on the half-shell (see A Note about Shellfish Safety, 489). See below for shucking instructions. Good oysters are expensive, and even those with strong flavors are readily tamed by heat. If you are cooking oysters, buy relatively inexpensive, preshucked oysters, which are usually Eastern oysters from the South. Keep the cooking times as short as possible; as soon as the edges begin to curl, they are done.

Where found: Ubiquitous.

To buy: Oyster beds are certified and inspected; ask to see the tag if you want to be sure of your purchase. Shells should be tightly closed, impossible to budge. In some states, preshucked oysters have a packing or "sell by" date on the container.

To store: Not in a sealed plastic bag, where they will suffocate. Preferably in a bowl or mesh bag, in the refrigerator, covered lightly with a damp towel. Ice is not necessary; mollusks stay alive for days at 40°F.

To clean: Use a stiff brush and scrub the shells thoroughly, in particular the often-encrusted Eastern and European oysters (Pacific oysters tend to be cleaner).

To shuck: Hold the oyster, deep shell down, firmly in a folded kitchen towel over a bowl. Insert the point of an oyster knife, which has a strong pointed blade and protective shield, into the hinge between the shells at the pointed end of the oyster. Turn the knife to pry open and lift the upper shell enough to cut through the hinge muscle. Run the knife point between the shells to open, shown above. Once open, scrape the oyster from its shell, but do not remove it. Nestle the shells in some ice or rock salt to keep them from tipping over. Strain any liquor in the bowl and pour it over the oysters. Serve raw on the half-shell with Mignonette Sauce, 506. You can steam, microwave, or grill or roast oysters open. And, if you are careful, you can catch them before they cook through, so they will still retain good flavor and texture.

Best cooking techniques: In stews, chowders, and soups, grilling or broiling, deep-frying.

Substitute: Hard-shell clams.

When is it done? When the edges curl, almost immediately. An overcooked oyster is tough, dry, and rubbery, and it can reach that state in less than 5 minutes.

ABALONE

The abalone is an ear-shaped univalve. Its delicious meat resides within its beautiful shell, which is iridescent mother-of-pearl inside, pink, red, green, or black outside. Wild American abalone, native to the Pacific

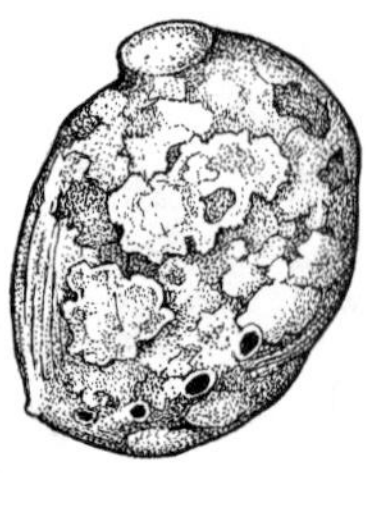

Abalone

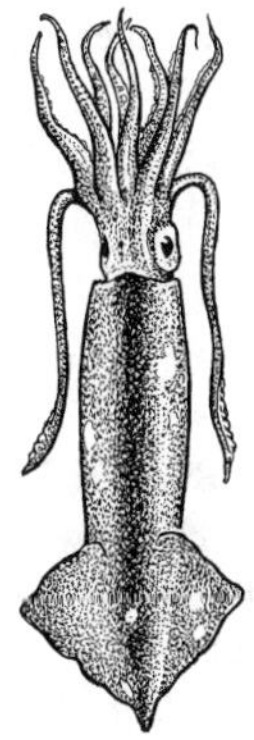

Squid

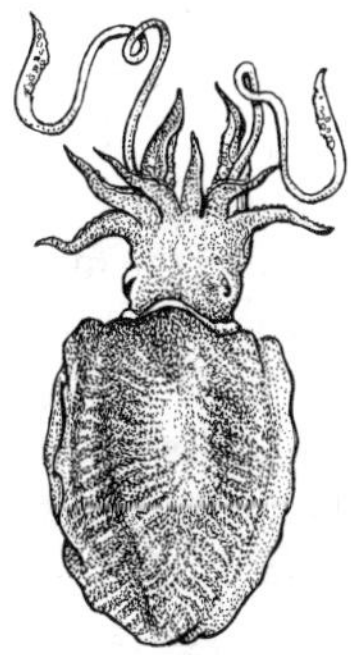

Cuttlefish

off Alaska and California, is in dwindling and controlled supply, but baby varieties are farmed in Hawaii and California. Abalone is rare and always expensive. If you are fortunate enough to find it live, enjoy the meat and save the gorgeous shell.

Where found: Live, occasionally in California. Canned or frozen in Asian stores throughout the country. Prepounded frozen abalone can be very good.

To buy: If in the shell, it must be alive and the meat should glisten.

To store: If alive, refrigerate and eat within a day.

To clean: If alive, shuck and trim off innards; you eat only the large muscle.

Best cooking techniques: As for conch (thinly slice and eat raw) or squid (cook for a minute or two).

Similar shellfish: Conch.

When is it done? Almost instantly.

SQUID

Squid, with its mild, sweet, and nutty flavor, is easy to cook, freezes beautifully, and is in good supply on both the East and West coasts. The trick to cooking squid is timing. To preserve its tenderness, squid needs to be cooked either quickly over very high heat, as when fried or grilled, or very slowly over low heat, as when braised. Anything in between, and it will be tough and chewy.

Cuttlefish, shown above right, which is closely related to squid, is widely eaten in Europe and Asia and occasionally makes its way to our markets. Its flavor and texture are similar to those of squid, and it can be prepared in the same way.

Where found: Worldwide. Sold frozen everywhere, fresh in coastal markets but spottily elsewhere.

To buy: As with shrimp, frozen (and cleaned) if top-quality fresh is not available. Figure at least 8 ounces raw, cleaned squid per person, as it shrinks formidably during cooking.

To store: If frozen, do not thaw until the day before you are ready to cook it. If fresh or thawed, keep on or in a bed of ice, with drainage for melting ice. Keep iced until ready to cook. Squid is more perishable than most seafood.

To clean: Grasp the squid's head and innards as far inside the body as you can; pull gently. If the translucent "quill" remains inside, remove it by itself. Using the dull edge of a knife, scrape any remaining

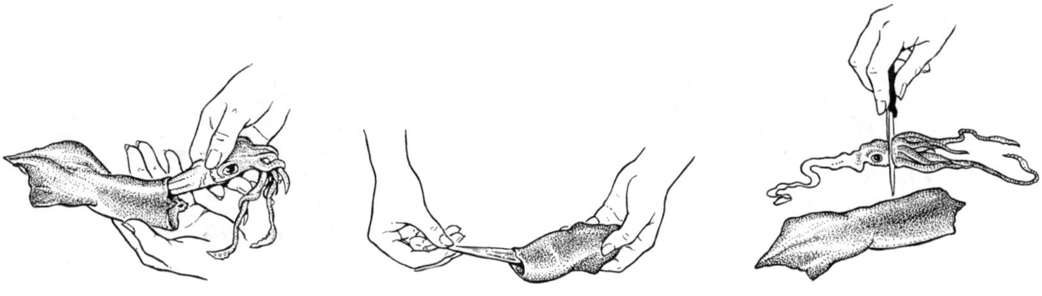

Cleaning a squid

innards from the body. Just above the squid's eyes is a hard ball, called the "beak," which creates a slight bulge. Cut the tentacles above that bulge, then squeeze them until the beak pops out. Discard the beak, head, and innards and reserve the tentacles. With your fingers, peel the mottled purple skin off the body—it usually comes off in one or two pieces—and off of the tentacles of large squid. Rinse the tentacles and bodies and dry well. The bodies can be sliced into rings, good for most preparations, or left whole to be stuffed. The tentacles can be divided into smaller pieces or left whole for most preparations, or chopped to make stuffing.

Best cooking techniques: Quickly: deep-frying, grilling, poaching, pan-grilling, sautéing, or broiling. Slowly: poaching, braising, or stewing.

Similar shellfish: Octopus, cuttlefish.

When is it done? When it is tender, from 2 to 3 minutes or over 60 minutes, but not at times in between.

OCTOPUS

Octopus is meaty, tender (when properly cooked), and delicious. Almost always sold cleaned (and often frozen), it only needs to be cooked. Most octopus at the market weigh in at 2 to 3 pounds; look for larger ones if possible, because shrinkage is formidable.

Octopus must be precooked to tenderize it (there are other methods—hurling it against rocks or the kitchen sink, or grating it with radish; but precooking is most reliable). To do so, simmer it in water to cover with 1 tablespoon of salt, 1 bay leaf, 2 crushed garlic cloves, and a few peppercorns. Test for tenderness after 45 minutes by piercing it with a thin-bladed knife; when the knife meets little resistance, the octopus is ready. It may take up to twice that long to become tender, so be patient. Remove from the water, then chill or proceed with any of the recipes in this chapter.

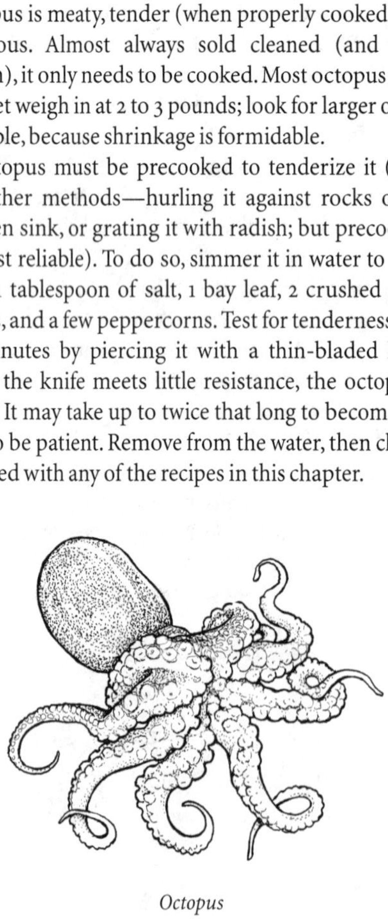

Octopus

Where found: Worldwide; shipped, usually frozen, to all markets.

To buy: Buy frozen if possible. If thawed, smell to ensure freshness.

To store: If frozen, in the freezer; thaw in the refrigerator or in cold water. If thawed, keep in the refrigerator on ice; use as soon as possible. Or precook and store, well wrapped and refrigerated, for a day or two.

To clean: Most are sold cleaned. If not, turn the head inside out and all its contents. Wash well. The skin is edible, although most of it will come off during cooking.

Best cooking techniques: After precooking, grilling or stewing.

Similar shellfish: Squid, cuttlefish.

When is it done? When tender.

SEA URCHIN

Sea urchins are an elusive luxury—you eat only about a quarter of their innards (the tan to orange roe or gonads), which usually means less than a mouthful per urchin. Still, at their best, they have a subtle yet briny and complex flavor, something like an undiscovered species of oyster. Like oysters, they are eminently enjoyable, especially with a squeeze of lemon.

Where found: Along all coastlines; fished commercially in Maine.

To buy: It is worth opening one sea urchin before buying; make sure the smell is good and that, indeed, there is roe.

To store: In the refrigerator, covered with a damp cloth or paper towel, for a day or two.

To open: Use scissors to enlarge the urchin's existing hole and remove a flap to gain access to the interior. Discard all but the tan or orange roe.

Best cooking techniques: Best raw.

CONCH AND WHELK

Conch and whelk are different, but in the kitchen they can be treated the same. In effect, they are both large

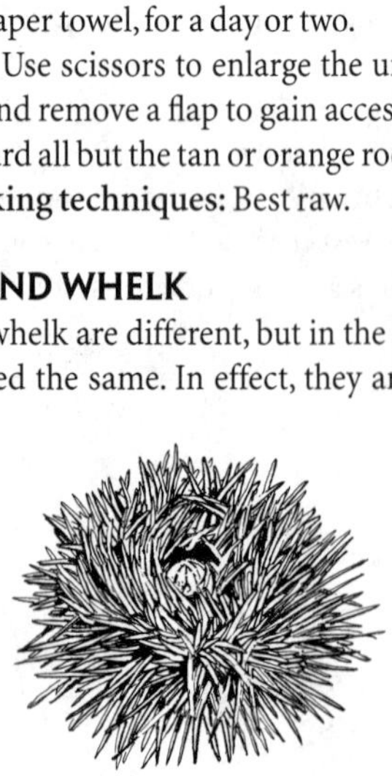

Sea urchin

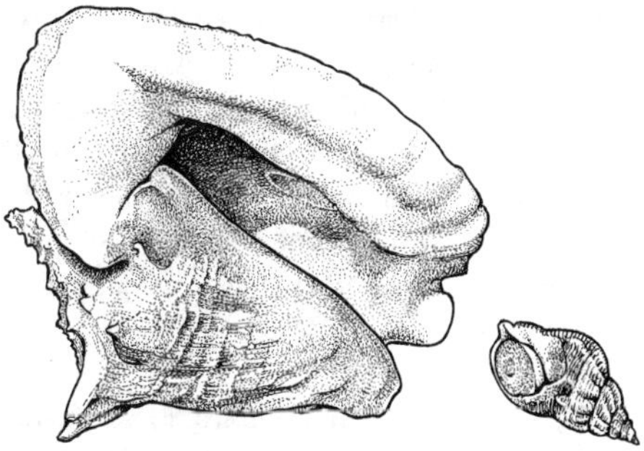

Conch and whelk

Periwinkles

snails and often are referred to as "sea snails." Most are cooked before being removed from the shell. If you buy them alive, just poach them in boiling water to cover for 3 to 5 minutes; once they are cooked, you can easily grab the meat with a fork or skewer and pull it out. (Or you can do as the Chinese do: Smack the shell with a heavy hammer and remove the meat.) Usually, each piece is quite substantial—4 ounces or so.

Conch and whelk are tender and delicious when raw or when cooked minimally. More often people cook the meat until it toughens and then becomes fairly tender again—like squid. Much whelk (especially when sold as scungilli, the Italian name for it) is removed from the shell, precooked to the point of near-tenderness, and frozen. This, of course, takes little work to prepare further.

Where found: Worldwide; usually sold frozen.

To buy: If whole, the "foot" will move when touched. If removed from the shell, it should be cooked and/or frozen.

To store: Alive, in the refrigerator, covered with a damp cloth or paper towel, for up to 3 days. Cooked, on ice, for a day or two.

To clean: See above for instructions on removing sea snails from their shells. Be sure to remove the hard protective disk (the operculum) attached to one end, for it is inedible.

Best cooking techniques: Raw, poached, cut up and incorporated into fritters, soups, stews, sauces, and chowders.

Similar shellfish: Hard-shell clams.

When is it done? When tender, or nearly so—after minimal cooking or up to an hour of simmering.

PERIWINKLES AND GARDEN SNAILS

The first of these are the tiny sea snails you can gather along the Atlantic Coast or sometimes find in markets; the second are the kind frequently sold in cans which are easier to handle (they are precooked), but not as flavorful. Periwinkles are delicious but take a bit of work. Cook them for 3 to 5 minutes in boiling water to cover, then remove them with a pin. Peel off the hard end of the meat (the operculum), if it has not fallen off already, and dip them in garlic butter before eating as a very light appetizer. Or chill and serve with Traditional Mayonnaise, 72. Garden snails, which have already been removed from their shells, can simply be roasted in garlic butter until heated through.

Where found: Atlantic Coast, limited availability.

To buy: If you do find them in a store, smell them first—the scent should be wonderfully briny. Check to see that most of them are alive; they are hardy and will move their "foot" if you touch it.

To store: In the refrigerator, covered with a damp cloth or paper towel, for up to a day.

To clean: Just rinse.

To shuck: Boil for 3 to 5 minutes, no longer, then refrigerate or eat hot. Remove from their shells with a pin or skewer.

Best cooking techniques: Boiling.

When is it done? When easily removed from the shell, just a few minutes.

FROGS' LEGS

The legs of large frogs do indeed taste like chicken—wings, to be specific—although some liken them to lobster.

Where found: Fresh, rarely, in the South and Midwest. Frozen in some supermarkets and fish stores.

To buy: Fresh, they must be fresh smelling (the faint scent of mud is acceptable). Frozen, without freezer burn. Figure at least six pairs per person.

To store: If fresh, refrigerate and eat within a day.

To clean: No preparation is needed.

Best cooking techniques: Fried or sautéed with butter and garlic.

When is it done? When firm and opaque throughout.

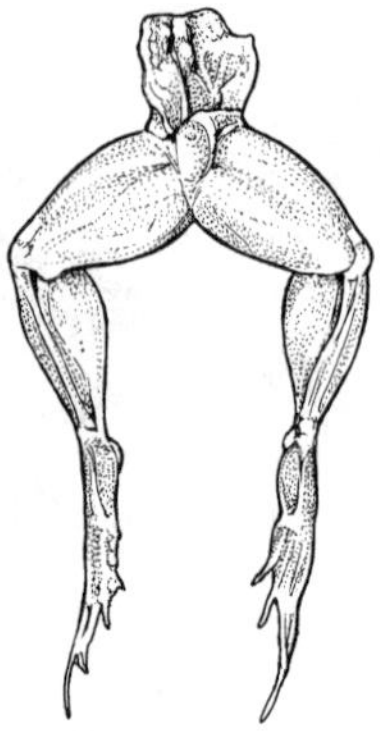

Frogs' legs

ABOUT RAW SHELLFISH

Raw shellfish is one of the world's great luxuries. This is especially true of oysters, which vary considerably in flavor and texture. But it is impossible to say this without mentioning that more illnesses are caused by eating raw shellfish than by eating all other fish combined. Please read A Note about Shellfish Safety, 489.

MIGNONETTE SAUCE

About ½ cup, enough for 24 oysters

This sauce is classic with oysters on the half-shell, but it is good with any raw shellfish.

Mix together well in a small bowl:

½ cup red wine vinegar
4 teaspoons finely chopped shallots
1 tablespoon finely chopped fresh parsley
2 teaspoons cracked black peppercorns
Salt to taste

Serve chilled or at room temperature. This sauce will keep, covered and refrigerated, for 2 to 3 days.

RASPBERRY MIGNONETTE

Prepare Mignonette Sauce, above, substituting raspberry vinegar for the red wine vinegar and adding 2 tablespoons fresh lemon juice.

CHAMPAGNE MIGNONETTE

Prepare Mignonette Sauce, above, substituting ¼ cup Champagne and ¼ cup Champagne vinegar for the red wine vinegar.

SCALLOP SEVICHE

4 servings

Seviche is "cooked" in the sense that the acid in the marinade changes the texture of the scallop just as heat would, but it is not "cooked" in the sense that all bacteria is destroyed. Use only perfectly fresh, carefully handled scallops and treat them as you would any food you plan to eat raw.

There are many directions in which you can take this basic recipe. Garnish with parsley if you use lemon juice, or scallions if you add soy; add ½ teaspoon or more red pepper flakes; top with minced fresh or sliced pickled ginger; or surround with Tomato Concassé, 433.

Cut into ⅛- to ¼-inch slices or small chunks:

1 pound sea or bay scallops, tough opaque part removed

Combine with:

½ cup fresh lemon or lime juice, or a combination
1 tablespoon soy sauce (optional)
½ teaspoon red pepper flakes, or to taste (optional)

Refrigerate until they are opaque, 30 to 60 minutes but no longer than 90 minutes.

Season with:

Salt and ground black pepper to taste

Garnish with:

Minced fresh parsley, cilantro, chives, or scallions

ABOUT GRILLING OR BROILING SHELLFISH

Please read About Broiling or Grilling Fish, 543, since most of that advice applies to shellfish as well.

Generally speaking, shellfish do not stick to the grill, or do so only minimally, so they are much easier to grill than finfish. And you have more latitude in timing when broiling or grilling shellfish, because they are much more forgiving. If you overcook most finfish, they will fall apart on the grill. Overcook shellfish, however, and they will simply dry out; you will lose some of their pleasures, but at least you will still be able to serve them. Broiling, of course, remains a near-perfect alternative to grilling.

It is difficult to make a grill or broiler too hot for shellfish; by the time you char their exterior, they are invariably done. So use plenty of charcoal or preheat the gas grill or broiler for a good 15 minutes.

Because grilled shellfish are rich and enormously flavorful, it makes sense to keep sauces (if any—usually a squeeze of lemon is sufficient) as light as possible. Those incorporating some acidity, in the form of tomatoes, vinegar, wine, or citrus juice, are usually most successful. Try, for example:

Tomato Concassé, 433, or Fresh Tomato Sauce, 305
Salsa Verde, 81
Any light vinaigrette, 236 to 238

BROILED OR GRILLED SHRIMP OR SCALLOPS

4 servings

These present no more challenge than a steak and, as with steak, it is important not to overcook them. Since shrimp and scallops cook in just about the same amount of time and complement each other nicely, you can cook some of each if you like. It is nice to place them on skewers, alternating a shrimp and a scallop. Since scallops have a tendency to stick to the grill, use a thin spatula to loosen them before turning; do not worry about them falling apart. Shrimp can be grilled with their shells on or off.

Prepare a medium-hot charcoal or wood fire or preheat a gas grill or broiler. Make sure the grill rack is clean and place it as close to the heat source as possible. Toss to coat in a shallow bowl:

1½ to 2 pounds sea scallops or large or extra-large shrimp, peeled, deveined if desired, or a combination

2 tablespoons extra-virgin olive oil

1 tablespoon sherry vinegar or other vinegar (optional)

Grill or broil as close to the heat as possible. Turn the shrimp after the first side becomes pink, 2 minutes or so; turn the scallops when the first side becomes opaque, 2 to 3 minutes. Season liberally with:

Salt and ground black pepper to taste

Grill or broil until the second side is pink or opaque; test one of the pieces by cutting into it to make sure it is cooked through. Serve hot or at room temperature with:

Lemon wedges, minced fresh parsley or cilantro, and extra-virgin olive oil (optional); or Scandanavian Mustard-Dill Sauce, 79

BROILED OR GRILLED SHRIMP OR SCALLOPS WITH CHILI PASTE

4 servings

If you like fiery food, use more red pepper; if you prefer milder food, omit it altogether—the chili powder will add plenty of flavor by itself.

Prepare a medium-hot charcoal fire or preheat a gas grill or broiler. Make sure the grill rack is clean and place it as close to the heat source as possible. Mix together into a paste in a large, shallow bowl:

1 tablespoon minced garlic

1 tablespoon chili powder (the fresher the better), or to taste

½ teaspoon ground red pepper, or to taste

1 tablespoon peanut, olive, or other oil or as needed to make a moist paste

Salt and ground black pepper to taste

Add and toss to coat well:

1½ to 2 pounds sea scallops or large or extra-large shrimp, peeled, deveined if desired, or a combination

Place on the grill or under the broiler as close to the heat as possible. Turn the shrimp after the first side becomes pink, 2 minutes or so; turn the scallops when the first side becomes opaque, 2 to 3 minutes. Grill or broil until the second side is pink or opaque; test one of the pieces by cutting into it to make sure it is cooked through. Serve hot or at room temperature with:

Lime wedges and minced fresh parsley or cilantro, or Citrus Sauce, 54

BROILED OR GRILLED SHRIMP OR SCALLOPS, BASQUE STYLE

4 servings

Prepare a medium-hot charcoal fire or preheat a gas grill or broiler. Make sure the grill rack is clean and place it as close to the heat source as possible. Mix together in a serving bowl:

½ cup fresh lemon juice

⅓ cup extra-virgin olive oil

1 tablespoon minced garlic

¼ to ½ teaspoon hot red pepper sauce, or to taste

½ cup coarsely chopped fresh herbs (any combination of parsley, sage, thyme, basil, marjoram, oregano, chervil, etc.)

Salt and ground black pepper to taste

Toss to coat in a shallow bowl:

1½ to 2 pounds sea scallops or large or extra-large shrimp, peeled, deveined if desired, or a combination

2 tablespoons extra-virgin olive oil

Place on the grill or under the broiler as close to the heat as possible. Turn the shrimp after the first side becomes pink, 2 minutes or so; turn the scallops when the first side becomes opaque, 2 to 3 minutes. Grill or broil until the second side is pink or opaque; test one of the pieces by cutting into it to make sure it is cooked through. Add the hot shellfish to the herb mixture, toss gently, and serve immediately.

BROILED SHRIMP OR SCALLOPS WITH PERSILLADE

4 servings

Persillade is a coating of parsley and garlic, traditionally placed on a rack of lamb. It is also wonderful on broiled seafood.

Position the broiler rack about 4 inches from the heat source. Preheat the broiler. Mix together by hand or in a small food processor:

1½ cups fresh breadcrumbs

½ cup fresh parsley leaves

1 clove garlic, peeled

Salt and ground black pepper to taste

Toss to coat in a shallow roasting pan:

1½ to 2 pounds sea or bay scallops or large or extra-large shrimp, peeled, deveined if desired, or a combination

2 tablespoons extra-virgin olive oil

Place under the broiler as close to the heat as possible. Turn the shrimp after the first side becomes pink, 2 minutes or so; turn the scallops when the first side becomes opaque, 2 to 3 minutes. Spread the breadcrumb mixture all over the shellfish, then broil, this time about 4 inches from the heat source, until the breadcrumbs are browned but not burned, 3 to 4 minutes. Serve hot with:

Lemon wedges

BROILED OR GRILLED SHRIMP OR SCALLOPS WITH COCONUT CURRY SAUCE

4 servings

You can also make this sauce for Grilled Squid, below.

Combine in a saucepan:

½ cup unsweetened coconut milk
¼ cup fresh lime juice
1 tablespoon curry powder
1 teaspoon minced peeled fresh ginger

Bring to a boil over high heat, then immediately reduce the heat to low. Simmer, uncovered, for 30 minutes, stirring occasionally.

Meanwhile, prepare a medium-hot charcoal fire or preheat a gas grill or broiler. Make sure the grill rack is clean and place it as close to the heat source as possible. Stir into the sauce:

1 teaspoon dried red pepper flakes, or to taste

Place on the grill or under the broiler as close to the heat as possible:

1½ to 2 pounds sea scallops or large or extra-large shrimp, peeled, deveined if desired, or a combination

Turn the shrimp after the first side becomes pink, 2 minutes or so; turn the scallops when the first side becomes opaque, 2 to 3 minutes. Season liberally with:

Salt and ground black pepper to taste

Grill or broil until the second side is pink or opaque; test one of the pieces by cutting into it to make sure it is cooked through. Remove to a serving bowl, gently warm the coconut sauce if necessary, pour it over the top, and sprinkle with:

2 scallions, minced
1 tablespoon sesame seeds, toasted

GRILLED OR BROILED SHRIMP OR SCALLOPS WITH HOISIN OR BARBECUE SAUCE

4 servings

Take care not to burn the sauce once you brush it on; if necessary, move the shellfish to a cooler part of the grill or lower the broiler rack a couple of inches.

Combine in a shallow bowl:

1½ to 2 pounds sea scallops or large or extra-large shrimp, peeled, deveined if desired, or a combination
2 tablespoons soy sauce
1 tablespoon sake or white wine

Prepare a medium-hot charcoal fire or preheat a gas grill or broiler. Make sure the grill rack is clean and place it about 4 inches from the heat on a grill or 2 or 3 inches from the broiler heat. Remove the shellfish from the soy mixture, pat dry, and place on the grill or under the broiler. Grill or broil until beginning to brown, about 2 minutes. Turn, then brush the top side with:

Hoisin sauce or ketchup-based barbecue sauce

Grill or broil for 2 minutes more. Turn again, move the shellfish to a cooler part of the grill or adjust the broiler rack down a notch, and brush again with sauce. Turn and brush every minute for 3 to 4 minutes, until the shellfish has developed a nice glaze and is cooked through. Serve hot or at room temperature, garnished, if you like, with:

Minced scallions or chopped walnuts

GRILLED SQUID (OR CUTTLEFISH)

4 servings

The ingredients for grilling squid (or its close relative, cuttlefish) are the same as those for grilling shrimp or scallops, but the technique is somewhat different, largely because few broilers get hot enough to do the job. Build the hottest fire you can (preferably of hardwood charcoal) and place the grill rack as close to the heat as possible. The idea is to sear the squid before it has a chance to become rubbery.

Prepare a hot charcoal or wood fire or preheat a gas grill. Make sure the grill rack is clean and place it as close to the heat source as possible. Toss to coat in a shallow bowl:

2 pounds cleaned squid, tentacles skewered, bodies left intact or skewered
2 tablespoons extra-virgin olive oil
1 tablespoon sherry vinegar or other vinegar (optional)

(Or use any of the flavor treatments suggested for shrimp and scallops in the recipes above.) When the fire is good and hot, place the squid as close to the heat as possible. Grill about 1 minute, 2 at most, until the surface facing the flame is firm and seared. Turn and cook another 1 to 2 minutes. Be careful—overcooking will make the squid quite tough. Serve immediately with:

Several drops of sherry or other vinegar, or lemon wedges and minced fresh parsley, or Salsa Verde, 81

GRILLED, BROILED, OR ROASTED SOFT-SHELL CRABS

4 servings

To grill these delicious creatures, it is best to use a moderately hot fire and keep the grill rack at least 4 inches from the heat source; or use a covered grill and indirect heat. Or simply roast them in the oven. To clean soft-shell crabs, see page 494.

Prepare a medium-hot charcoal fire or preheat a gas grill or broiler. Make sure the grill rack is clean and place it about 4 inches from the heat on a grill or 2 or 3 inches from the broiler heat. Or preheat the oven to 500°F.

Mix:

3 tablespoons melted butter or olive oil
1 teaspoon minced garlic (optional)
Salt and ground black pepper to taste

Brush the butter mixture over both sides of:

8 soft-shell crabs, cleaned and patted dry

Grill or broil, taking care not to burn the shells (especially the claws), until bright red and firm, 4 to 6 minutes each side. Or place in a roasting pan and bake, without turning, for about 10 minutes. Serve hot with:

Lemon or lime wedges and hot red pepper sauce (optional), or Lemon Beurre Blanc, 58

GRILLED OR BROILED SPLIT LOBSTER WITH OLIVE OIL, GARLIC, AND LEMON

4 servings

Split lobster cooks just a little faster than whole lobster, but the smoky flavor of the grill permeates the meat better. Also try whole or split lobster tail, now readily available.

Prepare a medium-hot charcoal fire or preheat a gas grill or broiler. Make sure the grill rack is clean and place it as close to the heat source as possible. Kill with a knife, 491:

4 lobsters (at least 1¼ pounds each)

Split the lobsters in half, 491, leaving them attached by a hinge of their shell. Remove the head sac and intestines. Crack the claws and legs slightly with the back of a knife. Sprinkle the open bodies and tails with:

Salt and ground black pepper to taste
1 teaspoon to 1 tablespoon red pepper flakes (optional)

Combine in a small bowl:

⅓ cup extra-virgin olive oil
1 tablespoon minced garlic

Brush the lobsters with the oil mixture and place them shell side down on the grill or broiler rack. If grilling, cover the lobsters with an inverted pie pan or roasting pan. Grill or broil until the flesh is opaque, the tomalley is hot, and any roe is bright orange-red, about 10 minutes. Baste with the remaining oil mixture, and serve with:

Minced fresh parsley
Lemon wedges

ROASTED SCALLOPS OR SHRIMP WITH TOMATO

4 servings

Consider cooking these, or serving them, in large scallop shells, but they are equally delicious in a gratin dish. Preheat the oven to 500°F. Combine:

2 cups chopped seeded peeled fresh tomatoes
½ cup minced onions
2 tablespoons extra-virgin olive oil
1 teaspoon paprika
¼ teaspoon ground red pepper, or to taste
Salt and ground black pepper to taste

Place in a gratin or other shallow baking dish. Roast until bubbly, about 8 minutes. Top the tomato mixture with:

1½ to 2 pounds sea or bay scallops or large or extra-large shrimp, peeled, deveined if desired, lightly rinsed and dried

Roast until the scallops are opaque on the outside but still translucent in their centers or the shrimp are pink and firm, 5 to 10 minutes. Serve very hot, garnished with:

Minced fresh parsley

MARINATED AND GRILLED OCTOPUS

4 servings

Please read Octopus, 504, for directions on precooking. Once you have done that, this recipe is quite simple.

Combine:

1 octopus (at least 3 pounds), precooked, 504
⅓ cup fresh lemon juice
⅓ cup extra-virgin olive oil
1 medium onion, chopped
1 clove garlic, lightly mashed
2 tablespoons minced fresh marjoram, oregano, mint, or basil, or a combination

Refrigerate for 1 to 24 hours.

Prepare a medium-hot charcoal fire or preheat a gas grill or broiler. Make sure the grill rack is clean and place it as close to the heat source as possible. Cut each of the tentacles from the octopus body and cut the body itself into 2 or 3 pieces. Skewer the pieces if you like or simply place them on the grill. Cook, brushing with the marinade, until beginning to brown and crisp all over, 8 to 15 minutes. Serve hot, at room temperature, or cold, with a drizzling of:

Extra-virgin olive oil

Serve with:

Lemon wedges

CLAMBAKE

12 to 15 servings

Devised by Native Americans (most likely the Wampanoag tribe of Massachusetts and Connecticut) prior to the arrival of the first European settlers, the clambake is America's premier culinary celebration. This ritual feast has many variations, but it always involves cooking seafood—always clams, usually lobster, very often mussels, and sometimes shrimp—along with vegetables—always corn on the cob, usually potatoes and onions—in a pit dug on the beach. The heat is supplied by rocks that in turn have been heated by a driftwood fire, and layers of seaweed both cushion the food from direct heat and provide steam to assist in the cooking.

A clambake is not a meal that you cook for two people, nor is it something you whip up on the spur of the moment. It takes both advance planning and considerable time but, like the Southern pig roast or a Hawaiian luau, it is fun and, when you taste the food, you will know it was well worth the effort.

In addition to the food, for a clambake you will need several bushels of seaweed. Rockweed is best, because its little sacks full of water provide a lot of steam. If there is no rockweed on the beach, use any seaweed you can find. You will also need enough driftwood (or cordwood) to build a large fire, about fifteen large rocks to heat in the fire, and a large tarp to place on top of the food so the heat and steam are trapped inside the pit.

Dig a pit in the sand about 2 feet deep, 2 feet wide, and 3 feet long. Line the bottom of the pit with large stones, then build a large fire on top of the stones. Feed the fire to keep it going for 1 to 2 hours, then allow it to burn down until all the wood has burned to coals, about 2 hours. Meanwhile, wrap up in cheesecloth to make flat packets.

3 pounds medium potatoes or sweet potatoes
8 quarts littleneck or cherrystone clams
2 dozen ears sweet corn with husks on
2 pounds large onions
8 quarts mussels (optional)
12 chicken thighs or 3 pounds spicy sausages (optional)

When the fire is all coals, cover the stones with a 6- to 8-inch layer of seaweed, preferably rockweed. Stack the packets of potatoes, clams, corn, onions, mussels, and chicken (in that order) on top of each other on the coals, adding thin layers of seaweed in between if desired. Add:

12 live 1-pound lobsters

Top with a 3- to 4-inch layer of seaweed. If using seaweed other than rockweed, pour about 8 cups seawater over the last layer of seaweed. Cover the pit completely with a large canvas tarp that has been thoroughly soaked with seawater. Cover the tarp with stones to hold it in place, then add a ½-inch layer of sand. Cook until all the foods are cooked, 1 to 1½ hours. Remove the food packets and lobsters from the pit and serve hot, with plenty of:

Melted butter

ABOUT COOKING SHELLFISH WITH OR IN LIQUID

Please read About Cooking Fish in Liquid, 553; for much of that advice appies to shellfish as well. But for many shellfish—especially soft-shell clams, mussels, and lobsters—cooking in or over liquid is the easiest and often best choice. These foods are so flavorful that they can be steamed with no seasonings whatsoever and still produce a superb broth. Sometimes their poaching or steaming liquids are seasoned, and sometimes not; but in either case, they should never be discarded. The broth from steaming clams, mussels, or lobsters (or even a broth made from simmering shrimp shells) can be used in place of fish stock in any recipe or used on its own to make a wonderful risotto or the base for a fish soup or stew. See A Note About Liquids for Cooking Shellfish, 511.

The key to successful cooking of unshucked clams, oysters, and mussels in liquid is thorough cleaning. There are few things worse than a gritty mussel or a muddy broth, and both can be avoided by diligent cleaning. Wash soft-shell clams and mussels as thoroughly as you would salad greens: in repeated changes of water, until it looks clear. Scrub hard-shell clams and, especially, oysters until their shells are free of mud and grit.

As noted elsewhere, clams, mussels, lobsters, shrimp, and some other shellfish clearly signal you when they are fully cooked. Clams and mussels, for example, pop open; shrimp turn pink. But some shellfish, such as scallops—which are already shucked—do not have these built-in indicators. And although steaming and poaching are fairly gentle cooking processes which help seafood retain its intrinsic moisture, they are also fairly quick cooking processes, and overcooking is possible.

A NOTE ABOUT LIQUIDS FOR COOKING SHELLFISH

In these and many other shellfish recipes, some liquid is needed to begin or finish the cooking. You may choose from a variety of liquids or combine them as you like. Generally speaking, these are, in order of preference:

Fish Stock, 41
Water from steaming lobsters or hard-shell clams, reduced for more flavor if desired
Shrimp Stock, 41
Water from steaming soft-shell clams (steamers) or mussels, well strained, reduced for more flavor if desired
Chicken or vegetable stock, preferably on the light side
Dry white wine
Water

BASIC STEAMED CLAMS (STEAMERS)

4 servings

You can steam any clam you like (in fact, you can steam any mollusk you like), but soft-shell clams (steamers) are traditional. (Razor clams usually are steamed also, but they are hard to find.) To a great degree, soft-shell clams are steamed because it is difficult to purge them entirely of sand. If you steam them, the resulting broth gives you a flavorful dip in which you can rinse the clams clean before popping them in your mouth or dipping them in melted butter. Steam as many or as few as you like.

Rinse:

4 to 8 pounds soft-shell steamers or razor clams

in several changes of water until the water runs clear and there is little or no sand at the bottom of the sink or pot. Place the clams in a large pot with an inch or so of water. Cover the pot, turn the heat to high, and cook the clams, shaking occasionally, until they are all open, 5 to 10 minutes. Meanwhile, melt in a small pan over low heat:

½ pound (2 sticks) salted butter (optional)

When the clams are done, remove them to a large bowl. Strain the broth, then taste and season with:

Salt and ground black pepper to taste

Put bowls of the broth on the table. Serve the clams so that everyone can dip them in the broth and then in the butter. Or serve them plain or with:

Cocktail Sauce, 70, or Mojo, 79

STEAMED HARD-SHELL CLAMS WITH GARLIC

4 servings

Unlike steamers, hard-shell clams, such as littlenecks, barely need to be washed before steaming. This makes it possible to steam them and serve them in the same liquid.

Combine in a large, deep skillet:

2 tablespoons olive oil
1 tablespoon minced garlic
1 small dried chili pepper, or 1 jalapeño or other fresh chili pepper, seeded and minced

Cook, stirring occasionally, over medium heat until the garlic begins to color, about 5 minutes. Add:

24 to 36 littleneck clams, washed and drained

Increase the heat to high and cook, stirring, for about 1 minute. Add to the skillet:

1 cup dry white wine or other liquid (see A Note About Liquids for Cooking Shellfish, above), or a combination

Cover the skillet and cook, shaking the pan occasionally, until nearly all the clams are open (some are always a little more stubborn than the rest). Remove the chili pepper. Taste the broth and season with:

Ground black pepper to taste

Serve the clams with the broth poured over them. Garnish with:

Minced fresh parsley or cilantro
Lime wedges

THAI CLAM POT

4 to 6 servings

Here are clams at their spiciest and most delicious.

Have ready:

8 cloves garlic, thinly slivered
8 scallions, cut into 2-inch lengths, then lengthwise in half
1 teaspoon red pepper flakes
1 cup rice wine mixed with 1 cup water
3 pounds small littleneck clams, well washed and drained
1 cup fresh basil leaves, cut into thin strips
2 tablespoons fish sauce

When ready to cook, bring to a rolling boil in a large pot:

12 to 16 cups water

Add and cook until done, 2 to 3 minutes:

4 ounces thin somen noodles or angel-hair pasta

Drain immediately in a strainer and rinse lightly to remove starch. While the noodles are cooking, heat a heavy pot large enough to hold the clams over high heat until hot. Add:

2 tablespoons peanut oil

Heat, swirling, until very hot but not smoking. Add the garlic, scallions, and red pepper flakes. Stir for about 15 seconds. Standing back, add the wine mixture, cover, and bring to a boil. Add the clams, cover, and return the liquid to a boil. Immediately reduce the heat to medium and cook until the clams have just opened, 7 to 8 minutes, shaking the pot 3 or 4 times to ensure that the clams cook evenly.

Add the basil and stir it thoroughly into the liquid. Cover and cook for 30 to 45 seconds. Add the fish sauce and stir thoroughly. Divide the noodles among individual bowls, add the clams, and pour the broth over them. Serve immediately.

STEAMED LOBSTER *4 servings*

There is only one good reason to boil lobsters instead of steaming them: If you are cooking lobsters in batches—say, eight or more, so there is no way you can fit them all into the pot at once—each one flavors the broth for the ones that follow. But for the average meal, steaming is faster and easier (if you can steam broccoli, you can steam lobster). You can use this same procedure for king crab legs or Dungeness crab as well.

Have ready:

4 lobsters (at least 1¼ pounds each)

Fill the bottom of a pot large enough to hold the lobsters with a good inch of water. Add:

1 tablespoon salt (better still, use seawater)

Cover and bring to a boil. Add the lobsters and cover. Cook 1½-pound lobsters for about 15 minutes, until they are bright red. Add 2 to 3 minutes for every ¼ pound increase in weight; that is, steam 2-pound lobsters for 20 minutes, 2½-pound lobsters for 25. (All of this assumes that the water continues to boil as you add lobsters; if you are cooking more lobsters or you leave the lid off for more than 30 seconds or so, add a couple of minutes to the cooking time.) Serve with:

Melted butter and/or lemon wedges

LOBSTER THERMIDOR *2 servings*

This is a celebratory dish whose origins are certainly French, though the specifics have long since become a mystery. Pieces of lobster are mixed with a rich cheese sauce, Dijon mustard, and a lobster broth, then are returned to their shells and broiled until bubbling hot. Inventive chefs have added truffles, mushrooms, or even spinach, as we do here.

Kill with a knife, 491:

2 lobsters (1½ pounds each)

When they are still, tie the lobsters together, belly to belly, with kitchen string. Be sure to secure the tails to each other so that they do not curl during cooking.

Fill the bottom of a steamer or large pot with a lid into which a colander just fits with 2 inches water. Cover and bring to a full boil. When ample steam has collected, place the lobsters on the steamer rack or in the colander. Cover, and steam without peeking for 7 minutes. Remove the lobsters and immediately cool under cold running water. Remove the claws from the lobsters. Crack the claws and knuckles, remove the meat, and cut it into chunks. Lay a lobster on its back on your cutting board. With a sharp knife, cut through the belly shell of the lobster, leaving the top shell intact. Remove the tail meat from the shell and cut into 1½-inch chunks. Repeat with the second lobster and place all of the lobster meat in a small bowl.

Discard the small legs and intestines from the lobster shells so that the large shells are completely empty. Using kitchen scissors, trim the tail shells so that the thinner bottom shells of the tails are removed. Rinse the shells and pat dry. With the palm of your hand, press open the tail and body of each lobster shell so that it remains flat and open. Set the shells on a baking sheet or broiler pan.

Preheat the broiler. Heat in a small skillet over medium-high heat:

1 tablespoon butter

Add:

1 pound spinach, tough stems removed, washed and dried

¼ teaspoon freshly grated or ground nutmeg

¼ teaspoon salt

Cook, stirring, until the spinach is wilted, about 2 minutes. Let cool, then transfer to a cutting board and coarsely chop. Divide the chopped spinach between the lobster shells and pat into an even layer over the length of the shells. The spinach will prevent the sauce from leaking out of the shells. Bring to a boil in a small saucepan:

1½ cups heavy cream

Cook down for 10 to 12 minutes. You should have about ⅔ cup cream. Add:

2 teaspoons dry sherry

Cook for 30 seconds. Remove from the heat and add:

½ cup grated Gruyère cheese

Whisk until melted, then whisk in:

1½ teaspoons Dijon mustard

¼ teaspoon salt

Set ¼ cup sauce aside. Stir the remaining sauce into the lobster meat along with:

⅛ teaspoon salt

Divide this mixture between the lobster shells. Top with the remaining sauce. The lobsters can be prepared up to this point 1 day ahead; cover and refrigerate, then bring to room temperature for about 20 minutes before broiling.

Sprinkle with:

½ cup grated Gruyère cheese

Broil the lobsters about 5 inches from the heat until hot, bubbling, and golden brown, 4 to 5 minutes. If the sauce begins to burn before the lobsters are hot, cover with aluminum foil.

STEAMED BLUE CRABS *3 to 5 servings*

The delightfully messy traditional way to serve these is to dump them in the center of a large table covered with newspaper—outside if possible. Hand out small hammers, rolling pins, or nutcrackers and nut picks. Plan on about 5 crabs per person, or as many as 10 if you are serving hearty eaters. Omit the seafood seasoning or crab boil (available at fish stores) if you are not planning to serve the crabs in their shells.

Fit a tall-footed rack or slotted lift-out basket into the bottom of an 8-gallon stockpot. Pour into the pot:

2 cups cider vinegar

Add water to come two-thirds of the way up to the bottom of the rack or basket. Bring the vinegar and water to a boil. Rinse quickly under cold water:

24 live blue crabs

Arrange in no more than six layers on the rack, sprinkling each layer with:

1 tablespoon coarse salt

1 tablespoon commercially prepared seafood seasoning or crab boil (optional)

Bring the vinegar and water to a rapid simmer, cover the pot tightly, and steam the crabs until they turn bright pink and their legs can be pulled from the sockets fairly easily, 15 to 20 minutes. Serve with:

Melted butter and/or lemon wedges

STEAMED MUSSELS *4 servings*

If you wash the mussels well, 493, you can steam them in their own seasonings and serve them with the broth. This makes it easy to vary seasonings. You also can add cut-up pieces of sausage, such as linguiça or chorizo, to the pot, or use a cup or so of chopped tomato in place of or along with the wine.

Wash and debeard, 498:

4 to 6 pounds mussels

Place them in a large pot and add:

½ cup dry white wine

½ cup minced fresh parsley, chervil, or basil, plus more herbs if you like

2 tablespoons chopped garlic

Cover the pot, place it over high heat, and cook, shaking the pot occasionally, until most of the mussels are opened, about 10 minutes. Use a slotted spoon to remove the mussels to a serving bowl, then strain the cooking liquid over them. Drizzle over the mussels:

1 tablespoon extra-virgin olive oil

Juice of 1 lemon

Serve with:

Plenty of crusty bread

STEAMED MUSSELS WITH TARRAGON CREAM SAUCE *4 servings*

Just a tiny step beyond simple steamed mussels, and the result is heavenly.

Prepare:

Steamed Mussels, above

Remove them to a serving bowl, cover, and keep warm in a very low oven. Strain the cooking liquid into a saucepan and boil over high heat until reduced to 1 cup. Reduce the heat to low and whisk in:

2 tablespoons butter, cut into small pieces

Add:

2 teaspoons minced fresh tarragon or 2 tablespoons minced fresh chervil

1 cup heavy cream

Heat, stirring, but do not boil. Season with:

Salt and ground black pepper to taste

Pour the sauce over the mussels and serve immediately.

STEAMED SCALLOPS OR SHRIMP WITH SOY SAUCE *4 servings*

Steam, covered, for 5 minutes:

1 leek (white and green parts), cleaned thoroughly, and cut into matchsticks

1 medium carrot, peeled and cut into matchsticks

Meanwhile, have ready:

1 pound bay or sea scallops, lightly rinsed and cut into ½-inch-thick slices, or 1 pound large shrimp, peeled, halved lengthwise, deveined if desired

Place the shellfish slices on top of the vegetables and sprinkle everything with:

1 to 2 tablespoons top-quality soy sauce

If your soy sauce is very strong, dilute it with a little water or white wine. Steam, covered, until the scallops are opaque but still very tender or the shrimp are pink, 3 to 7 minutes. Garnish with:

Grated peeled fresh ginger

Snipped fresh chives

NO-FAIL BOILED SHRIMP

4 servings

If you wish, prepare the shrimp in plain water.
In a large saucepan, combine:

- **10 cups water**
- **2 celery stalks, cut into 2-inch lengths**
- **1 medium onion, cut into eighths**
- **1 small lemon, quartered**
- **½ bunch fresh parsley**
- **8 black peppercorns**
- **2 bay leaves**
- **1 tablespoon salt**
- **½ teaspoon ground red pepper**

Bring to a boil, reduce the heat, and simmer, uncovered, for 10 minutes. Strain the liquid and return it to the pan. Add:

- **2 pounds shrimp, any size, fresh or frozen, preferably in their shells for best flavor**

Return the liquid to a boil, reduce the heat, and simmer, uncovered, for 2 minutes exactly. Drain the shrimp, remove to a platter, and let cool. Serve with:

- **Cocktail Sauce, 70**
- **Sauce Rémoulade, 73**
- **Tartar Sauce, 73**

POACHED SHRIMP WITH CARROT JUICE AND THAI SPICES

4 servings

This delicate dish will delight and enchant you. If you use canned carrot juice, the entire operation will take less than 15 minutes. A dish created by the innovative chef Jean-Georges Vongerichten.
Bring a small saucepan of water to a boil. Add:

- **1 cup diced peeled carrots**

Cook for 4 minutes, then drain and plunge into cold water to stop the cooking. Drain again. Place the carrots in a large saucepan or skillet. Add:

- **2 cups carrot juice**
- **2 tablespoons finely chopped lemon grass or lemon zest**
- **2 tablespoons fresh lime juice**
- **1 teaspoon minced lime zest**
- **1 small jalapeño pepper, seeded and minced, 1 small dried chili pepper, or ¼ teaspoon ground red pepper**

Bring to a boil over high heat, then add:

- **24 large shrimp, peeled, deveined if desired**

Reduce the heat to medium and simmer, uncovered, until pink, 3 to 5 minutes. Reduce the heat to low and add:

- **2 tablespoons chopped fresh cilantro**
- **2 tablespoons chopped fresh mint**

If you wish, whisk in:

- **3 tablespoons butter, cut into small pieces**

Ladle into bowls and garnish with:

- **Fresh mint sprigs**

STEAMED SHRIMP TORTILLAS WITH COCONUT CURRY SAUCE

4 servings

Like any "sandwich," these are infinitely variable; you can add any minced vegetable you like, or cooked rice noodles, or sliced avocado. You can also use a soy-based dipping sauce or wrap the mixture in rice paper.
Peel, and devein if desired:

- **16 large shrimp**

Place them in a steamer or boiling salted water to cover in a saucepan and cook until pink, firm, and cooked through, 3 to 5 minutes. Plunge into ice water to stop the cooking, then drain, dry, and cut lengthwise in half.
Place in a small saucepan:

- **2 cups unsweetened coconut milk**

Bring to a boil over high heat, reduce the heat to medium, and cook for 5 minutes, stirring occasionally.
Stir in:

- **1 tablespoon fish or soy sauce**
- **1 teaspoon curry powder, or to taste**
- **½ teaspoon ground red pepper, or to taste**
- **Salt and ground black pepper to taste**

Let cool. Divide the shrimp among:

- **4 flour tortillas**

Top each with:

- **½ cup shredded lettuce or cabbage**
- **¼ cup Tomato Concassé, 433, or chopped fresh tomatoes**
- **4 to 6 sprigs fresh cilantro or mint**
- **4 long, thin strips cucumber**
- **Shredded peeled carrots**
- **Shredded scallions**

Do not overfill. Roll up the tortillas, then serve them with the sauce.

CRAYFISH OR SHRIMP ÉTOUFFÉE

4 servings

This Louisiana classic is rich, complex, and intense. If you use crayfish, which look like small lobsters, be sure to scoop out the little bit of fat between the tail meat and the body and add it to the sauce.
Bring to a boil in a large saucepan or deep skillet over high heat:

- **4 cups water**
- **1 bay leaf**
- **1 onion, quartered**
- **2 cloves garlic, lightly crushed**
- **1 teaspoon fresh thyme leaves, or ½ teaspoon dried thyme**

1 teaspoon ground black pepper
10 coriander seeds
1 small dried chili pepper

Add:

3 pounds large shrimp or crayfish, in their shells

Return the liquid to a boil (it need not completely cover the shellfish), reduce the heat to medium, cover, and cook for 1 minute. Remove from the heat and let the shellfish cool in the liquid for 10 minutes. Remove the crayfish or shrimp with a slotted spoon (you can serve them at this point, hot or cold, with lemon wedges and hot sauce). Strain the liquid into a clean saucepan and boil until reduced to about 2 cups. Meanwhile, peel the shellfish (if using crayfish, reserve 4 whole ones for garnish).

Heat in a large saucepan over medium heat until hot:

3 tablespoons peanut or other oil

Stir in:

3 tablespoons all-purpose flour

Cook, stirring often, until the flour turns brown, about 10 minutes. Stir in:

1 red or yellow bell pepper, minced
1 medium onion, minced
1 jalapeño or other fresh pepper, seeded and finely minced (optional)
1 tablespoon minced garlic

Cook for 1 minute. Gradually whisk in the reduced stock and cook, stirring, over medium-low heat until thickened. Stir in the peeled shellfish along with:

4 scallions, minced
2 tablespoons butter, cut into small pieces
1 tablespoon fresh lemon juice
Ground red pepper to taste (optional)
Salt and ground black pepper to taste

Heat through and taste and adjust the seasonings. Garnish with the reserved whole crayfish, if using. Serve with:

Hot cooked rice

SHRIMP AND BEANS
4 servings

If you can remember to double the recipe the next time you make Classic Tuscan Beans, 284, this is a 10-minute operation.

Prepare:

Classic Tuscan Beans, 284

Add to the beans as they cook:

10 fresh sage leaves, minced, or 1 teaspoon dried sage, crumbled

When the beans are done, stir into the pot:

1½ pounds shrimp, peeled, deveined if desired, and cut into small pieces
8 ounces Italian sausage, cut into bits and browned (optional)
1 tablespoon minced garlic

Cook, stirring, over low heat until the shrimp is cooked, the garlic is mellowed, and the flavors are blended, 5 minutes or so. Garnish with:

Plenty of minced fresh parsley
Several fresh sage leaves, minced

CURRY SHRIMP
4 servings

Slow-cooked onions and shrimp stock make this curry rich and flavorful.

Place in a large, heavy saucepan or large, deep skillet:

2 large onions, sliced

Cover the pan and cook over medium-low heat, stirring every 10 minutes, until the onions begin to brown and almost stick to the pan, about 30 minutes. Meanwhile, peel, and devein if desired:

1½ to 2 pounds medium to large shrimp

Simmer the shells in just enough water to cover for about 10 minutes. Strain and measure 1 cup stock. Add to the onions:

2 tablespoons peanut or vegetable oil
Salt and ground black pepper to taste

Increase the heat to medium and cook, stirring occasionally, until the onions are deep brown and very tender, almost falling apart. Add the shrimp stock along with:

2 ripe tomatoes, peeled, seeded, and chopped
1 red or yellow bell pepper, chopped
1 tablespoon minced garlic
2 tablespoons minced fresh cilantro
1 tablespoon fresh lemon juice
1 tablespoon ground cumin
1 teaspoon ground coriander
1 teaspoon ground black pepper
1 teaspoon ground turmeric
½ teaspoon ground fenugreek
Ground red pepper to taste
Salt to taste

Bring to a boil over medium-high heat. Reduce the heat to medium-low and cook, stirring occasionally, until the tomatoes break up and the mixture is very saucelike. Taste and adjust the seasonings. Stir in the shrimp and cook until pink and firm, 3 to 4 minutes. Garnish with:

Minced fresh cilantro

Serve with:

Hot cooked rice

STEWED OCTOPUS, SQUID, OR CUTTLEFISH, PROVENÇAL STYLE

4 servings

If you use octopus here, it must be precooked, 504, for the octopus must be quite tender for this recipe. Squid and cuttlefish need only be cleaned, 503.

Combine in a large, heavy saucepan or large, deep skillet:

3 tablespoons extra-virgin olive oil
1 large onion, chopped

Cook, stirring, over medium-high heat until the onion is softened, about 5 minutes. Add:

2 cups chopped seeded peeled tomatoes
½ cup dry red wine
¼ cup chopped pitted Kalamata or other black olives
¼ cup chopped fresh parsley or basil
2 tablespoons capers, drained
2 tablespoons minced anchovies (optional)
1 tablespoon minced garlic
1 teaspoon fresh thyme, or ½ teaspoon dried
½ teaspoon minced fresh rosemary, or ¼ teaspoon dried, crumbled
Salt and ground black pepper to taste

Bring to a boil, stirring often. Reduce the heat and simmer, uncovered, about 15 minutes, until the tomatoes break up and the mixture becomes a sauce. Meanwhile, cut into bite-sized pieces:

1 octopus (about 3 pounds), precooked, 504, or 3 pounds squid or cuttlefish, cleaned, 503

Stir the seafood into the sauce and simmer until it is hot and tender, less than 5 minutes. Taste and adjust the seasonings. Garnish with:

Minced fresh basil, parsley, or fennel leaves

Serve with:

Crusty bread or hot cooked rice or pasta

OVEN-BRAISED SQUID WITH TOMATO SAUCE

4 servings

You may fill squid with almost any stuffing you like. Take care not to overstuff it, because squid shrinks a great deal when cooked.

Clean, 503, without splitting open the bodies:

8 medium to large squid (about 2 pounds)

Chop the tentacles. Preheat the oven to 325°F. Lightly oil a 2-quart baking dish. Combine:

2 tablespoons extra-virgin olive oil
1 tablespoon minced garlic

Cook over medium heat until the garlic begins to color. Stir in the tentacles and cook for 1 minute. Stir in:

1 cup fresh breadcrumbs
½ cup minced fresh parsley

Cook until the breadcrumbs are golden. Stir in:

⅓ cup grated aged pecorino cheese (optional)
¼ cup minced onions
1 tablespoon minced anchovies

Season with:

Salt and ground black pepper to taste

Stuff the squid bodies loosely with the breadcrumb mixture and seal each open end with a toothpick. Place the squid side by side in the baking dish. Top with:

2 to 3 cups Italian Tomato Sauce, 304

Cover the dish with aluminum foil. Bake until the squid is tender, about 45 minutes. Garnish with:

Minced fresh parsley

Serve with:

Crusty bread or hot cooked pasta

MIXED SHELLFISH IN TOMATO SAUCE

4 to 6 servings

Make this on the moist side, by adding extra tomatoes or reducing the cooking time a bit, if you would like to serve it over pasta.

Combine in a large, heavy saucepan or large, deep skillet:

3 tablespoons olive oil
1 small dried chili pepper, or to taste
3 cloves garlic, mashed or coarsely chopped

Cook, stirring, over medium-high heat just until the garlic begins to brown. Discard the pepper and garlic. Remove from the heat for a couple of minutes to reduce spattering. Add:

3 cups chopped seeded peeled tomatoes
1 teaspoon minced fresh rosemary, or ½ teaspoon dried, crumbled
Salt and ground black pepper to taste

Cook, stirring occasionally, over medium heat, until the tomatoes break up and the mixture becomes fairly dry. Stir in:

1½ to 2 pounds mixed shellfish (peeled shrimp, cleaned squid, 503, and/or cooked whelk, 505, or octopus), 504, cut into small pieces
2 pounds well-washed mussels and/or hard-shell clams (optional)

Cover the pan, reduce the heat to medium-low, and cook until the shellfish are cooked and the mollusks, if using, are opened, 5 to 10 minutes. If the sauce is too moist, increase the heat to medium high and cook, stirring, for a little longer. Garnish with:

Minced fresh parsley or basil

Serve with:

Crusty bread or hot cooked rice or pasta

MIXED STEWED SHELLFISH WITH MUSHROOMS AND GREENS

4 servings

You can add finfish to this wonderful stew, but none described as "soft" or "delicate." Use any greens you like.

Combine in a large, heavy saucepan or large, deep skillet:

¼ cup olive oil
2 cups chopped mixed mushrooms
1 tablespoon minced garlic

Cook, stirring, over medium heat, until the mushrooms begin to soften, about 5 minutes. Add:

4 cups young greens (dandelion, chard, kale, and/or collards), washed, dried, stems and leaves coarsely chopped
2 cups liquid (see A Note About Liquids for Cooking Shellfish, 511)

Increase the heat a bit and cook until both greens and mushrooms are softened and the liquid has reduced by about half, about 10 minutes. Stir in:

1½ to 2 pounds mixed shellfish (peeled shrimp, cleaned squid, 503, and/or cooked whelk, 505, or octopus), 504, cut into small pieces
2 pounds well-washed mussels and/or hard-shell clams (optional)

Cover the pan, reduce the heat to medium-low, and cook until the shellfish are cooked and the mollusks, if using, are opened, 5 to 10 minutes. Season with:

Salt and ground black pepper to taste

Spoon the shellfish, mushrooms, and greens into serving bowls and pour a little of the cooking liquid over them. Drizzle over the top a little:

Extra-virgin olive oil

ABOUT SAUTÉING AND PAN-GRILLING SHELLFISH

Please read Sautéing and Pan-Grilling Fish, 556. Do not be afraid to use high heat when cooking shellfish on top of the stove, unless you are concerned about burning seasonings such as garlic or the cooking medium (a real concern with butter). The shellfish themselves can take superhigh heat, because by the time their exterior begins to dry out, their interior is invariably cooked through. And although they may toughen, they will never fall apart on you, as will many fish fillets.

Pan-grilling is a wonderful alternative to sautéing, but does produce volumes of smoke. Try the combination of pan-grilling and broiling (see Pan-Grilled Shrimp, Scallops, or Squid, below); if it works well for you, you can use the technique for almost any meat or sturdy fish.

PAN-GRILLED SHRIMP, SCALLOPS, OR SQUID

4 servings

If you cannot grill for one reason or another and your broiler never seems to get hot enough, but you want shellfish with a charred exterior and want to keep fat to a minimum, pan-grilling is the answer. If you use a nonstick skillet, you can eliminate the oil entirely.

If you do not have an exhaust fan, preheat the oven—preferably with a baking stone in it—to its maximum setting for at least 15 minutes before beginning cooking. Heat a large, heavy skillet over medium-high heat for 3 to 4 minutes. Toss to coat well:

2 tablespoons olive oil
1½ to 2 pounds large or extra-large shrimp, peeled, deveined if desired; scallops; or cut-up cleaned squid, 503

Turn on the exhaust fan. Increase the heat under the pan to high for 30 seconds if your stove is gas, 1 minute if electric. Add the shellfish in small handfuls to the skillet, distributing them evenly so that they are all touching the pan's surface. If you do not have an exhaust fan, place the pan in the oven as soon as it begins to smoke. Otherwise, begin to turn the shellfish 1½ to 2 minutes after the first ones have hit the pan. Brown the second side for an equal amount of time, until firm. If necessary, reduce the heat a little bit and cook for another minute or two. Shellfish finished in the oven will be done in a similar amount of time, about 4 minutes. Sprinkle with:

Fresh lemon juice or sherry vinegar
Minced fresh parsley, cilantro, or mint

SAUTÉED SHRIMP OR OTHER SHELLFISH IN OLIVE OIL

4 servings

This is the way to make shrimp "scampi." Do not skimp on the olive oil, for it is an important ingredient.

Rinse and pat dry:

1½ to 2 pounds large or extra-large shrimp, peeled, deveined if desired; scallops; cut-up cleaned squid, 503, or cooked octopus, 504, or whelk, 505

Combine in a large skillet:

½ cup extra-virgin olive oil
1 tablespoon minced garlic

Cook, stirring occasionally, over low heat until the garlic is golden, about 10 minutes; do not rush it. Increase the heat to medium-high and add the shrimp. Cook until they turn pink on the bottom and turn them over. Add:

¼ cup minced fresh parsley
1 teaspoon minced garlic (optional)

Cook until the shrimp are firm and pink, about 5 minutes total. Sprinkle with:

1 tablespoon fresh lemon juice
Minced fresh parsley

SAUTÉED SHRIMP WITH POLENTA *4 servings*

If at all possible, use fresh Hungarian paprika in this recipe; its flavor is incomparable.

Prepare:

Polenta Toast, 249

Cut the polenta into ½-inch by 3-inch slices and brown in a skillet. Remove to a serving platter, cover with aluminum foil, and keep warm in a low oven while you prepare the shrimp.

Rinse and pat dry:

1½ to 2 pounds large or extra-large shrimp, peeled, deveined if desired

Combine in a large, heavy skillet over medium heat:

3 tablespoons extra-virgin olive oil
1 large clove garlic, lightly crushed

Cook until the garlic is golden, then remove and discard it. Add the shrimp, increase the heat to medium-high and stir in:

¼ cup chopped fresh basil leaves
3 tablespoons minced fresh marjoram
3 tablespoons minced fresh parsley

Cook, tossing until the shrimp begins to turn pink. Add:

2 teaspoons sweet or hot paprika

Stir for 5 seconds, then add:

⅔ cup dry white wine

Cook over medium-high heat until the shrimp is just firm, 2 to 3 minutes more. Season with:

Salt and ground black pepper to taste

Spoon the shrimp over the polenta and serve.

SHRIMP WITH PARSLEY PESTO *4 servings*

Combine in a small saucepan:

¼ cup vegetable oil
¼ cup olive oil
2 cloves garlic, unpeeled

Cook over low heat until the garlic is softened, about 8 minutes. Remove to a measuring cup (with a pouring lip) and refrigerate until cool. Peel the garlic cloves and place them in a blender. Add:

1 cup packed fresh parsley leaves
¼ cup pine nuts, toasted
2 tablespoons cold water
½ teaspoon salt

Pulse until the parsley leaves are well chopped. You will have to stop the blender several times to stir the ingredients. With the machine running, very slowly pour the oil into the blender until the sauce begins to emulsify, then add the remaining oil more quickly. You can make the pesto 1 day in advance; cover and refrigerate. If using immediately, remove to a serving bowl and let stand at room temperature.

Butterfly, 490:

1¼ pounds large shrimp, in their shells

Season with:

¼ teaspoon salt
Ground black pepper to taste

Heat in a heavy skillet over high heat until the oil is smoking:

1 tablespoon olive oil

Add as many of the shrimp shell side up as will fit in the pan without crowding. Cook for 1 minute, turn the shrimp, and cook just until firm and pink, about 1 minute more. Remove to a serving platter and keep warm. Repeat with the remaining shrimp, adding to the skillet:

1 tablespoon olive oil per batch

Stir into the pesto just before serving:

1 teaspoon fresh lemon juice

Serve with the shrimp as a dipping sauce.

SPICE-DUSTED SHRIMP OR OTHER SHELLFISH ON GREENS *4 servings*

You can control the spice level of this dish simply by changing the proportions of spice and cornmeal. Save the shrimp shells for shrimp stock, 41.

Rinse and pat dry:

1½ to 2 pounds large or extra-large shrimp, peeled, deveined if desired; scallops; or shucked hard-shell clams, oysters, or mussels

Warm in a large skillet over low heat:

3 tablespoons peanut or other oil

Meanwhile, combine:

½ cup cornmeal
½ cup chili powder, ground cumin, curry powder, or other spice mixture of your choice

Toss the shellfish a few pieces at a time in this mixture and shake to remove the excess. Place on a rack or wax paper until all are coated.

When you are ready to cook, increase the heat under the oil to medium-high and heat for 1 minute.

Add the shellfish a few at a time to the skillet, increase the heat to high, and turn them as they begin to brown.

Season well with:

Salt and ground black pepper to taste

Total cooking time will be about 5 minutes. Remove the shellfish to a plate and keep warm. Pour into the skillet:

¼ to ½ cup liquid (see A Note About Liquids for Cooking Shellfish, 511)

Cook, stirring, over high heat until reduced by about half. Stir in:

2 tablespoons vinegar
Salt and ground black pepper to taste

Remove from the heat and return the shellfish to the pan. Spoon them with the sauce over:

4 to 6 cups mixed salad greens, washed and dried

Serve.

SHRIMP IN CREOLE SAUCE *4 servings*

Heat in a large, heavy saucepan over medium heat:

1 tablespoon unsalted butter
1 tablespoon olive oil

Add:

1 medium onion, cut into ½-inch pieces
1 red bell pepper, cut into ½-inch pieces
1 green bell pepper, cut into ½-inch pieces
1 celery stalk, cut into ½-inch pieces
1 bay leaf
2 teaspoons dried thyme
½ teaspoon salt

Cover and cook, stirring occasionally, until the vegetables are softened, about 10 minutes. Add and cook, stirring, for 2 minutes:

3 cloves garlic, minced

Add and cook, stirring, for 1 minute:

2 tablespoons tomato paste

Add and cook for 5 minutes more:

1 cup canned crushed tomatoes

Add:

1½ cups chicken or fish stock
1 teaspoon salt

Bring to a simmer, cover, and simmer for 25 minutes. The sauce can be made 1 day ahead; in fact, the flavors tend to blend and mellow overnight.

Shortly before serving, heat in a large, heavy pan over high heat until the oil is smoking:

1 tablespoon olive oil

Meanwhile, dust:

1¼ pounds large shrimp, in their shells

with:

½ teaspoon ground red pepper
¼ teaspoon salt

Add about half the shrimp to the hot oil and cook until the shells turn red, about 1 minute per side. Remove the shrimp. Heat in the same pan:

1 tablespoon olive oil

Cook the remaining shrimp and remove. Let the pan cool for a few minutes. Return the shrimp to the pan and add the sauce along with:

6 ounces smoked ham, sliced thick and cut into ½-inch pieces

Bring to a simmer and cook just until the shrimp are done, about 2 minutes. Stir in:

3 tablespoons dry sherry
½ teaspoon hot red pepper sauce

Top with:

2 tablespoons chopped yellow celery leaves

Serve with:

Hot cooked rice

STIR-FRIED SHRIMP, SCALLOPS, OR SQUID WITH BASIL AND GARLIC *4 servings*

Like all stir-fries, this one is fast and easy. Adjust the proportion of basil to hot pepper to suit your own taste.

Rinse and pat dry:

1 to 1½ pounds shrimp, peeled, deveined if desired; scallops, halved if large; or squid, cleaned, 503, and cut into bite-sized pieces

Heat a wok or large skillet over high heat. Pour in:

2 tablespoons peanut or other oil

Almost immediately add:

1 tablespoon minced garlic
1 tablespoon minced peeled fresh ginger
1 teaspoon red pepper flakes, or to taste

Cook, stirring once or twice, until the garlic begins to color, about 15 seconds. Add the shellfish and cook until it is opaque. Season with:

Salt and ground black pepper to taste

Add:

¼ to ⅓ cup chopped fresh basil or cilantro
¼ to ½ cup liquid (see A Note About Liquids for Cooking Shellfish, 511)

Stir; taste and adjust the seasonings. Garnish with:

Minced fresh basil, cilantro, chives, or scallions

Serve with:

Hot cooked rice

STIR-FRIED CLAMS OR MUSSELS WITH OYSTER OR HOISIN SAUCE *4 servings*

Use small littleneck clams or very well-washed mussels for this stir-fry. Usually, mollusks produce enough liquid that you will not have to add any to make a sauce, but if you find the mixture a bit dry at the end, add ½ cup or so stock or water.

Wash well and pat dry:

4 pounds littleneck clams or mussels, debearded

Heat a wok or large skillet over high heat. Pour in:

2 tablespoons peanut or other oil

Almost immediately add:

1 tablespoon minced garlic

1 teaspoon minced peeled fresh ginger

Cook, stirring once or twice, until the garlic begins to color, about 15 seconds. Add the shellfish and stir once or twice. Cover and cook for 2 minutes, still over high heat. Uncover and cook, stirring, until the mollusks open, a few minutes more. Add:

2 tablespoons soy sauce

2 tablespoons oyster or hoisin sauce

1 tablespoon dry sherry or white wine

2 tablespoons chopped scallions

Cook, stirring, for about 30 seconds. If the mixture seems dry, add:

¼ to ½ cup liquid (see A Note About Liquids for Cooking Shellfish, 511)

Garnish with:

Minced fresh scallions, chives, or cilantro

Serve with:

Hot cooked rice

STIR-FRIED SQUID, SHRIMP, OR SCALLOPS WITH BLACK BEANS

4 servings

Chopped fresh tomatoes provide most of the liquid for the sauce in this stir-fry.

Combine and let stand for about 10 minutes:

2 tablespoons fermented black beans

2 tablespoons dry sherry, white wine, or water

Meanwhile, rinse and pat dry:

1 to 1½ pounds shrimp, peeled, deveined if desired; or scallops, halved if large; or squid, cleaned, 503, and cut into bite-sized pieces

Heat a wok or large skillet over high heat. Pour in:

2 tablespoons peanut or other oil

Almost immediately add:

1 tablespoon minced garlic

1 tablespoon minced peeled fresh ginger

Cook, stirring once or twice, until the garlic begins to color, about 15 seconds. Add the shellfish and cook, stirring, for 15 seconds. Add the black bean mixture along with:

1½ cups diced seeded peeled tomatoes

¼ cup chopped scallions

Cook, stirring, until the tomatoes begin to break up, 2 to 3 minutes. Add:

2 tablespoons soy sauce

Cook for 30 seconds. Garnish with:

Minced scallions or chives, or Tomato Concassé, 433

Serve with:

Hot cooked rice

STIR-FRIED LOBSTER WITH CHIVES

4 servings

This stir-fry uses lobster claws and tails only; reserve the bodies (you can parboil, 491, and freeze them if you like) for Lobster Bisque, 112.

Kill with a knife or by parboiling, 491:

3 or 4 lobsters (1 to 1½ pounds each)

Cut each tail through the shells into 3 or 4 pieces. Separate the claws and knuckles and crack each section with a sharp blow from the back of a thick, heavy knife or cleaver. Heat a wok or large skillet over high heat. Pour in:

2 tablespoons peanut or other oil

Almost immediately add:

1 tablespoon minced garlic

1 teaspoon minced peeled fresh ginger

Cook, stirring once or twice, until the garlic begins to color, about 15 seconds. Add the lobster pieces in their shells and stir once or twice. Cover and cook for 2 minutes, still over high heat. Uncover and cook, stirring, until the shells are bright red, 2 to 3 minutes. Add:

½ cup 1- to 2-inch pieces fresh chives

2 tablespoons oyster sauce

2 tablespoons soy sauce

1 teaspoon paprika (optional)

Cook, stirring, for about 30 seconds. If the mixture seems dry, add and heat for 10 seconds:

¼ to ½ cup liquid (see A Note About Liquids for Cooking Shellfish, 511)

Finish the dish by drizzling over it:

1 tablespoon toasted sesame oil

Garnish with:

Snipped fresh chives

Serve with:

Hot cooked rice

CRABCAKES

4 servings

Buy fresh lump crabmeat if you can find it, and give yourself time to refrigerate the cakes after you shape them so that they will hold together better when you cook them.

Gently pick over for bits of shell and cartilage:

1 pound fresh lump crabmeat

In a skillet over medium heat, warm:

2 tablespoons butter or olive oil

When the butter foam has subsided, add:

1 tablespoon finely diced red bell peppers (optional)

½ cup diced scallions
1 teaspoon minced garlic

Cook, stirring, until the mixture is tender but not browned, about 10 minutes. Set aside. In a large bowl, mix the crabmeat with:

1 egg, lightly beaten
¼ cup mayonnaise
1 tablespoon Dijon mustard
Salt and ground black pepper to taste
¼ teaspoon ground red pepper (optional)
¼ cup minced fresh parsley, cilantro, or dill
2 tablespoons fresh breadcrumbs, toasted

Add the sautéed vegetables and blend well. Place on a plate:

1 to 2 cups fresh breadcrumbs, toasted

Shape the crab mixture into 8 small or 4 large cakes and, 1 at a time, coat each of the cakes in the breadcrumbs, pressing lightly to make sure the crumbs coat evenly. Place the cakes on a rack, or on a plate covered with wax paper, and refrigerate for 1 to 2 hours if you have the time. When you are ready to cook, heat in a large skillet over medium heat:

¼ cup butter, clarified butter, 1069, or oil

When the fat is hot, add the cakes, 1 at a time; do not crowd—it is fine to cook them in two batches. Adjust the heat so that the fat is sizzling but not burning the breadcrumbs. Rotate the cakes from side to side once or twice so that they brown evenly before turning them over after about 5 minutes. Cook until both sides are nicely browned; smaller cakes need a total of 8 to 10 minutes of cooking, larger ones 12 to 15 minutes. Keep any finished cakes warm in a 300°F oven while you complete the cooking. Serve hot with:

Lemon wedges, Aïoli, 74, a seasoned mayonnaise, 73 to 75, or Salsa Fresca, 61

ABOUT DEEP-FRYING SHELLFISH

Please read Deep-Frying, 1050. Although there are different rules for preparing each type of shellfish for deep-frying, the procedure is essentially the same, and it is quite simple. The oil should be fresh, deep, and heated to about 365°F. Keep the coating light; heavy batter overwhelms seafood (fritters, which are not really fried seafood but fried seafood-flavored batter, are the exception). Do not crowd the pieces in the pan. It is perfectly acceptable, if less than ideal, to keep the food warm in a low oven while you finish frying (although it is better, if your social conditions allow it, to simply serve the morsels as you pull them from the oil and drain them).

Clams: Shuck soft-shells, cut off the tough "neck" skin, 000, and rinse well. "Frying clams" are soft-shells sold already shucked. Keep the meats whole and dry well.

Shrimp: Peel and dry. Devein, and butterfly, 490, if desired.

Scallops: Halve horizontally if very large. Dry well.

Squid: Cut bodies into rings; leave tentacles whole unless very large. Dry as thoroughly as possible, for they are notorious for spattering. Cook in a covered fryer if possible.

Oysters: Do not use very large ones. Shuck them and dry well.

FRIED CLAMS, SHRIMP, SQUID, OR OYSTERS WITH CORNMEAL COATING

4 servings

Heat in a deep-fat fryer or deep, heavy pot over medium-high heat to 365°F:

3 inches vegetable oil

Prepare for deep-frying, above:

1½ to 2 pounds shellfish

Pour into a shallow bowl:

1 cup milk or buttermilk

Mix in a second shallow bowl:

1½ cups cornmeal
½ cup all-purpose flour
2 tablespoons ground cumin, chili powder, or curry powder (optional)
1½ teaspoons salt
Ground black or red pepper to taste

Dip the shellfish in the milk, drain thoroughly, then coat with the seasoned cornmeal. Let stand on a rack or wax paper until all are coated and the oil is hot. Add a few pieces at a time to the oil, keeping the heat high in order to maintain a fairly consistent temperature. Do not crowd. Cook until golden brown, stirring occasionally (large pieces may need to be turned individually). Drain on paper bags or paper towels. Serve with:

Lemon wedges and hot red pepper sauce, Tartar Sauce, 73, Aïoli, 74, or a seasoned mayonnaise, 73 to 75

FRIED SHRIMP, SCALLOPS, OR OYSTERS WITH BREADCRUMB COATING

4 servings

Substitute unsweetened dried coconut for the breadcrumbs for a terrific variation.

Prepare for deep-frying, 521:

1½ to 2 pounds shellfish

Be sure to dry the pieces well. Mix in a shallow bowl:

2 cups dry bread or cracker crumbs

Salt and ground black pepper to taste

Whisk together in a second shallow bowl:

3 large eggs

Dip the shellfish in the eggs, then coat with the seasoned crumbs. Refrigerate on a rack or baking sheet lined with wax paper for 1 to 2 hours.

When you are ready to cook, heat in a deep-fat fryer or deep, heavy pot over medium-high heat to 365°F:

3 inches vegetable oil

Add a few of the shellfish pieces at a time, keeping the heat high in order to maintain a fairly consistent temperature. Do not crowd. Cook until golden brown, stirring occasionally (large pieces may need to be turned individually). Drain on paper bags or paper towels. Serve with:

Lemon wedges and hot red pepper sauce, Tartar Sauce, 73, Aïoli, 74, or any seasoned mayonnaise, 73 to 75

FRIED CLAMS, SHRIMP, SCALLOPS, SQUID, OR OYSTERS WITH FLOUR COATING

4 servings

When you fry with no moisture in the coating, as in this recipe, you get a very light, transparent crust. It is not as crunchy as other crusts, but it allows more of the shellfish's flavor to come through.

Heat in a deep-fat fryer or deep, heavy pot over medium-high heat to 365°F.

3 inches vegetable oil

Prepare for deep-frying, 521:

1½ to 2 pounds shellfish

Pour into a shallow bowl:

1½ cups milk or buttermilk

Mix in a second shallow bowl:

2 cups all-purpose flour

Salt and ground black pepper to taste

Dip the shellfish in the milk, drain thoroughly, then coat with the seasoned flour, shaking off the excess. Add a few pieces at a time to the oil, keeping the heat high in order to maintain a fairly consistent temperature. Do not crowd. Cook until golden brown, stirring occasionally (large pieces may need to be turned individually). Drain on paper bags or paper towels. Serve with:

Lemon wedges and hot red pepper sauce, Tartar Sauce, 73, Aïoli, 74, or a seasoned mayonnaise, 73 to 75

CLAMS, SHRIMP, SCALLOPS, SQUID OR OYSTERS TEMPURA

4 servings

Add a few pieces of cut-up vegetables to this mixture, and you can have a full meal of tempura. There are a few unusual procedures in making tempura batter, which results in a thin, lacy coating that is exceptionally light and crisp. Like most fried food, tempura is best served as soon as possible, but it will hold for a few minutes in a low oven.

Heat in a deep-fat fryer or deep, heavy pot over medium-high heat to 365°F:

3 inches vegetable oil

Prepare for deep-frying, 521:

1½ to 2 pounds shellfish

Be sure to dry the pieces well. Prepare the batter just before frying. Place in a bowl:

Scant 2 cups ice water

Sift over it:

2 cups self-rising cake flour (low-gluten, with baking soda and salt added)

Stir to mix slightly; there should be lumps in the batter. Test the oil: a few drops of batter should sink slightly, rise and puff quickly, but not color immediately. Dip the shellfish 1 piece at a time in the batter and gently lay them in the oil. Do not crowd; you can cook in batches if necessary. Keep the heat high in order to maintain a fairly consistent temperature. Let them fry, undisturbed, for about 1 minute. Turn and fry for another minute. When done, the shellfish will be opaque and the batter crisp but barely colored. Remove to a rack or paper bags or paper towels to drain. If pieces of batter separate and float to the top of the cooking oil, strain them out with a mesh strainer. Keep warm, if necessary, in a low oven. Serve with:

Lemon wedges or Ginger Soy Sauce, 84

CARIBBEAN STYLE CLAM, SQUID, OR WHELK FRITTERS

8 or more appetizer servings

This is a great recipe for tough, inexpensive clams, such as the minced clams sold in containers in supermarkets. It is also fine for chopped squid (even leftovers) and precooked whelk. Beer batter makes the lightest, crispest fritters.

Mix in a large bowl:

1½ cups all-purpose flour

½ teaspoon baking powder

1½ teaspoons salt

1 teaspoon dried thyme

½ teaspoon ground black pepper

¼ teaspoon ground red pepper, or to taste

¼ teaspoon ground allspice
¼ teaspoon ground cinnamon
⅛ teaspoon freshly grated or ground nutmeg

Add and stir just until well blended:

One 12-ounce bottle beer
1 tablespoon fresh lemon juice

Stir in:

1 cup minced clams, squid, or cooked whelk or conch, 505

Heat in a deep-fat fryer or deep, heavy pot over medium-high heat to 365°F:

3 inches vegetable oil

Spoon about ¼ cup batter for each fritter into the oil. Make only a few fritters at a time; do not crowd. Fry for 2 to 3 minutes, until lightly browned, turning the fritters if necessary (sometimes they turn themselves). If pieces of batter separate and float to the top of the cooking oil, strain them out as you cook. Drain the fritters on paper bags or paper towels. Keep warm, if necessary, in a low oven. Serve with:

Lime wedges
Hot red pepper sauce

GEODUCK CLAM FRITTERS WITH PINEAPPLE SALSA

6 servings

You will need 2 pounds clam meat for these fritters. Steam the geoducks just until they open easily, then remove and discard the siphon and stomach from each clam. If geoduck clams are not available, use whatever fresh clams you find at your local fish store.

Place in a small saucepan over high heat:

¼ cup sugar

Heat, without stirring, until a light brown caramel has formed, about 4 minutes. Watch the sugar carefully to make sure it does not overbrown; remove the pan from the heat a moment before you think the sugar is done, as it will continue to cook off the stove. Cool briefly, then return the pan to the burner. Add:

2 tablespoons Champagne vinegar or rice vinegar
¾ cup pineapple juice

Cook, stirring, over medium heat for 3 minutes. Stir in:

1 tablespoon *sambal oelek* (Indonesian chili paste), 2 teaspoons Chinese chili paste, or 1 teaspoon hot red pepper sauce
½ cup diced pineapple, preferably fresh

Cook for 2 minutes. Add:

1 medium tomato, peeled, seeded, and diced
1 teaspoon salt

Cook for 1 minute. Mix together, then stir in:

1 tablespoon plus 1 teaspoon cornstarch
2 tablespoons water

Simmer gently until the salsa is lightly thickened, about 5 minutes. Remove from the heat and keep warm.

Combine in a food processor:

2 pounds geoduck clam meat, cut on a diagonal into slices
1 medium onion, quartered
2 tablespoons chopped fresh parsley
1 teaspoon snipped fresh chives
2 teaspoons salt
1½ teaspoons ground white pepper

Pulse until the mixture is evenly chopped. Remove to a bowl and stir in:

1 large egg

Gradually stir in, then mix very well:

1 cup all-purpose flour

Heat in a deep-fat fryer or a deep, heavy pot over high heat to 375°F:

12 cups vegetable oil

Beat until soft peaks form:

2 large egg whites

Fold gently into the clam mixture. Spoon 1 heaping tablespoon batter for each fritter into the oil. Cook in batches without crowding. Fry, turning once, until the fritters have floated to the top of the oil and are golden, about 3 minutes. Drain the fritters on paper towels. Sprinkle with:

Salt

Serve immediately with the salsa.

FRIED SOFT-SHELL CRABS WITH GINGER, LEMON, AND BLACK BEANS

6 servings

Cut in half through the top of the shell:

6 soft-shell crabs, cleaned, 494

Measure into a bowl:

½ cup cornstarch

Dip the cut part of the crabs in the cornstarch and set aside. Combine:

¼ cup finely shredded peeled fresh ginger
1 tablespoon shredded lemon zest
2 small fresh red chili peppers, shredded
3 scallions, cut into 1-inch lengths

Set aside. In a separate bowl, combine:

1½ tablespoons minced garlic
1 tablespoon salted and fermented black beans
1 tablespoon Shaoxing wine or dry sherry

Set aside. In another bowl, combine:

1½ cups chicken or fish stock
1 tablespoon grated lemon zest

2 tablespoons oyster sauce
1 tablespoon light soy sauce
1 teaspoon sugar
Pinch of salt

Set aside. In another bowl, combine:

1½ tablespoons cornstarch
¼ cup water

Set aside. In a deep, heavy pot, heat until very hot but not smoking, about 365°F:

3 inches peanut oil

Add half the crab pieces. Cook for 2 to 4 minutes, turning them in the oil until red and crisp. Remove and drain on a rack or paper towels. Repeat with the other pieces. Heat a clean wok or skillet over high heat and add:

¼ cup peanut oil

When it is hot but not smoking, add the ginger mixture and cook, stirring, until just fragrant, about 10 seconds. Add the black bean mixture and cook, stirring, another 20 seconds. Add the seasoned stock and bring to a boil. Give the cornstarch and water a quick stir and add it to the sauce. Cook, stirring, until the sauce is thickened and glossy. Arrange the crabs on a serving platter, pour the sauce over, and garnish with:

Cilantro sprigs

LOBSTER NEWBURG
4 servings

A classsic American dish, this preparation takes full advantage of every delicious bit of the lobster.

Kill with a knife, 491:

3 lobsters (1½ pounds each)

When they are still, separate the tail and claws from the bodies and set aside. Split each lobster body. With your fingers or a paring knife, remove and discard the vein-like intestinal tract along the length of the lobster tail. Remove the small sac from behind the eyes. Remove the tomalley (the greenish gray liver) and the dark red coral (if the lobster is female). Press half of the tomalley and roe through a strainer to remove any lumps and set aside. Discard the other half. Cut each lobster body into 4 pieces.

Pour 2 inches water into the bottom of a steamer or large pot with a lid into which a colander just fits. Cover and bring to a full boil. When ample steam has collected, place the lobster claws and tails on the steamer rack or in the colander. Cover and steam without peeking for 4 minutes. Remove the lobsters and immediately cool under cold running water. Remove the tail meat from the shells and cut into 1½-inch chunks. Crack the knuckles and claws, remove the meat, and cut into chunks.

Heat in a large saucepan over high heat until smoking:

2 tablespoons vegetable oil

Add the lobster body pieces and cook, stirring, for 5 minutes. Add and cook for 5 minutes more:

3 medium shallots, coarsely chopped
2 tablespoons tomato paste
1 teaspoon paprika

Add and bring to a boil:

6 tablespoons dry white wine

Boil until almost evaporated, 1 to 2 minutes, then stir in:

1½ cups chicken or fish stock
1½ cups heavy cream
1 teaspoon salt

Bring the cream to a boil, reduce the heat, and simmer gently for 15 minutes. Meanwhile, melt in a large skillet over medium heat:

1 tablespoon unsalted butter

Add:

6 ounces small mushrooms, wiped clean and quartered

Cook, stirring occasionally, until softened and all of the liquid has evaporated, about 5 minutes. Strain the lobster sauce into the skillet, pressing on the shells to extract their flavorful liquid. Stir in the lobster meat and bring to a simmer. Add:

2 tablespoons dry sherry

Simmer for 30 seconds. Whisk together in a small bowl the reserved tomalley and roe and 2 tablespoons of the cream sauce along with:

1 large egg yolk
2 tablespoons heavy cream

Whisk this mixture into the lobster sauce and bring just to a simmer over low heat. Do not let the sauce boil. Stir in:

1½ tablespoons chopped fresh tarragon
1½ tablespoons chopped fresh parsley

Serve with:

Hot cooked rice

SEA SCALLOP GRATIN (COQUILLES SAINT-JACQUES AU GRATIN)
4 appetizer or 2 main-course servings

Combine and rub together with your fingertips until blended:

2 tablespoons unsalted butter, melted
¾ cup fresh breadcrumbs
6 tablespoons grated Parmesan cheese
2 tablespoons minced fresh parsley
2 teaspoons chopped fresh thyme
¼ teaspoon salt
Ground black pepper to taste

Melt in a medium skillet over medium heat:

1 tablespoon unsalted butter

Add:

2 shallots, minced

2 cloves garlic, minced

Cook, stirring, until softened but not browned, about 2 minutes. Add:

8 ounces small mushrooms, wiped clean and quartered

1 teaspoon salt

Cook, stirring occasionally, until softened, about 7 minutes. Add:

¼ cup dry white wine

Increase the heat and simmer until the wine is almost evaporated, about 3 minutes. Add:

1 cup heavy cream

Boil until thickened, about 5 minutes. The sauce can be prepared up to this point several hours in advance and refrigerated until use.

Preheat the broiler.

Shortly before serving, bring the sauce to a simmer and add:

12 ounces medium sea scallops, cut horizontally in half

Cook just until they are no longer translucent, about 1½ minutes. Remove the pan from the heat and stir in:

1 teaspoon fresh lemon juice

Spoon the mixture into scallop shells or individual gratin dishes. Sprinkle the breadcrumb mixture over the scallops and sauce. Broil until golden brown on top and bubbling around the edges, about 1½ minutes.

BAKED STUFFED LOBSTER *4 servings*

Position a rack in the upper third of the oven. Preheat the oven to 375°F. Spread over a large baking sheet:

3 cups fine fresh breadcrumbs

Toast in the oven, stirring every minute or so, until they have just begun to color, 2 to 5 minutes. Remove to a medium bowl and toss with:

½ cup chopped fresh flat-leaf parsley

1 tablespoon pressed or finely minced garlic

1 teaspoon salt

1 teaspoon ground black pepper

Split lengthwise in half, 491, leaving them attached by a hinge of their shell:

Four 1½- to 2-pound live lobsters

Be sure to collect the juices of the lobsters when they are cut. Remove the head sacs and intestines. Arrange the lobsters cut sides up in a single layer on the baking sheet. Lightly press the breadcrumb mixture into the chest cavities and tails of the lobsters. Using a fork, bring some of the flavorful tomalley up into the stuffing, and moisten the stuffing of each lobster with 1 tablespoon of the lobster juices. Drizzle over each lobster:

¼ cup olive oil

Use about 1 teaspoon oil to coat the claws and the rest to moisten the stuffing. Pour into the bottom of the baking sheet:

1½ cups dry white wine

Bake the lobsters for 25 to 30 minutes, basting the claws two or three times with pan juices. If the stuffing looks dry, moisten it with pan juices, but do not add more than a teaspoon or two, or the stuffing will become soggy. The lobsters are done when the stuffing is very hot and browned on top and the tail meat feels firm when pressed with your finger. Serve immediately.

BAKED STUFFED JUMBO SHRIMP *4 servings*

These are delicious with a dry white wine and a tomato salad.

Position a rack in the upper third of the oven. Preheat the oven to 450°F.

Have ready:

14 raw colossal shrimp (2 pounds or more), unpeeled

Butterfly, 490, 12 of the shrimp. Season lightly with:

Salt and ground black pepper

Peel the remaining 2 shrimp, coarsely chop, and combine with:

1½ cups fine fresh breadcrumbs

6 tablespoons (¾ stick) butter, melted

¼ cup finely chopped fresh flat-leaf parsley

2 teaspoons pressed or finely minced garlic

¼ teaspoon salt

¼ teaspoon ground black pepper

Arrange the shrimp in a single layer in a shallow baking dish and top with the stuffing mixture, pressing it lightly. Pour into the baking dish, just enough to cover the bottom of the pan:

¾ to 1 cup dry white wine

Bake the shrimp until piping hot, 10 to 12 minutes; be careful not to overcook. Spoon a bit of the juice from the baking dish over each shrimp and serve immediately.

ESCARGOTS IN SHELLS *3 to 4 servings*

Snail shells can be bought at fish stores. If washed and dried thoroughly after use, they can be reused for many years.

Preheat the oven to 425°F.

Have ready:

Snail Butter, 77

Rinse well and drain thoroughly:

18 snail shells

One 4½-ounce can escargot (18 snails)

Place the snails in the shells and pack the shells firmly with the snail butter so that only the herbed butter is visible at the opening. You can chill the snails for later use, or bake them at once in the preheated oven just until piping hot, 3 to 5 minutes. Serve immediately with long, closely tined forks to remove the meat.

SEAFOOD À LA KING

4 servings

You will need a total of 3 cups cooked seafood. Use whatever combination you like best or just one kind.

Preheat the oven to 375°F. Melt in a small saucepan over medium heat:

1 tablespoon unsalted butter

Cook until the butter turns brown. Add:

⅓ cup minced onions

2 cloves garlic, minced

Cook for 1 minute. Scrape into a small bowl and add:

¾ cup fresh breadcrumbs

2 hard-boiled eggs, finely chopped

2 tablespoons minced fresh parsley

¼ teaspoon salt

Ground black pepper to taste

Rub the mixture together with your fingertips until blended.

Heat in a medium skillet over medium heat:

1 tablespoon unsalted butter

Add:

8 ounces small mushrooms, wiped clean and quartered

1 red bell pepper, diced

Cook, stirring occasionally, until softened, about 7 minutes. Add:

8 ounces medium shrimp, peeled, deveined if desired, and cut into ½-inch pieces

8 ounces sea scallops, cut into ½-inch pieces

Cook just until the seafood is firm, about 2 minutes. Drain the seafood and vegetables, allowing the liquid to drain into a measuring cup. Add:

Enough milk to measure 2 cups

Melt in a medium saucepan over medium heat:

2 tablespoons unsalted butter

Whisk in:

2 tablespoons plus 1 teaspoon all-purpose flour

Cook for 30 seconds. Whisk in the milk mixture and cook until thickened, about 3 minutes. Stir in:

1 tablespoon fresh lemon juice

1½ teaspoons Worcestershire sauce

1½ teaspoons salt

Add the seafood mixture to the sauce. Stir in:

1 cup diced cooked lobster meat

1 cup frozen peas

4 scallions, sliced

Spread the mixture evenly in an 11-inch gratin dish and top with the breadcrumb mixture. Bake until hot and bubbling and the top is golden brown, about 25 minutes.

DEVILED CRAB GRATIN

4 servings

Preheat the oven to 375°F. Melt in a small saucepan over medium heat:

1½ tablespoons unsalted butter

Add and cook, stirring, for 1 minute:

2 cloves garlic, minced

Do not let the garlic brown. Whisk in and cook for 30 seconds:

1½ tablespoons all-purpose flour

Whisk in and boil until thickened, 2 to 3 minutes:

1 cup milk

Stir in and boil for 30 seconds more:

1 tablespoon Pernod or aniseed

Stir in:

1 tablespoon whole-grain mustard

1 tablespoon minced fresh parsley

1 tablespoon minced fresh tarragon

¾ teaspoon salt

¼ teaspoon ground red pepper

Gently fold in:

1¼ pounds jumbo lump crabmeat, picked over for shells and cartilage

Remove to 4 individual gratin dishes and top with:

¾ cup grated Parmesan cheese

Bake until hot and bubbling, about 15 minutes, then broil just until the cheese turns golden brown, 1 to 2 minutes. Serve immediately.

FISH

Cooking fish is simple, as the recipes in this chapter will demonstrate. The best fish dishes are as elementary as the best meat dishes: They begin with a few top-notch ingredients and finish with a basic technique. Nutritionists recommend that we eat three or more servings of fish per week on the basis of many studies demonstrating links between higher fish intake and low rates of coronary heart disease and cancer. The fat in fish is of the Omega-3 variety, which seems to keep blood from getting sticky and to decrease the likelihood of having a stroke.

WHERE DOES FISH COME FROM?

More than half of the shrimp eaten in the United States was raised on a farm. Salmon, now grown in nearly every northern country with access to cold, deep water, has moved ahead of cod on the list of most-eaten fish. Catfish has replaced cotton as the most important crop in both Mississippi and Alabama; it, too, is on the "top-ten list," although it was rarely eaten more than fifty miles from the Mississippi River just twenty years ago. Highly treasured bay scallops, found in the wild in a limited area between Long Island and Cape Cod, are now exported by the ton from farms in China.

All of this means that there are few "traditional" fish. Cod is no longer a North Atlantic fish, nor salmon a North Pacific fish. Each are harvested in season, wherever they are found, and shipped to markets all over the world. The net effect means that fish are like vegetables: There are no longer any seasons. What you find in your fish market is an eclectic combination of what is available that week, not from your local waters, but from all waters. As good as this aquaculture is, it has caused challenging environmental problems all over the world, and fully satisfactory solutions have not yet been found.

Whenever you have a choice, buy wild fish; the flavor is always superior. In addition, you are buying one of the last remaining truly wild, naturally organic foods remaining on Earth.

MAINTAINING QUALITY AT HOME

More fish spoils at home than anywhere else. Refrigerators are not cold enough to store fish, which keeps almost twice as well at 32° or 33°F (its temperature when buried in ice) as it does at 40°F, the temperature of most refrigerators. Fill the vegetable bin or a baking pan with ice (or ice packs, which are neater) and do your best to bury your wrapped fish in there; you will maintain the quality of your fish for far longer.

Still, it pays to cook fish as soon as possible—although some fish will retain their quality for as long as eight or even ten days, many of those days are usu-

HOW TO BUY FISH

There are some simple rules you can follow that will help you bring home high-quality fish:

1. *Buy fish from a reputable fishmonger where you can see and smell the fish easily.*
2. *Never buy fish that is not stored at 33°F. It should be on ice or in a refrigerated case with a thermometer.*
3. *Trust your instincts: Good fish looks good, has firm, unmarred flesh, and smells like fresh seawater. The surface of the fish should be bright, clear, and almost translucent. It should not have spots of pink (which are usually bruises) or brown (which indicates spoilage), and it should have no areas of deep red or brown. Whole fish gives you more signals than fillets or steaks. Look for red gills, bright, reflective skin, firm flesh, an undamaged layer of scales, and no browning anywhere. Again, the smell—even in the body cavity—should be sweet. The best whole fish look alive, as if they just came out of the water.*
4. *When buying frozen fish, make sure there are no signs of freezer burn—the meat will look dry and almost chalky—a sure sign that the fish has lost so much moisture that its taste and texture will be markedly inferior.*

ally spent in getting the fish from the water to your home. Even a farm-raised fish, which is harvested according to schedule and shipped within a day, is probably at least three days old by the time it reaches your supermarket counter.

So it makes the most sense to buy fish the day you are going to eat it, or at most the day before. If your plans change and you find that you are not going to be cooking it, freeze it. (There are also times when you have too much fish—you overbought accidentally or because the fish was on sale or you or a friend had a plentiful catch.) Home freezing of fish is eminently practical, as long as you see it as a short-term process. With a few exceptions—shrimp among them—frozen fish does not keep as well as frozen meat; it is best to use it within a month or at the most two. To freeze, simply wrap cleaned and rinsed fish tightly in plastic wrap, then wrap again. Make sure your freezer holds a temperature of 0°F or lower.

To thaw the fish, place it on a plate in the refrigerator 24 hours or so before you want to cook it; to hurry the process, place it in cold water to cover, changing the water often. Once it is thawed, store it on or in ice in the refrigerator and cook it as soon as possible.

HOW TO CLEAN FISH

There is not a single fish-preparation technique that you cannot perform at home, as long as you have a few good knives.

Whenever you clean fish, you should be reserving anything that has meat attached to it—fins, tail, head (minus the gills), and bones—for the stockpot. As is the case with any food scraps, you can freeze these pieces until you have enough of them to make a large quantity of stock, or simply simmer them for 20 minutes in water to cover while you are going about your business. Strain the stock and use it on the spot or freeze it for later use.

Removing the Fins: Assuming you start with a whole fish to which nothing has been done, the first task is to remove the fins. These sharp, bony appendages can cut you and are ultimately destined for the stockpot. The easiest way to remove fins is with heavy scissors.

Removing the Scales: You must scale almost all fish before going any further. (If you are going to fillet the fish and remove its skin, you need not scale it; but if you are going to fillet it and leave the skin on, scale it now—it is easier.) Although scaling is messy, it is easy enough. You can use a spoon, a dull knife or the back of a knife, or a fish scaler sold in all sporting-goods stores. Hold the fish by its tail, and simply run the tool up the length of the fish, from the tail toward the head. You will get the hang of it instantly, and the scales will soon be flying.

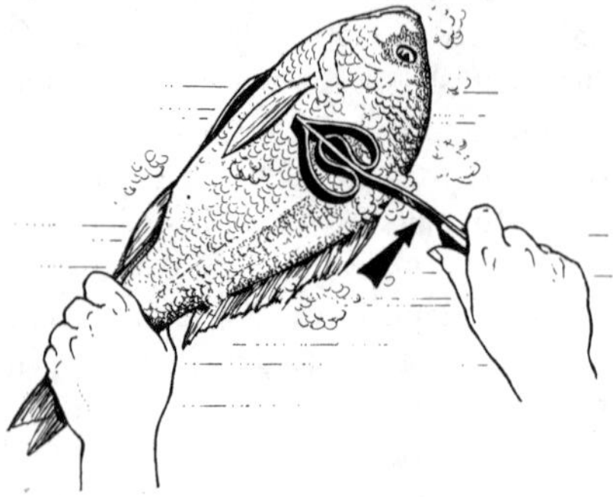

Scaling a fish

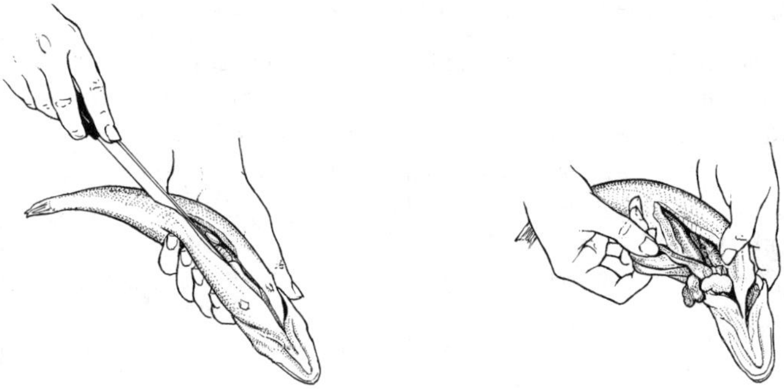

Removing the innards

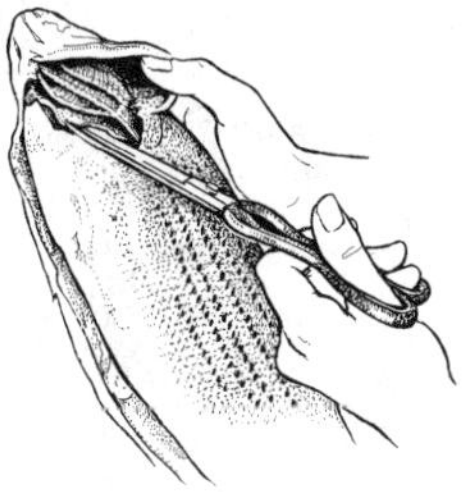

Removing the gills

To reduce the mess of scaling: Scale outside, where flying scales do not matter; scale in a deep sink, under running water; or scale into a clear, large plastic bag.

Removing the Innards: Next, remove the guts from the fish: Cut along the length of the fish's belly, from under the gills to the anal opening, then simply pull out the innards, shown above left. Roe is edible, so you might reserve it and cook it separately (see About Shad Roe, 566). Scrape out any guts that cling to the bones, such as the kidneys. Discard the innards and wash the fish.

If you are cutting the fish into steaks or fillets, proceed to those steps, below. If you are serving a whole fish, remove the gills and, if necessary, the head and tail.

Removing the Gills: Gills are inedible and must be removed and discarded. Using the same opening you make to remove the innards, above, cut them out with scissors, shown above right. Be careful—they are sharp.

Removing the Head and Tail: If you are roasting, grilling, or broiling the fish, or if the fish will fit whole in your cooking pan, leave the head and tail on—they make it easier to handle the fish, the head has good meat in it, and the presentation is more attractive. If, however, your pan or pot is too small, or you do not want to look at the head or tail, remove them, shown below left.

Cut the tail off. Some fish have thick bones that run all the way down to the tail, so you may have to use a heavy knife and some arm muscle. The tail goes in the stockpot.

As for the head, on smaller fish, you can cut through the "neck," using a sturdy knife. On larger fish, you may need a larger knife, and it may help to whack it through the center bone with a wooden or rubber mallet, rolling pin, or similar object. Or cut partway through the neck, then bend the head sharply over the cutting surface, snapping the bone. The head, with the gills removed, is the prime ingredient for the stockpot.

CUTTING STEAKS

Once you have removed the fins, scales, and innards from a large fish, you can cut it into steaks. Just use a sharp, heavy knife, shown below right. If necessary, whack it through the center bone with a wooden or rubber mallet, rolling pin, or similar device. You can remove the belly flaps if you like—they will go into the stockpot. Or you can turn large steaks into two small fillets each: With a sharp, thin-bladed knife, cut along the inside of the skin and the bone of one fillet, shown 530. Repeat on the other side. You can cut off the thin ends if desired.

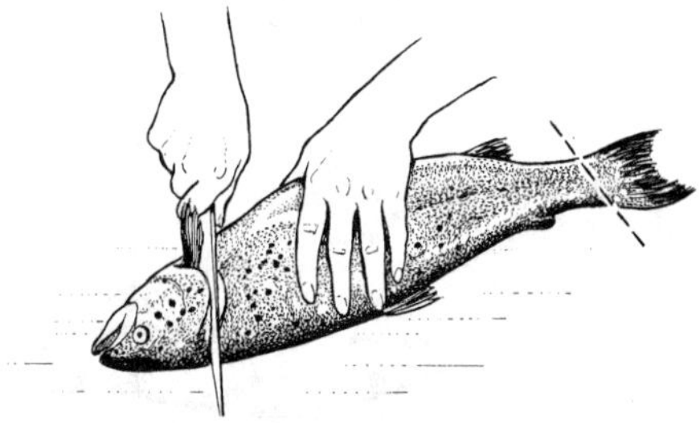

Removing the head and tail

Cutting a large fish into steaks

A NOTE TO THOSE WHO CATCH THEIR OWN FISH

Although the cleaning procedure is the same whether you buy or catch your own fish, there are certain steps that you can take on a boat or shoreline to make sure that your fish stays as fresh as possible.

The ideal way to kill a fish is to make a cut along its throat and place it in a bucket of ice water. It will bleed and cool down at the same time. Next, gut it and pack it in ice. Keep it there until you get it home, then clean it further.

If this is impractical, do whatever you can to cool the fish down quickly after capture. Gutting it and packing it in ice (put ice in its body cavity too) works well. If you don't have the time for even that, you might kill the fish with a sharp blow to the head and pack it in ice, or let it remain alive in a bucket of cold water until you get a chance to deal with it.

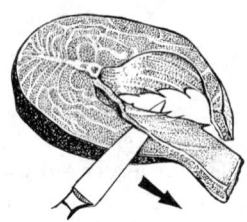

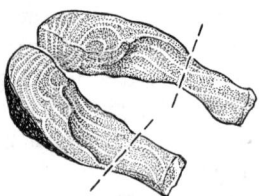

Cutting large steaks into fillets

FILLETING

Filleting roundfish, shown below, is easy. Start by cutting around the base of the head and across the tail with a sharp, thin-bladed knife (do not, however, cut either off completely). Then make a cut along the back from gill cover to tail, following the line of the central bone, shown below left. Now cut down behind the gill cover until you feel the bone, and turn the knife parallel to the fish and the cutting board, with the cutting edge toward the tail. Cut with a sliding motion along the backbone until you have released the fillet in one piece, shown below right. Repeat on the other side.

Remove the thin belly flap for stock, or just use a knife to bone it (in salmon, especially, the meat here is quite delicious). Use tweezers, needle-nose pliers, or your fingers to remove any stray bones or pin bones, which run down the center of some fillets, shown 531.

To fillet flatfish, shown 531, score the outline of the fillets with a sharp, thin-bladed knife, cutting to the bone behind the head and straight down the center of the fish, tail to head. Then hold the knife parallel to the fish and cutting board and cut the fillet away from the ribs, using a stroking motion. Repeat on the second fillet, then turn the fish over and repeat on the other side (these fillets may be slightly thinner).

SKINNING

To skin fillets—not always necessary or recommended—place the fillet skin side down. Hold the tail firmly with your free hand and cut through the fillet

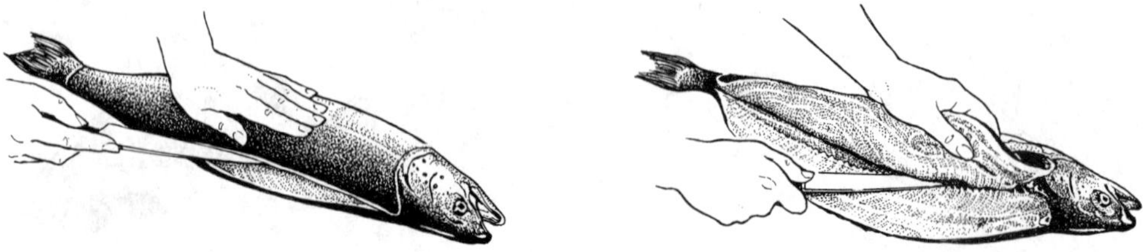

Filleting roundfish

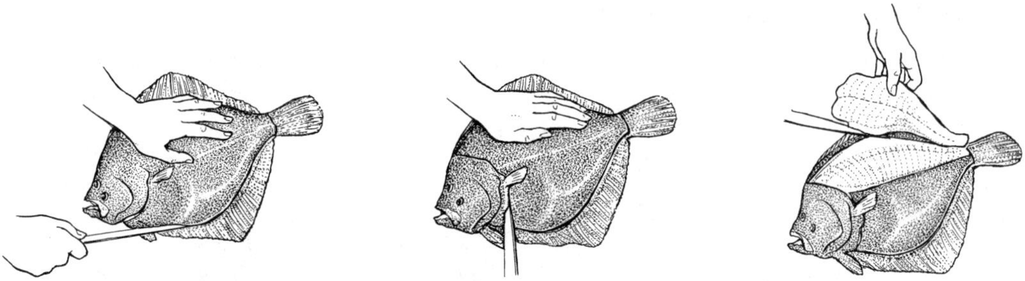

Filleting flatfish

down to the skin about ½ inch up from the tail end. Now just hold that flap tightly and run a sharp, thin-bladed knife up the length of the fillet, angling it so that it scrapes the skin but does not cut it, shown below right. You will probably succeed quite well the first time you try it. (Remember that you can almost always remove skin after cooking too, with no trouble at all.)

THE FISH

Here are details about the fish you are most likely to find in the market or catch yourself.

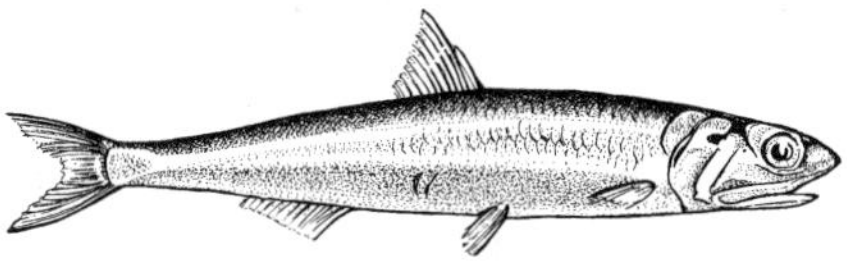

European anchovy

Common Name: Anchovy
Local to: Worldwide
Special preparation techniques: When packed in salt, rinse and pick over first; when in oil, rinse if you wish and reserve the oil for use in cooking; when fresh, debone like sardines (shown 559).
Best cooking techniques: When canned or salted, as flavoring in other dishes; when fresh, grilling or broiling (if large), sautéing, roasting, or pickling

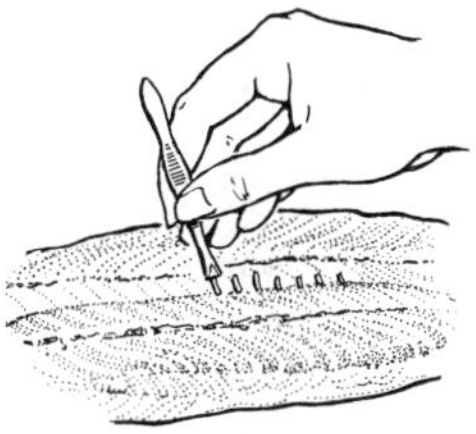

Removing stray bones

Texture: Soft, delicate flesh
Flavor/Color: Strong/Dark
Fat content: Moderate to low
Notes: When fresh, often confused with sardines and herring; no matter, they are all pretty much interchangeable.

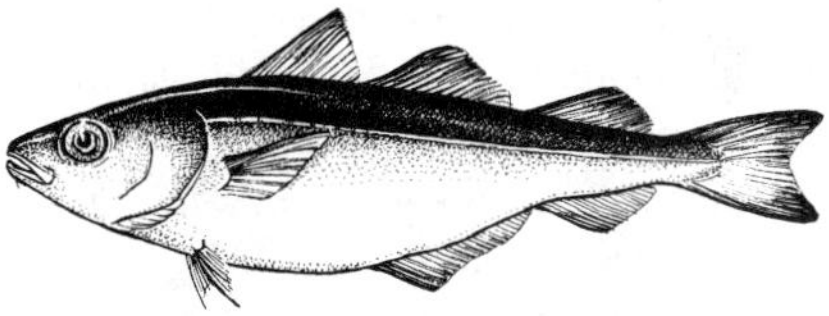

Atlantic pollock

Common Names: Atlantic Pollock, Boston Blue
Local to: Northeast
Best cooking techniques: Sautéing, broiling, cooking with liquid, deep-frying
Texture: Moderately firm, with large, codlike flakes
Flavor/Color: Mild/Off-white (becomes lighter when cooked)
Fat content: Low
Notes: Much like cod but a little darker, more flavorful, and somewhat sturdier. Pacific (or Alaskan) pollock is more delicate.

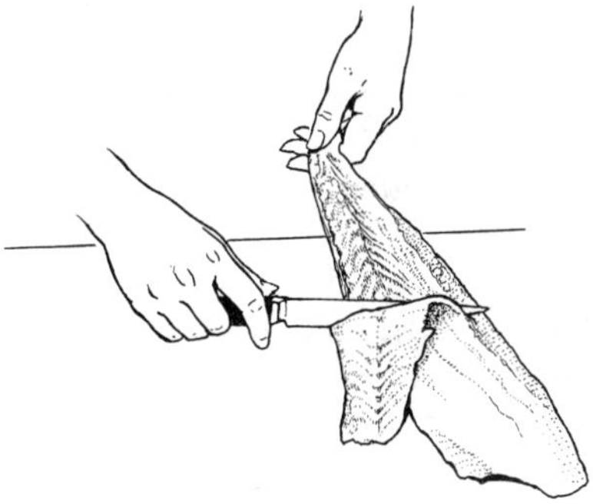

Skinning a fillet

HOW TO KNOW WHEN FISH IS DONE

To cook fish well, all you need to know is that most fish are best treated simply. The Canadian Cooking Theory, a timing technique popularized by the late cooking authority James Beard, advises cooking fish for 10 minutes per inch of thickness regardless of cooking method, cut, or species of fish. This is about as good as generalizations get. But if you follow it religiously, your fish will often be overcooked and occasionally undercooked. (You would never cook a sirloin steak by the clock, would you?) As a general guideline, 8 to 9 minutes per inch of thickness works a little better than 10—but only as a guideline.

Timing gives an approximate sense of when a fish is likely to be done, but you have to check it all the while. Even under the best of circumstances, cooking is inexact. And many things can affect the speed at which fish cooks: The actual temperature of the oven, grill, or skillet; the shape, thickness, density, and temperature of the flesh; and the presence or absence of liquids, for example.

Almost all recipes—including those here—give some timing guidelines for knowing when fish is done. But you will soon learn to recognize the signs of doneness: a firming up of texture; the beginnings of flakiness; an opaque, whiter look throughout.

In addition, there are two surefire ways to determine whether fish is done: interior appearance and interior temperature. When a fish is opaque throughout, it is done. When you begin to suspect that a piece of fish has nearly finished cooking, take a thin-bladed knife and gently prod between the flakes of fillets or steaks, or cut between flesh and bone. Do not be afraid to poke around while fish is cooking; if you like your salmon or swordfish just underdone or your tuna medium-rare, learn what it looks like inside. Remove the fish just before it reaches the stage at which you want to eat it; it will finish cooking between kitchen and plate.

Just as accurate is an instant-read thermometer. Insert it into the thickest part of the fish. All fish is cooked through at 137°F. Usually, 135°F leaves just a hint of translucence and more moisture and is done enough for most people. For tuna and other fish that you might prefer less well-done, try 120°F for starters. Use the knife-peeking technique to double-check the thermometer if you are unsure.

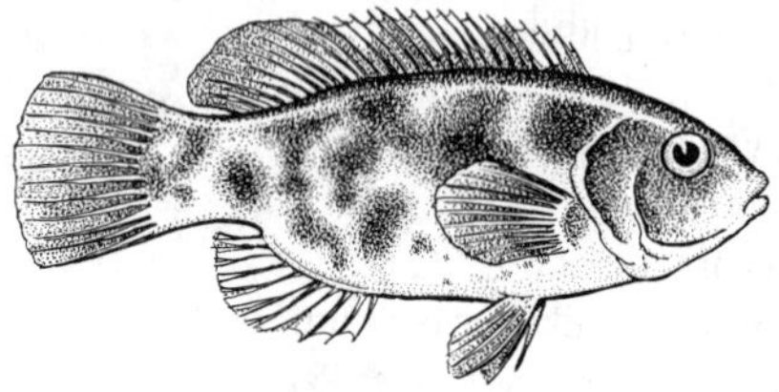

Blackfish or tautog

Common Names: Blackfish, tautog
Local to: Northeast
Special preparation techniques: Skin must be removed.
Best cooking techniques: Grilling (with care), broiling, sautéing, cooking with liquid
Texture: Quite sturdy
Flavor/Color: Mild/Pinkish white
Fat content: Low
Notes: One of the few white fillets that can be grilled.

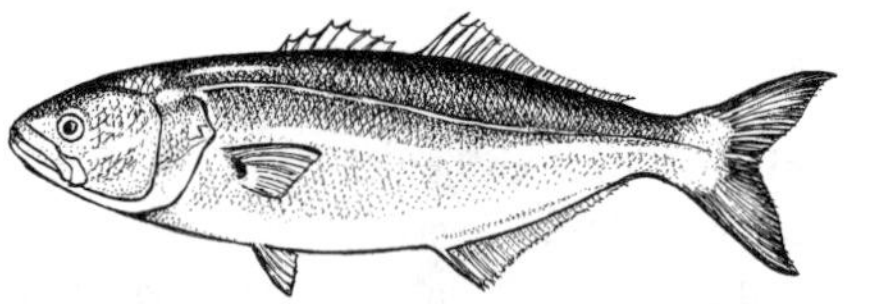

Bluefish

Common Name: Bluefish
Local to: Atlantic coast
Special preparation techniques: Dark center line of fillets can be cut out. Cook with acid to cut through fish's natural fat
Best cooking techniques: Broiling, grilling (whole fish, with care), sautéing
Texture: Soft
Flavor/Color: Rich and full/Dark grayish blue when raw, tan when cooked
Fat content: High
Notes: Highly perishable, so keep cold religiously; good for smoking.

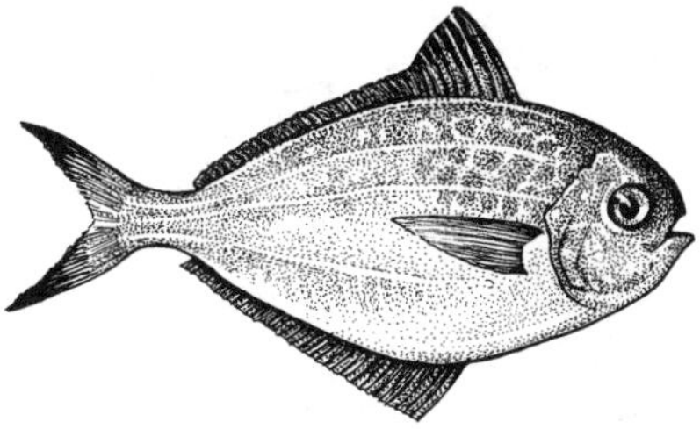

Butterfish

Common Name: Butterfish
Local to: Worldwide
Special preparation techniques: Needs no scaling
Best cooking techniques: Pan-frying
Texture: Meaty
Flavor/Color: Full-flavored (somewhat buttery)/Off-white
Fat content: Moderate
Notes: Tiny fish, frequently weighing less than 4 ounces each; excellent eating.

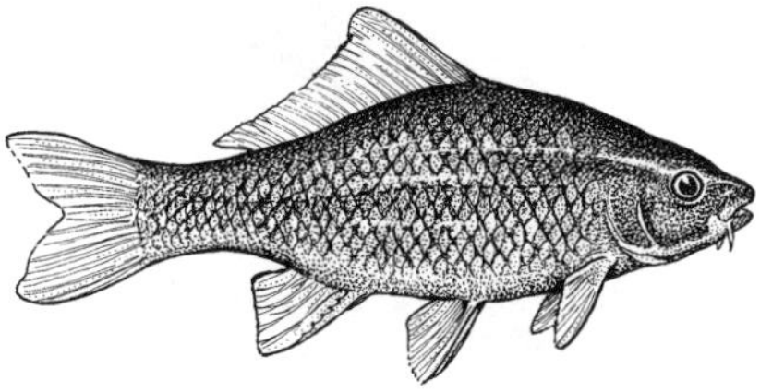

Carp

Common Name: Carp
Local to: Freshwater fish, farm-raised all over the world
Special preparation techniques: Trim dark flesh before cooking.
Best cooking techniques: Cooking with liquid, frying
Texture: Firm
Flavor/Color: Mild/Off-white
Fat content: Low
Notes: Juicy and meaty when cooked with liquid; classic Chinese braised fish.

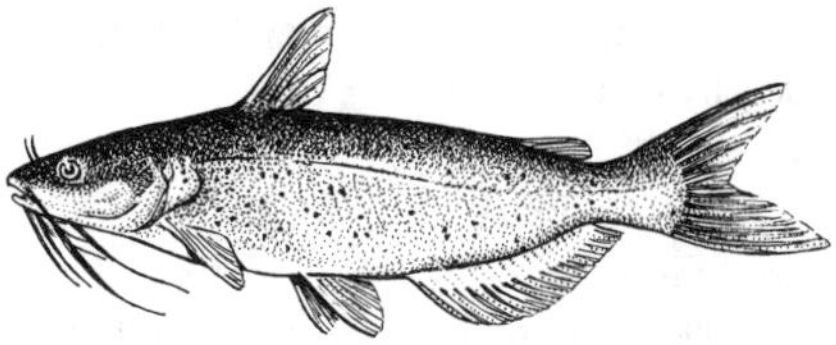

Catfish

Common Names: Catfish, Channel Cat, Bullhead
Local to: Central United States (especially the Mississippi), but now farm-raised almost everywhere
Best cooking techniques: Frying, sautéing, cooking with liquid, broiling
Texture: Moderately firm
Flavor/Color: Mild to muddy/White
Fat content: Low
Notes: Sturdier than many other white-fleshed fish.

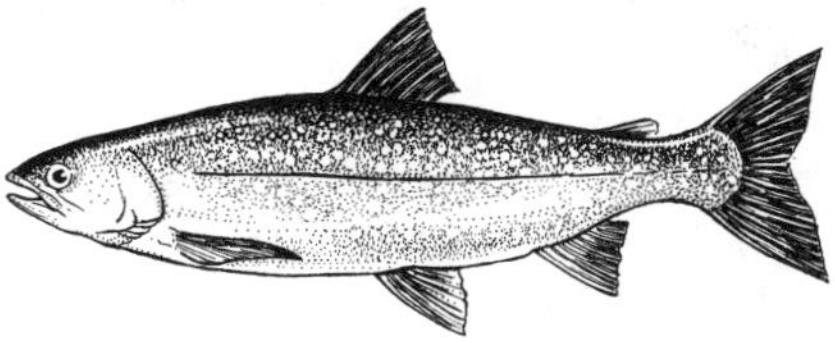

Arctic char

Common Names: Char, Arctic Char
Local to: Farm-raised in Northern waters
Best cooking techniques: As for salmon
Texture: Moderately firm
Flavor/Color: Buttery and rich/Orange
Fat content: High
Notes: Troutlike fish that is virtually indistinguishable from salmon.

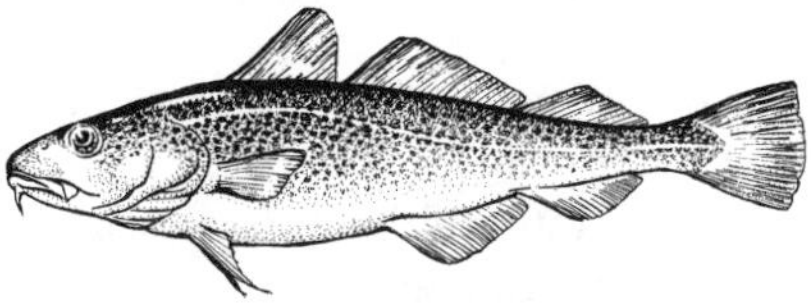

Cod

Common Names: Cod, Atlantic Cod, Scrod, Pacific Cod
Local to: The North Atlantic (Atlantic Cod) and North Pacific (Pacific Cod)
Special preparation techniques: Thick fillets are preferable.

Best cooking techniques: Everything but grilling, for which it is too delicate
Texture: Soft
Flavor/Color: Mild/White
Fat content: Very low
Notes: The quintessential delicate white-fleshed fish. Beautiful, large flakes, very tender. Salted (to make salt cod), dried (to make stockfish), and cured with lye (to make lutefisk).

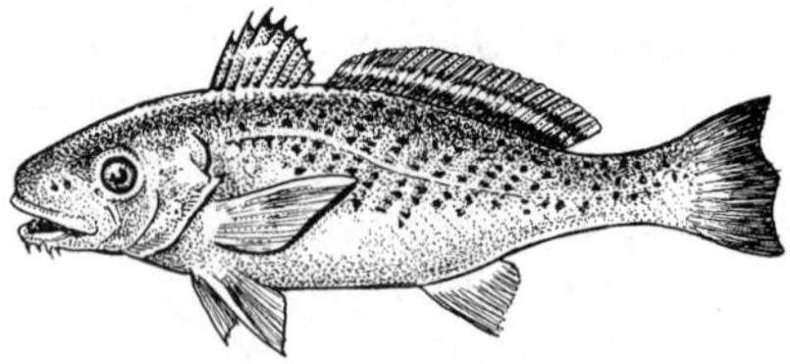

Croaker

Common Names: Croaker, Drum, Hardhead, Blackmouth
Local to: Worldwide
Best cooking techniques: Pan-frying (whole or fillets), cooking with liquid, frying
Texture: Fairly soft
Flavor/Color: Sweet and mild/White
Fat content: Low
Notes: Names come from booming sound they are capable of making. Delicious fish. Similar to porgy and spot.

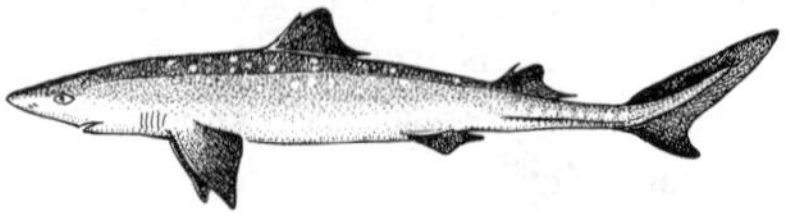

Dogfish

Common Names: Dogfish, Cape Shark, Rock Cod
Local to: Worldwide
Special preparation techniques: Must be skinned.
Best cooking techniques: Frying, sautéing, broiling, roasting
Texture: Moderately firm
Flavor/Color: Mild/Pinkish white
Fat content: Low
Notes: Classic fish-and-chips fish.

Eel

Common Name: Eel
Local to: All Atlantic waters
Special preparation techniques: Sometimes sold live; must be skinned by a professional.
Best cooking techniques: Broiling, grilling, cooking with liquid
Texture: Firm and very oily
Flavor/Color: Meaty, full, and rich/Grayish white
Fat content: High
Notes: Wonderful smoked.

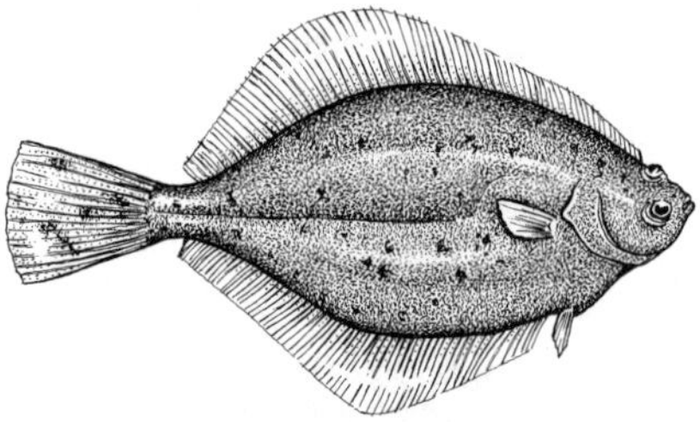

Winter flounder

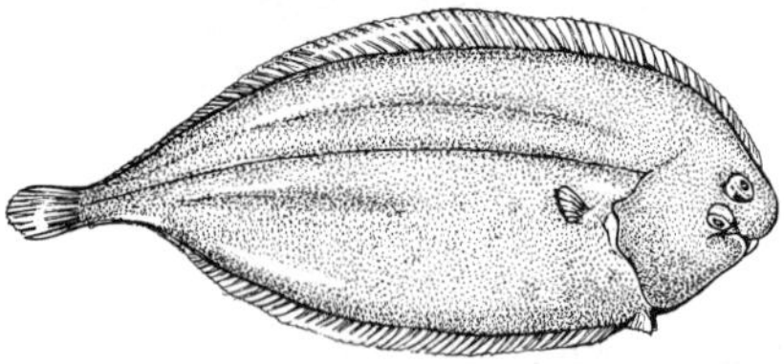

Dover sole

Common Names: Flounder, Dab, Plaice, Sole, Fluke, etc.
Local to: Worldwide
Best cooking techniques: Grilling (whole fish only), pan-grilling, broiling, sautéing, roasting, cooking in liquid (gently and briefly)
Texture: Extremely delicate
Flavor/Color: Mild/White to whitish gray
Fat content: Extremely low
Notes: Excellent cooked whole. Fillets are extremely delicate; cook for no more than 3 or 4 minutes.

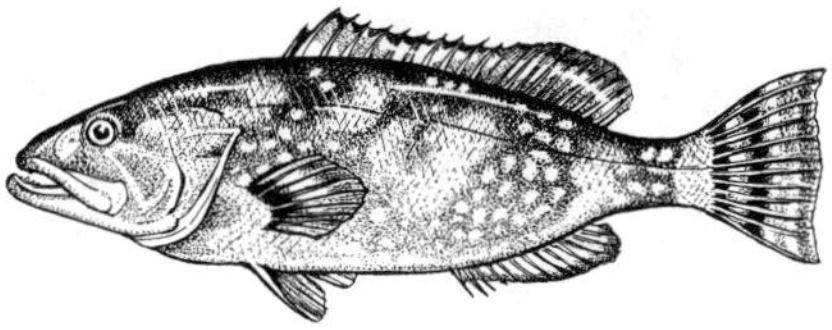

Red grouper

Common Names: Grouper, Rock Cod, Sea Bass, Jewfish
Local to: Worldwide in warm waters
Best cooking techniques: All-purpose; fillets can be grilled with care.
Texture: Moderately firm
Flavor/Color: Mild/White
Fat content: Low
Notes: Large fish of 10 pounds or more are more likely to carry ciguatera poisoning and should be avoided.

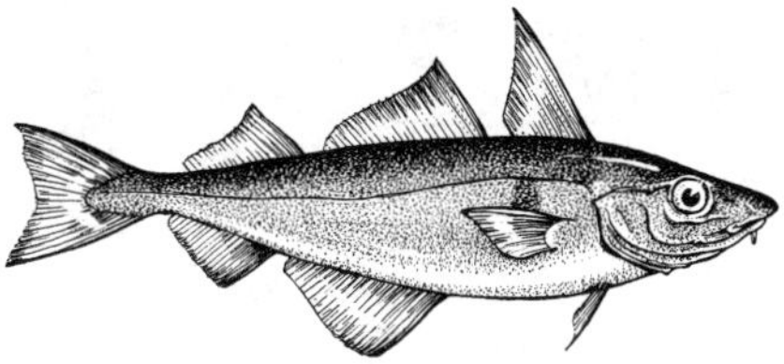

Haddock

Common Names: Haddock, Scrod
Local to: Western North Atlantic
Best cooking techniques: As for cod, except for grilling
Texture: Delicate
Flavor/Color: Mild/White
Fat content: Low
Notes: Usually sold with skin on, which has an easily recognizable black line running through it.

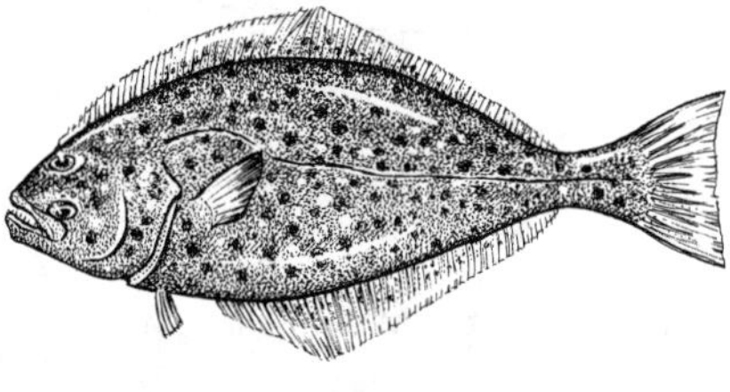

Atlantic halibut

Common Name: Halibut
Local to: North Atlantic and (to some extent) Pacific
Best cooking techniques: Grilling, broiling, roasting, sautéing (gently), cooking in liquid
Texture: Moderately firm
Flavor/Color: Mild/White
Fat content: Low
Notes: The largest flatfish; sold as both steaks and fillets. Atlantic species are superior but increasingly rare.

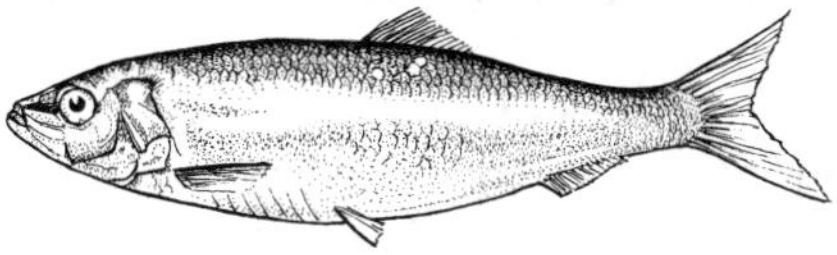

Herring

Common Names: Herring, Alewife, Sardine
Local to: Worldwide
Special preparation techniques: Small specimens can be boned like sardines, shown 559
Best cooking techniques: Grilling (if large), broiling, pickling, roasting
Texture: Soft
Flavor/Color: Strong but clean/Brownish blue
Fat content: High

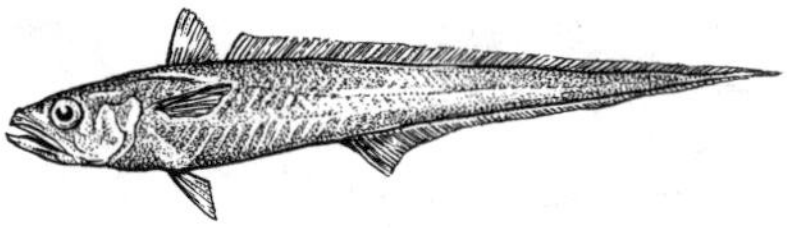

Hoki

Common Names: Hoki, New Zealand Cod
Local to: New Zealand
Special preparation techniques: Almost always frozen before sale; best to buy still frozen or just thawed.
Best cooking techniques: As for cod
Texture: Delicate
Flavor/Color: Mild/White
Fat content: Low
Notes: Sold as a cod substitute; not a topflight eating fish.

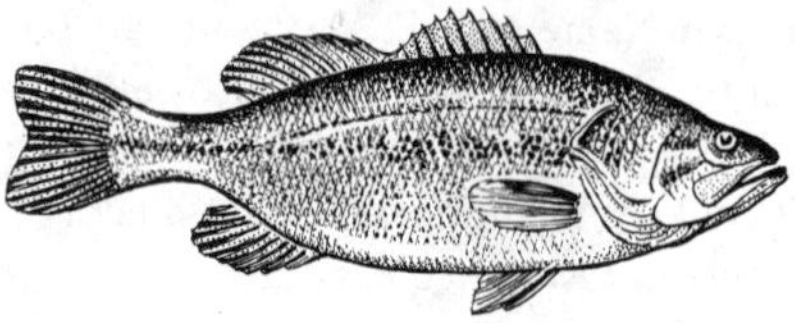

Largemouth bass

Common Names: Largemouth or Smallmouth Bass
Local to: Lakes of the United States
Best cooking techniques: Grilling and broiling, pan-frying, roasting, sautéing
Texture: Moderately firm
Flavor/Color: Sweet and mild/White to grayish white
Fat content: Low
Notes: One of the most popular freshwater game fish, almost never sold in markets.

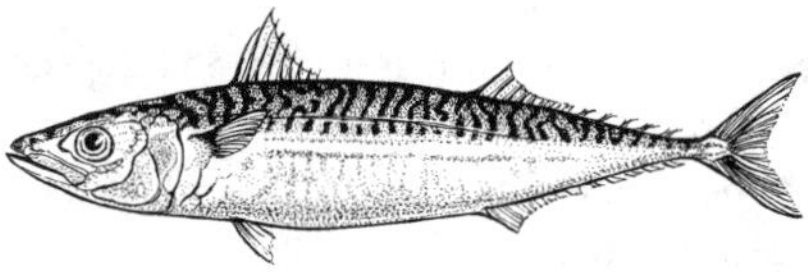

Common mackerel

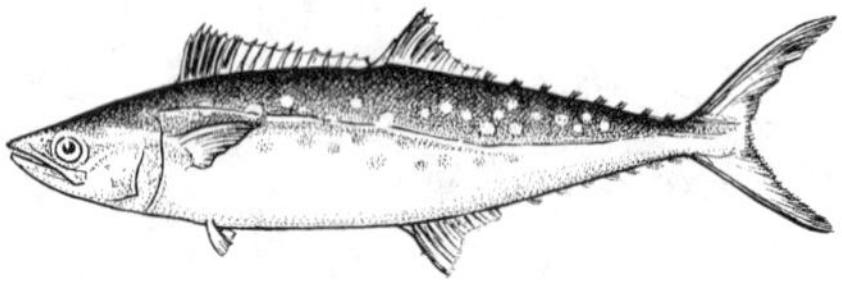

Spanish mackerel

Common Names: Mackerel, King Mackerel, Kingfish, Spanish Mackerel, Tinker, Cavalla
Special preparation techniques: Cook with acid to cut through fish's natural fat.
Best cooking techniques: Grilling (with care), broiling, roasting, pickling
Texture: Moderately soft
Flavor/Color: Mildly to strongly "fishy"/Blue to blue-gray
Fat content: High
Notes: Highly perishable, so keep cold religiously. Very easy to fillet or eat off the bone.

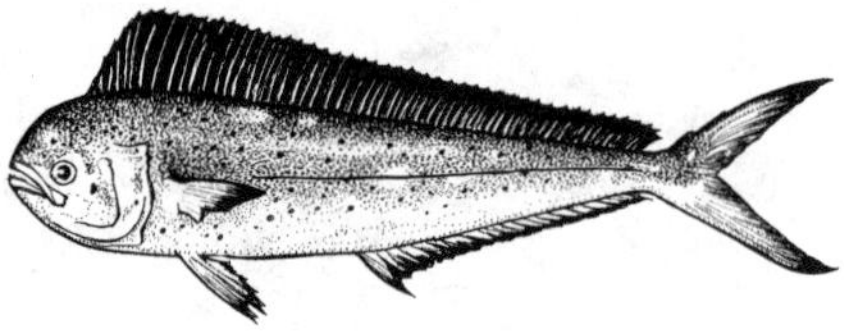

Mahi-mahi

Common Names: Mahi-mahi, Dolphin, Dorado
Local to: Worldwide in warm waters
Special preparation techniques: Fairly oily, so keep added fat to a minimum and cook with acid.
Best cooking techniques: Virtually all-purpose
Texture: Firm and meaty
Flavor/Color: Mildly fishy, somewhat sweet/Gray to ivory when raw, white when cooked
Fat content: Moderate
Notes: Not to be confused with the mammalian dolphin, which is not a relative.

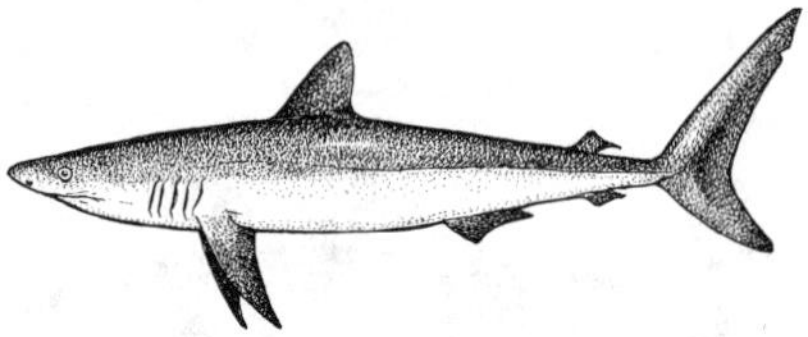

Mako shark

Common Names: Mako Shark, Bonito Shark
Local to: Worldwide
Special preparation techniques: Remove skin and any dark spots.
Best cooking techniques: Grilling, broiling, sautéing, cooking with liquid
Texture: Very meaty
Flavor/Color: Mild/Pinkish to ivory
Fat content: Low
Notes: Good substitute for swordfish.

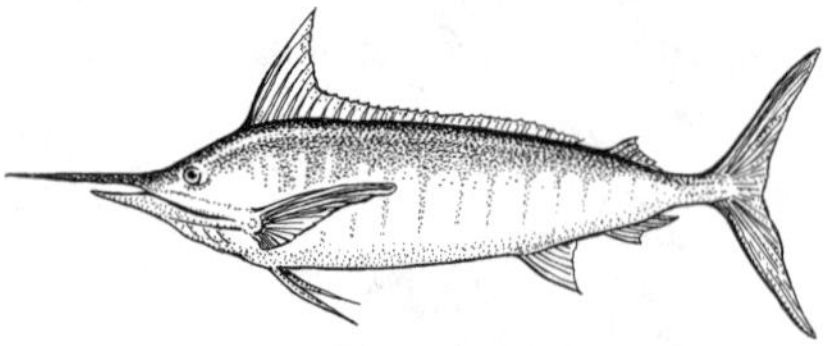

Blue marlin

Common Names: Marlin, Blue Marlin, Striped Marlin
Local to: Worldwide

Best cooking techniques: As for tuna, for which it is a good substitute
Texture: Firm
Flavor/Color: Mild but rich/White
Fat content: Moderate
Notes: A sport fish that is rarely sold in markets.

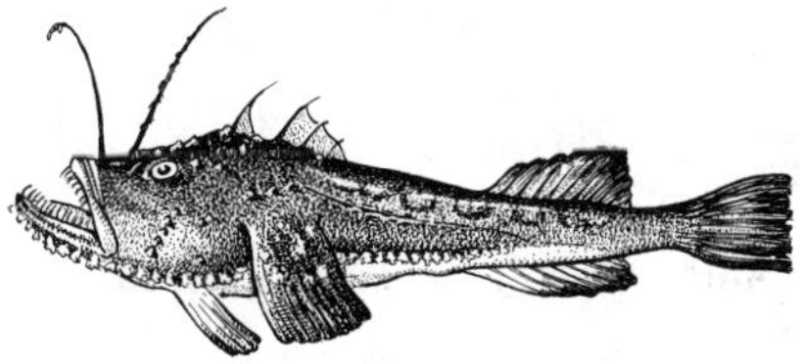

Monkfish

Common Names: Monkfish, Anglerfish, Lotte, Roger, Goosefish, Allmouth
Local to: North Atlantic and Mediterranean
Special preparation techniques: Remove the thin gray membrane that covers the flesh before cooking.
Best cooking techniques: Grilling, broiling, pan-grilling, roasting, sautéing, cooking in liquid
Texture: Very meaty
Flavor/Color: Mild/White
Fat content: Moderate
Notes: Since it has a center cartilage, monkfish "fillets" are truly boneless. Sometimes called "poor man's lobster" because of its wonderfully meaty texture. Can be cooked whole or cut. Monkfish fillets are covered with a thin gray membrane. Remove it with a paring knife, then cut the monkfish into medallions if you like, shown below.

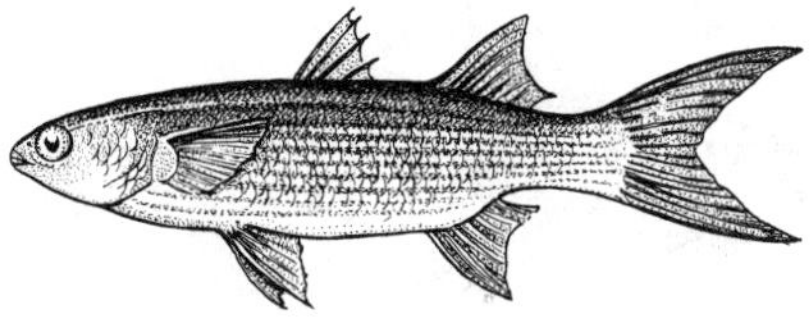

Striped mullet

Common Name: Mullet
Local to: Gulf of Mexico
Best cooking techniques: Roasting, pan-frying, frying
Texture: Soft
Flavor/Color: Clean but a little fishy/Gray to white
Fat content: High
Notes: Not the mullet called for in European recipes (use sea bass or ocean perch for those). Extremely fragile, does not ship well; good smoked.

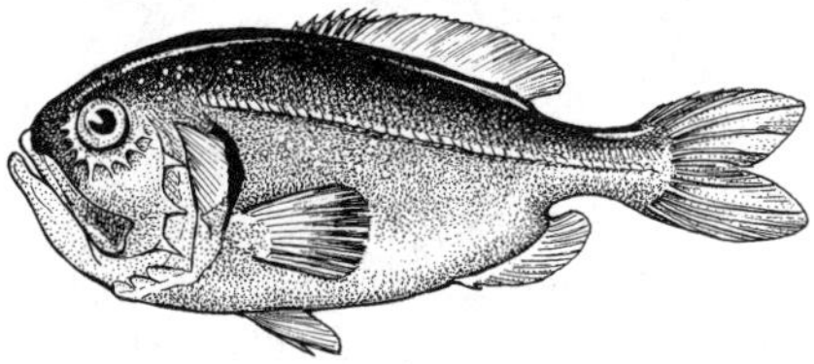

Orange roughy

Common Name: Orange Roughy
Local to: Worldwide, but mostly Southern Pacific
Special preparation techniques: Usually shipped frozen; buy frozen if possible or recently thawed.
Best cooking techniques: As for cod
Texture: Delicate
Flavor/Color: Mild/White
Fat content: Low
Notes: A substitute for cod.

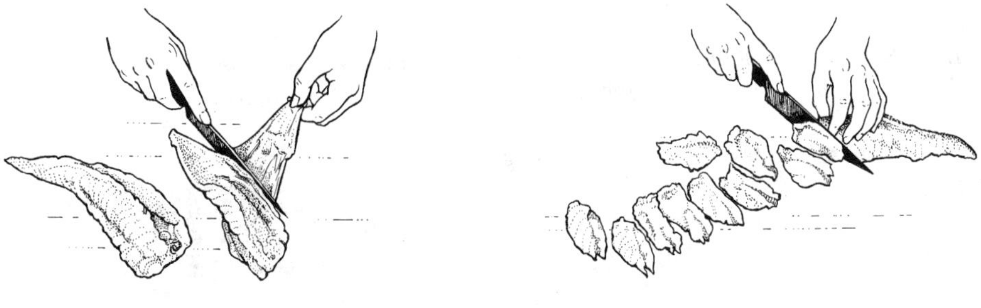

Remove the thin gray membrane from the monkfish fillets, then cut into medallions.

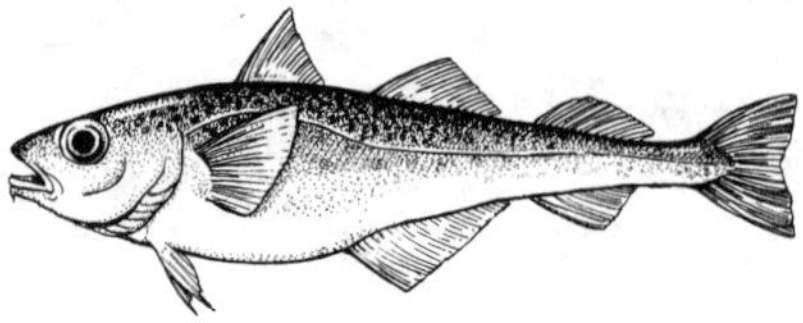

Pacific pollock

Common Names: Pacific Pollock, Alaskan Pollock
Local to: Northern Pacific
Best cooking techniques: As for cod
Texture: Delicate
Flavor/Color: Mild/White
Fat content: Low
Notes: Whiter and more delicate than Atlantic pollock; often frozen.

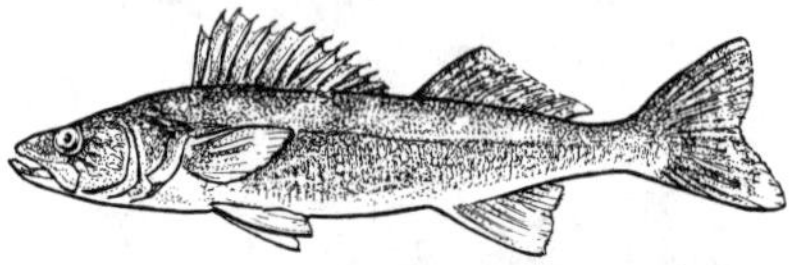

Walleye

Common Names: Perch, Yellow Perch, Walleye
Local to: Freshwater lakes of United States
Best cooking techniques: Pan-frying, roasting, sautéing
Texture: Moderately firm
Flavor/Color: Mild and sweet/White
Fat content: Low
Notes: Excellent-eating freshwater game fish; walleye especially is highly prized, and in the Midwest is sold in stores.

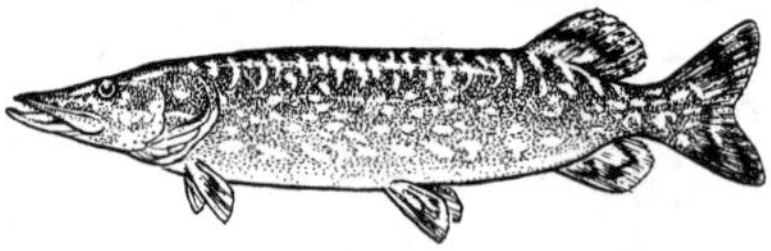

Northern pike

Common Names: Pike, Pickerel, Northern Pike
Local to: Freshwater lakes of Northern United States
Best cooking techniques: Pan-frying, roasting, sautéing
Texture: Moderately firm
Flavor/Color: Mild and sweet/White
Fat content: Very low
Notes: Good-eating freshwater game fish.

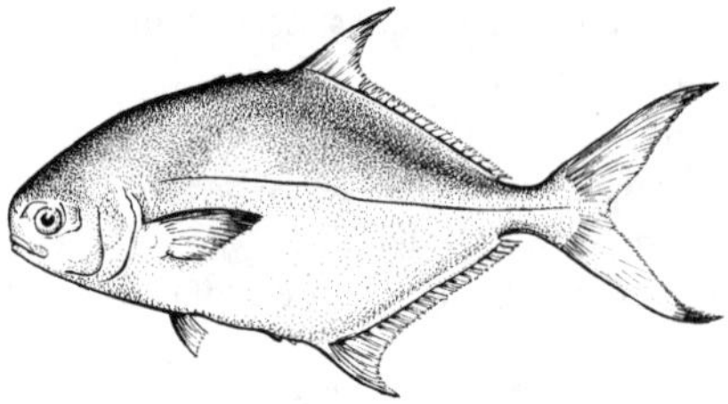

Jack

Common Names: Pompano, Jack, Yellowtail, Pomfret
Local to: Pompano is an Atlantic fish; yellowtail is Pacific; jacks are found worldwide.
Best cooking techniques: Among the best fish for grilling whole; also good for roasting, cooking with liquid (gently), sautéing.
Texture: Firm
Flavor/Color: Full/Gray to white
Fat content: Moderately high
Notes: Easy to cook and eat whole. Pompano is a very fine fish.

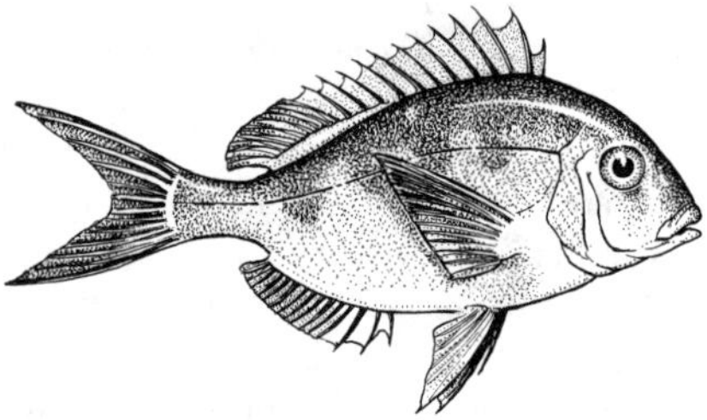

Porgy or scup

Common Names: Porgy, Scup, Sheepshead
Local to: Worldwide
Best cooking techniques: Pan-frying, roasting, cooking with liquid, broiling, frying
Texture: Moderately firm
Flavor/Color: Mild and sweet/Off-white
Fat content: Low
Notes: Very bony fish; good flavor. Interchangeable with croaker and spot.

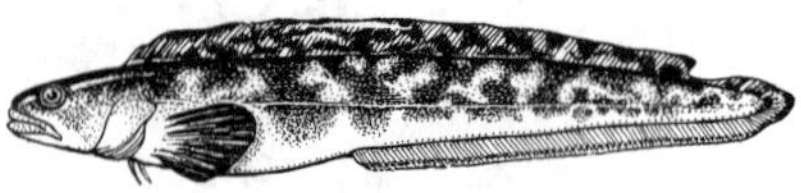

Ocean pout

Common Names: Pout, Ocean Pout
Local to: Northern Atlantic
Best cooking techniques: With liquid
Texture: Slightly mealy but moderately firm
Flavor/Color: Mild/White
Fat content: Low
Notes: A dry, tough fillet that needs added moisture during cooking; not a topflight eating fish.

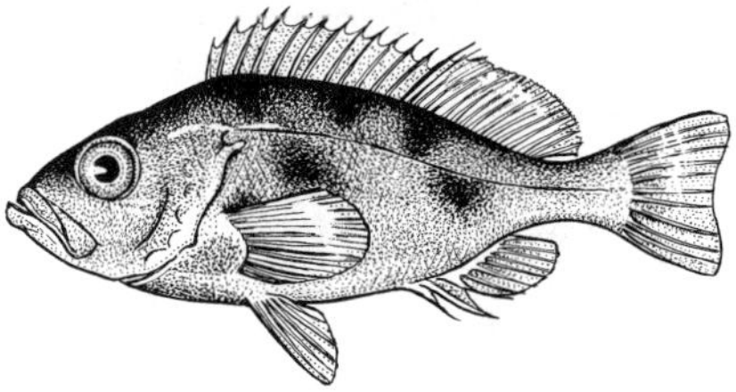

Ocean perch

Common Names: Rockfish, Ocean Perch, Rock Cod
Local to: Mostly Pacific, but ocean perch is Atlantic.
Special preparation techniques: Larger, thicker fish usually have firmer flesh.
Best cooking techniques: All-purpose, except for grilling (they are delicate), good in fish stews
Texture: Fairly delicate
Flavor/Color: Mild/Pinkish white
Fat content: Low
Notes: Often sold as a substitute for red snapper, rockfish is softer. Excellent fish.

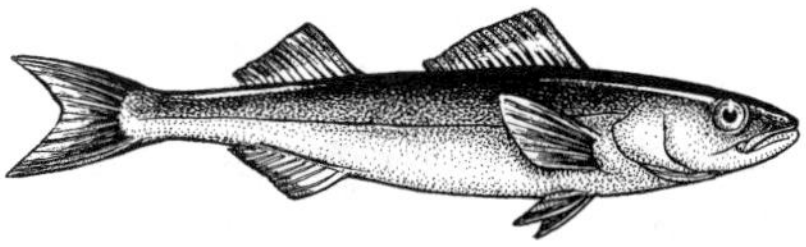

Black cod

Common Names: Sable, Sablefish, Black Cod, Butterfish
Local to: Northern Pacific
Best cooking techniques: Grilling, broiling, pan-grilling, cooking in liquid
Texture: Delicate, with large flakes; codlike
Flavor/Color: Rich and buttery/Stark white
Fat content: High
Notes: Has furry skin that must be removed or scrubbed. Fantastic flavor.

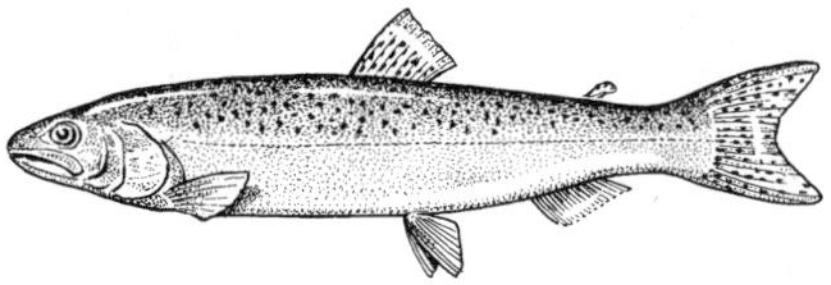

King salmon

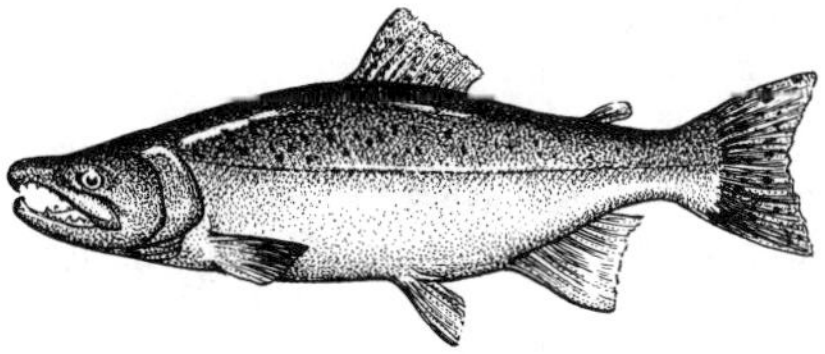

Silver salmon

Common Names: Salmon—Coho (Silver), King (Chinook), Sockeye (Red), Chum, Dog, Pink, etc.
Local to: Northern waters; farm-raised throughout the world
Special preparation techniques: Remove pin bones from fillets, shown 531.
Best cooking techniques: Any and all
Texture: Soft to firm
Flavor/Color: Mild to full/Pink to orange
Fat content: High
Notes: Gorgeous fish when whole; king, sockeye, and coho are choice wild fish, available fresh from spring through fall. Atlantic salmon is only available farm-raised—it is consistent but not highly flavorful. "Norwegian" salmon is simply farm-raised Atlantic salmon from Norway.

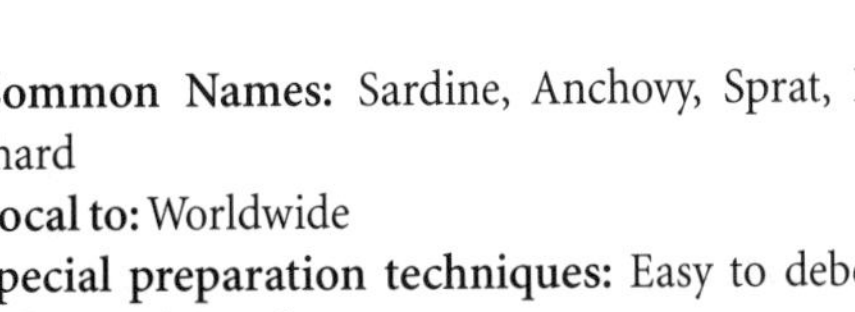

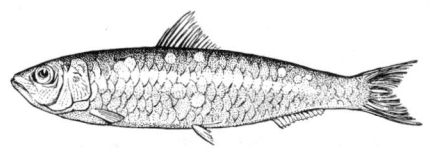

Sardine (European pilchard)

Common Names: Sardine, Anchovy, Sprat, Pilchard
Local to: Worldwide
Special preparation techniques: Easy to debone before cooking, shown 559
Best cooking techniques: Broiling, roasting, pickling, sautéing; cook with acid to cut through fat
Texture: Moderately soft
Flavor/Color: Full, sometimes "fishy"/Gray to brown

Fat content: High
Notes: Often confused with and sold as anchovies or herring; excellent broiled.

Common Name(s): Scrod, cod, haddock
Local to: Northern Atlantic
Best cooking techniques: As for cod
Texture: Delicate
Flavor/Color: Mild/White
Fat content: Low
Notes: There is no such fish as scrod; all scrod is cod, haddock, pollock, or another codlike fish.

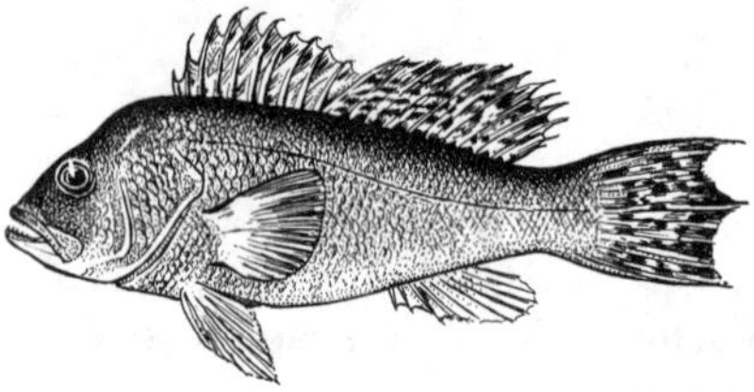

Black bass

Common Names: Sea Bass, Rockfish, Black Bass
Local to: Worldwide
Best cooking techniques: Broiling, roasting, pan-grilling, sautéing, cooking with liquid; smaller fish are excellent steamed
Texture: Quite firm
Flavor/Color: Mild/White
Fat content: Moderate
Notes: Sea bass has a simple bone structure which makes it easy to eat whole; it is a wonderful fish. "Chilean sea bass" is actually a grouper.

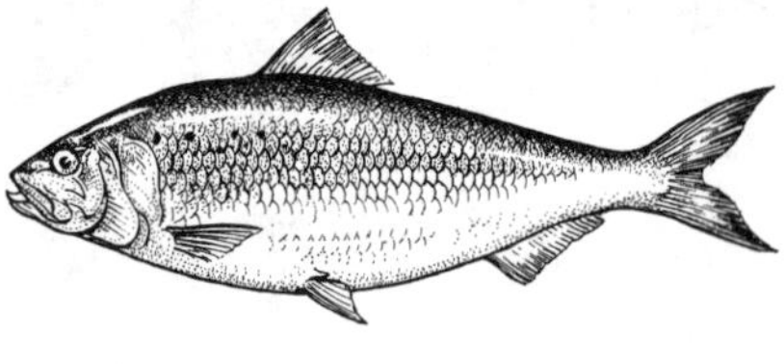

Shad

Common Name: Shad
Local to: East and West coasts, usually in rivers
Special preparation techniques: Filleting requires a learned technique and much practice; buy it filleted or cook it whole.
Best cooking techniques: Broiling, roasting, sautéing
Texture: Soft
Flavor/Color: Sweet and full/Pink
Fat content: High
Notes: Whole fish are often slow-cooked in an attempt (usually futile) to dissolve bones. Roe is highly prized, as it should be.

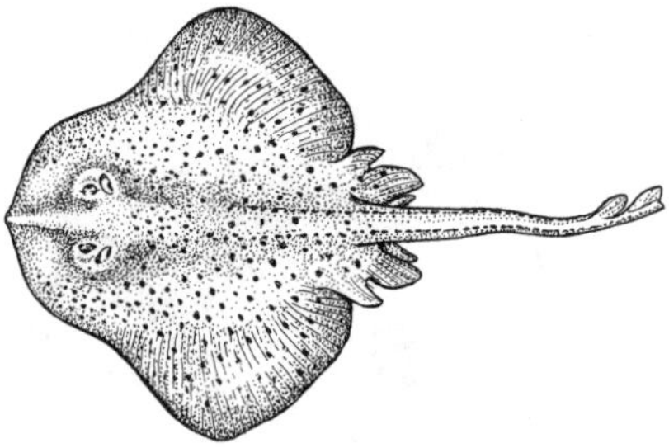

Skate or ray

Common Names: Skate, Ray
Local to: Worldwide
Special preparation techniques: Skinning and filleting should be done by a fishmonger.
Best cooking techniques: Cooking with liquid (sometimes followed by sautéing), sautéing
Texture: Firm and chewy
Flavor/Color: Mild/White
Fat content: Low
Notes: An excellent eating fish. You can buy fillets or poach the fish, see page 553. Once the fish is cooked, its cartilage comes out easily.

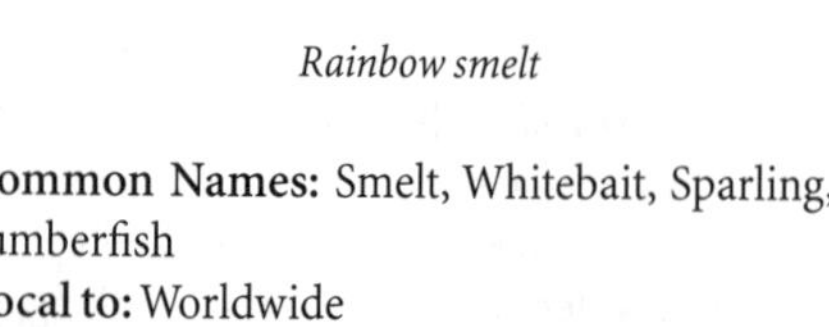

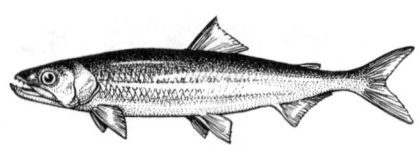

Rainbow smelt

Common Names: Smelt, Whitebait, Sparling, Cucumberfish
Local to: Worldwide
Special preparation techniques: The tiniest, an inch or two long, are eaten whole; others are best eaten like corn on the cob, nibbling around the bone
Best cooking techniques: Sautéing, frying, broiling
Texture: Soft
Flavor/Color: Mild and sweet to slightly muddy/Grayish
Fat content: Moderate

Notes: Some smelts are caught in freshwater, others in saltwater.

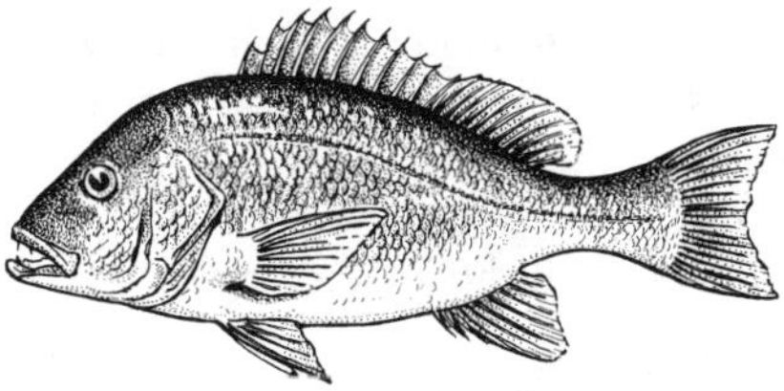

Red snapper

Common Names: Red Snapper, Yellow Snapper, Vermillion Snapper, Mutton Snapper, etc.
Local to: Worldwide
Best cooking techniques: All-purpose; true red snapper is firm enough to grill
Texture: From soft to firm
Flavor/Color: Mild/White to off-white
Fat content: Moderate
Notes: Red snapper, which can be almost as high as it is long, is among the best eating fish.

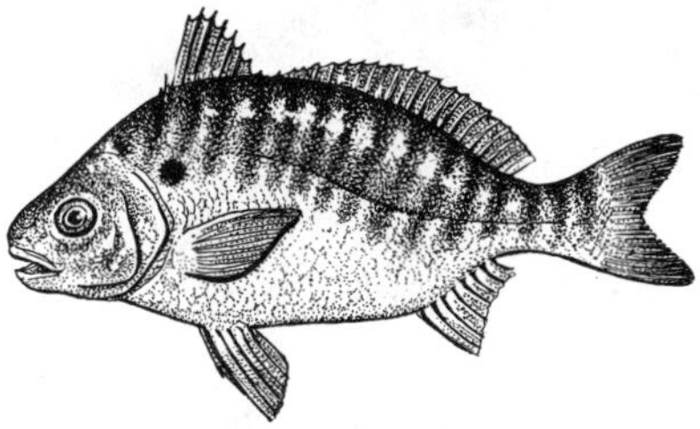

Spot

Common Name: Spot
Local to: Worldwide
Best cooking techniques: Pan-frying (whole or fillets), cooking with liquid, frying
Texture: Fairly soft
Flavor/Color: Sweet and mild/White
Fat content: Low
Notes: Interchangeable with croaker and porgy.

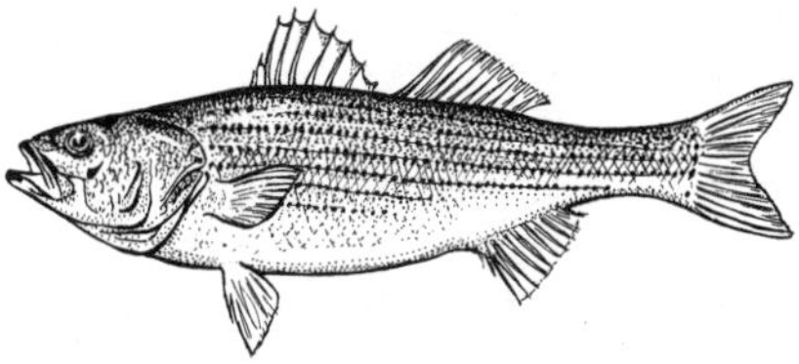

Striped bass

Common Names: Striped Bass, Rockfish
Local to: East and West Coasts
Best cooking techniques: All-purpose, sturdy enough to grill (with care)
Texture: Firm
Flavor/Color: Mild/Off-white
Fat content: Moderate
Notes: A great favorite of sportsmen, this is also one of the great eating fish. Farm-raised striped bass (sunshine bass) is actually a hybrid and can be quite good.

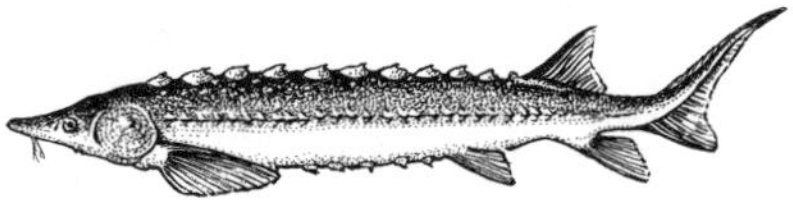

Sturgeon

Common Names: Sturgeon, Hackleback
Local to: Worldwide
Special preparation techniques: Skin is inedible.
Best cooking techniques: Grilling, broiling, cooking with liquid, sautéing, all gently
Texture: Very firm
Flavor/Color: Rich/Off-white
Fat content: High
Notes: A fish two hundred million years old, with cartilage instead of bones, making filleting a snap. So firm it can be used as a substitute for chicken breast or veal. Farm-raised sturgeon are of very high quality (and expensive). The precious roe of this fish is used to make caviar.

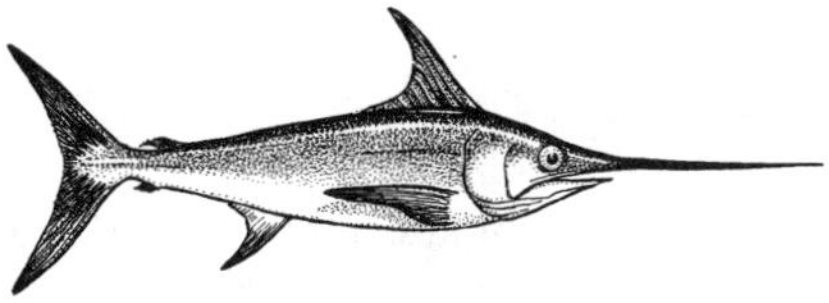

Swordfish

Common Name: Swordfish
Local to: Worldwide, but most popular in Mediterranean and United States
Special preparation techniques: Skin is tough.
Best cooking techniques: Grilling, broiling, roasting, sautéing, cooking with liquid (all briefly)
Texture: Firm and meaty
Flavor/Color: Rich and juicy/Off-white
Fat content: High
Notes: Terrific eating fish. Some specimens have

been found to contain high levels of mercury, so eating it more than a few times a week is not recommended.

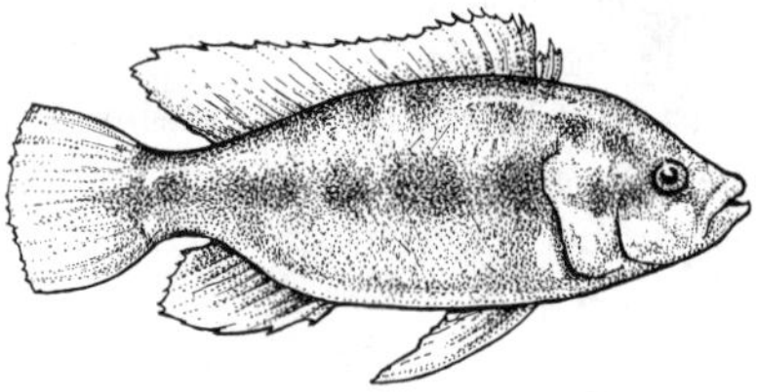

Tilapia

Common Names: Tilapia, Nile Perch
Local to: Worldwide, in freshwater
Best cooking techniques: Cooking with liquid, roasting, broiling
Texture: Soft
Flavor/Color: Mild/White
Fat content: Low
Notes: Farm-raising has made this fish popular, but its quality is still not up to that of many wild fish.

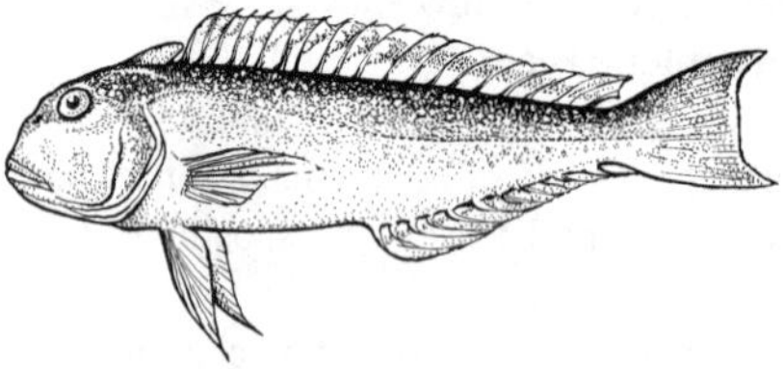

Tilefish

Common Name: Tilefish
Local to: Western Atlantic
Best cooking techniques: Any way but grilling
Texture: Moderately firm
Flavor/Color: Mild/White
Fat content: Low
Notes: A superb fish, like cod but firmer.

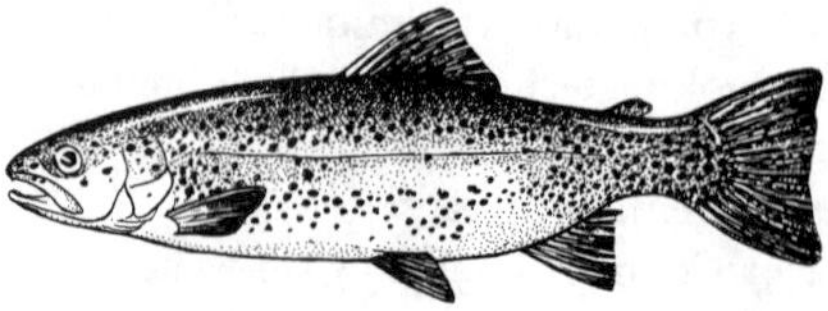

Rainbow trout

Common Names: Trout—Rainbow, Brook, Steel-Head, etc.
Local to: Freshwater lakes and streams
Best cooking techniques: See the recipe for Blue Trout, 556. Also roasting, grilling (very carefully), broiling, pan-frying
Texture: Soft
Flavor/Color: Rich/Pink or orange (salmonlike) to off-white
Fat content: Moderate
Notes: Some farm-raised trout look exactly like salmon and can be treated as such.

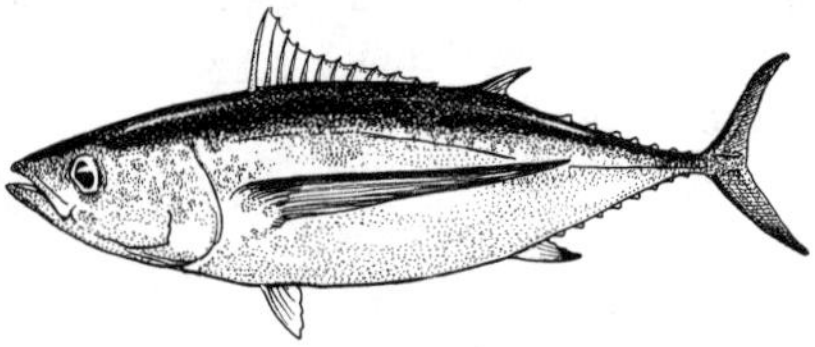

Albacore tuna

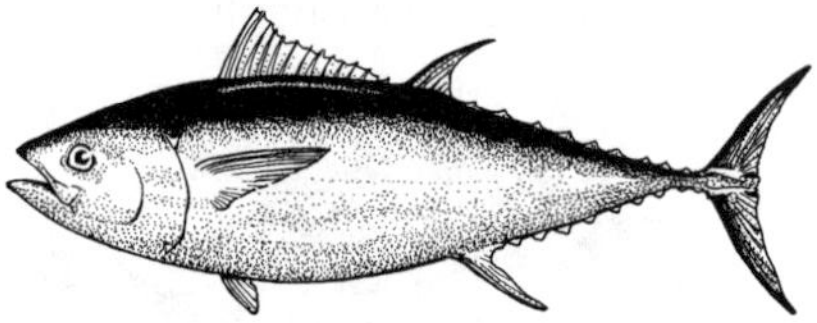

Bluefin tuna

Common Names: Tuna, Albacore, Bluefin, Yellowfin, Skipjack, etc.
Local to: Worldwide
Special preparation techniques: Skin is inedible; many people remove dark areas on the flesh because they have a bitter taste.
Best cooking techniques: Excellent raw. Otherwise, grilling, broiling, roasting, pan-grilling, sautéing
Texture: Firm
Flavor/Color: Mild to bold/Pale pink to deep red
Fat content: High
Notes: Bluefin is the best but increasingly rare. Yellowfin is a good choice. Albacore, bigeye, and skipjack are all good.

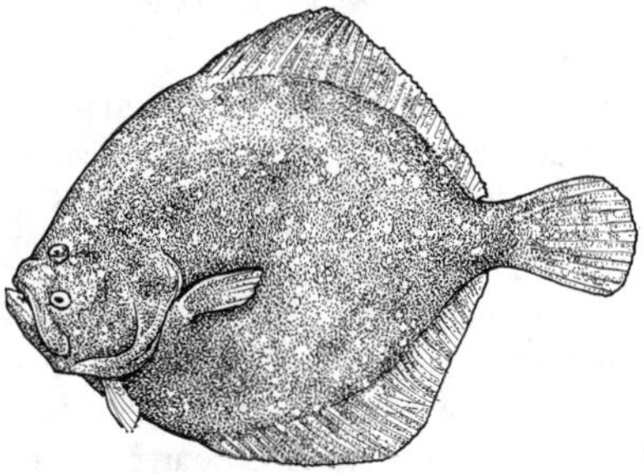

Turbot

Common Name: Turbot
Local to: Northern Atlantic
Best cooking techniques: As for halibut
Texture: Soft to firm
Flavor/Color: Mild/White
Fat content: Low
Notes: A delicious and noble flatfish. The best wind up on European tables.

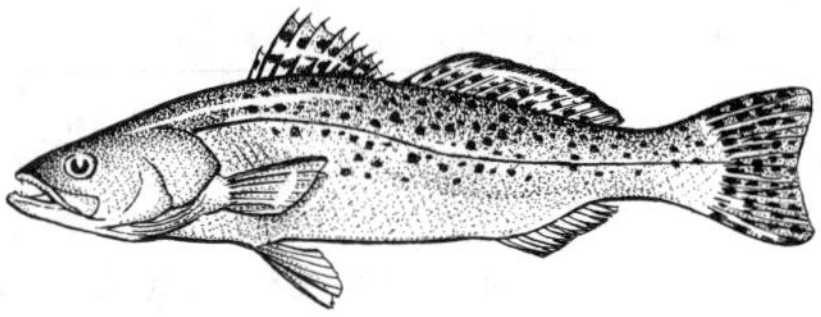

Sea trout

Common Names: Weakfish, Sea Trout, Speckled Trout
Local to: Atlantic and Gulf coasts
Best cooking techniques: Sautéing, broiling, roasting, cooking in liquid, frying
Texture: Soft
Flavor/Color: Mild/Pink to ivory to white
Fat content: Low
Notes: Very soft fish whose fillets are fried in the Southeast. Good eating.

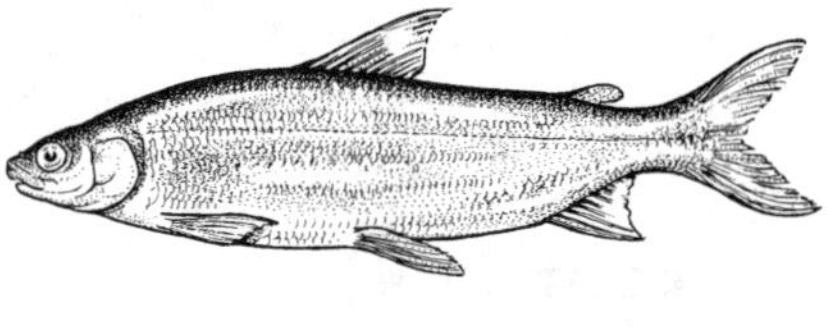

Whitefish

Common Name: Whitefish
Local to: Great Lakes, other fresh waters
Best cooking techniques: Roasting, cooking with liquid, broiling, sautéing
Texture: Soft
Flavor/Color: Full/Off-white
Fat content: High
Notes: Often smoked. Delicious flaked into a salad.

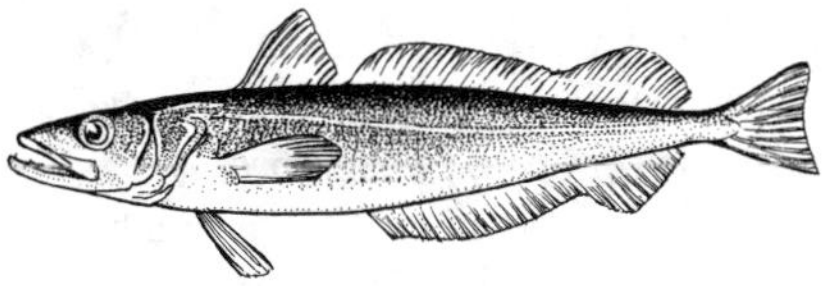

Hake or whiting

Common Names: Whiting, Hake, Silver Hake, Red Hake, etc.
Local to: Western Atlantic
Best cooking techniques: Cooking with liquid, frying, sautéing, roasting
Texture: Soft
Flavor/Color: Mild/White
Fat content: Low
Notes: Highly delicate but delicious.

Wolf fish

Common Names: Wolf Fish, Ocean Catfish
Local to: Northern Atlantic
Best cooking techniques: Sautéing, grilling (with care), broiling, cooking with liquid
Texture: Fairly meaty, halibutlike
Flavor/Color: Mild/White
Fat content: Low
Notes: Fish with good flavor and texture.

ABOUT BROILING AND GRILLING FISH

Broiling and grilling are ideal techniques for cooking many fish. The intense heat complements the flavor of the fish by charring its surface; often, little more added flavor is needed, so you can keep seasonings to a minimum.

When to broil, when to grill? Remember that these are two sides of the same coin. In broiling, the heat is above the food, in grilling beneath it. Unless you use hardwood charcoal, the good flavor comes from the interaction of intense heat and the food itself, not from the fuel. So you do not lose much by broiling, which is often easier. Certain fish—especially most delicate white fish and thin fillets—are virtually impossible to grill; they simply fall apart when you try to turn them over. Some whole fish are also tricky. Best for grilling are thick steaks of swordfish, salmon, tuna, and the like; small, firm whole fish such as mackerel, pompano, and red snapper; and, of course, many shellfish (see About Broiling or Grilling Shellfish, 506).

Generally, you want to grill fish over a hot fire (see Grilling, 1055). Make sure the grill grates are clean and do not use too much oil on the fish (it causes flare-ups). When applicable, start grilling the fish skin side down, then let the skin firm up for a couple of minutes before you try turning the fish (or, if it is a not-too-thick fillet, cover the grill and do not turn it at all). If you lose the skin to the grill rack, do not worry—it beats losing the fish. A fish grilling basket can make grilling fillets easier.

You can broil any cut of fish at all, with the exception of whole fish larger than three pounds (these are best roasted, see page 549). It is a simple technique, especially because you can adjust not only the level of heat but the distance of the fish from the heat source. Preheat the broiler for 15 minutes or so. (If you have an electric oven in which the broiler cycles on and off, preheat the oven to its maximum heat, then switch to the broiler just a couple of minutes before beginning to cook the fish.) Position the rack as close to the heat source as you can, use a lightly oiled baking sheet or 13 x 9-inch roasting pan; and, unless the fish is more than an inch thick, do not turn it, for there is enough ambient heat in the oven to cook the bottom of the fish and you want to give the top ample time to brown. If the fish is thick and will take more than 5 minutes or so to broil, you can baste it with marinade, cooking liquid, or a simple flavoring mixture, such as a vinaigrette; if it is thin, this is not necessary.

In addition to the recipes here, you can serve almost any simply broiled or grilled fish with:

- Flavored Butters, 76 to 78
- Flavored Oils, 78 to 79
- Citrus Sauce, 54
- Lemon Beurre Blanc, 58
- Beurre Blanc, 57
- Tomato Concassé, 433, or Fresh Tomato Sauce, 305
- Salsa Verde, 81
- Vinaigrettes, 236 to 239

BROILED FILLETS WITH OLIVE OIL AND LEMON

4 servings

This is the most basic of fish recipes and probably the most useful. Substitute butter for the olive oil if you like. When broiling dark fillets, such as bluefish or mahi-mahi, use a teaspoon or two of lemon juice (or vinegar) in place of the oil to cut through some of the fish's natural fat. Preheat the broiler for 15 minutes before cooking. Adjust the rack so that it is approximately 2 inches from the heat source if the fillet is under 1 inch thick, 4 inches from the heat if the fillet is thicker. Lightly oil a baking sheet or shallow roasting pan.

Place on the baking sheet or roasting pan:

1½ to 2 pounds fish fillets, skin on or off, in 1 or more pieces, rinsed and patted dry

Brush lightly with:

1 to 2 tablespoons extra-virgin olive oil or melted butter

Sprinkle with:

Salt and ground black pepper to taste

Place the fish under the broiler and broil, undisturbed, for 4 minutes. If the fillets are ½ inch thick or less, they are done as soon as the exterior turns opaque. If they are thicker, check after 6 minutes; fish up to 1 inch thick probably will be done at this point. Thicker fillets will need another couple of minutes and should be basted with a little more oil. Those over 1½ inches thick should be turned and cooked another 5 or 6 minutes. (To check for doneness, see page 532.)

Sprinkle with:

2 teaspoons fresh lemon juice

Serve with:

Minced fresh parsley and lemon wedges or any of the suggested accompaniments, above

BROILED FILLETS WITH HERBS

Prepare Broiled Fillets with Olive Oil and Lemon, above, stirring 2 tablespoons chopped fresh herbs (any combination of parsley, chervil, basil, thyme, or fennel) into the olive oil. If the fillets are ½ inch thick or less, spread this paste on them before broiling. Rub thicker fillets with some olive oil and spread the herb paste on them 3 or 4 minutes before they are done.

BROILED FILLETS WITH SEASONED BREADCRUMBS

Heat in a skillet over medium heat until the oil is hot or the butter is melted and the foam has begun to subside:

3 tablespoons olive oil or butter

Add:

¾ cup fresh breadcrumbs

Salt and ground black pepper to taste

Cook, tossing, until the crumbs have darkened and become crisp, about 1 minute. Drain on paper towels. Prepare Broiled Fillets with Olive Oil and Lemon, above. If the fillets are ½ inch thick or less, spread the breadcrumb mixture on them before broiling. Rub thicker fillets with some olive oil or melted butter and spread the breadcrumb mixture on them 3 or 4 minutes before they are done. Serve with parsley and lemon wedges or with any of the suggested accompaniments on page 544.

GRILLED FILLETS WITH OLIVE OIL AND LEMON

4 servings

You will get the best results if you use firm fish fillets that are at least 1 inch thick.

Prepare a medium-hot charcoal fire or preheat a gas grill. Make sure the rack is clean and place it about 4 inches from the heat.

Brush:

1½ to 2 pounds fish fillets, with the skin on, rinsed and patted dry

with:

1 tablespoon extra-virgin olive oil

Sprinkle with:

Salt and ground black pepper to taste

Place the fillets skin side down on the grill. Cover the grill if you like; check after 8 minutes. (To check for doneness, see page 532.) Or do not cover the grill and turn very carefully, with a wide spatula, after no less than 3 minutes. Serve immediately with:

Lemon wedges, several drops of vinegar, or any of the suggested accompaniments on page 544

GRILLED OR BROILED SALMON, TUNA, SWORDFISH, OR OTHER THICK STEAKS

4 servings

These are a pleasure to grill, for they tend not to stick too much and are easy to turn. Salmon is at its best when still a little translucent inside, and tuna is best a little on the rare side. But even if you prefer them cooked through, remove them from the grill just before the interior is opaque (they will continue to cook off the heat). These steaks should be more than an inch thick so that they will not cook too quickly; if possible, buy two large ones rather than four small ones. Consider serving this or any grilled or broiled fish with Basic Vinaigrette, 236, slightly warmed in the microwave or over low heat.

Prepare a medium-hot charcoal fire or preheat a gas grill or the broiler. Make sure the grill rack is clean and place it about 4 inches from the heat on a grill, or 2 to 3 inches from the broiler heat.

Brush:

1½ to 2 pounds fish steaks (2 large or 4 small), at least 1 inch thick, rinsed and patted dry

with:

1 tablespoon extra-virgin olive oil

Sprinkle with:

Salt and ground black pepper to taste

Place them on the grill or under the broiler. Grill or broil until browned, 3 to 6 minutes; turn and grill the other side until browned, 3 to 5 minutes more. (To check for doneness, see page 532.) Serve immediately with:

Lemon wedges, several drops of vinegar, any of the suggested accompaniments on page 544, or Tart Corn Relish, 65

TERIYAKI GRILLED SALMON, TUNA, SWORDFISH, OR OTHER THICK STEAKS

4 servings

A technique often used in Japan with yellowtail, a fish usually not available here. Teriyaki literally means "glaze-grilling." The secret to really succulent teriyaki is to apply the glaze bit by bit toward the end of the grilling process so that it browns but does not burn. This technique also works well with eel, as well as boneless chicken breasts. You can gain a similar effect by substituting hoisin sauce for the soy sauce and mirin mixture.

Combine in a small saucepan:

⅔ cup soy sauce

½ cup mirin

1 tablespoon sugar

Cook, stirring, over medium heat until the sugar is dissolved. Increase the heat slightly and cook, stirring occasionally, until foamy. Reduce the heat and simmer, stirring constantly, until the mixture is reduced by half. Let cool, then remove half of it to a glass jar to store in the refrigerator for future use, as the whole recipe makes enough glaze for about 10 servings.

Marinate:

4 salmon or other fish steaks (6 to 8 ounces each), at least 1 inch thick, rinsed and patted dry

in:

1 cup sake

for about 15 minutes, turning 2 or 3 times.

Meanwhile, prepare a hot charcoal fire or preheat a gas grill or the broiler; the fire should be good and hot.

Make sure the grill rack is clean and place it about 4 inches from the heat on a grill, or 2 to 3 inches from the broiler heat.

Remove the fish from the wine and pat dry. Place on the grill rack or a broiler pan and sprinkle very lightly with:

Coarse salt

Grill or broil for 2 minutes, until the fish begins to brown. Turn, then grill or broil for 2 minutes more. Move the fish to a cooler part of the grill or move the broiler rack down a notch. Brush the fish with the teriyaki glaze, then grill or broil, with the glaze facing the heat, until the glaze dries, about 1 minute. Brush the other size and grill or broil until the glaze dries. By this time, the fish will be done or nearly so. (To check for doneness, see page 532.) If it needs another minute, repeat the brushing and cooking procedure once or twice. Serve hot or at room temperature.

BROILED SALMON WITH TOMATOES, BASIL, AND MINT

4 servings

Combine, cover, and let stand for 30 to 40 minutes:

2 very ripe beefsteak tomatoes, cored, seeded, and cut into ½-inch dice
5 tablespoons extra-virgin olive oil
3 tablespoons soy sauce
2 tablespoons fresh lemon juice
1½ cups fresh basil leaves, torn into pieces if large
2 teaspoons finely chopped fresh mint
½ teaspoon cracked black peppercorns

Preheat the broiler.

Generously brush all sides of:

4 salmon fillets (6 to 7 ounces each)

with:

2 tablespoons olive oil

Season well with:

Salt and ground black pepper to taste

Place on a sheet of aluminum foil:

Eight ⅛-inch-thick slices onions

Brush with:

Olive oil

Season with:

Salt and ground black pepper to taste

Place the fish on a broiler pan. On each fillet, overlap 2 onion slices. Broil about 8 inches from the heat until the onions have wilted and caramelized, 12 to 15 minutes. Do not worry if the onions char here and there, but if they blacken, cover them with foil. Check the fish for doneness: It should look rosy, not deeply salmon-colored. Remove the fish to plates. Stir the tomato salsa and spoon it generously over the salmon.

GRILLED SALMON WITH A CHILI SPICE RUB

5 to 6 servings

This recipe makes enough spice mixture for several dinners. Store it in an airtight container and use it with chicken, beef, lamb, or pork as well as salmon.

Prepare a hot charcoal fire in a 22½-inch or larger charcoal grill.

Stir together in a small nonstick skillet:

¼ cup sweet paprika
1 tablespoon chili powder
1 tablespoon ground cumin
1 teaspoon salt
¼ teaspoon ground cinnamon
¼ teaspoon ground red pepper

Heat, stirring constantly, over medium heat for 2 minutes. Remove from the heat. Pat 2 tablespoons of the spice mixture over the flesh side of:

One 2½-pound salmon fillet

Drizzle over the top:

1½ tablespoons olive oil

When the coals are covered with a thin layer of white ash, push half of the coals to one side of the grill and the other half to the other side so that there are no coals in the center. Place the grill grate over the coals and, with long-handled tongs, rub the grill with a wad of paper towels dipped lightly in:

Vegetable oil

Lay the fillet, flesh side down, over the middle of the grill grate where there are no coals. Cover and grill for 7 minutes. Turn the fillet with two spatulas and grill skin side down for 7 to 8 minutes. (To check for doneness, see page 532.) Remove from the grill with the two spatulas, cut into portions, and serve hot with:

Lime wedges

GRILLED OR BROILED CHUNKS OF SWORDFISH OR OTHER FISH ON SKEWERS

4 servings

Precut chunks of fish may be more or less expensive than steaks, depending on whether they are simply cut-up steaks or trimmings. If they are less expensive, fine, but make sure they have not been sitting for too long; the more surface area that is exposed to the air, the faster the fish loses its quality. If you have a thriving rosemary plant, use freshly cut foot-long branches as skewers and omit the herb from the marinade.

Rinse, pat dry, and cut into 1½-inch cubes:

1½ to 2 pounds thick fish steaks or fillets

Whisk together in a large bowl:

¼ cup extra-virgin olive oil

¼ cup fresh lemon or lime juice
1 teaspoon minced fresh thyme, 1 tablespoon minced fresh basil or 1 bay leaf, crumbled
Salt and ground black pepper to taste

Add the fish and toss to coat well. Let stand.

Prepare a medium-hot charcoal fire or preheat a gas grill or the broiler. Make sure the grill rack is clean and place it about 4 inches from the heat on a grill, or 2 to 3 inches from the broiler heat.

Thread the fish onto 4 metal or wooden skewers (if you use wood, it is best to soak them in water while you marinate the fish); do not crowd. If you like, alternate the fish chunks with:

Cherry tomatoes, small onion wedges, cucumber chunks, mushroom slices, and/or other vegetables
Bay or basil leaves

Grill or broil the skewers, turning as each side browns and brushing occasionally with any remaining marinade. Total cooking time will be 10 to 15 minutes; be especially careful not to overcook salmon, as it will begin to fall from the skewers. (To check for doneness, see page 532). Serve as is or with:

A vinaigrette, 236 to 239

GRILLED OR BROILED SWORDFISH AND NECTARINE SKEWERS

4 servings

Here are fish skewers with a novel touch. The result is delightful. Best with swordfish, these are also good with tuna, mako shark, or monkfish.

Rinse, pat dry, and cut into 1½-inch cubes:

1½ to 2 pounds thick fish steaks or fillets

Whisk together in a small bowl:

½ cup balsamic vinegar
¼ cup fresh lemon juice
1 teaspoon minced garlic
½ teaspoon sugar
Salt and ground black pepper to taste

Whisk together in a large bowl:

⅓ cup olive oil
¼ cup fresh lemon juice
⅓ cup coarsely chopped fresh basil
1 tablespoon minced garlic
Salt and ground black pepper to taste

Add the fish to the large bowl and toss to coat well. Add and toss to combine:

2 nectarines or peaches, pitted, quartered, and each quarter halved crosswise
2 red bell peppers, stemmed, seeded, quartered, and each quarter halved crosswise
2 red onions, cut into 8 wedges each

Prepare a medium-hot charcoal fire or preheat a gas grill or the broiler. Make sure the grill rack is clean and place it about 4 inches from the heat on a grill, or 2 to 3 inches from the broiler heat.

Thread the fish, nectarines, bell peppers, and onions onto 4 metal or wooden skewers (if you use wood, it is best to soak them in water while you marinate the fish); do not crowd. If you have more basil, intersperse a few leaves on the skewers with the other ingredients.

Grill or broil the skewers, turning as each side browns and brushing occasionally with any remaining marinade. Total cooking time will be 10 to 15 minutes. (To check for doneness, see page 532.) Remove from the grill, drizzle the balsamic vinegar mixture over the skewers, and serve immediately.

GRILLED OR BROILED MONKFISH AND TOMATO SKEWERS WITH MOROCCAN FLAVORS

4 servings

Often overlooked, monkfish is the one pure-white-fleshed fish that always stands up to the grill.

Rinse, pat dry, and cut into 1- to 1½-inch cubes:

4 to 6 filleted small monkfish tails (about 1½ pounds), fine membrane removed

Combine in a wide bowl:

¼ cup minced fresh cilantro
¼ cup minced onions
1 tablespoon ground cumin
1 teaspoon ground coriander
¼ teaspoon ground cinnamon
Salt and ground black pepper to taste

Moisten with:

¼ cup olive oil

Stir to make a paste. Add the fish and toss to coat well. Refrigerate for up to 2 hours.

When you are ready to cook, prepare a medium-hot charcoal fire or preheat a gas grill or the broiler. Make sure the grill rack is clean and place it about 4 inches from the heat on a grill, or 2 to 3 inches from the broiler heat.

Thread the fish onto 4 metal or wooden skewers (if you use wood, it is best to soak them in water while you marinate the fish), alternating with:

About 24 cherry tomatoes

Do not crowd. Grill or broil the skewers, turning as each side browns and brushing occasionally with any remaining marinade. Total cooking time will be about 12 minutes; monkfish is at its best when all traces of translucence are gone from the center. (To check for doneness, see page 532.)

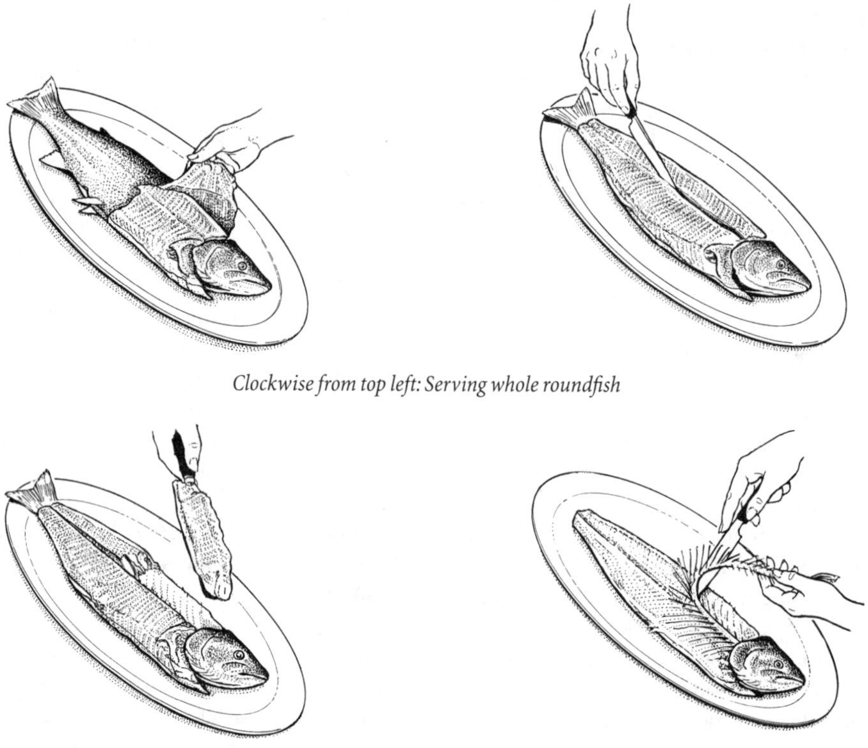

Clockwise from top left: Serving whole roundfish

GRILLED OR BROILED WHOLE RED SNAPPER OR OTHER FISH *4 servings*

A grilled or broiled whole fish can be a delight to eat but not to cook. To ensure success, begin with a relatively firm-fleshed fish such as red snapper, pompano, or sea bass. Keep the fish size within reason; if you go over 2 pounds or so, the fish will be difficult to turn. Again, it is best to broil (or even roast, 549) until you are completely comfortable cooking whole fish.

Prepare a medium-hot charcoal fire or preheat a gas grill or the broiler. Make sure the grill rack is clean and place it about 4 inches from the heat.

Rub:

2 red snappers or other fish (1½ to 2 pounds each), rinsed inside and out and patted dry

with:

2 tablespoons extra-virgin olive oil

Mix:

2 tablespoons minced fresh parsley or fennel leaves
1 teaspoon coarse salt
Ground black pepper to taste

Rub this mixture all over the fish, inside and out. Place the fish on the grill or under the broiler; cover the grill if possible. Cook, undisturbed, until the side facing the heat is brown and blistered, about 8 minutes. Turn carefully (do not fret if you lose some of the skin) and cook on the other side until the meat near the bone has lost its translucence, 8 to 10 minutes. (To check for doneness, see page 532.)

To serve, shown above, remove the skin from the top of the fish with your hands or a fork. With a thin-bladed knife, make an incision along the back of the fish. Work a spatula or turner under the fillet, gently loosening it from the skeletal structure and removing it completely. Next, lift the whole skeletal structure off the bottom fillet, starting with the tail and holding down the bottom fillet with the knife or the back of a fork. The second fillet is now ready to be served.

Serve immediately with:

Lemon wedges, Beurre Blanc, 57, or a vinaigrette, 236 to 239

GRILLED OR BROILED WHOLE RED SNAPPER WITH GINGER SOY VINAIGRETTE *4 servings*

Prepare a medium-hot charcoal fire or preheat a gas grill or the broiler. Make sure the grill rack is clean and place it about 4 inches from the heat.

Combine in a bowl:

¼ cup toasted sesame oil
¼ cup peanut or other oil
¼ cup rice or other mild vinegar

¼ cup fresh lime juice
¼ cup soy sauce
4 to 6 dashes hot red pepper sauce
½ cup chopped fresh cilantro
2 tablespoons minced peeled fresh ginger
Salt and ground black pepper to taste

Toast in a small dry skillet over medium-high heat just until the aroma rises:

¾ cup coriander seeds
2 tablespoons red pepper flakes

Pulverize the mixture with the flat side of a heavy knife or coarsely grind in a spice mill. Season with:

Salt and ground black pepper to taste

Rub the spice mixture all over:

2 red snappers or other fish (1½ to 2 pounds each), rinsed inside and out and patted dry

Place the fish on the grill or under the broiler; cover the grill if possible. Cook, undisturbed, until the side facing the heat is brown and blistered, about 8 minutes. Turn carefully (do not fret if you lose some of the skin) and cook on the other side until the meat near the bone has lost its translucence, 8 to 10 minutes. (To check for doneness, see page 532.) Serve immediately with the vinaigrette.

GRILLED OR BROILED WHOLE MACKEREL OR TROUT WITH BACON *4 servings*

These two fish are similar in shape and size. If you catch your own trout, there is nothing better, but if you are shopping, fresh mackerel is the tastier and less expensive choice. Mackerel or trout are also wonderful simply grilled or broiled and served with any sharply seasoned flavored butter, 76 to 78, or acidic vinaigrette, 236 to 239, or salsa, 61 to 63.

Prepare a medium-hot charcoal fire or preheat a gas grill or the broiler. Make sure the grill rack is clean and place it about 4 to 6 inches from the heat.

Sprinkle:

4 mackerel or trout (1 to 1¼ pounds each), rinsed and patted dry

with:

Salt and ground black pepper to taste

Wrap each fish in:

1 or 2 slices bacon

Place the fish on the grill or under the broiler; cover the grill if possible. Cook, undisturbed, for 3 to 4 minutes, taking care not to burn the bacon (move the fish to a cooler part of the grill or lower the broiler rack if necessary). Turn and continue to cook. Turn again if necessary. The fish is done when the bacon is crisp and there are no longer any traces of blood in the body cavity. Total cooking time will be about 12 to 15 minutes.

ABOUT BAKING AND ROASTING FISH

Baking implies more moderate heat—350°F or even lower—than roasting, which takes place at 450°F or higher. Both are useful for cooking fish: Baking allows more leeway in cooking times and is better for preserving the fish's moisture; roasting is faster, of course, delivers a nice crust to fish, and adds flavor by browning.

You will find both kinds of recipes here; each allows you to minimize preparation time and fat content, cook the fish without constant attention, and add vegetables to the dish without much extra work. Generally, these methods are best for whole fish, steaks, and thick fillets. You can roast any fish whole—size is no limit. Very large fish roast just as well as 1-pounders, maybe better, because the longer cooking time allows the skin to become crispy. Thick steaks and fillets also roast long enough to become brown, but thin fillets may dry out before they brown and are better run under the broiler.

Generally, it is best to roast whole fish at very high heat, 500°F or higher, and without much liquid. But if the fish is very large—over 3 pounds or so—reduce the heat to 450°F to prevent the skin or seasonings from scorching. You also should reduce the temperature if you want to roast vegetables along with the fish; it does not take much to thinly slice some eggplant and tomatoes, for example, and use them as a bed for the fish. They will absorb any liquid the fish gives off during cooking, become tender in the same amount of time it takes to cook the fish, and provide you with a flavorful side dish.

Whenever you roast whole fish, cut 3 or 4 crosswise slashes in each side. This allows added flavors to permeate the flesh and hastens cooking. It also makes it easy to determine when the fish is done—just take a look into the slits and see if the flesh has turned opaque down to the bone.

QUICKLY ROASTED FISH FILLETS *4 servings*

If you have little time and just want the pleasing, intrinsic flavor of fish, perhaps sparked by a squeeze of lemon, this is the least fussy way to get it. The technique works with any fillet. Those of flatfish are done nearly as soon as you put them in the oven, in 3 to 5 minutes; they will not brown but in every other way will be delicious. Fillets of cod and other delicate white fish will be done at a rate of about 8 minutes per inch of thickness; those of sturdier white fish, such as red snapper, or of dark-fleshed fish, such as mackerel, at perhaps 9 to 10 minutes per inch of thickness. In any case, remove the fish from the oven just as the last traces of translucence begin to disappear, and you will avoid overcooking.

Preheat the oven to 500°F. Grease a baking sheet or shallow roasting pan with a little oil or butter.

Lay in the pan:

1½ to 2 pounds fish fillets, in 1 to 4 pieces, rinsed and patted dry

Brush with:

1 tablespoon extra-virgin olive oil or melted butter

Season with:

Salt and ground black pepper to taste

Place in the oven and roast, undisturbed, until done. (To check for doneness, see page 532.) Serve with:

Minced fresh parsley and lemon wedges, Sauce Bercy, 49, Sauce Soubise, 47, Beurre Blanc, 57, a flavored butter or flavored oil, 78 to 79, or a vinaigrette, 236 to 239

ROASTED FISH FILLETS SPENCER

4 servings

This time-honored method of roasting fillets produces results similar to frying but with far less fuss and considerably less fat. Serve with lots of lemon or with Tartar Sauce, 73, Salsa Verde Cruda, 62, or Mustard Sauce, 47.

Position a rack in the upper third of the oven. Preheat the oven to 550°F. Lightly oil a baking sheet or shallow roasting pan.

Mix in a shallow bowl:

½ cup milk, warmed

1 teaspoon salt

Spread in a second shallow bowl:

1 cup fresh breadcrumbs, toasted

Dip first in the milk mixture, then coat with the breadcrumbs:

1½ to 2 pounds cod or other thick white fillets, in 1 or 2 pieces, rinsed and patted dry

Make sure the fillets are well coated, patting to help the crumbs adhere. Place the fillets on the baking sheet and drizzle over them:

2 tablespoons extra-virgin olive oil, melted butter, or melted bacon drippings

Roast for 8 to 12 minutes, depending on the thickness of the fillets. (To check for doneness, see page 532.) Garnish with:

Minced fresh parsley

Lemon wedges

ROASTED FISH FILLETS ON A BED OF VEGETABLES

4 servings

Use your judgment to substitute different vegetables for the eggplant and tomatoes here. Extremely soft, quick-cooking vegetables, such as tender greens, need no precooking at all; roast firmer ones, such as potatoes or broccoli, for 20 to 30 minutes before adding the fish.

Cut crosswise into ¼-inch slices and salt, 372:

1 eggplant (1 to 1½ pounds)

Cut into ¼- to ½-inch slices:

3 or 4 medium to large ripe tomatoes

Cut into ¼-inch or thinner slices:

1 large or 2 medium onions

Preheat the oven to 450°F. Rinse the eggplant and pat dry. Spread over the bottom of a 13 x 9-inch baking pan:

2 tablespoons extra-virgin olive oil

Spread the onions on the bottom, followed by the eggplant, and finally the tomatoes. Sprinkle with:

1 teaspoon minced fresh thyme or 1 tablespoon minced fresh cilantro

Season lightly with:

Salt and ground black pepper to taste

Drizzle over the top:

1 tablespoon olive oil

Roast, undisturbed, until the tomatoes are beginning to bubble, 10 to 15 minutes. Place on top of the vegetables:

1½ to 2 pounds cod or other thick white fillets, in 1 or 2 pieces, rinsed and patted dry

Season the fish with:

Salt and ground black pepper to taste

Brush with:

1 tablespoon olive oil

Sprinkle with:

½ teaspoon minced fresh thyme or 1 teaspoon minced fresh cilantro

Roast for 10 to 20 minutes, depending on the thickness of the fillets. (To check for doneness, see page 372.) Garnish with:

Fresh thyme or cilantro sprigs

SLOW-BAKED SALMON FILLETS WITH HERBED OLIVE OIL

4 servings

You can drizzle almost anything over this easy-to-cook salmon: soy sauce warmed with a little sesame oil and several drops of vinegar; Pesto, 307, thinned with oil or broth; Fresh Tomato Sauce, 305; or even Mashed Potatoes, 408. The gentle cooking ensures that the fish remains moist and tender.

Preheat the oven to 325°F. Coat a shallow baking dish with:

1 teaspoon extra-virgin olive oil

Place in it, skin side up:

2 center-cut salmon fillets (about 12 ounces each), about 1¼ inches thick at the thickest point, rinsed and patted dry

Place the fish in the oven and bake for 12 minutes. Meanwhile, heat in a small saucepan over low heat:

3 tablespoons extra-virgin olive oil
1 tablespoon chopped fresh tarragon or chervil
½ clove garlic
Salt and ground black pepper to taste

After 15 minutes, check the internal temperature of the salmon with an instant-read thermometer. When the temperature reaches 125°F, remove the fish from the oven and let stand for 3 minutes. Remove the skin (it will come off easily) and turn the fillets over. Strain the herbed oil over the top and serve.

SALMON FILLETS ROASTED IN BUTTER

4 servings

High heat gives the salmon fillets a lovely bit of crust but makes overcooking a danger here: Be sure to remove the fish from the oven before its center is completely opaque. The combination of butter and oil is both rich and fragrant, but you can use all butter or all olive oil if you wish.

Preheat the oven to 500°F. Heat in a small saucepan over medium-low heat until the butter is melted:

2 tablespoons butter
2 tablespoons extra-virgin olive oil
½ teaspoon salt

Spread half of the butter mixture over the bottom of a shallow roasting pan. Place in the pan, skin side up:

1½ pounds salmon fillets, in 1 or 2 pieces, 1¼ to 1½ inches thick at the thickest point, skin on or off, rinsed and patted dry

Sprinkle with:

Salt and ground black pepper to taste

Drizzle the remaining butter mixture over the fish. Roast for 5 minutes and carefully turn the fish. Roast until the interior is nearly but not completely opaque, about 5 minutes more. (To check for doneness, see page 532; salmon is still somewhat translucent in its center at 125°F.) Remove the salmon to a platter and pour all the pan juices over it. Garnish with:

Minced fresh parsley

BAKED SWORDFISH "BIRDS"

4 servings

You can stuff "scaloppine" of swordfish (or salmon or tuna, following the same procedure) with almost any mixture of moistened grains and seasonings, such as couscous tossed with mushrooms, kasha with caramelized onions, or a tabbouleh-like mixture of bulgur, tomatoes, and mint or parsley. Be careful not to overstuff.

Heat in a small skillet over medium-high heat:

2 tablespoons olive oil

Add:

½ cup chopped onions

Cook, stirring, until softened, about 5 minutes. Add:

½ cup chopped fresh parsley
1 tablespoon minced garlic
1 tablespoon drained capers
1 teaspoon minced fresh rosemary, thyme, or winter savory, or scant ½ teaspoon dried
Salt and ground black pepper to taste

Cook, stirring, for 2 minutes. Combine 2 tablespoons of the onion mixture with:

1½ cups chopped seeded tomatoes
1 tablespoon extra-virgin olive oil
Salt and ground black pepper to taste

Combine the remaining onion mixture with:

1 cup fresh breadcrumbs
2 tablespoons dry white wine, Fish Stock, 41, or water
3 tablespoons pine nuts, toasted
Salt and ground black pepper to taste

Preheat the oven to 350°F. Cut horizontally in half for four ½-inch-thick steaks:

2 swordfish steaks (12 ounces each), about 1 inch thick each, skinned

Press down on the top of the fish with one hand while you slice with the other and try to keep the thickness consistent. Place each steak between 2 pieces of plastic wrap and, using a rolling pin, rubber mallet, small pan, or whatever is handy, pound gently until the fish is about ¼ inch thick or less all around. Remove from the wrap.

Spread one-quarter of the breadcrumb stuffing on each piece of the fish, leaving a ½-inch border around the edges. Start at the shortest edge and roll up evenly, tucking in the sides. Seal the "birds" with toothpicks if necessary.

Spread half of the tomato mixture on the bottom of a shallow roasting pan just large enough to hold the birds. Place them on top of the tomato mixture, then season lightly with:

Salt and ground black pepper to taste

Spoon the remaining tomato mixture on top of the fish. Bake until the center of the fish is cooked through, 30 to 40 minutes. Serve immediately.

ROASTED WHOLE RED SNAPPER OR OTHER FISH

4 servings

Red snapper, grouper, blackfish, rockfish, or any other meaty fish is wonderful when roasted.

Preheat the oven to 500°F. Cut 3 or 4 slashes in each side of:

1 red snapper or other fish (3 to 4 pounds), rinsed inside and out and patted dry

Combine and rub the fish inside and out with:

1 tablespoon extra-virgin olive oil

1 tablespoon sherry or other vinegar or fresh lemon juice

Season inside and out with:

Salt and ground black pepper to taste

Make sure to get some flavoring into the slashes. Line a shallow roasting pan with aluminum foil (to ease cleanup) and place the fish on a rack in the pan. Roast, undisturbed, until the meat is translucent right down to the bone, 25 to 35 minutes. (To check for doneness, see page 532.) Serve with:

Minced fresh parsley and lemon wedges, or a vinaigrette, 236 to 239

ROASTED WHOLE BLACKFISH, GROUPER, OR OTHER FISH WITH MEDITERRANEAN FLAVORS

4 servings

You can use almost any Mediterranean herbs here and vary the flavors: Try branches of fennel, rosemary, or oregano; bunches of cilantro, basil, or parsley; fresh bay leaves, mint, or chives. You also can substitute orange for the lemon or add a few slices of onion.

Preheat the oven to 500°F.

Cut 3 or 4 slashes in each side of:

1 blackfish or other fish (3 to 4 pounds), rinsed inside and out and patted dry

Rub the fish inside and out with:

1 tablespoon extra-virgin olive oil

Season inside and out with:

Salt and ground black pepper to taste

Make sure to get some flavoring into the slashes. Tuck into the body cavity:

12 branches fresh thyme

16 thin slices lemon

1 large clove garlic, thinly sliced

Line a shallow roasting pan with aluminum foil (to ease cleanup) and place the fish on a rack in the pan. Roast, undisturbed, until the meat is translucent right down to the bone, 25 to 35 minutes. (To check for doneness, see page 532.) Garnish with:

Fresh thyme sprigs

Lemon slices

ROASTED WHOLE SALMON

8 to 10 servings

This recipe also works very well on a grill. Follow the directions below but grill over indirect heat. You can use a smaller fish if you like, but a 7-pounder is the largest salmon that will fit comfortably into a standard oven or a 22½-inch kettle grill.

Preheat the oven to 475°F.

Rinse and pat dry:

1 salmon (7 pounds), cleaned, with head and tail on

Rub the salmon inside and out with:

2 tablespoons olive oil

Sprinkle inside and out with:

Salt and ground black pepper

Stuff the cavity with:

1 small lemon, sliced

Several sprigs fresh thyme (optional)

Loosely wrap the head and tail of the fish in aluminum foil. Roast on a rack set on a jelly-roll pan until cooked through but slightly translucent at the bone, about 45 minutes. When the salmon is cooked, remove it to a serving plate with two spatulas. Remove the foil. Cut the skin around the head and tail, and down the top of the back, and gently pull off. Use a blunt knife to push out the line of little bones that run along the top of the back. Then push out the bones that run along the bottom of the belly. Gently cut off the brown flesh. Garnish the plate with:

Chopped fresh parsley, fresh thyme, and lemon wedges

To serve, see page 548.

ROASTED MONKFISH WITH GARLIC AND HERBS

4 servings

Monkfish is so meaty that you can make it into veal-like scaloppine, or treat it like pork tenderloin as is done here. Monkfish tails are sold almost always with the center cartilage removed; if yours is not, simply cut around it with a knife—as easy as pitting a peach.

Preheat the oven to 450°F.

Remove the membrane from:

4 monkfish tails (about 6 ounces each), rinsed and patted dry

Mince together:

½ cup packed parsley, chervil, basil, or cilantro leaves

2 teaspoons coarsely chopped garlic

1 teaspoon coarse salt

Cut a few small slits in each of the monkfish tails and insert a pinch of this seasoning into them. Combine the remaining seasoning with:

½ cup all-purpose flour
Ground black pepper to taste

Coat the fish lightly with this mixture. Spread over the bottom of a shallow roasting pan:

1 tablespoon extra-virgin olive oil

Add the fish; roast for 5 minutes, then turn. Add:

1 cup dry white wine or fish or chicken stock

Cook, turning the fish in the liquid occasionally, until the fish is cooked through (completely opaque) and tender, about 20 minutes. Remove the fish and keep warm. Add to the roasting pan:

1 cup dry white wine or fish or chicken stock

Cook, stirring and scraping, over medium-high heat until the liquid is reduced by about half. Spoon the sauce over the monkfish. Garnish with:

Several sprigs parsley, chervil, basil, or cilantro

Serve with:

Hot cooked rice or Basic Pilaf, 257

FISH BAKED IN SALT *4 servings*

Baking fish in coarse salt is one of the finest, most flavorful, and simplest ways to prepare fish, for the salt crust acts as a moist "oven," enveloping the entire fish, baking it gently and evenly.

Preheat the oven to 500°F. Cover the bottom of a baking dish that is just large enough to hold the fish with a ½-inch layer of:

Coarse or sea salt

Rinse and pat dry:

1 center-cut piece fish (2 to 3 pounds), such as salmon, or 1 whole fish (2 to 3 pounds), such as red snapper, grouper, porgy, tilefish, rockfish, or any other white-fleshed fish

The fish need not be scaled but should be gutted and gilled. Lay the fish on the salt and pour enough salt over and around the fish to cover all of its surfaces by at least ¼ inch. Place in the oven and bake, undisturbed, for at least 30 minutes. Poke through the salt into the thickest part of the fish with an instant-read thermometer. At 130°F, the fish is done; this likely will take 10 to 15 minutes more.

Remove the pan from the oven and let stand for 5 minutes. Remove the fish to a platter and brush off all the salt; some of it will have caked, but all of it will come off easily. Remove to a clean plate and remove the skin; it, too, will come off easily. Serve the fish by spooning it off the bone. Garnish with:

Lemon wedges

Drizzle over the top:

Extra-virgin olive oil

or serve with:

Sauce Bercy, 49, Sauce Soubise, 47, or Lemon Beurre Blanc, 58

ABOUT COOKING FISH WITH LIQUID

Cooking with liquid cannot give a fish a nice brown crust, but it does have several advantages. The liquid gives more flexibility in timing, because the fish does not dry out as quickly. The liquid also eliminates the need for some or all of the cooking fat you would use with other methods. Finally, cooking with liquid allows you an easy way to combine one or more fish in the same dish—most fish stews are examples of this. In fact, the only types and cuts of fish that do not take well to cooking in liquid are the delicate fillets, which fall apart easily.

There are several different ways to cook with liquid. The most obvious is poaching, in which the fish is simply simmered in water or other liquid until it is done. This is best for soups, stews, and whole pieces of fish that will be served cold with a sauce, such as salmon. "Poaching" usually implies that you will discard or reserve the cooking liquid; "stewing," on the other hand, indicates that you are intending to season the liquid and serve the fish in it.

Steaming has a similar effect to poaching, but you can use a minimum of seasoning because it is diluted by nothing other than the fish juices. Small to medium whole fish that have good flavor and texture—sea bass is the perfect example—are wonderful steamed with a few spices.

Braising—cooking in a small amount of flavorful liquid, often after initially browning the fish—is a wonderful way to add flavor, color, and a number of other ingredients to a whole fish. Because you can braise in the oven, it eliminates some of the hassle and mess of cooking large fish on top of the stove.

Finally, there is cooking *en papillote,* that is, in little foil or parchment-paper packages. This is essentially a kind of steaming with very little liquid. The same kind of results can be achieved by cooking in a covered casserole or saucepan with much less fuss.

A word about equipment: You do not need a poacher to poach fish, nor do you need a steamer to steam it. Either can be improvised using equipment you have on hand. The only rule to remember is that when you steam fish, it should not be in contact with the steaming liquid; find a way to elevate it a couple of inches, and you are all set.

POACHED SALMON

4 servings

Salmon, the most commonly poached fish, must not be overcooked. This easy method consistently results in a moist piece of fish, and works as well with a whole fish, a section of a whole fish, or a sizable fillet; if you want to poach steaks, however, see Fish Steaks Poached in White Wine, below. Make sure to use abundant water.

Rinse and scale if desired:

1 salmon (about 3 pounds), 1 center-cut piece of salmon (2 to 3 pounds), or 1 large thick salmon fillet (2 to 3 pounds)

Place in a pot large enough to hold it, then cover with cold water. Add:

1 tablespoon salt

Bring to a boil over high heat, then immediately remove from the heat. Let stand for 10 minutes. Remove the fish from the water, drain, and refrigerate. Before serving, bring the fish to room temperature and peel off the skin. Season with:

Salt and ground black pepper to taste

Garnish with:

Fresh herb sprigs

Serve with one or several of:

A mayonnaise, 71 to 75, thinned, if you like, with sour cream, Scandanavian Mustard-Dill Sauce, 79, Sauce Hongroise, 47, and/or Asian Black Bean Sauce, 83

BRAISED WHOLE FISH WITH RED WINE SAUCE

4 to 6 servings

The ideal fish for this dish are red snapper, grouper, or carp, all of which are found easily in larger sizes; striped bass is another possibility. Serve this with plenty of crusty bread for mopping up the sauce.

Heat gently in a deep skillet, casserole, or roasting pan large enough to hold the fish:

¼ cup vegetable oil

Mix:

About 1 cup all-purpose flour
Salt and ground black pepper to taste

Coat with the seasoned flour:

1 red snapper or other whole fish (3 to 5 pounds), scaled, rinsed, and patted dry

Increase the heat under the skillet to high and heat the oil until hot. Add the fish and brown for about 5 minutes on each side, turning only once (carefully) and making sure that a nice dark crust develops.

Meanwhile, soak in hot water to cover:

1 to 2 tablespoons dried porcini mushrooms

Remove the fish to a platter. Pour the fat from the pan and wipe it out with paper towels. Heat the pan over medium heat. Add:

2 tablespoons extra-virgin olive oil or butter
8 ounces mushrooms, wiped clean and sliced

Cook, stirring, for a minute or two. Drain the porcini, straining the soaking water through a fine sieve lined with a dampened paper towel. Chop the porcini and add them with 2 tablespoons of the water to the cooking mushrooms. Add:

1 cup chopped onions
1 teaspoon minced garlic
1 teaspoon fresh thyme leaves, or scant ½ teaspoon dried
Salt and ground black pepper to taste

Cook, stirring occasionally, until the onions are softened, about 8 minutes. Add the remaining porcini water along with:

1 cup dry red wine
1 bay leaf

Bring to a boil and stir. Reduce the heat to medium-low, set the fish in the liquid, and cover. Cook gently until the fish is done, 15 to 20 minutes for a 3-pound fish, 25 to 30 minutes for a 5-pound fish. (To check for doneness, see page 532.) Carefully remove the fish to a platter. If the sauce is thin, boil, stirring, over high heat, until reduced to a saucelike consistency. Remove the bay leaf, spoon the sauce over the fish, and serve, garnished with plenty of:

Minced fresh parsley

FISH STEAKS POACHED IN WHITE WINE

4 servings

Use any fish steaks you like in this recipe: Salmon, cod, sturgeon, turbot, and halibut are all good. If you prefer, you can poach the fish in Court Bouillon, 39. Whatever you choose, the poaching liquid can be reused. After you are finished cooking, boil it for 2 minutes, cool, strain, and refrigerate up to 3 days or freeze indefinitely. It pays to brighten it a bit with fresh herbs, spices, and vinegar each time you use it.

Place in a deep skillet or casserole large enough to hold the fish in a single layer:

2 cups dry white wine
2 cups water
2 tablespoons rice, sherry, or white wine vinegar
1 teaspoon salt
10 peppercorns
10 coriander seeds
2 whole cloves

1 bay leaf
1 clove garlic
Several sprigs fresh parsley, thyme, or tarragon, or
½ teaspoon dried

Bring to a boil, uncovered, over high heat; reduce the heat and simmer for 5 minutes. Place gently in the poaching liquid:

1½ to 2 pounds fish steaks (4 small or 2 large), rinsed and patted dry

Cover the pan and adjust the heat so that the liquid is gently simmering; cook for 8 minutes, then check for doneness (see page 532). Remove the fish when the flesh still clings a little bit to the bone and is slightly translucent. Serve hot, at room temperature, or chilled with:

A mayonnaise, 71 to 75, a vinaigrette, 236 to 239, or Sauce Mousseline, 56

STEAMED FISH STEAKS OR WHOLE FISH, CHINESE STYLE

4 servings

This preparation is great for small fish, such as sea bass.

Combine:

2 cloves garlic, thinly slivered
One 1-inch piece fresh ginger, peeled and thinly slivered
2 scallions, minced
1 tablespoon soy sauce
1 tablespoon dry sherry

Rub this mixture all over:

2 halibut or other steaks (about 1 pound each), well rinsed and patted dry; or 2 whole fish (1½ to 2 pounds each), cleaned and scaled, 2 or 3 slashes cut in each side

Place the fish on a plate and pour any remaining mixture over it. If you like, you can cover the fish and let it marinate in the refrigerator for up to 2 hours. When you are ready to cook, place the fish on a heatproof plate set on a rack over gently simmering water (or use a bamboo steamer, still keeping the fish on a plate) and steam until cooked through, about 10 to 12 minutes for the steak, 15 minutes or longer for whole fish. Serve the fish with the accumulated juices.

FISH FILLETS OR STEAKS IN PACKAGES OR CASSEROLE

4 servings

Traditionally, cooking *en papillote* means sealing portions of meat or vegetables with seasonings and liquid in little packages made from parchment paper. In recent years, the same effect has been achieved using aluminum foil. But the packages need not be individual—you can seal everything in a covered casserole and not bother with dividing ingredients into four separate packages.

Of course, it is fun to serve individual packages to each diner, so if you wish, simply divide the ingredients into four portions and seal each one in a package made of aluminum foil or parchment paper. Cooking time will be about the same.

This technique can be used with any combination of vegetables and seasonings placed under the fish; just make sure that they all will cook in about the same amount of time as the fish. (In order to achieve this, you may have to blanch harder vegetables such as broccoli or potato.)

Preheat the oven to 400°F.

Layer in the order listed in a 13 x 9-inch glass casserole:

2 tomatoes, cut into ½-inch slices
1 medium onion, cut into ¼- to ⅛-inch slices
2 tablespoons minced fresh basil leaves or fresh parsley

Sprinkle with:

Salt and ground black pepper to taste
1 tablespoon extra-virgin olive oil
½ cup dry white wine, Fish Stock, 41, or water

Top with:

4 fillets or steaks of any fish you like (about 6 ounces each)

Cover the casserole and bake until the fish is cooked and the vegetables are softened, 12 to 20 minutes, depending on the thickness of the fish. (To check for doneness, see page 532.)

SMALL FISH, FILLETS, OR STEAKS POACHED IN SOY SAUCE

4 servings

Combine in a large skillet or casserole with cover:

2 scallions, minced
1 tablespoon minced peeled fresh ginger
1 tablespoon minced garlic
1 tablespoon sugar
¼ cup soy sauce
¼ cup mirin
¼ cup water
1 tablespoon rice vinegar or other mild vinegar

Bring to a boil over medium-high heat. Reduce the heat and lay in a single layer in the liquid:

1½ pounds fish fillets or steaks (4 small or 2 large), or 4 small fish (12 to 16 ounces each), rinsed (cod, halibut, mackerel, salmon, butterfish, or any other fish that is not too delicate)

Reduce the heat to low and cover the pan. Cook for 5 minutes for ½-inch-thick fillets, up to 15 minutes for thick steaks or small whole fish. (To check for doneness, see page 532.) Remove the fish to a platter. If the sauce seems too thin, boil over high heat until slightly thickened.

BLUE TROUT (TRUITE AU BLEU)

4 servings

For trout to turn blue and curl onto itself, it must be freshly killed—an hour before cooking at most—and it must not be washed (it is the trout's protective coating that turns it blue). Blue trout is traditionally served with plain boiled potatoes, 407, and minced parsley; because it is boiled in a vinegar solution, it is nice to serve it also with a rich, mild sauce, such as Hollandaise Sauce, 55, or, better still, Sauce Mousseline, 56.

Combine in a pot large enough to hold the fish and bring to a boil:

12 cups water
3 cups white wine vinegar, rice vinegar, or other white vinegar
2 bay leaves
1 carrot, coarsely chopped
1 celery stalk, coarsely chopped
1 onion, quartered
2 cloves
1 teaspoon salt
10 peppercorns
10 coriander seeds
Several parsley stems

Reduce the heat and simmer while you prepare the trout. Kill and gut:

4 freshly caught trout (at least 8 ounces each)

Lower them all into the simmering liquid, increase the heat, and bring to a boil again. Cover, remove from the heat, and let stand for 5 to 10 minutes, no longer.

Remove the fish to a serving platter and serve hot with:

Boiled potatoes, 407
Minced fresh parsley
Hollandaise Sauce, 55, Sauce Mousseline, 56, or Traditional Mayonnaise, 72, thinned with cream or sour cream

ABOUT MICROWAVING FISH

For simple fish recipes that are most like steamed fish, in very small quantities, the microwave does a credible job. The rules are straightforward: Get used to your own microwave so that you can get a sense of how long the cooking will take (the alternative is opening the oven door every 30 seconds); cook small portions, never more than a pound and preferably less; do not use a lot of liquid; and keep added ingredients few—the more you include, the more likely that half the dish will be done and the other half not.

MICROWAVED FISH FOR TWO

Here is a basic recipe for using the microwave to cook fish. Try making Steamed Fish Steaks or Whole Fish, Chinese Style, 555, or Fish Fillets or Steaks in Packages or Casserole, 555, in the microwave, using the timing here as a starting point.

Arrange on a plate with the thickest edge toward the outside:

8 to 12 ounces fish fillets, preferably in 2 pieces, up to 1 inch thick, rinsed and patted dry

Season the fish with:

Salt and ground black pepper to taste

Sprinkle with:

1 tablespoon Fish Stock, 41, dry white wine, or fresh citrus juice

Cover with another plate or plastic wrap. Microwave on high for 3 minutes (2 minutes if you are using flounder or other flatfish, 4 minutes if the fillets approach an inch in thickness. To check for doneness, see page 532). If the fish is nearly done, just re-cover it and let it stand for a minute; it will finish cooking. If it needs more time, continue to microwave in 1- to 2-minute intervals to avoid overcooking.

Drizzle over the fish:

Extra-virgin olive oil

Serve with:

Lemon wedges

SAUTÉING AND PAN-GRILLING FISH

Sautéing is a simple process: Heat enough fat to come into contact with one side of the fish, coat the flesh with something that will become crisp—such as a batter, some breadcrumbs, some flour or cornmeal—and sear the fish on both sides. Since most fish cooks quickly, this may be all you need. For thick pieces that take longer to cook than to brown, reduce the heat and finish the cooking without much further browning, turning occasionally. Or, easier still, brown the fish on both sides and finish the cooking in a hot oven.

Sautéing is one of the best cooking techniques for fillets, which tend to dry out when roasted or even grilled or broiled. But it is also suitable for steaks and whole fish. In fact, the traditional American method for cooking most smaller whole fish—those under 1½ pounds or so—is to coat them in cornmeal or flour and pan-fry—that is, sauté—them.

You can use any fat you wish for sautéing: Olive oil is a very popular choice and rightly so, but a combination of olive oil and butter is more flavorful. All butter is an especially delicious treat. Clarified butter, 1069, does not burn as easily. Peanut oil, with its distinctive flavor, is at its best when used in Asian-style dishes. Bacon fat and lard are flavored too strongly for cooking most fish. Other oils—corn, safflower, sunflower, and especially canola—are good when you are looking for a fat to contribute crispness without adding flavor.

Pan-grilling is cooking at high heat on top of the stove with no fat or liquid. It is ideal for fish that contains a bit of its own fat: salmon, for example, or tuna, swordfish, pompano, mackerel, and so on; these fish have moisture that will not evaporate immediately when subjected to high, dry heat. The technique itself is easy: Preheat a nonstick skillet over medium-high heat until it is good and hot—usually 2 to 5 minutes, depending on your stove—and add the fish. Brown it, turn it, brown it again. If the fish has enough flavor and enough fat, drizzle lemon juice or vinegar over it, and you are done. Pan-grilled fish is also wonderful on a bed of other foods: cooked vegetables, raw greens, beans or lentils, well-seasoned grains, and so on.

No matter how much you like pan-grilling, however, there are times when you must sauté. You crave that crunch, or you have a piece of fish which is so lean that it cries out for some added fat.

PAN-GRILLED FISH FILLETS OR STEAKS

4 servings

Pan-grilling fillets is ideal when the fish has its skin, especially if that skin is good to eat, but it is also wonderful with steaks. Another option is to turn steaks into small "fillets": Use a small knife to carefully cut the fish away from the center bone, then turn it on its side, shown 530.

Heat a large nonstick skillet over medium-high heat for 3 minutes. Meanwhile, lightly brush:

1½ to 2 pounds salmon or other fish, steaks or fillets (2 large or 4 small), scaled, rinsed, and patted dry

with:

1 tablespoon olive or other oil

Lay the fish skin side down in the skillet and cook, undisturbed, until the skin is nice and brown, 4 to 5 minutes. Sprinkle with:

Salt and ground black pepper to taste

Turn the fish and cook for 1 to 2 minutes for medium-rare salmon, 3 to 4 minutes for almost cooked through salmon, 5 minutes or more for well-done salmon. (To check for doneness, see page 532.) If desired, serve with:

Fresh Tomato Sauce, 305

Garnish with:

Minced fresh parsley

Lemon wedges

PAN-GRILLED FISH FILLETS OR STEAKS WITH SORREL SAUCE

4 servings

It was the famed Troisgros brothers who first paired sweet salmon with a tart sorrel sauce in their three-star French kitchen. See for yourself how delicious their world-famous idea is.

Combine in a saucepan:

½ cup dry white wine

½ cup water

2 celery stalks, coarsely chopped

1 medium carrot, coarsely chopped

1 medium onion, quartered

2 cloves garlic

4 sprigs fresh thyme, or ½ teaspoon dried

6 sprigs fresh parsley

3 fresh sage leaves, or generous pinch of dried, crumbled

2 teaspoons tomato paste

Bring to a boil over medium-high heat, then reduce the heat to low. Cook, covered, for 20 minutes. Strain through a sieve, pressing the solids to release all of their juices. Return the liquid to the saucepan; there should be about ½ cup. Over very low heat, gradually whisk in:

8 tablespoons (1 stick) butter, softened, cut into pieces

Season with:

Salt and ground black pepper to taste

Stir in:

2 cups fresh sorrel, washed, tough stems removed, torn into 1-inch pieces

Keep warm. Prepare:

Pan Grilled Fish Fillets or Steaks, above

Serve with:

Boiled potatoes

Spoon a bit of the sorrel sauce over all.

PAN-GRILLED SWORDFISH OR TUNA STEAKS AU POIVRE

4 servings

These are the two fish that can be treated most easily like meat and can make the most devoted steak eaters enjoy themselves eating a creature of the sea.

Press:

2 tablespoons coarsely cracked black peppercorns or mixture of black, white, green, and pink peppercorns

onto the outside of:

4 tuna or swordfish steaks (6 to 8 ounces each)

Heat a cast-iron or other heavy skillet over medium-high heat for 5 minutes; it should be really hot. Add the steaks to the pan, increase the heat to high, and sear them for 2 minutes on each side. At this point, smaller tuna steaks will be done if you like them rare; cook thicker steaks, such as swordfish, for another 2 minutes per side. (Alternatively, sear them on one side, then move them, without turning, to the broiler and broil until done.) Remove to a warmed platter and reduce the heat to medium. Add to the pan:

1 cup dry red wine
1 tablespoon minced shallots

Cook, stirring, until the wine is reduced by about one-third and the shallots are softened, about 2 minutes. Stir into the sauce:

1 or 2 tablespoons butter, softened
1 teaspoon salt

When the butter is incorporated, add:

1 teaspoon minced fresh tarragon, pinch of dried tarragon, or 2 tablespoons minced fresh parsley

Spoon the sauce over the fish and serve.

SAUTÉED FISH FILLETS

4 servings

Best with flounder, sole, or other flatfish, this basic sautéing technique is also fine for thicker fillets, such as those of cod. Use the biggest skillet you have, do not skimp on the fat, and cook in batches if necessary, keeping the first batch warm in the oven while you cook the second.

Preheat the oven to 200°F. Heat a large nonstick skillet over medium heat for 3 to 4 minutes.

Mix in a shallow bowl:

1 cup all-purpose flour
Salt and ground black pepper to taste

Coat with the seasoned flour:

1 to 1½ pounds thin white fillets (about 8 pieces), such as flounder or sole, less than ½ inch thick, skinned, picked over for stray bones, rinsed and patted dry

Shake off the excess flour. Add to the skillet and heat until hot:

4 tablespoons butter, oil, or a combination

Add the fillets without crowding to the skillet. Increase the heat to high and sauté, shaking the pan from time to time, until the bottom of the fish is nicely browned, about 3 minutes. Turn and brown the other side. Remove the fillets to a plate and keep warm in the oven. Sauté the remaining fillets in the same fat or replace it if it has burned. When all the fish is done, garnish with:

Minced fresh parsley
Lemon wedges

SAUTÉED FISH FILLETS WITH WINE SAUCE AND CAPERS

Prepare:

Sautéed Fish Fillets, above

Keep the fillets warm in the oven. Add to the skillet:

1 cup dry white wine

Cook, stirring, over high heat until reduced by about one-third. Stir in:

1 tablespoon butter, softened (optional)
2 tablespoons drained capers

Serve the fish with the sauce.

PARMESAN-CRUSTED SAUTÉED FISH FILLETS

This is best made with "medallions" cut from monkfish tails or with meaty fillets of catfish, dogfish, grouper, blackfish, or red snapper.

Prepare:

Sautéed Fish Fillets, above

Instead of coating the fish with flour, dip first in a mixture of:

1 large egg, lightly beaten
2 tablespoons milk

Then coat in a mixture of:

1 cup fresh breadcrumbs, toasted
½ cup grated Parmesan cheese
¼ cup minced fresh parsley

Sauté as directed, taking care not to burn the coating.

COD IN GREEN SAUCE

4 servings

This is not exactly a sauté, because the heat is kept fairly low and the exterior of the fish never becomes crisp, but it is a wonderful take on fish cooked in oil. If you use a moist, delicate fish for this dish—cod is traditional, but whiting, halibut, haddock, and hake are all equally good—the juices combine with the abundant olive oil to make a delicious, deceptively creamy sauce.

Warm over low heat in a large skillet until the garlic begins to color, at least 10 minutes:

½ cup olive oil
1 tablespoon minced garlic

Add:

1½ to 2 pounds cod or halibut fillets or steaks, in 2 or 4 pieces, rinsed and patted dry

Increase the heat to medium-low, and gently cook the fillets for 3 minutes or the steaks for 4 to 5 minutes. Carefully turn the fish. Add to the pan:

1 cup coarsely chopped parsley

Cook, shaking the pan gently, until the fish is done, 8 to 12 minutes. Serve, garnished with:

Chopped fresh parsley

PAN-FRIED WHOLE FISH
2 servings

This is the basic recipe for panfish, useful for everything from tiny smelts or sardines to midsized butterfish (which weigh less than 8 ounces each) all the way up to "large" croaker and porgy (which weigh in at over a pound). Allow 8 to 12 ounces of whole fish per person, as the yield is just about 50 percent; anyone accustomed to eating whole fish can easily finish a fish that weighs more than a pound.

If you do not wish to soak the fish in milk first, simply coat it well with flour or cornmeal before sautéing it. You also can add other seasonings to the coating medium if you like: chili or curry powder, minced fresh herbs, lots of ground black pepper, or some cinnamon.

Soak for 15 minutes:

1 to 2 pounds whole small fish, cleaned, scaled, and rinsed well

in:

1 cup milk or cream, or as needed

Mix in a shallow bowl:

1 cup cornmeal or all-purpose flour
Salt and ground black pepper to taste

Coat the fish with the seasoned cornmeal.

Heat a large nonstick skillet over medium-high heat for 2 to 3 minutes. Add to the skillet:

½ cup olive, peanut, or canola oil, oil mixed with butter, bacon drippings, or lard

Heat until the fat is hot. Add the fish and fry on each side until browned, adjusting the heat so that the fat is always bubbling but not burning. Usually these fish are done when each side is golden, but check the interior of larger fish to make sure no blood remains. Drain well on paper bags or paper towels. Serve hot or at room temperature with:

Minced fresh parsley and lemon wedges, or Salsa Fresca, 61, or Tartar Sauce, 73

Or keep the fish warm while you make this light sauce. Pour off all but 1 tablespoon fat from the skillet, then add:

1 tablespoon minced shallots or 1 teaspoon minced garlic

Cook, stirring, over medium heat, until softened, about 1 minute. Add:

1 teaspoon minced fresh tarragon, or scant ½ teaspoon dried
1 cup dry white wine, Fish Stock, 41, or water

Increase the heat to medium-high and cook, stirring, until the liquid is reduced by about half, about 5 minutes. Stir in:

1 tablespoon fresh lemon juice or vinegar

Cook for another 30 seconds. Taste and adjust the seasonings and serve with the fish.

PAN-FRIED SMALL FISH, SWEDISH STYLE
4 servings

In Sweden, these little fish "sandwiches" are made with Baltic herring, but you can make them with any small fish from which you can remove the backbone, such as smelts, anchovies, and sardines.

To bone these fish, shown below, snap down on the head and pull it off in a downward direction; some of the innards will come out along with it. Use your finger to open the fish up from the front and remove the remaining innards, then grasp the backbone between your fingers and pull it out. You will be left with two tiny fillets joined by the skin. Plan to make 8 of these—4 sandwiches—for each serving.

Stir together:

½ cup Maître d' Hôtel Butter, 77
1 teaspoon Dijon mustard
Salt and ground black pepper to taste

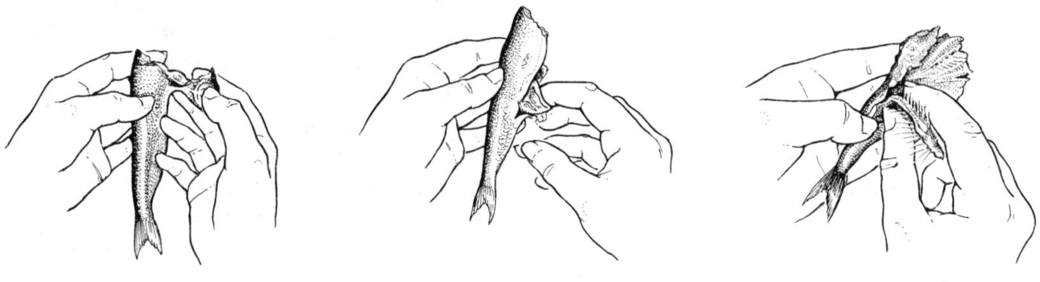

Boning small fish

Let it soften slightly at room temperature. As described above, remove the heads and backbones of:

32 sardines, anchovies, small herrings, or smelts

Rinse and dry them well. Spread a small amount of the dill butter on the inside of half of the fish, then top with the other half, making 16 fish sandwiches.

Whisk together in a shallow bowl:

2 or 3 large eggs

Spread in a second shallow bowl:

1½ cups fresh breadcrumbs, toasted

Heat in a large nonstick skillet over medium-high heat:

4 tablespoons (½ stick) butter, or a combination of butter and olive oil

Dip each sandwich first in the eggs, then coat with the breadcrumbs. Add to the skillet and cook until lightly browned on both sides, less than 5 minutes. Adjust the heat so that the fat is bubbling but not burning. Serve hot, cold, or at room temperature with:

Minced fresh dill and lemon wedges, or Tartar Sauce, 73

SWORDFISH OR TUNA SAUTÉED WITH OLIVES, CAPERS, PEPPERS, AND TOMATO

4 servings

Only strong-tasting fish such as swordfish, tuna, bluefish, or king mackerel can stand up to this highly spiced sauce from the Italian region of Calabria. Use the best olives you can find—they will make a difference.

Heat in a large skillet over low heat until the garlic turns pale gold, 15 to 20 minutes:

3 tablespoons extra-virgin olive oil
3 large cloves garlic, thinly sliced

Remove the garlic with a slotted spoon to a small bowl. Increase the heat to medium-high and add:

½ cup thinly sliced red onions

Cook for about 2 minutes. Add:

1¼ to 1½ pounds swordfish, tuna, or other dark-fleshed fish, skinned, cut into 1-inch-wide strips

Increase the heat to high and quickly sear the fish on all sides, while seasoning it with:

1 tablespoon minced fresh basil
1 tablespoon minced fresh mint
1 teaspoon minced fresh oregano or marjoram
Salt and ground black pepper to taste

Cook until the fish is done to your liking, 2 to 5 minutes. Remove the fish to a hot platter or warm oven. Return the garlic to the skillet along with:

1 cup chopped seeded peeled tomatoes, fresh or canned
½ cup Gaeta, Kalamata, or other good dark olives, pitted if you like
1 tablespoon capers, drained
Generous pinch of red pepper flakes, or to taste

Cook for just a minute, stirring occasionally. Spoon over the fish. Garnish with:

Minced fresh basil
Minced fresh mint

SKATE WITH "BLACK" BUTTER

4 servings

Usually you can buy skate off the wing—that is, filleted—but in the event that you cannot (or that you caught the skate yourself), this recipe begins with whole skate.

If you have skate fillets, proceed directly to the flouring step. If not, place in a deep skillet or casserole:

1 skate wing (about 2 pounds)

Cover with water and add:

1 tablespoon salt
1 bay leaf
Several sprigs fresh thyme (optional)

Bring to a boil, reduce the heat, and simmer gently until you can lift the meat off the cartilage at the thickest point. Remove the skate, immediately plunge it into a bowl of ice water, and let cool completely. Drain the fish and gently lift each fillet off the center cartilage. Dry thoroughly.

Mix in a shallow bowl:

1 cup all-purpose flour
Salt and ground black pepper to taste

Coat the skate fillets with the seasoned flour. Heat a nonstick skillet large enough to hold the skate in a single layer over medium heat for about 3 minutes.

Add and heat until the butter foam subsides:

1 tablespoon olive oil
2 tablespoons butter or additional olive oil

Add the skate, increase the heat to high, and brown quickly on both sides; the skate is done when you easily can separate one segment from its neighbor (this will take about the same amount of time as it does to brown it). Remove the skate to a warm oven, wipe out the skillet, and return it to medium heat. Add:

3 tablespoons butter

Heat until the butter foams, then stir in:

2 tablespoons capers, drained
1 tablespoon white wine vinegar

Cook about 10 seconds. Pour the sauce over the skate and garnish with:

Minced fresh parsley

CRISP AND SPICY SAUTÉED FISH FILLETS

4 servings

This produces a fillet with an almost deep-fried crust and as much spicy flavor as you like. Do not use delicate fish here—stick with catfish, dogfish, blackfish, grouper, or red snapper.

Mix together:

1½ cups all-purpose flour
1½ cups water
1 tablespoon or more spice mixture of your choice (curry powder, Garam Masala, 1061, chili powder, or another spice mixture)
Salt and ground black pepper to taste

Rub:

1½ pounds fish fillets, in 2 or 4 pieces, rinsed and patted dry

with:

Fresh lime or lemon juice or vinegar

Heat a large skillet over medium heat. Pour in:

⅛ inch peanut, corn, or canola oil

Dip each of the fillets in turn into the spice mixture and let the excess drip off. Place them in the skillet and increase the heat to medium-high. Cook, turning once, until nicely browned on both sides, adjusting the heat as needed to keep the oil bubbling but not burning. Drain on paper bags or paper towels. Serve with:

Minced fresh cilantro
Lime wedges

BLACKENED FISH STEAKS OR FILLETS

4 servings

The original blackened fish was redfish, the spice mixture and accompanying technique was created by New Orleans chef Paul Prudhomme, and the result was a craze that vaulted Prudhomme to national fame. Fortunately, you can make this dish with any firm-fleshed steak or fillet, such as swordfish, red snapper, grouper, or catfish. *Do not make this dish unless your stove has a functional exhaust fan.* And turn off the smoke detectors.

Mix together in a shallow bowl:

1 tablespoon minced fresh thyme, or 1 teaspoon dried
1 tablespoon minced fresh oregano or marjoram, or 1 teaspoon dried
1 tablespoon paprika
1 teaspoon ground red pepper
1 teaspoon coarsely cracked black or white peppercorns
1 teaspoon coarse salt

Place a large cast-iron skillet over high heat. Turn on the exhaust fan. Have ready:

½ cup clarified butter or olive oil
4 firm-fleshed fish fillets or steaks (6 to 8 ounces each), rinsed and patted dry

When the pan begins to turn white, after 5 to 10 minutes, brush both sides of the fish with a little butter or oil, then dip into the herb mixture. Place in the pan and drizzle over each piece a little of the melted butter or oil. Fry for 3 minutes, turn the fish, and drizzle over a little more butter or oil. Cook for 3 to 6 minutes, depending on the thickness of the fish. Reduce the heat if necessary to keep the herb mixture from burning. Serve hot with:

Lemon wedges

ABOUT DEEP-FRYING FISH

See Deep-Frying, 1050. Fish deep-fries very quickly; if the coating is brown, chances are the fish is done. If you want to use a fat that contributes pleasant flavor, use olive or peanut oils; if you want to minimize the flavor of the cooking medium, use canola or other seed or vegetable oil.

DEEP-FRIED FILLETS, SOUTHERN STYLE

4 servings

When you deep-fry whole fish, you must have a suitably large vessel and plenty of oil. This simple technique is fast and easy; just be sure to use firm-fleshed fish—catfish, red snapper, blackfish, dogfish, grouper, and the like, are best—and properly heated oil.

Heat in a deep-fat fryer or deep, heavy pot over medium-high heat to 375°F:

2 inches corn, canola, olive, peanut, or other oil

Mix in a shallow bowl:

1 cup cornmeal or all-purpose flour
1 tablespoon chili powder (optional)
Salt and ground black pepper to taste

Coat with the seasoned cornmeal:

1½ to 2 pounds fish fillets, rinsed and thoroughly patted dry

Pat the cornmeal onto the fish to help it adhere. Add the fish 1 piece at a time to the hot oil and increase the heat to high to maintain the temperature. Cook the fish in batches if the pot becomes crowded—it will not take long. Stir once or twice just to make sure the fillets are not sticking anywhere. Remove the fillets when they are golden brown. Drain on paper bags or paper towels. Serve immediately with:

Hushpuppies, 780
Tartar Sauce, 73
Lemon wedges

FISH AND CHIPS *4 servings*

Dogfish, now being sold as "cape shark" (it has always had other names in attempts to boost its popularity, although it is a fine fish), is classic in fish and chips. Any white-fleshed fish is suitable, although the firmer ones are less likely to fall apart than delicate fish such as cod.

Place in a bowl and soak in cold water to cover for 30 minutes:

4 large baking potatoes, peeled and sliced into 2¼ x ⅜-inch strips

Stir together in a medium bowl:

1 cup all-purpose flour
1 teaspoon baking powder
1 teaspoon salt
½ teaspoon ground black pepper
½ teaspoon ground cinnamon (optional)

Add and stir until smooth:

1 cup milk, water, or a combination
1 large egg

Let stand. Heat in a deep-fat fryer or deep, heavy pot over medium-high heat to 330°F:

3 inches peanut or other vegetable oil

Drain the potatoes and dry them well. Drop the potatoes—about 1 cup at a time—into the hot oil and fry until the spattering ceases, about 2 minutes. Remove with a slotted spoon and drain on a paper bag or paper towels. Let stand for 10 minutes. Meanwhile, increase the temperature of the oil to 350°F.

In the interests of frugality, you can fry the fish in the same oil, before finishing the potatoes, but you risk having burnt bits of batter among your chips, even if you skim carefully. Better to use separate batches of oil. Heat in a second deep-fat fryer or deep, heavy pot over medium-high heat to 365°F:

2 inches peanut or other vegetable oil

Stir the batter, then dip into it 1 piece at a time:

1½ pounds dogfish or other white-fleshed fillets, in 6 or 8 pieces, rinsed and thoroughly patted dry

Let the excess batter drip off, then place the fish carefully in the oil. Increase the heat to high to maintain the temperature. The fish is done when the batter is golden brown. Drain on paper bags or paper towels.

To finish the chips, fry the potatoes in small batches in the 365°F oil in a frying basket, if you have one, to ensure quick and easy removal. Fry until they are golden brown, 2 to 3 minutes, then remove the basket, or remove the chips from the oil with a slotted spoon and drain on paper towels. Serve with the fish and accompany with:

Malt or other vinegar, lemon wedges, and/or Tartar Sauce, 73

THAI FISH CAKES (TOD MAN PLA) *4 servings*

These are fragrant, spicy, crisp, and fresh-tasting. Serve with a spicy, vinegary cole slaw or cucumber salad.

Puree in a food processor:

1 dried red chili pepper, seeded, or 1 teaspoon red pepper flakes
1 shallot, coarsely chopped
2 cloves garlic, coarsely chopped
One ½-inch piece fresh ginger or galangal, peeled and coarsely chopped
2 tablespoons fish sauce
1 teaspoon grated lime zest or 2 kaffir lime leaves
1 teaspoon salt
1 teaspoon sugar

Add:

1 pound white fish fillets, picked over for bones, rinsed and patted dry
1 large egg

Process until the mixture is quite pasty. Add:

2 tablespoons chopped fresh cilantro
2 scallions, coarsely chopped

Pulse the machine a few times to combine. Heat in a deep-fat fryer or deep, heavy pot over medium-high heat to 350°F:

2 inches corn, canola, olive, peanut, or other oil

Knead the fish mixture with your hands until it is smooth, then shape it into 1-inch balls or 2-inch cakes. Gradually add them to the hot oil and increase the heat to high to maintain the temperature. Cook until nicely browned, 4 to 5 minutes. Drain on paper bags or paper towels. Serve hot, garnished with:

Minced fresh cilantro
Lime wedges

RECIPES USING UNUSUAL TECHNIQUES OR UNUSUAL OR LEFTOVER FISH

SEVICHE *6 servings*

Seviche is raw fish marinated in citrus juice. Though the fish is not technically cooked, it turns opaque and firms up so that it does not seem raw. Fish options here include grouper, halibut, flounder, and snapper; be sure to use only the freshest ocean fish available. For a less saucelike version suitable for serving on lettuce leaves as a first course or on tostadas for a pass-around appetizer, reduce the tomato juice to a tablespoon or two.

Remove all of the bones and skin from:

1 pound very fresh firm-fleshed fish fillets

Cut the fillets into small cubes, about 3/8 inch each, and place in a glass or stainless-steel mixing bowl. Stir in:

1/2 cup fresh lemon juice
1/2 cup fresh lime juice

Cover with plastic wrap and refrigerate, stirring occasionally, until the fish is opaque throughout (break open a piece to test it), 4 to 6 hours. Thoroughly drain the fish. (It can be refrigerated at this point for up to 18 hours before serving, if desired.) To serve, mix the drained fish with:

1 cup tomato juice
1 1/2 tablespoons olive oil
1 medium, ripe tomato, cored, and diced
1 small onion, finely diced
1/4 cup coarsely chopped pitted green olives
2 tablespoons chopped fresh cilantro
1 to 2 fresh jalapeño peppers, seeded and minced
1 teaspoon dried oregano
1/2 teaspoon salt, or to taste
1/2 to 1 teaspoon sugar, to taste

Taste and adjust the seasonings and refrigerate until serving time. Serve in small bowls garnished with:

Fresh cilantro sprigs
Diced avocado (optional)

SHRIMP SEVICHE

Prepare Seviche, above, substituting for the fish fillets 1 pound cooked peeled medium-large shrimp, cut into 1/4-inch bits. Reduce the lemon and lime juices to 3 tablespoons each and reduce the initial refrigerating time to about 1 hour. Drain, then stir in the remaining ingredients as directed.

GRAVLAX (SALMON CURED WITH SALT, SUGAR, AND DILL)

At least 15 servings

This traditional Swedish method of curing salmon is easy to do at home. This fish must be impeccably fresh. Gravlax keeps well, covered and refrigerated, for several days.

Fillet or have filleted by the fishmonger, leaving the skin on:

1 salmon (4 to 5 pounds)

Mix together:

2 1/2 cups sugar
1 1/2 cups salt
1 tablespoon ground black pepper

Rub the fillets all over with this mixture. On the flesh side of one of the fillets, lay:

2 cups coarsely chopped fresh dill, including stems

Sprinkle with:

2 tablespoons brandy, aquavit, plain or lemon-flavored vodka, or other spirits

Lay the other fillet flesh side down on top of the dill-covered fillet. Wrap in plastic wrap or cheesecloth, sprinkling the outside with any scraps of dill and remaining salt mixture. Place on a plate, cover with another plate, and top the whole package with 3 or 4 pounds of weight. Refrigerate.

Twice a day, open the package and baste the fish all over with the juice it has exuded. The gravlax is done when it is opaque, usually in 3 days but it could be 2 or 4. Thinly slice. Serve with:

Mustard Sauce, 47, or Mustard Mayonnaise, 73, thinned with cream or sour cream

ESCABÈCHE OF FISH

6 appetizer servings

Escabèche was brought to Mexico by the Spaniards. It is basically a pickle, originally conceived as a way to preserve the fish with spices, vinegar, and oil. The fish is fried and submerged in the marinade. Any mild firm-fleshed white fish works well.

Combine well in a small saucepan:

1 cup white vinegar
1 cup water
1 tablespoon minced garlic
1 tablespoon sugar
1 teaspoon ground cumin
1 small fresh jalapeño or other fresh chili pepper, seeded and minced
Salt and ground black pepper to taste

Bring to a boil over high heat, then remove from the heat.

Mix in a shallow bowl:

1/2 cup all-purpose flour
1 teaspoon salt
1 teaspoon cracked black peppercorns

Coat with the seasoned flour:

1 pound cod, snapper, or halibut fillets

Heat in a large skillet until hot but not smoking over medium-high heat:

1/4 cup vegetable oil

Place the fillets in the pan and fry until golden brown on the outside and completely opaque at the center, 3 to 4 minutes each side. Remove to a wide, shallow bowl. Pour the vinegar mixture on top and sprinkle with:

1/4 cup chopped fresh cilantro
Juice of 2 limes

Serve hot or at room temperature.

FISH LOAF

4 servings

Be sure to use some of a more oily fish so that the loaf is moist—even a 4-ounce can of tuna or salmon works. Avoid softer fishes such as sole or flounder, since the fillets tend to break up too much when they are combined with the other ingredients. In a pinch, you can certainly use all canned tuna or salmon.

Heat in a small skillet over medium-low heat:

2 tablespoons unsalted butter

Add:

1 small onion, minced
1 celery stalk, minced

Cover and cook, stirring occasionally, until the vegetables are very soft, about 10 minutes. Add:

¾ teaspoon curry powder

Cook, stirring, for 1 minute more. Scrape into a large bowl. Stir in:

½ cup heavy cream
2 large eggs, lightly beaten
6 tablespoons fresh breadcrumbs
2 tablespoons minced fresh parsley
2 tablespoons minced fresh tarragon
2 tablespoons snipped fresh chives
¾ teaspoon salt
Ground black pepper to taste

Add:

1½ pounds cooked fish (salmon, snapper, cod, and/or halibut), flaked

Mix gently until well combined. Refrigerate the mixture for 15 minutes.

Preheat the oven to 375°F.

Shape the fish mixture into a loaf, about 8 inches long and 4 inches wide, on a nonstick, heavy baking sheet. Bake until a knife inserted in the center of the loaf for 20 seconds is hot to the touch, 45 to 50 minutes. Let cool slightly, cut into thick slices with a serrated knife, and serve.

GEFILTE FISH

8 servings

Gefilte means filled or stuffed. This was originally a dish of fish skins stuffed with the ground fish mixture which is now simply formed into ovals or balls. Traditionally made with freshwater fish—carp, whitefish, and pike—this is just as good with fish from the sea. You can mix in some darker fish, such as bluefish and even salmon, although it is not traditional. Some fish markets will grind the fish and onions together for you, which saves a bit of time. Good, strong horseradish is the essential accompaniment. Prepare this a day before you want to serve it.

Combine in a stockpot:

2 to 3 pounds fish heads, bones, and skin
1 large onion, with skin, quartered
3 carrots, coarsely chopped
2 teaspoons salt

Add water to cover and bring to a boil. Reduce the heat to low and simmer for 30 minutes, skimming the residue from the surface, while you prepare the fish balls. If the broth goes below the level of the top of the fish and vegetables, add some fresh water. Strain the stock, rinse out the pot, return the stock to the pot and bring to a simmer. Meanwhile, combine in a food processor:

3 large onions, peeled and chopped
3 to 3½ pounds assorted fish fillets (carp, whitefish, and pike), carefully picked over for bones, rinsed and patted dry

Pulse until coarsely chopped; do not overprocess. Remove to a mixing bowl and stir in:

3 large eggs
¾ cup cold water
¼ cup matzo meal
1 tablespoon sugar
1½ tablespoons salt
½ tablespoon ground black pepper

If the mixture seems dry, add about ¼ cup more water; it should be light and almost fluffy. Wet your hands and shape the mixture into 4-inch-long ovals (about ½ cup each) or into 1- to 1¼-inch balls (about 3 tablespoons each). Drop each of the ovals or balls into the simmering stock, raising the heat if necessary to keep the liquid gently bubbling. Cover the pot and simmer very gently for 1 to 1½ hours. Add to the pot 30 minutes before the fish balls are done:

3 carrots, peeled and sliced into ½-inch-thick rounds

When done, turn off the heat and allow the fish to cool in the liquid. Remove the fish balls and the carrots to a deep platter or bowl; if there are more than 4 cups of stock, reduce it to 4 cups over high heat. Strain it over the fish balls, cover the platter, and refrigerate. Serve the fish cold, with a bit of the jelly, the carrot slices, and plenty of:

Grated red or white horseradish or any prepared horseradish

SALMON CROQUETTES

4 servings

Combine in a medium bowl:

1 pound cooked or canned salmon
1½ cups mashed potatoes
¼ cup heavy cream

1 tablespoon chopped fresh parsley
1 teaspoon snipped fresh chives
1 teaspoon snipped fresh dill
¼ teaspoon ground red pepper
Salt to taste

Spread in separate shallow bowls:

2 cups fresh breadcrumbs
2 cups all-purpose flour

Whisk together in a third shallow bowl:

4 large eggs

Shape the salmon mixture into 8 patties. Working with 1 patty at a time, coat lightly with the flour and shake off the excess. Dip quickly into the eggs and let the excess drip off, then coat with the breadcrumbs.

Heat in a large nonstick skillet over medium heat until sizzling:

2 tablespoons unsalted butter

Add as many of the croquettes as will fit comfortably. Cook, stirring, until golden on both sides, about 2 minutes each side. Remove and repeat with the remaining croquettes.

BRANDADE DE MORUE (CREAMY SALT COD DIP)

Deceptively simple, this Provençal dish is a real powerhouse of flavor. It is traditionally made with a lot of raw garlic, but you can mellow the flavor by cutting back on the raw garlic or gently poaching the garlic in the cream or milk for about a minute before starting.

Soak in cold water to cover:

1 pound salt cod, preferably boneless

Refrigerate, changing the water every 6 to 8 hours, for 24 hours. Rinse one last time, drain, and remove any skin and bones. Place the fish in a saucepan with water to cover, bring to a boil over medium-high heat, and turn off the heat. Let stand for 10 to 15 minutes, then drain and pat dry. Place the fish in a food processor (or you can use a mortar and pestle) along with:

¼ cup extra-virgin olive oil
¼ cup heavy cream, half-and-half, or milk
1 to 6 cloves garlic, peeled

With the machine running, add through the feed tube, alternating the two:

½ cup extra-virgin olive oil
½ cup heavy cream, half-and-half, or milk

Process until the mixture has the consistency of creamy mashed potatoes. Season to taste with:

Fresh lemon juice
Ground black pepper
Freshly grated or ground nutmeg

Heat the brandade in the top of a double boiler or in a covered casserole in a 300°F oven. Serve warm—not hot—with:

Croutons, pita bread, crackers, crusty bread, or vegetable sticks

SUNDAY SUPPER FISH CAKES WITH HORSERADISH CREAM

4 servings

As for Fish Loaf, 563, use some of a more oily fish so the cakes are moist. A 4-ounce can of tuna or salmon will do the trick; you can also use all canned fish.

Stir together in a medium bowl:

1½ cups sour cream
2 tablespoons drained horseradish
Juice of ½ lemon
1 teaspoon hot red pepper sauce
2 tablespoons coarsely chopped fresh dill
Salt to taste

Refrigerate this sauce while preparing the fish cakes.

Mix well in a large bowl:

1½ pounds cooked fish (salmon, snapper, cod, or halibut), flaked
5 tablespoons mayonnaise
2 celery stalks, minced
2 tablespoons chopped fresh parsley
1 egg yolk
1 tablespoon fresh lemon juice
1½ teaspoons Old Bay seasoning
¼ teaspoon ground red pepper
¾ teaspoon salt
Ground black pepper to taste

Spread on a large plate:

2 cups fresh breadcrumbs

Shape the fish mixture into 8 cakes, pressing the ingredients firmly together. Press the patties into the breadcrumbs on all sides to coat evenly. Shake off any excess.

Heat in a large skillet over medium heat:

2 tablespoons vegetable oil
1 tablespoon unsalted butter, or more if needed

Add as many of the fish cakes as will fit comfortably. Cook until browned on both sides, about 2 minutes each side. Serve with the sauce.

KEDGEREE

4 servings

Bring to a boil in a medium saucepan:

1 cup heavy cream

Add:

¼ teaspoon ground red pepper
¼ teaspoon turmeric
½ teaspoon salt

Simmer for 2 minutes. Add and heat through:

3 cups cooked long-grain rice, preferably basmati or jasmine

Cut on a diagonal into thin slices:

4 scallions, whites and greens separated

Fold the scallion whites into the rice mixture along with:

4 smoked trout fillets (about 8 ounces total), at room temperature, broken into 1-inch pieces

Remove the kedgeree to a 5-cup soufflé dish or casserole. Top with the scallion greens along with:

3 large hard-boiled eggs, chopped

Alternatively, butter the dish, pack with kedgeree, and unmold onto a serving plate. Top with the scallion greens and chopped eggs.

ABOUT SHAD ROE

These days prize roes more often are exported than consumed domestically, with one exception—that of shad. And shad roe, a sac of millions of tiny eggs held together by a tough, gossamer membrane, is in demand every spring, when the shad begin running in coastal rivers.

You need a pair of shad roe for two people; it is so filling that it would be hard to eat an entire pair alone. Shad roe should be cooked just until pinkish red in the center, for it continues to cook after it is removed from the heat.

SAUTÉED SHAD ROE

2 servings

The most delicate preparation. As always with shad roe, slight undercooking is essential.

Heat in a large nonstick skillet over medium-high heat until the foam subsides:

3 tablespoons butter or olive oil

Lay gently in the fat:

1 pair shad roe, separated and gently dried with paper towels

Brown each side for 2 to 5 minutes, seasoning with:

Salt and ground black pepper to taste

Either serve immediately with the cooking butter drizzled over the roe and accompanied with:

Lemon wedges

Or add to the pan:

2 tablespoons capers, drained

1 tablespoon wine or sherry vinegar

Cook for about 30 seconds. Spoon or pour this sauce over the roe. Garnish with:

Minced fresh parsley

POULTRY

Properly defined, the term poultry means a farm-raised, as opposed to wild, bird produced for meat or eggs. Thus all guinea fowl, quail, partridge, and pheasant that have been bought rather than shot are poultry, for, by federal law, any bird offered for sale in the United States must be farm-raised. However, since these birds are still popularly associated with the wild, they are dealt with in the Game chapter, leaving only chicken, turkey, duck, and goose for this chapter. This is just as well. Today, many Americans eat poultry several times a week, and recipes for our common domesticated birds have multiplied to keep pace.

ABOUT POULTRY PRODUCTION

With the emergence of the modern poultry farm after World War II, chicken and turkey, once fairly expensive and reserved for Sunday and holiday dinners, became increasingly affordable, everyday foods. Unfortunately, as poultry production moved from the barnyard to the processing plant, both the quality and the safety of our poultry were compromised. Chicken has suffered the most. In order to remain profitable in a highly competitive industry, producers rush their chickens to market less than forty days after hatching, which is simply not enough time for the birds to develop flavor. In addition, producers raise their chickens in crowded, sometimes squalid, conditions. To prevent the spread of disease, most add antibiotics to the feed, the long-term effects of which on consumers are unknown. And while antibiotics stave off epidemics in the coop, they do not kill off some infections, such as salmonellosis, quickly spread by overcrowding.

In response to the problems associated with mass production, a secondary poultry industry has emerged, providing the consumer with "free-range," "organic," and "natural" poultry. However, since these terms are only vaguely defined, if at all, by law, some producers, intentionally or not, use them in ways that can be misleading.

By USDA standards, free-range chickens and turkeys must have ready access to the out-of-doors. However, this does not mean that the birds roam freely. A small flock of barnyard chickens will come to no harm if permitted to wander, but chickens raised in large groups become extremely aggressive when allowed to range at liberty. Thus, a free-range chicken is often one that has lived out its life in a coop with a single door leading to a small enclosed pen.

Contrary to what many consumers believe, free-range chickens are not necessarily fed an organic diet. However, almost all "organic" chickens are—not by law but by producer choice—free-range. Because the USDA does not recognize the term "organic" at this time, the industry generally follows the so-called California definition. To be organic, the chicken must be raised without antibiotics on feed grown on fields that have not been treated with pesticides or chemical fertilizers for at least three years.

The USDA does recognize and regulate the term "natural," but its definition is extremely broad. By current USDA standards, any minimally processed bird can be called "natural," regardless of what it has been fed or how it has been raised. This means that only such products as precooked marinated chicken parts and additive-injected "self-basting" turkeys are excluded. Any other poultry product—from a premium poussin nurtured by a small producer to an ordinary supermarket package of boneless, skinless chicken breasts—can be labeled "natural" by USDA definitions. But some poultry producers mean something more specific by the term. Some define a "natural" chicken or turkey as one that was fed a pesticide-free, antibiotic-free diet, much like an organic chicken. Others call a bird "natural" if it tests antibiotic-free at slaughter, which may be accomplished by withdrawing antibiotics from the chicken's feed ten days before processing.

Kosher chickens are processed according to Jewish dietary laws. Rabbis supervise their production all along the way, making sure they are in topnotch condition, and perform the ritual slaughtering. After slaughter, the chickens undergo a three-hour process of cold-water defeathering, soaking, brining, and drying that is designed to draw out as much blood as possible. The salt used in brining permeates the bird, causing the cooked meat to taste pleasantly seasoned.

With the increase in the Muslim population in this country, halal chickens are showing up in supermarkets across the country. Unlike ordinary supermarket chickens, which are usually machine-slaughtered by stunning or suffocation, halal chickens are hand-slaughtered by someone of the Islamic faith.

BUYING POULTRY

First and foremost, be sure to check the "sell by" date on the package. Don't buy poultry whose time is nearly up, unless you plan to eat it right away. If the package contains an unusual amount of liquid, feels sticky, or has even the faintest off-odor, the contents are suspect, regardless of what the expiration date may be. Avoid icy poultry from the back of the case. Since most poultry has already been frozen by the time it comes to the store, this has been, in effect, frozen twice, with damaging consequences to texture and flavor.

The color of poultry skin is not an indication of quality. Rather, producers manipulate skin color through feed and processing in order to satisfy consumer preferences. Consumers in the Northeast have long preferred yellow-skinned chickens, though golden chickens now trigger a negative response in some shoppers, who associate this color with butter and, therefore, a high-fat content. Producers in the South cater to their customers' predilection for pale, almost white chickens. Of course, as skinless parts become more the norm, skin color becomes less of an issue.

Most consumers assume that the chickens in their supermarket meat case are fresh, not frozen, and that turkeys, ducks, and geese, when sold as fresh at the premium price that fresh commands, have not been frozen. But indeed matters are not so simple. Until recently, federal law permitted poultry to be "stored" at temperatures as low as 0°F and still be called "fresh." The law has been changed, but consumers are only slightly better off. Now, if it is to be labeled "fresh," poultry need only be stored at temperatures above 26°F, which means that it may—and often does—arrive at the supermarket having been kept below 32°F, the freezing point as it is understood by most of us outside the poultry industry, for several weeks before we buy it. Nearly all the "fresh" turkeys sold at Thanksgiving, in fact, have been slaughtered several weeks beforehand and kept at high freezing temperatures. Meanwhile, the new law stipulates that poultry stored at temperatures between 0° and 26°F cannot be labeled either fresh or frozen. In other words, if the label on a package of chicken does not explicitly claim that the contents are "fresh," the chicken may actually have been frozen at 0°F for an indefinite period and then thawed before being offered for sale. Is there any such thing as frozen poultry? Yes. According to current law, it is poultry that has been held at temperatures below 0°F.

Where does this leave the consumer? Since poultry tastes best when it has been stored for the shortest length of time, "fresh" is still the best, for even though fresh poultry, generally speaking, has been frozen, it has not been frozen for long. (Poultry is perishable in the 26° to 32°F temperature range and cannot be held for longer than a few weeks.) As for those chickens at the supermarket that are not labeled either fresh or frozen, you can be assured that most have been processed fairly recently, since the high demand for chicken ensures a rapid turnover.

STORING AND FREEZING POULTRY

Poultry should be stored in the back of the refrigerator, where the temperature is coldest, and cooked and eaten within a day or two of purchase. Leave it in its original packaging. If poultry proves to have a slight off-odor when you open the package, it can be refreshed. Rinse it well under cool running water, then place it in a bowl with cold water to cover and add 1 tablespoon vinegar or lemon juice and 1 teaspoon salt for every cup of water. Refrigerate the poultry from 1 to 4 hours, then proceed with the recipe. Since the skin is especially prone to spoilage, it is advisable to remove it.

Any poultry that cannot be eaten promptly should be frozen. Leave it in its original packaging. (If the bird is wrapped in butcher's paper, leave it in the wrap and place it in a self-sealing plastic bag.) Assuming a freezer temperature of 0°F or lower, frozen poultry will remain safe to eat for a year or longer, but, for the best taste and texture, cook it within a month.

Frozen poultry must be thawed before cooking, either in the refrigerator or, for quicker results, in *cold* water. If thawing in the refrigerator, set the bird, still in its original packaging, on a baking sheet and defrost 1 day for every 6 pounds. If thawing in cold water, enclose the poultry, in its original packaging, in a sealed plastic bag (or a trash bag for a turkey), place it in water, and weight it with a plate or pot to keep it submerged. Defrost for 1 to 8 hours, depending on weight, changing the water periodically. Poultry can appear to be thawed before it really is. Do not declare it fully defrosted until the flesh feels pliable and squashy to the touch and the legs and wings move freely at the joints when wiggled. In the case of birds that are to be roasted whole, underthawing is disastrous, for the birds will cook through on the outside while the center remains virtually raw. Should a refrigerator-thawed whole bird prove to be stiff and icy on the day you plan to roast it, transfer it to cold water to finish defrosting. *Thawed poultry is highly susceptible to spoilage and must be cooked promptly. Unless you can be absolutely certain that it never reached a temperature above 40°F during thawing, do not refreeze.*

Most frozen *processed* poultry—for example, already-stuffed whole birds—must be transferred directly from the freezer to a hot oven. Follow the package instructions to the letter.

Contrary to popular belief, the undercooking of poultry is rarely the cause of salmonella illness. (Stuffed whole poultry is an important exception; see Roasting Whole Poultry, 572.) Salmonella is seriously compromised at 140°F, a temperature at which poultry remains nearly raw, and is completely eradicated at 160°F, the lowest temperature at which most people would ever think of cooking a chicken or turkey, unless, for some odd reason, they liked the meat bloody. Rather, the usual way in which people contract a salmonella infection is by eating a raw or lightly cooked food that has come into contact with infected raw poultry or its juices. To reduce the chances of contamination, never store raw poultry, even when wrapped, next to an unwrapped food that will be eaten raw, such as salad greens or bread. And after cutting up or otherwise handling raw poultry, always wash your hands, cutting board, counter surface, knives, poultry shears, and so on, in hot sudsy water before preparing another food.

HOW TO CUT UP POULTRY

Using a reasonably sharp knife, any home cook can easily cut a whole chicken, turkey, duck, or goose into serving pieces with just a little practice. By cutting up a bird yourself, you not only save a considerable amount of money but also ensure that you will have precisely the right parts, cut just the way you want them. Of course, for most cooks, the parts available at the supermarket will do just fine, but the supermarket does not always provide for special needs. Supermarkets never offer butterflied chickens, perfect for stuffing under the skin and roasting, and they rarely offer halved and quartered chickens, which are nice grilled or broiled. Supermarkets detach the "oysters," the delicious nuggets of meat that lie on either side of the small of the back, from the thighs, and they jumble large and small parts from different chickens together in the same pack, which creates problems for a cook who wants to broil or fry, techniques that require small parts.

The back, neck, heart, and gizzard from a cut-up bird will make 2 to 3 cups of excellent stock. These pieces can all be wrapped and frozen for future use.

To Butterfly or Split a Bird: These two procedures are related. To butterfly a bird, cut through the ribs on either side of the backbone with shears and remove the bone, shown 570 (top left). Turn the bird breast side up, place your palm over the breastbone, and press hard to flatten the bird completely, shown 570 (top center). To keep the legs in place during cooking, make ½-inch slits on either side of the breast tip, then insert the ends of the drumsticks into each of these openings, shown 570 (top right).

To split a bird, remove the backbone and flatten as for butterflying. Place the bird skin side down and pry out the reddish breastbone and attached cartilage with your fingers. Cut the bird in half at the seam where the breastbone has been removed.

To Cut a Bird into Six, Eight, or Ten Pieces: This is how one makes so-called poultry parts. Generally

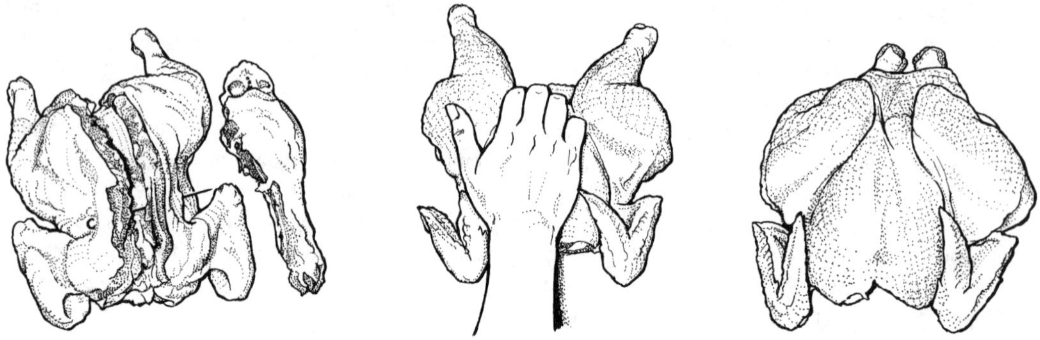

Butterflying a bird

speaking, only chickens and turkeys are cut into eight or ten pieces. Ducks, if cut at all, are separated into six pieces: two whole legs, two whole wings, and two breast halves. Geese are rarely cut up, except for confit.

Start with the legs. Lay the bird on its side, pull the leg away from the body, and cut into the skin with the knife held close to the thigh so that you will not remove too much of the breast skin, shown below (top left). As you cut, continue to pull up on the leg until the thighbone pops out of its socket, shown below (top right). Now, press the tip of a paring knife against the backbone just behind the thigh joint and dig out the little nugget of meat, called the oyster, shown below (bottom right). Slice through the skin from the tip of the oyster to the opposite corner of the thigh and detach the leg, shown below (bottom left). If you wish, you can leave half or all of the tail attached to the thigh skin. Repeat with the other leg. To separate the drumstick and thigh, flex the leg and crack the ball joint, shown 571 (upper left). Place the leg on a cutting board with the inner side facing up and cut exactly at the thin line of fat separating the drumstick and thigh.

The wings can be removed cleanly at the joint or, to make a more ample serving, with a small piece of breast meat attached. To remove the wing at the joint, lay the chicken on its side, pull the wing away from the body until the joint is exposed, and cut, shown 571 (bottom left). To leave a piece of breast attached to the

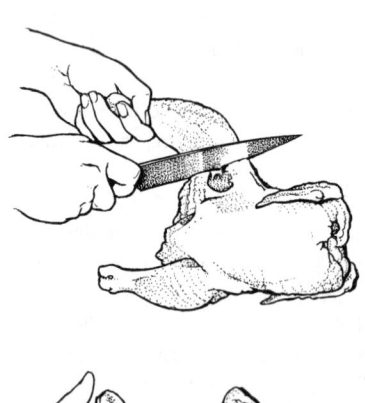

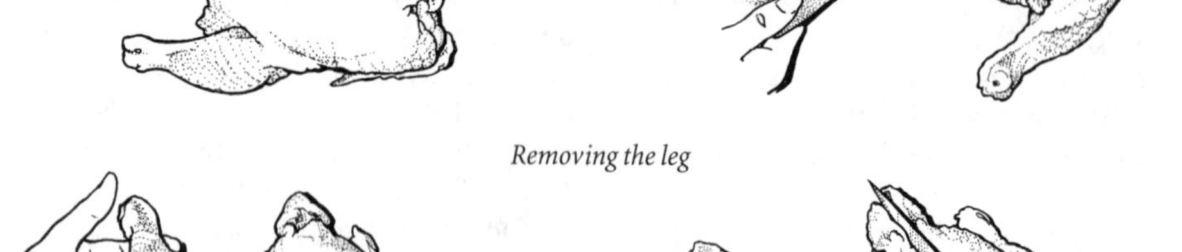

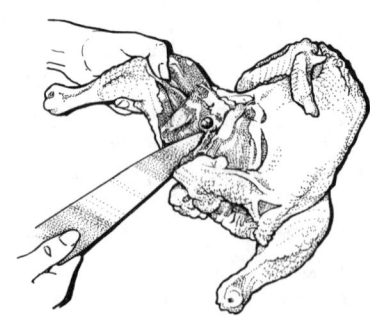

Removing the leg

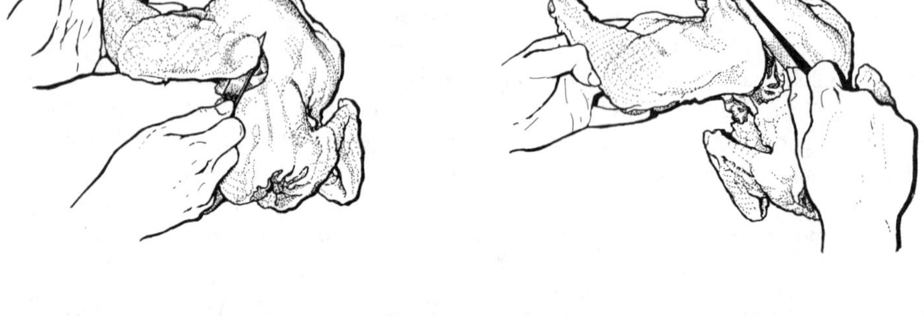

HOW TO KNOW WHEN CHICKEN AND TURKEY ARE DONE

The following remarks pertain to rock Cornish hens, chickens, capons, and turkeys. Doneness for ducks and geese is discussed separately; see About Duck, 618, and About Goose, 622. To test whole roasted birds for doneness, please read Roasting Whole Poultry, 572.

We smile when we come across a recipe that calls for cooking chicken or turkey "until tender." Nowadays, with chickens and turkeys coming to the market within weeks of hatching, all birds are tender from the outset. Today's birds, when very thoroughly cooked, do not become tender but simply fall apart into dry shreds. That said, chicken and turkey do need to be cooked to the done stage, that is, to the point where the meat releases clear, not pink, juices when pricked to the bone with a fork. For the dark meat—that is, the legs—this correlates with an internal temperature of 170°F on an instant-read thermometer. For the white meat—that is, the breast—doneness is reached at an internal temperature of 160°F. The dark meat, in addition to requiring more cooking than the white meat, also has a greater tolerance to overcooking than the white meat. That is to say, the dark meat, while fully cooked at 170°F, can be cooked to considerably higher temperatures and still remain palatable. The white meat, of course, is an entirely different matter. The breast, which is perfectly juicy and tender at 160°F, becomes hard and dry at any temperature above 165°F.

Given the differences in cooking results between the dark and white meat, it obviously makes sense to prepare chicken and turkey dishes with breasts only or legs only whenever possible. Alternatively, in the preparation of some dishes, you can prevent the white meat from overcooking by adding it to the pot later or taking it out earlier than the dark meat. Some cooks fry the white and dark meat in separate skillets to ensure that both are perfect.

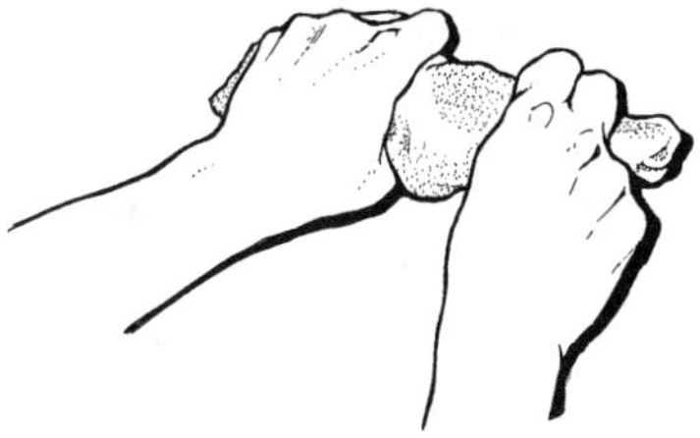

Separating the drumstick and thigh

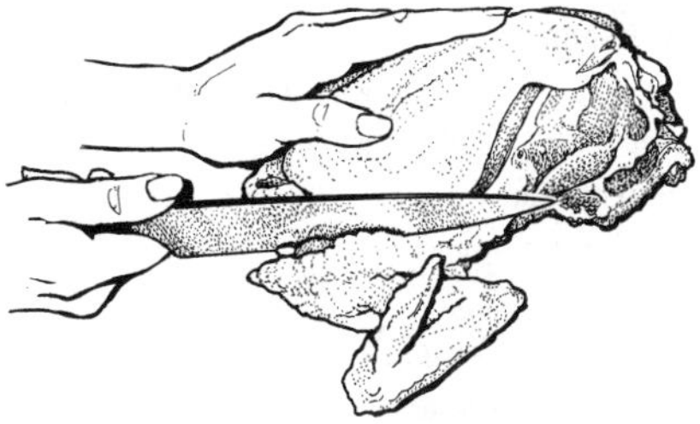

Removing the wing with a piece of breast meat attached

wing, lay the bird on its side and make a cut into the breast about 1 inch up from the top of the wing joint, parallel to the ribs. Pulling the wing away from the body, cut against the ribs until you reach the ball joint, then cut through the joint and detach the wing, shown above right.

To separate the breast from the back, cut through the rib bones on either side of the backbone with poultry shears or a sharp knife, shown below right. Be sure to cut close to the backbone, or you will lose the underside of the breast to the back. Reserve the back for stock.

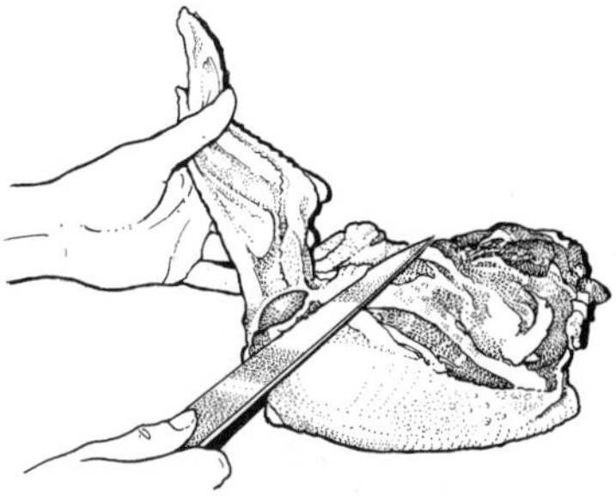

Removing the wing at the joint

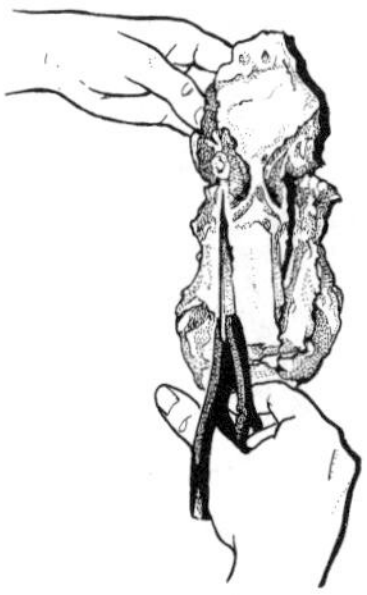

Separating the breast from the back

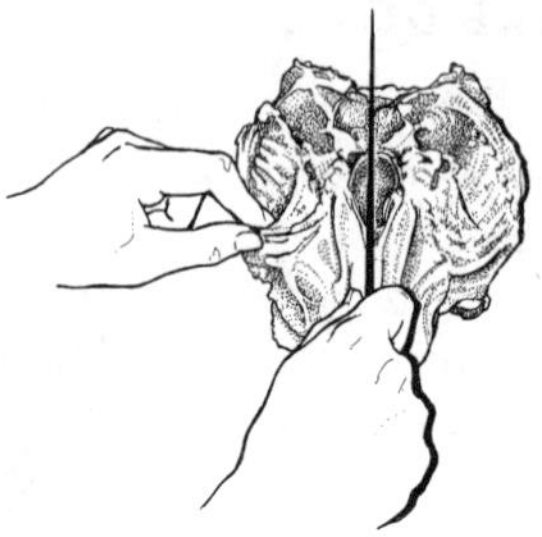

Cutting down the middle of the breast through the breastbone

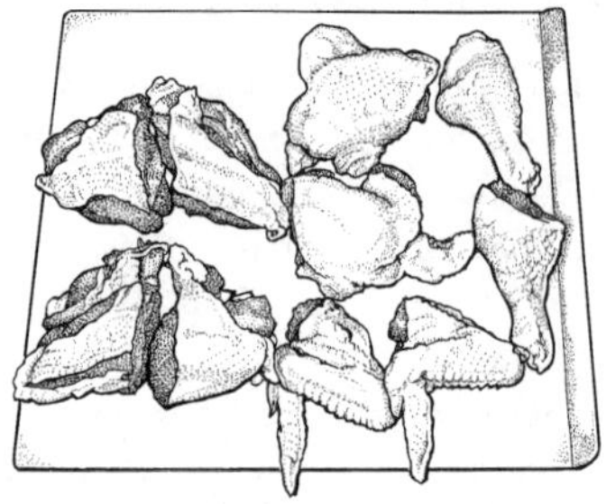

Bird cut into 10 pieces

Before cutting the breast, locate the wishbone at the thick end (opposite the cartilage tip), scrape it free from the surrounding flesh with the tip of a paring knife, and pull it out. Stretch the breast skin smoothly over both halves of the breast, then turn the breast skin side down. Using a sharp knife, cut down the middle of the breast, through the reddish breastbone, to make two halves, shown above. For some chicken dishes, you may want to cut the breast into 4 serving pieces. Turn one breast half skin side up and, arching your free hand over the knife and stretching the skin between your fingers, cut the breast in half diagonally through the bone, shown below. (If you will be quartering the breast of a small chicken, you should remove the wings at or very near the joints, or else the back breast pieces will be rather bony.)

ROASTING WHOLE POULTRY

The following remarks on the trussing, stuffing, doneness testing, and carving of whole birds pertain primarily to chickens and turkey. Except for stuffing procedures, duck and goose are handled differently; see About Duck, 618, and About Goose, 622.

Trussing: Properly speaking, to truss a bird means to bind its legs and wings to the body, either by sewing through the joints with a trussing needle and twine or by simply tying the appendages into place. The closing of the body and neck cavities—which is necessary only if the bird is stuffed—is a separate procedure. Today, many people lump both operations under the rubric of "trussing," but when a recipe in *Joy* calls for trussing, the binding of the bird, not the closing of the cavities, is what is meant. Trussing is rarely obligatory, but it does facilitate the handling of the bird, especially in those recipes that require turning during roasting, and it gives the bird a handsome shape.

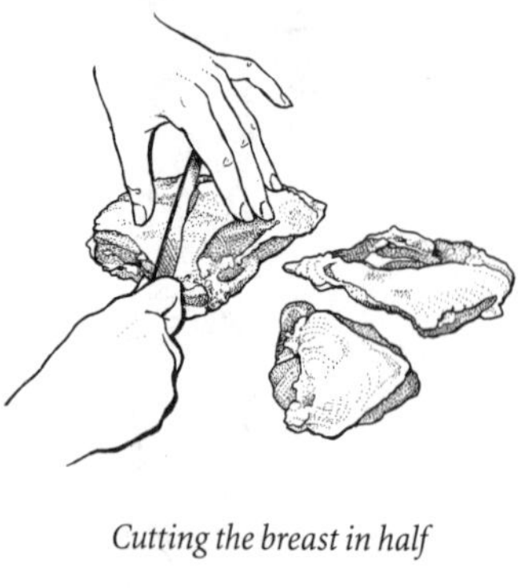

Cutting the breast in half

The classic method of trussing involves sewing the bird with a trussing needle and twine. The procedure has two steps. First, you sew a loop of twine through the tips of the drumsticks and through the back, near the tail; when you tie this loop tightly, the legs are bound together and drawn down toward the tail. Next, you sew a long piece of twine into one wing, through the body cavity, and out the other wing, and then through the thigh, into the breast tip, and out the opposite thigh. When you draw this loop taut and tie, the entire bird miraculously stiffens, and the wings and thighs hug the body. This classic method of trussing produces the most attractive bird, but it has major disadvantages. The heavy-gauge 8- to 12-inch needle that is required is rarely stocked by cookware stores, and the procedure is time-consuming. Cooks who truss only once a year, when preparing the Thanksgiving turkey, often find they forget how to do it. But the most serious drawback of the classic truss is that it binds the legs so tightly to the body that the inner thighs often remain pink long after the breast has cooked through.

In the interest of delivering to the table a handsome, evenly cooked bird with a minimal expenditure of time and effort, we prefer the following technique, which we call a "simple truss." Cut a long piece of sturdy kitchen twine—about 18 inches for rock Cornish hens, 30 inches for chickens, and 48 inches for turkeys. Tie the center of the twine around the bird's

RULES FOR STUFFING BIRDS

1. *Always stuff the bird just before roasting*—never *ahead of time, which would give any harmful bacteria that might be present in the cavity ample time to breed.*

2. *Have the stuffing* hot *and* pack it loosely *in the body and neck cavities. The stuffing must reach a temperature of 160°F during roasting to ensure that any possible pathogens are killed. If it is cold and packed tightly into the bird, it will not heat to this point until long after the bird is cooked through.*

3. *You must close the cavities in order to keep the stuffing in place. The quickest and most efficient way to do this is by sewing the cavities shut with a trussing needle and twine. If you do not own a trussing needle, secure the body cavity with small skewers and lacing (kits for this purpose are sold at kitchen shops) and close the neck cavity with toothpicks.*

4. *When the bird has cooked through, take the temperature of the stuffing by plunging the stem of the thermometer deep into the body cavity. If the stuffing has not yet reached 160°F, simply take the bird out of the oven, scoop the stuffing into a buttered casserole, and bake it in the hot oven while the bird stands before carving.*

5. *Finally, always take all the stuffing out of the cooked bird as soon as you begin to carve. Stuffing left inside a large turkey may remain warm for several hours, even if the bird is refrigerated, providing a perfect environment for bacterial growth.*

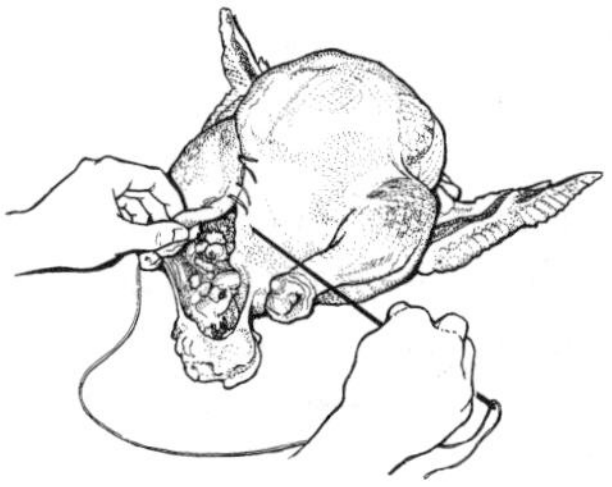

Sewing body cavity shut with a trussing needle and twine

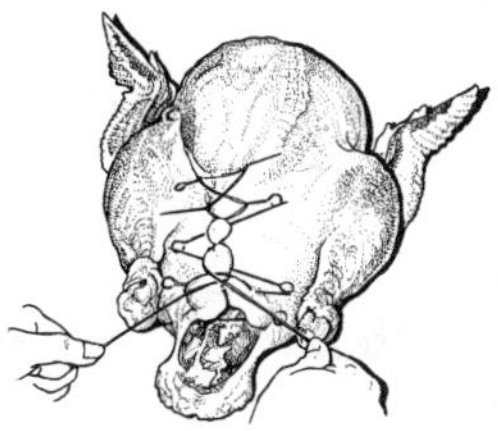

Securing body cavity with small skewers and lacing

ankles, binding the legs together, shown below left. Bring the ends of the twine over the backs of the legs and lower breast. Loop the twine once around the wings at the elbow joint (that is, the joint between the two meaty parts), shown below center. Bring the ends of the twine over the lower third of the breast and tie as tightly as possible, shown below right.

Stuffing: In the past few years, stuffing, once considered by many to be the best part of the Thanksgiving bird, has acquired a controversial reputation. Some warn that stuffing can cause illness, that it soaks up fat, and that it causes the bird to overcook. Furthermore, they say, no one has the time, skill, or equipment necessary to stuff a bird properly. These voices miss the

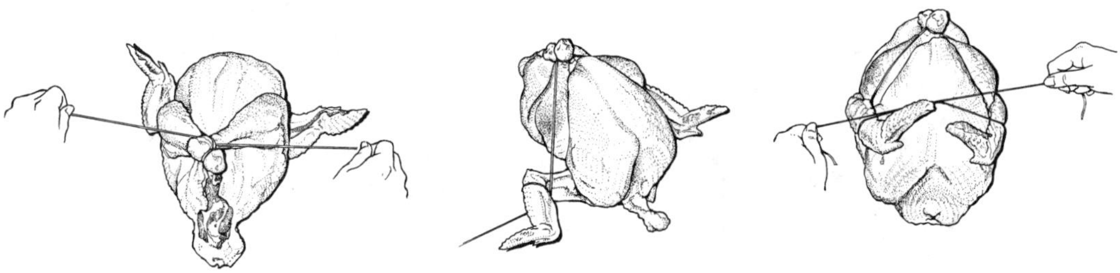

Performing a simple truss

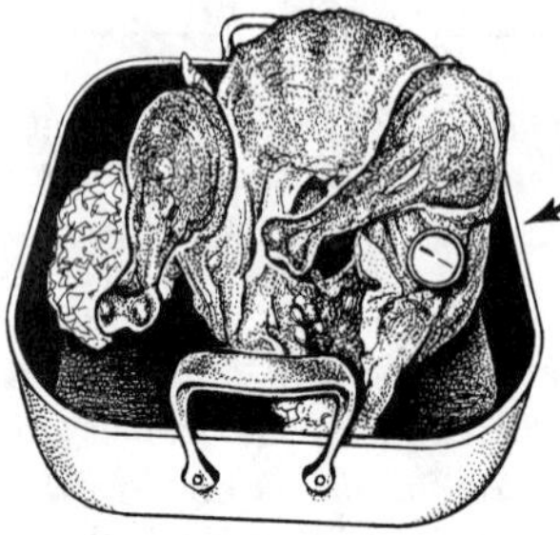

Checking the leg for doneness

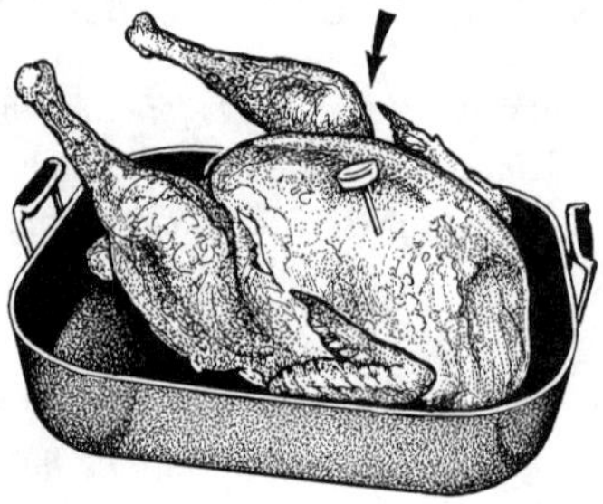

Checking the breast meat for doneness

point. The whole purpose of stuffing is precisely to soak up the wonderfully flavorful juices that leach into a bird's cavity during roasting. And we stress the word *juices.* The fat is in the skin. Poultry meat—even the meat of ducks and geese—is lean, and it is the juices of the meat that the stuffing blots up. All this said, we will admit that stuffing presents its own set of challenges, but these are hardly insurmountable, even for the cook who is stuffing a bird for the very first time (see Rules for Stuffing Birds, 573).

Testing for Doneness: The hard truth is that it is practically impossible to judge the doneness of a whole roasted bird without using an accurate instant-read thermometer.

To check the breast meat, insert the stem of the thermometer parallel to the breastbone deep into the neck end of the breast, where the meat is thickest, shown above left. If the thermometer registers between 160° and 165°F, the breast meat is perfectly cooked, but that doesn't mean that the leg is fully cooked or that the stuffing, if there is one, has reached the safe temperature of 160°F. Test the stuffing as directed in rules for stuffing birds, 573. To check the leg, stick the stem of the thermometer into the thickest part of the thigh just beneath, but not touching, the bone, reaching all the way down to the joint, shown above right. If you like juicy, tender breast meat, consider the leg done at 170°F. At this temperature, the inside of the thigh, when pulled away from the body, will reveal a faintly ruddy glow, the meat will be on the firm side, and the leg joint will be slightly stiff and pinkish. If you find this unappealing, roast the bird until the leg reaches a slightly higher temperature, around 175°F. Those who do not like the slightest trace of pink in a bird should roast until the leg reaches 180°F. The result of such thorough roasting, however, is that the breast is inevitably overcooked.

Resting: Whole roasted poultry must be allowed to rest outside the oven before carving so that the meat will become firm enough to slice neatly. For a chicken, duck, or goose, a 10- to 15-minute rest is sufficient. A 15-pound turkey should rest for about 20 minutes, and larger turkeys should be allowed to rest for 2 minutes longer for each additional pound. Do not tent the bird with foil as the skin will become soggy. The bird will release juices during resting. If you are making a sauce or gravy, be sure to add these delicious juices to it. Otherwise, spoon the juices over the carved meat or stir them into a vinaigrette for a salad served with the bird.

Carving: Preparations for carving should start before the bird goes into the oven. Lift the skin of the raw bird at the neck end and, using the point of a paring knife,

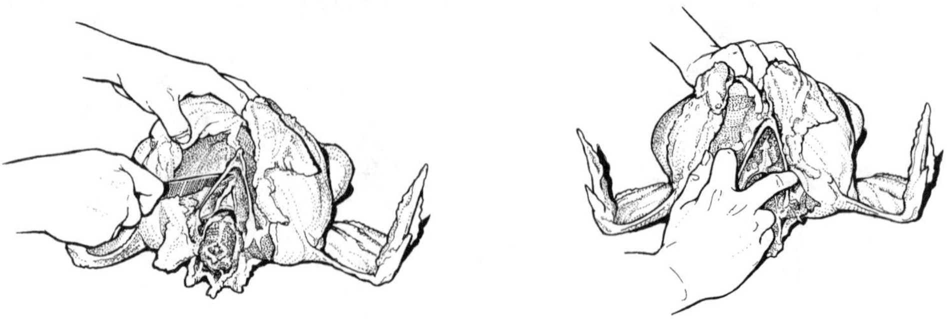

Removing the wishbone

scrape against the wishbone until it is mostly freed from the surrounding flesh, shown 574, bottom left. Hook the wishbone on either side with two fingers and pull it out, shown 574, bottom right. With the wishbone removed, you will be able to carve the breast of the cooked bird in unbroken slices from end to end.

Once the cooked bird has rested and you are ready to carve, remove the trussing twine. If the bird is stuffed, open the cavities, spoon the stuffing into a serving dish, and return it, covered, to the still-warm oven while you dismantle the carcass.

The first task is to remove the legs. Holding the bird in place with a large fork (or with your hand), cut through the skin where the leg is attached to the breast. Push the leg away from the body with the blade of the knife (or pull down on the leg with your hand) until the thighbone pops out of its socket, shown below. The treasured oysters, two nuggets of meat lodged on the back and attached to the thigh by skin, can be removed with the leg by making a lateral cut, toward the neck, before detaching the leg from the body. But don't bother with this tricky maneuver unless you are carving a small chicken, whose thigh will be served whole. When carving larger birds, simply cut off the leg, then tilt the carcass to one side and scrape the oyster free, shown above left. Transfer the legs to a carving board and separate the drumstick and thigh by cutting through the ball joint. The leg meat of large chickens, capons, and turkeys should now be carved off the bone. Fastidious—and experienced—carvers manage to cut thin slices of meat parallel to the bone, holding drumsticks upright by the ankle and carving thighs on a board. Most people, however, are content to cut the meat in rather rough chunks.

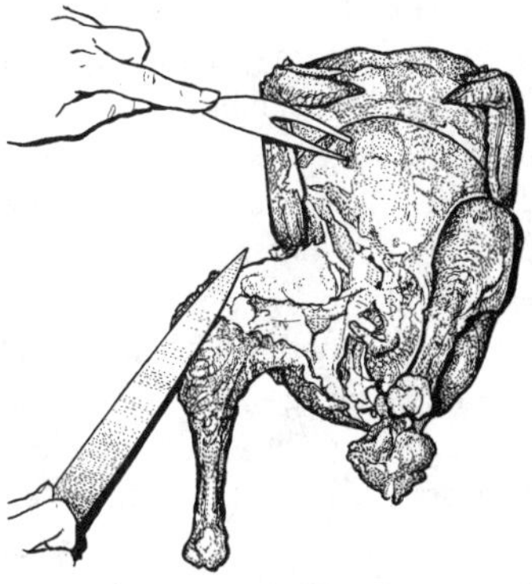

Pushing the leg away from the body until the thighbone pops out of its socket

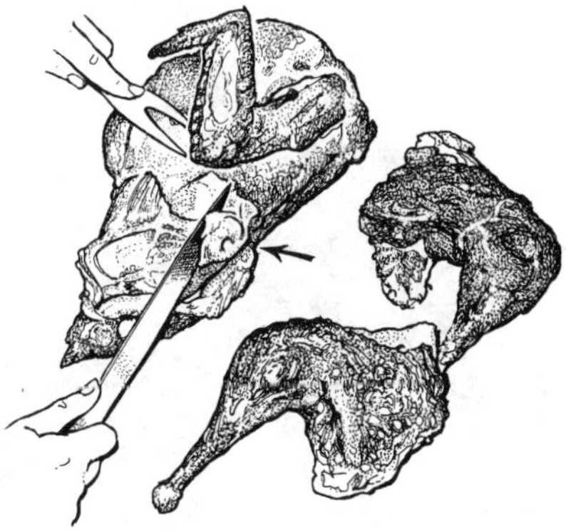

Scraping the oyster free

Next, tackle the wings. If you are carving a small chicken, cut into the breast about 1 inch up from the top of the wing joint, then cut down, scraping against the ribs, until you sever the joint. In this way, you will leave a small piece of breast meat attached to the wing, making a nice serving, shown below right. In the case of large chickens, capons, and turkeys, pry the wing away from the body with a fork (or your hand) until the joint is exposed, then cut through the joint. How you handle the wings of large birds depends on the formality of the occasion. At a family Thanksgiving, guests will feel perfectly comfortable gnawing on a whole wing. At a dinner party, guests will be inclined to eat more daintily, so transfer the wings to the carving board and cut them into pieces at the joints. Place only the meatier pieces on the serving platter and save the tips for stock.

There are two ways to carve the breast. The traditional way is to cut long, thin slices from one end to the other, parallel to the breastbone, shown 576. A more contemporary way is to remove an entire breast half from the bone, place it skin side up on a carving board,

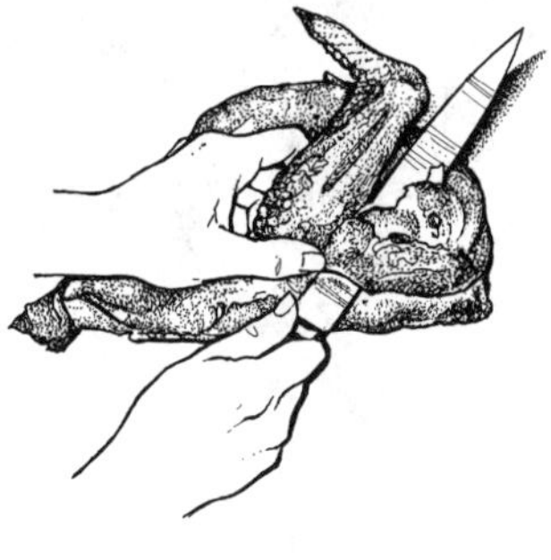

Removing the wing

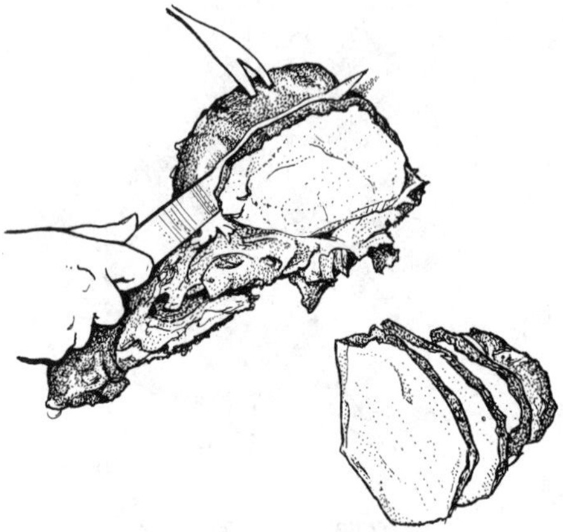

Cutting the breast meat parallel to the breastbone

and cut it crosswise on a diagonal into thickish slices, as one would slice a chicken breast for fanning on a plate, shown below. While there is an undeniable elegance in long, thin slices, thicker slices are less prone to drying out and becoming cold. Whichever method you choose, if you have a large turkey and a small crowd, you may prefer to wait until second servings are called for before carving the second half of the breast so that the meat will still be warm.

WHOLE CHICKENS

Any chicken, from a 1-pound poussin to a 10-pound capon, can be roasted. As a general rule, figure on 1 pound chicken per person.

On the small end of the scale are the rock Cornish hen and the poussin. Rock Cornish hens are a crossbreed of white Plymouth Rock and Cornish strains. Regardless of their lineage, they taste like all other chickens. Poussins, which are also called squab broilers (not to be confused with squab, a game bird), are simply very young chickens. Rock Cornish hens used to run about 1¼ pounds, a perfect size for an individual serving, but for economic reasons, producers are now bringing them to market in the 1½- to 1¾-pound range. Choose the smallest rock Cornish hens you can find when you want to serve one per person. A large rock Cornish hen, either roasted whole or split and broiled, makes a perfect dinner for two persons of modest appetite. At a diminutive 1 pound apiece, poussins may eventually displace rock Cornish hens as the birds of choice for single-serving presentation. Poussins are expensive and, in some areas, are available only through butchers or mail order.

Cutting the breast meat crosswise

Today, most chickens weighing 2 to 3¼ pounds are sold to restaurants. What is left for supermarket sale are chickens at the heavier end of the midsized range, weighing between 3½ and 4¾ pounds. Usually these are labeled simply "whole chicken." If you do see one called a broiler/fryer, don't get too excited, for it probably will turn out to be a fairly large chicken like all the rest. If you are buying a whole midsized chicken for roasting, assume that it will feed four people, generously if it weighs over 4 pounds, modestly if it weighs less. If you are buying the chicken to cut up and broil or fry, try to find one weighing 3½ pounds or less.

Large chickens—generally those weighing 5 to 7 pounds, though some producers include chickens weighing as little as 4 pounds in this category—are marketed today as roasting chickens or roasters. They are often perfect candidates for roasting (allow 1 pound per person), but they can also be cut up and baked, fricasseed, or stewed. But do not broil or fry them, for they will char on the outside before cooking through.

A capon is a castrated young male chicken. His loss causes him to swell to a weight of 8 to 10 pounds, enough for eight or more generous servings. Traditionally, these birds are fed milk and bread the last ten days before processing, making their meat extremely white and tender. Capons come to the supermarket only at holiday time but are available through a butcher year-round.

There are two types of stewing hen, also called fowl: those that are raised for eggs, and those that are raised to lay eggs for hatching. The former are a leaner breed and, when slaughtered for sale as meat, used to be called "light" stewing hens. In recent years, these hens have been genetically redesigned to be even leaner, and, therefore, are no longer sold for meat at the retail level. The hatchers, formerly known as "heavy" stewing hens, still come to market as dressed whole birds. Stewing hens are much too tough to roast. The usual treatment is to stew them slowly for a long time, but, no matter how they are cooked, the meat is dry and distinctly stringy. Stewing hens make excellent stock and soup.

CHICKEN PARTS

The remarks that follow pertain to standard chicken parts, which are cut from midsized chickens weighing 3¼ to just under 5 pounds. Most supermarkets now also carry parts cut from large roasting chickens in the 5- to 7-pound weight range. Roasting chicken parts look larger than standard parts, and they are always prominently labeled. Large parts are not suitable for broiling or frying, but otherwise, they can be used in the same dishes as standard parts. Just remember to adjust cooking times upward.

Mixed Parts: Even if a package of mixed chicken parts is labeled "whole cut-up chicken," the parts contained inside always come from a number of different chickens. So select packs whose parts look to be of more or less equal size. A leg from a 5-pound chicken will take much longer to cook than one from a 3½ pounder. Producers label mixed parts in a variety of different ways, and they sometimes exclude parts, such as wings, that a consumer might expect to find. Again, check the package carefully. A pack that is suspiciously inexpensive relative to the others in the case is likely to contain the back and/or giblets, which you probably do not want unless you are making stock.

Quartered Chicken: The idea behind quartering is to make four equal-sized servings of chicken. As defined by most packagers, a quartered chicken consists of two breast halves, with the wings detached, and two whole legs. This combination is well suited to broiling, and packages of quartered chicken often suggest on the label that the chicken is "for broiling." But sometimes a quartered chicken turns out to be a quartered breast, with the two front pieces attached to the legs and the two back pieces attached to the wings. Chicken cut in this way will not broil successfully but can be baked or braised.

Breast: Chicken breast can be prepared in virtually any way imaginable. Just be very careful not to overcook it. As soon as the juices run clear when the meat is pricked with a fork, the breast is done. Further cooking will only turn the meat hard and dry.

Whole Chicken Breast: This is the whole breast of a chicken, with skin and bone attached. It can be roasted, broiled, baked, poached, or used to make a creamed dish, pot pie, or casserole. With one whack of a heavy, sharp knife down the center, a whole chicken breast becomes a split chicken breast. Split breasts can be used in the same ways as whole breasts and, because they are smaller, also can be braised or fried. Skinless split chicken breasts are simply split breasts without the skin and are equally versatile. Boneless chicken breasts come with the skin still attached but the bones removed. They are sold both whole and split. Although boneless chicken breasts can be used in the same ways as all other breasts, people usually buy these for broiling and grilling. The skin not only protects the meat during these heat-intensive procedures but also crisps up and chars slightly to delicious effect. Whole boneless chicken breasts can also be stuffed and folded over, the skin making a natural wrapping.

Boneless, Skinless Chicken Breasts: Also called chicken breast cutlets or simply chicken cutlets, boneless, skinless chicken breasts are split chicken breasts with all skin and bone removed. Quick-cooking and low in fat, they are the most popular poultry cut in the United States. Boneless, skinless chicken breasts are most often sautéed or grilled over fairly high heat or poached and used to make chicken salad, pot pie, or casserole. However, they also can be cut into strips or bite-sized pieces before cooking and then stir-fried, skewered, or prepared as chicken fingers or nuggets. The chicken breast "tenders" sold at supermarkets usually turn out to be simply boneless, skinless chicken breasts that have been cut into strips; and not, as one might assume, chicken breast tenderloins, which are the long, thin pieces of meat that lie beneath either side of the breast. Since boneless, skinless chicken breasts are very expensive and tenders even more so, you may find it worth your time to bone and skin whole chicken breasts yourself.

How to Bone and Skin a Chicken Breast: First, peel off the skin with your fingers. Locate the wishbone at the wide end of the breast (opposite the cartilage tip), scrape it free of the surrounding flesh with the tip of a paring knife, and pull it out. Place the breast skinned side up on your work surface and press down firmly with the heel of your hand to break the membrane covering the reddish breastbone and cartilage tip. Turn the breast over. Using the point of a paring knife, cut around the shoulder bones attached to the breastbone at the wide end of the breast and remove them, shown 578 (top left). Free the breastbone and cartilage from the flesh with your fingers, then pull both out, shown 578 (top center). Slip your fingers or a paring knife beneath the rib bones and work them free of the flesh,

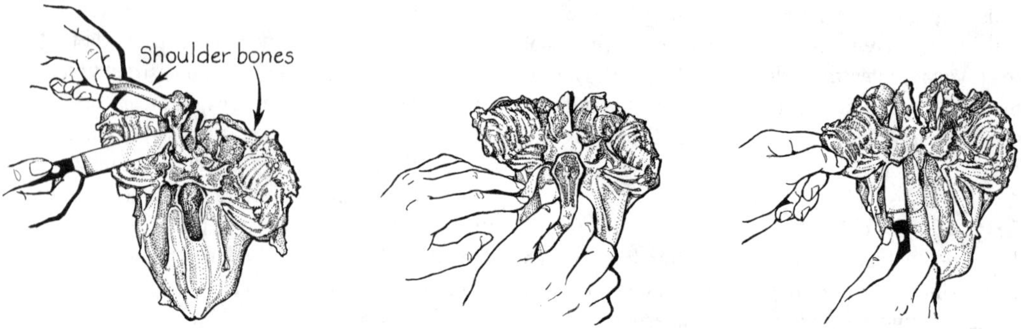

Boning a chicken breast: Remove the shoulder bones, pull out the breastbone and cartilage, then work the rib bones free of the flesh.

shown above (top right). Cut the breast in half at the breastbone line then trim any ragged edges, shown below left. You should remove the long white tendon that runs through each tenderloin, especially if it is thick. With the breast placed tenderloin side up, pull the thick end of the tenderloin away from the breast and lay it on your work surface. Holding the tip of the tendon down, scrape against the tendon with a knife until it detaches from the flesh, shown below right. If you wish, reserve the bones and skin for making stock.

Legs: Chicken legs comprise not only the drumsticks but also the thighs. Unlike the breast, chicken legs are tolerant of long, thorough cooking. For this reason, they are good for fricassees, stews, and other braised dishes. But legs take well to virtually any cooking treatment, including baking, broiling, frying, and grilling. Despite their firm texture and meaty flavor, legs do not appeal to most Americans. Dark-meat lovers will find legs a bargain at the supermarket.

In addition to whole chicken legs, supermarkets carry many kinds of leg parts. Chicken thighs are plumper and meatier than the drumsticks. Buying skinless chicken thighs with bones is a needless expense since removing the skin from a chicken thigh is as easy as peeling a banana. Do not buy them unless they are no more expensive than skin-on thighs. Boneless, skinless chicken thighs are the dark-meat lover's alternative to boneless, skinless chicken breasts. Thighs take longer to cook than breasts, but otherwise they can be prepared in exactly the same ways. This includes dishes that use cut-up chicken, such as stir-fries, kebabs, and chicken fingers and nuggets. Chicken drumsticks are ideal for picnics or any other finger-food occasion. They take well to all cooking treatments, pan- or oven-frying in particular.

Wings: Wings consist of three joints: the meaty first joint, the somewhat less meaty, double-boned second joint, and the tip. They are available in three forms: whole, whole but with the tips removed, and first and second joints cut apart. Packs of mixed joints are often labeled "drumettes" or "buffalo wings," even though logically only the first joint can be considered a drumette. Whole wings are always the cheapest. Since

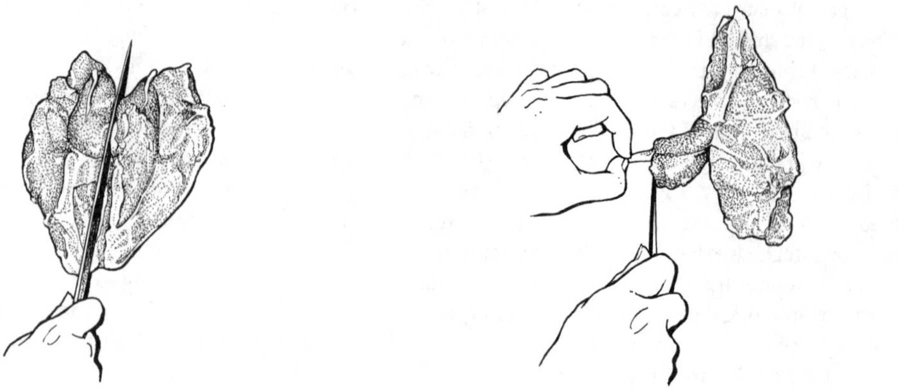

Cut the breast in half, then scrape the tendon free of the flesh.

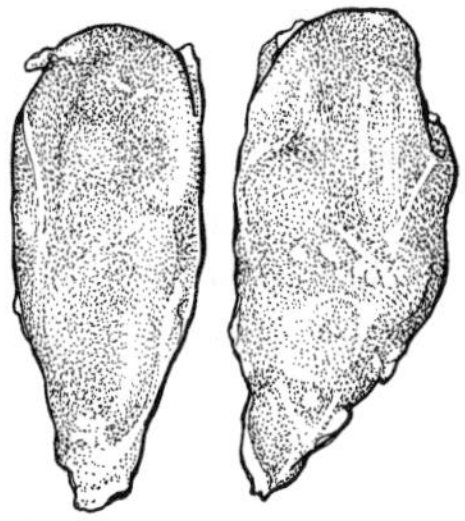

Boneless, skinless chicken breasts

it takes only a moment to cut them apart at the ball joints, it makes sense to buy whole wings even if you only want the first and/or second joints. Save the tips for stock.

Back and Feet: If available at your supermarket, chicken backs and feet are usually very inexpensive and perfect for stock. Rinse feet thoroughly before use. Hack or snip backs into 2-inch pieces with a chef's knife or heavy-duty kitchen shears before putting them into the pot. If the "oysters," the little nuggets of meat lodged in the backbone, are still attached, you can pry them out and fry them up as a snack.

Gizzards, Hearts, and Livers: These organs are referred to collectively as the giblets. The gizzards and hearts make a savory stew, and the livers are delicious sautéed. See About Poultry Giblets, 729.

Ground Chicken: See About Ground Turkey and Chicken, 618.

ABOUT ROASTED CHICKEN

Roasting a chicken does not require the skills of a restaurant chef. You will get perfectly good results if you proceed as your grandmother did. Simply arrange the chicken breast side up on a rimmed baking sheet or in a shallow roasting pan (deep pans interfere with browning) and roast it until the thigh releases clear juices when pricked with a fork. This is our recipe for Roasted Chicken, below, and it produces a bird that far surpasses the average take-out specimen.

If you are looking for perfection, you might consider trying the technique outlined in Turned Roasted Chicken, 580. This recipe calls for arranging the chicken on a rack (preferably a V-rack) and roasting it first on one side, then on the other, and finally breast side up. When a chicken is roasted on its sides, the dark meat is exposed to the reflected glare of the hot oven roof while the sensitive breast is turned toward the cooler oven walls. This serves to cook the dark meat at a faster rate than the breast, which is precisely what one wants, as the dark meat is done at an internal temperature of 170° to 180°F, while the white meat is cooked through at the much lower temperature of 160°F and begins to dry out and harden if heated much beyond 165°F. There is also gravity to consider. When a chicken sits breast side up throughout cooking, gravity inevitably draws the juices down toward the back and into the roasting pan. Flipping the chicken reverses the flow of the juices.

ROASTED CHICKEN

4 to 7 servings; about 1 pound chicken per person

This is the simplest way of roasting a chicken. For the brownest skin, roast the bird on a rimmed baking sheet or in a shallow roasting pan.

Position a rack in the center of the oven. Preheat the oven to 400°F. Lightly oil a shallow roasting pan or baking sheet.

Remove the neck and giblets from, then rinse and pat dry:

1 whole chicken (4 to 7 pounds)

Generously rub the body and neck cavities and sprinkle the skin with:

Salt

Arrange the chicken breast side up in the pan. Brush the breast and legs with:

2 to 3 tablespoons melted butter

Put the chicken in the oven and roast. If you prize moist breast meat, consider the chicken done when the thickest part of the thigh exudes clear juices when pricked deeply with a fork and registers 170° to 175°F on an instant-read meat thermometer. If you like the dark meat falling off the bone and are willing to risk a dry breast, roast until the thigh registers 180°F. The total roasting time for a 4-pound bird will be 55 to 65 minutes. For larger birds, figure 1 hour for the first 4 pounds, plus about 8 minutes for each additional pound. Remove the chicken to a platter and let stand for 10 to 15 minutes. Meanwhile, if you wish, make:

Poultry Pan Sauce or Gravy, below

Carve and serve.

POULTRY PAN SAUCE OR GRAVY

About 1 cup; 4 servings

These proportions are for a chicken weighing around 4 pounds. For a larger chicken or capon, double all ingredients.

After removing the chicken to a platter, pour into the roasting pan:

¼ cup dry white wine, sherry, port, Madeira, or water

Place the roasting pan on two burners over medium-high heat. Bring the juices to a simmer and, using a wooden spoon, scrape up the browned bits on the bottom of the pan. Pour the mixture into a short drinking glass, let the fat rise to the top, skim off the fat with a spoon, and discard. (You can also use a gravy separator.) Return the mixture to the roasting pan or pour it into a small saucepan. Add the juices that have accumulated around the chicken along with:

¾ cup chicken stock

Bring to a simmer. If you wish to thicken the sauce into a gravy, mix to a smooth paste:

1 tablespoon unsalted butter, softened
1 tablespoon all-purpose flour

Whisk the paste bit by bit into the simmering mixture and cook until thickened. Season with:

Several drops of fresh lemon juice or vinegar to taste
Salt and ground black pepper to taste

TURNED ROASTED CHICKEN

4 to 7 servings; about 1 pound chicken per person

This recipe calls for turning the chicken twice during cooking in order to ensure that the breast will still be tender and juicy by the time the dark meat is done.

Position a rack in the center of the oven. Preheat the oven to 400°F.

Remove the neck and giblets from, then rinse and pat dry:

1 whole chicken (4 to 7 pounds)

Generously rub the body and neck cavities and sprinkle the skin with:

Salt

Set a V-rack or flat wire rack, shown 643, in a shallow roasting pan, place the chicken on the rack, and brush the skin all over with:

2 to 3 tablespoons melted butter

Position the chicken on its side, that is, with a leg facing up. If you are using a flat rack, you may need to prop the chicken up with balls of aluminum foil to keep it from toppling over. Roast for 25 minutes for the first 4 pounds, plus 3 minutes more for each additional pound. Insert a wooden spoon or large metal spoon into the body cavity or grasp the chicken at both ends, with your hands protected with paper towels. Turn the chicken over on its other side, again propping with foil balls if necessary. Roast again for 25 minutes for the first 4 pounds, plus 3 minutes for each additional pound. Turn the chicken breast side up and roast 15 to 30 minutes more. The chicken is done when the thickest part of the thigh exudes clear juices when pricked deeply with a fork and registers 170° to 175°F on an instant-read thermometer. (If you prefer very well-done chicken, roast until the thigh registers 180°F. Remove the chicken to a platter and let stand for 10 to 15 minutes. Meanwhile, if you wish, make:

Poultry Pan Sauce or Gravy, 579

Carve and serve.

ROASTED CHICKEN WITH HERBS AND GARLIC

4 to 7 servings

Use these proportions for a chicken weighing 4½ pounds or less. Double the ingredients for a larger bird.

Position a rack in the center of the oven. Preheat the oven to 400°F.

Combine:

2 teaspoons minced fresh rosemary or thyme, or ¾ teaspoon dried, crumbled
1 teaspoon grated lemon zest (optional)
2 to 3 medium cloves garlic, minced
¼ teaspoon red pepper flakes
½ teaspoon salt

Remove the neck and giblets from, then rinse and pat dry:

1 whole chicken (4 to 7 pounds)

Generously rub the body and neck cavities and sprinkle the skin with:

Salt

Arrange in a roasting pan or on a rack in a roasting pan and brush with butter as directed for:

Roasted Chicken, 579, or Turned Roasted Chicken, above

Using your fingers, loosen the skin and spread the herb mixture over the meat of the breast, thighs, and drumsticks. Roast as directed.

ROASTED CHICKEN AND VEGETABLES

4 to 7 servings

Prepare the smaller amount of vegetables and other ingredients when roasting a 4- to 5-pound chicken, the larger amount when roasting a bigger bird. Since the vegetables should be cooked in a single jumbled layer, you will need to use a wide pan such as a 12 x 16 x ½-inch baking sheet. Because the vegetables will absorb most of the chicken drippings, it is not possible to make a pan sauce or gravy. Still, there will be a few browned bits on the bottom of the pan, which it will be worth your while to dissolve in a little chicken stock and pour over the chicken.

Position a rack in the center of the oven. Preheat the oven to 400°F.

Toss together to coat and combine:

Two to three 2- to 3-inch boiling potatoes, peeled and quartered
2 to 3 medium carrots, peeled, halved lengthwise, and cut into 1-inch pieces
Two to three 2-inch onions, peeled and quartered lengthwise
2 to 3 medium celery stalks, trimmed and cut into 1-inch pieces
2 to 3 tablespoons melted butter or vegetable oil
½ to ¾ teaspoon dried thyme
½ to ¾ teaspoon salt
Ground black pepper to taste

Remove the neck and giblets from, then rinse and pat dry:

1 whole chicken (4 to 7 pounds)

Generously rub the body and neck cavities and sprinkle the skin with:

Salt

Arrange in a roasting pan or on a rack in a roasting pan and brush with butter as directed for:

Roasted Chicken, 579, or Turned Roasted Chicken, 580

The vegetables need to cook for about 1 hour. If you are roasting a 4-pound chicken, scatter the vegetables over the roasting pan in a single layer as soon as the chicken goes into the oven. If you are roasting a larger chicken, add them to the pan about 1 hour before you estimate that the chicken will be done. (If the chicken happens to cook more quickly than you anticipate, continue to roast the vegetables while the chicken stands before carving.) Stir the vegetables every 15 to 20 minutes during cooking. Remove the vegetables to a platter and, if feasible, remove any fat in the pan. Pour into the pan:

⅓ to ½ cup chicken stock

Set the pan on two burners over medium heat, bring the liquid to a simmer, and scrape with a spoon until the browned roasting bits are dissolved. Carve the chicken, arrange on the platter with the vegetables, and drizzle the deglazing liquid over all.

ROASTED STUFFED CHICKEN OR CAPON

6 to 10 servings; about 1 pound chicken per person

When you want a festive stuffed bird, you should start with a chicken weighing 6 to 7 pounds or a capon. The cavities of smaller birds simply do not have enough space to accommodate a decent amount of stuffing.

Position a rack in the center of the oven. Preheat the oven to 400°F.

Remove the neck and giblets from, then rinse and pat dry:

1 whole chicken (6 to 7 pounds), or 1 whole capon (8 to 10 pounds)

Generously rub the body and neck cavities and sprinkle the skin with:

Salt

Prepare and have *hot:*

½ recipe Basic Bread Stuffing or Dressing or a variation, 482 to 483, or ½ recipe Basic Corn Bread Stuffing or a variation, 484

Loosely pack the stuffing into the body and neck cavities (see Roasting Whole Poultry, 572). Sew or lace up the body cavity, sew the neck vent, or secure with small skewers or toothpicks. If you wish, perform a simple truss, see page 573. Roast as directed for Roasted Chicken, 579, or Turned Roasted Chicken, 580. The stuffing may increase the total roasting time by 10 to 20 minutes.

ROASTED ROCK CORNISH HENS OR POUSSINS

4 servings

Just like the rest of us, rock Cornish hens seem to put on a little weight with each passing year. If you can find hens in the 1¼- to 1½-pound weight range that used to be the norm, allow a whole bird per serving. Otherwise, buy two heavier hens and split each one to make two servings.

Position a rack in the center of the oven. Preheat the oven to 400°F. Lightly oil a baking sheet or shallow roasting pan large enough to allow several inches of space between the birds.

Remove the neck and giblets from, then rinse and pat dry:

4 small rock Cornish hens or poussins (under 1½ pounds), or 2 large rock Cornish hens (1¾ pounds or more)

Mix together, then rub into the body cavity and over the skin:

1½ teaspoons dried thyme
1 teaspoon salt
1 teaspoon ground black pepper

Arrange the birds breast side up on the pan. Brush the exposed skin with:

2 to 3 tablespoons melted butter

If you wish, place in each cavity:

1 small sprig fresh thyme or rosemary

Roast until the thickest part of the thigh exudes clear juices when pricked and registers 170° to 175°F on an instant-read thermometer, 25 to 30 minutes for small hens, 35 to 40 minutes for larger ones. (If you prefer your poultry very well done, roast a few minutes more, until the thigh registers 180°F. Remove the birds to a platter and let stand for 10 minutes. Meanwhile, if you wish, prepare:

Poultry Pan Sauce or Gravy, 579

If you have roasted larger birds, divide each one in half with a sharp knife or poultry shears before serving.

GLAZED, STUFFED, ROASTED ROCK CORNISH HENS OR POUSSINS

6 servings

Filled with a savory stuffing and burnished with a slightly sweet glaze, these are classic birds for a party. Since you will be serving a whole bird to each person, choose the smallest rock Cornish hens you can find at the market or use poussins.

Position a rack in the center of the oven. Preheat the oven to 400°F.

Remove the neck and giblets from, then rinse and pat dry:

6 small rock Cornish hens or poussins (under 1½ pounds)

Sprinkle the body and neck cavities and skin with:

Salt

Stuff each bird with a scant ½ cup of:

Rice Stuffing with Almonds, Raisins, and Middle Eastern Spices, 485, Couscous Stuffing with Dried Apricots and Pistachios, 486, Wild Rice and Porcini Stuffing, 486, or Rice Stuffing with Chorizo and Hot Chili Peppers, 486

Tie the legs together at the ankles. Arrange the birds breast side up on a rack set in a shallow roasting pan and roast for 25 minutes. Meanwhile, make a glaze by heating in a small saucepan over low heat:

⅓ cup fruit jelly, seedless jam, or strained preserves or marmalade

2 tablespoons soy sauce or balsamic vinegar

After 25 minutes' roasting, remove the birds from the oven and brush generously with the glaze. To prevent smoking, coat the bottom of the roasting pan with ⅛ inch water. Return the birds to the oven and roast until the thickest part of the thigh exudes clear juices when pricked and registers 170° to 175°F on an instant-read thermometer, about 15 minutes for poussins, 20 to 25 minutes for rock Cornish hens. (If you prefer your poultry very well done, roast a few minutes more until the thigh registers 180°F.) Remove the birds to a platter and let stand for 10 minutes. Meanwhile, if you wish, prepare:

Poultry Pan Sauce or Gravy, 579

Serve one whole bird to each person.

ROASTED CHICKEN STUFFED UNDER THE SKIN

4 servings

Position a rack in the center of the oven. Preheat the oven to 400°F.

Remove the neck and giblets from, then rinse and pat dry:

1 whole chicken (about 3½ pounds) or 2 rock Cornish hens (at least 1½ pounds each)

Prepare:

Spinach Ricotta Stuffing, 487, or Duxelles, 387

Butterfly the bird(s) (see How to Cut Up Poultry, 569). Inserting your hand at the wing end of the breast, loosen the skin over the breast and around the thigh and drumstick, shown below left. Generously pack the stuffing under the skin, first pushing it over the drumstick and thigh and then over the breast, shown below center. Cut a ½-inch slit in the skin on either side of the breast, about 1 inch from the tip, and slip the end of 1 drumstick into each opening, shown below right. Smooth the stuffing with your hands to give the bird(s) a plump but natural shape. Place the bird(s) skin side up on a rack in a shallow roasting pan. Brush with:

1 to 2 tablespoons melted butter

Roast until the thickest part of the thigh exudes clear juices when pricked deeply with a fork and registers 170° to 175°F on an instant-read thermometer, 45 to 50 minutes for the chicken, 25 to 30 minutes for the hens. Let stand for 10 minutes.

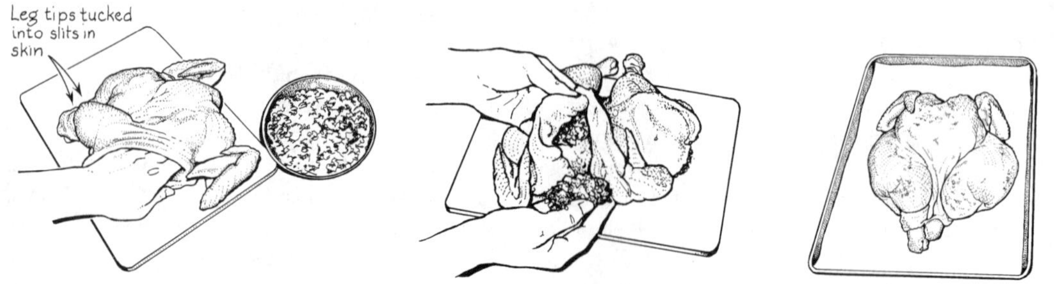

Stuffing a chicken under the skin

CASSEROLE-ROASTED CHICKEN WITH FORTY CLOVES OF GARLIC

4 or 5 servings

Because it is cooked in a covered casserole with a small amount of liquid, this chicken steams as it roasts, so the flesh ends up moist and succulent. Forty cloves may seem like a lot of garlic, but garlic loses much of its pungency and becomes nutty and sweet when roasted. Serve the unpeeled garlic cloves along with the chicken and let everyone have fun squeezing them out of their jackets.

Remove the neck and giblets from, then rinse and pat dry:

1 whole chicken (3½ to 4 pounds)

Rub the skin with:

Olive oil

Mix together, then rub into the body cavity and over the skin:

1 teaspoon dried thyme, crumbled
1 teaspoon dried sage, crumbled
½ teaspoon salt
½ teaspoon dried rosemary, crumbled
½ teaspoon ground black pepper

Place in the cavity:

1 lemon, quartered

If you wish, perform a simple truss (see Roasting Whole Poultry, 572). Arrange the chicken breast side up in a casserole, cover, and refrigerate for 2 to 24 hours.

Position a rack in the center of the oven. Preheat the oven to 375°F.

Add to the casserole with the chicken:

3 heads garlic, cloves separated but not peeled
1¼ cups chicken stock
1 cup dry white wine

Bring to a boil, cover the casserole and roast the chicken for 25 minutes. Increase the oven temperature to 450°F, uncover the casserole, and roast the chicken until the thigh exudes clear juices when pricked deeply with a fork and registers 170° to 175° on an instant-read thermometer, 35 to 60 minutes more. Check to make sure there is always some liquid in the bottom of the casserole; add a little more wine or stock if needed. Remove the chicken and garlic from the casserole and keep warm. Skim as much fat as possible from the pan juices with a spoon. If the pan juices are watery or weak in flavor, boil them down over high heat to concentrate. (Transfer the juices to a saucepan if your casserole cannot withstand direct heat.) If you wish, peel 6 or more of the garlic cloves, mash to a paste, stir into the sauce, and boil for 1 minute. Remove the sauce from the heat and stir in, if you wish:

2 tablespoons minced parsley or finely shredded basil or 2 teaspoons minced fresh thyme, tarragon, or rosemary

Season with:

Salt and ground black pepper to taste

Cut the chicken into serving pieces and arrange on a platter. Spoon the pan juices over it and scatter the garlic cloves around it.

ABOUT BROILED CHICKEN

For broiling, small chickens are wanted. Large chickens simply take too long to cook through; by the time they are done, the skin has charred and the kitchen has filled with smoke. In years past, a cook proposing to broil a chicken would buy a so-called broiler/fryer, that is, a small chicken weighing 2½ to 3 pounds. Today, alas, chickens in this weight range rarely appear at supermarkets, and the term broiler/fryer has lost its meaning, for it is often applied to chickens weighing as much as 4½ pounds. To make the best of this imperfect situation, buy a 3½-pound chicken, or the smallest one you can find, and split it or divide it into parts yourself. If you must use chicken parts, buy the smallest ones available and examine the package to make sure that it does not contain an oversized leg or breast half. (The parts in a package do not necessarily come from the same chicken.) Another alternative is to broil rock Cornish hens. Split the hens, removing the backbones, and serve a half to each person.

Broiling recipes are inevitably inexact because the broiling elements of home ranges vary greatly in the intensity of their heat. As a general rule, chicken should be placed 6 to 8 inches beneath the preheated element and broiled for 15 minutes on the bone side and then for 10 to 15 minutes on the skin side. (Always broil the bone side first, or the skin will become soggy.) When ranges with very hot broilers are used, however, it may be necessary to move the chicken much farther from the heat to prevent charring, and when the chicken is moved away from the heat, it may take somewhat longer to cook through.

Since barbecued and grilled chicken tastes divine when rubbed with herbs and spices or coated with a flavorful herb or spice paste, it would seem logical to treat broiled chicken in the same way. Unfortunately, things are not so simple. When you prepare chicken on an outdoor grill, you can prevent charring by moving the chicken away from the coals, damping the fire, or covering the grill rack. But the broiling elements of most indoor ranges have only one setting—high—and many gas ranges do not permit the cook to set the

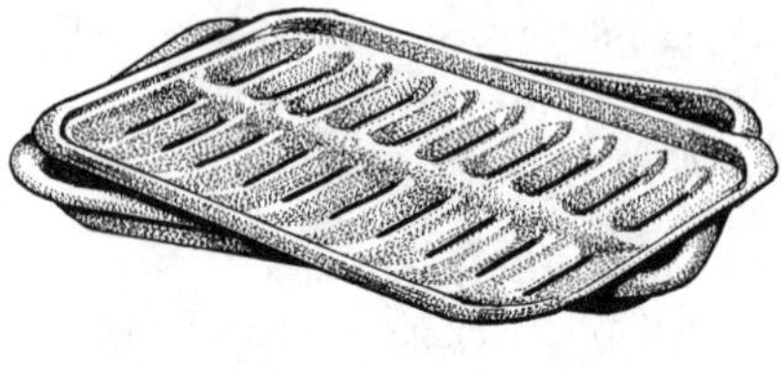

Two-piece broiling tray with a slotted tray

chicken lower than 8 inches from the broiling element. The inevitable result is that rubs and pastes burn. If you want to apply a rub or paste, you are better off baking the chicken and then crisping the skin under the broiler, if you wish (see Chicken with Chili Pepper Garlic Spice Paste and its two variations, 587). Marinades, glazes, and sauces also tend to blacken and require special handling. If you want to use a marinade, choose one that does not include sugar or a sweet ingredient such as molasses, honey, jelly, or jam. Any garlic in a marinade should be put through a garlic press or minced almost to a paste, or else it will leave unpleasant blackened bits on the chicken skin. Sauces and glazes, which often contain ingredients easily charred, must be applied separately to each side of the chicken shortly before that side is cooked through.

Always broil chicken in a two-piece broiling pan with a slotted or perforated broiling tray, shown above, which allows dripping fat to drain away and collect in the pan below. When chicken is broiled in a flat pan, on a cake rack set in a pan, or in a ridged disposable foil pan, the fat is directly exposed to the heat and will smoke and may even catch fire.

BROILED CHICKEN OR ROCK CORNISH HENS

4 servings

Preheat the broiler.

Rinse and pat dry:

1 chicken (about 3½ pounds), 2 rock Cornish hens (1½ to 1¾ pounds), or 3½ pounds chicken parts

If broiling a whole chicken or hens, cut the bird(s) in half, removing the backbone, and make a shallow incision on the inside of each leg at the drumstick/thigh joint to help the heat penetrate. Arrange the pieces skin side down on a broiler tray and brush the exposed side with:

2 tablespoons melted butter or olive oil

Sprinkle liberally with:

Salt and ground black pepper to taste

Place the pan 7 to 8 inches beneath the broiler element and broil 15 minutes for the chicken, 10 minutes for the hens, and 12 to 15 minutes for the chicken parts. Turn the pieces skin side up and brush with:

1 to 2 tablespoons melted butter or olive oil

Sprinkle with:

Salt and ground black pepper

Broil until the skin is browned and crisp and the thigh releases clear juices when pricked deeply with a fork, 15 to 20 minutes for the chicken, 6 to 8 minutes for the hens, and 8 to 10 minutes for the chicken parts. (If the skin begins to char before the cooking time is up, move the pan farther from the heat). Remove the broiled pieces to a platter. If you wish, prepare:

Poultry Pan Sauce or Gravy, 579

To maximize the flavor of the sauce, slowly pour the wine (or water) and stock used to make the sauce over the broiling tray, still set over the bottom pan, all the while scraping the rack with a wooden spoon to dissolve the browned bits.

BROILED CHICKEN WITH BARBECUE SAUCE

Prepare Broiled Chicken or Rock Cornish Hens, above. About 2 minutes before the chicken or hens are fully cooked, brush both sides with about 1 cup barbecue sauce. Return to the broiler skin side up and broil until the skin and sauce have charred slightly and the flesh is done. If the sauce threatens to burn, move the pan farther from the heat.

BROILED LEMON GARLIC CHICKEN

4 servings

Combine in a large bowl:

¼ cup strained fresh lemon juice
¼ cup olive oil
1 to 2 tablespoons pressed or very finely minced garlic
1 tablespoon Dijon mustard
½ teaspoon dried thyme
1 teaspoon salt
1 teaspoon ground black pepper

Rinse, pat dry, and cut up the chicken or hens as directed for:

Broiled Chicken or Rock Cornish Hens, above

Place the pieces in the bowl with the marinade, turn to coat well, and refrigerate, covered, for 1 to 3 hours. Broil, brushing with the marinade instead of butter or oil and omitting the salt and pepper. Remove the broiled pieces to a platter. If you wish to make a pan sauce, pour over the broiling tray (still set over the broiling pan), all the while scraping with a wooden spoon:

½ cup dry white wine or chicken stock

Remove the broiling tray and skim the fat off the juices in the broiling pan with a spoon. Place the pan on two burners over medium heat and boil the juices until concentrated and flavorful. Spoon the sauce over the chicken and sprinkle with:

2 tablespoons minced fresh parsley

BROILED TERIYAKI CHICKEN

Prepare Broiled Chicken or Rock Cornish Hens, 584, brushing the pieces with vegetable oil and omitting the salt and pepper. Prepare Teriyaki Sauce, 86, and simmer, stirring, in a small saucepan over medium heat until slightly thickened. About 2 minutes before the chicken or hens are fully cooked, brush both sides with about ¾ cup of the sauce. Return to the broiler skin side up and broil until the skin is lightly charred. If the pieces threaten to burn before they are cooked through, move the pan farther from the heating element. Remove the broiled pieces to a platter. Skim the fat off the pan juices with a spoon, then pour the juices over the chicken or hen pieces.

ABOUT BAKED CHICKEN

The term "baked chicken" always implies a dish prepared with chicken parts. (A whole chicken, when baked, is said to be roasted.) Baking is certainly the easiest technique for cooking chicken parts and produces excellent results. If you are lucky enough to be cooking for a crowd that unanimously prefers either white or dark meat, bake breasts or legs only. This way, you will not have to worry about the breasts drying out while the legs finish cooking. If you are preparing drumsticks and/or thighs only, you can bake them just until the juices run clear or, if you prefer, until the meat falls off the bones. Breasts, though, should be removed from the oven as soon as the flesh is no longer pink, or else the meat will be dry.

BAKED CHICKEN WITH ONIONS, GARLIC, AND ROSEMARY

4 to 5 servings

This simple but delicious dish is Greek in inspiration, so you might serve it in the Greek style with oven-roasted potatoes cooked with olive oil, garlic, and herbs.

Position a rack in the center of the oven. Preheat the oven to 400°F.

Rinse and pat dry:

3½ to 4½ pounds chicken parts

Season liberally with:

Salt and ground black pepper to taste

Toss together:

3 medium onions, cut into rings
6 to 12 cloves garlic, thinly sliced
2 tablespoons olive oil
4 teaspoons minced fresh rosemary, or 2 teaspoons dried, crumbled

Spread half of the onion mixture in a shallow baking dish or roasting pan just large enough to hold the chicken pieces in a single layer. Arrange the chicken pieces skin side up on top, then cover with the remaining onion mixture. Drizzle over the chicken:

2 tablespoons olive oil

Bake the chicken until the dark meat pieces exude clear juices when pricked deeply with a fork, 45 to 55 minutes.

CHICKEN BREASTS BAKED ON MUSHROOM CAPS

4 to 6 servings

Baking chicken breasts on a bed of mushroom caps makes a quick, delicious, and elegant dish. For the most attractive presentation, use the caps of portobello, shiitake, or large button mushrooms. Otherwise, buy any kind of smaller mushroom in a quantity sufficient to cover the bottom of the baking dish.

Position a rack in the center of the oven. Preheat the oven to 400°F.

Rinse, pat dry, and trim any excess fat from:

6 bone-in or boneless chicken breast halves (with skin)

Season with:

1 teaspoon dried thyme
Salt and ground black pepper to taste

Lightly oil a 13 x 9-inch baking pan or shallow baking dish just large enough to hold the chicken pieces in a single layer. Remove the stems from:

6 large portobello mushrooms or 12 to 18 large shiitake or button mushrooms, wiped clean

Or cut into ¼-inch-thick slices:

Enough smaller mushrooms to cover the bottom of the pan

Arrange the mushrooms, gill side down and overlapping if necessary, in the pan. Sprinkle with:

1 tablespoon minced garlic
Salt and ground black pepper to taste

Pour over the mushrooms:

2 cups dry white wine

Lay the chicken breasts skin side up on top of the mushrooms. Brush lightly with:

Olive oil

Bake, uncovered, until the chicken skin turns golden brown, about 20 minutes. Check to see that there is some liquid in the pan; if not, add more wine. Baste the chicken with pan juices and turn the pieces over. Bake until the chicken is firm and fully cooked, 10 to 20 minutes more. Using a slotted spoon, remove the chicken and mushrooms to a platter, arranging the chicken skin side up on the mushrooms. Pour the pan juices into a small saucepan and skim the fat off the top with a spoon. For a low-fat sauce, add:

Enough water or chicken stock to measure 1 cup

For a more luxurious sauce, add:

½ to 1 cup heavy cream

Boil the sauce over high heat until reduced to a syrupy consistency. Taste and adjust the seasonings. Spoon some of the sauce over the chicken and pass the rest separately. If you wish, sprinkle the chicken with:

2 tablespoons minced fresh parsley

BAKED CHICKEN WITH ORANGE JUICE

4 servings

A perfect quick after-work dinner.

Position a rack in the center of the oven. Preheat the oven to 375°F.

Rinse and pat dry:

1 chicken (about 3 pounds), quartered, or 3 pounds chicken parts

Smear the skin with:

4 teaspoons Dijon mustard

Arrange the chicken skin side down in a shallow roasting pan or baking dish just large enough to hold it in a single layer.

Sprinkle the pieces with:

½ cup finely chopped onions
2 tablespoons unsalted butter, cut into bits
Salt and ground black pepper to taste

Pour around the chicken:

1½ cups orange juice

Bake, basting once, for 30 minutes. Turn the chicken skin side up and sprinkle with:

¼ cup firmly packed dark brown sugar

Bake until the chicken is tender and golden, 15 to 20 minutes more. Add more orange juice if the pan seems dry. Remove the chicken to a serving platter. Pour the juices into a small saucepan and boil over high heat until syrupy. Spoon the sauce over the chicken and serve.

BAKED CHICKEN WITH TOMATOES, HAM, AND MADEIRA

4 to 5 servings

Position a rack in the center of the oven. Preheat the oven to 350°F.

Rinse and pat dry:

3 to 4 pounds chicken parts

Season with:

Salt and ground black pepper to taste

Combine:

4 ounces smoked ham, diced (about ½ cup)
1 medium onion, thinly sliced
1 cup chopped seeded peeled tomatoes, fresh or canned
2 cloves garlic, chopped
1 tablespoon whole-grain mustard
½ cup Madeira or sweet sherry
¼ cup dry white wine
1 tablespoon olive oil
1 teaspoon dried marjoram or oregano
½ teaspoon salt
¼ teaspoon ground black pepper

Spread this mixture in the bottom of a shallow roasting pan or baking dish just large enough to hold the chicken in a single layer. Place the chicken pieces skin side up on top and brush lightly with:

Olive oil

Bake, uncovered, for 45 to 60 minutes, basting every 15 minutes with the pan juices and adding a little wine, water, or chicken stock if the pan seems dry. The chicken is done when the dark meat pieces exude clear, not pink, juices when pricked deeply with a fork. Remove the chicken to a platter. Tilt the roasting pan and skim as much fat as possible from the pan juices. Taste and adjust the seasonings, then pour the sauce over the chicken. If you wish, sprinkle the chicken with:

Grated Parmesan cheese
Chopped fresh parsley

OVEN-BARBECUED CHICKEN

4 servings

This recipe could not be easier.

Position a rack in the center of the oven. Preheat the oven to 350°F.

Rinse and pat dry:

3½ to 4½ pounds chicken parts

Season liberally with:

Salt and ground black pepper

Have ready:

1 cup barbecue sauce

Place the chicken in a shallow roasting pan or baking dish, brush with two-thirds of the sauce, and arrange skin side down in a single layer. Bake for 20 minutes. Using tongs, turn the chicken skin side up. Paint with the remaining barbecue sauce and bake until the dark meat pieces exude clear juices when pricked deeply with a fork, about 20 minutes more. If you wish to crisp and color the skin, run the chicken briefly under a hot broiler.

BAKED MUSTARD CHICKEN

4 servings

Position a rack in the center of the oven. Preheat the oven to 350°F. Lightly oil a baking sheet.
Rinse and pat dry:

3½ to 4½ pounds chicken parts

Brush the chicken pieces liberally with:

About ⅓ cup Dijon mustard

Combine in a wide, shallow bowl:

2 cups dry unseasoned breadcrumbs
¼ cup minced fresh parsley
2 tablespoons unsalted butter, melted
2 cloves garlic, minced
1 teaspoon salt
½ teaspoon ground black pepper

Coat each piece of chicken with the crumb mixture, patting with your fingers to make the crumbs adhere. Place the chicken skin side up on the baking sheet. Bake until the coating is nicely browned and the dark meat pieces exude clear juices when pricked with a fork, 45 to 60 minutes. For a crispier crust, run the chicken briefly under a hot broiler. Serve immediately or at room temperature.

BAKED CHICKEN WITH CHILI-GARLIC SPICE PASTE

4 servings

A taste thrill for those who like their chicken highly seasoned.
Rinse and pat dry:

3½ to 4½ pounds chicken parts

Using about 2 tablespoons per piece, coat the chicken on all sides with:

1 cup Chili-Garlic Spice Paste, 88

Cover and refrigerate for 2 to 24 hours.
Position a rack in the center of the oven. Preheat the oven to 350°F. Lightly oil a shallow roasting pan or baking sheet.
Arrange the chicken pieces skin side down in the pan. Bake for 20 minutes. Using tongs, turn the chicken skin side up and bake until the dark meat pieces exude clear juices when pricked deeply with a fork, about 20 minutes more. If you wish to crisp the skin, run the chicken briefly under a hot broiler.

BAKED CHICKEN WITH ASIAN-GINGER SPICE PASTE

Pungent and gingery.
Prepare Baked Chicken with Chili-Garlic Spice Paste, above, substituting 1 cup Asian-Ginger Spice Paste, 88, for the chili paste.

BAKED CHICKEN WITH THAI GREEN CURRY PASTE

Prepare Baked Chicken with Chili-Garlic Spice Paste, above, substituting 1 cup Thai Green Curry Paste, 88, for the chili paste.

ABOUT BONELESS, SKINLESS CHICKEN BREAST HALVES

Chicken breasts that have been boned, skinned, and split down the middle—also known as chicken breast halves or cutlets or, in French, *suprêmes de volaille*—are the most popular poultry cut in the United States. The esteem that they enjoy is only partly accounted for by the fact that we are a nation of white-meat chicken lovers. Boneless, skinless chicken breasts are also low in fat, quick and easy to prepare, and amenable to a wide range of cooking treatments, including sautéing, frying, grilling, poaching, creaming, and baking. The important thing to remember about boneless, skinless chicken breasts is that they are easy to overcook. Cook them just to the point where they release clear juices when pricked with a fork, or they will be disappointingly dry and firm.

You can save yourself some money by preparing this cut yourself from bone-in, skin-on chicken breasts (see Chicken Parts, 577).

SAUTÉED BONELESS, SKINLESS CHICKEN BREASTS (BASIC RECIPE)

2 to 4 servings

Sautéed chicken breasts should be a rich nut-brown on the outside, tender and veritably bursting with juice inside. Stephen Schmidt, a cookbook author and cooking teacher and great friend to *Joy*, has discovered the secret to success. It is high heat—not so high as to burn the fat, but pretty close. At low heat, the chicken simply dries out and turns to leather. If the pan is hot enough, the chicken will take—more or less exactly—4 minutes per side to cook through. Sautéed boneless, skinless chicken breasts are delicious on their own but even better when served with a simple sauce made in the pan, 579.
Rinse and pat dry:

4 boneless, skinless chicken breast halves (about 1½ pounds)

Trim any fat around the edges. If you wish, remove the white tendon running through the tenderloins. Sprinkle both sides with:

Salt and ground black pepper to taste

Spread on a plate:

¼ cup all-purpose flour

Coat the chicken on both sides with the flour, pressing to make the tenderloins, the thin strips of meat on the undersides of the breasts, adhere. Gently shake off the excess flour, holding the chicken tapered side up to avoid detaching the tenderloins. Heat in a heavy 10- to 12-inch skillet over medium-high heat until fragrant and nut-brown:

1½ tablespoons unsalted butter

Add:

1½ tablespoons olive oil

Swirl the butter and oil together. Arrange the chicken tenderloin side down in the skillet and sauté for exactly 4 minutes, keeping the fat as hot as possible without letting it burn. Using tongs, turn the chicken and cook until the flesh feels firm to the touch and milky juices appear around the tenderloins, 3 to 5 minutes more. Serve immediately, or remove to a platter and keep warm in a very low oven while you prepare one of the recipes that follow.

SAUTÉED BONELESS, SKINLESS CHICKEN BREASTS PICCATA

2 to 4 servings

Prepare and keep warm in a 200°F oven:

Sautéed Boneless, Skinless Chicken Breasts, 587

Remove all but about 1 tablespoon of the fat in the skillet, heat over medium heat, and add:

2 to 3 tablespoons minced shallots or scallions

Cook, stirring, until wilted, about 1 minute. Increase the heat to high and add:

1 cup chicken stock

Bring to a boil, scraping the bottom of the skillet with a wooden spoon to dissolve the browned bits. Add:

3 to 4 tablespoons strained fresh lemon juice
2 tablespoons nonpareil capers, drained

Boil until the mixture is reduced to about ⅓ cup, 3 to 4 minutes. Add any accumulated chicken juices and reduce again. Remove from the heat and swirl in:

2 to 3 tablespoons unsalted butter, softened

Pour the sauce over the chicken and serve immediately.

SAUTÉED BONELESS, SKINLESS CHICKEN BREASTS WITH SHERRIED MUSHROOM CREAM SAUCE

2 to 4 servings

Prepare and keep warm in a 200°F oven:

Sautéed Boneless, Skinless Chicken Breasts, 587

Remove all but about 2 tablespoons of the fat in the skillet, heat over medium heat, and add:

2 to 3 tablespoons minced shallots or scallions

Cook, stirring, until wilted, about 1 minute. Increase the heat to high and add:

8 ounces mushrooms, thinly sliced (about 2⅓ cups)

Cook, stirring, until the mushrooms are softened and lightly browned, 2 to 3 minutes. Add:

⅓ cup sweet or dry sherry

Boil until the sherry is nearly evaporated, about 1 minute. Add:

1 cup heavy cream
½ cup chicken stock

Boil until the sauce is thick enough to lightly coat a spoon, about 5 minutes. Add any accumulated chicken juices and reduce again until thick. Stir in:

2 tablespoons finely chopped fresh parsley
Pinch of freshly grated or ground nutmeg or ground mace
Salt and ground white or black pepper to taste

Season with:

Several drops of fresh lemon juice

Spoon the sauce over the chicken and serve immediately.

SAUTÉED BONELESS, SKINLESS CHICKEN BREASTS WITH TOMATOES, CAPERS, AND BASIL

2 to 4 servings

Prepare and keep warm in a 200°F oven:

Sautéed Boneless, Skinless Chicken Breasts, 587

Remove all but about 2 tablespoons of the fat in the skillet, heat over medium heat, and add:

⅓ cup minced shallots or scallions

Cook, stirring, until the shallots are softened, about 1 minute. Increase the heat to high and add:

¼ cup dry white wine or vermouth

Boil, scraping the bottom of the skillet with a wooden spoon, until the wine is almost evaporated. Stir in:

1 pound tomatoes, seeded and chopped (about 2 cups)
2 tablespoons nonpareil capers, drained
1 tablespoon minced garlic

Cook, stirring constantly, until the tomatoes have given up their juice, creating a thick chunky puree, about 2 minutes. Add any accumulated chicken juices and boil the sauce until thick.
Remove from the heat, and stir in:

2 tablespoons finely shredded fresh basil
Salt and ground black pepper to taste

Spoon the sauce over the chicken and serve immediately.

SAUTÉED BONELESS, SKINLESS CHICKEN BREASTS WITH BALSAMIC CITRUS SAUCE

2 to 4 servings

Prepare and keep warm in a 200°F oven:

Sautéed Boneless, Skinless Chicken Breasts, 587

Remove all but about 1 tablespoon of the fat in the skillet, heat over medium heat, and add:

3 to 4 tablespoons minced shallots or scallions
1 heaping tablespoon honey
Pinch of ground allspice

Cook, stirring, until the shallots are wilted, 1 to 2 minutes. Increase the heat to high and add:

1 cup chicken stock
1 tablespoon strained fresh lemon juice

Boil, scraping the bottom of the skillet with a wooden spoon, until reduced to about ½ cup. Add:

¼ cup heavy cream

Boil until the sauce is slightly thickened, about 1 minute. Add:

1 tablespoon balsamic vinegar
Salt and ground black pepper to taste

Return to a boil, then spoon the sauce over the chicken and serve immediately.

BREADED CHICKEN CUTLETS

2 to 4 servings

Easy to make and always a crowd pleaser.

Rinse and pat dry:

4 boneless, skinless chicken breast halves (about 1½ pounds)

Trim any fat around the edges. If you wish, remove the white tendon running through the tenderloins. Place the cutlets 1 at a time between sheets of wax paper and gently pound with a mallet or the side of an empty bottle to flatten slightly. Combine in a wide, shallow bowl:

1 cup dry unseasoned breadcrumbs
¼ cup grated Parmesan cheese (optional)
1 tablespoon minced fresh parsley or basil or 1 teaspoon dried rosemary, thyme, or oregano, crumbled (optional)
1 teaspoon salt
½ teaspoon ground black pepper

Whisk together in a shallow bowl:

1 large egg
1 teaspoon water

Spread on a plate:

¼ cup all-purpose flour

Coat the chicken with the flour and shake off the excess. Dip in the egg mixture and then coat with the breadcrumb mixture, patting with your fingers to make the crumbs adhere. Heat in a heavy 10- to 12-inch skillet over medium-high heat until shimmery and fragrant:

⅓ cup olive oil

Add the chicken and sauté until lightly browned, 2 to 3 minutes. Using tongs, turn the cutlets and cook, 2 to 3 minutes more, adding a little more oil if the pan looks dry. Quickly blot the chicken with paper towels. Serve immediately or at room temperature.

DEVILED BONELESS, SKINLESS CHICKEN BREASTS

6 servings

Rinse, pat dry, and trim any excess fat from:

6 boneless, skinless chicken breast halves

If desired, remove the white tendon running through the tenderloins. Arrange the breasts in a baking dish large enough to hold them in one layer. Pour over the chicken breasts:

Soy-Sherry Marinade, 85

Roll the breasts until they are completely coated with marinade, then cover the dish and refrigerate, turning the chicken once or twice, for at least 2 hours or up to 12 hours.

When ready to cook, position a rack in the center of the oven. Preheat the oven to 375°F. Mix together with a fork in a small bowl:

1 cup fresh breadcrumbs
2 tablespoons unsalted butter, melted
½ teaspoon ground black pepper

Drain and discard any excess marinade from the chicken, leaving the breasts in the dish. Cover the chicken evenly with the breadcrumb mixture and bake, uncovered, until the chicken and crumbs are browned and the chicken is firm when pressed, 20 to 30 minutes. Serve with:

Béarnaise Sauce, 56 (optional)

CHICKEN PARMIGIANA

2 to 4 servings

The Italian-American classic that everyone loves. This dish can be assembled early in the day, refrigerated, and then baked when needed.

Prepare:

Breaded Chicken Cutlets, above

Position a rack in the center of the oven. Preheat the oven to 350°F. Lightly oil a 13 x 9-inch baking pan or shallow baking dish. Spoon into the pan:

½ cup Italian Tomato Sauce, 304

Arrange the chicken cutlets over the sauce, slightly overlapping them. Sprinkle with:

3 to 4 tablespoons grated Parmesan cheese

Spoon over:

1 cup Italian Tomato Sauce, 304

Top with:

6 ounces mozzarella cheese, thinly sliced
½ cup grated Parmesan cheese

Cover the pan with aluminum foil and bake until heated through, 20 to 30 minutes. If you wish to brown the top, remove the foil and run the dish briefly under a hot broiler. Serve hot, sprinkled with:

Chopped fresh parsley (optional)

CHICKEN CORDON BLEU

2 to 4 servings

This classic has never lost its appeal.

Rinse and pat dry:

4 boneless, skinless chicken breast halves (about 1½ pounds)

Trim any fat around the edges. If you wish, remove the white tendon running through the tenderloins. Place the chicken breasts 1 at a time between sheets of wax paper and gently pound with a mallet or the side of an empty bottle until about ⅜ inch thick. Season with:

Salt and ground black pepper to taste

Cover half of the underside of each chicken breast with:

1 thin slice ham or prosciutto

Leaving a small space around the edges, top the ham slice with:

1 thin slice Gruyère or other Swiss cheese

Fold the chicken breast in half over the ham and cheese and press the edges firmly to seal. Make a ⅛-inch cut along the folded edge of the breast to help prevent the packet from opening during cooking. Combine in a wide, shallow bowl:

1 cup dry unseasoned breadcrumbs
¼ cup minced fresh parsley
1 teaspoon salt
½ teaspoon ground black pepper

Whisk together in a shallow bowl:

1 large egg
1 teaspoon water

Spread on a plate:

¼ cup all-purpose flour

Working 1 at a time, press both sides of each packet in the flour, then dip in the egg mixture and coat with the breadcrumb mixture, patting with your fingers to make the crumbs adhere. Heat in a heavy 10- to 12-inch skillet over medium-high heat until fragrant and nut-brown:

1½ tablespoons unsalted butter

Add:

1½ tablespoons olive oil

Swirl the butter and oil together. Place the packets in the skillet and sauté, until nicely browned, 3 to 4 minutes. Using tongs or a spatula, turn the packets and cook for 3 to 4 minutes more. Drain on paper towels and serve immediately.

GORGONZOLA-STUFFED CHICKEN BREASTS

4 servings

If you have the time, refrigerate the coated chicken breasts, covered, for up to 4 hours. This will help the crust adhere while the chicken is cooking.

In a medium, heavy skillet, heat:

3 tablespoons olive oil

Add:

3 medium onions, sliced

Reduce the heat to low and cook until deep brown, about 25 minutes. Transfer the onions to a bowl and let cool. Stir in:

½ cup crumbled Gorgonzola cheese
⅓ cup chopped walnuts, toasted

Cover and refrigerate until ready to use.

Lay smooth side down on a work surface and flatten to a ¼-inch thickness shown below:

4 boneless, skinless chicken breast halves (about 1½ pounds)

Spoon one-quarter of the filling onto each breast and spread to within ½ inch of the edges. Fold about ½ inch of each long side over the filling. Press down firmly. Roll the breasts starting with the narrow end and keeping the folded edges tucked in. Secure with a toothpick.

Combine in a wide, shallow dish:

½ cup finely chopped walnuts
½ cup cornmeal
Salt and ground black pepper to taste

Roll the chicken breasts in:

3 tablespoons butter, melted

Then roll in the cornmeal mixture to cover, pressing the coating with your hands. In a medium skillet, heat until foaming:

2 tablespoons butter
1 tablespoon olive oil

Add the breasts, seam side down. Cook, turning them every few minutes, until the crust is well browned and the chicken feels firm when pressed, about 18 minutes.

CHICKEN KIEV

4 to 8 servings

This justly famed entrée consists of thinly pounded boneless, skinless chicken breasts that are rolled around fingers of seasoned butter and then breaded and fried.

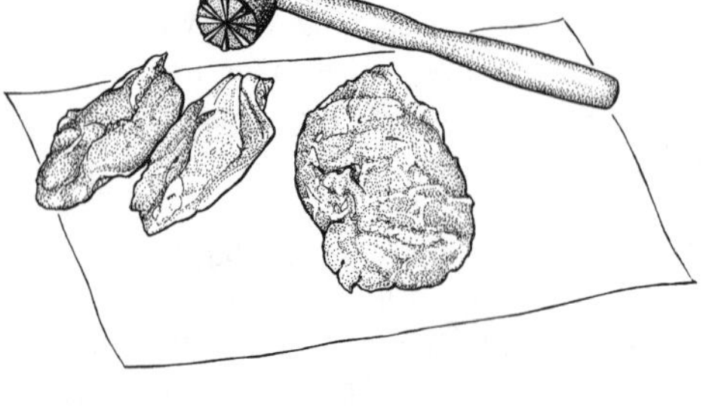

Pounding the cutlets to ¼ inch thick

When the rolls are cut, the melted butter spurts out, creating a moment of high culinary drama. Obviously, the key to success in preparing this dish is to seal the chicken packets tightly and to bread them with care so that the butter does not leak out during cooking.

Using the back of a wooden spoon, cream together in a medium bowl:

½ pound (2 sticks) unsalted butter, softened
2 tablespoons strained fresh lemon juice
1 tablespoon minced fresh parsley
1 tablespoon finely snipped fresh chives, or 2 teaspoons dried (optional)
1 teaspoon minced garlic
½ teaspoon salt
¼ teaspoon ground black pepper

On a sheet of wax paper, shape the butter into a 6 x 3-inch cake and refrigerate for 2 hours.

Rinse and pat dry:

8 boneless, skinless chicken breast halves (about 3 pounds)

Trim any fat around the edges. If you wish, remove the white tendon running through the tenderloins. Place the breasts 1 at a time between sheets of wax paper and gently pound with a mallet or the side of an empty bottle until ¼ inch thick, shown 590. Season with:

Salt and ground black pepper to taste

Divide the chilled butter crosswise into 8 fingers, each 3 inches long. Arrange the chicken tender side up on a work surface. Place 1 finger of butter crosswise on each breast about one-third of the way up from the tapered end, shown below (top left). Fold the tapered end over the butter, shown below (top right) then roll the butter up inside the remainder of the breast, tucking in the sides to enclose the butter completely, shown below (bottom right, left). Combine in a wide, shallow bowl:

2 cups dry unseasoned breadcrumbs
1 teaspoon salt
1 teaspoon ground black pepper

Whisk together in a shallow bowl:

2 large eggs
2 teaspoons water

Spread on a plate:

½ cup all-purpose flour

Coat the chicken packets in the flour, being sure to cover the tucked-in ends. Roll the packets in the egg mixture, then coat on all sides with the breadcrumb mixture, patting with your fingers to make the crumbs adhere. Place the rolls on a rack, cover loosely with wax or parchment paper, and refrigerate for 1 to 8 hours.

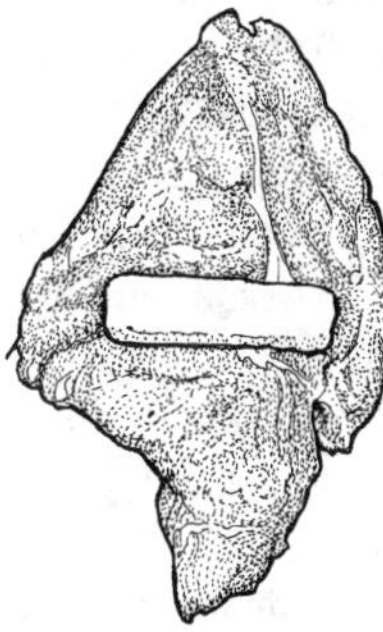

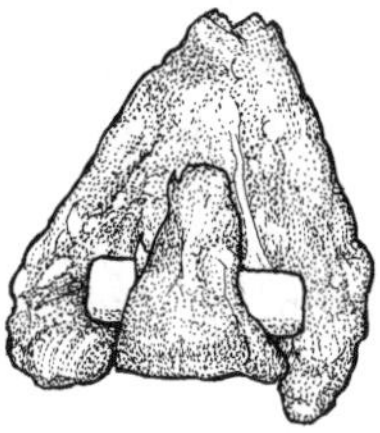

Clockwise from top left: Preparing Chicken Kiev

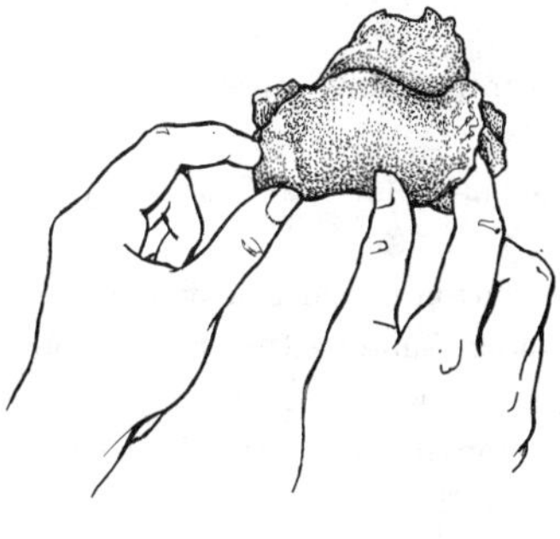

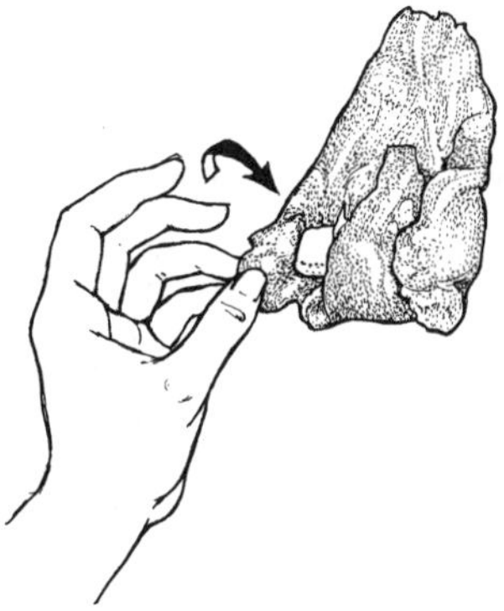

Position a rack in the center of the oven. Preheat the oven to 350°F.
Heat in a skillet large enough to hold the rolls in a single layer over medium-high heat until shimmery:

½ cup vegetable oil

Arrange the rolls in the skillet and sauté until the first side is nut-brown, 2 to 3 minutes. Turn carefully with a slotted spatula and brown the second side in the same manner. Using the spatula, transfer the rolls to a baking sheet and bake for 15 minutes. Serve immediately.

BAKED STUFFED BONELESS CHICKEN BREASTS

6 to 8 servings

This recipe can be prepared using boned, split chicken breasts without the skin or with the skin still attached. The skin becomes brown and crisp and keeps the delicate meat moist.
Position a rack in the center of the oven. Preheat the oven to 350°F.
Rinse and pat dry:

8 boneless chicken breast halves (about 3 pounds), with or without the skin

Trim any fat around the edges. If you wish, remove the white tendon running through the tenderloins. Place the chicken breasts 1 at a time between sheets of wax paper and gently pound with a mallet or the side of an empty bottle until about ⅜ inch thick. Season with:

Salt and ground black pepper to taste

Heat in a small skillet over medium-high heat until the foam begins to subside:

2 to 3 tablespoons unsalted butter

Add and cook, stirring, until tender but not brown, about 5 minutes:

⅓ cup finely chopped onions

Stir in and cook for 30 seconds:

1 teaspoon minced garlic

Remove the mixture to a bowl and stir in:

2 cups dry unseasoned breadcrumbs
¼ cup grated Parmesan cheese
¼ cup finely chopped fresh parsley
½ teaspoon dried rosemary, crumbled
½ teaspoon dried sage, crumbled
½ teaspoon salt
½ teaspoon ground black pepper

Stir in:

⅓ to ⅔ cup chicken stock

The stuffing should be just moist enough to hold together in a crumbly ball when squeezed firmly in the hand. Do not overmoisten. Taste and adjust the seasonings.
Lightly oil a 13 x 9-inch baking pan. Place ¼ cup stuffing on the center of the underside of each breast and press lightly to compact it. Bring the top and bottom flaps of the chicken up over the stuffing, slightly overlapping the ends, then fold up the sides to enclose the stuffing completely. Lay the packets seam side down in the pan and brush with:

Olive oil

Season with:

Salt and ground black pepper to taste

Bake until the chicken is lightly browned and feels firm when pressed, 20 to 30 minutes. Serve immediately.

BAKED STUFFED BONELESS CHICKEN BREASTS SICILIAN STYLE

Prepare Baked Stuffed Boneless Chicken Breasts, above, decreasing the breadcrumbs to 1½ cups and adding to the finished stuffing ¼ cup oil-cured black olives, pitted and chopped; ¼ cup raisins, lightly chopped, or dried currants; ¼ cup pine nuts or finely chopped walnuts; 3 to 4 anchovy fillets, rinsed, dried, and finely chopped (optional); and 2 tablespoons drained nonpareil capers.

BONELESS, SKINLESS CHICKEN BREASTS BAKED IN FOIL WITH SUN-DRIED TOMATOES AND OLIVES

4 servings

This method of cooking, called in French *en papillote,* entails baking boneless, skinless chicken breasts in sealed foil packages. The foil traps the juices, resulting in moist and tender meat.
Position a rack in the center of the oven. Preheat the oven to 450°F.
Rinse and pat dry:

4 boneless, skinless chicken breast halves (about 1½ pounds)

Trim any fat around the edges. If you wish, remove the white tendon running through the tenderloins. Season with:

Salt and ground black pepper to taste

Combine:

10 Kalamata or other black olives, pitted and finely chopped
8 sun-dried tomato halves in oil, cut into thin strips
3 tablespoons sun-dried tomato oil (from the jar of tomatoes) and/or olive oil
2 tablespoons finely shredded fresh basil or minced fresh parsley

Cut four 12-inch squares of aluminum foil. Fold each square in half to make a crease at the center. Unfold the foil and lightly oil the shiny side. Lay each breast on the shiny side of the foil just to one side of the crease. Spoon the tomato mixture over each breast, leaving a ¼-inch border around the edges. Loosely fold the foil over the chicken, then crimp the edges of the packet to seal tightly. Place the packets on a baking sheet and bake for 20 minutes. Remove from the oven and let stand for 5 minutes. To avoid being burned by steam, cut a slit in the packets before opening them.

SOUTHWESTERN CHICKEN BAKED IN FOIL OR PARCHMENT

4 servings

Rinse and pat dry:

4 boneless, skinless chicken breast halves (about 1½ pounds)

Lay on a work surface with the smoother side up. Make an incision about 3 inches long and 2 inches deep in the middle of the thick side to create a pocket. In a small bowl, combine:

4 ounces mild goat cheese, at room temperature
2 medium fresh jalapeño peppers, seeded and minced
3 sun-dried tomato halves in oil, minced

Spoon one-quarter of the filling into each pocket. Press to seal the edges. Generously season each chicken breast with:

Salt and ground black pepper to taste

Refrigerate for at least 15 minutes.

Meanwhile, combine:

2 cups cooked black beans (about ⅔ cup dried), 271, rinsed and drained if canned
1 small red onion, finely chopped
⅓ cup chopped fresh cilantro
3 tablespoons olive oil
1 teaspoon ground cumin
1 teaspoon red wine vinegar
Pinch of ground red pepper

Preheat the oven to 375°F.

Cut four 15-inch squares of aluminum foil or parchment paper and crease them in half on the diagonal. Spoon about ½ cup of the black bean mixture on one side of each piece of foil or parchment; top with a chicken breast and sprinkle with:

Hot paprika

Fold the empty half of the foil or parchment paper over the chicken to cover. Fold the edges of the foil or parchment together all the way around, closing the packet tightly. Set on baking sheets and bake until the packets are browned and puffed, about 25 minutes. Serve with:

Lime wedges

ABOUT STIR-FRYING

Stir-frying is one of the basic methods of Chinese cooking. It involves three essential elements: the use of very high heat for a brief cooking time; using just enough peanut oil to cook the dish well; and the cutting of all the ingredients to a more or less similar size so that they cook in about the same amout of time. If the cooking time of ingredients is very different although they have been cut to approximately the same size, they may be cooked separately and then combined all at once at the end. In every case, stir-frying involves flipping and stirring the ingredients very rapidly in a wok or skillet. It is always important not to overcook; both the meat and other ingredients should emerge very hot but full of flavor.

STIR-FRIED GARLIC CHICKEN

2 to 4 servings

A tangy dish that comes together very quickly.

BEFORE COOKING:

In a medium bowl, mix together thoroughly:

1 tablespoon cornstarch
1 tablespoon Chinese cooking wine or dry white wine
2 teaspoons light soy sauce
2 teaspoons oyster sauce
1 teaspoon salt
1 teaspoon sugar

Cut into 1½ x ½-inch pieces (this is more easily done if the chicken is partially frozen):

1½ pounds boneless, skinless chicken thighs

Toss in the soy sauce mixture. Cover with plastic wrap and let stand for 20 to 30 minutes. On a small plate, place:

4 teaspoons finely minced garlic
1 tablespoon finely minced peeled fresh ginger

On another small plate, place:

20 snow pea pods, trimmed
1 medium onion, cut into ¼-inch-thick slices

In a small bowl, mix together thoroughly:

1 tablespoon hoisin sauce
1 tablespoon ketchup
1 tablespoon toasted sesame oil
1½ teaspoons dark soy sauce
½ teaspoon red pepper flakes

Have ready:

⅔ cup chicken stock
3 scallions, sliced lengthwise into thin strips, then cut into 2-inch sections

TO COOK:

Heat a wok or large skillet over high heat until hot.

Add:

2 tablespoons peanut oil

Swirl the oil around the pan until very hot but not smoking. Add the minced garlic and ginger and stir briefly until the garlic is very slightly browned. Add the chicken and quickly stir and flip in the oil to separate the pieces. Continue to toss and cook for about 3 minutes. Add the chicken stock and swirl until the stock is heated through. Add the snow peas and onions, stir once, cover, and cook for 2 minutes. Uncover the pan and add the soy sauce mixture. Stir lightly until all pieces are thoroughly coated. Sprinkle with the scallions, stir lightly, and remove to a serving dish. Serve immediately.

STIR-FRIED GINGER CHICKEN *4 servings*

Quick and easy, this is chicken raised to a new level by a tasty sauce.

BEFORE COOKING:

In a medium bowl, mix together thoroughly:

1 egg white, lightly beaten
1½ tablespoons cornstarch
½ teaspoon salt

Cut into ¾-inch cubes (this is more easily done if the chicken is partially frozen):

3 boneless, skinless chicken breast halves

Toss in the egg white mixture. Let stand for 20 to 30 minutes.

Place on a small plate:

3 scallions, cut into ¼-inch pieces
2 tablespoons finely minced peeled fresh ginger

In a medium bowl, mix together thoroughly:

2 tablespoons plus 2 teaspoons sugar
½ teaspoon salt
2 tablespoons ketchup
4 teaspoons white vinegar
4 teaspoons Chinese cooking wine or dry white wine
2 teaspoons dark soy sauce

In a cup, mix together thoroughly, leaving the spoon in for later:

2 teaspoons cornstarch
2 teaspoons cool water

TO COOK:

Heat a wok or large skillet over high heat until hot. Add:

½ cup peanut oil

Swirl the oil around the pan until very hot but not smoking. Add the chicken and quickly stir and flip in the oil to separate the pieces. Cook lightly. Remove with a slotted spoon, leaving the oil in the wok or skillet. Set aside.

Reheat the wok or skillet over high heat. Swirl the remaining oil around the pan (there should be 2 to 3 tablespoons) until it is very hot but not smoking. Add the scallions and ginger. Stir and toss vigorously until slightly brown, about 30 seconds. Add the soy sauce mixture and stir until heated through. Stir the cornstarch mixture, then pour it slowly into the sauce, stirring constantly. Cook, stirring until the mixture is thickened. Return the chicken to the wok or skillet. Cook, stirring thoroughly to mix, until heated through. Remove to a serving dish. Serve immediately.

ABOUT CHICKEN FRICASSEES, STEWS, AND OTHER BRAISED DISHES

The world's cuisines boast a wealth of fricassees, stews, and ragouts made with chicken. Definitions of these dishes overlap, but all involve braising chicken in liquid. After cooking, the liquid becomes a flavorful sauce or gravy, which can be thickened with flour or egg yolks or enriched with cream. Many of these dishes were originally made with hens past their egg-laying prime, whose tough, stringy flesh required slow braising in order to become tender. Today, with hens in short supply at the supermarket, most cooks choose ordinary young chickens instead.

Braising is perhaps the easiest and most forgiving of all cooking methods for chicken. Most people consider roasted, broiled, fried, or sautéed chicken disappointing when the white meat has been cooked to the point of becoming firm and dry. But they are happy with a thoroughly cooked braised chicken breast, because the sauce or gravy with which the chicken is served succeeds in masking the meat's dryness.

CHICKEN FRICASSEE *4 or 5 servings*

This delicate and creamy dish of chicken and vegetables has long been an American favorite.

Rinse and pat dry:

3½ to 4½ pounds chicken parts

Separate the legs into thighs and drumsticks; cut each breast half diagonally in half through the bone. If you wish, remove the skin. Sprinkle the chicken with:

Salt and ground black or white pepper to taste

Heat in a heavy 8- to 10-inch skillet over medium heat until fragrant and golden:

4 tablespoons (½ stick) unsalted butter

Place as many chicken pieces in the pan as will fit comfortably and cook, turning once, until pale golden, 3 to

5 minutes on each side. Remove the chicken to a plate and brown the remaining pieces in the same manner. Add to the fat in the pan:

1½ cups chopped onions

Cook, stirring occasionally, until the onions are tender but not browned, about 5 minutes. Stir in:

⅓ cup all-purpose flour

Cook, stirring, for 1 minute, then remove the pan from the heat and whisk in:

2 cups hot water
1¾ cups chicken stock

Whisking constantly, bring the mixture to a boil over high heat. Add:

8 ounces mushrooms, sliced (2⅓ cups)
3 medium carrots, peeled and diced (1 cup)
2 large or 3 medium celery stalks, diced (1 cup)
½ teaspoon dried thyme
1 teaspoon salt
½ teaspoon ground black or white pepper

Return the chicken pieces with all accumulated juices to the pan and bring to a simmer. Reduce the heat so that the liquid barely bubbles. Cover tightly and cook until the dark meat pieces exude clear juices when pricked with a fork, 20 to 30 minutes. Skim off the fat from around the sides of the pan with a spoon. If you wish, stir in:

¼ to ½ cup heavy cream

Season to taste with:

Salt and ground white or black pepper
Several drops of fresh lemon juice

The sooner the chicken is served, the juicier it will be. However, the dish can be made ahead. To serve within 1 hour, simply cover the pot and slide to a warm corner of the stove. Otherwise, let the chicken cool to tepid, then cover and refrigerate for up to 3 days.

CHICKEN AND DUMPLINGS

4 or 5 servings

Prepare, undercooking the chicken slightly:

Chicken Fricassee, above

Degrease the pan juices and season the fricassee. Push the chicken pieces down so that they are submerged in gravy and drop in spoonfuls over the top:

Dumplings, 321, or Cornmeal Dumplings, 322

Cover and cook as directed for dumplings. Serve immediately.

CHICKEN ÉTOUFFÉE

4 to 6 servings

This is the classic Cajun way of making chicken fricassee. To give this dish its characteristic dark color and deep flavor, brown the chicken pieces thoroughly and cook the roux until nearly as dark as chocolate.

Rinse and pat dry:

4 to 5 pounds chicken parts

Mix together:

1 teaspoon paprika
1 teaspoon dried thyme
1 teaspoon salt
½ teaspoon ground black pepper
½ teaspoon dried basil
¼ teaspoon ground red pepper

Rub the spice mixture all over the chicken pieces. Pour into a doubled brown paper bag:

1 cup all-purpose flour

Shake 4 pieces chicken at a time in the bag to coat with flour; remove and shake off the excess. Repeat until all the chicken is coated. Reserve the flour. Heat in a wide, heavy skillet over medium-high heat until shimmery:

3 tablespoons vegetable oil

Add as many pieces of chicken to the skillet as will fit without crowding and brown on both sides to the color of dark toast, about 5 minutes each side. Remove the chicken, brown the remaining pieces in the same manner, and then remove them from the skillet as well. Remove all but about 3 tablespoons of the fat in the skillet. Reduce the heat to medium. Using a wooden spoon, stir in 3 tablespoons of the reserved flour. Cook, stirring constantly, until the roux is almost as dark as milk chocolate. This may take as long as 20 minutes. Stir in:

1 cup chopped onions
½ cup chopped celery
¼ cup chopped red bell peppers
¼ cup chopped green bell peppers
¼ cup chopped andouille sausage or smoked ham

Cook, stirring, until the vegetables are golden brown, 5 to 6 minutes. The roux will continue to darken to a deep mahogany color. Add:

2 tablespoons chopped garlic
¼ teaspoon dried sage, crumbled
¼ teaspoon dried thyme

Stir well and cook for 1 minute more. Stir in:

2 cups chicken stock
3 tablespoons tomato paste
1 tablespoon Worcestershire sauce
¼ teaspoon hot red pepper sauce, or to taste

Stirring constantly, bring the sauce to a simmer. Return the chicken pieces with all accumulated juices to the skillet and bring the liquid back to a simmer. Reduce the heat so that the sauce bubbles gently. Cover the pan and cook, turning the pieces occasionally, until the chicken exudes clear juices when pierced with a fork, about 30 minutes. Remove the chicken to a plate. Skim the fat from the sauce with a spoon. Add:

½ cup finely chopped scallions
¼ cup chopped fresh parsley

Boil until the sauce is thickened. Season the sauce generously with:

Salt and ground black pepper to taste
Hot red pepper sauce

Return the chicken to the pan and heat through. Serve with:

Hot cooked rice

COUNTRY CAPTAIN

4 servings

Versions of this fragrant, subtly sweet chicken curry have been prepared in American kitchens since colonial times.

Rinse and pat dry:

3½ to 4½ pounds chicken parts

Separate the legs into thighs and drumsticks; cut each breast half diagonally in half through the bone. Coat the chicken pieces on all sides with:

⅔ cup all-purpose flour

Heat in a wide, heavy pan over medium-high heat until fragrant and golden:

3 tablespoons unsalted butter

Add as many chicken pieces to the pan as will fit without crowding and brown to a deep golden color on both sides, 3 to 4 minutes each side. Remove the chicken to a plate and brown the remaining pieces in the same manner. When all the chicken has been browned and removed, add to the fat and cook until tender and golden around the edges:

2 cups chopped onions
1 large green bell pepper, diced

Stir in:

1 tablespoon curry powder
1 teaspoon ground ginger
½ teaspoon ground cinnamon
¼ teaspoon ground cloves
¼ teaspoon freshly grated or ground nutmeg

Cook slowly, stirring, for 1 minute. Add:

One 14- to 16-ounce can whole tomatoes, with juice
⅔ cup chicken stock
⅔ cup dried currants or raisins
3 tablespoons strained fresh lemon juice
1 tablespoon packed dark brown sugar
2 to 3 cloves garlic, minced
½ teaspoon dried thyme
½ teaspoon salt
¼ teaspoon ground black pepper

Using a wooden spoon, lightly mash the tomatoes against the sides of the pan and scrape the bottom to dissolve the browned bits. Return the chicken to the pan and bring the liquid to a simmer over high heat. Reduce the heat so that the liquid barely bubbles. Cover tightly and cook, turning the pieces occasionally, until the chicken exudes clear juices when pricked deeply with a fork, 20 to 30 minutes. Remove the chicken to a plate. Skim the fat from the pan gravy with a spoon; if the gravy seems watery, boil it down over high heat. Return the chicken to the pan and heat through. Serve with:

Hot cooked rice

BRUNSWICK STEW

6 to 8 servings

This Southern specialty is commonly served as a side dish with barbecue but can easily stand on its own as a main course. Chicken, lima beans, and corn are the main ingredients, with such meats as rabbit, pork, or even squirrel sometimes added to the pot as well. This version includes barbecue sauce, which makes it especially rich and thick. For a delicious twist, remove the cooked chicken from the pot, cover it with foil, and prepare Cornmeal Dumplings, 322, in the sauce.

Rinse and pat dry:

5 pounds chicken parts

Season with:

Salt and ground black pepper to taste
½ teaspoon ground red pepper (optional)

Heat in a large, heavy Dutch oven over medium-high heat until shimmery:

2 tablespoons bacon fat or vegetable oil

Add the chicken pieces in small batches and brown on all sides; remove them to a plate as they are done. Remove all but 2 tablespoons of the fat in the pan. Reduce the heat to medium and add:

1 cup chopped onions
1 cup chopped celery

Cook, stirring occasionally, until the vegetables are just tender, 5 to 7 minutes. Return the chicken with the accumulated juices to the pan. Add:

3 cups lima beans, fresh or frozen
2 cups barbecued pork or smoked ham, cut into ½-inch chunks (optional)
1½ to 2 cups chopped seeded peeled tomatoes, fresh or canned
1 cup barbecue sauce
1 cup tomato puree
1 cup chicken stock or water
1 tablespoon minced garlic (optional)
2 bay leaves
Salt and ground black pepper to taste
Ground red pepper to taste

Bring the stew to a boil over high heat. Reduce the heat to low, cover the pan, and simmer gently until the chicken is nearly tender, 35 to 45 minutes. Add:

3 cups corn kernels, fresh or frozen

Simmer, uncovered, for 10 minutes more. Skim any fat from the gravy with a spoon. Season the stew to taste with:

Salt and ground black pepper
Several drops of Worcestershire sauce
Several drops of hot red pepper sauce

If you wish, sprinkle the top with:

Minced fresh parsley
Toasted fresh breadcrumbs

CHICKEN CACCIATORE

4 servings

Cacciatore means "hunter's style" in Italian, and there are countless versions of this dish. Italian hunters who cook always seem to have tomatoes and olives handy. Flavors blossom when this dish is cooked a day ahead, just be sure to undercook slightly and reheat slowly to finish cooking. Rabbit can also be used in this dish. The flavor and aroma produced by the simple combination of its basic ingredients—chicken or rabbit, tomatoes, onions, and sometimes mushrooms—must not be missed. Polenta is a traditional companion.

Rinse and pat dry:

3½ to 4½ pounds chicken parts

Season with:

Salt and ground black pepper to taste

Heat in a large, heavy skillet over medium-high heat until shimmery and fragrant:

3 tablespoons olive oil

Add the chicken pieces in small batches and brown on all sides; remove them to a plate as they are done. Remove all but 2 tablespoons of the fat in the pan. Reduce the heat to medium and add:

1 cup chopped onions
1 bay leaf
1½ teaspoons chopped fresh rosemary, or ½ teaspoon dried, crumbled
1 teaspoon minced fresh sage leaves, or ½ teaspoon dried, crumbled

Cook, stirring, until the onions are golden brown, about 5 minutes. Add:

1 large clove garlic, minced

Cook about 30 seconds more, being careful not to brown the garlic. Return the chicken to the skillet and pour in:

½ cup dry red or white wine

Cook over medium-high heat until all the wine is evaporated, turning the chicken and scraping up the browned bits on the bottom with a wooden spoon. Add:

8 ounces canned whole tomatoes, with juice, crushed with your hands
¾ cup chicken stock

Reduce the heat to low, cover, and simmer gently for 25 minutes. Add:

½ cup oil-cured black olives, pitted and sliced (optional)
8 ounces mushrooms, sliced

Cook, covered, for 10 minutes. Uncover the pan and boil the pan juices over high heat until slightly thickened. Taste and adjust the seasonings.

COQ AU VIN

4 servings

When the old rooster, or *coq*, lost his crow, he would find himself the main ingredient in this classic French country fricassee. This dish is most commonly made with red wine, but white wine also can be used. If you would like to try a white, choose one that is flavorful and fruity, such as Riesling or Chardonnay.

Rinse and pat dry:

3½ to 4½ pounds chicken parts

Season with:

Salt and ground black pepper to taste

Cut into sticks ¼ inch wide:

4 ounces thick-cut bacon

Fry the bacon in a large, heavy Dutch oven over medium-high heat until it is nicely browned and most of its fat is rendered. Remove the bacon to a plate. Add as many pieces of chicken to the pan as will fit without crowding and brown until deep golden on both sides, about 7 minutes. Remove the chicken pieces and brown the remaining pieces in the same manner. Remove all but about 3 tablespoons of the fat in the pan. Add:

1 cup chopped onions
½ cup chopped peeled carrots

Cook, stirring occasionally, until the vegetables are tender, about 10 minutes. Stir in:

3 tablespoons all-purpose flour

Reduce the heat to low. Cook, stirring constantly, until the roux just begins to turn light brown, about 5 minutes. Stir in:

3 cups dry red wine
1 cup chicken stock
2 tablespoons tomato paste
2 bay leaves
½ teaspoon dried thyme
½ teaspoon dried marjoram or oregano, crumbled

Increase the heat to high and bring the sauce to a boil, stirring constantly. Return the bacon and chicken with any accumulated juices to the pan. Return the sauce to a boil, then reduce the heat so that the liquid barely simmers. Cover and cook until the chicken exudes clear juices when pricked with a fork, 25 to 35 minutes. Meanwhile, measure:

1 to 2 cups pearl onions

Cut a tiny slice from both ends of each onion. Cover with boiling water and let stand for 1 minute. Drain in a sieve, rinse with cold water, and pinch off the skins. Heat in a wide skillet over medium-high heat until fragrant and golden:

2 to 3 tablespoons unsalted butter

Add the onions and cook, stirring often, until they are lightly browned and just tender, 5 to 8 minutes. Add:

8 ounces mushrooms, sliced

Cook, tossing, until the mushrooms give up their juices. Remove from the heat. Remove the cooked chicken to a platter and cover with aluminum foil to keep warm. Bring the sauce to a boil over high heat and reduce until syrupy, using a spoon to skim off the fat as it accumulates. Add the onions and mushrooms with all juices to the sauce and heat through. Season with:

Salt and ground black pepper to taste

Pour the sauce over the chicken. If you wish, sprinkle with:

2 to 3 tablespoons minced fresh parsley

Serve with:

Boiled potatoes or noodles

BASQUE CHICKEN

4 servings

A favorite French bistro dish.

Rinse and pat dry:

3½ to 4 pounds chicken parts

Heat in a wide, heavy Dutch oven over medium-high heat until fragrant:

3 tablespoons olive oil

Lightly brown the chicken in 2 batches in the hot oil, removing the browned chicken to a plate. Remove all but 3 tablespoons of the fat in the pan. Return the chicken to the pan and add:

2 pounds red and/or yellow bell peppers, cut into ½-inch strips
4 small fresh jalapeño peppers, seeded and minced
Four 2-ounce slices ham, cut into ½-inch squares
¼ cup chopped garlic (about 12 cloves)
¾ teaspoon salt
½ teaspoon ground black pepper

Place the pan over low to medium heat, cover tightly, and cook at a quiet sizzle, stirring often, until the chicken is cooked through and the peppers are soft, about 45 minutes.

Meanwhile, prepare the sauce. Heat in a large saucepan over medium-high heat until fragrant:

2 tablespoons olive oil

Add:

2 to 3 cups chopped onions

Cook, stirring often, until the onions are tender but not browned, about 7 minutes. Add:

2 pounds fresh tomatoes, peeled, seeded, and chopped, or one 28-ounce can whole tomatoes, with juice, seeded and crushed
½ teaspoon salt
½ teaspoon ground black pepper

Bring to a boil, then reduce the heat to medium. Simmer, stirring often, until the sauce has thickened, about 20 minutes. Skim off any excess fat from the chicken with a spoon. Season both the chicken and sauce with:

Salt and ground black pepper to taste

Spoon onto a serving platter or divide among 4 plates:

4 to 6 cups cooked white rice

Arrange the chicken and pepper mixture over the rice.

CHICKEN PAPRIKASH (PAPRIKÁS CSIRKE)

4 servings

This rich and delicious dish requires genuine Hungarian paprika, which is available both sweet and hot. Sweet paprika is what you want, though you can add a little hot if you like spice. Once opened, Hungarian paprika must be stored tightly closed in the refrigerator or, even better, in the freezer to maintain freshness.

Rinse and pat dry:

3½ to 4½ pounds chicken parts

Season generously with:

Salt and ground black pepper to taste

Heat in a wide, heavy skillet over medium-high heat until fragrant:

2 tablespoons butter or lard

Add as many pieces of chicken to the skillet as will fit without crowding and cook until golden on both sides, about 5 minutes. Remove the chicken to a plate and brown the remaining chicken in the same manner. Add to the fat remaining in the skillet:

3 cups very thinly sliced onions

Reduce the heat slightly. Cook, stirring, until the onions just begin to color, about 10 minutes. Sprinkle over the onions:

¼ cup sweet Hungarian paprika
2 tablespoons all-purpose flour

Cook, stirring, for 1 minute. Stir in:

1½ cups chicken stock
1 tablespoon minced garlic
1 large bay leaf
½ teaspoon salt
½ teaspoon ground black pepper

Bring the mixture to a boil, stirring constantly. Return the chicken with all accumulated juices to the skillet. Reduce the heat so that the liquid barely bubbles, cover the skillet, and cook, turning the chicken once or twice, until the dark meat pieces release clear juices when pricked with a fork, 20 to 30 minutes. Remove the chicken to a plate. Discard the bay leaf. Let the sauce settle, then skim the fat off the surface with a spoon. Boil the sauce over high heat until very thick, almost pasty. Remove the skillet from the heat and blend thoroughly into the sauce:

1 to 1½ cups sour cream

Return the sauce to high heat and boil until thickened. Season to taste with:

Salt and ground black pepper
Several drops of fresh lemon juice

Return the chicken to the skillet and heat through. Serve with:

Hot cooked noodles or spätzle

ARROZ CON POLLO (CHICKEN AND RICE)

4 servings

In this popular dish, chicken and rice are cooked together, blending into a savory whole. With a salad, arroz con pollo becomes a complete meal.

Rinse and pat dry:

3½ to 4½ pounds chicken parts

Separate the chicken legs into thighs and drumsticks; cut each breast half diagonally in half through the bone. Season the chicken pieces with:

Salt and ground black pepper to taste

Heat in a wide, heavy pan large enough to hold the chicken pieces in a single layer over medium-high heat until shimmery:

2 tablespoons vegetable or olive oil

Add the chicken pieces and brown well on all sides, 7 to 10 minutes. Remove the chicken from the pan. Pour off all but 3 tablespoons of the fat. Reduce the heat to medium-low and add:

2 cups chopped onions
1 green bell pepper, diced (optional)
4 ounces smoked ham, finely diced (about ½ cup)

Cook, stirring occasionally, until the onions are tender but not brown, about 5 minutes. Add:

2 cups medium- or long-grain white rice

Cook, stirring, until the grains are coated with fat. Add:

1 tablespoon minced garlic
1 tablespoon paprika
1 teaspoon salt
½ teaspoon ground black pepper

Cook, stirring, for 1 minute. Add:

3 cups chicken stock
½ teaspoon dried oregano (optional)
¼ teaspoon loosely packed saffron threads (optional)

Bring to a boil over high heat, scraping the bottom of the pan with a wooden spoon to loosen the browned bits. Nestle the chicken pieces in the rice and pour in any accumulated juices. Cover the pan tightly and simmer over medium-low heat for 20 minutes. Stir in:

1 cup cooked fresh peas or unthawed frozen peas
⅓ cup drained bottled pimientos or roasted red peppers, cut into thin 1-inch-long strips
¼ cup chopped pitted brine-cured green olives

Cover and cook until the rice is tender, about 10 minutes more. Taste and adjust the seasonings.

CHICKEN CHILI VERDE

4 servings

Chili verde can be served with rice, beans, and corn tortillas or used as a filling for burritos, tacos, or enchiladas. You can make this recipe with 2 to 3 cups leftover chicken or turkey and 2 cups canned chicken broth.

Combine in a medium pan:

2½ pounds chicken thighs and/or drumsticks, or mixed chicken parts
4 cups chicken stock, or 4 cups water and 1 teaspoon salt

Bring to a boil over high heat, then reduce the heat so that the liquid simmers gently. Cook, partially covered, for 30 minutes. Remove the chicken from the broth and let stand until cool enough to handle. Remove the skin and bones, keeping the meat in the largest chunks possible. Skim the fat from the stock with a spoon. (For an especially flavorful dish, chop the bones with a cleaver and return with the skin to the stock; simmer for 1 hour and degrease.)

Heat in a large, heavy pan over medium heat until shimmery:

2 tablespoons vegetable oil

Add:

1 cup chopped onions
¼ cup chopped celery
1 tablespoon chopped garlic

Cook, stirring occasionally, until the vegetables are tender, about 5 minutes. Sprinkle with:

2 teaspoons chili powder
1 teaspoon ground cumin
½ teaspoon dried oregano
½ teaspoon salt

Cook, stirring, until fragrant, about 1 minute. Remove the pan from the heat. Have ready:

1 cup canned tomatillos or 4 large or 6 medium fresh tomatillos

If using canned tomatillos, drain and chop. If using fresh, drop into about 6 cups of rapidly boiling water, boil for 1 minute, slip off the papery husks, and rinse well; cut out and discard the cores and dice the flesh. Add the tomatillos to the vegetable mixture. Separate the leaves and stems of:

1 large bunch cilantro

Finely chop the cilantro stems and leaves separately. Add the stems to the pan. Add 2 cups of the chicken stock along with:

3 fresh Anaheim or poblano peppers, roasted, 402, peeled, and chopped, or one 7-ounce can diced green chilis, drained
2 fresh jalapeño peppers, seeded and finely chopped (optional)

Gently simmer the sauce, uncovered, for 10 minutes. Add the reserved chicken and ½ cup of the chopped cilantro leaves along with:

2 tablespoons fresh lime juice

Simmer for 5 to 15 minutes more, depending on how tender you prefer the chicken. Season with:

Salt to taste

Garnish with the remaining cilantro leaves.

CHICKEN TAGINE WITH CHICKPEAS

4 servings

Tagine refers to the cooking vessel in which Moroccan cooks prepare this and other similar stews. A hint of cinnamon provides a characteristically North African flavor. This dish is quickly and easily prepared in a single pot with ingredients that you are likely to have on hand.

Remove the skin from, rinse, and pat dry:

3½ to 4 pounds chicken parts

Heat in a large, heavy pan over medium-high heat until fragrant and golden:

2 tablespoons unsalted butter

Lightly brown the chicken in 2 batches in the hot butter and remove to a plate. Add to the pan:

2 cups chopped onions
½ cup chopped scallions

Cook, stirring often, until the onions are tender, 5 to 7 minutes. Stir in:

One 19-ounce can chickpeas, drained and lightly rinsed
1 cup water
1 tablespoon minced garlic
1 teaspoon ground ginger
¾ teaspoon salt
½ teaspoon ground black pepper
½ teaspoon ground cinnamon
⅛ to ¼ teaspoon ground red pepper

Return the chicken pieces with all accumulated juices to the pan and gently turn to coat.

Bring the mixture to a boil, then reduce the heat so that the liquid just simmers. Cover tightly and cook, turning the chicken once or twice, until the dark meat releases clear juices when pierced with a fork, 35 to 45 minutes. Remove from the heat and stir in:

½ cup chopped fresh parsley and/or cilantro

Season with:

Salt and ground black pepper to taste

CHICKEN CURRY

4 servings

All of the flavors work together here; no spice is obvious, yet all are essential to the balance of this true Indian chicken curry.

Remove the skin from:

3½ pounds chicken parts

Separate the legs into thighs and drumsticks; cut each breast half diagonally in half through the bone. Rinse the chicken and pat dry. Heat in a heavy, wide skillet over medium-high heat until shimmery:

2 tablespoons vegetable oil

Add and cook, stirring occasionally, until golden brown, 7 to 10 minutes:

1 large onion, thinly sliced

Add and cook, stirring, for 30 seconds:

2 teaspoons very finely minced garlic
2 teaspoons very finely minced peeled fresh ginger
1½ teaspoons Garam Masala, 1061
1 teaspoon ground turmeric

Add the chicken and cook, stirring, until the chicken loses its raw color, 2 to 3 minutes. Stir in:

½ cup low-fat yogurt

Cook, stirring occasionally, over high heat until the liquid has reduced and thickened and the oil separates and pools, 3 to 5 minutes. Stir in:

1 cup water
2 tablespoons chopped fresh cilantro
1 fresh serrano or jalapeño pepper, quartered lengthwise
¾ teaspoon salt

Reduce the heat so that the liquid bubbles gently, cover, and cook until the dark meat pieces release clear juices when pierced with a fork, 30 to 40 minutes. Remove the chicken to a platter or wide bowl and cover to keep warm. If the sauce is thin and runny, uncover the pot and boil over high heat to reduce and thicken it. Pour over the chicken. Serve with:

Hot cooked rice
Coriander and Mint Chutney, 66

DORO WAT (ETHIOPIAN CHICKEN IN RED PEPPER SAUCE)

4 servings

Doro wat is chicken stewed slowly in a thick, spicy, scarlet sauce. The dish depends on two staples of the Ethiopian kitchen: *niter kibbeh,* or spiced butter, and *berbere,* a mixture of ground red pepper and spices, which may be bought at grocery stores catering to an African clientele. The *berbere* outlined in this recipe has been toned down for the Western palate. If you wish to make a more authentic version, substitute additional ground red pepper for some—or all—of the paprika. The slow caramelizing of the onions in a dry pot requires patience and vigilance but is essential to the flavor of the dish.

Melt in a small, heavy saucepan over low heat:

8 tablespoons (1 stick) unsalted butter, cut into pieces

Add:

3 tablespoons coarsely chopped onions
1 tablespoon minced garlic
1 tablespoon minced peeled fresh ginger
One 1-inch piece cinnamon stick
¾ teaspoon ground turmeric
Heaping ¼ teaspoon whole cloves
⅛ teaspoon freshly grated or ground nutmeg
1 cardamom pod, crushed (optional)

Simmer, uncovered, until the sediment falls to the bottom of the pan and the onions are brown, 15 to 25 minutes. Strain through a fine sieve. Rinse:

3½ to 4½ pounds chicken parts

Remove and discard the skin. Separate the legs into thighs and drumsticks; cut each breast half diagonally in half through the bone. Rub the chicken pieces with:

½ lemon

Sprinkle generously with:

Salt

Cover loosely with wax paper and let stand at room temperature. Place a very large, heavy pan or Dutch oven over medium heat. Add to the dry pan:

3 to 4 cups finely chopped onions

Cook, stirring constantly, until the onions are very dry and beginning to brown, about 10 minutes. Reduce the heat and slowly pour in:

¼ cup water

Cook, stirring, until the onions are colored deep brown, about 10 minutes longer. Be very careful not to let the onions burn. Remove the pan from the heat. In a separate bowl, make *berbere* by mixing:

¼ cup paprika
1 to 3 teaspoons ground red pepper to taste
1 teaspoon ground ginger
½ teaspoon ground cinnamon
¼ teaspoon ground cloves or allspice
¼ teaspoon ground coriander (optional)

Stir into the onions, then add, making a smooth paste:

½ cup warm water

Stir in the spiced butter along with:

1 tablespoon minced garlic
1 tablespoon minced peeled fresh ginger
1 teaspoon freshly grated or ground nutmeg
1½ teaspoons salt

Over medium heat, bring to a simmer, and cook, stirring, for 1 minute. Add the chicken and turn to coat well. Return to a simmer, then reduce the heat so that the sauce barely bubbles. Cover and cook for 30 minutes, stirring often to prevent sticking. Stir in:

1½ cups dry wine or water
1 teaspoon ground black pepper
4 to 6 hard-boiled eggs, peeled (optional)

Cook, covered, until the chicken is very tender and the butter begins to rise to the top, about 10 minutes. Stir the butter back into the sauce. Serve with:

Hot cooked rice

CHINESE SOY-BRAISED CHICKEN

4 main-course or 8 appetizer servings

When braised slowly in soy sauce, sugar, and spices, chicken takes on a beautiful deep brown color and an irresistible sweet-salty flavor. This dish can be served as a main course but is more commonly presented as an appetizer. Chinese chefs typically hack the cooked chicken through the bone into small pieces with a cleaver. If you wish to do the same, you must use a thin, lightweight, razor-sharp cleaver. The heavy cleavers commonly used in American home kitchens will splinter the bones.

Remove the skin, then rinse and pat dry:

2 large rock Cornish hens or 3 to 3½ pounds mixed chicken parts or thighs

If using hens, divide the birds in half, removing the backbones. Combine in a large, heavy Dutch oven:

4 cups water
¾ cup soy sauce
⅓ cup sugar
⅓ cup Chinese black vinegar or balsamic vinegar
¼ cup chopped peeled fresh ginger
4 large cloves garlic, lightly mashed and peeled
2 large whole star anise or 4 teaspoons star anise pieces or fennel seeds
One 3-inch cinnamon stick
¼ teaspoon red pepper flakes
Strained juice and ½ rind of 1 medium orange

Bring to a boil over high heat, then reduce the heat and simmer, covered, for 5 minutes. Add the chicken to the pan and reduce the heat so that the liquid barely bubbles. Cover and cook for 35 minutes. Remove from the heat and let stand for 30 to 60 minutes. Remove the chicken to a cutting board and brush liberally with:

Toasted sesame oil

Arrange on a platter or individual plates:

6 to 8 cups mixed baby salad greens

Top the greens with the chicken. Drizzle some of the poaching liquid over and garnish with:

Sesame seeds, toasted
Chopped scallions
Fresh cilantro leaves

ABOUT FRIED, DEEP-FRIED, AND OVEN-FRIED CHICKEN

You can produce fried chicken in a variety of ways, including baking it in the oven. Fried chicken is defined not so much by the cooking process as by the result, which should be juicy, succulent chicken covered in a crispy crust that is not at all greasy.

PAN-FRIED OR SAUTÉED CHICKEN *4 servings*

The quickest and simplest of all fried chicken recipes. Because it is not coated with flour, the chicken does not have a true crust, but the skin is deliciously brown and crispy.

Rinse and pat dry:

3½ to 4 pounds chicken parts

Season generously with:

Salt and ground black pepper to taste

Heat in a large, heavy skillet over medium-high heat until golden and fragrant:

1 tablespoon unsalted butter
1 tablespoon vegetable oil

Arrange the chicken pieces skin side down in a single layer in the skillet. Fry until the chicken is nicely browned on the bottom and detaches itself easily from the skillet, about 5 minutes. Turn the chicken with tongs and cook until nicely browned on the second side, about 5 minutes more. Reduce the heat to medium and continue to cook the chicken, turning often, until the dark meat pieces exude clear juices when pricked with a fork, about 20 minutes more. Remove the chicken to a platter. If you wish, prepare in the pan:

Poultry Pan Sauce or Gravy, 579, or a sauce for Sautéed Boneless, Skinless Chicken Breasts, 587 to 588

FRIED CHICKEN *4 servings*

This chicken has the crackling crisp skin and distinctive mahogany color that are the hallmarks of this dish as prepared by the best Southern cooks. The buttermilk marinade promotes tenderness. Use a cast-iron skillet if possible, for it allows the chicken to achieve the prized deep color without charring. Frying the chicken in vegetable shortening rather than oil gives the crust a snapping crispness and, because shortening is more highly refined than oil, the odor-causing compounds are removed and it leaves less odor in the kitchen. A final important tip: The crust will stay crisper longer if you drain the chicken on a rack rather than on a paper bag or paper towels.

Rinse and pat dry:

3½ to 4 pounds chicken parts

Separate the chicken legs into thighs and drumsticks; cut each breast half diagonally in half through the bone. Stir together in a large bowl:

1½ cups buttermilk
1 teaspoon salt
½ teaspoon ground black pepper

Add the chicken and turn to coat well. Cover the bowl with plastic wrap or remove the chicken and buttermilk to a sealable plastic bag. Refrigerate for 2 to 12 hours. Shake to mix in a doubled brown paper bag:

2 cups all-purpose flour
2 teaspoons salt
1 teaspoon ground black pepper
Pinch of ground red pepper (optional)

Shake the chicken a few pieces at a time in the bag until well coated. Let dry on a rack at room temperature for 15 to 30 minutes. Place a deep, heavy skillet, preferably cast iron, large enough to hold the chicken pieces in a single layer over medium-high heat and add:

3 cups solid vegetable shortening

There should be enough shortening in the skillet to measure about ½ inch. Heat until a small corner of a chicken piece causes vigorous bubbling when dipped into the fat, about 350°F on a deep-fry thermometer.

Being careful not to spatter yourself, gently lay the chicken pieces skin side down in the hot fat and cover. Cook for 10 minutes, checking after 5 minutes and moving the pieces if they are coloring unevenly or turning the heat down if the chicken is browning too quickly. (At this point, the fat should be bubbling and register between 250° and 300°F on a thermometer.) Turn the chicken pieces with tongs and cook, uncovered, until the second side is richly browned, 10 to 12 minutes more. Remove the chicken to a rack set over a baking sheet. If not serving immediately, remove the chicken, still on the rack, to an oven warmed at the lowest setting. If you wish, prepare in the pan:

Poultry Pan Sauce or Gravy, 579

Chicken that is not to be served hot may be safely held at room temperature, still on the rack and loosely covered with wax paper, for several hours. It will be crisper and juicier than if chilled. Leftovers, of course, must be refrigerated.

CRISPY-CRUNCHY DEEP-FRIED CHICKEN

4 servings

If plain fried chicken is not crusty enough to suit your taste, try this instead. This chicken is almost as much crust as it is meat. For this recipe, you might consider buying a small chicken and cutting it into ten serving pieces yourself (see How to Cut Up Poultry, 569). Packs of mixed parts often contain oversized pieces, which can become excessively dark on the outside before the chicken has cooked through.

Rinse and pat dry:

3½ pounds chicken parts, or 1 whole chicken (about 3½ pounds), cut into 10 serving pieces

Separate the legs into thighs and drumsticks; cut each breast half diagonally in half through the bone. Sprinkle the chicken very generously with:

Salt and ground black pepper to taste

Whisk thoroughly in a medium bowl:

2 large eggs
⅓ cup plus 1 tablespoon milk
1 teaspoon salt

Mix together on a plate:

1½ cups all-purpose flour
2 teaspoons salt
2 teaspoons ground black pepper

Heat in a deep-fat fryer or deep, heavy pot to 350°F:

3 pounds solid vegetable shortening

There should be at least 2 inches fat in the pot. Toss the breast pieces and wings in the flour mixture, then remove to the egg mixture and turn until thoroughly moistened on all sides. One at a time, lift the pieces out of the egg, letting the excess drip off, roll in the flour mixture until completely coated, and slip into the hot fat. Fry for 10 minutes, turning the pieces several times with tongs and keeping the fat between 320° and 360°F. Remove the pieces to a baking sheet lined with paper towels, quickly turn to blot up the excess oil, then slip into a barely warm oven. Repeat the same procedure with the thighs and drumsticks, frying the pieces for 15 minutes rather than 10. The liver may be coated and fried just until golden, about 2 minutes. Serve immediately. If you wish, accompany with:

Sauce Rémoulade, 73, or warm honey

OVEN-FRIED CHICKEN WITH PARMESAN CHEESE

4 to 6 servings

Crisp, savory, and quickly made, this oven-fried chicken is equally good hot or cold.

Position a rack in the center of the oven. Preheat the oven to 350°F. Lightly oil a baking sheet. Rinse and pat dry:

12 chicken drumsticks, thighs, or breast halves, or a combination

Mix in a medium bowl:

1 cup whole-milk or low-fat yogurt
1 cup sour cream
½ cup Dijon mustard
1 tablespoon minced garlic

Combine in a wide, shallow bowl:

3 cups dry unseasoned breadcrumbs
1 cup grated Parmesan cheese
1 teaspoon ground sage
1 teaspoon dried oregano
1 teaspoon salt
½ teaspoon ground black pepper

Coat each piece of chicken with the yogurt mixture, then roll in the crumb mixture, patting with your fingers to make the crumbs adhere. Arrange the chicken on the baking sheet. Bake until the coating is nicely browned and the dark meat pieces exude clear juices when pricked with a fork, 45 to 60 minutes. Serve immediately or at room temperature.

OVEN-FRIED CHICKEN WITH A CORNMEAL CRUST

4 servings

Oven-frying delivers a crisp, crunchy crust with a minimum of fat. This chicken is terrific served at room temperature as part of a summer picnic. If serving it cold, you can remove the skin before coating and baking, which also reduces the fat substantially. The marinated chicken baked without the coating is also delicious and quick to prepare.

Rinse and pat dry:

3½ pounds chicken parts

Whisk together in a bowl large enough to hold the chicken:

¾ cup buttermilk or whole-milk or low-fat yogurt
¼ cup strained fresh lemon juice
¼ cup olive oil
2 tablespoons finely minced shallots
1 tablespoon finely minced fresh thyme or rosemary, or 1 teaspoon dried
2 teaspoons salt
2 teaspoons chili powder
1 teaspoon grated lemon zest (optional)

Add the chicken to the yogurt mixture and turn to coat. Cover and refrigerate for 2 to 4 hours.

Position a rack in the upper third of the oven. Preheat the oven to 425°F. Lightly oil a baking sheet.

Combine in a wide, shallow bowl:

⅔ cup grated Parmesan or aged Monterey Jack cheese
½ cup dry unseasoned breadcrumbs
½ cup cornmeal
3 tablespoons minced fresh parsley
1 teaspoon chili powder
1 teaspoon salt
½ teaspoon ground black pepper

Remove the chicken from the marinade and shake off the excess. Whisk together in a shallow bowl:

2 large eggs
2 tablespoons melted butter

Dip the chicken pieces in the egg mixture, then coat with the cornmeal mixture, patting with your fingers to make the crumbs adhere. The chicken can be prepared to this point up to 3 hours in advance and kept, uncovered, in the refrigerator. Arrange the chicken skin side up on the baking sheet. If you wish, drizzle over the chicken:

2 to 3 tablespoons melted butter or olive oil

Bake until the chicken is crisp and golden, 35 to 40 minutes. Serve immediately or at room temperature.

OVEN-FRIED CHICKEN WITH A CORN FLAKE CRUST

4 servings

To reduce the fat, remove the chicken skin before coating.

Position a rack in the upper third of the oven. Preheat the oven to 350°F. Lightly oil a baking sheet.

Rinse and pat dry:

3½ pounds chicken parts

Season with:

Salt and ground black pepper to taste

Whisk together in a shallow bowl:

2 large eggs
¼ cup milk

Combine in a wide, shallow bowl:

2½ cups crushed corn flakes
2 teaspoons salt
½ teaspoon ground black pepper

Dip the chicken pieces in the egg mixture, then coat with the corn flake mixture, patting with your fingers to make the crumbs adhere. The chicken can be prepared to this point up to 3 hours in advance and kept, uncovered, in the refrigerator. Arrange the chicken skin side up on the baking sheet. If you wish, drizzle over the chicken:

2 to 3 tablespoons melted butter

Bake until the chicken is crisp and golden, 45 to 60 minutes. Serve immediately or at room temperature.

ABOUT CREAMED CHICKEN AND TURKEY DISHES, POT PIES, CASSEROLES, AND CROQUETTES

Creamed chicken or turkey consists of boneless, skinless pieces of white or dark meat cloaked in a thick, rich sauce made from butter, flour, poultry stock, and milk. Creamed poultry can be either served as a dish unto itself or used as the base for a pot pie or casserole. In the former guise, it is almost always served over rice or pasta, on toast, or in puff pastry patty shells.

Creamed chicken or turkey can be prepared from scratch by poaching chicken parts or boneless, skinless chicken or turkey breast meat in chicken stock. In this case, the flavorful poaching liquid provides the base for the sauce. But when preparing creamed poultry dishes with leftover roasted chicken or turkey, there is no poaching liquid. Homemade chicken stock or canned chicken broth can be substituted.

CREAMED CHICKEN OR TURKEY

4 to 6 servings

Serve this on toast, over rice or pasta, or in puff pastry patty shells, or combine it with other ingredients to make a pot pie or casserole. This recipe includes directions for poaching raw poultry. You can also use 4 cups diced or shredded skinless cooked poultry. Just substitute 2 cups canned chicken broth for the reserved poaching broth.

3½ pounds chicken parts or 1½ pounds boneless, skinless chicken breast or turkey breast cutlets or tenders

Place the chicken in a Dutch oven. Add:

1¾ to 2 cups chicken stock

Pour in just enough water to cover the pieces. Chicken parts may require as much as 3 cups water to be covered, while boneless, skinless breasts may not need any at all. Bring to a simmer over high heat, then reduce the heat so that the poaching liquid barely bubbles. Partially cover and cook until the meat releases clear juices when pierced with a fork, 25 to 30 minutes for chicken parts, 8 to 12 minutes for boneless, skinless chicken or turkey breast. Remove the meat from the stock and let stand until cool enough to handle. If using chicken parts, remove and discard the skin and bones. Cut or shred the meat into bite-sized pieces. Skim the fat from the stock with a spoon. Melt in a large saucepan over medium-low heat:

4 tablespoons (½ stick) unsalted butter

Add and whisk until smooth:

⅓ cup all-purpose flour (for a creamed dish), or ½ cup (for a pot pie or casserole)

Cook, whisking constantly, for 1 minute. Remove the pan from the heat. Add 2 cups of the chicken stock and whisk until smooth. Whisk in:

1½ cups whole milk, half-and-half, or light cream

Increase the heat to medium and bring the mixture just to a simmer, whisking constantly. Remove the pan from the heat, scrape the inside of the saucepan with a wooden spoon or heatproof rubber spatula, and whisk vigorously to break up any lumps. Return the pan to the heat and, whisking, bring to a simmer and cook for 1 minute. Stir in the cooked poultry along with:

2 to 3 tablespoons sherry (optional)

Cook for 1 minute more. Remove from the heat and season to taste with:

Several drops of lemon juice
Salt and ground white or black pepper
2 to 3 pinches of freshly grated or ground nutmeg

CHICKEN OR TURKEY À LA KING

4 to 6 servings

Delicate and delectable if made with care. The classic enrichment of egg yolks and cream can be omitted.

Prepare, using ⅓ cup flour:

Creamed Chicken or Turkey, above

Heat in a medium skillet over medium-high heat until the foam subsides:

1½ tablespoons unsalted butter

Add:

8 ounces mushrooms, sliced (2⅓ cups)

Cook, stirring, until all the liquid in the skillet is evaporated. Stir the mushrooms into the creamed chicken.

Bring the chicken to a simmer, stirring occasionally. Serve immediately, or for a richer, more velvety sauce, whisk together in a medium bowl:

2 large egg yolks
⅓ cup heavy cream

Remove the chicken from the heat. Gradually stir 2 cups of the hot chicken and sauce into the egg yolk mixture, then pour this into the remaining chicken and stir thoroughly. Return to the heat and, stirring constantly, heat to the first bubble of a simmer. The sauce should thicken slightly. Serve in:

Bouchées (puff pastry patty shells), 911

or over:

Hot cooked rice or toast

If you wish, sprinkle with:

¼ cup sliced or slivered almonds, toasted
2 tablespoons minced fresh parsley

CHICKEN OR TURKEY POT PIE

6 to 8 servings

This pot pie has a top crust only, which may be either biscuit or pie pastry. Sautéing the vegetables separately instead of cooking them with the chicken ensures that they will retain their texture and color.

Prepare, using ½ cup flour:

Creamed Chicken or Turkey, above

Prepare the dough for:

Basic Rolled Biscuits, 789, Buttermilk Biscuits, 790, Quick Drop Biscuits, 790, ½ recipe Flaky Pastry Dough, 859, or ½ recipe Deluxe Butter Flaky Pastry Dough, 862

Position a rack in the upper third of the oven. Preheat the oven to 400°F. Butter a 13 x 9-inch baking pan or other shallow baking dish.

Heat in a large skillet over medium-high heat until the foam begins to subside:

2 tablespoons unsalted butter

Add and cook, stirring often, until barely tender, about 5 minutes:

1 medium onion, chopped
3 medium carrots, peeled and sliced ¼ inch thick
2 small celery stalks, sliced ¼ inch thick

Stir the vegetables into the creamed chicken along with:

¾ cup frozen peas, thawed
3 tablespoons minced fresh parsley

Pour the chicken mixture into the prepared pan. If using a rolled biscuit dough, cut the dough into biscuits and arrange on top of the chicken, overlapping the biscuits if necessary. If using a drop biscuit recipe, simply drop small biscuits on top. If using pie dough, roll it out into the shape of the pan, place on top of the chicken, and tuck the edges in against the pan sides. For a golden brown glaze, brush the top with:

2 tablespoons beaten egg (½ large)

Bake until the chicken is bubbly and the topping is nicely browned, 25 to 35 minutes.

CHICKEN OR TURKEY TETRAZZINI

6 to 8 servings

This dish was created nearly a century ago by the great French chef Auguste Escoffier in honor of the legendary opera star Luisa Tetrazzini. It has lost none of its appeal since. If you are using leftover pasta for this dish, you will need about 4 cups cooked.

Prepare, using ½ cup flour:

Creamed Chicken or Turkey, 604

Position a rack in the center of the oven. Preheat the oven to 400°F. Butter a 13 x 9-inch baking pan or other shallow baking dish.

Heat in a medium skillet over medium-high heat until the foam begins to subside:

1½ tablespoons unsalted butter

Add and cook, stirring, until tender, about 5 minutes:

8 ounces mushrooms, sliced (about 2⅓ cups)

Stir the mushrooms into the creamed chicken. Cook until tender in a large pot of boiling salted water:

8 ounces spaghetti, macaroni, or egg noodles

Drain the pasta well, then stir it into the chicken mixture along with:

½ cup slivered or sliced almonds, toasted

Pour the mixture into the prepared pan and sprinkle with:

½ cup grated Parmesan cheese

Bake until the sauce is bubbly and the cheese is golden brown, 25 to 35 minutes.

SESAME CHICKEN

4 servings

In a large pot, bring to a rolling boil:

16 cups water

Add:

3 bone-in chicken breast halves (with skin)

and cook until no longer pink, 8 to 10 minutes. Remove to a plate and let cool.

Thoroughly combine in a medium bowl:

¼ cup toasted sesame paste or smooth peanut butter
2 to 3 tablespoons toasted sesame oil (enough to liquefy the sesame paste or peanut butter)
2½ tablespoons light soy sauce
1 tablespoon white vinegar
½ to 1 tablespoon hot chili pepper oil, or to taste
1 teaspoon sugar
2 teaspoons minced peeled fresh ginger
1 scallion, finely chopped

Remove the bones from the cooled chicken breasts. By hand, tear the chicken meat along the grain to make rough shreds 2½ inches long by ½ inch thick. Place in a serving bowl. Pour the sesame paste sauce over the chicken shreds and mix thoroughly to coat. Place on a small plate:

1 medium cucumber, halved and seeded then cut diagonally into slices ¼ inch thick

If desired, cover the chicken and cucumbers separately and refrigerate for up to 24 hours. Bring both the chicken and cucumber to room temperature before serving.

To serve, pile the cucumber slices on top of the chicken and serve.

CHICKEN OR TURKEY CASSEROLE WITH GREEN VEGETABLES

6 to 8 servings

If prepared with broccoli, this casserole becomes the classic and delicious chicken or turkey divan.

Prepare, using ½ cup flour:

Creamed Chicken or Turkey, 604

Position a rack in the center of the oven. Preheat the oven to 400°F. Butter a 13 x 9-inch baking pan or other shallow baking dish.

Steam in a basket over briskly simmering water until tender but still bright green, about 5 minutes:

3 cups broccoli florets or 1-inch pieces tender asparagus

Cool the vegetables under cold running water until no longer warm, then drain thoroughly. Spread the vegetables in the prepared pan and top with the creamed chicken. Sprinkle with:

½ cup grated Parmesan cheese or 1 cup grated Cheddar cheese

Bake until the sauce is bubbly and the cheese is golden brown, 25 to 35 minutes.

CHICKEN OR TURKEY CHILI PEPPER CASSEROLE

6 to 8 servings

A delicious, contemporary twist on the traditional casserole theme.

Prepare, using ½ cup flour:

Creamed Chicken or Turkey, 604

Stir in:

One or two 4½-ounce cans chopped mild or hot green chili peppers, drained
¼ teaspoon ground cumin

Position a rack in the center of the oven. Preheat the oven to 400°F. Butter a 13 x 9-inch baking pan or other shallow baking dish.

In the prepared pan, layer the creamed chicken alternately with:

4 ounces tortilla chips, lightly crushed (2 to 3 cups)
2 cups lightly packed grated Cheddar cheese (8 ounces)

Top with a final layer of tortilla chips sprinkled with cheese. Bake until the sauce is bubbly and the cheese is golden brown, 25 to 35 minutes.

CHICKEN OR TURKEY AND RICE CASSEROLE

6 to 8 servings

A favorite treatment for Thanksgiving leftovers.

Prepare, using ½ cup flour:

Creamed Chicken or Turkey, 604

Position a rack in the center of the oven. Preheat the oven to 400°F. Butter a 13 x 9-inch baking pan or other shallow baking dish.

Heat in a medium skillet over medium-high heat until the foam begins to subside:

1½ tablespoons unsalted butter

Add and cook, stirring, until tender, about 5 minutes:

8 ounces mushrooms, wiped clean and sliced (about 2⅓ cups)

Stir the mushrooms into the creamed chicken along with:

3 cups cooked white rice or wild rice blend
½ cup chopped walnuts or pecans, toasted

Pour the mixture into the prepared pan. Mix:

⅓ cup dry unseasoned breadcrumbs
2 tablespoons grated Parmesan cheese
1 tablespoon melted butter

Sprinkle over the top of the casserole. Bake until the sauce is bubbly and the crumbs are golden brown, 25 to 35 minutes.

CHICKEN OR TURKEY CROQUETTES

4 servings

A classic croquette is a mixture of very thick velouté sauce and cooked chicken or turkey that is shaped, breaded, and deep-fried. This old-fashioned but extremely satisfying dish may be served with a sauce or a squeeze of lemon juice. Accompany the croquettes with a green vegetable and mashed potatoes or rice.

Prepare using 4 tablespoons unsalted butter and ¼ cup flour:

½ recipe Velouté Sauce, 48, or 1 recipe Sauce Béchamel, 46

Melt in a medium saucepan over medium-low heat.

1 tablespoon unsalted butter

Stir in:

1 cup chopped onions

Cook, stirring often, until tender but still crunchy, 7 to 10 minutes. Add the reserved sauce and cook for 1 minute. Scrape the sauce into a large bowl and combine thoroughly with:

2½ cups chopped skinless, cooked chicken or turkey
¼ cup chopped fresh parsley
½ teaspoon ground white or black pepper
½ teaspoon dried thyme
⅛ teaspoon ground nutmeg
Salt to taste

Press a sheet of plastic wrap directly on the surface of the mixture and refrigerate until very cold and firm, at least 2 hours. Spread in an even layer on 2 separate plates:

1½ cups fresh breadcrumbs
½ cup all-purpose flour

Whisk together in a wide shallow bowl:

2 large eggs

Drop a generous ¼-cup scoop of the croquette mixture onto the flour and gently roll until the rough ball is evenly coated. Roll in the beaten egg, then transfer to the breadcrumbs and roll until coated on all sides. While rolling, shape the croquette into an oval, cylinder, or pyramid. Set aside on a plate. Repeat with the remaining mixture to make 8 croquettes.

Heat to 375°F in a deep-fryer or deep, heavy pot over medium-high heat:

8 cups vegetable oil or 3 pounds solid vegetable shortening

Gently drop 4 croquettes in the hot fat and fry until deep brown on all sides, 3 to 4 minutes. Remove with a slotted spoon and drain on paper towels. Fry the remaining croquettes in the same manner. Arrange on 4 plates or on a platter and serve with:

Lemon wedges or Whole Cranberry Relish, 64

ABOUT CHICKEN AND TURKEY COOKED ON AN OUTDOOR GRILL

The grilling techniques that yield perfect burgers and steaks do not always work for chicken. Burgers and steaks really need nothing more than a red-hot fire, but grilled chicken—with its bones and skin and combination of light or dark meat—requires a more complicated management of heat.

The same hot fire that gives a steak its pleasing brown crust will char bone-in chicken pieces before cooking them through, and chicken fat dripping onto the hot coals will quickly spark a conflagration. No wonder so many of today's cooks opt for boneless, skinless chicken breasts—no pesky bones, no fatty skin, no irregular shapes to contend with—but the perks have their price. Both bones and skin add flavor to the meat, and the skin also protects the meat from the harsh heat and, when cooked to the proper crispness, adds richness and welcome textural contrast.

Chicken is cooked on an outdoor grill in one of two ways: either directly over the hot coals (grilling) or *opposite* the coals, which are arranged on the grill bottom across from the chicken (grill-roasting or barbecuing). Grilling requires a rather cool fire and an unheated spot on the grill to which the chicken may quickly be pulled in the case of flare-ups. It also demands the cook's undivided attention. Grill-roasting is much less bothersome, but it does not crisp and brown the chicken skin, and it imparts a milder flavor and softer, more barbecuelike texture than grilling. For those who want the flavor of grilling and the ease of grill-roasting, a combination of both techniques can be used, much like oven-searing at a high temperature, then roasting at a lower temperature to ensure even cooking. The chicken is cooked over moderately hot coals until its skin begins to crisp and render fat; then it is removed to a spot opposite the fire, covered, and allowed to cook through by indirect heat.

Butterflied whole chickens and skin-on chicken parts can be grilled, grill-roasted, or cooked by a combination of techniques, as you choose. But because of their short cooking time, boneless, skinless chicken parts, whether light or dark meat, should be grilled. (They also benefit from a marinade, which offers the flavor and protection normally provided by the skin.) Whole chickens, however, must be grill-roasted, or else they will burn before cooking through.

Chicken and vegetable kebabs are festive, colorful, and low in fat. Composed of chunks of marinated boneless, skinless chicken, either white or dark meat, and an array of multicolored vegetables, they are best grilled over direct heat. Since vegetables, generally speaking, cook rather slowly, cut them in pieces no bigger than the chicken chunks. (Most cooks tend to do the opposite.) Although less eye-pleasing, segregating chicken and vegetables on separate skewers guarantees that both will be cooked just right. Whatever you do, be sure to thread the chicken and vegetables on the skewers loosely, for neither will cook evenly in cramped quarters.

Although the recipes in this section are written for use with a coal-fired grill, they can be adapted for use with a gas grill as well. Turn both burners on high to preheat the grill rack (this takes about 10 minutes), then turn off one of the burners. If grilling, place the chicken on the heated side, reserving the opposite side as a safety area should flare-ups occur. If grill-roasting, place the chicken on the unheated side of the rack and cover the grill; the turned-on burner will provide the heat. If the grill is equipped with an upper rack set above the grill rack, you can turn both burners on and grill-roast on the upper rack or use this rack as a safety area when grilling.

GRILL-ROASTED WHOLE CHICKEN *4 servings*

Grill-roasting produces a chicken with perfectly cooked breast meat and a delicious smoked taste. No seasoning other than salt is really required, but if you wish, you can rub the chicken with herbs and garlic (see Roasted Chicken with Herbs and Garlic, 580). Alternatively, you can brush the chicken with barbecue sauce after it has roasted for 45 minutes. Before beginning, please read About Chicken Cooked on an Outdoor Grill, 607.

Remove the neck and giblets from, then rinse and pat dry:

1 whole chicken (3½ to 4½ pounds)

Generously rub the neck and body cavities and sprinkle the skin with:

Salt

Perform a simple truss, 573, or tie the legs together. Brush the chicken all over with:

2 tablespoons olive oil or melted butter

Open the vents on the bottom of the grill completely. Ignite 55 to 65 charcoal briquettes and heat until covered with white ash. Divide the coals in half and push half to each side of the grill. Replace the grill rack and arrange the chicken breast side up directly on the rack midway between the two piles of coals. Cover the grill and open the cover vents completely. After 45 minutes, you can brush the chicken with:

½ to 1 cup barbecue sauce

Roast until the thigh exudes clear juices when pricked deeply with a fork and registers 175° to 180°F on an instant-read thermometer, 60 to 80 minutes. Let the chicken stand for 10 to 15 minutes before carving.

GRILL-ROASTED WHOLE TURKEY *12 servings*

It is fun to grill-roast a whole turkey outdoors, and the results are excellent. Turkeys in the range of 11 to 14 pounds work better here than larger ones. You can omit the brining, but this step yields an especially moist, well-seasoned bird and is worth the effort. This method is not good for stuffed birds.

Remove the neck and giblets, then rinse and pat dry:

1 turkey (11 to 14 pounds)

In a clean bucket or other container large enough to hold the turkey, mix until the salt dissolves:

2 pounds salt (2 cups table salt or 4 cups kosher salt)
2 gallons water

Submerge the turkey in the solution. If the turkey is not completely covered, prepare additional brine using a ratio of 1 pound salt to 1 gallon water. Set the turkey in a very cool spot for 4 to 6 hours. Remove the turkey from the brine. Thoroughly rinse inside and out, then pat the skin and both cavities dry. Arrange the turkey breast side down on a V-rack or wire rack set inside a large disposable roasting pan. If you are using a flat rack, you may need to prop the turkey up with balls of aluminum foil. Brush the back and legs with:

2 tablespoons melted butter

Pour into the roasting pan:

½ cup water

Open the bottom vents of the grill completely. Ignite about 75 charcoal briquettes and heat until covered with white ash. Divide the coals in half and push half to each side of the grill. Replace the grill rack and set the turkey in the pan between the two piles of coals. Cover the grill and open the cover vents completely. Roast for 1 hour. Meanwhile, about 40 minutes into roasting, heat another 35 briquettes in a chimney starter. After 1 hour of roasting, remove the turkey from the grill, remove the grill rack, stir up the coals, and add half of the new hot coals to each pile; replace the grill cover. Protecting your hands with paper towels, grasp the turkey at both ends and turn breast side up. Baste the breast with:

2 tablespoons melted butter

If the pan is dry, add more water. Return the turkey to the center of the grill, replace the lid, and cook until a meat thermometer inserted into the thickest part of the thigh registers 175° to 180°F, 60 to 80 minutes more. Remove the turkey to a platter and let stand for at least 20 minutes. If you wish, prepare:

Giblet Gravy, 615

CHICKEN KEBABS

8 kebabs; 4 to 6 servings

Remember to soak wooden or bamboo skewers in water for at least 30 minutes before use to prevent them from charring. If you thread the poultry and vegetables onto two parallel skewers in the making of each kebab, the pieces will stay put when the kebabs are turned, ensuring even cooking. The vegetables suggested below are the usual choices, but almost any vegetable will work. Firm vegetables such as carrots, potatoes, cauliflower, and broccoli should be steamed until nearly tender before being used. Before beginning, please read About Chicken and Turkey Cooked on an Outdoor Grill, 607.

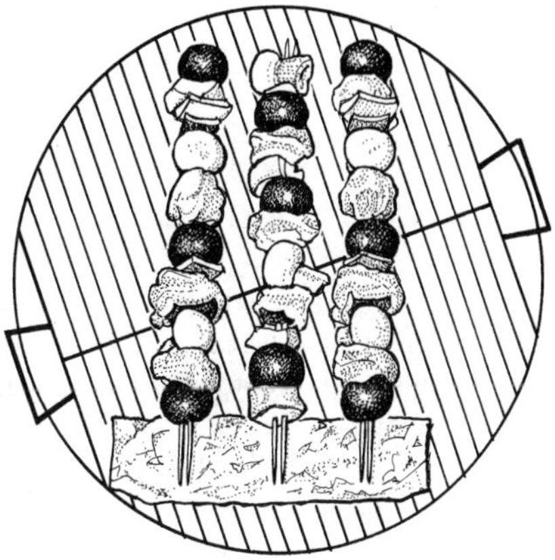

Chicken kebabs

Prepare:

¾ cup Fresh Herb Vinaigrette, 237, or ¾ cup Green Peppercorn Vinaigrette, 237, or ¾ cup Ginger-Soy Vinaigrette, 238

Or stir together in a medium bowl:

½ cup olive oil
3 tablespoons strained fresh lemon juice
2 to 3 cloves garlic, minced
1 teaspoon salt
1 teaspoon ground black pepper

Pour half of the marinade into another medium bowl. Rinse and pat dry, then dip into the marinade and turn to coat well:

4 boneless, skinless chicken breast halves or 6 boneless, skinless chicken thighs, cut into 1-inch cubes

Cover and refrigerate for at least 30 minutes or up to 2 hours. When you are ready to grill the kebabs, add to the remaining marinade and turn to coat:

1 large red onion, cut into ½-inch chunks
16 small mushrooms
16 cherry tomatoes
1 red, yellow, or green bell pepper, cut into 1-inch pieces, or 2 small zucchini or summer squash, halved lengthwise and sliced ½ inch thick

Thread the meat and vegetables onto 8 skewers, leaving a little space between the pieces to allow for even cooking.

Heat about 50 charcoal briquettes until covered with white ash. Spread the coals on one side of the grill to make a medium-hot fire. Replace the grill rack and cover the grill until the rack is hot, about 5 minutes. Arrange the skewers on the hot rack opposite the coals and place a strip of aluminum foil under the exposed ends of the skewers. Grill for 4 minutes, then turn and grill until the vegetables are crisp-tender and browned along the edges and the chicken is opaque throughout, 3 to 4 minutes more.

ASH-ROASTED CHICKEN THIGHS

3 to 6 servings

In this recipe, chicken thighs are triple-wrapped in foil and cooked directly on hot coals rather than on a grill rack. On a wintry night, when outdoor grilling is a distant pleasant memory, you might try cooking the chicken in your fireplace, burying the chicken in the embers *surrounding* the fire, not directly under it. The same technique can be employed with a campfire. This recipe can be multiplied to serve as many people as you wish, but wrap only two thighs per packet to guarantee easy handling. Before beginning, please read About Chicken and Turkey Cooked on an Outdoor Grill, 607.

Rinse, pat dry, and remove the skin from:

6 bone-in chicken thighs

Sprinkle generously with:

Salt and ground black pepper to taste

Have ready:

¼ cup minced fresh parsley
6 cloves garlic, thinly sliced
1 lemon, very thinly sliced

Cut a sheet of wide, heavy-duty foil about 18 inches long. Place 2 thighs in the center of the sheet, sprinkle with parsley and garlic, and top with 2 or 3 lemon slices. Cover with a second sheet of foil, also 18 inches long. Crimp the edges of the two sheets to seal securely, then roll the edges in toward the center to make an 8- to 9-inch square packet. Wrap the packet in a third sheet of foil to seal completely. Repeat with the remaining thighs, making 3 packets altogether.

Heat 55 to 65 charcoal briquettes until covered with white ash. Push the coals to one side of the grill, arrange the chicken packets in a single layer over the bottom of the grill, and scatter the coals in an even layer over the top of the packets. Cook for 35 minutes. Remove the packets from the coals with tongs and let stand for 10 minutes. Open the foil carefully to avoid being burned by the steam.

GRILLED CHICKEN DIJON

4 servings

Before beginning, please read About Chicken and Turkey Cooked on an Outdoor Grill, 607.

Rinse and pat dry:

3½ to 4½ pounds chicken parts

Mix in a large bowl:

⅓ cup olive oil
⅓ cup strained fresh lemon juice
3 tablespoons Dijon mustard
2 to 3 cloves garlic, minced
¾ teaspoon salt
½ teaspoon ground black pepper

Add the chicken pieces to the marinade and turn to coat well. Cover and refrigerate for 2 to 24 hours.

Heat 55 to 65 charcoal briquettes until covered with white ash. Spread the coals over one side of the grill to make a medium-hot fire. Replace the grill rack and cover the grill until the rack is hot, about 5 minutes. Place the chicken parts skin side down directly over the coals and cook, moving the pieces around as needed to avoid charring, until the skin is crisp and golden, 8 to 10 minutes. Move the chicken opposite the coals and turn skin side up. Cover the grill and cook until the meat is opaque throughout, 10 to 15 minutes more.

SPICY CHICKEN HOBO PACK WITH LIME AND CHILI PEPPERS

4 servings

Roasting food in the embers of a dying fire is one of the easiest and oldest ways of cooking in the world—and it is still a favorite technique in Boy Scout and Girl Scout camps throughout the United States, where foil-wrapped meals are known as "hobo packs." Chris Schlesinger and John Willoughby, authors of *The Thrill of the Grill*, gained hobo pack skills as scouts and perfected the method over the course of hundreds of meals cooked on the beach. There is an element of unpredictability in cooking these packets (which can contain just about any combination of meat and vegetables), but that's part of the fun, and there is no denying the intrinsic appeal of this method to the primitive cook in all of us.

Combine in a large bowl and toss well:

4 bone-in chicken breast halves, skin removed
8 small new potaotes
12 garlic cloves, unpeeled
1 lime, sliced into very thin rounds
⅓ cup chopped fresh cilantro or parsley
1 teaspoon minced fresh chili peppers
¼ cup olive oil
Salt and ground black pepper to taste

Place in the center of a sheet of heavy-duty aluminum foil about 2 feet long. Cover with a second sheet of foil and roll the edges together on all sides to seal. Place in the center of a third length of foil and fold it up around the pack.

Prepare a medium-hot charcoal fire.

Place the pack on the bottom of the grill or fireplace, and pile coals up on all sides. Cook for 30 to 35 minutes, depending on the intensity of the coals. Remove from the coals, unroll the foil carefully, and serve at once.

GRILLED SPICE-RUBBED CHICKEN WITH LEMON AND GARLIC OIL

4 servings

This recipe calls for bone-in breasts, but mixed chicken parts or boneless, skinless breasts or thighs can be substituted. Since boneless, skinless parts cook more quickly, grill them directly over the coals until completely done, 4 to 5 minutes on each side. If you like, you can omit the spice rub and simply salt the chicken before grilling. Before beginning, please read About Chicken and Turkey Cooked on an Outdoor Grill, 607.

Mix:

1½ teaspoons fennel seeds
1½ teaspoons ground coriander
¾ teaspoon dry mustard
¾ teaspoon salt
¼ teaspoon ground cinnamon
¼ teaspoon ground red pepper

Rinse and pat dry, then rub the spice mixture all over:

4 bone-in chicken breast halves (with skin)

Heat 55 to 65 charcoal briquettes until covered with white ash. Spread the coals over one side of the grill to make a medium-hot fire. Replace the grill rack and cover the grill until the rack is hot, about 5 minutes. Place the chicken skin side down over the coals, cover the grill, and cook until the skin is crisp and golden brown, 8 to 10 minutes. Move the chicken to the opposite side of the grill and turn skin side up. Cover the grill and cook until the meat is opaque throughout, 10 to 15 minutes more. Meanwhile, mix in a small bowl:

¼ cup olive oil
¼ cup minced fresh cilantro or parsley or 1 tablespoon minced fresh thyme or oregano
3 tablespoons strained fresh lemon juice
1 small clove garlic, minced
¼ teaspoon salt

Remove the chicken to a serving platter, spoon the lemon-garlic oil over the pieces, and serve.

GRILL-SMOKED JAMAICAN JERK CHICKEN

6 to 8 servings

Chicken, pork, and fish all can be cooked in the unique Jamaican style known as "jerk." The cornerstone of all jerk dishes is a vinegary, intensely hot paste of dried herbs and habanero peppers, which are some five times hotter than jalapeños. If you cannot find these peppers, a habanero-based hot sauce makes a good substitute. You can cook the chicken immediately or marinate it, covered and refrigerated, for up to 12 hours. Before beginning, please read About Chicken and Turkey Cooked on an Outdoor Grill, 607.

Puree in a food processor or blender:

⅓ cup fresh lime juice
10 fresh habanero or Scotch bonnet peppers or ¼ cup habanero-based hot sauce
2 tablespoons white vinegar
2 tablespoons fresh orange juice
3 scallions, coarsely chopped
2 tablespoons dried basil
2 tablespoons dried thyme
2 tablespoons yellow mustard seeds or 1 tablespoon dry mustard
2 teaspoons ground allspice
1 teaspoon ground cloves
1 teaspoon salt
1 teaspoon ground black pepper

The mixture should have the consistency of thick tomato sauce. If needed, thin with additional:

Lime juice, vinegar, or orange juice

Rinse and pat dry, then brush this mixture over:

8 whole chicken legs, or 8 bone-in chicken breast halves (with skin)

Prepare a medium-hot charcoal fire. When the coals are covered with white ash, push them over to one side of the grill. Replace the grill rack. Arrange the chicken pieces skin side down opposite the coals. Cover the grill and cook for 20 minutes. Turn the chicken and cook until the meat is opaque throughout and pulls away from the bone, 30 to 60 minutes more, depending on the size of the chicken parts and the temperature of the fire.

TANDOORI CHICKEN

4 servings

In Indian cooking, "tandoori" refers to cut-up chickens, meat kebabs, and flatbreads that are cooked in a tandoor, a fiercely hot, charcoal-fired vertical oven. Before cooking, chicken and meat are always marinated in an aromatic mixture of yogurt and spices. This marinade is tinted with a natural dye, which imparts to tandoori chicken its characteristic orange-yellow color. An excellent tandoori-style chicken can be prepared in a covered grill using a very hot fire. To ensure that the outside does not char before the chicken cooks through, use the smallest chicken parts you can find or cut a 3½-pound chicken into parts yourself (see How to Cut Up Poultry, 569). Two split rock Cornish hens also work well.

In lieu of grilling, you can roast the chicken on a lightly oiled baking sheet in a 500°F oven for 25 to 30 minutes, but be prepared for a smoky kitchen. Before beginning, please read About Chicken and Turkey Cooked on an Outdoor Grill, 607.

Prepare:

Tandoori Marinade, 85

Remove the skin from:

3½ pounds chicken parts or 2 split rock Cornish hens

Add the chicken pieces to the marinade, turn to coat well, cover the bowl, and refrigerate for 4 to 6 hours. Prepare a hot charcoal fire. When the coals are covered with white ash, push them over to one side of the grill. Replace the grill rack and cover the grill until the rack is hot, about 5 minutes. Arrange the chicken parts bone side down on the hot rack over the coals, cover the grill, and cook for 15 minutes. Turn the chicken and place it opposite the coals, replace the grill cover, and cook until the juices run clear when the meat is pricked with a fork, 10 to 15 minutes more.

ABOUT TURKEY

Despite the best efforts of turkey producers and their advertisers, most Americans still serve turkey, whole and roasted, only at holiday time. The whole turkeys available at the supermarket generally weigh between 10 and 25 pounds. Those weighing under 18 pounds are usually hens, while those weighing more are almost always toms. There is no appreciable difference in quality between female and male turkeys, so select a size according to the number of people you will be serving, allowing about 1 pound per person, plus, if you wish, a margin for leftovers. Even though most "fresh" turkeys have actually been held for several weeks at subfreezing temperatures before you buy them (see Buying Poultry, 568), they taste markedly better than frozen turkeys, which often have been stored much longer. Fresh turkeys, then, are worth their higher price. Whether or not a turkey labeled "organic," "free-range," "natural," or "minimally processed" is worth the money is a complicated question; see About Poultry Production, 567.

Self-Basting Turkeys: These have been injected with broth or vegetable oil or butter plus seasonings and flavor enhancers to increase moistness and improve the flavor. If the solution makes up 3 to 8 percent of the total weight, the label may read simply "basted," "marinated," "added flavoring," or some other such term. If the solution is more than 8 percent by weight, the precise percentage and the method of preparation must be stated on the packaging.

Wild Turkeys: Wild turkeys are quite different from the common supermarket type. They are much smaller—the hens usually weigh 5 to 7 pounds and the toms 9 to 11 pounds—and their breasts are thin rather than plump. Most significantly, all of their meat, including the breast, is dark, just like goose. This bird is quite expensive, running eight to ten times higher in price than supermarket turkeys.

TURKEY PARTS

Breast: A whole turkey breast with bone and skin generally weighs between 4 and 7 pounds. For Thanksgiving or some other festive occasion, you might want to consider a "hotel style" whole turkey breast, which comes with the wings attached and a packet of giblets for making gravy. Whole turkey breast takes about the same time to roast as a whole chicken of comparable weight. It often comes with a pop-up timer set to go off at an internal temperature of about 163°F, at which point the meat will be juicy and tender. The whole breast can also be grill-roasted or used to make a turkey salad, creamed dish, pot pie, or casserole. A boneless half turkey breast, with or without the skin attached, is often called turkey London broil at the supermarket. As the name implies, this is a perfect cut for broiling or outdoor grilling. To prevent the breast from drying out, marinate it or oil the surface generously before cooking, especially if the skin has been removed. Slices of boneless, skinless turkey breast are called turkey cutlets or, if sliced very thin, turkey scaloppine. Turkey cutlets can be used in any recipe calling for either boneless, skinless chicken breasts or veal cutlets or scaloppine. They cook in a flash, and though they are expensive, they cost much less than veal. Finally, supermarkets sometimes carry packs of turkey tenderloins or tenders, the 4- to 6-ounce strip of breast meat that is nestled on either side of the breastbone. Their chewy white tendons having been removed at the processing plant, these little morsels are perfect for cutting into cubes and skewering or stir-frying. They can also be sautéed whole, with or without a breading, or pounded between sheets of wax paper and turned into cutlets.

How to Make Boneless, Skinless Turkey Breast and Turkey Cutlets: Peel the skin off a whole turkey breast. Turn the breast bone side up and locate the wishbone at the wide end. Scrape around the wishbone with the point of a paring knife, then pull the wishbone out. Turn the breast skinned side up. Using a sharp knife (or a boning knife if you happen to have one), slit the breast along the breastbone from one end to the other. To bone each breast half, cut along the side of the breastbone and then over the ribs until the meat is detached, always scraping the knife as close as possible to the bones, shown below left. Repeat with the remaining breast half. Turn each breast half skinned side down and scrape away the long, white tendon that runs along the tenderloin.

While it is possible to slice turkey cutlets from a boned, skinned breast half, the procedure is easier if you start with a whole breast on the bone. Peel off the skin, then remove the wishbone (see above). To ensure even slices, freeze the breast until it is firm and icy but not frozen solid, 2 to 4 hours. Using a very sharp knife, cut the breast parallel to the center bone in slices about ⅜ inch thick, angling the knife to make the longest, widest slices possible, shown below right. The outermost and innermost slices will be thin and narrow. If you wish, you can cut these slices slightly thicker and then pound them gently between sheets of wax paper to make them similar to the others. When you get to the tenderloin, which is nestled against the breastbone, peel it off in one piece and scrape away the tendon. Divide the tenderloin in half or in thirds, depending on its size, and pound each piece.

Legs: Whole turkey legs, turkey drumsticks, and turkey thighs are all available in single packages for those who love dark meat. The legs can be baked or grill-roasted, and they make delicious soups and stews. The thighs can also be skinned, boned, and cut into cubes for stir-fries and kebabs.

Wings: Turkey wings are usually sold whole. They roast and grill well and make excellent stock. The meaty first and second joints can be prepared in the same ways as chicken wings.

Gizzards, Hearts, and Livers: These organs are referred to collectively as the giblets. They usually end up in giblet gravy—supermarkets package them separately around the holidays for just that purpose—but the gizzards and hearts can also be braised. See About Poultry Giblets, 729.

Ground Turkey: See About Ground Turkey and Chicken, 618.

ABOUT ROASTED TURKEY

Turkeys are really just oversized chickens, so if you can roast a chicken, you can roast a turkey too.

Roasting Methods: Of course, there are good and better ways to roast a turkey. The simplest method is to roast the turkey breast side up in a moderate oven until done, basting it now and then with the pan drippings to encourage the skin to brown. This will deliver a respectable bird to the table but not a perfect one. The problem is the breast. To be tender and juicy, the breast needs to be cooked to an internal temperature no greater than 165°F. The legs, meanwhile, must be cooked to 175° to 180°F, or else they will remain chewy and disturbingly pink. In roasting a turkey, then, the object is to encourage the legs to cook at a faster rate than the breast. Unfortunately, when you roast by the simple breast-up method, precisely the opposite happens. Exposed throughout roasting to the glaring heat of the oven roof and drained of juice by gravity's downward tug, the breast inevitably overcooks and dries out by the time the legs are done and the stuffing has heated through.

A generous ladling of good gravy will make even the driest breast meat palatable, and if you are content to solve all problems via sauce, you need read no further. But if you are intent on producing a moist, succulent breast that needs no gravy, we have outlined two special roasting methods that will help you. Both entail roasting the turkey with the delicate breast turned

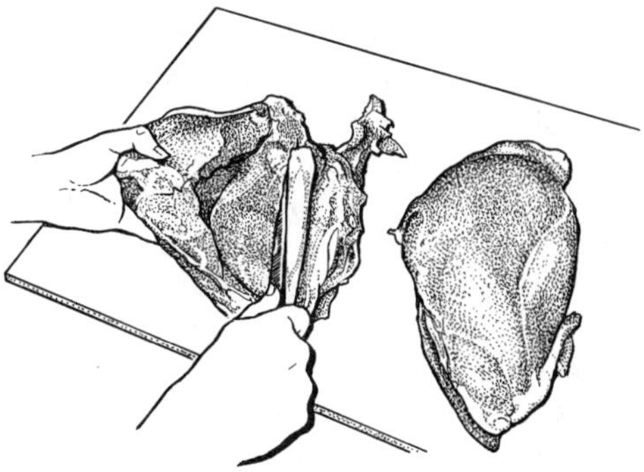

Boning a turkey breast half

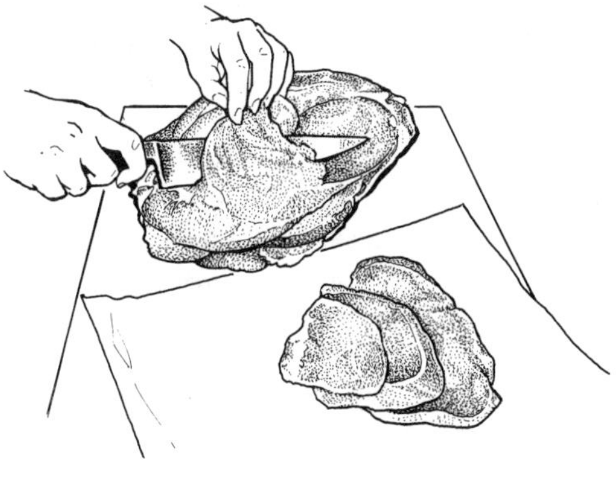

Slicing turkey cutlets from a whole breast on the bone

away from the oven roof during most of the cooking. In other words, the turkey goes into the oven arranged in the pan in an unconventional way, with either its back or one leg pointing up. Since the breast will not brown unless eventually turned top side up, both methods require the cook to turn the turkey during roasting, a maneuver that sounds scary to the uninitiated but that proves quite manageable once tried. Otherwise, the two methods work on divergent principles. The linchpin of Roasted Brined Turkey, 616, is soaking the turkey in a strong salt solution, which saturates the flesh, yielding a remarkably juicy bird. The secret of High-Heat Roasted Turkey, 616, is flipping the bird from side to side in a superhot pan. This, in effect, fries the legs, bringing them to the high temperature that they require, while the breast remains relatively cool.

Which method should you choose? If you prepare Roasted Brined Turkey, you will have to allocate time for soaking (though there is considerable flexibility), but you will end up with the juiciest bird imaginable, pleasantly seasoned throughout by the brine. High-heat roasting requires that you turn the bird over every 30 minutes during cooking (a brined turkey needs be turned only once) and so is feasible only with turkeys weighing under 15 pounds. High-heat roasted turkeys are browner, have a stronger roasted flavor, and produce a darker, richer gravy than roasted brined turkeys, but they are never as drippingly moist. In short, neither method is perfect, but both come pretty close.

Gravy: Everyone loves gravy, but everyone is terrified of making it. No wonder. Generations of cooks have been taught to make gravy directly in the roasting pan by stirring flour into the drippings and then adding water or stock. Unfortunately, the all-too-usual result is a lumpy, greasy glop. The problem is that the flour will mix smoothly with the fat but not with the juices and roasting particles. This causes lumps. Meanwhile, there is too much fat for the flour to fully absorb. When liquid is added, the excess fat separates and floats to the top of the gravy.

The three gravy recipes that begin on page 615 are constructed in an entirely different way and are guaranteed to produce smooth, delicious, and reduced-fat results. Quick Turkey Gravy, 615, is made entirely in the roasting pan. Giblet Gravy, 615, and Reduced-Fat Giblet Gravy, 616, require the preparation of a giblet stock, but this can be done ahead, even a day or two before roasting. The browned bits and sticky brown substance remaining in the roasting pan are the keys to perfect gravy, so be certain not to discard any of these precious elements when skimming the fat from the juices.

Leftovers: Many people feel that if they do not have leftovers, they have not had a true Thanksgiving. Leftover turkey can be put to many uses besides the usual turkey sandwiches and salads. For some traditional and still excellent ideas, see About Creamed Chicken and Turkey Dishes, Pot Pies, Casseroles, and Croquettes, 603. Or turn the turkey into an elegant salad by tossing cubes or strips of meat with a relish, salsa, or chutney, 67 to 68, and serving over a bed of mixed baby greens.

The carcass, meanwhile, can be recycled to make an excellent turkey stock. Give someone the job of picking the leftover meat off the bones immediately after the meal, then prepare the stock as soon as possible, even Thanksgiving night. The longer the carcass sits in the refrigerator, the less likely it is ever to end up in the pot. The leg, thigh, and wing bones will easily fit into the pot, but the rib and back must be hacked up or ripped apart. (A cooked carcass separates quite easily.) Cover the bones with water and toss in a quartered onion and a small carrot and/or celery stalk, if you happen to have them. A bay leaf, a little dried thyme, and a few sprigs of parsley would not hurt either. Bring the stock to a simmer, skimming the foam off as it rises to the top. Reduce the heat and simmer the stock, uncovered, at a bare bubble for 2 hours. Strain the stock into a large bowl, let cool to room temperature, then cover and refrigerate. Skim off any fat that congeals on the surface of the broth.

ROASTED TURKEY

10 to 25 servings; 1 pound turkey per person

If you choose not to stuff your bird, you may wish to fill the cavity with a handful of chopped onions, carrots, and celery and a few sprigs of parsley, sage, or thyme. These aromatics will subtly perfume the meat and will also flavor the juices of the bird, making for a better gravy. Before beginning, please read About Turkey, 611, and About Roasted Turkey, 613. For information on removing the wishbone, stuffing, trussing, testing for doneness, and carving, see Roasting Whole Poultry, 572.

Position a rack at the lowest level of the oven. Preheat the oven to 325°F.

Remove the giblets and neck from, then rinse inside and out and pat dry:

1 turkey (10 to 25 pounds)

To facilitate carving, you may wish to remove the wishbone. Generously rub the body and neck cavities and sprinkle the skin with:

Salt

If you wish to stuff the bird, prepare and have *hot:*

Bread Stuffing or Dressing or a variation, 482 to 483, or Corn Bread Stuffing or a variation, 484

Loosely pack the body and neck cavities with the stuffing and close the vents. Perform a simple truss, 572. Arrange the turkey breast side up on a rack set in a roasting pan. Brush the skin all over with:

3 to 6 tablespoons melted butter, depending on the size of the turkey

Basting every 30 minutes with additional melted butter or pan drippings, roast the turkey until an instant-read thermometer plunged into the thickest part of the thigh registers 175° to 180°F, 10 to 12 minutes per pound if the bird is not stuffed, 12 to 15 minutes per pound if it is. To be safe to eat, the stuffing must register at least 160°F. If the bird is done but the stuffing is not, remove the stuffing from the bird and bake it in a buttered casserole while the bird stands. Remove the turkey to a platter and let stand for at least 20 minutes before carving. Meanwhile, if you wish, make:

Quick Turkey Gravy, below, Giblet Gravy, below, or Reduced-Fat Giblet Gravy, 616

QUICK TURKEY GRAVY

4 cups; about 12 servings

If preparing this gravy for a crowd, increase all ingredients by half or double the recipe.

Remove the rack from the roasting pan. If the juices in the turkey pan have evaporated, leaving only fat and browned bits on the bottom of the pan, carefully pour out the fat and discard it, retaining all browned bits. If there is juice, tilt the pan and skim as much fat as possible off the juice with a spoon. Set the pan over two burners set on medium heat. Pour in:

4 cups chicken stock

Bring the mixture to a simmer, all the while scraping the bottom of the pan with a wooden spoon to loosen the browned bits. Reduce the heat and cook slowly for 5 minutes. Mix to a smooth paste:

¼ cup water
3 tablespoons cornstarch

Whisking constantly, gradually pour this mixture into the simmering broth, then cook for 1 minute. Season to taste with:

Sherry, port, or Madeira (optional)
Salt and ground black pepper

Pour into a gravy boat and serve with the turkey.

GIBLET GRAVY

4 cups; about 12 servings

When increasing this recipe by half or doubling it to serve a crowd, you may wish to buy extra giblets, as those packed inside a large turkey may have belonged originally to a smaller bird.

Rinse and pat dry:

1 turkey neck, heart, and gizzard

Chop the neck into 2-inch pieces. Cut the heart lengthwise in half and divide the gizzard at the lobes. Heat in a wide, heavy saucepan over medium-high heat until shimmery:

2 tablespoons vegetable oil

Add the turkey parts to the pan, then scatter around them:

½ to 1 cup chopped onions

Reducing the heat slightly if the ingredients begin to char, cook, without stirring, until the turkey parts are richly browned on the first side, 5 to 10 minutes. Turn and brown the second side in the same manner. Add:

4 cups chicken stock
½ cup dry white or red wine
¼ cup finely chopped peeled carrots (optional)
¼ cup finely chopped celery (optional)
2 small sprigs parsley (optional)
1 large bay leaf
½ teaspoon dried thyme, or 2 to 3 sprigs fresh
4 whole cloves or allspice berries or pinch of ground cloves or allspice (optional)

Partially cover the pan and simmer very slowly until the meat is tender, about 1 hour. If you wish, add and simmer until stiffened, about 5 minutes:

1 turkey liver, rinsed

Strain the stock through a fine sieve and add enough water to measure 4 cups. Finely chop the turkey neck meat and cut the giblets into tiny dice. Add the neck meat and giblets to the stock. Discard the vegetables in the sieve. Heat in a large saucepan over medium-high heat until foaming:

3 tablespoons unsalted butter

Add and cook for 1 minute, whisking constantly:

⅓ cup all-purpose flour

Remove the pan from the heat. For an especially silky gravy, remove the giblet stock to a saucepan, bring it to a furious boil, and then pour it all at once into the roux, whisking as you pour. Otherwise, simply whisk the unheated stock into the roux, blending thoroughly. Whisking constantly, bring the gravy to a simmer over medium heat and cook for 1 minute. Remove from the heat and cover. If you will be finishing and serving the gravy within a few hours, let it stand at room temperature; otherwise, refrigerate it.

Remove the rack from the roasting pan. If the juices in the pan have evaporated, leaving only fat and browned bits on the bottom of the pan, carefully pour out the fat and discard it, retaining all browned bits. If there is juice, tilt the pan and skim as much fat as possible off the juice with a spoon. Set the pan on two burners over medium heat. Pour in:

½ cup sherry, Madeira, port, dry white wine, or water

Bring the mixture to a simmer, all the while scraping the bottom of the pan with a wooden spoon to loosen the browned bits. Pour the drippings into the gravy. Place the gravy over medium heat and simmer, stirring occasionally, for 5 minutes to blend the flavors. Season with:

Salt and ground black pepper to taste

Pour into a gravy boat and serve with the turkey.

REDUCED-FAT GIBLET GRAVY

This gravy is lighter on the tongue, darker in color, and slightly more intense in flavor than a traditional roux-thickened gravy.

Prepare Giblet Gravy, above, through the combining of the giblet stock with the chopped neck meat and giblet dice. Turn the mixture into a saucepan. Prepare the pan drippings as outlined for the gravy and pour into the stock. Bring to a simmer. Mix 3 tablespoons cornstarch and ¼ cup water or chicken stock until smooth. Whisking constantly, gradually pour the cornstarch slurry a little at a time into the simmering stock, adding only as needed to thicken the gravy to your taste. Season and serve.

ROASTED BRINED TURKEY

10 to 25 servings; 1 pound turkey per person

Brining—that is, soaking the turkey in a solution of water and salt—helps the bird retain moisture and seasons the meat throughout. This recipe calls for a 4- to 6-hour soak. If it better suits your schedule, you can decrease the salt by half (in proportion to the water) and soak the turkey for 12 to 18 hours. Do not brine self-basting turkeys or kosher turkeys, both of which already have been treated with salt. Before beginning, please read About Turkey, 611, and About Roasted Turkey, 613. For information on removing the wishbone, trussing, testing for doneness, and carving, see Roasting Whole Poultry, 572.

Remove the giblets and neck from, then rinse:

1 turkey (15 to 25 pounds)

In a clean bucket or other container large enough to hold the turkey, mix until the salt dissolves:

2 pounds salt (2 cups table salt or 4 cups kosher salt)
2 gallons water

Submerge the turkey in the solution. If the turkey is not completely covered, prepare additional brine using a ratio of 1 pound salt to 1 gallon water. Set the turkey in a very cool spot for 4 to 6 hours.

Position a rack at the lowest level of the oven. Preheat the oven to 325°F.

Remove the turkey from the brine. Thoroughly rinse inside and out, then pat the skin and both cavities dry. To facilitate carving, you may wish to remove the leg tendons and wishbone. Place in the large cavity:

1 onion, peeled and quartered
1 carrot, peeled and cut into 1-inch chunks
1 small celery stalk, cut into 1-inch chunks
1 teaspoon dried thyme, or 8 sprigs fresh (optional)

See Turned Roasted Chicken, 580. Perform a simple truss, 572; there is no need to close the cavities. Brush the turkey skin all over with:

4 to 6 tablespoons melted butter, depending on the size of the turkey

Place a V-rack or sturdy wire rack in a roasting pan and arrange the turkey breast side down on the rack. If you are using a flat rack and the turkey topples over, prop it up with balls of aluminum foil. Pour into the roasting pan:

¾ cup water

Roast the turkey breast side down for 2 hours if it weighs 18 pounds or less, 2½ hours if it weighs between 18 and 21 pounds, and 3 hours if it weighs more than 21 pounds. Baste the back and legs once or twice with:

2 to 3 tablespoons melted butter

Remove the turkey from the oven. Protecting your hands with paper towels, grasp the turkey at both ends and turn breast side up. Return the turkey to the oven and roast, basting once or twice with pan drippings, until an instant-read thermometer plunged into the thickest part of the thigh registers 175° to 180°F, 30 to 90 minutes more, depending on the turkey's size. (If the turkey approaches doneness before the breast has browned, increase the oven temperature to 400°F for the last 5 to 10 minutes of roasting.) Remove the turkey to a platter and let stand for 20 to 40 minutes. Meanwhile, if you wish, make:

Quick Turkey Gravy, 615, Giblet Gravy, 615, or Reduced-Fat Giblet Gravy, above

HIGH-HEAT ROASTED TURKEY *12 to 15 servings*

This high-heat roast delivers a beautifully browned, intensely flavorful bird, and it only requires attention to a few details. Because the turkey must be flipped from side to side every 30 minutes, only a relatively small bird is feasible. And because the turkey is cooked directly on the pan, not on a rack, the pan must be nonstick, preferably heavy. Before beginning, please read About Turkey, 611, and About Roasted Turkey, 613. For information on removing the wishbone, stuffing, trussing, testing for doneness, and carving, see Roasting Whole Poultry, 572.

Position a rack at the lowest level of the oven. Preheat the oven to 425°F.

Remove the giblets and neck from, then rinse inside and out and pat dry:

1 turkey (12 to 15 pounds)

To facilitate carving, you may wish to remove the wishbone. Generously rub the body and neck cavities and sprinkle the skin with:

Salt

If you wish to stuff the bird, prepare and have *hot:*

Bread Stuffing or Dressing or a variation, 482 to 483, or Corn Bread Stuffing or a variation, 484

Loosely pack the body and neck cavities with stuffing and close the vents. Perform a simple truss, 572. Place the turkey in a heavy nonstick roasting pan and brush all over with:

4 to 5 tablespoons melted butter

Arrange the turkey so that it rests on one of its sides, that is, with a drumstick pointing up. If the turkey topples over, prop it up with balls of aluminum foil. Roast for 30 minutes. Remove the turkey from the oven. Protecting your hands with paper towels, grasp the turkey at both ends and turn it onto its other side, again propping it up with foil if necessary. Baste all exposed skin with pan drippings, then roast for 30 minutes. Turn and baste twice more so that the turkey roasts twice on each side, for a total of 2 hours. Turn the turkey breast side up, baste, and roast until an instant-read thermometer plunged into the thickest part of the thigh registers 175°F, 10 to 30 minutes more. (To be safe to eat, the stuffing must register at least 160°F. If the bird is done but the stuffing is not, remove the stuffing from the bird and bake it in a buttered casserole while the bird stands.) Remove the turkey to a platter and let stand for at least 20 minutes before carving. Meanwhile, if you wish, make:

Quick Turkey Gravy, 615, Giblet Gravy, 615, or Reduced-Fat Giblet Gravy, 616

ABOUT DISHES MADE WITH TURKEY PARTS

When you prepare turkey breast and turkey legs as separate dishes, you can give each cut the kind of cooking treatment that it responds to best. To be at its juicy, tender finest, the breast needs to be roasted, grilled, broiled, poached, or cut into scallops and sautéed. As soon as the meat has lost all traces of pink—that is, at an internal temperature of around 160°F—it is done. The legs, by contrast, require long, slow cooking. Roasting, either on the whole bird or off, is fine, providing that the legs reach an internal temperature of at least 170°F. But the legs take even better to slow cooking in liquid, producing delicious braised dishes and stews.

ROASTED TURKEY BREAST

5 to 9 servings; about 12 ounces turkey per person

If you have two ovens, you can roast a whole turkey in one and a turkey breast in the other, ensuring that the white-meat lovers at your Thanksgiving table will have plenty.

Position a rack in the center of the oven. Preheat the oven to 350°F.

Rinse and pat dry:

1 whole turkey breast (4 to 7 pounds)

Season both the skin and bone sides generously with:

Salt and ground black pepper to taste

Arrange the breast skin side up on a baking sheet or in a shallow roasting pan. Brush the skin with:

2 tablespoons melted butter

Roast until the meat releases clear juices when pricked deeply with a fork and registers 160°F on an instant-read thermometer, 15 to 20 minutes per pound. Let stand for 20 minutes before carving. If you wish, prepare:

Quick Turkey Gravy, 615, or Poultry Pan Sauce or Gravy, 579

BRAISED TURKEY THIGHS WITH OLIVES

4 or 5 servings

A deeply flavorful dish.

Rinse and pat dry:

2½ pounds boneless, skinless turkey thighs

Combine in a heavy Dutch oven over medium heat:

¼ cup olive oil

4 cloves garlic, slightly bruised

Cook the garlic until just beginning to brown, then discard the garlic. Add the turkey thighs and brown on all sides. Stir in:

1 cup chopped onions

¼ cup chopped sun-dried tomatoes, drained if oil-packed

1 tablespoon chopped fresh rosemary, or 1 teaspoon dried, crumbled

Cook for 2 minutes. Stir in:

2 cups turkey or chicken stock

1½ cups sliced pitted Kalamata or other brine-cured black olives
1 cup dry white wine
⅛ teaspoon red pepper flakes

Cover and simmer gently over low heat until the turkey is very tender, 1½ to 2 hours, adding a little water or stock if needed. Skim the fat from the sauce with a spoon. Stir in:

1 to 3 tablespoons finely chopped fresh parsley

Season with:

Salt and ground black pepper to taste

TURKEY IN SIMPLE RED MOLE *6 servings*

Pass plenty of hot corn tortillas when serving this version of mole, Mexico's classic fiesta dish. Leftover sauce can be frozen, but to regain the smooth texture, you may need to process it in the blender before reheating it.

Heat a medium, heavy skillet or griddle (preferably cast iron) over medium heat until hot. Add:

8 large cloves garlic (unpeeled)

Roast, turning occasionally, until the garlic is soft, about 15 minutes. Let cool, then peel the garlic. Remove the stems and seeds from:

8 medium dried ancho peppers (4 ounces)

Tear the peppers into flat pieces. In the hot skillet, lightly toast the peppers while pressing them flat with a metal spatula for about 10 seconds on each side. Remove to a bowl and add hot water to cover; submerge them with a plate and let soak for about 30 minutes. Drain the peppers, remove to a blender along with the garlic, and add:

⅔ cup turkey or chicken stock
1½ teaspoons dried oregano
½ teaspoon ground black pepper
⅛ teaspoon ground cloves

Process the mixture until smooth, then press it through a medium-mesh sieve into a bowl. Heat in a Dutch oven over medium heat until hot:

1½ tablespoons vegetable oil

Add:

½ cup whole almonds

Cook, stirring constantly, until lightly toasted, about 3 minutes. Remove the almonds with a slotted spoon to the blender. To the remaining hot oil, add:

1 small onion, thinly sliced

Cook, stirring occasionally, until nicely browned, about 8 minutes. Remove the onion with the slotted spoon to the blender. To the hot pan, add:

¼ cup raisins

Cook, stirring constantly, until the raisins are puffed, about 30 seconds. Scoop the raisins into the blender. To the blender, add:

2 slices firm white bread, toasted and torn into pieces
1 cup turkey or chicken stock
½ cup drained canned tomatoes
¼ cup chopped Mexican chocolate or 2 tablespoons unsweetened cocoa
¼ teaspoon ground cinnamon

Process the mixture until very smooth. Heat in the same Dutch oven over medium heat until hot:

1 tablespoon vegetable oil

Add the strained ancho mixture and cook, stirring, until the mixture darkens and becomes very thick, about 5 minutes. Stir in the almond mixture and cook until very thick, about 5 minutes. Stir in:

4 cups turkey or chicken stock

Reduce the heat to low, partially cover, and simmer, stirring often, about 45 minutes. Taste and season with:

2 to 2½ teaspoons salt, depending on the saltiness of the broth
1 tablespoon sugar, or to taste

Preheat the oven to 325°F. Heat a large, heavy skillet over medium-high heat until hot, then add and heat until hot:

1 tablespoon vegetable oil

Rinse and pat dry, then add:

1 boneless turkey breast half (about 2 pounds) or 2 to 2¼ pounds bone-in turkey thighs

Brown the turkey nicely on all sides, about 10 minutes total. Remove the turkey from the pan and nestle it into the seasoned mole. Bake, covered, until an instant-read thermometer inserted in the thickest part of the meat registers about 160°F, about 40 minutes. Remove the turkey from the mole, cut into thick slices, and serve with a generous amount of the sauce and a garnish of:

Fresh parsley leaves
Sesame seeds, toasted

ABOUT GROUND TURKEY AND CHICKEN

Ground turkey comes in three styles: regular (7 to 10 percent fat), lean (about 3 percent fat), and ground breast (about 1 percent fat). Ground chicken comes in only one form; it is often labeled "lean" but actually has a fat content comparable to that of "regular" ground turkey. For many people, ground turkey and chicken make perfectly acceptable substitutes for ground beef, particularly in highly seasoned dishes like chili and tacos. When substituting ground poultry for beef in mild dishes, you may want to increase the spice.

GROUND TURKEY OR CHICKEN LOAF

4 servings

You can cook this delicious mixture as a loaf, as burgers, or as meatballs.

Position a rack in the center of the oven. Preheat the oven to 350°F. Lightly oil a 4- to 5-cup loaf pan.

Heat in a medium skillet over medium heat until fragrant:

1 tablespoon olive oil

Add:

½ cup chopped onions
1 clove garlic, minced

Cook, stirring, until the onions are tender but not browned, 5 to 7 minutes. Remove to a medium bowl and add:

1 pound ground turkey or chicken
1 large egg
¼ cup grated Parmesan cheese
2 tablespoons milk
2 tablespoons dry unseasoned breadcrumbs
1 tablespoon tomato paste
1 tablespoon chopped fresh basil, or 1 teaspoon dried
1 tablespoon chopped fresh parsley, or 1 teaspoon dried
1½ teaspoons salt
½ teaspoon ground black pepper

Thoroughly combine the mixture, then pat into the prepared pan. Bake until the center feels firm when pressed, about 35 minutes. Let stand for 10 minutes, then unmold from the pan if you wish. Serve hot.

TURKEY OR CHICKEN MEATBALLS

Prepare the mixture for:

Ground Turkey or Chicken Loaf, above

Form into 1-inch balls and roll in:

½ cup cornmeal

Heat in a large, heavy skillet over medium-high heat until fragrant and hot but not smoking:

2 tablespoons olive oil

Add the meatballs and brown on all sides, about 10 minutes. Serve with a vegetable or with pasta and tomato sauce.

ABOUT DUCK

Duck has a reputation for being fatty. Actually, nearly all of the fat is under the skin or in the openings of the body and neck cavities. The meat itself is fairly lean. Since you can, if you cook the bird with care, render most of the fat out of the skin, leaving the skin crisp and delicious, there is no reason to think of duck as a forbidden treat to be reserved for special occasions only.

Supermarket ducks generally weigh between 4½ and 5½ pounds. Since a great deal of that weight is skin, fat, and bones, you should buy the heaviest duck available. Even then, you will end up with only enough meat for four modest servings. Indeed, most restaurants serve a half duck per person. Formerly, ducks usually came to market frozen, but many supermarkets now carry fresh ducks wrapped in such a way as to permit storage of a week or longer. If you buy one of these, check the expiration date on the package and be sure to cook it by that date.

In recent years, specialty breeds, especially Moulard and Muscovy ducks, have become available. These ducks have a meatier flavor than the ordinary supermarket type, and Muscovy ducks, in particular, have considerably larger breasts. These ducks must be specially ordered and are expensive. Producers offer both whole birds and separately packaged breasts and legs. Cook specialty ducks as you would supermarket ducks, allowing a little extra time if the ducks are large.

COOKING DUCK IN PARTS

Unlike chickens and turkeys, whose breasts have white meat and whose legs have dark, ducks are entirely dark meat. That said, the breast and legs of duck are quite different. The breast is tender, delicate, and very lean, while the legs are firm and tough. This means that the breast, while delicious when roasted to the well-done stage on the whole bird, is, to many tastes, even better when cooked separately to just rare or medium-

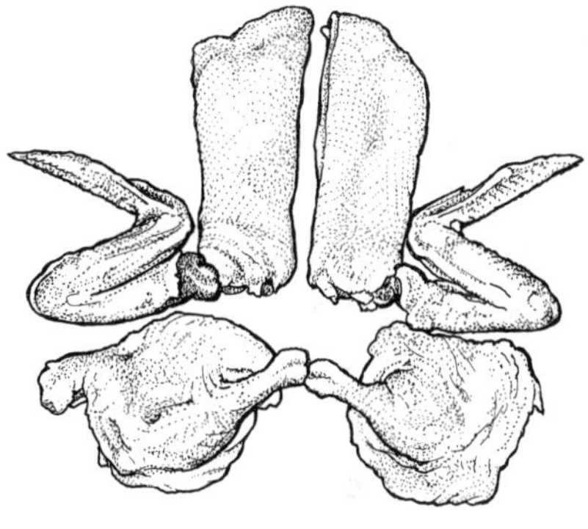

Duck cut up in pieces

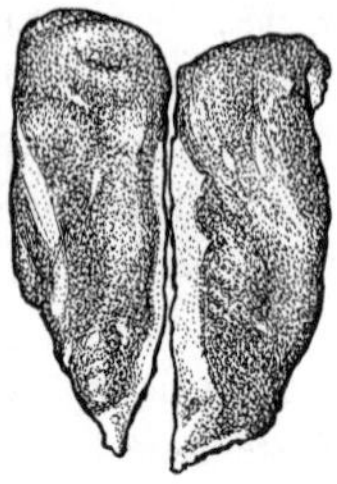

Boneless, skinless duck breasts

rare. The legs, by contrast, require thorough cooking, whether roasted on the whole bird or prepared on their own.

The French, who are always fastidious in such matters, have long insisted that the breast and leg of duck require separate treatments. Typically, a French chef will bone and split the breast, making two *magrets*; sometimes she will also remove the skin and fat. She will then sauté or grill the breast just until rare and braise or bake the legs or use them to make confit. When a French chef roasts a whole duck, she may slice off the breast meat while it is still rosy and serve it as a first course. Then, while the breast is being consumed, she will cut off the legs and wings, bake or broil them until tender, and present them as a second course.

Boneless, skinless duck breasts, boned duck breasts with skin, and duck legs can be bought from specialty producers or prepared at home. If you wish to cut up a duck yourself, start by cutting off the legs and wings (see How to Cut Up Poultry, 569). Try to keep the oysters connected to the legs; sever the wings as close to the body as possible. Before removing the breast, pull up the skin at the neck end of the body and locate the wishbone. Free the wishbone from the surrounding flesh with the point of a paring knife and pull the bone free. To remove the breast, slit the breast from one end to the other alongside the breastbone. Scrape the knife down the side of the breastbone and over the ribs to remove one side of the breast. Repeat to remove the other side. If you wish, pull the skin off the breast halves, then carefully trim any clinging bits of fat and membrane. (The membrane, nearly invisible when the breast is raw, is unsightly once the breast is cooked.) You can cook the wings with the legs or chop them up and combine them with the carcass and giblets to make duck stock. Follow the directions for turkey stock, 39.

CRISPY ROASTED DUCK

2 to 4 servings

Slow-roasting in a very low oven ensures that the delicate breast meat will remain moist and that the skin will be crispy and without fat. Pricking the skin helps to release melted fat. Be sure to insert the skewer or knife tip into the skin without puncturing the meat itself, or else juices from the meat will leak out and stain the skin.

Position a rack in the center of the oven. Preheat the oven to 250°F.

Remove the neck and giblets from, then rinse and pat dry:

1 duck (about 5 pounds)

Pull out all large pieces of fat from the openings of the body and neck cavities, shown 621 (top left). Rub the body cavity and sprinkle the skin with:

Salt

Holding a sharp metal skewer or the point of a paring knife almost parallel to the duck to avoid puncturing the meat, pierce the skin all over in 20 to 30 places, shown 621 (top right). Place the duck breast side down on a rack in a large roasting pan. Roast for 3 hours, giving the skin a few extra pricks with the skewer or knife every hour or so. After 3 hours, drain the fat out of the roasting pan, turn the duck breast side up, and increase the oven temperature to 350°F. Roast for 45 minutes more. The skin should be nice and crispy. Remove the duck to a platter and let stand for 10 minutes.

To serve 2, cut the duck in half through the breastbone and back with a very sharp knife or poultry shears. To serve 4, cut off the legs and divide them at the thigh/drumstick joint. Cut off the wings and divide them in half. Cut each breast half from the bone, then divide each half into half. Serve each person a drumstick or thigh, half a wing, and a piece of the breast meat.

CRISPY ROASTED DUCK WITH QUICK ORANGE SAUCE

2 to 4 servings

Prepare:

Crispy Roasted Duck, above

Combine in a small saucepan:

½ cup orange marmalade
2 tablespoons soy sauce
2 tablespoons orange liqueur, such as Grand Marnier, Cointreau, or Triple Sec (optional)
1 tablespoon white wine vinegar

Bring to a boil over medium heat and cook briefly until the sauce is the consistency of light syrup. If it becomes too thick, dilute it with stock or water. Season with:

Salt and ground black pepper to taste

Serve the sauce with the duck.

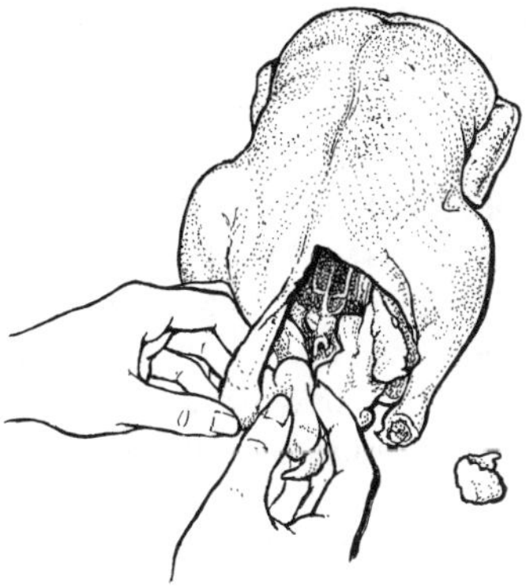
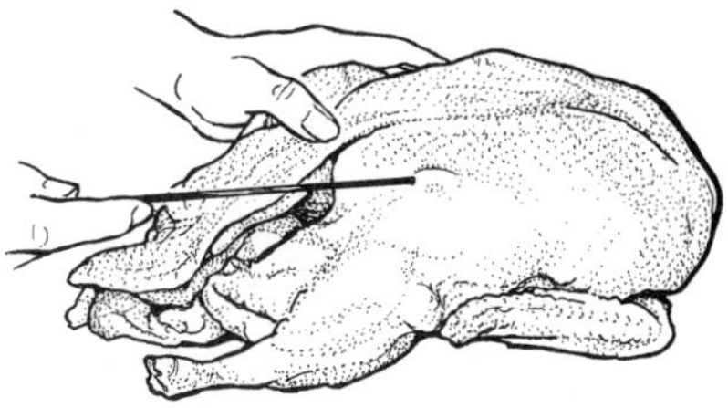

Preparing Crispy Roasted Duck for roasting

CRISPY ROASTED DUCK WITH OLIVES

2 to 4 servings

Americans usually serve roast duck with a sweet sauce, but this savory French sauce with olives is worth investigating.

Prepare:

Crispy Roasted Duck, above

Rinse and pat dry:

2 pounds chicken wings, backs, or drumsticks

Heat in a heavy Dutch oven over medium-high heat until shimmery:

2 tablespoons vegetable oil

Add the chicken and brown on all sides until the color of dark toast. Remove the chicken to a plate and add to the oil:

2 cups chopped onions

Cook, stirring, over medium-high heat until browned and crisp around the edges, 12 to 15 minutes. Sprinkle over the onions:

2 tablespoons all-purpose flour

Cook, stirring, for 1 minute more. Return the chicken to the pan and add:

6 cups chicken stock
2 cups dry white wine
1/3 cup tomato paste
1 bay leaf
12 large sprigs fresh parsley
1/4 teaspoon dried thyme
1/4 teaspoon fennel seeds
1/4 teaspoon ground black pepper

Simmer gently, uncovered, for 2 hours, periodically skimming off the fat with a spoon. Strain the sauce through a sieve, discarding the solids, then return it to the pan and boil over high heat until thickened to a saucelike consistency. Bring to a boil in a medium saucepan over high heat:

4 cups water

Add:

1 cup pitted brine-cured green olives

Boil the olives for 2 minutes, then drain. Taste. If the olives seem very salty, repeat. Add the olives to the sauce and simmer gently for 10 minutes. Serve the sauce with the duck.

CHINESE ROASTED DUCK

2 to 4 servings

With its crispy, lacquered-looking skin, this is similar to the famous Peking Duck but requires much less time and effort.

Remove the neck and giblets from, then rinse and pat dry:

1 duck (about 5 pounds)

Pull out all large pieces of fat from the openings of the body and neck cavities. In a pot large enough to hold the duck, bring to a boil:

5 cups water
1/2 cup soy sauce
1/4 cup honey

Place the duck in the boiling mixture for 1 minute, turning it with 2 wooden spoons to coat it evenly. Remove the duck from the pot, drain, and pat dry. Place the duck on a rack set on a baking sheet. Refrigerate, uncovered, for 24 hours, or set the duck in front of an electric fan in a cool location for 2 to 3 hours to dry the skin well.

Position a rack in the lower third of the oven. Preheat the oven to 425°F.

Place the duck breast side up on a rack in a roasting pan. To prevent the fat from smoking, pour into the pan:

2 cups water

Roast the duck for 20 minutes, then turn breast side down and roast for 20 minutes more. Remove from the oven and reduce the oven temperature to 350°F. Pour all the fat and water out of the roasting pan. Prick the duck skin thoroughly with a fork or metal skewer, holding the fork or skewer almost parallel to the duck and being careful not to pierce the meat. Stir together:

¾ cup orange juice
¼ cup rice vinegar
3 tablespoons soy sauce
2 tablespoons honey
½ teaspoon five-spice powder (optional)

Turn the duck breast side up, brush with the orange mixture, and roast for 20 minutes. Turn the duck breast side down, brush again with the orange mixture, and roast for 20 minutes. Turn the duck breast side up again, give it another brushing, and roast for 20 minutes more. Let the duck stand for 10 minutes, then carve as directed for Crispy Roasted Duck, 620.

PAN-SEARED BONELESS, SKINLESS DUCK BREASTS

6 servings

Boneless, skinless duck breasts are similar to a lean red meat cutlet and always are served rare or medium-rare. In addition to being pan-seared, they can be broiled or grilled.

Rinse and pat dry:

6 boneless, skinless duck breast halves

Combine in a glass or ceramic bowl large enough to hold the duck:

3 tablespoons raspberry or other fruit-flavored vinegar
2 tablespoons olive oil
2 tablespoons minced onions, shallots, or scallions
2 tablespoons honey
1 tablespoon minced garlic
½ teaspoon dried marjoram or oregano
½ teaspoon dried sage, crumbled
½ teaspoon dried thyme
¼ teaspoon ground allspice
½ teaspoon salt
½ teaspoon ground black pepper

Turn the duck breasts in the marinade to coat well, then cover the bowl with plastic wrap and refrigerate for 2 to 12 hours. Remove the duck breasts from the marinade, scrape off the solids, and pat dry. Brush both the breasts and a large, heavy skillet with:

Olive oil

Heat the skillet over medium-high heat until the oil begins to smoke. Add the duck breasts and cook until the bottom is lightly browned, 2 to 3 minutes, depending on size. Using tongs, turn the breasts and cook for 2 to 3 minutes more. Serve immediately.

PAN-SEARED DUCK BREASTS WITH FIG AND RED WINE SAUCE

6 servings

This sauce can be made a week ahead and kept in a covered container in the refrigerator. If possible, use the large Calimyrna or Smyrna figs rather than the smaller, darker Mission figs, which are softer and less flavorful.

Combine in a medium saucepan:

2 cups fruity dry red wine, such as Zinfandel
¼ cup duck or chicken stock
2 tablespoons sugar
½ teaspoon dried thyme
One 2-inch strip lemon zest
1 large clove garlic, minced
1 bay leaf
Pinch of ground cloves or allspice

Stirring, bring the mixture to a boil over high heat, then add:

16 dried figs, stems removed

Return the mixture to a boil, then reduce the heat. Cover, and simmer gently until the figs are very soft but still retain their shape, about 45 minutes. If the pan becomes too dry, add a little more wine or stock. Remove the lemon zest and bay leaf. Puree 3 of the figs with about one-third of the poaching liquid in a food processor or blender, then stir this mixture back into the remaining fig sauce. If needed, thin the sauce with wine or stock. Prepare:

Pan-Seared Boneless, Skinless Duck Breasts, above

Warm the sauce through and serve with the duck.

ABOUT GOOSE

Goose is entirely dark meat, but unlike most other dark-meat birds, it does not taste in the least bit gamy. Rather, goose tastes very much like well-done roast beef. Indeed, in seventeenth-century England, certain cuts of roast beef were known, fancifully, as goose.

Dressed geese generally weigh 9 to 12 pounds. Buy the largest one you can find, as there is a great deal of skin, fat, and bone in proportion to the meat. Except at holiday time, most geese come to market frozen, a process that they withstand quite nicely. You will find geese in all sizes and shapes. Some are long and slim, with thighs that protrude above the breastbone; others are wide and squat, with thighs tucked against the body. These variations have no relation to the quality of the goose and do not affect cooking.

Goose is famously fat—a single bird may release a quart or more of fat into the pan during roasting—but, as with all poultry, the fat is under the skin, not in the meat itself, which is lean. Before roasting, goose needs to be scalded and dried to tighten the skin so that it squeezes out fat during cooking. The end result is crisp, fairly lean skin as irresistibly delicious as that of Peking duck.

Despite frequent advice to the contrary, goose really should be stuffed. The stuffing does not absorb fat, and since there is relatively little meat on a goose, a stuffing is needed in order to amply serve eight people. Goose is carved in the same basic way as chicken and turkey, but its leg and wing joints are harder and tighter and are located closer to the back. In other words, goose is best carved in the kitchen rather than at the table (but do exhibit it at the table first), for disjointing the bird is inevitably a bit of a struggle. While you are at it, you might consider making up individual plates of meat, skin, stuffing, and gravy in the kitchen, rather than bringing everything out to the dining room in serving dishes. This way, you can portion out the scarce meat and prized skin evenly and round out servings with generous helpings of stuffing.

Cut-Up Goose: Goose is usually roasted whole, but it can be cut into six serving pieces (two drumsticks, two thighs, and two breast halves) and cooked in parts. Cut off the legs and wings, leaving the oysters attached to the legs and severing the wings as close to the body as possible (see How to Cut Up Poultry, 569). Cut the legs into two pieces at the thigh/drumstick joint. Pull up the skin at the neck end of the body and locate the wishbone. Free the wishbone from the surrounding flesh with the point of a paring knife and pull the bone free. If you wish to prepare bone-in breast halves for confit, 624, cut out the backbone with poultry shears, then divide the breast lengthwise in half, through the breastbone, with a heavy knife. If you wish to make boneless breast halves, slit the breast from one end to the other alongside the breastbone. Scrape the knife down the side of the breastbone and over the ribs to remove one side of the breast. Repeat to remove the other side. If you wish, pull the skin off the breast halves, then carefully trim away any clinging bits of fat and membrane. Chop up the wings and combine them with the carcass and giblets to make stock, following the directions for turkey stock, 39.

Goose parts can be substituted in any recipe calling for duck breasts or legs, 622. If the goose is large, a quarter breast will be sufficient for one serving.

ROASTED STUFFED GOOSE WITH GIBLET GRAVY

8 servings

Note that the drying of the skin, essential for crispness, requires one to two days. Before beginning, please read About Goose, 622, and Roasting Whole Poultry, 572.

Remove the neck and giblets from, then rinse and pat dry:

1 goose (10 to 12 pounds)

Reserve the neck and giblets for gravy. Snip the wing tips off and reserve them for gravy as well. Pull out any lumps of fat from around the cavities. Using small pliers, pull out any quills in the skin. Pull up the skin at the neck end and locate the wishbone. Scrape along the wishbone with a paring knife until the bone is exposed, then cut the bone free and pull it out. Using a sharp skewer or trussing needle, prick the skin all over, especially over the thighs and breast, holding the skewer nearly parallel to the bird to avoid puncturing the meat.

Bring a large pot of water to a rapid boil. Protecting your hands with rubber gloves, submerge the neck end of the goose in the boiling water for 1 minute, shown below. Pull the goose out, then submerge the tail end for 1 minute. Remove the goose from the water, drain, and pat as dry as possible, inside and out. Set the goose breast side up on a flat rack set in a roasting pan and refrigerate, uncovered, for 24 to 48 hours to dry the skin. Meanwhile, using the goose neck and giblets, prepare through the step where it is thickened with roux:

Giblet Gravy, 615

Let cool, then cover and refrigerate until needed.

Position a rack in the center of the oven. Preheat the oven to 325°F.

Prepare and have *hot:*

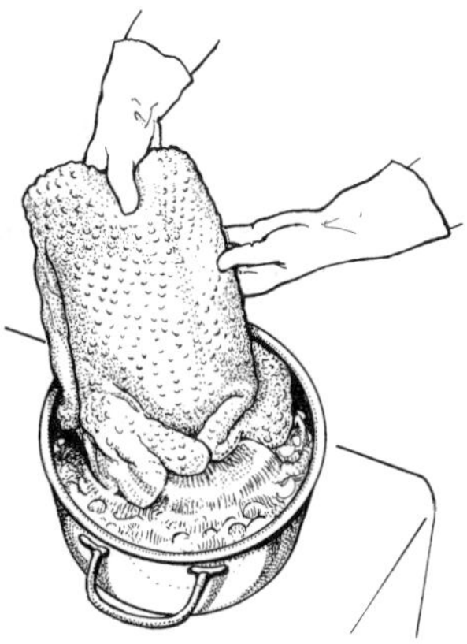

Submerging the neck end of a goose in boiling water

Bread Stuffing with Sausage and Apples, 483, Bread Stuffing with Toasted Nuts or Chestnuts and Dried Fruit, 483, or Herbed Mashed Potato Stuffing, 485

Loosely pack the body and neck cavities of the goose with stuffing and close the vents. Bake any leftover stuffing in a buttered dish. Place the goose breast side down on the rack in the roasting pan and cook for 1½ hours. Remove the goose from the oven and spoon out most of the fat in the roasting pan, being careful not to discard juices and browned bits. Turn the goose breast side up, return to the oven, and roast until the flesh of the drumsticks feels soft when pressed and the skin has puffed around the breast and tops of the thighs, 1¼ to 1½ hours longer. If you wish extra-crispy skin, set the goose, still on its rack, on a baking sheet. Increase the oven temperature to 400°F and roast the goose for 15 minutes more. Remove the cooked goose to a cutting board and let stand for 30 minutes.

Meanwhile, carefully pour, then spoon, the fat out of the roasting pan, retaining all juices and browned roasting particles. Set the pan on two burners over medium heat. Pour in:

½ cup Madeira or port

Bring the mixture to a simmer, all the while scraping the bottom of the pan with a wooden spoon to loosen the browned bits. Pour the drippings into the giblet gravy base. Place the gravy over medium heat and simmer, stirring occasionally, for 5 minutes to blend the flavors. Season with:

Salt and ground black pepper to taste

Let the goose stand for 15 minutes, then remove the stuffing and carve the meat. Cut any skin that becomes detached from the meat into strips. Serve the stuffing, meat, and skin with the gravy.

CONFIT

12 first-course or 6 to 8 main-course servings

Confit is poultry or meat poached slowly in fat and then stored in the fat until needed. Confit was originally devised as a preparation method, and so the meat, before cooking, was given a full-scale curing in salt. Since confit is now made solely for its taste, this recipe uses only enough salt to flavor the meat, which means that the confit should not be kept longer than a month in your refrigerator. Goose confit, a classic ingredient in cassoulet, is traditionally prepared with legs only, but this recipe starts with a whole goose because that is what most home cooks are likely to have. Of course, four to six goose legs can be substituted, as can eight to ten duck legs. To cut up a goose, please see About Goose, 622.

Rinse, pat dry, and cut into 6 pieces:

1 goose (10 to 12 pounds)

Combine:

⅓ cup kosher salt
2 tablespoons ground black pepper
2 teaspoons dried thyme
¼ teaspoon ground allspice

Rub the mixture evenly over the goose pieces, place them in a shallow pan, cover tightly, and refrigerate for 1 to 3 days.

Place in a heavy pot large enough to hold the goose pieces and lard:

2 medium onions, sliced
10 cloves garlic, unpeeled
10 sprigs fresh thyme, or 1 teaspoon dried

Add:

7 pounds lard

Heat, stirring, over low heat until the lard melts, then remove from the heat. Rinse the goose well and pat dry. Carefully slip the goose pieces into the fat. They should be completely submerged. If they are not, add:

1 to 3 pounds additional lard or solid vegetable shortening

Cook, uncovered, over the lowest possible heat until the goose legs feel tender when pierced with a knife, 1½ to 2 hours. The fat should be kept at a very lazy bubble, about 200°F on a thermometer, or the meat will turn stringy. If necessary, place the pot on a flame-tamer device.

Using a slotted spoon, remove the goose to a plate. Increase the heat to medium-high and cook the fat until it stops sputtering, 5 to 10 minutes. Strain the fat through a very fine sieve and discard all solids. Place the goose in a crock (or in the wiped-out cooking pot) and cover with the strained fat. Let cool to room temperature, then cover and refrigerate. The goose will keep for up to 1 month. If you take out a piece, remelt some of the fat from the pot (or additional fat) and cover the spot. To serve confit, broil or pan-fry it rather slowly until it is heated through and the skin crisps up.

GAME

America was built on game. Long before domesticated sheep and cattle grazed tamed acreage, first Native Americans, then European settlers set out daily to bring down wild creatures for the evening meal. Until the end of the nineteenth century, in fact, game was the most abundant meat on the American table. Only with the coming of the twentieth century, with its ever more efficient systems of animal husbandry (and storage and distribution), did domesticated birds and beasts take over the dinner table.

Today, however, there is renewed interest in game—encouraged partly by gastronomic exploration and partly by the realization that the meat of most game birds and animals is significantly lower in saturated fat than that of their domestic counterparts. For example, quail, pheasant, and guinea hen all possess 40 percent fewer calories and 60 percent less fat, pound for pound, than chicken. As demand for game increases, however, the definition of game has changed. The term used to mean only birds or animals caught in the wild; today, "game" includes birds and animals once caught in the wild that are now raised domestically, such as quail, rabbit, deer, and so on.

Game birds and animals are both ranched and farmed. Ranched game is raised under free-range conditions, developing a more complex flavor, with less excess body fat. Farmed game is typically milder to the taste and somewhat fattier. Game raised by either method is usually more tender than wild game and, although lacking the assertive gamy character of animals from the wild, may be more consistently pleasing in flavor. It is also far more convenient—both because of regular availability and because it comes to market already dressed and often already cut into serving pieces.

Hunting remains a popular sport in almost every state in the union. If you choose to hunt, remember that proper handling of game will greatly enhance its flavor; if you're a novice, contact your local cooperative extension service or State and Federal Fish and Wildlife Agencies for information on safe and proper handling of game before you hunt. When cooking wild game, follow the recommendations for its farm-raised counterpart, but remember that wild game is almost always leaner and often must be barded and basted so that it does not dry out (see Marinating and Barding Game, 626).

When cooking wild fowl, if you are at all doubtful that a bird is young or prime, do not hesitate to use a moist-heat method of cooking. At the extreme, very old birds are fit only for the stockpot or soup pot or for making hash, sausages, and sauces. With younger wild birds, often only the breasts are served, and the tougher legs are simmered with the wings, neck, and giblets for stock. This stock is most useful, for in no cooking is less gravy naturally produced than in that of game.

BUYING GAME

Not every supermarket carries game, but many meat departments and butcher shops can special-order it on a few days' notice. There are also mail-order companies that will deliver game to your door. In judging the quality of game, use the same standards as for other meats and poultry: Look for moist, well-shaped cuts that are firm to the touch and without slime, discoloration, or dry spots. Meat should smell fresh, not sour or "off." The skin on game birds should be smooth and supple, the wing tips moist and pliable, and the breastbone firm. While fresh products are generally preferred, properly frozen game is far superior to poorly handled fresh specimens. For best results, thaw frozen game slowly in the refrigerator.

COOKING GAME

The most common error in cooking game is overcooking it. Because game is lower in fat than domestic meats, it cooks more quickly and dries out faster. In addition, game meats raised domestically do not necessarily need to stew for hours in order to become tender. In general, the red meat of venison and buffalo is best when cooked not beyond medium-rare. Game birds should be tested for doneness by piercing the skin of the fleshy thigh; the juices of light-fleshed birds should run clear, while those of dark fowl should retain a slight pink hue. More specific cooking instructions follow with the recipes.

MARINATING AND BARDING GAME

Many kinds of game, especially hooved varieties like venison and boar, were traditionally marinated in red wine and spices to counterbalance stronger flavors and tenderize the meat. It isn't necessary to marinate domestic game, though many cooks still do for added flavor; if you do marinate, don't overdo it, especially with delicately flavored light-fleshed game. (*Do not serve uncooked marinade.*) Another common practice in earlier times was barding game—wrapping it in bacon or another form of pork fat—to compensate for its natural leanness. Barding was especially popular for lean game birds, including partridge and guinea hen, and certain cuts of venison and boar, such as the leg, round, and bottom round.

Wild game birds always should be barded, but barding may or may not be necessary with commercially raised game, which often has a little more fat. Follow recommendations given in the recipes. To bard, use bacon or thin (1/8- to 1/4-inch) slices of pork fat (or fatback), cut into small squares or lengths. As you truss the fowl, 572, slip pieces of bacon or fat into place on either side between the breast and legs to cover the breast, shown below left. Alternatively, cover the entire trussed bird—legs and all—with bacon or fat and tie securely, shown below right, making sure all exposed surfaces are blanketed. After cooking, discard the barding. Bear in mind that the barding fat will prevent the surface from browning. To remedy this, remove the barding 10 minutes or so before the bird is finished roasting.

An alternative to traditional barding is to rub the bird all over with softened butter before roasting. A flavored butter, 76 to 78, or plain softened butter may be used to baste the bird and boost the flavor at the same time. Gently loosen the skin around the breast and thighs of the bird and work the softened butter under the skin and then over the outside of the bird before roasting. (See Roasted Guinea Hen with Chili Butter,

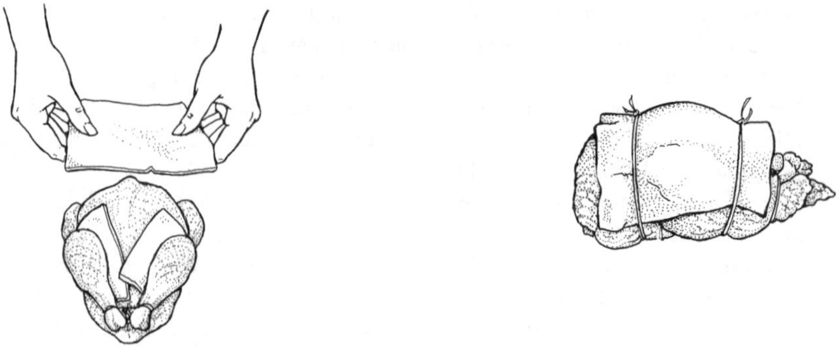

To bard, slip pieces of bacon or fat into place between the breast and legs, or cover the entire trussed bird with bacon or fat and tie securely.

below.) Butter not only helps keep the bird moist but it also promotes attractive browning of the skin.

Another option for keeping the breast meat moist on a wild game bird is to roast it upside down on a rack in a roasting pan. Gravity will pull the juices into the breast meat. Simply turn the bird right side up for the last 10 minutes to brown the top.

ABOUT HANGING GAME BIRDS

Hanging game birds, specifically partridge, duck, grouse, and pheasant, for a few days before cooking tenderizes the lean, tougher meat of a truly wild game bird. At the same time, the longer a game bird hangs, the richer and more pronounced the flavor. While the questions of exactly how to hang game birds and for how long is largely a matter of personal preference, there are some general guidelines. Old birds are usually hung longer than young ones, as more time is needed to tenderize the tougher, more mature flesh. A second consideration is the weather. In muggy or hot climates, ripening is accelerated. Whatever the case, if you find yourself with a brace of freshly shot game birds, we recommend keeping the birds in a cool, airy place and consulting your local cooperative extension service or State and Federal Fish and Wildlife Agencies for specific recommendations. Since commercially raised game birds are raised and harvested to ensure tenderness and flavor, hanging becomes unnecessary.

ABOUT GUINEA FOWL

Guinea fowl or guinea hen, also known as African pheasant, has been commercially raised for centuries in many parts of the world. The tender flesh is light and delicate, with a taste similar to that of pheasant (to which it is related). Any recipe for pheasant or chicken will work equally well with guinea fowl. This bird is very lean and may be barded, 626. It is also delicious braised, stewed, or sautéed. Guinea fowl generally weigh between 1 and 4 pounds. Roast the smaller birds, allowing one per person; the larger ones may be split or even quartered (to serve two or four, respectively) and stewed or braised.

ROASTED GUINEA HEN WITH CHILI BUTTER *4 servings*

If only smaller 2-pound birds are available, buy 2 and roast them initially for just 10 minutes at 450°F; the cooking time remains the same at 350°F. The hens may be prepared up to 2 hours ahead of cooking time and refrigerated until use.

Prepare:

Chili Butter, 77, softened

Preheat the oven to 450°F.

Rinse and pat dry:

1 guinea hen (3 to 3½ pounds), dressed

Being careful not to tear it, loosen the skin around the breast and thighs and force the butter mixture under the skin with your fingertips. Rub any remaining chili butter on the outside of the bird. Place it breast side down on a rack in a roasting pan and roast for 20 minutes. Reduce the oven temperature to 350°F and turn the bird breast side up. Add to the pan:

¼ to ½ cup dry white wine (optional)

Roast, basting often, until a meat thermometer inserted in the thickest part of the thigh registers 160°F and the juices from the thigh are clear when the skin is pierced, 25 to 30 minutes more. Transfer to a cutting board, cover loosely with aluminum foil, and let stand for 10 minutes before carving. Carve and pour the pan juices over the hen.

ROASTED BREAST OF GUINEA HEN *4 servings*

Preheat the oven to 425°F.

Rinse and pat dry:

4 boneless guinea hen breasts (7 to 9 ounces each) with a wing drumette attached

Rub with:

Salt and ground black pepper to taste
2 tablespoons butter, softened

Place them in a roasting pan, set the pan in the oven, and immediately reduce the heat to 350°F. Roast, basting often, until the breasts are tender and the juices are clear, 30 to 40 minutes. If desired, top each with a slice of:

Maître d'Hotel Butter, 77

Drizzle the pan juices over each breast and serve.

ABOUT QUAIL

Quail is one of the sweetest and most tender of all game birds and also, since it is widely farm-raised, one of the most readily available. Quail is sold both fresh and frozen (in which form it is quite acceptable). It is the smallest game bird commonly eaten in the United States, weighing between 4 and 8 ounces each, with only a few ounces of breast meat per bird. Two quail make a main course, one an appetizer. We love quail served hot off the grill or spit, to be picked up and eaten with the fingers, but they can be roasted whole or boned and then broiled or sautéed. ("Boned" quail has the backbone and breastbone removed, but the tiny wing and leg bones remain; we recommend asking the butcher to bone the birds or doing it yourself, rather than buying them preboned.) Quail are best cooked simply, with no potent seasonings to mask their delicate flavor. They also take well to full-flavored marinades and sauces.

SPICY MAPLE ROASTED QUAIL

4 main-course or 8 appetizer servings

Serve these quail as an appetizer or as a main course accompanied by sautéed greens and rice. The marinade may be used with game hens, chicken, and pork tenderloin as well.

Rinse and pat dry:

8 quail

Season inside and out with:

Salt and ground black pepper to taste

Whisk together in a shallow bowl:

⅓ cup maple syrup
¼ cup soy sauce
2 tablespoons red wine vinegar
2 tablespoons chili paste with garlic
8 cloves garlic, finely chopped
½ teaspoon five-spice powder

Marinate the quail in the mixture, covered and refrigerated, for at least 4 hours or up to 8 hours.

Preheat the oven to 475°F.

Drain the quail, reserving the marinade, and place them on a rack in a roasting pan. Fold the wingtips under the birds and tie the legs together. Roast for 10 minutes, then reduce the oven temperature to 375°F. Roast, basting twice with the marinade, until the juices from the thigh are slightly pink when the skin is pierced and the flesh is still juicy, about 10 minutes more. Cover loosely with aluminum foil and let stand for 5 minutes before serving. Remove the string and serve.

QUAIL BROILED WITH MUSTARD BUTTER

4 servings

Any small bird can be prepared this way.

Rinse and pat dry:

8 boned quail, 627

Prepare:

½ recipe Mustard Butter, 77

Melt the butter and brush it thoroughly inside and out the quail. Marinate the quail, covered and refrigerated, for 4 hours.

Preheat the broiler.

Place the quail, breast side down, in a shallow roasting pan. Broil 4 inches from the heat for 5 minutes, brush with the marinade, and turn over. Broil until golden brown on the outside but still juicy, 3 to 5 minutes more. The juices from the thigh should still be slightly pink when the skin is pierced. Remove the quail and cover to keep warm. Place the pan over high heat and add:

⅔ cup chicken stock

Boil, whisking constantly, until slightly thickened and reduced to about ½ cup. Taste and season with:

Salt and ground black pepper to taste

Spoon the sauce over the quail and garnish with:

Watercress sprigs

ABOUT PHEASANT

Pheasant, which has been farm-raised for centuries in both Europe and America, is one of the most popular of game birds. The pinkish white meat of domestic birds has a very mild, delicate flavor and texture and is one "exotic" meat that really does resemble chicken. Wild pheasant, on the other hand, has a rich gamy flavor, often accentuated by aging. Whole pheasants weigh between 2 and 3 pounds and will serve two people. The small bones of a pheasant mean a high ratio of meat to bone. The leg and thigh meat tends to be a bit darker and firmer than the tender breast meat, but the two served together offer a good balance of flavor and texture. These small birds can be used in any chicken recipe with the understanding that, in spite of the thin coating of fat protecting the breast meat of farm-raised pheasant, it is quite a bit leaner than chicken, so the cook must avoid overcooking, which renders the meat dry and tasteless. Barding the breast, 626, before roasting will keep it moist and is especially recommended for the leaner wild pheasant. Alternatively, wild pheasant can be cut up before cooking and the tougher thighs and legs braised or stewed, while the more tender breast meat is grilled, sautéed, or roasted.

ROASTED PHEASANT

2 servings

The regal "pheasant under glass," considered the ultimate in upscale dining in an earlier era (it was served beneath a glass dome, which helped keep it moist between oven and table), was traditionally stuffed with wild rice and mushrooms. Pheasant can also be stuffed with a chestnut or sausage dressing, and can be roasted quite successfully with no stuffing at all. The classic sauce for pheasant is Sauce Smitane, 49, but it is equally delicious with Sauce Chasseur.

Preheat the oven to 400°F.

Rinse and pat dry:

1 young pheasant (2 to 3 pounds)

Season inside and out with:

Salt and ground black pepper to taste

Truss, 572, and bard the bird, 626, if desired. Place it on a rack in a roasting pan, set the pan in the oven, and reduce the oven temperature to 350°F. Roast until the juices from the thigh are clear when the skin is pierced, 25 to 30 minutes a pound if stuffed or 20 to 25 minutes a pound if unstuffed. Remove the trussing strings and barding fat, if using, and carve the pheasant into serving pieces. If desired, serve with:

Sauce Smitane, 49 or Sauce Chasseur, 51

PHEASANT BRAISED WITH GIN AND JUNIPER

2 servings

Slow braising guarantees a moist bird. Use a good-quality gin for optimum flavor.

Rinse and pat dry:

1 pheasant (2 to 3 pounds)

Season inside and out with:

Salt and ground black pepper to taste

Truss the bird, 572, or tie the legs together. Wrap completely, 626, in:

2 ounces pork fat or bacon, thinly sliced

Tie the barding fat around the bird securely. Heat in a Dutch oven over medium-high heat:

2 tablespoons vegetable oil

Add the pheasant and cook, stirring, until golden on all sides, 5 to 10 minutes. Remove it to a plate. Add to the pan and cook, stirring, until golden, 3 to 5 minutes:

½ cup sliced shallots

Add the pheasant along with:

1 cup Game Stock, 40, or chicken stock
⅔ cup gin
¼ cup dry sherry
½ teaspoon crushed juniper berries
2 bay leaves

Bring to a boil, cover the pan, reduce the heat to low, and simmer until the pheasant is tender and the juices from the thigh are clear when the skin is pierced, 35 to 40 minutes. Remove the pheasant to a platter and keep warm. Strain the sauce, skim off the fat, and return the sauce to the pan. Boil over medium-high heat until slightly thickened, 3 to 5 minutes. Remove the bay leaves. Stir in:

3 tablespoons minced fresh parsley
2 tablespoons butter (optional)
Salt and ground black pepper to taste

Remove the barding fat and trussing strings from the pheasant. Carve into serving pieces, spoon the sauce over, and serve.

ABOUT PARTRIDGE AND GROUSE

In the South, bobwhite quail is sometimes called partridge; elsewhere, the name is applied to ruffed grouse. However, most commercially raised partridge in America today is the variety known as Chukar partridge. These are small birds, appreciated for their tender, tasty, lean breast meat, which is similar to that of pheasant but a little firmer and not as delicate. Grouse, a close cousin of partridge, is not farmed and remains a true game bird; any found in United States' markets is imported. Grouse, considered by many to be the finest of game birds, with darker and more flavorful meat than partridge, is so highly prized in England and Scotland that the much anticipated opening day of grouse season in mid-August is known as "The Glorious Twelfth." Partridges generally weigh a bit less than 1 pound apiece, so serve 1 bird per person. Grouse may range from a pound or so to as much as 5 or 6 pounds; whatever the size of the bird, about 1 pound per person is sufficient. Because of their lean meat, partridge and grouse are often best barded, 626, before cooking and frequently basted to keep their meat moist. Small partridge and grouse can be roasted or cut into pieces and grilled, sautéed, or braised.

ANDALUSIAN PARTRIDGE

2 servings

In the spirit of Spanish tapas, serve this dish at room temperature for an appetizer. Other small game birds can also be cooked this way.

Preheat the oven to 325°F.

Rinse and pat dry:

2 partridge (¾ to 1 pound each)

Loosely fill the cavities with about two-thirds of:

1 medium red onion, thinly sliced

and:

2 bay leaves

Truss the birds, 572, or tie the legs together. Rub them all over with:

2 tablespoons sherry vinegar
Salt and ground black pepper to taste

Place the birds in a casserole or Dutch oven. Add the remaining sliced onions along with:

¾ cup dry sherry
¼ cup chicken stock
½ cup olive oil
2 tablespoons sherry vinegar

¼ cup golden raisins
3 large cloves garlic, peeled
3 bay leaves
6 whole cloves
12 black peppercorns
½ teaspoon salt

Bring to a boil, cover, and cook in the oven until the birds are very tender, 1½ to 2 hours. Let the birds cool in the cooking liquid. Discard the bay leaves, remove the birds, and serve at room temperature with a small amount of the cooking liquid spooned over the partridge.

ROASTED GROUSE

4 servings

Preheat the oven to 400°F.
Rinse and pat dry:
4 young grouse (about 1 pound each)
Season inside and out with:
Salt and ground black pepper to taste
Divide among the cavities:
1 small apple, quartered
1 small onion, peeled and quartered
1 celery stalk, cut into 4 pieces

Truss, 572, and bard the birds, 626. Place them on a rack in a roasting pan, set the pan in the oven, and reduce the oven temperature to 350°F. Roast, basting often, until the juices from the thigh are lightly pink when the skin is pierced, 25 to 35 minutes. Remove the birds from the oven and cover to keep warm. Prepare:
For Pan Gravy Poultry, 52
Remove the trussing strings and serve, if desired, with:
Whole Cranberry Relish, 64

ABOUT SQUAB, PIGEON, AND DOVE

The birds we call squab, pigeon, and dove are basically the same animal; all are doves—of which there are some three hundred species. Though *pigeonneau* (literally, young pigeon) is highly regarded in France, Americans consider pigeons to be nuisance birds, not gastronomic treats. Neither pigeon nor dove is sold commercially under those names in this country. Squab, on the other hand, is readily available, and squab is *pigeonneau*—farm-raised young pigeons that have not yet learned to fly. Their meat is dark, rich, tender, and succulent. In order to best appreciate its flavor and texture, squab should be served medium-rare, at which stage the juices run pink and the meat remains slightly rosy and moist. If cooked longer, the meat takes on a distinctively "livery" flavor. Squab adapts well to many cooking methods and can be roasted or braised whole, or split and boned and then broiled, grilled, or sautéed. Always begin cooking squab by browning the breast, skin side down, so that the thin layer of fat beneath the skin bastes the meat as it cooks. Squab are generally sold at a weight of ¾ to 1 pound—enough to serve one person. They may also be split for an appetizer for two.

BROILED SQUAB

2 servings

Preheat the broiler. Grease a broiler pan.
Rinse and pat dry:
2 squab (about 1 pound each)
Remove the backbone with poultry shears. Spread the squab out, skin side up, on the broiler pan. Brush well with:
2 tablespoons butter, melted
Broil the squab 4 inches from the heat, turning once, until the juices from the thigh are lightly pink when the skin is pierced, 15 to 20 minutes. Season with:
Salt
Hot or sweet paprika
If desired, serve on:
Buttered toast
Pour any drippings over the squab. Serve immediately, garnished with:
Chopped fresh parsley

GRILLED SQUAB

Prepare a medium-hot charcoal fire. Prepare Broiled Squab, above, substituting olive oil for the butter. Grill the squab starting skin side down. Serve hot topped with a slice of flavored butter, 76 to 78.

SALMI OF SQUAB

2 to 3 servings

A venerable French classic, a true salmi is a laborious two-step preparation for wild duck, pheasant, partridge, or woodcock. First the game bird is roasted until just barely rare, then the meat is cut from the bone and set aside so that the carcass can be crushed in a duck-press or mortar and pestle to form the basis for the sauce. Once the sauce is made and enriched with classic Sauce Demi-Glace, 50, mushrooms, Cognac, and even truffles, the meat is warmed tableside in a chafing dish with great ceremony and served at once. Needless to say, this dish is rarely presented in its original form any longer. For the sake of convenience, our version relies on a quick reduction of stock. Pheasant or partridge can easily be substituted.
Rinse and pat dry:
2 squab (about 1 pound each), backbone removed, split in half
Season inside and out with:

Salt and ground black pepper

Heat in a large skillet over medium-high heat:

2 tablespoons olive oil

Add the squab, in batches if necessary, skin side down and cook until crispy and brown, 5 to 6 minutes. Turn over and cook for 3 to 4 minutes more. Remove and set aside. To the same pan, add and cook, stirring, until the mushrooms begin to brown, about 8 minutes:

1 pound mushrooms, preferably cremini, wiped clean and sliced

Remove the mushrooms and set aside. To the same pan, add and cook over medium heat until softened, about 2 minutes:

1 tablespoon olive oil

½ cup sliced shallots

1 tablespoon fresh thyme, or 1 teaspoon dried

Add and cook, stirring to loosen the browned bits, until almost evaporated:

3 tablespoons Cognac

Add and cook until reduced by half:

1½ cups dry red wine

Add and cook until reduced by half:

1½ cups Game Stock, 40, or beef stock

Return the squab to the pan and simmer for 20 to 25 minutes, turning the birds halfway through cooking. Remove the pan from the heat and transfer the birds to a plate to cool slightly. Pull off and discard the skin of the birds, then pull the meat from the bones and add it to the pan. Discard the bones. Add the reserved mushrooms and reheat over medium heat. Stir in:

2 tablespoons butter (optional)

Salt and ground black pepper to taste

2 tablespoons chopped fresh parsley

Heat for 2 to 3 minutes more and serve over:

Polenta Toast, 249, or cooked fresh pasta

HOME-SMOKED SQUAB CHINESE STYLE

4 servings

You can smoke any small bird this way, but be careful not to overcook it and dry the meat out.

Puree in a blender or food processor:

Grated zest of 1 lemon

Grated zest of 1 orange

½ cup light soy sauce

⅓ cup oyster sauce

2 tablespoons honey

1 tablespoon chopped fresh cilantro

1 teaspoon finely chopped peeled fresh ginger

2 cloves garlic, finely chopped

1 bay leaf

½ teaspoon ground black pepper

Pour into a shallow pan. Rinse, pat dry, and add to the pan:

4 squab (about 1 pound each), whole or halved with backbone removed

Marinate, covered and refrigerated, for at least 6 hours or up to 12 hours, turning occasionally.

Prepare a covered grill for hot smoking, 1056. Hot-smoke the squab until the juices from the thigh run slightly pink when the skin is pierced, about 45 minutes to 1½ hours, depending on how hot the fire is. Baste with the marinade every 15 minutes and add 8 to 10 coals to the fire halfway through the cooking time to maintain an even heat. Serve immediately. Do not serve uncooked marinade.

ABOUT WILD TURKEY

Even when "wild" turkey is farm-raised, as it is today in many states, it retains a flavor and texture quite distinct from those of its more common, plump-breasted supermarket relatives. Wild turkeys have more leg meat and less breast meat than the domestic kind, and like many other game birds, all of their meat, including the breast, is dark. Despite its leanness, wild turkey can be quite succulent and rich in flavor (imagine a cross between domestic turkey and squab). Unfortunately, fresh wild turkeys tend to appear in the marketplace only at Thanksgiving and Christmas. Frozen ones are sometimes available at other times and make a suitable substitute, but they must be thawed slowly in a refrigerator to maintain juiciness. It is rare to find wild turkeys, whether farm-raised or wild, at more than 12 to 15 pounds, and the younger hens—often considered the best—are sold at 6 to 10 pounds. On average, figure 1 to 1½ pounds per person. We recommend barding the breast, 626, before roasting to keep the lean meat moist; if you choose to spit-roast the bird, baste it frequently. Wild turkey can be used in place of domestic turkey in any recipe, but be very careful not to overcook it, as it can become almost inedibly dry.

WILD TURKEY ROASTED IN A BAKING BAG

10 to 12 servings

It was a hunter's wife of our acquaintance who discovered that roasting wild turkey in a bag would keep it from losing precious juices. Roast wild turkey with or without stuffing, as you desire.

Preheat the oven to 325°F. Have ready a 23½ x 19-inch roasting bag.

Rinse and pat dry:

1 wild turkey (8 to 12 pounds)

Rub with:

Salt and ground black pepper to taste

If desired, stuff with:

Basic Bread Stuffing, 482, or Bread Stuffing with Sausage and Apples, 483

or:

3 celery stalks, cut into 1-inch pieces
1 onion, quartered

Truss the bird, 572, or tie the legs together. Insert a meat thermometer in the center of the thigh muscle. Put the turkey in the roasting bag, tie the bag closed, and place it in a roasting pan. Roast until the thermometer registers 165°F and the juices from the thigh are just slightly pink when the skin is pierced, 10 to 12 minutes per pound if unstuffed, 12 to 14 minutes per pound if stuffed. Remove from the oven and let stand for about 20 minutes before removing from the roasting bag and carving. If you would like a gravy, carefully transfer the juices in the bag to a saucepan. Mix together:

2 tablespoons cornstarch
2 tablespoons water

Gradually pour into the juices, whisking constantly, and bring to a boil. Season with:

Salt and ground black pepper to taste

ABOUT RABBIT AND HARE

Rabbit and hare, though closely related, are quite different in size and flavor. Rabbit, which is primarily farm-raised, has smooth-textured white meat with a mild, delicate, slightly sweet taste, very much like that of chicken. Smaller rabbits, referred to as fryers, generally weigh between 2 and 4 pounds (anything larger is called a roaster). Regardless of size, all commercially raised rabbits have a much greater proportion of meat to bone. They are commonly cut into 6 or 8 pieces—2 forelegs, 2 hind legs, and 2 to 4 sections of saddle or loin. The saddle or loin sections offer the tenderest meat and can be sautéed, grilled, or roasted either on the bone or in boneless fillets. The legs are usually tougher, especially on larger rabbits, and are better suited for stewing or braising. The front legs often offer so little meat that they end up in the stockpot but should be included if the rabbit is stewed or braised. A 3- to 4-pound rabbit will serve four people. Rabbit can be substituted for chicken in almost any dish, treating the saddle as the breast meat and the legs as drumsticks. Because rabbit has less fat than chicken, however, be very careful not to overcook it and dry it out.

Hare can weigh up to 14 pounds, and its meat is usually very dark—regardless of the color of its fur, which varies from species to species, from white to dark brown. The most common wild hare in America is the jackrabbit, but some varieties of European hare are now being farm-raised in America. Hare should be cut up as rabbit, but it is often marinated before cooking. Smaller, younger hare are often roasted, while larger animals should be stewed or braised. Because hare is known to carry tularemia, wear gloves when you handle it. Rabbit and hare are often sold with giblets intact. These should be removed and can be used in pâtés, sausages, and stuffings.

BRAISED MARINATED RABBIT WITH PRUNES

4 servings

Combine in a large bowl:

3 cups hearty red wine
3 tablespoons olive oil
1 cup thinly sliced red onions
½ cup finely diced carrots
2 teaspoons fresh thyme leaves, or ¾ teaspoon dried
2 large bay leaves

Add and marinate, covered and refrigerated, for up to 24 hours:

1 rabbit (3 to 3½ pounds), cut into serving pieces, giblets reserved if desired

Heat in a large Dutch oven or casserole over medium-high heat:

2 tablespoons olive oil

Add and cook, stirring, until vegetables are lightly browned, about 15 minutes:

1 cup pearl onions, peeled
8 ounces whole small mushrooms

Remove with a slotted spoon and set aside. Add and lightly brown, about 10 minutes:

4 ounces bacon, diced

Remove with a slotted spoon to paper towels to drain and set aside. Remove the rabbit from the marinade and pat dry. Season well with:

Salt and ground black pepper to taste

Add the rabbit pieces to the pan and lightly brown, 3 to 5 minutes each side. Remove and set aside. Add to the pan and cook, stirring, over low heat until the flour starts to color slightly, 2 to 3 minutes:

1 tablespoon all-purpose flour

Strain the marinade through a fine-mesh sieve into the pan and whisk to blend with the flour. Bring to a boil and add the bacon and rabbit. Reduce the heat, cover, and simmer for 25 minutes. Add the reserved pearl onions and mushrooms along with:

12 ounces pitted prunes

Cover and simmer until the rabbit is tender, about 20 minutes more. Remove the rabbit, vegetables, and prunes to a deep serving dish and cover to keep warm. If the sauce is thin, boil the liquid over high heat until slightly thickened, 5 to 8 minutes. Finely chop the giblets, if using, and add to the pan along with:

2 tablespoons raspberry vinegar
2 teaspoons red currant or apricot preserves (optional)
Salt and ground white pepper to taste

Simmer the sauce, stirring, for 5 minutes more. Pour the sauce over the rabbit and serve immediately.

RABBIT IN ALMOND SAUCE

4 servings

Season:

1 rabbit (3 to 3½ pounds) cut into 8 serving pieces

with:

Salt and ground black pepper to taste

Heat in a large sauté pan or skillet with a lid over medium heat:

2 tablespoons olive oil

Add and cook, stirring, until the onions are lightly colored, 7 to 10 minutes:

2 cups chopped onions
¼ cup rabbit or chicken livers
2 tablespoons slivered garlic
24 whole blanched almonds

Remove to a blender or food processor. Add:

½ teaspoon ground cinnamon
½ teaspoon saffron threads
½ teaspoon salt
¼ teaspoon red pepper flakes
8 white peppercorns
2 whole cloves

Puree until smooth, stopping to scrape down the sides as necessary. Set the mixture aside. Add to the sauté pan and heat over medium-high heat:

2 tablespoons olive oil

Add the rabbit pieces and lightly brown, 3 to 5 minutes each side. Add the onion mixture along with:

1 cup dry white wine
1 cup Game Stock, 40, or chicken stock, or more if needed
2 bay leaves

Cover and simmer gently until the rabbit is tender, about 45 minutes, turning the pieces over halfway through cooking time. Remove the rabbit pieces to a warmed serving platter and cover to keep warm. Add to the pan and whisk until smooth:

¼ cup dry sherry

Bring to a boil and cook until the sauce is reduced to about 2 cups, 10 to 15 minutes. Remove the bay leaves and season, if desired with:

Salt and ground black pepper to taste

Pour the sauce over the rabbit. Garnish with:

2 tablespoons chopped fresh parsley

LAPIN À LA MOUTARDE (RABBIT WITH MUSTARD)

4 servings

This a French bistro classic. Serve it on a bed of sautéed cabbage with onions or with buttered noodles.

Mix together in a small bowl:

⅓ cup Dijon mustard
1 tablespoon fresh thyme leaves, or 1 teaspoon dried

Generously brush it over:

1 rabbit (3 to 3½ pounds), cut into 8 serving pieces

Season with:

Salt and ground black pepper to taste

Heat in a large sauté pan or skillet with a lid over medium heat:

3 tablespoons olive oil

Add the rabbit pieces, in batches if necessary, and lightly brown, about 5 minutes each side. Remove the rabbit pieces to a platter. Reduce the heat to medium-low. Add to the pan and cook, stirring, until lightly browned, 1 to 2 minutes:

2 tablespoons chopped shallots

Add and bring to a boil, scraping up the browned bits:

1½ cups chicken stock or vegetable stock
1 cup dry white wine
½ cup heavy cream (optional)

Reduce the heat and simmer for about 5 minutes. Return the rabbit to the pan, cover, and cook gently until tender but still moist, about 45 minutes. Remove the rabbit from the sauce, cover to keep warm, and strain the sauce carefully through a fine-mesh sieve. Stir in:

1 tablespoon chopped fresh parsley, chives, tarragon, and/or chervil
2 teaspoons yellow mustard seeds, lightly toasted (optional)

Bring to a boil over high heat and cook until the sauce is reduced to about 2 cups, about 6 minutes.

Season with:

2 to 3 drops fresh lemon juice
Salt and ground black pepper to taste

Spoon the sauce over and around the rabbit pieces and serve immediately.

ABOUT VENISON

We usually use the term "venison" to mean deer meat, but the word, derived from the Latin *venari*, "to hunt," properly refers to all large antlered game animals, including elk, caribou, and antelope, as well as deer. Currently, all four are raised commercially in America. In general, their meat is more tender and less gamy than that of their wild counterparts. Differences in species, diet, age, and methods of rearing and processing may account for differences in taste and texture, but all venison is lean red meat.

Deer remains the most popular and common of venisons and is both farmed and ranched extensively, domestically and abroad. Much of the venison available today is the meat of farm-raised red deer from New Zealand, often marketed under the name Cervena—a trademark name that guarantees the meat is from animals under three years of age. Fallow deer is also farm-raised. Other varieties, including axis and sika deer, are ranched, roaming freely on large-game compounds. Farm-raised deer are more uniform in size and flavor than wild or free-range ranched deer, but the latter are leaner, and their flavor may be more complex.

Antelope meat is delicate and deliciously flavored, a bit lighter than other venison—almost like veal. It is best cooked and served simply. Both nilgai (or nilgi) and black buck antelope are ranched; the former is larger and has a milder flavor. Caribou, which have been domesticated in Alaska for years, is juicy and flavorful. Elk is considered by some connoisseurs to be the best venison of all and is sometimes compared to prime beef.

COOKING VENISON

Venison of any type, unfortunately, is all too easy to ruin in the kitchen. Since there is very little intramuscular fat or marbling in venison, it loses moisture quickly in the heat of the oven or skillet; without fat to coat its protein, it quickly turns tough and chewy. Remember this simple axiom for cooking venison: Cook the tender cuts from the saddle, loin, tenderloin, and hind leg over high heat for a short time, and stew or braise the tougher cuts from the shoulder or neck. As with lamb or beef, the most tender (and most popular) cuts are the center and top portions, sold in the form of steaks, chops, or strip loins. In addition, many processors bone, trim, and butcher the hind leg into a convenient assortment of 7 or 8 cuts, referred to as the Denver leg, all of which make excellent steaks, medallions, and small roasts.

All naturally tender cuts are best broiled, sautéed, or grilled quickly to rare or medium-rare. (Venison should remain crimson; if it's gray, it's overcooked.) Tougher cuts of venison, such as the shoulder, neck, and stew meat of commercially raised game, or large roasts from wild animals, should be seared over high heat to brown, then slowly roasted in a 225° to 250°F oven or braised in liquid until tender. It is not necessary to marinate commercially raised venison, but wild venison often benefits from marinating, which increases tenderness and enhances flavor. Red wine marinades are traditional, but buttermilk or yogurt marinades, 85, offset the stronger gamy flavor of wild venison, and the milk proteins tenderize the meats quite efficiently. Do not overmarinate; 1 hour at room temperature or up to 24 hours in the refrigerator is usually sufficient. (*Do not serve uncooked marinade.*) Ground venison is best when combined with a little ground beef or pork or beaten eggs to keep it moist when grilled. Venison burgers may be cooked without additions by quickly browning them over high heat (either on a grill or in a pan), and then cooking them, covered, with a little broth or wine. Avoid overcooking as they will taste leathery.

ROASTED LEG OF VENISON

8 to 12 servings if boneless; 6 to 8 servings if on the bone

This recipe works equally well with venison saddle or rib roast. Serve with Mashed Potatoes, 408, if desired.

Preheat the oven to 450°F.

Melt in a small saucepan over low heat:

8 tablespoons (1 stick) butter

Add and cook without browning for 5 to 6 minutes:

2 tablespoons chopped fresh parsley
1 tablespoon minced garlic
1 teaspoon dried sage
1 teaspoon dried oregano

Season:

1 boneless or bone-in venison roast (6 to 8 pounds)

with:

Salt and ground black pepper to taste

Place the roast on a rack in a roasting pan and pour the butter mixture over it, spreading evenly over the meat with your hands. Roast for 20 minutes. Reduce the oven temperature to 325°F and add to the pan:

2 cups finely chopped onions
2 cups dry red wine

Roast, basting often until a meat thermometer inserted in the thickest part of the roast registers 130 to 140°F, for medium-rare, about 15 minutes per pound if boneless, about 12 minutes per pound if on the bone. Remove the roast to a platter and cover to keep warm. Set the roasting pan over medium-high heat and add:

3 cups Game Stock, 40, or chicken stock

Boil, scraping up any browned bits, until the sauce is reduced to 1½ to 2 cups. Carefully strain through a fine mesh sieve into a saucepan. Set over high heat and add:

½ cup red currant jelly
¼ cup brandy or Cognac

Skim off any fat and boil for 2 to 3 minutes until slightly thickened. Season with:

Salt and ground black pepper to taste

Slice the roast and serve with the warm sauce.

ROASTED LOIN OF VENISON WITH A NUT CRUST

6 to 10 servings

Combine in a small bowl:

1 cup ground hazelnuts, pecans, or walnuts
½ cup fresh breadcrumbs
2 tablespoons chopped fresh parsley
2 tablespoons vegetable oil
2 teaspoons ground black pepper
½ teaspoon salt

Preheat the oven to 425°F.

Place on a rack in a roasting pan:

1 boneless venison loin roast (3 to 5 pounds), well trimmed

Rub all over with:

1 tablespoon vegetable oil

Coat the venison with the nut mixture on all sides, pressing to make it adhere. Roast the loin until a meat thermometer inserted in the center of the roast registers 110° to 115°F for rare, about 7 minutes per pound, 120° to 125° for medium-rare, about 8 minutes per pound, or 130° to 135°F for medium, about 10 minutes per pound. Let the roast rest for 5 minutes before slicing.

VENISON POT ROAST

Use the less tender cuts of venison, including the shoulder or blade roasts as well as cuts from wild venison, either in a single large piece or cut into small ones, but be sure to remove all fat. Place the meat in a marinade, 84 to 86, cover, and refrigerate it for at least 12 hours, or up to 48 hours, turning it from time to time. Pat dry. Prepare as for Beef Pot Roast, 667, adding some of the marinade to the cooking liquid if desired. Cook as directed for pot roast until tender; the length of time will depend on the size and shape of the cut of venison as well as the oven heat.

SAUTÉED VENISON STEAKS

6 servings

Be sure to use steaks cut from the loin or tender portion of the leg for this recipe.

Gently pound and flatten with a meat pounder or the bottom of a small, heavy pan to an even thickness of about ½ inch:

6 venison loin steaks (6 to 7 ounces each)

Heat in a large, heavy skillet over medium heat:

3 tablespoons olive oil

Add and quickly brown:

4 cloves garlic, slightly crushed

Discard the garlic, leaving the oil. Increase the heat to high and very quickly brown thc mcat, 2 to 3 minutes each side. Season well with:

Salt and ground black pepper to taste

Remove and cover to keep warm. Add and simmer briskly, uncovered, until the tomatoes are soft and reduced to a pulp, 5 to 10 minutes:

2 pounds ripe tomatoes, seeded and chopped
1 to 2 tablespoons fresh oregano leaves
Pinch of red pepper flakes

Stir in:

¼ cup chopped pitted Kalamata or Niçoise olives or 2 tablespoons drained capers
½ cup dry white wine

Season with:

Salt and ground black pepper to taste

Serve immediately over the steaks.

ABOUT BUFFALO (BISON)

Bison, or American buffalo, is an animal indigenous to North America that once roamed in huge herds over the plains of this country, providing both food and shelter for Native Americans. Buffalo is now raised for meat on numerous ranches around the United States, and the meat has significant advantages over beef: It is high in protein and extremely low in cholesterol (approximately 30 percent less than beef), and it has about half the calories and fat of beef. It is also delicious—not unlike beef, but rather coarsely textured and sweet. Since buffalo meat is not marbled with fat like beef, it cooks more quickly (fat acts as insulation). Regardless of the cooking method, buffalo meat should only be cooked rare to medium-rare; well-done meat will prove dry, chewy, and flavorless. The best cuts are steaks, chops, and roasts from the rib, loin, and sirloin. Trim any visible external fat before cooking buffalo. If grilling buffalo steaks or chops, cook them quickly at least 6 inches from the heat source, basting to keep the meat moist. Ground buffalo, like ground venison, is best combined with a little ground pork or beef. Buffalo may be used in virtually any beef recipe as long as you are careful not to cook the meat past medium-rare.

BUFFALO RIB ROAST WITH ORANGE MOLASSES GLAZE

10 to 14 servings

Carefully trim to remove all but a thin layer of fat, and tie securely, if desired:

1 boneless buffalo rib or top sirloin roast (7 to 9 pounds)

Place on a rack in a roasting pan. Prepare:

Orange Molasses Glaze, 89

Generously brush the roast with the glaze and let stand for about 1 hour at room temperature or cover and refrigerate for up to 24 hours. (Bring to room temperature before roasting.) Reserve any remaining glaze to baste the meat while it roasts.

Preheat the oven to 450°F.

Roast the meat for 15 minutes. Reduce the oven temperature to 325°F and roast, basting occasionally with the glaze, until a meat thermometer inserted in the thickest part of the roast registers 120° to 130°F for rare, about 8 to 10 minutes per pound, or 130° to 140°F for medium rare, about 10 to 12 minutes per pound. Be careful not to overcook as the meat will be dry and chewy.

Remove the roast from the pan and cover to keep warm. Add to the pan:

1½ cups beef stock

¾ cup dry red wine

Boil, scraping up any browned bits, until reduced to about 2 cups and slightly thickened. Strain through a fine-mesh sieve and season with:

Salt and ground black pepper to taste

Slice the roast and serve with the warm pan sauce.

ABOUT BOAR

Boar, which has been hunted extensively in Europe for centuries, is a cousin of the domesticated hog, but its meat is leaner and more flavorful. In America, boar can be many things, from Russian boar imported to these shores, to razorback hogs that have escaped into the wild, to the native American wild pig called peccary or javelina. Boar can range in flavor from very mild and delicate to distinctly gamy, depending on the season and the animal's diet. In general, younger animals are preferred for flavor and tenderness. The most popular cuts come from the loin or saddle; tougher, less expensive cuts, such as the hind leg, are best braised or stewed. Wild boar may be prepared like pork. It always should be thoroughly cooked and never eaten rare.

ABOUT OSTRICH AND EMU

Although classified as poultry, ostrich and emu taste and are cooked very much like venison. Both of these farm-raised birds have deep red meat that is extremely low in fat, especially saturated fat, with very little cholesterol. The main difference between the two is that the meat of the emu, which is a smaller animal, is finer grained. The best cooking methods are sautéing or quickly grilling over hot coals to medium-rare. As with venison and buffalo, overcooking turns the meat dry and tough. For grilling, rub the meat with a little olive oil and season with salt and pepper. Although the different cuts of ostrich and emu are confusing, the most tender portions are the cuts referred to as the fan fillet, inside strip, tenderloin, and oyster; next in tenderness are the tip, top loin, and outside strip. The tougher cuts come from the leg area. Use any recipes for lean venison or for beef in preparing ostrich or emu.

MEAT

According to the United States Department of Agriculture, the term *meat* refers to the muscle of cattle, pigs, sheep, and goats. Of these, beef and pork have long prevailed in North America, and their popularity has risen steadily since the first settlers brought over a few pigs and cows. While initially pork overshadowed beef, the boom of western cattle ranches along with the introduction of refrigerated rail transport began a hunger that has yet to be quelled—America's voracious appetite for beef. Changes in economics and taste may cause dips and peaks in the popularity of various meats over the years, but one thing does not change: per capita meat consumption continues to rise. Today, meat remains the most common source of protein in our diets, providing a richness of vitamins and minerals as well.

The way meat is produced and consumed has changed dramatically in recent decades. Growing health concerns about dietary fat have led consumers to demand less fat in food, and the meat industry has responded accordingly. It is estimated that beef sold today is 27 percent leaner than it was twenty years ago, while today's pork, which was once valued as much for its lard as its meat, is closer to 50 percent leaner than in days of old. While this may be good news for our cardiovascular systems and waistlines, it presents a new set of challenges for the cook. Anyone who has ever savored a well-marbled, juicy rib-eye steak knows how fat lubricates meat, making it more tender and moist. Since fat has a direct effect on flavor and juiciness, these new leaner meats must be handled differently. Lean meats are easily dried out and made unpalatable with overcooking, and you can assume that unless a cookbook was written in the past ten years, its cooking times and temperatures for meats are outdated.

The other significant change in the meat industry is that the knowledgeable, helpful butcher has been replaced by an unseen presence that mysteriously slices, grinds, and wraps behind a partition or by bins full of prepackaged meat straight from processing plants. In the past, meat was shipped to market as hanging carcasses, sides, or large pieces known as primal cuts. A butcher's ability to fabricate retail cuts like steaks, roasts, stew meat, and hamburger relied on his knowledge of the anatomy of each animal and his understanding of the distinctions in muscle structure and texture. Skilled butchers could easily help customers identify the best cuts for flavor or tenderness and offer cooking and handling advice. All this changed in the 1970s with new technology that allowed producers to ship beef more efficiently and economically to market by precutting and packaging individual cuts—a method commonly referred to in the industry as *boxed meat*. Today, butchers are no longer required to understand the entire musculature and skeleton of any type of meat; they simply need to be able to trim and slice large cuts into small pieces. We now also can buy large cuts of *boxed beef* still in its factory vacuum-packed seal at the popular wholesale clubs and large retailers. The difficulty for the consumer when purchasing a vacuum-packed meat is that the bag contains quite a bit of fluid, which makes it difficult to judge the color and quality of the meat inside and adds a fair amount of unusable weight. When opening a package of vacuum-sealed meat, bear in mind that it may appear darker than normal and give off an unpleasant odor when it first comes into contact with oxygen. Let the meat air for a few minutes; the color will return to normal, and any unpleasant smell will dissipate.

If you are lucky enough to have a knowledgeable, experienced butcher nearby, by all means give him or her your business and tell your friends. If not, the best tool for understanding the variety of cuts available is to learn a bit about meat cuts in general.

ABOUT MEAT INSPECTION AND GRADING

Meat products are among the most highly regulated and supervised products in our food supply. The Pure Food and Drug Act passed in 1906 and The Wholesome Meat Act implemented in 1967 are intended to assure consumers that all the meat they buy is inspected and approved as wholesome. Under the guidance of the United States Department of Agriculture (USDA), both federal and sometimes state, meat inspectors oversee the processing and distribution of all meat to ensure that it meets standards of safety and sanitation. Despite this control, there are still instances of contaminated meat making its way to the consumer, because harmful bacteria, such as *E. coli* and salmonella, are invisible to the naked eye and can go undetected under current inspection practices. This poses a challenge for the meat industry (a challenge it is trying to meet) and underscores the need for every consumer and cook to handle all meats in a safe and sanitary manner.

Meat labeled as kosher indicates an additional inspection. Kosher meats are processed according to rabbinical law by a specially trained *shoehet,* and the term kosher translates to mean correct or proper. A "kosher" stamp certifies cleanliness, not quality.

While the USDA inspection system ensures that our meat supply is safe, it neglects matters of taste, tenderness, and other characteristics we associate with a good cut of meat. For most consumers, tenderness matters above all else. Unfortunately, tenderness depends not only on the comparative youth of the animal but also on the species to which it belongs and the way it was fed—facts we are rarely privy to. For this, we must rely on grading, a voluntary system instituted by the USDA in 1927 to provide consumers with an indication of the palatability and tenderness of meat. Under this system, packing houses and processors hire federal meat graders to evaluate their meat according to consistent and uniform standards for overall tenderness, juiciness, and flavor determined largely by the age and condition of the animal and the amount of marbling, or intramuscular fat. While there are slight differences in the grades for beef, veal, and lamb (pork is not graded), the rankings are similar.

The highest grade, prime, generally goes to specially raised animals with a high degree of marbling. The meat is tender, finely textured, and well flavored, but it is also quite expensive and scarce. The highest-quality grade usually available in supermarkets and butcher shops is choice, indicating meat from young animals with moderate to minimal marbling. Choice is the broadest grade of meat and can include quite a variation. Some producers attempt to pinpoint choice more exactly with labels such as "high choice" or "top choice," but these are not official grades. Lower grades, good or select, are assigned to the leaner, less tender meat, often from lesser breeds or less well-fed animals. The lowest grades, such as standard, commercial, utility, cutter, and canner, are given to meat with a coarser appearance than other grades and no marbling. However, these grades are rarely seen in retail markets; they are primarily used in commercial and manufactured meat products. For more specific information on how each meat is graded and what that grade implies for a recipe you want to cook, refer to the introductory notes for each type of meat in this chapter.

Since grading is not mandatory and meat processors must pay extra to have their meat graded, a small percentage (less than 15 percent) of the meat sold in our supermarkets is ungraded. Bear in mind as well that some meats which seem to be ungraded in fact fall into the good or select category but are not labeled as such; ask to be sure. The best shopping strategy when dealing with ungraded or unlabeled meat is to look for well-shaped cuts with clean, pure-looking fat and compact, evenly grained muscle. Some large meat packers and supermarket chains have developed their own in-house "grades," which are used in place of or in addition to USDA grades. These in-store grades can be misleading, bearing such names as "butcher's choice," "star," or other fanciful designations.

ABOUT NATURAL AND ORGANIC MEATS

Despite having a food supply that scientists and industry experts often describe as the safest in the world, many American consumers remain concerned about the pesticides, antibiotics, and steroids used by conventional meat producers to control disease and promote growth. The USDA monitors the use of these drugs and chemicals; in order to pass federal inspection, all meat must be free of any residue of drugs or chemicals. Since 1993, the USDA has regularly tested our meat supply for volatile residues of antibiotics and other animal drugs and has reported that there is virtually no incidence of violation of its National Residue Program.

A growing number of producers sell their meat as "natural" and "organic." As defined by the USDA in 1982, "natural" has no bearing on how an animal was raised—it refers to any meat that has been minimally processed and contains no artificial flavorings, colorings, preservatives, or other synthetic ingredients. This definition, then, allows all conventional meat to be labeled "natural." It rules out only canned hams and other processed meats with water or chemical additives. At present, the USDA does not recognize the term "organic," although several states have their own programs, which adhere to the 1994 California definition. To be labeled "organic," meat must be raised on certified organic farms without antibiotics, pesticides, or steroids, and must be processed by certified handlers in ways that minimally affect the environment.

ABOUT MEAT CUTS AND TENDERNESS

It is no mystery that different cuts of meat cook differently. The mystery is how to know the difference when shopping for a certain recipe. Some cuts are tough and coarse and require special handling to become tender; others are naturally buttery soft—ideal for quick grilling or roasting. While the grade or brand of the meat may give you an indication of its overall tenderness, different cuts from the same grade or brand of meat differ widely in how they cook—as anyone who has ever compared a tender rib steak with a chewy chuck steak knows. Fortunately, there is an easy logic that applies to beef, pork, lamb, and veal.

Meat is muscle, and the character of that muscle defines its quality. Well-protected, less-stressed muscles, such as the tenderloin and loin, will have a fine, close-grained texture. These prize cuts are known to be naturally tender, meaning they can be simply broiled, grilled, sautéed, or roasted to rare or medium doneness, at least in grades of choice and above. Well-exercised muscles, such as the neck, shoulder, and leg, are leaner, more coarse grained, and generally tougher. The toughness is due largely to a class of proteins recognized as connective tissue, sinew, and gristle. Connective tissue, also referred to as collagen, can be softened through cooking, but only when cooked very slowly with moist heat for a long time. Thrown on the grill, a piece of meat high in collagen will remain as tough as leather, yet when treated to a gentle, slow braise, it will emerge fork-tender and delectable. The so-called tougher cuts, they can be incredibly flavorful—more so than some of the mild-tasting tender cuts—and, of course, they are generally inexpensive. It is worth noting that many of these once-neglected tougher cuts, such as shank and breast, are now becoming popular in some of our finest restaurants for their slow-cooked succulence.

Younger animals such as veal and lamb will be more tender overall than the mature ones. Compare a fork-tender, mild-tasting veal scallop with the more robust top round steak. These are the same cuts from animals of different ages. As the animal matures, the texture of the meat becomes progressively coarser and the color darkens. The distinction between tough and tender cuts is much more pronounced in beef that it is in veal or lamb. For example, a veal shoulder can be successfully roasted, while the same cut of beef would be miserably tough and chewy if roasted.

When shopping for meat, the best way to distinguish a tough or tender cut is to read the label. Each carcass is broken up into like muscle groups known as *primal* or *major cuts,* shown 647, 679, 687, and 709, and almost all supermarket labels bear the name of the primal cut. The tenderest (and most expensive) cuts of all are the middle and top, known as the rib, loin, and sirloin. These are easily recognizable by their fine grain and neat, single eye muscle. The tenderloin is found in the loin and is the tenderest and mildest-tasting of all the cuts. There is a distinct separation between the loin and the sirloin, despite their similar names. The loin is the saddle section beneath the ribs, and the sirloin is the hip area—a part of the animal that gets a fair amount of exercise. Whereas both the loin and sirloin are good for roasting or cooking as steaks, the loin is the more tender of the two. Cuts from the sirloin are recognizable by their more complicated bone and muscle structure.

The tougher, richer-tasting primal cuts are from the well-exercised muscle groups toward the head, neck, and breast known as chuck, shoulder, brisket, shank, short plate, and breast. These cuts are characterized by their coarser grain, but many also have a complicated structure composed of a few different smaller muscles linked together with connective tissue. Of these cuts, the chuck is prized for its great flavor. The in-between cuts—not too tender, not too tough—come from the hindquarter, known as the rump, round, or leg. Many meat lovers prefer these in-between cuts for the meaty flavor they offer without being too tough. Please see the individual sections on beef, veal, pork, and lamb for information on cooking specific cuts.

Over the years, markets created over a thousand fanciful names for retail cuts intended to promote the sale of a certain cut rather than to provide consumers with the information they need. The National Livestock and Meat Board has recently published a listing of uniform retail meat identity standards in an attempt to help the consumer make sense of the variety of meat available. We have used these names throughout the chapter.

ABOUT COOKING MEAT

The primary change that occurs when meat cooks is that it loses moisture and becomes firmer. When properly controlled by the cook, this renders meat tastier and more digestible. The muscle fibers in raw meat are composed of protein and water—up to 75 percent water. When the internal temperature of meat goes up, these muscle fibers shrink and the water is squeezed out. The sizzle of a steak in the skillet or the steam rising off a hamburger on the grill are both examples of this loss of water. As meat cooks, the fibers become increasingly shorter, squeezing out more and more water. The higher the heat, the faster this process occurs. The results can be clearly seen and felt in an overcooked piece of meat that looks shrunken and feels quite firm to the touch. The lost water carries with it flavor and nutrients, and the meat becomes dry and bland.

Factors other than heat influence the amount of shrinking and drying in meat. First, all meat contains some fat, both through and around the actual meat. For the cook, the fat that runs through the muscle, known as marbling or intramuscular fat, is the most significant. Marbled fat actually separates the protein fibers and inhibits the process of shrinking and drying out. In addition, the fat melts as the meat cooks, which adds to the succulence and juiciness. In the end, a well-marbled piece of meat will retain more moisture than a lean cut of meat when they are cooked side by side.

ABOUT DRY- AND MOIST-HEAT COOKING

Naturally tender meats are best cooked by dry-heat cooking methods, such as grilling, broiling, and roasting. Tough cuts are best handled by moist-heat cooking methods, including braising and stewing. Dry-heat cooking can be done at high or low temperatures; moist-heat cooking is done only at low temperatures. Another way to think of the difference is to cook naturally tender meats by temperature and tougher meats by time. Tender meats are cooked to a certain internal temperature according to the desired degree of doneness. For example, a beef roast at 130°F will be medium-rare and juicy and at 170°F will be gray and less moist. While most professionals can judge the doneness of a roast by touch (it becomes firmer as it cooks through), most of us are better armed with an accurate instant-read thermometer.

The second category of meats, the not-so-tender class, requires time to break down the collagen-filled muscle structure; these meats are considered done after a certain amount of time on the stove or in the oven. The objective when cooking tougher meats is to soften the collagen so that it is no longer chewy or tough, and this occurs most effectively in the presence of moist heat in the range of a low simmer (185°F and below). Higher temperatures will continue to soften the collagen but will render the rest of the meat unbearably tough. When properly stewed or braised, potentially tough meats emerge fork-tender. The softened collagen gives body and richness to the pan sauce or cooking liquid, providing that irresistible character of a slow-cooked stew. Since all proteins lose moisture as they cook, stewed or braised meat will never be as juicy as a rib roast and will not have a pink center. Instead, they get moisture from the rich, concentrated pan juices.

In addition to the collagen, many tougher cuts contain some sinew and gristle, which is made up of elastin. Unlike collagen, elastin will not soften under any circumstances and must be trimmed away before cooking (collagen is intertwined with the actual meat and cannot be trimmed away before cooking).

ABOUT BRAISING, STEWING, AND POT-ROASTING MEAT

A well-made braise or stew offers fork-tender meat with a gloriously deep-flavored, glossy sauce. The distinctions between these two methods has to do with the amount of liquid and the cut of meat. Braising refers to cooking, covered, in a small amount of liquid. A pot roast is a braise made with a 3- to 5-pound piece of meat. Smaller cuts, such as steaks and chops, can also be braised as long as only the smallest amount of liquid is used—enough to come no more than 1 inch up the sides of the pot. A stew is made with ½- to 3-inch cubes of meat and enough liquid to cover. Stews are served directly in their cooking liquid, much like a thick soup, while the cooking liquid for a braise becomes highly concentrated and deeply flavored and is served with the meat as a sauce or gravy. Stews take less time to cook than braises, because the meat is entirely submerged, which cooks it more quickly, and because the pieces of meat are generally smaller. The ideal pan for both methods is a heavy pan, like a Dutch oven, with a tight-fitting lid. Some cooks like to cover the pan with aluminum foil before adding the lid to create an extra-tight seal.

Every step in a recipe for braised or stewed meat is intended to enhance either the flavor or the body of the final dish. The first step for all stews and braises (unless the sauce is intended to be "blonde," as in an Irish stew, 716) is to brown the seasoned meat and vegetables in fat. Besides promoting the even browning of the meat and vegetables, fat also carries flavor, so whatever fat you use will infuse the entire dish with flavor. There are many fats from which to choose, from fruity olive oil to sweet butter to the savory fat of rendered bacon or the melted fat from bits of leftover ham. Many old-time recipes simply call for melting a piece of the fat trimmed from the meat to underscore the integral flavor of the dish.

The deep, caramelized flavors that develop from careful browning of meat and vegetables become the base for the entire dish, and no amount of seasoning later will make up for their absence. Good browning takes time, patience, and vigilance. The pan needs to be hot enough to sizzle but not so hot that it scorches what is put into it. The ideal is a rich, deep brown crust on the meat without producing a pan with a blackened bottom.

For all but the smallest recipes, the meat and vegetables should be browned separately to not overcrowd the pan and to best manage the different times it takes to brown meat and vegetables. Beyond the classic trinity of onions, carrots, and celery, you can add leeks, mushrooms, spices, and herbs. Many recipes call for adding more vegetables later to give a fresh flavor note.

Following the browning is the opportunity to add a liquid for flavor. Common choices are stock and wine (red or white), beer, the juice from canned tomatoes, or other juice. Water can certainly be used, but the resulting sauce will have less flavor. Whatever the choice, scraping up the browned bits left on the bottom of the pan as soon as the liquid is added ensures that they will blend with the liquid to deepen its flavor.

The body and texture of the sauce or cooking liquid are paramount. As with developing flavor, there are several ways to give body and texture to the liquid. The commonest is simply to rely on the natural collagen present in tougher cuts of meat. In the gentle, moist heat of a stew pot or Dutch oven, the collagen melts and turns to soft, velvety gelatin, which gives body and viscosity to sauces. The cuts with the highest proportion of collagen are the shank, breast, and beef oxtail. The sumptuous and shiny character of some braises is often achieved by adding a chunk of pork rind, a calf's foot, or a pig's ear—items that do not necessarily end up in the final dish but contribute an impressive amount of collagen.

In addition to relying on collagen to thicken a sauce, we sometimes use flour both at the start of cooking and at the end. Coating meat with flour before browning accomplishes two things: A light dusting of flour helps create an evenly brown crust; and the few tablespoons of flour that adhere to the meat gradually thicken the liquid as the dish cooks. Once the stew or braise is thoroughly cooked, the sauce can also be thickened by whisking in a few tablespoons of kneaded butter, 44, at the ratio of 1 to 2 tablespoons each flour and butter per cup of liquid. Some people dislike the matte appearance that flour can give to a sauce. The alternatives are to serve the sauce unthickened or to remove the meat and simmer the liquid until it cooks down to a saucelike consistency.

ABOUT ROASTING MEAT

Tender, juicy, delectable roast meat depends as much on buying the right cut as it does on how you cook it. In general, buy the highest grade of meat possible for roasting—ideally, prime or choice—and look for well-marbled, well-shaped cuts. The cuts most suitable for roasting come from the rib, back, sirloin, and hindquarters of the animal; each area yields slightly different results. Your choice should be determined by the occasion, your pocketbook, and your own preference.

All roasts should be trimmed of sinewy membrane and excess fat, either at the meat market or once you get it home. Just leave a thin layer of surface fat to baste the roast as it cooks. Roasts are sold both bone-in and boneless. Many cooks find that bone-in roasts stay moister and flavorful and shrink less during cooking, although they take a bit longer to cook. Others prefer the convenience of carving and serving a completely boneless roast. For a bone-in roast, figure on 10 to 12 ounces per person, and for boneless, 5 to 8 ounces. Because larger cuts tend to shrink less and stay juicier, it is always best to have too much rather than too little.

There are three possibilities when it comes to roasting: high heat, low heat, or moderate heat. It is only a matter of matching the temperature to the cut of meat.

High-temperature roasting (anything over 400°F) produces a crispy brown crust that cannot be duplicated at lower temperatures. High-temperature roasting is fast and abrupt—the meat stays in the oven just long enough for the inside to reach the desired state of doneness. The downside of high-temperature roasting is that it will succeed only with modest-sized cuts of good-quality beef, lamb, and veal. Large cuts of meat (over 6 inches in diameter) suffer badly at high temperatures, because by the time the center reaches the desired doneness, the exterior has become overly charred and dry. High temperatures also cause problems for finely grained pork, which quickly becomes tough and dry. Likewise, cuts of beef with less marbling and more connective tissue, such as the round or sirloin, need more time than high temperatures allow in order to soften and tenderize the connective tissue.

Low-heat roasting is the second method and our favorite for all but the tenderest and most well-marbled meat. Low-heat roasting involves a two-step process in which the meat is first seared in a hot (450°F) oven and then cooked slowly and gently at low heat (250°F). The initial burst of high heat provides some of the lovely brown crust, and the slow, gradual finish minimizes shrinking and keeps the meat moist and tender all the way through. This method is especially useful for leaner roasts and roasts from the in-between cuts from the shoulder or rump.

The third method, and the one familiar to most of our grandmothers, is the moderate roast. While we prefer either high- or low-heat roasting for most meats, moderate roasting (between 325° and 350°F) best suits large, meaty cuts such as pork shoulder or leg of lamb. Experience has shown us that the texture of these cuts suffers dramatically when roasted at temperatures too high or too low.

ABOUT ROASTING PANS AND RACKS

When choosing a roasting pan, the most important consideration is size. The pan should be just large enough to hold the roast and no larger. If the pan is too large, the juices and drippings will burn, giving an acrid flavor to the roast and ruining any pan gravy or juice that you might make. A heavy, high-sided roasting pan with sturdy handles is ideal, but simple baking pans work just as well. Ideally, the sides of a roasting pan should be 3 to 5 inches high (low sides are best for small roasts, high sides for large roasts). Anything higher than the actual roast will hide the meat from the oven heat, distorting the cooking times and inhibiting the browning.

A roasting rack, either a V-shaped rack or a flat grid-type rack, is a good investment if you like to roast meat. Setting the meat on a rack keeps it off the bottom of the pan and promotes even browning by allowing the hot, dry oven air to circulate around the entire roast. Without a rack, the bottom of the roast will begin to stew in the accumulating pan drippings. Another advantage of a roasting rack is that the pan juices are cleaner, so it is easy to make a pan sauce. For lean meats, it is helpful to oil the roasting rack lightly to prevent sticking. Bone-in rib roasts and racks of lamb or other meats need no roasting rack, since the natural arc of the rib bones holds the meat up off the bottom of the pan. For other roasts, some cooks prop the meat up with a few carrots and celery sticks in place of a rack.

Depending on the size of your oven and whether or not you are using a roasting rack, we recommend positioning an oven rack in the lower third of the oven for larger roasts and in the center for smaller roasts so that the top of the roast will be in the upper-middle part of the oven. This allows maximum air circulation for even cooking and is especially important when roasting at high temperatures.

HOW TO TIE MEAT FOR ROASTING

Tying a roast gives it a neat, compact shape and ensures even cooking. While tying is optional with the more expensive single-piece roasts from the loin and rib, it is obligatory for any roast that has been boned or butchered in such a way that it will not hold together on its own. Many markets sell roasts already rolled and tied, but it is a simple enough process to do yourself. First compress the meat into a neat package and tuck in any loose flaps or thin end pieces that would cook too quickly if left out. Then secure the meat with butcher twine tied at 1½- to 2-inch intervals. Finish by

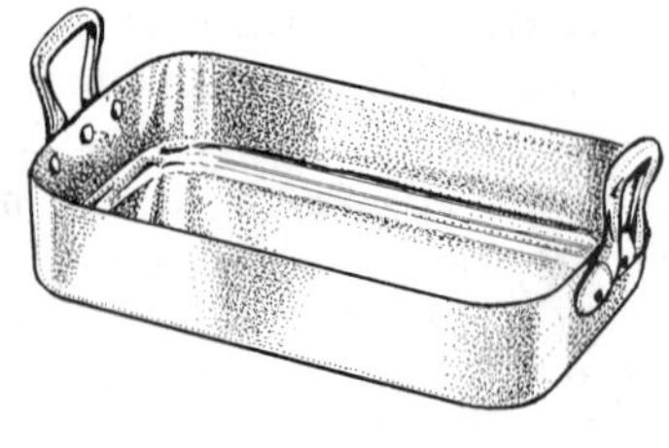

Roasting pan

wrapping the twine around the length of the roast and end with a secure double knot. After roasting and before carving, snip the strings and remove them.

HOW TO DETERMINE DONENESS OF ROASTS

Except in the cases of stews and braises, which are simply cooked until tender, the most accurate way to determine the doneness of any cooked meat is by temperature. While most recipes offer guidelines as to how many minutes per pound to cook a certain piece of meat, there are too many variables for these to be precise. Factors such as the shape and thickness of the meat, the temperature of the meat before cooking, the size and accuracy of your oven, the shape of the roasting pan, and the fat and bone content of the meat all influence the time meat takes to reach the desired degree of doneness. Use the recommended cooking times in a recipe for a rough idea of when to begin checking the internal temperature. After that, use the chart on page 644 to determine which temperature corresponds to how you like your meat.

The best tool for checking the internal temperature of meat is an instant-read thermometer. The thin stem and accuracy of these thermometers gives them a definite advantage over the old-fashioned meat thermometers. To check meat, insert the thermometer into the thickest part of the meat, away from any fat or bone, and wait about 20 seconds for it to register correctly. Once the meat is within 15 degrees of your target temperature, begin monitoring every 10 minutes or so, since the temperature can climb quite rapidly.

In determining doneness, bear in mind that any piece of meat over ½ inch thick benefits from a 10- to 30-minute standing time after cooking and before carving and that the temperature can continue to rise during this time. This rest renders the meat moister by allowing the juices to be redistributed. Meat should be loosely covered with aluminum foil as it stands. When cooked at high heat, expect the internal temperature of a roast to rise 5 to 10 degrees during the standing time (larger cuts hold more heat, and the temperature rises more). Cooked at low or moderate heat (250° to 350°F), the temperature of meat will rise only 4 to 5 degrees. It is best to let thick steaks and chops stand for 3 to 5 minutes before carving.

The recommended final temperatures in the chart are used by cooks and chefs for steaks, chops, roasts, and other unground cuts of meat. In recent years, the public's concern for food safety has prompted the USDA to publish cooking temperatures that are conservatively higher than those listed here. Fortunately, when properly stored and handled, unground meat poses very little health risk even when cooked to rare or medium-rare. For more information about meat safety, please refer to About Meat Storage and Safety, 645.

ABOUT BROWNING MEAT

In recent years, the once widespread belief that searing meat seals in juices has been universally debunked by food scientists and cooks. Regardless of this change of opinion, browning remains one of the most important steps in cooking meat. Browning gives meat a richer, more pronounced, more complex flavor. Compare the taste and appeal of a crispy, well-browned crust on a rib roast to a gray, pallid piece of boiled beef.

Browning is a chemical reaction that can only occur in a dry-heat environment at temperatures above 300°F. This happens when we grill, broil, sauté, or roast at high heat, as long as the meat has been patted dry (wet meat does not brown, it steams). The difficulty arises with the gentler cooking methods (including braising, stewing, and low-heat roasting) when the meat never gets hot enough to brown. Even though the oven temperature for a braise may be 350°F, the temperature inside a closed pot containing a liquid cannot climb above 212°F. While this gentle heat protects the

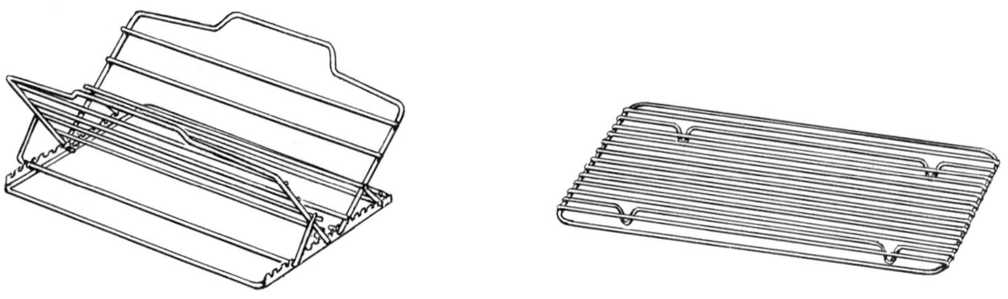

V-shaped and flat roasting racks

FINAL TEMPERATURES FOR COOKED MEAT

BEEF AND LAMB		PORK		VEAL	
Rare	120° to 130°F	Medium	155° to 165°F	Medium	145° to 155°F
Medium-Rare	130° to 135°F	Well-Done	180° to 185°F		
Medium	140° to 150°F				
Medium-Well	155° to 165°F				
Well-Done	170° to 185°F				

meat from drying out and turning tough, it does nothing to brown the meat. The solution used in nearly every stew and braise recipe is to first brown the meat evenly before adding liquid and covering the pot. This first step creates the flavor foundation on which the entire dish is based. Not only will the actual pieces of meat taste better with a browned crust, but the dark, caramelized juices stuck to the bottom of the pan after browning provide the rich, meaty flavor base for the entire dish.

The keys to browning meat successfully are to always start with dry meat and to brown it over high heat. Overcrowding the pan is a mistake, because it lowers the temperature and causes the meat to steam, not sear. The heat should be kept high enough so that the meat sizzles but not so high that it begins to scorch. Turn the meat so that all sides brown evenly. Done properly, browning takes time: Expect a large piece of meat, like a pot roast, to take 15 to 20 minutes, while smaller chunks of stew meat take 10 to 15 minutes.

ABOUT GRINDING AND POUNDING MEAT

Tough cuts of meat are sometimes tenderized by mechanical means. When meat is ground, finely chopped, or even pounded, the coarse, tough fibers that make it chewy are physically cut or smashed. The resulting meat is easy to chew and perceived as tender.

Now that the food processor is a fundamental tool in most kitchens, it is very easy to grind or chop your own meat. By chopping your own meat at home, you have complete control over cleanliness, and you have a better guarantee of freshness and fat content, depending on the meat you buy. The best cuts to use are shoulder or chuck. Trim away visible fat and cut the meat into 1-inch cubes. Keep the meat thoroughly refrigerated before and after chopping. If your kitchen is exceedingly warm, you can also chill the processor workbowl and blade. Place enough meat in the bowl of the processor to cover the blade by 1 inch, no more. Pulse the processor until the pieces of meat are uniformly small (about ⅛ inch). Remove the chopped meat from the bowl and repeat the process until all the meat is done. Use this meat in any recipe calling for ground or chopped beef. For more information on buying ground meat, please read About Ground Meat, 720.

Medallions, cutlets, and chops from lean meats such as veal and pork are often tenderized by pounding to break down the tough fibers of the meat. Pounding can be done with the flat side of a meat cleaver, a macerating hammer, a wooden or rubber mallet, or any smooth object such as a wine bottle or the heel of your hand. If you are using a smooth-sided pounder, place the meat between two sheets of plastic to prevent it from sticking to either the tool or the board. With a macerating hammer (which has a rough grid on one side), moisten the surface of the hammer to prevent sticking. Whatever tool you use, strike the meat with a glancing blow to prevent the meat from tearing, especially when pounded paper-thin, as in Weiner Schnitzel, 684. If you are using a cleaver, hold it with both hands and make sure its handle projects beyond the edge of the cutting board so that you do not whack your fingers.

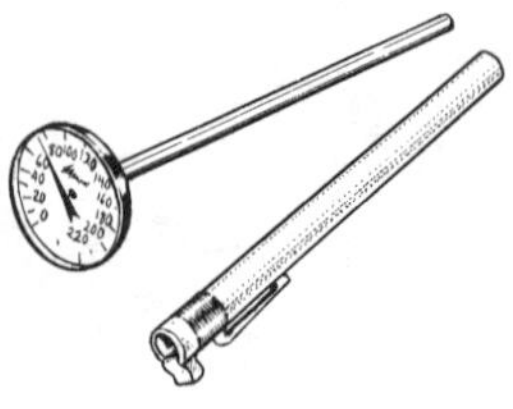

Instant-read thermometer

ABOUT SEASONING AND MARINATING MEAT

Seasoning is perhaps the most interpretive and personalized aspect of meat cooking. While there is some disagreement about when to salt meat, either before cooking or after, there is no disagreement about the value of salt as a seasoning. Salt enhances the natural flavor of meat and should be used judiciously. When meat is salted before cooking, the taste is more rounded and full than if the meat is cooked unsalted.

The argument against salting food before cooking stems from salt's ability to draw moisture from the meat. In reality, with the exception of salt-cured meats, the small amount of salt used to season a steak or a roast will have little effect on the actual moisture content of meat. The real problem with presalting meat is that the small amount of moisture that comes to the surface is enough to make it difficult to brown small cuts like steaks, chops, cubes, and medallions evenly. This is much less of a problem with roasts, since the dry heat of an oven dries any moisture quite efficiently. The solution for both flavor and browning is to dry the meat first with paper towels and then, at the very last second before browning, sprinkle the meat with salt.

Pepper is a different matter. Freshly ground pepper contains very volatile flavor compounds that dissipate and fade during cooking. If you really enjoy the flavor of freshly ground pepper, we recommend peppering the meat twice: once before cooking so that the flavors penetrate the surface slightly, and again after the meat is cooked to add the taste of freshly ground pepper.

Besides the obligatory salt and pepper, there are plenty of other ways to enhance the flavor of meat before cooking, from a simple marinade, 84, to a complex spice rub. The fundamental difference between marinades and spice rubs is that marinades are traditionally made with an acidic liquid, such as vinegar, wine, or citrus juice, and can alter the texture of the meat. While a marinade cannot transform a tough shoulder steak into a fork-tender filet mignon, it will soften and tenderize the surface of the meat. This occurs because the acid actually breaks down the fibrous proteins that make meat tough in the first place, and the stronger the acidity of a marinade, the more it will soften the meat—but only on the surface. Marinades do not penetrate more than ¼ inch into the meat, so the center of any cut thicker than ½ inch remains unaffected. Some cooks try spearing the meat with a fork, and some have even gone so far as to inject the marinade into the meat, but neither method offers much success. We are satisfied with a well-seasoned exterior and a natural-tasting center.

Marinades should have enough liquid to cover the meat, and we recommend turning the meat once or twice as it marinates. The longer meat sits in marinade, the more flavor it will absorb. For most dishes, a marinating period of 4 to 24 hours is sufficient. Regardless of the length of marinating time, always marinate meat in the refrigerator, and never serve uncooked marinade. Many recipes advocate marinating meat at room temperature for maximum flavor transfer. Our experience has shown that any benefit of a more rapid infusion of flavor is not worth the potential risk of bacterial growth. If you enjoy a little marinade as sauce to serve with cooked meat, set some aside before the marinade comes into contact with the raw meat, or bring the marinade to a boil before serving.

Spice rubs and pastes are best described as a dry marinade. They can be rubbed on immediately before cooking or in advance and refrigerated overnight. Since there is no acidic liquid in a rub, there is little worry about altering the texture of the meat. Instead, the spice rub or paste gives the meat a highly flavorful, slightly crunchy crust on the exterior, while the interior retains the original flavor of the meat.

To use spice rubs or pastes, simply take small handfuls of the mix and rub it over the entire surface of the food you are going to cook, using a bit of pressure to make sure it adheres to the food. Once you have started to cook, do not worry if the rub begins to turn dark brown; as long as the spices do not begin to smoke, the food is safe.

Another alternative for adding flavor to meat is to make small incisions over the surface of a large cut of meat and stuff them with assertive ingredients such as slivers of garlic, slices of anchovy, bits of onion, or a mix of spices and herbs. As the roast cooks, these little flavor pockets perfume the surrounding meat. Take care that no bits of garlic remain on the surface of the meat, for garlic burns easily and can give a bitter, burnt flavor to the meat.

ABOUT MEAT STORAGE AND SAFETY

Fresh meat is quite perishable and should be stored in the coldest part of the refrigerator, between 34° and 40°F. Single cuts of meat, including steaks and roasts, are the stablest, while ground meat, fresh sausage, and variety meats are the most perishable, in terms of both flavor retention and safety. In general, pork is slightly less stable than beef, lamb, and veal, because it contains a higher level of unsaturated fat (which spoils more quickly than the saturated fats found in most meats). As a general rule, the larger the piece of meat, the longer it will keep.

Store fresh meat in the package it comes in. Meat wrapped in butcher paper should be stored with the paper loosened for ventilation; the plastic wrap used at the supermarket allows meat to breathe. Roasts will hold for 3 to 5 days, steaks and chops for 2 to 4 days, and cubes, stew meat, ground meat, fresh sausage, and variety meats for 2 days. Leftover meat should be cooled quickly after cooking and transferred to a sealed container or be well wrapped and refrigerated for 3 to 5 days. Always check raw meat for freshness before cooking. It should have no off-odors, and the surface should be moist but never slimy.

Any meat that cannot be cooked and eaten within the recommended time should be frozen. In order to freeze meat properly, leave it in its original package. If it is wrapped in butcher paper, leave it in the wrap and place it in a sealable plastic bag. Assuming the freezer is 0°F or lower, beef, lamb, and veal steaks or roasts will keep for 1 year; pork chops and roasts for 4 to 8 months; ground meat for 3 months; and sausage for less than 3 months. Most home freezers, however, are slightly warmer. Also, for the best taste and texture, do not keep meats frozen for more than 1 month. Never refreeze previously frozen meats.

Frozen meat should be completely thawed before cooking, and the best method is in the refrigerator. Set the meat in its original package on a baking sheet to catch any drips. Steaks and chops will thaw in 1 day's time, while larger roasts may take as long as 3 days. Thawing meat under running water speeds up the process but can compromise flavor and texture. To thaw meat in cold water, tightly seal the meat in a plastic bag, place it in a large bowl of cool (never warm) water, and weight it with a plate or pot to keep it submerged. Change the water occasionally to ensure that it stays below 40°F. Attempting to cook large cuts of meat that are only partially thawed begs disaster. The frigid interior will remain raw even when the outside becomes well done. Harmful bacteria grow easily in the partially cooked meat inside and can cause illness.

While many cookbooks and food experts recommend bringing meat to room temperature before cooking, we encourage you to follow the safer practice of keeping meat refrigerated right up to the last minute before cooking. While room-temperature meat will cook more quickly, there is not enough benefit to outweigh the risks of tempting bacteria even for a short time.

When storing and handling raw meat, take care to avoid contaminating other already cooked foods or foods that will be eaten raw, such as salad greens or fruits. In the refrigerator, store raw meat away from cooked foods and always set it on some sort of tray or pan to catch any drippings. After cutting or handling raw meats, always wash your hands, cutting board, counter surface, knives, and other utensils in hot sudsy water before handling other food.

In recent years, the issue of meat-borne illness has put a spotlight on the health risks associated with eating undercooked *ground* meat. Any common cooking method for even the rarest steak or roast will kill the bacteria on the surface of the meat. The inside may remain a lovely rosy 135°F, while the well-browned exterior will be above 300°F—definitely hot enough to kill any troublesome bacteria. The problems arise with ground meat when the outside surface, which may have been contaminated, is ground up and mixed with the inside. Any contamination present will now be spread throughout the hamburger and no longer be killed by simply charring the outside. To eliminate any risk, hamburgers and other ground-meat products must be cooked to 155°F—at which temperature there will be little sign of pink or juiciness left to the hamburger. If you do prefer to eat hamburgers less than well done, lessen the risk by buying top-grade beef, have it ground to order, and cook it immediately after purchase. Best of all, buy fresh top-grade meat and grind it yourself, 644, just before cooking.

ABOUT BEEF

Steaks, chops, roasts, stews, and burgers—beef has been an American favorite for centuries. From the westward cattle drives to Chicago's thriving livestock industry, this nutritious and flavorful meat has contributed enormously to the history of this country. What started with a few cattle brought over from Europe by the earliest explorers and settlers has now become our most complex and extensive livestock industry. Through crossbreeding and advances in animal husbandry, there are now ninety breeds of cattle raised for beef (compared with only thirty-five to forty in the late 1970s).

Beef sold today is 27 percent leaner than it was twenty years ago. Producers have cut fat not only by trimming beef more heavily before sale but also by breeding leaner cattle. Without the advantage of the built-in tenderizer marbling provides, lean beef can quickly become dry and tough if overcooked. The solution is to monitor cooking temperatures closely and to use moist-heat cooking methods for all but the tenderest cuts.

Another modern characteristic of beef is that producers strive to get cattle to market faster. An estimated 99 percent of the beef is less than twenty months old at maturity. This younger meat will generally be tenderer than that of more mature cattle. Turn-of-the-century recipes for beef stews suggest cooking the meat all day to tenderize it. While such legendary toughness is no longer a real concern, such tenderer beef also has a milder flavor. One solution is to enhance the flavor of beef with marinades, spice rubs, and condiments.

When buying beef, look for a good, deep red color, with no more than ¼ inch of smooth, white external fat. Steaks that have marbling, or intramuscular fat, should have small specks of fat evenly distributed throughout the muscle. Look for even, well-shaped cuts with no signs of discoloration.

ABOUT BEEF GRADES

Beef has more grade levels than other animals—eight—because beef cattle have greater variation in quality and yield. Of these eight grades, the average consumer need only be concerned with three of them—prime, choice, and select. Prime, the highest grade, is scarce. Less than 2 percent of all graded beef is prime, and most of that ends up in expensive steakhouses. If you are lucky enough to have a butcher or market that sells prime, expect to pay a lot for it. Prime-grade beef has abundant marbling and comes from young, well-fed cattle. Prime steaks are quite often dry-aged as well, an expensive process. Choice is generally the highest quality sold in most supermarkets. Below choice, much of supermarket beef is graded select. Select meat has less marbling and less juiciness than prime or choice. Because the meat is lean, it can dry out easily when overcooked, especially steaks and roasts, but when cooked properly, it can be quite satisfying.

The remaining grades for beef are used in commercial and manufactured meat products such as canned meats or soups. These are in descending order of quality: standard, commercial, utility, cutter, and canning. These grades come from older cattle and have a coarser appearance than other grades, no marbling, and very little external fat.

ABOUT AGING BEEF

Aging is a process intended to tenderize and develop flavor in meat. Under controlled temperatures, the tissue will relax, yielding a less resilient piece of meat that is easier to chew and more pleasurable to eat. The original method of aging, called dry-aging, is becoming increasingly rare and is most often done only with prime-grade beef for a very limited market. To dry-age beef, a carcass or large cut is hung in a temperature-controlled (34° to 38°F) cooler for three weeks or longer. During this time, the beef loses moisture and develops flavor. After dry-aging, besides the reduction of carcass weight from moisture loss, there is a great deal of trimming to be done to cut away the dried-out surface. The results: deliciously tender, yet firm, steaks with incomparable flavor at a very high cost.

Instead of dry-aging, most of our beef today undergoes wet-aging. The fresh cuts of meat are vacuum-packed in plastic bags, a process known as *Cryovac*, and are then allowed to sit at temperatures between 34° and 38°F for 7 to 28 days. Inside the plastic, the beef does age and become tenderer, but there is none of the

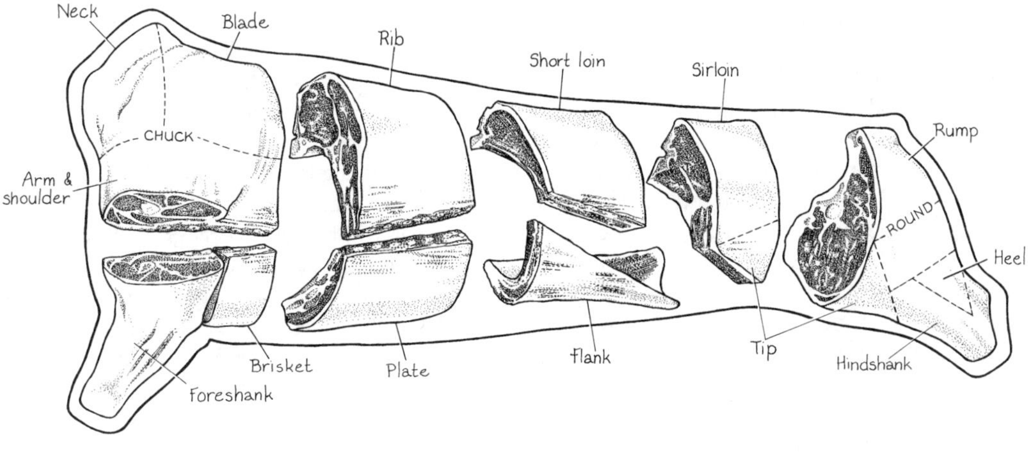

Major cuts of beef

flavor development or moisture loss that distinguishes dry-aging.

ABOUT ROASTING BEEF

Roast beef should be well seared (nicely browned) on the outside while remaining juicy and tender inside. For roasts less than 5 inches across from naturally tender cuts, such as tenderloin or a smaller, well-trimmed rib-eye roast, this is best achieved by high-heat roasting. Larger cuts, such as standing rib roast, would become charred on the outside without cooking through at such high temperatures. These are best cooked by a combination of high and low heat—first in a hot oven for 10 minutes to sear the outside and then slowly roasted to perfection at 250°F. When it comes to roasts from the less tender cuts, such as beef round and sirloin, you can choose between high and low heat, depending on how you like your roast beef. The aggressive heat of high-temperature roasting can cause some toughening and drying of the already less-than-tender meat. Slow-heat roasting, though, does not produce the deeply seared crust that so many of us love. In the end, both methods produce beautifully cooked roast beef. If you prize tenderness above all else, roast at low heat. If you love the flavor of a richly browned crust, stay with high heat all the way through.

Final internal temperature, after its rest once out of the oven, for rare beef is 120° to 130°F; medium-rare is 130° to 135°F; medium is 140° to 150°F; medium-well is 155° to 165°F; and well-done is 170° to 185°F. In the recipes that follow, we take into account the fact that the internal temperature of meat will continue to rise after it is taken out of the oven, so we remove the roast at temperatures 5 to 10 degrees lower than desired. For more information, please see About Roasting Meat, 641.

ABOUT MAKING A JUS FOR A BEEF ROAST

A simple method for boosting the flavor and enhancing the juiciness of roast beef is to make a quick jus, or juice, with the pan drippings as soon as the roast comes from the oven. First remove the cooked roast from the roasting pan and set it aside, loosely covered, to stand. Pour off any excess grease (reserve it for Yorkshire pudding, 787, if you wish). Place the roasting pan over medium heat and add ½ to ¾ cup of any flavorful stock, 40 to 41, preferably beef or mushroom, or canned stock, preferably low-sodium. Bring the liquid to a boil and scrape the bottom of the pan with a wooden spoon until the roasting particles are all dissolved. Season with salt and pepper and drizzle the jus over the sliced beef. Bear in mind that a jus does not preclude the use of a more robust sauce—it simply enhances it.

ABOUT RIB ROASTS

The most traditional cut of beef for an elegant and impressive roast beef dinner is the standing rib roast, also called a rib roast or prime rib—although this last name is misleading, since the beef may not necessarily have earned the prime-quality grade. This grand, naturally tender, well-marbled cut comes from the rib section starting just behind the shoulder and running along the backbone to where the ribs end, shown 647; smaller partial roasts are also sold. A full standing rib roast contains seven rib bones; these act as a natural roasting rack and give the roast its impressive appearance. The less meaty ends of the rib bones, known as the short ribs, are generally trimmed off, although they may be left on and "Frenched" (stripped of fat and gristle) for presentation purposes. Most markets will remove the backbone, or chine bone—a task accomplished only with a meat saw. Be sure to request this, or you will be miserable come carving time. Sometimes the chine bone is left on but scored with vertical cuts to allow you to carve through it easily. While this method is certainly serviceable, we find that having the chine bone completely removed promotes more even cooking. The cap fat is the thick layer of fat that covers the top of a rib roast; it should be trimmed to just a thin layer covering the outside of the roast.

There is an important distinction between the ribs closest to the shoulder, known as the large end or chuck end, and the ribs toward the loin, also known as the small end or better end. As the ribs progress away from the shoulder, the eye meat—the center nugget of prized rib meat—becomes more recognizable and tenderer. Toward the shoulder, the roast may be larger, but it is composed of several lateral muscles, referred to as cap meat, lifter meat, or blade meat, that vary in tenderness and flavor and are separated by layers of fat. When buying less than a full rib roast, ask for a roast cut from the loin end, where you will find the largest part of the rib eye and the greatest tenderness.

For convenience and ease of carving, there are also boneless, well-trimmed rib roasts, referred to as rolled rib roasts. While these lack the festive appearance of a standing rib roast, carving them is simple. These are sold with an external layer of fat tied around the exterior to keep the meat moist as it roasts and to give the roast a neat, compact shape. Some meat markets cut the rib bones off the meat but tie them back on the roast to protect the eye meat during roasting. The strings and fat, and bones if present, are then removed before serving. Further trimming to remove all the cap meat, leaving only the tender eye meat, produces the most expensive of all roasts—a boneless rib-eye roast.

We do not recommend roasting anything smaller than a two-rib roast, weighing about 4 to 5 pounds, perfect for serving four to six people. For larger roasts, expect each additional rib to allow two or three more servings—that is, a three-rib roast for six to nine servings, a four-rib roast for eight to twelve servings, and so on. For boneless rib roasts, figure on 5 to 8 ounces of trimmed meat per person.

ABOUT CARVING STANDING RIB ROASTS

Carving is an easy task as long as the chine bone, or backbone, has been removed before roasting. There are two methods for carving a standing rib roast. The first may be the simplest, although a bit less dramatic: Begin by steadying the roast with a meat fork with the ends of the rib bones pointing up and slice the meat away from the bones in one chunk. (Be sure to serve the ribs alongside the meat for those who like to gnaw on crisp, meaty bones!) Then set the roast fat side up and cut it vertically into slices as thick or thin as you like—¼-inch slices are typical. The second method, also known as the English method, is to set the roast on its side and cut it horizontally from the fat side toward the rib into thicker (⅜ to ½ inch) slices, removing the rib bones one at a time with a vertical cut as you carve off the slices.

SLOW-ROASTED BEEF RIB ROAST

8 to 10 servings

Request a rib roast cut from the "small end" of the rib, that is, the part nearest the loin. Be sure that the chine bone, or backbone, is removed by the butcher; the rib bones should remain intact. Please read About Roasting Beef, 648, and About Rib Roasts, 648.

Position a rack in the lower third of the oven. Preheat the oven to 450°F.

Pat dry:

One 4-rib beef roast (7 to 9 pounds), trimmed

Season liberally with:

Salt and ground black pepper to taste

Place the roast rib side down in a roasting pan and roast for 10 minutes. Reduce the oven temperature to 250°F and roast until an instant-read thermometer inserted in the thickest part of the roast reads 115° to 125°F for rare, 125° to 130°F for medium-rare, or 135° to 145°F for medium, 15 to 30 minutes per pound (the temperature will continue to rise 5° out of the oven). Remove the roast to a platter, cover loosely with aluminum foil, and let stand for 15 to 30 minutes before carving. Make a jus as directed on page 648. Please read About Carving Standing Rib Roasts, above. Drizzle the jus over the sliced meat. If desired, serve with:

Sauce Demi-Glace, 50, Sauce Madère, 50, American Horseradish Cream, 79, or Pan Gravy for Meat, 52

SLOW-ROASTED BEEF RIB ROAST WITH DRY MUSTARD MARINADE

Before preparing Slow-Roasted Beef Rib Roast, above, mix ¼ cup Dijon mustard, 1 tablespoon dry mustard, 1 tablespoon sugar, and salt and ground black pepper to taste, and rub this over the surface of the trimmed raw roast. Refrigerate for at least 2 hours before proceeding.

BEEF RIB-EYE ROAST (HIGH-TEMPERATURE METHOD)

8 to 10 servings

The elegant, well-trimmed boneless rib-eye roast responds beautifully to high-heat roasting, producing a nicely seared crust and tender, juicy slices of beef. It does take a bit longer to roast than other leaner boneless roasts such as the sirloin or tenderloin.

Position a rack in the center of the oven. Preheat the oven to 425°F.

Pat dry:

1 boneless rib-eye roast (about 4½ pounds), well trimmed and tied at 2-inch intervals

Season liberally with:

Salt and ground black pepper to taste

Place the roast fat side up on a rack in a roasting pan and roast until an instant-read thermometer inserted in the thickest part of the roast reads 110° to 120°F for rare, 120° to 125°F for medium-rare, or 130° to 135°F for medium, 15 to 20 minutes per pound (the temperature will continue to rise 10° out of the oven). Remove the roast to a platter, cover loosely with aluminum foil, and let stand for 15 to 30 minutes before carving. Make a jus as directed on page 648. Remove the strings and carve the roast into ⅛- to ½-inch slices. Drizzle the jus over the slices. If desired, serve with:

Sauce Demi-Glace, 50 Sauce Madère, 50, American Horseradish Cream, 79, or Pan Gravy for Meat, 52

SLOW-ROASTED RIB-EYE ROAST

The exterior will not be as crisp with this method, but the interior will be juicier. Prepare Beef Rib-Eye Roast, above, reducing the oven temperature to 250°F after the first 10 minutes. Roast the beef until the internal temperature is 115° to 120°F for rare, 125° to 130°F for medium-rare, or 135° to 140°F for medium, 20 to 30 minutes per pound (the temperature will continue to rise 5° out of the oven).

HERB- OR SPICE-RUBBED RIB-EYE ROAST (HIGH-TEMPERATURE METHOD)

High-heat roasting is best to give these well-seasoned roasts a crispy, zesty crust. Before preparing Beef Rib-Eye Roast, above, mix 2 tablespoons olive oil, 1 tablespoon minced garlic, 1 tablespoon dried thyme, 1 teaspoon dry mustard, 1 teaspoon salt, and ½ teaspoon ground black pepper and rub this over the trimmed and tied raw roast. Alternatively, rub the roast with ½ cup Mediterranean Garlic Herb Paste, 87, Mustard Paste for Roast Meats, 87, or Peppery Dry Rub, 86. Refrigerate for at least 2 hours before proceeding.

BEEF STRIP LOIN ROAST (HIGH-TEMPERATURE METHOD)

8 to 10 servings

A strip roast, also referred to as top loin or shell roast, comes from the short loin—the muscle that runs on either side of the backbone from the ribs to the hip, or sirloin, area. Cut into steaks, the strip loin makes strip steaks or shell steaks. Left whole, this boneless, evenly shaped cut yields a tender, delicious, easily carved roast, perfect for entertaining. A strip loin is even tenderer and milder in flavor than a rib roast. The only tenderer cut of beef is the tenderloin itself. Many markets now sell full strips at an economical price, packaged in Cryovac and weighing 10 to 12 pounds each. Although you can roast an entire strip, we recommend dividing it into 2 smaller roasts. Alternatively, after cutting off a piece large enough to roast, slice the rest into ¾- to 1-inch-thick shell or strip steaks. Because a strip loin is narrow and not very thick, it is ideal for high-heat roasting and cooks very quickly.

Position a rack in the center of the oven. Preheat the oven to 425°F.

Pat dry:

1 boneless beef strip loin roast (about 4½ pounds), fat trimmed to ¼ inch, tied at 1½-inch intervals

Season liberally with:

Salt and ground black pepper to taste

3 tablespoons dried thyme and/or rosemary (optional)

Place the roast fat side up on a rack in a roasting pan and roast until an instant-read thermometer inserted in the thickest part of the roast reads 110° to 120°F for rare, 120° to 125°F for medium-rare, or 130° to 140°F for medium, 8 to 15 minutes per pound (the temperature will continue to rise 10° out of the oven). Remove the meat to a platter, cover loosely with aluminum foil, and let stand for 15 to 30 minutes before carving. If desired, make a jus as directed on page 648. Remove the strings and carve the roast into ⅛- to ½-inch slices. Drizzle the jus over the slices. If desired, serve with:

Sauce Demi-Glace, 50, Sauce Madère, 50, Béarnaise Sauce, 56, or Pan Gravy for Meat, 52

ORANGE-MOLASSES GLAZED STRIP LOIN ROAST

Before preparing Beef Strip Loin Roast (High-Temperature Method), above, brush the trimmed and tied roast with Orange Molasses Glaze, 90, and omit the optional seasoning. Refrigerate for 3 to 5 hours before roasting. Line the roasting pan with aluminum foil for easier cleanup. Roast as directed, basting the meat several times with glaze as it cooks.

MUSTARD-SEED-CRUSTED STRIP LOIN ROAST

Before preparing Beef Strip Loin Roast (High-Temperature Method), above, omit the optional seasoning and rub the trimmed and tied roast with olive oil, season with salt and pepper, and roll in ¼ cup whole yellow mustard seeds before roasting.

SLOW-ROASTED STRIP LOIN ROAST

Champions of the slow roast happily forsake a degree of crisp exterior for a slightly more tender interior. Prepare Beef Strip Loin Roast, above, reducing the oven temperature to 250°F after the first 10 minutes. Roast the beef until the internal temperature is 115° to 120°F for rare, 125° to 130°F for medium-rare, or 135° to 140°F for medium, 10 to 20 minutes per pound (the temperature will continue to rise 5° out of the oven).

SLOW-ROASTED BEEF SIRLOIN

8 servings

Not nearly as majestic as the more expensive cuts of beef, but full of rich beef flavor and a good deal less expensive. Slow-roasting the sirloin maximizes its tenderness and retains the moist juices. If you are serving just a few people, buy a tri-tip (triangle tip) roast, a small, flavorful, moderately tender piece cut from the bottom of the sirloin, weighing from 1 to 3 pounds. For larger gatherings, buy a top sirloin, top butt, or center-cut sirloin roast, which are from the top of the sirloin. Individual meat markets may cut these into smaller portions and name them otherwise. Figure on 5 to 8 ounces of boneless, trimmed sirloin per person. Because roasts from the sirloin include several kinds of muscles, there may be some variation in levels of doneness throughout the roast.

Position a rack in the center of the oven. Preheat the oven to 450°F.

Pat dry:

1 boneless beef sirloin roast (about 3½ pounds), preferably top sirloin, well trimmed and tied at 1½-inch intervals

Rub the beef with:

2 tablespoons olive oil

Season liberally with:

Salt and ground black pepper to taste

Place the roast fat side up on a rack in a roasting pan and roast for 10 minutes. Reduce the oven temperature to 250° and roast until an instant-read thermometer inserted at several spots in the roast reads 115° to 125°F for rare, 125° to 130°F for medium-rare, or 135° to 145°F for medium, 20 to 30 minutes per pound (the temperature will continue to rise 5° out of the oven). Remove the meat to a platter, cover loosely with aluminum foil, and let stand for 15 to 20 minutes before carving. If desired, make a jus as directed on page 648. Remove the strings and carve the roast into ⅛- to ½-inch slices. Drizzle the jus over the slices. If desired, serve with:

Red Onion-Garlic Ketchup, 70, Sauce Chasseur, 51, Béarnaise Sauce, 56, or Pan Gravy for Meat, 52

GARLIC-AND-HERB-STUDDED SIRLOIN ROAST

Before preparing Slow-Roasted Beef Sirloin, above (omitting the oil and seasonings), toss 2 large cloves garlic, thinly slivered, with 1½ teaspoons crumbled dried thyme, 1½ teaspoons salt, and 1 teaspoon ground black pepper. Make slits in the roast and insert the seasoned garlic slivers. Rub the remaining seasonings over the meat, then marinate the meat, covered, for at least 30 minutes or up to 2 hours at room temperature, or up to 24 hours in the refrigerator. Roast as directed.

ROASTED SIRLOIN (HIGH-TEMPERATURE METHOD)

Expect to sacrifice a bit of tenderness to gain a good deal of flavor from a more heavily seared crust—especially nice with the Garlic-and-Herb-Studded Sirloin Roast, above. Prepare Slow-Roasted Beef Sirloin, above, in an oven preheated to 425°F without reducing the oven heat and roasting the beef until the internal temperature is 110° to 120°F for rare, 120° to 125°F for medium-rare, or 130° to 140°F for medium, 10 to 20 minutes per pound (the temperature will continue to rise 10° out of the oven).

SLOW-ROASTED BEEF ROUND *6 to 8 servings*

Cuts of beef from the round, or hind leg, are less tender than loin and rib cuts but far more economical. They can also make fine roasts if handled with care. The best choices are the top and bottom round and the rump. The eye round, while an attractive compact shape, is quite firm. These roasts need to be sliced thinly for tenderness; they are the beef most often used for roast beef sandwiches. In order to be sliced thinly enough, round roasts are best cooked to medium-rare and a bit beyond, 135° to 140°F. If roasted very rare, they will be too soft to slice thinly. If roasted to medium or beyond, however, the meat becomes tough, dry, and coarse. Cuts from the round should only be slow-roasted, for they fare poorly under high heat.

Prepare as directed for Slow-Roasted Beef Sirloin, above or Garlic-and-Herb-Studded Sirloin Roast, above:

1 boneless beef round roast (about 3 pounds), trimmed and tied

When cold, these roasts make excellent roast beef sandwiches. If desired, serve with:

A salsa, 61 to 63, a relish, 63 to 65, or a flavored mayonnaise, 72 to 75

ABOUT FILET OR TENDERLOIN OF BEEF

The choicest, tenderest cut, known as the filet or tenderloin, is the lean, club-shaped muscle that runs along either side of the backbone, tucked underneath the strip loin and sirloin. Because of its tenderness, neat shape, fine texture, and mild flavor, the meat from the filet can be utilized in many ways. It is often sold cut into small portions, but we have found that it is most economical to purchase an entire filet, which weighs 6 to 8 pounds. The whole tenderloin can be roasted or easily cut into smaller portions as described below and used in a variety of recipes. For most recipes, figure on 5 to 8 ounces trimmed meat per person.

The various parts of this prized cut have their own designations. The butt section comes from the sirloin, or butt, end and weighs between 2 and 3 pounds. It is perfect as a small roast for four to six people. For a larger group, if you cannot find a whole filet, consider buying two tenderloin butts to serve eight to twelve. The tenderloin butt can also be cut into two or three 1½-inch filet steaks. In the second half of the tenderloin butt lies the chateaubriand, 5 or 6 inches long, which is most often roasted or grilled whole and then sliced thickly to feed two or three people. The remainder of the filet is cut into 1- to 2-inch filet steaks, tournedos, and filet mignon, or small filets. Finally, the tip or tail section can be trimmed and used for beef Stroganoff, beef stir-fry, or beef kebabs.

Cooking times vary for these cuts, depending on their size and thickness. The two constants are never to cook beef filet past medium and to use only dry-heat cooking, such as roasting, grilling, sautéing, and broiling, with the exception of the poached Beef on a String, 655. A marinade, spice rub, or simply a nicely charred crust are excellent ways to give the very mild meat a flavorful exterior while preserving the tender interior.

ABOUT TRIMMING AND TYING A WHOLE FILET OR TENDERLOIN OF BEEF

If you buy an entire filet, you will need to do a bit of trimming before cooking by any method. Begin by cutting and pulling away all of the external fat to expose the meat. Some markets leave the long, thin, coarse-grained muscle attached to the side of the filet. This is known as the side muscle or chain muscle; it should be removed (use it in soup or stew), as it is much tougher than the filet. With a sharp, pointed knife, remove the thin, tough, bluish membrane underneath the fat, known as the silver skin. Cut the skin off in long strips, angling the knife away from the meat so as not to cut into the meat. To cook the filet whole, most cooks tuck the thin tail end under the roast and tie it to equalize the thickness. Alternatively, you can simply cut off the 6-inch tail and slice it into strips for beef Stroganoff or stir-fry. Likewise, the flap of meat at the thick end can be tied to secure it or trimmed off and used with the trimmed tail. In any case, it is best to tie the entire roast with butcher twine at 1½-inch intervals for an even shape.

ROASTED FILET OR TENDERLOIN OF BEEF (HIGH-TEMPERATURE METHOD)

10 to 12 servings

If roasting less than a whole tenderloin, buy a piece from the butt, or thicker, end. The roasting time will be about the same as for a whole tenderloin. Be sure to use a shallow roasting pan just big enough for the filet.

Position a rack in the center of the oven. Preheat the oven to 425°F. Lightly oil a roasting pan.

Pat dry:

1 filet of beef (about 5 pounds), well trimmed and tied, as above

Mix together and rub the entire surface with:

2 tablespoons olive oil or softened butter
1½ teaspoons salt
1 teaspoon ground black pepper

Place the tenderloin in the roasting pan and roast until an instant-read thermometer inserted in the thickest part of the roast reads 120°F for rare, 125° to 130°F for medium-rare, or 135° to 140°F for medium, 25 to 45 minutes (the temperature will continue to rise 5° to 10° out of the oven). Cover the roast loosely with aluminum foil and let stand for 15 to 20 minutes. Remove the strings and cut the tenderloin into ½-inch slices. If desired, serve with:

Béarnaise Sauce, 56, Sauce Marchand du Vin, 51, or Sauce Bordelaise, 51

SPICE-RUBBED ROASTED FILET OF BEEF

Prepare Roasted Filet or Tenderloin of Beef (High-Temperature Method), above, substituting 1 cup Peppery Dry Rub, 86, or Chili-Garlic Spice Paste, 88, for the oil and seasonings. If desired, serve the beef with Chimichurri, 80, Red-Onion Garlic Ketchup, 70, or another sauce.

GARLIC-AND-HERB-ROASTED FILET OF BEEF

Prepare Roasted Filet or Tenderloin of Beef (High-Temperature Method), above, studding the trimmed and tied filet with thin slivers of garlic sliced from 2 cloves garlic. Rub with 2 teaspoons each chopped fresh rosemary and thyme mixed with the oil, salt, and pepper. If desired, serve with Béarnaise Sauce, 56, Sauce Foyot, 56, Sauce Bordelaise, 51, or another sauce.

MARINATED FILET OR TENDERLOIN OF BEEF WITH MUSHROOMS (HIGH-TEMPERATURE METHOD)

10 to 12 servings

Use a good-quality Cabernet Sauvignon for the marinade, preferably the same wine used to make the sauce. It is best to roast the beef in a roasting pan just wide enough to hold the meat, because the juices tend to burn if the pan is too wide.

Combine in a small bowl:

¼ cup dry red wine
2 tablespoons balsamic or red wine vinegar
2 tablespoons minced fresh rosemary, or 2 teaspoons dried
2 teaspoons salt
1½ teaspoons ground black pepper

Gradually whisk in:

¼ cup olive oil

Place in a heavy roasting pan just large enough to hold it:

1 filet of beef (about 5 pounds), well trimmed and tied, 652

Prick the meat all over with a fork. Pour the marinade over the meat, turn to coat, and rub the marinade in with your hands. Cover the meat loosely with wax paper and marinate in the refrigerator for 2 to 24 hours, basting and turning from time to time.

Position a rack in the center of the oven. Preheat the oven to 425°F.

Without wiping off the marinade, roast the meat until an instant-read thermometer inserted in the thickest part of the roast reads 120°F for rare, 125° to 130°F for medium-rare, or 135° to 140°F for medium, 25 to 45 minutes (the temperature will continue to rise 5° to 10° out of the oven). Remove the meat to a platter, cover loosely with aluminum foil, and let stand for 15 to 20 minutes before carving.

Meanwhile, heat in a large, heavy skillet over high heat until the butter begins to brown:

1½ tablespoons butter
1½ tablespoons olive oil

Add half of:

1½ pounds mushrooms, preferably shiitake and oyster, stems removed, wiped clean and halved

Cook, tossing constantly with a wooden spoon, until softened and lightly browned, 3 to 4 minutes. Add half of:

1½ tablespoons very finely minced garlic

Toss several seconds more, then remove the mushrooms to a warmed pan. Return the skillet to the heat and add:

1½ tablespoons butter
1½ tablespoons olive oil

Repeat with the remaining mushrooms and garlic. Cut the filet of beef into ½-inch slices and arrange the slices on warmed plates. Add the sautéed mushrooms to the roasting pan along with any juices lost during carving and heat the mushrooms over high heat.

Season with:

Salt and ground black pepper to taste

Spoon the mushrooms over the slices of beef and, if desired, top with:

Sauce Marchand du Vin, 51, or Beurre Rouge, 57
Chopped fresh parsley

GRILLED FILET OR TENDERLOIN OF BEEF

10 to 12 servings

Those who find filet of beef too bland have not tasted it cooked over a charcoal fire. Searing the meat over a hot fire and then pushing the coals to the side, covering the grill, and cooking it over indirect heat gives it a deliciously crusty exterior with a tender, moist interior. You can be somewhat less fastidious when trimming a tenderloin for grilling, since a little external fat will simply add to the wonderful char-broiled flavor.

Prepare a very hot charcoal fire. Season:

1 filet of beef (about 5 pounds), well trimmed, 652

with:

1 tablespoon salt
2 teaspoons cracked black peppercorns

Sear the beef well on both sides, about 10 minutes per side. Remove the meat from the grill and push all the coals to one side of the grill. Place the meat on the side without the coals, cover the grill, leaving the vents open a bit, and cook, turning once or twice, until an instant-read thermometer inserted in the thickest part of the meat reads 120° to 125°F for rare, 130° to 135°F for medium-rare, or 140° to 150°F for medium, 25 to 35 minutes (the temperature will continue to rise 5° off the grill). Remove the roast from the grill, cover loosely with aluminum foil, and let stand for 15 to 20 minutes before carving. Cut the tenderloin into ½-inch slices. If desired, serve with:

Red Onion-Garlic Ketchup, 70, Chimichurri, 80, or American Horseradish Cream, 79

SPICE-RUBBED OR MARINATED GRILLED FILET OR TENDERLOIN OF BEEF

Prepare Grilled Filet or Tenderloin of Beef, above, substituting for the salt and pepper 1 cup Peppery Dry Rub, 86, or West Indies Dry Rub, 87, or marinate the meat in Red Wine Marinade, 85. Let the filet stand, covered, for up to 1 hour before grilling as directed.

STUFFED BUTTERFLIED FILET OR TENDERLOIN OF BEEF

8 to 10 servings

It is best to trim off the thin tail of the tenderloin and use it for another dish.

Position a rack in the center of the oven. Preheat the oven to 425°F.

Heat in a medium skillet over medium heat:

2 tablespoons olive oil

Add and cook just until softened, about 5 minutes:

2 medium onions, chopped

Add and cook until heated through, about 5 minutes:

4 ounces pancetta or ham, finely chopped
1 cup cooked spinach, well drained and chopped
⅓ cup chopped pitted black olives, preferably Kalamata
2 cloves garlic, chopped
2 tablespoons chopped fresh basil, or 2 teaspoons dried

2 teaspoons chopped fresh parsley
1 teaspoon ground black pepper
½ teaspoon salt

Let cool. Add:

⅔ cup fresh breadcrumbs

Cut away the last 4 to 6 inches from the narrow end of:

1 filet of beef (about 5 pounds), well trimmed, 652

Make a long, straight cut down the center of the filet just to the center of the meat. Then, starting inside that cut and holding the knife at a slight angle, make a cut to the left and a cut to the right, both about 1½ inches deep. This is called a "Y" cut, because if you could see a cross section of the meat, it would look like an inverse "Y." Lay the filet open and cover it with the spinach mixture. Reshape the meat and tie it at 1½-inch intervals. Toss together:

24 very thin slivers garlic
1 teaspoon chopped fresh thyme, or scant ½ teaspoon dried
1 teaspoon salt
½ teaspoon ground black pepper

Make 24 slits in the filet and insert the seasoned garlic slivers. Rub the meat with:

2 tablespoons olive oil

Place the filet in a roasting pan and roast until an instant-read thermometer inserted in the thickest part of the meat reads 120°F for rare, 125° to 130°F for medium-rare, or 135° to 145°F for medium, 25 to 45 minutes (the temperature will continue to rise 5° to 10° out of the oven). Remove the roast from the oven, cover loosely with aluminum foil, and let stand for 15 to 20 minutes before carving. Cut into ¾-inch slices and serve.

BEEF WELLINGTON

6 to 8 servings

An entire filet of beef embellished with pâté and sautéed mushrooms and baked in a pastry crust is a preparation reminiscent of grander times. In the classic method, the beef gets roasted twice—once before being wrapped in pastry and once after—with the unfortunate result of either overcooked beef or undercooked pastry. In the following recipe, we skip the preliminary roasting and instead wrap the uncooked meat directly in pastry. This one-step method promises moist, rosy-centered beef surrounded by a crisp pastry crust.

Position a rack in the center of the oven. Preheat the oven to 400°F.

Season:

1 center-cut filet of beef or chateaubriand (about 3 pounds), well trimmed, 652

with:

Salt and ground black pepper to taste

Combine in a medium bowl:

5 ounces (½ cup) foie gras or duck, goose, or chicken liver pâté, 725, mashed until smooth
1½ cups Duxelles, 387, cooled
3 tablespoons Madeira

Spread the pâté mixture over the entire filet. Roll out to a ¼-inch-thick rectangle large enough to wrap easily around the entire filet with some overlap, about 13 x 9 inches:

Brioche dough, 764, or 1 pound Food Processor Puff Pastry dough, 908, lightly chilled

Lightly whisk together:

1 large egg
1 tablespoon water
1 tablespoon milk

Place the filet in the center of the dough. Gently pull the pastry up and around the roast, wrapping the entire filet in a neat package. Trim off any excess dough and seal the edges by brushing them with the egg wash and pressing them together. Lightly grease a baking sheet. Place the wrapped filet seam side down on the pan and brush the top with egg wash. Use the trimmed dough to make decorative leaves or scrolls, if desired. Cut 2 or 3 small, neat holes evenly spaced in the top of the pastry to allow steam to escape as the filet cooks and to allow you to insert a meat thermometer without breaking the crust. Bake until the crust is golden brown and an instant-read thermometer tucked in the thickest part of the roast registers 120° to 125°F for rare, 125° to 130°F for medium-rare, or 135° to 140°F for medium, 35 to 55 minutes (the temperature will continue to rise 5° to 10° out of the oven). If the pastry begins to get too brown during baking, cover it loosely with aluminum foil. Remove the roast from the oven and let stand, uncovered, for 15 to 20 minutes. Carve the roast at the table, using a serrated knife to cut ¾-inch-thick slices. If desired, consult the sauce chapter for sauce ideas or serve with:

Sauce Marchand du Vin, 51, or Sauce Bordelaise, 51

BEEF WELLINGTON FOR TWO

Prepare Beef Wellington, above, using instead a 10- to 12-ounce filet steak and 2 ounces pâté, ⅓ cup duxelles and 1 tablespoon Madeira. Roast for about 30 minutes at 425°F.

BEEF ON A STRING (BOEUF À LA FICELLE)

4 to 6 servings

This flavorful and luxuriously tender French classic takes its name from the string (*ficelle*) used to tie the beef so that it can be easily lowered into simmering stock and suspended as it gently cooks. A truly elegant dish, its simple preparation requires no added fat. It is wonderful served either warm or cold. Unlike other boiled beef dishes, which tend toward toughness, the gentle poaching in this recipe delivers beef that is rosy-centered, moist, and tender. A boneless rib-eye roast can easily be substituted for the filet, although the results will be slightly less tender. Afterward, strain the enriched stock and freeze it for up to 6 months to have handy as a base for soups and sauce.

Heat in a fish poacher or pot large enough to hold the meat:

12 cups beef stock, or enough to cover the beef
1 onion, peeled and quartered
1 carrot, peeled and quartered
1 celery stalk with leaves, cut into 4-inch lengths
1 bay leaf
3 sprigs fresh thyme, or 1 teaspoon dried
1 clove garlic, crushed

Bring to a boil. Reduce the heat and simmer, partially covered, for 30 minutes. Add:

2½ pounds filet of beef or boneless rib-eye roast in one piece, well trimmed, 652, and tied at 2-inch intervals, leaving enough string at each end to dangle over the sides of the pot

Cover and simmer gently until an instant-read thermometer inserted to the thickest part of the beef registers 120°F for rare, or 125° to 130°F for medium-rare, 15 to 20 minutes (the temperature will continue to rise a few degrees after cooking). Remove the beef from the stock, cover loosely with aluminum foil, and let stand for 10 to 15 minutes. Remove the string, cut into ½-inch slices, and season with:

Salt and ground black pepper to taste

Serve warm or cold with:

American Horseradish Cream, 79, or Bavarian Apple and Horseradish Sauce, 79 (optional)
Boiled potatoes
Steamed vegetables, such as carrots, beets, or green beans

STEAK TARTARE

6 servings

The one essential ingredient for this classic dish of finely chopped and highly seasoned raw beef is top-quality, fresh, lean beef. Do not purchase already ground beef for Steak Tartare. Steak Tartare is best made from tenderloin, top round or sirloin. Trim away every speck of fat and membrane, and plan to serve the meat immediately after chopping. The classic accompaniments—onions, parsley, capers, lemon juice, anchovies, and egg yolk—are then mixed in with the meat at the table to taste. Alternatively, combine the chopped meat with the egg yolks and half of the measure of onions, shallots, parsley, and capers called for in the recipe and serve the meat preseasoned. Extra seasonings can be passed separately. *Caution:* Chopped meat is a very good culture medium for potentially dangerous bacteria because of its large surface area. Unless you can be absolutely certain that the meat you are eating is clean, eating raw meat can be hazardous to your health.

Place in a food processor fitted with the metal chopping blade:

1½ pounds boneless lean beef from the tenderloin, top round, or sirloin, well trimmed and cut into ½-inch cubes

Pulse the processor and off until the meat is chopped into ⅛-inch pieces, about 7 to 10 seconds. Do not over-process the meat. Use a fork and a spoon to remove the meat to a chilled platter or individual plates and gently form it into 6 individual mound shapes. If desired, make a spoon-shaped indentation on top of each mound and crack into each one:

1 egg yolk

Divide and arrange in small piles around each serving:

½ cup minced onions
½ cup minced shallots
½ cup minced fresh parsley
¼ cup minced drained capers
8 to 12 anchovies, minced (optional)

Serve immediately and pass separately:

Fresh lemon juice
Worcestershire sauce
Dijon mustard
Hot pepper sauce
Freshly ground black pepper
Salt

Each diner will need two forks to mix in his or her seasonings.

ABOUT STEAK

By definition, a steak is a slab of meat (or fish, for that matter), anywhere from ¾ inch to 3 inches thick, cut across the muscle grain and intended for high-heat cooking by grilling, broiling, pan-broiling, or sautéing. In the case of beef, success relies on a naturally tender cut of meat, so only certain parts should be cooked as steaks. Tender, mild-flavored steaks come from the top and middle sections, while less tender but more flavorful steaks come from the front and hind quarters. It is also important to consider the grade of the beef. Most prime- or choice-grade steak will be tenderer and more flavorful than the same cut from a select grade of beef. If cooking steaks from select cuts, do not cook past medium doneness.

The most popular, and most expensive, steaks come from the short loin, shown 647. When boned for roasts, the little-exercised muscles of the short loin are recognizable as the familiar strip loin or top loin and the prized filet or tenderloin, 651. As steaks, these tender and finely grained cuts are ideal choices for grilling and broiling, if somewhat milder than the beefy rib and sirloin cuts. Cutting the short loin into bone-in steaks yields several popular steaks. The larger of the two is porterhouse steak, followed by T-bone steak. Both are characterized by a larger section of top loin than filet and a round eye of tenderloin separated by the telltale T-shaped bone. The porterhouse is the more expensive because it has a larger section of tenderloin than the T-bone. Short-loin steaks with no tenderloin at all are called top loin, strip loin, shell, or strip steaks, as well as the more colloquial Delmonico steaks or the confusing title sirloin strip (sirloin is another cut altogether). When sold boneless, top loin steaks are often referred to by less standard names, such as Kansas City steak, New York strip steak, and boneless club steak. The term club steak refers specifically to the last steak from the rib end of the short loin. Then from the short loin, there are the more expensive steaks from the tenderloin alone, also called filet steaks, as discussed in About Filet or Tenderloin of Beef, 651. These steaks are quite tender and mild, and their smaller size makes them suitable for sautéing as well as broiling and grilling.

Rib steaks and boneless rib-eye steaks, sometimes called Spencer steaks (and, confusingly, Delmonico steaks), are cut from the rib section of beef. These have finely grained eye meat and often have more fat marbling than the top loin. While they are slightly less tender than the top loin, they are generally rich, juicy, and full-flavored. The French call these entrecôtes. Rib steaks and rib-eye steaks are excellent choices for grilling and broiling.

The sirloin is the hip section between the short loin and the rump. From this cut come several desirable steaks. The sirloin is one of the most confusing of all cuts of beef, since it is made up of many muscle groups and can be cut in several different configurations. The best cuts come from the top portion of the sirloin and are sold as top sirloin steak, sometimes called top butt steak, hip sirloin, or center-cut sirloin. These make fine grill steaks and are sometimes cut large enough to serve three or four people apiece. A smaller steak from the top sirloin, known as top sirloin cap steak, or culotte steak, is great for sautéing and grilling. Sold bone-in, these sirloin steaks are easily identified by the shape of the hip bone, sometimes referred to as the pin bone, the flat bone, or the wedge bone.

From the bottom of the sirloin, known as the bottom sirloin butt or simply the bottom butt, comes the increasingly popular sirloin tri-tip, also called triangle steak or triangle roast. It has less marbling and is less tender than the top sirloin steak, but it has a fine meaty flavor and makes a great steak as long as it is not cut less than ¾ inch thick and care is taken to avoid drying it out. Other steaks from the bottom sirloin are the ball tip and flap steaks.

From the hind leg portion come top round steaks. For many steak lovers, the robust top round offers the best combination of texture and flavor. Other popular round steaks are the bottom round and round tip steaks, also called knuckle steaks. Avoid the lean, compact, but disappointingly tough eye-of-the-round steaks—these are best braised until tender.

You might also consider a blade steak from the chuck, or shoulder, section. Surprisingly, these are one of the five tenderest cuts of all. They have a great deal of flavor and are inexpensive. This steak has a line of tough connective tissue down the middle that can be removed before or after cooking. Also from the chuck are chuck-eye steaks, which have fine flavor but can be quite tough.

London broil is a much misused term. Originally used to describe a method for quickly pan-broiling flank steak, the term is now widely used to describe any thin, less tender cut from the flank, round, or even shoulder that is best quickly broiled and thinly sliced across the grain. Flank steak is a lean, flat, boneless cut from the underside of the beef, just below the sirloin and short loin. It has tremendous flavor but must be cooked quickly and thinly sliced across the grain to be at all tender. It takes well to marinades and pan-broiling.

Skirt steak is a long, narrow steak from the short plate, or breast, of the beef. Also referred to as fajita steak, the skirt steak is tenderer with more fat than flank steak. Like flank and top round, skirt steak is also best quickly broiled and takes well to marinades.

ABOUT COOKING AND SERVING STEAK

On some occasions, individual steaks are the thing, while at other times, a few large steaks make easy work of serving a crowd. For a bone-in steak, figure on between 12 and 16 ounces per person, depending on the rest of the menu and the appetites. For boneless steaks, count on 6 to 8 ounces per person, less for lean cuts like tenderloin steaks, more for steaks with a good deal of external fat such as rib steak. Before cooking by any method, trim all but a thin ¼-inch layer of fat from the outside of the steak.

Please read the "About" sections for specific directions and recommendations for each cooking method. The easiest way to check for doneness is to make a small cut in the thickest part of the steak and take a peek at the inside. For bone-in steaks, cut into the meat right near the bone. Some experts claim that cutting into the meat will cause it to leak precious juices. It won't. To check for doneness, pull the steak from the heat when it appears just short of the desired doneness. For example, if you like your steak medium-rare, stop cooking when it still looks somewhat rare inside. A thick steak will continue to cook for a few minutes after you remove it from the heat, and the juices will be redistributed, giving it the perfect degree of doneness. Many seasoned cooks judge doneness simply by feel. This takes some practice, but you can start by feeling a raw steak—it will be squishy and soft. Steaks cooked to rare yield less but remain quite soft. At medium-rare, the meat will feel springier with a slight bit of firmness. The meat continues to firm up (and toughen) as it cooks; a well-done steak will feel hard and unyielding. With thick steaks (over 1½ inches), it is possible to use an instant-read thermometer to check for doneness by inserting it several inches deep into the side of the steak without hitting any bone; look for 120° to 130°F for rare, 130° to 135°F for medium-rare, 140° to 150°F for medium, and 155° to 165°F for medium-well. Bear in mind that steaks cooked past medium tend to dry out and be tough—especially if the beef is lean.

After cooking, steaks should stand for 5 minutes before carving to even out the color and juices in the meat. Carving a steak into thick slices is fine for naturally tender steaks, but the less tender cuts, such as the sirloin and top round, should be sliced thinly and at an angle for maximum tenderness. In flank or skirt steak, the muscle grain runs contrary to that of other steaks, so be sure to cut across the grain to make the meat easier to chew.

A steak is enhanced easily by the addition of a hot or cold sauce. Consider placing a slice of flavored butter, 76 to 78, on a hot-off-the-grill steak. The seasoned butter will melt on the way to the table, turning into a quick and savory sauce. Or serve a small bowl of tangy-sweet chutney, 66 to 68, or fiery salsa, 61 to 63, to complement the rich taste of beef. Consult Stocks & Savory Sauces and Condiments, Marinades, & Rubs chapters for other sauce ideas.

STEAK KNIVES

Most steak (and veal, pork, lamb, et cetera) is tender enough to be eaten without a special steak knife. Nonetheless, some hosts like the look and ceremony of a special piece of cutlery for steaks. If you are among them, choose attractive knives with partially serrated blades. (Avoid ones with deep sawlike teeth, which tend to rip rather than cut the meat.) Steak knives with handles longer than their blades are useful when any serious cutting has to be done, since they allow the user to exert more direct pressure on the meat.

ABOUT GRILLING AND BROILING STEAK

There is no finer treatment for a thick, naturally tender steak than to toss it onto the grill or under the broiler. The high heat of these two methods delivers the desired crisp, charred exterior while leaving the inside juicy, all with minimal effort and very little time. In the supermarket, look for steaks at least ¾ inch thick. When buying steaks from a butcher, request them cut 2 inches thick for best results. Steaks thinner than ¾ inch tend to dry out and toughen quickly; they are best pan-broiled or sautéed. When grilling, we prefer to cook without a cover, since covering the grill tends to overwhelm the meat with a smoky flavor. The grill rack should sit 4 to 6 inches above a bed of luminous coals. For steaks thicker than 1 inch, it is sometimes helpful to shift the steak to a cooler spot on the grill once both sides are well seared if the outside begins to burn before the inside cooks through.

For broiling, be sure to preheat the broiler and broiler pan, positioning the broiler pan closer to the heating element for thin steaks and farther away for thicker steaks. As with grilling, if the outside of the steak begins to burn, simply move the broiling pan away from the heat by lowering it.

Consult the chart below for approximate cooking times. All steaks should be flipped just past the halfway point in the recommended cooking time, since the second side will cook a bit faster than the first. For steaks of varying thickness, add or subtract about 1 minute total for every ½-inch difference in thickness. The recommended cooking times are based on steaks straight from the refrigerator. Expect room-temperature steaks to cook a few minutes faster.

APPROXIMATE TOTAL COOKING TIMES FOR GRILLED AND BROILED STEAKS

STEAK TYPE	THICKNESS	RARE	MEDIUM-RARE	MEDIUM
Tenderloin, filet, flank, or skirt steak	1 inch	6 to 8 minutes	8 to 10 minutes	10 to 12 minutes
	2 inches	12 to 14 minutes	14 to 18 minutes	18 to 20 minutes
Boneless top loin, rib, sirloin, top round, or chuck steak	1 inch	6 to 8 minutes	8 to 10 minutes	10 to 12 minutes
	2 inches	16 to 18 minutes	18 to 20 minutes	20 to 22 minutes
Bone-in T-bone, porterhouse, rib, top loin, or sirloin steak	1 inch	10 to 12 minutes	12 to 16 minutes	16 to 18 minutes
	2 inches	18 to 20 minutes	20 to 24 minutes	24 to 28 minutes

GRILLED OR BROILED STEAK

4 servings

The best cuts for broiling and grilling are T-bone, porterhouse, top loin, sirloin, and tenderloin steaks. Cooking times for grilling and broiling are approximate and depend on the many variables of steaks and cooking temperatures.

Prepare a medium-hot charcoal fire or preheat the broiler and broiler pan. If broiling, position the broiler pan 4 to 5 inches from the heating element.

Pat dry:

4 small beef steaks (6 to 12 ounces each) or 2 larger steaks (¾ to 1½ pounds each), 1¼ to 2 inches thick

Season both sides with:

Salt and ground black pepper to taste

If desired, rub with the cut side of:

1 clove garlic, halved

Grill or broil the steaks, turning them once just past the halfway point in the cooking time. Consult the chart above, for cooking times. To check for doneness, make a small incision in the steak and check the center. The interior should be slightly less done than desired. Thicker steaks may require broiling farther from the heat or moving the steak to a cooler section of the grill to complete the cooking. For sauce ideas, please read About Cooking and Serving Steak, above.

MARINATED OR SPICE-RUBBED STEAK

Choose from among the spice rubs, herb pastes, and marinades on pages 84 to 88, or marinate the streaks in one of the following:

Teriyaki Marinade, 86, Mediterranean Garlic Herb Paste, 87, Red Wine Marinade, 85, or West Indies Dry Rub, 87

Cover and let the seasoned steak marinate, refrigerated, for at least 1 hour or up to 24 hours. If using a wet marinade, dry the steaks before cooking. Cook as directed for Grilled or Broiled Steak, above.

SPICE-CRUSTED SIRLOIN WITH LEMON GARLIC BUTTER

For the lemon garlic butter, prepare Maître d'Hotel Butter, 77, adding 1 teaspoon minced garlic. Shape the butter into a cylinder and refrigerate until solid, about 1½ hours. Meanwhile, rub all sides of a 2-inch-thick sirloin steak, 1½ to 2 pounds, with ½ cup Peppery Dry Rub, 86. Cook as directed for Grilled or Broiled Steak, above. Serve the steak by cutting it into ½-inch-thick slices and topping each serving with about 1 tablespoon of the lemon garlic butter.

RIB-EYE STEAK WITH ORANGE CHIPOTLE GLAZE

2 servings

A red-hot hardwood fire is the best way to cook this steak, but any hot grill will do. Some devotees of open-fire cooking actually cook the steak in the middle of the fire—directly on a log that has caught fire at the edges but still provides a flat surface. The steak cooks quickly in the surrounding flames.

Prepare a very hot charcoal fire or preheat the broiler and broiler pan. If broiling, position the broiler pan 4 to 5 inches from the heating element.

Simmer until reduced by almost half:

1 cup Orange-Pineapple-Chipotle Baste, 89

Combine in a small bowl:

2½ tablespoons cumin seeds, preferably toasted
2 tablespoons cracked black peppercorns
2 tablespoons coarse salt, or scant 1½ tablespoons salt

Pat dry:

2 beef rib-eye steaks (6 to 10 ounces each), 1 to 1½ inches thick

Rub the steaks with the spice mixture and grill or broil for 7 to 8 minutes each side for medium-rare. Make a small incision and check the center. The interior should be slightly less done than desired, for it will continue to cook somewhat off the heat. Cook each side for 1 to 2 minutes more for medium. Remove the steak from the heat and let stand for about 5 minutes. Brush with the orange glaze, passing any extra on the side.

CHILI-CRUSTED FLANK STEAK WITH MANGO SALSA

3 or 4 servings

This recipe is best with pure ground chili peppers made from toasted dried ancho, pasilla, or guajillo peppers, but ordinary chili powder can also be used.

Prepare a hot charcoal fire or preheat the broiler and broiler pan. If broiling, position the broiler pan 4 to 5 inches from the heating element.

Combine in a small bowl:

2 tablespoons ground dried chili peppers
2 tablespoons cracked black peppercorns
1½ tablespoons ground cumin
1½ tablespoons coarse salt, or 1 tablespoon salt

Pat dry:

1 beef flank steak (about 1½ pounds)

Rub the entire surface of the steak with the spice mixture and grill or broil for 4 to 6 minutes each side for medium-rare. Make a small incision and check the center. The interior should be slightly less done than desired, for it will continue to cook somewhat off the heat. Cook each side for 1 to 2 minutes more for medium. Remove the steak from the heat and let stand for about 5 minutes. Thinly slice the steak across the grain. Serve immediately, topped with:

Mango Salsa, 63

GRILLED OPEN-FACED STEAK SANDWICH WITH QUICK PICKLED ONIONS

4 servings

A tri-tip sirloin is a less expensive cut that makes remarkable steak sandwiches, especially when the beef and bread are grilled over a charcoal fire. If tri-tip is unavailable, choose any thick steak cut from the top round or sirloin.

Prepare and set aside:

Quick Red Onion Pickle, 65

Build an extra-large charcoal fire and, before grilling, spread the fire so that one side of the grill is very hot and the other side is not hot at all. The very hot side should be so hot that you can hold your hand 6 inches above the coals for only 3 seconds. You should be able to hold your hand over the cooler side for twice as long. Pat dry:

1 beef tri-tip roast (1½ to 2 pounds) or 1½- to 2-inch-thick top round or sirloin steak, excess fat/membrane trimmed

Rub the entire surface of the meat with:

¼ cup Southern Dry Rub for Barbecue, 86

Sear the meat on the very hot side of the grill for 3 to 4 minutes each side. Move it to the cooler side of the grill and cook each side for 8 to 10 minutes more for medium-rare. Make a small incision and check the center. The interior should be slightly less done than desired, for it will continue to cook somewhat off the heat. Cook each side for 1 to 2 minutes more for medium. Remove the steak from the grill and let stand, loosely covered, for 5 minutes. Meanwhile, grill over the cooler side of the grill until lightly toasted, about 2 minutes each side:

4 slices crusty white bread

Thinly slice the steak, about ¼ inch thick, across the grain. If desired, spread each slice of toasted bread with:

Red Onion-Garlic Ketchup, 70, or Tomato Chutney, 68

Lay the steak slices on the toast. Top with the pickled onions and serve.

T-BONE OR PORTERHOUSE STEAK WITH SOUTH AMERICAN STEAK SAUCE

2 to 3 servings

This simple uncooked sauce, a variation of the Argentinean condiment Chimichurri, adds a wonderful vibrant flavor to the mighty T-bone or porterhouse. When carving, be sure that each person gets a little of both the tenderloin and the strip loin.

Position the broiler pan 4 to 5 inches from the heating element. Preheat the broiler and broiler pan.

Combine in a small bowl:

⅓ cup olive oil
¼ cup chopped fresh parsley
1 tablespoon minced garlic
1 teaspoon red pepper flakes
1 teaspoon salt

Pat dry:

1 beef T-bone or porterhouse steak (1½ to 2 pounds), about 1½ inches thick

Rub the entire surface of the steak with:

2 teaspoons salt
2 teaspoons cracked black peppercorns

Place the steak on the broiler pan. Cook for 6 to 8 minutes on the first side, then turn and cook the second side for 4 to 6 minutes. Make a small incision and check the center. The interior should be slightly less done than desired, for it will continue to cook somewhat off the heat. Cook each side for 1 to 2 minutes more for medium. Remove the steak from the broiler and let stand, loosely covered, for 5 minutes. Cut the steak off the bone and then into thick slices. Serve each person a few slices of each section of the steak. Top with the garlic sauce and:

Juice of 1 lemon

BROILED TENDERLOIN STEAK WITH SHERRIED MUSHROOMS

2 servings

The rich, meaty flavor of the broiled mushrooms makes them a perfect complement to the tenderloin steaks.

Position the broiler pan 4 to 5 inches from the heating element. Preheat the broiler and broiler pan.

Combine in a small bowl:

¼ cup olive oil
1 tablespoon minced garlic
1 teaspoon cracked black peppercorns
1 teaspoon salt

Add and toss to coat:

2 cups small mushrooms, wiped clean, stems trimmed

Pat dry:

2 beef tenderloin or filet mignon steaks (6 to 8 ounces each), 2 inches thick

Immediately before cooking, rub all sides of the meat with:

2 teaspoons salt
2 teaspoons cracked black peppercorns

Place the steaks and mushrooms on the broiler pan. Cook for 8 to 12 minutes, turning the steaks and mushroom caps once halfway through cooking. Make a small incision and check the center. The interior will be slightly less done than desired, for it will continue to cook somewhat off the heat. Cook each side for 1 to 2 minutes more for medium. Remove the steaks and mushrooms from the broiler and let the steaks stand, loosely covered, for 5 minutes. Remove the mushrooms to a small bowl and toss with any accumulated meat juices from the broiler pan along with:

2 tablespoons dry sherry

ABOUT PAN-BROILING STEAK

Pan-broiling, or dry-skillet cooking, is a simple and convenient method for cooking any steak up to 2 inches thick. It is especially useful for steaks less than ¾ inch thick, which fare poorly if grilled or broiled. As an added advantage, pan-broiling is an excellent method for achieving a good crisp crust. The only disadvantage is that the high heat used for pan-broiling creates smoke and splattering, but this is easily solved by opening a window or turning on the kitchen exhaust fan.

Pan-broiling is best done in a well-seasoned heavy skillet or griddle or nonstick skillet. Specially designed ridged cast-iron pans are ideal but not necessary. Steaks should be patted dry and seasoned well with salt, pepper, and other spices immediately before cooking: salting too far in advance makes the surface too moist for the meat to brown evenly. Do not hold back on seasoning: pan-broiling, after all, is the technique used to produce spicy "blackened" steaks. It is important to get the pan hot enough that the meat sizzles the instant it hits the pan: lower temperatures will not produce the desired crust. With a well-seasoned pan, additional oil or fat is unnecessary when cooking well-marbled steaks. For leaner cuts, we recommend a light coating of vegetable oil. Do not overcrowd the pan and cook steaks uncovered, turning them occasionally. Pour off any fat that accumulates to keep from frying the steaks.

BASIC PAN-BROILED STEAK

4 servings

Pan-broiled steaks tend to smoke, so turn the exhaust fan on high or open the windows.

Pat dry:

4 small beef steaks (2 to 12 ounces each) or 2 larger steaks (¾ to 1½ pounds each), ¾ to 1½ inches thick

If the meat is very lean, brush it with:

Olive oil

Season both sides of the steaks with:

Salt and ground black pepper to taste

Heat a large, heavy skillet or griddle over medium-high heat. You may need 2 skillets if the steaks are large. To determine when the pan is hot enough, touch a corner of the steak to the pan; it should sizzle briskly. Once the pan is hot, sear the steaks on one side, without crowding, for about 5 minutes. Turn them over and sear the other side for 3 to 4 minutes for rare, 5 to 8 minutes for medium. You may need to turn the steak more than once if one side gets too brown before the steak is done. Pour off any fat that accumulates during cooking. For sauce ideas, please read About Cooking and Serving Steak, 657.

BLACKENED STEAK

The key to this favorite from New Orleans kitchens is a

heavy coating of Cajun Spice Rub, which caramelizes as it cooks to form a tangy, crispy black crust around the moist, tender steak meat.

Generously coat a 1- to 1½-inch-thick steak with ¼ cup Cajun Dry Rub, 86, and follow the directions for Basic Pan-Broiled Steak, above.

PEPPER STEAK WITH BRANDY CREAM SAUCE

4 servings

The rich brown crust from high-heat searing combined with the pan sauce prepared after the steaks are cooked makes for a grand steak dinner. Green peppercorns can easily be substituted for some or all of the black peppercorns, but green peppercorns do tend to pop and splatter as they cook. Serve one thick steak per person for meat lovers; lesser appetites can easily share.

Pat dry:

2 to 4 boneless beef strip steaks (12 to 14 ounces each), 1½ to 2 inches thick, excess fat trimmed

Rub all sides of the meat with:

4 tablespoons cracked black peppercorns, green peppercorns, or a mix of the two

1 tablespoon salt

Heat a large, heavy skillet, preferably cast iron, over high heat until quite hot. To determine when the pan is hot enough, touch a corner of the steak to the pan; it should sizzle briskly. Once the pan is hot, sear the steaks, without crowding, for 6 to 7 minutes each side. Make a small incision and check the center. The interior should be slightly less done than desired, for it will continue to cook somewhat off the heat. Cook each side 1 minute more for medium. Remove the steaks from the pan and let stand, loosely covered.

Pour off any excess fat from the pan and heat the pan over medium-high heat. Add:

¼ cup chopped shallots or red onions

Cook, stirring, just until barely softened, about 15 seconds. Remove the pan from the heat and carefully add:

¼ cup brandy

If the brandy flames, let it burn itself out. Return the pan to medium-high heat and cook until the liquid is almost evaporated. Add:

1 cup beef or veal stock

Boil until reduced by half, about 5 minutes. Add:

¼ cup heavy cream

Bring to a boil and cook until reduced by half, about 4 minutes. Remove the pan from the heat. Add:

2 tablespoons chopped fresh parsley

Salt and cracked black peppercorns to taste

Serve immediately over the steaks.

LONDON BROIL

3 or 4 servings

Flank steak is the traditional cut for London broil. It is well flavored, is easy to cook, and has no waste. London broil refers to a quick pan-broiling over high heat and thinly slicing the meat across the grain before serving. It is ideal for cooking lean, tougher steak cuts, such as shoulder and round, as well as flank steak. For best results, never cook London broil beyond medium-rare, or it becomes tough and dry.

Pat dry:

1 boneless beef flank steak (about 1½ pounds) from the chuck blade, top round, or flank, not less than ¾ inch thick

Rub each side with the cut side of:

1 large clove garlic, halved

Season generously with:

1 teaspoon dried oregano

Salt and ground black pepper to taste

Heat a large, heavy skillet or griddle over high heat. To determine when the pan is hot enough, touch a corner of the steak to the pan; it should sizzle briskly. Once the pan is hot, sear the steak on one side for 4 to 5 minutes. Turn it over and sear the other side for 3 to 4 minutes. Make a small incision and check the center. It should be slightly less done than desired. Remove the steak from the pan and let it stand for 5 minutes, then carve it diagonally across the grain into ¼-inch slices.

PAN-SEARED TOP ROUND STEAK WITH SMOKY ONIONS AND RED WINE

4 to 6 servings

This bold recipe turns a little-appreciated cut of beef into a first-class main course. The smoky flavor of the onions marries beautifully with the flavors of the steak and red wine. The high heat of the pan puts out a good amount of smoke, so be sure your kitchen exhaust fan is working.

Pat dry:

1 beef top round steak (1½ to 2 pounds), 1½ inches thick

Rub all sides of the meat with:

2 tablespoons cracked black peppercorns

1 tablespoon salt

Heat a large, heavy skillet, preferably cast iron, over high heat until quite hot. To determine when the pan is hot enough, touch a corner of the steak to the pan; it should sizzle briskly. Once the pan is hot, sear the steak about 6 minutes on each side. Make a small incision and check the center. It should be slightly less done than desired, for it will continue to cook somewhat off the heat. Remove the steak from the pan and let it stand, loosely covered. Heat the pan over medium-high heat.

Add:

3 medium, red onions, halved and thinly sliced

Cook, stirring constantly, until well colored, 2 to 3 minutes. Expect the onions to look somewhat scorched; this is what gives the dish its smoky flavor. Add:

1½ cups dry red wine

Boil until reduced by half, 3 to 4 minutes. Remove from the heat and stir in:

4 tablespoons (½ stick) cold butter, cut into pieces

Once the butter is no longer visible, add:

⅓ cup chopped fresh parsley

Salt and ground black pepper to taste

Very thinly slice the steak across the grain and spoon the onion sauce on top.

ABOUT SAUTÉED STEAKS

Sautéing is the method preferred in France and Italy for cooking steaks and is especially well suited for tender, lean steaks such as filet, sirloin, and strip. The steak is browned in a small amount of fat over medium-high heat, not quite as ferocious a heat as when pan-broiling. This popular cooking technique turns out steaks with an evenly browned exterior and lends itself to making tasty pan sauces quickly and easily. For more sauce ideas, please read About Gravy and Pan Sauces, 51. Sautéing becomes pan-frying when more fat is added to the pan in the case of regional specialties like Chicken-Fried Steak, 663.

SAUTÉED STEAK

4 servings

Ideal for boneless top loin, tenderloin, or top sirloin cap steaks.

Pat dry:

4 boneless beef steaks (6 to 8 ounces each), ¾ to 1¼ inches thick

Season both sides with:

Salt and ground black pepper to taste

Heat in a large, heavy skillet over medium-high heat:

1 tablespoon olive oil

Put the steaks in the pan and sauté for about 5 minutes each side for medium-rare, less time for rare or more for medium. Make a small incision and check the center. It should be slightly less done than desired, for it will continue to cook somewhat off the heat. Remove the steaks to a warmed platter and let stand for 3 to 4 minutes before serving. If desired, pour off all but 1 tablespoon of fat from the pan and make a pan sauce, 51 to 55, to serve with the steak.

SAUTÉED STEAK WITH RED WINE HERB SAUCE

Prepare Sautéed Steak, above, pouring off all but 1 tablespoon of fat from the pan and placing the pan over medium-high heat. Add 2 tablespoons chopped shallots and cook for 1 minute. Add ½ cup each dry red wine and chicken or beef stock, and 1 teaspoon chopped fresh rosemary or scant ½ teaspoon dried. Increase the heat to high and boil the sauce, scraping up any browned bits, until it is reduced to about ¼ cup. Add any accumulated meat juices from the steaks. For a richer sauce, swirl in 1 tablespoon butter off the heat. Season with salt and pepper to taste and serve immediately.

STEAK DIANE

4 servings

This recipe also works nicely with medallions of pork.

Prepare Sautéed Steak above, removing the cooked steaks to a warmed platter and pouring off any fat in the pan. Return the pan to medium-high heat. Add and heat until hot:

2 tablespoons butter

Add and cook, shaking the pan, until softened, about 2 minutes:

½ cup chopped shallots or scallions (white part only)

Stir in:

¼ cup beef stock

¼ cup brandy

1 tablespoon Dijon mustard

2 teaspoons fresh lemon juice

1 teaspoon Worcestershire sauce

Salt and ground black pepper to taste

Boil for 1 to 2 minutes, scraping up any browned bits. Add any juices from the steaks. If desired, remove from the heat and add, swirling the pan until melted:

2 tablespoons butter, softened

Garnish with:

2 tablespoons snipped fresh chives

2 tablespoons chopped fresh parsley

Pour the sauce over the steaks and serve immediately.

HOISIN-GLAZED SKIRT STEAK WITH SCALLION GINGER SLAW

4 servings

A widely misunderstood cut of beef, the skirt steak is similar to flank steak but narrower in shape and a bit less lean and, therefore, more tender. Flank steak will do if skirt is unavailable. The flowery flavor of basmati rice makes an excellent accompaniment to this steak.

Combine in a medium bowl:

¼ cup rice vinegar

2 tablespoons fresh lime juice

2 tablespoons grated peeled fresh ginger
1½ tablespoons soy sauce
1½ tablespoons sesame seeds, preferably toasted
1 tablespoon toasted sesame oil
1 teaspoon sugar
¼ teaspoon hot chili oil, or more to taste (optional)

Add and toss to coat:

8 scallions, cut into 2-inch lengths, then into thin strips
1 red bell pepper, cut into 2-inch lengths, then into thin strips
½ cup rinsed sliced water chestnuts

Combine in a small bowl:

½ cup hoisin sauce
¼ cup soy sauce
1½ tablespoons white wine vinegar
1 tablespoon sugar

Pat dry:

1½ to 2 pounds beef skirt or flank steak

Rub both sides with:

Salt and ground black pepper to taste

Heat in a large, heavy skillet over medium-high heat until almost smoking:

2 tablespoons olive oil

Add the steaks and sauté about 5 minutes each side for medium-rare, less time for rare or more for medium. Make a small incision and check the center. It should be slightly less done than desired. Brush both sides of the steaks with the hoisin glaze and cook each side for 30 seconds more. Remove the steaks to a platter and let stand for 3 to 4 minutes. Thinly slice the steaks across the grain. Serve with the scallion slaw and extra hoisin glaze on the side.

PAN-FRIED CHUCK STEAK WITH TOMATOES AND CHIVES

4 servings

Chuck steaks have wonderful flavor and are quite inexpensive. If you can find top blade steaks, they will be the tenderest. Steaks from the round can also be substituted. Purchase choice- or prime-grade beef for best results.

Pat dry:

1½ to 2 pounds beef chuck steaks (2 large or 4 small), ¾ to 1 inch thick

Season both sides with:

Salt and ground black pepper to taste

Heat in a large, heavy skillet over medium-high heat:

1 tablespoon olive oil

Put the steaks in the pan and sauté for 4 to 5 minutes each side for medium-rare, less time for rare or more for medium. Make a small incision and check the center. It should be slightly less done than desired, for it will continue to cook somewhat off the heat. Remove the steaks to a warmed platter and let stand for 3 to 4 minutes. Pour off all but 1 tablespoon of fat from the pan and heat over medium heat. Add and cook just until softened, 3 to 4 minutes:

1 onion, thinly sliced

Add and cook for 1 minute:

1 tablespoon chopped garlic
1 teaspoon fresh thyme, or scant ½ teaspoon dried

Add and simmer for about 5 minutes:

One 15-ounce can plum tomatoes, drained and chopped, or 1½ cups chopped seeded peeled fresh tomatoes
½ cup beef stock or dry red wine

Add:

½ cup chopped pitted black olives, preferably Kalamata
¼ cup chopped fresh parsley or basil
Salt and ground black pepper to taste

Add the steaks along with any accumulated juices to the sauce and warm briefly, about 30 seconds. Serve immediately.

CHICKEN-FRIED STEAK

4 servings

This dish is battered and fried like Southern fried chicken. Cooking a thin piece of tough meat this way is popular in the South and Southwest, where it is prime truck-stop fare. Do not use cube steak; look for bottom round or rump steak instead.

Using the flat side of a cleaver or a meat mallet, pound to ⅓ inch thick:

1 beef round or rump steak (about 1½ pounds)

Cut into 4 serving pieces. Mix in a shallow bowl:

1 cup all-purpose flour
2 teaspoons ground black pepper
1½ teaspoons salt
¾ teaspoon ground red pepper

Whisk together in a second shallow bowl:

¼ cup milk
1 large egg

Coat each steak with the seasoned flour, dip into the egg mixture, then coat with the seasoned flour again and shake off any excess. Let dry on a rack for 15 minutes. Heat in a large, heavy skillet over medium-high heat:

½ inch vegetable oil, shortening, or lard

To determine if the fat is hot enough (350° to 360°F), dip a corner of the steak into it; it should sizzle and sputter. Carefully add the steaks and fry, turning once, until golden brown, 2 to 3 minutes each side. Remove the steaks to a warmed platter, pour off all but 2 to 3 tablespoons of fat from the pan and return to medium heat. Stir in, and cook until softened, about 5 minutes:

1 onion, thinly sliced

Add, stirring, and cook for 2 to 3 minutes:

2 tablespoons all-purpose flour

Stir in and bring to a boil, scraping up any browned bits:

1 cup milk

Reduce the heat and simmer until thickened, 3 to 5 minutes. Season with:

Salt and ground black pepper to taste
Dash of hot red pepper sauce (optional)

Pour over steaks and, if desired, serve with:

Mashed Potatoes, 408

ABOUT COOKING BEEF CUBES, STRIPS, AND TIPS

A quick and economical way to make a beef dinner is to cut any tender steak into cubes or strips and quickly sauté or stir-fry the meat over high heat. In addition to being convenient, these dishes are especially popular with those who enjoy the taste of beef but prefer to avoid a large slab of steak. Because the beef in these dishes is cooked quickly over high heat, success depends on starting with naturally tender cuts; no amount of marinating will tenderize a tough cut enough for satisfactory results. Although many markets sell small trays of precubed or sliced "kebab" or "stir-fry" meat, we recommend buying steaks from the tenderloin, loin, sirloin, or top round and cutting them yourself. Top blade steaks from the chuck are also a good choice as long as you trim out the center line of tough connective tissue. This ensures that you get the high-quality, tender meat you want and often saves money.

BROILED OR GRILLED BEEF KEBABS *4 servings*

Shish kebab originated as a Turkish dish of skewered, marinated lamb grilled over a charcoal fire, but today, we cube and skewer just about anything, from beef to vegetables, and call them kebabs. There is plenty of room for improvisation when assembling kebabs, but combine foods that will cook at the same rate of speed. Quick-cooking, delicate vegetables such as mushrooms and tomatoes are best skewered separately from the meat. Create your own versions by using marinades or basting sauces, such as Teriyaki Sauce, 87, or Orange Molasses Glaze, 89. Other meats and seafood (chicken, lamb, shrimp) can be used; simply adjust the cooking time accordingly. If using bamboo skewers, soak them in water for at least 30 minutes to prevent them from burning. The meat and vegetables are first lightly oiled and seasoned to prevent sticking. As with all tender cuts, beef kebabs should not be cooked beyond medium, or they will become tough and dry.

Cut into 1- to 1½-inch cubes:

One 1- to 1½-pound beef top loin, sirloin, filet, or top round steak, 1 inch thick

Mix in a large bowl:

2 tablespoons vegetable oil
1 tablespoon red wine vinegar
2 teaspoons Dijon mustard
1 teaspoon grated lemon zest
1 teaspoon chopped fresh thyme or rosemary, or scant ½ teaspoon dried
1 teaspoon minced garlic
1 teaspoon salt
½ teaspoon ground black pepper

Add the beef along with:

1 medium bell pepper, cut into 1-inch pieces
1 onion, cut into small wedges

Toss to coat the beef and vegetables, cover, and marinate in the refrigerator for 2 to 24 hours.

Preheat the broiler and broiler pan or prepare a medium-hot charcoal fire. If broiling, position the broiler pan 3 to 4 inches from the heating element. Thread the meat and vegetables on skewers. Broil or grill for 8 to 10 minutes, turning the skewers occasionally. Make a small incision in a cube of meat and check the center. It should be slightly less done than desired, for it will continue to cook somewhat off the heat. Serve immediately with:

Basic Pilaf, 257, or couscous, 266 to 267

HERB-CRUSTED SIRLOIN KEBABS WITH TOMATO BASIL RELISH *4 servings*

Preheat the broiler and broiler pan or prepare a very hot charcoal fire. If broiling, position the broiler pan 3 to 4 inches from the heating element.

Combine in a medium bowl:

2 medium tomatoes, cored and diced
½ cup chopped pitted brine-cured black olives, preferably Kalamata
¼ cup balsamic vinegar
¼ cup olive oil
1 tablespoon minced garlic
½ teaspoon salt
½ teaspoon ground black pepper

Cut into 1½-inch cubes:

1½ to 2 pounds beef steak, preferably sirloin tip

Rub the meat with:

1 cup Mediterranean Garlic Herb Paste, 87

Have ready:

2 small red onions, cut into small wedges

2 bell peppers, preferably 1 red and 1 green, cut into 1-inch pieces

Thread the meat and vegetables on 8 skewers, evenly distributing the peppers and onions. Broil or grill for 8 to 10 minutes, turning the skewers occasionally. Make a small incision in a cube of meat and check the center. The interior should be slightly less done than desired, for it will continue to cook somewhat off the heat. Spoon the tomato relish onto 4 dinner plates and top each with 2 kebabs.

SAUTÉED STEAK STRIPS WITH MUSHROOMS

4 servings

This light and quick dish uses very little meat to create a tasty sauce for pasta or rice. Try it over wide pappardelle or bow-tie-shaped farfalle. The basic recipe can be embellished with the addition of other herbs, spices, and vegetables. Use lean tender cuts of beef such as tenderloin, sirloin, or top round.

Combine and let soak until softened, about 1 hour:

1 ounce dried porcini or shiitake mushrooms

1 cup hot water

Drain, reserving the soaking liquid. Strain the liquid through a sieve lined with a dampened paper towel. Set aside.

Cut into thin strips, about 2 x ¼ inch:

¾ to 1 pound beef steak, about ¾ inch thick

Toss the beef strips with:

1 teaspoon finely chopped garlic

½ teaspoon dried thyme

½ teaspoon salt

¼ teaspoon cracked black peppercorns

Heat a large nonstick skillet over medium-high heat. Add the meat strips and sauté, shaking the pan constantly to avoid sticking, until the meat is seared but still pink inside, 2 to 3 minutes. Remove the meat strips. Add to the skillet:

8 ounces mushrooms, wiped clean and sliced

1 teaspoon finely chopped garlic

Pinch of salt

Ground black pepper to taste

Sauté the mushrooms and garlic until the mushrooms just begin to brown, about 2 minutes. Remove. Add the porcini mushrooms and the soaking liquid to the skillet. Stir in:

½ cup beef stock

1½ tablespoons tomato paste

Boil until the liquid is reduced by half. Return the beef and mushrooms to the pan. Taste and adjust the seasonings. Serve over:

12 ounces fresh pasta, or 8 ounces dried, cooked

Sprinkle with:

Freshly grated Parmesan cheese

BEEF AND VEGETABLE STIR-FRY

4 to 6 servings

Stir-frying is the Chinese technique of using a little oil and an Asian flavor base to cook meat, fish, and vegetables. This method is quick and easy; a Chinese wok is handy, but a large skillet also will do. This is a basic recipe and can be varied with different combinations of vegetables and seasonings. Any cut of lean, tender beef, such as flank steak, sirloin steak, sirloin tip, skirt steak, or top sirloin cap steak, can be used. Lean pork, lamb, or chicken can be substituted for the beef.

BEFORE COOKING:

Mix in a medium bowl:

¼ cup soy sauce

2 tablespoons dry sherry or Chinese rice wine

1 tablespoon water

1 tablespoon sugar

1 tablespoon cornstarch

2 teaspoons toasted sesame oil

Add and toss to coat:

1 pound beef steak, sliced across the grain into 2 x ½-inch strips

Marinate the beef for at least 20 minutes.

On a large platter, place in separate piles:

1 medium onion, chopped

2 bell peppers, preferably 1 green and 1 red, chopped

1 cup mushrooms, preferably shiitake, wiped clean, stemmed, and cut into ½-inch strips

4 scallions, cut into 2-inch lengths

1 cup snow peas, trimmed, cooked for 30 seconds in boiling water, rinsed, and drained

Combine in a small bowl:

2 tablespoons minced peeled fresh ginger

1 tablespoon minced garlic

⅓ to 1 teaspoon chili oil, or more to taste (optional)

Have ready:

2 to 4 tablespoons chopped fresh cilantro or chopped scallions

1 tablespoon fermented black beans, rinsed, drained, and chopped (optional)

1½ teaspoons red pepper flakes, or more to taste (optional)

Remove the beef from the marinade. Add to the marinade and set aside:

⅓ cup chicken stock or water

TO COOK:

Heat in a wok or large, heavy skillet over very high heat until hot but not smoking:

2 tablespoons peanut oil

Add the ginger mixture and stir-fry until fragrant but not browned, about 30 seconds. Add the beef and cook, quickly stirring and flipping it in the oil to separate the slices, until browned, about 2 minutes. Remove and reserve the beef, ginger, and garlic.

Heat the wok or skillet over high heat until hot. Add:

1 tablespoon peanut oil

Heat until hot but not smoking. Add the onion, peppers, and mushrooms and stir-fry until crisp-tender, about 2 minutes. Add the 2-inch scallion pieces, the snow peas and the Chinese black beans and red pepper flakes, if using. Return the meat to the pan along with any accumulated juices and the marinade mixture. Toss for 10 seconds over high heat. Serve with:

Hot cooked rice or Chinese noodles

Garnish with the cilantro or scallions.

STIR-FRIED BEEF WITH ASPARAGUS

4 to 6 servings

Both the beef and the vegetable take on rich flavor in this popular dish.

BEFORE COOKING:

Mix well in a medium bowl:

2 tablespoons Chinese cooking wine or dry white wine
2 tablespoons oyster sauce
1 tablespoon cornstarch
2 teaspoons light soy sauce
1½ teaspoons salt
1½ teaspoons sugar

Cut across the grain to make very thin 2 x 1-inch slices (this is more easily done if the meat is partially frozen):

1 pound flank steak

Add the meat to the soy mixture, cover with plastic wrap, and marinate for at least 30 minutes.

Place in cold water to cover:

1½ pounds medium-thick asparagus, trimmed and cut into 1-inch pieces

Place on a small plate:

2½ tablespoons fermented black beans, rinsed lightly under cold water and mashed to a paste
1 tablespoon finely minced garlic
1 teaspoon red pepper flakes (optional)

Mix well in a small bowl:

¾ cup chicken stock
½ teaspoon salt
½ teaspoon sugar

Mix well in a cup:

3 tablespoons cool water, leaving mixing spoon in for later
2 tablespoons cornstarch

Have ready:

1 tablespoon toasted sesame oil

TO COOK:

Heat a wok or large, heavy skillet over high heat. Add and heat until very hot but not smoking:

2 tablespoons peanut oil

Add the beef and cook, quickly stirring and flipping it in the oil to separate the slices, until browned, about 2 minutes. Drain in a strainer or colander.

Heat the wok or skillet over high heat until hot. Add:

2 tablespoons peanut oil

Heat until very hot but not smoking. Add the black beans, garlic, and pepper flakes. Briefly cook, stirring, until the garlic browns very slightly.

Drain the asparagus, add it to the wok, and cook for 2 minutes. Stir in the chicken stock mixture and bring to a boil. Cook the asparagus for 1 to 2 minutes more, depending on thickness.

Return the beef to the wok or skillet. Stir and toss quickly to mix completely.

Stir the cornstarch mixture, then pour it gradually into the sauce while stirring. Cook, stirring, until the sauce is thickened. Add the sesame oil, give a final stir, and serve immediately.

BEEF STROGANOFF

4 to 6 servings

The enduring appeal of this dish lies in its simplicity. Since its origin in Russia in the eighteenth century, there have been many variations on the theme of sautéed beef slices in a cream-based sauce. Some recipes include onions and mushrooms, and others spice the sauce with mustard. In our version, the beef is cooked with onions for flavor, but then the onions are discarded so as not to interfere with the taste of slices of tender beef in a simple roux-thickened cream sauce. Sautéed mushrooms and rice pilaf are good side dishes. Stroganoff is an elegant way to use up any leftover tenderloin pieces cut from the whole filet.

Cut into thin 2 x ¼-inch strips:

1½ pounds beef tenderloin, top loin, or sirloin tip, well trimmed

Season with:

Salt and ground black pepper to taste

Melt in a small saucepan over medium heat:

1½ tablespoons butter

Add and stir with a whisk until smooth:

1 tablespoon all-purpose flour

Add, whisking constantly to prevent lumps, 3 to 4 minutes:

1 cup beef stock, 40, heated to a simmer

Simmer until the sauce is smooth and thickened. Set aside and keep warm. Heat in a large skillet over medium-high heat:

2 tablespoons butter

Add the beef along with:

1 onion, thinly sliced

Cook quickly, shaking the pan and stirring, until evenly browned, 1 to 2 minutes. The meat should remain pink in the center. Remove the meat to a warmed platter with a slotted spoon and discard the onion. Return the sauce to medium heat, stir in, and heat briefly without boiling:

3 tablespoons sour cream
1 teaspoon Dijon mustard
Salt and ground black pepper to taste

Add any accumulated juices from the cooked meat. Spoon the sauce over the meat and serve immediately with:

Egg Noodles, 318
Basic Pilaf, 257
Sautéed Mushrooms, 385

ABOUT POT ROAST

Slowly cooked and richly flavored, pot roasts are the ultimate in home-cooked food. While many a good cook has a version of this dish, the method stays more or less the same—first brown a 3- to 5-pound cut of beef, then brown an aromatic mix of vegetables, add stock, wine, beer or water, cover, and braise until the roast is fork-tender. The key to a moist and tender pot roast is to cook the meat at a gentle simmer. Please see About Braising, Stewing, and Pot-Roasting Meat, 640, for a more detailed explanation of technique.

The best cuts for pot roast are from the chuck and rump, and the chuck is the more desirable of the two. In order of preference, look for chuck top blade roast, also called top chuck roast, chuck shoulder pot roast, or chuck mock tender roast. All of these are well marbled enough to cook into a tender, juicy, richly flavored pot roast. Most cuts from the round are too lean and may turn out dry when braised. The exception is bottom round rump roast, which makes first-rate pot roast. Boneless cuts are easier to handle and serve than bone-in pot roasts, but make sure the boneless roast is tied into a neat, compact shape before cooking, for any loose or excessively thin parts will overcook before the whole roast is tender.

Pot roasts generally come in two shapes: high and round like a loaf or wide and flat. The wide, flat roasts cook a bit faster and should be turned about every 20 minutes so that the bottom does not cook faster than the top. Flat-shaped roasts take 1½ to 2½ hours to cook. Loaf-shaped roasts can be turned less often, every 35 minutes or so, and generally take closer to 3 to 4 hours to cook. A good test for doneness is to cut two thin slices from one end of the roast and taste the inside slice. A pot roast is done when it is firm-tender and still somewhat moist. If the pot roast has been cooked gently enough, there may even still be a faint tinge of pink in the center. If the meat is still tough and hard, let it cook a little longer. Avoid the common mistake of overcooking a pot roast until it becomes coarse, dry, and stringy.

BEEF POT ROAST (BASIC RECIPE)

6 to 10 servings

As with other moist, slowly cooked meats, leftover pot roast tastes superb. The best method for rewarming is to heat slices of meat gently in the sauce with additional stock, wine, or water on the stove or in a microwave.

Pat dry:

1 beef chuck or rump roast (3 to 5 pounds), neatly tied if boneless

Season with:

Salt and ground black pepper to taste

Heat in a heavy Dutch oven with a tight-fitting lid over medium-high heat:

2 to 3 tablespoons vegetable oil, rendered beef fat, or lard

Add the roast and brown on all sides, about 15 to 20 minutes. Maintain the heat so that the meat sizzles but does not burn. Remove the meat to a plate. Pour off all but 2 tablespoons of fat from the pan and heat over medium-high heat. Add:

2 cups finely chopped onions
½ cup finely chopped celery
½ cup finely chopped carrots

Cook the vegetables, stirring occasionally, just until they begin to color, about 5 minutes. Add:

1 cup beef or chicken stock, dry red wine, or water

Bring to a boil and add:

1 bay leaf
1½ teaspoons fresh thyme, or ½ teaspoon dried

Return the roast to the pan and cover. Reduce the heat to its lowest setting. Cook the roast slowly so that the liquid just barely simmers. Turn the roast every 30 minutes or so. Flat roasts will take 1½ to 2½ hours to cook; round or oblong roasts may take as long as 4 hours. Make sure there is always some liquid in the pot and add more as needed. When the meat is tender, remove the roast to a platter and cover with aluminum foil to keep warm. Skim off any fat from the surface of the liquid. Strain the liquid. To thicken the sauce slightly, bring the liquid to a boil. For each cup liquid, stir together and whisk in:

1 tablespoon all-purpose flour
1 tablespoon butter, softened

Simmer, stirring constantly, until thickened. Serve with:

Potato Pancakes, 410, Egg Noodles, 318, or boiled new potatoes

ITALIAN POT ROAST (STRACOTTO)

6 to 8 servings

A classic of home cooking, *stracotto* changes from one part of Italy and one family to another. The braising juices can be used to sauce pasta, and leftover *stracotto* makes excellent hot sandwiches on chewy rolls, moistened with pan sauce.

Mince together:

3 large cloves garlic
¼ cup tightly packed fresh parsley leaves
4 fresh sage leaves, or 1 teaspoon dried
1 tablespoon fresh rosemary, or 1 teaspoon dried

Set aside half the mixture and mix the rest with:

1 tablespoon olive oil
¼ teaspoon ground black pepper

Make about 10 deep slits in:

1 beef rump roast (3½ to 4 pounds)

Stuff the slits with the oil and herb mixture. Heat in a 6-quart heavy pot over medium-high heat:

3 tablespoons olive oil

Add the roast and brown on all sides until dark and crusty, about 20 minutes. Maintain the heat so that the meat sizzles but does not burn. Remove the roast from the pot and pour off all but 2 tablespoons of fat. Sprinkle the roast with:

1 teaspoon salt

Return the pot to the heat and add:

1 onion, chopped
1 carrot, chopped
1 celery stalk with leaves, chopped
4 ounces mushrooms, wiped clean and thinly sliced
1 bay leaf, broken

Cook, stirring, until the onion is lightly browned. Stir in the remaining herb mixture and cook for 30 seconds. Add and boil until almost dry:

½ cup dry red wine
2 tablespoons tomato paste

Stir in and boil until reduced to less than ½ cup:

1 cup dry red wine
1 cup beef or chicken stock

Add the roast along with:

One 28-ounce can whole tomatoes, drained and crushed
1 cup dry red wine
1 cup beef or chicken stock

Bring to a gentle simmer and cover the pot. Reduce the heat to its lowest setting. Cook the roast slowly, so that the liquid just barely simmers, for about 2½ hours. Turn the roast every 30 minutes or so. When the meat is tender, remove it to a platter and cover it with aluminum foil to keep warm. Skim off any fat from the surface of the liquid. Taste and adjust the seasonings. If the sauce seems weak, boil it down for a few minutes. Slice the meat about ¼ inch thick and moisten it with the braising liquid. Serve with:

Soft Polenta with Butter and Cheese, 249, or boiled potatoes

SAUERBRATEN

6 to 10 servings

This German/American classic gets its distinctive flavor from a 2- to 4-day marinade in spiced vinegar. We still recommend using the tenderer pot roast cuts such as boneless chuck top blade roast, rump roast, or chuck shoulder pot roast.

Combine in a saucepan and bring to a boil:

1 cup red wine vinegar
1 cup dry red wine
1 medium onion, sliced
2 bay leaves
1 teaspoon black peppercorns
1 teaspoon caraway seeds
6 juniper berries, crushed, or 1 ounce gin

Let cool, then pour into a large, heavy plastic bag or a large bowl. Add and turn to coat:

1 boneless beef pot roast (4 to 5 pounds), rolled and tied

Close the bag or cover the bowl. Refrigerate for 2 to 4 days, turning the roast every so often. The longer you marinate the roast, the more intense the flavors will be. When you are ready to cook, remove the meat and pat dry. Strain the marinade and discard the solids. Season the meat with:

Salt and ground black pepper to taste

Heat in a large Dutch oven over medium-high heat:

2 tablespoons vegetable oil

Add the roast and brown on all sides, about 20 minutes. Maintain the heat so that the meat sizzles but does not burn. Remove the meat and pour off all but 2 tablespoons of fat from the pan. Add:

½ cup finely chopped onions
½ cup finely chopped carrots
¼ cup finely chopped celery
Generous pinch of ground ginger

Cook, stirring, over medium heat until the vegetables begin to soften, about 10 minutes. Sprinkle with:

2 tablespoons all-purpose flour

Stir until smooth and cook until the flour begins to color, about 3 minutes. Pour in the reserved marinade along with:

½ cup beef stock
1 bay leaf

Bring to a boil, stirring constantly and scraping up any browned bits from the bottom of the pan. Return the roast to the pan. Cover and cook gently for 1½ to 2 hours, as directed for Beef Pot Roast (Basic Recipe), above. When the meat is tender, remove it from the pan and keep it warm. Skim off the fat from the surface of the liquid and reduce the liquid over high heat to 2 to 3 cups. Stir in:

½ cup crushed gingersnap cookies

Cook, stirring, until the sauce begins to thicken. If you want a smooth sauce, strain it. If you wish, enrich the sauce by stirring in, off the heat:

¾ cup sour cream
1 tablespoon red currant jelly or brown sugar

Slice the meat and serve it on a platter. Pour some of the sauce over the top and pass the rest. Serve with:

Potato Dumplings, 322, Dumplings, 321, or Potato Pancakes, 410
Braised Red Cabbage with Apples, 356

ABOUT BEEF STEW AND OTHER BRAISED BEEF DISHES

The key to a good beef stew is balance. Well-browned beef and slow-simmered stock or wine provide the undertones of meaty flavor, while ingredients such as pungent herbs, fresh vegetables, and zesty seasonings create sharper flavors to brighten the entire dish. As with so many full-flavored, slow-cooked dishes, beef stews are just as good (some say better!) made 1 or 2 days in advance. As the stew sits undisturbed in the refrigerator, layers of flavors begin to meld, creating the flavor that makes leftovers so pleasing. In addition, any excess fat in the stew will rise to the surface when it cools and can be easily skimmed off. Reheat stews gently, adding a bit more liquid (wine, stock, beer, juice, or water) if necessary. Serve stew in wide bowls with pasta, rice, potatoes, fresh bread, dumplings, or biscuits.

The best beef stew is made with the more flavorful, less tender cuts, including chuck, rump, short rib, cross-rib, brisket, blade, and shoulder. Round and rump roasts also hold up over long, slow cooking, although the leaner meat tends to be a bit less moist. Shank, or shin, meat can also be used, but it adds much more texture than it does flavor. We recommend buying steaks or roasts and trimming and cutting them yourself into ½- to 3-inch cubes; the prepackaged, precut meat labeled "Beef Stew Meat" is often overpriced, and you never know what you are getting. Size is a matter of preference. The smaller the cube, the faster the stew will cook. Small cubes will also give the stew a thicker, more homogenous character, while large chunks maintain their shape. The longer cooking time required to cook larger pieces means more opportunity to develop the marvelous slow-cooked flavors of a stew. Large or small, any piece of meat will shrink somewhat during cooking and should be considered done when tender enough to cut with a spoon.

Other favorite slow-cooked beef dishes are made by braising whole pieces of short ribs, brisket, and oxtail. These sometimes neglected cuts of meat impart a wonderful beef flavor and become fall-apart tender when stewed, creating incomparable and inexpensive beef dishes.

BEEF STEW (BASIC RECIPE) *6 to 8 servings*

By altering the vegetables or the proportions, the recipe variations are limitless. For a fresher flavor, add more vegetables or herbs toward the end of cooking. For a deeper flavor, use a few spoonfuls of Meat Glaze, 38, to enrich the sauce.

Pat dry:

2 pounds boneless stewing beef, such as chuck, short-rib meat, or bottom round, cut into 2-inch cubes

Season the meat with:

½ to 1 teaspoon dried herbs (thyme, marjoram, savory, oregano, and/or basil)
½ teaspoon salt
½ teaspoon ground black pepper

Dredge the meat with:

½ cup all-purpose flour

Shake off any excess flour. Heat in a Dutch oven over medium-high heat:

2 tablespoons olive or vegetable oil, bacon fat, beef drippings, or other fat

Add the meat in batches and brown on all sides, being careful not to crowd the pan or scorch the meat. Remove with a slotted spoon. Pour off all but 2 tablespoons of fat from the pan (add more if needed). Add:

½ cup chopped onions
¼ cup chopped carrots
¼ cup chopped celery
¼ cup chopped leeks (optional)
2 tablespoons chopped garlic (optional)

Cover and cook, stirring often, over medium heat until the onions are softened, about 5 minutes. Add:

2 bay leaves
½ to 1 teaspoon of the same herbs used to season the meat
½ teaspoon salt
½ teaspoon ground black pepper

Add enough to cover the meat at least halfway:

2 to 3 cups beef or chicken stock, dry red or white wine, or beer

Bring to a boil. Reduce the heat, cover, and simmer over low heat until the meat is fork-tender, 1½ to 2 hours. Add:

2 to 3 carrots, peeled and cut into 1-inch chunks
3 or 4 boiling potatoes, peeled and cut into 1-inch chunks
2 turnips, peeled and cut into 1-inch chunks
2 parsnips, peeled and cut into 1-inch chunks

Cover and cook until the vegetables are tender, 35 to 40 minutes. Remove the pan from the heat and skim off any fat from the surface. Taste and adjust the seasonings. If you wish, thicken the sauce by stirring together and whisking into the stew:

1 to 1½ tablespoons Kneaded Butter, 44

Simmer, stirring, until thickened. Garnish with:

Chopped fresh parsley

HUNGARIAN GOULASH (PÎRKÎLT)

8 to 10 servings

Try to find fresh Hungarian paprika, combining hot and sweet to suit your taste.

Brown in a large Dutch oven over medium-high heat:

4 ounces lean bacon, smoked ham, or Hungarian paprika sausage, diced

Remove to a small bowl. Pat dry and cut into 1-inch cubes:

3 pounds boneless beef chuck, or 1½ pounds boneless beef chuck and 1½ pounds pork or veal shoulder

Season the meat with:

Salt and ground black pepper to taste

Lightly dredge the meat in:

½ cup all-purpose flour

Shake off any excess flour. Heat the fat in the pan over medium-high heat. If there is not enough fat, add:

Vegetable oil or bacon drippings

Add the meat in batches and brown on all sides, being careful not to crowd the pan or scorch the meat. Remove the meat with a slotted spoon. Add to the remaining fat in the pan:

3 cups thinly sliced onions

Cook over medium heat until the onions are lightly colored and quite soft. Add:

6 cloves garlic, chopped

Cook for 1 minute more. Add:

½ cup (2 ounces) sweet Hungarian paprika or a combination of sweet and hot paprikas

Stir well, coating the onions and garlic thoroughly. Cook for 2 minutes more. Add:

3 red bell peppers, diced
1 cup diced carrots
1 tablespoon dried marjoram
1 teaspoon caraway seeds
1 teaspoon ground black pepper
3 bay leaves

Toss briefly with the onions and garlic. Add:

2 cups beef or chicken stock
1 cup dry white wine or beer
1 pound sauerkraut, drained (optional)
¼ cup tomato puree or 2 tablespoons tomato paste

Bring to a boil, scraping up any browned bits, and add the browned meat and bacon. Reduce the heat to low and simmer, covered, stirring occasionally, until the meat is tender, 1½ to 1¾ hours. If the sauce needs thickening, remove the meat and vegetables with a slotted spoon and keep warm. Skim off the fat from the surface of the liquid. Boil the sauce just until it begins to thicken. Remove from the heat and stir in:

½ to 1 cup sour cream or crème fraîche (optional)
Salt and ground black pepper to taste

Stir the meat and vegetables back into the sauce. Serve with:

Spätzle, 322, Egg Noodles, 318, or boiled potatoes with melted butter

BOEUF BOURGUIGNONNE

6 to 8 servings

Based on local ingredients and local wine, this robust stew typifies the earthy, full-flavored cooking of the gastronomic capital of France—Burgundy. Originally made with the rather lean and coarse beef from the region's Charolais cattle, this dish can be made with any good stew cut. Choose a light, dry red wine such as

Pinot Noir (the grape of Burgundy) or Beaujolais and marinate the beef overnight for the most flavor—it will emerge purplish and wine soaked. The great Burgundian chef, Paul Bocuse, adds pork rind and a calf's foot to his stew to give the sauce an exquisite deep gloss and texture.

Cut into 2-inch chunks:

2 pounds boneless beef chuck, short-rib meat, or bottom round

Place the meat in a large bowl and add:

2 cups dry red wine
¼ cup olive oil
1 onion, chopped
1 carrot, peeled and chopped
1 clove garlic, chopped
1 bay leaf
2 tablespoons chopped fresh parsley
1 teaspoon fresh thyme, or scant ½ teaspoon dried
1 teaspoon cracked black peppercorns
½ teaspoon salt

Stir to combine and coat the meat. Cover and marinate in the refrigerator for 1 hour or up to 24 hours, turning the meat occasionally. Drain the beef and pat dry. Strain the marinade and reserve it and the vegetables separately. Heat a large Dutch oven over medium-high heat. Add and brown:

4 ounces bacon, diced

Remove the bacon, leaving the fat in the pan. You should have 2 tablespoons. If not, add vegetable oil. Return the pan to medium-high heat. Add the beef in batches and brown on all sides, being careful not to overcrowd the pan. Remove with a slotted spoon. Add the reserved vegetables and cook until lightly browned, about 5 minutes. Stir in:

2 tablespoons all-purpose flour

Cook, stirring, until beginning to brown, about 1 minute. Stir in the marinade, then return the beef and bacon to the pan. Bring to a boil. Reduce the heat to low and cook, covered, until the meat is fork-tender, 1½ to 2 hours. Add:

8 ounces mushrooms, wiped clean and quartered
8 ounces small boiling onions (about 2 cups), peeled

Cover and cook until the vegetables are tender, about 20 minutes. Skim off the fat from the surface. Add:

¼ cup chopped fresh parsley
Salt and ground black pepper to taste

If you wish, thicken the sauce by whisking in:

1 to 1½ tablespoons Kneaded Butter, 44

Simmer, stirring, until thickened. Serve with:

Boiled new potatoes

BEEF DAUBE WITH MUSTARD, HERBS, AND WHITE WINE
4 to 6 servings

The word *daube* comes from daubière, the French word used for a covered casserole. Prevalent in farmhouse kitchens throughout France, daubes are said to have originated in the vibrant region of Provence. The following recipe is a refreshing change from the heartier and heavier flavors that we often associate with beef stew.

Pat dry and cut into 3-inch cubes:

2 pounds boneless beef stew meat, such as shoulder, chuck, blade, rump, or brisket

Season with:

Salt and ground black pepper to taste

Heat in a Dutch oven over medium-high heat:

3 tablespoons olive oil

Add the meat in batches and brown on all sides, being careful not to crowd the pan or scorch the meat. Remove with a slotted spoon and set aside. Pour off all but a light film of fat from the pan. Add:

One 750-ml bottle dry white wine, such as Chardonnay

Bring to a boil, scraping up any browned bits on the bottom of the pan. Reduce the heat and gently simmer, uncovered, until the wine is reduced by about half, 7 to 10 minutes. Add and whisk to blend:

2 tablespoons Dijon mustard

Return the beef and any accumulated juices to the casserole. Add:

One 16-ounce can plum tomatoes, with juice
3 medium onions, halved and sliced
3 cloves garlic, halved
Bouquet garni: 4 sprigs each fresh parsley, thyme, and tarragon, and 1 bay leaf, tied in a bundle

Cover and simmer over low heat until the meat is fork-tender, 2 to 3 hours. Remove and discard the bouquet garni. With a slotted spoon, remove the beef, onions, and tomatoes to a platter. Increase the heat to high and boil the sauce until slightly thickened and reduced by one-third, about 10 minutes. Reduce the heat to medium, return the solids to the sauce, and reheat gently. Serve the daube in warmed shallow soup bowls.

BEEF CHILI (CHILI CON CARNE)
6 to 8 servings

For more flavor in this dish, make your own chili powder. As a rule of thumb, use smaller amounts of hotter peppers, such as arbol or serrano, and larger amounts of the mild and midrange varieties, such as ancho, mild New Mexico (red Anaheim), and guajillo.

Toast in a skillet over medium heat for 1 to 2 minutes:

1 recipe New Mexican Chili Powder, 1060, or 1 cup store-bought chili powder

Set aside. Pat dry:

3 pounds beef chuck, trimmed and cut into ½-inch cubes

Season with:

1 to 2 teaspoons salt

Heat in a cast-iron skillet over medium-high heat:

1 tablespoon olive oil

Brown the meat in batches, adding more oil if needed. Remove the browned meat to a Dutch oven. Add to the cast-iron skillet:

1 tablespoon olive oil
2 large onions, minced
10 cloves garlic, minced
7 fresh jalapeño peppers, stemmed, seeded, and minced
½ teaspoon salt

Cook, stirring often, over medium-high heat until the vegetables are softened, 6 to 8 minutes. Remove to the Dutch oven with the meat. Stir the toasted spices into the meat mixture and cook for 2 minutes over medium-high heat. Add:

One 28-ounce can plum tomatoes, with juice
1 tablespoon red wine vinegar
6 cups water

Season with:

Salt to taste

Simmer, uncovered, until the meat is tender and the sauce is reduced and thickened, about 1½ hours. Serve with:

Hot cooked rice
Sour cream

CHILI WITH MEAT AND BEANS *8 to 10 servings*

Prepare Beef Chili, above, stir in 6 cups cooked black or pinto beans (1 pound dried beans, cooked), and heat through.

MACLEID'S ROCKCASTLE CHILI *8 to 10 servings*

This is camp chef extraordinaire and good friend Matt MacLeid's Saturday-night staple on Ethan Becker's camping trips to the Rockcastle River Gorge.

Sauté in a large skillet until cracklings are golden brown:

½ pound bacon, diced

Remove the bacon using a slotted spoon. In the drippings, sauté briefly:

1½ pounds round steak, coarsely ground or chopped in a food processor
6 to 12 large cloves garlic, coarsely chopped
2 large onions, coarsely chopped

Deglaze the skillet, 51 to 52, until foam disappears, with:

One 12-ounce bottle dark beer

Remove all to a large pot or Dutch oven. Stir in:

One 32-ounce can tomatoes, with juice
One 16-ounce can kidney beans, with juice
One 16-ounce can great northern beans, with juice
One 16-ounce can pinto beans, with juice
6 tablespoons ancho chili powder
2 tablespoons ground cumin
1 tablespoon ground black pepper
1½ cups water or another 12-ounce bottle dark beer

Simmer for about 3 hours, covered, stirring occasionally to prevent sticking. Season to taste with:

Salt and ground black pepper
Red pepper sauce

Serve with:

Southern Corn Bread, 777
Diced sharp Cheddar cheese

CINCINNATI CHILI COCKAIGNE *6 servings*

There are hundreds of so-called original recipes for John Kiradjieff's Cincinnati Chili that he served for the first time in Cincinnati's first chili parlor, The Empress. We particularly like this version of our hometown obsession, and we can guarantee without question that it is *not* one of myth.

In a 4- to 6-quart pot, bring to a boil:

1 quart water

Add:

2 pounds ground chuck

Stir until separated and reduce heat to a simmer. Add:

2 medium onions, finely chopped
5 to 6 cloves garlic, crushed
One 15-ounce can tomato sauce
2 tablespoons cider vinegar
1 tablespoon Worcestershire sauce

Stir and add:

10 peppercorns, ground
8 whole allspice, ground
8 whole cloves, ground
1 large bay leaf
2 teaspoons salt
2 teaspoons ground cinnamon
1½ teaspoons ground cayenne pepper
1 teaspoon ground cumin
½ ounce unsweetened chocolate, grated

Bring back to a boil, then reduce to a simmer, for 2½ hours cooking time in all. Cool uncovered and refrigerate overnight. Before serving, skim all or most of the fat and discard. Reheat the chili and serve over:

Cooked spaghetti

For a 2-Way. Add:

Cheddar cheese, grated (optional)

For a 3-Way. Sprinkle on:

Chopped onion (optional)

For a 4-Way. Top each serving with:

¼ cup cooked red kidney beans, 274 (optional)

For a 5-Way. Traditional sides also include:

Oyster crackers (optional)

Red pepper sauce (optional)

OHIO FARMHOUSE SAUSAGE CHILI

4 to 6 servings

A delicious "warmer-upper" after a fine tramp in the woods on a chilly day.

Brown in a large skillet:

1 pound pork sausage

1 large onion, chopped

Toward the end of the browning, add:

1 celery stalk, diced

When the celery is softened, add:

One 28-ounce can (3½ cups) whole tomatoes, chopped

2 cups tomato juice or chicken broth or a mixture of the two

1 to 2 tablespoons maple syrup or molasses

2 teaspoons ground cumin

1½ teaspoons powdered sage

½ teaspoon ground black pepper

Simmer for 20 minutes. Add:

3½ to 4 cups cooked red kidney beans, 274, drained and rinsed

Simmer for 15 minutes more. Serve with:

Sharp Cheddar cheese, cubed

Northern Corn Bread, 777, or Buttermilk Biscuits, 790

OXTAILS SMOTHERED IN ONIONS

6 servings

For the cook, the tough, coarse-grained oxtail meat demands special treatment—it takes the gentle, slow heat of a braise to soften the high percentage of connective tissue, or collagen, present. For the diner, this means a fall-apart tender dish with rich beef flavor and a lush, velvety sauce. Oxtails are usually sold in 1- to 3-inch cross sections and, because of the amount of bone, you should buy at least 1 pound per person. Pieces from the very narrow tip of the tail yield almost no meat at all and are best saved for the stockpot.

Preheat the oven to 325°F.

Pat dry:

6 pounds meaty oxtails, cut into 2-inch pieces

Season with:

Salt and ground black pepper to taste

Coat with:

¼ cup all-purpose flour

Shake off the excess. Heat in a large Dutch oven over medium-high heat:

¼ cup olive oil

Add the oxtails in batches and brown evenly on all sides, about 8 minutes. Remove with a slotted spoon. Pour off all but 2 tablespoons of fat from the pan. Return the pan to medium heat. Add and cook, stirring, until lightly browned, 3 to 4 minutes:

4 large onions, thinly sliced

Add:

3 cups dry red wine

Bring to a boil, scraping up any browned bits on the bottom of the pan. Add:

6 cloves garlic, peeled

Bouquet garni: 1 bay leaf and 1 sprig each fresh parsley and thyme, tied in a bundle

Arrange the oxtails on top and pour in any meat juices. Cover, and place in the oven. Cook until the meat pulls easily away from the bone, 3 to 4 hours. Remove the oxtails to a warmed platter, top with the onions and garlic, and cover loosely. Discard the bouquet garni and, if necessary, skim the fat from the surface of the cooking liquid. Return the pan to medium-high heat and simmer until the liquid is reduced by two-thirds, 5 to 7 minutes. Taste and adjust the seasonings and spoon the sauce over the oxtails. Serve with:

Mashed Potatoes, 408

SWISS STEAK

4 to 6 servings

These braised steaks, referred to in England as smothered steak, are best made with beef bottom round or round steak. Do not buy pretenderized meat—it turns to mush. In fact, we do not recommend pounding the meat, as many traditional recipes suggest. Long, slow cooking will tenderize the most ornery slab of meat; pounding simply destroys the texture. Swiss steak is entirely unlike Salisbury steak, which is a broiled hamburger patty.

Preheat the oven to 325°F.

Pat dry:

2 pounds beef bottom round or round steak, ¾ inch to 1¼ inches thick, excess fat trimmed

Sprinkle with:

1 teaspoon minced garlic
½ teaspoon salt
½ teaspoon ground black pepper

Cut the meat into serving pieces or leave the steak whole. Dredge in:

½ cup all-purpose flour

Shake off the excess. Heat in a large, deep ovenproof skillet or Dutch oven over high heat:

2 tablespoons vegetable oil or bacon drippings

Add the steak and sear until nicely browned on both sides, 6 to 8 minutes. Remove the meat from the pan and keep warm. Add:

1 cup diced onions
1 cup chopped carrots
½ cup diced celery

Reduce the heat and cover the pan. Cook, stirring occasionally, until the vegetables are softened but not browned, 5 to 10 minutes. Add:

1 cup beef or chicken stock
½ cup dry wine or beer (optional)
2 tablespoons tomato paste
1½ teaspoons chopped fresh thyme, basil, or oregano, or ½ teaspoon dried
2 bay leaves

Return the meat to the pan. Cover and bake until the meat is tender, about 1½ hours for individual steaks, or 2 to 2½ hours for one large steak. Remove the meat to a warmed platter. Skim off the fat from the surface of the sauce. Season with:

Salt and ground black pepper to taste

Pour the sauce over the steak. Serve with:

Mashed Potatoes, 408
Glazed Parsnips, 394

STEAK AND MUSHROOM PIE

4 to 6 servings

This version of the English pub classic, steak and kidney pie, is made with mushrooms, whose rich and earthy flavor complements the beef. We recommend a top crust only, baked on or added at the last minute.

Preheat the oven to 350°F.

Pat dry and cut into 2-inch pieces:

2 pounds beef round, rump, or chuck steak

Season with:

1 teaspoon salt
1 teaspoon ground black pepper

Dredge in:

½ cup all-purpose flour

Shake off the excess. Heat in a large skillet over high heat:

3 tablespoons butter, rendered beef fat, or vegetable oil

Add the meat in 2 batches and brown well on all sides, being careful not to crowd the pan, about 3 to 4 minutes. Remove the meat with a slotted spoon. Reduce the heat to medium. If the pan is dry, add:

2 tablespoons butter

Add and cook, stirring, until browned, about 2 minutes:

1 pound portobello, cremini, or white mushrooms, wiped clean and thickly sliced

Remove and set aside. Return the pan to medium heat. Add and cook until softened, about 3 minutes:

3 tablespoons butter
2 cups finely chopped onions
Pinch of salt
Pinch of ground black pepper
Pinch of dried thyme

Add and cook, stirring, until evenly incorporated:

3 tablespoons all-purpose flour

Add to the pan:

2 cups dry red wine or ale
1 cup beef stock

Bring to a boil, reduce the heat, and simmer until slightly thickened. Butter an 8- to 10-inch ovenproof casserole with a 2- to 3-quart capacity. Spoon the meat into the bottom and cover with the mushrooms. Pour the thickened stock and onion mixture over all. Bake, covered, for 1 to 1½ hours. Taste and adjust the seasonings. If desired, add:

¼ cup chopped fresh parsley
2 tablespoons snipped fresh chives

Cool completely. At this point, the filling can be refrigerated for up to 2 days.

To finish the pie, preheat the oven to 425°F.

Roll out and cover the filling in the casserole with:

½ recipe Deluxe Butter Flaky Pastry Dough, 862, ½ recipe Food Processor Puff Pastry, 908, or the dough for Quick Drop Biscuits, 790

Whisk together and brush lightly over the top of the dough:

1 large egg
2 tablespoons milk

Bake until the pastry is golden and fully cooked, 25 to 30 minutes. Serve at once.

BRAISED SHORT RIBS (BASIC RECIPE)

4 servings

Beef short ribs are simply the meaty tail ends of the beef ribs from the rib, chuck, and brisket portion. Short ribs are sold in slabs of varying lengths and widths, depending on the butcher. Unlike back ribs, which are more bone than meat, short ribs offer a good amount of beefy-tasting meat that is also high in connective tissue. They also tend to be quite fatty, so besides trimming any external fat before cooking, it is best to brown the ribs before cooking to render excess fat and intensify the meat flavors. By substituting different dry rubs or herb pastes, 86 to 88, for the herbs and salt and pepper in this basic recipe, you can produce a host of variations. You can also change the vegetables and the braising liquid.

Preheat the oven to 350°F.

Pat dry:

3 pounds beef short ribs, from the chuck or rib section, excess fat trimmed

Season with:

1 teaspoon salt
1 teaspoon ground black pepper
½ teaspoon dried herb (marjoram, oregano, rosemary, savory, thyme, or sage)

Heat in a Dutch oven or large, heavy skillet with a lid over medium-high heat:

2 tablespoons vegetable oil, rendered beef fat, or bacon fat

Add the ribs in batches and brown well on all sides, being careful not to crowd the pan. Remove the ribs with a slotted spoon. Pour off all but about 2 tablespoons of fat from the pan. Add and cook, stirring, over medium heat just until they begin to color, about 10 minutes:

2 cups chopped onions
½ cup chopped celery
½ cup chopped carrots
¼ cup chopped shallots (optional)
3 tablespoons chopped garlic
1½ teaspoons ground black pepper
½ teaspoon salt
Pinch of same herb used to season the meat

Add:

1½ cups beef or chicken stock

Bring to a boil and return the short ribs to the pot. Add:

2 or 3 bay leaves

Bake, covered, until the ribs are tender and the meat pulls away easily from the bone, 1½ to 2 hours. Remove the ribs and cover to keep warm. Skim off any fat from the surface of the liquid and reduce the liquid over high heat until the sauce is syrupy. Serve the ribs with the sauce and:

Mashed Potatoes, 408, or hot cooked rice

OVEN-BROWNED OR GRILLED SHORTRIBS

4 servings

Once the short ribs are braised to perfect tenderness as in the basic recipe, above, they can be briefly roasted or grilled to render them crisp and savory. This blast of high heat just before serving produces an irresistibly crusty exterior while leaving the inside tender and moist. Serve these ribs with plenty of napkins.

Prepare:

Braised Short Ribs (Basic Recipe), above

Preheat or increase the oven temperature to 450°F. Place the cooked ribs on a roasting rack in a pan. Sprinkle with:

Salt and ground black pepper to taste

Or brush the ribs with:

Dijon mustard or barbecue sauce

Bake until the surface is browned and the edges are crispy, 10 to 12 minutes. Meanwhile, reduce the braising liquid as directed in the recipe. Pour the sauce over the top. Serve at once with:

Mashed Potatoes, 408, or Soft Polenta with Butter and Cheese, 249

SWEET & SOUR BRISKET

6 to 8 servings

You can serve this immediately, but it is much better if prepared a day ahead and chilled, as in this recipe.

Preheat the oven to 350°F.

Have ready:

3½ pounds trimmed first-cut or thin-cut brisket

Spread with:

3 cloves garlic, minced
Ground black pepper to taste

Heat in a flame-proof roasting pan over medium-high heat:

1 tablespoon vegetable oil

Brown the brisket about 3 minutes each side. While it is searing, add to the pan:

2 large onions, sliced

When browned on both sides, remove the brisket. Reduce the heat to medium and cook the onions until very brown, about 4 minutes more. Add:

½ cup red wine
½ cup beef stock

Cook for 1 minute, scraping up the browned bits. Stir in:

1 cup chili sauce
½ cup apple cider vinegar
½ cup packed dark brown sugar
1 bay leaf

Taste the sauce and adjust the seasoning. Return the meat to the pan and spoon the sauce over it. Cover the pan tightly with aluminum foil. Roast until the brisket is fork-tender, 2 to 3 hours. Remove the pan from the oven, uncover, and let cool in the pan. Refrigerate overnight. Slice the meat and return it to the sauce. Reheat in a 350°F oven for 25 to 30 minutes. Serve with:

Tzimmis, below
Potato Pancakes, 410, and applesauce

DRIED FRUIT VARIATION

Omit chili sauce and add ½ pound whole dried apricots and ½ pound whole pitted dried prunes about 30 minutes before the end of roasting.

TZIMMIS WITH POTATO KNAIDLE

6 main-course servings

The Yiddish word *tzimmis* has come to mean "fuss," as in "Don't make such a tzimmis." Tzimmis is basically any form of meat, potato, and vegetable casserole, sometimes including fruit. A really excellent, old-fashioned tzimmis requires patience, as it has to be cooked very slowly for a long time, basting from time to time so that all the flavors meld together. This recipe is for tzimmis with potato knaidle, potato pancakes in the form of a dumpling.

Heat in a large Dutch oven over medium heat:

2 tablespoons chicken fat or canola oil

Brown both sides, about 5 minutes each side, of:

One 2- to 3-pound brisket

Add:

2 onions, peeled and chopped

3 cloves garlic, chopped

Cook until lightly browned, 10 to 15 minutes. Deglaze pan with enough water to cover the meat. Add:

2 teaspoons salt

½ teaspoon ground black pepper

¼ teaspoon freshly grated or ground nutmeg

Bring liquid to a boil, then reduce the heat, cover, and simmer for 1½ to 2 hours, until the meat is tender. At this point, the meat can be sliced and returned to the pot or left whole.

Preheat the oven to 350°F.

Add to the pot:

2 pounds carrots, peeled and cut into ¼-inch rounds or julienned

3 large sweet potatoes, peeled and cut into ½-inch wedges

⅓ cup brown sugar

Juice of 1 lemon

Cover and bake in the oven for 1½ to 2 hours, basting from time to time, until the vegetables are tender. Taste for seasoning. If the liquid in the pot is very watery, or there is a lot of it, you can thicken the liquid. Heat in an ungreased skillet until lightly browned and nutty-smelling, being very careful not to burn, 3 to 5 minutes:

2 to 3 tablespoons all-purpose flour

Add 1 cup of the cooking liquid, mix until smooth, and return the mixture to the pot.

For the potato knaidle, combine:

3 large potatoes, grated, liquid squeezed out

1 small onion, grated

1 tablespoon matzo meal or flour

1 tablespoon chicken fat or oil

Mix well. Drop heaping tablespoonfuls of the knaidle on the vegetables and in the pockets of stew (not covering the stew). Bake, uncovered, for 30 to 60 minutes until the knaidle are cooked through. Serve immediately.

POTATO AND DRIED FRUIT TZIMMIS:

Prepare Tzimmis, above, omitting the carrots and sweet potatoes and substituting 2 large potatoes, peeled and cut into ½-inch wedges, and ½ pound large pitted prunes or dried apricots, or a combination of the two.

CORNED BEEF OR CORNED BEEF AND CABBAGE

8 to 10 servings

Before refrigeration, Americans depended on cured and salted meats through the winter months. The name is a reference to the corn-sized crystals of salt used to brine large cuts of beef brisket and sometimes beef round. In addition to the salt, spices such as garlic, allspice, black pepper, and bay leaves were added. The corned beef sold in our markets is still a salt-and-spice brine-cured cut of beef brisket or round. In New England, where corned beef remains popular, it is still possible to find a "gray-cured" brisket, referring to the color of corned beef made without chemicals to preserve its rosy color. In most supermarkets, corned beef is sold in vacuum-sealed bags that contain some of the brine and seasonings used during curing. It needs to be cooked before serving. Corned beef makes some of the greatest sandwiches ever and, of course, there is also Corned Beef Hash, 677.

Wash under running water to remove the surface brine:

1 corned beef brisket (about 4 pounds)

Place the brisket in a large pot and add water to cover. Drop in:

20 black peppercorns

2 bay leaves

Simmer, covered, until a fork can easily penetrate to the center, about 3 hours. If desired, add to the pot for the last 15 to 20 minutes of cooking:

1 head green cabbage, cut into wedges

Remove the meat and let stand for 15 minutes. Drain the cabbage and keep warm. Cut the brisket into thin slices against the grain and remove to a platter. Pass:

American Horseradish Cream, 79, or prepared horseradish
Whole-grain mustard and/or hot English-style mustard

Serve with:

Boiled potatoes

Serve leftover corned beef cold in sandwiches with the above condiments or, better still, heat thin slices in a steamer or microwave. Serve as a hot corned beef sandwich or in a Reuben Sandwich, 190.

CANDIED CORNED BEEF

8 to 10 servings

After cooking a corned beef, bake it with the following glaze for a dramatic-looking dish.

Prepare:

Corned Beef, above, without the cabbage

Place it on a baking sheet lined with aluminum foil. Preheat the oven to 350°F.

Mix well:

3 tablespoons packed brown sugar
1½ tablespoons soy sauce
1½ teaspoons dry mustard
1 teaspoon ground ginger

Spread over the cooked brisket. Bake until the topping has set and turned golden brown, about 15 minutes. Let stand for 15 minutes before thinly slicing the meat across the grain. Pass the same condiments as for corned beef. Serve with:

German Potato Salad, 221, and/or Cole Slaw, 222
Buttered Egg Noodles, 318

NEW ENGLAND BOILED DINNER

10 to 12 servings

A cold-weather tradition in New England, this humble and hearty dish has gained popularity across the country. Fresh brisket can be used in place of corned beef, but you will miss the tangy nuances of the cured beef. This is a delectable dinner if composed only of beef, onions, and cabbage, but for authenticity, we add more vegetables.

Prepare:

Corned Beef, above, without the cabbage

Meanwhile, cook separately until tender, then cool, peel and quarter:

10 to 12 medium beets

When the brisket is cooked, remove it from the pot. Add to the stock:

10 baby or pearl onions, peeled
6 carrots, peeled and quartered
6 medium potatoes, peeled and quartered
3 parsnips, peeled and quartered
3 turnips, peeled and quartered

Simmer, uncovered, for 30 minutes. Add:

1 head green cabbage, cut into wedges

Simmer until tender, 10 to 15 minutes. Return the meat to the pot just to reheat it. Slice and serve immediately, surrounded by the beets and the drained vegetables from the stock. Garnish with:

Chopped fresh parsley

If there are leftovers, use them for Red Flannel Hash, below.

CORNED BEEF HASH

4 to 6 servings

New Englanders say that this hash must be put together from the leftovers of New England boiled dinner. However, it can be made quite successfully with corned beef bought from a deli. Ask for a slice that is thick enough to be cut into ½-inch cubes. A well-seasoned cast-iron skillet gives the hash a good brown crust, but a nonstick skillet makes unmolding easy. The quantities and pan size depend on the amount of leftovers you have, but the following are approximate measurements.

Add to a large, heavy skillet over medium-high heat:

3 tablespoons vegetable oil
1 cup chopped onions

Cook, stirring, until the onions are lightly browned, about 3 minutes. Add:

3 cups cooked Corned Beef, above, cut into ½-inch cubes (about 2 pounds)
2 to 3 cups leftover vegetables, excluding the beets, from New England Boiled Dinner, above, or 2 to 3 cups cooked potatoes, cut into ½-inch cubes

Stir once, reduce the heat to medium, and press down with a spatula to compress the hash. Cook, without disturbing, until the bottom is well browned, 10 to 15 minutes. Slide or invert the hash onto a serving plate. Garnish with:

Chopped fresh parsley

Serve with:

poached eggs, 129, or fried eggs, 128

RED FLANNEL HASH

Beets give this hash its color and its name.

Prepare Corned Beef Hash, above, adding 2 or 3 beets, cooked, peeled, and cut into ½-inch cubes, to the other vegetables.

ABOUT STUFFED AND ROLLED BEEF

Whether they are called braciole, beef rolls, beef birds, roulades, or paupiettes, the concept is the same: Slices of beef are rolled around a stuffing and then braised in a savory liquid. They are served whole or sliced, depending on the size. This variation of braised beef is an excellent choice for the more flavorful but less tender, and less expensive, cuts from the rump and round. Consult Stuffing, 481, for more stuffing ideas. When shopping for beef to stuff and roll, buy a cut of meat composed of a single muscle, such as rump, bottom round, top round, or flank.

BEEF BRACIOLE

4 servings

Braciole, an Italian specialty, is best made from thin slices of beef rump, top round, or bottom round. Pork cutlets can be substituted for the beef in this dish. The individual slices are stuffed, rolled, tied, and braised in a combination of wine, stock, and tomatoes. Stuffings vary slightly from household to household, so feel free to improvise.

Purchase from a butcher or slice from a roast:

Four ¼-inch-thick slices rump, bottom round, or top round steak (4 to 5 ounces each)

Using the flat side of a cleaver, pound the slices about ⅛ inch thick, taking care not to tear the meat. Trim any excess fat and pat dry. Season lightly with:

Salt and ground black pepper to taste

For the stuffing, mix together:

1 cup soft breadcrumbs from day-old bread
4 ounces ground beef, veal, or pork
½ cup grated Parmesan cheese
¼ cup chopped fresh parsley
¼ cup finely chopped prosciutto, dry salami, or hot or mild dry coppa
¼ cup finely chopped shallots, onions, or scallions
1 large egg, lightly beaten

Lay the meat slices out flat and season with:

1 teaspoon salt
1 teaspoon ground black pepper

Spread evenly with the stuffing, leaving at least a 1-inch border all around. Roll up, tucking in the sides and forming a tight, neat packet. Tie securely with string, crosswise and lengthwise. Dredge the rolls with:

½ cup all-purpose flour

Shake off the excess. Heat in a large, heavy skillet with a lid over medium-high heat:

2 tablespoons olive oil

Add the meat packets and brown carefully on all sides. Remove the rolls with a slotted spoon and pour off all but 2 tablespoons of fat from the pan. Add to the pan:

½ cup finely chopped onions
¼ cup finely chopped carrots
2 teaspoons minced garlic

Cover and cook the vegetables over medium-high heat for 5 minutes. Add:

½ cup beef stock
½ cup dry red or white wine
½ cup tomato puree or 2 tablespoons tomato paste
1 bay leaf
½ teaspoon dried thyme

Bring to a boil and return the beef rolls to the pan. Reduce the heat, cover, and simmer until the beef is fork-tender, 1 to 1½ hours. Remove the rolls to a platter and keep warm. Skim off the fat from the surface of the liquid. Reduce, if necessary, over high heat just until it turns syrupy. Season with:

Salt and ground black pepper to taste

Remove the strings from the rolls and cut into 1-inch slices or leave whole. Pour the sauce over the meat. Serve with:

Soft Polenta with Butter and Cheese, 249, buttered noodles or pasta, or risotto, 260

ABOUT VEAL

Veal has been considered a special dish since Biblical times, when the return of the prodigal son was celebrated by cooking a fatted calf. Today, veal is a rare luxury. Veal is the meat of young calves. Ideally, veal calves come to market between the ages of eight and twelve weeks, at a weight of 150 to 250 pounds, though some are as old as sixteen weeks and weigh close to 400 pounds. Formerly, top-quality veal was produced from calves that were fed milk exclusively, but today, most calves are raised instead on highly enriched formulas intended to produce very pale, almost white meat, similar to milk-fed—the single most important criterion of quality. Whatever the animals are fed, they must be raised in such a way as to limit their movement to keep the meat tender and pale. In recent years, this has led to concerns about the excessive confinement of veal calves. In response, most producers have redesigned their methods of production to be more humane.

Many supermarkets sell precut portions of veal from a brand-name producer. Some butchers also carry brand names, but most buy generic veal in primal cuts, which they then butcher into roasts, chops, or scaloppine. Veal can be graded, like beef, but it rarely is. Look for meat that is very pale, with white, creamy fat. The flesh should be firm, dense, and uniform in color, without streaks of fat or marbling; the bones should be white on the outside and bright red at the center. Veal meat that is distinctly reddish in color has likely come from older calves that were partially fed on grain. Reddish veal will have a stronger flavor and tougher texture and is acceptable for stews or braises. Buy only the palest veal for roasts, chops, and scaloppine.

When buying veal, it is best to plan ahead and order what you need. There is typically very little veal available in supermarkets except the most popular cuts. Most of the time, you will find scaloppine or veal stew meat. Occasionally, stores will carry veal chops, breast, and ground veal. Very rarely will you find a roast, and if you do, it is probably from the shoulder. All cuts of light-colored veal meat are relatively tender, but some are more tender than others. The neck meat is considered the toughest and is used for stewing or braising. The shoulder is tender enough to roast, though it can be stewed or braised as well. The chuck, behind the neck, is fattier and best used for stewing or braising. Along the center back of the animal are the rib (or rack) and the loin, the tenderest and most expensive parts of the veal. These sections are usually cut into chops (the loin chops are choicer, for they include a nugget of the tenderloin), but they also can be prepared as roasts, bone-in or boneless. Rib and loin veal are best cooked by a dry-heat method—that is, grilled, roasted, or pan-fried—and served slightly pink. Behind the loin is the sirloin, a chewy piece of meat that is usually boned, then braised, stewed, or cut or pounded into scaloppine. The meat of the upper back legs, the top round, can be roasted, but its prime use is as scaloppine. The shanks of the back legs and, less desirably, the foreshanks can be braised whole or cut into sections and braised as for Osso Buco alla Milanese, 686. Finally, there is the veal breast, a chewy, bony, but highly flavorful cut that can be stuffed and roasted or cut into pieces and used to make stewed or braised dishes.

With the exception of veal breast and chuck, which have fat layered in the muscle that keeps it moist during cooking, veal is an extremely lean meat. Because of its leanness, it is easy to overcook, and a tender, juicy piece of meat will become bland and dry if not handled carefully. The cuts to watch the closest when cooking are the rib and loin, roasted whole or cut into chops, and also veal top cut into scaloppine. Scaloppine literally take less than a minute to cook in a hot skillet. The roasting times in this chapter produce a pink center with lots of juice.

ABOUT ROASTING VEAL

Veal can be roasted by high or low heat. High heat delivers a browned outside and pink juicy inside, and slow heat produces a uniformly pink roast without deep browning on the outside. While both methods produce fine results, we find that high heat works best with the more expensive rib and loin cuts, the tenderest cuts of veal. For the slightly less tender and leaner shoulder, breast, and leg, we recommend slow roasting. With little fat to keep them moist at high temperatures, these cuts retain more moisture and emerge tenderer at low temperatures.

Depending on the occasion and your budget, you can choose from several cuts of veal for roasting. Veal rib roast consists of the ribs closest to the loin. A whole rib roast is nine ribs, but you can order any size that you like. If you want a partial rib roast with only three or four ribs, make sure it is cut from the loin end, not the shoulder end, which contains the central eye muscle that shrinks and breaks up. Have the butcher remove the chine bone (backbone), which will ease slicing greatly. Allow one rib per serving and simply cut between the rib bones after roasting. A boneless loin roast usually weighs 3 to 4 pounds and consists of a single muscle, the top loin. The tenderloin is removed

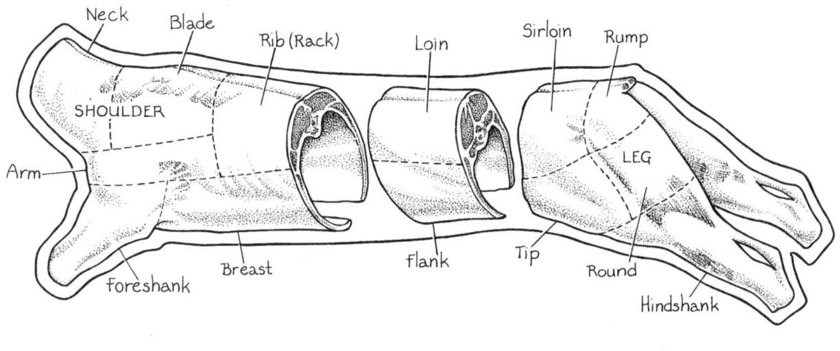

Major cuts of veal

when the loin is boned out and is generally sold separately, either whole, thinly sliced for scaloppine, or ground. The loin can be rolled and tied, or untied but trimmed of all extra flaps and fat. When rolled and tied, the loin muscle is often covered with a flap of meat to keep it moist during cooking. The rib and loin cuts of veal can be roasted by high or low heat. Both techniques work very well. The shoulder (arm) and chuck roasts and the leg roast, or top round, are best slow-roasted, while veal breast, with its higher amount of fat to keep it moist, roasts well at a moderate 325°F. Again, not all veal roasts are routinely carried in stores, but they can easily be ordered.

VEAL ROAST (HIGH-TEMPERATURE METHOD)

6 servings

Use this method for veal loin and rib roasts only. These cuts are the most expensive of the veal roasts and are great choices for a party; they are easy to carve, and there is very little waste. High-heat roasting creates a nice outer crust and keeps the meat pink, moist, and juicy in the center. If you prefer a roast that is more evenly pink without the browned exterior, follow the procedure for Slow-Roasted Veal, below. Both methods of roasting produce very tender results. If using a rib roast on the bone, have the butcher remove the chine bone (backbone).

Position a rack in the center of the oven. Preheat the oven to 425°F.

Pat dry:

1 boneless veal loin or rib roast (3 to 4 pounds), or one 6-rib veal roast on the bone (5 to 7 pounds)

If using a boneless roast, tie it in a neat, compact shape with butcher twine. If using the rib roast on the bone, leave as is. Rub all surfaces with:

2 tablespoons olive or vegetable oil

Season generously with:

Salt and ground black pepper to taste

Place the veal fat side up on a rack in a shallow roasting pan. Roast until an instant-read thermometer inserted in the thickest part of the meat registers 145°F, about 45 to 60 minutes for the boneless roast, 1¼ to 1½ hours for the bone-in roast (the temperature will continue to rise about 10° out of the oven). Remove the roast to a platter, cover loosely with aluminum foil, and let stand for 15 to 20 minutes. Set the roasting pan over high heat and pour in:

⅓ cup dry white wine

⅓ cup chicken stock

Bring to a boil, scraping up the browned bits with a wooden spoon, and boil for 1 minute. Slice the veal, cutting the bone-in roast between the ribs, and arrange the meat on the platter. Season with:

Salt and ground black pepper to taste

Drizzle the sauce over the veal and serve.

SLOW-ROASTED VEAL

6 servings

All veal roasts do well with this roasting technique, remaining pink throughout and extremely juicy.

Position a rack in the center of the oven. Preheat the oven to 450°F.

Pat dry:

1 boneless veal shoulder, leg (top round), loin, or rib roast (3 to 4 pounds)

Tie the roast in a neat, compact shape with butcher twine. Rub all surfaces with:

2 tablespoons olive or vegetable oil

Season generously with:

Salt and ground black pepper to taste

Place the veal fat side up on a rack in a shallow roasting pan. Roast for 10 minutes. Reduce the oven temperature to 250°F and roast until an instant-read thermometer inserted in the thickest part of the meat registers 145 to 150°F, 1¼ to 1¾ hours (the temperature will continue to rise about 5° out of the oven). Remove the roast to a platter, cover loosely with aluminum foil, and let stand for 15 to 20 minutes. Set the roasting pan over high heat and pour in:

⅓ cup dry white wine

⅓ cup chicken stock

Bring to a boil, scraping up the browned bits with a wooden spoon, and boil for 1 minute. Slice the veal and arrange the meat on the platter. Season with:

Salt and ground black pepper to taste

Drizzle the sauce over the veal and serve.

VEAL ROAST WITH PROSCIUTTO AND HERBS

Before preparing Veal Roast (High-Temperature Method), above, or Slow-Roasted Veal, above, make slits all over the roast with the tip of a paring knife. Either with a large knife or in a food processor, mince together to form a paste 6 slices (about 3 ounces) prosciutto, 3 cloves garlic, and ½ teaspoon each dried rosemary and thyme. Push the paste into the slits. Proceed as directed.

VEAL RIB ROAST WITH GARLIC CRUMBS AND MUSTARD CREAM (HIGH-TEMPERATURE METHOD)

6 servings

Cooking this roast coated with garlic crumbs in a hot (425°F) oven gives it a nice crust. To serve, slice the roast between the rib bones and serve as chops. Have the butcher remove the chine bone (backbone) for easier carving. For a variation, substitute Dijon mustard flavored with green peppercorns, horseradish, or herbs. For a more elegant presentation (but with less finger-licking), you can French the roast, which involves trimming the rib bones completely. For full instructions, please see How to Trim and French a Rack of Lamb, 713.

Position a rack in the lower third of the oven. Preheat the oven to 425°F.

Using a fork, mix together in a bowl:

1½ cups fresh breadcrumbs
2 tablespoons unsalted butter, melted
2 cloves garlic, minced
Salt and ground black pepper to taste

Make sure the crumbs are evenly coated with butter. Pat dry:

One 6-rib veal roast (5 to 7 pounds)

Brush the entire surface with:

¼ cup Dijon mustard

Coat all surfaces of the roast with a thin layer of the breadcrumb mixture. Place on a rack in a shallow roasting pan. Roast until an instant-read thermometer inserted in the thickest part of the meat registers 145°F, 1¼ to 1½ hours (the temperature will continue to rise about 10° out of the oven). If the coating begins to brown too much during roasting, cover loosely with aluminum foil. Remove the roast from the oven and let stand for 15 to 20 minutes in the roasting pan.

While the meat roasts, bring to a boil in a saucepan over medium-high heat:

1 cup heavy cream
1 cup chicken or veal stock

Reduce the heat and simmer until reduced to 1 cup. Whisk in:

¼ cup Dijon mustard

Simmer for a few minutes more to blend the flavors. Season with:

Salt and ground black pepper to taste

Slice the roast and arrange the meat on plates or a platter. Gently reheat the sauce if necessary and spoon some over the veal. Pass the remaining sauce at the table. Sprinkle the chops with:

2 tablespoons snipped fresh chives

ITALIAN STUFFED ROASTED VEAL BREAST FOR A CROWD

8 to 12 servings

This is a beautiful presentation and makes a perfect company dish. Have the butcher prepare the breast for stuffing by slicing a horizontal pocket along the bones (between the meat and the bones) and cutting through the rigid cartilage between the rib bones from underneath the breast (not the meat side) without cutting into the meat. This cracks the bones, which will make carving the roast easier. You will need a pan that is at least 17 x 11½ inches to accommodate the entire veal breast. When made without pancetta or bacon, this is a typical Eastern European dish.

Heat in a medium skillet over medium-low heat:

2 tablespoons olive oil

Add:

2 medium onions, finely chopped
1 clove garlic, minced

Cook, stirring often, for 15 minutes. Add:

4 ounces pancetta or bacon, thinly sliced and cut crosswise into ¼-inch pieces (optional)

Cook until the pancetta browns, 6 to 8 minutes. Remove the mixture to a large bowl. Add to the onion mixture:

7 cups fresh breadcrumbs
2 tablespoons water
1 tablespoon red wine vinegar
2 large eggs, lightly beaten
3 tablespoons chopped fresh parsley
1 tablespoon chopped fresh sage
1 tablespoon fresh thyme leaves
Salt and ground black pepper to taste

Mix thoroughly. Place in a large roasting pan:

6 carrots, peeled and sliced
4 leeks (white and green parts), cleaned thoroughly and quartered

Position a rack in the lower third of the oven. Preheat the oven to 325°F.

Pat dry:

1 whole veal breast (12 to 14 pounds), prepared for stuffing by butcher (see above)

Season the meat with:

Salt and ground black pepper to taste

Fill the pocket with the stuffing, spreading it in an even layer. Place the breast in the roasting pan. To keep the breast moist during roasting, brush with olive oil or arrange on top of the meat:

12 ounces pancetta or bacon, thinly sliced (optional)

Roast, uncovered, until the exterior is deeply browned and the inside is no longer pink when you make a small incision near the bone, 2½ to 3 hours. Remove the meat to a platter and let stand for 15 to 20 minutes. Remove the carrots and leeks to a bowl with a slotted spoon, spoon the fat from the pan juices, and add:

2 cups dry white wine

Set the roasting pan over high heat and bring to a boil. Reduce the heat and simmer until the sauce is reduced by half. Slice the veal and spoon the sauce over the slices. Serve with the roasted carrots and leeks if desired.

VITELLO TONNATO *4 servings*

This is a classic Italian dish of cold sliced veal served with a tuna mayonnaise-style sauce spiked with capers and anchovies. It is best when the veal is cooked ahead and well chilled. You can use any cut of veal that is easily sliced, preferably a boneless loin roast. The sauce is also good over roast turkey or pork.

Refrigerate until cold:

1 to 1½ pounds cooked veal roast

Prepare:

Tuna Sauce, 81

Cut the veal into thin slices and arrange on plates or a platter. Spoon a generous amount of the tuna sauce over the slices and serve with:

Lemon wedges

ABOUT SCALOPPINE (SCALLOPS), CUTLETS, AND SCHNITZEL

These names may seem confusing, but where veal is concerned, scaloppine, cutlet, and schnitzel are all synonymous terms for thin slices of veal from the same cut of leg meat: top or bottom round, which is sometimes referred to as veal top. Since this cut is most familiar through its use in Italian recipes, it is typically called scaloppine. Ideally, scaloppine are cut across the grain from a single muscle of the leg (veal top), which yields the widest pieces. Too often, however, scaloppine are cut with the grain from a different cut of veal (typically the chewier sirloin) using two or more muscles, and as a result, they shrink and buckle in the pan. When top round is sliced across the grain, scaloppine will remain flat during cooking and in one piece, juicy, tender, and succulent. It is important that scaloppine not be cut superthin, for they will inevitably be overcooked—dry and leathery—by the time the surface is browned. If you live near an Italian market, you should be able to buy scaloppine that are well cut. If you have to rely on supermarket scaloppine, which are often cut irregularly at best, avoid any paper-thin slices. Look for slices that are smooth on the surface, not with a bumpy texture or lines that look like stripes, which indicates that they were cut with the grain.

Alternatively, you can buy a whole veal top and cut your own scaloppine. You will have to order the veal top, which weighs between 3 and 4 pounds. To cut your own scaloppine, place the veal top on a work surface and, using a very sharp, long-bladed knife, slice it crosswise. You will see the direction the grain runs; cut in the opposite direction. Where the veal top is thin and tapering, make your cuts almost ½ inch thick; otherwise, slice the meat just over ¼ inch thick. Place the slices between sheets of wax or parchment paper and gently pound them to just under ¼ inch in thickness. You can use a smooth-surfaced meat pounder or even the heel of your hand, but a broader implement such as a small rolling pin or an empty wine bottle often produces more even scaloppine. To ensure that the scaloppine will not curl, make a few cuts around the edges, each about ⅛ inch deep. Wrap the scaloppine that you will be using in plastic, stacking and separating the slices between pieces of wax or parchment paper. To freeze any extra scaloppine, tightly wrap the slices individually in plastic. Stack them in serving-sized batches for one, two, or four. Then wrap the stacks in aluminum foil, label them, and freeze. Use them within 2 to 3 months.

VEAL SCALOPPINE *4 servings*

Serve simply, as in this recipe, or try with any of the variations that follow.

Preheat the oven to 180°F. Have ready an ovenproof platter.

Have ready:

1 pound veal scaloppine slices (8 to 12), cut a little more than ¼ inch thick and pounded to slightly less than ¼ inch

Season with:

Salt and ground black pepper to taste

Dredge in:

½ cup all-purpose flour

Shake off the excess. Heat in a large skillet over high heat:

1 tablespoon olive oil

1 tablespoon unsalted butter

Cook the scaloppine in batches, being careful not to crowd the pan. Brown quickly, 30 to 60 seconds each side. Remove to the platter and keep warm in the oven. Repeat, adding more oil and butter to the pan as needed, until all the scaloppine are cooked. Season with:

Salt and ground black pepper to taste

Serve immediately.

VEAL PICCATA

Prepare Veal Scaloppine, above, and keep warm in the oven. Add ¼ cup dry white wine and ⅓ cup fresh lemon juice to the pan. Bring to a boil, scraping up the browned bits with a wooden spoon. Reduce the heat and simmer until slightly reduced, about 5 minutes.

Turn off the heat and quickly whisk in 4 tablespoons softened unsalted butter. Season to taste with salt and pepper and 2 tablespoons chopped fresh parsley. Spoon the sauce over the scaloppine and serve immediately.

VEAL MARSALA

Although many variations of this classic dish include mushrooms, this traditional recipe does not.

Prepare Veal Scaloppine, above, without placing the veal in the oven after browning. After the scaloppine have been cooked, set them aside and add ⅔ cup dry Marsala to the pan. Bring to a boil, scraping up the browned bits with a wooden spoon. Reduce the heat and simmer until cooked down to about ½ cup. Whisk in 2 tablespoons softened unsalted butter. Continue to simmer until the sauce becomes thicker and velvety. Return the veal to the pan along with 2 tablespoons chopped fresh parsley and simmer the meat in the sauce so that it warms through, about 1 minute. Remove from the heat and serve immediately.

VEAL SALTIMBOCCA

4 servings

Saltimbocca means "jump into the mouth," which is precisely what these delicious stuffed, sauced cutlets do. Prosciutto and sage are the traditional stuffing, but contemporary chefs often add a slice of cheese as well. The Italians make saltimbocca with veal cutlets, but turkey breast is also very good.

Have ready:

1 pound veal scaloppine slices (8 to 12), cut slightly more than ¼ inch thick and pounded to slightly less than ¼ inch

Season with:

Salt and ground black pepper to taste

Leaving a ¼-inch border around the edges, divide among the scaloppine slices:

2 ounces paper-thin slices prosciutto

8 to 12 large fresh sage leaves

Cover the prosciutto with:

3 ounces thinly sliced plain or smoked mozzarella cheese

Fold the cutlets in half and secure with toothpicks. Heat in a large, heavy skillet over medium-high heat until fragrant and golden:

1 tablespoon olive oil

1 tablespoon unsalted butter

Add the veal packets and sauté, turning once, until lightly browned, about 3 minutes each side. Remove to a platter and cover with aluminum foil to keep warm. Add to the hot pan:

2 tablespoons minced shallots or scallions

Cook, stirring, until wilted, about 1 minute. Pour in:

½ cup dry white wine

Scraping the bottom of the pan with a wooden spoon to loosen the browned bits, boil until the wine is almost evaporated. Add:

1 cup chicken or veal stock

1 tablespoon strained fresh lemon juice

Boil over high heat until reduced to about ½ cup. Remove the skillet from the heat and swirl in:

2 tablespoons unsalted butter, softened

Taste and adjust the seasonings, adding a bit more lemon juice if you like. Pour the sauce over the veal packets. If desired, sprinkle with:

Chopped fresh parsley

VEAL PARMIGIANA

Prepare Chicken Parmigiana, 589, substituting veal scaloppine for the chicken cutlets.

VEAL FRANCESE

4 servings

This dish is very popular in home-style and family restaurants. Some cooks like to cover the veal for the last 2 minutes of cooking, which softens the outer crust of the batter. Others prefer a slight crisp to the coating.

Preheat the oven to 180°F. Have ready an ovenproof platter.

Have ready:

1 pound veal scaloppine slices (8 to 12), cut slightly more than ¼ inch thick and pounded to slightly less than ¼ inch thick

Dredge in:

½ cup all-purpose flour

Shake off the excess. Beat together in a bowl until frothy and thick:

3 large eggs

6 tablespoons grated Parmesan cheese

1½ tablespoons chopped fresh parsley

½ teaspoon salt

¼ teaspoon ground black pepper

Heat in a large skillet over medium-high heat:

1½ tablespoons olive oil

1½ tablespoons unsalted butter

Dip the floured scaloppine into the egg batter and place in the hot pan. Cook the scaloppine in batches, being careful not to crowd the pan. Cook until nicely browned, 1½ to 2 minutes each side. Remove to the platter and keep warm in the oven. Repeat, adding more oil and butter to the pan as needed, until all the scaloppine are cooked. When they are all done, return them to the pan and sprinkle with:

Juice of 1 large lemon (¼ to ⅓ cup)

Reheat, either covered or uncovered, and cook for 1 minute more to blend with the lemon. Season with:

Salt and ground black pepper to taste

Serve immediately with:

Chopped fresh parsley
Lemon wedges

WIENER SCHNITZEL

4 servings

This Austrian specialty is breaded veal scaloppine, although the Germans make it with pork cutlets. Traditionally browned in lard, these schnitzel are cooked in vegetable oil.

Preheat the oven to 180°F. Have ready an ovenproof platter.

Have ready:

1 pound veal scaloppine slices (8 to 12), cut slightly more than ¼ inch thick and pounded to slightly less than ¼ inch thick

Season with:

Salt and ground black pepper to taste

Spread on a plate:

½ cup all-purpose flour

Beat together in a shallow bowl:

2 large eggs
1 tablespoon milk

Spread on another plate:

2 cups fresh breadcrumbs

Dredge the veal slices lightly in the flour mixture and shake off the excess. Dip into the egg mixture, then coat with the crumbs, pressing down on the crumbs slightly to help them adhere to the veal. Heat in a large skillet over medium-high heat:

3 tablespoons vegetable oil

Cook the schnitzel in batches, being careful not to crowd the pan, until nicely browned, 1 to 1½ minutes each side. Remove to paper towels to drain, then keep warm on the platter in the oven. Repeat, adding more oil to the pan as needed, until all the schnitzel are cooked. Sprinkle with:

Salt and ground black pepper to taste

Serve with:

Lemon wedges

ABOUT VEAL CHOPS AND MEDALLIONS

Veal chops can be cut from the rib or loin. Rib chops have one curved bone, while loin chops are distinguished by their T-bone shape, with the loin muscle on one side and the tenderloin on the other. Both the rib and loin chops have a thin layer of fat around the edges. You can trim this fat if you wish, but we like to leave at least ¼ inch of fat to keep the chops moist during cooking. Veal shoulder chops, or blade steaks as they are sometimes called, are a bit tougher and are generally reserved for braising. Medallions are individual round steaks cut from the boneless loin of veal, which has been trimmed of fat and connective tissue. What remains is a perfectly clean, solid piece of tender meat that makes an elegant presentation. The best techniques for cooking veal chops and medallions are grilling or pan-frying; broiling is not recommended, because the chops will dry out before they have a chance to brown. Chops for grilling are best cut about 1½ inches thick so that the center remains pink and juicy while allowing time for the meat to cook near the bone. Pan-fried chops are ideal when cut 1 inch thick; they do not burn or dry out. Veal medallions are sliced about ¾ inch thick and cook very quickly in a hot skillet. Grilled veal chops can be cooked and served simply with a wedge of lemon, but their hefty appearance and mild taste allows for novel enhancements. Try a herb or spice rub or serve with a vinaigrette, chutney, relish, or other chunky, rustic sauce or condiment. Pan-fried chops and medallions are perfect for making pan sauces that can be put together just a few minutes after the meat is cooked. You also can make a sauce ahead and reheat it gently either in the skillet or in a separate pan. Consult Stocks & Sauces, 35, for ideas.

GRILLED VEAL CHOPS

4 servings

If you have a bottled authentic well-aged balsamic vinegar, serve a few drops of it with each chop.

Prepare a medium-hot charcoal fire.

Pat dry:

4 rib or loin veal chops, cut 1¼ to 1½ inches thick

Rub the chops with:

2 tablespoons olive oil

Sprinkle with:

Salt and ground black pepper to taste

Place the chops over the hottest area of the grill and sear for 2 minutes on each side. Move the chops to a cooler spot and finish cooking, 8 to 10 minutes, turning halfway through the cooking time. The chops will be well browned and give only slightly when pressed firmly with a finger. Remove to a platter or plates and serve with:

Lemon wedges

SAUTÉED VEAL CHOPS

4 servings

Pat dry:

4 rib or loin veal chops, cut 1 inch thick

Season with:

Salt and ground black pepper to taste

Heat in a large skillet over medium-high heat:

2 tablespoons unsalted butter

Add the chops and sear until golden on the bottom, about 2 minutes. Turn and sear the second side. Reduce the heat to medium and cook for 3 to 5 minutes, turning the chops halfway through cooking. Remove to plates and let stand. Increase the heat to high and add:

½ cup chicken or veal stock

Boil, stirring, until the sauce is syrupy and glazelike, 1 to 2 minutes. Spoon the sauce over the chops and serve.

SAUTÉED VEAL CHOPS WITH WILD MUSHROOMS

Soak 1 ounce dried porcini mushrooms in ⅔ cup hot water for 30 minutes. Remove the mushrooms from the liquid, squeeze out the excess liquid, and chop. Strain the soaking liquid, measure ¼ cup, and reserve. Wipe clean, stem, and coarsely chop 8 ounces each shiitake and portobello mushrooms. Heat 4 tablespoons unsalted butter in a large skillet over medium-high heat. Add all the mushrooms and sprinkle with ½ teaspoon salt and some ground black pepper. Sauté for about 5 minutes, stirring often. Add 4 cloves garlic, minced, and 2 tablespoons chopped fresh parsley; cook for 5 minutes more. Add the reserved porcini liquid and ¼ cup veal or chicken stock; cook until the mushrooms are glazed, 5 to 10 minutes. Prepare Sautéed Veal Chops, above, omitting the chicken or veal stock. Remove the chops to plates, add the mushroom mixture to the skillet, reheat it, and spoon over the chops.

SAUTÉED VEAL CHOPS SERVED AGRODOLCE

Heat 2 tablespoons olive oil in a medium skillet over medium heat. Add 3 cups chopped onions and salt and ground black pepper to taste. Cook, stirring, until golden, about 10 minutes. Stir in 1 tablespoon tomato paste, then add ¼ cup balsamic or red wine vinegar, ½ cup veal or chicken stock, 2 tablespoons raisins, 1 tablespoon sugar, and ½ teaspoon dried thyme. Cook until the juices are reduced and coat the onions. Season with salt and pepper to taste. Prepare Sautéed Veal Chops, above, omitting the chicken or veal stock. Remove the chops to plates, add the onion mixture to the skillet, reheat it, and spoon over the chops.

SAUTÉED VEAL CHOPS WITH ARTICHOKES AND BLACK OLIVES

Thaw one 9-ounce box frozen artichoke hearts, and chop. Melt 2 tablespoons olive oil in a medium skillet over medium-low heat. Add 1 onion, chopped, 2 cloves garlic, minced, and salt and ground black pepper to taste. Cook for 5 minutes and add the artichokes. Cook for 10 minutes more, stirring often. Add ¼ cup chopped pitted Kalamata olives, 2 tablespoons fresh lemon juice, and 2 tablespoons chopped fresh parsley. Cook for 1 minute more to heat the olives through, then set aside. Prepare Sautéed Veal Chops, above. After deglazing the pan, drizzle the sauce over the chops. Add the artichoke mixture to the skillet, reheat it, and spoon over the chops.

SAUTÉED VEAL MEDALLIONS

4 servings

Position a rack in the lower third of the oven. Preheat the oven to 180°F. Have ready an ovenproof platter.

Pat dry:

8 veal medallions, cut ¾ inch thick from the center loin

Season with:

Salt and ground black pepper to taste

Heat in a large skillet over medium-high heat:

2 tablespoons unsalted butter

Add the medallions in batches, being careful not to crowd the pan, and sear until golden on the bottom, about 2 minutes. Turn and sear the second side. Remove to the platter and keep warm in the oven. Repeat, adding more butter to the pan as needed, until all the medallions are cooked. Increase the heat to high and add to the skillet:

¼ cup chicken or veal stock

Boil, stirring, until the sauce is syrupy and glazelike, 1 to 2 minutes. Spoon the sauce over the medallions and serve.

SAUTÉED VEAL MEDALLIONS ON ARUGULA TOMATO SALAD

Whisk together in a small bowl ¼ cup extra-virgin olive oil, 2 tablespoons fresh orange juice, 2 tablespoons fresh lemon juice, 1 teaspoon grated orange zest, and salt and ground black pepper to taste. Toss together in a large bowl 6 cups torn arugula leaves and 2 medium tomatoes, cored and diced. Prepare Sautéed Veal Medallions, above, without making the pan sauce. Thinly slice the meat when cooked. Toss the arugula with the orange dressing and arrange the salad on 4 plates. Divide the veal and arrange it over the salads. Sprinkle with salt and pepper to taste and drizzle the pan sauce over the veal.

ABOUT VEAL STEWS AND BRAISED VEAL

Veal is particularly well suited to stewing and braising, a moist-heat technique, because it has so much collagen that melts to natural gelatin and gives the finished gravy tremendous body and texture. The best cuts for stewing and braising are the tougher, more flavorful ones including the neck, chuck, shoulder, breast, sirloin, and shank. For stews, buy or cut cubes of meat from the neck, chuck, or shoulder. For braising larger cuts, look for whole pieces of boneless chuck, shoulder or veal breast, which can be braised on the bone or boneless, rolled and tied into a neat loaf—ideal for stuffing. Veal shanks should be cut into thick crosswise slices to expose the marrow, which is considered a special treat in the Italian braised veal dish Osso Buco, below (*osso buco* means "bone cavity"). The best are the hind shanks, for they are meatier and more tender than the smaller foreshanks. As with all stewed and braised dishes, the flavor improves after a day. Please see About Braising, Stewing, and Pot-Roasting Meat, 640.

OSSO BUCO ALLA MILANESE

4 servings

Literally translated, osso buco is a bone with a hole, and that hole contains marrow. In this classic north Italian dish, a seasoning mixture, gremolata, is added at the end. Gremolata typically includes parsley, garlic, and lemon zest, but excellent variations include anchovies and orange zest in place of the lemon zest. If possible, choose veal hind shank slices, which are meatier than the foreshank.

Position a rack in the lower third of the oven. Preheat the oven to 325°F.

Pat dry:

8 very meaty slices veal shank, cut 1 to 1½ inches thick

In a large Dutch oven with a tight-fitting lid, heat over medium-high heat:

2 tablespoons olive oil

Add the shanks in batches and brown well on all sides, adding more oil as needed. Remove to a plate. Reduce the heat to medium-low and add to the pan:

⅓ cup diced carrots
⅓ cup diced onions
⅓ cup diced celery
4 cloves garlic, crushed
1 small bouquet garni, 37

Cook, stirring, until the vegetables are softened, 5 to 10 minutes. Return the shanks to the pan and arrange in a single layer as best you can. Add:

1 cup dry white wine
1 cup veal or chicken stock
Ground black pepper to taste

The liquid should reach about halfway up the shanks. Increase the heat to high, bring to a boil, and cover with the lid. Place in the oven and braise for 1 hour. Have available:

1 to 2 cups veal or chicken stock

Turn the shank slices over and add stock if needed to keep the level halfway up the shanks. Braise until the meat is tender and offers no resistance when pierced with the tip of a sharp knife, about 1 hour more.

Meanwhile, to prepare the gremolata, mix together in a small bowl:

2 tablespoons chopped fresh flat-leaf parsley
2 cloves garlic, minced
2 teaspoons grated lemon zest

When the veal is cooked, remove the shanks to an ovenproof serving platter and keep warm in the oven with the door ajar. Spoon off any fat from the braising juices; strain the juices into a saucepan, and boil over high heat until slightly thickened. Add the gremolata and season with:

Salt and ground black pepper to taste

Spoon the sauce over the veal. Serve with:

Risotto Milanese, 260, or Soft Polenta with Butter and Cheese, 249

ABOUT PORK

American pork is not the same meat it used to be—it is both tenderer and leaner. Modern pork producers feed their livestock a diet of grain supplemented with protein, vitamins, and minerals, and bring them to market at six to seven months old—young enough to be tender and mild-flavored. In addition, breeders, responding to market demands, have turned pork from a fatty meat into a lean one. This is good news for health-conscious diners, but it raises problems for cooks. Without the fat of yesteryear, which basted the meat and kept it moist as it cooked, pork can easily dry out, becoming tough and tasteless. To get the most in flavor and tenderness from today's pork, we need to adapt to different cooking times, internal temperatures, and techniques. For instance, we once recommended cooking pork roasts and chops to an internal temperature of 170° to 185°F, but we now endorse temperatures in the range of 150° to 160°F for slightly rosy, tender, juicy roasts and chops. For detailed cooking information, please refer to the sections about specific cuts.

These new recommended internal temperatures for cooked pork upset the long-standing prejudice in this country against eating pork that shows even the faintest blush of pink. The tendency to cook pork until it is gray and dry comes from a fear of trichinosis, which was once associated with eating undercooked pork. Fortunately, modern production practices have vastly improved the safety and wholesomeness of pork. At any rate, the trichinosis organism is destroyed at 137°F—well below recommended internal cooking temperatures.

Of the pork produced in this country, about one-third is consumed as fresh pork, meaning roasts, chops, medallions, ribs, and such. All the rest gets processed and cured into the variety of hams, bacons, sausages, and cold cuts sold in our markets. For more information on cured pork, please read About Cured Pork, 703.

The cuts of fresh pork sold in markets throughout the country are standardized. The most popular are from the loin—the meat that runs along either side of the backbone, starting in the shoulder blade area and running all the way to the leg. Unlike beef, veal, and lamb, whose ribs, loin, and sirloin are divided into separate sections, the pork loin contains the ribs, the loin, and the sirloin, shown below. There are two loins per pig; each weighs 15 to 20 pounds before boning and trimming. Retail cuts from the loin include rib and loin roasts and chops, the tenderloin, and the back and country-style ribs. Country-style ribs are cut from the shoulder blade end of the loin. Back ribs are cut from the center section of the loin and also from the shoulder end. So prized is the loin that, over the years, breeders have increased its length. In fact, pigs have been bred to have one more rib than beef, veal, or lamb. Whole pork loins can be cut in a number of ways, and the names of these cuts are sometimes confusing. For example, a cut labeled in one market as pork loin center-cut chops may be labeled in another as rib chops or loin chops, and all are correct. "Center-cut" is simply a more specific name indicating the best cuts from the center of the loin, where the eye-muscle meat is the largest.

The shoulder, sometimes called New York-style shoulder, is the large front arm and shoulder blade section. It weighs 15 to 25 pounds and is rarely seen whole. Instead, each shoulder is divided into two smaller cuts. The arm section of the shoulder is referred to as the picnic shoulder. It weighs 7 to 9 pounds and is sometimes found cut in half, yielding both shank end and shoulder end pieces of about equal weight. Picnic shoulder roasts are delicious roasted fresh, though they are most often sold smoked as hams. The upper part of the shoulder, closer to the loin and containing the shoulder blade bone, is the Boston-style shoulder, also known as pork butt or Boston butt. A whole Boston-style shoulder, or butt, averages 8 to 9 pounds bone-in, 5 to 7 pounds boneless, and is flavorful, meltingly tender, and very juicy from its higher proportion of fat. It is a great cut for many cooking methods, but you may need to special-order it. Most often, it is ground into fresh sausage or ground pork. When left whole, Boston-style shoulder is best braised to keep it moist and tender.

The leg is available fresh and is sometimes called fresh ham. The whole bone-in leg weighs between 15 and 25 pounds and is also available boneless and tied, as well as cut into bone-in and boneless roasts or leg steaks. From the underside of the pig come spareribs and bacon.

When buying pork, look for meat that is moist and attractively pink, not gray or red. Expect little mar-

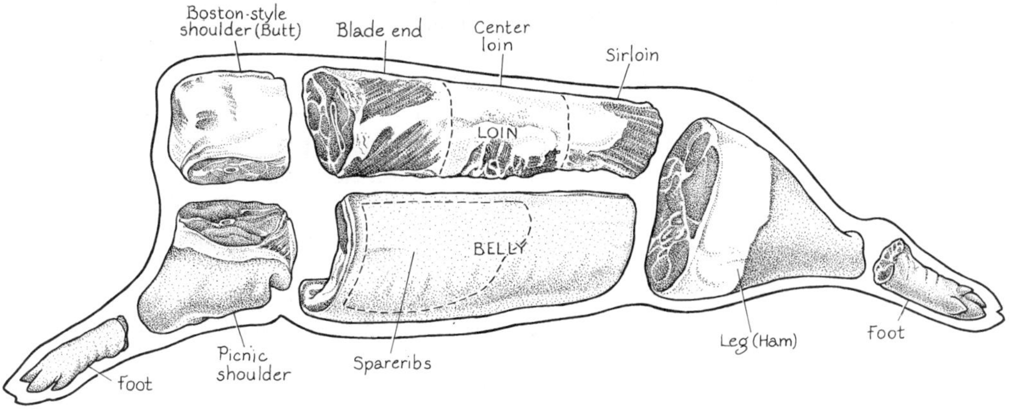

Major cuts of pork

bling and choose neat-looking cuts with a fine-grained texture. Any external fat should be smooth and white, not chalky or discolored. It will keep well wrapped in plastic for 2 to 4 days in the refrigerator. For longer storage, freeze pork in heavy plastic bags, plastic wrap, or aluminum foil. Wrap the meat tightly, removing as much air as possible. Roasts, steaks, and chops will keep in the freezer for 3 to 6 months; ground pork and sausage, 1 to 3 months. Thaw pork slowly in the refrigerator for the least amount of moisture loss.

As with beef, veal, and lamb, there are two methods for cooking pork—dry heat and moist heat. Dry-heat methods, such as roasting, grilling, sautéing, pan-frying, and stir-frying, are reserved for the naturally tender cuts from the loin and tenderloin. Bear in mind that these lean cuts fare best when cooked to medium, with a faint blush of pink. The tougher shoulder and leg cuts are cooked to tenderness by the slow, moist heat of a braise or stew—although they can be slow-roasted in the oven if basted frequently.

Because the flavor of pork is relatively delicate, it works well with many spices and seasoning mixtures, including dry rubs and marinades, 84 to 88. The cooking times for all the recipes in this section are based on meat directly from the refrigerator, not meat at room temperature.

ABOUT ROASTING PORK

Roasts from the loin require one method and those from the leg and shoulder another. For a juicy and tender loin roast, we have had the best results using the slow-roasting technique of starting at 450°F to brown, then reducing the oven temperature to 250°F to finish the meat slowly. The maximum internal temperature recommended for a boneless pork loin roast is 150°F, while a bone-in roast needs a little extra time and should cook until it reaches 155° to 160°F—the temperature of all roasts will continue to rise 5° to 10° out of the oven.

Boneless center-cut roasts generally weigh 3 to 4 pounds but can be cut to any size. Also called the loin eye, this is a single muscle of tender meat with very little fat covering it. More pork loin is sold boneless now so that the tenderloin can be sold separately. Bone-in roasts can always be ordered; be sure to have the butcher cut through the backbone, or chine bone, so that you can carve the roast easily after cooking. A rack of pork is a bone-in pork loin with the backbone removed. A crown roast is one or two pork racks tied into the shape of an upright crown. Less expensive roasts are the sirloin roasts, from the hip end of the loin. These run 5 to 7 inches in length and are easiest to carve when bought boneless; they have a relatively complicated bone structure. From the other end of the loin come the blade loin roasts, sometimes called rib-end roasts, containing 5 to 7 ribs. The blade and sirloin ends of the pork loin are redder, with more flavor, but are also chewier. The center cut is a paler color with a milder flavor and a tenderer grain.

Picnic shoulder and leg roasts are cooked in an entirely different manner than pork loin roasts: roasted slowly at 325°F to an internal temperature of 185°F. Because of their size, entire legs, also known as fresh hams, take some time to roast, anywhere from 3 to 6 hours, but are a terrific choice for a large party. Picnic shoulder roasts come with the skin on and can be roasted with or without it. Latin American cooks leave the skin on to keep the meat moist, basting it with water to soften the skin for eating. Others remove the skin before roasting, then baste to keep the meat moist and tender. Either technique produces a fine roast.

Test for doneness with a meat thermometer. If you do not have a thermometer, check for doneness by feel and color of the meat and juices. For pork loin roasts, look for a pale pink blush and lots of clear juice; for shoulder and leg roasts, the meat should be very tender and falling off the bone. Remember to let all roasts stand for about 15 minutes before carving, to allow the juices to redistribute. The internal temperature of a roast will continue to rise 5 to 10 degrees during the rest period, cooking the meat perfectly.

SLOW-ROASTED BONELESS PORK LOIN

6 servings

Boneless pork loin is best slow-roasted, but it is difficult to give exact cooking times, since pork loins vary widely in diameter. In general, a 3-pound boneless pork loin should take 1¼ to 1½ hours total cooking time. If the roast is very small, less than 2 inches in diameter, check the internal temperature after it has cooked at 250°F for 30 minutes. Otherwise, begin checking at 45 minutes. For the best results, test for doneness with an instant-read meat thermometer. After roasting, make a quick pan sauce by adding stock or wine to the pan or simply serve the meat with the defatted pan juices. Roast pork is also delicious served with Buttered Cider Sauce, 1049.

Position a rack in the center of the oven. Preheat the oven to 450°F.

Mix together:

1 tablespoon olive oil
1 tablespoon dried thyme, sage, oregano, or rosemary
1 teaspoon salt
½ teaspoon ground black pepper

Rub evenly over the entire surface of:

1 boneless center-cut pork loin roast (about 3 pounds)

Place the meat on a rack in a roasting pan. Roast for 10 minutes. Reduce the oven temperature to 250°F and roast until a meat thermometer inserted in the thickest part of the meat registers 150° to 155°F, 45 to 80 minutes (the temperature will continue to rise about 5° out of the oven). Remove to a cutting board, cover loosely with aluminum foil, and let stand for 15 minutes. Skim off the fat in the roasting pan, leaving behind all the pan juices. If desired, place the pan over medium-high heat and add:

½ to 1 cup chicken stock or dry white wine

You want about 1 cup of liquid. Boil, scraping up any browned bits, until slightly thickened. Cut the meat into ¼- to ½-inch slices and arrange on plates. The roast should be slightly pink and very juicy. Spoon the pan juices or pan sauce over the meat and serve.

PORK ORLOFF COCKAIGNE

Ethan Becker fell in love with Veal Orloff while he was a student at the Cordon Bleu in Paris. Back in Cincinnati, he had a difficult time finding a good veal roast and improvised on a classic with a pork roast. Substituting pork for veal makes a wonderful dish that is a standout on its own.

Prepare:

Slow-Roasted Boneless Pork Loin, above

While the loin is in the oven, prepare:

1½ recipes Becker Duxelles, 387

When the roast is done, spread a thin layer of the duxelles in the serving platter. Slice the roast. Spread the pork slices with the duxelles and reassemble the roast. Finish with a line of duxelles along the top of the roast. Garnish with:

Chopped fresh parsley or chopped watercress

Serve at once with:

Sautéed Tiny New Potatoes, 412

BONELESS PORK LOIN WITH ROASTED RED PEPPER GRAVY

6 servings

A garlicky spice-rubbed pork loin served with a gravy made with pureed roasted red peppers.

Prepare:

Roast Red Pepper Sauce, 58

Set aside.

Position a rack in the center of the oven. Preheat the oven to 450°F.

Mix together:

1 tablespoon sweet paprika
1 teaspoon salt
½ to 1 teaspoon ground red pepper, or to taste
½ teaspoon ground cinnamon

Drop in and mix well to coat:

24 very thin slivers garlic (3 to 4 cloves)

Make 24 small incisions in:

1 boneless center-cut pork loin roast (about 3 pounds)

Stuff the incisions with the garlic slivers and rub the remaining spice mixture evenly over the entire surface of the roast. Roast for 10 minutes. Reduce the oven temperature to 250°F and roast until a meat thermometer inserted in the thickest part of the meat registers 150° to 155°F, about 45 to 80 minutes (the temperature will continue to rise about 5° out of the oven). Remove the roast to a cutting board, cover loosely with aluminum foil, and let stand for 15 minutes. Skim the fat off the pan juices. Pour the reserved red pepper sauce into the pan, set the pan over low heat, and scrape up any browned bits from the bottom with a wooden spoon. Season with:

Salt to taste

Slice the meat and serve with the sauce. Garnish with:

Snipped fresh chives

FLORENTINE BONELESS ROAST PORK (ARISTA DI MAIALE)

6 servings

Arista derives from the Greek word *aristos*, meaning "best," as in "aristocrat." According to Italian gastronome Pelligrino Artusi (1820–1911), the name was first applied to this dish by Greek Orthodox clergymen who were served Tuscan-style roast pork at a council in Florence in 1430: "Arista! Arista!" they reportedly exclaimed when they first tasted it. Arista is equally delicious served warm or cold.

Position a rack in the center of the oven. Preheat the oven to 450°F.

Mix together:

4 large cloves garlic, minced
4 teaspoons chopped fresh rosemary
1 teaspoon fennel seeds, crushed (optional)
½ teaspoon salt
½ teaspoon ground black pepper

Make deep incisions in:

1 boneless center-cut pork loin roast (about 3 pounds)

Stuff the incisions with the garlic mixture and spread any remaining over the entire surface of the meat. Rub with:

2 tablespoons olive oil

Roast for 10 minutes. Reduce the oven temperature to 250°F and roast until a meat thermometer inserted in the thickest part of the meat registers 150 to 155°F, about 45 to 80 minutes (the temperature will continue to rise about 5° out of the oven). Remove the roast to a cutting board, cover loosely with aluminum foil, and let stand for 15 minutes. Skim the fat off the pan juices. Slice the meat and serve with the pan juices.

ALMOND-CRUSTED ROASTED BONELESS PORK LOIN

6 servings

The spicy yogurt marinade keeps the pork loin moist, and the toasty chopped almond crust produces an appealing contrast of texture and flavor.

Whisk together in a small bowl:

¾ cup yogurt
2 cloves garlic, minced
2 tablespoons olive oil
1 tablespoon fresh lemon or lime juice
1 teaspoon dry mustard
½ teaspoon ground black pepper

Place in a shallow baking dish:

1 boneless center-cut pork loin roast (about 3 pounds)

Pour the marinade over the roast and roll to coat all sides. Cover and refrigerate for at least 6 hours or up to 24 hours.

Position a rack in the center of the oven. Preheat the oven to 450°F.

Mix together:

1 cup finely chopped almonds
½ cup fresh breadcrumbs
½ teaspoon salt

Scrape off most of the marinade from the roast, then roll in the nut mixture and press the crumbs into the meat. Roast for 10 minutes. Reduce the oven temperature to 250°F and roast until a meat thermometer inserted in the thickest part of the meat registers 150 to 155°F, about 45 to 60 minutes (the temperature will continue to rise about 5° out of the oven). Remove the roast to a cutting board, cover loosely with aluminum foil, and let stand for 15 minutes. Skim the fat off the pan juices. Slice the meat and serve with the pan juices.

SEED-CRUSTED ROASTED BONELESS PORK LOIN

For an alternative flavor with the same appealing crunch, make a seed crust using your favorite spice, alone or in combination with other spices.

Prepare Almond-Crusted Roasted Boneless Pork Loin, above, omitting the almonds and increasing the breadcrumbs to 1 cup. Mix 1 to 2 tablespoons whole seed spices, such as fennel, sesame, mustard, caraway, poppy, or cumin, with the crumbs.

STUFFED BONELESS PORK LOIN WITH APPLES

6 servings

Dried apples vary greatly in tenderness and moisture content; the natural variety, sold at health-food stores, requires longer cooking and more liquid than supermarket dried apples. Some natural dried apples also "balloon" during cooking, producing half again as much stuffing as you need. Any extra stuffing can be baked in a small casserole alongside the pork and basted with a little butter, apple juice, or chicken stock.

Melt in a large skillet over medium-low heat:

4 tablespoons (½ stick) unsalted butter

Add:

2 cups finely chopped onions

Cook, stirring often, until softened and golden brown, about 15 minutes. Add:

6 ounces moist supermarket-type dried apples, or 4 to 5 ounces natural dried apples, chopped
1 to 1½ cups apple cider or apple juice
½ cup fruity white wine, such as Riesling

Bring to a boil. Reduce the heat to low, cover, and cook until the apples are no longer chewy but still retain some texture, about 20 minutes. If the liquid cooks off before the apples are done, add more cider or juice; if there is still liquid in the pan when the apples are done, boil it off. The mixture must be very dry. Remove from the heat and stir in:

¼ to ¾ cup fine fresh breadcrumbs

The mixture must be stiff enough to hold its shape when formed into a ball. Add:

2 to 3 teaspoons finely shredded fresh sage
½ teaspoon salt
¼ teaspoon ground black pepper
¼ teaspoon freshly grated or ground nutmeg

Position a rack in the center of the oven. Preheat the oven to 450°F.

Make 24 incisions in:

1 boneless center-cut pork loin roast (about 3 pounds)

Toss together:

24 very thin slivers garlic (3 to 4 cloves)
4 teaspoons finely shredded sage leaves
1 teaspoon salt
¼ teaspoon ground black pepper

Stuff the incisions with the herbed garlic and rub the remaining herb mixture over the roast. Turn the roast fat side down. Make a long, straight cut lengthwise down the center of the loin just to the center of the meat. Then, starting inside that cut and holding the knife at a slight angle, make a cut to the left and a cut to the right, both about 1½ inches deep. This is called a "Y" cut, because if you could see a cross section of the meat, it would look like an inverse "Y." Spread about 2 cups of the stuffing inside the roast and reshape it. (Bake extra stuffing in a buttered dish with the roast.) Tie the roast at 2-inch intervals and place it upside down on a rack in a roasting pan. Roast for 10 minutes. Reduce the oven temperature to 250°F and roast for about 1 hour. Then turn the roast right side up and cook until a meat thermometer inserted in the thickest part of the meat registers 150 to 155°F, 10 to 20 minutes more (the temperature will continue to rise about 5° out of the oven). Remove the roast to a cutting board, cover loosely with aluminum foil, and let stand for 15 minutes. While the pork roasts, make a sauce. Combine in a saucepan:

1 very large or 2 medium Golden Delicious or Granny Smith apples (10 to 12 ounces), cut into ½-inch chunks with peel and core
1½ cups apple cider or apple juice

Bring to a boil. Reduce the heat, cover, and simmer until translucent, about 20 minutes. Strain through a fine sieve or food mill set over a bowl, pushing the apple pulp through with a spoon if using a sieve. Return the liquid and apple pulp to the saucepan and add:

2 tablespoons sugar

Bring to a boil, then reduce the heat and cook until it thickens and begins to sputter, 10 to 15 minutes. When the roast is done, remove to a cutting board, cover loosely with aluminum foil, and let stand for 15 minutes. Skim off the fat from the pan juices, place the roasting pan over medium heat, and add:

⅓ cup Cognac or brandy

Bring to a boil, stirring to loosen and dissolve any browned bits, then add the liquid to the apple puree and boil down if necessary to thicken. Stir in:

2 tablespoons unsalted butter

Season to taste with:

Fresh lemon juice
Salt and ground black pepper

Slice the pork, pour the sauce over the slices, and serve.

STUFFED BONELESS PORK LOIN WITH PRUNES

Prepare Stuffed Boneless Pork Loin with Apples, above, substituting pitted prunes for the dried apples, prune juice for the apple cider, and a fruity red wine, such as Beaujolais, for the white wine. Omit the apple puree. Deglaze the roasting pan with ⅓ cup Armagnac or Cognac. Add enough chicken stock to measure 1 cup pan juices and reduce to about ¾ cup or until slightly thickened. Whisk in 2 to 4 tablespoons softened unsalted butter. Taste and adjust the seasonings and spoon over the sliced pork.

BONE-IN PORK LOIN ROAST *6 servings*

Pork loin roasted on the bone has more flavor than a boneless loin roast but needs to cook slightly longer. Have the butcher cut the chine bone (backbone) for easy carving through each chop. Rack of pork, a rib roast on the bone with the chine bone completely removed (the cut used for a crown roast), is also available, but it is not as flavorful. You can substitute any of the rubs or seasoning mixtures for boneless pork loin roast for the one given here.

Position a rack in the lower third of the oven. Preheat the oven to 450°F.

Mix together:

1 tablespoon olive or other vegetable oil
2 teaspoons dried thyme
2 teaspoons ground allspice
1 teaspoon salt
½ teaspoon ground black pepper

Rub the mixture over the entire surface of:

1 bone-in center-cut pork loin roast (about 5 pounds)

Place the roast directly in a roasting pan. There is no need for a roasting rack, because the roast rests on the flat chine bone. Roast the pork initially for 15 minutes, then reduce the oven temperature to 250°F and roast until a meat thermometer inserted in the thickest part of the meat registers 155 to 160°F, about 80 to 90 minutes more. Remove the roast to a cutting board, cover loosely with aluminum foil, and let stand for 15 minutes. Skim the fat off the pan juices. If desired, add stock to the pan juices and boil to thicken as in Slow-Roasted Boneless Pork Loin, 689. Slice the roast and serve with the pan juices or pan sauce.

PORK LOIN BRAISED IN MILK *6 servings*

Pork cooked by this Italian method was popularized in this country by the great Italian cooking teacher and cookbook author Marcella Hazan. Use a pork loin from the shoulder or sirloin end, as they are more succulent than the center cut. You can also use Boston butt, shoulder, or sirloin roast, and the pork can be either boneless or bone-in. Boneless is best for even browning of the meat, but with bone-in pork, the sauce will have enormous flavor. If you buy boneless pork, ask the butcher for a couple of bones and add them to the pot.

Heat in a heavy pot, just large enough to hold the pork, over medium heat:

1 tablespoon unsalted butter

Add:

2½ pounds boneless pork loin or 3 pounds bone-in pork loin, or other cut

Brown the meat evenly on all sides, about 10 minutes total. If the butter browns too much, reduce the heat. Add:

1 cup milk

Bring to a boil, reduce the heat to low, and simmer, with the cover just slightly askew, for 1 hour, turning the meat occasionally. The milk will reduce and caramelize. Add:

2 cups milk

Bring back to a boil, reduce the heat to low, cover the pot completely, and simmer for 1½ to 2 hours more, turning the meat occasionally, until it is very tender when pierced with the tip of a sharp knife. Remove the meat to a cutting board and let stand. Spoon off the fat from the surface of the sauce and bring to a boil. Cook until browned and thickened slightly, about 5 to 10 minutes. You will see lots of milk clusters, which will brown as well; if you cook the sauce down too far and it becomes too thick, add a couple of tablespoons of water and stir. Season the sauce, if desired, with:

Salt and ground black pepper to taste

Slice the meat and arrange on a platter. Season the slices with salt and pepper to taste, spoon the sauce over the meat with all the clusters of milk, and serve.

PORK CROWN ROAST

10 to 12 servings

Most butchers will prepare a crown roast for you, but make sure the roasts used are of uniform size so that they cook evenly. Crown roasts are sometimes cooked stuffed; we prefer to bake the stuffing separately in a casserole. This makes it easier to transfer the roast to a platter, and yields plenty of juices for gravy.

Have ready:

1 pork crown roast (8 to 10 pounds)

Prepare and place in a casserole:

Basic Bread Stuffing, 482, Bread Stuffing with Sausage and Apples, 483, Bread Stuffing with Toasted Nuts or Chestnuts and Dried Fruit, 483, or Sweet Potato and Apple Stuffing, 485

Position a rack in the lower third of the oven. Preheat the oven to 450°F.

Mix together:

2 tablespoons vegetable or olive oil
4 teaspoons dried thyme
4 teaspoons ground allspice
2 teaspoons salt
1 teaspoon ground black pepper

Rub the mixture over the surface of the crown roast and roast for 15 minutes. Reduce the oven temperature to 250°F and roast until a meat thermometer inserted in the thickest part of the meat registers 155° to 160°F, 2 to 3 hours (the temperature will continue to rise 5° out of the oven). After 1½ hours of roasting, bake the stuffing in a separate covered casserole until heated through. Remove the roast to a cutting board, cover loosely with aluminum foil, and let stand for 15 minutes. Skim the fat off the pan juices and add to the roasting pan:

½ cup Madeira or dry white wine

Bring to a simmer, scraping up the browned bits on the bottom of the pan. Remove to a saucepan and add:

1½ cups chicken stock

Bring to a boil and cook to concentrate the flavor if the juices taste thin and weak. If you want to thicken the juices to make gravy, mix together in a small bowl:

2 tablespoons cornstarch
2 tablespoons cold water

Reduce the heat and pour the cornstarch mixture into the simmering, not boiling, juices, whisking until smooth. Bring to a boil to thicken, adjust the seasoning, and serve with the roast cut into chops and a spoonful of stuffing.

ROASTED PORK SHOULDER WITH LEMON GLAZE

8 servings

You can substitute lime, orange, or tangerine juice, alone or in combination, for the lemon juice if you wish.

Position a rack in the lower third of the oven. Preheat the oven to 325°F. Line a roasting pan with aluminum foil and place a rack in it.

Combine in a small saucepan:

1 cup fresh lemon juice
1 cup sugar

Bring to a boil over medium heat to dissolve the sugar. Remove to a bowl. Remove the skin from:

1 picnic shoulder (about 7 pounds)

Score the fat and flesh 1 to 1½ inches deep and place the roast on the rack in the pan. Roast for 30 minutes, then baste with the lemon glaze. Roast, basting every 15 to 20 minutes with the glaze, until a meat thermometer inserted in the thickest part of the meat reads 185°F, 4 to 4½ hours total cooking time (the temperature will continue to rise about 5° out of the oven). Let the roast stand, loosely covered with aluminum foil, for 20 minutes before carving. Cut into slices and season with:

Salt and ground black pepper to taste

LATIN ROASTED PORK SHOULDER *8 servings*

The picnic shoulder is among the tastiest of pork roasts. Here it is seasoned in the traditional Latin manner with oregano and garlic. Brushing the skin with water during roasting makes the crisp, brittle skin tender enough to eat.

Mash to a paste with a mortar and pestle or very finely chop with a knife:

12 large cloves garlic
2 tablespoons salt

Remove the mixture to a bowl and stir in:

2 tablespoons dried oregano
1 tablespoon ground black pepper

Moisten to a pastelike consistency with:

1 to 2 tablespoons red wine vinegar

With a paring knife, cut deep tunnels into the exposed fleshy ends of:

1 picnic shoulder (about 7 pounds)

Push two-thirds of the paste into the pockets with your fingers. Loosen the skin in several places and spread the rest of the paste underneath the skin and over the surface of the roast where there is no skin. Wrap the roast tightly in 2 layers of aluminum foil and refrigerate for 24 to 48 hours.

Position a rack in the lower third of the oven. Preheat the oven to 325°F.

Arrange the roast on a rack in a roasting pan and roast to an internal temperature of 185°F, 4 to 4½ hours (the temperature will continue to rise 5° out of the oven), brushing the skin every 15 to 20 minutes with cold water to help keep it soft. Let the roast stand, loosely covered with aluminum foil, for 20 minutes before carving. Skim off the fat from the pan juices and add:

1 cup chicken stock, or ½ cup chicken stock and ½ cup white wine

Bring to a boil, scraping up the browned bits on the bottom of the pan. Cook over high heat for 2 to 3 minutes to dissolve the roasting particles. Remove the skin from the meat and cut it into strips or squares. Slice the meat, arrange on a platter, and pour the sauce over it. Arrange the skin around the meat and serve.

PULLED PORK SANDWICHES *About 12 sandwiches*

In many parts of the country, this is what is meant by barbecue. Pulled pork is pork shoulder cooked until it is tender enough to be shredded with a fork. After being pulled apart, it is mixed with a sauce and served on a bun.

Trim the excess fat from:

1 boneless Boston butt or pork shoulder blade roast (about 4 pounds)

Rub the meat with:

Southern Dry Rub for Barbecue, 86

The meat can be cooked at once or wrapped in 2 layers of aluminum foil and refrigerated for up to 24 hours.

Position a rack in the center of the oven. Preheat the oven to 325°F.

Heat a heavy ovenproof pot large enough to hold the meat over medium heat. Add and heat:

2 tablespoons lard or vegetable oil

Add the meat and brown well on all sides. Cover the pot tightly with foil or a lid, place in the oven, and bake until the meat is tender enough to be shredded easily with a fork, 3 to 3½ hours. Skim off the fat from the pan juices. Shred the meat into strings with a fork and mix with the pan juices. Stir in:

1½ to 2 cups barbecue sauce

Have ready:

Cole Slaw, 222
12 hamburger buns

If necessary, gently reheat the pork over medium-low heat. To make each sandwich, spoon the pork on the bottom half of the buns, top with some slaw, and cover with the top half of the buns.

PULLED PORK, NORTH CAROLINA-STYLE

In North Carolina, cooks season pulled pork with a tangy vinegar-based sauce in place of barbecue sauce. Prepare Pulled Pork Sandwiches, above, replacing the barbecue sauce with a combination of ¾ cup white vinegar, ¾ cup cider vinegar, 1 tablespoon hot red pepper sauce or more to taste, 1 tablespoon sugar, 2 teaspoons crushed red pepper flakes, and salt and cracked black peppercorns to taste.

ROASTED LEG OF PORK OR FRESH HAM

15 to 20 servings

A whole pork leg, also known as fresh uncured ham, is a perfect dish for feeding a large crowd and great for holidays. Cooking times are approximate because the weight of fresh hams is variable; for best results, use a meat thermometer. If your fresh ham weighs more than 20 pounds, increase the cooking time accordingly. Plan on about 1 pound per person, less if there are numerous side dishes. Ask your butcher to remove most of the skin, leaving that around the shank. Score the fat and meat deeply and rub with seasonings to obtain a crisp, savory crust.

Position a rack in the lower third of the oven. Preheat the oven to 425°F.

Remove the skin, up to but not including the shank from:

1 bone-in pork leg or fresh ham (15 to 20 pounds)

Score the fat and meat 1 to 1½ inches deep in a diamond pattern 1 to 1½ inches apart.

Mix together:

2 tablespoons olive or other vegetable oil
1 tablespoon salt
2 teaspoons dried sage, thyme, savory, oregano, or crumbled rosemary
2 teaspoons ground black pepper

Rub this mixture over the entire surface of the ham. Scatter in a large roasting pan:

2 large onions, cut into 1-inch slices
4 carrots, cut into 1-inch slices
4 celery stalks, cut into 1-inch slices
1 bay leaf

Place the fresh ham on the bed of cut vegetables. Roast for 30 minutes, then reduce the oven temperature to 325°F. Roast for 1 hour more, then pour over the meat:

2 cups dry white wine

Roast, basting every 20 to 30 minutes, until a meat thermometer inserted in the thickest part of the meat registers 185°F, 2½ to 3½ hours more, 4 to 5 hours or longer if the fresh ham is large (the temperature will continue to rise 5° to 10° out of the oven). Remove the ham to a large platter, cover loosely with aluminum foil, and let stand for 30 to 60 minutes. Pour off the fat from the pan. Add to the pan:

2 cups chicken stock

Bring to a simmer, scraping up the browned bits on the bottom of the pan. Strain the juices into a saucepan and boil until slightly thickened. Taste and adjust the seasonings. If you want to thicken the juices to make a gravy, mix together:

3 tablespoons cornstarch
3 tablespoons cold water

Whisk into the simmering, not boiling, juices. Bring to a boil, whisking to thicken. To carve the meat, cut it into slices starting at the shank end, keeping the knife perpendicular to the bone. Then make one long slice with your knife along the bone to separate the slices from the leg. Arrange the slices on a platter and serve with the pan juices or gravy, if desired.

ROASTED SUCKLING PIG

8 to 12 servings

Have the butcher prepare the pig for you by cleaning it well and removing all organs, including the kidneys. If you want to put a small apple, lemon, or lime in the cooked pig's mouth, you will need to prop open the mouth with a piece of wood or a ball of aluminum foil before cooking. Some butchers will open the mouth for you if you ask. There is not as much meat on a suckling pig as you would expect. A 15- to 20-pound pig, while large, yields just enough meat for eight to twelve people; most of the weight is in the head and bones. The taste and texture of the meat is heavenly, melting in the mouth. If you have a standard oven about 23 inches wide, you will have no problem. If your oven is smaller inside, you may have to prop the head up to fit the pig in. A 20-inch roasting pan is ideal, but anything 17 inches or larger will work. Do not use a disposable aluminum pan, for it will collapse under the weight of the pig. The pig is simply stuffed, seasoned, and roasted with some white wine for basting. The stuffing can be prepared up to a day ahead and refrigerated.

Generously oil a 20-inch roasting pan. If the pan is smaller (no smaller than 17 inches), have ready a loaf pan and lots of heavy-duty aluminum foil.

The day before or just before roasting, prepare one of the following stuffings (you will need 12 cups):

1½ recipes Basic Bread Stuffing, 482, 1 recipe Bread Stuffing with Toasted Nuts or Chestnuts and Dried Fruit, 483, 1½ recipes Sweet Potato and Apple Stuffing, 485, or 3 recipes Couscous Stuffing with Dried Apricots and Pistachios, 486

Position a rack at the lowest rung of the oven. Preheat the oven to 450°F.

Place in the sink:

1 suckling pig (15 to 20 pounds)

Check to make sure that no bristles or hairs remain; if any do, shave them off with a razor blade or singe them off with a flame. Rinse the pig well inside and out and pat dry. Turn the pig on its back and fill the cavity loosely with the stuffing. Truss with string or skewers about 2 inches apart. Tie the hind legs together and pull them forward over the belly. Keep the legs side by side, not crossed; the legs will act as a roasting rack. Pull the front legs back, placing one on either side of the hind legs. Tie all 4 legs together under the pig, keeping them side by side. Turn the pig over. Slash the skin on either side of the backbone in long parallel diagonal cuts about 2 inches apart to release the fat and prevent the skin from swelling and breaking during cooking and also to allow the fat to baste the meat. Avoid cutting below the layer of back fat and into the meat. Mix together:

½ cup extra-virgin olive oil
2 tablespoons salt
1 tablespoon ground black pepper

Rub over the entire pig. Remove the pig to the roasting pan, resting it on its haunches and keeping it upright. If your pan is too small, arrange the pig diagonally in the pan and prop its head up with a loaf pan under its chin. Arrange heavy-duty aluminum foil extending out from the roasting pan under the head and loaf pan to catch the juices and let them flow back into the pan during cooking. If the pig has a tendency to lean, prop it with balls of aluminum foil where needed. Alternatively, lay the pig on its side; this method requires turning the pig during cooking. Cover the ears and tail with pieces of foil. If desired, pry open the pig's mouth with a screwdriver and prop open with a ball of aluminum foil or a wooden block. Place the pig in the oven and roast for 30 minutes. Reduce the oven temperature to 350°F. Pour into the roasting pan:

3 cups dry white wine

Rub the pig all over with:

½ cup olive oil

Roast the pig until a meat thermometer inserted in the thickest part of the rump reads 165° to 170°F, 2 to 2½ hours more (the temperature will continue to rise 5° to 10° out of the oven). Baste the pig every 20 minutes with the wine and pan juices. When the pig is done, carefully remove it to a platter and let stand for 30 to 60 minutes. Skim off the fat from the pan juices. Place the roasting pan over medium-high heat and add:

2 cups chicken stock

Bring to a simmer, stirring to scrape up the browned bits on the bottom of the pan. Pour the juices into a saucepan. If you want to thicken the juices to make a gravy, mix together:

¼ cup cornstarch
3 tablespoons water

Whisk into the simmering, not boiling, juices. Bring to a boil, whisking, to thicken. If the gravy tastes weak, cook it down until it is flavorful. Season with:

Salt and ground black pepper to taste

Remove the foil from the pig's ears and tail. Gently roll it on its side and remove the string and/or skewers. Return the pig to its right-side-up position. Remove the foil ball or wooden block if using. If desired, place in the pig's mouth:

1 apple, lemon, or lime

and in the eyes:

2 prunes or cranberries

Arrange around the pig:

A bed of greens

After presenting the pig at the table, carve by removing the forelegs and hindquarters and arranging these on a platter. Cut the skin into squares. Remove the loin meat and cut into slices. Arrange the slices and skin on the platter and let the guests pick at the rest. Quickly reheat the pan juices or gravy and pass in a sauceboat.

ABOUT PORK TENDERLOIN

Pork tenderloin was traditionally sold attached to a bone-in loin roast, hiding beside the backbone. Since the 1980s, though, it has been increasingly available as a separate cut. Tenderloin is very low in fat—nearly as low as skinless chicken breast—and very tender, with good flavor. It cooks quickly and is best suited to such dry-heat techniques as pan-frying, pan-roasting or -broiling, grilling, sautéing, and deep-frying. It can also be roasted, but only at 500°F; because it lacks fat, lower temperatures dry out the meat before it is cooked through and browned. Tenderloin can be cooked whole or cut into medallions; medallions can be pounded into thin cutlets or scaloppine. Cut these from the thicker end of the tenderloin and save the tails for pan-frying or pan-broiling in one piece. Tenderloin is also perfect cut into cubes or strips for kebabs, satays, or stir-fries. Another possibility is to butterfly the tenderloin, either whole or in two or three pieces (see Kentucky-Fried Pork Tenderloin, below) for even quicker cooking. Because tenderloin is so lean, take care not to overcook it—it should always remain juicy with a pale pink color. Cook a whole one as you would a loin roast, to an internal temperature of 150° to 155°F, let stand for a few minutes, and serve. Cut-up tenderloin cooks in just a few minutes per side, depending on its thickness. Tenderloins are generally sold prepackaged with two whole ones in each package. The best tenderloins are the smaller ones, about 8 to 12 ounces each, generally enough for two servings.

SAUTÉED PORK TENDERLOIN MEDALLIONS

4 servings

A classic brown sauce or a variation, 48 to 50, is a wonderful accompaniment to these quickly cooked pork tenderloin medallions; or make a pan sauce.

Pat dry and cut crosswise into 1-inch-thick slices:

1 pound pork tenderloin, the thicker ends

Season with:

Salt and ground black pepper to taste

Heat in a large skillet over high heat:

1½ teaspoons butter
1½ teaspoons olive oil

Add the tenderloin medallions in batches and pan-fry for 2 minutes, being careful not to crowd the pan. Cook for 1½ to 2 minutes. They will be well browned on the outside and moist and slightly pink in the center. Remove to plates or a platter. Pour off the excess fat from the pan and, if desired, serve with:

Sauce Piquant, 51, or Buttered Cider Sauce, 1049

Spoon the sauce over the medallions and serve.

PORK TENDERLOIN SCALOPPINE WITH CITRUS BALSAMIC SAUCE

4 servings

These scaloppine are cut thinner than medallions and cook very quickly, so do not walk away after you put them in the pan.

Pat dry:

1 pound pork tenderloin, cut crosswise into ½-inch-thick slices

Pound them to a little less than ¼ inch thick. Season with:

Salt and ground black pepper to taste

Heat in a large skillet over high heat:

1½ teaspoons butter
1½ teaspoons olive oil

Cook the scaloppine in batches for 30 to 60 seconds each side. They will be well browned on the outside and moist and slightly pink in the center. Remove the scaloppine to a warmed platter. Place the skillet over medium-high heat and add:

3 to 4 tablespoons minced scallions or shallots
1 tablespoon honey
Pinch of ground allspice

Cook, stirring, until the scallions or shallots are soft, 1 to 2 minutes. Increase the heat to high and add:

1 cup chicken stock
1 tablespoon strained fresh lemon juice

Boil, scraping up the browned bits from the bottom of the skillet with a wooden spoon, until reduced by half. Add and boil until the sauce thickens slightly, about 1 minute:

¼ cup heavy cream

Add:

1 tablespoon balsamic vinegar
Salt and ground black pepper to taste

Return the sauce to a boil, then spoon over the pork and serve immediately.

KENTUCKY-FRIED PORK TENDERLOIN

6 servings

In Kentucky, this spicy pork dish is usually served for breakfast, but it also makes a terrific sandwich or main course at dinner. Grill the tenderloin instead of pan-frying for a smokier taste.

In a small bowl, combine:

1 tablespoon sweet paprika
1½ teaspoons salt
1½ teaspoons ground black pepper
½ teaspoon garlic powder
½ teaspoon dried sage
½ teaspoon dried oregano
½ teaspoon dry mustard
½ teaspoon ground red pepper

Pat dry:

2 pork tenderloins (about 12 ounces each), cut into 6 crosswise pieces

Butterfly each piece by making a lengthwise cut along the side of the meat, holding the knife parallel to the surface. Do not cut all the way through the meat; leave a ½ inch intact on one side to form a hinge as you fold the piece open like a book and flatten it gently with your hand. Sprinkle evenly with the spice mixture and rub it in. Marinate for 30 to 60 minutes in the refrigerator. Heat in a large skillet over medium-high heat:

¼ inch vegetable oil

Dredge each tenderloin piece in:

½ cup all-purpose flour

Shake off the excess. Add the pieces to the skillet in batches and fry until nicely browned on one side, 3 to 4 minutes. Turn over and fry on the other side for 3 to 4 minutes. They should be well browned on the outside and moist and slightly pink in the center. Remove the pork to a platter and keep warm. Pour off all but 2 tablespoons of fat from the pan. Add:

1 cup milk

Heat just to a boil, scraping up any browned bits on the bottom of the pan. Pour the gravy over the pork. You can strain it if you wish. There is no need to add thickener; the flour from the pork is enough to create a gravy. For breakfast, serve with:

Biscuits, 789 to 791

For lunch, on:

Soft rolls

with:

Cole Slaw, 222
Sliced tomatoes

For supper, with:

Gratin Dauphinois, 412
Steamed or braised kale, chard, or mustard greens

PAN-ROASTED TENDERLOIN *4 servings*

Whole pork tenderloin is kept moist by being browned in a pan on top of the stove first, then simmered until done. If your tenderloins weigh more than 8 ounces, adjust the cooking times accordingly. A savory fruit sauce makes a fine accompaniment.

Pat dry:

2 pork tenderloins (8 to 12 ounces each)

Season with:

Salt and ground black pepper to taste

Heat in a large skillet over high heat:

1½ teaspoons unsalted butter

1½ teaspoons olive oil

Brown well on all sides. Reduce the heat to medium and cook, turning once or twice, until an instant-read thermometer inserted in the thickest part of the meat reads 150° to 155°F, 10 to 15 minutes (the temperature will continue to rise 5° to 10° off the heat). Remove to a plate, cover loosely with aluminum foil, and let stand for 5 to 10 minutes before slicing. If a sauce is desired, pour off all the fat from the skillet. Place over medium-high heat and add:

Blackberry Sage Sauce, 54, or Orange and Ginger Sauce, 54

Bring to a boil, scraping up any browned bits from the bottom. Cook until hot. Slice the meat, spoon the sauce over the tenderloin, and serve.

SAUTÉED BRAISED PORK TENDERLOIN WITH QUICK PAN SAUCE *4 servings*

This technique is similar to pan-roasting, except the pan is covered after the meat is browned, giving the cook lots of juices with which to make a sauce when the tenderloin is done. The crust doesn't lose much of its glaze, and the meat emerges moist and tender. For a simpler presentation, skip the sauce and spoon the pan juices over the sliced meat.

If desired, choose one of the following pan sauces and have the ingredients ready for:

Pan Sauce with Leeks, Orange, and Rosemary, 53, or Basic Herb Pan Sauce, 52

Pat dry:

2 pork tenderloins (8 to 12 ounces each)

Season with:

Salt and ground black pepper to taste

Heat in a large skillet over high heat:

1½ teaspoons butter

1½ teaspoons olive oil

Brown well on both sides, cover the pan, and reduce the heat to low. Cook until the internal temperature reads 150° to 155°F, 15 to 20 minutes (the temperature will continue to rise 5° to 10° off the heat). Remove the tenderloins to a plate, cover loosely with aluminum foil, and let stand for 5 to 10 minutes while you prepare the sauce with the juices in the skillet, if desired. Slice the tenderloins and serve with the pan sauce, if using, or with the pan juices seasoned to taste with:

Salt and ground black pepper

GRILLED PORK TENDERLOIN *4 servings*

Grill tenderloin whole, in medallions, or cut into large cubes for kebabs; anything smaller dries out too quickly. Remember that gas grills are not as hot as charcoal grills and so require longer cooking times. Please read Grilling, 1055, for more information. Sauces for grilled tenderloin can be a barbecue sauce, a flavored butter, or a more contemporary dry rub, condiment, dipping sauce, vinaigrette, glaze, or salsa. See the Stocks & Savory Sauces or Condiments, Marinades, & Rubs chapters for ideas.

Prepare a medium-hot charcoal fire.

Pat dry:

2 pork tenderloins (about 8 to 12 ounces each), left whole or cut crosswise into 1-inch-thick medallions

Rub the tenderloin with:

1 tablespoon olive or other vegetable oil

Season with:

Salt and ground black pepper to taste

Grill the whole tenderloins for 8 to 10 minutes on each side until an instant-read thermometer inserted in the thickest part of the meat reads 150° to 155°F (the temperature will continue to rise 5° to 10° off the grill). Let stand, loosely covered with aluminum foil, for 5 to 10 minutes before slicing. Medallions take about 2 minutes each side.

Season with:

Salt and ground black pepper to taste

If desired, serve with:

Pear Chutney, 68, Salsa Fresca, 61, or lemon wedges

SPICE-RUBBED GRILLED PORK TENDERLOIN

Prepare Grilled Pork Tenderloin, above, omitting the oil, salt, and pepper. Rub the tenderloin with Southern Dry Rub for Barbecue, 86, or West Indies Dry Rub, 88, 2 to 24 hours before you plan to serve it. Refrigerate, covered, until ready to grill.

ROASTED SESAME PORK TENDERLOIN *6 servings*

This is a much leaner version of those glistening strips of pork, called *char su,* displayed in shops throughout

Chinatowns. This tasty, crunchy meat can be eaten hot or at room temperature. Serve leftovers on a bed of stir-fried vegetables.

Combine:

¼ cup soy sauce
¼ cup hoisin sauce
¼ cup honey
2 tablespoons packed brown sugar
1 tablespoon toasted sesame oil
1 tablespoon grated peeled fresh ginger
1 teaspoon minced garlic

Trim:

2 pork tenderloins (about 12 ounces each)

Place tenderloins in a large, heavy plastic bag or a shallow baking dish. Add the marinade and turn to coat evenly. Close the bag or cover the dish and marinate for at least 2 hours or up to 24 hours in the refrigerator. Position a rack in the center of the oven. Preheat the oven to 500°F.

Spread on a plate:

½ cup sesame seeds

Remove the meat from the marinade, drain off the excess, and roll in the sesame seeds to coat. Remove to a rack in a shallow roasting pan. Roast the tenderloin until an instant-read thermometer inserted in the thickest part of the meat reads 150° to 155°F, 20 to 25 minutes (the temperature will continue to rise 5° to 10° out of the oven). Let the pork stand, loosely covered with aluminum foil, for 5 to 10 minutes, then slice.

ABOUT PORK CHOPS, STEAKS, AND CUTLETS

The terms chops, steaks, and cutlets are somewhat interchangeable, but you can most often expect a chop to be a single-serving, thick cut of meat from the pork loin with the bone in—although they may be sold boneless. The term steak is used a bit more loosely for any thick slice of meat, and cutlets refer to thinner boneless cuts from the loin or leg. Pork chops cut from the pork loin have a variety of names. Starting at the shoulder end are pork loin blade chops (also called blade steaks). Next, from the center section, come rib chops and loin chops, the latter containing the tenderloin and resembling a T-bone or porterhouse beef steak. The tenderest pork chops are cut from the center section of the pork loin; these are sold in varying thicknesses. After the center section come the sirloin chops, which are larger and sometimes cut thin for a cutlet. Pork steaks can be cut from the leg, shoulder, or loin. The leg offers tip, top, bottom, and eye steaks from different muscles and a whole crosswise center slice for a larger steak.

Pork chops from the loin are best cooked by dry-heat methods—pan-frying, pan-broiling, sautéing, or grilling. When sautéing chops that are 1 inch thick or thicker, it is best to begin by browning the chops over high heat, then reducing the heat and covering for 4 to 5 minutes to cook through without drying out the surface. Braising works for blade and sirloin chops and for shoulder and leg steaks, but not for classic pork loin chops, which can easily become overcooked and tough when cooked in liquid. Look for pork loin chops that are about 1 inch thick, though they can be slightly thicker or thinner. For cutlets, we suggest ¼ to ½ inch of thickness, and for stuffing, 1½ to 2 inches. We also sometimes find pork loin medallions, which are slices of boneless center loin cut any thickness. Sauté quickly if thin or cook slowly, covering and reducing the heat after browning, if 1 inch or thicker. Pork chops and medallions, pan-fried or sautéed, are good choices if you want a sauce, for pan sauces are easily put together right in the skillet, dissolving the caramelized juices into the sauce, after the chops have cooked. Or you can prepare a sauce ahead and have it ready to reheat. See Stocks & Sauces, 35, or Condiments, Marinades, & Dry Rubs, 60, for pan sauce or other, sauce ideas.

SAUTÉED PORK CHOPS *4 servings*

The technique of first sautéing over high heat to give the meat a crust and then finishing by covering the pan and reducing the heat works best for all pork chops 1 inch thick, cut from the loin.

Pat dry:

4 center-cut pork loin chops (bone-in or boneless), 1 inch thick

Season with:

Salt and ground black pepper to taste

Heat in a large skillet over high heat:

1½ teaspoons unsalted butter
1½ teaspoons olive or vegetable oil

Brown for 1 minute, turn, and brown for 1 minute more. Reduce the heat to low, cover the pan, and cook the chops for 5 minutes, 4 minutes if boneless. Turn the chops over, cover the pan again, and cook for 5 minutes more, 4 minutes if boneless. They will be well browned on the outside and slightly pink in the center. Remove to a warmed platter or plates. Increase the heat to high and boil down the pan juices. If desired, make a pan sauce or reheat a prepared sauce such as Sauce Marchand de Vin, 51, in the juices.

STUFFED PORK CHOPS

4 servings

Our grandmothers used to braise stuffed pork chops, but chops from today's leaner pork turn dry when cooked by this method. Sautéing first over high heat and then covered over low heat works wonderfully here.

Heat in a small skillet over medium heat:

1 tablespoon olive oil

Add:

1 small onion, chopped
1 small clove garlic, minced
Salt and ground black pepper to taste

Cook for 5 minutes to soften the onion a bit. Remove to a bowl and add:

¼ cup packed finely chopped dried peaches, apricots, or pitted prunes
1 tablespoon chopped fresh basil, or 1 teaspoon dried
1 slice white bread, crumbled
2 tablespoons heavy cream

Mix together with a fork to make a stuffing. With a sharp paring knife, trim the excess fat and cut pockets in:

4 bone-in center-cut pork loin chops, 1 to 1½ inches thick

Make the cut parallel to the cutting board in the middle of the meat and cut almost to the bone. Fill the chops with the stuffing and close with toothpicks. Season with:

Salt and ground black pepper to taste

In a large skillet, melt over high heat:

½ tablespoon butter
½ tablespoon olive or vegetable oil

Place the stuffed chops in the pan and brown for 1 minute on each side. Reduce the heat to low, cover the pan, and cook the chops for 5 minutes more on each side if 1 inch thick or 7 minutes more if 1½ inches thick. Remove to plates. Increase the heat to high to reduce the pan juices if you like. Spoon the pan juices over the chops and serve.

SAUTÉED THIN PORK CHOPS OR MEDALLIONS

4 servings

Use this quick, high-heat method for any chops or medallions that are less than ¾ inch thick.

Pat dry:

8 center-cut pork loin chops, ½ inch thick, or 1 pound boneless center-cut pork loin, cut into ½-inch-thick slices

Season with:

Salt and ground black pepper to taste

Heat in a large skillet over high heat:

1½ teaspoons unsalted butter
1½ teaspoons olive or other vegetable oil

Sauté for 1 minute on each side. If cooking boneless medallions, remove them from the pan, for they are done. They will be well browned on the outside and moist and slightly pink in the center. If the chops are on the bone, reduce the heat to low and cook 2 to 4 minutes more, turning once. If necessary, do this in two batches, adding more butter and oil if needed. Remove to plates. If desired, make a pan sauce, 52 to 54, to spoon over the pork.

PAN-FRIED PORK SCALOPPINE

4 servings

In some parts of the world, delicate pork scaloppine are more common than veal scaloppine. In fact, ordering a Wiener Schnitzel, 684, in Germany will get you a pork cutlet pounded thin, lightly breaded and pan-fried. Make the butter sauce ahead so that the scaloppine do not cool too much.

Prepare:

Beurre Noisette, 57, or a variation, such as Sauce Polonaise, 57

Cook as directed for Sautéed Thin Pork Chops or Medallions, above:

1 pound boneless center-cut pork loin, cut slightly more than ¼ inch thick and pounded to slightly less than ¼ inch thick

Cook the scaloppine for 30 to 60 seconds each side. Remove to plates and season with:

Salt and ground black pepper to taste

Serve with the prepared butter and:

Lemon wedges

BREADED PORK CHOPS OR CUTLETS

4 servings

Thin slices of pork loin or thin pork chops on the bone make tender, juicy breaded chops. Add other herbs or spices to the breadcrumbs for more flavor.

Pat dry:

8 center-cut pork chops, cut ½-inch thick, or 1 pound boneless center-cut pork loin, cut into 1-inch-thick slices

Season with:

Salt and ground black pepper to taste

Mix on a plate:

¾ cup fresh breadcrumbs
1 teaspoon crushed fennel seeds, dried thyme, or oregano

Dredge the chops in:

½ cup all-purpose flour

Shake off the excess and dip in:

1 large egg, lightly beaten

Coat the chops with the seasoned crumbs and set aside on a plate. Heat in a large skillet over medium-high heat:

1 tablespoon unsalted butter

1 tablespoon olive or other vegetable oil

Cook as directed for Sautéed Thin Pork Chops or Medallions, above.

If desired, serve with:

Beurre Noisette, 57

Lemon wedges

GRILLED PORK CHOPS

4 servings

For a cool and vibrant accompaniment, try a relish or salsa from the Condiments, Marinades, & Rubs chapter, such as Mango Salsa, 63, Red Onion Marmalade, 67, or Mojo, 79.

Prepare a medium-hot charcoal fire.

Pat dry:

4 center-cut pork loin chops (bone-in or boneless), ¾ to 1½ inches thick

Rub the chops with:

2 tablespoons olive or other vegetable oil

Season with:

Salt and ground black pepper to taste

Grill over hot coals for 5 to 8 minutes each side for bone-in, or 4 to 6 minutes each side for boneless, depending on thickness. Remove to plates. Serve with the sauce if using.

SPICE-RUBBED GRILLED PORK CHOPS

Prepare Grilled Pork Chops, above, omitting the salt, pepper, and oil. Rub the chops with Southern Dry Rub for Barbecue, 86, or West Indies Dry Rub, 87. 2 to 24 hours before you plan to serve them. Refrigerate, covered, until ready to grill.

ABOUT RIBS

Each of the three main types of pork ribs has its devotees. Spareribs come from the side or underbelly of the pig. They have the least amount of meat of the three types but are very flavorful; plan on 1 pound of spareribs per person. (St. Louis-style ribs are further trimmed spareribs with the breastbone removed.) Back ribs are cut from the loin section, or the back, of the pig, and are sometimes called loin back ribs. These are meatier than spareribs and not as fatty. Baby back ribs are simply a narrower slab of back ribs cut from the rib end and are sometimes called riblets. A whole rack of back ribs weighs between 1½ and 1¾ pounds; count on 1 pound of back ribs per person. Country-style ribs are the meatiest of all ribs, with much less bone than the other types; they are even sometimes sold boneless. Like back ribs, they are cut from the loin section of the pig. Figure on 8 to 12 ounces of country-style ribs per person.

Ribs can be baked, grilled, or braised. The two most important factors in cooking ribs well are time—plenty of it—and temperature—very low. Oven-cooked ribs are best cooked at 300° to 325°F. On the grill, ribs fare best over indirect heat, with the coals pushed to the sides. Ribs are considered done when you can just loosen, or wiggle, the bone from the meat with little effort and the meat is very tender. Ribs take seasonings well and are delicious sauced or covered with a spice rub. If using a sauce on the grill, baste only during the last 30 minutes of cooking: most of these sauces contain some type of sugar or sweetener and tend to burn. Ribs sauced in the gentler heat of the oven can be brushed from the beginning of cooking.

OVEN-ROASTED SPARERIBS

6 servings

These are dry, savory spareribs rather than the sweet, sticky kind made with barbecue sauce.

Pat dry:

2 sides pork spareribs (about 6 pounds)

Combine:

2 teaspoons ground sage

2 teaspoons salt

1 to 2 teaspoons ground black pepper

1 teaspoon dried thyme

6 juniper berries, finely crushed (optional)

Rub the mixture over both sides of the ribs. Arrange the ribs bone side up on a broiler pan or on a rack set in a roasting pan. Cover loosely with wax paper or plastic wrap and refrigerate for 1 to 12 hours.

Position a rack in the center of the oven. Preheat the oven to 350°F.

Roast the ribs for 45 minutes, then turn them meat side up and roast until the ribs are nicely browned and very tender, 45 to 60 minutes more. Remove from the oven and let stand for 15 minutes. Slice between the bones and serve.

COUNTRY-STYLE RIBS BAKED IN BARBECUE SAUCE

6 to 8 servings

After 4 hours of cooking, these ribs become fall-apart tender and deeply infused with the flavor of barbecue sauce. During the final hour, the ribs are cooked uncovered to thicken the sauce and give them a shiny glaze.

Position a rack in the center of the oven. Preheat the oven to 300°F.

Arrange in a 13 x 9-inch baking dish:

4 pounds country-style ribs

Whisk together in a bowl:

1½ cups barbecue sauce

1 cup orange juice

Pour the sauce over the ribs and turn them to coat completely with the sauce. Cover the dish tightly with aluminum foil and bake for 3 hours. Uncover, increase the oven temperature to 350°F, and bake the ribs for 1 hour more, turning them once after 30 minutes. Do not worry if they fall apart a little when turning them over. Remove the ribs to a warmed platter and let stand for 15 minutes. Spoon off the fat from the sauce and serve the ribs with the sauce.

BARBECUED SPARERIBS *6 servings*

You will need a sturdy base of charcoal to remain burning gently for the 2 to 2½ hours it takes to cook these ribs. The best flavor comes from hardwood charcoal lit without lighter fluid. The addition of hickory smoking chips will give these ribs real down-home flavor.

Pat dry:

2 sides pork spareribs (about 6 pounds)

Rub both sides with:

⅔ cup Southern Dry Rub for Barbecue, 86

Refrigerate for 1 to 2 hours or, for a stronger flavor, wrap in plastic and refrigerate for 12 to 24 hours. Prepare a large charcoal fire in a clean 22-inch kettle grill. When the coals are covered with a light ash, push them to one side of the grill. Open the bottom vents of the grill completely. Wrap 2 cups hickory smoking chips in aluminum foil, poke small holes in the foil with a fork, and lay the package on the coals. Put on the grill rack, arrange the rib slabs side by side on the rack as far from the charcoal as possible, and cover with the lid, leaving the top vent two-thirds open. Cook the ribs for 2 to 2½ hours, turning them every 30 minutes. If the fire threatens to die out, add a few more briquettes as far away from the ribs as possible. The ribs are done when the bones begin to pull away from the meat and feel slightly loose when twisted. Immediately wrap the ribs in aluminum foil and let stand for 15 minutes. If you wish, swab the ribs lightly and/or serve them with:

Barbecue Sauce, 90

ABOUT BRAISING AND STEWING PORK

Braising (cooking a whole piece of meat in a small amount of liquid) and stewing (cooking smaller pieces of meat in more liquid) are perfect for the less tender cuts of pork from the shoulder and leg. The cuts from either end of the loin—the blade end or the sirloin end—are best cubed and stewed. Like most braised and stewed dishes, pork prepared this way often tastes better the next day. For more information on stewing and braising, please see About Braising, Stewing, and Pot-Roasting Meat, 640.

BRAISED PORK WITH SAUERKRAUT *8 servings*

The addition of fresh cabbage to the traditional pairing of pork and sauerkraut gives this dish an added dimension of flavor. Use fresh sauerkraut rather than canned if you can find it.

Mix together:

2 teaspoons sweet paprika

1 teaspoon salt

1 teaspoon ground black pepper

½ teaspoon dried sage

½ teaspoon dried thyme

¼ teaspoon dry mustard

Pat dry and rub all over with the spice mix:

4 pounds Boston-style pork shoulder, butt, or blade roast, excess fat trimmed

Marinate the meat for 2 to 24 hours in the refrigerator. Position a rack in the center of the oven. Preheat the oven to 325°F.

Heat in a large, heavy Dutch oven over medium heat:

2 tablespoons olive oil or bacon fat

Add the meat and brown on all sides. Remove to a plate. Pour off all but 2 tablespoons of fat from the pan and add:

4 cups shredded cabbage

2 cups thinly sliced onions

½ cup diced carrots

½ cup thinly sliced leeks (white part only)

Cover the pan and cook, stirring occasionally, over medium heat until the vegetables are softened and the cabbage is wilted, about 10 minutes. Add:

1 tablespoon minced garlic

Cook for 1 minute more. Add:

1 pound sauerkraut, rinsed and drained

1 cup chicken stock

12 ounces dark beer

1 teaspoon caraway seeds

1 teaspoon dried savory

2 bay leaves

Bring to a boil. Return the meat to the pan, nestle it into the cabbage mixture, and cover the pan. Braise it in the oven for 2 hours. Check the meat; it should be fork-tender. If not, cook for 30 to 60 minutes more. Remove the meat from the pan and skim off any fat from the pan juices. Slice the meat and serve with the vegetables and pan juices.

RED-COOKED PORK SHOULDER *8 servings*

Red-cooking is a popular Chinese technique for slow-cooking meat, poultry, and even tofu in a soy-based liquid to give it a deep reddish brown color. Traditionally, the cooking liquid is reserved and used repeatedly, as its flavor intensifies with each use. The meat need not be browned: it gets plenty of color and flavor from the soy sauce. Use a good-quality, naturally fermented soy sauce if you can find one. Plain white rice is an ideal accompaniment.

Heat in a large, heavy Dutch oven over medium-high heat:

1 tablespoon oil

Add and toss in the oil just until heated through, about 1 minute:

4 scallions, cut crosswise in thirds
2 large cloves garlic, crushed
One 1-inch piece fresh ginger, thinly sliced

Add:

4 cups water, or 2 cups chicken stock and 2 cups water
1 cup dark soy sauce
¾ cup rice wine, Scotch, or sherry
¼ cup packed brown sugar
4 star anise, or 1½ teaspoons anise seed
One 3-inch cinnamon stick

Bring to a boil, then add:

1 pork picnic shoulder (about 7 pounds)

Turn the meat to cover it with liquid and color it. Reduce the heat and cover the pan. Simmer, turning the meat every hour and basting it, until it is fork-tender, 3 to 4 hours. Remove the meat from the pan and spoon off the fat from the pan juices. Slice the meat. Serve with the pan juices and:

Hot cooked rice

PORK ADOBO *6 servings*

Adobo is a marinade of chili peppers, paprika, and vinegar commonly used in Spanish-speaking cultures, most often with pork. This is a style of adobo popular in New Mexico; it can also be made with beef. In New Mexico, the stew would be served with rice and sopapillas (fried bread), but flour or corn tortillas can be substituted.

Cover with boiling water in a bowl:

4 dried ancho or 6 dried New Mexico (red Anaheim) chili peppers

Let soak for 20 minutes. Drain the peppers, reserving the water. Slit the peppers open and discard the stems and seeds. Put the peppers and ¼ cup of the soaking liquid in a food processor or blender. Add:

⅓ cup apple cider vinegar
4 cloves garlic, peeled
1 teaspoon salt
1 teaspoon cumin seeds
½ teaspoon dried oregano
½ teaspoon ground black pepper
¼ teaspoon ground coriander
Pinch of ground cinnamon

Process to a smooth paste. Pour the paste into a large bowl and add:

3 pounds Boston-style pork shoulder or butt, boned, trimmed and cut into 2-inch cubes; or 4 pounds country-style ribs, trimmed; or 3½ pounds pork shoulder blade steaks

Toss to coat the meat with the marinade and cover the bowl with plastic wrap. Refrigerate for at least 12 hours or up to 3 days, occasionally turning the meat in the marinade. Heat in a large, heavy Dutch oven over medium heat:

2 tablespoons vegetable oil

Add:

1 cup chopped onions

Cover and cook, stirring often, until the onions are softened but not browned, about 5 minutes. Add the pork with all the marinade along with:

1½ cups seeded peeled chopped fresh or canned tomatoes

Reduce the heat, cover the pan, and simmer until the pork is tender, 1½ to 2 hours. Remove the meat to a bowl and keep warm. Spoon off the fat from the sauce, then boil the sauce over high heat to thicken it a bit. Taste and adjust the seasonings. Pour the sauce over the meat and stir to coat it. Serve with:

Hot cooked rice or warmed flour or corn tortillas

PORK VENDALOO *4 to 6 servings*

Vendaloo, or Vindaloo, is a vibrant, spicy stew from the southwest coast of India. Perfumed with spices, this dish can be made fiery hot to suit your taste. An equal amount of skinless, boneless chicken thighs can be substituted for the pork.

Process in a blender until smooth:

⅓ cup white wine vinegar
2 tablespoons olive oil
6 large cloves garlic, peeled
3 tablespoons chopped peeled fresh ginger
1½ tablespoons curry powder
1 tablespoon mustard seeds, preferably black
2 teaspoons ground cumin
¾ teaspoon ground cardamom
¼ teaspoon ground cloves
¼ teaspoon red pepper flakes, or to taste

Remove the mixture to a large bowl. Add and toss to coat well:

2 pounds trimmed pork loin or shoulder, cut into 1-inch cubes

Cover and refrigerate for at least 1 hour or up to 8. Heat in a large, heavy pan over medium-high heat:

2 tablespoons olive oil

Add and cook, stirring, until golden, about 5 minutes:

2½ cups chopped onions

Add the seasoned pork and cook, stirring, until lightly browned, about 3 minutes. Add:

One 14½- to 16-ounce can diced tomatoes, with juice
One 3-inch cinnamon stick

Bring to a boil. Reduce the heat, cover the pan, and simmer, stirring occasionally, until the pork is tender, about 1 hour. Season with:

Salt and ground black pepper to taste

Stir in:

2 teaspoons mustard seeds, preferably black

Simmer, uncovered, until the liquid is slightly thickened, about 10 to 15 minutes. Remove the cinnamon stick and stir in:

¼ cup chopped fresh cilantro (optional)

Serve hot with:

Hot cooked rice

ABOUT CURED PORK

Throughout history, homesteaders and urban dwellers alike have relied on a rich variety of cured pork. Whether it is ham, bacon, pancetta, salt pork, or any other type of cured pork, we still find it in kitchens and markets everywhere. In fact, cured pork products account for over 65 percent of all the pork eaten in this country. Curing, a process that uses salt to retard bacterial growth, was originally developed to preserve pork, but it is now used primarily to enhance the flavor and texture of the meat. A processor keeps his or her individual method a well-guarded secret. Curing can be done by one or a combination of three methods: dry-curing, rubbing salt and spices directly into the meat; pickling and brining, immersing the meat in a brine and spice solution; or injecting a brine solution into the meat itself—the quickest and commonest technique in commercial packing-houses today. After curing, cuts such as bacon and ham are often smoked to further dry the meat and add flavor, color, and character to the meat. This step is skipped for milder-tasting cured pork. While curing will preserve pork, it does not always eliminate the need for refrigerating or cooking the meat. If in doubt as to whether a cured pork product needs refrigeration, ask the person who sold it to you, or be on the safe side and refrigerate it.

ABOUT HAM

Someone once defined eternity as a ham and two people. The definition probably dates from the days when the term *ham* only applied to the small mountain of meat we now call a whole ham, which is technically the entire back leg portion of the hog that has been cured or smoked. (Fresh ham is the fresh hind leg that has not been smoked or cured.) Now that there is a wide variety of cuts and sizes available, eternity has shortened somewhat and ham is no longer reserved for large holiday celebrations. Today, the term *ham* is used for a variety of pork cuts from either the back leg or front shoulder that are processed through salt-curing and sometimes smoking and aging.

Ham is usually labeled one of two ways: "Partially Cooked" or "Fully Cooked." Whichever you buy, follow scrupulously the packer's instructions on the label. Partially cooked hams—also labeled "Cook Before Eating"—need to be roasted to an internal temperature of 155° to 160°F. Fully cooked hams—also called "Ready to Eat" or "Ready to Serve"—can be eaten as is, with no further preparation, but they will taste better and have a more appealing presentation if baked and glazed, as in Baked Ham, 706. The U.S. Department of Agriculture requires that fully cooked ham must have been exposed to an internal temperature of 148°F for 30 minutes to minimize any danger of disease. Smoking is the preferred method for accomplishing this, as it produces a richly flavored, juicy ham at the same time. Although most hams in this country are smoked, you might also find milder, less expensive hams that have been precooked by other methods. Heavy cold-smoking is used for expensive specialty hams, such as the domestic Smithfield and the European

Westphalian; this process does not cook the ham but does destroy microorganisms and also dries the meat, resulting in the characteristic firm texture of top-quality hams. Cold-smoked hams are drier with a deeper color and richer flavor owing to the lengthy aging process; they are often enjoyed sliced paper-thin and eaten raw.

Both partially and fully cooked hams come in several sizes and shapes. The whole ham, a 10- to 15-pound hind leg of pork with bone intact, is the most flavorful and least wasteful cut. It will serve twenty to thirty people generously, probably with leftovers. The best have a short plump shape, with a stubby rather than an elongated shank, or pointed end. For smaller meals, you can buy a section of the whole ham, either the rounded part called the rump half, or butt portion—the upper thigh of the animal, or the lower shank half. The rump half is somewhat more meaty but relatively difficult to carve. Either section can weigh from 4 to 7 pounds—enough to serve ten to twelve people. Smaller steaks and ham roasts are also available cut from the center of the leg (where the rump and shank are divided). These center ham slices or roasts generally weigh under 2 pounds and are quick to cook and serve, as in Baked Ham Steak, 707.

Spiral-cut hams are cured, fully cooked hams that are elaborately presliced so that they hold together for a dramatic presentation but are very easy to serve. The term "spiral" refers to the way hams are cut to the bone by a specially designed machine that spins the ham while cutting continuously to produce evenly thin slices. Increasing in popularity for large buffets and parties, spiral hams are now widely available in supermarkets. The patent that protected the original machine and recipe for these hams expired in 1957, and now they are produced by a growing number of companies and stores.

Besides the typical ham from the hind leg, there are other bone-in hams that tend to cost less while providing excellent taste. A picnic ham is the smoked arm section of the shoulder and, although flavorful, is slightly tougher than ham from the hind leg. Because it contains more fat, bone, and skin in proportion to lean meat, you must figure on almost a pound of picnic ham per serving. Another shoulder ham, known as Boston butt, cottage ham, or daisy ham, comes from the Boston-style shoulder, and though tender and tasty, it may be quite fatty. A long narrow piece is usually preferable to a short plump selection; it will serve three or four people. Cut into slices, it makes a delicious alternative to bacon. It can be broiled, sautéed, roasted, or simmered.

Fully cooked ham is available in many boneless forms: whole, in halves, or in chunks of various sizes. After boning, the meat may be shaped by the packer and rolled and packaged in airtight wrappers. Such hams are meant to be eaten sliced for sandwiches, at home or in the delicatessen. The deli hams found thus packaged are made with lean, cured meat with most of the external fat removed and may contain added water and phosphates. The best contain no added water or other ingredients and are simply labeled ham. Others in descending order of quality are ham with natural juices, ham with water added, and ham-and-water product.

The wide assortment of canned hams offers the instant convenience one needs when the house is suddenly flooded with unexpected guests. When you buy canned hams, check the label for perishability and suggested refrigeration. Most of the larger canned hams, including the superior types imported from Denmark, Holland, and Poland, must be kept under refrigeration before being opened and can be stored thus for a few months. Some of the smaller canned hams can be stored without refrigeration. These hams have been sterilized in the canning process, at the expense of texture and taste.

Less frequently prepared in this instant-everything age is the time-honored country ham, sometimes called Virginia, Kentucky, or Tennessee ham. All country hams are dry-cured and heavily salted and require soaking followed by long simmering. Perhaps the best-known example of the country hams is the Smithfield-style ham of Virginia and North Carolina, but the flavor and aroma of any true country ham are worth the extra time and effort. While 90 percent of American hogs are corn-fed, producers of specialty country hams assume the extra expense of feeding their pigs a diet of acorns or peaches or peanuts—the latter being the diet of the famous Smithfield hogs. This different feed produces nuances of flavor in hams from one area to another. Many country hams are sold by mail order.

Ham should be served warm or cool but never chilled. Do not worry if a rainbow iridescence appears on sliced ham—it is merely light refraction on a thin fatty film. The rule for storage is that all hams must be kept refrigerated, with two exceptions: small unopened canned ham not labeled perishable, and dry-cured ham—the country or Smithfield type, which can be kept in a cool, dry, dark place (or in the refrigerator). For best results, uncanned whole hams should not be stored longer than a week in the refrigerator before cooking; small portions should be kept no longer than 3 to 5 days. Sliced ham is best used within 2 days. Freezing any ham is not recommended because of rapid deterioration in quality and flavor; canned ham is especially vulnerable because of its high water content.

BACON

Bacon is made from trimmed hog bellies, also called sides, that have been cured in brine and then smoked until partially cooked. Bacon is a fatty cut, and although there are leaner varieties, the fat that remains is integral to its flavor and texture. Most bacon sold in the supermarket is sliced—thick or thin. Unsliced bacon, or slab bacon, is usually found in specialty stores and is ideal anytime you want thick pieces, which the French call *lardon*. (Lardons are ½-inch-thick strips of bacon that are fried crisp and added to salads.)

All bacon loses flavor with time and should be used within a week or so of purchase. It can be frozen, but only for one or two months. When cooking bacon under the broiler or in a frying pan, start with a cold grill or pan to prevent curling. Do not cook bacon over high heat, since it can go from browned to burnt in a matter of seconds. Low to medium heat works best. Separating slices of bacon in the pan as it warms helps prevent tearing of individual slices.

CANADIAN BACON

Canadian bacon bears little resemblance to standard bacon, because it comes from the meatier, leaner loin of the pig and is more thoroughly trimmed before curing. Although most Canadian bacon is brined and smoked and closely resembles ham, it is also sold uncooked. Slice the cooked variety as you would regular ham, for cold cuts or pan-frying. The uncooked variety comes rolled in cornmeal and is typically baked; for a special treat, try thick slices grilled outdoors and served on a sandwich roll.

PANCETTA

Pancetta is the Italian version of bacon from the pork belly (*pancia*). The most commonly found pancetta is curled into a tight roll and secured in a natural casing to preserve its cylindrical shape. Flat pancetta, which closely resembles slab bacon, is hard to find here but is the normal kind in Italy. Pancetta is not smoked, so it is moister and has a mellower flavor than bacon. The incomparable spicy-sweet taste of pancetta comes from the mixture of salt, black pepper, and spices used to cure the pork. Pancetta is commonly used as a flavoring for stews and braises by rendering the fat and using it to cook other ingredients. It is also a fine savory addition to stuffings of all sorts. If you substitute bacon for pancetta, blanch it first in boiling water to subdue the smoky flavor.

PROSCIUTTO

Prosciutto means "ham" in Italian, and it is exquisite ham. Hogs are specially raised on a diet of chestnuts or, in the Parma region, on the whey from the local Parmesan cheese production. The hind legs are dry-cured and air-dried for a minimum of ten months, giving the meat a firm, dry quality with an exquisite flavor. Prosciutto needs no cooking and, in fact, can become dry and tough if cooked. Instead, it is added at the end of cooking for flavor and is commonly served sliced paper-thin with sliced melons or figs or used sparingly to season soups and stews. Look for prosciutto di Parma imported from Italy and avoid domestic varieties of unsmoked, salt-cured ham, which do not compare.

SERRANO HAM

Serrano ham comes from the Spanish for "mountain ham"—*jamón serrano*. Similar to prosciutto from Italy, serrano hams are from the mountainous regions of Spain where raw hams are cured by air-drying in the cool, dry alpine air. The best serrano ham is quite rich in flavor and firm in texture and should be eaten alone as an appetizer or used in small quantities to flavor cooked dishes.

TASSO

A heavily spiced and smoked cured ham, tasso is a Creole and Cajun specialty that can be difficult to find outside of Louisiana. Made primarily from the pork shoulder, tasso is first cured with a salt brine, then rubbed with a pungent mix of spices and cold-smoked until it becomes quite dry. The resulting ham is often chopped and added for flavor to gumbo, jambalaya, étouffée or other Louisiana dishes.

FATBACK

Fatback is unprocessed fat taken from the belly or back and sold in slabs or thin sheets to be rendered into fat for cooking or larding meats. Because it is not cured or smoked, fatback has a pure, mellow flavor. Cracklings are little pieces of fatback that have been fried until crispy.

SALT PORK

From the fatty part of the belly, knuckle, or even shoulder comes this heavily salted unsmoked product prized for its fat, which is commonly rendered for cooking in the South and Northeast. A chunk of salt pork added to a soup or a pot of beans during cooking lends a savory richness to the entire dish. The salt pork is typically removed before serving. Salt pork is often soaked before being used to cut down on its saltiness. Bacon can be substituted without first presoaking.

HAM HOCKS

Ham hocks are pieces of lower leg containing bone, lean meat, fat, and rind. They are most often found salted and heavily smoked, although fresh ones are sometimes available. They are a great contribution to slow-cooked stews and bean soups, adding an earthy, smoky flavor and enriching the texture of the cooking liquid.

PORK RIND

Pork rind is trimmed from the edges of bacon, salt pork, fatback, or hocks and, because of its high collagen content, adds sumptuous texture to stocks, soups, stews, and braises. Deep-fried pork rind, or chitlins, is also enjoyed as a snack food.

ABOUT HAM GLAZES AND ACCOMPANIMENTS

Traditionally, ham has been served with a fruit-based sauce or garnish to balance the salty, sometimes smoky, flavor of the meat. Beyond fruit, many ingredients and flavors make great partners for ham, such as chili peppers, onions, and fresh herbs. A few ideas are given below for sauces and glazes to cook and serve with baked ham or ham steak. Consult Stocks & Sauces, 35, or Condiments, Marinades, & Dry Rubs, 60, for other ideas and experiment with classic or new sauces, relishes, salsas, chutneys, glazes, and pastes.

BAKED HAM

10 to 12 servings

Baked ham is great for entertaining and perfect for a buffet. Whole hams weigh between 10 and 15 pounds, and half hams (called rump or shank end) range from 5 to 7 pounds. Fully cooked hams need only be warmed through, by bringing the internal temperature to 140°F. Partially cooked hams need to be fully cooked to an internal temperature of 155° to 160°F. For an attractive and delectable, crisp crust, crosshatch the top of the ham with the point of a sharp knife and glaze it during the last hour of cooking.

If you wish to glaze the ham, have ready one of the Glazes for Baked Ham and Roasted Poultry, 90.

Position a rack in the lower third of the oven. Preheat the oven to 325°F.

Place in a shallow roasting pan:

One 5- to 15-pound half or whole bone-in ham, fully or partially cooked

Bake the fully cooked ham until an instant-read thermometer inserted in the thickest part of the meat reads 140°F, 10 to 12 minutes per pound (the temperature will continue to rise 5° out of the oven). Bake the partially cooked ham until an instant-read thermometer inserted in the thickest part of the meat reads 160°F, 15 to 20 minutes per pound (the temperature will continue to rise 5° out of the oven). If you are glazing the ham, remove the ham from the oven 45 minutes before it is done, score the top of the ham by making a grid pattern with the tip of a sharp knife, cutting through just the skin (about 1/16 inch), then brush the ham with the glaze. Return the ham to the oven and finish baking. When it is done, remove the ham to a platter, cover loosely with aluminum foil, and let stand for 10 to 15 minutes, then carve. Alternatively, bake the ham without a glaze and serve with:

English Cumberland Sauce, 80

BAKED COUNTRY HAM

40 to 60 servings

Country hams can be quite salty to the uninitiated, but the taste is incomparable. It takes some time to extract enough salt to make the ham palatable, but the end result is well worth the effort. Country ham needs to be soaked at least 24 hours and then scrubbed if necessary to remove any mold before cooking. Older hams should be soaked for 48 hours. Once the ham is soaked and scrubbed, it needs to be simmered until cooked through. The ham then can be very thinly sliced for sandwiches and such or, as in this recipe, baked and glazed for a magnificent main course.

Place in a large pot:

1 country ham (16 to 20 pounds)

Cover with water and soak for 24 to 48 hours, changing the water once or twice. Drain and scrub off any mold with a stiff brush or scrape it off. Rinse the ham thoroughly and return it to the large pot. Cover with cold water and bring just to a boil. Pour off the water. Cover again with fresh cold water and bring just to a boil. Reduce the heat and simmer, partially covered, until the bone is loose, 2½ to 3 hours. Turn off the heat and let the ham cool in the cooking liquid. Remove the ham to a baking sheet or a platter and remove the skin and as much of the fat as desired. Let stand for about 30 minutes. At this point, the ham can be baked, chilled, cut into paper-thin slices like prosciutto, and served.

For baking, position a rack as low as possible in the oven. Preheat the oven to 350°F.

Arrange the ham meaty side up on a rack in a roasting pan and sprinkle it with:

1 cup brown sugar
Several cracked black peppercorns to taste

Bake until glazed, 20 to 30 minutes. Let stand for 30 minutes, cut into paper-thin slices like prosciutto, and serve with plenty of:

Basic Rolled Biscuits, 789, or Buttermilk Biscuits, 790

BROILED OR GRILLED HAM STEAK

4 servings

The high heat of the grill or broiler caramelizes the glaze to a lovely crisp crust surrounding the tender ham steak. Feel free to experiment with other sauces or glazes.

Position the broiler pan 2 inches from the heating element and preheat the broiler, or prepare a medium-hot charcoal fire.

Pat dry:

1 fully cooked ¾- to 1-inch-thick ham steak (1½ to 2 pounds)

Spread one side of the steak with one-half of:

½ cup Southwestern Apricot Glaze, 89, or barbecue sauce

Broil with the glazed side facing the heat for 5 to 7 minutes or grill glazed side down for 2 minutes. Spread the other side with the remaining glaze or sauce and broil for 5 to 7 minutes more or grill for 2 minutes more, depending on which side is facing the heat. The steak should be well browned on both sides and heated through. Serve with:

Cole Slaw, 222
American Potato Salad, 220

BAKED HAM STEAK

4 servings

A quick way to dress up a ham steak. This recipe lends itself to improvisation with your own sauces or glazes as well.

Position a rack in the lower third of the oven. Preheat the oven to 325°F.

Place in a baking dish:

1 fully cooked ¾- to 1-inch-thick ham steak (1½ to 2 pounds)

If desired, spread the steak with:

½ cup Orange Molasses Glaze, 89, or ¼ cup Mediterranean Garlic Herb Paste, 87, or to taste

Bake, uncovered, until heated through and nicely browned on top, about 20 minutes. Remove the steak to a platter with any accumulated juices and serve with:

Franconia, or Browned Potatoes, 411

SAUTÉED HAM STEAK

4 servings

Melt in a large skillet over medium-high heat:

1½ teaspoons unsalted butter

Add:

1 fully cooked ¾- to 1-inch-thick ham steak (1½ to 2 pounds)

Sauté the steak until nicely browned, 3 to 5 minutes each side. Remove to a platter and season with:

Ground black pepper to taste

HAM STEAK WITH RED-EYE GRAVY

A Southern classic.

Prepare Sautéed Ham Steak, above, cutting the ham slices only ¼ to ½ inch thick. After the ham is cooked, remove it to a warmed platter and return the skillet to the heat. Add 1 cup of brewed coffee to the skillet and boil, stirring, until it turns slightly red. Add ½ cup of heavy cream, reduce the heat, and simmer until slightly thickened, about 10 minutes. Season with salt and ground black pepper to taste.

SAUTÉED BACON

When cooking bacon, cook to your own personal taste; the longer bacon cooks, the more fat is rendered out of it. Count on about 2 to 3 slices bacon per person. Starting the bacon in a cold skillet prevents it from curling. If the bacon is very thinly sliced and threatens to tear when separated, wait until it warms up and coax the slices apart with a spatula.

Place in a large cast-iron or other heavy skillet:

2 or 3 slices bacon per person

Do not overlap the slices; cook in batches if necessary. Place the pan over medium-low heat and slowly cook the bacon until browned. Turn the bacon often and monitor the heat to avoid burning the bacon. Spoon off the fat if over ¼ inch accumulates in the pan during cooking. Remove the slices to paper towels to drain.

BROILED BACON

A cold broiler pan prevents the bacon from curling. Position the broiler pan 4 to 6 inches away from the heating element. Preheat the broiler but not the broiler pan.

Arrange on the cold broiler pan:

2 or 3 slices bacon per person

Place the pan under the broiler. Cook, turning often, until browned and crisp, 10 to 15 minutes. Remove to paper towels to drain.

MICROWAVED BACON

The microwave does an excellent job of cooking bacon more quickly and with less mess than other methods. It also requires less tending, which frees you to do other things. Since individual microwaves vary in power and efficiency, the method below provides only an approximate time. Work out the timing for your own oven and desired degree of doneness.

Spread 3 or 4 layers of paper towels on a plate and arrange on the towels:

2 or 3 slices bacon per person

Place in the microwave oven and cook on high for 3 minutes. Touch the bacon and, if not crisp enough, continue cooking, checking for doneness every 30 seconds. Pat the surface of the bacon with paper towels and serve.

SAUTÉED CANADIAN BACON

Canadian bacon is boneless pork loin that has been brine-cured and smoked. Typically, it is sold sliced and ready for sautéing just like regular bacon but is also available in a solid piece that you can slice at home.

Melt in a large skillet over medium heat:

1½ teaspoons butter or vegetable oil

Add:

2 or 3 slices Canadian bacon per person, ⅛ to ¼ inch thick

Cook the slices, turning often, until browned and heated through, 3 to 5 minutes. Remove to plates and serve.

HAM HOCKS AND GREENS

6 servings

In this old Southern recipe, ham hocks are slow-cooked with spices and hearty greens until they emerge fall-apart tender. Save any extra liquid to use as a soup base. Either fresh or smoked ham hocks can be used, but smoked will give you intenser flavor.

Place in a large stockpot:

8 smoked or fresh ham hocks

Cover with water, bring to a boil, and skim off any scum that raises to the top. Add:

2 large onions, sliced
4 carrots, sliced
2 celery stalks, sliced
4 cloves garlic, crushed
½ bunch parsley sprigs
1 bay leaf
1 tablespoon dried thyme
2 teaspoons salt
1 teaspoon red pepper flakes
Ground black pepper to taste

Simmer, uncovered, skimming as needed, for 1 hour. Add:

2 pounds kale, collards, mustard greens, Swiss chard, or a combination, tough stems removed, washed well, and cut crosswise into 3- to 4-inch pieces

Simmer, uncovered, until the greens and hocks are fall-apart tender, 1½ to 2 hours. Pour off most of the cooking liquid (if desired, save it for another use), leaving enough to keep the greens and meat moistened. Season the hocks and greens to taste with:

Cider vinegar
Salt and ground black pepper
Red pepper flakes

Place one or two ham hocks in each bowl of greens, moisten with cooking liquid, and serve immediately. Pass hot pepper sauce and cider vinegar on the side.

ABOUT LAMB

Most lamb comes to market between five and seven months of age, with a dressed weight of 50 to 65 pounds. The smallest lamb, sometimes referred to as hothouse or milk-fed lamb, can be less than four weeks old and weigh as little as 8 pounds. Known for their tenderness and delicate flavor, lambs of this size are generally roasted whole. Other small lambs, between 20 and 50 pounds, are often sold under the name of spring or Easter lamb, although they are now available year-round thanks to new breeding techniques.

Mutton, the meat of sheep over two years old, is rarely available in the United States—which is unfortunate, because it can be quite good, despite its bad reputation. Cuts of mutton are similar to those of lamb; they are larger, darker in color, and richer in flavor but lack lamb's delicacy and tenderness. Mutton tends to have more fat than lamb and should be well trimmed before cooking. Prepare mutton according to lamb recipes, allowing extra time to compensate for the larger cuts.

Lamb is currently produced in every state in the Union, with flocks concentrated in the West, especially Colorado and California. Besides American lamb, both Australian and New Zealand lamb are widely available, either frozen or deep-chilled. New Zealand lamb tends to be the smallest but not necessarily the mildest or tenderest. We prefer American lamb, because the individual cuts are bigger, with more meat in proportion to the bone. Lamb is graded prime, choice, and good. Marbling with fat is not a factor in grading lamb as it is with beef; instead, the highest grade goes to lamb with thick, well-shaped eye muscles in the loin and rib cuts. Less than 10 percent of lamb meat is graded prime. The vast majority is choice, with only a tiny fraction graded good. When buying lamb, look for meat that is moist and bright, not slimy or sticky. The color may range from pinkish rose to pale red, depending on the age of the animal. The fat should be waxy white and not discolored, brittle, or chalky-looking.

Large cuts of lamb are covered with a white, papery membrane called the fell, which must be removed, by either the butcher or the home cook. Not only is the fell indigestible, it also prevents seasonings and even heat from penetrating the meat. Beneath the fell, lamb has a fair amount of fat, which is best trimmed away as it can have a strong, tallowlike taste that will overwhelm the delicate flavor of the meat. Leave only a few streaks of fat to baste the meat as it cooks. As with all meats, before searing or browning lamb cuts, pat them dry with paper towels to remove excess moisture.

The most popular cuts of lamb—leg, chops, rack, and loin—are tender enough for dry-heat cooking by roasting, broiling, sautéing, and grilling. Lamb cooked this way is best rare or medium-rare so that it does not become greasy-tasting and tough. To determine doneness, insert an instant-read thermometer into the thickest portion of the meat without touching any bone. The final temperature for medium-rare lamb is 130° to 135°F, while medium is 140° to 150°F. Bear in mind that the internal temperature of large cuts will rise about 5°F as the meat stands before carving. The less tender cuts, including the shoulder, shanks, and breast, are best braised or stewed until tender. Please see About Stewing, Braising, and Pot-Roasting Meat, 640.

With its pronounced, sweetish flavor, lamb stands up very well to assertive seasonings, from pungent herbs to spice rubs to curry sauces.

ABOUT LEG OF LAMB

The naturally tender and extremely flavorful leg of lamb is best roasted, whether whole, boneless, or stuffed. Boned and butterflied leg of lamb and smaller, thinner cuts from the leg, such as lamb steaks, leg chops, or kebabs, can also be grilled, broiled, or sautéed with great success. The flavor and texture of lamb are best when not cooked past medium. The tender, lean leg meat does not hold up well to the long cooking of a stew. Better choices for stewing are the tougher, fattier (and cheaper) cuts like shoulder, neck, or breast.

Leg of lamb comes in several forms. The commonest is the whole leg with the bone in. These generally weigh from 7 to 9 pounds untrimmed, but may weigh as little as 5½ pounds (or even less in the case of New Zealand lamb). Figure on 8 to 10 ounces per person of bone-in lamb. Each leg has three bones: the hip or pelvis, the thigh, and the shank. Your butcher will remove all or some of these. Even if you want a bone-in leg, we recommend asking the butcher to remove the hip bone to make carving easier or doing it at home (see below). A fully boneless leg is most often opened and laid flat as a butterflied leg of lamb—perfect for stuffing and rolling or simply grilling flat like a large steak. When buying a boneless leg, figure on 6 to 8 ounces per person. Some markets also sell "short legs," which have the wider top section of the leg removed. These are easier to carve than whole legs, but we regret the loss of the fine sirloin meat along with the bone.

As a general rule when cooking leg of lamb, figure on 10 to 13 minutes per pound for a large leg (over 7

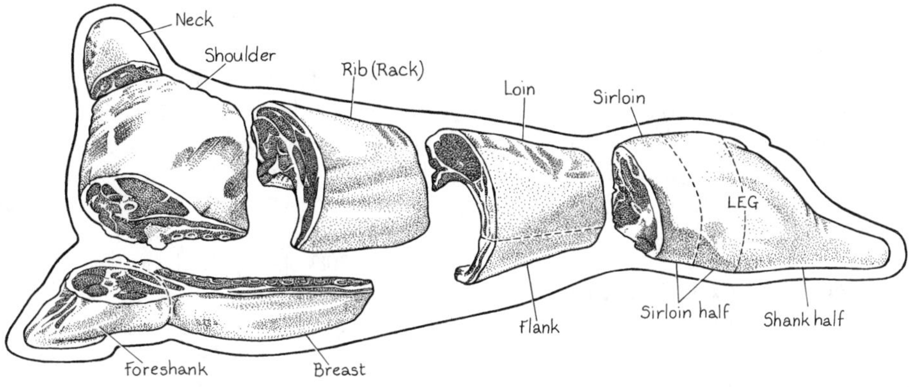

Major cuts of lamb

pounds), 8 to 9 minutes per pound for a smaller leg (5 to 7 pounds).

HOW TO TRIM A LEG OF LAMB

Although you can ask your butcher to trim the leg for you, chances are that you will have to do some trimming at home before roasting it. If you are planning to butterfly the leg of lamb, please read the instructions below before trimming the meat. However you plan to cook it, all the fell and most of the fat must be removed first. Start trimming by poking a sharp knife under the fat at the wide end of the leg until you find a place where the fell and the fat will come free in a single solid flap, exposing the meat. Pull of the flap of fell and fat with one hand, cutting away at the membrane that connects it to the meat as you go. Take care always to hold the knife blade against the membrane, not the meat. Once you have removed this neat layer of fell and fat, shave away at any remaining fat, holding the knife parallel to the leg to avoid cutting into the meat; leave only a few streaks of fat to keep the meat moist. If you wish to remove the hip bone before roasting for ease of carving later, see How to Remove the Hip Bone below.

HOW TO REMOVE THE HIP BONE

This will ease carving. Place the lamb on a large cutting board with the hip bone facing up. There may be a small, sickle-shaped extension protruding from the side of the leg. This is the tailbone, and you will need to cut around it and break it off. You are faced with the hip bone proper, a large, blade-shaped bone attached to the main leg bone by a ball-and-socket joint. Begin by cutting around the edges of the exposed bone to loosen it, always holding the knife against the bone to avoid cutting into the muscle. Continue scraping away the meat, exposing and freeing the bone by cutting under and around it, until you reach the thigh joint. Then lift and bend the hip bone back toward the rest of the leg, applying enough pressure to expose the ball-and-socket joint. Cut through the tendons inside and around the joint and scrape away any meat to remove the hip bone. Stop here for a whole leg of lamb, using a trussing needle or small skewers to neaten the loose flaps of meat, if desired, for even cooking and a neater presentation.

HOW TO BUTTERFLY A LEG OF LAMB

A butterflied leg of lamb is completely boned and then spread flat and trimmed, making it ideal for a stuffed roast or for quick grilling or boiling, much like a large steak. Most butchers will butterfly a leg of lamb for you, but it is a straightforward task you can perform yourself. Figure on 6 to 8 ounces boneless meat per person, a bit less if you plan to stuff it. Begin by trimming the fell and only the thickest layer of fat from the outside of the leg. Leave some membrane in order to prevent the leg from falling apart once it is boned. The first step is to remove the hip bone, if it is in place.

Then turn the leg bone side up. Begin to remove the thigh bone by making a straight cut down through the meat from the hip joint, along the thigh bone, to the next joint. Your goal is to cut the meat away from the bone by opening it out like a book, leaving as much of the meat as possible in one piece. With your knife against the thigh bone, you will feel this next joint where the thigh bone connects with the shank bone. Work the point of the knife around the thigh bone without cutting all the way through the meat until the bone is completely exposed and loosened. Make small, scraping cuts to avoid cutting into the meat. Cut the meat away from the joint and continue downward to free the shank bone so that both bones can be lifted out and removed. Lay the boneless leg flat and cut away the kneecap, the small white disk of cartilage that is found toward the shank end of the meat. Then carefully trim away any lumps of fat and sinew. Finally, even out the thickness of the meat by making lengthwise cuts about 1 inch deep in the thicker sections of the meat and spreading them open like a book (or butterfly). The butterflied leg should be approximately the same thickness—2 to 2½ inches—all over. The flat side of a meat mallet or the bottom of a small, heavy pan can be used to further flatten any thicker portions. For a neat presentation and ease in flipping the meat on a grill or under a broiler, run 2 or 3 skewers crosswise through the meat to secure any loose flaps. After cooking, carve a butterflied leg of lamb by slicing it on the diagonal in ¼- to ½-inch slices much as you would carve a steak.

HOW TO CARVE A BONE-IN LEG OF LAMB

You have a choice. For large, thin, flat, slices, grab the shank, or narrow end, of the roast with a towel or heavy cloth napkin and raise it at an angle off the platter. With a sharp carving knife held parallel to the bone, begin cutting away from you to carve flat, ¼-inch-thick slices from the meatiest part of the leg. Continue until you reach the leg bone. Then turn the leg over and use the same slicing method until you reach the bone again. Finally, carve away any meat left attached to the bone. If the hip bone is still attached, again hold the shank with a towel or heavy cloth, with the meatiest part of the leg facing up. With a sharp carving knife, start at the shank end and make vertical slices down to the bone. Then turn the knife parallel to the bone and cut the slices free from the bone. Continue slicing toward the wide end of the leg. Rotate the leg as you go to carve the meat off all sides. As you reach the hip bone, carve around it.

ROASTED BONE-IN LEG OF LAMB *10 servings*

A simply seasoned roast leg of lamb needs no sauce—though some people insist on a bit of mint jelly or English Fresh Mint Sauce, 80, or enjoy Greek Avgolemono, 82, served on the side.

Pat dry:

1 whole bone-in leg of lamb (7 to 8 pounds), preferably with hip bone removed, excess fat/membrane trimmed, 710

Position a rack in the lower third of the oven. Preheat the oven to 450°F.

Combine in a mixing bowl:

1 tablespoon ground black pepper
2 teaspoons salt
1 teaspoon finely minced fresh rosemary, or scant ½ teaspoon finely crumbled dried

Rub the wide end of the leg with half of the seasoning mixture. Add to the remaining seasoning mixture and toss to coat:

2 large cloves garlic, cut lengthwise into slivers

Cut 15 to 20 evenly spaced slits in the roast and insert the seasoned garlic slivers. Rub the surface of the roast with:

3 tablespoons olive oil

Rub any remaining seasoning mixture over the roast and arrange it meatier side up on a rack in a roasting pan. Place it in the oven and immediately reduce the oven temperature to 325°F. Roast until an instant-read thermometer inserted in the thickest part of the meat reads 125° to 130°F for medium-rare or 135° to 145°F for medium, 1¼ to 1¾ hours (the temperature will rise about 5°F out of the oven). Remove from the oven, cover loosely with aluminum foil, and let stand for 15 to 20 minutes. For carving, please see How to Carve a Bone-In Leg of Lamb, above.

GLAZED BONE-IN LEG OF LAMB

Prepare Roasted Bone-In Leg of Lamb, above, omitting the rosemary, garlic, and olive oil. Instead, brush the trimmed leg with either 1 cup of Vermouth Baste, 89 or 1¼ cups Orange Molasses Glaze, 89, at least 1 hour before roasting. Marinate, covered, for at least 1 hour in the refrigerator or up to 24 hours. Baste the lamb several times during roasting with more glaze.

ROASTED BONE-IN LEG OF LAMB WITH CAPER SAUCE *10 servings*

Prepare Roasted Bone-In Leg of Lamb, above. While roasting the lamb, prepare a lamb stock by simmering for 1 hour, partially covered, 3 cups beef or chicken stock with 1 pound meaty lamb bones or stewing bones. Strain, defatten, and set aside. When lamb is roasted, remove to a platter to stand and add the lamb stock to the roasting pan with ⅓ cup dry white wine or vermouth. Bring to a boil, scraping up any browned bits, and cook down to 1½ cups. Add ⅓ cup nonpareil capers and 1 tablespoon balsamic vinegar; season with salt and ground black pepper to taste. Thicken, if desired, with 1 tablespoon cornstarch dissolved in 1 tablespoon cold water, whisked into the sauce and boiled.

STUFFED BUTTERFLIED LEG OF LAMB *8 to 10 servings*

Please read How to Trim a Leg of Lamb, 710.

Position a rack in the lower third of the oven. Preheat the oven to 375°F.

Pat dry:

1 butterflied leg of lamb (4 to 5 pounds), trimmed to an even thickness of 2 to 2½ inches

Season the boned side of the meat with:

2 tablespoons chopped garlic (optional)
1½ teaspoons salt
1 teaspoon ground black pepper

Spoon onto the boned surface of the lamb:

4 cups Spinach, Mushroom, and Ground Meat Stuffing, 487, made with ground lamb or pork, or 4 cups Couscous Stuffing with Dried Apricots and Pistachios, 486

Starting from a longer side, roll the lamb to enclose the stuffing. The stuffed leg should be longer than it is wide. With butcher twine, tie the leg securely at 2-inch intervals to give it a snug, compact, cylindrical shape. You may need to sew the small end with a trussing needle or secure it with small skewers. With the point of a paring knife, make 20 to 25 slits about 2 inches apart over the surface of the lamb. Push into the slits:

3 cloves garlic, cut lengthwise into slivers

Rub the surface with:

3 tablespoons olive oil
1 teaspoon salt
½ teaspoon ground black pepper

Place the stuffed leg seam side down on a rack in a roasting pan and roast until an instant-read thermometer inserted in the thickest part of the meat reads 130° to 135°F, 1½ to 1¾ hours (the temperature will rise about 5° out of the oven). Remove from the oven, cover loosely with aluminum foil, and let stand for 10 to 15 minutes. Just before serving, remove the string and cut into ½- to ¾-inch-thick slices (the roll may come apart). Pass separately, if desired:

Avgolemono, 82, Lemon Egg Sauce, 82, or Sauce Piquant, 51

TAPENADE-STUFFED BUTTERFLIED LEG OF LAMB

Prepare Stuffed Butterflied Leg of Lamb, above, omitting the salt inside the lamb. Substitute 1 recipe Tapenade, 161, for the ground meat stuffing and spread it evenly over the boned surface of the lamb. Reduce the cooking time by about 15 minutes.

BROILED OR GRILLED BUTTERFLIED LEG OF LAMB

8 to 10 servings

Pat dry:

1 butterflied leg of lamb (4 to 5 pounds), trimmed to an even thickness of 2 to 2½ inches

Rub the entire surface with:

½ cup Peppery Dry Rub, 86, or West Indies Dry Rub, 86

or a mixture of:

3 tablespoons minced fresh rosemary, or 1 tablespoon dried
2 tablespoons minced garlic
1 teaspoon salt
1 teaspoon ground black pepper

Marinate in the refrigerator for at least 1 hour or up to 24 hours.

Position the broiler pan 4 to 5 inches away from the heating element and preheat the broiler and broiler pan, or prepare a medium-hot charcoal fire.

To cook, place the lamb skinned side up on the broiler pan or skinned side down on the grill rack. Cook until well seared on the outside but still juicy and pink on the inside, about 12 minutes each side. Cook for a few minutes more each side for medium. Let the lamb stand for 6 to 8 minutes, loosely covered with aluminum foil, then cut into ½-inch-thick slices. Serve immediately with, if desired:

Red Onion Marmalade, 66
Roasted Tomato-Chipotle Salsa, 62

MARINATED BUTTERFLIED LEG OF LAMB

Before preparing Broiled or Grilled Butterflied Leg of Lamb, above, marinate the butterflied meat, lightly covered, in the refrigerator for 6 hours in 1½ tablespoons olive oil, ¾ cup dry red wine, 1 tablespoon grated lemon zest, 2 crumbled bay leaves, 2 crushed cloves garlic, and 2 teaspoons dried oregano. Pat dry before broiling or grilling as directed.

LAMB KEBABS

The best meat for lamb kebabs is leg meat cut into 1- to 1½-inch cubes. Follow the procedure for marinating and cooking described in Barbecued Kebabs, 165. Good choices for marinades are Tandori Marinade, 85, Red Wine Marinade, 85, or Mediterranean Garlic Herb Paste, 87.

ABOUT RACK OF LAMB

The rack is the rib section of the lamb, extending from the shoulder to the loin, and is nothing more than the lamb chops left in one piece. There are usually seven rib bones, although some butchers include an eighth rib from the shoulder end to provide an even number. As the ribs get closer to the shoulder, the eye meat, or center nugget, gets smaller. An average trimmed rack weighs between 1¼ and 2½ pounds and feeds two or three people, figuring two to three chops per person. With the smaller racks from New Zealand or especially large appetites, figure on three to four chops per person.

HOW TO TRIM A RACK OF LAMB

When you buy a rack of lamb, make sure that the backbone, or chine bone, has been removed or deeply scored to allow you to cut through it to serve individual chops. This sturdy bone holds the individual chops securely in place but makes it nearly impossible to carve the finished roast into neat chops. Unless you are adept with a meat cleaver or meat saw, removing the chine bone yourself is difficult and even dangerous.

Anytime you buy an untrimmed rack of lamb, you will need to remove the heavy blanket of fat and meat covering the rib bones and the center eye of meat that accounts for as much as ⅓ of the weight of the rack. Start at the heavier end of the rack and use a sharp knife to free the outer layer of fat and meat, then grab it with one hand and pull—it should lift off in one piece. Finish by trimming all but a thin layer of fat protecting the center eye meat.

HOW TO FRENCH A RACK OF LAMB

Trimming a rack of lamb so that the ends of the rib bones are exposed is called Frenching. Rack of lamb is often sold already Frenched, but if it is necessary to do it yourself, place the rack bone side down on a cutting board and, with a sharp knife held perpendicular to the rib bones, make a long cut through the fat layer about 2 inches from the end of the bones and above the eye meat. (Do not cut too close to the eye meat, or you will detach it.) Angle the knife into the cut and slide the knife away from the eye meat toward the ends of the bones. Keep the blade flush with the bones and remove the layer of fat covering them. Use the point of a small knife to cut out the meat between the bones. Scrape the exposed ribs free of any fat or tendon. The bones must be absolutely clean, or the adhering fat and meat will burn during roasting. (This can also be prevented by covering them with aluminum foil.) Once the rib bones are cleaned, trim away all but a thin layer of fat from the eye meat.

ROASTED RACK OF LAMB

3 or 4 servings

For average domestic lamb, one 7- or 8-rib rack will weigh close to 2 pounds and feed 3 to 4 people, but for smaller racks from baby lamb or New Zealand lamb that may weigh as little as 1 pound, figure on 2 to 3 servings per rack. Also, expect the cooking time to be relative to the size of the rack—a larger rack may take as long as 25 minutes. Searing the rack of lamb before roasting gives it a crisp, brown exterior and helps melt any untrimmed fat. If you choose to skip this step, add 5 to 8 minutes to the cooking time.

Position a rack in the center of the oven. Preheat the oven to 425°F.

Pat dry:

1 rack of lamb (7 or 8 ribs), trimmed, leaving a thin layer of fat on the surface, and Frenched, above

Season with:

1 teaspoon salt

½ teaspoon ground black pepper

Heat a large, heavy, ovenproof skillet without fat over high heat. Add the lamb meat side down and sear well, about 2 minutes. Using tongs or a meat fork, turn it and brown the other side, about 4 minutes total. Pour off any fat in the pan, set the lamb bone side down in the skillet, and place the skillet in the oven. Roast until a meat thermometer inserted in the thickest part of the meat registers 125°F for rare or 130°F for medium-rare, about 15 to 20 minutes (the temperature will rise about 5° out of the oven). Remove from the oven, cover loosely with aluminum foil, and let stand for 5 to 10 minutes. Cut between the bones and serve 2 or 3 chops per person. If desired, serve with:

Red Wine and Sour Cherry Sauce, 53

Red Onion Marmalade, 66

ROASTED RACK OF LAMB WITH MUSTARD COATING

Prepare Roasted Rack of Lamb, above, through the searing. Mix together 2 tablespoons Dijon mustard, 2 tablespoons olive oil, 1 tablespoon fresh lemon juice, 2 teaspoons chopped fresh rosemary, or ¾ teaspoon dried, 1 teaspoon salt, and ¼ teaspoon ground black pepper. Using a pastry brush, coat the entire surface of the seared lamb with the mustard mixture and roast as directed.

ROASTED RACK OF LAMB WITH MOROCCAN SPICE RUB

Mix well with a fork in a small bowl 2 tablespoons olive oil; ¼ cup chopped fresh mint; 2 tablespoons chopped fresh parsley; 1½ teaspoons ground ginger; ½ teaspoon each ground allspice, ground cinnamon, ground black pepper, paprika, ground coriander, and salt; and large pinch each of ground red pepper and ground cloves. Have ready a rack of lamb as for Roasted Rack of Lamb, above. Instead of seasoning with salt and pepper and searing the rack, rub the paste all over it and marinate for 30 to 60 minutes in the refrigerator. Roast as directed and serve.

ABOUT LOIN OF LAMB

Lamb loins run along either side of the backbone, starting at the last rib and extending to the hindquarters, or sirloin. When still attached to the backbone, the loins are referred to as the saddle. Roasted saddle of lamb with a parsley garlic crust was once considered a grand dish to be served in the most elegant private homes; regrettably, it has now gone out of fashion, and lamb saddle has become quite difficult to find. Instead, butchers most often cut the loin into loin chops. The only differences between loin chops and rib chops are that loin chops come without rib bones and can be slightly larger and tenderer. When not cut into chops, the loin can be boned and roasted whole for an elegant dinner.

ROASTED LOIN OF LAMB

4 servings

For a special meal, order a boneless loin of lamb and roast it to medium-rare. A single boned and trimmed loin ranges in size from ¾ pound for New Zealand or baby lamb to 2 pounds for average domestic lamb.

To avoid drying out the very small loins and to have enough to serve 4 to 6 people, buy two boneless loins if they are under 1 pound and have the butcher tie them together into one compact cylinder. Roast as for one whole 2-pound loin. Even when roasting one whole loin, tie it with butcher twine so that it holds its shape. We recommend leaving a ¼-inch layer of fat on the roast to keep it moist while roasting. Rubbing the roast with olive oil before roasting is also a good idea.

Preheat the oven to 425°F.

Pat dry:

1 boneless loin of lamb (1½ to 2 pounds), trimmed and tied at 1½-inch intervals

Season with:

1 teaspoon salt

½ teaspoon ground black pepper

Heat a heavy, ovenproof skillet without fat over high heat. Add the lamb and brown on all sides, about 3 minutes. Place the skillet in the oven. Roast until a meat thermometer inserted in the thickest part of the meat registers 125°F for rare or 130°F for medium-rare, about 25 minutes (the temperature will rise 5° out of the oven). Remove from the oven, cover loosely with aluminum foil, and let stand for 5 to 10 minutes. Remove the strings and cut into ¾-to 1-inch-thick medallions. If desired, serve with:

Red Wine and Sour Cherry Sauce, 53, or Sauce Marchand de Vin, 51

ROASTED LOIN OF LAMB WITH PERSILLADE

Persillade is a mixture of parsley and garlic that is often added to a dish as a last-minute seasoning. Here it is combined with breadcrumbs and used to coat a loin of lamb.

Prepare Roasted Loin of Lamb, above, through the searing. In a small bowl, combine ½ cup chopped fresh parsley, ⅓ cup fresh breadcrumbs, 1 tablespoon minced garlic or to taste, and 2 tablespoons olive oil, or enough to make a rough paste. Roll the lamb in the parsley mixture and press firmly to make the paste adhere. Roast as directed.

ABOUT LAMB CHOPS AND STEAKS

The most popular, but expensive, lamb chops are loin and rib chops, prized for their tenderness and good-sized nugget of eye meat. Rib chops are recognizable by the "handle" of rib bone extending from the eye. Loin chops are more compact and somewhat meatier, resembling a tiny T-bone steak. Either can be grilled, broiled, pan-broiled, or sautéed; as with all tender cuts of lamb, however, they are best when not cooked past medium. Chops at least ¾ inch thick are best, as thinner ones are easy to overcook. Figure on two or three chops per person, depending on size.

Chops from the arm and shoulder are labeled as shoulder chops, arm chops, or blade chops. Unlike rib and loin chops, these less expensive chops have lines of fat laced through the muscle and varying amounts of connective tissue. Shoulder and arm chops are often braised to tenderize them. We have also had good luck marinating them before grilling or broiling. While never as tender as rib or loin chops, they have excellent flavor and will not dry out when cooked past medium. Allow one 6- to 8-ounce chop per person, a bit more if the chops have a lot of bone.

Loin and leg chops tend to be larger than rib or loin chops and less fatty than shoulder chops. Many cooks (and diners) consider chops from the upper leg, or sirloin, among the best cuts of lamb; these can be grilled or braised. They will not be as tender as rib and loin chops, but they have a marvelous rich flavor. Leg chops can vary greatly from market to market, however, so it is best to specify that you want steaks from the sirloin and not from the smaller, less tender parts of the leg. Large steaks from farther down the leg are recognizable by the cross section of leg bone, much like a ham steak. These can be cooked by dry-heat methods such as grilling or broiling, although they might be a bit chewy. Figure on 6 to 8 ounces leg meat per serving, a bit more if the steaks have a lot of bone.

SAUTÉED LAMB CHOPS

4 servings

Pat dry:

8 lamb chops, preferably from the rib or loin, about 1 inch thick

Season with:

1 teaspoon salt

½ teaspoon ground black pepper

Heat in a large, heavy skillet over medium-high heat until the butter begins to turn light brown:

1 tablespoon butter

1 tablespoon olive oil

Arrange the lamb chops in the pan. For medium-rare, sauté the chops for 4½ to 5 minutes on each side. Sauté the chops for 1 minute more for medium. Remove the chops to a warmed platter or plates and serve immediately. If desired, serve with:

Basic Herb Pan Sauce, 52, Pan Sauce with Leeks, Orange, and Rosemary, 53, or chopped fresh parsley

PAN-BROILED LAMB CHOPS

A method using no fat and higher heat.

Prepare Sautéed Lamb Chops, above, omitting the oil and butter and, instead, heating a well-seasoned cast-iron or nonstick skillet over high heat. Add the chops and cook for 3½ to 4 minutes each side.

LAMB CHOPS WITH ROASTED GARLIC AND COGNAC

4 servings

Prepare:

Sautéed Lamb Chops, above

When chops are cooked, remove them to a serving platter and set aside in a warm place. Pour the fat from the skillet, being careful not to pour out any juices or browned bits. Place the skillet over high heat and add:

⅓ cup brandy

Boil for 1 minute, scraping the bottom of the pan with a wooden spoon to loosen and dissolve the browned bits. Add:

½ cup beef or lamb stock

Boil until reduced by half. Whisk in any lamb juices that have accumulated along with:

2 tablespoons pureed Roasted Garlic, 378

Bring the sauce back to a boil, stirring. Remove from the heat and whisk in 1 tablespoon at a time:

1 to 3 tablespoons softened butter

Add:

1 tablespoon fresh thyme leaves, lightly chopped (optional), or 1 teaspoon dried
1 tablespoon snipped fresh chives (optional)
Salt and ground black pepper to taste

Pour the sauce over the chops and serve immediately.

BROILED OR GRILLED LAMB CHOPS

4 servings

Make sure the chops are close enough to the heat to brown well but not so close that they char; 3 to 4 inches is usually ideal.

Preheat the broiler and broiler pan or prepare a medium-hot charcoal fire.

Pat dry:

8 lamb chops, preferably from the rib or loin, about 1 inch thick

Rub both sides with:

2 tablespoons olive oil
1 teaspoon salt
½ teaspoon ground black pepper

Place the chops on the broiler pan or grill rack and cook for 4½ to 5 minutes each side for medium-rare. Cook the chops for 1 minute more for medium. Remove the chops to a warmed platter or plates and serve immediately. If desired, serve with:

Saffron Garlic Mayonnaise, 75, Anchovy Butter, 77, or Roasted Tomato-Chipotle Salsa, 62

BROILED OR GRILLED LAMB STEAKS

4 servings

Whisk together:

¾ cup olive oil
½ cup dry red wine
1 teaspoon salt
½ teaspoon ground black pepper

Pour the mixture over:

2 pounds lamb steaks or shoulder chops, about ¾ inch thick

Cover and marinate in the refrigerator for at least 1 hour and up to 24 hours.

Preheat the broiler and broiler pan or prepare a medium-hot charcoal fire. Place the meat on the broiler pan or grill rack and cook for 3 to 4 minutes each side for medium-rare. Cook for 1 minute more for medium. Remove the steaks to a warmed platter or plates and serve immediately. If desired, serve with:

Tapenade, 161, or Anchovy Butter, 77

BROILED OR GRILLED LAMB STEAKS WITH MEDITERRANEAN GARLIC HERB PASTE

Prepare as for Broiled or Grilled Lamb Steaks, above, omitting the red wine marinade and, instead, rubbing the lamb steaks generously with 1½ cups Mediterranean Garlic Herb Paste, 87. Marinate in the refrigerator for at least 1 hour or up to 24 hours before broiling or grilling as directed.

TANDOORI LAMB CHOPS

4 servings

The assertive, almost sweet flavor of lamb pairs beautifully with the aromatic yogurt-based Tandoori marinade. Do not leave the lamb chops in the marinade for more than 6 hours, or the acidity of the yogurt will overtenderize the meat.

Prepare:

Tandoori Marinade, 85

Pour the marinade over:

8 to 12 lamb chops, preferably from the rib or loin, about 1 inch thick

Marinate for 4 to 6 hours in the refrigerator, turning the chops occasionally.

Prepare a medium-hot charcoal fire. Arrange the lamb chops on the grill rack and grill for 4 to 5 minutes each side for medium-rare. Grill for 1 minute more for medium. If desired, serve with:

Raita I, 83, or Raita II, 83
Naan, 753

ABOUT LAMB STEWS AND BRAISES

Lamb stew meat sold in the supermarkets generally comes from the shoulder, neck, breast, shank, or leg. Of these, meat from the shoulder and neck have the best flavor; leg meat is the mildest, but it can become dry when stewed or braised. The whole shoulder is also often available, boned and rolled, and can be braised slowly as for a pot roast, 667. Shoulder chops are ideal for braising on top of the stove. Lamb neck pieces are another fine choice for slow, moist cooking, and although they are less meaty than some cuts, the flavor is tremendous. Unlike roasted and sautéed lamb dishes, stewed and braised lamb should be cooked gently in a bit of wine, stock, tomato juice, or some combination of these until the meat is well done and very tender. In addition to the recipes that follow, lamb can be substituted for beef, pork, and veal in any slow-cooked stew or braise. Please see About Braising, Stewing and Pot-Roasting Meat, 640.

PAN-BRAISED SHOULDER CHOPS

4 servings

Unlike tender rib and loin chops, these flavorful chops fare best when braised in a mixture of wine and stock.

Pat dry:

4 lamb shoulder chops, preferably arm or blade (2½ to 3 pounds), about ¾ inch thick

Season with:

1 teaspoon salt
½ teaspoon ground black pepper

Heat in a large, heavy skillet over high heat until the butter begins to turn light brown:

1 tablespoon butter
1 tablespoon olive oil

Brown the lamb chops evenly and sauté about 2 minutes each side. Remove the chops and pour off all but about 1 tablespoon fat from the pan. Place the pan over medium heat and add:

3 cloves garlic, coarsely chopped
1 teaspoon dried herbes de Provence or scant ½ teaspoon each dried thyme, rosemary, and basil

Cook, stirring, until garlic is soft but not brown. Add:

1 cup dry white wine

Simmer, scraping up any browned bits on the bottom of the pan, until reduced by half. Add and reduce again by half, or until smooth and slightly thickened:

½ cup Lamb Stock, 40, or chicken stock
1 cup tomato puree

Return the chops to the pan. Reduce the heat to low, cover, and simmer, turning once, until the chops are tender, 40 to 45 minutes. Remove from the heat and skim off any fat from the surface of the sauce. If desired, add:

½ cup halved pitted Niçoise olives

Taste and adjust the seasonings. Garnish with:

Chopped fresh parsley

If desired, serve with:

Mashed Potatoes, 408

IRISH STEW

4 to 6 servings

The potatoes in this recipe are cut in two different ways because they serve different purposes. Those that are sliced break down during the long cooking and thicken the stew without the addition of flour. The halved potatoes cook to tender and add soft bite to the stew. As in a French blanquette, the meat is not browned.

Preheat the oven to 325°F.

Heat in a Dutch oven over medium heat:

2 tablespoons vegetable oil or unsalted butter

Add and cook without browning, until softened:

2 medium onions, chopped

Stir in:

3 pounds boneless lamb stew meat, cut into 1-inch cubes, or 3 pounds lamb shoulder chops
2 teaspoons fresh thyme leaves, or ¾ teaspoon dried
Salt and ground black pepper to taste

Mix in:

2 medium boiling potatoes, peeled and sliced
3 cups chicken stock or water
½ teaspoon Worcestershire sauce

Add:

4 medium potatoes, peeled and halved

Cover tightly and bake for 1 hour. Remove from the oven and add, stirring:

8 medium carrots, peeled and cut diagonally into ½-inch slices
¼ cup pearl barley
¼ cup heavy cream

Cover and return to the oven. Bake until the meat is fork-tender and barley is softened, 45 to 60 minutes more.

Season with:

Salt and ground black pepper to taste

Serve sprinkled with:

Chopped fresh parsley

LAMB CURRY WITH TOMATO *4 servings*

This fiery hot, royal red curry has a richly reduced tomato sauce. Eat it with a flat bread such as pita. For a milder dish, reduce the ground red pepper to ¼ teaspoon.

Drain, reserving the juice, and coarsely chop:

One 28-ounce can whole tomatoes

Heat in a Dutch oven over medium heat:

¼ cup vegetable oil

Add and cook, stirring, until softened and evenly golden brown, 5 to 7 minutes:

1 medium onion, thinly sliced

Increase the heat to medium-high and add and cook, stirring, for 30 seconds:

2 teaspoons ground cumin
2 teaspoons ground coriander
1½ teaspoons minced garlic
1½ teaspoons grated peeled fresh ginger
1 teaspoon ground turmeric
½ teaspoon ground red pepper

Add ½ cup of the chopped tomato and ¼ cup of the tomato juice along with:

1½ pounds boneless lamb stew meat, trimmed and cut into 1- to 1¼-inch cubes

Simmer, stirring occasionally, until the liquid is cooled down and thickened slightly, 5 to 7 minutes. Stir in the remaining tomatoes and juice. Season with:

¾ teaspoon salt

Cover and reduce the heat to maintain a simmer. Cook until the lamb is tender, 45 to 60 minutes. Remove the meat with a slotted spoon and keep warm. Skim any fat from the surface of the liquid, increase the heat, and simmer briskly until the sauce is cooked down and thickened. Return the meat to the sauce and stir in:

2 tablespoons chopped fresh cilantro (optional)

If desired, serve with:

Hot cooked rice
Indian Lentil Puree, 284
Naan, 753

BRAISED SHOULDER OF LAMB *8 servings*

Lamb shoulder has great flavor and becomes tender when braised. Most markets sell boneless lamb shoulder roasts rolled and tied; the irregularly shaped shoulder bones are difficult to manage when it comes time to carve. If you prefer a bone-in shoulder roast for more flavor, cook it until the meat falls off the bone.

Preheat the oven to 425°F.

Pat dry:

1 lamb shoulder (4 to 5 pounds boneless, or 8 to 9 pounds bone-in), rolled and tied for easy carving

Season with:

1 teaspoon salt
½ teaspoon ground black pepper

Heat in a Dutch oven over high heat:

2 tablespoons olive oil

Add the lamb and brown on all sides. Remove the lamb from the pan, reduce the heat, and remove all but 2 tablespoons fat from the pan. Add:

1 medium onion, diced
1 celery rib, diced
1 carrot, peeled and diced
1 small turnip or parsnip diced
1½ teaspoons salt
1 teaspoon ground black pepper
½ to 1 teaspoon mixed spices (ground coriander, ground cumin, turmeric, saffron, fenugreek, and/or curry powder)

Cook slowly, scraping up any browned bits, until starting to soften, about 10 minutes. Meanwhile, bring to a boil in a saucepan over high heat:

2 cups of beef, lamb, or vegetable stock
1 cup tomato puree

Return the lamb to the pan with the vegetables. Add the boiling stock mixture along with:

1 bay leaf

Cover the pan, bring to a simmer, and place in the oven. Immediately reduce the oven temperature to 325°F and cook until the meat is fork-tender, 2 to 2½ hours (up to 3½ hours if bone-in). Remove the meat from the sauce and keep warm. Skim off the fat from the surface of the sauce. Taste and adjust the seasonings. Cut the strings from the meat and serve it in chunks or slices with plenty of sauce. If desired, serve with:

Buttermilk Mashed Potatoes, 409, or Gratin Dauphinois, 412

BARBECUED LAMB SHOULDER *8 servings*

This dish can be made a few days in advance and simply reheated in a gentle oven (350°F), with a bit of water or more sauce added if it looks dry.

Position a rack in the center of the oven. Preheat the oven to 325°F.

Pat dry:

4 pounds boneless lamb shoulder, cut into 2 or 3 large pieces, lightly pounded to an even thickness of 1½ to 2 inches

Heat in a large, heavy skillet over medium-high heat until hot but not smoking:

2 tablespoons olive or other vegetable oil

Add the meat in batches and brown well on both sides, being careful not to overcrowd the pan, about 5 minutes for each piece.

Line a baking sheet with three 24-inch pieces of heavy-duty aluminum foil, and loosely shape the foil into a packet. Spoon into the foil half of:

2 cups barbecue sauce

1 large onion, halved and thinly sliced

Arrange the meat on top and cover it with the remaining sauce and onions. Close the packet, crimping the edges to prevent leaks. Cut another sheet of foil and wrap a second time if necessary. Bake for 2½ hours. Let stand for 5 to 10 minutes before opening the packet, then carefully unwrap the foil, letting the sauce run onto the baking sheet. Thinly slice the meat and coat the slices with the sauce. Arrange the sauced meat on a platter and serve.

ABOUT LAMB SHANKS

Lamb shanks are the shin portion of the legs. The foreshanks are the meatiest and the easiest to find, because the rear shanks are usually only sold attached to the whole leg of lamb. Front or back, most lamb shanks are cut longer than the more familiar veal shanks and have enough meat attached so that one per person is a satisfying portion. The shank contains a good deal of connective tissue which, when cooked by the slow, moist heat of a braise, produces a velvety sauce. Substitute lamb shanks in any recipe for braised veal shank or beef short ribs or oxtail.

BRAISED LAMB SHANKS

4 servings

Middle Eastern and Mediterranean cultures have long appreciated lamb shanks.

Preheat the oven to 300°F.

Trim most of the external fat from:

4 meaty lamb shanks (about 3 to 4 pounds total)

Season with:

1 teaspoon salt

½ teaspoon ground black pepper

½ teaspoon ground ginger

½ teaspoon sweet or hot paprika

Heat in a large Dutch oven over high heat:

2 tablespoons olive oil

Add the shanks and brown on all sides, about 5 minutes. Remove the shanks and keep warm. Pour off all but 2 tablespoons of fat from the pan. Add:

2 onions, halved and thinly sliced

2 tablespoons chopped garlic

Reduce the heat to medium, cover, and cook, stirring often, until the onions are quite soft. Sprinkle with:

1 tablespoon chopped fresh mint, or 1 teaspoon dried

1 teaspoon sweet or hot paprika

1 teaspoon ground coriander

1 teaspoon ground cumin

½ teaspoon ground black pepper

¼ teaspoon ground ginger

Pinch of ground cinnamon

Pinch of ground allspice

Stir well to coat the onions. Add:

2 cups chicken or lamb stock or water

1 cup dry white wine

⅓ cup tomato puree

Increase the heat and bring to a boil. Return the lamb shanks to the pan, cover, and bake until the meat is almost falling off the bone, 1 to ½ hours. Add:

2 cups 1-inch pieces carrots

2 cups diced, peeled winter squash, such as butternut or Hubbard

Cover and bake until the vegetables are tender, about 15 minutes more. Remove the meat and vegetables to a platter and cover with aluminum foil to keep warm. Skim off the fat from the surface of the sauce. Add:

2 tablespoons fresh lemon juice

2 to 3 tablespoons chopped fresh mint, or 2 tablespoons dried

2 teaspoons Harissa, 82, or to taste (optional)

Taste and adjust the seasonings and pour the sauce over the meat and vegetables. Serve with:

Cooked orzo, Basic Pilaf, 257, braised lentils, or white beans

SHEPHERD'S PIE

4 servings

Finely chopped or ground lamb covered with mashed potatoes is favorite pub food in England and Ireland. It is equally good whether made with fresh or leftover ground lamb. Chopped or ground beef substituted for the lamb makes the dish cottage pie.

Place in a large pot of cold water over medium heat:

1½ pounds all-purpose potatoes, peeled, quartered, and well rinsed

Bring to a boil and cook until tender, about 15 minutes. Drain, reserving ½ cup of the cooking water. Mash the potatoes with a fork or potato masher, adding the cooking water along with:

1 tablespoon butter
Salt and ground white pepper to taste

Beat with a wooden spoon until fluffy.
Preheat the oven to 400°F.
While the potatoes are cooking, heat in a medium skillet over medium-low heat:

3 tablespoons vegetable oil

Add:

1 medium onion, chopped
1 carrot, peeled and chopped
1 celery stalk, chopped

Cook, stirring occasionally, until softened, about 15 minutes. Increase the heat to medium and add:

1 pound leftover cooked lamb, finely chopped, or raw ground lamb

Cook for about 5 minutes, stirring to brown evenly. If using raw lamb, cook for 10 minutes more, stirring and breaking up the meat with a wooden spoon. Spoon off any fat. Add:

1 tablespoon all-purpose flour

Cook, stirring, for 2 to 3 minutes. Add:

¾ cup beef or vegetable stock
1 tablespoon chopped fresh thyme, or 1 teaspoon dried
1 tablespoon chopped fresh rosemary, or 1 teaspoon dried
Pinch of ground nutmeg
Salt and ground black pepper to taste (leftover lamb or beef many not need seasoning)

Reduce the heat to low and simmer, stirring occasionally, until thickened, about 5 minutes. Let cool slightly, then remove to a 9-inch pie plate or baking dish. Spread the mashed potatoes over the top, making irregular peaks with the tines of a fork. Scatter over the top:

2 tablespoons cold butter, cut into small pieces

Bake until potatoes are browned and the dish is heated all the way through, 30 to 35 minutes. Let cool slightly, then serve directly from the baking dish.

ABOUT GOAT OR KID

The meat of young goat, or kid, has long been savored by cultures in the Mediterranean, the Middle East, Central and South America, and the Caribbean—almost everywhere, it seems, but here. This is our loss, because it is lean, delicate-tasting meat, similar to lamb in texture but milder in flavor. You can find kid at Hispanic, Greek, Italian, and West Indian meat markets, especially around Easter, and premium markets occasionally sell it as well. It is labeled "chevron," the French word for kid, by U.S. government ruling. Most kid comes to market under four months of age, with a dressed weight of between 12 and 30 pounds. The smaller the animal, the more subtle-tasting and tender the meat. Whole kid is traditionally spit-roasted until the meat is almost falling off the bone. If you buy individual cuts, braising and stewing are the best cooking methods. Tenderer cuts from the rib and loin can be cooked by dry heat, such as roasting or grilling, but even these tend to be tough. Use kid in any stewed or braised lamb or beef recipe.

JAMAICAN CURRIED GOAT *6 servings*

Considered by many the national dish of Jamaica, this curry is fiery-hot when made with the Caribbean habanero pepper, or Scotch Bonnet. Use milder jalapeño peppers for less heat. Lamb or pork can be substituted for the goat.
Combine in a large bowl and toss to coat evenly:

2 pounds goat meat, trimmed and cut into 1-inch cubes
2 tablespoons curry powder
2 fresh chili peppers, such as habanero or jalapeño, seeded and minced
2 cloves garlic, minced
1 teaspoon salt
1 teaspoon ground black pepper

Cover and refrigerate for at least 1 hour or up to 12 hours. Remove the meat from the marinade, pat dry, and reserve any juices that may have accumulated. Heat in a Dutch oven over medium-high heat:

2 tablespoons vegetable oil

Add the meat and brown on all sides, in batches if necessary, 5 to 6 minutes. Remove the browned meat with a slotted spoon. Add and cook over medium heat, stirring often, until the onions begin to brown, about 5 minutes:

1 medium onion, chopped
1 celery stalk, chopped

Add any reserved marinade juices along with:

2½ cups vegetable stock or water
1 bay leaf

Bring to a boil. Cover and simmer over low heat for 1 hour. Add:

3 to 4 boiling potatoes, peeled and cut into 2-inch chunks

Cover and cook until potatoes and meat are fork-tender, 20 to 40 minutes. Remove from the heat and skim off any fat from the surface. Adjust the seasonings and serve with:

Hot cooked rice

ABOUT GROUND MEAT

By far the most popular ground meat in America is ground beef. Different cuts contain varying levels of fat. Ground chuck has the best flavor and is the best for hamburgers, 186, while ground chuck or the leaner, milder ground round can be used for meat loaf and meatballs. Since these recipes include eggs, breadcrumbs, and other ingredients to bind the meat together and add flavor, look for pale red or pink meat; too red meat may mean that a dishonest butcher has added blood or federally restricted sodium sulfite to heighten the color. While extremely lean meat may appeal to our health-consciousness, it is important to note that a little fat is necessary to prevent the meat from drying out and becoming overcooked. Conversely, very pale pink meat is often high in fat and will literally shrink and cook away. Untreated ground beef will naturally darken with exposure to light, but this darkening is not harmful. Ground beef should smell fresh, not sour, and should be moist but not slimly.

Ground turkey and chicken have become recent favorites and are discussed in Poultry, 567. Other ground meats include veal, pork, and lamb. Ground veal should be almost white or very pale pink—the redder the meat, the tougher and older the calf. Veal contains very little fat and is generally combined with either beef or pork for meatballs, burgers, and meat loaf to make up the difference. Ground pork should be nicely pink. Today, hogs are bred leaner and are not as fatty as in the past. Very pale pink or white pork is high in fat and not recommended for meatballs and meat loaf; it can be used for pâtés and terrines, 724. Ground lamb should be pale red or dark pink and is generally ground from the shoulder.

Do not store any uncooked ground meat for more than 24 hours. For information on grinding your own meat, see About Grinding and Pounding Meat, 644.

GROUND BEEF WITH POTATOES AND SPICES (KEEMA ALU)

4 servings

This dish of beef, tomatoes, and potatoes makes a satisfying meal when paired with cooked lentils and pita bread.

Heat in a large cast-iron or other heavy skillet over medium-high heat:

3 tablespoons vegetable oil

Add and cook, stirring, until golden brown, 5 to 7 minutes:

1 medium onion, finely chopped

Add and cook quickly, stirring, just until well mixed:

2 teaspoons minced garlic
2 teaspoons grated peeled fresh ginger
2 teaspoons ground cumin
2 teaspoons ground coriander
1 teaspoon turmeric
¼ teaspoon ground red pepper, or to taste

Add:

1 pound lean ground beef or turkey
½ cup chopped canned tomatoes, drained, plus 1 tablespoon juice
¾ teaspoon salt

Cook, stirring, until the meat is no longer pink and all the liquid is evaporated, leaving the meat to sizzle in oil, 8 to 10 minutes. Stir into the meat mixture and cook for 2 minutes:

12 ounces boiling potatoes, peeled and cut into ½-inch cubes

Add:

1 cup water

Cover, reduce the heat to low, and simmer until the potatoes are tender, 15 to 20 minutes. Uncover, increase the heat, and cook until all the water is evaporated. Taste and adjust the seasonings. Sprinkle with:

2 tablespoons chopped fresh cilantro
1 fresh serrano or jalapeño pepper, seeded and cut into thin strips (optional)

If desired, serve with:

Pita bread
Dal, 284
Raita, 82

PICADILLO

4 servings

This dish is sometimes served as is, with bowls of garnish such as grated cheese, shredded lettuce, guacamole, and chopped tomatoes. But it is perhaps best as a filling for tortillas—enchiladas, tacos, tostados, and the like. One of the most spectacular ways to use it is as a stuffing for chili peppers, as in Baked Chile Rellenos with Cheese, 405.

Place in a frying pan and cook until the beef starts to brown, mashing down to crumble the meat:

1 pound ground beef
1 cup chorizo

If too much fat is released, drain on paper towels and put back in the pan. Add:

1 onion, chopped
1 clove garlic, minced

Cook for a few minutes, then add:

1 cup chopped tomatoes
1 tablespoon vinegar
1 teaspoon ground cinnamon

¼ teaspoon ground cumin
Pinch of sugar
Pinch of ground cloves
1 bay leaf

Simmer, covered, for 30 minutes. Add:

½ cup raisins
½ cup slivered blanched almonds (optional)
½ cup pitted black olives, chopped (optional)

Cook, uncovered, for 10 to 15 minutes.

ETHAN'S LAMB PATTIES *4 to 6 servings*

If you love lamb, you'll love these hors d'oeuvres hot off the grill.

Combine in a large bowl and mix well, using your hands:

1 pound ground lamb
Zest of ½ lemon
Juice of ½ lemon
2 teaspoons sherry
2 teaspoons soy sauce
1½ cloves garlic, finely minced
1 teaspoon dried thyme, crushed
1 teaspoon salt
1 teaspoon ground black pepper
2 dashes hot red pepper sauce

Shape the mixture into 2-inch patties. In a skillet, heat over medium-high heat:

2 tablespoons olive oil

Fry patties for 2 minutes, flip, and sprinkle with additional:

Soy sauce

Fry for 1 minute more. Remove skillet from heat, cover, and let stand 1 minute. Serve with:

French bread, or
Toast rounds

ABOUT MEAT LOAF AND MEATBALLS

A hearty meat loaf with plenty of mashed potatoes and gravy reminds us of home and times gone by. Many restaurants are capitalizing on our nostalgic passion for meat loaf, and this once homely dish now appears on some of the finest tables.

Interesting meat loaves can be made with more than one kind of meat, and although differing ratios of beef, pork, and veal are specified in recipes, they can be varied to suit your own taste. A fairly coarsely ground meat is best so that the loaf will have some texture, not unlike a country pâté. Raw sausage meat can be substituted for pork; keep in mind that both pork and sausage generally are fattier than beef, so a combination of meats is always best. Ground turkey or chicken as discussed in the Poultry chapter, 567, can also be included as part of the meat mixture, although it is too lean to use on its own. No matter what combination of meats you choose, make sure the total amount of meat in relation to the other ingredients remains the same and do not overmix or overwork the mixture, or it will become heavy and tough. The idea is to work the ingredients just enough so that they are evenly mixed; the best tools for this are your hands. Most meat loaf recipes contain some egg to enrich and bind the mixture and some breadcrumbs or grain to lighten the texture.

Part of the pleasure of making meat loaf is that it is entirely unfussy and open to interpretation. It can be mounded on a greased baking sheet with a rim to catch the juices or put into a greased ring mold or loaf pan. Some cooks pour about ½ cup ketchup in the bottom of a loaf pan before filling it with the meat, while others pour about 2 tablespoons chili sauce over the meat loaf when it is half-baked to create a light crust. Meat loaf is sometimes baked in two layers with a stuffing in between. Small, individual meat loaves can be baked in muffin tins—they take only 20 to 30 minutes. Cover a single large meat loaf with a piece of aluminum foil during cooking to keep it moist, but uncover it for the last 15 minutes of baking.

Meat loaf baked in a ring mold makes a cheerful presentation filled with spicy greens or browned potatoes. Or serve it sliced and cold with flavorful homemade condiments. Leftover meat loaf is never a problem. There is nothing like cold meat loaf between slices of tangy rye bread with thinly sliced onions and lots of mayonnaise—it makes one of the world's great sandwiches.

Meat loaf is highly suited to being either frozen raw for cooking later or cooked and frozen to reheat. Sometimes if meat loaf containing a lot of tomato or coated in ketchup is wrapped in foil, the acidity may create small pinholes in the foil. It is not harmful or toxic and can be safely eaten. However, as a preventive measure, wrap it in plastic first, then aluminum foil. Regardless of freezing or storage, meat loaf should be cooked thoroughly to 160°F. Do not overcook it; it should be firm but not dry. A 9 x 5-inch loaf will generally serve six to eight people.

Meatballs are similar to meat loaf in everything but form. They are made with seasoned ground meat enriched by egg, breadcrumbs, minced onions, and other ingredients. Meatballs can be simmered in stock or browned and then added to a sauce or gravy. Uncooked meatballs can be frozen on a baking sheet, then placed in a plastic bag and kept frozen for up to 3 months. Any meat loaf recipe can be used for meatballs; shape the meat into ¾- to 1-inch balls and cook as meatballs.

CLASSIC MEAT LOAF

8 servings

A good meat loaf should be both firm and juicy; it should not crumble or fall apart when sliced. This meat loaf is cooked in a bread pan, which gives a juicier result; it can also be molded into a freeform loaf on a baking sheet.

Position a rack in the center of the oven. Preheat the oven to 350°F. Lightly grease a 9 x 5-inch (8-cup) loaf pan.

Combine in a large bowl:

12 ounces ground beef chuck
12 ounces ground beef round
1½ cups finely chopped onions
1 cup quick-cooking rolled oats or breadcrumbs
⅔ cup ketchup
⅔ cup finely chopped fresh parsley
3 large eggs, lightly beaten
1 teaspoon ground thyme
1 teaspoon salt
½ teaspoon ground black pepper

Knead the mixture with your hands until everything is well blended. Do not overmix.

Fill the loaf pan with the meat mixture, mounding the top. Place the pan on a baking sheet and bake until the meat is firm to the touch and has shrunk from the sides of the pan or until an instant-read thermometer inserted in the center of the loaf reads 160°F, 1 to 1¼ hours. Pour off the excess fat and let stand for 15 minutes. Serve, if desired, with:

Pan Gravy for Meat, 52
Mashed Potatoes, 408

SOUTHWESTERN MEAT LOAF

Prepare Classic Meat Loaf, above, adding with the other ingredients:

1 large green bell pepper, chopped
½ cup chopped raisins
½ cup pine nuts, toasted
¼ cup finely chopped garlic
2 tablespoons chili powder
1 tablespoon ground cumin
1 teaspoon ground red pepper
1 teaspoon dried oregano
½ teaspoon ground cinnamon

ITALIAN MEAT LOAF

Prepare Classic Meat Loaf, above, adding with the other ingredients:

2 cups shredded fresh mozzarella cheese
1 cup grated Parmesan cheese
3 tablespoons finely chopped garlic
1½ teaspoons dried oregano

Decrease the salt to ½ teaspoon.

ADDITIONS TO MEAT LOAF

Meat loaf is often bound with egg, cracker crumbs, breadcrumbs, or oats, but different ingredients can also be added for flavor and texture. If you are experimenting with new ingredients, you may want to first mix a very small batch and fry up a hamburger of the mixture to taste it before mixing and cooking the entire loaf. To one 8-cup recipe, you can add vegetables such as:

½ cup finely grated carrots, potatoes, or sweet potatoes

The vegetables must be finely grated or chopped so that they fully cook inside the loaf. It is best to cook some additions first, such as:

½ cup thinly sliced sautéed mushrooms, or ½ cup cooked rice

For crunch, you can add:

¼ cup coarsely chopped almonds, pecans, or walnuts

For a little spice, add:

2 teaspoons chili sauce, 1 tablespoon Dijon mustard, or 1 tablespoon drained horseradish

The key is to season highly. Be brave! Add more garlic if your family likes garlic or try another herb combination. For each 1 tablespoon parsley, substitute:

1 tablespoon chopped fresh thyme, 1 tablespoon snipped fresh chives, or 1 tablespoon chopped fresh basil

Do no overmix meat loaf, or it will be too dense. When making additions, it is always best to cook a small amount first to see if the mixture will hold together and that it is seasoned properly. Make a small patty and sauté it in a skillet, let it cool slightly, and taste. If the mixture falls apart, add another egg; if it is bland, add more seasonings.

HAM LOAF

4 servings

Make this with smoked ham for a more distinctive flavor, but any cooked ham will do. Leftovers make good sandwiches.

Preheat the oven to 350°F.

Combine in a large bowl:

1 pound cooked ham, ground or finely chopped
½ pound ground pork
1 onion, finely chopped
1 apple, peeled, cored, and finely chopped
½ cup cracker crumbs or dry breadcrumbs
½ cup sour cream
2 eggs
1 teaspoon dry mustard
¼ teaspoon ground allspice
¼ teaspoon ground nutmeg
¼ teaspoon ground black pepper

Mix together with your hands until everything is well blended. Place the mixture in a lightly greased 9 x 5-inch (8-cup) loaf pan or shape it into a loaf in a shallow baking pan. If desired, mix together in a small bowl:

3 tablespoons red currant or grape jelly
2 tablespoons prepared horseradish

Bake until an instant-read thermometer inserted in the center of the loaf reads 155°F, about 1½ to 2 hours. During baking, baste the loaf with the jelly mixture, if using. Serve warm.

GERMAN MEATBALLS WITH CAPER SAUCE (KÖNIGSBERGER KLOPSE) *4 servings*

Place in a large bowl and add just enough water to cover:

1 cup slightly stale coarse breadcrumbs

When well softened, place the bread in a large bowl with:

1 pound ground lean beef
½ pound ground pork

Work with clean hands to make a smooth paste. Stir in until well mixed:

1 tablespoon minced shallots
1 anchovy, minced
½ tablespoon drained juice from a jar of capers
½ teaspoon lemon juice
½ teaspoon salt
¼ teaspoon grated lemon zest
Pinch of ground white pepper

Add and work until smooth:

1 large egg, beaten

Use spoons or moist hands to form the meat into about twelve 2-inch meatballs. In a large pot over high heat, bring to a boil:

6 cups beef or veal stock

When boiling rapidly, add the meatballs in batches so as not to crowd the pot. Cook until the meatballs rise to the top, about 12 to 15 minutes. Remove from the broth with a slotted spoon and set aside to keep warm. Strain the broth and reserve it to make the caper sauce. Melt in a skillet over medium heat:

2 tablespoons butter

Add and cook until soft:

1 tablespoon minced shallots

Stir in:

2 tablespoons all-purpose flour

Cook, stirring, until the flour bubbles. Slowly stir in 1¼ to 1½ cups strained broth and simmer, stirring occasionally, until smooth and thick.

In a small bowl, beat until pale-colored:

1 large egg yolk

Slowly whisk into the yolk a few tablespoons of reserved broth. This will lightly warm (temper) the yolk and prevent it from curdling when added to the sauce. Reduce the heat to low and whisk the yolk and broth mix into the sauce. Cook, stirring constantly, until the sauce is slightly thickened. Be careful not to boil the sauce. Add:

½ tablespoon capers
Several drops of lemon juice
Salt and ground black pepper to taste

Add the meatballs to the sauce and add more broth, if needed, to thin out the sauce. Serve hot.

SWEDISH MEATBALLS *About 90 meatballs*

The trick to making authentic Swedish meatballs is to beat the ground meat with water until fluffy and smooth. Serve these as an hors d'oeuvre (enough for 12 to 16 guests) or as a main course (for 6 to 8) accompanied by mashed potatoes and cranberry sauce.

Melt in a small, heavy skillet over medium-high heat:

1 tablespoon butter

Add and sauté, stirring often, until soft, about 1 to 2 minutes:

1 tablespoon minced onions

Remove from the heat and set aside. In the large bowl of an electric mixer, combine and let stand until soft, about 1 to 2 minutes:

⅔ cup fresh breadcrumbs
1 cup water

Add the reserved onions along with:

¾ pound lean ground beef
¾ pound lean ground pork
2 large egg yolks
1 teaspoon salt
¼ teaspoon ground black pepper
¼ teaspoon grated nutmeg
¼ teaspoon ground allspice

Beat on low speed until smooth. Turn the mixer to high

speed and beat until the mixture is light in color and fluffy, about 10 minutes. Using two spoons dipped in cold water, shape the meat into 1-inch balls. Heat in a large skillet over medium heat:

4 tablespoons butter

Cook the meatballs in batches of about 15 to 20 at a time and brown on all sides. Remove with a slotted spoon and drain briefly on paper towels before removing to a warmed serving platter. Cover to keep warm. When all the meatballs are cooked, reduce the heat to low and add to the skillet:

2 tablespoons all-purpose flour

Cook, stirring, until lightly browned. Slowly add:

2 cups beef stock

Cook, whisking, until the gravy is thick and smooth. Strain, if desired. Pour the gravy over the meatballs and serve hot.

ABOUT PÂTÉS AND TERRINES

Pâtés and terrines are the stars of a cold buffet and are basically no harder to make than meat loaf. What distinguishes them is the sometimes luxurious quality of their ingredients. The typical richness of a pâté can come from ground liver, cream, eggs, spices, or even truffles. The texture may be smooth, if all the meat is finely ground, or patterned, if the more colorful ingredients, such as green pistachios or strips of ham, are diced to show decoratively when the loaf is cut. Endless combinations are possible to develop your own pâté maison.

Pâté de campagne, or pâté maison, refers to the rustic character of a coarsely ground mixture of meat. This can be baked in round or oval pans and is simply fancy meat loaf. Another famous pâté is pâté de foie gras, made from the fattened liver of geese or ducks. These livers are often marinated in Cognac, and the mixture is typically flavored with truffles. Fresh fattened duck liver is now produced and sold in the United States.

Although the terms *pâté* and *terrine* are now used interchangeably in both French and English, there was a difference in the past. Pâtés were traditionally forcemeat or meat mixtures wrapped and baked in pastry, such as Food Processor Puff Pastry, 908, or Brioche, 764, which protects the delicate meat mixture from direct heat. (Indeed, the word pâté shares the same origins as patty, pastry, and paste.) This is now most commonly referred to as pâté en croute, or pâté in a crust. Oftentimes, "terrine" will simply refer to a coarsely ground, rustic pâté.

The ingredients for pâtés and terrines should be very fresh. Handle liver with care, remove the gall bladder if present and all veins and blood. Wash thoroughly in cold water before using. Some meats can be bought ground, or you can ask your butcher to grind them for you. If you grind or puree your own, keep the meat well chilled and keep everything impeccably clean, washing and drying the equipment thoroughly before and after use.

Cook pâtés and terrines until the juices run clear when pierced with a skewer or to an internal temperature of 160°F. Set on a rack to cool. The temperature will continue to rise 5° to 10°F. Let cool to room temperature, then place the terrine on a baking sheet (with sides to catch any juices) and weight it to give a compact texture: Simply place a board or smaller pan directly on the terrine and place several cans on top. Refrigerate until firm, for at least 12 hours but preferably for 3 to 4 days to mature. A properly made, properly refrigerated pâté or terrine will safely keep 7 to 8 days in the refrigerator.

Lean meats, such as rabbit, can also be used, but they require the addition of lard or another animal fat.

PÂTÉ MAISON

10 servings

A pâté de campagne, the texture and robust country flavors make for a great first course when the pâté is sliced and served with cornichons, the tangy small French pickles. Our version has a slightly smoky flavor from the bacon.

Position a rack in the center of the oven. Preheat the oven to 325°F.

Line the bottom and sides of a 9 x 5-inch (8-cup) loaf pan with:

12 to 16 slices bacon

Combine in a large bowl:

1 pound ground veal
1 pound ground calf's or chicken liver
2 large eggs, lightly beaten
½ cup heavy cream
1 tablespoon finely chopped garlic
2 teaspoons dried thyme
1½ teaspoons salt
1½ teaspoons ground black pepper
1 teaspoon freshly grated or ground nutmeg
1 teaspoon sweet paprika
½ teaspoon ground sage

Mix until well combined. Heat in a small saucepan:

⅓ cup brandy or Cognac

If using electric heat, ignite with a match; if using gas heat, tilt the pan to catch the flame. Pour the flaming brandy into the meat mixture and mix well to combine. Fill the lined loaf pan with the meat mixture and spread evenly. Place over the top:

5 or 6 slices bacon

Butter a piece of aluminum foil and place on top of the bacon to seal. Place a dish towel in a 13 x 11-inch roasting pan. Fill the pan halfway with water for a hot-water bath and place the loaf pan in the water bath. Place the pan in the oven and cook until the juices run clear and an instant-read thermometer inserted in the center registers 160°F, about 1½ to 2 hours. Remove to a rack to cool completely. Place a small board or another loaf pan on top of the foil and weight with 2- or 3-pound cans. Refrigerate until firm, at least 12 hours or up to 4 days.

To serve, remove the bacon from the top. Run a sharp knife around the edge, and turn the pâté out onto a serving platter or cutting board. Remove the bacon from the bottom and sides of the pâté and slice into approximately ¾-inch slices. Serve with:

Cornichons
Mustard, preferably Dijon
French bread

CHICKEN LIVER PÂTÉ

8 servings

The technique for this pâté differs slightly in that the liver is cooked and then pureed. The pâté is bound with heavy cream and butter and does not require any further cooking or lengthy weighting down.

Cut into small pieces and place in the freezer:

8 tablespoons (1 stick) butter

Melt in a large skillet over medium-low heat:

2 tablespoons butter

Add:

2 large shallots, finely chopped

Cook until softened, 2 to 3 minutes. Add:

1 small Golden Delicious apple, peeled, cored, and grated

Cook, stirring constantly, until softened, about 3 minutes. Remove to a food processor. Rinse and pat dry:

1 pound chicken livers, trimmed and halved

Heat in the same skillet until the foam subsides:

1 tablespoon butter

Add the chicken livers and season with:

Salt and ground black pepper to taste

Sauté over high heat until brown on the outside but still pink in the center, about 2 minutes each side. Remove the pan from the heat. Pour in:

3 tablespoons Calvados or Cognac

If using electric heat, ignite with a match; if using gas heat, tilt the pan to catch the flame. Return the pan to the heat and swirl until the alcohol has burned off. Remove to the food processor with the apple mixture. Add:

2 tablespoons heavy cream

Process until smooth. With the machine running, drop the pieces of the cold butter 1 at a time down the feed tube. Taste and adjust the seasonings. Scrape into a small crock or bowl and smooth the top with a spatula. Press plastic wrap directly on the surface and refrigerate until firm, at least 2 hours. Serve cold or at room temperature.

ABOUT SAUSAGE

If sausage has the vestiges of a murky reputation in this country, it is probably because of our long-held (and usually mistaken) belief that sausage is made from "parts"—not just various internal organs but the ears, lips, or tails of the animals. Most of what is available in America today, no matter what its ethnic origin, is made from nothing more than meat, fat, and spices—and the commercial sausage industry is highly regulated. Some types of sausage admittedly do contain additives that some may wish to avoid, such as MSG or sodium nitrite, but sausages made from high-quality meats and spices and without additives are increasingly available.

Pork is the traditional sausage meat in most of the world, with beef and veal also favored, but in recent years, sausages made from game, poultry, and even seafood have begun to gain popularity. Sausages made from turkey, chicken, or a blend of the two are now particularly appreciated in America. No matter what their base meat, most sausages fall into one of three main categories.

Fresh sausages are made from raw meat, sold raw, to be cooked before eating. These are usually based on ground or chopped meat, with a slightly coarse texture, combined with spices and herbs. Sausages of this type can be bought in casings or in bulk. You can find fresh country-style or breakfast sausage, Italian sausage, chicken and apple sausage, bratwurst, and kielbasa, among others, in the market. Because they are raw, these sausages are quite perishable; they should be refrigerated immediately and must be eaten within 2 days.

Precooked sausage can be smoked or precooked by other methods. The texture of sausages in this category range from very fine, emulsified types, such as hot dogs, bologna, and knockwurst, to coarser types like smoked kielbasa and cooked salami. Boudin blanc, a fine-textured white sausage made from veal and chicken, and boudin noir, a blood sausage, are both

GRILLED SAUSAGE

Sausages are easy to grill, but it is important to employ a few basic techniques to reduce the chance of fat dripping onto the fire and flaming:

Grill over medium-hot coals. Try to keep the open flames to a minimum. A covered kettle-type barbecue works best, because the cover cuts down on flare-ups.

Poach raw sausages, such as Italian sausages, before grilling.

Do not prick sausages before or during cooking. This will reduce the amount of fat dripping onto the coals. If flare-ups do occur, spray the flames with water from a spray bottle and immediately cover the grill if possible.

For best results, turn sausages often to ensure even browning.

Smoked sausages and poached fresh sausages should take no more than 7 to 10 minutes total on the grill. Thinner sausages, hot dogs for example, cook more quickly. Do not overcook the sausages. If you do cook raw sausages directly on the grill, they will take 12 to 15 minutes. To be completely sure sausages are cooked through, cut one in half. A cooked sausage will be firm to the touch, hot all the way through, and no longer pink in the center.

examples of sausages that are cooked but not smoked. All precooked sausages in this category are completely safe to eat as is, but most are vastly improved if heated through before eating. Since these sausages are perishable, they should be refrigerated immediately and eaten within 3 to 5 days of purchase.

Partially dried and fully cured sausages may be made of raw meat, as in salami, but cured with salt and dried to prevent bacterial growth. Fully cured sausages, such as dry salami or pepperoni, will keep unrefrigerated for several months but will become hard. Semidry, partially cured types, such as summer sausage, thuringer, and Spanish chorizo, are more perishable but will keep in the refrigerator for 2 to 3 weeks. Both types can be sliced and eaten cold but also are used to flavor hot dishes, such as paella, 262, and pizza, 195.

ABOUT COOKING SAUSAGES

Fresh, raw sausages are best slowly pan-fried, or poached or simmered and then grilled or broiled. The preferred method for preparing precooked sausages with a fine texture, such as frankfurters, is to poach them in hot water. Coarse-textured smoked sausages, such as kielbasa, are best pan-fried, grilled, or broiled. The coarser, precooked sausages can also be baked in the oven, but since they dry out easily, care must be taken not to overcook them. If you must microwave a precooked sausage, it is best to submerge it in water or stock in a closely covered container to keep the skin from turning tough and papery. Fresh sausages should never be microwaved, lest they burst.

PAN-FRIED SAUSAGE

4 servings

This method of cooking sausage drains off most of the fat. Thick fresh sausages are best cooked this way.

Cut into individual links and place in a large, heavy skillet:

8 raw sausages

Add:

½ cup boiling water or beer

Cover the pan and simmer gently until the sausages are almost done, 8 to 10 minutes. Pour off the liquid and discard. Return the sausages to the pan. Cook them over low heat, shaking the pan occasionally until evenly browned. Drain. Serve with:

Mustard

PAN-BROILED SAUSAGE

4 servings

For delicately seasoned fresh sausage and for most smoked or precooked sausages, this method is preferable to pan-frying, since poaching these in water before browning tends to leach out juices and flavor. The sausages should not be too thick, or they will not cook through before browning.

Heat a large, heavy skillet over medium heat. Add:

1 teaspoon oil

8 raw or precooked sausages

Cover and cook, turning the sausages often, until evenly browned. Precooked sausage will take 5 to 6 minutes to brown and warm through. Raw sausage will take 10 minutes or so to cook through completely and brown. Serve with:

Mustard or another condiment of choice

BOILED SAUSAGE *4 servings*

This is a misnomer, since the sausage is actually poached in hot water that should not be allowed to reach a boil after the sausage is added.

Bring to a boil in a lidded pot:

8 to 12 cups water

Add:

8 smoked or precooked sausages, such as frankfurters or white knockwurst

Turn off the heat and cover the pot. Let the sausages stand until firm to the touch and heated through, 10 to 15 minutes. Remove the sausages and serve on:

Rolls

Accompany with:

Mustard or another condiment of choice

Or serve them alongside:

Braised Red Cabbage with Apples, 356, or Alsatian Sauerkraut, 357

MAKING SAUSAGE AT HOME

It is quite easy to make fresh, country-style (without casings) homemade sausage patties, especially with a food processor. The advantage of making your own sausage is that you control everything: the freshness, the amount of fat and salt, the quality and type of meat, the spice blend—the ultimate flavor.

When making sausage at home, remember these rules for safety and hygiene:

- Do not taste the raw meat mixture; instead, fry a small patty and taste that to check the seasonings.
- Keep the meat refrigerated before and between all steps.
- Do not leave any meat sitting in the grinder. Wash all utensils and equipment at once, even if you are only going to take a short break.
- Wash your hands frequently.
- If fresh sausage will not be eaten within 3 days, freeze it.

COUNTRY OR BREAKFAST SAUSAGE

Makes 2 pounds

Cut into strips if using a meat grinder or 1-inch dice if using a food processor:

1½ pounds pork butt

8 ounces pork fatback, trimmed of rind

Grind the meat and fat together in the meat grinder fitted with a ¼-inch plate, or coarsely chop in the food processor. Mix together in a large bowl with:

2 teaspoons salt

2 teaspoons coarsely ground black pepper

1½ teaspoons dried sage

½ teaspoon dried marjoram

¼ teaspoon dried savory, crumbled

⅛ teaspoon ground ginger

Pinch of ground cloves

Pinch of ground red pepper

¼ cup cold water

Using your hands, knead and squeeze the mixture until well blended. Leave in bulk or form into patties as needed. If not used immediately, fresh sausage can be frozen for up to 2 months.

CHICKEN AND APPLE SAUSAGE *About 2 pounds*

This sausage can be used as a substitute for Country or Breakfast Sausage, above. Although it has less than half the fat of conventional breakfast sausage, it remains juicy if it is not overcooked. One of our favorite ways to serve these sausages is with French Toast, 808, smothered with Buttered Apple Slices, 448.

In a small pan, boil down to 2 to 3 tablespoons syrup:

1 cup apple cider

Remove the bones from:

2¼ pounds chicken thighs

Cut the chicken into strips if using a meat grinder or 1-inch dice if using a food processor. Grind the chicken and skin together in a meat grinder fitted with a ⅜-inch plate, or coarsely chop by hand or in a food processor along with:

1½ ounces dried apples

Mix the chicken and apple mixture and syrup in a large bowl with:

2½ teaspoons salt

1 teaspoon ground black pepper

1 teaspoon dried sage

½ teaspoon dried thyme

⅛ teaspoon ground cinnamon

⅛ teaspoon ground ginger

Using your hands, knead and squeeze the mixture until well blended. Leave in bulk or form into patties as needed. If not used immediately, fresh sausage can be frozen for up to 2 months.

ABOUT VARIETY MEATS

Variety meats include organ meats like sweetbreads, brains, kidney, and liver; muscle meats like heart, tongue, and tripe; bony meats like knucklebones and their marrow centers; and extremities such as ears, feet, and head. Although variety meats are rarely prepared at home, it is not difficult to do so, and they are, in general, quite economical. We recommend shopping for them at ethnic markets or ordering ahead from a full-service meat market. Variety meats are the most perishable parts of any animal, and it is essential that they are impeccably fresh when you buy them and are cooked within 24 hours.

ABOUT LIVER

Liver from young animals is preferred, as it is mildest and tenderest. Real calf's liver is delicate, delicious, and fairly expensive. It is paler in color than the redder, more mature "baby beef" liver. Choose the palest liver you can find, for it will have the mildest flavor. Often baby beef liver is labeled calf's liver in the supermarket. For true calf's liver, ask your butcher or buy it from a reputable "gourmet" supermarket. Baby beef liver, although slightly stronger in flavor than calf's liver, can be very good and is preferable to actual beef liver. Beef liver from a full-grown animal is dark red, almost brown, and strength of color corresponds to strength of flavor. Although beef liver is readily available, it is generally considered too strong for simple preparations. Some cooks soak beef liver for several hours in the refrigerator in milk or a flavorful spicy marinade such as White Wine Marinade, 85, before cooking to soften the intense flavor. The liquid is discarded and the liver is patted dry before cooking. Lamb liver, which can be hard to find, is tender, well flavored, and almost sweet. Pork liver, also hard to find, is strong in taste, although very tender. Marinating or soaking in milk as for beef liver mellows its taste. All liver is an excellent source of iron and B vitamins, and because it is very tasty when properly cooked, it should be a regular part of a healthful diet. Chicken liver is discussed in About Poultry Giblets, 729.

As with all other variety meats, liver should be impeccably fresh, with no slimy or dry patches and with a clean scent. If preparing a whole liver, wipe it first with a damp cloth. With a sharp knife, remove any exposed veins, ducts, or connective tissue. Using your fingers, peel away the thin outer membrane without tearing into the liver itself. Slice on a diagonal to the desired thickness, anywhere from 1/4 to 1 inch, depending on your recipe. Presliced liver can be purchased and is more commonly available than whole liver. If your butcher has not done so, remove the outer membrane on the slices. Once liver is sliced and the outer membrane removed, make 1/8-inch cuts at 1-inch intervals around the outside of the slices. Liver has a tendency to shrink and curl when it is cooked; these cuts will help keep the pieces flat. Liver should be cooked until pink yet firm in the center. Overcooking and excessively high heat will toughen it. Since liver is richer in flavor than other meats, a 4-ounce serving is an ample main course for most appetites.

SAUTÉED CALF'S LIVER (BASIC RECIPE)

4 servings

This classic presentation reminds us that simplicity is often the best approach. However, augment and garnish this basic recipe as you please. Liver has a natural affinity for Madeira, white wine, sour cream, nutmeg, and thyme.

Remove the membrane and cut into 1/4-inch-thick slices:

1 pound calf's liver

Season each slice with:

Salt and ground black pepper to taste

Dredge in:

All-purpose flour

Shake off the excess flour. Heat in a heavy skillet or frying pan over medium-high heat:

2 tablespoons vegetable oil or butter or a combination

Add the liver in batches and brown quickly on both sides, 1 to 2 minutes. Do not crowd the skillet and add more oil or butter as needed. Remove to a warmed platter as it is done. Do not overcook.

LIVER AND ONIONS

4 to 6 servings

This is one of the tastiest and most traditional of all calf's liver dishes. The essential element in this recipe is the long, slow cooking of the onions to bring out their natural sugars.

Heat in a large skillet with a lid or a Dutch oven over medium-low heat:

3 tablespoons olive oil

Add:

3 to 4 large onions (1½ to 2 pounds total), halved and thinly sliced

Generous sprinkling of salt and ground black pepper

Cover the pan and cook, stirring often, over low heat until the onions are very soft but not colored, 20 to 30 minutes. Meanwhile, remove the membrane from and cut into 1/2-inch slices:

1½ pounds calf's liver

Season all sides with:

Salt and ground black pepper to taste

Dredge in:

All-purpose flour

Shake off the excess four. Heat in a large skillet over medium-high heat:

¼ cup olive oil

Add the liver in batches and sauté for 2 to 3 minutes each side. Remove the liver to a warmed platter as it is done. Spoon the liver over the cooked onions and serve immediately.

VENETIAN-STYLE LIVER AND ONIONS

Prepare Liver and Onions, above, cutting the meat into ½-inch-thick slices rather than chunks. Sauté in batches for 1 to 2 minutes each side. Pour into the skillet over high heat ⅓ cup balsamic vinegar, or ⅓ cup red wine vinegar and a pinch of sugar. Boil, scraping up the browned bits on the bottom of the pan, until the vinegar is reduced to 3 to 4 tablespoons. To serve, spoon the onions over the liver and sprinkle with the vinegar.

ABOUT POULTRY GIBLETS

The giblets are the gizzard, heart, and liver of any fowl. Although these morsels are lumped together under the same rubric, they are rarely cooked together except in the making of giblet gravy. Gizzards and hearts require long, slow braising in order to become tender. Poultry livers, by contrast, respond best to quick cooking and should be served while still pink and creamy on the inside. Generally speaking, only chicken giblets are sold in bulk at the supermarket, though turkey gizzards and hearts sometimes show up at holiday time. The gizzards and hearts usually come mixed together. The livers come in plastic tubs.

To prepare chicken livers for cooking, turn them into a colander, rinse lightly, and then pat dry with paper towels. If the livers are destined for a delicate sauté, you may want to remove the strings that connect the lobes. One at a time, place the livers on a cutting board and, while gently holding down one lobe, press against the opposite lobe with the blade of a paring knife until the string pulls out of the lobe you are holding; now, press the string against the board and press against the other lobe with the knife blade until the string releases. To prepare the gizzard for cooking, rinse, then cut away and discard the flap of tough skin that connects the two lobes.

SAUTÉED CHICKEN LIVERS

3 or 4 servings

The trick to sautéing chicken livers is to cook them in small batches in a very hot pan using an ample quantity of fat. This ensures that they will brown lightly and cook evenly.

Turn into a colander and rinse lightly:

1 pound chicken livers

Remove the connective strings, separating the lobes. Pat as dry as possible. Season generously with:

Salt and ground black pepper to taste

Heat in a large skillet over high heat until lightly browned and fragrant:

3 tablespoons unsalted butter

Add half of the livers to the skillet and quickly spread them in a single layer with a slotted spoon or spatula. Sauté, undisturbed, for 1 minute, then nudge them over onto their uncooked side and sauté until firm and beginning to release juices into the pan, 1 to 2 minutes more. Remove the livers to a plate and sauté the remaining livers in the same manner, adding more butter to the skillet if needed. Add to the remaining fat in the skillet:

½ cup very finely minced shallots or onions

Cook, stirring, until the shallots are brown and crisp around the edges, about 2 minutes. Stir in:

½ cup dry white wine or apple juice

Scraping the bottom of the skillet with a wooden spoon to loosen the browned bits, boil until the liquid is reduced by half. Add:

½ cup chicken stock

Boil again until reduced by half and slightly syrupy. Return the livers with accumulated juices to the skillet and heat, stirring, just until the sauce bubbles. Remove from the heat and stir in:

2 tablespoons minced fresh parsley

Season to taste with:

Salt and ground black pepper
Several drops of vinegar

Serve at once with:

Hot cooked rice or Mashed Potatoes, 408

CHICKEN OR TURKEY GIBLET RAGOUT

4 or 5 servings

Giblets make a delicious stew that can be enjoyed over rice or pasta.

Rinse and pat dry:

2 pounds chicken or turkey gizzards and/or hearts

Remove and discard the tough membrane connecting the two lobes of the gizzards. Cook in a heavy skillet over medium-high heat until lightly browned:

2 ounces pancetta or 2 slices bacon, diced

Add the giblets and cook, stirring, until lightly browned, about 5 minutes. Add:

1 teaspoon dried basil
½ teaspoon fennel seeds
Salt and ground black pepper to taste

Stir well and cook for 1 minute. Stir in:

2 cups chicken or turkey stock
2 cups seeded peeled chopped tomatoes, fresh or canned
1 cup dry red wine
1 tablespoon tomato paste
2 bay leaves

Simmer gently, uncovered, over medium-low heat until the giblets are very tender, 1½ to 2 hours. If the sauce becomes too thick, add more stock or water. If too watery, boil it down over high heat. Serve the giblets with:

Hot cooked Rice or pasta

Accompany with:

Freshly grated Parmesan cheese

ABOUT FOIE GRAS

Foie gras is French for fattened liver, and it is, indeed, the liver of a duck or goose that has been enlarged to stupendous proportions by means of specialized feeding and production techniques. (In their natural state, the livers of ducks and geese are comparable in size to those of chickens and turkeys, but a duck foie gras generally weighs around a pound and a goose foie gras twice as much.) In this country, only ducks are raised for foie gras, and only duck foie gras is available fresh. All goose foie gras is imported and, by law, must be sold cooked or processed as pâté. Foie gras is very mild in taste, more like butter than liver. Traditionally, birds raised for foie gras are force-fed, a practice that many people regard as cruel; but the production of American duck foie gras does not entail force-feeding. Rather, the birds are kept in low-lit sheds, which encourages them to gorge on their own.

Fresh duck foie gras must be specially ordered and is always very expensive. Usually it is sold whole, but you can sometimes buy either the larger or the less desirable smaller lobe separately. It is packed in Cryovac and will keep for quite some time, though not indefinitely. In handling foie gras, remember that it is largely fat. It will chip and crumble if cut when too cold and simply melt away to nothing if cooked excessively. To prepare foie gras for cooking, leave it at room temperature for about 1 hour to soften slightly. Carefully pull apart the two lobes with your hands and pull out as much of the connective string and other matter as you can with your fingers. Don't be overzealous, or you will end up breaking the foie gras. In traditional practice, foie gras is deveined, but this complicated procedure is quite unnecessary if you plan to slice and pan-sear the foie gras (the usual method of preparation in America) rather than to poach, steam, or bake it in one piece. If you would like to draw excess blood from the foie gras, submerge it in water and ice and refrigerate it for 1 hour. Once the foie gras has been cleaned, it can be tightly wrapped in plastic and refrigerated for a day before cooking.

Before slicing the foie gras, let it stand at room temperature for 1 hour. (If you are proceeding directly from cleaning to slicing without an intermediary soaking, it has already softened enough.) Provide yourself with a pitcher filled with very hot water, a stack of paper towels, and a thin, sharp knife. Cut each lobe of the foie gras crosswise into slices just over ½ inch thick, dipping the knife in hot water each time and thoroughly wiping the knife clean after each cut. Arrange the slices in a single layer on a baking sheet lined with wax paper. If you are not ready to sauté the foie gras at once, cover it with another sheet of wax paper and refrigerate it for up to 12 hours.

Pan-seared foie gras is always served rare and creamy in the center. It cooks in a flash and must be served at once, so have all ingredients, cooking equipment, and serving plates—as well as your guests—assembled before you begin. Pan-seared foie gras is usually served on a bed of something—we have suggested polenta, sautéed fresh corn, or mangoes or peaches finely diced—but it is equally delicious served simply on small, thin rounds of toasted brioche or corn bread. Cold foie gras is traditionally served with a Sauterne, but hot fois gras is equally good with a strong, fruity Chardonnay or Riesling.

PAN-SEARED FOIE GRAS

8 to 10 first-course servings

Clean and, if you wish, soak:

1 whole duck foie gras (at least 12 ounces)

Let the foie gras stand at room temperature for 1 hour, then cut into slices a little more than ½ inch thick. Season with:

Salt and ground black pepper to taste

Have at the ready a large plate on which to put the foie gras slices as they are cooked and a bowl into which you can drain excess sautéing fat. Brush a wide, heavy skillet with a very thin film of:

Vegetable oil

Heat the skillet over very high heat until the oil begins to smoke. Place 4 to 6 slices foie gras in the skillet. Sauté just until the foie gras pulls in slightly on the underside and releases fat into the pan, about 15 seconds. Turn the slices with a spatula and sauté about 15 seconds on the second side. Remove the foie gras to the plate and pour the fat into the bowl. Repeat until all the foie gras is cooked. Leaving about 2 tablespoons of fat in the skillet, pour in:

½ cup port or Madeira

Scraping the bottom of the skillet with a wooden spoon to loosen the browned bits, boil the wine over the highest heat possible until nearly evaporated. Add:

½ cup apple juice or cider

Boil until the liquid is reduced by half and syrupy. Add:

2 tablespoons veal glaze dissolved in ⅓ cup warm water, or 1 cup rich veal or duck stock reduced to ⅓ cup

1 tablespoon wine vinegar or strained fresh lemon juice

Boil the sauce until slightly syrupy, then remove from the heat. If you wish, divide among 8 to 10 serving plates:

Soft Polenta with Butter and Cheese, 249, or 3 cups fresh corn kernels sautéed in butter, or 3 cups diced peeled peaches or mangoes

Arrange the foie gras on top and moisten with the sauce. Serve at once.

ABOUT SWEETBREADS

Their delicate flavor and soft texture make sweetbreads popular even among those who do not enjoy other variety meats. Sweetbreads take on a flavor of what they are cooked with; a nice sauce enhances their richness. Sweetbreads are not brains, as is commonly believed. They are the thymus and sometimes pancreatic glands of young animals. Sweetbreads usually come in pairs and are quite rich. Calf sweetbreads are the most sought after. Lamb sweetbreads, hard to find, are also very good.

Sweetbreads should be compact in texture and white or pale in color, with no dark patches or discoloration. Like all variety meats, sweetbreads are highly perishable and should be cooked as soon as you buy them.

HOW TO PREPARE SWEETBREADS FOR COOKING

To give them a milky-white color, some cooks first soak sweetbreads in a large quantity of cold water mixed with the juice of 1 lemon (acidulated water) in the refrigerator for 1 to 2 hours, changing the water two or three times. This process releases any blood and is purely cosmetic. Next, all sweetbreads must be blanched: Cover with cold water mixed with the juice of 1 lemon. Bring slowly to a boil, and simmer, uncovered, for 2 to 5 minutes, depending on the size. Drain and plunge them at once into cold water. Let cool, then drain again. Using your fingers, remove any cartilage, tubes, ducts, and tough outer membrane that remain. Blanching firms them for further cooking without destroying their delicate texture.

After blanching, place the sweetbreads between two plates, place a weight on top, and refrigerate until much of their water has been released and they have firmed up, at least 2 hours. Leave the sweetbreads whole, slice to the desired thickness, or break them into smaller sections or nuggets.

Sweetbreads must be cooked quickly to maintain their tenderness, a process that takes less than 5 minutes. Cooking sweetbreads for a longer period of time will harden their texture, turning them slightly chalky. Allow one pair for two servings, 2 ounces per first-course serving, or 3 to 5 ounces per main-course serving.

SAUTÉED SWEETBREADS *4 to 6 servings*

After you have mastered these few techniques, you will be comfortable experimenting on your own. If the breading seems too complicated, simply coat the slices with seasoned flour and sauté, eliminating the egg wash and breadcrumbs.

Cut into ¼-inch-thick slices:

1 pound sweetbreads, prepared as above

Whisk together in a shallow bowl:

1 large egg, lightly beaten

2 to 3 teaspoons water or milk

Spread in a second shallow bowl:

¾ cup dry unseasoned breadcrumbs

Spread in a third shallow bowl:

½ cup all-purpose flour

Pat the sweetbread slices dry and season with:

Salt and ground black pepper to taste

Dredge the slices lightly with the flour and shake off the excess. Slide the flour-coated slices through the egg mixture, making sure the entire surface is covered. Then coat the slices with the breadcrumbs, pressing the crumbs with your fingers. Handle very gently so that the coating does not crack. Heat in a medium skillet over medium-high heat:

⅛ to ¼ inch olive oil

Add the sweetbread slices in batches and cook until brown on one side, about 1½ to 2 minutes. Turn and brown on the other side, about 30 seconds. Do not overcook. Remove to a paper-towel-lined plate and pat off the excess oil. Serve with:

Boiled new potatoes

Garnish with:

Watercress
Lemon slices

SAUTÉED SWEETBREADS WITH BACON AND CURLY ENDIVE

Prepare Sautéed Sweetbreads, above.

Toss 1 cleaned head curly endive, washed, dried, leaves separated, and torn into bite-sized pieces, with Basic Vinaigrette, 236, made with balsamic vinegar. Divide the salad among 4 plates. Top with sautéed sweetbreads and 5 slices bacon, coarsely chopped and cooked crisp.

ABOUT BRAINS

Brains are the most delicate and creamy organ meat. They contain no muscle fiber at all, so when cooked, they have a texture almost like a very thick sauce. As with all other organ meats, calf brains are generally best, but sheep, lamb, pork, and beef brains can also be used. Brains can be substituted in all recipes calling for sweetbreads, although the two are different organs, and as with sweetbreads, they must be very fresh. Keep refrigerated and cook within 24 hours, for they are very perishable.

Brains should be compact and white in color with very little blood or discoloration. They should smell clean and fresh, not sour.

HOW TO PREPARE BRAINS FOR COOKING

Because brains are very delicate, always handle them with care; they have a tendency to fall apart. To prepare, soak them for 1½ to 2 hours in cold water to free them of all traces of blood. Some recipes and palates prefer a very creamy texture for cooked brains, and they can be cooked at this point to achieve this. For less creamy brains, firm them by poaching: Put the brains in a saucepan and cover with water mixed with the juice of 1 lemon or a splash of white vinegar. Bring to a slow simmer and cook for about 10 to 12 minutes for calf brains, 15 for others. Be sure the water does not boil. Drain and rinse carefully with cold water. Like sweetbreads, it is best to place brains between 2 plates and weight them slightly to press out some of the water and firm them. Refrigerate the weighted brains for 1 to 2 hours.

The soft, texture and delicate taste of brains makes them adaptable to many recipes. They are often paired with eggs as in the Southern breakfast dish of scrambled eggs and brains. Other regional specialties put fried brains with bacon or even in a sandwich, while more sophisticated dishes pair brains with sweetbreads in ragout and soufflés. Allow 1 pound of brains for five servings or 1 set for two servings.

SAUTÉED BRAINS IN BROWN BUTTER SAUCE

4 servings

A classic preparation—the dark nutty flavor of the browned butter complements the delicate taste of the brains.

Cut lengthwise in half:

2 sets calf or lamb brains, prepared as above, poached, and weighted

Pat dry. Season with:

Salt and ground black pepper to taste

Dredge in:

½ cup all-purpose flour

Shake off the excess flour. Melt in a large skillet over medium heat until fragrant:

4 tablespoons (½ stick) butter

Add the brains and cook for about 3 minutes each side. Cover, reduce the heat to medium, and cook for 3 to 4 minutes more, until the brains are somewhat firm and browned. Remove to a warmed platter. Serve with:

Beurre Noisette, 57
Lemon wedges

Garnish with:

1 to 2 teaspoons chopped drained capers (optional)

ABOUT KIDNEYS

Calf kidneys have long been valued for their tender texture and delectable taste. Lamb kidneys are somewhat soft and slightly less flavorful but are especially suited for grilling. Pork and large beef kidneys tend to be hard and strong in flavor and need soaking first for 2 hours in milk or cold salted water. All other kidneys should not be soaked or washed, for they absorb liquid easily. Off-flavors can be withdrawn by blanching, 1052, in water with a little vinegar or lemon juice for 20 minutes; or, after soaking and drying, the kidneys can be sautéed briefly over brisk heat and allowed to cool partially before further cooking. Most often, kidneys are not served on their own; they are best mixed with other ingredients, such as a stew of mushrooms and wine or in a creamy sauce of mustard and shallots. Their neat shape and firm texture make them ideal for skewering and grilling.

Kidneys should be fresh, with no smell of ammonia. Calf kidneys should be deep pink in color, not red. Pork and beef kidneys should be red but not brown or black. Kidneys are sometimes sold with a surrounding layer of fat. Calf and lamb kidneys are sometimes roasted whole in their fat.

HOW TO PREPARE KIDNEYS FOR COOKING

The white membrane should be removed from all kidneys before cooking. Curved scissors are convenient for this. Snip the membrane and fat where it is connected to the core and peel away the membrane with your fingers. The membrane can also be removed by first sautéing the kidneys in fat for about 1 minute, discarding the rendered fat, and pulling away the membrane. With a sharp knife, remove the veins and ducts from the center. Larger kidneys are often cut into cubes before cooking.

Calf and lamb kidneys should be cooked for as short a time as possible over medium heat. Do not overcook. The center should be firm yet pink. Exposure to high heat will toughen them. Do not let kidneys boil in a sauce. Always taste the pan juices before making a pan sauce—sometimes they will be bitter. If so, discard the juices and serve with freshly melted butter or sour cream. Allow 1 medium calf kidney or 2 to 3 lamb kidneys per person.

SAUTÉED KIDNEYS WITH MUSTARD

3 or 4 servings

This traditional French preparation pairs the pungent mustard that originated in the French city of Dijon with capers and a bit of cream.

Prepare as above:

3 calf or 6 lamb kidneys

Cut the calf kidneys crosswise into ½-inch slices or the lamb kidneys lengthwise in half. Remove all white tissue. Season with:

Salt and ground black pepper to taste

Melt in a large, heavy skillet over medium heat:

2 tablespoons butter or vegetable oil

Add the kidneys in batches and brown, about 1½ minutes on each side. Remove the kidneys from the pan and keep warm. If the fat is gone, add to the pan:

2 tablespoons butter or vegetable oil

Cook over medium heat until softened, 3 to 4 minutes:

½ cup chopped shallots or onions
1 teaspoon chopped garlic

Pour in:

½ cup dry white wine
½ cup chicken stock
1 teaspoon chopped fresh rosemary or thyme

Bring to a boil, scraping up the browned bits on the bottom of the pan. Boil over high heat until reduced to about ⅓ cup. Turn off the heat. Stir in and mix thoroughly:

2 tablespoons heavy cream
1 tablespoon chopped drained capers
1½ teaspoons Dijon mustard

Season with:

Salt and ground black pepper to taste

Return the kidneys and their juices to the pan to coat with the sauce. Serve with:

Hot cooked rice

ABOUT TONGUE

Tongue is popular in many cultures, and its popularity in America is thanks, no doubt, to its similarity to our much-loved cold cuts. No matter what the source—beef, calf, lamb, or pork—the smaller tongues are usually better. The best flavored, whether fresh, smoked, or pickled, is beef tongue. For tenderest texture, it should be under 3 pounds. Fresh tongue should be moist and pink or pale red in color. Before cooking, scrub the tongue well using a kitchen brush. If it is smoked or pickled, blanch it first by simmering it in water to cover for about 10 minutes to remove the excess salt and smoked or pickled taste. Drain and immerse the tongue in cold water. After draining, cook as for Boiled Fresh, Smoked, or Pickled Beef Tongue, below. Cook tongue until tender when pierced with a two-pronged fork and the bone at the root pulls away from the meat.

If the tongue is to be served hot, drain it, plunge it into cold water for a moment so that you can handle it, then skin it. With a paring knife, make a small cut at the tip and peel away the skin. If it comes off easily at this point, continue to skin it completely, but if not, let it cool longer. Trim the tongue by removing the small bones and gristle. Return it very briefly to the hot cooking water to reheat before serving. If the tongue is to be served cold, let it cool enough to handle. Drain the tongue, skin it as described above, then cut it away from the bones. Trim the small bones and gristle, then return it to the pot to cool completely in the cooking liquid.

To carve tongue, place it on its side and, starting at the tip, cut large diagonal slices. Allow 4 to 6 ounces per main-course serving.

BOILED FRESH, SMOKED, OR PICKLED BEEF TONGUE

6 to 8 servings

To remove some of the brine or smoky taste from a pickled or smoked tongue, blanch it as described above.

Place in a large kettle or stockpot:

1 fresh, smoked, or pickled beef or calf tongue (about 3 pounds)

Add:

2 medium onions, halved
1 large carrot, peeled
3 or more celery stalks with leaves
6 black peppercorns
2 bay leaves

Barely cover these ingredients with boiling water. Bring to a boil and reduce the heat. Skim off the scum on the surface after the first 5 minutes. Simmer the tongue, uncovered, until tender, 2½ to 3 hours. Let the tongue cool in the liquid until it can be handled. Skin the tongue as above, then carve into slices.

Return the tongue to the liquid and reheat it. Serve it hot with:

Sauce Piquant, 51

Or refrigerate the sliced tongue in its liquid until cold and serve with:

Russian Horseradish Cream, 73, or whole-grain or smooth French-style mustard

ABOUT CHITTERLINGS

Chitterlings, also known as "chitlins," the small intestine of a hog, are most popular in the South or in places where authentic soul food is on the menu. So popular are they in Sally, South Carolina, that each year, the town hosts a festival known as the Chittlin' Strut. Chitterlings are also the base for *andouillette,* a tripe and chitterling sausage, very popular in France.

To be specific, chitterlings are the small intestines of a young pig, which are emptied while still warm, turned inside out, and thoroughly cleaned. The mucous covering is scraped away and completely removed, then they are washed repeatedly in cold salted water and refrigerated overnight in cold salted water to cover. Chitterlings are very strong in both flavor and odor. They are generally sold cleaned, but another rinse or two in cold salted water will not hurt. Once they are thoroughly cleaned, either coarsely chop them or cut into 2-inch lengths. Typically, chitterlings are boiled and served with collard or turnip greens or are buttered and deep-fried.

SAUTÉED CHITTERLINGS

4 to 6 servings

After simmering for 3 to 4 hours, the chitterlings are sautéed over high heat until browned and seasoned with a dash of tangy vinegar.

Place in a large pot with enough water to cover:

2 pounds cleaned chitterlings, chopped

Bring slowly to a boil. Cover, reduce the heat, and simmer until very tender, 3 to 4 hours. Stir occasionally to prevent sticking. Drain well and pat dry. Season with:

Salt and ground black pepper to taste

Heat in a large skillet over high heat:

2 tablespoons vegetable oil

Add the chitterlings and sauté until golden brown, 5 to 8 minutes. Season to taste with:

Apple cider vinegar
Salt and ground black pepper

Serve with:

Southern Corn Bread, 777, or Black-Eyed Peas, 273

ABOUT MARROW

Marrow is high in flavor, nutrients, and fat. A classic ingredient in French cuisine, it is found in the center of the long leg bones of animals, generally beef. Marrow bones should be fresh, clean, and free of blood. Marrow itself is slightly off-white. It should be firm and well chilled.

Marrow can be prepared in several different ways. Bone marrow can be removed from split large bones. Use a cleaver to crack the bone, and pull it apart, separating the split bone; remove the marrow from the center. Cut the marrow into ½-inch slices and soften in the top of a double boiler over simmering—not boiling—water. You also can gently poach the slices in stock for 1½ to 2 minutes. Once cooked, marrow is slightly firm to the touch. Marrow must not be overcooked, as it is very fatty and simply melts and disintegrates under too much heat. Serve the poached slices on small toast rounds for an appetizer.

Alternatively, shorter 3-inch marrow bones can be poached for 1½ to 2 minutes in water, stock, or Court Bouillon, 39, or seasoned with salt and pepper and baked in the bone in a preheated 300°F oven for about 1 hour. Serve (with marrow spoons or other long spoons) with toast rounds and an accompaniment such as chutney. See Osso Buco alla Milanese, 686.

YEAST BREADS

Bread is as old as the Stone Age. Yeast-risen bread dates back almost four thousand years to ancient Egypt, whose bakers discovered the secret of yeast and learned how to control it (they were also among the first brewers of beer, another yeast-fermented product) and also developed ovens for baking several loaves at a time. In medieval England, the term for "dough kneader" developed gradually into the word "lady"—an indication of the justified respect, we have always thought, with which bread bakers have long been regarded.

The tradition of baking bread in the home kitchen nearly disappeared in America in the mid-twentieth century—and commercial loaves degenerated, for the most part, into sugar-dosed presliced white bread. Many Americans grew up never having tasted a home-baked, much less whole-grain, loaf. The revival of professional interest in artisanal baking in the latter part of the century has spurred home cooks to try their hand at baking once again.

The following pages offer some secrets of the bread maker's craft, along with a few simple rules and a number of proven recipes. Some of these are scaled to work in bread machines, those modern technological marvels that have made it possible for even the impatient to make bread at home. Others, made with sourdough starters, require time and plenty of patience, and also the improvisation of a hearth in your oven. Also provided are a number of excellent breads for those on gluten-free diets. Hearth-style breads are hand-shaped and baked in a home oven on an improvised hearth or baking stone, without pans or forms. In this chapter, the sourdough bread recipes give full instructions for producing these rustic breads. For discussion of flours and yeast, please read pages 1071 to 1075.

ABOUT EQUIPMENT

Mixers: Heavy-duty (at least 300-watt) electric mixers—equipped with removable bowls and interchangeable mixing paddles, including dough hooks—can eliminate the physical labor and reduce the time involved in mixing and kneading doughs. However, motors burn out quickly if doughs are too tough (this is usually caused by an inadequate amount of liquid) or if there is too much dough in the machine. Refer to the machine's instructions for mixing guidelines and capacity. Some home bakers like to start mixing dough with the flat paddle and then change to the dough hook when the dough reaches a firmer consistency. Sometimes it is best to start a dough in the mixer and then finish it by hand on the table. Never walk away and leave mixers unattended. They can "walk" off countertops, and dough likes to climb the hook; when this happens, stop the machine, scrape the dough off

RULES FOR YEAST BREADS

Find a clean surface (2 feet square is adequate) at a comfortable height for mixing and kneading.

Use bottled spring water if your local water is hard or overly chlorinated.

To ensure freshness, store whole-grain flours, nuts, seeds, and other ingredients containing oil in dated airtight containers in a cool, dark place or, for longer periods, in the freezer.

Use high-gluten bread flour whenever called for, especially if the dough includes nongluten products (oatmeal or cornmeal, for example) or low-gluten grains like rye. Unbleached flour is preferred.

Bring ingredients to room temperature before mixing.

Measure accurately.

Test for proper rising by pressing two fingers gently into the dough; if indentations remain, the dough is fully risen.

Preheat the oven (unless a cold oven is specified to increase rise) and use an oven thermometer to check your oven for temperature accuracy and hot spots.

Introduce steam into the oven during the first few minutes of baking with a spray bottle or by pouring water into a preheated pan placed on the oven bottom or lowest rack.

Rotate the loaves in the oven during baking from top to bottom and back to front.

Test for doneness by thumping the bottom of the baked loaf; a hollow sound indicates doneness.

For best taste and texture, let freshly baked bread cool for at least 20 minutes before slicing.

Always let bread cool completely before wrapping it for storage.

the hook and back into the bowl with a rubber spatula, and then continue to mix. Water and flour both can be added during mixing to achieve the proper consistency.

Food Processors: Those with plastic dough blades can mix and knead bread dough in less than 2 minutes. Larger machines will handle 7 to 8 cups flour for 2 loaves of bread. Some smaller machines will handle 3 to 3½ cups flour for 1 loaf of bread. (Check the machine's instructions to determine capacity.) The high speed at which food processors operate can overheat dough. One remedy is to lower the temperature of the liquids to be added. To mix and knead yeast bread dough in a food processor, put solid ingredients including shortening in the workbowl. Process to mix, about 20 seconds. Dissolve active dry yeast in warm liquid (105° to 115°F). Combine with the remaining liquids chilled to about 40°F. With the machine running, add the liquids through the feed tube to form a dough. Process until the dough forms a mass and cleans the sides of the bowl, adding flour as needed through the tube to achieve a dough that is soft and satiny but not sticky. An alternate method is to briefly process instant dry yeast (see About Yeast, 1074) with flour and other dry ingredients in the workbowl. Then, with the machine running, add cold liquids through the feed tube as described to form a dough. A third technique is to pulse all the ingredients to mix, let them rest in the workbowl for 5 to 20 minutes, and finish by processing until the dough is ready, about 30 seconds. The rest period allows the gluten to set up without excessive mixing. For notes on bread machines, see page 759.

Ovens: All kinds of ovens, gas and electric, conventional and convection, can produce good bread. Convection ovens should be set 50°F lower than conventional ovens, as the airflow increases the efficiency of heat distribution and shortens the baking time. Electric ovens often have exposed coils, which generate direct bottom heat; if the bottoms of the loaves are routinely burned in your electric oven, buffer them with an empty pan placed on a lower shelf or a baking sheet placed directly under them. Every oven has its hot and cold spots, which can cause uneven baking; for this reason, it is usually necessary to rotate breads 180 degrees and from one shelf to another to compensate. It is also helpful to use an oven thermometer to check the accuracy of the thermostat and also the baking differences between shelves.

Baguette pans, bannetons, couches: Baguette pans are long metal pans that join two half-cylinders along one long side, providing the proper curve for two traditional baguettes. The shaped dough rises and bakes in the same pan. Bannetons are small wooden baskets used in artisanal bakeries for shaping bread. The loaf rises upside down in the floured basket and is taken out just before baking. Banneton shapes include round and oblong. These special baskets are especially useful with soft dough that will not hold a shape if left free form. Bannetons are relatively expensive; use stainless-steel mixing bowls or inexpensive wicker or woven bread baskets sprayed with vegetable oil and dusted with flour as substitutes.

Couches (pronounced "coosh") are burlap, canvas, or linen cloths upon which dough for hearth breads can rise. The dough does not stick to the cloth, which can be bunched between the loaves to provide support, allowing the doughs to rise up rather than spreading sideways. Most home bakers let baguettes and oblong loaves rise on a sheet pan without such support, but clean dish towels, dusted with flour, can be used in place of a *couche* if desired.

Bread and Baking Pans: Bread pans, also called loaf pans, are made in different sizes and materials including tin, steel, aluminum, and glass. Each of these substances conducts heat differently; glass generally bakes bread faster than metal. Always spray or grease bread pans lightly but evenly before putting in the dough for its final rise. Even so-called nonstick or glazed pans will work better if lightly greased. The dough should equal about half the volume of a loaf pan, so that when baked it will rise just above the top, doming evenly rather than mushrooming out over the sides. Pans vary in size, but here are some general guidelines: a large 9 x 5 x 3-inch loaf pan holds about 2 pounds of dough; a medium 8 x 4 x 2-inch loaf pan holds about 1½ pounds of dough; a small 7 x 3 x 2-inch loaf pan holds about 1 pound of dough. You will lose 11 to 12 percent of the weight due to evaporation in the oven (about 2 ounces for each pound of dough); for example, use 18 ounces dough to yield a 1-pound loaf.

A *pain-de-mie* mold, called a Pullman pan in this country, is a long loaf pan with its own lid. The lid creates a perfectly square loaf and a very even and fine crumb structure. Improvise by placing a baking sheet, well greased on the bottom, on top of your loaf pan, and weighing it down with a heavy cast-iron skillet during baking. Pans can be lightly greased but should also be sprinkled with semolina, polenta, or cornmeal before the dough is put in. Better still, use readily available baking parchment paper, cut to fit the pan. This does not need to be greased, but it should be dusted with cornmeal.

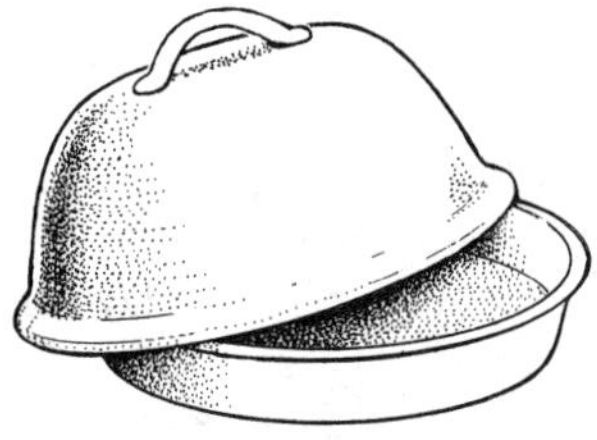

A cloche

Cloches and Stones: *Cloches* are small clay ovens large enough for baking one loaf of bread. They can be placed in home ovens to replicate in miniature a brick or adobe hearth oven. Shaped like a bell (*cloche* in French) with a round plate and a dome lid, a cloche works like a baking stone and also traps the steam, creating a shiny crust. Because it takes time for oven heat to penetrate the clay, the bread rises longer in the oven, increasing in size by as much as 20 percent. To get the best results with a *cloche*, increase the heat by 25° to 50°F above what is called for in the recipe, and add 10 to 15 minutes to the baking time. Clay stones, bricks, or quarry tiles may also be used to replicate the floor of a brick oven. The most convenient way is a commercial pizza stone—a thick, flat stone that can be placed either on the floor of a gas oven or on a rack in an electric oven to conduct radiant heat into the loaf and produce a superior crust. You can improvise by inverting a heavy baking sheet on a rack and allowing it to preheat along with the oven.

Scoring Tools: Professional bakers use a sharp curved razor called a *lame* for scoring bread. You can improvise by using a single-edged razor blade or by placing a popsicle stick through the center slots in a traditional,

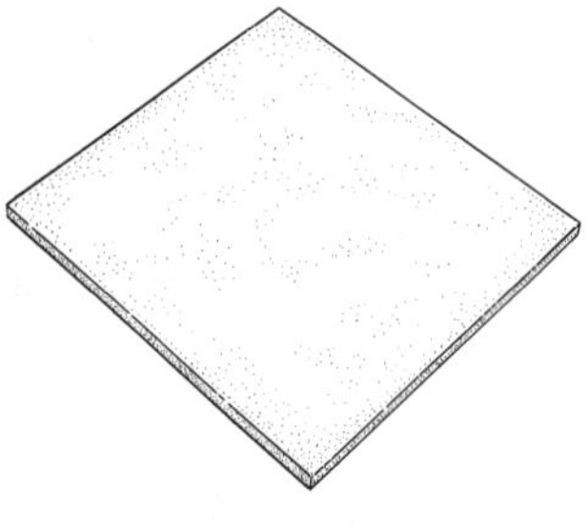

Pizza stone

flat double-edged razor blade. Other tools for scoring bread include serrated knives, sharp kitchen knives, scissors, and matte knives (see Scoring, 742).

Proofing Bowls: Bread dough will rise successfully in glass, ceramic, plastic, or stainless-steel bowls, but do not use bowls of aluminum or other reactive metals. While not essential, a light spraying of oil makes it easier to remove dough from the bowl. Always use a bowl large enough to accommodate the dough after it has doubled in size. Cover proofing bowls with either lightly oiled plastic wrap or a damp, clean dish towel to keep the dough's surface from drying out.

Spray Bottles (Spritzers): Inexpensive plant misters can be used to spray loaves during the first few minutes of baking. This is an easy way to improvise at home the steam-injected ovens of commercial bakeries. Spray the oven walls to create steam, but be very careful to keep the spray away from the oven lightbulb: Any water on the bulb may cause it to shatter. Many home bakers prefer to preheat a pan on the bottom of the oven and pour hot water into it just before placing the loaves in the oven.

Pastry or Dough Scrapers: These gadgets make cleanup easier, especially if you are kneading by hand. Most pastry scrapers are square and made of plastic or stainless steel. They are convenient for cutting dough and for scraping the work surface to lift up dough and prevent sticking. You can also use a plastic hand spatula, which is flat on one side and rounded on the other—especially good for scraping out bowls.

Baker's Peels: These are flat wooden or metal paddles with long handles for placing shaped dough in the oven and removing the finished loaf. The traditional long-handled variety is often seen in pizza parlors, but short-handled peels for home bakers are now available. You may also use the back of a baking or cookie sheet as an improvised peel. Always remember to dust the surface of the peel with cornmeal or semolina so that the dough will slide off it easily.

Scales: Battery-powered baking scales or small spring scales are very useful to home bakers, because weight is a more accurate measure than volume. Flour expands and contracts according to the humidity in the air, and everyone scoops and packs ingredients in a measuring cup a little differently—but a pound remains a pound. The best baking scales handle at least 5 pounds.

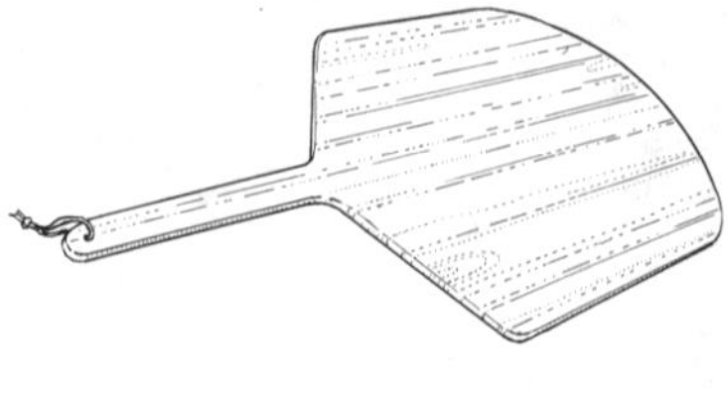

Baker's peel

Thermometers: Bakers have been baking bread without thermometers for centuries, but an instant-read thermometer is a sure way to determine quickly if water for dissolving yeast or the bread dough is at the proper temperature. An oven thermometer lets you know how accurate your oven's thermostat is and where the hot spots are.

Timers: Most recent-model ranges have built-in timers; however, a portable timer can be invaluable for keeping tabs on dough at various stages when you're not in the kitchen. Some digital timers track three different times at once. There are even some models designed to hang around your neck so you will not miss the alert.

MIXING BREAD DOUGH

There are two methods for mixing the basic ingredients to make dough: the direct or Straight Dough Method, and the indirect or Sponge Method. In the Straight Dough Method, all ingredients are mixed together to form a dough that is ready to knead. In the indirect or Sponge Method, small quantities of the main ingredients are combined and allowed to ferment before the rest of the ingredients are added. Both direct and indirect doughs can be mixed by hand, in a mixer or food processor, or in a home bread machine.

STRAIGHT DOUGH METHOD

To mix by hand, stir two-thirds of the flour and all the other dry ingredients together in a large bowl. In a separate small bowl, dissolve active dry yeast in warm (105° to 115°F) liquid by letting it stand for 5 minutes. Add the remaining liquid and whisk to mix. Add the yeast mixture to the flour mixture and stir with a large, sturdy spoon until all the flour is incorporated. Gradually stir in as much of the remaining flour as is needed for the dough to clean the sides of the bowl and form a cohesive mass. The dough is now ready to be turned out onto a floured surface and kneaded.

In a heavy-duty electric mixer, using the paddle blade, mix two-thirds of the flour and all the other dry ingredients on low speed for 2 to 3 minutes while slowing adding the liquid yeast mixture. Add as much flour as is needed for the dough to clean the sides of the bowl. Replace the paddle blade with the dough hook and knead, adding additional flour to keep the dough from sticking.

In a food processor fitted with a dough blade, place two-thirds of the flour and all the other dry ingredients in the workbowl and pulse to mix. Add the dissolved yeast combined with the other liquids through the feed tube and pulse to mix until the dough forms a cohesive mass that cleans the sides of the bowl; add more flour, a little at a time, as needed. Let the dough rest for several minutes, then process for about 30 seconds to knead. For additional mixing techniques, see Food Processors in About Equipment, 736.

For bread machines, follow the manufacturer's directions for your particular model.

SPONGE OR STARTER METHOD

In contrast to the relatively quick-rising yeast breads made by the direct or Straight Dough Method, breads made by the indirect or Sponge Method often take days to complete. However, the sponges or starters used to extend fermentation times allow the development of complex flavor and the unique texture that characterizes traditional European hearth-style breads. Sponges are made with flour, liquid (usually water), and yeast. Once the sponge is made, it is allowed to ferment for up to several days, during which time it is periodically "fed" with additional flour and water. When the sponge is fully developed, part of it can be reserved as a starter for future loaves. For starter recipes and instructions, see Breads Made with the Sponge or Starter Method, 755.

KNEADING

Kneading converts flour, water, and leavening into a smooth and elastic bread dough, by developing the protein called gluten. Gluten is a tight but elastic cellular web formed when two of the proteins in flour, gliadin and glutenin, combine with liquid. When the bread dough is kneaded, the elastic bands stretch and loosen. Yeast causes the dough to ferment, which produces carbon dioxide; this gas gets trapped as bubbles in the gluten strands, and the dough rises. Kneading may be done in an electric mixer with a dough hook or in a food processor, but because the process is so sensual and, some think, relaxing, many bakers prefer to knead by hand the old-fashioned way. Even sensualists, however, may find that kneading by machine is preferable for certain very wet or sticky doughs (such as rye dough).

All doughs, though, should be slightly sticky when first turned out from the mixing bowl onto the lightly floured board or kneading surface. When kneading by hand, grease or flour your hands to prevent sticking, then work the dough with the heels of your hands, using firm pressure and pushing it against the work surface so the dough folds over itself as you work. Continue in this way, pushing the dough away from yourself, peeling it off the surface, re-forming it into a loose ball, and giving it a quarter turn (use a pastry scraper to help turn the dough if it is supposed to be soft), for about 10 minutes, until the gluten has developed. When finished, most doughs should be smooth and elastic, and tacky rather than sticky. To test, slowly and gently stretch a small piece of dough, turning it in a circular motion as you pull so that it stretches evenly. The dough should hold together without tearing until it forms a sheer membrane, thin enough to let light come through. (Alternately, you may simply test the temperature of the dough with an instant-read thermometer; the center of the dough should measure 77° to 80°F.)

When kneading by electric mixer, you will need a fairly powerful one with a dough hook, unless your dough is very wet. Make sure that the mixer bowl is large enough to hold the dough with room left over. Work the dough on low speed for about 3 minutes, until the dough is smooth and cleans the sides of the bowl. Continue to knead for about 7 minutes more. Knead the dough for a minute or two longer if necessary, but do not overdo it. Food processors mix and knead dough like lightning, in less than 2 minutes. Caution should be taken when using a food processor not to ruin a dough by overmixing. (See Food Processors in About Equipment, 736, and Straight Dough Method, 738.)

RISING

When the dough has been kneaded, place it in a clean bowl that has been lightly coated with oil and cover the bowl with oiled plastic wrap or a damp, clean dish towel. Set it aside to rise in a draft-free room at a temperature of 70° to 85°F. If the room is cold, place the bowl of dough on a rack over a pan of warm water or near (but not on) a radiator or other heat source. You may also place the bowl in an oven that has been preheated for less than 1 minute until just warmed (or in a pilot-lit oven). Do not force the rise by overwarming it; this will result in inferior bread. If the bread is to have a moist crumb, the dough should approximately double in volume on the first rise; this should take 1 to 2 hours. If it rises more than that, it will fall back into the bowl. Do not permit this to happen unless the recipe calls for it, as it may result in a coarse, dry bread. (Dough will rise more rapidly at high altitudes and may overrise if not watched carefully.) To make sure the dough has risen sufficiently, poke it with a fingertip; if it is ready, the impression will remain in the dough. Next, punch down the dough with a balled hand. Work the edges to the center and turn the bottom to the top. Some bread recipes call for a second kneading and another rise, to yield a finer grain. The second rise may be done in the same bowl.

SHAPING

After the dough has risen, it must be shaped. Punch down the dough, turn it out onto a work surface, and knead briefly to remove any gas bubbles. Using a knife or pastry scraper, divide the dough into the desired number of pieces and let rest for a few minutes before shaping. This brief rest period, called "bench proofing," allows the gluten to relax slightly for easier shaping. Quick-rising doughs and those made with a sponge starter are best baked in loaf pans or other shaped molds. Slower-rising bread doughs and sourdough breads are best baked without a mold or in a loose one, such as a baguette pan, to best develop their natural crustiness.

Loaf Pan Breads: To choose an appropriate loaf pan, see Bread and Baking Pans in About Equipment, 737, and About Bread Crust, 742. Begin to form the loaf by firmly throwing down one of the resting dough pieces onto the counter to deflate any remaining gas bubbles. Using your hands or a rolling pin, press the dough evenly into a circle and fold the outer curves toward the center to make a rectangle before shaping the loaf. Or you may treat the dough like a thick scroll, rolling it up and pressing it together with the heels of your hands. Pinch the seam closed, sealing it with your fingers and tucking under any excess dough at the same time. Place the shaped dough, seam side down, in a greased loaf pan. The loaf should be long enough to touch both ends of the pan and should be even across the top.

Cover the pan with lightly oiled plastic wrap or waxed paper or a damp, clean kitchen towel. The dough will eventually rise to fill out the corners of the pan, almost doubling in size, cresting above the pan and forming a smooth, even dome. If you press your finger into the dough, a slight impression should remain. Be sure your oven is preheated and follow the baking instructions in the recipe you are using. For pan placement in the oven, see Baking, 742.

Round Loaves (Boules): On an unfloured work surface, gently shape and rotate one loaf-sized piece of dough with both hands. Pull down against the side of the dough with your left hand and gently push up with your right hand so the dough rotates counterclockwise. As you rotate the dough, lightly push under the dough with the sides of both hands. As you do this, much of the dough is worked under and the top surface becomes smoother, tighter, and dome shaped. Do not overstretch or tear the dough. Let the dough rest for about 10 minutes, covered loosely with a sheet of oiled plastic wrap so a crust does not form, while shaping the second piece of dough. After all the pieces of dough have rested for at least 10 minutes, shape them for a minute or two more. Next, sprinkle proofing baskets (or plain baskets lined with fabric) liberally with flour to prevent sticking and turn the loaves, dome side down, gently into the baskets. The part of the dough facing up does not have to be smooth, as it will later become the bottom of the loaf. Pinch the seams in the dough together until they are sealed. If you do not have baskets, spray the loaves lightly with vegetable oil, cover the rounds with plastic wrap, and let them rise, dome side up, on a flat surface. The loaves may flatten out slightly during proofing, because they have no basket to help them hold their shape, but not enough to lessen their appeal by much. Soft doughs, which have a tendency to spread sideways, can be placed in greased round cake pans—the sides will provide structure. You may also create support by encircling the loaf with a lightly greased 1-inch band of aluminum foil. Remove the foil after the bread has risen halfway.

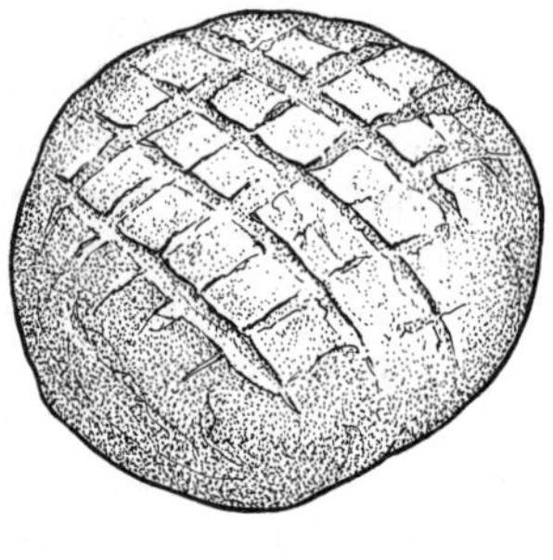

Round loaf or boule

Baguettes: Baguettes are one of the few traditional breads you can make with the straight dough method and commercial yeast. Quick-Rising White Bread dough, 744, will work too, but Slow-Rising White Bread dough, 744, or a starter-based dough, 757 to 758, will result in a crustier and tastier loaf. Baguettes can be held in shape either by baking in a baguette pan, 737, or, as is done by professional bakers, by proofing in a *couche,* 737, and then carefully moving it to a floured peel just before baking. You also can shape the loaves and proof them with no mold at all, but they will not end up quite as cylindrical and plump. The time needed for proofing will depend on whether you have used yeast or a starter. The baguettes will be tastier if the loaves rise in a cool place or, better yet, if you give them an overnight rise in the refrigerator.

Divide the dough into the desired number of pieces. On an unfloured work surface, gently shape and rotate the pieces to round them slightly. Cover the mounds of dough with plastic wrap or a clean dish towel and let rest for 15 minutes. Next, on a floured work surface, flatten each piece by hand or with a rolling pin into a 7 x 5-inch rectangle. Fold the short ends of the rectangle over each other as though you were folding a business letter in thirds. Press down on the rectangle to flatten it slightly and fold one long side about two-thirds down; roll and pinch the seam together to seal. Roll the dough with the flats of both hands until it stretches out slightly, then fold down the long side one more time and pinch again. Continue gently stretching and rolling, while tapering the ends, until the loaf is about 16 inches long. The dough will stretch about an inch as you move it to the baguette pan. If your baguette pans are larger or smaller, adjust the size of the loaves accordingly. If the dough does not stretch as you roll it, cover it with plastic wrap and let rest for 10 minutes before continuing. Repeat with the other pieces of dough.

If using baguette pans, wipe the pans lightly with oil and gently lower in the baguettes with the seam facing down. If using a *couche,* place the well-floured cloth on a baking sheet. Place one of the baguettes, seam side up, along one end of the cloth and gently fold up the cloth so that it forms a wall of cloth next to the baguette (later you will turn the loaf over onto the baking stone). Place another baguette next to the first, with the cloth separating the two, and repeat until you have used all the dough.

Thick Baguettes (Bâtards): These loaves, shorter and stubbier than baguettes, keep better and are easier to slice. These loaves are too wide for most baguette pans, so you will need a basket about 9 to 12 inches long and 4 to 5 inches wide to use for proofing. You can also use a *couche* or cloth as described for baguettes or simply proof the loaves directly on a floured baking sheet or peel; they may spread a little but will still be quite good. They are baked in the same way as baguettes but take longer.

Thin Baguettes (Ficelles): Shaped in the same way as baguettes (if you like them a lot, buy a *ficelle* pan, just like a baguette pan but narrower), these are the perfect loaves for crust-lovers. The dough should be divided and shaped into very thin, long loaves. *Ficelles* are baked in the same way as baguettes but for less time.

Bread Sticks: Any bread dough may be used for bread sticks. The dough is not left to rise after it has been shaped but is instead allowed to rise twice (it is punched down after the first rise). When the dough has doubled in volume a second time, it is shaped into bread sticks and immediately baked. To make bread sticks, use any of the recipes beginning on page 744. Preheat the oven to 500°F. Use the flat of your hand to push the dough into a ½-inch-thick rectangle about 24 x 7 inches. Liberally sprinkle 2 baking sheets with semolina flour, cornmeal, or all-purpose flour. With a knife, cut the dough crosswise into ½-inch-thick strips. Transfer the strips to pans, arranging them with about ½ inch between them. They will stretch to the width of the pan, 12 inches, as you transfer them. Bread sticks can be topped by lightly brushing with water and sprinkling with coarse salt, seeds, herbs, spices, or grated cheese. Just before baking, open the oven door a crack and, using a spray bottle, spritz about 5 times with water. Wait 1 minute and quickly slide in the pans of bread sticks. Bake at 400° to 450°F until well browned, about 15 minutes. Let them cool on a rack.

Rolls: Almost any bread dough can be used to make rolls of various shapes and styles. See individual recipes, beginning on page 750, for instructions on shaping.

FINAL RISING

Once you have shaped the dough into loaves, cover them loosely (so they can still rise) with lightly oiled plastic wrap or waxed paper or a damp, clean kitchen towel. Let rise at room temperature or in a warm place (75° to 80°F). Bread dough made with a large amount of commercial yeast may begin to rise visibly in 10 minutes, while that made with a starter may take an hour or more to begin. (The warmer the temperature, the faster the rise.) As with the first rising, verify that the dough has risen enough by pressing it with a fingertip; if it is ready, the impression will remain in the dough. If your dough is not quite fully risen but needs to be baked quickly, put it in a cool oven rather than a preheated one. This works best for pan breads, not free-form loaves.

REFRIGERATING DOUGH

You may sometimes find it more convenient to refrigerate the dough to retard rising, to fit your baking schedule. The process also helps flavors develop and may improve crusts. Dough may take anywhere from

12 to 24 hours to rise in the refrigerator, and in some very cold ones may become dormant and not rise at all. Retarded doughs may be kept in a refrigerator at 40°F or lower for up to 2 days. Above that temperature, dough might overrise. When refrigerating dough, it is best to cover it loosely with plastic wrap or to place the loaves in a large plastic bag. If the retarded dough stops rising before reaching the desired size, set it out at room temperature for an hour or two until it "wakes up" and begins rising again.

SCORING

Most country loaves and baguettes are scored (slashed across the top) just before going into the oven, both for decoration and to aid rising. If bread is baked without scoring, the pressure of the expanding dough will tear the crust in an irregular pattern—or, worse, the dough will be trapped by its own crust and rise very little. Slashes should be made with a *lame*, a single-edged razor, a sharp knife, or any of the other tools suggested on page 737. The slashes should be about ½ inch deep. For round loaves, make a single cut into the dough at a 45 degree angle, working it about two-thirds around the loaf. You can also make a crisscross pattern by making about 6 slashes from side to side an inch apart across the surface of the loaf and then another 6 at a slight diagonal to these. Baguettes require a series of parallel diagonal cuts, while thick baguettes are usually marked with a single long, diagonal slash.

BAKING

When loaves in pans have doubled in size, they are ready for the oven. Bake a single loaf in the middle of the preheated oven. Bake two loaves side by side. When baking more than two loaves, rotate loaves during baking from top to bottom and front to back so they brown evenly.

When hearth-style loaves have doubled in size, turn them out, seam side down, onto a baking sheet or baker's peel well sprinkled with a thin, even layer of semolina flour or cornmeal shaken through a sieve. You can sprinkle the tops of the loaves themselves with bread flour so that, as the bread bakes, the flour browns and gives the breads a lovely rustic look. If you are setting more than one loaf on a baking sheet or baking stone, bear in mind that the loaves will increase in size by almost half, so leave plenty of space—almost the size of a whole loaf—in between.

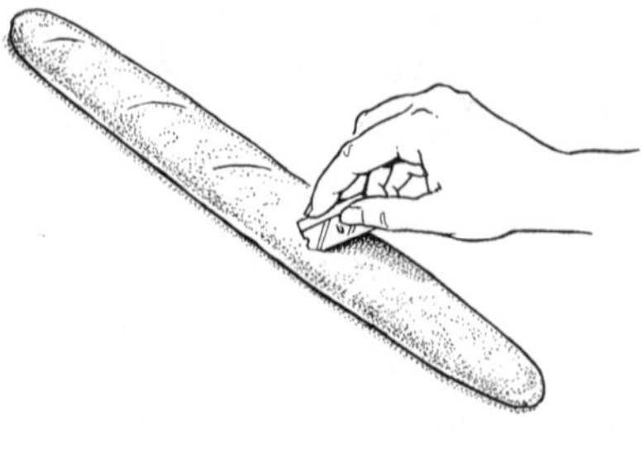

Scoring a baguette

Controlling heat and humidity in your oven is essential for successful bread baking. Most oven surfaces are made of light sheet metal, which retains heat poorly; every time you open the oven door, the temperature drops and your bread suffers. Placing a baking stone or tiles on the bottom rack of your oven helps. You can also lean unglazed tiles along the sides of the oven to stabilize temperature further. Because tiles and baking stones take a long time to get hot, remember to start preheating the oven for at least 45 minutes before baking.

Humidity is important first of all to keep the crust from setting too quickly in the hot oven. Professional ovens have special steam injectors that fill the oven with steam during the first few minutes of cooking, but at home we need to improvise by spraying the inside of the oven with a spray bottle. This also helps produce a crisp crust. Immediately before baking, quickly open the oven door only a crack and spray about 5 spritzes on the sides and bottom of the oven with water using a spray bottle. Wait about 30 seconds, then slide the loaves onto the baking stone or tiles and close the oven. Wait 2 minutes, barely crack open the oven door, and quickly shoot in 5 more spritzes of water. Try not to get water directly on the loaves (or on the light bulb). Spritz again in 2 more minutes. Don't open the oven door for the next 15 minutes of baking or you'll let out the humidity. You may also use a hot empty pan into which you pour 1 cup hot water just after loading your loaves.

ABOUT BREAD CRUST

A thick, brown crust may be acheived in glass, darkened tin, black steel, silicone-coated, stoneware, and dull aluminum pans. Glass pans require a slightly lower temperature, because they conduct heat more efficiently. Hard rolls, Vienna, French, and rye breads should be baked either in parchment-covered pans or on lightly greased baking sheets sprinkled with cornmeal, polenta, or semolina to prevent them from sticking. Milk, either in the dough or brushed on at the end of the baking period, gives crusts a good brown color through caramelization of the milk's natural sugars.

Cream or butter also may be brushed on for color up to 10 minutes before baking is done. Introducing steam into the oven during the first few minutes of baking or brushing partially baked loaves with salted water (1 teaspoon salt to ½ cup water) also helps produce nice crusts.

TESTING BREADS FOR DONENESS

A loaf is done when it has shrunk from the sides of the pan, has a hollow sound when thumped on the bottom, and feels firm all around. An instant-read thermometer can also be inserted into the center of a roll or loaf; if it reads above 195°F and the loaf passes the thump test, it can come out of the oven. If a loaf is not done, return it to the oven, in or out of the pan, for a few minutes until it is finished. When hearth bread looks done (hard, golden brown crust), it still needs more time for the center to evaporate moisture. Otherwise, the crust will soften as it cools and lose its crackle. Turn the oven off and let the loaves remain in the oven for 5 to 10 minutes. This cool-down technique helps retain the crust without overbaking or burning the bread. Hearth breads should have an internal temperature of 200° to 210°F.

COOLING AND STORING BREAD

Always let bread cool completely before wrapping it for storage; there should be no warmth radiating from the loaf. If it is wrapped while still warm, condensation may encourage molding. Let bread cool on a rack so the moisture can escape. Do not cut into a loaf until it has been out of the oven for at least 20 minutes, and wait an hour if possible (less for rolls and small breads). Bread always tastes best after it has cooled to an internal temperature of 85°F or less. Keep bread away from drafts, which will dry it out and cause shrinkage. All loaves, even crusty hearth breads, can be stored in plastic wrap, though the crust will soften. Bread boxes and dry, cool, ventilated drawers or containers are also acceptable. Use a baking soda solution or bleach water to cleanse storage areas of any possible off-odors, which bread could easily absorb. Refrigeration tends to dry out bread, but well-wrapped loaves can be frozen for up to 3 months. Once thawed, however, they dry out more rapidly than fresh baked bread.

ADDITIONS TO YEAST DOUGHS

Eggs: In addition to protein and other nutritional value, eggs contribute a small amount of leavening and dilute the gluten, softening the crumb. They also add richness of color to both the crumb and the crust.

Fat: Butter, margarine, lard, vegetable shortening, and vegetable oil are sometimes added to bread dough to enrich flavor and soften the crumb. Fat also extends the shelf life of bread by holding moisture in the loaf while protecting it against mold.

Dairy Products: Ingredients such as buttermilk (fresh or dried), whole and skim milk (fresh or dried), yogurt, and sour cream also soften the crumb and promote browning in the crust, as well as contributing protein and other nutrients.

Sugars: Many kinds of sugar are added to promote fermentation and to lend flavor. Sugar also softens dough by diluting the gluten and promotes caramelization of the crust. (Doughs with added sugar should be baked at lower temperatures, so they do not brown too quickly before the center of the loaf is done.)

Salt: Although we tend to think of it as essential to bread, salt was not used widely in baking until the eighteenth century, when it became an affordable commodity. Today, of course, almost all breads—some Italian and Spanish breads are the exception—require salt, for flavor, texture, and color and also to slow the fermentation process so that the yeast does not act too quickly. By affecting the water absorption of the yeast and gluten cells, salt also firms dough and increases elasticity. Whichever salt is used—fine or coarse, iodized table salt, sea salt, or kosher salt—the correct amount is about 2 percent of the weight of the flour. Be careful not to let the yeast and salt come into direct contact before mixing, as the salt can quickly kill the yeast.

Herbs and Spices: Rosemary, thyme, marjoram, cayenne, caraway, fennel seeds, and black pepper—alone or in combination—are delicious additions to bread when used moderately; delicate herbs, such as parsley, basil, or chervil, are apt to be overwhelmed by other ingredients. Herb and spice breads offer a variety of options, but a guiding principle is to remember that a little herb goes a long way. Their purpose is to enhance or magnify flavors, not to dominate. A general guideline for using strong dried herbs such as rosemary, celery seeds, caraway seeds, oregano, summer savory, thyme, sage, and dill or dill seeds is no more than 1 tablespoon per loaf. With some milder dried herbs, like parsley and chervil, you can add 2 or even 3 tablespoons. When using fresh herbs, which are not as intense in flavor as dried herbs, you may use 3 or 4 times the amount. Intense spices such as nutmeg, dried ginger, cloves, allspice, and mace are always best used in small amounts, and in combination with one another—use no more than 1 teaspoon per loaf.

Other Additions: Raisins, dates, dried fruits, nuts, sesame and sunflower seeds, lightly sautéed onions, olives, bean or grain sprouts, grains, toasted wheat germ, and brewer's yeast are among the other ingredients added to yeast doughs to increase flavor and nutritional value. These are seldom used in quantities greater than 25 percent of the weight of the flour. Unless otherwise specified, mix the basic ingredients of the dough thoroughly before adding any of these items. Fruits and other sticky additions can be dusted lightly with flour to keep them from sticking together. Remember that some whole grains like rice and barley should be cooked before being added to bread. Smaller coarse grains like rolled oats and polenta can be used as is or pulverized in a blender if desired.

BREADS MADE WITH THE STRAIGHT DOUGH METHOD

FAST WHITE BREAD

One 8½ x 4½-inch loaf

This is the easiest and quickest yeast bread we know.

Stir together in a large mixing bowl or in the bowl of a heavy-duty mixer:

2 cups bread flour
1 tablespoon sugar
1 package (2¼ teaspoons) quick-rising active dry yeast
1¼ teaspoon salt

Add:

1 cup very warm (115° to 125°F) water
2 tablespoons melted butter or margarine

Mix by hand or on low speed for 1 minute. Gradually add ¼ cup at a time until the dough is moist but not sticky:

¾ to 1 cup bread flour

Knead for about 10 minutes by hand or with the dough hook on low to medium speed until the dough is smooth and elastic. Transfer the dough to an oiled bowl and turn it over once to coat with oil. Cover the bowl loosely with plastic wrap and let rise in a warm place (75° to 80°F) until doubled in volume, 30 to 45 minutes.

Grease an 8½ x 4½-inch (6-cup) loaf pan. Punch the dough down, form it into a loaf, and place seam side down in the pan. Cover loosely with oiled plastic wrap. Let rise in a warm place until doubled in volume, 30 to 45 minutes.

Meanwhile preheat the oven to 450°F. Bake the loaf for 10 minutes. Reduce the heat to 350°F and bake until the bottom of the loaf sounds hollow when tapped, about 30 minutes more. Remove the loaf from the pan to a rack and let cool completely.

QUICK-RISING WHITE BREAD

Two 8½ x 4½-inch loaves

Combine in a large mixing bowl or in the bowl of a heavy-duty mixer and let stand until the yeast is dissolved, about 5 minutes:

1 package (2¼ teaspoons) active dry yeast
¼ cup warm (105° to 115°F) water

Add:

3 cups bread flour
2 cups warm (105° to 115°) water
1 tablespoon melted butter, margarine, or vegetable shortening
2 tablespoons sugar
1 tablespoon salt

Mix by hand or on low speed for 1 minute. Gradually add ½ cup at a time until the dough is moist but not sticky:

3 to 3½ cups bread flour

Knead for about 10 minutes by hand or with the dough hook on low to medium speed until the dough is smooth and elastic. Transfer the dough to an oiled bowl and turn it over once to coat with oil. Cover loosely with plastic wrap and let rise in a warm place (75° to 80°F) until doubled in volume, 1 to 1½ hours.

Grease two 8½ x 4½-inch (6-cup) loaf pans. Punch the dough down, divide it in half, and form into 2 loaves. Place seam side down in the pans. Cover loosely with oiled plastic wrap and let rise in a warm place until doubled in volume, 1 to 1½ hours.

Meanwhile, preheat the oven to 450°F. Bake the loaves for 10 minutes. Reduce the heat to 350°F and bake until the bottoms of the loaves sound hollow when tapped, about 30 minutes more. Remove the loaves from the pans to a rack and let cool completely.

SLOW-RISING WHITE BREAD

Two 8½ x 4½-inch loaves

Prepare Quick-Rising White Bread, above, substituting 1 teaspoon active dry yeast dissolved in 1 tablespoon warm (105° to 115°F) water for the yeast and cold (50°F) water for the 2 cups warm. Before the first rise, refrigerate the dough for at least 5 hours or up to 12 hours. Take the dough out of the refrigerator and let rise at room temperature until doubled in volume, about 6 hours. Shape, let rise, and bake as directed.

WHITE SANDWICH BREAD

Two 8½ x 4½-inch loaves

This classic all-purpose white bread stales slowly and slices well for sandwiches.

Combine in a large mixing bowl or in the bowl of a

heavy-duty mixer and let stand until the yeast is dissolved, about 5 minutes:

4 teaspoons active dry yeast
¼ cup warm (105° to 115°F) water

Warm to 105° to 115°F:

1 cup milk

Add to the milk and stir to dissolve the sugar:

1 cup warm (105° to 115°F) water
2 tablespoons (¼ stick) butter or shortening, softened
2 tablespoons sugar or honey
1 tablespoon salt

Stir the milk mixture into the yeast. Have ready:

4½ to 5 cups bread flour

Add 3 cups of the flour to the yeast mixture and mix by hand or on low speed for 1 minute. Gradually add the remaining flour until the dough is moist but not sticky. Knead for about 10 minutes by hand or with the dough hook on low to medium speed until the dough is smooth and elastic. Transfer to an oiled bowl and turn it over once to coat with oil. Cover loosely with plastic wrap and let rise in a warm place (75° to 80°F) until doubled in volume, 1 to 1½ hours. Knead the dough briefly, return it to the bowl, and let rise again until doubled, about 1 hour. (You may skip this step if under time constraints, but the bread will be better with the second rise.)

Grease two 8½ x 4½-inch (6-cup) loaf pans. Punch the dough down, divide it in half, and form into 2 loaves. Place seam side down in the pans. Cover loosely with oiled plastic wrap and let rise in a warm place until the loaves crest above the pan, making a nice dome, about 1 hour.

Meanwhile, preheat the oven to 450°F. Bake the loaves for 10 minutes. Reduce the heat to 350°F and bake until the bottom of the loaves sound hollow when tapped, about 30 minutes more. Remove the loaves from the pans to a rack and let cool completely.

WHOLE-WHEAT BREAD

Whole-wheat bread is made the same way as white bread but with whole-wheat flour substituted for some of the white flour. (A loaf made entirely with whole-wheat flour won't have sufficient rising power and will come out disappointingly heavy.) Bakers tend to disagree about the ideal proportions of whole-wheat flour to white; we favor one part whole-wheat to two parts white. Any of the white bread recipes on page 744 can be adapted for whole-wheat bread.

FAST WHOLE-WHEAT BREAD

One 8½ x 4½-inch loaf

Prepare Fast White Bread, 744, substituting 1 cup whole-wheat flour for 1 cup of the bread flour.

QUICK-RISING WHOLE-WHEAT BREAD

Prepare Quick-Rising White Bread, 744, substituting 1½ cups whole-wheat flour for 1½ cups of the white bread flour and increasing the yeast to 2½ teaspoons.

SLOW-RISING WHOLE-WHEAT BREAD

Prepare Slow-Rising White Bread, 744, substituting 1½ cups whole-wheat flour for 1½ cups of the white bread flour and increasing the yeast to 2½ teaspoons.

WHOLE-WHEAT SANDWICH BREAD

Prepare White Sandwich Bread, 744, substituting 2 cups whole-wheat flour for 2 cups of the white bread flour and increasing the yeast to 4¼ teaspoons.

VARIATIONS ON WHOLE-WHEAT AND WHOLE-GRAIN BREADS

Many grains may be added to bread doughs to add flavor, textures, and/or nutritional value. As long as the total amount of whole-grain flours equals no more than one-third of the total flour (the other two thirds being bread flour), you can create an infinite number of variations. Oats, rye, barley, amaranth, millet, quinoa, corn, triticale, and dehydrated potatoes may be added uncooked. Rice can be added as a flour or as a cooked grain. Grains larger than millet—that is, larger than tiny pellets the size of bird seed—should be cooked first.

RYE BREADS

While the traditional rye breads of Europe are usually made with a starter, and care must be taken to compensate for rye flour's low gluten content, these versions, made by the straight dough method, are excellent:

BASIC RYE BREAD

Prepare Fast White Bread, 744, Quick-Rising White Bread, 744, or White Sandwich Bread, 744, replacing one-fourth to one-third of the bread flour with an equal amount of light rye flour or pumpernickel (coarse) flour. The more rye flour used, the denser the finished bread.

SPECIALTY BREADS

MILK BREAD

One 8½ x 4½-inch loaf

This is one of the simplest and most satisfying white breads. The milk, egg, and butter impart a delicate rich flavor, tender crumb, and soft golden brown crust. The dough is also easily shaped into rolls.

Combine in a large mixing bowl or in the bowl of a heavy-duty mixer and let stand until the yeast is dissolved, about 5 minutes:

1 package (2¼ teaspoons) active dry yeast
3 tablespoons warm (105° to 115°F) water

Add:

1 cup whole or low-fat milk, warmed to 105° to 115°F
5 tablespoons melted butter or margarine
3 tablespoons sugar
1 large egg
1 teaspoon salt

Mix by hand or on low speed for 1 minute. Gradually stir in:

2 cups bread flour

Gradually add until the dough is moist but not sticky:

1½ to 2 cups all-purpose flour

Knead for about 10 minutes by hand or with the dough hook on low to medium speed until the dough is smooth and elastic. Transfer the dough to an oiled bowl and turn it over once to coat with oil. Cover loosely with plastic wrap and let rise in a warm place (75° to 80°F) until doubled in volume, 1 to 1½ hours.

Punch the dough down, knead briefly, and refrigerate covered for 30 minutes. At this point the dough may be shaped into rolls, 750 to 752. Or grease an 8½ x 4½-inch (6-cup) loaf pan, form the dough into a loaf, and place seam side down in the pan. Cover loosely with oiled plastic wrap and let rise in a warm place until doubled in volume, 1 to 1½ hours.

Preheat the oven to 375°F. Brush the top of the loaf with:

Melted butter or milk

Bake until the crust is deep golden brown and the bottom of the loaf sounds hollow when tapped, 40 to 45 minutes. Remove the loaf from the pan to a rack and let cool completely.

CINNAMON RAISIN LOAF

One 8½ x 4½-inch loaf

A favorite breakfast treat.

Prepare Milk Bread, above, through the first rise. While the dough is rising, place in a small saucepan with enough cold water to cover by ½ inch:

½ cup raisins

Bring to a boil, drain well, and let it cool. Stir together:

2 tablespoons sugar
2 teaspoons ground cinnamon

Grease an 8½ x 4½-inch (6-cup) loaf pan. Punch the dough down. Using a rolling pin, roll the dough into an 8-inch-wide rectangle, about ½ inch thick. Brush the surface of the dough with:

1½ teaspoons melted butter

Sprinkle all but 2 teaspoons of the cinnamon mixture over the dough, then spread the raisins evenly over the surface. Starting from one 8-inch side, roll up the dough as you would a jelly roll. Pinch the seam and ends closed. Place seam side down in the pan. Cover loosely with oiled plastic wrap and let rise in a warm place until doubled in volume, 1 to 1½ hours.

Preheat the oven to 375°F. Whisk together and brush over the top of the loaf:

1 egg
Pinch of salt

Sprinkle the top of the dough with the remaining cinnamon mixture. Bake until the crust is deep golden brown and the bottom of the loaf sounds hollow when tapped, 40 to 45 minutes. Remove the loaf from the pan to a rack. While the bread is still hot, brush the top with:

2 teaspoons melted butter

Let cool completely before slicing.

CHALLAH

1 braided loaf

This traditional Jewish Sabbath bread, blessed and served before Friday-night dinner, is a sort of butterless brioche, 764. It is particularly good at breakfast time.

Combine in a large mixing bowl or the bowl of a heavy-duty mixer and let stand until the yeast is dissolved, about 5 minutes:

1 package (2¼ teaspoons) active dry yeast
½ cup warm (105° to 115 F) water

Add:

½ cup all-purpose flour
2 large eggs, lightly beaten
2 egg yolks, lightly beaten
3 tablespoons vegetable oil
3 tablespoons sugar
1¼ teaspoons salt

Mix by hand or on low speed until thoroughly blended. Gradually stir in:

2½ cups bread flour

Knead for about 8 minutes by hand or with the dough hook on low to medium speed until the dough is smooth and elastic and no longer sticks to your hands or the bowl. Transfer the dough to an oiled bowl and turn it over once to coat with oil. Cover with plastic wrap and let rise in a warm place (75° to 80°F) until doubled in volume, 1 to 1½ hours. Punch the dough down, knead briefly, and refrigerate covered until it has again nearly doubled in volume (a three-quarter rise is sufficient), 4 to 12 hours. The dough is now ready to be shaped.

THREE-STRAND BRAIDED CHALLAH

Anyone who has braided hair or rope will have no trouble here. In fact, you can divide the dough into as many strands as you like and braid accordingly, but this one is a simple 3-strand braid.

Weigh and divide the dough equally into 3 pieces. On an unfloured work surface, roll into balls and let rest, loosely covered with plastic wrap, for 10 minutes. Grease a baking sheet and sprinkle it with cornmeal. Roll each ball into a 13- to 14-inch-long rope, about 1½ inches thick and slightly tapered at the ends. Dust the 3 dough ropes with rye flour so they will be more distinctly separated. Place the 3 dough ropes side by side and pinch the top ends together. Lift the left dough rope and place it between the right and middle ropes. Lift the right rope and place it between the left and middle ropes, then the left rope between the right and middle ropes and so on until you reach the ends. Tuck both ends of the braid underneath the loaf and set it on the baking sheet. Whisk together and brush over the top of the loaf:

1 egg
Pinch of salt

Loosely cover the braid with lightly oiled plastic wrap and let rise in a warm place until not quite doubled, about 45 minutes.

Preheat the oven to 375°F. Brush the loaf again with egg wash. If desired, sprinkle with:

1 tablespoon poppy or sesame seeds

Bake until the crust is golden brown and the bottom of the loaf sounds hollow when tapped, 30 to 35 minutes. Let cool completely on a rack.

FOUR-STRAND BRAIDED CHALLAH

Weigh and divide the dough equally into 4 pieces. On an unfloured work surface, roll into balls and let rise, loosely covered with plastic wrap, for 10 minutes. Roll the balls of dough into long ropes about 1 inch thick and 20 inches long, slightly tapering the ends. Dust the ropes of dough with rye flour so they will be distinctly separated. Arrange the 4 ropes side by side and pinch the top ends securely together.

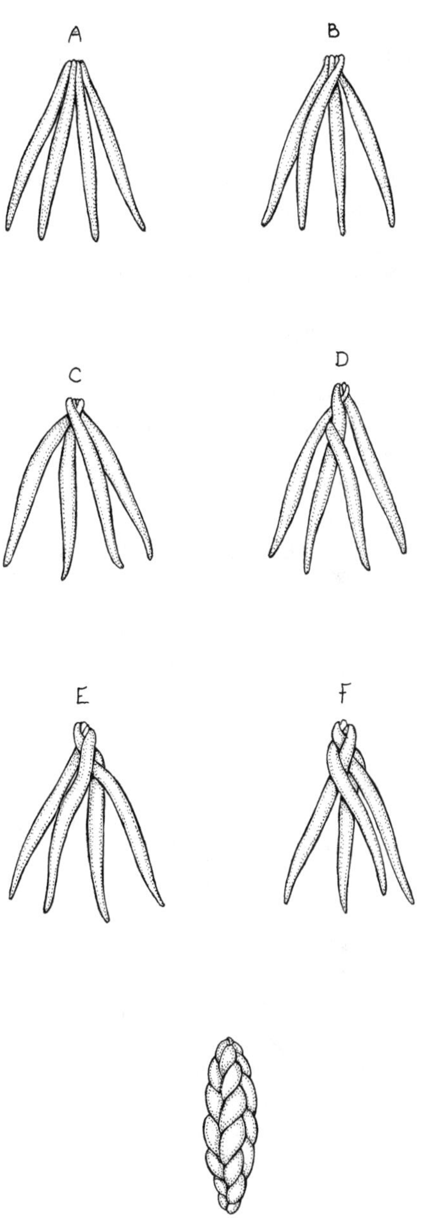

Braiding four-strand challah

Braid the strips of dough in the following sequence, as shown above: Lift and place the fourth strand over the second, B. Lift and place the first strand over the third, C, then lift and place the second over the third, D. Repeat this sequence, placing the strand that is now the fourth over the second, E, the first over the third, F, then the second over the third. Continue braiding until you reach the end of the strands. Pinch the bottom ends together and tuck both top and bottom ends underneath the braid. Finish as directed for Three-Strand Braided Challah, 747.

DILL BREAD

One 9 x 5-inch loaf

This is an updated version of the Dill Batter Loaf that has been a longtime *Joy* favorite. Fresh dill can now be found the year around in most supermarkets and is much preferable to dried dill or dill seeds.

Combine in a small bowl and let stand until the yeast is dissolved, about 5 minutes:

1 package (2¼ teaspoons) active dry yeast
½ cup warm (105° to 115°F) water

Combine in a large mixing bowl or the bowl of a heavy-duty mixer:

3 cups bread flour
½ cup finely chopped onions
3 tablespoons chopped fresh dill, or 1 tablespoon dried dill or dill seeds
2 tablespoons sugar or honey
1 tablespoon wheat germ, toasted
1 teaspoon salt

Add the yeast along with:

1 cup large-curd cottage cheese
1 large egg

Mix by hand or on low speed until the dough comes together, adding additional flour or warm water if needed. Knead for about 10 minutes by hand or with the dough hook on low to medium speed until the dough is smooth and elastic. Transfer to an oiled bowl and turn it over once to coat with oil. Cover loosely with plastic wrap and let rise in a warm place (75° to 80°F) until doubled in volume, 1 to 1½ hours.

Grease a 9 x 5-inch (8-cup) loaf pan. Punch the dough down, form into a loaf, and place seam side down in the pan. Cover with oiled plastic wrap and let rise in a warm place until doubled in volume, about 1 hour.

Meanwhile, preheat the oven to 350°F. If desired, brush the top of the loaf with:

1 egg, lightly beaten, or 1 tablespoon melted butter

Sprinkle lightly with:

½ teaspoon coarse salt or a few dill seeds

Bake until the crust is deep golden brown and the bottom of the loaf sounds hollow when tapped, 35 to 40 minutes. Remove the loaf from the pan to a rack and let cool completely.

OATMEAL MOLASSES BREAD

2 loaves

This dough also makes delicious rolls.

Combine in a medium saucepan:

1½ cups water
1 cup steel-cut or rolled oats
1 tablespoon butter
¾ teaspoon salt

Cook, stirring occasionally, over a medium-low heat until the oatmeal is soft, smooth, thick, and free of lumps, about 20 minutes. Let cool, stirring occasionally, until tepid and no warmer than 115°F.

Combine in a large mixing bowl or the bowl of a heavy-duty mixer and let stand until the yeast is dissolved, about 5 minutes:

1 package (2¼ teaspoons) active dry yeast
¼ cup warm (105° to 115°F) water

Add to the yeast the oatmeal mixture along with:

½ cup room-temperature water
⅓ cup molasses

Stir until well blended. Gradually stir in until the dough is moist but not sticky:

3¾ cups to 4 cups all-purpose flour

Knead for 10 to 15 minutes by hand or with the dough hook on low to medium speed until the dough is smooth and elastic. Transfer the dough to an oiled bowl and turn it over once to coat with oil. Cover the bowl with plastic wrap and let rise in a warm place (75° to 80°F) until doubled in volume, 1 to 1½ hours. Punch the dough down and knead briefly.

Grease a baking sheet or two 8½ x 4½-inch (6-cup) loaf pans. Divide the dough in half. On an unfloured work surface, roll each piece into a ball, loosely cover with plastic wrap, and let rest for 30 minutes. Form into 2 free-standing round loaves (see Shaping, 740) or loaves for the loaf pans. Place seam side down and well spaced on the baking sheet or in the loaf pans. Cover loosely with oiled plastic wrap and let rise in a warm place until doubled in volume, 1 to 1½ hours.

Preheat the oven to 375°F. Slash the round loaves before baking (see Scoring, 742). Bake until the bottoms of the loaves sounds hollow when tapped, 40 to 45 minutes. Remove from the pans to a rack and let cool for at least 30 minutes before serving.

BUTTERMILK POTATO BREAD

Two 9 x 5-inch loaves

Prepare:

¾ cup freshly cooked potatoes riced through a potato ricer or mashed with a fork

In a large mixing bowl or in the bowl of a heavy-duty mixer, stir into the still-hot potatoes:

8 tablespoons (1 stick) butter, very soft

Add and mix well:

4 teaspoons active dry yeast
2 cups buttermilk, at room temperature
2 large eggs, lightly beaten
2 tablespoons sugar
2½ teaspoons salt

Gradually stir in until the dough is moist but not sticky:

6¼ to 6½ cups bread flour

When the dough comes together, knead for 10 to 12 minutes by hand or with the dough hook on low to medium speed until the dough is smooth, soft, and elastic. Transfer the dough to an oiled bowl and turn it over once to coat with oil. Cover with plastic wrap and let rise at room temperature until doubled in volume, 1 to 1½ hours.

Grease two 9 x 5-inch (8-cup) loaf pans. Punch the dough down, divide it in half, and form into 2 loaves. Place seam side down in the pans. Cover with oiled plastic wrap and let rise until nearly doubled in volume, 1 to 1½ hours.

Preheat the oven to 375°F. Brush the top of the loaves with:

1 egg, lightly beaten with a pinch of salt

If desired, sprinkle with:

1 tablespoon poppy seeds

Bake the loaves until the crust is golden brown and the bottoms sound hollow when tapped, 40 to 45 minutes. Remove the loaves from the pans to a rack and let cool for at least 30 minutes before serving.

CHEESE BREAD

Two 8½ x 4½-inch loaves

Do not add the cheese too early in the mixing. Either roll it up in the risen dough before shaping or knead it into the dough in the final turns. For variation, add a sprinkling of fresh or dried herbs, such as thyme or marjoram, with the cheese. You may also add chopped onions or garlic or diced scallions or green olives when you roll up the loaves.

Combine in a large mixing bowl or the bowl of a heavy-duty mixer:

5½ cups bread flour
3 packages (2 tablespoons plus ¾ teaspoon) active dry yeast
2 tablespoons wheat bran (optional)
2 tablespoons sugar
1 tablespoon salt

Add:

1¼ cups buttermilk, at room temperature
2 tablespoons melted butter
1 cup finely chopped red bell pepper or well-drained pimientos (optional)

Mix by hand or on low speed until the dough comes together, adding more buttermilk or flour if needed. Knead for about 10 minutes by hand or with the dough hook on low to medium speed until the dough is smooth and elastic. Add during the final 2 minutes of kneading or work in later:

1½ cups shredded Cheddar, Swiss, or provolone cheese

Transfer the dough to an oiled bowl and turn it over once to coat with oil. Cover loosely with plastic wrap and let rise in a warm place (75° to 80°F) until doubled in volume, about 1½ hours.

Grease two 8½ x 4½-inch (6-cup) loaf pans. Punch the dough down and divide it in half. If the cheese is already in the dough, form into 2 loaves and place seam side down in the pans. If you have not yet added the cheese, roll out the 2 pieces of dough into 8-inch-wide rectangles and sprinkle the cheese evenly on top. Starting from one 8-inch side, roll up each rectangle as you would a jelly roll. Pinch the seams and ends closed. Place seam side down in the pans. Cover loosely with oiled plastic wrap and let rise in a warm place until doubled in volume, about 1½ hours.

Preheat the oven to 350°F. Bake the loaves until the crust is golden brown and the bottom sounds hollow when tapped, 45 to 50 minutes. Remove the loaves from the pans to a rack and let cool completely.

BEER BREAD

One 8½ x 4½-inch loaf

Bread and beer are cousins: Both are based on yeast-fermented grain. Beer can also be substituted for water or milk in many other bread recipes for the flavor its hops and malted barley add. Strong ales or dark stouts are excellent choices.

Combine in a large mixing bowl or the bowl of a heavy-duty mixer:

3½ cups bread flour
¼ cup cooked brown or white rice
2 tablespoons packed light or dark brown sugar
1 tablespoon plus ¾ teaspoon active dry yeast
1 tablespoon wheat bran
1½ teaspoons salt

Add:

1 cup strong beer, ale, or stout, at room temperature
¼ cup milk or buttermilk, at room temperature

Mix by hand or on low speed until the dough comes together, adding additional milk or flour as needed. Knead for about 10 minutes by hand or with the dough hook on low to medium speed until the dough is smooth and elastic. Transfer the dough to an oiled bowl and turn it over once to coat with oil. Cover loosely with plastic wrap and let rise at room temperature until doubled in volume, about 1½ hours.

Grease an 8½ x 4½-inch (6-cup) loaf pan. Punch the dough down, form into a loaf, and place seam side down in the pan. Cover loosely with oiled plastic wrap and let rise at room temperature until doubled in volume, about 1½ hours.

Preheat the oven to 350°F. Bake the loaf until the crust is golden brown and the bottom sounds hollow when tapped, about 45 minutes. Remove the loaf from the pan to a rack and let cool completely.

YEAST ROLLS

Hard rolls are made from lean bread doughs, while the softer rolls we give here come from the enriched milk doughs, tenderized further with butter, oil, or buttermilk. Hard crusts can be delicious, but we often make these softer rolls to serve with dinner. They keep for several days without going stale.

MILK BREAD POMPONS

18 rolls

Prepare the dough for Milk Bread, 746, through the first rise. Divide the dough equally into 18 pieces, about 1 ounce each. Grease a baking sheet. On an unfloured surface, roll the dough pieces into balls and place them 2 inches apart on the baking sheet. For the egg wash, whisk together 1 egg and a pinch of salt, and brush over the tops of the rolls. Cover with oiled plastic wrap and let rise in a warm place until doubled in volume, about 1 hour.

Preheat the oven to 425°F. Brush the pompons again with the egg wash. If desired, sprinkle with coarse or granulated sugar. Bake the rolls until the crust is golden brown and the bottom sounds hollow when tapped, about 15 minutes. Serve freshly baked and warm or reheat in a 400°F oven for 4 to 6 minutes.

JOINED FINGER ROLLS

18 rolls

Prepare the dough for Milk Bread, 746, through the first rise. Divide the dough equally into 18 pieces, about 1 ounce each. Grease a baking sheet. On an unfloured surface, roll the dough pieces into balls, then, working from the center outward, elongate them into plump oblong-shaped rolls, about 3 inches long, 1½ inches wide at the center, and slightly tapered at the ends. Place the elongated rolls in a straight line and about ½ inch apart on the baking sheet so that they join together during rising. Finish as directed for Milk Bread Pompons, above.

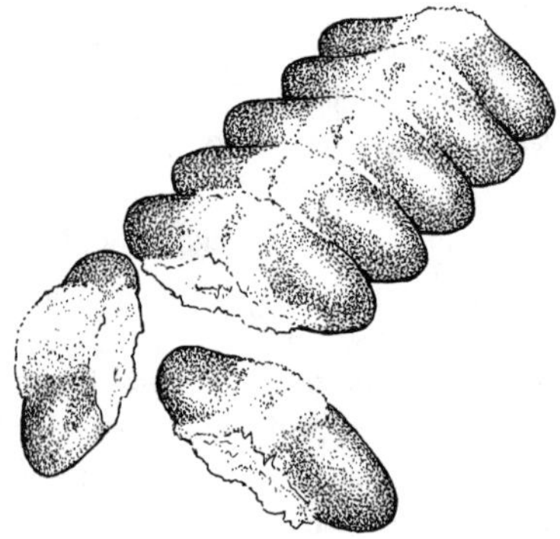

Joined Finger Rolls

Milk Bread Pompons

PARKER HOUSE ROLLS

18 rolls

These soft rolls, invented by a baker at the Parker House Hotel in Boston in the 1850s, have become an American classic.

Prepare the dough for Milk Bread, 746, through the first rise. Divide the dough equally into 18 pieces (about 1 ounce each). On an unfloured work surface, roll the dough pieces into balls. Loosely cover with oiled plastic wrap and let rest for 10 minutes. Grease a baking sheet. With a rolling pin or a dowel, roll just the center of each round to create an oval (do not roll over the edge as the edges should be slightly thicker than

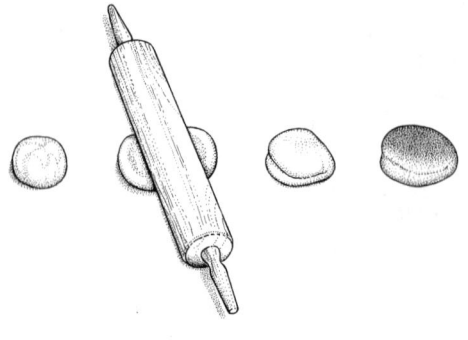

*Forming Parker House Rolls—
a baked Parker House Roll is at far right*

the center). Brush the tops lightly with melted butter and fold the ovals in half so the two elongated ends meet. Place the rolls in rows 2 inches apart on the baking sheet. Cover with oiled plastic wrap and let rise in a warm place until doubled in volume, about 1 hour.
Preheat the oven to 425°F. Brush the tops of the rolls with melted butter or milk. Bake until golden brown, about 15 minutes.

HOT CROSS BUNS
18 buns

These originated in medieval England as simple tea rolls, flavored with dried fruit and spices and crossed with sugar, to commemorate Good Friday. An easy way to make these is to add flavorings to the Milk Bread dough, 746, and shape into rolls, but you may also make these rolls using the enriched doughs for Stollen and Panettone, 763 to 764.
Place in a small saucepan with just enough water to cover by ½ inch:

½ cup dried currants or raisins

Bring the water to a boil, then drain well. Transfer the currants to a small bowl and sprinkle with:

2 tablespoons water

Cover and let soak at least 30 minutes.
Stir together:

¼ teaspoon ground cinnamon
⅛ teaspoon freshly grated or ground nutmeg
⅛ teaspoon ground ginger

Prepare:

Milk Bread dough, 746

adding the spice mixture to the bread flour, and adding the drained currants toward the end of the kneading. Proceed and bake as directed for Milk Bread Pompons, 750, brushing with the egg wash but omitting the sugar.
While the rolls are baking, make a glaze by stirring together:

½ cup powdered sugar
1 tablespoon fresh lemon juice, orange juice, or milk

While rolls are still slightly warm, decorate each one with glaze in the shape of a cross.

CLOVERLEAF ROLLS
12 rolls

Buttermilk Potato Bread dough, 748, also makes lovely cloverleaf rolls. Prepare the dough for Milk Bread, 746, through the first rise. Divide the dough equally into 12 pieces (about 1½ ounces each). On an unfloured surface, roll the dough pieces into balls. Loosely cover with oiled plastic wrap and let rest for 10 minutes. Grease a standard 12-muffin pan. Divide each ball into 3 pieces and roll each piece into a tiny ball. Place 3 balls in each of the muffin cups. Cover with oiled plastic wrap and let rise in a warm place until doubled in volume, about 1 hour.

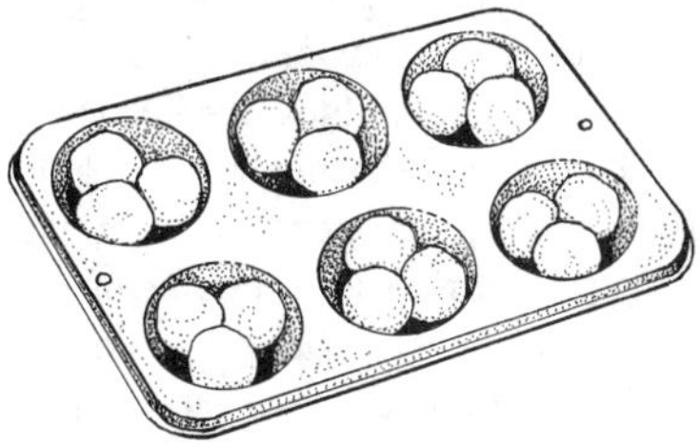

Making Cloverleaf Rolls

Preheat the oven to 425°F. Brush the tops of the rolls with melted butter or milk. Bake until golden brown, about 15 minutes.

OATMEAL MOLASSES ROLLS
Twenty-four 2-inch rolls

Prepare the dough for Oatmeal Molasses Bread, 748, through the first rise. Lightly grease 2 baking sheets. Divide the dough equally into 24 pieces, about 1½ ounces each. On an unfloured work surface, roll each piece into a ball and place the balls 2 inches apart on the baking sheets. Loosely cover with oiled plastic wrap and let rise in a warm place until doubled in volume, 1 to 1½ hours.
Preheat the oven to 400°F. Bake the rolls until browned, 20 to 25 minutes. Serve freshly baked and warm or reheat for 4 to 6 minutes in a 400°F oven.

CHEESE ROLLS
24 rolls

Prepare the dough for Cheese Bread, 749, through the first rise, setting the cheese aside to add later. (The whole recipe will yield 24 rolls, or you may cut the recipe in half to yield 12 rolls.) Punch the dough down, knead briefly on an unfloured surface, and divide the dough in half. Cover with oiled plastic wrap and let rest for 10 minutes.
Grease 2 baking sheets. Using a rolling pin, roll each piece of dough into a 15 x 8-inch rectangle. Cut each rectangle crosswise into thirds and lengthwise once to

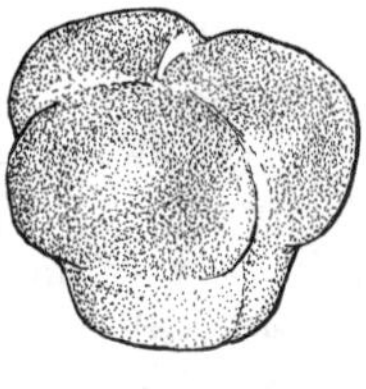

Baked Cloverleaf Rolls

form six 5 x 4-inch rectangles (12 total). Cut each rectangle in half diagonally, forming 24 triangles. Sprinkle about 1 tablespoon shredded Cheddar cheese in the center of each triangle. Starting from the longest side of the triangle, roll to the opposite point. Place each rolled triangle point side down on one of the baking sheets and repeat, spacing the rolls about 2 inches apart. Gently turn the ends inward to form a crescent shape. Cover with oiled plastic wrap and let rise in a warm place until doubled in volume, about 1 hour.

Preheat oven to 400°F. Bake the rolls until golden brown, about 15 minutes. Serve freshly baked and warm or reheat in a 400°F oven for 4 to 6 minutes.

HARD ROLLS OR VIENNA ROLLS

Twelve 2¼-inch rolls

These rolls have a harder crust than some Viennese-style rolls but are lighter and softer than rolls made from starter-risen bread doughs. The beaten egg whites give them a lighter crumb. These are best baked on a stone; remember to preheat it in the oven for 45 minutes before baking.

Combine in a large mixing bowl or the bowl of a heavy-duty mixer and let stand until the yeast is dissolved, about 5 minutes:

1 package (2¼ teaspoons) active dry yeast
¼ cup warm (105° to 115°F) water

Add:

1 cup warm (105° to 115°F) water
2 cups all-purpose flour
2 tablespoons vegetable shortening
1 tablespoon sugar
1¼ teaspoons salt

Mix by hand or on low speed until thoroughly blended. Beat until soft peaks form:

2 large egg whites

Fold into the dough. Gradually stir in until the dough is moist but not sticky:

1¾ to 2 cups all-purpose flour

Knead for about 7 minutes by hand or with the dough hook on low to medium speed until the dough is smooth and elastic. Transfer the dough to an oiled bowl and turn it over once to coat with oil. Cover with plastic wrap and let rise in a warm place (75° to 80°F) until doubled in volume, 1 to 1½ hours. Punch the dough down, knead it briefly, and let rise again until doubled, about 1 hour.

Punch the dough down and divide it equally into 12 pieces. On an unfloured work surface, roll each piece into a ball. Loosely cover the balls of dough with plastic wrap. Lightly dust a baking sheet with cornmeal. Place the rolls 2 inches apart on the baking sheet. Loosely cover with oiled plastic wrap and let rise in a warm place until doubled, about 1 hour.

Preheat the oven to 425°F. Just before baking, place a 13 x 9-inch baking pan filled with ½ inch of boiling water in the bottom of the oven and spray the oven walls with water a few times with a spritzer (avoid the bulb). Bake the rolls for 15 minutes, keeping the oven door closed throughout, then remove the pan of water. Bake until the rolls are golden brown and crusty, 5 to 7 minutes longer. Serve freshly baked and warm or reheat for 4 to 6 minutes in a 400°F oven.

FLATBREADS

Flatbreads can be leavened or unleavened and appear in varying degrees of thinness, as opposed to thicker raised breads such as rolls or loaves.

LEAVENED FLATBREADS

BASIC PIZZA DOUGH

Two 12-inch crusts

As you become an avid pizza baker, you will, no doubt, come up with your own style of crust and your own favorite toppings (for our favorite toppings, see pages 195 to 196). This is the dough that will get you started. For baking and serving instructions, see page 195.

Combine in a large mixing bowl or the bowl of a heavy-duty mixer and let stand until the yeast is dissolved, about 5 minutes:

1 package (2¼ teaspoons) active dry yeast
1⅓ cups warm (105° to 115°F) water

Add:

3½ to 3¾ cups all-purpose flour
2 tablespoons olive oil
1 tablespoon salt
1 tablespoon sugar (optional)

Mix by hand or on low speed for about 1 minute to blend all the ingredients. Knead for about 10 minutes by hand or with the dough hook on low to medium speed until the dough is smooth and elastic. Transfer the dough to a bowl lightly coated with olive oil and turn it over once to coat with oil. Cover with plastic wrap and let rise in a warm place (75° to 80°F) until doubled in volume, 1 to 1½ hours.

Preheat the oven to 475°F. Grease and dust 2 baking sheets with cornmeal; or place a baking stone (if you have one) in the oven and preheat it for 45 minutes. Punch the dough down and divide it in half. Roll each piece into a ball and let rest, loosely covered with plastic wrap, for 10 to 15 minutes. At this point prepare the desired toppings (see pages 195 to 196).

Flatten each ball of dough 1 at a time on a lightly floured work surface into a 12-inch round, rolling and stretching the dough. Place each dough circle on a prepared baking sheet; if using a baking stone, place them on baker's peels dusted with cornmeal. Lift the edge and pinch it to form a lip. To prevent the filling from making the crust soggy, brush the top of the dough with:

Olive oil

Use your fingertips to push dents in the surface of the dough (to prevent bubbling) and let rest for about 10 minutes. The pizza is now ready to be topped.

FOCACCIA

Two 10-inch focaccia

Like pizza, focaccia is essentially a large disk or slab of slightly risen bread dough—but focaccia is more bread and less topping. A simple way to make focaccia is to use pizza dough, divide and roll each piece out to ½-inch-thick round, and transfer these to well-oiled 10-inch cake pans. Let rise, covered with plastic wrap, for 1½ hours.

Preheat the oven to 400°F. Ten minutes before baking, dimple the dough with your fingertips and drizzle evenly with olive oil (as much as ½ cup—authentic focaccia is quite oily). Top with a small amount of grated cheese, a sprinkle of dried herbs, or coarse sea salt. Bake the focaccia until golden, about 25 minutes. Remove from the pans to cool on a rack and serve warm or at room temperature. If you leave off the toppings, halve the finished focaccia horizontally and use it as sandwich bread. Or fill it with your favorite exotic fixings, then slice it into small finger sandwiches called *panini*, "little breads."

PITA BREAD

8 pitas

This ancient flatbread, also called pocket bread, is common all over the eastern Mediterranean. This bread not only can be divided into two round sandwich sides but is also excellent for scooping up dips and sauces—especially Middle Eastern ones such as Hummus, 164, or Baba Ghanoush, 164, but also guacamole as well.

In this recipe, you can substitute any amount of whole-wheat flour for white flour, according to your preference, although the dough may require additional water to be soft and pliable. You may also spray the top of the rolled-out pita rounds with water and sprinkle with sesame seeds before baking.

Combine in a large mixing bowl or the bowl of a heavy-duty mixer:

3 cups bread flour
1½ tablespoons sugar
1½ teaspoons salt
4 teaspoons active dry yeast

Add:

2 tablespoons melted butter
1¼ cups room-temperature water

Mix by hand or on low speed for about 1 minute to blend all the ingredients. Knead for about 10 minutes by hand or with the dough hook on low to medium speed until the dough is smooth, soft, and elastic. Add flour or water as needed; the dough should be slightly tacky but not sticky. Transfer the dough to an oiled bowl and turn it over once to coat. Cover with plastic wrap and allow to rise at room temperature until doubled in volume, 1 to 1½ hours.

Punch the dough down, divide equally into 8 pieces, and roll the pieces into balls. Cover and let rest for 20 minutes. Preheat the oven to 450°F. If you do not have a pizza or baking stone, place a baking sheet upside down on an oven rack to serve as a hearth.

On a very lightly floured surface, roll out each ball of dough into a thin round, about 8 inches in diameter and ⅛ inch thick. Spray the stone or baking sheet with a mist of water, wait 30 seconds, then place as many dough rounds as will fit without touching directly onto the hearth. Bake until the dough puffs into a balloon, about 3 minutes, wait 30 seconds, then remove each bread to a rack to cool. If you leave the breads in the oven too long, they will not deflate to flat disks.

NAAN

4 naan

This is the delicious soft Indian flatbread traditionally baked in red-hot tandoor ovens, but you can make it at home with a baking stone or inverted baking sheet.

Combine in a large mixing bowl or the bowl of a heavy-duty mixer:

2 cups bread flour
½ teaspoon salt
1¼ teaspoons active dry yeast

Add:

2 tablespoons melted butter or vegetable oil
¾ cup yogurt or buttermilk, at room temperature
1 teaspoon to 1 tablespoon water as needed

Mix by hand or on low speed until a soft ball of dough is formed. Knead for about 10 minutes by hand or with the dough hook on low to medium speed until the dough is smooth and elastic. Transfer the dough to an oiled bowl and turn it over once to coat. Cover with plastic wrap and let rise at room temperature for about 1½ hours.

Punch the dough down and divide equally into 4 pieces. Roll into balls, cover, and let rest for 10 minutes.

Place a baking stone or inverted baking sheet in the oven and preheat to 475°F. Roll out each ball of dough into an oval 8 to 10 inches long and ¼ inch thick. Brush the tops:

1 to 2 tablespoons melted butter

If desired, sprinkle on top:

2 tablespoons minced scallions or 2 teaspoons sesame or poppy seeds

Place the dough topping side up with as many ovals as will fit without touching directly onto the baking stone or sheet and bake until each oval gets puffy and just begins to turn golden, 6 to 7 minutes. Remove from the oven and bake the remaining dough. Drizzle over the baked bread:

1 tablespoon melted butter (optional)

Fold the naan in half and place in a cloth-lined basket. Keep covered and serve warm.

UNLEAVENED FLATBREADS

FLOUR TORTILLAS

Eight 6- to 8-inch tortillas

Tortillas are surprisingly easy to make.

Combine in a large mixing bowl or the bowl of a heavy-duty mixer:

2 cups bread flour
1 teaspoon salt
¼ cup vegetable shortening or lard
¾ cup warm (105° to 115°F) water

Mix by hand or on low speed until the dough comes together. Knead by hand or with the dough hook on low to medium speed until smooth, 4 to 6 minutes. Divide the dough equally into 8 pieces and roll them into balls. Cover and let rest for 20 minutes.

Place a baking stone or an inverted baking sheet in the oven and preheat the oven to 450°F. Roll out each ball of dough into a 6- to 8-inch round, ⅛ inch thick. If the dough is resistant, move to the next piece and return later to finish rolling. Place as many dough rounds as will fit directly on the baking stone and bake for about 3 minutes. When the tortilla puffs or balloons, remove it to a rack to cool. For crisp tortillas, flip them over and bake the second side as well.

CORN TORTILLAS

Sixteen 5-inch tortillas

Because tortilla dough dries out quickly, the unused portion must be kept covered until used, but you may always readjust the consistency by kneading it with additional water if necessary—extra kneading does not harm the finished product. Tortillas are not made with salt, as they often accompany savory, well-seasoned dishes.

Mix with your hands, adjusting the quantity of water, to form a soft dough:

2 cups masa harina
1¼ to 1⅓ cups hot (120° to 125°F) water

Cover with plastic wrap and let rest at least 30 minutes before forming tortillas. Knead the rested dough with your hands, adjusting the consistency with additional water or masa until the dough is soft, smooth, and pliable but neither sticky nor crumbly. Place 2 heavy ungreased skillets on the stove, or use a griddle large enough to cover two burners. Adjust the heat under 1 skillet (or one side of the griddle) to medium-low and the second to medium-high.

Break off a piece of dough and roll it into a ball 1½ inches in diameter. Cover the remaining dough to keep it from drying out. Place the dough ball between 2 pieces of heavy plastic such as a plastic freezer bag cut open and then cut in half. In a tortilla press or with the bottom of an unheated heavy skillet, press the dough firmly, turning it 180° in the tortilla press and pressing again, until it is uniformly 1/16 inch thick. Peel off the top piece of plastic and lift the bottom piece to invert the tortilla onto the palm of your other hand. Peel off the plastic. (If the tortilla crumbles, the dough is too dry; if it sticks to the plastic, the tortilla is too thin or the dough is too wet. Adjust the consistency of the rest of the dough accordingly before continuing to shape the tortillas.) Lay the tortilla on the cooler of the two skillets until it begins to release itself from the pan but before the edges curl, about 20 seconds. Flip the tortilla over onto the hotter skillet and cook until the underside is lightly browned in spots, 20 to 30 seconds. Flip the tortilla over and finish browning the first side. If the pan is hot enough and the dough properly moist, the tortilla should puff up like a pillow (you may encourage this by pressing it with your fingers or the back of a spatula). When browned, remove the tortilla to a clean towel (it will deflate) and cover it. Form and cook each tortilla the same way, stacking the hot tortillas on top of each other and covering the stack each time. Serve the tortillas warm. Reheat leftovers wrapped in foil in the oven or wrapped in wax paper in the microwave until soft and pliable.

CRACKERS

Almost any bread dough may be turned into crackers. Simply roll the dough out ⅛ inch thick, cut crackers to the desired size and shape, and place about 1 inch apart on a lightly greased baking sheet. You can brush the tops with melted butter or beaten egg and sprinkle sesame, poppy, or any favorite seeds on top before cutting. For crisp crackers, use doughs such as Basic Pizza Dough, 752, or Naan, 753, although any lean bread dough will do. For richer, more buttery crackers, do the same with Brioche dough, 764. Experiment with different types of dough to find your favorite. Bake the crackers on the baking sheet in a preheated 450°F oven until they begin to turn light or golden brown, 6 to 9 minutes.

BREADS MADE WITH THE SPONGE OR STARTER METHOD

The best-quality European-style breads are made by the indirect method, using sponges or starters to extend fermentation times. A starter is a medium for yeast that will promote fermentation. Made with flour, liquid, and commercial or wild yeast, it ferments in as little as 6 hours or as long as 5 days, after which time it must be "fed" with additional flour and water. This process results in more texture and flavor in the loaves eventually made from it. In general, a sponge starter is thinner, and more liquid, and is the quickest to make and use. A sourdough starter, made with commercial or wild yeast, is firmer and takes longer to make and use. (However, traditional bakers the world over make their own exceptions to all these rules.)

Such breads require more time and commitment than those made by the straight dough method, but they are becoming increasingly popular as more home cooks discover the joys of freshly baked European-style bread and seek to recreate them at home. The following recipes include breads made with commercial yeast starters and sourdough starters. Starters are really quite simple to make once you get used to the additional steps required—and once you make one, you can keep it on hand and replenish it indefinitely.

Here are some guidelines for the care and feeding of starters:

- The consistency of the feeding cycle is very important. Micro-organisms develop a "memory" of their own and prefer regular intervals between feedings. However, you may refrigerate a starter for months without feeding it. It will go dormant, the acids will dissolve the gluten, and a grayish liquid, called the liquor, will separate from the flour and float on top. To reactivate the starter, merely pour off the liquid, throw out some of the dormant starter, and build it back through a couple of regular feedings as outlined below. It should begin to bubble and percolate within 2 days and be ready for baking.
- The standard feeding of a starter doubles it in volume, so that if you have 2 cups starter, you will build it first to 4 cups, then to 8, and so on. If you eventually have more starter than you can use, give some away or throw some out. When making bread, always leave enough starter behind so you can build it back up in time for your next batch. You also may freeze a starter, but you must give it at least 24 hours at room temperature to reactivate it.
- It is not usually necessary to sterilize your starter crock, jar, or container to prevent contamination. The dominant bacteria and yeast in a starter tend to fend off invaders. However, if the starter becomes discolored or foul smelling, it should be discarded.

SPONGE STARTER

1 cup

These starters, called *poolishes* in France and *bigas* in Italy, have the thinnest consistency and are the quickest to make. Any starter can be made into a sponge starter simply by increasing the proportion of water. This recipe is made with commercial yeast and requires only 6 hours of fermentation. You can ripen the starter faster by letting it rise in a warm place, but we recommend slow rising at room temperature for more flavor. Refrigerated rising overnight is even better. Except for the straight dough method, this is the quickest way to make bread and will result in loaves with some of the rustic qualities—including crustiness and a hearty crumb—that make starter-raised breads so inviting.

Combine in a medium mixing bowl and let stand until the yeast is dissolved, about 5 minutes:

½ teaspoon active dry yeast
½ cup lukewarm (100°F) water

Add:

¾ cup bread flour

Stir rapidly with a clean wooden spoon until you notice elastic strands pulling away from the sides of the bowl, about 2 minutes. Cover the bowl tightly with plastic wrap and let rise at room temperature until bubbly and tripled in volume, about 6 hours. Or let the starter rise for about 14 hours (overnight) in the refrigerator. If making bread with a sponge that has just come out of the refrigerator, remember to use warm water (105° to 115°F) for making the dough. When the starter has tripled in volume and begins to collapse slightly, it must be used immediately to make bread or be fed with ¾ cup bread flour and ½ cup water to keep the yeast from starving and the starter from weakening.

YEAST-LEAVENED SOURDOUGH STARTER

2 cups

It takes at least 3 days to prepare a starter with natural wild yeasts, but a starter that provides some of the same flavor and texture also can be made from commercial yeast, in 6 to 8 hours. The starter may be matured more slowly by letting it rise for 24 hours in the refrigerator or by chilling it in the refrigerator for about 4 hours and then letting it slowly warm and rise at room temperature.

Combine in a large mixing bowl or the bowl of a heavy-duty mixer until the yeast is dissolved, about 5 minutes:

2 tablespoons lukewarm (100°F) water
⅛ teaspoon active dry or instant yeast

Stir into the yeast mixture:

¾ cup room-temperature (72° to 75°F) water
2 cups bread flour

Mix by hand for about 5 minutes or on medium speed for 2 minutes until the dough is smooth and firm. Place the dough in a lightly greased medium ceramic, glass, or plastic bowl. Cover the bowl tightly with plastic wrap and let rise at room temperature until tripled in volume, 6 to 8 hours. Punch the risen starter down and roll into a ball. Use it immediately or return it to the bowl, cover, and refrigerate for up to 48 hours before using.

NATURAL SOURDOUGH STARTER

About 2 cups

A natural starter contains wild yeasts instead of the commercially packaged variety. The simplest traditional recipes for natural starters, such as this one, combine flour and water and allow the wild yeasts contained in the air and flour slowly to reproduce. However, wild yeast starters can be made with a variety of ingredients. Some natural sourdough starters are made with a combination of cooked or raw potatoes to which water, salt, and cornmeal or flour are added. Some use a combination of fresh or dried hops, potatoes, and cornmeal. And some use milk, yogurt, and flour. Some bakers use nonairborne wild yeasts, such as those found on organically grown grapes. (If you look closely at a fresh grape, you'll notice a thin white film covering its skin—this is composed of wild yeasts.)

But the following recipe is ideal for the home baker. This traditional starter begins with a small piece of dough made from flour and water. It is fed on a daily basis with fresh flour and water until the "wild" yeasts reproduce enough so that the starter can be used to make bread. During this slow fermentation process, bacteria in the starter also reproduce and cause the starter to sour. The starter can be maintained indefinitely with twice-daily feedings or allowed to go dormant in the refrigerator and fed only once a week. Some recipes for starter require up to 2 weeks of initial growth, but we have developed a method for making a sourdough starter in 3 days. However, if your starter stubbornly refuses to sour, it may take a day or two longer.

Stir together in a very clean small mixing bowl:

½ cup bread flour
¼ cup barely lukewarm (about 80°F) water

Turn it out onto a clean (unfloured) work surface and knead the dough using the heel of one hand until it is smooth and elastic, 3 to 5 minutes. Return the dough to the bowl and cover tightly with plastic wrap. Poke 4 or 5 holes in the plastic with the tip of a sharp knife. Let stand at room temperature away from drafts for 12 to 15 hours.

Mix thoroughly into the starter:

½ cup bread flour
¼ cup room-temperature water

Re-cover the bowl and let stand for another 12 to 15 hours. Transfer the starter to a clean medium bowl and continue the feeding by mixing in:

½ cup bread flour
¼ cup room-temperature water

Re-cover the bowl and let stand at room temperature for 24 hours without disturbing it. Look at the starter. If at this point it has not risen and started bubbling, discard it and start over. If it has, continue to feed the starter on a regular schedule as follows. (With each feeding the consistency loosens into a sponge and bubbling activity increases.) Mix into the starter:

½ cup bread flour
¼ cup room-temperature water

Cover the bowl tightly with a fresh piece of plastic wrap and do not poke holes in it this time. Let stand at room temperature until it rises and the surface has bubbles all over, for about 12 hours. Feed the starter once with:

½ cup bread flour
¼ cup room-temperature water

Cover with plastic wrap and let stand until risen and very bubbly, 4 to 8 hours. There should be a faint sour tang in the aroma. The starter is now ready to use in sourdough bread recipes. If the starter does not look very active at this time, continue the same feeding schedule (every 12 hours) for 2 more days until it builds enough leavening strength to rise bread dough.

Maintaining the Starter: It is best to use the starter for making bread 4 to 8 hours after the last feeding at room temperature. If you use the starter just before feeding, the yeast may be hungry and less active; if you use your starter just after feeding, you will have diluted it somewhat and it may rise a bit more slowly. Starter kept covered at room temperature must be fed twice daily at 12-hour intervals. If you find that you are using the starter infrequently, keep it covered in the refrigerator and feed it just once a week.

MIXED STARTER *2 cups*

This is a useful method if you like the flavor and texture of country-style bread but do not want to maintain a separate sourdough starter. All you need to do is save a piece of bread dough from a batch that has just finished fermenting. When you are ready to bake, you knead the leftover dough with flour and water, let it rise, and work this starter into your bread dough. When the dough is finished fermenting—just before you shape it into loaves—pinch off a piece of dough and reserve it for the next time. More and more flavor will develop in your bread as you keep repeating this process. If making this starter for the first time, include an additional ⅓ cup water and ⅔ cup flour in your first batch of bread to compensate for the piece of dough you are going to remove before baking. If you continue to use leftover bread dough for making your breads, you will notice that the bread dough takes longer and longer to rise. This is because after several generations the yeast weakens. While this slow fermenting will improve the flavor of your bread, there comes a point where the rising simply takes too long. At this point, dissolve ⅛ teaspoon fresh yeast in 1 teaspoon warm water and add this to your mixed starter before setting it aside to rise.

Remove from a fully risen batch of bread dough and reserve tightly wrapped for a day or two in the refrigerator (or in the freezer for up to 3 months):

¾ cup (after deflating, or 6 ounces) dough

When ready to make bread, thaw the bread dough if it has been frozen. Place the dough in a large mixing bowl or the bowl of a heavy-duty mixer and add:

⅔ cup warm (105° to 115°F) water

1½ cups bread flour

Mix by hand or on medium speed for 2 minutes. Knead by hand for 7 to 10 minutes or with the dough hook on medium speed for 3 minutes.

Transfer the dough to an oiled bowl and turn it over once to coat. Cover tightly with plastic wrap and let rise at room temperature for 8 to 12 hours or in a warm place (75° to 80°F) for 4 to 6 hours until slightly more than doubled in volume. The starter is now ready to use in a bread recipe or can be refrigerated overnight before using.

FINAL RISE FOR BREADS MADE WITH STARTERS

Once the dough is shaped (see Shaping, 740), you need to let the loaves rise until about doubled before baking. Remember that a longer, slower rise (at lower temperatures) will make a tastier loaf. Loosely but thoroughly cover the dough with oiled plastic wrap, so that the plastic does not stick to the dough. Let the dough rise in a warm place (75° to 80°F) for about 2 hours or at room temperature for about 4 hours until it has doubled in volume. If you poke it with a fingertip, the impression will remain. These rising times will vary somewhat, depending on the kind of dough and the exact temperature of the rising area.

WHITE BREAD WITH A SPONGE STARTER *2 loaves or 4 baguettes*

This sponge-based version of basic white bread is more flavorful than that made by the direct method, 744.

Mix in a large mixing bowl or the bowl of a heavy-duty mixer until the dough cleans the sides of the bowl:

1 cup Sponge Starter, 755

2 cups room-temperature (72° to 75°F) water

4½ cups bread flour

Sprinkle in:

1 tablespoon fine sea salt or salt

If necessary, adjust the consistency of the dough by adding flour or water. The dough should feel sticky to the touch but should not actually stick to your hands. Knead for about 10 minutes or with the dough hook on low to medium speed until the dough is smooth and elastic. Transfer the dough to an oiled bowl and turn it over once to coat with oil. Cover the bowl with plastic wrap and set aside to let rise until doubled in volume, about 3 hours in a warm place (75° to 80°F) or about 6 hours at room temperature.

Either divide the dough in half and shape each half into a round loaf or thick baguettes (see Shaping, 740), or divide the dough equally into 4 parts and shape into baguettes. Place the shaped loaves in baskets or on floured cloths or in oiled pans as directed in the shaping directions. Cover with oiled plastic wrap and let rise at room temperature until doubled in volume, 2 to 4 hours.

Preheat the oven to 450°F. If using a baking stone, preheat it on the center oven rack for 45 minutes.

To bake loaves directly on the hot stone, you will need a baker's peel sprinkled with cornmeal for the transfer. Flip the risen loaves on the peel, spacing them several inches apart. Score the risen loaves (see Scoring, 742). Spritz the preheated oven with water from a spray bottle (avoid the bulb), wait 1 minute, and quickly slide in the loaves. Wait 2 minutes and spritz the oven walls again. Bake baguettes for about 30 minutes, thick baguettes for about 35 minutes, and round loaves for about 40 minutes. The loaves will be browned and the bottoms will sound hollow when tapped. To further set the crust, turn off the oven and leave the baked loaves in the oven for 5 minutes. Let cool completely on a rack.

WHITE BREAD WITH YEAST-LEAVENED STARTER

Prepare White Bread with a Sponge Starter, above, substituting 2 cups Yeast-Leavened Sourdough Starter, 756, for the Sponge Starter, and reducing the water to 1¾ cups (use warm water if the starter is cold from the refrigerator).

WHITE BREAD WITH MIXED STARTER

Prepare White Bread with a Sponge Starter, above, substituting 2 cups Mixed Starter, 757, for the Sponge Starter, and reducing the water to 1¾ cups (use warm water if the starter is cold from the refrigerator). This dough will be firmer than those made with the sponge or yeast-leavened starters, so that free-form loaves should not lose their shape prior to baking. Remember to save ¾ cup (6 ounces) of the risen dough for the next batch.

SOURDOUGH WHITE BREAD

2 loaves or 4 baguettes

Because of the time needed for making the sourdough starter, you will need to plan your baking at least 3 days in advance for this loaf, but the results are worth it. For sourdough whole-wheat bread, substitute 2 cups whole-wheat flour for 2 cups of the bread flour.

Combine in a large mixing bowl or the bowl of a heavy-duty mixer:

2 cups Natural Sourdough Starter, 756
1½ cups lukewarm (100°F) water
4 cups bread flour

Mix by hand or on low speed until a sticky dough forms. Cover the bowl with plastic wrap and refrigerate the dough for 12 to 14 hours, letting it rise until almost doubled. Let warm at room temperature for 2 hours. Add:

½ cup bread flour
4 teaspoons fine salt, preferably sea salt

Knead by hand for 7 to 10 minutes or with the dough hook on low to medium speed until smooth and elastic but sticky to the touch. Cover loosely with plastic wrap and let rest for 10 minutes.

Shape, let rise, and bake the dough as directed for White Bread with a Sponge Starter, 757.

RYE BREAD WITH A SPONGE STARTER

2 loaves

Unless you want a lighter loaf, use medium rye flour, which is darker and has more rye flavor than the more common white rye flour.

Combine in a large mixing bowl or the bowl of a heavy-duty mixer:

1 cup Sponge Starter, 755
2½ cups room-temperature (72° to 75°F) water
3½ cups medium rye flour
3½ cups bread flour

Stir rapidly with a wooden spoon or on medium speed for about 2 minutes. Adjust the consistency of the dough by adding flour or water. Work in by hand for 2 minutes or with the dough hook on the mixer:

4 teaspoons fine salt, preferably sea salt

Knead by hand or with the dough hook on low to medium speed until the dough is smooth, elastic, and firm, about 7 minutes. Transfer the dough to an oiled bowl and turn it over once to coat. Cover the bowl tightly with plastic wrap and let rise in a warm place (75° to 80°F) for 1½ hours. The dough will rise only very slightly; do not leave it longer, or it will overferment the starter, which will make the bread heavy (yeast cells eat rye flour very quickly).

Divide the dough in half and shape each half into a round loaf (see Shaping, 740). Place the loaves in 2 round proofing baskets or in two 1½-quart bowls lined with oiled plastic wrap or on greased baking sheets sprinkled with:

Cornmeal

as free-standing loaves. Cover with oiled plastic wrap and let rise in a warm place for 1½ hours. Preheat the oven to 450° F. If using a baking stone, preheat it on the center oven rack for 45 minutes. If the loaves are not already on baking sheets, sprinkle the back of a baking sheet with a thin layer of cornmeal (use a baking sheet instead of a peel because the sticky dough sometimes clings to the peel). Quickly flip the bowls of dough onto the baking sheet, leaving several inches of space between them, and gently pull away the bowls and peel the plastic wrap away from the dough. Score the risen loaves (see Scoring, 742). Spritz the preheated oven with water from a spray bottle, wait 1 minute, and quickly slide in the loaves. Spritz the oven walls again. Bake until well browned and the bottom of the loaf sounds hollow when tapped, about 45 minutes. Let cool on a rack.

CLASSIC TUSCAN SALTLESS LOAF *1 large loaf*

This is a rough and ready bread, satisfying on its own, ideal for Bruschetta, 167 to 168, and as a foundation for bread soups. The leisurely risings ensure two things: You build the bread around your own schedule, and slow risings yield a bread full of deep wheat flavor. Use organic stone-ground flours and good-tasting spring water if possible.

Mix in a large mixing bowl or the bowl of a heavy-duty mixer for 1 minute:

2 cups lukewarm (80° to 90°F) water
1 cup whole-wheat flour
¾ cup bread flour
2 teaspoons active dry yeast

Cover the bowl with plastic wrap and let rise at room temperature for 8 to 12 hours.

Stir in:

2½ to 3½ cups all-purpose flour
1 tablespoon olive oil

Adding flour as needed, mix until a soft, slightly sticky dough comes together. Knead by hand for 15 minutes or with the dough hook on low to medium speed for 7 minutes. Add flour as needed; the dough should be very elastic but still a bit sticky.

Transfer the dough to an oiled bowl and turn it over once to coat. Cover the bowl with plastic wrap and let rise at room temperature until doubled in volume, about 2 hours. Punch down the dough and knead briefly. Shape into an oval loaf by stretching and tucking dough underneath itself as for a round loaf (see Shaping, 740). Lightly oil a baking sheet and sprinkle with:

Cornmeal

Transfer the loaf to the pan, cover with oiled plastic wrap, and let rise at room temperature until more than doubled, about 1½ hours. The loaf is ready to bake when the indentation from a gentle finger poke does not spring back.

Thirty-five minutes before baking, preheat the oven to 425°F. Set a broiler pan on the lowest oven rack. Score, 742, the risen loaf in a crosshatch pattern and place the baking sheet in the oven. Immediately add 1 cup water to the broiler pan and shut the oven door. Bake until the bottom of the loaf sounds hollow when tapped, about 40 minutes. Let cool on a rack.

BREAD MACHINE BREADS

An automatic bread machine that kneads, proofs, and bakes can never rival the quality of bread made the old-fashioned way. But for convenience, especially using the automatic timer that gives you warm, fresh bread ready when you want it, a bread machine cannot be beat. Look for a bread machine with a large capacity (at least 1½ pounds) so you can make good-sized loaves of bread. Although manufacturers label their machines as capable of producing either 1-pound, 1½-pound, or 2-pound loaves, you really need to look at the capacity of the containers. A good 1½-pound machine will have a 12-cup container—any smaller and you risk overflowing and sticking. Also, look for a machine with a standard rising and baking cycle of at least 3½ hours total. Machines that are designed only to produce bread more quickly turn out inferior loaves. The best bread machines offer programs for producing several different types of loaves—white; French; a type that has added fruit, nuts, or other ingredients; they also have a cycle that merely mixes the dough for you and beeps to let you know it is ready. The dough can then be shaped however the cook chooses—baguettes, boules, focaccia, dinner rolls, pizza crusts—and baked in a conventional oven. An automatic cooling function to keep baked loaves from becoming soggy is a must.

Breads made in bread machines are almost always straight dough or direct method loaves. Besides being convenient, these machines can produce beautiful, light, airy loaves when desired (or denser loaves if the dough is firmer). The following recipes work in any brand of machine, but it is important to read the instructions for your machine regarding the order of ingredients, as each brand has its own technique programmed into the computer chip that operates it. It is also important to note the temperature at which ingredients should be added to your particular machine. Ingredients in the following recipes are listed for both 1-pound machines and 1½-pound machines; the measurements for the larger machine are in parentheses.

BREAD MACHINE PAIN DE MIE *1 loaf*

You may add a few tablespoons of cracked wheat or sesame seeds to this bread for texture, as well as a few tablespoons of grated Parmesan cheese. Add 1 tablespoon water for each tablespoon wheat, seeds, or cheese added.

Add the following ingredients to the bread machine at the temperature and in the order recommended by your bread machine manufacturer:

2 (3) cups bread flour
½ (¾) teaspoon salt
2 (3) tablespoons nonfat dry milk
2 (3) teaspoons sugar
1 (1½) teaspoon active dry yeast, or ¾ (1) teaspoon quick-rising yeast
1 (1½) tablespoon vegetable oil
¾ cup plus 2 tablespoons (1¼) cup water

Process on the bread cycle until baked. Let cool before serving.

BREAD MACHINE PIZZA DOUGH

Two 14-inch pizza crusts

Very good pizza dough can be made in a bread machine. See the Sandwiches, Burritos & Pizzas chapter, 181, for toppings and cooking ideas.
Add the following ingredients to the bread machine at the temperature and in the order recommended by your bread machine manufacturer:

2½ (3¾) cups bread flour
½ (¾) teaspoon salt
1 (1½) teaspoon(s) active dry yeast, or ¾ (1) teaspoon quick-rising yeast
2 (3) tablespoons olive oil
1 (1½) cup(s) water

Process on the dough cycle. Use this dough as you would any pizza dough or follow the shaping and baking directions for Basic Pizza Dough, 752.

BREAD MACHINE BRIOCHE *1 loaf or 8 buns*

Cut into tablespoon-sized pieces and let soften:

6 (9) tablespoons unsalted butter

Add the following ingredients to the bread machine at the temperature and in the order recommended by your bread machine manufacturer:

2 (3) cups bread flour
2 (3) tablespoons sugar
½ (¾) teaspoon salt
1 (2) large egg(s)
1 (1) large egg yolk
1 (1½) teaspoon(s) active dry yeast, or ¾ (1¼) teaspoon(s) quick-rising yeast
½ (¾) cup water

Process on the bread cycle. As the machine kneads the dough into a ball, gradually add the butter 1 piece at a time, placing it on the dough not on the side of the container. Wait 30 seconds between each addition and continue until all the butter is blended into the dough. If making the single loaf, let the machine continue to process and bake the dough.
This dough can be removed from the machine and finished by hand for small brioche and kouglof (kugelhopf). A 1-pound machine will make 8 individual *brioche à tête.* Shape and bake as directed, 765. For kouglof, knead in by hand:

½ (¾) cup currants or raisins, soaked and drained, as for Kouglof, 766

Arrange in the pan and bake and directed for Kouglof.

BREAD MACHINE MULTIGRAIN AND SEED BREAD *1 loaf*

When sliced, this bread makes wonderful breakfast toast. You may substitute sesame, flax, or hulled pumpkin seeds for the sunflower seeds. Soy, rye, and quinoa flour also may be used in place of the cornmeal or oats.
Add the following ingredients to the bread machine at the temperature and in the order recommended by your bread machine manufacturer:

1½ (2¼) cups bread flour
¼ (⅓) cup whole-wheat flour
2 (3) tablespoons quick-cooking or old-fashioned rolled oats
2 (3) tablespoons cornmeal or polenta
2 (3) tablespoons nonfat dry milk
1 (1¼) teaspoon(s) salt
2 (3) teaspoons active dry yeast, or 1¼ (2) teaspoons quick-rising yeast
1 (2) tablespoon(s) grated orange zest
2 (3) tablespoons honey
1 (2) tablespoon(s) butter or margarine, softened
¾ cup plus 2 tablespoons (1¼ cups) water

Process on the bread cycle. After 10 minutes of kneading or when the beeper sounds, add:

½ (¾) cup hulled sunflower seeds

At the end of the baking cycle, transfer the bread to a rack and let cool completely.

GLUTEN-FREE BREADS

Many people are unable to eat conventional wheat breads because of gluten intolerance. Gluten intolerance, manifested in a medical condition known as celiac or sprue, is a challenge to home bakers because it is gluten that provides the structural strength that allows bread to support and maintain a rise. But there are an increasing number of gluten-free baked goods and baking products available, and you can make delicious breads that everyone can enjoy. There are many ways in which gluten intolerance manifests itself and also many degrees of sensitivity. For further gluten-free baking information, ingredients, and equipment, useful resources include:

Red Star Yeast: 800-4CELIAC
Gluten-Free Pantry: 800-291-8386
ENER-G-FOODS: 800-331-5222
Celiac Sprue Association/USA, Inc.: 402-558-0600

INGREDIENT SUBSTITUTIONS

Breads made without gluten will have a different texture than wheat-based breads, but through the use of certain vegetable gums, a structural fabric can be created to trap carbon dioxide and thus leaven the bread. Besides wheat, other grains that contain gliadin, the offending component of gluten, include rye, oats, barley and barley malt, and triticale. Recent medical research indicates that many of those who are gluten intolerant can eat oats, but we do not use oats in these recipes. Use caution in buying millet because it may be mixed with wheat. Similarly, although buckwheat is a relative of rhubarb and not a grain, it may still be contaminated with wheat. Gluten-free baking works best when rice flours are used, combined with smaller amounts of tapioca flour, potato starch, defatted soy flour, rice polish, corn flour, cornstarch, and sweet rice flour (glutinous rice). Xanthan and guar gum are the two most widely used gum emulsifiers in gluten-free breads. They are both available from natural foods stores and by mail order. Xanthan gum, which we recommend, has strong gelling properties, and so only a small amount is needed. One teaspoon xanthan gum is used for every cup of gluten-free flour in breads, and ½ teaspoon per cup of flour in cakes and cookies. It is developed from a controlled fermentation process of corn sugar by the bacterium *Xanthomonas campestris*. It is a nondigestible cream-colored powder and is used in various foods as a stabilizer, thickener, and emulsifier.

OTHER TIPS FOR MAKING GLUTEN-FREE BREADS

- A heavy-duty mixer is necessary for mixing the softer, stickier gluten-free dough. Bread machines also work well.
- Smaller items, such as muffins and rolls, bake up taller and lighter than bread loaves.
- Gluten-free products tend to dry out faster than wheat products, so store them tightly wrapped in the freezer or refrigerator.
- Consider adding eggs, dry milk, cottage cheese, or other cheeses to increase both flavor and nutritional value.
- In yeast products 1 teaspoon gluten-free vinegar or ¼ teaspoon ascorbic acid per 4 cups gluten-free flour helps with flavor and rise.
- Buy gluten-free flours from a store that has a rapid turnover or from a specialty mail-order company. Store them in the freezer so they will not become rancid. For frequent use, store gluten-free flours in canisters with tight-fitting lids to protect them from pests.
- Avoid buying gluten-free grains from bulk bins as there is a risk of contamination from gluten-containing grains stored nearby or previously stored in the same container.
- Note that bread machine yeast contains ascorbic acid, so omit any ascorbic acid called for in the recipe if using this type of yeast.

GLUTEN-FREE FRENCH BREAD *2 baguettes*

Have all ingredients at room temperature. Grease or oil 2 baguette pans.
Mix on low speed in a heavy-duty mixer bowl with the paddle attachment for 1 minute:

1¼ cups white rice flour
1 cup brown rice flour
¾ cup tapioca flour
¼ cup potato starch
⅔ cup nonfat dry milk
2 tablespoons sugar
3¼ teaspoons xanthan gum
1 tablespoon egg replacer
1 tablespoon plus 2 teaspoons active dry or quick-rising yeast
1½ teaspoons salt
¼ teaspoon ascorbic acid (or 1 teaspoon rice vinegar added with the liquid ingredients)

Add and mix on low speed for 1 minute:

1 large egg
2 large egg whites
1½ cups warm (105° to 115°F) water

Increase the speed to medium-high and mix for 4 minutes. Spoon about half the flour evenly into each baguette pan and smooth the top. Brush the tops with:

2 tablespoons melted butter

Cut 3 or 4 diagonal slashes about ½ inch deep across the top (unlike wheat-flour baguettes, this bread must be scored before it rises). Cover loosely with a clean kitchen towel and let rise at room temperature until puffy, about 35 minutes.
Preheat the oven to 350°F. Using a spray bottle, mist the baguettes with water and place in the oven. Bake 2 minutes and spray the baguettes again. Repeat a third time 2 minutes later. Bake until the loaves are golden brown, about 25 minutes more. Let the loaves cool in the pans for 10 minutes, then remove to a rack and let cool for 30 minutes before serving.

GLUTEN-FREE PIZZA DOUGH

1 pizza crust

You can get a toasted rice flavor by heating 1 cup brown rice flour in a 325°F oven for 30 minutes. Let the flour cool to room temperature before using.

Have all ingredients at room temperature.

Mix on low speed in a heavy-duty mixer bowl with the paddle attachment for 1 minute:

1 cup brown rice flour, toasted if desired
1 cup white rice flour
1½ cups tapioca flour
½ cup potato starch
1 tablespoon xanthan gum
1 tablespoon sugar
1 teaspoon salt
2 tablespoons active dry or quick-rising yeast

Add and mix on low speed for 1 minute:

1 cup buttermilk
3 tablespoons olive oil
1½ teaspoons rice or apple cider vinegar
2 large eggs
1 large egg white
¼ cup very warm (115° to 125°F) water

Increase the speed to medium-high and mix for 4 minutes. Grease or oil a 12-inch round nonstick pizza pan (for thick crust) or 14-inch round nonstick pizza pan (for thinner crust). Sprinkle with:

2 tablespoons cornmeal or polenta

With wet hands, press the batter onto the pan and spread it evenly. Cover loosely with a clean kitchen towel and let rise at room temperature until puffy, about 20 minutes.

Preheat the oven to 400°F. Prick the pizza crust all over with a fork and bake for 15 minutes. Cover with sauce and other toppings (except cheese) and continue baking for 10 minutes for thin crust or 15 minutes for thick crust. Cheese may be sprinkled on for the last 5 minutes of baking.

GLUTEN-FREE PIE CRUST

Two 9-inch pie shells

Professional baker Jane Davis enjoys the challenge of creating gluten-free recipes for her daughter Liz. Jane loves this crust because it is easy to make, freezes well, and tastes like French tart dough. Liz sprinkles the scraps with cinnamon and sugar and bakes them into cookies.

The dough is easily made in a standard food processor. Remember to have the cream cheese and eggs at room temperature before you start.

Pulse 4 or 5 times in a food processor to combine:

1 cup white rice flour
¾ cup potato starch
½ cup tapioca flour
1 tablespoon sugar
1 teaspoon salt
¼ teaspoon xanthan gum

Add and process until well blended:

4 ounces cream cheese, softened, cut into cubes
½ cup vegetable shortening

Add and process until a smooth dough forms:

1 large egg, at room temperature
2 large egg yolks, at room temperature
1 teaspoon gluten-free vanilla
3 tablespoons very cold tap water

You may shape and bake the pie crusts immediately or freeze the dough.

To bake immediately, lightly grease two 9-inch pans. With wet hands, place half the dough in each pan. Evenly pat the dough across the bottom and up the sides, and form a rim at the top. Decorate the rim by pressing it with the back of a fork. Prick the shell all over with a fork. Freeze while preheating the oven to 425°F. Bake until the edges are golden brown, about 15 minutes.

To freeze and bake at a later date, divide the dough in half and place each half on a large sheet of plastic wrap. Pat each into a ½-inch-thick-disk. Cover tightly with the plastic wrap, place in freezer bags, and freeze for up to 3 months. When you are ready to use it, thaw the dough for about 1½ hours at room temperature. Sprinkle potato starch lightly over a large sheet of parchment paper and a rolling pin. Place one disk of dough on the parchment and roll from the center out to a 10-inch round. Invert a 9-inch pie pan over the dough and invert the parchment with the dough into the pan. Pat the dough evenly in the pan, removing the paper. Shape a rim and prick all over with a fork. Bake as directed above.

GLUTEN-FREE RAISIN DROP SCONES

14 scones

These are delicate and flavorful with a hint of orange. One of the secrets of the flavor and moistness is soaking the raisins in orange zest and orange juice.

Have all ingredients at room temperature.

Combine in a small bowl and let stand at least 30 minutes:

1 cup raisins, dried currants, or dried cherries
¼ cup freshly squeezed orange juice
1 teaspoon grated orange zest

Mix on low speed in a heavy-duty mixer bowl until combined:

1 cup white rice flour
½ cup tapioca flour
½ cup potato starch

2 tablespoons sugar

2 teaspoons gluten-free baking powder

1 teaspoon salt

½ teaspoon baking soda

½ teaspoon xanthan gum

Add 1 tablespoon at a time while mixing on low speed:

8 tablespoons (1 stick) unsalted butter, softened

Mix until the mixture resembles coarse crumbs. Add and mix on medium speed for 1 minute:

1 cup buttermilk

1 large egg, lightly beaten

1 teaspoon gluten-free vanilla

Add the raisin mixture and mix on low speed for 30 seconds.

Preheat the oven to 425°F. Line 2 insulated or heavy cookie sheets with parchment paper or coat with vegetable oil spray. Using a ¼-cup measuring cup, scoop the batter onto the cookie sheets 2 inches apart. Whisk together and brush over the tops:

1 large egg, lightly beaten

1 tablespoon water

Sprinkle each scone with:

½ teaspoon sugar

Bake until lightly browned, about 12 minutes. Remove to a rack to cool. Serve warm or at room temperature. Cooled scones can be wrapped and stored at room temperature for up to 2 days or in the freezer for up to 3 months.

RICH AND HOLIDAY BREADS

Breads with high sugar and fat content are called rich breads. This category includes many of the popular breads we associate with holidays and feast days. The doughs for these breads are tender and almost cakelike, and the yeast fermentation may take longer than for other breads. Many holiday breads are similar to each other and often vary more in shape than ingredients.

STOLLEN

1 large loaf

Originally from Dresden, Germany, stollen is traditionally served during the Christmas holidays, but it is so enjoyable that many of us bake it year-round. The shape and folds of the dough are said to represent the folds of the blanket of the baby Jesus. Stollen is similar to brioche, but it contains more sugar and has a slightly coarser texture, as well as nuts and candied fruits to give it a festive tone.

Place in a small saucepan with enough cold water to cover by ½ inch:

1 cup raisins

Bring the water to a boil, then drain well. Transfer the raisins to a medium bowl. Add:

¼ cup ¼-inch cubes citron

¼ cup ¼-inch cubes candied orange peel

Sprinkle with:

3 tablespoons dark rum or other liquor or simple syrup, 1010

Cover and let the fruits soak for at least 30 minutes or up to 3 days. Meanwhile, to prepare the sponge, combine in a large mixing bowl or the bowl of a heavy-duty mixer:

1 tablespoon active dry yeast

¾ cup whole milk, warmed to 105° to 115°F

Let stand until the yeast is dissolved, about 5 minutes. Add:

1½ cups all-purpose flour

¼ cup sugar

Mix by hand or on low speed until the dough is smooth. Cover with plastic wrap and let rise in a warm place (75° to 80°F), until doubled in volume, about 1½ hours. Add to the sponge:

2 large eggs, lightly beaten

1 tablespoon vanilla

Grated zest of ½ lemon

1 teaspoon salt

Mix by hand or on low speed. Stir in:

1½ cups bread flour

When the dough comes together, knead by hand for about 10 minutes or with the dough hook on low to medium speed until the dough is smooth and elastic and no longer sticky. Work in:

14 tablespoons (1¾ sticks) very soft butter

Vigorously knead in the butter until completely incorporated and the dough is once again smooth. Add the raisin mixture along with:

⅓ cup coarsely chopped almonds

Knead just until the fruits and nuts are incorporated. The dough should be soft and moist. Place the dough in a buttered large bowl. Cover with plastic wrap and let rise until nearly doubled in volume, 1 to 1½ hours. Punch the dough down and knead briefly. Cover and refrigerate for at least 30 minutes or up to 12 hours.

On an unfloured work surface, roll the dough into a ball, loosely cover with plastic wrap, and let rest for 10 to 15 minutes. Grease a baking sheet. Using a rolling pin, roll out the dough into a ½-inch-thick oval about 16 inches long and 9 inches wide. Do not roll out to the edges of the oval, so that the edges remain thicker than the center. Brush the top of the dough with:

1 tablespoon melted butter

Fold the dough oval slightly less than half lengthwise so the long edges of the dough are about ½ inch apart. Tuck the two short ends (about 1 inch on each end) underneath the loaf. Place the stollen on the baking sheet. Loosely cover with oiled plastic wrap and let rise in a warm place (75° to 80°F) for about 45 minutes. This dough does not have to fully double in volume; a three-quarter rise is enough.

Preheat the oven to 350°F. Bake the stollen until deep golden brown and a knife inserted in the middle of the loaf comes out clean, 50 to 60 minutes. Brush with:

1 tablespoon melted butter

Sift over the top:

Powdered sugar

Return to the oven for about 3 minutes. Sift again with:

Powdered sugar

Transfer to a rack and let cool before serving.

PANETTONE

1 loaf

This Italian Christmastime treat is baked in a special tubular mold (originally made of grease-proof paper), but a coffee can may be substituted.

Place in a small saucepan with enough cold water to cover by ½ inch:

½ cup golden raisins

Bring the water to a boil, then drain well. Transfer the raisins to a small bowl. Add:

2 tablespoons ¼-inch cubes citron

2 tablespoons ¼-inch cubes candied orange peel

Sprinkle with:

3 tablespoons dark rum, other liquor, or simple syrup, 1010

Cover and let soak for at least 30 minutes or up to 3 days. Meanwhile, to prepare the sponge, combine in a large mixing bowl or the bowl of a heavy-duty mixer:

1 package (2¼ teaspoons) active dry yeast

½ cup milk, warmed to 105° to 115°F

Let stand until the yeast is dissolved, about 5 minutes. Add:

½ cup all-purpose flour

½ cup bread flour

1 tablespoon sugar

Mix by hand or on low speed until the dough comes together. Transfer the dough to a buttered bowl, cover with plastic wrap, and let rise in a warm place (75° to 80°F) until doubled in volume, about 1½ hours.

Whisk together in a large mixing bowl or the bowl of a heavy-duty mixer:

⅓ cup sugar

1 large egg

2 large egg yolks

1 teaspoon vanilla

1 teaspoon grated lemon zest

1 teaspoon grated orange zest

1 teaspoon salt

Add the sponge along with:

1 cup bread flour

Mix until the dough comes together. Knead by hand for about 7 minutes or with dough hook on low to medium speed for about 4 minutes. The dough should be smooth and elastic and no longer stick to your hands or the mixing bowl. Add:

5 tablespoons very soft butter

Vigorously knead in the butter until completely incorporated and the dough is once again smooth. Add the raisin mixture and knead just until the fruits are incorporated. The dough should be soft and moist. Place the dough in a buttered large bowl. Cover with plastic wrap and let rise until nearly doubled in volume, for about 1½ hours.

Butter a tall 6-cup panettone mold or use instead a clean empty 24- or 26-ounce coffee can. Punch the dough down and roll into a ball on an unfloured work surface. Loosely cover with plastic wrap and let rest for 10 to 15 minutes. Gently press down on the top of the dough to flatten it slightly. Place the dough in the buttered mold, cover with plastic wrap, and let rise in a warm place until nearly doubled in volume, 45 minutes to 1 hour.

Preheat the oven to 350°F. Brush the top of the dough with:

1½ teaspoons melted butter

Bake until deep golden brown and a knife inserted in the center of the loaf comes out clean, 45 to 55 minutes. Unmold the panettone onto a rack and let cool before serving.

BRIOCHE

1 loaf or 10 buns

This classic is a simple yeast dough that is enriched with eggs and lots of butter. The high butter content gives the impression that the dough is wetter than it actually is, leading to the temptation—which you

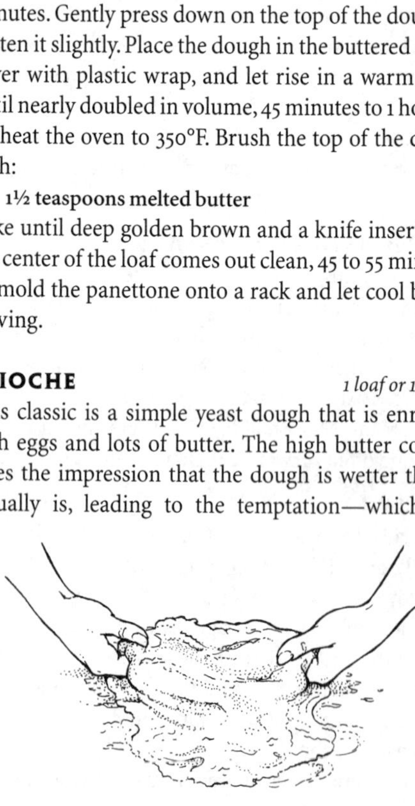

Brioche and Kouglof doughs are very moist and sticky before kneading.

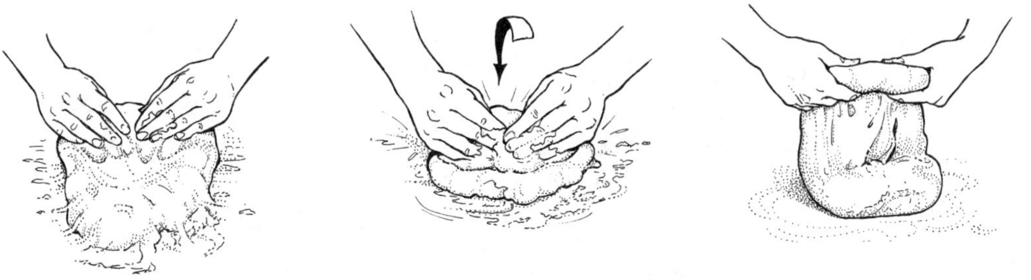

Kneading Brioche

must resist—to add more flour. This dough is easily braided, following directions for Challah, 746.

Combine in a large mixing bowl or the bowl of a heavy-duty mixer and let stand until the yeast is dissolved, about 5 minutes:

1 package (2¼ teaspoons) active dry yeast
⅓ cup whole milk, warmed to 105° to 115°F

Add:

1 cup all-purpose flour
3 large eggs, lightly beaten
3 tablespoons sugar
2 tablespoons whole milk
1 teaspoon salt

Mix by hand or on low speed. Gradually stir in:

1¾ cups bread flour

Mix for about 5 minutes until all the ingredients are blended. Knead by hand for about 15 minutes or with the dough hook on low to medium speed for 7 to 10 minutes until the dough cleans the sides of the bowl. Because this is a rather sticky dough, kneading by hand requires a particular technique: Slap the dough down on the work surface, lift half of it upward with both hands (part of it will remain stuck to the table, which is normal), and slap it down over onto itself. Repeat this until the dough is smooth and elastic and no longer sticky. Add:

12 tablespoons (1½ sticks) butter, softened

Vigorously knead in the butter until completely incorporated and the dough is once again smooth. Place the dough in a buttered large bowl, cover with plastic wrap, and let rise in a warm place (75° to 80°F) until doubled in volume, about 1½ hours.

Punch the dough down, knead briefly, and refrigerate, covered, for 4 to 12 hours. If the dough has doubled, punch it down and shape it. If it has not yet doubled, let it finish rising in a warm place, then punch it down, refrigerate for 30 minutes, and shape it.

BRIOCHE À TÊTE (TOPPED BRIOCHE)

Brioche à tête, literally "with a head," has a small topknot that sits on a larger base. It is traditionally baked in fluted molds that flare at the top.

Roll the dough on an unfloured work surface into a ball. Cover with plastic wrap and let rest for 10 minutes. Butter ten ½-cup fluted brioche molds, muffin cups, deep tartlet pans, or ramekins. Divide the dough equally into 10 pieces and roll each piece into a ball. Shape the dough using the edge of your hand (like a karate chop) to divide partially, without separating, each ball into 2 parts, one twice as big as the other. Set each piece of dough into a mold with the larger (base) part on the bottom; push the top section down so that it is deeply nestled in the base. Whisk together and brush over the dough:

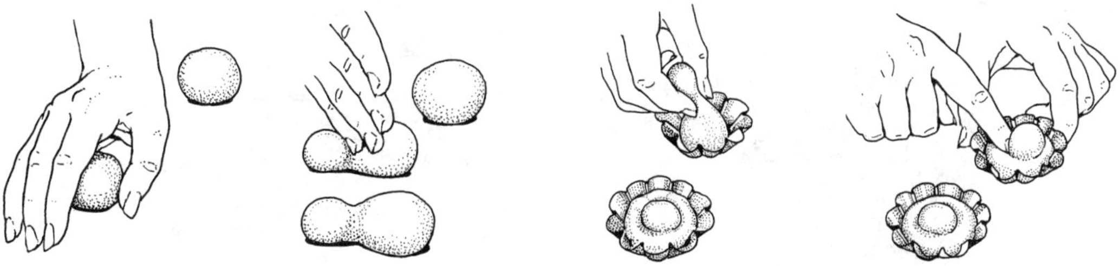

Forming Brioche à Tête

1 egg
Pinch of salt

Cover loosely with oiled plastic wrap and let rise in a warm place until doubled in volume, about 1 hour.

Preheat the oven to 375°F. Dip a sharp pair of scissors in cold water (to prevent the blades from sticking to the dough) and cut four or five ½-inch-deep incisions in the dough at the crease where the top joins the base. This will help the dough rise evenly without tearing or losing its shape during baking. Brush the risen dough again with egg wash. Bake until deep golden brown and a knife inserted in the center of one brioche comes out clean, about 20 minutes. Unmold the brioches onto a rack and let cool. Serve slightly warm or cool.

SECTIONED BRIOCHE LOAF

1 large loaf

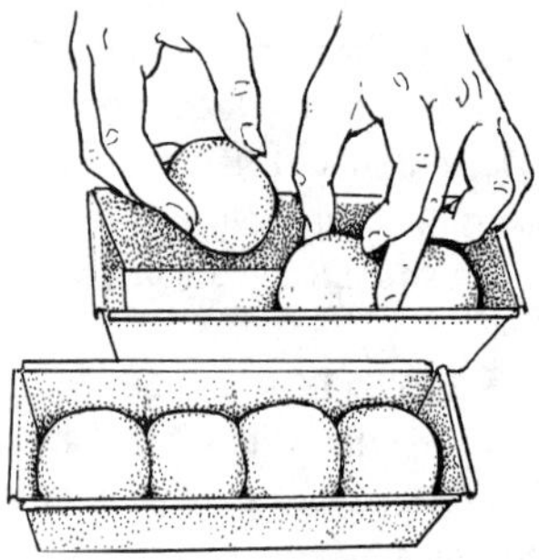

Making a Sectioned Brioche Loaf

Brioche is such a luxurious treat that it is worth making the extra effort to give it a dramatic shape. Here the dough is divided into quarters and each quarter rolled into a round. The rounds are nestled together in a loaf pan, and the result is an especially pretty loaf.

Butter a 9 x 5-inch (8-cup) loaf pan. Divide the brioche dough equally into 4 pieces. Roll each piece into a ball, cover with plastic wrap, and let rest for 10 minutes. Stand the balls of dough on their sides in the loaf pan so they are touching. Whisk together and brush over the top:

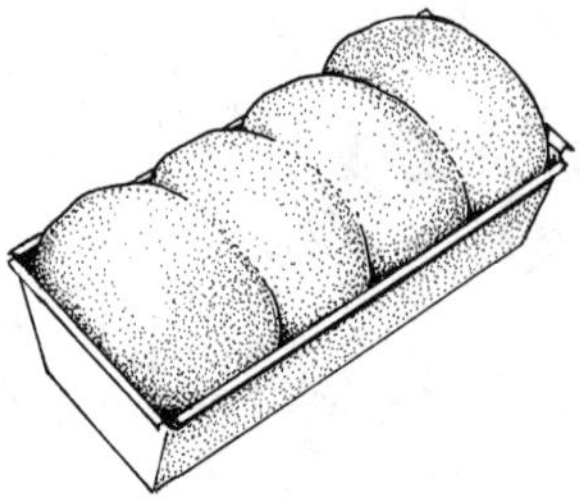

Baked Sectioned Brioche Loaf

1 egg
Pinch of salt

Cover loosely with oiled plastic wrap and let rise in a warm place until the dough is doubled in volume and fills the pan, about 1 hour.

Preheat the oven to 375°F. Brush the loaf again with the egg wash. Bake until golden brown and a knife inserted in the center of the loaf comes out clean, about 30 minutes. Unmold the loaf onto a rack and let cool. Serve slightly warm or cool.

KOUGLOF (KUGELHOPF)

1 loaf

Not as rich with butter as brioche, this slightly sweet decorative loaf comes from the Alsace region of France. Kouglof should be baked in a fluted ring mold. An earthenware mold is traditional, but metal or glass molds work just as well. The mold helps the kouglof to bake evenly; you can also use a plain tube or Bundt pan. This makes a wonderful breakfast bread.

Place in a small saucepan with enough cold water to cover by ½ inch:

½ cup currants

Bring the water to a boil, then drain well. Transfer the currants to a small bowl and sprinkle with:

2 tablespoons rum or water

Cover and let soak for at least 30 minutes or up to 3 days.

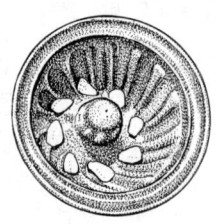

Sprinkle the bottom of the Kouglof mold with slivered almonds or place whole almonds in the indentations in the bottom of the mold.

Forming Kouglof

Combine in a large mixing bowl or the bowl of a heavy-duty mixer and let stand until the yeast is dissolved, about 5 minutes:

1 package (2¼ teaspoons) active dry yeast
½ cup whole milk, warmed to 105° to 115°F

Add:

1 cup all-purpose flour
3 large eggs, lightly beaten
¼ cup sugar
1 teaspoon salt

Mix by hand or on low speed until blended. Gradually stir in:

1¾ cups bread flour

Mix for about 3 minutes until all the ingredients are blended. Knead by hand for about 20 minutes or with the dough hook on low to medium speed for about 7 minutes.

Because this is a rather sticky dough, hand kneading requires a particular technique: Slap the dough down on the work surface, lift half of it upward with both hands (part of it will remain stuck to the table, which is normal), and slap it down over onto itself. Repeat this until the dough is smooth and elastic and no longer sticky. Add:

10 tablespoons (1¼ sticks) very soft butter

Vigorously knead in the butter until completely incorporated and the dough is once again smooth. Drain the soaked currants and knead them into the dough just enough to incorporate them. Place the dough in a buttered large bowl, cover with plastic wrap, and let rise in a warm place (75° to 80°F) until doubled in volume, about 1½ hours.

Punch the dough down, knead briefly, and refrigerate, covered, for 4 to 12 hours. If the dough has doubled, punch it down and shape it. If it has not yet doubled, let it finish rising in a warm place, then punch it down and refrigerate for 30 minutes. Roll the dough on an unfloured work surface into a ball. Cover with plastic wrap and let rest for 10 minutes. Butter a 7- to 8-cup kouglof mold or tube or Bundt pan. Sprinkle the bottom of the mold with:

¼ cup slivered almonds

Or place in the indentations in the bottom of the mold:

Whole almonds

Lightly dust the center of the dough ball with flour. Make a small hole in the center with your fingertips and gently stretch the dough to enlarge the hole just enough so that it fits around the tube in the center of the mold. Place the dough ring in the mold, cover with plastic wrap, and let rise in a warm place until doubled in volume, about 1 hour.

Preheat the oven to 375°F. Bake the kouglof until golden brown and a knife inserted in the middle of the loaf comes out clean, about 45 minutes. Immediately unmold the kouglof onto a rack. Dust the top with:

Powdered sugar

Let cool completely. Just before serving, dust the top a second time with more:

Powdered sugar

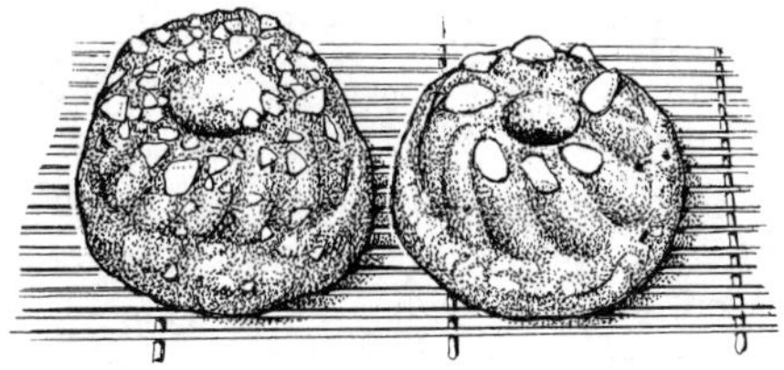

Baked Kouglof

SAVARIN AND BABAS

The dough for savarins and babas is the same but the shapes are different, and babas contain raisins or currants. Savarins can be large or small and are baked in individual doughnut-shaped molds or in large savarin molds or Bundt pans. Unlike savarins, babas contain raisins and are baked in individual cup-shaped molds. Savarins and babas have a cakey texture when they come out of the oven, but they are then thoroughly soaked in simple syrup, 1010, and doused with rum or other spirits. The finished product is a deliciously moist rum-soaked cake. An aromatic, flavorful rum, such as dark rum from Martinique or Jamaica, is traditional, but babas and savarins can be flavored with almost any liquor—unsweetened fruit brandies like kirsch, Poire William, framboise, and mirabelle—or with coffee.

SAVARIN

1 loaf cake

Combine in a large mixing bowl or the bowl of a heavy-duty mixer and let stand until the yeast is dissolved, about 5 minutes:

1 package (2¼ teaspoons) active dry yeast
¾ cup warm (105° to 115°F) water

Add:

⅔ cup all-purpose flour
⅔ cup bread flour
1 tablespoon sugar
½ teaspoon salt

Mix by hand or on low speed until blended. Gradually stir in:

2 large eggs, lightly beaten
1⅓ cups bread flour

Mix until the dough comes together, about 2 minutes. Knead by hand for 10 minutes or with the dough hook on low to medium speed for about 6 minutes, until the dough is smooth and elastic and no longer sticks to your hands or the bowl. Gradually knead in:

¼ cup melted butter, cooled

Continue to knead until the butter is completely incorporated and the dough is soft and pliable. Place the dough in an oiled large bowl, cover with plastic wrap, and let rest in a warm place (75° to 80°F) about 15 minutes.

Lightly oil a savarin mold or a 7- to 8-cup fluted tube or Bundt pan (oil is used because butter can pit the surface of the savarin). Gently place the dough in the mold, spreading it with your fingers so it fills the mold evenly. Cover with plastic wrap and let rise in a warm place until doubled in volume, about 1 hour.

Preheat the oven to 350°F. Place the pan on a baking sheet and bake until the savarin, including the sides, is golden brown all over and a knife inserted in the center comes out clean, about 45 minutes. Immediately unmold the savarin onto a rack and let cool completely. The savarin can be stored in a well-sealed plastic bag for up to 4 days in the refrigerator or for up to 2 weeks in the freezer.

When you are ready to serve the savarin, soak it with a light simple syrup. To make the syrup, bring to a boil in a saucepan:

1 cup sugar
2 cups water
Grated zest of ½ lemon
1 vanilla bean, split (optional)

Remove from the heat. If not using a vanilla bean, stir in:

1 teaspoon vanilla

Place a rack on a clean baking sheet. Place the savarin on the cooling rack and ladle the hot syrup over the top (which was the bottom as it baked) until the entire savarin is well soaked with the syrup. The simple syrup must be hot, so the savarin can quickly absorb it without becoming soggy or losing its shape. The syrup that runs off onto the baking sheet can be rewarmed and ladled over the cake again. Let the thoroughly moistened savarin drain for about 10 minutes. Brush it with:

½ cup dark rum or other liquor or liqueur

If desired, lightly glaze with:

Strained warmed apricot jam

Just before serving, fill the center of the savarin with:

Chantilly cream, whipped cream, or pastry cream

Top with:

Strawberries or other fresh or macerated fruits

BABAS AU RHUM

12 babas

Place in a small saucepan with enough cold water to cover by ½ inch:

½ cup currants or ½ cup raisins

Bring to a boil then drain well. Transfer the currants to a small bowl and sprinkle with:

¼ cup rum

Cover and let soak for at least 30 minutes or up to 3 days. Prepare the dough for Savarin, above, draining the currants and kneading them into the dough just after the butter. This can be done by hand or with the dough hook. Let rest in a warm place (75° to 80°F) for about 15 minutes.

Lightly oil 12 traditional baba molds (cylindrical cup-like molds) or the 12 cups of a standard muffin tin. Dividing the dough equally, fill each cup halfway with dough. Cover loosely with oiled plastic wrap and let rise in a warm place until the dough has doubled in volume and fills the molds, about 30 minutes.

Preheat the oven to 350°F. Bake until golden brown and a knife inserted in the center comes out clean, about 30 minutes. Steep the cooled babas as for Savarin. Serve the soaked babas plain or fill by cutting them horizontally in half and spreading the bottom layer with:

Whipped cream, chantilly cream, or pastry cream

Cover with the top baba layers. If desired, brush the tops with:

Strained warmed apricot jam

Decorate with:

Almonds and/or candied fruits

YEAST-LEAVENED COFFEECAKE AND BUNS

YEASTED COFFEECAKE

1 loaf or 8 buns

Here is a simple and popular multipurpose yeasted coffeecake to serve as a breakfast loaf with streusel topping or as sticky buns.

Combine in a large mixing bowl or the bowl of a heavy-duty mixer and let stand until the yeast is dissolved, about 5 minutes:

1 package (2¼ teaspoons) active dry yeast
¼ cup warm (105° to 115°F) water

Add:

½ cup cake flour
⅓ cup sugar
1 teaspoon salt
2 large eggs, lightly beaten
¼ cup milk
1 teaspoon vanilla

Mix by hand or on low speed until blended. Gradually stir in:

2 cups bread flour

Mix for 1 minute until the dough comes together. Knead by hand for about 10 minutes or with the dough hook on low to medium speed for 5 to 7 minutes until the dough is smooth and elastic and no longer sticks to your hands or the bowl. Add:

6 tablespoons (¾ stick) very soft butter

Vigorously knead in the butter until completely incorporated and the dough is once again smooth. Place the dough in a large buttered bowl. Cover with plastic wrap and let rise in a warm place (75° to 80°F) until doubled in volume, about 1½ hours.

Punch down the dough, knead briefly, and refrigerate, covered, until doubled again, 4 to 12 hours. Punch down the dough and shape it. If it has not yet doubled, let the dough finish rising in a warm place, punch it down, and refrigerate for 30 minutes.

COFFEECAKE LOAF WITH STREUSEL

One 9 x 5-inch loaf

Prepare:

Yeasted Coffeecake, above

Butter a 9 x 5-inch loaf pan. Prepare:

⅔ cup Streusel I, 1011 or Streusel II, 1011

Using a rolling pin, roll out the dough to a 12 x 9-inch rectangle, about ⅓ inch thick. Brush the surface with:

1½ teaspoons melted butter

Sprinkle evenly with half the streusel topping along with:

⅓ cup chopped nuts, such as pecans or walnuts (optional)

Starting from one short side, roll up the dough as you would a jelly roll. Place seam side down in the loaf pan, cover loosely with plastic wrap, and let rise in a warm place until doubled in volume, about 1½ hours.

Preheat the oven to 375°F.

Whisk together and brush over the top of the loaf:

1 egg
Pinch of salt

Sprinkle the remaining streusel topping over the dough. Bake the loaf until golden brown and a knife inserted in the center comes out clean, about 45 minutes. Unmold the loaf onto a rack and let cool.

STICKY BUNS

8 buns

These longtime breakfast favorites have recently become something of a mania. Many bakeries skimp on the pecans, but you need not.

Prepare:

Yeasted Coffeecake, above

Butter a 13 x 9-inch baking pan. Bring to a boil in a small saucepan over medium heat, stirring to dissolve the sugar:

1 cup packed dark brown sugar
8 tablespoons (1 stick) butter
¼ cup honey

Remove from the heat and stir in:

¾ cup chopped pecans (optional)

Pour the hot syrup into the baking pan and spread it evenly. Let cool. Using a rolling pin, roll out the dough to a 16 x 12-inch rectangle. Brush the dough with:

1 tablespoon melted butter

Sprinkle with:

⅓ cup packed dark brown sugar
2 teaspoons ground cinnamon

Starting from one long side, roll up the dough as you would a jelly roll. Cut crosswise into 8 slices. Arrange the slices cut side down in the prepared pan, spacing the slices equally in the pan. Cover the pan with plastic wrap and let rise at room temperature until doubled in volume, about 1 hour.

Preheat the oven to 350°F.

Bake until the buns are golden brown and the syrup is bubbling hot, about 30 minutes. Let the buns cool in the pan for 5 minutes, then invert the pan onto a baking sheet to collect the hot syrup; you may want to line the sheet with aluminum foil. Serve warm or at room temperature, pulling the sticky buns apart at the seams.

QUICK BREADS

Quick breads are so called because they are quickly mixed and, with the absence of yeast, need no lengthy rising time before baking. Thus gratification is never delayed. These breads encompass not only sweet and savory loaves to serve as mealtime accompaniments or teatime temptations in lieu of yeasted breads, but also corn breads with savory fillings, spoon breads, sweet morning coffeecakes, muffins, tender biscuits, and fanciful flavored scones.

So very easy to make, these delightful breads are literally a busy person's "rabbit from a hat." Homemade hot biscuits can transform the simplest meal, fresh muffins will turn a cup of coffee into breakfast good enough for a guest, and a homemade scone at four o'clock will attract the envy of workmates. For more elaborate occasions, any home cook can enhance a table with an astonishing array of quick breads in remarkably short order.

Most quick breads are mixed in one of three ways. Understanding the mixing methods is your key to success.

MIXING METHODS

THE MUFFIN METHOD

This is the simplest of all. The method for mixing most muffins and corn breads, many quick loaves, and some coffeecakes can be described in three steps involving "dry" ingredients and "wet," or liquid, ingredients:

First, mix the dry ingredients (flour, salt, leavening, sugar, etc.) thoroughly with a whisk to distribute the leavening and salt and to aerate or fluff up the flour so that it will mix easily with the wet ingredients in the last step. If the baking powder or baking soda is caked or lumpy in the container, strain or pinch out the lumps before adding it—there is nothing worse than tasting a lump of soda or baking powder in an otherwise delicious muffin.

Second, whisk the wet ingredients together thoroughly. These ingredients may include eggs; melted butter or oil; honey, molasses, or brown sugar; and the main liquid—milk, yogurt, sour cream, buttermilk, or fruit juice. Although brown sugar is technically a dry ingredient, it is often included with the wet ingredients because it blends more easily.

Third, combine the two mixtures (wet and dry) by mixing or folding briefly—just enough to moisten the dry ingredients. Use a wooden spoon or rubber spatula (our preference) with a light hand and use as few strokes as possible. Do not worry if the texture of the batter is uneven or appears lumpy. Do not mix or beat the batter until smooth. Overmixed batters yield tough, rubbery muffins and breads with uneven shapes.

Since the final mixing is necessarily brief, we emphasize that both wet and dry ingredients should be mixed thoroughly before they meet. Otherwise poorly distributed ingredients may remain so. Chopped nuts or fruits and other little pieces are either tossed with the dry ingredients or folded gently into the batter near the end of the mixing.

THE CREAMING METHOD

Some muffins, coffeecakes, and quick loaves are mixed with an electric mixer, using the same technique that is used for a butter cake: All ingredients must be at room temperature. The butter is beaten with the sugar until lightened in color and texture. The eggs are beaten in, followed by one-third of the dry ingredients at a time, alternating with the main liquid. For a more complete explanation of this technique, see page 236. Quick breads mixed this way are often richer and have a finer cakelike texture than other breads.

THE BISCUIT METHOD

Most biscuits and scones, some quick breads and coffeecakes are mixed by this simple method. The dry ingredients are mixed thoroughly as for muffins; then cold butter is cut into the flour before the wet ingredients are mixed in. For details, see About Biscuits and Scones, 787.

IDEAS AND SUBSTITUTIONS FOR QUICK BREADS

In general, you may make the following kinds of recipe changes with most quick breads. Substitute whole-wheat or whole-wheat pastry flour for up to one-third of the all-purpose flour in a recipe; use sugar and brown sugar interchangeably; substitute up to ¼ cup of honey, golden syrup, molasses, or pure maple syrup for an equal or lesser quantity of the sugar; or substitute melted butter for oil and vice versa. You can add, subtract, or exchange chopped nuts, raisins, chocolate chips, and diced dried fruit. You can introduce savory ingredients such as shredded or diced cheese, chili peppers, ham, or bacon and experiment with herbs and spices—see Ideas for Corn Bread, 776, and Ideas for Biscuits, 788.

ABOUT BAKING QUICK BREADS

Quick bread, coffeecake, and corn bread batters all can be baked in a muffin pan. The general rule for baking quick breads, no matter what the shape, is to bake until a toothpick inserted in the center comes out clean. This will take anywhere from 25 to 40 minutes for a loaf. If your loaf pan is larger than the one called for, note that the baking time will be shorter; if it is smaller, the baking time will be longer.

The bleary-eyed cook who cannot read a recipe in the morning can assemble and mix all dry ingredients and wet ingredients separately the night before. Cover both bowls, then refrigerate the wet bowl and store the dry bowl on the counter. Preheat the oven and stir the contents of the bowls together while the coffee is brewing.

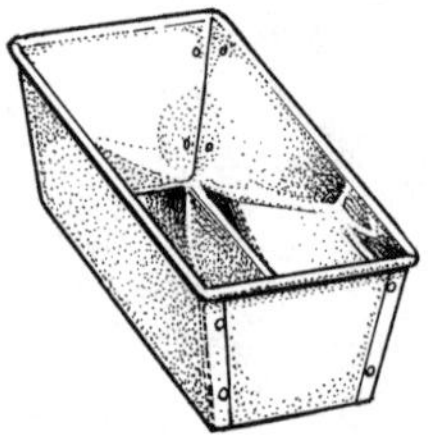

Loaf pan

ABOUT STORING QUICK BREADS

Quick breads and cakes can be stored at room temperature or frozen. For instructions, please read About Storing Cakes, 929, and About Freezing and Thawing Cakes, 930.

IRISH AMERICAN SODA BREAD *8 servings*

The American idea of Irish soda bread looks like a giant golden brown scone studded with raisins and caraway seeds. It is richer, sweeter, and more cakelike than authentic Irish soda bread, which we are assured never made the acquaintance of a raisin or a caraway seed either. When this batter is made with the greater amount of sugar and baked in a loaf pan, it becomes a fine crusty tea bread that stays moist for 3 to 4 days.

Position a rack in the center of the oven. Preheat the oven to 375°F, 350°F if you are baking in the loaf pan. Grease a large baking sheet or an 8½ x 4½-inch (6-cup) loaf pan.

Whisk together thoroughly in a large bowl:

1⅔ cups all-purpose flour
2 tablespoons sugar, or 5 tablespoons for the tea loaf
1 teaspoon baking powder
½ teaspoon baking soda
½ teaspoon salt

Stir in:

1 cup raisins
2 teaspoons caraway seeds

Whisk together in another bowl:

1 large egg

⅔ cup buttermilk, or 1 cup for the tea loaf

4 tablespoons (½ stick) warm melted unsalted butter

Add to the flour mixture and stir just until the dry ingredients are moistened. The batter will be stiff but sticky. Scrape the batter onto the baking sheet in a mound 6 to 7 inches in diameter or scrape it into the loaf pan and spread evenly. Use a sharp knife to slash a large X about ½ inch deep on top of the batter. Bake until golden brown and a toothpick inserted in the center comes out clean, 25 to 30 minutes on the baking sheet, 45 to 50 minutes in the loaf pan. Transfer the bread to a rack to cool completely before serving. Or, if using a loaf pan, let cool in the pan on a rack for 5 to 10 minutes before unmolding to cool completely on the rack.

POPPY SEED LOAF

Position a rack in the lower third of the oven. Preheat the oven to 350°F. Grease an 8½ x 4½-inch (6-cup) loaf pan. Prepare Irish American Soda Bread, above, in the loaf pan, using ¼ cup sugar and increasing the buttermilk to 1 cup. Substitute 1 tablespoon plus 2 teaspoons poppy seeds for the raisins and caraway seeds. Scrape the batter into the pan and spread evenly. Bake as directed for 35 to 40 minutes.

SWEET WHEAT BREAD

8 to 10 servings

We like this bread so much that our attempts to make a less sweetened version failed. It makes excellent toast.

Position a rack in the lower third of the oven. Preheat the oven to 375°F. Grease a 9 x 5-inch (8-cup) loaf pan.

Whisk together thoroughly:

2½ cups whole-wheat flour

2 teaspoons baking powder

1 teaspoon baking soda

½ teaspoon ground cinnamon

¼ teaspoon salt

Whisk together in a large bowl:

1 large egg

½ cup light molasses

¼ cup packed light or dark brown sugar

¼ cup vegetable oil

1 teaspoon grated orange or lemon zest

Add the flour mixture in 3 parts, alternating with, in 2 parts:

⅔ cup yogurt or buttermilk

After each addition, stir or fold just until the dry ingredients are moistened. Do not overmix; the batter will be thick. Scrape the batter into the pan and spread evenly. Bake until a toothpick inserted in the center comes out clean, 35 to 40 minutes. Let cool in the pan on a rack for 5 to 10 minutes before unmolding to cool completely on the rack.

BROWN BREAD

16 servings

This is the moist, dark molasses bread traditionally served with Boston Baked Beans, 284.

Grease two 4- to 5-cup molds, such as pudding molds, small heatproof bowls, or 8½ x 4½-inch (6-cup) loaf pans. Have ready a steamer, Dutch oven, or kettle with a lid large enough to hold both molds, or 2 smaller pans with lids to hold 1 mold each.

Whisk together thoroughly in a large bowl:

1 cup yellow cornmeal

1 cup rye flour

1 cup whole-wheat flour

2 teaspoons baking soda

1 teaspoon salt

Whisk together in another bowl:

2 cups buttermilk

1 cup chopped raisins

¾ cup light or dark molasses

Add to the dry ingredients and stir until the batter is well blended. Divide the batter between the molds. If the pudding molds have lids and clips, grease the inside of the lids and secure the clips. Otherwise cover the molds with a double thickness of greased aluminum foil, greased side down, and secure tightly with kitchen string. Set the molds on a trivet or a folded towel in the steamer. Pour boiling water into the steamer until it reaches halfway up the sides of the molds. Cover the steamer and turn the heat to high. (If the cover fits loosely, you can weight it with another pot or pan to keep the steam from escaping.) When the water boils, adjust the heat so that the water simmers gently. Steam loaf pans for 2 hours and deeper containers for as long as 3 hours. Replenish the water in the steamer as necessary. The bread is done when a toothpick inserted in the center comes out clean. Transfer the containers to a rack, uncover the breads, and let cool for about 20 minutes before unmolding. Serve warm or let cool completely on the rack before wrapping to store. The loaves can be reheated in a 300°F oven or slipped back into their molds and resteamed before serving. To slice without crumbling, use a tough string or dental floss and a sawing motion.

BANANA BREAD

8 servings

An unusual mixing method produces a tender cakey loaf with excellent banana flavor.

Have all ingredients at room temperature, 68° to 70°F. Position a rack in the lower third of the oven. Preheat the oven to 350°F. Grease an 8½ x 4½-inch (6-cup) loaf pan.

Whisk together thoroughly:

1⅓ cups all-purpose flour
¾ teaspoon salt
½ teaspoon baking soda
¼ teaspoon baking powder

In a large bowl, beat on high speed until lightened in color and texture, 2 to 3 minutes:

5⅓ tablespoons unsalted butter
⅔ cup sugar

Beat in the flour mixture until blended and the consistency of brown sugar. Gradually beat in:

2 large eggs, lightly beaten

Fold in just until combined:

1 cup mashed very ripe bananas (about 2)
½ cup coarsely chopped walnuts or pecans

Scrape the batter into the pan and spread evenly. Bake until a toothpick inserted in the center comes out clean, 50 to 60 minutes. Let cool in the pan on a rack for 5 to 10 minutes before unmolding to cool completely on the rack.

PUMPKIN BREAD

10 to 12 servings

You can make this loaf with any cooked mashed squash, yams, or sweet potatoes.

Have all ingredients at room temperature, 68° to 70°F. Position a rack in the lower third of the oven. Preheat the oven to 350°F. Grease a 9 x 5-inch (8-cup) loaf pan.

Whisk together thoroughly:

1½ cups all-purpose flour
1½ teaspoons ground cinnamon
1 teaspoon baking soda
1 teaspoon salt
1 teaspoon ground ginger
½ teaspoon ground nutmeg
¼ teaspoon ground cloves
¼ teaspoon baking powder

Combine in another bowl:

⅓ cup water or milk
½ teaspoon vanilla

In a large bowl, beat until creamy, about 30 seconds:

6 tablespoons unsalted butter

Gradually add and beat on high speed until lightened in color and texture, 3 to 4 minutes:

1⅓ cups sugar, or 1 cup sugar plus ⅓ cup packed light or dark brown sugar

Beat in 1 at a time:

2 large eggs

Add and beat on low speed just until blended:

1 cup pumpkin puree

Add the flour mixture in 3 parts, alternating with the milk mixture in 2 parts, beating on low speed or stirring with a rubber spatula until smooth and scraping the sides of the bowl as necessary. Fold in:

½ cup coarsely chopped walnuts or pecans
⅓ cup raisins or chopped dates

Scrape the batter into the pan and spread evenly. Bake until a toothpick inserted in the center comes out clean, about 1 hour. Let cool in the pan on a rack for 5 to 10 minutes before unmolding to cool completely on the rack.

ZUCCHINI CHEDDAR BREAD

10 to 12 servings

We make this bread whether or not the garden runneth over! Serve with soup or salad for lunch or add to an assortment in a breadbasket. This is lovely toasted the next day.

Position a rack in the center of the oven. Preheat the oven to 350°F. Grease a 9 x 5-inch (8-cup) loaf pan.

Whisk together thoroughly in a large bowl:

3 cups all-purpose flour
4 teaspoons baking powder
1 teaspoon salt
½ teaspoon baking soda

Add and toss to separate and coat with flour:

1 cup coarsely shredded zucchini
¾ cup shredded sharp Cheddar cheese
¼ cup chopped scallions
3 tablespoons chopped fresh parsley
1 tablespoon snipped fresh dill, or 2 teaspoons dried

Whisk together in another bowl:

2 large eggs
1 cup buttermilk
4 tablespoons (½ stick) warm melted unsalted butter or vegetable oil

Add to the flour mixture and mix with a few light strokes just until the dry ingredients are moistened. Do not overmix; the batter should not be smooth. Bake until a toothpick inserted in the center comes out clean, 55 to 60 minutes. Let cool in the pan on a rack for 5 to 10 minutes before unmolding to cool completely on the rack.

ORANGE LOAF WITH DRIED CRANBERRIES OR APRICOTS AND PECANS

10 to 12 servings

Almost cake, this close-grained, sweet bread slices beautifully. Dressy enough for the buffet table or a fancy tea party, it stays moist for at least 3 days.

Have all ingredients at room temperature, 68° to 70°F. Position a rack in the lower third of the oven. Preheat the oven to 350°F. Grease an 8½ x 4½-inch (6-cup) loaf pan.

Whisk together thoroughly:

1½ cups all-purpose flour
1 teaspoon baking powder
¼ teaspoon salt

Combine in another bowl:

¼ cup milk
¼ cup orange juice
Grated zest of 1 small lemon
Grated zest of 1 orange

In a large bowl, beat on high speed until lightened in color and texture, 2 to 3 minutes:

6 tablespoons (¾ stick) unsalted butter
⅔ cup sugar

Gradually beat in:

2 large eggs, lightly beaten

Add the flour mixture in 3 parts, alternating with the milk mixture in 2 parts, beating on low speed or stirring with a rubber spatula just until incorporated and scraping the sides of the bowl as necessary. Fold in:

⅔ cup coarsely chopped pecans
⅓ cup finely chopped dried cranberries or apricots

Scrape the batter into the pan and spread evenly. Bake until golden brown and a toothpick inserted in the center comes out clean, 45 to 50 minutes. Let cool in the pan on a rack for 5 to 10 minutes before unmolding to cool completely on the rack.

DATE NUT BREAD

18 servings

Choose relatively dry dates rather than Medjools, which are too soft here.

Position a rack in the lower third of the oven. Preheat the oven to 350°F. Grease one 9 x 5-inch (8-cup) loaf pan or four 5½ x 3-inch (2-cup) loaf pans.

Cut into quarters (sixths if the dates are large) and place in a medium bowl:

1½ cups packed pitted dates

Stir together, then pour over the dates:

1 teaspoon baking soda
1 cup boiling water

Let stand until the mixture is lukewarm, about 20 minutes. Whisk together thoroughly:

1⅔ cups all-purpose flour
½ teaspoon salt
½ teaspoon baking powder

Whisk together in a large bowl:

2 large eggs
¼ cup vegetable oil
1 cup packed light or dark brown sugar
1 teaspoon vanilla

Stir in the cooled date mixture. Stir in the flour mixture just until blended. Fold in:

2 cups coarsely chopped walnuts

Scrape the batter into the pan(s) and spread evenly. Bake until a toothpick inserted in the center comes out clean, 35 to 40 minutes for small loaves, 55 to 65 minutes for the large loaf. Let cool in the pan(s) on a rack for 5 to 10 minutes before unmolding to cool completely on the rack.

PEAR AND PECAN BREAD

10 to 12 servings

This fragrant loaf remains moist for days. Use any type of well-ripened flavorful pear.

Position a rack in the lower third of the oven. Preheat the oven to 350°F. Grease a 9 x 5-inch (8-cup) loaf pan.

Whisk together thoroughly:

1½ cups all-purpose flour
1 cup sugar
1 teaspoon baking soda
½ teaspoon salt
½ teaspoon ground cinnamon
¼ teaspoon ground nutmeg

Whisk together in a large bowl:

1 large egg
½ cup vegetable oil
1 teaspoon vanilla
1 teaspoon grated lemon zest
1 tablespoon fresh lemon juice
1½ cups grated peeled ripe pears, with juice

Add the flour mixture and fold until about three-quarters of the dry ingredients are moistened. Add:

1 cup coarsely chopped pecans

Fold just until the dry ingredients are moistened. Scrape the batter into the pan and spread evenly. Bake until a toothpick inserted in the center comes out clean, 1 hour 15 minutes to 1 hour 20 minutes. Let cool in the pan on a rack for 5 to 10 minutes before unmolding to cool completely on the rack.

QUICK BEER BREAD

8 servings

This super-quick wheat bread has a marvelous yeasty fragrance in the oven and the intriguing, slightly bitter flavor of hops. Serve with hearty soups or stews and mild or strong cheeses. Slices are good toasted, or you can rewarm the whole loaf in the oven for a crisp outer crust. This bread lasts for 2 to 3 days.

Position a rack in the lower third of the oven. Preheat the oven to 400°F. Grease an 8½ x 4½-inch (6-cup) loaf pan.

Whisk together thoroughly in a large bowl:

1 cup whole-wheat flour
1 cup all-purpose flour

½ cup old-fashioned rolled oats
2 tablespoons sugar
2 teaspoons baking powder
½ teaspoon baking soda
½ teaspoon salt

Add:

1½ cups light or dark beer (but not stout), cold or at room temperature but not flat

Fold just until the dry ingredients are moistened. Scrape the batter into the pan and spread evenly. Bake until a toothpick inserted in the center and all the way to the bottom of the pan comes out clean, 35 to 40 minutes. Let cool in the pan on a rack for 5 to 10 minutes before unmolding to cool completely on the rack.

BEER, CHEESE, AND SCALLION BREAD

Prepare Quick Beer Bread, above, adding ½ cup finely diced sharp Cheddar or aged Monterey Jack cheese and ¼ cup sliced scallions to the flour mixture. You can also add 2 teaspoons caraway seeds, if you wish.

MEDITERRANEAN OLIVE BREAD

8 to 10 servings

Enjoy this easy-to-make bread with a salad or served with a creamy goat cheese or soft mozzarella. It will stay moist for 2 to 3 days and makes good toast.

Position a rack in the lower third of the oven. Preheat the oven to 350°F. Grease an 8½ x 4½-inch (6-cup) loaf pan. Whisk together thoroughly:

1½ cups all-purpose flour
¾ cup whole-wheat flour
2½ teaspoons baking powder
¾ teaspoon dried rosemary, or 1 teaspoon chopped fresh
½ teaspoon salt

Whisk together in a large bowl:

2 large eggs
1 cup milk
¼ cup olive oil

Add the flour mixture and fold until about three-quarters of the dry ingredients are moistened. Add:

⅓ cup finely chopped walnuts
⅓ cup chopped pitted imported olives

Fold just until the pieces are distributed and the dry ingredients are moistened; the batter will be stiff. Scrape the batter into the pan and spread evenly. Bake until a toothpick inserted in the center comes out clean, 40 to 45 minutes. Let cool in the pan on a rack for 5 to 10 minutes before unmolding to cool completely on the rack.

ABOUT CORN BREADS

Anyone who grew up on southern corn bread knows the hankering for its rich brown crust, crunchy edges, and slightly gritty bite. The ultimate southern experience demands both stone-ground meal *and* a preheated heavy pan to supply the required crustiness. The cakier northern corn bread also reaches its pinnacle with stone-ground meal.

When making corn bread at high altitudes, reduce the baking powder or soda by one-quarter, but do not reduce the soda to less than ½ teaspoon for each cup of buttermilk or sour cream used.

IDEAS FOR CORN BREAD

Whether you bake corn muffins, corn sticks, or corn bread, you can vary the cornmeal and flour proportion, within a 2-cup limit, to your own taste. You can always substitute whole-wheat flour for up to half of the all-purpose flour. We include a number of new savory recipes with chili peppers that we are especially proud of. Do not forget to try sweet and savory ingredients together, such as sautéed onions, raisins, and chili peppers with a touch of cinnamon.

Fold dry additions, such as chopped nuts, raisins, and shredded cheese, into the batter after it is complete. Mix moist ingredients, such as honey, corn kernels, and cooked chili peppers or onions, with the liquid ingredients. Stir fine dry ingredients, such as herbs and spices, into the flour mixture.

You can always substitute honey or molasses for sugar, mixing it in with the liquid, or omit sweeteners altogether. You can also substitute oil, bacon grease, or other fats for the butter. Flavorful additions may include any one or more of the following:

Canned chipotle peppers in adobo: 3 to 4 drained, stemmed, and finely chopped or pureed
Jalapeño peppers: 1 to 2 fresh or roasted and skinned, minced
Mild green chili peppers: up to one 4-ounce can, drained and diced
Sun-dried tomatoes: ½ cup diced
Corn kernels: up to 1 cup fresh or frozen or 1 cup canned creamed corn
Cheddar or Monterey Jack cheese: up to 1 cup grated
Crisp bacon or ham: ½ cup diced
Peanut butter: ¼ cup
Raisins: up to 1 cup
Sunflower seeds or roasted pumpkin seeds: ½ cup

SOUTHERN CORN BREAD *8 servings*

Real southern corn bread is made only with stone-ground cornmeal (tradition dictates white), buttermilk, eggs, leavening, and salt—no flour and no sugar. Some southern cooks stir in a tablespoon of bacon fat. The bread is moist, crusty, and tastes of the essence of corn. Rush this bread from oven to table. It begins to dry out almost at once.

Position a rack in the upper third of the oven. Preheat the oven to 450°F. Place in a heavy 9-inch skillet, preferably cast-iron, or less desirably, an 8 x 8-inch glass baking pan:

1 tablespoon bacon fat, lard, or vegetable shortening

Whisk together thoroughly in a large bowl:

1¾ cups stone-ground cornmeal, preferably white
1 tablespoon sugar (optional)
1 teaspoon baking powder
1 teaspoon baking soda
1 teaspoon salt (¾ teaspoon if using buttermilk with salt)

Whisk until foamy in another bowl:

2 large eggs

Whisk in:

2 cups buttermilk

Add the wet ingredients to the dry ingredients and whisk just until blended. Place the skillet or pan in the oven and heat until the fat smokes. Pour in the batter all at once. Bake until the top is browned and the center feels firm when pressed, 20 to 25 minutes. Serve immediately from the pan, cut in wedges or squares, with:

Butter

Leftovers, though dry, are nice enough if wrapped in foil and rewarmed in a low oven.

CORN STICKS

Prepare Southern Corn Bread, above. Generously brush a cornstick pan with oil or melted shortening and heat in a preheated 450°F oven until the fat smokes. Fill the cups two-thirds full. Bake for 10 to 15 minutes. Pry out onto a rack with a knife or fork. Brush out any crumbs, regrease, and continue with the rest of the batter. The yield will vary depending on the pan you use.

NORTHERN CORN BREAD *10 to 12 servings*

A mixture of cornmeal and flour, an additional egg, and a combination of milk and buttermilk yields a lighter bread with a more cakey texture than Southern Corn Bread.

Position a rack in the center of the oven. Preheat the oven to 425°F. Grease a 9 x 9-inch pan or a standard 12-muffin pan or line the muffin pan with paper cups. Whisk together thoroughly in a large bowl:

1¼ cups stone-ground cornmeal
¾ cup all-purpose flour
1 to 4 tablespoons sugar
2 teaspoons baking powder
½ teaspoon baking soda
½ teaspoon salt

Whisk together in another bowl:

2 large eggs
⅔ cup milk
⅔ cup buttermilk

Add the wet ingredients to the dry ingredients and stir just until moistened. Fold in:

2 to 3 tablespoons warm melted unsalted butter or vegetable oil

Scrape the batter into the pan and tilt (if using a square pan) to spread evenly. Bake until a toothpick inserted in the center comes out clean, 10 to 12 minutes in a muffin pan, 20 to 25 minutes in a square pan. Serve hot.

BUCKWHEAT CORN BREAD

Prepare Southern Corn Bread, above, or Northern Corn Bread, above, substituting ½ cup buckwheat flour for ½ cup of the cornmeal. Add ¼ cup hulled sunflower seeds, if you like.

CORN BREAD WITH RAISINS, NUTS, AND SPICES

Prepare Southern Corn Bread, above, or Northern Corn Bread, above, using 2 tablespoons sugar and ¾ teaspoon salt and adding to the dry ingredients:

¾ teaspoon ground cinnamon
¼ teaspoon ground nutmeg
¼ teaspoon ground ginger
¼ teaspoon ground cardamom (optional)

Fold into the completed batter:

⅔ cup raisins
½ cup coarsely chopped walnuts or almonds

CORN BREAD WITH ROSEMARY AND PINE NUTS

Prepare Southern Corn Bread, above, or Northern Corn Bread, above, omitting the sugar and adding to the wet ingredients:

2 tablespoons honey
½ cup fresh or frozen corn kernels (optional)

Fold into the completed batter:

½ cup pine nuts, lightly toasted
1½ teaspoons chopped fresh rosemary, or ½ teaspoon dried

CORN BREAD WITH RAJAS

Rajas are delectable strips of roasted chili peppers. Here they are diced and combined with sautéed onions.
Prepare and let cool:

1 poblano pepper, roasted until the skin is blackened, skinned, seeded, and diced
1 medium onion, diced and sautéed until golden brown in 2 teaspoons butter or olive oil

Prepare Southern Corn Bread, 777, or Northern Corn Bread, 777, using 1 tablespoon sugar and ¾ teaspoon salt. Fold the prepared ingredients into the completed batter.

CORN BREAD WITH JALAPEÑO OR SMOKED CHILI PEPPERS

Prepare Southern Corn Bread, 777, or Northern Corn Bread, 777, using 1 tablespoon sugar and adding to the wet ingredients:

1 to 2 fresh jalapeño peppers, seeded or unseeded and minced, or 3 to 4 canned chipotle peppers in adobo sauce, drained, stemmed, seeded, and minced or pureed

Sprinkle over the batter and fold in:

1 cup grated sharp Cheddar or Monterey Jack cheese (optional)

SMOKY BACON, CHEESE, AND ROASTED HOT PEPPER CORN BREAD

Very spicy, robust, and satisfying—possibly the best hot and spicy corn bread of them all. To reduce saturated fat, use oil instead of butter, omit the bacon, and substitute smoked Cheddar cheese for the plain Cheddar to recoup some of the smoky bacon flavor.
Prepare and let cool:

2 fresh jalapeño peppers, roasted until the skins are blackened, skinned, seeded, and diced
1 red bell pepper, roasted until the skin is blackened, skinned, seeded, and diced
6 slices bacon, diced, fried until crisp, drained, and blotted

Combine in a medium bowl and toss with:

¾ cup shredded sharp Cheddar cheese

Prepare Southern Corn Bread, 777, or Northern Corn Bread, 777, using 1 tablespoon sugar and adding to the dry ingredients:

1 tablespoon chili powder

Fold the prepared pepper mixture into the completed batter.

BUTTERMILK CRACKLING CORN BREAD

8 servings

This cornbread has an almost puddinglike interior, a crunchy top, and golden brown edges.
Preheat the oven to 425°F.
Rinse quickly, then pat dry:

4 ounces fatty salt pork

Slice off and discard the rind, then cut the pork into ¼-inch dice. (If the pork is too soft to cut easily, freeze it for 30 minutes.) Turn into a heavy 9- or 10-inch skillet, preferably cast-iron, and cook over medium heat until very brown and crisp and the fat is rendered. Remove the skillet from the heat.
Whisk together thoroughly in a large bowl:

¾ cup cornmeal
¾ cup all-purpose flour
1½ tablespoons baking powder
1 tablespoon sugar
½ teaspoon baking soda
½ teaspoon salt

Whisk until foamy in another bowl:

2 large eggs

Whisk in:

1½ cups buttermilk

Add the wet ingredients to the dry ingredients and stir just until moistened. Fold in the cracklings and all but 1 tablespoon of the fat in the skillet. Set the skillet over high heat until the fat smokes. Remove from the heat and pour in the batter all at once. Immediately set in the oven and bake until a toothpick inserted in the center comes out clean, 15 to 25 minutes. Serve at once, either plain or with:

Jam or sorghum syrup

ABOUT SPOON BREADS

These corn breads are soft enough to eat with a spoon or fork. Serve them as a starch with any main dish—such as chicken or ham. For a light meal, sprinkle with grated cheese or add a dollop of sour cream and spicy salsa on the side and serve with a green salad. For additions to spoon breads, see Ideas for Corn Bread, 776.

SPOON BREAD

6 to 8 servings

For added richness, substitute half-and-half for all of the milk.
Position a rack in the center of the oven. Preheat the oven to 375°F. Grease an 8 x 8-inch baking dish.

In a large, heavy saucepan, bring to a simmer:

2½ cups milk
2 tablespoons unsalted butter
1 teaspoon salt

Reduce the heat to low. Add in a slow, steady stream, whisking constantly to prevent lumps:

1 cup cornmeal

Increase the heat to medium and cook, stirring constantly, until the mixture is thick and shiny, 3 to 4 minutes. Remove from the heat and set aside to cool for 3 to 4 minutes. Whisk together:

3 large egg yolks
½ cup cream or milk

Stir gradually into the cornmeal mixture. Beat on medium speed until the peaks are stiff but not dry:

3 large egg whites
⅛ teaspoon cream of tartar (optional)

Fold one-quarter of the egg whites into the cornmeal mixture to lighten it, then fold in the remaining whites. Scrape the batter into the baking dish and spread evenly. Bake until the bread has risen like a soufflé, with a golden brown surface, and a knife inserted in the center comes out clean, 25 to 35 minutes. Serve immediately.

CUSTARD-TOPPED SPOON BREAD *8 servings*

In the oven, this quick and easy batter is transformed, as if by magic, into moist corn bread topped with a layer of golden-crusted creamy custard that takes our breath away. Serve it with bacon or sausage for breakfast, or even all alone—but try this luxurious dish at least once with pure maple syrup.

Position a rack in the lower third of the oven. Preheat the oven to 350°F. Place an ungreased 8 x 8-inch baking dish in the oven to heat.

Whisk together thoroughly:

1 cup all-purpose flour
¾ cup cornmeal, preferably stone ground
1 teaspoon baking powder
½ teaspoon baking soda

Whisk together in a large bowl:

2 large eggs, lightly beaten
2 cups milk
2 tablespoons warm melted unsalted butter
2 tablespoons sugar
1½ tablespoons white vinegar
½ teaspoon salt

Add the dry ingredients to the wet ingredients and stir just until the batter is smooth and free of lumps. Add to the heated baking dish and tilt to coat the bottom:

2 teaspoons butter, softened or melted

Scrape the batter into the baking dish and spread evenly. Set the dish on the oven rack. Pour over the batter slowly, without stirring:

1 cup heavy cream

Bake until the custard layer on top is puffed and golden brown but still quivery and a knife inserted in the center comes out clean, 45 to 50 minutes. Remove from the oven and let stand for about 10 minutes before serving. Serve hot or warm.

JONNYCAKES *Ten 3-inch pancakes; 4 servings*

Jonnycakes are a form of corn pone, America's original cornbread, made only with cornmeal, water, and salt. In the days of fireplace cooking, corn pone was prepared in a variety of ways. When fashioned into boiled dumplings, it became corn dodgers; when wrapped in corn husks and baked in embers, it became ash cake; and when baked before the fire on a tilted-up plank, it was often known as jonnycake. Once the stove replaced hearth cooking, corn dodgers were transferred to the oven, while jonnycakes came to be made in a skillet, like pancakes. These are extraordinary skillet corn cakes, crusty, almost crackly, on the outside, moist and creamy within, like polenta. In Rhode Island, the center of the modern jonnycake universe, jonnycakes are usually eaten at breakfast, either with pure maple syrup or butter and jam. They are delicious with pot roast, with chicken fricassee, or topped with a salsa, corn relish, or roasted garlic cream. Use only stone-ground cornmeal and serve the cakes as quickly as possible.

Combine in a large bowl:

1½ cups stone-ground cornmeal
1 teaspoon salt
1 teaspoon sugar

Pour over slowly, stirring constantly to prevent lumps:

2¼ cups boiling water

Set aside for 10 minutes. Set 2 very large skillets over medium heat. (You can also use a medium-hot griddle, set to about 325°F.) Add to each skillet:

1 tablespoon butter

When the butter begins to color, dip the batter by ¼ cupfuls. The cakes should be thick (about ¾ inch) and no more than 3 inches across. Smooth the top lightly with your fingertips if necessary. Let cook at a quiet sizzle, without allowing the butter to become darker than a pale nut brown, until the underside is a very deep golden brown, 6 to 11 minutes. Cut into extremely thin pats:

1 to 1½ tablespoons unsalted butter

Lightly press one pat onto each jonnycake, flip with a

spatula, and let cook on the other side until deep golden brown, 6 to 11 minutes more. Keep warm in a 200°F oven. Repeat with the remaining batter.

HUSHPUPPIES

About 12 hushpuppies

Fishermen used to fry this savory corn batter in the same lard as the catfish. Legend has it that they threw some to their clamorous dogs with the admonition, "Hush, puppy!" These morsels consist of a crusty, golden brown exterior surrounding a tasty corn-and-onion flavored center. They go particularly well with fried fish and barbecued dishes.

Have ready a baking sheet lined with paper towels.

Whisk together thoroughly in a large bowl:

1⅔ cups cornmeal, preferably stone ground
⅓ cup all-purpose flour
2 teaspoons baking powder
1 teaspoon sugar
1 teaspoon ground black pepper
¾ teaspoon salt
½ teaspoon baking soda
⅛ teaspoon ground red pepper, or more to taste (optional)

Whisk together in another bowl:

2 large eggs, lightly beaten
1 cup buttermilk
½ cup grated onions

Add to the cornmeal mixture and stir just until the dry ingredients are moistened. Pour into a wide skillet—a 10-inch cast-iron skillet works well—and heat to 360°F:

1 inch vegetable oil or shortening

Using a measuring tablespoon, gently drop the batter into the hot fat. Adjust the heat so the batter turns golden brown on one side in about 45 to 60 seconds. Fry several hushpuppies at a time, without crowding, turning them with a slotted spoon, until golden brown on both sides. Transfer to the baking sheet and keep warm in a 200°F oven. Repeat with the remaining batter. Serve immediately.

ABOUT COFFEECAKES

Coffeecakes are a nice excuse for eating cake any time of day. We subscribe to the illusion that cinnamon and nuts—in the form of streusel—or blueberries have the power to transform the richest cake into breakfast fare. The inimitable sour cream coffeecake is a hard standard to topple—for it is really a superb butter cake with topping. Hotel pastry chefs tell us that people welcome familiarity rather than surprise for breakfast—so we go gently with coffeecake. We add apples or cranberries to streusel or a little chocolate in the filling. Yogurt in place of sour cream offers a little less fat, and everyone enjoys the spiced coffeecake with oil, which is lower in saturated fat and the quickest of all our coffeecakes to make. We find that oil-based cakes taste better after cooling and that a neutral-flavored oil, such as corn oil, works best. To vary recipes on your own, see Ideas for Quick Breads, 772.

SOUR CREAM OR YOGURT COFFEECAKE

12 to 16 servings

Fluffy and light, yet rich and not overly sweet.

Have all ingredients at room temperature, 68° to 70°F. Position a rack in the lower third of the oven. Preheat the oven to 350°F. Grease a 13 x 9-inch pan.

Prepare and set aside:

Streusel I, 1011, or Streusel II, 1011

Whisk together thoroughly:

2 cups all-purpose flour
1 teaspoon baking powder
1 teaspoon baking soda
½ teaspoon salt

Combine in another bowl and set aside:

1¼ cups sour cream or yogurt
1 teaspoon vanilla

In a large bowl, beat on high speed until lightened in color and texture, 3 to 4 minutes:

4 tablespoons (½ stick) unsalted butter
1 cup sugar

Beat in 1 at a time:

2 large eggs

Add the flour mixture in 3 parts, alternating with the sour cream mixture in 2 parts, beating on low speed or stirring until smooth and scraping the sides of the bowl as necessary. Scrape the batter into the pan and spread evenly. Sprinkle with the streusel. Bake until a toothpick inserted in the center comes out clean, 25 to 30 minutes. Let cool briefly in the pan on a rack. Serve warm.

CRANBERRY OR APPLE STREUSEL COFFEECAKE

Prepare Sour Cream or Yogurt Coffeecake, above, increasing the sugar to 1¼ cups. If using cranberries, add 1 tablespoon grated orange zest, if desired, to the sour cream mixture. Sprinkle 2½ cups cranberries or diced peeled apples over the batter in the pan. Sprinkle the streusel over the fruit. Bake for 40 to 45 minutes.

COFFEECAKE WITH MARBLED FILLING

Grease an 8- to 10-cup fluted tube or Bundt pan. Prepare Chocolate Fruit Filling, 1011, and set aside. Prepare

Sour Cream or Yogurt Coffeecake, above, Spoon one-quarter of the batter into the pan and spread evenly. Sprinkle with half of the filling. Top with half of the remaining batter and sprinkle with the remaining filling. Top with the remaining batter. Marble the cake and filling with a small spoon by scooping batter from the bottom of the pan up to the top 5 to 6 times, moving around the tube with each scoop. Spread the surface of the batter evenly. Bake until a toothpick inserted in the center comes out clean, 45 to 50 minutes. Let cool in the pan on a rack for 5 to 10 minutes. Rotate and tap the pan until the cake is loosened on all sides. Invert the cake onto the rack to cool. Serve warm or at room temperature sprinkled with:

Powdered sugar

SPICED COFFEECAKE WITH OIL (REDUCED FAT AND EGG FREE)

8 servings

The best reduced-fat coffeecake we know.

Position a rack in the lower third of the oven. Preheat the oven to 350°F. Grease an 8 x 2-inch round pan. Prepare and set aside:

Streusel II, 1011

Whisk together thoroughly in a large bowl:

1 cup all-purpose flour
⅔ cup sugar
¾ teaspoon baking soda
½ teaspoon ground cinnamon
¼ teaspoon ground nutmeg
¼ teaspoon salt

Combine in another bowl:

⅓ cup nonfat or low-fat yogurt
⅓ cup orange juice
3 tablespoons vegetable oil
2 teaspoons grated orange zest
1 teaspoon vanilla

Pour over the flour mixture and stir just until the dry ingredients are moistened. Do not overmix; the batter will not be smooth. Scrape the batter into the pan and spread evenly. Sprinkle with the streusel. Bake until a toothpick inserted in the center comes out clean, 25 to 30 minutes. Let cool in the pan on a rack for 5 to 10 minutes before unmolding to cool completely on the rack.

BLUEBERRY CRUNCH COFFEECAKE

8 to 10 servings

The batter for this superb coffeecake is mixed like biscuit dough. Brown sugar and almonds in the bottom of the pan are transformed into a cloak of crunchy toffee over a tender coffeecake.

Position a rack in the lower third of the oven. Preheat the oven to 350°F. Grease an 8½ x 4½-inch (6-cup) loaf pan. Combine and sprinkle in the bottom of the pan:

¼ cup sliced almonds
¼ cup packed dark brown sugar

Whisk together thoroughly in a large bowl:

1½ cups all-purpose flour
⅔ cup sugar
1 tablespoon baking powder
½ teaspoon salt
¼ teaspoon ground nutmeg

Add:

5 tablespoons cold unsalted butter, cut into pieces

Cut in the butter with 2 knives or a pastry blender until the mixture resembles coarse crumbs. Do not allow the butter to melt or form a blended paste with the flour. Whisk together in another bowl:

1 large egg
½ cup milk
1 teaspoon vanilla

Pour over the flour mixture and stir until about three-quarters of the dry ingredients are moistened. Add:

1 cup fresh or frozen blueberries

Fold just until the dry ingredients are moistened and the berries are distributed. Spoon the batter into the pan and spread evenly. Bake until a toothpick inserted in the center comes out clean (other than juice from the berries), 55 to 60 minutes. Let cool in the pan on a rack for 5 to 10 minutes. Loosen the edges, if necessary, and invert onto the rack. Serve warm or, for the crunchiest topping, let cool before serving.

DELUXE SUNDAY MORNING COFFEECAKE

8 to 10 servings

This is a moist coffeecake with an extravagantly crumbly top. A portion of the dry ingredients becomes a streusel topping, while the rest is turned into a rich cake with the addition of buttermilk and an egg.

Have all ingredients at room termperature, 68° to 70°F. Position a rack in the center of the oven. Preheat the oven to 350°F. Generously grease the bottom and lightly grease the sides of a 10-inch springform pan. Sprinkle the bottom of the pan with:

Dry breadcrumbs

and turn lightly to coat. Tap out the excess crumbs.

In a large bowl, whisk together until well blended:

2 cups all-purpose flour
1 cup plus 2 tablespoons sugar
1 teaspoon salt

Add and cut in with a whisk until the mixture resembles coarse crumbs:

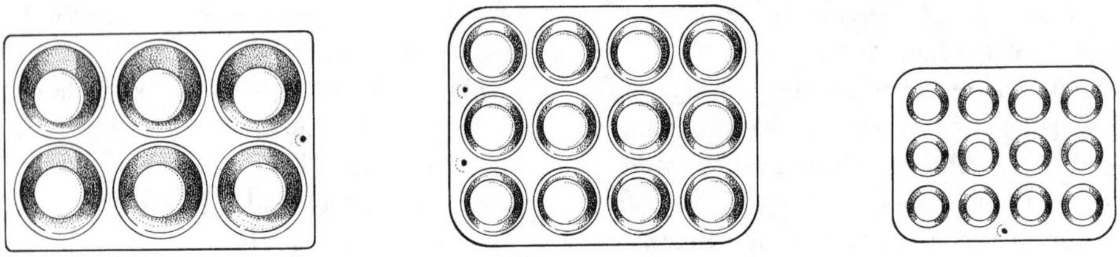

Jumbo muffin tin, standard muffin tin, and mini muffin tin. Quick breads can be baked in any size tin with small adjustments to baking time.

10 tablespoons (1¼ sticks) unsalted butter

Remove 1 cup of the crumbs to a separate bowl and set aside. Add to the mixture remaining in the large bowl and whisk thoroughly:

1 teaspoon baking powder
½ teaspoon baking soda

Add:

¾ cup buttermilk or full-fat or low-fat yogurt
1 large egg
1 teaspoon vanilla

Whisk vigorously until the batter is smooth and fluffy, 1½ to 2 minutes. (The batter is heavy. If you prefer, beat on medium-high speed for about 1 minute.) Scrape the batter into the prepared pan and smooth the top.

For the streusel topping, add to the reserved crumbs and toss with a fork until blended:

¾ cup walnuts or pecans, finely chopped
½ cup firmly packed dark brown sugar
1 teaspoon ground cinnamon

Sprinkle the crumbs over the batter. Bake until a wooden skewer inserted in the center comes out clean, 50 to 65 minutes. Let cool in the pan on a rack for 5 to 10 minutes. Slide a slim knife around the cake to detach it from the pan. Remove the pan side. Let cool on the rack for 1½ hours before serving.

DELUXE COCONUT CHOCOLATE CHIP COFFEECAKE

Prepare Deluxe Sunday Morning Coffeecake, above, stirring 1 cup miniature chocolate chips into the batter. For the streusel topping, decrease the nuts to ½ cup, omit the cinnamon, and add 1 cup lightly packed sweetened flaked dried coconut.

DELUXE RASPBERRY ALMOND COFFEECAKE

Prepare Deluxe Sunday Morning Coffeecake, above, adding 1 teaspoon almond extract along with the vanilla. Scrape the batter into the prepared pan and smooth the top. Stir ½ cup seedless raspberry jam until smooth and fluid, then carefully spread over the batter. For the streusel topping, omit the cinnamon and substitute ½ cup sugar for the dark brown sugar and ¾ cup ground almonds for the chopped walnuts or pecans. Add 1 large egg yolk and 1 teaspoon almond extract to the crumbs and mix with a fork, then firmly knead the mixture with your fingers until the color is uniform. Sprinkle the crumbs over the jam and bake as directed.

ABOUT MUFFINS

The simplest method—and most predominant—for mixing muffins is described in detail on page 771, as it applies to quick breads as well. Remember that muffins invite substitutions and inventive flavoring, and that any coffeecake, quick loaf, or corn bread batter can be made into muffins as well.

Most muffin batters can be mixed, spooned into the pan, and refrigerated overnight to be baked in the morning. Muffins can also be frozen before baking or after. To freeze before baking, simply scoop the batter into paper-lined muffin pans and freeze. Transfer the frozen muffins to a plastic freezer bag with a note to remind you of the oven temperature and baking time called for in the recipe. To bake, plop the still-frozen muffins into a muffin pan and bake for about 5 minutes longer than specified in the recipe to compensate for the cold batter. To freeze baked muffins, cool thoroughly, then bag and freeze. To reheat, place the frozen muffins on a cookie sheet in a 350°F oven or toaster oven for 5 to 10 minutes until hot. Microwave heating is effective also, but you will not have a crisp crust or crunchy edges.

Muffin pans should be greased or lined with paper cups. In either case, grease the top surface of the pan if you are making giant muffins with mushrooming tops. Nonstick spray is the easiest way to grease muffin pans, but many people prefer the flavor of butter.

Fill the muffin cups to any level you wish. The standard is about two-thirds full, but you can fill them to the rim or even heap thick batter above the rim for giant muffins. Batter for 12 standard muffins will make 48 miniature muffins, but only 6 to 8 jumbo muffins!

Muffin pan sizes vary, and baking times vary with them: a mini muffin will take 10 to 12 minutes, a standard-sized muffin 15 to 18 minutes, and a jumbo muffin 22 to 25 minutes.

The richer and sweeter the muffin, the longer it stays moist. Reduced-fat muffins and muffins that contain only 4 tablespoons or less butter or oil are best consumed freshly baked or as soon as possible, for they go stale quickly.

BASIC MUFFINS WITH MILK OR CREAM

12 muffins

With this basic recipe one can create a myriad of muffins by adding berries or chopped fresh fruit, dried fruit, nuts, etc. You can substitute up to 1 cup whole-wheat flour or whole-wheat pastry flour for an equal measure of all-purpose flour. You can add spices or toppings as you desire. Note that the liquid ingredient is infinitely variable, from nonfat or low-fat milk to the richest cream! The flexible amount of butter or oil allows you to control the richness of the muffins with the following advice: Muffins made to be consumed immediately—very fresh and warm from the oven—are perfectly delicious with only 4 tablespoons butter or oil. If muffins must be made hours before they will be consumed, or even the day before, you are wise to use 6 to 8 tablespoons butter or oil.

Position a rack in the center of the oven. Preheat the oven to 400°F. Grease a standard 12-muffin pan or line with paper cups.

Whisk together thoroughly in a large bowl:

2 cups all-purpose flour
1 tablespoon baking powder
½ teaspoon salt
¼ teaspoon ground nutmeg (optional)

Whisk together in another bowl:

2 large eggs
1 cup milk or cream
⅔ cup sugar or packed light brown sugar
4 to 8 tablespoons (½ to 1 stick) warm melted unsalted butter or vegetable oil
1 teaspoon vanilla

Add to the flour mixture and mix together with a few light strokes just until the dry ingredients are moistened. Do not overmix; the batter should not be smooth. Divide the batter among the muffin cups. Bake until a toothpick inserted in 1 or 2 of the muffins comes out clean, 12 to 15 minutes (or longer for variations with fruit). Let cool for 2 to 3 minutes before removing from the pan. If not serving hot, let cool on a rack. Serve as soon as possible, preferably within a few hours of baking.

BASIC YOGURT, BUTTERMILK, OR SOUR CREAM MUFFINS

Prepare Basic Muffins with Milk or Cream, above, adding ½ teaspoon baking soda to the dry ingredients and substituting 1 cup yogurt (nonfat, low-fat, or full-fat), buttermilk, or sour cream for the milk or cream.

BASIC REDUCED-FAT MUFFINS

12 muffins

When these muffins are served warm from the oven, most people would not guess that they contain less than 4 grams of fat. You can substitute up to ⅔ cup whole-wheat pastry flour for an equal measure of all-purpose flour or use brown sugar instead of sugar. Reduced-fat muffins are prone to toughness unless the batter is mixed minimally—we find a rubber spatula and a folding stroke to be the most efficient. To avoid overmixing when making muffins with berries or other fruit or nut pieces, add the pieces when the dry ingredients are only about two-thirds moistened, then continue to fold until all of the ingredients are moist and the pieces are distributed. Yogurt makes a particularly thick batter—simply keep folding gently until the flour is moistened. In general, this batter holds its shape when spooned into cups; do not try to spread or smooth the batter evenly in the cups before baking.

Position a rack in the center of the oven. Preheat the oven to 400°F. Grease a standard 12-muffin pan or line with paper cups.

Whisk together thoroughly in a large bowl:

2 cups all-purpose flour
½ to ⅔ cup sugar
4 teaspoons baking powder
½ teaspoon salt
¼ teaspoon baking soda, if using yogurt instead of milk
¼ teaspoon ground nutmeg (optional)

Whisk together in another bowl:

1 large egg
3 tablespoons vegetable oil or 3½ tablespoons warm melted unsalted butter
1 teaspoon vanilla
1 cup nonfat milk or nonfat yogurt

Add to the flour mixture and mix together with a few light strokes just until the dry ingredients are moistened. Do not overmix; the batter will be light but fairly stiff and it will not be smooth. Divide the batter among the muffin cups. Sprinkle the tops with:

Cinnamon and sugar (optional)

Bake until a toothpick inserted in 1 or 2 of the muffins comes out clean, about 12 minutes (or longer for variations with fruit). Let cool for 2 to 3 minutes before removing from the pan. If not serving hot, let cool on a rack. Serve as soon as possible, preferably within a few hours of baking.

BLUEBERRY MUFFINS

Prepare Northern Corn Bread, 777, using 1/3 cup sugar, Basic Muffins, 783, or Basic Reduced-Fat Muffins, above. Fold 1½ cups fresh or frozen blueberries into the batter. Sprinkle with cinnamon and sugar before baking.

RASPBERRY MUFFINS

Prepare Blueberry Muffins, above, substituting frozen raspberries for the blueberries and omitting the pecans. If you wish, add ¼ teaspoon almond extract to the wet ingredients. Sprinkle the top of each muffin with a few sliced almonds and a little sugar before baking.

LEMON POPPY SEED MUFFINS

Prepare Basic Yogurt, Buttermilk, or Sour Cream Muffins, 783, adding 1 tablespoon grated lemon zest to the wet ingredients and 1½ tablespoons poppy seeds to the dry ingredients. For the reduced-fat version, prepare the recipe for Basic Reduced-Fat Muffins, above, using the yogurt and 2/3 cup sugar and increasing the amount of baking soda by 1/8 teaspoon. Add lemon zest and poppy seeds as directed above.

DOUGHNUT MUFFINS OR BUTTER PUFFS

Plain muffins dipped in melted butter and rolled in cinnamon and sugar taste just like cake doughnuts. You can dip and roll the entire muffin (baked in a greased pan without paper liners) or cut the amounts of butter, sugar, and cinnamon for dipping in half and dip or brush just the muffin tops.

Prepare Basic Yogurt, Buttermilk, or Sour Cream Muffins, 783, or Basic Reduced-Fat Muffins, above, using the optional nutmeg. While the muffins are baking, melt 8 tablespoons (1 stick) unsalted butter and place it in a bowl just large enough to hold a muffin. Combine ½ cup sugar and 1 teaspoon cinnamon in a small but shallow bowl. As soon as the muffins are done, dip them 1 at a time in the melted butter and then roll in the sugar mixture. Set on a rack to cool.

APPLE WALNUT MUFFINS

12 muffins

Allowing the apples to render their juices with the sugar and eggs makes tender, flavorful muffins.

Position a rack in the center of the oven. Preheat the oven to 400°F. Grease a standard 12-muffin pan or line with paper cups.

Whisk together thoroughly:

1½ cups all-purpose flour
2 teaspoons baking powder
1½ teaspoons ground cinnamon
1 teaspoon baking soda
Scant ½ teaspoon salt

Whisk together in a large bowl:

2 large eggs
¾ cup sugar

Stir in and let stand for 10 minutes:

1½ cups packed coarsely grated or finely chopped peeled apples (about 2 medium), with juice

Stir in:

5 tablespoons warm melted unsalted butter
½ cup coarsely chopped walnuts or pecans

Add the flour mixture and fold just until the dry ingredients are moistened. Do not overmix; the batter should not be smooth. Divide the batter among the muffin cups. Bake until a toothpick inserted in 1 or 2 of the muffins comes out clean, 14 to 16 minutes. Let cool for 2 to 3 minutes before removing from the pan. If not serving hot, let cool on a rack. Serve as soon as possible, preferably the day they are baked.

BANANA NUT MUFFINS

12 muffins

Tender banana muffins enhanced with walnuts and just enough whole-wheat flour or (our preference) wheat bran for extra flavor.

Position a rack in the center of the oven. Preheat the oven to 375°F. Grease a standard 12-muffin pan or line with paper cups.

Whisk together thoroughly:

1½ cups all-purpose flour
½ cup whole-wheat flour or wheat bran
2 teaspoons baking powder
1 teaspoon ground cinnamon
½ teaspoon baking soda
¼ teaspoon salt
1/8 teaspoon ground nutmeg

Stir in:

2/3 cup coarsely chopped walnuts

Whisk together in a large bowl:

1 large egg
¾ cup packed light brown sugar
1 1/3 cups mashed ripe bananas (2 to 3)

6 tablespoons vegetable oil
1 teaspoon vanilla

Add the flour mixture and mix together with a few light strokes just until the dry ingredients are moistened. Do not overmix; the batter should not be smooth. Divide the batter among the muffin cups. Bake until a toothpick inserted in 1 or 2 of the muffins comes out clean, about 18 minutes. Let cool for 2 to 3 minutes before removing from the pan. If not serving hot, let cool on a rack. Serve as soon as possible, preferably the day they are baked.

BANANA MUFFINS II (REDUCED FAT/LOW CHOLESTEROL) *12 muffins*

You may simply omit the nuts from Banana Nut Muffins, above, and reduce the oil to ¼ cup for a muffin with less than 6 grams fat. With only 2 grams fat, the following muffin has loads of banana flavor.

Position a rack in the center of the oven. Preheat the oven to 350°F. Grease a standard 12-muffin pan or line with paper cups.

Whisk together thoroughly:

2 cups all-purpose flour
¾ cup sugar
1 teaspoon baking soda
½ teaspoon salt

Whisk together in a large bowl:

1 large egg
1⅓ cups mashed ripe bananas (2 to 3)
1 tablespoon vegetable oil

Add the flour mixture and mix together with a few light strokes just until the dry ingredients are moistened. Do not overmix; the batter should not be smooth. Divide the batter among the muffin cups. Bake until a toothpick inserted in 1 or 2 of the muffins comes out clean, about 30 minutes. Let cool for 2 to 3 minutes before removing from the pan. If not serving hot, let cool on a rack. Serve as soon as possible, preferably the day they are baked.

CARROT MUFFINS *12 muffins*

Mildly spicy and moist.

Position a rack in the center of the oven. Preheat the oven to 400°F. Grease a standard 12-muffin pan or line with paper cups.

Whisk together thoroughly:

1½ cups all-purpose flour
1 teaspoon baking powder
1 teaspoon baking soda
1 teaspoon ground cinnamon
½ teaspoon salt
½ teaspoon ground nutmeg
¼ teaspoon ground cloves
¼ teaspoon ground allspice

Whisk together in a large bowl:

2 large eggs
¾ cup sugar

Stir in and let stand for 10 minutes:

1½ cups packed finely shredded carrots

Stir in:

¼ cup orange juice
5 tablespoons warm melted unsalted butter or vegetable oil
½ cup coarsely chopped walnuts or pecans
½ cup golden raisins

Add the flour mixture and fold just until the dry ingredients are moistened. Do not overmix; the batter should not be smooth. Divide the batter among the muffin cups. Bake until a toothpick inserted in 1 or 2 of the muffins comes out clean, 15 to 18 minutes. Let cool for 2 to 3 minutes before removing from the pan. If not serving hot, let cool on a rack. Serve as soon as possible, preferably the day they are baked.

CORN MUFFINS *12 muffins*

Any flavored corn bread batter based on either Southern Corn Bread, 777, or Northern Corn Bread, 777, makes superb savory muffins. Plain muffins are best served hot, as they dry out quickly as they cool.

For corn muffins that stay moist for several hours, substitute 3 to 4 tablespoons corn oil for the melted butter. Savory corn breads with moist additions such as corn kernels, creamed corn, or diced chili peppers will be moister than those that are plain. For moister sweet corn muffins, increase the sugar (or honey) to ¼ or ⅓ cup.

Position a rack in the center of the oven. Preheat the oven to 400°F. Grease a standard 12-muffin pan or line with paper cups. Prepare Southern Corn Bread, 777, or Northern Corn Bread, 777. Divide the batter among the muffin cups. Bake until a toothpick inserted in 1 or 2 of the muffins comes out clean, 16 to 20 minutes, depending on the additions to the batter. Let cool for 2 to 3 minutes before removing from the pan. Serve immediately.

OAT BRAN MUFFINS *12 muffins*

A light-colored, very satisfying, somewhat dense muffin with a touch of orange flavor.

Position a rack in the center of the oven. Preheat the oven to 350°F. Grease a standard 12-muffin pan or line with paper cups.

Whisk together thoroughly:

2 cups all-purpose flour
1⅓ cups oat bran or wheat bran
1½ teaspoons baking powder
½ teaspoon baking soda
½ teaspoon salt

Whisk together in a large bowl:

2 large eggs
½ cup packed light brown sugar
1⅓ cups buttermilk
8 tablespoons (1 stick) warm melted unsalted butter
1 tablespoon light or dark molasses
2 teaspoons grated orange zest

Stir in:

½ cup raisins
½ cup coarsely chopped walnuts (optional)

Add the flour mixture and mix together with a few light strokes just until the dry ingredients are moistened. Do not overmix; the batter should not be smooth. Divide the batter among the muffin cups. Bake until a toothpick inserted in 1 or 2 of the muffins comes out clean, 20 to 22 minutes. Let cool for 2 to 3 minutes before removing from the pan(s). If not serving hot, let cool on a rack. Serve within a few hours of baking.

BRAN MUFFINS

24 muffins

The batter for this mahogany-colored muffin can be refrigerated for up to 1 week to be scooped into pans and baked as needed.

Position a rack in the center of the oven. Preheat the oven to 400°F. Grease 2 standard 12-muffin pans or line with paper cups.

In a large bowl, combine and let stand for 15 minutes:

1⅔ cups wheat bran
1 cup boiling water

Whisk together thoroughly in another bowl:

1¾ cups whole-wheat flour
½ cup all-purpose flour
2½ teaspoons baking soda
½ teaspoon salt

Whisk into the bran mixture:

¾ cup honey
⅓ cup light molasses
6 tablespoons vegetable oil
¼ cup packed light brown sugar
1 teaspoon grated orange zest

Whisk in:

2 large eggs

Stir in:

1⅓ cups raisins
1 cup coarsely chopped walnuts

Add the flour mixture and fold just until the dry ingredients are moistened. The batter will be thick but soupy. Divide the batter among the muffin cups. Bake until a toothpick inserted in 1 or 2 of the muffins comes out clean, 15 to 18 minutes. Let cool for 2 to 3 minutes before removing from the pans. If not serving hot, let cool on a rack. These muffins are moist enough to be enjoyed the next day.

DOUBLE CHOCOLATE MUFFINS

12 muffins

One person's afternoon snack is another's ideal breakfast! These muffins are mixed like a typical butter cake—so do not substitute oil for the butter.

Have all ingredients at room temperature, 68° to 70°F. Position a rack in the center of the oven. Preheat the oven to 350°F. Grease a standard 12-muffin pan or line with paper cups.

Melt and let cool:

2 ounces unsweetened chocolate

Whisk together thoroughly:

1¾ cups all-purpose flour
1 teaspoon baking soda
¼ teaspoon salt

Combine in another bowl:

1 cup buttermilk
1 teaspoon vanilla

In a large bowl, beat until creamy, about 30 seconds:

8 tablespoons (1 stick) unsalted butter

Gradually add and beat on high speed until lightened in color and texture, 4 to 5 minutes:

1 cup packed light brown sugar

Beat in:

1 large egg

Beat in the chocolate just until blended. Add the flour mixture in 3 parts, alternating with the buttermilk mixture in 2 parts, beating on low speed or stirring with a rubber spatula until smooth and scraping the sides of the bowl as necessary.

Stir in:

1 cup semisweet chocolate chips

Divide the batter among the muffin cups. Bake until a toothpick inserted in 1 or 2 of the muffins comes out clean, 25 to 30 minutes. Let cool for 2 to 3 minutes in the pan before removing to cool completely on a rack. Serve at room temperature.

POPOVERS

8 large or 12 medium popovers

Baking advice for these high, crusty, hollow beauties varies widely. Miraculously, perfect popovers can be made started in a cold or a preheated oven, though we prefer the latter. It is important to bake popovers until they are well browned and crusty, or else they will collapse. If you are using ovenproof custard cups instead of a muffin pan or popover tin, grease the cups lightly and dust with flour, sugar, or grated Parmesan cheese (depending on the flavor of the batter) so that the batter will have something to climb as it rises.

Have all ingredients at room temperature, 68° to 70°F. Position a rack in the center of the oven. Preheat the oven to 450°F. Grease a popover tin, standard 12-muffin pan, or twelve 6-ounce custard cups. If using custard cups, dust as directed above.

Whisk together thoroughly in a large bowl:

1 cup all-purpose flour
½ teaspoon salt

Whisk together in another bowl:

2 large eggs
1¼ cups milk
1 tablespoon warm melted unsalted butter

Pour over the flour mixture and fold just until blended. A few small lumps may remain. Fill the cups two-thirds to three-quarters full. Fill any unfilled cups one-third full with water so that the pan does not burn. If using custard cups, place them well apart on a baking sheet. Bake for 15 minutes at 450°F, then reduce the oven temperature to 350°F and bake for 20 minutes more, until well browned and crusty. Do not open the oven to check the popovers until the last 5 minutes to avoid deflating them. Remove from the oven, unmold onto a rack, and puncture the sides with a sharp knife to let steam escape. Serve immediately or return to a turned-off oven for up to 30 minutes for extra crispness.

CHEESE POPOVERS

Have ready ½ cup grated Parmesan cheese or 2 ounces cream cheese or soft fresh goat cheese cut into 8 cubes (1 for each popover). Divide half the Popover, 786, batter equally among the cups, filling them about one-third full. Divide the cheese among the cups and cover with the remaining batter. Bake as directed above.

YORKSHIRE PUDDING *4 to 6 servings*

Crusty on the outside, custardy on the inside, Yorkshire pudding was, in the days before cholesterol concerns, cooked in the pan with the roast beef, allowing the drippings to be absorbed into it. Now we cook it in a separate pan and make it either with the drippings or with melted butter.

Preheat the oven to 450°F.

Whisk together:

1 cup minus 1 tablespoon all-purpose flour
½ teaspoon salt

Whisk together in a large bowl:

2 large eggs
1 cup milk

Add the flour mixture and beat until well blended. Heat a 13 x 9-inch baking pan, preferably glass or ceramic, for 10 minutes and add:

¼ cup beef drippings or 4 tablespoons warm melted unsalted butter

Pour in the batter all at once. Bake for 15 minutes. Reduce the oven temperature to 350°F and bake until puffy and deep, golden brown, 15 to 20 minutes more. Cut into squares and serve immediately. It deflates quickly.

ABOUT BISCUITS AND SCONES

Experienced cooks know that biscuits are quick and easy, but, frankly, anyone who has never made a biscuit is apt to be daunted by the mystique. How easy can it be to attain biscuits that are tender, flaky, and light?

A survey of good biscuit recipes proves that biscuits are quite forgiving. Some cooks use twice the amount of baking powder. Some use four times the amount of butter. Even the size of the fat pieces cut into the flour varies. Nor is there a precise proportion of liquid to flour, for good rolled biscuits seem to be made from both fairly stiff and soft doughs.

Biscuits rise in the oven to become light and flaky not only from baking powder but also from the tiny flake-shaped pieces of butter or fat in the dough. These melt in the oven, leaving pockets of air that fill with steam from the moisture in the dough as it bakes. Baking powder produces tenderness in biscuits as well, but the dough must also be mixed just briefly to avoid developing the gluten in the flour, which toughens the biscuits. The Basic Rolled Biscuits recipe, 789, describes the technique for making biscuits successfully, safeguarding the precious butter pieces and avoiding overmixing.

For novice cooks, it is worth noting that the easiest biscuit of all is the drop biscuit, which requires no rolling or cutting—and less cleanup afterward.

At high altitudes, biscuits should require no adjustment of leavening.

MIXING BISCUITS AND SCONES

MIXING THE DRY INGREDIENTS

Mix the dry ingredients (flour, leavening, and salt) very thoroughly with a whisk or fork at the outset. If baking powder in the can is packed or caked, sift it before adding it to the flour. Poorly mixed baking powder produces biscuits with brown spots or a bitter salty taste when you bite into a pocket of the unmixed leavening. Once liquid is added, the batter should be mixed very little, so mix the dry ingredients thoroughly while you can.

CUTTING IN THE FAT

Incorporating the butter or fat into the flour is called "cutting in" the butter or fat. Butter must be cold, but shortening or lard can be at room temperature, since it does not melt so readily. Add the fat to the dry ingredients in a lump or several pieces and then cut it into increasingly smaller pieces with two knives, a fork with widely spaced tines. or a hand tool called a pastry blender, tossing with the flour to coat and separate the pieces as you work. Some cooks use their fingertips instead, breaking the fat into smaller and smaller pieces and rubbing them lightly into the flour. In either case, the butter should not be blended into a paste with the flour and should not be allowed to melt. You can cut the fat into uniformly small pieces that resemble coarse crumbs to make soft, fluffy biscuits, or you can leave some of the butter pieces as large as peas for flaky biscuits or scones with a layered structure almost like a croissant and a little crunch at the edges!

ADDING AND MIXING THE LIQUID

Pour the liquid into the flour and fat mixture all at once—some cooks first make a depression or a well in the center of the dry ingredients to receive the liquid. Once the liquid touches the flour, mixing must be kept to a minimum to avoid developing the gluten in the flour, which will, in turn, produce tough biscuits. Mix—with a wooden spoon, fork, rubber spatula, or your fingers—just until the dry ingredients are moistened or nearly moistened. Do not expect or attempt to make a completely smooth dough.

Experienced cooks can alter the liquid slightly to produce a dough that is precisely the consistency desired for rolling. At high altitudes and in desert regions, flour may be very dry and require 1 to 2 tablespoons extra liquid for a soft dough to be formed. However, there is nothing especially critical in these adjustments; one has leeway, and it is best for the beginner not to fuss. Should one go overboard with liquid and find that the dough is too sticky to roll without a significant addition of flour, make Quick Drop Biscuits, 790, rather than try to correct the flour; too many adjustments will result in overmixing, which damages the biscuits more than a less-than-perfect amount of liquid.

KNEADING THE DOUGH

For rolled biscuits, gather the dough into a ball and knead it gently, very few times, just until all of the dry pieces of dough are incorporated and the dough is a cohesive mass. We prefer to knead in the bowl to avoid incorporating extra flour. Kneading is meant to flatten the pieces of fat into flakes, not to blend completely with the flour. Do not knead excessively—if in doubt, stop. You will know this point instinctively after a batch or two of biscuits. A very soft dough can be patted to the proper thickness before cutting; otherwise roll it out with a lightly floured rolling pin.

MIXING BISCUITS AND SCONES IN A FOOD PROCESSOR

Cut the butter into tablespoon-sized pats, cut each pat into 4 cubes, and freeze until hard, 20 to 30 minutes. Pulse the dry ingredients in a food processor fitted with the steel blade to mix thoroughly. Add the frozen butter cubes. For scones or for biscuits with a flaky, layered structure, pulse just until the largest butter pieces are the size of peas and the smallest resemble breadcrumbs. For classic fluffy biscuits, continue to pulse until all of the butter pieces resemble breadcrumbs. Add the wet ingredient(s) and pulse just until the dough comes together as one mass, not longer. Do not allow the butter to melt or form a blended paste with the flour. Turn out the dough onto a lightly floured board and knead a few times. Shape as directed.

IDEAS FOR BISCUITS

The recipe for Basic Rolled Biscuits, 789, describes how to shape and cut essentially any shape you like. We like square and rectangular shapes because they eliminate most scrap. Plain biscuits (rolled or dropped) can be sprinkled with cinnamon and sugar, grated Parmesan, paprika, or ground red pepper before baking.

Rolled biscuits can also be filled like tiny sandwiches: Roll the dough into a square or rectangle ¼ inch thick. Cut in half and spread or sprinkle one-half with any flavorful sweet or savory mixture such as jam or preserves, streusel or coffeecake filling, nuts and raisins, chutney, pesto or tapenade, anchovy paste, goat cheese and herbs, etc. Top with the second half of the dough, cut, and bake as usual. The recipe for Pinwheel Biscuits, 790, offers another method for filling biscuits. Drop biscuits and rolled biscuits can be used to top a casserole; both can be enhanced with additions such as those listed below.

ADDITIONS TO BISCUITS AND SCONES

In general, add moist ingredients, such as ham or drained diced chili peppers, with the wet ingredients in the recipe, and add dry ingredients such as herbs to the dry ingredients. If in doubt, mix in the flavor ingredient after cutting in the butter and before adding the liquid.

Ham or prosciutto: 5 to 6 tablespoons finely chopped
Sun-dried tomatoes: 5 to 6 tablespoons finely chopped
Chives: ¼ cup snipped fresh
Rosemary: 1 teaspoon minced fresh, or ½ to ¾ teaspoon crumbled dried
Parmesan cheese : ⅓ to ½ cup grated, added to the dry ingredients. Reduce the salt slightly, if desired, and bake at 425°F instead of 450°F.
Cheddar or Monterey Jack cheese: ¾ cup finely shredded, added after the butter is cut in. Reduce the salt slightly if desired and bake at 425°F.
Chili peppers: ¼ to ⅓ cup drained canned diced green chili peppers. Also add to Cheddar or Monterey Jack biscuits to make chili cheese biscuits.
Watercress: 1 cup chopped leaves

BASIC ROLLED BISCUITS

Twenty 2-inch biscuits

Position a rack in the center of the oven. Preheat the oven to 450°F. Have ready a large ungreased baking sheet.
Whisk together thoroughly in a large bowl:

2 cups all-purpose flour
2½ teaspoons baking powder
½ to ¾ teaspoon salt

Drop in:

5 to 6 tablespoons cold unsalted butter, cut into pieces

Cut in the butter with 2 knives or a pastry blender, tossing the pieces with the flour mixture to coat and separate them as you work. For biscuits with crunchy edges and a flaky, layered structure, continue to cut in the butter until the largest pieces are the size of peas and the rest resemble breadcrumbs. For classic fluffy biscuits, continue to cut in the butter until the mixture resembles coarse breadcrumbs. Do not allow the butter to melt or form a paste with the flour.
Add all at once:

¾ cup milk

Mix with a rubber spatula, wooden spoon, or fork just until most of the dry ingredients are moistened. With a lightly floured hand, gather the dough into a ball and knead it gently against the sides and bottom of the bowl 5 to 10 times, turning and pressing any loose pieces into the dough each time until they adhere and the bowl is fairly clean.
To shape round biscuits: Transfer the dough to a lightly floured surface. With a lightly floured rolling pin or your fingers, roll out or pat the dough ½ inch thick. Cut out 1¾- to 2-inch rounds with a drinking glass or biscuit cutter dipped in flour; push the cutter straight down into the dough and pull it out without twisting for biscuits that will rise evenly. You can reroll the scraps and cut additional biscuits (they are never as tender as the first-cut) or freeze for Pinwheel Biscuits, 790.
To shape square biscuits (with virtually no scraps): Roll out the dough ½ inch thick (¼ to ⅜ inch if cooking on a griddle) into a square or rectangle. Trim a fraction of an inch from the edges of the dough with a sharp knife before cutting into 2-inch squares.
To bake biscuits in the oven: For browner tops, you can brush the biscuit tops with:

Milk or melted butter

Place the biscuits on a baking sheet at least 1 inch apart for biscuits with crusty sides or close together for biscuits that are joined and remain soft on the sides. Bake until the biscuits are golden brown on the top and a deeper golden brown on the bottom, 10 to 12 minutes. Serve hot.
To cook biscuits on a griddle: To avoid completely charring the outside before the inside is sufficiently cooked, roll out the biscuit dough just ¼ to ⅜ inch thick. Cook at least 1 inch apart on a lightly greased, medium-hot griddle or frying pan until brown on one side, 3 to 4 minutes; turn and cook until brown on the other side and cooked in the center. Serve hot.

CORNMEAL BISCUITS

Prepare Basic Rolled Biscuits, above, reducing the flour to 1½ cups and the baking soda to 2 teaspoons; adding ½ cup cornmeal, 2 tablespoons sugar, and ½ teaspoon baking soda; and substituting buttermilk for the milk.

WHOLE-WHEAT BISCUITS

Prepare Basic Rolled Biscuits, above, reducing the all-purpose flour to 1½ cups and adding ½ cup whole-wheat flour.

REDUCED-FAT BASIC ROLLED BISCUITS

Preheat the oven to 425°F. Prepare Basic Rolled Biscuits, above, reducing the baking powder to 2 teaspoons and the butter to 2 tablespoons.

FLUFFY OR SHORTCAKE BISCUITS

Prepare Basic Rolled Biscuits, above, using ¾ teaspoon salt and adding 1 tablespoon sugar to the dry ingredients. Use half-and-half instead of milk for added richness. Roll out the dough a scant ¾ inch thick. (For shortcakes, cut 2½-inch squares or 3-inch rounds. After baking, cool and split the biscuits horizontally with a fork before filling.)

BUTTERMILK BISCUITS

Prepare Basic Rolled Biscuits, above, reducing the baking powder to 2 teaspoons, adding ½ teaspoon baking soda, and substituting buttermilk for the milk.

CREAM BISCUITS

Twenty 2-inch biscuits

Position a rack in the center of the oven. Preheat the oven to 450°F. Have ready a large ungreased baking sheet.

Whisk together thoroughly in a large bowl:

2 cups all-purpose flour
2½ teaspoons baking powder
½ to ¾ teaspoon salt

Add all at once:

1¼ cups heavy cream

Mix with a rubber spatula, wooden spoon, or fork just until most of the dry ingredients are moistened. Knead, shape, and bake as directed for Basic Rolled Biscuits, 789. Serve hot.

QUICK DROP BISCUITS

About 24 biscuits

Extra-moist batter dropped directly on a baking sheet, like cookie dough, eliminates kneading, rolling, and cutting. The biscuits are moist and tender inside with a toothsome, rough, crunchy, golden brown crust. Any rolled biscuit can be made into a drop biscuit by adding ¼ to ⅓ cup milk to the wet ingredients in the recipe to form a thick, sticky batter.

Prepare Basic Rolled Biscuits, 789, or any other rolled biscuit in this section, increasing the milk to 1 cup. Add the milk to the dry ingredients and stir until the dry ingredients are well moistened. The batter should be moist and sticky but not smooth. Use a teaspoon to form walnut-sized scoops of batter; use another spoon to scrape the batter onto the baking sheet, spacing the biscuits about 1½ inches apart. Bake as directed until the bottoms are deep golden brown, about 12 minutes. Serve hot.

DROP BISCUITS MADE WITH OIL (NO CHOLESTEROL)

About 24 biscuits

These are remarkably acceptable, especially if one adds other flavorful ingredients (see page 789). For biscuits to accompany savory dishes, consider olive oil instead of vegetable oil and flavor with rosemary, sun-dried tomatoes, or other Mediterranean flavorings.

Position a rack in the center of the oven. Preheat the oven to 475°F. Have ready a large ungreased baking sheet.

Whisk together thoroughly in a large bowl:

1⅔ cups all-purpose flour
1 tablespoon baking powder
½ teaspoon salt

Whisk together in another bowl:

⅔ cup milk
⅓ cup vegetable oil

Add to the flour mixture and stir just until the dry ingredients are moistened and the batter pulls away from the sides of the bowl. It will be very thick and sticky—not smooth. Use a teaspoon to form walnut-sized scoops of batter; use another spoon to scrape the batter onto the baking sheet, spacing the biscuits about 1½ inches apart. Bake until the bottoms are deep golden brown, about 8 minutes. Serve hot.

PINWHEEL BISCUITS

Twelve 3-inch biscuits

Brown sugar, butter, and pecans rolled up with biscuit dough look and taste for all the world like sticky buns. If you have saved biscuit scraps in the freezer, thaw and add them to this fresh dough just before rolling out. If you add a significant amount of scrap, roll a little larger than the 10-inch square called for and increase the butter and sugar amounts a bit as well.

Position a rack in the center of the oven. Preheat the oven to 450°F. Grease a large baking sheet or a 13 x 9-inch pan. Prepare the dough for Basic Rolled Biscuits, 789, Buttermilk Biscuits, 790, Fluffy or Shortcake Biscuits, 790, Cream Biscuits, 790, or Whole-Wheat Biscuits, 789. Transfer the dough to a lightly floured surface. With a lightly floured rolling pin, roll out the dough into a 10-inch square ¼ inch thick. Spread evenly with:

5 tablespoons unsalted butter, softened

Sprinkle evenly over the surface:

1 cup coarsely chopped walnuts or pecans
⅔ cup packed dark brown sugar
½ cup raisins

Roll the dough up fairly tightly (it will lengthen slightly as you roll). Cut crosswise into 12 equal slices, each about 1 inch wide. Place the slices, cut side down, on the baking sheet or in the pan. Bake until golden brown, 10 to 12 minutes on the baking sheet, about 14 minutes in the pan. Remove from the oven and invert onto a plate to unmold. Serve warm, sticky side up.

BEATEN BISCUITS

Twenty-four 2-inch biscuits

A Southern specialty, beaten biscuits look and taste like a creamy soda cracker. In order to break the gluten in the flour and thus ensure a tender, flaky texture, the dough must be thoroughly beaten. Originally this was done with a wooden mallet or the broad side of an axe. In the 1870s, this arduous labor was rendered obsolete by the introduction of the biscuit brake, an ingenious device consisting of hand-cranked rollers mounted on an iron base. Antique biscuit brakes can sometimes be picked up at yard sales, but, thankfully, a food processor does the job wonderfully. Serve beaten biscuits as a cocktail tidbit, with a savory spread, or, in Southern fashion, with butter and thin slices of country ham.

Position a rack in the center of the oven. Preheat the oven to 325°F. Have ready a large ungreased baking sheet.

Combine in a food processor and process for 5 seconds:

2 cups all-purpose flour
2 teaspoons sugar
½ teaspoon salt
¼ teaspoon baking powder

Add and process until the mixture resembles coarse crumbs, about 10 seconds:

6 tablespoons (¾ stick) unsalted butter or lard, cut into small pieces

Add and process for 3 minutes:

½ cup milk

The dough will be soft and puttylike, something like melted mozzarella. Wrap the dough in plastic and let rest for 10 minutes. Turn out onto an unfloured surface and roll out to a little more than ⅛ inch thick. Fold the dough in half, making two layers, and roll lightly to a thickness of about ⅜ inch. Cut out 2-inch rounds with a biscuit cutter. Knead the scraps together, then roll, fold, and cut in the same manner. Arrange the biscuits on the baking sheet so they are close together but not touching. Prick all over with a fork. Bake until the tops are golden brown and the bottoms are deep brown, 30 to 40 minutes. Turn off the oven and let the biscuits stand inside until cold. Beaten biscuits can be stored, airtight at room temperature, for up to 3 weeks.

CLASSIC CURRANT SCONES

8 large or 12 small scones

Scones are sweet, rich biscuits that are usually made with cream as well as butter. Eggs add flavor, rich color, and a slightly cakey texture, but delicious flaky scones can also be produced by omitting the egg in this recipe and increasing the cream to 1 cup.

Position a rack in the center of the oven. Preheat the oven to 425°F. Have ready a large ungreased baking sheet. Whisk together thoroughly in a large bowl:

2 cups all-purpose flour
⅓ cup sugar
1 tablespoon baking powder
½ teaspoon salt

Drop in:

6 tablespoons (¾ stick) cold unsalted butter, cut into pieces

Cut in the butter with 2 knives or a pastry blender, tossing the pieces with the flour mixture to coat and separate them as you work, until the largest pieces are the size of peas and the rest resemble breadcrumbs. Do not allow the butter to melt or form a paste with the flour.

Stir in:

½ cup dried currants or raisins

Whisk together, then add all at once:

1 large egg
½ cup heavy cream
1 teaspoon grated orange zest (optional)

Mix with a rubber spatula, wooden spoon, or fork just until the dry ingredients are moistened. Gather the dough into a ball and knead it gently against the sides and bottom of the bowl 5 to 10 times, turning and pressing any loose pieces into the dough each time until they adhere and the bowl is fairly clean. Transfer to a lightly floured surface and pat the dough into an 8-inch round about ¾ inch thick. Cut into 8 or 12 wedges and place at least ½ inch apart on the baking sheet. Brush the tops with:

2 to 3 teaspoons cream or milk

If desired, sprinkle the tops with:

Cinnamon and sugar

Bake until the tops are golden brown, 12 to 15 minutes. Let cool on a rack or serve warm.

CREAM SCONES

Heavy cream provides both the fat and the liquid in this simplest of all scone recipes.

Prepare Classic Currant Scones, above, omitting the butter and egg and increasing the heavy cream to 1¼ cups.

APRICOT, BLUEBERRY, CRANBERRY, CHERRY, OR GINGER SCONES

Prepare Classic Currant Scones, above, or Cream Scones, above, substituting for the dried currants or raisins ½ cup dried fruit—blueberries, cranberries, cherries, chopped apricots, or chopped pears—or ¼ cup finely chopped crystallized ginger (or candied ginger in syrup, drained and patted dry). If the fruit pieces stick together, lightly toss with the dry ingredients to separate them before adding the liquid. We like to add 1 to 2 teaspoons grated orange zest with dried cranberries or apricots and lemon zest with dried blueberries or ginger.

LEMON SCONES

Prepare Classic Currant Scones, above, substituting for the dried currants or raisins ¼ cup chopped best-quality candied lemon peel or ½ cup chopped dried apricots, dried blueberries, or slivered blanched almonds. Increase the sugar by 1 tablespoon and use 1 tablespoon grated lemon zest in place of the optional orange zest.

CHOCOLATE-CHIP ORANGE SCONES

Prepare Classic Currant Scones, above, substituting for the dried currants or raisins ½ cup semisweet or white chocolate chips and increasing the orange zest to 3 to 4 teaspoons.

OATMEAL SCONES WITH RAISINS OR DATES

8 large or 12 small scones

Extra simple to make, these satisfying scones are made with melted rather than cold butter.

Position a rack in the center of the oven. Preheat the oven to 450°F. Have ready a large ungreased baking sheet.

Whisk together thoroughly in a large bowl:

1½ cups all-purpose flour
¼ cup sugar
1 tablespoon baking powder
½ teaspoon salt

Stir in, using your fingers if necessary to separate the fruit:

1¼ cups old-fashioned rolled oats
½ cup raisins or chopped dates

Whisk together, then add all at once:

1 large egg
10 tablespoons (1¼ sticks) warm melted unsalted butter
⅓ cup milk

Mix with a rubber spatula, wooden spoon, or fork just until the dry ingredients are moistened. The batter will be quite sticky. Transfer the dough to a lightly floured surface. With floured fingers, pat the dough into an 8-inch round about ¾ inch thick. Cut into 8 or 12 wedges. If the dough is too sticky to move the wedges intact, wait 1 to 2 minutes. Using a spatula, place the wedges at least ½ inch apart on the baking sheet. Bake until lightly browned, 10 to 12 minutes. Let cool on a rack or serve warm.

DRIED FRUIT AND BUTTERMILK DROP SCONES (REDUCED FAT/LOW CHOLESTEROL)

Twelve 3-inch scones

Moist, light scones with a golden crusty exterior. Buttermilk produces a pleasantly tangy flavor that complements any dried fruit.

Position a rack in the center of the oven. Preheat the oven to 400°F. Lightly grease a large baking sheet.

Whisk together thoroughly in a large bowl:

2 cups all-purpose flour, or 2½ cups if using oil instead of butter
¼ cup sugar
4 teaspoons baking powder
½ teaspoon salt
¼ teaspoon baking soda

Whisk together, then add all at once:

1 large egg
1 cup low-fat buttermilk
3½ tablespoons warm melted unsalted butter or 3 tablespoons vegetable oil
½ cup raisins, or dried currants, blueberries, cherries, or cranberries, or chopped dried apricots or pears

Mix with a rubber spatula, wooden spoon, or fork just until the dry ingredients are moistened. The batter will be quite sticky. Use a soupspoon or ice cream scoop to drop the batter in mounds 2½ inches in diameter at least 1 inch apart on the baking sheet. Sprinkle the tops with:

Cinnamon and sugar

Bake until the tops are golden brown, 12 to 15 minutes. Let cool on a rack or serve warm.

PANCAKES, WAFFLES, FRENCH TOAST & DOUGHNUTS

In 1889, at an exposition in St. Joseph, Missouri, the predecessor of Aunt Jemima pancake mix was introduced. Since then, pancakes have never relinquished their favored position on the American menu. National dietary trends notwithstanding, pancakes have actually become richer in butter and eggs than they were twenty years ago. Perhaps because we eat pancakes less often now, we want them to be as rich and tender as possible when we do indulge.

MIXING PANCAKE BATTERS

Basic pancake batter is extremely simple—it contains nothing more than flour, leavening, and sugar (the dry ingredients) and milk, eggs, and melted butter (the wet ingredients)—and easy to mix. (The technique for mixing pancakes and waffles is similar to that used for muffins, 771.)

To start, mix the dry ingredients in a bowl, stirring them together with a whisk to ensure that everything is well blended. There is rarely a need to sift dry ingredients, although you should always make sure that baking powder and baking soda are free of lumps—if you find lumps, pinch them between your fingers. You can mix the dry ingredients in advance and store them in a sealable plastic bag or an airtight container for up to 2 weeks in a cool cupboard or 1 month in the freezer.

The wet ingredients are mixed together in another bowl. You can mix the wet ingredients together ahead of time and store them, covered, in the refrigerator for up to 24 hours.

When you are ready to make the pancakes, combine the dry and wet ingredients by mixing them together, preferably with a rubber spatula or a wooden spoon, using a light hand and mixing only until the ingredients are combined. It is better to have a few small lumps than to overwork the batter, activate the flour's gluten, and end up with a tough cake.

All pancake recipes can be doubled or tripled without making adjustments to the proportions.

THE TEXTURE OF PANCAKES

The words used most often to describe pancakes are "light" and "fluffy." However, making pancakes with different flours or with additional ingredients will inevitably change the consistency. Basic pancakes, with their soft crust and light inner sponge that soaks up syrup, are the ones we know best. But some pancakes, like those made with oatmeal or rice, are more substantial, and others, especially those raised with yeast, resemble soft, thin bread.

INGREDIENTS AND SUBSTITUTIONS

Flour gives pancakes their basic structure. Milk is the primary liquid in most pancake batters. Skim, low-fat, or whole milk can be used interchangeably in pancake recipes, though, of course, the richer the milk, the richer the pancake. In savory pancakes, broth can be substituted for all or some of the milk. In both sweet and savory pancakes, sour cream and yogurt (full-fat, low-fat, or even nonfat) can be used interchangeably, and a combination of three parts yogurt and one part milk can be substituted in recipes calling for buttermilk.

It is not necessary to separate the eggs when making pancakes, but for extra fluffiness, the whites can be beaten until stiff but not dry. If this is done, the beaten whites should be folded into the batter at the last moment. Pancakes can be made with egg whites only—add 1 beaten egg white for every 2 egg yolks you eliminate—but these will be a bit drier.

The batter needs melted butter for tenderness. You can use oil, especially if you are making savory pancakes, but butter adds the most agreeable flavor. Skimping on butter robs pancakes of moistness.

Finally, you can substitute brown sugar for white sugar in any recipe or substitute up to 3 tablespoons of honey, molasses, or pure maple syrup for an equal or lesser quantity of the sugar.

EQUIPMENT

Although a skillet can be used, pancakes are most easily made on a flat griddle, shown 795. Some kitchen ranges have a built-in griddle. If yours does not, a stovetop griddle is a good substitute. The most efficient of these fit over two burners, shown 795, providing enough room to cook 6 pancakes at a time. Griddles are available both with nonstick surfaces and in cast iron, which is a wonderful and durable material but one that needs to be seasoned before its first use. (To do this, rub the surface generously with corn or peanut oil and then wipe off the excess oil.) Never scour a griddle after use, whether it is cast iron or nonstick. Wipe a cast-iron griddle clean with a paper towel or, if necessary, wash it gently with soap and water and dry it immediately and thoroughly. Rub it with a thin coating of oil before each use. Nonstick griddles should be wiped clean or washed gently and dried thoroughly after each use.

A griddle should always be heated before use. You will know it is ready when a few drops of cold water flicked onto the surface bounce and sputter; if the water just sits and boils, the griddle is not hot enough, and if it evaporates immediately, it is too hot. Over-the-burner griddles work best at medium heat in most cases. After the first few pancakes, you will gain a feel for the griddle and heat source and will be able to adjust your stove accordingly.

An electric griddle is another possibility. Often large enough to accommodate 6 pancakes at a time and equipped with a temperature control that allows heat low enough for warming and hot enough for cooking bacon, these are especially handy if you like to prepare pancakes at the table. For pancakes, electric griddles should be heated to between 350° and 375°F.

For making blini or silver-dollar-sized pancakes (also known as Swedish pancakes), nothing beats a platar, shown 796. Made of cast iron (which must be seasoned), a platar is a flat pan with seven round indentations, each about 3 inches wide and ½ inch deep. The pan shapes the pancakes perfectly, producing a firmer crust than a griddle. Any griddlecake can be made in a platar.

A crucial tool in pancake-making is a metal spatula. An offset spatula, shown 796, is especially efficient. Its blade is positioned slightly below the handle, which allows the cook to slip it under the pancakes easily when turning them.

KEEPING PANCAKES HOT

Pancakes can be kept for as long as 20 minutes before serving in a preheated 200°F oven. As the pancakes come off the griddle, place them on a heatproof platter or baking pan, one slightly overlapping the last, and cover them very loosely with aluminum foil. For added tenderness and moistness, brush both sides of each pancake with a little melted butter before putting it in the oven.

FREEZING PANCAKES

Leftover pancakes can be allowed to cool, then sealed in an airtight container and frozen for up to 1 month. To reheat, brush both sides of the pancakes with a little melted butter, place them in a single layer on a baking sheet, and warm them through in a preheated 350°F oven for about 10 minutes. Pancakes reheated in a microwave tend to toughen, but frozen pancakes can be popped into a regular toaster or toaster oven, though this produces a thicker, darker crust than oven warming. Just be careful that "toasted" pancakes don't burn. Reheated pancakes will never have the tenderness and suppleness of freshly made ones but are still awfully good—and convenient.

COOKING PANCAKES

To begin, lightly butter, oil, or spray your griddle, if needed, and heat over medium heat. If you are using an electric griddle, preheat it to 350°F.

Pancake batter should be spooned, ladled, or poured slowly and steadily from a height of 2 to 3 inches onto the griddle, shown below. To get a nice round pancake, hold the spoon, ladle, or pitcher steady so that the batter falls in the same spot. Depending on the consistency of the batter, it will either spread into a round by itself or need a little nudge with the back of a ladle or spoon or a metal spatula. It is always a good idea to make one test pancake first to check the batter's consistency and judge how much space each one will need. If, for example, a recipe produces 4-inch-round pancakes, you will need to pour the batter onto the griddle at intervals of 5 to 6 inches, thus allowing room for each pancake as well as an inch or two of breathing room between them. Of course, if a couple of pancakes run together, it is not a tragedy, since they can be cut apart easily with the edge of a spatula.

Pouring the pancake batter onto the griddle

Most pancakes are "bubblers." When the top of the pancake is speckled with bubbles, some bubbles have popped, and the underside of the pancake is golden brown (lift an edge with your spatula and peek at the underside to make sure), slide your spatula under the pancake and turn it, taking care not to let it fold over on itself. Cook the pancake until the second side is lightly browned—it won't get as dark as the first side—which will take only about half as long as the first side did. It is best to turn pancakes just once.

Suggested pancake sizes and yields are provided with the recipes that follow, but these are only guidelines. If you are serving pancakes as part of a large meal, for instance, you might want to make them in the popular silver-dollar size, using only about 2 tablespoons of batter for each pancake. Alternatively, for a more dramatic presentation, you might want to increase the amount of batter and serve up pancakes as wide as a plate.

BASIC PANCAKES

About twelve 5-inch cakes

Tried and true, these pancakes are right for every day and any topping.

Prepare and preheat your griddle, 794.

Whisk together in a large bowl:

1½ cups all-purpose flour
3 tablespoons sugar
1½ teaspoons baking powder
½ teaspoon salt

Whisk together in another bowl:

1½ cups milk
3 tablespoons unsalted butter, melted
2 large eggs
½ teaspoon vanilla (optional)

Pour the wet ingredients over the dry ingredients and gently whisk them together, mixing just until

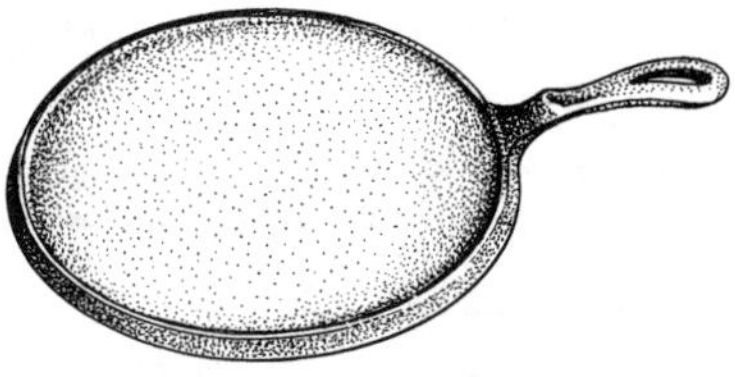

Circular flat griddle

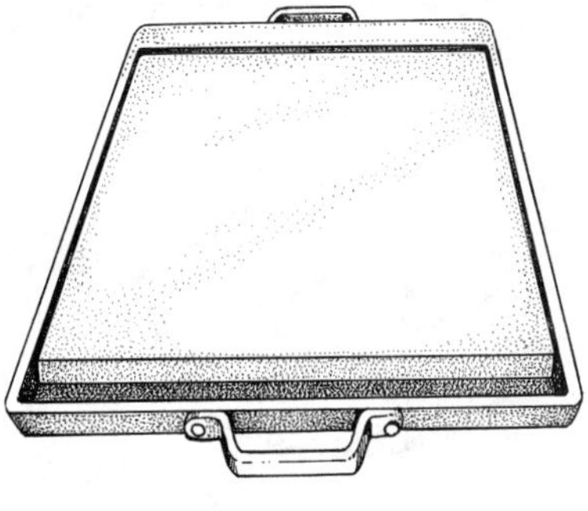

Rectangular stovetop griddle

combined. If you wish, fold in one or more of the following:

- ½ cup plump raisins or other very finely diced soft dried fruit
- ½ cup fresh or frozen blueberries or raspberries
- ½ cup finely chopped nuts, toasted
- ½ cup thinly sliced ripe bananas
- ½ cup crumbled cooked bacon
- ½ cup shredded cheese
- ¼ cup shredded sweetened dried coconut
- ¼ cup grated semisweet or milk chocolate

Spoon ⅓ cup batter onto the griddle for each pancake, nudging the batter into rounds. Cook until the top of each pancake is speckled with bubbles and some bubbles have popped open, then turn and cook until the underside is lightly browned. Serve immediately or keep warm in a 200°F oven while you finish cooking the rest. Serve with:

- Pure maple syrup or honey
- Pats of butter

BASIC BUTTERMILK PANCAKES

Prepare Basic Pancakes, above, adding ½ teaspoon baking soda to the dry ingredients and substituting buttermilk for the milk.

CORNMEAL PANCAKES

About sixteen 5-inch cakes

Prepare and preheat your griddle, 794.

Whisk together in a large bowl:

- 1¼ cups yellow cornmeal, preferably stone ground
- ¾ cup all-purpose flour
- 1¾ teaspoons baking powder
- ¾ teaspoon salt

Whisk together in another bowl:

- 1⅔ cups milk
- 4 tablespoons (½ stick) unsalted butter, melted
- ¼ cup pure maple syrup
- 2 large eggs

Pour the wet ingredients over the dry ingredients and gently whisk them together, mixing just until combined. The batter will be very thin. Stir in:

- ¾ cup fresh, frozen, or drained canned corn kernels (optional)

Spoon ¼ cup batter onto the griddle for each pancake, leaving room for spreading. This is a thin, runny batter that forms irregularly shaped rounds before it sets, but the pancakes will look fine when you flip them over. Cook until the top of each pancake is speckled with bubbles and some bubbles have popped, then turn and cook until the underside is lightly browned. Serve immediately or keep warm in a 200°F oven while you finish cooking the rest. Serve with:

- Pure maple syrup, honey, or fruit syrup
- Yogurt

JALAPEÑO CORNMEAL PANCAKES

For a spicy, savory pancake, prepare Cornmeal Pancakes, above, folding into the batter 1 jalapeño pepper, seeded and minced, 2 tablespoons finely minced fresh cilantro (optional), ½ teaspoon hot red pepper sauce, ¼ teaspoon chili powder, and ground black pepper to taste.

FOUR-GRAIN FLAPJACKS

About eighteen 4½-inch cakes

Prepare and preheat your griddle, 794.

Whisk together in a large bowl:

- 1 cup whole-wheat flour
- ¾ cup all-purpose flour
- ⅓ cup cornmeal, preferably stone ground
- ¼ cup old-fashioned or quick-cooking rolled oats
- 2 tablespoons sugar
- 2 teaspoons baking powder
- 1 teaspoon salt
- ½ teaspoon baking soda
- ½ teaspoon ground cinnamon (optional)
- Pinch of freshly grated or ground nutmeg

Whisk together in another bowl:

- 1¾ cups milk
- 4 tablespoons (½ stick) unsalted butter, melted
- ¼ cup honey
- 3 large eggs

Pour the wet ingredients over the dry ingredients and gently whisk them together, mixing just until combined. Spoon ¼ cup batter onto the griddle for each

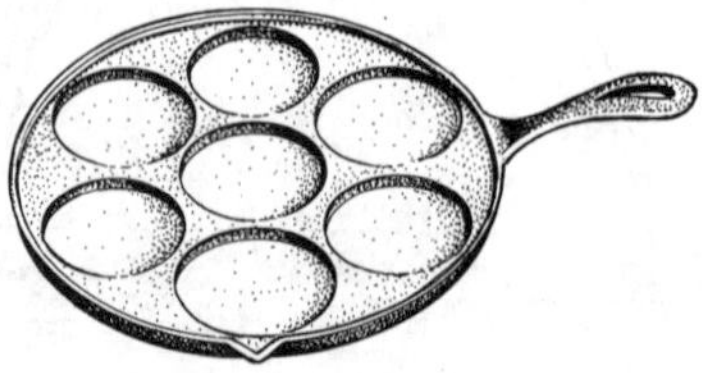

Platar

Offset spatula

pancake, nudging the batter into rounds. Cook until the top of each pancake is speckled with bubbles and some bubbles have popped, then turn and cook until the underside is lightly browned. Serve immediately or keep warm in a 200°F oven while you finish cooking the rest. Serve with:

Pure maple syrup or honey
Cottage cheese

COTTAGE CHEESE PANCAKES

About twelve 5-inch cakes

Cottage cheese gives these thick pancakes a tender sponge, which, when just off the griddle, is soft and almost puddinglike. Although the pancakes will lose their puff and puddingness as they cool, their sweet, wholesome flavor will remain. Plump currants by soaking them in boiling water to cover for 15 minutes. Drain before using.

Lightly butter, oil, or spray your griddle, if needed, and preheat it over medium heat. If you are using an electric griddle, preheat it to 350°F. Preheat the oven to 200°F if you do not plan to serve the pancakes hot off the griddle.

Whisk together in a large bowl:

1⅓ cups all-purpose flour
⅓ cup sugar
2 teaspoons baking powder
½ teaspoon baking soda
½ teaspoon ground cinnamon or pinch of ground nutmeg (optional)
¼ teaspoon salt

Whisk together in another bowl:

1 cup milk
1 cup full-fat or low-fat cottage cheese
3 tablespoons butter, melted
2 large egg yolks
1 teaspoon vanilla

Pour the wet ingredients over the dry ingredients and gently whisk them together, mixing just until combined. Stir in:

⅓ cup finely chopped walnuts (optional)
⅓ cup dried currants, plumped (optional)

Beat until the peaks are stiff but not dry then fold into the batter:

2 large egg whites

The batter will be thick and bubbly—similar to cake batter. Spoon ⅓ cup batter onto the griddle for each pancake, nudging the batter into rounds. These are thick and might take a little longer to cook than most other pancakes. Cook until the top of each pancake is starting to dry around the edges—you will get a few bubbles here and there—then turn and cook until the underside is lightly browned. These will keep in a 200°F oven while you finish making the rest, but they are best served immediately, when they are at their lightest and puffiest. Serve with:

Pure maple syrup or honey
Plain yogurt (optional)

SAVORY COTTAGE CHEESE PANCAKES:

Prepare Cottage Cheese Pancakes, above, omitting the sugar, cinnamon or nutmeg, vanilla, walnuts, and currants and adding 1 small shallot, very finely minced, ¼ cup thinly sliced scallion (white and tender green parts only), 2 tablespoons finely minced parsley, and 1 tablespoon finely snipped dill.

BLUEBERRY BUTTERMILK PANCAKES

About twelve 4½-inch cakes

Prepare and preheat your griddle, 794.

Whisk together in a large bowl:

1 cup all-purpose flour
½ cup yellow cornmeal, preferably stone ground
¼ cup sugar
1¼ teaspoons baking powder
¼ teaspoon baking soda
¼ teaspoon salt

Whisk together in another bowl:

1¼ cups buttermilk
4 tablespoons (½ stick) unsalted butter, melted
2 large egg yolks
1½ teaspoons finely grated lemon zest

Pour the wet ingredients over the dry ingredients and gently whisk them together, mixing just until combined. Beat until the peaks are stiff but not dry then fold into the batter:

2 large egg whites

Fold in:

1 cup fresh or frozen blueberries

Spoon ⅓ cup batter onto the griddle for each pancake, nudging the batter into rounds. Cook until the top of each pancake is speckled with bubbles and some bubbles have popped, then turn and cook until the underside is lightly browned. Serve immediately or keep warm in a 200°F oven while you finish cooking the rest. Serve with:

Pure maple syrup, honey, or blueberry sauce

RAISED BUCKWHEAT BLINI

About fifteen 3-inch cakes

Dark, nutty buckwheat flour is the basis for blini—small, yeast-risen pancakes that serve as the traditional "bread" for caviar and smoked fish in Russia and

Ukraine. A version made from a combination of buckwheat and white flour is slightly more refined. Blini are particularly associated with Maslenitsa (literally "butter festival"), the week preceding Lent, when they are eaten with melted butter, caviar or smoked fish, and *smetnana* (soured cream). This recipe will make large, stack-'em-up pancakes for breakfast or small blini that look like Swedish pancakes. For pancakes, ladle the batter onto a hot griddle; for blini, use a cast-iron platar, shown 796, to produce perfectly round, beautifully browned cakes.

Combine in a saucepan:

1½ cups milk
4 tablespoons (½ stick) unsalted butter

Heat until the butter is melted, then let cool to between 105° and 115°F. Sprinkle with:

2 teaspoons active dry yeast

Let stand until the yeast is dissolved, about 5 minutes. Whisk together:

⅔ cup all-purpose flour
⅔ cup buckwheat flour
2 tablespoons sugar
1 teaspoon salt

Pour the wet ingredients over the dry ingredients and gently whisk them together, mixing just until combined. Cover the bowl tightly with plastic wrap and let rise in a warm place until doubled in volume, about 1 hour. When the batter has risen, you can make the pancakes immediately or refrigerate the covered bowl for up to 24 hours. If the batter is refrigerated, let stand at room temperature for 20 minutes before proceeding. Stir to deflate the batter and whisk in:

3 large eggs, lightly beaten

Prepare and preheat your griddle or platar, 794.

If you are using the platar, spoon about 2 tablespoons batter into each mold. Cook until the top of each blini is speckled with bubbles and some bubbles have popped, then turn and cook until the underside is lightly browned. (The easiest way to turn blini is to spear them with a thin skewer, nail, or knitting needle; you can also slip a narrow icing spatula under the cakes.) If you're making these on a griddle, spoon a scant ¼ cup batter onto the griddle for each pancake, leaving room between the pancakes for spreading, and cook as directed above. Serve immediately or keep warm in a 200°F oven while you finish cooking the rest. Serve with:

Melted butter or caviar and sour cream or crème fraîche

Or treat like breakfast pancakes and serve with:

Pure maple syrup

SOURDOUGH PANCAKES

About twelve 5-inch cakes

A surprising treat to wake up to. Do not be impatient; an overnight rest is the key to success for these tart, moist pancakes.

Whisk together:

2½ teaspoons active dry yeast
½ cup warm (105° to 115°F) water

Let stand until the yeast is dissolved, about 5 minutes. Whisk in:

1½ cups warm (105° to 115°F) milk
3 tablespoons unsalted butter, melted

In a large bowl, whisk together:

2 cups all-purpose flour
3 tablespoons sugar

Pour the wet ingredients over the dry ingredients and gently whisk them together, mixing just until combined. Cover the bowl tightly with plastic wrap and set in a warm place for 1 hour. Let the mixture increase in volume by at least half and become bubbly. Uncover and stir the batter down, then cover the bowl again. Let rise overnight at room temperature or in the refrigerator. (The batter can be refrigerated for up to 48 hours, but it will become tangier.) If the batter is refrigerated, let stand at room temperature for 20 minutes before proceeding.

Stir to deflate the batter and whisk in:

2 large eggs, lightly beaten
1 teaspoon salt

Prepare and preheat your griddle, 794.

Spoon ¼ cup batter onto the griddle for each pancake, leaving room for spreading. This is a thin, runny batter that forms irregularly shaped rounds before it sets, but the pancakes will look fine when you flip them over. Cook until the top of each pancake is speckled with bubbles and some bubbles have popped, then turn and cook until the underside is lightly browned. Serve immediately or keep warm in a 200°F oven while you finish cooking the rest. Serve with:

Pure maple syrup or honey
Pats of butter

LEMON PANCAKES

About twelve 4-inch cakes

Prepare and preheat your griddle, 794.

Whisk together in a large bowl:

1 cup all-purpose flour
⅓ cup sugar
1½ teaspoons baking powder
½ teaspoon baking soda
¼ teaspoon salt

Whisk together in another bowl:

¾ cup sour cream
⅓ cup milk
¼ cup fresh lemon juice
3 tablespoons unsalted butter, melted
1 large egg
1½ teaspoons vanilla

Pour the wet ingredients over the dry ingredients and gently whisk them together, mixing just until combined. Fold in:

Finely grated zest of 2 lemons

The batter will be thick and bubbly—similar to a cake batter. Spoon ¼ cup batter onto the griddle for each pancake, nudging the batter into rounds. Cook until the top of each pancake is speckled with bubbles and some bubbles have popped, then turn and cook until the underside is lightly browned. Serve immediately or keep warm in a 200°F oven while you finish cooking the rest. Serve with:

Honey
Sweetened sour cream or crème fraîche

LEMON POPPY SEED PANCAKES

Prepare Lemon Pancakes, above, folding in ½ cup poppy seeds along with the lemon zest.

CHOCOLATE CHOCOLATE-CHIP PANCAKES

About eighteen 4-inch cakes

These are surprisingly good at room temperature, when the chocolate chips are firm and the pancakes begin to taste like devil's food cake.

Prepare and preheat your griddle, 794.

Whisk together in a large bowl:

1 cup all-purpose flour
½ cup sugar
⅓ cup unsweetened cocoa, sifted
2 teaspoons baking powder
¼ teaspoon baking soda
¼ teaspoon salt

Whisk together in another bowl:

1¼ cups milk
4 tablespoons (½ stick) unsalted butter, melted
2 large egg yolks
1½ teaspoons vanilla

Pour the wet ingredients over the dry ingredients and gently whisk them together, mixing just until combined. Stir in:

¾ cup miniature semisweet chocolate chips or finely chopped semisweet or bittersweet chocolate

Beat until the peaks are stiff but not dry then fold into the batter:

2 large egg whites

Spoon ¼ cup batter onto the griddle for each pancake, nudging the batter into rounds. Cook until the top of each pancake is speckled with bubbles and some bubbles have popped, then turn and cook until the underside is lightly browned. Serve immediately or keep warm in a 200°F oven while you finish cooking the rest. Serve with:

Sweetened sour cream or crème fraîche and chocolate sauce

SILVER DOLLAR HOTS

About 40 mini pancakes

Super light and fluffy describes these delicate treats. Hot off the griddle is the best way to eat them.

Prepare and preheat your griddle or platar, 794.

Lightly beat:

2 large eggs

Whisk in:

1 cup sour cream
¼ cup all-purpose flour
1½ tablespoons sugar
½ teaspoon salt
¼ teaspoon baking soda

If you are using the platar, spoon 1 tablespoon batter into each mold. If you are making these on a griddle, spoon 1 tablespoon batter onto the griddle for each pancake, nudging the batter into 2½-inch rounds. Cook until the top of each pancake is speckled with bubbles and some bubbles have popped, then turn over and cook until the underside is lightly browned. Serve immediately with:

Pure maple syrup or fresh fruit

DUTCH BABY

One 10-inch cake; 2 to 4 servings

Sometimes called a German or puff pancake, this batter is poured into a skillet looking like a heap of scrambled eggs and emerges from the oven puffed and wondrously golden. Serve this straight from the oven with a dusting of powdered sugar, a spoonful of the best fruit preserves you can lay your hands on, or some sliced fruit sautéed in butter and splashed with brandy or dark rum.

Preheat the oven to 425°F.

Whisk together until smooth:

½ cup milk
½ cup all-purpose flour
¼ cup sugar
2 large eggs, at room temperature

Melt in a 10-inch ovenproof skillet (cast iron is ideal) over medium heat:

4 tablespoons (½ stick) unsalted butter

Tilt the pan so that the butter coats the sides. Pour the egg mixture into the skillet and cook, without stirring, for 1 minute. Place the skillet in the oven and bake until the pancake is puffed and golden, 12 to 15 minutes. Serve immediately, for the pancake loses its puff, and therefore its drama, almost immediately.

DOUBLE DUTCH PANCAKE

For twice as many servings, double the recipe for Dutch Baby, above. Melt the butter in a 12 x 9-inch ovenproof glass baking pan in the preheated oven. Pour in the batter and bake as directed for 15 to 17 minutes.

ABOUT WAFFLES

Waffles are light, leavened cousins of the ancient Communion wafer, which, like waffles, were once baked in irons and had the same honeycomb pattern that characterizes all members of the wafer/waffle family. The earliest waffle irons were probably produced in thirteenth-century Germany or Holland. Consisting of two hinged iron plates attached to long wooden handles, the irons were designed to be held over the embers of a hearth fire. The ancient plates were far more elaborate that those of today's waffle irons, often embossed with family initials, religious symbols, coats of arms, figures, or landscape scenes. Today, the usual pattern is simply a grid, often shallow but better, especially for Belgian waffles, when deep. Most contemporary waffle irons are square or rectangular in shape, but look for those shaped like a Five of Hearts—a circle composed of five shallow-gridded hearts—a form once popular among the Pennsylvania Dutch. Waffles were brought to America by the Dutch settlers of the 1600s, but they were probably not widely known until sometime in the next century. In the late 1700s, Thomas Jefferson traveled to France and brought back a French waffle iron at considerable trouble and expense.

Waffle batters are similar to pancake batters. To mix the batter, see Mixing Pancake Batters, 793.

A waffle batter needs butter and a fair amount of it. The butter both tenderizes a waffle and helps keep it from sticking to the iron. You can substitute oil for butter in a recipe without changing the texture—of course, this will affect the flavor—but you cannot make waffles without either butter or oil.

EQUIPMENT

The simplest waffle irons are those that resemble the earliest ones—long-handled hinged plates to be held over a stovetop burner or a campfire. Today, electric waffle irons, shown below, are the most popular tools for the purpose, and with good reason, for they are efficient, reliable, and long-lasting. Our family still turns out championship waffles with a model my folks received as a wedding present in 1932! All that the older models are missing is the nonstick coating—which makes it easier to lift the waffles off the iron and is easier to clean. The Belgian waffle iron, shown below, right, yields waffles with the deepest "pockets."

USING A WAFFLE IRON

If you are using a stovetop cast-iron waffler, seasoning is a must. Rub the baking surfaces lightly with corn or peanut oil and wipe off any excess oil.

If you have an electric waffle iron with a nonstick finish, there is probably no need to season the grids; simply follow the manufacturer's instructions. Even if seasoning is not required, the iron may smoke when it is first heated. This is normal, but it is usually a good idea to think of the first couple of waffles that come off

Waffle iron

Belgian waffle iron

BAKING WAFFLES

You can bake any waffle recipe in any waffle iron, but the amount of batter you will need for each waffle and the number of waffles the recipe yields will change. In all likelihood, in fact, you will have to make adjustments for your own iron—you may need less of a thinner batter, more of a thicker one. Try a sample waffle or two to be safe. Because batters have different consistencies, some will spread across the iron's grids by themselves, while others will need a little cajoling with the back of a metal spatula, wooden spoon, or ladle. Batters, self-spreaders or otherwise, should be poured or spread to within ¼ inch of the edge of the grids; when the iron is closed, the top plate will push the batter to the edge to fill the space. If you have overfilled the grids or spread the batter too far, try baking with the iron open for 30 seconds; this may stop any overflow. Once the iron is closed, do not open it until the steam has subsided. Waffles usually take 4 to 5 minutes to cook. If after that time the lid is difficult to open, do not force it, for the waffle is not yet baked.

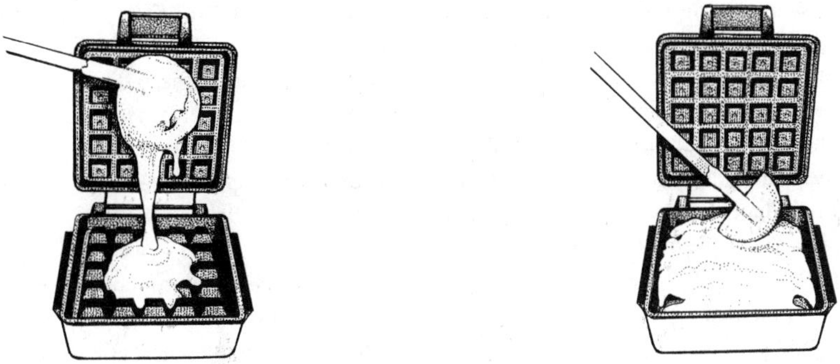

Pouring the waffle batter onto the iron

a brand-new iron as your testing set. (In our family these were reserved for Joy, Ethan's dog.)

A properly seasoned waffle iron, with or without a nonstick coating, doesn't need to be greased every time you use it, since most waffle batters contain enough butter to keep the waffles from sticking. If you feel it is necessary to grease your iron, rub with corn or peanut oil, vegetable oil spray, or melted butter before heating the iron. If, after a few batches, the waffles begin to stick, grease again very lightly. After making waffles, unplug the iron, let it cool, then wipe it down with a soft towel. If any crumbs stick to the grids, use a soft brush—we use an old toothbrush—to remove them. Never scrub a waffle iron with an abrasive cleaner or scouring pad and, of course, never immerse an electric iron in water.

KEEPING WAFFLES HOT

Waffles can be kept warm for as long as 20 minutes in a 200°F oven, spread out in a single layer directly on the oven rack (stacking makes them soggy). Because waffles freeze and reheat well, we plan for leftovers and multiply the recipe, wrapping cooled waffles airtight and storing them in the freezer. To reheat, place the still-frozen waffles directly on the rack of a preheated 350°F oven and bake until heated through, about 10 minutes.

BASIC WAFFLES

12 6-inch waffles

We give you three choices to prepare this recipe: use 4 tablespoons butter for a reduced-fat waffle, 8 tablespoons for a classic light and fluffy waffle; or 16 tablespoons for the crunchiest most delicious waffle imaginable.

Preheat your waffle iron.

Whisk together in a large bowl:

1¾ cups all-purpose flour
1 tablespoon baking powder
1 tablespoon sugar
½ teaspoon salt

Whisk together in another bowl:

3 large eggs, well beaten
4 to 16 tablespoons (½ to 2 sticks) unsalted butter, melted
1½ cups milk

Make a well in the center of the dry ingredients and pour in the wet ingredients. Gently whisk them together with a few swift strokes. (The batter should have a pebbled look, similar to a muffin batter). If you wish, fold in one or more of the following:

½ cup plump raisins or other very finely diced soft dried fruit
½ cup fresh or frozen blueberries or raspberries
½ cup finely chopped nuts, toasted
½ thinly sliced ripe banana
½ cup crumbled cooked bacon
½ cup shredded cheese
¼ cup shredded sweetened dried coconut
¼ cup grated semisweet or milk chocolate

Spoon ½ cup batter (or the amount recommended by your waffle iron's manufacturer) onto the hot iron. Spread the batter to within ¼ inch of the edge of the grids, using the back of a metal spatula, wooden spoon, or ladle. Close the lid and bake until the waffle is golden brown. Serve immediately or keep warm in a single layer on a rack in a 200°F oven while you finish cooking the rest. Serve with:

Pure maple syrup or jam
Pats of butter

BASIC BUTTERMILK WAFFLES

Prepare Basic Waffles, 801, adding ¼ teaspoon more baking soda to the dry ingredients and substituting buttermilk for the milk.

CORNMEAL WAFFLES

Eight 6½-inch round waffles

Terrific at breakfast with syrup and sausages, these can also be cut into wedges and served with roasted chicken, grilled shrimp, smothered pork chops, or hearty beef stew. Think of these as flat, crisp corn bread.

Preheat your waffle iron.

Whisk together in a large bowl:

1 cup all-purpose flour
1 cup cornmeal, preferably stone ground
2 teaspoons baking powder
¾ teaspoon salt
½ teaspoon baking soda

Whisk together in another bowl:

2 cups buttermilk
¼ cup pure maple syrup
5 tablespoons unsalted butter, melted
2 large egg yolks, at room temperature

Pour the wet ingredients over the dry ingredients and gently whisk them together, mixing just until combined. Beat until the peaks are stiff but not dry then fold into the batter:

2 large egg whites

Spoon a rounded ½ cup batter (or a little more than the amount recommended by your waffle iron's manufacturer) onto the hot iron. Spread the batter to within ¼ inch of the edge of the grids, using the back of a metal spatula, wooden spoon, or ladle. Close the lid and bake until the waffle is golden brown. Serve immediately or keep warm in a single layer on a rack in a 200°F oven while you finish cooking the rest. Serve with:

Pure maple syrup
Bacon

BELGIAN WAFFLES

Twelve 6-inch waffles

Nowadays, any waffle with very deep pockets is often called a Belgian waffle, but when Belgian waffles were introduced to Americans at the 1964 World's Fair in New York City, they were yeast-raised and served with sweetened whipped cream. This recipe is in the spirit of the original Belgian waffle.

Whisk together:

1 envelope (2¼ teaspoons) active dry yeast
¼ cup warm (105° to 115°F) milk

Let stand until the yeast is dissolved, about 5 minutes.

Whisk together in a large bowl:

3 large egg yolks
¼ cup lukewarm milk
12 tablespoons (1½ sticks) unsalted butter, melted and cooled to lukewarm

Whisk in the yeast mixture along with:

½ cup sugar
1½ teaspoons salt
2 teaspoons vanilla

Add, in 3 parts:

4 cups all-purpose flour

alternating, in 2 parts, with:

2½ cups warm (105° to 115°F) milk

Beat until soft peaks form then fold into the batter:

3 large egg whites

Cover the bowl tightly with plastic wrap and let rise in a warm place until doubled in volume, about 1 hour. Stir to deflate the batter.

Preheat your waffle iron.

Spoon ½ cup batter (or the amount recommended by your waffle iron's manufacturer) onto the hot iron. Spread the batter to within ¼ inch of the edge of the grids, using the back of a metal spatula, wooden spoon, or ladle. Close the lid and bake until the waffle is golden brown. Serve immediately or keep warm in a single layer on a rack in a 200°F oven while you finish cooking the rest. Serve with:

Pats of butter and powdered sugar or fresh fruit and whipped cream

FRENCH TOAST WAFFLES

5 pieces

This is a shortcut for preparing waffles.

Preheat your waffle iron.

Whisk together in a large bowl:

3 large eggs, lightly beaten
¼ cup milk
2 tablespoons unsalted butter, melted
⅛ teaspoon salt

Cut into pieces to fit a waffle iron:

5 slices bread

Coat the bread well in the egg mixture. Place on the hot iron and close the lid. Bake until the bread is a light golden brown. Serve immediately or keep warm in a single layer on a rack in a 200°F oven while you finish cooking the rest. Serve with:

Pure maple syrup
Pats of butter

HONEY BRAN WAFFLES

Six 6½-inch round waffles

Whole-wheat flour and coarse bran, also known as miller's bran, are available at natural foods markets. Try these with slices of sharp Cheddar cheese.

Preheat your waffle iron.

Whisk together in a large bowl:

¾ cup all-purpose flour
¾ cup whole-wheat flour
½ cup coarse bran
2 teaspoons baking powder
½ teaspoon salt
¼ teaspoon baking soda

Whisk together in another bowl:

1½ cups buttermilk
⅓ cup honey
4 tablespoons (½ stick) unsalted butter, melted
2 large eggs
½ teaspoon vanilla

Pour the wet ingredients over the dry ingredients and gently whisk them together, mixing just until combined. The batter will be thick and bubbly. Spoon a rounded ½ cup batter (or a little more than the amount recommended by your waffle iron's manufacturer) onto the hot iron. Spread the batter to within ¼ inch of the edge of the grids, using the back of a metal spatula, wooden spoon, or ladle. Close the lid and bake until the waffle is golden brown. Serve immediately or keep warm in a single layer on a rack in a 200°F oven while you finish cooking the rest. Serve with:

Honey or pure maple syrup
Pats of butter

CHOCOLATE MARSHMALLOW WAFFLES

Five 6½-inch round waffles

Even if your waffle iron is nonstick or well seasoned, you'll need to butter, oil, or spray the grids before you start these—even then, a marshmallow or two will probably stick.

Preheat your waffle iron.

Whisk together in a large bowl:

1 cup all-purpose flour
⅓ cup unsweetened cocoa, sifted
⅓ cup sugar
1½ teaspoons baking powder
¼ teaspoon baking soda
¼ teaspoon salt

Whisk together in another bowl:

1¼ cups milk
2 large egg yolks
4 tablespoons (½ stick) unsalted butter, melted
1 teaspoon vanilla

Pour the wet ingredients over the dry ingredients and gently whisk them together, mixing just until combined. Stir in:

½ cup miniature semisweet or bittersweet chocolate chips
½ cup miniature marshmallows

Beat until the peaks are stiff but not dry then fold into the batter:

2 large egg whites

Stir the batter to make sure the chips and marshmallows are evenly distributed, then spoon a scant ⅔ cup batter (or a little more than the amount recommended by your waffle iron's manufacturer) onto the hot iron. Spread the batter to within ¼ inch of the edge of the grids, using the back of a metal spatula, wooden spoon, or ladle. Let the batter bake on the grids for 30 seconds, then close the lid and bake until the waffle is set. Serve immediately or keep warm in a single layer on a rack in a 200°F oven while you finish cooking the rest. Serve with:

Whipped cream or ice cream

ABOUT CRÊPES AND BLINTZES

An ancient European dish, crêpes were brought to America by the first English settlers of the seventeenth century and continued to be enjoyed until the time of the Civil War. Early Americans knew crêpes by their old English name, pancakes, which in the late 1800s became the usual name for the puffy, chemically leavened griddle cakes so beloved today. Meanwhile, as fluffy pancakes soared in popularity in the late nineteenth century, thin pancakes, that is, crêpes, became rare in the American scene until the 1930s, when they were reintroduced from France, primarily as the famous crêpes Suzette. Since then, their fortunes have risen, then fallen, then risen again. But in one form or another, they appear to be here to stay. They are simply too good to forget.

MIXING CRÊPES AND BLINTZES

The batters for crêpes and blintzes are thinner than those used for pancakes and are best made at least 30 minutes ahead so that the flour can absorb all the liquid. Batters can be made up to 2 days ahead, in fact, and kept in a bowl, covered, in the refrigerator. Give the batter a good stirring before you start.

EQUIPMENT

Crêpes and blintzes are most easily made in a crêpe pan—a short-sided skillet about 7½ inches across, shown below. (You can also use a regular skillet of the same size.) If your pan is nonstick, you may not have to season it—simply follow the manufacturer's instructions. New crêpe pans always need to be seasoned. Rub the cooking surface lightly with corn or peanut oil, then wipe off any excess oil. Once seasoned, crêpe pans do not have to be washed; a quick wipe with a paper towel should keep them in good shape. Even if your crêpe pan is nonstick, however, you will want to use at least ½ teaspoon butter for each crêpe, as much for flavor as for ease of preparation.

Crêpe pan

MAKING CRÊPES AND BLINTZES

You'll need only 2 to 3 tablespoons of batter for each crêpe or blintz. The easiest and neatest way to get this small amount of batter into the pan is to pour it from a pitcher or from a ladle that holds just the right amount. Heat a crêpe pan over medium to medium-high heat and grease it lightly by rubbing the end of a stick of butter on the cooking surface. Lift the pan off the heat and pour in the batter, tilting and rotating the pan as you do so that the batter covers the entire bottom of the pan in a very thin, even layer. It is an odd movement, but you will get the hang of it after a crêpe or two. Cook the crêpe on one side until it sets and starts to bubble (the underside should be golden brown). Run a blunt, thin knife or metal spatula around the edge of the pan, lift the crêpe up, and turn it over. (If you can stand the heat, fingers are the best tools for turning.) Cook the second side just until it is speckled with golden dots; it will never be as brown as the first side. For blintzes, cook just the first side.

KEEPING AND FREEZING CRÊPES AND BLINTZES

Crêpes and blintzes can be served as soon as they are made but typically are kept aside to be served all together or stored for later use. If you want to finish cooking the batch before serving the first one, place the first crêpe or blintz on a plate and cover it with a square of wax paper. Continue layering the crêpes between sheets of wax paper as they are cooked. To store, either cover the plate with plastic wrap and refrigerate overnight or wrap them airtight and freeze for up to 1 month. Crêpes and blintzes can be thawed, still wrapped, overnight in the refrigerator or warmed in a microwave for a few seconds—just long enough to make them soft enough to peel from the wax paper without tearing.

BASIC SWEET CRÊPES *About twelve 7½-inch crêpes*

Combine in a blender or food processor until smooth:

½ cup all-purpose flour
½ cup milk
¼ cup lukewarm water
2 large eggs
2 tablespoons unsalted butter, melted
1½ tablespoons sugar
Pinch of salt

Pour the batter into a pitcher or other container with a pouring lip. Cover with plastic wrap and let stand for 30 minutes or refrigerate for up to 2 days. (This allows the flour to thoroughly absorb the liquid and gives the gluten in the flour a chance to relax.)

Place a nonstick or seasoned crêpe pan over medium heat. Coat the pan with a little:

Unsalted butter

Stir the batter and pour about 2 tablespoons into the pan, lifting the pan off the heat and tilting and rotating it so that the batter forms an even, very thin layer. Cook until the top is set and the underside is golden. Turn the crêpe over, using a spatula or your fingers (fingers work best here) and cook until the second side is lightly browned. Remove the crêpe to a piece of wax paper. Continue cooking the rest of the crêpes, buttering the pan and stirring the batter before starting each one. Stack the finished crêpes between sheets of wax paper. Use immediately or let cool, wrap airtight, and freeze for up to 1 month.

BASIC SAVORY CRÊPES

Prepare Basic Sweet Crêpes, above, omitting the sugar and increasing the salt to ½ teaspoon.

BUCKWHEAT CRÊPES

About 16 crêpes

Buckwheat crêpes, a.k.a. *galettes de sarrasin,* are a little thicker than regular wheat-flour crêpes and lot more assertive, thanks to the strong, nutlike flavor of buckwheat. Rarely used in desserts, buckwheat crêpes can be used in any savory crêpes recipe. The batter needs to rest for an hour before cooking, so be sure to factor this into your schedule.

Combine in a blender or food processor until smooth:

½ cup buckwheat flour
½ cup all-purpose flour
1 cup milk
¾ cup water
3 large eggs
2 tablespoons vegetable oil
1 teaspoon salt

Scrape down the sides of the container with a rubber spatula and process until thoroughly blended, about 15 seconds more. Pour the batter into a pitcher or other container with a pouring lip. Cover with plastic wrap and let stand for 1 hour or refrigerate for up to 1 day. Proceed as for Basic Sweet Crêpes, 804.

CRÊPES SUZETTE

12 crêpes; 6 servings

Henri Charpentier, a young chef at the Hôtel de Paris in Monte Carlo in the late nineteenth century, is said to have invented this dessert by accident. One day when he was composing a complicated crêpe sauce for his patron, Albert, Prince of Wales, the cordials accidentally caught fire, and he thought both he and his sauce were ruined. Quickly he plunged the crêpes into the boiling liquid, added more of the cordials, and let the sauce flame again. The dish was a triumph. Below is an approximation of Henri's crêpe batter and sauce. The easiest way to make the sauce for crêpes Suzette is in a large skillet in the kitchen; it can then be transferred to a chafing dish in the dining room so that when the last bit of warmed brandy is ladled over the crêpes and set aflame, no one will miss a thing.

Place in a large skillet or chafing dish over medium heat:

4 tablespoons (½ stick) unsalted butter
½ cup fresh orange juice
⅓ cup sugar
1 teaspoon fresh lemon juice
Grated zest of 1 small orange (optional)

Bring the mixture to a boil, stirring to melt the sugar, then continue to boil just until slightly thickened, 2 to 3 minutes. Stir in:

2 tablespoons Grand Marnier
2 tablespoons Cognac

Return the sauce to a boil and boil for 30 seconds. One by one, place in the sauce:

12 Basic Sweet Crêpes, 804

Allow each one to heat through and soak up some of the sauce, about 15 seconds. Using tongs, fold the crêpe into quarters, so that it forms a ruffle-edged triangle with the brownest side out, and transfer it to a warmed dessert plate. Arrange 2 crêpes on each plate so that they overlap each other slightly in the center. Continue heating and arranging the crêpes. When you are ready to serve, pour a little of the remaining sauce over the crêpes, then heat in a saucepan or ladle until barely warm:

½ cup Grand Marnier

Spoon over the crêpes and, standing well back, ignite with a long wooden match. Serve still flaming.

CRÊPES WITH CARAMELIZED APPLES

12 crêpes; 6 servings

The cider syrup can be kept for a week and is worth making on its own to serve with other pancakes and waffles.

For the cider syrup, stir together in a small saucepan:

1 cup apple cider
3 tablespoons light corn syrup
1 tablespoon light brown sugar
1 tablespoon fresh lemon juice

Bring to a boil, then reduce the heat to medium and boil, stirring occasionally, until the mixture is reduced by half, about 10 minutes. Remove the pan from the heat and swirl in, piece by piece:

2 tablespoons cold unsalted butter, cut into 6 pieces

Serve immediately or let cool, pour into a jar, and refrigerate for up to 1 week. Reheat (but do not boil) before using.

To prepare the apples, peel, halve, and core:

3 Golden Delicious or other firm, sweet apples (1 to 1¼ pounds)

Cut each half into 6 wedges. In a large skillet, preferably nonstick, melt over medium heat:

2 tablespoons unsalted butter

Add the apples and cook, stirring frequently, until the apples release their juices and start to soften, about 5 minutes. Sprinkle with:

2 tablespoons sugar

Stir to mix. Continue cooking the apples, turning them occasionally, until they have a light crust and are golden caramel in color, 10 to 15 minutes. Use the apples immediately or cover and keep at room temperature for up to 2 hours. Reheat before using.

To assemble the dessert, place a seasoned crêpe pan or skillet over medium heat and coat it with a little:

Unsalted butter

One by one, add:

12 Basic Sweet Crêpes, 804

Heat one side only in the hot pan for about 30 seconds. Fold the crêpe into quarters, so that it forms a ruffle-edged triangle with the brownest side out, and transfer it to a warmed dessert plate. Arrange 2 crêpes on each plate so that they overlap each other slightly in the center. Continue heating and arranging the crêpes, rubbing the pan with a little butter before heating each one. Divide the hot caramelized apples among the plates and spoon the warm syrup over all. Serve immediately as is or topped with:

Lightly sweetened whipped cream, crème fraîche, or vanilla ice cream

CRÊPE CAKE

6 servings

Colonial Americans ate their crêpes stacked into a layer cake, as do the Norman French to this day. For an especially high and dramatic cake that will serve 8 to 10 people, prepare a double recipe of crêpes.

Prepare the batter for:

Basic Sweet Crêpes, 804

Make the batter into large crêpes, about 8 inches in diameter. Stack the crêpes like a layer cake on a heatproof platter, spreading each with a thin layer of:

Jelly or jam, applesauce, or Rich Hot Lemon Sauce, 1043

Sprinkle the top with:

Sugar

Set aside at room temperature for up to 8 hours. To serve, place in a 250°F oven for about 15 minutes, or until warmed through. If you wish, heat until barely warm:

¼ cup brandy or rum

Pour over the crêpes and, standing well back, ignite with a long wooden match. Cut into wedges. If you wish, serve with:

Whipped cream

BLINTZES

About twelve 7½-inch blintzes

Combine in a blender or food processor until smooth:

1 cup all-purpose flour
1 cup milk
3 large eggs
2 tablespoons unsalted butter, melted
2 teaspoons sugar
Pinch of salt

Pour the batter into a pitcher or other container with a pouring lip. Cover with plastic wrap and let stand at room temperature for 30 minutes or refrigerate for up to 2 days. (This allows the flour to thoroughly absorb the liquid and gives the gluten in the flour a chance to relax.)

Place a nonstick or seasoned crêpe pan over medium heat. Coat the pan with a little:

Unsalted butter

Stir the batter and pour 2½ to 3 tablespoons into the pan, lifting the pan off the heat and tilting and rotating it so that the batter forms an even layer. Cook until the top is dry and set and the underside is golden. Remove the blintz to a piece of wax paper. Continue cooking the rest of the blintzes, buttering the pan and stirring the batter before starting each one. Stack the finished blintzes between sheets of wax paper. Use as soon as they are cool enough to fill and roll, or let cool, wrap airtight, and freeze for up to 1 month.

SWEET CHEESE BLINTZES

8 filled blintzes; 4 servings

Farmer's cheese is a drier relative of cottage cheese. These blintzes are delicious accompanied with mixed berries or a warm dried fruit compote or with thick slices of bacon or ham.

Combine in a blender or food processor until smooth:

1¼ cups (10 ounces) farmer's cheese or drained small-curd cottage cheese
2 ounces cream cheese
1 large egg
1 tablespoon sugar
1 teaspoon vanilla
¼ teaspoon salt
Grated zest of ½ orange (optional)

Transfer to a bowl and stir in:

½ cup plump raisins (optional)

Spoon the filling in the center of the uncooked side of:

8 Blintzes, above

Fold the sides of each blintz around the filling to form a rectangular package. (At this point, the filled blintzes can be wrapped airtight and frozen for up to 1 month.) In a large skillet, preferably nonstick, heat over medium heat:

2 tablespoons unsalted butter

1 tablespoon vegetable oil

When the butter is melted and the bubbles subside, add the blintzes, seam side down, and cook until golden brown on both sides. Transfer the blintzes to paper towels to drain for a moment. Serve immediately with:

Sour cream (optional)

and any other topping or accompaniment of your choice.

BLUEBERRY BLINTZES *6 filled blintzes; 6 servings*

These plump blintzes are traditionally served with sour cream but are also lovely with a thinned ginger-flavored custard or a spoonful or two of lemon curd.

Combine in a medium saucepan:

1 cup fresh or frozen blueberries

Juice and finely grated zest of ½ lemon

2 tablespoons sugar

½ teaspoon ground ginger

¼ teaspoon ground cinnamon

Bring to a boil over medium heat, stirring constantly, then continue to boil until most of the berries have popped and the mixture is the consistency of jam. Add:

1 cup fresh or frozen blueberries

Cook and stir for 1 minute. Transfer to a bowl and let cool to room temperature. Spoon the filling in the center of the uncooked side of:

6 Blintzes, above

Fold the sides of each blintz around the filling to form a rectangular package. (At this point, the filled blintzes can be wrapped airtight and frozen for up to 1 month.) In a large skillet, preferably nonstick, heat over medium heat:

2 tablespoons unsalted butter

1 tablespoon vegetable oil

When the butter is melted and the bubbles subside, add the blintzes, seam side down, and cook until golden brown on both sides. Transfer the blintzes to paper towels to drain for a moment. Serve immediately with the topping of your choice.

PALATSCHINKEN *8 rolled pancakes*

Palatschinken come from Austria and Hungary and might be thought of as a cross between a crêpe and a blintz. They are delicious rolled around a filling of warm apricot jam and sprinkled with chopped nuts and powdered sugar.

Whisk together in a large bowl:

1 cup all-purpose flour

3 tablespoons sugar

Pinch of salt

Add and whisk until smooth:

1 cup milk

2 large eggs

½ teaspoon vanilla

Pour the batter into a pitcher or other container with a pouring lip. Let stand while you prepare the filling or cover and refrigerate for up to 2 days.

In a small saucepan, bring to a boil:

1 cup apricot jam

1 tablespoon brandy or Grand Marnier

Remove from the heat. Place a nonstick or seasoned crêpe pan over medium heat. Coat the pan with a little:

Unsalted butter

Stir the batter and pour about ¼ cup into the pan, lifting the pan off the heat and tilting and rotating it so that the batter forms an even layer (thicker than for a crêpe or blintz). Cook until the underside is golden, then turn and cook the other side briefly, just until lightly browned. Remove the pancake to a warm plate. Continue cooking the rest of the pancakes, buttering the pan and stirring the batter before starting each one. While the next pancake is cooking, spread the last pancake with a spoonful of jam and roll it up. Place the rolled-up pancake on a baking sheet and sprinkle with:

Finely chopped walnuts (optional)

Keep warm in a 250°F oven while you finish cooking the rest. Serve immediately as is or with:

Sweetened whipped cream

ABOUT FRENCH TOAST

Americans eat French toast for breakfast, but the French serve it for dessert (and call it *pain perdu,* or "lost bread"). White bread makes the lightest French toast, but whole-wheat and rye breads work too. Not surprisingly, French bread is fine for this dish, and brioche and croissants are superb. American cooks have developed a number of variations on the basic theme, such as stuffing French toast with rich filling, baking it with a honey glaze, and even soaking the bread overnight, then baking it to golden goodness the following day.

FRENCH TOAST *6 slices*

When hungry breakfasters call out for French toast, this is what they hope they will get—plump slices of bread soaked in a rich bath of eggs and cream and sautéed to a honey-brown crispness in unsalted butter.

Whisk together in a shallow bowl:

⅔ cup whole milk, heavy cream, or half-and-half
4 large eggs
2 tablespoons sugar or pure maple syrup
1 teaspoon vanilla
¼ teaspoon salt

One or two at a time, add:

6 slices white or egg bread, with or without crusts

Turn the slices in the egg mixture until thoroughly saturated but not falling apart. In a skillet, melt over medium heat:

2 tablespoons unsalted butter

Add as many slices of bread to the skillet as will fit without crowding and cook until the underside is golden brown. Turn the bread and cook until the second side is golden. Serve immediately or keep warm in a 200°F oven while you finish cooking the rest. Dust each slice with:

Powdered sugar

and serve with:

Pure maple syrup
Bacon, ham, or sausages

HONEY-BUN FRENCH TOAST *6 slices*

An oven-baked version of French toast, toasty on one side, syrupy on the other.

Preheat the oven to 400°F.

In a 12 x 9-inch glass baking pan, place:

4 tablespoons (½ stick) unsalted butter
3 tablespoons honey

Heat in the oven until the butter is melted and the honey is bubbling. Do not allow the mixture to take on any color. Remove the pan from the oven, stir to mix the honey and butter, and sprinkle over the surface:

1 cup chopped pecans

While the butter and honey are melting, whisk together in a shallow bowl:

⅔ cup apple cider
4 large eggs
¼ teaspoon ground cinnamon
¼ teaspoon salt
Pinch of ground allspice (optional)

One or two at a time, add:

6 thick slices white or egg bread, with or without crusts

Turn the slices in the egg mixture until thoroughly saturated but not falling apart. Arrange the soaked bread over the nuts in the baking pan. Bake until the top is golden brown and the bottom is bubbly, 15 to 20 minutes. Serve immediately with:

Honey or pure maple syrup

HONEY-BUN ORANGE FRENCH TOAST

Prepare Honey-Bun French Toast, above, substituting fresh orange juice for the apple cider.

FILLED FRENCH TOAST *8 slices*

For variety, mix the cream cheese with thick fruit preserves or spiced apple butter.

Preheat the oven to 400°F. Lightly butter a baking sheet.

Whisk together:

8 ounces cream cheese, softened
¼ cup packed light brown sugar
¼ cup honey or pure maple syrup
1 teaspoon vanilla
Grated zest of ½ orange (optional)
Pinch of ground cinnamon
Pinch of salt

Stir in:

¼ cup finely chopped nuts (such as almonds or pecans), toasted, or shredded sweetened or unsweetened dried coconut (optional)

Trim the crusts from:

One 1-pound loaf white bread, preferably egg bread

Cut the loaf into 1-inch-thick slices; you probably will get 8 slices. Carefully work the knife into one side of each slice of bread to create a pocket that you can open with your fingers. Spoon an equal amount of filling into each pocket. Whisk together in a shallow bowl:

1 cup milk
3 large eggs
¼ cup all-purpose flour
3 tablespoons sugar
2 teaspoons baking powder
2 teaspoons vanilla
¼ teaspoon salt

One or two slices at a time, soak the bread in the egg mixture until thoroughly saturated but not falling apart. In a skillet, heat over medium-low:

1 tablespoon unsalted butter
1 tablespoon vegetable oil

Add as many slices of bread to the skillet as will fit without crowding and cook until the underside is just lightly golden. Turn the bread and cook until the second side is lightly golden. As each slice is cooked, transfer it to the baking sheet. Continue cooking the French toast, adding more butter and oil as needed.

Bake the sautéed slices until puffed and beautifully golden, about 6 minutes. Serve immediately with:

Powdered sugar, pure maple syrup, or honey

OVERNIGHT BAKED FRENCH TOAST *8 slices*

A great dish when guests are expected the next morning for brunch. The overnight soak produces very creamy and fluffy French toast. Whisk together in an 8 x 8-inch baking dish:

1 cup heavy cream, half-and-half, or whole milk
6 large eggs
¼ cup pure maple syrup
2 tablespoons packed light brown sugar
1 teaspoon vanilla
¼ teaspoon salt

Trim the crusts from:

8 slices white or egg bread

One slice at a time, turn the bread over in the egg mixture to coat it, then fit the coated bread into the pan in a double layer. Very gently press the bread with the back of a fork to compress the slices slightly. Cover with plastic wrap and press on the plastic to help the bread soak up the egg mixture. Refrigerate overnight.

Preheat the oven to 400°F. Lightly butter a baking sheet, preferably nonstick.

Using a wide spatula, lift the bread, slice by slice, out of the soaking mixture, allowing the excess liquid to drip back into the pan, and place on the baking sheet. Bake until puffed and golden, 12 to 15 minutes, turning the slices over halfway through the baking. Serve immediately with:

Pure maple syrup
Sliced fresh fruit (optional)

EGGLESS MAPLE FRENCH TOAST *6 slices*

Because this recipe contains neither eggs nor cream, it is not French toast as we know it—but it is irresistibly good and a model of simplicity.

Trim the crusts from:

6 slices white or egg bread

Measure:

¾ cup pure maple syrup

Brush 1 tablespoon of the syrup over each side of each slice of bread, stacking the slices on top of each other on a plate. Cover with a piece of wax paper and gently press on the paper to help the bread soak up the syrup. Let stand for about 5 minutes. Check that the bread is saturated before proceeding.

In a skillet, preferably nonstick, melt over medium heat until bubbly:

2 tablespoons unsalted butter

Add as many slices of syrup-soaked bread to the skillet as will fit without crowding. Cook the bread until golden and crispy on both sides, adding more butter as needed and taking care not to allow the butter to burn. Serve immediately or keep warm on a baking sheet in a 200°F oven while you finish cooking the rest. Serve with:

Pats of butter

MIXING AND CUTTING

Like cake batters, doughnut doughs are best made with room-temperature ingredients, and like pastry doughs, they are best handled minimally and chilled before rolling and cutting. The dough should be rolled or patted (most doughs will be soft enough to pat into shape) between ¼ and ½ inch thick and cut with a well-floured doughnut cutter—a double cutter with a handle. If that implement is unavailable, two biscuit or cookie cutters—one about 2½ to 3 inches in diameter and the other about 1 inch in diameter—will do as well. Once they are cut, transfer the doughnuts to a piece of wax paper and let them air-dry for about 10 minutes; the slight crust they will develop will reduce the amount of fat they will absorb during frying.

ABOUT DOUGHNUTS AND BEIGNETS

The doughnut harks back to the Dutch *Olie-Koechen* (fried cake), which probably came to America with Dutch settlers of the 1640s but may have arrived even earlier, with the Pilgrims, who spent several years in exile in Holland before making their way to Plymouth.

Yeast-based doughnuts require no adjustment for high altitudes. For quick-leavened doughnuts, reduce the baking powder or soda by one-quarter but do not use less than ½ teaspoon baking soda for each cup if sour milk or sour cream is used.

FRYING AND SERVING

You can fry doughnuts in any oil or solid shortening. Most important, the fat must be impeccably fresh and clean. Using a deep skillet, saucepan, or fryer—an electric deep fryer with a rotating basket is highly recommended—heat about 3 inches of fat to a steady temperature of 360° to 370°F, unless otherwise specified. To keep the fat at a constant temperature, fry no more than 2 or 3 doughnuts at a time, being careful not to crowd them. The easiest way to slip a doughnut into fat is to dip a metal spatula into the hot fat and then lift the doughnut with the spatula from the counter into the pan, once again immersing the spatula. It is hard to give exact cooking times. Color is a better indicator than the clock, so fry doughnuts until they are deeply golden on one side, then flip them over. When the doughnuts are done, remove them from the fryer with tongs or a long-tined fork and transfer them to a triple layer of paper towels to drain, patting off any excess fat. As soon as one doughnut comes out of the fryer, another should go in. If you want to sugar the doughnuts, shake them in a bag of granulated sugar while they are still warm or dust them with powdered sugar after they cool a bit. Doughnuts taste best while they are still warm or no more than an hour or two out of the fryer.

YEAST DOUGHNUTS

About twenty-four 2¾-inch doughnuts

This easy dough (ideal for making jelly doughnuts) has the perfect sponge for sopping up a honey dip and possesses a flavor mild enough to take a topping or stand on its own. It behaves much like a brioche dough, meaning that it will fall apart as you mix it and then come together. It is important that after each addition the dough be beaten until it comes together and cleans the sides of the bowl.

Stir together in a medium bowl:

1 cup warm (105° to 115°F) water

2 envelopes (2¼ teaspoons each) active dry yeast

Let stand until the yeast is dissolved, about 5 minutes. Add and stir until the mixture is smooth:

1 cup all-purpose flour

Cover the bowl tightly with plastic wrap and let rise in a warm place until bubbly, 30 to 60 minutes.

In a large bowl, beat until creamy, about 30 seconds:

10 tablespoons (1¼ sticks) unsalted butter

Gradually add and beat until light and fluffy:

⅔ cup sugar

Add, one at a time, beating for about 1 minute after each addition:

3 large eggs

Add and beat until blended:

2 teaspoons vanilla

1 teaspoon salt

Grated zest of ½ lemon or ¼ orange (optional)

Add the yeast mixture along with:

3½ cups all-purpose flour

Mix until the flour is fully incorporated and the dough, which will be very soft and golden, wraps around the dough hook or paddle and comes away from the sides of the bowl. (If you do not have a heavy-duty mixer, the batter can be beaten by hand with a wooden spoon.) Butter a large bowl, add the dough, and turn it so that its entire surface is lightly coated with butter. Cover the bowl tightly with plastic wrap and let rise in a warm place until doubled in volume, 1½ to 2 hours. Punch the dough down, wrap tightly in plastic and then a large plastic bag, and refrigerate for at least 3 hours or overnight. (The dough will rise some and may pop out of its plastic wrap, which is the reason for the large plastic bag. You don't want the dough to be exposed to the air and develop a crust.)

Working on a lightly floured surface with half of the dough at a time, pat or roll the dough out ½ inch thick. Cut with a well-floured doughnut cutter and place the doughnuts and holes on a sheet of wax paper. Repeat with the remaining half of the dough. Let rise, uncovered, in a warm place until soft and puffy to the touch, about 30 minutes.

Drop the doughnuts and holes, 2 or 3 at a time, into deep fat heated to 365°F, 809. Fry until golden on both sides. Drain well on paper towels and either dust with:

Powdered sugar

or shake in a bag with:

Sugar

Serve while still warm or within a few hours of frying.

JELLY DOUGHNUTS

Prepare the dough for Yeast Doughnuts, above. Pat or roll it out ¼ inch thick and cut into rounds instead of rings. Place in the center of each half of the rounds:

Heaping 1 teaspoon jelly or jam

Brush the edges of the filled rounds with:

1 large egg white, lightly beaten

Then top each with a plain round and pinch the edges together to seal. Repeat with the other rounds. Let rise until puffy and fry as directed above. Dust with:

Powdered sugar

HONEY-DIPPED DOUGHNUTS

Prepare Yeast Doughnuts, above. Pour into a small saucepan to a depth of 2 inches:

Honey

Bring to a boil. As soon as the doughnuts are removed from the fryer and drained, poke a few holes in their sides with a toothpick. Place each doughnut in the boiling honey, count about 15 seconds, then turn it over and give the second side similar treatment. Transfer to a rack placed over a piece of wax paper. Repeat with the remaining doughnuts, replenishing the honey as needed. Serve the doughnuts when the dip has dried.

BUTTERMILK POTATO DOUGHNUTS

About thirty 2¾-inch doughnuts

Potatoes passed through a ricer yield the most velvety doughnuts.

Peel and cut into small cubes:

2 medium baking potatoes

Boil the potatoes in a large quantity of lightly salted water until they can be pierced easily with the point of a knife. Drain the potatoes very well, then push them through a ricer, 408. Measure 1 cup riced potatoes; keep any leftovers for another use. Whisk together in a medium bowl:

3¾ cups all-purpose flour
2½ teaspoons baking powder
1 teaspoon salt
½ teaspoon baking soda
¼ teaspoon freshly grated or ground nutmeg

In a large bowl, beat until foamy:

2 large eggs

Gradually add and beat until thoroughly blended:

⅔ cup sugar

Stir in until blended:

1 cup buttermilk
4 tablespoons (½ stick) unsalted butter, melted
1 teaspoon vanilla

Stir in the riced potatoes. Add the dry ingredients and stir just until incorporated. The dough will be very soft. Pat the dough into a disk, wrap it in plastic, and refrigerate for at least 2 hours or up to 2 days. The dough will never become firm but it will be workable when cold. Working on a lightly floured surface with half of the dough at a time, pat or roll the dough out ½ inch thick. Cut with a well-floured doughnut cutter and place the doughnuts and holes on a sheet of wax paper. Repeat with the remaining half of the dough. Drop the doughnuts and holes, 2 or 3 at a time, into deep fat heated to 365°F, 809. Fry until golden on both sides. Drain well on paper towels and either dust with:

Powdered sugar

or shake in a bag with:

Sugar

Serve while still warm or within a few hours of frying.

SOUR CREAM CAKE DOUGHNUTS

About twelve 2¾-inch doughnuts

These doughnuts have an inviting tang and a firm crumb that will put you in mind of your favorite sour cream coffeecake.

Whisk together in a medium bowl:

2 cups all-purpose flour
2½ teaspoons baking powder
½ teaspoon baking soda
½ teaspoon salt
½ teaspoon ground cinnamon

In a large bowl, beat until foamy:

2 large eggs

Gradually add and beat until thoroughly blended:

½ cup sugar

Stir in until blended:

½ cup sour cream
1 teaspoon vanilla

Add the dry ingredients and stir just until incorporated. The dough will be very soft. Pat the dough into a disk, wrap it in plastic, and refrigerate for at least 2 hours or up to 2 days. The dough will never become firm but it will be workable when cold.

Working on a lightly floured surface, pat or roll the dough out ½ inch thick. Cut with a well-floured doughnut cutter, keeping the doughnut holes too. Drop the doughnuts and holes, 2 or 3 at a time, into deep fat heated to 365°F, 809. Fry until golden on both sides. Drain well on paper towels and either dust with:

Powdered sugar

or shake in a bag with:

Sugar or cinnamon and sugar

Serve while still warm or within a few hours of frying.

BEIGNETS

About 15 beignets

Beignets are a specialty of New Orleans, where they are traditionally served with chicory-flavored coffee.

Combine in a medium saucepan and bring to a steady boil:

½ cup water
4 tablespoons (½ stick) unsalted butter
1 tablespoon sugar
½ teaspoon salt

Add all at once:

½ cup all-purpose flour

Stir vigorously, without stopping, over medium heat until the mixture comes together and takes on a shine. Continue to cook, stirring constantly, for 2 minutes. When you remove the pan from the heat, you will notice that the flour has formed a light crust on the bottom of the pan. Transfer the mixture to a bowl. Add, one at a time, beating on medium speed for 2 to 3 minutes after each addition and scraping down the sides of the bowl:

4 large eggs

The mixture should be smooth, shiny, and fold over on itself in a ribbon when the beater is lifted. Beat in:

2 teaspoons vanilla

Immediately drop the dough, a scant tablespoon at a time, into deep fat heated to 365°F, 809. Fry 4 or 5 beignets at a time until puffed and golden on both sides. Drain well on paper towels and dust with:

Powdered sugar

COOKIES

The smell of baking cookies is one of life's most satisfying pleasures. Making cookies at home is so popular because it is so easy. Once you know a few simple secrets, they require only very basic ingredients, equipment, and techniques.

MIXING COOKIES

The method used to mix a dough is directly related to the texture of the finished cookie. Unlike cakes, which can all be made with an electric mixer, cookies can be made with an electric mixer, in a food processor, or by hand with a wooden spoon. For best results, follow the instructions in each recipe. Unless otherwise specified, it's best to let butter, flour, eggs, nuts, and other ingredients warm up almost to room temperature before using. If a recipe calls for "softened" butter, make sure it's not too cold and firm (which will make it too stiff and lumpy to fluff up or "cream" properly) or nearly melted (which will make it too thin to fluff up at all). If the butter is too cold or too warm, it can even change the temperature of the dough enough to significantly alter baking time. Once you add flour to the wet ingredients in a recipe, don't overbeat the dough; this can result in tough cookies, especially in reduced-fat recipes.

ABOUT INGREDIENTS AND SUBSTITUTIONS

Quite satisfactory results can be obtained by replacing up to half the butter with the same amount of regular nondiet stick margarine in the recipes. Do not substitute margarine for butter in shortbreads or butter cookies, though, because the flavor of these cookies depends so much on a truly buttery richness. Bleached flour produces a more tender, buttery cookie than unbleached flour, and has a less wheaty flavor. If you like to use whole-wheat flour, start with highly flavored cookies (those with molasses or chocolate, for instance), and replace no more than a third of the all-purpose flour with whole-wheat flour. If you can find it, whole-wheat pastry flour is best. However, cookies made even with this whole-wheat flour will always be slightly darker and heavier than the all-purpose-flour variety.

HANDLING DOUGH FOR ROLLED AND SHAPED COOKIES

Resist the temptation to add extra flour to make a cookie dough more manageable during shaping or rolling, as you might if you were making bread. To prevent most cookie doughs from sticking to your work surface and rolling pin, roll portions between sheets of wax or parchment paper, occasionally checking the underside of the paper and smoothing any creases, shown 826. Then keeping the paper attached, layer the dough on trays and chill until slightly firm. Molasses doughs are too sticky to be rolled between paper, but letting them rest at room temperature for several hours before rolling out tames them enough to allow you to get by with minimal added flour. With short, rich doughs that seem too soft to handle, on the other hand, just the right amount of chilling will bring them under control. Refrigerate them until they are firm enough to hold their shape, but remove them before they become too cold and stiff. For doughs that warm up and soften very rapidly, start with only a portion of the dough, keeping the rest refrigerated until needed.

When cutting or otherwise shaping cookies, try to keep them all about the same size and thickness, so that they bake evenly. And remember that if you choose to make cookies larger or smaller than the recipe specifies, the amount of spreading, the baking time, and the recipe yield will vary. The more you make cookies, the more adept you will become at dropping exact amounts of cookie dough and rolling dough to an even thickness each time, so that eventually your yields will be closer to those listed in the recipes.

BAKING COOKIES AT HIGH ALTITUDES

In general, up to 3,000 feet, no adjustments are necessary to obtain attractive, properly textured cookies. When baking above 3,000 feet, reduce the oven temperature by about 25 degrees, which helps the cookies retain moisture. It also helps to reduce the sugar in the recipe by 2 tablespoons for every 1 cup. For rich chocolaty or very sweet doughs, slightly reducing the baking powder may be helpful. Above 5,000 feet, it is sometimes necessary to reduce baking powder by half and sugar by about 2 tablespoons for every cup. In sour cream doughs, the baking soda should not be reduced beyond ½ teaspoon for every cup of sour cream.

REDUCED-FAT COOKIES

Because some fat is essential for flavor, tenderness, proper crisping, and browning in almost every kind of cookie (meringue kisses are a rare exception), we've significantly reduced fat without eliminating it entirely. Cookies that might originally have contained 4 to 8 grams of fat apiece now contain 1½ to 3½—enough to maintain good flavor and an attractive texture. We've also de-emphasized butter in favor of canola and corn oil. Some butter is usually needed to produce a manageable consistency and a hint of buttery taste, however, so we've left in a little bit.

Please don't be tempted to substitute low-fat margarine or "spread" for butter, since these products tend to have a high water content, which can turn cookie dough runny and yield a flattened-out and overdone end result. If you insist on avoiding butter, use regular nondiet stick margarine instead. You'll lose some flavor, but at least the consistency should be right. Wherever possible, our reduced-fat recipes also cut down on the number of egg yolks used. If a recipe does call for egg yolks, though, it's because they're essential for tenderness or flavor.

It is particularly important not to overbeat reduced-fat cookies, as this can turn lean doughs tough. Pay close attention to recommended baking times, too, and remove cookies from the oven the instant they're done, as lower fat means less moisture and these cookies can dry out quickly.

DECORATING COOKIES

We've always liked the idea of decorations that provide a clue to a cookie's flavor: a sprinkling of cinnamon and sugar to advertise a hint of spices; a few coconut shreds to signal a coconut filling. Coarsely chopped nuts or chocolate chips are wonderful toppings for big, flavorful, rough-textured cookies, but would be out of place on delicate wafers and crisps. Likewise, fine piping, tiny nonpareils, crystal sugar, or dainty dabs of jam are fine for tea cookies, but would seem fussy on hefty drop cookies and bars.

To ensure that nonpareils and other garnishes will stay on top of cookies, press them firmly into the dough before baking (use a wide-bladed spatula if the cookies are flat)—or secure them after baking with Royal Icing, 1009. Cookies can also be decorated with food-coloring paint. To paint cookies before baking, whisk together an egg yolk, about ¼ teaspoon water, and a drop of the desired food coloring. (Remember that blue coloring will turn green when mixed with the yellow yolk; for a true blue, use egg white instead.) For paint to be applied after baking, simply combine a drop of food coloring with a bit of water to dilute it to the appropriate intensity. (This color wash only shows up well on Springerle, sugar cookies, and other light-colored cookies.) Apply the paint in either case with a soft, fine-tipped paintbrush—or a small pastry brush if detail isn't important.

Don't overdo it, though. A good general rule is to keep cookie decorations simple.

BAKING COOKIES

Preheating the Oven: Always turn the oven on 20 minutes before baking.

Pans: Use medium- to heavy-gauge, shiny, rimless metal cookie sheets, shown below. They are specifically designed so that heat can circulate evenly over the cookies. Dark sheets may cause overbrowning or burning. A pan with high sides will both obstruct the flow of heat and make the cookies difficult to remove. Cookie sheets come in many sizes. But for most modern ovens, sheets in the 17 x 14-inch range are perfect. They can accommodate 12 to 16 medium cookies.

If your cookies burn on the bottom, even with shiny sheets, the first thing to do is invest in an oven thermometer to make sure the oven's setting and the interior temperature agree. It is surprising how many ovens are off in one direction or the other—sometimes by as much as 30 or 40 degrees! If this is not the problem, the most economical aproach is to try double panning—baking with one sheet on top of another. If this does not work, the final step might be buying very heavy-gauge pans or ones with an air-cushion inset, shown below.

Rimless cookie sheet

Preparing Cookie Sheets: Unless a recipe gives other instructions, always grease baking sheets with butter or shortening or coat with nonstick spray. Several varieties of cookies—shortbreads and other kinds that contain no eggs but have a high percentage of fat, for instance—can be baked on ungreased sheets. And a few, such as meringue kisses and others with a large proportion of egg whites and little or no fat, will stick tenaciously unless baked on parchment paper or on generously greased and floured cookie sheets.

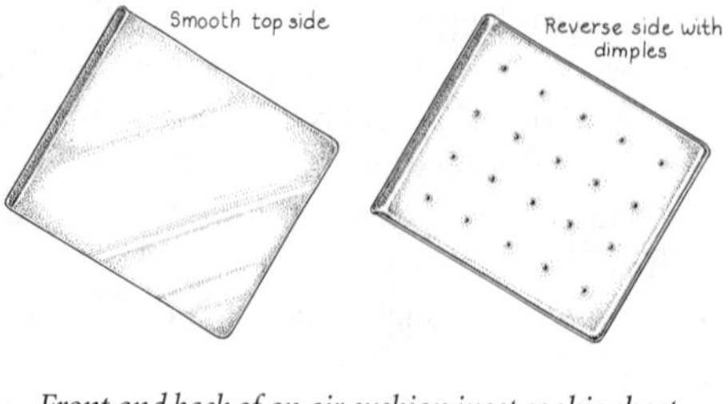

Front and back of an air cushion inset cookie sheet

Unless your oven is very large and your cookie sheets very small, bake only one sheet of cookies at a time. If you do bake more than one sheet at once, make sure the sheets are identical. Do not bake partial sheets of cookies, and do not leave large gaps between cookies; doing either may affect spreading, browning, crisping, and baking time. If there is only enough dough left for a few cookies, switch to a very small baking sheet, a 12-inch pizza pan, or an inverted metal pie pan, so the cookies can be spaced the required distance apart. This will ensure that the heat from the pan is absorbed evenly and that the amount of dough is right for the baking surface. Also, when a recipe specifies baking in the upper, middle, or lower third of the oven, be sure to follow instructions. Finally, rotate the cookie sheets halfway through baking, turning them front to back, to ensure even browning. (Note: This direction is repeated in those recipes where it is especially important.)

Use an inverted metal pie pan for the last bit of cookie dough

Timing: Many factors can affect baking time, so a range of suggested times is given in the recipes that follow. Always set your kitchen timer to the minimum time specified; it's easy to reset it and bake longer if necessary, but once a pan is forgotten and cookies are overbaked or burned, there is no remedy.

Removing Cookies from Sheets to Cool: When the cookies are done, remove the cookie sheet from the oven immediately. As soon as the cookies can be moved without crumbling or tearing, gently lift them one at a time with a wide, fine-bladed spatula and place them flat on racks until completely cool. Usually this will be in a minute or two, but it is a good idea to check by trying to lift a test cookie with a spatula every 30 seconds or so. Very tender, short cookies (those containing a lot of butter) may require considerable standing time, while thin, brittle ones may need almost none. (Where it's necessary to work very fast, we've noted this right in the recipe.) In any case, it is important not to dally when the cookies are ready, as they will continue to bake until removed from the cookie sheet and some may become rigid and stuck. Whenever cookies have inadvertently cooled and hardened, instead of prying them up and risking breakage, return the baking sheet to the oven for a few minutes to soften them again.

Cookie sheets should also be cooled completely between batches to keep the dough from warming too much, which can cause the cookies to flatten and spread and in some cases can even cause the butter in the cookies to melt. To avoid any problems, have a couple of extra cookie sheets on hand and rotate among them.

STORING COOKIES

Packaging: Plastic storage containers and sealable plastic bags keep cookies airtight. Still, as long as their lids fit tightly, old-fashioned cookie tins do the job nicely and have a lot more charm. Never store cookies in any kind of container until they have completely cooled. Warm cookies will produce steam, which will cause the entire batch to soften, and eventually to spoil. If cookies have been iced or painted, let the icing or coloring set up and dry completely before storing them.

Separating Flavors: Cookies can generally be stored at room temperature for 1 to 2 weeks. Pack each type of cookie in a separate container. Otherwise, butter cookies and mild bars will quickly take on the flavors of the spicy, citrusy kinds, and snaps and crisps will go soft from moisture borrowed from thicker, chunkier ones. For extra-large cookies and oversized bars, store individually in small sealable plastic bags.

Freezing: Although cookies have a well-deserved reputation for keeping better than other baked desserts, most are truly at their peak of flavor in the first few days. Even with cookies that benefit from some mellowing, like the spicy honey kinds, fresh flavors begin to fade after several weeks. And cookies laden with butter and nuts may develop off-flavors as the butterfat and the oil in the nuts go stale. Fortunately, most cookie varieties freeze well, staying moist and retaining their just-baked flavor for a month if packed in airtight containers. Brownies, chocolate chip and sugar cookies, and thin, crispy varieties freeze particularly well. If freezing bar cookies, pack them away uncut, then cut into servings when partially thawed. Cookies that are sprinkled with or rolled in sugar, or that are to be frosted or glazed, should be frozen without these enhancements. Allow them to defrost completely before sugar coating, glazing, or frosting.

If you want to eat frozen cookies right away, lay them on baking sheets and warm in a preheated 300°F oven for a few minutes. Homemade, or even store-bought, cookies that have gone limp from exposure to humidity can also be rejuvenated and crisped this way. When setting cookies out to thaw, it is best to leave them partially unwrapped so they can breathe and condensation doesn't build up. Loosen the lids of plastic boxes or metal tins and untie and partially open plastic bags. Do not let cookies stand out long if the weather is very humid—the crispy varieties, in particular, may begin to droop. Cookies that have dried out and hardened can also be refreshed. Slip a piece of apple or dampened paper towel into an open sealable plastic bag or loosely crumpled piece of aluminum foil. Insert into the container of cookies and close the lid tightly. In a few days the cookies will have softened and the apple or towel should be removed.

PACKAGING COOKIES FOR SHIPPING

The best choices are small and medium cookies, at least ¼ inch thick and firm in consistency. Although softer, brownies, blondies, and other bar cookies also usually ship well—with the exception of bars with sticky fillings or icings. (Cut bar cookies into portions and wrap individually in plastic wrap, then pack in airtight containers before shipping.)

More delicate varieties can also be mailed successfully if they are packed carefully in tins or tough plastic boxes with plenty of crumpled wax or parchment paper added to keep them from jostling each other. Extremely thin, brittle cookies and tender, crumbly ones do not travel well, nor do cookies with sticky glazes or with moist fillings such as jam or buttercream. Chewy-soft or fragile meringue kisses and other egg white cookies are likewise an unwise choice; in fact, they may disintegrate completely if thrown about.

After cookies are placed in durable rigid containers, they then need to be packed in larger boxes filled with Styrofoam bits, plastic bubble sheets, crumpled newspaper, or other airy filler to cushion the goodies inside from bumps and knocks. As added insurance that the cookies will arrive at their destination unbroken, consider shipping by air.

PACKAGING COOKIES FOR GIFT GIVING

Pretty metal cookie tins, ceramic cookie jars, clear glass storage jars, and decorative wooden boxes all make a gift of home-baked cookies more special. Secure containers with loose lids by tying them up with a beautiful ribbon. If you have a modicum of sewing ability, you can also present cookies in fabric sacks tied with ribbon or fancy twist-ties made with wire ribbon. (Slip a plastic bag, cut down to size if necessary, inside the fabric for an airtight liner.) Small, dainty cookies can also be tucked in colored bonbon papers or mini-cupcake cups in flat candy boxes. For a special touch, tie a ribbon around the gift bag or box and secure a cookie cutter in the bow.

CHRISTMAS COOKIES AS ORNAMENTS

To prepare a cookie ornament for hanging, use a toothpick to poke a hole through the uncooked shaped dough. When the cookie is baked, remove the toothpick, wiggling it a bit if necessary to widen the hole. Loop ribbon, colored yarn or string, rickrack, or even fine braid or lace trim through the hole and tie in a pretty bow. The "snow"-covered gingerbread house, 842, also makes a charming decoration for the table or mantelpiece.

ABOUT BAR COOKIES

Since these are simply spread in a pan, baked, and cut into serving pieces, the time normally taken up with forming dozens of individual cookies is completely eliminated. Still, there can be a lot of variety in bars. They can range from soft-cakey to chewy-gooey to crunchy and brittle. They can also be left plain, or topped with nuts, powdered sugar, or icing; and cut into squares, from very small to very large, or sliced into narrow strips.

When making bar cookies, pay close attention to the size of the pan called for in each recipe. Variations will throw off the baking time and may affect the texture as well. If the pan is too large, the dough may dry out and the bars will be too thin. If the pan is too small, the bars may become gummy in the center or more cakey than they should be.

A number of bar recipes call for lining the pan with aluminum foil, leaving enough overhang on two opposing ends to use as handles, shown above. The easiest way to shape the foil is to turn the pan upside down, then smooth the foil around its contours until the right shape is achieved. Foil not only makes cleaning up easy, but means the cooled slab can be lifted from the pan and transferred to a board for cutting in one fell swoop. For bars pretty enough to set out on a buffet table, use a large, sharp knife, and trim away the dry edges before cutting them, wiping bits of cookie off the knife with a damp paper towel as you work.

Aluminum-foil-lined pan for bar cookies

BROWNIES COCKAIGNE

Sixteen 2¼ x 2¼-inch or twenty-four 2¼ x 2-inch bars

This recipe has appeared in *Joy* since the original 1931 edition.

Have all ingredients at room temperature, 68° to 70°F. Position a rack in the center of the oven. Preheat the oven to 350°F. Line a 13 x 9-inch baking pan with greased aluminum foil, allowing it to overhang the 2 narrow ends of the pan by about 2 inches.

In a large, heavy saucepan over very low heat, melt, stirring constantly until the mixture is smooth:

4 ounces unsweetened chocolate, coarsely chopped
8 tablespoons (1 stick) unsalted butter

Set aside to cool completely. Stir in:

2 cups sugar
2 teaspoons vanilla

Stir in until well combined:

4 large eggs

Stir in just until combined:

1 cup all-purpose flour
1 cup chopped walnuts or pecans

Scrape the batter into the pan and spread to the edges. Bake until the center is almost firm when lightly pressed and a toothpick inserted in the center comes

ESPECIALLY FOR CHRISTMAS

We have placed a Christmas tree symbol ▲ next to the recipes for cookies traditionally made during the holiday season.

out clean, but still moist at the bottom, 23 to 28 minutes. Remove the pan to a rack and let stand until completely cool. Using the overhanging foil as handles, lift the brownie to a cutting board. Carefully peel off the foil. Cut into bars.

CHEESECAKE BROWNIES

Twelve 2 x 2-inch bars

Position a rack in the center of the oven. Preheat the oven to 350°F. Line an 8 x 8-inch baking pan with greased aluminum foil, allowing it to overhang 2 opposing ends of the pan by about 2 inches.

Whisk together thoroughly:

1 cup all-purpose flour
¼ teaspoon salt
¼ teaspoon baking soda

Melt, stirring constantly, in a large, heavy saucepan over very low heat:

6 ounces bittersweet chocolate, or 5½ ounces semisweet and ½ ounce unsweetened chocolate, coarsely chopped
4 tablespoons (½ stick) unsalted butter

Let cool to barely warm. Add and beat with a wooden spoon until well blended:

⅔ cup sugar
2½ teaspoons vanilla

Beat in 1 at a time until well combined:

2 large eggs

Stir in:

2 tablespoons light corn syrup

Stir the flour mixture into the chocolate mixture until well blended and smooth. Scrape the batter into the pan and spread to the edges. Bake for 12 minutes.

Meanwhile, combine in a food processor until well blended:

12 ounces cream cheese, softened and cut into chunks
½ cup sugar
2 tablespoons unsalted butter, melted
1 large egg
1 teaspoon vanilla
¼ teaspoon finely grated lemon zest

Spread the cream cheese topping evenly over the chocolate layer. Reduce the oven temperature to 325°F.

Return the pan to the oven. Bake until the cheesecake layer is just tinged with brown and beginning to crack on top and a toothpick inserted in the center comes out clean, but still moist and fudgy at the bottom, 32 to 36 minutes. Remove the pan to a rack and let stand until completely cool. Refrigerate until well chilled before slicing. Using the overhanging foil as handles, lift the brownie to a cutting board. Carefully peel off the foil. Cut into bars.

CHEWY BROWNIES (REDUCED FAT)

Twelve 2¾ x 2-inch bars

These brownies contain just under 4 grams of fat apiece.

Position a rack in the center of the oven. Preheat the oven to 350°F. Line an 8 x 8-inch baking pan with greased or nonstick spray-coated aluminum foil, allowing it to overhang 2 opposing ends of the pan by about 2 inches.

Whisk together thoroughly:

¾ cup all-purpose flour
1½ tablespoons unsweetened nonalkalized cocoa, sifted
¼ teaspoon baking soda
¼ teaspoon salt

Melt, stirring constantly, in a large, heavy saucepan over very low heat:

4 ounces semisweet or bittersweet chocolate, coarsely chopped
2 teaspoons corn or canola oil

Remove from the heat and stir in until well combined:

½ cup packed light brown sugar
¼ cup sugar
2 tablespoons light corn syrup
1 tablespoon water
2 teaspoons vanilla

Add and stir until the sugar is dissolved:

2 large egg whites

Stir the flour mixture into the chocolate mixture until well blended and smooth.

Scrape the batter into the pan and spread to the edges. Bake until the center of the top is almost firm when lightly pressed and a toothpick inserted in the center comes out clean, but still moist and fudgy at the bottom, 20 to 25 minutes. Remove the pan to a rack and let stand until completely cool.

Using the overhanging foil as handles, lift the brownie to a cutting board. Carefully peel off the foil. Cut into bars.

BLONDIES

Twelve 2 x 2-inch bars

Position a rack in the center of the oven. Preheat the oven to 350°F. Line an 8 x 8-inch baking pan with greased aluminum foil, allowing it to overhang 2 opposing ends of the pan by about 2 inches.

Toast, stirring occasionally, in a baking pan until very lightly browned, 5 to 8 minutes:

1 cup chopped pecans

Set aside to cool. Whisk together thoroughly:

1 cup all-purpose flour
¼ teaspoon baking powder
⅛ teaspoon baking soda
⅛ teaspoon salt

In a large, heavy saucepan, melt, then boil, stirring constantly, until light golden brown, about 4 minutes:

8 tablespoons (1 stick) unsalted butter

Remove from the heat and stir in until well blended:

⅔ cup packed light brown sugar
¼ cup sugar

Let cool to barely warm. Stir in until well combined:

1 large egg
1 large egg yolk
1 tablespoon light corn syrup
1½ teaspoons vanilla

Stir in the flour mixture and the pecans until well blended. Scrape the batter into the pan and spread to the edges. Bake until the top is golden brown and a toothpick inserted in the thickest part comes out clean, 28 to 33 minutes. Remove the pan to a rack and let stand until completely cool. Using the overhanging foil as handles, lift the blondie to a cutting board. Carefully peel off the foil. Cut into bars.

DREAM BARS (ANGEL BARS)

Twelve 2¾ x 2⅓-inch bars

Many a copy of *Joy* has been sold on the strength of this recipe.

Have all ingredients at room temperature, 68° to 70°F. Position a rack in the center of the oven. Preheat the oven to 350°F. Line an 11 x 7-inch or similar 2-quart rectangular baking pan with greased aluminum foil, allowing it to overhang the 2 narrow ends of the pan by about 2 inches.

Beat on medium speed until very fluffy and well blended:

4 tablespoons (½ stick) unsalted butter, softened
2 tablespoons sugar
1 large egg yolk
¼ teaspoon vanilla

Stir in, then knead until well blended and smooth:

¾ cup all-purpose flour

Firmly press the dough into the pan to form a smooth, even layer. Bake for 10 minutes; set aside to cool slightly.

Toast, stirring occasionally, in a baking pan until the coconut is very lightly browned, 7 to 10 minutes:

1½ cups chopped pecans or walnuts
1 cup flaked or shredded sweetened coconut

Beat on medium speed or with a wooden spoon until well combined:

2 large eggs
1 cup packed light brown sugar
1½ tablespoons all-purpose flour
¼ teaspoon baking powder
⅛ teaspoon salt
1½ teaspoons vanilla

Stir the nut mixture into the egg mixture. Spread the mixture evenly over the baked layer. Bake until the top is firm and golden brown and a toothpick inserted in the center comes out slightly wet, 20 to 25 minutes. Remove the pan to a rack to cool slightly. While the bar is still warm, stir together:

2 tablespoons unsalted butter, softened
⅔ cup powdered sugar
2 teaspoons fresh lemon juice
½ teaspoon vanilla

If necessary, stir in enough water to yield a spreadable consistency. Spread the icing evenly over the top. Let stand until completely cool and the icing is set. Using the overhanging foil as handles, lift the bar to a cutting board. Carefully peel off the foil. Cut into bars.

CHOCOLATE-GLAZED TOFFEE BARS

Twenty-four 2⅔ x 1-inch bars

A cookie made up of a chewy brown sugar-pecan toffee layer spread over shortbread and topped with chocolate.

Grease an 8 x 8-inch baking pan.

Whisk together thoroughly:

⅔ cup all-purpose flour
1½ tablespoons sugar
⅛ teaspoon salt

Sprinkle over the top:

4 tablespoons (½ stick) cold unsalted butter, cut into small pieces

Using a pastry blender, 2 knives, or your fingertips, cut in the butter until the mixture resembles fine crumbs. Sprinkle over the top and stir in to blend:

2 teaspoons milk

Knead until the milk is distributed and the particles begin to hold together. If necessary, add a teaspoon or two more milk, until the mixture holds together but is not wet. (Alternatively, in a food processor, process the dry ingredients and butter in on/off pulses until the mixture resembles coarse crumbs; be careful not to overprocess. A bit at a time, add the milk, and process in on/off pulses until the particles begin to hold together; if necessary, add just enough additional milk so the mixture holds together but is not wet.) Firmly press the dough into the pan to form a smooth, even layer. Refrigerate for 15 minutes.

Meanwhile, position a rack in the center of the oven. Preheat the oven to 350°F.

Bake the chilled dough for 10 minutes; set aside to cool slightly. Toast, stirring occasionally in a baking pan, until very lightly browned, 5 to 8 minutes:

1½ cups chopped pecans

Set aside to cool. Combine in a medium, heavy saucepan and, stirring frequently, bring to a boil over medium heat:

5 tablespoons unsalted butter, cut into pieces
½ cup packed light brown sugar
2 tablespoons clover or other mild honey
1 tablespoon milk
⅛ teaspoon salt

Boil the mixture, uncovered, for 3 minutes; remove from the heat. Stir in the toasted pecans along with:

1 teaspoon vanilla

Spread the mixture evenly over the baked layer. Bake until the crumb mixture is bubbly, golden brown, and just slightly darker at the edges, 17 to 20 minutes. Remove the pan to a rack to cool slightly. Sprinkle over the top:

¼ cup semisweet chocolate chips

Let stand for several minutes until the chocolate chips partially melt, then smooth across the surface with a table knife to partially spread the chocolate. (The surface should not be completely covered with chocolate.)

Sprinkle over the top:

2 tablespoons finely chopped pecans

Let the chocolate cool until thickened but still slightly soft, then cut into bars; let cool completely before lifting the bars from the pan. Retrace the cuts to separate the bars, if necessary.

LEMON CURD BARS COCKAIGNE

Eighteen 3 x 2-inch bars

Ethan Becker loves lemon in any form but is especially partial to these bars.

Position a rack in the center of the oven. Preheat the oven to 325°F. Have ready a 13 x 9-inch baking pan.

Sift together into a large bowl:

1½ cups all-purpose flour
¼ cup powdered sugar

Sprinkle over the top:

12 tablespoons (1½ sticks) cold unsalted butter, cut into small pieces

Using a pastry blender, 2 knives, or your fingertips, cut in the butter until the mixture is the size of small peas. Using your fingers, press the mixture into the bottom of the pan and ¾ inch up the sides to avoid leaking during baking. Bake until golden brown, 20 to 30 minutes. Set aside to cool slightly. Reduce the oven temperature to 300°F.

Whisk together until well combined:

6 large eggs
3 cups sugar

Stir in:

Grated zest of 1 lemon
1 cup plus 2 tablespoons fresh lemon juice (about 5 lemons)

Sift over the top and stir in until well blended and smooth:

½ cup all-purpose flour

Pour the batter over the baked crust. Bake until set, about 35 minutes. Remove the pan to a rack to cool completely before cutting into bars.

RASPBERRY STREUSEL BARS

Twenty 2½ x 2⅛-inch bars

Generously grease a 13 x 9-inch baking pan.

Sift together into a large bowl:

2 cups all-purpose flour
¼ cup sugar
¼ teaspoon salt

Sprinkle over the top:

12 tablespoons (1½ sticks) cold unsalted butter, cut into small pieces

Using a pastry blender, 2 knives, or your fingertips, cut in the butter until the mixture resembles fine crumbs.

Stir together:

3 tablespoons milk
1 teaspoon almond extract

Sprinkle the milk mixture over the flour mixture. Lightly stir to blend. Knead until the milk is distributed and the particles begin to hold together. If necessary, add a teaspoon or two more milk, until the mixture holds together but is not wet. (Alternatively, in a food processor, process the dry ingredients and butter in on/off pulses until the mixture resembles coarse crumbs; be careful not to overprocess. A bit at a time, add the milk mixture, and process in on/off pulses until the particles begin to hold together; if necessary, add just enough additional milk so the mixture holds together but is not wet.)

Firmly press the dough into the pan to form a smooth, even layer. Refrigerate for 15 minutes.

Meanwhile, position a rack in the center of the oven and another in the upper third. Preheat the oven to 375°F.

Bake the chilled dough in the center of the oven until

barely firm in the center, 12 to 15 minutes. Spread evenly over the hot crust:

1 cup seedless raspberry preserves or jam

To prepare the streusel, whisk together thoroughly:

1¾ cups all-purpose flour
⅔ cup sugar
½ teaspoon ground cinnamon
¼ teaspoon salt

Sprinkle over the top:

8 tablespoons (1 stick) cold unsalted butter, cut into small pieces

Using a pastry blender, 2 knives, or your fingertips, cut in the butter until the mixture is well blended. (Alternatively, combine the flour, sugar, cinnamon, and salt in a food processor. Sprinkle the butter over the top. Process until the mixture is well blended. Turn out into a bowl.) Using a fork, stir into the flour mixture 1 at a time:

¾ cup sliced blanched or unblanched almonds
½ cup old-fashioned rolled oats

Beat together lightly and stir into the flour mixture until the streusel is moistened and forms small clumps:

1 large egg
2 tablespoons milk

(If necessary, add a teaspoon or two more milk, until the mixture is just moist enough to clump.) Sprinkle the streusel evenly over the raspberry preserves, breaking up any large clumps with a fork or your fingertips. Bake in the upper third of the oven until the streusel is nicely browned and the raspberry mixture is bubbly, 25 to 30 minutes. Remove the pan to a rack to cool completely. Cut into bars.

SCOTTISH SHORTBREAD

Twenty-four 2⅔ x 1-inch bars

Fragrant with butter, this cookie is easy to make. Some shortbread lovers substitute rice flour or cornstarch for a portion of the all-purpose flour. Unlike wheat flour, rice flour and cornstarch do not develop gluten, and therefore produce an especially crumbly and tender shortbread. If desired, substitute ⅓ cup rice flour or cornstarch for an equal amount of all-purpose flour.

Position a rack in the center of the oven. Preheat the oven to 300°F. Have ready an 8 x 8-inch baking pan or a rectangular shortbread mold.

Beat on medium speed until very fluffy and well blended:

10 tablespoons (1¼ sticks) unsalted butter, softened
¼ cup powdered sugar
1½ tablespoons sugar
¼ teaspoon salt

Gradually sift over the top while stirring:

1½ cups all-purpose flour

Lightly knead until well blended and smooth. If the dough is too dry to hold together, sprinkle a few drops of water over it, adding only enough to hold the particles together and being careful not to overmoisten it. Firmly press the dough into the pan or mold to form a smooth, even layer. If baking in a pan, pierce the dough deeply with a fork all over in a decorative pattern. Bake until the shortbread is faintly tinged with pale gold and just slightly darker at the edges, 45 to 50 minutes. Remove the pan to a rack and let cool until barely warm. Cut almost through the dough to form bars. If desired, sprinkle with:

1 to 2 teaspoons sugar

Let stand until completely cool. Gently retrace the cuts and separate into bars.

CHOCOLATE SHORTBREAD

Fifteen 3 x 2½-inch bars

Our friend Mildred Kroll used to make this quick version of shortbread as a snack for her kids when they went off to college.

Position a rack in the center of the oven. Preheat the oven to 300°F. Have ready a 13 x 9-inch baking pan.

Beat on medium speed until very fluffy and well blended:

½ pound (2 sticks) unsalted butter, softened
½ cup superfine sugar

Melt, stirring often, in the top of a double boiler or in a microwave on medium:

2 ounces semisweet or bittersweet chocolate

Remove from the heat and let cool slightly. Sift over the top:

2 cups all-purpose flour

Add the melted chocolate, then stir until well blended. Press the dough into the pan to form a smooth even layer. Bake until the top is firm when lightly pressed and a toothpick inserted in the center comes out clean, about 40 minutes. Remove the pan to a rack and let cool until barely warm. Cut into bars and transfer to a rack to cool.

MOTHER KROLL'S LEBKUCHEN

Twenty-four 2 x 2-inch bars

These German cookies date back to the Middle Ages, when honey was the everyday sweetener. This recipe was given to us by Carolyn Reidy, the president of our publishing company. Carolyn's mother, Mildred Kroll, comes from a long line of cookie bakers, and this is a family favorite at Christmas.

Position a rack in the center of the oven. Preheat the oven to 400°F. Line a 13 x 9-inch baking pan with greased aluminum foil, allowing it to overhang the 2 narrow ends of the pan by about 2 inches.

Bring to a boil in a large, heavy saucepan:

⅓ cup honey

Remove from the heat and let cool completely. Stir in:

¾ cup packed light or dark brown sugar
1 large egg, lightly beaten
1 tablespoon fresh lemon juice
1 teaspoon grated lemon zest

Combine and sift over the honey mixture:

2½ cups sifted all-purpose flour
½ teaspoon baking soda
1 teaspoon ground cinnamon
1 teaspoon ground cloves
½ teaspoon ground allspice
½ teaspoon ground nutmeg

Stir together:

⅓ cup chopped blanched almonds
⅓ cup chopped citron

Add to the honey mixture and stir until well blended. Firmly press the dough into the pan to form a smooth, even layer. Bake until a toothpick inserted in the center comes out almost clean, 18 to 20 minutes.

Meanwhile, stir together until smooth:

1 cup powdered sugar
2 tablespoons fresh lemon juice
¼ teaspoon vanilla

If necessary, stir in enough water to yield a spreadable consistency. While the bar is still warm, spread the icing evenly over the top. Immediately mark into squares and decorate by placing in the center of each square:

1 candied cherry

Arrange around each cherry in an X shape originating from each corner:

4 whole blanched almonds

Remove the pan to a rack and let stand until completely cool and the icing is set. Using the overhanging foil as handles, lift the bar to a cutting board. Carefully peel off the foil. Cut into bars. If possible, let the cookies age for at least 2 weeks to allow the spices to ripen. Lebkuchen will keep for months in an airtight container.

ABOUT DROP COOKIES

Except for bars, drop cookies are the easiest cookies to make, because shaping usually involves nothing more than dropping dough from a spoon. A few recipes call for patting down the dough or spreading it out with the tip of a knife. In most cases, drop cookies are very forgiving: if the mixture is slightly stiffer or softer than expected, no harm is done; the results will just be a little flatter or puffier than usual.

Occasionally, however, when the batter must be very fluid, as with Pecan Lace, 823, the consistency has to be just right for the desired amount of spreading. When working with this kind of batter, you may want to test bake a cookie or two. If the finished cookie is too thick or has spread too much during baking, stir in a little liquid or flour to thin or stiffen the mixture.

The recipes call for dropping dough or batter from a *measuring* teaspoon or tablespoon. This is for the sake of precision and helps ensure that recipe yields and baking times are accurate.

CLASSIC CHOCOLATE CHIP COOKIES

About 3 dozen 2½-inch cookies

Position a rack in the center of the oven. Preheat the oven to 375°F. Grease cookie sheets. Whisk together thoroughly:

1 cup plus 2 tablespoons all-purpose flour
½ teaspoon baking soda

Beat on medium speed until very fluffy and well blended:

8 tablespoons (1 stick) unsalted butter, softened
½ cup sugar
½ cup packed light brown sugar

Add and beat until well combined:

1 large egg
¼ teaspoon salt
1½ teaspoons vanilla

Stir the flour mixture into the butter mixture until well blended and smooth. Stir in:

1 cup semisweet chocolate chips
¾ cup chopped walnuts or pecans (optional)

Drop the dough by heaping measuring teaspoonfuls onto the sheets, spacing about 2 inches apart. Bake, 1 sheet at a time, until the cookies are just slightly colored on top and rimmed with brown at the edges, 8 to 10 minutes; rotate the sheet halfway through baking for even browning. Remove the sheet to a rack and let stand until the cookies firm slightly, about 2 minutes. Transfer the cookies to racks to cool.

OATMEAL CHOCOLATE CHIP COOKIES (REDUCED FAT)

About 3 dozen 2½- to 2¾-inch cookies

These cookies have 3.3 grams of fat apiece.

This recipe was developed to give chocolate chip cookie lovers a lean alternative.

Position a rack in the center of the oven. Preheat the oven to 375°F. Coat cookie sheets with nonstick spray.

Whisk together thoroughly:

1¼ cups all-purpose flour
¾ teaspoon baking soda
¾ teaspoon baking powder
¼ teaspoon salt

Beat on medium speed until well blended:

¼ cup corn or canola oil
2 tablespoons unsalted butter, softened
1 cup packed dark brown sugar
1 large egg
1 large egg white
⅓ cup light or dark corn syrup
1 tablespoon skim milk
2½ teaspoons vanilla

Stir into the batter:

2 cups old-fashioned rolled oats
1 cup reduced-fat semisweet chocolate chips

Let the mixture stand for 10 minutes so the oats can absorb some moisture. Stir in the flour mixture; the dough will be slightly soft. Drop the dough by heaping measuring tablespoonfuls onto the sheets, spacing about 2½ inches apart.

Bake, 1 sheet at a time, until the cookies are tinged with brown all over and the centers are just barely firm when lightly pressed, 7 to 10 minutes; be careful not to overbake. Remove the sheet to a rack and let stand until the cookies firm slightly, about 2 minutes. Transfer the cookies to racks to cool.

CLASSIC OATMEAL COOKIES

About 3½ dozen 3-inch cookies

These are homey and nubby-textured and have a mild brown sugar and oats flavor.

Position a rack in the upper third of the oven. Preheat the oven to 350°F. Grease cookie sheets.

Whisk together thoroughly:

1¾ cups all-purpose flour
¾ teasooon baking soda
¾ teaspoon baking powder
½ teaspoon salt
½ teaspoon ground cinnamon
½ teaspoon ground nutmeg

Beat on medium speed until well blended:

½ pound (2 sticks) unsalted butter, softened
1½ cups packed light or dark brown sugar
¼ cup sugar
2 large eggs
2½ teaspoons vanilla

Stir the flour mixture into butter mixture until well blended and smooth. Stir in:

1 cup raisins, chopped
3½ cups old-fashioned rolled oats

Drop the dough by heaping measuring tablespoonfuls onto the sheets, spacing about 3 inches apart. With lightly greased hands, lightly press the cookies down to form ½-inch-thick rounds. (If necessary, wipe off your hands and regrease to prevent the dough from sticking to them.) Bake, 1 sheet at a time, until the cookies are lightly browned all over and almost firm when lightly pressed in the center of the top, 6 to 9 minutes; rotate the sheet halfway through baking for even browning. Remove the sheet to a rack and let stand until the cookies firm slightly, about 2 minutes. Transfer the cookies to racks to cool.

TUILES (FRENCH ALMOND WAFERS)

2½ to 3 dozen 3-inch wafers

These curled wafers are often brought to the table at the end of a special dinner and served with chocolate truffles, coffee, and brandy. Their name is the French word for tiles, because they are shaped like the curved terra-cotta roof tiles so prevalent in the south of France. Almost paper thin, with a subtle almond flavor, tuiles are curled by being draped, while still warm and pliable, over a rolling pin until cool and firm. The step that requires attention is removing them from the baking sheet. The trick is to use a wide spatula with a very thin blade and to work very quickly. Cookie sheets need to be clean and cool before you make a new batch.

Have all ingredients at room temperature, 68° to 70°F. Position a rack in the upper third of the oven. Preheat the oven to 350°F. Very generously grease cookie sheets or cover with parchment paper or well-greased

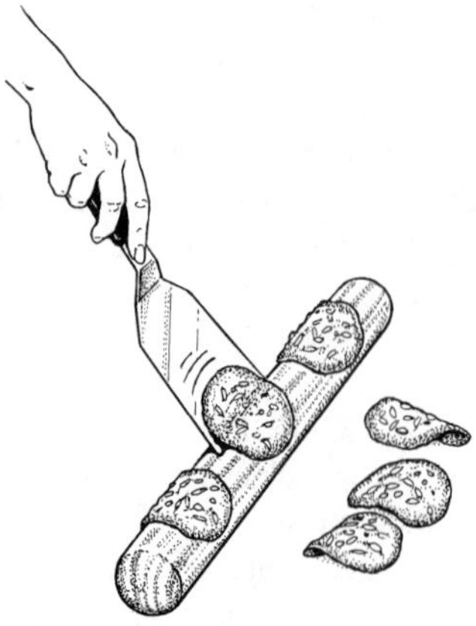

aluminum foil. Have ready several rolling pins or bottles the same width as the rolling pin to shape the wafers.

Warm, stirring constantly, over very low heat until very soft but not thin and runny:

5 tablespoons unsalted butter

Whisk together until very frothy:

2 large egg whites
⅛ teaspoon salt
⅓ cup plus 1 tablespoon sugar
¼ teaspoon almond extract
¼ teaspoon vanilla

Gradually whisk in:

½ cup sifted cake flour (not self-rising)

A bit at a time, whisk in the softened butter until the mixture is well blended and smooth.

Drop the batter by heaping measuring tablespoonfuls onto the sheets, spacing about 3 inches apart. Don't crowd, as the wafers will spread a great deal. Using the tip of a knife and working in a circular motion, spread each portion into a 3-inch round. Very generously sprinkle the rounds with:

½ to ⅔ cup sliced blanched or unblanched almonds, coarsely chopped

Bake, 1 sheet at a time, until the wafers are rimmed with ½ inch of golden brown, 6 to 9 minutes; rotate the sheet halfway through baking for even browning. Remove the sheet to a rack and let stand for a few seconds. As soon as the wafers can be lifted without tearing, loosen them with a thin-bladed wide metal spatula and slide them, bottom side down, onto rolling pins or bottles. (Remove the wafers to the rolling pins 1 at a time, so the others remain warm and pliable. If some of the wafers cool too quickly to shape on the rolling pins, return the sheet to the oven briefly to warm and soften them.) As soon as the tuiles are firm, transfer to racks to cool.

PECAN LACE

About 6 dozen 3¼-inch wafers

Since much of the appeal of these see-through wafers is in their brittle, caramelized texture, make them on a dry day.

Have all ingredients at room temperature, 68° to 70°F. Position a rack in the upper third of the oven. Preheat the oven to 350°F. Grease cookie sheets or cover with well-greased aluminum foil.

Toast, stirring constantly, in a baking pan until very lightly browned, 5 to 6 minutes:

½ cup finely chopped pecans

Set aside to cool. Increase the oven temperature to 375°F.

Melt in a medium saucepan over medium heat:

10 tablespoons (1¼ sticks) unsalted butter

Adjust the heat and boil the butter gently, stirring occasionally, until the solids on the bottom of the pan turn light brown, 3 to 4 minutes. Remove from the heat and stir in until well blended:

1 cup packed light brown sugar
¼ cup light corn syrup
1 tablespoon milk
¼ teaspoon salt

Stir in until well combined:

1½ cups old-fashioned rolled oats
2 tablespoons all-purpose flour
2 teaspoons vanilla

Stir in the nuts. Drop the batter by scant measuring teaspoonfuls onto the sheets, spacing about 3 inches apart. Don't crowd, as the wafers will spread a great deal. The batter will stiffen as it cools. Bake, 1 sheet at a time, until the cookies are golden brown all over and slightly darker at the edges, 6 to 8 minutes; rotate the sheet halfway through baking for even browning. Remove the sheet to a rack and let stand until the cookies firm slightly, about 1 minute. Gently transfer the cookies to racks to cool. If they become too cool and brittle to be removed easily, return them to the oven a minute to soften.

ALMOND MACAROONS

About 2½ dozen 1¾-inch cookies

Have all ingredients at room temperature, 68° to 70°F. Position 2 racks in the middle of the oven. Preheat the oven to 350°F. Cover cookie sheets with parchment paper or well-greased aluminum foil.

Combine in a food processor and process until finely chopped, scraping the sides of the bowl as necessary:

7 ounces almond paste, cut into small pieces
1 cup powdered sugar

With the machine running, slowly pour through the feed tube and process until the mixture is smooth, about 1 minute:

3 large egg whites
¼ teaspoon almond extract (optional)

Transfer the mixture to a large, heavy saucepan. Cook, stirring constantly, over medium heat until slightly thickened, about 4 minutes. Refrigerate until cooled and slightly firm.

Drop by heaping measuring teaspoonfuls onto the sheets, spacing about 2 inches apart. Bake, 2 sheets at a time, just until the cookies are tinged with brown but still soft inside, 19 to 24 minutes; rotate the sheets halfway through baking for even browning. Remove the sheets to racks and let stand until the cookies cool. Carefully peel the cookies from the paper or foil and transfer to racks to dry out.

COCONUT MACAROONS

About 2 dozen 1½-inch cookies

All macaroons used to be based on almonds, but the coconut version has been popular for many decades.
Position a rack in the upper third of the oven. Preheat the oven to 325°F. Cover cookie sheets with parchment paper or well-greased aluminum foil.
Stir together until well combined:

⅔ cup sweetened condensed milk
1 large egg white
1½ teaspoons vanilla
⅛ teaspoon salt

Stir in until well blended:

3½ cups flaked or shredded sweetened coconut

Drop the dough by scant measuring tablespoonfuls onto the sheets, spacing about 2 inches apart. Bake, 1 sheet at a time, until the cookies are nicely browned, 20 to 25 minutes. Remove the sheet to a rack and let stand until the cookies are completely cool. Carefully peel the cookies from the paper or foil.

MERINGUE NUT KISSES (REDUCED FAT)

About 3 dozen 1½-inch cookies

Although we advise against putting 2 cookie sheets in the oven at once, meringues bake in a very low oven and brown only slightly—so in this case, you can bake 2 sheets at the same time. Because the only fat in these cookies comes from the nuts, they end up with less than 1 gram of fat per cookie.
Have all ingredients at room temperature, 68° to 70°F. Preheat the oven to 250°F. Cover cookie sheets with parchment paper.
In a medium bowl, beat on low speed until foamy:

4 large egg whites
⅛ teaspoon salt
⅛ teaspoon fresh lemon juice

Increase the speed to high and beat until the egg whites are frothy and just begin to form soft peaks. Gradually add and beat until well combined, scraping the sides of the bowl as necessary:

1 cup sugar

Reduce the speed to low and add:

2 teaspoons vanilla
½ teaspoon almond extract (omit if pecans are used)

Beat until the mixture is glossy and stands in very stiff peaks. Fold in:

½ cup finely chopped pecans, almonds, or skinned hazelnuts

Using a heaping measuring teaspoonful for each cookie, drop the batter onto the sheets in peaked mounds, spacing about 1½ inches apart. (Alternatively, pipe the batter into 1¼-inch kisses using a pastry bag fitted with a ½-inch-diameter open star tip.)
Bake, 2 sheets at a time, for 18 minutes. Rotate the sheets and switch racks. Bake for 18 minutes more. Turn the heat off and let the cookies stand in the oven for 30 minutes. With the cookies still attached to the paper, place on a flat surface until completely cool. Gently peel the cookies from the paper.

WHITE CHOCOLATE MACADAMIA MONSTERS

Fourteen 4½-inch or forty 3-inch cookies

Position a rack in the center of the oven. Preheat the oven to 325°F. Grease cookie sheets or cover with parchment paper or greased aluminum foil.
Beat on medium speed until very fluffy and well blended:

20 tablespoons (2½ sticks) unsalted butter, softened
1⅓ cups sugar
⅔ cup packed dark brown sugar

Beat in 1 at a time:

2 large eggs

Stir in:

½ teaspoon vanilla

Stir in just until combined:

2½ cups all-purpose flour
1 teaspoon baking soda
⅛ teaspoon salt

Stir in:

1 cup macadamia nuts
1 cup coarsely chopped white chocolate

Using ⅓ cup for each monster, drop the dough onto the sheets, spacing about 3 inches apart. Bake, 1 sheet at a time, until the cookies are golden brown, 20 to 25 minutes. For regular-sized cookies, drop by heaping measuring teaspoonfuls 1½ inches apart and bake for 15 to 17 minutes. Remove the sheet to a rack and let stand until the cookies firm slightly. Transfer the cookies to racks to cool.

ABOUT ROLLED COOKIES

Sugar cookies and gingerbread men are the best-known rolled cookies, but many ethnic and regional specialties, such as Sablés, 828, and Moravian Molasses Thins, 829, are shaped by this method, too.

Rolled cookies are usually cut into shapes with cookie cutters. These can be fun to collect, and an interesting assortment of cutters makes it possible to turn out eye-catching cookies with no extra effort. The rim of a glass or cup can be used if necessary, but it won't provide the variety of shapes or give the sharp, clean edges good tin cutters do. A compromise is to cut the rolled-out dough into diamonds, squares, triangles, or other geometric shapes with a sharp knife.

MAKING A TEMPLATE

You can also create your own shapes (a tree, bell, rocking horse, etc.) using the patterns below. Trace each figure on a separate piece of paper, then enlarge the image on a photocopier. Cut out the shape, paste it to a sturdy piece of cardboard, and cut out the template. To use the template, oil or grease one side lightly, then lay it gently, oiled or greased side down, on a portion of the rolled-out dough. Working carefully, cut around the template with a small, sharp paring knife, then remove the template and lift out the shaped dough.

To turn out first-rate rolled cookies, the dough needs to be firm and manageable enough to roll and cut out easily. Avoid overflouring or overworking the dough, though; inexperienced bakers often ruin rolled cookies by using too much flour in the rolling process. See Handling Dough for Rolled and Shaped Cookies, 812.

ICED SUGAR COOKIES

About 3 dozen 2-inch cookies

These sugar cookies take well to decorative icing.

Whisk together thoroughly:

3¼ cups all-purpose flour
1½ teaspoons baking powder
½ teaspoon salt

Beat on medium speed until very fluffy and well blended:

20 tablespoons (2½ sticks) unsalted butter, softened
1 cup sugar

Add and beat until well combined:

1 large egg
1 tablespoon milk
2½ teaspoons vanilla
¼ teaspoon finely grated lemon zest (optional)

Gradually stir the flour mixture into the butter mixture until well blended and smooth. Divide the dough in half. Place each half between 2 large sheets of wax or parchment paper. Roll out to a scant ¼ inch thick, checking the underside of the dough and smoothing any creases. Keeping the paper in place, layer the rolled dough on a baking sheet and refrigerate until cold and slightly firm, about 30 minutes.

Position a rack in the center of the oven. Preheat the oven to 375°F. Grease cookie sheets.

Working with 1 portion at a time (leave the other

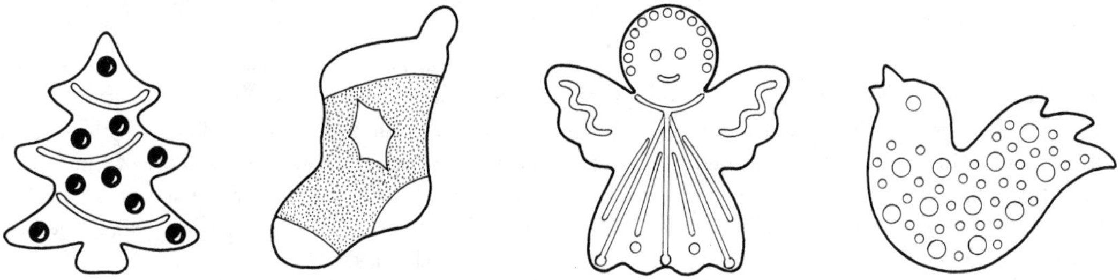

Patterns for templates (see above for instructions)

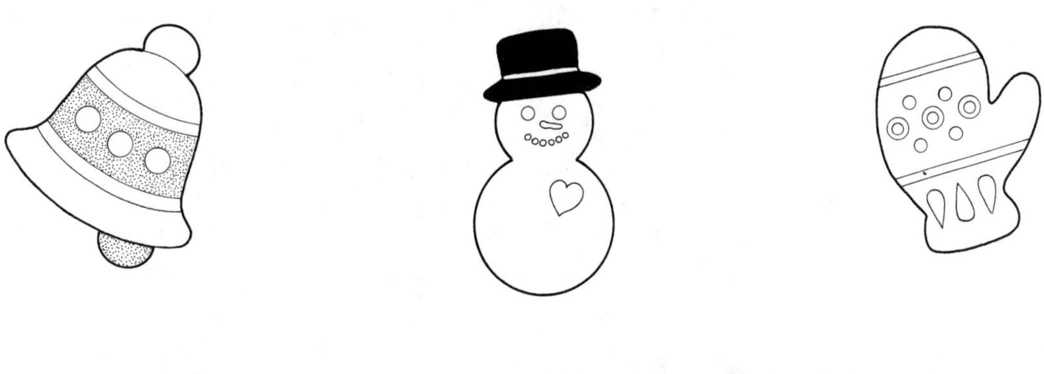

refrigerated), gently peel away and replace 1 sheet of the paper. (This will make it easier to lift the cookies from the paper later.) Peel away and discard the second sheet. Cut out the cookies using 2- or 3-inch cutters. With a spatula, transfer them to the cookie sheets, spacing about 1½ inches apart. Roll the dough scraps and continue cutting out cookies until all the dough is used; briefly refrigerate the dough if it becomes too soft to handle.

If not planning to ice the cookies, decorate with:

Colored sugar or nonpareils

Bake, 1 sheet at a time, just until the cookies are lightly colored on top and slightly darker at the edges, 6 to 9 minutes; rotate the sheet halfway through baking for even browning. Remove the sheet to a rack and let stand until the cookies firm slightly. Transfer the cookies to racks to cool.

FOURTEEN IN ONE (MASTER RECIPE)

About 7 dozen 2½-inch cookies

Simplicity itself. We love this recipe, especially at holiday time, because from just one easy cookie dough, you can make fourteen kinds of cookies. Putting the sugar through a food processor gives these cookies a wonderful lightness and fineness of texture.

Have all ingredients at room temperature, 68° to 70°F. In a large bowl, beat on medium speed until very fluffy and well blended:

½ pound (2 sticks) unsalted butter, at room temperature
1 cup sugar, processed in a food processor for 30 seconds, or superfine sugar
½ teaspoon salt

Add and beat until well blended:

1 large egg yolk

Add and beat until well combined:

1 large egg
2 teaspoons vanilla

Reduce the speed to low and beat in just until combined:

2½ cups all-purpose flour

Divide the dough in half and wrap in plastic. Refrigerate until firm, at least 1 hour. (The dough can be refrigerated for up to 2 days or it can be double-wrapped and frozen for up to 1 month.)

To bake, position a rack in the upper third and another in the lower third of the oven. Preheat the oven to 375°F. Remove 1 disk of dough from the refrigerator and cut in half. Return the unused portion to the refrigerator.

Either: Scoop the cookie dough into 1-tablespoon balls with a small ice cream scoop and roll each ball between your palms until smooth. Place the dough balls on parchment-lined cookie sheets, spacing about 2 inches apart. Using the bottom of a smooth, flour-coated glass, flatten each dough ball to about ⅛ inch thick.

Or: Lightly flour the work surface. Roll the dough to ⅛ inch thick, using an offset spatula to loosen the dough. Sprinkle the surface lightly with flour as needed to keep the dough from sticking. Cut the dough into desired shapes. Place the dough shapes on parchment-lined cookie sheets, spacing about ½ inch apart. Get as many dough shapes as you can out of each sheet, because the dough should be rolled only 2 times. Discard any leftover dough after the second rolling, or form the leftover dough into balls and flatten them to about ⅛ inch thick.

Bake, 2 sheets at a time, until the cookies are evenly golden brown, 6 to 8 minutes; rotate the sheets halfway through baking for even browning. Using a thin-bladed spatula, immediately transfer the cookies to racks to cool to room temperature. Decorate the cooled cookies, if desired, and transfer to an airtight container.

CORNMEAL CITRUS COOKIES

Follow the master recipe, adding 1 teaspoon finely grated lemon or orange zest to the creamed butter, sugar, and salt, and substituting 1 cup fine cornmeal for 1 cup of the flour.

CHOCOLATE-CINNAMON COOKIES

Follow the master recipe, adding 1 ounce melted and cooled unsweetened chocolate to the creamed butter, sugar, and salt. Substitute ¼ cup unsweetened cocoa for ¼ cup of the flour and add ¼ teaspoon ground cinnamon to the flour-cocoa mixture.

MARBLE COOKIES

Follow the master recipe, stirring 2 ounces melted and cooled semisweet or bittersweet chocolate into one-quarter of the master recipe dough. Divide the chocolate dough into 6 portions. Press into the remaining three-quarters of the master recipe dough. Knead the doughs together to create a marbled effect.

LEMON BUTTER COOKIES

Follow the master recipe, adding 2 teaspoons finely grated lemon zest to the creamed butter, sugar, and salt.

LEMON POPPY SEED COOKIES

Follow the master recipe, adding 2 teaspoons finely grated lemon zest to the creamed butter, sugar, and salt, and stirring 2 tablespoons poppy seeds into the finished dough.

ORANGE BUTTER COOKIES

Follow the master recipe, adding 1 teaspoon finely grated orange zest to the creamed butter, sugar, and salt.

ORANGE-NUT COOKIES

Follow the master recipe, adding 1 teaspoon finely grated orange zest and 1 cup finely ground walnuts, pecans, or skinned hazelnuts to the creamed butter, sugar, and salt.

COCONUT COOKIES

Follow the master recipe, stirring 1 cup flaked sweetened dried coconut, toasted, into the finished dough.

GINGER COOKIES

Follow the master recipe, adding 1 teaspoon ground ginger to the flour and stirring 6 tablespoons finely minced candied ginger into the finished dough.

BUTTERSCOTCH COOKIES

Follow the master recipe, substituting 1 cup packed light brown sugar for the sugar.

PEANUT BUTTER COOKIES

Because of the extra fat from the peanut butter, these cookies have a sandier, melt-in-your-mouth texture.

Follow the master recipe, creaming ⅔ cup peanut butter with the butter, sugar, and salt.

SPICE COOKIES

Follow the master recipe, substituting 1 cup packed light brown sugar for the sugar and adding ¾ teaspoon ground cinnamon, ½ teaspoon ground ginger, ¼ teaspoon ground nutmeg, ¼ teaspoon ground allspice, and ⅛ teaspoon ground cloves to the flour.

RAISIN-SPICE COOKIES

Prepare Spice Cookies, above, stirring ½ cup finely minced raisins or ½ cup dried currants into the finished dough.

RICH ROLLED SUGAR COOKIES

2½ to 3½ dozen 2½- to 3½-inch cookies

Christmas wouldn't be Christmas without an assortment of these. This is the dough just waiting for that collection of cookie cutters you have squirreled away. Have fun decorating the different shapes with colored sprinkles or sugar. For a more elaborate finish, pipe with Royal Icing, 1009.

Beat on medium speed until very fluffy and well blended:

½ pound (2 sticks) unsalted butter, softened
⅔ cup sugar

Add and beat until well combined:

1 large egg
¼ teaspoon baking powder
⅛ teaspoon salt
1½ teaspoons vanilla

Stir in until well blended and smooth:

2⅓ cups all-purpose flour

Divide the dough in half. Place each half between 2 large sheets of wax or parchment paper. Roll out to a scant ¼ inch thick, checking the underside of the dough and smoothing any creases. Keeping the paper in place, layer the rolled dough on a baking sheet and refrigerate until cold and slightly firm but not hard, 20 to 30 minutes.

Position a rack in the upper third of the oven. Preheat the oven to 350°F. Grease cookie sheets.

Working with 1 portion of dough at a time (leave the other refrigerated), gently peel away and replace 1 sheet of the paper. (This will make it easier to lift the cookies from the paper later.) Peel away and discard the second sheet. Cut out the cookies using 2- or 3-inch cutters. With a spatula, transfer them to the cookie sheets, spacing about 1 inch apart. Roll the dough scraps and continue cutting out cookies until all the dough is used; briefly refrigerate the dough if it becomes too soft to handle.

If desired, very lightly sprinkle the cookies with:

Colored sprinkles or colored sugar

Bake, 1 sheet at a time, just until the cookies are lightly colored on top and slightly darker at the edges, 6 to 9 minutes; rotate the sheet halfway through baking for even browning. Remove the sheet to a rack and let stand until the cookies firm slightly. Transfer the cookies to racks to cool.

If desired, decorate with:

Royal Icing

SABLÉS

About 4 dozen 2¼-inch cookies

Sablés, originally *galettes sablées,* are classic French rolled shortbread cookies, said to have originated in Normandy. Cutting the butter into the flour coats the flour with fat, creating the distinctive "sandy" (*sablé* in French) texture of the cookies.

Place in a large bowl:

½ pound (2 sticks) cold unsalted butter, cut into small pieces
2¾ cups all-purpose flour

Using a pastry blender, 2 knives, or your fingertips, cut in the butter until the mixture resembles fine crumbs. Beat together with a fork until well blended:

3 large egg yolks
¾ cup sugar
3 tablespoons powdered sugar
⅛ teaspoon salt
1½ teaspoons vanilla
2 or 3 drops almond extract (optional)

Stir the egg yolk mixture into the flour mixture, then knead to form a smooth dough. Divide the dough in half. Place each half between 2 large sheets of wax or parchment paper. Roll out to ¼ inch thick, checking the underside of the dough and smoothing any creases. Keeping the paper in place, layer the rolled dough on a baking sheet and freeze until cold and slightly firm, about 15 minutes.

Position a rack in the upper third of the oven. Preheat the oven to 350°F. Grease cookie sheets.

Working with 1 portion of dough at a time (leave the other in the freezer), gently peel away and replace 1 sheet of the paper. (This will make it easier to lift the cookies from the paper later.) Peel away and discard the second sheet. Cut out the cookies using a fluted or plain round 2-inch or slightly larger cutter (or the rim of a glass). With a spatula, transfer them to the cookie sheets, spacing about 1 inch apart. Roll the dough scraps and continue cutting out cookies until all the dough is used; briefly refrigerate the dough if it becomes too soft to handle.

Bake, 1 sheet at a time, just until the cookies are lightly colored on top and slightly darker at the edges, 12 to 16 minutes; rotate the sheet halfway through baking for even browning. Remove the sheet to a rack and let stand until the cookies firm slightly. Transfer the cookies to racks to cool.

LEMON SABLÉS

Prepare Sablés, above, adding 1¼ teaspoons finely grated lemon zest to the egg yolk mixture.

Gingerbread person

GINGERBREAD PEOPLE (REDUCED FAT)

About 2 dozen 5-inch-tall cookies

No one would ever guess that one of these contains only 3 grams of fat. If you like, make Quick Lemon Icing, 1009, or Royal Icing, 1009, to decorate the cookie.

Whisk together thoroughly:

3 cups all-purpose flour
1½ teaspoons baking powder
¾ teaspoon baking soda
¼ teaspoon salt
1 tablespoon ground ginger
1¾ teaspoons ground cinnamon
¼ teaspoon ground cloves

Beat on medium speed until well blended:

6 tablespoons (¾ stick) unsalted butter, softened
¾ cup packed dark brown sugar
1 large egg

Add and beat until well combined:

½ cup molasses
2 teaspoons vanilla
1 teaspoon finely grated lemon zest

Gradually stir in the dry ingredients until well blended and smooth. Divide the dough in half. Wrap each half in plastic and let stand at room temperature for at least 2 hours or up to 8 hours. (The dough can also be stored for up to 4 days, but in this case it should be refrigerated. Return to room temperature before using.)

To bake, position a rack in the upper third of the oven. Preheat the oven to 375°F. Grease cookie sheets.

Place 1 portion of the dough on a lightly floured work surface. Very lightly sprinkle flour over the surface of the dough and dust the rolling pin. Roll out to a scant ¼ inch thick. Lift the dough frequently and add a bit more flour to the work surface and rolling pin as necessary to prevent sticking. Cut out the cookies using a 4- or 5-inch-tall gingerbread boy or girl cutter. With a spatula, transfer them to the cookie sheets, spacing about 1½ inches apart. Roll the dough scraps and continue cutting out cookies until all the dough is used.

If desired, garnish with:

Raisins and/or red hots, for eyes and buttons

Bake, 1 sheet at a time, until the edges of the cookies are just barely dark, 7 to 10 minutes; rotate the sheet halfway through baking for even browning. Remove the sheet to a rack and let stand until the cookies firm slightly. Transfer the cookies to racks to cool.

MORAVIAN MOLASSES THINS

5½ to 7 dozen 2½-inch cookies

These gingery, paper-thin cookies are traditional in American communities settled by Moravian religious immigrants from central Europe. This recipe—an adaptation of one from Old Salem, North Carolina—has been modified to provide the option of substituting vegetable shortening, easier to find than good-quality lard. If you are adept at rolling the dough very thin, you may get 7 dozen cookies.

Whisk together thoroughly:

1 cup all-purpose flour
1½ teaspoons ground cinnamon
1 teaspoon ground ginger
½ teaspoon ground cloves
¼ teaspoon ground cardamom
½ teaspoon baking soda

Beat on medium speed until well blended:

⅓ cup molasses
¼ cup solid vegetable shortening or good-quality lard
½ cup packed dark brown sugar
1 teaspoon vanilla

Gradually stir the flour mixture into the molasses mixture, then knead until very smooth, 3 to 4 minutes. Divide the dough in half. Wrap each half in plastic and set aside in a cool spot (but not the refrigerator) for at least 6 hours and preferably 12 hours. (The dough can also be stored for up to 4 days, but in this case it should be refrigerated. Return to room temperature before using.)

To bake, position a rack in the center of the oven. Preheat the oven to 300°F. Grease cookie sheets.

Roll out half of the dough as thin as possible on a very lightly floured work surface. (The thinner the dough, the more cookies it will yield.) Lift the dough frequently and add a bit more flour to the work surface and rolling pin as necessary to prevent sticking. Cut out the cookies using a 2¼-inch fluted or plain round cutter. With a spatula, transfer them to the cookie sheets, spacing about 1 inch apart. Roll the dough scraps and continue cutting out cookies until all the dough is used.

Bake, 1 sheet at a time, until the edges of the cookies are just barely dark, 6 to 8 minutes; rotate the sheet halfway through baking for even browning. Don't overbake, as the cookies will be bitter. Remove the sheet to a rack and let stand until the cookies firm slightly. Transfer the cookies to racks to cool.

ABOUT HAND-SHAPED COOKIES

Hand-shaping is the art of forming dough into different shapes. It is the method that lends cookies a certain character and personality.

It is important to note that the dough should be handled as little as possible. Warm hands can affect the texture of the cookies, especially those with a high butter content. We have illustrated throughout this section some of the most common hand-shaping techniques. Many cookies begin as balls of dough that are rolled and then curved into crescents; flattened into rounds with the bottom of a glass, either oiled or dipped into sugar or water to prevent sticking; or pressed down with the tines of a fork, leaving an attractive crisscross pattern in the cookie surface. In the case of biscotti, dough is formed into logs or thin loaves, baked until almost firm, then cut crosswise on the diagonal into individual slices and baked again.

SNICKERDOODLES

About 3 dozen 3½-inch cookies

A New England favorite, these large, crinkly-topped sugar cookies are probably German in origin. Their name may be a corruption of the German word

Flatten balls of dough with the bottom of a glass or press them with the tines of a fork.

Schneckennudeln—which translates roughly as "crinkly noodles."

Position a rack in the upper third of the oven. Preheat the oven to 350°F. Grease cookie sheets.

Sift together:

2 cups all-purpose flour

2 teaspoons cream of tartar

1 teaspoon baking soda

¼ teaspoon salt

Beat on medium speed until very fluffy and well blended:

½ pound (2 sticks) unsalted butter, softened

1½ cups sugar

Add and beat until well combined:

2 large eggs

Stir the flour mixture into the butter mixture until well blended and smooth. Pull off pieces of the dough and roll between your palms to form generous 1¼-inch balls. Roll in a mixture of:

¼ cup sugar

4 teaspoons ground cinnamon

Space about 2¾ inches apart on the sheets. Bake, 1 sheet at a time, until the cookies are light golden brown at the edges, 8 to 11 minutes; rotate the sheet halfway through baking for even browning. Remove the sheet to a rack and let stand until the cookies firm slightly. Transfer the cookies to racks to cool. Let the cookie sheets cool between batches or the cookies may spread too much.

CHOCOLATE CHIP COOKIES COCKAIGNE

About 3 dozen 2½-inch cookies

The classic American cookie, with a twist: finely ground rolled oats, giving them a chewy crunch.

Position a rack in the upper third of the oven. Preheat the oven to 375°F. Grease cookie sheets.

Whisk together thoroughly:

1⅔ cups all-purpose flour

1¼ teaspoons baking soda

¾ teaspoon baking powder

¼ teaspoon salt

Beat on medium speed until lightened in color and creamy:

½ pound (2 sticks) unsalted butter, softened

Add and beat until well blended:

¾ cup sugar

⅔ cup packed light brown sugar

1 large egg

1½ tablespoons milk

2½ teaspoons vanilla

Stir the flour mixture into the butter mixture until well blended and smooth. Finely grind in a food processor or blender:

1⅓ cups old-fashioned rolled oats

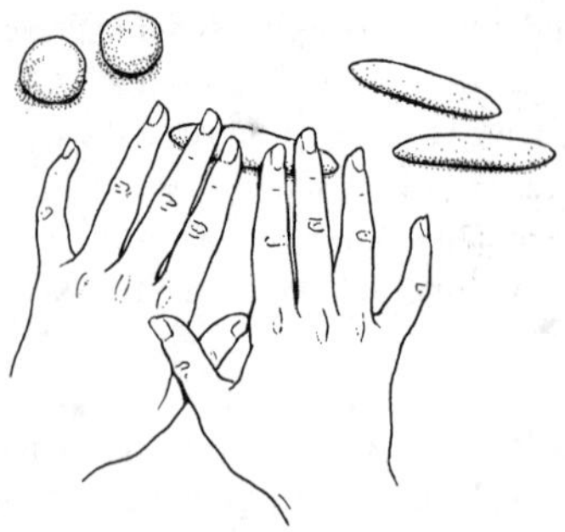

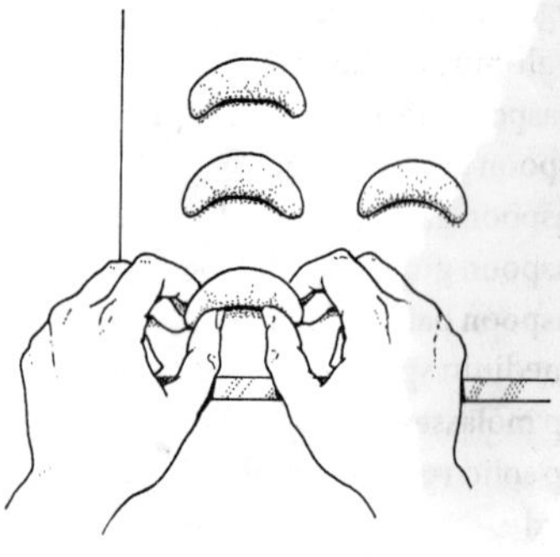

Rolling and shaping crescents

Stir into the dough along with:

1 cup semisweet chocolate chips

One 3-ounce milk chocolate bar, coarsely grated or finely chopped

¾ cup chopped walnuts or pecans (optional)

With lightly greased hands, shape the dough into generous 1½-inch balls. Space about 2 inches apart on the sheets. Pat down the tops of the balls just slightly.

Bake, 1 sheet at a time, just until the cookies are tinged with brown, 8 to 12 minutes; rotate the sheet halfway through baking for even browning. Be careful not to overbake. (The cookies should be soft in the center.) Remove the sheet to a rack and let stand until the cookies firm slightly. Transfer the cookies to racks to cool.

CLASSIC PEANUT BUTTER COOKIES

About 3 dozen 2½-inch cookies

Position a rack in the upper third of the oven. Preheat the oven to 350°F. Grease cookie sheets.

Whisk together thoroughly:

2½ cups all-purpose flour

1¼ teaspoons baking powder

½ teaspoon baking soda

¼ teaspoon salt

Beat on medium speed until very fluffy and well blended:

¼ cup corn or canola oil

⅔ cup smooth peanut butter

12 tablespoons (1½ sticks) unsalted butter, softened

⅓ cup powdered sugar (sifted after measuring if lumpy)

1 cup packed light brown sugar

Add and beat until well combined:

1 large egg

1 large egg yolk

2½ teaspoons vanilla

Stir the flour mixture into the peanut butter mixture until well blended and smooth. Let the dough stand for about 5 minutes to firm slightly. Pull off pieces of the dough and roll between your palms into generous 1-inch balls; it will be fairly soft. Space about 2 inches apart on the sheets. Using the tines of a fork, form a crosshatch pattern and press each ball into a 1½-inch round.

Bake, 1 sheet at a time, until the cookies are just tinged with brown at the edges, 9 to 12 minutes; rotate the sheet halfway through baking for even browning. Remove the sheet to a rack and let stand until the cookies firm slightly. Transfer the cookies to racks to cool.

PEANUT BUTTER CHUBBIES

Twenty-four 1¼-inch cookies

These intensely flavored peanut butter shortbread cookies are tender almost to the point of being crumbly. Their distinctive and appealing taste comes from the addition of peanut butter cups to the batter.

Position a rack in the center of the oven. Preheat the oven to 350°F. Grease a very large cookie sheet.

Whisk together thoroughly:

1 cup all-purpose flour

¼ teaspoon salt

Add and beat on low speed until the mixture just begins to hold together:

5½ tablespoons (⅔ stick) cold unsalted butter, cut into small pieces

3 tablespoons smooth or chunky peanut butter

½ teaspoon vanilla

Add and beat until well blended:

11 ounces peanut butter cups, chopped (about 14 peanut butter cups)

⅔ cup finely chopped unsalted peanuts

Shape into 1-inch balls. Space about 1¼ inches apart on the baking sheet. Bake until faintly tinged with brown, 15 to 18 minutes; rotate the sheet halfway through baking for even browning. Remove the sheet to a rack and let stand until the cookies are completely cool and firm; do not attempt to move the cookies beforehand, as they will be too crumbly.

BENNE SEED WAFERS (SESAME SEED WAFERS)

About 4½ dozen 2¼-inch cookies

West African for "sesame," *benne* is still used all over the South. Benne Seed Wafers are so nutty tasting that people often think they contain peanuts. Be sure to buy hulled sesame seeds, available in health food stores. Unhulled ones have a dull, brownish appearance.

Position a rack in the center of the oven. Preheat the oven to 375°F. Grease cookie sheets. Place in a large skillet over medium heat:

¾ cup sesame seeds

Toast the seeds, stirring them or shaking the pan every few seconds, until they just turn pale brown, 5 to 7 minutes. Immediately remove from the heat, continuing to stir for 30 seconds. Let cool completely.

Whisk together thoroughly:

1½ cups all-purpose flour

1¼ teaspoons baking powder

½ teaspoon baking soda

¼ teaspoon salt

Beat on medium speed until very fluffy and well blended:

8 tablespoons (1 stick) unsalted butter, softened

¾ cup packed light brown sugar

Add and beat until well combined:

1 large egg

1½ teaspoons vanilla

Stir the flour mixture and ⅓ cup of the sesame seeds into the butter mixture until well blended.

Pull off pieces of the dough and roll between your palms into 1-inch balls. Dip the top of each ball into the remaining sesame seeds to coat. Space the balls, seeded side up, about 2 inches apart on the sheets. Gently flatten the balls into 1½-inch rounds with the heel of your hand. Bake, 1 sheet at a time, until the cookies are just lightly browned at the edges, 6 to 9 minutes; rotate the sheet halfway through baking for even browning. Remove the sheet to a rack and let stand until the cookies firm slightly. Transfer the cookies to racks to cool.

MEXICAN WEDDING CAKES

About 5 dozen 1¼-inch cookies

In Mexico, where they're often served at weddings, these are known as *Pastelitas de Boda,* or Little Wedding Cakes. They are also known as Pecan Butter Balls.

Position a rack in the upper third of the oven. Preheat the oven to 350°F. Grease cookie sheets.

Toast, stirring occasionally, in a baking pan until lightly browned, 5 to 8 minutes:

1 cup coarsely chopped pecans

Set aside to cool completely, then grind until very finely chopped but not powdery or oily. Beat on medium speed until very fluffy and well blended:

½ pound (2 sticks) unsalted butter, softened

¼ teaspoon salt

½ cup powdered sugar

2 teaspoons vanilla

Gradually beat the pecans into the butter mixture. Sift over the top and stir in until well blended:

2 cups all-purpose flour

Pull off pieces of the dough and roll between your palms into generous 1-inch balls. Space about 1¼ inches apart on the sheets. Bake, 1 sheet at a time, until the cookies are faintly tinged with brown, 12 to 15 minutes; rotate the sheet halfway through baking for even browning. Remove the sheet to a rack and let stand until the cookies firm slightly. Transfer the cookies to racks to cool completely. Roll the cookies until coated all over in:

⅓ cup powdered sugar

VIENNESE CRESCENTS

About 4 dozen 2¼-inch cookies

Position a rack in the upper third of the oven. Preheat the oven to 350°F. Grease cookie sheets.

Beat on medium speed until lightened in color and creamy:

½ pound (2 sticks) unsalted butter, softened

Sift over the top and beat until well combined:

¾ cup powdered sugar

Stir in:

2 teaspoons vanilla

1 cup ground walnuts or ground blanched almonds

Gradually sift over the top while stirring:

2 cups all-purpose flour

Knead until well blended. Pull off generous 1-tablespoon pieces of the dough, roll with your hands into a short rope, and shape into crescents, shown 830. (If the dough is soft and hard to handle, refrigerate until slightly firm.) Space 1¼ inches apart on the sheets.

Bake, 1 sheet at a time, until the crescents are faintly tinged with brown and slightly darker at the edges, 13 to 16 minutes; rotate the sheet halfway through baking for even browning. Remove the sheet to a rack and let stand until the cookies firm slightly. Transfer the cookies to racks to cool. Sift over the cookies until evenly coated:

⅔ cup powdered sugar

KOURAMBIEDES

About 4 dozen 1¼-inch cookies

These Greek cookies are so buttery and fine in texture that they melt in the mouth. Handle gently, as these cookies are fragile.

Beat on medium speed until lightened in color and creamy:

¾ pound (3 sticks) unsalted butter, softened

¼ teaspoon salt

Beat in until very fluffy and well blended:

⅔ cup powdered sugar

1 large egg yolk

2 tablespoons brandy

1 teaspoon vanilla

Gradually add and stir until well blended and smooth:

3 cups all-purpose flour, sifted

Cover and refrigerate the dough until firm enough to shape into balls, about 1 hour.

To bake, position a rack in the upper third of the oven. Preheat the oven to 350°F. Grease cookie sheets.

Pull off pieces of the dough and roll between your

palms into generous 1-inch balls. Space about 1 inch apart on the sheets. If desired, garnish the balls by inserting into the top of each:

1 whole clove

Bake, 1 sheet at a time, until the cookies are faintly tinged with brown, 14 to 18 minutes; rotate the sheet halfway through baking for even browning. Remove the sheet to a rack and let stand until the cookies firm slightly. Gently transfer the cookies to racks to cool completely. Sift over the cookies until evenly coated:

½ cup powdered sugar

PFEFFERNÜSSE (PEPPERNUTS)

About 5 dozen 1-inch cookies

These cookies may firm up and even become hard during storage. To soften them slightly, add an apple slice wrapped in a paper towel or in an open plastic bag to the storage container. In a few days, the cookies will soften, and the apple can be discarded.

Whisk together thoroughly:

1 cup plus 1 tablespoon all-purpose flour
1 teaspoon ground cinnamon
½ teaspoon ground cardamom
¼ teaspoon ground cloves
¼ teaspoon ground nutmeg
⅛ teaspoon ground black pepper
¼ teaspoon baking powder
⅛ teaspoon baking soda
⅛ teaspoon salt

Beat until very fluffy and well blended:

4 tablespoons (½ stick) unsalted butter, softened
½ cup sugar

Add and beat until well combined:

1 large egg yolk

Stir in:

¼ cup slivered blanched almonds, finely chopped
¼ cup finely chopped candied orange peel
1 teaspoon finely grated lemon zest

Stir the flour mixture into the butter mixture in 3 parts, alternating with, in 2 parts:

3 tablespoons light or dark molasses
3 tablespoons brandy

Cover and refrigerate the dough for at least 8 hours or up to 2 days to allow the flavors to blend.

To bake, position a rack in the upper third of the oven. Preheat the oven to 350°F. Grease cookie sheets.

Pull off pieces of the dough and roll between your palms into scant ¾-inch balls. Space about 1 inch apart on the sheets. Bake, 1 sheet at a time, until the cookies are faintly tinged with brown on top and slightly darker at the edges, 12 to 14 minutes; rotate the sheet halfway through baking for even browning. Remove the sheet to a rack and let the cookies stand briefly. Roll the cookies until well coated in:

½ to ⅔ cup powdered sugar

Let cool completely. (If freezing, coat with the powdered sugar after the cookies have thawed.)

GINGER SNAPS

6 to 6½ dozen 2¼-inch cookies

For *very* crunchy cookies, overbake slightly; for more tender ones, underbake by a minute or two.

Position a rack in the upper third of the oven. Preheat the oven to 350°F. Grease cookie sheets.

Whisk together thoroughly:

3¾ cups all-purpose flour
1½ teaspoons baking powder
½ teaspoon baking soda
4 teaspoons ground ginger
1 teaspoon ground cinnamon
¼ teaspoon ground cloves
¼ teaspoon salt

Beat on medium speed until very fluffy and well blended:

12 tablespoons (1½ sticks) unsalted butter, softened
1⅔ cups sugar

Add and beat until well combined:

2 large eggs
½ cup dark molasses
2 teaspoons fresh lemon juice
¼ teaspoon finely grated lemon or orange zest

Stir the flour mixture into the molasses mixture until well blended and smooth. Pull off pieces of the dough and roll between your palms into generous 1-inch balls. Space about 1½ inches apart on the sheets. Pat down the balls to flatten the tops just slightly.

Bake, 1 sheet at a time, until the cookies are tinged with brown and just firm when lightly pressed in the center of the top, 10 to 13 minutes; rotate the sheet halfway through baking for even browning. (The cookies flatten and develop cracks during baking.) Remove the sheet to a rack and let stand until the cookies firm slightly. Transfer the cookies to racks to cool.

ORANGE GINGER WAFERS (REDUCED FAT)

About 4½ dozen 2½-inch wafers

These crispy wafers have less than 1.5 grams of fat each.

Position a rack in the upper third of the oven. Preheat the oven to 375°F. Coat cookie sheets with nonstick spray.

Whisk together thoroughly:

2 cups all-purpose flour
2 teaspoons baking powder
¼ teaspoon baking soda
½ teaspoon ground ginger
⅛ teaspoon ground cloves
¼ teaspoon salt

Beat on medium speed until well blended:

1 cup sugar
2½ teaspoons finely grated orange zest
1 teaspoon finely grated lemon zest
3 tablespoons corn or canola oil
2½ tablespoons unsalted butter, softened

Add and beat until well combined:

1 large egg
¼ cup light or dark molasses
2½ teaspoons vanilla

Gradually beat the flour mixture into the molasses mixture until well blended and smooth. Pull off pieces of the dough and roll between your palms into generous ¾-inch balls. Space about 2¼ inches apart on the sheets. Lightly oil the bottom of a large, flat-bottomed glass. Very lightly dip the glass into:

2 tablespoons sugar

Flatten the balls until ¼ inch thick, dipping the glass into the sugar before flattening each cookie. Wipe the buildup from the glass and reoil as necessary. Bake, 1 sheet at a time, until the cookies are faintly tinged with brown and slightly darker at the edges, 8 to 11 minutes; rotate the sheet halfway through baking for even browning. Remove the sheet to a rack and let stand until the cookies firm slightly. Transfer the cookies to racks to cool. Let the cookie sheet cool between batches, or the cookies may spread too much.

CLASSIC BISCOTTI (REDUCED FAT)

About 3 dozen 3 x ½-inch biscotti

Most plain biscotti are low in fat to begin with. These have less than 2 grams each.

Position a rack in the center of the oven. Preheat the oven to 375°F. Grease a cookie sheet.

Whisk together thoroughly:

3⅓ cups all-purpose flour
2½ teaspoons baking powder
½ teaspoon salt

Beat on medium speed until well blended:

¼ cup corn or canola oil
1¼ cups sugar
2 large eggs
2 large egg whites
1 teaspoon finely grated lemon zest
½ teaspoon finely grated orange zest
1 teaspoon anise extract or almond extract
1 teaspoon vanilla

Gradually stir the flour mixture into the egg mixture until well blended and smooth. Shape the dough into 2 smooth, evenly shaped 11 x 1½-inch logs, either by wrapping each log in plastic and rolling it back and forth until smooth, or by shaping it with lightly floured hands. Arrange the logs as far apart from one another as possible on the sheet and press to flatten slightly. Bake for 25 minutes. Remove the sheet to a rack. When the logs are just cool enough to handle, carefully transfer to a cutting board and cut crosswise, on a slight diagonal, into ⅜-inch-thick slices. Lay the slices flat on the sheet. Return to the oven and bake for 10 minutes. Turn the slices over and bake until lightly browned, 5 to 10 minutes more. Transfer the biscotti to racks to cool.

CHOCOLATE-COATED MOCHA BISCOTTI

About 3½ dozen 3 x ½-inch biscotti

If you wish to freeze these, coat with chocolate after thawing to room temperature.

Position a rack in the center of the oven. Preheat the oven to 350°F. Grease a cookie sheet.

Spread in separate small baking pans:

1⅓ cups whole blanched almonds
1⅓ cups whole hazelnuts

Toast, stirring occasionally, until the almonds are tinged with brown and fragrant, and the hazelnut skins are loosened, 8 to 12 minutes. Let cool, then rub the hazelnuts in a dish towel or between your palms to remove as much skin as possible. Coarsely chop the nuts.

Chop into small bits:

6 ounces bittersweet or semisweet chocolate

Whisk together thoroughly:

3 cups all-purpose flour
¼ cup unsweetened cocoa
2½ teaspoons baking powder
¼ teaspoon salt

Beat on medium speed until very fluffy and well blended:

8 tablespoons (1 stick) unsalted butter, softened
1 cup sugar

Beat in 1 at a time:

3 large eggs
1 large egg white

Add and beat until the coffee is dissolved:

1½ tablespoons light corn syrup
1 tablespoon instant coffee granules or powder
1¼ teaspoons vanilla
1¼ teaspoons almond extract (optional)

Gradually stir the flour mixture into the egg mixture until well blended and smooth. Stir in the nuts and chocolate.

Shape the dough into 2 smooth, evenly shaped 15 x 1½-inch logs, arrange on the sheet, and flatten either by wrapping each log in plastic and rolling it back and forth until smooth, or by shaping it with lightly floured hands. Bake for 35 minutes. Remove the sheet to a rack. When the logs are just cool enough to handle, carefully transfer to a cutting board and cut crosswise, on a slight diagonal, into ½-inch-thick slices. Lay the slices flat on the sheet. Return to the oven and bake until the slices are almost firm when lightly pressed on top, 16 to 20 minutes. Transfer the biscotti to racks to cool.

To prepare for adding the optional drizzled chocolate, arrange the slices in neat rows about ½ inch apart on the cookie sheet. Melt, stirring often, in the top of a double boiler over barely simmering water:

4 ounces bittersweet or semisweet chocolate, coarsely chopped
1 tablespoon corn or canola oil

Remove the top of the double boiler from the bottom and add, off the heat:

2 ounces bittersweet or semisweet chocolate, cut into ½-ounce pieces

Stir until the melted chocolate cools to just barely warm. Remove any unmelted chocolate. Immediately spoon the chocolate into a paper cone or a pastry bag fitted with a large writing tip. If using a paper cone, cut off the tip to allow a ⅛-inch-wide drizzled line. Quickly drizzle long zigzag lines back and forth until all the biscotti are decorated. Let stand, chocolate side up, in a cool room until the chocolate is completely set, about 30 minutes.

ABOUT FILLED COOKIES

Filled cookies—the fillings might be anything from jam tucked in the indentations of thumbprint cookies to thin chocolate mints sandwiched between golden wafers—are time consuming to prepare, but they always give the impression of being special.

Since there is so much variety in the shaping, handling, and baking of filled cookies, not many general rules apply. Simply follow the directions provided with each recipe.

CHOCOLATE MINT SURPRISES

About 2½ dozen 2¼-inch cookies

The filling for these sandwiches comes in the form of thin chocolate mints, about 1½ inches across and no more than ⅛ inch thick. Thicker kinds, such as miniature mint patties, don't melt enough to bond with the cookies.

In contrast to most sandwich cookies, which are assembled after the wafers are completely cool, these must be put together while the cookies are still hot from the oven, so the chocolate will melt and stick to the cookie layers.

Place in a large bowl:

½ pound (2 sticks) unsalted butter, chilled but not firm and cut into small pieces
2¼ cups all-purpose flour

Using a pastry blender, 2 knives, or your fingertips, cut in the butter until the mixture resembles fine crumbs.

Beat together with a fork until well blended:

2 large egg yolks
¾ cup sugar
¼ teaspoon salt
1 teaspoon vanilla

Stir the egg yolk mixture into the flour mixture, then knead to form a smooth dough. Divide the dough in half. Place each half between 2 large sheets of wax or parchment paper. Roll out to a generous ⅛ inch thick, checking the underside of the dough and smoothing any creases. Keeping the paper in place, layer the rolled dough on a baking sheet and freeze until cold and slightly firm, about 20 minutes.

Position a rack in the upper third of the oven. Preheat the oven to 350°F. Grease cookie sheets.

Working with 1 portion of at a time (leave the other in the freezer), gently peel away and replace 1 sheet of the paper. (This will make it easier to lift the cookies from the paper later.) Peel away and discard the second sheet.

Cut out the cookies using a fluted or plain round 2¼-inch cutter (or the rim of a small glass), or cut to a size just large enough that the thin mint candies will fit within them. With a spatula, transfer the cookies to the sheets, spacing about 1 inch apart. Roll any dough scraps between the paper and continue cutting out cookies until all the dough is used; if the dough becomes too warm to handle, chill it again briefly. Bake, 1 sheet at a time, just until the cookies are lightly colored on top and slightly darker at the edges, 9 to 14 minutes; rotate the sheet halfway through baking for even browning. Remove the sheet to a rack and let the cookies stand just until firm enough to lift but still hot. Turn half of the cookies bottom up on the cookie sheet. Immediately cover each bottom with:

1 thin square chocolate mint wafer (about 30 total)

Cover with the cookie tops, top up, and press down

lightly. Let the sandwiches stand on the cookie sheets until the mints melt. Transfer the sandwiches to racks until the cookies are cool and the filling is set; during the cooling process, adjust any sandwiches that slip askew.

ALMOND THUMBPRINT COOKIES (REDUCED FAT)

About 3½ dozen 1¾-inch cookies

These cookies contain only about 2 grams of fat apiece, and are festive enough for a tea table. Be sure to use thick, seedless jam or preserves, not jelly, so the filling will not be runny.

Position a rack in the center of the oven. Preheat the oven to 375°F. Grease cookie sheets.

Whisk together thoroughly:

1½ cups all-purpose flour
⅓ cup cornstarch
¼ teaspoon baking powder
¼ teaspoon baking soda
¼ teaspoon salt

Beat on medium speed until well blended:

3½ tablespoons unsalted butter, softened
3 tablespoons corn or canola oil
1 tablespoon light corn syrup
½ cup sugar
1 large egg
¼ teaspoon very finely grated lemon zest
2½ teaspoons vanilla
¼ teaspoon almond extract

Stir the flour mixture into the egg mixture just until combined. With lightly greased hands, pull off pieces of the dough and roll between your palms into ¾-inch balls; do not make them larger, as the cookies should be small and will puff and spread a bit during baking. Space the balls about 2 inches apart on the sheets. With your thumb (or knuckle), press down the center of each ball to make a large, deep well. Fill the wells with:

About ⅔ cup seedless fruit jam or preserves, such as cherry, apricot, damson plum, or raspberry

Very lightly sprinkle the tops of the cookies with:

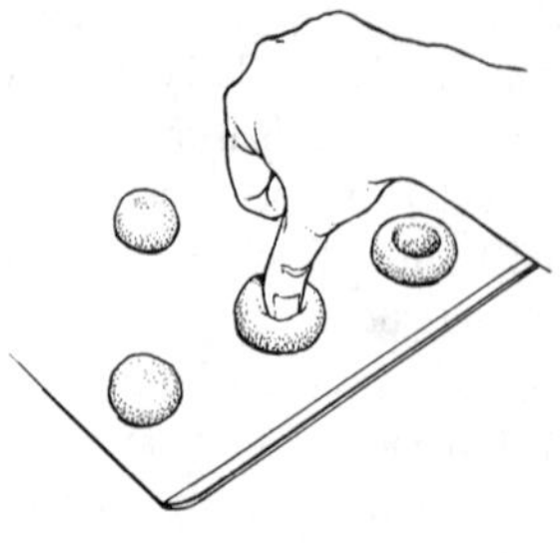

2 to 3 tablespoons chopped sliced blanched or unblanched almonds

Bake, 1 sheet at a time, until the tops are just barely tinged with brown, 6 to 9 minutes. Remove the sheet to a rack and let stand until the cookies firm slightly, about 2 minutes. Transfer the cookies to racks to cool.

DREI AUGEN

About 3 dozen 1½-inch cookies

Drei Augen means "three eyes" in German; the "eyes" are small holes in the top cookie, revealing the jelly within.

Beat on medium speed until very fluffy and well blended:

20 tablespoons (2½ sticks) unsalted butter, softened
⅔ cup sugar

Whisk together thoroughly:

2⅓ cups all-purpose flour
½ cup whole unblanched almonds, finely ground
1 teaspoon ground cinnamon

Stir the flour mixture into the butter mixture. Divide the dough into thirds. Place each third between 2 large sheets of wax or parchment paper. Roll out into a circle 11 inches in diameter and ⅛ inch thick, checking the underside of the dough and smoothing any creases. Keeping the paper in place, layer the rolled dough on a baking sheet and refrigerate for at least 2 hours or up to 24 hours.

To bake, position a rack in the center of the oven. Preheat the oven to 350°F. Grease cookie sheets or cover with parchment paper or greased aluminum foil.

Working with 1 portion of dough at a time (leave the remainder refrigerated), gently peel away and replace 1 sheet of the paper. (This will make it easier to lift the cookies from the paper later.) Peel away and discard the second sheet. Use a 1½-inch cutter to cut out rounds, then use the small end of a ⅜-inch plain pastry tip or a straw to cut out 3 small holes in half of the rounds. With a spatula, transfer the cookies to the sheets, spacing 1½ inches apart and baking the top and bottom cookies separately, as the cookies with holes bake faster. Bake, 1 sheet at a time, until the cookies are pale golden, 10 to 15 minutes. Remove the sheet to a rack and let stand until the cookies firm slightly. Transfer the cookies to racks to cool completely. Sift over the cutout cookies:

1 cup powdered sugar

Boil for 2 minutes:

1 cup red currant jelly

Cool to lukewarm. Turn over the solid cookies so the bottom side is up. Spoon ¼ teaspoon of the cooled jelly onto each cookie, then top with a cutout cookie. Press lightly so the jelly fills in the 3 holes.

LINZER HEARTS

Prepare Drei Augen, 836, using a heart-shaped cutter and substituting seedless raspberry preserves for the red currant jelly.

RUGELACH

About 30 rolled rugelach or 16 large or 32 small crescents

Always use jam or preserves, never jelly, with fruit and sugar listed as the first two ingredients on the label, to avoid leaking during baking.

Beat on medium speed until well blended, 15 to 20 seconds:

½ pound (2 sticks) unsalted butter, softened

6 ounces cream cheese, softened

Add all at once and beat on low speed just until the dough comes together, 10 to 15 seconds:

2¼ cups all-purpose flour

Divide the dough into thirds. Flatten each third into a 6 x 4-inch rectangle or 6-inch circle. Wrap in plastic and refrigerate for 1 hour. (The dough can be refrigerated for up to 1 week or packed airtight and frozen for up to 1 month.)

To bake, position a rack in the upper third of the oven. Preheat the oven to 350°F. Cover a cookie sheet with parchment paper.

Whisk together:

⅓ cup sugar

1 teaspoon ground cinnamon

Working quickly with 1 portion of dough at a time (leave the remainder refrigerated), generously sprinkle the work surface and the top of the dough with:

All-purpose flour

For rectangular rugelach: Shape by rolling each portion into a 16 x 10-inch rectangle, about ⅛ inch thick. Brush the excess flour from the top and bottom of the dough, and the work surface, and turn the rectangle so the long edge is parallel to the edge of the work surface. Leaving a ¼-inch border, spread 1 rectangle with:

¼ cup raspberry jam or apricot preserves

Along the edge of the jam on the long side nearest you, place a line of:

¼ cup raisins or chocolate chips

Sprinkle the rest of the surface with 2 teaspoons of the cinnamon and sugar and:

2½ tablespoons ground walnuts

Roll the dough, starting at the raisin edge, gently tucking and tightening as you go.

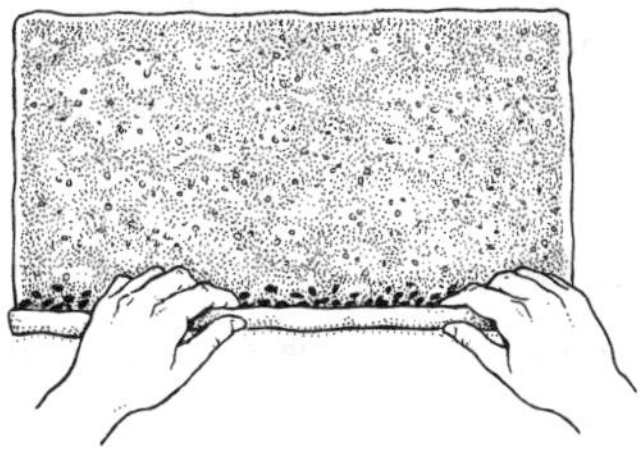

Finish with the seam of the roll facing down. Cut the roll into 1½-inch-thick slices. Repeat with the remaining rectangles.

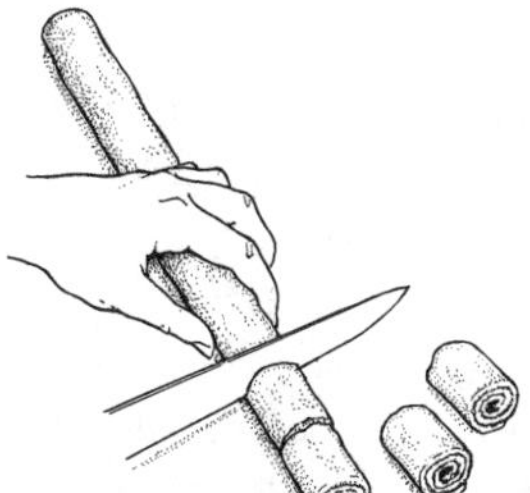

FOR CRESCENT RUGELACH:

Shape by rolling each portion into a circle about 14 inches in diameter and about ⅛ inch thick. Spread the jam in a thin layer, leaving a ¼-inch border, then sprinkle the entire surface with the raisins, cinnamon and sugar, and ground nuts. Cut the circle like a pizza, cre-

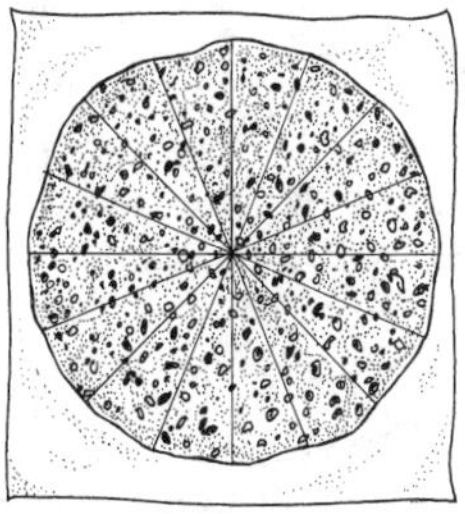

ating 8 (for large cookies) or 16 (for small cookies) even triangles. Roll up from the wide end to the point, tucking the point under. Repeat with the remaining circles.

With a spatula, transfer the rugelach to the cookie sheet. Sprinkle each cookie with ⅛ teaspoon of the cinnamon and sugar. Bake until the bottoms are light golden (the tops will still be blond), about 25 minutes. Remove the sheet to a rack and let stand until the rugelach firm slightly. Transfer the rugelach to racks to cool.

ABOUT ICEBOX COOKIES

What Irma Rombauer first called "icebox cookies" in the 1931 *Joy,* and Marion Becker renamed "refrigerator cookies" in the '50s, might most accurately be called "freezer cookies" today, since the freezer is where we now store logs of slice-and-bake dough. But we've gone back to Irma's term, because it brings to mind a bygone era.

Icebox cookies are convenient: The dough can be mixed when you have a few minutes, then formed into logs and stashed in the freezer (some for as long as 2 months) until you're ready to bake. There's little shaping time required, since the logs are simply cut crosswise into slices. Most kinds do not even have to be thawed before slicing—and actually slice best when very, very cold.

ICEBOX SUGAR COOKIES

3½ to 4 dozen 2½-inch cookies

These slice-and-bake logs are a cinch to make. Let the kids have a field day decorating them.

Whisk together thoroughly:

1½ cups all-purpose flour
1½ teaspoons baking powder
¼ teaspoon salt

Beat on medium speed until very fluffy and well blended:

10 tablespoons (1¼ sticks) unsalted butter, softened
⅔ cup sugar

Add and beat until well combined:

1 large egg
2 teaspoons vanilla
¼ teaspoon finely grated lemon zest (optional)

Stir the flour mixture into the butter mixture until well blended and smooth. Cover and refrigerate until slightly firm, 20 to 30 minutes. Place the dough on one end of a long sheet of wax or parchment paper. With lightly greased hands, shape into an even, 11-inch-long log. Roll up in the paper, twisting the ends of the paper to prevent unrolling. Place on a baking sheet and freeze until completely frozen, at least 3 hours. Use immediately or transfer to a sealable plastic bag and freeze for up to 1 month.

To bake, position a rack in the upper third of the oven. Preheat the oven to 375°F. Grease cookie sheets.

Gently peel the paper off the log and cut the log crosswise into ⅛-inch-thick slices. Transfer the slices to the cookie sheets, spacing about 2 inches apart. Bake, 1 sheet at a time, until the cookies are golden all over and just slightly darker at the edges, 7 to 10 minutes. The longer the baking time, the crisper the cookies. Remove the sheet to a rack and let stand until the cookies firm slightly. Transfer the cookies to racks to cool.

CREAM CHEESE ICEBOX COOKIES

About 3½ dozen 2¼-inch cookies

This is a forgiving, easy to handle dough that produces a cookie with outstanding flavor.

Whisk together thoroughly:

2 cups all-purpose flour
½ teaspoon salt
½ teaspoon baking powder
⅛ teaspoon baking soda

Beat on medium speed until very fluffy and well blended:

11 tablespoons unsalted butter, softened
1 cup sugar
1 large egg

Gradually beat in until well combined:

3 ounces cream cheese, softened and cut into chunks
1 teaspoon vanilla
¼ teaspoon finely grated lemon zest (optional)

Stir the flour mixture into the butter mixture until well blended and smooth. Refrigerate until slightly firm, about 1 hour. Place the dough on one end of a long sheet of wax or parchment paper. With well-greased hands, shape into a 12 x 2-inch log. Roll the dough up in the paper, twisting the ends of the paper to prevent unrolling. Place on a tray or baking sheet and freeze until completely frozen, at least 3 hours. Use immediately or transfer to a sealable plastic bag and freeze for up to 1 month.

To bake, position a rack in the upper third of the oven. Preheat the oven to 375°F. Grease cookie sheets.

Gently peel the paper off the log and cut the log crosswise into ⅛-inch-thick slices. Transfer the slices to the cookie sheets, spacing about 2 inches apart. Using stencils or tiny cutters as a design outline, sprinkle the tops with:

Colored sugar, cinnamon and sugar, or nonpareils

Press lightly to secure nonpareils in place. Bake, 1 sheet at a time, until the cookies are tinged with brown at the edges, 7 to 11 minutes. Remove the sheet to a rack and let stand until the cookies firm slightly. Transfer the cookies to racks to cool.

COFFEE SNAPS

50 cookies

The secret to this cookie is instant espresso powder mellowed with Kahlúa. The dough slices like a dream and freezes beautifully for up to 4 weeks.

Stir together in a small bowl:

4 teaspoons Kahlúa
2 teaspoons instant espresso powder

Whisk together thoroughly:

2½ cups all-purpose flour
¼ teaspoon ground cinnamon
⅛ teaspoon salt

Beat on medium speed until well blended and no lumps of sugar remain:

½ pound (2 sticks) unsalted butter, softened
¾ cups packed dark brown sugar

Add the espresso mixture and beat until blended. Gradually add the flour mixture, beating on low speed until blended and beginning to form a dough. Place the dough on a large piece of plastic wrap. Using the plastic wrap to help mold the dough, shape it into a 12 x 3 x 1-inch log. Wrap tightly in plastic and refrigerate until very firm, about 6 hours. Use immediately or transfer to a sealable plastic bag and freeze for up to 1 month.

To bake, position a rack in the upper third of the oven. Preheat the oven to 350°F. Line cookie sheets with parchment paper.

Gently unwrap the log and cut crosswise into ⅜-inch-thick slices. Transfer the slices to the cookie sheets, spacing about 1 inch apart. Bake, 1 sheet at a time, until the tops look dry and slightly brown around the edges, about 12 minutes. Remove the sheet to a rack and let stand until the cookies firm slightly. Transfer the cookies to racks to cool completely

ABOUT PIPED, PRESSED, AND MOLDED COOKIES

The distinguishing feature of this category of cookies is that they are shaped with molds, presses, or other special equipment not generally on hand in the kitchen. Each type of shaping device lends a different, distinctive, and decidedly handsome look.

A pastry bag and piping tube can be used to shape a large variety of doughs, which simply need to be soft enough to flow through the tip easily. Piped Spritz cookies, as well as a number of meringue cookies, can quickly be formed in this way.

For pressed cookies, such as Pressed Spritz, the dough can be short, but it must be chilled to just the right degree of firmness, or the cookie will not squeeze out neatly in the desired shape. Too much baking powder or soda will cause the cookies to puff excessively.

With molded cookies such as Springerle and Spekulatius, the dough must be fairly firm to facilitate shaping, and thus contains little or no butter or leavening. Too much of either causes the cookies to spread and puff up during baking, blurring the splendid designs. And although there is no real way to produce the attractive look of these cookies without the appropriate molds, the dough can be rolled to about ⅜ inch thick and shaped with cookie cutters—for equally delicious results! You can even try pressing a design into them with the head of an old-fashioned meat-tenderizing mallet, the surface of a deeply etched cut-glass bowl or tumbler, or even the tines of a fork.

PIPED AND PRESSED SPRITZ COOKIES

About 5 dozen 2-inch cookies

Both piping and pressing work with this dough. For those who have never formed cookies with either method, piping is likely to yield better results with less practice. In fact, most cooks can turn out rosettes and stars that look as fancy as store-bought on the first try. On the other hand, a press does yield cookies with a distinctive, charming appearance. Certainly if there is already a press in the house, it is fun and rewarding to put it to use. The key to success is to chill the dough just enough so the cookies can be forced through the press plate neatly and hold their shape during baking. Since most presses come with a variety of design plates—such as rosettes, stars, rigid strips, and Christmas trees—it is a good idea to try several and see which ones produce the most attractive results. (Keep in mind, with both piped and pressed cookies, any that do not come out quite right can be scooped up and formed again.)

Some Spritz cookies are soft and tender to the point of being cakelike, but these are more on the crisp-tender side.

Grease cookie sheets.

Beat on medium speed until very fluffy and well blended:

½ pound (2 sticks) unsalted butter, softened
¾ cup sugar

Add and beat until well combined:

2 large egg yolks
¼ teaspoon salt
1½ teaspoons vanilla
¾ teaspoon almond extract (optional)

Sift over the top and stir in until well blended and smooth:

2¼ cups all-purpose flour

TO PIPE THE COOKIES:
Stir in:

1½ to 2½ tablespoons milk

until the dough is soft enough to easily force through a pastry bag tube.
Position a rack in the upper third of the oven. Preheat the oven to 350°F.
Fit the piping bag with a ½-inch-diameter open star (or similar) tip. Fill the pastry bag no more than two-thirds full, twist the opening tightly closed, and squeeze out generous 1½-inch rosettes or stars, spacing about 1 inch apart on the cookie sheets. (For best results, keep the bag and tip perpendicular to the sheet, with the tip almost touching the sheet.)

TO PRESS THE COOKIES:
If the dough seems soft and difficult to handle, stir in

1 to 2 tablespoons all-purpose flour.

Cover and refrigerate the dough until slightly stiff but not at all hard, 30 to 40 minutes.
Position a rack in the upper third of the oven. Preheat the oven to 350°F.
Ready the press by inserting the desired design plate by sliding it into the head and locking it into place, or follow the manufacturer's instructions. If you are unsure whether the dough is of the right consistency, put a small amount in the press tube and press out several test cookies. Chill the dough further before continuing if it does not go through cleanly. When the consistency is right, fill the press tube with the dough, packing it down firmly. Press out the cookies, spacing

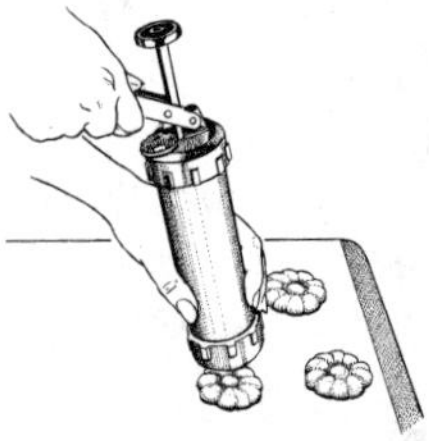

about 1 inch apart on the sheets. Keep the unused dough refrigerated as you work.
If desired, decorate piped or pressed cookies with:

Candied cherry or almond bits, colored sugar sprinkles, or nonpareils

Bake, 1 sheet at a time, until the cookies are just slightly golden and barely tinged with brown at the edges, 9 to 12 minutes. Remove the sheet to a rack and let stand until the cookies firm slightly. Transfer the cookies to racks to cool.

SPRINGERLE

2 to 3 dozen assorted 2- to 4-inch cookies

Springerle are striking-looking anise-flavored cookies made by stamping rolled-out dough with carved rolling pins or wooden molds. For a more pronounced anise flavor, add 1 to 2 teaspoons anise seeds to the storage container.
Have all ingredients at room temperature, 68° to 70°F.
Grease cookie sheets.
Whisk together thoroughly:

3¼ cups all-purpose flour
¼ teaspoon baking powder

Beat on high speed until lightened in color:

4 large eggs

Gradually add and beat until lightened in color, creamy, and thick enough that it drops in thick ribbons, about 3 minutes more:

1⅔ cups sugar
1 teaspoon finely grated lemon zest
1 teaspoon anise extract

Stir in the flour mixture until well blended and smooth.
Sprinkle a clean work surface with:

¼ cup all-purpose flour, plus more for the dough

Turn out the dough onto the work surface and sprinkle with a little more flour. Knead in enough flour to firm the dough and make it manageable. Divide the dough in half and place 1 portion in a sealable plastic bag to prevent it from drying out. Roll out the other portion ¼ inch thick, lifting the dough and lightly dusting the work surface and rolling pin as necessary. Lightly dust a Springerle carved rolling pin or cookie molds with flour; tap off the excess. Firmly roll or press the Springerle rolling pin or molds into the dough to imprint designs. Cut the designs apart using a pastry wheel or sharp knife. With a spatula, transfer the cookies to the cookie sheets, spacing about ½ inch apart. Gather up the dough scraps and knead into the reserved dough. Repeat the rolling and imprinting process until all the dough is used. Set the cookies aside, uncovered, for 10 to 12 hours.

To bake, position a rack in the center of the oven. Preheat the oven to 300°F.

If desired, sprinkle the cookies with:

2 to 3 tablespoons whole or crushed anise seeds

Bake, 1 sheet at a time, until the cookies are almost firm but not colored, 18 to 25 minutes. Transfer the cookies to racks to cool.

If desired, decorate the cookies by highlighting the designs with a food coloring wash as follows: Dilute vegetable food colorings with a bit of water and, using a small brush, apply a light wash of color to raised areas of the imprint. Or paint the raised areas of the imprint with edible gold leaf (available at specialty baking stores). Let the painted cookies stand until completely dry, about 2 hours.

SPEKULATIUS

1 to 2 dozen cookies depending on size of molds

A Christmas specialty from the Rhineland, these cookies are also a favorite in Holland, where they are called *speculaas* and are sometimes made into figures as tall as 2 feet and given to children on December 6, the Feast of Saint Nicholas.

Unlike Springerle molds, which imprint designs on the dough, Spekulatius molds serve as forms for it: a portion of the dough is pushed into the carved-out indentation; the mold is then rapped on the counter to release the dough. If you don't have Spekulatius molds, use ceramic cookie molds stocked by most kitchen stores at Christmastime.

Whisk together thoroughly:

2¾ cups all-purpose flour
1 tablespoon ground cinnamon
1¼ teaspoons ground allspice
¼ teaspoon ground nutmeg

Beat on medium speed until well blended:

12 tablespoons (1½ sticks) unsalted butter, softened
1¼ cups packed dark brown sugar
1 large egg
1 tablespoon milk
2 teaspoons vanilla
¼ teaspoon almond extract
½ teaspoon finely grated lemon zest

Stir in the flour mixture until well blended and smooth. Wrap the dough in plastic and refrigerate for at least 8 hours or up to 3 days. (The dough can also be frozen for up to 1 month. Thaw it completely in the refrigerator before using.)

To bake, position a rack in the center of the oven. Preheat the oven to 350°F. Grease cookie sheets.

Prepare the molds by lightly brushing vegetable oil over all the interior surfaces, being sure to reach all the crevices and indentations. Lightly sprinkle or sift flour over the molds, tipping the molds back and forth until all the crevices are coated. Tap out all the excess flour. The molds must be dusted after each cookie, but they do not need to be reoiled. Working with a small portion of the dough at a time (leave the remainder refrigerated), pull off pieces large enough to fill the mold, and press the dough into the form. Even if the dough seems too stiff at first, work with it; it will soften as the cookie is formed. When the interior is completely filled, press down all over to remove air pockets. Push any dough protruding over the edges back inside the edges of the mold. Cut away the excess dough so the cookie is flush with the back of the mold.

To remove the cookie from a wooden mold, hold the mold upside down and rap it repeatedly and sharply against a hard surface until the cookie loosens. For a ceramic mold, rap it a little more gently against a wooden board or other slightly softer surface to avoid chipping or breaking the form. When the cookie is loosened all over, tap or peel it out onto the sheet. If one particular section sticks, very carefully loosen it with the point of a knife. Space the cookies about 1½ inches apart.

Bake, 1 sheet at a time, until the cookies are tinged with brown at the edges, 15 to 25 minutes. Remove the sheet to a rack and let stand until the cookies firm slightly. Transfer the cookies to racks to cool.

BOURBON BALLS

About sixty 1-inch balls

These get even better as they age.

Sift together into a medium bowl:

1 cup powdered sugar
2 tablespoons unsweetened Dutch-process cocoa

Whisk together until well blended:

¼ cup bourbon
2 tablespoons light corn syrup

Stir into the cocoa mixture. Crush in a food processor or electric mixer:

2½ cups vanilla wafers

(Alternatively, put the wafers in a sealable plastic bag and crush with a rolling pin or the bottom of a heavy saucepan.) Mix with:

1 cup coarsely chopped pecans

Stir the pecan mixture into the cocoa mixture. Roll into 1-inch balls between your palms (the balls do not have to be even). Roll in:

½ cup powdered sugar

Store at room temperature between layers of wax or parchment paper in an airtight container for up to 3 weeks.

GINGERBREAD HOUSE

One 8-inch-wide x 9-inch-tall house

Although gingerbread houses are associated with Christmas, you can create a gingerbread Easter bunny hutch or Halloween witch's cottage just by changing the decorations in this recipe.

GINGERBREAD DOUGH

Whisk together thoroughly:

6 cups all-purpose flour
½ teaspoon baking powder
4 teaspoons ground ginger
4 teaspoons ground cinnamon
½ teaspoon ground cloves or allspice
½ teaspoon salt

Beat on medium speed until very fluffy and well blended:

12 tablespoons (1½ sticks) unsalted butter, softened
1½ cups packed light brown sugar

Beat in until well combined:

2 large eggs
1 cup dark molasses
1 tablespoon water

Beat half of the flour mixture into the molasses mixture until well blended and smooth. Stir in the remaining flour, then knead the mixture until well blended. If the dough is soft, stir in more flour until it is firmer and more manageable but not at all dry.

Place the dough in a sealable plastic bag or airtight plastic container. Set aside in a cool place, but not the refrigerator, for at least 2 hours or up to 6 hours. Or refrigerate the dough for up to 3 days; bring to room temperature before using.

CUTTING OUT PATTERN PIECES

Meanwhile, cut out pattern pieces using either graph paper or smooth, manila-folder-weight paper. Graph paper lines provide easy, automatic guides for measuring and cutting out pattern pieces, but slightly heavier paper yields sturdier patterns. Cut out and label the pattern pieces as follows, shown 843:

One 5½-inch-wide x 7½-inch-high piece for the front and back of the house
One 7-inch-wide x 6½-inch-high piece for the roof
One 5-inch-wide x 3-inch-high piece for the sides of the house

To form the peaked front and back: With a pencil, mark the center point on one of the short ends of the 5½ x 7½-inch rectangle to establish the top of the template. Starting at the lefthand bottom corner, measure 3 inches up the side and mark this point. Repeat on the righthand side. Using a ruler, connect the lefthand mark with the center top mark. Repeat on the righthand side, creating an inverted V. Cut along these lines to create the front and back peaked template.

For the chimney, cut out the pieces as follows:

One 1-inch-wide x 3-inch-high piece for the chimney front
One 1-inch-wide x 1½-inch-high piece for the chimney back
One 1-inch-wide piece, 2¾ inches high on one side and 1½ inches high on the other, shown 843

ROLLING OUT THE DOUGH

Position a rack in the center of the oven. Preheat the oven to 350°F. Have ready several cookie sheets.

Divide the dough in half. Working with 1 portion at a time (leave the other covered to prevent drying), roll out the dough to a scant ¼ inch thick directly on a large sheet of wax or parchment paper; keep the layer

Gingerbread house

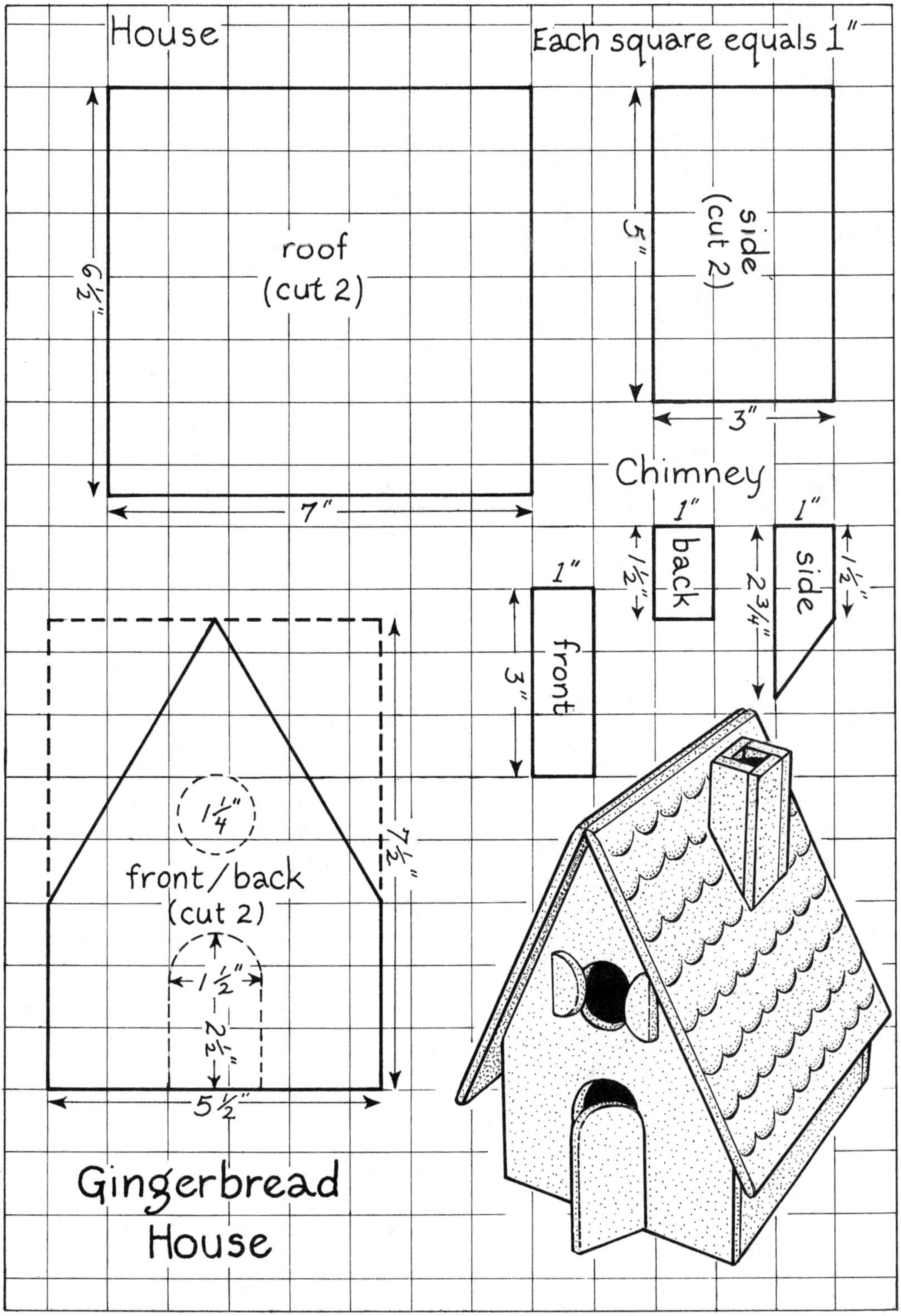
House
Each square equals 1"
roof
(cut 2)
6½"
7"
side
(cut 2)
5"
3"
Chimney
1"
back
1½"
1"
side
2¾"
1½"
1"
front
3"
1¼"
front/back
(cut 2)
1½"
2½"
7½"
5½"
Gingerbread
House

as uniform as possible. This is easier if you have a set of ¼-inch dowels to lay on all 4 sides of the dough and to use as guides, but these are not essential. If necessary, lightly dust the rolling pin with flour to prevent sticking.

CUTTING OUT THE HOUSE PIECES

Before placing pattern pieces on the dough, lightly rub the surface of the dough with a small amount of flour. Gently lay as many pattern pieces as will fit on the dough. Using a sharp knife, wiping the blade clean as you work, cut out the following pieces: house front, back, and 2 sides. Cut away the front door opening, reserving the door piece. If desired, also cut away the centered upstairs window; then split the cutout piece in half lengthwise to use as shutters. Also cut out the chimney front, back, and side pieces. For sides, cut around the angled pattern piece, then turn the pattern over and cut out again. Immediately lift the patterns from the surface of the dough to prevent sticking. Peel away the excess dough from around the cutout pieces and reserve the scraps in a sealable plastic bag to prevent drying. As necessary, cut apart the paper with scissors so individual house pieces (along with the paper) can be transferred to the cookie sheets; group large house pieces together on larger cookie sheets, and chimney, door, and shutter pieces, if using, together on a smaller sheet, spacing the pieces about 1 inch apart.

If wax or parchment paper is unavailable, roll the dough out on a lightly floured work surface, lifting the dough frequently and lightly dusting the rolling pin with flour as needed to prevent sticking. Using a wide thin-bladed spatula, gently transfer the pieces from the work surface to lightly greased cookie sheets, trying not to stretch them out of shape. If pieces do stretch, trim them back to the original pattern size using a paring knife; remove the scraps from the cookie sheets. Reserve all the scraps in a sealable plastic bag.

Continue rolling out the dough and cutting out until all the pieces are prepared. If desired, add a curved roof tile design to the roof pieces by pressing the curve of a flatware spoon into the dough surface to produce indentations at regular intervals. If desired, add clapboard texture to the house sides, front and back, by drawing the back of a fork horizontally across the dough surface so the tines produce lines.

BAKING THE HOUSE PIECES

Bake just until the pieces are tinged with brown and beginning to darken at the edges, 11 to 15 minutes for larger house pieces, 6 to 8 minutes for chimney, door, and shutter pieces; rotate the sheets halfway through baking for even browning. Remove the sheets to racks and let stand until the pieces are cool and firm, about 15 minutes. Transfer the pieces, along with the paper, to racks to cool.

MAKING THE ICING

Royal Icing is the glue for constructing your gingerbread house. Double the recipe on page 1009 to yield enough for both gluing and decorating the finished house with "snow" or other finishing piping.

CONSTRUCTING THE HOUSE

If you have a pastry bag and large writing tip, apply the icing glue with it. Otherwise, apply it as neatly as possible using a spoon or the tip of a knife. Working on a large wax- or parchment-paper-lined tray, start by putting the house front, sides, and back together. Pipe a line of icing on each end of 1 side piece. Place it between the front and back pieces, gently pressing at the joints to lightly hold it in place until the second side is added. Add icing to the second side piece and fit it in place between the front and back, adjusting as necessary to make the house square. Working on 1 side of the house at a time, pipe icing along the angled front and back edges. Grasp 1 roof piece by the edges and lay it against the piped edges, gently pressing to lightly hold it in place until the second roof piece is added. To finish the roof, pipe icing along the angled front and back edges as well as the top edge of the roof piece already in place. Press the second piece in place, adjusting so it fits snugly against the first roof piece to form a peak. Force additional icing into any seams that need reinforcing, wiping off the excess with your fingertip.

For the chimney, glue the 4 pieces together as for the house base. Before icing the base, set the chimney in place on the rooftop. If it does not sit up straight, carefully trim the chimney bottom with a sharp knife until the bottom angle aligns evenly with the rooftop. Then pipe icing on the base of the chimney and secure it in place on the rooftop. Let the house stand, uncovered, for at least 1 hour and preferably for 8 hours before decorating.

DECORATING THE HOUSE

Decorate according to the season. For Christmas, you may want to add Royal Icing, 1009, snow and icicles along the edges of the roof, and accent the house with candy canes, peppermint pinwheels, and other appropriate sweets.

CANDY

Most candy making is an art—and most candy recipes require a considerable degree of patience, time, attention, and practice to get right. Being well prepared is absolutely vital. Timing is crucial: Fudge can overcook in just the time it takes to retrieve the right spatula. Before beginning, check to make sure you have all the ingredients and equipment you need at the ready. Read through the recipe to see if there are any steps that must be done in advance, and make sure your equipment is very clean, to help avoid crystalization, also.

Accurate measurements are essential in candy making. One final basic counsel: Watch the weather report. Heat and humidity can adversely affect many candies. On humid days, candy must cook longer, to a temperature at least 2 degrees higher than on dry days, and you should dip chocolates or make cooked fondant, hard candy, divinity, and any candy that requires drying time on a rack only when it is cool and dry.

THE COLD WATER TEST

Most experienced candy makers use both a thermometer and the ice-cold water test. Exact temperature as measured by a thermometer is a useful guide in candy making, but a candy that will be ready at 250°F one day may need to be 3 degrees higher the next. To perform the ice-cold water test, use a clean wooden spoon or a metal spoon (run under hot water to warm it) to drop a small quantity of candy syrup—less than a teaspoonful—into a small container of very cold (not ice) water. Quickly gather the syrup between your fingers. The temperature to which the sugar has been cooked can be identified by the way the syrup reacts. As the water heats and evaporates, the concentration of sugar in the syrup rises; the higher the concentration of sugar, the harder the mixture will be upon cooling. The following table lists the stages of cooking, the temperature range for each one, the visual characteristics of each, and a few of the candies that are made at that stage.

Whether you should let the syrup continue cooking while you are using the ice-cold water test depends on how quickly you work. If testing takes you several minutes, remove the pan from the heat, remembering that doing so cools the syrup and can delay the cooking; if you are an old hand at this, leave the pan on the heat, as a few seconds won't make much difference.

ABOUT CHOCOLATE AND COCOA

Chocolate comes from almond-shaped beans that grow inside the pods of cacao trees in tropical areas near the equator. Cocoa beans, as they are known in the United States, develop their distinctive chocolate

THE STAGES OF COOKED SYRUP

STAGE		TEMPERATURE	VISUAL CHARACTERISTICS
Thread		215°F	Makes a brittle thread that can be stretched with the fingers
Pearl		220° to 222°F	Runs off a metal spoon in drops
Blow/ Soufflé		230° to 234°F	Makes a loose thread
			A SPOONFUL OF SYRUP DROPPED INTO ICE-COLD WATER WILL MAKE:
Soft Ball	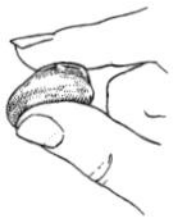	234° to 242°F	A limp, sticky ball that flattens when removed from the water
Firm Ball		244° to 248°F	A ball that holds its shape and will not flatten when removed from the water
Hard Ball		250° to 266°F	A hard ball that holds its shape when removed from the water but is still pliable
Soft Crack	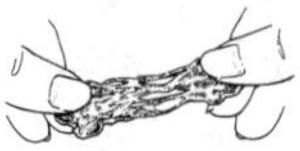	270° to 290°F	Firm strands that can be stretched or bent when removed from the water
Hard Crack		300° to 310°F	Stiff, firm threads that break easily when removed from the water

CARAMELIZED SUGAR

Light Caramel	320° to 338°F	Syrup changes from honey colored to light brown
Medium Caramel	356°F	Sugar turns a medium brown color
Dark Caramel	374°F	Sugar turns a dark brown color

Note: As with baking, altitude can make a difference in candy making. If you live above sea level, candy should come in 1 degree lower than indicated in the recipe for each increase of 500 feet above sea level. For instance, if you're making fudge that needs to cook to 234°F, your syrup should "fudge" at about 230°F at 2000 feet, and at about 224°F at 5000 feet.

ABOUT CRYSTALLIZATION

One of the greatest frustrations in candy making comes when a smooth, promising candy syrup turns with lightning speed into a grainy mass. This is often caused by sugar crystals that have formed on the sides of the pan in the process of being stirred down into the syrup. Here are several ways to prevent this from happening:

If the recipe calls for butter, grease the sides of the pan with some of it before putting in the other ingredients.

Brush down any crystals on the sides of the pan with a pastry brush dipped into hot water. With high-temperature syrups, it may be necessary to brush down the sides of the pan more than once if the syrup is boiling violently.

Avoid stirring the syrup once it begins to boil. (The rare exceptions to this rule are noted in individual recipes.)

Warm the candy thermometer before placing it in the hot syrup to avoid shocking the syrup with cold metal, which can also cause crystallization.

If you use the cold water test, be sure that your spoon is wooden or warmed metal and absolutely clean.

If you detect the beginnings of crystallization, add a small quantity of water to the pan and begin the cooking process over again. The finished product will not be adversely affected, and in the case of fudge, the texture will be even finer than usual.

When pouring or molding the finished syrup, avoid scraping the dregs from the pan. The crystallization rate of the syrup nearest the bottom of the pan, which has been exposed to the greatest heat, is faster than that of the free-flowing syrup from the upper portion. Adding the former to the latter can cause the entire batch to crystallize.

flavor, color, and aroma only after they have been fermented, dried, and roasted. To make chocolate, the roasted beans are chopped into small pieces called nibs. The nibs are rich in cocoa butter, a cream-colored, natural vegetable fat that melts during the grinding process producing a dark brown, fluid mass called chocolate liquor—the primary ingredient in all forms of chocolate (except white chocolate).

Chocolate liquor, also known as unsweetened, bitter, baking, or cooking chocolate, is pure chocolate with no added ingredients. It contains nearly equal parts cocoa butter and cocoa solids, the meat of the cocoa bean, which is why it imparts such a deep, rich chocolate flavor to anything you make with it. Unsweetened chocolate is always combined with sugar and other ingredients to make American-style cakes, brownies, frostings, and fudges.

Extra-bittersweet, bittersweet, semisweet, and sweet cooking chocolates are made of chocolate liquor, not more than 12 percent milk solids, cocoa butter, sugar, vanilla or vanillin, and lecithin. Bittersweet bars often have a deeper chocolate flavor than those labeled "semisweet," and they are apt to be less sweet (although the amount of sugar they contain is not regulated). These chocolates may be used interchangeably in most recipes, but their differences can alter the flavor, texture, and appearance of the finished product. For that reason, try to use the chocolate specified in the recipe.

Milk chocolate, America's favorite eating chocolate, is the sweetest of the sweet chocolates. It is lighter in color and less intensely chocolate flavored than dark chocolate because it contains less chocolate liquor and at least 3.39 percent butterfat and 12 percent milk solids. Milk chocolate is rarely used for baking because of its high sugar content and heat-sensitive milk solids.

White chocolate resembles milk chocolate in composition except that it contains no chocolate liquor, which is why it is ivory, not brown. The cocoa butter it contains gives it a very mild, milk-chocolate flavor and a creamy mouth feel. This product should not be confused with white confectionery coating, which is made with a vegetable fat other than cocoa butter. White chocolate is used most frequently in cheesecakes, light-textured cakes, mousses, and icings when a delicate chocolate flavor is desired.

Couverture, which means coating or covering, is a term that confectioners use to identify dark, milk, and white chocolates of the highest quality. Couvertures contain a high percentage of cocoa solids and cocoa butter, so they have a deep, rich flavor and a smooth, creamy texture. Confectioners regularly use them to enrobe pieces of candy in a thin coating of chocolate, to mold shapes, and to create luscious chocolate creations.

Chocolate chips come in various flavors and sizes and are formulated to withstand normal oven heat and to hold their shape in baked desserts without melting, even though the fat is fully melted. For that reason, they should not be substituted for bar chocolates in recipes that require melted chocolate.

Cocoa is pulverized, partially defatted chocolate liquor that contains 10 to 24 percent cocoa butter and absolutely no sugar. Two types of cocoa are available in supermarkets: nonalkalized (natural) and alkalized (Dutch-process). Nonalkalized cocoa is light in color and somewhat acidic with a strong, assertive chocolate flavor. Alkalized, or Dutch-process, cocoa has been processed with alkali to neutralize its natural acidity by raising its pH level. It is darker, milder in taste, and less acidic than nonalkalized cocoa. When buying Dutch-process cocoa, look for labels that say Dutch-process or European-style. Don't confuse cocoa powder, which is unsweetened, with instant cocoa, which usually contains 80 percent sugar, is precooked, and has an emulsifier added to make it dissolve readily in either a hot or a cold liquid. In baking, use nonalkalized cocoa in recipes that call for baking soda and alkalized cocoa in those that use baking powder as the primary leavener. In recipes where no leavening is required, the choice is a matter of taste and we call simply for unsweetened cocoa. For details about cocoa and chocolate as a beverage, see page 33. For dipping chocolate, see page 350.

SUBSTITUTIONS

Cocoa may be judiciously substituted for unsweetened chocolate in sauces and some other recipes by using 1 tablespoon butter or shortening and 3 tablespoons cocoa for each square or ounce of unsweetened chocolate called for. In baking, it is wiser to use recipes written either for chocolate or for cocoa, as cocoa has a flourlike quality that must be compensated for if chocolate is substituted, lest the texture of the finished product be compromised.

ABOUT STORAGE AND SHELF LIFE

Ideally, chocolate should be stored in a cool, odor-free place away from heat and direct sunlight at 60° to 70°F with a humidity of less than 50 percent. Fluctuations in temperatures may cause a gray cast (bloom) to appear on the chocolate, a superficial flaw that will disappear when the chocolate is melted. Under optimum conditions, dark chocolate will last at least one year, milk chocolate ten months, and white chocolate eight months.

If chocolate is stored in the refrigerator or freezer, wrap it in usable-size portions and do not unwrap the pieces until completely thawed or brought to room temperature. Condensation will form on the surface of any unwrapped cold or frozen chocolate left at room temperature, and this moisture will damage the appearance of the chocolate and prevent it from melting smoothly.

TO GRATE OR CHOP CHOCOLATE

We prefer to chop chocolate on a clean, dry cutting board with a large knife. Slightly chilled chocolate (do not refrigerate for long, as condensation will damage the chocolate) can be grated by hand or processed in a food processor. Grated or chopped, chocolate moves around a lot due to static electricity; use a large cutting board or grate into a large bowl to control the mess.

TO MAKE CHOCOLATE SHAVINGS

Warm the smooth back surface of a chocolate bar by setting it in a warm place or stroking it with your palm. To make shavings, scrape the blade of a paring knife across it at a 45 degree angle or use a vegetable peeler to do the same.

ABOUT MELTING CHOCOLATE

Chocolate is heat-sensitive and burns easily, especially when melted alone. Do not heat dark chocolate over 120°F or milk and white chocolates over 110°F. White chocolate is the most delicate of all. Containers and stirring utensils must be clean and perfectly dry; stray drops of water or condensation must not be allowed to touch the chocolate. Small amounts of water may cause melted chocolate to lose its gloss and tighten or "seize" instead of melting smoothly.

Water-Bath Method: Chop the chocolate into almond-size pieces with a sharp, dry knife. Place one-third of it in the top of a double boiler or in a bowl that fits snugly over the top of a saucepan. Fill the bottom pan with enough tap hot water (130°F) to touch the bottom of the top bowl, but not so much as to allow the bowl to float. Avoid splashing water into it. Begin stirring with a rubber spatula when the outside edges of the chocolate begin to liquefy. Gradually add the rest of the chocolate. Carefully lift the bowl of chocolate from the water bath when the chocolate is nearly melted, dry the bottom, and continue stirring the chocolate until it is smooth and shiny.

Microwave Method: Select a dry, microwave-safe plastic bowl and fill it no more than half full with chopped chocolate. Microwave 1 to 8 ounces of dark chocolate, uncovered, on medium power for 1½ minutes to 3½ minutes, depending on the amount. Use low power for milk and white chocolates. Stir it after the first 1½ minutes, even if it appears firm. If necessary, continue microwaving in increasingly shorter increments at the appropriate power level until most of the chocolate is melted. Stir until the chocolate is smooth and shiny.

ABOUT TEMPERING CHOCOLATE

Tempering is simply a matter of heating and cooling melted chocolate to predetermined temperatures so that the finished chocolate will have a glossy surface and a smooth texture when it dries. Chocolate is in that condition when it leaves the factory, and with proper handling and storage, it should still be in that condition when you buy it. Once you melt it, however, the tempering process must be repeated before you can use it to dip confections, mold novelty shapes, and make fanciful decorations. Tempering is not required when melted chocolate is used as an ingredient in a recipe. To verify the temperature of your chocolate, you will need a thermometer with a range of 70° to 130°F. A chocolate tempering machine is a practical investment only if candy making is more than an occasional project for you. Elaine Gonzalez, chocolate specialist and teacher, has simplified the tempering process for us in the two easy methods that follow.

Chunk-Tempering Method: Set aside 4 ounces chocolate cut into 1-inch chunks. Melt 1 pound chopped chocolate until smooth and shiny. (Melt blemished, untempered chocolate to 110° to 120°F.) Transfer the chocolate to another bowl and cool to 100°F. Add the chocolate chunks and stir with a rubber spatula until the temperature cools to a maximum of 88°F for milk and white chocolates and 90°F for dark chocolate. Remove the chunks, place them on a wax- or parchment-paper–lined baking sheet, and refrigerate until dry; they are reusable. The chocolate is now in temper and ready to be tested and used.

The Easiest Way to Temper Chocolate: (Controlled-Melt Method) Set aside 4 ounces chocolate cut into 1-inch chunks, in case you need it. Microwave 1 pound chopped dark chocolate, uncovered, in a microwave-safe plastic bowl on medium power for about 3 minutes; stir. Use low power for milk and white chocolates. Continue microwaving in increasingly shorter increments until two-thirds of the chocolate is melted. Stir gently to coax the remaining soft pieces to melt. Insert the thermometer. If the temperature is no higher than 90°F (88°F for milk and white chocolates), the chocolate is in temper and ready to be tested and used. If it is warmer, cool it with the reserved chunks until it reaches the proper temperature (see Chunk-Tempering Method).

ABOUT TESTING AND MAINTAINING THE TEMPER IN CHOCOLATE

To test tempered chocolate, chill a dab of tempered chocolate on a piece of wax paper for 3 minutes. If it is dry to the touch and evenly glossy, the chocolate is ready to use. To maintain the temper in a bowl of chocolate over an extended period, place it in a water bath up to 2 degrees warmer than the maximum temperatures allowed for tempered dark, milk, and white chocolates (90°F for dark, 88°F for milk and white chocolates). Or microwave in 5-second increments until warm. Be careful. If you exceed the maximum temperatures, you will break the chocolate's temper and have to begin again.

ABOUT MOLDING CHOCOLATE

Molding is fun, as long as you use tempered chocolate. Tempered chocolate sets up quickly, pulls away from the sides of the mold when it dries, and releases easily. Select shiny, scratch-free molds made of metal or food-grade plastic. They should be clean, dry, and at room temperature (68° to 70°F).

Flat Sheet Molds: Spoon the chocolate into the cavities, taking care not to overfill them. Rap the mold on the counter to settle the chocolate and release the air bubbles. If necessary, use a long, metal icing spatula to scrape the wet chocolate off the surface of the mold before it dries. Refrigerate the mold until the chocolate feels cold (10 to 30 minutes, depending on the size of the cavities). Invert the mold onto a wax- or parchment-paper–lined baking sheet, tapping the back lightly to release the chocolate. If it does not release, chill it for a few minutes longer. Refrigerate leftover melted chocolate on a wax- or parchment-paper–lined baking sheet until dry.

Molding a Hollow Bowl: Melt and temper 2 pounds chocolate. Pour 1 cup of the chocolate into the bottom of a 6- to 8-inch metal bowl, rotating it to coat all but the rim. Pour the excess into the bowl of tempered chocolate. Clean the rim and refrigerate for 5 minutes. Apply a second layer of chocolate; refrigerate it for about 20 minutes. To release the chocolate, grasp the top of the mold with both hands, invert it, and press. If it does not release, chill longer. Refrigerate leftover chocolate on a paper-lined baking sheet until dry.

Molding a Two-Part Chocolate Mold: Melt and temper 1 pound chocolate. To mold a hollow figure, paint both cavities with a thin layer of chocolate using a 1-inch-wide pastry or artist's brush. Spoon the chocolate into half the mold (the deepest half, if there is one), filling it to the rim. Rap it on the counter to settle the chocolate and release the air bubbles. Assemble the two halves, aligning the pin locks (if the mold has them) and securing the sides with clips. Immediately shake and rotate the mold vigorously to allow the filled half to coat the walls of the other half with chocolate. Refrigerate the mold, newly coated side down, turning it frequently as it cools. Release the clips after 10 minutes. Leave refrigerated for 10 to 20 minutes more, depending on the size of the mold. Remove the back half of the mold first. If it resists, chill longer. Trim the seams with a wire cheese slicer or a knife. Refrigerate leftover melted chocolate on a wax- or parchment-paper–lined baking sheet until dry.

ABOUT DIPPING CHOCOLATE

The centers to be dipped should be dry, firm, and 70°F, if possible. To dip fruit or cookies, hold them by the edge and immerse them halfway into a bowl of tempered chocolate; drain off the excess. Place them on a wax- or parchment-paper–lined baking sheet; refrigerate briefly. They will remain shiny and firm at room temperature. Reserve fork dipping for firm centers such as nuts, marzipan, and fondant balls. Dipping truffles is a challenging task for inexperienced dippers because the centers are too soft to handle unless they are chilled, but dipping cold truffles causes the chocolate surface to dry to a dull finish and be streaked with tiny cracks that ultimately leak. The hand-dipping method that follows eliminates most of these problems.

Dipping Truffles: Melt and temper 1 pound chocolate (enough for 35 truffles). Smear a handful of tempered chocolate on the palm of your left hand. (This works well if you wear tight-fitting latex gloves.) Place a truffle in your chocolate-coated palm and roll it around with the fingers of your right hand until it is completely covered. Place it on a wax- or parchment-paper–lined baking sheet to dry. Continue in that manner, coating your palm frequently with chocolate, until all the truffles have been dipped. (Alternatively, you may use a candy dipper. When the center is coated, tap the dipper on the side of the bowl to remove excess chocolate. Transfer them to a wax- or parchment-paper–lined pan to dry.) When they are dry, dip them again, this time placing them on a grid-style cooling rack. While they are still wet, roll them around the rack to rough up the surface. Transfer them to another wax- or parchment-paper–lined pan before they dry and refrigerate them for about 5 minutes. Refrigerate leftover melted chocolate on a wax- or parchment-paper–lined pan; it is reusable.

DARK CHOCOLATE TRUFFLES (BASIC RECIPE)

30 to 35 pieces

Truffles are the easiest chocolate candies to make, and the most sensually satisfying to eat—but use the best-quality chocolate you can afford, since there are very few added ingredients to boost the flavor of a mediocre one.

Chop into very tiny pieces and place in a medium mixing bowl:

8 ounces bittersweet or semisweet chocolate

Scald in a small saucepan over medium heat:

½ cup heavy cream

Pour the hot cream all at once over the chocolate and stir gently with a rubber spatula until the ganache mixture is smooth and thoroughly blended. Tightly cover, let cool to room temperature, and refrigerate until thick and quite stiff, 3 to 4 hours.

Refrigerate a baking sheet until cold; line it with wax or parchment paper. Use a melon baller or pastry bag fitted with a ½-inch plain tip to shape the ganache into ¾-inch balls on the lined baking sheet. Cover loosely with plastic wrap and refrigerate until firm, but not stiff, 2 to 3 hours. When the chocolate is firm, dust your hands with cornstarch and roll the centers into balls between your palms. Let the balls come to room temperature and keep them at room temperature until ready to dip, up to 12 hours.

Temper, 849:

1 pound bittersweet or semisweet chocolate couverture

Using your hands or a candy dipper, dip the centers, one by one. Place on a wax- or parchment-paper–lined baking sheet. Cover and refrigerate until set, 2 to 3 minutes. Place the truffles in candy cups. Serve right away or store between layers of wax or parchment paper in an airtight container in the refrigerator for up to 3 weeks or in the freezer for up to 2 months. If frozen, thaw for 24 to 48 hours in the refrigerator. Remove the truffles from the refrigerator 30 to 45 minutes before serving.

MILK CHOCOLATE TRUFFLES

Prepare Dark Chocolate Truffles, above, substituting 12 ounces milk chocolate for the bittersweet or semisweet chocolate and reducing the amount of cream to ½ cup. Place the chocolate and cream (unscalded) in the top of a double boiler over hot, not boiling, water and stir frequently until the ganache mixture is smooth. Proceed as directed.

ABOUT FUDGE

Fudge, a semisoft candy made from a cooked sugar syrup enriched with cream or butter, is a truly American candy—apparently invented in a small grocery store in Baltimore in 1886, by accident (like so many culinary successes), when a batch of caramel grained, or crystallized, prematurely.

DARK CHOCOLATE FUDGE

1¼ pounds, about 64 pieces

Combine in a large heavy-bottomed saucepan:

2 cups sugar
¼ cup light corn syrup
½ cup half-and-half
½ cup heavy cream
⅛ teaspoon salt

Stir over low heat until the sugar is dissolved, about 5 minutes. Bring to a boil and boil for 1 minute. Brush down the sides of the pan with a pastry brush dipped in warm water and remove from the heat. Stir in until melted and completely smooth:

6 ounces bittersweet or semisweet chocolate, finely chopped

Brush down the sides of the pan again, then set the pan over medium heat, place a warmed candy thermometer in the pan, and cook the mixture, without stirring, until it reaches 238°F, the soft-ball stage. Remove from the heat. Add but do not stir in (stirring at this point can cause graininess):

2 tablespoons unsalted butter, softened
1 teaspoon vanilla

Cool the candy to 110°F by placing the bottom of the pan in cold water to stop the cooking. Alternatively, pour it out onto a marble slab or baking sheet (inverted over a rack) sprinkled with cold water, without scraping the bottom of the pan.

When it is cool, stir the fudge in the pan with a wooden spoon or work it on the slab with a candy scraper just until it "snaps" and begins to lose its sheen. Or transfer the cooled fudge to the bowl of a heavy-duty mixer. Using the paddle attachment, beat the fudge on low speed until it begins to thicken and lose its sheen, 5 to 10 minutes. Watch the mixture carefully or it may thicken too much and become unworkable. Stir in:

1 to 1½ cups walnuts, coarsely chopped (optional)

Line an 8 x 8-inch pan with aluminum foil and butter the foil. Turn the fudge into the pan. Smooth the top with a spatula dipped in hot water as needed. Let stand for at least 1 hour. Using a large, heavy knife, score the fudge into 1-inch squares. Cover and refrigerate for at least 24 hours. Remove the fudge from the pan, peel off the aluminum foil, and finish cutting the fudge into squares. Serve in candy cups. Store the pieces between layers of wax or parchment paper in an airtight container. Fudge keeps well for up to 10 days at room temperature or for up to 1 month in the refrigerator.

CARAMEL CORN

About 6 cups

Microwave popcorn is too fragile in this recipe.

Pop and place in a large mixing bowl:

¾ cup popcorn

Melt in a medium, heavy-bottomed saucepan:

1½ tablespoons unsalted butter

Add:

1½ cups packed light brown sugar
6 tablespoons water

Stir over low heat until the sugar is dissolved. Bring to a boil over medium heat, then brush down the sides of the pan with a pastry brush dipped in warm water. Place a warmed candy thermometer in the pan and boil, without stirring, until it reaches 234°F, the soft-ball stage. Remove from the heat and pour over the popped corn. Stir gently with a wooden spoon until the corn is well coated, then turn it out onto a baking sheet lined with wax or parchment paper. When the corn is cool enough to handle, lightly butter your fingers and separate it into individual kernels or press it into balls or lollipops (with an embedded loop of thick string or a wooden stick). Caramel corn keeps well in an airtight container for about ten days.

CLEAR PEANUT BRITTLE

2 pounds

Oil a marble slab or oil and refrigerate a baking sheet to chill it. Combine in a large, heavy-bottomed saucepan:

4 cups sugar
½ cup water
⅛ teaspoon cream of tartar

Stir gently over low heat until the sugar is dissolved. Brush down the sides of the pan with a pastry brush dipped in warm water. Increase the heat to medium-high and bring the mixture to a boil. Place a warmed candy thermometer in the pan and cook, without stirring, until it reaches the light caramel stage, 320°F. Remove from the heat.

Quickly stir in with a lightly oiled wooden spoon:

2 tablespoons unsalted butter, cut into small pieces

2 cups roasted unsalted peanuts or other nuts

Carefully pour the syrup onto the marble slab or baking sheet. Quickly spread the mixture ¼ inch thick with a lightly oiled wooden spoon. Let cool completely, then break the brittle into pieces. Store between layers of wax paper in an airtight container at room temperature for up to 1 month.

ABOUT FONDANT

Fondant is a candy itself, and is also used to make other candies, either as filling or as coating. For example, fondant centers can be dipped in chocolate, and melted fondant can ice pastries and confections, especially the little teacakes called petits fours. Fondant is made from nothing more than water, sugar, and corn syrup or cream of tartar. You can enrich it by using milk or cream in place of the water if you wish, or by adding butter, or by substituting brown sugar for part of the sugar. Fondant is always cooked to the soft-ball stage (234° to 242°F). If cooked to a higher temperature, fondant will be too firm to handle upon cooling.

The key to a successful fondant is controlling the crystallization of the sugar—controlling, not preventing, because this mixture must crystallize, but in a predictable and controlled manner. After cooking, pour the sugar syrup onto a marble slab or baking sheet (inverted over a rack) lightly sprinkled with water. (Do not scrape out the bottom of the pan, for the sugar there will have a different texture.) Let the fondant cool undisturbed, being careful not to jostle the pan, lest it crystallize too soon. When it has cooled, stir the fondant in a figure-8 pattern. It will go through several stages as you stir, from clear to cloudy to opaque to very white. Once it thickens and becomes white in color, knead by hand until it is smooth and pliable. If the fondant is to be melted down, it can be used immediately; otherwise, it needs to ripen for 24 hours. Even professional candy makers sometimes overcook fondant so that it is too hard to knead. If this happens to you, simply place the mixture in the top of a double boiler over simmering water, add ⅔ cup hot water, and stir constantly until the fondant has thoroughly melted. Then return it to the heavy saucepan and bring it to a boil again. Brush down the sides of the pan with a pastry brush dipped in warm water, place a warmed candy thermometer in the pan, and boil the mixture, uncovered and without stirring, to the soft-ball stage, 234°F. Cool, stir, and knead the fondant as above. To ripen fondant, form it into a ball, cover it with a damp cloth or paper towel, seal it tightly with plastic wrap, and let cool to room temperature. Fondant can be stored in the refrigerator for 3 to 4 days, but be sure to bring it to room temperature before using.

To dip candy centers in fondant, melt the fondant in the top of a double boiler over barely simmering water, stirring frequently and making sure that the temperature does not rise above 140°F. Remove the double boiler from the heat but keep the fondant over the pan of water to keep it liquid. Drop a candy center into the fondant and turn to coat completely. Lift out the candy using a candy dipper or fork, let the excess drip off, and place it on a wax- or parchment-paper–lined plate. Refrigerate for 15 to 20 minutes to firm up. To cover petits fours or other pastries with fondant, place them on a rack over a baking sheet lined with wax or parchment paper. Melt the fondant in the top of a double boiler over barely simmering water, stirring frequently. If it seems too thick, add a little warm water until it is thin enough to pour over the pastries. Flavor and color the fondant, if desired, then pour it over the petits fours in a steady stream. Refrigerate petits fours for 15 to 20 minutes to set the fondant.

BASIC FONDANT

1¼ pounds

Bring to a boil in a large, heavy-bottomed saucepan:

1 cup water

Remove the pan from the heat, add, and stir until dissolved:

3 cups sugar

Return the pan to the heat and bring to a boil. Sprinkle with:

¼ teaspoon cream of tartar

This may make the syrup boil up, so be ready to stir with a long-handled wooden spoon. Brush down the sides of the pan with a pastry brush dipped in warm water. Place a warmed candy thermometer in the pan and boil, uncovered and without stirring, until it reaches 234°F, the soft-ball stage.

Meanwhile, sprinkle a marble slab or a baking sheet (inverted over a rack) with cold water. Remove the pan from the heat and pour the syrup onto the wet surface, without scraping the bottom of the pan. Let the syrup cool for 5 to 10 minutes. (If on a baking sheet, the mixture will be thicker and may take up to 30 minutes longer to cool.) When you can place your hand over the fondant and feel no heat rising, test a corner by touching it with a fingertip. If it holds the indentation, it is ready to work.

Use a spatula, a candy scraper, or even a clean putty knife to work the syrup by lifting and folding, always from the edges to the center, then stir in a figure-8 pattern, pushing the fondant back out to the sides. When the mixture begins to turn white, dust your hands with powdered sugar, gather the mixture into a ball, then push it outward with the heel of your hand. Draw it back in with a candy scraper and repeat the process until the surface is smooth and creamy looking.

After kneading the fondant, shape it into a ball and cover it with a damp cloth or paper towel. Tightly cover the ball with plastic wrap or place it in a sealable plastic bag. Let the fondant ripen in a cool place overnight; it gets better day by day. If not using it for several days, replace the damp cloth or towel whenever it dries out. To keep the fondant for several weeks or months, store it in the refrigerator. When ready to use the fondant, dust a work surface with:

Powdered sugar

To color fondant, place it on the work surface dusted with powdered sugar. Make several slashes in the mass and use a toothpick to dot in a few drops of food coloring paste. Knead and fold the mass to distribute the color evenly.

To flavor fondant, work in the flavoring the same way. Use one of the following:

1 to 2 teaspoons vanilla, almond extract, or rose or orange flower water
3 to 5 drops oil of peppermint or anise oil
1 tablespoon Grand Marnier, kirsch, framboise, or other liqueur
2 teaspoons grated orange or lemon zest
½ cup shredded sweetened dried coconut
2 to 4 ounces bittersweet, semisweet, milk, or white chocolate, melted
⅓ cup peanut or hazelnut butter
½ cup almonds or walnuts, toasted and chopped
⅓ cup finely chopped dried cherries, candied orange peel, or candied ginger

To shape fondant, make sure the mixture is at room temperature. Dust the work surface generously with:

Powdered sugar

You may find it easier to work with only half of the fondant at one time. Form it into a long cylinder by rolling it on the work surface, then cut into candy-size pieces or mold it into shapes. To use fondant as coating, heat it in the top of a double boiler set over barely simmering water. If it is too thick, add 1 tablespoon hot water at a time and stir until the proper consistency is reached. Be careful not to heat the fondant over 140°F or it will become too stiff.

UNCOOKED FONDANT

1½ pounds; about seventy-five 1-inch balls

This uncooked version of fondant for candies or candy centers is plenty fast, and foolproof, but not quite as creamy as the cooked variety. It can be colored or flavored just like Basic Fondant.

Beat until soft:

8 tablespoons (1 stick) unsalted butter
¾ teaspoon vanilla
½ teaspoon almond, mint, orange, or lemon extract (optional)
¼ teaspoon salt

Add very slowly and beat until very light:

⅔ cup sweetened condensed milk

Add, cup by cup:

5 cups powdered sugar, sifted

Dust a work surface with:

1 cup powdered sugar

Turn the candy out onto the work surface and work the sugar into the fondant. Shape it into 1-inch balls. Raisins, nuts, or bits of candied fruit may be used as centers. Refrigerate the balls to harden. The centers may be dipped in chocolate if desired, 850.

ABOUT PRALINE

Two distinct candies, both with the same name. The one that Americans pronounce PRAH-leen is a patty-shaped pecan candy from New Orleans. PRAY-leen is a French invention—a clear nut brittle, made with almonds or hazelnuts and pulverized for use in desserts. (Just to confuse things, praliné, pronounced prah-leen-AY, is the French word for confections made with praline powder.) New Orleans pralines have an unmistakable grain that comes from beating the sugar mixture while it is warm; that and the city's notorious humidity has inspired a softer, more fudgelike candy than the French brittle. New Orleans pralines are cooked to the soft-ball stage, about 236°F. French pralines are cooked to a much higher temperature, the medium caramel stage, about 356°F.

NEW ORLEANS PRALINES

1½ pounds; about 24 patties

Buttermilk gives these pralines their delectable tang.

Preheat the oven to 350°F. Spread in a baking sheet and toast in the oven, stirring occasionally until very lightly browned, 5 to 8 minutes:

2 cups pecan pieces

Line a baking sheet with wax or parchment paper, or with aluminum foil that is the lightly buttered. Combine in a large, heavy-bottomed saucepan:

2 cups sugar
½ cup packed light brown sugar
1 cup buttermilk
1 teaspoon baking soda
Pinch of salt

Stir over low heat with a long-handled wooden spoon until the sugar is dissolved. Brush down the sides of the pan with a pastry brush dipped in warm water. Add:

4 tablespoons (½ stick) unsalted butter, softened and cut into small pieces

Stir until the butter is completely melted. Increase the heat to medium, place a warmed candy thermometer in the pan, and cook, without stirring, until it reaches 236°F, the soft-ball stage. Remove from the heat. Quickly stir in the toasted pecans and:

1 teaspoon vanilla

Beat with a wooden spoon until the mixture begins to thicken and become opaque, about 1 minute. Drop tablespoonfuls onto the lined baking sheet, forming patties about 2 inches in diameter. Let the pralines stand until completely cool, about 30 minutes. Store between layers of wax or parchment paper in an airtight container for several days.

PRALINE *¼ pound; 1¼ cups*

A mixture of equal parts almonds and hazelnuts is traditionally, but other nuts may be substituted. Praline can be folded into cake batters, mousses, and custards. It can also garnish desserts; try pressing it onto the sides of a cake or sprinkling over vanilla ice cream.

Coat a 15 x 10-inch baking sheet with vegetable oil spray. Combine in a 4-cup, heavy-bottomed saucepan:

1 cup sugar
½ cup water
⅛ teaspoon cream of tartar

Stir over low heat until the sugar is dissolved. Brush down the sides of the pan with a pastry brush dipped in warm water. Bring to a boil. Place a warmed candy thermometer in the pan, increase the heat to medium-high, and cook, without stirring, until it reaches the medium caramel stage, 356°F. Add:

1 cup whole blanched almonds or skinned hazelnuts, or a combination, lightly toasted

Stir quickly with a wooden spoon to coat the nuts completely with the caramel. Remove from the heat and immediately pour the syrup onto the baking sheet. Let cool completely. Break into small pieces and pulverize in a food processor or crush with a rolling pin. Store in an airtight container at room temperature for up to 1 month or in the freezer for up to 1 year.

ABOUT ALMOND PASTE AND MARZIPAN

Almond paste and marzipan are both made from a mixture of finely ground almonds and sugar. The distinction between the two is a fine one: Almond paste has a higher proportion of nuts to sugar and is uncooked; marzipan is made with a cooked sugar syrup. Almond paste tends to be slightly grainier and stickier than marzipan, which is very smooth and pliable. Two kinds of almonds, sweet and bitter, are commonly used in candies and pastries. Bitter almonds, which are more flavorful, also contain harmful hydrocyanic acid, and although the acid is destroyed by processing, these almonds are banned in the United States. To compensate for the blander taste of sweet almonds, we add a dose of almond extract to both almond paste and marzipan. Other flavorings as well as color may be kneaded into both almond paste and marzipan.

ALMOND PASTE *2 pounds*

The high proportion of nuts to sugar makes this paste a good choice for flavoring cake batters or, Mediterranean style, for stuffing the cavities of dried fruits.

Combine in a food processor:

3 cups whole blanched almonds
1½ cups powdered sugar
1 cup sugar

Process until the nuts are very finely ground. If your food processor is not large enough, grind the nuts with the sugar in batches and finish the paste using a heavy-duty mixer. Add to the almond mixture:

½ cup light corn syrup
1 teaspoon almond extract

Process until the mixture is thoroughly blended and moist enough to hold together when pressed in your hand. If it seems a bit dry, add:

Up to 1 tablespoon water

Remove the paste from the processor and knead several times on a surface dusted with enough:

Powdered sugar

just to bring the paste together. The paste is now ready for use.

Store at room temperature, wrapped tightly in plastic wrap, for up to 1 week, refrigerate for up to 4 weeks, or freeze for up to 3 months. Bring to room temperature before using. If the paste seems very hard, knead it by hand—or in the bowl of a heavy-duty mixer with the paddle attachment—with a little corn syrup or liquid flavoring such as rose or orange flower water or fruit or nut liqueur.

MARZIPAN *3¼ pounds*

Because of its supple texture, marzipan is often molded into such shapes as fruits or animals. It is also sometimes rolled out into sheets and draped over cakes. Disks, balls, and logs of flavored marzipan can be dipped in chocolate if you like, and in Spain and Sicily, marzipan half-moons are often filled with thick, mild-flavored preserves.

Combine in a food processor:

3 cups whole blanched almonds
2½ cups powdered sugar

Process until the nuts are very finely ground. Combine in a large, heavy-bottomed saucepan:

3⅔ cups sugar
½ cup light corn syrup
½ cup water

Stir over low heat with a long-handled wooden spoon until the sugar is dissolved. Brush down the sides of the pan with a pastry brush dipped in warm water. Increase the heat to medium, place a warmed candy thermometer in the pan, and cook, without stirring, until it reaches 244°F, the firm-ball stage. Remove from the heat, turn on the food processor, and immediately pour the sugar syrup through the feed tube into the almond mixture. Grind to a fine paste, then add:

2 teaspoons almond extract

Pulse to blend the extract. Lightly coat a medium bowl with vegetable oil spray and remove the paste to the bowl. Place a damp dish towel over the top (to keep the paste from drying out) and let cool. The marzipan is now ready for use. If you like, knead in a few drops of food coloring paste or a little extra flavoring, such as rose or orange flower water or a fruit liqueur. Store at room temperature, tightly wrapped in plastic wrap in an airtight container for up to 3 months. Marzipan can also be frozen for up to 6 months. If frozen, bring to room temperature before using.

Marzipan shapes can be formed by hand, or pieces can be pressed into the same plastic decorative molds used for chocolate. Simply coat the molds lightly with vegetable oil spray, pinch off a piece of marzipan, knead for a moment to make it pliable and smooth, then press it into the mold. Repeat until all of the mold's depressions are filled. Use a small, sharp knife to trim any excess, so that the marzipan is level with the surface of the mold (be careful not to scratch the decorative depressions or the mold will no longer be useful for chocolate). Turn the mold over and rap sharply on the counter—the marzipan pieces should fall out; if not, gently prod them out with the tip of a knife. Kids are great at modeling freeform shapes and enjoy making fanciful creatures and surreal fruits. Shape marzipan by hand just as you would modeling clay; use a tiny dab of light corn syrup to affix one shape to another. Use whole cloves for fruit stems and the rough side of a grater to create the stippled skin of an orange—just look in your kitchen cupboards for inspiration. Marzipan can also be rolled thinly on a surface dusted with powdered sugar, then cut into various shapes with miniature cookie cutters or the tip of a small knife. To paint molded marzipan, use liquid vegetable food coloring. In a small bowl or cup, place a few tablespoons of clear liqueur (such as kirsch, framboise, or grappa) and add the food coloring little by little until you like the color. Prepare as many colors as you like in this manner. Use a tiny watercolor brush to paint the marzipan. Set aside to dry for 1 hour, then lightly glaze the candy for a sparkling finish and to help preserve its moistness.

To make the glaze, combine in a small saucepan:

½ cup light corn syrup
½ cup water

Bring the mixture just to a boil, then remove from the heat. While the syrup is still hot, lightly brush it over the candies and let stand until completely dry. Store in an airtight container in a cool spot or in the refrigerator for up to 1 month.

PIES & TARTS

Pies came to America with the Pilgrims, and our love affair with these desserts has continued ever since. Southerners dote on pecan, chess, and sweet potato pies, New Englanders adore pumpkin pie, and the Pennsylvania Dutch never need an excuse to make shoofly pie. But pie-making has kept pace with changing times as well. In this century, refrigeration made possible cream and chiffon pies, and as the century ends, pies are filled with chocolate (lots of it), peanut butter, caramel, coffee, ice cream, or any mousse imaginable. Though still based on traditional recipes, contemporary fruit pies contain more fruit and less sugar.

We used to think of tarts as small pies; they were usually open, and meant for individual servings. Today we call these tartlets, reserving the name tart for large pastries baked in tart pans and then unmolded before serving. While pie and tart methods overlap and crusts and fillings are often interchangeable, American tarts display a distinctly French style. Just as a French sandwich puts as much emphasis on the bread as it does on the filling, a French tart balances a small amount of filling with a superb crust. The wide, shallow tart shell provides an elegant base for arranging the fruit.

EQUIPMENT FOR PIES AND TARTS

There are two kinds of rolling pins—the American pin with handles, and the European pole. If you have never rolled out crust before, choose an American pin of a size and weight you find comfortable. European rolling pins are made either thick and uniformly cylindrical or slender and tapered at the ends. Once you get the hang of rolling out dough, you will want a tapered pin for the way it allows you to maneuver the dough to any effect, but many beginners find one awkward to work with. Wood is the perfect material for all rolling pins. Hollow metal pins filled with ice water sweat; glass pins are beautiful to behold but fragile.

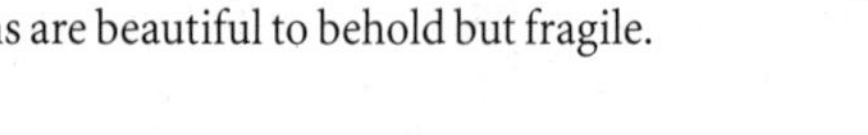

American-style rolling pin, with handles

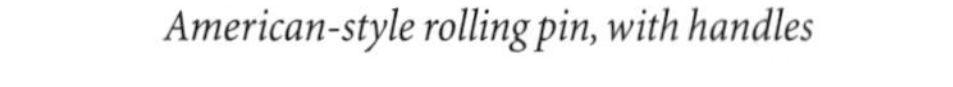

European tapered rolling pin

Pastry blender

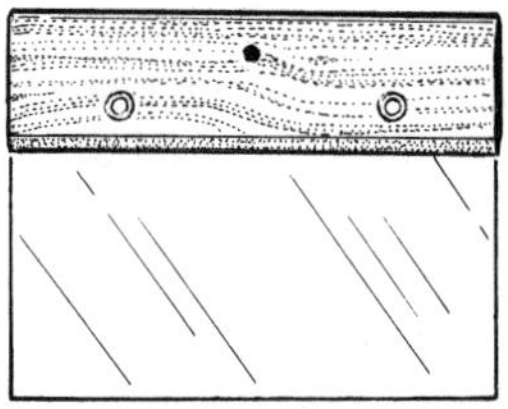

Metal dough scraper

A pastry blender, a tool consisting of five or six bowed metal blades for blending flour and fat in flaky pastry, is essential. Also useful are a ruler to measure the thickness and width of the dough, a fluted pastry wheel (pastry jagger) for cutting decorative lattices, and a metal dough scraper. For weighting unfilled "blind-baked" crusts, metal pie weights are a good alternative to raw beans or rice, which burn and grow musty with use. Some home bakers cover the edge of a pie with a shield to prevent overbrowning, but this has limited effect; the same benefit can be achieved with a ring cut from heavy aluminum foil.

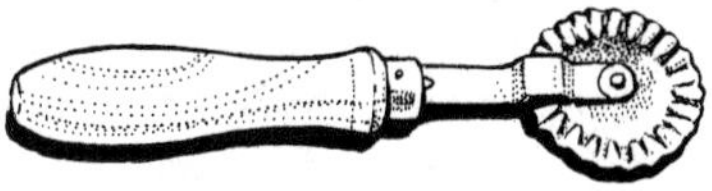

Fluted pastry wheel

American pie pans come in two standard diameters, 9 inches and 10 inches; the former has a capacity of around 4½ cups, and the latter, 6 cups. Glass pie pans produce wonderfully brown, crisp crusts, but heavy metal pans, whether matte, shiny, or black finish, are perfectly acceptable. Do not use deep-dish glass pie pans for an ordinary pie, because they lack the flared rim needed to form the edge of the crust. Also avoid the flimsy nonstick metal pans often sold in supermarkets; they are too shallow to hold a standard amount of pie filling.

We wish some enterprising manufacturer would

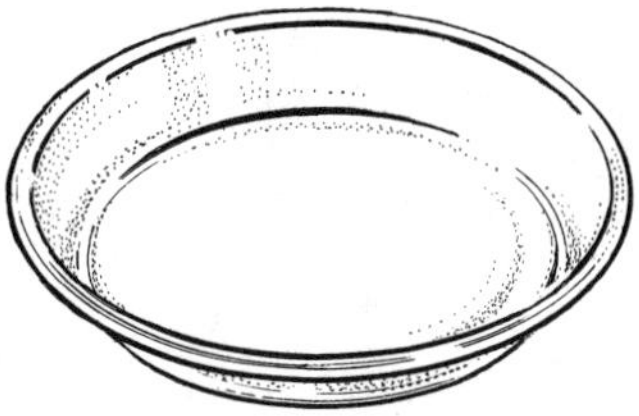

Pie pan

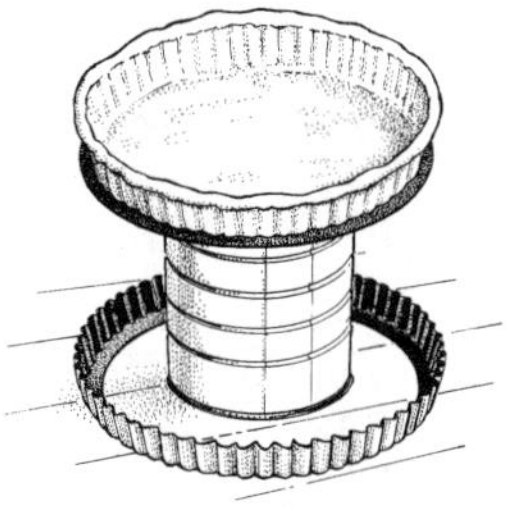

Two-piece tart pan. To unmold, balance the base on a coffee can and let the rim fall to the counter.

design tart pans that correlate precisely in capacity with standard American pie pans. Until that day comes, use a tart pan measuring 9½ or 10 inches across and 1 to 1¼ inches deep for 4 to 4½ cups filling, and a tart pan 11 inches in diameter and about 1 inch deep for 4½ to 6 cups filling. If you unmold a tart for serving, the pan must be a two-piece construction with a removable bottom. All two-piece tart pans are metal. Black-finish tart pans may produce slightly browner crusts, but crusts are less likely to stick in shiny metal pans.

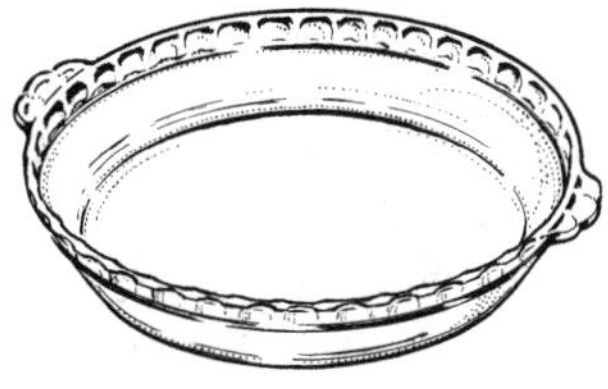

Deep-dish glass pie pan

Tartlet pans come in a great number of sizes, from 1½-inch miniature pans used to make hors d'oeuvre cases to 4½-inch pans for individual tartlets. They may be of one-piece or two-piece construction; they may have straight or sloping sides, and their sides may be either smooth or fluted. They are made in virtually every shape imaginable. Speaking broadly, buy wider shallow tartlet pans, as crusts tend to lose their shape

Tartlet pans

during baking when formed in deep, narrow pans. Muffin pans, ramekins, and baking cups can be substituted for tartlet pans. You can either line these molds with dough on the inside in the usual way, or turn them upside down and line the outside. If you choose the latter, use Flaky Cream Cheese Pastry Dough, 864; other doughs have a tendency to melt and split during baking.

ABOUT FLAKY PASTRY (PÂTE BRISÉE)

Well-made flaky pastry is a paradox—firm and crisp on the one hand but tender, light, and flaky on the other. It derives its strength from gluten, a tough, weblike molecule that forms when flour is moistened with water and then handled during the mixing and rolling of the dough. For tenderness, pie pastry depends on fat, which, if properly deployed, prevents too much gluten from developing and separates the dough into paper-thin sheets, helping to create the flaky effect. No one recipe can precisely convey a sense for the way the dough should look and feel at all stages nor confer the fabled "touch." This comes (and it does come) only with practice. Still, flaky pastry is much less difficult to make than someone who has never made a pie crust before often imagines. What follows is a step-by-step overview of the entire process.

MAKING FLAKY PASTRY DOUGH

There are two steps in the making of flaky pastry dough. In the first step, the goal is to cut the fat into the dry ingredients, usually with a pastry blender, leaving it in firm, separate pieces, some fine and crumblike and the rest the size of peas. The finer particles of fat coat the grains of flour, partially blocking the penetration of water and hindering the formation of gluten function.

Cut the fat into the dry ingredients with a pastry blender.

When the larger chunks of fat melt during baking, they leave gaps in the dough that fill up with steam and expand, separating the pastry into myriad flaky ledges. Inexperienced pie makers tend to overwork the flour and fat mixture into a soft, greasy paste, resulting in pastry that is mealy and dense, like shortbread, rather than crisp and flaky. The age-old advice remains the best: Have the butter or lard cold (vegetable shortening, which resists melting, may be at room temperature) and work quickly and purposefully.

In the second step, the binding of the dough with water, the trick is to add enough water to make the dough cohere but not so much as to cause gluten to form, which will produce pastry that is either hard or chewy and breadlike. The amount of water required varies depending on the moisture content of the flour, the type of fat used, the degree of blending of fat and flour, and the ambient temperature and humidity. As a general rule, the flour and fat mixture should be moistened only to the point where it forms small balls that hold together when pressed together with your fingers. If the mixture gathers into a mass on its own, without pressure, it is too wet. Beginners should probably err on the side of overmoistening, as a very dry dough will split or crumble when rolled.

About Fats Used in Flaky Pastry Doughs: Vegetable shortening is easy to work with, because it resists melting and disperses easily in dry ingredients. It also has a tenderizing effect on flour and thus assures a tender crust. Shortening, however, has little flavor, and for this reason, use it in combination with unsalted butter if you want more flavor in the crust. The recipe for Flaky Pastry Dough, 859, can be made with either shortening only or with equal parts shortening and butter. For a very buttery crust, make Deluxe Butter Flaky Pastry Dough, 862, which is almost entirely butter. Leaf lard, rendered from the fat of the pig that surrounds the kidneys, produces a wonderfully flaky crust and is traditional for covered fruit pies but is difficult to find.

Supermarket lard, which is processed from various parts of the animal, has a more pronounced flavor than leaf lard.

Sweetening and Flavoring Flaky Pastry Doughs: Our basic recipes for Flaky Pastry Dough, below, and Deluxe Butter Flaky Pastry Dough, 862, call for just a hint of sugar. However, both doughs can be sweetened more if you prefer. Except when used in tiny amounts, ordinary granulated sugar makes flaky pastry doughs sticky and hard to handle, so be sure to use powdered sugar instead. One-quarter to ⅓ cup powdered sugar to 2½ cups of flour will impart a light background sweetness; ¾ cup will make the crust noticeably sweet. Crusts made with more than ¾ cup powdered sugar may burn and turn out hard and crunchy rather than flaky.

You may flavor any flaky pastry dough by tossing the flour and other dry ingredients with one or more of the following. With all these additions, you should sweeten the dough with at least ¼ cup powdered sugar. These amounts are for a full recipe of Flaky Pastry Dough or Deluxe Butter Flaky Pastry Dough; use only half as much if you are halving the recipe or if you are making Flaky Cream Cheese Pastry Dough.

Nuts: ⅓ to ½ cup coarsely ground or finely chopped

Sesame or poppy seeds: 2 tablespoons

Anise, caraway, or coriander seeds: 1 tablespoon finely crushed

Orange or lemon zest: 1 to 2 teaspoons grated

Cinnamon, ginger, cardamom, or nutmeg: ¼ teaspoon ground

Moisture-proofing the Crust: Crusts that are to hold uncooked fillings and then be baked should be glazed with egg yolk to prevent sogginess. Crusts filled with cooked mixtures can be glazed with yolk or, if the filling is poured in cold, glazed with one of the following:

Fruit glaze: Melt jelly, jam, or preserves in a small saucepan over low heat, then strain out any solids. Brush the warm glaze over the bottom and the sides of the shell. If you are making a fresh fruit tart, you can daub the fruits on top of the tart with the same glaze that you applied to the shell.

Butter: Unsalted butter makes an effective and virtually unnoticeable protective coat. Soften about 2 teaspoons of unsalted butter to the consistency of mayonnaise, then brush or spread it very thinly over the bottom and sides of the baked shell.

Chocolate: Melt semisweet, bittersweet, milk, or white chocolate and spread it thinly over the inside of the crust with a knife or the back of a spoon. Refrigerate the crust until the chocolate hardens. Moisture-proof shells with chocolate only when its flavor is compatible with the pie or tart filling.

Chocolate Ganache Glaze or Frosting, 1003: This is as effective as chocolate in moisture-proofing a shell and, because it is soft, may be applied in a much thicker layer. Banana cream pie, peanut butter pie, and fresh raspberry tarts are particularly good with ganache-glazed shells.

FLAKY PASTRY DOUGH

Two 9-inch pie crusts, or two 9½- or 10-inch tart crusts, or one 9-inch covered pie crust

This dough makes a light, flaky crust that shatters at the touch of a fork. Before beginning, please read About Flaky Pastry, 858, and Making Flaky Pastry Dough, 858. If you want to make the dough in a food processor, see 866. If you need only a single pie or tart crust, decrease all ingredients by half or freeze half the dough for future use.

Using a rubber spatula, thoroughly mix in a large bowl:

2½ cups all-purpose flour

1 teaspoon white sugar or 1 tablespoon powdered sugar

1 teaspoon salt

Add:

1 cup solid vegetable shortening, or ½ cup shortening and 8 tablespoons (1 stick) cold unsalted butter

Break the shortening into large chunks; if using butter, cut it into small pieces, then add it to the flour mixture. Cut the fat into the dry ingredients by chopping vigorously with a pastry blender or by cutting in opposite directions with 2 knives, one held in each hand. As you work, periodically stir dry flour up from the bottom of the bowl and scrape clinging fat off the pastry blender or knives. When you are through, some of the fat should remain in pea-sized pieces; the rest should be reduced to the consistency of coarse crumbs or cornmeal. The mixture should seem dry and powdery and not pasty or greasy. Drizzle over the flour and fat mixture:

⅓ cup plus 1 tablespoon ice water

Using the rubber spatula, cut with the blade side until the mixture looks evenly moistened and begins to form small balls. Press down on the dough with the flat side of the spatula. If the balls of dough stick together, you have added enough water; if they do not, drizzle over the top:

1 to 2 tablespoons ice water

Cut in the water, again using the blade of the spatula, then press with your hands until the dough coheres. The dough should look rough, not smooth. Divide the dough in half, press each half into a round flat disk, and wrap tightly in plastic. Refrigerate for at least 30 minutes, and preferably for several hours, or for up to 2 days before rolling. The dough can also be wrapped airtight and frozen for up to 6 months; thaw completely before rolling.

HOW TO ROLL OUT PASTRY DOUGH

The secret to rolling dough is to lean into the pin rather than down on it: The goal is to enlarge the dough, not press and crush it. Use firm, decisive, sweeping strokes and try to get the job done as quickly as possible.

***Rolling the Dough:** Start by clearing a large work surface, as you will need lots of elbow room. You can roll dough on a wood or plastic pastry board or on a marble slab (which retains cold and thus helps keep the dough from softening) or directly on a clean smooth countertop. Do not roll dough next to the oven or in a hot corner of the kitchen, for the fat will melt. If the dough has been chilled for longer than 30 minutes, let it stand until it feels firm yet pliable, like modeling clay, when pressed. If too cold, the dough will crack around the edges when rolled. If the dough becomes too soft during rolling, loosen it from the work surface, slide a rimless cookie sheet beneath it, and refrigerate until it firms up.*

Flour the work surface—lightly if you are an experienced pastry maker but a bit more generously if you are starting out. Excessive flouring toughens dough, but sticking is a disaster. Place the dough in the center of the floured surface and flour the dough as well. Exerting even pressure on the pin, roll the dough from the center out *in all directions, stopping just short of the edge. In order to keep the dough in a circular shape, each stroke should be made in the opposite direction from the one that preceded it. You can do this by rotating the dough itself rather than by moving the pin. Be sure to check the dough for sticking by periodically sliding your hand beneath it; strew a little flour on the work surface as necessary. Seal cracks and splits by pushing the dough together with your fingers. If the split reopens, your dough is probably too dry. Dab the edges of the split with cold water, overlap the edges slightly, and press firmly with your fingertips, sprinkling a little flour over the repaired area if it feels moist and sticky. If the dough assumes an irregular shape, cut off the protruding piece, moisten the edge of the patch with cold water and press it over the short spot.*

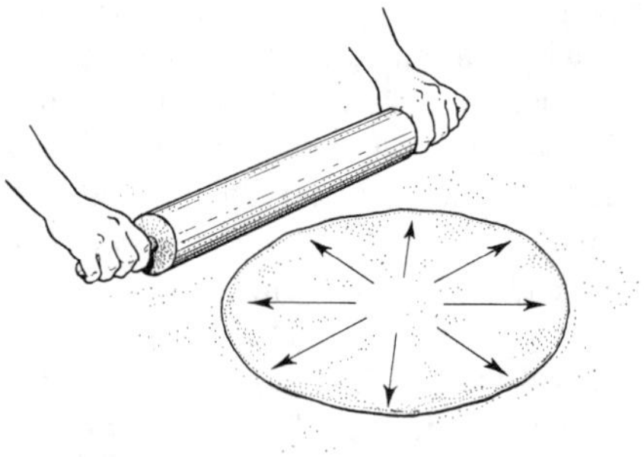

Roll the dough from the center out in all directions.

Roll the dough roughly 3 to 4 inches wider than your pan. This will allow plenty of dough for covering the entire pan and for constructing a rim. Place the pan (right side up for a tart pan, inverted for a pie pan) in the center of the dough to calculate the width by eye.

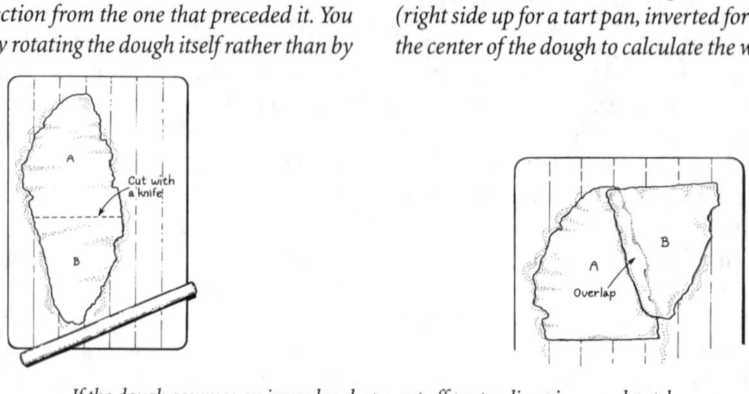

If the dough assumes an irregular shape, cut off protruding pieces and patch.

FITTING THE DOUGH INTO THE PAN AND RESTING

Fitting the Dough into the Pan: *To transfer the dough to the pan, roll it loosely around the pin, center the pin over the pan, and then unroll the dough. Alternatively, you can fold the dough in halves or quarters, place it in the pan, and unfold it to cover. If the dough ends up off center, slide your hand beneath it and carefully maneuver it into place. It is important to press the dough over the bottom and into the corners of the pan before you mold it against the pan sides. Otherwise, you will end up with stretched, webbed corners that may tear when the shell is weighted for prebaking or is filled. Patch any holes or cracks with dough scraps, first lightly moistening the scraps with cold water. When you are satisfied that the pan is completely covered, trim the edges of the dough with scissors, leaving an overhang of ¾ inch all around the sides of the pan. Wrap and refrigerate all scraps. These will come in handy if the shell shrinks or splits when baked.*

Transfer the dough to a pie or tart pan by folding it in half or quarters.

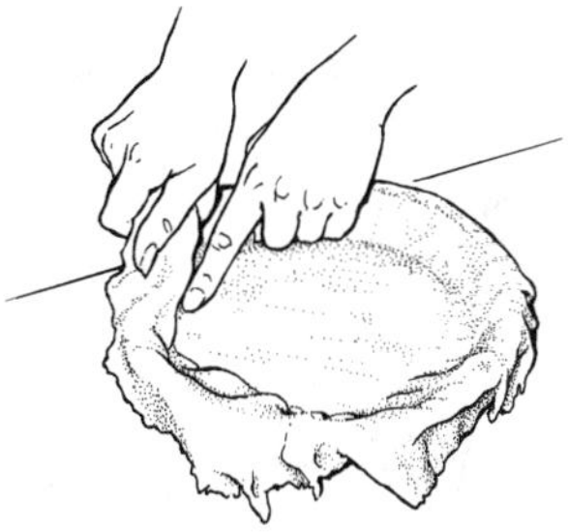

Press the dough over the bottom and into the corners of the pan.

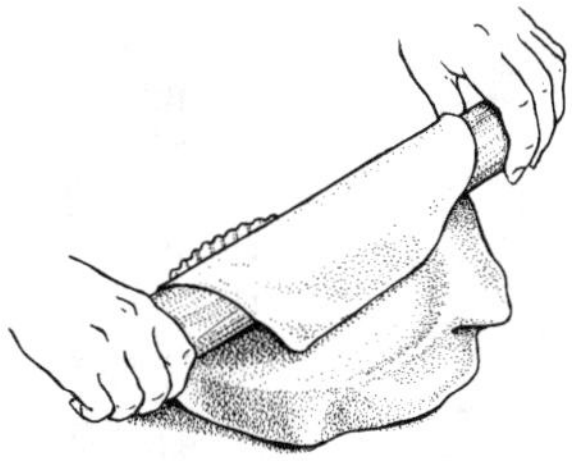

Transfer the dough to a pie or tart pan by rolling it around the pin.

Resting, Storing, and Freezing Unbaked Crusts: *In order to relax the dough and minimize shrinkage, pie and tart crusts must be chilled at least 30 minutes before baking. A rest of 3 to 24 hours is preferable if you have designed an elaborate crust rim, which may otherwise lose its shape during baking. Wrap crusts that are refrigerated for more than 3 hours in plastic or cover with the foil liner to be used in weighting the shell, 863. A crust may also be frozen for up to 6 months. Either freeze it in the pan, wrapped airtight, or freeze it solid, then pry it out of the pan and wrap. Frozen crusts need not be thawed before baking. They will require a few minutes longer in the oven.*

HOW TO MAKE A PIE CRUST

To Make a Pie Crust: *Tuck the overhanging dough underneath itself to make a doubled rim, then rest the rim on the flared edge of the pie pan. To crimp the rim, press it all around with the tines of a fork or the blunt side of a knife. For a fluted rim, press your thumb and index finger, held about 1 inch apart, against the outside of the rim, then poke a dent through the space from the inside of the pie crust with the index finger of your other hand. For a coiled or braided design, roll dough trimmings into long thin ropes, then twist or braid the ropes to your choosing. Flatten the rim of the pie crust against the edge of the pan, brush with cold water, and press the fancy rope into place.*

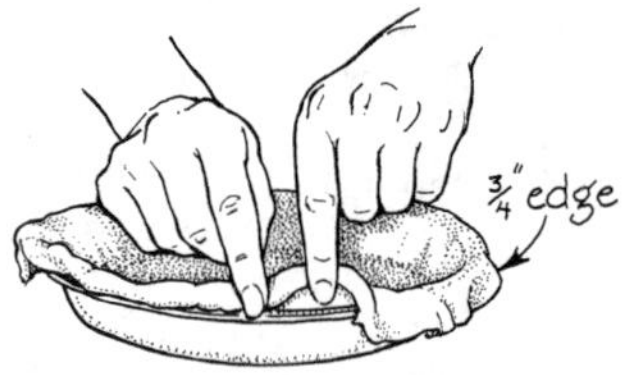

Tuck the overhanging dough underneath itself to make a double layer.

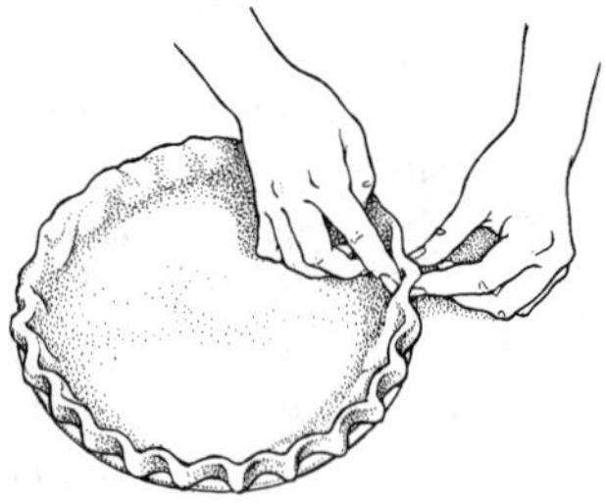

Forming a fluted rim

Crimping the rim

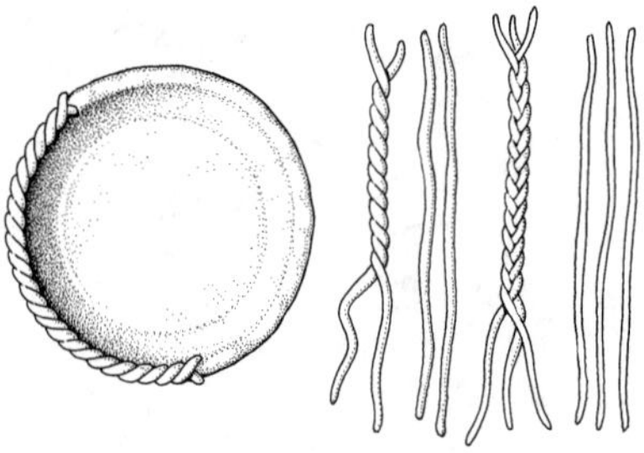

For a coiled rim, twist dough ropes as desired and press them along the rim of the pan.

LARD FLAKY PASTRY DOUGH

This very tender crust is best reserved for covered fruit pies.

Prepare Flaky Pastry Dough, above, substituting 1 cup of cold or frozen lard, cut into pieces, for the fat.

DELUXE BUTTER FLAKY PASTRY DOUGH (PÂTE BRISÉE)

Two 9-inch pie crusts, or two 9½- or 10-inch tart crusts, or one 9-inch covered pie crust

This dough is richer in fat than ordinary flaky pastry and is thus softer and more difficult to handle, but it yields a marvelously tender, flaky crust with a superb butter flavor. While it is possible to make this dough with butter only, a small amount of shortening makes it flakier without interfering with the buttery taste. Since this dough tends to puff out of shape during baking, you should not use it to make a crust with a tightly fluted or braided edge.

Before beginning, please read About Flaky Pastry, 858, and Making Flaky Pastry Dough, 858. If you want to make this in a food processor, see 866. If you need only a single pie or tart crust, decrease all ingredients by half or freeze half the dough for another pie.

Using a rubber spatula, thoroughly mix in a large bowl:

2½ cups all-purpose flour
1 teaspoon white sugar or 1 tablespoon powdered sugar
1 teaspoon salt

Working quickly to prevent softening, cut into ¼-inch pieces:

½ pound (2 sticks) cold unsalted butter

HOW TO MAKE A TART CRUST

To Make a Tart Crust: *Lightly brush the sides of the tart crust with cold water. Fold the dough overhanging the pan down over the sides and press firmly, doubling the thickness of the upper part of the crust wall. Squeeze any noticeably thicker parts of the sides with your fingers, then trim the protruding spots flush with the rest of the top using scissors.*

Fold the dough overhanging the tart pan back onto itself and press firmly.

Trim protruding spots flush with the rest of the top.

ABOUT PREBAKING CRUSTS & WEIGHTING

In previous editions, we called for only partial *prebaking of flaky pastry crusts that would be returned to the oven and baked again with the filling, as in pumpkin or pecan pie. Our theory was that the second baking would finish what the first had begun, but time and time again, our theory was refuted by a soggy, undercooked crust. We now believe that all prebaked pastry crusts must be* fully *baked before filling. Defying logic, the baked shells do not burn when baked a second time with their filling, though the edge does sometimes darken—a small price to pay for a deliciously crisp and flaky crust.*

Weighting the Crust: *When pastry crusts are baked unfilled—"blind baked"—they tend to puff up and slip down the sides of the pan unless weighted with raw beans or rice or metal pie weights during the first 20 minutes of baking. Instead of using weights, you may keep the dough in place by nesting a pie pan of identical size in the crust. If you choose this method, you must be content with a simple crimped rim, for the second pan will flatten a fluted or braided rim.*

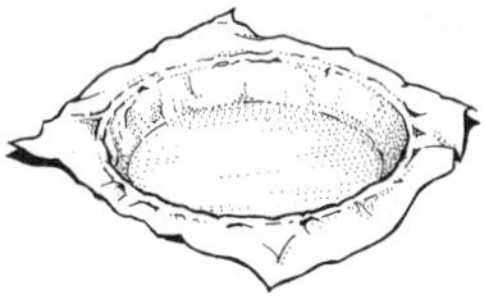

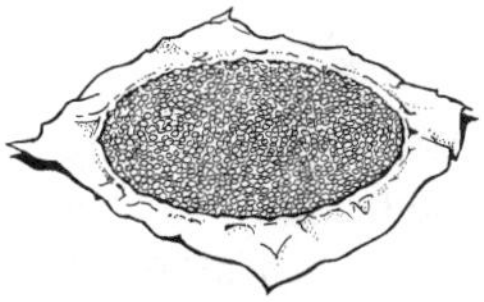

Weighting the crust

Add the butter to the dry ingredients. Using a pastry blender or two knives, chop the butter into pea-sized pieces. Add:

¼ cup solid vegetable shortening

With a few quick swipes of the pastry blender, cut the shortening into large chunks and distribute throughout the bowl. Continue to chop with the pastry blender until the mixture resembles coarse crumbs with some pea-sized pieces. Do not let the mixture soften and begin to clump; it must remain dry and powdery. Drizzle over the flour and fat mixture:

⅓ cup plus 1 tablespoon ice water

Cut with the blade side of the rubber spatula until the mixture looks evenly moistened and begins to form small balls. Press down on the dough with the flat side of the spatula. If the balls of dough stick together, you have added enough water; if they do not, drizzle over the top:

1 to 2 tablespoons ice water

PATCHING THE CRUST

Patching the Crust: *Pastry crusts sometimes develop a split along the bottom (usually during the weighted phase of baking) or shrink down the sides of the pan (usually after the weights have been removed and during the final baking). If the crust is to hold a thick, fully cooked mixture, as in cream, chiffon, or lemon meringue pie, small imperfections can be ignored. But if you are filling the crust with an uncooked liquid mixture, as in custard, pecan, chess, or pumpkin pie, all cracks need to be patched, or else the filling will leak through. Using your fingertips, press reserved dough scraps into the required shape, lightly moisten one side with water, and press the moistened side over the problem area of the baked crust. If you have no scraps, make a thick paste with flour and water and smear it over the tear with your fingers. The crust need be returned to the oven only long enough to harden and dry the patch, not to brown it and bake it through. If glazing the crust with egg yolk before filling, be sure that the edges of the patch are completely sealed with yolk.*

Patch a blind-baked crust with dough scraps.

Cut in the water, then press with your hands until the dough coheres. The dough should look rough, not smooth. Divide the dough in half, press each half into a round flat disk, and wrap tightly in plastic. Refrigerate for at least 30 minutes, preferably for several hours, or for up to 2 days before rolling. The dough can also be wrapped airtight and frozen for up to 6 months; thaw completely before rolling.

CORNMEAL FLAKY PASTRY DOUGH

Cornmeal adds both crunch and lightness to crusts. Use it for fresh fruit tarts made with berries, peaches, or nectarines.

Prepare Deluxe Butter Flaky Pastry Dough, above, substituting ¾ cup yellow cornmeal for ¾ cup of the all-purpose flour and increasing the powdered sugar to ⅓ cup.

NUTTED FLAKY PASTRY DOUGH

Prepare Deluxe Butter Flaky Pastry Dough, above, adding ½ cup finely chopped or coarsely ground walnuts or pecans to the dry ingredients and increasing the powdered sugar to ⅓ cup. You can also add 1 teaspoon grated lemon zest with the nuts.

SWEET FLAKY PASTRY DOUGH (PÂTE SUCRÉE)

This pastry is delicious but burns easily. Use it only for pies and tarts that require little or no baking after being filled, such as Lemon Meringue Pie and fresh fruit tarts.

Prepare Deluxe Butter Flaky Pastry Dough, above, increasing the powdered sugar to ¾ cup.

WHOLE-WHEAT FLAKY PASTRY DOUGH

Prepare Deluxe Butter Flaky Pastry Dough, above, substituting 1 cup of whole-wheat pastry flour for 1 cup of the all-purpose flour and increasing the powdered sugar to ⅓ cup. For extra tenderness, beat 1 large egg yolk with the first addition of ice water (⅓ cup plus 1 tablespoon) and add it to the dough.

FLAKY CREAM CHEESE PASTRY DOUGH

One 9-inch pie crust or 9½- or 10-inch tart crust

Cream cheese pastry is rich and tangy, and it seems to turn out tender and flaky no matter what. To make this in a food processor, see 866. This recipe can be doubled and used to make a covered or lattice-top pie.

Whisk together thoroughly in a large bowl:

PATTING THE DOUGH IN THE PAN

Patting the Dough into the Pan: *Although patting out a crust is a simple procedure, it must be done carefully if the crust is to be of an even thickness. If the dough is soft and sticky, refrigerate it until it becomes manageable; if it is cold and hard, let it stand at room temperature until malleable, like modeling clay. Pat the dough into an even 4-inch disk and set it in the center of your pie or tart pan. Always working from the center out, press down on the dough in all directions until it covers the entire bottom of the pan in an even layer. To form the sides of the crust, again press the dough from the center of the pan until an even ring of dough builds up against the pan sides. Flatten the dough ring against the pan sides to form the crust sides. In forming a pie crust, you can push the top of the sides slightly beyond the rim of the pan and crimp or flute the crust edge. For a tart crust, press down on the top of the sides with the thumb of one hand while pressing against the inside edge with the forefinger of your other hand. You will thus make the top of the sides flat and of the same thickness as the base, which not only strengthens the sides but also gives the crust an attractive look.*

The Option of Rolling: *If you are comfortable and proficient with the pin, you may find it easier to produce a crust of an even thickness by rolling the dough rather than patting it. Flatten the dough into a 4-inch disk, then refrigerate it until it becomes firm but malleable, like modeling clay. Since these doughs tend to be sticky, soft, and crumbly, they must be rolled between sheets of wax paper. Lightly flour both sides of the dough, set it between two 12-inch squares of wax paper, and, working from the center out, roll the dough into a 12-inch circle. If the paper wrinkles as you roll, peel it off and smooth it back into place. Remove the top sheet of wax paper. Holding the bottom sheet by the corners, pick up the dough and flip it, paper side up, into the pan, then carefully peel off the paper. The dough may not end up perfectly centered in the pan, and it may well tear and crumble in any number of places, but none of this matters. Simply press the dough into the pan's contours and then repair any holes by pushing the dough together with your fingers. Finish the edge of the crust as directed above.*

To form the sides of a pat-in-the-pan pie or tart crust, flatten the dough against the pan sides.

For a pie crust, push the top of the sides slightly beyond the rim of the pan.

Forming a pat-in-the-pan tart crust edge

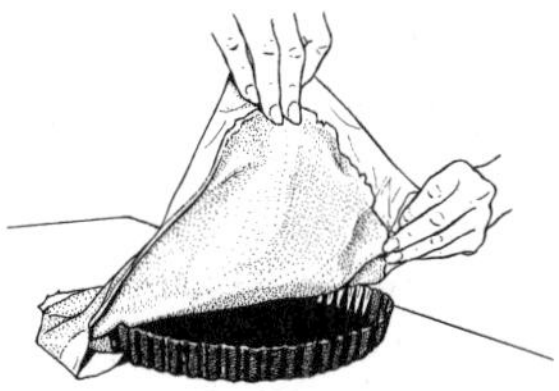

Flip the rolled pat-in-the-pan dough into the pan.

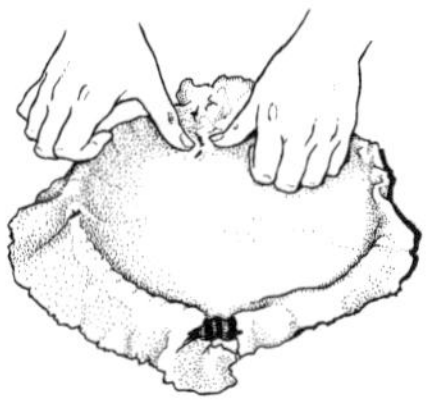

Patching tears in rolled pat-in-the-pan dough

1 cup plus 2 tablespoons all-purpose flour
1 tablespoon white sugar or 2 tablespoons powdered sugar
¼ teaspoon salt

Cut into ¼-inch pieces and add:

6 tablespoons (¾ stick) cold unsalted butter
3 ounces cold cream cheese

Using a pastry blender or 2 knives, cut the butter and cream cheese into the dry ingredients until the mixture resembles coarse crumbs with some pea-sized pieces. Drizzle over the top:

2 to 3 tablespoons cold heavy cream

Cut with the blade side of a rubber spatula or stir with a fork until the dough begins to gather into moist clumps. Press the dough into a flat disk, wrap tightly in plastic, and refrigerate for at least 1 hour or up to 2 days.

TO MAKE FLAKY PASTRY DOUGH USING A FOOD PROCESSOR

The food processor is fast and efficient, but its speed needs to be treated with caution. Use 1- to 2-second pulses rather than letting the machine run, and check the dough frequently. These instructions pertain to Flaky Pastry Dough, 859, Deluxe Flaky Pastry Dough, 862, and their variations, as well as to Flaky Cream Cheese Pastry Dough, 864.

Have all fats, including solid vegetable shortening, ice cold, preferably frozen; have cream cheese cold. Combine the dry ingredients in the food processor and process for 10 seconds. Cut the fat (and cream cheese) into ½-inch chunks and, with the machine off, scatter over the dry ingredients. Pulse in 1- to 2-second bursts until most of the fat is the size of peas. With the machine turned off, drizzle ⅓ cup plus 1 tablespoon ice water (or 2 tablespoons cream for cream cheese pastry) evenly over the top. Pulse until no dry patches remain and the dough begins to clump into small balls. Try to press the dough together with your fingers; if it will not cohere, sprinkle on a bit more ice water (or cream), pulse, and try again. Do not allow the dough to gather into a single mass during processing. Wrap and refrigerate as directed.

BAKED FLAKY PASTRY CRUST

One 9-inch pie crust or 9½- or 10-inch tart crust

The pastry doughs listed here are all-purpose doughs and may be used interchangeably in any recipe calling for a baked flaky pastry crust. Use the variations on these doughs if they are specified in a recipe or if they appeal to you for use with a particular filling.

Before beginning, please read How to Roll Out Pastry Dough, 860, and About Prebaking Crusts, 863.

Prepare:

½ recipe Flaky Pastry Dough, 859, ½ recipe Deluxe Butter Flaky Pastry Dough, 862, or 1 recipe Flaky Cream Cheese Pastry Dough, 866

Roll out the dough and fit it into a 9-inch pie pan or 9½- or 10-inch two-piece tart pan. Refrigerate the crust for at least 30 minutes.

Position a rack in the lower third of the oven. Preheat the oven to 400°F.

Smooth a sheet of heavy-duty aluminum foil, shiny side down, over the bottom and sides of the crust, flaring the excess foil, like an awning, over the crust edge to keep it from overbrowning. Fill the liner with raw beans or rice or metal pie weights, banking the weights against the sides of the crust if you do not have enough to fill the crust to the brim. Bake the crust for 20 minutes with the weights in place to set the pastry. Carefully lift out the foil with the weights inside. Prick the crust thoroughly with a fork, return it to the oven, and bake until the crust is golden brown all over, 5 to 10 minutes more. Check the crust periodically; if it puffs along the bottom, prick it with a fork, then press down *gently* with the back of a spoon. If you are filling the crust with an uncooked mixture that requires further baking, whisk together, then brush the inside with:

1 large egg yolk
Pinch of salt

Return to the oven until the egg glaze sets, 1 to 2 minutes. Fill the shell at once, while still hot, or let cool as specified in the recipe.

BAKED FLAKY PASTRY TARTLET CRUSTS

About nine 3½-inch or six 4½-inch crusts

Tartlet pans come in myriad sizes, shapes, and designs (see Equipment for Pies and Tarts, 856). The following instructions assume that you will be using 3½- to 4½-inch pans with shallow, straight sides, which produce crusts of a size suitable for individual first-course or dessert tartlets. If you are using smaller, slope-sided pans to make dessert-tray tartlets or hors d'oeuvre cases, roll the dough thinner (1/16 inch, if you can manage it) and do not double the crust sides. Obviously, the baking times and yield will also vary.

While it is possible to make tartlet crusts with Flaky Pastry Dough, 859, or even Deluxe Butter Flaky Pastry Dough, 862, both tend to both puff and shrink down the sides of the pans during baking, diminishing the holding capacity of the crusts. These problems can be solved by prebaking the crusts with weights, as one

does for large shells—but this is a real nuisance. On balance, we prefer cream cheese pastry dough for tartlet shells, since it holds its shape better during baking.
Prepare:

Flaky Cream Cheese Pastry Dough, 866

On a lightly floured work surface, roll the dough about ⅛ inch thick, then cut into rounds wide enough to cover the bottom and sides of your tartlet pans, with 1 to 1½ inches extra dough to spare. Press the dough rounds into the pans, then fold the overhanging dough back on itself over the crust sides, doubling their thickness. Press the doubled dough firmly to seal, then thoroughly prick the sides and bottoms with a fork. Arrange the crusts on a baking sheet and refrigerate for at least 30 minutes.
Position a rack in the center of the oven. Preheat the oven to 400°F.
Bake the crusts for 5 to 7 minutes, then prick the bottoms of any that have puffed. Continue to bake until the crusts are golden brown and firm to the touch, 12 to 15 minutes more.

ABOUT PAT-IN-THE-PAN CRUSTS

The succes of flaky pastry depends upon the expert management of gluten. Pat-in-the-pan doughs are made in such a way that virtually no gluten develops. The fat is softened and thoroughly blended into the flour, not cut in as for flaky pastry dough. As a result, the flour ends up moisture-proofed by the fat and cannot absorb the liquid needed to produce gluten. All pat-in-the-pan crusts are crumbly like shortbread, rather than flaky.

Pat-in-the-pan crusts are usually baked before they are filled. Therefore they cannot be used to make covered fruit pies, though shortbread doughs can be used to make *crostate*, or "crostatas," and galettes. Note also that these crusts *must* be glazed with egg yolk when they are to be filled and further baked, as in pecan or pumpkin pies; otherwise, the crusts will soak up the filling and adhere to the pan.

PAT-IN-THE-PAN BUTTER CRUST

One 9-inch pie or 9½- or 10-inch tart crust

Those who are daunted by flaky pastry will find this simple alternative more than satisfactory.

This dough will also make about eight 3½-inch tartlet crusts. Press the dough into the tartlet molds and bake until firm and golden, about 15 minutes, pricking several times during baking with a fork.
Position a rack in the center of the oven. Preheat the oven to 400°F.
Whisk together in a bowl or process for 10 seconds in a food processor:

1½ cups all-purpose flour
½ teaspoon salt

Add:

8 tablespoons (1 stick) unsalted butter, softened, cut into 8 pieces

Mash with the back of a fork or process until the mixture resembles coarse crumbs. Drizzle over the top:

2 to 3 tablespoons heavy cream

Stir or process until the crumbs look damp and hold together when pinched. Transfer the mixture to a 9-inch pie pan or 9½- or 10-inch two-piece tart pan. Pat evenly over the bottom and sides with your fingertips. If making a pie, form a crust edge and crimp or flute. Prick the bottom and sides with a fork. Bake until the crust is golden brown, 18 to 22 minutes, pricking the bottom once or twice if it bubbles. If you are filling the crust with an uncooked mixture that requires further baking, whisk together, then brush the inside with:

1 large egg yolk
Pinch of salt

Return to the oven until the egg glaze sets, 1 to 2 minutes.

VEGETABLE OIL CRUST

One 9-inch pie or 9½- or 10-inch tart crust

This firm, sandy-textured crust is easier to roll than to pat. The flavor of the oil tends to become pronounced with prolonged baking, so save this crust for pies that don't need to be baked after filling, such as cream pies, Key lime pie, or lemon meringue pie.
Position a rack in the lower third of the oven. Preheat the oven to 425°F.
Whisk together thoroughly:

1⅓ cups all-purpose flour
½ teaspoon salt

Mix in a cup until creamy:

⅓ cup plus 1 tablespoon vegetable oil
¼ cup cold milk

Pour the oil mixture over the dry ingredients and stir with a fork until blended. Pat the dough evenly over the bottom and sides of a 9-inch pie pan or 9½- or 10-inch two-piece tart pan, or roll it between sheets of wax paper and flip it into the pan (see About Pat-in-the-Pan Crusts, above). If making a pie, crimp or flute the edge. Thoroughly prick the sides and bottom with a fork. Bake until the crust is golden brown, 12 to 18 minutes. If you are filling the crust with an uncooked mixture that requires further baking, whisk together, then brush the inside with:

1 large egg yolk
Pinch of salt

Return to the oven until the egg glaze sets, 1 to 2 minutes.

SHORTBREAD CRUST

One 9-inch pie or 9½- or 10-inch tart crust

This rich, sweet dough resembles a shortbread cookie. Use it for a cream pie, a lemon tart, a fresh fruit tart with pastry cream, or any other pie or tart with a creamy or buttery filling, or to make approximately eight 3½-inch tartlet crusts. For tartlets, press the dough into your molds and bake until firm and golden, about 15 minutes, pricking with a fork several times during baking.

If you make this in a food processor using cold butter, it will be firm enough to form into a crust at once; if made by hand with softened butter, the dough will require brief chilling before forming.

Position a rack in the center of the oven. Preheat the oven to 400°F. Grease or butter the bottom, but not the sides, of a 9-inch pie pan or 9½- or 10-inch two-piece tart pan. Dust the pan with flour, tilt to coat the bottom, then tap out the excess. (If using a tart pan, pop out the bottom, wedge it between your palms, and tap.)

Whisk together in a bowl or process for 10 seconds in a food processor:

1¼ cups all-purpose flour
⅓ cup sugar
1 teaspoon grated lemon zest (optional)
¼ teaspoon salt

Add:

8 tablespoons (1 stick) unsalted butter, softened if working by hand, cut into 8 pieces

Mash with the back of a fork or process until the mixture resembles coarse crumbs. Add:

1 large egg yolk

Mix with a spatula or process just until the dough comes together in a ball. If the dough is too soft and sticky to work with, refrigerate for at least 30 minutes or up to 2 days. Pat the dough evenly over the bottom and sides of the prepared pan, or roll it between sheets of wax paper and flip it into the pan (see About Pat-in-the-Pan Crusts, 867). Do not attempt to crimp or flute the edge. Thoroughly prick the bottom and sides with a fork. Bake until deep golden brown, 18 to 22 minutes. If you are filling the crust with an uncooked mixture that requires further baking, whisk together, then brush the inside with:

1 large egg yolk
Pinch of salt

Return to the oven until the egg glaze sets, 1 to 2 minutes.

ABOUT CRUMB AND NUT CRUSTS

The sweet crunchiness of these easy-to-make crusts provides a delicious contrast to creamy fillings. Graham crackers are the usual base, but chocolate and vanilla wafers, gingersnaps, and zwieback also make wonderful crumb crusts. If you are starting with crackers or cookies, grind them in a food processor or put them in a sturdy plastic bag and pulverize them with a rolling pin. The crumbs must be quite fine, or the crust is likely to crumble when cut. You can freeze these crusts for 20 minutes before filling and not bake them, but they are indisputably crunchier and more flavorful when baked. Measure the butter and sugar carefully. If there is too little of either, the crumbs will not cohere when patted into the pan. If there is too much, the crust may slip down the sides of the pan during baking and turn out hard and candylike. (Should the crust slip or bubble during baking, it can usually be smoothed into place with the back of a spoon.) To prevent sticking, lightly grease or oil the pan. If the crust sticks nonetheless, set the bottom of the pan in a bowl of warm water for 1 minute.

CRUMB CRUST

One 10-inch pie crust

The proportions here are ample for a 10-inch pie pan or a 10- to 12-inch springform pan, and very generous for a 9-inch pie pan or an 8- to 9-inch springform pan. For the smaller size pans, you can reduce quantities to 1¼ cups crumbs, 5 tablespoons butter, and 3 tablespoons sugar.

If you wish to bake the crust, preheat the oven to 350°F. Lightly grease or oil a pie pan or springform pan.

Mix together with a fork or pulse in a food processor until all the ingredients are moistened:

1½ cups fine crumbs made from graham crackers, chocolate or vanilla wafers, or gingersnaps
6 tablespoons (¾ stick) melted butter, warm or cool
¼ cup sugar
¼ teaspoon ground cinnamon (optional)

Spread the mixture evenly in the pan. Using your fingertips or the flat bottom of a drinking glass, firmly press the mixture over the bottom and ½ inch up the sides of a pie pan or over the bottom of a springform pan. Freeze for 20 minutes or bake until the crust is lightly browned and firm to the touch, 10 to 15 minutes.

Let cool thoroughly if filling with a cooked mixture, but use hot if filling with a mixture that requires baking.

NUT CRUST

One 10-inch pie crust

To make this crust in a food processor, combine nut halves or pieces with the butter, sugar, and salt and pulse until the nuts are finely chopped.

Preheat the oven to 375°F. Grease a 9- or 10-inch pie pan or an 8- to 10-inch springform pan.

Chop to the consistency of coarse crumbs:

2 cups walnuts or pecans

Add and mix with a fork until uniformly moistened:

4 tablespoons (½ stick) unsalted butter, softened
3 tablespoons sugar
¼ teaspoon salt

Using your fingertips or the flat bottom of a drinking glass, press the mixture evenly over the bottom and sides of a pie pan or over the bottom and ½ inch up the sides of a springform pan. Bake until the crust is richly browned, 10 to 15 minutes. Check periodically during baking; if the crust has slipped down the sides of the pan, smooth it into place with the back of a spoon. Let cool before filling.

ABOUT MERINGUE CRUSTS

Pure white, sweet, crisp, and fat-free, meringue is an excellent crust for ice cream and frozen yogurt pies or for tarts made with fresh fruit and whipped cream. Meringue shells can be made in small pans of any size or formed on a baking sheet using a spoon or a pastry bag. Note the long baking—and long storing—time. To cut the sweetness, flavor the meringue with coffee or cocoa.

MERINGUE PIE CRUST

One 10-inch pie crust

Position a rack in the lower third of the oven. Preheat the oven to 225°F. Very generously grease, with solid vegetable shortening, both the inside *and the rim* of a 10-inch pie pan, preferably glass. Dust the pan with flour, tilt in all directions to coat, then tap out the excess. Prepare:

Soft Meringue Topping I or II, 1012

Spread the meringue over the bottom and sides of the prepared pie pan with the back of a spoon. Bake until the interior of the meringue seems just slightly sticky when probed with the point of a paring knife, 1½ to 2 hours. Turn off the oven and let the crust cool completely inside the oven. Wrap the crust airtight and store at room temperature until needed. It will keep indefinitely. If it becomes soft during storage, bake unwrapped in a 200°F oven for 1 hour to recrisp.

ABOUT COVERED FRUIT PIES

A hundred years ago, when pies were often eaten at breakfast as well as supper, many American housewives baked a dozen or more fruit pies every week. Today many home bakers have never made a covered fruit pie, and for them we give a general orientation. We urge you not to judge your fruit pies against the picture-perfect specimens shown in magazine photographs. Under real home conditions, fruit pies often bubble over during baking, brown unevenly, stick to the pan, and yield somewhat runny slices. And no matter what you do, the undercrust always turns out slightly soft on the side facing the fruit. None of this should deter you. Fruit pies are simple, homey desserts, meant for eating, not display. And they are indeed delicious.

The Filling: A covered fruit pie is simply fruit baked between two crusts, the upper one of which is a single pastry sheet or multiple strips of pastry arranged in a lattice. Other than the fruit, which may be canned, frozen, dried, or precooked as well as fresh and raw, the filling usually contains sugar and a thickener such as flour, cornstarch, or quick-cooking tapioca.

Older recipes, our own included, generally call for 4 cups of sliced fresh fruit or berries for a 9-inch fruit pie, which is the approximate amount that a standard 9-inch pie pan will hold when lined with pastry. However, since raw fruit shrinks when cooked, we now prefer to start with 5 cups of fruit, or even more in the case of apples, to ensure that the top crust will not sink and the filling will seem ample. The measuring cup should be leveled, not heaped. Although it is possible (and tempting) to mound 6 to 7 cups of fruit into a 9-inch crust, it is not wise to do so, for the pie is certain to gush juices as it bakes, and it may not hold together well when sliced.

Ideally, the amount of sugar and thickener added to the filling should be adjusted according to the sweetness, acidity, and juiciness of the fruit. Sugar is a simple issue, but deciding how much thickener to add is tricky. In general, we lean toward the lesser quantity of thickener suggested in the recipes when there is a choice given. However, if you are partial to pies that slice neatly and are willing to risk a slightly solid filling, add the greater amount of thickener called for.

While flour is still a popular choice for thickener among home cooks, cornstarch or quick-cooking tapioca produces clearer fillings and a smoother, more melting consistency. The exception is apple pie, which seems to benefit from the creaminess that flour imparts. Of course, you may thicken any fruit pie with flour. Use as much flour as cornstarch or tapioca.

Baking the Pie: Fruit pies must be baked as soon as they are filled and assembled, or the juicy filling will begin to soften the bottom crust. Thoroughly preheat the oven and place the pie on the lowest oven rack to brown and crisp the undercrust and prevent the upper crust from becoming too dark. Fruit pies made with raw fillings are baked at a high temperature for 30 minutes to set the crust, then baked about 30 minutes more at a moderate temperature to cook the filling. Pies made with precooked fillings are baked at a high temperature throughout, generally for somewhat less time than for raw fruit fillings. The downfall of untold fruit pies is a flabby, underbaked crust. Do not declare the pie done until the top has turned a deep, rich brown, almost the color of a hazelnut shell, and *thick* juices bubble enthusiastically through the steam vents or lattice. Remember that pies glazed with egg, milk, or cream will often brown within the first 30 minutes of baking, long before they are baked through. You can slow, though not stop, the browning process by laying a sheet of aluminum foil loosely over the top crust. Fruit pies are apt to char around the edge, especially when the pies spill over. Do not worry. A charred rim is a small price to pay for a well-baked crust.

Freezing Fruit Pies: Fruit pies, except those made with custard, freeze surprisingly well. For best results, freeze the pies before baking. Form the pie in a pan lined with plastic wrap. Do not cut steam vents in the top or apply a glaze. Freeze the pie solid, then pry it out of the pan and peel off the wrap. Wrap the pie airtight in foil, seal it in a plastic bag, and freeze for up to 6 months. When you are ready to bake the pie, return it, still frozen but unwrapped, to its original pan and glaze it if you wish. Bake the pie at 425°F for 10 minutes, cut vents in the top, and bake for 20 minutes more. Reduce the oven temperature to 350°F and bake the pie until thick juices bubble through the vents, about 1 hour longer.

To freeze a baked pie, cool the pie thoroughly, then wrap it airtight, still in the pan. Before serving, let the pie thaw, then set it in a 325°F oven until a knife inserted through a steam vent comes out warm, about 15 minutes.

How to Make a Pie with Any Fruit: Once you develop a feel for making fruit pies, you can virtually dispense with recipes. A 9-inch pie needs about 5 cups of fresh fruit or berries plus sugar, thickener, and a little butter. You will seldom go wrong if you use the following formula:

5 cups sliced fruit or berries
¾ cup sugar
3 tablespoons quick-cooking tapioca or cornstarch
1 tablespoon strained fresh lemon juice
⅛ teaspoon salt
2 to 3 tablespoons unsalted butter, cut into small pieces

There are, of course, special cases. Tart fruits such as sour cherries, rhubarb, cranberries, gooseberries, blackberries, fresh currants, and green tomatoes require 1 to 1½ cups sugar. Apples need only half as much thickener, while juicy berries may require one-third more, especially if they are heavily sweetened. Mix the fruit, sugar, thickener, lemon juice, and salt and let stand for 15 minutes before pouring it into the pie crust. Dot the butter over the filling, then cover with the top crust or lattice. Bake the pie in the lower third of a 425°F oven for 30 minutes; then slip a baking sheet beneath it, reduce the oven temperature to 350°F, and bake the pie until thick juices bubble through the vents, about 30 minutes more.

Combination Fillings: Fruit pies filled with combinations of fruits and berries are infinite in possibility and often magical in result. However, those who demand predictability should not venture out onto this limb. It is tricky to gauge the thickening and sweetening required by combination fillings, and the colors are sometimes startling. Create your own fillings or try the following suggestions:

3½ cups sliced peeled pears and 1½ cups raspberries, cranberries, or dark raisins
3½ cups sliced peeled peaches and 1½ cups blueberries or raspberries
3 cups sliced peeled apples and 2 cups sliced green tomatoes
3½ cups sliced peeled apples and 1½ cups raspberries, blackberries, or fresh currants
2½ cups pitted sour cherries and 2½ cups diced rhubarb
4 cups pitted sour or sweet cherries and 1 cup dark raisins
2½ cups sliced strawberries and 2½ cups gooseberries
4 cups diced fresh pineapple and 1 cup dark raisins or sliced strawberries
2½ cups sliced bananas and 2½ cups blueberries or sliced strawberries

Fillings with Frozen Fruit: If you buy frozen fruits such as peaches, cherries, or berries, choose those that are "individually frozen" or "dry-packed," meaning that they have been processed without sugar and come in loose pieces rather than a block.

Follow any recipe calling for fresh fruit, substituting an equal volume of frozen fruit. Since frozen fruit resists settling in the cup, it must be measured by a special procedure. Separate the pieces and knock off clinging ice, but do not thaw. Pour the fruit into a 4-cup measure, shake to settle it as much as possible, and measure 4 level cups. Measure out 1 more cup in a 1-cup measure. Toss the still-frozen fruit with the other ingredients, using the maximum amount of thickening called for, and spoon the filling into the crust at once, without the usual 15-minute standing time. If the fruit is allowed to thaw, it will release a flood of juice and make the crust soggy. Do not glaze the top crust with sugar or egg. Bake the pie at 400°F for 50 minutes; then slip a baking sheet beneath it and bake at 350°F until thick juices bubble through the vents, 25 to 40 minutes more.

Canned Fruit: Canned fruits, preferably packed in unsweetened juice, make acceptable pies. For Cherry Pie with Canned or Bottled Fruit, see 875; for Winter Peach Pie, see 876. Otherwise use the following generic formula: Slice pears and peaches, halve apricots, and cut pineapple into chunks; leave plums whole.

Prepare:

Flaky Pastry Dough, 859

Roll half of the dough into a 13-inch round, fit it into a 9-inch pie pan, and trim the overhanging dough to ¾ inch all around. Refrigerate. Roll the other half into a 12-inch round for the top crust and refrigerate it. (If you wish to make a lattice top, see 872.)

Position a rack in the lower third of the oven. Preheat the oven to 425°F.

Pour into a sieve set over a bowl:

3 pounds canned fruit

Shake the fruit lightly to drain. Measure 3½ cups fruit and ½ cup juice and combine in a bowl with:

½ to ¾ cup sugar

3 tablespoons quick-cooking tapioca or cornstarch (use cornstarch for a lattice pie)

2 tablespoons strained fresh lemon juice

Let the mixture stand for 15 minutes, then pour into the bottom crust. If the crust seems too full to be covered with a pastry lid, remove a little of the fruit and liquid. Dot with:

2 tablespoons unsalted butter, cut into small pieces

Brush the overhanging edge of the bottom crust with cold water. Cover with the top crust or lattice, then seal the edge, trim, and crimp or flute. If using a closed top crust, cut steam vents. Bake the pie for 30 minutes. Slip a baking sheet beneath the pan, reduce the oven temperature to 350°F, and bake until thick juices bubble through the vents, 25 to 35 minutes more. Let cool completely on a rack before serving.

ABOUT FORMING A COVERED FRUIT PIE

Crusts for covered fruit pies must be made with a flaky pastry dough. Flaky Pastry Dough, 859, made either with shortening or with a combination of butter and shortening, and Deluxe Butter Flaky Pastry Dough, 862, are suitable for any fruit pie. Lard Flaky Pastry Dough, 862, is particularly good with apple pies but works as well with other fruit pies, so long as you appreciate the flavor of lard. Flaky Cream Cheese Pastry Dough, 866, is also a good all-purpose dough, though you may find it a bit too tangy with tart fruits such as sour cherries and rhubarb. If you like, use Cornmeal Flaky Pastry Dough, 864, for blueberry or blackberry pies or Nutted Flaky Pastry Dough, 864, with stone fruits, such as peaches or cherries. Be aware, however, that these doughs tend to leak during baking. Sweet Flaky Pastry Dough, 864, is not good for covered fruit pies, as it is likely to char during the long baking.

In preparing the dough for a covered fruit pie, it is better to add slightly more water (or cream) than is needed rather than too little. If the dough is dry and crumbly, the filling is likely to seep through the bottom crust, even when there are no visible cracks or holes. When you divide the finished dough before wrapping and chilling, allow a slightly larger portion for the bottom crust than for the top. The bottom crust needs to be rolled a tad thick to withstand the juices released by the fruit during baking.

Once mixed, fruit pie fillings should not stand longer than 15 minutes before being turned into the crust, or else they may become too juicy. Line the pie pan with the bottom crust and roll out the top crust *before* you prepare the filling. Refrigerate both bottom and top crusts until the filling is complete and you are ready to assemble the pie. Glass pie pans seem to produce an especially crisp and brown undercrust, and they also let you to check on its progress during baking. However, any 9-inch pie pan will do.

Roll out the bottom crust, fit it into the pan, and trim the overhanging dough to ¾ inch all around (see How to Roll Out Pastry Dough, 860). Patch any holes, tears,

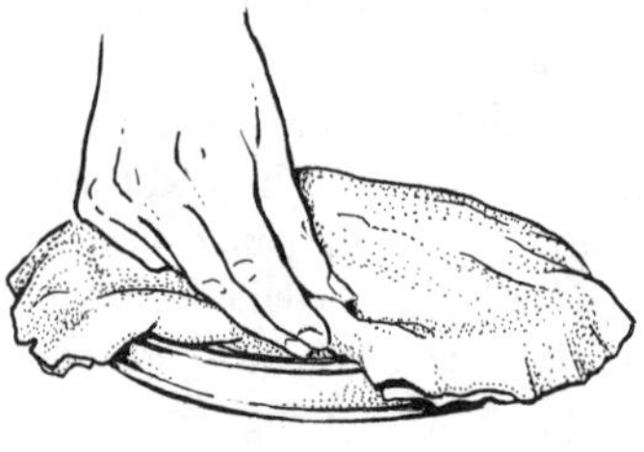

Tuck the overhang of the doubled edge underneath itself so that it is flush with the rim of the pie pan.

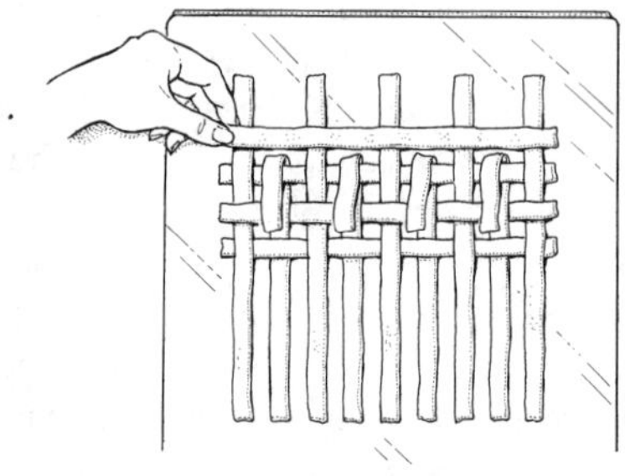

Forming a woven lattice top

or thin spots with dough scraps, dabbing them on one side with cold water and then firmly pressing them, moistened side down, into place. Cover any short spots in the overhang in the same manner; if the pie is to be well sealed, you must have a wide overhang all around. Carefully transfer the lined pan to the refrigerator. Roll the remaining half of the dough into a 12-inch round, slip a rimless cookie sheet beneath it, and refrigerate it. (To make a lattice top, see below.)

Remove the bottom crust from the refrigerator and fill it. Dot the top with butter if your recipe calls for it. Brush the overhanging edge of the bottom crust with cold water and place the top crust over the pie. Firmly pinch the edges of both crusts together with your fingers to seal. Trim the doubled edge to make an even overhang of ¾ inch, then tuck the overhang underneath itself so that the folded edge is flush with the rim of the pie pan. Crimp or flute the edge as for a single-crust pie (see 862); a high fluted rim will help to contain any juices that bubble through the top crust. Using a sharp paring knife, make three or four 2-inch slashes in the top crust to allow steam to escape during baking. If you wish, cut scraps of dough into decorative shapes, brush lightly with cold water, and press onto the top crust.

To Make a Lattice Top: Lattice tops are fun to construct. A plain lattice, which simply entails laying

Cutting vents in the top crust

strips of dough in a crisscross pattern over the top of the pie, requires less patience than a woven lattice, but both are eminently doable. Since tapioca granules that are exposed in the spaces of a lattice sometimes fail to soften, it is wise to thicken fillings for lattice-top pies with cornstarch (or flour) instead.

To Form a Plain Lattice Top: For a 9-inch pie pan, roll the dough reserved for the top crust into a 13½-inch round and trim the round to make a 10-inch square. Cut the square of dough into 18 strips, each about ½ inch wide. Spoon the filling into the bottom crust of the pie and brush the edge of the bottom crust with cold water. Place 9 of the dough strips ½ inch apart on top of the pie, then arrange the remaining dough strips over these, either on a diagonal or in a perpendicular crisscross pattern. Trim the lattice strips so that they hang over the edge of the bottom crust at least ¼ inch on each end. Press the strips against the bottom crust. Fold the edge of the bottom crust up, covering the ends of the lattice strips, then crimp or flute the edge.

To Form a Woven Lattice Top: Woven lattices tend to soften and become juice soaked when formed directly on the pie, so construct them on a cookie sheet and then transfer them, chilled, to the pie. For a 9-inch pie pan, roll the dough reserved for the top crust into a 13½-inch round and trim the round to make a 10-inch square. Cut the square into eighteen ½-inch strips. Arrange 9 of the strips ½ inch apart on a floured rimless cookie sheet (or on the back of a baking pan). Fold every other strip halfway back, making the ends meet, then place 1 strip crosswise just beyond the folded edge. Return the folded strips to their original flat position over the perpendicular strip. Fold back the strips that you just left flat and then place a second strip crosswise just beyond the folded edge. Unfold strips over the second perpendicular strip. Repeat until you have woven 5 crosswise strips into the lattice, completing one half. Now weave the remaining 4 crosswise strips into the lattice starting on the other side of the center crosswise strip, completing the other half. Refrigerate the lattice until firm. Fill the bottom crust of the pie and brush the exposed edge with cold water. Slide the lattice off the sheet onto the pie. Trim the lattice strips so that they hang over the edge of the bottom crust at least ¼ inch on each end. Press the strips against the bottom crust. Fold the edge of the bottom crust up, covering the ends of the lattice strips, then crimp or flute the edge.

APPLE PIE I *One 9-inch pie; 6 to 8 servings*

We like using Golden Delicious apples in this pie because they retain their texture and do not flood the pie with juice. Gala and Fuji are also good. Classic alternatives are: Newton Pippin, Rhode Island Greening, Winesap, Northern Spy, and Jonathan. We do not recommend Granny Smiths; although crisp when raw, all too often they turn mushy when baked in a pie with both a top and a bottom crust.

Apple pie is best with a rich crust. A lard crust is superb; an ordinary flaky pastry crust made entirely with vegetable shortening makes a surprisingly close facsimile. Deluxe Butter Flaky Pastry Dough, 862, is also very good. Because the filling starts out heaped, a lattice top is not feasible; if you want a lattice, make Apple Pie II, below, in which the filling is partially cooked before going into the pie. It is crucial to slice the apples about ¼ inch thick, measured at the thicker end. If the slices are thinner, the filling is apt to turn mushy; if thicker, the pie will not hold together when cut. Resist the temptation to add other spices or flavorings. A hint of cinnamon is all that is needed.

Before beginning, please read About Covered Fruit Pies, 869.

Prepare:

Flaky Pastry Dough, 859, Lard Flaky Pastry Dough, 862, or Deluxe Butter Flaky Pastry Dough, 862

Roll half the dough into a 13-inch round, fit it into a 9-inch pie pan, and trim the overhanging dough to ¾ inch all around. Refrigerate. Roll the other half of the dough into a 12-inch round for the top crust and refrigerate it.

Position a rack in the lower third of the oven. Preheat the oven to 425°F.

Peel, core, and slice ¼ inch thick:

2½ pounds apples (5 to 6 medium-large)

Measure 6 cups. Combine the apples with:

¾ cup sugar

2 to 3 tablespoons all-purpose flour

1 tablespoon strained fresh lemon juice (optional)

½ teaspoon ground cinnamon

⅛ teaspoon salt

Let stand for 15 minutes, stirring several times, so that the apples soften slightly and will better fit into the crust. Pour the mixture into the bottom crust and gently level with the back of a spoon. Dot the top with:

2 tablespoons unsalted butter, cut into small pieces

Brush the overhanging edge of the bottom crust with cold water. Cover with the top crust, then seal the edge, trim, and crimp or flute. Cut steam vents in the top crust and sprinkle with:

2 teaspoons sugar

⅛ teaspoon ground cinnamon

Bake the pie for 30 minutes. Slip a baking sheet beneath it, reduce the oven temperature to 350°F, and bake until the fruit feels *just* tender when a knife or skewer is poked through a steam vent and thick juices have begun to bubble through the vents, 30 to 45 minutes more. For the filling to thicken properly, the pie must cool completely on a rack, 3 to 4 hours. If you wish to serve the pie warm, place it in a 350°F oven for about 15 minutes. The pie is best the day it is baked, but it can be kept for 2 to 3 days on the counter.

APPLE PIE II *One 9-inch pie; 6 to 8 servings*

Because raw apples shrink a great deal during baking, apple pies tend to develop a gap between the top crust and fruit, causing the top crust to crumble when the pie is sliced. In this recipe, the filling is precooked and thus preshrunk, eliminating the gap and producing a beautifully full, compact pie that slices like a charm. Precooking also allows you to cover the pie with a lattice top if you choose. As one would expect, this pie is slightly softer than one made with raw apples, and the filling has a certain smoothness on the tongue. On the other hand, since the filling requires no thickener, the pie has a lovely fruity taste. To select apples for a pie, please read Apple Pie I, above.

Before beginning, please read About Covered Fruit Pies, 869.

Prepare:

Flaky Pastry Dough, 859, Lard Flaky Pastry Dough, 862, or Deluxe Butter Flaky Pastry Dough, 862

Roll half the dough into a 13-inch round, fit it into a 9-inch pie pan, and trim the overhanging dough to ¾ inch all around. Refrigerate. Roll the other half into a 12-inch round for the top crust and refrigerate it. (For a lattice top, see 872.)

Peel, core, and slice a little thicker than ¼ inch:

3 pounds apples (6 to 8 medium-large)

Measure 7 cups. In a very wide skillet or pot, heat over high heat until sizzling and fragrant:

3 tablespoons unsalted butter

Add the apples and toss until glazed with the butter. Reduce the heat to medium, cover tightly, and cook, stirring frequently, until the apples are softened on the outside but still slightly crunchy, 5 to 7 minutes. Stir in:

¾ cup sugar
½ teaspoon ground cinnamon
⅛ teaspoon salt

Increase the heat to high and cook the apples at a rapid boil until the juices become thick and syrupy, about 3 minutes. Immediately spread the apples in a thin layer on a baking sheet and let them cool to room temperature.

Position a rack in the lower third of the oven. Preheat the oven to 425°F.

Pour the apple mixture into the bottom crust. Brush the overhanging edge of the bottom crust with cold water. Cover with the top crust or lattice, then seal the edge, trim, and crimp or flute. If using a closed top crust, cut steam vents. Bake until the crust is richly browned and the filling has begun to bubble, 40 to 50 minutes. Let cool completely on a rack, 3 to 4 hours. If you wish to serve the pie warm, place it in a 350°F oven for about 15 minutes. The pie is best if eaten promptly, but it can be kept at room temperature for 2 to 3 days.

BLUEBERRY PIE

One 9-inch pie; 8 servings

If you are constructing a lattice, use the greater amount of cornstarch suggested to prevent a watery filling from bubbling over the strips.

Before beginning, please read About Covered Fruit Pies, 869. To use frozen blueberries, see 871.

Prepare:

Flaky Pastry Dough, 859, Lard Flaky Pastry Dough, 862, Deluxe Butter Flaky Pastry Dough, 862, Cornmeal Flaky Pastry Dough, 864, or double recipe Flaky Cream Cheese Pastry Dough, 866

Roll half the dough into a 13-inch round, fit it into a 9-inch pie pan, and trim the overhanging dough to ¾ inch all around. Refrigerate. Roll the other half of the dough into a 12-inch round for the top crust and refrigerate it. (For a lattice top, see 872.)

Position a rack in the lower third of the oven. Preheat the oven to 425°F.

Combine and let stand for 15 minutes:

5 cups blueberries, picked over
¾ to 1 cup sugar
3½ to 4 tablespoons quick-cooking tapioca or cornstarch (use cornstarch for a lattice pie)
1 tablespoon strained fresh lemon juice
1 teaspoon grated lemon zest (optional)
⅛ teaspoon salt

Pour the mixture into the bottom crust and dot with:

1 to 2 tablespoons unsalted butter, cut into small pieces

Brush the overhanging edge of the bottom crust with cold water. Cover with the top crust or lattice, then seal the edge, trim, and crimp or flute. If using a closed top crust, cut steam vents. Bake the pie for 30 minutes. Slip a baking sheet beneath it, reduce the oven temperature to 350°F, and bake until thick juices bubble through the vents, 25 to 35 minutes more. Let cool completely on a rack. The pie is best the day it is baked, but it can be stored at room temperature for up to 1 day.

CHERRY PIE

One 9-inch pie; 8 servings

Sour cherries make the best pie, but ripe Bing cherries will certainly do. A cherry or olive pitter, a device that looks like a paper punch, is a welcome time-saver here. Before beginning, please read About Covered Fruit Pies, 869.

Prepare:

Flaky Pastry Dough, 859, Lard Flaky Pastry Dough, 862, Deluxe Butter Flaky Pastry Dough, 862, or double recipe Flaky Cream Cheese Pastry Dough, 866

Roll half the dough into a 13-inch round, fit it into a 9-inch pie pan, and trim the overhanging dough to ¾ inch all around. Refrigerate. Roll the other half into a 12-inch round for the top crust and refrigerate it. (For a lattice top, see 872.)

Position a rack in the lower third of the oven. Preheat the oven to 425°F.

Combine and let stand for 15 minutes:

5 cups pitted sour or Bing cherries (2 to 2½ pounds)
1¼ cups sugar for sour cherries, or ¾ cup sugar for Bing cherries
3 to 3½ tablespoons quick-cooking tapioca or cornstarch (use cornstarch for a lattice pie)
2 tablespoons water
1 tablespoon strained fresh lemon juice
¼ teaspoon almond extract
1 to 2 drops red food coloring (optional)

Pour the mixture into the bottom crust and dot with:

2 to 3 tablespoons unsalted butter, cut into small pieces

Brush the overhanging edge of the bottom crust with cold water. Cover with the top crust or lattice, then seal the edge, trim, and crimp or flute. If using a closed top crust, cut steam vents. Bake the pie for 30 minutes. Slip a baking sheet beneath it, reduce the oven temperature to 350°F, and bake until thick juices bubble through the vents, 25 to 35 minutes more. Let cool completely on a rack before serving. Store at room temperature for up to 1 day.

CHERRY PIE WITH CANNED OR BOTTLED FRUIT

One 9-inch pie; 8 servings

Canned or bottled sour cherries make a more flavorful pie than canned or bottled sweet ones. Adjust the sugar depending on which type you have and whether they are packed in plain water or in a syrup.

Before beginning, please read About Covered Fruit Pies, 869.

Prepare:

Flaky Pastry Dough, 859, Lard Flaky Pastry Dough, 862, Deluxe Butter Flaky Pastry Dough, 862, or double recipe Flaky Cream Cheese Pastry Dough, 866

Roll half the dough into a 13-inch round, fit it into a 9-inch pie pan, and trim the overhanging dough to ¾ inch all around. Refrigerate. Roll the other half into a 12-inch round for the top crust and refrigerate it. (For a lattice top, see 872.)

Position a rack in the lower third of the oven. Preheat the oven to 425°F.

Pour into a sieve set over a bowl:

3 pounds bottled or canned cherries

Shake the cherries lightly to drain. Measure 4 cups fruit and ½ cup juice and combine with:

½ cup sugar for sweet cherries in syrup, ¾ cup sugar for sour cherries in light syrup, or 1¼ cups sugar for sour cherries packed in water

3 tablespoons quick-cooking tapioca or cornstarch (use cornstarch for a lattice pie)

1 tablespoon strained fresh lemon juice

¼ teaspoon almond extract

Let stand for 15 minutes, then pour into the bottom crust and dot with:

2 to 3 tablespoons butter, cut into small pieces

Brush the overhanging edge of the bottom crust with cold water. Cover with the top crust or lattice, then seal the edge, trim, and crimp or flute. If using a closed top crust, cut steam vents. Bake the pie for 30 minutes. Slip a baking sheet beneath it, reduce the oven temperature to 350°F, and bake until thick juices bubble through the vents, 25 to 35 minutes more. Let cool completely on a rack before serving. Store at room temperature for up to 1 day.

PEACH PIE

One 9-inch pie; 8 servings

Whether freestone or clingstone, yellow or white, peaches make a luscious pie. To peel peaches easily, drop them into boiling water for about 1 minute, then slip off the skins.

Before beginning, please read About Covered Fruit Pies, 869. To use frozen peaches, see 871.

Prepare:

Flaky Pastry Dough, 859, Lard Flaky Pastry Dough, 862, Deluxe Butter Flaky Pastry Dough, 862, or double recipe Flaky Cream Cheese Pastry Dough, 866

Roll half the dough into a 13-inch round, fit it into a 9-inch pie pan and trim the overhanging dough to ¾ inch all around. Refrigerate. Roll the other half into a 12-inch round for the top crust and refrigerate it. (For a lattice top, see 872.)

Position a rack in the lower third of the oven. Preheat the oven to 425°F.

Peel, pit, and slice ¼ inch thick:

2½ pounds peaches

Measure 5 cups and combine with:

½ to ¾ cup sugar

3 to 3½ tablespoons quick-cooking tapioca or cornstarch (use cornstarch for a lattice pie)

3 tablespoons strained fresh lemon juice

¼ teaspoon almond extract (optional)

⅛ teaspoon salt

Let stand for 15 minutes, stirring occasionally. Pour into the bottom crust and dot with:

2 to 3 tablespoons unsalted butter, cut into small pieces

Brush the overhanging edge of the bottom crust with cold water. Cover with the top crust or lattice, then seal the edge, trim, and crimp or flute. If using a closed top crust, cut steam vents. Lightly brush the top of the pie with:

Milk or cream

Sprinkle with:

2 teaspoons sugar

Bake the pie for 30 minutes. Slip a baking sheet beneath it, reduce the oven temperature to 350°F, and bake until thick juices bubble through the vents, 25 to 35 minutes more. Let cool completely on a rack before serving. This pie is best the day it is baked, but it can be stored at room temperature for up to 1 day.

PEACH RASPBERRY PIE

Used by themselves, raspberries make a runny and rather seedy pie. Try them this way instead.

Prepare Peach Pie, above, substituting 2 cups of raspberries for 2 cups of the peaches. Use the maximum amounts of sugar and thickener and decrease the lemon juice to 1 tablespoon.

WINTER PEACH PIE *One 9-inch pie; 8 servings*

This pie can also be made in the summer with 5 cups sliced fresh peaches in place of the canned. It is gorgeous with a lattice top.

Before beginning, please read About Covered Fruit Pies, 869.

Prepare:

Flaky Pastry Dough, 859, Lard Flaky Pastry Dough, 862, Deluxe Butter Flaky Pastry Dough, 862, or double recipe Flaky Cream Cheese Pastry Dough, 866

Roll half the dough into a 13-inch round, fit it into a 9-inch pie pan, and trim the overhanging dough to ¾ inch all around. Refrigerate. Roll the other half into a 12-inch round for the top crust and refrigerate it. (For a lattice top, see 872.)

Position a rack in the lower third of the oven. Preheat the oven to 425°F.

Pour into a clean sieve set over a bowl:

2½ pounds canned sliced peaches, "packed in juice"

Shake the peaches lightly to drain. Measure 3 cups fruit and ½ cup juice and combine with:

⅔ cup dark raisins
⅔ cup firmly packed light brown sugar
3 tablespoons quick-cooking tapioca or cornstarch (use cornstarch for a lattice pie)
2 tablespoons strained fresh lemon juice
½ teaspoon ground ginger
¼ teaspoon ground cinnamon
¼ teaspoon ground mace or freshly grated or ground nutmeg
⅛ teaspoon ground cloves

Let stand for 15 minutes, then pour into the bottom crust and dot with:

2 to 3 tablespoons unsalted butter, cut into small pieces

Brush the overhanging edge of the bottom crust with cold water. Cover with the top crust or lattice, then seal the edge, trim, and crimp or flute. If using a closed top crust, cut steam vents. Whisk together, then lightly brush the top of the pie with:

1 large egg yolk
⅛ teaspoon water

Bake the pie for 30 minutes. Slip a baking sheet beneath it, reduce the oven temperature to 350°F, and bake until thick juices bubble through the vents, 25 to 35 minutes more. Let cool completely on a rack before serving. Store at room temperature for up to 1 day.

RHUBARB PIE *One 9-inch pie; 8 servings*

If possible, make this pie early in the season, when the stalks are still thin skinned, pink, and no thicker than your thumb. Only mature rhubarb will require the greater amount of sugar suggested.

Before beginning, please read About Covered Fruit Pies, 869.

Prepare:

Flaky Pastry Dough, 859, Lard Flaky Pastry Dough, 862, Deluxe Butter Flaky Pastry Dough, 862, or double recipe Flaky Cream Cheese Pastry Dough, 866

Roll half the dough into a 13-inch round, fit it into a 9-inch pie pan, and trim the overhanging dough to ¾ inch all around. Refrigerate. Roll the other half into a 12-inch round for the top crust and refrigerate it. (For a lattice top, see 872.)

Position a rack in the lower third of the oven. Preheat the oven to 425°F.

Without peeling, cut into 1-inch lengths:

1¾ to 2 pounds rhubarb stalks

Measure 5 cups and combine with:

1¼ to 1½ cups sugar
¼ cup quick-cooking tapioca or cornstarch (use cornstarch for a lattice pie)
Grated zest of 1 orange (optional)
¼ teaspoon salt

Let stand for 15 minutes, stirring occasionally. Pour into the bottom crust and dot with:

2 tablespoons unsalted butter, cut into small pieces

Brush the overhanging edge of the bottom crust with cold water. Cover with the top crust or lattice, then seal the edge, trim, and crimp or flute. If using a closed top crust, cut steam vents. Lightly brush the top of the pie with:

Milk or cream

Sprinkle with:

2 teaspoons sugar

Bake the pie for 30 minutes. Slip a baking sheet beneath it, reduce the oven temperature to 350°F, and bake until thick juices bubble through the vents, 25 to 35 minutes more. Let cool completely on a rack before serving. This pie is best eaten on the day it is baked, but it can be stored at room temperature for up to 1 day.

STRAWBERRY RHUBARB PIE

This tastes more of strawberries than of rhubarb and generally pleases even the rhubarb-wary.

Prepare Rhubarb Pie, above, substituting 2½ cups strawberries, hulled and halved lengthwise, for 2½ cups of the rhubarb. Decrease the sugar to 1 cup and omit the orange zest.

ABOUT MINCE PIE

Mince pie dates back to medieval English baking and came to America with the first settlers. Until the late nineteenth century, Americans considered it the choicest of all pies—an obligatory dessert at Thanksgiving and Christmas. Originally, the central ingredient was minced or finely chopped meat, usually beef but sometimes veal or venison, and in our grandmother's day meatless mince pies were still the exception rather than the norm.

MINCE PIE

One 9-inch pie; 8 servings

A handsome pie with a delicious flavor quite unlike that of commercial mincemeats.

Before beginning, please read About Covered Fruit Pies, 869.

Prepare:

Flaky Pastry Dough, 859, or Deluxe Butter Flaky Pastry Dough, 862

Roll half the dough into a 13-inch round, fit it into a 9-inch pie pan, and trim the overhanging dough to ¾ inch all around. Refrigerate. Roll the other half into a 12-inch round for the top crust and refrigerate it. (For a lattice top, see 872.)

Combine in a medium, heavy pot or saucepan:

3 medium-large Golden Delicious apples, peeled, cored, and cut into ¾-inch chunks
1½ cups dark raisins, coarsely chopped
1 cup walnuts or pecans, coarsely chopped
1 cup sugar
¼ cup apple juice or cider
¼ cup brandy or apple juice
4 tablespoons (½ stick) unsalted butter
Grated zest of ½ lemon
Strained juice of ½ lemon
1 tablespoon cider vinegar
1 teaspoon salt
1 teaspoon ground cinnamon
½ teaspoon freshly grated or ground nutmeg
¼ teaspoon ground cloves

Bring to a boil over high heat. Reduce the heat to low and gently simmer, stirring frequently, until the bottom of the pot is almost dry and the fruits are glazed with a thick, molasses-like syrup, 20 to 30 minutes. Let cool to room temperature.

Position a rack in the center of the oven. Preheat the oven to 400°F.

Pour the filling into the bottom crust. Brush the overhanging edge of the bottom crust with cold water. Cover with the top crust or lattice, then seal the edge, trim, and crimp or flute. If using a closed top crust, cut steam vents. Whisk together, then brush the top of the pie with:

1 large egg yolk
⅛ teaspoon water

Bake the pie for 30 minutes. Reduce the oven temperature to 350°F and bake until the crust is richly browned, 30 to 40 minutes more. Let cool completely on a rack, then refrigerate for up to 1 week. Before serving, warm the pie in a 300°F oven for about 20 minutes. Serve with:

Hard Sauce, 1007, or vanilla ice cream

ABOUT DEEP-DISH FRUIT PIES

Deep-dish pies are simply covered fruit pies baked without a bottom crust. Despite their name, these pies should be baked in dishes that are relatively wide and shallow rather than narrow and deep, so that there is enough crust in relation to fruit. The 10-inch Pyrex dishes made expressly for deep-dish pies—they lack the flared rim of ordinary pie pans—are serviceable for recipes made with up to 6 cups fruit. For pies with more generous fillings, choose a glass or ceramic casserole.

Any fruit pie in this chapter can be baked as a deep-dish pie. Since the filling need not be firm enough to slice—deep-dish pies are served with a spoon—you can decrease the thickening by up to half. For the top crust, use a half recipe of any flaky pastry dough, 859 to 864, or a full recipe of Flaky Cream Cheese Pastry Dough, 866. Roll the dough the same shape as, but a little wider than, the top of the dish, lay it over the filling, and tuck the edges against the inside of the dish. Cut steam vents in the top. If you wish, sprinkle the crust with sugar or glaze with an egg yolk beaten with ⅛ teaspoon water. Set the pie on a baking sheet and bake in the center of a preheated 375°F oven until the crust is nicely browned and juices bubble through the vents, about 1 hour.

DEEP-DISH PEAR PIE WITH CRANBERRIES AND APPLES

8 to 10 servings

Prepare:

½ recipe Flaky Pastry Dough, 859, or ½ recipe Deluxe Butter Flaky Pastry Dough, 862

Position a rack in the center of the oven. Preheat the oven to 375°F.

In a 10- to 12-inch casserole (3½ to 4½ quarts), combine:

3½ pounds firm ripe pears (7 medium-large), peeled, cored, and cut into ¼-inch-thick slices
1½ pounds firm tart apples (3 medium-large), peeled, cored, and cut into ⅛-inch-thick slices
2½ cups (8 ounces) cranberries, picked over
1⅓ cups sugar
⅓ cup all-purpose flour
1 tablespoon strained fresh lemon juice
⅛ teaspoon salt

Stir gently until well blended. If you wish, dot the top with:

2 to 4 tablespoons unsalted butter, cut into small pieces

Roll the dough to fit the top of the dish, lay it over the filling, and tuck in the edges. Cut 3 or 4 steam vents in the crust. Brush the top with:

2 tablespoons beaten egg (½ large)

Place the pie on a baking sheet and bake until the crust is golden brown and juices bubble through the vents, about 1 hour. Let cool on a rack. The pie can be stored at room temperature for up to 1 day. Serve warm or at room temperature with:

Vanilla ice cream

DEEP-DISH APPLE PIE WITH CHEDDAR CRUST

8 servings

Combine and toss together:

¾ cup lightly packed grated extra-sharp Cheddar cheese
⅔ cup all-purpose flour
6 tablespoons (¾ stick) cold unsalted butter, cut into ¼-inch pieces

Chop the mixture with a pastry blender to the consistency of coarse crumbs, then press together with your fingers and knead in the bowl until a cohesive dough forms. Flatten the dough into a 4-inch disk, wrap in plastic, and refrigerate until firm but malleable, 30 to 60 minutes. Flour the dough lightly, then roll into a 9-inch round between sheets of wax paper. Slip a rimless cookie sheet beneath the dough and refrigerate until firm, about 30 minutes.

Position a rack in the center of the oven. Preheat the oven to 375°F.

Heat over high heat in a very wide skillet (not cast iron) until sizzling and fragrant:

6 tablespoons (¾ stick) unsalted butter

Add:

2 pounds Golden Delicious, Gala, Fuji, or Newton Pippin apples (about 4 medium-large) peeled, cored, and sliced ¼ inch thick

Toss with a wooden spoon until the apples release their juice and are just tender, 5 to 7 minutes; reduce the heat if the apples begin to color. Stir in:

1 cup dark raisins (optional)
½ cup chopped walnuts or pecans
½ cup sugar
Grated zest of 1 large lemon
Strained juice of 1 large lemon
¼ cup brandy (optional)
¼ teaspoon ground cinnamon
½ teaspoon freshly grated or ground nutmeg
½ teaspoon salt
¼ teaspoon ground cloves

Boil over high heat, stirring occasionally, until the juices thicken to the consistency of maple syrup. Pour the mixture into a 9-inch pie pan. Peel the top sheet of wax paper off the dough, then flip the dough onto the filling and peel off the bottom sheet. Let the dough soften slightly, then tuck the edges inside the rim of the pan and cut two 2-inch steam vents. Place the pie on a baking sheet and bake until the crust is golden brown and the filling is bubbly, 30 to 40 minutes. Let cool slightly before serving. The pie can be made up to 12 hours ahead and warmed in a 350°F oven for 10 to 15 minutes. Accompany with:

Vanilla ice cream

ABOUT SINGLE-CRUST FRUIT PIES AND FRUIT TARTS

While covered fruit pies demand a rolled crust made from flaky pastry dough, the crusts of open fruit pies and tarts can be made, if you choose, with a simpler pat-in-the-pan dough. Open fruit pies and tarts are meant to beguile the eye as well as the palate. So unless the fruit will be obscured by streusel, arrange it with as much care and precision as your patience allows.

FRESH STRAWBERRY (OR RASPBERRY) PIE

One 9-inch pie; 8 servings

One of America's most popular desserts, this pie is filled with uncooked berries bound together with a thickened berry puree. This is only as good as the berries you start with.

Prepare in a 9-inch pie pan:

Baked Flaky Pastry Crust, 866, Pat-in-the-Pan Butter Crust, 867, or Crumb Crust, 868, made with graham crackers or vanilla wafers

Pick over:

6 cups strawberries or red or black raspberries

Rinse, dry, and hull the strawberries; cut any very large ones in half. Do not rinse the raspberries. Measure 4 cups of berries and set aside. Puree the remaining 2 cups berries in a blender or food processor. Whisk together in a medium saucepan:

1 cup sugar

¼ cup cornstarch

⅛ teaspoon salt

Whisk in:

½ cup water

Stir in the pureed berries along with:

2 tablespoons strained fresh lemon juice

2 tablespoons unsalted butter, cut into small pieces

Bring the mixture to a simmer over medium-high heat, stirring constantly, and cook for 1 minute. Pour half of the reserved berries into the crust and spoon half of the hot berry mixture over them. Gently shake the pie pan to coat the berries evenly. Cover with the remaining berries, spoon the remaining hot berry mixture over them, and gently shake the pan as before. Refrigerate the pie for at least 4 hours to set. This pie is best served the day it is made. Serve with:

Whipped cream

OPEN-FACED PEACH CUSTARD PIE

One 9-inch pie; 8 servings

A *Joy* classic.

Prepare in a 9-inch pie pan, glazing with the egg yolk:

Baked Flaky Pastry Crust, 866

Position a rack in the lower third of the oven. Preheat the oven to 400°F.

Whisk together until well blended:

1 large egg or 2 large egg yolks

¾ cup sugar

6 tablespoons (¾ stick) unsalted butter, melted

⅓ cup all-purpose flour

1 teaspoon vanilla

¼ teaspoon salt

Arrange in a single layer, cut side down, over the bottom of the crust:

3 to 4 fresh peaches, peeled and halved, or 6 to 8 drained canned peach halves

Pour the egg mixture over the peaches. Bake the pie for 10 minutes. Reduce the oven temperature to 300°F and bake until the custard is brown and crusty on top and appears firmly set in the center when the pan is shaken, about 1 hour longer. Let cool on a rack. Serve warm or at room temperature. The pie can be stored refrigerated for up to 1 day. If you wish, accompany with:

Whipped cream

APRICOT FRANGIPANE TART

One 9½- or 10-inch tart; 8 servings

Fresh apricots make a spectacular tart filling, especially when paired with a rich almond custard.

Prepare in a 9½- or 10-inch two-piece tart pan, glazing with the egg yolk:

Baked Flaky Pastry Crust, 866, or Shortbread Crust, 868

Let cool completely.

Position a rack in the lower third of the oven. Preheat the oven to 350°F

Spread on a baking sheet:

1 cup slivered blanched almonds

Toast the nuts, stirring once or twice, until golden, about 7 minutes. Let cool to room temperature, then coarsely chop. In a medium bowl, cream with the back of a wooden spoon until light and fluffy:

4 tablespoons (½ stick) unsalted butter, softened

⅓ cup sugar

⅛ teaspoon almond extract

Beat in thoroughly:

1 large egg, at room temperature

Stir in the nuts. Spread the mixture over the bottom of the tart crust. Pit and slice ¼ inch thick:

4 large or 6 medium apricots

Arrange the apricots in concentric circles over the nut mixture, overlapping the slices slightly. Brush with:

2 to 3 tablespoons strained warmed apricot jam

Bake the tart until the nut custard is set, 20 to 25 minutes. Let cool on a rack. Serve slightly warm or at room temperature. Store refrigerated for up to 1 day.

RASPBERRY STREUSEL TART

One 9½- or 10-inch tart; 8 servings

You can make this tart with any summer berry or with a mixture of berries.

Prepare in a 9½- or 10-inch two-piece tart pan, glazing with the egg yolk:

Baked Flaky Pastry Crust, 866, or Shortbread Crust, 868

Let cool completely.

Position a rack in the center of the oven. Preheat the oven to 350°F.

Stir together just until combined:

3 cups raspberries

½ cup sugar

2 tablespoons cornstarch

1 tablespoon strained fresh lemon juice

Distribute the raspberry mixture evenly in the tart crust. Sprinkle over the berries:

Streusel I, 1011

Bake the tart until the streusel has browned and thick juices bubble up near the center, 45 to 60 minutes. Let cool completely on a rack. Serve the tart the day it is made.

PEAR STREUSEL TART

One 9½- or 10-inch tart; 8 servings

Prepare in a 9½- or 10-inch tart pan, glazing with the egg yolk:

Baked Flaky Pastry Crust, 866, or Pat-in-the-Pan Butter Crust, 867

Let cool completely.

Position a rack in the center of the oven. Preheat the oven to 350°F.

Peel, core, and slice ¼ inch thick:

1½ pounds firm ripe pears (about 3 medium-large), preferably Bosc or D'Anjou

Measure 3 cups pears and toss with:

⅓ cup sugar

2 tablespoons all-purpose flour

Distribute the pear mixture in the tart crust. Cover evenly with:

Streusel I, 1011

Bake the tart until the pears feel tender when pierced with a fork, 40 to 50 minutes. Let cool completely on a rack. Serve the tart on the day it is made.

FRESH FRUIT PASTRY CREAM TART

One 9½- or 10-inch tart; 8 servings

A fresh fruit pastry cream tart consists of uncooked berries or thinly sliced fruit artfully arranged over a thin layer of pastry cream in a tart crust. Almost any ripe berry or fruit or any combination of berries and fruits will do, including raspberries, strawberries, blueberries, plums, peaches, nectarines, kiwis, and star fruits. Avoid only very juicy fruits such as melon, hard or crisp fruits such as apples and pears, and bananas, which blacken. You can bake the crust and prepare the pastry cream up to 2 days in advance, but do not assemble the tart until shortly before serving, lest the crust soften and the fruit wilt.

Both flaky pastry and shortbread crusts are suitable. If you prefer the former, make the crust with Deluxe Butter Flaky Pastry Dough, 862, or Sweet Flaky Pastry Dough, 864.

Prepare in a 9½- or 10-inch two-piece tart pan, glazing with the egg yolk:

Baked Flaky Pastry Crust, 866, or Shortbread Crust, 868

Let cool completely. To moisture-proof the crust, brush over the bottom:

3 tablespoons currant, raspberry, or strawberry jelly, melted, or 1 tablespoon unsalted butter, softened

Refrigerate the shell for 10 minutes to set the glaze or butter. Spread evenly over the crust:

1 cup Pastry Cream, 996, or Frangipane Pastry Cream, 997

Arrange over the cream in a single layer:

2 cups whole small berries, sliced strawberries, or thinly sliced fruit

If you wish, brush the fruit lightly with:

2 to 3 tablespoons jelly, melted

Otherwise, just before serving, dust the tart very lightly with:

Powdered sugar

If not serving immediately, store in the refrigerator for no longer than 6 hours.

FRESH FRUIT CREAM TARTLETS

Prepare Fresh Fruit Pastry Cream Tart, above, substituting Baked Flaky Pastry Tartlet Crusts, 866, for the large tart shell. Depending on the exact size and shape of your tartlet shells, you may need slightly more or less glaze, pastry cream, and fruit.

TARTE TATIN *8 servings*

This classic French upside-down apple tart is named for the Tatin sisters, who served it at their hotel in the Loire Valley. The apples are cut in quarters and arranged in circles over the bottom of a skillet containing sugar and melted butter. The apples are cooked on the stove in a cast-iron skillet over high heat until their juices begin to darken and then covered with a pastry crust and baked. When the tart is turned out of the skillet, the crust becomes a base for dazzling concentric circles of translucent, caramelized apples.

Prepare tarte Tatin in any ovenproof, deep, heavy skillet measuring 7 to 8 inches across the bottom and 10 to 11 inches across the top. The filling does not react with cast iron, but you may find a cast-iron skillet cumbersome and heavy to flip when unmolding the tart. Pans made specially for tarte Tatin are available at some cookware stores.

Prepare:

½ recipe Deluxe Butter Flaky Pastry Dough, 862

Roll the dough into a 12-inch round, slip a rimless cookie sheet beneath it, and refrigerate.

Position a rack in the upper third of the oven. Preheat the oven to 375°F.

Peel, core, and quarter lengthwise:

Arrange a circle of apple quarters against the sides of the pan, then fill in the center; flip them with a fork or paring knife.

6 medium-large Golden Delicious apples (about 3 pounds)

Melt in the skillet chosen for the tart (see note above):

8 tablespoons (1 stick) unsalted butter

Remove from the heat and sprinkle evenly over the bottom:

1 cup sugar

Arrange a ring of apple quarters against the sides of the pan, standing the apples on the thin edge of their cut side so as to fit as many as possible. Fill in the center of the skillet with the remaining apple quarters. You may have a piece or two of apple left over.

Place the skillet over the highest possible heat and cook, stirring, until the juices turn from butterscotch to deep amber, 10 to 12 minutes. Remove the skillet from the heat, spear the apples with a fork or the point of a paring knife, and flip them onto their uncooked sides. Return the skillet to high heat and boil 5 minutes more. Remove the skillet from the heat and slide the prepared crust onto the apples. Being careful not to burn your fingers, gently tuck the edges of the dough against the inner sides of the skillet.

Bake the tart until the crust is richly browned, 25 to 35 minutes. Let cool on a rack for 20 minutes, then loosen the sides with a knife and invert the tart onto a serving plate that can withstand heat. Return any apples that stick to the skillet to their proper place on top of the tart. Serve immediately or let stand at room temperature for up to 8 hours. When ready to serve, warm the tart to tepid in an oven heated at the lowest setting.

Accompany with:

Sour Cream Whipped Topping, 1040, crème fraîche, or vanilla ice cream

LINZERTORTE

One 9½-inch torte; 8 to 10 servings

Named after the Austrian town of Linz, the traditional linzertorte is a lattice-top tart made with a rich and crumbly nut crust and filled with raspberry or currant jam. Other jams, preserves, and marmalades can be substituted, as can fruit butters. Linzertorte actually improves in flavor for 2 to 3 days after baking and keeps for at least 1 week.

Position a rack in the center of the oven. Preheat the oven to 350°F.

Spread on a baking sheet:

¾ cup slivered blanched almonds or whole hazelnuts

Toast in the oven, stirring occasionally, until golden, 5 to 7 minutes. If using hazelnuts with skins, rub the nuts a handful a time in a thick towel to remove as much of the skins as possible. Turn off the oven. Let the nuts cool completely, then finely grind in a blender or food processor. Remove to a large bowl and whisk in thoroughly:

1⅓ cups all-purpose flour
½ cup powdered sugar
1 tablespoon unsweetened cocoa (optional)
1 teaspoon ground cinnamon
¼ teaspoon ground cloves
¼ teaspoon salt

Add:

10 tablespoons (1¼ sticks) unsalted butter, softened
2 large egg yolks
Grated zest of 1 medium lemon

Mix on low speed with an electric mixer or cream with the back of a wooden spoon until a smooth dough forms. Press the dough into a flat disk, wrap in plastic, and refrigerate for at least 2 hours or up to 2 days.

Position a rack in the center of the oven. Preheat the oven to 350°F. Have ready a two-piece 9½- or 10-inch tart pan.

Let the dough warm at room temperature until malleable but firm, 30 minutes to 1 hour. Set aside one-quarter of the dough for the lattice. With your hands, press the remaining dough evenly over the bottom and sides of the tart pan. Roll the remaining dough into a

10-inch square between 2 sheets of plastic wrap or wax paper. Remove the top sheet of plastic or paper and cut the dough into 8 to 12 strips of equal width. If the strips are too soft to handle, refrigerate or freeze them until firm. Spread evenly over the crust:

1½ cups raspberry jam

The layer should be about ¼ inch thick. Carefully arrange half of the dough strips on the tart at equal distance from each other; pinch the ends onto the crust. Arrange the remaining strips on top at right angles to those beneath, forming a crisscross lattice. If the strips break during handling, simply piece them together; they will fuse during baking. Bake until the lattice is golden brown, 40 to 45 minutes. Let cool completely on a rack. Remove the side of the pan, leaving the bottom in place beneath the torte. Wrap airtight and store in the refrigerator for up to 1 week or freeze for up to 1 month. Let warm to room temperature before serving *mit Schlag,* that is, with:

Whipped cream

ABOUT GALETTES

A galette—or in Italian, a *crostata*—consists of a flat crust of pastry or bread dough covered with sugar, pastry cream, or a thin layer of fruit. The famed *Galette des Rois,* or Twelfth Night cake, is made with puff pastry. Sometimes it is baked with an elaborately decorated top crust and filled with a rich almond cream. Most galettes, however, are more simply made and rustic in look. They are, in effect, dessert pizzas. Since galettes are baked on a flat sheet rather than in a pie or tart mold, they may be made in any shape that appeals to you. If the filling is juicy, bring the edge of the crust over the filling to catch drips; otherwise, simply double up the crust edge, then crimp or flute if you wish. The recipes that follow convey the basic technique. Use them to create your own variations, remembering that the topping should be spare so as not to overwhelm the crust.

FRUIT CROSTATA

8 servings

In Italy, cherished recipes for this favorite rustic tart are handed down from generation to generation. Use ripe fruit picked at the peak of the season to appreciate the simple perfection of this recipe.

Prepare the dough for:

Shortbread Crust, 868

Refrigerate the dough until firm but malleable, like modeling clay.

Position a rack in the lower third of the oven. Preheat the oven to 375°F.

Fruit crostata

Lightly flour the dough, then roll it into an 11-inch round between 2 sheets of parchment paper. Peel off the top sheet of paper. Lift the dough on the bottom sheet of paper onto a large baking sheet. Leaving bare a 1-inch border at the edge, spread evenly over the crust:

¼ cup raspberry or other jam

Fold over the border to form a rim. Toss together gently:

4 medium plums or 2 peeled medium peaches or 2 medium nectarines, pitted and cut into ½-inch pieces
½ cup raspberries or blueberries (optional)
2 tablespoons sugar
1 tablespoon plus 1 teaspoon all-purpose flour

Distribute the fruit mixture over the jam. Bake the *crostata* until the crust is golden brown and the fruit juices have thickened, 25 to 35 minutes. Let cool slightly before serving.

HALF-COVERED BERRY OR PEACH GALETTE

8 servings

In making this galette, you roll the crust extra wide and then fold the edges over the fruit, leaving the fruit exposed in the center. A cornmeal crust works well here.

Prepare:

½ recipe Cornmeal Flaky Pastry Dough, 864, or ½ recipe Deluxe Butter Flaky Pastry Dough, 862

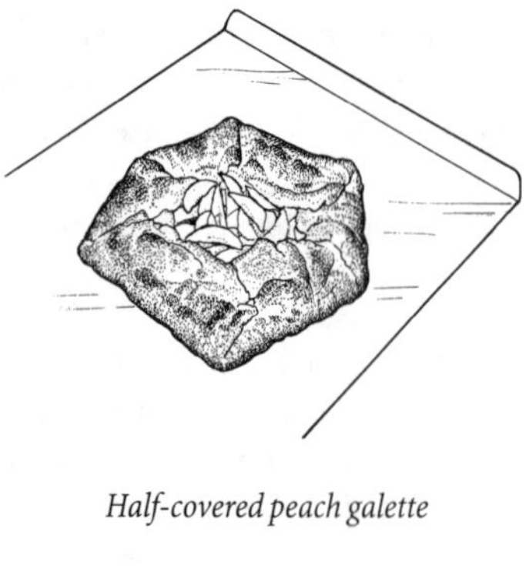

Half-covered peach galette

Position a rack in the lower third of the oven. Preheat the oven to 400°F.

On a well-floured work surface, roll the dough into a 13-inch round. Carefully slide a rimless cookie sheet beneath the dough, letting the edges of the dough overhang the sides of the sheet. Leaving bare a 2- to 3-inch border at the edge, arrange in the center:

1½ cups blueberries, raspberries, or thinly sliced peeled peaches

Scatter evenly over the fruit:

2 tablespoons sugar

1 tablespoon cold unsalted butter, cut into small pieces

Fold the border of dough over the fruit, forming a pleated half cover, with the fruit exposed in the center. Light brush the dough with:

Milk

Sprinkle with:

1 to 2 teaspoons sugar

Bake the galette until golden brown, 25 to 35 minutes. Let cool on a rack. Serve warm or at room temperature. The galette is best served the day it is made.

APPLE GALETTE

8 servings

This is a bit like a pizza, with thinly sliced apples on a buttery crust.

Prepare:

½ recipe Deluxe Butter Flaky Pastry Dough, 862

Position a rack in the lower third of the oven. Preheat the oven to 425°F.

On a sheet of parchment paper or aluminum foil, roll the dough into an 11- to 12-inch round. Pick up the edges of the paper and transfer with the dough to a baking sheet. Melt and cool to lukewarm:

3 tablespoons unsalted butter

Brush a thin coat of butter over the pastry, reserving the rest. Sprinkle the pastry with:

1 tablespoon sugar

Peel, core, and slice ⅛ inch thick:

2 large firm apples, such as Golden Delicious

Leaving bare a 1-inch border at the edge, arrange the apple slices in slightly overlapping concentric rings on the pastry. Fold the border of dough over the edge of the apples. Brush or drizzle all but about 2 teaspoons of the remaining melted butter over the apples. Combine, then sprinkle over the apples:

3 tablespoons sugar

⅛ teaspoon ground cinnamon

Bake until the pastry begins to color, 15 to 20 minutes. Reduce the oven temperature to 350°F and bake until the pastry is golden brown and sounds crisp when poked with a skewer, 20 to 30 minutes more. Set the pan on a rack, brush the apples with the remaining butter, and let cool. Serve warm or at room temperature. The galette is best served the day it is made.

ABOUT CREAM PIES

Cream pie filling is simply a cornstarch pudding made on top of the stove and enriched with egg yolks. In order to avoid scorching, stir the filling constantly as it cooks with a wooden spoon or heatproof rubber spatula, reaching all corners of the saucepan. To prevent lumps, remove the filling from the heat as it approaches the simmer and begins to thicken, and whisk vigorously. After whisking, return the filling to the heat, bring it to a full simmer, and cook for 30 seconds. If this is not done, amylase, an enzyme in the egg yolks, will react with the starch, thinning out and discoloring the filling within 24 hours. The filling is also likely to thin out if allowed to cool before being poured into the crust, so spoon the filling into the crust immediately after cooking. Contrary to popular belief, hot filling does not cause the crust to become soggy. The following cream pies can be made up to 1 day ahead and refrigerated.

VANILLA CREAM PIE

One 9-inch pie; 8 servings

This not only is a scrumptious pie on its own but also provides the base for four classic variations.

If topping the pie with meringue, position a rack in the center of the oven and preheat the oven to 325°F.

Prepare in a 9-inch pie pan:

Baked Flaky Pastry Crust, 866, a pat-in-the-pan crust, 867 to 868, or Crumb Crust, 868

Whisk in a medium, heavy saucepan until well blended:

⅔ cup sugar

¼ cup cornstarch

¼ teaspoon salt

Gradually whisk in:

2½ cups whole milk

Vigorously whisk in until no yellow streaks remain:

5 large egg yolks

Stirring constantly with a wooden spoon or heatproof rubber spatula, bring the mixture to a bare simmer over medium heat. Remove from the heat, scrape the corners of the saucepan with the spoon or spatula, and whisk until smooth. Return to the heat and, whisking constantly, bring to a simmer and cook for 1 minute. Off the heat, whisk in:

2 to 3 tablespoons unsalted butter, cut into small pieces

1 tablespoon vanilla

Spoon the filling into the prepared crust and press a sheet of plastic wrap directly on the surface. If you are covering the pie with meringue, proceed at once to prepare:

Soft Meringue Topping I or II, 1012

Remove the plastic wrap and spread the meringue over the top of the pie, anchoring it to the crust rim on all sides. Bake the pie for 20 minutes, let cool completely on a rack, and then refrigerate. If not using a meringue, simply refrigerate the pie for at least 3 hours to firm the filling. Shortly before serving, remove the plastic wrap and cover the pie with:

Whipped cream

BANANA CREAM PIE

Prepare the crust and filling for Vanilla Cream Pie, above. Thinly slice 2 to 4 firm ripe bananas, enough to measure 1½ to 2 cups. Spoon a third of the filling into the pie shell and scatter half of the bananas over the top. Cover with another third of the filling and then the rest of the bananas. Spread the remaining filling over the top.

BUTTERSCOTCH CREAM PIE

Prepare Nut Crust, 869, made with pecans. Cook 6 tablespoons unsalted butter and 1 packed cup light brown sugar in a medium, heavy saucepan over medium heat, stirring until melted and bubbly, 3 to 5 minutes. Gradually stir in ½ cup heavy cream or evaporated milk. (Do not use regular milk; it may curdle.) If necessary, return briefly to the heat to melt the butterscotch. Let cool slightly. Prepare the filling for Vanilla Cream Pie, above, but omit the sugar, decrease the milk to 2 cups, add the brown sugar mixture along with the milk, and omit the butter.

CHOCOLATE CREAM PIE

We can never decide if we prefer this old-fashioned pie with a meringue or a whipped cream topping. Whipped cream has the edge for those who like to decorate the top with grated semisweet chocolate.

Prepare Vanilla Cream Pie, above, but increase the sugar to 1 cup and decrease the cornstarch to 3 tablespoons. Finely chop 4 ounces unsweetened baking chocolate, add it with the butter, and stir until the chocolate melts.

COCONUT CREAM PIE

Wonderful served with a chocolate or caramel sauce.

Spread 1 to 1⅓ cups shredded sweetened dried coconut in a 9-inch cake pan and toast, stirring occasionally, in a 300°F oven until golden brown, 20 to 30 minutes. Prepare Vanilla Cream Pie, above, adding the coconut to the filling along with the butter. If topping the pie with whipped cream, you can reserve 2 to 3 tablespoons of the coconut for sprinkling on the top.

ABOUT CHIFFON AND MOUSSE PIES

If the filling is based on a custard sauce stiffened with gelatin, you have a chiffon pie; otherwise, call the filling a mousse. All of the pies in this sprawling category have a light and airy texture imparted by whipped cream, beaten egg whites, or marshmallows. The secret is a deft, gentle hand in folding the whipped cream or other aerated mixture into the filling. Mousse pies soften quickly at room temperature and become impossible to slice neatly, so leave them in the refrigerator until just before serving.

LEMON OR LIME CHIFFON PIE

One 9-inch pie; 6 to 8 servings

Tart and sprightly, this has long been America's favorite chiffon pie.

Before beginning, please read about uncooked eggs, 122.

Prepare in a 9-inch pie pan:

Baked Flaky Pastry Crust, 866, a pat-in-the-pan crust, 867 to 868, or Crumb Crust, 868

Pour into a small, heavy saucepan:

¼ cup water

Sprinkle over the top and let stand for 5 minutes:

1 envelope (2¼ teaspoons) unflavored gelatin

Whisk in:

½ cup water
½ cup strained fresh lemon or lime juice
1 teaspoon grated lemon or lime zest
⅓ cup plus 1 tablespoon sugar
4 large egg yolks

Stirring constantly with a wooden spoon or heatproof rubber spatula, heat over medium heat until the mixture begins to steam and coats the spoon or spatula fairly heavily. Do not allow to simmer, or it will become grainy. Immediately pour the mixture into a large bowl and refrigerate for 45 minutes to 1 hour, or until it forms little mounds when dropped from a spoon. Be careful not to let it set. Beat on medium speed until foamy:

4 large egg whites

Add:

¼ teaspoon cream of tartar

Continue to beat until soft peaks form, then gradually beat in:

½ cup sugar

Increase the speed to high and beat until the peaks are stiff and glossy. Using a large rubber spatula, gently fold the egg whites into the gelatin mixture. Spoon the filling into the crust, mounding it in the center, and refrigerate for at least 4 hours or up to 1 day.

BLACK BOTTOM PIE *One 10-inch pie; 8 to 10 servings*

Marjorie Kinnan Rawlings, in her classic 1942 cookbook, *Cross Creek Cookery*, proclaimed this pie "so delicate, so luscious, that I hope to be propped up on my dying bed and fed a generous portion. Then I think that I should refuse outright to die, for life would be too good to relinquish."

Before beginning, please read about uncooked eggs, 122.

Prepare and bake in a 10-inch pie pan:

Crumb Crust, 868, preferably made with gingersnaps

Pour into a small cup:

¼ cup cold water

Sprinkle over the top and let stand for 5 minutes:

1½ teaspoons (¾ envelope) unflavored gelatin

Place in a small bowl:

6 ounces bittersweet or semisweet chocolate, finely chopped, or 1 cup semisweet chocolate chips

Whisk together thoroughly in a medium, heavy saucepan:

⅓ cup sugar

4 teaspoons cornstarch

Gradually whisk in:

2 cups light cream, or 1 cup milk and 1 cup heavy cream

Vigorously whisk in until no yellow streaks remain:

4 large egg yolks

Stirring constantly with a wooden spoon or heatproof rubber spatula, bring the mixture to a simmer over medium heat and cook for 30 seconds. Immediately stir 1 cup of the mixture into the chocolate. Add the softened gelatin to the remaining mixture in the pan and stir for 30 seconds to dissolve the gelatin. Vigorously stir the chocolate mixture until smooth; if the chocolate fails to melt completely, set the bottom of the bowl in very hot water. Spread the chocolate mixture evenly over the bottom of the pie crust and refrigerate. Stir into the custard in the pan:

2 tablespoons dark rum

2 teaspoons vanilla

Beat on medium speed until foamy:

3 large egg whites

Add:

¼ teaspoon cream of tartar

Continue to beat until soft peaks form, then gradually beat in:

⅓ cup plus 1 tablespoon sugar

Increase the speed to high and beat until the peaks are stiff and glossy. Using a large rubber spatula, gently fold the egg whites into the custard mixture. Spoon the filling over the chocolate mixture. Refrigerate for at least 3 hours or up to 1 day. Shortly before serving, beat on medium speed until thickened:

1 cup cold heavy cream

Add:

¼ cup powdered sugar

½ teaspoon vanilla

Beat until the peaks are stiff. Spread the whipped cream over the top of the pie. If you wish, sprinkle with:

1 ounce bittersweet or semisweet chocolate, grated or shaved

Store refrigerated for up to 1 day.

CHOCOLATE MOUSSE PIE

One 10-inch pie; 10 servings

This pie has become an American favorite. A plain chocolate mousse makes a soft, lush filling; a chocolate mousse with gelatin yields a slightly stiffer filling and neater slices.

Prepare and bake in a 10-inch pie pan:

Crumb Crust, 868, made with chocolate wafers

Let the crust cool completely, then fill with:

Chocolate Mousse, 1030, or Chocolate Mousse with Gelatin, 1030

Refrigerate the pie for at least 3 hours to set the filling. Shortly before serving, beat on medium speed until thickened:

1 cup cold heavy cream

Add:

¼ cup powdered sugar

½ teaspoon vanilla

Whip until stiff peaks form. Spread the whipped cream over the top of the pie. If you wish, sprinkle with:

1 ounce bittersweet or semisweet chocolate, grated or shaved

Store refrigerated for up to 1 day.

CHOCOLATE ALMOND CANDY BAR PIE

One 10-inch pie; 10 servings

A gooey chocolate mousse in a thick, crunchy crust made from cream-filled chocolate sandwich cookies.

Position a rack in the center of the oven. Preheat the oven to 400°F. Lightly butter a 10-inch pie pan.

Place in a sturdy plastic bag:

30 cream-filled chocolate sandwich cookies

Crush with a rolling pin to coarse ¼-inch pieces. Transfer to a mixing bowl and combine well with:

6 tablespoons (¾ stick) unsalted butter, melted

Pat the mixture over the bottom and sides of the pie pan. Bake for 7 minutes, then let cool completely on a rack. Tear or snip into quarters:

24 large marshmallows

Chop into ¼-inch pieces:

1 pound milk chocolate candy bars with almonds

Stirring with a wooden spoon or heatproof rubber spatula, bring to a boil in a large saucepan over medium heat:

1 cup heavy cream

Set aside 3 tablespoons of the chopped chocolate bars for decorating. Add the remaining to the boiling cream and stir until the chocolate melts. Remove the pan from the heat, stir in the marshmallows, tightly cover, and let stand for 5 minutes. Very gently fold the softened marshmallows into the chocolate mixture, retaining as much air in the mixture as possible. (There may be a few unblended bits of marshmallow.) Pour the filling into the crust and refrigerate for 4 hours. If not serving the pie at once, press a sheet of plastic wrap directly onto the surface and refrigerate for up to 2 days. Shortly before serving, beat on medium speed until thickened:

1 cup cold heavy cream

Add:

¼ cup powdered sugar

½ teaspoon vanilla

Whip until stiff peaks form. Spread the whipped cream over the top of the pie. Sprinkle with the reserved chopped chocolate.

PEANUT BUTTER PIE *One 10-inch pie; 8 to 10 servings*

This may sound like kids' stuff, but it's not. The filling is mousselike and surprisingly subtle in flavor, and the chocolate glaze gives the pie a finished, elegant look.

Prepare and bake in a 10-inch pie pan:

Crumb Crust, 868, made with graham crackers or chocolate wafers

Beat on medium speed just until smoothly blended:

8 ounces cream cheese, softened

1 cup chunky or smooth peanut butter

½ cup sugar

2 teaspoons vanilla

In a separate bowl, beat on medium-high speed until stiff peaks form:

1 cup cold heavy cream

Using a large rubber spatula, fold half of the whipped cream into the peanut butter mixture to lighten it, then fold in the remaining cream. Spread the mixture evenly in the pie crust. Press a sheet of plastic wrap directly on the surface and refrigerate until firm, about 4 hours. Stirring, bring to a boil in a medium saucepan over high heat:

⅓ cup heavy cream

2 tablespoons unsalted butter

Remove from the heat and immediately stir in:

4 ounces bittersweet or semisweet chocolate, finely chopped

Let cool to lukewarm, then pour the glaze over the top of the pie and spread evenly. If you wish, sprinkle with:

⅓ cup chopped salted peanuts

Refrigerate for at least 1 hour or up to 3 days. Accompany with:

Whipped cream

ABOUT CUSTARD PIE

Like all custards, fillings for custard pies need to be baked at a relatively low temperature to keep from curdling; but the crust tends to become soggy unless the pie is baked at a high heat. In our 1975 edition we suggested baking the custard and crust separately in 2 pie pans of identical size and then slipping the filling into the shell just before serving. This sleight-of-hand works surprisingly well, but we have since discovered that it is possible to make custard pie in a more conventional way and still get excellent results. The trick is to have both the custard and the crust hot when the pie is assembled. This allows the custard to set quickly at the comfortably low temperature it favors, and thus the crust does not become soaked. For this trick to work, you must use a flaky pastry crust, fully baked and carefully moisture-proofed with egg yolk; pat-in-the-pan crusts inevitably become sodden. To prevent the filling from overcooking and turning grainy around the edges, custard pie must be removed from the oven when the center is still quivery, like gelatin. The filling will continue to cook on stored heat as the pie stands and will thicken further upon cooling. Because custard pie is highly susceptible to spoilage, refrigerate it as soon as it has cooled to room temperature. Serve the pie within a day of baking, or the crust will soften.

CUSTARD PIE *One 9-inch pie; 6 to 8 servings*

A thoroughly satisfying pie that has changed little since its first appearance in American cookbooks nearly two centuries ago.

Position a rack in the center of the oven. Preheat the oven to 325°F.

Prepare in a 9-inch pie pan, preferably glass, glazing with the egg yolk:

Baked Flaky Pastry Crust, 866

If the crust has cooled, warm it in the oven for up to 10 minutes while you prepare the filling. Whisk together just until blended:

3 large eggs
2 to 3 large egg yolks
½ cup sugar
1 teaspoon vanilla
⅛ teaspoon salt

Stirring, bring to a simmer in a small saucepan over medium heat:

2 cups whole milk

Gently whisking all the while, gradually add the milk to the egg mixture. Immediately pour the hot custard into the warmed crust. Dust the top with:

½ to 1 teaspoon freshly grated or ground nutmeg

Bake until the center of the custard seems set but quivery, like gelatin, when the pan is nudged, 25 to 35 minutes. Let cool completely on a rack, then refrigerate for up to 1 day. Let warm to room temperature for 1 hour before serving.

CHOCOLATE-FROSTED CUSTARD PIE

A great favorite in our grandmother's day and overdue for a revival.

Prepare Custard Pie, above, omitting the nutmeg; let cool to room temperature. Finely chop 3 ounces bittersweet or semisweet chocolate. Bring ⅓ cup heavy cream and 2 tablespoons sugar to a boil in a small saucepan, stirring to dissolve the sugar. Remove from the heat, add the chocolate, and stir until melted. Let cool slightly, then spread over the top of the pie. Refrigerate until the glaze sets.

COCONUT CUSTARD PIE

Prepare Custard Pie, above, sprinkling the crust with 1 to 1¼ cups shredded sweetened dried coconut or finely shredded fresh coconut before pouring in the custard.

ABOUT PUMPKIN, SWEET POTATO, AND SQUASH PIES

Although these pies are made with cooked vegetable purees, structurally speaking they are actually custard pies and should be handled in a similar way. To set the filling quickly and thus prevent a soggy crust, have the filling at room temperature and the crust warm. If the pie is overbaked, the filling will be coarse and watery around the edges, so remove the pie from the oven as soon as the center quivers like gelatin when the pan is nudged. The pie will continue to set up as it cools. Eat the pie within a day of baking, or the crust will soften.

Fresh Pumpkin: Jack-o'-lantern pumpkins make poor pies, so look instead for an eating variety (there are many) at a specialty market. You will need 5 to 6 pounds pumpkin to make 4 cups of puree, or enough for 2 pies. Split the pumpkins into quarters with a cleaver or heavy knife. Cut out the stem, scrape out the stringy pulp, and hack into 4-inch pieces. Place the pumpkin, rind side down, in an oiled roasting pan, cover tightly with aluminum foil, and bake at 325°F until very soft, about 1½ hours. Scrape the flesh free of the rind and puree in a food processor or force it through a food mill or fine sieve. If the puree seems loose and wet, pour it into a colander lined with cheesecloth, bring the ends of the cheesecloth up over it, and cover with a cake pan and a 5-pound weight. Let the pumpkin drain for 30 to 60 minutes, or until it reaches the same consistency as the canned kind.

Fresh Winter Squash: Prepare fresh squash as for pumpkin, above, using a firm, dense, sweet variety such as butternut or Hubbard. Squash is quite moist and requires thorough draining in cheesecloth as directed above.

PUMPKIN PIE

One 9-inch pie; 8 servings

Use 3 eggs for a soft, custardy filling, 2 for a firmer pie with a pronounced pumpkin flavor.

Position a rack in the center of the oven. Preheat the oven to 375°F.

Building up a high fluted rim, prepare in a 9-inch pie pan, preferably glass, glazing with the egg yolk:

Baked Flaky Pastry Crust, 866, or Pat-in-the-Pan Butter Crust, 867

Whisk thoroughly in a large bowl:

2 to 3 large eggs

Whisk in thoroughly:

2 cups freshly cooked or canned pumpkin puree or cooked squash puree
1½ cups light cream or evaporated milk, or ¾ cup milk and ¾ cup heavy cream
½ cup sugar
⅓ cup firmly packed light or dark brown sugar
1 teaspoon ground cinnamon
1 teaspoon ground ginger
½ teaspoon freshly grated or ground nutmeg
¼ teaspoon ground cloves or allspice
½ teaspoon salt

Warm the pie crust in the oven until it is hot to the touch, letting the filling stand at room temperature in the meantime. Pour the pumpkin mixture into the crust and bake until the center of the filling seems set but quivery, like gelatin, when the pan is nudged, 35 to 45 minutes. Let cool completely on a rack, then refrigerate for up to 1 day. Serve cold, at room temperature, or slightly warmed. Accompany with:

Whipped cream and/or Hot Brandy Sauce, 1042

SOUR CREAM PUMPKIN PIE

One 9-inch pie; 8 servings

A tangy pie with a light, soufflélike texture.

Position a rack in the center of the oven. Preheat the oven to 350°F.

Building up a high fluted rim, prepare in a 9-inch pan, preferably glass, glazing with the egg yolk:

Baked Flaky Pastry Crust, 866, or Pat-in-the-Pan Butter Crust, 867

In a large, heavy saucepan, whisk together thoroughly:

1½ cups freshly cooked or canned pumpkin puree
8 ounces (scant 1 cup) sour cream
¾ cup sugar
3 large egg yolks
1 teaspoon ground cinnamon
½ teaspoon ground ginger
½ teaspoon freshly grated or ground nutmeg
¼ teaspoon ground cloves or allspice
¼ teaspoon salt

Whisking constantly, heat over medium heat until just warm to the touch. Beat on medium speed until foamy:

3 large egg whites, at room temperature

Add:

¼ teaspoon cream of tartar

Continue to beat until soft peaks form, then gradually beat in:

¼ cup sugar

Increase the speed to high and beat until the peaks are stiff and glossy. Using a large rubber spatula, gently fold the egg whites into the pumpkin mixture. Pour the filling into the prepared crust. Bake until the top has browned lightly and feels softly set when touched, 40 to 50 minutes. Let cool completely on a rack. At this point the pie can be refrigerated for up to 1 day. Let warm at room temperature for 30 minutes before serving. Serve with:

Whipped cream

SWEET POTATO PIE

One 9-inch pie; 8 servings

A moist and creamy version of this southern favorite.

Position a rack in the center of the oven. Preheat the oven to 400°F.

Building up a high fluted rim, prepare in a 9-inch pie pan, preferably glass, glazing with the egg yolk:

Baked Flaky Pastry Crust, 866, or Pat-in-the-Pan Butter Crust, 867

Peel deeply, removing both skin and the pale, fibrous layer beneath it:

2 pounds sweet potatoes

Cut crosswise into 1-inch chunks and steam in a basket over boiling water until very tender, about 20 minutes. Puree in a food processor or force through a clean fine-mesh sieve with the back of a spoon. Measure 1⅓ cups puree. Whisk together thoroughly in a medium bowl:

4 large eggs
½ cup sugar

Whisk in the sweet potato puree, then whisk in:

1 cup light cream or evaporated milk, or ½ cup milk and ½ cup heavy cream
4 tablespoons (½ stick) unsalted butter, melted
4 teaspoons strained fresh lemon juice
1½ teaspoons vanilla
¾ teaspoon ground cinnamon
¾ teaspoon freshly grated or ground nutmeg
½ teaspoon salt

Warm the pie crust in the oven until it is hot to the touch. Pour in the filling and bake for 20 minutes. Reduce the oven temperature to 325°F and bake until the center of the filling seems set but quivery, like gelatin, when the pan is nudged, about 20 minutes more. Let cool completely on a rack, then refrigerate for up to 1 day. Serve at room temperature or warmed. Accompany with:

Whipped cream

SWEET POTATO PUDDING

Double the recipe for Sweet Potato Pie, above, omitting the crust. Pour the filling into a buttered shallow 2- to 3-quart baking dish. Bake at 350°F in a water bath (see About Baked Custards, 1013) until firm in the center, 45 to 60 minutes. Serve with Hot Brandy Sauce, 1042.

ABOUT PECAN, CHESS, AND SHOOFLY PIES

The filling of pecan pie is actually a sort of custard composed of sugar, butter, and eggs, and like all custards, it will curdle and break if subjected to excessive heat. The trick is to pull the pie from the oven as soon as the filling has thickened to a gelatin-like consistency in the center. Although soft coming out of the oven, the filling will firm up nicely by the time the pie has cooled to room temperature.

Chess pies, now chiefly a southern specialty, are essentially pecan pies without the nuts. There are countless varieties, but all are rich and intensely sweet, approximating candy. Chess pies, like pecan pies, are highly heat sensitive, and the same precautions must be observed when baking them. Shoofly pie, a famous dessert of Pennsylvania Dutch country, is a distant relative of the pecan and chess family. Because the filling is thickened by a sort of streusel, it more closely resembles cake than custard and is not prone to curdling.

PECAN PIE *One 9-inch pie; 8 servings*

Made with white sugar and light corn syrup for a mild, sweet, buttery flavor. For a dark pecan pie with a caramel-like taste, substitute light or dark brown sugar and/or dark corn syrup.

Building up a high fluted rim, prepare in a 9-inch pie pan, preferably glass, glazing with the egg yolk:

Baked Flaky Pastry Crust, 866, or Pat-in-the-Pan Butter Crust, 867

Position a rack in the center of the oven. Preheat the oven to 375°F.

Spread on a baking sheet:

2 cups pecans, coarsely chopped

Toast the nuts in the oven, stirring occasionally, until golden and fragrant, 6 to 10 minutes. Whisk until blended:

3 large eggs
1 cup sugar
1 cup light corn syrup
5 tablespoons unsalted butter, melted
1 teaspoon vanilla or 1 tablespoon dark rum
½ teaspoon salt

Stir in the toasted nuts. Warm the pie crust in the oven until it is hot to the touch, then pour in the filling. Bake until the edges are firm and the center seems set but quivery, like gelatin, when the pan is nudged, 35 to 45 minutes. Let cool on a rack for at least 1½ hours. Serve warm or at room temperature with:

Whipped cream or vanilla ice cream

The pie can be made up to 2 days ahead. Store in the refrigerator, but let warm to room temperature or warm in a 275°F oven for 15 minutes before serving.

CHOCOLATE PECAN PIE

Chop 6 ounces bittersweet or semisweet chocolate; melt in the top of a double boiler over barely simmering water, or microwave on medium (50% power) for 1½ to 2 minutes. Prepare Pecan Pie, above, decreasing the corn syrup to ½ cup and the butter to 1 tablespoon. Whisk one quarter of the filling into the melted chocolate, then blend the result into the remaining filling. Stir in the nuts. Proceed as directed. Bake until the edges of the pie are slightly puffed and the center seems set but still soft, 25 to 30 minutes.

CHOCOLATE CHIP OR CHUNK PECAN PIE

Softer and lighter in texture than Chocolate Pecan Pie but even richer.

Prepare Pecan Pie, above, decreasing the pecans to 1 cup and stirring in 1 cup chocolate chips or 2 ounces *each* dark, milk, and white chocolate, cut into ¼-inch chunks, along with the nuts. Bake as directed. Refrigerate the pie until cold and hard, then slice. Before serving, warm the slices in a 275°F oven until the chocolate just begins to soften.

CHESS PIE *One 9-inch pie; 8 servings*

Egg yolks give this filling a sparkling translucency and a smooth, soft, and melting texture.

Prepare in a 9-inch pie pan, glazing with the egg yolk:

Baked Flaky Pastry Crust, 866

Position a rack in the center of the oven. Preheat the oven to 275°F.

Warm the pie crust in the oven while you prepare the filling. Whisk in a heatproof bowl just until no yellow streaks remain:

1 large egg
4 large egg yolks
⅔ cup sugar
⅔ cup firmly packed light brown sugar
½ teaspoon salt

Whisk in:

⅔ cup light cream or evaporated milk, or ⅓ cup milk and ⅓ cup heavy cream

Scatter over the top:

6 tablespoons (¾ stick) unsalted butter, cut into small pieces

Bring 1 inch of water to a simmer in a skillet. Set the bowl in the skillet and gently whisk the mixture until shiny and warm to the touch. Stir in:

½ to ¾ cup chopped walnuts or pecans, toasted (optional)

Pour the filling into the crust. You now have two options. For a pie without meringue, bake until the edges are firm and the center looks set but quivery, like gelatin, when the pan is gently nudged, 50 to 65 minutes. For a pie with a meringue, as soon as the pie goes into the oven, measure out all the ingredients (and prepare the cornstarch paste) for:

Soft Meringue Topping I or II, 1012

Bake the pie just until the center resembles corn syrup in consistency when the pan is nudged, 25 to 40 minutes. Remove the pie from the oven, increase the oven temperature to 325°F, and proceed at once to finish the meringue. Spread a band of meringue around the edges of the pie, where the filling is firmest, anchoring the meringue to the crust at all points. Drop the remaining meringue in dollops over the center of the filling and gently spread it to make a smooth, cohesive topping. Return the pie to the oven and bake for 20 minutes. Let cool completely on a rack. Store the pie in the refrigerator for up to 3 days but bring to room temperature before serving. If you have not topped the pie with meringue, you may wish to accompany it with:

Whipped cream

BUTTERMILK CHESS PIE

To some southerners, this is the only true chess pie. Prepare Chess Pie, above, substituting ⅔ cup additional granulated sugar for the brown sugar and ⅔ cup buttermilk for the light cream. Stir ½ cup *each* chopped raisins and chopped pecans or walnuts into the filling.

LEMON CHESS PIE

Lemon Chess Pie filling tastes very much like lemon curd. Prepare Chess Pie, above, but substitute ⅔ cup additional sugar for the brown sugar, the grated zest of 1 lemon for the salt, ⅓ cup heavy cream plus ⅓ cup strained fresh lemon juice for the light cream or evaporated milk. Omit the nuts, or stir in ½ cup shredded sweetened dried coconut. Decrease the baking time to 25 to 40 minutes. If using a meringue, apply it after 10 to 15 minutes' baking.

SHOOFLY PIE

One 9-inch pie; 8 servings

There are both "dry-bottom" and "wet-bottom" versions of this Pennsylvania Dutch specialty. The former are almost like soft gingerbread in a crust, while the latter consist of a tender molasses custard topped with crumbs. This version is "wet."

Prepare in a 9-inch pie pan:

Baked Flaky Pastry Crust, 866, or Pat-in-the-Pan Butter Crust, 867

Position a rack in the center of the oven. Preheat the oven to 400°F.

Combine in a bowl:

1 cup all-purpose flour
⅔ cup firmly packed dark brown sugar
5 tablespoons unsalted butter, softened

Mash with a fork or chop with a pastry blender until crumbly. In a separate bowl, beat with a large spoon until blended:

1 cup light molasses
1 large egg
1 teaspoon baking soda

Stir in thoroughly:

1 cup boiling water

Stir half of the crumb mixture into the molasses mixture and pour into the prepared crust. Sprinkle the remaining crumb mixture evenly over the top. Bake for 10 minutes. Reduce the oven temperature to 350°F and bake until the pie has puffed around the sides and feels firm in the center, 20 to 30 minutes more. Let cool completely on a rack. Store at room temperature for up to 3 days. Accompany with:

Whipped cream

ABOUT LEMON AND LIME PIES

If you are going to make a lemon or lime pie from scratch, you might as well take the time to grate zest and squeeze juice from fresh citrus fruits. Citrus zest, with its pungent oils, is essential to a well-flavored filling, and fresh juice tastes incomparably better than frozen or bottled juices, in which flavor is compromised by pasteurization and preservatives.

LEMON MERINGUE PIE

One 9-inch pie; 8 servings

Prepare in a 9-inch pie pan:

Baked Flaky Pastry Crust, 866, or a pat-in-the-pan crust, 867 to 868

Position a rack in the upper third of the oven. Preheat the oven to 325°F.

Whisk thoroughly in a medium saucepan:

1¼ cups sugar
⅓ cup cornstarch
⅛ teaspoon salt

Whisk in, blending well:

1½ cups water
½ cup strained fresh lemon juice (from 2 to 3 lemons)
2 to 3 teaspoons grated lemon zest

Whisk in until no yellow streaks remain:

4 large egg yolks

Add:

2 to 3 tablespoons unsalted butter, cut into small pieces

Stirring constantly with a wooden spoon or rubber spatula, bring the mixture to a simmer over medium heat, then cook for 1 minute. The filling should be very thick. Pour the filling into the pie crust and press a sheet of plastic wrap directly on the surface. Immediately prepare:

Soft Meringue Topping I or II, 1012

Remove the plastic wrap from the pie and spread the meringue on top, anchoring the meringue to the edge of the crust at all points. Bake for 20 minutes. Let cool completely on a rack, then refrigerate. The pie can be stored for up to 3 days in the refrigerator. Serve at room temperature or cold.

OHIO LEMON PIE *One 9-inch pie; 8 servings*

This pie is often associated with the Shakers, a nineteenth-century religious group, though it was popular among all Americans by the time the Shakers adopted it. The filling consists of whole lemons, including the white pith, sliced paper-thin and macerated in sugar until tender and sweet. The pie sounds odd, but don't be afraid of it.

Before beginning, please read About Covered Fruit Pies, 869.

Prepare:

Flaky Pastry Dough, 859, or Deluxe Butter Flaky Pastry Dough, 862

Roll half the dough into a 13-inch round, fit it into a 9-inch pie pan, and trim the overhanging dough to ¾ inch all around. Refrigerate. Roll the other half into a 12-inch round for the top crust and refrigerate it. Grate the zest from:

2 large or medium lemons

Slice the lemons paper-thin, removing the seeds as you do so. In a glass or stainless-steel bowl, combine the lemon slices and grated zest with:

2 cups sugar

¼ teaspoon salt

Cover and let stand at room temperature for 2 to 24 hours, stirring occasionally. The longer the lemons macerate, the better.

Position a rack in the lower third of the oven. Preheat the oven to 425°F.

Whisk until frothy:

4 large eggs

Whisk in:

4 tablespoons (½ stick) butter, melted

3 tablespoons all-purpose flour

Stir the lemon mixture into the egg mixture. Pour the filling into the bottom crust and level with the back of a spoon. Brush the overhanging bottom crust with cold water. Cover with the top crust, trim, and crimp or flute the edge. Cut steam vents in the top crust. Bake the pie for 30 minutes. Reduce the oven temperature to 350°F and bake until the top crust has puffed and a knife inserted into the center comes out clean, 20 to 30 minutes more. Let cool completely on a rack. The pie can be stored in the refrigerator for up to 2 days, but let it warm to room temperature before serving.

LEMON TART *One 9½- or 10-inch tart; 8 servings*

This staple of French patisseries is an elegant dinner-party dessert. It is much richer than other lemon pies and tarts.

Prepare in a 9½- or 10-inch two-piece tart pan, glazing with the egg yolk:

Baked Flaky Pastry Crust, 866, made with Deluxe Butter Flaky Pastry Dough or Sweet Flaky Pastry Dough; or Shortbread Crust, 868

Position a rack in the center of the oven. Preheat the oven to 350°F.

Combine in a heatproof bowl:

1 cup sugar

8 tablespoons (1 stick) unsalted butter, cut into small pieces

Bring 1 inch of water to a bare simmer in a skillet. Set the bowl in the skillet and stir until the butter is melted. Remove the bowl from the skillet. Add and beat until no yellow streaks remain:

8 large egg yolks

Stir in:

½ cup strained fresh lemon juice (from 2 to 3 lemons)

Return the bowl to the skillet and, stirring gently, heat the mixture until thickened to the consistency of heavy cream (lightly coats a spoon), 6 to 8 minutes. Strain the lemon mixture through a clean fine-mesh sieve into a bowl, then stir in:

1 tablespoon grated lemon zest

Pour the filling into the tart crust. Bake the tart until the center looks set but still very quivery, like gelatin, when the pan is nudged, 15 to 20 minutes. If overbaked, the tart will be grainy around the edges. Let cool completely on a rack. Lightly oil a sheet of plastic wrap and press it directly on the filling. The tart can be stored in the refrigerator for up to 1 day. Let warm to room temperature before serving. If you wish, accompany with:

Fresh Raspberry Sauce, 1048

KEY LIME PIE *One 9-inch pie; 8 servings*

If you do find the smaller Key limes, you may need as many as a dozen to yield ½ cup of juice.

Prepare in a 9-inch pie pan:

Baked Flaky Pastry Crust, 866, or Crumb Crust, 868, made with graham crackers and baked

Position a rack in the center of the oven. Preheat the oven to 325°F.

Whisk together until well blended:

One 15-ounce can sweetened condensed whole, low-fat, or skim milk

4 large egg yolks

½ cup strained fresh lime juice (3 to 4 limes)

3 to 4 teaspoons grated lime zest

The mixture will thicken as the milk reacts with the acidic citrus juice. Pour the filling into the pie crust. For a pie without a meringue topping, bake the pie until the center looks set but still quivery, like gelatin, when the pan is nudged, 15 to 17 minutes. Let cool completely on a rack, then refrigerate until cold or for up to 1 day. Shortly before serving, whip until thickened:

¾ cup cold heavy cream

Add:

¼ cup powdered sugar

Whip until stiff peaks form. Spread the whipped cream over the pie and serve.

For a pie with a meringue topping, let the unbaked pie stand at room temperature while you measure the ingredients (and prepare the cornstarch paste) for:

Soft Meringue Topping I or II, 1012

Bake the pie until the filling thickens just enough to support the topping, 5 to 7 minutes, but no longer. Meanwhile, finish the meringue. Spread a band of meringue around the edges of the filling, anchoring it to the crust at all points. Dollop the remaining meringue over the center and smooth the top. Bake for 20 minutes more. Let cool completely on a rack, then refrigerate until cold or for up to 1 day.

UNBAKED EGGLESS KEY LIME PIE

Prepare Key Lime Pie, above, with the crumb crust, omitting the egg yolks. Refrigerate for 4 hours to set the filling completely. Though soft, the filling is sliceable. Top with whipped cream.

ABOUT CHOCOLATE AND CARAMEL PIES AND TARTS

The tarts in this section are different in their basic structure but similar in their richness and intensity. Bittersweet Chocolate Tart, below, and Chocolate-Glazed Caramel Tart, below, are elegant confections that make suitable desserts for a fancy dinner party.

BITTERSWEET CHOCOLATE TART

One 9½- or 10-inch tart; 8 to 10 servings

Prepare in a 9½- or 10-inch two-piece tart pan:

Shortbread Crust, 868

Position a rack in the lower third of the oven. Preheat the oven to 375°F.

In a small saucepan, bring to a simmer:

1 cup heavy cream

Remove from the heat and add:

8 ounces bittersweet or semisweet chocolate, finely chopped

Whisk until the chocolate is completely melted and the mixture is smooth, then whisk in:

1 large egg, lightly beaten

Pour the chocolate mixture into the tart shell. Bake until the center seems set but still quivery, like gelatin, when the pan is nudged, 15 to 18 minutes. Let cool on a rack. Serve slightly warm or at room temperature with:

Whipped cream

The tart is best served the day it is made but it can be refrigerated for 2 to 3 days. Let warm to room temperature before serving.

CHOCOLATE-GLAZED CARAMEL TART

One 9½- or 10-inch tart; 10 to 12 servings

Serve this tart in small slices. It is almost candy.

Prepare in a 9½- or 10-inch two-piece tart pan, glazing with the egg yolk:

Baked Flaky Pastry Crust, 866, or Shortbread Crust, 868

Position a rack in the lower third of the oven. Preheat the oven to 325°F.

Spread on a baking sheet:

½ cup slivered blanched almonds

Toast in the oven, stirring occasionally, until golden, 5 to 7 minutes. Let cool, then coarsely chop. Place in a medium, heavy saucepan:

1½ cups sugar

Drizzle evenly over the top:

½ cup water

Place the pan over medium heat and, without stirring, very gently swirl the pan by the handle until a clear syrup forms. It is important that the syrup clarify *before* the boil is reached, so slide the pan on and off the burner as necessary. Increase the heat to high and bring the syrup to a rolling boil. Cover the pan tightly and boil for 2 minutes. Uncover the pan and cook the syrup until it begins to darken. Once again gently swirl the pan by the handle and cook the syrup until it turns a deep amber. Remove the pan from the heat. Standing back to avoid possible spatters, pour in:

1¼ cups heavy cream

Stir until smooth. If the caramel remains lumpy, place the saucepan over low heat and stir until smooth. Let the mixture cool for 10 minutes. In a medium bowl, whisk until frothy:

1 large egg
1 large egg yolk
1 teaspoon vanilla
⅛ teaspoon salt

Gradually whisk in the caramel mixture. Pour the filling into the prepared tart crust and bake until the edges darken and begin to bubble and the center looks almost set, 45 to 55 minutes. Let cool completely on a rack.

Heat in the top of a double boiler over gently simmering water or in a microwave on medium until melted and smooth:

3 ounces bittersweet or semisweet chocolate, finely chopped
2 tablespoons heavy cream

Spread the chocolate glaze over the caramel filling and sprinkle with the toasted almonds. Refrigerate the tart until firm or for up to 2 days. Serve cold with:

Whipped cream

ABOUT ICE CREAM PIES

Pies filled with ice cream—or frozen yogurt, sherbet, or sorbet—are quick and simple to assemble, and you can create as many different varieties as there are flavors of ice cream in your grocer's freezer case. Start with a Crumb Crust, 868, or Meringue Pie Crust, 869; other crusts are flavorless and rock hard when frozen. Freeze the pie shell thoroughly before filling it, or the ice cream will melt along the bottom, soaking into the crust and fusing it to the pie pan. It is essential to use a premium brand of ice cream. Bargain brands are fluffed up with air and will deflate, losing as much as half their volume, when softened and packed into the shell. Let the ice cream or other frozen product soften to the point where it can easily be packed into the shell, but do not let it liquefy, or it will turn coarse and icy when it refreezes. If, as often happens, the pie sticks to the pan when sliced, hold the bottom of the pan in a bowl of warm water for about 30 seconds.

ICE CREAM PIE

One 10-inch pie; 8 to 10 servings

Use this basic recipe as a starting point and give your imagination free rein.

Bake in a 10-inch pie pan:

Crumb Crust, 868, or Meringue Pie Crust, 869

Let cool to room temperature, then freeze for at least 1 hour before filling. Meanwhile, let stand in the refrigerator until just soft enough to pack:

1½ to 2 quarts ice cream, frozen yogurt, sherbet, or sorbet

If you wish, have ready:

1 to 1½ cups crushed cream-filled chocolate sandwich cookies, chopped nougat-filled candy bars, or chocolate-covered peanut butter cups

Working quickly, pack half of the ice cream into the shell with the back of a large spoon. If you are using them, sprinkle half of the crushed cookies or chopped candies over the top and press in firmly. Pack the remaining ice cream in the shell, mounding it in the center, then sprinkle with the rest of the cookies or candies and again press them in. Smooth a sheet of plastic wrap on the surface of the pie and freeze until solid, at least 2 hours or up to 2 days. About 30 minutes before serving, transfer the pie to the refrigerator to allow it to soften slightly. If you wish, use a pastry bag fitted with a large star tip to pipe over the top of the pie:

Whipped cream

Decorate with:

Crushed cookies, chopped candies, or toasted nuts (optional)

Serve the pie with:

A chocolate sauce, a caramel or butterscotch sauce, a fresh fruit sauce, or a cooked fruit sauce

AMERICAN FRUIT DESSERTS

We love the names Americans have given their homey fruit-and-dough desserts over the years—pandowdy, cobbler, crisp, brown betty, crunch, slump, grunt, buckle. These desserts seem descended from puddings on one side and pies on the other. They may be based on biscuit dough, pie dough, dumplings, breadcrumbs, a crumbled flour-based topping, or cake; the fruit may be cooked under, over, or inside the dough or between dough layers. However they are made, these are plain, uncomplicated desserts—almost folklore, passed down from one generation to the next—made with whatever ingredients are available.

All these desserts are best enjoyed the day they're made. Reheat them in the oven if needed, as the microwave steams and destroys a crisp topping. Serve warm with ice cream or unsweetened whipped cream or scoop into a bowl and pass a pitcher of cream or rich milk.

PANDOWDIES

A pandowdy is a dish of cooked fruit, typically apples, baked under a crust of pie or biscuit dough. Originally pandowdies were eaten for breakfast, having baked overnight in the embers of the family hearth. The origin of the name is unknown but may refer to the act of "dowdying" the pastry—slashing or breaking the partially baked crust to submerge it in the juicy filling as it finishes baking. (For best results, the pastry must be partially baked dry before it is moistened.) Serve pandowdy warm from the oven, or reheat, covered with aluminum foil, at 325°F.

APPLE PANDOWDY

6 to 8 servings

Apple pandowdy is traditionally sweetened with maple syrup, molasses, or cider, but you may also use brown or white sugar. After cutting the partially baked pastry into squares, baste with the pan juices to flavor and glaze the crust. Empire or Gravenstein apples give this dish an especially soft, lush texture. Other apples to try are Gala and Russet.

Position a rack in the lower third of the oven. Preheat the oven to 400°F. Have ready an unbuttered 8 x 8-inch baking dish.

Prepare:

½ recipe Deluxe Butter Flaky Pastry Dough, 862, or Flaky Pastry Dough, 859

On a lightly floured surface, roll out the dough into a 10-inch square, ⅛ inch thick. Transfer to a baking sheet, cover with plastic wrap, and refrigerate while you prepare the filling. Peel, halve, and core:

4 medium to large apples (2 to 2½ pounds)

Place the apples cut side down on a cutting board and slice crosswise ¼ inch thick. Combine the apples with:

½ cup maple syrup, molasses, packed brown sugar, or white sugar
2 tablespoons cornstarch or ¼ cup all-purpose flour
½ teaspoon ground cinnamon
¼ teaspoon ground nutmeg
¼ teaspoon salt
⅛ teaspoon ground allspice

Spread the apple mixture evenly in the baking pan. Dot with:

2 tablespoons unsalted butter, cut into small pieces

Remove the dough from the refrigerator and let stand for a few minutes, until pliable. Fold the dough in half and unfold over the top of the apples, covering them. Trim the dough around the pan, leaving a ½-inch overhang. Fold the edges of the dough under to fit inside the dish and press the dough gently against the apples (around the edge only). Bake until the top has browned lightly, about 30 minutes. Remove the dish from the oven to a level area. Reduce the oven temperature to 350°F. With a knife, score the crust, as you would a pan of brownies, into 2-inch squares. Baste the crust squares by tilting the pan all around and spooning some of the apple juices over the squares, basting the middle squares as well. You can also submerge the squares in the juices with the back of the spoon. Do not worry about crushing or tearing the crust, for doing this is part of the character of the dish. (The crust will also sink slightly into the juices while cooking.) Return the dish to the oven and bake until the apples are tender when pierced with a skewer, the filling has thickened slightly, and the crust is golden brown, about 30 minutes more. Let cool for 15 minutes before serving. Serve warm in deep bowls with:

Heavy cream, softly whipped cream, or vanilla yogurt

To store, cover and refrigerate. Reheat, covered with aluminum foil, in a 325°F oven for about 20 minutes.

BLUEBERRY PANDOWDY

Prepare Apple Pandowdy, above, with the following substitutions: For the crust, use ½ recipe Cornmeal Flaky Pastry Dough, 864; for the filling, substitute 3 pints blueberries for the apples, light brown sugar for the maple syrup, and ¼ teaspoon ground cinnamon for all the ground spices (cinnamon, nutmeg, and allspice). Do not dot the fruit with butter.

ABOUT COBBLERS

Nobody knows where the name *cobbler* came from, but we have always liked to think that it might once have referred to a cook cobbling, or patching together (like a shoemaker), the ingredients for this casually crafted dessert. Cobblers are simply deep-dish single-crusted fruit pies; the crust is usually on the top, though occasionally it is on the bottom. Cobblers used to be made with pie dough, but a sweet, rich biscuit dough is more common today. For a tender crust, do not overmix the dough; stir in the liquid quickly and knead gently a few times to form the dough. Cobblers can be made in square, round, or rectangular pans, but a 12-inch oval gratin dish works especially well. Almost any type of fruit or combination of fruits can be used, but berries are traditional. Unsweetened frozen berries can be substituted when fresh ones are out of season; use them directly from the freezer without thawing, and increase the baking time as needed to cook the dough through. You may add a pinch of spice to the fruit, such as cinnamon, nutmeg, or allspice, but usually the filling is simply a mixture of sugar and a small amount of thickener for the juices from the fruit. Serve a cobbler warm from the oven alone or with a pitcher of cream, a dollop of whipped cream, or a scoop of ice cream or frozen yogurt.

BASIC COBBLER BISCUIT DOUGH

1 cobbler topping

This recipe makes the perfect amount of dough for one cobbler recipe and may be varied with other ingredients, such as cornmeal or sour cream. You can cover fruit with a whole piece of dough, cut the dough into shapes, or spoon nut-sized pieces of it off and roll into small balls. While heavy cream makes the richest cobbler biscuit dough, milk is a fine substitute.

Have ready an unbuttered enameled cast-iron, earthenware, or glass baking pan of about 2-quart capacity and 2 inches deep, such as an 8 x 8-inch or 11 x 7-inch pan; a 12-inch oval gratin; or a 9 x 2-inch or 10 x 2-inch glass pie pan.

Whisk together in a bowl:

1⅓ cups all-purpose flour
2 tablespoons sugar
1½ teaspoons baking powder
½ teaspoon salt

Add:

5 tablespoons cold unsalted butter, cut into small pieces

Toss with the dry ingredients. Using a pastry blender or 2 knives, cut the butter into the dry ingredients (as for Basic Rolled Biscuits, 789) until the mixture resembles coarse breadcrumbs. Add:

⅔ cup heavy cream or ½ cup milk

Mix with a wooden spoon, rubber spatula, or fork only until the dough comes together and can be rolled or patted. Gently knead the dough in the bowl 5 to 10 times if needed, turning and pressing any loose pieces into the dough. Dust the top and bottom of the dough with a little flour, then roll or pat the dough with your hands to the shape of the top of the baking dish, between ¼ and ½ inch thick. Cut the dough into circles, squares, rectangles, or pie wedges, into 1-inch strips for a lattice, or trim the edges and leave it whole. You may also gently roll small pieces of the dough into balls, flatten each one slightly, and place on the fruit. If making a lattice, arrange the strips in opposite directions, weaving them if you like. If leaving the dough whole, cut 3 small holes for steam vents. Place the biscuit dough on the fruit. Lightly brush the top with:

1 to 2 tablespoons melted butter, cream, milk, or lightly beaten egg

Sprinkle with:

About 1 tablespoon sugar

Bake the cobbler as directed in each recipe, typically 45 to 50 minutes.

CORNMEAL COBBLER BISCUIT DOUGH

Prepare Cobbler Biscuit Dough, above, substituting ⅓ cup cornmeal for ⅓ cup of the flour.

SOUR CREAM COBBLER BISCUIT DOUGH

Prepare Cobbler Biscuit Dough, above, substituting a mixture of ¾ teaspoon baking powder and ¼ teaspoon baking soda for the baking powder, and a mixture of ½ cup sour cream and ¼ cup heavy cream for the heavy cream or milk. Whisk the creams together before adding to the flour mixture.

STRAWBERRY RHUBARB COBBLER

6 to 8 servings

An egg wash gives this cobbler topping a shiny, golden glaze when baked.

Position a rack in the lower third of the oven. Preheat the oven to 375°F. Have ready an unbuttered enameled cast-iron, earthenware, or glass baking pan of about 2-quart capacity and 2 inches deep, such as an 8 x 8-inch or 11 x 7-inch pan; a 12-inch oval gratin; or a 9 x 2-inch or 10 x 2-inch glass pie pan.

Without peeling, cut into 1-inch lengths:

1¼ pounds rhubarb stalks

Place in a large bowl (you should have about 4 cups). Wash and pat dry:

1 pint strawberries

Hull and halve the berries; quarter if very large. Add them to the rhubarb. Stir together, then toss with the fruit:

½ cup sugar

1 tablespoon cornstarch or 2 tablespoons all-purpose flour

Spread evenly in the baking dish. Prepare:

Cornmeal Cobbler Biscuit Dough, above

Roll, pat out, shape into balls, or cut into desired shapes, as described. Brush with the glaze of your choice and sprinkle with:

Sugar

Arrange the dough over the fruit. Bake until the top is golden brown and the juices are bubbling, 45 to 50 minutes. Let cool for 15 minutes before serving. Serve with:

Softly whipped cream or vanilla ice cream

BLUEBERRY COBBLER

6 to 8 servings

Lime zest brings out the flavor of blueberries.

Position a rack in the lower third of the oven. Preheat the oven to 375°F. Have ready an unbuttered enameled cast-iron, earthenware, or glass baking pan of about 2-quart capacity and 2 inches deep, such as an 8 x 8-inch or 11 x 7-inch pan; a 12-inch oval gratin; or a 9 x 2-inch or 10 x 2-inch glass pie pan.

Wash and pat dry:

3 pints blueberries

Combine and toss with the berries:

½ cup sugar

2 tablespoons cornstarch or ¼ cup all-purpose flour

1 teaspoon grated lime zest

Spread evenly in the baking dish. Prepare:

Sour Cream Cobbler Biscuit Dough, above

Roll, pat out, shape into balls, or cut into desired shapes, as described. Brush with the glaze of your choice and sprinkle with the sugar. Arrange the dough over the fruit. Bake until the top is golden brown and the juices have thickened slightly, 45 to 50 minutes. Let cool for 15 minutes before serving. Serve in shallow bowls with:

Chilled heavy cream, softly whipped lightly sweetened cream, or lemon ice cream

PEACH RASPBERRY COBBLER

6 to 8 servings

This cobbler has a cakelike batter that is spooned over the fruit. Buttermilk makes a flavorful and tender dough with less fat than usual. Baking soda (instead of baking powder) works with the acidic buttermilk to give the batter lift. You may peel the peaches if you like, but the skins add a lovely color to the juices.

Position a rack in the lower third of the oven. Preheat

the oven to 350°F. Have ready an unbuttered enameled cast-iron, earthenware, or glass baking pan of about 2-quart capacity and 2 inches deep, such as an 8 x 8-inch or 11 x 7-inch pan; a 12-inch oval gratin; or a 9 x 2-inch or 10 x 2-inch glass pie pan.

Wash and wipe dry:

6 medium, ripe peaches (1½ to 1¾ pounds)

Cut in half and remove the pits. Cut each half into 5 wedges and spread evenly in the baking dish. Cover with:

2 cups fresh or frozen raspberries

Sprinkle evenly over the top and set aside:

¼ cup sugar

Whisk together thoroughly:

1 cup all-purpose flour
1 teaspoon baking soda
¼ teaspoon salt

In a separate bowl, beat until light and fluffy:

4 tablespoons (½ stick) unsalted butter, softened
⅓ cup sugar

Beat in:

1 large egg

Add half of the dry ingredients and beat on low speed just until incorporated. Beat in:

¼ cup buttermilk

Add the remaining dry ingredients and beat just until the batter is smooth. Drop spoonfuls of the batter on top of the fruit to cover it, leaving a ½-inch border all around the edge of the dish to leave room for expansion during cooking. Bake until the top is golden brown and the fruit is tender when pierced with a skewer, 40 to 45 minutes. Let cool for 15 minutes before sewing. Serve with:

Softly whipped cream

ABOUT SHORTCAKES

It is difficult to imagine a more definitively American dessert than shortcake. Shortcakes are made of rich biscuits or scones split open, or layers of sponge cake baked and cut into rounds, filled with sugared fresh fruit, and topped with lots of softly whipped cream. A number of doughs will work well for shortcake—Fluffy or Shortcake Biscuits, 790, Cream Biscuits, 790, Cream Scones, 791, for traditional shortcakes, or Dried Fruit and Buttermilk Drop Scones (Reduced Fat/Low Cholesterol Scones), 792, for a lighter dish. Or try Cornmeal Biscuits, 789, as the base for a blackberry or peach shortcake. Roll the biscuit dough a scant ¾ inch thick; if any thinner, it will not rise enough to split easily. Any sponge cake, including Hot Milk Sponge Sheet, 953, or Génoise, 948, makes a great shortcake too. To serve eight shortcakes, cut the sponge into sixteen 1- to 1½-inch-thick rounds, triangles, hearts, or other shapes. Prepare the fruit and cream no more than 2 hours ahead of serving and keep both chilled. The cream will separate slightly in the refrigerator but will reblend if given a few swift whisks.

STRAWBERRY SHORTCAKE

8 servings

You can use any berries you wish or sliced peaches or nectarines; you can also substitute chilled or hot stewed fruit for the fresh fruit and sugar. Whipped and lightly sweetened crème fraîche or a combination of half sour cream and half whipping cream can be substituted for the plain whipped cream.

Prepare:

Eight 3-inch Fluffy Shortcake or Biscuits, 790, or 3-inch Cream Scones without currants, 791, dough patted or rolled ¾ inch thick before cutting, or 16 pieces sponge cake

Wash, pat dry, and hull:

3 pints strawberries

Crush one-quarter of the berries and slice the remaining. Combine the sliced and crushed berries with:

¼ cup sugar, or more to taste

Refrigerate until serving time.

Just before serving, reheat the biscuits or scones in a 250°F oven for 10 minutes (do not heat sponge cake if using). Split each biscuit horizontally in half with a fork. Place the bottom of each biscuit or a layer of sponge cake on each of 8 dessert plates or shallow bowls. Spoon the berry mixture over and top with the biscuit tops or another layer of cake. Prepare:

1½ recipes Whipped Cream, 995

Spoon a generous dollop of cream on top of each shortcake. Serve immediately.

ABOUT GRUNTS AND SLUMPS

Grunts and slumps, both descended from puddings cooked in pots over the fire, are steamed fruit topped with dumplings. Grunts are steamed in a mold inside a kettle full of water and inverted when served; the result is something like a warm fruit shortcake. Slumps are cooked in a covered pan and served dumpling side up in bowls—more like a hot, sweet soup or stew under a dumpling. If the grunt is perhaps named for the sound it makes when unmolded, the name *slump* seems to describe the eventual fate of the dumplings. Grunts are best steamed in a soufflé dish, but pudding molds or heatproof bowls work as well; metal molds are not recommended, as they may overcook the fruit and impart a metallic taste. Cook slumps in stainless-steel, enameled cast-iron, or glass saucepans, but make sure the vessel has a tight-fitting lid to contain the steam. If the pan is uncovered before the dumplings are done, they will collapse into toughness.

APRICOT CHERRY SLUMP

6 to 8 servings

Cherries bring out the gentle flavors in apricots.

Whisk together thoroughly in a medium bowl:

1½ cups all-purpose flour
2 teaspoons baking powder
½ teaspoon salt

Add and stir just until the dry ingredients are moistened:

1 cup milk
4 tablespoons (½ stick) unsalted butter, melted

In a large, heavy-bottomed saucepan or Dutch oven with a tight-fitting lid, stir until dissolved:

1 cup water
½ cup sugar

Wash and pat dry:

8 medium, ripe apricots (about 1 pound)
1 pint Bing cherries

Cut the apricots in half, remove the pits, and add the apricots to the sugar water. Pit the cherries and stir them in with the apricots. Cover and bring to a boil over high heat. Reduce the heat and simmer for about 10 minutes. Do not lift the lid during this time. Remove the lid and quickly cover the fruit with spoonfuls of batter. Replace the lid and simmer over low heat for 20 minutes. Check the dumplings for doneness. They should look firm and feel dry to the touch. If not, cover and continue steaming for 5 to 10 minutes more. Check quickly so that little steam escapes. Slump is best served right away, but if you need to wait 10 minutes or so, cover the pan with a clean dish towel placed under the lid to absorb excess moisture. Serve in soup plates or shallow bowls with:

Softly whipped cream or lemon or vanilla yogurt

PEACH SLUMP WITH RICOTTA DUMPLINGS

6 to 8 servings

This filling is especially dense with fruit to balance the rich hazelnut dumplings. In the winter months, try this slump with pears or apples or a combination of the two.

Preheat the oven to 350°F.

Spread on a baking sheet:

⅓ cup hazelnuts

Toast until fragrant and golden brown under the skin, 7 to 10 minutes. While the nuts are still hot, rub them in a towel to remove as much of the skins as possible. Let cool. Grind or finely chop the hazelnuts. Transfer to a medium bowl and whisk together thoroughly with:

1 cup all-purpose flour
2 tablespoons sugar
1 teaspoon baking powder
½ teaspoon salt

Whisk together:

1 cup whole-milk or part-skim ricotta cheese
2 large eggs
¼ cup milk

Add the milk mixture to the dry ingredients and stir just until the dry ingredients are moistened. In a large, heavy-bottomed saucepan or Dutch oven with a tight-fitting lid, stir until dissolved:

1 cup water
½ cup sugar

Rinse and wipe dry:

7 medium, ripe peaches (about 2 pounds)

Cut in half and remove the pits. Cut each half into ½- to 1-inch chunks and add to the sugar water. Cover and bring to a boil over high heat. Reduce the heat and simmer, covered, for 10 minutes. Do not lift the lid while simmering until you are ready to spoon on the dumplings; lots of steam will escape. As soon as the fruit is ready, remove the lid and quickly cover the fruit with spoonfuls of the batter. Replace the lid and simmer over low heat, without removing the lid, for about 30 minutes. Check the dumplings for doneness. They should look firm and feel dry to the touch. If not, continue steaming for 5 to 10 minutes more. Check quickly so that little steam escapes. Slump is best when served right away, but if you need to wait 10 minutes or so, cover the dish with a clean dish towel placed under the lid to absorb excess moisture. Serve in shallow bowls.

BLACKBERRY RASPBERRY GRUNT

6 to 8 servings

This dish is like a warm shortcake. Try it also with blueberries or strawberries in any combination of berries.

Butter a 6-cup baking dish, such as a soufflé dish or pudding mold. Have ready a covered Dutch oven or pot large enough to hold the soufflé dish or mold with ample room around it.

Wash in a bowl of cold water and pat dry:

1 pint raspberries
1 pint blackberries

In a medium bowl, toss the berries with:

½ cup sugar

Pour into the buttered mold and spread evenly. Whisk together thoroughly:

1¼ cups all-purpose flour
2 tablespoons sugar
1¼ teaspoons baking powder
½ teaspoon salt

Add:

3 tablespoons cold unsalted butter, cut into small pieces

Using a pastry blender or 2 knives, cut the butter into the dry ingredients (as for pie dough, 859) until the mixture resembles coarse crumbs. Add:

½ cup milk

Stir just until the dry ingredients are moistened. With a lightly floured hand, gather the dough into a ball and knead it gently against the sides and bottom of the bowl 5 to 10 times, turning and pressing any loose pieces into the dough each time, until they adhere and the bowl is fairly clean. Dust the top and bottom of the dough with a little flour. On a work surface, pat the dough into a round just large enough to cover the top of the fruit. Cover the fruit with the dough. Tear off a piece of aluminum foil large enough to cover the top and reach halfway down the sides of the mold. Butter an area in the center of the foil the same size as the dough. Cover the mold with the foil, butter side down and fold the foil down against the outside of the mold. Tie a string around the foil to secure it. Place a second piece of foil, folded in half, in the bottom of the Dutch oven. Set the mold on the foil. Place a plate on top of the foil-covered mold. Place the Dutch oven over low heat and pour in enough boiling water to come halfway up the sides of the mold. Cover the pot with a tight-fitting lid and simmer for 1½ hours, replenishing the water as needed to maintain the water level.

Remove the mold from the Dutch oven. Remove the plate. Cut the string and carefully remove the foil. The dough will resemble a swollen biscuit. A knife inserted in the biscuit will come out hot and dry. Run the knife around the biscuit to loosen it from the sides of the dish. Carefully unmold the dessert onto a large platter deep enough to hold the juices. Serve warm in deep bowls with:

Vanilla Bean Custard Sauce, 1041, vanilla ice cream or yogurt, or softly whipped cream

ABOUT FRUIT DUMPLINGS AND TURNOVERS

Any pie dough, puff pastry, or biscuit dough can be used to make fruit dumplings or turnovers. Dumplings are formed by gathering the edges of the dough up around the filling like a purse or pouch; the resulting packets may be baked or boiled. (The texture of baked pastry contrasts particularly nicely with the filling.) Turnovers are made by folding the dough over the filling and can be formed in any size from miniature to large. The dough can be made well ahead and kept chilled until ready to use. These little "pies" are best eaten the day they are baked.

APPLE DUMPLINGS *6 servings*

This dessert is made with whole apples filled with brown sugar and cinnamon, which are then wrapped and baked in biscuit or pie dough. Look for small apples (about 4 ounces each) for a nice serving size, but you can also make them with larger apple halves. Both biscuit and pie dough are delicious; biscuit dough holds its shape well, while the pie dough is rich and luxurious. The apples are cooked in a flavored syrup and basted for the last 15 to 20 minutes of baking, so that they emerge glistening from the oven. For added convenience, assemble, wrap, and chill the apples several hours before baking. You may substitute jam or preserves for the brown sugar filling.

Prepare:

Fluffy Shortcake or Biscuit dough, 790, Flaky Cream Cheese Pastry Dough, 866, ½ recipe Flaky Pastry Dough, 859, or ½ recipe Deluxe Butter Flaky Pastry Dough, 862

Refrigerate the dough for at least 30 minutes.

Preheat the oven to 425°F. Generously butter a baking dish with sides large enough to fit the dumplings with 1 to 2 inches between each one, such as an 11 x 7-inch rectangular dish or a 12-inch oval gratin dish.

Peel and core:

6 small flavorful apples (about 4 ounces each) or 3 large apples (about 8 ounces each)

Halve the large apples lengthwise, if using. Mix with a fork until blended:

½ cup packed dark brown sugar
1 teaspoon ground cinnamon
¼ teaspoon salt

Add:

4 tablespoons (½ stick) unsalted butter, softened

Mix well. Fill the hollowed apples with the brown sugar mixture. Pat any remaining mixture on top of the fruit. If using apple halves, fill the hollow with the mixture and save any remaining mixture for later. On a lightly floured surface, roll the dough into an 18 x 12-inch rectangle, about ⅛ inch thick. Cut into six 6-inch squares, then roll each a square a little larger into a 7-inch square. Lightly brush with:

1 egg, lightly beaten

Place an apple in the middle of each square. If using apple halves, place cored side down and spread with the remaining sugar mixture over the rounded tops of the apples. For each square, bring the 4 corners of the dough up around the apple and pinch the corners and edges of the dough together. Prick the top of each pastry several times with a fork and place in the baking dish. Bake for 10 minutes.

While the dumplings bake, make the syrup. Whisk together in a saucepan:

1 cup water
½ cup packed light brown sugar
2 tablespoons unsalted butter
1 teaspoon ground cinnamon
¼ teaspoon salt

Add:

1 small lemon, thinly sliced and seeded

Bring to a boil and boil for 5 minutes. Pour the boiling syrup over the dumplings when they begin to color, 10 to 15 minutes into the cooking time. After the dumplings have baked for 10 minutes, pour the syrup over them. Reduce the oven temperature to 350°F and bake until the apples are tender when pierced with a small knife or toothpick, 30 to 35 minutes more, depending on the size and type of apple. Baste the apples with the syrup every 10 minutes or so to form a glaze and flavor the crust. Let cool slightly. Serve warm with:

Heavy cream, softly whipped cream, or vanilla ice cream

ABOUT CRISPS AND CRUNCHES

These simple and popular desserts consist of sweetened fruit—usually lightly thickened to produce syrupy juices—baked with crumbly toppings of flour, butter, and sugar and sometimes oats, cookie or cake crumbs, nuts, and spices. For a crisp, the flour, butter, and sugar are mixed together like pie dough before the liquid is added, and the mixture scattered over the top like a streusel or crumb topping. An approximate ratio of three parts fruit to one part topping makes a perfect crisp. A crunch is fruit sandwiched between two layers of sweetened, buttered crumbs; it is served cut into squares, like bar cookies, but is a bit more fragile. Keep the butter cold for crisps and crunches and handle lightly to assure that the toppings will be both crisp and tender. When completely cooled, crunches may be eaten by hand; if still warm, a dish is necessary. *Crumble* is the British name for a crisp or crunch with oatmeal in the topping.

For any of these desserts, choose a 2-quart baking dish that is 1¾ to 2 inches deep. It may be a 9- or 10-inch deep-dish pie pan, an 8 x 8-inch or 9 x 9-inch pan, a 12-inch oval gratin, or an 11 x 7-inch rectangular pan.

APPLE CRISP

6 to 8 servings

Select a tart, crisp apple to balance the sweetness of the topping. Gravenstein, Pippin, and Braeburn are good choices, but local apples in season may be the best choice of all.

Position a rack in the lower third of the oven. Preheat the oven to 375°F. Have ready an unbuttered 2-quart earthenware or glass baking dish, 2 inches deep.

Peel and core:

8 medium apples (about 2½ pounds)

Cut the apples in half and then into 1-inch chunks. Spread them evenly in the baking dish. Combine:

¾ cup all-purpose flour
¾ cup sugar
½ teaspoon salt
½ teaspoon ground cinnamon
¼ teaspoon ground nutmeg

Add:

8 tablespoons (1 stick) cold unsalted butter, cut into small pieces

Using a pastry blender or 2 knives, cut the butter into the dry ingredients (as for Basic Rolled Biscuits, 789) until the mixture resembles coarse breadcrumbs. Or do this with a mixer or in a food processor, taking care not to blend the butter too thoroughly. Scatter the topping evenly over the fruit. Tap the dish on the counter once or twice to settle in the crumbs. Bake until the topping is golden brown, the juices are bubbling, and the apples are tender when pierced with a skewer, 50 to 55 minutes. Serve warm with:

Softly whipped cream or vanilla ice cream

APPLE ALMOND CRISP

Prepare Apple Crisp, above, adding ½ cup sliced almonds, coarsely crumbled in your hand, with the flour.

MANGO PEAR CRISP

6 to 8 servings

Mango adds perfume and subtle background flavor to the pears, and crystallized ginger in the topping piques the taste buds with a little exotic heat. Bosc or Bartlett pears are the best choice for this dessert.

Position a rack in the lower third of the oven. Preheat

the oven to 375°F. Have ready an unbuttered 2-quart earthenware or glass baking dish, 2 inches deep.
Peel and core:

6 medium, firm ripe pears (about 2 pounds)

Slice pears in half and then each half into 4 wedges. Place in the baking dish. Peel, and cut into ½-inch slices, 466:

2 slightly firm ripe mangoes (about 1¼ pounds)

Toss with the pears. Stir together:

¾ cup all-purpose flour
½ cup sugar
½ teaspoon salt

Add:

8 tablespoons (1 stick) cold unsalted butter, cut into small pieces

Using a pastry blender or 2 knives, cut the butter into the dry ingredients (as for Basic Rolled Biscuits, 789) until the mixture resembles coarse breadcrumbs. Or do this with a mixer or in a food processor, taking care not to blend the butter too thoroughly. Stir in:

¼ cup diced crystallized ginger (about 1½ ounces)

Scatter the topping evenly over the fruit. Tap the dish on the counter once or twice to settle in the crumbs. Bake until the topping is golden brown, the juices are bubbling, and the fruit is tender when pierced with a skewer, about 45 to 50 minutes. Serve warm.

CRANBERRY CRUNCH

6 to 8 servings

Reminiscent of bar cookies, these squares are chewy and sweet yet nicely tart.
Position a rack in the lower third of the oven. Preheat the oven to 350°F. Butter an 8 x 8-inch baking dish.
Combine:

1 cup old-fashioned or quick-cooking rolled oats
1 cup packed dark brown sugar
½ cup all-purpose flour
½ teaspoon salt

Add:

8 tablespoons (1 stick) cold unsalted butter, cut into small pieces

Using a pastry blender or 2 knives, cut the butter into the dry ingredients (as for Basic Rolled Biscuits, 789) until the mixture is crumbly but holds together when pressed. Spread half over the bottom of the baking dish and press gently with your hand, packing the mixture slightly. Cover with:

3 cups fresh or frozen cranberries, picked over

Sprinkle with:

½ cup sugar

Top evenly with the remaining crumb mixture. Bake until the fruit is tender and the crunch is firm and well browned, 50 to 60 minutes. Let cool for 20 to 30 minutes. Cut into squares and serve warm with:

Caramel ice cream

ABOUT BROWN BETTIES

Nobody remembers who Betty was, but a brown betty is both layered and topped with sweet buttered crumbs. The crumbs should be dry, so that they will absorb the juices in the middle and bottom layers and remain crunchy on the top. (For homemade breadcrumbs, dry sliced bread in a 225°F oven until firm to the touch and crisp, about 1 hour. Let cool, then break up the dried bread with your hands or chop with a knife into about 1-inch square pieces. Crush with a rolling pin to produce a fine meal or process in a food processor. Store in an airtight container. For graham cracker crumbs, crush graham crackers either on a work surface with a rolling pin or in a food processor.) Another style of betty blends a pastry-cream custard with the fruit, then layers the mixture with the crumbs.

APPLE BROWN BETTY

6 servings

Lots of tart lemon juice and sweet brown sugar.
Position a rack in the lower third of the oven. Preheat the oven to 350°F. Have ready an unbuttered 8 x 8-inch baking dish, a 9-inch pie pan, or a 10 x 6-inch oblong glass baking dish.
Peel, core, and slice:

3 medium apples (about 1 pound)

Stir together with a fork in a small bowl:

1½ cups dry unseasoned breadcrumbs (see About Brown Betties, above)
6 tablespoons (¾ stick) unsalted butter, melted

Sift if lumpy; otherwise, whisk together thoroughly in another bowl:

1¼ cups packed dark brown sugar
1 teaspoon ground cinnamon
¼ teaspoon ground nutmeg
¼ teaspoon ground cloves

Spread one-third of the crumb mixture evenly in the bottom of the baking dish. Distribute half of the apples in the dish. Sprinkle with half of the sugar mixture and then with:

1½ tablespoons fresh lemon juice

Cover with another third of the crumb mixture, the remaining apples, the remaining sugar mixture, and:

1½ tablespoons fresh lemon juice

Cover with the remaining crumb mixture. Cover the dish with aluminum foil and bake until the apples are nearly tender when pierced with a skewer, about 40 minutes. Uncover the dish. Increase the oven temperature to 400°F and bake until the betty is browned, about 15 minutes. Serve warm in bowls with:

Vanilla Bean Custard Sauce, 1041, or vanilla ice cream

BANANA BROWN BETTY

6 to 8 servings

The sweet crumbs and custard filling balance perfectly with slightly acidic bananas. Choose firm fruit with yellow skins and no brown spots.

Position a rack in the lower third of the oven. Preheat the oven to 350°F. Have ready an unbuttered 8 x 8-inch baking dish, a 9-inch pie plate, or a 10 x 6-inch oblong glass baking dish.

Stir together:

1½ cups graham cracker crumbs
¼ cup sugar
6 tablespoons (¾ stick) unsalted butter, melted

Peel and cut into ½-inch slices:

4 firm ripe bananas

In a medium, heavy saucepan, bring to a simmer over medium heat:

1½ cups milk
½ vanilla bean, split (or add ½ teaspoon vanilla extract later)

While the milk heats, beat in a medium bowl until thick and pale yellow:

1 large egg
¼ cup sugar
1 tablespoon all-purpose flour
1 tablespoon cornstarch
¼ teaspoon salt

Remove the vanilla bean if using. Gradually whisk half the milk into the egg mixture, then whisk this mixture gradually into the milk remaining in the pan. Cook, whisking constantly and scraping the bottom and sides of the pan, over medium heat until the center bubbles and the mixture has thickened. Remove from the heat and stir for 1 minute to cool. (Add the vanilla extract if using.) Fold the bananas into the hot custard. Gently press half the crumb mixture over the bottom of the baking dish. Spoon the banana mixture evenly over the crumbs and cover evenly with the remaining crumb mixture. Bake until the top has browned and the filling is warm, 25 to 30 minutes. Let cool on a rack for 20 minutes before serving. To serve, spoon into bowls and top with:

Fresh Strawberry Sauce, 1048
Vanilla ice cream

To store, cover and refrigerate for up to 2 days. Remove from the refrigerator at least 15 minutes before serving. This dish does not reheat well.

ABOUT KUCHENS, BUCKLES, CLAFOUTIS, AND UPSIDE-DOWN CAKES

Kuchen is the generic German word for cake, but in America it refers specifically to a breakfast pastry (equally delicious for dessert) filled with cheese or fruit and usually made from yeast dough. Our streamlined variation, however, is raised with baking powder. Before baking, kuchen is sometimes topped with streusel, 1011. A buckle is another type of cake with fruit folded into the batter before baking and a generous crumbly streusel topping. The cake buckles, or crumples, in spots from the weight of the topping before the batter sets, creating pockets of caramelized sugar and butter. A buckle may be kept covered at room temperature for up to 2 days or refrigerated for up to 3 days. (Remove from the refrigerator 30 minutes before serving or reheat, covered with aluminum foil, in a 325°F oven until the center is warm, about 20 minutes.) A clafouti is a simple French country dessert. It is similar to an old American dessert called batter pudding and is another example of a quick batter made with fresh fruit. An upside-down cake, is, as its name implies, inverted after baking. The cake batter is first poured over a layer of fruit that has been generously covered with sugar, melted butter, and spices; this forms its own syrupy sauce over the whole cake when the baked cake is inverted.

FRESH FRUIT KUCHEN

8 servings

This versatile summer fruit-topped cake can be made with apricots, plums, cherries, raspberries, blueberries, or a combination of these instead of the peaches or nectarines.

Have all ingredients at room temperature, 68° to 70°F. Position a rack in the lower third of the oven. Preheat the oven to 350°F. Grease a 9 x 2-inch round pan.

Whisk together thoroughly:

1 cup all-purpose flour
1 tablespoon baking powder
⅛ teaspoon salt

In a large bowl, beat on medium to high speed until light and fluffy, 3 to 4 minutes:

8 tablespoons (1 stick) unsalted butter
¾ cup sugar

Beat in 1 at a time just until blended:

2 large eggs

Stir in the flour mixture just until incorporated. Scrape the batter into the pan and spread evenly. Scatter on top:

2 cups sliced peeled peaches or unpeeled nectarines (2 large)

¼ cup coarsely chopped pecans (optional)

Combine and sprinkle over the fruit:

1 tablespoon sugar

¼ tablespoon ground cinnamon

Bake until the topping is golden brown and a toothpick inserted in the center of the cake (avoiding the fruit) comes out clean, 40 to 45 minutes. Let cool to room temperature before serving.

BOYSENBERRY AND PEACH BUCKLE

8 servings

A hint of ground nutmeg adds interest to the crumb topping.

Position a rack in the lower third of the oven. Preheat the oven to 350°F. Have ready a buttered and floured 10 x 2-inch round cake pan or 9 x 9-inch baking dish.

Whisk together thoroughly in a medium bowl:

½ cup sugar

6 tablespoons all-purpose flour

¼ teaspoon ground nutmeg

¼ teaspoon salt

Add:

4 tablespoons (½ stick) cold unsalted butter, cut into small pieces

Using a pastry blender or 2 knives, cut the butter into the dry ingredients (as for pie dough, 859) until the mixture resembles coarse crumbs. Or do this with a mixer or in a food processor, taking care not to blend the butter too thoroughly. Set the topping aside.

Wash and wipe dry:

1 medium to large ripe peach (8 to 12 ounces)

Cut in half and remove the pit. Cut the peach into chunks the size of boysenberries and transfer to a bowl. Wash, pat dry, and add to the peach chunks:

1½ cups boysenberries

Whisk together thoroughly in a large bowl:

1¾ cups all-purpose flour

2 teaspoons baking powder

½ teaspoon salt

Combine in another bowl:

4 tablespoons (½ stick) unsalted butter, half melted

1 cup sugar

1 cold large egg

½ teaspoon vanilla

Beat until slightly fluffy. Gradually beat in:

½ cup milk

Add to the flour mixture and stir just until the dry ingredients are moistened and the batter is smooth. Gently fold the reserved fruit into the batter. Spoon into the prepared pan and spread evenly. Sprinkle the topping evenly over the batter. Bake for 40 to 45 minutes, until the top springs back slowly and a toothpick inserted in the center comes out clean. Let cool in the pan on a rack for at least 20 minutes before serving. Serve warm or at room temperature with:

Orange or lemon sherbet or softly whipped cream

ALMOND PEAR BUCKLE

8 servings

Almonds add a delicate floral overtone to baked pears.

Position a rack in the lower third of the oven. Preheat the oven to 350°F. Butter and flour a 10 x 2-inch round cake pan or 9 x 9-inch baking dish.

Spread evenly in a pie or cake pan and toast until lightly browned, 6 to 8 minutes:

½ cup sliced almonds with their skin

Let cool. Whisk together thoroughly in a medium bowl:

½ cup all-purpose flour

½ cup packed light brown sugar

¼ teaspoon ground cinnamon

¼ teaspoon salt

Add:

4 tablespoons (½ stick) cold unsalted butter, cut into small pieces

Using a pastry blender or 2 knives, cut the butter into the dry ingredients (as for Basic Rolled Biscuits, 789) until the mixture resembles coarse breadcrumbs. Or do this with a mixer or in a food processor, taking care not to blend the butter too thoroughly. Stir in the reserved toasted almonds. Peel, halve, and core:

2 medium to large ripe pears (12 to 16 ounces)

Cut each half into 4 wedges, then cut the wedges crosswise in half. Toss with:

1 tablespoon fresh lemon juice

Cover with a sheet of plastic wrap in direct contact with the fruit. Set aside while you make the cake. Whisk together thoroughly in a large bowl:

1¾ cups all-purpose flour

2 teaspoons baking powder

½ teaspoon salt

Combine in another bowl:

4 tablespoons (½ stick) unsalted butter, half melted

¾ cup packed light brown sugar

1 cold large egg

½ teaspoon vanilla

¼ teaspoon almond extract

Beat until slightly fluffy. Gradually beat in:

½ cup milk

Add to the flour mixture and stir just until the dry ingredients are moistened and the batter is smooth. Gently fold the pears into the batter. Spoon into the prepared pan and spread evenly. Sprinkle the topping evenly over the batter. Bake for 40 to 45 minutes, until the top springs back slowly and a toothpick inserted in the center comes out clean. Let cool in the pan on a rack for at least 20 minutes before serving. Serve warm or at room temperature with:

Pear sherbet or softly whipped cream

ALMOST CLASSIC CHERRY CLAFOUTI

6 servings

This custardlike dessert comes from the Limousin region of France. Classically made with unstoned black cherries, on the theory that the cherry pits add flavor to the cake, this version is called "almost classic" because you have the option of using pitted cherries, a blessing to the unsuspecting. The mixture for a clafouti resembles a thick pancake or crêpe batter and for this reason, according to *Larousse Gastronomique,* the Academie Francaise defined the clafouti as a "sort of fruit flan." Under protests from residents of the Limousin, the definition was changed to a "cake with black cherries," even though other types of cherries—and even other fruits—are often used.

Preheat the oven to 375°F. Butter a 10-inch deep-dish pie pan.

Beat until frothy, about 2 minutes:

4 large eggs
¾ cup sugar

Add and beat until smooth:

1 cup milk
1 tablespoon Cognac or rum (untraditional, but good with the custard)
2 teaspoons vanilla

Stir in:

¾ cup all-purpose flour
Pinch of salt

Distribute over the bottom of the pie pan:

1 pound sweet cherries, pitted or not (frozen cherries, thawed and patted dry, or canned cherries, drained and dried, can be used)

Pour the batter over the cherries and place the pie pan on a baking sheet. Bake the clafouti for 10 minutes; reduce the oven temperature to 350°F and bake until the top has puffed (it will sink on cooling) and a toothpick inserted in the center comes out clean, about 35 minutes more. Transfer to a rack and cool for about 20 minutes. Dust with:

Powdered sugar

Serve in wedges.

FRUIT CLAFOUTI

An equal amount of peeled, cored, and finely cubed apple or pear can be substituted for the cherries. Similarly, the clafouti can be made with moist, plump prunes, pitted or not. If you use the prunes, substitute 1 tablespoon Armagnac for the Cognac.

PINEAPPLE UPSIDE-DOWN CAKE

8 servings

Traditionally baked in a cast-iron skillet or "spider," this sweet, gooey-topped cake was devised to promote canned pineapple. The best variations we know are fresh apricots, peaches, or plums, cut in slim wedges, or ½-inch slices of tart apple with a few chopped walnuts between them and ¼ teaspoon cinnamon mixed into the brown sugar topping. For a gooier topping (one of the joys of this cake), you have two options: Either increase the butter in the pan to 6 tablespoons and the brown sugar to 1 cup, or bake the cake in an 8-inch pan and increase only the butter to 4 tablespoons.

Have all ingredients at room temperature, 68° to 70°F. Preheat the oven to 350°F. Have ready one 9-inch skillet or a 9 x 2-inch round pan.

Drain and place in 1 layer on paper towels to absorb the excess juice:

7 slices canned unsweetened pineapple (one 20-ounce can)

Place in the skillet or cake pan:

3 tablespoons unsalted butter

Place the pan in the oven just until the butter is melted, or melt it on the top of the stove. Tilt to coat all sides with butter. The extra butter will settle in the bottom of the pan. Sprinkle evenly over the bottom of the pan:

¾ cup packed light or dark brown sugar

Place 1 pineapple ring on the brown sugar in the center of the pan and arrange 6 more around it. In the center of each ring and in the spaces between them, place any of the following, best side down:

19 maraschino cherries, 19 cooked pitted prune halves or quarters, or 19 pecan halves

Whisk together with a fork:

2 large eggs
2 tablespoons buttermilk
½ teaspoon vanilla

Mix for a few seconds with an electric mixer in a large bowl:

1 cup all-purpose flour
¾ cup sugar

¾ teaspoon baking powder
¼ teaspoon baking soda
¼ teaspoon salt

Add:

6 tablespoons (¾ stick) unsalted butter, softened
6 tablespoons buttermilk

Beat on low speed just until the flour is moistened. Increase the speed to medium, or high speed with a hand-held mixer, and beat for exactly 1½ minutes. The batter will be stiff. Add one-third of the egg mixture at a time, beating for exactly 20 seconds and scraping the bowl after each addition. Scrape the batter over the fruit in the pan and spread evenly. Bake until a toothpick inserted in the cake comes out clean, 35 to 40 minutes. Remove the cake from the oven and tilt the pan in all directions to detach it from the sides of the pan. Let cool for 2 to 3 minutes before unmolding. Invert a serving platter on top of the pan. Cover your hands with oven mitts and turn the cake onto the platter. Lift off the pan. If any fruit or nut pieces are askew, use a fork to push them back into place. If brown sugar is left in the pan, scrape it up and spoon it over the cake. Serve warm or cool, plain or with:

Whipped cream

PUFF PASTRY, STRUDEL & DANISH PASTRIES

European pastries are the most ethereal delights in all of baking. Think of pillowy croissants, puff pastry turnovers filled with warm spiced apple, or Danish spirals with sweet cream cheese. All may sound as intimidating as they do delicious, but they need not if you start with recipes such as Food Processor Puff Pastry, 908, perfected for the home cook, or Danish Pastry, 915, and use them to bake crisp and buttery classics such as Croissants, 913, Apple Strudel, 917, and Cream-Cheese Danish Spirals, 916. These doughs are not only quite approachable but also far superior to anything you can buy.

ABOUT LAYERED PASTRY DOUGHS

Layered pastry doughs, such as puff pastry, Danish pastry, and croissant dough, are composed of literally hundreds of layers, which can be seen to separate (and sometimes puff) as the dough is baked. The ingredients are no different from those in other basic doughs; it is the manipulation of ingredients that creates the layers. A flaky pie dough has short, randomly distributed layers, produced by mixing small bits of fat (lard, butter, vegetable shortening) with flour; a flaky layered dough is made up of continuous parallel layers produced over a period of several hours by repeatedly rolling out and folding a giant malleable pat of butter enclosed in dough. (Puff pastry can be made with oil instead of butter, and some Provençal and Italian chefs prefer olive oil to butter for the task, but this is uncommon.) Each time the ensemble of butter and dough is rolled out and folded—pastry cooks call this a *turn*—the number of layers is multiplied geometrically. When the pastries are baked, the moisture in the dough turns to steam, which pushes the layers apart. Meanwhile, the butter melts, coating and tenderizing each layer while imparting its incomparable flavor.

ABOUT MAKING LAYERED DOUGHS

It is indeed best to choose a cool dry day on which to make layered dough; heat and humidity both cause problems. The tools and equipment required for making layered doughs are the same as those needed for pie crusts, 856; a cool marble work surface is ideal but not essential. Keep in mind that these are the most challenging and delicate of pastries, and proceed the way porcupines, according to the old joke, are said to make love: very, very carefully.

To make any kind of layered dough, a large block of butter, wrapped in the dough like a package, must be rolled out and folded, rerolled and refolded. The idea is to create thin, even layers of butter between distinct layers of dough rather than integrating dough and butter. For this to work, the butter and the dough must be similar in temperature and consistency so that they move together at an even pace under the pressure of the rolling pin. If the butter is too cold and hard, the pressure of the rolling pin may push it through the dough layer instead of extending it, resulting in nonuniform layers. Fortunately, it is possible to see and feel the butter cracking in the dough as it is rolled out, enabling the cook to stop and let the dough rest and the butter soften a bit. Butter that is too soft is even worse though: The dough and butter merge under pressure from the rolling pin instead of maintaining their separate identities. If the dough seems to squishy and/or the butter oozes from it as you roll, stop and refrigerate them until firm but still pliable. And at no point allow the dough to absorb excess moisture or dry out.

To roll the dough, flour the work surface and the dough or the rolling pin lightly. (Use only as much flour as needed to prevent sticking, for excess flour will toughen the pastry and turn it gray.) Always position the dough with the short end in front of you. Roll the dough with even pressure to maintain an even thickness. Keeping the pin parallel to the work surface, roll from the center of the dough away from you and then from the center of the dough back toward you, lifting the pin after each roll. Rolling back and forth without lifting the pin develops the gluten in the dough, making it tough and elastic. Never roll the pin over the edge of the dough. Roll the dough the long way to the desired length and then adjust the width if necessary. As you roll the pastry to the desired size, maintain the dough's rectangular shape, keeping the corners square, the sides of the dough as straight as possible, and the thickness even. Straighten the sides of the dough occasionally with your hands, as though straightening a stack of papers, or press the sides with a pastry scraper or rolling pin. If the dough becomes misshapen, correct it with the rolling pin, rolling specifically on the side that is uneven before proceeding. If a small area of butter becomes uncovered when the dough is being rolled, gently pat a little flour over the butter spot and brush off any excess flour. Brush excess flour from the dough with a dry pastry brush before folding.

The folding technique and the number of turns required vary according to the type of pastry. Classic puff pastry is given 3 sets of 2 turns each, for a total of 6 turns, and the folding is always in thirds, like a business letter; this is called a single fold. Food processor (the recipe we give here) and quick puff pasry are given 4 turns, but 3 of these are double folds. In a double fold, the top and bottom of a long rectangle are folded to the center; the rectangle is then folded in half. Croissant dough is given 4 turns with single folds, and Danish pastry dough, 5 turns with single folds.

To avoid excess gluten development, the dough should be rotated after every single turn so that the gluten strands are stretched in a different direction with each successive turn. The dough is wrapped in plastic wrap, refrigerated, and allowed to rest for 30 to 60 minutes (depending on the pastry) between the turns. The rest relaxes the gluten strands and lets them adjust to their new length; chilling firms the butter, which helps keep the layers of dough and butter distinct. (Do not allow the butter to turn hard or brittle while chilling; if this occurs, remove the dough from the refrigerator and let it sit on the counter for 10 minutes or so until the butter reaches a pliable state.) The dough is chilled again after the finished dough has been rolled into a sheet and before it is cut into shapes—and often still again just before baking. (Read each recipe for specific instructions.) It is surprisingly easy to lose track of how many turns you have given the dough as it rests. Professional bakers make a shallow fingertip imprint in the dough, one for each turn, before they refrigerate the dough for its resting period.

ABOUT PUFF PASTRY

Puff pastry is the flakiest pastry imaginable, which is not surprising when you consider that it actually contains more butter than flour. Puff pastry, in its myriad shapes or sizes, can be filled with practically anything to create countless desserts and an encyclopedia of savory foods, from appetizers to main courses. Puff pastry is baked in the lower third of the oven at 400°F for part of its cooking time (to push the pastry to maximum height), then at 350°F (to ensure that the pastry will be thoroughly baked without overbrowning). Read About Making Layered Doughs, 906, for detailed mixing and handling instructions. Once the dough is made, we recommend working with no more than 1 pound of it at a time, for greater control and easier rolling. Since the puff pastry recipe here makes more than that, freeze the excess for future use, according to the instructions below. Save all puff pastry scraps and trimmings too, freezing them similarly. Accumulated scraps can be rolled together when thawed, then folded as if you were giving the dough a single turn before rolling out and using. Rolled scraps of puff pastry can be used for napoleons, twists, minitarts, palm leaves, or any other pastry for which full height is not crucial.

CUTTING AND DOCKING PUFF PASTRY

After rolling out the dough to the desired thickness, trim the pastry edges (reserving the scraps for another use) before cutting desired shapes. Always cut puff pastry with a sharp knife, pressing straight down through the dough. Dragging the knife prevents the edges of the pastry from rising evenly or to full capacity. Since even a sharp knife compresses a few top layers, puff pastry will rise higher and straighter if it is turned upside down after cutting. Thus, we invert pastry pieces for turnovers and bouchées but not for napoleons, which should not rise to capacity.

Sometimes it is important to control rather than promote the rise of puff pastry. Docking is the term for piercing a pastry all over with the tines of a fork (or a spiky tool called a pastry docker) to inhibit the rise but maintain flakiness. Napoleon layers are docked to keep them very thin but still flaky. The bottoms but not the sides of vol-au-vents and tart shells are docked to achieve thin-bottomed shells with high-rising sides. After cutting, turn pieces of pastry upside down before docking (except napoleons).

GLAZING PUFF PASTRY

For a shiny golden surface, brush puff pastry with beaten egg wash or a combination of milk and sugar before baking. Glaze only flat pastry surfaces; never brush or allow the glaze to drip over cut edges, where it can prevent the layers from rising to full height. Baked puff pastry may, alternatively, be glazed with a light sugar syrup as it emerges hot from the oven.

STORING PUFF PASTRY

Blocks of puff pastry can be refrigerated for up to 2 days or frozen for up to 6 months. Wrap in plastic and then aluminum foil, then slip the packets into a sealable plastic bag, pressing out the air before sealing. If freezing, thaw the pastry, without unwrapping, overnight in the refrigerator. Or freeze puff pastry after it is rolled out, either in sheets or cut into shapes. After rolling, chill until firm, cut into shapes if desired or leave sheets whole, then wrap. Stack cut pieces with wax paper between each layer before wrapping and freezing. For the best rise, bake frozen (unfilled) cut pieces without thawing. The latter is our preference, since shapes are ready to bake at a moment's notice. If freezing sheets, thaw them over-night in the refrigerator before cutting. Unbaked but filled puff pastry shapes such as turnovers can be covered and refrigerated for up to 8 hours before baking.

For maximum flakiness and crispness, puff pastry should be consumed the day it is baked. Filled and baked puff pastry desserts, such as turnovers, are best served warm from the oven, although they can be reheated. Individually assembled puff pastry desserts (such as bouchées and napoleons) should be eaten immediately after they are assembled. Napoleons that are made whole and then sliced should be eaten within 6 hours of being assembled. Puff pastry desserts with cream fillings should be refrigerated to prevent spoilage. Store baked puff pastry pieces at room temperature.

FOOD PROCESSOR PUFF PASTRY *2¾ pounds*

In this modernized puff pastry recipe, both the dough and the butter block are mixed in the food processor, and the dough is given 4 turns—1 single fold plus 3 double folds—in lieu of the usual 6 single folds and turns. The results are flaky, even more tender than classic puff pastry, and very high rising.

Pulse to combine in a food processor:

2⅓ cups all-purpose flour

1¼ teaspoons salt

Scatter over the flour:

5 tablespoons cold unsalted butter, cut into ½-inch cubes

Pulse until the mixture resembles coarse crumbs. Stir to combine:

½ cup ice water

2 tablespoons fresh lemon juice

1 large egg yolk

Drizzle the mixture over the contents of the processor. Pulse just until the dough begins to come together. Scrape the dough onto a sheet of plastic wrap and form it into a 5-inch square. Wrap the dough and refrigerate for 1 hour.

Cut into ½-inch slices and freeze for 2 minutes:

28 tablespoons (3½ sticks) unsalted butter

Place in a food processor:

1 cup all-purpose flour

Distribute the butter slices over the flour and pulse just until the mixture looks like fine gravel; it should not be processed to a paste. Scrape the mixture onto a sheet of

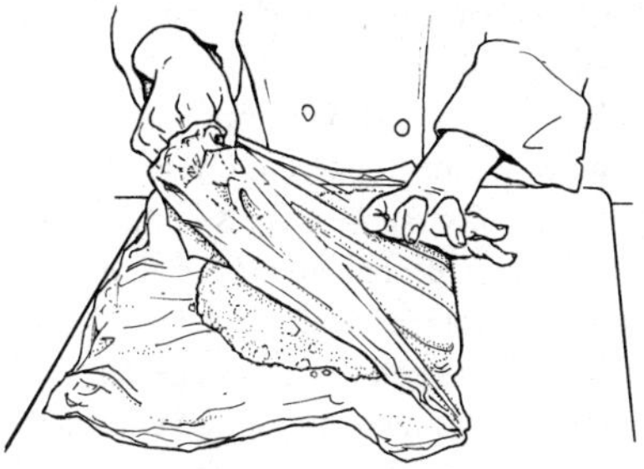

Scrape the mixture onto a sheet of plastic wrap, cover, and shape into a 6-inch square.

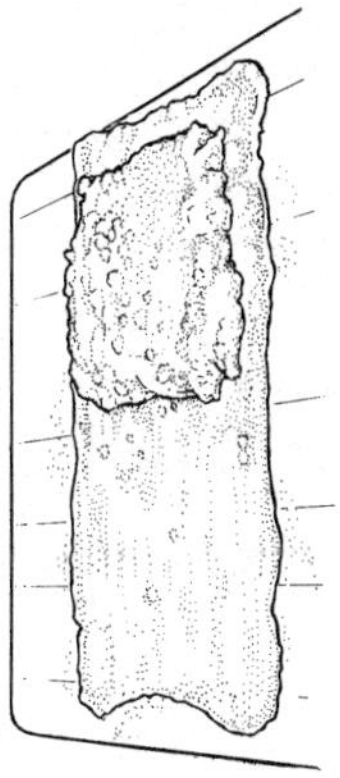

Center the butter patty on one half of the dough.

plastic wrap, cover, and shape into a 6-inch square. Wrap and refrigerate while rolling out the dough.

Remove the 5-inch dough square from the refrigerator. Place it on a lightly floured surface and roll into a 13 x 8-inch rectangle, keeping one 8-inch side facing you. Brush off the excess flour. Remove the butter patty from the refrigerator, unwrap it, and center it on one half of the dough. Fold the dough over the butter, completely covering it. Press the dough together on the 3 open sides. Turn the dough so that the folded edge is on the left, with one of the sealed sides (where the dough was pressed together) on the right to change the direction of the pastry for the next roll. The dough is now ready for turns.

Roll the dough package into a 17 x 7½-inch rectangle, keeping one short side of the rectangle facing you. Slide a metal dough scraper or spatula under the bottom third of the dough and fold it up. Slide the spatula under the top third of the dough and fold it down on top of the first third, as though you were folding a business letter. This rolling and folding is called a single turn. Rotate the dough so that the folded edge is on the left and the open edge is on the right (like a book about to be opened). Roll the dough once more into a 17 x 7½-inch rectangle. This time fold the bottom end up and the top end down to meet in the center (rather than overlapping), then fold the dough in half so that the folded ends meet to make 4 layers of dough. This double fold is the second turn. Mark the dough with 2 imprints to remind yourself that you have given the dough 2 turns. Wrap the dough and refrigerate for 45 minutes.

With the folded edge on the left and the open edge on the right, roll the dough out again to 17 x 7½ inches. Repeat the double fold for the third turn. Mark with 3 imprints, wrap the dough, and refrigerate for 45 minutes. Roll the dough out and repeat the double fold for the fourth turn. Mark the dough with 4 imprints, wrap, and refrigerate for at least 1 hour or up to 24 hours. The puff pastry is ready to use.

CLASSIC NAPOLEON (MILLE-FEUILLE)

6 to 8 servings

A classic napoleon, or mille-feuille (thousand leaves), is made up of 3 layers of puff pastry coated with apricot jam and filled with vanilla pastry cream. Serve the napoleon within a few hours of making it. If you make

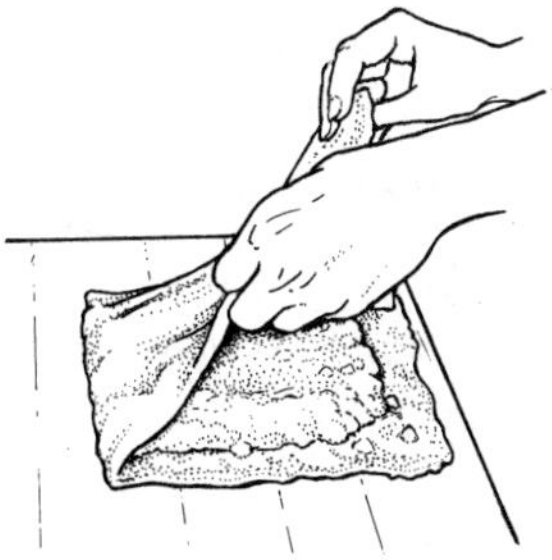

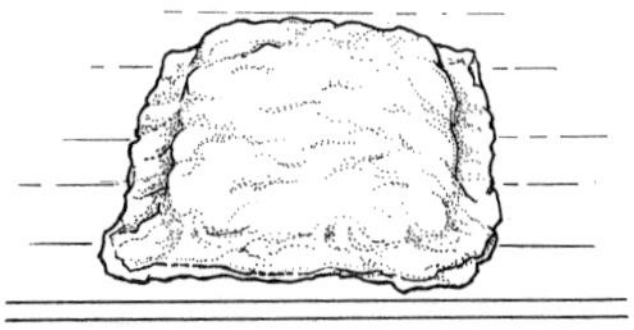

Fold the dough over the butter and press the dough together on the 3 open sides.

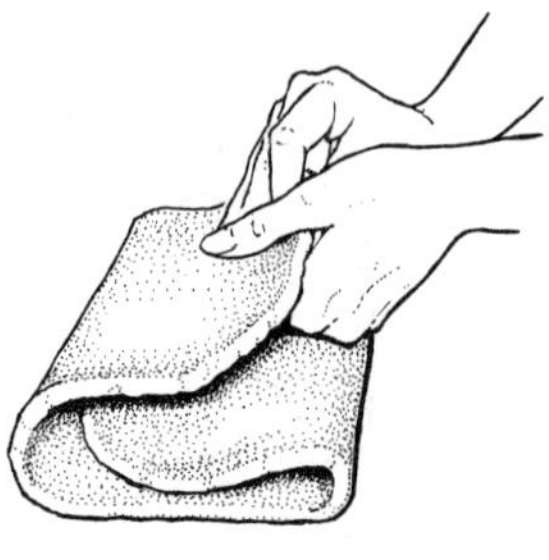

Puff pastry: First turn.

a napoleon with saved puff pastry scraps, you need not weight the layers during baking.

Prepare and chill:

2 cups Pastry Cream, 996

Have ready an unbuttered baking sheet.

Roll out 1/16 to 1/8-inch thick into a 17 x 13-inch rectangle:

1 pound Food Processor Puff Pastry, 908

Transfer the pastry to the baking sheet. Prick it all over with a fork. Cover and refrigerate for at least 30 minutes or wrap airtight and freeze until ready to use.

If the dough is frozen, let it thaw for a few minutes before trimming. Quickly transfer the dough to a cutting board and trim ½ inch from all the sides to make a 16 x 12-inch rectangle. Return it to the baking sheet and the refrigerator while the oven preheats.

Position a rack in the lower third of the oven. Preheat the oven to 400°F.

Invert a wire rack directly on the surface of the dough to prevent it from rising high in the oven while baking but to allow it to cook through. Bake until golden brown, 20 to 25 minutes. After 10 minutes of baking time, remove the rack, prick the pastry all over, replace the rack, and finish baking. Remove the rack for the final 2 to 3 minutes' baking time to dry and cook the top layers. Slide the pastry onto a wire rack that is not hot and let cool to room temperature.

Using a sharp serrated knife, saw the pastry gently lengthwise into three 16 x 4-inch strips. Brush 2 of the strips with:

1½ tablespoons apricot jam, warmed

Spread half of the pastry cream over one of the jam-covered pastry pieces. Place the second jam-covered piece on top and cover with the remaining pastry cream. Turn the last puff pastry strip upside down and place it over the pastry cream. Refrigerate until ready to serve but no longer than 6 hours. Use a sharp serrated knife and a sawing motion to cut the napoleon into individual servings. Dust the top of each serving with:

Powdered sugar

PUFF PASTRY FRUIT SQUARES *6 servings*

This is a puff pastry dessert for bakers who do not want to fuss: simply baked squares of pastry served with berries scattered over them. Any summer fruit can be substituted for the berries: Use less sugar than called for if the fruit is unusually sweet, and add a tablespoon or so of orange or raspberry liqueur to the fruit if you wish. Assemble the squares just before serving.

Have ready an unbuttered baking sheet.

Roll out into a 17 x 13-inch rectangle, 1/16 to 1/8 inch thick:

1 pound Food Processor Puff Pastry, 908

Transfer the pastry to the baking sheet. Prick it all over with a fork. Cover and refrigerate for at least 30 minutes or wrap airtight and freeze until ready to use.

If the dough is frozen, let it thaw for a few minutes before cutting. Quickly transfer the dough to a cutting board, trim ½ inch from all the sides to make a 16 x 12-inch rectangle, and cut into twelve 4-inch squares. Return it to the baking sheet, separating the squares slightly. Refrigerate while the oven preheats.

Position a rack in the lower third of the oven. Preheat the oven to 400°F.

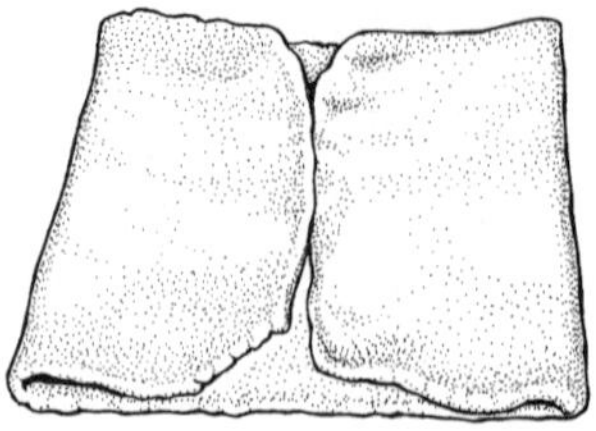

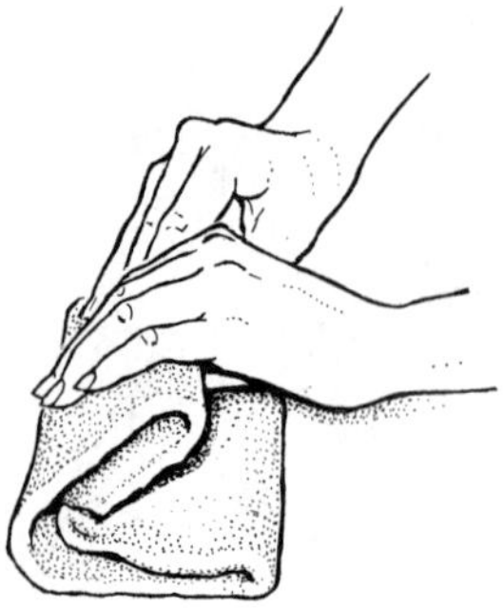

Puff pastry: double fold for second, third, and fourth turns.

Invert a wire rack directly on the surface of the dough to prevent it from rising high in the oven while baking but to allow it to cook through. Bake until golden brown, 20 to 25 minutes. After 10 minutes of baking time, remove the rack, prick the pastry all over, replace the rack, and finish baking. Remove the rack for the final 2 to 3 minutes' baking time to dry and cook the top layers. Slide the pastries onto a rack that is not hot and let cool to room temperature.

Mix gently and let macerate for 10 minutes:

3 cups berries (any combination of blackberries, sliced strawberries, raspberries, or blueberries)
3 tablespoons sugar
2 tablespoons fresh orange juice

Place 6 puff pastry squares on plates. Divide the berry mixture among the pastries. Top with:

1 cup crème fraîche or whipped cream

Sprinkle the tops of the remaining pastry squares with:

Powdered sugar

Place a pastry square askew on top of each napoleon. Serve immediately.

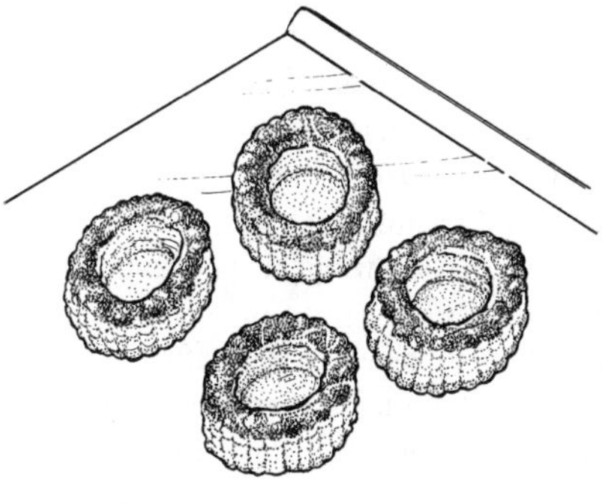

Bouchées

BANANA BOUCHÉES *6 servings*

Bouchées (mouthfuls) are individual patty shells—deep puff pastry shells baked and then filled with sweet or savory fillings. A large pastry of the same shape is called a vol-au-vent (flight in the wind) and is almost always savory. (Chicken à la King is traditionally served in one.) The banana filling here is heavenly.

Have ready an unbuttered baking sheet. You will also need two round pastry cutters, one 4 inches and the other 2 to 2½ inches.

Cut in half:

1 pound Food Processor Puff Pastry, 908

Refrigerate half of the puff pastry. Roll out the other half into a 13 x 9-inch rectangle, about ⅛ inch thick. Place the pastry on one side of an unbuttered baking sheet. Repeat with the second half of the dough and place on the other side of the baking sheet. Cover and refrigerate for at least 30 minutes, or wrap airtight and freeze until ready to use.

If the dough is frozen, let it thaw for a few minutes before cutting. Quickly transfer the pastry rectangles to a cutting board and, using a 4-inch round pastry cutter, cut six 4-inch circles from each rectangle; you will have 12 rounds. Using a 2- or 2½-inch round cutter, cut centers from 6 of the rounds to make rings. (Save the centers for another use.) Turn the whole 6 rounds upside down and return to the baking sheet. Lightly brush over the rounds:

1 large egg, lightly beaten

Turn the rings upside down and press them onto the rounds. Brush the rings with a little egg wash. With a fork, prick only the centers of the shells, not the rings. Cover and refrigerate while the oven preheats.

Position a rack in the lower third of the oven. Preheat the oven to 400°F.

Bake the shells until they begin to brown, about 10 minutes. To allow more space for the filling, deflate the centers again (and only the centers) by pricking them with a fork. Reduce the oven temperature to 350°F and continue to bake until golden, 15 to 20 minutes. Remove to a rack and let cool.

Just before serving, whip until soft peaks form:

½ cup heavy cream
2 tablespoons sugar
2 teaspoons dark rum (optional)
¼ teaspoon vanilla

Stir gently together in a separate bowl:

2 medium, ripe bananas, cut into ⅛- to ¼-inch dice
2 tablespoons light brown sugar
1 tablespoon dark rum
1 tablespoon fresh lime juice

Divide the banana mixture among the pastry shells. Spoon some of the whipped cream on top and off to one side. Or fold the banana mixture into the cream and spoon the banana cream into the shells. Serve immediately.

APPLE TURNOVERS *8 turnovers*

Called *chaussons aux pommes* in French, these classic pastries are a favorite Parisian snack. Golden Delicious, Braeburn, Fuji, and Gala are good apples to use here.

Have ready 2 unbuttered baking sheets.

Cut in half:

1 pound Food Processor Puff Pastry, page 908

Refrigerate half of the puff pastry. Roll out the other half into an 11-inch square, about ⅛ inch thick. Place

the pastry on a baking sheet. Repeat with the second half of the dough and place on the second baking sheet. Cover and refrigerate for at least 30 minutes, or wrap airtight and freeze until ready to use.
Cut into ¼-inch dice:

1 pound firm apples (about 3), peeled and cored

If the dough is frozen, let it thaw for a few minutes before trimming and cutting. Quickly transfer the pastry squares to a cutting board and trim ½ inch from all the sides to make two 10-inch squares. Cut each into four 5-inch squares (or circles if you prefer, using a cutter); you will have 8 squares. Turn each piece upside down. Toss well with the apples:

¼ cup sugar
1 teaspoon all-purpose flour
½ teaspoon ground cinnamon
¼ teaspoon fresh lemon juice
Pinch of salt

Spoon the apple mixture, dividing it equally, onto the center of the pastry squares. Lightly brush a ½-inch border on 2 adjacent edges of each pastry square with:

1 large egg, lightly beaten

Form a triangular turnover by folding the dry corner of the pastry over the apples to the egg-washed corner; press the corner and edges together with the flat tines of a fork to seal them. Brush the top of each turnover with egg wash. Cut 3 small slits in the top of each one. Arrange the turnovers at least 1 inch apart on the baking sheets. Refrigerate until firm, about 30 minutes.
Position a rack in the lower third of the oven. Preheat the oven to 400°F.
Bake the turnovers until they begin to brown, about 15 minutes Reduce the oven temperature to 350°F and bake until golden, about 20 minutes more. Serve warm. If you wish, accompany with:

Crème fraîche, whipped cream, or
Caramel Sauce Cockaigne, 1046

PALM LEAVES

48 small cookies

Palm leaves (*palmiers* in French) usually measure about 3 inches in diameter; when they are 5 to 6 inches across, they become elephant ears. We prefer the smaller ones, as they are more apt to be caramelized all the way through. Puff pastry scraps are ideal for this recipe.
Have ready 1 or 2 unbuttered baking sheets.
Measure:

1 to 1½ cups sugar

Roll out into a 12 x 5½-inch rectangle on a lightly sugared surface:

8 ounces Food Processor Puff Pastry, 908

Sprinkle about ¼ cup of the sugar over the dough and roll lightly with the rolling pin to embed the sugar. With the short edge closest to you, fold the dough into thirds, like a business letter. Turn the dough so the folded edge is on the left and the open edge is on the right (like a book about to be opened). Roll out into a 13 x 7-inch rectangle with one short edge facing you. Sprinkle about 2 tablespoons of the sugar over the dough and roll lightly with the rolling pin to embed the sugar. Fold each long side of the dough toward the center, leaving a ¼-inch space in the middle. Lightly brush the top of one folded side with:

1 large egg white, lightly beaten

Sprinkle the other folded side with about 1 tablespoon of the sugar. Fold the dough lengthwise in half, so that the sugared surface meets the egg white, and press the 2 halves together. Place the pastry on an unbuttered baking sheet. Cover and refrigerate the dough for at least 30 minutes, or wrap airtight and freeze until ready to use.
Position a rack in the lower third of the oven. Preheat the oven to 425°F. Butter the baking sheets generously.
If the dough is frozen, let it thaw for 5 to 10 minutes before cutting. Quickly transfer the dough to a cutting board. Spread some of the sugar in a shallow bowl. Cut the dough crosswise into ¼-inch-thick slices. Press one cut side of each slice into the sugar and place sugar side down and at least 3 inches apart on a baking sheet. If necessary, push each slice back into shape. Sprinkle sugar over the tops. If you wish, make the palm leaves in 2 batches. Bake for 5 minutes, until the cookies begin to brown around the edges. Sprinkle again with sugar. Turn each cookie over with metal spatula and sprinkle the second side with sugar. Bake until golden brown and caramelized all over, 2 to 5 minutes longer. Watch carefully, for the cookies burn quickly. Remove to a rack and let cool completely before serving.

Palm leaves

CINNAMON SUGAR STICKS

Prepare Cheese Straws, 152, substituting 6 tablespoons sugar mixed with 2 teaspoons ground cinnamon for the cheese and salt and ground black pepper. Before cutting the strips, sprinkle the top of the dough with sugar and roll to press it in. Cut twist, and bake until light brown, 10 to 15 minutes. These cook faster than the cheese straws because of the sugar, so watch carefully.

ABOUT CROISSANTS

Although *croissant* still suggests "breakfast in Paris" to many of us, its origins are actually Hungarian. In 1686, Hungarian bakers working the night shift to prepare morning pastries heard Turkish invaders tunneling under the city. Thanks to the bakers' warning, the Hungarian army was able to rally and defeat the Turks. The Hungarian government rewarded the bakers with a mandate to create a pastry in the shape of the crescent symbol on the Turkish flag. Soon all of Europe was nibbling on the symbol of Turkish defeat. *Croissant* is, of course, the French word for crescent. A croissant can be made plain or baked with a filling, such as jam, almond paste, or even a savory food such as ham. Filled with chocolate, it is called *pain au chocolat,* chocolate bread.

CROISSANTS DE BOULANGER

Eighteen 3½-inch-long croissants

If you wish, divide this recipe in half and use half to make croissants and half to make Pains au Chocolat, 914.

Place on a work surface:

¾ pound (3 sticks) cold unsalted butter

Measure:

3 tablespoons all-purpose flour

Sprinkle the butter with a little of the flour and begin to beat it with a rolling pin. Scrape the butter from the work surface and the rolling pin as needed and fold it over itself into a heap. Continue to work the butter until it is a smooth and malleable mass (without any hard lumps). Knead the remaining flour into the butter with your hands, working quickly to keep the butter cold. Place the butter on a sheet of plastic wrap and shape it into a 9 x 6-inch rectangle. Wrap and refrigerate the butter while you make the dough.

Whisk together and let stand until the yeast is dissolved, about 5 minutes:

1 cup warm (105° to 115°F) whole milk

2½ teaspoons active dry yeast

1 tablespoon sugar

Mix together in a large bowl:

2¾ cups all-purpose flour

1 teaspoon salt

2 tablespoons unsalted butter, softened and cut into small pieces

Make a well and add the warm milk mixture. Mix with a fork or your fingers to make a dough. Transfer to a lightly floured surface and knead for a few seconds until smooth. Let the dough stand for 5 minutes. Sprinkle the top of the dough with flour and roll into a 15½ x 8-inch rectangle, sprinkling additional flour underneath it as needed to prevent sticking. Position the dough so that one of the short ends is facing you. Cover the upper two-thirds of the dough with the rectangle of butter, leaving a 1-inch border of dough along the sides and at the top. Fold the bottom third of the dough over the butter. Fold the top third of the dough, with the butter on it, down over the first third, as if you were folding a business letter. Press the edges of the dough together on all 3 sides to seal in the butter. Rotate the dough so that the folded edge is on the left and the sealed edge on the right to change the direction of the pastry for the next roll.

Sprinkle the dough lightly with flour and press it gently with the rolling pin to flatten it slightly. Roll into an 18 x 8-inch rectangle, keeping the short side of the rectangle facing you. Fold the bottom third up and the top third down, as if folding a business letter. This rolling and folding is called a single turn. Rotate the dough so that the folded edge is on the left and the open edge is on the right (like a book about to be opened). Give the dough one more single turn, rolling it an 18 x 8-inch rectangle and folding it in thirds. (Sprinkle the work surface lightly with flour as needed to prevent the dough from sticking. If at any time the butter gets soft, refrigerate it for 10 to 15 minutes.) Mark the dough with 2 imprints to remind yourself that you have given the dough 2 turns. Wrap the dough loosely in plastic and refrigerate for 30 minutes.

Place the dough so the folded edge is on the left and the open edge is on the right, and give it another turn. Rotate and give the dough its final, fourth turn. If at any time the butter gets soft, refrigerate it for 10 to 15 minutes. When the 4 turns are completed, make 4 imprints to remind yourself that it is done, wrap the dough loosely in plastic, and refrigerate for 1 hour to overnight. (At this point the dough can also be frozen, wrapped in plastic, then aluminum foil, then in a plastic bag with the air removed. If frozen, thaw overnight in the refrigerator before proceeding.)

To Cut and Shape: Roll the dough into a 24 x 12-inch rectangle, about ¼ inch thick. Let stand for 5 minutes, to relax the gluten and prevent shrinkage when cut. Cut the dough lengthwise into two 24 x 6-inch rectangular strips. Refrigerate 1 rectangle. Position the remaining rectangle with one long side in front of you, parallel to the edge of the counter. Starting from the left, mark the

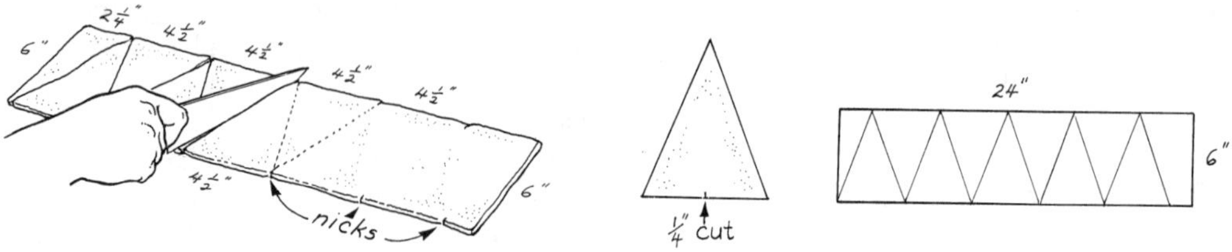

Cutting triangles for croissants

bottom edge of the dough by nicking it with a knife at 4½-inch intervals. Mark the top edge of the dough once 2¼ inches from the left edge, then continue to mark it at 4½-inch intervals. To cut the dough into triangles, cut from the bottom left corner of the dough to the first mark at the top, then from the first mark at the top to the first mark at the bottom, then from the first mark at the bottom to the second mark at the top, and so forth, until all 9 triangles are cut. In the middle of the shortest side of each triangle make a nick, ¼ inch long.

To form a croissant, stretch the short side of a triangle by pulling the corners gently as you begin to roll the stretched edge tightly (but not too tightly) toward the opposite point of the triangle. Finish rolling the croissant so that the point of the triangle is on the bottom of the roll. Shape the other croissants in the same manner. Repeat the cutting and shaping procedure with the second rectangle.

Place the croissants at least 2 inches apart on baking sheets, curving the ends to form crescent shapes. (Unbaked croissants can be refrigerated overnight; they will rise partially, for the yeast continues to work slowly in the chilled environment. Let them finish rising at room temperature before baking. They also can be frozen. Thaw overnight in the refrigerator before proceeding.) Cover the croissants with a towel or plastic wrap. Let rise at room temperature until increased in volume by almost half, 1 to 1½ hours.

To Bake the Croissants: Position a rack in the lower third of the oven. Preheat the oven to 375°F.

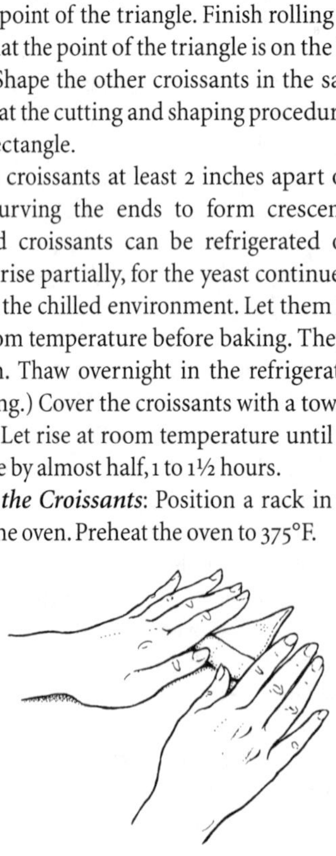

Rolling a croissant

Brush each croissant lightly with some of:

1 egg, lightly beaten

Bake on the unbuttered baking sheets until golden brown, 20 to 25 minutes. Transfer the croissants to the rack and let cool completely. Croissants are best served on the day they are baked.

RASPBERRY CROISSANTS

Any jam may be used in place of the raspberry jam—try apricot, blueberry, or black currant jam or apple-butter.

Prepare Croissants de Boulanger, above, placing 1½ teaspoons raspberry jam ¾ inch from the nick at the wide end of each triangle before rolling up the croissant. On the first roll, pinch around the jam to seal it in.

ALMOND CROISSANTS

Prepare Croissants de Boulanger, above, placing 1½ teaspoons almond paste ¾ inch from the nick at the wide end of each triangle before rolling up the croissant. After brushing with the egg wash, sprinkle the tops with sliced almonds.

PAINS AU CHOCOLAT

Twenty-four 3½-inch-long pains au chocolat

Little flaky rolls of croissant pastry filled with dark chocolate are a traditional *gouter* (teatime or afterschool snack) for schoolchildren all over France.

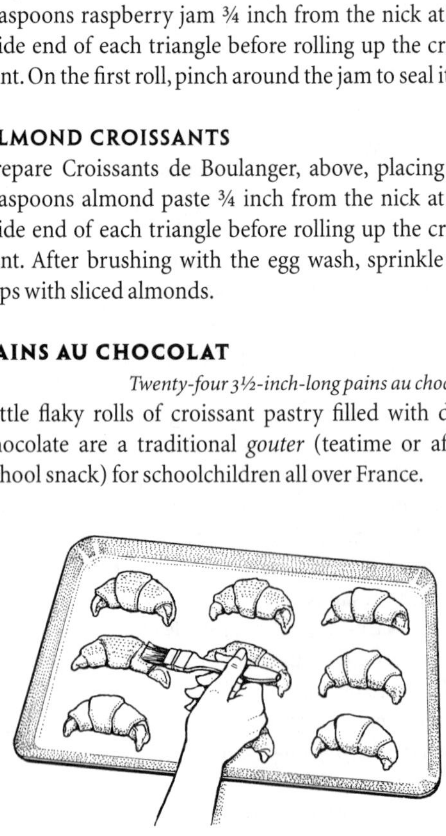

Crescent-shaped croissants

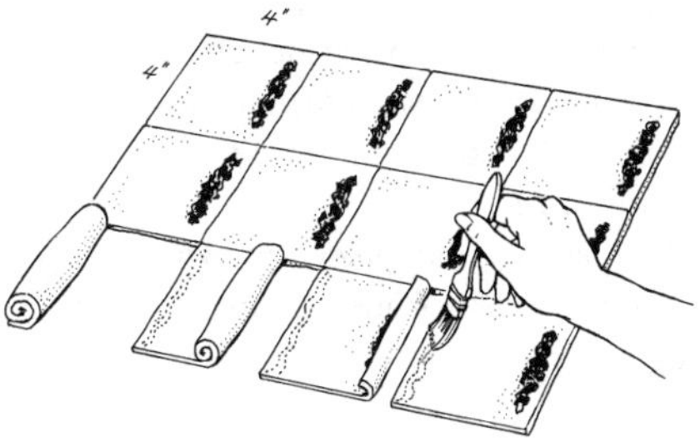

Cutting, filling, and shaping Pains au Chocolat

Have ready:

12 ounces semisweet or bittersweet chocolate, coarsely chopped, or 12 ounces large chocolate chips

Prepare the dough for:

Croissants de Boulanger, 913

Divide in half and refrigerate one half. Roll the other half into a 16 x 12-inch rectangle. Cut the rectangle into twelve 4-inch squares. Arrange ½ ounce of the chocolate in a 2-inch-long mound, parallel to and about ½ inch from one edge of each dough square. Lightly brush the opposite edge of the square with a ½-inch band of:

1 large egg, lightly beaten

Fold the edge of the dough closest to the chocolate over the chocolate and continue to roll the dough up to form a cylinder. Place the rolls seam side down at least 2 inches apart on baking sheets. Repeat with the remaining dough and chocolate. Let rise and bake as directed for Croissants de Boulanger, 913.

ABOUT DANISH PASTRY

This rich, buttery breakfast pastry—a cross between rich bread and buttery puff pastry—is a revelation, so much better than store-bought Danish as to seem like a different species altogether. Read About Making Layered Doughs, 906, before beginning, remembering in particular to refrigerate the dough if the butter becomes soft or if the dough is difficult to roll. The ideal temperature for letting dough rise is between 70° and 80°F. Danish pastry dough is egg-enriched and somewhat less flaky than croissant dough, but the procedure for making it is quite similar. Bake Danish pastries on unbuttered baking sheets, unless you are making filled, rolled, sliced ones—which are baked on their sides with the filling touching the baking sheet; in this case, butter is essential. Danish pastries are best eaten on the day they are baked.

DANISH PASTRY

About eighteen 3-inch pastries

Place on a work surface:

½ pound (2 sticks) cold unsalted butter

Measure:

2 tablespoons all-purpose flour

Sprinkle the butter with a little of the flour and begin to beat it with a rolling pin. Scrape the butter from the work surface and the rolling pin as needed and fold it over itself into a heap. Continue to work the butter until it is a smooth and malleable mass, without any hard lumps. Knead the rest of the flour into the butter with your hands, working quickly to keep the butter cold. Place the butter on a sheet of plastic wrap and shape it into an 8 x 5½-inch rectangle. Wrap and refrigerate the butter while you make the dough.

Whisk together and let stand until the yeast is dissolved, about 5 minutes:

½ cup warm (105° to 115°F) whole milk
2½ teaspoons active dry yeast
1 tablespoon sugar

Mix together:

2 cups plus 2 tablespoons all-purpose flour
2 tablespoons sugar
½ teaspoon salt
½ tablespoon unsalted butter, softened and cut into small pieces

Make a well and pour the yeast mixture into it. Mix lightly with a fork to form a thin batter in the well. Beat together and add to the well:

1 large egg
1 large egg yolk

Mix with a fork or your fingers to make a dough. Transfer to a lightly floured board and knead for a few seconds, until smooth. Let the dough stand for 5 minutes. Place the dough on a lightly floured work surface and sprinkle the top with flour. Roll out into a 14 x 8-inch rectangle, sprinkling additional flour underneath it as needed to prevent sticking. Position the dough so that one of the short ends is facing you. Cover the upper two thirds of the dough with the rectangle of butter, leaving a 1-inch border of dough along the sides and at the top. Fold the bottom third of the dough over the butter. Fold the top third of the dough, with the butter on it, down over the first third, as if you were folding a business letter. Press the edges of the dough together on all 3 sides to seal in the butter. Rotate the dough so that the folded edge is on the left and a sealed edge on the right to change the direction of the pastry for the next roll.

Sprinkle the dough lightly with flour and press it gently with the rolling pin to flatten it slightly. Roll into

a 16 x 8-inch rectangle, keeping the short side of the rectangle facing you. Fold the bottom third up and the top third down, as if folding a business letter. This rolling and folding is called a single turn. Rotate the dough so that the folded edge is on the left and the open edge is on the right (like a book about to be opened). Give the dough one more single turn, rolling it into a 16 x 8-inch rectangle and folding it in thirds. (Sprinkle the work surface lightly with flour as needed to prevent the dough from sticking. If at any time the butter gets soft, refrigerate it for 10 to 15 minutes.) Mark the dough with 2 imprints, to remind yourself that you have given the dough 2 turns. Wrap the dough loosely in plastic wrap and refrigerate for 30 minutes.
Give the dough 2 more single turns, always making sure that the folded edge is on the left and the open edge is on the right before beginning the next roll. Make 4 imprints, wrap in plastic, and refrigerate for 30 minutes. Give the dough a final single turn, imprint it with 5 marks, wrap, and refrigerate it for at least 30 minutes. (At this point the dough can be frozen or refrigerated overnight. Before freezing, wrap in plastic, then aluminum foil, then airtight in a plastic bag. Thaw overnight in the refrigerator before rolling.)

RASPBERRY DANISH PINWHEELS

Eighteen 3-inch pastries

Have ready an unbuttered baking sheet.
Roll out into an 18 x 9-inch rectangle:

½ recipe Danish Pastry, 915

Cut into eighteen 3-inch squares. Lightly brush the squares with:

1 large egg, lightly beaten

Dollop each center with:

1 teaspoon raspberry jam

Make a 1½-inch slit from each corner toward the center. Starting at the bottom left, fold one corner of each triangle to the center and press it down, forming a pinwheel.
Sprinkle with:

Sugar

Place the pinwheels 2 to 3 inches apart on the baking sheet. Let the Danish rise until puffy, 30 to 60 minutes.
Position a rack in the lower third of the oven. Preheat the oven to 375°F.
Bake the pastries until golden brown, 20 to 30 minutes. Remove to a rack and let cool completely before serving.

PRUNE OR APRICOT DANISH

Eighteen 3-inch pastries

Have ready an unbuttered baking sheet.
Place in a saucepan and bring to a boil:

8 ounces dried prunes or dried apricots, cut in half
1 cup water or cider
¼ cup sugar
Pinch of salt

Reduce the heat and simmer until the prunes are very soft, 20 to 30 minutes. (Some fruits are drier than others—add more liquid and cook a bit longer if necessary to soften.) Stir in:

2 tablespoons lemon juice
2 tablespoons Armagnac or Cognac (optional)

Transfer to a blender or food processor and puree. Remove to a small bowl. Prepare:

Raspberry Danish Pinwheels, above

without cutting slits in the dough squares and substituting the prune filling for the jam. Place a scant tablespoon of prune or apricot filling in the center of each square in place of jam. Gather up the 4 corners of the dough and pinch together above the filling. Place the pastries 2 to 3 inches apart on the baking sheet. Let rise until puffy, 30 to 60 minutes.
Position a rack in the lower third of the oven. Preheat the oven to 375°F.
Bake the pastries until golden brown, 20 to 30 minutes. Remove to a rack and let cool completely before serving.

CREAM-CHEESE DANISH SPIRALS

Sixteen 3½-inch pastries

Have ready a buttered baking sheet.
Beat until smooth:

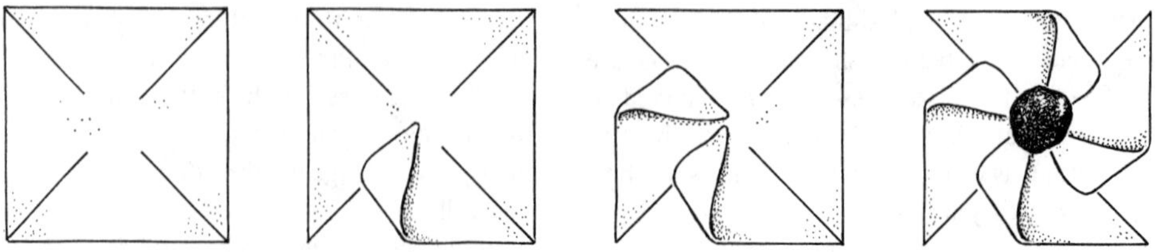

Forming pinwheels

6 ounces cream cheese, softened
¼ cup sugar

Add and stir until blended:

1½ teaspoons ground cinnamon (optional)
1½ tablespoons heavy cream

Roll out into a 17 x 12-inch rectangle:

½ recipe Danish Pastry, 915

Spread the cream cheese mixture evenly over the dough, leaving a ¼-inch border on all sides. Roll the dough into a log, starting at one long edge. Place the log seam side down on a baking sheet and freeze for 15 minutes. Place the log on a cutting board and trim the ends by ½ inch. Cut the log into sixteen 1-inch-thick slices, wiping the knife clean between cuts if necessary. Arrange the slices cut side down 2 to 3 inches apart on the baking sheet. Tuck the ends underneath. Let the Danish rise until puffy, 30 to 60 minutes.

Position a rack in the lower third of the oven. Preheat the oven to 375°F.

Lightly brush the Danish with:

1 large egg, lightly beaten

Bake the pastries until golden brown, 20 to 30 minutes. Remove to a rack. While the pastries are still hot, stir together and brush over the tops:

3 tablespoons powdered sugar
1 teaspoon water

Let cool completely before serving.

ABOUT STRUDEL AND PHYLLO DOUGH

In puff pastry or Danish pastry dough, the layers are formed within the dough itself; strudel and phyllo (or filo) doughs are first rolled into tissue-thin, almost transparent sheets, which are layered when the pastry is constructed. Strudel dough is usually formed into a single large sheet, covered with filling, and rolled; phyllo sheets are smaller and are stacked, often with filling between them. Both emerge crispy and golden from the oven, with a multitude of thin layers. If you are not concerned with authenticity, you can use strudel and phyllo doughs interchangeably.

APPLE STRUDEL

10 to 12 servings

The strudel can be formed, wrapped tightly in buttered aluminum foil, and frozen for up to 2 months before baking, but the pastry will lose crispness. We added some cider vinegar to the dough (a secret imparted by Deidre Davis), which yields a very tender strudel.

Cover a table at least 3 feet square with a cloth or sheet. Make sure there is enough room to walk around the table. Do not flour the cloth.

Melt and set aside in a small bowl:

8 tablespoons (1 stick) unsalted butter

Sift together in a large bowl:

1½ cups all-purpose flour
½ teaspoon salt

Make a well in the center of the flour mixture. Whisk together, then pour into the well:

1 large egg
⅓ cup room-temperature water
1 tablespoon of the melted butter
1 teaspoon cider vinegar

Working from the inside of the well, mix the wet ingredients quickly into the dry ingredients with your fingers or a fork. When all the liquid is incorporated, knead the dough on a lightly floured work surface until it is silky, pliable, and no longer sticky, about 10 minutes. Form the dough into a ball and brush with some of the melted butter. Let rest in a covered bowl in a warm place for 30 to 60 minutes.

Cut into wedges, then slice crosswise into ¼-inch pieces (about 6 cups):

6 medium, tart, dry apples such as Gravenstein, Braeburn, Gala, or Fuji, peeled and cored

Preheat the oven to 350°F. Toast in a cake pan in the oven until browned, 10 to 15 minutes:

¾ cup coarse fresh breadcrumbs

Remove half of the breadcrumbs to a medium bowl. Add and stir together:

1 cup sugar
½ cup walnuts, toasted and finely chopped
⅓ cup currants
1 tablespoon grated lemon zest
2 teaspoons ground cinnamon

Increase the oven temperature to 400°F. Butter a baking sheet.

Roll the dough as thinly as possible before transferring it to the cloth-covered table. Lightly flour the surface as you roll the dough only as necessary; try rolling it without flour. The dough will be soft and responsive to the touch. Remove any rings and drape the edges of the dough over the backs of your hands (palms downward and fingers halfway clenched). Stretch the dough gently at the table, pulling it away from the center and moving your hands apart at the same time. Stretch one section of the dough at a time and work slowly around the table. Take your time; patience will reward you with a thinner dough. Try not to tear the dough or make holes in it. Stretch the dough into a square, 30 to 35 inches each side, letting it drape over the edge of the table if it is bigger. Anchor the corners of the dough with a small plate if the square stretches back a bit

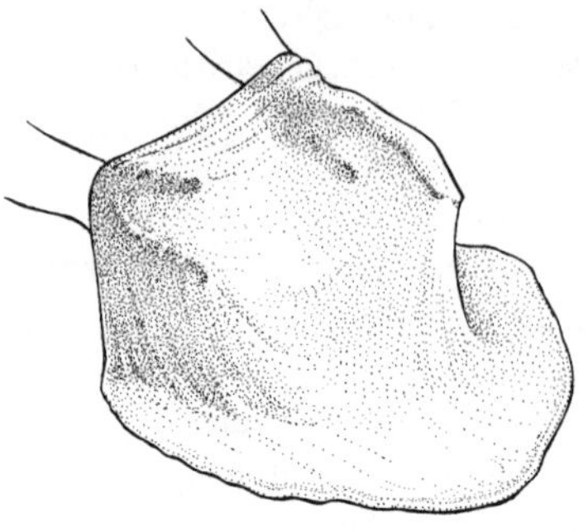

Drape the edges of the strudel dough over the backs of your hands.

while you work on the other edges. Trim the thicker edges of dough with scissors and use the trimming to patch any holes if needed. Let the dough stand and dry for 10 minutes so that it will not stick to itself during rolling.

Brush the entire surface of the dough gently with some of the melted butter. Leaving a 3-inch border of dough along one edge, sprinkle the remaining toasted breadcrumbs in a strip next to the border, covering one third of the dough. The remaining two thirds of the dough will form the layers. Mix the apples with the sugar mixture. Again leaving the 3-inch border of dough along the edge, spread the apple filling over the crumbs. Keep the filling together. Fold the 3-inch border over the filling. Pick up one end of the cloth underneath the strudel with both hands, one on either side, and let the strudel roll slowly over onto itself. It should not be tightly rolled. Continue to lift the cloth underneath the strudel and let the strudel roll onto itself to the end.

Place the rolled strudel on the prepared baking sheet, curving it into a horseshoe shape. Brush the strudel with two-thirds of the remaining melted butter. Bake for 20 minutes. Brush with the remaining butter. If necessary, rotate the strudel in the oven for even coloring. Bake until the strudel is golden brown, 20 to 25 minutes more. Slide onto a rack and let cool completely.

Dust the strudel with:

Powdered sugar

Slice on a diagonal with a serrated knife. Strudel is best served on the day it is made. You can freeze baked strudel; after thawing, reheat it in a 350°F oven for 15 to 20 minutes.

ABOUT PHYLLO

Phyllo, literally leaf in Greek, can be made by hand, but we do not recommend it; it is an arduous and tricky process that yields results no better than what is commercially available frozen in most grocery stores or fresh from Greek and Middle Eastern bakeries. Store-bought phyllo is easy to work, but it is essential to keep the thin sheets from drying out. If using frozen phyllo, thaw it slowly, without unwrapping, in the refrigerator for several hours or overnight. Once it is thawed, unwrap the phyllo and remove only the number of sheets required for the recipe; rewrap the remaining sheets in plastic wrap and return them to the refrigerator or freezer. Stack the sheets to be used on a tray or a sheet of plastic wrap, cover the stack with a sheet of plastic wrap, and cover the wrap with a damp towel. (Do not allow the damp towel to touch the phyllo, or it will dissolve into paste.) A sheet of phyllo left uncovered dries out in just a minute and will crack when you try to use it. Remove from the covered stack only the number of sheets of phyllo immediately called for and quickly re-cover the stack before proceeding.

BAKLAVA

About 30 squares or diamonds

Baklava is a dessert of Turkish origin, dating from the fifteenth century, today popular also in Greece and throughout the Middle East. Layered with nuts and drenched in sugar syrup (traditionally scented with orange- or rose-flower water) or honey, it is the best known of all phyllo pastries. In Greece it was originally an Easter specialty, made with 40 layers of pastry representing the 40 days of Lent. Chopped nuts are the traditional filling, but dried fruits, sesame seeds, coconut, or pineapple may be substituted for a nontraditional version.

Preheat the oven to 325°F. Butter the bottom and sides of a 13 x 9-inch baking pan.

Finely chop or coarsely grind:

3 cups coarsely chopped nuts (walnuts, pistachios, almonds, and/or pecans), toasted

Stir together in a small bowl:

¼ cup sugar
1 teaspoon grated lemon zest
½ teaspoon ground cinnamon

Melt:

½ pound (2 sticks) unsalted butter

Stack flat on a work surface:

1 pound phyllo dough

Trim the phyllo into 13 x 9-inch sheets, saving the scraps for another use. Cover the stack with plastic wrap and a damp towel. Place 2 phyllo sheets in the baking pan and brush the top sheet evenly with the melted butter. Add 2 more sheets and brush with the butter, then repeat once more for a total of 6 sheets. Sprinkle with half of the nuts and then half of the sugar mixture. Cover the filling with 2 phyllo sheets, butter the top sheet, and repeat until there are 6 sheets on top of the filing. Cover with the remaining nuts and sugar mixture. Cover with all of the remaining phyllo sheets, adding them 2 at a time and buttering only the second sheet each time. Brush the top with the remaining butter. Using a sharp serrated knife so that the pastry will not be crushed, cut through all of the layers to make 2-inch diamonds or squares. This is important because you will not be able to cut the baklava once it is baked without crushing the pastry; it also allows the syrup to soak in and around each piece. Bake for 30 minutes. Reduce the oven temperature to 300°F. Continue to bake until the baklava is golden brown, 45 to 60 minutes. During the last 30 minutes of baking, combine in a saucepan:

1⅓ cups sugar
1⅓ cups water
⅓ cup honey
1 tablespoon fresh lemon juice
Zest of 1 orange, removed in large strips

Bring the mixture to a gentle boil, reduce the heat, and simmer, uncovered, for 15 minutes. Strain the hot syrup and pour evenly over the baked baklava. Let cool completely, at least 4 hours, at room temperature before serving.

PHYLLO CUPS WITH RASPBERRIES AND PISTACHIO CREAM

6 servings

Individual phyllo cups are versatile. To maintain their crispness, fill them just before serving with ice cream and sauce, mousse, pudding or custard, or fruit. Baked unfilled phyllo cups can be stored in an airtight container for up to 2 days before using.

Position a rack in the lower third of the oven. Preheat the oven to 350°F. Butter the insides and the rims of 6 large muffin cups.

Melt:

4 tablespoons (½ stick) unsalted butter

Measure:

¼ cup sugar

Stack flat and cover with plastic wrap and a damp towel:

4 sheets phyllo dough

Place 1 sheet of phyllo on a work surface. Brush the sheet evenly with one quarter of the melted butter and sprinkle 1 tablespoon of the sugar evenly over it. Cover with a second sheet of phyllo and butter and sugar put on in the same manner. Repeat until all 4 sheets of phyllo have been used, ending with a layer of butter and sugar. Cut the stack of phyllo sheets into twelve 4½-inch square stacks (3 strips down and 4 across). Place 1 square stack in 1 muffin cup, easing it in with the backs of your fingers so that it covers half the bottom and rises to hang over the side of the cup. Ease in a second stack, slightly overlapping the first, to cover the other half of the muffin cup. Repeat to make 5 more phyllo cups. Bake until the pastry is golden brown, 10 to 15 minutes. Let cool completely, then carefully remove from the muffin cups.

Whip until almost stiff:

⅓ cup heavy cream
⅓ cup sour cream
2 tablespoons sugar
¼ teaspoon vanilla

Fold in:

¼ cup pistachios, toasted and chopped

Just before serving, place a phyllo cup on each of 6 plates. Divide the pistachio cream between the cups. Divide and top with:

3 cups fresh raspberries

Serve immediately.

ABOUT CHOUX PASTE (PÂTE À CHOUX)

Choux is French for "cabbages," and these little dollops of puff paste indeed expand in the oven to resemble tiny cabbage heads. Choux paste can be formed into a variety of shapes and filled with an even greater variety of fillings and creams. It is the basis for cream puffs and éclairs. Cream puffs filled with ice cream and cloaked in chocolate sauce are called profiteroles. Unsweetened choux paste is baked and filled with savory fillings, or mixed with cheese and baked to make simple or fancy hors d'oeuvres such as *gougères*, 162.

Like other pastry doughs, choux paste consists of flour, butter, and water. Unlike others, it is cooked on top of the stove before it is shaped and baked, with milk added for color and richness, and it is leavened primarily with eggs. (Choux paste to be used with savory fillings is often made with chicken stock or a mixture of chicken stock and water as the liquid.) The cooked flour paste must be allowed to cool slightly before the eggs are added to prevent the eggs from cooking prematurely, but if the paste is too cold when the eggs are added, they will not blend in smoothly. The finished paste should be shiny, smooth, and very thick but not stiff.

Choux paste can be made by hand or with an electric mixer. Bake small puffs, profiteroles, and éclairs on ungreased baking sheets. Larger puffs or large éclairs are easier to remove when baked on greased and floured sheets. After piping the choux paste onto the sheets, lightly glaze with an egg wash, taking care to keep the egg from touching the baking sheet (which would inhibit rising). The paste is baked in a hot oven for the first few minutes to cause quick expansion; the temperature is then reduced to finish the baking and dry out the hollow shells.

If you wish to further dry out the shells and allow more room for the filling, turn off the oven and let the puffs dry for about 10 minutes. For small puffs and éclairs, pop them off the sheets, poke a small hole in the bottoms (or ends for éclairs) with a skewer or the tip of a small, sharp knife, and turn them upside down on the sheets for drying. For larger shapes and rings, slide a spatula under the shapes to loosen them and poke them in a few places on the sides. Or slice off the tops horizontally, place the tops upside down on the baking sheet, remove any soft dough inside, and let the puffs dry and crisp. Let the puffs cool on racks.

To fill the puffs, use the hole that you have poked and fill the cooled puffs with pastry cream or whipped cream. If using pastry cream, fill a pastry bag fitted with a ¼-inch tip or spoon the cream into open puffs. If using whipped cream, pipe it into open puffs with a huge star tip for an attractive presentation or spoon it in. Whipped cream does not retain its texture when piped through a small tip.

Once baked and filled, choux pastries should be served immediately or refrigerated and served within a few hours. However, unfilled baked shells can be frozen for up to 1 week in an airtight container.

ABOUT FORMING CHOUX PASTE

Choux paste can be piped into almost any shape or size with a pastry bag or spooned out in simple round shapes.

Fit a pastry bag with a ½-inch plain tip for small shapes and a 1-inch plain tip for large shapes. Pipe or spoon shapes 2 inches apart as follows:

Miniature éclairs: pipe logs 2½ inches long and ½ to ¾ inch wide or spoon and shape into logs
Large éclairs: pipe logs 5 inches long and 1½ inches wide or spoon and shape into logs
Profiteroles: pipe puffs 1 inch wide and 1 inch high or spoon out a scant tablespoon each
Cream puffs: pipe puffs 2½ inches wide and 1 inch high or spoon out ¼ cup each

To use a pastry bag, fit a pastry tip in the bottom of the bag. Twist and stuff the bottom of the bag into the tip to prevent the choux paste from leaking out before you are ready to pipe. If you are right-handed, hold the bag in your left hand (if you are left-handed, use the opposite hand throughout). Fold the top 3 to 4 inches of the pastry bag down over your hand like a cuff. Scoop the choux paste into the bag, filling it no more than two-thirds full. (You can also place the bag in a 2-cup glass measure, leaving both hands free to fill the bag.) Unfold the cuff and squeeze the bag to push the choux paste toward the tip. Twist the top part of the bag. Unstuff the lower part of the bag from the tip and push the paste farther into the tip.

To pipe round shapes for profiteroles or cream puffs, hold the bag with the tip at a 90-degree angle to the baking sheet. To pipe logs for éclairs, hold the bag with the tip at a 45-degree angle. With the tip of the bag just above the pan, squeeze gently and evenly with your right hand while guiding the tip of the bag with your left hand. Use gentle pressure to form a shape no wider than the width of the tip; use greater pressure and move the bag slower for thicker shapes. (You can practice piping different shapes and return the paste to the bag to be reused.)

To stop piping, release pressure from the bag before lifting the tip, then push the tip down and quickly jerk it upward to end the shape without a tail. Pipe shapes about 2 inches apart to allow for expansion. After piping all the shapes, eliminate tails, if any, and smooth out the points with a finger dipped in cold water. As the bag is depleted, slide your hand forward, pressing the paste toward the tip.

If you do not have a tip the right size, measure the small opening of the pastry bag. Some types of pastry bags can be cut to a specific size opening; others are hemmed with an opening of about 1 inch. If your bag is close to ½ or 1 inch or can be cut to size, simply use the bag without a tip it to pipe the paste. If you don't have a pastry bag, snip off the corner of a plastic bag and use it to shape the paste. Alternatively, spoon out shapes and smooth them with a finger dipped in cold water.

CHOUX PASTE

About 2½ cups

Position a rack in the lower third of the oven. Preheat the oven to 400°F.

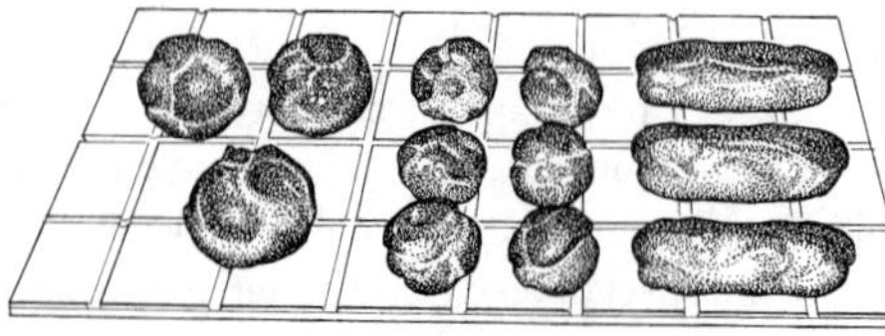

Round and log-shaped choux

Measure:

1 cup sifted all-purpose flour

Combine in a large saucepan:

½ cup water
½ cup whole milk
8 tablespoons (1 stick) unsalted butter, cut into small pieces
½ teaspoon salt

Bring the mixture to a full boil over medium heat. Add the flour all at once and stir vigorously with a wooden spoon until the mixture pulls away from the sides of the pan. Continue to cook and stir the mixture for about 1 minute, to eliminate excess moisture. The butter may ooze out, which is fine; it simply means that the moisture is evaporating. Transfer to a bowl and let cool for 5 minutes, stirring occasionally. Beat in 1 at a time by hand, with a wooden spoon, or on low speed with a mixer:

4 large eggs

Make sure that the paste is smooth before adding the next egg. Beat the dough until it is smooth and shiny. Choux paste can be covered and refrigerated for up to 4 hours. When it is cold, you do not need to bring the paste to room temperature before shaping.

CHOCOLATE ÉCLAIRS

8 to 10 large or about 48 miniature éclairs

Position a rack in the lower third of the oven. Preheat the oven to 400°F. Butter and flour a baking sheet if making large éclairs or have ready 2 unbuttered baking sheets if making miniature éclairs.

Prepare:

1 recipe Choux Paste, 920

Scoop the paste into a large pastry bag fitted with a 1-inch tip for large éclairs or a ½-inch tip for miniatures. Shape the paste into 8 to 10 large or 24 miniature éclairs, as directed in About Forming Choux Paste, 920. Bake the éclairs for 15 minutes. Reduce the oven temperature to 350°F and bake until golden brown and very firm to the touch, 10 to 15 minutes more for miniatures or 25 to 30 minutes more for large éclairs. Turn off the oven, poke the short end of the éclairs, and let dry in the oven for 10 minutes. (Read About Choux Paste, 919, for more drying information.) Remove the éclairs to a rack and let cool completely.

Prepare:

3 cups Pastry Cream, 996, or lightly sweetened whipped cream

Fill a pastry bag fitted with a ¼-inch tip with the pastry cream. Poke the pastry tip into the drying hole in each eclair and pipe full. Or cut off the top third of the éclairs horizontally with a serrated knife for the lids. Remove any uncooked dough and spoon the filling into the éclairs. This method works best for whipped cream. Dip the top of each éclair (either the lids or the whole éclair) into:

Bittersweet Chocolate Glaze or Frosting, 1003, or Chocolate Ganache Glaze or Frosting, 1003

Replace the tops on the cut éclairs. Refrigerate the éclairs, chocolate side up, until the glaze is set or until ready to serve. Éclairs are best on the day they are made.

CREAM PUFFS

15 puffs; 6 servings

These larger shells are a very quick way to make an attractive dessert. Fill just before serving, set the tops slightly askew, and dust with powdered sugar.

Position a rack in the lower third of the oven. Preheat the oven to 400°F. Have ready an unbuttered baking sheet.

Prepare:

½ recipe Choux Paste, 920

Scoop the paste into a pastry bag fitted with a ½-inch plain tip. Shape the paste into 15 puffs on the baking sheet, as directed in About Forming Choux Paste, 920. Bake the puffs for 15 minutes. Reduce the oven temperature to 350°F and continue to bake until golden brown and very firm to the touch, 20 to 25 minutes more. Turn off the oven. Poke the bottom of each puff, turn upside down on the baking sheet, and let dry in the oven for 10 minutes. (Read About Choux Paste, 919, for more drying information.) Remove to a rack and let cool to room temperature.

Prepare:

2 cups lightly sweetened whipped cream, flavored or plain, or Pastry Cream, vanilla or another flavor, 996 to 997

Slice the tops from the puffs, remove any uncooked paste, and fill with the cream. Place the tops slightly askew and dust the puffs with:

Powdered sugar

PROFITEROLES

24 profiteroles; 6 servings

Vanilla is traditional, but any ice cream flavor or a combination can be used.

Position a rack in the lower third of the oven. Preheat the oven to 400°F. Have ready an unbuttered baking sheet.

Prepare:

½ recipe Choux Paste, 920

Scoop the paste into a pastry bag fitted with a ½-inch plain tip. Shape the paste into 24 profiteroles on the baking sheet, as directed in About Forming Choux Paste, 920. Bake the profiteroles for 15 minutes. Reduce the oven temperature to 350°F and continue to bake until golden brown and very firm to the touch, 10 to 15 minutes more. Turn off the oven. Poke the bottom of each profiterole, turn upside down on the baking sheet, and let dry in the oven for 10 minutes. (Read About Choux Paste, 919, for more drying information.) Remove to a rack and let cool to room temperature.

Prepare:

Chocolate Ganache Glaze or Frosting, 1003

Whisk the glaze until smooth. If desired, thin it with a little:

Heavy cream

Keep warm in the top of a double boiler (or reheat in a microwave just before serving).

To serve, slice the profiteroles horizontally in half. Remove any uncooked dough. Place 4 bottoms on each of 6 plates. Place a small scoop of:

Vanilla ice cream (24 scoops total)

in each bottom half. Cover with the top halves and drizzle with some of the chocolate glaze. Serve immediately with the remaining glaze on the side.

CAKES, TORTES & CUPCAKES

Baking a cake is culinary magic. Nowhere else in cooking is the transformation of a few simple ingredients so profound and so appreciated. Happily, baking can be learned from a book. The rewards are great. The fame of many a host or hostess is built on "that great cake."

Baking has the reputation of being more difficult than cooking—the specter of chemistry frightens some people. And baking *is* different from cooking. A great cook may create dishes intuitively, almost casually, working with what is in the larder and refrigerator, tasting and correcting the work in progress. A great cake baker is attentive to technique, details, and timing. Unable to taste, correct, and create along the way, the baker is a stickler for measurements, insistent on proper pan sizes, and fussy about the temperature of everything from the oven to the butter. Because the same ingredients combined in a different order, mixed differently, or even used at different temperatures result in quite different cakes (or failures), good bakers are dedicated to the small things that produce beautiful cakes that taste heavenly.

ABOUT CAKE PANS

Sturdy medium-weight aluminum pans with dull surfaces or professional pans made of tinned steel are best for cakes. Avoid stainless steel, which does not conduct heat evenly. Heavy dark metal and glass pans absorb and hold more heat, resulting in heavy, dark crusts. If you bake in these pans, reduce the oven temperature by 25 degrees and expect the baking time to be approximately the same. Pan materials do affect baking time, so always check cakes early to be safe.

Layer cake pans work best if they have straight sides and are filled no more than one-half to two-thirds full. Loaf and tube pans can be filled a little fuller.

The results predicted in each recipe will be achieved only by using the pan size(s) specified in each recipe. If you bake in a larger pan, you will have a thinner cake that will bake in less time; if the sides of the pan are too tall, it may not brown well. If you bake in a pan that is much too small, you will have a coarse-textured cake or one that overflows the pan.

If you do not have a pan that corresponds to the size and shape called for in the recipe, see the chart, 925, to find a pan with a similar surface area (the same number of square inches). A recipe calling for a 9-inch round pan (about 64 square inches) can be baked in an 8-inch square pan (also 64 square inches). Note that a 9-inch round pan equals only about three-quarters of the area of a 9-inch square pan. A recipe that calls for two 9-inch layer pans can be baked in one 13 x 9-inch pan, but it will come out slightly higher than the layers (twice 64 inches is 128, while the 13 x 9-inch pan has an

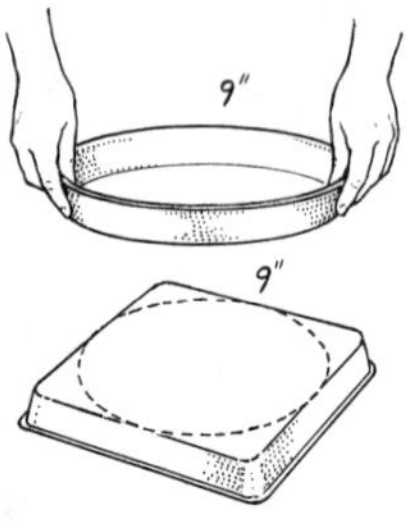

A 9-inch round pan equals about three-quarters of the area of a 9-inch square pan.

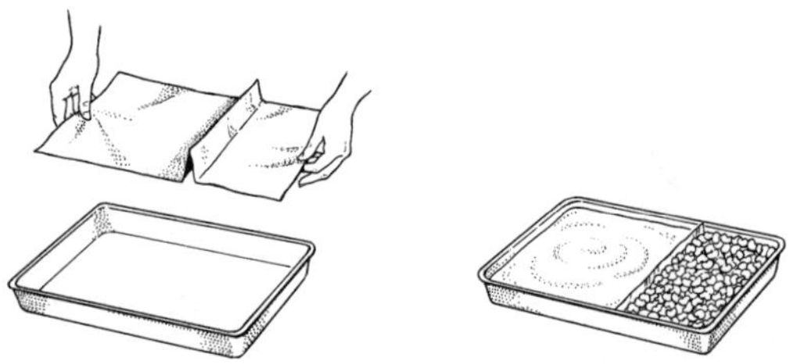

Reduce the pan size with an aluminum foil barrier, weighted on one side.

area of 117 inches). Should a square or rectangular pan be too large, you can reduce the size of it with a divider made of folded aluminum foil, shown above, right. The batter holds the divider in place on one side. Dried beans or rice can be used to weight the other side.

ABOUT PAN SIZES

Pans from different manufacturers differ in exact measurement, and pan capacities vary depending on whether the pan sides are straight or tapered. The chart measurements reflect the top inside dimensions of the pans or the sizes actually marked on the pans. The capacities are approximate.

To determine how much batter to mix for oddly shaped pans or molds, first measure their volume with water. Then make up two-thirds as much batter as the amount measured.

The texture of butter cakes, especially, varies with the depth of the batter in the pan. Thin layers baked in separate pans turn out with a lighter texture at best but are prone to drying out. The same cakes baked in loaf, Bundt, or tube pans are usually moister and more velvety textured. In spite of this, American home bakers are accustomed to dividing batters for layer cakes to make two to three very thin layers in separate pans. While this is acceptable so long as cakes are not overbaked, better results can be obtained from batters poured at least 1 inch deep in the pan. Professional bakers bake layer cakes in 2-inch-tall layer cake pans, filling them 1 to 1½ inches deep. The finished cakes, 1½ to 2 inches tall, are then cut horizontally into thin layers for layer cakes. You can duplicate this technique by, for example, filling a 9 x 2-inch round pan two-thirds full instead of dividing the batter between two or three shallower pans of the same diameter. Remember that the baking time for a deeper cake will be longer.

ABOUT PAN PREPARATION

Angel cakes, chiffon cakes, and most sponge cakes and tortes are baked in ungreased pans so that the batter can climb up and cling to the sides of the pan for support during baking and cooling. While most other types of cake are traditionally baked in greased or greased and floured pans, there is no imperative to do so for most layer cakes with flat bottoms and smooth sides. We prefer and recommend the simplicity of lining only the pan bottoms with wax or parchment paper. Once baked, the cake is released from the sides of the pan, as with angel and sponge cakes, with the use of a thin knife or metal spatula pressed close to the sides of the pan to avoid tearing the cake.

Except in rare cases, parchment paper does not need to be greased in order for it to release from a cake. However, jelly-roll pans can be lightly greased before lining with parchment simply to keep the parchment from slipping.

Bundt pans, fluted tubes, and decorative molds are another story. These must be prepared so that the cake will release perfectly without the aid of a knife, which would damage the cake's surface. The same is true for layer cakes that will not be iced on the sides. In these cases, bakers are divided in their preference for grease only or grease and flour. A floured pan produces a slight crust on the surface of the cake; a greased pan produces a tenderer surface.

For a greased pan, use vegetable oil spray or solid shortening applied in a thin layer with a piece of wax paper or a pastry brush, or even your fingers. Margarine does not release cakes as well as shortening does, and though the flavor of butter is superior, it does not always release perfectly.

For a greased and floured pan, sprinkle a tablespoon or so of flour into a greased pan and tap and rotate the pan until the greased surfaces are completely and evenly coated. Invert the pan over the sink or another

ROUND LAYER PANS AND SPRINGFORM PANS WITH STRAIGHT SIDES

SIZE	SURFACE AREA IN SQUARE INCHES	CAPACITY
6 x 2 inches	28	4 cups
8 x 2 inches	50	7 cups
8 x 2½- or 8 x 3-inch springform	50	9 to 10 cups
9 x 2 inches	63	9 cups
9 x 2½- or 9 x 3-inch springform	63	11 to 13 cups
10 x 2 inches	79	11 cups
10 x 2½- or 10 x 3-inch springform	79	14 to 16 cups
12 x 2 inches	113	16 cups
14 x 2 inches	154	22 cups

SQUARE, RECTANGULAR, AND JELLY-ROLL PANS WITH STRAIGHT OR TAPERED SIDES

SIZE	SURFACE AREA IN SQUARE INCHES	CAPACITY
8 x 8 x 2 inches	64	8 to 9 cups
9 x 9 x 2 inches	81	10 to 12 cups
11 x 7 x 1½ inches	77	8 cups
13 x 9 x 2 inches	117	16 cups 15½
x 10½ x 1-inch jelly roll	163	10 cups
17½ x 11½ x 1-inch jelly roll	201	12 cups

LOAF PANS

SIZE	CAPACITY
5½ x 3⅛ x 2¼ inches	2½ cups
7½ x 3¾ x 2¼ inches	4 cups
8½ x 4½ inches	6 cups
9 x 5 x 3 inches	8 cups
10 x 4 x 3 inches	7½ cups

PLAIN AND FLUTED TUBE PANS AND BUNDT OR KUGELHOPF PANS

SIZE	CAPACITY
6¼ x 3¼-inch fluted tube or Bundt	5 cups
8¼ x 3¼-inch fluted tube or Bundt	6 to 7 cups
8 x 4-inch fluted tube or Bundt	8 to 10 cups
10 x 3¾-inch fluted tube or Bundt	12 to 14 cups
9½ x 4¼-inch plain tube (angel cake pan)	17 cups
9¾ x 4¼-inch plain tube (angel cake pan)	19 cups

pan to be dusted and tap out the excess. Do not flour pans for cakes that will be cooled, stored, and served in the baking pan—flour coatings turn pasty when the cake is left in the pan.

If using nonstick pans, follow the manufacturer's suggestion; wax or parchment paper can still be used in the bottom.

ABOUT MEASURING AND SIFTING

Nowhere in cooking is accurate measuring as important as in baking. While some recipes are more forgiving than others, you will not achieve consistently excellent results in cake making with haphazard measurement. The most critical measurements are for flour, liquids, and leavenings, but if you wish to duplicate results from one time to the next, you will measure every ingredient accurately. Reduced-fat recipes are especially vulnerable: a little too much flour can transform a good cake into a dry, leaden one. Weighing ingredients on a scale is the easiest way to measure accurately. If you prefer to use measuring cups, be sure to sift flour before measuring when sifted flour is called for, because 1 cup of unsifted all-purpose flour weighs 5 ounces, while 1 cup of sifted all-purpose flour weighs only 4 ounces. Whether or not the recipe calls for sifted flour, do not pack the flour into the measuring cup—simply spoon it in lightly. For dry ingredients such as flour and sugar, use dry measuring cups in the exact increments you are measuring: a half-cup measure to measure ½ cup, a quarter-cup measure to measure ¼ cup, etc. Level the ingredients by sweeping a knife across the top of the cup. Measure small quantities of dry ingredients, such as leavenings, with measuring spoons, precisely leveled off; don't use your tableware. Use clear glass or plastic measuring cups marked off in increments for measuring liquids. Check the level of the liquid at eye level; looking down at the cup is not accurate. If we sound like fuddy-duddies, just taste our cakes!

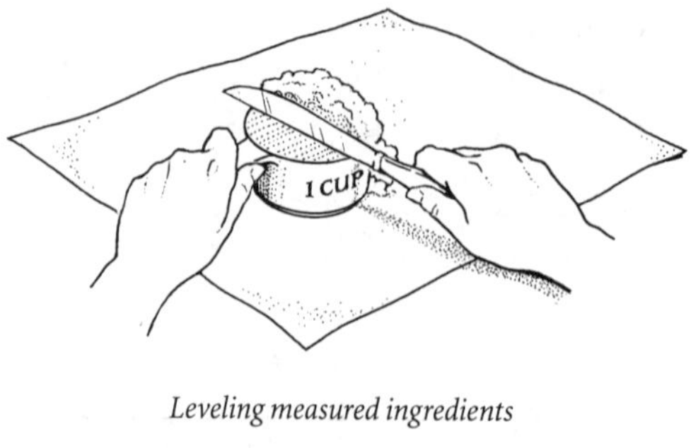

Leveling measured ingredients

Sifting flour accomplishes several aims, one of which is to render volume measurements more consistent by eliminating the difference between a canister of loosely packed flour and a sack of flour that the kids have been sitting on. When flour is measured after sifting (by sifting onto wax paper and pouring or spooning lightly into the cup before leveling), it makes no difference how packed or loose the flour was to start. If you measure flour by weight, you need not sift first (5 ounces of flour is 5 ounces of flour regardless of whether or not it has been sifted), but you may want to sift it after weighing in order to combine it with other dry ingredients and aerate it so that it mixes more easily into batters.

ABOUT THE TEMPERATURE OF INGREDIENTS

In general, all ingredients should be at room temperature (68° to 70°F), or at about 65°F in a very warm kitchen or hot climate. This is especially important with butter cake recipes, where the butter, liquid, and eggs are meant to form an emulsion during the mixing steps. Emulsions can break or curdle (like a sauce) if some ingredients are colder than the rest. When this happens, the batter loses its ability to trap air, and the cake will be heavy.

Butter should be cool and firm but malleable when squeezed, not soft and squishy. Butter that is too soft or melted will not trap air and will collapse with prolonged beating. Your fingers are the best guide. Butter of the proper consistency may range in temperature from 60° to 70°F.

Cold eggs cause problems in sponge and foam recipes, because they do not increase in volume as much as room-temperature or warm eggs when beaten. Cold eggs also spell trouble for chocolate recipes, as they are too cold to blend smoothly into melted chocolate or batters containing large quantities of melted chocolate.

Spur-of-the-moment bakers can transform cold dairy products into room-temperature ingredients quickly with judicious use of the microwave, a few seconds at a time, on low power. Break eggs and separate or beat them lightly before microwaving, and stir before checking the temperature each time. Liquids at 68° to 70°F feel quite cool, not warm, to the touch, and butter is malleable but firm. If you are not sure of what this temperature feels like, an inexpensive instant-read thermometer can be used to verify your judgment. Absent a microwave, place whole eggs or a bowl of broken eggs in a bowl of warm water to bring them to room temperature. Do the same for liquids.

Heavy-duty stand mixer

ABOUT MIXING

Whether you mix a cake by hand or with an electric mixer (often you will do both for the same recipe), mixing affects leavening and therefore the volume and texture of a cake. (For information on leaveners, see page 1074.) Different methods of mixing, creaming, stirring, beating, and folding are used for different ingredients and with different goals.

Mixing times and speeds given for electric mixers apply to most portable hand-held mixers with two beaters as well as to ordinary stand mixers. Heavy-duty or quasi-professional stand mixers are considerably more powerful, generally performing tasks in 25 to 75 percent less time and at lower speeds. Consult the owner's manual for details. When making cakes, do not use a blender or hand-held immersion blender (a light-duty portable mixer with only one beater) or a food processor in place of an electric mixer.

Times and speeds are given for many mixing tasks, to provide guidance for new cooks and bakers. However, the most important signals emanate from the bowl. Learning to bake is learning to recognize when egg yolks and sugar are thick and pale yellow or when butter beaten with sugar has lightened in color and texture, regardless of the clock or the mixer switch.

BEATING (CREAMING) THE BUTTER AND SUGAR UNTIL LIGHT

This is the essential first step in mixing many batters, from butter cakes and cookies to frostings: beating butter and sugar together until the mixture appears lighter in color and texture because of the incorporation of air. Well-creamed butter and sugar creates the initial structure of the batter, enabling the addition of other ingredients without causing that structure to collapse. Start with butter at 65° to 70°F for the proper friction necessary to beat air into the mixture without overly softening or melting it.

By Hand: Begin mashing the butter against the side of the bowl with a wooden spoon, using a rocking and sliding motion and keeping the butter in a limited area of the bowl, rather than spreading it all over the bowl, shown below. Scrape the mass together as necessary and repeat the mashing, sliding, and rocking motion until the butter is softened. Add the sugar gradually and work the butter and sugar together until the mixture is light in color and texture. It will look like sugary frosting. If it is curdled or frothy, you have worked it too long and the oil in the butter has separated. The result will be a coarse-grained cake. Correct the situation by refrigerating the mixture for 5 to 10 minutes before continuing to beat.

By Machine: Beat the butter at low speed for about 30 seconds until it is creamy. Add the sugar gradually and, if using a hand-held mixer, beat at high speed until the mixture is light in color and texture and resembles a sugary frosting. This usually requires from 3 to 7 minutes, depending on quantities. If using a heavy-duty mixer that offers a choice between a whisk and paddle, use the paddle and beat on medium speed for less time. If the mixture looks curdled or begins to ooze melted butter, you have mixed too long, or your ingredients were too warm. Correct the situation by refrigerating the mixture for 5 to 10 minutes before continuing to beat.

TO STIR INGREDIENTS INTO A BATTER

Stirring is used to incorporate dry and/or wet ingredients gently but thoroughly into another mixture, without overmixing or beating, which may toughen the mixture.

By Hand: Using a wooden spoon or rubber spatula, begin at the center of the bowl, mixing with a circular

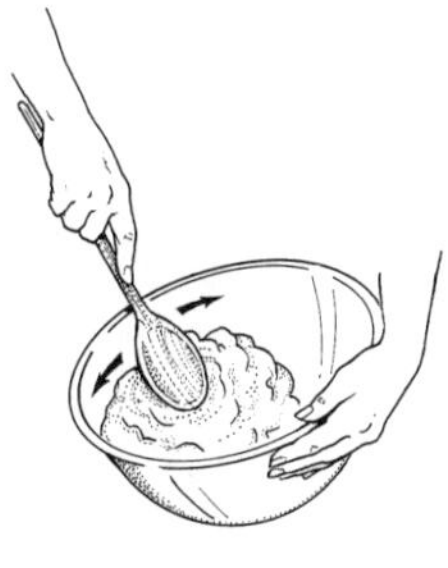

Mash the butter using a rocking and sliding motion.

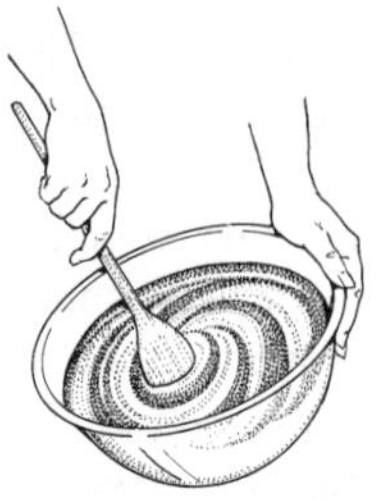

Stir ingredients in a circular motion.

motion in an ever-widening pattern as the ingredients become blended, shown above. Scrape the sides of the bowl from time to time as necessary.

By Machine: At low speed, mix just until the ingredients are smoothly blended. Do not overdo it. Scrape the sides of the bowl with a rubber spatula as necessary.

TO BEAT OR WHIP

Beating or whipping means to mix energetically with the goal of trapping air in the batter and increasing its volume.

By Hand: Use a long thin or balloon-shaped whisk for beating cream or egg whites; use a wooden spoon or rubber spatula for batters. Beat with a brisk sweeping motion that brings batter from the bottom to the top of the mass with every stroke, and lift the whisk or spoon up and out of the batter each time. Your wrist should move as though you were twirling a lasso, and you should hear the whisk or spoon striking the bottom of the bowl with each stroke, shown below. Increase your speed as you work.

By Machine: Beat on medium to high speed until the desired state, or smoothness, or volume is reached. If you have a choice of whip or paddle attachment on your mixer, choose the whip for egg whites and cream and the paddle for batters and doughs.

Beat or whip using a brisk sweeping motion.

HOW TO BEAT EGG WHITES

Egg whites can increase by as much as nine times in volume when beaten correctly, so choose a bowl large and deep enough. Avoid plastic bowls, which in spite of careful washing tend to retain a slight grease film, preventing the full volume from being achieved. Unlined copper bowls have a well-deserved reputation for turning out stable, voluminous whites, but they are costly and require scrubbing before each use with salt and white vinegar (one part to four parts), followed by rinsing and drying. For cooks without copper bowls, a pinch of cream of tartar (¼ teaspoon for every 4 whites) will help stabilize the foam. Always be sure that bowl, beater, and scraper are absolutely free of grease and detergent. If in doubt, wipe with lemon juice or vinegar, rinse, and dry carefully.

Egg whites can be beaten by hand or in an electric mixer. Do not use a blender or food processor. If beating by hand, be prepared to give your forearm a workout—about 300 strokes in 2 minutes for 2 egg whites. Using a thin-wired, flexible whisk, begin slowly and lightly with a very relaxed wrist motion and beat steadily until the egg whites lose their translucency and become foamy. At this point, gradually increase the beating tempo, using large hand motions to incorporate the maximum air, and continue without stopping until the whites are airy and have reached the desired stage of firmness. Follow the same principle with an electric mixer, starting on low speed and increasing speed as the whites become foamy and then begin to stiffen. When working with a hand-held mixer, push the beaters around the bowl, moving them up and *through* the whites to incorporate more air and similarly starting on low speed and progressing to high. The key to a successful egg foam is to stop beating when the eggs are stiff but not dry. Overbeating causes the whites to turn grainy and brittle, making it difficult to incorporate them into a batter without rupturing the air cells. To determine if the whites are beaten sufficiently, some cooks use the inverted bowl test: the whites should cling tenaciously to the bottom of the upside-down bowl. A less risky method is to lift your whisk or beater to check the condition of the peaks of the egg whites; the foam should be just stiff enough to stand up in well-defined, unwavering peaks. In the making of meringues and some cakes, sugar is beaten into the egg whites when they have reached the soft-peak stage. Add the sugar gradually to ensure that it will dissolve. Although sugar reduces volume slightly, it produces a sturdier foam.

Beaten egg whites do not hold up well, so start beating only when all other ingredients are mixed and ready. If the beaten egg whites are headed for the oven, have the oven preheated. To preserve their volume when incorporating them into a soufflé or batter, beaten whites need a firm but gentle hand. See How to Fold Egg Whties, below.

HOW TO FOLD EGG WHITES

Folding is a delicate technique used to mix or incorporate ingredients thoroughly into a batter without deflating either the batter or the ingredients or mixture folded into it. It is always done by hand, with a rubber spatula, rather than with a mixer. Cut down into the center of the batter and sweep the spatula up the side of the bowl, scooping up batter from the bottom of the bowl and bringing it to the top. Repeat the folding stroke, giving the bowl a partial turn after each, until the batter is uniform, shown below. Folding beaten egg whites into a batter is required in many recipes and is an important skill to master.

To fold beaten egg whites into a batter: Be sure to choose a bowl that is large enough. Some cooks fold with a whisk; we prefer a large rubber spatula. Use the spatula to scoop about one-quarter of the egg whites onto the top of the batter. Use the edge of the spatula to cut through the middle of the egg whites down to the bottom of the bowl. Draw the spatula toward you, scraping a big scoop of batter up the side of the bowl, and lift and turn the spatula so that the batter falls gently back on top of the egg whites in the center. Rotate the bowl slightly and repeat the steps, always cutting into the center of the biggest mass of egg whites as you proceed. When these first egg whites are well incorporated, scrape all of the remaining egg whites on top of the batter and fold them in as described.

ABOUT OVEN RACK PLACEMENT

Position the oven rack in the lower third of the oven unless otherwise noted. This means that a cake pan will be just below the center of the oven rather than in the upper half, which would be the case if the rack were positioned in the center.

TESTING CAKES FOR DONENESS

Some cakes are ready to be removed from the oven when they are still gooey in the center. Others are done when they spring back when pressed lightly on the surface and/or when the top is golden brown, the sides are just beginning to pull away from the pan, and a toothpick inserted in the center comes out clean. Follow the instructions in each recipe.

We prefer wooden toothpicks or wooden skewers rather than metal cake testers or skewers. Uncooked batters and gooey crumbs cling better to wood than to metal, enabling you to make a better judgment about how the cake is progressing toward doneness. This is especially important for those gooey cakes and desserts that are done when the tester comes out with moist crumbs rather than perfectly clean.

Because ovens and cake pans vary, always begin to test a cake for doneness early. Should you forget to set a timer, you will begin to smell the cake when it is about two-thirds to three-quarters of the way done.

ABOUT STORING CAKES

Unless a cake is perishable and requires refrigeration, store it at room temperature under a cake dome or in a box. If the cake has been cut, you can press a piece of plastic wrap or wax paper against the cut edges to keep it from drying out. Refrigerated cakes are best stored

Folding egg whites

in airtight plastic containers to keep them from absorbing odors and flavors from other foods.

ABOUT FREEZING AND THAWING CAKES

Most cakes can be frozen for 4 to 6 months with little loss of quality. Many sources say 6 to 8 months, but we take a conservative stance, to allow for the temperature variability and high traffic in and out of home freezers—and to prompt the reader to enjoy cakes in their prime. The richer the cake, the better it retains flavor and texture after freezing and thawing. Thus butter cakes, cheesecakes, and rich chocolate tortes freeze especially well. Cakes with little or no fat, such as angel cakes, many sponge cakes, and most reduced-fat cakes, lose quality after 6 to 8 weeks. Spice cakes may diminish in flavor after about 6 weeks in the freezer as well.

The faster cakes freeze, the better they are wrapped, and the less air there is in the package, the better results you will have. To this end, chill cakes completely before freezing, then wrap airtight using freezer paper or heavy-duty aluminum foil alone or in combination with plastic wrap or plastic bags specifically designated for the freezer. Many successful freezer jockeys wrap first in plastic, which conforms softly to the item being frozen, and then in heavy-duty foil or plastic freezer containers for a second barrier.

Thaw cakes without unwrapping or removing them from the freezer container, thereby allowing the condensation that forms on all thawing items to collect on the surface of the wrapper or container rather than directly on the cake. Thaw cakes that are to be served cold over several hours, or overnight, in the refrigerator. Thaw cakes to be served at room temperature at room temperature.

ABOUT BIRTHDAY AND SPECIAL CAKE PAN SHAPES

We are blessed with the availability of cake pans in a myriad of shapes from rabbits to rocket ships. Fill these pans no more than two-thirds full of batter, bake at the temperature called for, and use the test for doneness described in the recipe. Note that the baking time for 1- to 1⅓-inch-deep batter in a single pan will be longer than it would be to bake the same amount of batter, poured less deep, in two or three layer pans. To predict the amount of batter needed for a given pan, measure the capacity with water to determine how many cups the pan holds and plan to make one-half to two-thirds that amount of batter. In general, recipes that call for two 8- or 9-inch round layer pans, an 8- to 10-cup fluted tube or Bundt pan, or a 9-inch flat-bottomed tube pan will yield 6 to 7 cups of batter. Recipes that call for a 6-cup fluted tube or Bundt pan yield about 4 cups of batter. For example, the Devil's Food Cake Cockaigne recipe yields 6 to 7 cups of batter, as do the Buttermilk Layer Cake and Lady Cake. The White Cake yields about 9 cups of batter. Quick and one-bowl cakes that call for an 8 x 8-inch pan yield 4 to 5 cups of batter.

ABOUT QUICK CAKES AND GINGERBREAD

Quick cakes and gingerbread are never as fine or delicate as classically made sponge or butter cakes, but they are satisfying and delicious because the ingredients are fresh and genuine. By all means make them when you are in a hurry, and use them to teach your children to bake. Any of the following cakes can be mixed in one bowl in a matter of minutes. Use an electric mixer or mix by hand as directed. (These are specially devised cakes; do not try to use the one-bowl method for just any recipe.)

Contrary to our usual insistence on sifting before measuring flour, we give unsifted flour measurements for quick cakes and gingerbread both in order to save a step and because these batters are somewhat forgiving. Sifting the dry ingredients together or shaking them through a large medium-mesh sieve after measuring does make it easier to mix them into the batter without lumps; however, in the name of speed you will also succeed simply by stirring the dry ingredients together with a fork or whisk to mix and aerate them prior to combining them with the batter.

TO UNMOLD QUICK CAKES AND GINGERBREAD

To unmold, slide a thin knife around the cake to detach it from the pan. Invert onto a rack. Peel off the wax or parchment paper, if using, and turn right side up to cool. Unless otherwise noted, let cool completely before wrapping airtight or frosting.

LIGHTNING CAKE

8 servings

This is a German Blitztorte, named for the speed with which it can be produced. It is a quite simple lemon-scented yellow cake, delicious with or without the topping, or frost it with any powdered-sugar or quick icing, 1006 to 1010, or Chocolate Satin Frosting, 1004.

Have all ingredients at room temperature, 68° to 70°F. Preheat the oven to 350°F. Grease and flour one 8 x 2-

inch round pan or line the bottom with wax or parchment paper.
Whisk together thoroughly:

1 cup all-purpose flour
1 teaspoon baking powder
¼ teaspoon salt

In a large bowl, beat until creamy, about 30 seconds:

8 tablespoons (1 stick) unsalted butter

Gradually add and beat on high speed until lightened in color and texture, 3 to 5 minutes:

1 cup sugar

Beat in 1 at a time:

3 large eggs

Beat in:

1 teaspoon grated lemon zest
2 tablespoons fresh lemon juice

Stir in the flour mixture just until smooth. Scrape the batter into the pan and spread evenly. If desired, sprinkle the top with a mixture of:

⅓ cup chopped or sliced natural (unblanched) almonds or other nuts
1 heaping tablespoon sugar

Bake until a toothpick inserted into the center comes out clean, 30 to 35 minutes. Let cool in the pan on a rack for 10 minutes. Slide a thin knife around the cake to detach it from the pan. Invert the cake and peel off the paper liner, if using. Let cool right side up on the rack.

SOUR CREAM CHOCOLATE CHIP CAKE

8 servings

We sometimes substitute nuts, raisins, dried cranberries, or chopped dried apricots for some or all of the chips. Revive stale slices by toasting.

Preheat the oven to 350°F. Grease and flour one 9 x 5-inch (8-cup) loaf pan or line the bottom with wax or parchment paper.

Melt, then pour into a large mixing bowl and let cool slightly:

5 tablespoons unsalted butter

Add and stir together until smooth:

⅔ cup sugar
1 teaspoon vanilla
¼ teaspoon salt
1 cup sour cream
1 large egg

Add in pinches to break up any lumps and whisk in:

¾ teaspoon baking soda
¾ teaspoon baking powder

Stir in just until combined:

1½ cups all-purpose flour

Stir in:

¾ cup miniature or regular semisweet chocolate chips

Scrape the batter into the pan and spread evenly. Bake until a toothpick inserted into the center comes out clean, 40 to 45 minutes. Let cool in the pan on a rack for 10 minutes. Slide a thin knife around the cake to detach it from the pan. Invert the cake and peel off the paper liner, if using. Let cool right side up on the rack. Serve dusted with:

Powdered sugar

or frost with:

Quick Orange Icing, 1006

SOUR CREAM FUDGE CAKE

8 servings

This not-too-sweet chocolate cake has a tender, soft grain. Excellent gussied up with chocolate frosting; remarkably satisfying served plain with coffee.

Preheat the oven to 350°F. Grease and flour two 8 x 8-inch pans or two 9 x 2-inch round pans or one 13 x 9-inch pan or line the bottom(s) with wax or parchment paper.

Melt in the top of a double boiler or in a microwave on medium just until melted and smooth:

3 ounces unsweetened chocolate, coarsely chopped

Sift together into a large bowl:

1¾ cups cake flour
1½ cups sugar
1 teaspoon baking soda
1 teaspoon salt

Add and beat on high speed for exactly 2 minutes:

1 cup sour cream
6 tablespoons (¾ stick) unsalted butter, softened

Add the melted chocolate along with:

2 large eggs
1 teaspoon vanilla
¼ cup hot water or coffee

Beat for exactly 2 minutes. Scrape the batter into the pan(s) and spread evenly. Bake until a toothpick inserted into the center comes out clean, 20 to 25 minutes in square or round pans, 25 to 30 minutes in a 13 x 9-inch pan. Let cool in the pan(s) on a rack for 10 minutes. Slide a thin knife around the cake to detach it from the pan(s). Invert the cake and peel off the paper liner(s), if using. Let cool right side up on the rack. If desired, frost with:

Chocolate Satin Frosting, 1004

or serve plain, sprinkled with:

Powdered sugar

or accompany with:

Whipped cream

CHOCOLATE SHEET CAKE (TEXAS SHEET CAKE)

12 to 16 servings

We mix this cake by hand and serve from the pan frosted, or served with whipped cream, Coffee Whipped Cream, 995, or Mocha Whipped Cream, 995.

Preheat the oven to 375°F. Grease and flour one 13 x 9-inch pan.

Sift together into a large bowl:

- **2 cups sugar**
- **2 cups all-purpose flour**
- **1 teaspoon baking soda**
- **½ teaspoon salt**

Combine in a medium saucepan and bring to a boil, stirring constantly:

- **1 cup water**
- **½ cup vegetable oil**
- **8 tablespoons (1 stick) unsalted butter**
- **¼ cup unsweetened nonalkalized cocoa**

Pour the hot mixture over the dry ingredients and stir together just until smooth.

Whisk together, then stir into the batter:

- **2 large eggs, lightly beaten**
- **½ cup buttermilk**
- **1 teaspoon vanilla**

Scrape the batter into the pan and spread evenly. Bake until a toothpick inserted in the center comes out clean, 20 to 25 minutes. Let cool briefly in the pan on a rack. While still warm, spread with:

- **1½ to 2 cups Quick Mocha Icing, 1006, or Quick Chocolate Icing, 1006 (optional)**

and sprinkle the top with:

- **1 cup chopped pecans or walnuts (optional)**

OATMEAL SHEET CAKE

12 to 16 servings

This sweet, moist cake with a broiled topping has a loyal following. Make it a day or two before serving.

Combine and let stand for at least 20 minutes:

- **1 cup old-fashioned rolled oats**
- **1½ cups boiling water**

Have all remaining ingredients at room temperature, 68° to 70°F. Preheat the oven to 350°F. Grease one 13 x 9-inch pan.

Whisk together thoroughly:

- **1⅓ cups all-purpose flour**
- **1 teaspoon baking soda**
- **1 teaspoon ground cinnamon**
- **½ teaspoon freshly grated or ground nutmeg**
- **½ teaspoon salt**

In a medium bowl, beat on high speed until lightened in color and texture, 4 to 6 minutes:

- **8 tablespoons (1 stick) unsalted butter**
- **1 cup sugar**
- **1 cup packed light or dark brown sugar**

Beat in:

- **2 large eggs**
- **1 teaspoon vanilla**

Beat in the oat mixture, then the flour mixture. Scrape the batter into the pan and spread evenly. Bake until a toothpick inserted in the center comes out clean, about 30 minutes. Let cool briefly in the pan on a rack. While still warm, ice with:

- **About 2 cups Broiled Icing, 1011**

and broil as directed.

DAIRY-FREE CHOCOLATE CAKE (VEGAN)

8 servings

This is a delightful simple chocolate cake whether or not you observe dietary restrictions.

Preheat the oven to 350°F. Grease and flour one 8 x 8-inch pan or line the bottom with wax or parchment paper.

Sift together into a large bowl:

- **1½ cups all-purpose flour**
- **1 cup plus 2 tablespoons sugar**
- **6 tablespoons unsweetened nonalkalized cocoa**
- **1 teaspoon baking soda**
- **⅛ teaspoon salt**

Combine and add:

- **1 cup cold water**
- **¼ cup vegetable oil**
- **1 tablespoon white vinegar**
- **2 teaspoons vanilla**

Stir until smooth. Scrape the batter into the pan and spread evenly. Bake until a toothpick inserted into the center comes out clean, 25 to 30 minutes. Let cool in the pan on a rack for 10 minutes. Slide a slim knife around the cake to detach it from the pan. Invert the cake and peel off the paper liner, if using. Let cool right side up on the rack. Serve plain, dusted with:

- **Powdered sugar**

or frost with:

- **Quick Cookie Icing flavored with rum, brandy, or coffee liqueur, 1009**

ULTRA-ORANGE CAKE (VEGAN)

8 servings

This is moist and sweet and orangey. For a less sweet cake, decrease the sugar by 2 tablespoons.

Preheat the oven to 350°F. Grease and flour one 8 x 8-inch pan or line the bottom with wax or parchment paper.

Whisk together thoroughly in a large bowl:

1½ cups all-purpose flour
1 cup sugar
1 teaspoon baking soda
½ teaspoon salt

Add and stir together until smooth:

1 cup orange juice
⅓ cup vegetable oil
1 tablespoon grated orange zest
1 tablespoon white or cider vinegar
1 teaspoon vanilla

Scrape the batter into the pan and spread evenly. Bake until a toothpick inserted into the center comes out clean, 30 to 35 minutes. Let cool in the pan on a rack for 10 minutes. Slide a thin knife around the cake to detach it from the pan. Invert the cake and peel off the paper liner, if using. Let cool right side up on the rack.

ORANGE RUM CAKE

8 servings

This subtle cake has the lightness of a sponge cake and the butteriness of a pound cake.

Preheat the oven to 375°F. Grease and flour one 8 x 2-inch round pan or line the bottom with wax or parchment paper.

Melt and let cool:

3 tablespoons unsalted butter

In a large bowl, beat on high speed until thick and pale yellow, about 4 minutes:

1 cup sugar
⅛ teaspoon salt
3 large eggs
Grated zest of 1 large orange

Sift over the top and fold in:

1¼ cups all-purpose flour
1½ teaspoons baking powder

Stir in the melted butter along with:

⅓ cup heavy cream

Scrape the batter into the pan and spread evenly. Bake until a toothpick inserted into the center comes out clean, 30 to 35 minutes. Let cool in the pan on a rack for 10 minutes. Slide a thin knife around the cake to detach it from the pan. Invert the cake and peel off the paper liner, if using. Let cool right side up on the rack.

Puncture the cake all over with a wooden skewer. Spoon over:

5 tablespoons dark rum

Let cool completely. Glaze with:

Bittersweet Chocolate Glaze, 1003

or dust with:

Powdered sugar

ORANGE ALMOND CAKE

Prepare Crunchy Almond Topping, 1011, in the cake pan before making the Orange Rum Cake, above. Add ⅛ teaspoon almond extract to the batter with the eggs.

APPLE SPICE CAKE

8 servings

This cake tastes spicier once it has cooled and rested for a couple of hours, but if you like your apple cake on the spicy side and enjoy eating it warm, increase all of the spices by just a pinch. We use tart green apples with the skins left on.

Preheat the oven to 350°F. Grease and flour one 8 x 8-inch pan or line the bottom with wax or parchment paper.

Whisk together thoroughly in a large bowl, pinching out any lumps in the brown sugar:

1½ cups all-purpose flour, or a combination of all-purpose and whole-wheat flour
1 cup packed dark or light brown sugar
1 teaspoon baking soda
1 teaspoon ground cinnamon
½ teaspoon ground cloves
½ teaspoon freshly grated or ground nutmeg
½ teaspoon salt

Add and stir together until smooth:

1 cup buttermilk
½ cup vegetable oil
2 tablespoons rum or brandy (optional)
1 teaspoon vanilla

Stir in:

1 cup chopped apples
½ cup chopped walnuts or pecans

Scrape the batter into the pan and spread evenly. Bake until a toothpick inserted into the center comes out clean, 40 to 45 minutes. Let cool in the pan on a rack for 10 minutes. Slide a thin knife around the cake to detach it from the pan. Invert the cake and peel off the paper liner, if using. Let cool right side up on the rack. Serve warm plain or with:

Vanilla ice cream

or let cool completely and frost with:

Quick White Icing, 1006, or Quick Butterscotch, or Penuche, Icing, 1007 (optional)

CARROT CAKE

12 to 16 servings

Carrot cake is now as American as apple pie. Ours is medium-spicy, moist but not heavy, and flavorful enough to enjoy without frosting.

Have all ingredients at room temperature, 68° to 70°F. Preheat the oven to 350°F. Grease and flour two 9 x 2-

inch round pans or two 8 x 8-inch pans or one 13 x 9-inch pan or line the bottom(s) with wax or parchment paper.
Whisk together thoroughly in a large bowl:

1⅓ cups all-purpose flour
1 cup sugar
1½ teaspoons baking soda
1 teaspoon baking powder
1 teaspoon ground cinnamon
½ teaspoon ground cloves
½ teaspoon freshly grated or ground nutmeg
½ teaspoon ground allspice
½ teaspoon salt

Add and stir together well with a rubber spatula or beat on low speed:

⅔ cup vegetable oil
3 large eggs

Stir in:

1½ cups finely grated peeled carrots
1 cup finely chopped walnuts
1 cup golden raisins (optional)
½ cup crushed pineapple, lightly drained (optional)

Scrape the batter into the pan(s) and spread evenly. Bake until a toothpick inserted into the center comes out clean, 25 to 30 minutes in round or square pans, 30 to 35 minutes in a 13 x 9-inch pan. Let cool in the pan(s) on a rack for 10 minutes. Slide a thin knife around the cake to detach it from the pan(s). Invert the cake and peel off the paper liner(s), if using. Let cool right side up on the rack. Fill and frost with:

Cream Cheese Frosting, 1007, Quick White Icing, 1006, or Quick Brown Butter Icing, 1007

ABOUT GINGERBREAD

These spicy cakes, which appeal to the modern cook for the speed and ease of their preparation, predate modern times by thousands of years; they can be traced back further than any other baked good with the exception of bread.

Although the spices in any one recipe may reflect certain ethnic or regional influences, you can vary them at whim; add a little ground black or red pepper, the grated zest of an orange or a lemon, a tablespoon of brandy. We make our gingerbread with light molasses. You can vary the molasses flavor by replacing a portion of it with honey, golden syrup, or dark corn syrup. You can add nuts. You can augment or replace ground ginger with minced fresh ginger and/or chopped crystallized ginger. Gingerbread is wonderful served warm or at room temperature, simply dusted with powdered sugar or accompanied with whipped cream, crème fraîche, yogurt, or sour cream. Fresh or poached fruit makes a fine partner as well.

Gingerbread batters are often thin and liquid. For those made with melted butter, we obtain the tenderest results by mixing the batter entirely by hand, using a whisk. If you do use an electric mixer, avoid overmixing: Scrape the bowl often to minimize the amount of mixing required to blend the ingredients, and use low speed to blend in the dry ingredients.

OLD-FASHIONED GINGERBREAD *8 servings*

Dark, moist, and spicy.
Have all ingredients at room temperature, 68° to 70°F.
Preheat the oven to 350°F. Grease and flour one 9 x 9-inch pan or line the bottom with wax or parchment paper.
Sift together:

1¾ cups all-purpose flour
1 teaspoon baking soda
1 tablespoon ground ginger
2 teaspoons ground cinnamon
¼ teaspoon ground cloves
¼ teaspoon salt

In a large bowl, beat until creamy, about 30 seconds:

8 tablespoons (1 stick) unsalted butter

Gradually add and beat on high speed until lightened in color and texture, 2 to 3 minutes:

1 large egg
½ cup packed light brown sugar

Gradually beat in:

1 cup light molasses

Add the flour mixture and stir just until combined. Stir in:

½ cup boiling water
3 tablespoons finely chopped crystallized ginger (optional)

Scrape the batter into the pan. Bake until a toothpick inserted into the center comes out clean, 35 to 40 minutes. Let cool in the pan on a rack for 10 minutes. Slide a thin knife around the cake to detach it from the pan. Invert the cake and peel off the paper liner, if using. Let cool right side up on the rack.

APPLESAUCE GINGERBREAD *8 servings*

This mildly spicy, light, and very moist gingerbread contains no milk products or butter.
Preheat the oven to 325°F. Grease and flour one 8 x 8-inch pan or line the bottom with wax or parchment paper.
Bring to a boil in a medium saucepan:

1 cup applesauce

Remove from the heat and stir in:

½ cup light molasses
1 teaspoon baking soda

The mixture will foam and bubble vigorously. Let cool slightly. Meanwhile, sift together:

1½ cups all-purpose flour
1 teaspoon ground ginger
¾ teaspoon ground cinnamon
¼ teaspoon ground cloves
¼ teaspoon salt

In a large bowl, beat on high speed until thick and pale yellow, 3 to 4 minutes:

2 large eggs
⅔ cup sugar

Gradually beat in:

⅓ cup vegetable oil

Fold in the flour mixture in 3 parts, alternating with the applesauce in 2 parts. Scrape the batter into the pan. Bake until a toothpick inserted into the center comes out clean, 40 to 45 minutes. Let cool in the pan on a rack for 10 minutes. Slide a thin knife around the cake to detach it from the pan. Invert the cake and peel off the paper liner, if using. Let cool right side up on the rack.

FRESH GINGER CAKE

8 servings

Some of the best cooks we know swear by versions of this cake. The large quantity of fresh ginger (don't be afraid) and the absence of other spices produces a sophisticated cake.

Preheat the oven to 350°F. Grease and flour one 9 x 9-inch pan or line the bottom with wax or parchment paper.

Whisk together thoroughly:

1½ cups all-purpose flour
1 teaspoon baking soda
¼ teaspoon salt

Whisk together in a large bowl:

½ cup packed light or dark brown sugar
¼ cup light molasses
¼ cup dark corn syrup, golden syrup, honey, or light molasses
1 large egg

Whisk in:

½ cup finely minced fresh ginger

Combine in a saucepan and heat until the butter is melted:

8 tablespoons (1 stick) unsalted butter
½ cup water

Whisk into the molasses mixture. Stir in the flour mixture just until smooth. Scrape the batter into the pan. Bake until a toothpick inserted into the center comes out clean, 25 to 30 minutes. Let cool in the pan on a rack for 10 minutes. Slide a thin knife around the cake to detach it from the pan. Invert the cake and peel off the paper liner, if using. Let cool right side up on the rack.

HONEY CAKE

10 to 12 servings

This version is typical of the eastern European cake known in Yiddish as *lekach.*

Preheat the oven to 350°F. Grease and flour one 13 x 9-inch baking pan (glass is best).

Cook, stirring gently, over low heat until well blended:

1½ cups dark honey
¾ cup vegetable oil
1 cup coffee
2 teaspoons vanilla

Remove from the heat and set aside to cool. Whisk together thoroughly in a large bowl:

3¾ cups all-purpose flour
1½ teaspoons baking soda
1 teaspoon baking powder
2 teaspoons ground cinnamon
½ teaspoon ground ginger
¾ cup raisins (optional)
¾ cup chopped walnuts (optional)

In a medium bowl, beat on high speed until thick and pale yellow, 4 to 5 minutes:

3 large eggs
¾ cup sugar

Beat the cooled honey mixture into the eggs. Add the dry ingredients and beat until well blended. Scrape the batter into the pan and spread evenly. Bake until a toothpick inserted into the center comes out clean, 35 to 40 minutes. As soon as the cake is removed from the oven, use a fork to prick holes all over the surface. Heat:

¾ cup dark honey

Using a large spoon, pour and spread the honey over the surface of the cake. Let the cake cool completely in the pan on a rack before cutting.

ABOUT BUTTER CAKES

Butter cakes may be the glory of the American cake repertoire. The mother of all butter cakes is surely the English pound cake made with a pound each of flour, sugar, butter, and eggs—a heavy but satisfying cake adopted by the French and aptly named *quatres-quarts* (four quarters) for its simple ingredient ratio. The discovery of baking powder in the nineteenth century opened the door to a lighter, moister cake, and considerable liberty with the original four-quarter recipe.

Properly made, with care and attention to the details, even the plainest butter cake approaches a kind of simple perfection that brings pride to the most accomplished baker.

For flavor and texture, butter is our strong preference. Shortening and margarine yield cakes with higher volume, but the loss of flavor is not an equal trade. Some may argue that in a spice or even a chocolate cake it does not matter, but we cannot agree.

Regular sugar (also called fine granulated sugar) varies in coarseness from region to region in the United States. Sugar that is too coarse may cause butter cakes to collapse in the oven—especially those made by the creaming method. If the sugar you are using looks significantly coarser than table salt, process it for 1 to 3 minutes in a blender or food processor, or buy sugar that is labeled superfine or extra fine.

The defining structure, velvety texture, and flavor of a butter cake are derived from the high proportion of butter in relationship to the eggs and other ingredients in the recipe. Butter cakes are leavened by baking powder and/or baking soda, which produce carbon dioxide to expand the air bubbles beaten into the batter. Success depends on the temperature of the ingredients and a sequence of mixing steps designed to create a stable batter with enough air trapped in it to rise and set properly in the oven.

There are three methods of mixing butter cakes successfully. Each yields a slightly different texture. While each method has its dedicated followers, we use different methods for different cakes. However, any butter cake can be mixed according to the method of your choice.

THE CREAMING METHOD

This is the classic method. Have all ingredients measured, the pans prepared, and the oven preheated, so that the mixing sequence is not interrupted from one step to the next until the cake is safely in the oven. All ingredients should be at 68° to 70°F, or slightly lower, 65°F, in a very hot kitchen or climate. Butter at this temperature is pliable but still very cool and firm, not melted or squishy. Cold butter will not disperse properly; melted butter will not trap air. (See About the Temperature of Ingredients, 926.)

The butter or shortening is beaten with the sugar until lightened in color and texture; this creaming takes from 3 to 10 minutes on medium to high speed, depending on the quantity of ingredients and the type of mixer. (For heavy-duty mixers with a choice of paddle or whisk, use the paddle; the lower times and speeds given in a recipe will apply.) Then the whole eggs, often first whisked lightly together, are added to the sugar and butter gradually, so as to preserve the volume and avoid breaking the emulsion of the ingredients. The eggs are beaten in at medium-low to medium speed; if liquid ingredients are added too fast, or if they are too cold, the emulsion of the batter "breaks," or curdles, volume is lost, and the cake may suffer in texture. Turning the mixer briefly to a higher speed can sometimes smooth out the batter and restore the emulsion.

After the eggs are incorporated, the sifted dry ingredients (flour and leavenings, sometimes cocoa and spices) are added in three parts, alternating with two additions of the wet ingredients (milk or water, or buttermilk, yogurt, or sour cream, and any liquid flavorings). To keep the mixture as stable as possible, start and end with the dry ingredients. Thus, first add one-third of the flour mixture, followed by half of the liquid, then another third of the flour, followed by the rest of the liquid, then the rest of the flour. Low speed is used for adding dry ingredients, a slightly higher speed for wet ingredients. Scrape the sides of the bowl as necessary to ensure that the batter is smooth. Mix the added ingredients only enough to incorporate; overmixing during this stage can develop too much gluten in the flour, toughen the cake, and result in too fine a crumb. For this reason, some careful bakers like to mix in the dry and wet ingredients by hand with a rubber spatula.

THE COMBINATION, OR SEPARATED-EGG, METHOD

The creaming method is followed with these changes: The eggs are separated and only the yolks are added to the beaten butter and sugar. After the wet and dry ingredients are added to the butter mixture, the egg whites are beaten with a little sugar until stiff but not dry and folded gently into the batter for extra lightness.

A variation of the combination method turns up in chiffon cake recipes in which the fat (oil) acts as the liquid and in very rich chocolate tortes, for which the butter is melted with the chocolate rather than beaten with the sugar. In the latter, the egg whites are often the only source of leavening.

THE BLENDING METHOD

This method is borrowed from bakeries and other establishments that make cakes in high volume, using shortening. In *The Cake Bible*, Rose Levy Beranbaum adapted and perfected the method for home bakers, using butter instead of shortening. The method is faster and less delicate than the creaming method. Advocates praise its finer grain, velvety texture, and supreme tenderness, while others find the results denser and heavier than the creaming method.

In the blending method, the mixing is done in two stages. In the first, the dry ingredients are beaten together for about 2 minutes with softened butter and just enough liquid to form a smooth mixture. The flour particles are thus immediately coated with fat, which prevents gluten development and toughening in the finished cake. In the second stage of mixing, the beaten eggs and remaining liquid are added in three parts and beaten for 20 to 30 seconds after each addition.

TO UNMOLD BUTTER CAKES

To unmold, slide a thin knife around the cake to detach it from the pan. Invert onto a rack. Peel off the wax or parchment paper, if using, and turn right side up to cool. If using a fluted tube or Bundt pan, rotate and tap the pan against the counter until the cake is loosened on all sides. Invert the cake onto the rack to cool. Unless otherwise noted, let cool completely before wrapping airtight or frosting.

IDEAS FOR BUTTER CAKES

While inexperienced bakers are advised not to tamper with the structure of cake recipes, you can vary flavorings and extracts or spices to suit your taste. You can fold up to ¼ cup plain or macerated finely chopped dried fruits, raisins, nuts, chocolate bits, or grated citrus zest into most butter cake batters. Do not add or subtract liquids, especially acid liquids, such as lemon or other fruit juices, which will upset the balance of leavening; and do not count on success if you simply add chocolate or cocoa to a batter—this type of alteration may require additional modifications.

Any butter cake that is baked in thin layers can also be baked in loaf or tube pans, or as a single thick layer, should you wish to serve the cake like a pound cake or teacake without frosting. As a rule of thumb, fill loaf and fluted tube or Bundt pans two-thirds to three-quarters full. If you have no idea how much batter a recipe yields or which loaf or tube pan to choose, set aside pans of several capacities before you start. Scrape the batter into a 16-cup glass measuring bowl, then select the pan with a capacity of 1⅓ to 1½ times the liquid measure of the batter. Baking time will be longer than for thin layers. Loaves often take 50 to 60 minutes or longer to bake; cakes baked in 6- to 8-cup fluted tube or Bundt pans take approximately 40 to 50 minutes, as do layers in 2-inch-deep 8- and 9-inch pans filled two-thirds full. Cakes baked in 9- and 10-inch flat-bottomed tube pans and 12-cup fluted tube or Bundt pans take close to an hour, or more. Use the toothpick test and check early every time. The texture of cakes baked in deeper pans will be closer-grained and more velvety, like moist pound cake, than those baked in thin layers. You can also bake butter cake batter in individual pans or molds, such as cupcake tins, madeleine pans, or tartlet or shell-shaped molds.

Try baked Crunchy Almond Topping, 1011, or Broiled Icing, 1011, with butter cakes.

WHITE CAKE

10 to 12 servings

This recipe is a good candidate for a traditional white wedding cake, 969, as it is easily multiplied eight times or more with results as fine as the basic small recipe. Try filling it with any of the tangy lemon or orange fillings, 998 to 999, or make a Lady Baltimore Cake, 965.

Have all ingredients at room temperature, 68° to 70°F. Preheat the oven to 375°F. Grease and flour three 8 x 2-inch round pans or line the bottoms with wax or parchment paper.

Sift together twice:

3½ cups sifted cake flour
1 tablespoon plus 1 teaspoon baking powder
½ teaspoon salt

Combine:

1 cup milk
1 teaspoon vanilla
¼ teaspoon almond extract (optional)

In a large bowl, beat until creamy, about 30 seconds:

½ pound (2 sticks) unsalted butter

Gradually add and beat on high speed until lightened in color and texture, 3 to 5 minutes:

1⅔ cups sugar

Add the flour mixture in 3 parts, alternating with the milk mixture in 2 parts, beating on low speed or stirring with a rubber spatula until smooth and scraping the sides of the bowl as necessary. In another large bowl, beat on medium speed until soft peaks form:

8 large egg whites
⅜ teaspoon cream of tartar

Gradually add, beating on high speed:

⅓ cup sugar

Beat until the peaks are stiff but not dry. Use a rubber spatula to fold one-quarter of the egg whites into the butter mixture, then fold in the remaining whites. Divide the batter among the pans and spread evenly. Bake until a toothpick inserted into the center comes out clean, about 25 minutes. Let cool in the pans on a rack for 10 minutes. Slide a thin knife around the cake to detach it from the pans. Invert the cake and peel off the paper liners, if using. Let cool right side up on the rack. Fill and frost as desired.

LEMON COCONUT LAYER CAKE

Prepare 2 layers of White Cake, above, fill with Lemon Curd, 998, and cover the top and sides with Seven-Minute Frosting, 1001. Press 1 to 2 cups flaked sweetened dried coconut into the frosting.

LADY CAKE

Grease and flour one 9-inch tube pan, two 8½ x 4½-inch (6-cup) loaf pans, or two 6-cup fluted tube or Bundt pans or line the bottoms of the loaf pans with wax or parchment paper.

Prepare White Cake, above, increasing the butter to 1½ cups. Substitute 1 teaspoon almond extract and the grated zest of 2 lemons for the vanilla. Use only 6 large egg whites. Bake until a toothpick inserted into the center comes out clean, 45 to 50 minutes in loaf or fluted tube or Bundt pans, about 60 minutes in a tube pan. Let cool in the pan(s) on a rack for 10 minutes. Slide a thin knife around the cake to detach it from the pan(s), or tap the sides of the tube or Bundt pan(s) against the counter to loosen the cake. Invert the cake and peel off the paper liners, if using. Let cool, right side up or inverted, on the rack. Serve sprinkled with powdered sugar or iced with Quick Lemon Icing, 1006, or icing of your choice.

GOLD CAKE

10 to 12 servings

This very rich and tender cake is nicely complemented by any orange or chocolate filling or frosting. We occasionally use it as the base of an ultrarich Boston Cream Pie, 966. Consider preparing this with the egg yolks left over from making Basic Angel Cake, 952, White Cake, 937, or Lady Cake, above.

Have all ingredients at room temperature, 68° to 70°F. Preheat the oven to 375°F. Grease and flour three 9 x 2-inch round pans or line the bottoms with wax or parchment paper.

Sift together 3 times:

2½ cups sifted cake flour
2½ teaspoons baking powder
¼ teaspoon salt

In a large bowl, beat until creamy, about 30 seconds:

12 tablespoons (1½ sticks) unsalted butter

Gradually add and beat on high speed until lightened in color and texture, 2 to 4 minutes:

1¼ cups sugar

In another large bowl, beat on high speed until thick and pale yellow:

8 large egg yolks
1 teaspoon vanilla
1 teaspoon fresh lemon juice or grated lemon zest

Beat into the butter mixture. Add the flour mixture in 3 parts, alternating with, in 2 parts:

¾ cup milk

beating on low speed or stirring with a rubber spatula until smooth and scraping the sides of the bowl as necessary. Divide the batter among the pans and spread evenly. Bake until a toothpick inserted into the center comes out clean, about 20 minutes. Let cool in the pans on a rack for 10 minutes. Slide a thin knife around the cake to detach it from the pans. Invert the cake and peel off the paper liners, if using. Let cool right side up on the rack. Fill and frost with:

Quick Orange Icing, 1006

or sprinkle with:

Powdered sugar

and accompany with:

Fruit and whipped cream

1-2-3-4 YELLOW CAKE

10 to 12 servings

Use your imagination with fillings and frostings—this cake goes well with almost anything from lemon to chocolate, peanut butter to pastry cream.

Have all ingredients at room temperature, 68° to 70°F. Preheat the oven to 350°F. Grease and flour three 8 x 2-inch or 9 x 2-inch round pans or line the bottoms with wax or parchment paper.

Sift together twice:

2⅔ cups sifted cake flour
2¼ teaspoons baking powder
½ teaspoon salt

Combine:

1 cup milk
1½ teaspoons vanilla, or 1 teaspoon vanilla and ½ teaspoon almond extract

In a large bowl, beat until creamy, about 30 seconds:

½ pound (2 sticks) unsalted butter

Gradually add and beat on high speed until lightened in color and texture, 3 to 5 minutes:

1½ cups sugar

Beat in 1 at a time:

4 large egg yolks

Add the flour mixture in 3 parts, alternating with the milk mixture in 2 parts, beating on low speed or stirring with a rubber spatula until smooth and scraping the sides of the bowl as necessary. In another large bowl, beat on medium speed until soft peaks form:

4 large egg whites
Scant 1/4 teaspoon cream of tartar

Gradually add, beating on high speed:

1/4 cup sugar

Beat until the peaks are stiff but not dry. Use a rubber spatula to fold one-quarter of the egg whites into the egg yolk mixture, then fold in the remaining whites. Divide the batter among the pans and spread evenly. Bake until a toothpick inserted into the center comes out clean, 25 to 35 minutes. Let cool in the pans on a rack for 10 minutes. Slide a thin knife around the cake to detach it from the pans. Invert the cake and peel off the paper liners, if using. Let cool right side up on the rack. Fill and frost as desired.

SIX-LAYER CAKE

Prepare either Gold Cake, 938, or 1-2-3-4 Yellow Cake, 938, slicing each layer in half horizontally. Fill and frost the top and sides with about 6 cups Chocolate Satin Frosting, 1004.

BUTTERMILK LAYER CAKE

10 to 12 servings

This is a sensational butter cake, tender and light as a feather, with the complex flavor that only buttermilk seems to impart. Fill and frost with any chocolate frosting or Cream Cheese Frosting, 1007.

Have all ingredients at room temperature, 68° to 70°F. Preheat the oven to 350°F. Grease and flour two 9 x 2-inch or 8 x 2-inch round pans or line the bottoms with wax or parchment paper.

Sift together:

2 1/3 cups sifted cake flour
1 1/2 teaspoons baking powder
1/2 teaspoon baking soda
1/4 teaspoon salt

In a large bowl, beat until creamy, about 30 seconds:

12 tablespoons (1 1/2 sticks) unsalted butter

Gradually add and beat on high speed until lightened in color and texture, 2 to 4 minutes:

1 1/3 cups sugar

Whisk together, then gradually beat in, taking about 2 minutes:

3 large eggs
1 teaspoon vanilla

Add the flour mixture in 3 parts, alternating with, in 2 parts:

1 cup buttermilk

beating on low speed or stirring with a rubber spatula until smooth and scraping the sides of the bowl as necessary. Divide the batter between the pans and spread evenly. Bake until a toothpick inserted into the center comes out clean, 25 to 30 minutes in 9-inch pans, 30 to 35 minutes in 8-inch pans. Let cool in the pans on a rack for 10 minutes. Slide a thin knife around the cake to detach it from the pans. Invert the cake and peel off the paper liners, if using. Let cool right side up on the rack.

FLO BRAKER'S POUND CAKE

8 to 10 servings

The true pound cake, made with equal weights of each key ingredient is considered too dry and heavy for today's tastes, but the memory of a perfect pound cake continues to haunt us. We think this superb cake captures the rich buttery flavor and texture of the pound cake.

Have all ingredients at room temperature, 68° to 70°F. Preheat the oven to 325°F. Grease and flour one 9 x 5-inch (8-cup) loaf pan or line the bottom with wax or parchment paper.

Resift twice:

2 cups sifted cake flour

Whisk together in a medium bowl:

5 large eggs
1 teaspoon vanilla
1/2 teaspoon almond extract
1 teaspoon grated lemon zest
1 teaspoon grated orange zest
1/2 teaspoon ground mace (optional)

In a large bowl, beat until creamy, about 30 seconds:

1/2 pound (2 sticks) unsalted butter

Gradually add:

1 1/3 cups sugar
1/4 teaspoon salt

Scrape the sides of the bowl and beat on high speed until lightened in color and texture, 3 to 5 minutes. Gradually dribble in the egg mixture, about 1 tablespoon at a time, and beat until light and fluffy, 3 to 4 minutes. Add the flour in 3 parts, beating on low speed or stirring with a rubber spatula until smooth and scraping the sides of the bowl as necessary. Scrape the batter into the pan and spread evenly. Bake until a toothpick inserted into the center comes out clean, 1 hour to 1 hour 10 minutes. Let cool in the pan on a rack for 10 minutes. Slide a thin knife around the cake to detach it from the pan. Invert the cake and peel off the paper liner, if using. Let cool right side up on the rack.

SEED CAKE

Prepare Flo Braker's Pound Cake, above, omitting the almond extract and citrus zests and adding 1 teaspoon lightly crushed caraway seeds to the dry ingredients.

MACE POUND CAKE

Prepare Flo Braker's Pound Cake, 939, omitting the almond extract and citrus zests and adding 1½ teaspoons ground mace to the dry ingredients.

ROSE LEVY BERANBAUM'S LEMON POPPY SEED POUND CAKE

8 servings

A tender, buttery pound cake with the texture of velvet.

Have all ingredients at room temperature, 68° to 70°F. Preheat the oven to 350°F. Grease and flour one 6-cup fluted tube or Bundt pan or one 8½ x 4½-inch (6-cup) loaf pan or line the bottom of the loaf pan with wax or parchment paper.

Whisk together in a medium bowl:

3 large eggs
3 tablespoons milk
1½ teaspoons vanilla

Whisk together thoroughly in a large bowl:

1½ cups sifted cake flour
¾ cup sugar
3 tablespoons poppy seeds
1 tablespoon grated lemon zest
¾ teaspoon baking powder
¼ teaspoon salt

Add half of the egg mixture to the flour mixture along with:

25 tablespoons (3 sticks plus 1 tablespoon) unsalted butter

Beat on low speed until the dry ingredients are moistened. Increase the speed to high and beat for exactly 1 minute. Scrape the sides of the bowl. Gradually add the remaining egg mixture in 2 parts, beating for 20 seconds after each addition. Scrape the sides of the bowl. Scrape the batter into the pan and spread evenly. Bake until a toothpick inserted into the center comes out clean, 35 to 45 minutes in a fluted tube or Bundt pan, 55 to 65 minutes in a loaf pan.

Shortly before the cake is done, combine in a small saucepan and cook, stirring, over medium heat until the sugar is dissolved:

¼ cup strained fresh lemon juice
6 tablespoons sugar

As soon as the cake comes out of the oven, place the pan on a rack, poke the cake all over with a wooden skewer, and brush it with half of the syrup. Let cool in the pan for 10 minutes. Slide a slim knife around the cake to detach it from the pan, or tap the sides of the fluted tube or Bundt pan against the counter to loosen the cake. Invert onto a greased rack and peel off the paper liner, if using. Poke the bottom of the cake with the skewer and brush with some of the syrup. Invert onto another greased rack and brush the remaining syrup over the sides of the cake. Let cool, right side up or inverted, on the rack. Wrap airtight and store for at least 24 hours before serving.

LIQUOR-SOAKED POWDERED SUGAR POUND CAKE

8 servings

Liquor-soaked pound cakes are popular holiday fare and great homemade gifts. Ours keeps for 2 weeks in a cool place or up to 1 month in the refrigerator. Vary the liquor according to taste. You can double this recipe.

Have all ingredients at room temperature, 68° to 70°F. Preheat the oven to 300°F. Grease and flour one 6-cup fluted tube or Bundt pan or one 8½ x 4½-inch (6-cup) loaf pan or line the bottom of the loaf pan with wax or parchment paper.

Measure:

1½ cups sifted cake flour

In a large bowl, beat until creamy, about 30 seconds:

12 tablespoons (1½ sticks) unsalted butter

Gradually sift in and beat on high speed until lightened in color and texture, 4 to 5 minutes:

1¾ cups powdered sugar

Beat in 1 at a time:

3 large eggs

Beat in:

½ teaspoon vanilla

Gradually add the flour, beating on low speed or stirring with a rubber spatula until smooth and scraping the sides of the bowl as necessary. Scrape the batter into the pan and spread evenly. Bake until a toothpick inserted in the center comes out clean, 35 to 45 minutes in a fluted tube or Bundt pan, 55 to 60 minutes in a loaf pan. Meanwhile, combine in a medium saucepan and cook, stirring, over medium heat until the mixture comes to a simmer:

1 cup sugar
½ cup water
¼ cup light corn syrup

Stop stirring and bring to a boil. Cover and boil until the sugar is dissolved, about 1 minute. Remove from the heat (do not stir) and let cool, uncovered, for about 5 minutes. Gently stir in:

⅔ cup rum, brandy, or other liquor

Let cool in the pan on a rack for 5 minutes. (If using a loaf pan with a paper liner, slide a thin knife around the cake to detch it from the pan. Invert the cake and peel off the paper then return the cake to the pan.) Poke holes halfway through the cake with a wooden skewer, spacing them ½ inch apart. Pour the syrup over the cake and let cool on the rack for about 30 minutes before unmolding. To unmold a fluted tube pan or Bundt pan, rotate and tap the pan against the counter to loosen the cake on all sides. Invert the cake onto a serving platter. Serve a loaf cake right side up. Serve warm or cool.

LIQUOR-SOAKED CHOCOLATE POUND CAKE

Prepare Liquor-Soaked Powdered Sugar Pound Cake, above, melting 2½ ounces coarsely chopped bittersweet or semisweet chocolate and letting it cool slightly. Decrease the sugar to 1½ cups. Beat in the melted chocolate before adding the eggs. Decrease the water for the syrup to ⅓ cup and increase the liquor to ¾ cup.

SOUR CREAM POUND CAKE COCKAIGNE

10 to 12 servings

A rich "plain cake" with a nuance of sour cream and a spectacular crackly brown top. Leftovers stay moist for close to a week.

Have all ingredients at room temperature, 68° to 70°F. Preheat the oven to 325°F. Grease and flour one 9-inch tube pan.

Sift together:

3 cups sifted cake flour
¼ teaspoon baking soda
¼ teaspoon salt

Combine:

1 cup sour cream
2 teaspoons vanilla

In a large bowl, beat until creamy, about 30 seconds:

½ pound (2 sticks) unsalted butter

Gradually add and beat on high speed until lightened in color and texture, 3 to 5 minutes:

2 cups sugar

Beat in 1 at a time:

6 large egg yolks

Add the flour mixture in 3 parts, alternating with the sour cream mixture in 2 parts, beating on low speed or stirring with a rubber spatula until smooth and scraping the sides of the bowl as necessary. In another large bowl, beat on medium speed until soft peaks form:

6 large egg whites
¼ teaspoon cream of tartar

Gradually add, beating on high speed:

½ cup sugar

Beat until the peaks are stiff but not dry. Use a rubber spatula to fold one-quarter of the egg whites into the sour cream mixture, then fold in the remaining whites. Scrape the batter into the pan and spread evenly. Bake until a toothpick inserted into the center comes out clean, 1 hour 10 minutes to 1 hour 20 minutes. Let cool in the pan on a rack for 10 minutes. Slide a thin knife around the cake to detach it from the pan. Invert the cake, then let cool right side up on the rack.

YOGURT CAKE (REDUCED FAT)

8 to 10 servings

A delicious white cake with a gentle tangy flavor. You can add to the batter ½ cup each chopped nuts and raisins, or 1 cup diced dried fruits, or fold in up to 2 cups fresh blueberries or cranberries.

Have all ingredients at room temperature, 68° to 70°F. Preheat the oven to 350°F. Grease and flour one 6-cup fluted tube or Bundt pan or two 8 x 2-inch round pans or line the bottoms of the round pans with wax or parchment paper.

Sift together:

2¼ cups sifted cake flour
1 teaspoon baking powder
½ teaspoon baking soda
½ teaspoon salt

In a large bowl, beat until creamy, about 30 seconds:

5 tablespoons unsalted butter

Gradually add and beat on high speed until lightened in color and texture, 2 to 3 minutes:

1 cup sugar

Whisk together, then gradually beat in:

1 large egg
2 large egg whites
1 teaspoon vanilla

Add the flour mixture in 3 parts, alternating with, in 2 parts:

1 cup nonfat yogurt

beating on low speed or stirring with a rubber spatula until smooth and scraping the sides of the bowl as necessary. Scrape the batter into the pan(s) and spread evenly. Bake until a toothpick inserted into the center comes out clean, 25 to 40 minutes in a fluted tube or Bundt pan, 25 to 30 minutes in round pans. Let cool in the pan(s) on a rack for 10 minutes. Slide a thin knife around the cake to detach it from the pans, or tap the sides of the fluted tube or Bundt pan against the counter to loosen the cake. Invert the cake and peel off the paper liners, if using. Let cool, right side up or inverted, on the rack. Fill and frost plain layers with:

Chocolate Frosting (Reduced Fat), 1004, or Classic Lady Baltimore Filling and Frosting, 1001

or glaze fruit and nut versions with:

Strong Liquor Splash, 1010, or Translucent Sugar Glaze, 1010, made with rum

CHOCOLATE MARBLE CAKE (REDUCED FAT)

8 to 10 servings

Grease and flour a 6-cup fluted tube or Bundt pan.
In a small bowl, whisk together until smooth:

⅓ cup unsweetened Dutch-process cocoa
⅓ cup sugar
¼ cup water

Prepare Yogurt Cake, 941, stirring 1½ cups of the batter into the cocoa mixture. Using a large spoon, scoop three-quarters of the plain batter into the bottom of the pan without smoothing the surface. Spoon all of the chocolate batter over the plain batter, without smoothing the surface. Distribute the remaining plain batter on top, spacing the dollops so that some of the chocolate batter shows through. Use a table knife to marble the two batters gently without blending them completely.

MARZIPAN CAKE

8 to 10 servings

The crunchy almond topping is all the decoration this elegant cake needs. Serve it with fresh fruit or Fresh Raspberry Sauce, 1048.
Have all ingredients at room temperature, 68° to 70°F. Preheat the oven to 325°F. Prepare Crunchy Almond Topping, 1011, in the pan if desired; otherwise grease and flour one 8 x 2-inch round pan or line the bottom with wax or parchment paper.
Crumble into a large bowl:

7 to 8 ounces almond paste, 854, or marzipan, 855

Add and beat until soft and well blended:

6 tablespoons (¾ stick) unsalted butter

Gradually add and beat on high speed until lightened in color and texture, 2 to 3 minutes:

⅔ cup sugar

Whisk together, then gradually beat in, for a total of 3 minutes:

3 large eggs
1 tablespoon kirsch or brandy
¼ teaspoon almond extract

Add in pinches to break up any lumps and beat in:

¼ teaspoon baking powder

Fold in with a rubber spatula:

⅓ cup all-purpose flour

Scrape the batter into the pan and spread evenly. Bake until a toothpick inserted into the center comes out clean, 35 to 40 minutes. Let cool in the pan on a rack for 10 minutes. Slide a thin knife around the cake to detach it from the pan. Invert the cake onto the rack to cool. If you did not prepare the almond topping, invert the cake and peel off the paper liner, if using. Let cool right side up on the rack. Sprinkle with:

Powdered sugar (optional)

COCONUT PECAN CAKE

10 to 12 servings

To make an Italian Cream Cake, fill and frost with Italian Cream Frosting, 1008.
Have all ingredients at room temperature, 68° to 70°F. Preheat the oven to 350°F. Grease and flour two 8 x 2-inch round pans or one 10- to 12-cup fluted tube or Bundt pan or line the bottoms of the round pans with wax or parchment paper.
Measure:

1½ cups sifted cake flour

Combine:

⅔ cup buttermilk
¾ teaspoon baking soda
1 teaspoon vanilla

In a large bowl, beat until creamy, about 30 seconds:

8 tablespoons (1 stick) unsalted butter

Gradually add and beat on high speed until lightened in color and texture, 4 to 6 minutes:

1⅓ cups sugar

Beat in 1 at a time:

3 large egg yolks

Add the flour in 3 parts, alternating with the buttermilk mixture in 2 parts, beating on low speed or stirring with a rubber spatula until smooth and scraping the sides of the bowl as necessary. Stir in:

1 cup sweetened shredded dried coconut
⅔ cup chopped pecans

In a medium bowl, beat on medium speed until soft peaks form:

3 large egg whites
⅛ teaspoon cream of tartar

Gradually add, beating on high speed:

¼ cup sugar

Beat until the peaks are stiff but not dry. Use a rubber spatula to fold one-quarter of the egg whites into the buttermilk mixture, then fold in the remaining whites. Scrape the batter into the pan(s) and spread evenly. Bake until a toothpick inserted into the center comes out clean, 30 to 35 minutes in round pans, 55 to 65 minutes in a fluted tube or Bundt pan. Let cool in the pan(s) on a rack for 10 minutes. Slide a thin knife around the cake to detach it from the round pans, or tap the sides of the fluted tube or Bundt pan against the counter to loosen the cake. Invert the cake and peel off the paper liners, if using. Let cool, right side up or inverted, on the rack.

VELVET SPICE CAKE

10 servings

This is a mildly spicy cake with a light, delicate texture. For a denser and yet more velvety texture, beat all of the sugar with the butter and add the eggs whole instead of separated.

Have all ingredients at room temperature, 68° to 70°F. Preheat the oven to 350°F. Grease and flour one 9-inch tube pan or one 8- to 10-cup fluted tube or Bundt pan. Sift together twice:

2⅓ cups sifted cake flour
1½ teaspoons baking powder
½ teaspoon baking soda
1 teaspoon freshly grated or ground nutmeg
1 teaspoon ground cinnamon
½ teaspoon ground cloves
½ teaspoon salt

In a large bowl, beat until creamy, about 30 seconds:

12 tablespoons (1½ sticks) unsalted butter

Gradually add and beat on high speed until lightened in color and texture, 2 to 4 minutes:

1¼ cups sugar

Beat in 1 at a time:

3 large egg yolks

Add the flour mixture in 3 parts, alternating with, in 2 parts:

¾ cup plus 2 tablespoons yogurt or buttermilk

beating on low speed or stirring with a rubber spatula until smooth and scraping the sides of the bowl as necessary. In another large bowl, beat on medium speed until soft peaks form:

4 large egg whites
⅛ teaspoon cream of tartar

Gradually add, beating on high speed:

¼ cup sugar

Beat until the peaks are stiff but not dry. Use a rubber spatula to fold one-quarter of the egg whites into the egg yolk mixture, then fold in the remaining whites. Scrape the batter into the pan and spread evenly. Bake until a toothpick inserted into the center comes out clean, 45 to 55 minutes. Let cool in the pan on a rack for 10 minutes. Slide a thin knife around the cake to detach it from the pan, or tap the sides of the fluted tube or Bundt pan against the counter to loosen the cake. Invert the cake, then let cool, right side up or inverted, on the rack.

RAISIN OR PRUNE SPICE CAKE

Prepare Velvet Spice Cake, above, adding 1 teaspoon allspice along with the spices. Beat the butter with 1½ cups sugar and beat in the 3 whole eggs rather than adding the yolks and whites separately; omit the cream of tartar. Fold 1½ cups raisins, chopped, or soft prunes, cut into small pieces, into the batter.

APPLESAUCE CAKE

8 servings

We like this best with slightly chunky homemade applesauce. The 9-inch pan yields the lightest-textured cake; the loaf cake is denser. Use white sugar for a more pronounced apple flavor, brown for a stronger spice cake flavor.

Have all ingredients at room temperature, 68° to 70°F. Preheat the oven to 350°F. Grease and flour one 9 x 2-inch round pan, one 6-cup fluted tube or Bundt pan, or one 8½ x 4½-inch (6-cup) loaf pan or line the bottom of the round or loaf pan with wax or parchment paper. Whisk together thoroughly:

1½ cups sifted all-purpose flour
¾ teaspoon baking soda
1 teaspoon ground cinnamon
½ teaspoon ground cloves
½ teaspoon ground allspice (optional)
⅛ teaspoon freshly grated or ground nutmeg (optional)
⅛ teaspoon ground mace (optional)
½ teaspoon salt

In a large bowl, beat until creamy, about 30 seconds:

8 tablespoons (1 stick) unsalted butter

Gradually add and beat on high speed until lightened in color and texture, 3 to 5 minutes:

¾ cup plus 2 tablespoons white or packed light brown sugar

Beat in:

1 large egg

Add the flour mixture in 3 parts, alternating with, in 2 parts:

1 cup thick applesauce, preferably unsweetened

beating on low speed or stirring with a rubber spatula just until incorporated and scraping the sides of the bowl as necessary. Stir in:

1 cup finely chopped walnuts
1 cup raisins or dried currants (optional)

Scrape the batter into the pan and spread evenly. Bake until a toothpick inserted into the center comes out clean, 25 to 30 minutes in a round pan, 40 to 45 minutes in a fluted tube or Bundt pan, 1 hour to 1 hour 10 minutes in a loaf pan. Let cool in the pan on a rack for 10 minutes. Slide a thin knife around the cake to detach it from the pan, or tap the sides of the fluted tube or Bundt pan against the counter to loosen the cake. Invert the cake and peel off the paper liner, if using. Let cool, right side up or inverted, on the rack. Frost with:

Old-Fashioned Caramel Frosting, 1000, or Quick Brown Butter Icing, 1007

or sprinkle with:

Powdered sugar

BANANA CAKE

8 servings

Have all ingredients at room tmperature, 68° to 70°F. Preheat the oven to 350°F. Grease and flour a 9-inch springform pan or line the bottom with wax or parchment paper.

Combine in a food processor and process briefly just until blended:

2 large ripe bananas
2 tablespoons sour cream

Add and process until well combined:

2 large eggs
2 teaspoons grated lemon zest
1½ teaspoons vanilla

In a large bowl, beat on low speed for 30 seconds:

2 cups cake flour
¾ cup plus 2 tablespoons sugar
1 teaspoon baking soda
¾ teaspoon baking powder
½ teaspoon salt

Add half of the banana mixture along with:

10 tablespoons butter, softened

Beat on low speed just until the dry ingredients are moistened. Increase the speed to medium and beat for 1½ minutes, scraping the sides of the bowl as necessary. Gradually add the remaining banana mixture in 2 batches, beating for 20 seconds after each addition. Scrape the batter into the pan and spread evenly. Bake until a toothpick inserted into the center comes out clean and the cake springs back when lightly pressed, 30 to 40 minutes. Let cool in the pan on a rack for 10 minutes. Slide a thin knife around the cake to detach it from the pan; remove the pan side. Let cool on the rack. Dust with:

Powdered sugar

or frost with:

Chocolate Ganache Glaze or Frosting, 1003

DEVIL'S FOOD CAKE COCKAIGNE

10 to 12 servings

This is a classic and always satisfying chocolate cake. Try it with half white and half brown sugar. For special occasions, fill with Whipped Ganache Filling, 1005, and glaze with Chocolate Ganache Glaze, 1003, or Bittersweet Chocolate Glaze, 1003.

Have all ingredients at room temperature, 68° to 70°F. Preheat the oven to 350°F. Grease and flour one 9-inch tube pan or two 9 x 2-inch round pans or line the bottoms of the round pans with wax or parchment paper.

Whisk together:

1 cup sugar
½ cup unsweetened nonalkalized cocoa
½ cup buttermilk or yogurt

Sift together:

2 cups sifted cake flour
1 teaspoon baking soda
½ teaspoon salt

Combine:

½ cup buttermilk or yogurt
1 teaspoon vanilla

In a large bowl, beat until creamy, about 30 seconds:

8 tablespoons (1 stick) unsalted butter

Gradually add and beat on high speed until lightened in color and texture, 3 to 5 minutes:

1 cup sugar

Beat in 1 at a time:

2 large eggs

Beat in the cocoa mixture. Add the flour mixture in 3 parts, alternating with the buttermilk mixture in 2 parts, beating on low speed or stirring with a rubber spatula until smooth and scraping the sides of the bowl as necessary. Scrape the batter into the pan(s) and spread evenly. Bake until a toothpick inserted into the center comes out clean, 30 to 35 minutes in round pans, 45 to 55 minutes in a tube pan. Let cool in the pan(s) on a rack for 10 minutes. Slide a thin knife around the cake to detach it from the pan(s). Invert the cake and peel off the paper liners, if using. Let cool right side up on the rack.

GERMAN CHOCOLATE CAKE

12 servings

This well-loved American cake is not the legacy of our German immigrants but the contribution of a man named German, who invented German sweet cooking chocolate. Some good cooks add the three egg whites left over from the filling to the four in the cake batter—a thrifty impulse that begets a fluffier cake. For the most traditional presentation, fill with Coconut Pecan Filling, 999.

Have all ingredients at room temperature, 68° to 70°F. Preheat the oven to 350°F. Grease and flour three 8 x 2- or 9 x 2-inch round pans or line the bottoms with wax or parchment paper.

Sift together:

2¼ cups sifted cake flour
1 teaspoon baking soda
½ teaspoon salt

Combine and stir until the chocolate is melted and smooth:

4 ounces sweet baking chocolate, finely chopped
½ cup boiling water

Combine:

1 cup buttermilk or sour cream
1 teaspoon vanilla

In a large bowl, beat until creamy, about 30 seconds:

½ pound (2 sticks) unsalted butter

Gradually add and beat on high speed until lightened in color and texture, 4 to 6 minutes:

1¾ cups sugar

Beat in 1 at a time:

4 large egg yolks

Add the melted chocolate and beat just until incorporated. Add the flour mixture in 3 parts, alternating with the buttermilk mixture in 2 parts, beating on low speed or stirring with a rubber spatula until smooth and scraping the sides of the bowl as necessary. In another large bowl, beat on medium speed until soft peaks form:

4 large egg whites
Scant ¼ teaspoon cream of tartar

Gradually add, beating on high speed:

¼ cup sugar

Beat until the peaks are stiff but not dry. Use a rubber spatula to fold one-quarter of the egg whites into the egg yolk mixture, then fold in the remaining whites. Divide the batter among the pans and spread evenly. Bake until a toothpick inserted into the center comes out clean, 25 to 30 minutes in 9-inch pans, 30 to 35 minutes in 8-inch pans. Let cool into the pans on a rack for 10 minutes. Slide a thin knife around the cake to detach it from the pans. Invert the cake and peel off the paper liners, if using. Let cool right side up on the rack. Spread between the layers and on the top, leaving the sides bare:

Coconut Pecan Filling, 999

or fill and frost as desired.

ABOUT FOAM CAKES

Sponge cakes, angel cakes, and chiffon cakes are all called foam cakes. They contain a high proportion of eggs in relation to other ingredients, and they rely on eggs or egg whites beaten to a foam for their delicate structure and their leavening. Leavening occurs when the air trapped in the foam is heated and expands in the oven, aided by the steam produced as the moist batter bakes. Although some foam cakes contain baking powder for additional leavening, the creation and handling of the egg foam is critical to the success of all foam cakes: mixing and folding must be done with skill, to preserve as much of the air in the foam as possible. Follow the recipe instructions carefully and review the techniques for beating egg whites, 928, and folding, 929.

Do not be deceived by the light and airy texture of foam cakes; some are as rich in fat as butter cakes, others contain no fat at all. Sponge cakes, which may or may not contain butter, vary in richness depending on how many egg yolks they contain. Chiffon cakes are low in cholesterol but contain a generous amount of oil. Only angel cakes are fat-free (save for any flavor additions that might contain fat), because they are made with the whites of eggs and contain no butter, oil, or egg yolks.

ABOUT SPONGE CAKES

Sponge cakes are foam cakes based on well-beaten whole eggs (cold or warmed) or on separated eggs, with beaten egg whites contributing the principal foam. Some recipes are butterless, others are enriched with melted butter added toward the end of mixing. Sponge cake purists scorn baking powder, but many recipes include it for extra volume and a finer texture. Whether leavening is added or not, and whether butter is present or not, the success of the cake depends upon the cook's ability to fold dry ingredients thoroughly into a delicate foam, with as little loss of volume as possible. Even in cakes for which beaten egg whites supply the majority of the volume, the egg yolks are also beaten well (until thick and pale yellow), to trap air and to lighten them for easier blending with other ingredients. To the same end, we fluff and aerate flour by triple sifting so that it will fold more easily into the delicate foam. (Review the techniques for beating eggs, 928, and folding, 929.)

There are two styles of sponge cake: American and European. American sponge cakes are relatively high in eggs and sugar and rarely contain butter. Some, but not all, include leavening and some, but not all, are made with separated eggs. American-style sponge cakes are moist, tender, and usually open-grained. They make delicious eating plain, as well as embellished with frosting or fruit and cream. We enjoy nutted and Passover variations as well.

The European sponge cake, known as *biscuit* in French, is proportionately higher in eggs and flour. With less sugar and no butter, it is drier and less tender than the American sponge cake. The génoise, enriched with a little butter, is richer and moister than the *biscuit,* though it is used similarly. These cakes are rarely served plain—instead they are components of more elaborate cakes and desserts. In the form of ladyfingers, they are dry and crisp or dry and spongy—perfect for soaking up liquor with custards and creams in desserts from charlottes to trifles to tiramisù. In the form of cake layers, they are "sponges" for soaking with liquor syrups and then assembling into opulent European-style layer cakes.

The most delicate sponges are baked in pans, often tube pans, that are ungreased, so that the batter can cling to the clean pan sides (and the tube) for support as it rises and as it cools. These cakes are cooled upside down, like angel cakes (see page 950), to set the structure before unmolding. Sturdier sponge cakes are cooled right side up.

TO UNMOLD SPONGE, CHIFFON, AND ANGEL CAKES BAKED IN TUBE PANS

To unmold, slide a thin knife around the cake to detach it from the pan, pressing the knife against the pan to avoid tearing the cake. Using the same procedure, detach the cake from the tube. If the pan has a removable bottom, pull the tube upward, to lift the cake from the pan side. Slide the knife under the cake, to detach it from the bottom. If the pan does not have a removable bottom, invert and tap the pan against the counter to loosen the cake. Allow the cake to drop onto your hand, a rack, or a serving platter. Peel off the wax or parchment paper, if using. Let cool right side up on a rack. Unless otherwise noted, let the cake cool completely before wrapping airtight or frosting.

AMERICAN SPONGE CAKE *8 to 10 servings*

Easy to make, this gloriously moist, light cake, sometimes known as Feather Sponge for its texture or Sunshine Cake for its lovely golden color, has the characteristic open grain and tender texture of the best American sponge cakes. To a purist, this is a true sponge cake, for it contains no leavening. It is delicious unadorned, with Quick Orange Icing, 1006, or Quick Lemon Icing, 1006, or accompanied with strawberries and cream.

Have all ingredients at room temperature, 68° to 70°F. Preheat the oven to 325°F. Have ready 1 ungreased 9-inch springform pan or 10-inch tube pan.

Sift together 3 times and return to the sifter:

1 cup sifted cake flour
¼ teaspoon salt

In a medium bowl, beat on high speed until thick and pale yellow, 2 to 3 minutes:

⅔ cup sugar
7 large egg yolks
1 teaspoon vanilla

Beat in:

1 teaspoon grated lemon zest (optional)
1 teaspoon grated orange zest (optional)
3 tablespoons water or fresh orange juice

Scrape the egg yolk mixture into a large bowl. Sift the flour mixture evenly over the top, but do not mix it in. In another large bowl, beat on medium speed until soft peaks form:

7 large egg whites
½ teaspoon cream of tartar

Gradually add, beating on high speed:

⅓ cup sugar

Beat until the peaks are stiff but not dry. Use a rubber spatula to fold one-quarter of the egg whites into the egg yolk mixture, then fold in the remaining whites. Scrape the batter into the pan and spread evenly. Bake until the top springs back when lightly pressed and a toothpick inserted into the center comes out clean, 40 to 45 minutes. Let cool upside down for at least 1½ hours, setting the tube over a bottleneck or resting the pan on 4 glasses. To unmold the cake from the tube pan, see above; to unmold the cake from the springform pan, slide a slim knife around the cake to detach it from the pan. Remove the pan side and bottom. Let cool right side up on the rack.

PASSOVER SPONGE CAKE *10 servings*

Have all ingredients at room temperature, 68° to 70°F. Preheat the oven to 350°F. Have ready 1 ungreased 10-inch tube pan.

Sift together 3 times:

⅔ cup matzo meal
⅓ cup potato starch
¼ teaspoon salt

In a medium bowl, beat on high speed until thick and pale yellow, about 2 minutes:

9 large egg yolks
1 cup sugar

Beat in:

1 teaspoon grated orange zest
1 teaspoon grated lemon zest
¼ cup fresh orange juice
1 tablespoon fresh lemon juice

Gradually add the dry ingredients, beating on low speed just until smooth. Scrape the batter into a large bowl and set aside. In another large bowl, beat on medium speed until soft peaks form:

9 large egg whites
½ teaspoon cream of tartar

Gradually add, beating on high speed:

½ cup sugar

Beat until the peaks are stiff but not dry. Use a rubber spatula to fold one-quarter of the egg whites into the egg yolk mixture, then fold in the remaining whites. Spoon the batter gently into the pan and spread evenly. Bake until the top springs back when lightly pressed and a toothpick inserted into the center comes out clean, 50 to 55 minutes. Let cool upside down for at least 1½ hours, setting the tube over a bottleneck or resting the pan on 4 glasses. To unmold, see page 946.

PASSOVER NUT SPONGE CAKE

Prepare Passover Sponge Cake, above, folding in 1 cup finely chopped or ground walnuts or pecans with the second addition of egg whites.

HOT-MILK SPONGE CAKE *8 servings*

This tender, moist sponge cake can be used in place of the drier, comparatively coarse-textured génoise. It also makes a perfectly flexible sponge sheet, 953, for jelly rolls.

Have all ingredients at room temperature, 68° to 70°F. Preheat the oven to 350°F. Grease and flour the bottom of one 9 x 2-inch round pan or line the bottom with wax or parchment paper.

Sift together 3 times and return to the sifter:

¾ cup sifted cake flour

1 teaspoon baking powder

Heat in a small saucepan until the butter is melted:

¼ cup milk

2 tablespoons unsalted butter

In a large bowl, beat until light-colored, tripled in volume, and the consistency of softly whipped cream (3 to 4 minutes in a heavy-duty mixer with the whisk attachment, 10 to 15 minutes with a hand-held mixer):

¾ cup sugar

5 large eggs

Reheat the butter and milk until steaming hot. In 3 additions, sift the flour mixture over the top of the egg mixture and fold in. Add the hot milk mixture all at once and fold in until well combined. Scrape the batter into the pan and spread evenly. Bake until the top springs back when lightly pressed and a toothpick inserted into the center comes out clean, 20 to 25 minutes. Let cool in the pan on a rack for 10 minutes. Slide a thin knife around the cake to detach it from the pan. Invert the cake and peel off the paper liner, if using. Let cool right side up on the rack.

CHOCOLATE SPONGE CAKE *10 servings*

A tall, moist sponge cake with great cocoa flavor. You can cut this cake into layers, sprinkle the layers with rum or a liqueur of choice (optional), and spread them with Whipped Ganache Filling, 1005. Frost with additional filling or glaze with Bittersweet Chocolate Glaze, 1003.

Have all ingredients at room temperature, 68° to 70°F. Preheat the oven to 350°F. Have ready 1 ungreased 10-inch tube pan.

Sift together 3 times:

⅔ cup sifted cake flour

⅓ cup unsweetened Dutch-process cocoa

¼ teaspoon salt

Combine in a large bowl:

6 large eggs

2 teaspoons vanilla

2 teaspoons instant coffee powder

Beat on high speed until the consistency of softly whipped cream, about 10 minutes. Gradually beat in 1 tablespoon at a time, beating for about 3 minutes:

1 cup sugar

Sift about one-fifth of the cocoa mixture over the top and fold in. Sift and fold in the remaining cocoa mixture in 4 more additions. Scrape the batter into the pan and spread evenly. Bake until the top springs back when lightly pressed and a toothpick inserted into the center comes out clean, about 45 minutes. Let cool upside down for at least 1½ hours, setting the tube over a bottleneck or resting the pan on 4 glasses. To unmold, see page 946. Serve plain or with:

Whipped cream

EUROPEAN SPONGE CAKE (BISCUIT) *8 to 10 servings*

This is the classic unleavened sponge layer used in fancy European layered cakes. It is a light, dry-textured sponge, meant to be soaked with syrups before being filled with buttercreams, mousses, or other fillings. This recipe yields two 1-inch layers or one 2-inch layer that can be sliced into two or three thin layers.

Have all ingredients at room temperature, 68° to 70°F. Preheat the oven to 325°F. Grease and flour the bottom(s) of two 9 x 2-inch round pans or one 9-inch springform pan or line the bottom(s) with wax or parchment paper.

Sift twice and return to the sifter:

1 cup plus 2 tablespoons sifted cake flour

In a medium bowl, beat on high speed until thick and pale yellow, 2 to 3 minutes:

6 large egg yolks

¼ cup sugar

1 teaspoon vanilla

Scrape into a large bowl. Sift the flour evenly over the top but do not mix it in. In another large bowl, beat on medium speed until soft peaks form:

6 large egg whites

¼ teaspoon cream of tartar

Gradually add, beating on high speed:

⅓ cup sugar

Beat until the peaks are stiff but not dry. Use a rubber spatula to fold one-third of the egg whites not quite thoroughly into the egg yolk mixture. Fold in the remaining whites in 2 additions. Scrape the batter into the pan(s) and spread evenly. Bake until the top springs back when lightly pressed and a toothpick inserted into the center comes out clean, 20 to 25 minutes in round pans, 35 to 40 minutes in a springform pan. Let cool in the pan(s) on a rack for 10 minutes. Slide a thin knife around the cake to detach it from the pan(s); remove the side of the springform pan, if using. Invert the cake and peel off the paper liner(s), if using. Let cool right side up on the rack.

LADYFINGERS

Thirty-six 4-inch ladyfingers

These light sponge fingers are a delicious nibble, but most find their way into refrigerator desserts such as Tiramisù, 966, or Charlotte Russe, 1031.

Preheat the oven to 350°F. Grease and flour 2 large baking sheets or line the bottoms with wax or parchment paper.

Prepare the batter for:

European Sponge Cake, 947

Scrape the batter into a large pastry bag fitted with a ⅝-inch plain tip. Pipe 4-inch fingers at least 1 inch apart on the baking sheets. Sift lightly over the ladyfingers:

Powdered sugar

Bake until golden brown, 10 to 15 minutes. Transfer the ladyfingers or slide the parchment paper onto a rack to cool completely. Store in an airtight container.

GÉNOISE

10 servings

This is the layer cake of Europe, an unleavened whole-egg sponge cake with a delicate butter flavor and a dryish crumb. Properly made, it tastes good on its own, but a génoise comes into its glory sliced into thin layers and brushed with liquor syrups for flavor and moisture, then filled with rich buttercreams. This recipe makes two 1-inch layers or one 2-inch layer that can be split horizontally into three or four thin layers.

Have all ingredients at room temperature, 68° to 70°F. Preheat the oven to 350°F. Grease and flour the bottom(s) of two 9 x 2-inch round pans or one 9-inch springform pan or line the bottom(s) with wax or parchment paper.

Sift together 3 times and return to the sifter:

1¼ cups sifted cake flour

¼ cup sugar

Melt in a small saucepan:

⅓ cup clarified butter, 1069

Whisk together in a large heatproof bowl:

6 large eggs

¾ cup sugar

Set the bowl in a skillet of barely simmering water and whisk constantly until the mixture is warm to the touch (about 110°F). Remove the bowl from the heat and beat on high speed until the mixture is light-colored, has tripled in volume, and is the consistency of softly whipped cream (3 to 5 minutes in a heavy-duty mixer with the whisk attachment, about 15 minutes with a hand-held mixer). In 3 additions, sift the flour mixture over the top and fold in with a rubber spatula. Reheat the butter until it is hot and transfer to a medium bowl. Fold into the batter with a rubber spatula until completely incorporated about 1½ cups of the egg mixture along with:

1 teaspoon vanilla

Scrape the mixture into the remaining egg mixture and fold in. Scrape the batter into the pan(s) and spread evenly. Bake until the cake begins to pull away from the sides of the pan(s) and the top springs back when lightly pressed, about 15 minutes in round pans, 30 minutes in a springform pan. Let cool in the pan(s) on a rack for 10 minutes. Slide a thin knife around the cake to detach it from the pan(s); remove the side of the springform pan, if using. Invert the cake and remove the paper liner(s), if using. Let cool right side up on the rack.

CHOCOLATE GÉNOISE

10 servings

Have all ingredients at room temperature, 68° to 70°F. Preheat the oven to 350°F. Grease and flour the bottom(s) of two 9 x 2-inch round pans or one 9-inch springform pan or line the bottom(s) with wax or parchment paper.

Sift together 3 times and return to the sifter:

½ cup plus 1 tablespoon sifted cake flour

½ cup plus 1 tablespoon unsweetened cocoa

Melt in a small saucepan:

⅓ cup clarified butter, 1069

Whisk together in a large heatproof bowl:

6 large eggs

1 cup sugar

Set the bowl in a skillet of barely simmering water and whisk constantly until the mixture is warm to the touch (about 110°F). Remove the bowl from the heat and beat on high speed until the mixture is light colored, has tripled in volume, and is the consistency of softly whipped cream (3 to 5 minutes in a heavy-duty mixer with the whisk attachment, about 15 minutes with a hand-held mixer). In 3 additions, sift the flour mixture over the top and fold in with a rubber spatula. Reheat the butter until it is hot and transfer to a medium bowl. Fold into the batter with a rubber spatula until completely incorporated about 1½ cups of the egg mixture along with:

1 teaspoon vanilla

Scrape this into the remaining egg mixture and fold in. Scrape the batter into the pan(s) and spread evenly. Bake until the cake begins to pull away from the sides of the pan(s) and the top springs back when lightly pressed, about 15 minutes in round pans, 30 to 35 minutes in a springform pan. Let cool in the pan(s) on a rack for 10 minutes. Slide a thin knife around the cake to detach it from the pan(s); remove the side of the springform pan, if using. Let cool right side up on the rack.

ABOUT CHIFFON CAKES

Chiffon cakes were invented in 1927 by Harry Baker, a Hollywood insurance salesman who catered cakes for private parties on the side. Twenty years later, Baker sold the secret recipe for his chic new cake, made with oil instead of shortening, to General Mills. Chiffon cakes enjoy renewed interest today, as we look for ways to enjoy desserts with less cholesterol and saturated fat. Method and texture convince us to consider chiffon cakes in the foam cake category, despite the fact that these unique cakes are inherently as rich in fat and sugar as some butter cakes.

The fat in chiffon cakes is liquid (oil) rather than solid. In contrast to butter or shortening, it is impossible to beat much air into oil. Instead, air is beaten into the egg whites and folded into the rest of the batter. The result is a cake that is very light and fluffy, and very tender. Chiffon cakes are less sweet than angel cakes and much moister than sponge cakes. A precise mixing method—and the addition of baking powder to augment the rise from the beaten egg whites—makes chiffon cakes the easiest foam cakes to master.

Oil gives chiffon cakes great moistness and keeps them soft even when refrigerated, tender even when frozen. Thus a chiffon cake is a good choice for filling or layering with ice cream.

Choose oil that has as little flavor as possible and contains no silicates (check the ingredients label), as silicates inhibit foaming. Safflower, peanut, corn, and sunflower oils are good choices. Since oil does not contribute the flavor of butter, chiffon cakes need lots of flavor from other ingredients, such as tangy citrus juice and zest, spices, chocolate or cocoa, or toasted nuts.

Cakes made with oil are specially formulated. Do not try to substitute oil for butter or shortening in other types of cakes, and do not stray from the method for chiffon cakes.

IDEAS FOR CHIFFON CAKES

All chiffon cakes can be served with a simple dusting of powdered sugar. To add spark to the flavor, drizzle a citrus or liquor sugar glaze, 1010, over the cake. You can customize these cakes by changing the flavors—varying the spices, extracts, and citrus zest, changing the liquids from water to fruit juice or coffee, and/or adding finely chopped nuts or miniature chocolate chips.

Slice chiffon cakes horizontally into three layers and fill with softened ice cream, sorbet, or frozen yogurt. Refreeze for at least several hours, or overnight, before serving with a complementary or contrasting sauce, such as chocolate or a fruit puree, or top with whipped cream and toasted nuts.

BASIC CHIFFON CAKE *12 to 14 servings*

Our basic chiffon is tall and light, moist and lemony. Ice as suggested or serve with ice cream and fresh berries.

Have all ingredients at room temperature, 68° to 70°F. Preheat the oven to 325°F. Have ready 1 ungreased 10-inch tube pan with a removable bottom.

Sift together twice into a large bowl:

2¼ cups sifted cake flour
1¼ cups sugar
1 tablespoon baking powder
1 teaspoon salt

In another bowl, beat on high speed until smooth:

5 large egg yolks
¾ cup water
½ cup vegetable oil
1 teaspoon grated lemon zest
1 teaspoon vanilla

Stir into the flour mixture until smooth. In another large bowl, beat on medium speed until soft peaks form:

8 large egg whites
½ teaspoon cream of tartar

Gradually add, beating on high speed:

¼ cup sugar

Beat until the peaks are stiff but not dry. Use a rubber spatula to fold one-quarter of the egg whites into the egg yolk mixture, then fold in the remaining whites. Scrape the batter into the pan and spread evenly. Bake until the top springs back when lightly pressed and a toothpick inserted into the center comes out clean, 55 to 65 minutes. Let cool upside down for at least 1½ hours, setting the tube over a bottleneck or resting the pan on 4 glasses. To unmold, see page 946. Ice with:

Quick Lemon Icing, 1006, or Quick Orange Icing, 1006

or serve with:

Fresh berries and whipped cream

ORANGE CHIFFON CAKE

Prepare Basic Chiffon Cake, above, substituting ¾ cup orange juice and 2 tablespoons grated orange zest for the water and lemon zest. Emphasize the orange flavor by icing with Quick Orange Icing, 1006, or use Translucent Sugar Glaze, 1010, made with rum.

BANANA CHIFFON CAKE

Lighter than most banana cakes but very moist.

Prepare Basic Chiffon Cake, above, substituting 1¼ cups mashed very ripe bananas (2 to 3 medium) for the water and omitting the lemon zest. If you wish, add ½ teaspoon ground cinnamon and ¼ teaspoon freshly grated or ground nutmeg with the dry ingredients, and/or fold in ¾ cup finely chopped walnuts or pecans with the second addition of egg whites.

PUMPKIN CHIFFON CAKE

A delicately spiced cake with a moist spongy texture and pumpkin color. Ice with Cream Cheese Frosting, 1007, or serve with vanilla ice cream.

Prepare Basic Chiffon Cake, above, adding 1½ teaspoons ground cinnamon, ¾ teaspoon ground ginger, ½ teaspoon freshly grated or ground nutmeg, and ¼ teaspoon ground cloves to the dry ingredients, substituting 1¼ cups pumpkin puree for the water, and omitting the lemon zest. If you wish, fold in ¾ cup finely chopped walnuts or pecans with the second addition of egg whites.

NO-CHOLESTEROL CHIFFON CAKES

Make the following changes for Basic Chiffon Cake, above, and Orange Chiffon Cake, above: Sift the flour with only ¾ cup sugar. Increase the oil to ⅔ cup. Omit the egg yolks and increase the egg whites to 9. Increase the sugar beaten into the egg whites to ½ cup.

FUDGE CHIFFON CAKE *12 to 14 servings*

This is like a moist, light sponge cake with a surprising amount of chocolate flavor.

Have all ingredients at room temperature, 68° to 70°F, except for the water. Preheat the oven to 325°F. Have ready 1 ungreased 10-inch tube pan with a removable bottom.

Whisk together until smooth and set aside to cool:

¾ cup boiling water
½ cup unsweetened nonalkalized cocoa
1 tablespoon plus 1 teaspoon instant coffee powder

Sift together twice into a large bowl:

1¾ cups sifted cake flour
1¼ cups sugar
2 teaspoons baking powder
¼ teaspoon baking soda
½ teaspoon salt

Combine in a medium bowl:

½ cup vegetable oil
5 large egg yolks
1 teaspoon vanilla

Add the cooled cocoa mixture and beat until smooth. Stir into the flour mixture until smooth. In another large bowl, beat on medium speed until soft peaks form:

8 large egg whites
½ teaspoon cream of tartar

Gradually add, beating on high speed:

¼ cup sugar

Beat until the peaks are stiff but not dry. Use a rubber spatula to fold one-quarter of the egg whites into the cocoa mixture, then fold in the remaining whites. Scrape the batter into the pan and spread evenly. Bake until the top springs back when lightly pressed and a toothpick inserted into the center comes out clean, 55 to 65 minutes. Let cool upside down for at least 1½ hours, setting the tube over a bottleneck or resting the pan on 4 glasses. To unmold, see page 946. Ice with:

Quick Orange Icing, 1006, Quick Mocha Icing, 1006, any chocolate frosting, or sweetened or flavored whipped cream (optional)

ABOUT ANGEL CAKES

Angel cakes are sponge cakes without egg yolks or butter. Fat-free, pristinely white, airy, and delicate, they are enchanting accompanied with fruit, ice cream, or sauces, or topped with icings or frostings, from tart lemon to rich chocolate.

The home baker willing to follow instructions can produce heavenly angel cakes in blissful ignorance of the enormous volume of research done in the name of this seemingly simple cake. The main sources of leavening in angel cakes are air and steam. There are no chemical leaveners such as baking powder or baking soda, so the volume of air beaten into the egg whites is of supreme importance, as is the care with which other ingredients are folded into them.

The egg whites should be at least 3 days old (no problem for urbanites). Egg whites that have been frozen and thawed produce a less stable foam, and so are best avoided by the beginner. Be sure that the bowl and all utensils are perfectly clean and dry, and completely free of grease.

Do not exceed medium speed on either hand-held or heavy-duty mixers; overbeating the whites is the single most common mistake made in the production of angel cakes. Cold egg whites, straight from the refrigerator, help to prevent overbeating and produce a greater number of small sturdy air bubbles, rather than fewer more fragile large ones. Unlike the whites in most other meringues, egg whites for angel cakes should never be beaten stiff; they may even seem dangerously soft and underbeaten to anyone familiar with meringue making. The finished batter should be soft enough to pour, rather than scrape, into the cake pan.

Cream of tartar is used to keep the cake white and to stabilize the egg whites. Be sure that it has been stored in a closely covered container. We use regular granulated sugar, a portion of which is sifted with the flour to keep the sugar dispersed and prevent clumping as it is folded in. The remaining sugar is beaten into the egg whites. Folding is done by hand with a rubber spatula, never with the electric mixer. If your mixer bowl is tall and narrow, you will have better results if you transfer the batter to a very large wide bowl just before folding. Do not rush the addition of ingredients. For a review of folding technique, see page 929.

An angel cake pan is a flat-bottomed tube pan with or without a removable bottom. The light batter is supported by the sides and the central tube as it rises during baking. Do not grease or flour angel cake pans (for baking in jelly-roll pans, see page 953). A clean, dry, grease-free pan is essential for the cake to rise properly; scrub your pan with detergent before use if it is

Set the angel cake pan over the neck of a bottle to cool.

less than perfectly clean. When the cake is done, it must be inverted immediately to cool upside down, in the pan, to prevent it from sinking. Use the feet of the pan to hold it above the surface of the table or, better yet, prop it higher by setting the tube over a bottle or resting the pan on 4 glasses. To avoid last-minute panic, set up the cooling equipment while the cake is baking. Let the cake cool upside down for at least 1½ hours, until it is thoroughly set and thus unlikely to sink when turned right side up.

A special cake "comb" resembling a fork with several long, thin, widely spaced prongs, is ideal for cutting angel cakes; otherwise use a serrated knife and a sawing motion, to avoid compacting the tender cake. Angel cakes keep well for 2 to 3 days. They do not freeze as well as butter cakes or other sponge cakes; do not count on freezing them for more than a week.

IDEAS FOR ANGEL CAKES

Plain white angel cakes are complemented by tangy bright flavors. Try Translucent Sugar Glaze, made with lemon or orange, 1010, drizzled over the top. Fresh berries and whipped cream are natural partners. You can cut the cake into three or four horizontal layers or bake in a sheet for a roll cake and fill with Lemon Curd, 998, or any mousse, Bavarian cream, ice cream, sorbet, or flavored whipped cream and frost with whipped cream. For a richer effect, fill either Basic Angel Cake, below, or Cocoa Angel Cake, below, with Whipped

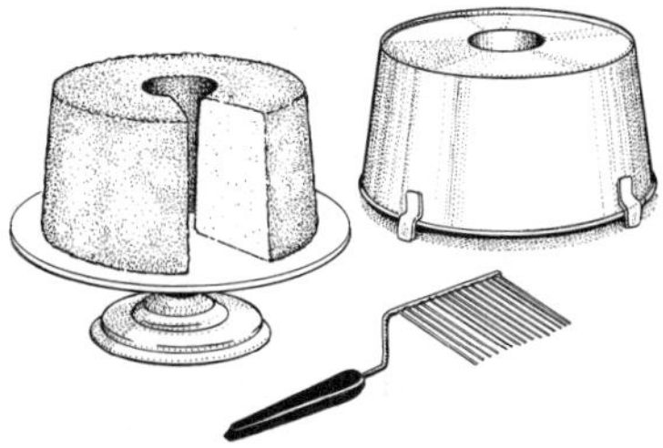

Clockwise from top right: The feet on the pan hold a cooling angel cake above the table surface; a cake divider; and a finished angel cake.

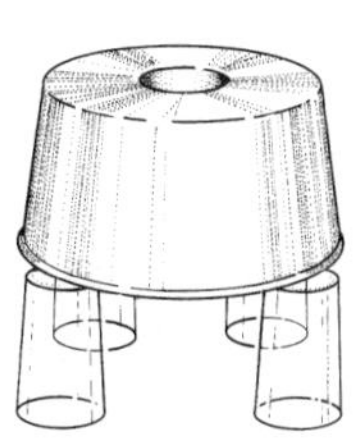

Rest the edges of the angel cake pan on four drinking glasses to cool.

Ganache Filling, 1005, and glaze with Bittersweet Chocolate Glaze, 1003, or fill and frost with Chocolate Mousse Frosting, 1005, or Mocha Buttercream, 1002, sprinkled with toasted pecans.

BASIC ANGEL CAKE *12 servings*

A high, very moist and tender angel cake that dissolves quickly on the tongue. For a less sweet cake with a slightly drier texture, decrease both sugar measures to ⅔ cup; the finished cake will be a tad shorter.

Egg whites should be cold. Preheat the oven to 350°F. Have ready 1 ungreased 9- or 10-inch tube pan.

Sift together 3 times:

- **1 cup sifted cake flour**
- **¾ cup sugar**
- **½ teaspoon salt**

In a large bowl, beat on low speed for 1 minute:

- **1½ cups cold egg whites (about 12 large whites)**
- **1 tablespoon water**
- **1 tablespoon fresh lemon juice**
- **1 teaspoon cream of tartar**
- **1 teaspoon vanilla**
- **¼ teaspoon almond extract (optional)**

Increase the mixer speed to medium (not high) and beat until the mixture increases in volume 4½ to 5 times and resembles a bowl of slightly translucent soft foam composed of tiny bubbles. (This takes anywhere from 1½ to 3 minutes.) The foam will hold a very soft, moist shape when the beaters are lifted. Beat in gradually (on medium speed), 1 tablespoon at a time, taking 2 to 3 minutes:

- **¾ cup sugar**

When all the sugar has been added, the foam will be creamy white and hold soft, moist, glossy peaks that bend over at the points; do not beat until stiff. If the mixer bowl is nearly full, transfer the mixture to a wide 4- to 6-quart bowl for easier folding. Sift a fine layer of the flour mixture (about one-eighth of the total) evenly over the surface of the batter and fold gently with a rubber spatula only until the flour is almost incorporated. Do not stir or mix. Repeat 7 more times, folding in the last addition until no traces of flour are visible. Pour the batter into the pan and tilt or spread to level the top. Bake until a toothpick inserted in the center comes out clean, 35 to 40 minutes. Let cool upside down for at least 1½ hours, setting the tube over a bottleneck or resting the pan on 4 glasses. To unmold, see page 946.

SPICED ANGEL CAKE

Prepare Basic Angel Cake, above, adding 1 teaspoon ground cinnamon, ½ teaspoon freshly grated or ground nutmeg, and ¼ teaspoon ground cloves to the flour mixture. Frost with Coffee Whipped Cream, 995, or Seven-Minute Frosting, 1001, to which you can add 1 to 2 teaspoons instant coffee powder.

COFFEE-FLECKED OR -FLAVORED ANGEL CAKE

Crush 3 tablespoons freeze-dried instant coffee with a rolling pin or in a coffee grinder. Sprinkle over Basic Angel Cake, above, batter and fold in with the last addition of flour (the coffee will not disperse completely). For coffee flavoring throughout the cake, instead of flecks, replace the water in the recipe with 3 tablespoons cold extra-strong coffee or espresso. You can also add as much as 1 tablespoon finely ground coffee or espresso beans to the flour mixture before folding it in. Serve plain or frost with whipped cream or any chocolate icing or glaze.

CANDY ANGEL CAKE

Crush with a rolling pin or finely chop with a knife enough peppermint sticks, sour lemon drops, toffee bars, or peanut butter cups to make ⅓ cup. Fold into Basic Angel Cake, above, batter with the last addition of flour. Frost with whipped cream or Seven-Minute Frosting, 1001, to which you can add more crushed candy.

COCONUT ANGEL CAKE

Prepare Basic Angel Cake, above, adding ½ teaspoon coconut extract to the unbeaten egg whites. Fold ½ cup shredded sweetened dried coconut into the batter with the last addition of flour. Frost with whipped cream and sprinkle with more coconut, or ice with Quick Lemon Icing, 1006, or Quick Orange Icing, 1006, or Translucent Sugar Glaze, 1010, made with rum.

LEMON OR ORANGE ANGEL CAKE

Prepare Basic Angel Cake, above, substituting 1 teaspoon lemon or orange extract for the almond extract. Stir 1 teaspoon grated lemon zest or 2 tablespoons grated orange zest into the flour mixture. Frost with Quick Lemon Icing, 1006, Quick Orange Icing, 1006, Translucent Sugar Glaze, 1010, made with rum, or Chocolate Ganache Glaze or Frosting, 1003, if desired.

COCOA ANGEL CAKE

Prepare Basic Angel Cake, above, substituting ½ cup (unsifted) unsweetened cocoa for ½ cup sifted cake flour. Dissolve 1 teaspoon instant coffee or espresso powder (optional) in the water. If desired, fold 6 tablespoons finely chopped semisweet or bittersweet chocolate into the batter with the last addition of cocoa and flour.

NUTTY ANGEL CAKE

Fold ¾ cup chopped or finely ground nuts into either Basic Angel Cake, above, or Cocoa Angel Cake, above, batter with the last addition of flour.

EXTRA-CHOCOLATE ANGEL CAKE

Pulverize in a food processor or finely chop 1 to 2 ounces semisweet or bittersweet (or even unsweetened) chocolate. Fold into Basic Angel Cake, above, or Cocoa Angel Cake, above, batter with the last addition of flour. Serve with whipped cream or ice with any chocolate frosting.

MARBLE ANGEL CAKE

Prepare Basic Angel Cake, above, or Cocoa Angel Cake, above. Alternate the batters in 2 ungreased 9- or 10-inch tube pans, swirling with a knife to marble. Bake as directed for Basic Angel Cake.

SPONGE, CHIFFON, AND ANGEL SHEETS

Almost any foam cake can be made into a sheet for jelly rolls simply by spreading the batter in a 17½ x 11½ x 1-inch pan (lined with wax or parchment paper) and baking it for just 10 to 15 minutes. In addition to the classic sponge, chiffon, and angel cake batters, we make rolled cakes from some flourless cocoa and chocolate batters that resemble thin soufflé cakes.

Thin cake sheets have a reputation for burning on the edges and for cracking when rolled. We used to deal with these problems by trimming the crisp edges and rolling up the hot cake sheet in a damp dish towel to "train" it; when cool, the cake would be unrolled, filled, and rerolled. But the real secret to a perfect cake roll does not involve trimming or wrapping in damp towels. Burnt or crisp edges result when the batter is not spread evenly all the way to the edges of the pan. Edges that are too thin burn before the rest of the cake is done. If the batter is ½ inch deep in the center of the pan, it should reach ½ inch up the sides of the pan all around as well. An offset spatula is the best tool for spreading batters evenly in shallow pans. Cake sheets crack while rolling if they are overbaked and dry; thin cake sheets become overbaked and dry much faster than thick sheets. Test early, and take the cake out of the oven as soon as the top springs back when lightly pressed or the cake meets the test specified in the recipe. A properly baked cake sheet can be allowed to cool flat, even in the pan, and still remain flexible enough to roll.

HOT-MILK SPONGE SHEET *10 servings*

A delightfully tender, moist, close-grained sponge that rolls beautifully without cracking. You can fill and ice with almost any filling or frosting, or make Old-Fashioned Jelly Roll, 964, Bûche de Noël, 967, or Sicilian Cassata, 968.

Have all ingredients at room temperature, 68° to 70°F. Preheat the oven to 400°F. Grease one 17½ x 11½-inch jelly-roll pan and line the bottom with wax or parchment paper.

Prepare the batter for:

Hot-Milk Sponge Cake, 947

Scrape the batter into the pan and spread evenly. Bake until the top is golden brown and springs back when lightly pressed, 8 to 10 minutes. While the cake is still hot, run a knife along the edges to release it from the pan. Immediately invert the cake onto a sheet of aluminum foil and remove the pan. Let the cake cool completely before peeling off the paper liner. The cake will stick to the foil as it cools. Peel off the paper liner. Lift the foil and turn the cake right side up onto another sheet of foil, with the old foil still stuck on top. Peel off the top sheet of foil, removing the brown "skin" from the cake as you do so.

Spread the cake with the desired filling. Roll (see How to Roll and Tighten a Cake Sheet, 964) and refrigerate for at least 1 hour until firm. If desired, frost or sift over the cake before serving:

Powdered sugar

GÉNOISE OR CHOCOLATE GÉNOISE SPONGE SHEET

Fill and frost to make a classic Bûche de Noël, 967. Vary the liqueur and buttercream flavors to create your own signature cake roll; you can also cut the sheet in four pieces to make a rectangular layer cake.

Preheat the oven to 350°F. Grease one 17½ x 11½-inch jelly-roll pan and line the bottom with wax or parchment paper.

Prepare the batter for:

Génoise, 948, or Chocolate Génoise, 948

Scrape the batter into the pan and spread evenly. Bake until the top springs back when lightly pressed, 15 to 20 minutes. While the cake is still hot, run a knife along the edges to release it from the pan. Immediately invert the cake onto a sheet of aluminum foil and remove the pan. Let the cake cool completely before peeling off the paper liner. The cake will stick to the foil as it cools.

Peel off the paper liner. Lift the foil and turn the cake right side up onto another sheet of foil, with the old foil still stuck on top. Peel off the top sheet of foil, removing the "skin" from the cake as you do so.

Moisten the cake, 989, then spread it with the desired filling. Roll (see How to Roll and Tighten a Cake Sheet, 964) and refrigerate for at least 1 hour until firm. If desired, frost or sift over the cake before serving:

Powdered sugar

CHIFFON CAKE SHEET

Fill with 2 to 2½ cups lightly whipped cream, or simply use to make any jelly roll.

Preheat the oven to 325°F. Grease one 17½ x 11½-inch jelly-roll pan and line the bottom with wax or parchment paper. Prepare half of the batter for:

Any chiffon cake, 949 to 950

Scrape the batter into the pan and spread evenly. Bake until the top is pale golden and springs back when lightly pressed, about 15 minutes. Let the cake cool completely in the pan on a rack. Run a knife along the edges to release the cake from the pan. Invert the cake onto a sheet of aluminum foil that has been sprinkled with:

Powdered sugar

Peel off the paper liner. Spread the cake with the desired filling. Roll (see How to Roll and Tighten a Cake Sheet, 964) and refrigerate for at least 1 hour until firm. If desired, frost or sift over the cake before serving:

Powdered sugar

ANGEL CAKE SHEET

Fill with 1½ cups Reduced-Fat Lemon Curd, 998, for a reduced-fat jelly roll or use to make any jelly rolls.

Preheat the oven to 350°F. Grease one 15½ x 10½-inch jelly-roll pan and line the bottom with wax or parchment paper.

Prepare half the batter for:

Basic Angel Cake, 952

Scrape the batter into the pan and spread evenly. Bake until the top springs back when lightly pressed, about 15 minutes. Let the cake cool completely in the pan on a rack. Run a knife along the edges to release the cake from the pan. Invert the cake onto a sheet of wax paper and remove the pan and paper liner. The cake will stick to the wax paper. Lift the wax paper and turn the cake right side up onto a sheet of aluminum foil. Peel off the wax paper, removing the top "skin" from the cake as you do so.

Spread the cake with the desired filling. Roll (see How to Roll and Tighten a Cake Sheet, 964) and refrigerate for at least 1 hour until firm. If desired, frost or sift over the cake before serving:

Powdered sugar

FLOURLESS CHOCOLATE SOUFFLÉ SHEET

10 to 12 servings

A thin, moist, and chocolaty sheet that is more like a layer of fallen chocolate soufflé. Severe cracking is inevitable as you begin to roll this fragile cake—but by the time the roll is completed, the cracks are gentler, and the overall effect is very tempting indeed. Whipped cream is a perfect filling, or make Double-Chocolate Roll, 964. No frosting is needed.

Have all ingredients at room temperature, 68° to 70°F. Preheat the oven to 375°F. Grease one 17½ x 11½-inch jelly-roll pan and line the bottom with wax or parchment paper.

Combine in a medium, heatproof bowl:

6 ounces bittersweet or semisweet chocolate, coarsely chopped
3 tablespoons water or strong coffee
1 teaspoon vanilla

Set the bowl in a large skillet of barely simmering water and stir often, until the chocolate is melted and smooth but not hot. Remove from the heat. In a large bowl, beat on medium speed until soft peaks form:

6 large egg whites
¼ teaspoon cream of tartar

Gradually add, beating on high speed:

¾ cup sugar

Beat until the peaks are stiff but not dry. Whisk into the warm chocolate mixture:

6 large egg yolks

Use a rubber spatula to fold in one-third of the egg whites. Scrape the mixture onto the egg whites and fold together. Scrape the batter into the pan and spread evenly. Bake for 10 minutes at 375°F, then reduce the oven temperature to 350°F, and bake until the top of the cake is firm to the touch, 5 to 7 minutes more. Let the cake cool completely in the pan on a rack. (The cake will sink dramatically as it cools.) Run a thin knife along the edges to release the cake from the pan. Invert the cake onto a sheet of aluminum foil that has been liberally sprinkled with:

Unsweetened cocoa

Peel off the paper liner. Spread the cake with the desired filling. Roll (see How to Roll and Tighten a Cake Sheet, 964) and refrigerate for at least 1 hour until firm. If desired, sift over the cake before serving:

Unsweetened cocoa or powdered sugar

REDUCED-FAT CHOCOLATE SOUFFLÉ SHEET

Although this cake sheet is still rich (37 percent calories from fat), there are no egg yolks and therefore it has no cholesterol.

Prepare Flourless Chocolate Soufflé Sheet, 954, omitting the egg yolks and decreasing the sugar to ½ cup.

ABOUT MERINGUE AND DACQUOISE PASTE

In the broadest sense, the term *meringue* refers to any baked or unbaked mixture of beaten egg whites with sugar. Meringue is frequently a component; it is folded into cake batters before baking, as well as into mousses, Bavarian creams, sauces, pancakes, and soufflés, or whenever an infusion of air or lightness is needed.

In this section, however, we are concerned with meringue in its finished baked form. Baked meringues can be crisp and dry throughout, crisp on the outside and marshmallowy within, or dry with a cakelike texture. They may be plain, flavored, or nutted. Dacquoise, also called Japonaise, Broyage, and Succès, is a crisp sheet of meringue with ground nuts and often a little flour or starch. Meringue and dacquoise, 957, are used as cake layers, on their own or alternated with thin sponge or génoise layers. Filled and frosted with buttercream, these make elegant European-style layer cakes such as Fresh Strawberry Dacquoise, 968. Crisp meringue is also used to make cookies and meringue mushrooms and meringue pie shells, meringues glacées, showy vacherins, and Windtortes to be filled with fruit and cream or ice cream.

Meringues are crisp or soft depending upon the ratio of sugar to egg whites and the temperature at which the meringue is baked. Crisp meringues are made with up to 2 cups of sugar for each cup of egg whites. They are baked in a very low oven (200° to 225°F) for as long as 2 hours, to dry them completely without browning or coloring. Then they are left to cool in the turned-off oven to ensure dryness; in former times, an overnight rest in an oven with a pilot light was the sure way to get perfect meringues. The same meringue base baked at 275°F for half the time is crisp on the outside and marshmallowy within. We encounter these types of meringues garnished with whipped cream and fruit in Schaumtortes. Soft meringue pie toppings, 000, and soft dry nut meringue cake layers are made with about half as much sugar and bake at higher temperatures for shorter periods of time.

Crisp dry meringue keeps for several weeks in airtight containers. We have tasted forgotten meringue mushrooms that were only slightly stale after being stored in a tin for 1 year! Do not refrigerate or freeze.

Crisp dry meringue shells or layers to be filled with whipped cream, custard, mousses, or any other moist fillings should be filled just before serving if they are to remain crisp. Otherwise, moisture from the filling will soften and ultimately disintegrate the meringue. This effect is sometimes desirable in dacquoise desserts, where a mousse or cream filling is meant to merge with the dacquoise by partially dissolving it. Meringues filled with ice cream or frozen desserts are called meringues glacées. These can be filled in advance and returned to the freezer, for up to 4 days, until serving; freezing protects the meringues from disintegration. Crisp meringue or dacquoise layers layered with buttercreams do not lose their crispness, though they mellow slightly, because the high fat content of the buttercream protects the layers from moisture.

As all meringues and variations are based on beaten egg whites, see page 928 for the proper beating technique. Crisp meringues can be made of granulated sugar beaten into the egg whites or of a combination of granulated and powdered sugar; some is folded rather than beaten in at the end. At their very best, both formulas produce a dry, light, tender meringue. Granulated sugar alone has the purest taste, but it is less forgiving and may turn out heavy from time to time. Mixing sugars consistently produces a light, tender meringue, but one with a slight taste and texture of starch from the cornstarch in the powdered sugar. Either type of meringue can be made using a warm method, wherein the egg whites, granulated sugar, and cream of tartar are combined and warmed to dissolve the sugar before the mixture is beaten. This is a good method for beginners, as it eliminates the guesswork of when to begin and how fast to add the sugar.

MERINGUE I (GRANULATED SUGAR)

12 servings

Have all ingredients at room temperature, 68° to 70°F. Preheat the oven to 225°F. Line cookie sheets with plain parchment paper for free-form meringues or individual meringue shells. To make layers, trace two 8- or 9-inch or three 7-inch circles on parchment, leaving an inch between them, and turn it upside down so that the tracing shows through but cannot transfer to the meringue.

In a large bowl, beat on medium speed until soft peaks form:

TO FORM AND BAKE MERINGUES AND DACQUOISE

To form individual meringues or kisses: Drop shapely dollops of meringue onto the prepared baking sheet with a soupspoon. Or pipe large "kiss" shapes using a pastry bag fitted with a large star tip.

To form individual shells: Drop large dollops of meringue onto the prepared baking sheet and use the back of a spoon to hollow out a nest in each one.

To form layers with a spatula: Divide the meringue evenly among the traced circles and spread with a spatula, making sure that the thickness of the meringue is as uniform as possible. Neaten the edges of each circle by tracing around them with your finger.

To form meringue layers with a pastry bag: Scrape the meringue into a large pastry bag fitted with a plain tip with a ⅜- to ½-inch opening. Starting in the center of each circle, pipe a widening spiral of meringue until each circle is covered with a coiled rope of meringue.

To form a pie shell: Spread the meringue in a greased pie pan and swirl and shape the meringue with the back of a spoon, making sure the edges are attractive. Pipe out and bake any extra meringue; it can be used to test for doneness.

Bake for 1½ to 2 hours. Remove a test shape from the oven and let it cool for 5 minutes. If it is dry and crisp to the bite, then similarly sized meringues are done. Larger meringues can also be tested by probing with the tip of a sharp paring knife. If the center of the meringue seems only slightly sticky, it will crisp as it cools. If meringue kisses are to be filled, you can make a depression in the flat side of each one with your finger while they are still slightly sticky inside and return them to the oven. (When cool, fill the depressions with whipped cream or ice cream and sandwich two kisses.) If in doubt, bake for the full 2 hours, or even a little longer. Leave the meringues in the turned-off oven to cool. If not using immediately, store airtight. Meringue layers are fragile. Cut the excess parchment paper from around each one and store still attached to the paper for protection. To remove it from the parchment, slide a slender metal spatula under the layer.

½ cup egg whites (about 4 large whites)
1 teaspoon vanilla (optional)
½ teaspoon cream of tartar

Very gradually add 1 tablespoon at a time, beating on high speed:

1 cup superfine sugar

Beat until the meringue holds very stiff peaks. Shape and bake as directed in To Form and Bake Meringues and Dacquoise, above, or recipe.

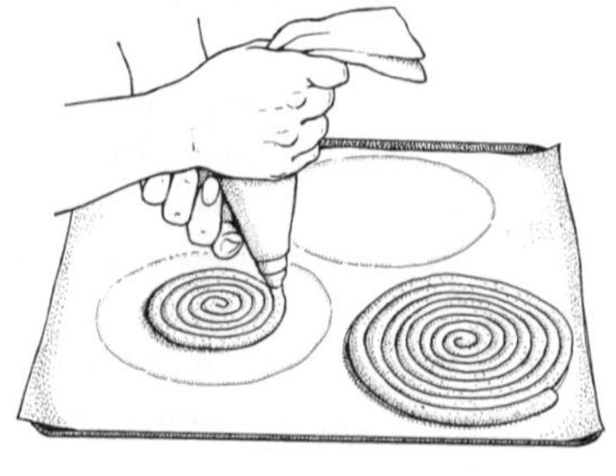

Form meringue layers by piping a widening spiral of meringue.

MERINGUE II (GRANULATED AND POWDERED SUGAR)

Prepare Meringue I, 955, reducing the superfine sugar to ⅔ cup. After beating it in, sift ⅔ cup powdered sugar over the meringue and fold in with a rubber spatula.

WARM-METHOD MERINGUE

Use this method for either Meringue I, 955, or Meringue II, above.

Whisk together the egg whites, superfine sugar, and cream of tartar in a large heatproof bowl. Set the bowl in a skillet of gently simmering water and whisk until the whites are warm, not hot, to the touch (110° to 115°F). Remove the bowl from the skillet and beat on high speed until the whites are stiff. If using the powdered sugar variation, fold in the powdered sugar.

COFFEE-FLAVORED MERINGUE

Prepare Meringue I, 955, Meringue II, 956, or Warm-Method Meringue, 956, stirring 2½ teaspoons instant espresso powder or pulverized freeze-dried instant coffee into the granulated sugar before adding it to the egg whites.

COCOA MERINGUE

Prepare Meringue II, 956, or Warm-Method Meringue, 956, sifting 3 tablespoons unsweetened cocoa with the powdered sugar before folding it into the meringue.

DACQUOISE

12 servings

This crisp nutted meringue is used to make torte layers that can be filled with buttercream or alternated with sponge cake or génoise layers before filling. Use from ½ to ¾ cup nuts, depending on how much nut flavor you wish.

Have all ingredients at room temperature, 68° to 70°F. Preheat the oven to 200°F. Line cookie sheets with parchment paper. Trace two 8- or 9-inch or three 7-inch circles on the parchment, leaving at least an inch between them, and turn it upside down so that the tracing shows through but cannot transfer to the meringue.

Combine in a food processor:

½ to ¾ cup whole nuts or pieces
⅓ cup sugar, preferably superfine
1 tablespoon cornstarch

Pulse until the mixture has the consistency of fine cornmeal; do not overprocess, or the nuts will become oily. In a large bowl beat on medium speed until soft peaks form:

½ cup egg whites (about 4 large whites)
½ teaspoon cream of tartar

Very gradually add 1 tablespoon at a time, beating on high speed:

½ cup sugar, preferably superfine

Beat until the meringue holds very stiff peaks. Fold in the nut mixture. Shape and bake the layers as directed in To Form and Bake Meringues and Dacquoise, 956.

MERINGUE MUSHROOMS

4 to 5 dozen mushrooms

It is best to use the warm method when preparing the meringue for these mushrooms, as it will hold its shape longer while you pipe the caps and stems.

Preheat the oven to 200°F. Line 2 baking sheets with parchment paper.

Prepare:

Meringue I, 955, Meringue II, 956, or Warm-Method Meringue, 956

Scrape the meringue into a large pastry bag fitted with a ½-inch plain tip. Pipe thin pointed "kiss" shapes about 1 inch tall to make stems. Pipe round button shapes onto the baking sheets to make mushroom caps. Use your finger to smooth the tops of the caps if necessary. Dust lightly with:

Unsweetened cocoa

Bake until crisp and completely dry, about 2 hours. Let cool in the turned-off oven. Melt in the top of a double boiler or in a microwave on medium:

2 ounces semisweet or bittersweet chocolate, coarsely chopped

Spread a little melted chocolate on the flat side of each meringue mushroom cap. Use a sharp knife to cut off and discard the pointed ends of the meringue stems, and attach the stems to the caps while the chocolate is still soft. Let stand until the chocolate is set. The mushrooms can be stored in an airtight container for up to 4 weeks.

SCHAUMTORTE

10 to 12 servings

Schaum means foam, which of course refers to the meringue. Of German origin, Schaumtorte recipes can be traced as far back as the 1870s in Wisconsin, where it is still a special-occasion cake. The torte was originally made with whipped cream; by the 1950s recipes also mentioned ice cream. The taste of cold creamy ice cream or whipped cream against sweet crisp meringue is raised to considerable heights with the addition of fresh berries and even more whipped cream.

Have all ingredients at room temperature, 68° to 70°F. Preheat the oven to 225°F. Grease and flour the sides of two 8-inch springform pans and line the bottoms with wax or parchment paper.

Prepare using the optional vanilla:

1½ recipes Meringue I, 955, Meringue II, 956, or Warm-Method Meringue, 956

Divide the meringue between the pans and spread

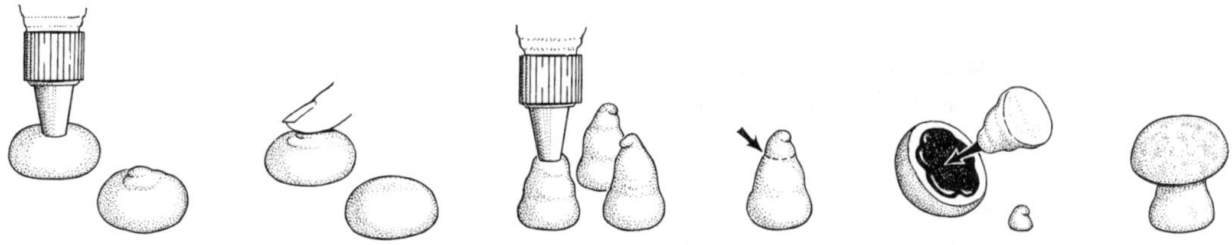

Forming meringue mushrooms

evenly. Bake for 2 hours. Turn off the oven and let the meringues cool in the oven. Slide a slim knife around the meringue to detach it from the pans; remove the pan sides. Invert the meringue and peel off the paper liners. Wash and dry 1 pan and return one of the layers to it. Spread with:

1 pint ice cream, slightly softened, or 1 cup heavy cream, whipped, sweetened to taste, and flavored with rum if desired

Place the second layer on top, pressing down gently. Wrap airtight and freeze if using ice cream, or refrigerate. To serve, unmold the torte and transfer it to a serving platter. Top with:

Whipped cream
Sliced or whole strawberries
Chocolate Sauce, 1045

ABOUT NUT TORTES AND CHOCOLATE TORTES

In Austria and Germany, the word *torte* refers to any round cake, plain or fancy, regardless of its ingredients or method of production. In America, *torte* is used to describe any cake that seems European or otherwise imported, or almost any cake that is considered "fancy." Yet a third definition refers to cakes from the Austro-Hungarian tradition that are made of ground nuts and crumbs in place of all or most of the flour. These nut tortes, and also chocolate tortes, are presented in this section.

Classic nut tortes are high in eggs, like sponge cakes, and are often made without dairy fat such as butter or cream, though we may serve them up with mountains of whipped cream. They are normally moist and not too sweet. The technique for preparing them resembles that of sponge cakes: Egg yolks and sugar are beaten until thick and pale yellow before flavorings and nuts are added. Stiffly beaten egg whites are folded in, often providing the only leavening, as opposed to baking soda or baking powder.

Chocolate nut tortes (with very little or no flour), and flourless and nutless chocolate tortes too, are related in method to nut tortes, in that leavening is usually provided by beaten egg whites. Without the structure provided by flour, all these cakes tend to sink in the center and remain moister than other cakes. They are ultrarich, not only in eggs but also in butter, chocolate, and nuts. Although chocolate nut torte recipes look similar to those for other nut tortes, there are marked differences in texture and crumb depending on whether the recipe contains small amounts of both flour and nuts, a larger amount of nuts with just a little flour, or a large quantity of nuts only. At the extreme, chocolate tortes with neither nuts nor flour actually resemble cheesecakes more than anything else.

Tortes are baked in springform or solid pans, usually with ungreased sides; the cakes rise and cling to the sides of the pans like sponge cakes. Let them cool right side up in the pan, then detach the cake from the pan after cooling.

HOW TO LEVEL AND UNMOLD A TORTE

To unmold, slide a thin flexible knife or small metal spatula around the edges of the cake, pressing it against the pan to avoid tearing the torte. With the cake still in the pan, level it by pressing down and compacting the raised edges with your fingers, so the center and edges of the torte are the same height, shown below. Invert and remove the paper liner, if using.

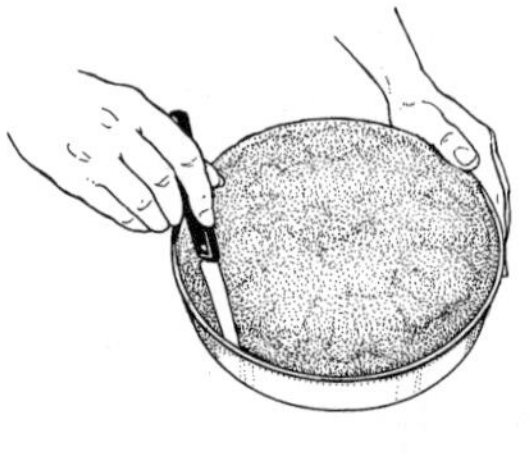

Slide a slim knife around the cake to detach it from the sides of the pan.

We often serve nut tortes right side up, without leveling them, simply sprinkled with powdered sugar. The natural depression in the center is inconsequential when served in this informal manner. You can pass a bowl of whipped cream separately. Or pipe or heap the cream dramatically in the center of the torte to cover the depression. For a more formal presentation, level the top of the torte before unmolding, then invert and stencil it, using a doily or hand-cut stencil, 992, or glaze with a chocolate glaze.

Press down the edges of the torte with your fingers.

ALMOND TORTE COCKAIGNE

10 servings

This traditional German Mandeltorte is not too sweet and is delightfully moist and light, with just the right hint of citrus.

Have all ingredients at room temperature, 68° to 70°F. Preheat the oven to 325°F. Grease and flour the bottom(s) of two 8 x 2-inch round pans or one 8-inch springform pan or line the bottom(s) with wax or parchment paper.

Finely grind:

¾ cup whole natural (unblanched) almonds

In a large bowl, beat on high speed until thick and pale yellow, about 2 minutes:

¾ cup sugar
6 large egg yolks

Stir in the almonds along with:

½ cup toasted fresh or dry unseasoned breadcrumbs
Grated zest and juice of 1 lemon or 1 small orange
1 teaspoon ground cinnamon
¼ teaspoon almond extract

In another large bowl, beat on medium speed until soft peaks form:

6 large egg whites
¼ teaspoon cream of tartar

Gradually add, beating on high speed:

¼ cup sugar

Beat until the peaks are stiff but not dry. Use a rubber spatula to fold one-quarter of the egg whites into the almond mixture, then fold in the remaining whites. Scrape the batter into the pan(s) and spread evenly. Bake until a toothpick inserted into the center comes out clean, about 20 minutes in round pans, 40 to 45 minutes in a springform pan. Let cool completely in the pan(s) on a rack; the center will sink as it cools. Slide a thin knife around the torte to detach it from the pan(s). Level and invert the torte (see page 958) before frosting with:

Whipped Cream, 995, Coffee Whipped Cream, 995, or Bittersweet Chocolate Glaze, 1003

Or if using a springform pan, simply remove the pan side, invert, remove the paper liner(s), if using, and serve right side up sprinkled with:

Powdered sugar

Layers can be filled with:

Flavored whipped cream, a mixture of whipped cream and Lemon Curd, 998, or Lemon-Orange Custard Filling, 999

HAZELNUT TORTE

Prepare Almond Torte Cockaigne, above, substituting either whole unblanched hazelnuts or toasted peeled hazelnuts for part or all of the almonds. Omit the citrus zest and juice, cinnamon, and almond extract.

FLOURLESS MATZO ALMOND TORTE

Prepare Almond Torte Cockaigne, above, substituting ½ cup matzo meal for the breadcrumbs.

QUEEN OF SHEBA (CHOCOLATE ALMOND TORTE)

10 to 12 servings

Moist and rich with brandy and almonds, this French standard is a well-known part of the American repertoire today. There are countless variations. In fact, the brown sugar called for is an American touch. You can substitute walnuts, pecans, toasted hazelnuts, or even peanuts for the almonds and select a compatible liqueur. And, yes, you can simply omit the alcohol. For an even more bittersweet cake, substitute 1 ounce unsweetened chocolate for 1 ounce of the semisweet or bittersweet.

Have all ingredients at room temperature, 68° to 70°F. Preheat the oven to 375°F. Grease and flour the bottom of one 9-inch springform pan or line the bottom with wax or parchment paper.

Combine in a large heatproof bowl:

9 ounces semisweet or bittersweet chocolate, coarsely chopped
12 tablespoons (1½ sticks) unsalted butter, cut into small pieces

Set the bowl in a large skillet of barely simmering water and stir often until the chocolate and butter are warm, melted, and smooth. Meanwhile, finely grind:

⅓ cup all-purpose flour
¼ cup whole natural (unblanched) almonds

In a medium bowl, whisk together until thick and pale yellow:

6 large egg yolks
½ cup sugar
⅓ cup brown or white sugar
¼ cup brandy (optional)
⅛ teaspoon almond extract

Remove the chocolate mixture from the heat and whisk in the egg mixture. In another medium bowl, beat on medium speed until soft peaks form:

6 large egg whites
¼ teaspoon cream of tartar

Gradually add, beating on high speed:

¼ cup sugar

Beat until the peaks are stiff but not dry. Use a rubber spatula to fold one-quarter of the egg whites into the chocolate mixture, along with the nut mixture. Fold in the remaining whites. Scrape the batter into the pan and spread evenly. Bake until a toothpick inserted 1 inch from the edge of the cake comes out clean, 35 to 40 minutes; the center will remain moist and gooey. Let cool completely in the pan on a rack; the center will sink as it cools. Slide a thin knife around the torte to detach it from the pan. Level and invert the torte (see page 958) before glazing or frosting with:

Bittersweet Chocolate Glaze, 1003, or Chocolate Ganache Glaze, 1003

Or simply remove the pan side, invert, remove the paper liner, if using, and serve right side up sprinkled with:

Powdered sugar

and accompanied with:

Whipped cream or Custard Sauce, 1041 (optional)

Store and serve at room temperature.

INDIVIDUAL MOLTEN CHOCOLATE CAKES

6 to 8 cakes

These are flourless, ultrarich, sauce-in-the-center, bittersweet chocolate cakes baked in a muffin tin and served warm. They are worthy of an elegant dinner party. You can make the batter ahead, scrape it into the muffin tin, and cover and refrigerate overnight before baking.

Have all ingredients at room temperature, 68° to 70°F. Preheat the oven to 400°F. Butter and sugar 8 muffin cups.

In the top of a double boiler or in a microwave on medium, heat, stirring often, until the chocolate and butter are melted and smooth:

6 ounces bittersweet or semisweet chocolate, coarsely chopped

6 tablespoons (¾ stick) unsalted butter

Remove from the heat and sift in:

¼ cup unsweetened cocoa

Stir until smooth. In a medium bowl, beat on medium speed until soft peaks form:

4 large egg whites

⅛ teaspoon cream of tartar

Gradually add, beating on high speed:

2 tablespoons sugar

Beat until the peaks are stiff but not dry. Use a rubber spatula to fold one-quarter of the egg whites into the chocolate mixture, then fold in the remaining whites. Fill the muffin cups about three-quarters full. Bake until the cakes are cracked on the top but still gooey in the center, 7 to 8 minutes (a minute or so longer if the batter has been stored in the refrigerator). Let sit for 2 to 3 minutes; the cakes will shrink slightly from the sides of the pan. Place a rack over the cakes and invert to unmold. Serve hot, accompanied with:

Whipped cream

FLOURLESS CHOCOLATE DECADENCE

12 to 14 servings

It is hard to find an elegant restaurant in the United States that does not offer a flourless or nearly flourless chocolate cake today. Choose a fine-quality chocolate, as chocolate is the star ingredient. Serve in very small wedges with whipped cream and fresh raspberries or Fresh Raspberry Sauce, 1048.

Have all ingredients at room temperature, 68° to 70°F. Preheat the oven to 325°F. Grease an 8 x 2-inch round pan (not a springform) and line the bottom with wax or parchment paper.

Combine in a large heatproof bowl:

1 pound bittersweet or semisweet chocolate, coarsely chopped

10 tablespoons (1¼ sticks) unsalted butter, cut into 10 pieces

Set the bowl in a large skillet of barely simmering water and stir often until the chocolate and butter are warm, melted, and smooth. Remove from the heat and whisk in:

5 large egg yolks

In another large bowl, beat on medium speed until soft peaks form:

5 large egg whites

¼ teaspoon cream of tartar

Gradually add, beating on high speed:

1 tablespoon sugar

Beat until the peaks are stiff but not dry. Use a rubber spatula to fold one-quarter of the egg whites into the chocolate mixture, then fold in the remaining whites. Scrape the batter into the pan and spread evenly. Set the pan in a large shallow baking dish or roasting pan, set the baking dish in the oven, and pour enough boiling water into it to reach halfway up the sides of the cake pan. Bake for exactly 30 minutes; the top of the cake will have a thin crust and the interior will still be gooey. Set the cake pan on a rack to cool completely, then refrigerate until chilled or overnight. To unmold, slide a thin knife around the cake to detach it from the pan. Invert the cake and peel off the paper liner. Reinvert onto a serving platter. Using a doily or hand-cut stencil, 992, if desired, sprinkle with:

Powdered sugar

Store in the refrigerator, but remove 1 hour or more before serving to soften. Serve with:

Whipped cream and fresh raspberries or Fresh Raspberry Sauce, 1048

CHOCOLATE MOUSSE CAKE (REDUCED FAT)

12 servings

Only 1¼ inches tall, this confection has the texture of mousse, with the intensity of a bittersweet chocolate truffle. Do use a good-quality chocolate and the best Dutch-process cocoa you can find.

Have all ingredients at room temperature, 68° to 70°F. Preheat the oven to 350°F. Grease the sides of one 8 x 2-inch round pan (not a springform) and line the bottom with wax or parchment paper.

Place in a large heatproof bowl:

5 ounces bittersweet or semisweet chocolate, coarsely chopped

Combine in a small, heavy saucepan:

⅔ cup sugar
½ cup unsweetened Dutch-process cocoa
2 tablespoons all-purpose flour

Stir in enough to make a paste, then stir in the rest:

¾ cup low-fat milk

Bring to a simmer over medium heat, stirring constantly with a wooden spoon to prevent scorching. Reduce the heat and simmer very gently, stirring constantly, until the mixture is slightly thickened, about 1 minute. Immediately pour the hot mixture over the chopped chocolate and whisk until the chocolate is melted and the mixture is completely smooth. Whisk in:

2 large egg yolks
1 teaspoon vanilla

In a medium bowl, beat on medium speed until soft peaks form:

4 large egg whites
¼ teaspoon cream of tartar

Gradually add, beating on high speed:

¼ cup sugar

Beat until the peaks are stiff but not dry. Use a rubber spatula to fold one-quarter of the egg whites into the chocolate mixture, then fold in the remaining whites. Scrape the batter into the pan and spread evenly. Set the pan in a large shallow baking dish or roasting pan, set the baking dish in the oven, and pour enough boiling water into it to reach halfway up the sides of the cake pan. Bake for exactly 40 minutes. The top of the cake will feel firm and the interior will still be gooey. Set the cake pan on a rack to cool completely, then refrigerate until chilled, or overnight. To unmold, slide a thin knife around the cake to detach it from the pan. Invert the cake and peel off the paper liner. Reinvert onto a serving platter. Using a doily or hand-cut stencil, 992, if desired, sprinkle with:

Powdered sugar

ABOUT CUPCAKES AND MINIATURE CAKES

You can transform any cake batter into cupcakes by baking it in muffin pans lined with fluted paper liners or pans that are greased and floured (even for sponge and angel cake batters, which are normally baked in ungreased pans). Paper liners are easy and neat; they also keep cupcakes moist and fresh longer. Children enjoy eating cupcakes that have been baked in flat-bottomed ice cream cones (set the cones on a cookie sheet before baking).

Fill muffin cups or ice cream cones about two-thirds full and bake at the temperature recommended for the batter you have chosen. Baking time will be about 20 minutes (25 minutes for cones), depending on the quantity and type of batter. It is always best to check early and watch carefully. Bake until the tops spring back when lightly pressed and a toothpick inserted into the center of a cupcake comes out clean. Let cool in the pan for about 5 minutes before unmolding or removing.

In addition to cupcakes, you can transform rich butter cake batters into sophisticated miniature cakes, to be eaten like cookies. Bake in small decorative molds such as small round or rectangular tartlet pans, madeleine molds, or scallop shell molds. Grease and flour the molds and fill them about half full. Baking time will be about 10 minutes, more or less, depending on the size of the molds. Serve sprinkled with powdered sugar or glaze with Translucent Sugar Glaze, 1010, made with rum, or Quick Lemon Icing, 1006, and serve with coffee or tea.

FROSTING AND DECORATING CUPCAKES

Choose any icing or frosting for cupcakes. Stiff or creamy icings can be spread with a small knife or spatula. To apply a chocolate glaze, hold cupcakes upside down and dip the tops. For a pointed swirl on top, dip into a soft, fluffy topping such as Seven-Minute Frosting, 1001, and twist as you lift and turn the cupcake right side up.

ESPECIALLY FOR CHILDREN

Decorate cupcakes with faces, using raisins, nuts, and/or candies for the features. Or stick a small inexpensive plastic doll in each cupcake up to its waist and frost the cakes to resemble fancy ball gowns or tutus. Use candies, colored sugars, or shot for sequins and jewels. For a children's party activity, supply a variety of decorations and let each child create his or her own miniature cake.

PEANUT BUTTER CUPCAKES *18 cupcakes*

Faster than lightning to make. Frost with Chocolate Satin Frosting, 1004, or Peanut Butter Frosting, 1008, and sprinkle with chopped peanuts.

Preheat the oven to 350°F. Line muffin pans with paper liners.

Combine in a food processor:

1¼ cups all-purpose flour
¾ cup packed light or dark brown sugar
1½ teaspoons baking powder
½ teaspoon salt
¾ cup milk
⅓ cup creamy peanut butter
1 large egg
1 tablespoon unsalted butter, softened
1 tablespoon vegetable oil
1 teaspoon vanilla
¾ cup semisweet chocolate chips

Pulse for a few seconds to mix. Scrape the sides of the bowl and the blade and pulse until smooth. Fill the muffin cups about two-thirds full. Bake until a toothpick inserted in the center of a cupcake comes out clean, 25 to 30 minutes. Remove from the pan and let cool completely on a rack before frosting.

BLACK BOTTOM CUPCAKES *16 cupcakes*

Moist, dark chocolate cupcakes with a heart of cream cheese and chocolate chips.

Preheat the oven to 350°F. Line muffin pans with paper liners.

In a medium bowl, beat until smooth:

8 ounces cream cheese, softened

Dipping the tops of cupcakes into glaze

⅓ cup sugar

Add and beat until smooth:

1 large egg

Stir in:

1 cup semisweet chocolate chips

Whisk together thoroughly in a large bowl:

1½ cups all-purpose flour
1 cup sugar
¼ cup unsweetened nonalkalized cocoa
1 teaspoon baking soda
½ teaspoon salt

Add:

1 cup water
⅓ cup vegetable oil
1 tablespoon white vinegar
1 teaspoon vanilla

Stir with a rubber spatula just until smooth. Fill the muffin cups about half full. Place a heaping tablespoon of the cream cheese mixture in the center of each. Bake until a toothpick inserted into the cakey part of a cupcake comes out clean, 20 to 25 minutes. Remove from the pan and let cool completely on a rack before frosting.

MADELEINES *About 24 teacakes*

These buttery French teacakes, something between a sponge cake and a butter cake in texture, are traditionally baked in scallop-shaped madeleine molds, but you can use miniature muffin tins or small tartlet pans in any shape.

Have all ingredients at room temperature, 68° to 70°F.

Preheat the oven to 450°F. Using melted butter, generously grease 2 madeleine pans, each with 12 molds.

Sift together and return to the sifter:

1½ cups sifted cake flour
½ teaspoon baking powder
¼ teaspoon salt

In a medium bowl, mash and beat with a wooden spoon or rubber spatula until very soft and creamy:

12 tablespoons (1½ sticks) unsalted butter, cut into small pieces

Warm the bowl by dipping it into hot water if necessary to hasten the softening of the butter. In a large

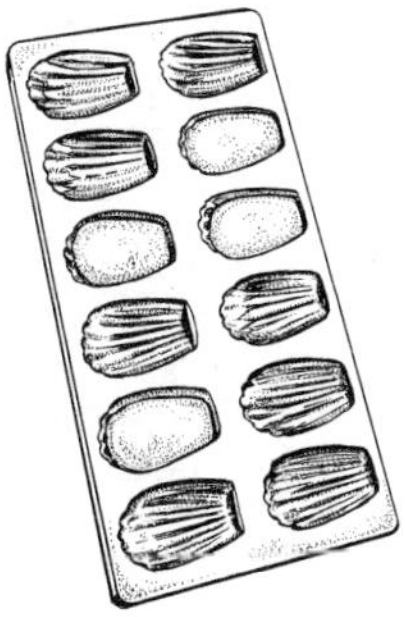

Madeleine pan

Glazing petits fours

bowl, beat on high speed until thick and pale yellow, about 2 minutes:

3 large eggs
1 large egg yolk
¾ cup sugar
1½ teaspoons vanilla

Sift the flour mixture over the top and fold in with a rubber spatula. Fold a dollop of the egg mixture into the butter. Scrape the butter mixture back into the remaining egg mixture and fold together. Let rest for at least 30 minutes.

Fill the molds three-quarters full; set any remaining batter aside. Bake until the cakes are golden on the top and golden brown around the edges, 8 to 10 minutes. Immediately loosen each cake with the tip of a slim knife and unmold onto a rack to cool. If necessary, wipe the molds clean, let cool, rebutter them, and repeat the baking process with the remaining batter. These are best the day they are made, but can be stored in an airtight container for a day or two.

ABOUT PETITS FOURS

Traditional petits fours are made of white cake (such as Lady Cake, 938), split and filled with jam and iced with white, pink, and green fondant. You can create interesting and equally elegant petits fours from any cake, filling, and frosting you choose.

The Cake: Hot-Milk Sponge Sheet, 953, or any cake or sponge sheet normally baked in a jelly roll is a very good choice. However, you can bake any cake batter in a 17½ x 11½-inch jelly-roll pan lined with wax or parchment paper. Baking time will be 10 to 15 minutes, at the temperature recommended for the cake. Watch carefully and bake just until the top of the cake springs back when lightly pressed and a toothpick inserted into a few places comes out clean. Let cool completely in the pan on a rack before filling and frosting.

Filling the Cake: If the finished cake is ½ inch tall or less, cut it in thirds crosswise and spread two of the pieces with jam (heated and strained or pureed for easy spreading) or a filling or buttercream of your choice. Stack the layers with the uncoated piece on top. If the finished cake is 1 inch or more tall after baking, cut it into thirds to make it easier to handle, then cut each piece into two or three layers with a serrated knife before filling. (If the cake is rich, don't bother splitting or filling it—simply cut and glaze it.) Place the filled cake strips on a cookie sheet and cover the top and sides with plastic wrap. Place a second cookie sheet on top and weight with canned goods to level and compact the layers so they will not come apart when cut into small shapes. Refrigerate for several hours, until firm, or wrap and freeze for up to 3 months.

Cutting and Glazing the Petits Fours: If desired, first brush hot strained preserves over the filled cake strips and top with a ⅛-inch-thick layer of rolled marzipan. With cookie or canapé cutters, cut the cake into small squares or diamonds, rounds or hearts, or other shapes. If you have not covered the cake with preserves and marzipan, you can brush the top and sides of each cut shape with hot preserves now, or spread a thin coat of buttercream on the tops and sides. Refrigerate to set the coating before glazing. Place the cakes slightly apart on a wire grid or a rack set on a baking sheet. Spoon Bittersweet Chocolate Glaze, 1003, Chocolate Ganache Glaze, 1003, or Fondant Icing, 1000, over each one, shown above. Once the glaze or fondant is set, you can decorate the petits fours with pieces of candied violets or rose petals, candied fruits, dragées, sliced almonds or pistachios. Or pipe dainty designs with melted chocolate or tinted fondant. If you like, serve in pleated paper cups. Petits fours can be completed up to 24 hours in advance.

ABOUT COMPONENT CAKES

To the serious baker, butter cakes and sponges, crisp meringues, mousses, creams, and custards are more than simply delicious in their own right. Along with frostings, fillings, buttercreams, sauces, and toppings, each is a building block. The simplest component cake—a filled and frosted birthday cake—has only two elements, cake and icing. At the other end of the spectrum, a European layer cake may be fashioned from as many as four different components.

The canny host who seems to produce showstopping desserts without breaking a sweat most likely relies on a well-stocked freezer, refrigerator, and pantry. With components prepared in advance, impressive desserts can be quickly assembled.

HOW TO ROLL AND TIGHTEN A CAKE SHEET

Here is how to roll a cooled cake sheet tightly so it keeps a nice round shape. Before filling any cake sheet, let it cool completely, peel off the paper liner, and transfer the cake to a sheet of aluminum foil (not wax paper or plastic wrap) exactly as described in the individual cake sheet recipe. Rolled cakes, like sleeping bags, must be rolled tightly at the beginning to ensure a compact shape at the finish. Fold and press an inch or so of the cake firmly up over the filling at one end to get started. Even if the cake cracks at first, keep these first turns especially tight; cracking will diminish as the diameter of the roll increases. Use the sheet of foil under the cake to help roll the cake. When the cake is rolled, use two hands to move the roll carefully back to the center of the foil. Wrap the back of the foil over the cake so that it overlaps the front portion of foil, covering the roll completely. Place the edge of a yardstick or a cookie sheet on top of the foil right in front of the long end of the cake roll facing you. Tighten the cake roll by pressing the yardstick or cookie sheet at an angle toward the counter while you grasp the bottom sheet of foil, shown above, right. Then wrap the tightened cake roll in the foil and fold the ends. Refrigerate to firm the roll before unwrapping and serving.

OLD-FASHIONED JELLY ROLL *10 to 12 servings*

This may be as simple as cake rolled up with jam, but we like it best with the addition of whipped cream or pastry cream. If the sponge is brushed with a little brandy or rum before it is filled, you will have created a trifle in the form of a jelly roll.

Prepare:

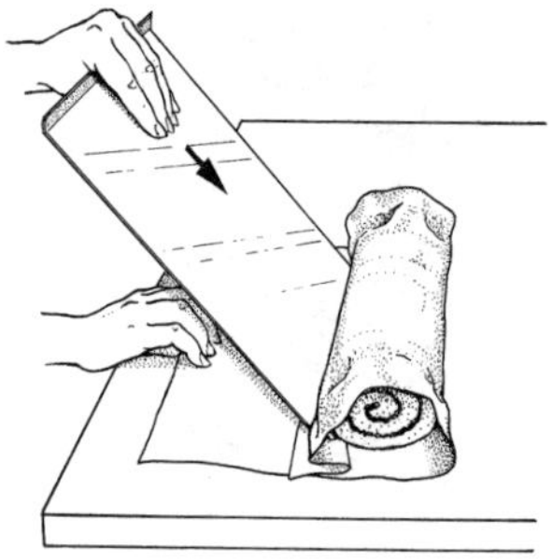

Tightening the cake roll

Hot-Milk Sponge Sheet, 953, or Angel Cake Sheet, 954

When cool, sprinkle with:

Powdered sugar

Spread with:

About ¾ cup jam or preserves, and/or 2 to 2½ cups lightly sweetened plain or flavored whipped cream, or 1½ to 2 cups Pastry Cream, 996

Starting at a long edge and using the foil to help roll, roll and tighten the cake, above (it may crack at first). Wrap and refrigerate for at least 1 to 2 hours until firm, or up to 24 hours before serving. To serve, sprinkle with:

Powdered sugar

LEMON JELLY ROLL

Substitute 1⅓ to 2 cups Lemon Curd, 998, or Lemon Filling, 998, for the fillings listed. For those who like their cake moistened with liquor, sprinkle or brush Old-Fashioned Jelly Roll, above, with a little dark rum before filling. Sift powdered sugar over the roll before serving.

CHOCOLATE-FILLED JELLY ROLL

Prepare Old-Fashioned Jelly Roll, above, filling with 2 to 3 cups Whipped Chocolate Ganache, 1005, Cocoa Whipped Cream, 996, or Mocha Whipped Cream, 995, or 1½ to 2 cups Chocolate Buttercream, 1002, Chocolate Custard Filling, 997, or Mocha Filling, 998. Sift unsweetened cocoa or powdered sugar over the roll before serving.

DOUBLE-CHOCOLATE ROLL *10 to 12 servings*

Prepare:

Flourless Chocolate Soufflé Sheet, 954

When cool, transfer to a sheet of aluminum foil that has been sprinkled with:

Unsweetened alkalized Dutch-process cocoa

Spread with:

2 to 3 cups Whipped Chocolate Ganache, 1005, Cocoa Whipped Cream, 996, or Mocha Whipped Cream, 995, or 1½ to 2 cups Chocolate Buttercream, 1002

Starting at a long edge and using the foil to help roll, 964, roll up and tighten the cake (it may crack at first). Wrap and refrigerate for at least 1 to 2 hours until firm, or up to 24 hours before serving. To serve, sprinkle with:

Unsweetened alkalized Dutch-process cocoa or powdered sugar (optional)

BAKED ALASKA

Miraculously, a little cake on the bottom and a covering of soft meringue is enough to insulate ice cream, even as the topping is browned in a hot oven. Use a homemade ice cream or parfait, or simply buy ice cream, sorbet, or frozen yogurt. The sky's the limit on flavors. Traditionally the cake is a génoise or sponge cake, but you can use angel cake, chiffon cake, or even a layer of brownies. Baked Alaska can be flambéed for a dramatic presentation. We also like to pass a pitcher of warm chocolate or caramel sauce.

The simplest Baked Alaska is made by positioning a solid frozen brick of ice cream (1½ pints or even ½ gallon) on top of a layer of cake, at least ½ inch thick and slightly larger all around than the ice cream. The cake can first be sprinkled lightly with rum, brandy, or a liqueur of choice or brushed liberally with a combination of Simple Syrup, 1010, and liquor. Trim the cake to match the dimensions of the ice cream and slip an aluminum-foil-covered double layer of cardboard under the cake. The ice cream can be topped with a second thin layer of cake, if desired. Return the dessert to the freezer until needed. To serve, preheat the oven to 425°F. Frost the dessert with a thick layer of Soft Meringue Topping I, 1012, or Soft Meringue Topping II, 1012, making sure to cover the lower edge of the cake on all sides. Swirl the topping decoratively with the back of a spoon, or pipe it onto the ice cream with a pastry bag and a large star tip. Sift powdered sugar over the topping and brown it according to the instructions in the topping recipe. (If the ice cream was frozen solid, the Baked Alaska can wait for a few minutes—but just a few—before serving.)

For a dome- or melon-shaped Baked Alaska, soften the ice cream slightly and mold it in a bowl or melon-shaped mold lined with plastic wrap; then freeze the cake or roll solid before proceeding. You can even fill a layer cake or jelly roll with softened ice cream and freeze hard before proceeding. A layer of brownies substituted for cake is best if assembled with the hard ice cream less than an hour before topping and browning; if frozen solid with the ice cream, the brownie layer will be too hard to eat.

To flambé successfully, choose a liquor with a high alcohol content—80 proof or higher. Wash half of an eggshell and, before browning the dessert, embed it like a small cup in the meringue. Just before serving, place ¼ cup liquor and a ladle in a small saucepan. Heat the ladle and the liquor just until the liquor begins to bubble (do not allow the liquor to boil off, or it will not stay lit when you need it to). Immediately ask someone to turn out the lights. Ladle part of the liquor into the eggshell and ignite it with a match. As the liquor burns, fill the warmed ladle half full with more of the warmed liquor and drizzle it slowly into the eggshell, raising the ladle as high as you safely can. The flame will go out by itself when the alcohol burns off.

LADY BALTIMORE CAKE

10 to 12 servings

This cake, filled with fruit and nuts and frosted with mountains of fluffy frosting, was served in the Lady Baltimore Tea Room in late-nineteenth-century Charleston, South Carolina. It remains a southern specialty. Try our Neoclassic Lady Baltimore Filling, made with freshly whipped cream.

Prepare:

White Cake, 937, or Lady Cake, 938, baked in three 8-inch layers

Classic Lady Baltimore Filling and Frosting, 1001, or Neoclassic Lady Baltimore Filling and Frosting, 996

Spread the filling between the cake layers. Frost the top and sides with the remaining frosting. Serve the classic version at room temperature within a few hours of frosting. Refrigerate the whipped cream version in a covered container for up to 24 hours in advance. Remove it from the refrigerator 1 hour before serving for the best texture and flavor.

LANE CAKE

10 to 12 servings

Emma Rylander Lane, of Eufala, Alabama, published a version of this popular southern cake in her 1898 edition of *Some Good Things to Eat.* The addition of pecans, coconut, dates, and cherries—even kumquats—to Mrs. Rylander's original filling of yolks, butter, sugar, and raisins is testimony to a cook's natural inclination to embellish and create.

Prepare:

White Cake, 937, or Lady Cake, 938, baked in three 8-inch layers

2¼ cups Lane Cake Filling, 1000

Spread two-thirds of the filling between the cake layers and frost the top with the remainder. Store at room temperature in a covered container for up to 24 hours before serving.

BOSTON CREAM PIE *10 to 12 servings*

Dessert history was made at Boston's Parker House Hotel in the 1850s, when a German pastry chef added a dark chocolate topping to the classic two-layer custard filled sponge cake known as Boston Pie. The Boston Pie is long forgotten, but the Boston Cream Pie is popular once again. We prefer the sponge cake, but you can use one of the butter cakes suggested here.

Prepare:

Hot-Milk Sponge Cake, 947 (or use 2 layers 1-2-3-4 Yellow Cake, 938, or Gold Cake, 938)
1 to 1½ cups Pastry Cream, 996
½ cup Bittersweet Chocolate Glaze, 1003

If using the sponge cake, split it in half to make 2 layers. Spread the pastry cream between the cake layers. Pour the glaze on the top, spreading it gently so that it drips randomly down the sides if desired. Refrigerate in a covered container for up to 24 hours before serving. Remove from the refrigerator 30 to 60 minutes before serving.

TIRAMISÙ *10 to 12 servings*

Tiramisù is Italian for "pick me up"—and how could ladyfingers soaked in espresso and brandy and slathered with sweetened Marsala-laced mascarpone fail to do so?

Prepare:

24 Ladyfingers, 948, or 1 European Sponge Cake, 947, or Génoise, 948, baked in two 8 x 8-inch pans

Preheat the oven to 350°F. If using the sponge cake or génoise, use only 1½ layers. Cut 1 layer into 8 strips and the half layer into 4. Cut all the strips in half. Arrange the ladyfingers or cake strips on a baking sheet. Bake until golden brown and crisp, 8 to 10 minutes. Let cool. Meanwhile, in a medium heatproof bowl, beat on high speed until thick and pale yellow, about 2 minutes:

5 large egg yolks
⅓ cup sugar

Whisk in:

⅓ cup sweet Marsala
1 tablespoon water

Set the bowl in a large skillet of barely simmering water and whisk or beat on low speed until the mixture reaches 160°F. Remove the bowl from the skillet and let cool for about 15 minutes, stirring from time to time.

Beat until soft peaks form:

½ cup heavy cream
2 teaspoons vanilla

Place in a large bowl:

12 to 14 ounces mascarpone cheese, softened

Fold in the whipped cream and the cooled egg yolk mixture. Combine in a shallow dish:

¾ to 1 cup cooled espresso or extra-strong coffee
2 to 3 tablespoons rum or brandy
2 to 3 tablespoons sugar

Dip half of the ladyfingers or cake strips into the espresso mixture and arrange in a serving dish, leaving a little space between each. Spread half of the mascarpone filling over and between the ladyfingers or cake strips. Sprinkle with half of:

5 ounces bittersweet or semisweet chocolate, grated

Dip the remaining ladyfingers into the remaining espresso mixture and arrange on top. Spread the remaining filling over and between the ladyfingers and sprinkle with the remaining chocolate. Sift over the top:

1 tablespoon unsweetened cocoa

Cover and refrigerate for at least 1 hour or up to 24 hours before serving.

TRIFLE *12 to 14 servings*

Traditionally this English dessert features vanilla custard and raspberries. Remember, you may use fresh, frozen, or canned fruit; omit the wine in favor of coffee or fruit juice or puree; or add amaretti crumbs, or chopped chocolate.

Prepare:

24 to 30 Ladyfingers, 948, Génoise, 948, or any sponge cake, cut into pieces of any size, or the equivalent quantity of any leftover cake
1½ recipes Custard Sauce, 1041, 9 egg yolks, ¾ cup sugar, 1½ cups whole milk, and 1½ cups heavy cream

Refrigerate until cold.

Arrange half of the ladyfinger or cake pieces in the bottom of a 2- to 3-quart serving bowl. (If the bowl is glass, make sure that each layer of ingredients touches the sides of the bowl so that the colors and textures can be seen.) Sprinkle with:

2 to 4 tablespoons sweet wine (such as sherry, muscat, Marsala, or Sauternes), brandy, or rum

Spread with half of:

½ to ¾ cup preserves

Sprinkle with half of:

2 cups fresh berries or sliced fruit

Top with half of the custard and sprinkle with:

2 tablespoons sliced or slivered blanched almonds, toasted

Repeat the assembly with the remaining ladyfinger or cake pieces, liquor, preserves, fruit, and custard. Whip until nearly stiff:

¾ cup heavy cream
2 to 3 teaspoons sugar
½ teaspoon vanilla

Spread the cream or pipe it decoratively on top of the trifle. Sprinkle with:

2 tablespoons sliced or slivered blanched almonds, toasted

Cover and refrigerate for at least 3 hours (longer is better) or up to 24 hours before serving.

LATIN SPONGE CAKE WITH "THREE MILKS" (TRES LECHES)

8 to 10 servings

This Latin American dessert is a simple sponge cake drenched with a sweet mixture of three types of milk and cream, which forms a rich interior sauce. It is traditionally topped with sweet soft meringue; replace the meringue with whipped cream if you prefer.

Have all ingredients at room temperature, 68° to 70°F. Preheat the oven to 350°F (325°F if the baking pan is glass). Grease one 9 x 9-inch pan or one 11 x 7-inch pan. Sift together:

1 cup all-purpose flour
2 teaspoons baking powder

In a large bowl, beat on medium speed until soft peaks form:

3 large egg whites
⅛ teaspoon cream of tartar (optional)

Gradually add, beating on high speed:

1 cup sugar

Beat in 1 at a time:

3 large egg yolks

Add one-quarter of the flour mixture at a time, beating on low speed or stirring with a rubber spatula just until incorporated and scraping the sides of the bowl as necessary. Add and beat just until the mixture is smooth and evenly mixed:

¼ cup milk

Scrape the batter into the pan and spread evenly. Bake until the top springs back when lightly pressed and a toothpick inserted into the center comes out clean, 25 to 30 minutes. Let cool in the pan on a rack for 10 minutes. Meanwhile, combine:

1 cup heavy cream
One 12-ounce can evaporated milk
One 14-ounce can sweetened condensed milk

Leaving the cake in the pan, prick it with a toothpick at 1-inch intervals. Pour the milk mixture slowly over the cake, including the corners and the edges. Refrigerate for at least 1 hour before serving or overnight.

To make the meringue topping, combine in a 2½-quart heatproof bowl (preferably stainless steel):

⅔ cup light corn syrup
2 large egg whites

Bring about 1 inch of water to a gentle simmer in a wide, deep skillet. Set the bowl of egg whites directly in the hot water. Immediately begin beating on low speed, moving the mixer all around the bowl, until the mixture reaches 140°F. If you must stop beating for any reason, remove the bowl from the hot water until you can resume, to prevent the egg whites from scrambling. Beat on high speed for 5 minutes; the mixture will be billowy and hold a stiff shape. Remove the bowl from the skillet and beat for 2 to 3 more minutes until the meringue is cool. To serve, leave the cake in the pan or slide a slim knife around the cake to detach it from the pan. Invert the cake onto a large shallow serving platter with enough of a rim to hold the excess milk that will gradually collect around the cake like a sauce. Spread or pipe the meringue topping over the cake. Cut into squares to serve.

BÛCHE DE NOËL

12 to 14 servings

The traditional Yule Log Cake is a work of art, complete with meringue mushrooms and sprigs of pine. Ours serves as a stunning holiday centerpiece until the moment of serving. Instead of coffee, flavor the buttercream filling with crushed or ground toasted or caramelized nuts. Or, instead of buttercream, try folding whipped cream into Lemon Curd, 998, for a light tangy filling, or use Whipped Ganache Filling and Frosting, 1005.

Prepare:

Hot-Milk Sponge Sheet, 953, or Chocolate Génoise Sponge Sheet, 953
3 cups Classic Buttercream, 1001, or Swiss Meringue Buttercream, 1002

Stir together until the coffee is dissolved:

1½ teaspoons instant espresso or coffee powder
1 teaspoon water

Flavor 1⅔ cups of the buttercream with as much of this mixture as you wish. Combine in a medium bowl:

8 to 9 ounces bittersweet or semisweet chocolate, finely chopped
⅓ cup boiling water

Stir until the chocolate is melted and the mixture is smooth. Stir into the remaining plain buttercream. Refrigerate until needed. Combine:

½ cup Simple Syrup, 1010
¼ to ⅓ cup brandy or rum

Place the sponge sheet right side up on a large sheet of aluminum foil. Brush generously with the liquor syrup. Spread with the coffee buttercream. Starting at a short edge and using the foil to help roll, roll up the cake tightly and wrap in the foil. For easiest handling, freeze for at least 3 hours until semifrozen, or for up to 3 months.

When ready to decorate, let the chocolate buttercream come to room temperature and stir until smooth. Spread most of the buttercream roughly over the cake roll, and texture it with a fork to look like tree bark. Use a sharp knife dipped in hot water to cut a 2-inch slice from each end of the roll. Set the cake roll on a serving plate. Place the reserved slices on either side of the cake roll to resemble stumps, using the remaining buttercream to cover the joints. Decorate the log with:

Meringue Mushrooms, 957

Refrigerate for up to 48 hours before serving (mushrooms on the bûche may soften—keep extras in an - airtight container at room temperature to serve separately). Remove the bûche from the refrigerator 2 to 3 hours before serving for the best flavor and texture.

SICILIAN CASSATA

12 to 16 servings

Cassata is Sicily's special-occasion cake. The lightest of sponge cakes is flavored with sweet rum syrup and filled with lush ricotta cheese studded with spicy candied citron, cinnamon, and vanilla. The whole is enveloped in sheets of marzipan and gilded with candied fruits. Creamy fresh ricotta makes all the difference here. Also, the candied fruit sold in big chunks often has better flavor than the diced supermarket kind.

Prepare:

Hot-Milk Sponge Sheet, 953

Combine in a small saucepan and simmer until the sugar is dissolved:

⅓ cup water
¼ cup rum
⅓ cup sugar

Remove from the heat. Puree in a food processor until perfectly smooth, 3 to 4 minutes:

2 pounds whole-milk ricotta cheese

Add and pulse until combined:

1 cup powdered sugar
⅔ cup finely chopped candied citron or candied orange peel
1 teaspoon vanilla
¼ teaspoon ground cinnamon (optional)

Have ready one 8-inch springform pan.

Cut two 8-inch round layers and two 13 x 1½-inch strips from the cooled sponge cake. Brush generously with the rum syrup. Place 1 cake layer, moist side up, in the bottom of the springform pan. Line the sides of the pan with the strips, moist sides facing in. Trim the strips to fit snugly. Scrape the ricotta filling into the pan and spread evenly. Place the second cake layer, moist side down, on top of the filling. Press to level. Cover the pan and refrigerate for at least 2 hours or overnight.

Remove the pan and invert the cake onto a serving platter (or leave it on the pan bottom). Refrigerate until needed. Combine in a small saucepan and bring to a simmer:

⅔ cup apricot jam
3 tablespoons water

Strain. Knead until smooth and pliable:

14 ounces marzipan, 855

Use a rolling pin to roll a little less than half of the marzipan between 2 sheets of wax paper into a smooth 9½-inch round. To avoid creases, peel off and reposition the wax paper now and then. Brush the top and sides of the cake generously with the warm apricot glaze. Center the marzipan, best side facing up, on top of the cake, smoothing the surface and pressing the edges over and against the sides of the cake. Roll the remaining marzipan into a rough 8 x 12-inch rectangle. Cut 4 neat strips, each 7 inches long and exactly as wide as the cake is tall. One by one, press the strips smoothly against the sides of the cake, overlapping the edges neatly. Arrange on top of the cake in a geometric pattern:

Candied fruit

Refrigerate for at least 2 hours or up to 8 hours before serving.

FRESH STRAWBERRY DACQUOISE OR MERINGUE WITH WHIPPED CREAM AND CHOCOLATE

12 to 14 servings

Crunchy and creamy, sweet and tart, this is a grand dessert. Have your way with it: Vary the nuts in the dacquoise, omit the chocolate coating on the layers, substitute fresh whole raspberries for the sliced strawberries. For a singularly American twist, try bananas and cream between layers of peanut dacquoise, topped with chocolate-dipped strawberries.

Prepare:

Three 9-inch layers (1½ recipes) Meringue I, 955, Meringue II, 956, Warm-Method Meringue, 956, or Dacquoise, 957, made with almonds

Choose 12 of the best-looking berries from:

2 pints strawberries, hulled

Dip them halfway into:

1 cup Bittersweet Chocolate Glaze, 1003

Set on a cookie sheet lined with wax or parchment paper and refrigerate. Spread both sides of each meringue or dacquoise layer with the remaining glaze. Set coated layers on wax or parchment paper and refrigerate to set the chocolate. Slice the remaining strawberries. Whip until thickened:

2 cups heavy cream or crème fraîche

Add and beat just until almost stiff:

1 to 2 tablespoons sugar

1 teaspoon vanilla

Fold the sliced berries into 2 cups of the whipped cream. Spread 1 chocolate-coated layer with about half of the strawberry filling. Top with a second layer. Spread with the remaining filling. Top with the third layer. Frost the top and sides of the stack with whipped cream. Press into the sides:

¾ cup sliced blanched almonds, toasted

If there is any cream remaining, use a pastry bag fitted with a medium star tip to pipe a border of rosettes around the top edge of the cake. Decorate the top with the chocolate-coated strawberries. Refrigerate for 2 to 4 hours before serving.

CHOCOLATE CHERRY TORTE *14 to 16 servings*

Crème fraîche instead of whipped cream makes this chocolate variation of a famous torte even more complex.

Prepare:

One 9-inch Chocolate Génoise, 948, cut into 3 layers

Combine:

½ cup Simple Syrup, 1010

¼ cup kirsch

Thaw and drain:

Two 10- to 12-ounce packages frozen cherries, preferably unsweetened

Combine in a small bowl:

6 ounces bittersweet or semisweet chocolate, finely chopped

¼ cup boiling water

Stir until the chocolate is melted and the mixture is smooth. Place 1 génoise layer on a cardboard cake round or the bottom of a 9-inch springform pan. Brush liberally with kirsch syrup. Whip until soft peaks form:

4 cups heavy cream or crème fraîche

4 to 5 tablespoons sugar

2 teaspoons vanilla

Fold ⅓ cup of the whipped cream into the chocolate mixture, then fold in another ½ cup. Immediately spread the chocolate cream over the moistened génoise. Moisten the top of another layer with syrup and place it moist side down on the chocolate cream. Press to level. Moisten the top of the layer. Arrange the cherries in a single layer, without packing them tightly; you will have some cherries left over. Beat the remaining whipped cream until almost stiff. Spread about 2 cups of it over and between the cherries. Moisten the last génoise layer and place it moist side down on the cherries and cream; press gently to level. Refrigerate the cake, as well as the remaining whipped cream and cherries until firm, at least 30 minutes. Frost the top and sides of the cake with the remaining whipped cream. Use a pastry bag fitted with a large star tip to pipe 12 to 16 whipped cream rosettes or a border of whipped cream around the top edge of the cake. Blot the remaining cherries dry and place 1 on each rosette. Decorate the center of the cake with:

Chocolate shavings

Refrigerate for at least 12 hours or up to 24 hours before serving.

CHOCOLATE RASPBERRY CREAM CAKE

Prepare Chocolate Cherry Torte, above, substituting two 5-ounce cartons (about 2½ cups) fresh raspberries for the cherries and framboise (raspberry eau-de-vie) for the kirsch. Or substitute ¾ cup raspberry liqueur for the kirsch mixture.

BLACK FOREST CAKE

Prepare Chocolate Cherry Torte, above, omitting the melted chocolate and filling both layers with cherries and plain whipped cream.

MAKING A THREE-TIER WEDDING CAKE

Making a wedding cake at home is a glorious undertaking.

We have chosen a very traditional white cake, with three 2-layer tiers, to serve 75 or more. For up to 40 additional servings, you can make a 2-layer "back-up" sheet cake. Our suggestions for filling and frosting do not require refrigeration, although it helps to chill the cakes during the icing and decorating stage if possible. Regardless, you will need a cool place to store the cake up to overnight before the wedding. You can choose any other filling or frosting if you wish, taking perishability and the need for refrigeration into account.

Our wedding cake was designed to be made in a single home oven, with an ordinary stand mixer and/or a good sturdy hand-held electric mixer with two beaters (not one) and one set of pans. The recipe must be baked twice to complete all the layers for each tier. (Additional baking is required for the back-up sheet cake.)

If you have never made a large special-occasion cake, allow yourself plenty of time and choose the simplest decoration options (which are often the prettiest anyway). If you like, frost the cake with a swirly or deliberately "homemade" texture rather than attempting smooth perfection, and decorate with unsprayed nontoxic fresh flowers and blossoms rather than buttercream roses and fancy frills. Practice piping simple borders on the backs of cake pans or on wax or parchment paper, with a pastry bag and star tip, until you have the knack—these borders are simple to master and provide the perfect finishing touch for the bottoms of cake tiers.

AN OVERVIEW OF WEDDING CAKE ENGINEERING

To prevent the cake from becoming the Leaning Tower of Pisa, each tier is supported by several pieces of ¼-inch-thick wooden dowel or plastic drinking straws sunk into the tier below. Each tier is also supported by a stiff lightweight cardboard base to prevent the frosting from buckling or cracking when the cake is moved and to enable the tiers to be removed as the cake is served. A plywood or Masonite "presentation board" 4 inches larger than the bottom cake tier, wrapped in florists' foil or foil wrapping paper, also serves as a sturdy carrying board.

TRANSPORTING THE CAKE

Sliding is the biggest danger in transporting wedding cakes.

Many wedding cake experts "stake" their cakes by driving a long sharpened dowel through the center of the entire cake before travel, 972, to prevent shifting en route. For short distances, the cake can travel on a tray. Place 2 or 3 large loops (sticky side out) of thick or double-sided adhesive tape on the tray to anchor it to the presentation board, or line the tray with a sheet of foam rubber about ⅜ inch thick. Keep the tray from sliding in the car by wedging it between heavier items or setting it on a thick foam rubber mat.

For longer-distance transport, especially on warm days, transport the cake in a box. Ideally it should be the exact size of the diameter of the presentation board, so that the cake sides will not come in contact with the sides of the box. If the box opens from the top, cut it with a utility knife so that the cake can be loaded from the side instead, then tape the box shut. Travel with a utility knife to open the box.

Always travel with extra frosting, a spatula, and a pastry bag and tip for repairs. With luck, you will never need them.

FROSTING QUANTITIES NEEDED FOR A THREE-TIER WEDDING CAKE PLUS A BACK-UP SHEET CAKE

To fill, frost, and decorate a three-tier wedding cake, you will need a total of 16 cups frosting (4 to 5 cups to fill the layers and 10 to 11 cups to frost the top and sides and to pipe the borders). To fill and frost a 2-layer 13 x 9-inch back-up cake, you will need an additional 4 to 5 cups (1 to 1½ cups to fill the layers and 3 to 3½ cups to frost the top and sides). Consult the individual filling or frosting recipes and increase the quantities to yield these amounts.

If you wish, fill the layers with one type of filling or frosting and frost the cake with another, using the breakdowns given above to plan the quantities of each filling or frosting you will need.

Keep in mind that buttercreams made with egg yolks, custard-based fillings, and whipped cream require refrigeration, and so will the wedding cake if you decide to use them.

TO FILL THE LAYERS AND ASSEMBLE THE TIERS

Each tier consists of 2 cake layers with filling or frosting between them. The layers must be completely cool before assembling the cake. Slide a rimless cookie sheet under large cake layers to move them without cracking. If layers are not flat, or if the top crust is tough or dry, trim with a serrated knife.

To assemble the 14-inch tier, put a couple dabs of frosting on the 14-inch cardboard cake round to keep the cake from sliding. Center 1 of the 14-inch layers right side up on the cardboard. Spread the layer with 2 to 2½ cups frosting. Top with the second cake layer, upside down. Spread a very thin crumb coat, 990, of frosting over the top and sides of the cake to cover cracks and secure crumbs. Refrigerate or set aside in a cool place so the frosting will set.

Assemble the 10-inch tier on the 10-inch cardboard round, filling the layers with about 1¼ cups frosting. Assemble the 6-inch tier on the 6-inch cardboard round, filling with about ⅓ cup frosting. Refrigerate each tier in a cool place or set aside.

GETTING READY TO MAKE THE WEDDING CAKE

SCHEDULE

Cake layers can be baked up to 3 weeks ahead, wrapped, and frozen. Or bake them up to 3 days ahead and wrap them airtight in plastic wrap or aluminum foil.

A week or more in advance:

Buy or borrow supplies and nonperishable ingredients, such as flour and sugar

Early in the week of the wedding:

Be sure all supplies and staple ingredients are on hand
Buy perishable ingredients, such as butter, milk, and eggs
Free up refrigerator space
Order or arrange for flowers needed to decorate the cake, or make buttercream roses and leaves
Make the presentation board: wrap an 18-inch plywood round with florists' foil or foil wrapping paper. Secure the foil to the underside of the board with tape.
Set up and tape a cardboard transport box if necessary.

Up to 3 days before the wedding:

Bake the layers, if you have not frozen them
Make the filling and frosting or buttercream

Up to 1 day before the wedding:

Assemble and frost the cake
Decorate the cake (if using buttercream flowers)

On the day of the wedding:

Decorate with fresh flowers

SUPPLIES/EQUIPMENT

Cake pans (check the recipe)
Large bowls (check the recipe)
A large professional-sized rubber spatula (optional but very convenient)
A metal icing spatula with an 8- to 10-inch blade
An angled (offset) metal icing spatula with an 8- to 10-inch blade (optional for frosting the top of the larger tiers)
A pastry bag with star tip #2 or #3 (does not require a coupler) for piping borders
A flower nail #7, coupler, and round tip #12, rose tip #103 or #104, and leaf tip #67 or #352 if you plan to make roses and leaves from frosting
One 18-inch, ¼-inch-thick, plywood or Masonite round for the "presentation board"
Gold or silver foil wrapping paper or florists' foil to wrap the board
A lazy Susan or cake-decorating turntable (optional but very useful)
One 14-inch cardboard cake round, one 10-inch cardboard cake round, and one 6-inch cardboard cake round
Thick adhesive or double-sided adhesive or foam tape
About a dozen plastic drinking straws or about 5 feet of ¼-inch wooden doweling
If necessary for transport: a corrugated cardboard box 18 inches square and 15 to 18 inches deep and tape for setting it up; foam rubber sheets for anchoring if needed; a utility knife

TO FROST THE TIERS

Place 3 or 4 pieces of double-sided adhesive tape on the presentation board, about 4 inches in from the edges. Frost the top and sides of the 14-inch tier, as smoothly as possible or with a swirly texture. If you have a long, extra-wide pancake turner with a stiff rather than flexible blade, use it to lift and transfer the tier to the wrapped board. Otherwise, slide a sturdy metal icing spatula under the tier and tilt it up so that you can slide your hand under for support. With one hand and the spatula supporting the tier, lift it over the center of the presentation board. Set the front edge (farthest from you) down first, 2 inches from the edge of the board. Pivot the cake to the left or right to center it before lowering the back edge. Slide the spatula out. Refrigerate if possible to set the frosting.

Frost the top and sides of the other 2 tiers. Refrigerate if possible to set the frosting before continuing.

TO STACK THE TIERS

Cut a circle of wax or parchment paper 8 inches in diameter. Center it on top of the 14-inch tier. Insert a plastic drinking straw or a piece of wooden dowel straight down into the cake at one edge of the paper

Use a rimless cookie sheet to move large layers without cracking them.

Insert the supports into the cake at even intervals.

circle. Mark the straw or dowel at the surface of the frosting, remove it, and cut at the mark to make a support. (Use pruning shears to cut a wooden dowel.) Cut 5 more supports identical in length. Insert the supports into the cake, evenly spaced around the perimeter of the paper circle. Put a generous teaspoon of frosting in the center of the paper circle.

Cut a circle of wax or parchment paper 4 inches in diameter. Center it on top of the 10-inch tier. Mark and cut 4 or 5 supports and insert them evenly around the perimeter of the paper circle. Put a small dollop of frosting in the center of the paper circle.

Do not install supports in the 6-inch tier.

Lift the 10-inch tier with the long pancake turner or your hand and hold it centered over the paper circle on the 14-inch tier. Lower the front edge (opposite you) first, with a friend guiding you if possible. In place of your hand and the spatula put a small paring knife or the small offset spatula, which will be easier to remove without damaging the frosting, on the lower tier; lower the tier into place. Carefully remove the paring knife blade.

Transfer the 6-inch tier to the center of the 10-inch tier, using the procedure described above. If you are planning to "stake" the cake, do so now.

TO "STAKE" THE CAKE FOR TRAVEL

Cut a length of ¼-inch wooden dowel slightly shorter than the height of the cake. Whittle a long sharp point in one end, or use a pencil sharpener. Drive the stake straight down into the center of the cake, tapping with a hammer. (You will cover the hole in the top of the cake with decoration.)

TO DECORATE THE CAKE

If you have a lazy Susan or a turntable, set the cake on it. Adjust the consistency of the frosting or buttercream as necessary (see page 989) so that it holds a good stiff shape when piped. Fit the star tip into the pastry bag and fill the bag no more than half full with frosting or buttercream. If you need practice, set an empty cake pan on a plate and pipe a border that covers the seam where the edge of the pan meets the plate. When satisfied, pipe a border around the base of the top tier where it meets the tier below. Pipe a similar border to cover the seam between the 10-inch tier and the bottom tier. Refrigerate the cake to set the frosting before decorating. The cake is now ready to decorate with buttercream roses and leaves or fresh flowers.

TO MAKE BUTTERCREAM ROSES

You can make the roses in advance, piping them onto squares of wax or parchment paper, and refrigerate or freeze until needed. Use the pastry bag and coupling, round tip #12, rose tip #103 or #104, and flower nail #7. The buttercream (or other frosting) must be as stiff as

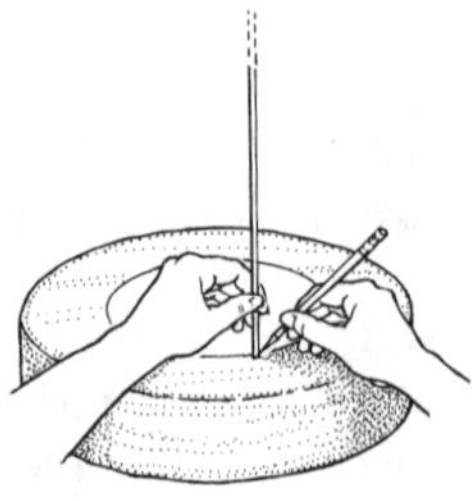

Mark the dowel or straw at the surface of the frosting.

Lower the 10-inch tier onto the 14-inch tier.

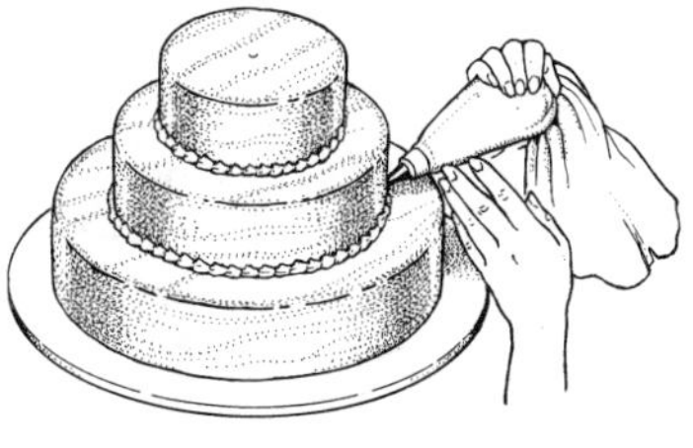

Pipe frosting or buttercream to cover the seams.

possible. Some cake decorators use Quick White Icing, 1006, adding ¼ cup solid vegetable shortening to the butter in the recipe for more stability. Color the frosting judiciously with food coloring if desired; colors deepen with time, so it is better to tint subtly.

Attach a 2-inch square of wax paper to the top of the flower nail with a dot of frosting. Make a cone-shaped base for the rose, shown 974: Hold the pastry bag fitted with the round tip #12 perpendicular to and touching the center of the paper square. Squeeze without lifting the bag until the tip is partially buried in a shallow mound of icing, about ½ inch in diameter. Continue to squeeze as you gradually raise the tip to form a cone of icing 1½ times as high as the opening of the rose tip (#104) used to make the petals.

Start the rose: Hold the bag at a 45-degree angle to the nail top, with the back of the bag pointing over your shoulder. The wide end of the tip should be just below the top of the cone, with the narrow end tilted over the point. Turn the nail counterclockwise one full turn as you squeeze and raise the tip up and away from the dome and then down around the base, overlapping your starting point and diminishing pressure toward the end. A ribbon of frosting should be wrapped around the cone like a rosebud.

Pipe the first row of 3 petals: Hold the bag at a 45-degree angle to the nail top, with the wide opening touching the bud at midheight and the narrow end pointing straight up. Turn the nail about one-third of a turn while moving the tip up and back down to touch the base; form a half-circle-shaped petal. Stop squeezing and lift the tip away. Make the second and third petals the same way, beginning the second petal at the end of the first. Begin the third petal overlapping the end of the second and end it overlapping the beginning of the first. Repeat the procedure to pipe a second outer layer of petals and then a third, shown 974. Remove the rose on the square of wax paper and refrigerate or freeze until needed. After refrigerating, the roses can be transferred to the cake with a small pair of scissors: Open and then partly close the blades under the rose to lift it off the wax paper. Position the rose on the cake and close the scissors to release the rose. All of this takes practice!

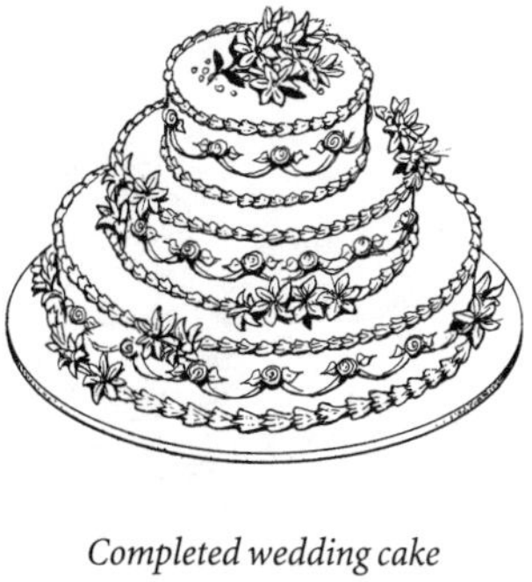

Completed wedding cake

TO PIPE BUTTERCREAM LEAVES

Use leaf tip #67 or #352. Pipe leaves directly onto the cake or onto wax or parchment paper, to be refrigerated or frozen until needed. The buttercream or frosting should not be as stiff as for the roses: stir buttercream over a pan of warm water to soften; thin powdered sugar icings with a few drops of milk. Tint with green food coloring. Hold the bag at a 45-degree angle to the surface. Start squeezing without moving the tip at first, to let the icing fan out. Diminish pressure gradually as you pull the tip away and draw the leaf to a point. The faster you move the tip, the longer the leaf. If the leaf tip is broken instead of pointed, thin the icing a little more. Transfer chilled leaves to the cake with the tip of a paring knife.

TO DECORATE A CAKE WITH FRESH FLOWERS

Decorate the cake only with unsprayed nonpoisonous flowers, such as roses, stephanotis, baby's breath, pear and apple blossoms, citrus leaves and blossoms, jasmine, acacia, lilac, miniature carnations, scented geraniums, borage flowers, daylilies, English daisies, hollyhocks, honeysuckle, lilac, pansies, petunias, nasturtiums, and violets and hibiscus. Avoid lilies of the valley, which are poisonous. Flowers should be as fresh-looking as possible. Keep the flowers in water until just before using and snip them, and any leaves you plan to use, just before putting them on the cake. Flowers may be simply laid on the surface of the cake, or short stems can be sunk into florists' vials filled with water and the pointed ends of the vials inserted in the cake. Roses that are at least partly closed are a good

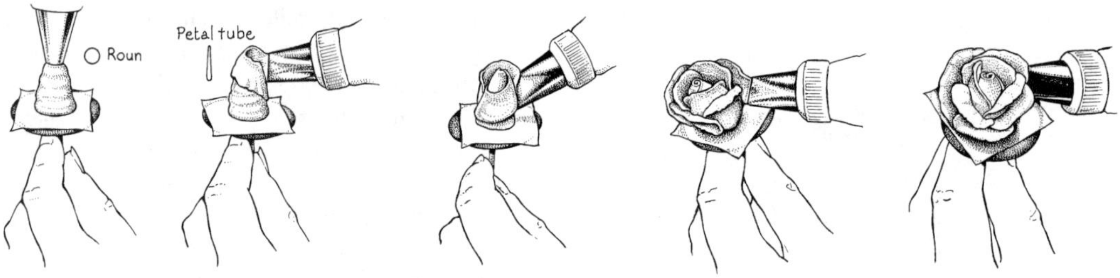

Piping a buttercream rose

choice when flowers must remain on the cake for several hours without water. Pinch off outer petals if they are bruised or too open. Fresh or crystallized flowers and leaves—even those that are unsprayed and nonpoisonous—should never be eaten by guests unless they were specifically cultivated as food. Remove and set them aside when the cake is served.

SERVING THE WEDDING CAKE

The bride and groom traditionally cut and serve each other a small wedge of cake from the bottom tier. Before cutting the guests' servings from the bottom tier, use a long serrated knife to cut a ring around the base of the second tier, straight down into the bottom tier. Servings are then cut 2 inches long (from the edge of the bottom tier to the base of the second tier). For a total of 75 servings, cut each wedge about 1⅝ inches wide at the edge, tapering to about 1⅜ inches wide. For 100 servings, cut pieces only about 1 inch wide at the edge. When the outer ring of the bottom tier has been served, remove and set aside the top tier for the bride and groom. Using the mark left by the base of the top tier as a guide, cut straight down into the middle tier to create another ring of cake; cut wedges of cake, as before. Remove the support pieces in the middle tier and the paper circle and cut servings from the small remaining core. Lift off the cardboard base, pull out the support pieces, and remove the paper circle from the bottom tier. Cut straight down into the tier 2 inches from the edge all around to create another ring, cut servings as before, then cut servings from the small core.

EQUIPMENT

14 x 2-inch, 10 x 2-inch, and 6 x 2-inch round pans
Oven large enough to hold the 14-inch pan on one rack and the other pans on the rack above
A stand mixer and/or a sturdy two-beater hand-held electric mixer
In addition to the large bowl of the stand mixer or a 2½- to 3-quart bowl for the hand-held mixer, an additional 2½- to 3-quart bowl for egg whites and a large bowl with at least an 8-quart capacity for the final mixing
An extra-large professional-sized rubber spatula (optional)
Cooling racks big enough for all the layers

THREE-TIER WHITE WEDDING CAKE

This recipe makes 3 round layers—14, 10, and 6 inches—each about 1½ inches tall, *so you will need to make the recipe twice to provide the 2 layers needed for*

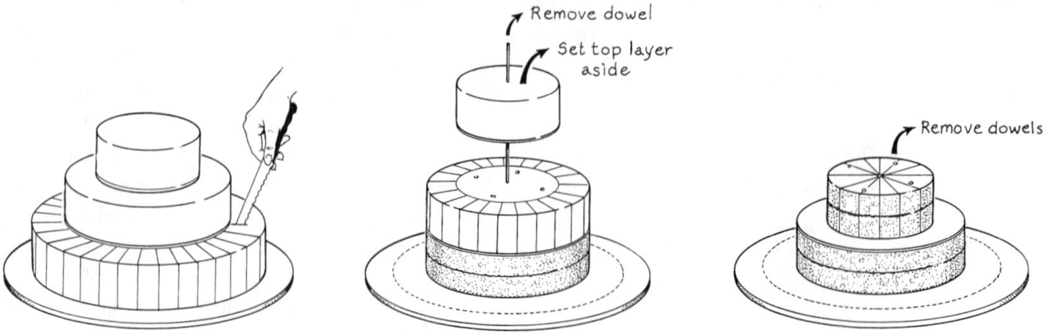

Cutting the wedding cake

each of the tiers. After filling and frosting, each tier will be about 3½ to 4 inches tall. The cake will make 75 servings, each 2 inches long by 1½ inches wide, or 100 servings, each 2 inches long by 1 inch wide, exclusive of the top tier—which can be saved for the bride and groom or cut into 9 to 14 additional servings. For 40 to 50 additional servings, make the recipe a third time, dividing the batter between two 13 x 9-inch pans to make a 2-layer 13 x 9-inch back-up sheet cake.

Fill and frost this cake with 16 cups Quick White Icing, 1006, or Quick Lemon Icing, 1006, or Swiss Meringue Buttercream, 1002, flavored as desired; or fill and frost as desired.

With a stand mixer, begin in the largest mixer bowl and then transfer the batter to the 8-quart bowl before folding in the egg whites. Complete the mixing with a hand-held mixer. With a hand-held mixer from the beginning, it is best to start in a 2½- to 3-quart bowl (to avoid chasing the butter and sugar all over the larger bowl) and then transfer to the large bowl later.

Have all ingredients at room temperature, 68° to 70°F. Position 1 rack just above the center of the oven and another rack just below the center, with at least 3 inches between them. Preheat the oven to 350°F. Grease and flour the sides and line the bottom of one 14 x 2-inch, one 10 x 2-inch, and one 6 x 2-inch round pan with wax or parchment paper.

Sift together twice:

7 cups sifted cake flour

2 tablespoons plus 2 teaspoons baking powder

1 teaspoon salt

Combine:

2 cups milk

2 teaspoons vanilla

⅜ teaspoon almond extract (optional)

In the large bowl of a stand mixer or a 2½- to 3-quart bowl (for a hand-held mixer), beat until creamy, a minute or so:

1 pound (4 sticks) unsalted butter

Gradually add and beat on high speed until lightened in color and texture, 6 to 7 minutes:

3⅓ cups sugar

Scrape the mixture into the 8-quart bowl. Add the flour mixture in 4 parts, alternating with the milk mixture in 3 parts, beating on high speed after each addition until thoroughly combined and scraping the sides of the bowl as necessary. In a clean, dry 2½- to 3-quart bowl, beat on medium speed until soft peaks form:

8 large egg whites

⅜ teaspoon cream of tartar

Gradually add, beating on high speed:

⅓ cup sugar

Beat until the peaks are stiff but not dry. Use a clean rubber spatula (avoid getting any of the butter mixture into the egg white bowl) to scrape half of the egg whites onto the butter mixture and set that spatula back in the egg white bowl. Use the largest rubber spatula you have to fold the egg whites into the butter mixture. Use the spatula in the egg white bowl to scrape the remaining egg whites on top of the mixture, but do not fold them in. Then add to the egg white bowl and beat on medium speed until soft peaks form:

8 large egg whites

⅜ teaspoon cream of tartar

Gradually add, beating on high speed:

⅓ cup sugar

Beat until the peaks are stiff but not dry. Scrape the egg whites onto the butter mixture and fold in. Divide the batter among the pans and spread evenly. Put the largest layer in the center of the lower rack and the other 2 layers on the upper rack, with the smallest toward the front; the pans should not touch each other or the sides of the oven. Bake until a toothpick inserted into the center of each cake comes out clean, 25 to 30 minutes for the 6-inch layer, 30 to 35 minutes for the 10-inch layer, and 35 to 40 minutes for the 14-inch layer. Let cool in the pans on racks for 5 to 10 minutes for the smaller layers and 10 to 15 minutes for the largest layer. Slide a thin knife around the cake to detach it from the pans, pressing the knife against the sides of the pan to avoid tearing the cake. Invert the layers onto the racks. Peel off the paper liners and turn right side up to cool. Let cool completely before filling and frosting.

ABOUT FRUITCAKES

Traditional fruitcakes are butter cakes embellished with a mixture of dried and candied or glacéed fruits and nuts. Today we freely interchange these additions, and many of us omit the candied and glacéed fruits altogether, replacing them with chopped dried apricots, pears, or dates, along with the traditional raisins or currants.

If you do like glacéed or candied fruits, you will be rewarded by spending a little extra on the best quality, often imported, available from specialty stores. Larger pieces are usually fresher and better. The diced offerings in the supermarket come in assorted colors but all taste alike, and are not very distinguished at that. Use oiled scissors to snip candied or dried fruits rather than trying to cut them up with a knife—a sticky procedure at best. Do not worry about uniformity in the sizes of pieces, as the knife that slices the cake will cut any fruit or nut in its path and the many shapes and colors in cross section make an attractive mosaic. Fruitcakes can be lightly studded with fruit or so loaded that there is only enough cake to hold them together.

Aging fruitcake allows the moisture from the fruit to permeate the cake. For an even moister cake, some cooks soak the fruit pieces in liquor before adding them to the batter, while others puncture and douse the cakes in liquor afterward and wrap them in liquor-soaked linens to ripen. Such cakes, well wrapped and stored in airtight tins, are reputed to remain enjoyable for as long as twenty-five years; we have not sampled one. In lieu of spirits, you may soak fruits in fruit juice, or not at all.

Bake fruitcakes in shiny metal pans rather than dark or glass ones, to prevent excessive browning of the cake and the fruit pieces that touch the pan during the long, slow baking period—as long as 3½ hours. Line the bottoms and sides of pans with wax, parchment, or brown paper to further insulate the batter and ensure that the heavy but fragile cake will emerge from the pan without sticking or breaking. If you use a tube pan, line the bottom with paper by cutting a hole to allow for the tube; use wide strips of paper to line the sides and tube as well. Grease pans first to hold the paper in place. It is not necessary to grease wax or parchment paper.

For a 2½-pound cake, use an 8-inch ring mold or an 8½ x 4½-inch (6-cup) loaf pan, and fill either one about 2½ inches deep. Do not overlook the possibility of baking miniature loaves, or using small fluted molds or disposable aluminum pans for gifts.

Hot fruitcakes are heavy and have a tendency to break apart; to be safe, let them cool for at least 20 or up to 60 minutes in the pan on a rack, before unmolding them very carefully. After unmolding, peel off the paper liner and allow the cake to cool completely right side up on the rack. When the cake is cool, you can puncture it a few times with a skewer and very slowly pour up to 1 cup (for a 2½-pound cake) hot, but not boiling, liquor—such as brandy, bourbon, rum, or wine—over the cake, allowing it to absorb the liquid.

ABOUT STORING FRUITCAKES

To store fruitcakes, wrap them in plastic wrap or in clean brandy- or wine-soaked linens. Wrap the cloth-wrapped cakes in plastic or place them in heavy-duty sealable plastic bags. Do not use aluminum foil to wrap liquor-doused fruitcakes, with or without spirit-soaked linens—the alcohol-and-fruit combination tends to dissolve foil. Foil can, however, be used for cakes first wrapped in plastic.

FRUITCAKE COCKAIGNE

Thirty-two ½-inch slices

The fruits stay light in color in this white pound cake.
Have all ingredients at room temperature, 68° to 70°F.
Preheat the oven to 325°F. Grease and line the bottoms and sides of two 8½ x 4½-inch (6-cup) loaf pans with wax or parchment paper.
Measure:

4 cups sifted all-purpose flour

Mix ½ cup of the flour with 4 cups fruits and nuts; we particularly like this combination:

1⅓ cups pecans or hickory nuts
1⅓ cups golden raisins
1⅓ cups chopped preserved kumquats or dried apricots

Resift the remaining flour with:

1 teaspoon baking powder
½ teaspoon salt

In a large bowl, beat until creamy, about 30 seconds:

12 tablespoons (1½ sticks) unsalted butter

Gradually add, beating on high speed until lightened in color and texture, 5 to 7 minutes:

2 cups sugar

Whisk together, then gradually beat in:

5 large eggs
1 teaspoon vanilla

Gradually beat in the flour mixture, scraping the sides of the bowl as necessary, until thoroughly combined. Divide the batter between the pans and spread evenly. Bake until a toothpick inserted in the center comes out clean, about 1 hour. Let cool in the pan on a rack for 20 to 60 minutes. Invert the cake and peel off the paper liners. Let cool right side up on the rack. To store, see About Storing Fruitcakes, above.

CURRANT CAKE

Prepare Fruitcake Cockaigne, above, substituting 1 to 1½ cups dried currants for the preserved kumquats or dried apricots.

WHITE FRUITCAKE

Prepare Fruitcake Cockaigne, above, substituting for the suggested fruit and nut mixture 1 cup chopped nuts (preferably slivered blanched almonds), 1 cup golden raisins, ½ cup thinly sliced candied citron or candied orange or lemon peel, ¼ cup candied pineapple, ¼ cup candied cherries, and ½ cup shredded sweetened dried coconut, if desired.

DARK FRUITCAKE *40 to 60 thin slices*

Better than any other we have sampled. Some say this is best stored for at least 1 month before serving, but we have enjoyed it quite fresh as well.

Have all ingredients at room temperature, 68° to 70°F. Preheat the oven to 300°F. Grease and line the bottom and sides of one 10-inch tube pan with wax or parchment paper.

Sift together:

- **3 cups all-purpose flour**
- **1 teaspoon baking powder**
- **½ teaspoon baking soda**
- **¼ teaspoon salt**
- **1 teaspoon ground cinnamon**
- **1 teaspoon freshly grated or ground nutmeg**
- **½ teaspoon ground mace**
- **½ teaspoon ground cloves**

In a large bowl, beat until creamy, about 30 seconds:

- **½ pound (2 sticks) unsalted butter**

Gradually add and beat on high speed until lightened in color and texture, 3 to 5 minutes:

- **2 cups packed light or dark brown sugar**

Beat in:

- **½ cup dark or light molasses**
- **Grated zest and juice of 1 orange**
- **Grated zest and juice of 1 lemon**

Add the flour mixture in 3 parts, alternating with, in 2 parts:

- **¾ cup brandy**

beating on low speed or stirring with a rubber spatula just until blended and scraping the sides of the bowl as necessary. Stir in:

- **2½ cups diced mixed candied fruits (citron, pineapple, cherries, kumquats, and/or orange and lemon peel)**
- **2 cups coarsely chopped walnuts**
- **1½ cups chopped dates**
- **1½ cups currants**
- **1½ cups golden raisins**

Scrape the batter into the pan and spread evenly. Bake for 3½ hours. The cake may appear done at 2½ hours; simply ignore this. If the cake is getting too dark on top, tent it loosely with aluminum foil for the last 30 to 60 minutes. Let cool in the pan on a rack for about 1 hour. Invert the cake and remove the paper liner. Let cool right side up on the rack. To store, see About Storing Fruitcakes, 976.

CALIFORNIA FRUITCAKE *18 thin slices*

This cake resembles a confection more than a cake—there is only enough batter to hold the delicious morsels together. Only nuts and dried fruits need apply—candied and glacéed fruits are banished. Substitute dried pears or peaches for some or all of the apricots or dates if you like. Most fruit and nut pieces go into the batter whole, so there is very little work for the cook. We never soak this cake with liquor, yet, well wrapped, it keeps for weeks. Slice very thin.

Preheat the oven to 300°F. Grease and line the bottom and sides of one 9 x 5-inch (8-cup) loaf pan with wax or parchment paper.

Stir together in a large bowl:

- **¾ cup all-purpose flour**
- **¼ teaspoon baking soda**
- **¼ teaspoon baking powder**
- **½ teaspoon salt**

Add and mix thoroughly with your fingers:

- **¾ cup packed light or dark brown sugar**
- **3 cups walnut halves**
- **2 cups quartered dates**
- **1 cup packed dried apricot halves**

In a small bowl, beat until thick and pale yellow:

- **2 large eggs**
- **1 teaspoon vanilla**

Pour the egg mixture over the dry ingredients and mix until all the fruit and nut pieces are coated (your hands are the best tools for mixing here). Scrape the batter into the pan and spread evenly. Bake until the top is deep golden brown and the batter clinging to the fruit and nut pieces is set (cover loosely with a tent of aluminum foil if the top browns too early), 1 hour 30 minutes to 1 hour 40 minutes. Let cool in the pan on a rack for 10 minutes. Invert the cake and remove the paper liner. Let cool right side up on the rack. To store, see About Storing Fruitcakes, 976—and try to store for at least a few days before serving!

ABOUT CHEESECAKES

The two main cheesecake camps are cream cheese and ricotta or curd-style cheese. Then there are fans of creamy versus dry, dense versus light. Factions exist as well for and against different types of crust (or any crust at all), toppings other than sour cream, any flavors other than plain. We offer several kinds so you and your guests can choose—and then keep arguing.

Cheesecakes are really very rich cheese and egg custards—not cakes at all. As such, they require low heat and proper timing to avoid the big cheesecake faults: cracking, shrinkage, and overbaking around the edges. Overmixing is the culprit in some cases, below, but most of the time the causes are baking too long or at too high a temperature and/or cooling too quickly. To make matters worse, cracking and shrinking do not become obvious until the cheesecake is out of the oven and cooling.

The remedy for most cheesecake problems is to keep baking temperatures low (300° to 325°F, with some exceptions), to check the accuracy of your oven, and to learn to take the cake out of the oven when it is still jiggly in the center. Remember that cheesecakes do not set until completely cool or even chilled. Cool a cheesecake slowly on the counter with a large bowl or pot inverted over it to keep the environment warm and moist. We also take care to grease the sides of the pan before filling it so that the cake lets go of the pan as it cools and shrinks instead of cracking in the center. Baking the cheesecake in a water bath, below, is also a powerful weapon against all cheesecake faults.

MIXING CHEESECAKES

If your mixer offers the choice of paddle versus whisk, use the paddle to achieve the best-textured cake. Cheesecake batter must be well mixed but not overbeaten. If too much air is beaten into a cheesecake batter, the cake will puff like a soufflé as it bakes and then fall dramatically and crack as it cools. Even more excessive overbeating—which most often happens in the food processor—results in thin, dense batters that may not rise.

The food processor is the best possible tool for transforming cottage cheese, ricotta cheese, and other curd cheeses into perfectly smooth purees when indicated. Process for a full 3 to 4 minutes, scraping the sides of the bowl and the blade several times. This is much easier and more effective than the traditional method of forcing curd cheeses through a fine sieve. We rarely use the processor for mixing cream cheese and other ingredients, however, as overprocessing can break down the cheese and produce a thin, heavy batter that does not rise at all. When we use the processor, we add the cream cheese—very well softened—last, so that it blends quickly with the other ingredients.

Lumps in the batter mar a good cheesecake; to avoid them, have the cream cheese at room temperature, or soften it in the microwave (20 to 30 seconds on high for an 8-ounce package) before beating. If you start with cold cream cheese, you are more likely to overbeat the cheese while trying to eliminate the lumps. For most recipes, beating the cream cheese with the sugar is the last chance you have to remove lumps. Once eggs and other liquid ingredients are added, any lumps in the cheese are likely to remain there. The sides of the bowl and the beaters should be scraped frequently during all stages of mixing, as the stiffer cheese mixture clinging to the beaters or bowl will not blend with the thinner mixture after the eggs and liquids are added. If the recipe calls for whipped cream or beaten egg whites, these are always folded in last, and by hand.

CHEESECAKE BAKING METHODS

The Traditional Method: Moderate to low heat can result in perfectly smooth, intensely flavored cheesecakes without cracks, so long as the batter is mixed properly, the oven temperature is accurate, the baker's timing is impeccable, and the cooling is slow. Cheesecakes with crusts on the bottom and sides have the best chance with this method because the crust tends to insulate the batter somewhat. Alas, having so many variables, this method is the trickiest, and so it often yields cracked and overbaked cheesecakes. But when it's good, it's great.

The New York Method: A low-heat method in wolf's clothing, this takes some of the guesswork out of the hands of the baker. The cake goes into the oven at 500° for 15 minutes, the oven temperature is reduced to 200°F for about an hour more of baking, and finally the cake is left in the turned-off oven with the door ajar. Remarkably, this yields a cheesecake with a golden brown surface and a creamy smooth interior—or a dry, creamy interior, depending on the recipe.

The Water Bath Method: Here the cake pan is placed in a pan of hot water when it goes into the oven. This method insulates the cake pan from extreme heat and allows the center and the edges of the cake to cook at about the same rate. It almost guarantees that the cake will be as creamy around the sides as it is in the center, and it promotes a gentle, even rise with very little shrinkage. The water bath is very forgiving: 10 minutes of extra baking are unlikely to damage the texture of the cake. We have never seen a cracked cake emerge from a water bath. This is an excellent method for reduced-fat cheesecakes, which tend to become grainy around the edges unless baked very gently.

You may ask why we do not recommend baking all cakes in the water bath. Cheesecake crusts do not emerge as crisp if baked in a water bath, and some cheesecake lovers demand a certain dense, dry, creamy texture and intense cheese flavor that cannot be produced with a water bath. To each cheesecake maven his or her own, and *vive la différence!*

HOW TO BAKE A CHEESECAKE IN A WATER BATH

If you are baking in a springform pan, you must wrap the bottom and sides to prevent water from seeping into the seams and soaking the cake. Set the pan on a wide sheet of heavy-duty aluminum foil. Fold the foil up the sides of the pan, making sure there are no rips or holes. For the water bath, choose a baking dish or roasting pan that is at least 3 inches wider, but that is no deeper, than the cheesecake pan. Put a kettle of water on to boil when you preheat the oven. After filling the cheesecake pan, set it in the baking dish. Slide the oven rack partway out and set the baking dish on it. Carefully pour boiling water around the cheesecake pan to a depth of about 1 inch. Slide the oven rack back gently to avoid sloshing.

If you use a solid cake pan, line the bottom with a round of wax or parchment paper and grease the sides (there is no need to wrap the pan in foil). Bake in the water bath as described. Cool and then chill the cake completely before unmolding.

TO UNMOLD CHEESECAKES BAKED IN SPRINGFORM PANS

Cheesecakes baked in springform pans can be unmolded while still slightly warm, but they are less fragile if chilled first. If the cake has pulled away cleanly from the pan, simply release the spring and carefully remove the pan side. Otherwise, slide a thin knife blade around the sides of the cake to detach it from the pan, pressing the blade against the pan to avoid tearing the cake, before releasing and removing the side. Serve the cake directly on the pan bottom, or chill it thoroughly before attempting to transfer it to a serving platter or cardboard cake circle.

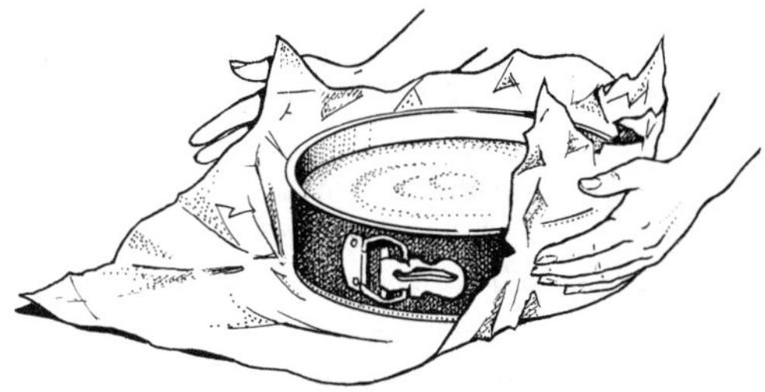

Fold foil up the sides of a springform pan.

Pour boiling water to a depth of 1 inch.

TO UNMOLD CHEESECAKES BAKED IN SOLID PANS

Cover the top of the pan with tightly stretched plastic wrap. Place a piece of cardboard or a lightweight baking sheet on top of the plastic wrap. Invert the pan and cardboard and rap the edge of the pan gently until the cheesecake is released. Remove the pan and peel off the paper liner. Place a cake circle or serving plate on the cake and carefully invert the cake so that it is right side up. Remove the plastic wrap.

STORING AND SERVING CHEESECAKES

The flavor and texture of all cheesecakes profit by thorough chilling before serving, preferably 24 hours; 48 hours intensifies the cheese flavor and the density of the cake as well. Store cheesecakes, covered, in the refrigerator. Remove an hour or so before serving to bring out the flavor and soften the texture.

IDEAS FOR CHEESECAKES

Specialty cheesecakes come in every conceivable flavor, and anyone who can make a plain cheesecake can invent a fancy new one. Start by varying the crust with nuts or spices. Toppings beyond sour cream can include Coconut Pecan Filling, 999, any chocolate or fudge frosting, Lemon Curd, 998, caramel sauce, crushed toasted or caramelized nuts, fresh fruit, or preserves. Fold into plain cheesecake batter fresh berries rolled in sugar, liquor-soaked raisins or chopped dried fruit, crystallized ginger, caramelized nuts, or bits of drained chestnuts in syrup; layer or fold in broken chocolate cookies or cubed brownies. You can flavor batters with nut pastes or praline powder, cocoa or instant coffee powder, citrus zest, or liquor;

marble them with Lemon Curd, 998, or Orange Curd, 999, preserves, or sweetened chestnut puree. You can substitute brown sugar or maple sugar for a portion of the white sugar and add nuts and a little bourbon for a praline caramel effect. You can bake almost any cheesecake with or without a crust, and you can alter the texture of a conventional cheesecake by baking it in a water bath or by trying the New York method.

CHEESECAKE COCKAIGNE

12 to 16 servings

One of the simplest and best. This old-fashioned sour cream–topped cake, only about 1¼ inches tall, tastes wonderfully homemade.

Prepare and bake in a 10-inch springform or cake pan:

Crumb Crust, 868, made with graham crackers

Have all ingredients at room temperature, 68° to 70°F. Preheat the oven to 300°F.

In a medium bowl, beat until creamy, about 30 seconds:

1½ pounds cream cheese

Gradually beat in:

1 cup sugar
1 teaspoon vanilla or ¼ teaspoon almond extract

Beat in 1 at a time, just until incorporated, scraping the sides of the bowl and the beaters after each addition:

3 large eggs

Scrape the batter into the crust and smooth the top. Place on a cookie sheet. Bake until the center just barely jiggles when the pan is tapped, 45 to 55 minutes. Let cool in the pan on a rack for at least 1 hour. Combine and spread over the cake:

1 cup sour cream
¼ cup sugar
1 tablespoon vanilla
⅛ teaspoon salt

Let cool completely in the pan on a rack before unmolding (see page 979). Cover and refrigerate for at least 3 hours, preferably 24 hours, before serving. Serve with fresh strawberries.

NEW YORK CHEESECAKE

15 to 20 servings

For many New Yorkers, this is the biggest and best cheesecake of all. (If you are baking for New Yorkers, go easy on the lemon zest or leave it out entirely.) Do not be afraid of the extreme oven temperature—the surface of the cake will be golden, with a creamy interior.

Preheat the oven to 400°F. Lightly grease a 9-inch springform pan.

Prepare the dough for:

Shortbread Crust, 868

Press one-third of the dough, or slightly less, over the bottom as evenly as possible. Prick the dough all over with a fork. Bake until the crust is light golden brown, 10 to 15 minutes. Let cool completely on a rack. Press the remaining dough about ⅛ inch thick around the sides of the pan, making sure that it is attached to the bottom crust all around. Brush the bottom and sides of the crust with:

1 egg white, well beaten

Refrigerate the crust if you are not filling it right away.

Have all the ingredients at room temperature, 68° to 70°F. Preheat the oven to 500°F.

In a large bowl, beat until creamy, about 30 seconds:

2½ pounds cream cheese

Scrape the sides of the bowl and the beaters well. Gradually add and beat until smooth and creamy, 1 to 2 minutes:

1¾ cups sugar
3 tablespoons all-purpose flour (optional)

Beat in:

1 teaspoon grated lemon zest
½ teaspoon vanilla

Beat in 1 at a time, just until incorporated, scraping the sides of the bowl and the beaters after each addition:

5 large eggs
2 large egg yolks

On low speed, beat in:

½ cup heavy cream

Scrape the batter into the crust and smooth the top. Bake for 15 minutes at 500°F, then reduce the oven temperature to 200°F and bake for 1 hour more. Turn the oven off, prop the oven door ajar with the handle of a wooden spoon, and let the cake cool in the oven for 30 minutes. Remove to a rack and let cool completely in the pan before unmolding (see page 979). Cover and refrigerate for at least 6 hours, preferably 24 hours, before serving. (The cheese flavor is even more intense after 48 hours.)

CREAMY WATER-BATH CHEESECAKE

12 to 16 servings

Baking in a water bath yields an ultracreamy cheesecake with a texture that is consistent from the edges to the center. You can bake any crustless cheesecake this way.

Have all ingredients at room temperature, 68° to 70°F. Preheat the oven to 325°F.

Coat the bottom and sides of a 9-inch springform pan with:

1 tablespoon unsalted butter

Sprinkle with:

¼ cup graham cracker crumbs

Tilt and tap the pan to spread the crumbs evenly over the bottom and sides. In a large bowl, beat just until smooth, 30 to 60 seconds:

2 pounds cream cheese

Scrape the sides of the bowl and the beaters well. Gradually add and beat until smooth and creamy, 1 to 2 minutes:

1⅓ cups sugar

Beat in 1 at a time, just until incorporated, scraping the sides of the bowl and the beaters after each addition:

4 large eggs

Add and beat on low speed just until mixed:

¼ cup heavy cream

¼ cup sour cream

1 teaspoon grated lemon zest

2 teaspoons vanilla

Scrape the batter into the pan and smooth the top. Set the pan on a length of wide heavy-duty aluminum foil. Fold the foil carefully up the sides of the pan without tearing it. Set the pan in a large baking dish or roasting pan. Set the baking dish in the oven and pour in enough boiling water to reach halfway up the sides of the cheesecake pan. Bake until the edges of the cheesecake look set but the center jiggles slightly when the pan is tapped, 55 to 60 minutes. Turn off the oven, prop the door ajar with the handle of a wooden spoon, and let the cake cool in the oven for 1 hour. Remove to a rack and let cool completely in the pan before unmolding (see page 979). Cover and refrigerate for at least 6 hours, preferably 24 hours, before serving.

FRESH RASPBERRY WATER-BATH CHEESECAKE

Roll ½ pint raspberries, rinsed and patted thoroughly dry, gently in 2 tablespoons sugar, or enough to coat. Prepare the batter for Creamy Water-Bath Cheesecake, above, and scrape three-quarters of it into the pan. Sprinkle the sugared berries over the top, scrape in the remaining batter, and smooth the top. Rap the pan on the counter to eliminate any bubbles. Bake as directed. After refrigerating, spread the top with 1 cup sour cream and arrange ½ to 1 pint raspberries on top.

VANILLA CHEESECAKE (REDUCED FAT)

10 to 12 servings

With only 32 percent of calories from fat and about 200 calories per serving, this cheesecake is dense, creamy, and satisfying. Serve it plain or with fresh berries. Be sure to process the cottage cheese for the full amount of time to ensure a silky-smooth texture.

Have all dairy ingredients cold. Grease one 8-inch springform pan.

Place in a strainer set over a bowl:

1 pint 2% low-fat cottage cheese

Refrigerate for at least 30 minutes to drain excess moisture.

Preheat the oven to 350°F.

Scrape the drained cheese into a food processor and process, scraping the sides of the bowl and the blade as necessary, until the cheese feels perfectly smooth on your tongue, 2 to 3 minutes. (Leave in the processor.)

Soften in the microwave on high for 30 seconds or in a bowl set in a skillet of barely simmering water:

8 ounces Neufchâtel cheese

Stir with a rubber spatula until creamy and smooth. Scrape the cheese into the processor bowl along with:

1 cup sugar

2 teaspoons vanilla

1½ teaspoons strained fresh lemon juice

¼ teaspoon salt

Pulse briefly 2 or 3 times. Scrape the sides of the bowl and the blade with a spatula and pulse again only if necessary to obtain a smooth batter; overprocessing will thin the batter. Scrape the batter into the pan and smooth the top. Set the pan on a length of wide heavy-duty aluminum foil. Fold the foil carefully up the sides of the pan without tearing it. Set the pan in a large baking dish or roasting pan. Set the baking dish in the oven and pour in enough boiling water to reach halfway up the sides of the cheesecake pan. Bake until the edges of the cake are puffed but the center still looks moist and jiggles when the pan is tapped, 40 to 45 minutes. Let cool completely in the pan on a rack before unmolding (see page 979).

Press:

¼ cup graham cracker crumbs

against the sides of the cake. Cover and refrigerate for at least 12 hours, preferably 24 hours, before serving.

CHOCOLATE MARBLE CHEESECAKE (REDUCED FAT)

Prepare the batter for Vanilla Cheesecake, above. In a small bowl, dissolve 3 tablespoons unsweetened Dutch-process cocoa, 1 tablespoon sugar, and ¼ teaspoon instant espresso or coffee powder in 3 tablespoons warm water. Stir 1 cup of the cheesecake batter into this mixture. Scrape the remaining batter into the pan. Pour the cocoa mixture over the plain batter in a wide ring about 1 inch from the edge of the pan. Use a teaspoon to marble the batters by gently stirring them in small looping circles until they are intermingled but not blended. Bake as directed.

After the cake is unmolded, press chocolate cookie crumbs around the sides instead of graham cracker crumbs, if desired.

LEMON CHEESECAKE (REDUCED FAT)

Prepare Vanilla Cheesecake, above, adding 1 teaspoon grated lemon zest to the batter with the lemon juice. Spread the top of the chilled cake with Reduced-Fat Lemon Curd, 998.

MOCHA CHEESECAKE (REDUCED FAT)

Prepare Vanilla Cheesecake, above, adding ¼ cup unsweetened cocoa and 1 tablespoon plus 2 teaspoons instant coffee or espresso powder to the food processor with the cottage cheese. Increase the sugar to 1 cup plus 2 tablespoons.

RICOTTA CHEESECAKE

10 to 12 servings

For the creamiest and best cheesecake of all, buy fresh whole-milk ricotta from an Italian market. If you use part-skim ricotta, you can make it creamier and less gritty by pressing it through a fine sieve or processing it for 3 to 4 minutes in a food processor.

Grease one 9-inch springform pan.

Prepare the dough for:

Pat-in-the-Pan Butter Crust, 867

Fit the dough into the pan so that it comes a bit more than halfway up the sides of the pan; it should be ⅛ inch thick. (The dough can be rolled out with a rolling pin or simply pressed into the pan with your fingers). Refrigerate for at least 30 minutes.

Preheat the oven to 400°F.

Prick the dough with a fork and press a sheet of aluminum foil over the bottom and up the sides of the pan. Fill with rice or pie weights and bake for about 15 minutes. Carefully remove the foil and weights and bake until the crust is golden brown, about 15 minutes more. Let cool completely in the pan on a rack. Patch any cracks or holes with scraps of dough before filling.

Have all ingredients at room temperature, 68° to 70°F.

Preheat the oven to 375°F.

Toss together:

3 tablespoons pine nuts, toasted
2 tablespoons chopped blanched almonds, toasted
2 tablespoons chopped candied citron or candied orange or lemon peel (optional)
2 tablespoons chocolate chips (optional)
1 tablespoon all-purpose flour

In a large bowl, beat on high speed until thick and pale yellow, 1 to 2 minutes:

4 large eggs
1 cup sugar
1½ teaspoons vanilla

Stir in:

3 cups (22 ounces) whole-milk or part-skim ricotta cheese (see headnote)

Stir in the nut mixture. Scrape the batter into the crust and smooth the top. Bake for 30 minutes, reduce the oven temperature to 325°F, and bake until a knife inserted about 2 inches from the edge of the cake comes out clean, 20 to 25 minutes more. The center will be softer and the cake will seem too jiggly, but it will set after it has cooled. Let cool completely in the pan on a rack before unmolding (see page 979). Cover and refrigerate for at least 6 hours, preferably 24 hours, before serving.

ALICE MEDRICH'S CHOCOLATE CHEESECAKE

12 to 16 servings

Richer than rich; for chocolate lovers only. This recipe is from the accomplished baker and author Alice Medrich.

Prepare and bake in a 9-inch springform or cake pan:

Crumb Crust, 868, made with chocolate wafers

Have all ingredients at room temperature, 68° to 70°F.

Place a loaf pan or cake pan filled with water on the bottom rack of the oven to moisten the air. Preheat the oven to 350°F.

Place in a small bowl:

8 ounces bittersweet or semisweet chocolate, finely chopped

Add:

⅓ cup boiling water

Stir until the chocolate is melted and smooth. In a large bowl, beat just until smooth, 30 to 60 seconds:

1 pound cream cheese

Scrape the sides of the bowl and the beaters well. Gradually add and beat until smooth and creamy, 1 to 2 minutes:

⅔ cup sugar
1 teaspoon vanilla

Beat in 1 at a time, just until incorporated, scraping the sides of the bowl and the beaters after each addition:

3 large eggs

Beat in:

2 cups sour cream
1 tablespoon unsweetened cocoa

Add the warm chocolate mixture and beat on low speed just until well blended. Scrape the batter into the crust and smooth the top. Place on a baking sheet. Bake until the edges of the cake have puffed but the center still looks moist and jiggles when the pan is tapped, 35 to 40 minutes. Turn the oven off, prop the door ajar with the handle of a wooden spoon, and let the cake cool in the oven for 1 hour. Remove to a rack and let cool completely in the pan before unmolding (see page 979). Cover and refrigerate for at least 6 hours, preferably 24 hours, before serving. (The flavors are even more intense after 48 hours.)

PUMPKIN CHEESECAKE *10 to 12 servings*

Warm fall pumpkin pie spices in a rich cheesecake.

Prepare and bake in an 8-inch springform or cake pan:

Crumb Crust, 868, made with graham crackers, or
Nut Crust, 869, made with pecans

Have all ingredients at room temperature, 68° to 70°F. Preheat the oven to 350°F. Place a loaf pan or cake pan filled with hot water in the oven to moisten the air. Combine:

⅔ cup packed light or dark brown sugar
¾ teaspoon ground cinnamon
¼ teaspoon ground cloves
¼ teaspoon ground ginger
⅛ teaspoon freshly grated or ground nutmeg

In a large bowl, beat just until smooth, 30 to 60 seconds:

1 pound cream cheese

Scrape the sides of the bowl and the beaters well. Gradually add the sugar mixture and beat until smooth and creamy, 1 to 2 minutes. Beat in 1 at a time until well blended, and scraping the sides of the bowl and the beaters after each addition:

2 large eggs
2 large egg yolks

Add and beat in just until mixed:

1 cup pumpkin puree

Scrape the batter into the crust and smooth the top. Set the pan on a baking sheet. Bake for 30 minutes at 350°F, reduce the oven temperature to 325°F, and bake for 10 minutes longer, or until the edges of the cheesecake are puffed but the center still looks moist and jiggles when the pan is tapped, 10 minutes more. Meanwhile, whisk together until well blended:

1 cup sour cream
¼ cup packed light brown sugar
1 teaspoon vanilla

Scrape on top of the hot cake and tilt the pan to spread the topping evenly. Return to the oven for 7 minutes. Place the pan on a rack and cover the pan and rack with a large inverted bowl or pot so that the cake cools slowly; let cool completely before unmolding (see page 979). Cover and refrigerate for at least 6 hours, preferably 24 hours, before serving.

ABOUT BAKING CAKES AT HIGH ALTITUDES

If you are new to high-altitude baking, bake recipes especially devised for your altitude or region, such as those in this section. For additional information and recipes, consult the cooperative extension service of a nearby university, a high school home economist, or the state agricultural service, or contact the U.S. Government Printing Office for booklets on high-altitude baking. Read the food pages of the closest regional newspaper and talk to other home cooks.

To adapt your favorite sea-level recipes, you will have to experiment. There are no hard and fast rules for successful adaptation. Read about the problems caused by high altitudes and the techniques we use to counter them, then launch forth; keep good notes as to what works best for your favorite recipes.

At altitudes over 3,000 feet, decreasing air pressure and low humidity can cause variations in cake batters. Cakes may rise too high and either overflow the pan or fall. Cake textures may be crumbly, porous, and dry. Since water boils at lower temperatures as altitude increases, batters lose too much moisture during baking. Moisture loss leads to higher concentrations of sugar in the batter, which exacerbates the problem of falling cakes: excessive sugar weakens the structure of cakes, as does excessive fat. Cakes baked at high altitudes also have a greater tendency to stick to the pan.

Our recipe modifications are designed to prevent excessive rising, compensate for moisture loss, and strengthen the cake or set the structure by baking the cake before excessive rising occurs. Repeated experimentation will give you the best results for each recipe.

GENERAL HIGH-ALTITUDE ADJUSTMENTS FOR CAKE BATTERS

Underbeat eggs and egg whites to keep cakes from rising too high at altitudes from 3,000 feet up. Use cold eggs rather than room-temperature ones, because cold eggs do not trap as much air when beaten and so expand less during baking. Increase baking temperatures by 15 to 25 degrees, to set the structure before too much rising occurs. For very rich batters, try decreasing the fat by 1 to 2 tablespoons and/or adding an egg. Do not fill pans more than half full.

Except when baking angel and sponge cakes, grease cake pans, especially decorative ones, well (and flour them if you wish) to counteract the tendency of cakes to stick; line all flat-bottomed pans with wax or parchment paper for easiest removal.

Use the chart, 985, as a starting point for additional adjustments depending on specific altitude. Always try the smallest adjustments first.

TECHNIQUES FROM UNOFFICIAL SOURCES

We talked to cooks who report success in adapting recipes at high altitudes simply by increasing the liquid by up to ¼ cup per cup called for and using a pan with higher sides to compensate for extra rising. Some cooks do not increase the oven temperature, because cakes dry out so quickly at high altitudes: baked goods may take longer to bake, they say, but higher temperatures can cause cakes to overcook in an instant. One cook we know who lives at 7,000 to 8,000 feet adapts her favorite recipes successfully merely by using three-quarters the amount of baking powder or baking soda called for, adding 1 tablespoon flour and 1 egg, decreasing the butter by a few tablespoons, and increasing the oven temperature by 25 degrees.

HIGH-ALTITUDE ANGEL CAKE *12 servings*

This recipe is for baking at 5,000 feet. If baking at 7,000 feet, add 1 tablespoon flour and decrease the sugar by 2 tablespoons; if baking at 10,000 feet, add 2 tablespoons flour and decrease the sugar by ¼ cup. (For general information about angel cakes, see page 950.)

Keep the egg whites refrigerated until needed. Preheat the oven to 375°F. Have ready 1 ungreased 10-inch tube pan.

Sift together 3 times and return to the sifter:

1 cup plus 2 tablespoons sifted cake flour
½ cup sugar
½ teaspoon salt

In a large bowl, beat on low speed until foamy:

1½ cups egg whites (about 12 large whites)
1½ teaspoons cream of tartar

Increase the speed to high and beat until the egg whites are glossy and form peaks that just barely fall over when the beaters are lifted. Using a rubber spatula, gradually fold in:

1 cup sugar

Using the mixer, beat until fluffy and meringuelike. Beat in:

1½ teaspoons vanilla

Sift about one-quarter of the flour mixture over the egg whites at a time, folding gently until each addition is nearly incorporated; do not stir or mix. Then continue to fold in the last addition until no traces of flour are visible. Scrape the batter into the pan and draw a thin spatula through the batter to eliminate large air pockets. Spread evenly. Bake until a toothpick inserted in the center comes out clean, about 40 minutes. Let cool upside down for at least 1½ hours, setting the tube over a bottleneck or resting the pan on 4 glasses. To unmold, see page 946.

HIGH-ALTITUDE CHOCOLATE ANGEL CAKE

Prepare High-Altitude Angel Cake, above, decreasing the sifted flour to 1 cup. Increase the sugar to ¾ cup and add ¼ cup unsweetened cocoa before sifting the dry ingredients.

HIGH-ALTITUDE SPICED ANGEL CAKE

Prepare High-Altitude Angel Cake, above, adding ¼ teaspoon ground cloves, ½ teaspoon freshly grated or ground nutmeg, and 1 teaspoon ground cinnamon to the dry ingredients before sifting. See pages 951 to 953 for other suggested angel cake flavorings.

HIGH-ALTITUDE BUTTER CAKE *8 servings*

The cake works well at altitudes from 5,000 to 9,000 feet.

Have all ingredients at room temperature, 68° to 70°F, except for the egg whites, which should be refrigerated. Preheat the oven to 375°F. Line the bottom of one 9 x 2-inch round pan with wax or parchment paper.

Sift together twice:

1½ cups sifted cake flour
1¼ teaspoons baking powder
¼ teaspoon salt

In a large bowl, beat until creamy, about 30 seconds:

8 tablespoons (1 stick) unsalted butter

Gradually add and beat on high speed until lightened in color and texture, 2 to 3 minutes:

¾ cup sugar

Beat in 1 at a time:

2 large egg yolks

Add the flour mixture in 3 parts, alternating with, in 2 parts:

1 cup milk
1 teaspoon vanilla

SPECIFIC ALTITUDE ADJUSTMENTS FOR CAKE BATTERS

ALTITUDE ADJUSTMENT	3,000 FEET	5,000 FEET	7,500 FEET	10,000 FEET
Decrease baking powder: for each teaspoon called for, decrease by	⅛ teaspoon	⅛ to ¼ teaspoon	¼ teaspoon	¼ to ½ teaspoon
Decrease sugar: for each cup called for, decrease by	0 to 1 tablespoon	0 to 2 tablespoons	1 to 3 tablespoons	2 to 3 tablespoons
Increase liquid: for each cup called for, add	1 to 2 tablespoons	2 to 4 tablespoons	3 to 4 tablespoons	3 to 4 tablespoons
*Increase flour: for each cup called for, add			1 to 2 tablespoons	1 to 2 tablespoons
Increase eggs				Add 1 egg

*Authorities do not agree on the wisdom of adding flour, except in foam cakes (sponge cakes, angel cakes, and chiffons), since additional flour has a drying effect that is unwelcome at altitudes where low humidity already makes for dry baked goods.

beating on low speed or stirring with a rubber spatula until smooth and scraping the sides of the bowl as necessary. In a medium bowl, beat on medium speed until soft peaks form:

2 large egg whites

Use a rubber spatula to fold one-quarter of the egg whites into the batter, then fold in the remaining whites. Scrape the batter into the pan and spread evenly. Bake until a toothpick inserted into the center comes out clean, about 40 minutes. Let cool in the pan on a rack for 10 minutes. Slide a thin knife around the cake to detach it from the pan. Invert the cake and peel off the paper liner. Let cool right side up on the rack. Frost as desired.

HIGH-ALTITUDE WHITE CAKE *10 to 12 servings*

This recipe is for baking at 5,000 feet. If baking at 7,500 feet, decrease the baking powder by ½ teaspoon; if baking at 10,000 feet, decrease the baking powder by 1 teaspoon.

Have all ingredients at room temperature, 68° to 70°F, except for the egg whites, which should be refrigerated until needed. Preheat the oven to 375°F. Grease and flour two 8 x 2-inch round pans and line the bottoms with wax or parchment paper.

Sift together twice:

2 cups sifted cake flour
1 cup sugar
2 teaspoons baking powder
½ teaspoon salt

Place in a large bowl:

8 tablespoons (1 stick) unsalted butter

Sift the flour mixture over the butter and add:

¾ cup milk
1 teaspoon vanilla

Beat on high speed for 2 minutes. In another large bowl, beat on medium speed until soft peaks form:

4 large egg whites

Gradually add, beating on high speed:

¼ cup sugar

Beat until the peaks are stiff but not dry. Add the egg whites to the butter mixture along with:

3 tablespoons milk

Beat for about 1 minute on medium-low speed. Divide the batter between the pans and spread evenly. Bake until a toothpick inserted into the center comes out clean, 25 to 30 minutes. Let cool in the pans on a rack for 10 minutes. Slide a thin knife around the cake to detach it from the pans. Invert the cake and peel off the paper liners. Let cool right side up on the rack.

HIGH-ALTITUDE FUDGE CAKE *12 to 16 servings*

This recipe is for baking at 5,000 feet. If baking at 7,500 feet, decrease the baking powder by 1 teaspoon; if baking at 10,000 feet, decrease the sugar by ¼ cup.

Have all ingredients at room temperature, 68° to 70°F, except for the eggs, which should be refrigerated until needed. Preheat the oven to 350°F. Grease and flour one 13 x 9-inch pan or two 9 x 2-inch round pans and line the bottom(s) with wax or parchment paper.

Melt in the top of a double boiler or in a microwave on medium, then set aside to cool to lukewarm:

4 ounces unsweetened chocolate, coarsely chopped

Sift together 3 times:

2 cups sifted cake flour
2 teaspoons baking powder
½ teaspoon salt

In a large bowl, beat until creamy, about 30 seconds:

8 tablespoons (1 stick) unsalted butter

Gradually add and beat on high speed until lightened in color and texture, 5 to 7 minutes:

2 cups sugar

Beat in 1 at a time:

3 large egg yolks

Beat in the melted chocolate. Add the flour mixture in 3 parts, alternating with, in 2 parts:

1½ cups milk

beating on low speed or stirring with a rubber spatula until smooth and scraping the sides of the bowl as necessary. In a medium bowl, beat on medium speed until soft peaks form:

3 large egg whites

Gradually add, beating on high speed:

¼ cup sugar

Beat until the peaks are almost stiff but not dry. Use a rubber spatula to fold one-quarter of the egg whites into the chocolate mixture, then fold in the remaining whites. Scrape the batter into the pan(s) and spread evenly. Bake until a toothpick inserted into the center comes out clean, about 35 minutes in round pans, 45 minutes in a 13 x 9-inch pan. Let cool in the pan(s) on a rack for 10 minutes. Slide a thin knife around the cake to detach it from the pan(s). Invert the cake and peel off the paper liner(s). Let cool right side up on the rack.

HIGH-ALTITUDE SPONGE CAKE *8 to 10 servings*

This recipe is for altitudes of 5,000 up to 10,000 feet. If baking at 10,000 feet, add 5 tablespoons sifted cake flour.

Have all ingredients at room temperature, 68° to 70°F, except for the eggs, which should be refrigerated until needed. Preheat the oven to 350°F. Grease and flour one 10-inch fluted tube or Bundt pan.

Resift twice and return to the sifter:

1¼ cups plus 1 tablespoon sifted cake flour

Combine in a medium bowl and beat on high speed until thick and pale yellow, 2 to 3 minutes:

6 large egg yolks
½ cup sugar
½ teaspoon salt
1½ tablespoons water
1 teaspoon vanilla

In a large bowl, beat on medium speed until soft peaks form:

6 large egg whites
¼ teaspoon cream of tartar

Gradually add, beating on high speed:

½ cup sugar

Beat until the peaks are almost stiff but not dry. Use a rubber spatula to fold one-quarter of the egg whites into the egg yolk mixture, then scrape the mixture back into the bowl with the remaining whites and fold together. Sift one-quarter of the flour over the mixture at a time and fold in just until incorporated. Fold in:

1 tablespoon grated lemon zest
1½ tablespoons fresh lemon juice

Scrape the batter into the pan and spread evenly. Bake until a toothpick inserted in the center comes out clean, about 35 minutes. Let cool in the pan on a rack for 5 minutes. Rotate and tap the pan against the counter to loosen the cake on all sides. Invert onto the rack and let cool completely.

FROSTINGS, FILLINGS & GLAZES

Fillings and frostings are the party clothes that transform simple cakes into celebrations. Birthday cakes, wedding extravaganzas, and memorable dinner party desserts are wrought from artful combinations of cake and frosting. These alluring sweet mixtures add moisture, creaminess, additional flavor, and enormous visual appeal. Combining cakes with fillings and frostings is an area of creativity for every baker. While we offer guidelines from our experience, we encourage you to experiment with combinations that strike your fancy.

In general, richer, denser frostings and glazes are used sparingly and spread thinner. Fluffy mixtures, including whipped cream, are used more lavishly. Pay attention to flavor, sweetness, coolness, creaminess, density, and richness when creating cake and filling and frosting combinations. You can complement or contrast the flavor, texture, and richness of a cake. Devil's Food Cake Cockaigne filled with Whipped Chocolate Ganache and glazed with Bittersweet Chocolate Glaze amply demonstrates the sublime results to be had by layering and reinforcing the same flavor—three different chocolate elements in a single dessert! Yet a tangy lemon cake with chocolate icing is equally impressive for its stark contrast of flavors.

Balance is the name of the game, but the rules are not always consistent. Whipped cream is an extraordinary partner for a variety of cakes, from the richest-of-the-rich flourless chocolate torte to the featheriest sponge cake. Elegant European cakes feature thin layers of light génoise, sponge cake, or meringue paired with the rich buttercreams, spread ultrathin. European nut and chocolate tortes are often served as a single thick layer, so rich or simply flavorful that filling and frosting are unnecessary; but a thin cloak of rich chocolate glaze adds emphasis and a touch of glamour. In place of the glaze, a dollop of whipped cream provides dramatic contrast.

Traditional American layer cakes feature thicker layers of rich butter cake filled generously with frosting. Fluffy frostings, such as Seven-Minute Frosting, 1001, delight those who love a marshmallowy texture and sweetness. Powdered-sugar icings, sweet and flavorful without being rich, enhance the rich flavor and texture of the cake. These icings are also convenient, because they require no refrigeration, and butter cakes are best enjoyed at room temperature. Powdered-sugar icings and glazes add sweetness and flavor as well to chiffon cakes and American-style sponge cakes.

Refrigeration is a point to consider when pairing cakes with frostings. Sponge cakes, chiffon cakes, and angel cakes do not harden in the refrigerator, and so they are compatible with fillings and frostings that might require refrigeration, such as custards, lemon curd, whipped cream, or buttercreams. Any cake filled and frosted with buttercream should be removed from the refrigerator an hour or more in advance of serving to restore its creamy glory. Butter cakes and rich chocolate tortes are diminished by refrigeration; flavor and fragrance are lost, and their velvety-rich and creamy textures harden. Should you pair one of these cakes with a filling or frosting that requires refrigeration, try to frost at the last minute, or remove the chilled cake from the refrigerator in advance of serving.

ABOUT FREEZING FROSTINGS AND FILLINGS

Dense frostings and fillings with high fat and low moisture freeze best. Thus buttercreams and powdered-sugar frostings (including those made from cream cheese) and nearly all chocolate glazes and frostings, including fudge, freeze well for at least 6 months.

Cream that has been frozen and thawed can be used in boiled mixtures, but it will not whip. Whipped cream that has been frozen cannot be spread or manipulated after thawing. However, if whipped cream rosettes or other shapes are piped before freezing, they can be transferred intact to a cake or dessert. In a pinch, you can freeze a cake that is frosted and/or filled with whipped cream, although we prefer not to.

Technically, pastry cream and other custards thickened with flour or cornstarch can be frozen, but we try to avoid it. Meringue toppings do not freeze successfully, either.

HOW TO FILL AND FROST A LAYER CAKE

Getting Ready

Cakes should be completely cool before being trimmed, cut, filled, and/or frosted. Warm cake layers melt frostings and cause layers to slip and slide.

To Cut a Single Tall Cake Horizontally into Thinner Layers

If the cake is just-baked and very tender, place it in the freezer for 20 minutes. Set the cake on a cardboard round, a piece of aluminum foil, or a decorating turntable or lazy Susan. If the cake is not level, trim it now. Cut a notch down one side of the cake so that you can line the layers up properly when you assemble the cake.

To divide a layer, place one hand flat on top of it. Hold the blade of a long serrated knife against the side of the cake where you wish to cut it. Turn the cake counterclockwise (clockwise if you are left-handed) while you saw a shallow groove all around the cake, always at an equal distance from the top of the cake, so the layer will be even. Do not try to cut all the way through the cake the first time around. After you have cut the groove, continue to rotate the cake while cutting deeper and deeper into the groove, until the layer is free. Alternatively, once the groove is cut, wrap a length of strong thread or dental floss around the groove, cross the ends in front, and pull them until the layer is cut through. Slide a piece of cardboard or a cookie sheet under the new layer and lift and set it aside. Repeat if necessary.

To Cope with Dome-Shaped Layers

Butter cakes may be slightly domed on top. In assembling a layer cake, the bottom and middle layers are usually placed dome side down and the top is placed dome side up. If the domes are very pronounced, trim them level and place them all upside down, since it is easier to spread frosting on an uncut surface.

Creating a Base for the Cake

A cardboard cake round or springform pan bottom the same diameter as the cake to be filled and/or frosted is a convenience that allows you to move the cake safely after you have completed it, simply by slid-

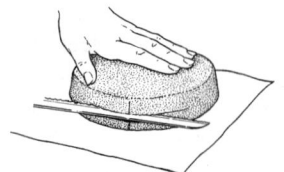

Cut a notch down one side of the cake, then saw a shallow groove all around the cake.

HOW MUCH FROSTING AND FILLING

Regard this as a general guideline; consider your own taste as well as the flavor, richness, and sweetness of the cake layers and the frosting. Whipped cream and Seven-Minute frostings are quite fluffy, and you can use the higher suggested amounts—or even more. For rich chocolate glazes or buttercreams in European-style cakes with thin layers, work with the smaller amounts and count on having some left over as well.

Top only (or filling for 1 layer):

For an 8- or 9-inch layer: ½ to 1 cup
For a 13 x 9-inch sheet: 1½ to 2 cups

Top and sides only:

For a 1-layer 8- or 9-inch cake: 1 to 1½ cups
For a 2-layer 8- or 9-inch cake: 1¼ to 1¾ cups
For a 3-layer 8- or 9-inch cake: 2 to 2½ cups
For a 13 x 9-inch sheet: 2½ to 3 cups

Top, sides, and filling:

For a 2-layer 8- or 9-inch cake: 2 to 3 cups
For a 3-layer 8- or 9-inch cake: 3 to 4 cups

Cupcakes:

For 12: 1 to 1½ cups

To fill a 17½ x 11½-inch jelly roll: 1½ to 3 cups

ing a metal spatula underneath it and lifting. Anchor the cake to the base with a dab of frosting, to keep it from sliding as you work. Otherwise, assemble and frost the cake directly on the serving platter. Slide wide strips of wax or parchment paper under the edges of the cake on all four sides to keep the platter clean. Remove the strips after the cake is frosted.

Using the Right Amount of Frosting and Filling

The amount of frosting and filling used for a particular cake depends on the style of cake and the richness of the filling. Fluffy frostings and whipped cream are spread thicker than denser, richer buttercreams. The buttercream between multiple thin layers in European cakes should be spread less than ⅛ inch thick (only ¼ to ⅓ cup of buttercream between 8-inch layers, ⅓ to ½ cup between 9-inch layers). Frostings and fillings between thicker American butter cake layers can be spread up to ¼ inch thick (up to 1 cup between layers). In other words, if the layers are thin, spread the filling thin; if the layers are thicker, spread the filling thicker. (See individual recipes or the chart, above, for general guidelines.) Each time you set a layer in place, make sure it is centered on the layer beneath it, sliding it as necessary.

Moistening a Cake with Soaking Syrup

European sponge layers and génoise are usually brushed, sprinkled, or sprayed with a flavored soaking syrup, 1010, to moisten them, add extra flavor, and create a liaison between the cake and the buttercream. Allow up to ¼ cup syrup for each 8-inch layer or up to ⅓ cup for each 9-inch cake layer (do not count any dacquoise or meringue layers, which are not moistened). The bottom cake layer is liberally moistened only on top with the entire amount of syrup allotted for the layer; other layers are moistened on the top and bottom, with half the syrup allotted to each side. Prepare the syrup according to your taste and the sweetness of the liquor. Sweet liquors may be mixed half and half with simple syrup (some of the sweetest liquors can even be used without syrup). For high-proof or stronger liquors, try one part liquor to three parts syrup and adjust from there. If the cake is very dry, use more syrup; if a génoise came out especially moist and tender, use less. Also consider how thick the layers are—use less syrup than is called for on ¼-inch-thick layers and up to the full amount on ½-inch-thick layers.

Adjusting the Consistency of Frostings and Buttercreams

The consistency of the frosting is critical to achieving the effect you want, in both filling and frosting the cake. Frosting that is too thick or stiff tears the cake and pulls up crumbs. Frosting that is too thin oozes out between cake layers, collapses into a puddle when piped, and may even slide off the cake. Modify the consistency of frostings according to need. Frostings rich in butter or chocolate can be softened or stiffened by placing the bowl in a pan of either warm or ice water and stirring to the desired consistency. Treat powdered sugar icings the same way, or beat in extra liquid to soften, powdered sugar to stiffen.

Whipped cream frosting works a little differently; do not try to soften or stiffen it once it is made, and do

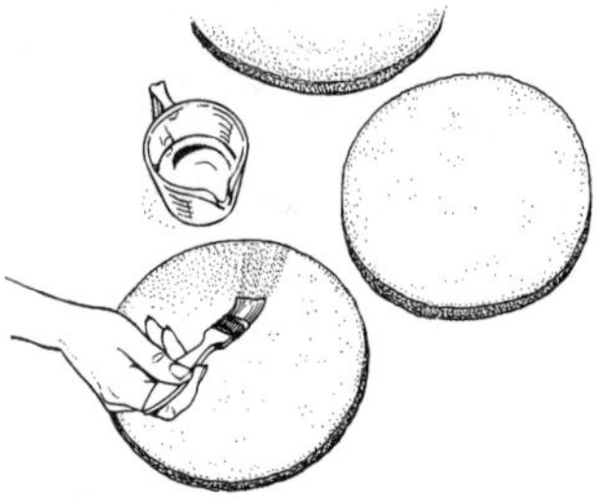

Moisten the cake layers with syrup.

not warm the spatula as you work, or you will break down the cream. If you are filling or frosting with whipped cream (or whipped ganache), underwhip the cream slightly. Spreading and smoothing the cream as you frost the cake will stiffen it adequately. If the cream is stiff before you begin, your finished frosting will look and taste overbeaten and grainy.

Dealing with Crumbs in the Frosting

Brush loose crumbs from the cake layers as necessary while you work. If a stiff frosting is tearing the cake and causing crumbs, adjust the consistency as directed, 989. Keep crumbs from "contaminating" the frosting in the bowl by scraping the spatula against another container each time before dipping it back into the frosting. Or divide the frosting between two bowls and work out of only one; save the other for the final frosting.

"Crumb-Coating" and Finishing the Cake

To keep crumbs from marring the finished frosting or glaze, seal the cake by first spreading a very thin coating of frosting, the "crumb coat," all over to smooth the surface and secure the crumbs. For the crumb coat, it is fine to use frosting that is already contaminated with crumbs. Some cakes are sealed with hot strained jam or preserves. You can refrigerate the cake for a few minutes to set the crumb coat before applying the final frosting. For chocolate butter glazes and ganaches, cool the glaze to the consistency of frosting for the crumb coat, then gently warm the remaining glaze to the correct temperature and fluidity for glazing.

With a clean, crumb-free spatula, spread the cake with a final attractive coat of frosting, smooth or in swirls as desired. You can texture the sides as directed, 991, or coat them with chopped nuts, or use the back of a spoon to make peaks and valleys in the frosting—see page 991 for decorating techniques.

Each pastry chef has different tools that he or she swears by. A stainless-steel spatula with an 8-inch blade is an excellent all-purpose tool for spreading frostings on cakes that are 8 or 9 inches in diameter. The spatula will enable you to spread a frosting smooth, in swirls, or with raised spikes; it also facilitates the spreading of poured chocolate glazes. A cake comb or serrated knife enables you to texture the sides and/or top of a cake. Perhaps not surprisingly, a perfectly smooth coat of frosting is the hardest texture to master. If you are determined to learn this technique, you will find it useful to acquire a decorating turntable or a lazy Susan to enable you to rotate the cake, holding the spatula steady as you smooth the frosting.

Any frosting or icing that is smooth and holds a shape can be piped with a pastry bag and a decorative pastry tip. Practice piping on the back of a cake pan.

Powdered-sugar icings and buttercreams should be stirred briskly with a rubber spatula before use and from time to time to eliminate air bubbles and keep the icing smooth.

HOW TO COAT A CAKE OR TORTE WITH CHOCOLATE GLAZE

Unlike lavishly spread frostings, which cover a multitude of imperfections on the surface of a cake, a poured chocolate glaze reveals all of them—from lopsided shapes to earthquake cracks. There are two great secrets to a perfectly glazed chocolate cake or torte: the preparation of the cake shape and surface, and the

Seal the cake by spreading it with a very thin coating of frosting, the crumb coat.

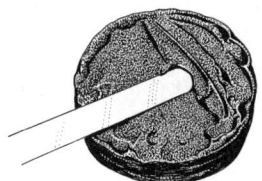

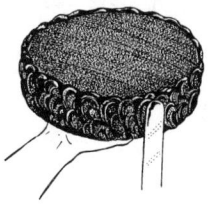

The spatula enables you to apply a smooth or textured frosting.

temperature at which the cake is stored and the glaze is poured.

The cake must be level. Trim sponge or butter cakes if necessary. Level those chocolate or nut tortes with a characteristic sunken center by pressing the edges and inverting the cake as directed on page 958. Place the cake on a rigid base such as a cardboard round or the bottom of a springform pan, so that the glaze will not crack or buckle when the cake is moved.

The cake surface must be smooth before glazing. In some classic European desserts, a coat of hot strained apricot or red currant jam is used to seal the cake or torte before glazing. An even more effective technique is to frost the cake very thinly with a little chocolate glaze that is first cooled to the consistency of frosting. As with frosted cakes, this is called "crumb-coating" the cake, because it smooths the surface, patches up cracks, and secures loose crumbs. Room-temperature cakes are crumb-coated at room temperature, and cakes that must be refrigerated or are to be served cold should be well chilled before crumb-coating. Once crumb-coated, a room-temperature cake should be refrigerated for 5 to 10 minutes, to set the crumb coat slightly without chilling the cake; remove the cake from the refrigerator even if you are not ready to glaze it. A cold cake should be returned to the refrigerator until you are ready to glaze it.

To glaze the cake, place it on a rack over a cookie sheet or on a lazy Susan or decorating turntable. Reheat the remaining glaze just until it is pourable (about 80°F). If it is too cool, it will immediately turn dull; if it is too warm, it will fall off the cake before coating it thickly enough. Pour the glaze on top of the cake and use a metal spatula to coat the top and sides completely, shown below. Gaps in coverage can be fixed by dipping a finger or the spatula into the excess glaze on the turntable or cookie sheet and touching the bare spot on the cake surface. Avoid spreading the glaze as it dries—this will dull the surface and cause streaks. The glaze on cold cakes starts to set immediately, so you must work quickly. For room-temperature cakes, let the glaze set naturally at room temperature; do not refrigerate the cake at any time. For cold cakes, return them to the refrigerator immediately after glazing and leave there until needed—which can be just before serving or up to 2 hours in advance of serving, depending on the nature of the cake.

In short, dull, mottled, or streaked glazes are caused by glaze poured at the wrong temperature or by cakes at the wrong temperature before or after glazing. Following these instructions will ensure gleaming, mirror-smooth glazed cakes.

DECORATIVE TREATMENTS FOR CAKES

To Texture the Top and Sides of a Frosted Cake

While the frosting or buttercream is still soft, dip a cake comb or serrated knife in hot water and wipe it dry. Hold it gently against the side of the cake at a 45-degree angle and, if you are using a turntable or lazy

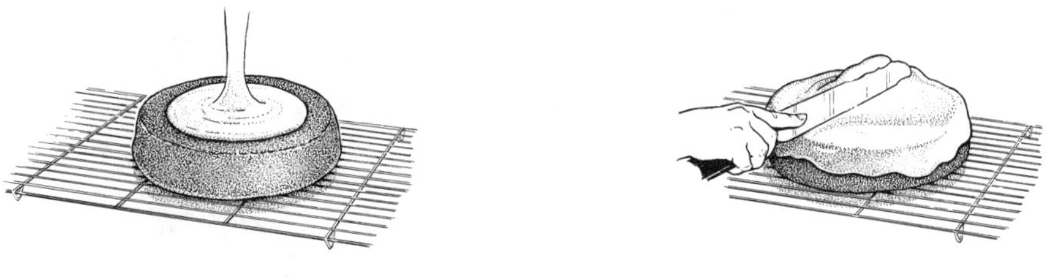

Pour all of the glaze in the center of the cake and spread it with a spatula

Fold a round of parchment or wax paper and cut a stencil.

Susan, rotate it slowly while holding the cake comb steady; otherwise, gently sweep the comb against the sides of the cake.

To Coat the Cake Sides with Nuts

While the frosting or buttercream is still soft, hold the cake (with one hand under the cardboard base) over a bowl of chopped nuts. Use your other hand to lift and press handfuls of nuts against the sides of the cake.

To Stencil the Top of the Cake

Refrigerate the cake to firm the frosting or buttercream. Use a paper doily, or make a hand-cut stencil: Fold a round of wax or parchment paper slightly larger than the surface of the cake into eighths or sixteenths and cut out small shapes along the folds (as for paper dolls). The shapes need not be specific or symmetrical. The advantage of a hand-cut stencil is that the cutouts are larger and more distinct than those of a lace doily and thus the design will show up better. No special design talent is necessary and you can enlist children to do the cutting. Flatten the stencil under a phone book if necessary before using. Lay the flattened doily directly on the surface of the cake. Use a fine-mesh sieve to sift a thin, even coating of powdered sugar or cocoa over the doily. Use both hands to lift the doily carefully off the cake without disturbing the pattern. Stencil cakes shortly before serving: the design will fade as sugar or cocoa is absorbed by the moist cake.

To Pipe Filigree or Write in Script

The best mixtures for fine piping are Royal Icing, 1009, and plain melted chocolate (thinned if necessary with drops of flavorless vegetable oil). Use a paper cone made of wax or parchment paper, shown 993. Or use a small sealable plastic bag. After filling, fold over and roll up the open end of the paper cone (like a toothpaste tube) or gather up and twist the plastic bag, forcing the frosting toward a bottom corner. Snip the end to make a tiny opening for piping. Test the size of the opening by practicing on a plate; snip the opening larger if necessary.

To Use a Pastry Bag

For piping borders, rosettes, stars, or other larger motifs with frosting, buttercream, or whipped cream, use a cloth or plasticized pastry bag. Choose a bag larger than you think you will need. Never fill the bag much more than half full; there should be plenty of empty bag to twist and seal off the filling.

Frostings and buttercreams to be piped should be stiff enough to hold a crisp shape. Stir them smooth with a rubber spatula before filling the bag. Whipped cream should be slightly underwhipped before piping, as forcing it through the bag and the tip will stiffen it further; stiffly whipped cream comes out of a pastry bag looking grainy and overbeaten. For best results, avoid piping whipped cream through a tip smaller than ¼ inch.

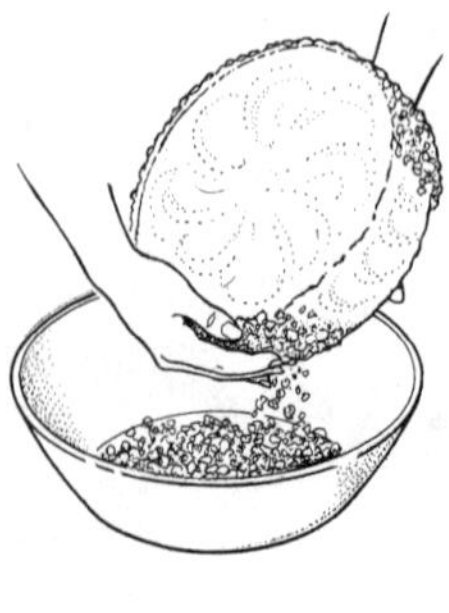

Coating cake sides with nuts

Sift an even coating of cocoa or powdered sugar over the doily.

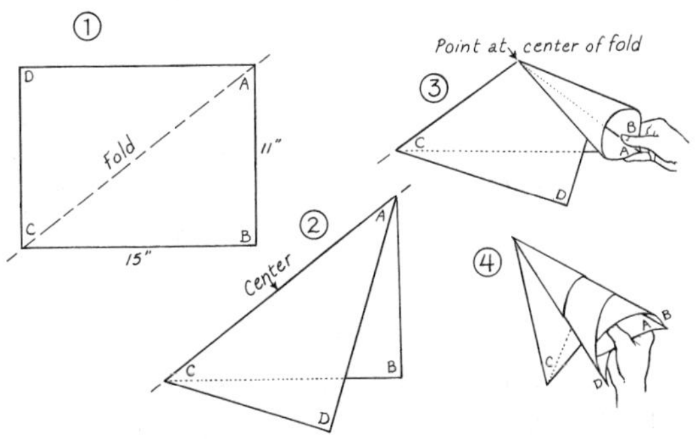

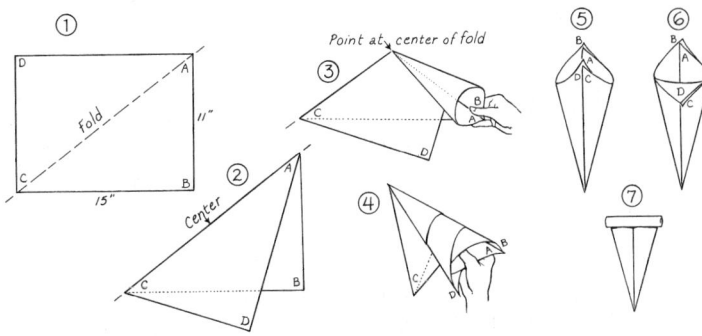

Making a paper cone

Each piped motif is the result of three factors: the angle of the bag and tip with respect to the surface of the cake, the timing and pressure of the squeeze, and the direction and speed of the stroke or movement. The bag and tip are held either at a 45-degree angle to the surface of the cake or at a 90-degree angle (meaning the bag is held straight up as you pipe on top of the

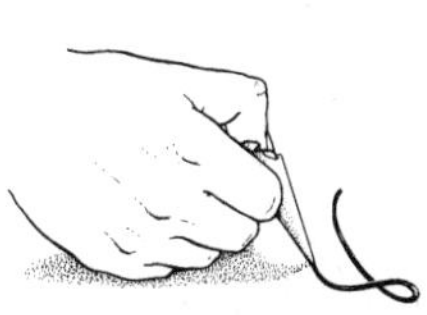

Using a paper cone to do fine piping

cake). Start to squeeze the bag a split second before starting to move the tip, and stop squeezing a split second before coming to a stop. If your motifs always trail off with an extra tail instead of ending crisply, it is because you are continuing to squeeze as you finish the stroke. The amount of squeezing before you begin to move the tip determines how full and fanned out the shape will be at the start. If you decrease pressure as you finish the stroke, it will taper off.

If you are having trouble achieving the shape you want, try altering any of these variables. Practice is the only way. There are two inexpensive and sturdy mixtures that can be used over and over again to practice piping. You can mix instant mashed potatoes with water to the desired consistency. As you practice, adjust the consistency of the potatoes with water as needed. Alternatively, make practice buttercream by beating 4 cups powdered sugar into 1½ cups vegetable shortening mixed with 2 tablespoons water and 1 tablespoon corn syrup. Practice on the backs of cake pans or on sheets of wax or parchment paper.

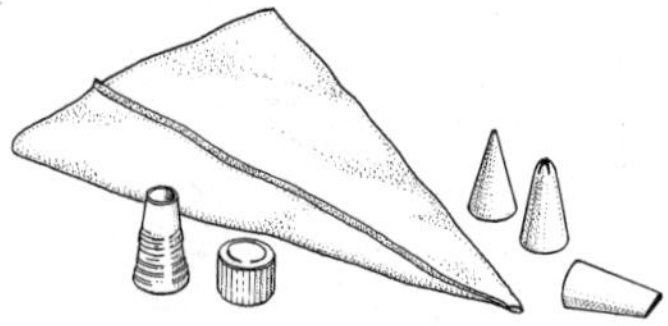

Pastry bag, coupler, and tips

Pastillage and Gum Paste

Pastillage and gum paste are malleable sugar pastes—related to fondant—used to create durable cake decorations and centerpieces for formal occasions from weddings to affairs of state. Plaques and architectural structures, figurines, flowers, remarkable replicas of lace, draped fabric, flowing ribbons, and ruffles fashioned from pastillage and gum paste transform cake into sculpture and showcase the pastry chef as an artist. Indeed, the pastes are worked with rollers, cutters, and carving tools much as sculptors work with clay or wax. Pastillage is used for larger, heavy pieces, gum paste for smaller, finer work such as flowers and lace. Pieces dry hard and brittle like unglazed china, with a slightly off-white color and matte finish. The

Fill the pastry bag half-full.

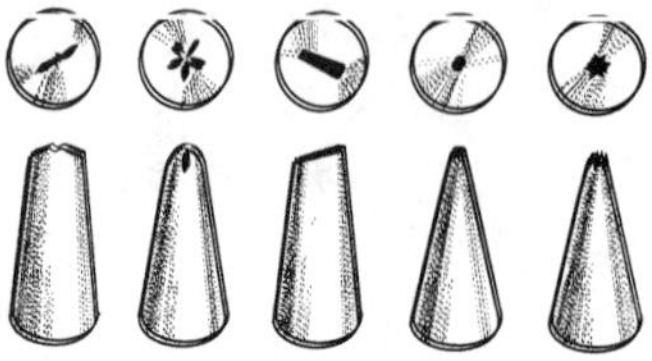

Piping tips

paste itself can be tinted or the finished work painted, or even gilded, after it has hardened. Although the pieces are technically edible, we do not expect or invite guests to nibble decorations made with gum.

Recipes for pastillage and gum pastes are simple, but the techniques for working with them take time and practice. For books, classes, and information about working with pastillage and gum paste, consult cake-decorating stores or mail-order houses that specialize in pastry and baking equipment.

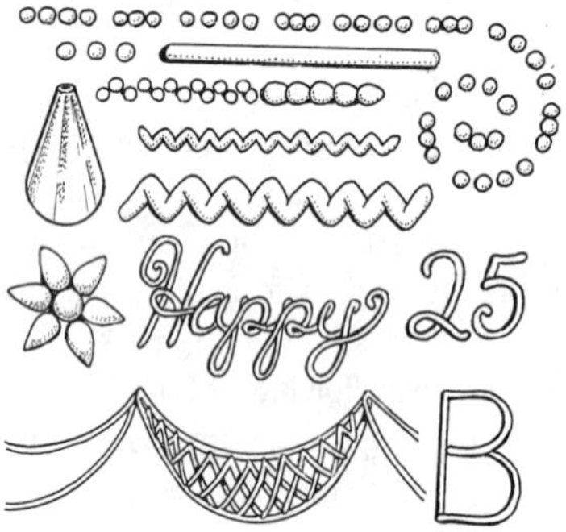

Piped motifs using a round tip

Piped motifs using a petal tip

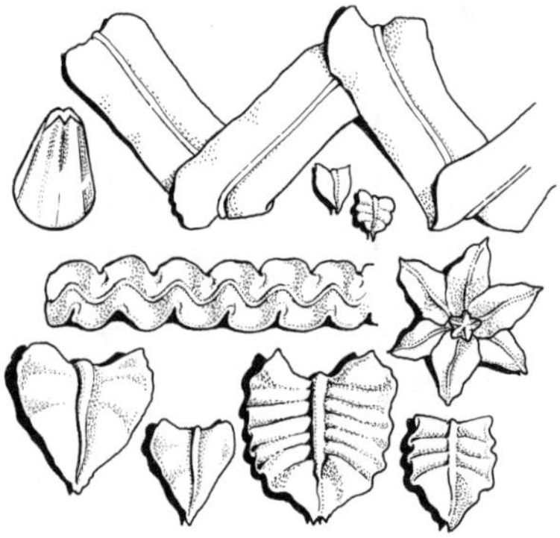

Piped motifs using a leaf tip

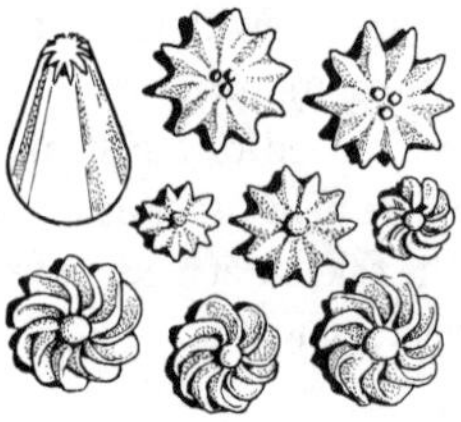

Piped motifs using a stellar drop tip

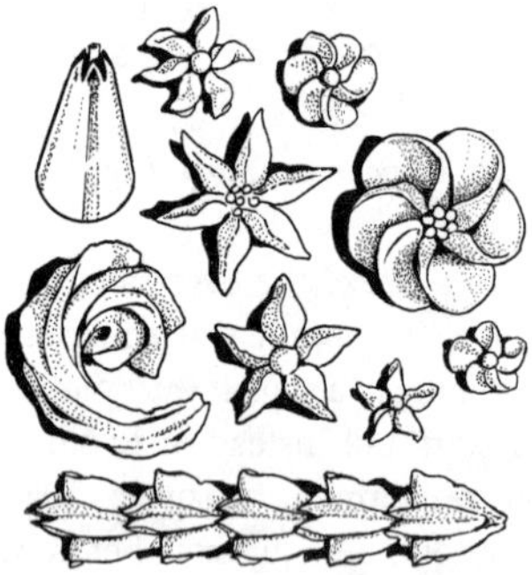

Piped motifs using a drop flower tip

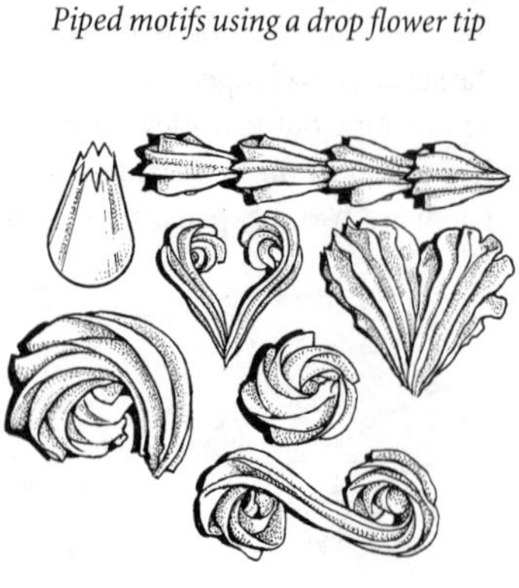

Piped motifs using a star tip

ABOUT WHIPPED CREAM

Cream must have a butterfat content of at least 30 percent to hold a stable, unseparated foam when whipped; for optimal stability, a butterfat content of 36 percent or more is preferable. In some areas, both 30 and 36 percent cream are available, the former sold as "medium" cream and the latter as "heavy." Confusingly, cream may be labeled either "whipping" or "heavy" with a butterfat content of either 30 or 36 percent. Our advice is simply to choose the heaviest cream available to you.

The cream must be cold or the butterfat will melt and the cream will refuse to aerate, thicken, and expand. When the weather is hot, it is a good idea to put the bowl and the beaters in the freezer for 5 minutes before beating. If your kitchen is very warm, set the bottom of the bowl of cream in ice water as you beat. Cream can be whipped by hand using a large balloon whisk, but it is certainly easier to use an electric mixer instead. Set a heavy-duty mixer on medium-high speed, a less powerful hand-held mixer at high speed. Beat the cream until it begins to thicken, and then add sugar and any flavorings. Continue to beat until the cream forms soft or stiff peaks, as you prefer. When stiffened to its maximum capabilities, the cream will begin to gather around the beaters. Watch it closely at this point, lest you inadvertently overbeat and turn the cream to butter. (If the cream has just begun to turn grainy and buttery, you can sometimes smooth it out by beating in ¼ cup cold milk or additional cream. The life of this whipped cream is precarious, so use as soon as possible.)

Perfectly whipped cream—billowy and stiff but still smooth—is frequently on its way to becoming butter by the time one has frosted a cake with it, spread it over a cake sheet for a jelly roll, or forced it through a pastry bag to make rosettes. This is because any manipulation of whipped cream, including stirring, spreading, or forcing it through a small opening, has the same result as continuing to beat it. The solution is to underwhip any cream to be used as a frosting, filling, or piped decoration. It is also advisable to underwhip cream whenever it must be refrigerated for several hours before use: whisk the cream briefly to the desired consistency just before use, to reincorporate any liquid that may have separated from it. A cake frosted or filled with whipped cream is best the day it is made.

WHIPPED CREAM

2 to 2½ cups

In a chilled bowl with chilled beaters, beat until thickened:

1 cup cold heavy cream

If you wish, add and beat to the desired consistency:

2 teaspoons to 2 tablespoons sugar, 1 to 4 tablespoons sifted powdered sugar, or 2 teaspoons honey (optional)

½ teaspoon vanilla (optional)

Use immediately or see About Whipped Cream, above, for storage information.

STABILIZED WHIPPED CREAM

The best-quality heavy cream has 38 to 40 percent butterfat content and can be used to fill or frost a cake, even a day in advance, without adding a stabilizer. But this type of cream is not available everywhere. Gelatin added to whipped cream gives it a firmer, mousselike texture and keeps it from weeping. It must still be stored in the refrigerator, but it will hold up longer on a buffet table, and you can fill or frost a cake with it a day in advance without worry.

Pour into a heatproof cup:

1 tablespoon cold water

Sprinkle with:

½ teaspoon unflavored gelatin

Let the gelatin soften, without stirring, for 5 minutes. Place the cup in a pan of simmering water until the gelatin is melted and the liquid is clear. Let cool to room temperature. Prepare Whipped Cream, above, adding the cooled (but not cold) gelatin mixture while you beat as the cream begins to thicken. Stabilized whipped cream can be flavored according to the variations, below, but do so as soon as possible—before the gelatin sets.

COFFEE WHIPPED CREAM

Prepare Whipped Cream, above, adding 2 teaspoons instant coffee or espresso powder to the cream with the vanilla. Use about 1 tablespoon plus 2 teaspoons sugar, or to taste.

LIQUOR-FLAVORED WHIPPED CREAM

Prepare Whipped Cream, above, adding 1 to 1½ tablespoons liquor to the cream with the sugar.

MOCHA WHIPPED CREAM

Prepare Whipped Cream, above, combining a small amount of the cream and the vanilla with 2 teaspoons instant coffee or espresso powder and 2 tablespoons unsweetened Dutch-process cocoa. Stir in the remaining cream and beat as directed, using 2 tablespoons sugar.

COCOA WHIPPED CREAM

Prepare Whipped Cream, above, combining a small amount of the cream and the vanilla with ⅓ cup sifted powdered sugar, 3 tablespoons unsweetened Dutch-process cocoa, and ⅛ teaspoon salt. Stir in the remaining cream and beat as directed, omitting the additional sugar.

NEOCLASSIC LADY BALTIMORE FILLING AND FROSTING

Prepare 2 recipes Whipped Cream, above. Fold into 2 cups of the whipped cream:

⅔ cup chopped pecans
⅓ cup chopped dried figs or dates
⅓ cup raisins
¼ teaspoon almond extract

Use to fill layers of White Cake, 937, and frost with the remaining whipped cream.

WHIPPED CREAM FILLING WITH FRUIT, NUTS, CANDY, OR COOKIES

If you are folding in wet ingredients, such as fruit puree, consider using Stabilized Whipped Cream, 995. Prepare but do not beat quite as stiff:

Whipped Cream, 995

Fold in any of the following:

½ cup chopped nuts
½ cup toasted or untoasted shredded sweetened dried coconut, mixed with 1 tablespoon rum (optional)
¼ cup praline paste, mixed with 1 tablespoon complementary liqueur (optional)
½ cup jam or marmalade
½ cup fresh, frozen, or canned fruit puree, mixed with 2 tablespoons kirsch or a complementary liqueur (optional)
¾ cup drained chopped fresh fruit
½ cup crushed or chopped candy, such as peppermint, toffee, nut brittle, or peanut butter cups
½ cup crushed chocolate wafer or sandwich cookies

ABOUT CAKE FILLINGS, CUSTARDS, AND CURDS

With some exceptions, cake fillings are less sweet than frostings. They offer a custardlike or puddinglike texture in contrast to the cake itself. Fillings are often starch based—like old-fashioned cornstarch pudding—or thickened with cooked whole eggs or yolks, like lemon curd or custard. We use two methods. In highly acidic fillings such as lemon, almost all the ingredients are combined and cooked over direct heat, because the acid in the lemon juice protects the eggs from curdling even when the mixture simmers. With less acidic fillings thickened with starch or flour in addition to eggs, the starch, sugar, and eggs are beaten together before being cooked with a hot liquid. This time, the starch protects the eggs from curdling as the filling cooks.

We cook most fillings over direct heat on the stove, rather than in the top of the once-favored double boiler, because it is essential that the starch actually cook so that the filling will taste as it should. Use heavy-bottomed pans and a whisk to help prevent burning or lumps (and if the mixture is acidic, be sure to use a stainless-steel or other nonreactive pan). It is wise to strain the finished mixture to remove any tiny bits of cooked egg white, which can mar the smoothness of the filling. Pay attention to the timing and heating details of any filling made with cornstarch or flour: Overcooking or overbeating can result in a disastrously thin filling, while an undercooked sauce may taste starchy or suddenly turn watery from the breakdown of starch caused by insufficiently cooked eggs. Egg safety is an issue in cooking custards. To avoid spoilage and salmonella contamination, be sure to scrape the finished cooked filling into a clean container (not one that has the remains of raw eggs in it), using a clean rubber spatula. Most custard-style fillings should be used within a day or two. Lemon curd can be kept refrigerated for up to 1 week.

PASTRY CREAM (CRÈME PÂTISSIÈRE)

About 2 cups

This is the vanilla custard filling for Boston Cream Pie, 966, custard éclairs, the best fresh fruit tarts, and countless other desserts. You can also add 1 to 2 tablespoons liqueur to any variation of this custard along with the vanilla if desired. For a lighter but richer filling, fold ¼ to ¾ cup Whipped Cream, 995, into this or any of the custard fillings that follow.

In a medium bowl, beat on high speed until thick and pale yellow, about 2 minutes:

⅓ cup sugar
2 tablespoons all-purpose flour
2 tablespoons cornstarch
4 large egg yolks

Meanwhile, combine in a medium stainless-steel or enamel saucepan and bring to a simmer:

1⅓ cups milk
1 vanilla bean, split (optional)

Fish out the vanilla bean if you used it. Gradually pour about one-third of the hot milk into the egg mixture, stirring to combine. Scrape the egg mixture back into the pan and cook, whisking constantly and scraping the bottom and corners of the pan to prevent scorching, over low to medium heat until the custard is thickened and begins to bubble. Then continue to cook, whisking, for 45 to 60 seconds. Using a clean spatula, scrape the custard into a clean bowl. If you have not used the vanilla bean, stir in:

¾ teaspoon vanilla

Cover the surface of the custard with a piece of wax or parchment paper to prevent a skin from forming. Let cool, then refrigerate before using. This keeps, refrigerated, for up to 2 days.

CHOCOLATE PASTRY CREAM

Prepare Pastry Cream, above, folding 3 to 5 ounces finely chopped semisweet or bittersweet chocolate into the hot custard along with the vanilla bean, if using. Stir gently just until the chocolate is melted and well blended.

COCOA PASTRY CREAM

Prepare Pastry Cream, above, combining ⅓ cup sugar and ⅓ cup unsweetened cocoa, preferably Dutch-process, in the saucepan before adding the milk. Whisk in just enough of the milk to form a smooth paste, then stir in the remaining milk and continue as directed.

COFFEE PASTRY CREAM

Prepare Pastry Cream, above, stirring 2 to 3 teaspoons instant coffee or espresso powder into the hot milk.

BANANA PASTRY CREAM

Prepare Pastry Cream, above, stirring 1 to 2 tablespoons rum into the hot custard if desired. Fold 2 or more bananas, thinly sliced, into the cold custard just before using.

HAZELNUT OR ALMOND PRALINE PASTRY CREAM

Prepare Pastry Cream, above. Fold ⅓ cup crushed hazelnut or almond praline, 854, into the cold custard just before using.

FRANGIPANE PASTRY CREAM

Prepare Pastry Cream, above, folding ⅓ cup ground blanched almonds and ⅛ teaspoon almond extract into the hot custard. Or fold ⅓ cup crushed almond macaroons into the cold custard just before using. Add 2 to 3 teaspoons minced candied orange peel if desired.

BUTTERSCOTCH PASTRY CREAM

Prepare Pastry Cream, above, substituting ½ cup packed light or dark brown sugar for the sugar and adding a pinch of salt.

REDUCED-FAT PASTRY CREAM

About 1¼ cups

In a medium bowl, beat on high speed until thick and pale yellow, about 2 minutes:

3 tablespoons sugar
1 tablespoon plus 2 teaspoons cornstarch
1 tablespoon all-purpose flour
1 large egg
1 large egg yolk

Meanwhile, bring to a simmer in a medium stainless-steel or enamel saucepan:

1 cup low-fat milk

Gradually pour about one-third of the hot milk into the egg mixture, whisking to combine. Scrape the egg mixture back into the pan and cook, whisking constantly and scraping the bottom and corners of the pan to prevent scorching, over low to medium heat until the custard is thickened and begins to bubble. Then continue to cook, whisking, for 45 to 60 seconds. Using a clean spatula, scrape the custard into a clean bowl and stir in:

½ teaspoon vanilla

Cover the surface of the custard with a piece of wax or parchment paper and refrigerate to thicken. This keeps, refrigerated, for up to 2 days.

REDUCED-FAT COCOA PASTRY CREAM

Prepare Reduced-Fat Pastry Cream, above, combining ¼ cup sugar and ¼ cup unsweetened cocoa, preferably Dutch-process, in the saucepan before adding the milk. Whisk in just enough of the milk to form a smooth paste, then stir in the remaining milk and continue as directed.

CHOCOLATE CUSTARD FILLING

About 1½ cups

Combine in a medium, heavy saucepan:

1 cup milk
¼ cup heavy cream
2 ounces unsweetened chocolate, finely chopped

Cook, stirring occasionally, over medium-low heat until the chocolate is melted and the mixture begins to simmer. Meanwhile, in a medium bowl, beat on high speed until thick and pale yellow, about 1 minute:

⅓ cup sugar
1 tablespoon cornstarch
1 tablespoon all-purpose flour

2 large egg yolks
1/8 teaspoon salt

Gradually pour about one-quarter of the hot chocolate mixture into the egg mixture, stirring to combine. Scrape the egg mixture back into the pan and cook, whisking constantly and scraping the bottom and corners of the pan to prevent scorching, over medium heat until the mixture is thickened and begins to bubble. Then continue to cook, whisking, for about 1½ minutes. Using a clean spatula, scrape the filling into a clean bowl and stir in:

1 teaspoon vanilla

Cover the surface of the filling with a piece of wax or parchment paper and refrigerate to thicken. This keeps, refrigerated, for up to 2 days.

MOCHA FILLING
About 1⅔ cups

Coffee lovers will appreciate the pronounced mocha flavor in this dark chocolate custard, which has the texture of thick pudding.

Combine in a medium, heavy saucepan:

¾ cup extra-strong coffee
⅓ cup heavy cream
1 ounce unsweetened chocolate, finely chopped

Cook, stirring occasionally, over medium-low heat until the chocolate is melted and the mixture begins to simmer. Meanwhile, in a medium bowl, beat on high speed until thick and pale yellow, about 1 minute:

¾ cup sugar
1½ tablespoons cornstarch
1/8 teaspoon salt
3 large egg yolks, or 1 large egg and 1 large egg yolk

Gradually pour about one-quarter of the hot chocolate mixture into the egg mixture, stirring to combine. Scrape the egg mixture back into the pan and cook, whisking constantly and scraping the bottom and corners of the pan to prevent scorching, over medium heat until the mixture is thickened and begins to bubble. Then continue to cook, whisking, for about 1½ minutes. Using a clean spatula, scrape the filling into a clean bowl. Let cool, without stirring. Cover the surface of the filling with a piece of wax or parchment paper and refrigerate to thicken. This keeps, refrigerated, for up to 2 days.

LEMON FILLING
About 1⅓ cups

Thickened with cornstarch, this has the taste and texture of lemon meringue pie filling.

Whisk together in a small stainless-steel or enamel saucepan:

¾ cup sugar
2 tablespoons cornstarch
1/8 teaspoon salt
Grated zest of ½ lemon
½ cup water or orange juice
¼ cup strained fresh lemon juice
3 large egg yolks, or 1 large egg and 1 large egg yolk

Add:

1 tablespoon unsalted butter

Cook, whisking constantly and scraping the bottom and corners of the pan to prevent scorching, over medium heat until the mixture comes to a simmer and thickens dramatically. Then continue to cook, whisking briskly, for about 30 seconds. Using a spatula, scrape the filling into a medium-mesh sieve set over a bowl and strain the filling into the bowl. Cover the surface of the filling with a piece of wax or parchment paper and refrigerate to thicken. Stir gently if necessary before using; do not beat. This keeps, refrigerated, for up to 2 days.

LEMON CURD
About 1⅔ cups

Tarter and tangier than Lemon Filling, above, this makes a sensational filling for sponge rolls or Basic Angel Cake, 952. You can also marble it into a plain cheesecake.

In a medium stainless-steel or enamel saucepan, whisk together until light in color:

3 large eggs
⅓ cup sugar
Grated zest of 1 lemon

Add:

½ cup strained fresh lemon juice
6 tablespoons (¾ stick) unsalted butter, cut into small pieces

Cook, whisking, over medium heat until the butter is melted. Then whisk constantly until the mixture is thickened and simmer gently for a few seconds. Using a spatula, scrape the filling into a medium-mesh sieve set over a bowl and strain the filling into the bowl. Stir in:

½ teaspoon vanilla

Let cool, cover, and refrigerate to thicken. This keeps, refrigerated, for about 1 week.

REDUCED-FAT LEMON CURD
About 1½ cups

Prepare Lemon Curd, above, decreasing the eggs to 2 and increasing the sugar to ¾ cup and the lemon juice to ⅔ cup. Omit the butter, or use just 2 tablespoons to reduce the tartness of this very tangy filling.

LEMON-ORANGE CUSTARD FILLING

About 1 cup

Whisk together in a small stainless-steel or enamel saucepan:

Grated zest of ½ lemon
Grated zest of ¼ orange
½ cup fresh orange juice
3 tablespoons fresh lemon juice
3 tablespoons water
½ cup sugar
2 tablespoons all-purpose flour
⅛ teaspoon salt
3 large egg yolks, or 1 large egg and 1 large egg yolk

Cook, whisking constantly and scraping the bottom and corners of the pan to prevent scorching, over medium heat until the mixture is thickened and begins to bubble. Then continue to cook, whisking briskly, for about 1 minute. Using a spatula, scrape the filling into a medium-mesh sieve set over a bowl and strain the filling into the bowl. Cover the surface of the filling with a piece of wax or parchment paper and refrigerate to thicken. Stir gently if necessary before using; do not beat. This keeps, refrigerated, for up to 2 days.

APRICOT CUSTARD FILLING

About 1½ cups

Combine in a small saucepan and simmer gently for 25 minutes:

½ cup gently packed dried apricots
1 cup water

Stir in:

1 tablespoon sugar

Simmer until the liquid is reduced to a glaze, 3 to 5 minutes. Puree the mixture until smooth.

Prepare:

Lemon-Orange Custard Filling, above

Stir the apricot puree into the hot filling.

ORANGE CURD

About 1⅔ cups

Blood oranges, if you can get them, are sensational in this filling.

In a medium stainless-steel or enamel saucepan, whisk together until light in color:

8 large egg yolks, or 4 large egg yolks and 2 large eggs
⅔ cup sugar
Grated zest of 1½ oranges

Add:

½ cup fresh orange juice
10 tablespoons (1¼ sticks) unsalted butter, cut into small pieces

Cook, whisking, over medium heat until the butter is melted. Then whisk constantly until the mixture is thickened and simmers gently for a few seconds. Using a spatula, scrape the filling into a medium-mesh sieve set over a bowl and strain the filling into the bowl. Let cool, cover, and refrigerate to thicken. This keeps, refrigerated, for about 1 week.

COCONUT PECAN FILLING

About 3¼ cups

Sweet and delicious, this is the traditional German Chocolate Cake, 944, filling and topping. The sides of the cake are left unfrosted.

Combine in a medium saucepan:

1 cup sugar
1 cup evaporated milk, half-and-half, or heavy cream
3 large egg yolks
8 tablespoons (1 stick) unsalted butter, cut into small pieces

Cook, stirring constantly, over medium heat until the mixture is thickened and bubbling gently around the edges. Reduce the heat to low and cook, stirring, for 1 to 2 minutes more. Remove from the heat and stir in:

1⅓ cups flaked sweetened dried coconut
1⅓ cups chopped pecans

Let cool until spreadable. This keeps, refrigerated, for about 1 week. Soften before using.

TOASTED WALNUT OR PECAN FILLING

About 1½ cups

Brown sugar and toasted nuts make a superb filling.

Combine in a small saucepan:

1 cup packed light brown sugar
4 tablespoons (½ stick) unsalted butter, cut into small pieces
2 tablespoons water
½ teaspoon salt

Cook, whisking, over low heat until the butter is melted and the mixture begins to simmer. Remove from the heat and whisk in:

2 large egg yolks

Return to low heat and cook, whisking constantly, until thickened, 1 to 2 minutes. Remove from the heat and stir in:

1½ cups chopped walnuts or pecans, toasted

Let cool before using. This keeps, refrigerated, for about 1 week. Soften before using.

LANE CAKE FILLING

About 2¼ cups

Whisk together in a medium, heavy saucepan:

8 large egg yolks
1 cup sugar
⅛ teaspoon salt
½ cup bourbon
8 tablespoons (1 stick) unsalted butter, cut into small pieces

Cook, stirring constantly, over medium-low heat until the mixture is thickened enough to coat the back of a spoon, about 10 minutes. Remove from the heat and stir in:

1 cup pecans, finely chopped
¾ cup shredded sweetened dried coconut
⅔ cup raisins, finely chopped
⅓ cup chopped dates or raisins
¼ cup chopped maraschino cherries (optional)
¼ teaspoon freshly grated or ground nutmeg

Let cool before using. This keeps, refrigerated, for about 1 week. Soften before using.

ABOUT COOKED ICINGS AND TRUE BUTTERCREAMS

Traditional American cooked icings include seven-minute frosting and the true fudge and caramel frostings—in short, any mixture that requires the cooking or boiling of sugar. We include classic buttercreams in this category, too, as any advice pertaining to cooked sugar is critical to these mixtures as well.

FONDANT ICING

Fondant Icing is Basic Fondant, 852, warmed and thinned to pouring or spreading consistency. Properly applied, it makes a slightly translucent satiny finish on petits fours and the tops of certain classic European-style cakes. The temperature and consistency of the fondant is important, as is the proper preparation of the items to be glazed. It takes a little practice to apply fondant perfectly.

For best results, warm the fondant very gently in a bowl set in a skillet of 110°F water, reheated as necessary on the stove to maintain the temperature. Stir the fondant gently with a rubber spatula, to avoid creating air bubbles, until the fondant reaches a temperature between 98° and 105°F. Stir in food coloring if desired and flavor to taste with extracts, lemon juice, instant espresso powder dissolved in a small amount of water, liqueurs, or the like. Thin the fondant judiciously with warm Simple Syrup, 1010, until it is the desired consistency—thinner for pouring over small sweets, such as petits fours, thicker for spreading on the tops of cakes; you can test the fondant on a spare piece of cake or a cookie.

Fondant will not hide cracks, unevenness, crumbs, or other imperfections, so cakes and petits fours must be properly prepared, neat, and smooth before the fondant is applied. A smooth thin coat of buttercream or hot apricot glaze spread or brushed on the top and sides of the item is the usual preparation. Chill or freeze (briefly) items to be coated with fondant so that the surface is firm and the fondant will set quickly.

Petits fours to be coated with poured fondant should be lined up, with spaces between them, on a wire grid or rack set on a baking sheet to catch the excess, which can be scraped up and reused as long as it is crumb free. Pour the fondant with a small pitcher or use a spoon. If spreading with a spatula, do so with a quick, sure stroke, as the fondant glazes over quickly and should not be reworked. You can also spear petits fours or small items from the bottom with a fork and dip them into the fondant to coat. To store fondant, cover the surface with a sheet of plastic wrap. This keeps for up to 1 week at room temperature or up to 6 months refrigerated.

CHOCOLATE FUDGE FROSTING

About 2½ cups

Whether your definition of a chocolate layer cake is traditional (yellow cake layers) or revisionist (chocolate cake, please), old-fashioned fudge frosting fits the bill. Warm leftovers to pour over ice cream.

Prepare Dark Chocolate Fudge, 851, omitting the walnuts or reserving them to sprinkle on top of the cake, if desired. In the final stage of beating, when the fudge begins to thicken and lose its sheen, beat in 1 tablespoon half-and-half just until blended. Remove the bowl from the mixer. Use a rubber spatula to scrape down and stir in the frosting from the sides and bottom of the bowl. Let the frosting stand and stiffen for 4 to 5 minutes before correcting the consistency. Adjust, if necessary, by stirring in a little half-and-half, 1 teaspoon at a time, until the perfect spreading consistency is obtained. Use immediately or cover the surface with a sheet of plastic wrap. This keeps for about 1 week at room temperature or about 3 weeks refrigerated. Or freeze for up to 6 months. Soften before using.

OLD-FASHIONED CARAMEL FROSTING

About 3 cups

For sweet tooths only. The flavor of brown sugar is a divine partner for Banana Cake, 944, or any spice cake. Sprinkle the frosted cake with chopped nuts if desired.

Combine in a medium, heavy saucepan and cook, stirring, over medium heat just until the mixture begins to simmer:

2 cups packed light or dark brown sugar
1 cup heavy cream

Stop stirring, cover, and simmer for 2 minutes to dissolve the sugar. Uncover and wash any sugar crystals from the sides of the pan with a wet pastry brush. Cook, uncovered, until the syrup reaches 238°F (soft-ball stage) on a candy thermometer. Remove from the heat and add, without stirring:

3 tablespoons unsalted butter

Set aside, without stirring, until the butter is melted and the mixture cools to 110°F, 45 to 60 minutes. Add:

1 teaspoon vanilla
1 to 2 tablespoons rum (optional)

Beat until the frosting cools and is thickened to a spreadable consistency. If the frosting becomes too thick, thin slightly with:

Heavy cream (optional)

If the frosting does not thicken, place the pan in a bowl of ice water and beat until it reaches the desired consistency. Use immediately or cover the surface with a sheet of plastic wrap. This keeps for up to 1 week at room temperature or about 3 weeks refrigerated. Or freeze for up to 6 months. Soften before using.

SEVEN-MINUTE FROSTING *About 4 cups*

This is the best of the traditional American fluffy white frostings, billowy and sweet—and, incidentally, fat free. For this recipe a stainless-steel bowl is recommended because crockery and glass are so slow to heat that the top of the meringue cools down before it is adequately heated. Be sure to rinse the stem of the thermometer in the simmering skillet water between readings to avoid contaminating the egg whites.

Have the egg whites at room temperature, 68° to 70°F.

Whisk together in a large stainless-steel bowl:

5 tablespoons water
¼ teaspoon cream of tartar
1⅓ cups sugar
2 large egg whites
1 tablespoon light corn syrup

Set the bowl in a wide, deep skillet filled with about 1 inch of simmering water. Make sure the water level is at least as high as the depth of the egg whites in the bowl. Beat the whites on low speed until the mixture reaches 140°F on an instant-read thermometer. Do not stop beating while the bowl is in the skillet, or the egg whites will be overcooked. If you cannot hold the thermometer stem in the egg whites while continuing to beat, remove the bowl from the skillet just to read the thermometer, then return the bowl to the skillet. Beat on high speed for exactly 5 minutes. Remove the bowl from the skillet and add:

1 teaspoon vanilla

Beat on high speed for 2 to 3 more minutes to cool. Stir in:

½ to 1 cup chopped nuts or shredded sweetened dried coconut (optional)

Use the day it is made.

SEVEN-MINUTE LEMON FROSTING

Prepare Seven-Minute Frosting, above, substituting 2 to 3 tablespoons fresh lemon juice for 2 to 3 tablespoons of the water and adding ¼ teaspoon grated lemon zest.

SEVEN-MINUTE ORANGE FROSTING

Prepare Seven-Minute Frosting, above, substituting ¼ cup fresh orange juice and 1 tablespoon fresh lemon juice for all of the water and adding ½ teaspoon grated orange zest.

SEVEN-MINUTE PENUCHE OR BROWN SUGAR FROSTING

Prepare Seven-Minute Frosting, above, substituting 1⅓ cups packed light or dark brown sugar for the sugar. Add ½ teaspoon maple, walnut, or pecan extract with the vanilla if desired.

CLASSIC LADY BALTIMORE FILLING AND FROSTING *About 4½ to 5 cups*

Macerate the fruits and nuts in sweet sherry for 30 minutes, then drain before using, if you like.

Prepare:

Seven-Minute Frosting, above

Fold in:

⅔ cup chopped pecans
⅓ cup chopped dried figs or dates
⅓ cup raisins
¼ teaspoon almond extract

CLASSIC BUTTERCREAM *About 3 cups*

Have all ingredients at room temperature, 68° to 70°F.

Combine in a medium, heavy saucepan and cook, stirring, over medium heat until the mixture begins to simmer:

1 cup sugar
½ cup water
¼ teaspoon cream of tartar

Stop stirring, cover, and simmer for 2 minutes to dissolve the sugar. Uncover and wash any sugar crystals from the sides of the pan with a wet pastry brush. Cook, uncovered, until the syrup registers 238°F (soft-ball stage) on a candy thermometer. Meanwhile, fill a wide, deep skillet with 1 inch of water and bring to a simmer. In a medium heatproof bowl, preferably stainless steel, beat on high speed until thick and pale yellow:

2 large eggs or 5 large egg yolks

Just before the syrup is ready, begin beating the eggs again on medium speed. Beating constantly, pour the hot syrup in a thin steady stream into the eggs at the edge of the bowl. Set the bowl in the skillet of simmering water and stir constantly with a whisk until the mixture registers 160°F on an instant-read thermometer. Remove from the heat. Wash the beaters, then beat the hot mixture until it cools to room temperature. Beat in 1 tablespoon at a time:

¾ pound (3 sticks) unsalted butter

beating until the buttercream is smooth and spreadable. If the mixture looks curdled at any time, continue beating until smooth. If the butter is added too quickly, the mixture may become soupy; refrigerate it briefly, then resume beating. This keeps, refrigerated, for up to 6 days. Or freeze for up to 6 months. To soften chilled or frozen buttercream, break it into chunks with a fork and place in a heatproof bowl in a pan of barely simmering water, or soften in a microwave on low for 15- to 30-second intervals, until some of the buttercream begins to melt. Stir with a rubber spatula until the buttercream is smooth and spreadable. If you oversoften it, you will have to refrigerate it again and resoften it again.

SWISS MERINGUE BUTTERCREAM *3 to 3½ cups*

This egg white buttercream is the easiest of the classic French buttercreams because it does not require a cooked syrup. A hand-held electric mixer is necessary; be especially careful to keep the cord away from the burner. Use a stainless-steel bowl, rather than glass or crockery, to ensure that the meringue is adequately heated. Be sure to rinse the stem of the thermometer in the simmering skillet water between readings, to avoid contaminating the egg whites.

Have the butter and egg whites at room temperature, 68° to 70°F.

Whisk together in a large stainless-steel bowl:

4 large egg whites
¾ cup sugar
2 tablespoons water
¼ teaspoon cream of tartar

Set the bowl in a wide, deep skillet filled with about 1 inch of simmering water. Make sure the water level is at least as high as the depth of the egg whites in the bowl. Beat the whites on low speed until the mixture reaches 140°F on an instant-read thermometer. Do not stop beating while the bowl is in the skillet, or the egg whites will be overcooked. If you cannot hold the thermometer stem in the egg whites while continuing to beat, remove the bowl from the skillet just to read the thermometer, then return the bowl to the skillet. Beat on high speed just until the mixture reaches 160°F, 2 to 4 minutes. Remove the bowl from the skillet and add:

1 teaspoon vanilla

Beat on high speed for 3 to 5 more minutes, to cool. The mixture should hold glossy marshmallowy peaks. In another large bowl, beat until creamy, about 30 seconds:

¾ pound (3 sticks) unsalted butter

Beat a large dollop of the meringue into the butter until well combined. Continue to beat in about half of the meringue in large dollops. Scrape the remaining meringue into the mixture and beat until smooth and fluffy. Beat in:

1 to 2 tablespoons liqueur (optional)

This keeps, refrigerated, for up to 6 days. Or freeze for up to 6 months. Soften as for Classic Buttercream, 1001.

COFFEE BUTTERCREAM

Dissolve 1 tablespoon instant coffee crystals or instant espresso powder in 1½ teaspoons water. Stir most of the mixture into Classic Buttercream, 1001, or Swiss Meringue Buttercream, above, then add the rest to taste.

MOCHA BUTTERCREAM

Melt 2 ounces chopped bittersweet or semisweet chocolate and let cool to lukewarm. Stir into Coffee Buttercream, above, along with 2 tablespoons coffee liqueur, if desired.

CHOCOLATE BUTTERCREAM *About 4½ cups*

Melt 8 to 12 ounces chopped semisweet or bittersweet chocolate with 1 tablespoon water for each 2 ounces chocolate (for example, 4 tablespoons water for 8 ounces chocolate). Let cool to lukewarm. Using a rubber spatula, stir into Classic Buttercream, 1001, or Swiss Meringue Buttercream, above, along with 2 or more tablespoons rum, brandy, or liqueur of choice, if desired.

PRALINE OR NUT BUTTERCREAM

Stir ⅓ to ½ cup nut or praline paste, chopped toasted nuts, or sweetened or unsweetened canned chestnut puree along with 1 to 2 tablespoons liqueur, if desired, into Classic Buttercream, 1001, or Swiss Meringue Buttercream, above.

ORANGE BUTTERCREAM

Stir 2 tablespoons grated orange zest, 1 teaspoon grated lemon zest, and 1 to 2 tablespoons orange liqueur into Classic Buttercream, 1001, or Swiss Meringue Buttercream, above.

LEMON BUTTERCREAM

Stir 4 teaspoons grated lemon zest into Classic Buttercream, 1001, or Swiss Meringue Buttercream, above. Or stir in Lemon Curd, 998, to taste.

LIQUOR-FLAVORED BUTTERCREAM

Gradually stir up to ½ cup liquor into Classic Buttercream, 1001, or Swiss Meringue Buttercream, above. The addition of liquid makes buttercream less stable: If the mixture begins to separate, stir briskly with a rubber spatula until smooth.

ABOUT CHOCOLATE GANACHE AND CHOCOLATE FROSTINGS AND GLAZES MADE WITH BUTTER AND CREAM

The sleek, rich chocolate coating on a European torte or an elegant restaurant dessert is apt to be chocolate ganache, as is the center of a rich chocolate truffle. *Ganache* is a French term that refers to any combination of chocolate and cream. Butter, and occasionally eggs or egg yolks, may be included; butter used in place of cream makes a variant of ganache, closely related in function and taste. Ganaches are versatile. We use them as fillings, frostings, and glazes. Often the very same recipe is a pourable glaze at 90°F and a spreadable frosting when cooled to room temperature. Some are whipped, some only stirred. Ironically, ganache is simpler and quicker to make than the powdered sugar icings traditionally called "quick icings." It is smoother on the palate and richer in both flavor and fat. The simplest ganache is made by stirring chopped chocolate into hot cream until melted and smooth, or by melting chocolate and butter together. In any case, the ingredients are few and the method is simple. Sugar is rarely needed for ganache, because the chocolate is sweetened.

CHOCOLATE GANACHE GLAZE OR FROSTING

About 1½ cups

Bring to a boil in a small saucepan:

¾ cup heavy cream

Remove from the heat and add:

8 ounces semisweet or bittersweet chocolate, finely chopped

Stir until most of the chocolate is melted. Cover and let stand for 10 minutes. Stir or whisk very gently until completely smooth. Stir in:

1 tablespoon liqueur, or more to taste (optional)

For a pourable glaze, let stand at room temperature, stirring occasionally, until the mixture cools to 85° to 95°F. For frosting, let stand until spreadable. If the frosting becomes too stiff, set the pan in a larger pan of hot water and stir until softened; or remelt and cool to 85° to 95°F for use as a glaze. This keeps for up to 3 days at room temperature or up to 1 week refrigerated. Or freeze for up to 3 months. Soften or melt before using.

BITTERSWEET CHOCOLATE GLAZE OR FROSTING

About 1 cup

A very sophisticated glaze or frosting to use on rich European chocolate or nut tortes. For an even more bittersweet effect, substitute 1 ounce unsweetened chocolate for 1 ounce of the bittersweet or semisweet chocolate.

In the top of a double boiler or in a microwave on medium, heat, stirring often, just until the chocolate is melted and smooth:

6 ounces bittersweet or semisweet chocolate, coarsely chopped
6 tablespoons water, freshly brewed coffee, or milk
Pinch of salt (optional)

Remove from the heat. With a rubber spatula, stir in 2 or 3 pieces at a time:

6 tablespoons (¾ stick) unsalted butter, cut into small pieces

Continue to stir (do not beat) until perfectly smooth. Stir in:

1 to 2 tablespoons liqueur (optional)

For a pourable glaze, let stand at room temperature, stirring occasionally, until the mixture cools to 90°F. For frosting, let stand until spreadable. If the frosting becomes too stiff, set the pan in a larger pan of hot water and stir gently with a rubber spatula; or remelt and cool to 90°F for use as a glaze. This keeps for up to 3 days at room temperature or up to 3 weeks refrigerated. Or freeze for up to 6 months. Soften or melt before using.

CHOCOLATE GLAZE (REDUCED FAT)

About 1 cup

Halfway between a chocolate sauce and a glaze, this is delectable drizzled over any chocolate tube cake or Bundt cake.

Combine in a medium, heavy saucepan:

⅔ cup sugar
⅓ cup unsweetened cocoa

Gradually add just enough:

⅔ cup low-fat evaporated milk

to make a paste, then stir in the rest. Cook, stirring constantly with a wooden spoon and reaching into the corners of the pan, over medium heat until the mixture comes to a boil. Boil gently, stirring, for about 2½ minutes. Remove from the heat and stir in:

2 ounces bittersweet or semisweet chocolate, finely chopped
½ teaspoon vanilla

Stir until the chocolate is completely melted and the glaze is smooth. Let cool until thickened before using. This keeps, refrigerated, for up to 1 week. Or freeze for up to 6 months. Warm gently before using, if necessary.

CHOCOLATE SATIN FROSTING

About 3 cups

Kids and adults love this shiny dark sweet chocolate frosting, which is easily made in a food processor. Keep any extra in a jar in the refrigerator and melt it for a quick ice cream sauce, or spread it on graham crackers or cookies.

Break or cut into 2 pieces:

6 ounces unsweetened chocolate

Bring to a boil in a small saucepan:

1 cup evaporated milk or heavy cream

Remove from the heat and add the chocolate pieces, without stirring. Cover and set aside for exactly 10 minutes. Scrape into a food processor or blender and add:

1½ cups sugar
6 tablespoons (¾ stick) unsalted butter, cut into small pieces
1 teaspoon vanilla

Process until the mixture is perfectly smooth, 1 minute or more. Transfer to a bowl. If necessary, set aside for a few minutes (longer if you have used cream), until thickened to the desired spreading consistency. This keeps, refrigerated, for up to 1 week if made with cream, or about 3 weeks if made with evaporated milk. Or freeze for up to 6 months. Soften before using.

CHOCOLATE SOUR CREAM FROSTING

About 2 cups

Very bittersweet and glossy. Use to fill and frost any chocolate butter cake. Prepare this just before using.

Melt, stirring often, in the top of a double boiler or in a microwave on medium:

10 ounces bittersweet or semisweet chocolate, coarsely chopped

Remove from the heat and stir in (do not beat) just until combined:

1 cup sour cream

Use immediately; if the frosting becomes too stiff or loses its gloss at any time, set the pan in a larger pan of hot water for a few seconds and stir to soften. This keeps, refrigerated, for up to 1 week. Or freeze for up to 6 months. Soften before using.

WHITE CHOCOLATE FROSTING

Prepare Chocolate Sour Cream Frosting, above, substituting white chocolate for the bittersweet or semisweet chocolate.

CHOCOLATE FROSTING (REDUCED FAT)

About 1 cup

Combine in a small, heavy saucepan:

½ cup plus 1 tablespoon sugar
½ cup unsweetened Dutch-process cocoa

Gradually add just enough:

½ cup low-fat milk

to make a paste, and then stir in the rest. Cook, stirring constantly with a wooden spoon and reaching into the corners of the pan, over medium heat until the mixture comes to a boil. Boil gently, stirring, for about 2 minutes. Remove from the heat and add:

½ teaspoon vanilla

Let cool for 5 minutes. Stir in until melted and smooth:

3 ounces milk chocolate, finely chopped

Cover the surface of the frosting with a piece of wax or parchment paper and let cool until spreadable. This keeps, refrigerated, for up to 1 week. Or freeze for up to 6 months.

CHOCOLATE TRUFFLE CREAM FROSTING

About 1¾ cups

Pastry chefs know that egg yolks are the secret to divinely rich and luxurious chocolate frostings, as well as to some of the world's finest chocolate truffles. To be safe, the eggs in this frosting are cooked.

Whisk together in a medium heatproof, preferably stainless-steel, bowl:

4 large egg yolks
¼ cup sugar
1 teaspoon instant coffee or espresso powder (optional)

Whisk in:

⅓ cup boiling water

Set the bowl in a large skillet of barely simmering water and heat, stirring constantly, until the mixture reaches 160°F on an instant-read thermometer. Remove from the heat and stir in:

6 ounces bittersweet or semisweet chocolate, finely chopped
8 tablespoons (1 stick) unsalted butter, cut into small pieces

Stir until the chocolate and butter are melted and the mixture is smooth. Let cool until spreadable. This keeps, refrigerated, for up to 6 days. Soften and stir until smooth before using.

CHOCOLATE MOUSSE FROSTING

About 3½ cups

This frosting has a light, appealing mousselike texture. Try it between layers of any angel cake, 952 to 953, a moist sponge cake, 946 to 948, or a devil's food cake, 944.

Whisk together in a medium heatproof, preferably stainless-steel, bowl:

2 large eggs
2 cups powdered sugar
½ cup milk, strong coffee, or water
⅛ teaspoon salt

Set the bowl in a large skillet of barely simmering water and heat, stirring constantly, until the mixture registers 160°F on an instant-read thermometer. Remove from the heat and stir in:

4 ounces unsweetened chocolate, finely chopped
6 tablespoons (¾ stick) unsalted butter, cut into small pieces
1 teaspoon vanilla

Stir until the chocolate and butter are melted and the mixture is smooth. Set the bowl in a larger bowl of ice water and beat on high speed until the frosting holds a shape. Use immediately or refrigerate for up to 4 days. Soften and beat until smooth before using.

WHIPPED GANACHE FILLING AND FROSTING

About 1½ cups

This is a light-colored but rich and creamy chocolate filling. Double the recipe to fill a 17½ x 11½-inch jelly-roll sheet generously. If you whip it until it is too stiff, warm the spatula with hot water to help in spreading. Start this at least several hours in advance.

Bring to a boil in a medium saucepan:

1 cup heavy cream

Remove from the heat and whisk in:

4 ounces bittersweet or semisweet chocolate, finely chopped

Cover and let stand for 10 minutes. With a rubber spatula, stir until perfectly smooth, scraping the bottom of the pan to be sure all of the chocolate is melted. Cover and chill for at least several hours. (The ganache can be refrigerated for up to 5 days or frozen for up to 6 months.) To use, beat on low to medium speed just until the ganache is thickened and begins to hold a shape; do not overbeat. Use immediately.

WHIPPED WHITE CHOCOLATE, MILK CHOCOLATE, OR MOCHA GANACHE FILLING AND FROSTING

Prepare Whipped Ganache Filling and Frosting, above, substituting white or milk chocolate for the bittersweet or semisweet chocolate or, for Mocha Ganache, substituting milk chocolate and adding 2 teaspoons instant coffee powder to the cream with the chocolate.

MILK CHOCOLATE MOCHA GLAZE OR FROSTING

About 1⅓ cups

Made with cinnamon, this glaze makes a grand topping for almost any cake.

Place in a small bowl:

9 ounces milk chocolate, finely chopped

Combine in a medium saucepan and bring to a simmer:

⅔ cup heavy cream
1 tablespoon light corn syrup
1 tablespoon instant coffee or espresso powder
⅛ teaspoon ground cinnamon (optional)

Immediately pour over the chocolate. Stir until the chocolate is melted and the mixture is smooth. For a glaze, let cool just to 100°F. To use as a frosting, let cool to room temperature and stir with a wooden spoon or rubber spatula until spreadable. If the frosting becomes too stiff, set the pan in a larger pan of hot water and stir gently with a rubber spatula, or remelt and cool to 100°F for use as a glaze. This keeps for up to 3 days at room temperature or up to 3 weeks refrigerated. Or freeze for up to 6 months. Soften or melt before using.

ABOUT POWDERED-SUGAR ICINGS, OR QUICK ICINGS

These traditional American icings are sweet, flavorful, and not too rich. The basic formula is easily remembered: 1 stick of butter to 1 box (1 pound) powdered sugar, and just enough liquid to correct the consistency. The quickest method entails beating softened butter with sifted powdered sugar, gradually adding liquids and flavorings until the desired consistency is obtained. The whole project takes but a few minutes.

All the icings in this section can be made in this very quick manner, but you will notice an extra heating step in Quick White Icing II, below. Some, but not all, powdered-sugar icings benefit from 5 to 8 minutes in the top of a double boiler, to eliminate the raw flavor (sometimes described as "metallic") of the cornstarch in the powdered-sugar. Heating also produces a creamier and more intensely flavored icing. The point is to expose the mixture to prolonged gentle heat, just enough to affect the starch but not enough to melt the sugar, which could turn the finished icing grainy. After heating, the mixture is beaten briefly to render it pourable (if a glaze is wanted) or several minutes to cool and thicken for spreadable icing.

Often the consistency of powdered-sugar icings is corrected by adding more powdered sugar to thicken or more liquid to thin. But since an icing of this type tends to thicken on its own if left undisturbed for a few minutes, and certainly if stirred over a bowl of ice water, we try one or both of these methods before adding powdered sugar, which can diminish the flavor and the texture of the icing as well. Make icing just before using, or press plastic wrap against the surface while storing, to prevent a crust from forming.

QUICK WHITE ICING I

About 1 cup

If you like your icing spread thin, this quantity will stretch to cover a 2-layer cake. This is the quickest of all.

In a medium bowl, beat together on medium speed:

2 cups powdered sugar, sifted if lumpy
4 tablespoons (½ stick) unsalted butter, softened, or 3 tablespoons hot heavy cream

Add and beat until smooth:

3 to 4 tablespoons milk, dry sherry, rum, or coffee
1 teaspoon vanilla
⅛ teaspoon salt

Correct the consistency if necessary, adding:

Additional powdered sugar or liquid of choice (optional)

To store, cover the surface of the icing with a sheet of plastic wrap. This keeps for up to 3 days at room temperature or up to 3 weeks refrigerated. Or freeze for up to 6 months. Soften and stir or beat until smooth before using.

QUICK WHITE ICING II

About 1 cup

It is important to watch this mixture very carefully as it cooks. Have everything measured before you begin.

Melt, or heat, in the top of a double boiler over low heat:

4 tablespoons (½ stick) unsalted butter or 3 tablespoons heavy cream

Remove from the heat and stir in:

2 cups powdered sugar, sifted if lumpy
3 tablespoons milk, dry sherry, rum, or coffee
⅛ teaspoon salt

Cook, stirring occasionally, over barely simmering water for 5 minutes. Remove from the heat and add:

1 teaspoon vanilla

Beat until cool and the desired consistency. (You can place the pan in a larger pan of ice water to quicken the process.) To store, cover the surface of the icing with a sheet of plastic wrap. This keeps for up to 3 days at room temperature or up to 3 weeks refrigerated. Or freeze for up to 6 months. Soften and stir or beat until smooth before using.

QUICK LEMON ICING

Prepare Quick White Icing I, above, grating the zest of 1 lemon directly into the bowl of ingredients and using 1 to 2 tablespoons fresh lemon juice for the liquid.

QUICK ORANGE ICING

Prepare Quick White Icing II, above, grating the zest of 1 small orange into the top of the double boiler and using 1 to 2 tablespoons fresh orange juice for the liquid.

QUICK MOCHA ICING

If you are in a hurry, prepare Quick White Icing I, above, but Quick White Icing II, above, produces a darker and more flavorful icing. Decrease the powdered sugar to 1⅓ cups and add 2 tablespoons unsweetened cocoa and 1 teaspoon instant coffee or espresso powder. Use water for the liquid.

QUICK CHOCOLATE ICING

About 1¼ cups

Melt in the top of a double boiler:

3 ounces unsweetened chocolate, coarsely chopped
3 tablespoons unsalted butter

Remove from the heat and stir in:

¼ cup hot strong coffee, light or heavy cream, or milk
1 teaspoon vanilla

If you are in a hurry, gradually add, beating until spreadable:

2 cups powdered sugar, or to taste

Otherwise, stir in the powdered sugar and heat over barely simmering water for 10 minutes; remove from the heat and beat until spreadable. To store, cover the surface of the icing with a sheet of plastic wrap. This keeps for up to 3 days at room temperature or up to 3 weeks refrigerated. Or freeze for up to 6 months. Soften and stir or beat until smooth before using.

QUICK MAPLE ICING

About 1 cup plus 2 tablespoons

Try this sweet icing on Banana Chiffon Cake, 950.

In a medium bowl, beat together on medium speed:

2 cups powdered sugar, sifted if lumpy
1 tablespoon unsalted butter, softened
½ teaspoon vanilla
¼ teaspoon salt
3 to 4 tablespoons milk, dry sherry, rum, or coffee

Gradually add, beating until spreadable:

⅓ to ½ cup pure maple syrup

To store, cover the surface of the icing with a sheet of plastic wrap. This keeps for up to 3 days at room temperature or up to 3 weeks refrigerated. Or freeze for up to 6 months.

QUICK BUTTERSCOTCH, OR PENUCHE, ICING

About 1½ cups

This icing is a pale coffee color with a creamy brown sugar flavor.

Heat, stirring, in the top of a double boiler until the mixture is smooth:

4 tablespoons (½ stick) unsalted butter
½ cup packed light or dark brown sugar
⅛ teaspoon salt
⅓ cup light cream or evaporated milk

Remove from the heat and let cool for about 5 minutes. Gradually add, beating until spreadable:

2 cups powdered sugar, sifted if lumpy
½ teaspoon vanilla or 1 teaspoon rum

If the icing seems thin, set the pan in a larger pan of ice water and beat until spreadable. If necessary, add more:

Powdered sugar (optional)

Stir in:

½ cup chopped walnuts or pecans (optional)

To store, cover the surface of the icing with a sheet of plastic wrap. This keeps for up to 3 days at room temperature or up to 3 weeks refrigerated. Or freeze for up to 6 months. Soften and stir or beat until smooth before using.

HARD SAUCE TOPPING

About 2½ cups

Slightly soften in a bowl set over simmering water:

Hard Sauce, 1042, made with brandy

then apply a thin layer to any cooled cake or coffeecake.

To store, cover the surface of the icing with a sheet of plastic wrap. This keeps for up to 3 days at room temperature or up to 3 weeks refrigerated. Or freeze for up to 6 months. Soften and stir or beat until smooth before using.

BROWN SUGAR FROSTING

About 1 cup

Delicious brown sugar flavor.

Combine in a small saucepan and cook, stirring, over low heat until the butter is melted and the mixture just begins to simmer:

1 cup packed light brown sugar
4 tablespoons (½ stick) unsalted butter
2 tablespoons water
½ teaspoon salt

Remove from the heat and whisk in:

2 large egg yolks

Return to low heat and cook, stirring constantly, until thickened, 1 to 2 minutes. Let cool to room temperature, then beat until spreadable. This keeps, refrigerated, for up to 4 days; do not freeze. Soften and stir or beat until smooth before using.

QUICK BROWN BUTTER ICING

About ¾ cup

The flavor of brown butter enhances plain butter cakes and spice cakes. The icing has little golden brown flecks in it. Make just before using.

Melt in a medium skillet over medium heat:

6 tablespoons (¾ stick) unsalted butter

Heat, stirring constantly, until deep golden. Gradually whisk in:

1¼ cups powdered sugar
1 teaspoon vanilla

Scrape into a bowl and beat until smooth and spreadable; do not attempt to thin with liquid. Use immediately.

CREAM CHEESE FROSTING

About 2 cups

There are two big secrets to perfectly smooth cream cheese frosting with enough body to spread in dramatic swirls or even pipe through a pastry bag. First, overbeating breaks down the cream cheese, and produces grainy looking frosting that is too soft to hold a shape. Second, cold (not softened) cream cheese produces the best texture in both of our methods. Have the butter, if you use it, at the temperature recommended for the method you choose, and sift the powdered sugar after measuring.

Feel free to vary the amount of powdered sugar to suit your taste: we have seen recipes with as little as 1 teaspoon and as much as ½ cup powdered sugar per ounce of cream cheese. The food processor method is the best and fastest method of all.

FOOD PROCESSOR METHOD

Have the cream cheese cold. The butter can be cold, but preferably at room temperature, 68° to 70°F.
Combine in a food processor and pulse just until smooth and creamy:

8 ounces cream cheese
5 tablespoons unsalted butter (optional)
2 teaspoons vanilla
2 to 2½ cups powdered sugar, sifted

If the frosting is too stiff, pulse for a few seconds longer. Do not overprocess. If desired, stir in additional flavoring to taste, such as:

Grated lemon or orange zest, ground cinnamon, or liqueur of choice

ELECTRIC MIXER METHOD

Have the cream cheese cold and the butter at room temperature, 68° to 70°F.
In a medium bowl, beat just until blended:

8 ounces cream cheese
5 tablespoons unsalted butter (optional)
2 teaspoons vanilla

Add one-third at a time and beat just until smooth and the desired consistency:

2 to 2½ cups powdered sugar, sifted

If the frosting is too stiff, beat for a few seconds longer. Do not overbeat. If desired, stir in additional flavoring to taste, such as:

Grated lemon or orange zest, ground cinnamon, or liqueur of choice

This keeps, refrigerated, for about 1 week. Or freeze for up to 3 months. Soften and stir until smooth before using.

ITALIAN CREAM FROSTING

About 4 cups

Prepare Cream Cheese Frosting above, increasing the cream cheese to 12 ounces, the butter to 12 tablespoons (1½ sticks), the vanilla to 1½ teaspoons, and the powdered sugar to 6 cups.

CHOCOLATE CREAM CHEESE FROSTING

About 2⅔ cups

In the top of a double boiler or in a microwave on medium, melt 5 ounces chopped semisweet or bittersweet chocolate with 3 tablespoons water or coffee. Stir often until smooth. Let cool to lukewarm. Stir into Cream Cheese Frosting, above.

REDUCED-FAT CHOCOLATE CREAM CHEESE FROSTING

About 1¼ cups

An excellent frosting for any chocolate cake. You will need a microwave for this.
In a 4-cup heatproof glass container, stir together until smooth:

1 cup powdered sugar
¼ cup unsweetened Dutch-process cocoa
3 tablespoons low-fat milk

Cover with plastic wrap and microwave on high until the mixture comes to a boil and rises to the top of the container, about 2 minutes. In a glass bowl, soften in the microwave for 10 to 20 seconds:

4 ounces Neufchâtel cheese

Stir with a rubber spatula until perfectly smooth and creamy. Stir a little of the hot cocoa mixture into the softened cheese, then gradually add the remaining cocoa mixture, stirring until smooth; do not whip or beat. Stir in:

½ teaspoon vanilla

Let cool until spreadable. This keeps, refrigerated, for up to 1 week. Or freeze for up to 3 months. Soften and stir until smooth before using.

PEANUT BUTTER FROSTING

About 2¼ cups

Stir in chopped peanuts to taste or sprinkle them over the finished cake, if desired. Try this frosting as a filling for any cake frosted or glazed with chocolate. See page 978 for tips about cream cheese in frostings.

FOOD PROCESSOR METHOD

Have the cream cheese cold. The butter can be cold, but preferably at room temperature, 68° to 70°F.
Combine in a food processor and pulse just until smooth and creamy:

½ cup smooth peanut butter
3 ounces cream cheese
1½ tablespoons unsalted butter
1 teaspoon vanilla
2⅔ cups powdered sugar, sifted

3 tablespoons light or heavy cream or milk
1 to 2 tablespoons bourbon or rum (optional)

If the frosting is too stiff, add:

1 to 2 tablespoons milk, light or heavy cream, or liquor

Process just to the desired consistency. Additional processing will thin the frosting.

ELECTRIC MIXER METHOD

Have the cream cheese cold and the butter at room temperature, 68° to 70°F.

In a medium bowl, beat just until blended:

½ cup smooth peanut butter
3 ounces cream cheese
1½ tablespoons unsalted butter
1 teaspoon vanilla
3 tablespoons light or heavy cream or milk
1 to 2 tablespoons bourbon or rum (optional)

Add one-third at a time and beat just until smooth and the desired consistency is reached:

2⅔ cups powdered sugar, sifted

If the frosting is too stiff, add additional liquid. Do not overbeat. This keeps refrigerated for about 1 week. Or freeze for up to 3 months. Soften and stir until smooth before using.

QUICK COOKIE ICING

About 1 cup

This is good for children's cookie-making. It can be tinted with food coloring and kept in small cups to be spread on gingerbread or sugar cookies. Mix up a thick batch for piping out of sealable plastic bags (cut off one bottom corner).

In a medium bowl, stir together until smooth:

4 cups powdered sugar
3 to 4 tablespoons water

Adjust the consistency as necessary with more:

Powdered sugar or water

Color as desired. To store, cover the surface of the icing with a sheet of plastic wrap. This keeps for up to 4 days at room temperature or about 1 month refrigerated.

QUICK LEMON ICING FOR COOKIES

Prepare Quick Cookie Icing, above, substituting fresh lemon juice for the water.

ROYAL ICING

About 6 tablespoons

This decorative icing dries hard like plaster and pure white unless tinted with food coloring. Made with a bit less sugar, it is spreadable (or you can add a little water); otherwise, it is stiff enough to pipe and makes beautiful filigree, lace, tiny dots, and string work on wedding cakes. Royal Icing is mostly sugar and not especially delicious, though it is used to ice certain traditional marzipan-covered wedding (and other) cakes. Our advice is to use it only when decoration is more important than taste and/or in very small quantities, as for the dainty work described above. Royal Icing is usually made by beating powdered sugar into raw egg whites. In our version, the egg whites are heated to 160°F as a safeguard against salmonella bacteria. It is a simple process. We also give a variation made with powdered egg whites that does not require heat.

Avoid making Royal Icing on humid days. Be sure that any container or utensil that comes in contact with the icing is grease free, and do not store the icing in a plastic container. While working, keep the bowl of icing covered with a damp dish towel and, when not piping, cover the tip of the icing bag as well to prevent drying. If you plan to ice an entire cake with this mixture or otherwise need it to remain a little softer, add about ¼ teaspoon edible glycerine per cup of sugar. *Caution: You must use edible glycerine, which is available at candy-making and cake-decorating supply stores. Topical glycerine, available at pharmacies, is toxic.*

ROYAL ICING WITH FRESH EGG WHITE

In a microwave-safe bowl, stir together until thoroughly combined:

1 large egg white
⅔ cup powdered sugar

Microwave on high until the mixture reaches 160°F on an instant-read thermometer (it should not exceed 175°F), 30 to 60 seconds. If you need to take more than one temperature reading, wash the thermometer thoroughly or dip it into a mug of boiling water before taking additional readings. Add and beat on high speed until the icing is cool and holds stiff peaks:

⅔ cup powdered sugar

If the icing is not stiff enough, add more:

Powdered sugar

Color, if desired, with liquid or powdered food coloring (the color will intensify as the icing stands). The icing can be stored in a covered container for up to 3 days; press a piece of wax or parchment paper directly against the surface to prevent drying. The icing can be rebeaten if necessary. To pipe, use a small pastry bag fitted with a fine tip, or cut off the corner of a sealable plastic bag or the tip of a parchment paper cone.

ROYAL ICING WITH POWDERED EGG WHITES

Beat together until stiff peaks form:

1⅓ cups powdered sugar
1 tablespoon powdered egg whites
2 tablespoons water

Color if desired with liquid or powdered food coloring. Use and store as directed above. Tightly covered, this keeps for up to 2 weeks.

ABOUT SUGAR SYRUPS AND SUGAR GLAZES

Here are syrups used to moisten and flavor cake layers for elaborate European layer cakes and rich pound cakes and for simple translucent glazes to top cakes or cookies. Exercise caution: Sugar syrups, especially those with a high ratio of sugar (such as caramel) boil at higher temperatures than water, and can cause severe burns. For richer, opaque sugar glazes, use Quick White Icing II, 1006, or either of its variations and beat only until well blended but still pourable.

TRANSLUCENT SUGAR GLAZE

About ½ cup

This glaze gives any plain cake a slightly shiny crust and a bit of extra sweetness. We use it on loaf and tube cakes. Double the recipe for a large Bundt or tube cake or sheet cake.

Stir together briskly until thoroughly combined:

1 cup powdered sugar, sifted if lumpy
2 to 3 tablespoons water, liquor, fresh lemon juice, or coffee
½ teaspoon grated orange or lemon zest (optional)
¼ teaspoon vanilla (optional)

Brush or use a spoon to drizzle over the cake. Do not store.

HONEY GLAZE

About ¼ cup

Spread or brush on cakes or cookies.

Combine in a small saucepan and bring to a boil:

¼ cup honey
2 tablespoons sugar
1 tablespoon unsalted butter

This keeps, refrigerated, for about 3 weeks. Reheat before using.

SIMPLE SYRUP

About 1 cup

Use this to dilute and sweeten liqueurs for moistening cake layers, such as Génoise, 948, before filling and frosting. A lighter syrup can be made using equal parts sugar and water.

Combine in a small saucepan:

1 cup sugar
⅔ cup water
¼ teaspoon cream of tartar

Cook, stirring gently with a wooden spoon, over low heat until the mixture is hot to the touch and most of the sugar is dissolved; do not stir again, or the syrup may crystallize as it cools. Brush down the insides of the pan with a wet pastry brush and bring to a simmer. Cover and simmer gently for 2 minutes. Remove from the heat and let cool, uncovered, before using. This keeps in a covered jar for up to 3 weeks at room temperature or up to 6 months refrigerated.

LEMON SYRUP

Prepare Simple Syrup, above, substituting fresh lemon juice for the water. Heat the mixture just until the sugar is dissolved. As soon as the cake comes out of the oven, place the pan on a rack, poke the cake all over with a wooden skewer, and brush it with half of the syrup. Let the cake cool in the pan for 10 minutes. Unmold and invert the cake onto a greased rack. Poke the bottom of the cake with the skewer and brush with some of the syrup. Turn the cake right side up on the rack and brush with the remaining syrup. Let the cake cool completely, then wrap and store for at least 24 hours before serving.

STRONG LIQUOR SPLASH

About ⅔ cup

This has a lot of alcohol flavor and is meant to penetrate only part of the way into the cake, not soak it entirely. For a sweeter, less alcoholic syrup, substitute liquor for the water in Simple Syrup, above.

Combine in a small saucepan and simmer for 2 minutes:

⅔ cup brandy, rum, or other liquor
¼ cup sugar

Apply as for Lemon Syrup, above.

COFFEE LIQUOR AND HONEY SOAK

About 1¼ cups

Moisten plain, walnut or pecan, or chocolate pound cakes or butter cakes with this sweet luscious syrup. Prepare Strong Liquor Splash, above, substituting coffee liqueur for the brandy and honey for the sugar. Simmer with ¼ cup water. Apply as for Lemon Syrup, above.

ABOUT BAKED AND BROILED TOPPINGS

Both homey and elegant. Consider the juxtaposition of warm toasted soft meringue on a cold dessert or crunchy caramelized toppings on soft, velvety textured cakes. Soft meringue topping makes an attractive nonfat frosting for cakes and a less sweet alternative to Seven-Minute Frosting, 1001. Simple to make, Crunchy Almond Topping, 1011, makes a plain or frosted butter cake sensational.

BROILED ICING *About 1 cup*

This topping can be used on warm or cooled cakes, coffeecakes baked in shallow pans, or cookies. Plain white, yellow, and spice cakes are enhanced by this treatment.

Stir together until smooth:

½ cup packed light or dark brown sugar
3 tablespoons heavy cream
3 tablespoons unsalted butter, melted
½ teaspoon vanilla
⅛ teaspoon salt
½ to 1 cup shredded sweetened dried coconut or chopped nuts, or a combination

Spread on the cake or cookies. Place 4 to 5 inches below the heat source in a preheated broiler. Broil until the topping is bubbly all over, 1 to 3 minutes; make sure it does not burn.

CRUNCHY ALMOND TOPPING *About 1⅓ cups*

This topping is really a crust, which bakes with the cake and becomes a topping after the cake is inverted and unmolded.

Preheat the oven to 325°F.

Toast until lightly browned, 5 to 10 minutes:

⅓ cup sliced blanched almonds

Let cool. Grease the cake pan liberally with:

2 teaspoons unsalted butter, softened

Press the toasted nuts into the butter on the bottom and sides of the pan. Sprinkle with:

2 to 3 teaspoons sugar

Mix the cake batter and carefully pour into the pan. Bake and unmold as directed.

STREUSEL I *About 2 cups*

Blend with a fork or pulse in a food processor until the mixture resembles coarse crumbs:

⅔ cup all-purpose flour
⅔ cup finely chopped walnuts or pecans
⅔ cup sugar or packed light brown sugar, or a combination
5 tablespoons unsalted butter, melted
1 teaspoon ground cinnamon
¼ teaspoon salt

STREUSEL II (REDUCED FAT) *About 2 cups*

Stir together:

⅓ cup Grape-Nuts cereal
⅓ cup finely chopped walnuts or pecans
⅓ cup packed light or dark brown sugar
2 tablespoons all-purpose flour
1 teaspoon ground cinnamon

Beat together in a separate bowl:

1 egg white
1 tablespoon vegetable oil
¼ teaspoon vanilla

Stir the egg white mixture into the cereal mixture with a fork.

CHOCOLATE FRUIT FILLING *About 2 cups*

Stir together until thoroughly combined:

⅔ cup finely chopped walnuts or pecans
⅔ cup packed light brown sugar
⅓ cup semisweet chocolate chips
2 tablespoons unsweetened cocoa
2 tablespoons instant coffee or espresso powder
2 teaspoons ground cinnamon
¼ cup dried cranberries, cherries, or chopped dried apricots

ABOUT SOFT MERINGUE TOPPING

Few things are as disappointing, or as frustrating, to a home baker as a meringue pie topping that weeps and puddles, and few kitchen conundrums have inspired as much theorizing and contradictory advice in the pages of cookbooks. In truth, undissolved sugar in the meringue, though often blamed, has little to do with this sad condition, and humid weather, another common suspect, has even less. The real culprit is egg white, with its characteristic sensitivity to heat. Most recipes direct you to spread the meringue over a cool or lukewarm filling and then brown the topping in a moderate oven for up to 20 minutes. The problem with this procedure is that it leaves the egg white nearly raw along the bottom, where it meets the tepid filling, but scorching hot on top, where it is exposed to the oven's heat. The undercooked part of the meringue simply melts as the pie stands, resulting in that infamous slippery puddle between filling and topping. Meanwhile, the overheated meringue on the surface breaks down and curdles, just like an overcooked custard, whereupon it weeps those unsightly little beads of sticky syrup.

The melting of the meringue along the bottom is easily prevented by simply having the filling hot, not warm, when you apply the meringue, so that the bottom of the meringue cooks on the heat released by the filling. If the filling has cooled before you are ready to apply the meringue, slip the pie into the oven for 5 minutes before you top it. Ideally, you will think to do this before you have finished preparing the meringue, because meringue does not like to sit once it is ready.

The overheating of the surface of the meringue and

the resulting beading is a more complex problem. Heating meringue over hot water, as one does in the making of a Swiss meringue or seven-minute frosting, serves to stabilize it and make it less prone to weeping. However, heated meringue tastes dry and sticky and tends to develop a leathery skin when further baked. A better solution, we think, is to stabilize the meringue with a cooked cornstarch paste, as indicated for Soft Meringue Topping I, below. Of course, the making of the paste entails an extra step that you may not have time to dispatch. So if you can live with a few beads, by all means use Soft Meringue Topping II, below, which is made in the conventional manner.

When applying a meringue to a pie or pudding, it is important to spread a band of topping around the edge of the crust or dish before you fill in the center. If you cover the center first, you are likely to displace some of the filling and cause it to spill over. Be especially careful to heed this advice when spreading meringue over a partially cooked and still liquid filling, as in the making of chess or Key lime pie. Pie meringue must be brought to the edge of the crust at all points or else it will shrink back. When applying a meringue to a crustless pudding, spread the topping to the edge of the dish. This may not prevent shrinking, especially if the dish is greased, but at least you tried.

Meringue Safety: If you wish to be certain that any possible pathogens in the egg whites have been killed, you must heat the meringue to 160°F. Follow the recipe as written, being sure that your pie filling is piping hot when you spread on the topping. After 20 minutes baking, carefully insert an instant-read thermometer sideways into the center of the meringue. If the temperature is shy of the mark, bake the meringue a little longer. Be careful, though, not to go much beyond 165°F, or the meringue will begin to break down even if stabilized by cornstarch.

SOFT MERINGUE TOPPING I

Covers one 9-inch pie

Because it is stabilized by starch, this meringue topping does not weep, leak, or deflate even when refrigerated for several days. Since your filling should be piping hot when the meringue is applied, it is wise to measure out your ingredients and prepare the cornstarch paste *before* you embark upon making the filling.

Before beginning, please read About Soft Meringue Topping, 1011.

In a very small saucepan or heatproof 1-cup measure, thoroughly mix:

1 tablespoon cornstarch

1 tablespoon sugar

Gradually stir in, making a smooth, runny paste:

⅓ cup water

Bring to a boil over medium heat, stirring briskly all the while, then boil for 15 seconds. Remove this thick, translucent paste from the heat and cover with a lid or saucer. In a clean, grease-free glass or metal bowl, beat on medium speed until foamy:

4 large egg whites (½ cup), at room temperature

Add and beat until soft but definite peaks form:

½ teaspoon vanilla

¼ teaspoon cream of tartar

Very gradually beat in:

½ cup sugar, preferably superfine

Beat on high speed until the peaks are very stiff and glossy but not dry. Reduce the speed to very low and beat in the cornstarch paste 1 tablespoon at a time. When all the paste is incorporated, increase the speed to medium and beat for 10 seconds. Immediately spread the meringue over a hot pie filling (or pudding), anchoring it to the edge of the crust (or dish) at all points. Bake as directed in your recipe.

SOFT MERINGUE TOPPING II

Covers one 9-inch pie

This conventional soft meringue topping is more quickly made than Meringue I but is not as stable. It is best served the same day it is made. Measure out the meringue ingredients *before* you embark upon making the filling.

Before beginning, please read About Soft Meringue Topping, 1011.

In a clean, grease-free glass or metal bowl, beat on medium speed until foamy:

4 large egg whites (½ cup), at room temperature

Add and beat until soft but definite peaks form:

¼ teaspoon cream of tartar

Very gradually beat in:

½ cup sugar, preferably superfine

Beat on high speed until the peaks are stiff and glossy but not dry. Beat in:

½ teaspoon vanilla

Immediately spread the meringue over a hot pie filling (or pudding), anchoring it to the edge of the crust (or dish) at all points. Bake as directed in your recipe.

CUSTARDS, PUDDINGS, MOUSSES & DESSERT SOUFFLÉS

ABOUT BAKED CUSTARDS

Whether the dessert is a simple cup custard or a burnished crème brûlée, the technique is the same: to heat eggs and milk or cream—the elements of all custards—just to the point where they solidify and become perfectly smooth and creamy. If, however, the custard exceeds a certain temperature—somewhere between 165° and 195°F, depending on the ingredients it contains—the gossamer net of solidified egg proteins shrivels into tiny lumps, giving the custard a hard, dry, grainy consistency. With prolonged overheating, these lumps fuse into solid clumps, expelling liquid like a wrung-out sponge. At this point, the custard is curdled—for what is left are curds of cooked egg aswim in a watery, translucent whey.

TEMPERING CUSTARDS

The proper management of heat, so crucial to the success of a custard, begins at the mixing stage. Generally speaking, the milk or cream for the custard is heated before it is mixed with the eggs, sugar, and other ingredients. Warming the milk speeds the setting of the custard and also dissolves the yolks and sugar, thereby liquefying the custard and allowing it to be strained, so that the chalazes—the tough bands that anchor the yolks—can be removed. It is important to acclimate the eggs to heat by pouring the hot milk or cream over them slowly, whisking all the while. We speak of this process as "tempering."

THE WATER BATH

The water bath, also known as the bain-marie or "Maria's bath," is the cook's principal means of managing heat during the cooking of custards, shown 1014. By baking a dish of custard in a larger pan of water, the cook partially insulates the custard from the oven's heat and thereby protects it from overcooking. To bake custards in a water bath, all you need is a roasting pan large enough to accommodate the custards comfortably. The cups should not touch one another or the hot pan walls. Either set a cake rack in the pan or cover the pan bottom with a dish towel or several layers of paper towels; the rack or towel(s) will prevent the custards from coming into direct contact with the hot pan bottom. Arrange the custards in the dry pan, slip the pan into a preheated 325°F oven, and immediately pour enough scalding-hot tap water into the pan to come one-half to two-thirds of the way up the sides of the custard dishes. (Some cooks prefer to pour the water into the pan before setting the pan in the oven. This is fine so long as you are able to hold the pan steady and level and thereby avoid splashing water into the custards.)

TESTING CUSTARDS FOR DONENESS

Most custards should be removed from the oven as soon as the center appears quivery, like firm gelatin, when the cup is gently shaken. Baking a custard until the center is completely firm may cause the periphery to overcook and turn slightly grainy. To be doubly sure that a custard is ready, tilt the cup up at a 45° angle. The center should remain firmly in place without flowing. Another test is to insert a knife two-thirds of the way from the side of the dish toward the center. The knife should come out clean or with just a tiny smudge of custard adhering. If you know from experience that your oven heats unevenly, it is a good idea to reverse the position of the pan midway through baking. This is particularly critical if you are preparing a single large custard rather than a number of cup custards; individual cups can always be removed from the oven as they are done, but a single large custard must cook through evenly. Custards will continue to cook by stored heat after they are removed from the oven. Therefore, if your custards have become slightly overdone, you should arrest the cooking process by immediately setting the custard dish or cups in cold water.

THE ROLE OF FAT IN CUSTARDS

Cooks who are concerned about fat and calories are often tempted to replace the whole milk, cream, and egg yolks called for in custard recipes with low-fat or skim milk and whole eggs or egg whites. Generally speaking, these substitutions can work well. Cream, whole milk, low-fat milk, and skim milk are interchangeable in any custard recipe. Do not expect a custard made with skim milk to be as thick and dense as one made with heavy cream. As for eggs, a good rule of thumb is that 1 whole egg has roughly the same thickening power as 2½ egg yolks or 1½ egg whites (or a scant 3 tablespoons).

Do be aware, however, that lean custards are more tricky to cook than rich ones. Custards thicken because the egg proteins, excited by heat, move about, collide, and stick to one another. This process, called coagulation, begins at around 150°F and continues with ever greater efficiency as the heat increases until, finally, the heat becomes so great that the agitated egg proteins fuse into lumps, curdling the custard. In a very rich custard like crème brûlée, there are so many fat molecules present that the egg proteins have trouble finding one another and bonding. Thus the custard will not curdle until it reaches a temperature past 190°F. In a lean custard, by contrast, there is nothing standing between the egg proteins, and so they may overcoagulate, curdling the custard, at a temperature as low as 170°F. When you make a cup custard with skim milk and egg whites, then the difference between perfection and breakdown is a mere 10 degrees. It is all too easy to overshoot the mark by leaving the custard in the oven a few minutes too long.

Of course, you need not feel compelled to choose between heavy cream and egg yolks on the one hand and skim milk and egg whites on the other. For most purposes, a "compromise custard" composed of whole milk (or skim or low-fat milk with a tablespoon of cream) and whole eggs will do just fine. If you do make your custard lean, be sure to add the maximum amount of sugar called for. Sugar, like fat, impedes the bonding of eggs, thus promoting tenderness, and its sweetness partially compensates for the loss of flavor caused by the reduction of egg yolks and other fat.

Custards in a water bath (bain-marie)

Cup custard with nutmeg and grater

CUP CUSTARD

5 servings

Delicious served in solitary glory—even when made with egg whites and skim milk. This can be readied for the oven in only a few minutes.

Preheat the oven to 325°F.

Whisk just until blended:

3 large eggs, or 1 large egg and 3 large egg whites
1/3 to 1/2 cup sugar
1/8 teaspoon salt

Heat in a small saucepan just until steaming:

2 cups whole, low-fat, or skim milk

Gradually whisk the hot milk into the egg mixture and stir gently until the sugar is dissolved. If you wish, strain the mixture through a fine-mesh sieve into a bowl or large measure with a pouring lip. Stir in:

3/4 teaspoon vanilla or scraped seeds from one 1-inch piece vanilla bean

Pour into five 6-ounce custard cups or ramekins. Dust with:

Freshly grated or ground nutmeg

Bake the custards in a water bath (see About Baked Custards, 1013) until set but still quivery in the center when the cups are shaken, 40 to 60 minutes. Let cool for 30 minutes, refrigerate until cold, and serve with:

Pure maple syrup, berries, Caramel Syrup, 1047, or a fruit sauce

Pot-de-crème cups

VANILLA POTS DE CRÈME

6 servings

The French interpretation of cup custard, is richer than the American version because it is made with egg yolks instead of whole eggs. *Pots de crème* are named for the individual lidded porcelain jars, or *pots*, in which they are traditionally baked, shown above.

Preheat the oven to 325°F.

Whisk just until blended:

6 large egg yolks
1/3 to 1/2 cup sugar

Stirring, bring to a simmer in a small saucepan:

2 cups whole milk or half-and-half

Gradually whisk the hot milk into the egg yolk mixture. Strain through a fine-mesh sieve into a bowl or large measure with a pouring lip. Skim off any foam with a spoon. Stir in:

1 teaspoon vanilla

Pour the mixture into six 4-ounce *pot-de-crème* cups or ramekins. Put the lids on the cups or seal each ramekin with a snug-fitting piece of aluminum foil to prevent a skin from forming. Bake in a water bath (see About Baked Custards, 1013) until set but still quivery in the center when the cups are shaky, 40 to 60 minutes. Take the custards out of the water bath and let cool for 30 minutes, then refrigerate for at least 2 hours before serving. If using *pot-de-crème* cups, serve with the lids on.

CHOCOLATE POTS DE CRÈME

This is something like a very rich chocolate cornstarch pudding.

Prepare Vanilla Pots de Crème, above, mixing the egg yolks with 1/2 cup sugar and stirring in 1/4 cup unsweetened cocoa. Add 2 ounces finely chopped bittersweet or semisweet chocolate to the simmering milk (or, better, half-and-half) and whisk until smooth. These will bake quickly, in 35 to 45 minutes.

FLAN (CRÈME CARAMEL)

8 servings

Flan is the preeminent dessert of Spain and Latin America, and it is also a favorite in France, where it is known as crème renversée au caramel or, popularly, crème caramel. Flan is a stiff egg custard baked in a mold with caramel at its bottom. It is turned out of its baking dish and served upside down. The caramel, which melts during baking, forms a lovely syrup that soaks the bottom of the custard and runs down onto the plate. Be aware that the baked custards must chill thoroughly.

Preheat the oven to 325°F.

Place in a small, heavy saucepan:

3/4 cup sugar

Drizzle evenly over the top:

1/4 cup water

Place the pan over medium heat and, without stirring, very gently swirl the pan by the handle until a clear syrup forms. It is important that the syrup clarify before it boils, so slide the pan on and off the burner as necessary. Increase the heat to high and bring the syrup to a rolling boil; cover the pan tightly and boil for 2 minutes. Uncover the pan and cook the syrup until it begins to darken. Gently swirl the pan by the handle once again and cook the syrup until it turns a deep amber. Quickly pour the caramel into eight 6-ounce custard cups or ramekins or a 2- to 2½-quart soufflé dish. Using a potholder, immediately tilt the cups or dish to spread the caramel over the bottom and halfway up the sides.

Whisk just until blended:

5 large eggs, or 4 large eggs and 3 large egg yolks
¾ cup sugar
⅛ teaspoon salt

Heat just until steaming:

3 cups whole or low-fat milk

Gradually whisk the milk into the egg mixture and stir gently until the sugar is dissolved. If you wish, strain the mixture through a fine-mesh sieve into a bowl or large measure with a pouring lip. Stir in:

¾ teaspoon vanilla

Pour into the caramel-lined cups or dish. Bake in a water bath (see About Baked Custards, 1013) until firmly set in the center, 40 to 60 minutes for individual cups, 1 to 1½ hours for a single dish. Refrigerate for at least 4 hours or up to 2 days. To unmold, dip the cups or dish briefly in hot water, loosen the edges with a knife, and invert onto individual plates or a large plate. The plate for a large flan must be either broad or deep to catch all the caramel.

COFFEE FLAN (CRÈME CARAMEL AU CAFÉ)

4 or 5 servings

This is France's best-loved flan, and when you taste it you'll know why: coffee and caramel make a celestial pair. For a mellow flavor and handsome buff color, use regular-roast coffee here, not dark roast or espresso.

Combine in a saucepan:

1½ cups water
¾ cup ground coffee beans

Bring to a boil, stirring, then remove from the heat. Let steep for 10 minutes, then drip through a coffee filter. Measure ¾ cup. Rinse out the pan, combine in it the coffee, 2 cups half-and-half, and ¼ cup milk, and gently heat through. Prepare Flan, above, substituting this mixture for the 3 cups milk.

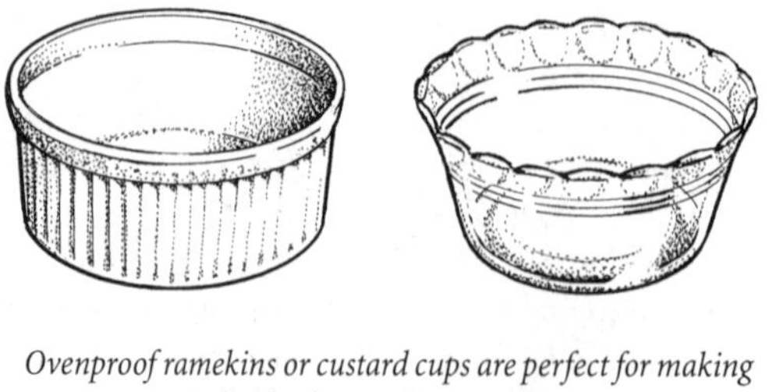

Ovenproof ramekins or custard cups are perfect for making individual custards or puddings.

LATIN AMERICAN FLAN WITH CONDENSED MILK (FLAN DE LECHE CONDENSADA)

8 servings

In Latin America, a favorite type of flan is made by simmering milk and sugar on the stove until reduced to a thick cream, then adding eggs. Since the cooking of the milk and sugar takes as long as an hour and requires nearly constant stirring, many cooks prefer instead to make this type of flan with sweetened condensed milk, which yields a similar result.

Preheat the oven to 325°F.

Line eight 6-ounce custard cups or ramekins or a single 2- to 2½- quart mold with caramel as directed for Flan, above. Combine in a saucepan:

One 14-ounce can sweetened condensed milk
1½ cups water
Zest of ½ lime removed in large strips
One 3-inch cinnamon stick
Pinch of salt

Bring to a boil, then reduce the heat and gently simmer for 5 minutes. Remove from the heat, cover, and let stand until just warm. Strain through a clean sieve into a bowl or large measure with a pouring lip. Whisk just until blended:

4 large eggs
3 large egg yolks
¾ teaspoon vanilla

Gradually whisk the milk mixture into the egg mixture. Pour into the caramel-lined cups or dish. Bake in a water bath (see About Baked Custards, 1013) until firmly set in the center, 40 to 55 minutes for individual cups, 50 to 70 minutes for a single dish. Refrigerate for at least 4 hours or up to 2 days. To unmold, dip the cups or dish briefly in hot water, loosen the edges with a knife, and invert onto individual plates or a large plate. The plate for a large flan must be either broad or deep to catch all the caramel.

ABOUT CRÈME BRÛLÉE

Crème brûlée is a rich custard covered with a hard caramel glaze that shatters delightfully under the pressure of a purposeful spoon. The caramel crust can be achieved many ways, each yielding a slightly different result. Thomas Jefferson's cook used a red-hot metal brand called a salamander to make "burnt cream." Today's home cooks can cover the custard with liquid caramel, which quickly hardens into a hard, mirrorlike glaze, or, for a more delicate and perishable effect, sprinkle the custard with sugar and then melt the sugar under the broiler or with a propane torch. Instructions for all follow.

CRÈME BRÛLÉE

6 to 8 servings

This crème brûlée is the most sumptuous we have ever tasted.

Heat almost to a simmer:

2 cups heavy cream

In a medium bowl, stir with a wooden spoon just until blended:

8 large egg yolks or 3 large eggs

½ cup sugar

Gradually stir in the cream. Strain through a fine-mesh sieve into a bowl or large measure with a pouring lip. Stir in:

¾ teaspoon vanilla

Pour into six to eight 4- to 6-ounce custard cups or ramekins and place in a water bath. Set the pan in the oven and set the oven temperature at 250°F. Bake until the custards are set but still slightly quivery in the center when the cups are gently shaken, 1 to 1½ hours. Remove the custards from the water bath and let cool to room temperature. Cover each one tightly with plastic wrap and refrigerate for at least 8 hours or up to 2 days. Shortly before serving, gently blot any liquid that has formed on the surface with paper towels, then caramelize the surface using one of the methods below.

CARAMEL GLAZE I

This method yields a hard, glossy, candylike glaze. The glaze may be applied to the custards up to 12 hours ahead without it softening.

Place a bowl filled with cold water near the stove. Measure into a small, heavy saucepan:

⅔ cup sugar

Drizzle evenly over the top:

¼ cup water

Set the sugar mixture over medium heat and, without stirring, very gently swirl the pan by the handle until a clear syrup forms. It is important that the syrup clarify before it boils, so slide the pan on and off the burner as necessary. Increase the heat to high and bring the syrup to a rolling boil; cover the pan tightly and boil for 2 minutes. Uncover the pan and cook the syrup until it begins to darken. Gently swirl the pan by the handle once again and cook the syrup until it turns a deep amber. Dip the bottom of the pan in cold water for 2 seconds to stop the cooking. Immediately spoon a scant tablespoon of the hot caramel over one of the custards and tilt the mold to cover the surface evenly. The caramel will bubble at first but will quickly settle into a glass-smooth glaze. Working quickly, glaze the remaining custards in the same manner. If the caramel continues to darken as you proceed, briefly dip the pan again in cold water to prevent it and the pan from burning. On the other hand, if the caramel becomes too thick to pour, stir it over low heat to liquefy it. Refrigerate the custards for at least 30 minutes or up to 6 hours.

CARAMEL GLAZE II

This method yields a delicate, brittle crust. The crust must be applied within an hour of serving or it will begin to melt into the custard.

Adjust a rack so that the tops of the custards will be about 2 inches from the broiler heating element. (If your rack cannot be set high enough, elevate the custards on an inverted roasting pan.) Preheat the broiler for 10 minutes. Measure:

⅓ cup granulated light brown sugar or ½ cup packed regular light brown sugar

If using granulated brown sugar, simply sprinkle it evenly over the surface of the custards. If using regular brown sugar, force the sugar through a sieve with your fingertips, covering the tops of the custards evenly; some sugar will inevitably spill over the sides. Arrange the custards on a baking sheet and transfer to the preheated broiler. Watching closely, broil the custards until the sugar melts and bubbles, turning the pan and/or moving the custards around if some cook more quickly than others. Do not expect even caramelization. Some sugar will remain unmelted and some spots will char; this is part of the charm. We prefer to serve these at once, while the glaze is still warm, but they may be refrigerated for up to 1 hour.

CARAMEL GLAZE III

This glaze is thinner and more delicate than Caramel Glaze I and harder, glossier, and more transparent than Caramel Glaze II.

Sprinkle evenly over the surface of each custard:

1½ to 2 teaspoons sugar

The coating should be no thicker than 1/16 inch. Caramelize the sugar with a propane torch, holding the flame about 2 inches above the surface of the custards and slowly rotating it to melt and color the sugar as evenly as possible. Serve at once, while still warm, or refrigerate for up to 1 hour.

GINGER CRÈME BRÛLÉE

Prepare Crème Brûlée, 1017, adding ¼ cup finely chopped peeled fresh ginger to the cream. Bring almost to a simmer, remove from the heat, and let steep for 5 minutes. Strain the egg mixture as directed, removing the ginger. Omit the vanilla. If you wish, sprinkle 1 teaspoon chopped crystallized ginger in the bottom of each cup before pouring in the custard.

MAPLE CRÈME BRÛLÉE

Prepare Crème Brûlée, 1017, substituting ⅔ cup pure maple syrup for the sugar.

RASPBERRY CRÈME BRÛLÉE

Prepare Crème Brûlée, 1017, placing 4 fresh raspberries in each cup before pouring in the custard.

ABOUT CORNSTARCH PUDDINGS

Pudding, to most Americans, means a creamy thick dessert in one of three flavors: vanilla, butterscotch, or chocolate. In truth, these beloved puddings are nothing more than milk, sugar, and cornstarch cooked together until the starch molecules bond, thickening the pudding into a smooth, satiny cream. To avoid lumping and scorching, the two most common problems, prepare cornstarch puddings in a heavy-bottomed saucepan, which provides gentle, even heat. The best stirring implement is a large, semiflexible, *heatproof* rubber spatula, which easily reaches the bottom, sides, and corners of the saucepan; the next best alternative is a wooden spoon. In mixing the pudding, be sure to dissolve the cornstarch thoroughly in a small amount of liquid, forming a lump-free runny paste, before adding the remaining liquid. The cooking is carried out in two distinct phases: the first over medium-high heat and the second over low. During the high-heat phase, stir the pudding in slow, sweeping circles, keeping the bottom, sides, and corners of the saucepan scraped clean so that heated pudding from the outside of the pan is constantly swept into the cooler center. When the pudding begins to thicken, immediately turn the heat down as low as possible—if using an electric stove, slide the pan off the heat briefly to allow the burner to cool—and begin stirring the pudding in quick little circles, rotating the spatula or spoon all around the pan. The pudding may look a little lumpy at this point, but if you stir fast enough, the lumps will soon smooth out. Bring the pudding to a sputtering simmer and then, still stirring, let it simmer for one full minute to cook the starch completely. Proceed at once to pour the pudding into cups, before it has a chance to congeal.

Pudding can be set in a single large dish or in individual cups. If you wish to unmold the pudding, you would be wise to set it in individual cups rather than in a large mold, since the pudding is rather soft and may split or warp when turned out if formed in a large size. If making an unmolded pudding, first coat the cups with vegetable oil spray or wipe them with a paper towel dipped in a mild vegetable oil. (This is safer than simply rinsing with water.) The unmolding process itself is simple: just invert the pudding over a plate and let it drop out. To prevent a skin from forming, press a piece of plastic wrap directly onto the surface of the warm pudding.

Finally, many of our readers have wondered why, on occasion, their puddings, after having thickened properly in the saucepan, suddenly thin out. This dismaying mystery has to do with the nature of cornstarch bonds, which are surprisingly fragile, especially once the pudding has begun to cool. If you break the bonds, your pudding turns to soup. In order to avoid this, do not beat, blend, or strain the pudding once you have taken it off the stove, even if it has lumped. Just pour it quickly, before it has a chance to cool and stiffen, into the serving dish and let it set undisturbed. And midnight snackers be warned: If you help yourself to a few spoonfuls of pudding from a fully set mold and then try to smooth the spot over, the pudding will betray your deed by liquefying.

VANILLA PUDDING

4 servings

An especially rich and creamy pudding when made with half-and-half but perfectly acceptable made with whole milk.

Have ready a 3-cup bowl or mold or four 5- to 6-ounce cups or ramekins. If unmolding the pudding, oil the mold(s).

Mix thoroughly in a heavy saucepan:

⅓ cup sugar
2 tablespoons plus 1½ teaspoons cornstarch
⅛ teaspoon salt

Gradually stir in, making a smooth, runny paste:

⅓ cup whole milk or half-and-half

Whisk in:

1⅔ cups whole milk or half-and-half

Stirring constantly, heat over medium heat until the mixture begins to thicken. Reduce the heat to low; stirring briskly, bring to a simmer and cook for 1 minute. Remove from the heat, then stir in:

2 teaspoons vanilla

Pour the pudding into the bowl or cups, then press plastic wrap directly onto the surface to prevent a skin.

Refrigerate for at least 2 hours or up to 2 days. Serve with:

Whipped cream or a fruit sauce

BUTTERSCOTCH PUDDING *4 servings*

The real thing, made with dark brown sugar cooked in butter.

Have ready a 3-cup bowl or mold or four 5- to 6-ounce cups or ramekins. If unmolding the pudding, oil the mold(s).

Melt over low heat in a small, heavy saucepan:

3 tablespoons unsalted butter

Stir in:

½ cup packed dark brown sugar

Cook, stirring, until melted and bubbly. Gradually stir in:

½ cup heavy cream (not milk)

Stir over low heat until the butterscotch is dissolved. Add and stir until blended:

1½ cups whole milk

Heaping ¼ teaspoon salt

Remove from the heat and let cool to barely lukewarm. Mix until smooth:

3 tablespoons cornstarch

3 tablespoons water

Stir into the milk mixture. Cook, stirring constantly, over medium-high heat until the mixture begins to thicken. Reduce the heat to low; stirring briskly, bring to a simmer and cook for 1 minute. Remove from the heat, then stir in:

1 teaspoon vanilla

Pour the pudding into the bowl or cups, then press plastic wrap directly onto the surface to prevent a skin. Refrigerate for at least 2 hours or up to 2 days. Serve with:

Whipped cream

CHOCOLATE PUDDING *4 or 5 servings*

Once you taste this rich, smooth, deeply chocolate pudding, you will never go back to a mix.

Have ready a 3-cup bowl or mold or four or five 5- to 6-ounce cups or ramekins. If unmolding the pudding, oil the mold(s).

Mix together thoroughly in a heavy saucepan:

½ cup sugar

⅓ cup plus 1 tablespoon unsweetened cocoa

⅛ teaspoon salt

Gradually stir in, making a smooth, runny paste:

⅓ cup warm water

Stirring constantly, bring to a boil over medium heat, then remove from the heat. For an especially thick and chocolaty pudding, add and stir briskly until melted:

1 ounce semisweet or bittersweet chocolate, finely chopped (optional)

Stir in:

1¾ cups half-and-half

Place in a bowl:

3 tablespoons cornstarch

Very gradually add, making a smooth paste:

¼ cup half-and-half

Thoroughly stir the cornstarch paste into the chocolate mixture. Cook, stirring constantly, over medium heat until the mixture begins to thicken. Reduce the heat to low; stirring briskly, bring to a simmer and cook for 1 minute. Remove from the heat, then stir in:

1½ teaspoons vanilla

Pour the pudding into the bowl or cups. If you do not want a skin to form, immediately press plastic wrap directly onto the surface of the pudding. Refrigerate for at least 2 hours or up to 2 days. Serve with:

Whipped cream

If you wish, sprinkle with:

1 ounce semisweet or bittersweet chocolate, grated

TREMBLEQUE (COCONUT MILK PUDDING) *8 servings*

Trembleque is a creamy pudding that "trembles" wonderfully when turned out of the mold. It is similar in texture to Vanilla Pudding but different in taste because it is made with coconut milk rather than cow's milk. (This also makes it a good choice for anyone who is lactose-intolerant.) Canned unsweetened coconut milk is not to be confused with the heavily sweetened "cream of coconut" used in mixed drinks. Don't be afraid if the milk looks lumpy. The lumps are simply solidified coconut cream and will quickly melt as the pudding heats.

Oil a 1½-quart soufflé dish or mold.

Mix together thoroughly in a heavy saucepan:

½ cup sugar

½ cup cornstarch

¼ teaspoon salt

Gradually stir in, making a smooth, runny paste:

½ cup canned unsweetened coconut milk

Stir in:

4½ cups canned unsweetened coconut milk

Stirring constantly, heat over medium heat until the mixture begins to thicken. Reduce the heat to low; stirring briskly, bring to a simmer and cook for 1 minute. Pour the pudding into the prepared dish, then press plastic wrap directly onto the surface to prevent a skin. Refrigerate for at least 12 hours. Invert onto a plate to unmold. Garnish with:

Cut-up fresh tropical fruits (such as pineapple, papaya, and mango)

If you wish, serve with:

A fresh fruit sauce

BANANA PUDDING

8 to 10 servings

Really a home-grown American trifle.

Mix together thoroughly in a heavy saucepan:

1 cup sugar
3 tablespoons cornstarch
¼ teaspoon salt

Gradually stir in, making sure to dissolve the cornstarch:

3 cups whole milk

Whisk in thoroughly:

3 or 4 large egg yolks

Add:

2 to 3 tablespoons unsalted butter, cut into pieces

Stirring constantly, heat over medium heat until the mixture begins to thicken. Reduce the heat to low; stirring briskly, bring to a simmer and cook for 1 minute. Remove from the heat, then gently stir in:

1½ teaspoons vanilla

Press plastic wrap directly onto the surface of the pudding and set aside. Have ready:

60 to 70 vanilla wafers

Peel and slice ¼ inch thick:

4 to 5 ripe but firm large bananas

Line the bottom and sides of a 10-inch glass pie pan or other wide 1½- to 2-quart dish with wafers. Cover with half the pudding and bananas. Arrange a layer of wafers over the top, then cover with the remaining pudding and bananas. Spoon pudding over any exposed bananas to forestall browning. Press plastic wrap directly onto the surface of the pudding and refrigerate for at least 4 hours and, just before serving, cover with:

Whipped cream

To make a traditional banana pudding, prepare:

Soft Meringue Pie Topping I or II, 1012

Preheat the oven to 425°F.

Spread the topping over the hot pudding, being sure it adheres to the cookies lining the sides of the dish, then brown the pudding in the oven for 5 minutes. Let cool to room temperature, then refrigerate for at least 2 hours or up to 24 hours. The longer the pudding is chilled, the softer the cookies become.

ABOUT RICE PUDDINGS

In classic European cuisine there exists a number of fancy rice puddings, some of which are molded in fancy shapes and then turned out onto silver trays. Most Americans, however, seem perfectly satisfied with rice puddings of a homier sort.

In former times, cooks often chose short- or medium-grain rice for rice puddings, as these types of rice are high in starch and thus give puddings an especially smooth and creamy texture. Unfortunately, short-grain rice is no longer sold in retail stores. Medium-grain can be found in markets catering to a Latin American clientele, but it is scarce elsewhere. (Arborio rice, a very starchy medium-grain rice sold for risotto, does not make good puddings.) That leaves only long-grain rice. This, happily, makes perfectly good puddings so long as it has not been "converted" or precooked (as in "instant" or "minute" rice). Do feel free to experiment with specialty long-grain rices, such as basmati, jasmine, and popcorn rice. Each will impart, in a subtle way, its own characteristic flavor.

RICE PUDDING

6 servings

The all-time favorite.

Have ready a serving bowl or six 5- to 6-ounce custard cups or ramekins.

Combine in a large, heavy saucepan:

¾ cup medium- or long-grain white rice
1½ cups water
Heaping ¼ teaspoon salt

Bring to a simmer over medium-high heat, then reduce the heat to low, cover, and simmer until the water has been absorbed, about 15 minutes. Stir in:

4 cups whole milk
½ cup sugar

Cook, uncovered, over medium heat for 30 to 40 minutes, stirring frequently, especially toward the end of cooking. The pudding is done when the rice and milk have amalgamated into a thick porridge. Do not overcook, or the pudding will be solid instead of creamy once cooled. Remove from the heat, then stir in:

½ teaspoon vanilla

Turn into the bowl or cups, then press plastic wrap directly onto the surface to prevent a skin. Serve warm, at room temperature, or cold. If you wish, sprinkle with:

Ground cinnamon

The pudding can be accompanied with:

Whipped cream or a fruit sauce

SWEDISH RICE PUDDING

8 to 10 servings

One of the greatest of all rice puddings—like a mousse, yet also creamy.

Prepare and keep hot:

Rice Pudding, above

Whisk together thoroughly:

2 large eggs

⅓ cup sugar

Gradually stir 2 cups of the hot pudding into the eggs, then stir the mixture back into the remaining pudding. Cook, stirring constantly, over the lowest possible heat just until it begins to thicken, 3 to 5 minutes. Do not allow the pudding to simmer, or the eggs will turn slightly grainy. Immediately turn the pudding into a serving bowl, then press plastic wrap directly onto the surface to prevent a skin. Refrigerate until cold. Whip until stiff peaks form:

1 cup cold heavy cream

Gently fold the whipped cream into the cold pudding. Serve at once or refrigerate for up to 2 days. Spoon into bowls or goblets. If you wish, sprinkle with:

⅓ cup chopped toasted almonds or hazelnuts

The pudding is lovely when drizzled with:

Fresh Raspberry Sauce, 1048

INDIVIDUAL BAKED RICE PUDDINGS

6 servings

These puddings are baked in little cups and can be unmolded. It is a delicious way to use up leftover rice in the refrigerator from the take-out delivery the night before.

Preheat the oven to 350°F. Butter six 6-ounce custard cups or ramekins.

Whisk together thoroughly:

2 large eggs

⅓ cup sugar

Grated zest of 1 lemon or orange

¼ teaspoon ground cinnamon

¼ teaspoon salt

Bring to a simmer:

1½ cups whole milk

Gradually whisk the hot milk into the egg mixture, then stir in:

1½ cups cooked white rice

½ cup dried currants

1 teaspoon vanilla

Pour into the prepared cups. Bake in a water bath (see About Baked Custards, 1013) until a knife inserted in the center comes out clean, 45 to 55 minutes. Let cool for at least 30 minutes before unmolding. Serve warm or cold with:

Whipped cream or a fruit sauce

The puddings can be made up to 2 days ahead; cover and refrigerate in the cups. To reheat, bake in a water bath at 300°F for about 15 minutes.

RICE PUDDING BRÛLÉE

Prepare Individual Baked Rice Puddings, above. Refrigerate until cold, then cover with Caramel Glaze I, II, or III, 1017. Since the glazes is meant for 8 cups rather than 6, you may not need quite all of it.

ABOUT TAPIOCA

Tapioca is derived from the root of the tropical cassava plant, which in many parts of the world is boiled and eaten as a starch. Most supermarkets today carry only quick-cooking tapioca, a precooked form that comes in tiny grains and is used not only to make tapioca custard but also to thicken fruit pie fillings. Some specialty food stores sell the traditional form called pearl tapioca, so named because it indeed resembles pearls. It comes in large-pearl and small-pearl types. Both must be soaked, and both require prolonged cooking. Although delightful, pearl tapioca is problematic, for it loses its thickening capacity when stored longer than a few months. Unfortunately, there is no way to determine the condition of pearl tapioca until you cook it. If your pudding refuses to thicken, you can always throw in a big handful of cooked rice and declare your dish a rice-and-tapioca pudding.

Tapioca should be cooked only until the grains (or pearls) become translucent (or nearly so) and no longer taste starchy or gritty. At this point, the pudding may still look thin, but it will continue to set up as it cools. Overcooked tapioca becomes gluey.

TAPIOCA CUSTARD

4 to 6 servings

Use the greater amount of tapioca if you like a thick pudding or if you are not adding egg.

Whisk together thoroughly in a heavy saucepan:

2½ cups whole or 2% low-fat milk

⅓ cup sugar

3 to 4 tablespoons quick-cooking tapioca

⅛ teaspoon salt

Let stand for 10 minutes, then slowly bring to a simmer over medium heat, stirring constantly. Simmer, stirring, for 2 minutes. Gradually whisk about half of the pudding into:

1 or 2 large eggs, well beaten (optional)

Thoroughly stir this mixture into the remaining pudding. Cook, stirring, over low heat just until you see the first sign of thickening. Remove from the heat at once and stir in:

1 teaspoon vanilla

Let cool in the saucepan for 30 minutes; it will thicken considerably. Turn into cups or bowls. Serve warm or chilled. If you wish, accompany with:

Whipped cream or a fruit sauce

EGGLESS TAPIOCA PUDDING

4 to 6 servings

Combine and let stand for at least 5 minutes:

1 cup water
¼ cup quick-cooking tapioca

Bring to a simmer in a large, heavy saucepan :

1½ cups water
½ cup sugar
One 3-inch cinnamon stick (optional)
⅛ teaspoon salt

Drop in:

2 large apples, pears, peaches, or nectarines (about 1 pound), peeled, cored or pitted, and cut into ¼-inch pieces

Simmer until tender, 2 to 5 minutes. Stir in the tapioca and very gently simmer, stirring, until the tapioca is translucent and the pudding has thickened like jelly, about 5 minutes. Let cool for 20 minutes. Pour into bowls or stemmed glasses and refrigerate until cold.

COCONUT PEARL TAPIOCA PUDDING

6 servings

This pudding is exceptionally good when made with pearl tapioca, with its chewy, creamy, slightly glutinous quality. However, you can use quick-cooking tapioca: reduce the amount of tapioca to ⅓ cup, soak it for only 10 minutes, and cook the pudding for just 2 minutes at a rolling boil.

Combine in a large, heavy saucepan:

⅔ cup small-pearl tapioca
2½ cups whole milk

Cover and refrigerate for at least 8 hours or overnight. Stir in:

One 15-ounce can cream of coconut
½ teaspoon salt

Bring the pudding to a simmer over medium-high heat, then reduce the heat and very gently simmer, stirring constantly, until the pearls are translucent and no longer gritty, 15 to 25 minutes. Be careful not to overcook the pudding, or it will be sticky. Remove from the heat. In a small bowl, whisk until frothy:

1 large egg

Gradually whisk in 1 cup of the hot pudding. Whisk this mixture into the remaining pudding in the pan and let stand for 5 minutes, covered. (The pudding will still be hot enough to cook the egg.) Transfer to a bowl or individual cups and press plastic wrap directly onto the surface. Refrigerate until thoroughly cold. Serve with:

Fresh fruit or a fruit sauce

ABOUT BREAD PUDDINGS

Bread puddings have recently regained the popularity they enjoyed a hundred years ago, when fashionable hostesses festooned them with meringues and served them up with fancy sauces. All modern bread puddings are fundamentally baked custards, but those that are light in bread but rich in eggs and cream will turn grainy and watery unless baked in a water bath. Those made with enough bread to soak the custard up may be baked directly on an oven rack.

Unlike many desserts, bread puddings accept a wide range of substitutions and additions. They may be made with virtually any bread or roll except those, like biscuits or muffins, that are leavened by baking powder or soda rather than yeast. Light egg breads such as challah or brioche produce bread puddings with a marvelously airy and spongy texture. Many of the recipes in this section call for generous quantities of cream and egg yolks, but these ingredients, too, should be regarded as flexible. Cream can always be replaced by half-and-half or even whole milk, and every three egg yolks can be replaced by one whole egg. Finally, never fear to add raisins, finely chopped dried apricots, chopped toasted nuts, chocolate chips, grated orange or lemon zest, or a few tablespoons of bourbon, brandy, or rum to a bread pudding. Bread puddings are like sponges. They can absorb almost anything.

BREAD PUDDING

6 servings

Sturdy but pleasantly soft and moist.

Butter a 2-quart baking dish.

Trim the crusts from and cut into ½-inch cubes:

12 to 16 ounces white bread, stale but not hard

You should end up with 4 to 5 lightly packed cups. Spread the bread evenly in the prepared baking dish, then scatter over the top:

¾ cup raisins (optional)

Whisk together thoroughly:

4 large eggs
¾ cup sugar
1 teaspoon vanilla
1 teaspoon ground cinnamon

½ teaspoon freshly grated or ground nutmeg

½ teaspoon salt

Whisk in:

3 cups whole or low-fat milk

Pour the mixture over the bread and let stand for 30 minutes, periodically pressing the bread down with a spatula to help it absorb the liquid.

Preheat the oven to 350°F.

Bake the pudding in a water bath (see About Baked Custards, 1013) until puffed and firm in the center, about 1¼ hours. Serve warm or cold with:

Whipped cream, milk, or heavy or light cream

The pudding can be made several days ahead; cover with aluminum foil and refrigerate. To reheat, bake for 15 minutes in a 325°F oven.

NEW ORLEANS BREAD PUDDING

10 to 12 servings

Like a warm sticky bun drenched in butter and bourbon.

Spread over a 13 x 9-inch baking pan, preferably glass:

3 tablespoons unsalted butter, softened

Cut into ½-inch-thick slices:

1¼ pounds French or Italian bread (1½ to 2 loaves)

Arrange the slices almost upright in tightly spaced rows in the prepared pan. Tuck between the slices:

1 cup raisins

Whisk until frothy:

3 large eggs

Whisk in:

4 cups whole milk

2 cups sugar

2 tablespoons vanilla

1 teaspoon ground cinnamon

Pour the liquid over the bread and let stand for 1 hour, pressing down now and then with a spatula to wet the tops of the slices.

Preheat the oven to 375°F.

Bake the pudding until the top is puffed and lightly browned, about 1 hour. Cover with:

Southern Whiskey Sauce, 1042

Let cool on a rack for 30 to 60 minutes, then cut into squares and serve. Leftover sauced pudding will keep for several days in the refrigerator and can be reheated in a 300°F oven for 15 minutes.

CHOCOLATE BREAD PUDDING

10 to 12 servings

Extravagant and luscious.

Cut into ½-inch-thick slices:

1 pound challah, brioche, or other light egg bread

Taking care to preserve as much of the crumb as possible, trim off and discard the crusts. Cut the bread into ½-inch cubes, making 6 to 7 cups. Bring to a boil, stirring constantly:

1 cup heavy cream

¾ cup sugar

⅛ teaspoon salt

Remove from the heat, then add:

12 ounces bittersweet or semisweet chocolate, chopped

Let stand for 2 minutes, then whisk until smooth. Whisk together thoroughly in a large bowl:

2 large eggs

2 large egg yolks

Add:

2 cups whole milk

1 tablespoon vanilla

Whisk in the chocolate mixture, then stir in the bread cubes. Let stand for 1 to 2 hours, gently stirring and pressing the bread down now and then with a spatula to help it absorb the liquid.

Preheat the oven to 325°F.

Generously butter a shallow 2-quart baking dish. Pour the pudding mixture into the prepared baking dish and smooth the top. Bake in a water bath (see About Baked Custards, 1013) until the center feels firm when pressed, 55 to 65 minutes. Let cool for 45 minutes, then serve with:

Southern Whiskey Sauce, 1042, or Warm White Chocolate Sauce, 1046

The pudding can be covered and refrigerated for up to 3 days. To reheat, bake in a water bath in a 300°F oven until a knife inserted in the center for 2 seconds comes out warm, 15 to 30 minutes.

MAPLE BREAD PUDDING

8 servings

A luxuriously rich yet ultralight bread pudding devised by a friend of ours, a New York pastry chef. If you can buy extra-flavorful Grade B or Grade A "dark amber" maple syrup, use it here.

Preheat the oven to 375°F. Lightly butter an 8 x 8-inch pan or a 9 x 2-inch round pan.

Trim the crusts from:

8 to 10 slices (10 ounces) egg bread or white loaf bread

Cut the bread into ½-inch squares, making about 4 cups. Spread on a baking sheet and toast to a rich golden brown, stirring several times. Turn the bread into the prepared pan. Reduce the oven temperature to 325°F. Whisk until blended:

9 large egg yolks

¾ cup pure maple syrup

Whisk in:

3 cups heavy cream

If you wish, strain the mixture through a fine-mesh sieve. Pour evenly over the bread and let stand for 20 minutes, pressing the bread down now and then with a spatula to help it absorb the liquid. Cover with a buttered sheet of aluminum foil. Bake in a water bath (see About Baked Custards, 1013) until firm in the center, 1 to 1¼ hours. Serve warm, drizzled with:

Pure maple syrup

Accompany with:

Vanilla or buttermilk ice cream

SUMMER PUDDING
5 or 6 servings

This traditional English-Irish pudding is made by lining a deep dish with bread and filling the bread casing with lightly cooked berries. The pudding is then weighted and refrigerated overnight so that the berries and bread can amalgamate, making the pudding solid enough to turn out onto a plate. The pudding is spongy, moist, and wonderfully fresh tasting, and it is very pretty as well.

Any combination of berries will work, so long as the total amount comes to 6 cups. Frozen berries work perfectly here.

Snugly line a 1½-quart soufflé dish or other cylindrical mold with plastic wrap.

Cut into ⅜-inch-thick slices:

1 pound egg bread (1½ to 2 pounds if the loaves are braided)

If your loaf is not as tall as your mold, slice the loaf lengthwise. Remove and discard the crusts. Cover the bottom of the mold with bread slices, trimmed to fit, then line the sides with additional bread, slightly overlapping the slices. Trim enough additional bread to make 2 layers inside the pudding and a final layer on top. Combine in a large saucepan:

1 pint sliced strawberries, or 12 ounces frozen unsweetened dry-pack strawberries, thawed
1 pint blueberries, or 12 ounces frozen unsweetened dry-pack blueberries, thawed.
1 pint raspberries, or 12 ounces frozen unsweetened dry-pack raspberries, thawed
1 cup sugar
3 tablespoons strained fresh lemon juice

Stir gently over medium heat until the mixture comes to a simmer and the berries begin to release their juice. Spoon one-third of the berries into the bread-lined mold and cover with a layer of bread. Repeat twice. Press plastic wrap over the pudding, then cover with a cake pan or tart pan bottom that fits *just inside* the mold. Set a 2-pound weight on top of the pan and refrigerate the pudding for at least 12 hours and up to 24 hours. To serve, remove the weight, pan or pan bottom, and plastic wrap; invert the pudding onto a plate and peel off the plastic. Cut the pudding with a wide, shallow spoon. Serve with:

Heavy or light cream

The pudding can be made up to 3 days ahead. After 24 hours, remove the pan or pan bottom and weight and cover the dish securely with aluminum foil.

ABOUT BAKED PUDDINGS

These lovely desserts are much firmer and more substantial than soft and creamy cornstarch puddings. This is because all baked puddings contain a high proportion of flour, breadcrumbs, cereal, or some other starch—indeed, so much that most baked puddings are virtually moist cakes. Baked puddings can be served either cold or hot and can be prepared in advance and reheated at serving time. While not obligatory, a sauce or accompaniment, such as Southern Whiskey Sauce, 1042, or a custard, lemon, or foamy sauce, 1043, is traditional with most baked puddings.

INDIAN PUDDING
6 servings

Indian pudding dates back to Pilgrim days, when cornmeal, the principal ingredient, was known as "Indian meal" in reference to America's native peoples, who taught the settlers how to grow corn. A truly warming dessert, with a taste and texture somewhat like pumpkin pie.

Preheat the oven to 275°F. Generously butter a heavy 8- to 9-inch (1½- to 2-quart) baking dish.

Measure into a large, heavy saucepan:

⅓ cup plus 1 tablespoon cornmeal

Stir in, very gradually at first to prevent lumps:

4 cups whole milk

Stirring constantly, bring to a boil over medium heat and cook for 3 minutes. Reduce the heat as low as possible and cook for 15 minutes, stirring frequently. Remove from the heat and whisk in:

½ cup light or dark molasses
4 tablespoons (½ stick) unsalted butter
2 tablespoons sugar
1½ teaspoons ground ginger
¾ teaspoon salt

Turn the pudding into the prepared dish. Bake until the center looks firm but still slightly quivery when the dish is shaken, 2½ to 3 hours. A dark crust will form on top. Let cool on a rack for 30 to 60 minutes, then serve with:

Vanilla ice cream or heavy or light cream

The pudding can be made up to 3 days ahead. Cool completely, cover with aluminum foil, and refrigerate. To reheat, bake, still covered with foil, in a 275°F oven for 45 to 60 minutes.

LEMON SPONGE CUSTARD
6 servings

This is a magical dessert. During baking, the batter mysteriously divides into a quivery layer of lemon custard on the bottom and a light and spongy cake on top.

Preheat the oven to 325°F. Lightly butter a 9 x 2-inch round pan or six 6-ounce custard cups or ramekins. Combine in a bowl and using the back of a wooden spoon, mash together until crumbly:

2 tablespoons unsalted butter, softened
⅔ cup sugar
⅛ teaspoon salt

Beat in:

3 large egg yolks

Add and mix until smooth:

3 tablespoons all-purpose flour

Gradually beat in:

¼ cup strained fresh lemon juice
2 to 3 teaspoons grated lemon zest

Stir in:

1 cup whole milk

Beat on medium-high speed until stiff but still moist:

4 large egg whites, at room temperature

The egg whites will look a little curdly. (Do not worry.) Gently whisk the whites into the milk mixture, blending just until no large lumps of whites remain. Ladle (do not pour) the batter into the prepared pan or cups; it is okay for it to reach the top. Bake in a water bath (see About Baked Custards, 1013) until a knife inserted in the center comes out nearly clean, 30 to 40 minutes for both small and large custards. Let stand for 10 minutes in the water bath. Serve warm, at room temperature or chilled, in the mold or turned out. If you wish, accompany with:

Fresh Raspberry Sauce, 1048

ORANGE SPONGE CUSTARD

Prepare Lemon Sponge Custard, above, reducing the lemon juice to 2 tablespoons, adding ¼ cup strained fresh orange juice, and substituting the grated zest of 1 orange for the lemon zest.

PERSIMMON BUTTERMILK PUDDING
8 servings

A soft, sweet pudding with an irresistible old-fashioned flavor. Be sure to use very ripe, mushy persimmons. To choose persimmons, see page 473.

Preheat the oven to 400°F. Butter a shallow 3-quart baking dish.

Cut lengthwise in half:

4 to 6 very ripe large persimmons

Remove the pits, then scrape the pulp free from the skins with a teaspoon. Puree the pulp in a blender or food processor. If it looks stringy, force it through a sieve with the back of a spoon. Measure 1½ cups persimmon pulp. In a large bowl, whisk until light:

4 large eggs

Whisk in the persimmon pulp, then whisk in:

2½ cups buttermilk
4 tablespoons (½ stick) unsalted butter, melted

Whisk together thoroughly in a separate bowl:

1½ cups sugar
1½ cups all-purpose flour
1½ teaspoons baking powder
1½ teaspoons baking soda
½ teaspoon ground cinnamon
½ teaspoon freshly grated or ground nutmeg
½ teaspoon salt

Add the dry ingredients to the persimmon mixture and whisk until well blended. Pour the batter into the prepared pan. Bake in a water bath (see About Baked Custards, 1013) until a toothpick inserted in the center comes out clean, 35 to 45 minutes. Serve the pudding warm or cold with:

Whipped cream, Rich Hot Lemon Sauce, 1043, or a foamy sauce, 1043 to 1044

PUMPKIN BUTTERMILK PUDDING

Prepare Persimmon Buttermilk Pudding, above, substituting 1½ cups canned pumpkin puree for the persimmon pulp.

ABOUT STEAMED PUDDINGS

Many cultures prepare steamed puddings, but most of those handed down in the United States are of English ancestry. Fruited suet puddings are dense, moist, and compact, something like soft fruitcake. Today only the great plum or Christmas pudding remains familiar.

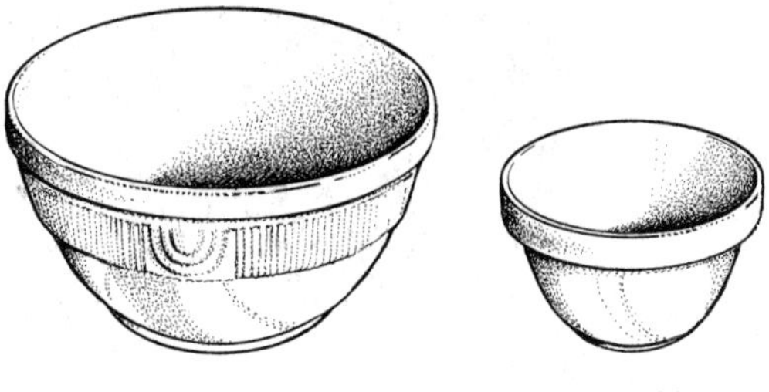

Pudding basins are classic molds for steamed puddings.

There is a plethora of light, fluffy steamed puddings, most of which are relatively modern inventions. Some of these taste much like dry, dense cake, while others have moist and soufflélike textures.

HOW TO STEAM A PUDDING

If you do not have a pudding basin—a deep bowl of heatproof ceramic—you may use any heatproof bowl with equally good results. The steep 4 to 5-quart metal bowls that come with heavy-duty mixers are good for particularly handsome large puddings. Grease these and all other metal bowls especially well, as puddings are more prone to sticking to metal than to glass or ceramic. Some specialty cookware stores carry fancy pudding molds. These are usually of a tube design and always come with a cover that snaps on tightly, shown below. Only plum pudding or other very firm puddings should be prepared in such molds. Lighter, more fragile steamed puddings will stick hopelessly and will collapse (or, worse, explode) if cooked tightly covered.

To steam a pudding, find a pot large enough to hold the pudding basin or bowl comfortably. If you are steaming several small plum puddings, a turkey roaster, set over two burners, is convenient. (Puddings must be steamed *in, not over*, simmering water, which rules out a double boiler.) To insulate the bottom of the pudding, set a trivet, rack, or folded dish towel in the bottom of your pot. Place the pudding in the pot, then pour in enough *boiling* water to reach halfway or to two-thirds the way up the sides of the pudding bowl. Bring the water to a boil over high heat, then turn the heat down to a brisk simmer. Cover the pot tightly and steam the pudding until done, checking the pot every 30 minutes and replenishing with boiling water as needed. When removing the cooked pudding from the pot, protect your hands with oven mitts or rubber gloves.

Pudding mold with snap-on cover.

ABOUT SUET

Ground or finely chopped beef suet is essential to certain steamed puddings, particularly plum pudding. Because it melts relatively late in the cooking process, after the starch in the batter has begun to set, suet leaves behind thousands of tiny spaces in the pudding. These spaces make the pudding soft and fine grained. Suet also imparts a special richness, without any beefy taste. You simply cannot make a good plum pudding with butter or shortening; it will end up greasy and heavy.

True beef suet is the pure pearly, crumbly fat that surrounds the kidneys. Beef fat from other parts of the animal, though often sold as suet, is not the same thing and should not be used. If possible, order suet from a butcher. Supermarket suet is intended primarily as bird food and may not be genuine or truly fresh.

Buy at least 10 ounces suet to yield 8 ounces cleaned. Cut away and discard any parts that are reddish or that look dried out, then crumble what remains between your fingers and remove any pieces of tough filament. (A certain amount of fine, papery filament will remain; don't worry about it.) Separate the pieces of suet and freeze solid in preparation for chopping. The suet must be chopped to a very fine, crumblike consistency, but it must not be allowed to melt and become pasty. If you work quickly, you will have no trouble doing this with a large chef's knife. Alternatively, you can grind the suet in a food processor fitted with the metal blade, being careful not to overprocess. Extra suet can be sealed in an airtight plastic bag and frozen for up to 6 months.

PLUM PUDDING (CHRISTMAS PUDDING)

1 large or 2 or 3 small puddings; 12 to 16 servings

Of all Christmas desserts, none is more traditional than a plum pudding, especially when brought to the table in a blue blaze of brandy flames. Plum is an old English term for raisins, hence the name. This dish is not a pudding in the modern sense. It more closely resembles a moist raisin-spice cake, served hot with a buttery sauce, than a modern pudding. See About Steamed Puddings, 1025, before you begin. Many cooks set aside a day for this project—a calm day early in the holiday season, for the pudding will only improve and mature while stored.

To make a single large pudding, use a 3-quart pudding mold, shown left, a 3-quart pudding basin, shown 1025, or a deep, heatproof glass or ceramic bowl with a capacity of 3 to 3½ quarts. To make smaller puddings, use 2 or 3 molds, basins, and/or baking dishes with a

total capacity of 3 to 4 quarts. Very generously grease each mold with solid vegetable shortening.
Divide in half and coarsely chop one-half:

2⅔ cups dark raisins

Combine all the raisins in a large, heavy pan with:

2 cups dried currants
2 cups water

Cover tightly and simmer gently for 20 minutes, then cook, stirring, until nearly all the liquid has evaporated. Let cool to room temperature, for at least 2 hours. Combine in a bowl:

1½ cups all-purpose flour
8 ounces ground or finely chopped beef suet (see About Suet, 1026)

Rub together lightly with your hands just until the suet particles are separated. Add:

1 cup firmly packed dark brown sugar
1½ teaspoons ground cinnamon
1½ teaspoons ground ginger
½ teaspoon ground cloves
½ teaspoon salt

Rub together just until blended. Whisk together thoroughly in a separate bowl:

4 large eggs
⅓ cup brandy or Cognac
⅓ cup cream sherry

Stir into the flour mixture, along with the cooked raisin mixture:

½ cup finely chopped dates (optional)
¼ cup finely chopped citron (optional)

Pour the batter into the prepared mold(s), leaving at least 1 inch of headspace for expansion. If you are using a fancy pudding mold with a cover, grease the inside of the cover and snap it in place. Otherwise, crimp a sheet of aluminum foil over the rim of the mold, allowing little or no overhang down the sides, and cover the foil with an inverted plate.
Arrange a rack or folded dish towel in the bottom of a large pot and set the mold(s) on top. Pour enough *boiling* water into the pot to come two-thirds of the way up the sides of the mold(s). Cover the pot tightly. Bring the water to a boil over high heat, then adjust the heat to maintain a brisk simmer. Replenishing the pot with boiling water as necessary, steam a single large pudding for 3½ hours, 2 smaller puddings for 2½ hours, or 3 small puddings for 2 hours. When done, the pudding should be firm at the center and dark around the edges. (At this point, a large pudding can be kept warm in the covered pot, with the heat off, for 3 hours; smaller puddings, for about 1½ hours.) Using oven mitts or rubber gloves, remove the pudding(s) and let stand at room temperature for 20 minutes. Invert onto a platter to unmold. If you wish to flame the pudding, warm to barely lukewarm in a small saucepan:

½ cup brandy or Cognac

Drizzle the liquor over the pudding, and then, standing back, ignite with a long wooden match. Serve with:

Custard Sauce, 1041, Hard Sauce, 1042, or Hot Foamy Sauce, 1044

To store the pudding, cool to room temperature, then turn out of the mold(s). Wrap first in plastic, then in aluminum foil; refrigerate for up to 1 month (it will become softer, darker, and more flavorful with age). To reheat, return the pudding to its original mold, well greased; steam again in briskly simmering water for 1½ to 2 hours for a large pudding, 1 hour for smaller puddings, or until a knife inserted in the center for 15 seconds comes out hot.

STEAMED CHOCOLATE FEATHER PUDDING

10 to 12 servings

Reminiscent of a chocolate soufflé, but more substantial. See About Steamed Puddings, 1025, before you begin.
Preheat the oven to 350°F.
Spread on a baking sheet:

1 cup fine dry unseasoned breadcrumbs

Toast, stirring 2 or 3 times, until richly browned, about 5 minutes. Let cool completely. Very generously butter a 4-quart heatproof bowl or pudding basin, shown 1025. Sprinkle the inside of the bowl with 2 tablespoons of the crumbs. Combine in a large, heatproof bowl:

8 ounces bittersweet or semisweet chocolate, chopped
½ cup heavy cream
4 tablespoons (½ stick) unsalted butter
2 tablespoons dark rum or strong coffee

Set the bowl in a skillet of almost simmering water and stir until the mixture is smooth. Remove from the heat and whisk in:

6 large egg yolks
1 tablespoon vanilla

In a separate bowl, beat on medium speed until foamy:

6 large egg whites, at room temperature

Add and beat until soft peaks form:

½ teaspoon cream of tartar

Gradually beat in:

½ cup sugar

Increase the speed to high and beat until the peaks are stiff and glossy. Using a large rubber spatula, fold the egg whites into the chocolate mixture. Sprinkle the remaining breadcrumbs over the top, along with:

2 tablespoons all-purpose flour

Fold until the crumbs and flour are incorporated. Turn the batter into the prepared mold and cover with an inverted plate. Set a rack or folded towel in the bottom of a pot large enough to hold the pudding comfortably. Set the pudding inside and pour enough *boiling* water into the pot to come halfway up the sides of the mold. Bring the water to a brisk simmer and tightly cover the pot. Replenishing the water as needed, steam the pudding until the top has flattened and the center feels firm, about 1¼ hours. Turn off the heat and let the pudding stand in the covered pot for 15 minutes. Invert the pudding onto a platter and serve with:

Whipped cream or a foamy sauce, 1043 to 1044

The uncooked pudding can be refrigerated for up to 12 hours before steaming.

ABOUT MOUSSES, BAVARIAN CREAMS, AND CHARLOTTES

These all refer to soft, light, airy desserts made with beaten egg whites or whipped cream. *Mousse,* which in French simply means froth or foam, is the broadest category of the three. Any dessert (or, for that matter, any savory dish) that has a frothy or foamy texture may be dubbed a mousse. A Bavarian cream, on the other hand, is a specific kind of mousse composed of two elements: a gelatin-bound custard, which gives the dessert its firmness and stability, and beaten egg whites and whipped cream, which make the dessert light. Bavarians are unmolded desserts. When set in a towering, crenulated mold and turned out onto a polished silver tray, a Bavarian makes a spectacular finale for a formal dinner party. The French distinguish between two types of dessert charlottes: those composed of a stiff fruit puree, typically apple, baked in buttered bread strips, and those that consist of a mousse (of any type) corseted in ladyfingers or cake or jelly-roll slices. There is a confusing muddle concerning charlotte and charlotte *russe*. The French consider a charlotte russe to be a plain vanilla charlotte molded in ladyfingers. Americans, however, have long used the term *charlotte russe* as simply a synonym for *charlotte,* as in the charlottes russe sold from pushcarts in New York in the 1930s, and thus American cookbooks give recipes for charlottes russe in flavors ranging from chocolate to peppermint.

HOW TO SERVE MOUSSES, BAVARIANS, AND CHARLOTTES IN DISHES

A French chef will tell you that only a mousse can be served in a dish, but Americans have long presented Bavarians and charlottes in dishes as well. A single large dessert is shown to best advantage in a cut-glass bowl; sherbet glasses, wine goblets, or champagne flutes make especially pretty individual dessert presentations. The so-called "cold soufflé" is another very attractive way of presenting a mousse, particularly one of the Bavarian type. Choose either a single large soufflé dish or individual porcelain ramekins with a total capacity about one-third less than the volume of the dessert. Fold a sheet of wax or parchment paper lengthwise in half (or, for small dishes, in quarters), then wrap it around the dish and fasten securely in place with kitchen string, a rubber band, or tape, making a "collar." Oil the inside of the collar, then fill the mold at least 1 inch above the rim. At serving time, unfasten and carefully peel off the collar, thereby creating a cap like that of a true soufflé.

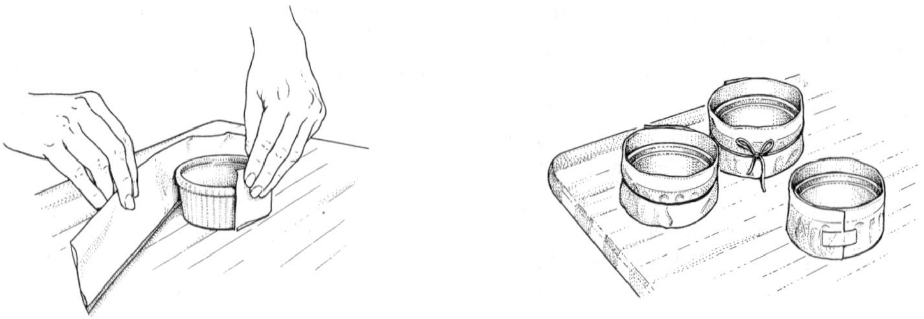

Make a "collar" around the soufflé dish or ramekin by wrapping folded wax or parchment paper around the dish. Secure the collar with kitchen string, a rubber band, or tape.

HOW TO MAKE UNMOLDED MOUSSES AND BAVARIANS

Unmolded desserts are a thrilling sight on the table. For a large dessert, use a soufflé dish, loaf pan, mixing bowl, charlotte mold (shown below), or a mold shaped as a ring, heart, star, or what have you. Coat the molds with neutral vegetable oil or cooking spray before filling. Refrigerate individual desserts for 3 to 4 hours and large desserts for at least 4 hours but preferably 12 to 24 hours if formed in high, narrow, or complex molds. (Gelatin continues to stiffen over a 24-hour period.) To release the dessert, dip the mold in a sinkful of very hot tap water. To avoid melting the surface of the dessert and obscuring any fancy patterns, leave a metal mold in hot water for no longer than a second or two. Thick molds made of ceramic, porcelain, or glass will require 5 to 10 seconds in hot water to warm through. To unmold, invert a plate over the top of the mold and then turn both over together. If the dessert is reluctant, tilt the mold up slightly at one side and pry a little part of the top away from the mold with a knife. Quickly withdraw the knife as soon as the dessert starts to descend. Mousses and Bavarians set in ring, heart, or star molds are less likely to end up rumpled or warped if you lightly oil the top (which will become the bottom) before unmolding.

HOW TO LINE A CHARLOTTE WITH LADYFINGERS

You will need a 2- to 2½-quart mold with a flat bottom, angled corners, and straight or only slightly sloping sides. The classic choice is the charlotte mold, shown below, which is shaped like a fez and has little heart-shaped handles. Charlotte molds come in a variety of sizes. For our recipes, you will need one that measures about 7 inches across the top and has a capacity of 2 to 2½ quarts. Our charlottes can also be prepared in 9 x 5-inch (8-cup) loaf pans, 2- to 2½-quart soufflé dishes, 8 x 8-inch pans, 9 x 2-inch round pans, or 8 x 3-inch springform pans.

Depending on your mold and on how you choose to line it, you will need between eighteen and thirty-six

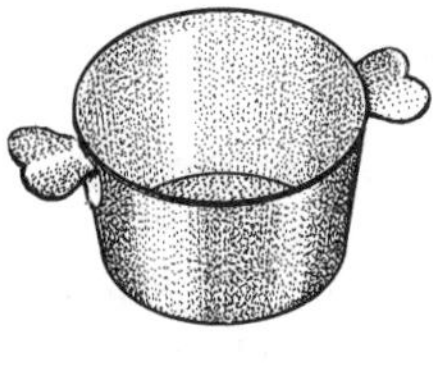

Charlotte mold

4-inch ladyfingers, either homemade, 940, or good-quality store bought. Do not use the hard, dry, crunchy ladyfingers sold for tiramisù. They are impossible to trim without crumbling.

To prepare the mold, lightly oil the interior, line the bottom with wax or parchment paper, and oil the paper as well. Snugly line the sides with ladyfingers, standing the fingers on their ends, with their flat sides facing the center. For a shallow mold, cut the ladyfingers in half and arrange them cut side up. If you are making the ladyfingers yourself, pipe them close together (about ¼ inch apart) on the sheet, so that they fuse during baking, then simply fit a strip of ladyfingers into the mold.

Now you must decide what to do about the bottom of the mold, which is to say, the eventual top of the dessert. If you are using a charlotte mold, a soufflé dish, or other deep round mold, the top is prettiest when left bare and adorned after the dessert is turned out with rosettes of whipped cream, each decorated with a coffee bean, a candied violet, chocolate shavings, and so on. If you are working with a shallow mold, you will probably want the top of the dessert to be covered. Square and rectangular molds are easy. Just arrange the ladyfingers over the bottom of the mold in rows, trimming as necessary. Round molds are more of a challenge. The traditional design is a sort of daisy, with a circle in the center and petals all around. To make the petals, trim the ladyfingers into teardrop shapes, using kitchen shears or a paring knife. Arrange the petals flat side up, with their pointed ends in toward the center; some of the petals will require further trimming to fit together tightly. When you have filled in the periphery, cut a circle out of another ladyfinger and place it in the middle. (If you are proficient with the pastry bag, you can pipe ladyfinger batter into a top that will fit your mold exactly. Pipe the batter as a daisy, in coils, or in any other design that appeals to you.)

You do not have to cover the top (which will be, after unmolding, the bottom) with ladyfingers, but if you have ladyfingers to spare, it is a good idea to do so: Charlottes that rest on a solid base are more stable and make neater slices than those with unlined bottoms. Trim the ladyfingers as necessary to make a neat fit. Use the leftover scraps from lining the bottom and sides of the mold as well. Arrange the ladyfingers, flat side up, inside the ends of the ladyfingers lining the sides of the mold. Trim the side lining flush with the bottom. If you have any moistening syrup left over, brush it over the bottom lining.

Charlottes can also be made in individual sizes. Oil eight to ten 8-ounce soufflé ramekins or small charlotte molds, cover the bottoms with wax or parchment paper, and oil the paper as well. Line the sides with ladyfingers that have been cut in half crosswise. Leave bare both bottom and top.

CHOCOLATE MOUSSE *6 servings*

With a soft, smooth, fluffy texture and a definite but not overpowering chocolate taste, this is the best chocolate mousse we know. For flavoring choose any liquor or liqueur that appeals to you. Alternatively, you can use strong coffee or simply water plus a little vanilla. This is a spooned mousse; if you wish to make the mousse slightly firmer so that it can be unmolded, see the direction below. This dessert is made with uncooked eggs; see page 122.

Heat 1 inch water in a large skillet over low heat until bubbles form along the bottom; adjust the heat to maintain the water at this temperature. Combine in a large heatproof bowl:

6 ounces semisweet or bittersweet chocolate, chopped
3 tablespoons unsalted butter
2 tablespoons liquor, liqueur, coffee, or water
1 teaspoon vanilla if using water

Set the bowl in the water bath and stir until the chocolate is melted. Remove from the water and set aside. Whisk together thoroughly in a heatproof bowl:

3 large egg yolks
3 tablespoons coffee or water
3 tablespoons sugar

Set the bowl in the water bath and, whisking constantly, heat the mixture until thick and puffy, like marshmallow sauce. Remove from the water bath and whisk thoroughly into the melted chocolate. Let cool to room temperature. In a separate bowl, beat on medium speed until foamy:

3 large egg whites, at room temperature

Add and beat until soft peaks form:

¼ teaspoon cream of tartar

Gradually beat in:

¼ cup sugar

Increase the speed to high and beat until the peaks are stiff. Using a large rubber spatula, stir one-quarter of the egg whites into the chocolate mixture to lighten it, then gently fold in the remaining whites. In another bowl, beat on medium-high speed until soft peaks form:

½ cup cold heavy cream

Gently but thoroughly fold the cream into the chocolate mixture. Turn into a 5-cup bowl or six 6- to 8-ounce individual cups. Refrigerate for at least 4 hours or up to 24 hours. Serve with:

Whipped cream

If you wish, sprinkle with:

1 ounce semisweet or bittersweet chocolate, grated (optional)

CHOCOLATE MOUSSE WITH GELATIN

When stiffened with a small amount of gelatin, Chocolate Mousse can be unmolded or used as a filling for a chocolate charlotte or a mousse cake.

Sprinkle 1½ teaspoons (⅔ envelope) unflavored gelatin over 3 tablespoons coffee or water and let soak for 5 minutes. Prepare Chocolate Mousse, above, substituting the gelatin mixture for the 3 tablespoons plain coffee or water added to the egg yolks. If you are making an unmolded chocolate mousse, be sure to oil your mold(s). Refrigerate this mousse for at least 6 hours to set.

CHOCOLATE CHARLOTTE *8 servings*

Following the directions on 1029, line a 2- to 2½-quart mold with ladyfingers.

Stir together in a small bowl until the sugar is dissolved:

¼ cup hot water or coffee
2 tablespoons sugar

Let cool to lukewarm. Stir in:

¼ cup liquor, liqueur, or coffee planned for the mousse

If the mousse is to be flavored simply with vanilla, double the hot water and sugar and add 1 tablespoon vanilla. Brush this sugar syrup onto the ladyfinger or cake lining. Prepare:

Chocolate Mousse with Gelatin, above

If you wish, fold in:

½ cup chopped toasted nuts

Fill the lined mold with mousse. If you have additional ladyfingers or cake slices, use them to cover the top of the mousse, then brush with any remaining syrup. Refrigerate for at least 6 hours or up to 3 days. Invert onto a plate and unmold. Serve with:

Whipped cream or a chocolate sauce, 1045 to 1046

WHITE CHOCOLATE MOUSSE WITH TOASTED ALMONDS *6 or 7 servings*

We have often found white chocolate mousses disappointingly faint in flavor, but this one, made with over

8 ounces of white chocolate, delivers a strong white chocolate taste. This mousse is firm enough to be unmolded, yet soft and creamy on the tongue.

Have ready six or seven 4- to 6-ounce stemmed glasses, ramekins, or bowls, or one 2-quart mold. Lightly oil the mold(s) if you wish to turn out the dessert.

Preheat the oven to 350°F.

Spread on a baking sheet:

1/3 cup slivered blanched almonds

Toast, stirring several times, until golden brown, 5 to 7 minutes. Let cool completely, then chop into 1/8-inch bits. Chop also into the same-size bits:

1 to 2 ounces white chocolate

Combine with the almonds and set aside. Measure into a small bowl:

3 tablespoons water

Sprinkle over the top:

3/4 teaspoon (1/3 envelope) unflavored gelatin

Let stand for 5 minutes to soften. Very finely chop or pulverize to a crumblike consistency in a food processor:

8 ounces white chocolate

If chopped, turn the chocolate into a bowl; if processed, leave in the work bowl of the machine. Stirring, bring to a rolling boil in a small saucepan:

1/2 cup heavy cream

Remove from the heat, add the softened gelatin, and stir for 30 seconds to dissolve the gelatin granules. Immediately pour this mixture over the chocolate and whisk or process just until smooth. Refrigerate the chocolate mixture until cold and thick enough to fall from a spoon in heavy, satiny ribbons, 15 to 45 minutes. Beat on medium-high speed until stiff enough to hold a firm shape on a spoon:

1 cup cold heavy cream

Fold the cream into the white chocolate mixture, then gently fold in the almond mixture. Turn into the glasses or mold and refrigerate for 2 hours, or at least 4 hours if unmolding. If you wish, decorate with:

1 to 2 ounces white chocolate, grated

The mousse can be accompanied with:

Fresh Raspberry Sauce, 1048

CHARLOTTE RUSSE

8 to 10 servings

Charlotte russe, a rich vanilla cream molded in ladyfingers, has been enjoyed in the United States since the 1830s. This dessert is always served with a light fruit sauce.

Line a 2- to 2½-quart mold with ladyfingers (see How to Line a Charlotte with Ladyfingers, 1029).

Stir over low heat until smooth:

1/2 cup seedless raspberry jam

3 tablespoons raspberry liqueur or water

Brush the syrup over the cake lining. The ladyfingers should be thoroughly soaked, but if they threaten to flop over, reserve some of the syrup for any ladyfingers that you use for the top. Pour into a large heatproof bowl:

3 tablespoons water

Sprinkle over the top:

1½ teaspoons (2/3 envelope) unflavored gelatin

Let stand for 5 minutes to soften, then whisk in:

6 large egg yolks

1/2 cup sugar

2 tablespoons vanilla

2 tablespoons brandy, Cognac, or water

Heat 1 inch of water in a large skillet over very low heat until small bubbles form along the bottom; adjust the heat to maintain the water at this temperature. Set the bowl with the egg yolk mixture in the water and, whisking constantly, heat the mixture until thick and puffy, like marshmallow sauce. (If you are concerned about eating uncooked eggs, periodically insert an instant-read thermometer for 15 seconds off the heat. When the temperature has reached 160°F, the eggs have been pasteurized.) Set the bottom of the bowl in cold water and, whisking now and then, cool to room temperature. Beat on medium speed until light and fluffy:

8 tablespoons (1 stick) unsalted butter

1/4 cup sugar

1/4 teaspoon salt

Beat in the egg yolk mixture by heaping tablespoons. Scrape the mixture back into the bowl used for the egg yolks. Beat on medium-high speed until stiff peaks form:

1½ cups cold heavy cream

Using a large rubber spatula, stir 1/2 cup of the cream into the egg yolk mixture, then gently but thoroughly fold in the remaining cream. Turn the mixture into the prepared mold. Cover the top with additional ladyfingers, if you have them, and brush with any remaining syrup. Refrigerate for at leaset 8 hours or up to 3 days. Invert onto a plate and unmold. Serve with:

Fresh Raspberry Sauce, 1048, or Cherries Jubilee, 1049

COLD LEMON SOUFFLÉ OR BAVARIAN CREAM

8 servings

This frothy, featherlight cream melts on the tongue. It can also be encased in ladyfingers and turned out, like a charlotte—but, being fragile, it will not yield neat slices. This dessert is made with uncooked eggs; see page 122.

For a cold soufflé, tie collars around oil eight 6-ounce ramekins or one 1½-quart soufflé dish (see How to Serve Mousses, Bavarians, and Charlottes in Dishes, 1028). For a Bavarian cream, oil eight 8-ounce individual cups or one 2½-quart charlotte or other mold.

Combine in a medium bowl.

½ cup strained fresh lemon juice
1 tablespoon grated lemon zest

Sprinkle over the top:

2¼ teaspoons (1 envelope) unflavored gelatin

Let stand for 5 minutes to soften. In a large bowl, whisk just until combined:

5 large egg yolks
⅓ cup sugar

In a medium, heavy saucepan, heat until bubbly around the edges:

1 cup whole milk

Gradually whisk the milk into the egg yolks, then return this mixture to the saucepan. Cook, gently stirring, over very low heat until almost as thick as heavy cream. The temperature must not exceed 170°F, or it will curdle. Immediately poor the hot custard over the gelatin mixture and stir for 1 minute to completely dissolve the gelatin granules. Rinse out the large bowl, then pour the custard into it through a clean fine-mesh sieve. Set the bowl in cool water and stir until the custard is no longer warm and thickens slightly. In a separate bowl, beat on medium speed until foamy:

3 large egg whites, at room temperature

Add and beat until soft peaks form:

¼ teaspoon cream of tartar

Gradually beat in:

⅓ cup plus 1 tablespoon sugar

Increase the speed to high and beat until the peaks are stiff but not dry. If the custard has stiffened, whisk until smooth. Whisk in one-third of the egg whites, then gently fold in the remaining whites with a large rubber spatula. Beat on medium speed until soft peaks form:

¾ cup cold heavy cream

Gently fold the cream into the egg white mixture. Turn into the prepared mold(s). Refrigerate the soufflé(s) for at least 4 hours, and the Bavarian(s) for 8 to 12 hours. Untie the collars from the soufflé(s) or unmold the Bavarian(s) onto plates. Decorate the soufflé(s) with:

Whipped cream

Serve the Bavarian(s) with:

Whipped cream, Fresh Raspberry Sauce, 1048, or Custard Sauce, 1041

COLD LIME SOUFFLÉ OR BAVARIAN CREAM

Like the filling of Key lime pie but lighter and tarter. Prepare Cold Lemon Soufflé or Bavarian Cream, above, substituting strained fresh lime juice and zest for the lemon juice and zest. If you wish, add 1 drop green food coloring when whipping the cream, to tint the dessert.

COLD ORANGE SOUFFLÉ OR BAVARIAN CREAM

Simmer 2 tablespoons grated orange zest and 1½ cups strained fresh orange juice in a small nonaluminum saucepan until reduced to just under ½ cup. Let cool completely, then add 1 tablespoon strained fresh lemon juice. Prepare Cold Lemon Soufflé or Bavarian Cream, above, substituting the orange reduction for the lemon juice and zest.

ABOUT DESSERT SOUFFLÉS

Soufflés have an undeserved reputation for difficulty. In fact, one reason they are popular with restaurant chefs is that they are so easy to prepare. Assuming that you have beaten your egg whites properly (see 928), a soufflé simply has to rise, for the air trapped in the beaten whites expands as the temperature increases. Additional puffing is provided by the steam generated as the milk, fruit juice, or other liquid in the batter evaporates. As soon as the soufflé is removed from the oven, the gas cools and contracts, making the soufflé fall, which means that a baked soufflé must be served at once. But that fact does not necessarily make soufflés entirely last-minute affairs. Most batters can be prepared several hours before baking and held in the refrigerator. Because they congeal upon cooling, chocolate soufflés can actually be made a full day ahead.

Like their savory counterparts, dessert soufflés are made by folding stiffly beaten egg whites into a thick, flavorful base. In traditional recipes, this base is a pastry cream, but in more contemporary recipes, the base may be a fruit puree or even simply fruit juice mixed with egg yolks and sugar. The airy mixture is usually baked in molds, though emptied orange or lemon rinds or the shells of passion fruit are sometimes used instead. When molds are used, they must be carefully prepared. Brush the mold with a *thick* coat of softened, not melted, butter, then sprinkle generously with sugar. Tilt the mold in all directions to spread the sugar evenly, then invert the mold and tap out the excess sugar. Be careful not to smudge the crust by inadvertently touching it with your fingers. When prepared in a properly coated mold, a soufflé will rise tall, straight, and even, and, even better, it will emerge from the oven with a delightfully crunchy, lightly caramelized crust.

A well-cooked soufflé should be firmly set but still moist and creamy in the center, not dry. Determining when this moment has been reached is a little tricky. At the minimum estimated baking time, open the oven door slightly and peek in. If the soufflé looks risen and browned on top, you can assume that it has set firm enough not to fall when tested. First, touch the top of the soufflé lightly with your hand. If it feels firm, the soufflé may well be cooked through. To be sure, insert a thin metal or wooden skewer at a 45° angle through the side of the soufflé into the center. It should come out dry or, if you prefer a creamy center, just slightly moist with a few curds of thick batter adhering. If it comes out wet, the soufflé needs to be baked longer. A baked soufflé will stay fully risen for at least a minute or two, giving you plenty of time to rush it to the table.

INDIVIDUAL CHOCOLATE SOUFFLÉS

6 servings

Unlike most chocolate soufflés, these are made without milk or starch. They are light yet moist, with an exceptional chocolate taste.

Preheat the oven to 375°F. Butter and sugar six 10- to 11-ounce ramekins (see About Dessert Soufflés, 1032) and arrange on a baking sheet.

Combine in a heatproof bowl:

8 ounces semisweet or bittersweet chocolate, chopped

6 tablespoons (¾ stick) unsalted butter

2 tablespoons rum, coffee, or water

Set the bowl in a skillet of hot, but not simmering, water and stir until the mixture is smooth. Let cool for 10 minutes and then whisk in:

6 large egg yolks

Beat on medium speed until foamy:

6 large egg whites, at room temperature

Add and beat on high speed until soft peaks form:

Heaping ¼ teaspoon cream of tartar

Gradually beat in:

½ cup sugar

Beat until the peaks are stiff but not dry. Using a large rubber spatula, stir one-third of the egg whites into the chocolate mixture, then gently but thoroughly fold in the remaining mixture. Divide the batter equally among the prepared ramekins and smooth the tops. Bake until risen and set, about 20 minutes. If you wish, after bringing the soufflé to the table, open a slit in the top of each soufflé with 2 forks held back to back and add:

Custard Sauce, 1041, or a white or dark chocolate truffle

The soufflés can be covered with plastic wrap and refrigerated for up to 24 hours before baking.

INDIVIDUAL APRICOT SOUFFLÉS

6 or 8 servings

Made without fat, yet deliciously rich in taste.

Preheat the oven to 350°F. Butter and sugar six 8-ounce ramekins or eight 6- to 7-ounce ramekins (see About Dessert Soufflés, 1032). Arrange on a baking sheet.

Combine in a medium, heavy saucepan:

1½ cups water

1 cup packed moist dried apricots

½ cup sugar

Bring to a gentle simmer, cover tightly, and cook for 20 minutes. Let cool, still covered, for at least 30 minutes. Spoon half of the apricots with half of the syrup into a blender. Add:

1 tablespoon strained fresh lemon juice

Puree thoroughly, scraping the sides of the container occasionally. The puree should be perfectly smooth and creamy, almost fluffy. If necessary, dribble in as much as:

1 tablespoon water

Turn the puree into a large bowl. Repeat with the remaining apricots and syrup, adding as before:

1 tablespoon strained fresh lemon juice

1 tablespoon water as needed

Add this puree to the first. Beat on medium speed until foamy:

5 large egg whites, at room temperature

Add and beat on high speed until soft peaks form:

¼ teaspoon cream of tartar

Gradually beat in:

¼ cup sugar

Beat until the peaks are stiff but not dry. Using a large rubber spatula, stir one third of the egg whites into the apricot puree, then gently but thoroughly fold in the remaining puree. Divide the batter equally among the prepared ramekins and smooth the tops. They should be filled to the brim. Bake just until well risen and beginning to brown, 11 to 14 minutes for large soufflés,

10 to 13 minutes for small ones. Be careful not to overbake, or they will fall and turn soupy in the center. If you wish, after bringing soufflé to the table, open a slit in the top of each soufflé with 2 forks held back to back and spoon in.

Custard Sauce, 1041

The soufflés can be covered with plastic wrap and refrigerated for up to 24 hours before baking; let warm at room temperature for 1 hour before putting them in the oven.

GRAND MARNIER SOUFFLÉ

6 servings

We never tire of this enduring classic.

Position a rack in the lower third of the oven. Preheat the oven to 375°F. Butter and sugar a 2-quart soufflé dish (see About Dessert Soufflés, 1032).

Melt in a saucepan over medium heat:

3 tablespoons unsalted butter

Whisk in until smooth:

2 tablespoons all-purpose flour

Cook, stirring, for 1 minute. Remove from the heat and stir in:

1 cup heavy cream
⅓ cup sugar
Grated zest of 1 large orange

Bring to a boil, whisking constantly, and remove from the heat. In a large bowl, whisk until slightly thickened:

5 large egg yolks

Very gradually whisk in the cream mixture, then stir in:

⅓ cup Grand Marnier

Beat on medium speed until foamy:

6 large egg whites, at room temperature

Add and beat until soft peaks form:

½ teaspoon cream of tartar
⅛ teaspoon salt

Increase the speed to high and beat until the peaks are stiff but not dry. Using a large rubber spatula, gently stir one-quarter of the egg whites into the egg yolk mixture, then fold in the remaining mixture. Turn the batter into the prepared dish and smooth the top. Bake until a skewer inserted sideways in the center comes out clean or just slightly moist, 35 to 45 minutes. Serve at once with:

Orange Liqueur Sauce, 1043

The soufflé can be set aside at room temperature, covered with an inverted bowl, for up to 1 hour before baking.

LEMON SOUFFLÉ

6 servings

Creamy and moist, with a sprightly lemon tang.

Position a rack in the lower third of the oven. Preheat the oven to 375°F. Butter and sugar a 2-quart soufflé dish (see About Dessert Soufflés, 1032).

Melt in a saucepan over medium heat:

3 tablespoons unsalted butter

Whisk in until smooth:

¼ cup all-purpose flour

Cook, stirring, for 1 minute. Remove from the heat and stir in:

1 cup light cream or ½ cup each whole milk and heavy cream
½ cup sugar
Grated zest of 2 lemons

Bring just to a boil, whisking constantly, and remove from the heat. In a large bowl, whisk until slightly thickened:

5 large egg yolks

Very gradually whisk in the cream mixture, then stir in:

⅓ cup strained fresh lemon juice

Beat on medium speed until foamy:

6 large egg whites, at room temperature

Add and beat until soft peaks form:

½ teaspoon cream of tartar
⅛ teaspoon salt

Increase the speed to high and beat until the peaks are stiff but not dry. Using a large rubber spatula, gently stir one-quarter of the egg whites into the egg yolk mixture, then fold in the remaining mixture. Turn the batter into the prepared dish and smooth the top. Bake in a water bath (see About Baked Custards, 1013) until a skewer inserted sideways in the center comes out clean or just slightly moist, 1 to 1¼ hours. Serve at once with:

Rich Hot Lemon Sauce, 1043, or Lemon Sabayon, 1045

The soufflé can be set aside at room temperature, covered with an inverted bowl, for up to 1 hour before baking.

ABOUT FLOATING ISLAND

Countless desserts are known as floating islands. All consist of some sort of puffy confection, typically (but not always) a meringue, floated on a sea of liquid custard or some other dessert sauce. In most floating islands, caramel, jelly, fruit, or a fruit puree is also involved, most commonly as a garnish or drizzle but sometimes as an ingredient in the puffs themselves. Americans have been enjoying floating island since colonial times, and various versions of the dessert have long been popular throughout Latin America as well. Today, however, the dish is best known in its two

French forms, île flottante and oeufs à la neige, both of which are outlined below. Île flottante, or "floating island," consists of a large baked meringue served on a custard sauce, often with a lacing of caramel over the top. Oeufs à la neige, or "eggs in snow," is similar, except that the meringue is formed in small egg shapes and is poached, not baked.

ÎLE FLOTTANTE (FLOATING ISLAND)

8 to 10 servings

One of the great desserts of classic cuisine. Baked in a water bath, the meringue has a surprising consistency—light, of course, but also firm and moist, almost creamy.

Lightly oil a heatproof 2½-quart bowl, preferably metal, or soufflé dish. Line snugly with aluminum foil, placed shiny side up, then oil the foil as well. Heat 1 inch of water in a large skillet over very low heat until small bubbles appear along the bottom; adjust the heat to maintain the water at this temperature. Combine in a large heatproof bowl:

¼ cup water
½ teaspoon cream of tartar

Whisk in thoroughly:

1 cup (7 to 8 large) egg whites
1¼ cups sugar

Set the bowl in the water bath and, whisking frequently, heat until the mixture begins to steam and feel uncomfortably warm to your fingers, about 140°F. This will take 3 to 5 minutes if using a metal bowl, 8 minutes or longer if using a heavy glass or ceramic bowl. Immediately remove from the heat and whisk in:

2 teaspoons vanilla

Beat on high speed until the mixture is very thick and the bottom of the bowl is barely tepid, 5 to 7 minutes. Spread a thick layer of the meringue around the inside of the prepared bowl, pressing to eliminate air pockets. Fill with the remaining meringue and level the top; it is okay if the meringue fills the bowl entirely. Using kitchen shears, trim any exposed foil flush with the top of the meringue. Bake in a water bath (see About Baked Custards, 1013) until the meringue has risen 3 to 4 inches or an instant-read thermometer registers 165°F when inserted dead center, 30 to 45 minutes. Let cool on a rack until deflated to its original height. Meanwhile, use the leftover egg yolks to prepare:

1½ recipes Custard Sauce, 1041

Invert the cooled meringue into a gratin dish, deep platter, or wide, shallow bowl, preferably glass. Pour some or all of the custard sauce around the base, saving the rest to pass separately. Serve at once or refrigerate for up to 12 hours. Just before serving, pour over the top of the island:

Caramel Syrup, 1047, Fresh Raspberry Sauce, 1048, or Fresh Strawberry Sauce, 1048

If you have chosen Caramel Syrup, you can sprinkle the top with:

1 to 2 tablespoons chopped nuts (optional)

OEUFS À LA NEIGE (EGGS IN SNOW)

5 or 6 servings

Until recently, this was one of the most popular desserts in good French restaurants in France and the United States alike, and we think it still should be.

Beat on medium speed until foamy:

4 large egg whites, at room temperature

Add and beat until soft peaks form:

1 teaspoon vanilla
¼ teaspoon cream of tartar
¼ teaspoon salt

Gradually beat in:

⅔ cup sugar, preferably superfine

Increase the speed to high and beat until the peaks are thick and glossy. Line a baking sheet with a thin dish towel or 2 layers of paper towels. Pour 2 inches of water into a large skillet and heat to 180°F or until tiny bubbles form along the bottom of the pan. Adjust the heat to maintain the water at this temperature; it must not simmer. Using a 3- to 4-ounce ice-cream scoop or a ⅓- or ½-cup measure, scoop up a slightly heaping mound of meringue. Round the top of the mound with your fingertips to form an egg shape. Drop the meringue into the skillet; if you are using a cup, scrape the meringue out with a rubber spatula. Preparing 5 to 8 meringues at a time (or for as many as will fit in the skillet), poach the meringues for 2 minutes on each side, turning once with a slotted spoon. When done, they should feel firm and bouncy all around. If soft spots remain, flip the meringues onto their undercooked sides and poach a bit longer. Remove the meringues from the skillet with the slotted spoon, briefly hold them aloft to drain, and set each one on the lined baking sheet. Poach all the meringues in the same manner. Prepare:

Custard Sauce, page 1041

Pour the sauce into a wide, deep glass dish or bowl, then float the meringues on the custard. For classic oeufs à la neige, prepare:

Caramel Glaze I, page 1017

Dip the bottom of the caramel pan in cool water for about 10 seconds, just until the caramel shows the first signs of thickening, then drizzle the hot caramel over the dessert by spoonfuls, waving the spoon to create a delicate filigree of threads. Serve at once or refrigerate for up to 12 hours. For a more contemporary version, instead of Caramel Glaze prepare:

Fresh Strawberry Sauce, 1048

Just before serving, drizzle a band of the strawberry sauce over each meringue and pass the remainder in a sauceboat.

ABOUT ZABAGLIONE AND SABAYON

Zabaglione is an Italian dessert made by whisking egg yolks, sugar, and Marsala over hot water until the mixture thickens into a luxurious, puffy cream. Sabayon is both the French name for zabaglione and a term that designates a wide range of desserts and sauces, both savory and sweet, made along the same lines. In making these foams, success hinges on heating the mixture rather slowly to a temperature of 160°F. If warmed too quickly, the foam will not thicken properly or acquire maximum volume. If overheated, the foam will contract and become heavy and sticky; eventually it will curdle. Heating is best done in a double boiler. If your double boiler is wider than 6 inches, be sure to use very gentle heat, as the mixture will be spread thin and thus be especially prone to overcooking.

For dessert sauce sabayons, see 1044 to 1045.

ZABAGLIONE

4 servings

Combine in the top of a double boiler:

4 large egg yolks
¼ cup sugar

Whisk vigorously until thick and pale yellow. Whisking constantly, gradually add:

½ cup dry Marsala

Scrape the sides of the double boiler clean with a rubber spatula, then set over, not in, very gently simmering water. Whisking constantly, heat the zabaglione to 160°F (insert in the center an instant-read thermometer off the heat), at which point it will have increased several times in volume and become thick enough to mound very softly on a spoon. The cooking should take 5 to 10 minutes. If the zabaglione appears to be heating too quickly, periodically remove it from the water and whisk vigorously to cool. Spoon into cups or stemmed glasses and serve immediately.

ABOUT GELATIN DESSERTS

Gelatin dishes will develop a grainy, rubbery skin and may refuse to set unless the gelatin is handled in two distinct steps. First, soak the gelatin in a small amount of *cold* liquid for at least 5 minutes to allow the granules to soften and swell; then dissolve the gelatin completely in *hot* liquid. If the mixture is transparent, you can tell if the gelatin has dissolved simply by dipping in a metal spoon and allowing the liquid to run off: The glaze on the spoon will be completely clear, without any sign of beading. In the case of an opaque mixture, stir until the spoon or spatula seems to slip and slide over the bottom of the bowl or pot. As long as the gelatin is fully softened and your liquid is steaming hot, the gelatin is virtually guaranteed to melt after 30 seconds of gentle stirring.

Assuming that the gelatin has been adequately dissolved, a gelatin that either fails to solidify or has an overly stiff, rubbery consistency is likely to be caused by inaccurate measuring, usually of the gelatin. Many recipes require a quantity that is either something more or less than a single premeasured envelope of unflavored gelatin, which contains approximately 2¼ teaspoons. Be certain that your measuring spoons are scrupulously leveled with a straight edge, or you will throw off the results. Many older recipes call for 1 tablespoon of gelatin when what they actually mean is a single 2¼-teaspoon envelope; this, inevitably, leads some cooks to measure out one-third more gelatin than the recipe requires. An envelope of gelatin has the capacity to thicken approximately 2 cups liquid. There are, of course, some variables. If, for example, the liquid has some inherent body—as in the case of milk or cream—an envelope will jell somewhat more than 2 cups. If the liquid is highly sweetened, a bit more gelatin than usual may be required, for sugar interferes with gelatin's setting properties. Terrines and other gelatin dishes meant to be stiff enough to slice may need two to three times as much gelatin as is customary, especially if they contain finely pureed fruits or vegetables—which, contrary to what it might seem, tend to interrupt the network of gelatin bonds. Finally, mixtures made with whipped cream or beaten egg whites often contain significantly less than one envelope of gelatin to 2 cups of liquid, for beating partially solidifies the cream or egg whites.

Gelatins studded with suspended fruits never fail to delight. The trick to making these is to chill the gelatin just to the point where it acquires enough body to float the fruit without, of course, making it set solid. If you are not in a hurry, simply place the gelatin in the refrigerator and check it periodically. To thicken the gelatin quickly, set the bowl in water and ice and begin to stir at the first sign of congealing. Generally speaking, gelatin is thick enough to hold solids when it has reached the consistency of raw egg white; at this point, it will fall from a spoon in sheets. All is not lost if you inadvertently let the gelatin set solid. Simply melt it over gently simmering water and start again. (Commercial gelatin, like the cat with nine lives, can be melted and reset nine times before its thickening capacities begin to break down.) One word of warning: Certain tropical fruits, such as pineapple, kiwi fruit, and papaya, contain an enzyme that prevents gelatin from setting. If you want to use these fruits, you must poach them first in a sugar syrup until they are completely tender. Canned pineapple, which is precooked, does not pose a problem, nor does raw mango, which does not contain the enzyme.

Gelatins usually become firm within 3 to 4 hours of refrigeration. Small gelatins set in simple molds may be turned out onto a plate at this point. However, large gelatins made in tall or complex molds, as well as all gelatin terrines, should be refrigerated for at least 8 hours and preferably up to 1 day to allow the gelatin to stiffen more completely. (Gelatin continues to set over a 24-hour period.) To loosen a gelatin from its mold, dip the mold into a sink filled with very hot tap water. Metal molds should be dipped for no longer than a couple of seconds, or the surface of the gelatin will melt, but thick molds of glass or ceramic may need to be warmed for as long as 10 seconds before they will release. Invert the gelatin onto a plate and marvel at its majesty.

RASPBERRY TEA GELATIN
4 to 6 servings

English breakfast tea makes a uniquely refreshing gelatin, welcome on a hot day.

In a medium bowl, gently whisk together until no longer granular:

One 3-ounce package raspberry-flavored gelatin
2 cups scalding hot English breakfast tea

Refrigerate until the gelatin is as thick as raw egg white, 1 to 1½ hours. Fold in:

1 cup fresh raspberries

Rinse a 3- to 4-cup bowl or mold with cold water, then shake out the excess. Pour in the gelatin mixture and refrigerate until set, about 3 hours. Dip the bowl for a few seconds into very hot water, then invert onto a plate, or serve from the bowl.

CHERRY MARSHMALLOW NUT GELATIN
4 to 6 servings

Marshmallows, nuts, and pieces of fruit are traditional and much-loved additions to gelatin desserts.

In a medium bowl, gently whisk together until no longer granular:

One 3-ounce package cherry-flavored or other red gelatin
1 cup boiling water

Stir in:

1 cup club soda

Refrigerate until the gelatin is as thick as raw egg white, 1 to 1½ hours. Fold in:

⅔ cup halved pitted fresh cherries or canned sweet cherries, well drained and halved
3 tablespoons chopped natural (unblanched) almonds
½ cup miniature marshmallows

Rinse a 3- to 4-cup mold with water, then shake out the excess. Pour in the gelatin mixture and refrigerate until set, about 3 hours. Dip the mold for a few seconds into very hot water, then invert onto a plate. If you wish, serve with:

Whipped cream

STRAWBERRY GELATIN CREAM
8 servings

Combining gelatin and ice cream was in fashion in the 1950s. The idea may sound odd, but the dessert that results is surprisingly elegant.

In a medium bowl, gently whisk together until no longer granular:

One 6-ounce package strawberry-flavored gelatin
2 cups boiling water

Add and mix until smooth:

1 pint strawberry ice cream
¾ cup plus 2 tablespoons sour cream

Refrigerate until the mixture begins to thicken. Fold in:

1½ pints hulled strawberries, chopped

Lightly oil a 9 x 5-inch (8-cup) loaf pan or other mold, then line snugly with plastic wrap. Pour in the strawberry mixture and refrigerate until completely set, about 3 hours. Invert onto a plate, peel off the plastic, and slice. If you wish, serve with:

Fresh Strawberry Sauce, 1048

PEACH GELATIN WHIP
6 servings

This dessert has a light and airy texture not unlike that of a mousse.

In a medium bowl, gently whisk together until no longer granular:

One 3-ounce package peach-flavored gelatin
1 cup boiling water

Stir in:

1 cup cold water

Refrigerate until the gelatin thickens slightly, 30 minutes to 1 hour. Lightly oil six 4-ounce custard cups, then line the bottoms with wax paper. Divide among the custard cups:

½ cup finely chopped peaches, fresh or canned

Beat on medium-high speed until soft peaks form:

½ cup cold heavy cream

2 teaspoons sugar

Gently whisk the gelatin until smooth, then fold in the cream. Pour into the cups and refrigerate until set, about 3 hours. Unmold by running a knife around the inside of each cup and inverting onto plates. Peel off the wax paper. If you wish, serve with:

Fresh Raspberry Sauce, 1048

STAINED GLASS GELATIN

8 to 12 servings

Among the most spectacular of all contemporary gelatin creations. Each serving resembles a pane of stained glass. If you mound this gelatin in a 10-inch crumb crust, you will have a stained-glass pie, plus enough extra filling for a separate small mold.

Prepare separately according to the package instructions:

One 3-ounce package lime-flavored gelatin

One 3-ounce package cherry-flavored gelatin

One 3-ounce package orange-flavored gelatin

Lightly oil three 8 x 8-inch pans. Turn the gelatins into the pans and refrigerate until firmly set. Cut the gelatins into ½-inch cubes, then return, still in the pans, to the refrigerator. In a large bowl, gently whisk together until no longer granular:

One 3-ounce package lemon-flavored gelatin

1 cup boiling water

Stir in:

½ cup cold water

Refrigerate until the gelatin just begins to set. Beat on medium-high speed until stiff:

1 cup cold heavy cream

Using a large rubber spatula, fold the cream into the lemon gelatin, then gently fold in the gelatin cubes. Turn at once into an oiled 13 x 9-inch baking pan and refrigerate until set, about 3 hours. If you wish, serve with:

Whipped cream

LAYERED CITRUS TERRINE

6 servings

This sophisticated gelatin dessert is molded in a loaf pan and served in slices. Vanilla, spices, and sweet wine add complexity. If you wish, replace the wine with orange or apple juice.

Place an 8½ x 4½-inch (6-cup) loaf pan or terrine in the freezer until needed. Working over a bowl and using a very sharp knife, remove both the skin and the white pith from:

5 navel oranges

2 pink grapefruits

Cut between the membranes to release the fruit sections. Pick out any seeds and drain the fruit in a sieve set over a bowl. Pour the juice into a measure, then add to make 2 cups exactly:

1 to 1⅓ cups orange or grapefruit juice

Pour into a small bowl:

⅓ cup cold water

Sprinkle over the top:

4½ teaspoons (2 envelopes) unflavored gelatin

Let stand for 5 minutes to soften. In a saucepan, combine the citrus juice with:

½ cup sugar

One 3-inch cinnamon stick

4 whole cloves

½ vanilla bean, split lengthwise (optional)

Slowly bring to a bare simmer over very low heat. Remove from the heat, add the gelatin, and stir for 1 minute to dissolve the gelatin thoroughly. Let stand for 30 minutes, then strain into a bowl and let cool to room temperature. Stir in:

¾ cup muscatel or other sweet white wine

1 teaspoon vanilla if not using the bean

Pour about one-quarter of the gelatin mixture into the frozen pan and refrigerate until completely set. Arrange a row of grapefruit sections against one of the long sides of the pan, placing the sections lengthwise, that is, end to end. Next to this, leaving a space of about ¼ inch between the lanes, arrange a row of orange sections in the same manner. Repeat, alternating the fruits, until the layer is covered, using about half of the sections. Carefully spoon enough gelatin over the sections to cover them, then refrigerate until completely set. Now make another layer of citrus sections in the same manner but start this time with orange sections. Cover with gelatin and refrigerate until completely set. Spoon any remaining gelatin over the top. Cover the pan with plastic wrap and refrigerate for at least 12 hours or up to 3 days. Dip the pan for a few seconds into very hot water, then invert onto a plate. Slice with a sharp knife dipped in hot water. Serve with:

Custard Sauce, 1041

If you wish, garnish with:

Finely chopped fresh mint

BLANCMANGE

6 servings

The original blancmange (pronounced BLAH-MANGE), or "white food," of medieval times was a rich porridge of minced capon breast, finely ground almonds, and cream, typically thickened with rice flour or breadcrumbs and seasoned with sugar and rose water. In seventeenth-century England, this elegant court dish began to evolve into a molded gelatin dessert based on almond milk, an infusion made by steeping ground almonds in milk or water. Gelatin blancmange became very popular in colonial America, and by the early nineteenth century numerous variations had developed. Most of these involved plain milk or cream rather than almond milk, and eventually the gelatin, too, was replaced by cornstarch, which had appeared on the market in the 1840s. As a result, in the United States blancmange, became simply a fancy name for vanilla cornstarch pudding, a meaning that it retained until the 1970s, when, after a run of nearly a thousand years, the term vanished. We give here a traditional blancmange made from almond milk and gelatin. This is an elegant pudding, silky in texture, delicate in taste, and white and translucent like fine bone china. Serve it with raspberries or peaches as a graceful ending to a rich meal, decorated, if you fancy, in the colonial fashion with tiny fresh violets or other edible flowers, 973.

Process in a food processor to tiny, moist clumps (about 3 minutes):

1 cup slivered blanched almonds

¼ cup sugar

With the machine running, slowly pour through the feed tube:

1¼ cups boiling water

Scrape down the sides of the work bowl and process for 30 seconds longer. Let steep for 3 minutes. Rinse a heavy cotton or linen napkin in hot water and wring as dry as possible. Set a sieve over a bowl, line the sieve with the napkin, and pour in the almond mixture. Let the almond milk drip through for 30 minutes, then carefully gather up the ends of the napkin and wring as much of the liquid out of the almonds as you can before discarding the debris. Pour the almond milk into a measure and add to make exactly 2 cups liquid:

About 1 cup whole milk

Turn into a bowl. Stir together in a small heatproof cup:

¼ cup heavy cream

2¼ teaspoons (1 envelope) unflavored gelatin

Let stand for 5 minutes to soften. Meanwhile, lightly oil six 4- to 6-ounce cups or molds. Set the cup with the gelatin in a skillet filled with nearly simmering water over low heat and stir gently until the mixture is thick and foamy, indicating that the gelatin has dissolved, about 3 minutes. Thoroughly stir the gelatin mixture into the almond milk. Stir in:

4 drops almond extract

4 drops rose water (optional)

Divide the blancmange among the prepared cups. Refrigerate until firm, about 4 hours. If not serving at once, press plastic wrap directly onto the surface and refrigerate for up to 3 days. Unmold onto plates and serve with:

Fresh raspberries and/or sliced fresh peaches

PANNA COTTA

6 servings

Like blancmange, to which, historically speaking, it is related, panna cotta, or "cooked cream," is a smooth, slithery gelatin cream, cool and light on the tongue, though not light in calories. This Italian dessert is not as magisterial as blancmange, but it is much less work to produce. Mold panna cotta in small ramekins or custard cups, then serve it turned out with a fruit sauce, fresh fruit, or both.

Lightly oil six 4- to 6-ounce cups or molds.

Pour into a small bowl:

3 tablespoons water

Sprinkle over the top:

2¼ teaspoons (1 envelope) unflavored gelatin

Let stand for 5 minutes to soften. Combine in a saucepan:

1½ cups heavy cream

1 cup whole milk

½ cup sugar

1 vanilla bean, split lengthwise (optional)

Stirring, bring to a boil over medium high heat. Remove from the heat and extract the vanilla bean. Add the gelatin and stir for 1 minute until completely dissolved. Stir in:

1 teaspoon vanilla if not using the vanilla bean

½ teaspoon almond extract (optional)

Pour the mixture into the prepared cups and refrigerate until firmly set, about 3 hours. Press plastic wrap directly onto the surface of each cream and refrigerate for up to 3 days. Unmold onto plates and serve with:

A fresh fruit sauce and/or sliced fresh fruit

DESSERT SAUCES

Never make a dessert sauce simply to dress up a plate. Choose one that will deepen and intensify the experience of the dessert. One way to do this is to create a provocative but pleasing contrast between dessert and sauce. For example, try pairing mousse, custard, ice cream, or any other sweet, creamy dessert with a tart fruit sauce or a subtly bitter chocolate or dark caramel sauce. With a light fruit dessert or gelatin, consider a rich and creamy but light-tasting sauce, such as whipped cream or sabayon. Cakes, bread puddings, baked puddings, and other desserts that are firm and dry take well to sauces that will soak in, such as custard sauces and hot butter-and-egg sauces. You need not, however, always strive for contrast. A rich chocolate bread pudding or chocolate cake is divine with an equally rich caramel, white chocolate, or southern whiskey sauce. And plum pudding, perhaps the richest dessert of all, is always accompanied with the butteriest of sauces, such as hard sauce, hot wine sauce, or hot foamy sauce.

Dessert sauces are indulgences, not health foods. Rather than skimping on butter, cream, and eggs, forgo rich sauces when you are watching calories.

ABOUT WHIPPED CREAM TOPPINGS

Please read About Whipped Cream, 995. Delicious with fruit, puddings, cakes, pies, ice creams, and so much more, nothing is easier to make or more universally loved than simple whipped cream.

SOUR CREAM WHIPPED TOPPING

About 2⅔ cups; 8 to 12 servings

A tangy topping that is lovely with a warm apple or pear tart.

Combine in a medium bowl:

1 cup cold heavy cream

½ cup cold sour cream

Beat on high speed until soft but definite peaks form. Do not attempt to whip until stiff. Use at once, or cover and refrigerate for up to 1 day.

ABOUT CUSTARD SAUCE (CRÈME ANGLAISE)

Although made from the same basic ingredients as flan, crème brûlée, and other dessert custards, custard sauce has a very different consistency. This is because the sauce is prepared on top of the stove and must be stirred constantly in order to prevent curdling at the bottom of the pan. The stirring disrupts the bonding of the eggs, resulting in a liquid rather than semisolid custard. The French call custard sauce *crème anglaise*, or English custard, a term that many American chefs have now appropriated.

The key thing is that custard sauce must be heated to

at least 160°F in order to thicken—but not past 170°F (or a few degrees more if made in part with cream) or it will curdle. (The boiling point is 212°F.) Use a heavy pan that will diffuse the heat evenly. Stir with a heatproof rubber spatula or a wooden spoon, both of which are more efficient than metal spoons at reaching all parts of the pan. Your heat must be low, preferably very low. The slower the custard heats, the thicker it will become and the less chance you will accidentally overshoot the curdle point. Finally, stir constantly but *gently* as the sauce heats, sweeping the entire pan bottom and reaching into the corners of the pan. Hard stirring damages the egg bonds and yields a runny sauce.

One of the first signs that the sauce is about to thicken is the dissipation of the foam on top. Next, you will feel a certain slipperiness beneath your spatula or spoon. Suddenly, the sauce will acquire body and a slight sheen. At this point, you should take the sauce off the burner and let the heat of the pan complete the cooking. Continue to stir the sauce off the heat for 2 minutes, or until it becomes thick enough to coat the spatula or spoon lightly if made with milk alone and fairly heavily if made in part with cream. You can return the sauce to the heat if it remains too thin; but remember that the sauce will be much thicker if served cold. If the sauce becomes grainy and dull as you stir, signs that it has begun to overheat, pour it through a fine-mesh sieve at once to arrest cooking. A slightly overcooked sauce will still be delicious, if a bit lacking in smoothness and finesse. Whirring it in a blender will partially restore its creaminess.

CUSTARD SAUCE (CRÈME ANGLAISE)

About 2 cups; 6 to 10 servings

A custard sauce can always be made with milk alone, but do consider enriching the sauce with cream when it is to accompany poached fruit or a gelatin dessert.

Whisk together in a medium bowl until slightly thickened:

6 large egg yolks
⅓ to ½ cup sugar

Pour into a medium, heavy saucepan:

2 cups whole milk, 1 cup whole milk and 1 cup light or heavy cream, or 2 cups half-and-half

Cook, stirring, over medium heat until bubbles form around the edges. Slowly whisk the hot milk into the egg yolks and sugar. Return this mixture to the saucepan. Rinse out and dry the mixing bowl, then set a fine-mesh sieve over the top. Place the saucepan over low heat. Using a heatproof rubber spatula or a wooden spoon, stir the sauce gently but constantly, sweeping the entire pan bottom and reaching into the corners. As soon as the sauce is slightly thickened, remove the pan from the heat and stir gently for 2 minutes to complete the cooking. The sauce should be the consistency of heavy cream and register around 170°F on an instant-read thermometer. Pour the sauce through the sieve and let cool for 10 minutes, stirring periodically to prevent a skin from forming. Stir in:

2 teaspoons vanilla

Serve warm or cold. If chilling, let the sauce become completely cold before covering, as condensation will cause it to thin. The sauce can be covered and refrigerated for up to 3 days. To reheat, set the container of sauce in water heated to 165°F and stir until warmed through.

CHOCOLATE CUSTARD SAUCE

About 2½ cups; 8 to 12 servings

Like thick, rich hot chocolate. Perfect with plain custards, fresh fruit, and angel or sponge cake, which would be overwhelmed by plain chocolate sauce.

Prepare Custard Sauce (Crème Anglaise), above, decreasing the vanilla to 1 teaspoon. Immediately after straining, add 4 ounces finely chopped semisweet or bittersweet chocolate. Wait a moment for the chocolate to melt, then gently whisk until smooth. If the slight froth bothers you, strain the sauce again.

COFFEE CUSTARD SAUCE

Prepare Custard Sauce (Crème Anglaise), above, using 1 cup strong coffee and 1 cup light or heavy cream. Decrease the vanilla to 1 teaspoon and add, if you wish, 1 to 2 tablespoons coffee liqueur.

VANILLA BEAN CUSTARD SAUCE

This is a special custard sauce with a deep, rich flavor.

Before preparing Custard Sauce (Crème Anglaise), above, cut 1 vanilla bean in half lengthwise. Scrape out the seeds and add along with the pod halves to the 2 cups milk or cream called for in the recipe. Bring to a simmer, then remove from the heat, cover, and let stand for 15 minutes. Rewarm the milk, then proceed with the recipe, straining out the seeds and pod halves at the end. Decrease the vanilla to 1 teaspoon.

ABOUT HARD SAUCE

In our childhood, hard sauce was, as the name implies, a hard cake of butter and sugar that could be cut with a knife. Today, however, most cooks prefer to whip hard sauce into a light, fluffy cream with a texture like that of a buttercream frosting. Modern hard sauce is a mixture of powdered sugar, butter, and spirits, usually brandy or dark rum. Those who wish to avoid alcohol can flavor the sauce with orange juice instead with excellent results.

HARD SAUCE

About 2½ cups; 16 servings

The classic accompaniment to plum pudding. When spooned onto the hot pudding, part of the sauce melts, bathing the plump fruits in a warm, buttery glaze, while the rest remains a delightfully cool and creamy froth, like whipped cream.

Combine in large bowl:

½ pound (2 sticks) unsalted butter, softened but cool
3 cups powdered sugar, sifted if lumpy
2 teaspoons vanilla
½ teaspoon freshly grated or ground nutmeg

Beat on high speed until light and fluffy but still thick enough to hold a firm shape, 6 to 10 minutes. Still beating, very slowly add:

¼ cup brandy, Cognac, dark rum, or fresh orange juice

Especially if you have opted for a nonalcoholic sauce, you may also wish to add:

Grated zest of 1 orange

Use at once or cover tightly and refrigerate for up to 3 days. Soften the cold sauce at room temperature until spreadable before transferring it to a serving bowl, or else it may deflate and thin out.

ABOUT HOT BUTTER-AND-EGG SAUCES

Brought from England by the first colonists, these buttery liquid custards were America's original hot dessert sauces. The sauces in this immense family are actually custards, but because their main ingredients are sugar and butter rather than milk or cream, they are translucent and syrupy rather than creamy. Since sugar and butter inhibit the binding properties of eggs, most, but not all, of these sauces can be boiled without curdling; indeed, most of them *must* be boiled in order to thicken properly. When made ahead and reheated, these sauces often separate or become slightly sugary. These problems are easily remedied by removing the sauce from the heat and whisking in a little warm water.

SOUTHERN WHISKEY SAUCE

About 1⅔ cups; 8 to 12 servings

This sauce is sumptuous spooned over plain or chocolate bread puddings, apple puddings, or any cake made with fruits or nuts. For a milder sauce, replace up to half of the spirits with water; for a very potent sauce, replace the water with additional spirits.

Melt over low heat in a small, heavy saucepan:

8 tablespoons (1 stick) unsalted butter

Stir in, using a heatproof rubber spatula or wooden spoon:

1 cup sugar
¼ cup bourbon or other whiskey
2 tablespoons water
¼ teaspoon freshly grated or ground nutmeg
⅛ teaspoon salt

Cook, stirring, until the sugar is dissolved and the mixture is blended. Remove from the heat. Whisk until light and frothy:

1 large egg

Vigorously whisk the egg into the liquor mixture. Set the sauce over medium heat and, stirring gently, bring to a simmer. Cook until thickened, about 1 minute. The sauce will not curdle. Serve at once, set aside at room temperature for up to 8 hours, or let cool then cover and refrigerate for up to 3 days. Reheat over low heat, stirring; if the sauce separates, remove from the heat and whisk in a little warm water.

HOT BRANDY SAUCE

Thanksgiving will never be the same once you try this on pumpkin pie.

Prepare Southern Whiskey Sauce, above, substituting brandy or Cognac for the bourbon.

HOT BROWN SUGAR SAUCE

A very nice nonalcoholic alternative to traditional whiskey sauce.

Prepare Southern Whiskey Sauce, above, substituting 1 cup packed light brown sugar for the sugar, omitting the bourbon, and increasing the water to ⅓ cup. When the sauce is done, remove from the heat and stir in 1 tablespoon vanilla.

HOT BUTTERED MAPLE SAUCE

About 1⅓ cups; 6 to 8 servings

When drenched with this sauce and then topped with vanilla ice cream, waffles become a showpiece.

Combine in a medium, heavy saucepan:

1 cup pure maple syrup
⅓ cup sugar

Stirring constantly with a wooden spoon, bring to a boil and cook until the last drop of sauce that falls from the spoon spins a short, wispy thread. This will take about 3 minutes. Remove from the heat and add:

6 tablespoons (¾ stick) unsalted butter, cut into pieces
2 tablespoons water
⅛ teaspoon salt

Stir briskly until the butter is melted and the sauce is thick and creamy. Whisk in a bowl until light and frothy:

1 large egg

Slowly whisk the hot maple mixture into the egg. Rinse out the saucepan, dissolving any sugar crystals, then dry the pan thoroughly. Return the sauce to the pan and cook, stirring constantly, over medium heat until the sauce comes to a simmer and is thickened. Serve at once, or let cool then cover and refrigerate for up to 3 days. Reheat over low heat, stirring; if the sauce separates, remove from the heat and whisk in a little hot water.

ORANGE LIQUEUR SAUCE

About 1½ cups; 6 to 10 servings

Lovely with any chocolate or orange dessert, especially soufflés.

Combine in a small, heavy saucepan:

⅔ cup sugar
⅓ cup orange liqueur
⅓ cup heavy cream

Whisk in until thoroughly blended:

3 large egg yolks

Add:

8 tablespoons (1 stick) unsalted butter, cut into pieces

Set over low heat. Stirring constantly but gently with a heatproof rubber spatula or wooden spoon, cook the sauce until thick enough to coat the spatula. Do not let the sauce simmer. Strain the sauce through a fine-mesh sieve. Serve at once, or let cool then cover and refrigerate for up to 3 days. Reheat over low heat or over hot water.

RICH HOT LEMON SAUCE

About 1⅓ cups; 6 to 10 servings

Similar to lemon curd but thinner, more transparent, and slightly sweeter, this sauce is traditional with gingerbread, pound cake, and angel cake. It is also delicious with virtually any dessert containing apples, blueberries, peaches, bananas, or coconut.

Combine in a small, heavy saucepan:

⅔ cup sugar
¼ cup strained fresh lemon juice
Grated zest of 1 lemon
2 tablespoons water

Whisk in until thoroughly blended:

3 large egg yolks

Add:

8 tablespoons (1 stick) unsalted butter, cut into pieces

Set over low heat. Stirring constantly but gently with a heatproof rubber spatula or wooden spoon, bring the sauce to a simmer and cook until thickened, about 1 minute. Strain through a fine-mesh sieve. Serve at once, or let cool then cover and refrigerate for up to 3 days. Reheat over low heat or over hot water.

RICH HOT LIME SAUCE

Especially good with banana or coconut desserts.

Prepare Rich Hot Lemon Sauce, above, substituting lime juice and zest for the lemon.

REDUCED-FAT CLEAR LEMON SAUCE

About 1½ cups; 6 to 8 servings

This is a pleasant low-fat alternative to Rich Hot Lemon Sauce, above. Use it in the same ways you would the richer sauce.

Combine in a small, heavy saucepan:

½ cup sugar
1 tablespoon cornstarch

Stir thoroughly, breaking up any lumps in the cornstarch. Stir in until well blended:

1 cup water or unsweetened apple juice
¼ cup strained fresh lemon juice
Grated zest of 1 lemon
Pinch of salt

Stirring constantly with a heatproof rubber spatula or wooden spoon, bring the sauce to a boil and cook until thickened. Stir in, if you wish:

1 to 2 tablespoons unsalted butter, cut into pieces

Serve the sauce at once, or let cool then cover and refrigerate for up to 1 week. Reheat over low heat, stirring.

REDUCED-FAT CLEAR LIME SAUCE

Prepare Reduced-Fat Clear Lemon Sauce, above, using water (not apple juice) and substituting lime juice and zest for the lemon.

ABOUT FOAMY SAUCES

In our grandmothers's day, foamy sauces were the most fashionable of all accompaniments for hot puddings. It is a pity they are so rarely seen today. As the name promises, these sauces are thick foams that melt into froths of fizzy bubbles when spooned onto hot desserts. Hot foamy sauces are hard sauces that are made with eggs and then whipped in boiling water until they thicken and foam. Dramatic and delicious, they are a bit nerve-racking for the cook, since they must be dispatched at the last possible minute. Cold foamy sauces are thick custards made frothy by the addition of whipped cream or a meringue. Though somewhat less special than their hot counterparts, they taste much the same and are more convenient, since they can be prepared several days ahead.

HOT FOAMY SAUCE

About 3½ cups; 12 to 16 servings

A very dressy accompaniment to Persimmon Buttermilk Pudding, 1025, Plum Pudding, 1026, or any bread pudding. Quantities can easily be halved.

Combine in a heatproof bowl, preferably metal:

12 tablespoons (1½ sticks) unsalted butter, softened
2½ cups powdered sugar
½ teaspoon freshly grated or ground nutmeg
½ teaspoon salt

Beat on medium-high speed until light and fluffy, 5 to 10 minutes. Whisk together thoroughly, preferably in a measuring cup with a pour spout:

2 large eggs, at room temperature
¼ cup brandy or Cognac

With the mixer running, pour the egg mixture into the butter mixture in a slow, steady stream. At this point, you may cover the mixture and set aside at room temperature for up to 3 hours or refrigerate for up to 3 days. Bring to room temperature before finishing the recipe. Set the bowl in a large pot and pour in enough water to come up to the level of the sauce in the bowl (*not* the top of the bowl). Bring the water to a boil. Whisk into the sauce:

¼ cup boiling water

Whisking constantly or beating on medium speed, heat the sauce until it reaches a temperature of 160°F and thickens into a light foam. Serve immediately.

COLD FOAMY SAUCE

About 3 cups; 12 to 16 servings

Delectable with Steamed Chocolate Pudding, 1019, Chocolate Bread Pudding, 1023, or warm chocolate cake. The recipe can be halved.

Whisk together thoroughly in a heatproof bowl, preferably metal:

2 large eggs
1 cup sugar

Pour 1 inch of water into a skillet and bring to a bare simmer. Set the bowl with the egg mixture in the water and, whisking constantly, heat until the mixture is thick and puffy and has reached a temperature of 160°F. Remove from the heat and add:

3 to 4 tablespoons brandy, Cognac, or dark rum
1 teaspoon vanilla

Beat on high speed until the bottom of the bowl no longer feels warm. In a separate bowl, beat on medium-high speed until stiff peaks form:

1 cup cold heavy cream

Gently fold the cream into the egg mixture with a rubber spatula. Use at once, or cover and refrigerate for up to 3 days. The sauce will separate slightly upon standing; gently fold to recombine.

ABOUT SABAYON SAUCES

The cooking of these light, delectable egg foams is discussed on page 1036. Zabaglione, an Italian dessert that is the mother of the sabayon sauce family, is always served freshly made and hot. Sabayon sauces, however, may be prepared ahead and served at room temperature or, if they contain whipped cream, cold. If you wish to prepare a sabayon ahead, stand the sauce in ice water immediately after cooking and whisk gently until it has cooled to room temperature. Otherwise, it will deflate. A sabayon will also deflate if stirred or otherwise disturbed when ice cold, so be sure to bring a refrigerated sabayon to room temperature before pouring it into a sauceboat or spreading it on fruit for a gratin. Hot sabayons are not really reheatable. However, once the sauce has reached room temperature, it can be set in a bowl of lukewarm tap water for 10 minutes to warm slightly.

SABAYON WITH WHITE WINE

About 2 cups; 6 to 8 servings

This is usually served over fruit or cake or used in the making of a fruit gratin.

In the top of a double boiler, whisk together vigorously until thick and pale yellow:

4 large egg yolks
¼ cup sugar

Whisking constantly, slowly add:

½ cup fruity white wine, such as Chardonnay or Riesling

Scrape clean the sides of the double boiler with a rubber spatula, then set over very gently simmering water. Whisking constantly, heat the sabayon to a temperature of 160°F, at which point it will have increased several times in volume and become thick enough to mound very softly on a spoon. The cooking should take 5 to 10 minutes. If the sabayon appears to be heating more quickly than this, periodically remove it from the water and whisk vigorously to cool. Serve at once, hot, or set the double boiler in ice water and gently whisk the sauce until cool to the touch. Cover and refrigerate for up to 1 day. Let the chilled sauce stand at room temperature for at least 2 hours before pouring it into a sauceboat or spreading on a fruit gratin. To warm slightly, set the sauce in lukewarm tap water for 10 minutes.

LEMON SABAYON *About 2 cups; 6 to 8 servings*

Grand on a lemon soufflé, especially when freshly made and spooned on piping hot. Also good on warm gingerbread and pound cake.

In the top of a double boiler, whisk together vigorously until slightly thickened:

2 large eggs

2 large egg yolks

⅓ cup plus 1 tablespoon sugar

Whisking constantly, slowly add:

¼ cup water

3 tablespoons strained fresh lemon juice

Whisk in:

Grated zest of 1 lemon

Cook and serve as for Sabayon with White Wine, 1044.

ABOUT CHOCOLATE SAUCES

Whether made with dark, milk, or white chocolate, most contemporary chocolate sauces are part of the family known as ganache, which means that their basic ingredients are simply chocolate and cream. The notable exception is hot fudge sauce, which is actually a sugar syrup with chocolate added that becomes delightfully chewy when spooned over ice cream. Chocolate sauces require the finest chocolate—deep and rich in flavor and, above all, absolutely smooth on the tongue, with no gritty or powdery residue. There is no need to resort to expensive European brands: many fine chocolates are now produced in the United States.

CHOCOLATE SAUCE *About 1 cup; 5 to 8 servings*

Simple to make but rich in taste. To make this sauce in a food processor, grind the chocolate to crumbs and then, with the motor running, add the simmering cream mixture. By the time the last of the cream has gone in, the sauce will be melted and smooth.

Combine in a medium, heavy saucepan:

½ cup light cream, or ¼ cup heavy cream and ¼ cup whole milk

1 to 2 tablespoons sugar

1 tablespoon unsalted butter

Stirring constantly, bring to a rolling boil. Remove the pan from the heat and immediately add:

4 ounces semisweet or bittersweet chocolate, finely chopped

Let stand for 1 minute, then whisk until smooth. Whisk in:

1 teaspoon vanilla, or 1 tablespoon dark rum or Cognac

Serve warm or cold; thin cold sauce with water as needed. The sauce can be covered and refrigerated for up to 2 weeks. Reheat over low heat, whisking in, off the heat, a little hot water if the sauce looks oily.

HOT FUDGE SAUCE *About 2½ cups; 8 to 10 servings*

This is the kind of hot fudge sauce that becomes firm and sticky-chewy when ribboned over ice cream. Vanilla ice cream is the classic vehicle for this sauce, but peppermint, coffee, strawberry, and chocolate ice cream are delicious too. Be sure that your ice cream is frozen hard.

Whisk together in a large, heavy saucepan, until blended:

½ cup sugar

¼ cup unsweetened cocoa

¼ teaspoon salt

Whisk in until well blended:

½ cup water

Bring to a simmer over medium-high heat. Remove the pan from the heat and whisk in:

1 cup heavy cream

1 cup light corn syrup

¼ teaspoon white vinegar

2 ounces semisweet or bittersweet chocolate, coarsely chopped

Return to medium-high heat and, whisking frequently, boil until the bubbles become small and the syrup is thick and sticky, about 225°F on a candy thermometer. This will take 5 to 8 minutes. Remove from the heat and add:

2 ounces semisweet or bittersweet chocolate, finely chopped

4 tablespoons (½ stick) unsalted butter, softened

1 tablespoon vanilla

Whisk until smooth. Serve at once, or let cool then cover and refrigerate for up to 2 weeks. Reheat in a heavy saucepan over low heat.

WARM DARK MOCHA SAUCE

About 1½ cups; 8 to 12 servings

The deepest, darkest mocha sauce we know. Wonderful with any chocolate mousse.

Combine in a small, heavy saucepan:

¾ cup freshly brewed espresso or strong coffee
3 tablespoons sugar

Cook, stirring, over very low heat until the sugar is dissolved and the mixture is steaming hot. Add:

8 ounces semisweet or bittersweet chocolate, finely chopped

Whisk until the chocolate is just melted and the mixture is smooth. Remove from the heat and whisk in:

2 tablespoons unsalted butter, softened

Serve at once or let cool, then cover and refrigerate for up to 2 weeks. Reheat over low heat, adding a little warm water if the sauce becomes oily.

WARM WHITE CHOCOLATE SAUCE

About 1½ cups; 8 to 12 servings

This falls from a spoon in satiny ribbons. Sublime with chocolate bread pudding. White chocolate will turn into a solid, grainy mass if overheated, so monitor the temperature of the water bath carefully.

Place a skillet of water over low heat and heat just until the water is hot enough to steam, about 145°F. You should be able to hold a finger in the water for 2 seconds without discomfort. Combine in a heatproof bowl:

9 ounces white chocolate, coarsely chopped or broken into small pieces
6 tablespoons (¾ stick) unsalted butter, cut into pieces
⅓ cup heavy cream

Set the bowl in the water bath and stir until the chocolate is melted. Remove from the heat and stir vigorously until smooth. Serve at once or cover and refrigerate for up to 2 weeks. Reheat by setting the sauce in hot water, as above, and stirring until thin.

WARM MILK CHOCOLATE SAUCE

Prepare Warm White Chocolate Sauce, above, substituting milk chocolate for the white chocolate.

ABOUT CARAMEL AND BUTTERSCOTCH SAUCES

Caramel is simply sugar cooked to the point where it melts and then begins to burn. Old cookbooks refer to it, appropriately enough, as burnt sugar. Butterscotch is similar, except that butter is added to the sugar as it caramelizes, resulting in the characteristic nutty taste. To convert caramel and butterscotch into sauces, a mixture of butter and cream, water, or some other liquid is added while the syrup is still hot. Otherwise, the syrup, once cooled, will become a hard candy.

Many professional chefs make caramel by stirring dry sugar in a pot over a flame. Home cooks, however, find the process easier when the sugar is first mixed with water. It is crucial that the sugar be fully dissolved before the syrup is allowed to boil: otherwise, the sugar may recrystallize once it reaches 238°F, leaving the cook with a white rock in the pan. (Actually, if the cook breaks the rock up with a spoon and continues cooking, caramel will eventually ensue, but we understand how unnerving a rock can be.) As the syrup approaches the caramelization point, the bubbles in the saucepan will become smaller and quieter. Then, around the edges of the pan, the first signs of darkening will appear. Begin swirling the pan by the handle to disperse the heated edges of the syrup toward the cooler center. Continue to cook the syrup until it becomes a deep amber color and begins to smoke, but stop before it becomes reddish or mahogany. If overcooked, the syrup will taste bitter and salty. Remove the syrup from the heat and immediately add butter and cream, water, or some other liquid to stop the cooking. Be prepared for the caramel to rear up into a sputtering, foaming mass. If adding water, as in the making of caramel syrup, stand back to prevent yourself from being spattered. Stir the sauce briskly to amalgamate it. If some of the caramel refuses to melt, set the pan over low heat and stir until the sauce smooths out.

CARAMEL SAUCE COCKAIGNE

About 1½ cups; 8 to 10 servings

One of the most luxurious versions of caramel sauce.

Place in a small, heavy saucepan:

1 cup sugar

Pour evenly over the top:

¼ cup water

Set over medium-high heat and swirl the saucepan gently by the handle until the sugar is dissolved and the syrup is clear. Avoid letting the syrup boil until the sugar is completely dissolved. Increase the heat to high, cover the saucepan tightly, and boil the syrup for 2 minutes. Uncover the saucepan and continue to boil the syrup until it begins to darken around the edges. Gently swirl the pan by the handle until the syrup turns a deep amber and begins to smoke. Remove from the heat and add:

8 tablespoons (1 stick) unsalted butter, cut into pieces

Gently beat until the butter is incorporated. Stir in:

½ cup heavy cream

If the sauce becomes lumpy, set the pan over low heat and stir until smooth. Turn off the heat and stir in:

2 teaspoons vanilla
Pinch of salt

Serve warm or at room temperature. The sauce can be covered and refrigerated for up to 1 month; it will become solid. Reheat in a double boiler or in a heavy saucepan over very low heat, adding a bit of water if it is too thick.

CHOCOLATE CARAMEL SAUCE

This would taste divine on old boot soles. When cold, it can be dipped into with a teaspoon and rolled in cocoa to make chocolate caramel truffles.

Prepare Caramel Sauce Cockaigne, above, using 4 tablespoons (½ stick) butter. Add 3 ounces finely chopped bittersweet or semisweet chocolate and stir until the chocolate is melted. Serve warm.

CARAMEL SYRUP

About 1 cup; 6 to 8 servings

The addition of water, instead of butter and cream, to hot caramel yields a thick syrup that is irresistible on ice cream, custard, or broiled, poached, or sautéed fruit.

Caramelize 1 cup sugar as directed for Caramel Sauce Cockaigne, above. Remove from the heat. Standing back, add ⅓ cup water, then stir until smooth. If the caramel remains lumpy, stir briefly over low heat. Serve at once or let cool, then cover and refrigerate for up to 6 months. Reheat over low heat, stirring in a little water if needed.

BUTTERSCOTCH SAUCE

About 1½ cups; 8 to 10 servings

The old-fashioned favorite, made with virtually the same ingredients as caramel sauce, only cooked in a different way.

Combine in a medium, heavy saucepan:

8 tablespoons (1 stick) unsalted butter
¼ cup water
2 tablespoons light corn syrup

Cook, stirring with a heatproof rubber spatula or a wooden spoon, over medium-low heat until the butter is melted. Add:

1 cup sugar

Continue to stir until all the gritty noises cease, indicating that the sugar is completely dissolved. Increase the heat to medium-high and, without stirring, boil the mixture until it begins to color around the edges, 4 to 8 minutes. Continue to stir this foamy, taffylike mass until it turns the color of a walnut shell and just begins to smoke. Remove from the heat and, standing well back to avoid being spattered, pour in:

½ cup heavy cream

Stir until smooth. If the sauce remains lumpy, stir briefly over low heat. Turn off the heat and stir in:

1 teaspoon vanilla
¼ teaspoon salt

Stir well to dissolve the salt. Serve at once, or let cool then cover and refrigerate for up to 1 month. Reheat the sauce in a double boiler or, if the container is heatproof, in a pan of simmering water.

ABOUT MARSHMALLOW SAUCE

The best kind of homemade marshmallow sauce is actually a meringue with melted marshmallows beaten in. It is softer and has more body than commercial marshmallow "creme" and is also less sweet.

MARSHMALLOW SAUCE

About 4 cups; 10 to 12 servings

Wonderful, of course, on a hot fudge sundae, but also delicious on sorbets, gelatin desserts, and chocolate cake.

Combine in a medium, heavy saucepan:

⅔ cup sugar
⅓ cup water

Stirring with a heatproof rubber spatula or a wooden spoon, bring to a rolling boil. Remove from the heat and immediately add:

20 large marshmallows

Stir gently until the marshmallows are melted. Stir in:

1 teaspoon vanilla

Cover tightly and set aside. Proceed at once to heat 1 inch of water in a large skillet over very low heat until it reaches 155° to 160°F; adjust the heat to maintain the water at this temperature. Dissolve in a heatproof bowl:

3 tablespoons water
¼ teaspoon cream of tartar

Whisk in thoroughly:

3 large egg whites
⅓ cup sugar

Set the bowl in the water bath and, whisking frequently, heat the mixture to 140°F. This will take 3 to 6 minutes if using a metal bowl, 8 to 10 minutes if using a heavy glass or ceramic bowl. Whisking gently, maintain the mixture between 140° and 155°F for 5 minutes. Beat the egg white mixture on high speed until the bottom of the bowl no longer feels warm, 4 to 8 minutes. Add the marshmallow mixture and beat for 30 seconds more. Use at once, or cover tightly and refrigerate for up to 2 weeks.

ABOUT UNCOOKED FRUIT SAUCES (COULIS)

Strained purees of uncooked berries and other fruits are often called today by the French name *coulis,* which means strained juice. Whatever their name, these are lovely sauces, fresh in flavor and vivid in color. They are also very easy to make. Frozen fruit works as well as fresh, but be sure to use so-called dry-pack frozen fruit, which usually comes in a plastic bag, not fruit that has been prepared with a syrup. For an elegant, restaurant-style presentation, prepare two or more fresh fruit sauces in contrasting colors and spoon them in a decorative pattern onto large white plates.

FRESH RASPBERRY SAUCE (RASPBERRY COULIS)

About 1 cup; 6 to 8 servings

The straining of fresh raspberry sauce requires some patience. Use a flexible rubber spatula to push the pulp through a sieve. Press firmly and periodically scrape the inside of the sieve clear of seeds, which will otherwise plug up the holes. Do not waste the precious pulp. Continue to press until you are left with just a heaping tablespoon of stiff, clumped-together seeds.

Puree in a blender or food processor:

1 pint raspberries, or 12 ounces frozen dry-pack raspberries, thawed
3 tablespoons sugar
2 teaspoons strained fresh lemon juice

Strain through a fine-mesh sieve, pressing firmly with a rubber spatula. Taste, then stir in a little more sugar or lemon juice if needed. Serve at once, either at room temperature or chilled, or cover and refrigerate for up to 3 days.

FRESH STRAWBERRY SAUCE (STRAWBERRY COULIS)

About 1½ cups; 6 to 12 servings

If using pale, underripe berries, you may find, after tasting, that the sugar and lemon juice need to be doubled.

Puree in a blender or food processor:

1 pint strawberries, or 12 ounces frozen dry-pack strawberries, thawed
3 tablespoons sugar
1 tablespoon strained fresh lemon juice

Do not strain. Taste, then stir in more sugar or lemon juice if needed. Serve at once, either at room temperature or chilled, or cover and refrigerate for up to 3 days.

FRESH BLUEBERRY SAUCE (BLUEBERRY COULIS)

About 1¼ cups; 6 to 10 servings

Because blueberries are high in pectin, a jelling agent, this sauce will thicken upon standing. Whisk and thin, if necessary, with water.

Puree in a blender or food processor:

1 pint blueberries, or 12 ounces dry-pack blueberries, thawed
3 tablespoons sugar
1 tablespoon strained fresh lemon juice

Strain through a fine-mesh sieve, pressing firmly with a rubber spatula. Taste, then stir in a little more sugar or lemon juice if needed. Serve at once, either at room temperature or chilled, or cover and refrigerate for up to 3 days.

FRESH MANGO SAUCE (MANGO COULIS)

About 1¼ cups; 6 to 10 servings

An unusual sauce with a tropical accent. Especially nice with banana and coconut desserts.

Have ready:

1 large soft but not mushy mango

Stand the mango on a narrow side and slice the flesh free from either side of the pit. Using a paring knife, score the flesh of each half down to the skin in ½-inch cubes. Push the skin inside out, popping up the mango dice and forming a mango "porcupine," then slice the flesh away from the skin. Peel the band of skin around the pit, then slice the flesh free and cut into chunks. Combine the mango in a blender or food processor with:

2 tablespoons sugar
2 tablespoons water
1 tablespoon strained fresh lime or lemon juice

Puree until smooth. If the sauce is too thick, thin with a bit more water; if not sweet enough, add a little more sugar. Serve at once, or cover and refrigerate for up to 3 days.

FRESH KIWI SAUCE (KIWI COULIS)

About 1 cup; 6 to 10 servings

Be careful not to blend the kiwi fruits too much when you puree the fruit, or the seeds will break up and turn the sauce brown. You can strain out the seeds, but we prefer a speckled look. For a luscious kiwi fool, spoon alternating layers of this sauce and sweetened whipped cream into four stemmed glasses.

Puree in a blender or food processor:

4 medium kiwi fruits, ends cut out, peeled and cut into 1-inch pieces
2 tablespoons sugar
2 teaspoons strained fresh lemon juice

Serve at room temperature or chilled. This is best used the day it is made, as the color fades.

ABOUT COOKED FRUIT SAUCES

These sauces are thicker and, if made with butter, richer than the raw-fruit coulis; they are usually served hot. The sauces make good low-calorie alternatives to whipped cream or custard sauce on hot puddings and cakes.

CHERRIES JUBILEE *About 2 cups; 6 to 10 servings*

This becomes an event when prepared in a chafing dish at the dining room table. It may be served over vanilla or chocolate ice cream, dark or white chocolate mousse, or virtually any cake. In the South, it is traditional with charlotte russe.

Place in a medium bowl:

3 cups (1 pound) fresh sweet red cherries, such as Bing, or well-drained canned or bottled sweet cherries, halved and pitted

Sprinkle with:

1/3 to 1/2 cup kirsch or cherry cordial

Cover and let stand for at least 30 minutes, preferably 3 hours or more, stirring occasionally. In a chafing dish or heavy skillet set over medium-high heat, combine the cherries and:

3/4 cup sugar

3 tablespoons strained fresh lemon juice

Boil until the juices are red and syrupy, about 5 minutes. Add:

1/2 cup brandy

Standing back, ignite with a long lighted match. Let the flames die off, then continue to boil until a thick, syrupy sauce results. If using the sauce with a warm or room-temperature dessert, stir in until incorporated:

3 to 6 tablespoons unsalted butter

Boil until rethickened. Turn off the heat and stir in:

2 tablespoons kirsch or cherry cordial

Serve at once, or let cool then cover and refrigerate for up to 3 days. If making the sauce ahead, reheat and add the kirsch just before serving.

HOT BLUEBERRY SAUCE

About 2 cups; 6 to 8 servings

A simple, nonalcoholic alternative to Cherries Jubilee, above. Lovely over vanilla ice cream, pound cake, or hot biscuits or corn bread.

Combine in a stainless-steel skillet:

1 pint blueberries, or 12 ounces frozen dry-pack blueberries, frozen or thawed

1/3 cup sugar

3 tablespoons strained fresh lemon juice

Cook over medium-high heat, stirring, until the berries soften and release their juice. Stir to a smooth paste:

1 tablespoon water

1 1/2 teaspoons cornstarch

Briskly stir the cornstarch mixture into the berries and cook until thickened, about 1 minute. If using the sauce with a warm or room-temperature food, stir in:

1 to 2 tablespoons unsalted butter (optional)

Serve at once, or let cool then cover and refrigerate for up to 3 days. Reheat over low heat.

HOT PEACH SAUCE

Prepare Hot Blueberry Sauce, above, substituting 2 cups diced peeled fresh peaches, or 12 ounces frozen dry-pack peaches, diced, for the blueberries.

BUTTERED CIDER SAUCE

About 1 1/4 cups; 6 to 8 servings

One of the most delicious and unusual sauces we know of, something like thin buttered applesauce with brandy. Terrific on gingerbread or warm pound cake. We even spoon it over roast pork.

Chop into coarse 1/4-inch pieces without peeling or coring:

1 large Granny Smith or other firm apple

Melt in a medium, heavy saucepan:

1 tablespoon unsalted butter

Add the chopped apple and cook over medium heat, stirring occasionally, until softened, about 5 minutes. Add:

1 1/2 cups cider or unsweetened apple juice, preferably unfiltered "natural"

1/4 cup sugar

1/4 cup honey

Simmer until the apple chunks are transparent, about 15 minutes. Pour through a sieve set over a bowl. Return the liquid to the saucepan. Force the apple pulp through the sieve with the back of a wooden spoon, discarding the skin and core left behind. Stir the apple pulp into the liquid and rapidly boil down over high heat, stirring, until the mixture reduces to about 1 cup of thin sauce. Remove from the heat and stir in:

3 tablespoons unsalted butter, softened

Scant 1/4 teaspoon freshly grated or ground nutmeg

1/8 teaspoon salt

When the butter is melted, add, if you wish:

2 tablespoons brandy, applejack, or Calvados

Serve at once, or let cool then cover and refrigerate for up to 1 week. Reheat over low heat, adding a bit more liquor if you like.

Cooking Methods

DRY-HEAT COOKING Cooking heats are generally known as dry or moist. Cooking with dry heat is achieved in a number of ways. Broiling or baking in an oven is one. Cooking directly on an ungreased griddle is another. Grilling over coals is a third. Most foods properly cooked with dry heat finish with a rich aroma, color, and flavor.

BAKING/ROASTING Baking is a general term we use to describe cooking food in an oven. Hot air is the working medium here, enveloping the food in radiant dry heat—perhaps with a little moisture released from the food and circulating as vapor in the oven. The technique is the same whether you are using a thermal—normal—oven or a convection oven, although the rapidly circulating air of a convection oven gives the most even results.

Roasting is a specific style of baking. Spit roasting in front of a hot fire is one of the oldest forms of cooking and the one from which all forms of roasting spring. Roasting is almost always done uncovered. A shallow pan permits the food to brown; not covering the pan and not adding liquid keeps the heat dry and allows the foods to brown and crisp; and setting meats and poultry directly on a rack keeps them from steaming in their own juices.

BROWNING As a preliminary cooking technique, browning meats and vegetables is generally achieved by quick sautéing, pan broiling, oven broiling, or even grilling. The term *searing* specifically refers to browning food, especially meat, over intense high heat. The goal is to add another layer of flavor before continuing with the recipe. As a finishing technique, browning a dish in an oven or under a broiler adds flavor, texture, and eye appeal. When the focus is browning sugar (either natural or added), we use the word *caramelizing*. To gratinée means to create a golden crust by covering the surface of a dish with breadcrumbs or grated cheese and browning it in the oven or under a broiler. Dishes prepared this way are referred to as *gratin de, au gratin*, or simply *gratiné*.

BROILING Whether you broil on a grill or in an oven, the principle is identical. The heat is direct and intense, and it differs from baking or roasting in that only one side of the food at a time is exposed to the heat source.

Generally you will want to broil foods that are quick cooking, inherently tender, relatively lean, and not too thick—chicken breasts, hamburger patties, and fish fillets are perfect candidates.

With household ranges, temperature control in broiling is exerted by the placement of the oven rack. The typical arrangement is for a 5- to 8-inch space between the source of heat and the top of the food. If browning fragile sauces or very thick meats—where the heat must have time to penetrate deeply without charring—you may find it best to lower the broiling rack. If you wonder why you cannot always reproduce the dishes you admire in some restaurant cooking, like steaks, remember that professional installations deliver much higher heats than home equipment can.

PAN BROILING/DRY SKILLET COOKING In pan broiling, a dry pan itself becomes the direct heat source. A well-seasoned cast-iron or nonstick pan is thoroughly heated dry, then the food (usually meat or fish) is laid in. (Some cooks like to sprinkle salt on the skillet to draw moisture to the surface of the meat quickly, creating a savory crustiness.) Once well browned on one side, it is turned to cook on the other. If any fat accumulates in the pan, it is tipped off, to keep the food from frying rather than broiling. If you have a ridged-bottom cast-iron skillet or griddle, the fat rendered from meat, fish, or poultry drips down into the ridges while the heat stays above it—a healthy method of cooking.

FLAMBÉING Flaming, or flambéing, is a technique of quickly enveloping a dish in flames by igniting a small amount of heated liquor poured over it. The food to be flamed needs to be warm, and the brandy or liqueur used to flambé it also needs to be warm—but well under the boiling point. For meat, do not attempt this process with less than 1 ounce of liquor per serving. For nonsweet food served from a chafing dish, pour the warmed liquor over the surface of the food and ignite by touching the edge of the pan with the flame of a match or taper. For hot desserts, sprinkle the top surface with granulated sugar, add the warm liquor or liqueur, and ignite.

HEAT FROM FAT COOKING Because fat contains no moisture, deep-frying, sautéing, and stir-frying are all technically dry-heat cooking methods. But our intuition tells us that these techniques are fundamentally different. Simply put, oil over any food protects it from drying out, especially in deep-frying, where submerging food in oil traps in moisture, steaming the food inside while browning the surface.

Deep-Frying: Done with care, a wide number of delicacies can emerge from hot oil crisp on the outside, moist within. Tender pieces of fish, shellfish, poultry, meat, vegetables, fruits, breads, and pastries can be deep-fried. Although intensely hot, the process is brief, so the food must already be tender. To add a crunchy coating or to protect the most fragile items, many foods are battered before frying.

Any deep kettle or saucepan, preferably a heavy one, serves nicely for deep-frying. The kettle should have a flat bottom, so that it sits securely on the heating unit. A short pot handle is desirable, to avoid the danger of accidentally overturning the hot oil. In case the fat should catch fire, have a metal lid handy to drop over the kettle. You may also smother the flame with salt or baking soda, but never use water, as this will only spread the fire.

It is not wise to skimp on the amount of fat. Always use fresh oil each time you fry. There must always be enough to cover the food and to permit it to move freely in the kettle. There must also be room for the quick bubbling up that occurs naturally when frying potatoes, onions, and other items with high moisture content. Never fill any container more than half full with fat. Remember also to heat the fat gradually (always uncovered) so that any unexpected moisture in it will have slowly evaporated by the time it reaches the required temperature.

Nothing is more important in frying than proper temperatures. For judging the temperature of the fat, use a deep-fry thermometer, no other. The proper temperature in most instances is 365°F—easy to remember. Above all, do not wait for the oil to smoke before adding the food. This is hard on the oil, since smoke indicates that it is breaking down, and the crust that forms on the food is likely to be overbrowned on the surface before the inside is cooked through. Food introduced into fat that is not hot enough to crust immediately, however, will tend to be grease-soaked.

After frying one batch of food, always let the oil temperature come up again to the required heat. Skim out bits of food or crumbs frequently as they collect in the fat during frying. If allowed to remain, they induce foaming, discolor the fat, and affect the flavor of the food. Have ready a supply of paper towels on which to drain the cooked food and so rid it of excess fat before serving.

Whenever possible, food should be at room temperature and as dry as possible when introduced into the kettle. Unbattered raw pieces, especially moist ones, should be patted between paper towels before cooking. It is generally best to immerse food gently. For good results, pieces of food to be fried should be uniform in size; small pieces, obviously, will cook through faster than large ones. Fry in several small batches rather than in one large one. The cooked food may be kept hot on a paper-lined pan in an oven set at very low heat.

FRITTER BATTER FOR VEGETABLES, MEAT, AND FISH

Enough to coat about 2 cups food

In a mixing bowl, mix together well:

1⅓ cups all-purpose flour or rice flour
1 teaspoon salt
¼ teaspoon ground black pepper
1 tablespoon melted butter or vegetable oil
2 beaten egg yolks

Add gradually, stirring constantly:

¾ cup flat beer

Allow the batter to rest, covered and refrigerated, 3 to 12 hours. Just before using, add:

2 egg whites, stiffly beaten (optional)

Sautéing: Sauter literally means "to jump," and if the French did not invent the technique, they certainly taught us the nuances. The cooking is done in a small amount of hot fat in an open shallow pan. The pan and the fat in it must be hot enough that, when the food is added, it sears it at once, preventing sticking. Food cut to a uniform thickness and size sautés best. To ensure a dry surface, food for sautéing is frequently floured or breaded. If cold, it will reduce the heat. If wet, it will not brown properly. Steam will also form if the pan is crowded; there must be space between the pieces of food you are sautéing. Fresh mushrooms, pounded slices of veal and turkey, fish fillets or steaks, and scallops are ideal for sautéing.

For most sautés use a combination of butter and oil. When the fat becomes very fragrant (but not smoking), it is time to start. With flat pieces, the handsomest side goes into the pan first; that first sizzle browning usually is not duplicated when the food is turned. Generally, meat or fish is cooked through when the juices rise to the surface of the cooked side. The exception is rare-cooked meat, which is done as soon as it has firmed slightly. Fish is turned as soon as the bottom half appears opaque, 1 to 4 minutes depending on thickness. If breaded pieces fail to brown, turn up the heat and, if necessary, add more fat to the pan. During cooking you may need to reduce the heat on the second side.

To serve sautéed food with a sauce, remove the food from the pan and keep it warm on a hot serving dish. Quickly deglaze the delicious residue on the bottom of the pan with stock or wine. Reduce the liquid into a sauce, season, and pour over the sautéed food.

Stir-Frying: In classic stir-frying, the food is always bite-sized, the stirring is ceaseless, and the heat is extremely high. In fact, on some home stoves it is hard to get the heat high enough to achieve the classic technique.

Familiarize yourself with the recipe, since you may not have time to stop and read once you are in action. You will want to allow yourself plenty of preparation time, since cutting food into small pieces to cook rapidly can be time-consuming. Have all ingredients within easy reach of the stove. Undercook rather than overcook—you can always return food to the heat.

On gas burners, either a round- or a flat-bottomed wok will work; for all other burners, a flat-bottomed wok is preferable. A 12- to 14-inch wok is ideal, but you can stir-fry beautifully in a skillet as long as it is heavy and large—the largest your burner will accommodate. The pan and surface must be capable of being heated empty over the highest heat without damage. Always heat the empty wok (or skillet) until it just begins to smoke, then add the oil and tip the wok to coat it before proceeding with the recipe.

MOIST-HEAT COOKING Moist-heat cooking can preserve the delicacy of fragile or subtle foods. Since fat is not part of the cooking medium and cooking liquids are not necessarily highly seasoned, foods cooked with these methods are generally lean, their flavors light and pure. Some long-simmered stews, however, are begun in a pan by browning; others, like the Irish variety, are not browned. Similarly, a braise, a fricassee, and a "smother" may all involve a preliminary browning followed by cooking in liquid.

SIMMERING AND BOILING While recipes often call for foods to be brought to the boiling point—that is, in liquid which has reached 212°F—or to be plunged into boiling water, they hardly ever demand boiling for a protracted period. Even "boiled" eggs are really simmered. Immersing food in simmering liquid ranks as one of the most important methods of cooking with moist heat. This technique gently cooks fragile foods and tenderizes tough ones.

Certain foods, of course, are truly boiled. Be sure to use enough water: adding foods to boiling water has the effect of reducing the water temperature and stopping the boil, unless the quantity of water is at least three times that of the food, which is exactly the proportions you need for boiling pasta, vegetables, and rice and other grains in some preparations. When boiling, the pan is always left uncovered.

A true simmer is the point at which bubbles rise gently and barely break the surface of the liquid—the best temperature for cooking soups, stews, and braises. The French say a simmer makes the pot smile. Some cookbook authors use the word *simmer* to indicate a gentle boil, while others mean liquid that barely bubbles.

BLANCHING/PARBOILING Blanching and parboiling are preliminary cooking techniques that employ boiling water or steam to soften textures, loosen skins, or remove strong flavors, saltiness, or smokiness—all with the goal of further utilizing the food in another recipe. Strongly flavored or salty foods such as salt pork, smoked bacon, and olives are often blanched in a large quantity of unsalted boiling water to remove excess salt or smoke flavor before they are used in a delicate dish.

STEWING AND BRAISING Stewing frequently involves browning small pieces of meat, poultry, or fish, then simmering them with vegetables or other ingredients in enough liquid to cover in a closed or partly closed pot, either in the oven, on the stovetop, or in a slow cooker.

Braising is usually done with one food—meat, fish, or a vegetable—and with less liquid. Butter or oil may be used along with a small amount of stock or other liquid. With the braising vessel closed, the liquid, as well as the juices from the food, condenses on the lid and supplies a measure of continuous basting.

Another kind of braising is smothering or cooking *à l'étouffée.* In this method, the main food items (such as pork chops, poultry, or seafood) are cooked in a small amount of liquid and are smothered under a blanket of aromatic vegetables in a covered pot; the flavor of the vegetables infuses the main food with flavor and moisture.

POACHING To poach means to cook a food completely covered in liquid. Usually, but not always, the liquid is maintained below the boiling point—nary a bubble should break the surface. Poaching is ideally suited to cooking in advance, since the food will be suffused with moisture. If you plan to serve the food cold, remove the pan from the heat when the food is on the brink of being done, then let it stand in the liquid until cool. This method makes chicken perfect for chicken salad. When poaching, a lid is not recommended since it traps heat and can easily raise the temperature of the liquid to a simmer.

DOUBLE-BOILER COOKING The purpose of a double boiler is to cook delicate sauces, usually egg-based, and other foods that cannot tolerate direct heat. To prevent the water in the bottom pan from boiling over, add no more than an inch of water (it should not touch the bottom of the upper container) and heat the water only to a gentle simmer. If you do not own a double boiler, choose any heat-resistant bowl that rests snugly on one of your saucepans, leaving 2 to 3 inches between the bottom of the bowl and the bottom of the pan.

WATER BATH/BAIN-MARIE See page 1013.

STEAMING Steaming is one of the gentlest ways to cook, since it is only the even, moist heat of the vapors—not simmering water—that envelops the food, allowing it to retain most of its natural juices and nutrients. Water is the most common steaming medium, though broth, beer, wine, or other herb-infused liquids can be used for an easy way to infuse flavor.

Ready-made stovetop steamers come in many sizes, shapes, metals, and prices, from the collapsible kind to the shallow insert of a spaghetti pot to the whole-fish-sized stainless-steel oval. Chinese tiered bamboo steamers are beautiful, but set in a wok as they were meant to be (they come with a top but not a bottom), they have to be watched so their rims do not burn. Rinse with hot water after each use and dry thoroughly before storing in an airy place. The multitiered Chinese aluminum steamers are more desirable. Either type is great for steaming a meal on one burner. The food that needs the most heat goes on the lowest tier, and the food that needs the least heat goes on top.

Always keep the top of the water an inch or so below the bottom of the steamer, and it is best to keep most foods an inch or so from the steamer sides. If the food will not render juices—vegetables, for example—the food goes in the steamer directly. If the food is juicy, steam it in a shallow bowl or deep plate to capture all the flavor.

Steam over moderate heat. A trick that alerts you to dwindling water is to put two or three marbles or coins in the bottom of your steamer. They will make a racket until the water is gone; silence means it is time to add water.

Remember that steam is scalding. And it is deceptive, since you cannot see all of it. Always lift the lid away from you, protecting your hands and arms from the steam.

PRESSURE COOKING No matter how high the heat source, boiling in water can never produce a temperature over 212°F. But, because pressure cooking traps a great volume of steam under a locked lid, temperatures as high as 250°F can be maintained at a gauge reading of 15 pounds pressure—the most common amount of pressure used in home cookers. Cooking at 15 pounds pressure takes only about one-third the total time—from putting the lid on the pressure cooker to the final release of pressure—that it takes to cook food in conventional ways at boiling temperatures. Time varies with each pressure cooker, so consult the book that comes with your pot.

When you are adapting recipes designed for conventional methods, in general you can use less liquid, because there will be no evaporation in cooking. Vegetables contain considerable moisture, so when you pressure-cook them (or stews with vegetables), you may add as little as ½ cup water to the pot—the minimum to produce steam.

Cooking with today's pressure cookers—indeed, with yesterday's pressure cookers—is not dangerous if you follow some commonsense guidelines. Before each use, hold the cover up to a light and look through the vent pipe to make sure it is open. Never fill the pressure cooker more than two-thirds to three-quarters full, depending on your model—consult the manual. Cook your dish *and cool it* according to the manual's or recipe's direction. For delicate foods or ones that might easily overcook, such as vegetables, bite-sized pieces of meat, and custards, the pot is set in the sink under cold running water until the pressure drops completely. For food that is dense—a big piece of meat or a thick soup or stew—the pressure is generally allowed to drop of its own accord.

Use the cooker's trivet when cooking vegetables to keep them out of the liquid and let them steam. You can also set vegetables in a collapsible metal steamer basket in the pressure cooker as long as no food pokes above the two-thirds level or the three-quarters level for some models.

Dried beans and dried whole (not split) green or yellow peas must be presoaked before going into the pressure cooker. If using a jiggle-top cooker, *always* add 1 tablespoon oil per cup of dried beans to control the foaming; if using a cooker with a stationary pressure regulator, the oil may be optional. Again, consult your owner's manual.

When cooking rice and dried beans (or soups or stews that include rice or dried beans), do not fill the cooker more than half full, since both rice and beans expand.

Always consult your manual if you are considering cooking foods that foam, froth, or sputter, since they might clog the vent. These include applesauce, cranberries, rhubarb, pearl barley, split peas, soup mixes containing dried vegetables, any form of noodles or pasta, and oatmeal or other cereals. Fresh fruit is generally too fragile for this cooking method, but reconstituted dried fruits, custards, and bread and rice puddings do beautifully in the pressure cooker.

WRAP COOKING Wrapping food before introducing it to heat is almost as ancient as cooking itself. Traditional peoples to this day surround pieces of food with all sorts of things to tenderize them and to protect them from burning. Native Americans baked fish, small animals, and birds in clay.

The wrapping you choose to work with will affect the finished food in several ways. Leaves add their own flavor to almost everything—whether it is the meat and rice mixture for stuffed cabbage or a whole brook trout; parchment and aluminum foil do not contribute flavor. Another consideration is the cooking method.

Leaf Wrappings: Certain fresh green leaves such as lettuce, cabbage, grape, and papaya create a flavorful *edible* wrap to food, while banana, palm, and taro leaves and cornhusks are inedible and only furnish protection (and flavor) during the cooking. As a rule, leaf-wrapped bundles have deeper flavor the day after cooking; they reheat beautifully because the leaves hold in their moisture. When you are collecting or buying leaves for wrapping, get extras; some will tear, and you may have more filling than you thought. Use any extra leaves to line the cooking dish or place extra leaves between the layers of bundles, or cover everything with leaves during cooking for added flavor.

Foil: An effortless way to steam food is to wrap it (butcher-wrap style) in heavy foil (shiny side in) and bake it. Due to the foil's insulating qualities, the wrapped food will take somewhat longer to cook. Either cook the food longer or raise the oven temperature and cook it the usual length of time. Whether over a campfire or barbecue, foil wrapping is an invaluable technique for the grill. As with all steam cooking, unless the food is browned first, colors will be pale, but the food will be flavorful and succulent.

Parchment Paper/En Papillote: Sealing a delicate fish fillet or veal chop along with aromatic herbs or vegetables in parchment and then popping the packet into a hot oven is called cooking en papillote. The packets are sealed by crimping the edges with a series of small, neat folds. In the oven, the parchment swells with steam. When cut open—usually done at the table by each diner—delicious aromas waft into the room.

Crust/En Croûte: In the case of pies and turnovers, the crust is as much the object of our attention as the filling. But in the case of dishes prepared *en croûte,* such as Beef Wellington, the crust functions for the most part as a protective wrapper.

BLACKENING Associated with Cajun cooking, blackening is a unique kind of pan frying that sears highly seasoned surfaces so intensely they form a crust. This method produces an enormous amount of smoke, so be prepared to deal with it. Setting your skillet over a very hot burner on top of the stove, or over a hot gas or charcoal grill or a large propane burner, will give you sufficient heat.

Heat a dry cast-iron skillet (no other) over very high heat until extremely hot, 5 to 10 minutes—when a white film just begins to appear in the center. Dip the food in melted butter, coating it thoroughly. Generously coat it all over with seasonings. At once, lay it in the skillet and drizzle the top with a little more butter (be careful, as it usually flares up). When a crust forms on the bottom, about 2 to 3 minutes, turn with a spatula and moisten again with butter. Blacken until done, about 2 to 6 minutes more depending on the thickness of the food you are cooking. Do not try to cook beef past medium—the exterior will burn and be bitter. After each pass, wipe the skillet completely clean with a thick cotton cloth.

DEGLAZING This is a technique for creating a simple sauce or gravy by dissolving—with wine, stock, or other liquid—the tasty browned bits left in the roasting pan or skillet in which you have cooked meat, poultry, or fish. Tilt the pan or skillet and skim off excess fat from any juices with a spoon. Add a generous splash of water, stock, or wine and gently cook for a few minutes, stirring and scraping up the precious residue from the bottom and sides.

REDUCING Reducing is the process of boiling down a liquid to thicken its consistency and concentrate its flavor. If you thicken a sauce by reducing, season it after it reaches the desired thickness; otherwise you may find it overseasoned or salty. Many tomato sauces demand long cooking and reducing; unless these sauces—or almost any thickened sauces—are reduced over very low heat, they will cook so fast that flavor and color will be impaired. Naturally, this technique is used only with sauces that contain no egg (which would curdle during cooking). Those that contain cream or flour must be stirred often to avoid scorching as they reduce. For perfectly smooth texture, many reduced sauces are strained before serving.

SWEATING To release flavor from finely chopped aromatic vegetables (onions, garlic, shallots, carrots, and celery, for example) before they are simmered in a sauce, stew, or braise, "sweat" them in a small amount of butter or oil in a covered pan over medium to low heat. After a few minutes—when the vegetables are tender but not browned and their juices have been released—they are ready. For a reduced-fat technique, butter and oil may be replaced with stock.

MICROWAVE COOKING The microwave is one of the most misunderstood appliances in the kitchen. There are a few basic facts to keep in mind: It is *not* a substitute for the stovetop and oven. It does *not* cook foods from the inside out. It cooks some things very well, but it cannot be used for all of your cooking needs.

In a microwave oven, electricity is converted into microwaves by the magnetron; the waves are spread throughout the oven cavity via a revolving "stirrer fan" in the oven. With a tight-sealing door and at least two interlocks, today's ovens are well within the U.S. Bureau of Radiological Health's safety standards. Microwaves can penetrate glass, ceramics, paper, and plastic, but they are deflected by metal, which is why microwave oven interiors are lined with metal.

When these aimless, fat little waves are scattered about the oven cavity they behave like billiard balls gone awry, bouncing off the walls and careening about until they land on something that is moist—water or food. At that point the waves will penetrate only ¾ to 1½ inches deep, but in so doing, they cause the water molecules they touch to vibrate, causing friction and thus producing heat. Once the water molecules are moving about, the food cooks by simple conduction, from the outside to the inside. Microwaves are the energy source, but the cooking process is the equal of what happens to food in a skillet over a burner or in the cavity of a hot oven: The heat is conducted from the outside of the food to the interior. But unlike in conventional cooking, it is the excited molecules that transfer the heat to the center of the food, rather than a heat source below or above it. Therefore foods do not brown in the microwave oven, and the devices that claim to brown food are usually ineffective and can be dangerous by concentrating heat on plastic surfaces.

Ingredients that have a high water content—most vegetables, virtually all greens, fish, and fruits—can be quickly cooked in a microwave oven. They will have a steamed quality to them, but without the excess moisture steam might leave behind. Fresh sweet corn cooks in seconds, artichokes in minutes, and a big winter squash requires only a fraction of the time it takes in a steamer or thermal oven. Wilted spinach salads—from cooking the bacon to finishing the dish—are ready to eat in moments. Peeling tomatoes or peaches is simple after a few seconds in the microwave, and, for melting cheese or chocolate or butter, nothing could be tidier.

In addition, microwaving fruits and vegetables preserves more nutrients than practically any other cooking method because you use little or no nutrient-leaching water and because it cooks faster than any other method. Defrosting in a microwave is healthful too, because it is fast—no meat or poultry sitting at room temperature encouraging bacteria to grow. Also less butter, oil, or other fat is required for microwave cooking, because these ingredients are used solely as flavorings, rather than to prevent sticking.

Timing: It is very tricky to adapt a conventionally cooked recipe to microwave cooking. The surest way is to find a microwave recipe that is comparable and use it for a model. Take all microwave recipe cooking times with a grain of salt. Your oven's wattage makes a difference; the higher the wattage, the faster the oven cooks. You can always put food back, but you cannot undo overcooking—and the microwave can overcook in a wink. There is no simple formula for adjusting time according to wattage, since minor fluctuations in voltage at your plug can also make a difference; have your microwave oven on a dedicated circuit. The oven's age is another factor in determining timing; an older oven may have not only lower wattage but decreased efficiency from repeated usage as well.

Covering Food: Covering keeps moisture in the food from evaporating too rapidly, thus helping the microwaves cook more evenly. Plastic wraps are routinely recommended for covering food in the microwave, particularly when abundant steam is needed for tenderizing and speeding the cooking along. But higher temperatures and prolonged contact with food—especially foods with high fat and sugar content—increase chances that the plastic will melt. When plastic wrap is called for, always provide an inch or more of space between the food and the wrap. And only microwave with plastic wraps that are clearly labeled safe for the microwave; ones not labeled as such may contain many plasticizers, which cause the plastic to melt quickly and possibly transfer unwanted chemicals to the food. Because of the buildup of steam, never tightly seal a dish with plastic wrap. If a recipe directs you to cover tightly during cooking, use a microwave-safe lid. If using plastic wrap, give the steam a way out: fold back an edge about an inch. When removing a lid or wrap, lift it from the side away from you to avoid the escaping steam, which can easily scald you. When neither trapping steam nor absorbing moisture is your goal (say, when microwaving a plate of leftovers), lay a sheet of wax paper on top of the dish. Paper towels and napkins are good for covering foods that splatter, such as melting butter.

Reheating: When reheating, it is especially important to turn and/or stir two or three times, to ensure even distribution of heat and avoid overcooking in spots. To heat bread, rolls, muffins, and sweet rolls, loosely wrap in a paper napkin and microwave in 5-second increments until the bread is warm—no further. Be aware that bread warmed in the microwave acquires an unpleasant rubbery texture as soon as it cools, and no amount of toasting can change it. For a whole plate of food, arrange thicker pieces toward the rim of the plate and quick-to-heat pieces toward the center. Cover with wax paper and heat in 1-minute increments. Meat sliced about ¼ inch thick heats best. Slices covered with gravy should then be covered with wax paper; slices without gravy should be covered with a paper towel. Heat on medium power in increments of 30 seconds.

Precautions: Be especially watchful with small portions of food; they can easily overcook and burn. If a doughnut or a Danish has a jelly center, be careful when you bite into it—sugar attracts the waves, remember, and that jelly can be scalding hot and cause painful burns. Never heat food in closed jars. Never heat fats and oils or try to deep-fry in the microwave—fat is a magnet for the little waves and can quickly overheat. Do not process food for canning in the microwave. Do not use a conventional meat thermometer—the metal will cause the sparking collision of microwaves called arcing. Pop popcorn only in bags or poppers designed for the microwave.

OUTDOOR COOKING Grilling is cooking food directly over live heat (either charcoal or gas), almost always uncovered and usually at fairly high temperatures. Barbecuing is a traditional, covered, slow-cooking method, usually for larger cuts of highly seasoned meats, employing relatively low, indirect heat from charcoal or wood. Grill roasting involves large cuts of meat, poultry, or whole fish cooked in a covered grill using indirect heat (the food is not directly over the coals). Smoking, originally a method of preserving meats and fish, often calls for a preliminary curing process and then either hot or cold cooking temperatures; hot smoking is a relatively short process, cold smoking a lengthy one.

GRILLING The central fact about grilling is that it is generally a high-heat cooking method, which involves cooking relatively tender foods quickly over a hot fire. When food is exposed to the direct heat of the flames, a seared crust develops on its exterior. Tender cuts of meat such as beef, pork, or lamb grill beautifully, as do shrimp, scallops, and firm-textured fish such as tuna, swordfish, and mahi mahi.

Steaks and chops are extraordinarily well suited to grilling. Avoid excessively thick cuts, which tend to char outside before they are cooked through; an inch and a half should be the thickness limit for individual servings. Oil the cooking grate before you begin grilling.

Equipment: Most outdoor grills fall into one of two categories: open or covered. Open grills range in size and portability from the simple, small hibachi to large built-in units. An open grill is most useful if it has a heavy grate (to transfer heat and give beautiful grill marks) and an adjustable firebox or grate (to help control the intensity of heat).

Covered grills come in many styles, but the covered kettle grill ranks high. Neither the charcoal grate on which the coals rest nor the cooking grate is adjustable, and the most popular units were designed to be used with the lid, to reduce the possibility of flare-ups and to speed cooking by circulating heat around the food.

Gas grills have come a long way in the last few years, most notably in burning fuel more efficiently and in their ability to achieve the higher temperatures crucial for a delectable brown crust.

Unfortunately the so-called "stovetop grills"—basically some variety of metal grid that fits over a stove burner, equipped with a pan to catch dripping grease—do not get hot enough to really grill. If you want to grill inside and you have a fireplace, consider the Tuscan grill. Although difficult to find, this handy device consists of a simple metal frame that holds an adjustable grilling grate, suitable for use in indoor fireplaces. To rig one of your own, remove the grill surface from any standard outdoor grill and support it in the fireplace above the coals with bricks.

Fuel for the Fire: Grilling has become synonymous with little pillow-shaped charcoal briquettes, available in every supermarket. Because they are not pure charcoal but rather a combination of charcoal, sawdust, powdered scrap lumber, starch, and additives, briquettes can impart unpleasant flavors. Hardwood lump charcoal, made by burning hardwood in a closed container with very little oxygen, is worth searching out in hardware and specialty stores. These chunks of almost pure carbon light more easily, give heat that is more responsive to changes in oxygen, and burn cleaner and hotter than briquettes. A wide variety of wood chips on the market, ranging from mesquite to cherry to hickory, can be added to glowing charcoal to give a smokier, wood-fire flavor. But unless the food spends more than a few minutes on the grill, the smoke from the chips will have little time to penetrate the food.

Starting the Fire: Starter fluid or presoaked charcoal briquettes should be avoided. Because fumes are released throughout the cooking process, the taste of the food can be affected.

To start a fire in the simplest fashion, crumple several sheets of newspaper in the bottom of the grill beneath the fire grate, set the grate back in place over the newspapers, and lay several handfuls of twigs or kindling on the grate. Next top the twigs with a rather loose tepee-shaped arrangement of slightly larger twigs (or several handfuls of charcoal, if that is your fuel of choice) and light the newspaper. When the wood or charcoal is well lit—about 5 minutes for wood, 15 minutes for charcoal—add additional fuel.

If the fuel is charcoal, you can start your fire with an electrical coil starter instead of paper and twigs. These electrical coils, attached to a power cord by means of a plastic handle, are reliable and consistent. The chimney starter, also known as a flue starter, is the paragon of efficiency, reliability, and economy. It is basically a sheet metal cylinder, open at both ends, with a grid set inside the flue several inches from the bottom. Fill the bottom section with crumpled newspaper, then fill the top with charcoal and light the newspaper. When the charcoal is red hot, dump it out and put as much additional charcoal as you want on top of it.

Whatever lighting method you use, light the fire far enough in advance to ensure an even, flameless fire of the proper temperature (15 to 40 minutes, depending on your fuel). Allow enough time for the fuel to get fiery red and then die down until it is just covered with gray ash. This is the point at which you are ready to cook.

Precautions: For safety's sake always set your grill on level ground in the largest possible open space, away from walls, wooden fences, overhanging eaves or tree branches, or anything else that might easily catch fire. Keep toddlers well away from the grill, and do not let older children run or play too close to the grilling area. If using any charcoal-fired equipment, do so with adequate ventilation, where the carbon monoxide fumes can be carried off completely; do not ever use charcoal grills in a house, tent, cabin, garage, or other enclosed area. Insufficient ventilation may prove fatal. Never light the fire with gasoline and never spray lighter fluid onto lit coals. It is always a good idea to have handy a fire extinguisher or a bucket of sand. Remember, fire goes out without oxygen, so that fires in covered grills can be extinguished by closing the lid and vents.

Spit-Roasting and Rotisserie Cooking: Spit and rotisserie cooking (the terms are interchangeable) are best for small or large fowl, whole joints like leg of lamb, and other chunky cuts of meat. Some grills include a spit, which is usually protected from wind by a metal shield on three sides. Consult the directions that come with a spit to determine the maximum weight it will support—probably ten pounds for roast meat and up to fifteen for fowl. Smaller birds should be strung traversely on the spit, larger ones head to tail along the spit's axis.

Remember that because of the high heat of spit roasting, the weight losses due to shrinkage can be great and flare-ups from dripping fat frequent. (In olden days, spit roasting was done in front of a fire, not over it, thus avoiding too strong a heat and any flare-ups.) Flare-ups can be avoided in part by careful trimming of surplus fat. Some short flare-ups may be desired for browning; unwanted ones can be doused with a spritz of water from a spray bottle.

GRILL ROASTING/INDIRECT GRILLING In this hybrid method, whole chickens, turkeys, legs of lamb, and the like are roasted by the indirect heat of the fire in a covered grill, as if in a smoky oven. To grill roast, build a fire in your grill in the usual manner and push all the coals to one side. On the other side, place a drip pan if you wish to collect juices or fill the cooking kettle with the steam from aromatic liquids. When you put the food on the cooking grate, place it over the side that has no coals and over the drip pan if you are using one. Then set the grill cover in place, making sure no portion of the item you are cooking is directly over the fire. Adjust the vents as necessary to maintain the temperature between 250° and 300°F; an oven thermometer, set close to the food, will help you determine the temperature of the environment.

COOKING IN ASHES Ash cooking is best done in a fireplace or campfire. The food you are preparing should be cut into relatively small pieces so that it will cook through before browning too much at the edges. And it is a good idea to keep the batches of food small, so the packets are not too unwieldy to take in and out of the coals. Although hamburger with potatoes and onions may be classic, bone-in chicken, root vegetables, sausages, and meaty fish—seasoned with herbs, garlic, and olive oil—are also wonderful candidates for ash cooking.

Wrapping the food properly requires three sheets of heavy-duty aluminum foil, each about 2 feet long. Start by spreading the food over the center of the first sheet, then lay the second length on top. Fold the edges of the two sheets together on all sides, closing the pack, then roll them up until they bump into the food, forming a ridge around its perimeter. Place the pack folded side up in the center of the third sheet of foil and fold the four sides over the top of the packet, one after the other.

Whether wood or charcoal is the fuel, the fire should have passed its peak of intensity and be dying down—nothing but glowing coals covered with gray ash. Sweep the coals to the side, leaving your "cooking surface" covered with hot ashes. Lay in the packets and surround with the coals. The only way to check for doneness is to open a packet and take a peek.

SMOKING Hot smoking is a relatively fast cooking process, intended to cook the food quickly. It is essentially grill roasting with the addition of wood chunks or chips. Cold smoking is slower, really not a cooking technique, but a drying and flavoring one. It often employs a preliminary salty brine or dry cure to compact the flesh and preserve it. Cold smoking cannot be accomplished in any covered grill, since it cannot maintain the appropriate temperatures of 80° to 115°F; you must use a cold smoker.

To improvise a hot smoker using a covered kettle grill, after lighting the coals, wrap six or eight wood chunks (or an equal amount of chips) in a double layer of aluminum foil. Pierce several small holes, then lay the foil-wrapped packet directly on top of the hot coals. Set the cooking grate in place and the food on top of the grate. As with grill roasting, a pan of aromatic liquid is frequently placed directly beneath the food. Put the lid on and adjust the vents to maintain a temperature of around 250°F.

BARBECUING While grilling is quick and hot, barbecuing is slow and low. Barbecuing involves cooking whole pigs or lambs or one of the large, tougher cuts of meat (such as beef brisket or pork shoulder) in an enclosed space with the hot smoke of a wood fire. The temperature is usually kept at around 220°F: the very slow cooking causes the meat's connective tissues, called collagen, to dissolve into tenderness. Because of the moisture in the enclosed space, barbecuing resembles the moist-heat method of pot roasting, transforming tough meat into a tender, smoke-tinged treat. The crusty, smoky exterior provides a satisfying chewiness that contrasts perfectly with the moist, richly flavored inner meat.

The role of sauce in barbecue is overrated. Whether based on ketchup, mustard, or vinegar, the sauce is really nothing more than the finishing touch. Like a condiment, it should complement rather than obscure the smoky flavor of the meat. Many cooks use a second sauce, called a mopping sauce, to baste the meat while it is cooking. Like finishing sauces, mopping sauces can vary from complicated mixtures of herbs, spices, and vinegar to just plain beer, all used to keep the meat moist as it cooks.

More important than either the finishing or the mopping sauce is the fire. Since the meat spends many hours in contact with smoky, hot air, only live fire can impart the proper taste. As fuel, charcoal briquettes will do in a pinch; hardwood charcoal is better; and the top choice is hardwood logs, particularly oak, hickory, mesquite, or any fruit wood.

To approximate true barbecue using a backyard grill, set up the grill as you would for grill roasting. Let the fire burn down to a medium-low heat. Cover the coals with a foil-

ALTITUDE ADJUSTMENTS

ADJUSTMENTS FOR HIGH-ALTITUDE CANNING

ALTITUDE (FEET)	BOILING WATER BATH: INCREASE PROCESSING TIME	PRESSURE CANNER: WEIGHTED GAUGE* (JIGGLE TOP) SETTING	PRESSURE CANNER: DIAL GAUGE SETTING
0-999	no change	10	11
1,000	5 minutes	15	11
2,000	5 minutes	15	12
3,000	10 minutes	15	12
4,000	10 minutes	15	13
5,000	10 minutes	15	13
6,000	15 minutes	15	14
7,000	15 minutes	15	14
8,000	15 minutes	15	15
9,000	15 minutes	15	15
10,000	20 minutes	15	15

*Above 1,000 feet, these canners must be set at 15 PSI, since they cannot be set higher.

wrapped packet of wood chips, as you would for smoking, above. Add a handful of charcoal or wood chunks every 20 to 30 minutes.

Pit Cooking: Pits may be small holes of just sufficient depth and width to take a bean pot, a three-legged kettle, or a true braising pot with a depression on top for coals. Or the pit may be big enough to accommodate all the makings of a king-sized luau, replete with suckling pigs. In direct pit-fire cooking (the original barbecue), hardwood embers are left in the pit and steel rods are put across it, a few inches above the fire, on rocks or logs set around its periphery; the rods, in turn, support a wire-mesh grid on which the food is cooked.

Moving from pit barbecuing to fireless pit cooking results in completely different culinary effects. Fairly large-scale cookery of the latter type requires digging a pit not less than 2 feet deep and 3 feet across. If pit cooking is more than occasional and the locale does not vary, you may find it more convenient to build a surface pit by constructing a hollow rectangle of concrete blocks, about the same height as a true pit is deep.

The next step is to line the bottom and sides of the pit with medium-sized flat rocks (*never* with shale, which may explode when heated). Toss in another loose layer of rock. Now spread over the rocks a substantial bonfire of hardwood deadfall or driftwood. Hickory, beech, maple, and ironwood are prime for this purpose, and grapevine cuttings lend grilled food special distinction. (The French, incidentally, regard food broiled over grape wood, or *sarments de vigne,* as extraordinarily choice.) When the fire has thoroughly heated the pit and completely burned down—this should take not less than 2 hours—rake out the red embers and the top rocks. Some pit roasters sprinkle a quart or so of water over the hot rocks remaining, and most add a 2-inch layer of fresh leaves—grape, fig, beech, pawpaw, or banana—or cornhusks or seaweed for a shore dinner. If you have remembered to bring along some handfuls of aromatic herbs, add them too.

Work quickly at this point, so that the rocks do not lose their stored heat. On the bed of packed foliage, arrange the elements of your meal: fish, cuts of meat, green peppers, onions, corn in its husks, unpeeled potatoes, acorn squash. Pile over them a second layer of green leafage and, if there is room, successive layerings of food and leafage. Cap it off with the remaining hot rocks, a tarpaulin, canvas, or metal cover, and 4 inches of earth or sand to cut off the air supply (which would fuel the embers) and insulate the chamber. How long the cooking will take in this steamy, smoky environment depends, of course, on what is cooking—maximum time will probably be required for a small pig; calculate about 20 minutes per pound and always check with a thermometer to ensure that the center of the meat has reached 170°F. In removing the covering when you are ready to serve, be extremely careful not to get food fouled up with sand or earth.

For shore dinners, with seaweed as filler, wire mesh is often placed over at least one layer to better support small crustaceans, clams, and oysters. For details of a clambake, see 510.

COOKING AT HIGH ALTITUDES Cooking and baking in the mountains have their quirks, but in our experience, there is practically nothing you cannot do at a mile high that you can do on the flats. In the kitchen, you must compensate for the effects of thinner, drier air; crackers and cookies stay crisp forever, but cakes and breads dry out quickly.

At high altitudes, liquids boil at a lower temperature than at sea level—the greater the elevation, the lower they boil.

TEMPERATURES AT WHICH WATER BOILS AT VARIOUS ELEVATIONS

Sea level	212°F	100°C
2,000 feet	208°F	98°C
5,000 feet	203°F	95°C
7,500 feet	198°F	92°C
10,000 feet	195°F	90°C
15,000 feet	185°F	85°C

To compensate for the lower boiling temperatures—which affect roasts as much as a pot of simmering beans—apply a little more heat or cook food longer. It is usual to add 15 to 20 degrees to a recipe's oven temperature or, for food cooked over a burner of a standard stove, a few more minutes than the recipe's suggested cooking time.

Here are guidelines for the typical changes you will need to make when cooking at around 5,000 feet. For higher altitudes, increase changes proportionately. When something is not mentioned—yeast breads, for example—you may notice things that behave a bit differently, but not enough to make alterations necessary.

If you do not know the altitude of your kitchen, consult the nearest county or state Cooperative Extension Service or Soil Conservation Service. Their information will prove useful for understanding any cooking alterations and will be especially essential for safe canning.

Baking: Higher baking temperatures are generally necessary. Do observe the general rule for stiffly beaten egg whites: Beat them only to soft peaks—too much air in the batter can cause a baked structure to fall. Flours will be drier at higher altitudes, so often a little extra liquid is needed; also, less baking powder or baking soda and, occasionally, less sugar are required. The only way to discover exact quantities for each change is through experimentation—or applying quantities from well-proven recipes to similar new ones.

Beans and Legumes, Dried: At 7,000 feet, beans will take about double the sea-level time. Above 8,000 feet, a pressure cooker may be the only way to cook them through.

Deep-Frying: If the exterior gets very brown while the interior is underdone, reduce the oil temperature 3°F for every 1,000 feet above sea level.

Frostings, Cooked: Above 2,500 feet, these may be ready faster than the recipe indicates.

Pastas: These need lots of furiously boiling salted water and more cooking time.

Pressure Cooking: Follow the manufacturer's directions. General rules: If the gauge is adjustable, increase pressure 1 pound for every 2,000 feet above sea level; if not, cook at full pressure. Above 2,000 feet, increase cooking time 5 percent for every 1,000 feet. Because times are increased, use proportionately more liquid in recipes.

Roasting: Use a slightly higher temperature.

Slow Cooking (Stews, Braises): For every 1,000 feet above 4,000 feet, allow 1 more hour on low and another 30 minutes on high.

Know Your Ingredients

ABOUT HERBS AND SPICES Seeds, leaves, flowers, stems, stamens, roots, fruits, bark, pods, and rhizomes of plants take on an almost magical aura when they become *herbs and spices.* When cooking with herbs, snip them with scissors or chop them by hand.

To substitute dried herbs for fresh, strengths vary in leaves, but the general rule is to use a generous ¼ teaspoon ground or 1 teaspoon crumbled dried leaves for every tablespoon of the fresh herb finely chopped.

Most fresh herbs are perishable, and careful keeping is crucial. Store bunches in the refrigerator, their stems in water. Pack loose leaves and flowers, and rhizomes such as ginger, in perforated plastic bags in the refrigerator crisper. If there is excess moisture in the leaves or tubers, before packing, pat them fairly dry, then crush a dry paper towel at the bottom of the bag and place the leaves on top. A little moisture helps keep plant parts fresh, but too much moisture promotes decay.

HOW TO DRY HERBS Optimum conditions for drying are temperatures above 85° and humidity below 60 percent. Tie stalks of herbs into skimpy bunches with cotton string and place each bunch upside down inside a large paper bag well punctured with air holes. Tie the neck of the bag tight and hang the bag with the leaves facing downward in a warm, airy place. The bag keeps light from degrading the leaves and flowers and catches any seeds that pop. Fresh leaves and seeds that have good flavor after drying include anise seeds, sweet basil, bay laurel, caraway seeds, celery seeds, dill seeds, fennel seeds, juniper berries, marjoram, mint, mustard seeds, oregano, poppy seeds, rosemary, sage, summer savory, tarragon, and thyme. Dried herbs and spices should be packed in tightly closed glass jars and kept in a cool, dark, dry place. (Glass best keeps aromas in—and out.)

Grind seeds fresh whenever possible in a small spice or coffee mill. The depth of flavor will amaze you—and whole spices will keep infinitely better than ground ones. The flavor of whole seeds is intensified when they are toasted first. This is best done in a dry skillet. Shake the seeds over medium heat until you can smell them. Be careful not to let them burn.

ALLSPICE (JAMAICAN PEPPER) *Berries:* Allspice berries taste principally of cloves, with whiffs of cinnamon, nutmeg, and ginger. Small, round, and reddish brown, the berries are from large evergreen trees, the finest of which are grown on the island of Jamaica. ***Alternative:*** cloves.

ANGELICA *Leaves:* Their flavor is a lightly sweet mix of licorice and fresh-cut hay. These might be lovage leaves, except they are dark green and even more serrated at the edges. ***Alternative:*** lovage.

ANISE (ANISEED) *Seeds:* Anise seeds look like those of caraway but are flatter. Bite into a seed and the flavor is sweet licorice, with heat. ***Alternative:*** fennel.

ANNATTO (ACHIOTE) *Seeds:* From spiny pods of the tropical lipstick tree come seeds that look like tiny chips of red brick. Used in small amounts, the seeds have no flavor—annatto can be used as food coloring for butter, margarine, or cheese because it does not affect the food's flavor. Used in quantity, the seeds taste musky, reminiscent of turmeric and saffron. Their color is released by heating in fat. ***Alternative:*** Safflower flowers.

BASIL *Leaves:* Like scented geraniums, basil leaves are spicy at bottom, then overlaid with delicious oils found in other plants. Sweet basils combine oils also in anise, orange blossoms, and lilacs.

Spicy basils have red stems, and their green leaves tend to be brushed with purple. Lemon basil is in a class of its own. To our taste, the blend of lemon and basil just may be the most brilliant marriage of flavors in all herb leaves. ***Alternative:*** Mint with a little marjoram; lemon verbena; or ground anise, cinnamon, or cloves.

BAY (BAY LAUREL) *Leaves:* From a graceful evergreen tree, these are long, narrow, pointed, dark, and leathery. Their flavor is pungent and complex—something between eucalyptus, mint, lemon, and fresh-cut grass. Do not confuse them with the far commoner California Bay, which is what is sold in this country as "bay leaves." European bay laurel leaves are labeled as imported. ***Alternative:*** Thyme.

BURNET *Leaves:* Burnet's dainty green leaves are round and pinked at the edges. Their flavor is astonishingly cucumber-like. It is important to select the youngest leaves you can find, because as the leaves age, they toughen. ***Alternative:*** Borage.

CALIFORNIA BAY *Leaves:* This leaf has the same shape as bay laurel, but when you feel the leaves, the bay laurel feels firm while the California bay, by comparison, feels soft. Bay laurel's flavor is smoky/spicy. This bay's flavor is pungent, sweet, lemony, spicy, with a trace of clove—and turpentine.

CAPERS *Buds:* These are the preserved buds of a white flower on a spiny Mediterranean shrub. Freshly picked, the buds are startlingly bitter, reminiscent of raw artichoke hearts. The smallest capers are called nonpareil. Capers are far better packed under salt but are usually found in brine. Always drain and rinse capers before using, however they are packed. ***Alternative:*** Chopped gherkins.

CARAWAY *Seeds:* From a flower that looks like Queen Anne's lace, these tiny, hard, brown seeds are ridged, tapered, and slightly curved. They are intensely aromatic and have a warm, nutty flavor touched with anise, dill, and sometimes lemon.

CARDAMOM *Seeds:* In tropical rain forests, tall plants in the ginger family produce small pods that contain a dozen or more bumpy seeds—among the world's most ancient spices. The pods are oval and green, even after drying in the sun. In this natural state, the seeds are at the peak of quality—near black in color, with a strong, spicy fragrance and fresh, sweet taste. However, some spice merchants like the pods paper white, so they bleach them, lightening not just the pods' but the seeds' color and blunting their intensity. If you cannot find green pods, bleached pods are preferable to ground seeds; the seeds quickly lose their vitality once crushed. Finely crush the hard seeds with a mortar and pestle as needed. Shake through a sieve to cull the pods. The aroma of ground cardamom is elusive—a ghost of ginger, hints of coriander, white pepper, and perhaps nutmeg. *Alternative:* Coriander.

CHAMOMILE *Flowers:* It is principally the yellow centers of these daisylike blossoms that are apple scented and, when dried, make legendary chamomile tea.

CHERVIL *Leaves:* Chervil looks like small, dark green ferns. Its flavor is slightly aniselike. *Alternative:* Tarragon leaves and fennel flowers for the flavor.

CHILI POWDER Based on ground dried chilies, this is a blend created to flavor Southwestern dishes. It is as individual as the person who prepares it. Sometimes it is very dark, sometimes a rusty red. Stir over the lowest heat until you can smell the spices.

NEW MEXICAN CHILI POWDER *About ½ cup*

Combine and toast in a skillet over medium heat for 2 minutes:

5 tablespoons ground mild chili peppers, such as New Mexico, pasilla, or ancho
2 tablespoons dried oregano
1½ tablespoons ground cumin
½ teaspoon ground red pepper, or to taste

CHIVES *Leaves:* The slim, tubular leaves of chives are diminutive versions of scallion leaves. The only concern about using chives is to cut and add them close to serving time to preserve their crisp texture and flavor. *Alternative:* Scallion tops.

CINNAMON AND CASSIA *Bark:* True cinnamon is the bark of a tree that flourishes in Ceylon and along the Malabar Coast. It is extremely mild, whether rolled in a tight quill or stick or in powdered form. Often the so-called cinnamon on the market is really cassia, a close but much less delicately flavored relative; cassia bark also is rolled into quills. *Alternative:* Ground cloves.

CLOVES *Buds:* The spicy, dried, rich red, unopened bud of the clove tree contains so much oil that you can express a drop with a fingernail. *Alternative:* Cinnamon.

CORIANDER *Seeds:* Coriander seeds—small (about 1/7 inch), round, ribbed, and light brown—are among the most venerable of spices. Their flavor is an exquisite blend of white pepper, cardamom, and cloves with a hint of orange. *Alternative:* Cardamom. *Leaves:* Commonly called **cilantro,** these leaves have a piercing flavor. Some perceive it as a blend hinting of flat-leaf parsley, juniper berries, mint, and lovage; others find it a mix of orange peel and sage. Cilantro leaves do not hold their flavor when dried. *Alternative:* Flat-leaf parsley for its shape or a spicy basil for its flavor.

CUMIN *Seeds:* Seeds of a plant native to the Nile Valley; the flavor is strong, hot, faintly bitter, with a touch of caraway. The seeds should be roasted in a dry skillet before using whole or grinding into a powder. *Alternative:* Caraway seeds.

CURRY POWDER Packaged curry powder was probably another British invention. Hoping to export to England the flavors they had enjoyed in India, the British likely took back with them one of the southern Indian spice mixtures—perhaps a *kari podi* (curry powder) or a *sambar podi* (*sambar* powder). This blend was added to Western-style flour-bound stews that were then dubbed curries. Indian cooks do not use a single spice mixture to flavor their cooking. Rather each dish is flavored individually with a combination of spices, called a masala, that may be simple or complex and that varies with the individual cook, the dish, and the region. Madras Curry Powder, below, is a variation on a Southern Indian *sambar* powder; a *sambar* is a soupy, southern Indian dish based on a legume such as lentils, mung beans, or pigeon peas with vegetables.

MADRAS CURRY POWDER *About 1⅓ cups*

Curry (or kari) leaves are the leaves of the kari plant, used to flavor the cooking of southern and southwestern India. Fresh leaves are sold at Indian specialty stores. You may substitute dried leaves, but their flavor is much less pungent.

Toast in a heated skillet over medium heat until a shade darker and fragrant, about 4 minutes:

6 tablespoons whole coriander seeds
4 tablespoons whole cumin seeds
3 tablespoons *chana dal* or yellow split peas
1 tablespoon black peppercorns
1 tablespoon black mustard seeds
5 dried red chili peppers
10 fresh or dried curry leaves (optional)

Combine the toasted spices with:

2 tablespoons fenugreek seeds

Grind the mixture to a powder in batches in a spice mill or electric coffee grinder. Mix well with:

3 tablespoons turmeric

Store in an airtight container in a cool place.

DILL *Leaves:* As feathery as fennel, these pungent and slightly tangy, somewhat caraway-flavored leaves are one of the best complements for fish, lamb, chicken, eggs, salad greens, beets, carrots, cucumbers, cabbages, and potatoes—and, of course, they are an integral part of dill pickles. Dried, the leaves are sold as dill weed. The leaves are best raw; when cooked, they lose strength. Because each leaf is not much thicker than a thread, the warm green leaves make a handsome garnish. *Seeds:* The small, flat, oval seeds bear a fine dill flavor and can be used every way the leaves are used. *Flowers:* Butter yellow and borne in inverted umbrellas, the tender flower heads can be used just like the leaves; in fact they are particularly appealing in a jar of pickles. *Alternative:* Caraway.

EPAZOTE *Leaves:* This pungent herb native to Mexico is commonly used in long-simmered dishes, such as black beans. There are green and purple varieties, though there is no discernible difference in the flavor of the two.

FENNEL *Leaves:* Both common (wild) and Florence (bulb)

fennel have wispy leaves fragrant with licorice, but it is common fennel that is used as an herb and source of aromatic seeds. *Seeds and flowers:* These have the same uses as the leaves, but the seeds (again, from common fennel, not the bulb familiar from supermarkets) have a more concentrated flavor and are wonderfully tasty in fresh sausages, meat loaf, tomato sauces, bread, candy, pickles, and fruit dishes with apples and pears. *Alternative:* Dill or caraway.

FENUGREEK *Leaves:* A member of the pea family; small leaves are borne three to a stem and look a bit like clover. The aroma is a pungent blend of celery and maple, and the flavor is bitter until cooked. *Alternative:* Lovage or celery.

FINES HERBES *Leaves:* The "fine" in "fines herbes" refers to the degree that they have been chopped. The term indicates equal parts finely chopped parsley, chervil, tarragon, and chives.

FIVE-SPICE POWDER The first three ingredients in this licorice-scented brown powder are star anise, Szechuan pepper, and fennel or anise seeds. Cinnamon and cloves bring the number to five, but two more may be added, chosen from licorice root, cardamom, and ginger. To prepare the mixture yourself, mix by grinding into a powder equal amounts of the spices chosen; if you lack Szechuan peppercorns, use black peppercorns instead. *Alternative:* Ground star anise.

GALANGAL *Rhizome, fresh:* Related to ginger, galangals come in two forms. Greater galangal's large rhizomes look like pale yellow ginger etched with thin crosswise stripes. In Thailand, their hot, ginger-pepper, sour flavor is preferred to ginger's. The texture is woody; pieces are thinly sliced (to be left, uneaten, on the plate) or finely pounded or grated. Select and store as for fresh ginger. Lesser galangal is a smaller rhizome with orange-red flesh and a stronger flavor. It is an ingredient in some bitters, liqueurs, and beers; in China, lesser galangal infusions are used medicinally. It is rarely available fresh. *Alternative:* Half ginger and half black pepper, in small amounts.

GARAM MASALA *About 1 cup*

This is the traditional blend of spices characterizing the flavor of Moghul and North Indian dishes, including Tandoori food.

To make 1 cup, put in a heavy plastic bag and smash with a rolling pin until lightly crushed:

½ cup green or black cardamom pods

Break open the pods and pull out the tiny seeds. Discard the pods and combine the seeds with:

⅓ cup whole cloves
Scant ¼ cup cumin seeds
Scant ¼ cup black peppercorns
5 hefty (about ⅓ inch thick) 3-inch-long cinnamon sticks

Grind the mixture to a powder in batches in a spice mill or electric coffee grinder. Store in an airtight container in a cool place.

GINGER *Rhizome, fresh:* Mistakenly called a root, ginger is a tropical rhizome that is thought to be native to Southeast Asia. If it is fresh and firm, it will keep for a week or so sitting on the counter. To keep it longer, it should go into the vegetable crisper in the refrigerator, inside a perforated plastic bag with a paper towel to absorb any moisture. When buying, select the hardest, heaviest rhizomes; those that have been sitting around will be wrinkled and light in weight. Check where the knobs have been broken: the longer the rhizome has grown before harvesting, the more fibrous it becomes, and the more fibers you will see at the break. Mature fresh ginger is hotter and to some extent more flavorful, but the fibers of an old rhizome may hinder the fine cuts required in Chinese cooking. *Rhizome, dried (ground ginger):* The indispensable spice for gingerbread, gingersnaps, ginger ale, and ginger beer. The ground spice can be substituted for fresh, but the spice is much hotter, so add it slowly as you taste.

HORSERADISH *Root:* This is a long, cream-colored, tapering root. The flavor of grated horseradish is that of radishes to the umpteenth power. Stirred into a paste with cider vinegar, finely grated horseradish is an incomparable finish for boiled beef, poached chicken, fish, shellfish, gefilte fish, potatoes, beets, and seafood cocktail sauce. (Place about 1 pound diced peeled root in a food processor. Process until finely chopped, then drizzle in cider vinegar until the mixture is of a spreadable consistency. Add salt and a few tablespoons sugar, to taste. This keeps several months in the refrigerator.) When the root is not in season (early spring), prepared horseradish sauce can be found in the grocery deli case.

HYSSOP *Leaves:* A hyssop plant looks like a small rosemary, except the green leaves are soft rather than leathery. This is one of the rare herbs with a truly bitter taste, yet there is a minty quality beneath the bitterness.

JUNIPER BERRIES *Berries:* Round and dark as a small blueberry, these dried berries of a juniper shrub smell like the forest when crushed. They also emit a whiff of gin, as they are one of the aromatics used to flavor gin. *Alternative:* A splash of gin.

LEMON GRASS *Leaves:* Lemon grass is an herb. Fresh lemon grass is sold by the stalk, which is gray-green, is 2 feet in length, and looks something like a scallion, though it is fibrous to the point of being woody. For this reason, unlike seasonings such as garlic and ginger, it is valued for the flavor it imparts rather than the substance it adds. Only the bulblike 6- to 8-inch base is used, after the top is trimmed and a layer of tough outer leaves is peeled off.

LEMON VERBENA *Leaves:* There is no getting bored with lemon verbena's sweet citrus fragrance. The oval, bright green leaves make exquisite tea. Because their flavor is delicate, be prepared to use rather a lot of fresh leaves. For example, if you wish to replace vanilla extract and infuse a custard with lemon verbena, it will take ½ cup finely snipped leaves for 1 teaspoon vanilla. *Alternative:* lemon grass or lemon zest.

LOVAGE *Leaves:* The leaves of this bold herb, whose stems can be candied like angelica or blanched and eaten like celery, are often used as a celery substitute; their flavor is spicier. *Alternative:* Celery.

MINT *Leaves:* The genus *Mentha* probably includes twenty-five distinct species, but these have hybridized among themselves so readily that over six hundred mints have been named. The true mints we commonly use for cooking are peppermint and spearmint. Peppermint is spicy, and its leaves are considered superior for drying. Pick mint leaves for drying before the plants flower. Cut off the stems at the ground, save the top two or three sets of leaves for cooking or garnish, then strip the remaining leaves and dry them. Dry leaves whole, being careful not to crumble until using them.

MUSTARD *Seeds:* Yellow, or white, mustard seeds are relatively large; most are ground into mustard powder and/or blended into prepared mustard. Their flavor is spicy and almost sweet. Brown mustard seeds come from another plant; their flavor is hot and slightly bitter. Toast either sort of seeds in a little butter or oil in a skillet until you can smell them. Tiny black mustard seeds are the most pungent. ***Alternative:*** Caraway seeds.

NUTMEG AND MACE *Seed:* Two spices come from the brown, oval seed of a fruit resembling an apricot, which grows on a tropical evergreen tree. Wrapped around the shell of the seed is a lacy sheath, which is ground before packing. A blade of mace is one segment of the lacy covering, called the aril. Scarlet when the fruit is opened, the aril dries to a shade of orange. Several weeks after harvest, when the kernel has shrunk in its shell, the thin shell is cracked and the kernel removed. This is nutmeg—brown, solid, and hard. Nutmeg is best freshly grated. As warm a spice as nutmeg is, mace is more refined and can be used in place of nutmeg.

OREGANO AND MARJORAM *Leaves:* These two herbs are listed together because they are so closely related and are easily confused. Both are members of the mint family. Oregano is earthier, and its leaves are larger and darker. Leaves are medium green and somewhat heart shaped, from ¼ to 1½ inches long. We hope the oregano will be Greek oregano and the marjoram, sweet marjoram. (Of the numerous varieties, Greek oregano and sweet marjoram set the standard.) Sweet marjoram is a summer herb—spicy, sweet, and intense yet light. ***Alternative:*** Sweet basil or mint.

PAPRIKA *Pods:* Finely ground dried ripe peppers constitute this spice. Depending on the pepper used, the color varies from light orange to deep red, the flavor from bland to rich but mild. *Sweet* paprika is ground from the flesh of particularly sweet peppers with most, if not all, of their seeds and ribs removed—these parts can be sharp tasting. By contrast, *hot* paprika is prepared with peppers whose flesh contains more heat; some seeds and ribs may be added. Most paprikas are blends that fall between sweet and hot. The best paprika has long come from Hungary, where paprika making is an important culinary tradition. ***Alternative:*** Ground red pepper—but just one-eighth the amount, for it is far hotter and not as sweet.

PARSLEY *Leaves:* In this country and in Britain, curly-leaf parsley is favored. In Europe, flat-leaf parsley—often called Italian parsley—is preferred for its richer taste. Curled or flat, parsley leaves can be vibrant or subtle. Stems are used in white stocks and sauces for their strength and because they do not color the sauce, as the leaves do. Because they contain so much chlorophyll, chewing the fresh leaves will destroy the scent of garlic and onion on your breath.

PEPPER *Berries:* Pepper is the fruit of a leafy green vine that has spikes of white flowers; the flowers become clusters of green berries. The soft green berries are usually preserved in vinegar in jars, although some are strung and shipped in their plump green state. Green peppercorns have a mild fresh flavor and are delicious chopped and creamed with butter as a seasoning or stirred into light sauces. Black peppercorns are green berries that are piled up and fermented for a few days, then dried in the sun, to become hard, wrinkled, and dark brown to black. Their flavor is rich and spicy, especially if the berries are Malabar peppercorns. Tellicherry is another fine berry. On the vine, the berries ripen to red. These are picked and soaked in water so the skin can be rubbed off, revealing a gray core. These are dried until they turn buff color—white peppercorns. White pepper has the hottest flavor, sometimes with a hint of ginger. It is the preferred pepper for light-colored foods—unless a color contrast is wanted. Try the French practice of combining equal parts black and white peppercorns in a mill; you will have the aromatic qualities of the black and the strength of the white. Peppercorns have different flavors, depending on how they are presented. Used whole to flavor soups and other long-cooking mixtures, their flavor is discreet; tie the whole berries in a cloth, then remove them before serving. When peppercorns are freshly crushed with a mortar and pestle, most of their oils are retained and the flavor is enormously pungent. Crushed pepper is wonderful pressed into the flesh of meats before grilling or sprinkled over pale fish and meats before serving. When ground in a mill, oils are dispersed and the pepper's flavor is light but still pungent. Because the oils are scattered to the air, ground pepper rapidly loses its quality. That is why you cheat yourself of flavor when you season with preground pepper. Pepper is not just for savory foods. Sneak a pinch of white pepper into cookies, cakes, and fruit dishes or try freshly ground black pepper on strawberries and discover the lift it gives. ***Alternative:*** Ground ginger.

QUATRE ÉPICES

This is a classic French combination of white pepper, nutmeg, ginger or cinnamon, and cloves. ***Alternative:*** Ginger.

For 1 teaspoon, mix together the following, freshly and finely grated or ground:

Rounded ½ teaspoon white pepper
Scant ¼ teaspoon nutmeg
Very scant ¼ teaspoon ginger or cinnamon
Generous pinch of cloves

RAS EL HANOUT

About ½ cup

Morocco's ras el hanout contains many different elements, from seeds, leaves, flowers, roots, and bark to Spanish fly beetle, a supposed aphrodisiac. It is usually added by the pinch or half teaspoon to stews of meat and poultry and to couscous dishes.

Mix together thoroughly:

2 tablespoons ground ginger
2 teaspoons ground black pepper
2 teaspoons ground allspice
2 teaspoons ground nutmeg

2 teaspoons ground mace
2 teaspoons ground cardamom
2 teaspoons ground cinnamon
2 teaspoons ground turmeric
1 teaspoon ground coriander
¼ teaspoon ground cloves
¼ teaspoon ground red pepper

ROSEMARY *Leaves:* From a distance, rosemary's leaves appear like diminutive pine needles on long, thin branches. The leaves are gray-green to green and sharp. No leaves are more pungent. Their fragrance and flavor might be described as pine mixed with mint. This is not an herb that can be subtle. Because the leaves are tough, chop them fairly fine. This releases even more of their flavor. The leaves dry well. ***Alternative:*** For their pungency, oregano or sweet basil leaves and flowers.

SAFFRON *Stigmas:* The golden red stigmas of the autumn crocus contribute extraordinary fragrance, aromatic flavor, and golden color. The tiny threads are strong. Just the right amount, and the dish is perfumed. Two or three stigmas too many, and the dish is bitter. When selecting saffron, the deeper the color, the finer the quality. The way to glean the most from the threads and to spread their color evenly is to make an infusion with liquid that can be used in the dish. Add the saffron called for to as much hot (not boiling) liquid as you can use—the more liquid, the farther the flavor will be carried. Let stand until the color is deep and bright and the aroma fills the kitchen. If the infusion is for rice or something similar, you may want to strain out and discard the stigmas—they will stain the food around them, giving a blotchy appearance. If you are baking with saffron, ¼ teaspoon steeped in 2 tablespoons hot water will suffice for 5 to 6 cups flour. Use only about ⅛ to ¼ teaspoon in 2 tablespoons hot water, stock, or white wine to season 6 to 8 servings of a sauce. Powdered saffron also is available, but it may be adulterated with false saffron. ***Alternative:*** For the color and some of the perfume, turmeric.

SAGE *Leaves:* The long, pebbled, gray-green leaves of common sage are among the best-loved herbs in this country. Their flavor is smoky and musky. Its astringent quality makes it excellent for cutting the richness of foods. The flavor of dried leaves is close to the fresh, but they soon lose much of their volatile oil. Dry the leaves carefully, as they are thick and mold easily. ***Alternative:*** Summer savory and thyme.

SANSHO (JAPANESE PEPPER) ***Pods:*** Sansho is the coarsely ground dried pods of a tree whose leaves are used as an herb, *kinome.* The tangy green-brown spice is sprinkled over food the way we sprinkle pepper, but it is not hot; "pepper" is a misnomer. ***Alternative:*** Lemon zest, for its tang.

SAVORY *Leaves:* Winter savory is a warming herb with small, thin, aromatic leaves. But it is summer savory's more delicate flavor that is preferred by most cooks. ***Alternative:*** Sweet marjoram.

SESAME *Seeds:* Sesame seeds grow in the pods of white or pink flowers on a medium-sized plant. The variety of the plant determines the color of the seeds. The flavor of the seeds is nutty and sweet. Black seeds are more flavorful and aromatic than the white. Brown sesame seeds are unhulled white seeds. All these seeds usually are toasted before using: stir constantly in a skillet over medium heat until the white and brown seeds are barely golden and the black begin to release their fragrance.

STAR ANISE From a small evergreen that grows in southwestern China and northern Vietnam, this striking-looking eight-pointed pod is one of the few spices used in Chinese cooking. Because of its more intense flavor and higher essential oil content, star anise is used in the West as a licorice flavoring more often than aniseed—by the French in anisette, for example. The Chinese use star anise in much the same way they use cinnamon, and sometimes in conjunction with it, whole, in meat and poultry dishes. It is also one of the six or seven components of five-spice powder. The Vietnamese add star anise pods to their beef soup called *phở*. Star anise is sold in plastic bags. Stored in a jar away from light and heat, it will keep for months.

SZECHUAN PEPPERCORNS The dried reddish-brown berries known as Szechuan peppercorns are not related to black peppercorns or chili peppers. The spice has a clean, spicy-woodsy fragrance that has made it popular in all regions of China for centuries. "Seasoned salt" (see below) is a popular accompaniment to fried and roasted foods. "Seasoned oil"—made by heating Szechuan peppercorns in peanut oil until they blacken, then straining the oil and discarding the peppercorns—makes a wonderful cooking oil for stir-fried dishes, or it may be used for dressing Chinese salads. Szechuan peppercorns are sold in plastic packages. They keep well in a covered jar.

To Make Szechuan Pepper: Toast Szechuan peppercorns in a dry skillet over medium heat until they begin to smoke (do not worry if a few blacken slightly) and then grind them in a mortar or spice grinder. Store excess powder in a jar.

To Make Seasoned Salt: Put 2 tablespoons Szechuan peppercorns, 3 tablespoons coarse salt, and 1 teaspoon white peppercorns in a dry skillet. Toast over medium heat, shaking the pan, until the Szechuan peppercorns begin to really smoke. Transfer to a mortar or spice grinder and grind to a coarse powder.

TARRAGON, FRENCH *Leaves:* The word *aromatic* especially suits tarragon. The components of its flavor are identical to those of anise—eating the long slender leaves is like eating leafy licorice. ***Alternative:*** Anise or fennel leaves.

THYME *Leaves:* Rare is the vegetable, meat, or poultry dish that cannot be enhanced by these tiny, pointed, gray-green leaves with their sweet wild-brush fragrance. Garden thyme is sometimes called English thyme. The French favor wild thyme for cooking, which, despite its name, is milder than garden thyme. Thyme is perfect for earthy cooking—rich stews, roasted game, thick pasta sauces. The only caution in pairing thyme with vegetables is to use less than you think you might need. Lemon thyme blends garden thyme's muted sweet flavor with clear lemon, a magnificent combination. Thyme leaves dry very well. ***Alternative:*** Young sage leaves and flowers.

TURMERIC *Rhizome:* A rhizome related to ginger. The dried ground spice is an intense gold and tastes musky, peppery, gingery, and warm. In small quantities, it can be used as coloring, often replacing saffron for this purpose. ***Alternative:*** Curry powder.

VANILLA *Pod:* The long, thin vanilla bean is a pod from the orchid flower of a tropical vine. When the unripe bean is picked, it has no flavor. In curing for several months, tiny fragrant white crystals called vanillin are secreted from the pod's lining. Eventually their aroma fills the inside of the pod as the crystals cover the outside. The pod wrinkles a bit and turns chocolate brown. When the pod is slit open lengthwise, black specks of seeds can be scraped from the center with the tip of a sharp knife. ***Extract:*** Pure vanilla extract is prepared by steeping the pods in alcohol.

ABOUT NUTS Nuts are large seeds of fruits, with hard external husks. (The exception is the peanut, which is a root legume used the same way nuts are.) Nuts contain concentrated protein and carbohydrates and a particularly high percentage of fats, mostly monounsaturated or polyunsaturated. A few varieties, such as Brazil nuts and chestnuts, contain fiber or starch or both, but most contain neither.

Because nuts contain oil, they turn rancid over time and are best stored in their shells. Most unshelled nuts will keep for at least 2 months and sometimes for up to 1 year in the refrigerator. They also will keep for a year or more in the freezer with little or no loss of quality. Shelled nuts should be stored, tightly covered, in a cool, dark, dry place or in the freezer. Unless frozen, these may become rancid in only a few weeks, so be sure to use them as quickly as possible. Unsalted nuts have a longer storage life than salted ones. Some nuts with particularly stubborn husks, like pecans and Brazil nuts, are more easily shelled if boiling water is poured over them and they are allowed to stand for 15 to 20 minutes. Be sure to discard any kernels that are moldy, shriveled, or dry, as they may prove bitter or rancid. Except for green almonds and pickled green walnuts, nuts are eaten ripe.

As a general rule, 1 pound nuts in the shell yields about ½ pound shelled.

BLANCHING NUTS In addition to the tough outer shell, some nuts, like hazelnuts and almonds, have a thin inner lining or skin that may need removing, as it can be bitter and somewhat unattractive. To do this, blanch them by pouring boiling water over the shelled nuts just before using. Drain the nuts, pour cold water over them, and drain again. You may have to let large quantities of nuts stand in the boiling water, but for only about a minute at the most. After blanching, pinch or rub off the skins. Peanuts, hazelnuts, and pistachio nuts also can be prepared by roasting in 350°F oven for 10 to 20 minutes; remove the skins by rubbing the nuts together in a dish towel to loosen the covering (this can be done when the nuts are hot or cool).

TOASTING NUTS Toasting nuts crisps them and brings out their flavor. To toast nuts in the oven: Spread them blanched or unblanched on an ungreased baking sheet and bake in a 325°F oven for 5 to 7 minutes, depending on the size of the nuts, checking and stirring often to prevent burning. To toast nuts on top of the stove: Place them in a dry skillet over medium heat and cook, stirring or shaking the pan frequently to prevent burning, until they just begin to release their fragrance, about 4 minutes.

To avoid loss of flavor and toughening, do not overtoast, as nuts tend to darken further and become crisper as they cool.

Let toasted nuts cool completely before processing them in a food processor or blender.

Toasted nuts can be stored, covered, in a cool, dry place for up to 2 weeks.

CHOPPING, PULVERIZING, AND MEASURING NUTS If large nut pieces are needed, simply break nuts like pecans and walnuts with your fingers. For finer pieces, use a chopping bowl and chopper or a very sharp knife. Gather the nuts together in a circle with a diameter almost as wide as the blade, and holding the top of the knife at the point, rock the blade briskly from point to hilt, gradually turning the knife toward you in a semicircle. (The crescent-shaped Italian chopping tool called a *mezzaluna* works well for this.) Gather the pieces together and repeat the process until the proper size is achieved. If you chop the nuts in a food processor, be very careful not to overprocess, because too many essential oils will be lost; nuts turn to butter in a flash. Process small batches as briefly as possible to achieve the desired fineness. Nuts are best grated with a special drum-style nut grater, rather than with a type that will crush them and release their oils. We also find that a clean, dry food processor bowl fitted with a reasonably sharp dry blade does a very fine job of pulverizing nuts without turning them oily or pasty—but, again, be careful not to overprocess them. A blender is not as effective as a processor; if you are stuck with one, pulverize only ¼ cup nuts at a time, making sure that the container and blade are dry before you start. Do not use a meat grinder, which crush the nuts and release the oils. Toasted nuts should be cooled completely before being pulverized.

It is the volume of nuts after grating or processing that should be measured, not the quantity of nuts you start with.

ABOUT OLIVES In the Mediterranean region, where most olives are grown, as much care is put into olive growing as into wine or cheese making; to classify olives as being simply green or black would not do justice to the wealth of piquant, nutty, sweet, and fruity olives available. If an olive is green, it has been harvested when it has grown to normal size but just before it has ripened. A black olive is allowed to fully ripen to a rich dark-purple hue before harvesting. Otherwise, the differences between types of olives are in how they are cured and processed. This involves either fermentation, the method used in Spain, where olives can then be stuffed with pimiento, onions, or almonds, or soaking the olives in brine, as is done in Greece and Italy, where other flavors like lemon or pepper are sometimes added. These processes produce crunchy, tart olives within a few weeks and chewy, sweeter olives within months. The American method used to produce "canned ripe olives" is an industrial, time-efficient method of soaking olives quickly in an alkaline solution, then boiling them in an iron compound, which ultimately strips the fruit of much characteristic taste and texture. Olives also can be dry- or oil-cured—that is, packed and aged in salt or oil—which produces a dry, wrinkled fruit that retains some bitterness.

Taste rather than size should determine your olive selection, so when considering olives for the table, martinis, or recipes such as aïoli or tapenade, explore the delicious array of Greek, Italian, French, Spanish, or Californian olives to find what best satisfies your palate. From Greece, the famous Kalamata olives are purple-black or maroon with a slender oval shape, soft texture, and rich flavor. The dark green naphlion are cracked before being cured, resulting in a crisp and fruity olive. Royal olives are cured with oil and vinegar and so are slightly chewy, with a similar flavor to Kalamatas but a more reddish hue.

From Italy, Gaeta olives are brownish black, smoothly soft, with a nutty, almost earthy, flavor. For a special treat try Sicilian green olives; they are tart and meaty and sometimes come spiced with red pepper or fennel. Less common Italian olives include the mellow tan-colored Calabrese, the salty and firm black Lugano, and the quite piquant and tart, brown-black Liguria.

The best-known French olive is certainly the Niçoise, which is a characteristic flavor of southern France. These olives are small, have a relatively large pit, and are often allowed to cure for several months until they are quite black and chewy. Niçoise olives can also be found cured in oil (sometimes with the addition of garlic and lemon), a process that serves to amplify their flavor and chewy texture. Picholine olives are greatly appreciated for their crisp, tart quality—these oblongs are best picked and cured when green and eaten relatively fresh. If you can find them, caillet roux, which are slightly red and peppery, plump black bouteillan, and the smaller, bitter brown Nyons olives are all worth a try. And do not neglect wrinkled black Moroccan olives or any type of Spanish olive, particularly black, firm, and nutty picual olives. Chilean black Alfonsos are soft-skinned and tender with a light vinegary taste, while Lebanese green Phonecia olives are packed in a robust, garlicky olive oil.

California also produces some fine olives. Try bottled Californian Greek-style black or green olives and dry-cured black olives, which are quite meaty and tender.

Buy olives that are uniform in color and free of surface blemishes and white spots. Keep loose olives in the refrigerator for several weeks; canned or bottled olives can be kept unopened on the shelf for up to two years and when opened should be refrigerated as loose olives.

ABOUT ASIAN INGREDIENTS

BEAN SAUCE Bean sauce is an essential ingredient in dishes of every region of China. (The beans are soybeans.) You can find it labeled as "whole bean sauce," which has a unique texture, or as "ground bean sauce," which tends to be saltier. All types of bean sauce can be stored indefinitely tightly covered in the refrigerator.

BONITO FLAKES Bonito flakes are dried, salted, fermented fish flakes. They keep indefinitely on a cool, dark shelf.

FISH SAUCE Called *nu'o'c ma'm* in Vietnam and *nam pla* in Thailand, fish sauce is made by packing fish, usually anchovies, in crocks or barrels, covering them with brine, and allowing them to ferment in the tropical sun over a period of months. The resulting brown liquid is drained off and used. Like olive oil, the first pressing (in this case siphoning), from which flows a clear amber liquid, is most highly prized and is usually reserved for dipping sauces. Fish sauce keeps indefinitely on the shelf.

HOISIN SAUCE This brownish red member of the soybean family is almost always sweet, garlicky, and spicy. It has the anise flavor of five-spice powder and is peppered with a little dried chili. The texture ranges from a creamy jam to a runny sauce. Store for up to 1 year in a dark cupboard away from heat.

KELP Sold as "Dashi Kombu," a 6-ounce package will be enough to make six batches of broth for 4 to 6 people. The whitish coating on kelp is okay. Kelp should never be washed, or it will lose flavor. Used dried or fresh, kelp may also be served as a vegetable. Kelp keeps indefinitely in a tightly sealed container.

MIRIN Sometimes called "sweet sake," mirin is rice wine with an 8 percent alcohol content and loads of sugar. Buy *hon-mirin*, which is naturally brewed and contains natural sugars, if you can find it. *Aji-mirin* is sweetened with corn syrup and may contain other additives. Mirin can be stored indefinitely on a cool, dark shelf.

MISO Miso, a fermented paste made from soybeans, comes in a variety of colors (from white to yellow to red) and textures (smooth or chunky), depending on the length of fermentation and the addition of grains such as barley or rice. As a general rule, the darker the miso, the longer it has been fermented and the stronger and saltier it will taste. Lighter miso, fermented for a shorter period, is sweeter. Barley miso is earthy and well aged. Although miso rarely spoils, it loses its flavor after a few months. Keep opened containers in the refrigerator.

NORI Nori are the paper-thin sheets of seaweed used to wrap sushi rolls. Keep nori in the freezer—the sheets thaw almost instantaneously and can be refrozen.

OYSTER SAUCE Originally made from oysters, water, and salt only, oyster sauce now contains added cornstarch and caramel color, to improve its appearance and also to thicken liquids in stir-fries. When buying oyster sauce, avoid the cheaper varieties, which contain fewer oysters and more cornstarch. You can store it in the refrigerator for years.

RICE PAPER Made from a dough of rice flour, water, and salt, rice paper is available in Asian markets. The sheets are brittle and must be handled with care. To soften, brush each sheet liberally on both sides with water. The sheets should then sit for a minute or two until they are soft and workable.

RICE WINE AND SAKE *Shaoxing (Shaoshing) Wine*, China's most famous rice wine, from Shaoshing in Zhejiang province, has been made, it is said, for over 2,000 years. Blended glutinous rice, rice millet, a special yeast, and local mineral and spring waters give this amber-colored beverage its unique flavor. More like sherry in color, bouquet, and alcohol content (18 percent) than like sake or a grape wine, it is aged about ten years in earthenware and in underground cellars. The finest varieties age a century or more. Like sake, Shaoshing is drunk warm and is rarely left out of a dish; it is vital to Chinese cooking. A top-quality dry sherry is a good substitute.

Sake is the stronger Japanese version of rice wine—any brand of sake is suitable for use in cooking except those labeled "cooking wine," which are made from inferior rice wines and may contain additives. Sake also acts as a tenderizer in marinades and removes strong odors in cooking. When looking for a substitute, try pale dry sherry or dry vermouth.

SALTED AND FERMENTED BLACK BEANS These soybeans, partially decomposed by means of a special mold, then dried and sometimes salted, predate soy sauce. Black beans have a pleasing winy flavor and when used properly are a wonderful complement to seafood and meats. Rinsing black beans is unnecessary. When buying the salted kind, simply take their saltiness into account when adding other seasonings. Depending on the dish, black beans should be chopped lightly or crushed a little with the side of a cleaver to release their flavor, then tossed with a tablespoon or two of Shaoshing wine or dry sherry, and chopped garlic and ginger if the dish calls for them, and set aside until ready to use.

Fermented black beans, often flavored with bits of ginger and sometimes orange peel, are usually sold in 8-ounce packages. After the package is opened, they should be transferred to a covered jar and stored away from light and heat. They will keep indefinitely.

SESAME OIL In China, sesame oil is considered too expensive to cook with, but it is highly prized as a seasoning sprinkled over dishes just at the end of cooking. The best and most flavorful sesame oil is pressed from seeds that have first been toasted; oil made from raw seeds cannot compare in flavor. In Japan, tempura oil may contain up to one-half sesame oil and is suitable for deep-frying; sesame oil on its own burns too quickly to stand up to this kind of heat. It is best bought in glass bottles or tins, in which it goes rancid much less quickly than in plastic. Keep for only a month or two in a cool cabinet.

SESAME PASTE Asian sesame paste is made from toasted and ground sesame seeds. It keeps well in the refrigerator, like fresh peanut butter; like fresh peanut butter, it tends to separate into oil and solid. Be sure to stir before using.

SOY SAUCE Soy sauce is a naturally fermented product made in several steps and aged up to two years. Typically, roasted soybean meal and a lightly ground grain, usually wheat, are mixed with an *Aspergillis* mold starter; the resulting culture takes a few days to grow. Brine is then added to the fermented meal, along with a *Lactobacillus* starter and yeast. The mash is then aged slowly. When the producer determines that it is ready, the soy sauce is then strained and bottled.

Chinese Soy Sauce: The Chinese invented soy sauce, and the Japanese learned the technology from them. The Chinese use both light and dark soy sauces. The latter is aged longer and toward the end of the processing is mixed with bead molasses, which gives it a dark caramel hue. Think of them as red and white wine, since as a rule, dark soy sauce flavors (and colors) heartier dishes, particularly those with red meat, whereas light soy sauce is used with seafood, vegetables, soups, and in dipping sauces.

Japanese Soy Sauce: The technique of aging and fermenting is the same for Japanese and Chinese soy sauces, but as a rule Japanese soy sauce (*shoyu*) contains more wheat and is thus a little sweeter and less salty. Standard to Japanese cooking is what they call dark soy sauce, which is labeled simply *soy sauce, shoyu,* or *koi-kuchi shoyu.* This sauce, on a Chinese scale of dark to light, would fall on the light end, and in a pinch could be substituted for light soy. The Japanese also market low-sodium soy sauces. Like salt, however, it is better to cut back on the amount of this most fundamental seasoning than to use an altered version of it.

TAMARI This Japanese term has been misapplied to Japanese-style soy sauces of varying quality. True tamari, rare in Japan, is a rich, dark soy sauce brewed without wheat. It is a remnant of the ancient soy sauce methods learned from the Chinese.

TONKATSU SOSU (DARK SPICY SAUCE) This soybean-based Japanese sauce is sweetened through the addition of tomatoes and fruit. The interesting underlying spice makes this sauce a favorite for barbecuing or for adding flavor to breaded fried fish and vegetables. Although the sauce does not spoil, it loses some flavor after several months; it can be kept on a cool, dark shelf.

WAKAME Wakame is seaweed. After they are soaked, the leaves of the plant are briefly cooked in soups or used to make a salad. It is sold dried and packaged, sometimes labeled *ito-wakame.* To reconstitute wakame, soak it in tepid water for 20 minutes, to maintain its flavor and high nutritional value. If the stem of the seaweed is present, it should be discarded.

WASABI Fresh wasabi, a 4- to 5-inch root indigenous to swampy earth next to cold mountain streams in Japan, is rarely available. Powdered wasabi should be mixed, half and half, with tepid water and then allowed to sit for 15 minutes to develop its flavor. Mix a small lump of this pungent green paste with a little soy sauce to make a dip for sushi. Once the package of wasabi is opened, it deteriorates quickly.

ABOUT VINEGAR In most cases the product of two stages of fermentation, vinegar can be made from almost any sugary liquid. In the first fermentation, the action of yeast converts the sugar to alcohol—grape juice becomes wine, for example. In the second fermentation, bacteria convert the alcohol to acetic acid—the wine becomes vinegar.

VINEGARS FROM FRUIT

Cider Vinegar: Depending on its quality and strength (which varies enormously), apple cider vinegar is good for almost all uses.

Balsamic Vinegar: Balsamic vinegars fall into two categories. Traditional, artisan-made balsamics that are far more liqueur than salad dressing, are made only in the provinces of Modena and Reggio in northern Italy's Emilia-Romagna region and are priced between $60 and $250 for 3½ ounces. Boiled-down grape must concentrates over years of passing through a series of wooden barrels in airy attics. By law artisan balsamic contains no wine vinegar. It is aged 12 years for "vecchio" (old), and 25 years for "extra vecchio." Its guarantee of authenticity is the word *tradizionale* on its label. Use traditional balsamic as an intense sauce, by the drop, on finished dishes, never on salad. It is extraordinary on vanilla ice cream.

Easily-had commercial balsamic can be produced anywhere and is usually wine vinegar with caramel added to it. Better examples have some boiled-down must. Quality ranges from poor to fine, as no regulations govern its production. Use commercial balsamic in marinades, in dressings, and cooked into recipes.

Champagne Vinegar: In France, Champagne used for vinegar is that which comes popping out with the sediment at what is called the degorgement stage. This is very close in flavor to white wine vinegar.

Sherry Vinegar: Olorosos, the sweet sherries we know as cream and golden, are fermented in oak casks until they turn to full-bodied brownish vinegars with sherry's raisiny warmth. These are like a cross between balsamic and red wine vinegars.

Wine Vinegar: Like sherry vinegar, the best wine vinegars are fermented in oak casks. Red wine vinegars fill the mouth with their bouquets; use them with red meats, red vegetables, and dark sauces. Some white wine vinegars are fruity, some are bone dry. Match their flavor with foods.

VINEGARS FROM GRAINS

Distilled White Vinegar: It is suited only to pickling.

Malt Vinegar: Malt is made of seeds of grain that have been partially germinated, which converts their starch to malt sugar, and then gently dried in a kiln. Barley is the grain of choice; others include rye, corn, or oats. The mash gives malt vinegar its deep amber color, slightly bitter flavor, and round full body, as it does to beer, ale, and whiskey. This robust vinegar is for sprinkling.

Rice Vinegar: Much of the white rice vinegar produced by Chinese or Japanese manufacturers these days is made from rice wine lees and alcohol. It is pleasant but weaker in flavor than American white vinegars, comparable instead to cider vinegar, less the fruitiness.

ABOUT FATS IN COOKING Both liquid and solid fats have the remarkable property of separating out their own flavor molecules and embedding them in what surrounds them. In soups and stews, fat can be added during cooking and later removed; its flavor remains. Other flavors, as from garlic or onions in sautéing, are easily absorbed by fats so that during cooking they are efficiently diffused. Because they are more slowly digested than other nutrients, fats give us a sustained feeling of satiety. Fats are derived from animal sources (butter, lard, and shortening) and vegetable sources (grain, seed, and nut oils). As a general rule, most fats that are solid when refrigerated and at room temperature come from animal sources; those that are liquid at room temperature are vegetable oils. Of primary concern in choosing fats for cooking is whether they are saturated, monounsaturated, or polyunsaturated. Saturated fats play a major role in raising blood cholesterol levels and should be eaten in moderation. These fats are derived mainly from animal products, although certain vegetable oils (coconut and palm) are also highly saturated. Animal fats also contain cholesterol, while those derived from vegetable sources do not. It was long believed that polyunsaturated fats, such as corn, soybean, and sunflower oils, were the most healthful, but now the consensus is that primarily monounsaturated oils, like olive and canola, are preferable because they may be capable of lowering blood cholesterol levels.

Also important in choosing which fats to use in cooking is the taste and texture they impart to foods. Nothing reveals the personality of a cuisine so much as the fat on which it is based. Olive oil evokes sunny Mediterranean cuisine, bacon arouses memories of the American South, and sweet butter brings forth memories of fine French dishes and well-browned homemade cakes and cookies. Not only flavors but food textures change with the use of different fats, whose characteristics are as individual as their tastes.

MEASURING FATS There is no mystery involved in measuring liquid fats or sticks of butter and margarine with measurements delineated on the wrapper. But for bulk fats, like shortening or tubs of butter, the displacement method works best. If you put these fats in dry measuring cups, pockets of air can form and throw off the measurement. Instead, if you want ½ cup shortening, fill a 1-cup liquid measure half full with water, then add the fat until the water reaches the 1-cup mark. Pour off the water.

Butter is 80 percent fat, so when substituting oil, which is 100 percent fat, use 80 percent of the butter's measure in oil; a robust olive oil should be kept to 75 percent. To substitute shortening for butter, replace it evenly, measuring by volume, as butter's water content equals the air in the shortening. However, if you are measuring by weight, use 15 to 20 percent less shortening than you would butter.

No matter the type of fat, each gram has 9 calories; each ounce has 250 calories. Measuring by volume is a less precise way to compare fats, because of the air, water, or other molecules they may contain. In general, per tablespoon, whipped butter has 70 calories, butter and soft or stick margarine have 108 calories; vegetable shortening has 111; lard has 117; and vegetable oils have 120 calories.

ABOUT OILS Oil magnifies the flavor of food and can be superb in baking. The flavors of olive and walnut oils come through beautifully in yeast bread in place of butter; or try fruity olive oil in a pie pastry to be used with a savory filling.

In cold pressing, raw materials are crushed and then pressed using minimal pressure and heat. Oils extracted in this way retain their natural flavors and textures and are without question the ones to buy when possible. Very few oils today, unfortunately, are produced by cold pressing, with the exception of "extra-virgin" olive oils, often made by small producers.

The next best choice is unrefined oils, which are produced with heat but subjected to minimal manipulation, resulting in rich flavorful oils. By definition, "virgin" olive oil is produced in this way. Other oils, particularly corn, nut, and peanut oils, can be found in their unrefined state and provide surprising flavor and color. Many oils that come from Asia—peanut, soybean, rapeseed, sesame, and coconut—are also unrefined. They have been produced in small batches with simple equipment and little or no heat, thus their flavor is relatively mild and true. Unrefined oils are fragile and break down with excessive heat, so keep them in a cool, dark place and do not use them for deep-frying.

Unfortunately, most of the commercially produced oils you might find in the supermarkets have been refined, neutralized, decolored and deodorized, resulting in tasteless products. Refining purges pressed oil of unwanted elements through the application of caustic chemicals, pressure, steam, heat, cold, filtering, washing, or drying.

Keep oils in airtight containers in a cool, dark place, preferably in opaque bottles that are tall and thin. Cold-pressed and refined oils will keep unopened in the refrigerator for 1 year, but once opened should be used within a few months. Refrigeration does not affect the flavor, and if the oil clouds or congeals, it will return to its clear and liquid state at room temperature. Costly cold-pressed nut oils should always be refrigerated, because they can start to break down within a month on the shelf. Refined oils should be kept for no longer than 1 year in a cool, dark cupboard. Monounsaturated and saturated oils cloud or congeal when cold; you might decant them into a bottle or closed pitcher that will hold as much as you will use in a week and keep the rest refrigerated. Discard any oil that smells fishy, cheesy, or musty, or that starts to foam, darken, or smoke excessively when heated; Discard any oil that has smoked, has darkened, smells rancid, or does not bubble when food is added.

When cooking with any oil, avoid heating it to the point where it begins to smoke—this signals that the oil is decomposing and possibly producing harmful substances. An oil's smoke point is determined by its fatty-acid content. Monounsaturated oils, such as sunflower, peanut, and canola oil, have the highest smoke points and are suitable for high-heat cooking like deep-frying. Polyunsaturated oils are less stable and deteriorate more quickly in high heat—use those for stir-frying and other techniques that require moderate heat. Unrefined oils are best used cold. Avoid cooking with metals that can cause oils to oxidize, such as copper, brass, or bronze; opt for stainless steel instead.

VEGETABLE SEED OILS Seed oils were mostly developed in response to demand for either polyunsaturated or inexpensive cooking oils. Corn oil, by far the most commonly used in this country, is a good all-purpose oil; it is primarily polyunsaturated, has a high smoke point, and makes sautéed and deep-fried foods crispy. Unrefined corn oil is less common, but it imparts a rich popcorn flavor to foods. Canola, or rapeseed, oil has gained favor because it is very low in saturated fat and high in monounsaturated, but it is relatively flavorless—add a drop of olive oil for flavor when cooking with canola. Canola oil is a primary component of commercial vegetable oil blends. Grape, safflower, and sunflower oils have high smoke points and are high in polyunsaturated fats, making them good all-purpose oils. Sesame seeds, whether toasted or not, provide intensely perfumed oils that are best added as a flavoring to dishes cooked with a more neutral oil. Cottonseed oil, which was used extensively at the beginning of the century in this country, is best avoided, as it is highly saturated and tends to contain some residual pesticides. Poppy seed oil has long been a staple in French kitchens and is called *huile blanche,* white oil, for its clarity. Mustard seed oil and pumpkin oil are interesting choices for flavor but can be expensive and so are used as condiments.

LEGUME AND NUT OILS Peanut oil varies greatly in quality. When it has not been cold pressed (and most domestic peanut oil has not been), there is little or no peanut flavor. At Asian markets, you can find cold-pressed oils with a true peanut taste. Oils extracted from roasted almonds, walnuts, hazelnuts, macadamia nuts, and pistachios are elegant and pure tasting but expensive and fragile: they go rancid quickly and must be refrigerated. They also have low smoke points and do not stand up well to excessive heat. Use nut oils as flavorings when you would use that nut itself.

OLIVE OIL The best grades of olive oil are made simply: The fruit is crushed and the oil collected. Buy the freshest olive oil possible. Pressing is done from midautumn to January, depending upon origin. Usually these oils reach the market by early spring. Store in a cool, dark place and use within 1 year. Keep oil away from heat and light.

Olive oils are graded according to how much acidity they contain and whether they are processed with or without solvents. As yet, the United States has no standard for imported Italian oils.

The following designations are those of the International Olive Oil Council, whose member countries account for 98 percent of the world's olive oil production. By its regulations these are the definitions of all olive oils exported to the United States:

Extra-Virgin Olive Oil: These oils are the premium ones that are pressed and processed without heat or solvents. Color is no indication of quality and ranges from gold to deep green, depending upon where and with what olives the oil is made. Clouded, unfiltered oils are prized by many for their sometimes fuller flavor. Lamentably the words "extra virgin" on the bottle do not guarantee good-tasting oil. If at all possible, sample before buying any quantity. Use extra-virgin oil for seasoning, salads, and cooking.

Fine Virgin Olive Oil: Pressed and processed without heat or chemicals. With flavor and character more subdued than extra-virgin oil, fine virgin oil is used by many cooks for cooking.

Olive Oil: Replaces what used to be called "pure olive oil." This oil is refined with solvents or chemicals, which are steamed off. It will gain color and flavor from blending with virgin olive oil.

"Light" Olive Oil: An American marketing title describing refined oil with little flavor or color; a culinary waste of time and money. Its caloric content is the same as all other olive oils, 120 calories per tablespoon.

Pumace Olive Oil: This oil comes from heating the paste left over from olives crushed to produce all the virgin oils. Heating and processing extracts the last remaining oil from the paste, which is then blended with virgin oil. Of no culinary interest.

FLAVORED OILS See page 78.

ABOUT BUTTER Butter is made by churning cream until it becomes smooth, thick, and rich. In this country, commercial butters are made from cow's milk, but the milk of sheep, goats, horses, and other mammals is also used in other countries. American butter has at least 80 to 82 percent milk fat, although some dairies offer richer butters with up to 86 percent milk fat. The rest of the butter is water, up to 16 percent, and milk solids, 1 to 1½ percent, with an optional 2 percent of salt. Salt is added to butter as a preservative, but it also changes the flavor slightly.

Always use store-bought butter, whether salted or unsalted, within 1 week of the date stamped on the carton. Because butter readily absorbs odors, store it well wrapped in the refrigerator and away from others foods. In general, unopened unsalted butter lasts about 8 weeks, salted up to 12. Use all opened butter within 3 weeks. You also can freeze butter for up to 6 months, although the flavor can sour slightly.

Clarified Butter: Butterfat that has been separated from its water and milk keeps about three times longer, does not burn in sautéing, and has a pure clean flavor. Cut unsalted butter into small pieces and melt over low heat without stirring and without allowing the butter to sizzle, then simmer for 10 to 15 minutes. Strain the mixture well and let the clear yellow liquid cool before covering. When chilled, clarified butter becomes grainy. It should not be used as a spread but only in cooking.

Ghee: Ghee is cooked longer than clarified butter, so the sugars in the butter are lightly caramelized, imparting an incomparably nutty flavor. Cook the butter over the lowest heat, keeping it below a simmer; 1 pound can take several hours or more. At this slow rate, the milk solids settle nicely, and straining the ghee is simple.

Originally a staple in humid climates with no refrigeration, ghee holds its quality for up to 2 months in a cool cupboard, 1 to 1½ months at room temperature, and up to 4 months in the refrigerator. Further refined than clarified butter, the smoke point of ghee is high enough for deep-frying.

Cultured Butter: The same bacteria that give buttermilk its velvety thickness and tang are added to the cream for this butter. The culture, lactic acid, causes the cream to ferment just enough to give it a faint elusive tartness.

Light Butter: In accordance with labeling restrictions, light or "lite" butter has 50 percent less fat as compared with a standard serving of traditional butter. Because of the high water content, light butter is inappropriate for cooking and baking and is useful only as a spread.

Whipped Butter: The butter is whipped while nitrogen is injected, usually 60 percent of the total volume—1 cup whipped butter weighs two-thirds as much as 1 cup traditional butter. The fat content is still 80 percent by weight.

ABOUT MARGARINES With the development of hydrogenation in 1905 it became possible to shift from animal to vegetable fats as a substitute for butter. Hydrogenation combines fatty acids with hydrogen in order to solidify oil, raise its melting point, and prevent it from going rancid. Hydrogenation also creates "trans" fatty acids in the product, which function similarly to saturated fats in raising blood cholesterol levels. Generally, the harder the margarine, the more trans fatty acids it contains and also the longer its shelf life. Margarines may contain animal products to lessen the need to hydrogenate; strict vegetarians should check the label. By law, only products that contain 80 percent fat, the same as butter, can be labeled margarine. Butter and margarine contain the same amount of calories as well.

ABOUT SHORTENINGS All fats have the ability to "shorten" gluten strands to give baked foods a more tender structure. Commercially produced shortenings are white, tasteless fats (unless real or artificial butter flavor and yellow color have been added) that are solid at room temperature. Designed for baking, they are processed from animal fats or refined and hydrogenated vegetable oils and whipped with air. Emulsified shortening has had an emulsifier added to help the mixing when a great deal of sugar is involved.

ABOUT LARD AND OTHER ANIMAL FATS Pure pork fat, known as lard, is softer, sweeter, and oilier than butter but is also drier because it contains less water. The finest lard, leaf lard, comes from the fat around the kidneys. As the fat in biscuits or pie pastry—anything that needs to be short and flaky—lard works wonders. Fats from turkeys, chickens, ducks, and geese tend to be more healthful than pork lard but are firmer and blander. Beef and lamb fat are also used, but their taste can overpower milder foods, and they are generally used only for cooking beef or lamb.

Rendering is the process of extracting and purifying fat from animal products and can easily be done at home. Begin by trimming off all the fat from the meat and cutting it into small pieces. Do not worry if there are a few bits of skin or meat attached—these can be strained after rendering. The two methods for rendering, dry and wet, produce slightly different results. Wet-rendered fat is pure and bland tasting, and dry-rendered fat tends to have a more savory flavor and a darker color. Dry-rendered fat will also smoke or burn at a lower temperature. Dry rendering occurs any time we fry bacon or sauté ground meat. The fat that appears in the pan as the meat cooks may be collected and used as a cooking fat. Typically, dry rendering is the first step of many meat soups and stews: toss a few bits of fatty bacon, beef trimmings, or chicken fat into a pot, heat it until the fat melts, and then proceed to add the other ingredients. Dry rendering may also be done in a moderate (350°F) oven. Wet rendering is generally reserved for accumulating a large amount of fat to be used at a later time. The trimmed fat is placed in a pot of water and brought to a gentle boil until all the fat melts. Then, as the liquid cools, the pure fat rises to the top, to be easily scraped off and used as cooking fat. In parts of France, rendered animal fat is sometimes flavored with garlic or sweet spices. Generally, store-bought lard in this country has been wet rendered and is flavorless, useful only in contributing texture to a dish. All animal fats should be stored in a covered container in the refrigerator.

ABOUT MILK Virtually all milk sold in the United States has been pasteurized, a process that involves heating milk to a high temperature and then cooling it rapidly in order to kill naturally existing bacteria and extend its shelf life. The most common method of pasteurizing commercial milks is high-temperature short-time (HTST) pasteurization, which involves heating the milk to 161°F and cooling it rapidly. This method is quite effective, but the milk may lose some flavor and nutrients as compared with traditional vat-pasteurized milk, which is heated to below boiling and held for 30 minutes before cooling. Choose the more fully flavored vat-pasteurized milk if you see it at the market. Ultra Heat Treatment (UHT) pasteurized milk is relatively new in this country, although it has been popular in Europe for years. In this process, milk is heated to very high temperatures, up to 302°F, and held for 2 to 6 seconds before being packaged in sterilized containers. The benefit of UHT milk is that it can be kept unrefrigerated for 2 to 3 months. The drawback is the flavor; although the high-heat treatment does not substantially affect the nutritional content of the milk, it tastes slightly bitter and scalded. Opened containers of UHT milk should be consumed within a day or two: it is particularly vulnerable to contamination but does not give the usual warning signs of curdling.

Most milk in this country is also homogenized, a mechanical process that shatters the fat particles in the milk so they do not rise to the top to form a layer of cream. You might find milk that has not been homogenized, or even milk that has not been pasteurized (raw milk) in areas where it is legal to sell raw milk. Considering that pasteurization serves to protect the consumer from the harmful bacteria that might be found in raw milk and do not adversely affect nutrient content or flavor, there is no reason to seek out raw milk. Raw milk does, however, produce superior cheese, and it *is* worth seeking out raw-milk cheese; any potentially harmful bacteria die during ripening.

In 1994, the government approved the use of Bovine Growth Hormone (BGH) to stimulate cows to overproduce milk—it is still undetermined what the effects are on people who drink milk produced by cows that have been given these hormones, but no serious health risks are anticipated. If you wish to avoid BGH, you have the option of buying certified organic milk.

The most important consideration when buying milk is the sell-by date on the container. Always buy the freshest milk you can find and refrigerate it below 40°F at all times. Although milk might last up to seven days after the sell-by date, a significant amount of flavor and body is lost well before. Buy milk in opaque containers rather than glass, to protect it from the oxidizing effects of sunlight and fluorescent light.

Whole Milk: If a container says simply "milk," then it is whole milk, containing not less than 3.25 percent milk fat and 8.25 percent milk solids.

Low-Fat Milk: Most dairies package partially skimmed milk—that is, milk with some but not all of the fat removed. These low-fat milks are labeled according to the percentage of fat by weight: 2 percent milk contains 2 grams fat per 100 grams and 1 percent milk contains 1 gram fat per 100 grams. These milks are slightly less rich than whole milk but contain the same nutrients with less fat and cholesterol. Low-fat milks are fortified with vitamin D, and vitamin A is also added to compensate for what is lost when the fat is removed.

Skim Milk: Skim, or nonfat, milk is what remains when you remove all of the fat from whole milk. It is bluish white in color and lacks much of the body and flavor of whole milk. Skim milk is also fortified with vitamins A and D.

Lactose-Reduced Milk: Many adults, especially those of non-European ancestry, find it difficult to digest lactose, the principal sugar in milk. These lactose-intolerant people experience bloating and gas after consuming fresh milk products. Milk can be treated with an enzyme that splits each lactose molecule into two simpler sugars, glucose and galactose, making it easier to digest. Lactose-reduced milk tastes sweeter than regular milk but is equal in nutritional value.

Flavored Milks: Chocolate and other flavored milks often contain additives as well as extra sugar or sweeteners, so while they may offer the same nutrients as regular milk, be wary of the added calories.

Evaporated Milk: Evaporated milk is whole, low-fat, or skim milk that has been evaporated to about one-half its volume. The milk is sealed in cans and heat sterilized. It can be reconstituted by adding to the milk an equal amount of water.

Condensed Milk: Condensed milk and condensed skim milk are similar to evaporated milks but contain added sugar. They cannot be substituted for evaporated milk. You may cut down the sugar in recipes calling for condensed milk to reduce sweetness.

Powdered Milk: Powdered or dry milk is made by removing water from skim milk. It reconstitutes easily. Simply follow the package instructions. Dry milk is handy in an emergency and for camping.

Goat's Milk: Goats produce milk that is whiter and richer-tasting than cow's milk, with a similar nutritional content. Although it is slightly lower in cholesterol, goat's milk contains more fat than cow's milk. The fat molecules in goat's milk are relatively small, so it does not need to be homogenized. Lactose-intolerant people and those allergic to cow's milk protein, however, need to avoid goat's milk as well. Goat's milk is not available in lower-fat varieties, nor is it fortified with Vitamin D, as commercial cow's milk is.

ABOUT CREAM Cream is made from the fat that rises to the surface of nonhomogenized milk. Sweet, or noncultured, creams are sold in pasteurized and ultrapasteurized forms.

Whipping Cream: Whipping cream that is labeled "heavy cream" contains at least 36 percent milk fat and is the richest cream available in most stores. It is normally used in desserts. Light whipping cream, often labeled simply "whipping cream," contains 30 to 36 percent butterfat. Unwhipped, it is added to sauces and soups and is used for ice cream. Whipped, it generally frosts or garnishes desserts. Sometimes is it difficult to make whipping cream mound properly. Buy heavy cream if you can.

Whipped Cream: To whip heavy cream or light whipping cream, first make sure the cream is cold and chill the bowl and the whisk or beaters for 2 hours in the refrigerator or for 10 minutes in the freezer. Using a wire whisk or electric mixer, beat the cream steadily at medium speed until the cream begins to thicken and stiffen. Stop beating when the cream is just stiff enough to hold itself up. Be careful not to beat too long, as the cream will begin to get grainy and finally soupy as butter particles form. A food processor with the regular steel blade can also be used. Fill the bowl less than half full and process for just a few seconds, until the cream stiffens and the surface rises in a doughnut-like curve. Be very careful of overbeating, as food processors tend to heat up their contents, which will hasten the forming of butter. Fresh heavy cream will double in volume. One of the advantages of vat-pasteurized over HTST or UHT cream is that it will stay whipped for days.

Light Cream: Light cream (also called coffee cream or table cream) has from 15 to 18 percent milk fat. It cannot be whipped.

Half-and-Half: Half-and-half is a mixture of cream and milk with between 10.5 and 18 percent milk fat. It is used mainly in coffee or on cereal, as is light cream, but can be substituted for cream in some recipes.

ABOUT SOUR AND CULTURED MILKS AND CREAMS Sour milks and creams play an important part in cooking. The presence of lactic acid gives them a more tender curd, and this in turn makes for a tenderer crumb in baking and a smoother texture in sauces.

Buttermilk: Buttermilk, once the residue left over from making butter, is today made by adding a bacterial culture to skim milk to produce the flavor, body, and acidity of the original product. Thus the word "buttermilk" today means cultured buttermilk.

Sour Cream: Sour cream is made by adding a bacterial culture to cream and incubating it at about 72°F until the lactose is converted to at least 0.5 percent lactic acid. The cultured cream is then packaged, chilled, and aged for 12 to 48 hours. When cooking with sour cream, remember that excessive heat readily causes curdling.

Crème Fraîche: French crème fraîche, like English clotted cream, results from a specific method of cream production that both thickens the cream and gives it its characteristic nutty flavor, similar to, but much more complex than, our sour cream. This homemade crème fraîche is a delicious facsimile of the real thing. You can flavor it with vanilla and sweeten it lightly to taste, whip it, and, generally, substitute it for heavy cream. If possible, avoid ultrapasteurized or sterilized cream. Combine in a small saucepan and heat to 110°F.

1 cup heavy cream
1 tablespoon buttermilk

Pour into a jar and keep in a warm place, loosely covered, until the cream is thickened and has a pleasant mildly sour flavor. This may take as little as 6 to 8 hours or as long as 3 days. Do not allow it to stand so long that the flavor becomes acidic or ammonia-like. (If you multiply the recipe, the culturing time may be longer.) Cover and refrigerate. The cream will thicken further when chilled. Crème fraîche keeps, refrigerated, for up to 3 weeks.

Clotted or Devonshire Cream: Clotted cream, a specialty of Devonshire, England, is a thick cream. To make clotted cream at home, use unpasteurized cream. Let fresh cream stand for 12 hours in winter or 6 hours in summer and then put on low heat until rings form on the surface but the cream does not boil. This heating will sterilize the cream. Store in a cold place for at least 12 hours. Skim the thick clotted cream from the surface to serve as a garnish for fresh fruits.

Yogurt: Yogurt is a mixture of milk, skim milk, and/or cream fermented by adding a culture and bacteria. The milk is incubated until the desired acidity is achieved and then chilled to stop fermentation. Some yogurts still contain "active cultures," which are thought to have healthful digestive benefits.

Like milk, yogurt is available in standard, low-fat, and nonfat varieties depending on the milk from which it is made. It may use natural or artificial sweeteners; check the label. Yogurt needs to be refrigerated below 40°F. It generally keeps for 10 days after the sell-by date but tastes better when fresher.

YOGURT CHEESE

About ½ cup

You can make a simple cheese for spreading on toast, topping mashed potatoes, or dipping vegetables.

Line a strainer or colander with cheesecloth or coffee filters and place a bowl beneath. Spoon in:

1 cup whole-milk plain yogurt

Cover with plastic wrap and refrigerate 6 hours or overnight. Discard the liquid. You can keep yogurt cheese in the refrigerator for up to a week. Pour off any liquid that accumulates.

BREADCRUMBS These are best made from good, stale bread. Place the slices on a baking sheet in a warm oven (about 200°F) for an hour or two to dry out; do not let them brown. The dry bread can be ground into crumbs with the grating blade of a food processor or with a hand grater. To toast, spread on a baking sheet in a 375° oven for 10 to 15 minutes.

SEASONED BREADCRUMBS Add ½ teaspoon salt to every 1 cup dry breadcrumbs; melt ⅓ cup butter per 1 cup crumbs in a skillet and toss the salted crumbs in the butter until browned. Spices, herbs, grated cheese, or minced cooked meats like bacon can be added while toasting. Cook until the butter is absorbed and the crumbs have turned golden brown.

CROUTONS These dried or fried seasoned fresh bread morsels come in all sizes. These are made by cutting bread, preferably simple French bread, into small or large dice or square slices, buttering them or rubbing them with olive oil, and toasting in a 375°F oven until crisp, 10 to 15 minutes. Oil-free croutons can be made by cutting up bread into small cubes and slowly drying them at 200°F. These are perfect for stuffings and poultry dressings.

FLOURING, BREADING, AND CRUMBING FOODS When dredging or lightly covering food with flour or crumbs or with a more elaborately bound coating, the ideal result is a thin, even, unbroken covering that sticks to the food. The food to be coated should be at about room temperature and dry. If the food is floury to begin with or is made with thickened sauce, the flouring may be omitted, but drying and flouring is essential for fish fillets, shrimp, meat, or anything else with a moist surface.

To prepare a simple breading, have ready finely sifted crumbs, flour, or cornmeal. Cornmeal gives the firmest coating. If the food is not fragile, simply put a small quantity of the seasoned coating mixture in a paper or plastic bag with the food you want to cover and shake. You will find that this method gives a very even, quick, and economical coating. Or prepare the following seasoned flour or crumbs.

I. Mix:

1 cup all-purpose flour, fine dry breadcrumbs, or finely crushed corn flakes

1 teaspoon salt
¼ teaspoon ground black pepper, or ½ teaspoon paprika
½ teaspoon ground ginger or nutmeg (optional)

II. Mix:
1 cup fine dry breadcrumbs or crushed corn flakes or crackers
3 tablespoons grated Parmesan cheese
½ teaspoon dried herbs, such as savory, chervil, chives, basil, or tarragon, or pinch of crumbled dried rosemary

TABLES OF EQUIVALENTS AND CONVERSIONS

In U.S. measuring systems the same word may have two meanings. For instance, an ounce may mean one-sixteenth of a pound or one-sixteenth of a pint; but the former is strictly a weight measure and the latter a volume measure. Except in the case of water, milk, or other ingredients of the same density, a fluid ounce and an ounce of weight are two completely different quantities. Most foreign cooks measure solid ingredients by weight. If you intend to use continental recipes frequently, a gram/ounce scale is a necessity.

U.S. MEASUREMENTS All these equivalents are based on U.S. "fluid" measure. In this book, this measure is used not only for liquids such as water and milk, but also for materials such as flour, sugar, and shortening, since the volume measure for these is customary in the United States.

LIQUID MEASURE VOLUME EQUIVALENTS

For U.S.-metric fluid volume, see chart, 1073.

A few grains	=	Less than ⅛ teaspoon
60 drops	=	1 teaspoon
1 teaspoon	=	⅓ tablespoon
1 tablespoon	=	3 teaspoons
2 tablespoons	=	1 fluid ounce
4 tablespoons	=	¼ cup or 2 ounces
5⅓ tablespoons	=	⅓ cup or 2⅔ ounces
8 tablespoons	=	½ cup or 4 ounces
16 tablespoons	=	1 cup or 8 ounces or 2 gills
8 tablespoons	=	1 teacup or 4 ounces
¼ cup	=	4 tablespoons
⅜ cup	=	¼ cup plus 2 tablespoons
⅝ cup	=	½ cup plus 2 tablespoons
⅞ cup	=	¾ cup plus 2 tablespoons
1 cup	=	½ pint or 8 fluid ounces
2 cups	=	1 pint or 16 fluid ounces
1 gill, liquid	=	½ cup or 4 fluid ounces
1 pint, liquid	=	4 gills or 16 fluid ounces
1 quart, liquid	=	2 pints or 4 cups
1 gallon, liquid	=	4 quarts

LINEAR MEASURES

For equipment comparison.

1 centimeter	=	0.394 inch
1 inch	=	2.54 centimeters
1 meter	=	39.37 inches

DRY MEASURE VOLUME EQUIVALENTS

Be careful not to confuse dry measure pints and quarts with liquid measure pints and quarts. The former are about one-sixth larger than the latter. Dry measure is used for raw fruits and vegetables, when dealing with fairly large quantities.

	DRY PINTS	DRY QUARTS	PECKS	BUSHELS	LITERS
1 Dry Pint	1	½	1/16	1/64	.55
1 Dry Quart	2	1	⅛	1/32	1.1
1 Peck	16	8	1	¼	8.8
1 Bushel	64	32	4	1	35.23
1 Liter	1.82	.91	.114	.028	1

COMPARATIVE U.S. AND BRITISH MEASUREMENTS
Many British or "Imperial" units of measurement have the same names as U.S. units, but not all are identical. In general, weights are equivalent but volumes are not. The most important difference for the cook, and one we were slow to realize until we had had consistent failures using English recipes with American measures, is noted below.

Also, the variable sizes of the British teaspoon and tablespoon created a further problem. Confronted with our dilemma, a British friend laughed and told us that there were no standard household British teaspoons and tablespoons. Her own teaspoons and tablespoons had been in the family since the fifteenth century and fit the family recipes perfectly. As a result the best we can recommend is experimentation. Below are differences between U.S. and British measuring cups:

An 8-U.S.-oz. U.S. measuring cup = 2 U.S. gills of 4 U.S. oz. each, or 16 U.S. tablespoons, or 48 U.S. teaspoons.
A 10-Imperial-oz. English measuring cup = 1 English breakfast cup or 2 Imperial English gills of 5 Imperial oz. each, or 20⅘ U.S. tablespoons, or 62½ U.S. teaspoons.

ABOUT METRIC CONVERSION

The charts below compare common kitchen measures from metric to American Standard and vice versa. To use, we give the following example: To determine the equivalent number of U.S. cups in a recipe that calls for 500 milliliters of liquid, look at the U.S. Metric Fluid Volume chart. Find 1 milliliter in the left column; follow across to cups to find .004. Multiply 500 by .004 and you will get the answer—2 cups.

U.S.—METRIC FLUID VOLUME

	FLUID DRAMS	TEA-SPOONS	TABLE-SPOONS	FLUID OUNCES	¼ CUPS	GILLS ½ CUPS	CUPS	FLUID PINTS	FLUID QUARTS	GALLONS	MILLI-LITERS	LITERS
1 Fluid Dram	1	¾	¼	⅛ .125	1/16 .0625	.03125	.0156	.0078	.0039	1/1024	3.70	.0037
1 Teaspoon	1⅓	1	⅓	1/16	1/12	1/24	1/48	1/96	1/192	1/768	5	.005
1 Tablespoon	4	3	1	½	¼	⅛	1/16	1/32	1/64	1/256	15	.015
1 Fluid Ounce	8	6	2	1	½	¼	⅛	1/16	1/32	1/128	29.56	.030
¼ Cup	16	12	4	2	1	½	¼	⅛	1/16	1/64	59.125	.059
1 Gill ½ Cup	32	24	8	4	2	1	½	¼	⅛	1/32	118.25	.118
1 Cup	64	48	16	8	4	2	1	½	¼	1/16	236	.236
1 Fluid Pint	128	96	32	16	8	4	2	1	½	⅛	473	.473
1 Fluid Quart	256	192	64	32	16	8	4	2	1	¼	946	.946
1 Gallon	1024	768	256	128	64	32	16	8	4	1	3785.4	3.785
1 Milliliter	.270	.203 or 1/5	.068	.034	.017	.008	.004	.002	.001	.0003	1	.001 or 1/1000
1 Liter	270.5	203.04	67.68	33.814	16.906	8.453	4.227	2.113	1.057	.264	1000	1

U.S.—METRIC MASS (WEIGHT)

	GRAINS	DRAMS	OUNCES	POUNDS	MILLIGRAMS	GRAMS	KILOGRAMS
1 Grain	1	.004	.002	1/7000	64.7	.064	.0006
1 Dram	27.34	1	1/16	1/256	1770	1.77	.002
1 Ounce	437.5	16	1	1/16	2835	28.35	.028
1 Pound	7000	256	16	1	"Lots"	454	.454
1 Milligram	.015	.0006	1/29,000	1/"Lots"	.1	.001	.000001
1 Gram	15.43	.565	.032	.002	1000	1	.001
1 Kilogram	15,430	564.97	.000032	2.2	1,000,000	1000	1

BRITISH—METRIC FLUID VOLUME

The British are presently using the metric system, but if you wish to use English recipes written before the early 1970s, you may find these tables a great help.

	FLUID DRAMS	FLUID OUNCES	¼ CUPS	GILLS ½ CUPS	CUPS	FLUID PINTS	FLUID QUARTS	MILLI-LITERS	LITERS
1 Fluid Dram	1	⅛	1/20 .05	1/40 .025	1/80 .0125	1/160 .006	1/320 .003	3.55	.0035
1 Fluid Ounce	8	1	¼	1/5 .2	1/10	1/20 .05	1/40 .025	28.4	.028
¼ Cup	20	2.5	1	½	¼	⅛	1/16	71	.07
1 Gill—½ Cup	40	5	2	1	½	¼	⅛	142	.14
1 Cup	80	10	4	2	1	½	¼	284	.28
1 Fluid Pint	160	20	8	4	2	1	½	568	.57
1 Fluid Quart	320	40	16	8	4	2	1	1136	1.13
1 Milli-liter	.28	.035	.014	.007	.0035	.0018	.0009	1	.001 or 1/1000
1 Liter	281.5	35.19	14.08	7.04	3.52	1.76	.88	1000	1

APPROXIMATE TEMPERATURE CONVERSIONS

	FAHRENHEIT	CELSIUS OR CENTIGRADE
Coldest area of freezer	-10°	-23°
Freezer	0°	-17°
Water freezes	32°	0°
Water simmers	115°	46°
Water scalds	130°	54°
Water boils—at sea level	212°	100°
Soft ball	234°	112°
Firm ball	244°	117°
Hard ball	250°	121°
Very low oven	250°–275°	121°–133°
Low oven	300°–325°	149°–163°
Moderate oven	350°–375°	177°–190°
Hot oven	400°–425°	204°–218°
Very hot oven	450°–475°	232°–246°
Extremely hot oven	500°–525°	260°–274°

To convert Fahrenheit into Centigrade, subtract 32, multiply by 5, divide by 9. To convert Centigrade into Fahrenheit, go into reverse: multiply by 9, divide by 5, add 32.

$100°C \times 9 = 900$

$900 \div 5 = 180$

$180 + 32 = 212°F$

NUTRIENT COMPOSITION OF FOODS AND INGREDIENTS

FOOD	SERVING SIZE	CALORIES	PROTEIN (G)	FAT (G)	MONO-FAT	SAT-FAT	CARBS (G)	FIBER (G)	VIT C (MG)	VIT E (MG)	FOLATE (μ)	IRON (MG)	CALCIUM (MG)
Almonds, raw, shelled	1 cup	795	27	71	45.8	6.7	28	15	1	32.4	79	4.9	359
Apple, raw, 2¾-inch diameter	1 item	81	0	1	0	0.1	21	4	8	0.4	4	0.3	10
Apple butter	1 tbsp	37	0	0	tr	0	9	0	0	tr	0	0.1	3
Apple juice	1 cup	117	0	0	0	0.1	29	0	2	0	0	0.9	17
Applesauce	½ cup	53	0	0	tr	0	14	1	1	0	1	0.2	4
Apricot, fresh	3 items	51	1	0	0.2	0	12	3	11	0.9	9	0.6	15
Apricot nectar, canned	½ cup	71	0	0	0.1	tr	18	1	42	0.1	2	0.5	9
Artichoke, globe, cooked, whole	½ cup	51	4	1	0	0.1	10	5	6	0.2	135	0.6	24
Artichoke, Jerusalem, whole	1 cup	114	3	0	tr	0	26	2	6	0.3	20	5.1	21
Asparagus, raw	1 cup	31	3	0	tr	0.1	6	3	18	2.7	172	1.2	28
Avocado	½ cup	185	2	18	11	2.8	9	6	9	1.5	71	1.2	13
Bacon, broiled, pan-fried, or roasted	1 slice	36	2	3	1.5	1.1	0	0	0	0	0	0.1	1
Banana	1 item	105	1	1	0.1	0.2	27	3	10	0.3	22	0.4	7
Barley, uncooked	1 cup	651	23	4	0.5	0.9	135	32	0	1.1	35	6.6	61
Baked beans, canned	1 cup	236	12	1	0.1	0.3	52	13	8	1.4	61	0.7	127
Baking soda	1 tsp	0	0	0	0	0	0	0	0	0	0	0	0
Baking powder	1 tsp	0	0	0	0	0	0	0	0	—	—	0	160
Beans, green, boiled	1 cup	44	2	0	0	0.1	10	4	12	0.2	42	1.6	58
Beans, kidney, boiled	1 cup	225	15	1	0.1	0.1	40	13	2	0.1	229	5.2	50
Beans, lima, boiled	1 cup	229	15	1	0.1	0.2	42	14	0	—	273	4.4	53
Beans, navy, boiled	1 cup	109	7	0	0	0.1	19	4	0	2.1	32	2.5	49
Bean sprouts	1 cup	31	3	0	0	0.1	6	2	14	0	63	1	14
Beef, dried	3 oz	140	25	3	1.4	1.4	1	0	0	0.3	9	3.8	5

FOOD	SERVING SIZE	CALORIES	PROTEIN (G)	FAT (G)	MONO-FAT	SAT-FAT	CARBS (G)	FIBER (G)	VIT C (MG)	VIT E (MG)	FOLATE (µ)	IRON (MG)	CALCIUM (MG)
Beef, filet mignon, raw	3 oz	259	22	18	7.9	7.3	0	0	0	0.2	6	2.2	9
Beef, lean, ground, raw	3 oz	224	15	18	7.6	7.1	0	0	0	0.2	7	1.5	7
Beef, rib roast, raw	3 oz	291	19	23	10	9.5	0	0	0	0.2	5	1.8	10
Beef, lean round roast, raw	3 oz	161	25	6	2.8	2.1	0	0	0	—	10	2.7	4
Beef, sirloin steak, lean, raw	3 oz	166	26	6	2.6	2.4	0	0	0	0.1	9	2.9	9
Beef, tongue, raw	3 oz	241	19	18	8.1	7.6	0	0	0	0.3	4	2.9	6
Beer	12 oz	146	1	0	0	0	13	1	0	0	21	0.1	18
Beet greens, chopped, cooked	1 cup	39	4	0	0.1	0.1	8	4	36	0.4	21	2.7	164
Beets, chopped, whole, raw	½ cup	54	2	0	0	0	12	4	14	0.4	114	1.1	20
Blackberries, whole, raw	1 cup	75	1	1	0.1	0	18	8	30	1	49	0.8	46
Blueberries	1 cup	81	1	1	0.1	0.1	21	4	19	1.5	9	0.3	9
Bologna sausage	1 slice	90	3	8	3.8	3	1	0	0	0.1	1	0.4	3
Bouillon, chicken	1 cube	10	0	0	0	0	1	0	0	—	—	0	0
Bran, oat	1 cup	276	15	5	—	0.9	4	13	0	1.4	0	4.2	47
Braunschweiger sausage	1 oz	102	4	9	4.2	3.1	1	0	0	0.1	12	2.7	3
Brazil nuts, shelled	1 cup	918	20	93	32.2	22.6	18	8	1	10.6	6	4.8	246
Bread, rye	1 slice	83	3	1	0.4	0.2	16	2	0	0.2	16	0.9	23
Bread, white	1 slice	67	2	1	0.4	0.2	12	1	0	0.1	9	0.8	27
Bread, whole wheat	1 slice	62	2	1	0.4	0.2	12	2	0	0.3	13	0.8	18
Broccoli, raw, chopped	1 cup	25	3	0	0	0.1	5	3	82	1.5	63	0.8	42
Brussels sprouts, raw	1 cup	87	7	1	0.1	0.1	18	8	172	1.8	123	2.8	85
Butter, salted	1 tsp	33	0	4	1.0	2.3	0	0	0	0.1	0	tr	1
Butter, unsalted	1 tsp	36	0	4	1.2	2.5	tr	0	0	0.1	0	tr	1

FOOD	SERVING SIZE	CALORIES	PROTEIN (G)	FAT (G)	MONO-FAT	SAT-FAT	CARBS (G)	FIBER (G)	VIT C (MG)	VIT E (MG)	FOLATE (μ)	IRON (MG)	CALCIUM (MG)
Cabbage, raw, chopped	1 cup	18	1	0	0	0	4	2	23	0.1	30	0.4	33
Cake, angel	2 oz slice	146	3	0	0	0.1	33	1	0	—	2	0.3	80
Cake, pound	2 oz slice	219	3	11	3.2	6.3	28	0	0	—	6	0.8	20
Cantaloupe, large (43.6 ounces)	1 item	392	11	1	0	0	98	14	461	—	0	2.6	160
Caramels, .5 ounce	2 pieces	43	0	0	0.1	0.1	10	0	0	0	0	0	3
Carrots, cooked, sliced	1 cup	70	2	0	0	0.1	16	5	4	0.7	22	1	48
Carrots, raw, sliced	1 cup	31	1	0	0	0	7	2	7	.3	10	0.4	19
Cashew nuts, dry roasted	1 cup	786	21	64	37.4	12.5	45	4	0	0.8	95	8.2	62
Cauliflower, cooked	1 cup	29	2	1	0	0.1	5	3	55	0.1	55	0.4	20
Caviar, sturgeon	1 tbsp	40	4	3	0.7	0.7	1	0	0	1.1	8	1.9	44
Celery, raw, chopped	2 stalks	13	1	0	0	0	3	1	6	0.3	22	0.3	32
Celery root, cooked, chopped	1 cup	50	2	0	0.1	0.1	12	2	10	0.5	10	0.9	56
Cereal, raisin bran	1 cup	170	5	1	0	0	43	7	0	0	100	4.5	40
Cheese, American	1 oz	105	6	9	2.5	5.5	0	0	0	0.1	2	0.1	172
Cheese, Camembert	1 oz	85	6	7	2	4.3	0	0	0	0.2	18	0.1	110
Cheese, Cheddar	1 oz	113	7	9	2.6	5.9	0	0	0	0.1	5	0.2	202
Cheese, cottage	1 cup	123	25	1	0.2	0.4	3	0	0	0.2	22	0.3	46
Cheese, cream	1 tbsp	51	1	5	1.4	3.2	0	0	0	0.1	2	0.2	12
Cheese, Parmesan, grated	1 tbsp	23	2	2	0.4	1	0	0	0	0	0	0.1	69
Cheese, ricotta	1 cup	360	28	24	—	16.0	12	0	0	—	—	0	600
Cheese, Roquefort	1 oz	103	6	9	2.4	5.4	1	0	0	0.2	14	0.2	185
Cheese, Swiss	1 oz	105	8	8	2.0	5	1	0	0	0.1	2	0.1	269
Cherimoya	1 item	514	7	2	—	—	131	13	49	—	—	2.7	126
Cherries	15 items	74	1	1	0.3	0.2	17	2	7	0.1	4	0.4	15

FOOD	SERVING SIZE	CALORIES	PROTEIN (G)	FAT (G)	MONO-FAT	SAT-FAT	CARBS (G)	FIBER (G)	VIT C (MG)	VIT E (MG)	FOLATE (μ)	IRON (MG)	CALCIUM (MG)
Chicken, dark meat, roasted	3½ oz	203	27	10	3.5	2.6	0	0	0	0.3	8	1.3	15
Chicken, breast, fried	1 item	322	58	8	3	2.2	1	0	0	0.7	7	2	28
Chicken breast, roasted, no skin	1 item	286	54	6	2.2	1.8	0	0	0	0.5	7	1.8	26
Chicken liver	4 oz	178	28	6	1.5	2.1	1	0	18	1.6	873	9.6	16
Chickpeas, cooked	1 cup	509	21	21	8.2	5.9	62	16	3	0.9	200	5.2	101
Chocolate, bittersweet	1 oz	138	2	10	3.4	5.9	16	2	0	—	—	1	11
Chocolate, milk	1 oz	153	2	9	2.9	5.6	16	1	0	—	2	0.4	59
Chocolate fudge	1 piece	65	0	1	0.4	0.9	14	0	0	0	0	0.2	7
Chocolate syrup	1 tbsp	51	0	0	0.1	0.2	12	1	0	—	—	0.3	3
Clams, raw	3 oz	63	11	1	0.1	0.1	2	0	11	0.9	14	11.9	39
Cocoa mix, powdered	2 oz	206	6	2	0.8	1.4	45	1	1	0.1	0	0.7	185
Coconut, raw, shredded	1 cup	283	3	27	1.1	23.8	12	7	3	0.6	21	1.9	11
Cod	3 oz	89	19	1	0.1	0.1	0	0	1	0.3	7	0.4	12
Coffee	1 cup	5	0	0	0	0	1	0	0	0	0	0.1	5
Collard greens, boiled, chopped	1 cup	61	5	1	0	0.1	12	5	45	0.9	129	1.9	357
Consomme, canned and prepared with water	1 cup	30	6	0	0	0	2	0	1	—	3	0.6	10
Corn, ear, cooked	1 item	83	3	1	0.3	0.2	19	2	5	0.1	36	0.5	2
Corn flakes	1 cup	110	2	0	0	0	26	1	15	0	100	8.4	0
Cornmeal, enriched, cooked	1 cup	212	3	1	0.1	0.1	26	2	0	0.8	16	1.4	2
Cornstarch	1 cup	488	0	0	0	0	117	1	0	0	0	0.6	3
Corn syrup	1 oz	99	0	0	0	0	23	—	—	—	—	0.1	1
Crab meat, Alaska, fresh, raw	4 oz	95	21	1	0.1	0.1	0	0	8	—	50	0.7	52
Cracker, graham, .25 ounce	1 item	30	0	1	0.4	0.2	5	0	0	0.1	1	0.3	2

FOOD	SERVING SIZE	CALORIES	PROTEIN (G)	FAT (G)	MONO-FAT	SAT-FAT	CARBS (G)	FIBER (G)	VIT C (MG)	VIT E (MG)	FOLATE (µ)	IRON (MG)	CALCIUM (MG)
Cracker, saltine, 2-inch square	1 item	13	0	0	0.2	0.1	2	0	0	0.1	1	0.2	4
Cranberries, raw, chopped	1 cup	54	0	0	0	0	14	5	15	0.1	2	0.2	8
Cream, half-and-half	1 tbsp	20	0	2	0.5	1.1	1	0	0	0	0	0	16
Cream, sour, cultured	1 tbsp	26	0	3	0.7	1.6	1	0	0	0.1	1	tr	14
Cream, whipped	1 tbsp	15	0	1	0	1	1	0	0	—	0	0	0
Cucumber, sliced	1 cup	14	1	0	tr	0	3	1	6	0.1	14	0.3	15
Dates	3 items	72	1	0	0	0	19	2	—	—	tr	0.3	12
Doughnut, plain glazed	1 item	192	2	10	5.4	2.4	23	1	0	—	5	0.5	27
Dressing, Thousand Island	1 tbsp	59	0	6	1.3	0.9	2	0	0	0.2	1	0.1	2
Dressing, French	1 tbsp	67	0	6	1.3	1.5	3	0	0	1.3	1	0.1	2
Duck, roasted, no skin	1 item	888	104	50	16.4	18.4	0	0	0	3.1	44	11.9	53
Egg, whole, poached	1 item	75	6	5	1.9	1.5	1	0	0	0.5	18	0.7	25
Egg yolk, raw	1 item	59	3	5	2	1.6	0	0	0	0.5	24	0.6	23
Egg white, raw	1 item	17	4	0	0	0	0	0	0	0	1	0	2
Eggplant, raw, whole	1 cup	21	1	0	0	0	5	2	1	0	16	0.2	6
Endive, raw, chopped	1 cup	9	1	0	tr	0	2	2	3	0.2	71	0.4	26
English muffin, plain	1 item	134	4	1	0.2	0.2	26	2	0	—	21	1.4	30
Fig, fresh	1 item	37	0	0	0	0	10	2	1	0.5	3	0.2	18
Flour, cake/pastry, enriched	1 cup	395	9	1	0.1	0.1	85	2	0	0.1	21	8	15
Flour, rye	1 cup	231	29	12	5.4	0.8	0	0	0	—	8.2	0.8	5.1
Flour, whole wheat	1 cup	407	16	2	0.3	0.4	87	15	0	1.5	53	4.7	41
Flour, white, all-purpose, enriched	1 cup	420	12	1	0.1	0.2	88	3	0	0.1	30	5.1	18

FOOD	SERVING SIZE	CALORIES	PROTEIN (G)	FAT (G)	MONO-FAT	SAT-FAT	CARBS (G)	FIBER (G)	VIT C (MG)	VIT E (MG)	FOLATE (µ)	IRON (MG)	CALCIUM (MG)
Flounder, baked	One 3.4-ounce piece	133	21	5	2.4	0.9	0	0	5	2.6	8	0.3	19
Frankfurter, beef and pork	1 item	182	6	17	7.8	6.1	1	0	0	0.1	2	0.7	6
Frog legs, raw	1 cup	165	37	1	0.1	0.2	0	0	0	2.3	34	3.4	41
Gelatin, plain	1 cup	142	4	0	0	0	34	0	0	0	0	0	5
Gin	4 oz	257	0	0	0	0	0	0	0	0	0	0	0
Ginger, raw, sliced	1 cup	66	2	1	0.1	0.2	15	2	5	0.3	11	0.5	17
Ginger ale	12 ounces	125	0	0	0	0	32	0	0	0	0	0.7	11
Goose, wild, roasted	4 oz	344	28	25	11.6	7.8	0	0	0	2	2	3.2	15
Gooseberries	1 cup	66	1	1	0.1	0.1	15	6	42	0.6	9	0.5	38
Grape juice	1 cup	154	1	0	tr	0.1	38	0	0	0	7	0.6	23
Grapefruit, white or red	1 item	118	3	1	0.1	0	29	18	188	—	0	0.7	113
Grapefruit juice, unsweetened	1 cup	94	1	0	0	0	22	0	72	0.1	26	0.5	17
Grapes, green, seedless	1 cup	58	1	0	0	0.1	16	1	4	0.3	4	0.3	13
Grits, hominy	1 cup	145	3	0	0.1	0.1	32	0	0	0.1	2	1.6	0
Guava	1 item	46	1	1	0.1	0.2	11	5	165	1	13	0.3	18
Haddock, broiled	One 3.1-ounce serving	95	21	1	0.1	0.1	0	0	0	—	11	1.2	36
Halibut, broiled	One 3-ounce serving	123	23	3	0.9	0.4	0	0	0	1	12	0.9	53
Ham, lean, roasted	3 oz	134	21	5	2.2	1.6	0	0	0	0.2	3	0.8	6
Herring, Atlantic, fresh, raw	One 3-ounce serving	134	15	8	3.2	1.7	0	0	1	0.9	9	0.9	49
Herring, pickled	1 piece	131	7	9	6	1.2	5	0	0	0.5	1	0.6	39
Hollandaise sauce	1 tbsp	80	1	7	2	3.6	3	tr	1	0.2	6	0.2	7
Honey	1 tbsp	74	0	0	0	0	17	0	0	0	0	0.1	1

FOOD	SERVING SIZE	CALORIES	PROTEIN (G)	FAT (G)	MONO-FAT	SAT-FAT	CARBS (G)	FIBER (G)	VIT C (MG)	VIT E (MG)	FOLATE (μ)	IRON (MG)	CALCIUM (MG)
Honeydew melon	1 cup	60	1	0	tr	0	16	1	42	0.3	10	0.1	10
Horseradish, raw	1 tbsp	13	0	0	tr	tr	3	0	12	tr	0	0.2	21
Ice cream, vanilla	1 cup	185	4	11	3	6.4	19	0	1	0.3	8	0.2	113
Icing, white boiled	1 cup	295	1	0	0	0	75	0	0	—	—	0	2
Jam	1 tbsp	48	0	0	0	tr	13	0	2	0	7	0.1	4
Kale, chopped, boiled	1 cup	42	2	1	0	0.1	7	3	53	1.1	17	1.2	94
Ketchup	1 tbsp	16	0	0	tr	tr	4	0	2	0.2	2	0.1	3
Kidneys, beef, raw	4 oz	121	19	3	0.8	1.1	2	0	10	0.2	91	8.4	7
Kiwi	1 item	46	1	0	0	0	11	3	75	0.9	29	0.3	20
Kumquat	1 item	12	0	0	tr	tr	3	1	7	0.1	3	0.1	8
Lamb chop, braised	One 3-ounce serving	237	30	12	5.2	4.3	0	0	0	—	19	2.3	22
Lamb shank, roasted	One 3-ounce serving	191	22	11	4.5	4.3	0	0	0	0.1	19	1.7	9
Lard	1 tbsp	115	0	13	5.8	5	0	0	0	0.2	0	0	tr
Leek	1 item	76	2	0	tr	0.1	18	2	15	1.1	80	2.6	73
Lemon	1 item	22	1	0	0	0	12	5	83	—	—	0.8	66
Lentils	1 oz	90	5	0	0	0	17	2	1	0.1	50	2.3	33
Lettuce, iceberg	1 head	120	6	1	0	0	21	9	27	—	0	2.4	0
Lime	1 item	20	0	0	0	0	7	2	20	0.2	5	0.4	22
Liver, beef, raw	4 oz	162	23	4	0.6	1.7	7	0	25	0.8	280	7.7	7
Liverwurst	1 slice	59	3	5	2.4	1.9	0	0	0	—	5	1.2	5
Lobster, raw	1 cup	204	43	2	0.7	0.4	1	0	0	1.4	36	0.7	109
Macaroni, plain, cooked	1 cup	155	5	1	0.1	0.1	32	2	0	0	—	1.7	11
Mackerel, king, broiled	3 oz	114	22	2	0.8	0.4	0	0	1	—	8	1.9	34
Mango	1 item	135	1	1	0.2	0.1	35	4	57	2.3	29	0.3	21
Maple syrup	1 tbsp	48	0	0	0	0	12	0	0	0	0	0.2	20

FOOD	SERVING SIZE	CALORIES	PROTEIN (G)	FAT (G)	MONO-FAT	SAT-FAT	CARBS (G)	FIBER (G)	VIT C (MG)	VIT E (MG)	FOLATE (μ)	IRON (MG)	CALCIUM (MG)
Margarine, corn oil	1 tsp	34	0	4	1.5	0.7	0	0	tr	2	0	0	1
Marmalade	1 oz	67	0	0	tr	tr	17	0	0	0	10	0	2
Marshmallows	5 items	115	1	0	0	0	29	0	0	0	0	0.1	1
Mayonnaise	1 tbsp	100	0	11	—	2	0	0	0	1.7	—	0	0
Melba toast	1 slice	16	1	0	0	0	3	0	0	0	1	0.2	1
Milk, buttermilk, 2%	1 cup	59	4	0	0	0	13	7	42	0.1	113	0.9	74
Milk, 1%	1 cup	102	8	3	1	1.6	12	0	2	0	12	0.1	300
Milk, 2%	1 cup	121	8	5	1.4	2.9	12	0	2	0.2	12	0.1	297
Milk, chocolate	1 cup	193	7	7	2.2	4.7	26	1	2	—	10	0.7	257
Milk, skim	1 cup	86	8	0	0.1	0.3	12	0	2	0.1	13	0.1	302
Milk, whole	1 cup	150	8	8	2.4	5.1	11	0	2	0.2	12	0.1	291
Molasses	1 tbsp	44	0	0	0	0	11	0	0	—	—	3.3	140
Muffin, corn	1 item	174	3	5	1.9	0.9	29	2	0	0.7	19	1.6	42
Mushrooms	1 cup	18	1	0	tr	0	3	1	2	0.1	15	0.9	4
Mustard greens, whole, boiled	1 cup	21	3	0	0.2	0	3	3	35	2.8	103	1	104
Nectarine	1 item	67	1	1	0.2	0.1	16	2	7	1.2	5	0.2	7
Noodles, egg, cooked	1 cup	213	8	2	0.7	0.5	40	2	0	0.1	11	2.5	19
Oatmeal, instant, cooked	1 cup	145	6	2	0.8	0.4	25	4	0	0.2	9	1.6	19
Okra, boiled	1 cup	32	2	0	0	0.1	7	3	17	0.7	46	0.5	64
Oil, corn	1 tbsp	120	0	14	3.3	1.7	0	0	0	2.9	0	0	0
Oil, olive	1 tbsp	119	0	14	10	1.8	0	0	0	1.7	0	0.1	0
Oil, peanut	1 tbsp	120	0	14	6.2	2.3	0	0	0	1.7	0	tr	0
Oil, safflower	1 tbsp	120	0	14	1.7	1.2	0	0	0	5.9	0	0	0
Oil, sesame	1 tbsp	120	0	14	5.4	1.9	0	0	0	0.6	0	0	0
Olives, green or black	1 large	10	0	1	0.8	0	1	0	0	—	—	0	0
Onion, raw, chopped	1 cup	61	2	0	0	0	14	3	10	0.2	30	0.4	32

FOOD	SERVING SIZE	CALORIES	PROTEIN (G)	FAT (G)	MONO-FAT	SAT-FAT	CARBS (G)	FIBER (G)	VIT C (MG)	VIT E (MG)	FOLATE (µ)	IRON (MG)	CALCIUM (MG)
Orange	1 item	62	1	0	0	0	15	3	70	0.3	40	0.1	52
Orange juice	1 cup	112	2	1	0.1	0.1	26	1	124	0.2	75	0.5	27
Oysters, raw	1 cup	134	12	4	0.4	1	13	0	11	—	41	13.1	100
Papaya, chopped	1 cup	55	1	0	0.1	0.1	14	3	87	1.6	53	0.1	34
Parsley, raw, chopped	1 tbsp	1	0	0	0	tr	0	0	5	0.1	6	0.2	5
Parsnips, sliced, boiled	1 cup	113	2	0	0.2	0.1	27	6	18	1.4	81	0.8	51
Peach	1 item	37	1	0	0	tr	10	2	6	0.6	3	0.1	4
Peanut butter	1 tbsp	95	4	8	3.9	1.7	3	1	0	1.6	12	0.3	6
Peanuts, dry, roasted, unsalted	1 cup	854	35	73	36	10.1	31	12	0	10.8	212	3.3	79
Pear	1 item	98	1	1	0.1	0	25	4	7	0.8	12	0.4	18
Prickly pear	1 item	42	1	1	0.1	0.1	10	4	14	0	6	0.3	58
Peas, black-eyed, boiled	1 cup	561	39	2	0.2	0.6	100	18	3	0.7	1056	13.8	184
Peas, green, fresh	1 cup	134	9	0	0	0.1	25	9	23	0.6	101	2.5	43
Peas, split, boiled with salt	1 cup	231	16	1	0.2	0.1	41	16	1	—	127	2.5	27
Pecans	1 cup	754	8	78	48.8	6.3	18	7	2	—	43	2.3	37
Pepper, chili, whole	1 item	10	0	0	0	0	2	1	9	—	—	0	0
Pepper, green	1 item	25	2	0	0	0	5	3	129	—	0	0.6	14
Pepperoni	1 slice	27	1	2	1.2	0.9	0	0	0	0	0	0.1	1
Persimmon	1 item	32	0	0	0	0	8	—	17	—	—	0.6	7
Pickle, dill, large	1 item	12	0	0	tr	0	3	0	1	0.1	1	0.4	6
Pineapple, fresh, diced	1 cup	76	1	1	0.1	0.1	19	2	24	0.2	16	0.6	11
Plum	1 cup	160	2	2	1.2	0.1	38	4	28	2.0	6	0.3	12
Pomegranate	1 item	105	1	0	0.1	0.1	26	1	9	0.9	9	0.5	5
Popcorn, popped, plain	1 cup	40	1	1	0.1	0.1	8	1	0	0	2	0.3	1
Pork, lean, roasted	4 oz	186	32	5	2.2	1.9	0	0	0	0.3	7	1.7	7

FOOD	SERVING SIZE	CALORIES	PROTEIN (G)	FAT (G)	MONO-FAT	SAT-FAT	CARBS (G)	FIBER (G)	VIT C (MG)	VIT E (MG)	FOLATE (μ)	IRON (MG)	CALCIUM (MG)
Pork chop, broiled	2.9 ounces	197	24	11	4.8	3.9	0	0	0	—	5	0.7	27
Potato, baked	One 7.2-ounce item	220	5	0	tr	0.1	51	5	26	0.1	22	2.8	20
Potato, boiled with skin	1 cup	212	5	0	tr	0.1	49	4	30	—	25	2.1	22
Preserves	1 tbsp	48	0	0	0	tr	13	0	2	0	7	0.1	4
Pretzels, thin stick	5 items	5	0	0	0	0	1	0	0	0	—	0.1	1
Prunes, dried	1 cup	339	4	1	0.5	0.1	88	10	5	0	5	3.5	72
Pumpkin, raw, cubed	1 cup	30	1	0	0	0.1	8	1	10	1.2	19	0.9	24
Rabbit, roasted	4 ounces	171	25	7	1.9	2.1	0	0	0	—	9	2	16
Radishes	3 items	2	0	0	tr	tr	0	0	3	0	4	0	3
Raisins	1 cup	435	5	1	0	0.2	115	6	5	1	5	3	71
Raspberries	1 cup	60	1	1	0.1	0	14	8	31	0.6	32	1	27
Red snapper, baked	One 3-ounce serving	109	22	1	0.3	0.3	0	0	1	—	5	0.2	34
Rhubarb, raw	1 cup	513	3	16	6.9	3.1	96	4	6	2.9	14	1.8	295
Rice, brown, cooked	1 cup	218	5	2	0.6	0.3	46	4	0	—	8	1	20
Rice, white, cooked	1 cup	242	4	0	0.1	0.1	53	1	0	—	4	2.8	6
Rice, wild, cooked	1 cup	166	7	1	0.1	0.1	35	3	0	0.4	43	1	5
Roll, hard white	One 2-ounce item	167	6	2	0.7	0.4	30	1	0	0.1	9	1.9	54
Root beer	12 oz	151	0	0	0	0	39	0	0	0	0	0.2	18
Rum	4 oz	257	0	0	0	0	0	0	0	0	0	0	0
Salami, dry, hard, pork	1 oz	115	6	10	4.5	3.4	0	0	0	0.1	1	0.4	4
Salmon, broiled	3 oz	262	29	15	6.5	3.6	0	0	5	—	40	1	32
Sardines, canned in oil	3 oz	177	21	10	3.3	1.3	0	0	0	0.3	7	2.5	325
Sauerkraut	1 cup	20	0	0	0	0	4	4	14	—	—	0	0

FOOD	SERVING SIZE	CALORIES	PROTEIN (G)	FAT (G)	MONO-FAT	SAT-FAT	CARBS (G)	FIBER (G)	VIT C (MG)	VIT E (MG)	FOLATE (µ)	IRON (MG)	CALCIUM (MG)
Sausage, pork, link	1 item	48	3	4	1.8	1.4	0	0	0	0	0	0.2	4
Scallop, large, raw	1 item	26	5	0	0	0	1	0	1	0.3	5	0.1	7
Seeds, pumpkin, dry, roasted, salted	1 oz	154	7	16	4.1	2.5	4	0	1	0.3	17	2.8	13
Seeds, sunflower, dry, roasted	1 oz	162	6	14	2.7	1.5	5	3	0	14.3	64	1.9	33
Sherbet, orange	1 cup	270	2	4	1.1	2.4	59	0	4	—	14	0.3	103
Sherry, dry	4 oz	159	0	0	0	0	9	0	0	0	1	0.5	9
Shrimp, boiled	3 oz	84	18	1	0.2	0.3	0	0	2	0.4	3	2.6	33
Sole, Dover	1 piece	149	31	2	0.3	0.5	0	0	0	2.4	12	0.4	23
Soybeans	1 cup	97	8	4	0	0	8	0	0	0	0	2	58
Spaghetti, plain, cooked	1 cup	197	7	1	0.1	0.1	40	2	0	0.1	10	2	10
Spareribs, roasted	One 3-ounce serving	208	24	12	5.3	4	0	0	0	—	4	1	44
Spinach, raw, chopped	1 cup	12	2	0	tr	0	2	2	16	1.1	109	1.5	55
Squash, boiled	1 cup	29	1	0	tr	0	8	3	8	0.2	30	0.6	23
Squash, butternut, baked	1 cup	82	2	0	0	0	22	7	31	—	39	1.2	84
Strawberries	1 cup	45	1	0	0.1	0	11	3	85	0.2	26	0.6	21
Sugar, brown	1 cup	827	0	0	0	0	214	0	0	0	2	4.2	187
Sugar, white	1 cup	774	0	0	0	0	200	0	0	0	0	0.1	2
Sweetbreads, veal, braised	One 3.1-ounce serving	153	28	4	1.3	1.3	0	0	65	0.7	1	1.8	3
Swordfish, broiled	One 3-ounce serving	132	22	4	1.7	1.2	0	0	1	—	2	0.9	5
Taco shell, baked	1 item	61	1	3	1.2	0.4	8	1	0	0.4	1	0.3	21
Tangerine	1 item	37	1	0	0	0	9	2	26	0.2	17	0.1	12
Tartar sauce	1 tbsp	76	0	8	1.7	1.6	1	0	0	1	1	0.1	3
Tea, instant, unsweetened	1 cup	2	0	0	0	0	0	0	0	0	1	0.1	5

FOOD	SERVING SIZE	CALORIES	PROTEIN (G)	FAT (G)	MONO-FAT	SAT-FAT	CARBS (G)	FIBER (G)	VIT C (MG)	VIT E (MG)	FOLATE (µ)	IRON (MG)	CALCIUM (MG)
Tofu, firm, raw	8 oz	329	36	20	4.4	2.9	10	5	0.5	—	66	23.8	465
Tofu, soft	8 oz	122	11	7	1.5	0	5	0	0	—	—	2	54
Tomato, ripe, raw	1 item	26	1	0	0.1	0.1	6	1	24	0.5	18	0.6	6
Tomato juice	1 cup	40	2	0	0	0	10	2	19	0.8	47	1.4	21
Tomatoes, canned	1 cup	46	2	0	0.1	0.1	11	2	34	0.8	19	1.3	72
Tongue, beef, raw	3 oz	241	19	18	8.1	7.6	0	0	0	0.3	4	2.9	6
Tortilla, corn	1 item	56	1	1	0.2	0.1	12	1	0	0	4	0.4	44
Trout, brook, broiled	One 3.5-ounce serving	196	24	11	2.8	1.5	0	0	1	0.5	17	1.1	218
Tuna, canned in water	4 oz	132	29	1	0.2	0.3	0	0	0	0.6	5	1.7	12
Tuna, raw	4 oz	117	25	1	0.2	0.4	0	0	1	—	10	1.4	33
Turkey breast, roasted, no skin	21.6 ounces	826	184	5	0.8	1.5	0	0	0	0.6	37	9.4	73
Turkey, roasted, dark meat	1 cup	262	40	10	2.3	3.4	0	0	0	0.9	13	3.3	45
Turnips, whole, boiled	1 cup	39	2	0	0	0	11	4	25	0.1	20	0.5	47
Vanilla extract	1 tbsp	44	0	0	0	0	4	0	0	—	—	0	0
Veal, braised chop	One 3-ounce serving	192	29	8	2.8	2.2	0	0	0	—	13	0.9	27
Veal, lean roasted sirloin	One 3-ounce serving	143	22	5	1.9	2.1	0	0	0	0.4	14	0.8	12
Venison, baked	1 pound	537	103	11	3	4.3	0	0	0	—	—	15.2	24
Vienna sausage, canned	1 item	45	2	4	2.0	1.5	0	0	0	0	1	0.1	2
Vodka	4 oz	257	0	0	0	0	0	0	0	0	0	0	0
Walnuts, chopped	1 cup	759	30	71	15.9	4.5	15	6	4	3.3	82	3.8	73
Watercress, chopped, raw	1 cup	4	1	0	tr	tr	0	1	15	0.3	3	0.1	41
Watermelon, sliced	1 cup	51	1	1	0.2	0.1	12	1	15	0.2	4	0.3	13

FOOD	SERVING SIZE	CALORIES	PROTEIN (G)	FAT (G)	MONO-FAT	SAT-FAT	CARBS (G)	FIBER (G)	VIT C (MG)	VIT E (MG)	FOLATE (µ)	IRON (MG)	CALCIUM (MG)
Wheat germ	1 tbsp	26	2	1	0.1	0.1	4	1	0	—	20	0.5	3
Whiskey	4 oz	257	0	0	0	0	0	0	0	0	0	0	0
Whitefish, broiled	3 oz	146	21	6	2.2	1	0	0	0	—	14	0.4	28
Wine, dry red or white	4 oz	119	0	0	0	0	1	0	0	0	1	0.5	9
Yams, boiled or baked	1 cup	158	2	0	tr	0	38	5	17	0.2	22	0.7	19
Yeast, brewers, dry	1 tbsp	25	3	0	0	0	3	3	0	tr	313	1.4	17
Yeast, compressed, fresh	1 oz	24	3	0	0.1	0	3	2	0	0	289	1.4	4
Yogurt, full-fat, plain	1 cup	139	8	7	2	4.8	11	0	1	0.2	17	0.1	274
Yogurt, nonfat, plain	1 cup	133	13	0	0	0	19	0	0	0.1	253	0	400
Zucchini, boiled	1 cup	29	1	0	tr	0	7	3	8	0.2	30	0.6	23

For this table we used the latest version of Nutritionist IV (June 1997). The numbers are rounded to the nearest whole number, except for monounsaturated fat, saturated fat, vitamin E, and iron, which were rounded to the nearest tenth, and "tr" represents trace value of less than .001. A dash indicates that there are no known values for this food. The foods listed are the most common whole foods. A few abbreviations are used: Mono-Fat = Monounsaturated Fat, Sat-Fat = Saturated Fat, Vit C = Vitamin C, and Vit E = Vitamin E.

Index

M

N

O

P

Q

R

T